Encyclopedia of Global Industries

FIFTH EDITION

Encyclopedia of Global Industries

FIFTH EDITION

Australia • Brazil • Japan • Korea • Mexico • Singapore • Spain • United Kingdom • United States

Encyclopedia of Global Industries, Fifth Edition

Product Management: Jenai Drouillard

Project Editor: Lynn M. Pearce

Editorial: Hillary Hentschel

Composition and Electronic Prepress: Evi Seoud

Manufacturing: Rita Wimberley

For product information and technology assistance, contact us at
Gale Custommer Support, 1-800-877-4253.
For permission to use material from this text or product,
submit all requests online at **www.cengage.com/permissions.**
Further permissions questions can be emailed to
permissionrequest@cengage.com

Gale, a part of Cengage Learning
27500 Drake Rd.
Farmington Hills, MI 48331-3535

ISBN-13: 978-1-4144-8689-5
ISBN-10: 1-4144-8689-8

This title is also available as an e-book.
ISBN-13: 978-1-4144-8690-1
ISBN-10: 1-4144-8690-1
Contact your Gale, a part of Cengage Learning, sales representative for ordering information.

Printed in Mexico
1 2 3 4 5 6 7 14 13 12 11

Contents

Alphabetic List of Industries

Introduction

Now in its fifth edition, the *Encyclopedia of Global Industries* continues to serve as a key source for inquiries into industry sectors on a global scale. No other publication or electronic database offers the same level of international breadth and industry depth as the *Encyclopedia of Global Industries,* and few rival it in currency and accessibility.

This volume contains 125 articles in 23 chapters spanning industry topics from agriculture and mining to semiconductors and engineering services. Each entry lays out an overview of current trends, background on past developments, and profiles of leading companies and countries. Significant data and trends are illustrated in tables and charts, and a list of references for further research is supplied for every topic.

For the convenience of experienced researchers, the encyclopedia continues to identify industry topics with corresponding categories from the U.S. government's Standard Industrial Classification (SIC) system; however, as many readers will note, this system is gradually being phased out by the government in favor of the North American Industry Classification System (NAICS) published in 1997, and industry profiles reflect and address the use of this system. Both systems are widely used by business and economic researchers to provide a common statistical and conceptual language for the study of industry. Although the encyclopedia's topics do not strictly follow either system, as in many cases the editors have fashioned the industry topics to best reflect the current structure of industry, a concordance between the two classification systems is provided as an appendix. To aid users in understanding the focus of each article, an industry definition paragraph appears at the beginning.

HOW TOPICS ARE CHOSEN

The present roster of 125 topics has evolved from two main sources, as well as through the development of past editions. Many were suggested by panels of business experts from academia and business libraries. The remainder were selected by the editors based on such criteria as the annual revenue size of the global industry, the popularity of the topic among researchers, and how well the topic represents the diversity of global economic activity.

CONTENT AND ARRANGEMENT

Despite the varied subject matter treated in this volume, industry narratives are presented following a standard set of topical themes. Every essay includes some or all of the following categories of discussion:

Industry Snapshot Identifies issues covered later in the article and highlights key facts to understanding the industry.

Organization and Structure Covers logistical and structural aspects of the industry, including definitions of leading products and services, regulatory and legal matters, and the international make-up of the industry.

Background and Development Introduces treatment of the industry's origins and past trends, including important innovations and the individuals who made them.

Current Conditions Provides important recent trends and statistics, including those with implications for the future.

Research and Technology Discusses recent advances in technology that may signal emerging trends for the industry in the future.

Work Force. Addresses demographics, compensation, and issues of the labor force.

Industry Leaders. Profiles major companies, including recent annual sales, historical notes, and specialties within the industry.

Major Countries in the Industry Provides country- or region-specific summaries of the industry.

Further Reading Lists sources for additional research, including specific books or articles that may be referenced in the entry as well as works offering general information on the industry.

STATISTICAL CHARTS AND TABLES

The *Encyclopedia of Global Industries* includes tables, graphs, and charts to highlight key statistics and themes. When all data in the table or graphic has come from a single, proprietary source, a reference is given at the bottom. Sources of data in the public domain or compiled or adjusted by the editors are generally not specified; however, readers may refer to the essay's Further Reading section for leads on where comparable data might be obtained.

ACCESS TOOLS

Indexes The *Encyclopedia of Global Industries* includes three indexes:

SIC Index. Provides a numerical listing of references based on four-digit Standard Industrial Classification (SIC) codes. The SIC codes may correspond fully or partially to the encyclopedia topics.

Geographic Index. Provides an alphabetic listing of countries and regions mentioned in the book and subdivided by industry. The index includes cross-references for variant names.

General Index. Provides an alphabetic listing of industries, companies, organizations, legislation, concepts, and prominent individuals referenced throughout the book. The complete list of the encyclopedia's industry topics may be found in this index, along with cross-references to common keywords and acronyms.

The publication also includes the following table to aid researchers of particular statistical categories.

NAICS Conversion Table. This numerical listing of five- and six-digit North American Industry Classification System (NAICS) codes enumerates NAICS categories associated in full or in part with the encyclopedia's entries.

COMMENTS AND SUGGESTIONS

Gale welcomes your comments and ideas pertaining to the *Encyclopedia of Global Industries*. Readers needing more information about this or other Gale business products for students are encouraged to contact the editor:

Managing Editor, *Encyclopedia of Global Industries*
Gale, a part of Cengage Learning
27500 Drake Rd.
Farmington Hills, MI 48331-3535
Telephone: (248)677-4253
Toll-Free: (800)347-GALE
Fax: (248)699-8070
Email: BusinessProducts@gale.com

AGRICULTURE

—■—

AGRICULTURAL PRODUCTION—CROPS

NAICS CODE(S)

111. Crop production provides the bulk of human nourishment. Primary categories in the industry include grains, general field crops, vegetables, and fruits. For the cultivation of plants underwater see **Aquaculture.**

INDUSTRY SNAPSHOT

Crop producers in the early 2000s had greater access to world markets as global trade agreements opened new markets worldwide and as incomes rose in developing countries. For example, the rapid growth of China's economy made that country the world's leading consumer of grain by 2005. Moreover, improved technology for storing, transporting, and producing crops has enhanced the trade and production potential of agricultural businesses around the world. However, fluctuations in the Asian and world economies were expected to continue to affect the long-term outlook for the grain, fruit, vegetable, and specialty agricultural markets. In addition, weather conditions and other events, such as the devastating tsunami that hit southern Asia in December 2004, are projected to have unpredictable impacts. The tsunami, for example, washed away topsoil and contaminated cropland with salt water, damaging thousands of kilometers of agricultural land. Some 50,000 hectares of farmland in Sumatra and 5,500 hectares in Sri Lanka were severely damaged, and the United Nations Food and Agricultural Organization (FAO) reported that about one-half of the food crop in the Maldives was destroyed. Although the global impact is not expected to be significant, local agriculture may take several years to recover.

The FAO reported in March 2002 that crop growers must find a way to grow more crops with less water because by 2030 the world's water supply would be unable to meet projected crop irrigation demands. Irrigation use would have to increase more than 80 percent by 2030 to satisfy projected global food demand.

One suggested solution to solve global hunger that was treated seriously is to stop the spoilage of tons of fruit and other produce that is wasted annually in countries where large numbers of people with nutritional deficiencies live. For example, in Pakistan, agricultural analysts estimate that up to 3 million tons of fruit and produce are wasted annually as a result of substandard harvesting and packing methods.

Cattle Network projected challenges for agricultural markets after it analyzed the October 10, 2008, USDA update for the World Agricultural Supply and Demand Estimates and Crop Production. One area of concern was that outside factors were expected to continue to have a strong influence on agricultural markets, resulting in "a tighter year for crop producers."

Grains.

Corn. Decreasing grain output in the early 2000s raised international concern. According to a September 2003 U.N. Wire report that year would be 93 million tons short of demand. The fourth consecutive year of shortfall would sink world reserves to their lowest levels in 30 years. Most of the blame was placed on drought caused by water shortages according to the USDA, while the Earth Policy Institute blamed climate change. Shortages in 2001 and 2002 were particularly acute in China, the world's most populous country, which became a net importer of wheat in

2004, reversing its position of the 1990s. Total grain harvests improved in 2004, reaching an estimated 1.85 billion metric tons, a positive trend that was expected to boost output to more than 2 billion metric tons in 2005.

According to the Economic Research Service of the USDA (ERS), as corn became the world's leading cash grain throughout the world, the crop was anticipated to reach 700.6 million metric tons (mmt) in 2005, more than 27 percent greater than the crop in 1992. Unlike wheat, most of the corn crop is used as feed for animals, with about 70 percent of the 1998 crop being used as feed. Corn exports also were rising, climbing to 90.7 mmt in 2005. Expanding agricultural economies in China, Argentina, and North Africa were expected to add to the demand as they required more grain to feed livestock. The United States dominated corn exports substantially in 2004 when corn exports were estimated at 50 mmt. Other countries with significant exports of corn in 2004 were Argentina with 9 mmt, China with 8 mmt, and Brazil with 5.5 mmt.

Wheat. Global output of wheat, which was the second leading grain in production volume, was just below that of corn and had once exceeded corn in total global production. Wheat production fluctuated slightly in the early 2000s, but averaged almost 580 mmt a year. Although only 566.96 mmt were harvested in 2003 552.83 mmt in 2004, production was projected to exceed 620.8 mmt in 2005. The leading wheat producers were the European Union, China, India, the United States, Russia, and Canada.

Rice. Rice ranked third globally in grain production in the early 2000s, with 389.2 mmt produced in 2004. Among the leading grains, rice production has grown the most steadily. China, which was undeniably the leading rice producing country, provided 35 percent of the world's rice, followed by India with 21 percent and Indonesia with 8 percent. Bangladesh and Vietnam were also significant producers of rice. According to the USDA, the global rice trade was expected to grow an average of 2.4 percent between 2004 and 2013, which represented 6 to 7 percent of all agricultural trade. In the early 2000s, rice in the United States was a US$1 billion industry, although it only amounted to about 2 percent of all grain production.

Soybeans. World soybean production rose from 189.2 mmt to 206.4 from 2003 to 2004. Brazil and Argentina, which had steadily increased production from 1997 through the early 2000s, accounted for almost 45 percent of world soybean production in 2003. The United States remained the single largest producer, with 66.78 mmt in 2004 and about 85.4 mmt in 2005. Brazil ranked second, with a projected crop of 644.5 mmt in 2005, followed by Argentina, with a projected crop of 39 mmt.

Fruit. Bananas were the largest single fruit crop in the world, followed by grapes, oranges, and apples. Global banana production exceeded 70.6 mmt in 2004, grape production topped 65.4 mmt, and orange production reached 63 mmt. Global apple production, which increased during the 1990s, exceeded 59 mmt in 2000 and remained relatively steady through 2004. China produced 20.5 mmt in 2004, the United States produced 4.2 mmt, and Chile produced 1.1 mmt. World pear production, which reached 17.9 mmt in 2004, was dominated by China, which raised 10.1 mmt. The European Union ranked second with 3 mmt.

Citrus. According to USDA economist Susan Pollack, Florida reported an 11 percent decline in citrus production, which she attributed mostly to disease. However, the 2004 and 2005 hurricane seasons caused significant damage to citrus groves.

Horticultural Products. According to the ERS, the value of total horticultural exports worldwide in 2003 exceeded US$12.3 billion. The largest importer and exporter of horticultural products was the European Union, followed by the United States, with imports valued at US$21.9 billion and exports at US$12.3 billion in 2003. Leading exporters were the Netherlands, Spain, Mexico, the United States, and China, while leading importers were the United States, Germany, Britain, and Japan.

Peanuts. Increased demand for peanuts in Eastern Europe, Asia, and the Middle East contributed to a 20 percent growth in world peanut trade between 1998 and 2004. China reported peanut exports of about 600,000 tons in 2003 according to the *People's Daily,* accounting for approximately 40 percent of global export volume. Other major exporters included the United States and Vietnam.

Of increasing worldwide concern was the potential negative effect of development projects. A natural gas pipeline from Bolivia to Brazil, completed in 2002, caused researchers to fear that wild peanut species native to the area could be destroyed. Scientists hoped that such species, many of which remained undiscovered, could help decrease the need for pesticides and prove resilient to drought and other adverse conditions. Because pipeline construction increased human settlement in remote regions, however, native peanut species faced extinction unless samples could be collected.

Oilseeds. The oilseed category includes soybeans, sunflower seeds, cotton seeds, flaxseeds, and canola seeds. Sesame seeds and poppy seeds are also included. The ERS predicted that oilseed trade would expand quickly in the twenty-first century. The United States was projected to continue to dominate the sector through 2005, accounting for 34 percent of the world crop in 2003 and supplying 40 percent of world exports. Brazil was the second largest producer, contributing 28 percent of global soybean production, followed by Argentina with 18 percent. China, the largest market for U.S. soybean exports, imported US$2.9 billion in 2003, followed by the European Union with imports of US$1.1 billion.

Field Crops. Field crops of global importance include sugar, cotton, coffee, and tobacco. World production of sugar cane reached 1.3 billion metric tons in 2004. Brazil remained the leading producer, with a harvest of 411 mmt. Other leading sugar cane producers were India (244.8 mmt), Thailand (63.7 mmt), Mexico (45.1 mmt), and Cuba (24 mmt). Global production of sugar beets, which was more than 237.8 mmt in 2004, was dominated by the European Union, with harvests of 125.7 mmt. Production in the United States was reported to be 27 mmt.

After a slight drop in the late 1990s, worldwide cotton production increased in the early 2000s and by 2004 reached an all-time high of 116.7 million bales, which was substantially more than the predicted level of 103 million bales. However, the USDA projected a 14-million-bale drop for 2005, the largest decline ever and the biggest percentage decline since 1992-93. Nevertheless, world consumption of cotton was expected to rise 3 percent. U.S. production reached 23 million bales in 2004.

After a dramatic jump in 1997, world coffee output declined significantly in the early 2000s. Production in 2003-04 reached about 105.3 million 60-kilogram bags, a drop of approximately 15 percent from 2002-03. Major producers were Brazil, the Ivory Coast, Indonesia, the Dominican Republic, India, Angola, and Vietnam.

The upward trend in tobacco production, which increased significantly through the early 1990s, was expected to continue at a slower rate. According to an FAO report from 2004, world production in 2000 had reached 6.137 mmt and was expected to grow to more than 7.1 mmt by 2010. Leading producers were China, India, Brazil, the United States, Turkey, Zimbabwe, and Mali.

ORGANIZATION AND STRUCTURE

The crop production industry encompasses small subsistence farmers, immense vertically integrated food conglomerates, and everything in between. Subsistence farmers generally operate small plots, while large organizations typically operate fields up to thousands of acres. Fields may be either owned or rented by a family or farming establishment.

The organizational levels within the farming community are geared toward moving raw ingredients from the farm to the end consumer. This chain can be short and direct when a farmer grows produce and his customer comes to the farm to make a purchase or the farmer takes his produce to a local market. More often, however, many marketing and processing levels are involved. A frequently employed intermediate step can be farm sales to granaries, processors, or wholesalers.

Farm transactions can be handled in several different ways. For example, the farmer may grow a crop, harvest it, and receive payment when it is delivered to market, or the farmer may make arrangements to sell his entire crop (or a predetermined percentage of it) at a specified price before he grows it.

Because a successful agricultural industry is essential for a successful political and social climate, many governments, especially those of the world's major crop producers, tend to carefully regulate the industry and offer price supports, including direct subsidies, low-interest loans, and guaranteed prices, to ensure its strong performance. However, agreements such as the General Agreement on Tariffs and Trade (GATT) call for the reduction of such practices, making farmers around the world more self-reliant and market dependent. In the mid- to late 1990s, large agricultural producers like the United States, the European Union, China, and Japan began implementing programs to eliminate and reduce many crop subsidies. Other countries, such as New Zealand, Sweden, and Australia, had privatized their agricultural industries in the 1980s that were successful in the 1990s.

By the early 2000s, only about a third of global agricultural land was used for crops. Nonetheless, world food production doubled in the last three decades of the twentieth century, largely because of increased yields rather than increased acreage. Although total food production kept pace with population growth, food shortages in many regions posed recurrent problems. Consequently, the leading producers, which included Australia, the European Union, Japan, and the United States, donated a portion of their output each year to help support these regions, especially Sub-Saharan Africa, Bangladesh, and India. Wheat was expected to continue to be the primary grain sent as food aid to developing countries. In addition, various organizations throughout the world, including the United Nations Food and Agriculture Organization, researched agricultural methods and crop hybrids that will increase productivity, shorten growing periods, and strengthen resistance to pests.

International Trade Agreements and Organizations. Agreements that regulated international trade included the General Agreement on Tariffs and Trade (GATT) and the North American Free Trade Agreement (NAFTA). In its original form, GATT governed trade from 1948 to 1994, when it was replaced by the Uruguay Round. According to GATT, participating countries may not introduce any new export subsidies, and U.S. and EU subsidies are subject to restrictions. The agreement called for the reduction and elimination of tariffs designed to protect domestic businesses from foreign competition. All participating countries agreed to cut tariffs 33 percent, and the United States, the European Union, Canada, and Japan decided to remove most of the tariffs inhibiting trade among these nations. GATT also established a formal organization to govern global trade policies, the World Trade Organization (WTO).

Implemented in 1994, the North American Free Trade Agreement (NAFTA) was expected to gradually eliminate trade barriers, such as tariffs and trade restrictions, between Canada, Mexico, and the United States. The United States and Canada negotiated their own trade accord, as well as individual agreements with Mexico. The combination of these agreements made up NAFTA, which phased out tariffs on most agricultural products and established initial trade quotas to prevent price dumping while the agreement was being implemented. Most of the safeguard tariffs and quotas expired in 2004 and the rest were eliminated by 2005, creating unrestricted trade among these countries.

The WTO was established in 1995 to oversee trade among nations participating in the Uruguay Round. The goals of the WTO were to liberalize trade and ensure stable and fair trading conditions for participating members. Based in Geneva, Switzerland, the WTO allowed any country to challenge the trade policies of any other country before its tribunal, the Dispute Settlement Body. As of 2005 the WTO had 148 members, including the leading agricultural producers, such as the United States, the European Union, Japan, Argentina, and Brazil.

One of the WTO's most urgent concerns in the early 2000s was the elimination of agricultural subsidies that protected farmers in wealthy countries, such as France and the United States, at the expense of farmers in developing countries. Analysts argued that such subsidies, estimated at some $300 billion annually, pushed down commodity prices, leading to overproduction and illegal dumping by selling goods to other countries at less than their cost of production. In 2004, the European Union, which was considered to implement the biggest protections for its domestic agriculture, agreed to eliminate all of its export subsidies, while the United States agreed to cut its $19 billion in annual subsidies 20 percent. These agreements were projected to contribute to increasingly equitable global trading conditions when they went into effect in 2006.

The Asia Pacific Economic Cooperation (APEC) forum supervised and assisted economic development in the industry's growing sector in the region. Formed in 1989, APEC not only encouraged growth in the region, but also sought to increase multilateral trade that benefited the region as well as the rest of the world.

BACKGROUND AND DEVELOPMENT

Some historians have equated the beginning of agriculture with the origins of civilization. Although they do not always agree on where crop cultivation originated, some possible places are China, India, the Middle East, South America, Sudan, and Southeast Asia. Some believe that agricultural techniques began in one place and spread throughout the world, while others believe that agriculture was developed independently in various locations.

Grains. One of the most important crop families in the global economy is grain, which includes wheat, rice, millet, sorghum, quinoa, and maize (corn). Grain cultivation began in prehistoric times when early farmers, perhaps relying on their experience with nature, selected seeds from useful plants and attempted to control where and how they grew.

According to some accounts, the first grain to be domesticated was probably wheat, which was important because of its unique gluten content. Gluten is the protein that gives wheat-based dough its ability to rise. Rising occurs when carbon dioxide produced during yeast fermentation becomes trapped in the dough. Gluten also gives dough elasticity and gives bread a chewy texture. Without wheat, there would be no leavened bread.

Another grain with a long history of cultivation is rice. Rice cultivation probably originated in mainland Asia before it was introduced to other areas. Cultivation of rice in the Philippines is thought to date back to between 4000 B.C. and 3000 B.C. When the indigenous people adopted rice, it probably supplemented domestic root crops like taro and sago. As it became more firmly established, it became valuable and was interwoven in the nation's culture.

In drought-susceptible regions of Africa, native crop production originally focused on millet and sorghum. When irrigation was possible, yields improved, which enabled farmers in drought-plagued areas to achieve self-sufficiency. One type of millet, commonly referred to as "pearl millet," was able to grow quickly in a short, rainy season, while sorghum was cultivated in tropical regions.

In the Andes mountains in South America the Incas cultivated, stored, and distributed grain harvests. Early grains included quinoa, kiwicha, and kaniwa. Quinoa, a versatile grain able to grow in rugged terrain and withstand extreme weather fluctuations, was one of the most popular early grains. When the Spanish arrived and conquered the local tribes, they sent the indigenous farmers to work in the gold mines, and the cultivation of native plants diminished. Subsequently, indigenous agriculture continued to be eroded by the large-scale wheat imports by Peruvian government officials.

Maize was important to early civilizations as a grain crop native to the Americas. The first maize was a tropical grass that may have originated in Mexico. Some historians place the origins of its domestication and cultivation in South America around 5000 B.C. Maize cultivation in North America began sometime in the first two centuries A.D. in what is now the Southwest United States. An indigenous population that presumably had prior knowledge of agricultural techniques began to cultivate it. By 800 A.D., maize was also being cultivated in the eastern part of North America.

Maize was unknown in Europe before Columbus allegedly discovered it in Cuba and carried seeds back to his home. By the mid-1500s, maize was popular in southern Europe. In northern Europe, maize was initially used for livestock rather than for human consumption. The grain was exported from Europe to the Philippines and Asia and was taken to Africa by Portuguese traders where it thrived because it could survive droughts. Over-reliance on maize, however, led to vitamin deficiencies for some African populations.

According to the Walta Information Center, beginning in 1960, rice consumption in Africa had grown at 5 percent per year, outpacing other crops on that continent. However, demand continued to exceed supply in sub-Saharan Africa.

Citrus Fruit. Citrus fruits, such as oranges, grapefruits, lemons, and limes, originated in Southeast Asia and in the East Indies. They were first introduced to Europeans during the twelfth century. Prior to the development of modern processing technology, citrus could only be sold in limited areas. Primary regions involved in commercial citrus production were North and South America, the Mediterranean, Australia, and South Africa.

In the 1940s, the development of citrus concentrate brought changes to the citrus industry. Other innovations were the ability to extend product storage life and improvements in transportation. Instead of being limited to a local market, growers were able to reach all corners of the world and overcome problems associated with their products' seasonality. Large-scale, modern commercial citrus producers generally grew their fruit in orchards on "composite" trees. Composite trees are trees with a rootstock that differed from their "scion," the upper portion of the plant that was grafted onto the rootstock. The rootstock was selected based on its ability to thrive in specific conditions. Important features included a natural resistance to diseases and pests and the ability to grow well in local soils. The scion was selected for the quality of its fruit.

Fruits, Vegetables, and Melons. Pineapples originated in the New World and are said to have been discovered by Columbus. Pineapples, which are considered native to Brazil, were spread throughout the tropical regions of the world. They were a staple in the diets of tropical South Americans during the fifteenth century. In the twentieth century an estimated 90 varieties of pineapple

were grown. Major pineapple-producing areas were Hawaii, the Philippines, Malaysia, Australia, South Africa, Puerto Rico, Kenya, Mexico, Cuba, and Taiwan. One of the most common ways in which pineapple-producing nations marketed the fruit was as a canned product. The United States, the United Kingdom, Germany, Canada, and Japan imported approximately 70 percent of the world's canned pineapple production. During the 1970s and 1980s, tropical fruits became increasingly popular for use in juices, with trade quadrupling and sales reaching US$4 billion in one decade. Developing countries played an important role in that growth, with production accounting for almost one-half of the total.

Indigenous to South America, tomatoes were introduced to Europe in the 1500s. The English believed that tomatoes were poisonous because of an early misclassification, so they did not begin to cultivate them until the early 1800s. However, some southern European countries began to cultivate them immediately, integrating them into their diet and treating them as a delicacy. Long before Europeans discovered the tomato, however, the Aztecs had mixed them with chili peppers, making salsa. By the twentieth century, tomatoes had become one of the world's most popular vegetables, in fresh and processed forms.

Potatoes also originated in the Americas, perhaps in Mexico, and spread south. Wild potatoes grew at least 13,000 years ago and have been cultivated for 9,000 to 10,000 years. During the sixteenth century, Spanish explorers took potatoes back to Europe. Seventeenth century British settlers brought them back to North America via Bermuda. Potatoes were introduced to Japan and China during the seventeenth century and to New Zealand during the eighteenth century.

Potatoes were popular among the poor in eighteenth and nineteenth century Europe because they could be grown easily in small family gardens and had high nutritional value. A farmer could feed about four times as many people per acre with potatoes as he could with wheat or rye. Sailors took potatoes with them on long voyages because they are high in vitamin C, which prevents scurvy. However, people depended too much on potatoes, causing potato famines like those in Ireland in the nineteenth century, when the potato crop was contaminated repeatedly by blight.

Despite blight and famines, potatoes became a favored crop in many places worldwide. Several varieties were developed to thrive in different growing conditions. In addition to being a nutritious and popular food, potatoes were used in several industrial applications. For example, during the nineteenth century, potato starch derivatives were used to make syrup and sizing agents, and manufacturers used potatoes in the production of paper, adhesives, and textiles. During World War II, the German military used potatoes to make an alcohol-based aircraft fuel, light streetlights, and power ground vehicles. Potatoes also have provided ingredients for cosmetics, pharmaceuticals, and even disposable diapers.

Field Crops. Field crops with global significance include sugarcane and sugar beets, both of which are used to produce sugar. Historians believe that sugarcane was first cultivated in prehistoric Asia and exported to Europe as early as the fifth century A.D. Sugarcane was grown in Egypt's Nile River Valley in the eighth century and was introduced to Central and South America during the sixteenth century. Sugarcane continues to be cultivated in tropical and semitropical regions. Sugar beets were first grown in southern Europe about 1800. There are many varieties of sugar beets, but *Beta vulgaris* is the most important commercially. Sugar beets are grown in the temperate climates of the European Union, the United States, and Russia.

CURRENT CONDITIONS

In the early 2000s, the future of farming in industrialized nations was reflected in the persistent decrease in the number of farms while production continued to grow. At the same time in the U.S. government, in the form of the USDA, began to address global climate change and the need for adjustments to land ecosytems. Liberal trade measures to make crop producers increasingly market dependent in the 1980s and 1990s produced positive agriculture conditions through the early 2000s. Trade pacts like the General Agreement on Tariffs and Trade (GATT) reduced trade barriers between many countries, and governments began to privatize their agricultural industries, eliminating government price supports and planting restrictions.

The general outlook for world agricultural production and trade looked positive as countries like China and Vietnam became highly competitive by raising crops in addition to rice. As the U.S. dollar strengthened in 2002, the United States faced diminishing sales for crops like wheat, and international buyers negotiated lower prices from countries with less solid currencies. With the elimination of approximately US$300 billion in annual farm subsidies in wealthy countries that was expected to go into effect in 2006, overall conditions for agricultural trade were expected to remain favorable. For example, the value of U.S agricultural exports, which fell to US$49 billion in 1999, exceeded US$62 billion in 2004 and was projected to reach US$59 billion in 2005.

In June 2008 an FDA advisory warned consumers in the United States to stop eating some varieties of red tomatoes because they were thought to be responsible for a salmonella outbreak that affected more than 1,000 people. Hot peppers later became suspect rather than tomatoes, but some tomato farmers never recovered, according to *USA Today*. As a result, the FDA's warning practices were called into question.

Vietnam was among nations that dramatically increased fruit and vegetable production in the early 2000s. At the start of 2002, the country's Ministry of Agriculture and Rural Development (MARD) predicted an end-of-year production of 11.4 million tons of fruit and vegetables with an export value of US$440 million. In addition, the government of Shandong Province, China, dedicated extensive land to grow green vegetables and be more competitive.

Grains. Used as food for humans and animals, corn (also known as maize) moved slightly ahead of wheat as the leading grain in the world in the early 2000s, according to the ERS. Global corn production soared from a high of 580.6 mmt to 622.5 mmt from 1997 to 2004 and was projected to reach 700.6 mmt in 2005. The United States by far remained the leading producer, with harvests of 256.9 mmt in 2004 and 299.9 mmt in 2005. In the United States, corn accounted for more than 90 percent of feed grain value, according to the ERS. U.S. corn acreage, which had been about 80 million acres in the late 1990s, was expected to increase gradually through 2013, while U.S. exports were expected to rise faster than global trade.

Although the ERS predicted continued slow growth in world wheat production through 2005, devastating heat waves in 2003 decimated the harvest in Eastern Europe, resulting in the smallest crop in 30 years. The USDA projected that this crisis would contribute to a decline in U.S. wheat exports through 2007, followed by a modest recovery through 2013. Population and income increases, combined with continued competition from Europe, Canada, Argentina, Australia, Russia, and the Ukraine, were expected to keep U.S. market share at about 23 percent. Leading wheat exporters in 2004 included the United States (31 mmt), Canada (16 mmt), and the European Union (7 mmt), while the leading importers included Egypt (6.3 mmt), Japan (5.8 mmt), and Brazil (5.6 mmt).

World rice production had increased steadily beginning in the early 1990s and was expected to reach 402 mmt in 2005, up from 389.2 mmt in 2004. Unlike most other grains, rice was used exclusively for human consumption. Even though world per capita consumption of rice was likely to continue falling through 2005, overall rice demand was anticipated to expand along with of population growth. Major rice exporters for 2004 were Thailand with an estimated 8 mmt, Vietnam with 4 mmt, the United States with 3 mmt, and China with 2.24 mmt. Primary importers were Indonesia with 2 mmt, Nigeria with 1.23 mmt, Iraq with 1.1 mmt, and Iran with 1 mmt.

In early 2005 the United States reached an agreement with the European Union, which was its top market for brown rice exports, to ensure market access for the crop that was worth $33 million annually.

Fruit. Global apple production in the early 2000s was dominated by China, which produced almost half of the world's total crop, and the United States. According to the FAO, global apple production reached a record high of 57.9 million tons in 2001, but declined the following year to 55.8 million tons. By 2004, however, global production surpassed 2001 levels to reach 59 million tons. China's crop in 2004 reached 20.5 million tons, while apple production in the United States, where harvests had declined in the early 2000s, rose to 4.2 million tons. Production also increased slightly in the European Union, exceeding 12.2 million tons. Although apple crops for South America's top producers, including Chile and Argentina, were expected to drive an increase in that sector's production to 4.4 million tons, levels fell short of the estimate, reaching only 3.2 million tons in 2002 and 3.5 million tons by 2004.

World production of canned peaches, which dropped to 858,000 tons in 2003 after a crop failure in Greece, was forecast to return to normal levels in 2005, reaching 1.1 million tons. Exports were expected to exceed 568,000 tons. Greece remained the leading exporter of peaches, followed by the United States, Spain, Italy, South Africa, Argentina, Chile, and Australia. Other major exporters were the United States, Spain, Italy, South Africa, Argentina, Chile, and Australia.

The 2008 California grape crop was projected to be slightly more than it had been in 2007 even though it had been damaged by spring frosts that had delayed the maturation of the vines, according to the *Sacramento Business Journal*. The USDA projected a 3.3 percent increase from the 2007 crop to 6.4 tons of grapes for the 2008–09 crop. The USDA also projected wine and raisin grape production to increase 3 percent and 1 percent, respectively.

Citrus Fruit. Citrus fruits, which include oranges, tangerines, grapefruit, and lemons, were the leading global fruit category by value. Oranges accounted for more than half of all citrus production. According to the USDA, world citrus production in 2004 increased almost 12 percent from 2003, reaching 73.3 million tons. Brazil and the United States, the two leading producers, along with Mexico, accounted for almost all of the increase.

Brazil, the leading orange grower, produced 18.2 million tons of oranges in 2004, an increase of almost 23 percent from 2002. Orange yields also increased in the United States to an estimated 12.3 million tons, almost 17 percent more than 2002, with a 79 percent share of the country's total citrus crop. U.S. citrus exports reached about 1.1 million tons in 2003, including 665,000 tons or oranges, 335,000 tons of grapefruit, 100,000 tons of lemons, and 15,000 tons of tangerines. Growth of about 2.3 percent annually was predicted for U.S. exports of fresh oranges through 2011, with the import market expected to grow 3 percent annually during that period. In China, citrus production rose slightly from 13.9 million tons in 2003 to 14.4 million tons in 2004. Citrus production in Spain reached a record high of almost 6.1 million tons in 2004, an increase of 6 percent from 2003. The orange crop was 2.93 million tons, tangerines 2.1 million tons, and lemons and limes exceeded 1 million tons for approximate increases of 4 percent, 3 percent, and 30 percent from the previous year, respectively.

In October 2008, a text message was sent to cell phones throughout China warning people, " Tell your families and friends not to eat oranges. Fruit fly maggots have been found (in oranges) in Guangyuan, Sichuan province." While maggots were found in a few oranges, it was not an epidemic. In addition, the maggots are harmful only to the fruit, not to humans. The problem is easily eradicated when the fruit is destroyed, but the panic that followed the text message caused consumers to stop buying the fruit. China Central Television reported that the loss citrus producers would be US$1.46 billion because oranges are the second largest fruit crop in China.

Vegetables and Melons. Vegetables and melons are grown throughout the world. Some of the leading crops are carrots, tomatoes, potatoes, and onions. The worldwide carrot harvest in 2004 was 23.6 mmt. Major producers included China, the United States, and Russia. World tomato production in 2002 totaled more than 108.5 mmt, a 10 percent increase from 1985, and grew to 115.9 mmt in 2004. World production of potatoes grew from 318.2 mmt to 328.8 mmt from 2003 to 2004. China, which continued to be the leading producer of potatoes, accounted for more than 20 percent of the global crop in 2002, reaching 75 mmt in 2004. The United States grew 20.4 mmt in 2004, while Canadian production reached 5 mmt. Revenues for potatoes and potato products were in a deficit for the first time in 2003, mostly because of increased imports from Canada. U.S. exports that year were valued at US$646 million, while imports reached US$682 million. Total onion production reached approximately 53.5 mmt in 2004, with China, India, the United States, Turkey, and Pakistan the leading producers. World cantaloupe and melon production reached 27.3 mmt in 2004 with China, Turkey, and the United States as the leading growers. Total production of watermelon, the leading U.S. melon crop, exceeded 92 mmt in 2004.

Oilseeds. The biggest disappointment for the United States in the early 2000s was the plunging market for some oilseeds, including peanuts, caused in part by record production levels in 2000 and 2001. World soybean production in 2004 reached 206.4 mmt, with the United States, Brazil, Argentina, and China the primary growers. In the United States, record soybean production in 2004 and 2005, along with decreased global demand, led to the largest soybean stock levels since 1985. The value of U.S. soybean exports in 2005 was expected to reach US$6.1 billion.

Global production of cottonseed, the second largest oilseed crop, reached 35.56 mmt in 2004 and was projected to increase to 44 mmt in 2005. Rapeseed production was just behind cottonseed, at a projected 43.6 mmt. Worldwide peanut production in 2005 was expected to reach 34.4 mmt, with 90 percent of the crop coming from developing countries, particularly in Asia and Africa. Sunflower seed harvests fell from 26.5 mmt in 2004 to a projected 25.35 mmt in 2005. Palm kernel production grew from 7.6 mmt in 2003 to a projected 8.5 mmt in 2005, while copra (the dried coconut from which coconut oil is derived) remained relatively unchanged from 5.33 mmt in 2004 to 5.48 mmt in 2005.

Field Crops. Global consumption of sugar was expected to exceed production in 2005 by an estimated 831,000 tons, marking the second consecutive year that demand was greater than supply. The FAO projected Latin American harvests to increase about 1.7 percent, led by Brazil. Asian output was projected to grow only about 1 percent, with severe droughts in China resulting in a 5.8 percent drop in production. Sugar production in the European Union was expected to be 42.6 mmt for 2005, up 2.3 percent from 2004. Adverse weather conditions in the United States, however, caused the projected harvest to decrease 30,000 mmt from 2003, reaching 8 mmt.

World cotton production grew from 94.9 million bales in 2004 to 116.7 million bales in 2005, an increase of 23 percent. U.S. production grew more than the world average, rising 26 percent from 18.2 million bales to 12 million bales from 2004 to 2005, while exports rose only 0.6 percent. U.S. exports fell 5.5 percent, largely because of reduced shipments to China.

A relatively poor coffee harvest in Brazil in 2003 contributed to a decrease in world exports of about 5 million bags from the previous year. Brazil, the top exporter, reported exports of about 24.5 million bags in 2004, down from 4.9 million bags in 2003. Production also fell in the Ivory Coast, Indonesia, the Dominican Republic, India, and Angola, but Vietnam had a production increase of 1.1 million bags. Stock in coffee-producing countries declined about 24 percent in 2004 to maintain the revised level of trade. World consumption, on the other hand, was projected to rise less than 1 percent. Small crops in Brazil and other

major producing countries, along with continued demand for high quality beans, resulted in increased prices in 2004. Arabica coffee futures were expected to average US$1 per pound in 2005, a 30 percent increase over prices in 2004.

In early 2005, the United States announced that it would rejoin the 2001 International Coffee Agreement. The United States is the largest consumer of coffee, with imports representing 24 percent of the global market. World exports of coffee reached 7.33 million bags in early 2005, a 13 percent increase over 2004. Brazil was the largest exporter, followed by Vietnam and Colombia.

World tobacco production dropped substantially in the mid-1990s, but global production began to grow steadily later in the decade. The United Nations expected growth to continue through 2010 based on projected demand in developing countries, where consumption was expected to increase to 5.09 mmt by 2010. In developed countries, however, declining demand was expected to decrease 10 percent between 1998 and 2010, reaching about 2.05 mmt by 2010. China's share of the global tobacco market was expected to remain steady at about 37 percent. Production was projected to increase in developing countries to meet increased demand.

RESEARCH AND TECHNOLOGY

Crop production research is conducted in several areas to improve yield, or the amount of harvest taken per unit of cultivated land. Some scientists have worked to develop plant varieties well suited to diverse growing conditions or varieties that are naturally resistant to pests and diseases.

The process of hybridization, cross-fertilizing two plant species to blend the best features of both, is commonly used to produce crops with improved yields. For example, the practice of cross breeding maize varieties enabled U.S. producers to experience a six-fold increase in maize yield. Other successes in genetic engineering of plants reduced the length of the rice-growing season. Rice production time fell from an average of 180 days to 110 days worldwide, resulting in three annual rice crops in some areas. Researchers estimated further refinements could increase rice production an additional 60 percent.

Some scientists completed research with potatoes, looking for increased efficiency in cultivation methods. Potatoes were planted from seed potatoes rather than from traditional seeds. Seed potatoes were bulky and heavy, which created storage problems and increased the potential for transmitting insects and diseases from one crop to the next. True potato seeds (TPS) were minuscule seeds produced by potatoes that needed to be grown in a nursery before they could be planted in the field. According to some researchers, if technological problems related to the use of TPS could be overcome, potato production could be made more economical.

Plant diseases were another major concern to researchers, especially the notorious potato blight. A nineteenth century naturalist, the Rev. M. J. Berkeley, discovered that the blight on the potato was not the result of disease but was the cause of the disease. The origin of the fungus responsible for blight, however, was not discovered until the middle of the twentieth century. Although chemicals were developed to keep blight at bay, they were expensive and not universally available. Subsistence farmers in developing nations, for example, typically did not have access to them.

To help combat potato blight, researchers sought to develop potatoes that were naturally resistant to blight. Dr. John S. Neiderhauser, winner of the 1990 World Food Prize, worked under the auspices of the International Potato Center in Lima, Peru, to examine the wild Andean potato gene pool and discover the genetic key to blight resistance. Neiderhauser's work with potatoes was credited with resulting in a four- to six-fold harvest increase over four decades in some developing countries, including Mexico, Pakistan, India, Turkey, and Bangladesh.

By the early 2000s, genetic research had led to new strands of genetically-modified (GM) food crops. Unlike traditional crossbred species, however, GM crops contain genes from entirely different organisms. For example, a plant might contain genetic material from an animal or a bacterium. Advocates of GM agriculture maintain that such crops can be tailored to resist pests or withstand climate extremes, but critics maintain that the safety of GM foods has not been proven. By 2003, GM crops were grown by at least 6 million farmers in 16 countries, including the United States, Argentina, Canada, and China. The major GM crops were soybeans, corn, cotton, and rapeseed. Use of GM crops remained controversial, however, and resistance was expected to affect world trade in the early 2000s. In 2004, the United Nations released a report stating that GM crops at that time were safe and that their use could help farmers in poor regions.

The Sacramento Bee (California) reported that the USDA had completed research on Owari Satsuma mandarin oranges grown in Placer County, California, showing that the fruit contained a natural antihistamine called synephrine, with the ability to relieve cold and allergy symptoms. The USDA study showed that Owari Satsuma juice had six times as much of the antihistamine as regular orange juice, which was the only other citrus tested for synephrine.

In addition to working to improve crop yields, researchers were developing ways to farm without causing damage to the environment, such as no-till crop methods that protect topsoil from erosion up to 98 percent. However, critics claimed that no-till methods caused other environmental damage because they required more chemicals, such as herbicides and pesticides. Proponents of no-till farming pointed out that improved pesticides killed targeted species by disrupting reproduction cycles without causing harm to other species.

MAJOR COUNTRIES IN THE INDUSTRY

China. China is a leading producer in many categories of crop farming. Economic liberalization that began in the 1980s made China dominate the industry in the 1990s. In the late 1980s when political changes led to decentralized agriculture, farmers were given the opportunity to develop small farms that ranged in size from one-half acre to three acres, instead of working on communal farms. In 2001 China led the world in apple production, and its estimated 1.5 billion bushels were more than the next seven competing countries or regions combined. In 1997 China led the world in wheat production (121 mmt), rice production (195 mmt), cotton production (4.2 mmt), tangerine production (6.07 mmt), and tobacco production (3.1 mmt). China also ranked as the world's second largest corn producer, with more than 105 mmt, behind only the United States, which produced 236.5 mmt.

In spite of China's enormous production, it has often failed to meet its domestic demand. In 1996, for instance, China produced 109 mmt of wheat, but domestic demand was 114 mmt, and the country was forced to import 4 mmt. Grain production fell significantly in the late 1990s and early 2000s, and in 2003 China had to import more wheat than it exported. The country faced the same problem with its other leading crops, either breaking even or importing heavily to satisfy demand. The ERS predicted that China would become a net importer of corn in 2007.

In 2005 the Chinese government announced that it would spend 5.5 billion yuan (about US$66 million) subsidizing agriculture to boost grain production and increasing farmers' incomes. China's wheat crop had faltered in the early 2000s but rose 9 percent in 2004 to 469 million tons, an upward trend that the country hoped to strengthen.

The United States. The value of combined U.S. agricultural exports reached a record of nearly US$60 billion in fiscal year 1996, before falling to $49.1 billion in 1999. However, exports recovered steadily in the early 2000s, reaching US$62.3 billion in 2004. However, global oversupply, lower prices, and increased competition led to a drop in the value of U.S. agricultural exports to US$59 billion. Steady economic growth and expanded international trade, however, were expected to boost export volume and prices for U.S. agricultural goods and reach US$78.6 billion by 2014. Countries in the Western hemisphere continued to be the major markets for U.S. agricultural goods. Canada was the primary importer of U.S.

crops, with an estimated US$10.2 billion in 2005. The next largest market was Mexico, with about US$8.5 billion, followed by Japan, the European Union, and China. At the same time, the United States remained a major consumer of agricultural imports. The value of total agricultural imports in 2005 was projected to be US$58 billion, which nearly matched the value of exports, and was projected to increase to US$76 billion by 2014.

Global grain shortages overseas worked to the advantage of the United States in the early 2000s, as exports of grain approached the record highs of 1996. In 2004, however, wheat exports fell to about 900 million bushels. The USDA projected slow growth of wheat exports after 2007, with U.S. market share remaining relatively steady at around 23 percent.

The United States remained the world leader in corn production, with exports reaching a projected 48 mmt in 2005. However, the value of U.S. corn exports reached US$5.8 billion in 2004, and then fell sharply in 2005 due to lower shipments and intense competition from Argentina. The total value of corn exports that year was projected at US$4.7 billion. The United States was also the world's leading wheat exporter and the leading producer and exporter of soybeans.

Although Brazil overtook the United States in commercial orange production in the late 1980s, the United States remained a major producer with a harvest of almost 12.3 mmt in 2004. Devastating hurricanes in Florida in late 2004, however, led to a decline of about 23 percent in 2005 U.S. citrus production. Florida's orange and grapefruit crops were expected to decrease about 27 and 63 percent, respectively. Slight increases in production were projected for California and Texas.

The United States was also a major sugar producer. Although some sugarcane was grown in regions around the Gulf of Mexico and Hawaii, most of the nation's sugar came from sugar beets. In 2003, the United States ranked fifth behind Brazil, India, the European Union, and China in sugar production, with 7.4 mmt. Top producing sugar beet states were California, Idaho, Minnesota, Colorado, Washington, North Dakota, Nebraska, and Michigan. In addition, the United States was among the leading producers of several other crops, including tobacco and apples. In 2002, the United States ranked third in global cantaloupe production and fourth in watermelon production.

The European Union. The European Union was another major producer of a number of crops, including sugar, wheat, corn, apples, and pears. In 2003 the European Union ranked third in global sugar production, with 18.3 mmt, and third in wheat exports. The European Union was also among the top producers of apples and peaches. In 2004 the

European Union admitted 10 member nations, for a total membership of 25 countries, which increased the number of farmers in the European Union almost 70 percent. Funding of EU5.8 billion was planned after expansion to assist farmers to modernize equipment, develop environmentally friendly farming practices, and improve marketing strategies. In 2004 the European Union was the world's largest food importer and the largest market for agricultural products from developing countries.

India. Although India usually trailed agricultural leaders, such as the United States and China, it constituted one of the world's major crop producers. In 2001 it ranked seventh among apple-producing nations, and in 2003 it ranked second in sugar production, with 19.45 mmt, and rice production, with 89 mmt. India also ranked among the world leaders in tobacco production.

Brazil. Brazil was one of South America's leading crop-producing nations, with sugarcane and coffee as major crops. By 2003 Brazil led the world in sugar production, with 22.7 mmt, and was also the leading grower of coffee, with production estimated at 32 million bags in 2004. After increasing its soybean acreage in the early 2000s, Brazil had increased its position in the soybean and soybean meal export market, which was expected to grow from 35 to 45 percent from the early 2000s to 2014.

In the early 1970s, the Brazilian government had subsidized farming and offered guaranteed assistance in land development. According to one estimate, one-half of the cost of land in Brazil was associated with clearing that land. As a result, Brazilian farming efforts increased dramatically as crop lands were carved out of forests. Government officials encouraged farmers to focus on growing crops for export, such as soybeans. During the 1990s Brazil was ranked second to the United States for soybean production and exports.

Brazil was also one of the world's major producers of citrus, primarily oranges. Brazil's orange crop for 2005 was expected to reach 18.4 mmt, a 23 percent increase from 2004. Favorable weather conditions, in addition to improved crop management, contributed to robust yields.

BIBLIOGRAPHY

Brown, Lester A. "Record Temperatures Shrinking World Grain Harvest." *Earth Policy Institute*, 27 August 2003. Available from www.earthpolicy.org.

"China Becomes Largest Exporter of Peanuts." *People's Daily*, 2004. Available from English.peopledaily.com.cn.

"Crop Productions & Outlook—The Demand Side." 20 October 2008. Available from www.cattlenetwork.com.

"EU Farm Ministers Mull Farm Subsidy Reforms." 19 November 2008. Available from www.abcnews.go.com.

Illovo Sugar. *Sugar Statistics, World of Sugar*, 2004. Available from www.illovo.co.za.

"Interim Trade Triumph Short on Hard Details." *The New York Times,* 2 August 2004.

Left, Sarah. "Public Urged to Join GM Debate," 3 June 2003. Available from www.guardian.co.uk.

"Modified Crops Help Farmers, UN Says." *Boston Globe,* 18 May 2004.

"Scientists Fear Irreparable Loss of Peanut Crop Biodiversity for World Food Supply." *Future Harvest,* 17 December 2004. Available from www.futureharvest.org.

Smith, Nathan. "2002 Peanut Situation and Outlook." The University of Georgia College of Agriculture and Environmental Sciences Cooperative Extension Service, 29 January 2002.

Soy Stats, 2004. Available from www.soystats.com.

"Two to Three Million Tons Fruits and Vegetables Going to Waste." *The Pakistan Newswire,* 12 March 2002.

United Nations Food and Agricultural Organization. *After the Tsunami,* 2005. Available from www.fao.org.

———. *Agricultural Data: FAOSTAT, 1997–2005.* Available from www.fao.org.

———. *Higher World Tobacco Use Expected by 2010,* 8 January 2004. Available from www.fao.org.

———. *Sugar Outlook,* December 2002. Available from www.fao.org.

U.S. Department of Agriculture, Economic Research Service. *International Baseline Projections to 2013,* 2004. Available from www.usda.gov.

———. *China's New Farm Subsidies.* 2005. Available from www.usda.gov.

U.S. Department of Agriculture, Foreign Agricultural Service. *Cotton: World Markets and Trade,* February 2005. Available from www.fas.usda.gov.

———. *Coffee Updates,* 2004. Available from www.fas.usda.gov.

———. *Grain: World Markets and Trade,* February 2005. Available from www.fas.usda.gov.

———. *Oilseeds: World Markets and Trade,* 2004. Available from www.fas.usda.gov.

———. *Oilseeds: World Markets and Trade,* February 2005. Available from www.fas.usda.gov.

———. *Outlook for U.S. Agricultural Trade,* February 2005. Available from www.fas.usda.gov.

———. *Rice: World Markets and Trade,* 2004. Available from www.fas.usda.gov.

———. *Situation and Outlook for Citrus,* 2004. Available from www.fas.usda.gov.

———. *Vegetables and Melons Outlook,* 2004. Available from www.ers.usda.gov.

———. *World Apple Situation,* 2003. Available from www.fas.usda.gov.

———. *World Cotton Production Rises Despite Low Prices,* 2001. Available from www.fas.usda.gov.

———. *World Pear Situation,* 2003. Available from www.fas.usda.gov.

———. *World Trade in Fresh Vegetables,* 2003. Available from www.fas.usda.gov.

U.S. Exports: FAPRI 2000 World Agricultural Outlook. Washington, DC, 2002. Available from www.fapri.org.

"Vietnam to Produce 11.4 Million Tons of Vegetables in 2002." *InfoProd,* 13 February 2002.

Walta Information Center. "Investment Key to Doubling Rice Production in Africa." *waltaInfo,* 5 November 2008. Available from www.waltainfo.com.

Walter, Bob. "Placer County Mandarins are Nothing to Sneeze at." *The Sacramento Bee (California),* 20 November 2008. Available from www.sacbee.com.

Weekly Outlook: Soybean Prices, University of Illinois College of Agricultural, Consumer, and Environmental Sciences, 24 February 2004. Available from web.aces.uiuc.edu/news.

Weise, Elizabeth. "Salmonella Warnings Shift Focus to Hot Peppers." *USA Today,* 10 July 2008.

"World Grain Harvest Short of Demand Four Consecutive Years." *U.N. Wire,* 17 September 2003. Available from www.unwire.org.

Zhe, Zhu. "Orange is a Lemon Not Sold Even for a Penny." *China Daily,* 13 November 2008. Available from www.chinadaily.com.

SIC 0200

AGRICULTURAL PRODUCTION— LIVESTOCK

NAICS CODE(S)

112. The livestock agriculture industry includes commercial farms, ranches, dairies, hatcheries, and other facilities that raise or tend animals to supply the world's food markets. Specific categories include dairy and beef cattle, goats, hogs, poultry, and sheep. (See also **Agricultural Production—Crops.**)

INDUSTRY SNAPSHOT

While overall food per capita demand is relatively fixed, the general economy determines the types and quantities of foods that are purchased. The livestock industry, which often mirrors the general economy, increases during economic expansion and decreases or stagnates in recessions. The Economic Research Service (ERS) of the U.S. Department of Agriculture (USDA) predicted average growth of 3 percent in gross domestic product (GDP) worldwide through 2005. In addition, the continued liberalization of global trade was expected to spur further growth in both production and cross-border trade.

An overall rise in meat production through the 1990s was fueled primarily by increased economic growth and demand in the United States, the European Union, and China. In 1997 the global meat supply, which was the largest market for livestock agriculture, was valued at US$500 billion. In 1997 global production of meat increased to approximately 220 million metric tons (mmt). The leading meats, including beef, veal, pork, poultry, lamb, mutton, and goat, climbed to 190 mmt, up from about 155 mmt in 1992, according to the Foreign Agricultural Service (FAS) of the USDA. After a sharp fall in 2001, global production of meat returned to 247 mmt in 2002 and reached 257.5 mmt in 2004, according to the United Nations Food and Agricultural Organization (FAO). Despite the overall increase in production, the World Bank indicated that meat production would have to increase 64 percent by 2020 to meet the needs of the world's swelling population.

Leading livestock-producing nations were China, the United States, the European Union, Australia, New Zealand, Brazil, and Canada, which had high-technology meat industries and sophisticated regulatory agencies. Each country was also a major exporter of packaged meat, carcasses, and live animals. Second-tier producers had well-developed meat and poultry industries and included Uruguay, Venezuela, Thailand, India, and some African countries.

Pork maintained its popularity among meat based on carcass weight produced, accounting for almost 40 percent of global meat production. In 2002 pork production was listed by the FAO at 95.3 mmt, and by 2004 it had reached 100.3 mmt. Poultry surpassed beef in the late 1990s as the second most popular meat, with 78.2 mmt produced in 2004. Beef production, which tapered off in 1997, totaled 58.7 mmt in 2004, while lamb, mutton, and goat meat reached 12.1 mmt.

Beef Cattle. The United States was the world's largest producer and second largest exporter of beef, according to the ERS. In 2004 the FAO reported beef production in the United States at 11.2 mmt, while Brazil, the second largest producer, produced 7.7 mmt. The USDA projected total beef exports at 6.2 mmt in 2004, with Brazil dominating the market at 1.6 mmt in exports in 2005. Australia's beef exports were anticipated to be 1.3 mmt, while U.S. exports were expected to reach only 272,000 tons for a 35 percent increase from 2004, but significantly lower than historical levels primarily as a result of bans on U.S. beef because of concerns about bovine spongiform encephalopathy (BSE contamination, commonly referred to as "mad cow disease"). Strong world demand, as well as favorable economic conditions, helped boost Argentina's beef exports to a projected 25-year high in 2005. New Zealand exports of beef rose to a record 413,000 tons in 2004 based on high demand from Asian markets, particularly Korea.

Australia's sheep farmers reaped the benefits of U.S. restrictions on imports of Australian beef following a World Trade Organization ruling. Australia shipped an estimated 72,000 mmt of mutton to the United States in 2002, up from 67,000 mmt in 2001, according to the USDA.

University of Wyoming Assistant Professor Chris Bastian anticipated a decrease in prices for cattle related to a

drop in demand for beef in 2009. He added that evidence of the link between the cattle market and corn production affected the price of cattle. When the cost of corn is low, it costs less to feed the cattle and the ranchers can get their stock to the slaughterhouse in less time. Ranchers net more from their cattle as the cost to get them to the slaughterhouse is decreased, resulting in lowered costs of beef.

Dairy Products. Worldwide milk production reached 613 mmt in 2003 and remained almost unchanged in 2004. The European Union led in global milk production with an estimated 146 mmt, followed by India, which dramatically increased milk production from about 70 mmt in 1997 to 90.4 mmt in 2004. The United States, which lagged behind India in the late 1990s, ranked third in 2004 with an estimated 77.5 mmt. The Russian Federation, with 31.1 mmt, came fourth. The European Union also dominated cheese production, with 5.55 mmt in 2003. Australia, with an output of 3.68 mmt, came second. The Organisation for Economic Co-operation and Development (OECD) reported that demand for dairy imports was likely to remain strong through 2005, especially in Asia.

In 2000 non-U.S. international markets experienced a 41 percent increase in nonfat dry milk (NDM), bringing the price in line with U.S. prices for NDM. This caused a corresponding drop in demand of about 40 percent. U.S. exports of NDM fell from 142 metric tons to 96 metric tons between 2000 and 2001, but rose to approximately 200 metric tons by 2004. U.S. sales of NDM were projected to reach 150 metric tons in 2005.

Poultry. In the mid- to late 1990s, poultry was the fastest growing segment of the global meat industry. In 2000, worldwide poultry meat production (including broiler chicken, duck, goose, turkey, and other poultry) reached 69.2 mmt, and by 2004, production had grown to 78.2 mmt. The leading producers, which included the United States, China, the European Union, and Brazil, contributed 65 percent of global production. Chicken remained the most popular poultry meat, accounting for about 85 percent of world production. In 2004 the United States was the leading producer of chicken meat (15.5 mmt), and turkey meat (2.4 mmt). China, however, dominated global production of duck meat (2.1 mmt) and goose meat (1.9 mmt).

In 2002 a few international markets had grown distrustful of U.S. chicken, claiming that hormones and growth-inducing drugs posed long-term adverse health effects for humans. When Russia became the first country to issue a ban on U.S. chicken, U.S. President George W. Bush announced intentions to overthrow the ban. Although in 2004 Russian authorities indicated that an agreement about poultry imports might occur in the near future, strict Russian quotas on poultry imports remained in effect throughout that year. In 2003 and 2004 poultry markets were shaken further when avian influenza (bird flu) broke out in many parts of Asia. The FAO estimated that potential losses up to US$10 billion could result from 2004 trade bans on poultry.

Eggs. Health concerns over egg consumption had hindered the growth of the egg industry beginning in the 1980s, especially in the United States and Europe. Studies had linked high intake of the dietary cholesterol that is abundant in eggs with high levels of blood cholesterol that in turn is related to increased risks for heart disease and other health problems. However, research in the late 1990s suggested that moderate cholesterol intake did not lead to substantially higher levels of blood cholesterol and egg sales started to increase in 1977. In 2001, Japanese consumption of eggs was the highest at 348 per capita annually. Next in annual per capita consumption were China (270 eggs), the United States (252), Malaysia (246), and Singapore (230). The average annual per capita egg consumption was 144 eggs worldwide.

Hogs. In 2005 pork remained the most popular meat in the world, with global production projected to be 91.6 mmt. China and the European Union were the primary producers, with China's output expected to reach 47.5 mmt and the European Union's expected to reach 21.1 mmt. China led in world consumption of pork as well, at about 47.1 mmt in 2005. However, per capita consumption of pork in Europe was greater than anywhere else. Worldwide pork exports were expected to reach a record 4.2 mmt in 2005. The European Union, with 25 member nations in 2005, continued to lead in world pork exports, followed by Canada, the United States, Brazil, and China.

ORGANIZATION AND STRUCTURE

International Trade Agreements and Organizations.

General Agreement on Tariffs and Trade. The General Agreement on Tariffs and Trade (GATT) was the key trade agreement governing international trade of livestock-related commodities. An older version of GATT was in place from 1948 until 1994, when a revision was adopted during the 1986–1994 Uruguay Round. Under the Uruguay Round, participating countries could not introduce any export subsidies, and U.S. and E.U. subsidies were subject to restrictions. GATT called for the reduction and elimination of tariffs designed to impede and control foreign competition in favor of domestic businesses. All participating countries agreed to cut tariffs 33 percent, and the United States, the European Union, Canada, and Japan removed most of the tariffs inhibiting trade among themselves. GATT also established the World Trade Organization as the formal organization for the implementation of systematic global trade policies.

World Trade Organization. The World Trade Organization (WTO) was established in 1995 to govern trade among nations participating in the Uruguay Round. The organization's objective was to liberalize trade and ensure stable and fair trading conditions for participating members. Based in Geneva, Switzerland, the WTO allowed any country to challenge the trade policies of any other country before its tribunal. In 2005 the WTO had 148 members, including leading agricultural producers like the United States, the European Union, Japan, Hong Kong, Argentina, and Brazil.

North American Free Trade Agreement. The North American Free Trade Agreement (NAFTA) took effect in 1994 and gradually removed trade barriers such as tariffs and trade restrictions among Canada, Mexico, and the United States, making trade between these North American countries more free by 2004. The United States and Canada renegotiated their 1989 limited free trade agreement and each signed separate agreements with Mexico, creating NAFTA. The agreement eliminated tariffs on most agricultural products and established initial trade quotas to protect individual countries from over-importing while the agreement was being implemented. Most of the safeguard tariffs and quotas had expired in 2004, and the rest had been eliminated by 2005, creating unrestricted trade among these countries.

Asia-Pacific Economic Cooperation. Headquartered in Singapore, the Asia-Pacific Economic Cooperation (APEC) is responsible for overseeing and assisting economic development in the Pacific region. Formed in 1989, APEC's goal was to stimulate multilateral trade within and outside the region. The 17 members of APEC were Australia, Brunei, Canada, Chile, China, Indonesia, Japan, Malaysia, Mexico, New Zealand, Papua New Guinea, the Philippines, Singapore, South Korea, Taiwan, Thailand, and the United States.

Market Segments.

Beef Cattle. The beef cattle industry thrives in countries with large areas of pasture, such as the United States, Argentina, Brazil, China, and New Zealand. A cow and her calf may be supported on as little as one acre of land in areas of abundant rainfall or irrigation or on as much as 600 to 700 acres on desert ranches.

Production of cattle, from birth to slaughter, takes between 18 months and 2 years. During the first 6 to 8 months, beef cows nurse their calves on a farm or ranch. As they are weaned, calves in most countries begin to graze on grassland until they are large enough to be slaughtered. In the United States, however, the vast majority of older yearling calves are confined in feedlots and fattened, or "finished," on a high-energy diet of grain. While the majority of U.S. beef is grown in feedlots, some foreign producers used feedlots to produce the highly marbled beef prized by many consumers, especially in Japan and the United States. For example, New Zealand opened its first commercial grain feedlot in 1991 to supply such beef to Japan. Demand for meat from grass-fed cattle, which is considerably leaner than feedlot beef, is increasingly in demand as healthy eating trends gain importance.

The number of cattle raised and their selling prices vary widely from year to year. In 1996, the world cattle inventory was 1.044 billion head, up slightly from 1995, and by early 2002 the count remained almost unchanged, according to Spectrum Commodities. Inventories declined significantly in the former USSR, however, dropping to about 50 percent of 1992 levels. At the same time, inventories in China rose to more than 150 million head. Most cattle are sold as beef.

A minority of world beef production is exported. Most beef is consumed in the nation where it is produced, although GATT had caused changes. Certain beef-producing countries had become dependent on exports. For example, New Zealand and Australia exported 81 and 63 percent of their 1997 beef outputs, respectively. In 2005, the United States led the world in beef production and remained a leading exporter. The second largest producer was Brazil, which was the primary exporter in 2005, although the country produced more hamburger than choice beef sections. Choice imported beef can cost up to one-half as much as domestic beef. U.S. imports of range-fed Latin American beef was used almost exclusively for hamburger.

Dairy Farms. Since milk must be continually refrigerated while it is processed and sent to retail outlets, dairy farms typically operate locally or regionally. While international trade in milk is limited, products made from milk, such as cheese, are widely exported. Milk production is more efficient in cooler climates, such as northern Europe and the northern United States. Milk consumption is largely a regional phenomenon, as a large share of the world's adult population is unable to digest it.

Poultry. The sharp increase in chicken consumption that began in the 1960s was a result of the low production and consumer costs of poultry compared to other meats. The world's poultry producers were able to drive down production costs by improving feed efficiency. Consumers also purchased more chicken because it was highly nutritious.

Poultry producers in many countries evolved into large, vertically integrated production–processing–marketing companies. Broiler chicks are bought in bulk, then housed and sold together to disrupt any potential disease cycles. In the United States, nearly all producers were vertically integrated.

While more than 50 countries were significant poultry producers, the top 12 accounted for 80 percent of world output. World poultry production is divided into three major segments: broiler chicken, turkey, and other poultry. Broilers account for around 68 percent of the world market, turkey accounted for 8.5 percent, and other poultry accounted for 24.5 percent.

Eggs. Some farms continue to produce eggs from "free range" chickens that are allowed to roam outside, but the majority of eggs are produced in vast factory farms where hens are kept in wire-floored cages. In the United States and other industrialized countries, technology plays a large role in egg production. Hens are bred carefully to maximize egg-producing characteristics such as early maturity, efficient use of feed, and production of white eggs. The laying house of the twenty-first century is typically automated with mechanized feeders, sanitizers, egg collectors, and temperature and light controls. An egg-production flock can be between 100,000 and 1 million hens. While most eggs are sold fresh in the shell, a growing percentage are pasteurized and sold in liquid, frozen, or dried forms. In 2003, there were about 278 million laying hens in the United States.

Hogs. Pork production traditionally has been highly segmented, with different farms and firms performing the separate functions of raising hogs, slaughtering, processing, and retailing. However, the global pork industry, like the chicken industry, consolidated functions and vertically integrated them in a small number of large firms. Hog farming also became increasingly industrialized, with a large number of hogs fed and housed in confinement rather than being free to roam outside. In order to manage high-volume hog farms, producers used sophisticated genetic breeding programs, nutritional science, and computerized record-keeping systems. Ownership of high-volume hog farms, particularly by large agricultural companies, was controversial in areas of the United States, such as Iowa, where small family farms continued to operate.

CURRENT CONDITIONS

Through the early 2000s global markets for meat were affected by several factors. Economic gains and increased meat consumption in the developing world spurred demand, but prices for U.S. meat decreased as the availability of livestock raised in competing markets continued to increase. In addition, health concerns affected trade. In 2001 global meat markets plummeted to their lowest level in 13 years after the discovery of bovine spongiform encephalopathy (BSE, or mad cow disease) in European beef. Although the beef industry recovered in 2002, an FAO report indicated that outbreaks of BSE in 2004 affected approximately one-third of global meat exports and threatened to affect US$10 billion in world trade.

Beef. Great Britain, and potentially all beef producers, had faced a beef production crisis in 1986 that escalated in late 1995 and continued to plague the industry in 2002. Researchers discovered that cows fed with animal parts could develop BSE. The European Union banned beef imports from Great Britain, and the British Agricultural Ministry ordered the slaughter of millions of British beef cattle, which cost the country US$10 billion. Scientists believed that consumption of diseased beef could lead to the development of a deadly strain of Creutzfeldt-Jacob disease (CJD) in humans. Consequently, the European Union persuaded Great Britain to stop using animal parts in livestock feed. By March 2002, more than 180,000 bovines had been slaughtered after contracting the disease or being exposed to it, according to *Post Graduate Medicine.* Japan had one confirmed case of a carcass infected with mad cow disease. In 2003 the disease surfaced in Canada, and the United States confirmed one case, which resulted in a ban that threatened that country's US$3.6 billion export business in beef and veal and restricted exports to Japan and Mexico. Although Mexico reopened its borders to U.S. beef in March 2004, the Japanese ban remained in effect through 2005. In October, 2004, Japan and the United States agreed to a trade framework that would reopen trade in beef beginning in 2006.

In the early 2000s, heightened demand in Russia and Brazil was expected to be a catalyst for industry growth, but demand and production began to shrink in the United States and the European Union. Moreover, rising income worldwide had led to greater per capita consumption of beef worldwide, especially in rapidly growing economies like China. The USDA also expected demand for imported beef to remain brisk in areas with limited agricultural resources and inefficient agricultural methods, such as the Pacific Rim and Russia. However, when domestic production increased enough to satisfy domestic demand, reliance on imported beef was expected to slow in emerging markets. Most of the major beef exporters, including Australia, Argentina, and the United States, were expected to increase their output through 2005, but the European Union's exports were projected to diminish.

Dairy Products. In 2004, world demand for dairy products exceeded exportable supplies, leading to significantly higher prices. USDA projections placed U.S. milk production at about 78.9 million tons for 2005, an increase of 2 percent from the previous year, while production in the European Union was expected to increase 0.6 percent to 131.1 million tons. Output in Australia was expected to reach 10.5 million tons, and New Zealand milk production, which grew 4.5 percent in 2004, was expected to increase another 2.5 percent to 15.4 million tons in 2005. After steady growth in the late 1990s and early 2000s of 5 to 6 percent annually, world exports of cheese were expected to increase about 1 percent in 2005.

Increased domestic consumption in E.U. countries contributed to slower growth of exports. World production of butter was expected to grow from 5.7 mmt in 2000 to 6.9 mmt in 2005. Exports were projected to increase 2.1 percent, with India increasing its sales to about 10,000 tons.

While the ERS projected dairy herd numbers to diminish slightly between 2000 and 2015, output per cow was expected to increase dramatically after 2006 when bovine growth hormone again became readily available.

Commodity prices for the dairy industry dropped during 2008 as the global economy weakened. Rabobank, a financial services provider specializing in the food and agriculture industries, predicted that as the global economy recovered, the dairy industry would experience a new era of inflated prices as consumers accepted significant increases in the price for milk. Rabobank senior analyst Hayley Moynihan expected New Zealand to "generate a substantial increase in milk supply" into 2009, which would help meet global demand for milk in the future.

Poultry. The poultry segment enjoyed considerable growth in the 1990s and early 2000s. In 2004 it was the second most popular meat in the world behind pork and represented the fastest growing segment in the global meat industry. In 2004, total production of poultry meat reached 78.2 mmt.

The majority of the poultry produced through the late 1990s and early 2000s was broiler meat, which in 1997 was estimated to be 37 mmt. Broiler exports continued to be a minority of the total output but grew significantly in the mid- to late 1990s. The United States led broiler exports, with 2.1 mmt in 1997, up sharply from 518,000 metric tons in 1990, followed by Hong Kong and China, with exports of 625,000 metric tons and 500,000 metric tons, respectively. Broiler meat exports fell worldwide in 2004 but were expected to rise to 6.2 mmt in 2005.

In 2002, growth hormones used in the United States and chemicals used in China by poultry producers resulted in export bans to Russia and the European Union, respectively. Outbreaks of avian influenza (bird flu) in 2003 and 2003 further affected global trade because of concerns that it could infect humans and lead to a pandemic. Infected birds were destroyed and export bans were imposed on affected countries. Asia was hardest hit, with more than 100 million birds destroyed in nine countries. Canada and the United States also reported cases of bird flu. According to the FAO, countries affected with bird flu accounted for 4 mmt (50 percent) of poultry export products. China's poultry exports in 2004 were expected to decline about 20 percent as a result of bird flu, and imports fell 25 percent. To meet import demands for poultry, nontraditional exporters, including Malaysia, the Philippines, and Brazil, increased their output and sales.

In 2004, Brazil surpassed the United States as the world's leading exporter of broiler meats, and market conditions in 2005 led to 10 percent growth for Brazilian exports. Growth was attributed to concerns about avian influenza, which had closed Asian markets to the United States and Canada, as well as competitive pricing, favorable exchange rates, and aggressive marketing strategies like an increase in value-added poultry meat. In addition, production costs in Brazil continued to be the lowest in the world among all major broiler meat producers.

Broiler meat output in the United States, which was the world's leading producer in the late 1990s and early 2000s, was anticipated to be 16 mmt in 2005, up 3 percent from 2004. Exports for 2005 were expected to increase 6 percent. After recovering from avian influenza outbreaks in 2003 and 2004, China increased its broiler meat production in 2005 to an estimated 10 mmt. With significantly increased shipments to Japan, China's total broiler exports were expected to reach 300,000 tons in 2005, an increase of 20 percent from 2004. China had requested approval to export cooked poultry meat to the United States, which would allow it to further expand its market share.

China's share of the industry was even more sizable when Hong Kong was included following its return to Chinese rule in 1997. Hong Kong produced less broiler meat than other leading exporters, such as Brazil and China, but exported a greater percentage of its overall production. However, four deaths in Hong Kong attributed to the H5N1 variety of strain A influenza transmitted by domestic poultry led to the slaughter and disposal of 1.2 million of the country's chicken flock in 1997. The ramifications of this disaster were expected to cripple Hong Kong's production and exportation into the 2010s, and Hong Kong's Agriculture and Fisheries Department announced plans to compensate producers for losses.

In 2005, broiler exports from the 25-member European Union, were expected to reach almost 8 mmt, an increase of less than 1 percent from 2004. Russia's broiler production fell rapidly after 1993 when output reached 540,000 metric tons. In 1997 Russia produced only 290,000 metric tons, a 46 percent drop, but improvements to the country's old, inefficient production facilities in the late 1990s began to reverse this trend. By 2004, Russia was expected to produce 640,000 tons of broilers, with production growing 13 percent in 2005. The decrease in poultry production resulted in Russia and former Soviet Union countries to become major chicken importers.

Argentina's broiler meat production and exports were expected to reach record highs in 2005, with production at 990,000 tons and exports reaching 90,000 tons. Heavy investment in plant upgrades, as well as overall economic recovery from a 2002 financial crisis, helped the country nearly double its broiler exports between 2002 and 2004. Major export markets included China, Chile, Saudi Arabia, and South Africa.

Eggs. Worldwide egg production grew from 50.1 mmt in 1997 to a projected 62.7 mmt in 2004. According to the International Egg Commission, global egg output could reach almost 90 mmt by 2030. China remained the primary producer of eggs, with 28.4 mmt in 2004, an increase of almost 160 percent from 1991. The United States, which ranked second in production, produced 73.18 billion table eggs in 2002, of which 48.1 million were exported at a value of US$30.5 million. U.S. production increased marginally in 2003 to 73.93 billion table eggs. Other major egg producers were Japan, Russia, India, and Brazil. The FAO projected rapid growth in egg production in developing countries, accounting for an estimated 77 percent of global production by 2030.

After melamine was discovered in exported Chinese eggs, consumers in Hong Kong were expected to keep paying inflated prices for fresh eggs in the foreseeable future to ensure that the eggs were free of melamine. The supply of eggs was not expected to meet demand in Hong Kong as imports from mainland China dropped 70 to 80 percent after the melamine discovery, resulting in increased prices.

Hogs. Global pork production rose from 83 mmt to 100.3 mmt between 1997 and 2004, primarily due to surging demand in China. In 1997 China produced 37.1 mmt of pork, and more than 47.7 mmt in 2004. In contrast, early in 2002 the United States had an excess of pork production, as higher hog birth rates and lower costs of beef decreased the market for pig meat to levels that even creative marketing could not overcome. However, the export restrictions on poultry and beef that followed outbreaks of avian influenza and BSE in 2003 and 2004, respectively, caused demand for pork to rise significantly in 2004.

Although U.S. pork production declined slightly in the late 1990s, the country remained the world's leading exporter. By 2004, U.S. pork products reported record-breaking sales by volume for the fourteenth consecutive year. According to the U.S. Meat Export Federation, the value of U.S. pork exports in 2004 exceeded US$2 billion. Pork exports by volume were more than 900,000 mmt. Although Mexico was the largest market for U.S. pork in tonnage (329,767 tons), exports to Japan, at US$893.7 million, had the highest value.

RESEARCH AND TECHNOLOGY

The Indiana Business Research Center reported a positive relationship between regulated livestock operations (RLOs) and property values in rural areas, especially for beef cattle.

MAJOR COUNTRIES IN THE INDUSTRY

The United States. The United States has long been a leader of the global livestock industry with a large and highly efficient agricultural economy. As in other major countries, the U.S. livestock sector maintained a complex relationship with the government, characterized by extensive regulation, heavy subsidies, price support programs, and other programs affecting the price, production, and exports of livestock products. However, there was a trend toward decreased levels of government involvement in the U.S. livestock business following passage of the Federal Agriculture Improvement and Reform Act of 1996, which included policies geared toward increasing the market dependency of U.S. farmers. In addition, trade agreements like GATT and NAFTA were slowly opening the United States and other international markets to increased competition through the elimination of farm subsidies, price supports, and trade restrictions.

The USDA projected that total U.S. meat exports would rise 6.4 percent to 3.5 million tons in 2005, although market share was expected to remain unchanged at 20 percent. Pork exports were projected to reach a record 959,000 tons, representing about 23 percent of the global market, but beef and veal exports dropped in 2004 and 2005 as a result of continued concern about BSE. U.S. broiler meat and turkey exports for 2005 were expected to reach almost 2.3 million tons, for 34 percent of the world market.

Beef. The United States was the largest producer of beef products worldwide in the 1990s and early 2000s, but ranked only fourth in total number of beef animals, due to the high efficiency of U.S. producers in obtaining the maximum amount of meat possible per animal. In 1997 the United States produced 11.5 mmt of beef from about 101 million head of cattle. Cattle inventory continued to decline in the early 2000s, reaching about 96.1 million head in 2003.

Although U.S. beef exports increased steadily through the 1990s, reaching a record volume of 2.57 billion pounds in 2003, export restrictions imposed after the late 2003 discovery of a BSE-infected cow from Oregon began a devastating decline. Every country except Canada banned U.S. beef in 2004, resulting in plummeting sales. Mexico resumed imports of U.S. beef later that year, but important Asian markets like Japan remained closed to U.S. beef exports. Negotiations in late 2004 established a time frame for the United States to resume beef sales to Japan in 2006.

Dairy Farms. The U.S. milk-per-cow average had increased over the years largely because of the controversial hormone bovine somatotropin (BST), which makes cows produce more milk. The trend was likely to further decrease the U.S. herd as fewer cows were able to produce larger quantities of milk. Under the Dairy Export Incentive program, cheese exports rose 10 percent in 1997 to 32.5 metric tons. The United States also exported large amounts of butter, dried milk, evaporated and condensed milk, and ice cream to Canada, Mexico, Japan, Korea, and China. The value of U.S. dairy exports, which reached US$982 million in 2003, was expected to increase to US$1.17 billion in 2004 and US$1.3 billion in 2005. California produced the most milk, with 33.1 billion pounds of milk in 2001, representing one-fifth of U.S. milk output.

Poultry. The United States led the world in production of broiler meat from chicken and turkeys. According to the National Turkey Federation, increased demand caused turkey production to grow more than 300 percent since 1970. By 2002, U.S. consumption of turkey was 17.7 pounds per person, an increase of 113 percent from 1970, fueled by demand from Asian countries, including Japan, Hong Kong, and Singapore. U.S. turkey exports for 2002 reached 438.5 million pounds. The value of turkey exports, however, rose only slightly in the early 2000s, from US$2.6 billion in 1994 to US$2.7 billion in 2003.

Hogs. Although the United States had a history of many small, independent pork producers, its pork industry became more vertically integrated and was concentrated in large company operations by the mid- to late 1990s. As in the broiler chicken industry, many pork companies controlled all phases of the production process, from birth to grocery store sales. These changes allowed pork producers to buy feed in larger quantities and spread costs over more hogs, resulting in increasingly efficient pork production. The United States reported 7.7 mmt of pork production in 1997, growing to 8.75 by 1999. Production fell slightly in 2000 and 2001, before climbing to about 8.71 in 2002 and 9.3 mmt in 2004. Since U.S. per capita pork consumption, which was about 51.4 pounds in 2003, was low compared to countries like Poland (84.3 pounds), the Czech Republic, France, Denmark, Spain, and Hong Kong, the United States exported a large percentage of its pork. Key markets for U.S. pork were China and other Pacific Rim countries, while Canada, Mexico, and Denmark were primary export competitors.

In March 2002, U.S. hog farmers continued to struggle as declining demand, shrinking prices, and steadily rising hog births combined to drive down prices. Readily available supplies of chicken, which was increasingly popular with consumers, led to a number of farm closings nationwide in 2001. About 1,000 of Indiana's 64,000 farms shut in 2001, many of which were pork-producing operations, according to the Purdue University Agricultural Service.

The European Union. In 2004 the European Union admitted 10 additional member nations, bringing the total to 25. This expansion led to many expected gains in the E.U. agricultural and livestock sectors.

Beef and Veal. In 2004, the European Union, which had been the second largest producer of beef and veal in the late 1990s and early 2000s, produced 8 mmt and fell behind Brazil. France and Germany were leading producers, with 1.59 and 1.2 mmt, respectively. In the European Union substantially less beef was typically consumed per capita than in the other leading beef producers, including the United States, Argentina, and Brazil. In 1997 E.U. per capita consumption was reported to be 19.5 kilograms. In 2001 and 2002, fear of mad cow disease seriously compromised British beef exports and led to increased pork production.

Poultry. Although the European Union lagged far behind the United States and China in poultry production in the mid- to late 1990s, it was the third largest producer of poultry meat with 10.7 mmt in 2004. The 2004 expansion of the European Union contributed to substantial gains for the E.U. poultry industry, which the USDA predicted would grow 3 percent in 2005. Exports of broiler meat increased 8 percent between 2003 and 2004, despite high competition from Brazil.

Hogs. With 21.5 mmt of pork produced in 2004, the European Union was also a major pork producer, trailing only China in overall production. Chief pork production areas in 2004 included Germany (4.3 mmt), Spain (3.3 mmt), France (2.2 mmt), and Poland (2.1 mmt). With an average per capita pork consumption of 46.6 kilograms in 1997, the European Union consumed more pork per capita than any other region. It produced enough pork to satisfy domestic demand, but consumption began a downward trend in the early 2000s that was expected to continue into 2005.

China. China had a long history of subsistence agriculture to feed its massive population. Protein sources were rare and were used primarily to supplement a steady diet of rice. Most Chinese livestock was kept in "backyard," or household, production that increasingly was altered by the economic liberalization of the 1980s. The agricultural economy of China began to focus on centralized production that resulted in the country becoming a primary global livestock and meat producer. By 2005 China was a world leader in the production of pork, sheep, duck, and goose meat.

Beef. Between 1993 and 1998, China's beef cattle herd had increased 40 million head to 147 million and its production had more than doubled, climbing to 5.8 mmt in 1998. In 2004 China continued to rank as one of the world's largest producers of beef, raising 6.2 mmt of beef and veal. Relatively low domestic consumption enabled China to export a significant portion of its output in the 1990s, but beef consumption rose significantly in the early 2000s, and China's export volume dropped proportionally, accounting for only about 1 percent of total production in 2001.

Poultry. China's poultry production also had expanded dramatically since the early 1990s, becoming one of the dominant global producers, behind only the United States. In 2004 China instituted stricter measures to ensure sanitary conditions and safe processing for broiler meat. Despite outbreaks of avian influenza in 2004, which caused both production and consumption to fall temporarily, China's production of broiler meat that year reached about the same levels as in 2003. China produced 13.6 mmt of poultry in 2004, most of which was from ducks and geese.

Hogs. China significantly expanded its lead as the world's top pork producer through the early 2000s. Although small farms continued to account for most production, large commercial operations with increased efficiency had expanded in the early twenty-first century.

Argentina. In 2001, Argentina's beef industry was hurt significantly by an outbreak of bovine foot and mouth disease. Argentina reported exports of US$323 million in the first half of 2003 after the country's herds were declared officially disease-free. Argentina's production tapered off in the 1990s and early 2000s, but the country remained an important low-cost producer and exporter of beef. In 1997 exports resumed to the United States, which had banned Argentine beef for almost seven decades, and Argentina regained its position as a leading beef producer and exporter. Disease-free status also made Argentina a formidable competitor for markets in Australia, North America, and Asia. Argentine beef production in 1997 dropped slightly to 2.5 million tons, while exports were estimated to be 430,000 metric tons. In 2004 production was estimated to be 2.7 mmt, with exports expected to reach 420,000 metric tons.

New Zealand. In the early 2000s, meat exports accounted for 15 percent of New Zealand's total exports. New Zealand exported 90 percent of its lamb, giving it a 53 percent share of that global market. In addition, New Zealand was a major cattle producer, with an output of 610,000 metric tons of beef in 1997 and 700,000 metric tons in 2004. The nation tended about 47.3 million sheep and 8.9 million cattle in 1997, while its human population numbered only about 3.6 million. In 2002 New Zealand was the fourth largest beef-exporting nation, with 321.7 million kilograms (kg) of frozen meat and 20.4 million kg of fresh meat. New Zealand's livestock and meat industry, which was the nation's largest employer, was highly dependent on exports. GATT provided New Zealand greater access to the U.S. market. Another major export region for New Zealand was the Middle East, which consumed large quantities of lamb. According to *Meat & Poultry,* New Zealand was the world's largest supplier of Halal slaughtered sheep meat, which was processed in accordance with Islamic religious requirements.

Brazil. Brazil increased its beef production in the early 2000s to become competitive with the United States as one of the world's main producers. In 2004 Brazil was the second largest producer and largest exporter of beef, with sales 40 percent higher by volume than in 2003. The USDA projected that Brazil's beef production would reach nearly 8.5 mmt in 2005, up about 6 percent from 2004. Brazil was also a significant producer and exporter of pork, with a projected output of almost 2.7 mmt in 2005. In 2004 Brazilian pork exports grew 3 percent in volume, but 41 percent in value. Despite a Russian ban on imports of Brazilian meat during most of 2004, Russia remained the primary destination for Brazilian pork products.

BIBLIOGRAPHY

Baxter, Tom. "Trade Fight Unhealthy for Poultry Producers." *Atlanta Journal and Constitution,* 10 March 2002.

Becker, Elizabeth. "Mexico Lifts Ban on Many U.S. Beef Products." *The New York Times,* 5 March 2004.

Bilgili, S. F. "Sarge." *Poultry Products and Processing in the International Marketplace,* 2001. Auburn University. Available from www.fass.org.

"Bird-Flu Fears Lead Hong Kong to Slaughter 1.2 Million Chickens." *The Wall Street Journal,* 29 December 1997.

Bishop, Diane. "Dairy Industry Poised for Strong Showing." *The Southland Times,* 11 November 2008. Available from www.stuff.co.nz.

"Brazil's Increased Pork Production Threatens U.S. Domestic Crop Markets." *Minnesota Issue Watch,* October 2001. Available from www.mnplan.state.mn.us.

"Commodity News." *Bloomberg News,* 27 March 2002.

Dorgan, Michael. "Food Safety Is Growing Problem in China, Say Consumers, Experts." *Knight Ridder/Tribune News Service,* 15 March 2002.

"Egg Industry Fact Sheet," June 2003. Available from www.aeb.org.

"Egg Prices May Fall with Oversupply." *The Nation,* 11 March 2002.

Egg Statistics. United Egg Producers, 2004. Available from www.unitedegg.org.

Estrada, Richard T. "Prices of Food Expected to Rise This Year." *Modesto Bee,* 27 March 2002.

———. "Finding the Milky Way." *Modesto Bee,* 23 March 2002.

"Food and Mouth Won't Affect Argentina Beef Status," 9 September 2003. Available from www.agriculture.com.

Mast, Tom. "Corn Price, Economy Will Affect Cattle Market." 9 November 2008. Available from www.casperstartribune.net.

———. "Stability Benefits Sheep Industry." 9 November 2008. Available from www.casperstartribune.net.

McCoy, David. "Pigmeat Production Forecast." *Belfast News Letter,* 16 February, 2002.

National Turkey Federation. *Turkey Statistics,* 2002. Available from www.eatturkey.com.

"New Zealand Beefs Up Exports." *Meat & Livestock Australia,* January 2005. Available from www.mla.com.au.

New Zealand Meat Exports. 2003. Available from www.marketnewzealand.com.

Spackman, Paul. "Long-term Dairy Outlook is Promising Despite Current Gloom, Report Says." Farmers Weekly Interactive, 11 October 2008. Available from www.fwi.co.uk.

Tucci, Louis A., and James J. Tucker III. "The General Agreement on Tariffs and Trade (GATT): Implications for Consumer Products Marketing." *Journal of Consumer Marketing,* Winter 1996: 35.

United Nations Food and Agricultural Organization. *Food Outlook: Meat,* May 2002. Available from www.fao.org.

———. "Animal Disease Outbreaks Hit Global Meat Exports," 4 March 2004. Available from www.fao.org.

U.S. Department of Agriculture Economic Research Service. *Agricultural Baseline Projections,* February 2004. Available from www.ers.usda.gov/.

———. *Livestock, Dairy, and Poultry Outlook,* 17 February 2004. Available from www.ers.usda.gov.

U.S. Department of Agriculture Foreign Agricultural Service. *Brazil: Livestock and Products, Semi-Annual Report, 2005,* 31 January 2005. Available from www.fas.usda.gov.

———. *China: Poultry and Products Semi-Annual 2005,* February 2005. Available from www.fas.usda.gov.

———. *Dairy: World Markets and Trade,* December 2004. Available from www.fas.usda.gov/.

———. *EU–25: Poultry and Products Semi-Annual 2005,* 31 January 2005. Available from www.fas.usda.gov.

———. *International Meat Review,* February 2003. Available from www.ams.usda.gov/.

———. *Livestock and Poultry: World Markets and Trade,* October 2004. Available from www.fas.usda.gov.

"U.S. Pork Industry Exports More Than $2 Billion for First Time." U.S. Meat Export Federation, 14 January 14, 2005. Available from www.usmef.org.

"Where's the Meat?: Pork." *American Farm Bureau Information,* 4 December 2001. Available from www.fb.com.

Wong, Adele. "Price of Eggs to Remain High As Supply Tightens." *The Standard,* 11 November 2008. Available from www.thestandard.com.

"World Agriculture Supply and Demand Estimates." *Bloomberg News,* 8 March 2002.

"World Growth at Less than 2 Percent Per Year." *International Egg Commission Newsletter,* April 2003. Available from www.internationalegg.com.

SIC 0182, 0273

AQUACULTURE

NAICS CODE(S)

111411, 112511. Unlike fisheries, which capture wild fish from open waters, the global aquaculture industry cultivates plants and animals in fresh water and salt water under a controlled environment in which producers can regulate reproduction, feeding, and climate.

INDUSTRY SNAPSHOT

Aquaculture began in ancient China, Rome, and Egypt. Since the 1970s modern aquaculture as an industry flourished throughout the world, particularly in inland nations. According to the United Nations Food and Agriculture Organization (FAO), world aquacultural production has grown by an average of 8.9 percent annually since 1970, more than any other animal-food producing sectors. In the mid-years of the first decade of the twenty-first century, the aquaculture industry enjoyed substantial global output increases, in part due to increasing dependence on fish by residents of China and also in large part because fishery waters in many parts of the world reached the limits of exploitation. Long-term predictions by the FAO pointed to the aquaculture industry as a significant economic player in world markets as an employer and producer of revenue. Most of the overall increase in world fishery production through 2010, the FAO said, would come from the rapid growth of aquaculture.

The raising of aquatic plants such as seaweed and animals such as fish and crustacea, particularly shrimp, continued to be dominated by Asian enterprises, but aggressive development of aquaculture production by other areas, and China's marketing strategy to raise more higher-value fish (reducing the higher tonnage of lower-value fish) slightly reduced that continent's share of the world market. However, Asia continued to dominate world aquaculture, with China being the dominant country by far. In 2006 China' total aquaculture production reached 52.5 million metric tons (mmt).

In spite of its rising importance in world markets, the aquaculture industry found itself coming under intense fire and scrutiny as environmental groups demanded stricter controls to protect wild fish species that could be lost due to intermingling with similar aquaculture species. In particular, the industry was being asked to demonstrate accountability as it increasingly cultivated genetically altered fish food species with an extra gene, which greatly increased the length and size of fish in shorter and shorter time periods. Environmentalists stressed the need for fish producers to produce sterile, single-sex fish used for consumption purposes only. Such polyploid aquatic animals have more chromosome sets than sexually normal fish, making them unable to produce and thereby saving their energy for growing meatier. In addition, scientific research published in 2004 found significantly higher levels of dioxins, PCBs, and other environmental carcinogens in farm-raised salmon than were found in captured fish, leading some specialists to recommend limiting intake of contaminated fish. Others, though, believed the risk was overstated.

Nonetheless, a number of experts at the Kyoto Conference predicted in their formal presentations that aquaculture production would increase significantly in spite of protests by some commercial fisheries and environmentalists. In the year 2010, industry experts predicted, aquaculture production might harvest 47 million tons of fish and seaweed, with about 33 million tons of fish and crustacea intended for food use.

A study in *Proceedings of the National Academy of Sciences* discussed dynamics related to aquaculture's significance, according to Natasha Real. It was a major finding that the industry was "set to reach a landmark in 2009, supplying half of the total fish and shellfish for human consumption." Real acknowledged farmed fish production had an increase in volume adding up to triple the approximate amount between 1995 and 2007.

ORGANIZATION AND STRUCTURE

Production Types and Methods. Aquaculture serves six primary functions: food, bait, aquarium stock, fee-fishing stock, biological supply, and lake stock. Food aquaculture was by far the leading form and included the fresh-water, brackish-water, and marine-water production of species such as catfish, shrimp, bass, trout, salmon, and tilapia. Characterized by many small operations, bait aquaculture raised minnows, suckers, goldfish, and crayfish for use as fishing bait. Limited mostly to warmer climates, aquarium aquaculture produced fresh-water and marine fish, such as guppies, gouramis, cichlids, clown fish, trigger fish, and goldfish, and plants used for aquariums. Featuring small, well-stocked ponds, fee-fishing aquaculture operations offered facilities primarily to sport fishers who paid to catch fish such as trout and catfish from stocked ponds or reservoirs. Some fee-fishing organizations functioned like hunting clubs, allowing members to fish as part of a membership, while others charged daily or hourly rates. Biological supply houses raised a host of aquatic organisms such as turtles, mollusks, and shrimp for research and educational purposes. Finally, lake-stocking aquaculture raised fish to replenish city and county lakes, and these operations produced bass, trout, walleye, and blue fish.

When raising fish and growing aquatic plants, producers must monitor the water quality constantly to ensure a successful harvest. Producers pay special attention to the water's temperature, since fish are cold blooded and their body temperatures conform to their environment. Different species of fish require different temperatures of water, yielding the classification of fish as cold water (which thrive in 48- to 60-degree water); cool water (which thrive in 55- to 75-degree water); and warm water (which thrive in 70- to 85-degree water). Other concerns are the water's alkaline (or acid) pH, ammonia contamination, and dissolved oxygen levels, as well as its mineral content and other chemical characteristics, such as chlorine if tap water is introduced. Suffocation of fish due to overcrowding or poor aeration, bacterial and parasitical infections, and diseases related to high quantities of fish excrement are problems that lead to unintended fish mortality and cause critics of the industry to call for reforms to institute more humane fish farming methods.

Producers use four general kinds of facilities for aquaculture: ponds, cages, raceways, and recirculating systems. Ponds include existing small bodies of water infused with aquaculture fish and plants as well as ponds specially designed for aquaculture. These can range in size from a quarter of an acre to more than 20 acres. To take advantage of existing bodies of water, producers also use cages to raise fish. The cages contain the fish but allow water to pass through; they come in rectangular, square, and round varieties ranging from four to eight feet in width and height. Raceways function largely as facilities for raising trout, and producers position them on slightly sloped areas of land, allowing the water to run down the raceways. Water re-circulating systems usually are indoor vats set up in a similar way to aquariums with a filtration and circulation system.

Industry analysts also distinguish between freshwater and marine aquaculture. In the mid-1990s, freshwater production dominated the industry, accounting for more than 65 percent of the world's total aquaculture harvest in 1995. However, some observers expected marine aquaculture—or mariculture—to continue to expand in subsequent years, as it did in the late 1990s, especially because 40 percent of the leading seafood species were caught faster than they could reproduce, according to the National Marine Fisheries Service. Although a number of countries farm fish along their coasts, maricultural technology allowed producers to cultivate fish further out in the ocean. Mariculturists placed large cages in the ocean and filled them with young fish and food. They then waited for the fish to mature and then harvested them. Leading species of fish for mariculture included red drum, red snapper, striped bass, and mahi mahi.

Contrary to claims otherwise, fish feed industry insiders said their industry is sustainable. Stanford University professor Rosamond Naylor had an article published in proceedings of the National Academy of Sciences that caused the controversy due to expressed beliefs that "growing demand for fish oil and fishmeal is ravaging fish stocks due to companies harvesting marine resources unstainably." Furthermore, Naylor called for stricter regulations in reduction of fish oil usage in aquaculture to "forment sustainable production of the prized product." The Global Organization for EPA and DHA Omega-3s Executive Director Adam Ismail countered that fish oil use in feed did not experience a major increase.

According to a Stanford University study, "aquaculture has grown to become the source for 50 percent of the fish consumed globally." An international team of researchers determined the industry was negatively impacting marine resources due to using substantial amounts of feed with wild fish harvested from the sea as a key ingredient. In 2006, it was estimated that approximately 20 million metric tons of wild fish were harvested for fishmeal production. "It can take up to five pounds of wild fish to produce one pound of salmon, and we eat a lot of salmon," explained lead research study author and professor of environmental earth system science at Stanford University and director of the Stanford Program on Food Security and the Environment Rosamond L. Naylor. Other options were cited, including reducing fishmeal use by following the lead of vegetarian fish farms and using plants for fish feed substitution or supplementation.

Trade Organizations. The World Aquaculture Society (WAS) advanced aquaculturists' education and the development of new techniques to make aquaculture a sustainable and profitable enterprise worldwide. With chapters in Japan, Southeast Asia, the United States, and Latin America, WAS provided technical information, research, and a forum for the enhancement of aquaculture. In addition, WAS worked with governments and industries to promote the ongoing success of aquaculture through legislation, agreements, and alliances.

Europe had its own support organization, the European Aquaculture Society (EAS). Founded in 1976, EAS members worked to improve aquaculture research, farming, education, promotion, and processing. EAS was based in Belgium and facilitated contact and information exchange between aquaculturists around the world.

In the United States, the National Aquaculture Association was the main aquaculture organization that looked out for the interests of members and served as an information source and ethical voice for environmental responsibility. In addition, other support organizations for aquaculture professionals in the United States tended to be active at the state level, such as the California Aquaculture Association and the Wisconsin Aquaculture Association. Other U.S. organizations tended to be grouped by specific fish species, such as the U.S. Trout Farmers Association.

BACKGROUND AND DEVELOPMENT

Some historians cite ancient manuscripts as proof that a form of freshwater aquaculture, the raising of carp, first was practiced in China between 3,100 and 4,000 thousand years ago. In addition, a primitive form of mariculture in China dates back about 2,000 years. China's reliance on aquaculture increased over the centuries so that in the twentieth century, China raised more fish than it caught via conventional means. Elsewhere in Asia, such as in India, Japan, and Indonesia, aquaculture expanded as well, becoming a significant source of food fish. These regions raised common carp in ponds. The ancient Romans also practiced a limited form of aquaculture raising oysters in ponds for gourmet appetites. Many European nations began practicing aquaculture in the Middle Ages and expanded the practice to include the scientific study of spawning, habitat, and feeding. In 1833, German aquaculturists developed methods for artificial fertilization of trout eggs and the raising of these fish under ideal conditions.

Aquaculture grew into a vital component of developing economies where low-cost seafood could be raised and harvested efficiently to help feed populations. Moreover, these countries began to rely on the proceeds of high-value seafood such as shrimp and prawns, which they could export for high profit.

The United States did not practice aquaculture until the mid- to late nineteenth century, when brood fish and fingerlings were first cultivated in small-scale operations. However, after the 1960s the United States began to raise fish other than trout and bait. Early U.S. endeavors were plagued by inexperienced aquaculturists, inadequate ponds, fish illnesses, and insufficient technology, which prevented expansion into other kinds of fish production. Starting in the late 1950s, catfish became a favorite of U.S. producers, especially in the South. Proof of aquaculture's twentieth-century origins in the United States is the fact that catfish production area increased from only 400 acres in 1960 to 161,000 acres by 1991 and 185,700 acres at the start of 2002, according to the United States Department of Agriculture (USDA). The leading U.S. catfish producers were Mississippi, Alabama, Arkansas, and Louisiana.

Aquaculture was one of the most rapidly growing sectors of food production at the beginning of the twenty-first century. Through the 1990s and the early years of the first decade of the 2000s, aquaculture output grew steadily. From 1990 to 1995, the total food output nearly doubled from 12.41 million metric tons (mmt) to 20.94 mmt. Continued growth was expected through 2010, with the FAO estimating outputs by that year of between 27 and 39 million tons. While global capture fishing rates remained relatively stable after 1995, aquaculture fishing increased. In 2002, world aquaculture production (including plants) totaled 51.4 million tons, an increase of 6.1 percent from 2000. In 1995 the world's aquaculture output, including seafood, aquatic plants, and ornamental fish, climbed to US$44.7 billion in value. In 1999 that figure rose to US$53.6 billion, and by 2002 it had grown to US$60 billion, 2.9 percent higher than in 2000. China was the leader in aquaculture production.

Trade regulations affected the aquaculture industry at the beginning of the twenty-first century. In 2004, according to an *Agence France* report, the International Trade Commission ruled that shrimp from Vietnam and other developing countries was being dumped in the United States, clearing the way for the U.S. Department of Commerce to impose tariffs later that year. U.S. shrimp farmers claimed that dumping by foreign competitors caused the value of U.S.-harvested shrimp to drop from US$1.25 billion in 2000 to only US$559 million in 2002.

With the appropriate technology, certain kinds of aquaculture can be practiced in any climate, and producers can raise fish in regions that cannot sustain crops. Leading aquaculture producers were developing countries with limited or over-exploited natural resources and large populations such as China, India, and Bangladesh. Because these countries obtained significant portions of their seafood from aquaculture, the natural fish supply in these areas was able to regenerate. At the same time, however, the environmental impact of aquaculture in these regions has raised increasing concern. Shrimp farming, for example, has resulted in the destruction of more than 50 percent of the world's mangrove forests, an ecosystem that offers natural protection from storms. When a devastating tsunami hit south Asia in December 2004, thousands of lives were lost and extensive tracts of cropland were destroyed. The impact would have been far less, according to a report on Indiatogether.org, if not for the negative impact on the shrimp farming industry.

As the world's population continued to increase and the global natural fish supply decreased due to over-exploitation, aquaculture constituted one method available to food producers to avoid shortages or depletion of certain popular species. The issue had some urgency, as a *Wall Street Journal* article highlighted, because fertility rates combined with agricultural production levels could lead to heightened world starvation by 2025.

However, the increasing availability of low-cost grain coupled with aquaculture expansion could help avert this worst-case scenario. Governments and institutions battling world hunger are hoping the twenty-first century will see more traditionally impoverished countries become producers of food protein with steadily increasing home-based aquaculture. One notable holdout was the continent of Africa, which had yet to begin large-scale aquaculture practices, although many of its nations had the coastline or inland waters essential to developing an aquaculture industry as, for example, India had done. The U.S. Agency for International Development committed assistance to help Tanzania, an African nation whose government expressed strong interest in adding aquaculture to its agricultural practices.

CURRENT CONDITIONS

The aquaculture industry saw tremendous growth from the mid-twentieth century to the early twenty-first century. By 2004, almost 60 million tons of product resulted from aquaculture worldwide, with a U.S. value of US$70.3 billion. Almost 70 percent of that total came from China, whereas about 22 percent originated from other Asia-Pacific countries. Other regions contributed also, with the least coming from Sub-Saharan Africa, although the region had natural potential, including the fact that tilapia was native to the continent.

Whereas wild catch in the oceans had dominated the world fisheries industry for decades, aquaculture was expected to increase worldwide throughout the mid- to late years of the first decade of the 2000s, according to the USDA. Reasons for this growth were a growing demand for seafood and the over-fishing of oceans. The most common fish grown in aquaculture environments worldwide as of 2007 were carp, oysters, clams, mussels, salmon, shrimp, and tilapia.

According to Luna Finnson in an August 2009 article in *IceNews*, the Memorandum of Understanding was signed by Norway and Sweden in 2009 in an effort to end their trade disputes and try to work collaboratively. Collaborative areas were projected to include exchange of experience on regulations, working together on research, providing joint access to insurance and finance, and tackling the issues of environmental sustainability. Teams representing each country were set to hold their first meeting in Scotland in 2010.

MAJOR COUNTRIES IN THE INDUSTRY

China. When it comes to being a solid leader, China has maintained its status in the aquaculture industry since 1989. Government data claims China provides 70 percent of total seafood products output for the world. In 1990, China earned distinction as the "first country in the world with a higher farmed fish output than wild fish output," noted Denise Recalde, writer and editor for Fish Information and Services (FIS), an online daily fishing, seafood, and aquaculture news site.

In 2006, China produced 52.5 mmt of aquaculture products, continuing a trend of yearly increases. The increase in production is attributed to the country's rapid economic growth, rising disposable incomes, and greater consumption of aquatic products. According to the 11th Five-Year Plan for Fishery Development (2006-2010) released by China's Ministry of Agriculture, total aquatic production is expected to increase by more than 3 percent annually to reach 60 mmt by 2010.

China's government paid little attention to aquaculture until the mid-1990s, emphasizing grain production. In the mid-1990s it began to implement measures to increase aquaculture production and stability by offering marketing and infrastructure support, as well as tax exemptions to new aquaculturists.

China's aquaculture industry has consisted of two key sectors: producers who cultivate inexpensive products for the local market, and companies and joint ventures that produce high-value products for the country's higher income consumers. Aquaculture production in the late 1990s increasingly began harvesting higher-value fish and shellfish. By the early years of the first decade of the 2000s, China had introduced more than 30 high-value species for freshwater cultivation.

In 1995, China devoted 4.6 million hectares of water to inland aquaculture and 653,500 hectares to marine aquaculture. By 2005, the total aquaculture area in China was 7.5 million hectares, including 5.85 million hectares of inland areas. There were 9,128 aquatic processing facilities in 2005, 383 more than the previous year. China's primary inland products were common carp, cyprinus, grass carp, bighead carp, silver carp, mud carp, and gold carp. Marine aquaculture in China centered primarily on shrimp, oysters, clams, seaweed, scallops, mussels, and other shellfish.

China's aquaculture industry faced several challenges in the mid-years of the first decade of the 2000s, including an increase in the rate of aquatic diseases, low technical innovation by the industry, and water utilization inefficiency. Despite these issues, the aquaculture industry in China was expected to continue to grow, especially in regard to exports. Aquatic exports, the largest category in all agriculture exports in China, reached US$7.2 billion in 2005. The largest importer of Chinese aquaculture products was Japan, followed by the United States.

After August 2009 floods, Pingtung County's aquacultural sector was given the opportunity to acquire low-interest loans from the Chinese government. Loan amounts varied depending on type of fish being farmed as determined by the Council of Agriculture. Loan terms included repayment in seven years with 1 percent interest. The Council claimed that its goal was "to help them so that their production will return to the current levels by 2012 and double by 2015."

India. India remained a leading aquaculture producer, with an output of 2.1 mmt (excluding aquatic plants) in 2002. Although carp, a freshwater species, accounted for 80 percent of cultivated fish in 1999, intensive shrimp farming grew in importance since the late 1990s. By the early years of the first decade of the 2000s, according to the United Nations Food and Agriculture Organization (FAO), shrimp farming in India employed about 200,000 people and generated about 1.6 percent of the value of India's export economy.

Although India's aquaculture industry achieved great success in the earlier part of the decade, it underwent intense government scrutiny of widespread misuse of chemicals, other environmental degradation, and wholesale fish losses. The future of the country's aquaculture industry depended on whether the government could convert the country's fish farms into a sustainable enterprise. Both the public and the private sectors initiated programs to exploit brackish-water aquaculture, especially in shrimp production.

Indonesia. Indonesia produced 5.11 million tons of fish and seafood products in 2003, up 5.2 percent from the previous year. Freshwater aquaculture was dominated by carp, catfish, tilapia, and others. A major concern for the near future was the lack of fry (hatchlings) for stocking freshwater areas. It might be necessary to increase investment in hatcheries to protect species from depletion.

In September 2009, Fish Information & Services (FIS) reported that the Philippines' Mindanao Economic Development Council issued a statement announcing that the Philippines and Brunei Darussalam would jointly build and operate a fish production and processing house at Maura Port in the latter aforementioned country. According to *Business World Online* the targeted completion date was May 2010. Plans called for four countries to unite and assume leadership for areas identified as small pelagic fish (Brunei), tuna production (Indonesia), high-value aquaculture (Malaysia), and seaweed (the Philippines).

Japan. Although Japan was fourth in the world for aquaculture products in the early years of the first decade of the 2000s, by 2007 production had fallen to 5.72 mmt and was expected to continue a downward trend. While other leading aquaculture producers concentrated primarily on freshwater production, in Japan, where inland waters were narrow, mariculture dominated. However, total inland water fishing and culture decreased by 10,000 metric tons, or 9.6 percent, in 2005. Some of the reasons for the decrease in aquaculture production in Japan were economic; other factors included the trend of young people to move away from agricultural areas to urban areas. In 2006 most male workers in the fishery industry were over 60 years old. Major mariculture products included seaweeds, oysters, scallops, yellowtail, and seabream. Inland fisheries primarily produced eels, carp, trout, and ayu sweetfish.

Thailand. Aquaculture in Thailand quadrupled from the 1980s through the 1990s, and placed the country as the fifth-largest aquaculture producer in 2001 when its output of aquaculture fish reached 742,000 tons. In 2002, however, fish output declined to 644,890 tons, placing Thailand in sixth place behind Bangladesh. The Thai government launched several programs to promote pond aquaculture in rural areas and to increase environmentally sound methods of shrimp production. Thailand remained the largest supplier of shrimp to the United States, with a value averaging about US$2.5 billion in 2003.

Vietnam. Vietnam made aquaculture a dominant industry, posting a mere 167,899 tons in 1992, compared to 518,500 tons by 2002. Inland waters, including the productive Mekong River, were intensively cultivated. About 75 percent of Vietnam's aquaculture production in the late 1990s came from various types of carp, with the remainder from catfish. By the middle of the first decade of the 2000s, Vietnam was also a major supplier of shrimp. The expansion of brackish-water culture, which began in the 1990s, was expected to continue.

VOV News, an online Vietnamese news site, broke the story about an outstanding increase for world demand related to tra fish. Projections called for exported volume to be 450,000 tonnes (metric tons, French) earning an amount adding up to US $900 million. Expectations included predicting Russia's dominance as a major importer would be made prevalent by importing approximately 40,000 tonnes in the fourth quarter and doubling its third quarter 2009 import total.

Chile. Chile, with aquacultural production (excluding plants) totaling only 86,442 tons in 1993, increased its output dramatically through the late 1990s. Production leaped from 391,587 tons in 2000 to 566,096 tons in 2001. The main fishery exports in the mid-years of the first decade of the 2000s were salmon and trout, valued at US$1.72 billion in 2005. More than 74 percent of the salmon exported went to Japan, Brazil, and the United States.

The United States. The United States dropped from its fifth-place ranking in aquaculture production in 1995 to tenth in the world in 2001. It remained in this position in 2002, with a harvest of 497,346 tons of fish and 47,183 tons of plants. The United States produced via aquaculture large amounts of several fish species, including catfish, trout, tilapia, crawfish, and ornamental fish. One reason for the decline was that the U.S. government and environmentalists spread awareness about the need for more environmentally friendly management methods. Though cultivated fish production in 2001 increased slightly from the previous year, reaching a total of 460,998 mmt, this amount remained below the 1999 harvest of 478,679 mmt. Despite relatively flat production, the value of U.S. aquaculture products increased from US$45 million in 1974 to more than US$978 million by 1998. The U.S. Department of Commerce's aquaculture policy for the early years of the first decade of the 2000s included initiatives that would significantly boost production and value of aquacultural production.

According to the U.S. Department of Agriculture (USDA), consumption of seafood in the United States will increase from its 2006 rate of 12 billion pounds of fish a year to 16.4 billion pounds by 2025. It is estimated that 50 percent of the U.S. seafood supply will come from aquaculture by 2020. In the middle of the first decade of the 2000s, about 70 percent of the seafood consumed in the United States was imported and at least 40 percent of that total was farm-raised.

The leading and most successful aquacultural product in the United States is catfish. Between 1990 and 1996, catfish production rose by over 30 percent. By 2005, the United States produced 638.4 million pounds of catfish worth US$449.9 million. Leading U.S. aquaculture states were Mississippi, Alabama, Arkansas, and Louisiana.

According to the USDA, 59.7 million pounds of trout, valued at US$62.6 million, were sold in 2005. The value of U.S. trout exports, which had reached US$1.2 million in 1999, fell to only US$1.5 million in 2000. Lower sales to Canada and Japan accounted for much of this decline. Although sales climbed dramatically in 2003, the following year, dramatically reduced shipments to Japan again lowered the total value of U.S. trout sales, which reached only US$2 million. Idaho, with approximately 75 percent of production, led the country, followed by North Carolina and California.

The United States consumed nearly 100 million pounds of tilapia per year, but the country itself only produced about 15 to 20 million pounds. Hence, the United States imported large quantities of tilapia from countries such as Taiwan and Costa Rica. Nonetheless, tilapia constituted one of the country's leading aquaculture products.

Crawfish production fell in the 1990s after reaching 71 million pounds in 1990. In 1996 production reached only 44.4 million pounds, down 20 percent from 1995, yet it was more than twice as much as the wild harvest, according to the USDA. After reaching 49 million pounds in 1997, crawfish production plummeted to 17 million pounds in 2000. However, the product's value, at US$28 million, remained unchanged from the previous year, when production reached 43 million pounds. Louisiana was by far the leading crawfish producing state. In 2003 the value of its farm-raised crawfish reached approximately US$47 million.

The United States also excelled in ornamental fish production. While production levels remained relatively flat through the 1990s and the early years of the first decade of the 2000s, value increased dramatically. The National Marine Fisheries Service estimated that the value of U.S. miscellaneous fish (including ornamentals) rose from US$75 million in 1995 to US$141 million in 2000. Production levels, which reached 23 million pounds in 1997, rose slightly to 26 million pounds in 2000. Ornamental fish alone, according to an Aquafeed industry report, accounted for U.S. exports worth US$5.1 million in the first half of 2004, a 16 percent increase from the same period in 2003. Canada is the largest market for U.S. ornamental fish exports.

Hubbs-SeaWorld Research Institute President Don Kent discussed criticism of plans related to the Institute's building and launch of "the largest offshore commercial fish farm in U.S. federal waters." The project vision was to have "a network of 24 fish-rearing pens or 'gravity cages' approximately five miles offshore of Mission Beach in water 100 to 300 feet deep." feeding striped bass fingerlings in the beginning and other species later. An ambitious goal aims to produce up to 6 million pounds of fish annually. This would exceed what San Diego County commercial fishermen brought in to docks three times over. Debate among industry insiders reflected the lack of 'real data' concluded the state aquaculture coordinator for the State Department of Fish and Game for California. Kent needed some private investors to cover first phase costs estimated to be approximately US$15 million. "We're breaking new ground, not only in the application of this technology for our nation, but in educating the resource agencies in permitting the technologies," Kent explained.

BIBLIOGRAPHY

Agence France Presse, 18 February 2004. Available from www. enaca.org.

Finnson, Laura. "Norway and Scotland Team up on Aquaculture." *IceNews*, 31 August 2009. Available from www.icenews.is.

Goodhue, David. "Half Of All Fish Consumed Now Come From Farms." *All Headline News*, 8 September 2009. Available from www. allheadlinenews.com.

Jain, Shubhanyu. "Promise of Plenty: MPEDA Steps Up Effort to Put India on the Global Seafood Map." *Seafood Business*, March 2007.

"Low-interest loans to be expanded for aquaculture." *China Post*, 31 August 2009. Available from www.chinapost.com.

Real, Natasha. "Aquaculture's rapid growth poses new challenges." 9 September 2009. Available from www.fis.com.

———. "Fish feed industry refutes unsustainability accusation." Fish & Info Services Ltd., 11 September 2009. Available from www. fis.com.

Recalde, Denise. "Chinese aquaculture leads world." Fish & Info Services Ltd., 23 August 2009. Available from www.fis.com.

———. "Fish facility borne out of bilateral." Fish & Info Services Ltd., 15 September 2009. Available from www.fis.com.

Rodgers, Terry. "Fish farm in the works." *La Jolla Light*, 10 September 2009. Available from www.lajollalight.com.

"Shrimp Media Monitoring, 2004." Network of Aquacultural Centres in Asia-Pacific. Available from www.enaca.org.

"Soy and Aquaculture." *Southwest Farm Press*, 12 March 2007.

"Stanford Study: Half of the fish consumed globally is now raised on farms." 14 September 2009. Available from media-newswire.com.

"Tsunami, Mangroves, and Market Economy." *India Together* January 2005. Available from www.indiatogether.org.

U.S. Census Bureau. "U.S. Private Aquaculture: Trout and Catfish Production and Value: 1998 to 2005," 20 March 2007. Available from www.census.gov.

U.S. Department of Agriculture, Foreign Agricultural Service. *Value of U.S. Exports of Trout, by Country, 1999–2004.* Available from fas.usda.gov.

————. "Chile Fishery Products Annual, 2006." *GAIN Report*, 22 September 2006. Available from fas.usda.gov.

————. "China Fishery Products Annual, 2006." *GAIN Report*, 31 December 2006. Available from fas.usda.gov.

————. "Indonesia Product Brief, Fish and Seafood, 2005." *GAIN Report*, 19 May 2005. Available from fas.usda.gov.

————. "Japan Fishery Products Annual Report 2006." *GAIN Report*, 4 October 2006. Available from fas.usda.gov.

————. "State of World Aquaculture," 2 April 2007. Available from fas.usda.gov.

————. "U.S. Seafood Imports Continue to Soar." *International Trade Report*, 8 July 2005. Available from fas.usda.gov.

"U.S. Seafood Consumption Losing Share to Meat; Growth Has to Come from Imports." *Aquafeed*, 8 October 2004. Available from www.aquafeed.com.

Vannuccini, Stefania. *Overview of Fish Production, Utilization, Consumption, and Trade*, May 2003. Available from www.fao.org/.

VOVNews. "Tra fish exports increase sharply." *VOV News*, 13 September 2009. Available from http://english.vovnews.vn.

Wright, James. "Task Force Calls for Responsible Aquaculture." *Seafood Business*, February 2007.

SIC 0910

FISHING, COMMERCIAL

NAICS CODE(S)

1141. This industry includes commercial harvesters of finfish, shellfish, and miscellaneous marine products from open waters, as opposed to aquaculture, which harvests fish from captive waters. For discussion of fish production from controlled habitats see **Aquaculture.**

INDUSTRY SNAPSHOT

Global fishery production between 1950 and 2004 increased from an estimated 20 million metric tons (mmt) to 90 mmt, with a record high of 95.6 mmt in 2000, according to the Food and Agriculture Organization (FAO) of the United Nations statistics. During this period, the number of participants in the industry also grew rapidly. As a result, more fishermen were attempting to catch fewer fish as fish stocks declined. Consequently, commercial fishing experienced accelerated competition from aquaculture fish farming because of greater control over fish production and because

of strained natural resources. By the middle of the first decade of the twenty-first century, major fishing countries such as China, Peru, and Chile were posting declines in total catches, while less developed fishing industries, such as in Morocco and South Africa, saw significant increases in production.

Two ocean regions play the largest roles in the commercial fishing industry. The world's three most productive areas, according to statistics compiled by the FAO, were the Pacific Northwest, the Pacific Southeast, and the Atlantic Northeast. These areas have large continental shelves with the ability to support substantial stocks of important fish species. After 1971, the Pacific Northwest was the most productive region for commercial fishing. The amount of fish caught in this region in 2000, according to FAO statistics, was 23 mmt, double the amount harvested there in the 1970s. The North Atlantic region and Pacific Southeast were also major fishing sites. In addition to their topography, the social conditions in the bordering coastal nations contributed to the development of robust fishing industries in the Northwest Pacific and North Atlantic. Japan, the Russian Federation, China, and South Korea were in close proximity to the Northwest Pacific. Norway, Denmark, Iceland, Canada, and the United States border the North Atlantic. Other major fishing regions were located in the Southeast Pacific, West Central Pacific, and inland Asia.

As a result of years of unrestrained fishing, the number of fish available began to shrink drastically in the 1990s as fisheries caught fish faster than they could reproduce. In particular, the number of ground fish (including black cod, ocean perch, lingcod, and Dover sole) plummeted in the 1990s. Furthermore, the FAO reported that companies had overfished two-thirds of the world's most popular marine species, including lobster, prawns, cod, and snapper. In response, national governments and the international community developed policies to make the industry sustainable. In order to meet the international demand for seafood, many of the leading seafood-producing countries started to promote aquaculture with government subsidies. Asia, the leading aquaculture region, achieved considerable success with the transition from catching to raising fish. Other countries, such as the United States, France, Peru, Chile, and Canada, also increased their aquaculture industries in response to dwindling wild fish stocks.

FAO studies concluded that the outlook for the global commercial fishing industry depended on the remedial measures taken to improve overfished regions. If fisheries could manage their production in a sustainable manner that allowed species to reproduce faster than they are caught, then the fishing industry was expected to have a chance to produce 105 million metric tons by 2010. However, if the global industry failed to improve fishing conditions worldwide, then the industry's output might drop to 80 million metric tons. Therefore, the commercial fishing industry could only expect slight growth at best through 2010, as aquaculture would most likely play a greater role in the world's overall fish output. In the twenty-first century, according to the FAO, it would be increasingly important to pay attention to the replacement of inadequate fleets, particularly in artisan waters, where post-harvest losses could total 20 to 50 percent of the annual catch. The fleets were expected to provide equipment to retard spoilage and to keep the catch fresh until brought to shore for processing and consumption.

While it was clear that some 30 percent of all popular food fishes in the sea were threatened and that at least some would never recover, the industry was expected to rebound as wasted catches were eliminated and stricter management controls were enforced by the seafood industry. "The demise of the fish industry has been proclaimed more than once, but in all likelihood, in 50 years our grandchildren will still be making a living from the sea and feeding an increasingly hungry world," according to the *National Fisherman*. However, should the industry tarry too long and allow the seas to be overfished by the unscrupulous, "the ocean's bounteous fisheries may become a distant memory," cautioned *Business Week*.

The National Oceanic and Atmospheric Administration announced the January 1, 2010, launch of its catch/share program for commercial group and title fish fisheries in the Gulf of Mexico. Major program goals include reducing overcapacity and improving profitability as well as working conditions for fisherman. Current practices meant fisheries were "managed by annual quotas and trip limits" spurring them to race ahead in unsafe conditions. The program will adapt one created for red snapper in the Gulf of Mexico in 2007, where, According to Roy Crabtree, Southeast administrator for the agency's fisheries service, red snapper industry conditions had "substanially improved." An additional benefit was that the program supported moving toward "ecosystem-based management" uniting all principal stakeholders.

In September 2009 RedOrbit, a Web site providing news and information about science, space, health, and technology, announced that approximately 91 nations throughout the world made a pact related to sea vessels. The nations agreed to sign a United Nations treaty that prevented vessels involved in illegal fishing trade from entering ports. Major countries vowing support included the United States, the European Union, Japan, Russia, and Brazil.

ORGANIZATION AND STRUCTURE

Traditionally, fishing was practiced by independent fishermen, often operating family-owned boats and fishing in the waters where their ancestors had fished. These fishermen operated under the control of fishing associations, local authorities, national governments, and regional treaties. When the industry became mechanized, larger corporate-owned vessels sailed to more distant waters. As a result, commercial fisheries came under the supervision of conventions, which existed by treaty, governing specific areas of the seas. One of the first conventions to be created was the Inter-American Tropical Tuna Commission (IATCC), established by treaty in 1949 for the purpose of studying tuna and tuna-like species in the eastern Pacific. The commission's first task was to make recommendations regarding efficient use of the Pacific's tuna resources.

The North Atlantic Fisheries Organization (NAFO), established in 1979, was given the task of governing fishing in the international waters of the northwest Atlantic. Contracting parties to the NAFO treaty included Bulgaria, Canada, Cuba, Denmark (in respect to the Faroe Islands and Greenland), Estonia, the European Community, Iceland, Latvia, Lithuania, Norway, Poland, Romania, the Russian Federation, and South Korea. One of NAFO's responsibilities was to protect overfished species, such as cod and flatfish, from exploitation. To preserve sustainable fish stocks, NAFO established and allocated catch quotas.

The South Pacific Forum Fisheries Agency (FFA), also established in 1979, was created to help increase cooperation among those fishing in the South Pacific, primarily for tuna. The FFA Convention was comprised of 16 independent member nations: Australia, the Cook Islands, the Federated States of Micronesia, Fiji, Kiribati, the Marshall Islands, Nauru, New Zealand, Niue, Palau, Papua New Guinea, the Solomon Islands, Tonga, Tuvalu, Vanuatu, and Western Samoa. The FFA provided its members with help in establishing fisheries policies, developing a system of licensing, and monitoring the activities of distant water fleets.

The Northeast Atlantic Fisheries Commission (NEAFC) was established in 1982. Its origins, however, extend to 1946 when the Convention for the Regulation of Meshes of Fishing Nets and the Size Limits of Fish was established. NEAFC membership included Cuba, Denmark (in respect to the Faroe Islands and Greenland), the European Community, Iceland, Norway, Poland, and Russia. The commission's responsibilities included conservation and ensuring optimum utilization of fishery resources within its jurisdiction, which included parts of the Atlantic and Arctic Oceans and the Baltic and Mediterranean Seas. Specific regulations governed types of permitted fishing gear, mesh sizes, fish size limits, area closures, fishing seasons, and catch quotas. Non-member nations operating within its territory included Belize, the Cayman Islands, Honduras, Panama, Sierra Leone, St. Vincent and the Grenadines, the United States, and Venezuela.

The European Community (subsequently known as the European Union) instituted its Common Fisheries Policy (CFP) in 1983. CFP governed access to fishing grounds, set catch limits, restricted time spent at sea, determined the number and type of vessels authorized to fish in certain areas, established the type of fishing gear able to be used, set minimum sizes, and created incentives to reduce by-catch losses. In January 1995, a licensing policy was created requiring that all boats operating in EC waters be licensed.

The Pacific Salmon Commission (PSC), formed as a result of the Pacific Salmon Treaty between the United States and Canada, was signed in 1985. The PSC was created to provide recommendations and advice regarding catches of migratory salmon in western U.S. and Canadian waters. The commissioners represented the interests of commercial fishermen as well as the interests of tribal governments and recreational fishermen.

Many other organizations operate to monitor fishery activities. For example, the International Baltic Sea Fishery Commission, with eight contracting parties—Estonia, the European Community (subsequently known as the European Union), Finland, Latvia, Lithuania, Poland, the Russian Federation, and Sweden—governed operations in the Baltic Sea. The Commission for the Conservation of Antarctic Marine Living Resources was initiated in 1982. It served to develop policies for the protection of marine life in Antarctica's waters. The North Atlantic Salmon Conservation Organization was established in the early 1980s to protect wild salmon. The Ocean Fisheries Commission monitored the activities of distant water fleets in the western Indian Ocean, and its members included Seychelles, Comoros Islands, Madagascar, and Mauritius.

In 1995, some 28 countries signed the Straddling Fish Stocks and Highly Migratory Fish Stocks Agreement. For years, countries battled over rights to fish that are born in one country's exclusive economic zones (EEZ) but migrate to another country's EEZ, where they are captured. Popular species, such as tuna, marlin, swordfish, sailfish, and frigate mackerel, are all highly migratory fish. The agreement established a set of obligations to replace the previous policy that allowed fishers to catch fish if they were found in their own EEZ—a first-come, first-serve policy. Participants also hoped that the accord would reduce by-catch (the unintentional taking of animals in addition to the targeted species), discards, and pollution, as well as promote fishery management based on scientific research. In addition, the agreement required its signatories to refrain from using any method, or taking any action, that had the possibility of destroying a stock's sustainability, until scientific evidence confidently supported its use.

In 2002, the Interim (which was later renamed International) Scientific Committee for Tuna and Tuna-Like Species in the North Pacific Ocean met in Japan to discuss ways to assure the sustainability of species such as the tuna and swordfish. The committee was made up of Japan, the United States, South Korea, Russia, and Taiwan. Absent from the meetings were China, Canada, and Mexico.

In 2002, the weekly science journal *Nature* challenged FAO figures that reported the world's catch was increasing by 700 million pounds annually. Its findings stated that the number of fish available for harvesting had decreased by about 800 million pounds annually. The news was indeed somber for the 54 million people employed in the fisheries industry, as well as for the industry itself, which might face worldwide collapse in 20 to 30 years. The report also was disturbing for the world, since a collapse of the fisheries industry would mean massive world hunger unless aquaculture industries could step up production far above 2002 totals. It was believed the only way to correct the depletion would be to severely limit the harvesting of fish, an action that might cause world catch totals to drop drastically by 2010, said fisheries expert Dr. Joshua S. Reichert.

BACKGROUND AND DEVELOPMENT

Although fishing is one of the most ancient professions known to mankind, the modern fishing era began in the fifteenth century. The discovery of the Grand Banks, attributed to John Cabot in 1497, led to the development of the cod industry in Labrador-Newfoundland (Canada) and in the New England area (of the subsequently named United States). During the seventeenth century, Atlantic fishery operations expanded to include additional species such as herring, mackerel, and capelin. In the eighteenth century, fishermen first observed a relationship between fish stocks in the North Atlantic and climactic variations. As the century closed, North Atlantic catch totals approached 140,000 tons. A century later, approximately 600,000 tons of fish were harvested from the North Atlantic.

Following World War II, the fishing industry experienced rapid growth. Mechanization and motorization led to increased yields and enabled fishermen to travel to distant waters. As demand for fishery products increased, fishermen looked for ways to improve productivity. Steam trawlers and purse seines—two types of fishing gear that later dominated the industry—were refined. Trawlers operate by pulling a catching device through the water near the bottom to scoop up fish. Purse seines are nets deployed around fish schools that can be closed in a manner similar to a drawstring purse and are retrieved using hydraulic power.

Purse seine fishing enabled catch rates per vessel to double. As a result, during the late 1950s and early 1960s, many bait boats were converted to purse seine vessels. Purse seines proved to be an economical means of providing large volumes of fish for massive canning operations. Purse seining also caused problems, however, because some types of dolphins swam near yellowfin tuna. When purse seiners set their nets around tunas and dolphins, dolphin injuries and drowning escalated. Although purse seines were efficient in catching large quantities of fish, they yielded catches of insufficient quality to meet the demands of fresh markets, such as Japan's sashimi market. To produce better quality fish, longlines were developed. Longlines employed hooked lines of vast lengths that were deployed and retrieved in waters where target fish populations were known to exist.

Other innovations leading to expansion within the fishing industry included the development of refrigeration equipment, factory freezer trawlers, and fish-finding equipment. Fish-finding equipment, using sonar and radar, enabled fishermen to accurately locate fish. The first fish finder was developed by British fisherman Ronald Balls, in 1933. Balls discovered that he could detect fish above the ocean floor using echo-sounding equipment. During the early 1950s, Norwegian whalers were the first fishing vessels to use the technology successfully. They were followed by Iceland's herring seiners, who used the equipment to locate schools of fish that could not be sighted from the surface. Catches increased dramatically. According to a NAFO estimate, annual fish catches in the Northwest Atlantic reached 1 million tons during the 1950s. The 1968 catch was judged to be 4.5 million tons.

In the United States, sensitive fish-finding equipment able to detect even individual fish was developed. Although early units were cumbersome and ill suited for use in a marine environment, by the 1970s they had become easier to use and more popular. As the computer age dawned, color displays enabled fishermen to locate school edges more precisely, and the need for recording paper was eliminated. Further refinements led to miniaturization, improved function, and reduced prices.

During the late 1960s and early 1970s, growing public concern about marine mammals, such as Canadian harp seals, whales, and dolphins, led to the passage of the Marine Mammal Protection Act in the United States in 1972. The act's goal was to reduce injury and mortality among marine mammals by commercial fishing operators. A ban on the importation of commercial fish and fish products taken by means that did not meet U.S. standards was among its provisions.

The ban led to a change in global fish distribution. Prior to its imposition, about 85 percent of the yellowfin tuna harvested from the Eastern Pacific was sold to the United States. By the early 1990s, the amount had dropped to about 10 percent. Following imposed embargoes, fishermen were forced to develop other markets. These included increased consumption by Latin American countries (Mexican consumption underwent a fivefold increase) and a growth in exports to other nations. As exports to other nations increased, surpluses developed, which depressed prices for Eastern Pacific fisheries products.

As Eastern Pacific fishing declined, fishing increased in the Indian Ocean. Seychelles, an island nation north of Mauritius in the Western Indian Ocean, gained independence from the United Kingdom in 1976 and expanded its exclusive economic zone (EEZ) to 200 miles in 1978. During the early 1980s, French tuna fishermen discovered rich tuna resources in the area. To accommodate foreign fishing fleets, the Seychelles government built the necessary infrastructure to provide marine support facilities to purse seiners and longliners from France, Spain, and the Soviet Union. The area within 60 miles of shore, however, was held exclusively for Seychelles fishermen.

Another change in global fishing patterns occurred during the 1970s. Negotiations to draft a new treaty regarding the international law of the sea began in 1973 and created a movement among coastal nations to adopt 200-nautical-mile-exclusive economic zones (EEZs). The EEZs afforded coastal countries an opportunity to protect valuable fishing grounds and regulate the operations of distant water fleets. One important exception to the widespread movement to adopt 200-mile EEZs occurred in the Mediterranean Sea, where such an action would have led to disputes as a result of overlapping zones. Malta, Morocco, and Egypt each instituted exclusive 25-mile zones; other countries adopted zones varying from 6 to 35 miles. The abundant waters of the Mediterranean Sea, with 46,000 kilometers of coastline and a total area of 2.5 million square kilometers, yielded nearly 100 different commercial species of fish and shellfish.

In the Pacific, climatic changes associated with El Niño (an ocean current with cyclical deviations) led to changes in South American fisheries operations. Peruvian anchovy stocks collapsed in 1971 and 1972 and did not begin expanding again until 1977. El Niño again negatively impacted eastern Pacific fisheries during 1982 and 1983, and the problem of reduced fish populations was compounded by high fuel prices. Fishermen responded by diversifying their catch among several species. Because other species responded differently to ocean conditions, catches of small pelagic (in open seas but not close to sea bottom) species became more stable. In 1970, Peruvian anchovies had represented 60 percent of the small pelagic harvest. In 1985 the largest single species taken was the South American sardine. It represented only 27 percent of global small pelagic catch.

While climatic conditions impacted some fisheries, over-exploitation began taking its toll on others. As important fish stocks became depleted, international tensions mounted. The issue of fishing rights was one of the concerns that led to the 1982 war between the United Kingdom and Argentina in the Falkland Islands. Fishing commissions began instituting policies to protect fish populations. In 1983, the European Community identified a restricted region, called the Shetland Box, off the northern coast of Scotland. Because the Shetland Box was known to be an important breeding ground, officials limited access to fishing in the area. In another region, the Norway Pout Box, part of the North Sea, was closed to industrial fishing vessels.

Regulators faced complex challenges in their efforts to make decisions aimed at protecting fish populations. Incomplete knowledge made it difficult to assess fish stocks accurately. Without reliable information about the numbers of fish available, however, projections to determine allowable catch quotas were uncertain. The task was further compounded by the necessity of getting governments to agree. As a result, some catch ceilings were set inappropriately. In addition to problems associated with overfishing, some fisheries experienced degradation as a result of pollution. Runoff from industrial and agricultural lands resulted in contamination of fisheries products by chemicals and pesticides. Areas suffering the greatest impact were located in estuaries and freshwater.

The 1980s also saw a reduction in the dominance of traditional fishing nations. At the beginning of the decade, fleets of developed countries were responsible for 53 percent of the global catch. By 1986, developing nations landed 52 percent of the total worldwide harvest.

According to an estimate made by the United Nation's FAO, 1986 saw a fishery harvest of almost 90 million metric tons, including fish, shellfish, and other aquatic products. The figure represented a 5 percent increase over 1985 and a 25 percent increase since the beginning of the decade. Most of the increase was attributed to the expanding participation of developing nations, particularly those in Asia and Latin America.

The largest single species taken in 1986 was Alaska pollock, representing 7 percent of the global catch. Other major species included Peruvian anchovy (6%), Japanese sardine and South American sardine (at 5%), and capelin, Atlantic cod, Chilean jack mackerel, Chub mackerel, and Atlantic herring (each representing 2%). Between 1983 and 1989, the estimated number of overexploited fishery stocks increased from 23 to 51.

During the early 1990s, the tuna catch in South Pacific waters represented approximately 40 percent of the worldwide annual tuna harvest. Fleets operating in the area were predominately from Japan, the United States, Taiwan, South Korea, and the Philippines. Because of different fish habits, South Pacific tuna does not associate with dolphin in the same way Eastern Pacific yellowfin tuna does. As a result, dolphin mortality was not a major issue for harvesters in the South Pacific. Eastern Pacific tuna, however, continued to represent about 25 percent of the global yellowfin tuna catch. Yielding to pressure from groups concerned with the safety of marine mammals, ten nations agreed to participate in an international program to reduce dolphin mortality associated with tuna fishing without turning to harvest methods that would potentially jeopardize other species such as sharks or sea turtles.

Annual global trade in fish and fish products (including aquaculture) reached US$58.2 billion in 2002, a 5 percent increase from 2002 and a 45 percent increase since 1992. Fish exports, according to the FAO, were an important source of foreign currency for many countries, especially developing nations; in some countries, earnings from fish sales accounted for as much as half of total export revenues. In the early years of the first decade of the 2000s, developing countries had begun to shift the focus of their fishing trade away from exports of raw material (usually destined to be processed in developed countries) and toward higher-value live fish or value-added products.

The world's commercial fisheries pinpointed the collective goal of finding ways to guarantee a protracted supply of fish and shellfish as food resources. According to the FAO, the overall world fish catch including crustaceans and mollusks was estimated at 90.3 million metric tons (mmt) in 2003, down slightly from 93.2 mmt the previous year. A decrease in production among some major fishmeal-producing regions accounted for this decline. Despite the smaller overall catch, however, bigger aquaculture harvests brought the total production of edible fish in 2003 to about 103 mmt, which the FAO determined was enough to meet the average per capita demand. Of the 2003 world capture totals, 81.3 mmt came from ocean waters and 9 mmt came from inland waters.

The most fertile marine fishing grounds in the middle of the first decade of the 2000s remained the northwest and southeast Pacific Oceans. Total catches however, showed a decline since 2000. Eastern central and southwest Atlantic catches also decreased substantially, but production increased in the tropical Pacific and Indian Oceans—a trend that the FAO predicted would continue. Catches in the northeast Atlantic and Mediterranean remained similar to production from previous years, while catches in the northwest Atlantic and the northeast Pacific increased.

The health of the fishing industry is directly related to the abundance of fish in the earth's waters. During the late 1980s and mid-1990s, many important fish stocks were threatened by overfishing. World production in 2000 led the FAO to conclude that about half of marine fish resources were at the very limit of a sustainable yield, about one-quarter of all ocean waters were dangerously depleted, and about another quarter could yield additional annual catches. The FAO's 2004 *State of World Fisheries and Aquaculture* report described an even more dire picture, stating that "the global potential for marine capture fisheries has been reached, and more rigorous plans are needed to rebuild depleted stocks and prevent the decline of those being exploited at or close to their maximum potential." To counter threats of overfishing, governments around the world began to impose restrictions and quotas to help preserve global fish stocks. Scientists also began trying to learn more about El Niño's Southern Oscillation effects, causing temperature changes in the world's waters that resulted in greatly diminished catches for the fisheries.

CURRENT CONDITIONS

China, the leading producer since 1992, continued to dominate production in 2004, with a catch of 16.8 million tons of fish from marine and fresh waters. Peru was second with 9.6 million tons, followed by the United States (4.95 mmt), Chile (4.93 mmt), Indonesia (4.81 mmt), Japan (4.40 mmt), and India (3.6 mmt).

In 2007 the U.S. Congress passed the Magnuson-Stevens Fishery Conservation and Management Act, which was intended to reduce overfishing and increase limited access privilege programs. The law was a follow-up to the 1996 Sustainable Fisheries Act, which was intended to prevent overfishing, rebuild stocks of depleted fish, protect habitat, reduce amounts of bycatch (fish unintentionally caught with a regular harvest and then discarded), and improve research and monitoring. According to a report from the National Marine Fisheries Service, by 2003 biomass of many species of groundfish—including Georges Bank haddock, Georges Bank yellowtail flounder, and Georges Bank and Gulf of Maine cod—had begun to increase. Yellowtail flounder spawning stock size, for example, increased from just over 2,000 mt in 1994 to 39,000 mt in 2001. In 2003, the NOAA Fisheries reported that the Gulf of Maine/northern Georges Bank silver hake was declared officially restored. It also reported that between 1997 and 2002, overfishing was corrected 26 times and stocks had been rebuilt above biomass thresholds 20 times, though the reverse occurred in 27 cases. The number of stocks that were overfished increased from 81 in 2001 to 86 in 2002, and the number of stocks not overfished decreased from 163 to 150. Fishing mortality thresholds were unknown, however, for 695 stocks.

In addition to gaining some control over the fishing industry in the United States, the Magnuson-Stevens Act included provisions for monitoring other nations' fishing activities. According to the National Sea Grant Law Center, "The Secretary may undertake activities to promote improved monitoring and compliance for high seas fisheries or fisheries governed by international fishery management agreements by several means, including sharing information on harvesting and processing capacity and illegal, unreported, and unregulated (IUU) fishing activities with relevant law enforcement organizations." Proponents were hopeful that the act would improve the situation. Bill Hogarth, director of NOAA Fisheries, explained that overfishing "jeopardizes both its [the fish stocks'] biological future and the future of those who depend on it for their livelihood."

In addition, the FAO predicted that population growth and higher incomes would cause demand for fish and fish products to expand by almost 50 million tons by 2015. Although this amount is high, it indicates annual growth of 2.1 percent compared to 3.1 percent during the last two decades of the twentieth century. Growth in fish production, however, is expected to decline from 2.1 percent annually between 2001 and 2010 to 1.6 percent annually between 2010 and 2015. Furthermore, all of the growth in total fish production will come from aquaculture. Capture fishing rates are expected to stagnate.

On September 1, 2009, the Pew Environment Group joined a massive effort encouraging the National Marine Fisheries Service rejection of a proposal to allow commercial longline fisherman to catch and sell more Atlantic bluefin tuna. The Pew Group stood in opposition with 14 fishing and conservation organizations plus more than 55,000 citizens. Although a ban on directed commercial fishing for bluefin tuna has been in effect since 1982, longline fisherman could keep up to three incidentally-caught bluefin tuna per trip when they ventured out for swordfish or yellowfin tuna.

RESEARCH AND TECHNOLOGY

To meet the challenges of the twenty-first century, several fisheries research programs were aimed at more accurately assessing fish stocks and determining how many fish could be harvested without further endangering fish populations. Because the job of setting and enforcing catch quotas was impeded by a lack of firm, reliable data, some analysts hoped that better information would lead to improved fisheries management and more efficient use of sea resources.

One such program, the Fisheries and Aquaculture Research Program (FAR), was established in 1987 by members of the European Community. Its original purpose was to investigate fisheries management, fishing techniques, industry products, and aquaculture (raising sea animals in a farming environment). Although initiated as a five-year program, many individual FAR projects continued beyond the expiration of the original funding commitment.

Advances in fishing technology sometimes seemed to conflict with the goals of fisheries management researchers. While some researchers looked for ways to protect fish populations, others developed equipment to help fishermen catch greater quantities of fish. Examples included temperature-probing equipment, night vision apparatuses, and on-board computers. Not all new gear was aimed at increasing catch sizes, however. Improvements in technology also included tools designed to help eliminate problems associated with bycatch. One device was created to let finfish escape capture by shrimp boats. Another, a time-release float mechanism, served to help retrieve lost crab pots and reduce unintentional crab mortality. Another device sounds an alarm to steer marine mammals away from gill nets and cod traps.

The 2009 Ecosystem Status Report revealed many species migrating away from the U.S. Atlantic. Commercial fishing and undersea climate change were considered to be major contributing factors.

According to Jeff Barnard, a study focusing on New Zealand and Australia fisheries was representative of "the scientific foundation" for catch share, a system of dedicating a secure share of fish catch among individual fishermen. The study was published in *Science* 2007. A major finding indicated "fishermen who owned a share of the harvest made more money fishing less while doing a better job of conserving the resource." Catch share provides a preferred alternative to the traditional race for fish. That tradition involved racing to meet overall quota and catching too many overfished species.

WORKFORCE

Fishing-Jobs.com, a Web site of the consulting firm HoganWest International providing information to people seeking work in the commercial fishing industry, shared insights about what it proclaimed was a very challenging and rewarding industry. This observation was believed to be a constant reality on both mental and physical levels. There were, however, also many benefits for "adventure seeker" commercial fisherman. Those benefits included great salaries, bonding with kindred spirits, extensive paid travel opportunities, and many options for career advancements.

Although commercial fishing was not necessarily a major national employer in the world's leading fishing nations, it was often a vital part of the economy in coastal regions where fishing provided both direct and indirect employment. According to one estimate, for every job at sea, four to five were needed on shore in boat yards, fish

processing plants, packaging operations, equipment manufacturers, and other industry suppliers.

According to the National Institute for Occupational Safety and Health (NIOSH), commercial fishing was consistently rated as one of the most dangerous jobs. The 2007 statistics showed commercial fishing had an annual fatality rate 28 times greater than the rate of all U.S. workers. Employment figures reflected between 80,000 and 160,000 fisherman on approximately 80,000 fishing vessels in the U.S. commercial fishing in Alaska was an area where harsh conditions had a severe impact on safety. However, United States Coast Guard safety requirements had an impact on the commercial fishing industry's success and operation.

Furthermore, in many countries, modernization, new technology, and depleted fish stocks were displacing traditional workers. According to one estimate, artisan fisheries required a workforce 20 times as large as modern industrial fisheries. Compounding the problems associated with worker displacement was the fact that in many areas where fishing was a traditional employer, relatively few alternate sources of employment existed. In some places, large foreign fleets had done little to employ people from the local population. As a result, some countries, such as the Pacific Island nations, initiated regulations requiring distant water fleets to hire a quota of local workers in order to maintain fishing rights within the EEZ.

INDUSTRY LEADERS

The industry was affected in the early years of the first decade of the 2000s when environmental groups seized hold of United Nations admissions that China, and possibly other Asian nations, had tremendously overestimated annual catches. This led activists and governments alike to demand universal limits on catches to assist badly depleted fish stocks in many parts of the world. Boycotts on purchasing fish from Chile in 2002 could spread to other parts of the world's fishing waters. International attention also was focused on overfishing in waters visited by Japanese fishing interests. Several Japanese companies moved away from fish caught by fleets of ships to aquaculture, and this clearly was also a trend in Korea and Thailand. Canada continued to keep a presence in the industry in spite of the collapsed cod catches. Norway, New Zealand, and Iceland also kept a determined presence and were alert for changes in fishing regulations, as the world's governments attempted to reconcile devastating estimates of the true numbers for the oceans' commercial fishes.

Fisheries Products International. Fisheries Products International (FPIL) is a St. John's, Newfoundland, fishing fleet giant. In February 2002 it attempted to consolidate its position as an even larger industry giant by taking over

Canada's other giant fleet, Clearwater Fine Foods of Bedford, Nova Scotia. The estimated US$321 million takeover was bitterly fought by the Canadian government, which clearly did not want Canadian Fisheries Products International to have such an overwhelming market share, and Clearwater survived the bid.

In the early years of the first decade of the 2000s, FPIL made substantial investments in new equipment to enhance its groundfish operations. It added a US$15 million groundfish freezer and trawler that year, and according to a Canada News Wire report, expected to invest more than US$20 million to modernize its processing plants. The company's revenues reached US$752.9 million in 2006.

Thai Union Frozen Products. Makers of the famous Chicken of the Sea brand, Thai Union Frozen Products posted slight profits, even in the face of declining world tuna populations and the falling sales of Heinz's Starkist tuna line that forced the manufacturer to close U.S. canning facilities in 2002. In 2003, the company's sales reached 40.3 billion baht (approximately US$1.05 billion). Largely due to reduction in tariffs on U.S. imports of Thai shrimp, the company expected to see revenues and profits increase. By 2008, they had risen to US$2 billion.

MAJOR COUNTRIES IN THE INDUSTRY

China. In almost every aspect, Asia dominated the commercial fishing industry. According to FAO figures for 2003, 85 percent of the world's fishing and aquaculture workers lived in Asia, with almost a third of the world total living in China. The fishing industry in China, the region's top producer, remained state owned. China's production in 1992 reached 8.3 mmt. However, it soared dramatically through the 1990s. In 1999, the country claimed a record high catch of 17.2 mmt. Amounts have decreased slightly since then, reaching 16.9 mmt in 2000 and 16.8 mmt in 2004. China's aquaculture production, by contrast, has increased; fish landings and aquaculture together gave the country an estimated 27.7 kg of fish protein per capita in 2003.

Peru. Peru has ranked second in total captured fish production since 1992. In 2004, the country's total catch reached 9.6 million metric tons—a substantial decrease from its production in 2000, when dramatic recovery of stocks of Peruvian anchoveta (small anchovy) boosted the total global catch by more than 2 million tons above normal levels. Most of Peru's catch consisted of small pelagic fishes such as sardines, anchovies, and mackerel; indeed, variations on anchoveta stocks are one of the most significant influences on the country's total

production levels. In 1987, the Peruvian government instituted the Fisheries Reactivation Fund with the goal of rebuilding and modernizing its fishing fleet. The government also created a state-owned fishing fleet and entered into joint venture agreements with other countries operating fishing vessels in Peruvian waters.

United States. In 2001, the U.S. commercial fishing industry moved ahead of Japan to become the third major producer, reporting a harvest of 4.9 mmt, slightly up from 4.7 mmt in 2000. Production rose again in 2002, when the total U.S. catch was reported at 4.9 mmt. By 2004 that figure had increased to nearly 5 mmt. In 2003, U.S. edible fish imports were valued at US$11.1 billion, an increase of US$974.2 million from the previous year. Shrimp imports, valued at US$3.8 billion, comprised 34 percent of total edible fish imports. Other major imports included salmon and tuna. U.S. edible fish exports in 2003 totaled US$3.1 billion, a slight increase from US$3 billion in 2002.

In March of 2004 the U.S. government banned commercial fishing for swordfish in the Pacific Ocean between the U.S. West Coast and Hawaii. This action was taken to protect endangered sea turtles, which are caught by longline hooks used for swordfish. The U.S. industry, however, accounted for only about 5 percent of swordfishing in the area. Other bans occurred around the nation; for instance, the Gulf of Mexico Fishery Management Council initiated an individual fishing quota (IFQ) for red snapper in 2006 and was considering a grouper IFQ.

Continued concern about mercury levels in some species of fish, including tuna, appeared to impact U.S. consumption levels in the mid-years of the first decade of the 2000s. Statistics from 2004 suggested a significant decline in canned tuna consumption, though some analysts disputed this trend. At the same time, other news reports in 2004 touted the health benefits of eating fish, including evidence that one meal of tuna per week can slow the narrowing of arteries in postmenopausal women. The FDA in 2004 approved the use of omega-3 health claims in the labeling of food products containing these fatty acids (plentiful in such fish as salmon and tuna), a development that the fishing industry hoped would boost consumer confidence and demand.

On August 20, 2009, the U.S. made what Ocean Conservancy Vice President Janis Searles Jones called a "landmark decision," according to Allison Winter writing for Scientific American magazine. It was a management plan impacting Artic fisheries by banning expansion of commercial fishing into areas experiencing ice melting. The Artic Fishery Management Plan makes 150,000 square nautical miles off limits. Winter claimed this area was five times larger than all U.S. national parks combined.

In *The Register-Guard* newspaper (Eugene, Oregon), Associated Press writer Jeff Barnard discussed dynamics and progress made related to NOAA efforts for a mandate ending all overfishing in U.S. waters by 2011 when the West Coast groundfish accord would go into practice. Out of the 244 fisheries that were assessed, 41 remained to be brought into line as of September 2009. Barnard described "catch share" as a new regulatory wave. A key factor was the "personal responsibility" aspect that awarded fishermen with shares of total catch while trusting them not to catch overfished species. They also were rewarded with "a promise of better prices for the fish they do haul up." NOAA statistics showed that commercial fishing in U.S. adds up to approximately US$28 billion per year.

Chile. Like Peru, the bulk of the Chilean fishery catch was anchovies, sardines, and mackerels. The country caught 4.93 mmt in 2004, up from 4.3 mmt in 2000 and significantly more than its disastrous harvest of only 3.2 mmt in 1998. As with Peru, the fate of Chile's commercial fishing industry remained uncertain because of years of overfishing its resources. To retain its role as a major seafood exporter, Chile started investing in aquaculture.

Indonesia. In 2004 FAO ranked Indonesia the fourth largest producer of captured fish with 4.81 mmt. The fishing industry in Indonesia was also predominantly traditional with many non-powered vessels such as dugouts and plank-built boats. However, the fleet also contained mechanized purse seines and modern longlining vessels that were introduced during the late 1960s and early 1970s. Purse seines were popular for catching Indian mackerel, and longlining was used predominantly for tuna in the eastern part of Indonesia, in the Indian Ocean, and Banda Sea. The waters off Indonesian shores supported a wide variety of fish habitats including continental shelves and deep sea waters. The nation's jurisdiction spanned 2.8 million square kilometers of internal waters, 300,000 square kilometers of territorial waters, and an EEZ comprising 2.7 million square kilometers. Indonesian fishermen landed 45 species of commercial fishes (including chub mackerel, sardine, scad, anchovy, skipjack tuna, and needle fish), eight types of crustaceans, and eight kinds of mollusks.

Japan. Although Japan led the industry in the late 1980s, it fell behind China, as well as Peru and Chile, in the 1990s and by 2001 ranked fifth in total capture production. In 2004 Japan reported a catch of 4.4 mmt, well behind its 1994 banner year total of 12 mmt. Japan remained the world's leading market for sashimi-grade tuna. Imports of tuna suitable for sashimi totaled 60,489 tons in 2003.

Japan's fishing industry remained privately owned and an efficient provider of food and jobs. Prior to the late 1970s, Japanese fishermen relied heavily on distant water catches. When foreign governments implemented 200-mile EEZs, Japan was forced to plan a new strategy for its fishing operations, and the nation's focus turned more toward its own offshore and coastal areas. During the mid-1980s, sardines taken from waters in the Sea of Japan and in the Pacific off the eastern coast of Hokkaido and the northern coast of Honshu represented the biggest increase in Japanese catch statistics. Changing industry conditions, however, continued to impact the profitability of Japanese fishing operations. When the Commonwealth of Independent States (CIS) restricted access to its waters and instituted a salmon fishing ban in 1992, one projection anticipated a 40 percent reduction in Hokkaido's fleet.

India. India's fishing industry saw significant growth in the early twenty-first century. Total capture figures rose from 3.9 mmt in 1999 to 4.8 mmt in 2004.

BIBLIOGRAPHY
"Announcement of Legislative Development, March 2007." National Sea Grant Law Center, 3 April 2007. Available from www.observernet.org.

Barnard Jeff. "The new catch share program aims to reduce overfishing while stablizing groundfish pieces." *The Register-Guard*, 8 September 2009 Available from www.registerguard.com.

Chea, Terence. "Feds Ban U.S. Commercial Swordfishing in Much of Pacific to Save Turtles." Associated Press, 12 March 2004. Available from www.enn.com.

Childers, Hoyt. "The 3 Keys to IFQs: Allocation, Allocation and Allocation." *National Fisherman*, April 2007.

Fishery Products International. *Annual Report*, 2004. Available from www.fpil.com.

Fishing Jobs. "The Industry." 2009. Available from www.fishing–jobs.com.

"FPI Limited Announces 2006 Annual Financial Results," 9 March 2007. Available from www.fpil.com.

Hogarth, Bill. "Meeting New Magnuson-Stevens Challenges." *National Fisherman*, March 2007.

Khari, Nate. "NOAA Warns of Change in Atlantic Ocean Fisheries." 3 September 2009. Available from www.ecofactory.com.

Moore, Kirk. "With Cuts in Fishing Time and Quotas, Fluke Alternatives Could Enter Market." *National Fisherman*, August 2006.

National Institute for Occupational Health and Safety. "Commercial Fishing in Alaska." Available from www.cdc.gov.

———. "Commercial Fishing Safety," 2009. Available from www.cdc.gov.

National Marine Fisheries Service, National Oceanic and Atmosphere Administration. *Implementing the Sustainable Fisheries Act: Achievements from 1996 to the Present*, June 2003. Available from www.nmfs.noaa.gov.

————. *Imports & Exports of Fisher Products: Annual Summary, 2003.* Available from www.st.nmfs.gov.

National Oceanic and Atmosphere Administration. "New program meant to make commercial fishing safer," 1 September 2009. Available from www.galvnews.com.

Thai Union Group Company Information. Available from www. thaiuniongroup.com.

Tuna Market Report. Rome, Italy: Globefish, June 2004 and December 2004. Available from www.globefish.org.

"UN Treaty Cracks Down On Illegal Fishing," 2009. Available from www.redorbit.com.

United Nations Food and Agricultural Organization, Fisheries Department. *Projection of World Fishery Production in 2010.* Available from www.fao.org.

————. *The State of World Fishers and Aquaculture 2004.* Available from www.fao.org.

————. *Yearbook of Fishery Statistics, 2004.* Available from ftp.fao.org.

Winter, Allison. "U.S. Bans Commercial Fishing in Warming Artic." *The New York Times*, 21 August 2009. Available from www.nytimes.com.

SIC 0800

FORESTRY

NAICS CODE(S)

113. Forestry organizations operate timber tracts, tree farms, forest nurseries, and related activities, such as reforestation services and the gathering of gums, barks,

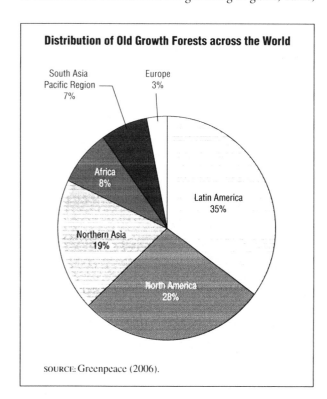

Distribution of Old Growth Forests across the World

SOURCE: Greenpeace (2006).

balsam needles, maple sap, Spanish moss, and other forest products. For discussion of logging and wood production, see **Logging.**

INDUSTRY SNAPSHOT

Forestry is the science of developing and managing woodlands and the water resources that sustain them. The purpose of forestry is to develop fuelwood (for fuel), sawlogs (for lumber), and pulpwood (for paper production) that can be extracted through logging. The production of fuelwood, sawlogs, and pulpwood grew steadily between 1960 and 2000, rising from 62 billion cubic feet in 1960 to 84 billion cubic feet in 1980, and 110 billion cubic feet in 1995. Global population growth increased demand for wood by 77 million cubic meters per year in the early 2000s. About half the wood harvested each year is used for fuel. By 2010, the United States timber industry was made up of over 10,000 companies with combined annual revenue of about US$10 billion.

Since forestry directly affects the environmental quality of every nation and involves the use of enormous amounts of public and private land, it is a focus of intense public debate in many countries. In most nations, the forest industry—which cuts timber—is also responsible for regenerating and maintaining the land. While intense worldwide debate continued over the extent and location of timber harvests, the forest industries of most major industrial nations have, for the most part, become more responsible and careful in their management of forest resources.

In 1960, the United States Forest Service was charged with the responsibility of managing the national forests according to a philosophy of sustaining the forest yield and multiple use: production of timber, preservation of fish and wildlife habitats, maintenance of watershed, mining, grazing, and recreation. However, by 1964, the growing demand for timber led the Forest Service to adopt the practice of clear cutting where vast forest tracks are stripped of all trees, leaving an unsightly bald area. Environmentalists claim that clear cut areas are susceptible to insect infestation, landslides, and erosion, and that runoff causes siltation of neighboring streams and spoils fish spawning grounds. Environmentalists have also blasted the ecologically disruptive effects of strip mining and overgrazing in the national forests and have urged restoration of blighted areas and pushed for a more equitable multiuse system in the future.

In some developing nations, the overcutting of land to create farmland, ranchland, or fuel continued to degrade the environment. While Southeast Asian nations producing tropical timber moved to check overcutting through regulation, taxation, and export bans, overcutting was said to continue despite safeguards. The loss of tropical rain forests in South America is a major example of this problem. Another problem was the massive damage done in Indonesia from 1997 through 2002, when fires—some deliberately set—ravaged lands where timber had been cut or where forests were being cleared for agriculture. The burnings were supposed to help prepare or clear the land for agricultural purposes, but once the fires were out of control, they created intense smog and haze that affected the entire region for months. Monetary damages from the fires and the haze they caused were estimated at US$4.4 billion in a study from the Economy and Environment Program for South East Asia (EEP-SEA) and the World Wildlife Fund (WWF).

Likewise, forest fires burned out of control in Mexico in May and June 1998. While these forest fires were attributed to extremely dry weather caused by the El Nino phenomenon, Mexican authorities were criticized for being unprepared for the disaster. The fires wiped out vast sections of Mexico's forestland, and the damage included the holdings of forest products companies. Fires have also been problematic in Chile. In 1999, fires flamed out of control to destroy 242,000 acres of forest. In 2002, some 93 fires in Chile threatened both forest preserves and cash-crop forests. In 2003, the Russian Federation lost 23.7 million hectares of forested land to fires; Australia, France, and Portugal also weathered significant fire losses that year. The biggest fire threat, however, is in sub-Saharan Africa, where the Food and Agriculture Organization of the United Nations (FAO) estimated that approximately 170 million hectares of forests are burned each year (about 10 percent of this, the FAO said, was necessary for woodland renewal). The costs associated with forest fires, which consume about 350 million hectares—the size of India—worldwide each year, are estimated by the FAO at several billion dollars annually. Between 2001 and 2010, there were over 68,000 forest fires reported within the U.S. By 2010, in the United States alone, more than 10 million acres of forest were burned annually, with the United States Forest Service reporting more than 100,000 wildfires every year. The control of forest fires had developed into an independent and complex science costing approximately US$100 million annually by 2010.

While forests exist in every nation on earth, the scientific management of forests tended to be concentrated in countries that produced large volumes of forest products although these countries did not necessarily have the most total forest area. For example, Finland and Sweden were leaders in forestry management and produced very high volumes of forest products, yet did not rank among the top 10 countries in terms of total forest area. Leading areas in terms of total forest cover were the Commonwealth of Independent States (formerly Soviet Union), North America, Scandinavia, continental Europe, Southeast Asia,

New Zealand, and Latin America. In Latin America, several companies established highly productive plantation forests (artificially planted forests intended for harvest at a specific time), particularly in Brazil and Chile.

Forest policies around the world differed based on each country's political history. In the United States, the federal and state governments own and manage substantial shares of forestland, especially in the West, but private corporations and individuals also own large woodland tracts, particularly in the South. In former communist countries, where forests were owned by the state, emerging market economies privatized forestry to varying degrees. Mixed ownership of woodlands, like that of the United States, is found throughout most of Asia, Western Europe, and South America. In Japan, most forests—a precious commodity in such a densely populated country—are state owned. In many African countries, tribal ownership is prevalent, a practice that can make modern forestry management difficult.

Although there are thousands of tree, plant, and shrub varieties growing in the world's forests, foresters cultivate a relatively small number of tree species. Most forestry activities focus on two broad varieties of trees: coniferous and nonconiferous (broadleaf). Coniferous trees, known as softwoods, include pines, spruces, firs and hemlocks, while nonconiferous trees are hardwoods that include oaks, maples, and beeches. Forested areas around the world also contain a large variety of woody shrubs and grasses (such as bamboo). In 2005, about 41 percent of the annual world harvest of wood was comprised of softwood species. Plantation forests accounted for only 4.7 percent of forestry acreage worldwide.

Forests regenerate naturally through seeding or sprouts that grow from the roots of cut trees or artificially by planting seedlings. Hardwood trees are usually allowed to regenerate naturally. Most softwoods do not sprout from the roots of cut trees and are most often replanted after harvest. In the early 2000s, according to USDA statistics, about 2.6 million acres of trees were planted annually in the United States, accounting for roughly 1.8 billion trees. The forest industry planted 45 percent of this total, and the national forest system planted 6 percent. Other government and industries accounted for another 7 percent, with the remainder planted by noncommercial owners. Reforestation is crucial to the forestry system within the global community. The use of timber within the rapidly growing world population makes it nearly impossible for forests to naturally keep up with the growing demand. Replanting forests and woodlands that have been depleted are essential factors in sustaining the delicate ecosystem of the earth, by absorbing pollution, mitigating global warming, and cleaning the air of carbon dioxide. Replanting by forest products companies and other groups created a net growth in the amount of forested land in most major countries. In Western Europe, for example, there was 30 percent more forested land in the mid-1990s than there was 50 years prior. From the early 1970s to the mid-1990s, the total acreage of trees growing in the United States increased by 20 percent.

Conflicting Demands. The global forestry industry has often struggled under the pressure of two conflicting demands: the world's growing population demanded more lumber, paper, and other wood products, and the environmental goal was to permanently preserve a larger share of the world's forests from commercial development.

Environmental groups, for example, argued that further use of wood resources would damage the environment. The timber industry contends that if timber production were reduced significantly worldwide, the use of more damaging wood substitute materials would likely increase. According to some sources, these substitute materials have substantially higher negative environmental impacts than tree harvesting and planting, an infinitely renewable process. For example, metals, cements, and other substitute materials would require environmentally damaging mining or quarrying activities. Also, the processing of most substitute products would require far more energy than is needed to create wood products.

The challenge of forestry is to create systems that are socially accepted while sustaining the natural resource and any other resources that might be affected. Forests absorb carbon dioxide through their natural photosynthesis, which in turn helps to mitigate global warming. Forest ecosystems are especially important to the global carbon cycle in two significant ways. First, they are responsible for moving approximately 3 billion tons of anthropogenic carbon every year. That amounts to about 30 percent of all global carbon dioxide emission from fossil fuels. Second, forest ecosystems are terrestrial carbon "sinks" that store large amounts of carbon which accounts for double the amount of carbon in the earth's atmosphere.

ORGANIZATION AND STRUCTURE

Major commercial forestry operations are concentrated in the forest product producing countries—mainly the United States; the Commonwealth of Independent States; and tree-rich countries with small populations, such as Sweden, Finland, and Canada. However, nontraditional forestry operations are growing fast in countries such as Brazil, Chile, and New Zealand. Also, Southeast Asian nations, such as Malaysia and Indonesia, having rapidly depleted their stands of virgin timber, were establishing large plantations to supply the many pulp and paper operations being built there.

Forestry operations are driven by the global demand for lumber and wood fiber, which was increasing at a rate parallel to or slightly greater than the increase in world population. In societies in which most of the population exists at a subsistence level, forestry management is based on the demands for firewood and cleared, arable land. In fact, more trees are used for firewood around the world than any other single use. In more industrialized countries, forestry focuses on growing trees to make building materials, paper, and other manufactured products.

Considerable tension remains between the world's desire for forest products and the demand for the permanent preservation of natural forests. Between 1960 and 1985, the amount of protected land worldwide grew from 100 million hectares (247 million acres) to 400 million hectares (988 million acres). In the United States, much of the battle over preservation focused on "old growth" timber, mostly in the Pacific Northwest. Old growth is the final stage in a forest's natural cycle of growth and renewal. It is characterized by large, old trees of varying heights and large, dead trees. Old growth timber is favored by sawmills since its extremely large trees produce exceptional timber products. Within the United States, it takes a hardwood forest one or two generations of trees— approximately 150 to 500 years—to reach old growth status, or approximately 150 to 500 years. In 2006, Greenpeace identified the world's remaining old growth forests. Thirty-five percent is located in Latin America, where the Amazon rainforest—located mainly in Brazil—clears a larger area of forest annually than any other country in the world. In North America, 28 percent of the world's old growth timber still grows. However, 10,000 square kilometers of these forests are harvested annually. Nineteen percent is located in northern Asia, home to the largest boreal—coniferous—forest in the world. Africa is home to 8 percent, while 7 percent is in the south Asia Pacific region, and less than 3 percent is in Europe.

According to the Finnish Forest Research Institute, about 27 percent of the world's 3.4 billion hectares of land area is covered with forests that have "closed" upper canopies. These closed forests consist of broadleaf and coniferous trees. "Open forests," also called savannas, usually contain woody shrubs and grasses and are usually found in tropical climates. Coniferous forests are usually found in cooler, drier areas, and broadleaf forests are more prevalent in warmer, moist regions. Tropical forests, such as those found in Southeast Asia, consist almost exclusively of broadleaf, hardwood species. Mixed broadleaf and coniferous forests are found near the boundaries between these two climatic areas, such as in the southern United States. About 42 percent of the world's forests are located in developed countries. The former Soviet Union contains 22 percent of overall forest area.

Coniferous forests are heavily concentrated in the Northern Hemisphere. In fact, 85 percent of all coniferous forests is found in North America and the Commonwealth of Independent States (CIS). Coniferous trees are generally favored for making lumber and pulp for paper products and tend to be intensively cultivated. Hardwood trees, while used to make furniture and paper pulp, tend to be less valuable than softwood.

In the 1970s and 1980s, several countries in the Southern Hemisphere took advantage of their superior tree-growing climate to expand production of several marketable tree species. For example, companies in Brazil established vast eucalyptus (a hardwood) plantations for use in making market pulp, which was then shipped to papermaking operations around the world. Likewise, Chile and New Zealand established large plantations of radiata pine (a softwood), which can be used to make lumber as well as pulp. In the 1990s, these plantations were turning Brazil and Chile, in particular, into formidable competitors in the global forest products industry. According to the World Forest Institute, South America ranked fourth in the industry by 1998. The Institute projected that Chile's wood fiber production would double by 2020 and that Argentina and Uruguay would become significant players early in the twenty-first century. Timber production on a tree plantation is generally higher than that of natural forests. While forests managed for wood production commonly create between one and three cubic meters per hectare per year, plantations of fast-growing species commonly yield between 20 and 30 cubic meters or more per hectare annually. A Grand Fir plantation in Scotland has a growth rate of 34 cubic meters per hectare per year, and Monterey Pine plantations in southern Australia can yield up to 40 cubic meters per hectare annually. In 2000, while plantations accounted for 5 percent of the global forest, they supplied about 35 percent of the world's timber.

One of the most controversial topics in global politics has been "sustainable development." This is the concept that human industry must be organized in such a way as to be able to sustain itself indefinitely without damaging the earth. The sustained yield concept is very important in forestry management where, according to this theory, a forest is managed in such a way that modest timber crops may be harvested indefinitely. Thus, foresters must precisely calculate net annual growth rates, including total forest growth minus harvesting and losses due to fire, insects, and disease. Sustainable yield focuses on optimal rotation, which is the age at which a crop of trees can be successfully harvested and used (this is different from the familiar concept of crop rotation in field crop agriculture).

Rotation varies widely by species and climate. Trees in subtropical areas which have a year-round growing season and a rich environment grow the fastest. For example, eucalyptus trees in tropical areas can be harvested for pulpwood in just seven years, while pine in the same area takes slightly longer. In the 1990s, advances in genetic research made those short rotations even shorter. In northern Europe and North America, however, the rotation for softwood for wood pulp can be as long as 50 years, although rotation for southern U.S. pine can be as short as 20 to 25 years. Softwood trees used for lumber need between 50 and 100 years of growth in northern climates, while hardwood trees can require as much as 200 years of growth before being used for sawlogs. Due to genetic research by major forest products companies, universities, and government agencies, growth rates in many species were dramatically increasing, which was expected to allow northern foresters to compete more effectively with their counterparts in the Southern Hemisphere.

Silviculture. The term "silviculture" describes the forestry science concerned with how trees are reproduced, planted, protected, and thinned as they grow to maturity. Silviculture can include natural regeneration of a cut stand from seed trees left standing after others are harvested or planting of seedlings on land that has been clear cut. Most silviculture by forest products companies focuses on the planting of seedlings, which allows foresters to alter and improve the genetic composition of trees. Many forest products companies have, through genetic manipulation, produced "super trees" that grow faster, resist insect damage, have fewer knots, and make forestland more productive.

Silviculture also addresses other concerns in the forestry industry. It is used to maintain wildlife habitats, create areas for recreation, and provide natural water quality management while creating or improving landscape issues. Silviculture can also be used to provide erosion control, enable watershed management, and preserve forests for atmospheric carbon dioxide dumping.

Softwood seedlings are grown in vast seed orchards before they are planted, either mechanically or by hand, in newly cut lands. Competing weeds and grasses are sometimes removed to help the trees grow faster. In the late 1990s and early 2000s, many companies increased the use of small doses of herbicides to control weeds that can retard seedling growth.

Wildlife management is also an important part of forestry. Every major change in a forest, such as wildfire, hurricanes, or harvesting, benefits some wildlife species and harms others. The Siberian tiger, for example, once roamed across huge areas of Northern Asia, but by 2010, it could only be found in a small area of intact forest near the Sea of Japan; only about 400 remained in the wild.

Critics of industrial forestry charge that creation of large tracts of artificially planted trees, often of the same species, inhibits biodiversity. Industrial foresters counter that while some species may be hurt by this approach, others thrive. Industrial forests may support as diverse a group of wildlife as forests that are allowed to grow, mature, and decline naturally.

BACKGROUND AND DEVELOPMENT

Tress have been grown from seeds or cuttings since biblical times. The Romans imported seedlings from elsewhere in the Mediterranean area and Germany. They planted large groves of trees such as those in Lebanon and Carthage and regulated the cutting and use of wood resources. However, when the Roman Empire fell, its forests were overcut and overgrazed. Fires destroyed many forested areas. When forests were overcut, the land was degraded by soil erosion and the subsequent silting of streams and harbors. Many of the forests became unusable scrubland.

In medieval Europe, forestry was the domain of feudal landowners who regulated forests to preserve hunting grounds. They allowed peasants to gather fuel and timber. The systematic management of forests began in the German states during the sixteenth century. Under the German system, each forest property was divided into sections for harvesting and regeneration on a regular rotation so as to ensure a sustainable timber yield.

Silviculture is believed to have begun in the 1500s in England, where landowners were urged to produce artificial tree plantations. By the 1990s, virtually all Britain's woodlands consisted of planted woodlands. While other countries maintained more of their natural forests, most forested areas in the heavily populated Northern Hemisphere had been cut by man at some time, leaving a very small amount of virgin forests. Formal education in forestry apparently began in the nineteenth century when Germany, France, and England founded private forestry schools. German foresters were particularly skilled and were highly sought after in many other countries.

The chief goals of forestry are to devise a means for cutting trees that provides the growth of a new forest crop and to ensure that adequate seeds of desirable species are set onto the ground and conditions are optimal for seed germination and the survival of saplings. The basic rule of timber management is to create a sustained yield—to cut each year a volume of timber no greater than the volume of wood that grew during that year. The twentieth century saw the steady growth of national forest laws and policies that protected woodlands and regulated the increased use of forest resources to satisfy the rapidly multiplying demand for timber and paper products. In the 1930s, countries in North America and Europe began repairing the extensive damage done by the relatively unregulated deforestation of the industrial revolution. Beginning in the 1940s, vast land reclamation was undertaken in the Mediterranean region, including Greece, Israel, Italy, Spain, and North Africa. These efforts were needed to save soil cover and protect watersheds. Some countries are fighting a losing battle in forestry. For example, in China, where forests once extended over 30 percent of the land, centuries of overcutting, grazing, and fires reduced forests to 7 percent of total land area.

CURRENT CONDITIONS

Despite the strain on wood supply that occurred in the mid-1990s as a result of logging bans in several countries, some experts were optimistic about the future of world forestry. They anticipated that after 2010, when many current plantations in the Southern Hemisphere would be ready for harvesting, wood supply might be plentiful. While there may be severe shortages in wood coming from the world's forests in the 2000s, supply should eventually catch up with demand. Some experts also felt that with prudent management, "super trees" that are hybridized to faster growth cycles, and a political solution to the debate over forest preservation, North America would likely be able to support increased harvests and should return to forestry self-sufficiency in the future.

Other observers, however, predicted that higher demand and restrictions on supply were likely to cause serious disturbances in the global timber supply system early in the twenty-first century, as supply was cut in some areas, such as North America, and increased in others, such as South America. Rapidly growing demand from China, for example, which imported 1.5 billion cubic feet of timber in 2003 and would become the world's largest consumer of wood by 2010, could pose a significant threat to world supply, according to WWF statistics published by CNN. While domestic consumption increased, China had been unable to meet demand because of logging bans that went into effect in parts of the country after devastating floods in 1998. The WWF called for China to improve its forest management to boost production, and to enforce regulations to hinder imports of illegally harvested logs. China's rapidly growing demand for paper and packaging products (it was the world's largest consumer in the early 2000s) was expected to lead to significant changes in that country's forestry industry. By 2005, China had created alliances with several African nations to export their timber to China. Africa has become a major timber supplier and China is poised to control access to this resource. Unlike the United States, which bans companies from doing business with outlaw regimes, Beijing has no qualms about dealing with Africa's most brutal and corrupt leaders.

As traditional supply sources are restricted and underused or newly developed resources are brought into the supply cycle, governments and forest products companies will need to make additional investments in global infrastructure, land/timber management, and environmental protection. All these factors are expected to drive up global costs for logs and pulpwood, according to some observers. In addition, wood product usage tends to go up considerably in times of economic plenty.

As with other industries in the twenty-first century, the forestry industry was expected to experience increasing numbers of consolidations similar to the takeover of U.S.-based Willamette by Weyerhaeuser Co. in January 2002. Following pressure put on Willamette stockholders and employees by Weyerhaeuser Co., Willamette Industries Inc. yielded and agreed to be taken over for a cash payment and assumption of debt service amounting to more than US$7 million. Weyerhaeuser's former chairman and chief executive officer, Steven Rogel, was a former Willamette employee, and his takeover bid was resented by some in Willamette's top management. In 2002, he told a University of Washington business class that consolidations had become the natural order of things in the cutthroat competition among forestry companies in the twenty-first century. The takeover and economic conditions in 2001 dropped earnings to about 50 percent of 2000 earnings, but by March 2001, Weyerhaeuser announced that its shares had jumped to US$64, an 18 percent increase that brought stock value to near-2000 levels. However, the company is in a volatile industry, especially when the global economy is in a decline. According to its 2009 Annual Report, total net sales and revenue of the Weyerhaeuser company decreased by nearly 50 percent between 2007 and 2009.

The Independent reported that Donegal Woodland Owners Society was launched in June 2008 to identify timber produce markers and maximize returns for the country's forest owners. The company is a result of partnership with Donegal County Council, the Donegal County Development Board and Teagasc. It will be able to provide substantially larger volumes and security of supply to potential timber buyers.

Deforestation Threats. While forest cover was gradually increasing in most parts of the Northern Hemisphere, the Southern Hemisphere continued to experience brisk deforestation. Between 1981 and 1990, over 15 million hectares of tropical rain forests were cut or burned out of a total forest area in the tropics of just under 2 billion hectares. A similar rate of destruction continued well into the 2000s. The destruction of the rain forest is a complex economic story and is largely separate from the establishment of tree plantations in the same area. Contrary to popular belief, most tree plantations in the Southern Hemisphere are on land that has already been cleared and used for agriculture.

The major causes of tropical deforestation appear to be poverty, inappropriate development, weak political institutions, monopolistic land ownership, low agricultural productivity, and rapidly expanding populations. Close to half the rain forest area lost each year is cleared by landless farmers who then move on to new tracts in following years. Land clearing for permanent agriculture is the second leading cause of deforestation, followed by the cutting of wood for heating and cooking. Another frequent use of cut wood by smugglers is in the form of plywood, which is easily loaded on ships for sale to unscrupulous merchants.

Much of the rain forest debate has focused on Brazil, which has the world's largest reserves of rain forest. One of the conflicts over the rain forest is between rubber tappers, who extract rubber from rubber trees without killing them, and ranchers and farmers who clear cut rain forest for pasture or cropland. In the early 1970s, the Brazilian government wanted to open rain forest areas for development. With the assistance of the World Bank, the government built roads and helped people buy land in the rain forests. Rubber tappers and nut gatherers, who traditionally worked this land, were removed. Some of the rubber tappers organized opposition groups. Farmers and ranchers reacted with violent, and sometimes murderous, confrontations. In the 1990s, however, the Brazilian government moved to further slow the destruction of rain forests, though results have been mixed. By the early 2000s, Brazil had increased its area of certified forests to slightly more than 1 million hectares.

Deforestation is often cited as one of the primary causes of the greenhouse effect. According to the Intergovernmental Panel on Climate Change, tropical deforestation is responsible for approximately 20 percent of the world's greenhouse emissions, mainly in tropical areas, and could account for up to one-third of total anthropogenic carbon dioxide emissions.

Southeast Asian nations also aggressively cut their huge forest reserves from the 1970s to the 2000s. Much of the output went to Japan, which, with its extremely limited forest resources and affluent population, had a seemingly insatiable demand for tropical hardwood. In the 1980s, Malaysia cut more tropical trees than any country except Indonesia and Brazil. The rate of forest clearance in Asia tripled from 1960 to the mid-1990s. Some countries in Southeast Asia have already felled the vast majority of their trees without replanting them.

While forests occupied 60 percent of the Philippines in 1950, just 10 percent remained forested in 1994; by 2005, this figure had fallen to about 7 percent, and the people are calling for a total ban on deforestation. However, as of 2010, the Philippine forests were still being pillaged at an alarming rate on both public and government-protected land. The situation was also urgent in Africa, home of the world's second-largest rain forest, which stretches across 700,000 square miles and six countries in the Congo River basin and represents approximately one-fifth of the world's remaining closed canopy tropical forest. By 2005, it was estimated that illegal logging and poaching in this region contributed to the loss of 3.7 million acres of forest land each year. In 2005, seven Central African countries, along with 40 governmental and nongovernmental agencies, signed a treaty aimed to preserve the remaining tracts of forest; in particular, nations agreed to streamline and enforce logging regulations. The Congo Basin Forest Partnership (CBFP) struggles to control many corrupt leaders in that sector who have made private deals with China to export much of their reserves, therefore it is doubtful that the treaty would prove effective.

In addition, attempts by Indonesia to change its forestry strategies in the 1990s apparently had been defeated in the 2000s. The Indonesian military government under President Suharto in the mid-1990s had required companies that acquired the right to cut trees on state land to replant areas that they cut, but lawlessness and corruption won following Suharto's ousting in 1998. In part because of corruption that allowed local province leaders to give permits to crooked loggers without restrictions, the forests of Tanjung Putting and Kalimantan were projected to disappear in the first decade of the twenty-first century. In large part, the blame for the depletion of forests and the resultant floods that have devastated parts of Indonesia can be shared by Malaysia, China, and Japan, which allowed shiploads of illegal shipments with impunity. Indonesia's exported wood products, valued at US$6.5 billion in 2002, are shipped in the form of plywood, sawmill-quality timber, pulp and wood products such as furniture. As world pressure on the Indonesians increased in the 2000s, exports diminished slightly to a projected US$4 billion. However, analysts contend that illegal logging continues almost unchecked. According to the environmental organization Rainforest Information Centre, as much as 90 percent of all industrial wood extraction in Indonesia in 2004 was illegal. While just under 7 million cubic meters was harvested legally under government quota, some 80 million cubic meters was cut that year for illegal export as plywood, pulp, and sawmill timber. In October 2010, the Indonesian government agreed to impose a moratorium on forest clearing in exchange for a US$1 billion grant from Norway to fund projects to curtail deforestation and land

degradation. Beginning in 2011, Indonesia has agreed to ban companies from clearing indigenous forests for two years. The timber and palm oil industries contribute to the destruction of approximately 2 million hectares of forests in Indonesia each year and are the leading cause of their greenhouse emissions.

For years, some environmental advocates argued that forestry practices, particularly in Indonesia, remained unsustainable. For example, the EEPSEA/WWF study of the 1997 forest fires in Indonesia found that the fires were promoted by several "poorly designed policies" including:

- a program to drain and convert one million hectares of peat forest to rice cultivation;

- confusing land ownership laws that encouraged people to clear land as a way of staking a claim to that land;

- weak enforcement of laws to regulate the use of fire for land clearing;

- policies that keep the prices of wood to processing mills low; and

- short-term leases of forest land to timber companies which leave them with little incentive to manage forest sustainability.

The EPPSEA/WWF study found that direct damages from the fires (not including the haze that blanketed the region) topped US$3 billion, including US$493 million in timber losses; US$470 million in foregone agricultural production; US$1.8 billion in ecological services provided by forests (such as food and medicine, water supply, and erosion control); and US$272 million for the contribution to global warming.

As a result of such problems, in the mid- to late 1990s, international pressure was growing for tropical timber producers to certify whether logs were produced using sustainable forestry methods. While producers initially resisted this demand, without certification they faced the prospect of losing sales in Europe and the UnitedStates—top markets for high-value wood products. Both Indonesia and Malaysia began certification procedures in the early 2000s.

Professionals from diverse parts of the world admired how Chinese people had the ability to change the world in visible ways by participating in tree planting programs. The 2006 Inner Mongolia project was a great success story for reforestation. Roots & Shoots Shanghai Director Tori Zwisler explained that the group was part of a team uniting farmers, nursery seedling suppliers, and school children. In addition to planting the trees, the team also monitored growth, value, and survival. Consequently a program was built that Zwisler projected would last for 45 years. Nevertheless, it was able to substantially address the organization's pledge to plant a million trees in the desert encroaching on Hare Banner in southeastern Inner Mongolia. The target for meeting that goal was set as 2016.

While reforestation is widely considered a laudable goal, not all reforestation projects are free of controversy. For example, the Environmental Defense Fund (EDF), a U.S. environmental group, attacked the World Bank's funding of a project to grow eucalyptus trees in India in the early 1990s. The eucalyptus tree, according to EDF, crowds out other vegetation, uses too much water, and is used exclusively for industrial purposes. According to the EDF, much of the eucalyptus crop in India was not being used for firewood and its cultivation was displacing subsistence farmers.

Effect of Recycling on Forestry. In the mid-1990s, Europe experienced a boom in paper recycling as the result of restrictive packaging laws. One of the reasons given for increasing paper recycling in Europe and elsewhere was to reduce the consumption of virgin fiber made from wood pulp. Ironically, however, increased recycling in Europe may have a negative effect on forest health, according to a report by the FAO. As recycling rates in Europe increased in the 1990s to meet stringent regulations, industries consumed increasing amounts of wastepaper and the demand and price for small diameter pulpwood decreased. In some areas, prices paid for small diameter trees dropped below the cost of harvesting them. This was one of the reasons that European forest landowners reduced their management of existing timber stands in the 1990s. Instead of thinning (cutting) small diameter trees, these trees were allowed to continue growing.

While this may seem to be a good thing, an unmanaged forest eventually produces a diminished value of forest products. According to foresters, a well-managed forest—one that is periodically thinned—will produce a larger volume of higher value forest products than an unmanaged forest. Stands that grow too thick may become "stagnant" with small-sized, low-quality trees competing for diminished nutrition and sunlight. Undesirable species of trees may also begin growing. A crowded forest is also more susceptible to fire, insects, and disease.

Effects of Cutbacks. Severe cutbacks on harvests in the U.S. Pacific Northwest begun in the early 1990s appeared to have become more or less permanent. Logging restrictions reduced the annual harvest of trees from federal land in the northwestern United States in the late 1990s to less than 20 percent of levels in the 1980s. Also, additional restrictions in British Columbia further curtailed timber cutting.

The growing shortfall in North American softwood supplies was expected to be made up by increased harvesting in other major wood producing regions, particularly in Western and Eastern Europe, the Nordic countries, and the Southern Hemisphere. While Japan has the potential for increased cutting, it was not expected to produce more softwood due to high operating costs, the structure of forest ownership, and high labor costs.

The shortfall in North American softwood production was further exacerbated by increased competition from softwood plantations in Chile, New Zealand, and Australia. To address this issue, Canada implemented a Forest 2020 initiative, which aimed to increase yields in Canadian forests through genetic improvements of tree stocks and through the introduction of fast-growth plantations.

RESEARCH AND TECHNOLOGY

The primary purpose of research in forestry is to produce hybrid trees that grow faster, are more resistant to disease, and produce better lumber. This science is called "high-yield forestry" and is particularly important in cooler climates, where trees grow much more slowly than in warmer areas.

Amid pressure to preserve more land, faster growing trees would allow the forestry industry to reduce the amount of forestland it needs to produce the same amount of wood. This would neutralize one of the arguments against using trees to make lumber and paper. However, developing more "super trees" will require major investments in plant biology and other high-tech genetic research. This area in particular will require more extensive networking between forestry companies, research institutions, and government agencies.

Another area of forestry research is carbon dioxide uptake. Excess carbon dioxide in the atmosphere, which contributes to global warming, is caused largely by the burning of fossil fuels. Young, growing trees consume large amounts of carbon dioxide and produce large amounts of oxygen. (As trees mature, this cycle is eventually reversed.) Planting billions of young trees may help fight global warming by capturing carbon dioxide.

An additional major research area in forestry is in the relatively new topic of biodiversity. This was one of the most publicized topics to emerge from the 1992 United Nations Conference on Environment and Development (The Earth Summit) held in Rio de Janeiro. Since then, there has been much discussion and research concerning the benefits of maintaining the maximum amount of biological diversity through preserving more of the world's forests.

A study of tropical forests (which contain 50 to 90 percent of the world's species) found that if deforestation continues at rates equal to those reached in the early

1990s, between 17 percent and 35 percent of the world's rain forests would be destroyed by 2040. If this occurs, between 7,300 and 27,000 plant and animal species (out of 10 million known varieties in the mid-1990s) would become extinct each year. In 2002, a special United Nations task force was launched to attempt to address the problem of threatened species due to deforestation of trees.

A report by the FAO in 2005 estimated that the global total forest area continued to decrease at about 13 million hectares per year. However, other groups claim that rainforests are being destroyed at an every-quickening pace. The Rainforest Foundation stated that the United Nations statistics were based on the definition of "forest" as being an area with as little as 10 percent actual tree cover, largely based on reporting from forestry departments of individual countries, and do not take into account unofficial activities such as the wide-spread illegal logging.

On July 1, 2008, UK Wildlife Minister Joan Ruddock announced wildlife projects throughout the world would benefit from funding for the next three years. The Darwin Initiative has earmarked funds for hundreds of conservation-related projects, including the Forest Restoration Research Unit of Chiang Mai University in Northern Thailand, a partnership with East Mailing Research and Wildlife Landscapes in the United Kingdom. The Unit's focus is restoring forests by selecting and planting an indigenous forest tree species diverse range to encourage seed dispersing wildlife that establish important species. The Darwin Initiative also agreed to provide funding for FORRU-CMU focused on spreading expertise to neighboring countries plus assisting foresters in forest restoration projects located in Laos, Cambodia, and China.

Also in 2008, the Australian Cooperative Research Centre for Forestry released a report showing about 6,300 Tasmanians are directly employed in the forestry sector. Approximately half of the forestry jobs were in downstream processing. Approximately 1,500 of those people were involved in silviculture.

MAJOR COUNTRIES IN THE INDUSTRY

Russia. In Russia, journalists have joked that money may not grow on trees, but the forestry industry could represent about US$20 billion annually to the economy of Russia. Russia's forestry industry plunged into crisis after the Communist regime was overturned in the early 1990s. Under chaotic economic conditions, Russian timber exports declined. Beginning in 1999, however, the industry saw a significant upward trend, with increased private investment in forestry infrastructure. As a result,

the Russian forestry industry took steps toward more efficient and transparent corporate management. Once forestry began to recover, however, competition among private investors in the sector led to several power scrambles between 2000 and 2004, which prevented the industry from achieving the higher production levels and profits that had been the goal of reform. In 2008, the profitability ratio of the forest industry in Russia decreased harshly according to the annual Top 50 Russian Forestry Industry rating published by Lesnaya Industriya. The total revenue in 2008 for the Russian forestry industry totaled US$7.19 billion.

Despite these challenges, some analysts saw significant opportunities for improvement in Russia's forestry sector in the early 2000s. Government investment and tax concessions, which have been periodically discussed, could boost output in many regions; the influx of cash from overseas investors, too, is expected to contribute to significant growth. There are vast areas of native forest in eastern Russia, and the terrain is relatively flat, making logging easier. Also, being in a very cold climate, Russian forests contain considerably less biodiversity than tropical forests, so damage to wildlife habitat is less controversial. Nevertheless, according to 2002 statistics published by *The Russia Journal,* Russia cuts only 15 percent of the 700 million cubic meters it could harvest annually.

Other aspects of Russia's eastern forests suggest that increased logging may cause serious environmental problems. Russia's eastern forests have a relatively low volume of timber per acre, meaning that very large areas would have to be logged in order to produce acceptable timber volume. In addition, it is difficult to regenerate timber in many eastern Russian forests, particularly in the colder regions in the north. This could raise the costs of forestry and perhaps tempt logging operations not to replant harvested forest areas. Lands that do not have an adequate forest cover for long periods can suffer severe environmental damage.

On June 28, 2008, *Novosti* reported that the presidents of Russia and Finland met to discuss forestry, one of their main areas of cooperation. Russian President Dmitri Medvedev and Finnish President Tarja Halonen discussed dynamics related to 20 percent of the Finnish timber industry working for Russian companies. In 2007, Russia had announced that it would raise export duties on timber up to 80 percent by 2011.

Canada. Canada has more than 307 million hectares of forests and other wooded lands in eight major forest zones from the Atlantic to Pacific Oceans. That represents about 50 percent of its total land area. Canada contains 10 percent of the world's forests and accounts for about 18 percent of the world's forest products exports. Canada's exports of lumber slipped in the 1990s in total value, in part because of U.S. reluctance to allow additional shipments of lumber exports in the country. The U.S. timber industry has argued that Canada's production and pricing unfairly subsidize Canadian logging, since most of the country's timber is cut from government-owned land and is sold below market value. Pressure from U.S. timber companies resulted in stiff tariffs on Canadian lumber, which in 2004 stood at 27 percent but were down to 17.18 percent in early 2005. Canada has strenuously rejected U.S. claims of subsidies and has sought adjudication of the matter through a NAFTA trade dispute panel.

Each year, about 1 million hectares—or 0.5 percent of Canada's productive forest land—is harvested, a level that may be permanently sustained. Canada's vast forest resources have been a key element of its economy for hundreds of years. As of the early 2000s, forest products were Canada's largest source of export income; they accounted for 20 percent of world trade in manufactured forest products in 2003. Forests support Canada's largest manufacturing industry, which exports pulp, paper, paperboard, and wood products to more than 100 countries. The forest industry is critical to Canada's economy, yet only one-third of 1 percent of its commercial forest area is actually harvested annually.

In Canada, 51 million hectares of forests have been removed from harvesting, an area equivalent to half the forest area of the European Union. In Canada's "heritage forests," 27 million hectares have been removed, and in its "protection forests," 24 million hectares have been removed. Another 193 million hectares are open forests with no commercial activity. Of the 209 million hectares classified as commercial, productive forests, 112 million hectares were managed for timber production as of 2004.

Of Canada's forestland, 80 percent was owned by the provincial governments, 11 percent by the national government, and 9 percent by private landowners. Forestry operations were inextricably tied to changes in government policy. Canada's high level of government ownership was a contrast to 40 percent public ownership in the United States and 28 percent in Sweden. In the 1990s, provincial governments in Canada responded to pressure from environmental groups by restricting logging on a greater percentage of public land. In British Columbia (BC), for example, the provincial government proposed banning logging on about 12 percent of BC forestland, up from about 8 percent. Environmental groups would like to increase that percentage further.

In the 1990s and 2000s, Canadian forest managers began adopting "ecosystem-based planning," an approach that attempts to balance the natural processes of forest ecosystems with sustainable economic benefits and includes the objectives of biodiversity conservation. In 1995, Canada adopted national certification standards for sustainable forest management, developed under the oversight of the Canadian Standards Association. Canadian forest managers were adopting new, lower-impact harvesting technologies and strategies that speed regeneration. Where appropriate, clear cutting was replaced by other harvesting methods, such as selective cutting and the use of "seed trees."

In June 2008, Phillip Hopkins reported that private forestry investment in Victoria was losing funding and the state government's private forestry unit faced closure. This projection involved both federal and state funding cuts for four private forestry development committees in Victoria viewed to have "largely fulfilled their goal," according to Agriculture Minister Joe Helper's spokesman. The private forestry funding came from the plantation's incentive strategy that was ending.

United States. Despite holding just 4 percent of the world's forestland, the United States is the world's leader in the production of wood and paper. Many U.S. forests are intensively managed for wood production. Despite its enormous appetite for wood, as of 2004 the United States still had 70 percent of the forests that stood in 1600.

In the United States about 67 percent of all forest lands, about the equivalent of 422 million acres, are owned by nearly 10 million private individuals, companies, individual states, or Native American tribes. The remaining lands are under the jurisdiction of four agencies of the federal government: the Forest Service, the Bureau of Land Management, the National Park Service, and the Fish and Wildlife Service. Many state, county, and municipal government organizations also control a share. The coalition was formed with the intent of protecting U.S. forests outside direct government control against losses due to building sprawl, industry cutting, and tree diseases. The coalition listed its intention of addressing present and future forest challenges identified by the National Research Council in a 1998 investigation of the state of the nation's forest areas. The ultimate goal was to assure future generations that all non-federal lands would be subject to proper stewardship practices or that accountability for violations would be assessed.

In the United States as of 2004, 247 million acres were reserved from harvest by law or were slow-growing woodlands unsuitable for timber production. Another 490 million acres are called timberlands—forests that can produce more than 20 cubic feet of wood per acre annually. Between 1952 and 1992, the amount of hardwoods growing in the United States increased 82 percent, from 184.1 million cubic feet to 335.7 million cubic feet, while the amount of softwoods increased 4 percent, from 431.8 million cubic feet to 449.9 million cubic feet.

With many forest products companies and government agencies sponsoring research into forestry practices, the United States is clearly a leader in world forestry. In the 1990s, as environmental demands grew, U.S. foresters began to examine the concept of sustainable forestry. In 1994, the forest products industry—through its trade group, the American Forest and Paper Association (AF&PA)—announced the Sustainable Forestry Initiative (SFI). This initiative binds member companies of the AF&PA to a set of forest principles and detailed guidelines that require companies to reforest harvested land promptly, provide for wildlife habitat, minimize the visual impact of harvesting, improve water quality and ecosystem diversity, and protect forestland of special ecological significance. The SFI requires detailed reporting of forest management practices by member companies, and the information is then released in annual reports to the public on the progress made toward achieving sustainable forestry. Under SFI, AF&PA members are committed to reforest their forestland within two years of final harvest by planting or direct seeding or within five years using planned natural regeneration. AF&PA has emerged as the leading voice for the forest industry. When any matter of major concern relating to the industry surfaces at the state, national, or international level, it is an active presence representing the industry interests.

Another matter of critical importance is the protection of forested lands from wildfires. In 2003, after catastrophic fires destroyed more than 1.8 million acres of forests in the western part of the country, President George W. Bush signed the Healthy Forests Initiative, which funded measures to thin dense undergrowth in public forests and thereby reduce the risk. According to a White House press release, more than 2.24 million acres of overgrown forests were thinned in 2002, and 2.57 million acres were slated for thinning in 2003. In 2006, according to a USDA report, the initiative was expected to reduce fire hazards and insect infestation on almost 4.3 million additional acres.

In 2005, the undisputed leader of the world forest industry was International Paper, which controlled more than 8 million acres of forests in the United States and 1.5 million acres in Brazil. Hard economic times and a general economic slowdown after the terrorist attacks of September 11, 2001, cut profits for the giant corporation, but it continued to show profit margins nonetheless. With operations in almost 40 countries worldwide, International Paper employed about 51,500 people in 2008 and posted total sales of US$22.3 billion.

Weyerhaeuser Company, with forest holdings of 6.4 million acres in the United States and 30 million acres of leased forests in Canada, remained one of the largest U.S. forest products producers. The company reported total 2008 sales of US$16.9 billion and employed 14,900 people in 2009 worldwide.

A World Resources Institute report from June 2008 concluded that the U.S. forestry industry would "gain more than it loses if it embraces the challenges that global warming poses for it." The report, entitled "Trees in the Greenhouse: Why Climate Change is Transforming the Forest Products Business," makes the case for sustainable forestry being an important part of climate change solutions in the future. The report warned readers that there would be an uncertain business climate for many years due to regulatory changes related to the advancement of climate science and cleaner technology.

BIBLIOGRAPHY

Canadian Department of Foreign Affairs and International Trade. *Building Momentum: Sustainable Development in Canada,* 1997.

"A Common Desire to Protect the Environment." 1 July 2008. Available from http://www.china.org.cn.

Consolidated Balance Sheet, Weyerhaeuser 2009 Annual Report and Form 20-K. Available from http://www.weyerhaeuser.com.

"Half of Forestry Jobs in Downstream Processing." ABC News, 27 June 2008. Available from http://abcnews.com.

Hopkins, Philip. "Changes Ahead for Private Forestry." *The Age,* 26 June 2008. Available from http://theage.com.au.

O'Brien, Declan. "Forestry Boost in Donegal" The Independent, 1 July 2008. Available from http://Independent.ie.com.

Reforestation: Growing Tomorrow's Forests Today. Washington, DC: American Forest & Paper Association, 1998.

"Renewed Commitment to Wildlife Will Help Poorer Communities Worldwide." Media-Newswire, 1 July 2008. Available from www.media-newswire.com.

"Russian, Finnish Presidents Discuss Forestry—Presidential Aide." *Novosti,* 28 June 2008.

Sandul, Irina, and Claire Bigg. "Russian Forestry Still a Thieves' Market." *The Russia Journal,* 7 March 2004. Available from www.therussiajournal.com.

"A Smart Forestry Industry Can Win from Climate: Report." Carbon Positive, 1 July 2008. Available from www.carbonpositive.net.

World Resources Institute. "Trees in the Greenhouse: Why Climate Change is Transforming the Forest Products Business." June 2008. Available from http://www.wri.org/publication/trees-in-the-greenhouse.

CHEMICALS

———————•———————

ADHESIVES AND SEALANTS

NAICS CODE(S)

325520. Adhesive and sealant makers produce such diverse bonding compounds as caulking, glues, epoxies, rubber cements, and related products for household and commercial use.

INDUSTRY SNAPSHOT

The adhesives and sealants industry was increasingly competitive during the middle of the first decade of the 2000s. Globally the industry reached a record US$36 billion in 2006, representing a 4 percent growth exceeding performance in the previous year. The greatest advancements occurred in Asia, which was responsible for 23 percent of global consumption and was growing about two-and-a-half times faster than developed areas. Contributing to this growth were emerging markets in China, India, Vietnam, Korea, and Malaysia.

Plagued by high raw materials and energy costs, in addition to uncertain auto and construction markets, companies in the industry were adapting products and expanding product lines to serve new market trends. While adhesive prices rose, the cost of raw materials had, in many cases, increased even more, offsetting revenue gains. This was one of the factors prompting mergers and acquisitions (M&A), which increased rapidly.

ORGANIZATION AND STRUCTURE

Makers of adhesives and sealants have historically located their production facilities at sites that combined three factors: ready availability of raw materials, customers' production facilities nearby, and a skilled workforce. For this reason, both the largest producers and consumers of adhesives and sealants are located in the most heavily industrialized countries of the world, notably Western Europe, the United States, and Japan.

The market is centered around several industries that use large amounts of adhesives and sealants: automobiles, housing, aircraft, and packaging. The United Nations' commodity export statistics on several categories of natural and manufactured adhesives reported US$6.5 billion in exports in 1991. With the exception of Europe, where a lingering recession led to continued sluggish sales through the mid-1990s, the overall market grew steadily toward the year 2000.

By 1995 almost all of the major consumers of adhesives and sealants showed signs of recovery from the recession of the early part of the decade. Most producers of sealants and adhesives, particularly those not heavily tied to European markets, experienced a very healthy 1994. Europeans and makers of bulk chemicals experienced overcapacity and subsequent low prices that hurt some companies and helped others.

Car sales boomed in the mid-1990s in the United States, as recovery from the recession of the early 1990s released pent-up demand and low interest rates gave consumers the ability to buy. U.S. auto sales in 1994 were 15.4 million units. Globally, auto sales were expected to move upward as improved economies in Latin America, the North American Free Trade Agreement (NAFTA), and growth in Southeast Asia boosted demand in those areas. Volkswagen AG of Germany, France's Peugeot-Citroën, and U.S.-based Chrysler Corporation and General Motors set up joint ventures in China to take advantage of lower labor costs and the expectation of rising demand in Asia for vehicles.

In construction, new housing starts in the United States shot up in the early 1990s as mortgage rates fell drastically during the recession. Buyers took advantage of the lowest mortgage rates since World War II, as well as considerable recession-driven price drops in major housing markets, such as Los Angeles and Washington, D.C. The largest builders of commercial and industrial projects saw their markets also recover and were predicting continued steady growth as long as interest rates remained low. Adhesive and sealant makers noted a strong pickup in the do-it-yourself market by the mid-1990s, as indicated by sales of existing homes. Both Europe and North America saw a recession-driven growth in the do-it-yourself markets as homeowners repaired or upgraded existing dwellings.

The headquarters of leading manufacturers of military and civilian aircraft are located in the United States, Europe, and the Commonwealth of Independent States. Components are made in many countries, mainly in the United States and Europe, but also in Canada, Asia, and Latin America. The military market, which had dropped since 1991, was extremely poor in the early and mid-1990s, with tens of thousands of workers in the United States alone being laid off, and major companies disappearing in acquisition deals. Demand for commercial aircraft rose after mid-decade, with flights increasing as the recession lessened. Asia, with its large population, was expected to grow at the most rapid rate, prompting U.S.-based Boeing and McDonnell Douglas to export some assembly work to China in attempts to gain market share there.

Forest products companies in North America and Europe were greatly affected by environmental laws that prompted large scale recycling, particularly of newsprint and consumer packaging. By the mid-1990s, pulp and lumber prices were still high, causing wood producers to increase their use of adhesives to turn more of the sawdust and short pieces into usable building products. Packaging companies, in turn, turned to newer specialty adhesives to help them keep profit margins up by offering niche or custom-made packaging.

Makers of household and office appliances, including computers, continued to see sales rise through the mid-1990s in North America. Improving economies and opening markets in developing nations sent major consumer goods manufacturers overseas in search of new markets by the turn of the century. Consumer goods makers like Avon, Gillette, Procter & Gamble, Duracell, and Colgate in the United States, Belgium's Alcatel Bell Telephone Manufacturing, and Japan's Matsushita Electronics Corporation, Hitachi TV Company, and Sanyo Electric, all entered the mainland China market, and several companies established joint ventures. Adhesive maker H.B. Fuller Company of Minneapolis (U.S.) also opened for business in China in 1986 and by 1992 began

to show a profit selling to packaging and consumer goods firms there. Unilever, a joint Netherlands/United Kingdom-owned company, announced plans in 1993 to open a manufacturing subsidiary in Korea to make Ablestik brand adhesives for electronics manufacturers in Asia. Unilever later sold its adhesives business to Imperial Chemical Industries.

BACKGROUND AND DEVELOPMENT

Adhesives and sealants have been used by many civilizations worldwide for thousands of years. Egyptians glued caskets shut in 3000 B.C. using animal byproducts; the Romans used albumin from dried blood; and casein, a milk protein, was used by the ancient Chinese and Mediterranean peoples. The first glue factory was built in 1690 in the Netherlands.

Adhesive substances have been and still are made from animal byproducts, including hide, bones, and blood; from vegetables, such as soybeans, cassava, corn and potatoes; from tree resins; and from fish. Anti-gelling agents are added during manufacturing to keep the glue from solidifying in the tube or can.

Synthetic resins, developed in the 1920s and first manufactured cheaply in the 1930s, changed many adhesive-dependent industries with their strength and durability. They are especially suitable for high stress applications, such as aircraft and automobiles, but one of the industry's key markets is the more mundane world of envelopes, cellophane tape, and packaging. Hot melt adhesives were invented to temporarily tack labels on canned food. Hot varnish emulsified in a casein solution was designed to resist water and allowed combatants in World War II to dump supplies into the South Pacific and float them ashore. Self-adhesive labels, consisting of a sandwich of paper, a release coating, an adhesive, and a paper liner, fit the needs of the computer age. U.S.-based Minnesota Mining and Manufacturing Co. (3M) had a strong, favorable response from the market when it introduced Post-its, small adhesive-backed memo slips of paper made up into pads that could be pulled off and stuck back on the pad again or attached to many other things.

Adhesives are also a critical ingredient in plywood and other manufactured construction components. They gained increasing use worldwide as a growing global population and a dwindling supply of forest products created demand for construction materials that wasted less of each tree and polluted less at any time during their cycle.

Leaders in the industry have been successful because they have had access to raw materials, chemistry know-how that was transferable to the related field of adhesives and sealants, and proximity to manufacturers needing the end product. Six of the eight countries leading in the production of adhesives and sealants had both oil production or refining capabilities and significant automobile and/or aircraft production facilities to buy the adhesives. Finland and Switzerland are adjacent to other European countries, such as France, Germany, Italy, Russia, and Sweden, that manufacture cars and aircraft.

The rise of synthetics meant an increasing dependence on oil, and the industry needed a reliable flow of petroleum at a reasonable price for the factories. The Oil Producing and Exporting Countries' (OPEC) oil embargo of the 1970s drove oil prices much higher, but more stable prices in the early 1990s contributed to a glut of product, pushing oil prices so low that oil industry profits suffered.

Fears of fluctuating oil prices began a move by the industry in the 1970s to develop non-petroleum based synthetics. The cyanoacrylates ("super glues") became popular, as did the two-part emulsion polymer isocyanate adhesives patented in Japan during that decade.

Another development of the 1970s that greatly affected the industry was an increasing awareness of the effects of man-made chemicals on the environment. Adhesives and sealants came under close scrutiny as possible contributors to "indoor pollution." Buildings constructed to be energy-efficient were sealed tightly from outside air, and particle board, paneling, window sealants, wallpaper paste, carpet and flooring adhesives, as well as fumes given off by adhesives, paints, and plastics in the appliances, furniture, and computers, came under suspicion as sources of possible toxicity. Criticism also came because petroleum-based adhesives required petroleum-based solvents to manufacture and be removed, and concern arose about the effects of solvents on air and water quality. State and national governments acted to control the use, manufacture, application, and disposal of adhesives and sealants, and manufacturers moved to change formulations whenever possible to water-based, rather than petroleum-based products.

By 2004 the world adhesives and sealants market had reached US$18.5 billion. While the industry had consolidated in the late 1990s and early years of the first decade of the 2000s, it remained fragmented with many small and mid-sized firms.

Due to weakening demand in various markets and high raw material costs, many companies in the industry set forth new business initiatives that included cost cutting, consolidation, global expansion, and product diversification. While the industry had looked to both the auto and construction markets for the majority of its sales in the past, new uses for adhesives continued to positively affect the North American and Western European markets. For example, demand for new adhesives applications in the medical industry, including use in transdermal drug patches, assembled disposable syringes, and tissue bonding and skin repair, forced major industry leaders, including Henkel, to spend heavily in research and development in order to take advantage of growth potential. In early 2002, Henkel, through its Loctite subsidiary, had tissue-bonding adhesives up for FDA approval. The products already had been cleared in Europe.

According to industry executives, portions of the medical adhesives market were growing by as much as 30 percent per year. The industry also continued to capture market share from mechanical fasteners. Sales growth in the electronics adhesives market was at 6 percent per year, up from the 2 to 4 percent adhesives average. The industry also was expected to benefit from changing demand in the construction industry, with more than an average of 4 percent annual growth expected through 2009. This would be caused by a shift to engineered wood that requires specialty adhesives, as well as the explosive growth of the market in China.

The industry's performance typically varied with both demand for its products and the cost of its raw materials. During 2003, the price of raw materials—from 20 to 80 percent—and energy costs were high, putting pressure on profit margins. As demand increased in new markets for new products, merger and acquisition activity continued in the first decade of the 2000s, but at a slower pace. Companies eyed acquisitions as a way to diversify product lines and expand into higher-margin product offerings, such as those in the medical industry.

CURRENT CONDITIONS

Within the US$36 billion adhesives and sealant industry in 2006, packaging captured the largest market share (28 percent) and was one of the fastest-growing market segments, along with construction. In 2006, construction and transportation each accounted for 17 percent of end use, followed by assembly (11 percent), tapes (9 percent), consumer (8 percent), and other (10 percent).

Environmental concerns continued to play a part in the industry as it moved toward the end of the first decade of the 2000s. In the construction market, the U.S. Green Building Council and Green Building Initiative were working for more environmentally friendly or "green" adhesives and sealants. These groups promoted the use of fewer volatile organic compounds (VOC) in adhesives and sealants. VOCs cause emissions that contribute to respiratory problems and poor air quality. Natural adhesives, such as those made from starch, sugar, and proteins, do not require hydrocarbons from crude oil and natural gas for their production and therefore do not produce harmful emissions. According to Lawrence Sloan, president of the Adhesives and

Sealants Council, "The nastiest stuff out there is made with a solvent base, which emits the VOCs. Over the years, we have replaced many of the solvent-based products with water-based products and hot melts, which do not emit any VOCs."

The U.S. demand for automotive coatings, adhesives, and sealants was expected to have a positive effect on the adhesives and sealants industry in the late years of the first decade of the 2000s. The Freedonia Group, an international market research firm located in Cleveland, Ohio, predicted a 4.1 percent annual increase in demand through 2010, reaching a value of $7 billion. Part of the expected growth was attributed to the increasing use and production of automobiles, as well as auto manufacturers' desire to increase fuel efficiency and reduce weight. To achieve the latter goal, manufacturers were choosing structural adhesives instead of mechanical fasteners. The use of sealants also contributes to consumers' demands for quieter and more insulated interiors.

RESEARCH AND TECHNOLOGY

One of the most compelling research areas in the adhesives industry has been developing new product formulations that meet environmental standards set by the European Union or the U.S. Environmental Protection Agency (EPA). In Europe, the adhesives and sealants industry was the second-largest consumer of solvents, and consequently has been greatly affected by volatile organic compound (VOC) directives. Such environmental initiatives as the 1997 Kyoto Protocol on Climate Change and the impending renewal of U.S. clean water legislation ensure that environmental issues will continue to press the industry toward lower solvent usage and more emission controls.

Thus, the biggest innovations as the industry entered the twenty-first century were product adaptations that met higher environmental standards and helped present the consumer with a product perceived as more environmentally friendly, perhaps using less packaging, fewer toxic adhesives, or no propellants. Companies were reducing solvents and VOCs to avoid polluting air and water and reducing the ozone content of the atmosphere. In Europe, Germany's "Green Dot" environmental laws (so named because companies in compliance are allowed to display a green dot in advertisements and on packages) have impacted nearly every country in the European Union, because companies exporting to Germany were affected as well as those German firms selling domestically. The laws limit packaging of consumer products, mandate packaging recycling, and will eventually require the recycling of automobiles. Green Dot laws were expected to spread throughout the European Union and perhaps to the United States. Therefore, companies such

as Apple Computer and Dow Chemical Co. began to meet Europe's standards and to develop plans for the eventuality of Green Dot laws in the United States.

After manufacturers recover the research and development costs involved in creating products that can replace solvent-based adhesives, the directives may actually improve profits. Water-based adhesives and those with a high solids percentage are more expensive and more profitable; new product lines give manufacturers another venue for continual upgrades that customers are likely to buy. Firms still specializing in solvent-based adhesives for applications requiring them may pick up jobs, product lines, or competitors abandoning that market.

By the mid-1990s, solvents were no longer used in consumer adhesives in Europe, and overall their use in Europe's adhesive and sealant manufacturing had declined. Solvent-based adhesives accounted for less than 10 percent of Henkel's adhesives sales, according to *Chemical Week* magazine, which annually publishes a special section on the global adhesive and sealant industry.

In the United States, solvent use also continued to decline and hot melts, and water-based products claimed larger market shares. By 1995, waterborne adhesives had a 61.7 percent share of the U.S. market, hot melts a 20.7 percent share, and solvents a 9.8 percent stake. Industry observers cited by *Chemical Week* felt that application limitations on the customer end would keep those proportions at roughly the same level for the foreseeable future.

Examples of companies responding to environmental pressures included National Starch, which was developing dispersible, vinyl-based, hot-melt adhesives for paper packaging makers that used recycled feedstock in hopes of alleviating gummed machinery and thereby increasing the recyclability of paper products. 3M introduced a water-based neoprene contact cement. H.B. Fuller developed a new water-based adhesive and a resin-based starch additive that would make adhesives waterproof, increasing the rigidity of cardboard shipping containers and thus cutting down on spoilage and waste. In the United States, a 1994 settlement between Sherwin-Williams Company and the state of California, fining the company US$1 million for violating limits on toluene, was expected to result in the reformulation of some of the company's products and very likely those of competitors. By the middle of the first decade of the 2000s, the majority of research and development in the industry was modifying existing products to meet new demands.

Other new technologies entering the market were those that improved the safety of manufacturing and using adhesives. Microwavable hot melts introduced by U.S.-based Loctite could replace hot glue guns, and

National Starch's new ethylene vinyl acetate-based hot melt was processed at lower temperatures and therefore was less risky to handle. TOTAL and Elf Atochem introduced heat resistant adhesives, while TOTAL's U.S. subsidiary, Bostik, developed a caprolactam-free polyamide powder for the automotive market.

Alternative Health Journal Community contributor Dan Dunlap allowed the shades of green to shine for "The Healthy Hospital Movement." A major finding of the National Association of Children's Hospitals and Related Institutions (NACHRI) and The Center for Health Design claimed research reflected "physical design of healthcare settings unintentionally contributes to negative outcomes." The group's "Evidence for Innovation" 2008 study conclusions reflected how the conscious efforts to improve the healthcare environment could have a positive impact on patients. Case studies served as proof for research findings. Among the positive moves listed for East Carolina Heart Institute and Lexington Medical Center was the selection of products with minimal harmful chemicals emissions from sealants. Dunlop concluded that the "Healthy Hospital Movement" was widespread and gaining momentum around the world. It was also noted that health-conscious initiatives could result in cost savings.

INDUSTRY LEADERS

Henkel KGaA. With estimated 2005 adhesive sales of US$5.8 billion, the chemical conglomerate Henkel KGaA led the German adhesive industry and was the world's largest adhesive manufacturer with operations in more than 60 countries. In 1997 it acquired U.S.-based Loctite Corporation, one of the United States' top five adhesives companies, and mid-sized Canada Adhesives Ltd. During the same year, Henkel made a pair of smaller acquisitions in the United States and initiated joint ventures in India with The Anand Group, a Delhi-based automotive contractor, and Chembond Chemicals Ltd., a metal chemicals firm in Bombay. The Indian ventures were mainly to serve the adhesive and chemical needs of that nation's automotive industry.

Upon entering the new millennium, Henkel continued to make small purchases to diversify its product line, and it also consolidated by divesting underperforming businesses. As part of this strategy, the company sold Cognis, its specialty chemicals business, and revamped its adhesives business under the Henkel Technologies Division. In 2005 Henkel acquired OSI, a large adhesives company. Company-wide sales rose to US$14.1 billion in 2005 with about 52,500 employees worldwide.

As Holger Elfes reported for *Bloomberg News* on August 5, 2009, Henkel's decision to raise its savings forecast related to its 2008 acquisition of ICI's National Starch adhesives unit. Resulting benefits added up to US$216 million that exceeded company goals. Tough times, however, led Henkel, who invented the glue stick in 1969 and manufactures it as the Pritt Stick, to lay off approximately 3,000 jobs in 2008. Plans for changing how it does business in Europe may lead to additional layoffs, Elfes continued.

Minnesota Mining and Manufacturing Company (3M). 3M ranks prominently in the United States' adhesive industry, as well as internationally. In the early years of the first decade of the 2000s the company produced about US$350 million worth of adhesives annually, much of which was used in its own production of various tapes and labels. By 2006, 3M's sales exceeded US$22.9 billion. At the start of the new millennium, the company retreated from some of its electronic media forays to focus on its core businesses: consumer/industrial products such as tape and Post-it notes, and medical supplies such as polymer wound sealants. Sales outside of the United States accounted for about two-thirds of the company's revenues in 2006.

3M Chairman, President, and CEO George W. Buckley indicated that there were three guideposts for the company during tough economic times. They were "preserving in its cash position, minimizing cost, and driving revenue where opportunities exist." Buckley saluted company employees and claimed "building" had occurred more than "cutting" since 2006.

H.B. Fuller Company. During the early years of the first decade of the 2000s, 92 percent of Fuller's sales stemmed from its adhesives, sealants, and coatings business. Company-wide sales reached US$1.4 billion in 2006, at which time the company had 4,000 employees. The firm's products are used by the automotive, converting, engineered systems, footwear, graphic arts, non-woven/hygienic, packaging, polymer, tobacco, window, and woodworking industries. Fuller operates in more than 36 countries in North America, Latin America, Europe, and the Asia/Pacific region. During 2001 the company reorganized into global business units and shut down approximately 20 percent of its worldwide capacity in order to cut costs. Fuller also continued to diversify its product line and focus on new technology.

Compared to its financial performance in 2008, H.B. Fuller acknowledged it was a more challenging time in 2009. It had, however, a strong second quarter.

National Starch and Chemical. Through its 1996 purchase of the major U.S. adhesive maker National Starch and Chemical, U.K.-based Imperial (ICI) vaulted into a leadership status within the adhesive industry. One of the world's largest paint manufacturers, ICI had total 2005 sales of about US$10 billion. National Starch, its primary adhesives holding, generated US$3.6 billion in 2006 sales and employed almost 10,000 people. In addition to non-adhesive products, National produces a wide range of adhesives for important industry segments including non-wovens, food packaging, paper converting, wood, building components, automotive, pressure sensitive products, and medical. Nearly 40 percent of company sales were derived from its adhesive business. North American operations accounted for nearly half of National's total sales.

Bostik Inc. Bostik Inc., a subsidiary of oil giant TOTAL S.A., was established when Bostik and Ato Findley were merged together during TotalFina's purchase of Elf Aquitaine. Bostik operates under three divisions: industrial adhesives, consumer, and construction. Sales for TOTAL S.A. in 2006 were US$175.1 billion; Bostik contributed US$1.5 billion of the total.

Creating a special alliance with equally special results, StarQuartz and Bostik joined together resulting in their creation called Bostik TruColor. The innovative "Water-based, urethane grout technology" can provide outstanding color-matching capabilities with the Hydroment or Durabond brands. It also offers features and benefits that are highly desirable for architects, builders and others supporting a green marketplace. According to Bostik Director of Sales and Marketing Robert McNamara, the distinctive partnership was set to become a long-term relationship. "The synergies in this relationship will uniquely position us to rapidly bring the most innovative systems to our industry," McNamara proclaimed.

As evidenced by a letter to its customers, Bostick is a proud member of the U.S. Green Building Council. In addition, the company is an avid supporter of the Rochester (New York) Institute of Technology's LEED (Leadership in Energy and Environmental Standards) initiative for the constructions materials industry. To that end, an attachment listing Bostick products that might assist with the qualification of projects seeking LEED-NC V2.2 certification accompanied the letter.

In August 2009, Bostick announced that it was stepping out into new territory. High Performance Latex (HPL) Wood Flooring Adhesive marked its establishing itself into a new market. HPL is designed to be "solvent free, has very low odor and VOC content, contains no hazardous chemicals, and is nonflammable."

Rohm and Haas Company. Rohm and Haas significantly increased its presence in the global adhesives and sealants industry with the purchase of Morton International in 1999. In 2006, total company sales were US$8.2 billion. The company established manufacturing plants in Brazil and Bombay in 2001 and also made two purchases to strengthen its position in the automotive and cold-seal adhesives markets. Rohm and Haas is focusing on product development related to food packaging, hot-melt technologies used in industrial lamination, and energy-cured adhesives. The company employed 16,500 people in 2006.

After administrative action affecting approximately 900 positions in all regions and businesses of the Rohm and Haas Company, it was acquired by Dow Chemical Company in April 2009. Consequently, Dow formed a new business tailor-made to become "the leading supplier of raw materials for architectural and industrial coatings in the world."

MAJOR COUNTRIES IN THE INDUSTRY

Asia/Pacific. With 23 percent of the global market for adhesives and sealants in 2006, Asia was growing fast, with development in such countries as China, India, Vietnam, Korea, and Malaysia contributing to the growth. Annual growth in China was estimated at about 10 percent. Overall, Asia averaged 6 percent annual growth, compared to a global growth rate of 3.5. to 5.5 percent, according to *Chemical Week*.

According to Kline & Company, the major worldwide consulting and research firm, a dramatic increase was expected for the "average volume growth of synthetic latex polymers." Conclusions featured in the study report entitled "Synthetic Latex Polymers 2009: China Business Analysis and Opportunities" reflected that growth in that market would be 7.5 percent between 2008 and 2013. Adhesives and sealants, along with paper plus paints and coatings, represent more than 75 percent of the volume linked to synthetic latex polymers for China.

Europe. Europe accounted for 34 percent of the adhesives and sealants industry in 2006 and was expected to grow by just under 3 percent per year through 2009. As prospects for future growth remained steady for Western Europe, the region's development of environmentally friendly adhesive technology was considered to be a step above U.S. efforts, which positioned the region to take advantage of future opportunities in this sector.

The United States. North America was responsible for 35 percent of industry production in 2006, and the ChemQuest Group, an international consulting firm specializing in the coatings/sealants/adhesives industries, estimated that the U.S. adhesives industry would grow at an annual rate of 3.9 percent per year, exceeding the GDP, through 2010. In 2005, U.S. sales of adhesives and sealants reached $11.6 billion, an increase of 6.4 percent from the previous year. Of the two major classes of adhesives, non-pressure-sensitive adhesives (NPSAs) accounted for 83 percent of industry sales, but pressure-sensitive adhesives sales were growing faster. According to the Adhesive and Sealant Council, the paper, board, and related products segment made up more than half of the entire adhesive and sealants market in North America in 2005, with demand reaching 3.6 billion pounds. Products in this segment include those used in the manufacturing of packaging (e.g., paper and plastic bags and envelopes), dry and wet lamination, bookbinding, nonwoven fabrics such as disposable diapers and surgical gowns, and pressure sensitive products, such as labels, tapes, decals, signs, and stamps. The building construction market was also strong, with sales of 1 billion pounds in 2005. A study by DPNA International attributed that growth to both an upturn in commercial building and rebuilding efforts due to Hurricanes Katrina and Rita in 2005.

BIBLIOGRAPHY

Adhesive and Sealant Council Inc. "2005—2007 North American Market Study for Adhesives and Sealants With a Global Overview," 2006 Edition, 15 May 2007. Available from www.ascouncil.org.

"The Adhesive and Sealant Market in the Americas." *Adhesives & Sealants Industry,* November 2004.

"Adhesives Growth to Stretch in Developing Regions." *Chemical Week,* 7 January 2004.

"Automotive Coatings, Adhesives, and Sealants Demand to Rise 4.1% Per Year Through 2010." All Business, 1 May 2006. Available from www.allbusiness.com.

"Big Surprise: Industry Sales Rise Despite Mounting Price Pressures." *Chemical Week,* 15 September 2004.

———. "Bostik Unveils its High Performance Latex (HPL) Wood Flooring Adhesive," 12 August 2009. Available from www.bostik-us.com.

Bostick. "Customer Letter," 13 November 2008. Available from www.bostik-us.com.

———. "StarQuartz and Bostik Alliance: Bostik, Inc. and StarQuartz Industries Announce Tile and Stone Industry Alliance." 2009. Available from www.bostik-us.com.

Blanchfield, Lindsey. "Adhesives, Sealants Face a Tough Market." *ICIS Chemical Business Americas,* 23 April 2007.

Colbert, Catherine. "Company Profile: Henkel KGaA." Hoover's Online, 2009. Available from www.hoovers.com.

"The Dow Chemical Company Forms Dow Coating Materials Following Acquisition of Rohm & Haas," 29 May 2009. Available from www.rohmhaas.com.

Dunlop, Dan. "Healthcare's Green Initiative: The Healthy Hospital Movement." *Alternative Health Journal,* 3 August 2009. Available from www.alternativehealthjournal.com.

Draper, Deborah J., ed. *Business Rankings Annual.* Detroit: Thomson Gale, 2004.

Elfes, Holger. "Henkel Raises Cost Saving Goals After Profit Triples." *Bloomberg,* 5 August 2009. Available from www.bloomberg.com.

Forrest, Wayne. "Demand Remains Strong, But Pricing Is Unsure." *Purchasing,* 2 November 2006.

"The Global Adhesive and Sealant Market." *Adhesives & Sealants Industry,* October 2004.

"H.B. Fuller Reports Second Quarter 2009 Results. Controllable Items Managed, End-Market Demand Still Challenged." 23 June 2009. Available from phx.corporate-ir.net.

"Henkel Creates Line for Supermarkets." *Marketing,* 5 February 2004.

"Hoover's Company Capsules." *Hoover's Online,* 2007. Available from www.hoovers.com.

"International Trade Statistics." World Trade Organization, 2003. Available from www.wto.org.

Kline & Company. "Emulsion Polymer Consumption in Construction in China Experienced Double-Digit Growth in 2008, According to Kline." *PR Newswire,* 13 August 2009. Available from News.prnewswire.com.

Lazich, Robert S., ed. *Market Share Reporter.* Detroit: Thomson Gale, 2004.

Lohan, Joseph. "North America Adhesives Demand to Rise Through '07." *ICIS News,* 4 August 2006.

Murad, Daniel S. "Global Adhesives and Sealants State of the Union." *Adhesives & Sealants Industry,* April 2007.

———. "The U.S. Adhesives Industry: Current Structure and Future Growth." *Adhesives & Sealants Industry,* October 2006.

"New Raw Materials: The Key to Industry Growth." *Adhesives & Sealants Industry,* April 2005.

"Rohm and Haas Company Announces Second Set of Actions in Response to Market Conditions," 20 January 2009. Available from www.rohmhaas.com.

Schmitt, Bill. "Margins on a Slippery Slope." *Chemical Week,* 2 April 2003.

"Sticking to Growth Markets." *Chemical Week,* 7 April 2004.

Walsh, Kerri, and Kate Phillips. "Developing Nations Drive Demand." *Chemical Week,* 11 April 2007.

SIC 8731

BIOTECHNOLOGY

NAICS CODE(S)

541710. Biotechnology firms harness living organisms and biological components at the molecular, sub-cellular, and cellular levels to create marketable products. Products include bacterial and viral vaccines; serums, plasmas, and various microbiological substances; and genetically engineered plants and animals. The industry also encompasses firms that perform related research services, such as genetic coding and forensic testing. Biotechnology is closely aligned with the pharmaceutical segment within the broader chemical industry. More information about the broader drug industry is provided in **Pharmaceuticals**.

INDUSTRY SNAPSHOT

After enduring difficult times during the early 2000s, when industry players struggled to keep research initiatives alive despite falling investment levels, the biotechnology industry showed signs of improvement. According to research by Ernst & Young (E&Y) the global revenues of public companies in the biotech field were US$41.4 billion, net losses were US$12.5 billion, and the industry employed 194,000 people. Although biotechnology industries were emerging in countries such as China, Singapore, Russia, Japan, and India, the United States continued to lead the global biotech industry on a single-country basis. U.S. industry revenues were US$53.5 billion in 2006, according to the Biotechnology Industry Organization (BIO), an association of companies, educational institutions, and state biotechnology centers.

Europe continued to be the second leading biotechnology market. However, some industry analysts were concerned that the European industry was in jeopardy of losing its luster as competition increased from emerging countries. Continued investment and the development of breakthrough biotechnology products were key to the region's leadership.

Biotech's emergence has been controversial. As the industry reports breakthroughs in cloning, stem cell research, and genetically modified foods, various social and political entities have responded with boycotts and bans, and in some extreme cases, violence. The United States is the world's largest producer and promoter of genetically modified crops, but most countries have been hesitant to accept even test fields of the products, with Thailand a notable exception. Despite the concerns of activists, many other countries were expected to follow, as large countries search for ways to more efficiently feed their populations and others try to compete for trade dollars.

A major joint study on biotechnology in agriculture was completed in 2008 by the United Nations and the World Bank. Titled the "International Assessment of Agricultural Knowledge, Science and Technology for Development," (IAASTD) the study involved 400 experts in various disciplines for four years. The study concluded that biotechnology held little potential for alleviating world poverty and hunger as some proponents had claimed. It supported an alternative view that biotechnology was a force for greater agricultural consolidation and profit in the wealthy nations. Representatives from the biotech firms Monsanto and Syngenta, who had been involved in the study, withdrew in protest before the findings were released.

Biotechnology-related debates continue to occur in other areas. In October 2010, the European Union (EU) proposed a ban on farm animal cloning, and prohibition of imports of meat and milk from cloned animals. The proposal was expected to be approved. David Edwards of the U.S.-based BIO claimed the decision went against "global scientific agreement that foods from livestock clones and their offspring are completely safe to eat." With the industry continuing to suggest that tremendous benefits are potentially available through continued biotech research, the debate should continue to take on interesting dimensions outside of the purely economic ones.

The recession of the late 2000s affected the biotech industry by restricting the flow of funds for new ventures and research. In November 2010, the *San Jose Mercury News* reported that conditions could be looking up, since 2010 had already seen 12 new Initial Public Offerings (IPOs) of biotech firms in the United States. There had only been three U.S. biotech IPOs in 2009 and just one in 2008. The alternative view was that the uptick was merely a result of new firms being unable to secure private, venture-capital-based financing and being left with little choice but to try the public stock markets.

ORGANIZATION AND STRUCTURE

The biotechnology industry was in the relatively early stages of development, but continued to grow globally in the 2000s. According to BIO, the United States was home to 1,473 companies with 198,300 employees in 2003, which was an increase from 1,466 companies with 194,600 employees in 2002. As of December 31, 2006, there were 1,452 biotech companies in the U.S. There were 180,000 people working in the sector. In 2007, the top five U.S. biotech companies invested an average of US$170,000 per employee in research and development. As of 2010, BIO reported more than 250 biotech health care products and vaccines in use. Over 13.3 million farmers worldwide were said to use biotech to increase production, fight pests, and reduce environmental impact.

A relatively advanced biotech sector also exists in Europe where 1,878 companies were active by 2002, primarily in the United Kingdom, Germany, and France. In other areas of the world, the number of biotechnology firms grew as governments provided necessary funding. By 2002, 601 firms were doing research in the Asia/Pacific region and 417 in Canada, which was significant in light of Canada's population in relation to other countries supporting the industry.

Biotech companies generally start with an idea for a promising new technology, such as a cure for acquired immune deficiency syndrome (AIDS) or a better method of testing DNA. The risk of failure is high, but success leads to potentially huge profits, status for the developing company and its researchers, and important benefits to society. A company developing a treatment for arthritis, for example, commonly spends two to four years identifying the biology of the disease and the potential therapeutic impact of a compound before spending another one to two years isolating a compound and figuring out how to get the substance to specific points in the human body. Another year or two may be spent designing a system to manufacture, modify, and purify the compound on a commercial scale. Thus, the company may have been laboring and investing for four to eight years with no product sales to support the research expenses. By 2005, there were more than 370 clinical trials in progress for vaccines and drugs connected with more than 200 human diseases including Alzheimer's, multiple sclerosis, and AIDS, according to BIO.

Biotech companies, which often begin with a few individuals, are typically funded with seed money contributed by venture capitalists. If early research and development efforts are encouraging, additional capital may be contributed by private investors during the first few years. If a firm can come up with what appears to be a promising product, a financial partner will inevitably step in, usually a large drug company that can support the start-up biotech firm with sizeable research expenses, as well as testing, government approval, and production. In return for its support, the drug company may receive compensation in the form of marketing and distribution rights to the new product. Some companies acquire additional funds by going public with their stocks. An increasing number of companies were obtaining government support for their research, particularly in Asia. Governments were seeing the potential social, economic, and political benefits of their countries holding the secrets to particularly useful biotechnological processes.

BACKGROUND AND DEVELOPMENT

Broadly defined, biotechnology has been applied commercially since at least 7000 B.C., when people began using fermentation to produce drinks, food, and fuel. A "second generation" biotechnology, which involved processes not completely understood by researchers at the time, emerged in the first half of the twentieth century. Scientists at that time began using microbiology and biochemistry to process waste and produce pharmaceuticals, chemicals, fuels, and food. In the 1930s, beef insulin, a protein, was used to treat diabetes, but it was one of only a few that humans were able to exploit until decades later because researchers were limited by their ability to extract a single protein from the hundreds of proteins that might be manufactured by a group of cells.

The pivotal breakthrough to biotechnology occurred in 1953, when British scientists James Watson and Francis Crick discovered the structure of DNA. That understanding led to a realization of the process by which proteins are produced by cells, which in turn led to the creation of the biotechnology industry. Another milestone was reached in DNA research in 1973 when U.S.

scientists Stanley Cohen and Herbert Boyer succeeded in snipping an individual piece of DNA out of an African clawed toad. They were able to splice that fragment into a common bacterium, where it began to function with the foreign gene, and the process of recombinant DNA was born. For their efforts, Cohen and Boyer received a Nobel Prize. The chief benefit of the breakthrough was that scientists discovered how to genetically alter microorganisms and produce large quantities of proteins that occurred naturally only in small quantities through fermentation. These proteins could be designed and manipulated for specific purposes.

A series of biotech advances followed the 1973 achievement beginning with the production of the first monoclonal antibodies in 1975. Monoclonal antibodies are essentially cloned cells that can be used to attack foreign toxins, viruses, and cancer cells. In 1976 the first working synthetic gene was developed, and in 1977 important methods for reading DNA sequences were discovered. By 1978, the first identification of the high-level structure of a virus and the first production of recombinant human insulin were achieved. The first human growth hormone was synthesized in 1979, and in 1980, biologists succeeded in transplanting the gene for human insulin into a bacterium. By the early 1980s, scientists were learning to transfer a number of newfound genes into bacteria to create large amounts of disease-fighting proteins. In 1981, scientists created the first Chimera, a creature carrying a gene placed there by humans rather than nature. That experiment, which involved a mouse, demonstrated how biotechnology could be used by humans to influence the genetic makeup of living creatures. It also proved that animals could be used to test human biotech treatments, following the precedent used in conventional medical experiments.

Although researchers in the United Kingdom, and later Europe, contributed to the biotechnology revolution during the 1960s and 1970s, scientists in the United States assumed an early and dominant lead in the emerging science. Significant early biotech start-ups were Cetus (1971), Genentech (1976), Genex (1977), Biogen (1978), Centocor (1979), and Amgen (1980), all based in the United States. These companies, along with a few others, capitalized on the belief of many investors that biotechnology was going to have a great impact on many areas of industry, medicine, food, energy, and agriculture. Although some of those companies made significant contributions to the burgeoning field of biotech, it was not until the 1980s that the industry boomed. The growth was largely the result of a U.S. Supreme Court ruling that allowed genetically engineered bacteria to be patented. For many, that ruling suggested the possibility of massive financial rewards for biotech innovators.

During the early and mid-1980s, growth in the biotech industry surged as new companies started and technology rapidly advanced. At the start of the 1980s, only 40 different genes had been identified, but by the end of the decade, as new genes were identified regularly, more than 4,000 had been discovered. Gene identification sparked enthusiasm about the potential to develop new treatments and cures for diseases, develop improved plants and foods, and create a range of industrial products that could, for example, clean up oil spills or produce substitutes for petroleum-based fuels. Although industry revenues were negligible early in the 1980s, the number of biotech start-ups was impressive. The United States led the world with about 50 start-up biotech companies in 1980. That figure grew to approximately 100 start-ups annually for most of the decade.

For reasons related primarily to politics and the attitude of the British financial community, the United Kingdom relinquished its early lead in biotechnology to the United States. However, the United Kingdom followed the U.S. industry's lead and became the second major global player during the 1980s. The first British biotech start-up, Celltech, was founded in 1980 as a combined effort between academic, government, and private-sector players. Similar start-ups that followed included Cambridge Life Sciences, Agricultural Genetics Co., British Biotechnology, and Delta. France and Germany followed with various government-supported biotech ventures. French start-ups included Transgene, Genetica, and G3. West Germany's interest in biotechnology was demonstrated in the 1970s by the creation of federally funded agencies, allowing the country to enter the industry relatively early compared to other continental European countries. By the late 1980s, Germany had become a rival of the United Kingdom for biotech investments.

After a slow start in the early 1980s, the Japanese government partnered with private industry to develop biotechnologies, including recombinant DNA and mass culturing of cells. Japan's biotech ventures were conducted through large companies rather than through entrepreneurial concerns. Japan made major investments and successfully converted some important technologies that had been developed elsewhere into marketable products, but did not produce many biotech innovations.

A surge in the biotech industry in the mid-1980s was largely a consequence of financial markets. Investors, excited by the possibility of huge returns from cancer-curing wonder drugs and other biotech products, made massive investments in promising biotech start-ups. Some of the cash flow was diverted to European companies, but most of it was infused in cutting-edge U.S. concerns. A combination of factors diminished cash flow beginning in 1987, and the industry was considered to be

reaping its just reward for overstating expectations. However, after a three-year lull, investor enthusiasm had returned, and the industry experienced explosive growth. Much of the rally was sparked by the successes of a few star players, especially U.S.-based Amgen, which introduced a successful drug designed to battle anemia. Funding for the U.S. biotech industry from all sources grew from about US$1.2 billion to US$4.4 billion between 1990 and 1991. Subsequently, the number of industry competitors in the United States and Europe surged to more than 1,500 by 1993, and the stock prices of publicly traded firms rose nearly threefold on average.

By 1993, the biotech industry was beginning to live up to its promise of providing life-enhancing, genetically engineered breakthroughs. A handful of companies, almost all of which were in the United States, succeeded in getting several important products approved for sale. Amgen, with huge sales and profits in 1993 and 1994, had the most products approved, followed by Biogen, which was pushing an Alpha interferon for hepatitis and cancer as well as a hepatitis B vaccine. In addition, biotech pioneer Chiron was marketing an anticancer agent and a treatment for multiple sclerosis, and Genentech was selling a human growth hormone and a treatment for cystic fibrosis.

Despite these encouraging success stories, some investors became disillusioned with the biotech industry. After years of large capital investments in research and development, many had become impatient waiting for returns. Their frustration was provoked by the number of big failures that consumed millions of dollars with little or no return. For example, Synergen, a U.S. firm, tried to create an antisepsis drug called Antril. Sepsis is an infection that floods the bloodstream of cancer and burn victims, affecting hundreds of thousands of people annually, often resulting in death. Armed with US$300 million in capital, Synergen built manufacturing plants and hired a sales force during the early 1990s, despite lackluster test results for Antril. The company eventually stopped developing the drug after losing US$165 million.

In December 2001, federal regulators refused to approve the cancer drug Erbitux that had been developed by ImClone Systems. By the end of January 2002, the price of the company's stock was about one-quarter of what it had been before the drug failed to gain approval.

Economic failures like Erbitux and Antril highlighted structural problems that plagued the biotech industry in the mid-1990s. Too much money was being spent on technology that was not working. Wary investors tightened their purse strings, suggesting a possible industry shakeout that would eliminate companies that were not producing results, reinforced by plunging biotech stock prices. Some industry observers considered part of the problem to be the high level of fragmentation in the industry. In the United States and parts of Europe, several companies were often competing to produce the same products. One result was that research and development efforts were overlapping, resulting in overall inefficiency. These and other dynamics indicated that the biotech sector might be entering a period of consolidation.

The net effect of industry turbulence in the mid-1990s was a shift of new capital from the investment community away from small, entrepreneurial start-ups with unproven technology to their established competitors who had a good chance of success. Shifting financial dynamics had numerous effects on the capital-intensive industry, including an increase in collaboration. Small firms that were faced with diminished access to funds compared to the early 1990s began to seek more joint ventures with large pharmaceutical firms, big brokerage houses, and other biotech firms with complementary technologies or operations.

Regardless of the state of the global biotech industry in the mid-1990s, the long-term outlook for the sector was good to excellent by the 2000s, once objections from some U.S. legislators were deflected. In the 1990s, new products entered the market, pivotal technologies advanced, and sales of approved drugs and vaccines rose rapidly. By 1995, about 1,800 biotech firms were operating in Europe and North America, with nearly 1,300 in the United States. In addition, a growing number of large pharmaceutical companies were becoming more active in biotechnology. In the United States, which continued to account for the majority of industry revenues and product introductions, biotech sales jumped from US$2.7 to US$7.7 billion between 1989 and 1994. Although aggregate industry losses increased from US$2.1 billion to about US$4.1 billion annually during the same period, employment and research spending was up significantly.

A number of successful biotech drugs came on the market and were being approved in 1995, validating positive projections for the global biotech industry. Effective cures or treatments were being marketed for diseases from hemophilia and heart disease to genital warts and kidney cancer. Some of the more significant biotech breakthroughs included Betaseron, a treatment for multiple sclerosis; Pulmozyme, a treatment for cystic fibrosis and possibly bronchitis; and a number of experimental compounds to treat AIDS.

The biotech industry reported advances in agriculture and forensics in the mid-1990s. For example, U.S. firm Calgene Corp. introduced a controversial genetically altered tomato that ripened on the vine and remained fresh for two weeks after picking. In addition, forensic pathologists could prosecute or clear criminals based on minute samples of body materials. However, infamous court cases such as that of O.J. Simpson, in which the defendant was acquitted despite DNA evidence, highlighted the tenuous status of such technology in courtrooms. Nonetheless, a number of cases in which prisoners or defendants were freed as a result of DNA testing indicated that such testing would become increasingly common during the twenty-first century.

Nevertheless, the biotech industry continued to focus on the development of drugs and gene therapy techniques in the mid-1990s. Few drugs had been developed by the biotech industry, but four of the top-selling drugs worldwide in 1994 were biotech drugs, an impressive proportion considering the size of the established pharmaceutical industry. Furthermore, a few biotech experiments suggested a promising future for the field of gene therapy. In 1994, researchers in Philadelphia cured a cholesterol disorder in a woman by injecting her with genetically engineered copies of genes that she lacked. Two girls with a genetic defect that disabled their immune systems were treated similarly.

By 1995, the biotechnology industry had spent more than US$25 billion in capital, most of which was invested in research and development. Biotech companies in the United States had raised additional capital at a rate of about US$5 billion annually in 1995, and the industry held the number one ranking worldwide in expenditures as a percentage of total revenues and total costs. After years of research and development (R&D), biotech pioneers in the mid-1990s had failed to produce the cancer cures and wonder foods that many investors and industry participants had expected. Nevertheless, research efforts were beginning to bear fruit, and a number of new development ventures suggested eventual breakthroughs. By 1995, biotech drugs were helping cystic fibrosis patients breathe more easily, reducing the number of heart attack related deaths by eliminating blood clots and diminishing the threat of hepatitis with vaccines and blood-screening tools.

AIDS was a key focus of research in the biotech industry in the mid-1990s. A cure for AIDS was not in sight, and the chance of finding one was estimated to be 1 in 10,000. The disease had quickly become resistant to all the potential cures that had been tested, but a number of therapies had been developed that were helping to mitigate its effects. Furthermore, a variety of government, private sector, and academic groups were teaming up to find a way to stop the AIDS virus. In 1993, 15 U.S. and European pharmaceutical companies joined forces to share information, drug supplies, and technologies in an effort to speed trials of different drug therapies. Some of the most important AIDS-related breakthroughs involved testing for the virus, including one product that could test for AIDS without a blood sample.

In addition to advances related to disease and human genetics, biotech research had produced breakthroughs in other segments of the industry. For example, the market for DNA testing equipment was exploding in 1995 as a result of new test kits that allowed multiple DNA tests to be conducted using one small sample of body tissue or fluid. Similar test kits were being marketed to cattle breeders, who used them to identify desired genetic traits in cattle. Potential markets for the bio-testing equipment were unlimited, including to identify the sex of small animals at an early age or to determine the exact origin of a piece of lumber that may have been cut from a government-protected forest.

Other breakthroughs investigated in the mid-1990s were related to slowing the aging process and extending human life. Scientists at Washington University had achieved surprising results identifying a gene known as Bcl-2 that prevented the death of cells. Researchers deleted the gene from laboratory mice, causing them to age extremely rapidly. Similarly, biotech researchers had made gradual gains in nerve regeneration, and companies had worked to develop nerve growth substances that could eliminate senility. Such substances had the potential to treat paralysis and mental disorders.

Important technological breakthroughs, new drugs, and significant increases in global biotech participation occurred in the late 1990s and the early 2000s. In 1997, Roslin Institute researchers in Scotland announced that a sheep named Dolly was the first mammal to be cloned with material taken from another. That development sparked international debate about the moral and ethical aspects of genetic engineering, particularly of human beings. Most countries agreed that cloning of human beings was not acceptable or desirable, and several signed a ban on cloning. By April 2002, the industry's biggest battlefield seemed to be in the U.S. Senate, where lobbyists for BIO fought against the Brownback bill, which banned not only the cloning of human beings, but also could lead to criminal charges against scientists who crossed certain boundaries of genetic research. Collaboration and consolidation among biotech and large pharmaceutical firms continued to characterize the U.S. industry.

Europe and Asia recognized the importance of biotechnology to health care and future economic prosperity. Europe recorded a 50 percent increase in the number of small biotech firms. Although Asia still trailed the United States and Europe in biotech development, several countries, notably Japan and China, made significant gains. Japan was developing its own pharmaceutical industry and had introduced several products to treat infections and detect diseases such as AIDS. Japanese researchers were also active in genetic engineering and

had successfully cloned a cow. China's biotech focus was largely on bioagriculture, although its pharmaceutical industry was growing. China produced several genetically engineered crops that included nutritious, disease-resistant tomatoes, wheat, and rice with a longer shelf life. The Chinese pharmaceutical industry was comprised of about 35 firms including joint ventures, which was expected to increase.

New biotech products appeared on the market as the time frame for government approval for new drugs decreased. The U.S. Food and Drug Administration (FDA) took an average of 18 months to review and approve new drugs, although a minimum of six months were required by law, and in the European Union, approval took about 12 months. An industry report by Ernst & Young International in the mid-2000s reported that Europe was the leader for the introduction of new medicines for originating companies and market arrivals. However, findings from the FDA claimed a turnaround closer to 15 months. The FDA indicated that priority drugs, especially for cancer, AIDS, and other viruses, usually received approval much faster than other drugs. Numerous drugs were introduced for the treatment of AIDS, cancer, Parkinson's, heart disease, and other conditions, and the rate of new drug treatments was continuing to rise rapidly. Most analysts agreed that the global biotechnology sector had finally emerged as a key economic player despite industry fluctuations. The long-range outlook for the industry moving into the twenty-first century was largely upbeat.

Biotechnology endured difficult times during the early 2000s. As capital investment levels declined, industry players struggled to keep their research and development initiatives alive with existing funds. BIO noted that while industry funding was US$38 billion in 2000, levels fell to US$15.1 billion in 2001 and US$10.5 billion in 2002. By 2003, conditions were improving as investors began to finance the biotechnology market. BIO indicated that funding levels began to increase in 2003, reaching US$16.9 billion. In addition, some companies benefited from increased funding related to going public, as well as mergers and acquisitions.

Research into vaccines against anthrax was promising in 2002 as companies anticipated worst-case scenarios similar to the deaths caused by anthrax-laced envelopes sent through the U.S. mail following the September 11, 2001, terrorist attacks against the United States. St. Louis University's Department of Molecular Microbiology and Immunology was developing a vaccine with a scaled-down, modified adenovirus that could provide immunity and stop the often fatal result of exposure to anthrax. In addition, the NIH had funded research for a vaccine that could similarly stop terrorist-induced hoof-and-mouth disease. One irony of the bioterrorism scare of the early 2000s was that it had mobilized university, government, and private sector researchers into a single team that discover ways to immunize humans and animals against deadly diseases.

According to a study by consulting firm Ernst & Young, three main issues faced the biotechnology industry. First, there were too many players in an industry that continued to lose money. Mergers and acquisitions had increased, especially for firms doing research in similar areas that sought economies of scale as funding became increasingly difficult. Companies that could not find funding and that chose not to seek a merger or acquisition were facing bankruptcy. For example, PPL Therapeutics, which had cloned Dolly the sheep in 1996, had filed for bankruptcy by 2004.

Second, the industry was starting to mature, resulting in specialization for firms that had once tried to diversify. Approximately one-third of companies were forming alliances with firms doing similar research with each firm responsible for a specific part of the process. Such alliances between large pharmaceutical companies and small biotech firms had become increasingly common. One successful alliance was between CuraGen Corporation and Bayer Pharmaceuticals to find treatments for diabetes and obesity. Previous investments in CuraGen allowed the company to enter the alliance that would allow it to profit from any drugs developed.

The third issue facing the biotechnology industry was globalization as companies expanded their markets and began to be listed on global stock exchanges to become more competitive and increase their investor base. An increase in government support also supported globalization in the biotech industry. For example, in March 2005, the United Kingdom announced a huge increase in funding for scientific research, especially for the growing area of stem-cell research. Successful research was also being completed in Cuba, where a vaccine for meningitis B was developed, leading to a biotech sector that was internationally successful.

The biotechnology industry had constantly struggled to find venture capital and had not kept pace with the more advanced biotech industry in the United States. Genmab, based in Denmark, and led by American Lisa Drakeman, was considered a rising star. The company had spent between US$300 and US$400 billion of its investors' money without producing any products for sale and without recording any profits. However, Genmab's clients agreed with Drakeman that drugs in clinical trials were of value. In 2006, GlaxoSmithKline agreed to a major licensing deal worth up to US$1.6 billion for Genmab's ofatumumab (HuMax-CD20) cancer and arthritis drug in clinical trials as long as the drug met

expectations. Mergers and acquisitions in Europe demonstrated increases, growing seven-fold from US$2.5 billion in 2007.

CURRENT CONDITIONS

The Competitive Enterprise Institute reported 250 million acres of bio-engineered crops were being grown globally, about seven percent of total production. Of this, the United States produced more than half—135 million acres. Furthermore, 90 percent of U.S. soybeans, 85 percent of cotton, and 50 percent of field corn was genetically modified (GM). Developing nations India and China used GM in almost 40 percent of their acreage. As their economies continued to grow at rapid rates, it was expected that their use of GM would grow faster than that of the developed world. Despite its ubiquity, biotechnology in agriculture continued to have its detractors, especially in Europe, where considerable legal restrictions had been enacted and GM food was much less common than in the United States.

Worldwide, biotech was rapidly adopted, however. In 2010, the fastest growing sector of agricultural biotech was transgenic crops. These promised to allow farmers to have greater yield per acre, reduce costs, and increase their crops' resistance to pest and disease. In 2009 alone, the acreage devoted to biotech crops rose by 333 million acres.

In medical biotech, Otsuka Holdings, Japan's second largest drug maker, planned to go public December 15, 2010, on the Tokyo Stock Exchange with a US$2.8 billion IPO, which would be the biggest biotech IPO to date. Funds would be used for global expansion and new drug research.

An interesting legal development occurred in 2010 when health care firm Myriad Genetics, which had patented two genes used in cancer testing, was sued. The judge in the case ruled that the genes in question could not be patented. Myriad asked the U.S. Justice Department to step in because the long-held position of the U.S. government was for easy patentability. In a surprise finding, the Justice Department agreed with the judge that the genes in question were not patentable. This finding was seen as a new direction on the issue by the Obama administration. Some industry representatives worried the new limits on cell patentability could restrict research by squeezing the profits firms might earn from successful products.

There were signs that the slowdown in U.S. biotech that came with the credit crunch and recession of the late 2000s eventually started to ease. In particular, an increase in biotech Initial Public Offerings (IPOs) in 2010, after two down years, had some feeling hopeful. Apart from the cyclical nature of the industry, biotechnology appears to be well entrenched in the present condition and future development of the global economy.

RESEARCH AND TECHNOLOGY

Publicly traded U.S. biotech companies spent US$27.1 billion on research and development in 2006 according to BIO. Biotech is one of the most research-intensive industries in existence. A number of important biotechnology developments occurred during the 1990s and 2000s that can be broadly categorized into three areas:

- chemistry-based technologies;
- genetic engineering technologies; and
- tissue engineering and biological products.

Chemistry-Based Technologies. Several important advances in drug development occurred during the mid-1990s, including a new screening technique called combinatorial chemistry, which used advanced robotics and synthesis techniques to develop new drug compounds. The technique essentially created new compound "libraries" that researchers analyzed to identify those displaying potential therapeutic benefits. One advantage of combinatorial chemistry was the significantly increased volume of compounds that could be initially screened in less time than the months or years required by traditional screening methods. The greater volume of compounds tested also resulted in a higher number of potentially beneficial compounds being identified and further analyzed. Many large pharmaceutical companies recognized the importance of combinatorial chemistry techniques. In early 1998, biotech leader Chiron Corporation and pharmaceutical giant Pharmacia & Upjohn formed a strategic partnership to identify molecule inhibitors of the hepatitis C virus. The partnership used Chiron's strengths in combinatorial chemistry, virology, high throughput assay development, and protein expression with Pharmacia & Upjohn's expertise in biology, medicinal chemistry, and knowledge of pre-clinical procedures. The corporations shared worldwide marketing rights.

Another important chemistry-based technique was the discovery of rational drug design, which involved the creation of a three-dimensional molecular image of a given protein in order to identify the location of its key functional sites. Once those sites are identified, new compounds could be designed that would bind to them. As with combinatorial chemistry, rational drug design significantly reduced screening time and increased the volume and accuracy of identifying potentially beneficial compounds. Agouron Pharmaceuticals and Vertex Pharmaceuticals were among the leading developers of rational drug design, using the technique to develop HIV protease inhibitor drugs.

A third chemistry-based technique, high-throughput screening (HTS), also used rapid automation of tests to identify possible compounds that would interact with certain proteins. As with the other chemistry-based techniques, millions of various compounds could be screened rapidly.

Signal transduction was the fourth important chemistry-based technique. It involved deciphering the way cells communicated within the human body. Researchers hoped to use the information to manipulate cell activity in relation to disease.

Genetic Engineering Technologies. Genetic engineering was a broad field in the 1990s. Several revolutionary advances were made in the 1990s, including the launch of a massive U.S. federal project to identify the entire human genome and gene therapy. Other discoveries were the appearance of the first cloned mammal; the emergence of xenotransplantation and transgenics; and the use of genetic engineering in forensics, criminal identification, paternity cases, anthropology, and wildlife management.

Human Genome Project. In addition to efforts in the private sector, large government-backed ventures to map the human genome were underway in the United States and Great Britain. Most notable was the Human Genome Project, an international effort spearheaded by the U.S. Department of Energy in partnership with various academic institutions. Funded by the United States' National Institutes of Health and the Department of Energy, the project was launched in 1990 to identify the approximately 100,000 genes that make up the human genome. By mid-1994, molecular descriptions of about 45,000 genes had been successfully developed and the project was moving aggressively to record and determine the function of the entire genome. Gene identification would enable scientists to develop therapies and techniques to prevent and treat diseases. Research was completed ahead of schedule in 2003. The nonprofit Institute for Genomic Research was working on a related effort that would make the findings of gene researchers available to the entire scientific community.

Cloning. The 1996 announcement of the birth of the first cloned mammal, a sheep named Dolly, astonished the world. Dr. Ian Wilmut, an embryologist at the Roslin Institute in Scotland, had cloned Dolly from a cell taken from the udder of an adult sheep. Dolly had been born on July 5, 1996, but her birth was not announced until seven months later. After being mated with a Welsh mountain ram, Dolly gave birth to a lamb in April of 1998. Dolly's cloning set off a maelstrom of worldwide reaction and concern about the possibilities for cloning human beings as well as debates about the moral and ethical considerations of such revolutionary technology. Responding to public opinion, then-U.S. President Bill

Clinton established the National Bioethics Advisory Commission (NBAC) to make recommendations on the moral, ethical, religious, legal, and regulatory aspects of cloning. In June 1997, the NBAC produced a report stating that cloning human beings would be "morally unacceptable" based on ethical and safety considerations. The U.S. National Bioethics Advisory Commission (NBAC) encouraged the president to continue the ban on using federal funds for human cloning for at least three to five years. In early 1998, the U.S. Food and Drug Administration (FDA), as regulator of human cloning activities, announced that cloning human beings without FDA approval would be a federal offense. Around the same time, approximately 20 European countries signed a human cloning ban, although the door remained open for other areas of cloning research with the potential for medical benefits. In March 2005, the United Nations General Assembly voted to approve a non-binding statement urging its members to adopt a total ban on all forms of cloning. Many nations abstained from voting or voted against the ban, citing that U.N. member countries were not in agreement about the validity of stem-cell research if it constituted the destruction of human life.

Xenotransplanting and Transgenics. Xenotransplanting and transgenics transplant organs and DNA, respectively, to an another organism for biological and medical research. Xenotransplants involve the transplantation of animal organs, tissues, and cells across species. Transgenics involves transplanting DNA into another organism. The animals most commonly used for these techniques are pigs, cows, goats, and sheep. For example, Diacrin, Inc., successfully transplanted cells from pigs into the brains of 23 patients suffering from Parkinson's disease. The company also used the technique for patients with Huntington's disease, Alzheimer's disease, focal epilepsy, and other neurological conditions.

Transgenics has also been applied to agriculture and aquaculture. For instance, as of October 2010 the U.S. Food and Drug Administration (FDA) was deciding whether to approve a transgenic salmon that could feed demand for seafood while helping wild salmon populations recover from overfishing. The transgenic salmon contains genetic material from an eel-like creature called a pout that causes it to grow twice as fast as regular farm-raised salmon.

Gene Therapy. Gene therapy techniques involved using recombinant DNA to correct hereditary disorders, such as cystic fibrosis and muscular dystrophy. A key difficulty in gene therapy is that a treated cell often adds random parts of DNA, making it impossible to predict the resulting chromosomes and ensure that the treated gene would accomplish its mission. In May 1998,

Japanese researchers announced that they had constructed an artificial chromosome about one-tenth the size of a human chromosome, which they believed might relieve the difficulty. That same month, Matrigen, Inc., and Prizm Pharmaceuticals announced that they would merge to form Selective Genetics, Inc. The merger created the first gene therapy company specializing in tissue repair and regeneration. In 2005, several advances in gene therapy were announced, including gene therapy's use against colon cancer and ADA deficiency.

Dr. V.K. Tripathi, head of the pharmaceutical firm Khandelwal Laboratories, claimed that mineral-based gene therapy could cure almost any illness. The process corrected the effects of illness and aging that made the human body weak. Even if a full cure for ailments did not occur after treatment, most patients benefited from increased energy and suffered no side effects. Treatment required lying in a bathtub for an hour with carefully selected minerals that repaired damaged genes as they were absorbed by the body. The human digestive system rendered oral minerals less effective.

Introgen Therapeutics was the first company to file for FDA approval of gene-based therapy. The company's drug, Advexin, altered the cancer cells found in head and neck cancer by delivering a deactivated cold virus to the cancer cells. Approval was also pending in Europe.

DNA Identification. Every living organism has its own unique DNA that is made up of two interwoven strands of chemicals. Those chemicals form the genes that determine the unique makeup of each organism. DNA typing uses a variety of tissue, such as hair strands, skin, or bodily fluids, and mixes it with enzymes that essentially "read" and "cut" the DNA wherever a specified combination is found. The resulting cut genetic pieces make up the DNA pattern that forms an individual organism's unique genetic fingerprint. DNA typing has enabled forensic scientists to identify remains, as in the case of Czar Nicholas II of Russia and his family. DNA samples from living descendants, including Prince Philip of the United Kingdom, were compared to DNA samples from the remains. DNA typing of suspected criminals was also increasingly common, although its universal credibility had not been established in the courts, where it was sometimes considered to be open to deliberate or inadvertent contamination to yield a particular result. If properly employed, it would substantially increase the accuracy of criminal convictions and could exonerate falsely accused individuals. Many U.S. states passed laws requiring criminals to submit to DNA typing, with the information entered into a statewide DNA database. DNA typing was also being used to determine paternity by comparing DNA samples from the mother, child, and alleged father. The mother and child's matching combinations were identified and eliminated, and the remaining combination was tested against that of the alleged father to determine whether or not there was a match. DNA typing was also used in anthropology to determine a variety of information about fossil remains, past historical eras, and antiquities like the Dead Sea Scrolls. As the number of endangered species continued to increase, DNA typing had become an important way to preserve species.

Tissue Engineering and Biological Products. Tissue engineering, also known as regenerative medicine, was an emerging biotechnology in the mid- to late 1990s. According to a study by Brown University, more than 2,600 people in 89 firms located in 15 countries were researching tissue engineering at the end of 2002. However, the number involved in the field had been decreasing since 2000, as many researchers moved into the related field of stem-cell research. Despite FDA approvals for a variety of procedures, including the use of a patient's own cartilage cells for later injection into damaged sites and growing new skin from cells taken from the foreskins of newborns for burn victims and patients requiring plastic surgery, the field had not produced a profitable product by the mid-2000s.

Nonetheless, at Swinburne University in Melbourne, Australia, Professor Yos Morsy, who conducted tissue engineering and heart valve research, expected the first quarter of the twenty-first century to be revolutionary for medical science based on positive results from research with skin, cartilage, and bone. Recipients of engineered tissues would benefit from continued growth as the recipient grows, which would be especially advantageous for young recipients.

A November 2010 *Nature* article reported on the successful attempt of researchers to turn human skin cells into blood. This was expected to be an important step toward producing a variety of types of tissue or cells from any other kind of cell without having to go through a stem cell stage. This process could lead to safer therapies than possible with stem cells.

Biological and Chemical Warfare. The biotech industry continued to play a key role in protecting the world from the threat of biological terrorist attacks in the mid-2000s. On July 21, 2004, U.S. President George W. Bush signed Project BioShield, which, according to BIO, "provides new tools to improve medical countermeasures protecting Americans against a chemical, biological, radiological, or nuclear (CBRN) attack." It is "a comprehensive effort to develop and make available modern, effective drugs and vaccines to protect against attack by CBRN weapons."

INDUSTRY LEADERS

Amgen. Amgen was started in 1980 by George Rathman, who had been working for U.S. research giant Abbott Laboratories and had become intrigued by recombinant DNA technology. Abbott Labs offered to fund 52 percent of his venture, but Rathman turned them down because he wanted his company to be free from corporate influence to achieve its goals. The company started with funding from venture capitalists before going public in 1983. Its research focus was on a chicken growth hormone that was designed to reduce feeding costs. Additional public offerings brought enough cash into Amgen's coffers to fund intense research and development efforts throughout the 1980s.

In April 2002, *Forbes* magazine informed readers that if they had purchased Amgen stock in 1983, they "would now be sitting on a 182-fold gain." In 2005, Amgen continued to be the unrivaled leader of the biotech industry. Three Amgen drugs—Epogen, Neupogen, and Procrit—topped the list of the world's 10 leading drugs based on 1996 worldwide sales of US$3.2 billion. By 2003, Epogen and Aranesp comprised one-half of Amgen's sales.

Amgen's main research and development efforts had focused on several areas, including inflammation, metabolic disease, osteoporosis, oncology, hematology, nephrology, and neurology. Epogen and Neupogen were developed as part of Amgen's research on hematopoiesis. Amgen's rapid growth during the late 1980s was a result of the introduction of Epogen, which was approved by the FDA to treat anemia associated with chronic renal failure. The company reported 1996 worldwide sales of nearly US$2 billion, and company stock jumped from US$19 million in 1981 to US$3 billion in 1996. Amgen soon received FDA approval for Neupogen, which stimulates the production of a specific white blood cell and can be used to treat cancer-related anemia. Following the introduction of Neupogen, Amgen's sales shot up to US$1.5 billion in 1993.

By 2004, the company had 24 programs in human clinical trials and approximately 40 programs in development. In 2004, Amgen's sales were nearly US$20.6 billion. In 2009, with the economy weak, revenue was US$14.6 billion. The company reported 17,000 employees at its U.S.-based research facilities and its worldwide manufacturing plants.

Genentech. Another global biotech leader, Genentech, was founded in 1976 by Robert A. Swanson and Herbert Boyer. The company focused on three main areas: oncology, cardiovascular conditions, and endocrinology. Headquartered in San Francisco, Genentech marketed and developed products based on human genetic information. It was the first company to splice a human gene into a bacterial cell to manufacture a usable protein. The company manufactured and marketed a number of products in the United States, including Protropin and Nutropin, and Nutropin AQ for the treatment of human growth deficiencies. Other products included Activase, a treatment for acute myocardial infarction (heart attack); Actimmune, for the treatment of infections from chronic granulomatosis (a deficiency of the immune system); Pulmozyme, a treatment for cystic fibrosis; Avastin, for the treatment of colon cancer; and Rituxan, for the treatment of non-Hodgkin's lymphoma. Genentech reported 13,000 employees in 2010. In March 2009, Genentech merged with the Roche Group, operating as an independent center within the group.

In 1995, Roche Holdings Ltd., of Basel, Switzerland, became Genentech's majority stockholder, and by 2004 it owned about 56 percent of the company. The agreement enabled Genentech to receive royalties from sales of its products in Canada and from sales of Pulmozyme in Europe. The company also received royalties on sales of its other products through various licensees in the United States and Canada. Genentech also received royalties on five products that originated from company research and were marketed worldwide by other companies. In 1992, Genentech opened the US$85 million Founders Research Center, the world's largest biotechnology research facility, which was dedicated to the company's two founding researchers.

Chiron/Novartis. Chiron Corporation, founded in 1981, had business units for blood testing, vaccines, and biopharmaceuticals for infectious diseases and cancer. The company generated revenues of more than US$1.7 billion in 2004, up 81.6 percent from 2002 revenues. By the end of 2004, the company employed approximately 5,400 workers in 18 countries on five continents. In addition to research centers in Emeryville, California; Seattle, Washington; and Siena, Italy, the company had manufacturing operations in the United States, the United Kingdom, Germany, Italy, the Netherlands, and India. Chiron was the first company in the United States to market a drug to treat multiple sclerosis, Betaseron, which reduced the frequency and severity of attacks caused by some forms of the disease.

Chiron was the world leader in blood testing systems for screening by blood banks. In 2004, the company was the fifth largest developer of vaccines worldwide, including a vaccine against meningococcal C disease. Chiron's growth in this area had been primarily the result of global acquisitions. The company also developed a range of therapeutic products for cancer and infectious and pulmonary diseases. In 2004, the company sought approval for Pulminiq, an inhalation solution for lung transplant

patients and Cubicin for skin and soft tissue infections. With one of the broadest and deepest product lines in the biotech industry, Chiron maintained collaborations with more than 500 research institutions and commercial organizations. Chiron was acquired by Switzerland-based Novartis in 2006. Novartis generated some US$44 billion in sales in 2009 and employed nearly 100,000 people in 140 countries.

Genzyme. Based in Cambridge, Massachusetts, Genzyme was founded in the early 1980s by a group of entrepreneurs with enzyme expertise. Because the company began by developing and manufacturing diagnostic products, it had an immediate source of revenue, unlike many other biotech start-ups. The company focused its research efforts in the areas of genetic diseases, disorders of the immune system, cardiovascular disease, and oncology.

In April 2002, Genzyme's stock value rebounded from US$2.31 to US$42.98 as its drug Renagel appeared to have life-saving benefits preventing heart disease deaths for dialysis patients. In 2002, *The Boston Globe* said that Renagel "could be the next billion-dollar drug." By 2004, the company was focused on developing treatments for rare genetic disorders. Despite increases in revenues, the company experienced several years of losses before achieving a net gain in 2004. At the end of 2004, the company acquired Ilex Oncology, which brought with it two FDA-approved cancer treatment drugs. In 2009, the company had revenues of US$4.5 billion and employed approximately 10,000 people worldwide.

Biogen Idec Inc. In November 2003, two of the world's leading biotech firms, Biogen Inc. and IDEC Pharmaceuticals Corp., merged to form Biogen Idec Inc. The merger was one of the signs that the biotech industry was maturing and emphasized the need for companies in the industry to strengthen their investor base while decreasing expenditures through the amalgamation of services. Biogen Idec concentrated on treatments for inflammatory and autoimmune conditions, as well as various forms of cancer. Based in Cambridge, Massachusetts, the company also had offices in Canada, Australia, Japan, and throughout Europe, employing approximately 4,000 people worldwide. In 2003, the company recorded sales of US$2.21 billion, a 225 percent increase over the previous year. Although this increase was matched with a relatively small net income figure of US$44 million, it was a significant improvement over the previous year's net loss of US$875.1 million. By 2009, revenue exceeded US$4 billion.

Biogen had been formed in 1978 when a group of biologists, who were leading researchers in the emerging field of genetic engineering, convened in Geneva, Switzerland. Two of the biologists had received Nobel Prizes for their discoveries, which led to products based on the alpha interferon gene and hepatitis B antigens.

IDEC Pharmaceuticals had been established in 1985 in San Francisco. During its early years, the company developed "anti-idiotype" monoclonal antibodies, which it described as a patient-specific, customized approach to treating non-Hodgkin's lymphoma. By 1991, the company had begun trading on the NASDAQ. IDEC's breakthrough cancer drug Rituxan for treatment of non-Hodgkin's lymphoma was approved by the FDA in 1997.

In early 2005, Biogen Idec had voluntarily suspended sales of its multiple sclerosis drug, Tysabri, after a patient died from a rare disease. The announcement had a negative affect on the entire industry, and Biogen Idec reported an immediate decline in the price of its shares of 44 percent.

MAJOR COUNTRIES IN THE INDUSTRY

Canada. According to a 2002 study by Ernst & Young, Canada ranked second to the United States on a per-country basis in terms of the number of companies doing business in the biotechnology industry. When compared with the size of its economy, Canada led the world with 0.65 companies per billion dollars in GDP, while the United States has about 0.15 companies and Europe had 0.2. A 2004 study by KPMG showed that in terms of clinical trial costs Canada had a 22.4 percent cost advantage over the United States, which ranked eighth in the study. In 2001, the health care sector of the industry accounted for 52 percent of biotech firms, followed by 17 percent for the agricultural biotech sector. Approximately 12,000 people were employed in the industry, with the vast majority working in companies of fewer than 50 employees.

Many Canadian firms had strong alliances with U.S. and other global companies, particularly for marketing and distribution. For example, in 2003, Cardiome, which made a cardiovascular drug, signed a US$68 million co-development and marketing agreement with the U.S. subsidiary of Japanese pharmaceutical company Fujisawa. In 2004, a similar agreement was signed between Canada's Xenon Pharmaceuticals Inc. and Switzerland's Novartis AG. A concern of Dr. Stelios Papadopoulos, vice chairman of SG Cowen investment bank, was that potential investors were looking for companies with strong management and well developed development pipelines, while most Canadian biotech firms were small.

Canadian organizations were responsible for the first publicly available draft sequence for the coronavirus, which was important for the development of diagnostic tests for Severe Acute Respiratory Syndrome (SARS).

Europe. In 2002, Europe was home to 1,878 biotech companies, ahead of the 1,466 in the United States. However, the region did not benefit from the same market vitality as the United States due to a difficult investment climate and complex funding. As Europe faced these and other challenges, including competition from the emerging Asian biotech industry, some industry analysts were uncertain if the region would remain a viable player. For example, in *Chemical Market Reporter,* E&Y UK Health Sciences leader William Powlett Smith said: "There is a real risk that in five to 10 years there may be virtually no biotech industry in Europe of any significance if there is not a scaling-up in the size of European biotech companies. Without an increasing number of larger companies, Europe will succumb to stronger companies from outside the region. This possible loss of control over European biotechnology is obviously a doomsday scenario. There are some exciting areas of bioscience in Europe, so the commercial potential is there. It is a question of whether it gains its fair share of the revenues from its own innovations."

United Kingdom. Despite Europe's challenging climate, the United Kingdom remained a biotech leader. According to The BioIndustry Association (BIA) of Britain, as of 2005, the United Kingdom accounted for 27 percent of Europe's private companies and 93 percent of the continent's publicly traded companies. More than 40,000 people worked in the industry in 2005, which was experiencing a 20 percent growth rate each year. By this time, 6 of Europe's 10 leading biotech companies were British. The United Kingdom was home to about 300 biotech companies with a US$13 billion market. In addition to private funding, the British government announced in March 2005 that it would spend approximately US$1.87 billion on biotechnology research by 2008.

Between 1975 and 1994, the United Kingdom contributed 14 percent of globally significant drugs. That development put the United Kingdom in second place behind the United States in terms of important drug development and made it a leader in the European biotech sector. Its strength in comparison to other European nations was derived partly from its early lead in biotech research and development. Beginning with the development of a smallpox vaccine in 1796, the United Kingdom boasts a long tradition of biotech-related innovations. In addition to the 1953 discovery of the structure of DNA, British scientists made other breakthrough discoveries, such as interferon findings (1957), the structure of insulin (1958), monoclonal antibodies (1975), and the cloning of the first adult mammal, Dolly the Sheep, in 1996. However, the United Kingdom has failed to find profitable ways to bring its discoveries to market. For example, although magnetic resonance imaging (MRI) was developed in the United Kingdom, it was the Americans who marketed the product.

Funding was in short supply in the United Kingdom, leaving many firms to seek mergers and acquisitions to find the money needed to continue their research. An increase in merger and acquisition activity in the U.K. industry in 2003 and 2004 led to the largest deal in the biotech industry in the country when Belgium-based UCB Pharma purchased CellTech Group for US$2.8 billion.

However, the U.K. biotech industry had an advantage over other European nations with ready access to venture capital. About half of all European biotech venture capital in the early 1990s was invested in the United Kingdom. In 1993, for example, venture capital investments in British biotechnology were about two times greater than those in Germany, which was ranked second in Europe in biotech venture capital funding. Biotech players in most countries outside the United States were forced to rely much more heavily on largely inaccessible public equity markets and government grants. To that end, the U.K. biotech community got a finance-related boost in 1993 when it convinced the London Stock Exchange to allow young biotech companies to be listed without having to prove profitability. By 2003, U.K. firms were attracting approximately US$157 million in venture capital funding. In 2004, a new company, PowerMed, was formed after receiving more than US$35 million in venture capital funding to develop DNA vaccines.

In 2010, the UK Biotech Database reported 1,586 companies in the U.K. The top three types were Professional Services and Consulting (401), R&D Services (347), and Public / Non-Profit (251).

Germany. Germany became active in the biotech industry with the 1974 creation of the Bundesministerium für Forschung und Technologie, a government effort aimed at promoting biotechnology. Most of the country's biotech research and development was carried out through large pharmaceutical companies and government-backed projects and consortiums. Major biotech powers in Germany included pharmaceutical giants Hoechst, Bayer, and BASF. Small companies are often created as specialty research arms of larger companies or with the help of venture capital from the United States and other countries.

By mid-2004, *Biopharm International* reported that the German government was actively helping the country increase its prominence in the biotech industry. The elimination of bureaucratic roadblocks helped to quiet fears regarding the use of genetically engineered crops, which had caused setbacks in the United Kingdom. In addition, the German government had matched private funds in order to expedite biotech growth.

According to a May 2004 report by E&Y, Germany had 350 biotechnology firms by 2003, employing 11,535 people, a continuing fall from 2001 levels of 365 companies employing 14,408. However, despite these decreases the number of products that had reached the preclinical to approval phase, known as the pipeline, increased by 14 percent over 2002 levels, a figure matched by a four percent increase in venture capital funding.

Several problems existed for the German biotech sector. First, there were a large number of small companies which lacked the monetary backing or number of employees needed for long-term existence. Second, because many of these firms focus only on the development of one product, they do not have a fallback in case of product failure, nor do they have other products to provide ongoing funding for research and development activities in other areas. Third, venture capital funding was not expected to last, in spite of slight increases in the mid-2000s. According to E&Y, only one-quarter of biotech firms in Germany had funds to last more than 12 months.

Denmark. By the end of 2003, Denmark was quickly approaching the United Kingdom in terms of the percentage of biotech revenues it was contributing to the European market (US$8.8 billion from Denmark versus US$9.4 billion from the United Kingdom). The region was often grouped with other Scandinavian countries for statistics as well as marketing purposes, with many biotech organizations spread over the region. Denmark was the top-performing country in terms of drug approvals and U.S. patents. A 2009 Ernst & Young study cited Denmark as the third largest pharmaceutical development pipeline in Europe.

Asia. Although the Asian biotechnology sector had lagged behind the United States and Europe, by the late 1990s most Asian countries had recognized the importance of the industry to future economic prosperity. In other Asian countries, microbes were being used in a number of innovative ways, such as to clean up man-made messes like oil spills and sewage, and to reduce landfill waste. In 2002, 601 companies were engaged in biotechnology research. Japan was the leader of Asia's biotech industry, but China, South Korea, the Philippines, and Indonesia were very active in the sector.

Japan. Despite its leadership position, Japan's biotech industry had gotten a late start, as Japanese chemical companies followed the U.S. lead. Because Japan's financial markets generally did not benefit high-risk start-up companies, large companies became the major participants in the industry. About 250 large Japanese companies were involved in biotech. Those organizations typically differed significantly from many U.S. and European biotechnology companies in that they emphasized bringing to market innovations that had been developed elsewhere. For example, a Japanese company may obtain a license from a U.S. firm to manufacture a biotech drug that the U.S. company developed and patented.

In the 1980s, the Japanese government teamed up with major companies to try to build a formidable biotech industry. These companies invested at home in research and development of proprietary drugs and products and purchased significant shares in some U.S. biotech companies to gain access to their research. In the late 1980s, many U.S. observers feared that Japan was going to overcome North America's lead and dominate the global biotech industry. By the early 1990s, however, Japan's biotechnology sector had failed to introduce even one significant product. By the mid-1990s companies that manufactured drugs licensed to them by U.S. companies like Amgen and Genentech were among the few Japanese biotech successes.

Pharmaceuticals continued to dominate the Japanese biotech industry in the late 2000s with several large firms investing heavily in new drug development. For example, one firm used pieces of human chromosomes in mice to develop antibodies against infections, and in 1997, Japanese researchers successfully cloned a cow. The use of microbes as "factories" in which to produce human growth hormones, proteins, and antibiotics was also on the rise among Japanese biotech firms.

By 2002, Japan's biotech industry was estimated to be worth approximately US$13.4 billion and was expected to reach US$230 billion by 2010, according to the *JETRO Japan Biotechnology Market Report (2004)*.

China. Ever mindful of its population and scarcity of arable land, China was one of the more aggressive countries developing and using biotechnology in Asia. Chinese researchers focused primarily on bioagriculture to develop nutritional and disease-resistant crops. They succeeded in producing a number of genetically altered crops such as peppers, rice, potatoes, and wheat. China was also developing pharmaceuticals, and some of the country's larger firms had successfully produced anti-cancer and hepatitis products. According to research completed by Datamonitor, China's biotechnology market was worth US$5.1 billion in 2003 and had reported growth of more than 20 percent per year since 1993.

Despite their overall support of biotechnology, many people in Asian countries continued to debate the wisdom of genetic engineering. Possible effects of transgenic animals and plants on the environment and the future of biodiversity were of concern. Most Asian governments agreed that replicating human beings by cloning was not acceptable. Nevertheless, some western biotech industry

players were concerned about the direction China might take with research initiatives for cloning. Even though China had banned reproductive cloning in 1998, there was skepticism about whether or not regulations would be enforced.

In 2002, *The Economist* reported that one researcher at the Peking University Stem Cell Research Centre said: "if Chinese scientists want to collaborate with foreign research groups, publish in international journals or attract overseas investment, they have to abide by international rules. Practicality, if not morality, will help to keep most scientists in line with international notions of acceptable biological research." In the late 1990s and early 2000s, Asian nations had attempted to remove barriers hindering biotechnology industry dominance, allowing university professors to work in private enterprise where formerly it was not government permitted.

In a November 2010 *Forbes* blog post, Dennis Gillings, CEO of Quintiles Transnational, raised the possibility that higher regulation in the U.S. could lead to China being the top nation for biotech by 2050.

The United States. The United States assumed an early lead in the global biotech industry partly because of its entrepreneurial environment, as well as efficient capital markets and strength in technologies related to biotechnology. The United States produced a number of biotech start-ups and technological breakthroughs during the 1970s and early 1980s, and the industry thrived during the mid-1980s. Even during the industry downturn of the late 1980s, investment and research efforts continued to increase. By the end of the decade, 1,275 U.S. biotech companies employed 140,000 workers and generated annual sales of US$13 billion, although net revenues exceeded US$17 billion when non-product income was included. Despite rising sales, the industry continued to post net losses of US$4 billion per year, due in large part to the US$9 billion invested annually in research and development.

Between 1975 and 1994, the United States had developed 45 percent of the world's most important drugs. The next largest pharmaceutical developer was the United Kingdom, which contributed 14 percent. The treatments targeted respiratory conditions, AIDS, Parkinson's, heart disease, stroke, hypertension, cancer, and non-Hodgkin's lymphoma. The United States led its overseas counterparts in major research efforts, such as a biotech cure for AIDS and identification of the human genome.

The U.S. biotech industry sales surged from about US$3 billion in 1990 to US$6 billion in 1992 to nearly US$8 billion in 1994. The number of start-ups that were not producing revenue, combined with U.S. biotech losses of about US$4 billion in 1994, caused many analysts to predict an industry shakeout and a consolidation of research and development operations during the late 1990s. Financial markets responded to those predictions by shifting funds from start-ups to established companies. In June 1994, a study showed that about half of all U.S. biotech companies did not have enough cash to last two years. By 1995, the number of biotech companies had increased to about 1,300, and total industry employment swelled to more than 100,000. By 1996, industry sales were nearly US$11 billion. The accounting firm E&Y tabulated 1996 industry revenues from a combination of product sales and payments from research partnerships at US$14.6 billion. By 1997, the number of firms had declined from 1,287 to 1,274, supporting predictions of consolidation, but it could not be considered a shakeout.

Financial turbulence in the U.S. biotech industry opened the door for several European competitors to boost their involvement in the industry in the mid-1990s. Many U.S. biotech companies, hungry for capital, had turned to large, cash-rich European pharmaceutical companies as development partners. The arrangement worked well for the European companies, many of which were lagging far behind their technologically superior U.S. counterparts. They also benefited from the unrivaled ability of U.S. companies to transfer biotechnology from the academic world to the private sector. At the same time, U.S. firms benefited from the familiarity that their European partners had with regulatory approval processes on the continent. In fact, many U.S. firms were seeking and gaining approval for their biotech products through less restrictive European regulatory bodies rather than through the comparatively strict U.S. Food and Drug Administration.

In 2004, a number of states were offering incentives to attract biotech companies, including Massachusetts, California, Maryland, New Jersey, and Pennsylvania, that offered a variety of grants, investments, and tax credits to support the formation or continued growth of their respective biotech industries.

By 2005, the United States continued to dominate the biotechnology industry. According to a 2004 study conducted by the Santa Monica, California-based Milken Institute, the city of San Diego was home to the leading U.S. biotechnology hub, ahead of Boston and San Francisco. In its June 14, 2004, issue, the *San Diego Business Journal* revealed that the city's biotech industry directly or indirectly accounted for US$5.8 billion in income, as well as 55,600 jobs. However, the publication indicated that aside from three large biotech companies (Genentech Inc., Chiron Corp., and Applied Biosystems), San Diego's biotech cluster was home to many small firms that depended heavily on venture capital. Moving forward, it was critical

for the city to produce FDA-approved drugs in order to maintain interest among investors.

In a November 2010 *Forbes* blog post touting the possibility of China assuming leadership in the world biotech market by 2050, a sign of erosion in the leadership of the United States was noted in the fact that Pfizer was getting 56 percent of revenue from outside the country. In addition, it was noted that virtually every big biotech company was looking to emerging markets like China for future growth.

BIBLIOGRAPHY

"About Amgen." Amgen, Inc. 14 November 2010. Available from www.amgen.com.

"About Biotechnology." Biotechnology Industry Organization, 14 November 2010. Available from bio.org.

"About Novartis." Novartis AG, 14 November 2010. Available from www.novartis.com.

"About Us." Biogen Idec, 14 November 2010. Available from www.biogenidec.com.

Aoki, Naomi. "Genzyme Pins Hopes on Dialysis Drug." *The Boston Globe,* 10 April 2002.

"Banking on Biotech." *Fortune,* 9 June 2003.

"Biotech Matures as Industry Shifts to Product-Driven Market." *Chemical Market Reporter,* 2 August 2004.

Biotechnology Industry Organization. "Biotechnology Industry Facts." Washington, D.C., 2004. Available from www.bio.org.

———. "Brownback Bill Would Criminalize Medical Research." Washington, D.C., 2005. Available from www. bio.org.

———. "Project BioShield Is Important Step Forward in Securing the National Defense." Washington, D.C., 19 May 2004. Available from www.bio.org.

———. "Welcome to the Gateway to Biotechnology." Washington, D.C., 2002. Available from www.bio.org.

"Biotech's Yin and Yang; Chinese Biotechnology." *The Economist,* 14 December 2002.

"Britons Attack US Cloning Ban Bid." BBC News, 29 August 2004. Available from news.bbc.co.uk.

Callaway, Ewen. "Cellular Alchemy Transforms Skin into Blood." *Nature,* 7 November 2010. Available from www.nature.com.

"Corporate Overview." Genentech 14 November 2010. Available from www.gene.com.

Daghlian, Marie. "Japan's Otsuka Plans Largest Biotech IPO in the World." *Seeking Alpha,* 14 November 2010. Available from seekingalpha.com.

"Database Info." *UK Biotech Database,* 14 November 2010. Available from www.ukbiotech.com.

Ernst & Young LLP. *Biotech Industry Report,* 2005. Available from www.eyi.com.

"First Gene Therapy for Heart Failure Offered in Clinical Trials." *ScienceDaily,* 19 June 2008. Available from www.sciencedaily.com.

Freese, Bill. "Biotech Snake Oil: A Quack Cure for Hunger." *Multinational Monitor,* September/October 2008.

"From Across the Divide: Europe's Biotech Firms Need to Think Big If They Are to Prosper, Says Lisa Drakeman of Genmab." *The Economist,* 12 June 2008. Available from economist.com.

"GM Salmon: Swimming Against the Regulatory Tide." The Heritage Foundation: The Foundry blog, 26 October 2010. Available from blogs.heritage.org.

Harris, Richard. "Feds Surprise Biotech Industry With Gene Patent Rule?" *NPR,* 4 November 2010. Available from www.npr.org.

Herper, Matthew. "Could China Steal America's Biotech Crown?" *Forbes:* The Medicine Show blog 5 November 2010. Available from blogs.forbes.com.

"Japan's Biotech Business Market to Top $202 Billion by 2010." *Japanese Biotechnology* & *Medical Technology,* April 2001.

Jarvis, Lisa. "Biotech Sector Enjoyed a Modest Recovery in 2003." *Chemical Market Reporter,* 15 March 2004.

Johnson, Steve. "Biotech Industry Cautiously Brings IPOs Back." *San Jose Mercury News,* 11 November 2010. Available from www.mercurynews.com.

Kilpatrick, Robert Lee. "Global Biopartnering: A Personal Perspective." *Biopharm International,* May 2004.

Langreth, Robert, and Zina Moukheiber. "Make Money In Biotech." *Forbes,* 15 April, 2002.

"Life Sciences: A Strong Biotech Cluster." Ministry of Foreign Affairs of Denmark, 14 November 2010. Available from http://www.investindk.com.

Miller, John W. "EU Nears Ban on Animal Cloning." *Wall Street Journal,* 20 October 2010. Available from online.wsj.com.

Milmo, Sean. "Hobbled By Financing, European Biotech Lags Behind the US." *Chemical Market Reporter,* 7 June 2004. Available from www.icis.com.

"Mineral Based Gene Therapy has Curative Powers: Scientist." *The Hindu,* 7 July 2008. Available from www.hindu.com.

Moorthie, Sowmiya, and Philippa Brice. "Regulatory Approval Sought for Cancer Gene Therapy Drug," 8 July 2008. Available from phg.foundation.org.

"New Research May Lead to Safer, More Effective Gene Therapy." *ScienceDaily,* 27 June 2008. Available from www.sciencedaily.com.

Newton, Alastair. "Europe's Biotechnology Hub: The United Kingdom." *Biopharm International,* November 2003.

O'Connell, Brian. "Have Biopharm Business, Will Travel: The Global Market for Biopharmaceuticals Points to a Healthy Future for Industry." *Biopharm International,* May 2004.

Olayiwola, Noimot. "Tissue Engineering Holds Hope for Healthcare: Expert," 26 June 2008. Available from www.gulftimes.com.

Roberson, Roy. "Biotechnology Driving Farm Growth." *Southeast Farm Press,* 5 December 2007.

Somers, Terri. "Biology Reborn." *San Diego Union-Tribune,* 17 June 2008. Available from www.signonsandiego.com

"Transgenic Crops Fastest Growing Sector in $12 bn Agricultural Biotechnology Market." *San Francisco Chronicle,* 12 November 2010. Available from www.sfgate.com.

Van Arnum, Patricia. "U.S. Biotechnology Industry: On the Rebound." *Chemical Market Reporter,* 7 June 2004.

Webb, Marion. "Biotech Execs Encouraged by New Study: Report Ranks S.D. as Top U.S. Hub Ahead of Boston and S.F." *San Diego Business Journal,* 14 June 2004.

"Who We Are." Genzyme Corporation, 14 November 2010. Available from www.genzyme.com.

SIC 2870

CHEMICALS, AGRICULTURAL

NAICS CODE(S)

3253. The agricultural chemicals industry manufactures the world's basic nitrogen and phosphate fertilizers, mixed fertilizers, pesticides, and related chemicals for agriculture. For coverage of other types of chemicals, see also **Chemicals, Industrial Inorganic**, and **Chemicals, Industrial Organic.**

INDUSTRY SNAPSHOT

The agricultural chemical industry is the smallest of all the chemical industries and includes production of both pesticides and fertilizers. By the mid-2000s, the pesticide market was in decline. In addition, according to the Food and Agriculture Organization of the United Nations (FAO), estimates on fertilizer usage during the next three decades were substantially lower than estimates made in the 1990s. According to the FAO study, lowered estimates in large part had to do with more efficient apportioning of fertilizers due to computer projections and because of more efficient use of available fertilizers. In addition, the health benefits of non-chemical, organically grown products led to a reduction in both pesticide and fertilizer usage. Fertilizer use, estimated to be about 138 million metric tons (mmt) in 2005, could rise as high as 199 mmt in 2030, or decline as low as 167 mmt, according to the study's authors. As of 2010, the agricultural chemicals manufacturing industry was comprised of over 700 companies with a combined revenue of US$30 billion annually. This represented just a portion of the US$1.79 trillion global chemicals market.

By the end of the 2000s, the top companies in the industry were Syngenta and Bayer, followed by DuPont, Dow, BASF, Agrium, and Monsanto, among others. While some of the top agricultural chemical manufacturers had spun off or sold their chemical operations by the early 2000s, others opted to concentrate on the briskly expanding market for biotechnology. The biotechnology industry, in part, strives to develop crops that are hardy and resistant with and without the aid of fertilizers, pesticides, and fungicides. Industry observers predicted increased interaction between genetically engineered crops and farm chemicals with the growing application of integrated pest management approaches to agriculture. (See also **Biotechnology**.)

The fate of genetically modified (GM) crops had not been decided by the mid-2000s. For example, industry leader Monsanto, which was restructured in late 2003 in

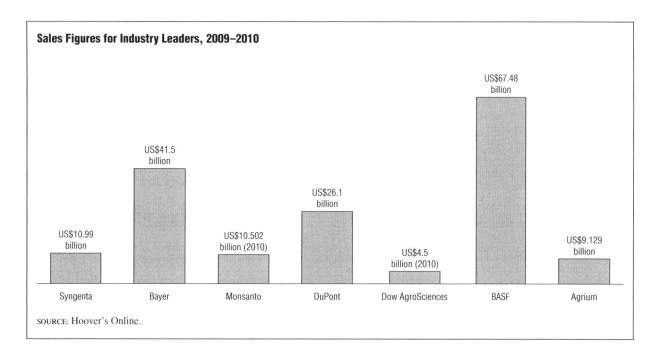

Sales Figures for Industry Leaders, 2009–2010

Syngenta: US$10.99 billion
Bayer: US$41.5 billion
Monsanto: US$10.502 billion (2010)
DuPont: US$26.1 billion
Dow AgroSciences: US$4.5 billion (2010)
BASF: US$67.48 billion
Agrium: US$9.129 billion

SOURCE: Hoover's Online.

order to concentrate on promoting the widespread use of GM crops, pulled the plug in 2004 on plans for GM wheat. While the company cited bottom-line issues, opponents of genetically engineered food claimed the industry was dying because it was unwanted and unneeded. GM crops have been slow to gain acceptance, especially outside the United States. In addition, a 2003 report based on USDA data found that in contrast to claims that GM crops required reduced pesticides, actual pesticide use had increased 23,000 tons during the previous six years.

ORGANIZATION AND STRUCTURE

The agricultural chemical industry produces chemicals for four principal end uses: pesticides, herbicides, fungicides, and fertilizers. Pesticides, which usually are organic chemicals, kill or discourage insects and other animal life that attack crops. Herbicides attack weeds that compete with crops for the nutrients in the soil, while fungicides kill fungus or prevent it from growing. Fertilizers replenish lost nutrients in the soil in order to make it more productive and raise crop yield.

Pesticides are manufactured in concentrated form and need to be mixed with adjuvants (inert ingredients designed to make pesticides more effective, such as attractants and extenders) before use. Certain manufacturers specialize in this mixing process, called formulation, to prepare a pesticide for the end user, who may be a farmer or home gardener. Adjuvant manufacturers supply their products to formulators and distributors, who prepare the product and market it.

Fertilizers include usable forms of three elements that all plants need to grow: nitrogen, phosphate, and potassium. The primary ingredient of most nitrogenous fertilizers is anhydrous ammonia, which may be reacted with nitric acid to produce ammonium nitrate. While it is an excellent fertilizer, ammonium nitrate is also highly combustible. Approximately 70 percent of the cost involved in producing ammonia covers the price of natural gas, one of its basic ingredients. Therefore, producers in countries with inexpensive access to natural gas, such as the Commonwealth of Independent States (an alliance of former Soviet republics), Canada, and Mexico, have a significant advantage over those in areas with high natural gas prices, such as Europe. Once the world's leading nitrogenous fertilizer, ammonium nitrate has lost market share to urea, which has a higher nitrogen content and is easier and safer to handle and store than ammonium nitrate.

Nitrogenous fertilizers accounted for about half of all fertilizer production in the 1990s, with phosphorous and potassium each holding a quarter of the market. As the fertilizer industry evolved, fertilizers became increasingly concentrated. Not surprisingly, all three types of fertilizers are often mixed in combination products. Manufacturers label such products with three numbers separated by hyphens, such as 15-10-5, which represent the mixture's percentages of nitrogen, phosphorus oxide, and potassium oxide, respectively.

Farmers usually test the chemical makeup of their soil before applying any kind of fertilizer. Government or privately operated laboratories test the soil and recommend a custom combination of fertilizers to suit its needs. Most fertilizers come in solid form to be spread on the ground, but some are liquids made for injection into the soil under pressure.

Environmental factors are extremely important in the manufacture, shipping, distribution, and use of pesticides. Increasingly strict environmental laws have contributed to the sluggish growth of the pesticide industry, and products have been subjected to stringent tests that measure their toxicity. According to the U.S. Department of Commerce, research and development (R&D) costs for just one new type of pesticide in the 1990s could top US$50 million, compared to about US$6 million in the 1970s. From the mid-1990s through the early 2000s, pesticide manufacturers spent as much as 10 percent of their sales revenue on R&D. Pesticide products, subjected to rigorous tests by governmental agencies, took as long as five years to complete. The total R&D process can take as long as ten years from "test tube to field," and only one in 20,000 substances tested is eventually produced on a commercial basis.

Governmental and private watchdogs in industrialized countries were on the lookout for damage done to the environment through pesticides and other pollutants. Pesticides impact the environment through accidental spills during transport; by leaching into the water supply; by affecting the growth of microorganisms in soil; and by being ingested by wild animals, causing death and deformity.

Industrialized countries have been concerned with indiscriminate use of pesticides and other agricultural chemicals in developing countries anxious to increase their level of food production. The spread of global trade means that a developing country's liberal use of pesticides on food crops could easily affect consumers living in another country. Consequently, developed countries have been searching for ways to diplomatically encourage developing countries to apply first-world policies to pesticide and herbicide use. Developed countries have also been forced to question their own policies of exporting to the Third World pesticides that are banned in their own countries.

In the mid-1990s, the European Union (E.U.) was developing its own standards for environmental testing, which included tracking the efficacy of pesticides. Intolerance for careless use of herbicides and pesticides was increasing worldwide. In Denmark, for instance, the Danish Environmental Protection Agency routinely sent employees into the fields to see if farmers were properly using atrazine, a pesticide intended to protect corn crops. Offenders were sternly warned the first time, but officials were known to levy fines on perennial offenders.

On the other hand, spokespersons for agribusiness argue that the use of pesticides has to be balanced against their benefits. Pesticide manufacturers have been developing products that let farmers manage their soil conservatively, resulting in less erosion as well as higher productivity. One significant advance is the introduction of pre-emergence herbicides, which attack weeds and invasive plants as they germinate. Nevertheless, the search for new products that are tough on weeds and bugs but kind to crops continues. Several trends expected to develop at the turn of the twenty-first century include the use of natural predators (bugs eating other bugs); products expressly developed to kill insects and plants that threaten only one or two crops; efforts to stay ahead of insects' ability to develop a tolerance for pesticides; substances that are effective at lower dosages; and packages that household users can more easily handle and store safely.

Patents are vital to the success of agricultural chemical producers in that one of the primary ways companies can earn profits is by developing a unique, successful product. However, when products once produced by a single company become generically available, their sales decline, leading to lower profits.

The permeability of national borders resulted in several intercompany and intercontinental alliances among major pesticide producers. For example, Hoechst Schering AgrEvo, a partnership between two German companies, Hoechst AG and Schering AC, headed up a North American venture (Hoechst Nor-Am AgrEvo).

Much of the world—100 countries, including the United States, Asia, and European nations such as Spain, Japan, Italy, and Greece—is battling desertification, a problem exacerbated, not caused, by fertilizers. Overgrazing, diversion of water supplies, and unwise farming practices have led to vast areas of land drying up throughout the world. According to the *International Herald Tribune*, the 2002 United Nations Secretariat of the Convention to Combat Desertification in Bonn told participating delegates that as the lands dry up, "chemical residues from fertilizers and pesticides [will] further degrade the land."

BACKGROUND AND DEVELOPMENT

The desire for the largest, highest-quality crop with the least amount of interference from insects and weeds has been a goal since early man first furrowed the ground to plant seeds. In order to grow properly, plants need carbon dioxide, water, and sunlight, as well as a very specific diet of other substances to develop according to their genetic program. Most plants also need a dose or two of magnesium, sulfur, calcium, potassium, phosphorus, and nitrogen. Moreover, some crops need trace elements such as chlorine, copper, and zinc. Heavily hybridized cash crops can quickly deplete soil of its natural balance of nitrogen, phosphorus, and potassium, leaving plants hungry for these elements.

Until manufactured fertilizers became commonly available, farmers would rotate crops that depleted the soil's stock of nutrients with crops that added elements back into the soil. Some organic farmers continue to manage crops in this manner. For example, alfalfa, clover, and legumes draw nitrogen from the air and release it back into the soil. At the end of the growing season, they are plowed back into the soil to enrich it for the next cycle. Manure, consisting of the excrement and soiled straw bedding of farm animals, was still used globally in the late 1990s. Although it is usually in plentiful supply (each year, farm animals in the United States alone produce more than 1 billion tons), manure is not necessarily the best fertilizer for a particular field or crop.

John Bennett Lawes, a British Victorian, dedicated his life to fertilizers and plant nutrition and has been considered to be the father of the fertilizer industry. Lawes experimented with different combinations of phosphoric acid, lime, bone dust, and other substances. Another pioneer was German Justus von Liebig, who described the importance of nitrogen in plant growth and developed a theory about plant growth and nutrition.

Widespread use of manufactured fertilizers came about indirectly as a result of the defense industry's buildup during World War II. Factories built to draw nitrogen from the air to use for explosives were easily converted after the war to make nitrogenous fertilizers. Because of the rapid adoption of commercial fertilizers, Western Europe became self-sufficient in terms of crop production, thus preserving European rural life.

In the 1940s, organic phosphates, including Malathion and Parathion, were briefly popular. Spraying pesticides from small, low-flying airplanes dramatically increased the efficiency of their application. Instead of taking hours to spread chemicals by hand on the ground, planes could dust 1,000 acres in just a few minutes. There are, however, no permanently effective pesticides as of 2010. Plants and insects alike adapt their tolerance for the chemicals in just a few generations; consequently, scientists must constantly monitor the effectiveness of the pesticides and develop new formulas.

Several innovations served to improve conditions in the industry. In 1944, 2/4-dichlorophenoxyacetic acid, a substance that selectively kills only broad-leafed plants, was commercially introduced. It turned out to be the first in a steady stream of more than 100 commercial herbicides introduced on the market in the subsequent 50 years.

Scientists also developed several chemicals to help farmers control the size of crops and the period when plants could grow, which allowed farmers to better time crops for market. By using certain hormones, fruit could even be kept from rotting before it was picked.

Although the farm chemical industry experienced robust sales worldwide in 1996 and 1997, prospects for 1998 were more subdued. Increased production of corn, soybeans, and wheat spurred growth in the farm chemical industry since producers required more chemicals to treat the greater amount of land farmed. Moreover, analysts predict that Asia's population growth will drive agricultural chemical sales in the future.

In 1996 and 1997, several of the world's largest agrochemical firms divested themselves of their general and specialty chemical divisions to focus on life science products. Two of the world's leading producers, Ciba-Geigy and Monsanto, both liquidated their chemical concerns during this period. In 1996 Ciba merged its life science division with drug maker Sandoz, Ltd., to form Novartis, while Monsanto completed its restructuring in 1997, giving up its chemical arm to make a concentrated foray into the budding life science business (and in 1998 merged with pharmaceutical maker American Home Products Corporation). Similarly, Hoechst, the parent company of AgrEvo, announced that it would sell its chemical operations by 2000, and top 10 farm chemical producer Rhône-Poulenc increased its commitment to the pharmaceutical industry by spinning off its chemical and fiber operations to form Rhodia in 1998. This restructuring marked the movement of the agricultural chemical industry away from the mainstream chemical industry and an increased alignment with the biotechnology and the food and nutrition industries, as companies began to focus on producing genetically enhanced crops in addition to conventional agrochemicals.

However, other leading farm chemical producers, such as Bayer, DuPont, and BASF, have reasoned that general chemical and biotechnology operations complement each other. Company executives have noted that such diversification balances the risks involved in both industries and allows them to benefit from advances in both fields.

Since the 1990s, pesticide and fertilizer manufacturers have faced flat or declining demand in many of the world's key markets, although increased crop production in the United States and Europe was expected to cushion pesticide sales, and increased demand from developing countries, particularly in Asia, was expected to bolster the market for fertilizers. In 2002, the U.S. Department of Labor attributed some decline of pesticides to the use of computers that help farmers and agribusinesses determine which specific areas of the farm to treat with chemicals, rather than simply covering a whole farm, as was formerly prevalent. In addition, some industrialized countries have been seeking ways to minimize dependence on commercial fertilizers. A small but influential trend toward organic agriculture has raised consumer awareness of the chemicals used to produce food.

In 2002 the United Nations Environment Program (UNEP) estimated that synthetic pesticides, such as fungicides, herbicides, and insecticides, had annual sales revenue of up to US$30 billion. Nonetheless, the UNEP cautions that improper application of such pesticides can and does have adverse effects on farmers' health, the environment, domestic animals, and food consumers.

Developing East Asian countries, such as China, Indonesia, India, Vietnam, Cambodia, Pakistan, Thailand, and Malaysia, have remained major growth markets for fertilizers. In 2003, the Asia-Pacific region's agricultural chemicals market reached US$291.26 billion and was expected to control 51.9 percent of the global market by 2008. These areas were expected to use more than 11 million metric tons (mmt) by 2005. Because agriculture in these areas is a major economic sector—for example, nearly two-thirds of Thailand's labor force is engaged in agriculture—and its structure follows the traditional family farm model, crop quality is crucial. In 2001 and 2002, South Korea shipped huge quantities of crop fertilizer to North Korea in an attempt to relieve massive food shortages, a move hailed by many world leaders as a small, important step toward reconciliation.

CURRENT CONDITIONS

The use of fertilizers and pesticides, particularly in China and India, is increasing at a faster rate than the world average due to government subsidies for fertilizer purchases. These two nations are perceived as very important to the international fertilizer market. Governments in the Middle East, China, and India subsidize fertilizer use, which partly explains the steady increase in demand in these regions. These policies are likely to remain, as most Asian countries have been under pressure to increase production from their arable land due to exploding population growth. In like manner, some governments in Africa distributed fertilizers and seeds to small rural farmers, the result being that some small success was claimed in 2002 at fighting hunger locally through the production of crops such as soybeans.

Shipments of fertilizers to Europe, on the other hand, continued to slow as heavy annual rains, particularly in 2002, affected agricultural regions. In 2002 countries such as Spain, Portugal, Greece, and Italy began fighting against the adverse effects of chemical residues on lands already ruined by unwise farming practices that cause desertification. In the United States, the amount of acreage exempted from crop production had a

significant impact on the demand for fertilizer. As in Europe, the Food and Agriculture Organization of the United Nations (FAO) expected overall consumption of fertilizers to remain flat with only slight increases. Latin America, on the other hand, was forecast to be a strong export region later in the first decade of the twenty-first century. The European agricultural chemicals market was worth US$107.85 billion in 2003, a slight increase in growth over the previous year. France, the largest market in this sector in Europe, reached a value of US$12.9 billion, up 1.2 percent over the previous year, but this was not expected to be the general trend over the next five years. The leading markets for agricultural chemicals through 2010 were projected to be Asia and South America, which have rapidly expanding economies and agricultural sectors.

Middle East countries without land to grow food on were turning to other countries for that resource, such as Pakistan and Sudan. The Middle East nations were desirable partners because they produced fertilizers needed to grow food efficiently. Global population growth meant there was a definite and intense demand for food. An HSBC study showed many Middle Eastern countries were short of food and water but continued to be large-scale exporters of fertilizers. In addition, companies throughout the regions with access to gas had an edge over others. Nevertheless, nitrogen-based fertilizers were considered to be major parts of global consumption. These fertilizers, unlike potash or phosphates, had to be reapplied on an annual basis.

RESEARCH AND TECHNOLOGY

Agricultural researchers began emphasizing integrated pest management (IPM) in the mid- to late 1990s. According to the American Crop Protection Association, integrated pest management (IPM) includes four major kinds of technology: biological (natural pest controls), cultural (crop rotation, cultivation, and pest monitoring), chemical (pesticides and insect growth regulators), and genetic (genetically engineered crops). Researchers continued to search for the most successful combinations of these crop protection methods. Following the IPM approach, researchers must consistently develop farm chemicals to meet the needs of the biological, cultural, and genetic methods.

A larger portion of the research in the latter part of the decade focused on chiral chemistry, which studies molecules with two structural forms that are mirror images of each other. These molecules often have similar chemical and physical properties but different biological properties, which in the pharmaceutical and farm chemical industries can produce different results. The importance of chiral chemistry to the farm chemical industry is that it can determine which molecular structures benefit crops the most, since one structure could be more effective than another.

In the mid-1990s, Responsible Agricultural Product Information and Distribution (RAPID) developed PowerAg, a computer network for the dissemination of information pertaining to farm chemicals and for the electronic distribution of farm chemicals. In 1997 more than 30 of the world's producers subscribed to PowerAg. The network allowed manufacturers to stay informed about safety and environmental regulations. Furthermore, PowerAg offered a venue for electronic commerce, letting producers reduce their inventories, which include about US$1.5 billion worth of unsold products each year. Users can also track orders and shipments with PowerAg.

Institutionalized composting was another endeavor that the industrialized agricultural economies flirted with in the mid-1990s. One method of efficiently delivering fertilizer used during this time is the use of biodegradable tapes placed at the plant's roots. Earthworms have also been used to replenish nutrient-stripped soil. As the worms eat through waste, they produce castings rich in nitrogen, phosphorous, and potassium. The French firm Sovadec developed a method called the Naturba Process, which separates recyclables from organic waste and then sterilizes the resultant waste to be sold as a fertilizer called "vermicompost."

In 2004, a model was introduced that was able to predict the effect of pesticides on animals. Researched for a quarter of a century, it was hoped the model would help crop growers assess the effect of such chemicals on the ecosystem in advance, because it could take factors such as climate into account in conjunction with animal physiology and behavior.

The U.S. Environmental Protection Agency (EPA) would not divulge information about the possible link of pesticides with the disappearance of millions of honeybees in the United States. Consequently, the Natural Resources Defense Council decided to review EPA studies needed for the approval of a Bayer CropScience pesticide, but had to file suit for access to the studies. Beginning in 2006, beekeepers reported an unexplained phenomenon known as "colony collapse disorder" that caused the loss of 30 percent or more of their hives. Scientists concluded the phenomenon was "linked to an onslaught of pesticides, mites, parasites and viruses, as well a loss of habitat and food." According to the U.S. Department of Agriculture, bees pollinate US $15 billion worth of U.S. crops, or approximately one-third of the human diet. The pesticide under critical review was called Clothianidin, a versatile part of the neonicotinoids pesticides class. Principal uses included coating corn, sugar beet, and sorghum seeds. After bee deaths occurred, France and Germany suspended

use of Clothianidin until further study was completed. In 2003, the EPA granted conditional registration for Clothianidin and required Bayer CropScience to submit studies about honeybees' chronic exposure to Clothianidin. The NRDC filed its lawsuit after an August 2008 deadline was missed by the EPA.

The USGS Toxic Substances Hydrology (Toxics) Program was designed to study the impact agricultural chemicals has on the environment from pesticides, fertilizers, veterinary medicines, and other sources. The Toxics Program investigates the processes of dispersal of the chemicals into the atmosphere, ground water, and surface water. It also studies the processes that determine the fate of nutrients in the environment, while identifying pesticide degradation instances. The studies also assess the impact of hypoxia (where it is deprived of oxygen), eutrophication (a process where a body of water builds its concentration of plant nutrients), and other processes on bodies of water that are used as drainage from agriculturally dominated watersheds.

INDUSTRY LEADERS

Syngenta. The world's biggest fertilizer company, Syngenta, was formed by the merger of Novartis and AstraZeneca. One of the biggest challenges for the company in the early 2000s was meeting demands from environmental action groups, most notably Greenpeace, that the company clean up massive quantities of chemical residues left by the companies Syngenta purchased. In January 2002, for example, Syngenta agreed to clean up a site near Katmandu, Nepal, although a spokesperson for the company stated that his company could not be held responsible for practices of another company two decades earlier. Instead, the problems were those of Sandoz AG and Ciba-Geigy, two companies that had been absorbed by Novartis, which itself was acquired by the firm known in 2010 as Syngenta.

In 2009, this global leader in chemicals had sales totaling US$10.99 billion and a net income of about US$1.766 billion. The number of employees in 2009 totaled over 25,900.

Novartis AG, a Swiss firm, had 2009 sales approaching US$44.27 billion. The company employed approximately 99,850 people in 2009. Novartis resulted from the merger of agrochemical leader Ciba-Geigy and prescription drugmaker Sandoz AG in 1996. Novartis had produced a wide variety of pharmaceuticals and medical and nutrition supplies, and it also had played a key role in the agricultural chemical industry. One of the world's most potent and controversial pesticides, DDT, was invented by a Geigy scientist. Ciba-Geigy was formed in 1970 by a merger of two prominent Swiss chemical companies. Geigy SA is the older of the two, with elements of the company dating back to 1758. Ciba, Ltd. was founded in the 1850s and was the largest chemical company in Switzerland by 1900. Ciba-Geigy has subsidiaries in Argentina, Australia, Austria, Belgium, Brazil, Canada, Chile, Colombia, Denmark, France, Italy, Japan, Korea, Lebanon, the Netherlands, Portugal, Spain, Sweden, the United Kingdom, and the United States.

The group formerly known as Zeneca Agrochemicals was part of the Zeneca Group that produced drugs for cardiovascular and cancer treatments, as well as herbicides, insecticides, and fungicides. In 1996 the company's revenues totaled US$9.1 billion, and farm chemicals accounted for 11 percent of its overall US$2.7 billion in sales. In 2004, Syngenta announced plans to purchase a majority stake in corn and soybean seed company Advanta from AstraZeneca. Along with the purchase of genetically modified corn technology from Bayer, the acquisition of Advanta was expected to put Syngenta at the forefront of the corn and soybeans market by 2005.

Bayer. Bayer AG, along with BASF and Hoechst, is heir to the German chemical cartel IG Farben. Originally founded in the late 1890s to produce synthetic dye, its 1996 sales totaled US$33.5 billion, 6 percent of which came from agrochemicals. The company is also involved in the production of pharmaceuticals, dyes, polyurethane, organic and inorganic chemicals, and synthetic rubber. As one the world's leading chemical producers, Bayer consists of 350 companies in 150 countries. In 2009, Bayer had sales of approximately US$41.5 billion. The company employed 108,400 people. In 2002 Bayer acquired the agrochemicals giant Aventis CropScience, which had been formed by a merger of France's Rhône-Poulenc and Germany's Hoechst, making Bayer the second largest company in the industry. In 2003, Bayer had 20 percent of the worldwide market, and was expecting to knock Syngenta out of the number one position by 2006. In 2004, France's ministry of agriculture banned Bayer's corn insecticide Gaucho, due to its potentially harmful effect on bees.

In 1982 Rhône-Poulenc was taken over by the French government. Just 11 years later, after suffering massive losses, it was re-privatized and by the mid-1990s the farm chemical powerhouse had more than 200 production plants and research labs around the world. In 1996 Rhône-Poulenc's sales totaled US$16.5 billion, with agrochemicals accounting for a 13 percent share, or US$2.2 billion. In addition to agrochemicals, Rhône-Poulenc is involved in pharmaceuticals, specialty chemicals, and plastics. In the agrochemical sector, the company produces herbicides, insecticides, seed protection, and genetic formulations. Rhône-Poulenc has subsidiaries in Australia, Austria, Belgium, Cameroon, Canada, Germany, Greece,

Guatemala, Indonesia, Italy, the Ivory Coast, Japan, Madagascar, Mexico, Morocco, the Netherlands, Portugal, Senegal, Spain, and Switzerland.

Hoechst AG of Germany had 1996 sales of US$33 billion, 7 percent of which was derived from agricultural chemicals. The company focuses on pharmaceuticals, but its AgrEvo division produces herbicides and insecticides as well as other chemicals used to keep crops and animals healthy. Hoechst began producing dye in 1863 in Frankfurt and is the largest of three chemical companies formed in 1952 by the disbanding of German chemical cartel IG Farben under the Allied postwar occupation. In 1987 Hoechst acquired Celanese Corp., one of the leading chemical producers in the United States. Hoechst has been criticized by environmentalists because of the company's production of chlorofluorocarbons (CFCs) but has since planned to produce an alternative called R134a. It also has begun to recycle and reduce solid waste and wastewater in its plastics facilities. In 1997 Hoechst announced it would restructure the company to focus on pharmaceuticals and agricultural chemicals.

Monsanto. Founded in 1901, Monsanto has conducted business in 130 countries. The creator of Roundup, the top herbicide worldwide, and NutraSweet, Monsanto withdrew from the chemical business in late 1997 to concentrate on life science products, including genetically engineered seeds and crops such as cotton and soybeans, as well as agricultural chemicals. To prepare itself for its new role, Monsanto began acquiring and forming alliances with life science operations between 1996 and 1997. Some of these companies included Calgene (a plant biotechnology leader), Asgrow Agronomics (a corn and soybean seed leader), Holden's Foundation Seeds Inc. (the world's largest foundation seed company), and DeKalb Genetics (the second largest U.S. seed company). In 1998 it agreed to merge with American Home Products Corp. In April 2002, Monsanto formed an agreement with DuPont and its subsidiary Pioneer Hi-Bred International to advance agricultural technologies for all three.

In 1997 Monsanto posted sales of US$7.5 billion, and farm chemicals contributed US$2.9 billion, or 38 percent, to this total. In the early 2000s, while involved in agriculture-related businesses other than pesticides, the company did considerable business in Latin America. However, it was estimating losses caused by the devaluation of the peso in Argentina. In 2010, Monsanto had sales of approximately US$10.502 billion and employed approximately 21,700 people.

E.I. du Pont de Nemours. In the mid-1990s, E.I. du Pont de Nemours and Company was the largest chemical company in the world with 1996 revenues of about

US$44 billion. Agricultural chemicals accounted for about US$2.5 billion of that total. Founded in 1802, the company began as a partnership in gunpowder and explosives. DuPont grew from a family business to a multinational conglomerate through the acquisition of companies and the diversification of product lines. In addition to agricultural herbicides and insecticides, DuPont is involved in producing various chemicals, plastics, petroleum products, fibers, and medical products, among others. In April 2002, DuPont, its subsidiary Pioneer Hi-Bred International, and Monsanto agreed to work together to develop agricultural technologies. Sales in 2009 were approximately US$26.1 billion. DuPont employed about 58,000 people at 220 sites with a presence in more than 75 countries.

In August 2008, DuPont revealed plans to enhance its seed business in Europe and open new research centers. Research center development reflects a US$5 million investment along with physical staff support. A DuPont subsidiary, Pioneer Hi-Bred, continues its effort of more than 50 years to deliver higher yielding products to European farmers. It planned to add 10 research positions at the new centers and transfer 25 research employees from other locations.

Dow AgroSciences. Dow Chemical Company, the parent company of Dow Agrosciences, took in nearly US$20 billion in sales in 1996 from its line of more than 2,000 products, half of which are basic chemicals. In addition to producing agricultural products, the company manufactures plastics, consumer products, and pharmaceuticals. Begun in 1890 by Herbert Dow to extract bromine from brine, the company came up with the revolutionary idea of using an electric current to separate bromides from brine. Dow eventually discovered chlorine bleach and pioneered the production of metal magnesium, used to manufacture automobiles after World War I. To produce agricultural chemicals, the company formed DowElanco, a joint venture with Eli Lilly, in 1989. DowElanco posted revenues of nearly US$2 billion in 1996, representing 10 percent of the parent company's sales. Dow AgroSciences was formed in 1997 after Dow Chemical bought out Eli Lilly & Company's 40 percent interest for US$1.2 billion. In 2010, Dow AgroSciences' annual sales topped US$4.5 billion.

Indianapolis-based Dow AgroSciences was encouraging scientists to help farmers grow bigger tomatoes, drought-resistant corn, and more productive dairy herds. Weather conditions around the world could be simulated in climate-controlled greenhouses, allowing Dow AgroSciences to grow plants year-round. The company aimed to become a bigger player in the US$48 billion seeds and agricultural chemicals market by helping farmers manage pests and grow improved crops.

In August 2008, Dow AgroSciences finalized its acquisition of Dairyland Seed Co. and Bio-Plan Research. "Dairylands Seed's investment in R&D, its product portfolio and brand will strengthen our corn, soybean and alfalfa business," said Jerome Peribere, president and CEO of Dow AgroSciences.

BASF. In 2000 German chemical manufacturer BASF became the third largest fertilizer manufacturer in the world after it acquired American Cyanamid. In 2009, total sales from all divisions reached approximately US$67.48 billion. Since the company's founding in 1865, Badische Analin und Soda Fabrik AG (later known as BASF) has been a major influence in the world chemical industry. BASF was one of three German chemical companies that comprised the cartel IG Farben. Best known in the United States for its video and audiocassettes, the company is involved in the production of plastics, chemicals, oil and gas, dyes, and finishing products. In March 2002, BASF insisted that it had no plans to sell off its 17 percent interest in Kali und Salz, its potash and fertilizer division. BASF admitted in 2002 that the company's plastics division had suffered in the generally stagnant European economy, incurring a loss of US$412 million during the fourth quarter of 2001.

BASF acquired American Cyanamid Corp. from American Home Products Corp. in 2000 for US$3.8 billion. Founded in 1907, American Cyanamid developed the first synthetic fertilizer for North American farmers. The company grew to have a significant presence in 145 countries around the world and was acquired by American Home Products Corp., a pharmaceutical and health care company. In 1996 the parent company reported sales of US$14 billion, and American Cyanamid accounted for 13 percent of revenues with US$1.9 billion.

BASF Crop Protection planned to invest more than US$225 million through 2010 to increase production capacity in Germany, France, Brazil, and the United States for fungicides, herbicides, and insecticides. The goal of BASF and BASF Crop Protection was to benefit from high demands for corn, soybeans, wheat, and canola crops.

Agrium. As of 2001, Agrium had 14 plants in North America and Argentina, producing not only nitrogen products, but also phosphate, potash, sulfate, and micronutrients used in fertilizers. Additionally, the company had about 225 fertilizer retail stores in the United States, and an additional 20 in Argentina. Approximately 55 percent of the company's total sales came from the wholesale market. In 2010, total sales were nearly US$9.129 billion, and the company employed roughly 6,000 people.

In the spring of 2002 Agrium was trying to establish its exact losses after the extreme devaluation of the peso in Argentina. The company had about 8 percent of its annual US$2.5 billion in revenue tied up in fertilizer shipments to Argentina. Argentina once had produced crops with little or no chemical fertilizers, but Calgary, Canada-based Agrium saw huge potential in Argentina in the early 1990s when pesticide sales in 1992 tripled from 1991 levels of US$286 million. Agrium was part of a corporate team that built a US$600 million urea fertilizer plant in the early 1990s, and had created one of the largest fertilizer corporations in the world in 1996 when it merged with Viridian Inc., for US$887.4 million.

In August 2008, Agrium's bid to build a nitrogen plant on Egypt's northeastern shore at Damietta was cancelled by the Egyptian cabinet following protests from local residents and feedback from an Egyptian parliamentary committee. Alternately, the state-owned oil company MOPCO agreed to acquire Agrium's Egyptian subsidiary and build the plant at a different location. Agrium had announced a joint venture with three Egyptian state corporations in early 2007. At the time the project was cancelled, the venture had already cost partners US$500 million and more than 40 percent of the plant had been completed.

MAJOR COUNTRIES IN THE INDUSTRY

North America. The United States began importing an increasing proportion of its potash fertilizers, importing a total of 10.4 mmt in 1996. However, nitrogen exports increased 6.5 percent to 5.1 million metric tons (mmt). The United States used 53.5 million tons of fertilizer in 1999, according to the FAO, and is second to China in nitrogen production. It produces as much as 20 mmt of ammonia, much of which is used as a fertilizer product. The United States also is a large potash producer, getting much of its potash from Canada and other nations.

Canada retained its status as a leading producer of potash, selling about 60 percent of its production to the United States. In 1996, Canada's production level grew and the country posted record exports. Domestic fertilizer consumption also increased in 1996. In 1999, Canada's fertilizer industry added US$1.6 million in domestic imports and exported US$2 billion worth of product.

The 2000s were a particularly hard time for the agricultural chemicals business, and in 2002 analysts said zero growth was expected for some time to come unless a blockbuster pesticide could be developed to increase business revenues. The United States and Canada accounted for 29 percent of the world's farm chemical market, with sales of US$8.98 billion in 1996. In the United States, total consumption of fertilizers and plant nutrients increased

from 24,877 tons in 1960 to 52,319 tons in 1994. Pesticide production was US$6.81 billion in 1993, according to the American Crop Protection Association, and pesticide consumption totaled US$6.35 billion. Fertilizer production in the country totaled US$318.7 million in 1994. However, in the mid-1990s, the use of nitrogenous fertilizers and potash declined 4 percent and use of phosphates declined 2 percent. The leading U.S. farm chemicals have traditionally been herbicides, which represented 65 percent of the country's market in 1996, followed by insecticides with 23 percent and fungicides with 7 percent. The U.S. market was valued at US$20.2 billion in 2002. A surge in the chemicals market in general occurred in 2004, with an 8.8 percent increase in the volume of agricultural chemicals in particular. Growth was then expected to slow to 1.3 percent in 2005, and 0.8 percent in 2006 in that market. With the growing economic recession, the industry growth fell flat through the remainder of the decade.

In Canada, pesticide bans nationwide challenged lawn-care companies. More than 140 municipalities, including Toronto and Vancouver, adopted bylaws prohibiting the use of pesticides for cosmetic purposes. Impacted areas included insecticides, herbicides, and fungicides that were, continued to be allowed on most golf courses and for non-cosmetic purposes. Many industry insiders were already feeling a strong need for additional organic products. Some companies were responding to bans by eliminating pesticide use or raising prices for services.

Europe. Fertilizer consumption fell 1 percent in Western Europe in 1996 to 17.7 mmt, reversing the previous year's advances. Fertilizer exports edged up that year 3.5 percent to 10 mmt and imports slowed to 12.4 mmt. Although production in Europe rose 2 percent to 17.6 mmt, imports continued to represent 70 percent of Western Europe's fertilizer consumption.

In Eastern Europe, fertilizer consumption continued its slow recovery, climbing 1 percent to 3.3 mmt. As the leading fertilizer user, Poland helped the regional increase, consuming 1.5 mmt in 1996, 6 percent above 1995 levels. Even though Bulgaria's use plummeted 43 percent, other countries, including Hungary, Slovakia, and the Czech Republic, experienced moderate increases, which offset Bulgaria's drop in use. Exports in the region grew the most. In 1996 they jumped 19 percent to 3.1 mmt, and overall fertilizer production rose 14 percent to 5.3 mmt.

In the 15 countries that make up the former Soviet Union (FSU), fertilizer consumption has fallen since 1990. In 1996 it dropped to 4.4 mmt. The FSU accounted for 3.4 percent of the world's fertilizer use in 1996, in contrast to 17 percent in 1990 before its political dismantling. Inflation, poor distribution networks, and loss of subsidies have suppressed fertilizer use in these countries. However, exports from FSU countries enjoyed considerable success in 1996, growing 20 percent to 11.8 mmt. In the late 2000s, the Russian Federation and the Ukraine led in fertilizer production and exportation.

Western Europe ranked second for crop protection chemical sales in 1996, representing 26 percent of the global market. In 1996 farm chemical sales rose 3 percent to US$8.2 billion in Europe. However, pesticide use in Europe declined 6 to 10 percent in the early 1990s and was not expected to rebound before 2000. Fertilizer consumption also had been dropping during this time and was predicted to continue doing so at about two percent per year throughout the decade. This trend was been brought about in part through the new Common Agricultural Policy (CAP) of the European Union. In 2001, the industry came under scrutiny following an explosion of a fertilizer plant at Toulouse, France, causing destruction and loss of life inside and outside the factory.

Despite the overall decline in the industry in Europe from 1999 through 2002, in 2003, the European fertilizers and agricultural chemicals market rose by 0.9 percent to reach a volume of 22.41 billion metric tones (bmt) and was valued at US$107.85 billion. The leading sector by volume in 2003 was nitrogenous fertilizers, accounting for 60 percent of market volume at 13.46 bmt, followed by the phosphate fertilizers sector, which accounted for 24.4 percent of market value at 4.02 bmt. The European market was projected to account for 17.6 percent of global market value with a value of US$105.34 billion by 2008, representing a decrease of 2.3 percent from 2003.

Deutsche Welle shared the inside story about how Greenpeace had "slammed" the German government about its use of pesticides after discovering large amounts of dangerous and prohibited substances in fruits and vegetables in Germany as well as in the entire E.U. The online version of *Der Spiegel* had originally broken the news. Greenpeace claimed 59 substances that were illegal in Germany were found in fruits and vegetables sold in that country. The conclusion was that German farmers were using the illegal and highly dangerous pesticides in such large quantities in order to save money. "The National Report on Food Monitoring," published in February 2008, contained a list of 14,942 foods compiled by the Ministry of Consumer Affairs and Food Safety. An investigation found that in 6,750 instances, samples exceeded the legal amount of a specific pesticide or contained a mix of several toxic substances. Approximately 2,176 of these products had a German origin.

Fresh herbs, potatoes, and raspberries were believed to contain the most illegal pesticides.

Asia. While Indonesia has been using increasingly larger amounts of fertilizers, higher prices for chemical fertilizers, urbanization, and decreasing agricultural growth in the 1990s and early 2000s led to lower fertilizer consumption in India, once the biggest consumer of chemical fertilizers. A governmental decision to deregulate fertilizers in 1992 led to escalating prices for phosphatic and potassic fertilizers that resulted in fewer shipments, according to a 2002 report in *India Business Insight.*

In 1996 Asia was the third largest market for agricultural chemicals, purchasing 22 percent of global sales. In South Asia, most countries experienced growth in fertilizer use. In 1996, India faced reduced subsidies of phosphate and potash fertilizers, resulting in a decrease in use of those fertilizers. In contrast, nitrogen fertilizer remained subsidized, and its use increased. Pakistan, the second largest consumer, expanded its use of fertilizers, especially potash, because of strong wheat and cotton prices.

Developed Asian countries such as Japan and South Korea consumed 2.6 mmt of fertilizer in 1996. However, Japan's agricultural labor problems led to a 4 percent drop in the production and consumption of fertilizer, while imports increased 4 percent. Exports from the region stood at only 700,000 metric tons, about 70 percent of which came from Korea.

Oceania reported a 3 percent rise in fertilizer consumption in 1996, 2.4 mmt of which was the result of an 11 percent increase in nitrogen fertilizer use in Australia. New Zealand's fertilizer use edged up 1 percent to 700,000 metric tons, while its production held at 300,000 metric tons. The region's imports climbed a dramatic 14 percent.

From 1999 through 2003 the compound annual growth rate in market volume was 1 percent. By 2003, the Asia-Pacific fertilizers and agricultural market had a total value of US$291.26 billion, up 2.2 percent from the previous year. Nitrogenous fertilizers are the top source of revenue in the region, making up 61.9 percent of market value. The Asia-Pacific region was expected to account for 51.9 percent of the global market for the industry by 2008, representing an increase of 1.2 percent since 2003.

According to *China View,* export duties on fertilizer in China were raised in an effort to keep prices low, protect farmers, and ensure agricultural production. This was considered a harsh move capable of pushing some domestic produces to the wall by eroding their profits. "Many producers have had no profit domestically. The new adjustment would make it even harder," concluded Guo Jing Pu, industry analyst with Cinda Securities.

South America. South America held 12 percent of the world pesticide market in 1996, with Brazil accounting for 40 percent of that amount. Argentina and Colombia were also major players in the industry, with the smaller countries in the region relying mostly on imports. In 1996 agricultural chemical sales climbed 13 percent to US$3.8 billion. Although the rate of fertilizer consumption in Latin America was lower than the world average, the industry outlook was optimistic for the region, particularly in Brazil, following the resolution of many economic problems of the 1980s. Adding to the positive forecast was the fact that many South American countries had abundant supplies of resources, such as phosphate rock and sulfur, to utilize in the future. Moreover, increasing privatization in the region was expected to boost industry competitiveness within South America as well as internationally. In early 2002, large fertilizer interests worldwide continued to assess exact losses following the devaluation of the peso in Argentina.

Stagnant and fragile economies in Latin America caused a 20 percent drop in shipments of fertilizer to the region in 2001 when compared to 2000. In 1996, Latin America consumed 8.7 mmt of fertilizer, down more than 5 percent from 1995. South America accounted for almost 75 percent of the 8.7 mmt total, and Brazil and Mexico accounted for 60 percent of the total. However, Brazil's use of fertilizer slipped in 1996 because of credit problems and Mexico's use dropped due to the devaluation of the peso, which drove up prices.

BIBLIOGRAPHY

"Asia-Pacific—Fertilizers & Agricultural Chemicals." *Datamonitor Industry Market Research,* 1 November 2004.

"Bayer CropScience Intends to Overtake Syngenta." *Chemical Week,* 10 September 2003.

Canadian Fertilizer Institute, 2011. Available from www.cfi.ca/

Clapp, Stephen. "Monsanto Wheat Decision Raises Questions about Future Products." *Pesticide & Toxic Chemical News,* 17 May 2004.

"Dow AgroSciences Completes Acquisition of Dairyland Seed Co.," 2 September 2008. Available from www.cattlenetwork.com.

Draper, Deborah J., ed. *Business Rankings Annual.* Detroit: Thomson Gale, 2004.

"DuPont Boosts Seed Research in Europe to Extend Leadership Position," 25 August 2008. Available from www.marketwatch.com.

"Egypt Cancels Agrium Fertilizer Plant." CBC, 5 August 2008. Available from www.cbc.ca.

"Europe—Fertilizers & Agricultural Chemicals." *Datamonitor Industry Market Research,* 1 November 2004.

"Fertilizer Export Duties Raised Again," 2 September 2008. Available from http://www.chinadaily.com.cn/bizchina/2008-09/02/content_6989583.htm.

"Fertilizer Growth Lower in 1990s." *India Business Insight,* 26 March 2002.

"Fertilizers and Pesticides in France, Germany, UK, US." *Euromonitor,* August 2004. Available from www.majormarketprofiles.com.

Food and Agriculture Organization of the United Nations. *Current World Fertilizer Situation and Outlook,* 2002. Available from www.fao.org.

"France—Fertilizers & Agricultural Chemicals." *Datamonitor Industry Market Research,* 1 November 2004.

"Global—Chemicals." *Datamonitor Industry Market Research,* 1 November 2004.

Guiro, Angela. "EU Clears BASF's Acquisition of Cyanamid." *Bloomberg News,* 5 December 2001.

"Hoover's Company Capsules." *Hoover's Online,* 2008. Available from www.hoovers.com.

"Illegal Pesticides Found in Germany's Produce." *Deutsche Welle,* 22 August 2008. Available from www.dw-world.de.

"International Trade Statistics." World Trade Organization, 2003. Available from www.wto.org.

James, Barry. "World Loses Ground to Deserts." *International Herald Tribune,* 4 April 2002.

Kay, Jane. "Lawsuit Seeks EPA Pesticide Data," *San Francisco Chronicle,* 19 August 2008. Available from www.sfgate.com.

Koprowski, Gene J. "Model Predicts Impact of Pesticides on Ecosystem." *Pesticide & Toxic Chemical News,* 9 February 2004.

"Middle-East Fertilizer Firms to Feed on Global Hunger." Commodity Online, 2 September 2008. Available from www.commodity online.com.

Pfenniger, Chantal. "Syngenta to Help Clean Up Pesticides." *Bloomberg News,* 16 January 2002.

———. "Syngenta 2001 Earnings Little Changed." *Bloomberg News,* 28 February 2002.

Russell, John. "Bold & Bountiful," 24 August 2008. Available from www.indystar.com.

Scott, Alex. "Bayer's Gaucho Insecticide Suspended in France." *Chemical Week,* 26 May 2004.

Sissell, Kara. "Argentine Uncertainties Hurt Agrium, Monsanto, and Eastman." *Chemical Week,* 13 February 2002.

Stewart, Monte. "Lawn-Care Industry Braces for Pesticide Bans." *Business Edge,* 5 August 2008. Available from www.businessedge.ca.

"Strong Growth May Moderate in 2005." *Chemical Week,* 15 December 2004.

"Syngenta Says Lumax Is a U.S. Success." *Chemical Week,* 13 August 2003.

U.S. Department of Labor. "Toxic Substance Hydrology Program." U.S. Geological Survey, October 2010. Available from http://toxics.usgs.gov.

Voith, Melody. "BASF to Boost Crop Protection Spending." ACS Publications, 5 August 2008. Available from pubs.acs.org.

Walsh, Kerri. "Syngenta and Private Equity Firm Buy Advanta Seeds." *Chemical Week,* 19 May 2004.

Warrington, Hannah, and Rudy Ruitenberg. "BASF Sees Difficult 2002." *Chemical Week,* 14 March 2002.

Winder, Robert. "A Growing Debate." *Chemistry and Industry,* 19 January 2004.

"Zimbabwe; Rural Farmers Make Inroads into Soybean Production." *Africa News,* 9 April 2002.

SIC 2810

CHEMICALS, INDUSTRIAL INORGANIC

NAICS CODE(S)

325. The industrial inorganic chemical industry extracts and processes a variety of chemicals and gases, often known as basic chemicals, from inanimate material of the earth's crust. Examples of industry products include alkalis, carbon dioxide, chlorine, nitrogen, numerous pigments, and a wide array of other chemicals for industrial use. For more information about the organic chemical industry, see also **Chemicals, Industrial Organic.**

INDUSTRY SNAPSHOT

Inorganic chemicals account for approximately one-quarter of total global chemical sales (not including allied products, such as plastic), which were hovering around US$1.94 trillion per year in 2003. The industrial inorganic chemical industry consists of four segments: alkalis and chlorine (or chloralkalis); industrial gases; pigments; and miscellaneous inorganic chemicals, which make up the bulk of industry output. Organic chemicals, which are derived from materials that contain carbon, make up most of the remainder of the industry. Because most leading companies and countries in the industry produce both organic and inorganic chemicals, the categories are closely intertwined statistically. Most inorganic (or basic) chemicals are building-block materials used to manufacture other compounds and products. Therefore, industry performance is closely tied to the health of the global economy.

A global economic slowdown throughout the 2000s forced many chemical firms to restructure operations.

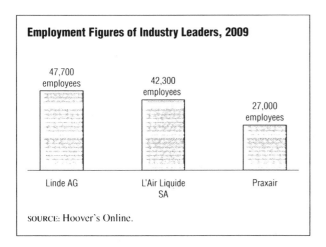

Employment Figures of Industry Leaders, 2009

47,700 employees — Linde AG
42,300 employees — L'Air Liquide SA
27,000 employees — Praxair

SOURCE: Hoover's Online.

Turbulent economies also brought on a wave of merger and acquisition activity. In 2001 the U.S. chemicals industry experienced its worst year since the early 1980s. The American Chemistry Council attributed the downswing to the faltering U.S. economy, rising energy costs, a strong U.S. dollar, overcapacity, weakening demand related to the consolidating manufacturing industry, and falling prices. By the mid-2000s, competition was rising from emerging economies, particularly China. The American Chemistry Council reported that by 2010, more than US$500 billion of chemistry products were being purchased each year worldwide. The products of chemistry are everywhere in everyday life, with more than 96 percent of all manufactured goods directly impacted by chemistry.

According to the *Oxygen, Nitrogen & Other Gas Manufacturing in the US* report, growth in revenue for the industrial inorganic chemical industry will be affected by not only the needs of its customers, but also by globalization and ongoing technological development. In addition, an increased awareness of the effect of chemicals on the environment was exerting a positive influence on the industry, which was working on the development of "green" chemicals.

The global market for this industry, which grew 10.9 percent in 2007, had a value of US$50.4 billion. The merchant gas segment captured 35.1 percent of market value, making it the largest segment. The Asia-Pacific region had the largest market for industrial inorganic chemical, with a 42.3 percent share. Research and Markets projected a market value of US$83.8 million for 2021, which would be a 62.2 percent increase from 2007.

ORGANIZATION AND STRUCTURE
Key Segments.

Chloralkalies. Examples of alkalis and chlorine are chlorine, sodium hydroxide (caustic soda), sodium bicarbonate, sodium chlorate, and various potassium compounds. Chlorine and caustic soda are major chloralkalies. They are created through the electrolysis of salt brine. Chlorine is used in the manufacture of numerous products, including paper (a controversial application because of its environmental impact); water and sewage treatment; fuel additives; and multiple other applications. Other major chemicals in the chloralkalies group are soda ash and sodium chlorate. Soda ash is primarily used in the production of glass, other chemicals, detergents, and soaps. Sodium chlorate can be used as a cleaner substitute for chlorine in many applications, particularly paper manufacturing. The United States is the largest global producer of chloralkalies, partly because of its dominance of the natural soda ash market. The U.S. annual capacity of soda ash was 13.1 million metric tons.

Industrial Gases. Industrial gases include the major gases nitrogen, oxygen, hydrogen, carbon dioxide, and argon. They also encompass more than 100 specialty gases, such as krypton and xenon, which are used in medicine, electronics, aerospace, and other industries. Nitrogen, the largest gas product by volume, is used in the production of other chemicals because of its inert "blanketing" qualities. It is also utilized in applications ranging from metal manufacturing to food processing. Oxygen is employed in a variety of applications as well, particularly chemical and glass manufacturing and medical care. Carbon dioxide is commonly used for refrigeration and freezing, as well as to carbonate beverages. Hydrogen is used in oil refining and ammonia production, among other applications. Gases are often sold in compressed liquid or solid form and then stored in cylinders or transported via pipelines.

The industrial gas sector differs from most other chemical segments in that it is dominated by four companies: Praxair Inc. (United States), Air Products and Chemicals, Inc. (United States), L'Air Liquide (France), and BOC Group PLC (United Kingdom). Each of those manufacturers controls a major portion of the global market for industrial gas. Both L'Air Liquide and Praxair controlled 18 percent of the worldwide industrial gas market, which was estimated at US$34.5 billion in 2001 by J.R. Campbell & Associates. BOC had a 14 percent market share, while Air Products secured an 11 percent share.

Inorganic Pigments. Inorganic pigments are used primarily to make paints and coatings. This category includes metallic oxides, metal powder suspensions, earth colors, and lead chromates. The largest selling pigment is titanium dioxide, which is consumed mostly by producers of paints and dyes, paper coatings and fillers, plastics, and rubber. According to the U.S. Geological Survey, worldwide titanium dioxide capacity was 4.3 million metric tons (mmt) per year. During 2000, complex inorganic pigments that could provide diverse characteristics like lightfastness and chemical resistance were growing in popularity. However, growth in heavy metal inorganic pigments was faltering due to environmental concerns. Major producers of pigments are U.S.-based Du Pont and U.K.-based Imperial Chemical Industries PLC.

Other Inorganics. Miscellaneous inorganic chemicals, which constitute the bulk of industry sales, include basic building-block chemicals used to make a plethora of other chemicals, compounds, and products. The most common industrial inorganic chemical was sulfuric acid,

with the United States producing almost 40 billion kilograms per year. Most sulfuric acid is used to produce fertilizer, but it is also used in numerous other applications ranging from oil refining to paper production. The U.S. Geological Survey estimated that nearly 75 percent of sulfuric acid used in 1999 was for phosphate fertilizer. Sulfuric acid is commonly consumed on the site at which it is produced.

Another major inorganic chemical is sulfur, most of which is used to make sulfuric acid. Major sulfur-producing countries included Poland, the United States, the Russian Federation (formerly the Soviet Union), and Canada. The United States is the world's largest consumer and producer of sulfur. Phosphoric acid is another important industrial inorganic. Most of it is used to make fertilizer, but it is also utilized in the manufacture of animal feed and food processing, as well as other industrial uses. Other important inorganics include ammonia (and ammonia nitrate and sulfate), nitric acid, and hydrochloric acid.

Production Dynamics. The industrial inorganic chemicals industry is more mature than the organic chemical industry. Most inorganic chemicals have existed commercially for several decades, and basic production techniques have changed little. Therefore, market growth closely parallels expansion of the major industrial sectors that consume the base inorganics: paper, construction, packaging, transportation, healthcare, paint and inks, and fertilizer industries. Overall, industry growth generally mimics overall economic health with the exception of a few segments like specialty gases. The industry was expecting growth in the developing Asian and Latin American countries, where industrialization was fueling demand for inorganics.

Because the industry is mature, particularly in industrialized countries, most of its products are produced on a very high-volume commodity basis. As a result, the industry is exceptionally consolidated with just a few producers in each geographic region dominating specific segments. Furthermore, it is characterized by low profit margins and emphasis on containing production costs. The most successful producers are those who can minimize labor and energy costs, obtain access to relatively low-cost raw materials, and minimize distribution costs (by locating near their primary customers, for example).

Environmental regulation has been a major industry issue since the 1970s, and particularly beginning in the 1990s, primarily because low production costs are crucial. The inorganic chemical industry creates more pollution than all other manufacturing businesses. To reduce detrimental impacts, all of the industrialized nations have implemented strict environmental controls that limit output and disposal of pollutants and by-products. Adherence to these regulations costs the industry billions of dollars annually and had forced many companies out of business by the mid-1990s. A corollary of increased production costs associated with environmental laws has been a reduction of competition between companies in industrialized nations and those in developing nations with less burdensome restrictions.

BACKGROUND AND DEVELOPMENT

Inorganic chemistry has its roots in the metallurgical and medical arts of ancient societies. The early Chinese and Egyptians were aware of simple alloys, such as metallic salts and mineral products, as well as chemical processes related to glassmaking, enameling, dyeing, and painting. It was not until the eighteenth century, however, that rapid advances in the inorganic chemical sciences occurred. In 1751 Sweden's Georg Brandt isolated cobalt, which was a pivotal discovery. Subsequent breakthroughs during the eighteenth century included the identification of hydrogen, discovery of water's chemical composition, and synthesis of nitric acid from moist air by British scientist Henry Cavendish.

Nicolas Leblanc of France is most often credited with giving birth to the chemical industry in spite of the enormous influence of scientists before and during his time. Leblanc differed from his peers and predecessors in that he was determined to find commercial applications for chemical processes. Near the beginning of the nineteenth century, Leblanc achieved his goal when he made sodium carbonate (soda ash) out of salt. He is recognized as the first person to deliberately convert one or more chemicals into other chemical products for economic purposes. Leblanc's goal to produce new and better chemical products economically continues to be the chief aim of the chemical industry in the twenty-first century.

While Leblanc's discovery was neglected in France, it became extremely important in England in the soap and textile industries. As British alkali producers advanced the inorganic chemical industry during the 1800s, they laid the foundation for the modern inorganics business. Important scientific breakthroughs of the late nineteenth century, including the formulation of the periodic law in 1869 by Russia's Mendeleyev and the discovery of the electron in 1897 by Sir Joseph J. Thompson of England, boosted industry success. Of equal consequence were two developments early in the twentieth century in Germany: the articulation of the

quantum theory by Max Weber in 1900 and the development of quantum mechanics in the early 1920s by Werner Heisenberg and Erwin Schrodinger.

During the first half of the twentieth century, World War I and World War II created massive demand for inorganic chemicals to feed the war machines. Although those wars drew attention to the importance of the inorganic chemical industry, they also were the source of the industry's decline in stature in relation to the organic chemical industry. The shortage of raw materials during the wars resulted in the chemical industry shifting its focus to the production of synthetic materials that could be created using organic chemicals.

Despite the emphasis on organic chemistry following World War II, the demand for inorganic chemicals continued to grow in the mid-twentieth century, particularly in the United States. The industry in the United States benefited from strong national economic and population growth and access to inexpensive raw materials. It also profited by supplying war-torn countries in Europe and Japan with inorganic industrial chemicals. By the 1950s the United States was supplying and consuming the majority of global industry output in most industry segments.

By the 1960s, the inorganic chemical industry had largely achieved technological maturity. Most of the known inorganics were being produced commercially. The only technological barriers that remained were related primarily to increasing the efficiency of extraction and processing. Furthermore, the massive U.S. inorganic chemical market was reaching maturity, meaning that demand growth in that key market was waning. As a result, demand and profit growth in the inorganics industry became closely linked with the health of the global economy, which was indicative of demand for inorganics by other industries, such as steel and textiles. In addition, the industry became more consolidated and increasingly focused on cutting production costs.

During the 1970s and 1980s the inorganics industry continued to become more competitive. The United States managed to keep its global market share at about 25 percent, but Western Europe and Japan lost markets to emerging economies. South America and the Pacific Rim, for example, boosted their share of both demand and supply. China's inorganic industry made gains during the 1980s and early 1990s as a result of a flourishing domestic industrial sector and improvements in its transportation infrastructure.

The inorganic chemical market emerged as a truly global industry in the 1990s and consequently experienced cyclical performances related to worldwide economies. In 1996 manufacturers experienced declining demand in most industrial chemical sectors, including inorganics, but in 1997 sales picked up and key producing countries in North America and Europe reported modest increases in total production and exports. However, East Asia faced economic problems, including currency devaluations, and skyrocketing debt in 1997 and 1998 thwarted domestic inorganic chemical production as well as trade. Asian countries, on the other hand, began to show improvement by the early 2000s.

During the 1990s chemical manufacturers looked to the increased liberalization of international markets through trade agreements like the General Agreement on Tariffs and Trade (GATT) and the North American Free Trade Agreement (NAFTA) to spur new growth, especially in developed nations. These agreements made it easier for established inorganic manufacturers from the United States and Europe to export their products to new markets and enabled developing countries to ship their chemicals to major industrial countries where they had the potential for pronounced price advantages over the domestically produced chemicals.

Following a mid-1990s trend, manufacturers in the chemical industry began merging and specializing in the late 1990s. This changed the look of companies from previous decades, when highly diversified chemical producers reigned and single companies manufactured agricultural chemicals, pharmaceuticals, organic chemicals, inorganic chemicals, and more. In the mid-1990s, firms in the agricultural chemical sector aligned with the life science industry and began divesting other concerns. Similarly, organic and inorganic chemical manufacturers began to concentrate on their core businesses, and smaller operations merged with larger ones.

Merger and acquisition activity was a prominent trend in the chemicals industry beginning in the late 1990s. During 1999, the global industry experienced mergers and acquisitions worth US$38 billion. In 2000, that number dropped to US$33 billion, but rose again in 2001 to US$37 billion. In 2001, 55 percent of all businesses acquired were European, 19 percent were based in the United States, and 26 percent were from Asia and the rest of the world. European buyers made the majority of purchases at 48 percent, while the United States accounted for 30 percent. Prospects for future merger and acquisition activity in Europe remained strong due to restructuring efforts.

A driving force behind this activity was the trend toward consolidation that had started in the 1990s. Highly dependent upon energy, the industry was exposed to high energy costs in 2000. Chemical manufacturers also were subject to continued government regulation and falling demand. Modest growth was projected for

the basic chemicals industry, due in part to its maturity. According to the Federal Reserve Board, production levels in the United States had changed only 0.1 percent from 1990 to 2000. However, from 1999 to 2000 production levels increased 3.8 percent.

Another trend in the chemicals industry was the increased use of the Internet as a sales venue. According to the American Chemistry Council, chemicals sales by electronic data interchange (EDI) reached US$7.2 billion in 2000, accounting for 1.6 percent of total chemical sales. The Council predicted that by 2006, 17 percent of total global chemical sales would be completed electronically, reaching US$382 billion. U.S. Internet sales of industrial chemicals were expected to reach US$54.1 billion by 2006.

The chloralkali segment struggled in the early 1990s due to an international recession, but manufacturers reported renewed growth by the mid-1990s because of increased demand for chlorine by vinyl producers. During the 1990s chlorine manufacturers also faced mounting resistance from environmental organizations, who called for a complete ban on chlorine production, as well as declining demand from paper manufacturers who switched to alternative methods of bleaching. (See also **Paper Mills**).

According to the Consulting Resources Corporation, an international management consulting firm, growth in the chlorine, caustic soda, and soda ash markets was expected to remain fairly stagnant. The company predicted that in the United States, with the world's largest supply of soda ash, production rates would increase 1.4 percent per year, from 39.7 million tons in 2002 to 42.5 million tons by 2007, and to 45.7 million tons in 2012. This industry segment is subject to maturing demand and is highly affected by fluctuating global economies. Exports of soda ash were 3.9 million tons in 2000, of which 44 percent went to Asian countries.

The industrial gases segment continued to grow moderately in the early 2000s, with worldwide sales of US$34.5 billion in 2001. This segment historically has performed well during industry downturns, and many companies with gas operations reported stronger earnings than their chemical counterparts. As with other segments of the chemical industry, competition increased as companies began to merge, although the 2001 acquisition of BOC by L'Air Liquide and Air Products was thwarted by antitrust laws, along with Linde's planned purchase of Messer Greisheim.

The Environmental Protection Agency released a Toxic Release Inventory (TRI) in 2001 stating that the chemical industry had reduced certain toxic chemical emissions as much as 56 percent from 1988 to 1999.

The American Chemistry Council claimed that the cost of complying with the TRI was approximately US$600 million in 2000.

The two chemical-producing regions most affected by environmental regulations since the 1970s have been North America and Western Europe. Chemical producers there were by far the largest contributors to global pollution. Regulatory measures enacted in the United States, where the chemical industry and the primary metal industry released the largest amounts of chemical waste, were typical of the enormous hurdles that inorganic chemical producers in most industrialized nations have had to overcome at the expense of billions of dollars annually.

Dominant legislation in the United States included the sweeping federal Clean Air Act, the Toxic Substances Control Act, the Clean Water Act, the Superfund, the Resource Conservation and Recovery Act, and the Occupational Safety and Health Act. Most of these initiatives were enacted during the 1970s and 1980s and have been amended to include new restrictions that serve to reduce pollutants released into the air, water, ground, and human body. They also established measures to fund the cleaning of existing waste sites and to take care of future problems caused by the chemical industry.

In addition to the core environmental laws, U.S. producers were subject to many supplementary regulations including the Chemical Divisions and Trafficking Act; the Pollution Prevention Act; the Safe Drinking Water Act; the Food and Drug Cosmetic Act; and the Federal Insecticide, Fungicide, and Rodenticide Act of 1972. When combined with complementary state legislation, such a regulatory environment posed a disadvantage for companies attempting to compete with manufacturers in less regulated developing regions, a reality that had prompted many European, Japanese, and U.S. producers to set up operations in countries with less restrictive environmental laws.

CURRENT CONDITIONS

As globalization of business accelerated in the early 2000s, chemical companies in the United States faced intense competition from manufacturers in emerging economies, where quality control had greatly improved while production costs remained low. According to Michael Arndt in the May 2, 2005, issue of *Business Week*, 70 U.S. chemical plants shut down in 2004, and at least 40 more closures were expected in 2005. At the same time, 120 major plants were under construction around the world, 50 of which were in China and only one of which was in the United States.

Dow Chemical planned to build a state-of-the-art membrane chloralkali production facility in Freeport,

Texas, because several existing plants were out of date. The new facility, which was expected to open in 2011, will provide a long-term reliable supply of for derivative products. Dow has projected a growth rate of approximately 4 percent from 2008 to 2012.

Growth in industrial gases was expected to continue due in part to new growth opportunities in the hydrogen, electronics, healthcare, and food markets. The growing use of noncryogenic production technology also boded well for industrial gas firms. Two types of noncryogenic production, membrane separation and pressure swing absorption, used less energy than the traditional cryogenic air separation process, in which air was cooled and pressurized until it took liquid form. The improvements could produce gas at nearly half of the cost of regular cryogenic procedures. Noncryogenic production technology thus created new application opportunities in the industrial gases industry that previously had been too expensive. As for hydrogen, new cleaner fuels regulations had prompted petroleum refiners in North America and Europe to use more hydrogen, stimulating demand from outside suppliers. Analysts expected hydrogen demand to grow more than 10 percent annually through 2008.

The U.S. color pigment segment, including organic, inorganic, and specialty pigments, was expected to grow 5 percent per year to US$3.6 billion in 2007. London-based Information Research claimed that demand in Western Europe for pigments, extenders, and fillers for coatings would grow 2.5 percent per year through 2006, while demand for titanium dioxide would grow 2.8 percent per year. While organic pigments had the strongest growth potential, heavy metal inorganic pigments were expected to experience slower growth due to their unfriendly environmental characteristics. However, according to the Freedonia Group Inc., the complex inorganic pigments market, producing pigments with better lightfastness, chemical resistance, and various performance characteristics, had promising growth opportunities.

Industrialized nations' market share of most other inorganic chemicals was projected to decline as developing nations became larger players in the chemical industry. Several factors contributed to increased inorganic production by emerging economies during the new millennium. Perhaps the greatest advantage that manufacturers in developing nations had over established producers was proximity to growing industrial sectors, which reduced distribution costs significantly. However, companies in less industrialized countries also benefit from inexpensive labor and cost advantages stemming from looser environmental regulations.

RESEARCH AND TECHNOLOGY

The industrial inorganic chemicals industry is characterized by a very low level of product research and development (R&D). However, many companies conduct and fund research related to the environment, most of which is aimed at developing cleaner production facilities and processes and minimizing the environmental impact of wastes. Most capital investment in the industry is oriented toward improving production and distribution processes. Such initiatives include factory automation and information systems designed to reduce labor and energy costs and improve customer service. According to the American Chemistry Council, the total U.S. chemicals industry spends more than US$22 billion annually in research and development.

In South Africa, the Chemical and Allied Industries' Association developed a questionnaire to guide interviews with key groups on their concerns about chemical hazards and their suggestions for improvements. Groups considered for the pilot study included government representatives, organizations, and customers.

A pilot study by ABIQUIM, the Brazilian chemical association and the University of Brazilia in Brazil utilized a Web-based questionnaire on the Internet with subjects covering availability of data. Target subjects included chemicals, education, and training courses on handling processes, and successful technology applications. The questionnaire was sent to more than 600 chemical companies, 200 government agencies, and departments of 12 major universities in Brazil with related interests. Results are expected to help outline an action plan under auspices of the National Commission on Chemicals Safety.

WORKFORCE

International employment figures for inorganic chemical production are inexact because not all countries separate inorganic from organic chemical manufacturing for statistical purposes. In the United States, approximately 98,000 people were employed in inorganic chemical production in 2000. These workers earned between US$13.91 and US$29.97 per hour. According to the U.S. Department of Labor, employment in the chemicals industry was expected to decline 17 percent from 2002 to 2012. According to the American Chemistry Council, there were approximately 800,000 workers in the pharmaceuticals, research, chemistry, and production sector of the chemicals industry in 2009, making it one of the largest U.S. industries in terms of employment. The average hourly wage in 2009 was US$20.30

Approximately three-fifths of the industry is employed in production, installation, maintenance, and repair. Just over one-fifth work in management, business, finance, and administration. The industry employs a relatively large number of skilled production workers compared to less mature industries and is characterized by a high degree of automation. Consequently, average wages tend to be higher than in other manufacturing industries. In addition, labor unions, particularly in Europe and the United States, are established within the industry and tend to boost wages and benefits.

The inorganic chemical industry workforce, which is characterized by generally high wages and comparatively good working conditions, has declined steadily since the 1970s and 1980s. Regardless of large increases in output, rampant automation and downsizing have reversed industry employment growth in industrialized nations. The downsizing effect was particularly pronounced in the early and mid-1990s, when European inorganics producers moved toward the practices that U.S. manufacturers had initiated in the early 1980s. The only employment gains were found in emerging countries, where wages are much lower and inorganics producers can afford to be much less automated. Overall, the inorganic chemicals industry was projected to lose nearly 16,000 jobs by 2010.

INDUSTRY LEADERS

As with workforce statistics, the value of inorganic chemical sales and profits is diluted by manufacturers' crossover activities, such as organic chemical and plastics production. All of the industry leaders are active in both the inorganic and organic chemical industries, and most are active in other businesses as well. With the exception of the industrial gas segment, the inorganic industry leaders are profiled in greater detail under the heading **Chemicals, Industrial Organic**.

Linde AG. Linde AG of Germany became the world's largest gas manufacturer when it acquired BOC Group in 2006. After the deal, Linde's gas & engineering business each account for half of company sales. The company is a leading producer of industrial and medical gases. Its engineering unit builds process plants for companies in the petrochemical, pharmaceutical, and gas manufacturing industries. Linde AG announced revenues of US$14.94 billion in 2009 with over 47,700 employees.

In September 2008, BOC announced that it had made a deal with LNG Refuellers, a consortium of seven Tasmanian transport operators, to supply liquefied natural gas to more than 120 gas powered heavy-vehicles. According to Consortium Chairman Ken Padgett, the project was expected to establish the first commercial pipeline-to-truck supply chain for the Australian heavy-vehicles transport sector.

In September 2008, BOC's Jamshedpur plant marked the 10th anniversary of the start of commercial production in Burmese mines. These mines have a production capacity of 1,290 tonnes of oxygen per day. In addition, BOC India could take advantage of the latest technology and had established support for its applications, which allowed the company to serve customers like Tata Steel. Since 1935, BOC India has been a leader in the country's gas market.

According to Tom Stundza in a September 10, 2008, article for *Purchasing*, the joint venture between the Linde Group and Sinopec Fujian Petrochemical would have a positive effect on the long-term supply of industrial gases to customers of the Fujian province in southeastern China. Fujian Linde-FPCL Gases announced plans for a US$141 million to produce and distribute nitrogen, oxygen, and argon. Aldo Belloni, a Linde executive board member, explained that the "collaboration is a further example of our long-term growth strategy in the emerging Asian nations."

L'Air Liquide SA. L'Air Liquide is the world's second-largest manufacturer of industrial gases. The French company generated revenues of US$15.97 billion in 2009, about 88 percent of which were attributable to gas sales. L'Air Liquide was founded in 1902 by Georges Claude, who had been a pioneer of acetylene technology by the time he was 26. Claude enjoyed success with his company throughout the early 1900s. After World War II, however, he was convicted of helping the Nazis to develop a "flying bomb" and was jailed until 1950.

L'Air Liquide continued to prosper during the middle of the twentieth century in spite of the absence of its founder. In the 1960s and 1970s, the company expanded in the United States and grew through mergers and acquisitions. Its global expansion into Japan, Australia, and numerous other overseas markets during the 1980s complemented its virtual lock on the French gas market and its strength in the United States.

Throughout the 2000s L'Air Liquide controlled about 18 percent of the global industrial gas market, had more than 130 subsidiaries in 65 countries, and employed a workforce of 42,300 by 2009. In 2004 Air Liquide's parent company acquired Messer Griesheim's North American, German, and U.K. business for more than US$3 billion. Air Liquide America supplies industrial gases to companies in the automotive, chemicals, food and beverage, and healthcare industries. Its specialties include oxygen, nitrogen, carbon dioxide, acetylene, and helium, which are shipped in cylinders or by pipelines, or are manufactured on site. In June 2004 Air Liquide America announced that it had signed an exclusive 15-year carrier gas supply agreement for a new 300 mm semiconductor manufacturing facility to be constructed in Richardson, Texas.

In August 2008, L'Air Liquide CEO Benoit Potier expressed confidence about the company's ability to continue to do well even in the event of an economic slowdown. Furthermore, Potier said that the company was targeting "a new improvement in the gas and services margin." When asked about possible U.S. acquisitions, Potier responded that there was the company was going to adopt a prudent attitude. In early 2008, L'Air Liquide entered a long-term agreement with Nest Oil"s Renewable Diesel Plant to supply hydrogen.

Potier planned to spend US$10 billion in 2011 on purchases and new factories to meet the growing demand in emerging markets for gases in the oil-refining and health industries. Potier said the company was on track to reach its goal of US $600 million in savings through 2010. The CEO attributed growth to "the strength of Air Liquide's business model." In February 2008, Potier doubled the maximum target for average sales growth to 10 percent, and announced plans to hire up to 30,000 people while targeting contracts in India, Russia, and the Middle East.

Praxair. Praxair of Danbury, Connecticut, is a leading provider of atmospheric gases. Its specialties include oxygen, nitrogen, and argon, and the company is also a major resource for carbon dioxide, helium, and hydrogen. In addition, it has expertise in building on-site gas plants and providing industrial gases in cylinders. In 2009, Praxair reported sales of just over US$9 billion, with 27,000 employees. In 2009, Praxair received two awards for outstanding environmental performance from the Compressed Gas Association.

Teresa Rivas described Praxair in the September 2, 2008, issue of *Barron's* as being a blend of "growth and defensiveness." The company stood out as an industrial gas supplier with end markets such as energy, health care, technology, metals and petrochemicals, with diverse customers and offerings. The offerings included atmospheric gases, such as oxygen and nitrogen, in addition to process and specialty gases, such as carbon dioxide, helium, and hydrogen. Approximately one-half of company sales were from outside of the United States, including Europe, Asia, and South America. Praxair earned high rankings for successfully securing long-term contracts, maintaining a high market share, and having disciplined management.

MAJOR COUNTRIES IN THE INDUSTRY

United States. The U.S. chemical industry, worth US$674.1 billion in 2009, is the largest producer and consumer of inorganic chemicals in the world. It supplied approximately 25 percent of global chemical output in 2003 when U.S. total exports of chemicals exceeded US$91 billion, according to the American Chemistry

Council, making chemicals the largest exporting sector in the country. Approximately 9,125 corporations made up the U.S. chemicals industry throughout the 2000s, of which about 1,725 produced and marketed industrial inorganic chemicals.

Basic inorganic chemical production rose 3.8 percent in 2000. However, in 2001 the U.S. chemical industry experienced its worst year overall since the early 1980s. Inorganic chemicals felt the brunt of high energy costs, overcapacity, and weakened demand. Production levels for aluminum sulfate fell 10.6 percent from 1999 to 2000; ammonia fell 4.5 percent; ammonium sulfate fell 0.3 percent; chlorine fell 1 percent; nitric acid fell 1.7 percent; phosphoric acid fell 5.9 percent; sodium hydroxide fell 8.2 percent; sodium sulfate fell 19.2 percent; and sulfuric acid fell 2.5 percent. Production levels rose for titanium dioxide, sodium chlorate, hydrochloric acid, and ammonium nitrate.

Production increased an average of 5.3 percent in all segments of the U.S. chemicals industry in 2004. Output of basic inorganics grew only 0.2 percent, but paints, coatings, and adhesives grew 5.4 percent. Helped by the relative weakness of the dollar, exports rose significantly in late 2004, and analysts predicted export growth of about 13 percent in 2005. Rising costs for raw materials contributed to price increases that raised the value of U.S. chemical shipments an average of 7.6 percent. Production growth was expected to moderate in 2005, reaching about 3.4 percent.

Employment in the U.S. chemicals industry has fallen consistently since 1998, when it reached 982,500 workers. This figure had been 907,900 in 2003 and dropped further to 891,000 in 2004, and to 800,000 in 2009. Even so, labor productivity rose about 5.1 percent. The trend toward more efficient production and lower overall employment was expected to continue, with the U.S. Department of Labor projecting an employment decline in the industry of about 17 percent from 2002 to 2012.

In emerging economies, inorganics producers continued to compete for shares of the U.S. import market in the early 2000s, particularly in the case of commodity inorganics because they could effectively undercut the prices of U.S. domestic output. As a result, many U.S. producers had shifted their focus to specialty organic chemicals that, unlike most inorganics, are not considered commodities. These specialties are harder to produce, require more sophisticated technology, and thus garner higher prices and wider profit margins than commodity chemicals. However, the United States was expected to benefit, at least in the short term, from proliferating demand for inorganics in emerging regions.

Demand for industrial and institutional cleaning chemicals in the United States was projected to grow to approximately US$10 billion by 2012. Market value was expected to continue to gain due to the increasing presence of environmentally compatible formulations and better performing, multifunctional cleaners offering sanitizing and other benefits. Widespread reports linked to tainted food supplies and ongoing concerns about disease transmission led to increased demand for industrial cleaning products, according to reportlinker.com on August 19, 2008.

Germany. Germany was replaced by China as the second-largest chemical-producing country in the world after suffering from a weak economy throughout the 2000s and experiencing relatively sluggish growth compared to other E.U. producers. The improved global economy in 2004, however, contributed to a 3.5 percent sales increase over 2003. Production also increased, with output of inorganic base chemicals growing 8 percent. Faced with rising costs for raw materials, however, the industry raised prices about 1 percent in 2004, and industry analysts expected further price increases in 2005. In 2009, Germany had US$212.8 billion in chemical shipments.

France. France's chemistry industry accounted for about 20 percent of the chemical industry in the European Union in 2005. It has been called "the cradle of modern chemistry," and has earned praise for major scientific and industrial development in the field. In 2000 exports to the United States increased 27 percent. In Central and Eastern Europe they rose 21 percent, and Asian growth eclipsed 20 percent. Of France's 130 major chemical companies, 43 produce inorganic chemicals, a segment that employed about 7,000 workers in 2004.

Increasing costs for raw materials contributed to production declines in the French chemical industry in the early 2000s, and the strong euro against the weak dollar resulted in reduced export profit margins through 2003. Nevertheless, France exported US$58.8 billion of chemicals in 2003. Because exports were more important than domestic sales to the French chemicals industry, manufacturers were worried about proposed regulations to tighten environmental safeguards, which were proposed to go into effect in January 2006. Analysts cautioned that the cost of compliance could adversely affect sales to major markets like the United States.

Growth in France's chemical industry in 2004 was led by such consumer products as soaps, perfumes, and household cleaning products. This sector was projected to grow about 4 percent in 2005. Inorganics were expected to grow 2.4 percent.

Emerging Nations. By 2000, one-third of global chemicals sales came from regions outside of the United States, Canada, Western Europe, and Japan. According to the American Chemistry Council, long-term industry growth rates from 1999 to 2010 for the major chemical regions per year were: China and East Asia, 7.5 percent; other Asia/Pacific countries, 6.25 percent; the Mideast, 5.5 percent; other Latin American countries, 5.25 percent; Mexico, 4.75 percent; Africa, 3.75 percent; Central and Eastern Europe, 3.5 percent; United States, 3.25 percent; Canada, 3.25 percent; Western Europe, 2.75 percent; and Japan, 2 percent.

Mexico's National Chemical Industry Association reported that the country's chemical industry registered a US$6 billion trade deficit in 2001. Exports fell approximately 3 percent from 2000 to 5.1 million metric tons. Chemical production fell, especially in the industrial inorganics sector, due to the weakening economy in the United States. India's chemical industry, including the agrochemical, petrochemical, and pharmaceutical segments, reached US$28 billion in 2004 accounted for about 12.5 percent of the country's total industrial output. India exports several inorganic and organic chemicals to the United States, the United Kingdom, and Taiwan. The Indian Chemical Manufacturers Association predicted that chemical demand in the country would grow approximately 11 percent per year through 2010. In Peru, the basic chemicals industry grew 3 percent. Mining investments in the country created increased demand for basic chemicals while imports of inorganic chemicals were expected to increase 5 percent during 2001.

Analysts at the 2002 Asia Plastics and Chemical Industry Meeting (APCIM) in Singapore predicted that the Asia/Pacific region would offer the most promising growth prospects for the industry during the first decade of the 2000s. These analysts also claimed that the region accounted for nearly one-third of global chemical consumption and that it would soon account for nearly half. The APCIM projected that the Asian industry would grow from US$260 billion in 2000 to US$1 trillion by 2010, and that Asia would account for approximately 40 percent of the US$2.6 trillion global chemical output by 2010.

Pigment had an active role as a "key, chemical product" due to its use in many diverse applications. According to reportlinker.com, China was both the biggest manufacturer and consumer of pigments in the world. It leads the way with output of iron oxide, lithopone, and organic pigment manufacturing around the world, but "Chinese pigment highly depends on overseas market and export proportion constituted around 45.9 percent of total output in 2007."

BIBLIOGRAPHY

"Air Liquide Lifts Net on Demand for Industrial Gases," 4 August 2008. Available from www.iht.com.

Arndt, Michael. "No Longer the Lab of the World: U.S. Chemical Plants Are Closing in Droves as Production Heads Abroad." *Business Week,* 2 May 2005.

"BOC and LNG Refuellers Reach Agreement Over Gas Supply," 3 September 2008. Available from www.fluidhandling.com.

"BOC Plant Turns 10." *The Telegraph* (Calcutta, India), 1 September 2008. Available from www.telegraphindia.com.

"BOC Signs Contracts to Supply Hydrogen to Chevron and Holly Oil Refineries." *Business Wire,* 23 June 2005.

The Business of Chemistry: Essential to Our Quality of Life and the U.S. Economy. American Chemistry Council, 2005. Available from www.accnewsmedia.com.

Chang, Joseph. "Global Chemistry Industry Completes $37 Billion in Transactions in 2001." *Chemical Market Reporter,* 25 February 2002.

"Chloralkali's Delicate Balance: Strong Worldwide Demand for PVC Is Driving Increased Chlorine Production." *Chemical Marketing Reporter,* 16 September 1996.

Denton, Timothy. "Reaching New Shades with High Performance Pigments." *Chemical Market Reporter,* 3 November 1997.

"Facts and Figures for the Chemical Industry." *Chemical and Engineering News,* 25 June 2001.

Freeburn, Christopher T. "Helium Suppliers Step In as Uncle Sam Steps Out." *Chemical Week,* 19 November 1997.

"Global E-Sales Take Off." *Chemical Business Newsbase,* 22 May 2001.

Graff, Gordon. "PVC Prices Are Inflating Despite Soft Demand and Overcapacity." *Purchasing,* 14 August 2008.

"Hoover's Company Capsules." *Hoover's Online,* 2009. Available from www.hoovers.com.

Hunter, David. "Industrial Gases: Getting a Lift from Recovery." *Chemical Week,* 18 February 2004.

"Industry Could Be Nearing Trough of Current Down Cycle." *Chemical Market Reporter,* 21 January 2002.

Johnson, Dexter. "Electronic Chemicals To Face Competition as Market Matures." *Chemical Market Reporter,* 17 November 1997.

———. "Industrial Gas Industry Is Driven by Economic, Environmental Forces." *Chemical Market Reporter,* 22 September 1997.

———. "Industrial Gases Move on Site." *Chemical Market Reporter,* 28 April 1997.

"Key Challenges and Issues Facing the Production and Market of Pigments in China," 19 August 2008. Available from reportLinker.com.

Layman, Patricia L. "Strong Exports of 1997 To Slow and Grow To Moderate in '98." *Chemical & Engineering News,* 15 December 1997.

Mitchell, Adam. "UPDATE: Air Liquide CEO Hasn't Observed Slowdown in Sector," 4 August 2008. Available from www.easybourse.com.

"Outlook for Pigments Demand Brightens Up." *Chemical Week,* 15 October 2003.

Peaff, George. "Mexico's Economy, Chemical Trade Still Robust." *Chemical & Engineering News,* 15 December 1997.

Rivas, Teresa. "A Stock That's Cookin' With Gas." *Barron's,* 2 September 2008.

Storck, William J. "U.S. Chemical Industry To See Modest Growth Next Year as Economy Cools." *Chemical & Engineering News,* 15 December 1997.

Stundza, Tom. "Linde Creates New Industrial Gases Joint Venture." *Purchasing,* 10 September 2008.

"Summary of Pilot Studies," 2002. Available from www.icca-at-wssd.org.

"Taking the Gas-Work Out of Demand." *MarketWatch,* 22 August 2008.

Tremblay, Jean-Francois. "Regional Economic Crisis, Capacity Additions Will Hurt Profits." *Chemical & Engineering News,* 15 December 1997.

U.S. Department of Labor Bureau of Labor Statistics. *Career Guide to Industries: Chemical Manufacturing,* 27 February 2004. Available from www.bls.gov.

Warren, Robert. "An Unsettled Japan: A Combination of Blossoming Asian Markets and Drooping Japanese Economy Is Forcing the Pace of Japan's Chemical Trade Evolution." *Chemical Market Reporter,* 19 February 1996.

Westervelt, Robert, and Ian Young. "Global Economic Slowdown Prompts More Profit Warnings." *Chemical Week,* 4 July 2001.

"World Chemical Outlook." *Chemical & Engineering News,* 10 January 2005. Available from www.pubs.acs.org.

Zack's Research. "Dow Chemical Under Pressure." 29 August 2008. Available from zacks-investment-research.duedee.com/2008/8/29/-Dow-Chemical-Under-Pressure-/39019/.

SIC 2860

CHEMICALS, INDUSTRIAL ORGANIC

NAICS CODE(S)

325. The organic chemical industry manufactures a large number of compounds for commercial and industrial uses. Important industry products include non-cyclic organic chemicals and their metallic salts; solvents; polyhydric alcohols and fatty acids; synthetic perfumes and flavoring materials; rubber processing chemicals; plasticizers; synthetic tanning agents; chemical warfare gases; cyclic crudes; dyes and organic pigments; and natural gum and wood chemicals.

Many industry firms also produce inorganic chemicals. For more detailed coverage of these businesses, see **Chemicals, Industrial Inorganic**.

INDUSTRY SNAPSHOT

Organic chemicals represent a significant segment of the global chemical industry, which reached nearly US$3 trillion in 2010. The European Union (EU) was the largest exporter (US$1.076 billion) of chemicals in 2009. The United States exported US$689.3 billion.

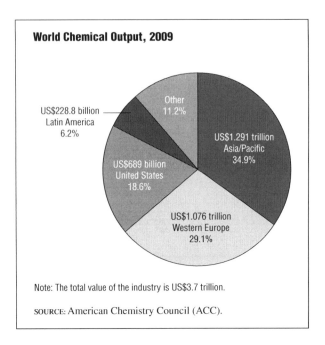

World Chemical Output, 2009

US$228.8 billion Latin America 6.2%

Other 11.2%

US$1.291 trillion Asia/Pacific 34.9%

US$689 billion United States 18.6%

US$1.076 trillion Western Europe 29.1%

Note: The total value of the industry is US$3.7 trillion.

SOURCE: American Chemistry Council (ACC).

Other major players in the industry were China (US$594.4 billion) and Japan (US$298.0 billion). The worldwide chemical industry was robust throughout the 2000s, with volumes, prices, profits, and chemical stock prices all increasing despite the high cost of raw materials and the rapidly rising cost of oil. The industry was expected to continue this trend into the next decade.

ORGANIZATION AND STRUCTURE

Chemical industry products are divided into organic and inorganic substances. Chemical companies make goods that fall into one or both categories. Inorganic chemicals, which are derived from the inanimate material of the earth's crust, include compounds such as sulfuric acid, sulfur, phosphoric acid, and hydrogen peroxide. Organic chemicals are mostly derived from substances that contain carbon, such as petroleum, coal, and natural gas. Petroleum-based chemicals, or petrochemicals, account for the large majority of organics industry shipments in the United States. For example, petrochemicals including ethylene and propylene were the largest organic chemicals in terms of volume. In 2000 production of ethylene was 55.4 billion pounds, while propylene accounted for 31.8 billion pounds.

The organic chemical industry serves one primary purpose: to take a relatively few fundamental raw chemicals that contain carbon and combine and transform them into new substances with desirable physical properties. Using carbon as a basic building block, chemists are able to unite other elements such as nitrogen, hydrogen, oxygen, sulfur, and chlorine to generate a multitude of different compounds. Furthermore, each resultant compound can be manipulated (with heat or additives, for example) to produce an infinite variety of characteristics and grades. Organics play an indispensable role in modern society. They are essential ingredients in plastics, synthetic fibers, rubber, adhesives, inks, dyes, explosives, and fertilizers, and provide vital support for the health, food, transportation, and communication industries.

The organic chemicals business is separated into three major segments: wood and gum chemicals; intermediates and pigments; and miscellaneous organics, which encompass the large majority of global output. Wood and gum chemicals represent the smallest sector of the industry. Such products are distilled from both softwoods and hardwoods and include natural dyes, fuels, tar and pitch, rosin, lacquers, solvents, alcohol, and oils. They are often sold in pure form, but may also be altered or used as additives to produce products ranging from wood treatments and paints to roof shingles and flame retardants.

Intermediate chemicals are distinguished from other organics by their closed-ring molecular structure, which allows them to combine with other chemicals to create a nearly infinite variety of intermediate compounds. The three primary "aromatic" chemicals manufactured by this sector are benzene, xylene, and toluene. They are used to create a multiplicity of intermediates. For example, benzene may be combined with sulfuric acid or other substances to make plastic resins, epoxy, rubber, nylon, and detergents. Xylene is often mixed with other chemicals to create gasoline additives, solvents, polyester fibers, plastic bottles and coatings, and high-tech engineering resins. Toluene is commonly used in the production of textiles, drugs, inks, adhesives, and photographic film. Toluene is also utilized in the manufacture of benzene. Organic dyes and pigments classified in this segment are usually obtained from petroleum through lengthy chemical processes. They are used to color food, clothing, and other goods.

The organic chemical industry also produces thousands of miscellaneous chemicals and resultant compounds that comprise the bulk of industry output of more than 70,000 different products. The most common category of organics is aliphatics, or olefins, which are straight-chain hydrocarbons. They can be made using either petroleum or (more usually) natural gas and turned into marketable products such as ethylene, propylene, and butadiene—the basic ingredients for most organic chemicals and synthetic materials. Ethylene, the largest industry product by volume, is used in the production of plastic, rubber, fibers, detergents, solvents, and anesthetics. Olefin is often used in the production of packaging, foam, gasoline, and fibers.

Butadiene is most commonly consumed by manufacturers of synthetic rubber and nylon. Synthetic methanol and methanol derivatives also comprise a significant portion of miscellaneous organic chemical industry output. For example, methyl tertiary butyl ether (MBTE), a gasoline oxygenate, is among the most common methanol derivatives.

International Standards and Organizations. In an effort to unify the global chemical industry, regional and international standards and organizations have been established. Chief among them are the International Union of Pure and Applied Chemistry (IUPAC) and the International Organization for Standardization (ISO). IUPAC was formed in 1919, relatively early in the development of modern chemistry, as a means of creating international standards for chemically related symbols, atomic weights, and nomenclature. It is a nonprofit organization composed of representative National Adhering Organizations (NAOs) in member countries, Associate National Adhering Organizations (ANAOs), and regional and international groups and consortiums such as the European Federation of Chemical Engineering. In 2010, IUPAC had 57 NAOs, four ANAOs, and nearly 1,000 chemists from around the globe who volunteered for its 37 commissions.

IUPAC has four primary goals: to promote international cooperation among chemists; to study issues of global importance, such as regulations and standards; to coordinate the efforts of other international chemical groups; and to advance chemistry in all aspects on an international scale. It achieves its goals through various ongoing programs and initiatives such as CHEMRAWN, a series of international conferences. Its seven main divisions include physical and biophysical chemistry; inorganic chemistry; organic and bio-molecular chemistry; macro-molecular chemistry; analytical chemistry; chemistry and the environment; and chemistry and human health. In the early 2000s IUPAC focused its attention on issues related to sustaining chemical production given the harmful environmental effects inherent to the chemical manufacturing process.

Unlike IUPAC, the International Organization for Standardization (ISO) is a multi-industry initiative that has been adopted in several international areas of business, including the chemical industry. The ISO adopted a set of standards designed to assure quality and standardization in product development and production for use in business-to-business contracts. For example, it establishes specific quality requirements for chemicals that must be met by registered members. Similarly, the ISO requires that chemical producers document processes to ensure that, even if all facility personnel were replaced, the company would continue to produce the exact same quality and grade of material.

Companies that demonstrate adherence to its standards may become certified by the ISO. Thus, customers that demand high-quality chemicals often prefer to deal with companies that are certified, or "licensed to compete," by the ISO. The cost of ISO registration is high, but it had become commonplace and nearly a necessity for competitors in the chemical industry by the new millennium. In 2009 the ISO had 162 national standards bodies, some 3,238 technical bodies, and more than 13,500 international standards and standards-type documents. The ISO claimed that in 2001 there were approximately 12 technical ISO-related meetings on each working day somewhere in the world.

BACKGROUND AND DEVELOPMENT

Chemicals have been produced for commercial use since ancient times. Ancient Egyptian and Chinese civilizations were the first to develop chemical processes related to dyeing, leather tanning, and glass making. It was not until the mid-1800s, after it was discovered that carbon was present in all organic chemicals, that the organic chemical industry began to develop.

Englishman William Henry Perkin, known as the father of the organic chemical industry, was the first chemist to synthesize an organic chemical for commercial use. Working in his father's house in 1856, the eighteen-year-old inventor accidentally created a synthetic dye using a piece of coal tar. Although he received a knighthood for his efforts, it wasn't until 1865 that the chemical structure of Perkin's dye was understood. In that year, German Friedreich von Kekule announced his breakthrough theory of the benzene ring. Building on Kekule's theory, chemists were able to build millions of new organic chemicals during the nineteenth and early twentieth centuries, many of which displaced natural materials and dyes. Chemists learned to synthesize petroleum and natural gas to create petrochemicals on a commercial scale in the early twentieth century.

The organic chemical industry was originally centered both in England and France. German chemists assumed a leading role in the industry in the early twentieth century, in part because of intense research efforts during World War I. During that period a huge demand arose for gasoline, rubber products, textiles, detergents, and plastics that could be created with petrochemicals. Germany assumed a dominant industry position with the formation of the government-supported IG Farben

conglomerate, which it created in 1925 through the combination of three large chemical companies.

It was during World War II that the organic chemical industry vaulted to international prominence. During the war, a shortage of natural and man-made materials resulted in massive industry expansion. For instance, production of synthetic rubber in the United States bolted from 72,000 tons in 1939 to more than 800,000 tons in 1945.

Japan and the United States joined their European counterparts during the early 1940s as leaders in the development and production of organic chemicals and related products. After the conclusion of the war, however, the U.S. organic chemical industry was the only one left largely intact. IG Farben was dismantled by the Allies, while many of the facilities of other countries had been battered in the conflict. As a result, U.S. chemical sales ballooned after World War II, as international customers looked to the United States to supply their chemical needs. The United States also benefited from strong domestic population growth and technological advances in other industrial sectors. By the 1950s, U.S. organic chemical manufacturers supplied and consumed well over half of global production.

To supply surging global demand, the U.S. organic chemical industry grew at a faster rate than any other U.S. industrial sector during the mid-1900s, with the exception of the automobile industry. The explosion of automobile production in industrialized nations during the 1950s, 1960s, and 1970s created a massive demand for chemicals utilized in the production of rubber, paint, and gasoline. Likewise, commercial and residential construction booms generated huge needs for paneling, roofing, insulation, carpet, draperies, upholstery, varnishes, and other chemical-based building materials. Defense and consumer products markets soared also.

The United States' share of the global market began to slip during the 1960s and 1970s, as war-torn European economies regained their strength. During the 1980s, both European and U.S. manufacturers ceded some markets to the Japanese organic chemical industry, which maintained an aggressive assault on global organic markets in the 1970s. In addition, manufacturers in emerging countries such as South Korea and Mexico began to vie for market share. At the same time, several other factors impacted the international industry. High petroleum prices during the early 1980s pummeled overall industry profits, while manufacturers in industrialized nations were hampered by a wave of costly environmental legislation that reduced their ability to compete against producers in less-regulated emerging nations. Finally, new technologies, particularly those related to automation and information systems, increased the efficiency of the industry.

These varied influences resulted in a major power shift in the international chemical industry during the 1980s. While Western Europe, Japan, and the United States all enjoyed demand, revenue, and profitability gains during the decade, especially the latter 1980s, their share of the global market slipped because of increased competition from emerging nations. For instance, while U.S. chemical sales ballooned nearly 100 percent between the early 1980s and early 1990s, the U.S. share of the global chemical export market slipped from about 17 percent to 15 percent. Even the vaunted Japanese organic chemical industry lost market share during the early 1990s. Perhaps the greatest success story in the global chemical industry during the 1980s was China, which led the world in percentage of GDP represented by chemical sales and in chemical industry growth rate among the leading 10 chemical-producing countries. China's chemical industry slumped with the global slowdown of the early 1990s, but its long-term potential was seen by some industry observers as phenomenal, particularly in the inorganic and commodity chemicals markets.

The winners in the new economic world order were manufacturers in emerging regions, particularly in the Pacific Rim, where companies found that they could produce low-tech, commodity-like organics much less expensively than could their counterparts in more industrialized nations. Labor costs were much lower than in industrialized nations, while emerging economies were also unencumbered by environmental laws that were costing competitors in the United States, Europe, and Japan billions of dollars every year. Such factors enabled developing countries to double their combined share of the global export market for all chemicals and allied products from 7 percent in 1980 to nearly 14 percent in the early 1990s.

With countries such as China and India competing in the world organic chemical market, traditional leaders, including the United States, lost shares of the market in the late 1990s. With low-priced dyes, China and India garnered significant exports throughout the 1990s in this segment of the industry. Environmental concerns and labor costs drove manufacturers in Europe and the United States to move production to Asia, in particular to China, Taiwan, and India. This trend was the most pronounced in the dye segment, since these countries also have strong textile and apparel industries that rely on dyes.

In the mid- to late 1990s, manufacturers in the chemical industry began to merge and specialize. Although diversified chemical producers thrived in previous decades, manufacturing agricultural chemicals, pharmaceuticals, organic chemicals, inorganic chemicals, and more, they began repositioning themselves during this period. The agricultural chemical sector aligned itself with the life science (pharmaceutical) industry and began divesting other concerns. Similarly, organic and inorganic chemical manufacturers started to concentrate on their core businesses, and smaller operations merged with larger ones. Global merger and acquisition activity continued into the new millennium, including Dow Chemical's US$9 billion merger with Union Carbide.

Organic chemical trade increased throughout the 1990s and beyond as established developers tapped emerging chemical markets and as industry newcomers from China, India, and South Korea began exporting large quantities of organic chemicals. The weakening U.S. economy actually benefited several foreign chemical industries. The United States' import levels in organic chemicals rose significantly between 1998 and 2001 due to the weakening economy and a strong U.S. dollar. U.S. products also began to lose their competitive edge during this time, making the region a lucrative export destination for foreign chemical manufacturers. In 1998, U.S. organic chemical imports were US$18.3 billion. By 2001 that number had climbed to more than US$30 billion.

By the early 2000s, the worldwide chemical industry was recording annual sales of around US$1.8 trillion. In what was deemed a turnaround year for the industry, global production rose more than 6.3 percent in 2004. That year, the United States accounted for US$506.5 billion in chemical shipments. In 2001, U.S. exports of organic chemicals were estimated at US$16.5 billion, a fall from US$17.9 billion registered in 2000. By 2003 the numbers were back up to US$20.5 billion, out of US$94.2 billion for the overall chemical industry. Japan exported US$51.3 billion, of which US$13.5 billion were organic chemicals.

In 2001 the chemical industry in the United States experienced its worst year since the early 1980s. Large players in the industry, including the European Union (EU), felt the pressure of weakening global economies. Production growth in the EU was 4.6 percent in 2000, but was estimated at negative 1.1 percent in 2001. Export growth also slowed in 2001 to 4.3 percent, just half of what it was in 2000. The European Chemical Industry Council (CEFIC) reported in December 2001 that the industry was having "rough times," and stated that petrochemicals and polymers, part of the segment that constitutes 57 percent of the EU's entire chemical industry, were declining.

In the United States, chemical shipments were valued at US$506.5 billion in 2004, an increase of more than 10.6 percent from the previous year. In Canada, the total increased to some US$35 billion. The European Union chemical output grew 2.4 percent in 2004. Research and development (R&D) spending was down throughout the industry.

Although the United States, the European Union, and Japan have traditionally supplied the majority of the world's organic chemicals, including petrochemicals, other countries continued to emerge as significant manufacturers. Countries in Asia, South America, Africa, and the Middle East had strong petrochemical capacities in the new millennium and analysts predicted that these emerging regions would gradually take market shares away from the developed leaders. China in particular was seeing explosive growth in demand for chemical products. In 2003 production of methanol in China rose nearly 42 percent over 2002 and was expected to continue to increase both demand and production well into the late 2000s.

CURRENT CONDITIONS

According to *Chemical and Engineering News,* the worldwide chemical industry started to improve in 2004 and continued on an upswing through the mid-2000s. In a July 2006 article, the journal reported that "higher pricing and cost cutting to offset rising raw material and energy costs, increased production, and growing world trade" were all factors in the growth of the chemical industry. Overall, in 2006 employment in the industry declined at many European companies but increased at Japanese and U.S. firms. Although employment actually decreased within the United States, worldwide employment for companies with U.S. headquarters increased. Worldwide, chemical production increased, although the United States saw a small decrease in production, partly due to the effects of Hurricanes Rita and Katrina.

The American Chemistry Council (ACC) put the total world chemical output at US$3.7 trillion in 2009, of which the United States accounted for about one-quarter. According to ACC figures, the Asia/Pacific region produced US$1.291 trillion, followed by the Western European region with US$1.076 trillion worth of product, the United States (US$689 billion), and Latin America (US$228.8 billion). Significantly smaller contributions were made by other parts of the world.

Environmental concerns continued to impact the chemical industry throughout the mid-2000s. In mid-2007 the EU's far-reaching environmental testing law, known as the Registration, Evaluation, and Authorisation

of Chemicals (REACH), took effect. The law requires manufacturers to register every product they make with the European Chemicals Agency. Of the approximately 30,000 chemicals produced in the EU, about 2,500 that may be hazardous will be required to undergo testing to ensure they can be used safely and do not present a danger to humans or the environment. The European Commission estimates that the direct cost to the chemical industry to register products under REACH will be about US$3.1 billion. In addition, indirect costs such as management and administration fees, new software implementation, safety data gathering, laboratory testing work, and legal services will also be added to the bill. On the other hand, producers are expected to gain tax benefits for participating in REACH, and as Seb Beloe, director of research and advocacy for Sustain-Ability (London), told *Chemical Week,* "There is growing pressure from consumer groups and retailers for certain chemicals to be removed from the supply chain. Wal-Mart may be the biggest downstream customer to launch programs aimed at eliminating chemicals of concern, but it is by no means the only one." REACH is expected to affect the chemical industry outside the EU as well, in that U.S. firms will have more leeway to decline to specify the potential hazards of a certain chemical, whereas EU companies will not have this option. Another issue is that REACH will require substances, rather than mixtures, to be identified, and countries outside the EU will need to have similar identification procedures in place so that chemicals can be dealt with as one substance under REACH.

RESEARCH AND TECHNOLOGY

The organic chemical industry invests a large portion of its revenues in R&D in comparison to most other industries. The U.S. chemical industry spent more than US$31 billion on R&D in 2001, and overall the industry accounted for nearly 11 percent of all industrial R&D spending in the United States. In addition, the United States typically spends more than twice as much money on R&D as Japan and more than four times as much as Germany, which is the third largest organic chemical-producing nation. R&D spending related to organic chemicals was slowing in the new millennium along with capital spending. As economies in major industry sectors remained unstable, chemical analysts predicted that future growth in R&D spending would remain unremarkable.

Japan made the greatest strides related to R&D spending during the 1980s, while R&D chemical spending by Germany and other Western European competitors languished. Japan's emphasis on R&D during this period was reflected by the number of U.S. chemical patents it received (the United States is the principal source of patents in the global chemical industry). Of the 29,433 chemical patents issued by the U.S. Patent & Trademark Office (PTO) in 1995, U.S. chemical manufacturers accounted for 52 percent, Japanese manufacturers for 21 percent, and German manufacturers for 8 percent. However, U.S., Japanese, Italian, and Dutch companies received fewer patents than in 1994. Taiwan and South Korea represented the fastest growing chemical patent recipients, advancing by 33 percent and 44 percent from 1994 to 1995, respectively.

In the 2000s, investment in research and technology increasingly focused on the design and production of high-profit chemicals. Automation and information systems that increased productivity and met stringent environmental regulations continued to be emphasized, but companies also tried to develop new molecular structures and compounds that would allow them to create new markets and sustain a technological edge over their competitors. Areas of emphasis included advanced chemicals used to make new pharmaceuticals, better fuel additives, high-performance resins and fibers, and environmentally friendly chemicals.

WORKFORCE

Despite a turnaround in business conditions in the industry in the mid-2000s, cost-cutting, downsizing, and outsourcing in the U.S. chemicals industry forced employment levels down. According to the American Chemistry Council, the U.S. chemicals industry employed about 802,800 workers in 2009, down from 1 million workers in 2001.

Global employment figures for this industry are scant because countries divide their chemical and allied product groups differently. For example, the delineation between organic chemical operations and biosciences (a category that includes pharmaceuticals and certain intermediates) has become increasingly blurred. Moreover, many companies produce both organic and inorganic chemicals, compounds, and related products, and they do so in several different countries. In the United States, which supplied about 27 percent of industry output in the early 2000s, approximately 120,000 people were engaged in activities specifically attributable to the organics industry. However, more than six times that number were engaged in all chemical and chemical-related industries.

About two-thirds of organic chemical industry workers in industrialized nations are production workers. The other third are engaged in management, administration, and research and development. Organic chemical manufacturers are major employers of highly educated workers such as scientists and researchers, raising the average

wages in the industry above those of most other manufacturing sectors. High wages also are a result of the strength of industry labor unions in Europe and the United States and the widespread use of skilled laborers. In 2009 wages in the United States ranged from US$26 per hour for a chemical engineer to more than US$20 per hour for a machine setter. In 2006 the average annual salary of a worker in the chemical industry in the United States was US$68,000.

Although the industry employs large numbers of workers at generally high wages, the chemical industry employment per pound of output, a key measure of productivity, plummeted in the mid-1990s. While production volume rose, many producers reduced their labor and management forces through restructuring, increasing automation, and moving production facilities to lower-wage labor markets. By the new millennium, employment in the industry was faltering because of these factors, along with increased consolidation through merger and acquisition activity.

INDUSTRY LEADERS

All of the leading international chemical producers by sales volume are located in Japan, the United States, and Western Europe. All are diversified chemical and chemical products manufacturers engaged in making both inorganic and organic chemicals and related goods. As with workforce statistics, the value of industry sales statistics is diluted by the lack of separation of inorganic and organic chemical manufacturing activities, and by sales potentially attributable to related industries such as plastics, drugs, and bioscience.

BASF. BASF of Germany operated as the world's largest chemical manufacturer in the mid-2000s, with more than US$67.57 billion in sales in 2009 and 104,780 employees. BASF, formed in the early 1860s, became a major supplier of dyes and fibers, and was integrated into the mammoth IG Farben cartel that dominated the global industry during the 1930s. After the dissolution of IG Farben, BASF emerged as a leader in the international production of mineral oil, natural gas, plastics, fibers, and intermediates. BASF has aggressively pursued U.S. markets in recent years, although it continues to secure nearly 60 percent of sales from its European operations. In the new millennium, the firm switched its emphasis from pharmaceuticals to its core chemical operations.

Dow Chemical. The Dow Chemical Company is the second largest global chemical concern and the largest in the United States. Dow was founded in 1890 as Canton

Chemical. The company initiated its reputation for industry innovation by using electric current to separate bromides from brine to distill other chemicals. It made other breakthroughs in rubber, plastic, and pharmaceutical manufacturing during the first half of the twentieth century, and profited handsomely from overseas operations, which accounted for more than half of its sales by the mid-1900s. After stumbling in the early 1980s, Dow reorganized, cut its workforce, and began to switch its focus to high-margin chemicals and products. The company generated revenues of more than US$44.875 billion from its operations in 2009 with 52,195 employees.

Du Pont. U.S.-based E.I. Du Pont de Nemours and Company ranked third in the global chemical industry with sales of US$26.1 billion and 58,000 employees in 2009. With operations in more than 70 countries, Du Pont was the largest chemical firm in the United States. Founded in 1802 by French immigrant and explosives expert Eleuthere Irenee Du Pont, the company dominated the U.S. explosives market by the early 1900s. Its experiments with nitroglycerin led it into other chemical-related businesses, particularly synthetic fiber production.

Du Pont's landmark invention of nylon in 1930 helped establish modern polymer-related industries. Explosive growth and continued product breakthroughs thrust Du Pont to the forefront of the chemical industry by the middle of the twentieth century. In the mid-1990s, Du Pont shifted its emphasis from commodity products to specialty high-tech chemicals and compounds. At the start of the new millennium, the firm restructured its operations and formed six business units consisting of coatings, crop protection chemicals and genetically modified seeds, electronic materials, polymers and resins, safety and security materials, and textiles and interiors.

ExxonMobil Chemical Company. Operating as the chemical subsidiary of Exxon Mobil, ExxonMobil Chemical posted 2009 sales of US$310.58 billion with a workforce of 79,900 employees. The company is active in petrochemicals manufacturing—a segment in which it ranks either number one or number two worldwide, depending on the specific chemical—polypropylene films, fuel additives, synthetic lubricant base stocks, and various other product manufacturing.

Bayer. Bayer AG of Germany, with 2009 sales of US$41.528 billion and 108,400 employees, was founded in the 1860s, became a world leader in dyestuffs, and pioneered the pharmaceutical industry early in the twentieth century. Bayer's development of aspirin around 1900 and

antibacterial drugs in the 1920s ensured continued growth. After the breakup of IG Farben, Bayer produced new insecticides, drugs, fibers, and plastics. It expanded globally during the 1960s, 1970s, and 1980s, with a strong emphasis on U.S. markets. By 2000, Bayer had more than 350 operating companies in Europe, the Far East, and North America. In 2004 Bayer agreed to pay a US$66 million fine for fixing prices on certain chemicals from 1995 to 2001. In 2005 the company spun off its chemical division into its own company, Lanxess. Lanxess had sales of US$8.4 billion in 2006.

MAJOR COUNTRIES IN THE INDUSTRY

Asia/Pacific. Japan's chemical industry suffered throughout the 2000s, as the region entered its fourth recession in 15 years. Japanese production of most organic chemicals fell from 2000 to 2001, including butadiene, ethylene, phenol, and styrene. Overall, the petrochemical sector was hit the hardest. The downtrend for many chemicals continued into the mid-2000s, especially for phenol-based products.

There was an upward trend in the chemical industries in other Asia/Pacific regions, including China, Taiwan, India, and South Korea. The Asian Development Bank estimates that China's gross domestic product increased by 9.3 percent during 2004, exceeding previous estimates of 7.9 percent earlier in the year. During 2001 it entered the World Trade Organization in order to strengthen its industrial industries. China exported US$15.2 billion worth of organic chemicals in 2006, an increase of 25.6 percent from 2005. South Korea enjoyed an increase in many organic chemicals in 2006, ranging from 1 percent (vinyl chloride) to 5.3 percent (propylene).

Taiwan's economy was on the upswing in the mid-2000s, with estimated GDP widely exceeding forecasts in 2004. The chemical industry in India was expected to grow at a rate of nearly 11 percent per year through 2010, according to the Indian Chemical Manufacturers Association. Even as the industry suffered from high energy costs, India's strong economy and growing demand were boding well for the nation's chemicals industry. In the midst of a strong economy, South Korea saw a major portion of its chemicals industry experience gains in 2004, including the organics segment, which reported an increase in production from 0.2 to 6.7 percent, with the exception of propylene, which fell 2.3 percent.

Europe. Most European nations experienced growth in the organic chemicals sector during the mid-2000s.

Particularly important to the European industry were the contributions of Germany and France.

During the early 2000s, Germany's chemical industry faltered due to the weak U.S. economy as well as a downturn in its domestic economy. Even though the country's export share fell throughout the 1990s, it remained tied with the United States as a leading global exporter of chemicals. Germany's reliance on exports to the United States, as well as its manufacturing operations there, left the country's chemical industry exposed to the U.S. downswing. Production in Germany fell in 2001, and industry sales were stagnant. Due to an improved global and national economy, however, German chemical production rose 6 percent in 2005 and almost 4 percent in 2006. In 2006 the German chemical industry enjoyed a 14 percent increase in orders for chemical plants, most of which involved modernization and capacity projects, and a 9 percent increase in foreign chemical orders.

The French chemical industry experienced growth in the early 2000s and continued to buoy the industry in Europe in the mid-2000s. Accounting for nearly 20 percent of the chemical industry in the European Union, France's chemical sales grew by 4.6 percent in 2000. The country's exports to the United States increased by 27 percent in 2000; in Central and Eastern Europe by 21 percent; and in Asia by 20 percent. France saw growth of 3.2 percent in 2004 and about 3 percent in 2006.

The United States. The United States continues as a leader in the global organic chemical industry. It accounts for 27 percent of global chemical and allied product sales, and its share of organic chemical sales is significant. In 2004, the country exported about US$25 billion worth of product, up from US$16 billion in 2001, and imported US$35 billion. Overall, the industry had one of its biggest growth years in 2004, with shipments of chemicals valued at US$506.5 billion in 2004, up 10.6 percent over the previous year. This figure increased another 5.3 percent between 2005 and 2006 to reach US$580 billion. The nation exported US$29.4 billion of organic chemicals in 2006, up from US$26.7 billion in 2005, and output of organic chemicals increased by 2.3 percent. The United States also had a competitive advantage during the mid-2000s in that it was less affected by rapidly climbing oil prices; most U.S. petrochemicals use natural gas feedstocks.

Much like the early 2000s, U.S. organics manufacturers had suffered setbacks during the late 1970s and early 1980s for reasons that ranged from increased foreign competition and high oil prices to environmental regulations. Industry competitiveness improved significantly during the 1980s and domestic manufacturers

were aided by both price and demand growth late in the decade. Although profitability improved, foreign competition continued to dilute global market share. A worldwide economic slowdown in the early 1990s posed serious setbacks for most manufacturers. Compounding U.S. organic industry woes in the early 1990s was excess production capacity, the result of expansion during the late 1980s and early 1990s. Oversupply still depressed organic prices entering the new millennium, thus eliminating profit growth. Despite its diminished dominance of global markets, the U.S. organic chemical industry was the largest, most advanced, and most competitive in the world in 2000. Its strength reflected a number of key advantages, including access to raw materials, an extremely advanced research and technology infrastructure, and unparalleled marketing expertise. Nevertheless, U.S. producers expect to continue facing stiff competition in commodity chemicals markets well into the mid-2000s, particularly from emerging Pacific Rim nations.

Latin America. After years of political and economic uncertainty, the Latin American region began to rebound in the petrochemical industry in the mid-2000s due to a greatly improved economy and high profits in this sector. The gross domestic product grew in Argentina (8.0 percent), Brazil (3.6 percent), Chile (5.2 percent), Mexico (3.7 percent), and Venezuela (17.9 percent) in 2006. Latin America had also received a boost in the sector due to large petrochemical projects in the region.

After rising in 2005, chemical output growth slowed somewhat in 2006 but continued to be strong. In Argentina, benzene production went from 158,000 metric tons in 2005 to 152,000 metric tons in 2006; in Brazil from 947,000 metric tons to 919,000 metric tons; in Mexico from 161,000 metric tons to 120,000 metric tons; and in Venezuela from 28,000 metric tons to 3,000 metric tons. Ethylene production, on the other hand, increased in all countries except Venezuela. Due to an increase in capacity, Brazil was expected to see strong growth in production throughout the mid- to late 2000s.

BIBLIOGRAPHY

"A Global Voice for the Chemical Industry." International Council of Chemical Associations, 2004. Available from www.icca-chem.org.

Alperowicz, Natasha. "Russia Posts Big Chemical Industry Earnings." *Chemical Week* (28 March 2007).

American Chemistry Council. "The Business of Chemistry," 15 May 2007. Available from www.ameicanchemistry.com.

———. "United States Chemical Industry Profile," 15 May 2007. Available from www.americanchemistry.com.

"Bayer Pleads Guilty to Price Fixing." *Chemical Week* (19 July 2004).

Berger, Helen. "Brazil Chem Exporters See Strong 2007." *ICIS Chemical Business Americas* (9 April 2007).

Blanchfield, Lindsey. "Firms Cultivate the Potential of e-Chemicals." *ICIS Chemical Business Americas* (7 May 2007).

"Chemistry Highlights 2006." *Chemical & Engineering News* (18 December 2006).

"Facts and Figures for the Chemical Industry." *Chemical & Engineering News* (10 July 2006).

"Hoover's Company Capsules." *Hoover's Online,* 2007. Available from www.hoovers.com.

"International Trade Statistics." World Trade Organization, 2003. Available from www.wto.org.

International Union of Pure and Applied Chemistry, 24 November 2010. Available from www.iupac.org.

"ISO in Figures for the Year 2009 (at 31 December)." International Organization for Standardization. Available from www.iso.org.

"Jobs and Wages, 2009." American Chemistry Council. Available from www.americanchemistry.com.

Kovac, Matt. "Singapore and China Battle to Be Top Chemical Hot Spot." *ICIS Chemical Business Americas* (9 April 2007).

Leblond, Doris. "Clouds Are Set to Lift for French Chemicals." *ICIS Chemical Business Americas* (26 March 2007).

Office of Industrial Technology. "Industry Profile." U.S. Energy Information Administration, 30 January 2004. Available from www.oit.doe.gov.

"Producers Face Policy Shift." *ICIS Chemical Business* (16 April 2007).

Scott, Alex. "Rough Seas Ahead." *Chemical Week* (28 March 2007).

"Strong Growth May Moderate in 2005." *Chemical Week* (15 December 2004).

Tomizawa, Ryuichi. "Japan's Chemical Industry: Today and Tomorrow." *Chemical Week* (9 May 2007).

Williams, Dede. "Record Orders Result in Delight for Germany's Chemical Contractors." *ICIS Chemical Business* (30 April 2007).

Winder, Robert. "Look to the Long Term." *Chemistry and Industry* (5 January 2004).

"World Chemical Outlook." *Chemical & Engineering News* (8 January 2007).

SIC 2833

MEDICINAL AND BOTANICAL PRODUCTS

NAICS CODE(S)

325411. Closely tied to the pharmaceutical industry, medicinal and botanical processors create saleable forms of organic and inorganic chemicals as well as botanical drugs and herbs.

INDUSTRY SNAPSHOT

Throughout the history of civilization, cultures have relied on the curative and preventive qualities of medicinal and botanical products. With little more than

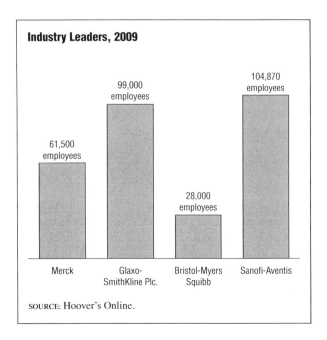

Industry Leaders, 2009

Merck: 61,500 employees
Glaxo-SmithKline Plc.: 99,000 employees
Bristol-Myers Squibb: 28,000 employees
Sanofi-Aventis: 104,870 employees

SOURCE: Hoover's Online.

word-of-mouth testimony, traditional folk concoctions and blends of herbal remedies reportedly cured the sick, perpetuated the aura of optimal health, drew your "true love" to you and supposedly released thousands from the clutches of fatalistic demons. However, as tales of these self-medicated, miraculous cures fueled communal fireside chatter, they also prompted rigorous scientific investigations to pinpoint the mysterious therapeutic values of herbal medicine. These investigations elevated the status of medicinal and botanical products from being of interest to a relatively narrow counterculture to being an industry that produced plant-derived prescription drugs valued at US$17 billion annually during the first decade of the twenty-first century. Not surprisingly, approximately one-quarter of drugs prescribed in the United States contain at least one compound derived from plants. The National Nutritional Foods Association estimated that 100 million people in the United States—more than one-third of the entire population—used herbal dietary supplements regularly.

Some observers estimate that two-thirds of the world's population uses medicinal botanicals as a primary source of health care. The Medical Association of South Africa reports that 80 percent of black South Africans rely on herbal healers. The Nepal Department of Drug Administration has 495 traditional herbal remedies on file, and 566 modern drugs. In Canada, surveys show that 57 percent of the population has used alternative therapies and 25 percent would trust an herbal remedy more than a medical prescription. In addition, representatives of the Centre for Scientific Research into

Plant Medicine (CSRPM), in Mampong, Ghana, in West Africa, has touted the economic benefits of plant-derived medicines in Ghana, which is home to an estimated 10 percent of available medicinal plants with a potential value of up to US$1.7 billion annually.

According to the World Health Organization (WHO), the global market for traditional medicines (often referred to as Complementary Alternative Medicine or CAM) has been increasing steadily. In 2002, 36 percent of adults in the United States reported using some form of traditional medicine, and by 2007 that number had grown to 38.3 percent of adults and 11.8 percent of children. In the early years of the first decade of the 2000s sales exceeded US$60 billion and were growing fast. Spending on traditional medicines in the United States reached US$17 billion, and sales in the United Kingdom totaled US$230 million. The U.S. market expected robust growth through the mid-years of the first decade of the 2000s, due to purchases by growing numbers of aging baby boomers in particular. In addition to comprising the largest segment of the population, baby boomers also were comfortable with plant-derived pharmaceuticals. The majority of the medicinal plants harvested for the multi-billion dollar industry were growing in the wild in the early and mid-years of the first decade of the twenty-first century, causing significant concern about species extinction.

ORGANIZATION AND STRUCTURE

Historically, most medicinal botanicals were drawn from ordinary wild plants that proved adaptable to cultivation outside their natural environment. Void of any fanfare, tribal healers, communal caretakers, herbal doctors, and other folk healers came to possess the knowledge of plant identification, location, and appropriate application. The fanfare emerged only after pharmaceutical companies validated the therapeutic values of herbal medicines and their related profits. Until the 1950s, almost all pharmaceutical research relied on vascular plants as sources for medicines. Interest in medicinal plants declined after the discovery of sulfa drugs, antibiotics like penicillin, and synthetic drugs. Pharmaceutical companies placed their hopes for miraculous cures in the accumulation of huge databases of synthetic chemicals, but the synthetics panacea did not have the expected impact on the drug market. Consequently, pharmaceutical companies returned, searching the world for new and expanded sources of herbal medicine.

Innovative methods of medicinal plant screening reflected several methodology refinements. During the 1960s, a standard screening assay to determine the potential of drugs for medicinal application consisted of injecting test material into a rodent and evaluating subsequent reactions. Modern bioassay, occasionally automated, produced more precise, less time-consuming feedback. For example, tiny amounts of material could be screened rapidly against an array of up to 60 distinct human tumor cell lines. Other assays determined the ability of an extract to influence the activity of a single enzyme involved in the biochemical interactions that underlie a disease. Once an extract displayed significant activity in a bioassay, investigators returned to the source site to collect bulk samples (normally 50 to 100 kilograms) of the original plant.

The medicinal and botanical industry in the mid-1990s consisted of a growing number of multi-sized companies involved in the research and manufacture of medicinal and botanical chemicals. Ethnobotanists, mostly from emergent countries, identified botanical medicinal sources. The industry investigated plant and herbal medicines frequently identified by consumers as alternative medicine, folk medicine, homeopathy, chiropractic, naturopathy, and sometimes even supernatural healing. According to the World Health Organization (WHO), medicinal plants are important because they serve as sources of direct therapeutic agents, function as a raw material base for the elaboration of more complex semi-synthetic chemical compounds, provide chemical structures usable as models for new synthetic compounds, and can be used as taxonomic markers for the discovery of new compounds.

Pharmaceutical raw materials include crude drugs such as botanical, animal, or other biological products; inorganic elements and compounds; and organic compounds. When a source substance is designated "official," the material has been the subject of a monograph in a pharmacopoeia or national formulary that specifies the minimum acceptable degree of chemical purity. The term "crude drug" applies to plant or animal organs and whole organisms or exudations, either fresh or dried, ground or not ground, that derive from cultivated or wild sources.

Production methods differ for inorganic and organic compounds. Organic compounds used as pharmaceuticals are either extracted from natural sources or prepared by chemical synthesis. In contrast to inorganic and organic materials, uncovering the therapeutics of crude drugs requires an extensive harvesting process. After identification of potential therapeutic value, a cleaning process removes direct and undesired plant components. Next, in order to activate the plant's therapeutic ingredients, plants are cured by sweating or drying for a period of up to a year. Either procedure halts the weakening effect of chemical reactions and reduces the weight and bulk of plants.

BACKGROUND AND DEVELOPMENT

The first verifiable hint of the use of plants as medicine came from ancient Chinese, Hindu, and Mediterranean civilizations. Around 2735 B.C. the Chinese emperor Shen Nung wrote an herbal (a book about herbs or plants) describing the anti-fever capabilities of a substance known as Ch'ang Shang (later proven to contain anti-malarial alkaloids). Later in Europe, the Greek physician Galen (around 130 A.D.) was reported to have included hyoscyamus, opium, squill, and viper toxin, among other drugs, in his apothecary shop.

There are many examples of crude plant and herbal remedies that have become basic home medications. Common treatments for constipation in ancient Egypt included senna pods and castor oil, along with caraway and peppermint to relieve indigestion. Up until 1900, when the much simpler compound benzococaine was introduced, cocaine had an essential use as the only available potent local anesthetic. Neither the Chinese nor the Central American Indians could explain the curative effects of fermented soybean curd for skin infections or fungi treatments on wounds, until Louis Pasteur's fermentation study led to the discovery of penicillin. Today penicillin and numerous other antibiotics, derived from fermenting mold, represent a major branch of the drug industry. Some of the more common popular natural products now are fish oil (omega 3), Echinacea, and flaxseed.

Despite the demonstrated therapeutic advantages of medicinal products, companies encounter several obstacles in the mass production of medicinal botanicals. One of the early problems of mass production was determining a uniform measurement of dosage. To solve this problem, researchers assumed that only a certain part of the crude drug, known as "the active principle," had the ability to act on the body. The active principle was identified and standardized so definite quantities could be converted to powders, tablets, capsules, and other medicinal vehicles. This knowledge also enabled physicians to prescribe precise drug quantities and to be aware of anticipated effects.

Obtaining financially worthwhile patents for botanical products was difficult within the industry. In 1994, the United States granted five patents related to plant medicinal products. Without patent protection, opportunities for clinical trials and funding are nearly impossible. In response, drug companies sometimes performed clinical trials in countries with fewer testing restrictions.

Pharmaceutical firms also test drugs abroad because they fear involvement with herbals might adversely affect regulatory approval of their conventional drugs. In some instances plants are not patentable, but their extracting processes are. Procedures to determine the efficacy of botanical products sold in the United States included clinical trials and safety testing for each constituent. The drug industry claimed that U.S. Federal Drug Administration (FDA) licensing procedures in the mid-1990s cost US$300 million. However, segments outside drug companies said that clinical trial cost was inflated, perpetuated by the drug industry's attempts to justify an unrealistic cost of doing business. Detection of modest but valuable benefits in botanical medicines requires random clinical trials conducted with 30,000 to 50,000 respondents at a cost of around US$231 million, according to some experts.

In the late 1990s several mainstream manufacturers were bought or subsidized as investments by such leading pharmaceutical manufacturers as Boehringer, Boots, and Ciba-Geigy. Eli Lilly & Co., a major California-based drug company, made a US$4 million equity investment in Shaman Pharmaceutical. The agreement included a four-year collaborative effort in developing drugs that worked against fungal disease. Shaman Pharmaceutical, a company less than five years old, wanted to combine drug development with an effort to preserve rainforest flora. The company sent teams of botanists and physicians to Latin America, Africa, and Asia to search for plants that would combat viruses, fungi, and diabetes, as well as those with sedative or analgesic properties. Once therapeutic benefits were identified, local people were hired to gather plants for commercial production. Of the 200 plants that passed preliminary stages, more than half showed activity against a targeted malady compared to less than 1 percent for mass screening. During a 16-month period, Shaman discovered an antiviral drug for childhood flu and brought it to the FDA for testing in humans. Shaman investigators also discovered an antiviral agent that works against drug-resistant herpes infections.

With the exception of a few plant-derived agents, herbal products were marketed in the late twentieth century as food additives, dietary supplements, or vitamins. Although consumers, including many physicians, used herbal products for a range of physical disorders, the lack of documented evidence on the effectiveness in alleviating or treating diseases was a concern worldwide. Governments found it especially difficult to control mail-order businesses that offered consumers little supervision for the uses of herbal medicines. In Ghana, an ethnobotany began to be compiled in 1996 by the Organization of African Unity and the Science and Technology

Research Committee. It will feature approximately 600 plants with photos and recipes for the products related to the disease they treat.

Chinese herbal medicine, rooted in a folk pharmacopoeia of more than 5,273 separate plants, offered a global potential for numerous botanical based remedies. Before the Chinese Cultural Revolution ended in 1976, the mysteries of Chinese medicine remained isolated from the world. In the latter decades of the twentieth century, China's guarded tolerance for capitalism resulted in aggressive promotion of herbal medicines worth more than US$1 billion.

In the mid-1990s most clinical studies in China were still conducted in hospitals. The hub of lab research was at the Chinese University of Hong Kong where Western-trained scientists began research to authenticate the chemical fingerprints of thousands of herbs in the early 1980s. However, lack of clinical testing was not the only factor that hampered the development of a world market for Chinese herbal products. While probing complex herbal mixtures containing hundreds of active compounds, scientists often found that isolated ingredients contained less potency than crude mixtures, precluding the consistent replication required for patenting. Undaunted, Chinese entrepreneurs continued to upgrade herb factories and diagnostic equipment at a cost of US$140 million.

Industry Regulatory Standards. In the early 1990s, several pieces of legislation heightened drug safety and consumer awareness in utilization of all drugs. The U.S. Dietary Supplement Health and Education Act of 1994 was enacted to facilitate integration of plant medicine in U.S. health care by mandating labels specifying the structure and function of various products. This expanded knowledge base was expected to increase sales and provide incentives for additional research funding and scientific validation of quality control for these products. The legislation was also intended to facilitate the marketing of dietary supplements, herbs, and botanicals by the drug companies. After drug safety and efficacy claims were validated, the new legislation permitted marketing opportunities without preclearance, provided the product claims conveyed the intrinsic values of the product to the public. While the FDA refrained from clarification or regulations regarding the act, it maintained that randomized, controlled testing reflected the best and most credible source of evidence for the efficacy of most therapies. International guidelines for herbal medicine assessment adhered to criteria established by the WHO.

Attention to environmental and humanitarian aspects of the industry was a particularly significant business objective of some botanical companies. As the search for medicinal and botanical industry products intensified, so did concern that tropical forests were being stripped of flora. Tropical plants from indigent countries comprised a primary source of botanical raw materials. These raw materials were profitable for drug companies, while plant-producing countries derived few, if any, benefits for their productivity or their knowledge. For example, research completed by Eli Lilly and Company on the wild rosy periwinkle plant from Madagascar led to production of vincristine and vinblastine. These chemotherapy drugs drastically reduced the mortality of childhood leukemia and produced a 19 to 80 percent remission rate in Hodgkin's disease patients. Since the 1960 discovery, these drugs have earned the company roughly US$100 million annually while Madagascar earned nothing. Such practices were not limited to Lilly. For more than 20 years, U.S. pharmaceutical drugs derived from naturally occurring compounds accounted for sales estimated at US$20 billion, with minimal benefits for the producing countries.

By the mid-1990s, host countries for botanical production were demanding more for their intellectual and biological contributions. The rationale was that indigenous people maintained intellectual property rights by virtue of possessing a wealth of esoteric knowledge about local plants. Conservationists argued that the wisdom of local inhabitants should be accorded an economic value. Scientists, on the other hand, maintained that their work to discover the usefulness of medicinal compounds in plants had to be protected. One notable effort to promote intellectual rights emerged from the 1992 Convention on Biological Diversity (the Rio Convention). Despite opposition from pharmaceutical companies, representatives from 167 nations persisted in recommending that less developed countries receive intellectual property rights for pharmacologically useful chemicals derived from their biological resources. Notwithstanding the ambiguities surrounding the issue of intellectual patents, the convention accentuated the conservation responsibilities of drug companies.

At least two U.S. drug companies, Merck & Co. and Shaman Pharmaceutical, took the lead in establishing a more equitable distribution of profits. These companies contracted with Latin American nations to gain access to virgin biological raw materials in exchange for a share of the profits from resulting products. Shaman further pledged to pass up endangered plants and committed to paying royalties from drug revenues to both the local government and the native communities where the plants were harvested. Merck agreed to pay US$1 million over a two-year period directly to Costa Rica's National

Institute of Biodiversity for collecting plants, insects, and microbes, as well as royalties for any pharmaceutical discoveries. In the mid-1990s, the U.S. National Institutes of Health (NIH) announced a five-year, US$12.5 million program to spur conservation and bioprospecting in Central America, South America, and Africa. Through alliances with organizations like Conservation International, local persons identifying medicinal plants would be eligible for patent and joint patent rights.

Intergovernmental and corporate efforts at the end of the twentieth century were considered to not be sweeping enough to stem the disappearance of both the land that produces these raw materials and the indigenous healers who know how to exploit them. According to the World Resources Institute, roughly 17 million hectares of rain forest are lost to deforestation annually. Loss of rain forest led to a loss of potential new drugs. In the mid-1990s, an investigator from the U.S. Environmental Protection Agency speculated that, given rates of extinction and the probability of a 5 in 10,000 chance that any plant would be the source of a marketable drug, the foregone value of lost drug products in 1992 alone was US$150 million. In addition, a burden was placed on a plant species after its medicinal efficacy was discovered. Conservationists worried that the Pacific Yew tree, an exclusive source for the cancer-fighting drug Taxol, would be eradicated in order to extract the compound. To ease concerns over the yew, Bristol-Myers Squibb, the sole purveyor of the drug, developed alternative Taxol sources. The dwindling group of traditional shamans, healers, and teachers was exacerbated by the extinction of rain-forest plant species. Recognizing the potential cultural loss, groups like the Association of Traditional Healers organized to train young people in the traditional use of plants in an effort to pass on generations of accumulated medicinal knowledge.

Similar to intellectual biodiversity rights, rainforest property rights also remained ill-defined and were not well enforced, primarily because these areas were held collectively or designated as government-owned reserves. Drug company participants defended their practice of foraging tropical forests by repeating that open access rainforest policies did not preclude anyone from searching for natural samples in developing countries. Void of enforceable property rights, rain forests were considered open access territory.

Before the Agreement on Trade-Related Aspects of Intellectual Property Rights (TRIPS) took effect in 2005, intellectual property law in India protected only the means of producing drugs without covering the medication. Consequently, Indian AIDS drug manufacturers could use unpatented production processes that allowed them to offer drugs at lower prices. The Indian government was concerned about the quantity of health care for its large population. In 1998, the government announced that it would promote a new awareness strategy that would make alternative health care options like Ayurveda, Unani, Shiddha, homeopathy, yoga, and naturopathy acceptable for its population. The government hoped to expand health care to all Indians, including those in rural areas who were thought to have difficulty seeing a traditional Western physician.

The Irish Association of Health Stores continued its campaign against "highly restrictive" laws that had been or were in the process of being implemented across the 27-member state bloc related to food supplement and functional foods. These laws covered health claims, permitted ingredients ,and dosage levels, as well as classification of medicinal and non-medicinal products. Association President Jill Bell said that industry leaders, manufacturers, and distributors would struggle if the directives passed, adding that the consumer's lack of ability to choose continued to being troublesome.

CURRENT CONDITIONS

Ethnobotanists have been primary sources for identifying therapeutic plants in the tropical areas of the world that are the most fertile grounds for medicinal plants and herbs. Botanists have estimated that 10 percent or less of the more than 250,000 flowering plant species in the world have been surveyed for pharmacological use. The gradual disappearance of these local healers, tribal medicine men, shamans, and other non-traditional caretakers is limiting the drug companies' resources. However, some family legacies were notable exceptions, offering a remedy for carrying on traditions. Michael Tierra, a well-known herbalist and author, taught his daughter, Shasta, who also worked with herbalist Christopher Hobbs and acupuncturist Miriam Lee. Shasta Tierra practiced traditional Chinese medicine in her San Jose, California, clinic. The father and daughter frequently wrote articles that were featured on Web sites for alternative and herbal medicines.

In 2004, the American Botanical Council (ABC) launched its first training and certification program. Offered via its website, the "ABC Herbal Information Course" is based on the *ABC Clinical Guide to Herbs.* Topics include history, regulation, trends, science, and insights about 29 commonly used herbs. After herb retailers and health practitioners are certified, they have complimentary access to one-page monographs for each herb discussed during the course.

In the January 10, 2004, edition of *New Scientist* Rob Edwards reported that two-thirds of the 50,000 medicinal plants in use in the early twenty-first century were harvested from the wild, causing increased concern about species extinction. Plantlife International found that 11 of 16 herbal remedy companies in the United Kingdom, including The Body Shop, obtained all the plants they sell from the wild. Ethnobotanists and activists called for companies using these plants to exercise caution when cultivating to ensure adequate future supplies. Among the plants in danger of being overharvested was the African cherry (*prunus africana*), valued for its bark that is used in Europe as a treatment for enlarged prostate conditions. Traditionally, less than half of a tree's bark would be taken, allowing the tree to survive. However, sudden high demand led to indiscriminate stripping and destruction of entire forests. As a result, exports of dried bark plummeted 50 percent between 1997 and 2000, and the main exporter, Plantecam, was forced to close its processing facility in Cameroon.

The European Union Traditional Herbal Medicinal Products Directive was enacted in 2005, requiring all herbal products classified as medicines to be registered by April 2011. However, the British Herbal Medicines Association felt it was imperative to encourage manufacturers to submit applications registering hundreds of botanical products before the deadline. The British Herbal Medicines Association said 100 registration applications had been filed by October 2007, making the United Kingdom the most advanced member state in terms of making applications.

On June 22, 2007, the U.S. Food and Drug Administration announced it had published final regulations for Good Manufacturing Practices for dietary supplements. The objective was to ensure products free of contamination that were accurately labeled. The new rules set to be phased in according to company size and were expected to take up to three years to completely go into effect.

According to the World Health Organization (WHO), in 2009 the medicinal, supplement, and botanical industry was valued at US$60 billion annually, with the related alternative medicine industry-at-large valued at US$34 billion. According to WHO, U.S. expenditures on complementary alternative medicine (CAM) totaled US$2.7 billion per year in 2009, and the European market for herbal remedies had a value of at least US$19.34 billion, after growing approximately 20 percent annually from 1994 to 2004.

Established pharmaceutical giants found themselves facing drastically reduced market share as a number of their patents expired as of 2005. The situation has placed immense responsibility on company researchers to replace the lost patent drugs with new discoveries in medicine that provide equivalent monies.

Significant long-term opportunities for this sector were expected to come from bulk analgesics, antibiotics, and digestives. However, FDA objections to claims made by some manufacturers for the benefits of their products had proliferated in the first decade of the twenty-first century, leading to bitter attacks on the FDA by some members of the industry. In all likelihood, protests for and against the industry will continue to be rancorous.

In the United States, the FDA improved its review procedure and approval of submissions. However, according to Alan Holmer of the Pharmaceutical Research & Manufacturers Association, the roughly US$800 million expense required to get a new medicine approved by the FDA and on the market has put the price of drugs out of reach for many consumers, particularly those who need them the most. The US$800 million figure, however, was considered to be highly inflated by consumer advocates, such as Michael Davis of Cleveland State University.

In many areas, tribal folklore medicine transcended local boundaries. Herbal apothecaries were no longer selling age-old remedies and secrets in unmarked bottles, and were replace by modern, high-class retail establishments, catering to average consumers and targeting wealthier clients who could afford to pay up to US$19,000 for a rare, wild Chinese ginseng root. At the other extreme, Wal-Mart Stores Inc. does a brisk business with its Nutrition Centers, offering a large assortment of value-priced therapeutic food supplements. In 2006 and 2007, sales of herbal dietary supplements rose more than 4 percent each year in the U.S. market, reaching approximately US$4.79 billion in 2007. The supplements, which typically had been perceived as an alternative form of health care, were being accepted by more consumers as part of the mainstream.

Entering the industry in early twenty-first century was not easy for entrepreneurs, partially because of the predominance of large-scale pharmaceutical companies with money and resources to survive the challenges of high start-up costs. In addition, in an effort to overcome entry barriers, many of the large companies were able to engage in various collaborative efforts with nonprofit botanical organizations and small drug companies. Monsanto Company, for instance, contracted with the Missouri Botanical Garden to supply several thousand plants from the United States and some tropical countries. Merck & Co. Inc. entered an arrangement with the New York Botanical Garden's Institute of Economic Botany and received plants from around the world for testing. Bionics, a small British start-up company, utilized a science broker approach and negotiated contracts to supply Glaxo and SmithKline Beecham with samples and chemical extracts from tropical plants. Some companies narrowed their search for new drugs by combing traditional pharmacopoeia to identify relatively nontoxic medicines. Similar approaches worked for Chemex Pharmaceutical of New Jersey, which won FDA approval in the 1990s to market Actinex (a drug derived from the creosote bush) as a treatment for precancerous skin lesions.

Despite the dominance of major pharmaceutical corporations, small start-up companies still saw opportunities in the market. MediMush, a Danish company founded in 2002, emerged in 2005 as a supplier of medicinal mushroom ingredients for the pharmaceutical and supplements industries. Mushrooms contain compounds used in treating cancer and are also widely used to enhance immune system function. According to company literature, MediMush has derived the world's first oral form of pure lentinan, a polysaccharide, from shiitake mushrooms. MediMush estimated that the global market for shiitake-based products was worth at least 400 million euros (about US$481.6 million).

In 2002 exports of traditional Chinese medicine (TCM) products declined 2.3 percent, some of which was due to aggressive growth of medicinal herbs in other countries. Nonetheless, exports in the first 11 months of 2001 earned US$478 million, slightly higher than the US$467 million reported for the same period in 2000. Most of the growth was in the western Sichuan and Gansu provinces, with 81.7 percent of China's exports. TCM had become fully integrated in the Chinese health care system by 2010, with 95 percent of hospitals offering TCM treatment. More than 800 manufacturers of herbal products report total annual revenues of US$1.8 billion.

In April 2004, a regulation intended to ensure quality was adopted by the European Union that required suppliers of herbal medicines to obtain the EU Good Manufacturing Product (GMP) certificate. China supplied US$108.3 million in traditional medicines to the European market, worth US$10 billion annually, in 2004. The new regulation caused exports to drop significantly, with the value of traditional medicine shipments from Shanghai to Europe falling 60 percent in May and more than 30 percent in June. While industry leaders in China acknowledged the initial negative impact of the regulation, they hoped that exports would grow over the long term. As Liu Zhanglin of the China Chamber of Commerce of Medicines & Health products Importers & Exporters told *China Daily* for the August 7, 2004, edition, the regulation "for the first time grants TCM legal status as medicines" and would open new European markets. Many medical experts conducted decades of

research and have concluded that traditional Chinese medicines have few side effects and are less expensive than most Western medicines.

In 2002, researchers seeking to help AIDS patients discovered a promising medicine known to the ancients as ayurveda. Although India's share of the export market for ayurveda was only 0.2 percent in 2002, the country was expected to become a leading exporter by 2010. In June 2004, African church leaders stated their commitment to "The 3 by 5 Initiative" calling for treatment of 3 million individuals with HIV/AIDS by 2005. Some 200 Protestant church leaders from 39 African countries showed support at the All Africa Conference of Churches (AACC) held in Nairobi, Kenya. AACC President Right Reverend Nyansanko Ni-Nku said approximately 40 percent of African health care facilities were owned by churches.

RESEARCH AND TECHNOLOGY

In the mid-1990s, scientists began tapping the medical potential of the marine environment. In the early 1990s nearly 2,000 compounds of marine origin were studied for possible use as antimicrobial, antiviral, or antitumor agents. Antibacterial and antiviral properties were identified in certain invertebrate species, such as sponges. Of the thousands of others investigated by the National Cancer Institute, about 4 percent demonstrated some antitumor effect. One marine compound under clinical trial at the time was Didemnin-B, isolated from the tunicate (sea squirt). Didemnin-B demonstrated properties as a potent killer of melanomas, as well as a measure of antiviral activity. The search for effective natural marine medicine aligned with the expertise described in traditional Asian pharmacopoeias. Asian folk cures were derived from dried seaweed, ground mollusk shells, and the vertebrae and livers of various species of fish. These folk medicines purportedly allayed diseases and a host of illnesses, such as high blood pressure, impotence, and insomnia. Although some remained unverifiable, a seaweed known as the Corsican weed contained an alpha-kainic acid that kills nerve endings and was reputed to be effective for intestinal worms. At least 37 compounds with sodium-channel blocking properties, proven effective for cardiovascular illness, were isolated from sea anemones and other marine life. The most notable of these discoveries were fish oils that contained eicosapentaenoic acid and docohexaenoic acid. These compounds proved to work well in the prevention of atherosclerotic heart disease. The oils of cold-water fish not only proved effective in reducing cholesterol and triglycerides, but also were beneficial for people with rheumatoid arthritis and diabetes.

Another promising development in the early years of the first decade of the 2000s was growing interest in plant sterols, a market worth US$75 million in Europe in 2003. Sterols, which are derived from soybeans and other plants and can lower cholesterol, are not sold directly to consumers, but are added to foods that can then be marketed as beneficial to health. These are known in Europe as functional foods and in the United States as nutraceuticals. In the early years of the first decade of the 2000s, regulatory agencies expanded the range of foods approved for sterol as an ingredient, leading to projections of significant growth by sterol suppliers. Sterols were one of the best-performing products for leading producer Cognis, which reported 8.9 percent growth in its Nutrition and Health unit in 2004. Rival supplier Raisio reported that sales of its Benecol sterol esters increased 66 percent in 2004. Rising demand from obesity-treatment and weight-loss markets was expected to spur further growth for sterol manufacturers.

In 2005, Canada became the first country to approve Sativex, a pain medication derived from cannabis (marijuana). Sativex, which targets nerve pain associated with MS, had been created by GW Pharmaceuticals. In 2003, GW sold marketing rights for Sativex to Bayer. In addition to a signature fee in the deal, GW received a share of Sativex revenues as well as additional fees up to £25 million (US$43.8 million) following approval of the drug in the United Kingdom.

INDUSTRY LEADERS

Merck & Co. Inc. Merck & Co. Inc. traces its beginnings to Freidrich Jacob Merck's 1688 purchase of an apothecary in Germany. Heinrich Emmanuel Merck began manufacturing drugs in 1827, with his first product, which was morphine. By the time he died in 1855, Merck products were used worldwide. The 24-year-old grandson of Heinrich Merck traveled to the United States and established his own business. In 1989, a plant site was acquired in Rahway, New Jersey, which in 2010 continued to house the corporate headquarters of Merck & Co. Inc. and four of its divisions. Merck operates 16 manufacturing plants and has established subsidiaries in Australia, Europe, South America, Africa, and the Middle East. It is one of the largest drug manufacturers in the United States and employs 61,500 people. Merck is tied with Glaxo Wellcome, Plc., as the world leader in prescription drugs. Along with drugs for cardiovascular health and pain management, Merck also produces vaccines for hepatitis A and B, as well as chickenpox.

In 2002, Merck Chairman and CEO Raymond V. Gilmartin was on the hot seat, as several key drug patents expired without equivalent new drugs being found to excite company shareholders. Nonetheless, the company's total 2009 revenue was US$22.5 billion, an increase of nearly 57 percent over the prior year.

In May 2004, Merck signed an agreement with DHL, an air express delivery leader, to expanding access to critically needed HIV medicines throughout sub-Saharan Africa. In June 2004 Merck announced plans to expand cooperation with Dutch pharmaceutical company H Lundbeck A/S for joint development and distribution of the sleep disorder compound gaboxadol. After working together in the United States, the companies expected to expand efforts to Japan. Also in June 2004 Merck announced its collaboration with Vertex Pharmaceuticals to produce a compound for cancer treatment. Merck would coordinate worldwide clinical development and commercialization of VX-680 and pay Vertex product royalties on sales. A third collaboration announced in June 2004 called for Merck to work with Alnylam Pharmaceuticals to jointly develop gene-suppression therapies for eye diseases. Terms involved a multiyear deal with potential to net Alnylam US$19.5 million.

In September 2004, Merck pulled its best-selling painkiller, Vioxx, off the market after a study indicated that it could double the risk of heart attack or stroke. Lawsuits were brought against the company alleging that patients had died after long-term Vioxx use. On the day that investigations completed by the U.S. Congress revealed that Merck officials had downplayed Vioxx's health risks, Merck CEO Raymond Gilmartin resigned. The controversy cost the company billions of dollars in legal fees and sales, with total sales in 2004 reaching only US$22.9 billion. Nevertheless, Merck continued cutting-edge research in 2005, including a possible vaccine for sudden acute respiratory syndrome (SARS) and a cervical cancer vaccine. In 2006, Merck was awarded FDA approval for its cervical cancer vaccine, Gardasil. For 2009, Merck reported sales of US$27.4 billion. In November 2009, Merck announced plans to merge with Schering-Plough, a major competitor, in a US$41 billion deal. The deal was considered a "reverse merger" in which Schering-Plough would assume the name Merck and continue its operations as a public corporation. The new company would operate under the name Merck in the United States and Canada, and under the name MSD elsewhere.

GlaxoSmithKline Plc. Glaxo began in the late nineteenth century in New Zealand as an independent company importing and exporting goods from whalebone to patent medicines. Moving to London, the company began to produce baby food products and expanded into Indian and South American markets. During the 1930s and 1940s, Glaxo began to produce pharmaceuticals and quickly grew through acquisition and consolidation in the following decade. The anti-ulcer medication Zantac was launched simultaneously in several European markets in the late 1970s, and by 1984 the medication had captured 25 percent of the new prescription market. In

2000 the company merged with SmithKline Beecham, becoming GlaxoSmithKline Plc (GSK). Total sales in 2001 were US$25 billion, and in 2003, reached US$38.2 billion, an increase of nearly 12 percent from the previous year. Revenue growth slowed considerably in 2004, however, when sales reached only US$39 billion. In June 2004, Glaxo entered an agreement with Thembalmi Pharmaceuticals, a joint venture between Adcock Ingram and Ranbax, the Indian pharmaceutical giant. The agreement involved a voluntary license for Thembalmi to make generic copies of patented medicines.

GSK's subsidiary, GlaxoSmithKline Biologicals s.a., develops vaccines for such diseases as hepatitis, influenza, rubella, and typhoid fever. It works with the World Health Organization (WHO) to improve access to medicines in underdeveloped regions. In 2009, GSK had developed a vaccine for the H1N1 influenza that was approved by the FDA. In 2009, GSK reported revenues of US$37.77 billion, with approximately 99,000 employees.

Bristol-Myers Squibb. In addition to being one of the most profitable pharmaceutical manufacturers in the world, Bristol-Myers Squibb is also recognized worldwide as a major producer and distributor of consumer products, such as toothpaste and drain opener. Two former fraternity brothers founded Bristol-Myers in 1887 with the investment of US$5,000 each in the failing New York-based Clinton Pharmaceutical Company. Selling medical preparations by horse and buggy to local doctors and dentists, the company began making profits in the early 1900s, with sales of such products as Sal Hepatica, a laxative mineral salt, and Ipana toothpaste, the first such product to contain a disinfectant.

During both world wars, the company was heavily involved in the production of pharmaceuticals like penicillin and other antibiotics. Through acquisitions, such as Clairol and Mead Johnson, Bristol-Myers continued to grow through the decades. In the 1970s, the company was the first pharmaceutical firm to invest in anticancer drugs, a move that garnered more than US$200 million in sales. Achieving success with its Excedrin and Bufferin brands, Bristol-Myers expanded its share of the analgesic market through a joint agreement with Upjohn (which became Pharmacia & Upjohn) that enabled it to introduce a new nonprescription pain reliever called Nuprin. Despite several tampering incidents, the company continued to grow as a manufacturer of prescription pharmaceuticals, moving into the area of acquired immune deficiency syndrome (AIDS) research. Merging with Squibb Corporation (which was founded in 1858 in the United States), Bristol-Myers Squibb posted sales of US$10.2 billion in 1997, with 40 percent coming from non-U.S. markets. In 2009 the company posted total sales of US$18.8 billion with a workforce of approximately 28,000 employees.

In May 2004 when U.S. Secretary of Health and Human Services Tommy Thompson addressed the need for increased treatment options for people with HIV/AIDS in developing countries, Bristol-Myers Squibb partnered with Gilead Sciences and Merck to develop fixed-dose combination medicines of three HIV drugs. The WHO applauded new government support expediting the process to review fixed-dose combination medicines and co-packaging of existing therapies for the treatment of HIV/AIDS in developing countries.

In 2005 Bristol-Myers Squibb announced plans to sell its consumer products divisions in the United States and Canada. The same year the company sold Swiss firm Novartis the rights to produce and market a range of over-the-counter brands worth US$258 million in annual sales. Therapeutic categories for the company included oncology, cardiovascular and metabolic disorders, infectious diseases, HIV/AIDS, and psychiatric disorders.

Sanofi-Aventis. Sanofi-Aventis, the third-largest pharmaceutical company, was formed in 2004 when French drug maker Sanofi-Synthélabo merged with another French giant, Aventis. In 2009 Sanofi-Aventis employed more than 104,870 people worldwide and posted sales of US$39.05 billion. It conducts research and development in cardiovascular disease, thrombosis, neurological disease, oncology, metabolic disorders, internal medicine, and vaccines. Among its major products are Copaxone, a treatment for MS; Lantus, an insulin injection; and Taxotere, a cancer treatment.

Aventis was the product of a merger of Hoechst and Rhône-Poulenc, both of which had been threatened with lawsuits for miscellaneous reasons. Rhône-Poulenc began in the nineteenth century, and its early history included a series of mergers and diversity. Started by a pharmacist named Etienne Poulenc, eventually uniting with the Société Chimiques des Usines du Rhône, a manufacturer of dyestuffs and raw materials for perfumes, the company had a strong commitment to research and development. Involved in agricultural and industrial chemicals, in addition to pharmaceuticals, the company was privatized in the early 1990s. By 1994 the public owned about half of the company, and a group of banks, employees, and the state owned the remainder. In the late 1990s, the company was subject to a series of lawsuits, and shared a US$670 million legal settlement with Baxter, Bayer, and Green Cross over blood products that infected hemophiliacs with HIV.

Hoechst sales came from dyestuffs in the nineteenth and early twentieth centuries. The company eventually gained control of the entire diuretic market and was a leader in oral medication for diabetics by the 1970s. Fueled by the increased production of antibiotics, serum, and steroids, Hoechst's pharmaceutical sales grew at a rate of 13 percent a year during this decade. Continuing its program of overseas expansion that began in the 1960s, Hoechst built a US$100 million plant in the United States and soon secured a large portion of the U.S. drug market, with 23 percent of its sales being generated in North America in 1993. In the early 1990s, the company was subject to freak chemical spills that caused it to divest its chlorofluorocarbon (CFC) business in 1993. In 1997, the company stopped making Seldane, which had come under attack, and replaced it with the popular product Allegra.

Aventis received a major blow in 2002 when the FDA refused to endorse Picovir as a cure for the common cold. The FDS maintained that Aventis failed to demonstrate a clinical benefit that would outweigh possible side effects from the drug.

BIBLIOGRAPHY

"African Heads of Churches Summit Commit to '3 by 5,'" 2005. Available from www.who.int.

"American Botanical Council. "Herb Supplement Sales Show Growth in Multiple Market Channels," 27 May 2008.

"American Botanical Council." HerbalGram, 2005. Available from www.herbalgram.org.

"American Botanical Council Launches First Online Training and Certification Course for Herb Retailers and Health Practitioners," 2005. Available from www.herbalgram.org.

Barrett, Amy. "Why Merck's Spin-Off Is No Cure." *Bloomberg News,* 31 January 2002.

"Bitter Medicine: Pills, Profit and the Public Health." *ABC News,* 29 May 2002.

Bleecher, Michele Bitoun. "Gold in Goldenseal: Healing Herbs Have Become a Cash Crop." *Hospitals & Health Networks,* 20 October 1997.

Datta, Mrinalini. "Aventis Pharma Expects Sales to Grow about 13 Percent This Year." *China Business,* 18 January 2002.

Edwards, Rob. "No Remedy In Sight for Herbal Ransack." *New Scientist,* 10 January 2004.

"Environment and Health Sector," 2005. Available from www.csir.org.gh.

"E.U. Regulation Affects TCM Exports." *China Daily,* 7 August 2004. Available from www.china.org.cn.

"Facts About Traditional Healing." World Health Organization. Available from www.independentliving.co.uk.

"FDA Publishes Final Rules for Good Manufacturing Practices for Dietary Supplements." American Botanical Society, 22 June 2007. Available from abc.herbalgram.org.

Fernandez, Edna. "Ancient Cures in a Global Market." *Financial Times,* 30 April 2002.

"Ghana; Nation Can Reap From Medicinal Plants." *Africa News,* 8 March 2002.

"Hoover's Company Capsules." *Hoover's Online,* 2005. Available from www.hoovers.com.

Krauskopf, Lewis. "Cure for Its (Merck) Blahs?" *The Record* (Bergen County, NJ), 30 January 2002.

Neimark, Jill. "On the Frontlines of Alternative Medicine." *Psychology Today,* January 1997.

Olson, Nigel. "Canada Becomes Sativex Country." *Cannabis Culture,* 19 April 2005. Available from www.medical marihuana.ca.

"Patent Pitfalls Unsettle Top Drug Makers." *The Business,* 30 January 2002.

Patton, Dominique. "Cognis Ramps Up Plant Sterol Capacity." *Nutra Ingredients,* 11 July 2004. Available from www.nutraingredients.com.

Starling, Shane. "100s of UK Herbals Face Ban as Registration Deadline Looms." *Nutra Ingredients,* 17 June 2008. Available from www.nutraingredients.com.

———. "Irish Health Group Welcomes 'No' to Lisbon Treaty." *Nutra Ingredients,* 16 June 2008. Available from www.nutrain gredients.com.

Stein, Lisa. "More Fallout from the Vioxx Mess." *U.S. News & World Report,* 16 May 2005.

"Swiss Pharmaceuticals Firm Acquires Key U.S. Drugs Portfolio." *Asia Intelligence Wire,* 16 July 2005. Available from www.hoovers.com.

Tierra, Shasta. "Increase Vitality and Productivity with Some Simple Food Tips." East West School of Herbology, 2005. Available from www.planetherbs.com.

"A Time of Ferment for Biopharmaceutical Contract Manufacturing." *Chemical Market Reporter,* 23 March 2001.

Wechsler, Jill. "More Changes and Challenges at FDA." *Pharmaceutical Executive,* February 1998.

"Use of Complementary and Alternative Medicine in the United States" National Center for Complimentary and Alternative Medicine, National Institutes of Health. Available from nccam.nih.gov.

"WHO Statement on US Proposal for Rapid Review of Fixed Combinations. 2005. Available from www.who.int.

SIC 2851

PAINTS AND COATINGS

NAICS CODE(S)

325510. The global paint industry produces paints and coatings for architectural (known in Europe as decorative), marine, packaging, transportation equipment, and many additional end uses. Industry products also include varnishes, lacquers, enamels, and shellac, as well as chemical paint removers and brush cleaners. Makers of pigments alone are discussed in **Chemicals, Industrial Inorganic** and **Chemicals, Industrial Organic** based on the specific pigment's chemical composition.

INDUSTRY SNAPSHOT

The paint industry has been a relatively small but rapidly growing segment of the broad chemical industry. Environmental pressures and regulations have been some of

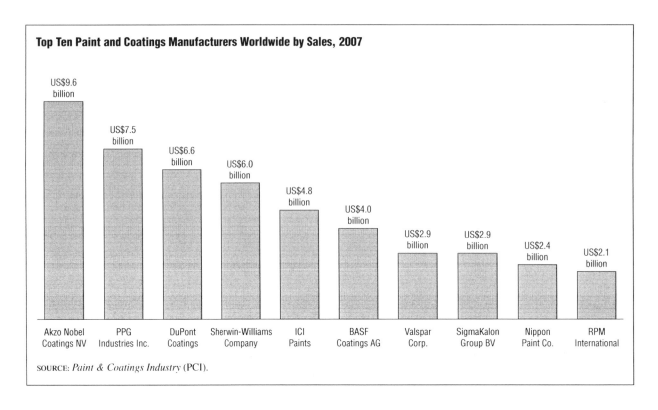

Top Ten Paint and Coatings Manufacturers Worldwide by Sales, 2007

SOURCE: *Paint & Coatings Industry* (PCI).

the biggest challenges faced by the industry. Skyrocketing prices of basic raw materials have also been a perennial concern, although by the late 1990s prices had stabilized somewhat. To counter increasing prices, paint manufacturers and suppliers worked together to formulate improved paints to justify price premiums. A simultaneous challenge for the industry was to incorporate the use of environmentally-friendly materials and abide by the regulations and pressures on volatile organic compounds (VOCs) and hazardous air pollutants (HAPs). Coatings generally were moving away from being solvent-based toward being water-based as of the mid-2000s.

Following the worldwide slump of manufacturing industries during the end of the 1990s and the beginning of the 2000s, the paints and coatings industry showed overall improvement by 2005, particularly in the architectural/decorative coatings segment, which grew 11 percent in value for U.S. manufacturers. Special purpose coatings declined slightly. While the product OEM (original equipment manufacturer) coatings segment improved worldwide, due in part to increased manufacturing in Asia and South America, the U.S. segment declined 13 percent in value.

Measured by consumption, North America and Asia are the world's largest paint markets, each consuming about 29 percent of world production. These regions are trailed by Western Europe at 22 percent, and other regions consume the remaining 19 percent. China showed the biggest growth in annual consumption from 1997 to 2002, with a 6.4 percent increase.

In 2007, the top 10 paint and coatings manufacturers worldwide, as ranked by *Paint & Coatings Industry (PCI)*, in terms of sales were Akzo Nobel Coatings NV, PPG Industries Inc., DuPont Coatings, Sherwin-Williams Company, ICI Paints, BASF Coatings AG, Valspar Corp., SigmaKalon Group BV, Nippon Paint Co., and RPM International.

Jessica Hinds observed that color choices were changing for paint selection. Caribbean homeowners had previously been choosing mainly greys, browns, and creams. In 2008, more and more houses in Barbados were being decked out in brighter shades. Paint companies were high on the list of those entities promoting the trend. Popular brighter colors include yellows, greens, and peaches. The harsh Caribbean climate offers a challenge to people who do not want their paint to fade. Paint companies are attempting to address that challenge by including synthetic instead of organic pigment in colorful paints.

ORGANIZATION AND STRUCTURE

Paints and coatings fall into three broad categories: architectural paints, original equipment manufacturer (OEM) paints, and special purpose coatings. Specialized paints such as skid-resistant paint, heat-reflective paints, heat-absorbent paints, phosphorescent paints, fluorescent coatings, electrically conductive/non-conductive paints, and temperature sensitive paints were used for a variety of purposes, especially in industry.

Architectural Paints. These paints are used for decorating and protecting homes, apartments, farm buildings, office buildings, and other commercial structures. Architectural paints include both solvent and water-based paints for interior and exterior surfaces. In industrial economies, such as those of Japan and Western Europe, architectural coatings are considered a mature market, with long-term growth projected at about 1 to 2 percent per year.

The "Fallingwater Inspired Colors" paint series was created to salute Frank Lloyd Wright's nature inspired palette featuring colors representative of materials found in his Pennsylvania home. There are 13 shades available that are linked to the restoration of Fallingwater by the Western Pennsylvania Conservancy restoration. Pittsburgh Paints created the colors emulating such things as concrete walls and fabric covering cantilevered living room couches.

According to Rohm and Paint Quality Institute, the most popular colors of exterior paint are white at 34 percent, beige at 28 percent, grey at 15 percent, blue at 7 percent, and green and yellow at 6 percent each. Choosing the wrong color could have a lasting impact or be costly to correct. An alternative to relying solely on paint chips is one designer's 27-item checklist to come up with possible color options for clients. That list includes roof color, the direction the house faces, the amount of decoration on neighboring houses, and the age and style of the home. Robert Schweitzer charges US$550 for home color consulting that includes diagrams for painters to use in order to make sure that they apply colors in the right places. Schweitzer advises clients across the country to try out the color on an area large enough to see it before confirming it is their choice for the job.

Original Equipment Manufacturer (OEM) Paints. OEM coatings, also known as industrial or product finishes, are typically used to protect and decorate durable and industrial goods. This group of paints is usually sold by paint companies to equipment manufacturers who apply the paints to their particular products, such as automobiles, trucks, aircraft, railroad equipment, home appliances, office machines, furnaces, and air-conditioning equipment.

Many of the paint technologies used in the early twenty-first century were developed for the OEM segment, where there was a growing focus on increasing the efficiency of application methods and reducing volatile solvents content to meet strict environmental regulations. A major challenge facing manufacturers of OEM coatings was the increased use of plastics in automobiles

and other durable goods. The need for OEMs to match the paint finish of steel body panels with plastic body panels that are painted separately was yet to be satisfied.

Special Purpose Coatings. This category includes paint products generally used for maintenance work and as coatings for the transportation aftermarket. They are designed for special applications and for withstanding unusual environmental conditions. Special purpose coatings are used widely in high specialty applications. These products include anti-corrosive paints, traffic and marine paints, weather resistant paints, spray paints in aerosol containers, and chemical resistant paints.

BACKGROUND AND DEVELOPMENT

The world's paint markets underwent a reversal of sorts in the 1990s, as some of the markets that had grown the fastest early in the decade had slowed by the late 1990s and early 2000s. In addition, some of the slowest markets had picked up speed, a trend that continued into the mid-2000s. Since 1995, demand growth had revived to about 3 percent annually, a pattern that was expected to continue through 2000, but then sputtered with a souring economy in 2001. A growth rate of 2 to 3 percent was expected again by 2003 as the global economy regained momentum. However, growth was not expected to come for U.S. manufacturers, who saw much of the industry moved to inexpensive offshore facilities, particularly in the product OEM sector. In fact, according to *Paints & Coatings Industry*, 2002 marked the first time in 70 years that chemical imports in general had a higher value than exports. Throughout the 2000s, Asia and South America were the world's most important growth markets.

Development of Paint Materials. Some of the earliest examples of painting occurred thousands of years ago, when Paleolithic artists devised elaborate cave paintings in blacks, yellows, reds, and whites at Lascaux, France. These early paints came from such substances as charcoal, iron oxide, clay, and calcite. Paints in the modern sense came into being when the early artists discovered that colors could be better applied when the pigments were mixed with binders such as egg whites, beeswax, gum arabic, and pitches and balsams from trees. Some of the main ingredients used in paints were pigments, binders, volatile solvents, and additives.

Pigments are materials that impart color and opacity to a paint film. White lead was the most important pigment used in paint from the end of the seventeenth century until early in the twentieth century, when titanium dioxide was introduced. Other pigments became popular in the mid-nineteenth century and led to the formation of multi-pigment paints.

Binder is the portion of the paint that holds the other ingredients together and serves to form the solid film of paint. Around the sixth century A.D., oils obtained from vegetable seeds and nuts began to be used as paint binders. Alkyd resins began to be used as paint binders around 1927. The excellent properties and great versatility of alkyd resins made their discovery and development one of the most important in modern paint technology. Numerous other resins and polymers were developed for highly specialized industrial and maintenance uses.

Volatile solvents or thinners are used in paints to facilitate their application. Turpentine was the first recorded thinner used in paint. Used by the ancient Egyptians, it was the most widely used paint thinner until the middle of the twentieth century when it was largely displaced by less expensive petroleum-based solvents, which were first used in the 1860s. With the increased use of latex paints and other water-borne coatings, water was also widely used as a solvent.

Additives are used in paints and coatings to perform specific functions not accomplished by the three major ingredients. Additives facilitate the performance of a variety of special functions, such as drying or hardening of paints, dispersing of pigment, preventing uneven color patterns, preventing pigment from settling, and resisting mildew growth on surfaces.

Origins of the Industry. A rudimentary chemical industry is said to have begun in the early seventeenth century with the production of wood tar that was used as pitch for the bottom of ships and potash that was used for making soap. The spread of industrialization outside of Europe and the United States as well as World Wars I and II acted as catalysts for the chemical industry.

Industrial growth in the United States increased civilian demand for chemicals, especially those used in bleaching and dyeing textiles. In 1867, D.R. Averill, from Ohio, patented ready-to-use paint, but quality ready-mixed paints were not produced until the 1880s. During both world wars, paint and varnish were vital to the U.S. military effort for protection and camouflage of equipment and personnel. The unique needs of the military compelled the development of specialized paints and coatings.

Time-tested technologies and processes are utilized for the production of conventional paints. The production process is composed of the mixing of primary materials followed by blending, testing, and filling operations. Unlike many basic and intermediate chemicals, paints

and coatings are sold under a brand name. Research and development and technological advances occur quite rapidly in a consumer environment, as has been the case in the paints and coatings industry.

The maturity of the paint business and increased technology requirements resulted in an extended period of industry consolidation. The growing burden of complying with government regulation, intense industry competition, and low profit margins contributed to a large number of mergers and acquisitions.

Environmental Challenges. Overcapacity and merger mania were not the only problems chemical companies confronted during the 1970s and 1980s. The industry faced an increase in government regulations and a growing environmental movement that saw chemical manufacturers as the prime villains. Many disasters that occurred within the chemical industry contributed to increasing environmental restrictions. Among these disasters were the Union Carbide tragedy in Bhopal, India; diseases caused by mercury contamination from the Chisso chemical company in Minamata, Japan; the 1976 explosion at a chemical plant in Seveso, Italy, that released a dioxin-contaminated cloud; and growing evidence that freon, used by DuPont in aerosol cans, was contributing to the destruction of the ozone layer.

These environmental concerns prompted the U.S. Congress to enact a series of laws regulating the entire chemical industry. The paint coatings industry was an integral part of the chemical manufacturing sector and was directly affected by these laws. The Environmental Protection Agency (EPA) was created to regulate the introduction, generation, transportation, treatment, and disposal of hazardous waste, and the Occupational Safety and Health Administration (OSHA) was created to monitor the workplace. In 1970 the Australian Government Paint Committee (GPC) was set up, in its present form, as an "onus of proof" scheme. It approved products for use by state and federal government departments and bodies.

Regulation of the industry accelerated dramatically during the environmentally conscious 1970s and 1980s when federal clean air regulations were adopted to encourage the production of less polluting and less toxic paints. Other environmental regulations included the Federal Insecticide, Fungicide and Rodenticide Act of 1972, the Toxic Substances Control Act of 1976, and the Comprehensive Environmental Response Compensation and Liability Act of 1980. The latter established a Superfund program for cleaning toxic waste sites, and the estimated bill for chemical manufacturers ran up to tens of billions of dollars. Since the Resource Conservation and Recovery Act (RCRA) had already classified paint wastes as hazardous materials, all paint manufacturers found themselves subject to fee collection under the Superfund.

The 1986 Emergency Planning and Community Right-to-Know Act led to the creation of the Toxic Release Inventory (TRI), a database containing releases of toxic substances into the environment by manufacturing companies. The TRI showed that the manufacturers were pouring several billion pounds of toxins into the environment each year. Chemical producers at the top of the list began to take steps to reduce their reported toxic releases.

The testing of six-eco-friendly paints showed that they had low- or no-VOC (volatile organic compounds), chemicals that helped to create the smell usually identified with fresh paint. The chemicals are essentially solvents that possibly contain formaldehyde, benzene, and other compounds linked to ozone depletion. Related medical problems have been identified as nausea and headaches, as well as ear, nose, and throat irritation. Some chemicals have even been linked to cancer. After the paint has dried, off-gasing, or the emission of VOCs, from paint may continue. In a non-scientific test, Benjamin Moore's low-VOC Aura paint offered superior coverage, low drips, and minimal smell. The test required one homeowner to open paint cans in her garage, sniff the paint, and try it on canvas. Colors and finishes can greatly affect how paint performs.

Lead. Once a primary component of paint, lead ranked as one of the top environmental threats to children's health in the 1990s. The effects of lead, which was also used in gasoline, ceramic finishes, plumbing and many other products, were discovered in the 1930s. White lead pigments were essentially eliminated from architectural paints in the 1940s, but it was not until 1977 that the use of lead-based paints was outlawed in the United States. Government and medical reports published in the late 1980s and early 1990s revealed evidence that lead poisoning could occur with much lower doses than was previously thought. The lead problem therefore turned out to be more pervasive than earlier believed. One of the most significant outcomes was that in 1993, all paint manufacturers in California were assessed on their past and present use of products containing lead and then given special fees based on the results of the assessment under the state's Childhood Lead Poisoning Act of 1991. According to *Forbes* and the Alliance to End Childhood Lead Poisoning, by the late twentieth century only one death from lead poisoning due to a child's eating of the substance had been reported, due to greater public awareness.

In the twenty-first century, *Forbes* predicted that paint manufacturers would likely find themselves in courtroom hot seats as firms such as Ness, Motley, Loadholt, Richardson & Poole follow through with civil suits against the paint and pigment industry for having relied so heavily on lead. Sherwin Williams' lead attorney denounced the suits and the Rhode Island attorney general for going ahead with a lawsuit against the company, according to *Forbes*. Others have pointed out that 30 years ago, lead also was present in certain containers and in gasoline. Now, socially conscious manufacturers are moving to water-based production as fast as possible.

Volatile Organic Compounds (VOCs). As paint dries, the organic solvents in the paint evaporate, thus releasing VOCs into the atmosphere. VOCs react with sunlight to contribute to smog. The U.S. Clean Air Act was introduced in 1977, which required that states regulate geographic areas that failed to meet air quality standards. There was growing pressure to reduce emissions of VOCs from the use of paints and the consumption of solvents, especially in original equipment and industrial applications. The paint industry is a major user of hydrocarbon solvents, accounting for about 25 percent of the demand.

Recycling. As a result of strict regulations and concern for the environment, recycling, a trend that took hold in the 1980s, also extended to the paint industry. Laidlaw Environmental Services of Canada was one of the pioneers in recycling old paint. It began running its US$3 million plant in Mississauga, Ontario, Canada, in 1992, which was the sole automated paint recycling facility worldwide at the time. Torrance, California-based Major Paint introduced Cycle II, the first recycled paint in the United States, which was composed of 50 percent post-consumer and post-industrial latex waste. Even the paint containers were recycled, yet it sold at half the cost of new paint. In one instance, Rasmussen Paint of Beaverton, Oregon, began to use recycled materials in all of its bulk paint containers.

Global Trade. In the early 2000s, more than US$18 billion worth of paints and coatings were traded among nations each year. In 2007, the U.S. exported US$1.6 billion in products, which was an increase of US$43 million over 2006. The U.S. posted a trade surplus of US$933 million in 2007, a 1 percent increase over the previous year and a 52 percent increase from 1997. Over 60 percent of all U.S. paint and coatings exports were sold to NAFTA partners in 2007. U.S. exports to Canada reached US$760 million, and Mexico reached US$245 million, with China filling the number three spot at US$60 million in 2007. That same year, Germany exported US$44 million in paints and coatings from the United States, and Japan exported US$40 million. In comparison to export market concentration, the top 10 importers purchased just over 50 percent of all paint imports, whereas the top 10 exporters controlled more than 75 percent of the market. There were approximately 54,600 establishments in the paint and coating sector in 2007.

CURRENT CONDITIONS

The top 10 companies in the industry worldwide all had increased sales in 2009, as did the majority of the top U.S. companies. By the mid-2000s, global companies were making abundant declarations that employee layoffs and other cost-cutting measures were a certainty as they sought a return to profitability. For example, according to *Paintings & Coatings Industry News,* Akzo Nobel, the world's giant in coatings production, promised to significantly scale back its global employee base in the areas of both chemicals and coatings. In 2007, there were 348,900 people employed in the U.S. paint and coating industry.

The paints and coating market in India started in 1902, and grew tremendously after that, focusing on decorative paints. By 2008, the focus of the Indian sector of the industry had expanded to include industrial paints and a technologically advanced market. Asian Paints led the Indian market, followed by Kansai, Berger, and ICI.

In Nigeria, more than 70 percent of raw materials used in the manufacture of paints and coatings are imported. In addition, Paint Manufacturers Association of Nigeria President Bola Olayinka said that the industry in Nigeria had to compete with imports of finished paints. In order to promote opportunities for survival, Olayinka urged Nigerian paints and coatings manufacturers to join forces with their counterparts around the world.

RESEARCH AND TECHNOLOGY

Environmental Regulation. A high proportion of research and development in the paints and coatings industry has been directed toward creating environmentally friendly products designed to comply with contemporary or anticipated government regulations. Funds have been diverted that might otherwise have been poured into technological innovations aimed at performance improvement.

The U.S. Environmental Protection Act (EPA) proposed reductions in volatile organic compounds (VOCs) in architectural coatings and industrial maintenance coatings that would be implemented in a three-step process beginning in 1996. Using 1990 as the base year, the first phase required a 25 percent reduction in VOC content by 1996, rising to 35 percent in the year 2000, and 45 percent by 2003. According to the U.S. National Paints and Coatings Association, a trade group, the VOC limits would affect 65 percent of the industry's volumes. The EPA also established a national program to train and accredit individuals and firms engaged in lead-based activities in September 1994.

The 1990 Clean Air Act (CAA), designed to eliminate VOCs, ozone depleters, and other hazardous air pollutants (HAPs), put limits on many organic solvents. In spite of attempts to develop "green" solvents, solvent sales have declined steadily since 1990, according to *Chemical Week* magazine. Sales of solvent were predicted to drop from 1993 to 1996 because of environmental regulations on chlorofluorocarbons (CFCs) and high-VOC solvents. It also was predicted that the market would recover slightly from 1996 to 2000, with increased demand for unregulated solvents. Odor regulations were another constituent of the Clean Air Act as paints and coatings producers were forced to reduce odor emissions by fall 1995. Since odors could not be classified as easily as VOCs, some confusion continued to exist about the impact of odor regulations.

According to *MarketWatch,* Green Seal updated its environmental standard for paint that had been classified as being a big contributor to indoor air pollution. The GS-11 provides a revised standard for certification with sticker guidelines to reduce VOC levels of colorants. Adjusting these levels makes it possible to ensure that even heavily tinted paints will contain a minimum amount of VOCs. The related test method produces accurate readings and is estimated to be ten times more effective in measuring exact VOC levels than before. "Consumers will soon be able to buy Green Seal certified paints with even more confidence," promised Green Seal President and CEO Dr. Arthur Weissman. Customers had previously been able to select Green Seal Paints made by Benjamin Moore, Dutch Boy, and Olympic Paints.

New Products and Processes. By the early 1990s, many companies had come to the conclusion that toxic reduction was not only a political and social necessity, but that it also made economic sense in terms of improved efficiency. The result was reduced solvent consumption, lowering the industry's unit growth rate, especially in the original equipment and special purpose paint categories.

Traditional paints contain low solids content—they have a high share of potentially hazardous chemical liquids that can evaporate into the air—and are based on environmentally harmful chemical solvents. Although their high use of solvents makes them the most environmentally damaging, in 1995, 40 percent of the world's paint still came from this class. While the industry was moving away from low-solids, solvent-based paints, they continued to represent about 30 percent of the market in 1999. More substantial reductions were expected in the early 2000s, when consumption was forecast to fall to 15 percent of all paints by 2005 and to 7 percent by 2010.

High-solids coatings, in which solids account for more than 60 percent of the paint by weight, are an example of the industry's efforts to reduce solvents. Water-borne coatings, where the solvent is primarily water, dominate the architectural coatings segment. Use of high-solids coatings that use solvents other than water is expected to decline entering the twenty-first century.

Powder coatings, which contain epoxy, polyester, and polyurethane resins, were replacing conventional solvent paints and other surface treatments, such as porcelain. Powder coatings were sprayed on dry and then electrically bonded to a surface. Since powder coatings contained no solvents, they complied with environmental standards. Major markets for powder coatings included metal finishing, 53 percent; appliances, 21 percent; automobile applications, 15 percent; lawn and garden, 8 percent; and architectural products, 8 percent. While powders accounted for just 8 percent of the world paint market in 1995, they were expected to reach 12 percent by 2000 and top 20 percent by 2010.

While the initial cost of equipment and materials necessary to convert from solvent paint manufacturing to powder coating production is high, factors such as increased material utilization, reduced energy and labor costs, and the elimination of solvent emissions that occur with the use of liquid coatings can more than offset the initial investment.

Radiation curing, which is the smallest of the alternative processes, involves the use of ultraviolet light or an electronic beam to harden a reactive liquid into a solid. Coatings are the largest market for radiation curing, at about 70 percent, and are used on plastics paper, wood, and metals, as well as for such electronic applications as optical fibers and printed circuit boards. Radiation curing claimed just 3.5 percent of the global coatings market in 1995, and its share was expected to rise slowly to 7.5 percent by 2010.

Technological Advancements. An article in *Japan Chemical Week* stated that the Japanese paint industry has increased its technological innovations to produce value-added products to cope with the economy. Nippon Paint and Kansai Paint developed transparent powdered paints for cars and competed to develop solvent-free powdered paints. The companies also accelerated unleaded electrodeposition paint technology as an answer to a U.S. ban on lead content in paint. Japanese paint manufacturers collaborated with companies in Turkey and China to produce electrodeposition auto coatings and bicycle-use coatings, with sales that were expected to double.

Magna Paints of Cape Town, South Africa, introduced a new fireproof paint, which can delay the spread of fire for at least an hour. The paint was made of ingredients that react at only 200 degrees Celsius. New or reformulated materials for paints and coatings exhibited at a New Orleans

Coating Technology show in October 1994 substantiated that 1994 was a breakthrough year for compliant technology, especially waterborne systems.

INDUSTRY LEADERS

Akzo Nobel N.V. The number one company in decorative paints worldwide, Akzo Nobel is based in Arnhem, the Netherlands. Akzo Nobel traces its roots back to a German rayons and coatings producer founded in 1899. The German company merged in 1929, creating Algemene Kunstzijde-Unie (AKU). In 1967, two Dutch companies merged to form Koninkijke Zout Organon (KZO), and in 1969 KZO merged with AKU, and Akzo was born. In the 1970s Akzo's main business was fibers. When Aarnout Loudon became chairman in 1982, Akzo's reliance on fibers was reduced, and in 1985, Akzo sold its largest U.S. fiber business to BASF. In the 1980s, the company began a major restructuring and reorganizing operation, centralizing management, reducing its workforce, and streamlining research and development.

In 1993, Akzo sold its paper and pulp business to Nobel Industries and got it back a few months later with an agreement to acquire Nobel from a Swedish government-owned holding company. In 1994, the merger was completed, creating Akzo Nobel, the world's second largest paint manufacturer. Since the merger, Akzo Nobel has concentrated on streamlining its operations, including eliminating duplicate positions. Akzo produced chemical products, man-made fibers, coatings, and health care products. International operations grew to include more than 60 countries.

Akzo Nobel's 1998 purchase of Courtaulds, which had been the world's eighth largest paintmaker, securely placed it at the industry's forefront in terms of sales volume, a position that it had long jockeyed with ICI to attain. Based on Akzo Nobel's 1997 paint sales of US$4.13 billion, the acquisition would add another US$1.2 billion in annual sales from Courtaulds, bringing Akzo Nobel's annual paint sales to more than US$5.3 billion. The company as a whole took in US$11.87 billion in 1997 revenues. While widely diversified in the coatings sector, in the late 1990s Akzo's main product lines included architectural/decorative paints, industrial coatings, and car refinishes. The Courtaulds line brought a variety of transportation equipment coatings to the mix, such as those for ships, airplanes, and motor vehicles, among other products. While architectural paints form Akzo's largest sales segment, that category accounts for a substantially lower proportion of sales at Akzo Nobel. Architectural paints accounted for less than 40 percent of Akzo's paint volume after the Courtaulds acquisition.

In 2001, with costs for oils and other base materials escalating, Akzo Nobel was reflecting a drop in other areas of the economy when its second quarter profits dropped 6 percent to US$217 million, in spite of rising sales, according to *Bloomberg News.* In 2009, sales rose to US$18.532 billion. The company employed 57,060 people as of 2009.

According to *International Herald Tribune* in July 2008 Akzo Nobel reported a drop in earnings that the company attributed to the troubled U.S. economy. "For the remainder of the year, we anticipate weaker economic conditions in some of our mature markets and raw material and energy price increases show no signs of easing," declared Chief Financial Officer Keith Nichols in a statement. Since 2007, Akzo Nobel was getting leaner in preparation for the future. It purchased Imperial Chemical Industries for a reported US$17.5 billion, and then sold that company's adhesives business to Henkel AG for US$5.7 billion. In 2009, Akzo Nobel divested Chemicals Pakistan to KP Chemical, and in 2010, it divested National Starch to Corn Products.

PPG Industries Inc. PPG Industries, based in Pittsburgh, Pennsylvania, is the world's second-largest coatings manufacturer. Pittsburgh Plate Glass (PPG) was founded in Creighton, Pennsylvania, in 1883 by John Ford and John Pitcairn. PPG became the first commercially successful U.S. plate glass factory. In 1924 PPG revolutionized the glass production process and in the 1930s and 1940s successfully promoted structural glass for use in the commercial construction industry. PPG was listed on the New York Stock Exchange in 1945, started producing fiberglass in 1952, and in 1968 it had adopted its present name, PPG Industries Inc.

PPG's second most profitable segment behind its relatively small chemicals division was coatings and resins, which generated about 43 percent of the company's operating profits as of 1997. Operating margins in PPG's coatings business hovered in the 18 to 19 percent range during the late 1990s. PPG has 72 major plants in the United States, Canada, Germany, Italy, Mexico, the Netherlands, Spain, Taiwan, and the United Kingdom. Its brands include Monarch, Lucite, and Olympic.

Since the mid-1990s, paints and resins have emerged as PPG's largest product segment, surpassing glass and fiberglass to contribute 55 percent of total revenues as of 2003. PPG Industries found itself contemplating layoffs and strategy changes in 2001 as fourth quarter income declined from the same period one year earlier to US$83 million. Net income for 2001 was US$387 million, a major downslide from 2000 net revenues of US$620 million, according to *Paint Coatings Industry News.* By

2009, sales were US$12.239 billion and the company employed 39,900 people.

A color trends event brought together PPG color experts to share their research and expertise on global color trends. "The big hot thing—is craving for color: great big, fun colors," claimed Pittsburgh Paints "Voice of Color," Artistic Director Josette Buisson. As part of PPG Chairman Charles Bunch's vision for improving collaboration between business units, the event was a success. For 2008 through 2009, colors were linked to the "green" movement. PPG offered colors such as those found on the "Eco-Echo" color palette, including Oakmoss and Pineapple Sage.

The Sherwin-Williams Company. The Sherwin-Williams Company was born in 1870, when Henry South bought out paint materials distributor Truman Dunham and joined with Edward Williams and A.T. Osborne in Cleveland, Ohio. Sherwin-Williams began making paints in 1871, and in 1877 patented a reclosable can. In 1880, the company introduced an improved liquid paint, making the Sherwin-Williams' brand the industry leader. In 1874, Sherwin-Williams introduced a special paint for carriages, beginning the concept of special-purpose paint. By 1900, Sherwin-Williams had introduced special-purpose paints for floors, roofs, barns, metal bridges, railroad cars, and automobiles. A dealership was established in Massachusetts in 1891 that was the forerunner of company-operated retail stores. In 1895 the "Cover the Earth" trademark was first used. In response to wartime restrictions, Sherwin-Williams developed a paint that was fast-drying and water-reducible, called Kem-Tone. The company also introduced the Roller-Koater, which was the forerunner of the paint roller.

In the 1960s the company continued to make acquisitions, and in spite of doubling sales, rising expenses kept earnings flat. In 1972, the company expanded its stores to include other decorating items. However, by 1977 the company lost US$8.2 million and suspended dividends for the first time since 1885. John Breen joined the company as CEO in 1979. He reinstated dividends, restructured management positions, closed inefficient plants, concentrated company store products on paints and wallpaper, and purchased Dutch Boy in 1980. Acquisitions in 1990 included the Krylon and Illinois Bronze aerosol operations from Borden, and DeSoto's architectural coatings business. In 1991, Sherwin-Williams purchased the Cuprinol brand of coatings and two coatings business units from Cook Paint and Varnish. In 2003 the company acquired Accurate Dispersions, and the following year the company acquired Duron.

The world's third largest paint-maker in terms of both sales and volume, Sherwin-Williams is the United

States' largest paint manufacturer, principally through its market leadership in architectural paints. It controls an estimated 25 percent of the U.S. paint market. The company is divided into two segments. The paint stores segment distributes architectural coatings, industrial maintenance products and finishes, and related items. The coatings segment consists of six divisions: coatings, consumer brands, automotive, transportation services, specialty, and international. Sherwin-Williams is also the leading maker of private-label paints, selling products to Sears, Roebuck and Co., Wal-Mart Stores Inc., and other retailers.

In 2007 Sherwin-Williams reported total sales of US$6.0 billion, of which about 40 percent came from manufactured shipments and about 60 percent from its 2,700 retail outlets. Architectural paints generated about 60 percent of Sherwin-Williams' sales.

In the 2000s, as Sherwin Williams became one of a number of major paint-makers likely to face lengthy and costly lawsuits over its one-time use of lead in paint, Morgan Stanley downgraded Sherwin-Williams' worth in spite of billions of dollars in annual sales, according to *Forbes*.

Fitch Ratings verified that Sherwin-Williams' outlook was stable when it acknowledged that the company continued to be in a leading market position in the architectural coatings industry. The company earned recognition for its unique distribution platform, diverse product offerings, focus on painting contractors and property maintenance managers, solid free cash flow generation and strong management team. On July 1, 2008, the Rhode Island Supreme Court overturned a February 2008 verdict in which a jury had found that the company and two others were liable for creating a public nuisance in a lead-based paint lawsuit brought by the State of Rhode Island.

Imperial Chemical Industries PLC. Imperial Chemical Industries (ICI) was created in 1926 through the merger of four British chemical companies: Nobel Industries Ltd.; Brunner, Mond and Company Ltd.; United Alkali Company Ltd.; and British Dyestuff Corporation Ltd. The most famous of these four companies was Nobel Industries, which was created as the British arm of Alfred Nobel's explosives empire. In 1929, ICI and DuPont signed a patents and process agreement, sharing research information. ICI, as Britain's representative in the chemical industry, plunged into research. ICI's skilled chemists, engineers, and managers created 87 products between 1933 and 1935 in its Dyestuffs Group Laboratory. Soon after the end of World War II, in 1952, the ICI-DuPont alliance crumbled. Faced with new competition, ICI added operations in Germany, the United Kingdom, and the United States in the 1960s. In spite of this, profits declined, and in 1980 ICI posted losses and cut its dividends for the first time.

Under the leadership of John Harvey-Jones in 1982, ICI was reorganized and shifted production from bulk chemicals such as soda and chlorine to high margin specialty chemicals, or "effect chemicals," such as pharmaceuticals and pesticides. Harvey-Jones purchased 100 companies from 1982 until his retirement in 1987. Some of ICI's major purchases were Glidden Paints in 1986 and Stauffer Chemicals in 1987, of which it sold all but the agricultural chemicals operations. The acquisition of Glidden was one of ICI's most important paint transactions and contributed to the company's rapid emergence as a paint industry leader. The wisdom of this purchase, however, was questioned in the 2000s after ICI became entangled in Glidden's lead paint suit and its stock dropped 5 percent, according to *Forbes*.

Throughout the 1990s, ICI maintained a rapid pace of acquisition and divestiture activities. Its overall strategy was to move from a commodity chemical manufacturer to a specialty chemical business. In the mid-1990s it sold its bioscience holdings to the Zeneca Group. By 1998, an estimated 38 percent of its revenues came from its specialty chemical line, which had been expanded with the purchase of a Unilever chemical division. In 1997, ICI also sold off its polyester and titanium dioxide (a key paint ingredient) business to DuPont and spun off its majority position in ICI Australia (renamed Orica) in a public offering. It also sold its explosives business that year. By 1998 ICI was already looking for buyers for segments of the Unilever acquisition that did not meet ICI's objectives. As of 1998, paints and coatings were considered solidly inside of ICI's business strategy.

Among the company's highly internationalized businesses, ICI's paint holdings in India were a particular priority because that nation's market was growing 10 percent or more annually in the mid- to late 1990s. ICI owned ICI India Ltd., a US$200 million operation (to which paints contribute 43 percent) that held about 14 percent of India's architectural paint market in 1997. In the mid- to late 1990s, paint production at ICI India, the country's third largest decorative paint manufacturer, was growing 27 percent annually as it gained market share, although growth was expected to taper off at the end of the decade. Another facet of ICI's Indian market penetration was a failed attempt to acquire a sizable stake in the country's leading supplier, Asian Paints Ltd. The move was blocked by Indian regulators.

In 2009, company revenue was US$4.835 billion. More than 91 percent of ICI's coatings volume was dedicated to architectural paints, with the remaining 9 percent devoted to metal container and industrial coatings.

E.I. du Pont de Nemours and Company. E.I. du Pont de Nemours and Company began as a family owned gunpowder and explosives partnership in 1802. The plant grew to be the largest of its kind and within several decades added dynamite, nitroglycerine, and guncotton. The outbreak of World War I generated about US$89 million in revenues, and the company diversified into paints, plastics, and dyes. Some of DuPont's most significant inventions include neoprene synthetic rubber (1931), Lucite (1937), and nylon and Teflon (1938). This chemical giant makes a variety of products classified into six principal segments: life sciences; chemicals—pigments, paints, and refrigerants; fibers—Stainmaster Plus and Lycra; polymers—polyester resins, Teflon, and packaging; petroleum—Conoco (acquired in 1981); and diversified business such as agricultural and medical products and electronics. The company placed considerable emphasis on its life science business in the late 1990s. DuPont, which is headquartered in Wilmington, Delaware, along with its subsidiaries, conducts business in some 70 countries worldwide. Its corporate sales were US$26.1 billion in 2009 with over 58,000 employees worldwide, but coatings accounted for only a small portion of that figure. The Coatings & Color Technologies Group was the world leader in coatings for the automotive market in 2003. Nearly half of DuPont's sales come from outside the United States.

BASF. BASF is the world's largest chemical manufacturer and the sixth largest paints and coatings manufacturer. The German conglomerate has six sectors: oil and gas, chemicals, agricultural products, plastics and fibers, dyestuffs and finishing products, and consumer products. Founded in Mannheim, Germany, in 1861, BASF was originally known as Badische, Anilin, and Soda Fabrik. A pioneer of coal tar dyes, in 1897 BASF successfully developed a synthetic indigo. BASF's synthetic dyes started replacing more expensive, inconvenient organic dyes. BASF, which had been largely dependent on sales of basic chemicals, expanded globally and diversified into related businesses mainly by way of acquiring chemicals, pigments, and paint and ink companies. In 1990 BASF became the first outsider to purchase a major chemical company in Eastern Europe. In the late 1990s it moved to refocus and restructure its coatings business by creating BASF Coatings AG, a new European unit to centralize its various paint businesses.

Total 2009 sales from all BASF businesses exceeded US$67.56 billion, but paints and coatings accounted for approximately 7 percent of this total. Producing about 1.14 million metric tons of paints and coatings annually, in 1997 BASF obtained US$2.19 billion from its coatings operations, which form the largest segment of its Colorants & Finishing Products division.

SigmaKalon Group BV. Europe's second largest decorative coatings manufacturer, SigmaKalon Group BV reported 2007 sales of US$2.9 billion. Based in the Netherlands, SigmaKalon was owned by TOTAL SA until 2003, when it was sold to Bain Capital, a private investment firm. The company derived three-fourths of its sales from decorative paints, with the remainder spread out among industrial, marine, and protective coatings. In 2003, the company acquired the largest paint manufacturer of Czech/Slovak, Primalex Brasy.

The Valspar Corporation Valspar was the world's eighth largest paint-maker by volume in 2003. The company was incorporated in Delaware in 1934. In the 1960s, 1970s, and 1980s, the company acquired a number of paints, glass, and plastics firms. Valspar, with its principal offices in Minneapolis, Minnesota, conducts operations at 21 locations. It manufactures and distributes a full line of latex acrylic and oil-based paints and varnishes marketed primarily under the names Valspar, Minnesota, Colony, BPS, Magicolor, Enterprise, and Masury. Other coatings businesses include product finishes for machinery, vehicles, composition board, wiring and containers, coil applications, metal equipment, leisure products, and other specialty items. The company also manufactures marine coatings, resins for use in paint and coating manufacturing, and color tinting systems. Paint sales in 1997 amounted to US$1.05 billion. In the latter half of the 1990s, the company produced about 440,000 metric tons of paint per year, giving it an estimated two percent share of the world market.

In 2000 Valspar purchased Lilly Industries for US$975 million. This increased Valspar's annual sales from US$1.4 billion to about US$2 billion. By 2007, the company reported US$2.94 billion in revenues, with about 75 percent of sales attributed to the United States.

Nippon Paint Co. Ltd. Established in 1881, Osaka, Japan-based Nippon Paint is Japan's oldest and largest paint company. With divisions in architectural, automotive, and industrial coatings, as well as in powder coating and chemical, the company reported sales of US$2.4 billion in 2007. In the United States, its subsidiary was Nippon Paint America (NPA), which manufactured both powder and automotive coatings.

Kansai Paint Co. Ltd. Kansai Paint was established in Japan in May 1918. Headquartered in Osaka, Japan, Kansai manufactured synthetic resin paint, odorless interior use paint, tin-free anti-fouling paint and other coatings for automobiles and trains. Kansai's largest paint segment by sales was automotive coatings, which claimed more than 40 percent of its annual paint sales. The company's other product groups included architectural paints (28 percent), metal coatings (18 percent), and marine/structural paints (12 percent).

In 2004 Kansai reported sales of US$2.74 billion, up 2.6 percent from the previous year. Within Japan alone, Kansai is bigger than rival Nippon, but Nippon had the lion's share of the international market. Kansai was pursuing a variety of international ventures, notably in China, Southeast Asia, and the United States, to fuel its growth. In 2001, the company launched a 51 percent joint venture with an Indonesian company for the making of automobile paints.

MAJOR COUNTRIES IN THE INDUSTRY

Asia. In 2002 Asia used about 29 percent of the world's paint. China exceeded Japan as the largest national consumer in Asia, accounting for nearly 30 percent of Asia's paint demand due to persistent economic woes in Japan that hurt the paint industry in the 2000s. The financial crisis that began to sweep the region in 1997 also temporarily diminished demand in some parts of Asia as construction projects were placed on hold and consumer spending on manufactured goods stagnated or declined.

Nonetheless, several Asian countries presented outstanding market conditions for paint-makers, and the region as a whole suffers from a capacity shortage that makes it dependent, at least in the short term, on imported paints. The region was estimated to need 200,000 metric tons of new paint production each year through the early 2000s. As local and multinational paint firms expanded their production facilities in Asia, many nations became more self-sufficient in paint production in the early 2000s. However, in certain places, especially China, local production continued to fall short on quality as well, forcing manufacturers to import high-performance coatings even when locally produced coatings were available. Therefore, at the same time that the region's paint capacity expanded, local manufacturers were likely to move toward new, sophisticated kinds of coatings that were formulated mostly by major Japanese, European, and U.S. chemical and paint conglomerates.

By 2002 more and more companies expressed confidence in China, although some problems remained. For example, Connecticut-based Arch Chemicals Inc., noting China's annual furniture exports of nearly US$3 billion each year, has increased coatings business operations in such areas as sales and support, according to *Paintings & Coatings Industry News.*

India has proven to be an exceptionally strong paint market in the region, although a slightly volatile one, and it continues to expand its domestic paint manufacturing base. India's per capita consumption of paint trails that of other developing nations in Asia. Whereas in the late

1990s Thailand consumed 1.2 kg per person annually and the Philippines consumed 6 kg per capita, India's much larger population purchased only 0.5 kg per capita. The country's largest producer is Asian Paints Ltd., which controls about 45 percent of India's architectural paint market, representing 70 percent of the nation's paints and coatings market, and has a strong presence in industrial coatings as well. Asian Paints has a net market share of 36 percent in India for all types of coatings and possesses that country's most extensive paint distribution network. From 1996 to 2000, Asian Paints embarked on an expansion plan that would add 80,000 metric tons of capacity to its plants. Goodlass Nerolac and ICI India Ltd. are the country's second and third largest paint companies, respectively.

Europe. In 2004, demand for paint in Western Europe totaled approximately 6.43 million tons and was expected to rise about 1 percent annually to 6.81 million tons by 2009. Western Europe continued to show low growth in the high-volume decorative paints sector, modest growth in industrial coating, and high growth in the architectural paints sector.

In the mid- to late 1990s, Europe was a comparatively lackluster paint market, and the German BASF conglomerate showed significant net sales drops by the 2000s. Late decade annual growth estimates for the region ranged from 1.5 to 2.5 percent, while such segments as conventional automotive refinishing paints actually experienced volume declines in 1996 and 1997. Other segments were virtually flat in 1997, with the notable exceptions of aerospace coatings and the environmentally friendly powder and radiation-cured coatings. In a number of cases, European production levels as of 1998 were at or below levels achieved in the late 1980s. A number of environmental laws that called for reductions in the amount of paint used in certain applications as a means of curtailing release of harmful toxins contributed to Europe's slack volume demand. The same laws, however, were fueling crossover sales of powder coatings and other low-polluting formulations in place of conventional coatings. Such attention to Europe's powder coatings, which were seen earlier in the decade as a promising high-margin specialty business, has unleashed fierce competition and price slippage to commodity levels, undermining the profitability of that segment. As a result, in Europe powder coatings have achieved twice the penetration rate than they have in the United States.

The United States. The US$19 billion U.S. paint industry under-performed in the general economy as measured by gross domestic product in the early and mid-2000s. Annual growth was in the range of 2 to 3 percent and actually dropped between 1997 and 2002 with economic faltering that occurred in related industries. As in other markets, however, certain U.S. segments have been considerably stronger than the market as a whole, particularly powder coatings, which have enjoyed annual increases of nearly 10 percent. Architectural paints make up about 48 percent of the U.S. market by volume, but only 38 percent in terms of value. This segment was valued at US$7.6 billion in 2003, and was projected to reach US$9 billion by 2008. A significant trend in architectural paints has been the rise of powerful mass merchandisers, such as The Home Depot Inc. and Wal-Mart Stores Inc., which have altered the pricing and marketing equations for U.S. paints. These stores demand low prices from manufacturers and wield the threat of dumping a paint brand if a coatings maker fails to meet their criteria. Such was the case with Sherwin-Williams' Dutch Boy paint, which Home Depot dropped from its 670 outlets in 1997 and replaced with ICI's Glidden brand.

BIBLIOGRAPHY

"2004 Top Companies Report." *Coatings World,* July 2004.

"Architectural Coatings Continue to Grow." *Paint & Coatings Industry,* 1 July 2004.

Bourguignon, Edward. "PCI 50." *Paint & Coatings Industry,* 1 July 2004.

Brezinski, Darlene. "2003 Bottom Line Improves." *Paint & Coatings Industry,* 1 July 2004.

D'Amico, Esther. "On an Expedition." *Chemical Week,* 26 November 2003.

Draper, Deborah J., ed. *Business Rankings Annual.* Detroit: Thomson Gale, 2004.

"Economic Contributions." American Coatings Association. Available from www.paint.org.

Freedman, Michael. "Turning Lead Into Gold." *Forbes,* 14 May 2001.

"Fitch Affirms Sherwin-Williams' IDR at 'A'; Outlook Stable." Fox Business, 9 July 2008. Available from www.foxbusiness.com.

"Global Top 10." Paint & Coatings Industry. Available from www.pcimag.com.

Hinds, Jessica. "Rainbow Colors." *Nation News,* 5 July 2008. Available from www.nationnews.com.

"Home Sales Drive Profits." *Chemical Week,* 20 October 2004.

"Hoover's Company Capsules," *Hoover's Online,* 2008. Available from www.hoovers.com.

Hume, Claudia, et al. "Paints and Coatings," *Chemical Week,* 18 October 2000.

Hunter, David. "Getting Creative with Additives." *Chemical Week,* 24 December 2003.

Idehen, Meshack. "Imported Paints are Killing Local Brands." *The Punch,* 5 July 2008. Available from www.punchng.com.

"Indian Paints and Coatings Market—Low Consumption Offers Growth Potential—www.companiesandmarkets.com Adds New Report." *PR Inside,* 16 July 2008. Available from www. pr-inside.com.

"Industrial Paints company Akzo Nobel Reports Lower 2Q Profit." *International Herald Tribune,* 29 July 2008. Available from www.iht.com.

"International Trade Statistics." World Trade Organization, 2003. Available from www.wto.org.

Lazich, Robert S., ed. *Market Share Reporter.* Detroit: Thomson Gale, 2004.

Milligan, Jessie. "Six Paints That Won't Raise a Stink." *Chicago Tribune,* 11 July 2008. Available from chicagotribune.com.

"Mixing and Matching." *Paint & Coatings Industry,* 1 July 2004.

"New Paint Standard Defines Green Leadership. Green Seal Launches Groundbreaking New Standard in the Paint Industry." *Market Watch,* 9 July 2008. Available from www.marketwatch.com.

"Paints & Coatings." *Chemical & Engineering News,* 3 November 2003.

"Paints and Coatings in France, Germany, UK, US." *Euromonitor,* August 2004. Available from www.majormarketprofiles.com.

"Pittsburgh Paint Manufacturer Shares Its Color Research." Trading Markets, 25 July 2008. Available from www.tradingmarkets.com.

Proctor, David. "Challenges Ahead for the Chemical Industry and Its Suppliers." *Paint & Coatings Industry,* 1 July 2004.

Ruitenberg, Rudy. "Akzo-Nobel Second-Quarter Net Seen Falling 6.2 Percent." *Bloomberg News,* 23 July 2001.

———. "ICI First-Quarter Profit Seen Falling." *Bloomberg News,* 2 May 2001.

U.S. Census Bureau. *Economic Census 2002,* 2005. Available from www.census.gov.

Walsh, Kerri. "Signs of Improvement After a Mixed Quarter." *Chemical Week,* 13 August 2003.

Warrington, Hannah. "BASF Probably Had Fourth-Quarter Loss." *Bloomberg News,* 7 March 2002.

Weber, Ann. "Ann Arbor Color Expert Urges Caution With Paint." *The Detroit News,* 19 July 2008.

———. "Choosing the Right Paint Colors for Your House." *Toledo Blade,* 26 July 2008.

"Western European Paint Demand to Hit 6.81 Million Tons by 2009." *Coatings World,* January 2005.

"World Paints and Coatings Demand to Reach 28.8 Million Tons in 2007." *Industrial Paint & Powder,* June 2004.

Yeager, Kim. "Chips Ahoy," 26 July 2008. Available from www.startribune.com.

SIC 2834

PHARMACEUTICALS

NAICS CODE(S)

325412. Pharmaceutical manufacturers produce a diverse range of preparations for human and veterinary treatment. The majority of these firms' products are produced in final form for consumption such as ampoules, tablets, capsules, vials, ointments, medicinal powders, solutions, and suspensions. Industry output consists of two important lines. Pharmaceutical preparations promoted primarily to the dental, medical, or veterinary professions are called "ethical" drugs, also known as prescription drugs. Those sold openly to the public are commonly described as "over-the-counter" (OTC) drugs. Industry firms may also

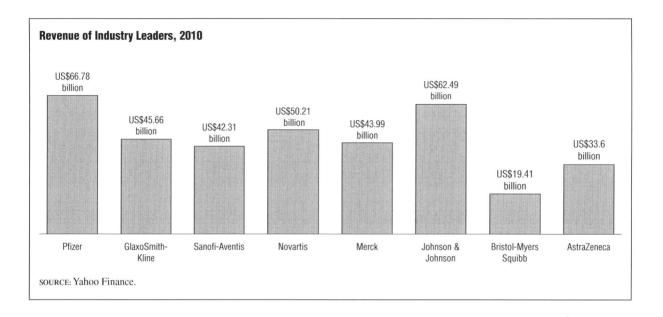

Revenue of Industry Leaders, 2010

US$66.78 billion — Pfizer
US$45.66 billion — GlaxoSmith-Kline
US$42.31 billion — Sanofi-Aventis
US$50.21 billion — Novartis
US$43.99 billion — Merck
US$62.49 billion — Johnson & Johnson
US$19.41 billion — Bristol-Myers Squibb
US$33.6 billion — AstraZeneca

SOURCE: Yahoo Finance.

produce therapies derived from genetic engineering or related biotechnology processes.

INDUSTRY SNAPSHOT

The pharmaceutical industry is one of the world's most dynamic and lucrative in terms of sales volume. Despite rising pressure from government agencies and employers to lower drug prices, worldwide pharmaceutical spending increased 11 percent in 2003. That year, spending totaled approximately US$500 billion, according to IMS Health, a company which provides market intelligence to the pharmaceutical and health care industries. Of this total, US$230 billion was attributed to the United States and Canada. By 2006, reports were that the global spending on prescription drugs topped US$643 billion, with the U.S. accounting for nearly half the global market with US$289 billion in annual sales. The European Union and Japan followed the U.S. in the global pharmaceutical market.

Mergers and product turnover continue to refashion the companies and products that lead the industry, but all of the top companies have historical ties to the industry often dating 50 years or longer. Because there are numerous specialties within the industry—numerous forms of cancer, AIDS, hypertension, cholesterol, and neurological drugs to name a few—many of the leading producers may at first only compete with one or two others on a product-by-product basis. This pattern derives in part from the enormous research costs usually involved with producing a new drug, a reality that has led many drug makers to specialize in a few therapeutic fields.

Until July 2007, Pharmerica was an AmeriSource-Bergen unit. Since going solo, it has further integrated with Kindred Pharmacy and improved profit margins. This relationship grew after AmeriSourceBergen and Kindred Healthcare combined their institutional pharmacy services businesses and spun them off. The company, energized by a growing use of generic drugs, processes and distributes drugs to facilities including nursing homes.

A source of continuing vigilance within the industry is the expiration of brand-name patents. While laws vary by country, in most world markets a new drug may be patented—that is, produced exclusively by its originator or firms authorized by the patent holder—for a fixed term. After the term expires, which is sometimes as long as 17 years, the compound is open to generic competition, and thus market forces usually bring prices down substantially from the levels obtained during the founding company's monopoly. In developing countries, they have the option of proving a substantial need that can override the patent issue and obtain cheaper versions of the drugs on a dire need basis. Pharmaceutical companies often offer the necessary drugs at no cost or a greatly reduced cost to developing countries in need.

In early 2004, IMS reported that while the overall pharmaceutical market was expected to experience single digit growth in 2004, generic drug sales would increase 20 percent, reaching US$34.8 billion. The research firm indicated that branded drugs would face noteworthy competition from generics through at least 2010. However, certain factors limit generics' ability to capture market share. Large patent holders can manufacture their own generics, force legal actions to protect intellectual property, or simply pay competitors to delay market launch of generics. A 2000 investigation by the U.S. Federal Trade Commission found Abbott Laboratories paying a generic drug maker US$4.5 million per month to delay a generic product. Occasionally, generic drugs reach the market only to find patent holders with new drugs ready to supplant their predecessors, rendering generics out-of-date before gaining market presence. However, with health care costs rising near double digit percentages, U.S. lawmakers were considering reducing patent protection times, among other remedies, to allow greater competition by generics.

IMS also shared insights about global biotech drugs prescription sales, which experienced an increase of 12.5 percent in 2007 soaring to US$75 billion. The expanding range of biotech products and their usage in multiple therapy areas was considered to be a major source of market growth. IMS forecasted that the global biotech market will evolve to more closely resemble the traditional pharmaceutical market. Highlighted key market dynamics influencing growth were identified as continued strong flow of innovative products, intensifying scrutiny by payers to demonstrate the effectiveness and value of biotech products, greater impact from product safety issues, growing competition from biotech products and emerging competition from biosimilars.

Another key issue for the industry is controlling the cost and duration of research and development (R&D). A rising share of company sales—more than 18 percent in the United States in 2002—are funneled into R&D, and development times have been on the upswing as well. The U.S. industry, the world's largest, averages 10 to 15 years to bring a new drug to the market. This is the key reason pharmaceutical companies are granted limited-term patents to produce and market their new drug exclusively in hopes to regain the cost of the R&D. As a result, a number of major firms engage in resource-sharing schemes such as joint ventures with other companies or undertake internal restructuring to arrive at a more cost-efficient workflow. Pharmaceutical consultants also push companies toward better data management. Successful manufacturers can feed back point-of-sale data to optimize current production, thus reducing inventory.

A continuing trend was the increasing percentage of marketing targeted directly to consumers. Following a softening of the U.S. Food and Drug Administration's (FDA) stance on the issue, for example, drug makers spent an estimated US$2.27 billion in 2000 on direct to consumer advertising, up 41 percent from 1999. According to a study by Harvard University and MIT, a 10 percent increase in direct-to-consumer advertising resulted in a 1 percent increase in sales.

Wall Street Journal reporter Vivek Wadhwa Washwa said the June 2008 Daiichi Sankyo bid for the Ranbaxy generic business was a forecast of things to come, reflecting that the Japanese were buying the energy, vitality and innovation of India's new research labs. Wadhwa said this signified "the beginning of a new wave of globalization." Further analysis showed India's role in the early stages of drug discovery made a strategic difference, while China was a key player in clinical trials. Indian and Chinese scientists were evolving to have the capacity for developing intellectual property. Wadhwa anticipated a world where more Western multinational pharmaceutical firms would set up working relationships with Chinese and Indian companies or acquire them.

On www.bizmology.com, the business blog posted each weekday by the editorial department of Hoover's, Inc., editor Anne Law discussed two other recent trends for the pharmaceuticals industry. The first one related to Japanese price cuts encouraging drug makers to branch out into new directions and markets. The second trend involved global countries traditionally focused on brand name drugs reaching toward new industries to balance lagging sales. This includes producing generic drugs or even partnering with other companies to streamline the enormous costs associated with research and development.

ORGANIZATION AND STRUCTURE

The global pharmaceutical market continues to consolidate. Notwithstanding high profile mergers and acquisitions by Pfizer, Glaxo, and Aventis, the single largest pharmaceutical company in 2001 accounted for only about 8 percent of the world's total market value by sales. As companies merged, they often shook off the "pharmaceutical" label for a more encompassing one—"life sciences." Many are chemical companies with separate divisions producing a wide range of products, from pharmaceuticals to agricultural chemicals.

Pharmaceutical preparations are commonly divided into two categories: ethical and over-the-counter (OTC). Worldwide, most ethical drugs are paid for by governments or consumers (patients) indirectly through third-party payers like health insurance companies.

Ethical Drugs. The top six classes of prescription drugs were central nervous system and sense organs; cardiovascular; digestive and genitourinary; neoplasms, endocrine and metabolic diseases; parasitic and infectious diseases; and respiratory.

These classes of finished-form drugs commanded the highest profit margins (30 percent of sales was commonplace), but also demanded high research and development and marketing expenses—15 percent and 24 percent of sales, respectively. Pharmaceutical firms used two primary methods to maximize the profit potential of their discoveries: marketing and patenting.

Specialized marketing techniques unique to the pharmaceutical industry evolved in the twentieth century. Since doctors usually made the purchase decision for the customer or patient, and (in most countries) ethical drugs could not be advertised to the general public, most pharmaceutical marketing was directed at general practitioners. Branding was a primary method of product differentiation. Knowledgeable sales forces made regular calls on doctors in an effort to sway their prescribing decisions. Most pharmaceutical firms also employed advertising in medical journals, direct mail, conference sponsorships, and promotional giveaways. In 2006, the top 20 pharmaceutical companies spent in excess of US$70.8 billion on research and development of ethical drugs, and over half the amount they spend on research and development goes into marketing the drugs to the consumer, with an increasing share of the U.S. marketing budget going to direct-to-consumer pushes. In the U.S. alone, nearly US$19 billion is spent annually on drug promotion.

A recent trend in pharmaceutical marketing is the rise of online drug stores and mail order pharmaceuticals. According to the pharmaceutical market research firm IMS Health, prescription drug orders to U.S. mail order pharmacies rose 27 percent to US$13.6 billion for the year ending in June 2000. The total market, including traditional retail pharmacies, rose 17 percent to US$82 billion. The typical mix of name brand to generic sales in those pharmacies is 59 percent to 41 percent, respectively. Mail order drug stores, however, typically fill name-brand prescriptions 72 percent of the time—a significant difference for maintaining or increasing brand market share. With health care costs rising dramatically in the United States at the end of the twentieth century, the FDA is also monitoring the rise of offshore online pharmacies, which offer pharmaceuticals at low prices, sometimes without a doctor's approval. The FDA bans such practices, but is unable to handle enforcement effectively due to the sheer volume of sites and the ephemeral nature of the World Wide Web.

Patenting was one of the most important aspects of the pharmaceutical industry. Most patents fell under two categories: product patents, which covered a given chemical substance, and process patents, which protected the manufacturing technique used. Until the mid-1950s, most countries found process patents sufficient to protect pharmaceutical preparations. But since circumventing these copyrights was relatively easy, many countries, including most of Europe and the United States, switched to product patents.

Although nominal patent life—the span of time from patent issue to expiration—exceeded 15 years in all countries that granted patents, effective patent protection began to grow shorter in the 1970s due in part to the often lengthy government approval process. The proliferation of so-called "me too" and derivative drugs shortened pharmaceutical companies' "pay back" period even further. By the early 1990s, all but 10 percent of patented drugs had a direct competitor, and some had more than one.

The 1962 Thalidomide scare precipitated more stringent global drug safety and approval standards. The United States had required federal inspection of new compounds since the beginning of the twentieth century and had toughened those controls with the formation of the FDA in the late 1930s. However, it was not until the 1960s that governments in industrialized nations began imposing the stringent pre-market approval systems that sometimes met with criticism during the 1990s. A German drug company had introduced Thalidomide as a "safe" sleeping pill in the 1950s. In the early 1960s, a U.S. drug company began testing the drug with a view to licensing it for sale in the United States. FDA tests observed that, when taken during a particular period of pregnancy, the drug caused severe birth defects. Although the drug never made it to market in the United States, the implications spurred more rigorous approval requirements, including clinical tests, in the United States and Europe. For better or worse, some industry observers have linked stronger pre-market regulations to the much-reduced flow of new drugs since 1960. The FDA also tightened controls in light of a number of drugs pulled from the market from 1997 to 2000. Approval times in 2000 rose to an average of 17 months, up from 12.6 months in 1999. Longer approval times shorten the effective patent protection of new compounds.

Out-of-patent or generic drugs gained considerable clout in the 1980s and remained strong into the first decade of the 2000s. Also known as multi-source drugs, generics were ethical drugs that had lost their patent protection. These compounds were then manufactured by smaller manufacturers and sold by prescription under a new brand name, usually at a lower cost. Intense price competition (30 percent to 70 percent below patented versions) and low profit margins characterized this segment of the pharmaceutical industry. Generic producers tended to limit their operations to domestic and regional markets. Nonetheless, in the United States, generics accounted for 47 percent of prescriptions written in 1999, up from 35 percent in 1992. By 2004, this rose to 56 percent, according to IMS Health figures cited by *USA Today*. Prices for prescription generics in the United States increased by 3.7 percent in 2003 and another 1.7 percent in 2004, reaching an average of US$28.71 per prescription, well below the name brand average of US$95.86.

Furthermore, approximately US$12 billion worth of name brand medications were scheduled to go generic in 2005, and still more as the patents of more medications expire. At the same time, intense competition from overseas manufacturers of generics, particularly in India, will likely pressure U.S. companies to keep prices down.

The proliferation of government funded health care programs, especially in Europe but to a lesser degree in the United States, helped promote the generic segment of pharmaceutical preparations. "Positive" and "negative" lists published by governments enumerated the prescription drugs that would or would not be reimbursed by social security programs, thereby exerting influence on doctors' prescribing practices. Managed care corporations produced formularies, lists of acceptable drugs for their members, which accounted for market comparisons on price and published efficacy studies of the drug and physicians' recommendations. These subtle methods of market control were used in most of Western Europe and to a limited extent in the United States, but not in Japan. As recently as the early 1990s, some industry observers prognosticated a massive shift toward generic drugs—to as much as 50 percent of the world market by 1995. By the late 1990s, it was evident that such a change would take longer, although the trend was decidedly toward generics.

In the early 1990s, many leading pharmaceutical producers began manufacturing their own "after-patent" versions of popular drugs by either affiliating with, acquiring, or forming their own generic firms in order to stop the profit margin squeeze. Although billions of dollars worth of patent drugs were slated to go generic by the turn of the century, some analysts speculated that the big pharmaceutical companies could retain their hegemony by introducing their own generic versions before the patents expired. Some of the largest "cash cows" slated to lose patent protection beginning in 2001 included Losec/Prilosec, Prozac, Zocor, Claritin, and Glucophage, each earning over US$1 billion in the United States in 2000.

Over-the-Counter Drugs. Over-the-counter (OTC) or non-prescription drugs were sold directly to consumers without a prescription. In general, these preparations had high advertising and low research expenditures, and few were genuinely new products. However, many over the counter medications toward the end of the 2000s were former prescription medications that had now become more main stream and considered to need less regulation. These included allergy and gastrointestinal medications.

While OTC drugs made a relatively small contribution to industry-wide sales and profits in the 1990s, they had the potential to increase faster than forecasted as consumers increasingly turned to self-diagnosis (i.e., at home pregnancy and cholesterol-testing kits) and self-medication. Prescription to OTC transfers also accelerated in the early 1990s. The British government, for example, converted 15 drugs from prescription to OTC status in 1993, whereas it had only made 11 such transfers in the previous decade. Consumption of OTC drugs

were forecast to grow fastest in developing nations, but would also remain strong in Europe and North America, as governments there transferred more prescription drugs to OTC status in order to shift costs to patients.

BACKGROUND AND DEVELOPMENT

Although some sources trace the pharmaceutical industry back only half a century, pharmaceutical practice evolved slowly over thousands of years of practical use of herbs, minerals, and other compounds. The word pharmacy derives from the Greek term "pharmakon," used by Homer in the *Odyssey* to describe a drug or charm. The discoveries of opium and hemlock have also been traced to ancient Greece. In spite of the spread of pharmaceutical knowledge throughout the Roman Empire, that civilization's decline and the onset of the Middle Ages suppressed pharmacological progress in the Western world. While Asian and Middle Eastern medical knowledge continued to develop during the ensuing 12 centuries, little of that information made its way to the West. The Renaissance revived pharmaceutical discovery beginning in the late fifteenth century. The discovery of the "New World" brought new plant-based medicaments, such as belladonna, ipecacuanha, Jesuit's bark, and cocoa. The sixteenth century witnessed the publication of the world's first pharmacopoeia, or guide to the preparation of known drugs and medicinal chemicals, in Germany. Pharmaceutical practices were professionalized with the 1617 establishment of the Society of Apothecaries in London. Some of the modern industry's largest companies grew from modest beginnings as small apothecaries, preparing treatments one dose at a time.

The modern pharmaceutical industry can be traced to the isolation and development of several potent medicinal compounds that could be mass-produced in the nineteenth century. The first of these were the alkaloids, which were derived from plant sources. Many of the powerful drugs in this group, including morphine, strychnine, quinine, nicotine, and cocaine, were still in use in the late twentieth century. The isolation of these compounds allowed for accurate dosing and testing of purity. Discernment of these drugs' chemical structure encouraged efforts at laboratory synthesis, and those experiments often yielded valuable related compounds. For example, in 1856, while trying to make quinine from aniline, William Perkins created the first artificial dye, aniline purple.

Germany, already the focal point of the chemical industry, became a pharmaceutical center as well. Researchers at chemical companies like Agfa, Bayer AG, and Hoechst AG formulated or isolated drugs from the by-products of their established businesses. Antipyretics (fever reducers) and analgesics (pain relievers) were distilled from coal tar, for example. The most familiar and enduring of these products, aspirin (acetylsalicylic acid), was discovered by Charles Gerhardt in 1853, but was not exploited until 1899 when Germany's Bayer recognized its therapeutic qualities. Hoechst sponsored Paul Erlich's groundbreaking discoveries in drug delivery and action at the turn of the twentieth century. Most notable was his isolation of Salvarsan, one of the first disease specific medicines, for the treatment of syphilis. Through investment in such fundamental research (as well as some questionable business practices), German chemical/pharmaceutical companies dominated the industry until World War I, when hostilities obliged many nations to establish their own manufacturers and research programs.

Independent research also contributed to the advancement of the pharmaceutical industry. Frenchman Louis Pasteur's conception of the germ theory of disease, combined with Briton Joseph Lister's application of that hypothesis in the use of antiseptics, has been called a "signpost to the modern pharmaceutical industry."

By the early twentieth century, patents were a familiar method used by European companies to protect their discoveries. Although the pace of drug development slowed in the first three decades of the twentieth century, the accidental rediscovery of sulphamides and their therapeutic qualities spurred increased research on the part of pharmaceutical companies, especially in the United States where original research had previously been limited.

The pharmaceutical industry followed a somewhat unique pattern of internationalization. Although some pharmaceutical companies began exporting before the turn of the twentieth century, most relied on licensing and marketing agreements as well as joint ventures to gain an international presence before World War II. Since many governments impeded the import of finished drugs with complicated testing and packaging requirements, pharmaceutical companies infiltrated foreign markets through the creation of affiliates. U.S. drug makers led the overseas postwar push through the establishment of subsidiaries. These companies could import the active ingredients from the overseas parent and then convert them into finished products under the laws of the new country.

World War II also marked the beginning of a period of intense competition to develop, patent, manufacture, and market new drugs. Many industry leaders—including Bayer and Hoechst in Germany; Roche Holding Ltd. and Ciba-Geigy AG in Switzerland; Pfizer Inc., Eli Lilly & Co., Merck & Co., Inc., and Abbott Laboratories in the United States; and Glaxo Holdings PLC, SmithKline Beecham, and Wellcome plc in the United Kingdom— were well established by this time. Fueled by intensified

research during the war, major pharmaceutical discoveries came in rapid succession. For example, methods for mass production of penicillin were discovered. Streptomycin, which was used in the treatment of tuberculosis, was brought to light in 1943. The first broad spectrum antibiotic, chloramphenicol, was discovered in 1947. Tetracyclines, corticosteroids, oral contraceptives, antihistamines, antidepressants, diuretics, semi-synthetic penicillins, and hundreds more were patented in the late 1940s and early 1950s. These developments transformed the pharmaceutical industry from a commodity chemicals business (in which pharmacists compounded the actual doses) into a field that relied on heavy investments in research and marketing to achieve the patents and brand names that drove sales. The 1960s and 1970s saw the advent of anticancer drugs, along with a nascent autoimmune therapy market.

CURRENT CONDITIONS

Worldwide pharmaceutical spending increased 9 percent in 2004, reaching nearly US$500 billion according to data from the research firm IMS Health. Of this total, nearly half was attributed to the United States and Canada. By 2008 the global pharmaceutical market was projected to exceed US$900 billion. And according to a 2007 report, global pharmaceutical spending is expected to experience an 8.7 percent annual growth upsurge through 2012, most notably in North America, Europe and the Asia Pacific region.

As the over-65 segment of the world's population continued to grow in the twenty-first century as the baby-boom generation reached retirement age, pharmaceutical companies stood to benefit from a related rise in chronic health conditions such as heart disease and diabetes. However, a number of roadblocks threatened industry profitability. In addition to an increase in the use of generic drugs, supported by expiring name-brand patents, fewer new drugs were being approved in the United States.

In early 2004, IMS reported that while the overall pharmaceutical market was expected to experience single digit growth in 2004, generic drug sales would increase 20 percent, reaching US$34.8 billion. The research firm indicated that branded drugs would face noteworthy competition from generics into the late years of the 2000s.

Perhaps the most significant industry challenge during the mid-2000s was rising pressure from governments to lower drug prices. As Ceci Connolly wrote in the March 16, 2004 issue of *The Washington Post,* "Pharmaceutical companies are facing rising anger over what many American consumers view as greed. Over the objections of the Food and Drug Administration, a few governors and mayors have begun helping constituents purchase medications from Canada, where the price can be 30 percent to 70 percent less than in the United States because of Canadian government price controls. A growing bipartisan coalition in Congress supports changing the law to make drug importation legal."

Pressure from the United States government increased during the late 2000s, following a drug benefit program for Medicare participants enacted in late 2003. In the April 5, 2004, issue of *B to B,* Richard T. Evans, a senior analyst with the New York firm of Sanford C. Bernstein & Co., indicated that when the Medicare drug program became effective in 2006, the government's portion of overall drug purchases would rise from 16 percent in 2004 to 45 percent. In fact, as Medicare Part D went into effect in 2006, revenues from the program were expected to be US$724 billion between 2006 and 2015.

Amid these conditions, a debate began between drug makers and consumers over obtaining drugs from other countries, namely Canada, where government price controls kept costs lower in comparison to the United States—sometimes as much as 60 percent. As states like California pursued legislation that would allow lower-cost pharmaceuticals to be imported into the United States, industry players argued that the practice was not safe, since quality and safety measures could not be assured. Furthermore, they charged that re-importation jeopardized research and development in the United States. Manufacturers reacted by changing the names of certain drugs in Canada, thereby creating confusion in pharmacies, and stepping up political action. In fact, some consumer groups were critical of the industry's contributions to political campaigns, charging them with "greasing" legislatures in an effort to preserve profits. The situation was further complicated in 2005 when Canada, citing the danger of potential domestic shortages, announced that it was drafting legislation that would limit bulk exports of essential drugs to the United States. By 2005, Canadian online pharmacies were exporting more than US$800 million worth of drugs annually to the United States.

During the mid-years of the 2000s, corporate mergers and acquisition activity continued at a strong pace. During the first half of 2004, Thomson Financial reported that mergers and acquisitions increased more than 43 percent from 2003, reaching US$896 billion. This high level of activity was bolstered by deals within the European pharmaceutical industry, as well as activity in Asia.

As pharmaceutical companies pursued mergers as one way to cut costs, some industry insiders were concerned about the strategy's implications. At a time when the development of new drugs was quite low, a number of observers argued that mergers only hurt the research and development process. This was because mergers often created distractions among workers as companies joined operations and concern about layoffs increased among staff.

Despite these concerns, research and development continued at a strong pace heading into the middle of the first decade of the 2000s. In 2004, Pharmaceutical Research and Manufacturers of America estimated that R&D spending increased approximately US$1 billion in 2003, reaching US$33.2 billion. That year, 86 drugs were granted FDA approval, including 21 new molecular entitles and 14 biologics. The association revealed that, among global pharmaceutical manufacturers, R&D spending was 40 percent higher in the United States than in Europe. This marked a departure from the previous decade, when European R&D spending was 50 percent higher than in the United States.

RESEARCH AND TECHNOLOGY

Because of its profound reliance on new product introductions, the pharmaceutical industry spends more than any other industry on R&D activities. An average of 20 percent of sales was earmarked for R&D budgets in 2000. According to Pharmaceutical Research and Manufacturers of America, R&D in the year 2000 topped US$25.7 billion, up from US$24 billion in 1999. Many of the mergers and acquisitions seen in the 1990s stem in large part from rising R&D bills and a commensurate lack of blockbuster drugs on the market. Those unable to keep their development pipeline full are usually the first to seek mergers. Research comes at a steep price, however. Only one in 5,000 compounds discovered actually reaches the market. Pressures from other companies, FDA approvals, and demographic trends are a few pieces of the tricky drug discovery and delivery puzzle.

Each year, only about 25 new chemical entities are actually approved for marketing. This is out of thousands being tested. This approval is the final outgrowth of years of study, test trials and heavy investment. The long and arduous process is a commitment to safety monitoring as well fine-tuning the effects of the drug. Because of this long-term process and the cost of research and development of drugs that are never approved, it is estimated that about US$1 billion (not including the cost of marketing) is needed to successfully develop a new drug. A study by the consulting firm Bain & Company reported that the actual cost for discovering, developing and launching (which includes marketing and overhead) a new drug actually rose over a five-year period to US$1.7 billion.

Although some industry representatives blamed the high cost of regulatory approval, which could consume up to two-thirds of an R&D budget, the increasing complexity of the industry's methods and goals also contributed to rising R&D expenses. In the 1980s, pharmaceuticals embraced genetic engineering and biotechnology as new methods of unraveling the causes and treatments of such complicated diseases as cancer and AIDS, which account for a major share of ongoing research efforts. Genomics or gene-based research is expected to drive up the drug discovery rate. Decisions Resources, Inc, a health care consultancy in Waltham, Massachusetts, estimated that genomics research will account for 20 percent of new central nervous system drugs in 2000. That number was expected to double by 2005. One-quarter of cardiovascular drugs will have roots in genomic research by 2000, and cancer drugs could expect to reach 50 percent by 2005. According to a report in *The Scientist,* biotech drugs accounted for about 7 percent of the pharmaceutical market in 2002 and were expected to comprise 12 percent by 2006. As of 2005, some 700 new genomic drugs were being tested, of which 200 were in late-stage trials.

In 2005, about half of the estimated 170 companies making biotech drugs were located in the United States, where manufacturing costs were high. With demand for biotech drugs expected to exceed production capacity by as much as 400 percent in 2005, analysts predicted that firms would look to overseas manufacturing facilities to boost output while containing costs.

The Promise of Proteomics? A new field of research building on genomics data, called proteomics, is the study of proteins and their functions. Once considered an unimaginably complex undertaking, the recent mapping of the Human Genome has given breadth to the possibility of understanding all known proteins and their functions through a thorough number-crunching of their genes. Although some leading scientists discount the hype around a field whose very term was coined in 1994, investors since mid-2000 have infused over US$700 million into proteomics companies, genomic companies, and pharmaceutical firms with proteomics divisions. Most in the field understand the focus on data intensive work, as evidenced by partnerships with corporations such as Oracle and Hitachi. The sheer vastness of describing a "proteome" involves data many times more voluminous than the human genome. However, small research initiatives have begun delving into small slices of the pie. Myriad Genetics, a genetics research firm in Salt Lake City, has identified 115,000 proteins derived from 157 different human tissues. With most large pharmaceutical companies already investing in proteomics divisions, it is clear that drugmakers realize the potential of these divisions to catalog and perhaps engineer proteins targeted toward specific tissues.

Race-Based Medicines. A new and controversial step in health care was taken in 2005 when the FDA approved the first medication intended for a particular racial group, BiDil. The drug, made by NitroMed of Lexington, Massachusetts, was shown to reduce heart failure deaths among African Americans by 43 percent, and was cleared for marketing to that target group. While geneticists expressed concern that the FDA was using "race as a crude shortcut for genetic typing," as *New York Times* writer Stephanie Saul reported, many African American political and scientific organizations welcomed the use of BiDil, which could significantly improve the odds for the 750,000 African Americans who suffer from heart failure. Financial analysts, furthermore, predicted that the drug might also be found to benefit other groups as well, and projected sales of between US$500 million and US$1 billion by 2010.

INDUSTRY LEADERS

Pfizer, Inc. With US$50 billion in 2009 revenues, Pfizer was the world's number one ranking pharmaceutical company in terms of sales, and the largest research-based drug enterprise with over 116,500 employees in 2010. The company's acquisition of Warner-Lambert in 1999 moved the company into a major presence in the pharmaceutical industry. Pfizer was founded in 1849 by cousins Charles Pfizer and Charles Erhart. Its first major product, santonin, was a treatment for parasites. Early in its history, the company was responsible for the mass production of citric acid, made from fermented sugar rather than expensive imported limes and lemons. It was also responsible for the successful mass production of penicillin, discovered earlier by Dr. Alexander Fleming. Its discovery of Tetracyn (tetracycline) in 1954, the first broad spectrum synthetic antibiotic, heralded the beginning of the pharmaceutical fight against bacterial infection.

Pfizer's products include Lipitor, a cholesterol-lowering drug; Viagra, which treats erectile dysfunction; Zithromax, an antibiotic; Celebrex, a treatment for arthritis, developed by Pharmacia and co-promoted by Pfizer; Norvasc, an anti-hypertensive; Zoloft, an anti-depressant; and Diflucan, an anti-fungal. In 2004, Pfizer was fined US$430 million when its Warner-Lambert division was charged with encouraging doctors to promote off-label use of the epilepsy drug Neurontin. David Franklin, a former employee who exposed the wrongdoing, was awarded more than US$26 million, according to the *CBS Evening News with Dan Rather.*

In 2005 Pfizer announced plans to acquire Vicuron Pharmaceuticals, Inc., a firm that develops anti-infective medications. Among Vicuron's potentially profitable medications were Andulafungin, a treatment for fungal infections; and Dalbavancin, a treatment for complicated skin and soft tissue infections.

Glaxo SmithKline. Glaxo was established as an offshoot of Joseph Nathan's New Zealand-based import-export business in 1873 to produce baby food, especially powdered milk sold under the Glaxo brand. Son Alec Nathan established the firm's marketing focus in Great Britain in the early twentieth century with the memorable slogan "Builds Bonnie Babies." The company expanded internationally after World War I, around the same time that it got into vitamin production. Glaxo entered the pharmaceutical market in 1927 with the launch of a liquid vitamin D concentrate, Ostelin. Acquisitions diversified the firm into veterinary medicine, medical instruments, and drug distribution in the post World War II era. Glaxo grew quickly in the 1980s on sales of its blockbuster anti-ulcer drug Zantac, and claimed 5 of the top 50 prescription drugs in the early 1990s.

Glaxo Wellcome's merger in 1999 with SmithKline Beecham to become Glaxo SmithKline followed similar pharmaceutical merger and acquisition fever in the late 1990s. By 2003, the company was the world's second-leading pharmaceutical enterprise. Its US$38.2 billion in total sales represented an increase of nearly 12 percent from 2002. Net income that year was US$8 billion, an increase of more than 26 percent from 2002. Sales grew by only 2.1 percent in 2004, however, reaching US$39 billion.

Based in the United Kingdom, Glaxo's overseas sales accounted for nearly 90 percent of the company's revenues in the early 1990s, and the United States continues to be its largest market. Although the company's anti-ulcer drug Zantac ranked as the world's top seller in the early 1990s, the company suffered predictable revenue losses when Zantac lost its patent in several major markets during 1997, and prices were halved.

The top three therapeutic areas for Glaxo SmithKline were treatments for respiratory, viral infection, and central nervous system disorders. Flagship products included Serevent, Ventolin, Flixotide/Flovent, and Becotide/Beclovent, all for the treatment of respiratory diseases. Combivir, Epivir, an anti-HIV drug, and Zovirax are leading antiviral products. SmithKline Beecham introduced the broad spectrum antibiotic Augmentin and its anti-depressant Seroxat/Paxil, to the Glaxo line. Avandia, a treatment for Type II diabetes, was introduced in 1999.

Through the 1990s and early years of the first decade of the 2000s, Glaxo continued extensive research and development of AIDS medications. With Vertex Pharmaceuticals, Inc., a biotech firm based in Cambridge, Masssachusetts, Glaxo developed two orally active HIV protease inhibitors and in 2005 received FDA fast track approval to study and develop a third.

In 2005, Glaxo entered a dual licensing agreement with Adherex Technologies, of Durham, North Carolina.

The terms allow Adherex to take over clinical development from Eniluracil, a Glaxo drug that improves effectiveness of oncology medications. Glaxo will retain rights to buy back the drug during the development. At the same time, Glaxo negotiated rights to license Adherex's tumor-fighting drug, ADH-1. The dual licensing deal was reported to be worth as much as US$200 million, plus royalties.

Elana Schor reported that Glaxo SmithKline was facing scrutiny in America after the British government inquiry finding it withheld data on the suicide risk of Paxil. Marketed in the United Kingdom as Seroxat, Paxil was the subject of suicide warnings b 2003. The British government told doctors not to prescribe it to young adults. Glaxo SmithKline added a warning about the effect to its U.S. labels in 2006. U.K. authorities subsequently concluded that Glaxo SmithKline failed to make appropriate disclosure of Paxil's suicide risk. A report by Harvard University psychiatrist Joseph Glenmullen, found Glaxo SmithKline inappropriately inflated the suicide risk of a placebo during clinical trials of the antidepressant. This concealed data hid the increased danger associated with Paxil. On June 12, 2008, a U.S. senator asked the Food and Drug Association to follow its U.K. counterpart in probing whether Glaxo SmithKline concealed clinical trial evidence. The company responded to concerns about accusations and Glenmullen's report by indicating the doctor looked at selected excerpts from their documents and jumped to conclusions.

In 2008, Glaxo SmithKline announced plans to lay off approximately 350 workers. The locations set to be impacted included U.S. headquarters in Philadelphia, the company's operations in North Carolina, and the company's worldwide headquarters in London and Italy. Anticipating the impact, the *Philadelphia Business Journal* noted most big pharmaceutical companies announced major cost-cutting efforts since the start of 2007. The companies had been impacted by severe competition from generic drugs and health scares such as the one Glaxo SmithKline experienced with Avandia. However, in 2009, GSK reported revenues of US$37.8 billion and a workforce of 99,000.

Debora MacKenzie, writing for *New Scientist*, discussed the new rating where Glaxo SmithKline ranked at the top of the list for pharmaceutical companies who treat the poor ethically. Access to Medicine Foundation released the rating on June 16, 2008. Innovest, a Dutch corporate social and environmental assessment firm, performed the assessment. MacKenzie explained how Access to Medicine Chairman Wim Leereveld made the connection between "ethical behavior" and profit. "Investors see ethical behavior as a sign of good long-term management," Leereveld said. "Also such companies are seen as being present in developing countries, where the future of the industry lies." Companies were rated on whether or not they take access issues seriously, grant licenses to patented medicines, help poor countries develop their own manufacturing capability, price drugs more cheaply in poor countries, and donate drugs and other aid to developing countries.

In 2010, Glaxo SmithKline announced plans to acquire Laboratorios Phoenix, an Argentine pharmaceutical company focused on developing and marketing branded generic products.

Sanofi-Aventis. One of the newest giants in the industry was formed in 1999 as Aventis, following the merger of Rhone-Poulenc and Hoescht's pharmaceutical, agricultural, and veterinary businesses. In 2004, Sanofi-Synthelabo acquired Aventis, forming Sanofi-Aventis, Europe's largest pharmaceutical company and the world's third largest.

Based in France, Sanofi-Aventis saw 2009 sales of US$39.09 billion, and reported a staff of over 104,870 worldwide. Top sellers for Sanofi-Aventis have included its antihistamine, Allegra, and its anti-thrombotic, Lovenox/Clexane, each of which reaped over US$1 billion in sales in 2000. Other key products include Taxotere, an anticancer agent; Amaryl, for type II diabetes; Arava, for the treatment of rheumatoid arthritis; and the thrombosis drug Plavix.

Rhone-Poulenc was formed through the 1928 merger of two chemical firms, the Etablissement Poulenc-Frères and the Société Chimiques des Usines du Rhône. Over-diversification and over-dependence on France's protective tariffs led to decline in the 1970s. Rhône-Poulenc was nationalized in 1982 by the French government after the company had endured a decade of decline. A government-appointed chairman, Loïk Le Floch-Prigent, reorganized the firm with an emphasis on pharmaceuticals and returned it to profitability for the first time in four years by the end of 1983. From 1986 to 1992, Rhône-Poulenc spent more than US$7 billion on acquisitions and sold at least 80 subsidiaries, thereby doubling sales from about US$7.5 billion to US$15.4 billion. The US$3.3 billion purchase of the U.S.-based Rorer Group Inc. ranked among the world's biggest transactions and sealed the conglomerate's position among leading pharmaceutical companies. By 1992, over 75 percent of the firm's business was outside France. In the late 1990s, the parent company moved to concentrate on its life sciences (including pharmaceuticals) business, spinning off its specialty chemicals operations as a new publicly quoted division named Rhodia. However, in the short term, Rhône-Poulenc's pharmaceutical division was delivering disappointing returns in the late 1990s. This fueled speculation that a merger or similar transformation would be necessary.

Hoechst was founded in 1863 to synthesize chemical dyes. The company was a pivotal force in the early pharmaceutical industry, supporting the development of Novocain and Salvarsan among other compounds. After the turn of the century, Hoechst also developed Adrenaline and Insulin. Hoechst was an affiliate of IG Farben, the German chemical industry cartel formed early in the twentieth century. Although IG Farben was disintegrated after the war, Hoechst continued to dominate the world's chemical industry until the 1980s. The company's pharmaceutical business grew rapidly in the 1960s and 1970s on strengths in diuretics, diabetic medicaments, antibiotics, and steroids.

Dow Jones Newswires reported in June 2008 that Sanofi offered about US$2 billion to buy outstanding shares of Zentiva. Sanofi already owned 25 percent of Zentiva, reflecting its interest in the generics business and Eastern Europe expansion. The company's major rival, Novantis, saw solid growth in its own generics unit called Sandoz. Eastern Europe countries where Zentiva made inroads were homes for upper middle income markets where drug manufacturers hoped to see growth across the board.

Novartis AG. Novartis, a leading pharmaceutical and consumer health company, had sales of US$44.27 billion in 2009, with 99,830 employees. Novartis supplied a broad range of products covering many disease areas. Key products included Exelon, a novel treatment for Alzheimer's disease; Diovan and Cibacen/Lotrel, anti-hypertensives; and Zometa and Gleevec, two anti-cancer drugs, which received FDA approval in late 2001. It also markets the controversial AD/HD drug Ritalin.

Headquartered in Basel, Switzerland, Novartis was formed in 1996 with the merger of two diversified chemical businesses, Ciba-Geigy and Sandoz, which had in fact previously been joined during the first half of the century.

Sandoz was founded as Kern and Sandoz in 1886 by Dr. Alfred Kern and Edouard Sandoz to manufacture the synthetic dyes that Kern, a leading chemist of his era, patented. In spite of early setbacks, the company expanded rapidly and was taken public in 1895 after the departure of the founders. In spite of Switzerland's isolation during World War I, the reorganized Sandoz and Company expanded quickly in the early decades of the twentieth century. Sandoz's pharmaceuticals division came to the fore in the post-World War II era, when ergotamine-based drugs Methergin (which inhibited postpartum hemorrhage), Gynergen (for the treatment of migraine headaches), and Delysid (or LSD, a hallucinogen) were developed. Acquisitions and organic expansion encouraged dramatic growth in the 1960s and 1970s. The firm's 1994 acquisition of Gerber Products

Co., the U.S. baby-food stalwart, fortified its standing in the nutrition market.

Ciba-Geigy's predecessor was founded to sell spices, natural dyes, and other organic products by Johann Geigy in 1758. The Geigy family's aggregate knowledge of dyestuffs came in handy in the mid-nineteenth century when synthetic dyes came to form the foundation of the modern pharmaceutical industry. Geigy joined Ciba, Switzerland's top chemical firm, and Sandoz in the inter-war period. Geigy and Ciba operated as competing companies during the 1950s and 1960s, expanding geographically and diversifying into agricultural chemicals. The two "re-emerged" in 1970 when intensifying global competition warranted the move. In the late 1980s and early 1990s, Ciba-Geigy invested in alternative research methods like biotechnology and genetic engineering. By 1995, the entire former cartel was reunited when Ciba-Geigy merged with Sandoz to create Novartis AG.

The year 2000 saw the spin-off of Novartis's agribusiness division to Zeneca to form a new company, Sygenta AG. In 2005, Novartis announced plans to acquire rights to Bristol-Myers-Squibb Company's over-the-counter portfolio, which includes the pain reliever Excedrin. The US$600 million deal further strengthened Novartis's position in the U.S. over-the-counter market.

According to the UN Children's Fund for Education, improvement is needed to protect and nurture African children, providing them with some of the basic necessities. On Africa Malaria Day in April 2007, Novartis delivered 4.7 million treatments of Coartem, an artemisinin-based combination treatment, to the Republic of Tanzania. "Novaritis will continue to offer Coartem to Africa's public sector without profit," said Hans Rietveld, Director of Global Access and Marketing for the Malaria Initiative at Novartis Pharma AG.

In 2009, the United States Department of Health and Human Services granted Novaris a US$486 million contract to construct the first U.S. plant to produce cell-based influenza vaccine, with the goal to have the capability of producing 150 million doses of pandemic vaccine within six months of declaring a flu pandemic.

Merck & Co., Inc. With US$27.4 billion in total 2009 revenues, Merck & Co., Inc. was among the top leaders in the world pharmaceutical industry. Merck initiated the 1990s trend toward purchasing drug distributors with its 1993 acquisition of Medco Containment Services Inc. for US$6.6 billion. By 1999, its Merck-Medco managed care program was contributing over US$15 billion in annual sales. Merck's three leading product areas include cholesterol, hypertension/heart failure, and osteoporosis. Its blockbuster anti-arthritis drug, Vioxx, tapped a market of aging baby boomers, but led the company into controversy in 2004 after a study

indicated that it could double the risk of heart attack or stroke. Lawsuits were brought against the company alleging that patients had died after long-term Vioxx use, and Congress demanded an investigation. On the day in September 2004 when hearings revealed that Merck officials had downplayed Vioxx's health risks, Merck CEO Raymond Gilmartin resigned. Merck pulled Vioxx, which had been its best-selling painkiller, off the market, and the controversy cost the company billions in sales and legal fees.

Merck traces its history across the Atlantic Ocean to Germany, where Freidrich Jacob Merck established an apothecary in 1668. A descendant, Heinrich Emmanuel Merck, started manufacturing drugs (including morphine, codeine, and cocaine) in 1827. Around the turn of the century, he sent his grandson, George, to the United States to set up operations there. The two companies were separated during World War I, when George Merck temporarily relinquished much of his firm's stock to the U.S. government in an effort to combat anti-German sentiment. After the war, the government returned corporate control to Merck, but the German and U.S. firms retained their separate entities. His successor and son, George W. Merck, established the company's reputation for innovative research. Some of the company's major discoveries included vitamin B12, cortisone, and streptomycin. Merck merged with another U.S. firm, Sharp and Dohme, Incorporated, in 1953 to beef up marketing and distribution. Those capabilities, combined with efficient production and continuing research, catapulted Merck to the top of the drug world in the late 1980s, where it remained in the first decade of the twenty-first century.

Merck's leading cholesterol drugs included Mevacor and Zocor. U.S. patent protection on these drugs expired in 2001 and 2005. The company's second largest product category in 1999 was hypertension/heart failure drugs, including Vasotec, Cozaar, and Hyzaar. A third area, osteoporosis, features Fosamax. These three categories of pharmaceuticals account for well over half of its drug sales. Cancidas, an anti-fungal, was new in mid-2001, and pipeline drugs include Invanz, an injectable antibiotic, and Etoricoxib, an anti-arthritic. During the early 2000s, approximately 14 percent of Merck's earnings came from foreign sales.

In May 2004, the company signed an agreement with DHL, an air express delivery leader, to work together to improve access to critically needed HIV medicines throughout sub-Saharan Africa. Also that year, Merck announced plans to expand its cooperation with Dutch pharmaceutical company H Lundbeck A/S regarding joint development and distribution of the sleep disorder compound gaboxadol, and to collaborate with

Vertex Pharmaceuticals to produce a compound for cancer treatment. Merck will coordinate worldwide clinical development and marketing of VX-680 and pay Vertex product royalties on sales. In yet another collaboration, announced in June 2004, Merck planned to work with Alnylam Pharmaceuticals to jointly develop gene-suppression therapies for eye diseases. Terms involved a multiyear deal with potential to net Alnylam a total of US$19.5 million, according to *Dow Jones Business News*. Among Merck's products under development in 2005 were a possible vaccine for sudden acute respiratory syndrome (SARS) and a cervical cancer vaccine.

Johnson & Johnson. With total 2009 sales of US$61.9 billion, Johnson & Johnson remained one of the world's leading pharmaceutical companies with over 118,700 employees. Johnson & Johnson produces consumer health care products as well as medical devices and diagnostics, but pharmaceuticals is its largest segment. In 1999 the company acquired Centocor, Inc., a leader in monoclonal antibody, vascular, and immunology research. By 2002, some 38 percent of the company's earnings came from foreign sales.

Johnson & Johnson's history dates to 1885 when brothers Robert Wood Johnson, James Wood, and Edward Mead Johnson founded a startup company in New Brunswick, New Jersey selling antiseptic surgical dressings. In 1891 they produced their first sterile product for surgeons. The year 1921 saw the introduction of Band-Aid bandages. With the spin-off of Ethicon in 1941, a separate business was created for surgical sutures and related products and equipment. In 1959 it purchased McNeil Laboratories, followed in 1961 by Belgium-based Janssen Pharmaceutical. Many companies followed in the 1980s, and by its hundredth anniversary, Johnson & Johnson was a well-established leader in healthcare supplies, equipment, and pharmaceuticals. Today Johnson & Johnson is comprised of 250 companies worldwide and markets health care products in more than 175 countries. Its brand names are well recognized—Tylenol, Aveeno, Mylanta, Motrin, and others. Its creation of a stanol ester designed to help control cholesterol levels is incorporated into various products under the brand name Benecol—an unusual foray into the foodstuffs market. Johnson & Johnson announced plans in 2005 to buy Guidant, a leading producer of cardiac care devices, for about US$25 billion.

In 2005, the Senate Finance Committee began investigating the company's alleged use of educational grants in the 1990s to fund a medical text promoting use of Propulsid, a heartburn medication, in pediatric patients despite evidence suggesting it was unsafe. The company pulled Propulsid from the market in 2000 after reports linked 80 deaths and 341 injuries to the product; in 2004, Johnson & Johnson paid US$900 million to settle lawsuits that claimed the drug caused 300 deaths and 16,000 injuries.

Bristol-Myers Squibb. With US$18.8 billion in total revenue for 2009, Bristol-Myers Squibb is a diversified company with interests in medical devices and household products as well as pharmaceutical preparations. Its early 1990s cash cow had been Capoten, a hypertension drug, but when it went generic, sales tapered off substantially. The late 1990s saw the rise of Pravachol, a cholesterol treatment, as well as its oncological products. Its anticancer agent Taxol was approved by the FDA in 1999 as a treatment for non-small lung cancer in combination with other pharmaceutical agents in patients where surgery and radiation therapy are not advisable. Other top anticancer names include Paraplatin, an anticancer agent specifically indicated in combination with other treatments for ovarian cancer; and Ifex, a treatment for testicular cancer. Other offerings include Vanlev, an anti-hypertensive, which differs from other anti-hypertensives by lowering both systolic and diastolic blood pressure. Glucophage/Glucovance is a successful treatment for Type 2 diabetes. The Gluco family held 39 percent of the market share as of late 2001, more than triple that of the nearest competitor.

Bristol-Myers Squibb also marketed a host of well-known OTC remedies such as Excedrin and Bufferin, and other consumer and medical products. The company garnered positive press in the late 1990s by being the first to gain FDA approval to market its OTC product Excedrin as an anti-migraine. But with prescription medications comprising the bulk of its sales in the early years of the first decade of the 2000s, the company decided in 2005 to sell its U.S. and Canadian consumer products operations. Novartis planned to purchase rights to its over-the-counter portfolio, which included the popular painkiller Excedrin, for US$600 million.

Bristol-Myers Squibb was formed in 1989, when Bristol-Myers acquired Squibb for US$12.7 billion. The older of the two companies, Squibb, was founded in New York City in 1858 by Edward Squibb. In the early years, the firm focused on the production of pure ether and chloroform. William Bristol and John Myers launched their firm in 1887 and initially named it for its hometown, Clinton, New Jersey. While Bristol-Myers (renamed in 1900) was an acquirer for much of its history, Squibb was often the object of acquisition. After the merger, the company shed many of its consumer products to concentrate on pharmaceuticals. Its primary therapeutic areas included anticancer and high blood pressure drugs. In the late 1980s, the company's Oncogen subsidiary began testing DDI, an AIDS treatment.

When the drug won FDA approval in 1991, it was released under the brand name VIDEX.

Roche Group. With about US$49.1 million in 2009 sales, Switzerland's Roche Holding Ltd. was another leader among the world's pharmaceutical firms. Some of the firm's total sales include revenues from diagnostic tests, including those used for DNA testing.

Roche was founded in 1894 by Fritz Hoffmann-La Roche to standardize production of pharmaceutical compounds. The founding family retained a controlling interest into the early 1990s. Roche had operations on four continents by the early 1910s and began synthesizing vitamins during the inter-war period. In anticipation of World War II, Roche split off its overseas operations under a holding company, Sapac. Roche created its most successful drug, Valium, in 1963. Valium, called "the world's first blockbuster prescription drug" in a 1994 *Forbes* article, dominated global pharmaceutical sales until 1981. During the 1970s, Roche was condemned for price fixing and for an industrial accident at one of its Italian plants. Problems continued in the 1980s when Valium went off patent, and Roche's annual sales were halved as a result. The Roche Group was formed in 1989 to reunite Sapac and F. Hoffman-La Roche. In the early 1990s, the firm concentrated on acquisition and R&D as its keys to growth. Top sellers for Roche in 2004 included Rocephin, an antibiotic; the anti-influenza drug Tamiflu; the obesity drug Xenical; and Roaccutan/Accutane, an anti-acne drug.

AstraZeneca plc. The April 1999 merger of Astra AB and Zeneca Group plc created AstraZeneca, a pharmaceutical and agricultural chemical products company. Total sales in 2009 were US$32.8 billion.

Astra was founded in 1913 in Sweden by Adolf Rising, Hans von Euler, and Knut Sjöberg. Its marketing of Xylocaine (lidocaine) in the late 1940s was one of its first worldwide breakthroughs. But its marketing of Neurosedyn, better known as thalidomide, under license from German-based Chemie-Grünenthal, nearly brought the company and its image to ruin in the 1960s.

Zeneca's history began in name in 1993 with the divestiture of the pharmaceuticals, agro and specialty chemicals divisions of U.K. based Imperial Chemical Industries. ICI's history began in the dyes and dyestuffs industries of the late 1850s.

AstraZeneca's top seller during the mid-2000s was Nexium, an anti-gastric medication. Its other offerings included drugs for cancer and cardiac care. In 2005 the company announced a partnership with Avanir, US, to license and research cardiovascular drugs. AstraZeneca agreed to pay Avanir an initial US$10 million, with as much as US$330 million in possible additional fees pending successful development of the drugs.

Research presented at the 2008 annual meeting of the American Society of Clinical Oncology discussed evolution of "personalized medicine." This practice plans treatments for individuals based on their genetic makeup. One example involved Genentech targeting breast-cancer drug Herceptin to the right patients by finding biomarker to identify patients.

MAJOR COUNTRIES IN THE INDUSTRY

The United States. The United States remained the world's top producer and consumer of pharmaceutical preparations, as well as the fastest-growing pharmaceutical market, with sales totaling US$216 billion in 2003. Seven of the top 15 drug companies were in the U.S. and in 2008, collectively they produced a staggering US$169 billion that year. Despite all of the challenges facing the pharmaceutical industry, analysts expected that the U.S. drug market would maintain its leadership position throughout the 2000s. Standard & Poor's projected that the U.S. market would grow at a compound annual rate of 10 percent from 2002 to 2007. The United Kingdom was expected to experience growth of 7 percent, followed by Germany (5 percent), France (4 percent), and Japan (2 percent).

According to U.S. Census Bureau data released in September 2004, U.S. pharmaceutical industry shipments were valued at nearly US$114 billion in 2002, up from US$100.3 billion in 2001 and US$88.7 billion in 2000. In 2002, the U.S. industry consisted of 723 companies. These firms operated a total of 901 establishments, 465 of which had 20 employees or more. California had the greatest number of establishments with 136, followed by New Jersey with 99, and New York with 98.

The October 2010 *IMS National Sales Perspectives* predicted that the global pharmaceutical sales would grow 5 to 7 percent through 2011, to US$880 billion, compared with the 4 to 5 percent growth pace for 2010. This IMS forecast predicts that divergent growth rates are expected for developed and pharmerging markets as countries begin to recover from the global economic crisis that plagued the late 2000s. According to IMS Senior Vice President, Murray Aitken: "We expect the pharmerging markets to continue their rapid expansion next year (2011) and remain strong sources of growth as we see the potential for several significant innovative treatment options that are becoming available for patients in areas that include metastatic melanoma, multiple schlerosis and acute coronary syndrome."

A key factor facing major drug companies in 2011 and 2012 will be the major shift once patents expire on some of the prominent drugs of the past decade. Some of the products with sales of more than US$30 billion that are expected to face the prospect of generic competition in major markets include, Lipitor, Plavix, Zyprexa, and Levaquin, which together accounted for more than 93 million prescriptions and generated over US$17 billion in total sales.

Health care reform topped the industry's list of concerns for the U.S. market starting in the 1990s, when government and popular criticism of high drug prices and profits sparked a call for controls. Although the Clinton administration's health care reform plan failed to pass in 1994, some industry observers noted that other market forces, including managed care providers—which serviced nearly half of the country's prescription drug customers—would bring about their own brand of price controls. Their effect began to be felt in the early 1990s when year-to-year prescription drug price increases slowed from 9.6 percent to 3.3 percent. Indeed, by 1996 the rate of U.S. pharmaceutical price inflation was slightly lower than that for the general economy. According to 1998 U.S. Department of Commerce figures, U.S. consumers spent an average of 64 cents a day on prescription drugs compared with 92 cents a day on electricity and US$1.05 a day on car repairs. Legislation on health care reform continued into the mid-years of the first decade of the 2000s under the administration of George W. Bush.

Since 1995 the United States has maintained a rising trade deficit in pharmaceuticals after years of trade surpluses. In 1997 U.S. exports were estimated at US$9.6 billion, while imports led at US$12.8 billion. This created a trade deficit of US$352 million. By 2004, U.S. exports of pharmaceutical products exceeded US$19.5 billion, and imports were valued at US$31.3 billion, leading to a trade imbalance of US$11.8 billion.

When Michigan Democratic Congressmen John Dingell and Bart Stupak asked for a two-year waiting period before drug makers advertised newly approved drugs to the general public, they only got part of what they wanted for policy. The time period drug makers agreed on was six months. Companies explained that the six-month time frame was already in effect due to educating doctors about new drugs before beginning to launch consumer ad campaigns. Companies agreed to follow the already established AMA guidelines for hiring actors to portray doctors. They didn't agree, however, to other requests. Notable among those denied requests was one to advertise products only after studies had shown they improved clinical outcomes. Past practices of advertising drugs approved solely based on surrogate markers were scheduled to continue.

Europe. Accounting for approximately 25 percent of worldwide pharmaceutical sales in 2003, Europe is the second largest market for pharmaceuticals. The rollout of the new European currency, the euro, in January of 2002, was seen as the beginning of quasi-national Europe's competition with the United States. The harmonization of drug approval processes in member countries is performed under the European Medicines Evaluation Agency based in London.

Global mergers and acquisitions were occurring at a strong pace during the mid-years of the first decade of the 2000s. Much of this activity was attributed to European firms. For example, the 2004 merger of French drug companies Sanofi and Aventis resulted in Europe's largest pharmaceutical enterprise and the world's third largest. The rise in market share for European pharmaceutical firms bodes well for continued competition in that market.

Europe announced its plans to launch the US$3.1 billion drug-discovery initiative called "Innovative Medicines Initiative." It provides financial grants to academic institutions and small companies to research ways to overcome bottlenecks in the drug development process. The focus will be on issues that are common to the drug development process and don't give any person or individual company a competitive edge. Europe wants to regain its status as a pharmaceutical industry leader. The European Commission is committed to contribute US$1.55 billion during the next seven years. Major European pharmaceutical companies are lined up to provide "in-kind" donations that may involve equipment and staff instead of just cash. The program will initially focus on diabetes, brain disorders and respiratory disease. Cancer and infectious diseases are scheduled for later investigation topics. The major goal is discovering better ways to predict the safety and efficiency of new pharmaceuticals. According to Reuters, this focus makes the initiatives Europeans have desired for a long time similar to the U.S. Food and Drug Administration's "Critical Path Initiative."

Japan. Holding about 12 percent of the world market in 2002, Japan ranked just behind Europe. As was the case with Europe, Japan accounted for a significant share of global mergers and acquisitions during the mid-years of the first decade of the 2000s. One example was the US$7.2 billion merger of Yamanouchi Pharmaceutical Co. and Fujisawa Pharmaceutical Co.

Japan's insular market was unique among the global leaders. Not one Japanese firm had made it into the industry's top 10 by the turn of the century. The growth of the Japanese pharmaceutical industry was based on a practice known as *bungyo,* wherein physicians prescribed and dispensed drugs and were reimbursed by the Japanese Ministry of Health, Labor, and Welfare. Japanese pharmaceutical manufacturers commonly sold their products to doctors at a lower price than the reimbursement rate, thereby encouraging over-all sales. By the late 1980s, Japan led the world in per capita drug consumption. Protectionist laws allowed the country's pharmaceutical firms to license foreign companies' preparations for domestic sale with little competition until the mid 1970s.

This provinciality came with a strategic cost, however. Japanese manufacturers lagged behind their U.S. and European competitors in R&D. Growth topped 23 percent in 1998, higher than the 17 percent rate of U.S. firms. Sales in Japan are only expected to increase 1.5 percent from 2000 to 2005, according to IMS Health.

Japan's Pharmaceutical Affairs Law, which went into effect in April 2005, removed restrictions that had limited outsourcing in drug manufacturing. The new law, requested by the pharmaceutical industry, creates a marketing authorization system similar to European and U.S. models, and allows companies to outsource up to 100 percent of manufacturing. The measure, which should enable pharmaceutical firms to reduce costs, is expected to improve the industry's competitiveness.

China. Legislation enacted in 2001, which standardized pharmaceutical drug procurement and distribution in China, was an effort to counteract a rise in drug counterfeiting and purchasing corruption. China, whose pharmaceutical market suffered under government decentralization of drug and medical device regulation, anticipates the law will provide greater open market competition. Data reported in the *People's Daily* showed that China's total pharmaceutical output reached US$54.4 billion in 2004. Even so, market share for the country's entire industry, comprised of more than 6,000 domestic companies, equaled that of only one top company, GlaxoSmithKline.

China, along with the rest of Asia, Africa, and Australia, comprises only 8 percent of the worldwide pharmaceutical market. However, China's pharmaceutical industry was poised for growth heading into the mid-years of the first decade of the 2000s, as the nation's economy boomed. By 2004, 20 of the leading 25 global pharmaceutical firms had established Chinese joint ventures, according to *Chemical Market Reporter.* As it became more modern and sophisticated, the industry was experiencing a flurry of consolidation and acquisition activity. This spurred Chinese citizens who had previously left the country, in pursuit of western education and employment, to return to China.

BIBLIOGRAPHY

Adiga, Aravind, et al. "Where to Look for Growth." *Money,* September 2001.

Beach, Marilyn. "China Opens Drug Market by Revising Pharmaceutical Law." *Lancet 257(9260),* 24 March 2001.

Boswell, Clay. "Rolling Out the Strategies of the Chemical Dot-Coms." *Chemical Market Reporter 257(16),* 17 April 2000.

Brichacek, Andra, and L.J. Sellers. "Flexing Their Budgets: Big Pharma Spend Trends." *Pharmaceutical Executive,* September 2001.

"Can Pfizer Keep It Up? Drug Giants Battle for Warner-Lambert." *Institutional Investor 34(1),* January 2000.

"Chinese Officials Stress IPR Protection in Pharmaceutical Sector." *People's Daily,* 20 July 2005. Available from http://english.people.com.cn.

"Chinese Pharma in Midst of Major Consolidation." *Chemical Market Reporter,* 29 March 2004.

Cohen, Jon. "The Proteomics Payoff." *Technology Review 104(8),* October 2001.

Connolly, Ceci. "2003 Drug Spending Up Despite Pressure to Cut Costs." *The Washington Post,* 16 March 2004.

"Durham-based Biotech Signs Deal with GlaxoSmithKline," *Herald-Sun* (Durham, NC), 17 July 2005.

"Europe's Plan to Narrow the Pharma Gap." *Seeking Alpha,* 17 June 2008.

The European Agency for the Evaluation of Medicinal Products (EMEA), 2005. Available from www.eudra.org.

"Fine Chemicals: Running at Full Throttle." *Chemical Week 162(7),* 16 February 2000.

Freidman, Katherine. "IMS Health Reports 27 Percent Rise in U.S. Mail Order Pharmaceutical Sales." *IMS Health Press Release,* London, 16 August 2000.

Goldstein, Jacob. "Drugmakers to Wait on Advertising New Drugs." 17 June 2008. Available from blogs.wsj.com.

———. "Sanofi's $2 Billion Generics Play." *WSJ Health Blog,* 18 June 2008 Available from http://blogs.wsj.com/health/2008/06/18/sanofis-2-billion-generics-play/.

Gundling, Richard L. "Discount Prescription Card Offers Medicare Benficiaries Temporary Relief." *Healthcare Financial Management,* September 2001.

"IMS Health Forecasts Global Pharmaceutical Market Growth of 5-7 Percent in 2011, Reaching $880 Billion." *BusinessWire,* 6 October 2010. Available from businesswire.com.

"IMS Health Report Global Biotech Sales Grow 12.5 Percent in 2007, Exceeding $75 Billion." IMS Health Incorporated, 17 June 2008. Available from imshealth.com.

Impact of Direct-to-Consumer Advertising on Prescription Drug Spending. The Henry J. Kaiser Family Foundation, June 2003. Available from www.kff.org.

Krauss, Clifford. "Canada Is Drafting Regulations to Curb Bulk Drug Exports to U.S." *New York Times,* 30 June 2005.

Law, Anne. "Indian Generic Firms Say, 'I Do' to Japanese Brand-Name Drugmaker." Bizmology, 16 June 2008. Available from www.bizmology.com.

Lipson, David. "A Five-Year Forecast: Clear Seas Ahead." *Pharmaceutical Executive,* October 2001.

Lowenbach, Janet. "New Outsourcing Law Readies Japanese Companies for Global Pharmaceutical Markets." OutsourcingAsia, Mach 2004. Available from www.outsourcing-asia

MacKenzie, Debora. "GSK Tops New Ethical Ranking for Investors." New Scientist, 16 June 2008. Available from www.newscientist.com.

McCook, Alison. "Manufacturing On a Grand Scale: As More Biotech Drugs Make It to Market, the Question Becomes

'Can They Be Made More Cheaply?'" *The Scientist,* 14 February 2005.

Milmo, Sean. "SKB and Glaxo Merger Creates a Powerhouse." *Chemical Market Reporter 257(4),* 24 January 2000.

Mirasol, Feliza. "IMS Reviews Pharma Growth and Outlines Future Trends." *Chemical Market Reporter 257(13),* 27 March 2000.

Nemes, Judith. "Industry Outlook: Medicare Drug Benefit, Election Hot Spots in '04." *B to B,* 5 April 2004.

Neondo, Henry. "Malaria, Diseases Kill More African Children Than Did Apartheid." *Africa Science News Service,* 17 June 2008.

Novak, Viveca. "The Assault on Generics." *Time 155(21),* 22 May 2000.

"Personalized Cancer Treatment on the Rise, Cutting Drug Speed." Fierce Healthcare, 3 June 2008. Available from www.fiercehealthcare.com.

"Pharma R&D Stats Released." *R&D,* March 2004.

"Pharmaceutical Products" Office of Trade and Industry Information, Manufacturing and Services, International Trade Administration, U.S. Department of Commerce, 2005. Available from tse.export.gov.

Pharmaceutical Research and Manufacturers of America. *Annual Report.* 2003-2004.

"PharMerica Up After Analyst Says Restructuring and Generic Drug Use Will Lift Profits." CNN Money, 12 July 2008. Available from money.cnn.com.

"Philadelphia Area to be Hit as GlaxoSmithKline Lays Off 350." *Philadelphia Business Journal,* 11 June 2008.

Pondel, Evan. "Pharmaceutical Firms Rush to Push Risks of Buying Drugs Abroad." *Daily News* (Los Angeles), 6 June 2004.

Rather, Dan, and Jim Axelrod. "Pfizer Fined Millions." *CBS Evening News with Dan Rather,* 13 May 2004.

"Report Shows Corporate Mergers, Acquisitions Picking Up in Global Market." *Kyodo News International* (Japan), 21 July 2004.

Saul, Stephanie. "FDA Approves a Heart Drug for African-Americans." *New York Times,* 24 June 2005.

———. "Senators Ask Drug Giant to Explain Grants to Doctors." *New York Times,* 6 July 2005.

Schmidt, Julie. "Generic Drug Prices Hold Steady." *USA Today,* 26 June 2005.

Schor, Elana. "Glaxo Smith Kline Faces U.S. Scrutiny Over Paxil Suicide Link." *The Guardian,* 12 June 2008. Available from guardian.co.uk.

Siegel, Robert. "Analysis: Continuing Mergers in the Pharmaceutical Industry Cause Problems for Research and Development of New Drugs." *All Things Considered (NPR),* 3 May 2004.

Standard & Poor's Industry Surveys. New York: Standard & Poor's, 26 June 2003.

"Strong Growth for Generic Drugs." *Chemical Week,* 17 March 2004.

U.S. Census Bureau. "Pharmaceutical Preparation Manufacturing: 2002." *2002 Economic Census.* Washington, D.C.: September 2004. Available from www.census.gov.

Wadhwa, Vivek. "Welcome, Global Pharma." *Wall Street Journal,* 17 June 2008. Available from online.wsj.com.

World Pharmaceutical Markets, Norwalk, CT: Business Communications Company, Inc., March 2004.

SIC 2841

SOAPS AND DETERGENTS

NAICS CODE(S)

325611. Industry manufacturers formulate personal and laundry soaps, synthetic organic detergents, inorganic alkaline detergents, and related compounds. The soap category includes granulated, liquid, cake, flaked, and chip soap; textile soap; scouring and washing compounds; and dishwashing compounds and presoaks. Manufacturers of shampoos and shaving preparations are discussed separately under **Toiletries and Cosmetics**.

INDUSTRY SNAPSHOT

Following a trend begun in the late 1990s, the middle years of the twenty-first century's first decade saw the global soap and detergent industry face tight competition in established markets and shift its focus to Asia, Eastern Europe, and Latin America for new growth. Amid a late 1990s economic downturn in several Asian markets—and a slowdown in Latin America—multinational soap makers found themselves squeezed for new markets. The tough market conditions of faltering economies in these regions, along with a slowdown in the United States, and fierce competition forced soap and detergent companies to develop new products while controlling costs and price. Many firms also looked to acquisitions or joint ventures to solidify their global position in the industry.

Among the established markets, such as Western Europe, Japan, Canada, and the United States, soap and detergent producers competed largely on price and their ability to satisfy changing consumer preferences, which varied from region to region. For example, liquid detergent sales continued to be stronger than powder sales in the United States, where washing machines were manufactured to work well with liquid detergents. However, demand in Europe for concentrated powder tablets continued to grow, especially in the United Kingdom. New products were often developed to appeal to a specific consumer region. A water-soluble capsule containing concentrated liquid detergent was launched in Europe by both Unilever and Proctor & Gamble—but was not marketed in North America.

Laundry detergents form the largest component of the industry in terms of sales value, accounting for as much as 50 percent of industry revenues in the United States and approximately 40 percent in Europe. In the United States alone, laundry detergent sales reached US$3.3 billion in 2004. Liquid detergents accounted for most sales by far, exceeding US$2.4 billion, while powders accounted for only US$850 million. World-wide, the laundry detergent market was worth about $35.8 billion in 2005, according to global market research company Euromonitor International (Chicago). Western Europe accounted for 29 percent of this total, followed by Asia/Pacific (25%), North America (18%), and Latin America (7%). Africa/Mideast and Australia accounted for only 5 percent and 1 percent of the market, respectively.

Although bar soap remained the most popular cleansing product among U.S. residents, with penetration in approximately 75 percent of the nation's homes, sales in that category were declining as consumers turned to newer forms of cleansers such as shower gels, body washes, and liquid soap. According to market research firm Research and Markets (Dublin), the U.S. market for soap and bath/shower products was worth about US$1.6 billion in 2006, with bar soap accounting for just under half of those sales. Although bar soap remained the largest segment, more growth was seen in the other segments.

ORGANIZATION AND STRUCTURE

The soaps and detergents industry is dominated by a handful of major multinational players originating in Europe and the United States. Although some are just regional powerhouses, a few leading firms are thoroughly internationalized and hold significant, and sometimes dominant, market positions in numerous countries. In most nations ,a second tier of companies usually operates on the national level and often produces for the low-price (or even generic brand) market.

Top-tier companies have found it necessary to compete in diverse global markets in order to sustain the growth rates and profits their shareholders seek. Often their home markets, such as Western Europe, are relatively saturated and afford few opportunities for growth. In a small number of cases, companies have pursued growth through acquisitions—sometimes simply at the product level rather than the company level—in order to better their stance in a particular product category or regional market. More often, however, leading soap and detergent manufacturers have battled one another for shares of these finite markets through discounting and product innovation, or have entered emerging markets where use of competitive products may be minimal.

Companies also keep track of distribution channels. Procter & Gamble (P&G) took the lead in developing a policy of everyday low pricing, reducing the traditional coupon and trade promotion discounts that retailers had long known. Such an arrangement encourages sales, especially to consumers who do not use coupons and who make purchase decisions based on in-store price comparisons. Although angry retailers initially reduced support for

affected P&G brands, because the lower prices were believed to also cut into the retailers' profit, product sales increased by about 4 percent in 1993; subsequently, about 90 percent of the firm's brands were similarly priced.

The soap and detergent industry is under pressure to reduce production costs due to rising competition from private label, or store brand, products. Though private labels continued to make inroads in the late 1990s, in most leading economies they still accounted for a relatively small share of the market.

Additionally, manufacturers deal with fluctuating costs for necessary raw materials, such as ethylene- and benzene-based ingredients. Europe, in particular, suffered from overcapacity for basic materials production, which depressed prices in that category. (Some soap and detergent makers produce raw materials as well, and thus can be hurt by low prices.) Other ingredients, notably phosphates, face environmental controversies, and some countries either have banned phosphate-based detergents or regulated their use.

BACKGROUND AND DEVELOPMENT

Traced back to ancient Rome, soap has been an integral part of human civilization. While the first soaps, made from wood ashes and animal fat, were used for medical purposes, by the second century A.D., soap was used to clean. During the Middle Ages, soap was still homemade but had developed into use for personal and laundry cleaning. In the late eighteenth century, soap evolved from a homemade product into a full-fledged industry, propelled by Nicholas LeBlanc's discovery of a method to manufacture soda ash from brine. It was not until the nineteenth century that cake soap went from being a luxury to a common-use item.

In 1806 William Colgate founded a company to make soap, starch, and candles. By 1906 the firm was producing 160 different types of soaps. In 1876 Fritz Henkel formed Henkel & Cie in Aachen, Germany, to manufacture a universal detergent. Just two years later, he launched "Henkel's Bleaching Soda." As early as the 1880s, Henkel was making water glass—a detergent ingredient. Henkel's "Persil" (a brand name later used by Unilever) eliminated the need to rub or bleach clothes and was brought to market in 1907.

William and James Lever presented the first packaged, branded laundry soap, Sunlight, in 1895. Initially serving Britain, Lever Brothers, the predecessor of today's Unilever, was marketing soaps in the United States, South Africa, and Australia less than 20 years later. Another industry milestone occurred in 1898 when J.B. Johnson launched Palmolive soap, which used palm and olive oils.

The worldwide soaps and detergents industry grew rapidly in the twentieth century. However, as with many other areas of life, it was forever changed during World War II when natural ingredients for soap became rare. Synthetic detergents were developed as substitutes for all soaps except those used for personal bathing. By the 1950s detergents surpassed the use of soaps in laundering and dishwashing. While the majority of the manufacturers sold their products in traditional markets, companies such as Amway Corp. revolutionized the industry when distributors sold products in-home rather than via traditional retail methods.

Heading into the 2000s, consumers throughout the world were demanding more than mere cleansing properties from soap products. Bath and shower products, worth US$20.5 billion in 2003, continued to meld with those traditionally found in the skin care category as people looked for soaps that exfoliated, moisturized, and toned their skin. In addition, a growing number of people looked for soaps that offered certain emotional benefits, namely relaxation. For example, a number of specially scented soaps offered so-called aromatherapy to bathers, or a "spa at home" experience. Some industry observers correlated the popularity of these products to rising levels of stress.

P&G and Unilever continued to hold a leading market share in the detergents sector. According to data from Chicago-based research firm Information Resources Inc., in 2003 U.S. laundry detergent sales totaled US$3.2 billion, US$2.4 billion of which was liquid detergent and US$869 million of which was powder. P&G's detergent sales were approximately US$2.0 billion, accounting for nearly 62 percent of all detergent sales. Unilever's sales totaled US$465 million, representing 14.5 percent of all sales. Together, the two companies controlled a sizable share of the broad personal care and household cleaning products industry. With sales growth tepid in many established markets, though, detergent companies sought product enhancements, such as new fragrances, that would strengthen the performance of leading brands. In 2005 Procter & Gamble introduced Tide with a Touch of Downy, which combined detergent with fabric softener. Company executives described this move as the biggest initiative since the introduction of Tide with Bleach in 1980.

Bar soap remained the most popular cleansing product among U.S. residents in 2003, with penetration into approximately 75 percent of the nation's homes. In its March 22, 2004 issue, *Mass Market Retailers Magazine* (*MMR*,) a global news source for the supermarket, drug, and discount chains, cited data from Information Resources Inc., a Chicago-based research firm, placing sales of bar soap at US$857.5 million for the 12 months ended

January 25, 2004. Of this total, non-deodorant soaps accounted for nearly 57 percent of sales, with the remaining 43 percent attributed to deodorant soaps. In the non-deodorant category, there were a number of clear brand leaders. These included Dove, with sales of US$219.4 million, Caress (US$50.5 million), Ivory (US$40.3 million), and Olay (US$33.7 million). Together, these four soaps accounted for nearly 71 percent of all non-deodorant bar soap sales.

As competitors tried to chip away at the leaders' shares during the early years of the first decade of the 2000s, the industry experienced an increase in merger and acquisition activity. In October of 2003, P&G announced that it would acquire the European detergent business unit of Colgate-Palmolive. Two years before, in 2001, Church & Dwight Co. Inc. purchased USA Detergents, increasing its U.S. laundry detergent market share to 9 percent and securing its position as the third-largest supplier in the United States.

The biggest merger of 2004 was Henkel KGaA's US$2.9 billion acquisition of Dial, which had put itself up for sale due to low earnings and increased competition. Henkel had previously established a joint venture with The Dial Corp. in 1999 to gain access to the U.S. market, but the deal was terminated in early 2001. Despite this, other joint ventures continued between the two companies, including one to market detergent tablets in the United States and one devoted to dry cleaning. The Dial acquisition contributed to a 20.8 percent increase in third-quarter sales for Henkel. In addition to its relationship with Dial, in 2000 Henkel had purchased the Mexican heavy-duty detergents business of Colgate-Palmolive and also acquired a majority interest in Pemos, a soap and detergent manufacturer based in Russia.

One leading trend in personal soaps during the first decade of the 2000s was the use of gels or body washes in place of conventional bar soap. These products have been especially successful in Japan and the United States. Manufacturers also prefer them because they allow more flexible formulations than do solid bars. According to Euromonitor data reported in *Global Cosmetic Industry*, worldwide sales of liquid soaps, body washes, and shower gels grew by 15 percent in value in 2003. By contrast, sales of bar soap fell by 4 percent. A related development has been the adoption of antibacterial soaps, which are marketed as convenient and effective preventives against tactile germ transmission. U.S.-based Dial Corp. is a major producer in this category. Compounds with similar properties have been offered in the dishwashing segment of the market.

Instant foaming hand soaps, which were introduced in 2001, were another important product development during the 2000s' first decade. In its February 2003 issue,

Soap & Cosmetics reported that foaming hand soaps had been introduced throughout the world by a number of industry leaders. Dial was among the first companies to introduce a foaming product, with its Dial Complete antibacterial foaming hand wash. Other product introductions included Colgate-Palmolive's Softsoap Foam Works, as well as products from Bath & Body Works. In addition to a foaming hand soap, Johnson & Johnson also unveiled a foaming hair detangler product for children. Foaming hand soaps also experienced adoption in other world markets, especially in Europe. In addition to the introduction of Carex Gentle Foaming Handwash by the United Kingdom's Cussons, Italy's Manetti & Roberts began introducing foaming hand soap products to the European market.

Going beyond the consumer sector, foaming hand soaps have made institutional inroads as well. In addition to adoption in restaurant, conference center, and shopping store bathrooms, foaming hand soap was being used by the airline industry. For example, Celeste Industries Corp., which supplies a number of international airlines, began offering its clients mechanical foamers for use in restroom cabins.

CURRENT CONDITIONS

Heading into the late years of the first decade of the 2000s, challenges for the soap and detergent industry included high energy, freight, and raw material costs. Although raising prices helped some producers offset costs, according to a report in *Chemical Week*, it was not enough. As a result, some companies turned to alternative energy and raw material sources. For example, Proctor & Gamble signed a US$1.8 billion contract with an Indonesia olechemical plant in 2006. (Oleochemicals are ingredients derived from the fats and oils of plants.) According to the firm, the plant will produce more than 200,000 tons a year of fatty alcohols, fatty acids, and glycerine, which will be used as raw materials in its shampoo and laundry detergents. Proctor & Gamble also had planned a joint venture with an olechemical plant in Malaysia. According to chemical marketing and technology consulting firm Colin A. Houston Associates, in 2007 expanded olechemical units in Indonesia, Malaysia, Thailand, the Philippines, China, and India would produce an additional 960,000 tons of detergent-grade long-chain alcohol products per year.

Many suppliers were focusing on innovation to increase their profit margins. In a January 30, 2009 article in *Chemical Week*, according to David Del Guercio, senior vice president and general manager of consumer specialties and household care at U.S.-based Evonik Goldschmidt Gmbh, an industrial and consumer chemical products company, watching consumer trends could help manufacturers of detergent and soaps create new products that were in demand. Said Del Guercio, "In addition to laundry detergents with bleach, we are seeing versions with fabric softener, for cold wash, for dark color wash, and with multiple fragrances and additives to enhance freshness." Mild detergents for people with sensitive skin were also in increased demand. On the other hand, fragrance was one of the fastest-growing sectors of the detergent market. According to the Freedonia Group, a global industrial research company based in Cleveland, Ohio, demand for detergent fragrances will increase about 9 percent to $265 million by 2009. Producers were also churning out more sophisticated fragrances, such as Seaside Escape and Sunshine Clean (from Henkel's Purex line).

Another detergent market trend in the mid-years of the first decade of the 2000s was the increased demand for biodegradable surfactants. Growth in this market was especially strong in Europe, where the European Union's Detergent Directive was enacted in 2005. The initiative requires all detergent and cleaning products to be biodegradable and derived from renewable resources.

RESEARCH AND TECHNOLOGY

Increased environmental concerns have led this industry to be constantly involved in research and technology, including the development of concentrated formulas and refillable containers. Leading environmentalists have called for an end to the pollution-causing detergent foam residues that coat the globe's waters. The problem is that while soap molecules break down, the molecules in synthetic detergents are too complicated to allow for similar breakdown. Manufacturers resolved this environmental issue by changing the structure of the hydrocarbon properties in soap ingredients.

Since the early 1950s, detergents containing phosphates have been causing water pollution. That problem was eased as manufacturers found biodegradable substitutes for detergent ingredients that were not harmful and allowed the phosphates to be more easily broken down and absorbed. In hard water, which contains major amounts of dissolved mineral salts, the molecules in the water can respond to the salts and form the notorious gray tub ring.

In the early 1990s Procter & Gamble introduced N-methyl glucosamide in its liquid detergents. This sugar-based surfactant is similar to the alkyl polygylcosides (APG) introduced by Henkel KGaA in 1992. The P&G product "is being marketed based on its biodegradability and claims of mildness," according to Robert Westervelt in *Chemical Week*. In 199, P&G brought to market its reformulated Tide with Carezyme.

Specific formulations to ensure that soap and detergents manufacturers' needs are met are underway. The U.S. surfactant industry grew almost 5 percent in 1994. However, petrochemical and oleochemical raw material costs grew in the second half of 1994. There is movement in the surfactant industry to use multifunctional raw materials to minimize chemical content. Specific and directed applications, such as hotel, restaurant, or a manufacturing facility's laundry, present separate and unique cleaning problems. This means that ingredient suppliers must work closely with industry customers.

Surfactant manufacturers developed several new products in the early years of the first decade of the 2000s to meet environmental and consumer concerns. Biosil Technologies, based in New Jersey, pioneered innovations in the use of silicone in surfactant systems. Its Biosil Basics Cocosil, as described by Nancy Jeffries in *Global Cosmetic Industry,* is "an amphoteric surfactant that is complexed with a silicone to yield a highly effective mild surfactant with softening and conditioning properties." Another surfactant company, Cognis, introduced Plantapon[R]LC 7, as well as a biodegradable surfactant from corn, which is useful in dishwashing detergents. Uniqema Americas has developed Avanel[R]150 CG, a mild surfactant suitable for facial washes for sensitive skin and acne. According to Jeffries, these new formulations will continue to offer the soap and detergent industry materials that "will target specific areas and specialized surfactants [that] will not only work to clean, but will protect, rebuild and even moisturize with a highly edited and diversely sourced ensemble of ingredients and system orchestration."

The next major laundry detergent innovation will likely be fueled by the adoption of new, energy-efficient washing machines. Such machines will use less water and electricity and will have lower water temperatures than their predecessors. However, they will require different detergent formulations that can function in reduced water and different machine cycles. In the low-water, low-temperature environment, detergents must be more soluble since they need to dissolve more easily, because both decreased temperature and less water reduce the rate at which detergent is dissolved. Current detergents would tend to leave residues or particles if used in such a process.

The introduction of foaming hand soaps in the early years of the first decade of the 2000s, according to an article by Martin Kleinman in the February 2003 issue of *Soap & Cosmetics,* was made possible by the development of new mechanical foam dispensers, which release soap with one touch. "These are proven, precision-engineered, high-performance engines that provide instant, perfect foam without the use of chemical propellants," explained Kleinman. "They allow a precise mixture of liquid and air with a single stroke of a smooth-action button. Their sophisticated valve technology ensures reliability and ease-of-use. The consumer gets soft, creamy foam from just one stroke of the pump. With state-of-the-art units now available, even shaking the product before use does not affect the quality of the foam. The foam is instant, easy to spread, easy to rinse and seems to wash better."

"An additional advantage to product developers and consumers alike is that these premium pumps can be fully filled and emptied completely, thanks to the design of the dip tube," continued Kleinman. "Further, product manufacturers can select from an appealing range of custom colors and container shapes, including square, triangular, domed, oval or flat."

INDUSTRY LEADERS

Unilever. One of the top-ranked companies in the soaps and detergents industry is Unilever, which has two headquarters: Unilever PLC, in London, and Unilever NV, based in Rotterdam. With US$40 billion in 2007 sales, the company and its affiliates were market leaders in many categories throughout Europe, North America, and parts of the Pacific Rim. Unilever reported having approximately 174,000 employees in about 100 countries.

During the 1990s, Unilever was plagued by competitive blunders, such as the Persil debacle in Europe and loss of market share to Procter & Gamble and other competitors. The Persil incident involved negative advertising by P&G promoting the discovery that Unilever's Persil detergent actually damaged fabrics. The embarrassing episode caused Unilever to reformulate its product, but it never recovered the lost market share. In the 1990s critics also charged that the company remained bloated and inefficient, prompting a number of restructuring initiatives.

These conditions led the company to implement its *Path to Growth* program, which involved reducing the number of brands to 400—down from 1,600—through a series of more than 50 divestment. It also created two major business segments, food and nonfood products. By 2003 the company's brand reduction strategy was well underway and its Home and Personal Care division, which includes such leading brands as Lifebuoy and Dove, accounted for nearly 43 percent of sales. Although growth in the laundry detergent category was flat that year, a number of the company's soap brands experienced double-digit growth. Dove, in particular, was a standout, achieving a remarkable growth rate of 21 percent.

However, by 2005 Unilever was forced to admit that its expectations for *Path to Growth* had not been met. Faced with tough market conditions, particularly in

Europe, total sales for the company in 2004 grew by only 0.4 percent, with top brands growing by only 0.9 percent. Nevertheless, Unilever's personal care segment performed relatively well in 2004, making the company the global leader in skin cleansers through brands such as Dove and Lifebuoy. On the other hand, detergents saw declining revenues, due primarily to lower prices. Despite gains for detergents in developing markets, declines in Europe and North America contributed to an overall decrease in market share for this segment. After Unilever's overall poor performance in 2004, the company announced a major corporate reorganization. One result was its sale in 2005 of its cosmetics unit to Coty for approximately US$800 million.

Unilever was founded in 1895 by William Hesketh Lever and his brother, James. Under the Lever Brothers name, they manufactured Sunlight, the first packaged and branded laundry soap and sold initially in Britain. A decade and a half later, the company was marketing its soap in the United States, South Africa, and Australia. Between 1906 and 1915, Lever acquired soap companies in Australia, Britain, and South Africa. The company also entered the plantation and trading company business to fill its requirements for vegetable oil, an ingredient in soap. Lever also expanded, dominating the U.S. market until 1946 when Proctor & Gamble introduced Tide, the first synthetic detergent. In Europe, however, Lever enjoyed resurgence and found markets green for new detergents, personal care products, and margarine. Along with the company's home and personal care products, it stands as a leading food concern in the global diversified foods industry.

When the going gets tough, the tough get going with high powered marketing campaigns. Tremendous activity in the lower-end segment led to an intense manufacturers' brand war, reported Abyssinia Lati. Unilever has been attracting attention with its campaign for its detergent Omo that was relaunched with "Multi Active" in 2006. In a sense, the company's own Sunlight low cost brand is a competitor for both detergents and bar soaps. Lati discussed AC Nielsen research study results related to market share volumes in detergents. A snapshot for March-April 2009 showed Omo's market share was at 42.6 percent while Sunlight was at 13.7 percent. The company's overall sales totaled US$54.4 billion in 2006.

The Procter & Gamble Company. Procter & Gamble (P&G), the leading U.S. manufacturer of household products, is responsible for a variety of soaps and detergents, including Ivory and Tide. The Cincinnati-based company was founded in 1837 by William Procter, a candle maker, and James Gamble, a soap maker. In 1879 they produced Ivory, touted as the "floating soap." This represented one of the first direct-to-the-consumer advertising campaigns.

Procter & Gamble was also responsible for the development of radio and television soap operas. In fact, Tide detergent was first introduced on a radio soap opera in 1947. P&G was a family-headed company until 1930, when William Deupree was named president and later chairman. Deupree helped steer the company to its position as the biggest producer of packaged consumer goods in the United States.

Procter & Gamble is a highly savvy competitor in all of its markets, a trait that has helped it maneuver market position away from established players when it enters new markets. P&G introduced Bold laundry detergent in Japan during August 2002, which captured almost 10 percent of the market and helped the company corner nearly 30 percent of the Japanese detergent market overall. P&G has also stepped up its presence in China. The company speculated that its sales in developing markets could reach US$70 billion by the early years of the second decade of the 2000s, equaling its sales in Western Europe and North America.

In 2006 P&G registered total sales of more than US$68.2 billion, up 20.2 percent from the previous year. In 2005 the firm purchased Gillette, the world leader in shaving supplies, in the company's biggest deal ever. By 2009, P&G's workforce had grown to 135,000 employees with sales of US$79 billion.

In her August 6, 2009, article in *The Wall Street Journal*, Ellen Byron describes Proctor & Gamble's decision to test Basic Tide in approximately 100 stores in southern U.S. states as a complicated one and a lesson in how Procter & Gamble was dealing with such issues as brand loyalty, maximum capabilities and effectiveness, product packaging and cost factors. Economic challenges for budget-conscious shoppers meant they were not always willing to pay premium prices when viable alternatives were present. Almost as good a product might get the job done well enough. Tide, however, had dependable sales with a loyal customer base adding up to an excess of US$3 billion of Proctor & Gamble's US$79 billion annual revenues. Nonetheless, executives started to seriously consider options for launching Basic Tide in November 2008. The company had previously sold low-end brands but spent minimal advertising efforts or dollars on them. As store or private label brands gained customers, major brands felt the impact. The Proctor & Gamble response involved creating a "portfolio" of products. That means there may be several versions of a product covering a price range. Since its launch in 1946, Byron claimed Tide had been promoted as "the first heavy-duty synthetic detergent, a technological breakthrough superior to all other soap." Tide Basic being tested in the marketplace by August 2009 was a product that Procter & Gamble admitted was inferior to the original. This being the case, Tide Basic was not deemed worthy of the orange color linked to traditional packaging for popular Tide family items. Test results would dictate whether there would be a massive rollout of the product encased in yellow and blue that was a new but not improved variation.

Henkel KGaA. Serving more than 125 countries in 2009, Henkel was continuing its tradition of sales and service from a Düsseldorf, Germany headquarters. Reported sales and employees for 2008 were US$19.9 billion and 52,303 respectively. The company's European operations account for nearly 70 percent of sales. Fritz Henkel formed Henkel & Cie. in 1876 in Aachen. Two years later he launched "Henkel's Bleaching Soda," credited as one of Germany's first brand name products. As early as the 1880s, Henkel was making water glass, a detergent ingredient.

By the 1920s Henkel was using newly introduced phosphates in its cleaning products. Henkel purchased Deutsche Hydrier-werke and Bohme Fettchemie. The latter had introduced a revolutionary synthetic detergent. Although most of Henkel's foreign holdings were lost during World War II, the company continued producing homemade soap. From the 1950s through the 1960s, Henkel was embroiled in a four-way battle with Colgate-Palmolive, P&G, and Unilever for market share on its home turf. While Henkel earned the number two position on some occasions, by 1968 it had rebuffed the triad and had a firm hold on 50 percent of Germany's soap and detergent business.

Henkel entered the U.S. market in 1960 when it acquired Standard Chemicals. The company earned a patent on a phosphate substitute and in 1971 acquired the chemical business division of General Mills Corp. Subsequent acquisitions included Nopco, a specialty chemical business; Ford Motor Co.'s Parker Chemical division; a metal surface pretreatment operation; and Emery, a leading oleochemicals manufacturer.

Henkel's largest national market consistently remains its home country, Germany, which is Europe's largest. While it holds a commanding position throughout much of the European market, Henkel was noticeably absent from the U.S. market until 2004, when it purchased the Dial Co. The company attributed much of the 28.9 percent growth in its laundry and home care sector in 2004 to the performance of its Dial and Clorox products. Henkel posted total sales just below US$20 billion in 2008.

In an August 2009 look at the German export business and economic situation, Jana Randow, writing for Bloomberg.com, included a brief update from Henkel AG. The company reported that "second-quarter profit

more than tripled." In addition, there was also a forecast calling for "slightly better" performance for its adhesive unit through November 2009. Major products for Henkel include Loctite glues and Persil detergent.

Kao. Kao Corporation is Japan's leading producer of soaps and detergents. Like Henkel, it has established itself primarily as a regional player. As behemoths like Unilever and P&G have focused on Asia, including Japan, Kao has seen its market share shrink at home and has faced stiffer competition in neighboring countries. Kao participates in the U.S. soap market chiefly through its Andrew Jergens Company subsidiary. For the fiscal year 2008, ending March 31, 2009, Kao posted revenues of almost US$13 billion. Its main brands included the laundry detergent Attack and dishwashing detergent Family Power Gel. As a result of increased competition, Kao was focused on increasing brand loyalty and strengthening its core products in the new millennium. An attempt to bolster its presence in the Japanese beauty segment by acquiring Kanebo ended in February 2004. Kao also participates in other industries, such as specialty chemicals, edible oils, and blank recording media.

Dial Corporation. With one of the United States' best selling bar soaps, Dial Corporation has emerged far from its roots. In 1914 Carl Eric Wickman used a passenger car to transport miners between the mines and a saloon. He expanded his transportation services and began working under the label of Northland Transportation in 1925. In 1928 his company added on the Great Northern Railroad and continued to add transit lines. In 1930 Northland Transportation changed its name to Greyhound and moved its headquarters to Chicago. In 1970 Greyhound acquired Armour & Co. for US$355 million. Not only did Greyhound pick up Armour's meat products, but it also acquired Dial, a leading U.S. deodorant soap.

Dial's 2004 sales reached US$1.3 billion, 4.9 percent above sales in 2003. During the early years of the first decade of the 2000s, the company's Dial brand and other soap products had a 20 percent market share in the U.S. soap industry. Its namesake Dial brand held status as the United States, leading antibacterial soap, with sales of some 1 million bars each day. In addition, Dial Corp.'s Purex laundry detergent was the nation's second-best-selling detergent brand. Dial became a subsidiary of Germany's Henkel KGaA in March 2004.

Colgate-Palmolive Company. The world leader in toothpaste and oral care products, Colgate-Palmolive also produces bar soaps, liquid soaps, and dishwashing and laundry detergents, as well as pet nutrition. Top brands include Irish Spring, Softsoap, Ajax, and Palmolive. Founded by William Colgate in 1806, Colgate & Company began as a manufacturer of chemical soaps and perfumes. One of its first products was Cashmere Bouquet, a perfumed bar soap, introduced in 1872. A year later the company introduced its first toothpaste; Colgate eventually discontinued its perfume operations. A rival company, B.J. Johnson Soap, introduced Palmolive Soap in 1898. The product, made from palm and olive oils instead of animal fats, was such a marketing success that the manufacturer changed its name to Palmolive. After merging with Kansas-based Peet Brothers, Palmolive became Palmolive-Peet. In 1928, a merger with Colgate resulted in the Colgate-Palmolive-Peet Company, later renamed Colgate-Palmolive.

To compete with rival P&G during the early years of television, Colgate-Palmolive sponsored afternoon soap operas, and was the sole sponsor of the program *The Doctors*. Among Colgate's popular early brands was Octagon, a laundry and all-purpose cleaning soap. In 1991 Colgate acquired Murphy Oil Soap, the top-selling wood cleaning product in the United States. By the early years of the first decade of the 2000s, Colgate operated in more than 200 countries and derived more than 70 percent of sales from international operations.

In 2005 the company finalized plans to sell its North American laundry detergent brands, including Fab, Cold Power, Dynamo, ABC, Arctic Power, and Fresh Start, to Phoenix Brands. Colgate posted total sales of US$15.3 billion in 2008, with 35,800 employees.

MAJOR COUNTRIES IN THE INDUSTRY

The United States. In 2004 the United States exported US$7.7 billion worth of soaps, cleaners, and toilet preparations; imports were valued at US$5.3 billion. Soap accounted for US$342.2 million in exports and US$427.1 in imports. Exports of detergents and cleaning agents reached US$1.6 billion, while imports were valued at US$608.3 million.

The U.S. market leader remained Procter & Gamble, maker of the top-selling detergent in both liquid and powder categories, Tide. Combined U.S. sales for Tide reached about US$1.2 billion in 2006. Unilever, Dial Corporation, Church & Dwight, and Colgate-Palmolive Co. were the other major companies in the detergent segment. Regarding the sale of soap, in 2006 the United States saw deodorant bar soap sales decline 10.8 percent, whereas non-deodorant bar soap sales increased 2.6 percent. However, sales of liquid hand soap saw even greater growth of about 7.4 percent, to US$260.1 million, and other liquid soaps increased 9 percent to about US$569 million. Irish Spring was the top-selling deodorant bar soap in the United States, garnering US$45.7 million in sales in 2006, followed most closely by Dial (US$44.2 million) and Lever 2000 (US$43.5 million). Along with

private labels sold by stores such as Wal-Mart, soaps and detergents are sold through distribution.

Japan. According to the March 25, 2003, issue of *Cosmetics & Toiletries & Household Products Marketing News in Japan,* figures from Japan's Ministry of Economy, Trade, and Industry revealed that sales volume within the Japanese soap and detergent industry was Yen 469.5 billion in 2002, an increase of 4 percent from the previous year. Of this total, solid bath soaps, liquid hand soaps, and other soaps totaled 12 percent of all sales. Synthetic detergents, including liquid and powder laundry soaps, represented about 55 percent of all sales. The remainder was attributed to fabric softeners, bleaches, acid/alkaline cleansers, and powder/liquid cleansers. According to the Japan Soap and Detergent Association, demand for special-care detergents, such as products for delicate or dry-clean-only fabrics, was growing significantly early in the first decade of the 2000s.

The Japanese market in the 1990s and the early years of the first decade of the 2000s was stable but not rapidly growing, owing to persistent recessive conditions in Japan's economy. Despite inroads made by P&G, Kao still controlled a majority share of the Japanese detergent market. Tokyo-based Lion Corporation joined Kao in that arena.

Europe. In its February 2003 issue, *Soap Perfumery & Cosmetics* reported that, on average, 64 percent of the population of the Big 5 European countries use shower gel each week, making it Europe's leading washing product. This especially was the case in Germany. Citing data from global market research firm Taylor Nelson Sofres, the publication indicated that shower gel had a market penetration of 63.8 percent in late 2002, followed by bar soap (52.3 percent), liquid soap (32.1 percent), bath liquids (21.6 percent), bath foam (17.1 percent), washes and scrubs (10.7 percent), all-over shampoo (7.2 percent), and body washes (2.2 percent). In 2002, Euromonitor reported that the bath and shower market was worth US$4.4 billion in both Western Europe and the United States, followed by the United Kingdom (US$846 million), Germany (US$733 million), Italy (US$713 million), France (US$613 million), and Spain (US$254 million). By 2003 Western Europe accounted for 28 percent of global sales of bath and shower products, overtaking Asia-Pacific as the top regional market.

Among Europe's largest players are Procter & Gamble, Unilever, Henkel, Beiersdorf, Cussons, and Sara Lee, although in the United Kingdom, especially, private/store labels have generated a rising share of industry sales. While Western Europe has traditionally provided a more reliable base of customers, Eastern Europe offered a higher growth potential for leading companies in the new millennium. Household laundry products account for the majority of industry sales in Europe, followed by industrial and institutional products, hard surface household cleaners, domestic maintenance products, dishwashing household products, soaps, and domestic bleach products.

BIBLIOGRAPHY

"Bar Soap Retains Broad Appeal." *MMR*, 22 March 2004.

Branna, Tom. "Suppliers Make Many Moves to Keep Innovations Rolling." *Household & Personal Products Industry*, March 2007.

Byron, Ellen. "Tide Turns 'Basic' for P & G in Slump." *Wall Street Journal*, 8 August 2009. Available from online.wsj.com.

Colbert, Catherine. "Company Profile: Colgate-Palmolive Company." *Hoover's Online*, 2009. Available from www.hoovers.com.

———. "Company Profile: Henkel KGaA." *Hoover's Online*, 2009. Available from www.hoovers.com.

———. "Company Profile: P&G." *Hoover's Online*, 2009. Available from www.hoovers.com.

de Guzman, Doris. "Detergents Get Healthy." *ICIS Chemical Business Americas*, 22 January 2007.

Graff, Gordon. "Buyers at Detergent Makers Leverage Natural Ingredients to Reduce Costs." *Purchasing*, 1 March 2007.

"High Hopes for Soaps." *Global Cosmetic Industry*, January 2005.

International Association for Soaps, Detergents, and Maintenance Products (AISE). "Market and Economic Data," 15 April 2007. Available from www.aise-net.org.

Jeffries, Nancy. "It All Comes Out in the Wash: Surfactants for Personal Care and Household Cleansers as Well as Detergents Add a Touch of Softness to Effective Cleaning Thanks to High-Tech Ingredients." *Global Cosmetic Industry*, January 2005.

———. "Wake Up and Wash: Soaps, Whether of the Household Variety or Those Intended for Personal Care, Do More Than Cleanse." *Global Cosmetic Industry*, December 2003.

Kao. "Company Outline," 2009. Available fromwww.kao.com.

Kleinman, Martin. "New Life in the Handsoap Market: A New Generation of Products Drives Re-invigoration of US$960 Billion Industry." *Soap & Cosmetics*, February 2003.

Lati, Abyssinia. "Detergent Makers Renew Turf Wars in High-end Market." *Business Daily Africa*, 12 August 2009. Available from www.businessdailyafrica.com.

MacDonald, Veronica. "Soap and Detergents: Going the World Over to Clean." *Chemical Week*, 26 January 2005.

———. "Soaps and Detergents: Shedding Extra Costs." *Chemical Week*, 1 February 2006.

"Making Waves: Manufacturers Are Focusing on Emotional Benefits of Ingredients to Drive Growth in the Bath and Shower Sector. SPC Reports. (Bath & Shower: Market Report)." *Soap Perfumery & Cosmetics*, February 2003.

Molaro, Regina. "Soap Specialties: Specialty Soaps Use Scent and Color to Enhance the Bath Experience. (Specialty Soaps)." *Soap & Cosmetics*, February 2003.

"Nondeodorant Bar Soap." *MMR*, 22 March 2004.

Prior, Molly. "Dove Spreads Its Wings into New Categories." *Drug Store News*, 21 June 2004.

Randow, Jana. "German Exports Jump the Most in Almost Three Years." *Bloomberg News*, 7 August 2009. Available from www.bloomberg.com.

"Sales of Soap & Detergents in 2002 (January-December)." *Cosmetics & Toiletries & Household Products Marketing News in Japan*, 25 March 2003.

"Soap Suppliers Make It New." *MMR*, 18 September 2006.

"The 46th Clean Survey: The Truth About Doing the Laundry." *Japan Soap and Detergent Association News*, September 2004. Available from www.jsda.org.

Unilever Annual Review 2004. Unilever plc, 2005. Available from www.unilever.com.

U.S. National Trade Data, 2004. Office of Trade and Industry Information, Manufacturing and Services, International Trade Administration, U.S. Department of Commerce, 2005. Available from tse.export.gov.

Walsh, Kerri. "Soaps and Detergents: Crossing the Atlantic to Find New Customers." *Chemical Week*, 28 January 2004.

SIC 2844

FLOUR AND OTHER GRAIN MILL PRODUCTS

NAICS CODE(S)

311211. Manufacturers in this industry mill flour or meal from various raw grains, excluding rice. The products of flour mills may be sold plain or in the form of prepared mixes or dough for specific purposes.

INDUSTRY SNAPSHOT

For the flour market (the primary end use of wheat), fluctuating wheat production imposes the most critical global ramifications. As of the middle of the twenty-first century's first decade, more than 60 percent of the world's wheat supply was converted to flour for making breads, biscuits, cakes, and other dough products. On a consumer level, flour and grain products constitute a substantial part of the world's staple diet, since they are basic ingredients of practically every meal consumed by the world's people. Fluctuating wheat production statistics largely portend the amount of food consumption and, in many parts of the world, the availability of food supply. In the United States, some 944.8 million bushels of wheat were ground for flour in 2000, but this number dropped steadily through the early years of the first decade of the 2000s, reaching 865.1 million bushels in 2004. This was the smallest amount in years, and represented the lowest per capita consumption since 1989. In 2005, however, IBIS World predicted industry revenue would grow at around 2.7 percent annually through 2009.

A key factor affecting companies' survival in the flour industry is the ability to compete within the fluid conditions of wheat production and consumption. Companies must maintain the structural and financial stability to weather fluctuations in national currencies, weather-induced wheat shortages and socioeconomic realities that figure so prominently in the industry. Many companies struggling to reinforce their market foothold attempt to expand their flour-based operations by acquiring new products or tapping new investment sources. Insufficient knowledge of consumer tastes and failure to take a long-term approach invariably lead to costly lessons for some companies, particularly those attempting to penetrate foreign flour markets.

ORGANIZATION AND STRUCTURE

The flow of wheat from field to table relies on a multitude of factors. The quality of a bountiful wheat crop ripe for the flour market industry depends on mild weather that lacks the extremes of cold or heat, rain or drought, wind, snow, or hail. Flour's various end uses derive from the milling process. In some parts of the world, even in the early years of the first decade of the 2000s, homemakers or local village millers still ground flour by crushing wheat between two stones or pounding wheat with a mortar and pestle. However, most modern mills employ sophisticated high-tech rollers, sifters, and purifiers for cleansing, grinding, separating, and blending wheat. Because individual flour mills normally grind only one wheat class prior to milling, several wheat varieties may be blended and tested. Hard wheats are primarily used for breads and rolls; soft wheats are used in sweet goods, crackers, and prepared mixes; and durum wheat is used in pasta noodles.

Two factors have largely determined flour utilization patterns: national food preferences and flour availability. Although wheat flour is the most popular, any grain can be converted to flour. Part of the universal appeal of wheat flour is that wheat cultivation adapts to a wide variety of climatic conditions. The global acceptance of wheat flour as a food staple resulted from its nutritional qualities. Wheat contains a unique protein called gluten. Mixed with water, gluten forms elastic dough capable of expanding several times its original volume during baking. The smaller amount of gluten protein contained in rye flour produces better dark rye breads, or, if blended with wheat flour, produces finer-textured light rye breads. Oat flour, the most nutritious flour, and oat meals are primarily used in breakfast food and granola-type products, while barley flour can be found in baby foods and malted milks. In some countries, large quantities of barley flour are used for bread making. Sorghum and millet flours are popular in India, Central America, and Ethiopia in the making of flat bread, tortillas, and pancakes. A small percentage of rice is converted to flour for use in baby foods and sauces. Buckwheat flour is often used in pancakes. Soybean technology has introduced soya flour and grits, which contain 50 percent protein and are adaptable to a variety of bakery products such as cereals, meat products, and soup mixes. Less appealing characteristics of soybean flour result from the multiplication of bacteria, especially during processing with steam and moisture. An excessively high bacterial count causes emission of off-odors and undesirable flavors. There has been continued research aimed to eliminate these adverse side effects.

All flour products must meet certain nutritional and cleanliness standards promulgated by various government agencies such as the U.S. Food and Drug Administration (FDA). The amount and type of additives, carbohydrates, protein, and other nutrients included in flour products derive from required nutritional and safety standards. By law, bread labeled "whole wheat" must be made from 100 percent whole wheat flour. U.S. legislation requiring truth-in-nutrition labeling mandates all food products to be labeled with a list of nutritional contents. The average composition of white flour includes 73.6 percent nitrogen-free extract and 13.5 percent water or other moisture. Millers can ill afford substandard products caused by too much or too little moisture, flour, or sugar, so most dough batches, under government controls, contain very small amounts of potassium bromate and other ingredients to enhance dough baking or other preservation qualities. Likewise, the differences between bleached and unbleached flour also affect color and baking quality: bleached flour adds to baking quality and color values while unbleached flour performs better for cookies, pie crusts, and crackers. Despite numerous changes in flour composition and uses, the U.S. public's preference for white flour or bread remains undiminished—probably a carry-over from past eras when white bread symbolized a status befitting royalty.

As a healthy alternative to white flour used by most consumers, The National Milling Company (NAMILCO), launched whole wheat flour, multigrain flour and toasted wheat germ products. They reflect the company's efforts to replace vitamins and minerals often lost in the milling process for making white flour. A major benefit of whole wheat flour is that it consists of "all three parts of the wheat grain—the bran, germ and endosperm." Multigrain flour combines wheat flour with eight types of grains.

Because grains are harvested close to the ground, sanitation factors largely determine the survival of flour mills. The FDA regulates sanitation controls for the United States' milling industry by defining levels for unavoidable, naturally occurring food defects considered non-hazardous to human health. High levels of flour bacteria are normally exterminated through numerous milling processes. It has been argued that the cleansing effectiveness of modern machinery not only removes all the bran and germ but also removes the part of the traditional bread flavor as well. On the other hand, some reports cite popular raw cookie dough as a contamination source because of the persistence of live microbes, apparently unaffected by milling heating or baking processes.

The primary structural change by the early years of the first decade of the 2000s was the worldwide shift of control over wheat and flour production and purchasing decisions from governmental agencies to private enterprises. In 1990, about 80 percent of these decisions where made by governments; in 1998, private millers and grain traders made 70 percent of such decisions. Latin America, in particular, underwent a very dramatic shift of this kind in just a few years. In most cases, privatization led to increased wheat consumption, quality-consciousness, and competition.

Major Uses of Flour. In the mid-years of the first decade of the 2000s the heaviest volume users were commercial bakers, who used more than 72 percent of the U.S. flour supply to make breads and cakes. Professional bakers buy flour by grades of refinement, while individual consumers purchase straight flour and convenience mixes. Typically, 100 pounds of wheat yield an average of 72 pounds of white flour, or depending on the variety, 100 pounds of wheat flour. Besides bread, flour is essential in the production of rolls and sweet goods (such as pastries, doughnuts, cakes, and cookies); tortillas, which account for one-fourth of the corn flour market, alongside corn chips and other snack foods; and pasta and noodles, for which the enrichment value ranks the highest of wheat flour-based products.

Perhaps the greatest impetus to guilt-free use of pre-packaged foods was the 1920 introduction of biscuit mix, which promised a convenient, tasty product by following a few simple steps. As popularity of mixes increased, flour mills began producing large unit volume mixes, which expanded commercial bakers' application of mixes for all types of products such as doughnuts, pastries, pie shells, cakes, and different breads. After a while, the lustrous period of mixes plummeted because flour marketers believed consumers lacked the time for and interest in traditional home baking. A Pillsbury official reiterated the potential of the flour mix market by reminding management that modern bakers are mostly mothers who crave convenience and easy-to-use products that are capable of producing homemade bread. The evidence was sufficiently convincing for Pillsbury to energize flour marketing and spark sales of bread machines and bread mixes by 1994. In the 1990s, 47 percent of volume baking mix users were homemakers with children aged 6 to 11.

BACKGROUND AND DEVELOPMENT

Perhaps more than any other food, wheat has survived consumer fickleness and food fads throughout the ages.

In the first decade of the 2000s, wheat continued to hold its 10,000-year-old status as the staff of life. Anthropologists have ascribed the cultivation and storing of wheat as a pivotal factor in stabilizing habitation patterns. This stability soon stimulated experimentation in expanding wheat as a food supply. Nomadic tribes discovered that using wheat as a food source increased their chances of survival. Archeological finds along the Nile River documented Egyptians applying various techniques of wheat harvesting and using the leavening process in bread making around 2600 B.C. The Romans improved the milling process and are acknowledged as the first people to make white bread. Bread became so important that it gained symbolic significance in some religions. As wheat and bread developed into more lucrative commodities, questions about the more unseemly aspects of bread consumption also arose. During the eighteenth century, for example, controversy erupted regarding the use of new versus old (aged) wheat preferred by French bakers. While the profit factors of new wheat appealed to traders, the public believed that new wheat caused diarrhea, pernicious gas, and possibly epidemic diseases. In addition, according to twentieth-century investigations, contaminated bread—allegedly a cause of psychosis—contributed to witchcraft persecution, which was prevalent during the eighteenth century in Europe.

One of the oldest types of wheat known is bulgur wheat, and the earliest means used to separate the parts of the wheat kernel involved rubbing the grain between the hands. Other methods included having hoofed animals walk over grains that had been spread on hard ground, and winnowing, a process in which grains were tossed in the air so that the chaff would blow away (removing the individual grains from the rest of the plant was necessary before milling could take place).

Grain milling practices were developed to separate the kernel components and make flour. The first types of milling procedures involved the use of rubbing stones, mortar and pestles, or querns. Querns were devices made from two stacked, disk-shaped stones. Wheat grains were poured into the quern through a hole in the top stone. As the two stones turned against each other with a rotary motion, the abrasive movement separated the parts of the wheat kernels and ground the endosperm into flour. The flour was then discharged between the stones.

The first continuous system for milling wheat into flour was developed during the last part of the eighteenth century by an American, Oliver Evans. Evans' mill design used steam technology and employed conveyors and bucket elevators to move the grain through a multi-phase milling process. Further advances in milling technology occurred during the nineteenth century. In 1865, Edmund La Croix developed a middlings purifier that separated the granular endosperm from the bran so that it could be reground to produce a better grade of flour. During the 1870s, the first roller mills were constructed in the United States.

Roller mills possessed several advantages: they eliminated the need to dress millstones; they were able to produce flour through a more gradual extraction process, which enabled millers to yield a larger percentage of better grade flour; and the greater efficiency of these mills made the construction of larger mills more feasible.

During the middle of the twentieth century, fundamental changes occurred in the primary location of mills. Prior to the 1950s, the cost of shipping wheat and the cost of shipping flour were approximately equal, and mills were frequently built close to wheat fields. During the early 1960s, the cost of shipping grain decreased following the introduction of hopper rail cars. At the same time, costs surrounding sanitation requirements increased the price of shipping flour. As a result, mills were constructed closer to end markets rather than near the wheat fields.

Granular flour, a product made with particles of a uniform size with carefully controlled amounts of atomized moisture to reduce clumping, was introduced during the 1960s. Although granular flour was more expensive than regular flour, it offered several advantages: there was less dust, it was easier to pour, it did not require sifting, and it dispersed in cold liquids.

During the 1970s, sales of household flour declined as developed societies moved away from home baking and homemakers demonstrated a preference for the convenience and consistency of prepared mixes. In addition, many mixes were less expensive than individual ingredients. Baking from "scratch" ceased to be an activity of necessity and was relegated to hobby status. Demographic information revealed that households with higher incomes were more likely to use flour than lower income households. Declines in flour use by households were partially offset by increases of flour sales to commercial bakers. Also during this period, the flour and grain mill industry was adversely affected when a nutrition-conscious population denounced starchy breads and tantalizing sugar products. Others rejected the reduced quality of commercial bakery products because of overuse of additives.

Acquisition activity and globalization continued to transform the industry, particularly as such activity was concentrated in emerging markets in Asia, Eastern Europe, and South America. China's transition from an agrarian economy to an industrial one posed opportunities for major international corporations such as U.S.-based Cargill Inc. and Archer Daniels Midland to make substantial inroads into that country. Middle Eastern countries continued to modernize their milling operations, allowing for the region's growing global presence within

the industry. Qatar's flour milling industry, for example, realized the effects of a healthy economy and improved technology and computer mechanization. As a consequence, grain-based food consumption in Qatar increased about 10 to 15 percent annually in the late 1990s.

Oat flour was gaining in popularity in spite of a shortage in Russia. Its status was soaring in large part due to views of it being a "wholesome" alternative with "beneficial properties". According to PAVA Commercial Director Angela Kiseleva, the company decided it was time for the Achinsk Mill to start oat flour production after conducting market analysis with current and prospective customers. The company had already reportedly received positive reviews for the oat flour available for delivery throughout Russia and elsewhere.

In the first decade of the 2000s, not all developing countries were greeting increased internationalization with open arms, however. Zambia, for instance, countered what it viewed as unfair foreign competition with a ban on flour imports in 2002. Indonesia, amid massive deregulation of its economy, maintained a flour consumption rate that was roughly a quarter that of the United States, which presented a significant market for potential growth to foreign corporations. But, as the market itself became privatized, the government implemented substantial tariffs on wheat flour to stave off foreign competition that could overpower domestic producers.

Such protective actions were not limited to developing nations. In the United States, the federal government took action against what it saw as harmfully high imports of wheat gluten.

Another issue of increasing prominence within the industry was health consciousness and quality control. Consumer demand for a nutritionally positive product dramatically altered the dynamics of the industry. As individual millers and companies assumed control of production and purchasing activities from governments, the focus shifted from the high quantity, low price demand that prevailed under governmental authority to the increased competition among industry players to offer consumers a high quality product at affordable prices. As a result, many companies invested substantial sums in research aimed at improving quality control. Grain quality includes an assessment of the physical characteristics of grain such as weight and moisture content, cleanliness and phytosanitary conditions (such as presence of weed seeds or pests), and an assessment of the intrinsic nutritional characteristics such as protein and gluten content. Reportedly less than a third of the world market demands these high wheat standards, but these markets include higher income groups that prefer protein, wholesome white bread, corn sweeteners, and tofu. Purchasing decisions may be affected by other factors, particularly price, but USDA studies found that grain importers most often base purchases on intrinsic characteristics. Purchases by state trading agencies in developing countries reportedly reflect less attention to quality and more to price. In the wake of world trade liberalizations such as the General Agreement on Tariffs and Trade (GATT), U.S. exporters may need to treat each market individually, dealing with importers' preferences almost on a retail basis.

CURRENT CONDITIONS

In 2006 world wheat flour exports reached 10.7 billion tons, making it the second biggest year on record. The all-time high was reached in 1997, when wheat flour exports totaled 11.6 billion tons. The European Union, traditionally the world's largest flour exporter, lost its leading spot in 2006 to Turkey. The E.U. was responsible for 2 million tons, whereas Turkey exported 2.25 million tons. The question of export subsidies for E.U. wheat remained controversial. In January 2005, the European Commission announced that subsidies, which had been suspended for 18 months, would resume for 2 million tons of wheat exports.

Kazakhstan, a member of the Commonwealth of Independent States, emerged as a leader in flour exporting in 2006 with 1.3 million tons. Argentina was also a major player, exporting 700,000 tons in 2006. Other countries seeing gains in flour exports included Brazil, Bolivia, Nigeria, Chile, Pakistan, and China. The United States, which at one time competed with the E.U. as a flour export leader, exported only 300,000 tons in 2006.

While the top exporters remain fairly constant, the names of the major importers change frequently. From 1998 to 1999, the top importers were Libya (with more than 800,000 tons imported) and Yemen (importing slightly over 1 million tons). Again from 1999 to 2000, these countries were the top importers; Libya imported a little over 1 million tons, and Yemen imported 700,000 tons. At various times, major importers have included the former USSR, Algeria, and Egypt. In 2004, Libya again led in flour imports with an estimated 1.2 million tons. According to International Grains Council (IGC) statistics, Libya's flour imports accounted for 17 percent of total world trade in 2003 and about 13 percent in 2004. Demand in Indonesia also continued to grow, making it a major importer of flour in 2006.

One trend affecting domestic flour sales in the mid-years of the first decade of the 2000s was the growing popularity of low-carbohydrate diets. This trend particularly affected bread and pasta manufacturers. In response, companies were introducing low-carbohydrate versions of these products in which some portion of

refined flour was replaced by a higher-protein ingredient, such as whole wheat flour, wheat germ, or soy protein.

The United States is recognized as having the most technologically advanced and most efficient grain handling industry. Since U.S. flour mills could not keep up with increased domestic demand through much of the late twentieth century, U.S. exports fell. But after reaching record levels in 2000, domestic consumption began to decline. Flour consumption in the U.S. dropped by 2.6 percent in 2001 and 2 percent in 2002. Though demand grew by 0.4 percent in 2003, per capita usage fell by about one pound from the previous year. This trend continued through 2004, with per capita consumption falling to a 16-year low. According to estimates from the U.S. Department of Agriculture's Economic Research Service (ERS), quoted on bakingbusiness.com, "much of the consumption gain posted in the last half of the final decade of the 20th century has been wiped out by the reductions posted thus far in the 21st century."

According to an article in the July 30, 2009, issue of the *Manila Bulletin,* Philippine Baking Industry Association President Walter Co joined bakers in strongly urging flour millers to reduce prices. Co noted that wheat prices on an international market basis had substantially increased, resulting in local millers charging higher prices. Price reductions for wheat could result in reduced cost per loaf, Co claimed during an address at the induction ceremony for Philippine Baking Association officers.

A 5 to 15 percent increase in the cost of processed food products was predicted, according to an August 2009 article published by *The Economic Times.* It was noted that prices had been rising for key ingredients including edible oils and wheat flour. Sharp increases in processed food products pricing, however, would undoubtedly result in consumers purchasing less of the items. Pickwick Hygienic Products General Manager Madhav Damle additionally admitted the wafer biscuit company had increased prices for some products in August 2009, a mere two months after raising prices for the same items.

In a July 27, 2009, article in the Toronto *Globe and Mail,* health and public policy writer and author Andre Picard shared background information about how the Canadian government adopted a mandatory policy of "fortifying flour-based products to prevent birth defects." White flour was on the list of impacted products. The program, which has been adapted by other countries, was credited with reducing neural tube defects, including spina bifida, by more than half, and sharply reducing "heart defects and a form of childhood cancer called neuroblastoma." These facts have prompted a move to further reduce those defects by doubling folic acid levels in food. However, there is concern, Picard explained, because Dr. Deborah O'Connor, director of clinical dietetics at the Hospital for Sick Children and principal author of research published in the Canadian Journal of Public Health, found that "pasta, breads and cereals can contain anywhere between 90 per cent and 377 per cent of folic acid claimed on the product label." The article also pointed out that although there are significant benefits from folic acid (vitamin B9), there are some risks from ingesting too much of it. "For example, excess folic acid can mask vitamin B12 deficiency, a common cause of anemia in the elderly, and it can interfere with drugs used to treat rheumatoid arthritis, psoriasis and malaria." Accurate folic acid content on product labels is also important because folic acid is essential in the first month after conception, when many women are not yet aware they are pregnant but are taking a daily prenatal multivitamin containing folic acid.

RESEARCH AND TECHNOLOGY

In the mid-years of the first decade of the 2000s, new flours and ingredients continued as research priorities for the flour and grain industry. Milo grain, a sturdy, nutritious variety of sorghum cultivated for about 30 percent less cost, was being studied as a wheat flour substitute for pancake mixes. The wet and dry milling process for milo offered tremendous potential as a top-quality wheat flour steeped in vitamins and minerals. Without the grittiness and bitter taste of whole grain, the palatability of milo grain products could possibly convert almost 40 percent of the population to whole grain products. By making whole grain flour more easily extruded, ConAgra planned to stimulate this virgin market with the introduction of ultra fine whole grain flour mixes in schools for making pizza crust, griddle mix, buttermilk muffins, and a host of other products. Genetic engineering and unconventional use of baker's yeast may possibly lead to wheat that produces a superior baking flour with more nutrients.

A United Nations report in 2004 blamed "alarming" deficits in IQs, productivity, and health across entire countries because of the lack of simple nutrients such as folic acid, niacin, and iron. Folic acid, a natural component of wheat and whole wheat products that is mostly lost in the milling process, is an essential vitamin that aids metabolic processes and produces red blood cells. The United States has, since 1998, required that food companies must add folic acid to most enriched bread, corn meal, flour, pasta, and rice products. Since then, incidents of two major birth defects, spina bifida and anencephaly, have declined by at least 20 percent. Flour is also routinely enriched in other western countries, but nutrients are not added to flour in developing countries, where grain is most often processed in small mills. To prevent vitamin deficiencies, which contribute to mental

impairment, birth defects, and other debilitating conditions, the United Nations has urged that developing countries increase their production of enriched foods such as flour.

Genetic selection and genetic engineering made up an area of concentration for researchers in the mid-years of the first decade of the 2000s. It has been found that protein content and overall quality of corn meal and other products can be enhanced by these means. In addition, debranning techniques, by which bran layers are stripped from the endosperm and hydrated before the milling process, came into play in the late 1990s. This technique allows for greater, more accurate control of finished flour moisture, which in turn improves bread quality and baking quality. A process to separate gluten and starch from wheat flour using ethanol instead of water may reduce waste treatment costs associated with the conventional process.

New Equipment. Excessively high or low moisture content signals a problem for the flour industry. Moisture content affects insect growth if moisture is below 14 percent and mold accumulation if it is higher than 14.5 percent. Wheat arrives at the mill with different moisture levels; therefore, without manual adjustment of moisture, mills have difficulty maintaining flour finish moisture of 14 percent. A U.S. company, Maple Leaf Flour Mill, installed a precise moisture control microwave-type system, which caused milling efficiency to increase 0.5 percent. Moreover, daily production of 550 tons of flour was maintained with 4.75 tons less wheat per day, which saved the company US$104,000 annually. Upon installation of new sifters capable of sifting diverse materials six days a week, the machine eliminated down time with a perfect reliability record.

INDUSTRY LEADERS

Archer Daniels Midland Company (ADM). Started as the Archer-Daniels Linseed Company in 1903, the Archer Daniels Midland Company spent its first two decades purchasing oil processing companies in the Midwestern United States. In 1930, the Commander-Larabee Company, a major flour miller, was purchased. By the company's fiftieth anniversary in 1952, Archer Daniels Midland (ADM) was manufacturing more than 200 standard products and had extended its operations overseas. ADM, whose grain milling division produces flour for bread, cakes, pasta, tortillas, and various ingredients for the baking industry, generated revenues of US$70 billion for the fiscal year ending June 30, 2008. ADM has approximately 27,000 employees with more than 230 processing plants serving markets in more than 60 countries. ADM's reputation was tarnished in the early years of the first decade of the 2000s by a federal investigation and subsequent lawsuits stemming from price-fixing allegations relating to high-fructose corn syrup. In 2004 the company agreed to pay US$400 million in damages to Coca-Cola, Pepsi Cola, and other food manufacturers that had brought claims against ADM.

In May 2009, Archer Daniels Midland Company Chairman and CEO Patricia Woertz, announced the introduction of "ADM Cares," an innovative program that focuses on social investment via three areas: "strong roots, strong communities, and bonds." Woertz linked the three areas to basic human needs for growth. "Whether we are helping to make sure certain farm families stay safe, promoting education in ADM hometowns or protecting environmentally sensitive habitats, ADM will seek out partnerships and programs that help ensure the responsible, sustainable development of agriculture," Woertz stated.

General Mills Inc. For more than 60 years, General Mills survived as an independent corporation by relying on its flour milling and breakfast cereals. Although incorporated in 1928, the company's origins date back to 1866, when Cadwallader Washburn opened a flour mill in Minnesota. His business, which soon became the Washburn Crosby Company, competed with local miller C. A. Pillsbury. In 1928, General Mills was formed, employing 5,800 workers and generating sales of US$123 million. Its strongest products at the time were Gold Medal Flour, Softasilk Cake Flour, and Wheaties, a then recently introduced ready-to-eat cereal. Also in 1928, Betty Crocker's name was introduced in connection with General Mills' consumer goods. Although the company through the years bought and sold such diverse entities as Eddie Bauer, Talbot's, and the Red Lobster and Olive Garden chains, in the late 1990s, General Mills again focused on food products as evidenced by its decision in 2001 to double its size by purchasing Pillsbury from Diageo. General Mills also produces its own flour, which it sells to bakeries. In 2009 sales continued their steady climb, reaching US$14.7 billion.

For those with celiac disease or simply searching for an alternative to wheat flour-based mixes, Betty Crocker has the answer. General Mills has introduced gluten-free desert mixes. The key ingredient substitution is rice flour. Blog writer mford tried out the gluten-free mix for brownies taste-tested by a group of 12-year-olds. The discerning young palates found these brownies to be tasty. It pleased the writer to discover that yellow and devil's food cake mix plus chocolate chip cookies were part of the Betty Crocker gluten-free line.

Cargill Inc. As a major U.S. private corporation, Cargill Inc. is one of the largest grain and commodities players in the world

and a longtime leader in the U.S. flour milling industry. William Wallace Cargill began his grain business in 1865 in Iowa. The business grew as it followed the expansion of the railroad in the period after the U.S. Civil War. During the Great Depression, Cargill invested heavily in the storage and transportation of grain, secure in the knowledge that a recovering economy would find Cargill reaping the benefits. By 1940, 60 percent of Cargill's business involved foreign markets. In 1955, the company opened a Swiss subsidiary to sell grain in Europe, and in the early 1960s, Cargill began its move into communist countries. In the 1990s, Cargill stepped up its foreign ventures, resuming trade with post-apartheid South Africa and expanding its Asian and Eastern European operations. By 2009, the company employed 160,000 people working in 67 countries.

ConAgra Foods Inc. ConAgra maintains a strong presence in nearly all areas of the U.S. food processing industry. Conceived in 1919 when a collection of mills consolidated to form Consolidated Mills Inc., the company steadily diversified and grew to become a national food powerhouse. In 1971, Consolidated Mills changed its name to ConAgra Inc., and then it grew consistently through the 1990s, by which time it had diversified heavily within the food industry and expanded into a global outfit, with employees in 32 countries. In the mid-years of the first decade of the 2000s, ConAgra was one of the largest food service manufacturers in the United States, providing poultry, French fries, and dough-based products for the food service industry. In 2006, ConAgra's revenues totaled US$11.5 billion. Only a small segment of this was attributed to agricultural processing, however, as the company's focus shifted to prepared foods in the late 1990s. ConAgra's top brands, such as Chef Boyardee, Banquet, Healthy Choice, and Van Camp's, generate approximately US$100 million in sales each year.

BIBLIOGRAPHY
"Archer Daniels Midland Company Announced ADM Cares Program." Archer Daniels Midland Company, 13 May 2009. Available from www.adm.com.
Athale, Gouri Agley. "Processed Foods to be Costlier." *The Economic Times*, 19 August 2009. Available from economictimes.indiatimes.com.
"Bakers say Millers can Still cut Flour Prices." Manila Bulletin Publishing Corporation, 2009. Available from www.mb.com.ph.
"Business Outlook: Flour Mill Product Manufacturing." *Food Magazine*, 24 February 2005.
China's Corn Output Reaches Record High." *Asia Pulse*, 14 March 2007.
Day, Sherri. "They Come to Praise the Carb, Not Bury It." *New York Times*, 4 February 2004.
"Flour Power." *Chemistry and Industry*, 2 October 2006.
"Hoover's Company Capsules." *Hoover's Online*, 2009. Available from www.hoovers.com.

"International Grains Council Says E.U. Flour Exports May Rise." bakingbusiness.com, 14 March 2005. Available from www.bakingbusiness.com.

Manor, Robert. "ADM to Pay $400 Million in Price Fixing Case." *Chicago Tribune,* 23 June 2004. Available from prorev.com.

"NAMILCO Launches Whole Wheat, Multigrain Flours." *Stabroeck News,* 17 August 2009. Available from www.stabroecknews.com.

"Opening Up New Markets for UK Wheat." *Farmers Guardian,* 20 March 2007.

"Pava Launches Oat Flour Production." PR-USA, 2009. Available from pr-usa.net.

Picard, André. "Labels on Fortified foods are wildly inaccurate." *Globe and Mail* (Toronto), 27 July 2009. Available from www.theglobeandmail.com.

Ramachandran, Arjun. "Flour Mill Product Manufacturing." *Food Magazine,* 1 February 2006.

Schlachter, Barry. "Giving Bread a Boost: New Additives Are Touted as a Way to Help Lower Bad Cholesterol, Aid Health." *Fort Worth Star-Telegram,* 4 April 2007.

Shelke, Kantha. "Grain-based Foods Fight Back." *Ingredients,* 2 April 2004. Available from www.foodprocessing.com.

Sosland, Morton. "IGC Estimates 3 Percent Decline in World Flour Exports in 2003-04." bakingbusiness.com, 8 March 2004. Available from www.bakingbusiness.com.

———. "Sharp Fall Affirmed in Total, Per Capita Flour Use." bakingbusiness.com, 30 March 2005. Available from www.bakingbusiness.com.

———. "Upturn in World Flour Exports as Kazakhstan Looms." *bakingbusiness.com,* 5 April 2007. Available from www.bakingbusiness.com.

———. "U.S. Flour Usage Increases for First Time since 2000." bakingbusiness.com, 5 April 2004. Available from www.bakingbusiness.com.

U.S. Census Bureau. "Flour Milling Products: 2005." *Current Industrial Reports,* June 2006. Available from www.census.gov.

U.S. Department of Agriculture, Economic Research Service and Foreign Agricultural Service. *Outlook for U.S. Agricultural Trade, 2005.* Available from www.fas.usda.gov.

U.S. Department of Agriculture, Foreign Agricultural Service. *Grain: World Markets and Trade,* March 2007. Available from www.fas.usda.gov.

———. *Turkey Grain and Feed Annual, 2005.* Available from www.fas.usda.gov.

———. *World Wheat, Flour, and Products Trade,* 9 March 2007. Available from www.fas.usda.gov.

COMPUTER HARDWARE AND SERVICES

COMPUTERS

NAICS CODE(S)

334111. The industry produces digital computers that may be in such configurations as mainframe computers, super computers, and personal computers. This diverse class of machines shares these common abilities:

- they store the processing programs and data necessary to execute programs;

- they can be freely programmed in accordance user requirements;

- they perform mathematical computations specified by the user; and

- they execute—without human intervention—a processing program requiring them to modify execution by logical decision during a processing run.

INDUSTRY SNAPSHOT

Japan, the United States, and Europe are the three mature world markets that accounted for the majority of global production and sales of computers and related products during the first decade of the twenty-first century. Between 2003 and 2005, the worldwide computer market grew 11.3 percent annually, and during the first quarter of 2005 alone, growth was 10.3 percent.

In the mid-2000s, Dell remained the worldwide market leader, with 18 percent of sales. HP commanded 16 percent, IBM garnered 7 percent, and Fujitsu had 4 percent. In the United States, Dell led with 33 percent of the market, followed by HP with 19 percent, Gateway and IBM with 6 percent each, and Apple with 4 percent.

Prices were dropping, largely due to market maturity and technological advances driving down the cost for parts. Aver Corporation and Lenovo Group entered the top 10 ranks in the late 2000s.

Due to the consumer drive for faster, lighter, gadget-driven computer, the trend toward digital technology was set to explode in the mid- to late 2000s with digital convergence, as technologies from different tech industries were merging. According to *Business Week,* the tech industries were poised for a "Big Bang" as the computer, consumer electronics, and communications industries merged technologies and products, forming new alliances and partnerships as well as new competitors. The computer industry is ever-evolving and new technologies emerge weekly, making the need to constantly upgrade systems or applications a virtual necessity to consumers desirous of staying on the cutting edge. The computer industry creates its own demand by constantly improving its supply.

The dreams of many young men have been realized as modern computer empires. For example, Bill Gates was a very young man when he started Microsoft, which made him one of the wealthiest men in the United States. Using profits from Microsoft, Gates created the Bill and Melinda Gates Foundation, which is one of the world's largest charities. Steve Jobs and Steve Wozniak of Apple computer fame were college students who were creative in the expression of their interest in high-tech sales. Jobs, who has also been called "Apple's messianic CEO," is considered to be the driving force for Apple.

ORGANIZATION AND STRUCTURE

Product Structure. The electronic computer industry can be divided into three categories: supercomputers, mainframes, and personal computers. Each category is distinguished by the speed with which a computer can process instructions and data.

Revenue of Industry Leaders, 2010

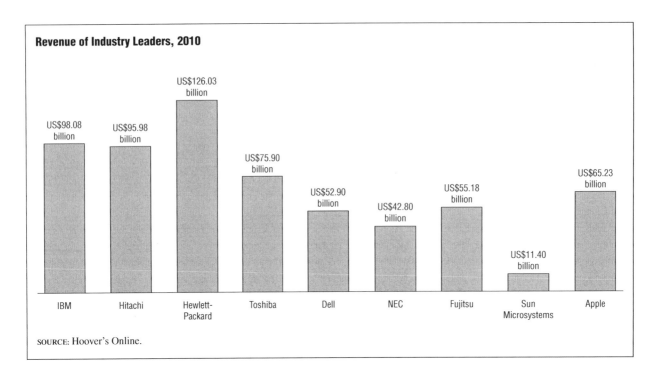

SOURCE: Hoover's Online.

Supercomputers. Supercomputers are the most powerful class of computers with extremely high bandwidth to provide users with the greatest possible capability for complex use by scientists, security experts, mapping professionals, theorists, and economics experts. Medical researchers use supercomputers to conduct research in cell studies and other uses that may save lives and prevent or reverse disease. A variety of professionals benefit from conducting theoretical and applied research enhanced with digital imaging. In the 1980s, the manufacturer Cray built powerful supercomputers and continued to have an enviable reputation for building complex, high-end supercomputers favored by many scientists and engineers into the late 2000s. During the early years of the twenty-first century, supercomputers were used for weather forecasting and in engineering research related to aerospace, automobiles, and nuclear science. In 2005, IBM had almost completed the Blue Gene/L. Housed at the Department of Energy at Lawrence Livermore National Laboratory, the Blue Gene/L ran at 135.3 trillion floating-point operations per second (TFLOPS) in March 2005 and was expected to reach 270 TFLOPS that summer, five times as fast at its closest competitor. About 50 times smaller than previous supercomputers, the Blue Gene/L was used for nuclear weapon simulations as well as for biochemical applications. Collectively, supercomputers in 2005 were about 1,000 times faster than their 1995 predecessors.

Mainframes. Mainframe computers are used to process high-volume general business applications where increased performance is required. They are large and powerful machines, although they have less bandwidth capacity than a supercomputer, and can hook up with other computers or terminals to allow dozens or even hundreds of employees to work at low security risk stations. In the early days of computers, the term referred to the "main frame" or "central processor unit" of a batch computer.

Personal Computers. A personal computer (PC) is a system with imbedded processing capabilities that is intended primarily for a single user. All are based on the microprocessor that manufacturers use to put an entire central processing unit (CPU) on one silicon chip. Businesses rely on personal computers for a variety of functions, including word processing, accounting, desktop publishing, and spreadsheet and database management applications. Microsoft typically sells all these functions in a single software package that many computer hardware sellers either install on the machine or sell to customers with the PC.

Personal computers first appeared in the late 1970s. One of the first and most popular personal computers was the Apple II, introduced in 1977 by Apple Computer. In the next four years, new models and competing operating systems seemed to appear daily, and some disappeared overnight. Then, in 1981 IBM became competitive with a personal computer, quickly dubbed a "PC." The IBM PC sold well, and attracted so-called IBM "compatible" machines or "clones" by makers such as Kaypro. Kaypro and others eventually went into rummage sale lots, but Apple Computer remained, and many "Mac Addicts" attached loyalty to the brand, which by 2002 relied on a popular operating system called the MAC OS X.

In the twenty-first century, one's personal computer was either a "Mac" or a PC that was a distant cousin of the first IBM PC. As distinctions fade, the newer, more powerful, video card-enhanced personal computers in the workplace and classroom have replaced what used to be slightly higher-end models called workstations. In the late 2000s, whether purchased off the shelf or with an upgrade, Macs and PCs are used for work and recreational uses, such as playing video games with startlingly real graphics, downloading music, and saving information and entertainment on DVDs and CDs.

Despite taking more than two decades for the number of personal computers in use to reach the 1 billion mark in the late 2000s, that number was expected to double by 2014. However, approximately 35 million computers were expected to end up in landfills as hazardous waste.

Market Structure. The United States and Japan were not only the largest supercomputer manufacturers but also had the largest markets. Although Japan was the second largest global market, it purchased most of its supercomputers from domestic sources, especially industry leaders NEC, Fujitsu, and Hitachi. Foreign suppliers had difficulty making advances in Japan's supercomputer market as a result of the Japanese government's support of its domestic industry; the Japanese industry's tendency to purchase from domestic manufacturers; and the Japanese industry's investment in Japanese-manufactured proprietary equipment and software. The United States was the source of almost all imports to Japan and accounted for 25 percent of Japan's computer hardware sales, approximately US$40 billion.

Due to the rise and development of client/server technology in the late 1980s and 1990s, mainframe sales decreased sharply. For example, U.S. mainframe sales were about US$12.4 billion in 1992 and fell to US$11.3 billion in 1993. However, the intense demand for the information generated by the Internet had created renewed interest in mainframe systems. Industry leader IBM still held 80 percent of the market, and mainframe revenues continued to grow. Sales of IBM's zSeries mainframes were up 14.9 percent from 2003 to 2004. IBM was being challenged by Japanese leaders Hitachi and Amdahl (that had been acquired by another major player, Fujitsu). U.S. leader Dell claimed US$312 million of the mainframe market in 1997 and was increasingly competitive in the 2000s.

In 1997 the midrange systems market was showing renewed growth, especially in foreign markets. As the economy strengthened and the role of midrange systems in client/server technology grew, sales began to increase. According to a report in *VARBusiness,* midrange systems were projected to become the hottest market in computing during the late 1990s. Major players in the industry included IBM and Hewlett-Packard. IBM continued to be the leader in midrange systems, and during the mid-2000s focused on making its platform competitive with other systems, such as Linux, and with other companies in terms of operational and development cost. Hewlett-Packard was a strong competitor, partnering with Intel to facilitate its growth in the market and using its economic clout to merge with Compaq for wider capabilities and marketing clout.

In 2004, worldwide revenues for the Internet server market grew 6.2 percent, and the market was valued at more than $49 billion. IBM and Hewlett-Packard accounted for 60 percent of sales. In terms of revenue, IBM remained the market leader, but HP shipped more servers. The total number of units shipped grew 19.3 percent in 2004. IDC reported a decline in the midrange and high-end server sectors, but other servers were realizing steady market growth, including Unix, Windows, and Blade servers. Linux servers remained the highest growth segment of the market, worth $1.3 billion in the fourth quarter of 2004.

Market Watch reported that on July 9, 2008, Mobile TeleSystems OJSC, Microsoft, and Fujitsu Siemens Computers announced plans to launch the first integrated 3G notebook solution in the Commonwealth of Independent States. The 3G notebook will be sold initially in Moscow before being offered in four additional cities. The joint operation was developed within the framework of the mobile broadband strategy MIS announced at the Mobile World Congress in Barcelona in February 2008.

Regulation. Environmental concerns played a major role in the electronic computer industry. In 1993 a collaborative report titled *A Workstation Life Cycle Environment Study* was produced by several government agencies. The study urged U.S. manufacturers to become more environmentally conscious and encouraged manufacturers to create efficient ways to recycle products and parts while reducing pollution created in the manufacturing process. U.S. President Bill Clinton issued an executive order in 1993 directing U.S. agencies to purchase computers that adhered to the Environmental Protection Agency's (EPA) Energy Star program. This program called for each part of a computer system, including some peripherals like printers, to enter a standby mode when not in use, which would reduce energy consumption. The EPA predicted that the Energy Star program requirements had the potential to reduce carbon-dioxide emissions enough to forestall the need for ten coal-burning power plants. Many U.S. computer manufacturers also followed the guidelines of the broader program and started to recycle processor boards, power supplies, and batteries.

BACKGROUND AND DEVELOPMENT

The computer was born several centuries ago out of a need to speed and aid computation. Although certainly not a computer by modern standards, the first such tool was a simple tabulation machine called the abacus, which originated in the Middle East. The first tabulation machine to have significant global impact was the mechanical calculator created by French mathematician Blaise Pascal in 1642. Built from a long wooden box and a combination of wheels and gears, numbers were entered into Pascal's calculator via six wheels located on the front of the machine, and the answers were displayed in windows above each wheel.

In the mid-nineteenth century, English mathematician Charles Babbage drafted designs for two calculating devices, the difference engine (1820s) and the analytical engine (1840s), neither of which were built. His designs for the analytical engine were enhancements based on the difference engine, which depicted the primary components of computers of the 1960s, such as programs stored on punch cards.

The concept was more fully developed later in the nineteenth century by Herman Hallerith, an American who created a machine that would sort and count cards based on the pattern of holes punched into them. Hallerith's machine was first used in the 1890 U.S. Census to aid in statistical analysis. Although the reading device certainly improved, Hallerith cards were used for inputting program instructions into computers well into the late 1970s and early 1980s. In 1896 Hallerith started a company called the Tabulation Machine Company. This company was one of three companies that later became International Business Machines Corporation (better known as IBM).

In the 1940s Howard Aiken developed what was considered the first electronic computer. Instead of using Hallerith cards, Aiken's machine used rolls of paper with instructions punched into them. Because it required extensive rewiring for each program entered into the computer, its design was limiting and time-consuming. The first general purpose computer was completed in 1946 and was used by the military. Although the electronic numerical integrator and calculator (ENIAC) still needed partial rewiring like its predecessor, it had far greater processing speed. Later in the 1940s, the concepts of Hungarian-American mathematician John von Neumann were used to create a computer that had the ability to internally store instructions, which reduced many of the problems found with Aiken's computer and the ENIAC.

In 1951 the U.S. Census Bureau purchased the first UNIVAC I. Created by J. Presper Eckert and John Mauchly, the UNIVAC I was the first computer that was commercially available. The two men later formed Remington Rand, one of IBM's first rivals. As advances were made in the 1950s, such as the development of transistors, which replaced vacuum tubes used in earlier computers, the electronic computer finally became a truly viable and useful business tool. Further advances that increased processing speed and memory were made in the 1960s and 1970s with the creation of the integrated circuit, which combined many transistors into a single compact unit; and the invention of the microprocessor, a further advancement of the integrated circuit. These advances continued to reduce both the size and cost of electronic computers, making them increasingly common in business, government, and education.

By the 1980s supercomputers, mainframe systems, and minicomputers had already infiltrated the world market. There were about 100 computers worldwide in the early 1950s, but by the 1980s there were millions in use, making it a lucrative market. Mainframe and minicomputer manufacturers earned high profit margins, some as much as 90 percent on a sale. These systems were proprietary in design—often only the manufacturer of a system provided the hardware, maintenance, and even the software needed for it. Once a company selected a system, it was very difficult and expensive to change to a system made by another manufacturer. However, with the advent of the personal computer and quicker, more powerful microprocessors, this trend changed.

Personal computers were low-cost, non-proprietary, and did not offer the high profit margins that mainframe and minicomputers did. When personal computers first became available, some computer manufacturers viewed them as low-profit, low-power machines with low market potential, and essentially ignored them. However, when linked together in a network, a group of personal computers could provide an inexpensive means of handling tasks previously performed by more powerful computers. This was especially true as personal computer technology increased in the 1980s and 1990s, and the lines that divided the various computer types became increasingly blurred. By the mid-1990s home PCs and even hand-held video games would have the graphics capabilities similar to the supercomputers of a decade before, and personal computers could no longer be ignored.

A volatile global economy and increasing competition impacted the global computer market. Another factor influencing the industry was the market's continuing movement away from large, expensive, nonstandardized (closed or proprietary) mainframes to small, inexpensive, standardized (open) computer systems. Since these smaller systems had a much lower profit margin than mainframes, revenues were greatly reduced and a higher quantity of sales became more important. In addition, government pressures caused computer manufacturers to make products more environmentally friendly as well as to create equipment and develop production methods that used less energy and emitted less radiation and other harmful pollutants.

In the booming 1990s, it seemed the growth rate in the computer industry would always be 20 percent annually or more. Analysts predicted that the industry would continue to grow in the new millennium, but by 2002 they had lowered some of these expectations for annual growth. Competition would continue to increase as manufacturers found new ways to produce computers more inexpensively and efficiently through automation. In addition, to improve sales volume and decrease costs, companies reduced prices to the consumer, decreased the workforce, and shared research and development costs with other companies. For example, Microsoft and Intel were collaborating on development of a Net PC, and were probably spurred on by Oracle's developments of a "thin client," or NC (network computer). As such alliances increased, more mergers between computer manufacturers were expected to take place, such as the merger of NEC's PC operations (except China and Japan) and Packard Bell, forming Packard Bell-NEC. Similarly, Compaq acquired Digital Equipment Corporation in 1998.

The impact of network computing was also being felt in the computer industry, especially the PC segment. Most growth in the PC market was expected to result from the rapidly increasing use of all networks—local area networks, wide area networks, intranets, and the Internet. Growth was especially strong in countries like France and Japan, which had been resistant to network technology. In tandem with the spread of client/server technology and networking as business tools, the market for PC servers was growing at a rate of 23 percent per year during the 1990s. Manufacturers were building servers with enough power to compete with (and replace) workstations.

The global market for personal computers in 1997 was US$67 billion, which was strong, yet represented a slowdown from its earlier 30 percent growth rate. The number of PC shipments worldwide increased 16.5 percent, from 17.4 million to 20.2 million units. The market for portable computers—handhelds, notebooks, and laptops—was expected to grow at a higher rate than desktop PCs.

In the late 1990s, another challenge to the computer industry was becoming readily apparent to businesses and computer manufacturers worldwide—systems that stored dates as only two digits, registering 1998 as "98," were destined to read the year 2000 as "00" or 1900. For businesses and agencies of all kinds, the year 2000 seemed

to spell disaster, but thanks to precautions worldwide, the "Y2K bug" was far less problematic than some computer viruses being circulated by unscrupulous or revenge-seeking computer users.

In March 2002 computer company executives were once again gaining confidence, and major companies like IBM, Oracle, and Macintosh began putting on trade shows in San Francisco again after a being completely stagnate in 2001. No one announced that the crisis was over, but many analysts were confident that the technology sales crisis of 2001 had been met head-on.

CURRENT CONDITIONS

According to *Market Share Reporter,* the commercial market in 2003 had the highest share of PC shipments in the United States, with 33 percent of the market. In contrast, the consumer market had 18 percent of the total. The business sector was expected to continue as the largest consumer into 2007. According to *Euromonitor,* the business sector would have US$26.1 billion of the total US$50.3 billion market. A number of Media Center PCs were introduced in 2004 from HP, Microsoft, and Gateway. The digital revolution was set to explode in a wave of new products in the mid-2000s, as the computer, electronic, and communications industries combined technologies.

Following several years of double-digit growth through 2005, Gartner Inc. reported that global shipment of PCs would slow, rising about 5.7 percent annually between 2006 and 2008 to reflect the global slowing economy. More than 60 percent of the projected growth was expected to come from emerging markets. According to the IDC, the replacement market for desktop computers was particularly strong, and demand was the highest in the Americas and Europe. Latin America, in particular, continued to grow more than 20 percent per year. A Gartner study found that in addition to the growing use of digital features in computers, the replacement market was expected to drive sales in the mid-2000s, with 120 million PCs set for replacement in 2005. The IDC expected total PC shipments to reach 199.2 million units in 2005 (up 11.4 percent) and 217 million units (up 9 percent) by 2006.

IBM dominated the supercomputer market, manufacturing half of the world's top 500 supercomputers as reported in "Top 500 Supercomputer Rankings." Five of the top ten computers on the list were based on IBM's Blue Gene/L supercomputer. As reported in *eWeek* in June 2005, HP's share dropped, and the company held 26 percent of the market, with 131 of the top supercomputers, down from 34 percent six months before. Silicon Graphics held 5 percent of the market with 24 supercomputers on the top 500 list, with Dell and Cray Inc. slightly behind. China also was increasing its share of the global market. When it entered the top 500 list in 2002, Chinese companies only had three supercomputers on the list, compared to 19 in 2005, just behind Japan with 23. In May 2005, Japan announced plans to build a machine capable of handing 1 quadrillion calculations a second by 2010.

RESEARCH AND TECHNOLOGY

Research and development plays a major role in the electronic computer industry, where some product cycles are measured in months and the power of the personal computers has doubled every 12 to 18 months. To help combat escalating expenses, some manufacturers have sought partnerships with other companies to share in the high cost of research.

One of the major areas of PC research was the rapid spread of analog to digital conversion in the electronics market. As a result, once separate industries cooperated as well as competed. Computers, telecommunications, consumer electronics, entertainment, publishing, and television companies all had a stake in digital technology, and all were devoting research and development resources in that direction. Digital technology affected PC technology by spurring the rapid growth of multimedia, which put video on computers. Moreover, digital technology allowed manufactures to begin development of hybrid PCs/televisions. In addition, computer manufacturers were engaged in efforts to expand communication bandwidth, an area of strong interest to entertainment and information content providers. The U.S. Federal Communications Commission was keeping a close eye on electronics, computer manufacturers, and broadcasters and issued standards for new digital televisions with specifications for the new technology.

WORKFORCE

All three mature markets—the United States, Japan, and Europe—maintained or slightly increased their workforce from 1996 to 1997. Following a period when companies were laying off employees to reduce costs, industry employers who hoped to hire skilled personnel were finding a shortage of qualified workers in the late 1990s. As a result of the downsizing trend of the mid-1990s and again in 2001, companies were not seeing much loyalty from computer industry employees, safe in the knowledge that they could easily find work elsewhere. While computer engineers were competing for a limited number of jobs earlier in the decade, employment in the area was expected to improve significantly through 2010 according to U.S. Department of Labor in 2002. Reasons for the rise in employment potential included a rebounding U.S. economy and computer systems with needs that were increasingly interconnected. Computer

engineers were responsible for not only designing hardware systems, but also for integrating software into established systems as new technologies were adopted.

In its April 2004 monthly jobs report, the U.S. Department of Labor reported a continuing increase in employment for computer professionals. Computer and electronic product manufacturing reported an increase of 2,600 jobs in the United States, for a total of more than 1.3 million. The management and technical services sector added 3,400 jobs the same month.

The DeAnza College held a Cybercamp Academy for US$700 for a week-long camp that featured computers, graphic design programs, and video game modification for 10- to 17-year-olds. Attendees would learn skills that they could transfer to possible careers or future studies. "About half of the day is spent working in front of computers, a quarter is spent being physically active, and another quarter is spent working in groups on projects," explained Davis Konrad, director of marketing for Cybercamps.

INDUSTRY LEADERS

IBM (International Business Machines Corporation). Charles Flint created Calculating-Tabulating-Recording (CTR) in 1910 by merging his two companies, International Time Recording Co. and Computing Scale Company, with a third company called Tabulation Machine Company, which was started by Herman Hallerith. In 1914, Flint hired Thomas Watson as general manager of CTR. Watson later became president and created a powerful business sales force that became known for its superior customer service. Under his leadership the company quickly expanded in both in sales and size, moving into Europe, Asia, and Latin America. In 1924 CTR came to be known as International Business Machines, focusing on large tabulation machines. By 1949 it had operations in 58 countries. IBM World Trade Corporation was created that same year, which enjoyed the same dominance in foreign markets as it did in the United States.

U.S. giant International Business Machines Corporation (IBM) was the world's largest producer of electronic computers in 1997 with $78.5 billion in sales. However, IBM was not alone at the top. Compaq quickly surpassed IBM in PC sales, and Hitachi closed in on the mainframe market. Due to its size, some experts believed that IBM was not able to react to the ever-changing computer market fast enough—its sales dropped, and IBM lost billions of dollars in profits between 1985 and the early 1990s.

In response to these problems, IBM began major restructuring efforts. To make it easier for multinational companies to conduct business with IBM and break down barriers between countries, a plan to have one contract and one discount cover them wherever they did business was implemented. In addition, efforts to unify its global operations shifted power from many managers who oversaw the operations of an entire country to only 14 managers of industry sectors. IBM's efforts seemed to be working, and in the first quarter of 1998 the company performed above analysts' projections. Hardware revenue for that period was down, but the loss was attributed to IBM's lower PC prices in response to PC price wars.

On March 1, 2002, IBM began what it hoped would become a return to greatness under a new chief executive, longtime IBM chieftain Samuel J. Palmisano. Palmisano was personally involved when the company's technology was mocked as inferior by upstart rivals and was unable to deliver products in a reasonable time in 2000, which had once been its crowning hallmark had become embarrassingly problematic, according to *Business Week*. Palmisano's first job was to stop the bleeding. In January 2002 IBM's once revered stock plunged more than US$5 in a single day. He promised to update the company and to build an Internet presence for sales for the first time. IBM shareholders were watching hopefully, albeit nervously, to see if the new CEO could turn the company around. Palmisano also faced the challenge of increasing software sales, which crept along at a 3 percent growth rate even as some rivals achieved up to 30 percent growth rates according to *Business Week*.

Palmisano and IBM shifted the company's focus during the early to mid-2000s, focusing more on global IT services, including application management and e-business hosting. By 2004, IBM was ranked first in IT services in the world, reporting $96.5 billion in revenues from all divisions and 8 percent growth over the previous year. Of that, global services revenue was $46.2 billion, software revenue was $15.1 billion, and hardware revenue was $31.2 billion, 10 percent higher than in 2003. The company's net income rose to $8.4 billion, an 11.2 percent jump over 2003 levels. IBM employed 319,273 people by the end of 2004 and was the world's leading computer hardware company. By 2010, IBM reported revenues of US$98.08 billion and employed roughly 399,000 people.

The Computer and Communications Industry Association (CCIA), an IT trade organization, was critical of IBM's acquisition of Platform Solutions. The two companies had competed in the mainframe market and IBM's acquisition of Platform Solutions ended lawsuits the companies had brought against each other. In November 2006, IBM accused Platform Solutions of patent infringement by creating computers enabling customers to run IBM's System z operating systems, and software on other vendors' mainframes. In January 2007, Platform Solutions filed a countersuit accusing IBM of antitrust violations and

unfair competition. CCIA President and CEO Ed Black said the deal meant the resulting market was one "with few prospects for anything but complete domination by IBM." CCIA called for U.S. and European authorities to review the merger, although the deal may have been below the financial threshold for mandatory review.

Hitachi. In 1910 Namihei Odaira created Hitachi in the Japanese city of the same name and produced electric motors. The company began manufacturing transistors in the mid-1950s and integrated circuits in the 1960s. In 1974 it created an IBM-plug-compatible computer that it sold worldwide through such companies as National Semiconductor, Olivetti, and BASF. In 1991 Hitachi began selling IBM notebook PCs under its own name in Japan, and in 1993 sold its first eight-processor mainframe computer. Hitachi was one of the leading semiconductor producers in the world and Japan's largest electrical machinery manufacturer. It was the second-largest company in the industry with US$68.7 billion in revenues and the industry's largest employer with 330,152 workers. Those figures increased to US$95,982 billion for revenues and 359,746 for employees in 2010.

Hitachi was the world's second largest dynamic random access mechanization (DRAM) chip producer and built many of IBM's mainframe systems. However, its reliance on the mainframe industry made it extremely vulnerable to changing consumer needs and it thus suffered losses. In response, Hitachi began to make advances with its 4 MB DRAM, which would be needed in the growing multimedia computer market, and entered into a joint venture with Mitsubishi Corp. to create flash-memory chips. In 1998 Hitachi released what it claims was "the world's fastest 3.5-inch hard disk drive, the DK3E1T-91 series, with the speed of 12,030-rpm." Also in 1998 the company introduced its first disk drive incorporating giant magneto-resistive (GMR) head technology. With an areal density of 3.9 Gigabits (Gb) per square inch, the DK228A-65 notebook drive provided a storage capacity of 6.48 Gb. This development established Hitachi as a leader in the rapidly growing computer storage industry, and in the words of *Business Week,* allowed the company to "eat IBM's lunch." In 2002 Hitachi positioned itself to become the true leader in new handheld technology, putting together a model with remarkable power for business, game, and personal use. For 2005 the company reported US$84.2 billion in revenue, a 3.4 percent increase over 2004.

Hewlett-Packard. Hewlett-Packard (HP), a U.S. company, was the fourth largest computer manufacturer in 1997 with US$42.9 billion in sales. It was the sixth largest employer in the industry with 121,900 employees worldwide. The company has operations in 17 countries worldwide, including France, Mexico, Germany, and

Japan. Of 1997 sales, 45 percent were generated inside the United States, 33 percent in Europe, and the remaining sales in other countries. Eighty-three percent of Hewlett-Packard's revenues were generated by sales of computers and computer services and support, making it the second-largest company (behind IBM) in terms of sales generated by computer operations.

In May 2002 HP's shareholders and management purchased Compaq Computer Corp. for US$18.69 billion in HP stock, the largest merger in the industry's history. The merger gave HP's sagging sales a tremendous boost, even as IBM was regrouping under a new CEO and Japanese competitors Hitachi and Toshiba were reeling with reports that the yen was going to continue to drop before that nation returned to prosperity. The combined company reported 2003 revenues of US$73.1 billion for a one-year growth of 29 percent. In 2004, Hewlett-Packard earned $79.9 billion in revenues, up 9.4 percent from 2003. The company employed more than 150,000 people. In 2010, HP reported revenues of US$126.03 billion and 310,000 employees following the acquisition of 3Com.

William Hewlett and David Packard officially created Hewlett-Packard (HP) in 1939, although they worked together earlier to create eight oscillators for the Walt Disney Studios. In 1966, HP created its first computer for internal use, never intending to enter the computer market. However, two years later it created the first desktop calculator capable of performing scientific calculations and by 1974 committed itself to moving into the computer industry with the HP3000. The HP-85, Hewlett-Packard's first personal computer, was released in 1985. Reaction to it was poor because it was not compatible with IBM's designs. This caused HP not only to create IBM-compatible PCs, but also to move toward making all of its computers, at least in part, cross-compatible. To better position itself for the global market, it increased cooperative efforts, and in the late 1980s HP entered into trade agreements with companies such as Hitachi, Canon USA Inc., and Sony.

Compaq was started in 1982 by three former Texas Instruments engineers, including Joseph "Rod" Canion. By 1983, the company went public and earned more than US$100 million. In 1991 Eckhard Pfeiffer replaced Canion as CEO. Compaq made its mark as a maker of PC clones, selling desktop PCs with standard computer components from Microsoft and Intel, among others. The company took this model and used it to venture into the corporate market, building servers that held mammoth amounts of data and were stealing business from microcomputers and mainframes. In January 1998, Compaq was named "Company of the Year" by *Forbes* magazine, citing its swift growth, great returns, and great strategic leadership by Eckhard Pfeiffer. In 1998 Compaq

also signed a deal to buy Digital Equipment Corporation for US$9.6 billion. Under the deal, Digital became a subsidiary of Compaq, but the merger proved disastrous, significantly hurting shareholder confidence after losses mounted going into the 2000s.

Although relatively new to the industry, Compaq had its best year as the world's largest PC maker in 1998. With US$24.6 billion in sales, Compaq ranked seventh in terms of gross revenues among the overall industry's top 10 companies. In 2002, Compaq claimed more than 13 percent of the global PC market, surpassing first-ranked IBM. Even so, PCs accounted for only half of Compaq's sales, with other products that included servers, disk drives, modems, workstations, monitors, and printers. Compaq employed 37,004 people, making it the eighth largest employer in the industry, but large numbers of layoffs and early retirements followed the HP purchase.

Gartner Research firm issued revised data from the first quarter of 2008 reflecting that IBM had 29.4 percent global market share for its server business, which meant that HP had not moved into first place over IBM as reported in preliminary May figures. Dell was ranked number three with 12.3 percent market share in the first quarter of 2008, with less than half of what its leading competitors made. HP held a 28.3 percent market share for comparable items in the same quarter.

According to *Business Week,* the HP TouchSmart IQ506 was proof that Hewlett-Packard was taking its slogan, "the computer is personal again," seriously. The TouchSmart was compared to Apple's iMac classification as another "all in-one computer" in the 2008 version that included many improvements over its first version. The IQ506 was approximately US$500 less expensive with much better touch software. With this model, HP has learned that "the common mistake in the design of touch interfaces is to treat the human finger as though it were some sort of mouse." The TouchSmart programs are distinctly different and very user friendly by assuming that it will be a home computer that families will share. Users have the ability to exchange typed, handwritten, or voice notes using an application based on a "Post-It Notes" metaphor. HP's IQ506 "might be worthy of the Jetsons' household" but lacked some power in its performance, according to *The Washington Post.* Its design was compared to a LCD TV, but was missing "some of the core inputs" that users might desire for "a home media hub." The IQ506 was a dynamic alternative computer choice but was not expected to be considered by users as a primary system.

Toshiba. Toshiba is a major manufacturer of portable computers. The company was created in 1939 by the merger of Japanese electrical equipment manufacturers

Hakunetsu-sha and Company and Tanaka Seizo-sho (Tanaka Engineering Works). In 1924 Hakunetsu-sha created Japan's first cathode ray tube and began creating computers in 1954. In 1985, it was the first company to manufacture one-megabit memory chips, and it began shipping laptop computers the following year. Toshiba had US$44 billion in sales in 1997 and was the world's fourth-largest computer manufacturer. It was the fourth-largest employer in the industry, employing 186,000 workers. Toshiba was the world's largest memory chip producer, a major supplier of color flat-screen displays used for many portable computers, and the third-largest maker of liquid screen displays. Its willingness and success in creating joint ventures with companies such as IBM and Apple made it one of the industry's strongest companies, despite the Japanese recession and an ever-increasing competitive worldwide market. However, Toshiba was losing market share in the notebook market, dropping from 30 to 20 percent of that market from 1996 to early 1998. The loss was attributed to stiff competition from IBM and Compaq in price and technology.

In March 2002, with sales stagnant and the Japanese economy suffering, Toshiba executives could wait no longer. According to *Electronic Buyers News,* Toshiba began to shut down a quarter of its 98 domestic plants and cut its Japanese workforce 12 percent to improve cash flow. By 2004 Toshiba's revenues were US$52.8 billion, an 11 percent increase over 2003, and net income was up 77 percent to US$273 million. In 2010, Toshiba reported revenues of US$75.9 billion.

Dell. Dell Inc. was new to the list of industry leaders in 1998, but along with Compaq was one of the fastest growing computer companies in the industry. By 2004, Dell was the world's leading direct sales computer company, with no retail store overhead, and was the largest PC maker in the world. The company reported 2005 revenues of US$49.2 billion, representing 18 percent growth from 2004. Dell employed more than 55,000 people. Of the top 10 PC makers worldwide, Dell was the only one that remained consistently profitable during the early to mid-2000s. In 2004, Dell retained 16.4 percent of the global PC market, up from 14.9 percent in 2003, as reported by Gartner Japan. Sales were attributed primarily to strong growth in Europe and Japan, according to *eWeek.* Surviving ups and downs and adjusting to the marketplace, Dell reported revenues of US$52.9 billion and 96,000 employees for 2010.

A May 1998 *Fortune* article titled "Michael Dell Rocks" claimed that Dell's CEO "has transformed his industry and enriched thousands of shareholders. Dell stock is up 29,600 percent this decade. And now the company looks stronger than ever." In 1997 Dell earned US$12.3 billion in revenue, up from US$7.75 billion in

1996. From 1995 to 1998, the company grew by an average of 53 percent annually. According to *Fortune,* Dell was growing at twice the rate of any of its competitors, including Gateway, Compaq, and IBM. Dell's stock rose from its initial public offering price of US$8.50 in 1988 to US$69.25 in mid-1998, which demonstrates the gains the company's shareholders made. Dell's success, which came after some hard learning experiences, was built on its direct made-to-order PC sales and its success using the Internet as a sales medium. Not limited to PCs, Dell also marketed servers, CD-ROMs, modems, network hardware, disk drives, and other peripheral equipment. The company had room for growth, however, as it claimed only 6 percent of the global PC market in 1998, behind Compaq and IBM, and generated 70 percent of its sales inside the United States.

Michael Dell founded "PCs Limited" in his dorm room at the University of Texas in 1984. He began buying excess computers from local retailers, enhancing them, and reselling them directly to consumers at low prices. It took him under a year to begin earning sales of US$50,000 per month, and Dell soon decided to devote all of his time to the company. In 1988 he renamed the company Dell Computer Corp. and took the company public. Dell's company employed more than 10,000 people worldwide in 1998. In 2001, with an aggressive TV and print marketing campaign, Dell kept its sales of PCs at a respectable level even as other rivals saw their share of the market fall or collapse.

In March 2008, when Dell was listed as one of *IndustryWeek*'s 50 Best Manufacturers of 2008, the company introduced a revised plan for the future. The plan outlined several actions targeted at reducing overall product costs for design, manufacturing, logistics, materials, and operating expenses to restore Dell's competitive advantage to its operating model. After accessing its global manufacturing and logistics network, Dell decided to close its manufacturing facility in Austin, Texas, reduce global employee headcount by at least 8,800, and reduce related operating expenses. Dell also confirmed plans to include the integration of software-as-a-service applications and remote management tools.

In June 2008, Dell celebrated the first year of its commitment to be 'green' by announcing a goal to produce notebooks and desktops that used 25 percent less energy by 2010. The company also planned to expand its "Plant a Tree for Me" program to encourage reforestation projects among the company and its partners. From 2006 through 2007, Dell increased the recovery of goods from its consumers 20 percent through its free pick-up program.

To prepare to market a laptop protection and data recovery service, Dell commissioned a study that found that more than 12,000 laptop computers are lost in U.S. airports each week, adding up to more than 600,000 laptops per year. Only 33 percent of those lost laptops are reclaimed, and 16 percent of business travelers claimed that they would do nothing if their laptops were lost, and 58 percent said they would not take any action until they had advice from their employers.

NEC. Japan's Nippon Electric Company (NEC), was created in 1898 as a joint venture between Western Electric of the United States and a group of Japanese investors. While it began as an importer of telephone equipment, it soon became a manufacturer and supplier. After struggling through the effects of an earthquake in 1923 and World War II, NEC entered the computer industry in 1954. By 1986 NEC had become Japan's second largest computer company, and was one of the largest manufacturers of semiconductors in the 1990s. In 1997 it had US$39.9 billion in sales, making it the world's fifth largest computer company. In Japan, NEC ranked first in sales of personal computers, holding 40 percent of Japan's domestic market and deriving 80 percent of its revenue there. By 2005 the company had US$45.29 billion in revenues, a slight decline from 2004, but net income rose 60 percent to $633 million. NEC's IT Solutions Business, which included systems integration, hardware, and software, was responsible for generating 44 percent of the company's revenues. NEC competed with Fujitsu for the number one spot in Japan. By 2010, its revenues were US$42.8 billion and the company had 142,358 employees.

Fujitsu. In 1935 Fuji Electric Co. Ltd. created Fujitsu to build telephone equipment. In 1954 it entered the data processing arena by developing Japan's first computer, which was called the FACOM 100. To ensure the success of its new computer industry, Japan's Ministry of International Trade and Industry (MITI) put up trade barriers. In addition, Japan sponsored the development of new computers through a public utility created in the 1950s called National Telephone and Telegraph, which essentially created a guaranteed market for Japanese-made computers. In the 1960s, MITI helped fund and direct Fujitsu's creation of mainframe systems. Despite these efforts, however, Fujitsu computers were still technologically far behind those of IBM. In 1972 Fujitsu invested money into the Amdahl Corporation, which was owned by the primary creator of IBM's extremely successful 360 series computers. In 1997 they bought the remaining 55 percent of Amdahl. This investment gave Fujitsu the technological knowledge it needed and put the company on level ground with IBM. The company shipped its first supercomputer in 1982 and by 1994 was the second largest maker of supercomputers.

Fujitsu was the world's sixth largest computer manufacturer in 1997 with US$36.37 billion in revenues. Counting 167,000 employees, it was the industry's fourth largest employer and Japan's second largest computer manufacturer. By 2004, the company rivaled NEC for Japan's number one spot, having reported US$45.1 billion in revenue for 2004, more than 17 percent more than in 2003. It also provided stiff competition to Hitachi as the world's second largest manufacturer of mainframes. In 1998 the company entered a joint venture with Computer Associates International Inc. to build Internet business systems for client/server systems. Fujitsu had operations in more than 400 locations around the globe, including Australia, the United States, Mexico, France, Colombia, Indonesia, and Zimbabwe. Fujitsu also entered the groupware market in the late 1990s with its Teamware, and was gaining market share in Japan, where Lotus Notes and Microsoft dominated. In 2002, as sales in all areas of the company slowed along with Japan's larger economic crisis, Fujitsu reduced its labor force by more than 25,000 workers. By 2010, the company had rebounded to earn US$55.18 billion with nearly 186,000 employees.

Sun Microsystems. Sun Microsystems was founded in 1982 by four young entrepreneurs, and has since grown into a *Fortune* 500 company with operations in more than 150 countries. Sun's first product was a high-performance Unix-based system computer. In 1997, it developed what was claimed to be one of the most powerful single-system servers. Taking another direction, in the late 1990s the company revolutionized the Internet software industry by developing the Java programming language.

Based in Palo Alto, California, Sun Microsystems was a leading manufacturer of network computing systems and Unix-based workstations. In 1997 Sun earned US$8.6 billion in revenue and employed 21,500 people, making it the world's tenth largest computer company and employer. Sun generated about half of its sales outside the United States, and demonstrated consistent 15 to 20 percent growth during the late 1990s. Sun's goal in 1998 was to transform itself into "an enterprise computing firm focused on global network computing." By 2009 the company was reporting US$11.4 billion in revenue and employing 29,000 people.

Sun Microsystems was acquired by Oracle in January 2010. Oracle's 2010 revenue was US$29.27 billion.

Apple Computer Inc. In 2002 executives at Apple had stopped reminiscing about the good old days when Mac's market share had climbed steadily. Instead, the company resisted the slump in PC sales with strong orders for G-4 laptops and the new iMac flat screen models. These models featured the company's most recent addition to the world of operating systems, OS X. Derived from the tried-and-true Unix program, the suddenly hot, new OS X, complete with splashy graphics, was introduced with more bells than bugs, and more flash than flaws. In 2002 the company's guru Steven Jobs announced that 40 percent of those entering the growing nationwide chain of Apple Mac stores say they were new customers to the Mac product line. During the fourth quarter of 2004, Apple shipped 836,000 Macintosh units (a 6 percent increase) and more than 2 million iPods (a 500 percent increase). Retail store revenues grew 95 percent from 2003 to 2004. Apple posted 33.4 percent growth in 2004, with US$8.27 billion in revenue. By 2010, revenues were posted as US$65.23 billion with 49,400 employees.

The U.S. Department of Justice conducted a two-year probe into backdated stock at Apple that resulting in a company confession that it had, in fact, backdated certain option grants, including two that had been awarded to founder and CEO Steven Jobs. The practice is not illegal as long as it is disclosed, which Apple had failed to do in the early 2000s.

Leander Kahney, author of *Inside Steve's Brain,* praised Steven Jobs for turning his distinctive personality traits into a unique business process at Apple. Jobs' control-freak tendencies were considered to be key reasons for Apple's ability to control "the entire experience of its products." Apple successfully controlled hardware, software, web services and advertising related to its products. In addition, while choice and flexibility were limited, Apple's products worked seamlessly together. Kahney concluded that Jobs on-going interest in consumers who were ordinary people helped Apple survive and excel. Kahney believed Jobs was "right in the sweet spot" for the early twenty-first century when all actions were "mediated by a computer or a smart device."

Gateway. A strong surge in sales in the 1990s catapulted Gateway into fourth place among personal computer sellers, but the company staggered due to consumer disinterest and a general economic slowdown in 2001. Gateway stocks fell to 1995 prices, dropping to US$4.24 one month after the September 11, 2001, terrorist attacks against the United States. In less than a year, Gateway lost its enviable 15 percent of the PC market and found itself with less than 9 percent of the market at the beginning of 2002. Much of Gateway's misfortune became rival Dell's good fortune as the rival muscled away Gateway's market share, according to nonprofit research company IDC. Unlike Dell, which has no store overhead, Gateway found itself at a disadvantage as it considered closing the stores that had been readily recognized with the trademark black and white logo. Gateway was also confusing buyers in 2001, as it changed its

selling mission regarding low-end buyers in mid-year. By 2004, Gateway had closed all of its stores and was selling products only through other retailers, directly over the phone, and on the Internet. The company acquired eMachines that year. In 2004 revenues were US$3.6 billion.

In order to align itself with new corporate parent, Acer Computers, Gateway decided to change its business model. The company decided to sell only through retail and e-tail partners. Retailers selling Gateway products included Best Buy, Costco, Wal-Mart, and several online retailers. The change was planned for the first weekend of August 2008 and would result in an undisclosed number of layoffs.

MAJOR COUNTRIES IN THE INDUSTRY

The United States. The United States was the world leader in the computer industry. In contrast to other major markets, the U.S. market was forecast to grow only 3.5 percent in 2007 due to market maturity and saturation according to *Euromonitor.* Consumer demand was expected to remain solid in the United States, with portable PCs generating the largest amount of demand. In June 2005 Current Analysis, a research firm, announced that for the first time in history, notebook computers outsold desktops, accounting for 53 percent of the total PC market, an increase of 46 percent. The change was expected to accompany growth in telecommuting and wireless network access. Sales were also facilitated by declines in laptop prices (17 percent) compared to declines in desktop pricing (4 percent). Desktop growth was expected to show low growth, if any, in the United States.

In 2002, in attempt to help the beleaguered computer industry, the federal government bowed to computer industry pleas and relaxed restrictions on computer exports. The industry was allowed to export computers to China, Russia, India, Pakistan, and others which had 190,000 millions of theoretical operations per second (Mtops), which was more than double previously allowable Mtops, according to *Electronic Engineering Times.* The move gave some nations with security limitations the ability to import far more powerful computers than previously allowed by the U.S. government.

European Union. The European market was hit hard during the first half of the 1990s by a weak economy. During the early 1990s, three of Europe's top computer manufacturers—Siemens Nixdorf, Olivetti, and Groupe Bull—each lost at least 12 percent in revenues over the previous year. Furthermore, European computer manufacturers had a difficult time competing in the global market because they lacked the research and development funding and strength found in their counterparts from the United States, and to a smaller degree, Japan, both of which continued to gain strength and dominance in the European market. As reported in a 1997 *Fortune* article, the outlook for European technology did not improve during the late 1990s.

In 2002 a soft economy, coupled with fallout from the September 11, 2001, terrorist attacks against the United States, the growth of the computer industry in Germany became chaotic. PC sales in 2001 plunged 7.3 percent from 2000, reaching US$6.42 million. Besides Germany, the European nations of Great Britain, France, Italy, and the Netherlands also had disastrous 2001 PC sales. As of early 2005, consumer demand gave the European market a boost, and laptop sales climbed almost 16 percent in January 2005. Most European nations reported double-digit growth, mainly in France, Spain, and Sweden. The Spanish PC market realized 24.7 percent growth during the first quarter of 2001, with the desktop market growing at almost the same rate as laptops in the country. Only Germany had declines in sales, falling 1 percent. Following the trend in the United States, laptop sales were expected to overtake desktop sales. Long-term growth in Europe was expected to be solid during the mid-2000s, due to increased mobility, updating aging systems, and increased market penetration. Moving into 2007, the U.K. market was expected to grow 47 percent, the German market was expected to grow 28 percent, and the French market was expected to grow 17 percent, according to *Euromonitor.*

Japan. In 2002 a depressed Japanese economy and a soft market for personal computers saw the nation's computer manufacturers in nail-biting mode. During the late 1990s Japan saw renewed growth in hardware purchasing, particularly in the networking area. Part of the reason for this surge in growth was the Japanese government's goal to achieve a "Fiber-to-the-Home" network that would connect all government offices, businesses, homes, and institutions by 2010. PC servers, workstations, and peripheral and networking interface systems were expected to be the best products for manufacturers hoping to market to Japan. During the 2000s, consumer demand was expected to boost growth in Japan, but slowing commercial growth was expected to limit growth overall.

Taiwan. One of the fastest growing markets in Asia during the late 1990s was Taiwan. According to *Business Week,* "As neighboring economies falter, this humming entrepreneurial dynamo is the envy of Asia." The country encouraged the start-up of new industries, in contrast to countries such as Japan and China, which relied on established large corporations to support their economies.

India. India, while still counted as one of Asia-Pacific's hottest growth areas, was experiencing difficulty in its domestic hardware industry due to increasing competition from multinational companies, which created price wars and stunted growth for domestic companies. Additionally, low import duties and devalued currency were narrowing profit margins for domestic companies. India was still seen as an area with enormous potential, however, and had remarkably low technology penetration, leaving much room for growth.

Latin America. Another region identified with high-growth potential was Latin America. Notebook PC shipments for the third quarter of 1997 were 935,000, and the regional PC market grew 32 percent from 1996 to 1997. Leading countries in the area were Venezuela (53 percent growth) and Chile (49 percent growth), while Argentina and Colombia also made substantial progress. The collapse of the Argentine economy in 2001 and slow sales in other Latin American nations contributed to general weakness in the computer industry in the early 2000s. *Business Wire* credited Compaq with 22.9 percent of computer shipments to Latin America in 2001. IBM, which provided high-end machines, reported the lion's share of 2001 revenues from computer sales, with 40 percent. Dell lost some money in 2001, but began to make its presence known in the region. As of 2005, Latin America was the fastest growing region in the global computer market.

BIBLIOGRAPHY
"3 of Top 10 PC Makers to Exit Market by 2007: Gartner." *Japan Computer Industry Scan,* 13 December 2004.

Baker, Stephen, and Heather Green. "Big Bang!" *Business Week,* 21 June 2004.

Burt, Jeffrey. "Big Iron Is Back" *eWeek,* 11 October 2004.

"Computer Shipments Rise in Q1." *Purchasing,* 19 May 2005. Available from www.purchasing.com.

"Current Analysis Reveals That Laptops Outsell Desktops in the US for the First Time." *Worldwide Computer Products News,* 6 June 2005.

"Dell Celebrates Green Year." IT Web Limited, 30 June 2008. Available from www.itweb.co.za.

"Desktop Personal Computers in Australia, China, France, Germany, Japan, South Korea, UK, US." *Euromonitor,* August 2004. Available from www.majormarketprofiles.com.

Gladstone, Darren. "HP TouchSmart IQ506 Desktop PC." *PC World,* 7 July 2008. Available from www.washingtonpost.com.

Glover, Tony. "Users Switch to Laptops." *MicroScope,* 4 April 2005.

Gross, Grant. "IBM Mainframe Acquisition Raises Antitrust Concerns." *IDG News Service,* 2 July 2008.

"Hoover's Company Capsules," *Hoover's Online,* 2008. Available from www.hoovers.com.

"HP Launched Media Center PC in China." *PC World,* April 2004.

Kahney, Leander. "Steve Jobs Nails It Again, and Again." *The Street,* 10 July 2008. Available from www.thestreet.com.

Lazich, Robert S., ed. *Market Share Reporter.* Detroit: Thomson Gale, 2004.

Leopold, George. "U.S. Relaxes Export Restrictions on PCs, MPUs." *Electronic Engineering Times,* 7 January 2002.

Menn, Joseph. "Gateway Stock Drops After Strategy Swing." *Los Angeles Times,* 1 March 2002.

"Microsoft Extends the Media Center PC." *PC Magazine,* 9 January 2004.

"MTS, Microsoft and Fujitsu Siemens Computers Partner to Deliver Mobile Broadband to CIS." *Market Watch,* 9 July 2008.

Musil, Steven. "Apple Escapes Charges in US Stock. Options Probe." CNET News, 14 July 2008. Available from news.cnet.com/.

Olenick, Doug. "Gateway Drops Direct-Sales Operation." *TWICE (This Week in Consumer Electronics),* 29 July 2008. Available from www.twice.com.

"PC Outlook Is Still Strong, According to IDC: Portable Adoption and Growth in Emerging Markets Remain Key Drivers." IDC, 16 June 2005. Available from www.idc.com.

"PC Recovery Continues, Fueled by Strong Performance in Europe and Moderate Enterprise Demand, According to IDC." IDC, 15 July 2004. Available from www.idc.com.

"Personal Computer Prices Industrywide Fell By 9 Percent During the First Three Quarters of 2003." *Purchasing,* 3 June 2004.

"The Personal Computer Threads The One Billon Mark." HP.com, 7 July 2008. Available from www.digital.com.

"Replacement Purchases Will Drive PC Industry." *Fairfield County Business Journal,* 31 May 2004.

"Revised Data Show IBM Ahead of Hewlett-Packard in Server Market." *Triangle Business Journal,* 7 July 2008.

Salkever, Alex. "Finally, a Chance for Apple to Flourish; Steve Jobs Certainly Has the Needed Pieces. The Key Question: Will its Hot Products and a Major Retail Effort Boost Market Share?" *Business Week,* 23 January 2002.

Scott, Stuart. "Internet Comes to Your Car." *Australian IT,* 7 July 2008. Available at www.australianit.news.com.au.

"Servers." *Information Age,* 10 March 2005.

"Strong PC Growth Seen in 2004." *Client Server News,* 1 March 2004.

Taylor, Josh. "Gateway Crashes the Living Room." *PC World,* April 2004.

Tompkins, Joshua. "Monster Mainframes Battle for Bragging Rights." *Popular Science,* June 2005.

"Top 500 Supercomputer Rankings Show IBM Surge." *eWeek,* 22 June 2005.

U.S. Department of Labor, Bureau of Labor Statistics. "Computer and Electronic Product Manufacturing," 23 July 2004. Available from www.bls.gov.

Wildstrom, Stephen H. "HP's Personal Touch." *Business Week,* 25 June 2008. Available from www.businessweek.com.

"Zeroes, Ones and Shameless Empire-Building." *The New Zealand Herald,* 7 July 2008. Available from www.nzherald.co.nz.

SIC 7374

DATA PROCESSING SERVICES

NAICS CODE(S)

518210. Data processing firms provide diverse computer-related services primarily to other businesses. Specialties within the industry include: Data entry; Database management; Text or graphics digitization; Payroll processing; Credit card transaction processing; Medical claims billing; Computer time leasing; and Off-site data management facilities.

Certain firms in the industry also perform computer systems design, hardware consulting, contract maintenance, on-site management, and integration services. For discussion of these activities, see **Computer Services.**

INDUSTRY SNAPSHOT

A key beneficiary of the global trend toward outsourcing non-core business functions, the data processing industry obtained double-digit sales growth in leading markets throughout much of the 1990s, and continued to grow well into the new millennium. According to the U.S. Bureau of Labor Statistics, the computer and data processing industry was the fastest growing industry in the U.S. economy, with employment projected to increase 86 percent between 2000 and 2010. During 2000, the information technology outsourcing market, a loose measure of data processing receipts, was nearly 20 percent of all outsourcing expenditures in the United States. According to market research firm International Data Corp., total global outsourcing spending was projected to reach US$151 billion by 2010.

Long-term prospects for the data processing industry worldwide remain strong. Trends supporting industry growth include a continued swing toward outsourcing for cost savings and, in some countries, a shortage of technologically savvy workers available to firms outside the information technology industries. The Outsourcing Institute reported that outsourcing related to e-commerce functions continued to be the fastest growing sector, with an annual growth rate of about 18 percent. The institute also claimed that demand for such support would continue to increase. By 2004, the institute reported that while the original intent of outsourcing was to save money, the reasons have ballooned to include the desire for access to the best providers in the industry, but on an as-needed basis.

By 2004, the outlook for data processing services was strong, as the outsourcing of IT services in general began an upswing. The U.S. Bureau of Labor Statistics reported more than 286,000 U.S. employees in the industry in 2003, the vast majority of whom worked in computer or administrative support positions.

ORGANIZATION AND STRUCTURE

Data processing companies perform services such as credit card authorization and billing, data entry, medical claims processing, payroll processing, and off-site data center management. Data processing services generally use their own facilities and proprietary software to process their customers' data. Many of the big data processing services tend to specialize. Historically, the largest segments of the industry by revenue were data center management, payroll processing, and credit card transaction processing, but with the proliferation of the Internet and the growing popularity of e-commerce, new sectors in the data processing services industry have become popular including online database management and Web site hosting and management.

Although many industry firms work with multi-year contracts, data processing services are often delivered on either a timesharing or a transaction basis. A timesharing service vendor usually sells customers a portion of time on a large computer. Timesharing is valuable to companies that need access to computing power that they could not otherwise afford. Companies also use timesharing services to handle part of their data processing needs in cases where their in-house facilities cannot accommodate the additional capacity, or when they are upgrading or building their own in-house computing systems.

Firms that provide transaction processing services assume responsibility for a company's high-volume office functions, such as payroll processing. Transaction providers base their rates on the number of transactions processed, rather than on the time it takes to process them (as with timesharing). One disadvantage for establishments that provide this kind of service is that transaction processing is sensitive to shifts in the economy. If a company offers payroll services, for instance, it may find that during a recession a client that trims its workforce needs fewer payroll checks processed.

Many companies turned to outsourcing in the late 1990s because of their increased need to consolidate operations, control costs, and make more efficient use of existing resources. Outsourcing continued to experience substantial growth into the early years of the first decade of the 2000s. Outsourcing has a particular appeal to companies that often spend hundreds of millions of dollars a year on data processing. Because computers generally account for between 3 to 5 percent of a company's operating budget, using an outsourcing vendor can lower costs significantly. The vendor is able to offer computerization on a large scale and can consolidate its data centers. The vendor will typically charge a fixed (or at least predictable) annual amount, and this gives the customer better control over costs.

The United States continues to command the greatest share of the world's data processing business. This is true in part because U.S. companies have been quicker to outsource various data management tasks, notably payroll management and credit card transaction processing, to independent services that specialize in the various kinds of data handling. The United States also has been quick to adapt to changing technologies brought on by the increased use of the Internet. Major industry participants in the United States, several of which lead the world in certain service categories, have also aggressively courted business worldwide and are market leaders within other countries, particularly in Canada and Europe. In addition to the leading companies that primarily sell computer services, the global market also is served by major hardware companies such as IBM, which have found that offering contract data management services can help cushion their profits during volatile periods in the hardware business.

Legal and Trade Issues. The U.S. government has placed a high priority on removing the barriers to cross-border trade and investment. Information service companies have benefited from implementation of both the North American Free Trade Agreement (NAFTA) and expansion of the General Agreement on Tariffs and Trade (GATT) to include services under the General Agreement on Trade in Services (GATS). Because its companies are so central to the world industry, the United States accrues a significant trade surplus in computer service revenues each year.

Provisions regulating telecommunications and intellectual property protection are important to the data processing industry. One of the greatest challenges facing the industry is the need to develop methods to protect personal privacy, security, and intellectual property. Industry firms process highly sensitive information for consumers and businesses—including paychecks, credit card transactions, and medical information—and thus data security is of paramount importance. As a larger portion of transactions began to take place either on the Internet or through company intranets, the need for security grew as data became susceptible to theft, credit card fraud, and computer viruses.

The International Chamber of Commerce (ICC) started to focus on security-related issues surrounding electronic commerce. The ICC created the Commission on Telecommunications and Information Technologies to develop policies on information security. The ICC also created the Electronic Commerce Project (ECP). The ECP consisted of experts from various other ICC commissions including Banking Technique and Practice, Telecommunications and Information Technologies, Financial Services and Insurance, Transport, and International Commercial Practice, and was created to promote safe and secure e-business transactions. In 2001 the project was divided into three major areas including the General Usage for Internationally Digitally Ensured Commerce (GUIDEC), the Electronic Trade Practices Working Group, and E-terms service. GUIDEC, a set of international rules, definitions, and guidelines for the use of electronic authentication techniques, was considered to be one of the first sets of global regulations for electronic commerce.

BACKGROUND AND DEVELOPMENT

Many of the world's leading data processing service companies began as early computer designers and manufacturers. Control Data Corporation (now known as Ceridian Corporation) was established in 1957 by a dozen former Sperry Rand engineers. Co-founder Seymour Cray, an American electronics engineer who designed early supercomputers, is regarded as one of the world's brightest and most influential computer designers.

World War II had a significant impact on the development of data processing companies because it hastened the conversion from office tabulating equipment to data processing. The computer industry grew after the conclusion of World War II, and a large number of companies formed that were devoted to data processing. The majority of these new companies specialized in the areas of payroll processing and banking.

A large portion of the companies in the computer and data processing and preparation service industry have strong historical ties to financial services. Some leading companies in the field grew out of the check and payroll processing area. Others like Control Data Corporation and TRW developed out of the defense industry, the military, and the scientific community.

One of the first major examples of outsourcing took place in 1989 when Eastman Kodak signed a 10-year contract with IBM. For the first time, outsourcing was seen as a viable alternative to in-house information systems. Other large companies followed suit, and by the late 1990s outsourcing, at least on a limited scale, was considered a norm in the United States and was a growing trend elsewhere in the world. By the early years of the first decade of the 2000s, outsourcing was one of the fastest growing segments in the computer and data processing services industry.

In addition, companies increasingly utilized processing companies for "front office" functions. Up until the mid-1990s, data processing services were used primarily for clerical, high-volume tasks like payroll processing, health care claims processing, and other general accounting and record keeping duties. Some organizations, however, began to take advantage of low-priced, higher performance computer technology to improve in areas such as customer service, fund transfers, materials replacement, or inventory requisition. As the Internet became a popular forum for business applications in the late 1990s and the early years of the first decade of the 2000s, most companies looked to data processing firms for their expertise in handling complex data processing systems.

The global computer outsourcing industry as a whole grew by as much as 13 percent annually in the latter half of the 1990s, according to published figures from International Data Corporation (IDC). Outsource-related spending reached US$99 billion in 1998 and was expected to grow to more than US$151 billion by 2003. In 1998, processing services including payroll, claims, and credit card processing were responsible for nearly 60 percent (US$59.5 billion) of global outsource spending.

CURRENT CONDITIONS

Revenue from data processing and related services is expected to continue to increase as new methods of data processing are introduced. The increasing need of companies to integrate multi-vendor systems is one reason for this growth. Corporations and other end users purchase hardware and software from multiple vendors. This means that organizations can build more cost-effective computer-based information systems. The complexity of designing and maintaining integrated systems has grown, and computer service firms help organizations with this. Specifically, data processing providers' staff provide the expertise to process the requirements, and work with other computer consultants to design the system.

Several factors led to the increased use of outsourcing in the data processing services industry, including globalization, privatization, deregulation, and technological advancement. The United States continues to dominate the industry, but the information systems and processing services segments in other countries were expected to experience steady growth. IDC estimated that in some countries, growth rates were reaching nearly 27 percent per year. IDC also believed that the Asia/Pacific region would increase its spending on outsourcing by 15 percent per year.

In the middle of the first decade of the 2000s, business continued to rise for this industry segment. Fueled by increasing activity in bank and merchant accounts, and coupled with the stabilizing economy and favorable business climate, the industry was growing steadily. By 2004, the health care industry had become a major market for processing accounts. The use of patient information cards, similar to credit and debit cards, but without payment functions, was on the horizon. In California, for example, insurance provider Spot Check offered medical cards with magnetic stripes. This card design allowed the patient to swipe it and give medical providers instant access to patient information such as insurance, doctor, and referrals.

RESEARCH AND TECHNOLOGY

Consumer demand for electronic data continued to grow during the mid-years of the first decade of the 2000s. Stimulants to growth in the industry included the expansion of e-commerce and a flood of new services related to developments in computer technology. Such services included computer mapping, computerized airline ticketing, electronic toll processing, Web site design, and online database management.

Data warehousing, the organization and assembly of data created from day-to-day business operations, became increasingly popular during the late 1990s. Companies that needed an efficient method of analyzing business transactions often turned to computer and data processing firms to manage the flood of data brought on by new technological advancements. This was extremely important for companies with online marketplaces. Having data placed in a warehouse allowed the company to retrieve important demographic and sales information that was beneficial to business and marketing plans. The need for data warehousing was expected to continue to grow as both brick and mortar companies and dot-com firms utilized advanced data management technology to analyze information, make business forecasts, and control inventory.

WORKFORCE

The U.S. Bureau of Labor Statistics reported that the computer and data processing services industry was the fastest growing industry in the economy in the new millennium. This industry was expected to account for 36.6 percent by 2006. Industry employment was expected to increase by 86 percent between 2000 and 2010.

Employees typically work in an office environment, telecommute, or work at a client's office. The majority of the workforce falls within the 25 to 34 age group, while the second largest group is 35 to 44 years of age. The largest occupational group in the industry is comprised of computer analysts, computer engineers, and computer programmers. The level of education needed for employment in this industry varies with each job and ranges from a high school diploma to a college degree, as well as specialized training.

INDUSTRY LEADERS

Electronic Data Systems Corp. The leading data processing company in the United States is Electronic Data Systems (EDS), which for more than 40 years has provided claims processing for the U.S. federal and state Medicaid and Medicare programs. In addition, the company is the primary provider of data processing services for General Motors. In 2004 EDS posted sales of US$20.7 billion and employed 117,000 people. Forty-three percent of sales stemmed from international operations. EDS also provides services related to systems integration, network and systems operations, data center management, application development, outsourcing, and management consulting. In 2005, EDS announced a joint venture company with Towers Perrin called ExellerateHRO (85% owned by

EDS), which combined EDS' payroll and related human resource outsourcing business with the pension, health, and welfare administration service business of Towers Perrin.

EDS was founded in 1962 by H. Ross Perot, a disgruntled IBM salesman. After presenting IBM executives with his idea of providing companies with electronic data processing management services, only to be turned down, Perot decided to do it himself. It took Perot five months to find his first customer. After that, Perot pioneered the long-term, fixed-price contract. At the time, service companies usually offered 60- to 90-day contracts. EDS contracts were written for a five-year period.

In the 1960s the company became involved in Medicare and Medicaid claims processing, insurance company data processing, and data management for banks. EDS eventually established itself as the number one service provider in all three of these market segments. Acquired by General Motors Corporation in 1984, EDS was later spun off as an independent company in 1996. Although EDS had long been highly diversified, services to General Motors still accounted for 9.5 percent of EDS's revenues in 2004, although this figure had been steadily falling.

In May 2007, EDS announced it was selected by the U.S. General Services Administration to provide end-to-end satellite communications services to all federal government agencies under the Satellite Services-II contract. Related services enable agencies to obtain satellite communications bandwidth plus experience many diverse applications. Those applications include distance learning, streaming video, Telemedicine, broadcast satellite service, plus engineering and maintenance support services.

Another May 2007 announcement spotlighted EDS's purchase of a 74.9 percent stake in the IT arm of KarstadtQuelle, Itellium Systems & Services GmbH. The agreement called for EDS to handle running, development, and maintenance of KarstadtQuelle's applications for eight years. Estimated value for the contract was US$1 billion.

Affiliated Computer Services Inc. Dallas, Texas-based Affiliated Computer Services (ACS) is a leading supplier of business process and information technology outsourcing, with local and state governments providing about 59 percent of its revenues in 2004. In the government sector, ACS provides focus on transaction processing and program management services such as child support payment processing, electronic toll collection, welfare and community services, and traffic violations processing. For commercial customers, in addition to systems integration and information technology outsourcing services, the company provides data processing services in the areas of healthcare claims processing and financial information processing. Total revenues in 2004 were US$4.1 billion. The company sold its federal business to Lockheed Martin Corporation in 2004. In 2005 the company reported having 52,000 employees. By 2006, business process outsourcing accounted for 75 percent of sales. Revenues were reported as being US$5.4 billion.

In April 2007, ACS announced that the Colorado Department of Health Care Policy and Financing awarded a three-year contact to continue operating the state's Medicaid Management Information System. ACS had operated the system since 1996. The contract calls for ACS to process more than 25 million claims annually. Additional services include providing systems development and maintenance, pharmacy benefits management, decision support services, fraud and abuse detection and recovery, claims processing, call center and program policy support, plus third-party recovery.

Another April 2007 announcement reflected that ACS had completed the acquisition of certain Albion Inc. company assets. Albion was a company specializing in integrated eligibility software solutions. The acquisition enhanced capabilities of ACS in the health and human services area.

Computer Sciences Corp. With 2005 revenues of US$14.1 billion, Computer Sciences (CSC) is a diversified computer services contractor to industry and governments worldwide. That year, 40 percent of company revenues stemmed from sources outside the United States, while 33 percent came from contracts with the U.S. federal government and 27 percent from U.S. commercial firms. Known for its strong position in the information technology services sector, the company provides outsourcing, management consulting, network design, and systems integration. CSC was ranked as the global market leader in insurance business process outsourcing (BPO). The company had 200 BPO customers and 20 BPO centers around the world in 2005.

By 2007, CSC had 77,000 employees. Its revenues totaled US$14.7 billion in 2006. CSC announced its plans to acquire Covansys for US$34 per share in an all-cash transaction valued at approximately US$1.3 billion. It was considered as an important move toward achieving the CSC strategic goal of increasing shareholder value and growing more business. The acquisition nearly doubled the size of CSC's workforce in India to approximately 14,000 employees. Both Convasys and CSC's operations in India were listed among the top 10 places to work for IT professionals in India.

First Data Corp. Posting US$10.1 billion in revenues during 2004, First Data Corp. originated as American Express Information Services Corp. in 1982; the name

was changed to First Data Corp. in 1992. In 1995 it merged with competitor First Financial Management Corp., which also held the Western Union chain of money transfer outlets. In the same year, First Data purchased Card Establishment Services, a major merchant credit card processing operation formerly held by Citicorp, making it the largest credit card transaction processor in the United States, a position it continued to hold in the early years of the first decade of the 2000s.

First Data's payment services business accounted for nearly 40 percent of sales prior to a restructuring announced in 2006. The company spun off Western Union plus related Orlandi Valuta and Vigo Remittance units. First Data provides check verification through Telecheck and ATM network operation through NYCE. In 2004, First Data further expanded when it acquired Cashcard Australia Limited. During 2005, the company had 33,000 employees, and Kohlberg Kravis Roberts agreed to buy First Data.

First Data agreed to use products from Vivotech, a contactless payments company responsible for developing Near Field Communication hardware. Those products include Near Field Communication terminals, wallets, and over-the-air provisioning systems for mobile commerce.

A green-sensitive trio launched an innovative, more environmentally friendly payroll program. Walmart, MasterCard Worldwide and First Data united to implement a plan resulting in Wal-Mart and Sam's Club associates in the United States experiencing reductions in amount of paper paychecks and stubs. The alternate solution utilizes an electronic pay program with the Money Network MasterCard Pay Card and electronic pay stubs. First Data's Money Network Payroll Distribution Service will share its expertise to provide processing and reloading of networks for the program.

First Data joined an alliance with LPP. The goal was fulfilling a terminal services agreement to provide terminals at 500 point-of-sale spots enabling card acceptance at 307 locations in about 220 municipalities throughout Poland.

Automatic Data Processing Inc. Operating as the world's largest payroll and tax filing processor, Automatic Data Processing (ADP) maintained a large global footprint. ADP's employer services unit accounted for two-thirds of its sales. The company proudly proclaimed it offered approximately 60 years of service. By 2009, ADP reported almost US$9 billion in revenues and 585,000 clients worldwide.

In addition to its payroll processing, ADP has a wide array of other data processing and related services, including brokerage services, inventory and data services for the auto and truck dealer industry, and accounting and insurance estimates for insurers. The company made nearly two dozen acquisitions from 1998 through early 2002 as part of its strategy to build its small business and Internet-related services.

ADP was founded in 1949 by Henry Taub as Automatic Payrolls, a payroll preparation service. During the 1950s the company continued selling its payroll services to new clients. The company changed its name to Automatic Data Processing in 1961 and went public. The following year, ADP bought its first computer and began offering back-office services to brokerage houses, beginning the automation of the company's manual accounting systems.

The 1970s marked an especially fertile time of growth for ADP. The company bought more than 30 firms engaged in data and payroll processing, shareholder services, computer networks, inventory control, or automated banking in the United States, Canada, and Germany. In 1971 revenues reached US$50 million. ADP has recorded per share earnings growth for 40 consecutive years.

In April 2007, ADP made the welcome announcement that it was hiring employees for its Northwest El Paso, Texas, facility. There were more than 200 part- and full-time positions available. A hiring fair was held to facilitate filling positions.

In May 2007, Visa USA announced a five-year agreement with ADP Employer Services to offer Visa-branded cards to its clients. The Visa ADP Total Pay card was issued by several Visa member financial institutions. Visa Payroll cards are accepted at the same outlets that accept Visa debit cards.

In 2009, ADP was placed in twelfth spot on *Training* magazine's "Training Top 125 for 2009." In 2008, ADP was in the 20th position on the same list. Being listed for the second consecutive year and moving up to a higher ranking were considered to be reflections of ADP's "ongoing associate training" and development.

In summer 2009, it was announced that ADP achieved the major distinction of reaching a "milestone" for HR/Benefits administration service. It services in excess of 115,000 employees for ADP's HR/Benefits Administration Service. The service allows a partnership to be established to function daily and stay prepared for crisis.

In September 2009, ADP announced its National Payroll Week Campaign. The campaign utilizes an American Payroll Association partnership "to educate American workers about paychecks, the payroll withholding system and other payroll-driven benefits by offering tips to help maximize payday." ADP Corporate Vice President Benito Cachinero-Sanchez pointed out that "direct deposit and pre-tax advantaged programs, such as Flexible Spending Accounts and employee savings plans, can provide significant financial benefits—now and for the future."

ADP purchased a Hoboken payroll service in 2009, according to the *Newark Star-Ledger.* Priority Payroll specializes in assisting small- to medium-sized businesses with up to 100 employees.

Capgemini. France's Capgemini became one of the world's top computer service outsourcing firms, and the largest in Europe, when it merged with Ernst & Young Consulting in 2000. In 2008, Capgemini, previously known as Cap Gemini Ernst & Young, employed more than 90,000 people and had revenues of about US$12.7 billion. It had operations in more than 30 countries. The firm provides management consulting, systems design and management, plus professional services to customers in Europe, North America, and the Asia/Pacific region. The company provided business process outsourcing services to many companies, including Canada's Hydro One (human resource and finance functions) and Australia's BlueScope Steel (accounting and human resources services). It takes pride in offering "the Collaborative Business Experience" model for working and the "Rightshore" global delivery model.

According to research by market research and consulting firm Kable Media Services, Inc., Capgemini rose from seventh to fourth place in rankings of the top suppliers to the public ICT market. Analysts acknowledged that Capgemini had experienced its first full year delivering a huge HMRC Aspire contract. It was among the leading service providers who had increased their influence at the expense of smaller generalists. Kable stressed that recent achievements did not guarantee ongoing success.

On September 15, 2009, Capgemini shared news about eight new members joining its North America Smart Grid advisory group. Their backgrounds make them uniquely qualified to assist utility clients. One of the main areas requiring support was implementing Smart Grid programs and addressing smart Grid Interoperability and Security Standards impacted by the American Recovery and Reinvestment Act introduced in 2009 by U.S. President Barak Obama. The Smart Grid team employs specialists to consult with major North American utilities and have significant impact on achieving Smart Grid goals.

Ceridian Corp. Ceridian is certainly a global business services organization leader. Its specialties include payroll outsourcing and payment innovation. As of 2006, sales were approximately US$1.6 billion. About three-quarters of its revenues came from the human resource solutions segment accounting for approximately 70 percent of the company's sales. In 2005, Ceridian reported having 9,433 employees.

The company sold off its defense electronics business to General Dynamics in order to concentrate on information services. Previously known as Control Data Corp., Ceridian sold some operations, closed others, and spun off its computer business as Control Data Systems in order to overcome substantial losses suffered in the 1980s. It also spun off Arbitron, its demographics research service, which was not considered part of data processing. Under its current structure, Ceridian has two main units: Human Resource Services and Comdata. Along with its payroll and tax processing business, the firm also provides benefits administration, human resource information systems, and training to clients in the United States, Canada, and the United Kingdom. Ceridian's Comdata operations were fortified by the firm's 1998 acquisition of a US$28 million per year service offered by competitor First Data Corp. In exchange, Ceridian sold Comdata's US$130 million gaming services business to First Data, a move lauded by analysts as signaling Ceridian's commitment to the data processing business. Through this segment, the company provides fuel cards, licenses, cash advances, vehicle escorts, and trucking industry-related services.

During the late 1990s, a growing share of Ceridian's data processing revenue came from foreign acquisitions. In 1998 it purchased the payroll processing units of two leading Canadian banks, Toronto-Dominion Bank and Canadian Imperial Bank of Commerce, valued at about US$77 million in annual receipts. The move made Ceridian the leading payroll-outsourcing firm in Canada. In the new millennium, Ceridian planned to diversify its product line by adding Internet-based services and also continued to look for key acquisitions.

In 2006, Ceridian experienced a challenge from its major investor. William Ackman, principal for Pershing Square Capital Management, ordered Ceridian to spin off its Comdata payment card business. The order was reportedly based on lagging sales and profits for the human resources division. Ackman felt spinning off Comdata would allow Ceridian to focus more on building the troubled division. Ceridian CEO Kathy Marinello instead announced that the company was planning a strategic review to determine the best option. In response, Pershing proposed an alternative slate of directors to challenge the company's nominees.

In April 2007, Ceridian admitted its responsibility for the leaking of confidential data to the Internet. Innovative Interactive, a New York advertising firm, unfortunately had confidential data released about its 150 employees to a Web site. The data included names, addresses, Social Security numbers, salary information, and checking account data. Ceridian claimed the information ended up on the Web site of a former employee who took the data by accident upon departing from the company in March 2006.

In May 2007, Ceridian announced that its Comdata subsidiary's card was being accepted at the Ambassador Bridge. That bridge was one of the international crossing points between the United States at Detroit, Michigan, and Windsor, Ontario, Canada. Drivers could swipe a Comdata Card in order to pay their tolls.

Another May 2007 announcement came after accusations that Comdata Executive Vice President Gary Krow had held unauthorized meetings with Pershing and revealed confidential information to third parties. Consequentially, Krow was fired. Pershing Founder Ackman claimed that Krow revealed contents of letters criticizing the performance of former CEO Ronald Turner. Pershing had planned to use those critiques in its campaign to remove company directors. Ultimately, CEO Marinello shared a five-point plan that may include offshoring jobs and consolidating facilities.

On September 14, 2009, Ceridian spread the news about Interface Security Systems selecting it to assist with improving efficiency and human resources management. Interface Security Systems Director of Finance Ray House said expectations called for Ceridian to help with increasing revenues, reducing costs and mitigating risks. Interface reportedly has 600 employees maintaining its presence at St. Louis corporate headquarters and 20 additional locations in 12 states.

MAJOR COUNTRIES IN THE INDUSTRY

In 2004, there were more than U.S. 30,000 companies providing data processing and preparation, according to Zapdata. Of this number, only 40 had more than 1,000 employees. But while the United States dominates the world data processing and preparation market, its foreign competitors are starting to gain market share. Most of the large U.S. data processing services providers have successful operations overseas.

A factor pointing toward growth in the Asia/Pacific data processing services industry is the increasing expansion of the information systems outsourcing market in that region. The region was expected to increase spending by 15 percent per year during the early years of the first decade of the 2000s. As more companies in various countries begin to utilize personal computers and the Internet, demand in the data processing services industry is expected to rise.

In the past, Japan possessed a comparatively underdeveloped data processing industry. This primarily was due to obstacles in Japanese trade legislation and the structure of the Japanese economy. Japanese companies were cautious about investing in multimedia and information delivery. They also had fewer resources to invest than they did before the prolonged recession of the 1990s, and directed much of the available capital into maintaining manufacturing competitiveness. The country did appear to be making headway in the industry in the new millennium, though. Japanese information technology providers began acquiring firms, both local and foreign, to beef up product lines and created international subsidiaries to provide data processing services.

BIBLIOGRAPHY

"ACS Awarded USD67m Contract by State of Colorado." *Telecomworldwire*, 27 April 2007.

———. "ADP Provides American Workers Tips to Maximize Their Paychecks," 9 September 2009. Available from www. adp.com.

"ACS Completes Acquisition of Assets of Albion." *Telecomworldwire*, 27 April 2007.

ADP. "ADP Named to 'Training Top 125' for Second Consecutive Year." 17 February 2009. Available from www.adp.com.

———. "ADP Reaches 115,000 Employee Milestone for HR/ Benefits Administration Services." 29 June 2009. Available from www.adp.com.

Baldwin, Carly. "Automatic Data Processing Buys Hoboken Payroll Firm." New Jersey Online, 1 September 2009. Available from www.nj.com.

"Brave EDS Move Could Backfire." *Computer Weekly*, 13 January 2004.

"Business Week in Review." *Star-Tribune* (Minneapolis-St. Paul, MN), 28 April 2007. Available from www. startribune.com.

Capgemini. "Capgemini North America Smart Grid Practice to Support Clients' Growing Needs for Technology and Regulatory Evidance," 15 September 2009. Available from www.capgemini.com.

"Capgemini and HP Gain Ground in Public Sector Marketplace." *Kablenet*, 2 May 2007.

Ceridian. "Leading Security Company Chooses Ceridian Solutions to Increase Revenue, Reduce Costs, Mitigate Risk" 14 September 2009. Available from www.ceridian.com.

"Comdata Card Now Accepted at Ambassador Bridge." *PR Newswire*, 9 May 2007.

"CSC to Acquire Convansys for $34.00 Per Share. Acquisition Increases CSC's India Delivery Capabilities, Accelerates Development of Strategic Offshore Offerings." *PR Newswire*, 25 April 2007.

"Dissident Shareholder: Ceridian Firing Completes Corporate House Cleaning." *Pioneer Press*, 14 May 2007. Available from www.twincities.com.

"EDS Selected by GSA for Satellite Communications Services Contract for Federal Agencies." *Canada Newswire English*, 4 May 2007.

First Data. "First Data and LPP sign agreement." 1 July 2009. Available from www.firstdata.com.

———. "Walmart Launches Associate Electronic Pay Program with MasterCard and First Data," 3 September 2009. Available from www.firstdata.com.

"Hoover's Company Capsules." *Hoover's Online*, 2007. Available from www. hoovers.com.

"Industry Report: Data Processing and Preparation (7374)." Dun & Bradstreet, 30 June 2005. Available from www. zapdata.com.

Kuykendall, Lavonne. "Volume on the Rise for Top Processors." *American Banker*, 22 July 2004.

"The New Workplace: Outsourcing in Japan." The Outsourcing Institute, 2001.

Park, Andrew. "Can the Buddy System Boost EDS?" *Business Week Online*, 14 January 2004. Available from www.businessweek.com.

Peterson, Susan E. "Ceridian Sees Strong Earnings." *Star Tribune*, 1 May 2007.

"The Processing Industry Views Health Care as a Major Market." *Cardline*, 9 January 2004.

Rosato, Donna. "ADP: Here's a Company That Will Benefit from the Economic Rebound—and Doesn't Have to Worry About Rising Interest Rates." *Money*, 1 June 2004.

Ryan, Vince. "First Data Invests in Mobile Commerce Outfit," 3 May 2007. Available from www.banknet360.com.

U.S. Census Bureau. *Service Annual Survey*. Washington, D.C.: 2004. Available from www.census.gov.

Wels-Maug, Cornelia. "EDS Buys a Majority Stake in Itellium Systems & Services." *Telecoms and Software News*, 9 May 2007. Available from www.ovum.com.

SIC 7371, 7373, 7378

INFORMATION TECHNOLOGY SERVICES

NAICS CODE(S)

541511, 541512, 811212. The information technology (IT) services industry provides a variety of services on a contract or fee basis, including:

- computer programming services;

- custom computer software design and analysis;

- modifications of custom software;

- training software end users and systems administrators;

- integrated systems design;

- computer maintenance and repair, including hardware and peripheral installations, upgrades, replacements, and troubleshooting; and

- hardware and software consulting.

Additional IT services include computer services outsourcing, disaster recovery, and overall facilities management, which involves on-site management of a customer's computer systems and networks, including computer maintenance and repair. Service firms that provide off-site data processing services are covered under **Data Processing Services,** and developers of mass-produced software are discussed in detail under **Packaged Software.** Some industry participants provide consulting services unrelated to information technology, which are included under **Management Consulting Services.**

INDUSTRY SNAPSHOT

The information technology services market experienced exceptional growth in the late 1990s. IT services recorded revenues of US$350 billion worldwide in programming, systems integration, consulting, outsourcing, education and training, and maintenance services in 1998. By 2004, this value had increased to US$607.8 billion, according to Gartner. The world leader in the IT service sector continued to be IBM, which accounted for 7.6 percent of the total sales worldwide.

Following the economic downturn of the early 2000s that lasted into 2003, the IT services industry suffered declining revenues and mass job insecurity. By 2004, industry consolidation was the norm, and *InternetWeek* reported 57 mergers and acquisitions in the first half of the year. Outsourcing was anticipated to increase, with more growth expected in management services. As of the mid-2000s, 59 percent of the market remained with U.S. companies.

Similarly, major European companies offering computer programming services find most clients within the European Union. For both Japanese and European companies, however, that is expected to change, and those firms are expected to begin competing more openly with the U.S. firms that have been leading the way in international expansion.

ORGANIZATION AND STRUCTURE

IT services constitute one of the largest, most rapidly changing, and relatively unregulated industries dealing with high technology. As a result, the rigid organization and structure of the early days, when mainframe computer manufacturers dominated the industry, has disintegrated into a conglomeration of mergers, alliances, and commercial relationships among manufacturers, independent service companies, and customers. Competition remained constant among manufacturers, retailers, and independent service companies of all sizes for IT services, along with increasing customer demands for service and reliability. Although IT service providers prefer to sign lucrative, comprehensive contracts as the sole service provider for their clients, most companies continued to use multiple vendors to meet IT service needs rather than rely on all-inclusive contracts.

New technology, competition in the industry, and growing demands from customers have blurred distinctions among programming, maintenance, and outsourcing services. Large mainframe manufacturers continued to rely on services for a large part of their revenues. For example, IBM created a separate division, IBM Global Services, to provide customers with network services for products from all IT manufacturers. IBM Global Service offers a product called ServicePacs through resale channels that provides maintenance, disaster recovery, and other services for small and midsize businesses. Two additional service-oriented products that were added in 1998 were

ServiceSuite, for midsize companies, and ServiceSelect, sold directly to IBM's largest customers. IBM also entered a partnership with J.D. Edwards to offer its outsourced energy resource planning services to IBM customers.

Other computer manufacturers concentrated on acquisition to bolster service offerings. Computer Associates (CA) offered clients total "end-to-end" product and service solutions. Wang Laboratories Inc. agreed to acquire Olivetti SpA's computer services business. Some believed that Compaq acquired of Digital Equipment Corporation (DEC) primarily because of DEC's services offerings. Other large companies, such as Hewlett-Packard, not only offered IT services to their customers but also outsourced those services to small service companies specializing in a particular area of expertise like help desk support or maintenance and repair. Customers calling the support numbers were not always aware that they were talking to a separate service provider.

Computer manufacturers are not the only companies heavily involved in IT services. For example, consulting firm Ernst & Young, in partnership with Microsoft, Oracle, and Sun Microsystems, offered an Advanced Development Center and Accelerated Solutions Environment where clients could plot strategy and acquire resources from software solutions to mainframe hardware. Xerox acquired a systems integration company to support document-management systems sales and a software vendor to support new application management and outsourcing services to be launched in summer of 1998. In addition, Big Six accounting firm Price Waterhouse merged with Coopers & Lybrand in July of 1998 to form PriceWaterhouseCoopers, which was the largest IT services firm in the world. The company generates more than US$13 billion in annual revenues, employs more than 160,000 people, and does business in more than 160 countries.

In response to the changing market, countries worldwide adopted the World Trade Organization's Information Technology Agreement, which in 2000 eliminated tariffs on many information and communication technology products, such as hardware, software, electronic components, and digital photocopiers. It was anticipated that countries participating in the agreement would experience job growth in almost every industry by accelerating technological development, lowering production costs, and increasing productivity. Twenty-eight countries signed the initial agreement at the Singapore Ministerial in 1996, representing almost 85 percent of the IT industry. By the beginning of 2001, the Information Technology Agreement had 40 participants, accounting for about 93 percent of the global IT industry. A few holdouts were expected to eventually sign the Information Technology Agreement.

BACKGROUND AND DEVELOPMENT

Computers revolutionized the workplace and made a dramatic impact on world markets for many goods and services only because of the programming that instructs computers what to do and how to do it. Over the years, a growing number of companies have come to rely on customized services to make computers perform specified functions and talk to other systems within the same organization on a network. The technology services industry has been altered by changes in technology and market conditions, including the rise in popularity of desktop computers and client/server systems; the increasing demand for new, improved, and less expensive technology from the business community; advances in packaged software; and the rise of Internet technology. The information technology services market is driven by the concept that the more computers do for the workplace, the more the workplace demands of computers.

In the late 1980s, networking became increasingly important to computer programming services, particularly as more local area networks (LANs) became connected to other LANs, mainframes, and minicomputers. Programmers increasingly were asked to customize network operating systems, workstation operating systems, and network shells (the software that determines whether user commands are processed by individual workstations or by the network). One of the challenges of network programming has been to follow the open system interconnection reference model that was developed by the International Organization for Standardization (ISO) for standard network protocols.

With the world economic recovery in the early and mid-1990s, the computer services industry emerged, reflecting the popularity of personal, laptop, and notebook computers and the rise of client-server systems. As prices dropped, stimulating competition, manufacturers were forced to embrace open systems, producing computers that could work in conjunction with other manufacturers' hardware. Sometimes customized services were offered as part of a package. However, it became more common for manufacturers to purchase equipment at the most reasonable cost and contract independent services firms to ensure that the components were compatible, customizing the software for specific user needs. Businesses were thus more likely to buy system components from different manufacturers and shop around among various software manufacturers to meet their needs. In this era of open computer architecture, the computer industry created demand for additional flexibility and all-around technical competence from computer service professionals. Therefore, workers who are able to work on many different types of systems and machines are in demand.

Heightened competition among hardware manufacturers not only led to lower prices for computing power but also led to better service, from longer warranty protection to promises of improved technical support, including help desks and on-site repair. Contracts increasingly required repair and maintenance firms to do more than simply keep machines running, especially among large clients. They also were asked to develop, integrate, maintain, and inventory hardware. For many major computer manufacturers, repair and maintenance and other post-sale services to customers, banded together under the general heading of "aftercare," accounted for to up to 50 percent of annual revenues. Many companies had started outsourcing, in which they contract with a third party that may or may not be the hardware supplier, to provide maintenance and service. In some cases, the third party brings in its own people and takes over an existing contract.

IT service professionals were asked to integrate software into the workplace and to improve interfaces and applications to make them more efficient and user-friendly. Most non-computer industry executives did not want to become technology experts, nor did they want their companies to become technology companies in order to obtain the systems and software to run their businesses. Rather, they want technology—particularly information systems and computer networks—to make the organization operate smoothly and efficiently and to help the people who work for the company, including the executives, do a better job. They want system-wide planning that not only allows workers to perform business functions, but also track how the system is being used and how it could be used more efficiently. Third-party independent service providers are able to handle the computer needs of more than one client, thus spreading technical overhead costs among a number of clients. This economy of scale helps computer purchasers limit maintenance and repair costs to less than 10 percent of the purchase price of the equipment. Many computer consumers arrange for maintenance and service from computer manufacturers, either as a package or as part of separate aftercare contracts. Increasingly, however, the trend among computer purchasers has been to shop for maintenance and repair service contracts, not only from the manufacturers, but also from other manufacturers and a growing number of independent IT service providers.

Competition among service providers has led to innovative packaging and marketing of IT services, including service contracts that bundle system development, programming, and maintenance with a variety of other services. One concept that has grown in popularity is the "turn-key" system, in which a corporation contracts with the service providers for a ready-to-operate computer system that includes all the hardware, software, training, maintenance, and repair support services necessary. The companies that offer outsourcing for computer maintenance and repair are able to do as much or more—and at lower cost—than in-house technicians.

Enterprise resource planning (ERP) software was a growing area of customized programming for corporate customers. ERP software was customized to help companies manage complete business, manufacturing, and communication functions within one system. Leaders in the development of ERP software included SAP AG, Oracle, Baan, and PeopleSoft. In 1997 Oracle released Oracle Applications, a suite of 30 software modules for financial and supply-chain management, manufacturing, project management, human resources, and sales and marketing, customized for each customer according to its industry. *Fortune* reported that ERP software helped corporate technology professionals automate manufacturing processes, organize accountants' books, and streamline departments like human resources, as well as many other functions. Companies that offered ERP design and implementation solutions were among the fastest growing in the IT industry. ERP's importance to business had grown because it handled all detail work for the client, from product planning to interactions with suppliers and tracking orders. ERP software was an e-commerce solution that kept businesses from having to juggle all their components and avoid the risk of crucial details falling through the cracks.

In the 1990s, one of the hottest sectors of the IT industry was system upgrades to accommodate the year 2000 (Y2K). In the late 1990s, companies hired outside vendors to develop strategies and implement system-wide fixes. The problem stemmed from the 1960s and 1970s when memory was costly and programmers saved a good deal by storing dates in systems and software as only the last two digits where, for example, 1975 was became 75. However, as 2000 approached, IT experts were concerned that computers worldwide would read 2000 as 1900, resulting in potentially crippling system failures globally. Concern centered on hardware, software, networks, legacy systems, and any machines that relied on a central processing unit with embedded clocks or dates. Because companies worldwide faced the same deadline, they all competed for the same resources to fix the problem—namely, programmers, who would isolate the problems and fix old code, and testing personnel. IT service providers cashed in on the problem, offering comprehensive Y2K solutions that helped companies identify and repair systems that were not Y2K compliant.

Another major conversion that put corporate resources in need of information technology services in the late 1990s and early 2000s was the adoption of the euro as the standard European currency unit of the European Union. The 12 participating EU member countries, including Austria, Belgium, France, Germany, Italy, Portugal, Spain, Luxembourg, Finland, Ireland, Greece, and the Netherlands (a few EU members opted out of the initial monetary union) began using the euro on January 1, 2002, when their national currencies became denominations of the euro rather than separately traded currencies.

Other national currencies were eliminated in 2002, which cost software developers up to US$300 billion. Banks and retailers needed software and system upgrades, with the conversion extending to manufacturers and almost all other sectors of not only the European Union, but also of companies and countries that did business with unified Europe. This major system change afforded IT services companies additional opportunity to offer comprehensive solution packages to companies doing business in Europe.

Although IT service revenues were predisposed to slump when the global economy falters, the industry continued to experience tremendous earnings growth during the late 1990s, although it slowed in the early 2000s. In part, this growth has been the result of a shortage of IT professionals, the sales of high-profit service contracts, and the growing demand for such services. After the economic downturn and terrorist attacks against the United States in 2001, IT services plummeted, along with many other industry segments. However, by 2002 demand from transportation and governmental entities had increased, and billing rates rose far higher than the actual cost of labor.

CURRENT CONDITIONS

In the early to mid-2000s, one of the most notable trends in IT was that consumer demand was driving technology. Traditionally, technological advances were developed and offered by the companies themselves, creating the demand for those products and services, which often were incompatible with competing offerings. However, in the more technologically advanced world of the new century, consumers knew what they wanted and companies scrambled to offer products and services to meet those desires.

Security issues continued to dominate the industry's projects. Financial companies in particular were seeking ways to improve the security of their data, but retailers had similar concerns, particularly as web-based purchase activity was increasing. However, consumer confidence in the safety of the systems was on the decline.

Gartner had estimated the value of the IT services industry to be US$607.8 billion in 2004, up 6.7 percent from 2003. The world leader in the industry continued to be IBM, which held 7.6 percent of the market. EDS held a 3.4 percent market share, while Fujitsu held 2.8 percent, and Hewlett-Packard, Accenture, and CSC each held 2.3 percent.

In 2005, Gartner predicted that IT outsourcing would grow globally from about US$20 billion in 2004 to about US$50 billion by 2007. However, increasing wage costs, coupled with increasing competition, had the potential for tight margins for IT service companies. Furthermore, the financial services industry was one of the largest users of IT services, spending 8.7 percent of their revenues on IT, according to Gartner, resulting in predictions that this sector would grow as it tried to compete in a world of increased consolidation and tightened regulations. India continued to expand its outsourcing capabilities, although China was expected to catch up quickly due to rapid economic growth in all industries.

RESEARCH AND TECHNOLOGY

Research in the IT services area during the late 1990s and early 2000s was focused on the issues facing companies as they approached the new millennium. These issues included the year 2000, the change in European currency, the rise of client/server and integrated systems, increased use of enterprise resource planning systems, and the integration of the Internet into complex business systems. Disaster planning also became an important part of the area of facilities management. When a computer system suffers a massive crash, either from an internal or external problem, such as natural disaster or criminal attack, repair and maintenance personnel are often called in to recover data and restore the system.

Following the September 11, 2001, terrorist attacks against the United States, as well as numerous break-ins into supposedly secure corporate and educational sites (including at *The New York Times* and Purdue University), information technology services companies increased their resolve to perfect encryption to lock out hacker assaults on client systems. In 2005, security issues and customized software development continued to be a leading component of IT service company offerings.

Companies offering programming services also dealt with the rapid expansion of new technologies, including the special challenges for programmers like the rapid conversion from analog to digital transmission in the electronics market. In addition, artificial intelligence (AI), including "smart" software and natural language processing, challenged the IT industry. Smart software had many applications, but the most important were the large programs that were financed by large corporations to administer computer networks. Typically, these networks were too vast and complicated for human management, and production had become highly automated. Some examples included the Internet, urban traffic systems, waste control systems, and aerospace production, as well as many other forms of manufacturing. All involved computer networks that communicated with, instructed, and monitored each other. Smart software not only made things work smoothly within a system, but it also could identify and resolve problems and system "bugs" before managers realized a there was a problem.

WORKFORCE

The IT services industry has been hampered by a shortage of professionals, which was expected to heighten. Globally, Gartner research was predicting in 2005 that the number of IT staff would decline 15 percent by 2010. The U.S. Department of Labor predicted industry growth of more than 35 percent through 2010. Other factors, such as integration of Internet applications, development of e-commerce, and the design and implementation of enterprise resource planning systems, all pointed toward increased demand for skilled professionals like programmers and project managers. According to *InformationWeek,* project management, business management, ERM/ERP, infrastructure, architecture, C++ programming language, data warehousing, Oracle programming, team-based work, and Unix programming were expected to be the top ten most sought after IT skills. By 2003, job prospects and salaries were increasing, but the hours were longer than they had been in the past.

In some respects, the shortage of programmers in the United States had created opportunities for workers from emerging countries, especially India, Pakistan, Indonesia, and China. Many engineers from Taiwan, China, Pakistan, India, and other nations in Southeast Asia have earned advanced degrees from U.S. colleges and universities. These engineers often work in Silicon Valley or for high-tech firms elsewhere in the United States. A number eventually return to their home markets or find work in other countries.

Whether in-house or on contract, computer programming services remain a significant part—typically one-third or more—of the average information systems budget for corporations. Other IT services accounted for an additional 20 percent of corporate budgets. Personnel costs were expected to remain high because so many companies wanted specific applications from customized customer support to management of inventory. The biggest outlays for custom programming services generally were for maintaining and upgrading aging applications. Spending on encryption services and ERP systems, as well as rising salaries, have seriously impacted corporate training budgets, and companies have not been able to offer as much training and tuition reimbursement as they have in the past.

INDUSTRY LEADERS

International Business Machines Corporation (IBM). Charles Flint created Calculating-Tabulating-Recording (CTR) in 1910 by merging two companies, International Time Recording Company and Computing Scale Company, with Tabulation Machine Company, which had been started by Herman Hallerith. In 1914 Thomas Watson was hired by Flint as general manager of CTR, later becoming company president. Watson created a powerful business sales force that became known for superior customer service and devoted most of the company's resources to the tabulator division. Under Watson's leadership, CTR quickly expanded in sales and size, moving into Europe, Asia, and Latin America. In 1924 the company was renamed International Business Machines and focused on large tabulations machines. By 1949 IBM had operations in 58 countries and had created IBM World Trade Corporation, which enjoyed the same dominance in foreign markets as it did in the United States.

International Business Machines Corp. (IBM) continued to be the world's largest provider of information technology services and computer products in 2004 with US$96.3 billion in revenues, with more than 369,000 employees worldwide. Prior to 1995, IBM support focused solely on IBM products, but in 1995 the company formed IBM Global Services by restructuring capabilities that had previously been managed by separate groups into an integrated global office. IBM Global Services was comprised of five units, including Integrated Systems Solutions Corp. (ISSC), IBM Global Network, Availability Services, the Consulting Group, and Education and Training. Since its inception, IBM's service groups have made profitable outsourcing deals with companies such as Rubbermaid, Kodak, and McDonnell Douglas. IBM Global Services, which accounted for about 48 percent of revenues in 2004, was one of the company's fastest growing divisions, in part because IBM capitalized on its experience as the world's largest computer manufacturer. In 2005, IBM continued to look for growth through acquisitions in companies providing key software and services, as well as those in emerging growth countries, such as China, Russia, India, and Brazil.

Electronic Data Systems Corp (EDS). EDS was founded in 1962 by H. Ross Perot with US$1,000 and an idea for a company to provide "information services," with a focus on improving clients' business. EDS helped companies meet business needs in systems and technology services, business process management, management consulting, electronic markets, and EDS' CoSourcing Service. The systems and technology area offered services such as systems development, systems integration, systems management and desktop services, and year 2000 conversion. Another area of high growth for EDS was its webmaster division. The company was awarded its first major contract in 1969 by Blue Shield of California, which was followed by the U.S. Navy and Xerox, for whom EDS continued to provide most IT needs. By 1973 EDS revenues reached US$100 million. In 1984 General Motors purchased EDS, and in 1996 General Motors spun off EDS. Services to GM still accounted for 30 percent of EDS revenues in 1997. Efforts to further global expansion included the 1990 acquisition of

SD-Scicon, a U.K. computer services company, and the 1995 acquisition of A.T. Kearney, a global management consulting firm. EDS was the one of the largest IT services provider in the industry, with earnings of US$21.5 billion in 1997, approximately one-third of which was generated by outsourcing services for computer systems and networks. The company employed 110,000 people worldwide, making it the industry's fourth-largest employer. The boost in the IT industry was expected to translate into great rewards for EDS in 1997 and 1998. In 1997 EDS was estimated to generate more than US$15 billion in new service contracts, almost double the amount booked in 1996 (US$8.4 billion). In 2001 EDS listed revenues of US$21.5 billion, an indicator of company health. However, in early 2002 EDS saw its stock plunge more than 6 percent due to management problems, according to the *American Banker*. EDS signed service contracts in the spring of 2002 worth around US$1 billion, a sign of customer support for EDS services. By 2003, company revenues of US$21.5 billion and 132,000 employees made EDS one of the largest companies in the industry.

Electronic Data Systems, better known as EDS, was the founder of the information technology outsourcing industry, and in 2005 continued to be the largest IT services provider in the United States. Employing 117,000 who worked in 60 countries in 2004, EDS earned revenues of more than US$20.7 billion that year. As one of the largest government contractors in the United States and the nation's largest supplier of Medicaid IT services, EDS had federal contracts of US$102 million and a US$48 million contract with the Massachusetts Medicaid program in the month of June 2005 alone. The company also owns management consultant giant A.T. Kearney. In addition, more than 26,000 contact center professionals delivered CRM Services in 48 languages on behalf of more than 450 clients from 155 locations in 26 countries.

More than 26,000 contact center professionals delivered CRM Services in 48 languages on behalf of more than 450 clients from 155 locations in 26 countries. In October 2008, EDS announced plans to terminate 75 application and outsourcing jobs as key customers were reducing their workloads. The company also announced the expansion of its Contact Center Managed Services to "integrate people, processes and technology, enabling clients to manage multiple vendors and improve the customer experience."

Fujitsu Limited. Fujitsu Limited, which was started as a manufacturing subsidiary of Fuji Electric in 1935, began producing computers in the 1960s. The world's third-largest IT services provider and the largest such provider in Japan, Tokyo-based Fujitsu earned revenues of about US$44 billion in 2004, about 44 percent of which could be attributed to its software and services division. About

70 percent of these revenues came from Japan, 13.3 percent were from Europe, 9.8 percent were from Australia, and 6.7 percent were from North America. The company was also a large supplier of computer hardware. For 2007, the company reported earnings of US$43.2 billion and 160,977 employees.

Fujitsu Services was one of the first Oracle User Group Partner of the Year Award Winners. The winners were selected by the Oracle community based on highest level of support provided during the past year. More than 1,000 customer votes were cast. Fujitsu had been an Oracle implementation partner for 15 years and served more than 2,000 global Oracle professionals.

Hewlett-Packard Company (HP). William Hewlett and David Packard officially created Hewlett-Packard (HP) in 1939, although they had worked together earlier to create eight oscillators for Walt Disney Studios. In 1966, HP created its first computer for internal use, never intending to enter the computer market. However, two years later the company created the first desktop calculator capable of performing scientific calculations, and by 1974 committed itself to moving into the computer industry with the introduction of the HP3000. The HP-85, Hewlett-Packard's first personal computer, was released in 1985, but reaction was poor because it was not compatible with IBM's designs. This caused HP not only to create IBM-compatible PCs, but also to move toward making all its computers, at least in part, cross-compatible. To better position itself for the global market, it increased cooperative efforts, and in the late 1980s HP entered into trade agreements with companies like Hitachi, Canon USA Inc., and Sony.

At the beginning of 2002, Walter Hewlett filed a lawsuit against the HP board and management team that the latter called spurious. In May, HP's shareholders and management purchased Compaq Computer Corp. for US$1.69 billion in HP stock.

By 2005, Hewlett-Packard (HP) was active in 178 countries serving 1 billion customers. It was ranked number 11 on the *Fortune* 500 list that year. In 2004, the company employed 151,000 people, of which about 65,000 worked in its services division. Although predominantly a hardware and software provider, HP's services division works with its other departments as well as local systems integrators to provide IT solutions to its customers. Most of its services were for outsourcing. Approximately 17 percent of the company's total revenues of US$79.9 billion in 2004 were attributed to its services division. By 2007, revenues were reportedly US $104,286 with 172,000 employees.

European trade unions launched protests against Hewlett-Packard in Italy and Germany in October 2008. The main reason for this effort was plans to cut thousands of jobs in the region. Related moves were part of its global cost cuts following the acquisition of EDS. Elected trade union representatives were reportedly consulting with EDS at the end of 2008.

Computer Sciences Corporation. California-based Computer Sciences Corporation (CSC) was founded in 1959 by Fletcher Jones of North American Aviation and Roy Nutt of United Aircraft as a small firm concentrating on services to government agencies. CSC provides IT management consulting and planning, as well as systems integration and outsourcing. The company grew to become the United States' third largest commercial outsourcing company with large IT management contracts as the federal government cut spending and reduced in-house programming services. William Hoover of the California Institute of Technology later joined the company and led CSC as it became a systems integration firm. Federal contracts continued to account for 30 percent of the company's business as of 1997. European operations accounted for 20 percent, or nearly two-thirds, of the company's international commercial business for 32 percent of 1997 revenues. CSC has opened subsidiaries worldwide and in an effort to diversity services, has made numerous acquisitions, including financial IT services firm, Continuum Company, and a healthcare consulting firm, American Practice Management. CSC was the target for acquisition in 1998, when Computer Associates made an unsuccessful hostile takeover bid. The company reported revenues of US$16.5 billion for the fiscal year ended March 2008 and employed about 89,000 people. Approximately one-third of its revenues come from federal agencies because it is a major government defense contractor.

Accenture. Accenture began as the consulting arm of accounting firm Arthur Andersen, but separated from its parent company because of conflicts with its consultants over pay. In 2000, an international arbitrator granted Accenture its independence. The company provides global management consulting and technology and outsourcing service. Accenture operates more than 100 offices in 48 countries with more than 100,000 employees. Revenues for 2007 were US$21.5 billion with 170,000 employees.

Capgemini. As Europe's leading IT services provider, Paris-based Capgemini provides IT consulting focusing on systems architecture, integration, and infrastructure. In addition, the company offers an outsourcing service, often managing all of a client's IT resources. The company has grown through a series of acquisitions, including Sesa (France, 1987), Hoskyns (United Kingdom, 1990), United Research (United States, 1990), Mac Group (United States, 1991), Volmac (the Netherlands, 1992), Programator (Scandinavia, 1992), Gruber Titze (Europe, 1993), and

Bossard (Europe, 1997). However, the company's largest acquisition was the purchase of Ernst & Young Consulting in 2000, which was initially known as Cap Gemini Ernst & Young. Revenues in 2004 were approximately US$7.6 billion, of which more than 76 percent came from Europe, 22 percent from North America, and the remainder from the Asia/Pacific region. In 2005, Capgemini had 59,000 employees in 30 countries.

In May 2008, Capgemini received Vodafone's Code of Ethical "Corporate Responsibility Engagement" Award, in recognition of its commitment to Vodafone's Code of Ethical Purchasing. The company was also involved with Vodafone's corporate responsibility issues as it developed its own corporate responsibility programs. Capgemini was also cited for "continually demonstrating its commitment to the global ethical standards in line with the expectations set by our Code of Ethical Purchasing and for objectivity and systematically aligning its corporate responsibility programme with their business values."

Atos Origin S.A. Paris-based Atos Origins provides its clients with consulting, operations management, and systems integration services, as well as facilities management, e-commerce consulting, and systems design, implementation and integration. The company acquired KPMG Consulting in the United Kingdom and the Netherlands in 2002. It became one of the leading global IT services companies when it purchased Sema Group from Schlumberger in 2004, adding 21,000 employees. Revenues for Atos Origin exceeded US$7 billion in 2006 with 49,847 employees. The company had more than 46,000 employees in 2005 and operated in 50 countries, although most operations were based in Europe.

Atos Origin collaborated with GlobeRanger to launch a real-time forensic tracking and tracing system for the Dutch Forensic Institute (NFI). The system makes it possible to track and trace the exact time, location, and movement of item-level criminal evidence during forensic analysis and processing at NFI. The collaboration called for an innovative Atos Origin's implementation of GlobeRanger's iMotion solution for NFI. "This system helps NFI ensure the high integrity of the crime scene evidence, thereby supporting law enforcement agencies in a timely manner, explained Atos Origin's RFID Competence Manager.

Getronics. Getronics started as Wang in 1951 by An Wang in Boston, Massachusetts. Wang's initial success was with minicomputers and word processors, but that business topped out in the mid-1980s. The company endured years of losses and restructuring, but came back after filing for bankruptcy in 1992. Wang's success in the mid-1990s was based on its offering of services to other companies and its strategy to build up those offerings by acquiring existing service companies. Acquisitions included

the 1995 purchase of Groupe Bull's U.S. systems integration services and the 1996 purchases of Dataserv Computer Maintenance and I-NET, a client/server, network, and desktop management services provider.

In 1997 U.S. industry leader Wang earned US$1.26 billion in revenues and employed 9,300 people. Wang agreed to acquire the computer-services segment (Olsy) of Italian Olivetti SpA in 1998 for approximately US$391 million to diversify its service offerings. The acquisition nearly tripled Wang's revenues and expanded its operations to Europe and Asia. Wang hoped to be able to compete more evenly with giants such as IBM and EDS. The company announced its name would be changing to Wang Global in March 1998. Beginning in 1993, Wang had focused on hardware and software consulting and installation services with about US$200 million of its revenues generated by the company's hardware (minicomputer) sales. Services provided included design and installation of systems and warranty, help desk, maintenance, and software support.

In 1999 the Dutch information technology company Getronics acquired Wang Global for US$1.8 billion. In 2001, the company reported losses of about US$920 million, and in March 2002, released its worst financial statement in 17 years and announced plans to reduce its staff 6 percent. By 2003, sales were up to US$3.4 billion, and the company reported a profit of about US$309 million. By 2006, revenues were reported at US$3.5 billion with 24,780 employees.

MAJOR COUNTRIES IN THE INDUSTRY

The United States. Most of the large global IT companies are based in the United States, although the domestic industry was highly fragmented. The top five companies of IBM, Fujitsu, Hewlett-Packard, EDS, and Computer Sciences Corp. accounted for about 18 percent of the total market. Industry growth from 2003 to 2004 was predicted to be more than 29 percent. The IT industry was served by the Information Technology Association of America (ITAA). With 500 domestic members and partners in 49 countries, the ITAA provided information and services to the industry and assisted with strategic planning and policy.

The United States has been an attractive market for companies from other countries, particularly those from emerging economies. A number of computer programming services companies from countries such as Pakistan and India, for example, have gained a foothold in the United States as subcontractors for larger firms with multinational contracts.

The United States dominates the IT services industry, and the international market helped a number of small U.S. computer software programming services grow. Companies in the industry include not only the small firms concentrating on specific services, but also computer giants that have branched out into these services. A number of major companies were reconfigured in the 1990s to put a new emphasis on professional computer services. NCR Corp., for example, created two service-oriented divisions, one of which concentrated on consulting and systems integration with a focus on helping customers move into open systems and develop system-wide architectures. U.S. giants IBM and Digital Equipment Corporation (later part of Compaq), which were two of the world's largest suppliers of networked computer systems, software, and services, each placed new emphasis on professional services during company reorganizations.

The computer consulting services market was valued at almost US$249 billion in 2003 by *Euromonitor*. Of this value, about half was attributed to the provision of systems integration services. By late 2003 and early 2004, a stabilizing economy and market growth in the United States supported demand for IT services across industry lines, particularly on a contract basis. Even so, many companies had already moved or were in the process of moving jobs offshore, making the immediate future somewhat uncertain for the labor force. Some industry analysts were concerned about the movement of white-collar jobs, following the mass movement of blue-collar employment. According to the ITAA, although the negative effect on domestic employment was clear, the offshore movement would still help the economy in general with inherent cost savings. The ITAA took a firm stand against government sector outsourcing, however. Overall, the IT industry was expected to need more than 500,000 new skilled workers by 2008, with more than half of the positions outsourced.

Japan. While several Japanese companies participated in the IT services industry, most of their business has been confined to the Japanese market, particularly to major corporate and industrial customers. Ventures into the international market were generally on behalf of domestic corporate and industrial clients. Japan had improved its global profile in software development and programming, largely at a giant research center in Tochigi, north of Tokyo. According to preliminary plans published by the Japan Personal Computer Software Association, the center will be open to cooperation with U.S. and other foreign software companies.

By 2003, the IT business in Japan was worth US$2.4 billion, but growth through 2008 was expected to exceed 30 percent. Most of the industry's growth in this area could be attributed Enterprise Resource Planning (ERP), which accounted for almost 67 percent of the market according to *Euromonitor*. ERP systems usually handle manufacturing, logistics, distribution, inventory, shipping, invoicing, and accounting. There was little competition in the market, and not much room for small firms, with leading players Oracle, SAP, and Fujitsu controlling almost 95 percent of the market.

India. Valued at about US$12.7 billion in 2004, India has one of the most vibrant IT services industries in Asia. Many global companies have outsourced their IT services to India, where costs can be reduced due to lower wages in the country.

China. The Chinese IT services industry was growing at the same dramatic rate as the country's economy. Between 2003 and 2008, the market was expected to grow more than 200 percent from almost US$6.6 billion to almost US$20.6 billion. Most of the firms in the industry were foreign, with IBM holding an 11 percent market share in 2003, according to *Euromonitor*. Altogether the top four firms of IBM, Accenture, Hewlett Packard, and Digital China held almost 32 percent of the market. Providing network services primarily to financial service companies was expected to be remain the largest sector in the industry in China.

The United Kingdom. More than half of the U.K.'s nearly US$46 billion market value in 2003 was attributed to outsourcing. *Euromonitor* reported that the industry in the United Kingdom was consolidating, although it remained fragmented. For example, Paris-based Atos Origins, was the U.K. leader in the IT industry, having grown through a series of acquisitions, including the IT services segment of Schlumberger in 2004. Other prominent players in the U.K. market include IBM, EDS, Accenture, and Capgemini.

Australia. Australia was reporting excellent industry growth, with a 2003 value of almost US$7.8 billion. Growth was expected to be more than 60 percent through 2008. Outsourcing and processing accounted for about 40 percent of the market, and were areas that were expected to increase another 5 percent by 2008.

BIBLIOGRAPHY
"2005 Trends: Analysts Predict Modest Growth IT Budgets To Hide Some Major Shifts Below Surface." *Syntelligence,* Vol.5, No. 1. Available from www.syntelinc.com.
"Atos Origin and Globe Ranger Announce Successful Launch of RFID Track and Trace Solution for Dutch Forensic Institute (NFI)." *Business Wire,* 22 October 2008. Available from www.businesswire.com.
Bickerton, Ian. "Getronics Positive Despite Its Worst Year on Record." *Financial Times* (London), 6 March 2002.
Bills, Steve. "EDS Follows Two Downgrades With $1B Package of Deals." *American Banker,* 1 April 2002.

Bray, Hiawatha. "Now Comes the Hard Part." *Boston Globe,* 1 April 2002.

"Capgemini Wins Vodafone's Corporate Responsibility Engagement Award 2008," May 2008. Available from www.capgemini.com.

Chabrow, Eric. "Slow Traffic in Tech IPOs." *InternetWeek,* 13 July 2004.

Day, Ron. "Oracle Shares Fall." *Bloomberg News,* 15 March 2002.

"EDS, an HP Company, Expands Contact Center Managed Services to Include Multivendor Management Capabilities," 21 October 2008. Available from www.eds.com.

Einhorn, Bruce. "Taiwan's Info-Tech Triumphs." *Business Week,* 15 June 2004. Available from www.businessweek.com.

"European Trade Union's Protest HP Job Cuts." Reuters, 21 October 2008. Available from www.reuters.com.

"Feel Good Factor." *Information Age* (London), 10 June 2004.

"Fujitsu Recognized With Top Oracle User Group Awards," 22 October 2008. Available from www.searchbyheadlines.com.

"Gartner Predicts That by 2010, the Number of IT Staff in the Profession Will Shrink by 15 Percent." Gartner press release, 24 May 2005. Available from www.gartner.com.

"Global IT Services Revenue Grows 6.2 Percent." *Weboptimiser,* 23 June 2004. Available from www.weboptimiser.com.

Hoffman, Thomas. "Demand for IT Contractors Rising Slowly." *Computerworld,* 5 April 2004.

"Hoover's Company Capsules." *Hoover's Online,* 2008. Available from www.hoovers.com.

Horvitz, Paul. "IBM Wins $1 Billion, 10-Year Invensys Services Contract." *Bloomberg News,* 22 March 2002.

Humer, Caroline. "American Express and IBM Sign $6.4 Billion Deal." *Toronto Star,* 26 February 2002.

"Inside the Debate Over Outsourcing Information Technology Service Jobs." *Manufacturing & Technology News,* 17 October 2003.

"IT Pay Still Flat, but Beginning to Recover." *Report on Salary Surveys,* May 2004.

Keefe, Bob. "HP Moves to Oust Dissident Director." *Atlanta Journal and Constitution,* 2 April 2002.

"Major Market Profiles (short profiles): Computer Consulting Services in Australia, China, France, Germany, Japan, South Korea, UK, and USA." *Euromonitor,* October 2004. Available from www.euromonitor.com.

Moschella, David. "Users Are Taking the Lead in IT." *Computerworld,* 31 May 2004.

Sharma, Mahesh. "HP Replaces Local EDS Directors." *Australia News,* 21 October 2008. Available from www.australianit. news.com.au.

"Survey Finds IT Services Business May Be Brightening," ITAA, 4 November 2002. Available from www.itaa.org.

Thibodeau, Patrick. "More IT Jobs to Go Offshore, Controversial ITAA Report Says." *Computerworld,* 5 April 2004.

Zarley, Craig. "IBM Dazzles Wall Street with Numbers." *ComputerWire,* 15 November 2001.

CONSTRUCTION MATERIALS AND SERVICES

ASPHALT PAVING AND ROOFING MATERIALS

NAICS CODE(S)

32412. This industry group encompasses firms that manufacture asphalt and tar paving mixtures, paving blocks made of asphalt, and various compositions of asphalt or tar with other materials. Using asphalt and tar, industry companies also produce, usually from purchased materials, rolls, shingles, and coatings for roofing. For coverage of concrete paving and building materials, see **Concrete, Gypsum, and Plaster Products.**

INDUSTRY SNAPSHOT

On March 31, 2009, the National Asphalt Pavement Association President Mike Acott made an appearance for a briefing to share insights about the asphalt paving industry with the U.S. Congress. Acott discussed current status and future projections with the House Science and Technology Subcommittee on Technology and Innovation. The industry was characterized as being proactive about reducing environmental impact. "Within five years, I believe you will see full deployment of warm mix, much higher rates of recycling and development and application of Perpetual Pavement and porous asphalt technologies leading to a substantial reduction of greenhouse gas emissions and other environmental and economic benefits within the asphalt pavement sector."

The fragmented asphalt paving and roofing materials industry comprises a diverse collection of corporations worldwide. In excess of 300,000 people were directly employed by the U.S. asphalt industry in the mid-2000s. More than 1 billion tons of asphalt are produced worldwide every year. A substantial portion comes from diversified global corporations loosely associated with the construction and oil industries. Asphalt companies compete with concrete producers for pavement materials market share, though many of the leading asphalt makers sell concrete as well. As of 2006, roughly 96 percent of roads in the United States alone were surfaced with asphalt. The U.S. industry accounted for US$20 billion of the worldwide industry, with 500 million tons of asphalt produced each year.

Environmentalism, particularly regarding the recycling of asphalt products, the most recycled U.S. product in 2006, continues to play a major role in the industry. Recycled asphalt pavement, which has won increasing favor in the United States and Europe, can often constitute up to 35 percent of an asphalt mix, saving taxpayers an estimated US$300 million annually. According to the Federal Highway Administration and the Environmental Protection Agency, by 2006 80 percent of the asphalt removed from road surfaces each year in the United States was recycled into new roads, roadbeds, shoulders, and embankments. Also, as environmental concerns increasingly became an issue of pressing global concern and publicity, a new competitive arena opened for companies to produce recyclable goods and practice efficient production methods. Environmentalism has also given rise to interest in cool roof systems that reduce roof temperatures in warm climates in an effort to lower energy costs and usage.

ORGANIZATION AND STRUCTURE

In the United States, more than half of the asphalt produced is used in highway and street pavement. An estimated 25 percent is sold commercially for use in private parking lots, driveways, and sidewalks, while the remainder is used for roofing materials and other applications. Most asphalt producers supply road materials and general road construction as well, and are often subsidiaries of larger diversified corporations. Asphalt paving companies not only compete with each other, but also often vie with concrete producers for contracts. While concrete's primary use in the field of road construction is for new roads, the battle for new construction was about evenly split in the late 1990s. With a 90 percent share, asphalt clearly dominated in terms of resurfacing projects. Similarly, asphalt roofing materials compete with wood, stone, and ceramic tile.

Traditionally, government agencies have dictated how pavement is to be constructed, including specification of the asphalt mix design. The late 1990s, however, witnessed a gradual transformation of this system, whereby road construction contractors have consolidated and initiated the design of asphalt pavement that utilizes the industry's advancing technology to tailor mix designs for particular geographic and logistic variables.

Several organizations, including the National Asphalt Pavement Association (NAPA) in the United States and the European Asphalt Pavement Association (EAPA), help to organize and oversee the industry, most prominently in the field of road construction but also in the research, development, and production of asphalt paving materials.

BACKGROUND AND DEVELOPMENT

The use of asphalt, a brownish-black hydrocarbon, dates back at least 5,000 years to the time when Mesopotamian cultures began mining naturally occurring bitumen. The Dead Sea was an ancient source of bitumen. Lumps of the substance often washed up on its shores, giving rise to the Dead Sea's original name, Lake Asphaltites. West Asian societies not only utilized bitumen as a sealant for reservoirs, but also exported it to Egypt, where it was used in that kingdom's famous mummification process. Asphalt further functioned as mortar and caulk and in paving, waterproofing, and paints. Trinidad's Pitch Lake, discovered by Sir Walter Raleigh, became the first large commercial source of bitumen. The first modern asphalt pavement was laid in Paris in 1854 using a natural rock bitumen from Switzerland. Within two decades, this type of road surfacing had spread to Great Britain, Germany, Switzerland, and the United States.

Asphalt shingles also date back to ancient times. These roofing materials, which are made of a paper-like core of felted organic fibers soaked with asphalt, are now described as organic-based asphalt shingles. The paper core of these roofing materials has since been replaced with recycled newspaper and sawmill scraps. Fiberglass-based asphalt shingles were developed in the United States in the 1950s. Their durability, low maintenance, and fire-resistance have made them the primary asphalt roofing product. Often referred to as a built-up roofing system, asphalt shingles dominated the roofing market from their inception in the mid-nineteenth century until the late 1980s.

The invention of the automobile lent a sense of urgency to previously haphazard road-building efforts. It soon became evident, both in Europe and the United States, which would become the top producers and consumers of asphalt, that the task would require the efforts of both industrialists and all levels of government. The sheer volume of roads needed to traverse the United States propelled many advances in large-scale (but not necessarily high quality) paving. This was especially true during the construction of the interstate highway system in the 1950s.

The development of the petroleum industry in the eighteenth, nineteenth, and twentieth centuries encouraged the gradual replacement of natural bitumen with asphalt refined from heavy oils and propelled corresponding shifts in the centers of production. Although sources of bitumen and asphalt are widely distributed around the world, deposits of heavy oil and tar sand are concentrated in the Western Hemisphere, especially in Venezuela, which claims half of the world's heavy oil, and Canada, which is endowed with a whopping 75 percent of global tar sand reserves.

U.S. manufacturers distinguish bitumen, the naturally occurring form of the substance, from asphalt distilled from heavy petroleum as a waste product of the oil refining process. Europeans, on the other hand, characterize both forms as bitumen. When applied in the paving industry, the term usually refers to asphalt combined with an aggregate of sand or gravel. Within that category, the end product may range from light road pavement to heavy, high-viscosity industrial asphalt.

Other important modern uses of asphalt include canal and reservoir linings, dam facings, and other harbor and sea works. These applications commonly use a thin, sprayed membrane of asphalt. Asphalt is also used in floor tile, soundproofing, and other building materials. Petroleum industry research, especially in the United States after World War II, contributed to the development of new products for the asphalt roofing industry, including rolled and membranous coverings.

After rising slowly and erratically in the 1980s, global asphalt production declined rapidly in the 1990s. By the late 1990s, however, production was high again.

In Europe, production has remained steady since the early 1990s.

Because of Europe's monetary unification in 1999 and the necessity of efficient international trade and transportation assuming increasing importance, the harmonization of European asphalt production and application standards has emerged as a pressing issue among European asphalt producers. In addition, as U.S. road contractors strive for more durable and cost-efficient asphalt pavement, they are looking to Europe, whose roads are internationally recognized as the model of durability, for production innovation. As a result of these factors, combined with the high proportion of worldwide asphalt production by the United States and Europe, the industry is likely to see increased international cooperation and uniformity of production methods and technology in the twenty-first century.

Several important environmental issues catalyzed change within the asphalt industry in the mid-2000s. Some U.S. states responded to environmental pressures to reduce emissions from asphalt plants by requiring enclosed facilities for asphalt production. Some industry observers speculated that this move signaled the possibility of additional environmental legislation affecting the industry, in particular regarding respiratory exposure to plant workers.

The technology behind cool roofs was being developed and implemented to reduce energy usage. The California Energy Commission (CEC), for example, led a campaign in 2001 to educate consumers about the technology and its cost and energy-saving benefits. Because this technology prevents the roof from becoming as hot as traditional roofs, less energy is required to keep the house or building cool in the summer. Other advantages of cool roofs include exceptional waterproofing and increased comfort within the buildings using these systems. Campaigns, such as the one sponsored by the CEC, informed consumers that the technology can decrease utility bills. In California, incentives were offered in 2001 to encourage people to try the cool roof technology. The Sacramento Municipal Utility District offered rebates directly to consumers, and the Tree Foundation offered rebates to contractors.

Another important environmental concern in this industry in the mid-2000s was recycling. An enormous amount of asphalt is recycled every year, saving waste disposal resources and cutting costs for contractors and, in turn, buyers. The estimated savings due to the use of recycled asphalt were US$300 million annually in the United States alone. Surprisingly, asphalt was the most recycled product in the United States in the mid-2000s. Interest in recycling tends to rise and fall with oil prices because the industries are so closely related. When oil prices start to rise, interest in recycled asphalt also rises.

Another major change in the asphalt production industry derived from emerging computer technology and an increasing awareness of specific weather and traffic effects on asphalt roads. As control over design specification moved into the hands of the contractors and developers, a methodological shift in the production approach occurred. Whereas asphalt production had in the past relied on an empirical, "recipe-based" mix design specification, innovations allowed for the widespread and rapidly proliferating use of performance-based specifications, whereby producers apply a volumetric mix design tailored to the specific needs of individual roads and regions.

CURRENT CONDITIONS

The Asphalt Pavement Alliance described why the material was so important when linked to energy and recycling. Less energy is required in production than with other pavements. The Alliance claimed recycling of asphalt saved U.S. taxpayers approximately US$1.8 billion annually. They also called it "the sustainable pavement."

The United States was by far the largest producer of hot mix asphalt in the mid-2000s, with 500 million tons produced in 2005. Japan was the second largest, with 57.3 million tons, and Germany was third with 57 million tons. As a whole, Europe was responsible for 320.7 million tons of hot mix asphalt in 2005.

The largest market for asphalt continued to be North America, accounting for 36 percent of total world demand in 2004, most of which was consumed in the United States. The Freedonia Group predicted world demand for asphalt products would increase 2.3 percent annually to 114 million metric tons by 2009. Eighty-five percent of asphalt consumed worldwide in the mid-2000s was used for paving, a trend that was expected to continue. Asphalt used for roofing was expected to increase 2.2 percent annually to reach 15 million metric tons by 2009, according to The Freedonia Group.

Prices were also on the rise. As oil prices rose to record levels in the mid-2000s, asphalt costs increased as well. According to a report in *The Plain Dealer* (Cleveland, OH), the per-ton cost of liquid asphalt in the United States rose from an estimated $190 to $270 in 2006. Some industry experts expected the price increases to have a negative effect on construction and road projects nationwide.

One of the new ideas being tested in the asphalt industry in the latter mid-2000s was the use of "warm mix" asphalt. Traditional hot mix asphalt is made by combining aggregates with liquid asphalt and keeping the mixture at 300 degrees F. The warm mix method uses an additive in the mix and keeps the temperature at 250 to 275 degrees F. The advantages of warm mix asphalt are that the paving season can be extended into the fall when temperatures are cooler and its production emits fewer gaseous odors and saves fuel by using less heat. Warm mix asphalt was already being used in Europe and had shown a 30 percent savings as compared to hot mix, but use of the product in the United States was still being tested in 2007.

RESEARCH AND TECHNOLOGY

Ever-increasing traffic demands and fluctuating petroleum stocks have forced asphalt producers to begin to examine the chemical composition of asphalt and work to obtain predictable results. In the late 1980s, the chemical composition of asphalt (about 90 percent carbon and hydrogen and 10 percent sulfur, nitrogen, oxygen, and trace metals) was finally pinpointed, allowing for a wealth of innovations and programs aimed at improving the quality of roads and the efficiency of asphalt production techniques.

Many of these initiatives originated in Europe, which is considered the leader in paving research. One of Europe's most celebrated innovations, stone matrix asphalt (SMA), was developed in Germany and Sweden in the 1960s. This material, which incorporates coarser, larger aggregates to form a "stone skeleton" within the asphalt binder, was created to withstand heavy European truck traffic. The product has proven more durable than conventional asphalt and is gaining favor in North American markets.

Although cold-mix asphalt, also known as asphalt emulsion concrete, has been in existence since the 1940s, it has recently been refined by Swedish engineers. The product's advantages over traditional hot-mix asphalt include lower energy costs and no unpleasant odor. True to its name, asphalt emulsion concrete uses emulsified asphalt, meaning that the asphalt binder is suspended in water to promote viscosity, instead of using heat to induce flexibility.

The U.S. government followed Europe's lead by establishing the Strategic Highway Research Program (SHRP) in 1987. The US$150 million initiative developed Superpave, a computer analysis system that can produce a set of volumetric asphalt mix design specifications for a given geographic area and traffic level. It was hoped that given the new knowledge of asphalt's composition, pavements could be made to last longer and perform better. And, as of the late 1990s, that hope was a reality, as states that had implemented and monitored these new developments reported that they had saved hundreds of millions of dollars on the rehabilitation and reconstruction of roads. In 2000 this computer technology was applied to recycling asphalt; as a result, computers were designed to manage the mix of discarded asphalt with hot rocks and gravel.

Recycling asphalt, especially asphalt used in road surfaces, has captured the attention of many in the industry.

The development and application of efficient, smoke-free manufacturing equipment for processing reclaimed asphalt pavement started in the late 1970s and has won increasing favor in recent years. In fact, asphalt pavement is the most recycled material in the United States, far outpacing other recyclables. Every year, an average of 73 million tons of asphalt is recycled, which amounts to almost double the volume of paper, glass, and plastic combined. This recycled asphalt is used in both paving and roofing. In the roofing industry, recycled asphalt void of ozone-depleting chemicals, called a "green" roof system, is popular among environmentally conscious professionals who hire contractors to construct residential or commercial buildings.

The use of rubberized asphalt is a hotly debated issue in the industry. The product was developed in the late 1960s in the United States. It incorporates bits of scrap rubber in the asphalt mix and has been embraced by environmentalists and tire industry representatives, who think it is the answer to their tire disposal problems. Proponents of rubberized asphalt maintain that the material is safer, more durable, and more cost-effective than standard asphalt. But opponents of the process said that augmenting asphalt with "waste material" such as scrap tires only renders it unrecyclable, thereby postponing its eventual arrival in the landfill. Still, asphalt rubber advocates, and some quiescent asphalt industry observers, asserted that expansion of their product's use is "inevitable."

Other pavement industry trends include limiting traffic noise and introducing quality assurance programs and performance guarantees in the form of warranties. Issues in the asphalt roofing industry include recycling, appearance, durability, low-odor asphalt, and cool roof technology. Many new shingles are made to resemble wood or slate or to give a more three-dimensional look. Laminated, or heavyweight, shingles have been developed to be more durable. Single-ply, or modified bitumen, roofing has been gaining popularity and market share, especially in commercial applications. Cool roof technology controls the temperatures that roofs can reach in the heat of the summer. A traditional roof can reach 170 degrees Fahrenheit on a 90-degree day, but a cool roof is likely to stay at 100 degrees. The idea behind this technology is relatively simple and is most easily understood by noting the difference between a black surface in the sun and a white one. Cool roofs are white, thereby increasing the solar reflectivity.

Overall quality of asphalt roofing installations has been significantly improved by utilizing modern equipment, according to the Quality Commercial Asphalt Roofing Council of the Asphalt Roofing Manufacturers Association (ARMA). ARMA Executive Director Reed Hitchcock acknowledged the necessity for skilled workforce to operate modern equipment. This combination had a dramatic impact on increasing success rates for fume recovery systems. Hitchcock concluded that asphalt roofing installations had changed substantially since 1977 due in large part to equipment improvements.

WORKFORCE

Technology works both for and against the asphalt paving and roofing workforce. While it enables a contractor to offer more, and better, options to a prospective client, it also requires that contractors stay abreast of the latest developments. Contractors must stay current on mixing improvements, environmental concerns, and computerization. Indirectly, technology in general has made it more difficult for contractors to find good workers. In the twenty-first century, young people are computer savvy and thus have skills they can use in office jobs. This is a challenge for contractors, who need young workers willing to put in long hours of hard work outside. As a result, contractors spend more time recruiting and training than they did in the past.

INDUSTRY LEADERS

Europe.

Lafarge SA. Lafarge SA, one of Europe's largest building materials groups, made substantial movement into markets throughout Europe, North and Latin America, and the Pacific Rim in the 1990s. With the acquisition of the United Kingdom company Blue Circle Industries, Lafarge became the world's largest cement manufacturer. One of North America's largest suppliers of building materials, Lafarge's total sales for 2006 reached more than US$22.3 billion, 35 percent of which was from the Western Europe market. The company employed 80,146 people in 2005.

Skanska AB. Skanska AB, a Swedish company, had net sales of US$18.3 billion in 2006. During the 1990s, the company reorganized into regional units to accommodate its rapid international expansion (especially into Europe and North America). As of 2007, Skanska had subsidiaries in more than 60 countries and employed 56,000 people.

The United States.

APAC Inc. APAC Inc. (formerly Ashland Paving and Construction), a subsidiary of Oldcastle Materials, was formed in 1879 when it supplied asphalt for the first commercial asphalt road in the United States. In the mid-2000s, the firm was one of the largest asphalt and concrete paving contractors in the United States, generating more than US$3.9 billion in 2006 revenue. APAC posted US$3.3 billion in sales in 2006 with 8,051 employees. The company is attempting to expand in the Midwest and Central states. It is also focusing on acquisitions.

Vulcan Materials Company. Vulcan Materials Company produces aggregates, asphalt, and ready-mix concrete in more than 220 plants in the United States and Mexico. The firm is the largest U.S. producer of construction aggregates, which accounts for about two thirds of its income.

CertainTeed Corp. Among asphalt roofing materials producers, CertainTeed Corp. of the United States is a major player and is highly regarded in the industry. It is a subsidiary of Saint-Gobain, a major French industrial company whose total income in 2006 exceeded US$7.1 billion. In 2007, CertainTeed owned 40 plants in North America. Diversified fiberglass manufacturer and designer Owens Corning Sales, another leading U.S. manufacturer of industrial asphalt (used primarily in commercial roofing), earned almost US$6.3 billion in total sales in 2006. CertainTeed Corp. products brand names include Bufftech, CertainTeed, Form-A-Drain, Prestige and Wolverine brands. By 2009, the company operated approximately 65 manufacturing plants in U.S. and Canada.

Canada.

Emco. Emco, a Canadian corporation, reported 2003 revenues of US$857 million, a portion of which was derived from its Building Products Group. Emco was purchased by Ontario Inc. in 2003.

MAJOR COUNTRIES IN THE INDUSTRY

The United States, with approximately 500 million tons of hot-mix asphalt produced in 2005, easily dominated the industry. The European Union followed, with 320.5 million tons, which represents the output of Germany (57 million), France and Italy (40.1 million each), Spain (41.5 million), and the United Kingdom (27.9 million). Europe remains a major center of asphalt and road construction innovation and design. Japan was also a leading manufacturer, with 57.3 million tons produced in 2005.

Roofing materials manufacturing experienced a slight three percent growth from 2007 to 2008. That growth was from US $10.6 billion to US $10.9 billion. In addition, *Roofing Materials in the U.S.* reported that asphalt shingles were in a place between "old school" and new materials. Older options, such as slate and clay, were "being repositioned as environmentally friendly." Newer options, such as green roofs and solar shingles, provided other asphalt alternatives.

BIBLIOGRAPHY

"Asphalt Demand Increasing." *Public Works,* February 2006.

"Asphalt Industry." Beyond Roads, 2005. Available from www.beyondroads.com.

Asphalt Pavement Alliance. "Asphalt: The Sustainable Pavement." Available from www.asphaltalliance.com.

"Asphalt Prices on the Rise." *Recycling Today,* August 2006.

Asphalt Roofing Manufacturers Association. "New Materials and Equipment Allows for Greater Control Over Asphalt Roofing Installations, Says QARC," 7 September 2007. Available from www.asphaltroofing.org.

Auburn University. "National Center for Asphalt Technology," 2004. Available from www.eng.auburn.edu.

Chang, Ivy. "New Technologies Promote Greater Use of Asphalt." *Construction Bulletin,* 6 October 2006.

European Asphalt Pavement Association. "Asphalt in Figures," 2005. Available from www.eapa.org.

Huchzemeyer, Laura. "APAC —Company Description." *Hoover's Online,* 2009. Available from www.hoovers.com.

"International Trade Statistics." World Trade Organization, 2005. Available from www.wto.org.

Moore, Walt. "Potential Benefits Heat Up as Temperature Cools." *Construction Equipment,* 1 March 2007.

National Asphalt Pavement Association. "NAPA President Briefs Congress on Breakthroughs in Sustainable Asphalt Technology," 31 March 2009. Available from www.hotmix.org.

Richardson, Mark. "CertainTeed—Company Description." *Hoover's Online,* 2009. Available from www.hoovers.com.

Roofing Materials in the U.S., 2nd Edition. Live-PR, 10 July 2009. Available from www.live-pr.com.

SIC 1622

BRIDGE, TUNNEL, AND ELEVATED HIGHWAY CONSTRUCTION

NAICS CODE(S)

237310. This industry includes general contractors who build bridges, viaducts, elevated highways, and tunnels for pedestrians, vehicles, and trains (excluding subways).

INDUSTRY SNAPSHOT

The market for bridge, tunnel, and elevated highway construction has become increasingly globalized since the 1980s. The dominant players in the industry—companies from North America, Western Europe, and Japan—have looked beyond these mature markets to seek out the opportunities for growth that are available in developing economies. However, funding for infrastructure construction projects such as bridges, tunnels, and elevated highways is quite dependent upon the economic health of a country, so economic weakness within these developing economies can cause the monetary resources in these markets to dry up or can shift resources away from infrastructure construction.

Even in mature and stable economies, infrastructure funding can be difficult to come by. Funding comes largely from public coffers, and many other concerns compete for these resources. Additionally, since the 1990s, governments

have been under pressure to balance their budgets, which emphasizes the finite nature of spending levels for infrastructure.

While developing economies need additional infrastructure in order to sustain their growth, the United States continued to be increasingly faced with the need to repair or replace existing bridges, tunnels, and elevated highways that were aged and deteriorating or inadequate to carry the current volume of traffic. With such needs and demands for these infrastructure projects, countered by the limited nature of public funding, modest growth is expected for the industry worldwide.

Although Asia's late 1990s economic crisis produced a chilling effect on heavy construction on much of that continent in the early years of the first decade of the twenty-first century, China was a significant exception, as astronomical development spurred the planning and execution of several monumental civil engineering projects.

ORGANIZATION AND STRUCTURE

As with general contractors in other construction sectors, companies involved in bridge, tunnel, and elevated highway construction bid on potential projects or "jobs" based on estimates of overhead costs, desired profit margin, and estimated time necessary to complete the job. Winning bidders are responsible for managing the construction project, although they may subcontract some or all of the project to other companies. Consequently, in some instances, the winning bidders may be companies that are known primarily as engineering firms rather than conventional construction contractors. (See also **Engineering Services.**)

Contracts to assume responsibility for construction of a bridge or tunnel (or most other types of construction) can take different forms. In cost-reimbursement contracts, builders are paid for reasonable costs incurred during the life of the project. Fixed-price contracts, on the other hand, require contractors to absorb cost overruns themselves. By the early years of the first decade of the 2000s, incentive-based contracts that reward builders for timeliness and quality of construction had become increasingly commonplace.

According to a report in *U.S. Industry & Trade Outlook,* across the construction industry in general, U.S. companies that win jobs overseas tend to use local labor through their foreign affiliates to carry out the work. Hence, U.S. construction firms generally export only their management and engineering skills, not their actual construction services.

Government budgets for new construction or renovation of existing structures are of great importance to the industry's vitality, as government contracts from around the world account for the vast majority of industry revenue. Government involvement in the construction process varies from country to country. In the United States, for instance, federal or state agencies are often involved in the execution of projects, as well as the funding. In less developed countries, such as those in Africa, parts of Asia, and Eastern Europe, funding sources often include the World Bank and regional development banks.

BACKGROUND AND DEVELOPMENT

Historic advances in this industry's development have resulted in some of the world's most notable architectural achievements. Led by European and U.S. builders who capitalized on the development of steel and other technological advances, bridge and tunnel construction has been characterized over the years by continuous improvement in design and execution. By building on the work of previous generations of architects, engineers, and builders, industry participants continue to devise ways to improve engineering and construction methods, as well as construction materials.

The early nineteenth century featured the introduction of several revolutionary bridge designs. In 1822, construction of the world's first iron railroad bridge was completed. It was followed three years later by the opening of the world's first wire suspension bridge in France. The first bridge of that type in the United States was opened in 1842 near Philadelphia, Pennsylvania. That bridge—25 feet wide and 358 feet long, with five wire cables on either side—cost US$35,000 to build. In 1845, the first wire cable suspension aqueduct bridge was opened over the Allegheny River at Pittsburgh, Pennsylvania. In 1849 the B&O Railroad bridge, which crossed the Ohio River and spanned 1,000 feet, became the world's longest bridge. By 1855, trains were able to cross a wire cable bridge that spanned Niagara Gorge between Canada and the United States.

Engineering and construction innovations continued through the latter part of the nineteenth century. The Brooklyn Bridge, the world's first steel-wire suspension bridge, opened in 1883 in New York City. Tunnel designs improved during this period as well. A railroad line completed in 1867 extended from Austria to Italy and included more than 20 tunnels to negotiate passage through the forbidding Brenner Pass. In the latter part of the nineteenth century much of the construction in the tunnel and bridge building industry centered on movable bridges that could accommodate river navigation. Numerous vertical-lift and swing-span bridges were built during the 1890s, which also featured the introduction of reinforced concrete bridges.

The industry continued to grow as the twentieth century began, although U.S. builders, long among the world leaders in bridge and tunnel construction, saw their fortunes sag immediately after the conclusion of World War I as labor strife and other problems diminished new business.

Meanwhile, in Europe it was necessary to rebuild after the war, but some European economies could not afford new construction given the high inflation and various social problems of the period.

The Detroit-Windsor Tunnel opened in 1930. The tunnel, which runs under the Detroit River and connects the United States and Canada, was built of prefabricated tubes floated over a trench and laid out in sections like pipeline. The celebrated Golden Gate Bridge, a 4,200-foot bridge that spans San Francisco Bay (the world's longest suspension bridge at the time), was completed a few years later. Halfway around the world in Sydney, Australia, a new structure, the Harbour Bridge, assumed the title of the world's longest arch bridge when it opened in 1932.

However, while bridge and tunnel construction accelerated around the world in the 1930s and 1940s, the industry's greatest growth was in the United States. Buoyed by the establishment of the Works Progress Administration (WPA) in 1935, industry contractors took advantage of the New Deal's economic environment, characterized by federal programs to stimulate economic growth, to secure building contracts across the United States. The surge in construction resulted in the creation of 78,000 bridges and more than 650,000 miles of public roads. The victory of the Allied forces in World War II further strengthened the bridge, tunnel, and elevated highway construction industry in the United States. The *Engineering News-Record* (*ENR*), McGraw-Hill Publishing Company's construction industry journal, noted that by the end of 1945, it had "identified a backlog of US$28 billion in proposed projects and half of those were already in the blueprint stage. Bridge construction rose by 220 percent in 1945. The postwar era also saw the introduction of the interstate highway system in the United States, which provided steady growth for the industry.

The industry outside the United States continued to grow as well, and the 1950s and 1960s were marked by new engineering marvels such as the Oosterscheldebrug Causeway in the Netherlands (1965), the Tagus River Bridge in Portugal (1966), and the Zdakov Bridge in Czechoslovakia (1967). In 1975 the Great Uhuru Railway was opened in Africa. This 1,160-mile rail line featured 300 bridges and 23 tunnels.

In the United States, meanwhile, the bridge and tunnel industry felt the effects of economic conditions that rocked the entire construction industry in 1970. Inflation had increased the cost of doing business; labor costs were particularly high. The *ENR* Construction Cost Index rose by 10.8 percent at this time.

In the 1980s, bridge and elevated highway construction took on increased importance in the United States. Construction of bridges and elevated highways accounted for more than 72 percent of public work in 1987, an increase of almost 10 percent over 1982. Tunnel construction, however, fell during that time, from almost 17 percent of total construction in 1982 to less than 10 percent by 1987. While the drop in tunnel building during this period dragged the figures down somewhat, U.S. participants in the industry registered a significant increase in total revenues. In 1982, a total value of US$2.82 billion was attributed to bridge, tunnel, and elevated highway construction in the United States. By 1987 the value of new construction in these areas had exploded to US$4.48 billion.

A new funding mechanism for U.S. construction projects was set up by Congress in 1995: state infrastructure banks (SIBs). These banks were to grant loans and other forms of credit to fund local transportation projects facing fiscal uncertainty. However, SIBs were not immediately created in all states. *ITS World* reported that the U.S. Department of Transportation estimated that about US$1.6 billion in projects had been financed by SIBs by the beginning of fiscal year 1998.

In the early years of the first decade of the 2000s, the transportation infrastructure in the United States had begun to age and deteriorate, and in some cases, the structures could not meet the needs and demands of usage. Bridges and other infrastructure aged rapidly due to increasing traffic and speeds and heavier vehicles. A 2003 national inventory of U.S. bridges estimated some 22.3 percent of the country's 286,195 interstate and state bridges had become structurally or functionally obsolete. Hence, there was an increased need to spend transportation dollars on repairing or replacing existing bridges, tunnels, and elevated highways (which might serve to divert a certain level of spending from the construction of new projects). According to *New Steel*, "federal government spending to build and maintain U.S. highways and bridges reaches about US$20 billion per year."

Two replacement projects of note link the cities of Port Huron, Michigan, and Sarnia, Ontario. A second Blue Water Bridge spanning the St. Clair River was completed in 1997, and, when repairs were completed on the original Blue Water Bridge, each bridge began to carry one-way traffic at this busy and often backed-up border crossing. According to *American City & County* magazine, the original bridge, built in the 1930s, had exceeded its traffic load capacity and was in need of structural renovation. Also, a new 1.1-mile rail tunnel below the St. Clair River was completed in 1995 at a cost of US$160 million. It replaced a leaking tunnel that had been built in 1890; the old tunnel had cost US$2.7 million to build. The new tunnel cuts travel time across (or rather, under) the river, as trains are able to travel at 60 mph, as opposed to 15 mph in the old tunnel, according to the *Flint Journal.* Furthermore, the new tunnel could accommodate double-decker and triple-decker vehicles. Previously, these vehicles were dismantled, loaded on barges, and ferried across the river, a process which took 12 hours. The *Flint Journal* reported that "General Motors officials have said that the new tunnel will save the company about a day's time hauling its new cars and trucks to Chicago from Oshawa, Ontario."

In 1994, transportation service began through the Channel Tunnel, or Chunnel, that runs beneath the English Channel and connects Great Britain to France. The Channel Tunnel was the second longest rail tunnel in the world, and the section that runs under the water (24 miles) is the longest undersea tunnel. The cost of this monumental 31-mile-long achievement exceeded US$17 billion.

Another noteworthy project was the Confederation Bridge, which connects the two Canadian provinces of New Brunswick and Prince Edward Island. This bridge, completed in 1997, spans 12,880 meters—about eight miles—and is among the longest in the world. In 1998, Japan opened the Akashi Kaikyo Bridge, which connects the islands of Honshu and Shikoku and is the longest suspension bridge in the world. The bridge, which took ten years to complete and cost about US$3.6 billion, involved more than 100 contractors. Japan is also home to the Seikan Tunnel, the longest (34-mile) railway tunnel in the world.

The biggest and most complex highway project in U.S. history began in 1991 in Boston, Massachusetts, and was completed in 2004. The "Big Dig," as the project was called, replaced the city's antiquated Central Artery, an elevated six-lane highway, with a larger underground expressway. It also extended Interstate 90 (the Massachusetts Turnpike) through downtown Boston to Logan Airport. The project included four major highway interchanges; a two-bridge, 14-lane crossing of the Charles River, including the widest cable-stayed bridge in the world; a tunnel under Boston Harbor; and a seven-building tunnel ventilation system. At its peak, the Big Dig employed about 4,000 construction workers. Originally funded at US$2.5 billion, US$14.6 billion had been spent on the project by 2006.

The economic growth, urbanization, and industrialization of developing economies requires the development of major infrastructure projects, includingbridges, tunnels, and elevated highways. In the late 1990s, the countries with the most promising growth prospects were in East Asia and the Pacific Rim, specifically China, South Korea, Malaysia, Vietnam, the Philippines, Indonesia, and Thailand. However, after slowdowns in some places during 1996, the region's severe economic crisis in 1997 began to negatively impact infrastructure construction in several countries. South Korea, Indonesia, and Thailand were hit particularly hard by the crisis and were being pressured by the international financial community to reform their economic, financial, and business practices. Similarly, fiscal tightening by Japan's government coincided with a downturn in the Japanese economy that left the region's largest and the world's second largest economy in what appeared to be early stages of recession in 1997 and 1998. As a result, government-funded construction projects were scaled back, causing lean times for the construction industry. Major companies in Japan looked increasingly to overseas projects in order to remain profitable. In 2001, Japan agreed to fund an extensive portable steel bridge project in Bangladesh. In 1994, the country had conducted a basic design study for the bridges, and two years later purchased the materials for 74 bridges to be constructed. In 1999, Japan began repairing another 80 Bangladesh bridges. Although the project was extensive, a bridge shortage remained, particularly in rural areas.

Twenty-First Century Developments. Despite some contraction for the market in Asia, demand for new infrastructure surged in China. In 2001 the country launched 48 railway, highway, tunnel, and bridge projects with combined contractual foreign funding of US$470 million. A cross-country highway linking Shanghai with the Kazakhstan city of Horgos, under construction in 2004, was expected to include the world's longest tunnel. Another major project was the Dong Hai Bridge, linking Shanghai's new port with Yangshan Island. Completed in late 2005, it is the longest oversea bridge in the world. Halcrow and NRS were among foreign contractors involved with the project, most of which was designed and built by Chinese construction companies. T. Y. Lin International, a U.S. engineering firm, designed two other major bridges in China and was joint contractor for construction of the Shibanpe Yangtze River Bridge, completed in 2006.

More bridge and tunnel projects in China were being awarded exclusively to domestic contractors. One such project was the Chaotianmen Bridge across the Yangtze River in Chongqing. The two-level bridge, begun in 2004 and scheduled for completion in 2008, will carry both light rail and six lanes of highway. China Harbour Engineering, the country's largest bridge building firm, is constructing the US$360 million project, which will be the world's longest arch bridge. Another project announced in 2005 was the Sutong Bridge, a cable-stayed bridge over the Yangtze River estuary at Nantong. With a central span of 1,088 meters, the Sutong Bridge would become the world's longest cable-stayed bridge. Total investment in the project, which was being built entirely by Chinese companies, was estimated at about US$725.77 million.

Additional projects being planned or under construction in the mid-years of the first decade of the 2000s were the Yichang-Wanzhou Railway, a US$2.1 billion project covering 378 kilometers and including 183 bridges and 114 tunnels, and the US$396 million Xiamen East tunnel, China's first undersea tunnel, due to be completed in 2010.

One of the few major infrastructure projects in Europe in the early years of the first decade of the 2000s was the Dublin Port Tunnel, completed in 2006. Japan's Nishimatsu Construction Company, Britain's Mowlem & Company, and Ireland's Irishenco Construction were all awarded contracts for the project. The Millau Viaduct Bridge in France, which connects the major highway between Paris and Barcelona, Spain, was built with private funds and opened in 2005. A single-span suspension bridge across the Strait of Messina, which would link Sicily with mainland Italy, was being planned in 2005. The 3.3 kilometer bridge would become the longest single-span bridge in the world and was expected to cost 6 billion euros. Construction began in late 2005 and was expected to be completed in 2011.

Greater potential for growth remained in Russia, the former Soviet republics, Eastern Europe, and South America—particularly in Brazil and Argentina. A Slovenian highway project that was to span the country from east to west and that includes several tunnels was funded by the European Bank for Reconstruction and Development as well as a gas tax. Russia's plan to improve transit in its relatively isolated far eastern regions, largely to facilitate cheaper shipment for raw materials such as coal, resulted in several major highway programs. In 2001, seven bridges were constructed in Sakhalin alone; numerous projects throughout eastern Siberia were planned through 2012. In Mexico, a major highway maintenance and restructuring plan financed by the World Bank began in the late 1990s and was extended well into the first decade of the 2000s. Upgrades of some 100 bridges will be included in the project. Venezuela's Economic Recovery Plan opened public works projects to foreign investors and builders.

CURRENT CONDITIONS

In the United States, funding for transportation construction, including bridges, tunnels, and elevated highways, was continued with passage of the Transportation Equity Act for the 21st Century (TEA-21) in 1998 and extended to 2003. The Safe, Accountable, Flexible, Efficient Transportation Equity Act: A Legacy for Users (SAFETEA-LU) was enacted in 2005 as a replacement of the TEA-21. It authorizes a federal program for highways, highway safety, and transit for the five-year period from 2005 to 2009. The Federal Highway Administration, addressing the ongoing problem of the nation's deteriorating transportation infrastructure, reported that 593,885 state and highway system bridges were deficient as of December 2004, estimating that it would cost US$50 billion to correct the problem.

The value of new U.S. highway and bridge construction increased by 16 percent to $76 billion in 2006. This was the largest increase since 1984, and analysts believed activity would stay elevated for a time due to the passage of the SAFETEA-LU. According to Kenneth Simonson, chief economist of the Associated General Contractors of America, "A lot of projects had either been deferred or had continued at prior-year levels; SAFETEA-LU ended that uncertainty about when the funding would come through." The SAFETEA-LU provides 38 percent more funding for transportation construction than the TEA-21.

Labor Day weekend of 2009 marked the 52nd annual Mackinac Bridge Walk. Michigan Governor Jennifer Granholm continued the tradition started by Governor G. Mennen Williams, when the state's top leader led thousands of people on a holiday stroll across the five-mile long landmark and major attraction. The first walk was part of the Bridge's dedication in June 1958. Labor Day 2009 also marked the celebration of the 150 millionth vehicle crossing the great bridge.

Associated Press writer Sudhin Thanawala pointed out, in a September 8, 2009, article that a repaired cracked bridge doesn't mean everything was mended and resolved because many questions remained unanswered about the 2009 Labor Day weekend closure of the 73-year-old San Francisco-Oakland Bay Bridge for a retrofit and detour of its replaced eastern span, during which the California Department of Transportation (Caltrans), in keeping with the Federal Highway Administration (FHA) requirement for bridge inspections to occur every two years, found a major crack in an eyebar, an important structural beam, of sufficient import to close the bridge on its own. The crack's cause and contributing factors were unknown, but fatigue cracks frequently occur in eyebars. Since the eyebar still sustained the bridge by managing some of the weight, it could not just be taken out and replaced with a newer model. Instead, Caltrans Engineer Brian Maroney designedcaps or "saddles" to brace it. C.C. Myers subcontractor Stinger Welding of Arizona constructed the braces. They arrived courtesy of a California Highway Patrol escort after being flown to California. Efficient assembly followed their arrival, and the bridge re-opened on September 8. "The bridge has been repaired and it's safer than it was when we closed it," said Caltrans Director Randy Iwasaki. The FHA did not inspect the repair, instead relying on state inspection reports to ensure that its guidelines were met. Thanawala also noted that the braces were of the same design used on the Interstate 35 bridge in Minneapolis, which had collapsed in 2007 and killed five people.

Less than two months later, on October 27, 2009, two steel rods and a metal section totaling about 5,000 pounds that had been supporting the saddle-shaped cap installed to strengthen the cracked eyebar broke off the bridge and rained down on rush hour traffic. There were no injuries, although three vehicles were damaged by the falling debris. The FHA sent engineers to help Caltrans engineers investigate why the recent repairs—which were supposed to last until the new bridge opened in 2013— failed in less than two months. Amid public anger and fear, the bridge reopened six days later, on November 2, 2009, after it first failed and then passed a stress test. A Caltrans spokesman said that "strong winds likely played a role in the failure, which heightened concerns by some experts about the integrity of the repair and the bridge's safety in an earthquake." Thanawala also quoted a University of California, Berkley civil engineering professor, who had studied the effects of the 1989 Loma Prieta earthquake on the bridge and called the Labor Day Weekend repair a "Band-Aid" and a very serious safety issue that "jeopardized public safety to get the bridge open quickly."

Denis Cuff, writing for the *Contra Costa Times,* described how the delay of "crucial" steel pieces ordered from China sources was impacting completion of the $6.3 billion new east span of the Bay Bridge. Bridge officials said the first of eight shipments of giant welded steel parts would be leaving China a year behind schedule because "the welds had to be redone in a Shanghai manufacturing plant that relies heavily on hand labor." The delay was causing a domino effect, preventing completion of other key aspects of Bay Bridge project. "Officials fear the delayed steel shipments will cause a backup in a sequence of bridge building segments." However, they said, it was "too early to say whether the new East Span completion will be bumped back into 2014 or later—something that would likely trigger cost overruns."

TripAdvisor, a Web site aimed at "helping people around the world plan and have the perfect trip," rated the five scariest bridges in the world. TripAdvisor's CEO pointed out that the bridges soared beyond the practical to be tourist attractions. Langkawi Sky Bridge in Kedan, Malaysia, was a cable pedestrian bridge providing "breathtaking views of the Andaman Sea and nearby islands." Capilano Suspension Bridge located in North Vancouver, British Columbia was another pedestrian bridge "high above a gorgeous canyon hosting North Vancouver's Capilano River." Carrick-a-Rede Rope Bridge in Antrim, North Ireland connected Carrick Island to the mainland. Trift Bridge in Gadmen, Switzerland, was the longest pedestrian bridge and reigned above the Triftsee Lake. Royal Gorge Bridge in Canyon City, Colorado, hung high in the balance at 1,000 feet above the Arkansas River. The majestic Grand Canyon area had a walkway made of planks.

RESEARCH AND TECHNOLOGY

The bridge, tunnel, and elevated highway construction sector has historically advanced in accordance with innovations and new developments in design, construction, and engineering. The industry continues to rely on these improvements—whether in the areas of construction materials, construction equipment, or engineering design—as it seeks ways to produce safer, more cost-effective, and (in some cases) more spectacular results.

In Japan, for example, three companies—Tokyo Electric Power Company, Taisei Corporation, and Ishikawajima-Harima Heavy Industries Company—joined forces to develop the world's first tunnel boring machine with the capability of turning 90-degree angles. The machine works, according to *ENR,* by using two shields. The smaller of the shields is located in a spherical housing at the front of the larger shield. The larger shield can tunnel either horizontally or vertically to the planned corner, whereupon the sphere at its front pivots and sends the smaller shield off in the desired direction. Such innovations provide the industry with continued vitality.

In the realm of bridge construction, builders around the world continually explore the feasibility of new techniques and methods. The DRC Consultants engineering firm, for example, designed widely instituted refinements in cable-stayed and segmental box girder bridge construction in the 1980s. An article published in *Civil Engineering* remarked, however, that innovative designs and construction methodologies are not always pursued with the same zeal in different regions of the world. In Europe, for example, supply-side engineering—in which designers and owners work closely together—has enabled firms to take a lead in innovative construction, whereas the United States lagged in this area—although by the mid-1990s it had begun to take steps in that direction.

Advances in the quality of materials also played a role in the steady development of the industry. Gall-Tough stainless steel, for example, has been used for bridge parts such as link hinge pins. Gall-Tough—an austenitic stainless alloy that is high in silicon and manganese content and is nitrogen-strengthened—possesses superior self-mated galling and metal-to-metal wear resistance. *Machine Design* noted that the alloy shows higher strength and high-temperature oxidation resistance compared to other stainless steel alloys with similar corrosion resistance. With a galling threshold rated 15 times higher than standard stainless steel, the alloy also has a high stress resistance, though it sacrifices a small amount of the corrosion resistance that other materials offer.

While steel remains a popular material for bridge and tunnel construction, industry researchers have also looked to other suitable materials such as aluminum and plastics where practical. In addition, alternatives to traditional welded-wire highway concrete reinforcements include fiber-reinforced concrete that uses acrylic, carbon, nylon, and polyethylene materials. Carbon steel plates and glass-fiber reinforced concrete have also been introduced in highway and bridge construction.

Several factors must be considered when choosing materials for bridge construction: cost, weight, life span, and reparability. The American Iron and Steel Institute (AISI) claimed in *New Steel* that, despite the dominance of concrete in the bridge market, "steel-supported bridges last longer, are easier to build and repair, and weigh less than bridges supported only by concrete.... If the concrete bridge deteriorates, it normally needs to be replaced altogether." The AISI stated further that, according to a study conducted by the Organization for Economic Cooperation and Development, steel bridges can last twice as long as concrete bridges without needing major repairs—50 years for steel as opposed to 25 years for concrete. Concrete bridges have been favored in the United States largely because they tend to be the cheapest, a trend some observers view as short-sighted.

The U.S. government has set up a program to spur the development of new types of steel for highway bridges. The goal is to lower the cost of bridge building. One result has been the development of "a low-carbon 70W steel processed via hot rolling reheat quench and tempering," according to *American Metal Market,* which will allow the elimination of one step of the fabricating process, thus reducing construction costs. This high-performance steel was expected to be used to construct a bridge in Tennessee and should reduce construction costs by 16 percent. This particular steel was developed jointly by three steel companies—U.S. Steel, Bethlehem, and Lukens—along with the U.S. Navy and the Federal Highway Administration.

The "Report Card for America's Infrastructure" 2009 grade was a "C." An examination of related conditions found that there was substantial room for improvement. U.S. Department of Transportation data showed 72,868 or 12.1 percent of 600,905 bridges throughout the United States "were categorized as structurally deficient" in December 2008. At the same time, another 89, 024 or 14.8 percent "were categorized as functionally obsolete." Furthermore, the American Association of State Highway and Transportation Officials (AASHTO) claimed "a combined investment from the public and private sectors of US$650 billion over 50 years" was needed to prevent the "backlog of deficient bridges to grow."

The National Science Foundation funds numerous research projects that aim to find new materials with which to construct bridges. One of the expected outcomes is to find a material that lasts longer than steel or concrete. In the early years of the first decade of the 2000s, work was being done by both Lockheed Martin Corporation and the University of California at San Diego's Dean of the Jacobs School of Engineering Frieder Seible, to develop bridges made of glass fibers. Building bridges with this lightweight material was expected to be quicker and less expensive than materials used at that time. Bridge maintenance with such a material would also be less costly.

In the latter part of the 1990s, high performance concrete (HPC) was put to the test, and by 2004, only six states had not used HPC in bridge specifications. HPC uses precast, high-strength concrete rather than conventional mixes. Because higher temperatures are required in the casting process, the concrete becomes stronger during casting. However, because the casts retain heat for longer periods, strength testing cannot occur for at least 56 days, compared to 28 days with traditional concrete products.

In 2001, the U.K. Highways Agency began to study the use of plastic as a building material. The plastic would be used in fiber-reinforced polymers (FRP) on bridge decks. According to *Presswire*, a press release distribution service also offering media databases, analysis and evaluation, FRP has the potential to provide a cost-effective alternative to conventional steel and concrete, as well as being strong, lightweight, and resistant to moisture and de-icing salts.

Other advances in the bridge building industry focus on worker safety and environmental protection. Steps taken to ensure worker safety during the construction of Canada's Confederation Bridge included doing 85 percent of the actual construction work on land using a 150-acre facility, providing food and heat at offshore work sites in case workers were stranded due to inclement weather or rough seas, and monitoring the whereabouts of offshore workers using electronic ID cards. In addition, the precautions taken to protect the environment and wildlife around the construction site earned this bridge project an environmental achievement award from the Canadian Construction Association.

INDUSTRY LEADERS

Early in the twenty-first century, U.S. companies dominated the bridge and tunnel construction industry. One of the largest U.S. companies in this industry in 2004 was Flatiron Construction Corp., the U.S. arm of Dutch company Royal BAM. Originally founded in 1947, Flatiron was bought by Hollandsche Beton Groep in the 1990s. When BAM acquired HBG, it formed HBG Constructors, but changed the company's name back to Flatiron in 2004. Flatiron Construction, which includes Flatiron Constructors and FCI Constructors, completed several major bridge and tunnel projects in the United States in the early years of the first decade of the 2000s, including the Ted Williams Tunnel in Boston and the Carquinez Suspension Bridge in California. As of 2005,

the company's projects included the San Francisco-Oakland Bay Bridge, valued at US$1.06 billion, and the Cooper River Bridge in South Carolina, valued at US$531 million.

Bechtel Group, Inc. The Bechtel Group was self-proclaimed the "world's No. 1 choice for engineering, construction, and project management." Based in San Francisco, California, the company employed about 44,000 people working in offices throughout the world. Though the company specialized in construction of petrochemical plants, it also worked on several major bridge and tunnel projects, including the Chunnel and the Big Dig. The company maintained a philosophy reflecting the belief that "every accident, and therefore every injury, is preventable." Sales reached US$31.4 billion in 2008. The company booked new work adding up to US$35 billion.

Peter Kiewit Sons', Inc. Another leading U.S. company was Omaha-based Peter Kiewit Sons'. The employee-owned firm had completed projects in 35 states, Canada, and Puerto Rico. Its network of offices spread throughout North America. Government contracts have accounted for more than 75 percent of its jobs, and about 50 percent of its sales have come from transportation contracts, including bridges and railroads as well as mass transit systems and highways. No matter how big or small a job might be, Kiewit asserts that it has the same goal: to "build it safely, on time, on budget and with no surprises." Sales in 2008 reached US$8 billion with 15,000 employees.

Besix. Belgium-based Besix, which constructed such projects as the Piet Hein tunnel in Amsterdam, saw earnings slip in the early years of the first decade of the 2000s but has turned increasingly to international projects to regain profitability. In the mid-years of the decade, it was engaged in major operations in Eastern Europe, the Middle East, Asia, and Africa. The company completed the Sheikh Khalifa Causeway Bridge in Bahrain and the Wadi Muddi Gillay tunnel in the UAR, among other projects. Sales for the company totaled US$522 million in 2005.

Balfour Beatty plc. Balfour Beatty plc, based in London, has provided engineering, construction, and project management services and worked on several major projects, including the Chunnel. The company is also responsible for repair and maintenance of more than 60 percent of London's busy subway system. It had approximately 27,600 employees in 2006. The company also acquired rival Birse Group in 2006. Balfour reported sales of almost US$12 billion in 2008.

North Texas Tollway Authority (NTTA) chose Balfour Beatty Infrastructure Inc. to be responsible for "a major design-build road project in the Dallas-Forth

Worth region." The U.S. civil engineering contractor affiliated with Balfour Beatty was considered to be an ideal choice for executing the joint venture with Fluor. This contract had an estimated value of US$415 million. A US$146 million tunneling contract near Boston in North Dorchester was another major project in the works for Balfour Beatty Infrastructure. As of August 2009, U.S. activities accounted for an estimated 30 percent of Balfour Beatty's revenue.

MAJOR COUNTRIES IN THE INDUSTRY

Companies from the United States, Western Europe, and Japan dominate the international market for bridge, tunnel, and elevated highway construction. While the United States has long held the preeminent position in this industry, Japan established a strong presence in the area of long-span bridge engineering. *ENR* noted that Japan recovered from a slow start in the construction of major suspension bridges—its first suspension bridges with spans over 500 meters were built more than 50 years after similar bridges had been constructed in Europe and North America—to take the lead in this segment of the industry.

According to ZanesvilleTimesRecorder.com, the American Recovery and Investment Act stimulus package was a funding resource for bridge deck replacements in Ohio. Complete General Contracting of Columbus was designated as the company to complete a contract project of US$1.6 million for Zane Grey Road Bridge and Moose Eye Road Bridge.

BIBLIOGRAPHY

American Road and Transportation Builders Association. *Transportation Construction Market Intelligence Reports.* Available from www.artba.com.

Balfour Beatty. "Balfour Beatty Joint Venture Selected for US$415 million Road Project in Texas," 24 August 2009. Available from www.balfour.beatty.com.

Bechtel Corporation. "Bechtel Corporation: Corporate Overview," 2009. Available from www.bechtel.com.

BESIX. "On the eve of our 100th anniversary, the Group BESIX is aiming at geographical diversification and new activities," 15 April 2008. Available from besix.com.

"Big Dig Facts." Available from www.bigdig.com.

"Bridge over Yangtze River Starting Construction." *China Daily,* 29 December 2004. Available from www.chinadaily.com.cn.

"Bridges/Report Card for America's Infrastructure," 2009. Available from www.infrastructurereportcard.org.

"China to Speed up Building Second Silk Road." *China View,* 15 April 2004. Available from news.xinhuanet.com.

"Companies Battle to Rebuild Iraq." *CNN News,* 14 January 2004. Available from www.cnn.com/WORLD.

"Congress Advances TEA-21 Renewal Prior to Easter Recess." *Transfer,* 25 March 2005. Available from www.transact.org.

Cuff, Denis. "Late Steel Threatens new Bay Bridge Construction Schedule," 9 September 2009. Available from www.mercurynews.com.

"Five Scariest Bridges in the World." 9 September 2009. Available from www.digitalcity.com.

"Hainan Mulls Bridge/Tunnel Link to Mainland." Xinhua News Agency, 3 February 2005. Available from http://www.china.org.cn/english/China/119799.htm

Huchzermeyer, Laura. "Peter Kiewit Sons', Inc. Company Capsule." *Hoover's Online,* 2009. Available from www.hoovers.com.

Hulse, Carl. "The President's Budget Proposal: Transportation; Senate Presses Confrontation on Costly Transportation Bill." *New York Times,* 3 February 2004.

Kiewit. "Overview: Jobs Done Well," 2009. Available from www.kiewit.com.

"Local Road, Bridge Projects get Funds From Federal Stimulus." *Zanesville Times Recorder,* 9 September 2009. Available from www.zanevilletimesrecorder. com.

Milacca, Andra. "Mackinac Bridge's Labor Day Bridge Walk and 150 Millionth Crossing This Weekend." Examiners, 2009. Available from www.examiner.com.

Monthly U.S. Transportation Construction Market Report, 22 March 2007. Available from artba.org.

"New Port to Benefit from Cross-Sea Link." *Bridge Design and Engineering,* 26 August 2003. Available from www.bridgeweb.com.

"N.J. Team Builds Bridges with Recycled Plastic." *Waste News,* 12 May 2003.

Richardson, Mark. "Bechtel Group, Inc. Company Capsule. 2009. Available from www.hoovers.com.

———. "Bechtel Group, Inc. Company Capsule". *Hoover's Online,* 2009. Available from www.hoovers.com.

Sigmund, Pete. "Road, Bridge Work to Sustain Industry in '07." *Construction Equipment Guide,* 11 December 2006.

Sleight, Chris. "Messina Plans Outlined." *KHL News,* 10 August 2004. Available from www.klh.com.

Thanawala, Sudhin. "Bay Bridge Crack Repair Raises Questions." *The Fresno Bee,* 8 September 2009. Available from www.fresnobee.com.

Triandafilou, Louis N. "HPC Bridge Response Favorable." *The Concrete Producer,* October 2004.

U.S. Department of Transportation, Federal Highway Administration. *Bridge Inventory,* December 2004. Available from www.fhwa.dot.gov.

SIC 3241

CEMENT, HYDRAULIC

NAICS CODE(S)

327310. The global cement industry manufactures various types of hydraulic cement, including portland, the most common form, as well as natural, masonry, and pozzolana cements.

INDUSTRY SNAPSHOT

Cement's highly cyclical demand is dependent on the world's construction markets. Where there are many new projects, the cement industry thrives. The regional economic recoveries and, in some places, the economic booms of the early and mid-1990s stimulated worldwide production growth spurts as high as 6.35 percent. By 2005, global production had reached 2.3 billion metric tons.

Fueling much of this growth was the briskly expanding Asian economies led by China, by far the world's largest cement producer and consumer. In the mid-1990s, the region found itself short of cement supply, and numerous firms within the region and around the world moved quickly to meet the excess demand. Growth was restrained by the 1997 financial crisis, however, as numerous companies, governments in the region scaled back construction projects, and as Asian cement manufacturers grappled with debt and cash flow problems. Into the mid-to late 2000s, China's economy was booming. By 2006 the nation was responsible for 45 percent of cement consumption worldwide, a number that was expected to reach 52 percent by 2020.

While the industry includes a number of sizable multinational companies, most cement production still occurs relatively close to its intended consumers because the logistics of handling cement over long distances are cost prohibitive for many manufacturers. Nonetheless, innovative firms such as CEMEX have helped stimulate a thriving regional trade, particularly in Asia and Central and South America.

ORGANIZATION AND STRUCTURE

Cement makers grind controlled mixtures of minerals, most often limestone and clay, in either a wet or dry environment to produce a powder. The powder is then heated in a kiln until it chemically changes into clinker pellets, which in turn are reground into a fine powder with additional minerals such as gypsum. This finished powder, the actual cement, may be mixed with water and sand or gravel, known as aggregate, to produce concrete. Various nations and trade associations prescribe minimum standards for cement composition and strength. Two widely recognized international standards for the industry are the American Society for Testing and Materials C150 specification and the British Standard Institution 12 specification; both specifications are revised periodically.

Portland cement, named after the British island of Portland and attributed to Englishman Joseph Aspdin, who obtained a patent for it in 1824, comprises by far the largest segment of the hydraulic cement market. It is the key ingredient in the concrete used in the construction of highways, dams, airports, sewage facilities, power plants, office buildings, and other structures. Although some concrete structures have stood a century or more, those made from portland cement paste are vulnerable to acids, sulfates, and some other salts. Portland cement is usually made from limestone or chalk and from clay or shale. Tetracalcium aluminoferrite contributes to its characteristic gray color. If a white cement is desired, use of tetracalcium aluminoferrite is kept down to about 1 percent.

Concrete can be mixed near the construction site or mixed at a central plant and transported by special agitator trucks, provided the operation can be completed within about 90 minutes. Transported concrete is known as ready-mixed.

While a number of international companies staked out greater control of some market segments entering the mid-1990s, the cement industry remained largely decentralized and competitive. Markets historically tended to be localized because of high transportation costs and the need for on-time delivery to construction sites. Because it is heavy and moisture-sensitive, cement requires special handling in transit as well. Thus, cement companies often own their own principal raw material quarries and locate their manufacturing plants at those sites to minimize material handling. Since clay and limestone are relatively abundant in many regions of the world, local production is usually feasible.

Cement production is a capital-intensive enterprise. The process requires continuous operations and utilizes a heating process that takes 4.4 million British thermal units (Btu) of heat to make one ton of cement. Facility shutdowns can be very expensive. Clinker and cement can be stored, but inventory maintenance can also be expensive. Moreover, cement production is a volume-sensitive industry in which any drop in sales has a disproportionately severe effect on profits. Because cement producers sell their product primarily to the construction industry, they are frequently buffeted by unpredictable, seasonal, and cyclical economic conditions felt by contractors.

In the early to mid-2000s, the United States was among the world's largest cement manufacturers. However, it ranked far below developing nations. Citing data from OneStone Consulting Group, *World Cement's World Review 2004* revealed that the North American region ranked fourth in cement production during 2003, at 105 million tons. By comparison, China produced 765 million tons, followed by Western Europe (including Turkey) with 236 million tons, and the Far East/Oceania region (excluding China, India, and Japan) with 215 million tons. In all, world production totaled nearly 1.9 billion tons in 2003.

On the consumption side, *World Review 2004* estimated that developing countries consumed nearly 75 percent of cement in 2003, based on estimates from J.P. Morgan. Of the total cement produced worldwide that year, China accounted for 973.8 million tons, followed by

Western Europe (226.2 million tons), North America (115.2 million tons), and Latin America (92.7 million tons).

While U.S. cement exports were negligible (totaling US$58.8 million in 2002), the United States was a sizable importer, with a total of US$940 million in 2002. Leading sources of U.S. imports included Canada, Spain, Mexico, and Venezuela. In general, most U.S. imports came from foreign facilities of companies also operating in the United States.

China constituted the world's largest cement maker, producing about 41 percent of world supply annually. By the mid-2000s, many of the nation's more than 500 cement and concrete additive producers were merging or forging alliances. In its *World Review 2004* report, *World Cement* indicated that China produced 765 million metric tons of cement in 2003, up 8.5 percent from the previous year. In addition, China was responsible for 43 percent of cement consumption worldwide, a number that was expected to top 50 percent by 2020.

By 2004, China's economy was booming. Following growth of 9.1 percent in 2003, Chinese Vice-Premier Zeng Peiyan revealed that the Chinese economy would achieve a growth rate of more than 10 percent in the first half of the year. This prompted the government to restrain credit and investment in fixed assets, amid concerns that the economy was "overheating," according to *The Australian.*

China exports a small share of its production to other nations, mostly elsewhere in Asia. However, Chinese exports have been at a disadvantage because the nation traditionally has not met international standards for strength and durability. Bringing cement up to standards is a priority for Chinese producers, who were focusing on research and development during the early and mid-2000s in order to bolster the country's export position.

In the April 2004 issue of *The Concrete Producer,* the Portland Cement Association (PCA) was optimistic for the portland cement sector heading into the mid-2000s. Edward Sullivan, the PCA's chief economist, estimated that nonresidential construction would surpass the residential sector as a growth leader, saying that "softer second-half residential construction activity is expected to be offset by marginally higher nonresidential and public spending activity.".

During the first half of 2004, the United States experienced a cement shortage. Twenty-three states were affected, and shortages were especially pronounced along the East Coast and in Florida. A number of factors contributed to this situation. Among them were strong residential construction levels supported by low interest rates and an uncharacteristically active winter construction season. These factors prevented the replenishment of cement inventories that normally occurs during the off-season. Hindering

imports was the booming Chinese economy, which was tapping much of the demand for bulk shipping and leading to increased shipping costs. In June of 2004, the PCA indicated that supply would likely improve during the second half of 2004, as interest rates began to rise, thereby slowing the construction market and reducing cement consumption. Shortages, however, were still prevalent in the first half of 2005, as prices surged an estimated 15 to 20 percent from the previous year. Price increases were due to domestic demand from increased building and greatly increased shipping costs to import supplies. More cement imported from Mexico, which was much less expensive, was one solution. Concrete prices stood at about US$90 a metric ton in 2005, up from US$75 in 2004, and demand was 120 million tons in the United States.

CURRENT CONDITIONS

Total global cement production in 2005 reached 2.3 billion tons. Into the later 2000s, China remained the largest producer of cement worldwide, producing 1.03 billion tons in 2005. India was second with 145 million tons, followed by the United States with 100 million tons. Other top cement-producing countries included Japan, Spain, South Korea, Russia, and Italy. Overall Asia contributed 65 percent of the world's production of cement and was home to 6 of the top 15 producing countries. China was also the leader in consumption, and the Freedonia Group estimated that by 2008 Chinese demand would exceed 1 billion metric tons, or about 44 percent of global demand.

In 2006 U.S. production of portland cement reached 94 million tons. Total cement capacity was about 115 million tons. Of all domestic cement sales, about 74 percent went to ready-mixed concrete producers, 14 percent to concrete product manufacturers, 6 percent to contractors (mainly road paving), 3 percent to building materials dealers, and 3 percent to other users. The top five U.S. producers were, in descending order, Texas, California, Pennsylvania, Florida, Michigan, and Alabama. These five states accounted for 48 percent of U.S. production.

Although U.S. cement plants were operating at about 91.5 percent in 2005, imports were necessary to keep up with consumption levels. The United States imported a record 33.7 million metric tons of cement and cement clinker in 2005, of which about 52 percent came from four countries: China, Canada, Thailand, and Greece. In 2005, imports from China increased to 6.6 million metric tons, thus causing China to replace Canada as the number-one importer of cement to the United States. The amount of cement imported into the United States increased again in 2006 to 42 million metric tons, and shortages previously experienced were reduced or eliminated. According to *Cement Americas,* total U.S. consumption of portland cement reached 122 million metric tons in 2006. Although a slowdown in housing starts was expected to affect the industry in the later 2000s, the market supply for cement and ready mixed concrete was expected to increase to meet demands in other end-use sectors, reaching possibly US$30 billion in 2010, up from US$25 million in 2005.

RESEARCH AND TECHNOLOGY

Cement production entails mixing ingredients in a long, rotating kiln, then gradually heating the blend to a temperature of about 1500 degrees centigrade by burning coal, oil, or other fuels. Consequently, high oil prices in the 1970s prompted cement producers to devise ways to reduce fuel consumption. One way was to convert plants to the so-called dry process manufacturing, wherein water is added to the mix after blending instead of before. The wet process (in which water is added before blending) requires much more fuel. First developed in Europe, the dry process added to the European producers' competitive advantage. Cement producers also cut energy costs by investing in either heating equipment that burned waste and solid fuels instead of oil and gas, or equipment that utilized fuel more efficiently.

Typically 100 to 150 meters long and 3 to 5 meters in diameter, cement kilns are capable of processing large volumes of materials. By the 1990s cement producers responded to the need to reduce energy costs and to provide cost-effective solutions to waste and environmental problems by putting cement kilns to work as waste disposal systems. The cement industry serves as a model for using tonnage materials facilities to recover or dispose of waste streams produced by others. Pressures from environmental organizations continued to push cement manufacturers to improve processes into the mid-2000s. Efforts are underway to establish uniform emissions standards and procedures for enforcing such standards. Many companies (especially the largest ones) are voluntarily taking steps to be environmentally responsible. Other areas of concern are handling of by-products and seeking alternatives to fossil fuels.

Producers can process and utilize waste from the cement-making process in three ways. First, they may substitute a by-product from another industrial operation for one or more of the original ingredients in the feedstream as long as the composition and performance of the cement product is unimpaired. Some say this process at times can yield better product. Among the by-products that manufacturers successfully use are spent sand from metal foundries, blast furnace slag (which supplies iron that cement requires and contains lime and silica in the ideal ratio), and gypsum (a required ingredient of cement) resulting from the "scrubbing" operation used

to clean the stack-gas emissions from power plants and other industrial facilities, including cement plants.

Second, cement producers have also fueled their kilns with the combustible by-products of other industrial operations. These fuels include waste oils, organic sludges, and spent solvents such as carbon tetrachloride, trichloroethane, and toluene left over from the manufacture of paint and other chemicals. Cement companies often obtain waste fuel at no cost and may actually receive payment for disposing of potentially toxic materials. When a material to be burned is classified as hazardous waste, though, the cement maker must keep careful records to document that all the hazardous materials are indeed destroyed.

Finally, cement producers can incorporate some waste materials into cement without impairing the quality of the product. Kilns' high temperatures can destroy certain toxic wastes by breaking them into benign elements and compounds that may be harmlessly encapsulated in the cement. Lubricating oil waste and sludge from steelmaking plants are two such materials. Within the United States, researchers explored ways in which the country's scrap tire dumps could be used. The U.S. scrap-tire stockpile increases by 275 million annually, so the supply is vast. Researchers have thus tested grinding them into powder and combining the powder with cement for roadways. In 1994 fatigue tests were underway on "rubcrete" (a cement containing up to 10 percent ground rubber); tests already showed that using rubcrete caused only minor changes in a pavement's durability and resistance to inclement weather.

Manufacturers in the United States were slow to pursue the potential use of cement kilns to recycle and dispose of other materials because energy was plentiful and cheap and solid wastes could be readily disposed. That was not the case in Japan or Western Europe. Countries there implemented extensive energy-saving and waste-recycling measures in their cement industries. Japan became a leader in incorporating various solid wastes, including steelmaking slag and coal-plant tailing, into feedstreams for cement kilns. The government also encouraged use of waste tires as a fuel for cement kilns. In 1992 Mitsubishi Materials burned more than 23,000 tons of tires at its cement plants.

The concrete made from cement underwent revolutionary formulation changes between 1980 and 1995. In the 1960s, high-strength concrete withstood a force of 5,800 pounds per square inch (psi). Thirty years later, high-performance concrete (HPC) produced strengths of 15,000 to 20,000 psi. HPC contains admixtures known as superplasticizers that help to drastically lower the ratio of water to cement, while maintaining enough workability to form a structure. HPC is favored for use in tall buildings, bridges, offshore structures, pavements, and other applications. Due mainly to transportation costs, however, ready-mixed HPC is available only in major metropolitan markets. Another concrete innovation is reinforced cement composites. These composites contain steel, carbon, polypropylene, glass, or fibers and provide better strength-to-weight ratios and energy absorption capacity than conventional concrete.

In 2003 the Strategic Development Council (SDC) released a research report entitled *Roadmap 2030: The U.S. Concrete Industry Technology Roadmap,* produced in cooperation with the U.S. Department of Energy (DOE). The report was a detailed follow-up to the SDC's report, *Vision 2030,* which was published in 2001. According to *The Concrete Producer,* in addition to reducing a 15-year lag between research and the development of actual technologies, the report identified four research areas as being a high priority for the industry. These included concrete production, delivery, and placement; constituent materials; design and structural systems; and repair and rehabilitation.

The DOE conducts industry research at the Oak Ridge (Tenn.) National Laboratory via the Concrete and Containment Technology Program. *The Concrete Producer* indicated that future research goals include a 500 percent increase in concrete recycling; a 60 percent reduction in jobsite material rejection; and a 20 percent reduction in power demand at cement plants. Another goal is to have structural concrete used to produce 50 percent of all new homes.

Inorganic polymer concrete (geopolymer) reportedly substitutes Portland cement with "fly ash" resulting in a "remarkably lower carbon footprint," according to Bryan Nelson. The new material resists corrosion, provides higher fire resistance and lowers shrinkage. In addition, greenhouse gas emission reduction occurs at a rate of 90 percent more than Portland cement. The benefits were extremely notable because Portland was one of the most widely produced man made materials on earth.

WORKFORCE

In 2005, the cement manufacturing industry employed 16,877 people, a figure that represents a 23 percent reduction since 1985. Seventy-six percent of employees were production workers, who earned an average of US$23.24 an hour. There were 115 portland cement plants in 37 states and Puerto Rico. The top five U.S. cement companies, which together accounted for about 56 percent of U.S. production, were Holcim Inc., Lafarge North America, CEMEX Inc., Buzzi Unicem USA, and Lehigh Cement Company.

INDUSTRY LEADERS

Lafarge SA. Lafarge originated in 1831 when Auguste Pavin de Lafarge, a French noble, established a small lime

kiln. There was nothing unique about the company's quarry, but the Lafarge family showed an ability to find markets for lime, which enjoyed an expanding range of industrial uses. In the 1840s Lafarge sold its product in far-flung regions, including the Mediterranean Basin. The company won a contract in 1864 to supply 110,000 tons of hydraulic lime for concrete blocks to form the jetties of the Suez Canal. During the nineteenth century, the company sought growth through acquisitions and established an organization able to supply markets in such far-flung world centers as New York City, Rio de Janeiro, and Saigon. The company's sales of cement products rose to 800,000 tons annually at the outbreak of World War I, making it the world's largest lime producer.

Lafarge Coppée's expansion in the early part of the twentieth century depended on its technical expertise in developing new cement products, for the invention of portland cement made hydraulic lime virtually obsolete. The stock market crash of 1929 contributed to an economic swamp wherein one-third of all workers in the French cement trade were laid off before 1936. During that period Lafarge obtained a number of failing competitors. World War II also created doldrums, but Lafarge emerged by 1959 to take the lead in the French cement industry with 3.2 million tons of cement produced annually.

In 1956 Lafarge entered Canada and in 1970 it merged with Canada Cement to form Canada Cement Lafarge. Canada Cement perfected the shift from cement production on the construction site to ready-mix concrete mixed at a central site and then transported to delivery points by bulk carriers. Lafarge gained prominence in the North American industry in 1981 when it merged Canada Cement Lafarge with Dallas-based General Portland to create a new subsidiary called Lafarge Corporation. By the 1990s Lafarge Corporation was the United States' second-largest cement maker. In 1989 Lafarge acquired Cementia of Switzerland and Asland of Spain and became the world's second-largest cement producer.

Renamed Lafarge SA in 1995, the company continued to pursue growth globally in the late 1990s largely through acquisitions. It moved swiftly into eastern European markets to glean sales from those nations' economic transitions and has continued to accumulate holdings in North and South America. In 1997 Lafarge succeeded in a hostile takeover bid for U.K. roofing tile maker and aggregate processor Redland PLC; the deal was the largest ever in the European building materials sector.

Lafarge's 2001 acquisition of Blue Circle Industries made it the world's largest cement maker. In addition, Lafarge SA holds a controlling interest in Lafarge North America Inc., one of the top cement makers in the United States. In the mid-2000s, the company's Cement

Division operated 117 cement factories and 24 grinding mills in 43 countries. In 2006, Lafarge's worldwide operations generated more than US$22.3 billion on the strength of approximately 77,000 employees, including nearly 36,000 in its Cement Division. More than half of the company's total revenue comes from cement production.

Lafarge believes the Ready Mix Concrete (RMC) market in India had "strong growth and value creation potential" and was willing to pay a hefty price for L & T concrete. The main goal is to introduce its value-added concrete products into the Indian market. While L & T agreed to sell its RMC business to focus on core businesses, Lafarge wanted to double its cement production capacity by 2014.

Holcim. Formerly known as Holderbank, Holcim was the second largest cement manufacturer in the world in the mid-2000s. It began its global expansion campaign in the early 1950s by buying a small Brazilian company and since then has selectively acquired numerous companies worldwide. Holcim avoided Asian countries where local companies were strong and concentrated instead on markets in Australia and New Zealand. The company entered the U.S. market by making several acquisitions, including Ideal Basic Industries, in the late 1980s. The assets of U.S. acquisitions were merged into Holnam Inc., the largest U.S. cement company.

Holcim's cement empire includes operations in more than 70 nations, with the bulk of its holdings in the Americas and Europe and a growing presence in Asia. During 2003, the company achieved increases in all of its global operating regions. The acquisition of a cement plant in Spain; the consolidation of operation in the Philippines; improved efficiency; and strong performance in Latin America, Asia Pacific, and Africa Middle East were all factors that allowed the company improve its net income—despite a generally weak economic climate.

In its 2008, annual report Holcim expressed concerns about 2009 being difficult for construction and building sectors. Predictions also reflected the belief there would be a cement industry benefit from "an economic upswing." Holcim-owned companies ACC and Ambuja Cement, both experienced "solid volume growth in 2008."

In August 2009, Holcim opened the doors for the United States' largest cement plant in Ste. Genevieve County, Missouri. The plant that is approximately 55 miles south of St. Louis has production capability of more than 12,000 metric tons of clinker per day and 4 million metric tons of cement each year. Cement demand declined during the recession. As a result, Holcim closed Michigan and Missouri plants.

On October 1, 2009, Holcim completed the acquisition of Cemex Australia. This acquisition furthers Holcim's goals to incorporate Australia into a mature market strategy promoting active involvement in the cement, aggregates and ready-mix concrete business.

Holcim Singapore has created a new "green concrete" formula reducing the necessity for sand which was experiencing rising costs resulting from shortages. The new products creation was considered to be proof of the company's commitment to Corporate Social Responsibility (CSR). Holcim belongs to the Singapore Compact for CSR, an approximately 240 member national society focused on developing and promoting ethical policies and practices

In 2008, Holcim's revenues totaled US$15 billion for cement sector. Number of sector related employees was cited as being 56,282. The company reported having 151 cement and grinding plants. Overall company net sales for 2008 were US$23,294. That total was up from US$22,543 in 2007.

CEMEX, S.A. de C.V. CEMEX was the third largest cement maker in the world as of 2006, behind Holcim and Lafarge. Its previous acquisition of Southdown, the second largest cement maker in the United States, was billed as important to the company's future, as was its 2005 purchase of cement giant RMC Group in the United Kingdom. CEMEX, founded in 1906, has in many ways set the industry leaders' pace by focusing largely on amassing market share in the world's rapidly growing economies and by leading in technological and logistical innovations. Its 1992 acquisition of two Spanish cement makers, Valenciana and Sanson, vaulted CEMEX into the arena with such world players as Holcim and Lafarge. The Spanish venture enabled CEMEX to skirt U.S. antidumping duties by exporting to the United States from Spain, which was not subject to the duties.

By December 2008, CEMEX had established a presence in more than 50 countries spreading throughout 5 continents. It had 64 cement plants and a minority participation in 15 others. CEMEX reported having 57,000 employees.

CEMEX is possibly the industry's most technologically advanced, in terms of both manufacturing plant and management infrastructure. It operates some of the world's most efficient and up-to-date cement facilities and supports production with an extensive information system for monitoring operations worldwide. CEMEX also has developed viable and profitable export channels to countries where it holds no plants, notably in Asia, where it acquired its first local stake in 1997. Via CEMEX Asia Holdings, the company has a 23.5 percent stake in PT Semen Gresik, Indonesia's top cement maker. Such diversification has helped insulate the CEMEX parent company from regional slowdowns, although some analysts still consider CEMEX to have considerable exposure to local market downswings.

CEMEX earned special recognition when it received the United Nations Habitat Award in the Accessible Housing Solutions category. Substantial assistance for low income families sprang from Patrimonio Hoy's micro financing and Centros Productivos de Autoempleo's (CPA) resources for developing basic materials utilized for construction or expansion of their homes. Recognition for the outstanding initiatives meant CEMEX was the only Latin American country honored in the competition.

In 2006, CEMEX achieved revenues of US$15.1 billion with 26,679 employees. Its annual cement production capacity was 98 million tons, and cement accounted for about 75 percent of revenues.

Taiheiyo Cement Group. Taiheiyo, Japan's leading cement company, is the result of the 1998 merger of Chichibu-Nihon and Onoda Cement Ltd. Chichibu-Nihon's emergence as a world leader largely occurred in the short span of the early to mid-1990s and is testimony to the high degree of consolidation and occasional instability in Japan's cement industry. Chichibu had been Japan's leading producer since it was formed in a 1994 merger with Onoda Cement Ltd. By 1997 it commanded more than 21 percent of the Japanese market share, some four percentage points higher than its next-closest rival did. Propelling it to the world scene was its 1997 agreement to merge with third-largest Nihon Cement Co., which itself had been Japan's leading cement maker until Chichibu and another rival displaced it. The merger was approved in 1998, and the two companies arrived at a new name, Taiheiyo. Within months of its announcement, the proposed Chichibu-Nihon transaction triggered another merger of cement operations between two smaller competitors, Mitsubishi Materials Corp. and Ube Industries Ltd.

By March 2009, Taiheiyo reportedly had 311 subsidiaries and 138 affiliates structured around four in-house companies targeting markets for cement, mineral resources, environmental and international business. Taiheiyo also produces ready-mix concrete and construction materials, which complement the company's real estate holdings. The company's interests are largely concentrated in Asia. It had 2,173 employees.

BIBLIOGRAPHY

"2006 Critical Trends in the North American Cement Industry." *Cement Americas,* 1 July 2006.

"Cement Industry Overview." *Economic Research,* November 2006.

"Cement Prices Continue to Fuel Surge in Construction Costs." *Knight-Ridder Tribune Business News,* 24 June 2005.

CEMEX. "This is CEMEX. At a Glance," 2009. Available from www.cemex.com.

"Chapter I: Introduction." *Chinese Markets for Cement Additives.* Asia Market Information & Development Co., December 2003.

"China Predicts 10pc Growth." *The Australian,* 7 July 2004.

"China's Cement Demand to Top 1 Billion Tons in 2008." *Cement Americas,* 1 November 2004.

"Concrete's Comeback." *Management Today,* 1 June 2007.

"Economist Gives Bullish Outlook." *The Concrete Producer,* April 2004.

"Forecast 2007." *Cement Americas,* 1 January 2007.

"Global Review of Operations." Nuevo Leon, Mexico: CEMEX, S.A. de C.V., 23 July 2004. Available from www.cemex.com.

Holcim. "Acquisition of Cemex Australia Successfully Completed," 1 October 2008. Available from www.holcim.com.

———. "Holcim at a Glance." 2008. Available from www. holcim.com.

Holcim opens nation's largest cement plant in MO." *St. Louis Business Journal,* 20 August 2009. Available from www. bizjournals.com/stlouis/.

"Hoover's Company Capsules." *Hoover's Online,* 2007. Available from www.hoovers.com.

International Trade Administration. "Portland Cement Sector." *U.S. Market Overview,* 2007. Available from http://trade.gov.

———. "U.S.–Mexico Agreement on Cement," 6 March 2006. Available from http://trade.gov/press.

Iyengar, Suresh P. "Holcim sees tough year ahead," *The Hindu Business Line,* 10 May 2009. Available from www.blonnet. com.

Klemens, Tom. "Questions, Answers, and Applications: High-Tech Research Is Yielding Concrete Results." *The Concrete Producer.* August 2003.

"Lafarge bets largely on ready mix now." *The Hindu Business Line,* 15 May 2009. Available from www.thehindubusinessline.com.

Luo, Serene. "More Companies Practice CSR." *The Straits Times* (Singapore), 4 October 2009. Available from www. straitstimes.com.

Nelson, Bryan. "New Cement Cuts Greenhouse Gases by 90%." *Mother Nature Network,* 29 September 2009. Available from www.mnn.com.

"No Cement Shortage in Alaska." *Knight-Ridder Tribune Business News,* 23 June 2005.

Owers, Paul. "Builders Ask for Help in Cement Shortage." *Palm Beach Post,* 30 June 2004.

"PCA: Cement Consumption Down." *Midwest Contractor,* 28 May 2007.

"PCA Forecasts Modest Gains Despite Mixed Outlook." *Cement Americas,* 1 May 2004.

"Prospects for Cement Shortage Relief Emerging." Skokie, Ill.: Portland Cement Association, 10 June 2004. Available from www.cement.org.

"Results for 2003: Holcim Improves Efficiency and Reports Significantly Higher Group Net Income Despite Weak Dollar." St. Gallen, Switzerland: Holcim Ltd, 9 March 2004. Available from www.holcim.com.

U.S. Census Bureau. *Annual Survey of Manufacturers,* January 2005. Available from www.census.gov.

———. *Statistics of U.S. Businesses: Cement Manufacturing.* Statistics of U.S. Businesses, 23 July 2004. Available from www.census.gov.

U.S. Geological Survey. "Cement." *Minerals Yearbook,* 2007. Available from http://minerals.usgs.gov.

"World Review 2004." *World Cement,* July 2004. Available from www.palladian-publications.com.

SIC 3270

CONCRETE, GYPSUM, AND PLASTER PRODUCTS

NAICS CODE(S)

327. Companies in this industry process and manufacture materials mostly for use in construction. The five major subsets are: concrete blocks and bricks; general concrete products; ready-mixed concrete; lime; and gypsum products.

Production of cement, a key ingredient in concrete, is discussed in greater detail under the heading **Cement, Hydraulic.**

INDUSTRY SNAPSHOT

The world's volatile building materials markets follow the trends set by the broader construction industry. In the early 2000s, the steel industry started losing revenue to the concrete industry when engineers and contractors more often chose concrete for their infrastructure needs. In the commercial and residential markets, new building construction and renovation drive global demand for the various concrete, lime, and gypsum products. Manufacturers of these products, like manufacturers of most building materials, are realizing the benefits of offering buyers more choices. In both the commercial and residential markets, buyers are looking for customized options. By 2004, innovations like self-consolidating concrete (SCC) allowed builders to make more elaborate concrete shapes by using forms and molds that were more elaborate than those used with traditional concrete.

China's economy was experiencing explosive growth in the mid- to late 2000s. As China's economy boomed, the nation's demand for construction-related materials caused shortages in other world markets—including the United States. Material shortages occurred for concrete, as well as gypsum products like drywall. While this shortage was partially attributed to a squeeze on available container ships, which slowed import activity worldwide, a considerable share of the shortage stemmed from the massive amount of construction materials China was consuming. By 2004, these factors caused all U.S. states, except Alaska, to experience shortages of the cement needed to make concrete. Shortages were especially pronounced along the East Coast and in Florida, where the residential construction market was booming. By 2006, the tight supply conditions had been alleviated due mostly to an increase in imports.

Environmental concerns affect the building materials industry more every year. Pressure from advocacy groups and legislators, along with the emerging technologies that result from that pressure, are making environmentally safe materials more available and affordable. In the gypsum industry especially, strides are being made to utilize recycled materials.

ORGANIZATION AND STRUCTURE

The industry's output, which constitutes a significant share of the world's nonwood, nonmetal building materials, comprises a number of diverse product categories. Most industry participants specialize in a few of these categories rather than producing the entire breadth of industry goods. A number of major companies operate in multiple stages of their products' supply chains, however, such as quarrying stone, processing it into cement, and then adding self-supplied aggregate (sand or gravel) to create concrete—the finished product—for customers. In this sense, some of the industry's largest firms are more vertically integrated than horizontally. Still, many building materials manufacturers obtain all of their raw materials from other firms.

While technological innovations in these building materials occur regularly, most are considered low-profit commodities best suited for mass production. Some technological entry barriers exist, however, for participation in world-class materials production. Certain material processing equipment requires significant capital investment, and hence cost precludes smaller firms from participating in those segments of the industry.

Concrete. In essence, concrete is a mixture of powder cement, water, and coarse or fine aggregate (gravel or sand, respectively). Its production is thus wholly dependent on the production of cement, which means that many of the leading cement companies (see **Cement, Hydraulic**) also produce concrete. Other concrete companies source their raw materials from unaffiliated manufacturers and perform their own mixing.

Concrete is used in diverse applications that cross virtually all subsets of the construction industry—some construction firms even manufacture their own. Leading uses include roads, bridges, airports, and buildings. To meet these end needs, concrete products may be delivered to customers as ready-mixed concrete to be poured on site or as preformed structures to be installed. Because of its widespread use in public structures such as roads, the concrete segment is more dependent on government public works spending than are other parts of the industry. Still, private construction demands a major share of the world's concrete as well.

Lime. The mineral by-product lime derives from quarried limestone, dolomite, and similar stones. Manufactured lime has numerous uses outside of construction, especially applications in the chemical and steel industries. In construction, lime is used to make mortar and plaster. Such construction uses account for a relatively small share of the world's lime production.

Gypsum. As with lime, gypsum comes from processed minerals. Unlike lime, however, the vast majority of gypsum is used for construction purposes, primarily in the fabrication of wallboard (also known as drywall or plasterboard). Over the course of the twentieth century, wallboard supplanted plaster in industrial countries to become the key material in residential walls, with a strong presence in nonresidential buildings as well. In addition, gypsum is sometimes used in plaster and other building materials. Gypsum plasters are, in actuality, a type of cement that is used widely in construction materials such as wallboard, slabs, flooring, and decorative moldings. These are made of a combination of gypsum and a dehydrated form of gypsum known as anhydrite. In addition, other chemicals can be added for properties needed in particular applications. For example, sulfate salts are added to some construction plasters to speed up the setting of the compound.

More so than in other building materials segments, gypsum product manufacturing is dominated by a handful of major producers that hold large shares of the market. In the late 1990s, for example, the largest U.S. wallboard maker controlled nearly a third of the U.S. market.

PR Newswire shared scoop on "major shift in the industry toward use of more synthetic gypsum." Environmental factors and financial challenges had reportedly made FGD gypsum a preferred option for cement companies that was actually more economical than other options. From 2006 until 2008, there was a 4 percent drop in gypsum world consumption. In the North American region, there was a 29 percent decline. The decline analysis did not translate into a loss of optimism for forecasters. Increased demand for gypsum applications in plaster and plasterboard were expected to soar from 80 Mt in 2008 to as much as 130 Mt by 2015.

BACKGROUND AND DEVELOPMENT

The raw materials from which building products are derived have been with humanity throughout the ages. Ancient Egypt first used gypsum as a building material 5,000 years ago. After heating, crushing, and remixing it with water, it was used as plaster on walls. Ancient cultures also combined these materials to make forms of cements and other types of plasters that could be used in conjunction with other common construction materials. The pyramids in Egypt, for example, were constructed of gypsum. Raw materials were plentiful and inexpensive and the products based on these minerals proved to have natural fire retardant properties.

The concrete block industry began in earnest in England in the mid-nineteenth century when bricklayer Joseph Aspdin created and patented Portland cement. Concrete block was prized as a construction material for its durability and price as well as its safety, compared to typical construction materials of that age, namely wood. Today, the primary use of cement and concrete products is by the construction industry.

Gypsum—also known in its purest form as the material alabaster—was initially sold as a fertilizer. In the late nineteenth century, changes in the composition of gypsum plasters, or plasters of paris, placed it in a position to compete with lime plasters.

One of the changes in the building materials industry was the invention of a gypsum material used primarily in the covering of framed structures as walls. It is known today by various names: drywall, plasterboard, wallboard, and by the trade name Sheetrock. Wallboard was invented in the United States in 1890 by Augustine Sackett and first marketed in 1894. The product is made from a layer of gypsum placed between two pieces of paper. The material has been utilized in construction because it is both fireproof and an excellent insulating material. In 1901, the U.S. Gypsum Company purchased the machine invented by Sackett as well as the proprietary information on its production and continued to make improvements. It was not until 1917 that production of the material was perfected. Army barracks used in World War I were among the first structures to use wallboard rather than fiberboard.

In the early 1900s, changes in transportation made a significant impact on these types of industries, such as the advent of trucks that could both deliver and mix concrete on site. In addition, more concrete and concrete products were needed in order to make easier travel possible.

In the 1920s, a price war in the United States wallboard industry drove prices down and a smaller company, CertainTeed Corporation, into compliance with the product guidelines and price controls set forth by U.S. Gypsum. Because U.S. Gypsum had patented the process of manufacturing wallboard, it was able to control the price under its licensing agreement with other manufacturing firms, including CertainTeed. One factor that allowed U.S. Gypsum to dominate the industry was its large size and the fact that the company was vertically integrated, a strategy that allowed it to control product costs from mining of the gypsum to shipping and even sales. It was also this position that caused problems decades later for the company. In 1940 the U.S. Justice Department charged wallboard manufacturers, including U.S. Gypsum, with price fixing as a result of cross-licensing. The decision put an end to price controls as well as the ability of U.S. Gypsum to license the patent to other wallboard manufacturers. The company was charged with price fixing again in 1973. However, this time, justice was not as lenient. The company settled for US$28 million and faced criminal indictment. The case was finally settled in 1980.

In Europe and the United States, the presence of several large, dominant producers in certain building materials segments—wallboard, in particular—meant relative stability throughout the 1990s for capacity. In fact, U.S. wallboard capacity utilization in the late 1990s was at extraordinarily strong levels, hovering in the 90 to 93 percent range from 1994 to 1998—and U.S. Gypsum was at 99 percent capacity in late 1997.

The reverse of this situation was in Japan and Southeast Asia in part as a result of the late 1990s financial crisis. Southeast Asia had been building up capacity to meet its own rapid expansion needs as well as to serve as an export base. The harsh fiscal climate stifled demand and battered some of the region's producers, who were struck with three potential setbacks: capacity for anticipated new demand that never materialized; declines in established demand; and internal debt, including any debt incurred to build new capacity and financial distress because of the currency and market declines. Consequently, at least for the short term, Southeast Asia's building materials companies grappled with overcapacity and falling prices in the late 1990s. Other parts of Asia, such as China and India, remained comparatively healthy.

Because industry products tend to be large, heavy, and relatively inexpensive, in most regions no substantial international trade has been realized (and when it has, it is usually between adjacent countries). More often, companies have entered foreign markets through establishment or acquisition of foreign affiliates that produce materials in the target country. However, building materials trade began to rise in the 1990s, and nonwood materials were among the fastest growing trade segments.

As Americans enjoyed a healthy economy in the late 1990s, they had the means to customize new buildings, both residential and commercial. After a slump, the economy began to rally again toward the end of 2001, and consumers were still interested in customized features for their building projects. While the concrete and gypsum industry is less affected than decorative industries by the desire for customization, the effect is worth mentioning. In 2001, The Bomanite Corporation (which specializes in concrete paving and flooring), for example, offered a wide variety of colored (100 patterns and 25 colors), textured, and imprinted concrete paving choices. Also in 2001, a psychiatric hospital in Pembroke Pines, Florida,

was renovated using a high-impact wallboard that is new to the industry. It installs easily, can be repaired easily, is fire-resistant, features a less institutional look, and is highly resistant to penetration. This is important because it creates a better atmosphere while minimizing the risk of escape. This facility serves as an illustration that all wallboard is not the same and that the expanding array of options available enables builders to make customized choices.

By 2004, China's economy was experiencing explosive growth. Chinese Vice-Premier Zeng Peiyan revealed that the Chinese economy would achieve a growth rate of more than 10 percent in the first half of 2004, following growth of 9.1 percent in 2003. According to *The Australian,* these conditions caused the government to restrain investment in fixed assets, as well as credit, amidst concerns that the economy was "overheating."

As China's economy boomed, the nation's demand for construction-related materials caused shortages in other world markets—including the United States. In addition to concrete, gypsum products like drywall, and steel, shortages of roofing materials and lumber also developed. Part of this shortage stemmed from a squeeze on available container ships, which slowed import activity worldwide. However, much of the shortage stemmed from the massive amount of materials China was consuming. For example, when construction of a 1.6 mile hydroelectric dam on China's Yangtze River called for the relocation of 1.5 million people, the Chinese government began building new cities for them to live in, requiring enormous supplies of concrete and steel.

Forty-nine U.S. states experienced a shortage of the cement needed to make concrete in early 2005. However, shortages were especially pronounced along the East Coast and in Florida. In June 2004, Florida's *Ocala Star-Banner* reported that while the United States imported 13 percent of its concrete from Asia and Europe, Florida was more susceptible to global shortages because the state's booming residential construction industry relied on imports to satisfy nearly 50 percent of concrete demand.

In addition to China's demand for building material, other factors contributing to the shortage of building products included strong residential construction levels fueled by low interest rates, as well as an uncharacteristically active winter construction season. In mid-2004, some industry observers noted that China expected to scale back its consumption of materials. Coupled with the prospect of rising interest rates, these conditions would likely correct the material shortages of 2004.

In 2003, *Cement Americas* reported on the results of a study conducted by economists with the U.S. Department of Labor Bureau of Labor Statistics. According to the study, prices for gypsum and cement increased by

17.4 percent and 15.4 percent, respectively, over the five-year period from 1996 to 2001.

CURRENT CONDITIONS

The industry's conditions are ever changing due to fluctuations in construction markets and internal industry dynamics alike. The industry passes through cyclical capacity and pricing conditions that factor into a given participant's sales and profits. When building materials manufacturers perceive an expanding market, many respond by investing in new plants to accommodate higher production levels. Once this new capacity is achieved, especially when several manufacturers expand simultaneously, it can create excess supply, which tends to induce price cuts. Lower prices, in turn, mean lost revenue and tighter profit margins. In highly competitive markets, manufacturers may introduce price cuts to lure market share from competitors, but this practice can reduce industry profitability in general when other firms respond in kind, and may not yield any market share to the initiating firm. Industry analysts therefore evaluate building materials companies in part by their discipline to expand capacity judiciously and to maintain sustainable pricing.

The U.S. concrete industry experienced a better year in 2005 than it had since the economic boom of the late 1990s. According to *The Concrete Producer,* concrete-related revenue increased almost 20 percent for the top 100 concrete contractors (CC100) in 2005. Total revenue for the CC100 that year reached US$15.4 billion, up from US$12.0 billion in 2004. Conditions looked good for the future as well. The Brookings Institute predicted that in 2030, about half of U.S. buildings will have been built after 2000, which means a lot of construction yet to come. The concrete industry hoped to build on that—literally. One expert told *Concrete Construction,* "By the year 2056, concrete construction will be the most prevalent form of building in the United States." Other factors expected to affect the industry in the United States included environmental concerns, climate, and increased populations. Bev Garnant said about the future, in the same article cited above, "We will do a better job of promoting concrete as a green product and will gain market share as a result. Concrete will also have a larger market share in response to issues like global warming, terrorism, seismic concerns, and our shrinking planet."

Compared to the United States, the concrete industry was doing even better globally. According to the Cement Bureau of Brussels, production worldwide grew by 6 percent in 2005 and 12 percent in 2006. The first quarter of 2007 showed even more promising figures. Due in part to a global construction boom, demand soared in the mid-2000s, and experts did not expect a slowdown before 2010. In 2006, the world consumed 2.5 billion tons of cement; the only commodity people use more of, stated an article in *Management Today,* is water. Much of the growth in the concrete industry is due to China; it accounts for about 50 percent of the world's cement consumption and more than 40 percent of its production. Other countries such as Malaysia and South Africa were experiencing strong growth as well. Even some unexpected European countries were getting in on the game, with the industry in Poland and Romania growing at around 20 percent annually.

Hinchcliff Drywall Construction has found a way to survive the tough times and continue to thrive in Hawaii. It combines determination, strategic awareness and innovation in a winning formula for success. The company connected with TexSton to become one of the exclusive distributors of its specialty plaster. That plaster has become a "staple finish on the wall in high end homes" according to Michelle Danihel-Kreusling, Hinchcliff's controller. The drive to survive led Hinchcliff to seek new sources of revenue plus reduce its operating expenses. As Danihel-Kreusling had pointed out, specialty plaster was highly adaptable. It was capable of serving as a duplicate for finishes and textures as diverse as marble and leather. Another Hinchcliff survival strategy called for it to partner with companies in different size ranges. The speed of payment or lack there of was sometimes linked to whether job was arranged as sub contract or direct connection.

RESEARCH AND TECHNOLOGY

When terrorists attacked the World Trade Center in New York City on September 11, 2001, people watched as the skyscrapers collapsed. As a result, many building material manufacturers asked themselves how they could improve the quality of their products. Researchers are working to create products that are sturdier, more durable, or more flexible. They are also focused on examining the ways in which their products fail (as they ultimately will, one way or another) so that they can take control of the ways they will break down, respond to destructive forces, or deteriorate.

Research began to address how materials could be improved and how those products' ultimate dilapidation could be controlled. Following the attacks, attention turned to the work of researchers such as the team at North Carolina State University who sought to create a high-performance, fiber-reinforced concrete (HPFRC) system that would improve the way buildings and other structures made with concrete react to destructive forces. This system capitalizes on the flexibility of mats constructed of recycled stainless steel fibers; these mats are then infused with concrete for application. Researchers note that this technology is not limited to new buildings because the mats can be fitted around existing supporting elements such as beams and columns or used to create new supporting structures by using the mats as tubular forms that can be filled with concrete.

Changing technology has made mining, refining, and manufacturing construction materials much easier. Bodies such as the American Society for Testing and Materials monitored minimum standards for concrete materials. The European Committee for Standardization planned to design criteria for building materials in the European Union. As the technology changed, so too did the criteria for the composition of these construction products. Industry was compelled to keep pace with these changes to remain competitive in the marketplace.

Continual and sometimes dramatic changes in science and engineering produced positive changes in the industry. The advent of automation meant that computers could be adapted to measure raw materials in the production of concrete as well as assist in packaging and transportation.

The rise of synthetic materials meant new developments in the manufacture and use of construction materials. There are plastic cements that have been developed for use as a construction binding material. Epoxy, polyester, and other resins have been used as well in conjunction with cement structures for joints as well as in the repair and protection of concrete.

The use of carbon as a conducting agent in concrete also opens up new possibilities. The introduction of special carbon fibers into concrete is being tested for use in heating buildings and paved surfaces, detecting earthquakes, and building submarines. The conductivity could make heating buildings more efficient, provide a safe lightning rod on the side of a building, and melt snow or ice on driveways and runways. Concrete containing these carbon fibers undergoes reduced conductivity when heavy pressure is applied. This is what makes the concrete act as a sensor as well as a building material. Possible applications of the sensory ability include weighing moving vehicles, providing electromagnetic shielding for security and privacy, and detecting earthquakes.

Many people are surprised at the possibility of using concrete to make submarines, but researchers are working to create just such a formula. A concrete submarine would have two important advantages over traditional steel vessels. First, it could go deeper into the ocean because concrete can withstand more pressure than steel; and second, it would be less detectable by sonar. Researchers continue to work toward a formula for bendable concrete, which would be valuable to the construction industry and the automotive and aircraft industries. A contributor to *The Economist* commented, "Unlikely as it may seem, concrete could be the wonder material of the future."

In Europe, increasingly tighter standards for emissions released into air and water were expected to particularly impact the precast concrete industry. Also, limits placed on mining activities were anticipated to result in supply problems for related industries in the late 1990s. As a result, research into the recycling of waste concrete was starting to allay supply problems.

However, not all of the production processes for these materials produced environmental problems. Some private industries, in partnership with government entities, are searching for new methods to responsibly manufacture materials as well as incorporate recycled goods into products. In eastern Germany, for example, wallboard factories were planned in six cities to convert some of the gypsum produced through desulphurization of brown coal power stations. Officials at Veag, the utility involved in the project, estimated that one power plant alone could produce 1 million tons per year of gypsum. The plasterboard factory at that site can only utilize 250,000 tons per year; the balance would be stored. Processing would continue well after the closure of the coal-burning power plants.

In the United States, USG has implemented a plan similar to the program in Germany and has begun drawing gypsum from coal-fueled power station smokestacks. In accordance with environmental regulations, utility companies using coal for fuel must scrub out their smokestacks to prevent pollutants from creating acid rain. The gypsum-rich chemical sludge that is scrubbed out of the smokestacks is a combination of smoke by-products and materials sprayed into the smokestacks to reduce air pollution. USG's decision to buy gypsum from utility companies benefits both parties; the utility company now makes money instead of spending it to have the waste taken to a landfill, and USG gets gypsum that is purer than what is mined out of the ground. In 2001, USG also introduced its Fiberock Brand Underlayment Aqua-Tough, an underlayment (sub-flooring) made completely of recycled gypsum and cellulose. Besides being environmentally sound, this product provides a moisture-resistant layer that is designed for indoor or outdoor use beneath virtually any type of flooring. Breakthroughs like this offer consumers the option to choose recycled materials without sacrificing function. The company benefits from extending the life of its product and also from presenting itself to the public as a company that takes steps toward preserving the environment. Other environmental initiatives by USG include using recycled newspapers and boxes to make ceiling panels and using steel mill slag to make ceiling tiles.

Canadian government officials and the private sector have also been working together to support and create the building of environmentally sound buildings with recycled materials. For example, in one demonstration project, colored chips of recycled glass were added to terrazzo floors; and drywall in the construction used the maximum available recycled materials. Another innovation may come from Dr. Bill Price of the University of Houston. His work toward creating transparent concrete was making progress in 2001, when he succeeded in creating partial transparency.

In 2003, the Strategic Development Council (SDC) released a research report entitled *Roadmap 2030: The U.S. Concrete Industry Technology Roadmap,* produced in cooperation with the U.S. Department of Energy (DOE). The report was a detailed follow-up to the SDC's report, *Vision 2030,* which was published in 2001. According to *The Concrete Producer,* in addition to reducing a 15-year lag between research and the development of actual technologies, the report identified four research areas as being a high priority for the industry. These included concrete production, delivery, and placement; constituent materials; design and structural systems; and repair and rehabilitation.

The DOE conducts industry research at the Oak Ridge (Tenn.) National Laboratory via the Concrete and Containment Technology Program. *The Concrete Producer* indicated that future research goals include a 500 percent increase in concrete recycling; a 60 percent reduction in jobsite material rejection; and a 20 percent reduction in power demand at cement plants. Another goal is to have structural concrete used to produce 50 percent of all new homes.

In January of 2004, *The Concrete Producer* reported that Texas EMC Products—a joint venture between the Dutch enterprise EMC Cement BV and the United States' Few Ready Mix Concrete Co.—was preparing to introduce an energetically modified cement (EMC) called CemPozz. Concrete producers could use the EMC as a 60 percent substitute for Portland Cement when mixing concrete. The EMC consisted of modified fly ash—a coal combustion byproduct—that produced a stronger concrete mixture at a lower cost. In addition, production required less energy, thereby benefiting the environment.

The patented process for producing EMC was developed in the early 1990s by Dr. Vladimir Ronin, a researcher at the Lulea University of Technology in Sweden. According to *Concrete Producer,* "CemPozz improves concrete's chemistry. Portland cement reacts with water to produce ordinary concrete. That chemical process, called hydration, forms two cementing compounds in the concrete—calcium silicate hydrate and calcium hydroxide."

"The calcium silicate hydrate gives concrete its strength and dimensional stability. The calcium hydroxide, which makes up about 25 percent of ordinary concrete, is relatively weak and porous. As a continuing part of the hydration process, CemPozz consumes the calcium hydroxide, turning it into additional hardened concrete.

This results in a denser, less permeable, and more durable concrete."

When it comes to earthen plaster, American Clay Enterprises is the ultimate resource for the special formula. The company earned a patent for its CEO and co-founder Croft Elsaesser's innovation. As a former sufferer of headaches and breathing problems believed to be linked to toxic substances in finishes, Elsaesser was inspired to create "an eco-friendly" plaster Elsaesser's proud parents were also industry innovators. Carol Sorensen-Baumgartel co-created American Clay Enterprises. Edward M. Sorensen acquired more than 20 patents.

One of CTS Cement Manufacturing Corporation's sales managers and three—decade—plus veterans suggested a modification that is resulting in classification change with major impact. Creighton Maher is credited with observing customer challenges with specifying specialty cement plasters. Maher concluded that the time was right for incorporating new alternatives to using Portland cement into the MasterFormat system design industry standard. The system was originally launched in 2004 for version currently in use but is revised on annual basis.

INDUSTRY LEADERS

USG. A division of the USG Corporation, U.S. Gypsum is the world's largest manufacturer of gypsum wallboard. Its main products are various wallboards, and its Sheetrock brand is the top-seller in the world. The company was formed in the late 1800s and early 1900s from a union of 35 gypsum manufacturers in the United States. At the time, the firm controlled half of the gypsum products market in the country. The company also had substantial assets in the production of lime products as well as other construction materials. The aftershocks of legal actions against the firm in the 1970s and 1980s, which ranged from antitrust matters to various claims from asbestos contaminated products, meant the company had to retrench fiscally. Although by 1998 USG was seen as a healthy and more disciplined company, its parent company filed Chapter 11 in 2001 to restructure in light of the significant financial implications of mounting asbestos claims. USG's Chairman, President, and CEO William Foote, explained in *Walls and Ceilings,* "The filing is not about restructuring our company's operating units or dealing with a liquidity crisis. Rather, the Chapter 11 process was our only alternative to prevent the value drain that has been occurring as U. S. Gypsum was forced to pay for the asbestos costs of other companies that have already filed Chapter 11." The company emerged from Chapter 11 in 2006. That year, the company had sales of US$5.8 billion and employed about 14,700 people.

BPB Industries. With some 40 percent of Europe's wallboard market and 9 percent of the North American market, U.K.-based BPB is a major player in the European market with a growing presence in North America and other parts of the world. Wallboard is a crucial product line for BPB, as it represented 64 percent of sales in 2004, up from 48 percent in 2001. The firm operates 90 plants in more than 50 countries. In 2006, revenues totaled US$4.3 billion. The company also produces paper and packing goods, which integrate well with its wallboard production.

Tarmac Ltd. One of the leaders in the U.K. construction materials trade only entered into the brick, tile, and assorted concrete products market in the 1980s. Tarmac Ltd. was founded on the creation of road material made from a combination of tar and slag; the company's name is still sometimes used as a generic reference to driving surfaces. Though primarily vested in interests in quarrying and sales of road-building materials as well as civil engineering, the company began positioning itself for growth in the brick and concrete markets in 1971. In the 1980s Tarmac began expanding into the global marketplace, and the purchase of The Hoveringham Group cemented Tarmac PLC's entry into the brick, tile, and assorted concrete products market as well as international commerce. The purchase, combined with subsequent purchases, gave Tarmac substantial holdings in quarrying and concrete production in the United States. The company registered 2001 sales of US$1.7 billion. Individual sales figures were not available in the late 2000s, by which time the company was a subsidiary of Anglo American, which registered overall earnings of US$29.4 billion in 2006.

Lafarge SA. France's Lafarge is one of the world's top building materials conglomerates. It has market-leading shares in several product categories and in several countries, but its international presence spans most parts of the world. Lafarge is the world's second-largest cement maker, but it also produces ready-mix concrete, aggregates, gypsum wallboard and other gypsum products, roofing tiles, and a variety of other building materials. In 1997 Lafarge transacted the largest acquisition ever in the European building materials industry when it bought out the United Kingdom's Redland PLC in a US$3.6 billion hostile takeover. Redland was a diversified aggregates, concrete, and roofing materials firm with a stronger market presence in the United Kingdom than Lafarge. The takeover was expected to have repercussions in the U.K. industry, particularly in the ready-mix concrete segment, and possibly lead to further consolidation. In 2001, Lafarge acquired Blue Circle Industries, propelling it to status as the world's leading cement producer. Lafarge had 2006 sales of US$22.3 billion, up 18 percent from the previous year. In 2006, cement accounted for approximately half of the company's sales.

BIBLIOGRAPHY

Aderinokun, Kunle. "Nigeria Plans to Export Cement by 2013." 21 October 2009. Available from allafrica.com/stories/2009 10210096.html.

"Building Materials Industry." *Value Line Investment Survey,* 2005.

"Cement Prices Continue to Fuel Surge in Construction Costs." *Knight-Ridder Tribune Business News,* 24 June 2005.

"Cement Shortages Threaten Construction Market." *Pit & Quarry,* June 2004.

Chiem, Linda. "Hawaii contractor builds success with new ideas." *Pacific Business News,* 22 October 2009. Available from pacific. bizjournals.com.

"Concrete and the Future." *Concrete Construction,* September 2006.

"Concrete's Comeback." *Management Today,* 1 June 2007.

CTS Cement Manufacturing Corporation. Concrete Producer Online, 21 October 2009. Available from www.theconcreteproducer.com.

"Concrete Contractors: A Very Busy Year." *The Concrete Producer,* September 2006.

"Forecast 2007." *Cement Americas,* 1 January 2007.

"Gypsum and Anhydrite: Global Industry Markets and Outlook (10th Edition, 2009)." PR Newswire, 20 October 2009. Available from in.sys.com.

"Hoover's Company Capsules." *Hoover's Online,* 2007. Available from www.hoovers.com.

Klemens, Tom. "Another Mix Option: Portland Cement Substitute Yields Economic, Environmental, and Durability Benefits." *The Concrete Producer,* January 2004.

———. "Questions, Answers, and Applications: High-Tech Research Is Yielding Concrete Results." *The Concrete Producer,* August 2003.

New Mexico Business Weekly. "American Clay earns patent for plaster formula." *Pacific Business News,* 18 February 2009. Available from pacific.bizjournals.com.

"No Cement Shortage in Alaska." *Knight-Ridder Tribune Business News,* 23 June 2005.

———. "Growing Big in the Residential Concrete Industry." *Concrete Construction Magazine,* 1 July 2006.

Stanfield, Frank. "Collision of Global, Local Growth Poses Problem for Ocala, Fla.-Area Builders." *Ocala Star Banner* (FL), 24 June 2004.

Sullivan, C.C. "For Liquid Stone, A Virtual Chisel: New Concrete Mixes Revive Classical Ornament." *Architecture,* August 2004.

"Survey: Cement, Gypsum are Price Increase Leaders." *Cement Americas,* 1 January 2003.

SIC 1540

CONSTRUCTION, NONRESIDENTIAL BUILDING

NAICS CODE(S)

2362. Nonresidential construction firms build, alter, remodel, repair, and renovate a wide range of commercial, industrial, and public buildings, including industrial buildings, warehouses, office buildings, churches and synagogues, hospitals, museums, schools, restaurants and shopping centers, and stadiums. See also **Construction, Residential Building** and **Engineering Services.**

INDUSTRY SNAPSHOT

The global construction industry is closely tied to general business and economic conditions. Consulting firm IHS Global Insight's Third Quarter Construction Briefing for 2009 showed the direction for U.S. construction spending was expected to be down for the year by 12 percent. In 2010, expectations called for a four percent drop. Double digit growth was predicted for 2011 and 2012.

Certain segments of the nonresidential building construction industry proved healthier than others amid the fluctuating economic trends of the first decade of the 2000s. While office building construction was plagued by oversupply in the early 1990s, economic conditions improved later in the decade. Despite problems like corporate downsizing, temporary work forces, and inventory reduction, the strong economy facilitated a rapid decline in office vacancies in the United States. The economic situation was particularly beneficial for smaller office building construction in smaller cities around the world, as many corporations began to decentralize their operations and moved divisional offices closer to manufacturing and distribution centers. Some corporations in search of lower costs abandoned large cities completely. This trend created an upturn in demand for new office buildings in some medium-sized cities in the southeastern United States. Furthermore, the industry, especially in the United States and parts of Western Europe, saw a shift in demographics in office building construction, as many businesses moved away from their traditional urban settings into suburbs and outlying areas.

The nonresidential building segment of the construction industry is aided by the fact that institutional building, like governmental buildings and schools, tends to remain relatively stable. Additionally, even in mature construction markets like the United States, new facilities, or at least upgrades to older facilities, are quite often needed to replace or refurbish aging schools, hospitals, and other publicly funded structures. In the case of schools, quite often increasing enrollment can bolster construction needs.

The rapid expansion of the Asian economies in most business sectors enabled construction companies worldwide to tap into this market. When companies established themselves in the Asia-Pacific region, construction contractors would then build the new facilities. Gains in the Asian market made it possible for international contractors to offset the more modest gains in the mature markets of Europe and North America, as well as regions with comparatively low demand such as Latin America,

the Middle East, and Africa. Asia (excluding Japan) was expected by most industry analysts to remain the leading region for new construction in the world early in the twenty-first century; areas such as Latin America and Eastern Europe were also predicted to grow, albeit somewhat more slowly.

ORGANIZATION AND STRUCTURE

International construction companies and the design firms that work closely with them are among the most independent of corporations. While international manufacturing corporations may diversify their products and services, builders tend to remain focused on construction. One division may specialize in high-rise office buildings while another will concentrate on petrochemical plants.

Most international construction companies and design firms manage their businesses independently of their respective governments. However, this does not mean that they are not regulated. Companies must build to local or national building codes and follow local or national environmental standards. They are usually monitored for safety on the work site by government departments and their own safety directors. In the United States, the Occupational Safety and Health Administration (OSHA) regularly issues and monitors rules that govern various aspects of the nonresidential building industry. In early 1995, for example, OSHA issued a safety regulation that mandated that all construction employees wear harnesses if working near the edge of a building. The harnesses, which are secured to the building, are designed to prevent the wearers from falling more than a few feet.

In the early years of the first decade of the 2000s, many of the largest construction firms were private companies, such as Bechtel Group Inc. and Parsons Corporation. Some companies were owned and headed primarily by their founding families. While many corporations hired for their higher management positions "business" people who often had little practical knowledge of the company, construction companies and engineering design firms were more typically headed by builders and engineers. Many in key positions in the industry began working in the field as project managers and subsequently learned how to run the business by working their way up.

BACKGROUND AND DEVELOPMENT

After reaching peak levels in 1998, due to strong economies in both North America and Europe, the nonresidential construction market began to decline in 2000 as a result of weakening economic trends. Companies in Europe, the United States, and Japan in particular saw significant reductions in new contracts, particularly for domestic projects. This downward trend, however, had begun to improve by 2004, when worldwide spending on construction, fueled in large part by surging demand in China and India, reached US$3.9 trillion. In the early years of the first decade of the 2000s, about 65 percent of the construction industry's business was in the form of new construction, while the remainder was derived from alterations, maintenance, and repair. While the United States remained a world leader in the nonresidential construction industry, about 80 percent of the world's construction activity took place outside U.S. borders.

Demand for office building construction increased when the dot-com boom of the late 1990s fueled numerous start-ups and expansion among existing businesses. However, in 2000, the growth in the office building market slowed considerably when the dot-com firms began disappearing and many technology firms began scaling back operations to weather the downturn. In fact, U.S. office building construction declined 22 percent in 2001, more than any other nonresidential construction sector. In comparison, the U.S. nonresidential building industry as a whole fell only 4 percent, from US$173.1 billion in 2000 to US$165.8 billion in 2001. According to *U.S. Construction Trends,* in a report released by construction industry research firm F. W. Dodge, "After a very strong 2000, the demand for office space was dampened by the dot-com correction, as a substantial amount of sublease space was put back on the market. The decline for office construction was especially pronounced in those cities that benefited from the high-tech boom, such as Washington D.C., Seattle, San Jose, and Dallas." More favorable economic conditions after 2004, however, began to reverse this downward trend. According to McGraw-Hill Construction, office building construction in January 2005 rose 11 percent nationwide (adjusted annual rate).

In the early years of the first decade of the 2000s, oil refinery and chemical plant construction around the world remained one of the fundamental cornerstones of the industry. Industry observers noted that, with China and other Asian countries, such as Vietnam, becoming more receptive to outside influence, the market for petrochemical plants was expected to remain steady early in the twenty-first century. U.S. companies particularly had the advantage in this market with decades of international experience building oil refineries. The rapid growth in global trade has also increased the need for projects such as port facilities and airports, especially in developing countries.

Construction of manufacturing plants has traditionally remained relatively steady over the years. Manufacturing plants, according to conventional wisdom, always need to be expanded, upgraded, rebuilt, and built in new locations. In fact, most of the construction activity in this industry segment is done to increase capacity, which was

expected to continue as companies expand globally and need greater capacity—with the caveat that cyclically, many manufacturing industries reach stages of overcapacity that spell lean times for construction firms. Manufacturing plant construction attracts a wide range of international expertise. However, the construction of huge manufacturing plants in the United States, such as those that assemble automobiles and trucks, was never again expected to rival the pace of construction achieved earlier in the twentieth century. Factories built at the end of the twentieth century were expected to last well into the next century, although renovation work on these facilities was likely to be done. In the United States, however, manufacturing over the last several decades of the twentieth century slowly declined as the country's economy became increasingly based on service industries. At the same time, the shifting of manufacturing jobs to developing countries, particularly in Asia, opened opportunities there for substantial growth in construction. In China, for example, construction investment—much of it for new factories—was projected to grow at about 7.9 percent through 2012. Even higher growth of 9.2 percent was projected for India.

One key to any developing country's efforts to build its own industrial base is access to electric power. While the construction of new electric generation plants in the United States slowed through the 1980s and 1990s, the world's hunger for power was expected to grow. China alone announced that it intended to double its electric power generating capacity over a five-year span. Doing that required the help of scores of international companies.

Although periodically threatened by tight budgets in the deficit-conscious 1990s, the construction of governmental and educational buildings was likely to remain one of the foundations of the nonresidential construction industry. Besides demographic trends that necessitated new school construction, the need to upgrade schools for Internet capabilities was a major challenge in the late 1990s and the first decade of the 2000s. This factor, combined with growing importance of school vouchers and other school choice programs, led to US$32.8 billion in school construction alone in the United States in 1996. As state and local governments began to approve the construction of new schools and the refurbishment of existing institutions, school construction soared to record levels in both 2000 and 2001. During the same period, the construction of transportation terminals grew 25 percent; courthouses and jails, 5 percent; and churches, 1 percent. The need for new or upgraded hospitals and related healthcare facilities, such as nursing homes, contributed to a 10 percent increase in construction in 2001; this growth trend was expected to continue through the 2000s as the U.S. population ages. In early 2005, the value of public construction of schools reached about US$64.6

billion and construction of public healthcare facilities was approximately US$6.6 billion.

Hotel and recreational facility construction benefits much from a healthy economy, as economic prosperity fosters more business and leisure travel. In addition, this industry segment has been boosted by the proliferation of gambling casinos, which are often integrated with hotels. When the economy weakens, however, construction dollars for these types of projects tend to evaporate more quickly than for other market sectors. In 2001, amusement-related projects, such as movie theaters, fell 14 percent in the United States. However, store and shopping center construction, which declined by only 9 percent, found the impact of the recessionary conditions offset a bit by those retail chains working to expand their reach despite a sluggish economy. As economic conditions improved through 2004 and 2005, investment flowed back into the hotel and recreation sector. Between December 2004 and January 2005, hotel construction grew by 34 percent, while building in the amusement sector increased by 75 percent.

In January 2009, The American Institute of Architects predicted U.S. hotel construction spending would decline by more than 20 percent in 2009 and another 12 percent in 2010. Furthermore, double digits declines were expected for construction of retail, office and industrial facilities. "This is not expected to turn around any time soon, and it's likely to get worse before it gets better," American Institute of Architects Chief Economist Kermit Baker stated.

The challenges facing the engineers, architects, and constructors who design and build these buildings, industrial plants, and manufacturing facilities are daunting. As the nonresidential construction markets in industrialized countries continued to mature and competition in those areas continued to intensify, many analysts recommended that industry players look to developing countries for new growth.

CURRENT CONDITIONS

The commercial construction industry was healthy in the mid-years of the first decade of the 2000s, especially in the United States. Nonresidential construction starts accounted for US$209 billion in 2006. Of this amount, about 47 percent was in commercial and industrial buildings and 51 percent was in institutional buildings (e.g., education and health care). The fastest growing type of construction was in the hotel market, which increased by about 50 percent in 2006. Construction of education buildings was also on the rise, following a decline that began in 2002. In 2001 education construction saw a record high of 273 million square feet, after which the industry slumped due to the economic recession of the

early years of the first decade of the 2000s. In 2004 construction of education buildings dropped 23 percent to 209 million square feet. The trend reversed, however, in 2005, and the industry showed an increase of 5 percent. In 2006 education square footage grew another 4 percent to 227 million square feet. Construction spending for malls, shopping centers, and large discount stores was also growing, and in December 2006 was almost 50 percent higher than it was at the same time in 2005. Office and manufacturing construction were also on the rise.

The increase in nonresidential construction in the United States also had a positive impact on the job market in the industry. According to Ken Simonson, chief economist for the Associated General Contractors of America (AGC), during 2006 nonresidential builders boosted employment by 160,000, or 5 percent. Wages for these workers also rose, netting an increase of 4.5 percent in 2006, as compared to 4 percent for all private industry production workers.

By 2009, U.S. nonresidential construction downturns were leading contractors to seek a quicker stimulus rollout. "We know from contractors' reports that stimulus money is beginning to flow, but what should be a torrent by now is only a trickle in most categories," concluded Associated General Contractors of America Chief Economist Ken Simonson. Simonson was making reference to the believed necessity for assistance from the U.S. federal government stimulus plan. According to Simonson, situations were becoming more dire due in part also to banks "keeping a tight lid on real estate lending."

RESEARCH AND TECHNOLOGY

The building construction industry has not been as motivated to develop new materials as other industries because steel and concrete are proven raw materials with well-known building properties. However, construction companies are expected to research new building materials as these become available due in part because of concerns about the ability of manufactured structures to withstand the tremendous force unleashed by periodic natural disasters. The major technical challenge is to find ways to construct earthquake-proof buildings. Even after years of research on how seismic forces affect buildings, some factors are still unknown. In Kobe, Japan, engineers were astonished to find that apartment buildings built on soft fill dredged up from the ocean floor survived the quake while carefully designed office buildings built on the mainland sometimes "pancaked" their center floors. The terrorist attacks on the World Trade Center in New York City on September 11, 2001, further underscored the need to continue researching methods for constructing buildings, particularly large ones, able to withstand various kinds of disasters.

A growing trend in the early years of the first decade of the 2000s was "green engineering," which aimed at minimizing the negative environmental effects of construction projects. Green buildings are often constructed using recycled or renewable materials and use energy-efficient technologies to reduce heating and cooling costs. The headquarters for Genzyme Corp., a global biotechnology company based in Cambridge, Massachusetts, is considered a model of green construction. The building uses no electricity for heating or cooling and is expected to use 33 percent less water and 40 percent less electricity than a conventional building of the same size. The building uses mirrors to bring natural light into office spaces, recycles rainwater, and relies on a computerized climate management system to maintain optimal interior conditions by automatically raising or lowering window blinds and louvers. While the US$140 million Genzyme building, which opened in late 2003 and accommodates 900 employees, cost about 16 percent more than a conventional building would, the company expected to realize significant savings in utilities costs. In addition, company officials said that the building's amenities would attract high-caliber employees. Though green technologies are more expensive than conventional construction, it is possible, according to the *Boston Globe,* to erect environmentally friendly buildings for as little as 2 percent above conventional costs. Furthermore, energy savings over the lifetime of the building could average 20 percent.

Interest in green building has skyrocketed in the United States since the late 1990s. In 2000, Seattle became the first metropolis in the nation to officially adopt a citywide sustainable building policy. Other cities soon followed, including Chicago, which in 2004 announced that all new public construction in the city would be certified by the U.S. Green Building Council. In 2003, products and services for green buildings across the nation reached about US$5.8 billion, up about 33 percent from 2002. Sustainable construction is also a major goal of the European Union, where many green building practices were pioneered. A partnership between the European Union and China, launched in 2003, aims to improve the environmental efficiency of major construction projects in China through the early 2000s, including the Beijing Olympic Village under construction for the 2008 summer games.

The design-build process, in which one firm contracts to design and build an entire project from scratch, began to take on increased significance in the late 1990s. By 2000, these projects accounted for roughly 25 percent of all nonresidential construction projects, up from about 6 percent in the late 1980s. The advantages of this type of contract include the single point of responsibility for the project, which lessens the risk and potential litigation expenses; faster project completion, as designs are implemented with a specific and familiar building technique in mind; and diminished administrative burden. However, some industry analysts have noted that such projects could pose potential problems in the face of increased globalization. Specifically, as international consortiums collaborate on projects, the design-build process may suffer from a lack of international design and building specifications and regulations.

WORKFORCE

The vast majority of construction companies are relatively small businesses, with fewer than ten employees, although some of the largest companies employ as many as 95,000 people worldwide. The United States—with more than 7.0 million wage and salary workers and 1.9 million self-employed workers (including small residential homebuilders) in 2004—boasted one of the largest construction labor forces in the world yet was still plagued by chronic labor shortages. Analysts forecast that by 2010 the industry would face as many as 2.4 million unfilled jobs for skilled and unskilled positions. Indeed, according to a *New York Times* article, Francis X. McArdle, managing director of the General Contractors Association of New York, predicted that, in response to acute demand, many workers would be pressed to work six- or seven-day weeks. Pay scales, however, would remain relatively high, reflecting the fact that construction workers are increasingly required to work with new technologies, including highly specialized equipment that incorporates computerized systems. In 2004, average wages for construction workers in the United States were about US$19.23 per hour. According to the U.S. Bureau of Labor Statistics, the number of construction jobs was expected to grow roughly 11 percent by the year 2014. Furthermore, it stated, "Employment in nonresidential construction is expected to grow a little faster because industrial construction activity is expected to be stronger as replacement of many industrial plants has been delayed for years, and a large number of structures will have to be replaced or remodeled." Also impacting this sector, according to the bureau, will be the growth in demand for nursing home and drug treatment facilities, as well as increased school enrollment.

U.S. construction workers were struggling to hang on in 2009, according to analysis of U.S. Bureau of Statistics data. That data reflected that approximately one-third of job loss in August 2009 was related to the industry. Associated General Contractors of America economist Simonson lamented that "There's nothing good in the report for the nation's construction workers." It was also acknowledged that construction employment throughout the nation declined by 65,000 in August.

Japan employed roughly 6 million construction workers in the late 1990s, but the industry saw a continued decrease in employment from 1998 through 2002, with an overall loss of 220,000 jobs after 1993. Japanese government figures suggested that this trend would continue. European construction employees in the late 1990s numbered more than 10 million, but a stagnant industry from the late 1990s through 2003 threatened significant job losses. Figures are harder to estimate in growing regions like Asia (excluding Japan), which continued to rely to a large degree on international firms for construction needs.

INDUSTRY LEADERS

VINCI. During the mid-years of the first decade of the 2000s, France-based VINCI was one of the largest construction companies in the world with approximately 133,500 employees and operations spanning more than 100 countries. The company has completed many extremely tall buildings, including a 700,000-square-meter residential and commercial complex in Kuala Lumpur, Malaysia. Company sales grew 17.6 percent in 2003 after the firm's acquisition of GTM Enterpose Ltd., which operated in over 90 countries and maintained a payroll of 67,000 employees, 33,872 of whom worked in building and civil engineering. The company posted revenues of US$25.5 billion in 2006.

Koninklijke BAM Groep nv. When Koninklijke BAM Groep (also known as Royal BAM) bought the giant Hollandsche Beton Groep (HBG) in 2002, the company became one of Europe's leading construction and engineering firms. While BAM's civil engineering divisions operated worldwide, its construction and property division remained in the Netherlands, Belgium, Great Britain, and Germany. In 2006 the company increased its residential construction activity when it bought the developer AM for more than US$1 billion. Sales for 2005 totaled US$8.79 billion, and the firm employed 27,190 workers. By 2008, those figures had increased to US$12.5 billion for sales and 30,338 employees.

Kajima Corporation. Kajima Corporation, based in Tokyo, was a leader in construction of skyscrapers in Japan and made major contributions to earthquake-proof building technologies. One of Japan's oldest and largest construction companies, Kajima was founded in 1840. In 2006 it listed total sales of US$15.09 billion and had 9,234 employees. Despite its primarily domestic focus, the firm maintained subsidiaries in North America, Europe, and in other Asian countries. As the Japanese construction market cooled in the early years of the 2000s' first decade, the company expanded its overseas operations and branched out into related services, such as environmental management.

Bouygues SA. Bouygues SA, founded in 1952 and headquartered in Cedex, France, employed 115,441 workers in 2006. Besides construction (its core business), Bouygues

engages in engineering, telecommunications, media, public utilities, and other activities. In the middle years of the first decade of the 2000s, the company owned 90 percent of the stock in Bouygues Telecom (France's third largest mobile phone carrier) and around 40 percent of TF1 (the number-one TV channel in France). Total revenues were US$31.9 in 2006, although only a portion of this came from the construction branch. Although it has grown increasingly diversified, the firm remains one of the largest construction companies in Europe and maintains 40 subsidiaries and affiliates in 80 countries. By 2007, the company had 137,500 employees. For 2008, its sales added up to about US$46.2

Bechtel Group, Inc. Based in San Francisco, California, the Bechtel Group was the largest construction company in the United States in 2007. Sales exceeded US$18.1 billion in 2005, and the firm had 40,000 employees. In 2003 it received contracts to reconstruct damaged infrastructure in post-war Iraq. As of November 2004, the company had completed renovations and repairs of 1,200 schools, 10 fire stations, and 52 health clinics, in addition to other infrastructure projects.

Kellogg Brown & Root, Inc. Founded in 1919, Brown and Root Inc. began operating as a subsidiary of Halliburton in 1962. In 1996, it split into three entities, one of which was named Brown and Root Engineering and Construction (BREC). When Halliburton acquired Dresser Industries in 1998, BREC was merged with Dresser's MW Kellogg division to form Kellogg Brown & Root, Inc., a global engineering and construction firm that builds petrochemical facilities and power plants, hotels, office buildings, shopping centers, hospitals, universities, correctional facilities, and other public buildings. The firm operated as a wholly owned subsidiary of Halliburton until April 2007, and reported sales of US$363.6 million in 2006.

MAJOR COUNTRIES IN THE INDUSTRY

The United States. In the United States, the value of nonresidential building construction fell from US$173.1 billion in 2000 to US$165.8 billion in 2001, and private spending for nonresidential construction fell by 15.9 percent in 2002. Office, retail, and hotel construction, which saw growth of more than 12 percent annually from 1993 to 2000, declined by 4.2 percent in 2001 and dropped by as much as 30 percent in 2002. Many leading U.S. nonresidential construction firms began looking to expand into emerging markets like Asia and Latin America. Most firms sought established businesses with which to partner in an effort to avoid some of the cultural barriers inherent in establishing a new business overseas. The decline in the industry ended in 2005, and by 2006 it had recovered as predicted. Overall, the value of U.S. construction starts (excluding residential projects) totaled $26.5 billion in January 2007, up 28.7 percent from January 2006. In 2009, times were challenging for U.S. nonresidential construction with the Associated General Contractors of America's Simonson describing the situation as "depression-like" conditions.

Europe. The construction market in Europe is characterized as very mature and offers little prospect for dramatic growth in the twenty-first century. Economic recession contributed to a flat performance for the industry through the early years of the first decade of the 2000s. Analysts forecast renewed but modest growth. Most new construction, though, is expected to occur in markets where significant economic reconstruction is taking place, including Ireland, Portugal, and Poland. Construction in Western Europe is projected to grow at about 3.9 percent annually through 2012, slightly below the projected world average of 4.8 percent.

In Germany, historically the largest construction industry in Europe, the economic recession of 2001 and 2002 hit construction companies hard. One of the country's leading firms, Philipp Holzmann AG, went bankrupt in 2002 after struggling with mounting debts since 1999. Industry analysts expected a further slump, including the loss of approximately 90,000 jobs in 2004, but predicted that the industry would recover.

Great Britain's construction industry in the early years of the first decade of the 2000s was the third largest in Europe and the fifth largest in the world, employing approximately 2 million people. Publicly funded projects such as hospitals, infrastructure, and housing accounted for most of Great Britain's domestic construction; international projects, however, especially in South and East Asia, accounted for a substantial part of earnings. Great Britain's construction industry was dominated by small companies, but analysts predicted a greater degree of consolidation in the early part of the decade.

Asia. Through the 1970s, 1980s, and 1990s, Japan's enormous construction industry faced criticism, especially from U.S. firms, that the market remained closed to foreign contractors. In 1994, yielding to demands for increased access, the Japanese government initiated its Action Plan on Reform of the Bidding and Contracting Procedures for Public Works. Many international contractors responded, mostly from the United States, South Korea, China, and France. U.S. contractors accounted for an overwhelming US$190 million of the total US$230 million in foreign contracts in the market in 1997. However, this total only reflected a small fraction of Japan's construction market. Like the United States and Europe, Japan was viewed as a

shrinking market with growing competition early in the twenty-first century. Indicative of these difficult conditions was the performance of four of Japan's largest general contractors in fiscal 2001: Shimizu Corp. and Obayashi Corp. posted losses, while Taisei Corp. and Kajima Corp. struggled to remain profitable. Though the decline in construction investment continued through 2003, the industry remained one of Japan's primary employers, with a labor force of almost 6 million workers.

The hottest region of the world for nonresidential construction in the early years of the first decade of the 2000s was Asia (excluding Japan). China, which was the second largest construction market in the world in 2005, accounted for the majority of new construction projects in the region. The largest construction firm in the nation, China State Construction, held only 2 percent of the Chinese construction market in 2000. In addition, the largest of the 500,000 firms engaged in some form of construction there only accounted for 10 percent of the industry. Analysts predicted strong demand for nonresidential construction in China through the 2010s. Among China's major projects in the early years of the first decade of the 2000s was the Olympic Village in Beijing, scheduled for completion for the 2008 summer Olympics. India and South Korea also were expected to emerge as major players in the global industry in the twenty-first century.

The devastating tsunami that hit southern Asia in December 2004 drove demand for much new building in the affected regions. Analysts predicted that construction needs would be substantial.

Africa. Africa continued to be a difficult market for international contractors to penetrate in great numbers, primarily due to the lack of business investment in the continent. The top 225 contractors conducted US$10.3 billion in business in the region in 1996. Africa's acute need for infrastructure, however, pointed to significant opportunities in the construction sector, which grew at an average of 4 percent per year on the continent after 1995. This performance varied considerably, however, from country to country, with underdeveloped nations such as Mozambique seeing growth of up to 14 percent, while more stable and well-developed countries such as Tanzania enjoyed growth of about 5 percent. Improvements in industry management also contributed to a positive outlook for the early years of the first decade of the 2000s. In Senegal, which instituted reforms that required open bidding on government contracts, construction costs in the late 1990s were cut by 40 percent. At the same time, these reforms led to the creation of 3,000 permanent construction jobs.

Growth in the tourism and manufacturing sectors was also expected to contribute to construction demand. In 1999, some 665 construction projects for tourist accommodations were built in Egypt alone. South Africa invested US$144 million in the expansion of the Johannesburg International Airport. According to *African Business,* at least 50 percent of all fixed capital investments in most African countries came from the construction sector alone, making it likely to remain one of the continent's strongest engines of economic growth through the early 2000s. Nevertheless, the region's need for foreign investment to fund large-scale building projects remained critical. In 2005, British Prime Minister Tony Blair announced a massive aid plan for Africa, including debt relief and increased trade to foster development. As the region increases its participation in the global economy through the early 2000s, demand will rise for new manufacturing plants, office complexes, health care facilities, schools, and other nonresidential buildings.

In 2007, construction of the King Shaka International Airport began in South Africa. The larger airport, with an estimated price tag of US$353 million, will replace the Durban International Airport and will be completed by 2010, in time for the international football tournament, the FIFA World Cup, which South Africa will host.

Latin America. In 1996, the top 225 international contractors in Latin America signed US$8.1 billion in construction business, continuing the steady incline of construction industry growth there during the 1990s. Many international contractors were optimistic about Latin America, however, as the economies of several nations in the region, including Colombia, Chile, Mexico, and Argentina, were expanding. By the end of the 1990s, yearly investment for infrastructure development in Latin America reached $40 billion, more than twice the amount allocated in 1995. In the early years of the first decade of the 2000s, Argentina announced a US$30 billion public works and housing project that was expected to give a much-needed boost to the construction sector. Venezuela implemented an Economic Recovery Plan that would allow foreign contractors to participate in several public works construction projects, including airports and hospitals. Industry observers expected Latin America to be a growth market well into the twenty-first century.

BIBLIOGRAPHY
Baker, Kermit. "Nonresidential Construction Poised for Solid Gains in 2005." *AIArchitect,* January 2005. Available from www.aia.org.

"Commercial Building Starts Soar." *Midwest Contractor,* 26 March 2007.

"Construction." European Commission. Available from europa.eu.int.

"Construction & Materials in Latin America." *Latin Sector Watch,* March 2005. Available from www.latin-sectors.com.

Construction Specifications Institute. "Construction Industry Statistics," 2003. Available from www.csinet.org.

"Construction Workers Account for One-Third of Job Losses." Dolan Media Newswires, 15 September 2009. Available from www.finance-commerce.com.

"Decline in U.S. non-residential construction sparks call for quicker stimulus rollout." *Daily Commercial News and Construction Record,* 4 September 2009. Available from dcnonl.com.

"Forecasts & Trends," McGraw-Hill Construction, 28 February 2005. Available from cotest.construction.com.

Haughey, Jim. "U.S. Construction Starts: Show Strength Early in 2006." *Business Credit,* June 2006.

"Hoover's Company Capsules." *Hoover's Online,* 2007. Available from www.hoovers.com.

"International Airport." *International Construction,* September 2006.

Japanese Ministry of Public Management, Home Affairs, Posts and Telecommunications. *Statistical Handbook of Japan.* Available from www.stat.go.jp.

Kennedy, Kim. "Education Construction Turns Upward." *Engineering News Record,* 9 April 2007.

"Lodging, Hospitals Fuel Nonres Growth." *Construction Equipment,* 1 January 2007.

"New Study Forecasts Improving Outlook for Global Construction Industry." Global Insight Inc., 9 June 2003. Available from www.globalinsight.com.

"Nonresidential Construction Growth Continues In '07." *Building Design & Construction,* 1 December 2006.

"Nonresidential Construction Jobs Grow." *Construction Bulletin,* 5 March 2007.

"Nonresidential Construction Seen Down in 2009." CNBC, 14 January 2009. Available from CNBC.com.

Palmer, Thomas C., Jr. "Building Green: Many More Developers Building Green." *Boston Globe,* 6 September 2004, p. D1.

"Profile: Japan's Construction Industry." *AsiaPulse News,* 14 October 2003.

Sarath, Patrice. "Bouygues-Company Description." *Hoover's Online,* 2009. Available from www.hoovers.com.

South Florida Business Journal. "Construction spending to keep falling." *Denver Business Journal,* 21 September 2009. Available from www.bizjournals.com/denver/.

"Turning Point for German Construction Industry Expected in 2005." *Europe Intelligence Wire,* 4 November 2003.

UK Trade and Investment Bureau. *Sector Profile: Construction.* Available from www.uktradeinvest.gov.uk.

U.S. Department of Labor, Bureau of Labor Statistics. *Career Guide to Industries,* 2005. Available from www.bls.gov.

"U.S. Real Estate and Construction Industry Overview, 2005." Plunkett Research Ltd., 2006. Available from www.plunkettresearch.com.

VINCI 2004 Financial Statements, March 2005. Available from www.vinci.com.

SIC 1520

CONSTRUCTION, RESIDENTIAL BUILDING

NAICS CODE(S)

2631. Contractors in this segment of the world's construction industry create new residential structures, including single- and multifamily dwellings, as well as additions, alterations, remodeling, and repairs to residential buildings. For details on other aspects of the construction trades, see also **Construction, Nonresidential Building** and **Engineering Services.**

INDUSTRY SNAPSHOT

While most residential buildings—whether for single families or multiple families—are constructed by local, domestic, small-scale operations, an estimated one-fifth of all construction worldwide is performed by large-scale companies. The international residential construction industry is dominated by well-funded U.S., European, and Pacific Rim (particularly Japanese) companies.

During the early years of the first decade of the 2000s, decline in the Japanese and other Asian economies hit their domestic construction markets hard. The most telling sign of the financial times was the dramatic reduction in the amount of money Japan spent on construction. While the industry was strong in the early 1990s, by 2002 the number of new building contracts had significantly declined—largely because of concerns about high vacancy rates. Analysts projected that investments in Japan's domestic construction industry would continue to decline. Nevertheless, employment in the construction industry and the number of new small construction companies entering the tough market rose due to the fact that the government spent US$550 billion on public works in the mid-1990s. The economy continued to suffer in subsequent years, however, because of this and other deficit spending.

By the mid-years of the first decade of the 2000s, the Asian housing market had started to bounce back; housing starts in Japan increased in 2006. China and India also showed growth.

In the United States, the already slowing economy took a downturn after the terrorist attacks of September 11, 2001. Many feared that this trend would take a catastrophic toll on the construction industry, since people in uncertain times generally stop looking to buy or build new homes, preferring the security of their existing housing. That the country witnessed widespread lay-offs seemed to ensure that housing projects would drop significantly. To the surprise of most industry analysts, however, residential construction proved quite resilient. In 2006, private housing starts in the United States totaled about 1.46 million units, after reaching the highest number since 1978 the year before (1.71 million). This growth, spurred by extremely low interest rates and an improving economy, reversed expectations of a market decline. According to figures reported by *Mortgage News,* the housing market—including spending from mortgage refinancing—contributed 33.8 percent of U.S. economic growth in 2003. In 2005 there were 1.6 million new housing starts, but the market slumped as expected in 2006.

Global Insight Inc. forecast that surging demand in India and China would drive global construction growth at about 5 percent through 2012. Construction in India was expected to grow at about 9.2 percent, with China close behind at about 7.9 percent. Though demand for industrial and commercial construction would initiate this growth, an influx of workers to new employment sites would stimulate demand for more residential construction. In the United States, the construction industry was expected to grow more moderately, at about 4.8 percent, while the European industry was expected to see growth of about 3.9 percent.

ORGANIZATION AND STRUCTURE

Residential construction includes single family houses, multifamily dwellings, and apartment buildings. The industry is highly fragmented: the United States and Japan combined hold approximately 1 million construction-related firms. The business also tends to be highly cyclical, reflective of changing demographic and economic factors like interest rates, property values, and the financial climate.

Residential builders are regulated in a variety of ways. Laws governing the habitats of wildlife (such as the Endangered Species Act in the United States) can impact builders, while regulations delineating criteria for energy efficiency, access for disabled persons, worker safety, and public safety also have to be taken into account. At the beginning of the new millennium, there was little concern in the industry regarding antitrust violations because none of the domestic leaders accounted for a large segment of the market activity. Although 2001 saw two notable acquisitions (Pulte bought Del Webb Corporation for US$1.8 billion, and Lennar Corporation bought U.S. Home Corporation for US$1.2 billion), there was still ample room for growth by individual companies.

In Germany, building plans for homes must conform to German industrial standards prescribing dimensions for stairways and other parts of a home. In some densely populated cities in Asia and elsewhere, however, evasion of building codes seemed almost a way of life, as owners and tenants thwarted safety plans through illegal subdivisions of apartments, obstruction of evacuation routes, and poor building maintenance.

Construction of housing, however, is a vitally important issue to virtually all countries, so most nations also support their residential construction industry through government programs and agencies. Many countries have institutions with responsibilities not unlike those of the Federal Housing Administration (FHA) in the United States. The FHA seeks to stimulate the residential home building industry by making houses more affordable through low-interest mortgages. Indeed, knowledgeable governments are aware that construction of all types accounts for increasing portions of the economic activity of developing countries.

Companies hoping to enter lucrative foreign markets typically boost their reputation and experience in three ways: by working first on public works projects, by building the overseas projects of domestic clients (particularly among Japanese companies), and by entering into joint ventures.

BACKGROUND AND DEVELOPMENT

The earliest known houses date back to 9000 B.C., although there is earlier evidence of more crude forms of shelter. Constructed of mud and reeds, these structures featured circular stone bases and conical roofs. The use of reeds as a building material ultimately led to the discovery of structural elements such as the frame, the column, the arch, and the vault. Baked mud bricks allowed greater flexibility in house design and enabled the first rectangular houses to be built in the Jordan valley around 7000 B.C. This design endured as the dominant shape for Western houses. Five thousand years later, more sophisticated dwellings featured second stories and balconies, elements designed to address the demands of urban life. The Romans introduced apartment buildings as a means of accommodating many people in a limited space; the earliest apartments were limited to five stories or less by decree and had no kitchen or bathroom facilities. These early structures demonstrated an awareness of the trade-offs between efficiency and customization.

While the principles of modularity and standardization reached their peak perhaps in the post-World War II houses of the suburban United States, the need to rebuild Europe and East Asia after that war helped turn construction into the international industry it was in the early years of the first decade of the 2000s. U.S. contractors controlled 90 percent of the global construction market by 1956. Soon, however, western European firms were able to offer similar quality at competitive prices. Japanese contractors needed to import technology, but when they did, their lower wages and increasing productivity made them keenly competitive, first domestically and then in neighboring countries. Some of the first substantial international joint venture projects for the Japanese construction industry arose from work done for the United States in Okinawa at the beginning of the Korean War. Japan eventually emerged as a significant player in the world marketplace, successfully competing with U.S. and European firms for the abundant Middle Eastern petroleum facility contracts of the 1970s despite language and geographical disadvantages. South Korea later used low bids and other practices to maneuver its way to a position of international relevance as well. Turkey, Mexico, India, and China were poised to follow on the strength of inexpensive, productive workforces.

After a period of growth in the mid- to late 1990s, the residential construction industry began slowing toward the end of the 1990s and into the first decade of the 2000s. This trend worsened considerably after the terrorist attacks against the United States on September 11, 2001. Nevertheless, the industry remained in relatively good health, and by 2003 analysts were projecting moderate global growth through 2012. Worldwide, spending on construction (including housing and other projects) reached US$3.9 trillion in 2004, according to Global Insight Inc., and residential construction grew by a projected 6.6 percent. In 2004, the US$882 billion-a-year U.S. construction industry accounted for almost 8 percent of the U.S. gross domestic product. The largest segment of this industry was in private sector residential construction, which generated more than US$453 billion worldwide in 2002.

CURRENT CONDITIONS

Despite the general economic slowdown at the beginning of the new millennium, the U.S. residential construction industry was on the rise. In 2003, U.S. Department of Housing and Urban Development figures showed that housing starts and project completions that year reached near-record levels. More than 1.78 million permits were taken out, and construction began on nearly 1.85 million new housing units. Much of this growth was attributed to very low mortgage rates. A surge of new housing starts in the United States in early 2005 again boosted construction more than expected. According to the U.S. Commerce Department, a record number of single-family dwelling starts contributed to the highest level of total housing starts since 1984. In January 2005, construction began on 2.159 million new housing units (adjusted annual rate). Single-family starts reached 1.76 million—the highest on record. Construction of multifamily housing rose to 399,000 units. Numbers rose again in February 2005, when single-family housing starts reached a record high of 1.77 million.

The year 2006 saw 1.6 million new housing starts, down 14.8 percent from 2005. According to Bernard Markstein of the National Association of Home Builders (NAHB), the downturn could be attributed to a rise in housing prices. Said Markstein, "All of a sudden, people stepped back and said, 'Wait, I can't afford this anymore,' so there was an oversupply. Then, when builders saw demand dropping off, they said, 'Wait a second, I can't afford to keep building like this.' Prices had just moved too high." The forecasting arm of NAHB, however, predicted the market would rebound.

Demographic factors influence the housing market to a great extent. Young families have traditionally been the primary buyers of new housing, and the number of newly formed families has risen significantly since the late 1980s. During the 1990s, about 12.5 million new households were started in the United States as members of "Generation X" reached adulthood. Demographers predicted that in the first decade of the 2000s, in large part because of high rates of immigration, new households will number between 13.4 and 15.4 million. Another significant factor in the growing demand for new construction is the aging of U.S. housing stock. According to the *Wall Street Journal,* the average U.S. house is about 33 years old, and about 25.8 million houses are more than 50 years old. As these dwellings wear out, many are torn down and replaced with new construction. One estimate suggested that about 7.4 million obsolete homes (about 740,000 per year) were demolished between 1985 and 1995. The U.S. Census Bureau cites a lower estimate of about 450,000 per year removed from the housing stock between 2005 and 2013.

Increased wealth in the early and middle years of the first decade of the 2000s also contributed to vigorous growth in the U.S. home construction industry. Sales of second homes, for example, increased dramatically as Baby Boomer families with the financial means sought vacation homes or investment properties. Analysts estimated that between 5 percent and 15 percent of the 2.82 million second homes sold in the United States in 2004 were newly constructed buildings.

In times of extended growth within the construction industry, increased demand typically leads to higher prices for building materials. Fortunately for contractors, however, the rapidly expanding international market and intense global competition have helped keep material prices in check; they remained relatively flat in the early years of the first decade of the 2000s. Near-record numbers of new housing starts in the United States in 2004 and 2005, however, contributed to shortages of some basic supplies, including brick, concrete (used primarily for basements), vinyl siding, and roof shingles.

One of the major trends in the residential construction industry, especially in the United States but also in western Europe, was the shift of construction activity from major urban centers to suburban and outlying areas. As businesses moved their offices out of big cities into the more serene suburban surroundings, people followed, exacerbating a move that began en masse with the proliferation of the automobile earlier in the twentieth century. In the United States, which continued to maintain a healthy amount of open space (especially in its Midwestern and Southwestern regions), this trend was expected to increase rapidly in the short term. At the same time, however, analysts also predicted a renewal of interest in urban housing, especially for new developments modeled on an "urban village" concept. Impatience with long commutes was cited as a significant factor influencing this trend. In response to growing concerns about suburban sprawl, states and municipalities changed zoning laws and created incentives for builders to site new housing near urban centers. Cambridge, Massachusetts, was one city that promoted new housing in densely built areas. Between 2004 and 2005, five major development projects were scheduled to begin in one neighborhood alone, adding a total of 4,500 new homes to a densely built section of the city. This was the largest number of new homes built in Cambridge since World War II. New York City has also seen record levels of new housing. In 2001 the city spent $US174 million on construction of new homes; in 2004 that amount rose to US$575 million.

Demand for urban lofts, townhouses, and condominiums has driven new construction and renovation projects in inner cities of the United States and Western Europe. The typical buyer of an urban loft is a young, single professional who wants to be close to work and nightlife by living very close to or right in the heart of a major city. Cities that have seen this trend include Atlanta, San Francisco, San Diego, Austin, Denver (where a hospital slated for demolition was saved to be renovated into lofts), and London. Industry experts observe that buyers are often willing to sacrifice square footage for features such as hardwood or concrete floors or granite countertops. Buyers' willingness to accept smaller units benefits builders because they are able to offer more lofts per building. New urban housing has also attracted "empty nesters," who find that the suburban homes in which they raised their families are too large for them once their children have grown up and moved away.

RESEARCH AND TECHNOLOGY

Most countries have been increasing the standardization of their building specifications. With globalization of the industry a reality, however, the issue of international standards is one that many industry analysts say needs to be addressed in the 2000s. Some important issues include building codes, which can dramatically affect costs of building (and hence, the affordability of housing) and safety regulations. In the United States, a major safety concern is the long-term health effects of mold. In 2001 the National Association of Home Builders received numerous inquiries from contractors and buyers about mold. In fact, this topic was the top-ranked subject of phone calls they received. This surge of interest in the topic forced builders to seek solutions to the problems of mold and to be proactive in addressing them.

Environmental concerns continued to impact new building projects and restorations. Not only was there an increasing desire on the part of buyers to live in environmentally friendly homes, but legislation was playing a greater role in dictating construction standards. These joint pressures kept researchers busy seeking solutions to real and potential environmental problems.

All residential building contractors—from the smallest operator to the largest international conglomerate—take note of technical innovations in construction. Industry analysts expect that increasing numbers of future homes will feature solar power and accommodations designed to meet the needs of older people, a population segment that grows each year.

In the late 1990s and early years of the first decade of the 2000s, the desire for customized houses was balanced with the need to reduce costs through standardization and universalizing of mass-produced modular elements. The support/infill concept, first developed in the Netherlands and later in Japan, epitomized this approach. This process allows customization decisions to be made later in the construction process, facilitating input from homeowners and allowing property managers to match market conditions more accurately.

Nontraditional materials were used with increasing frequency in the late 1990s and the early years of the first decade of the 2000s. Soaring wood prices made coldformed steel, which offers relatively stable prices but has not traditionally played a major role in the residential construction industry, an attractive alternative. Observers note that the transformation need not be dramatic; specifications and standards used for wood-frame building can be modified for steel-frame building without completely overhauling the guidelines. In addition, plastics manufacturers demonstrated that their recyclable products could be used as an energy-efficient alternative for roofing, window, siding, plumbing, and foundation construction, while fiber-cement proved a durable and efficient moisture-resistant material for siding and roofing in humid climates. Other structural materials were researched or improved, including engineered wood, laminated fiberboard, foam-core materials, and high-strength concrete.

The National Association of Home Builders reported an increase in demand for "green" buildings, which are energy-efficient in design and construction. Green buildings are often built using as many recycled and environmentally friendly materials as possible. Environmental conditions within and around houses—"green" or otherwise—receive the careful scrutiny of some architects. Environmentally conscious designs typically strive to maximize the positive effects of sunlight and good ventilation in a dwelling while minimizing energy costs through heavy insulation and the careful design of windows. The building materials themselves, as well as appliances, are also examined for possible toxic ingredients or emissions. In 2001, a study cited by the City of Seattle's Department of Planning and Development indicated that 96 percent of homebuyers would be willing to pay extra for "green" construction. Some 80 percent stated that they would not want old-growth lumber used in their homes, and more than 60 percent indicated a preference for sustainable harvested lumber.

Home buyers in the United States were becoming more technologically savvy in the early years of the first decade of the 2000s. It was common in upscale homes for an entertainment room to include cinema-style seats and a projection television system for viewing television and movies. These rooms are built to resemble movie theaters, complete with state-of-the-art sound and video systems. The growing demand for technology at home also feeds the market for "smart" housing. In these homes, owners can control lighting, security systems, heating and air conditioning, lawn watering, and appliances with a keyboard or remote control.

Another trend that demonstrates the ways in which people hope to get more out of their homes is the emergence of health-related housing features. In *The Futurist,* Battelle, a nonprofit technology research center, projected significant advances in the following areas by 2010: air quality, water quality, home power generators, and home security.

Earthquake and vibration control are other areas of enduring interest to building contractors. In Japan, which was victimized by the Kobe earthquake in the mid-1990s, visionaries sought to pioneer new horizons for the industry. Japan's heavily populated urban centers also contributed to that country's research efforts. In order to meet the housing needs of the world's increasing population, Japan's Ministry of Construction proposed the "hyper building" concept: structures 1,000 meters tall designed to last 1,000 years. Such buildings would fill their million square feet of space with both residences and offices. In the United States, contractors witnessed an increase in demand for "safe rooms" in residences. Such a room is reinforced with steel, has no windows, is centrally located in the floor plan, stores emergency provisions, and has a back-up power supply. The purpose of these rooms is to provide refuge in the event of an earthquake or other natural disaster.

WORKFORCE

Construction is one of the most labor-intensive industries in the world. In the United States alone, 7 million wage and salary earners and about 1.9 million self-employed people worked in construction in 2004. These numbers were expected to grow, with analysts predicting about 7.7 million wage-earners in construction by 2012. Construction is also a relatively high-paying industry in the United States, where wages increased faster than the average for other industries overall. In 2004, U.S. workers earned an average of US$19.23 per hour. In Germany, construction workers make almost US$20 per hour. In Italy unskilled laborers make US$13.68 per hour, and skilled laborers make US$15 per hour. In Japan a bricklayer earns US$150.76 in an eight-hour day, a carpenter makes US$161.28 per day, and a plumber makes US$137.81 per day. Other nations like Korea and Thailand do not provide such wages.

While compensation to employees in the construction industry was relatively high in the United States and other advanced economies, shortages of labor—particularly skilled labor—persisted, especially in developed countries. Health insurance coverage also added dramatically to labor costs, as did worker's compensation insurance in an industry that can be quite dangerous. In 2002, the U.S. construction industry had 1,121 work-related fatalities—more than any other industry; about 38,000 injuries were reported among workers in residential construction. Though construction work accounted for 20 percent of all work-related deaths, the industry ranked far below mining, agriculture, forestry, and trucking in the percentage of its total workforce (12.2) who were fatally injured on the job.

Labor shortages and discrepancies in wages have encouraged some contractors to import workers. In some areas, labor contractors pay illegal aliens much less than the going rate. Public outcry about hiring illegal aliens stems from two main objections: first, this practice takes jobs from legal workers, and second, illegal aliens are paid in cash and therefore pay no income tax on their earnings.

In the mid-years of the first decade of the 2000s, there were legal initiatives in place to address the labor shortage. Programs were available that offer training to individuals with few job prospects. These provide them with the skills necessary to enter a trade, while addressing the labor shortage in the industry. One such program is the Home Builders Institute's Project CRAFT (Community Restitution and Apprenticeship Focused Training), which trains juvenile offenders. This training provides a means of

rehabilitation for those who want it, and their entry into the job market addresses labor issues in the housing industry.

INDUSTRY LEADERS

Shimizu Corp. Shimizu Corporation of Tokyo has consistently won the industry's informal "triple crown"—work completed, new orders received, and profit. The company, which originated in the nineteenth century, was incorporated as Shimizu Gumi in 1915. It is involved in a wide range of engineering and construction projects, including both commercial and residential buildings. By the late 1990s it had become established as a global competitor with 15,300 employees, but by 2004 that number had dropped to 11,680. Of these, some 2,500 were licensed architects and 1,800 were licensed civil engineers. In 2008 Shimizu reported total sales of US$16.9 billion. With fewer contracts for extensive new domestic projects coming in, the company planned to increase its share of projects that involved remodeling existing buildings.

In the mid-years of the first decade of the 2000s, Shimizu completed major residential and nonresidential projects in Japan. Its chief overseas projects, however—including buildings in China, Indonesia, and the United States—were industrial and commercial buildings. Major projects have included the Tokyo Dome Hotel and the Paske Bridge in Laos.

Like its competitors, the company supports a variety of research interests. Shimizu was a proponent of support/infill projects. It also developed a computer-aided design system (operable in either Japanese or English) that allowed architects to cut design time 40 percent on some projects. Elaborate intelligent building systems that offer special amenities such as programmable aroma control (including lemon, nutmeg, and peppermint) were another specialty.

Taisei Corp. Taisei Corp. originated in the construction company Okuragumi Shokai, which was founded by Kibachiro Okura in 1873. Okura was a businessman, not a builder. He started a trading company, a leather and shoe factory, a brewery, a hotel, and many other enterprises. Okuragumi Shokai completed Japan's first railway station and became known as Taisei in 1946, after its shares were distributed to employees. Taisei's core business was construction, especially residential housing, but it was also highly active in civil engineering and real estate development. Based in Tokyo, Taisei maintained offices in the United States, Peru, England, Saudi Arabia, Turkey, and West Africa. The company was especially active in South and East Asia, where it had offices in China, Vietnam, Cambodia, India, Kuala Lumpur, Singapore, Myanmar, Thailand, Indonesia, Korea, India, and Pakistan. Although it remained one of Japan's top four construction companies, Taisei was forced to downsize some of its operations in the early years of the first decade of the 2000s because of difficult market conditions in Japan. By 2004 it had reduced its workforce to about 9,700 employees. Total sales in 2005 exceeded US$15.8 billion. For 2008, sales surpassed US $17.2 billion.

Obayashi Corp. Obayashi Corporation (formerly Ohbayashi) was founded by Yoshigoro Obayashi in 1892. The company's largest early projects were associated with the development of Osaka Harbor. In 1918, two of its engineers were sent to the United States to be trained by the Fluor Corporation in advanced construction techniques. After completing a Cambodian agricultural center, its first project outside Japan, the company revisited the United States in the 1960s to build a variety of civil works and residential projects. Obayashi also established itself as a builder of tunnels and dams; it constructed the world's largest suspension bridge over the Akashi Straits in Japan. The highly diversified company, which employed 13,377 people in 2004, also had interests in real estate, finance, and furniture manufacturing. Although 95 percent of its revenue came from construction operations in 2003, Obayashi expanded its operations into environmental services in response to the slowdown of Japan's construction industry in the early years of the twenty-first century's first decade. In 2005, the company posted total sales of US$13.0 billion. By 2006, it had 9,474 employees. The total sales for 2008 was US $17 billion.

Kumagai Gumi Co. Ltd. Kumagai Gumi Co. Ltd. was incorporated in 1938. Santoro Kumagai, the company's founder, began his construction career as a stonemason, crafting religious monuments and performing work for the expanding railway system. The company eventually became known for its ability to handle risky projects. It created additional markets through its build-own-transfer strategy, a means of privatizing the development of public works projects. Like its peers, the company has been active on a variety of civil engineering projects such as dams, tunnels, and highways. Kumagai also built a major Buddhist temple and a unique 3,300-unit housing project in Japan. The company has been particularly successful in Hong Kong and has landed substantial residential contracts in China. Kumagai's sales in 2008 totaled US$3 billion.

Since the 1990s, however, when Japan's real estate market dramatically weakened, Kumagai has experienced financial difficulties. In the early years of the first decade of the 2000s the company negotiated an unprecedented debt waiver—about 430 billion yen was forgiven by bank creditors—in order to stay afloat. It also abandoned its

announced merger with Tobishima Corporation, scheduled for early 2005.

D.R. Horton Inc. In fiscal 2005, D.R. Horton sold more than 51,000 homes in the United States. Most of its buildings are single-family homes aimed at first-time buyers, but it also constructs luxury-level dwellings. Horton, which bought Hawaii-based contractor Schuler Homes in 2001, has operations in 25 states. In 2008 total sales exceeded US$6.6 billion, on the strength of almost 3,800 employees.

Pulte Homes Inc. In 2006 Pulte Homes was one of the top four home builders (by number of units) in the United States. Pulte greatly expanded its business when it bought retirement community builder Del Webb in 2001, making the new company the largest residential construction firm in the country at that time. Pulte offers single-family homes, duplexes, townhomes, and condominiums at prices ranging from US$62,000 to more than US$3 million. A U.S. company, Pulte sells most of its residences in the western and eastern parts of the country, and also markets homes in Mexico and Argentina. In 2006 Pulte employed 13,400 people and earned revenues of US$14.27 billion.

Uniting to add up to 120 combined years of home building experience, Pulte Homes and Centex decided to merge in 2009. Shareholders of both companies overwhelmingly approved the merger. In a telephone press conference, Pulte CEO Richard Dugas said that the new company forms "America's largest and best positioned homebuilder." For the 2008 calendar year, Pulte and Centex had more than 39,000 closings and combined pro forma revenues of US $11.6 billion. Impacted brands included Fox & Jacobs Homes, Centex Homes, Pulte Homes, DiVosta Homes and Del Webb. Those brands received mention in the J.D. Power & Associates 2009 NewHome Builder Satisfaction Survey. In fact, Pulte Homes brands earned more top rankings than any other home builder.

Lennar. Lennar is one of the largest residential construction companies in the United States. In the early years of the first decade of the 2000s, it built more than 36,000 homes each year, including units in retirement communities, and also offers financial services associated with buying a home. In 2008, the company employed about 4,704 people and saw total sales of US$4.6 billion.

Centex Corp. Centex Corporation, among the largest construction companies in the United States, has made its Centrex Homes business one of the country's top residential builders. Centrex Homes, which operates in the United States and Britain, built about 49,000 homes in 2005. Centex Corporation, which is also involved with commercial contracting, mortgage banking, and commercial real estate, employed 13,867 people in 2006 and earned total revenues of US$16.26 billion.

MAJOR COUNTRIES IN THE INDUSTRY

Japan. Japan has historically been a leader in the global construction market. After years of dominating the world construction marketplace, Japan finally opened its markets to foreign contractors in the late 1980s under intense political pressure from the United States. The South Koreans proved most adept at penetrating this market initially, usually through joint ventures. Nevertheless, Japanese contractors experienced their biggest boom since the early 1970s, earning ¥750 billion (US$6 billion) a year on overseas contracts alone. An economic downturn in the late 1990s, however, took its toll on the Japanese construction industry. Government spending for public sector projects fell off, and as a result, new contracts among the country's top building companies declined by an average of 8.8 percent between 2001 and 2002. According to *AsiaPulse News,* some 5,863 Japanese construction companies went bankrupt in 2002—the third consecutive year in which more than 5,000 such companies failed. According to Japanese government figures, total investment in construction dropped 35.9 percent from 1992 to 2003. In 2004 the market rebounded somewhat; housing contracts were up 7 percent from the previous year.

In response to such market challenges, several top construction firms restructured, scaled back their labor force, or expanded into related services such as waste management. Another strategy was to focus on large urban renewal projects built around new technologies such as access to broadband communications. As a result, major construction firms weathered Japan's economic downturn relatively well. In 2003 the construction sector accounted for about 10.7 percent of the country's gross domestic product and employed about 10 percent of the Japanese workforce. By 2003, the picture had improved slightly for residential construction. That year, building started on 1.17 million new homes—the first increase in four years.

The top Japanese construction firms tend to be quite large compared to their counterparts in the United States, with extensive research and development investment. Japanese contractors have experienced greater success in the United States than U.S. firms have enjoyed in Japan. U.S. companies have battled to counter the perception in Japan that Americans are competitive in management and design but weak in the "dangerous and dirty" business of actual construction.

Russia. Russia is another major region in the global residential construction industry. However, the vast demand for housing has been hampered by shortages of materials, infrastructure problems, and lack of accessible financing. Although cooperative housing was a priority, it accounted for only a fraction of new building space commissioned.

Between 1930 and the breakup of the Soviet Union, Soviet engineers gained enough experience at home to export it to the world market. Although proven Soviet technologies were usually supplied, at times new designs were also offered. Like their Japanese counterparts, the Soviets often used a turnkey strategy, subcontracting project management to Finnish and Austrian companies and basic construction to local companies in the client country. Even during the cold war, however, the Soviets turned to Western companies to supply technology and equipment for more complex ventures.

Housing remained in relatively short supply in Russia in the early years of the first decade of the 2000s, and the government announced plans to increase residential units from 36 million in 2004 to 80 million by 2010. Shortage of housing in Moscow and St. Petersburg fueled residential construction growth of about 7.2 percent between 2003 and 2004. Yet the price of new housing built between 2000 and 2004 more than doubled, contributing to a slowdown in sales. To remain competitive with Western companies and to meet demand for new housing, Russian construction firms have expanded holdings so that they control companies that produce building materials, thus reducing costs. They have also added real estate financing to their services.

United States. In the United States, low interest rates and relatively poor returns on other investments boosted the market for residential real estate in the early years of the first decade of the 2000s. An increase in sales of second homes, for either vacation or investment purposes, contributed to high demand for residential construction. In 2005, nearly 2.16 million houses were started across the country. Single-family housing starts totaled about 1.76 million units. While domestic contracts were essential to residential contractors in the United States, U.S. contractors and their foreign subsidiaries also had a substantial share of international construction contracts.

Unlike Japan, the U.S. construction industry has a relatively high number of self-employed workers. In 2002, the country had about 792,000 construction companies, of which 237,000 were building contractors. The vast majority of these firms were small operations employing fewer than 10 workers. According to the U.S. Bureau of Labor Statistics, about 80 percent of construction workers in the United States are employed by companies of this size. However, industry analysts, such as Carl E. Reichardt of Banc of

America Securities, predicted that there would be more domestic mergers in the future of the industry. He estimated that there were 80,000 home builders in the United States and that the top 20 captured 30 percent of the business. These numbers are important because they indicate that the industry still has plenty of opportunity for consolidation before running into antitrust issues.

China. China experienced a boom in construction in the 1980s and 1990s, much to the benefit of developers in Hong Kong. The Chinese government sought to control this development—and accompanying inflation—by cutting down demand for materials and transportation. Thousands of projects, including some residential blocks, were suspended by the government in 1988 and 1989. This action cost hundreds of thousands of construction workers their jobs. The residential housing sector, however, was largely spared from these cutbacks because of the severe shortage of housing. The building boom in China also put a strain on the country's energy resources. Coal rationing resulted in many partially heated buildings. While such rationing conserved resources somewhat, it also undercut the energy-efficient designs of the buildings and boilers.

China's 28,000 construction companies have built millions of homes each year for the past 20 years. Demand for housing remained particularly high in cities, where populations skyrocketed due to an influx of workers from rural areas. According to *China Daily,* the number of homes sold in many Chinese cities exceeded the amount being built, and prices soared as a result. By 2003, the average urban Chinese resident spent 16.7 percent of his or her salary on housing, compared to 13.65 percent in the United States. Some analysts warned that greater government regulation would be necessary to curb prices and prevent a future glut in new home construction.

Europe. Europe's housing construction industry varies by country. The relatively low percentage of home ownership in Germany, for example, can be attributed in part to German culture. Families in that country commonly buy only one house in a lifetime; as a result, homes are often of elaborate construction and thus quite expensive. In Italy children tend to live in their parents' homes well into adulthood. In addition, industry analysts have noted that, for the sake of the European Monetary Union (EMU), some fiscal measures will have to be applied that will negatively affect the residential construction industry in the long run but that are not expected to have a lasting effect. Overall, Europe's construction market is characterized as very mature, making substantial growth unlikely. High real estate costs (which often account for 50 percent of residential housing costs) and construction expenses, however, have slowed any improvement in the situation.

An economic slowdown in the early years of the first decade of the 2000s contributed to a flat performance for the European construction industry in 2003. According to Global Insight Inc., however, Europe was expected to see construction growth averaging about 3.9 percent through 2012.

BIBLIOGRAPHY
"2007 Construction Activity Expected to Wane." *Bulk Transporter,* 26 March 2007.

Barnett, Megan. "Is It Boom Or Bust?" *U.S. News & World Report,* 5 September 2005.

Clark, Kim. "Construction," *U.S. News & World Report,* 21 March 2005.

Diesenhouse, Susan. "East Cambridge, Boomtown to Be." *Boston Globe,* 19 September 2004.

"Emerging Trends in Real Estate 2005." *Buildings,* January 2005.

"The Expert 400: Construction." *Gateway to Russia,* 2 December 2004. Available from www.gateway2russia.com.

Ford, Constance Mitchell. "What's Behind Hot Home Building Pace?" *Wall Street Journal,* 21 March 2005, p. 2.

Heavens, Alan J. "Builders' Blues," *Philadelphia Inquirer,* 27 March 2005.

"Hoover's Company Capsules." *Hoover's Online,* 2007. Available from www.hoovers.com.

"Housing Construction Reaches 21-Year High." *New York Times,* 17 February 2005.

"Housing: Where The Market Is Really Headed." *Business Week,* 10 July 2006.

"Housing: Will Surging Supply Pop The Bubble?" *Business Week,* 6 February 2006.

Japanese Ministry of Internal Affairs and Communications, Statistics Bureau. *Japan Statistical Yearbook,* 2006. Available from www.stat.go.jp/English.

"Kumagai Gumi, Tobishima Scrap Planned Merger." *Japan Times,* 16 November 2004.

"Major Trends Affecting the Real Estate & Construction Industry." Plunkett Research, 2004. Available from www.plunkettresearch.com.

"New Study Forecasts Improving Outlook for Global Construction Industry." Global Insight Inc., 9 June 2003. Available from www.globalinsight.com.

Nicholson, Jonathan. "U.S. Housing Starts Post Unexpected Rise in December." *Mortgage News,* 21 January 2004. Available from www.homebundmortgage.com.

"Overseas Investors Eye China's Housing Market." *AsiaPulse News,* 25 August 2003.

"Profile—Japan's Construction Industry." *AsiaPulse News,* 14 October 2003.

"Pulte and Centex Merge." P 18 August 2009. Available from premierbuilderusa.com.

Sigmund, Pete. "Road, Bridge Work to Sustain Industry in '07." *Construction Equipment Guide,* 11 December 2006.

Sleight, Chris. "Construction Europe." *KHL News,* 10 August 2004. Available from www.khl.com.

Strong Market Expected to Remain for Near Future." *TTJ: The Timber Industry Magazine,* 17 February 2007.

"Taylor Wimpey: Europe's Largest House Builder." *Construction Europe,* 26 March 2007.

Tulacz, Gary J. "World Construction Spending Nears $4 Trillion for 2004." *Engineering News Record*, January 3-10, 2005. Available from www.enr.com.

U.S. Department of the Census. *New Privately Owned Housing Units Authorized Unadjusted Units for Regions, Divisions, and States*, February 2005. Available from www.census.gov/.

U.S. Department of Commerce. *Building Projects and Construction.* International Trade Administration, 3 April 2007. Available from www.ita.dot.gov.

U.S. Department of Housing and Urban Development, Office of Policy Development and Research. *U.S. Housing Market Conditions Summary*, February 2004. Available from www.huduser.org.

U.S. Department of Labor, Bureau of Labor Statistics. *Career Guide to Industries.* 20 December 2005. Available from www.bls.gov.

———. *Fatal Occupational Injuries and Employment by Industry*, 2004. Available from www.bls.gov.

U.S. Housing Market Conditions, Fourth Quarter 2006. Washington, D.C.: HUD USER, February 2007. Available from www.huduser.org.

"U.S. Real Estate and Construction Industry Overview, 2005." Houston, Tex.: Plunkett Research Ltd., 2006. Available from www.plunkettresearch.com.

Zhongli, Yin, and Guo Jianbo, "House Market Needs Regulation." *China Daily*, 1 April 2005. Available from www.chinadaily.com.cn/English.

SIC 2411

LOGGING

NAICS CODE(S)

113310. The world's logging industry cuts timber to produce rough, round, or hewn wood for use as building materials, fuel, paper, and numerous other purposes. The logging industry is closely allied with forest management. For more extensive treatment of this topic, see **Forestry.**

INDUSTRY SNAPSHOT

In the early twenty-first century, industrial logging was taking place in virtually every major forested region in the world, including both temperate and tropical regions. Logging includes the harvesting of both coniferous trees, such as pine and spruce—called softwood—and deciduous trees, such as eucalyptus, maple, and oak—called hardwood. The United States led the world in total removals of industrial roundwood from forestland, with annual harvests of hardwood and softwood timber reaching 467 million cubic meters in 2003. This amount, however, represented a decrease from the 500 million cubic meters harvested in 2000. According to the U.S. Department of Agriculture Forest Service, approximately

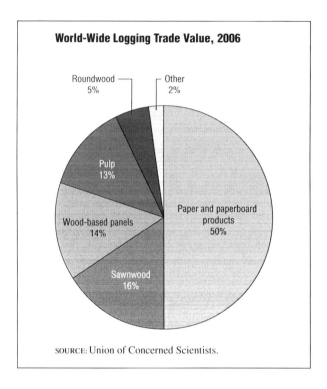

World-Wide Logging Trade Value, 2006

Roundwood 5%
Other 2%
Pulp 13%
Wood-based panels 14%
Sawnwood 16%
Paper and paperboard products 50%

SOURCE: Union of Concerned Scientists.

88 million cubic meters of lumber and 25 million cubic meters of structural panel product were produced in 2002. In 2006, the world total for all wood products imports was valued at US$159.6 billion.

Industrial wood in the rough consists of four elements: sawlogs, used to make lumber; veneer logs; pulpwood, used to make pulp for papermaking and wood-based panels; and other industrial wood. Removals of industrial wood in the rough from Western Europe, Eastern Europe, and the Nordic countries combined reached 434.5 million cubic meters in 2000. Removals of industrial roundwood totaled 399.1 million cubic meters in 2001, rising to 413.6 million cubic meters in 2002 and 488.3 million cubic meters in 2003. The Asia-Pacific region showed removals of 107.1 million cubic meters in 2000, due primarily to production declines in Asia. In 2003, developing nations in Asia harvested some 206 million cubic meters of industrial roundwood. Removals from the former Soviet Union rose steadily in the late 1990s and 2000s. About 95 million cubic meters were harvested in 1998, and some 143.6 million in 1999, an increase of more than 50 percent. Removals rose 10 percent in 2000, to 158.1 million cubic meters. Removals in 2001 were 164.7 million cubic meters, and in 2002 were 174.2 million cubic meters.

Some experts predicted a global shortage of wood production in the twenty-first century, particularly in softwoods. Total global production of industrial roundwood (industrial wood in the rough plus fuelwood, which is burned for heat and cooking) from softwoods was 935 million cubic meters in 1992. By 2010, soft-wood demand was expected to reach 1.14 billion cubic meters, a net increase of 10 percent over the period.

Most projections for softwood roundwood supply do not come close to matching anticipated demand. For example, annual softwood roundwood supply from the U.S. Pacific Northwest had been expected to drop 60 million cubic meters between 1992 and 2010, with an additional 10 million cubic meter decline from British Columbia. Government-imposed harvesting restrictions on public land in these regions were causing the declines. Over the same period, supply increases were expected from Eastern Europe (85 million cubic meters), fast-growing plantations in several countries (65 million cubic meters), Scandinavia and Western Europe (20 million cubic meters), and the U.S. South and the rest of Canada (10 million cubic meters). After factoring in the declines from other regions, these production increases were expected to produce a net increase in softwood supply of 110 million cubic meters by 2010, leaving softwood roundwood supply 95 million cubic meters short of the anticipated demand.

However, the global economy, particularly the North American economy, experienced a slowdown in the industry throughout the first decade of the twenty-first century. Forest product markets reached record highs in 2000, but declined in 2001. In addition, roundwood was in oversupply in Europe during 2000 following severe windstorms, which felled some 200 million cubic meters of timber. Wind-throw damages in Estonia in July 2001 drew attention to the fact that storm damage poses a permanent risk for roundwood markets and that practices may need to be modified to mitigate future storm damage.

The hardwood situation was not as critical as softwood, but hardwood supply was also expected to lag demand. World production of industrial hardwood roundwood was 440 million cubic meters in 1992. North America produced 36.6 million cubic meters and consumed 38.3 million cubic meters of sawn hardwood in 2000. By 2010, hardwood demand was expected to reach 550 million cubic meters, an increase of 110 million cubic meters. Under a realistic market forecast, several regions might produce hardwood roundwood increases totaling 55 million cubic meters annually by 2010. Fast-growing hardwood plantations were likely to contribute another 50 million cubic meters. However, hardwood production in Malaysia and Indonesia was expected to drop 45 million cubic meters by 2010, producing a net hardwood roundwood supply gain for the global market of just 60 million cubic meters, which would theoretically create a supply deficit of 50 million cubic meters by 2010.

The economic performance of the Asia-Pacific region was considered a critical factor in the industry's supply/demand outlook. The region was a net importer of fiber, and as the pulp and paper industry developed in such countries as Indonesia and Malaysia, those imports increased. Japan alone accounted for two-thirds of the world's total imports of woodchips by 2003.

China was a rapidly expanding market in the early twenty-first century, with retail lumber sales up by more than 10 percent in 2001. Total imports of roundwood in 2002 reached 16 million cubic meters, 11 times the amount imported in 1997. China imported 5.4 million cubic meters of sawnwood in 2002, up 33.5 percent from the previous year, and also imported 22 million cubic meters of roundwood. In 1998, China declared a 10-year logging moratorium after a series of massive floods exacerbated destructive logging practices throughout the region in previous decades. The increasing demand for lumber has led to illegal logging and deforestation in countries like Brazil. The growth of the logging industry in China has created stiff competition between the logging industry and the agricultural industry. Fueled by rising incomes and substantial investments in the housing sector, China's market for wood products is expected to continue sustained growth levels through the early twenty-first century. By 2010, China's demand for timber was expected to rise to 200 million cubic meters, of which half probably would be imported. China has approximately 1.65 million hectares of eucalyptus trees to sustain their logging industry. Many large international companies are moving into the region to take advantage of the bounty.

The ongoing depression of the Russian forest products industry was one of the major issues in world logging in the first decade of the twenty-first century. Harvesting of logs dropped dramatically as a result of the economic contraction in the Russian Federation and other former Soviet states. Environmental problems, organizational problems, lack of funds for infrastructure investments, and social and management problems contributed to disappointing results. In Russia, total removals of wood in the rough were 66.5 million cubic meters in 1996, far below levels in the 1980s. Despite these difficulties, Russia remained a major exporter of raw logs through the early 2000s. Exports, which were 20.9 million cubic meters in 1998, rose to 28.2 million the following year. Industrial wood exports reached 32 million cubic meters in 2000, 32.8 million in 2001, and 37.4 million in 2002. Although analysts predicted a gloomy future for the Russian logging industry through the first decade of the 2000s, Russian removal rates exploded in 1999, growing by 50 percent in one year. Harvests in Ukraine and Belarus also increased, bringing the total removals for the Commonwealth of Independent States (including Russia) from 109.7 million cubic meters in 1998 to more than 191.9 million cubic meters in 2002. During this period, Russian exports to Pacific Rim nations increased. By 2005, timber exports to China had increased about 31 times in volume, from 0.53 million cubic meters in 1996 to 17.02 million cubic meters in 2004. The average increase was more than 50 percent annually. In 2004, Russia exported 10.16 million cubic meters of sawn softwood, 10.2 million cubic meters of softwood logs, and 25.5 million metric tons of pulpwood. Exports for 2005 were projected at 11.6 million cubic meters of sawn softwood, 8.1 million cubic meters of softwood logs, and 25.6 million metric tons of pulpwood.

Several major controversies have engulfed the world logging industry. Global disputes included protests over the cutting of tropical timber in the Pacific Rim; federal court bans on harvesting from government-owned timberland in the northwest United States; boycotts of wood, pulp, and paper products from British Columbia; and protests over the cutting of forests in Chile. Throughout the early to mid-2000s, controversy continued, as did ongoing litigation in the courts of individual countries.

Problems also surfaced in the relatively new logging areas of the Pacific Rim and Latin America. Most of the growing stock in tropical hardwood forests either has low productive potential or is commercially inaccessible. Over-cutting of native Asia-Pacific forests without proper reforestation has greatly reduced the timber available for harvest. Environmental pressures to limit harvesting in Latin American tropical forests have been effective in reducing harvest levels there as well.

ORGANIZATION AND STRUCTURE

Companies of various sizes were involved in the logging industry. Large, integrated forest products firms, such as Georgia-Pacific in the United States and Stora in Europe, own large private timberland tracts and hold cutting rights on government forests, while small independent logging crews do much of the cutting for major companies. Large forest products companies often send their logs to company-owned sawmills, but small one-unit sawmills still survive in some countries. In less developed nations, thousands of individuals cut timber for use as firewood.

Most industrial logging is carried out according to complicated management plans established by the owners of the land. Owners of forests could be national, state, or provincial governments, forest product companies, or private landowners. Regulation of harvesting yields and methods vary widely from country to country, although in the early years of the twenty-first century it was generally accepted that replanting and management of cut stands was vital to sustainable forestry. A substantial share of logging is carried out by large forest products companies, although by the early 2000s many contracted more of the actual logging out to small, independent companies or to individual contractors. For example, most logging of pulpwood in the

southeast United States, which had been done by pulp and paper companies, was being subcontracted.

Individual forest management plans determine the yearly yield and the method of removing timber from forested land. Harvesting methods included clear-cutting all trees from large areas or selective cutting of individual trees or groups of trees. Much of the controversy over industrial forestry focused on the practice of clear-cutting, which involves cutting down all trees in a region. Loggers argued that it was, by far, the most efficient means of harvesting timber and was environmentally sustainable. Selective cutting, they claimed, was too expensive in some areas and would not necessarily lead to optimal growing conditions for new trees since the remaining large trees screened out much of the light that new trees needed to survive and grow. Environmental groups, however, lobbied heavily against clear-cutting. They alleged that clear-cutting and deforestation damaged an area's ecosystem and its biodiversity leading to the destruction of natural habitats and accelerating climate change.

As of 2010, clear-cutting had not been banned in major forest-producing countries. Nevertheless, logging companies began to use more selective cutting. They were also more careful in their selection of sites for clear-cutting, leaving "buffer zones" around rivers and lakes to prevent soil runoff; avoiding cutting near roads, centers of population and scenic areas; and using sophisticated computer models to select cuts that caused the least aesthetic and environmental disruption.

International Timber Trade. In the late 1990s and early 2000s, there was significant international trade in logs, although trading volume varied considerably in response to changing economic conditions. In a 2006 report by the Union of Concerned Scientists, 50 percent of the trade value of world-wide logging is in paper and paperboard products, 16 percent is in sawnwood, 14 percent is in wood-based panels, 13 percent is pulp for paper and recovered paper, 5 percent is roundwood, and 2 percent is other products. Europe exported 9.29 million cubic meters of softwood and hardwood logs (used for making lumber) in 1996 and imported 17.5 million cubic meters, while the United States exported 12.5 million cubic meters and imported 3.4 million cubic meters. There was also substantial international trade in pulpwood (used for making paper and some wood products). Europe exported 14.7 million cubic meters of pulpwood in 1996 while importing 28.8 million cubic meters. According to statistics from the European Commission, the market for pulpwood in Europe peaked in late 2000, but production and consumption had risen substantially by 2004. The United States, on the other hand, reported significant declines in production and exports of pulpwood and pulp products. Production of pulpwood was 193 million cubic meters in 2001, a 5.4

percent decrease from the previous year, with an additional decline of 1.4 percent in 2002, reaching 191 million cubic meters. Exports of paper and pulpwood products, which fell by 8 percent in 2001, increased by 0.5 percent in 2002. According to the U.S. Department of Agriculture Forest Service, the pulpwood market in the early 2000s was hit with its steepest declines since the 1970s. By 2002, industry earnings were down by approximately 50 percent from 2000 levels. The total for all wood products imports was US$159.6 billion in 2006. China and Japan imported the most roundwood, while the European Union and Canada imported the most veneer. Imports of Brazilian products are primarily wood pulp in the European Union and the United States.

The Asia-Pacific region, once a major exporter of logs, saw its export volume collapse in the mid-1990s. Asia-Pacific exports of tropical timber plunged from 21.3 million cubic meters in 1992 to 9.4 million cubic meters in 1996, 8.5 million cubic meters in 1997, and 7.9 million cubic meters in 1998. Exports grew moderately through the early 2000s, reaching 8.6 million cubic meters in 2003. Africa exported a substantial amount of tropical logs through the late 1990s with exports of industrial roundwood topping 5.3 million cubic meters in 1996 and 6 million cubic meters in 2000. Shipments fell to 4.2 million cubic meters in 2003. Almost all of Africa's timber comes from sub-Saharan countries.

Another factor affecting the international tropical timber trade was rapid economic growth in many Southeast Asian countries. This expansion produced an intense boom in residential, office, and industrial building construction. The net result of this activity was that more timber stayed in the country of origin. As a result, traditional importers of tropical timber began to buy from other sources. For example, Japan, the world's largest importer of tropical logs, replaced much of its import volume from the Pacific Rim with logs from Latin America and Africa. Japan also began substituting temperate, coniferous timber for applications that had traditionally used tropical wood, such as concrete forming.

North America, with its vast forestland, has long been a major producer, user, and exporter of logs. For many years, logging, lumber, and paper production were the dominant industries in areas such as the U.S. Pacific Northwest and British Columbia, Canada. However, growing demand for timber and environmental restrictions changed that situation. In the United States, controversy developed regarding the shipment of U.S. logs overseas. U.S. logging in the Pacific Northwest was cut dramatically in the 1990s, mainly due to environmental restrictions, and exports of U.S. roundwood fell sharply as well.

The Harvesting Process. Actual harvesting of logs consists of several processes, including felling (cutting), bucking (cross-cutting into logs), limbing, debarking, skidding (removing the logs from the cut site), and transporting logs to various industries. Felling is done by large machines, such as feller/bunchers, or manually, with large chain saws. Larger trees destined for the sawmill to be made into lumber are usually cut by chain saws. Smaller pulpwood trees that are used to make wood pulp are typically cut mechanically with such devices as the combine harvester, which shears trees off at the base. Another device, the feller/buncher, cuts and holds a group of trees together, then deposits the load onto a log truck.

Where possible, logs are loaded directly onto large log trucks. When necessary, logs are skidded to another site by tractors and steel cables or, in some countries, by animals. In rare cases, logs are removed with helicopters. After World War II, logging gradually became more mechanized, but areas existed where limited yields or difficult topography made the use of machinery too expensive or problematic. In these cases, human and animal labor were still used.

BACKGROUND AND DEVELOPMENT

Wood and logging have played a crucial role in the evolution of human civilization. Wood has been used for everything from providing heat and building carts and sailing vessels to creating housing, windmills, and mineshafts, as well as countless other applications. Plato wrote that all arts and crafts are derived from mining and forestry. Pioneer societies in many places of the world depended almost entirely on wood.

Civilizations have also tended to misuse wood resources, overcutting or burning large forest tracts and causing severe environmental consequences. The industrial revolution worsened deforestation in Europe and North America, and between 1800 and 1920, many of the great forests in those regions were completely cleared. However, modern forestry and logging methods were introduced in the 1930s and 1940s, accompanied by extensive reforestation in many countries. In general, total forest cover was maintained or increased after World War II in North America, Europe, and other major logging countries. However, deforestation continued to be a problem in less developed regions, such as Africa, South America, and Southeast Asia.

The global logging industry follows the boom and bust cycle of its principal customers, the lumber industry and the pulp and paper industry. Typically, as the housing market recovers after a recession, demand for lumber jumps and logging increases. The same is true of pulp and paper, where a more robust economy means increased demand for paper, which leads to the construction of large pulp and paper mills and the need for more pulpwood.

In the 1990s, however, this equation was altered by increased environmental restrictions on logging and increased production of recycled paper. Bans on logging in the Pacific Northwest and slowdowns in cutting in British Columbia, for example, depressed the logging industries there, put many loggers out of work, and drove up prices for finished lumber. A corresponding increase in the amount of recycled paper used in North America and Europe in the 1990s further depressed demand for pulpwood and made lasting structural changes in the way the logging industry operated in those regions. The financial crisis in the Asia-Pacific region, which began in 1996 and intensified rapidly in 1997, also reduced demand for imported logs and lumber, particularly from Canada. Poor economic conditions in Japan in the late 1990s led to decreased housing starts, resulting in reduced imports of Canadian lumber.

Canada's timber industry was hurt further in August 2001, when the U.S. Commerce Department, acting on a complaint by a group of U.S. lumber producers that claimed Canadian rivals were subsidized, imposed a 19.3 percent duty on Canadian softwood imports. In December 2003, however, the United States and Canada announced an agreement that eliminated the new tariff, which, according to CBC News, had cost the industry thousands of jobs and losses of as much as US$1.5 billion. The agreement, however, imposed limits on the amount of softwood that Canada could export duty-free to the United States. CBC News reported that this condition required Canada to reduce its share of the U.S. market from 33 percent to 31.5 percent. Canada brought the issue before NAFTA, which in 2004 rejected the U.S. argument that subsidized Canadian lumber imports were damaging the U.S. industry. Appealing this ruling, the United States set import duties on most softwood lumber from Canada at 21.2 percent. In early 2005, Canada proposed a negotiated settlement, offering to impose an export tax on softwood that would be reduced or eliminated as the country changed its method of harvesting from government land.

The effect of new environmental policies on logging volume is illustrated by changes taking place in North America, due in part to changes in forest practices to conserve biodiversity and to ensure a sustainable timber supply over the long term. In Canada, three British Columbia government programs reduced roundwood removals in the mid- to late 1990s: the 1995 Forest Practices Code, the Timber Supply Review, and the Protected Areas Strategy. Other reasons cited for the changes included overcutting in British Columbia's forests and lack of intensive reforestation from 1960 to 1990, environmental pressures, and public

demand for more parks and recreational lands. British Columbia forestry experts estimated that the Forest Practices Code would restrict the annual allowable cut in the province by 6 percent immediately and possibly by as much as 20 percent in the long term, reducing harvesting from 74 million cubic meters in 1996 to about 60 million cubic meters in 2000. In 2002, the province announced changes to the code to improve its administration.

In the United States, U.S. Forest Service timber sales dropped sharply beginning in 1986, as court decisions protected the habitat of such endangered species as the northern spotted owl essentially ended logging on vast areas of federal land in the Pacific Northwest. In 1986 the Forest Service sold about 50 million cubic meters of timber (which was cut by private companies), but by 1996 the volume was down roughly 70 percent to about 15 million cubic meters. In early 1997, warm, wet weather further reduced harvesting operations in the Pacific Northwest. New forestry guidelines stopped logging since the forest floor was wet and would be damaged by heavy motorized logging equipment.

Reduced harvest levels in the Pacific Northwest began when federal judges ruled in favor of environmental groups that had sued the U.S. Forest Service under the Endangered Species Act. The judges ruled that the Forest Service had to stop logging on vast areas of federal land until the agency drew up approved plans to protect the endangered spotted owl. The Clinton administration imposed a settlement in 1993-1994 that allowed some logging, although at only 15 to 25 percent of historic levels. The subject of lawsuits by both environmental groups and logging interests, the Clinton plan withstood several court challenges. However, the almost complete cutoff in harvesting of large, old-growth trees used mostly for lumber caused a massive closure of sawmills and extensive job losses.

In 2001 and 2002, the George W. Bush administration unveiled plans to relax the stricter policies of the previous decade. According to a 2001 article in the *National Journal*, Bush promised he would put the national forests "back to work" by approving more logging. Upon taking office, Bush filled key positions with pro-logging advocates who asserted that more timber sales would help prevent devastating and dangerous forest fires like the western U.S. wildfires of 2000. In 2001 the National Forest Service reported that some 50 million acres of federal forest lands were at high risk for fires.

In February 2002, Bush announced a plan that would give control of federal forest lands to local private management. Called the "charter forest," the U.S. Forest Service lands would be withdrawn from the Forest Service's control, and a "local trust entity" would be put in place to reduce management bottlenecks and costs. Environmental groups had long complained that the Forest Service focused too heavily on timber sales and oil leasing, rather than environmental preservation. Criticism became more heated after President Bush took office and froze a Clinton-era rule banning new roads needed for logging, drilling, and mining in one-third of all national forests.

Restrictions on logging in the Pacific Northwest appeared to be a boon for logging in the pine forests of the southeastern United States. Unlike the Northwest, most of forestland in the Southeast was not in federal hands, with nearly 60 percent owned privately, compared to 30 percent in the Northwest. However, environmental restrictions and wildlife preservation issues affected even private landholdings. Overproduction in the South, as well as oversupply of Canadian imports, resulted in depressed prices for timber in southern states in the early 2000s. According to a report from Mississippi State University, the value of Mississippi's timber harvest fell by 17.4 percent in 2001 and fell further after the terrorist attacks of September 11, 2001. In 2002, the decline was 3.6 percent, but by 2003 conditions had begun to improve. The value of timber production in Mississippi that year fell by less than 1 percent, due largely to increased housing starts.

The cutting and use of tropical timber in Asia and Latin America was also restricted for environmental reasons. Despite the growing importance of these regions in the pulp and paper industry, over-harvesting in the 1980s, restrictions on logging, and other factors combined to reduce the production of tropical forest products in the 1990s. For example, the total production of logs from these three regions was 139 million cubic meters in 1992, but by 1996 that total had dropped to 127 million cubic meters. The downward trend was caused by massive drops in the Pacific Rim, where log production dropped from 104 million cubic meters in 1992 to just 86 million cubic meters in 1996.

Production in Latin America increased from 28 million cubic meters in 1992 to 32 million cubic meters, and African production increased from 8 million cubic meters to 9.2 million cubic meters in the same period. While African production is low on a global scale, several nations of south central Africa derive a major share of their gross domestic product (GDP) from forest products, making the industry key to their national economies.

Some public and private groups developed certification programs that would identify timber produced in an environmentally responsible manner. Producers of tropical timber responded by moving away from cutting stands of virgin timber toward the concept of sustainable forest management, including the planting and harvesting of tree plantations using other tree species. To save endangered types of tropical timber, users of timber also replaced their use of tropical hardwood with temperate coniferous and nonconiferous species in many applications.

Removal Rates. Despite these restrictions, global production of wood continued to grow in the early 2000s. Economic conditions, however, produced the peaks and valleys typically associated with this industry. For example, weak demand for lumber and wood pulp caused removals of roundwood to decrease by 3.2 percent in Europe from 1995 to 1996. Furthermore, roundwood was in over-supply through 2000 and 2001, after devastating December 1999 windstorms felled enough lumber to account for nearly half the average annual production in most of Europe. However, roundwood removal was up to 443.5 million cubic meters in 2001, from 391 million cubic meters in 2000. Removals fell to 399 million cubic meters in 2001 but rose to 413.6 million cubic meters in 2002. Removals were expected to grow through 2004 at between 1.5 and 2 percent, but consumption was expected to increase by 4.1 percent annually.

In the Russian Federation, the decline of the forest industry continued in the mid-1990s. Softwood roundwood removals fell by 18.5 percent to 69.4 million cubic meters in 1996, reaching only 50 percent of levels in 1992. Hardwood removals also fell by 18.3 percent to 25.7 million cubic meters. Improvement occurred in 1998, however, when combined roundwood removals rose to 95 million cubic meters. The following year, total removals rose to 143.6 million cubic meters. Levels increased steadily through the early 2000s, reaching 158 million cubic meters in 2000 and 164.7 million cubic meters in 2001. Total roundwood removals for the Russian Federation reached 174.2 million cubic meters in 2002. According to the U.N. Economic Commission for Europe, forest products markets in Europe were expected to grow in 2004 and 2005, with volumes in Russia and former Eastern bloc nations approaching the levels they had reached prior to their economic transition in the early 1990s.

In the United States, roundwood removals wavered in the last half of the 1990s. As housing starts grew in the last few years of the twentieth century, the industry realized a slightly higher demand, and roundwood removals increased from 485.8 million cubic meters in 1997 to 500.1 million in 2000. Although removals dipped again the following year, totaling only 471 million cubic meters, the decline reversed in 2002, when removals reached 477.8 million cubic meters. Removals were steadier in Canada, which harvested 188.8 million cubic meters of roundwood in 1997, 176.9 million in 1998, 193.7 million in 1999, and 200 million in 2000. Levels remained at about 200 million cubic meters in 2001 and 2002, and grew by about 7.6 percent from 2003 to 2004. The *Journal of Forestry,* reported that the projected annual U.S. harvest of all species would rise 23 percent, about 4.2 billion cubic feet, from 1996 to 2050, with softwood harvests increasing by 3 billion cubic feet.

European pulpwood production (separate from log production, which is used for lumber) experienced a steep drop in 1996. After recovering over the next two years, the market reached a peak in late 2000. A significant increase in pulp production and consumption was expected in 2004, with slower growth in 2005. However, the United States experienced a substantial drop in pulpwood production, which by 2001 reached only 193 million cubic meters. The decline was attributed to the increasing use of recycled paper as a fiber source.

Trade Agreements. The international market for forest products was affected by trade agreements that went into effect in the first half of the 1990s, including the Uruguay Round of the General Agreement on Tariffs and Trade (GATT) and the North American Free Trade Agreement (NAFTA). Under GATT, tariffs on wood and paper products were expected to decrease more slowly than on other industrial products. Japan offered to cut its base rate tariffs by 50 percent during a five-year period, reducing tariffs on about 60 percent of Japanese wood and wood products by a margin of 2.6 to 10 percent. European countries offered to reduce tariffs by 44 percent, but with a long phase-in period. Major wood products exporters, such as the United States and Canada, wanted complete and rapid elimination of tariffs.

China's entry into the World Trade Organization, which by 2004 included 147 countries, was expected to boost world timber exports to meet increased demand in China's housing and furniture sectors. In 2001, China imported about 77 million metric tons of timber and timber products. From 2003 to 2004, the value of China's forest products market grew 24.8 percent, reaching US$32.3 billion. Exports were valued at US$16 billion, up 34 percent from the previous year, and imports were valued at US$16.34 billion, up 17.2 percent. Plywood exports increased by more than 110 percent in volume and 152 percent in value. The production of solid composite floor material was a significant segment of China's timber products industry. By 2004, China was manufacturing about 30 percent of world demand for solid composite floors, which totaled about 25 million square meters, all of which supplied domestic demand. Growth in this segment averaged about 40 percent annually between 2001 and 2004.

As international trade increased, concerns about illegal logging also grew. In 2003, the U.S. Department of State launched President George W. Bush's Initiative against Illegal Logging to provide assistance to countries that were fighting the sale and export of illegally harvested timber. The U.S. Department of State cited World Bank figures estimating that illegal logging cost developing countries between US$10 billion and US$15 billion per year. Illegal logging has also been linked to

environmental degradation. In late 2004, more than 1,000 people in the Philippines were killed by flash floods that sparked massive landslides on slopes where forests had been cut illegally. Illegal logging in the African rainforest was threatening the habitat of gorillas and chimpanzees.

Climate Change. The impact of global warming trends has brought significant changes to the international logging industry throughout the first decade of the twenty-first century. Warmer temperatures could weaken forests in temperate zones, which in 2002 accounted for about 77 percent of industrial timber production. Subtropical areas, however, where softwood trees can grow twice as fast as in temperate regions, could greatly expand production. According to an Ohio State University report, one analyst predicted that tropical timber plantations would increase by about 675,000 acres annually during the next 50 to 100 years. At the same time, softwood species in North America and Europe would migrate into northern hardwood forests, and some hardwood species would disappear. This shift could bode ill for the northern timber industry, as lumber from this deadfall would flood the market and depress prices.

CURRENT CONDITIONS

In the hardwood market, logs from North America and Europe accounted for a large share of total world production heading into the late 2000s. The United States produced approximately 61 million cubic meters of hardwood logs, 62 million meters of sawn softwood, and 27.8 million meters of sawn hardwood in 2005. China was the largest export market for North American hardwood, placing orders valued at US$328 million in 2006, an increase of 38 percent over the previous year. Europe was an important contributor to the worldwide logging industry, accounting for more than half of total exports, according to the United Nations Food and Agricultural Organization (FAO). The United Kingdom reported a decline in the industry, however, with the number of hardwood mills falling from 26 in 2001 to 18 in 2005. The number of softwood U.K. mills stood at 155 in 2005, according to the U.K. Forestry Commission. Growth in Eastern Europe was expected to be greater than that in Western Europe through 2020. Total forest area in Europe was also expected to increase about 5 percent annually through 2020, and increased demand for renewable energy was predicted to drive growth in the industry.

In 2007, a U.S. Congressional research project centered on the illegal timber trade, estimating that as much as 23 percent of hardwood timber and plywood traded internationally possibly came from illegal logging practices. As much as 80 percent of logging in the Brazilian

Amazon and 80 percent of forest products from Indonesia are considered illegal. According to some analysts, approximately US$23 billion of suspicious wood products traded annually prepressed the global prices between 7 and 16 percent. The World Wildlife Fund estimated that the European Union was spending approximately US$3.9 billion a year on illegal wood. In 2008, the European Commission estimated that 19 percent of European lumber imports could possibly come from illegal sources. Illegal wood imports to the United States is estimated to reach billions of dollars annually. The 2008 Farm Bill bans any importation of illegal lumber into the United States.

According to a 2009–10 report by the U.S. Department of Agriculture, recent climate changes have not met predictions, leading to expectations that the future ecosystem will change considerably, and making it imperative that significant ways are found to improve the health and sustainability of the earth's forests and grasslands. In 2002, the George W. Bush administration developed the Climate Change Science Program (CCSP) in an effort to coordinate and direct research efforts in the United States in the areas of climate and global change. Goals of the CCSP were reducing significant uncertainties in climate science, improving global observing systems, developing science-based resources, and communicating the findings globally in an effort to impact change.

INDUSTRY LEADERS

Leading logging and wood products companies also tended to be integrated forest products companies. They produced pulp, paper, and packaging, as well as wood products and lumber. The United States was by far the world leader in logging, and U.S. companies tended to be the largest forest and wood products companies.

Throughout the 2000s, International Paper Company was the world's largest forest products company. Although it owned 6.3 million acres of forested land in the United States during the early 2000s, as well as 1.2 million acres in Brazil and smaller tracts in New Zealand and Russia, by 2007 the company had sold much of its forested land, retaining about 500,000 acres in the United States and harvesting rights for about 1 million acres in Brazil and Russia. In 2008 International Paper posted total sales of US$22.3 billion, with paper and packaging accounting for about two-thirds of sales. That year the company employed 51,500 people.

Second behind International Paper was Georgia-Pacific Corporation, which was the world's largest producer of tissue products. Its major brands include Brawny, Quilted Northern, and Dixie. Sales in 2004 exceeded US$19.6 billion. Georgia-Pacific merged with Koch Industries in 2005 after a US$21 billion deal was offered.

Weyerhaeuser Company, which owned 6.4 million acres of timberland in the United States and leased about 30 million acres in Canada, was also licensed to harvest timber in Australia, New Zealand, France, and Ireland. In 2000 the company bought Canadian giant MacMillan Bloedel. In 2009 Weyerhaeuser's total sales had slipped to US$16.9 billion from US$21.8 billion in 2005, and the company employed a workforce of 14,900 people.

Boise Cascade Holdings produced building materials and paper and reported sales of US$5.9 billion in 2006 with 10,155 employees.

Swedish-based Stora Enso Oyj, which was formed by the merger of Stora with Finnish pulp and paper company Enso Oy in 1998, paid US$4.8 billion for U.S.-based Consolidated Papers Inc. in 2000, making the company the world's leading producer of paper and paperboard. Stora reported sales of US$15.7 billion in 2006.

Svenska Cellulosa Aktiebolaget SCA of Sweden, which acquired a majority stake in Papierwerke Waldhof-Aschaffenburg AG of Germany (PWA) in the 1990s, also had extensive forest products operations. It owned 5 million acres of forested land in Sweden and had operations in Africa, North and South America, Asia, Australia, and Europe. In 2009 the company realized US$11.8 billion in sales and reported a work force of 28,700 employees.

MAJOR COUNTRIES IN
THE INDUSTRY

The nontropical logging industry is dominated by the United States, the European Union, and Canada. At the start of the twenty-first century, the United States was, by far, the leading logging country in the world. It maintained a relatively steady removal rate in the late 1980s and early 1990s until the advent of bans on timber cut removals. Total U.S. production of coniferous and non-coniferous wood in the rough in 1996 totaled 414 million cubic meters. European production that year was 262 million cubic meters. In 2000, production had jumped to 500 million cubic meters in the United Sates and 434.5 million cubic meters in Europe. In 2003 Europe removed 488.3 million cubic meters of industrial roundwood, while the United States produced about 405 million cubic meters.

Coniferous softwood accounted for the majority of U.S. removals of wood in the rough at 289.6 million cubic meters in 2002, but the United States also produced a large amount of nonconiferous hardwood wood in the rough, 188 million cubic meters in 2002. Softwood, the more valuable of the two, is used to make lumber for housing construction, wood pulp, and other applications. In 2004, some 680 U.S. sawmills produced 27 million cubic meters of hardwood, compared to 33 million cubic meters produced by 1,000 sawmills in

1997. Because of improved efficiency sawmill turnover increased from about US$4.4 billion in 1997 to US$6.5 billion in 2004.

The southern United States, with its warm winters, flat land, and easy access to timberlands, is an easier place to log than the Northwest. Southern trees also grow faster than northern trees, improving the forest yield. With almost no old-growth timber, the South did not have as much environmental controversy as the Northwest.

Strong demand for pine products in 2003, which was tied to growth in residential construction, contributed to a stabilization of the timber industry in southern states. According to a report from Mississippi State University, the value of timber from southern states fell by 17 percent in 2001 and by 3.6 percent in 2002. By 2003, however, this decline had slowed to less than 1 percent. The U.S. timber industry also benefited from U.S. government purchases in 2003 of softwood panels and lumber for reconstruction after the war in Iraq. With U.S. housing starts surging in 2004 and 2005, consumption of sawn hardwood increased, and in 2006 was expected to continue its upward trend, although somewhat more slowly than in the early 2000s.

BIBLIOGRAPHY

Ali, Amina, et al. "Softwood Lumber Dispute." CBC News, 8 December 2003. Available from www.cbc.ca/news.

"ANU Forestry Market Report," March 2004. Available from http://sres.anu.edu.au.

Brack, Duncan. "Illegal Logging." Chatham House, March 2005. Available from www.illegal-logging.info.

"Canada Offers Wood Deal." *The New York Times,* 10 March 2005.

"China Wood Products Prices." *Global Wood,* 16–30 April 2005. Available from www.globalwood.org.

Forest Service Global Change Research Strategy, 2009–2019 Implementation, U.S. Forest Service. Available from www.fs.fed.us.

"Hoover's Company Capsules." *Hoover's Online,* 2007. Available from www.hoovers.com.

Howard, James L. *U.S. Forest Products Annual Market Review and Prospects, 2001–2005.* U.S. Department of Agriculture Forest Service. Available from www.fpl.fs.fed.us.

International Timber and Trade Review. Union of Concerned Scientists, Citizens and Scientists for Environmental Solutions, February 2009. Available from www.ucsusa.org.

"Market Report: Winds of Change?" *Forestry & British Timber,* 2 April 2007.

"New Developments in Logging." *E & P Magazine,* 20 August 2006.

"Pulp Projects by Country." Pulp Mill Watch. Available from www.pulpmillwatch.org.

"Traders Are Braced for Another Difficult Year." *TTJ: The Timber Industry Magazine,* 17 March 2007.

UNECE Trade and Timber Division. "Forest Products Statistics." *Timber Bulletin,* February 2007.

United Nations, Food and Agricultural Organization. "European Forest Sector Outlook Study," 2005. Available from www.unece.org.

———. "Forest Products Annual Market Review 2005–2006," 15 April 2007. Available from www.unece.org.

———. "Forest Products Statistics 2001–2005." Available from www.unece.org.

"U.S. Appeals NAFTA Ruling Against Tariffs on Canadian Lumber." *The New York Times,* 25 November 2004.

U.S. Department of State. "The President's Initiative Against Illegal Logging," 28 July 2003. Available from www.state.gov.

Warnook, Matt. "Environmental Agency Takes Action Against Timber Smuggling." *Wood & Wood Products,* September 2006.

ELECTRICAL AND ELECTRONIC EQUIPMENT

━━━━━━━━━━━ ■ ━━━━━━━━━━━

SIC 3630

APPLIANCES, HOUSEHOLD

NAICS CODE(S)

3352. The world's appliance manufacturers output an extensive range of consumer household devices. These include electric and non-electric cooking equipment such as stoves, ranges, and ovens (including microwaves); refrigerators and freezers; laundry equipment (such as washing machines, dryers, and ironers); electric housewares for heating (such as electric space heaters, electrically heated bed coverings, and portable humidifiers and dehumidifiers); electric fans; vacuum cleaners; water heaters; dishwashers; food waste disposal units; and sewing machines.

INDUSTRY SNAPSHOT

Although China had become the largest global supplier of so-called "white goods," the world appliances market included production by numerous nations all over the world and consumption by virtually every country. A unique aspect of this industry was that it offered something to almost every consumer, regardless of lifestyle or income. Within individual segments of the market were many choices and price ranges, making products accessible to almost anyone. The leading segments of the industry were refrigerators, stoves and ranges, washing machines, ovens, and dryers.

Because of maturing markets in the United States and western Europe, appliance manufacturers in these regions chose two avenues to expand sales: developing innovative products with time-and energy-saving features to lure new customers in existing markets, and tapping new markets. The emphasis on energy efficiency continues to be a major consideration for U.S. buyers. Features designed to save utility costs or help preserve the environment are popular. As economies in Asia, South America and eastern Europe expanded, manufacturers strove to capitalize on these areas' increasing disposable incomes and rising standards of living by developing export markets there and by forming joint alliances with manufacturers in these regions.

Waves of consolidation have characterized the U.S. industry, and a similar trend appeared later in Europe. U.S. consolidations left the country with only four major producers: Whirlpool, General Electric, Maytag, and Goodman Holding Company (Amana). In Europe, Electrolux and Bosch-Siemens started to acquire smaller manufacturers in an effort to achieve this kind of dominance and market positioning. Manufacturers in Asia, where appliance production has burgeoned, are forecast to consolidate or close down operations because of the faltering economy.

The European Committee of Manufacturers of Domestic Appliances (CECED) adopted Echelon Corporation technology as part of its Household Appliances Control and Monitoring Application Interworking Specification (AIS) standard. Echelon is a global networking company offering technology and solutions for controls, smart metering, and energy and environment management.It said that the CECED-approved standard "is an important step toward a mass market for smart appliances and home automation and control in Europe." The standard was viewed as a win-win benefiting both appliance manufacturers and consumers. There were projections that the standard would have a positive impact on growing the market for efficient smart homes.

ORGANIZATION AND STRUCTURE

Unlike industries with high fixed costs, appliance firms' costs are more variable because they are somewhat vulnerable to price changes in raw materials and parts. Company profits are enhanced by lower borrowing costs, market conditions that tolerate higher prices, and strong sales of high-end merchandise. Higher prices are not easily passed along to customers, especially since industry competition has increased significantly. One result of this heightened competitiveness has been an upsurge in industry consolidation.

Premium appliance models generally carry higher profit margins for industry manufacturers. Conversely, lower-end models have smaller profit margins. Washers, dryers, and refrigerators tend to be more profitable to appliance manufacturers than dishwashers and cooking equipment. The average life span of a major appliance is 10 to 15 years.

According to the Association of Home Appliance Manufacturers (AHAM), demand for household appliances varies from year to year depending on a number of economic and social factors: replacement demand, original purchase demand, saturation levels, state of the economy, and specific product demand.

Appliance Replacement. Replacement demand for a particular type of appliance depends on that appliance's average life span and, to a lesser extent, the rate of technological innovation that distinguishes new models from old. In some countries, replacement demand is a large percentage of total demand for household appliances. Home remodeling activity also influences replacement demand, for changes in a home's layout can often prompt consumers to upgrade from older models to newer ones for the sake of aesthetics and convenience.

Replacement demand tends to be stronger when real appliance prices remain constant over time, only rising at the general rate of inflation. As the costs of acquiring a new machine stay relatively constant, the desire to repair instead of replace the appliance typically decreases. The availability of affordable new appliances thus prompts greater replacement demand when the need to repair arises.

Original Appliance Market. In addition to replacement demand, new residential home construction is an important factor in the demand for household appliances. A typical new home can account for many different major units. Popular major units include dishwasher, refrigerator, oven, washer, dryer, and range.

Saturation Levels. Within each product category, saturation is defined as the presence of at least one unit of that particular appliance per household. In markets like the United States, saturation levels are high, resulting in lower levels of first-time home appliance purchases. In growing economies, such as in Asia and South America, saturation levels are comparatively low, and their markets present greater opportunities to companies seeking to increase their market share.

State of the Economy. Appliance sales trends usually mirror national economic growth trends. When an economy is in early recovery, the household appliance industry is one of the first to show signs of improvement. This reflects the crucial role of consumer discretionary income in fueling appliance purchases.

According to a Homewise agency research study data, 1 in 10 older people in Britain lived without basic household appliances such as refrigerators and washing machines. About 800,000 people over 65 years of age did not have the appliances. Viewed as clear evidence of "pensioner poverty" in Britain, the research results also revealed that older people living in the south of England were the least likely to own household appliances.

Specific Product Demand. Each type of appliance is affected differently by the cycles of the economy. For instance, range sales depend largely on housing starts because comparatively few are bought during the life of the home. Dishwashers, meanwhile, have shorter life spans and possess the lowest saturation levels. Refrigerators have a medium life expectancy and are less dependent on housing starts.

BACKGROUND AND DEVELOPMENT

The modern-day appliance industry traces its beginnings back to 1878 when Thomas Edison invented the light bulb. The Edison Electric Light Company became General Electric in 1892. Edison left the company in 1894 to go into mining, but the company went on to develop electric elevators, toasters, electric ranges, electric motors, various appliances, and light bulbs.

In 1908 W. H. Hoover formed the Electric Suction Sweeper Company to make vacuum cleaners after he saw his wife's cousin, J. Murray Spangler, demonstrate a homemade version of a crude vacuum cleaner that he created to help in his janitorial work. Spangler made the vacuum cleaner out of a fan motor, a broom handle, a soap box, and a pillowcase that collected dirt. Hoover was in the saddlery business at the time, which was being overtaken by the auto industry, but he was wise enough to see that such a product would meet the needs of everyone who cleaned. The vacuum was first sold in hardware stores, but its popularity surged after salesmen turned to home demonstrations. After World War I, the company went back to selling vacuums through dealers because of a change in consumer preferences.

During the course of the twentieth century, appliances such as refrigerators, stoves, freezers, dishwashers, clothes dryers, and microwave ovens became staples of households in industrialized nations. In the latter half of the twentieth century, the entry of more women into the workforce also led to an increase in the demand for household appliances that saved time in doing everyday chores—a huge factor in the popularity of the microwave oven.

In the United States, the domestic household appliance industry went through a period of rapid consolidation in the 1980s. Maytag Corp. bought Magic Chef and JennAir to round out its product line at differing price levels and to increase its overall sales. Whirlpool did the same in the 1980s, adding the KitchenAid and Roper names to its product line. These mergers helped U.S. firms compete internationally, while giving foreign firms the chance to enter into joint ventures and partnerships with U.S. firms.

In North America and Europe, the home appliance market began to stagnate toward the end of the 1990s after experiencing record sales in 1994 and 1995. Nonetheless, even with slight growth, U.S. appliance manufacturers reported record shipments in 1997. Because appliance ownership in these mature markets was already widespread, demand in the late 1990s was modest. Nevertheless, home appliance stores recorded total revenues of more than US$12 billion in 2000, a 7.1 percent increase over 1999.

During the late 1990s, higher growth was to be found in Asia and South America, which were much less saturated. Although many Asian economies suffered from currency depreciation and debt in 1997 and 1998, appliance sales still grew because of the low number of appliances per household. In particular, China's prodigious population drove the industry, while revenues grew limp in industrialized countries.

Environmental Issues. A U.S. statute called the National Appliance Energy Conservation Act of 1987 directed the U.S. Department of Energy to raise the environmental compliance standards for several types of appliances to meet tougher environmental goals. New energy efficiency standards were written for all types of appliances to encourage the use of more efficient motors, auxiliary water heaters, lower wash temperatures, reduced water usage, better insulation of components, and heat controlled shutoffs.

While energy efficiency was a concern for industry participants, chlorofluorocarbon (CFC) reduction became the leading issue for the appliance industry. CFCs, which had been used in freezers and refrigerators as coolants since the 1940s, provoked intense scrutiny because they were thought to damage the protective ozone layer of the earth's atmosphere. Under the Montreal Protocol of 1987, CFC production must end by the year 2000. In early 1992 scientific studies were released that described findings of higher levels of CFCs than expected in the North American stratosphere. These findings encouraged the United States to commit to halting CFC production by 1996.

The U.S. industry was relatively slow to convert to non-CFC coolants, however, compared to European household appliance manufacturers, which have been selling refrigerators and freezers without CFC coolants since the mid-1980s. In 1993 these new appliances were priced roughly 7 percent higher than appliances that contained CFCs. HFC-134a, a nonflammable agent, is the leading replacement for CFCs. It requires compressors to be redesigned for maximum efficiency.

The worldwide appliance industry is also being encouraged by governments to increase the recycling of old appliances. In the United States, congressional bills were introduced in 1992 that set measures for the recycling and packaging of major appliances. Mandates of the legislation covered recycling rates, the number of reuses of packaging, and the percentage of recycled content. Many in the industry contended that the new rules were not attainable. Analysts expected this struggle to balance the needs of the industry and the environment to continue in the twenty-first century.

The U.S. Department of Energy (DOE) issued program guidelines and funding for the Energy Efficient Appliances Consumer Rebate Program. Plans call for the program to be administered by state energy offices to support Consumers purchasing Energy Star appliances. The American Recovery and Reinvestment Act of 2009 will provide funding adding up to US$300 million. Key elements include efforts to "stimulate demand for home appliances, provide consumers with tremendous savings on the initial purchase cost and long-term utility costs of appliances and will also provide an important environmental benefit by way of a significant decrease in energy consumption." According to the AHAM (Association of Home Appliance Manufacturers), the DOE (Department of Energy) accepted "critical principles" and the Association made and incorporated them into plans.

Trends and Features. Features that provide convenience and simplicity of use have garnered much of the attention in the 1980s and 1990s, as opposed to radically new breakthrough products, which have been slow to develop.

Convenience features that proved successful included easy-to-clean induction cooking units, quieter dishwashers, greater appliance capacity, improved energy efficiency, and more appealing cosmetic appearances. Toward the close of the twentieth century, however, industry and consumer home shows revealed new products and future prospects to the public. Computer technology opened up new possibilities, and dramatic breakthroughs were already in application by the first decade of the 2000s.

Appliance manufacturers have also placed renewed emphasis on increasing speed in delivery of products. Historically, most retailers held large inventories of appliances to ensure that they were able to meet customer demand when the market for household appliances was strong. However, this was expensive and conflicted with retailers' interests in keeping overheads down. Retailers increasingly partnered with manufacturers to help them with the carrying costs of warehousing products. This trend triggered a surge in the use of appliance showrooms, where customers could place an order for an appliance and the product was shipped directly from the manufacturer to the customer the next day. Appliance manufacturers in the mid-1980s first developed this quick delivery system with parts suppliers to help cut the carrying costs of parts inventories.

CURRENT CONDITIONS

The appliances industry emerged from the recession of the early years of the first decade of the 2000s ahead of many other industry sectors. Improved consumer confidence levels, as well as low interest rates and strong housing starts, supported positive conditions by 2003. According to estimates from The Freedonia Group, a Cleveland, Ohio-based consultancy, global demand for major household appliances was projected to increase at an annual rate of nearly 4 percent from 2004 to 2007. This growth was expected to propel overall demand to 367 million units.

Although the major appliance manufacturers began to globalize in the 1990s, some of their products remained unique relative to the needs of target markets and regions. Because of cultural differences, manufacturers cannot always ship the same product to North America, South America, Europe, and Asia. Instead companies have to develop appliances suited to individual market demands. Hence, in many cases, the globalization of the industry meant consolidating the materials, component development, technology, and manufacturing to create technology and a basic manufacturing process common to all appliances.

Trade agreements such as the General Agreement on Tariffs and Trade (GATT) and the North American Free

Trade Agreement (NAFTA) made international trade increasingly accessible by removing tariffs and duties. By the early 2000s, these trade accords had made progress toward reducing barriers that previously hindered trade between the United States, the members of the European Union, Japan, South Korea, and developing economies around the world.

On 10 May 2007, the U.S. Department of Labor awarded a US$263,367 National Emergency Grant to assist approximately 80 workers impacted by closure of Whirlpool Corporation's Newton, Iowa, plant. On March 6, 2007, the department had awarded the city of Newton a Regional Innovation Grant of US$250,000 to conduct early planning offering assistance to impacted workers. The Labor Department for Trade Adjustment Assistance (TAA) previously certified those Whirlpool workers. Thus, they were eligible for training preparing them to find new jobs.

The United States. U.S. consumers enjoy state-of-the-art household appliances at relatively low prices because of intense competition brought about by both domestic and foreign firms. About 50 percent of the domestic market in many appliance categories is made up of imports. At the same time, many major U.S. appliance manufacturers have a global presence, too. Overall, however, the United States consistently imports more than it exports.

Writing for *USA Today* in an August 26, 2009, article, Kathleen Gray called rebate programs a "win-win situation" when describing how 60 utilities in states across the nation offered US$25 to US$50 for picking up and recycling old refrigerators and freezers. These programs started on the U.S. west coast in the 1990s and were progressively taking root in the east, according to Gray.

In June 2009 DTE's Detroit Edison subsidiary launched a "cash-for-clunkers" appliance recycling program. A primary goal of the program was to help customers make their homes more energy-efficient. Federal standards showed it was a good decision to get rid of old refrigerators or freezers and replace them with newer models. Those more recent options use approximately 450 kilowatt-hours compared to 1,500 kilowatt-hours annually for older models. "Refrigerators and freezers manufactured before 1990 typically use three times more electricity than new appliances and can cost an average of US$150 a year to run," Detroit Edison President and Chief Operating Officer Steven Kurmas explained. By August 2009, more than 1,000 old, running refrigerators had been turned in for a US$50 check received four to six weeks after collection of appliance. In addition to the financial incentive to replace and discard appliances correctly, it was noted that improperly discarded items can have a negative impact on the environment by expelling toxic substances impacting air and soil quality.

In her August 2009 article, Kathleen Gray also shared exciting news when describing the forthcoming cash for national appliances program. The program adapts a highly successful process used for the U.S. automotive industry's "cash for clunkers program" ending in August 2009. As Gray pointed out, however, it won't be essential to trade in an old model to take advantage of the rebate option for new ones with Energy Star seal designation. This federally-funded program involves the Department of Energy providing states with U.S.$300 million approved as part of U.S. President Barack Obama's US$787 billion stimulus plan. Both "clunker" programs were targeted at boosting the economy. "These rebates will help families make the transition to more efficient appliances, making purchases that will directly stimulate the economy and create jobs," acknowledged U.S. Energy Secretary Steven Chu when announcing the program, according to Gray.

Europe. Increasing market share in Europe remained as a difficult task for U.S. and Asian firms because the various cultural differences, languages, and even electrical standards in the region present significant challenges for any offshore company. Firms producing for Europe face the marketing challenge of trying to reach the most people in a way that is both economical and effective. Appliance manufacturers also must adapt to European demand for smaller and more efficient appliances.

In the spring of 2008, CECED sprang forth with its opposition to VAT (value added tax) reduction being used "to promote energy efficient appliances." Other financial incentives were suggested including revenue tax credits. CECED is a European representative body for affiliated companies in the household appliance industry.

Asia. If Asia's population of 2.6 billion were to achieve the same market penetration as that of the United States, Asian demand for refrigerators alone would top 70 million units per year, according to analysis published by *Appliance Manufacturer.* Similarly, if other appliances rose to this level, production and sales would escalate rapidly. By mid-2004, China was in the midst of an economic boom and had become the largest global supplier of so-called "white goods." This followed industry analyst predictions that China's world market share would rise from 8 percent in 2002 to 30 percent by 2005, according to *Modern Plastics.* Indeed, China's exports were expected to reach levels of US$10 billion by 2005.

Three Japanese conglomerates—Matsushita, Toshiba, and Hitachi—have historically controlled much of the Southeast Asian market, with pricing power and

distribution channel barriers that are hard to penetrate. Analysts expect these manufacturers to lead a wave of consolidations in the twenty-first century, similar to those in the United States and Europe, as local markets mature and exports increase.

RESEARCH AND TECHNOLOGY

Technology for household appliances focused on three primary objectives. First is the development of more energy-efficient and environmentally safe appliances; second is the development of "smart" appliances; and third is the development of better materials that are more lightweight, durable, and clean.

With pressure from environmental and governmental organizations and agencies, appliance manufacturers have been designing more efficient appliances that use less energy and fewer natural resources. Global demand for household appliances totals about a half billion units, which is good for the industry but potentially dangerous for the environment. Not only do appliances consume energy but they also must eventually be discarded. Researchers are studying both challenges, striving to reduce the amount of energy required to operate them and seeking safer, more recyclable materials.

An example of efforts to conserve energy is Maytag's Neptune washing machine. In conjunction with the U.S. Department of Energy, Maytag developed a front-loading horizontal axis washer that uses only 23 gallons of water per load, in contrast to 40 to 46 gallons used by conventional top-loading vertical axis washers. The Neptune also features an automatic water-level meter, which determines how much water is needed for each load. This feature prevents water from being wasted when users fail to set the water-level control for different size loads. U.S. consumer research indicates that almost 50 percent of all households do not change the water level, no matter what the size of the load, according to *Appliance Manufacturer.*

"Smart" appliances are unique in that they perform certain tasks automatically to streamline users' tasks. The key to smart appliances is that they are networked and connected, either to the Internet or to a central computer system. In an article for *Chain Store Executive with Shopping Center Age,* author Suzanne Barry Osborn remarks, "They aren't just appliances any more—they are infopliances." Economically, industry leaders hope that the more technologically advanced the appliances become, the more often people will replace them. To illustrate this point, consider the computer industry in which emerging technology creates constant motion in the buy cycle. Further, offering appliances that network to manufacturer software products creates an additional revenue stream for the manufacturers. Just as users of portable communication devices personalize them by buying various types of software or applications to meet their needs, so might users of Internet-connected household appliances purchase software to make their appliances meet their specific needs.

The kitchen is the room that gets the most attention from researchers working on smart appliances. After all, it is the room in which the most appliances are used. Whirlpool already offers a refrigerator that maintains an Internet connection with an online grocer, so that the user only has to punch some keys on the door to order groceries. There are also refrigerators that generate shopping lists when users scan bar codes of empty containers. Kitchen appliances are also available that can store favorite recipes. One interactive product being developed will supply recipes based on search criteria and subscribe to designated cooking magazines so that it can upload new recipes. It will even make wine suggestions.

Technology is under development that will create self-sufficient refrigerators and pantries. Armed with sensors, they will be able to detect when an item needs to be restocked. Then they will shop for it online, arrange for its delivery, and pay. In the future, a person could start dinner cooking in the oven from work by using e-mail or some other type of remote control device. Research on innovative materials is also projected as an important means of progress in future kitchens. Smart materials with sensors open up new possibilities. For example, consumers could have a tea kettle that changes color when the water reaches the desired temperature.

The laundry room is another area of appliance research. Whirlpool has introduced a washing machine that downloads its own instructions for stain removal. In fact, the user can e-mail the washing machine, so that the download is complete when he or she is ready to do laundry. This machine is designed to save time and money for the consumer in the long run.

Improved materials can be used in appliances in any room of the house. Dramatic advances in home appliance efficiency and ease of use have been made possible by the tough, lightweight, and corrosion-resistant properties of modern plastics. According to *Appliance Manufacturer,* the household appliance industry had increased its use of plastics from less than one percent of material content in the early 1960s to approximately 25 percent by weight, and more than 60 percent by volume, in the mid-1990s. Some analysts claim that without the high strength to weight ratio, corrosive resistance, and ease of fabrication properties of plastic, household appliances would cost about 25 percent more and consume 30 percent more energy, while losing 20 percent of storage space. Additionally, some analysts have reported that if plastic had not been introduced, corrosion would reduce the product life of clothes washers and dishwashers by about 50 percent.

The environmental aspect is relevant in materials development, and the need to recycle used plastics is still a daunting task. By 2007 refrigerator disposal alone is projected to yield approximately 125 million pounds of polyurethane foam and more than 200 million pounds of other plastics.

In a move away from secrecy and corporate protectionism, many household appliance manufacturers are sharing some of their research and development (R&D) efforts in this area. U.S. firms have joined with major universities, consulting firms, and major research firms to help them gain a more global perspective on all aspects of their industry. Utility-sponsored organizations, such as the Electric Power Research Institute and the Gas Research Institute, have assisted in efforts by U.S. firms to speed up the product development process as well. Accelerated production schedules increasingly demand input and contributions from sources outside company walls. By utilizing other sources of R&D knowledge, appliance manufacturers have also opened themselves up to other financing sources—often utility industry groups—for new products that never existed before. Research laboratories and universities can also be a great source of pooled resources.

According to the December 2003 issue of *Appliance Manufacturer,* the development of innovative, cutting edge appliance features continued during the early years of the first decade of the 2000s, despite a sluggish economy. For example, Italy's Merloni marketed Ariston Smart Tag appliances that were capable of reading embedded radio frequency identification (RFID) tags on clothing and food packaging. This capability enabled refrigerators to warn consumers when certain food products were about to expire. Whirlpool marketed a washer and dryer pair capable of communicating about specific wash loads, enabling the dryer to prepare for the next load and adjust its settings accordingly. Other developments included talking appliances from Electrolux.

Although research and development have long been important in developed markets like Europe and the United States, by mid-2004 they were also a growing concern in emerging economies like China. In its July 2004 issue, *Appliance Manufacturer* revealed that factors such as energy conservation, performance, and quality were quickly becoming more important to Chinese consumers than price. In fact, through a survey conducted by its Institute of Market Economy, the Development Research Centre of the State Council found that 85 percent of Chinese consumers ranked high performance and quality as being more important than cost in 2004.

In a July 29, 2009, article in *The New York Times,* writer Kate Galbraith indicated that a report from consulting firm McKinsey & Company revealed there was a need for the United States to invest US$520 billion in improvements including replacing inefficient household appliances to realize savings of US$1.2 trillion by 2020. This effort would reduce the projected energy use in 2020 by approximately 23 percent.

There was a consistent pattern of decreased energy consumption for 2008 major appliances shipments, according to AHAM research data. Compared to 2000 models, clothes washers experienced a 64 percent decrease of energy consumption per unit. During the same time period, tub capacity increased by 9 percent. This translated into enabling consumers to wash bigger loads of clothes while using smaller amounts of energy. Additional data results revealed refrigerators and dishwashers were over 30 percent more efficient than 2000 models.

INDUSTRY LEADERS

AB Electrolux. AB Electrolux was the world's largest household appliance manufacturer in 2005, and was known for its refrigerators, freezers, dishwashers, and washing machines. More than 55 million Electrolux products were sold in 150 countries every year. The company courted the South American market, where Whirlpool has a stronghold, in an effort to expand its international scope. Electrolux bought a 6 percent stake in Refrigeracao Parana SA, Brazil's second largest manufacturer of household appliances. The company also owned a subsidiary in Argentina that it used to distribute its household appliances under the Electrolux, Zanussi, and Frigidaire brand names. The company posted sales of more than US$18.2 billion in 2004, an increase of almost 6 percent from the previous year. Of total revenues, Sweden earned 3.6 percent, the rest of Europe earned 44 percent, North America earned 38.9 percent, and the rest of the world generated the remaining 13.5 percent of sales. Outside of Europe and North America, the company's largest international markets were in Brazil, India, China, and Australia. Consumer durables (mainly major appliances) accounted for 76 percent of Electrolux sales in 2004.

Electrolux announced its plans to execute a major advertising campaign to support launch of the Global Design Range incorporating cooling and washing categories plus other distinctive features. Efforts will include promotions involving print and TV ads plus a first-time attempt to utilize search and banner advertising.

Electrolux also advertised that it was looking for green appliance designs. The company held its fifth annual Electrolux Design Lab international student competition in 2007. The focus was for submissions featuring "eco-friendly and sustainable household appliances and solutions for the year 2020." According to Mairi

Beautyman in a June 1, 2007, article in *Interior Design,* entries were required to be commercially viable plus demonstrate energy and water efficiency as well as support new ways to foster sustainable behavior and product usage. The grand prize was approximately US$6,700 and a six-month internship at one of Electrolux's design centers.

Electrolux was expected to post a profit for the 2007–2008 fiscal year. Establishing Electrolux as a global brand was an important part of its strategy. Approximately 50 percent of its global sales came from the Electrolux brand compared to 15 percent in 2003.

Furthermore, as reported by Rupali Mukherjee in *The Times of India* in May 2007, in 2005, Electrolux divested its appliance business in India to Videocon. The action included three production facilities. The agreement also included the right for Videocon to use the Electrolux and Kelvinator brands in India.

During a May 17, 2007, interview with Debdatta Das in *The Hindu Business Line,* Peter Birch, CEO of Electrolux Major Appliances, Asia Pacific, stated that his company's "specific worldwide approach" was being "extremely consumer-oriented" and that this is why Electrolux attempted to determine the needs of diverse people throughout the world and address them. A focus on energy and water conservation was considered to be a common global concern. Birch also discussed plans for India including the May 2007 launch of an innovative four-door refrigerator and October 2007 launch of a range of frost-free refrigerators.

In a May 15, 2007, article on DNA India, an online international news and analysis Web site, Tanvi Shukla reported that Electrolux's refrigerator division accounted for 55 percent of the topline. The rest was broken down as AC at 20 percent, microwave at 10 percent and washing machines at 15 percent. AC and microwave carried the best margins in the consumer durable business. Consequently, Electrolux planned to be aggressive in those categories.

Electrolux launched a new line of products for the ecology conscious consumer that meets the toughest Australian and European standards for water and energy. It was appropriately named the Electrolux Eco-Range Collection. The line served as evidence of Electrolux's ongoing commitment to being "environmentally sensitive" and conscious of "environmental impact" of its products.

In an open letter, Electrolux President and CEO Hans Straberg shared some good news. Times were challenging but the second quarter 2009 report for Electrolux overall reflected "strong results." These results tied into being successful in all business areas. The company was also able to maintain a "very strong cash flow." This was impressive due to having made price increases in Europe and the U.S. Electrolux also successfully re-launched its Frigidare brand in North America.

Whirlpool Corporation. Whirlpool Corporation is consistently high on the list of the world's appliance industry leaders. It is headquartered in Benton Harbor, Michigan. Major brand names include Whirlpool, KitchenAid, Roper, and Bauknecht. The company is also involved in a number of joint ventures. In the mid-1990s it retained a 47 percent interest in Philips Electronics N.V., a leading European appliance maker. As of 2005 close to 68,000 people were employed by Whirlpool. By 2008, the company reported having annual sales of almost US$19 billion. It also claimed to have more than 70,000 employees working in manufacturing and technology research centers around the world.

Whirlpool was selected to serve on the Consensus Committee for the National Green Building Standard.The company will assist with efforts to transform the National Association of Home Builders' Model Green Home Building Guidelines into a national green building standard that will be certified by the American National Standards Institute. The voluntary guidelines outline fundamental ways to build more environmentally friendly and healthier homes.

The Whirlpool brand was selected as the 14th annual recipient of the Helen Keller Achievement Award saluting individuals and organizations involved in improving the quality of life for visually impaired. A specific acknowledgement was made for the company's Laundry 123 products. They were designed to accommodate the preferred practice of the visually impaired related to returning items to a specific place, aiding location recall.

In an effort to revitalize the Maytag brand it acquired in May 2006 for US$1.9 billion, Whirlpool launched a new advertising campaign. The campaign featured a younger and more proactive version of Maytag's popular repairman. The modern professional went out seeking alternative work instead of just sitting around due to his repair business being slow. Although Maytag had posted 2005 sales of US$4.9 billion, there was still considered to be room for growth. Another revitalization support-related decision enabled the return of Maytag products to Best Buy and Lowe's Home Improvement for sales availability through those national retailers.

When it comes to appliances, what is high-efficiency (HE) and what will it do for me? A Whirlpool-commissioned research survey revealed that almost 60 percent of survey respondents knew about HE laundry appliances. Another research result showed 40 percent were under the false impression that top-load washers had higher energy usage. "Historically, front-load laundry pairs have led the industry

in capacity and efficiency," stated Whirlpool Institute of Fabric Science Home Economist Mary Zeller.

Matsushita Electric Industrial Co. Ltd. The diversified manufacturing firm Matsushita Electric Industrial Co. Ltd. hasoperating units throughout the world. Based in Osaka, Japan, Matsushita is one of the world's top companies in audio/video equipment, home appliances, communication and industrial equipment, and electronic component manufacturing and is the second largest consumer electronics producer. By 2004, sales reached nearly US$81.4 billion, the majority of which were attributed to the Asian market.

According to a May 2007 article published in *The Asahi Shimbun,* Matsushita posted 217.1 billion yen in consolidated net profit. That amount was up 40.7 percent from 2005 due in large part to strong sales of flat-panel TVs and digital cameras.

There were fears thatprofits would be impacted by a recall of approximately 3 million home appliances because the products could possibly emit smoke and catch fire when used for extended periods due to soldering problems. The recall involved about 12 different types of microwave ovens, five models of refrigerators, and eight dryers. Another recall involved dryers supplied to Mitsubishi Electric Corporation.

MAJOR COUNTRIES IN THE INDUSTRY

While the United States remains a key market for household appliance manufacturers, it is not considered a high growth area for the industry. However, it is a crucial player in the global industry because of the billions of dollars spent on imports.

By 2004, foreign competitors such as BSH, Haier, LG, and Samsung were making stronger inroads in the United States, pressuring traditional domestic leaders. For example, in 2002 China's Haier established a US$40 million manufacturing facility in Camden, South Carolina, to produce refrigerators, with a goal of cornering10 percent of the U.S. full-size refrigerator market by 2005. This strategy was unprecedented among Chinese appliance firms. According to *Fortune,* although labor costs were cheaper in China, it was expensive to ship large appliances like refrigerators from Asia to the United States. In addition, Haier preferred to manufacture its products directly within local market areas. Therefore, it installed Chinese management and hired U.S. workers to produce its products domestically, further benefiting from a "Made in the U.S.A." label. Haier began expanding internationally after achieving a leading market share in China. In 2002 alone, the company held 26 percent of China's washing machine market and 29 percent of its refrigerator market, according to *Fortune.*

Alestron shared analysis related to the fourth global summit on household appliances initiated by Gome Electrical Appliances Holding Ltd. Gome is China's top home appliance retailer. Sales growth of communication devices and household appliances was rated as surpassing comparable figures for automobiles and furniture. Thus, consumer electronics were believed to be crucial to China's economic development.

Alestron also reported that Chinese household appliance companies were starting to take advantage of import market opportunities in Africa. This void had previously just been the focus of U.S., Japanese, and Korean companies. Some household appliance companies such as Chunian Group and Midea had reportedly witnessed rapid African market growth.

According to *Appliance Design,* the Freedonia Group's "Household Appliances in China" study estimated that the demand for major household appliances in China was expected to increase by 4.5 percent annually through 2010 to 138 million units. This high rate would outpace growth in other areas of the world. By 2010, China was expected to overtake the United States as the world's largest major household appliances market.

In decades past, the introduction of new products stimulated demand for industry products. Consumers in leading economies in the 1960s wanted dishwashers and dryers. During the 1970s and 1980s, households sought out microwave ovens. In the 1990s, however, such new product introductions slowed. Variations on existing products (such as a washing machine that cleans clothes with sonic technology instead of using water or a dryer that uses microwaves instead of conventional electric or gas heat to dry clothes) were unveiled, but these prototypes failed to attract a large following. With the emergence of computer technology in household appliances, however, consumers are intrigued by the potential new products and features for the future.

Most household appliance markets in the United States are fully mature. This has put pressure on companies to try and cut costs in the face of flat pricing environments. Often, price increases that can be passed along to consumers are just high enough to cover the increases in costs. Market share growth has in some cases been achieved solely through price competition.

In August 2009, British Retail Consortium (BRC) advised the U.K. government to launch a household appliances "scrappage" program. It was estimated the program would make a big difference by offering a small discount on the new equipment purchases. As a result, CO2 emissions would be reduced "by up to 1.3 million tonnes a year by 2020."

According to Geri Smith in an article on the Brazil Chamber of Commerce Web site, things were booming in Brazil. Purchases of food, clothing and household goods were up substantially. Increased demanded for appliances led Grupo Pao de Acucar to expand beyond just focusing on its supermarket chain to purchase Ponto Frito appliance retailer for US$422 million.

BIBLIOGRAPHY

Association of Home Appliances Manufacturers. "Doe Initiates Appliances Rebate Program to Assist Consumers with Purchase of Efficient Appliances." 14 July 2009. Available from www.aham.org.

———. "Home Appliance Energy Savings Quantified." 8 May 2009. Available from www.alwan.org.

Beatty, Gerry. "Major Appliance Biz Reflects (Not Always Happily) On Record Year." *HFN The Weekly Newspaper for the Home Furnishing Network,* 5 January 2004.

Beautyman, Mairi. "Electrolux Seeks Green Appliance Designs." *Interior Design,* 1 June 2007.

BSM Media. "Industry Group Names Whirlpool Brand Best Marketer to Moms." *PR Newswire,* 14 May 2007. Available from sev.prnewswire.com.

CECED. "CECED disagrees with using VAT reduction to promote energy efficient appliances as we believe other incentive schemes are more efficient." 14 April 2008.

"China to Focus On R&D." *Appliance Manufacturer,* July 2004.

"China's Consumer Goods Manufacturers Mounting a U.S. Assault." *The Kiplinger Letter,* 14 March 2003.

"Chinese Appliance Market." *Appliance Design,* December 2006.

"Chinese Household Appliances Makers Build Plants Abroad." *Alestron,* 18 April 2006.

Das, Debdatta. "Electrolux is Led by Consumer Insight." *The Hindu Business Line,* 17 May 2007. Available from www.thehindubusinessline.com.

"DoL Grants $263K to Aid Former Whirlpool Workers in Iowa." 2 June 2007. Available from www.reliableplant.com.

"DTE Energy Customers Turn in More Than 1,000 Old Refrigerators to Company's 'Cash-for-Clunkers' Appliance Recycling Program." *PR Newswire,* 12 August 2009. Available from news.prnewwire.com.

"Eco-friendly choices." *The Sun,* 18 May 2009. Available from www.sun2surf.com.

Electrolux. "Electrolux delivers strong results in a very tough market." 16 July 2009. Available from www.electrolux.com.

"Electrolux to Back Its Ranges With 'Strongest Ever' Ad Support." *Marketing Week,* 3 May 2007. Available from www.marketingweek.co.uk.

Galbraith, Kate. "McKinsey Report Cites $1.2 Trillion in Potential Savings from Energy Efficiency." *New York Times,* 29 July 2009. Available from www.greeninc.blogs.nytimes.com.

Gray, Kathleen. "Appliances get their own recycled clunkers program." *USA Today,* 26 August 2009.

Hampton, Stuart. "Whirlpool Company Description." *Hoover's Online,* 2008. Available from www.hoovers.com.

"Hitachi Appliances to Shift Focus to High-End Air Conditioners." *AsiaPulse News,* 10 May 2007.

"Household Appliances Giants Worry About Profits." *Alestron,* 19 April 2007.

"Household Spending Rose 1.1% in April." *Kyodo News,* 30 May 2007. Available from search.japantimes.co.jp.

International Trade Commission, Office of Trade and Economic Analysis. *U.S. Industry Sector Data,* 17 August 2004. Available from www.ita.doc.gov.

Koucky, Sherri. "Keeping It Green: Take a Look at How Appliance Manufacturers Are Addressing Environmental, Energy, and Performance Issues." *Machine Design,* 13 December 2001, 56-60.

"Matsuhita Electric to Recall 3 Min Home Appliances." *Forbes,* 3 May 2007. Available from www.forbes.com.

Moore, Stephen. "China Seeks to Expand Exports." *Modern Plastics,* May 2002.

Mukherjee, Rupali. "Top-End Focus: Electrolux Hopes to Net Profits in '08." *India Times,* 4 May 2007.Available from timesofindia.indiatimes.com.

"New European Standard for Household Appliances Includes Technology from Echelon." *Energy Resource,* 8 March 2007.

"Older People in 'Appliance Poverty.'" *Age Concern,* 16 May 2002.

Osborn, Suzanne Barry. "The TechnoHome." *Chain Store Executive with Shopping Center Age,* February 2001: 24.

Sanchez, Mark."Whirlpool Launches New Campaign for Maytag Man." *Business Review,* 27 May 2007.

Shukla, Tanvi."Electrolux Readies a Back-to-Black Strategy." Daily News & Analysis, 15 May 2007. Available from www.dnaindia.com/report.

Smith, Geri. "Brazil's Coming Rebound." Brazilian American Chamber of Commerce, 7 August 2009. Available from www.brazilcham.com.

Sprague, Jonathan. "China's Manufacturing Beachhead: No Foreign Brand Has Ever Made It Big in the U.S. Major-Appliance Market. But China's Top White-Goods Maker Is Determined to Change That." *Fortune,* 28 October 2002.

"Three Appliance Makers Post Record Profits." *The Asahi Shimbun,* 4 May 2007.

"UK government asked to introduce household appliance scrappage scheme." Financial News Network, 17 August 2009. Available from financial advice.co.uk.

Whirlpool. "One size does not fit all when it comes to high-efficiency laundry." 1 May 2009. Available from www.whirlpoolcorp.com.

"Whirlpool Corp. Appointed to Consensus Committee for National Green Building Standard." Multi-Housing News, 29 May 2007. Available from www.multi-housingnews.com.

SIC 3651

AUDIO AND VIDEO EQUIPMENT, HOUSEHOLD

NAICS CODE(S)

334310. The global household audio and video equipment industry manufactures a diverse number of electronic entertainment devices, including television sets; radio receivers (including automotive); compact disc (CD) and other digital disc players and recorders; tape players and recorders; amplifiers and speakers; phonographs; and videocassette players and recorders.

For discussion of makers of electronic components for such products, rather than the finished goods, see **Electronic Components**.

INDUSTRY SNAPSHOT

Audio/video equipment is a strong industry worldwide that grows with developing technology. With maturing markets in the United States, Europe, and Japan, digital and other high-tech products provided the highest growth rate in the 2000s. Some of these products included high-definition television sets (HDTV), digital television sets (DTV), digital versatile disc players (DVD), mini-disc (MD) players, digital video recorders (DVR) and Blu-ray discs (BD). Producers also targeted the emerging economies of Eastern Europe, Southeast Asia, and South America with basic model audio and video equipment. Areas of opportunity for mature markets were also available within the automotive industry.

The Consumer Electronics Association (CEA) predicted the total value of consumer electronics shipped would grow approximately 4 percent in 2005, earning just under $100 billion in worldwide revenue for the industry. In 2004 sales of consumer electronics in the United States exceeded US$113 billion, and were slated to top an industry record US$125.7 billion in 2005, representing a 10.7 percent growth over 2004. Digital products were expected to generate 70 percent of that revenue, according to Gary Shapiro, president of the CEA. Sales of DTV products reached US$10.7 billion in 2004, 78 percent higher than 2003. The CEA projected sales of more than 47 million DTV units by 2007, up from 7.3 million in 2004. In spite of a global economic crisis that slowed the industry growth in 2008 and 2009, by 2010 a much-needed upswing seemed to be on the horizon heading into the second decade of the twenty-first century.

The CEA's Home Technology Study estimated that 35,000 firms were installing home theaters. Furthermore, its Home Theater Opportunities Study claimed there was a multi-tiered market with several types of consumers ready to spend money on equipment and services.

ORGANIZATION AND STRUCTURE

Government Policy and Regulation. National governments have played a key role in the industry's development. The Japanese audio and video equipment industry was aided throughout the post-World War II years by the Japanese Ministry of International Trade and Industry (MITI). MITI provided subsidized loans to favored producers in the industry and facilitated research and development. MITI's activities were part of a broader strategy

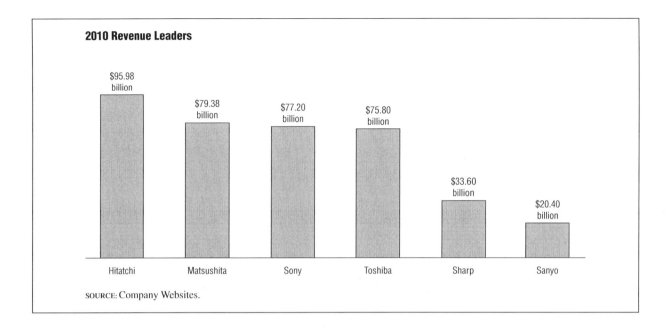

2010 Revenue Leaders

$95.98 billion — Hitatchi
$79.38 billion — Matsushita
$77.20 billion — Sony
$75.80 billion — Toshiba
$33.60 billion — Sharp
$20.40 billion — Sanyo

SOURCE: Company Websites.

of the Japanese government that sought to protect its domestic market from imports and to penetrate foreign markets by offering quality products at low prices.

In the United States, two government agencies, the International Trade Administration (ITA) and the U.S. International Trade Commission (ITC), are responsible for monitoring trade practices of foreign firms. The ITC identifies foreign firms that sell products below market value in the United States, a practice known as dumping. The ITC also determines whether U.S. industries have suffered material injury when the agency finds that dumping has taken place. Upon a finding of material injury, the ITA issues an antidumping order, which is enforced by the U.S. Customs Service.

Industry Associations. Japan's leading trade group, which includes as members all of the industry's leading companies, is the Tokyo-based Electronic Industries Association of Japan. Asian manufacturers are served by the Asia Electronics Union, established in 1968 and headquartered in Tokyo. The union publishes the English language bimonthly *Journal of AEU* and facilitates cooperation among its members in the areas of research, applications, and manufacturing techniques. Many Chinese producers of audio and video equipment are members of the China Audio Industry Association, the China Radio and T.V. Equipment Industry Association, or the China Electronics Chamber of Commerce. These three organizations were all established in the 1980s and are reflective of the relative newness of the consumer electronics industry in China. The U.S. industry is served by the Consumer Electronics Manufacturers Association of the Electronic Industries Association, established in 1924

and headquartered in Washington, D.C. Association publications include the *Electronic Market Data Book* and *U.S. Consumer Electronics Industry Today.*

BACKGROUND AND DEVELOPMENT

The household audio and video equipment industry originated in the late nineteenth century. Thomas Edison's development of the phonograph in 1877 and Guglielmo Marconi's use of wireless transmissions in 1895 were establishing innovations. Another important early innovation was Lee DeForest's vacuum tube, developed in 1906, which allowed electronic signals to be amplified.

The 1920s were important years of research and commercialization for the industry. Developments included the first commercial radio broadcast in 1922; the Western Electric Company's patents for electrical sound recording and the placement in radios of loudspeakers instead of headphones in 1924; the introduction of the alternating current (AC) radio in 1926; Philo Farnsworth's television patents and the introduction of automobile radios in 1927; and the first U.S. experimental television station permits, issued by the government in 1928.

The industry enjoyed rapid growth in the 1920s and 1930s. During that period more than 100 million radios were sold in the United States. The Federal Communications Commission (FCC) was established in the United States in 1934 to regulate broadcasting. The FCC authorized FM (frequency modulation) radio and television broadcasting in 1941, but these developments were forestalled by the country's entry into World War

II. By the end of World War II, there were nine commercial television stations, 46 commercial FM stations, and 943 AM (amplitude modulation) stations in the United States.

The late 1940s saw the industry return to its prewar patterns of rapid growth and innovation. In 1947 the first magnetic tape recorders were marketed, and Bell Telephone Laboratories demonstrated the first transistor. The transistor marked the birth of solid-state electronic components, commercialized in 1954 with the mass-marketing of the first "pocket" radio. Home audio hobbyists who put together their own systems revealed that the capacity for fidelity of sound-reproducing equipment far exceeded the fidelity of existing recordings. This led to the introduction of 45-rpm records and 33-rpm long-playing records in 1948. These records were the first mass-produced "hi-fi" or high fidelity recordings. Other important developments in these years included color television broadcasting in 1954, videotape recording for television stations in 1956, and stereophonic audio systems in 1958.

Sales of color televisions surged during the mid-1960s. The first solid-state color televisions were marketed in 1967. By the mid-1970s, solid-state color sets dominated the market. The first color videocassette recorders for household use were marketed in 1975, and sales increased rapidly after the early 1980s. The 1980s saw the introduction and rapid diffusion of digital technologies in household audio and video equipment. The industry developed compact disc and accommodating audio systems—first mass-marketed in 1983—that quickly supplanted phonograph and tape systems.

Japan's Emergence. One of the most important developments in the industry after World War II was the dramatic competitive success of Japanese producers, which progressively unseated U.S. manufacturers as the world's leading audio/video equipment producers. The foundations of Japan's ascendance were established in the immediate post-World War II years. The Japanese government's Ministry of International Trade and Industry (MITI) favored a handful of firms in the audio and video equipment industry, creating a powerful cartel. MITI's policy was to grant large low-interest loans to favored firms and deny credit to other firms. The Fair Trade Commission of Japan (FTCJ) argued that the consumer electronics cartel violated Japan's Antimonopoly Law of 1947. In a 1957 decision, the FTCJ ruled that Japanese firms had conspired to set prices. The FTCJ also stated in a 1970 decision that Japanese producers of consumer electronics were in violation of the Antimonopoly Law. In spite of these findings, however, the cartel continued to operate.

At the same time, foreign producers had great difficulty establishing a viable presence in the Japanese market. The domestic dominance of Japanese firms resulted in part from the common practice of granting exclusive retail dealerships. Retailers were given large rebates by affiliated manufacturers if they agreed to sell only that manufacturer's products. By the mid-1960s two-thirds of consumer electronics retailers in Japan were exclusive dealerships, and this share increased by the mid-1980s. Japanese producers of audio and video equipment also controlled the home market by purchasing wholesalers; by the 1970s, Japanese firms had acquired majority stakes in nearly all consumer electronic wholesale businesses in Japan.

Japan's trade policies helped buffer its audio/video equipment industry against foreign competition. The Foreign Exchange and Foreign Trade Control Law banned imports of a number of products, while the Law Concerning Foreign Investment prohibited foreign firms from establishing more than 10 wholly controlled facilities in Japan. Both of these laws were overturned in 1967. Until 1968, however, tariff rates on televisions were between 20 and 30 percent, but were reduced to 4 percent by 1973. Government regulations also required that all imports be paid for within four months of import.

MITI's control of foreign exchange enabled it to impose quantitative restrictions on imports. In the early 1960s, the Zenith Corporation of the United States attempted to market its television sets in Japan through a Japanese wholesaler. However, a letter from the wholesaler to Zenith stated that owing to the popularity of Zenith televisions, MITI would not allocate the foreign exchange required.

The Japanese government also facilitated research and development in the industry. In recent years, for instance, the government assessed a US$10 tax on every color television sold. The money was earmarked for research on high-definition television.

However, nongovernmental factors also contributed to the success of the Japanese audio and video equipment industry. In many cases, Japanese manufacturers were more efficient and more innovative than international counterparts, and this made their products more enticing to consumers in terms of both pricing and features.

Trade Dispute. U.S. producers argued that Japanese firms conspired to restrict competition among themselves, selling products at below market value to penetrate the U.S. market. In 1970 the National Union Electric Corporation of the United States filed suit under the Sherman Antitrust Act on behalf of U.S. producers Motorola Inc. and Sears, Roebuck and Co. The Zenith Radio Corporation joined the suit in 1974. The Japanese firms named in the suit were Hitachi Ltd., Matsushita Electric Industrial Company Ltd., the Toshiba Corporation, the Sony Corporation, the Mitsubishi Electric Corporation, Sanyo Electric Company Ltd., and the Sharp Corporation, all of which still rank as leading world companies. The case came before the U.S. Supreme Court in 1984 and became known as *Matsushita et al. v. Zenith Radio et al.* In a controversial 1986 ruling, the Supreme Court held that the Japanese firms had acted legally, affirming the position of the Reagan administration.

The U.S. International Trade Administration (ITA) continued to find evidence of price dumping by Japanese firms into the 1990s, however. Price dumping was measured by a "dumping margin," the difference between the home market price and export price expressed as a percentage of the export price. The ITA found that in 1991, the average dumping margin for Japanese televisions was 35 percent. The average dumping margin for all Japanese goods imported into the United States between 1980 and 1989 was estimated at 44 percent.

Events in the 1980s helped to solidify Japanese producers' gains and U.S. firms' marginalization. Japan's production expanded three times faster than U.S. production during the decade, and European output rose almost twice as fast. The U.S. hold on the market dropped from 44 percent in 1980 to 11 percent by decade's end. Not surprisingly, the U.S. trade deficit with Japan in consumer electronics stood at more than US$10 billion in 1990. However, the decline of U.S. consumer electronics firms could also be traced to factors within U.S. borders. The production of color television sets in the United States was hindered by the country's lag in integrated circuit technology. In the face of falling prices, U.S. producers responded with a short-run approach, cutting investment and increasing volume rather than emphasizing quality and productivity, the approach taken by their Japanese counterparts.

Japanese firms pursued similar strategies of market penetration in Europe. Some Japanese manufacturers turned to direct foreign investment in Europe as a means of circumventing import restrictions. Sony was the first Japanese consumer electronics firm to establish production facilities in the United States and in Europe. After Sony opened its television production plant in the United Kingdom in 1968, several other Japanese firms followed suit. Many of the television sets produced in the United Kingdom were shipped to other European countries. From 1979 to 1981, the Japanese share of the West German television market more than doubled. In the 1980s, Japanese penetration into the European market also was facilitated by the expiration of patents protecting broadcasting technologies. These patents were held by

the German firm AEG-Telefunken and applied to all western European countries except for France.

The production of consumer electronics in the newly industrializing countries of East Asia increased rapidly during the 1980s and 1990s, especially in South Korea, China, Singapore, Hong Kong, Malaysia, and Taiwan. Much of this production resulted from the foreign investment of European, U.S., and especially Japanese firms, which were attracted by the substantially lower wages paid to skilled workers in these countries. By the early 1980s, however, both South Korea and Taiwan had large, locally owned television production plants. Much of the production of consumer electronics in these countries was exported to other nations. These overseas sales further contributed to the highly competitive nature of the world market for audio and video equipment.

In 1994 the North American Free Trade Agreement (NAFTA) was implemented. The purposes of this agreement were to stimulate trade among the United States, Mexico, and Canada; to create jobs; to increase wages in Mexico; to improve environmental policies on the continent; and to generate goodwill among the nations. Among the effects of NAFTA is the growth of Mexico's television exports.

CURRENT CONDITIONS

By the mid-2000s, rapid growth caused DVD-player sales to outpace VCR sales. Jim Barry, a spokesperson for the Consumer Electronics Association (CEA), told the Associated Press that the rapid acceptance of DVD players resembled the quick acceptance of black-and-white television sets by Americans after World War II. By the mid-2000s, more than half of U.S. households contained a DVD player.

In 2003 DVD rental revenues topped VHS rentals for the first time, as reported by the Video Software Dealers Association. Spending by consumers on all video rentals was US$8.06 billion in 2004, off just 0.4 percent from 2003. DVD rental revenue, however, rose 39.2 percent to US$5.73 billion, about 70 percent of the total rental market. VHS rentals fell to US$2.33 billion.

Growth in consumer electronics was also powered by the transition to digital products in mature markets. A 2005 CEA study showed the analog to digital transition was influencing purchasing decisions as high-definition and flat-panel televisions gained market share, as did digital video recorders and DVD players. Portable MP3 players performed particularly well above expectations, doubling in the number of units shipped and tripling in revenue during 2004.

According to *Euromonitor,* the U.S. market for audio products was projected to increase 5.5 percent by 2008, and the market for video products was projected to increase 37.9 percent. By comparison, the French market for audio products was projected to increase 9 percent by 2008, and the market for video products was projected to increase 199 percent, largely due to DVD players. The German market for audio products was projected to increase 24 percent by 2008, with a 74 percent decrease expected for video products, largely due to market saturation. In the United Kingdom, audio products were expected to enjoy a market increase of 46 percent by 2008, with a 16 percent decline anticipated for video products.

RESEARCH AND TECHNOLOGY

HDTV (high-definition television) offers the picture quality of a 35-millimeter photograph combined with the sound quality of a compact disc player. Compared to conventional analog television, with its 525 horizontal lines, HDTV has 1,080 horizontal lines, providing far sharper images and detail. One of the factors hindering the sales of HDTV was standardization. The Advanced Television Advisory Committee of the U.S. Federal Communications Commission (FCC) fought for an HDTV standard but gave up the fight in 1997 and let private industry decide. Led by Dolby Laboratories and Zenith Electronics, the U.S. industry developed a standard incompatible with that of Europe. Consequently, U.S. and European manufacturers, using their different technologies, competed vigorously to win as many foreign customers as possible. In mid-1998, commercial U.S. television companies planned to begin broadcasting HDTV programs, and manufacturers anticipated full-scale HDTV set deliveries.

Wide-screen television was introduced into the United States in 1993 by a European manufacturer who marketed it under the name Pro Scan. The advantage of wide-screen television is that its width-to-height ratio of 16 to 9 was much closer to that of 35-millimeter movies than the standard set with its 4 to 3 width-to-height ratio. Wide-screen televisions are not high-definition, but are designed to be adaptable to HDTV. With the increased viewing of feature films on television—in large part a result of the popularity of pay television (see also **Cable and Other Pay-Television Services**), VCRs, and DVD players—the growth prospects of wide-screen television appear promising. One alternative to wide-screen television is the so-called letterboxing of broadcasts and videos. In this practice, the top and bottom parts of conventional sets are blocked out to accommodate 35-millimeter films. Films that are letterboxed, however, make use of only 60 percent of the conventional television's screen height.

As the Internet generation approached adulthood, the television industry was investigating the unique desires of this market. According to CEA research, members of Generation Y (children of the Baby Boomers, born between 1979 and 1994) were expected to find interest in accessing information about programming while watching. Examples include getting more information about a product, reviewing athletic statistics, or scanning movie reviews. There was interest expected in combining Internet features with television viewing, so users could check e-mail, shop online, or "surf" the Internet while watching television.

Another important development for the industry was the home theater, which integrates large-screen television sets with high quality audio systems. These products provided a significant boost to high-end producers of speakers and audio components. In 2002 Zenith introduced a 52-inch rear projection HDTV intended primarily for consumers with home theaters, thus responding to the market for wide-screen HDTVs with rear projection technology. To enthusiasts, this type of product represents the best of all worlds. The growth of the home theater market also led to several joint ventures between large furniture companies and producers of household audio and video equipment. LCD and plasma televisions were increasing in popularity as well. Technology advanced quickly during the early to mid-2000s, and price declines made the technology more affordable to consumers worldwide.

Statistics indicate that the majority of households with televisions also have VCRs. Unfortunately, the majority of VCR owners are unable to program their units and reap the full advantages of the device. This led to developments such as voice-activated programming that were designed to simplify programming procedures. Eight Japanese and two European VCR manufacturers developed a world standard for digital VCRs in an effort to avoid the incompatibility problems caused by the dual VHS and Beta videocassette formats. Digital VCRs were largely designed for use with high-definition television. The Zenith Electronics Corporation of the United States and Goldstar Ltd. of South Korea co-developed a digital VCR that used standard Super-VHS videocassettes and could record and play back in both HDTV and standard television formats.

Another answer to the difficulties of recording missed or concurrent programs is digital video recorder (DVR) technology. DVRs allow viewers to record any show on any channel at any time, without loading videotapes into the machine or programming it to record. Viewers simply set up the system to record whatever shows they choose, and every day the system records the appropriate program. This is convenient for recording new episodes and for episodes in syndication. The system also has the capability of matching viewer preferences with other shows not selected, in essence recommending new shows the viewer might enjoy. Another feature viewers enjoy about DVR technology is that it gives them the power to pause a show being watched without losing any of the show. Watching television then has the convenience of watching traditional videotapes that can be stopped, paused, rewound, and played at the touch of a button. The leader and originator of this technology is TiVo, whose customer satisfaction is so high that 97 percent recommend the system to friends. In 2002 the service was available through three different receivers. In January of the same year, TiVo introduced the TiVo Series 2 DVR, which offered greater recording capacity, lower cost, and entertainment features such as digital music, broadband video on demand, and video games.

In the late 1990s, DVD emerged as the successor to existing CD audio, CD-ROM, and laser videodisc formats. Pioneering manufacturers Matsushita, Sony, and others hailed it as the next revolutionary consumer electronics product. Robust sales of DVD players were anticipated as the format seemed likely to replace the VCR. With a 4.7 gigabyte capacity, DVDs can store an entire movie in stereo on a five-inch disk that allows speedy random access to any portion of the recording, as with the audio CD player, compared to videotape's slower and more cumbersome sequential access. Furthermore, manufacturers designed their DVD players to be backwards compatible—that is, to recognize older formats such as the audio CD and the CD-ROM. In the mid-2000s, sales of DVD players exceeded sales of VCRs.

Other innovations in audio formats included digital audiotape recorders (DATs), digital compact cassettes (DCCs), and minidiscs (MDs). These formats offered the same sound quality of conventional CDs, but also provided buyers with the additional ability to record. DCCs had the same copy-protection mechanism of the earlier-developed DATs, but their standard cassette format enabled the use of analog cassettes. Sales of DCC and MD audio equipment were slow in the early 1990s, and these technologies never blossomed as proponents expected.

By the mid-2000s, the development and inclusion of plastic computer chips in most electronic devices had become a reality. Not only is plastic cheaper than traditional glass or silicon chips, but it is also more durable. According to the independent research firm Gartner, plastic chips eventually will be produced with polymer inks, by any press or printer. When this occurs, specialized semiconductor manufacturing will not be needed, making plastic chip technology more available to a variety of companies and for a variety of applications. Some industry players projected the market for plastic chip technology will eventually reach a value of US$300 billion or more.

INDUSTRY LEADERS

Hitachi Ltd. Hitachi was established in 1910 and incorporated in 1920. Headquartered in Tokyo, the firm is one of the world's leading producers of electrical and electronic equipment and boasts a diversified global network. Hitachi Ltd.'s 2010 revenues were US$95.98 billion. The company employed more than 359,700 people worldwide as of 2010.

In March 2007, Hitachi announced its plans to close a parts factory in Guadalajara, Mexico, and cut 4,500 jobs, which would result in an estimated savings of US$300 million over five years. Related moves were part of restructuring measures focused at reviving the company's hard-disc drive business, which had been consistently in the red. Hitachi planned to shift production to developing countries in Asia by focusing on manufacturing hard-disc drives at its factory in Shenzhen, China. The company also planned to phase out production in Odawara, Japan, by the fourth quarter of 2007.

Toshiba Corp. Headquartered in Tokyo, the Toshiba Corp. has entered into cooperative arrangements with the General Electric Company of the United States, Siemens AG, and Olivetti of Italy. Toshiba's sales totaled US$75.8 billion in the fiscal year 2010. The company had 172,000 employees. Electronic devices were responsible for $12.2 billion in 2005, or 21 percent. Sales within Japan accounted for $46.8 billion, or 64 percent of revenue.

In January 2007, Toshiba announced its plans to appeal a European Union fine for price-fixing. Fines were issued against five European and five Japanese companies for fixing prices on switchgears used by power utilities. Toshiba protested, claiming it had "not engaged in illegal activity."

Toshiba also announced it had established a software research and development center geared toward digital consumer products in Vietnam. Toshiba Software Development Co. was established as a wholly owned subsidiary located in Hanoi and was scheduled to begin full operation in June 2007. A staff of about 20 was expected to grow to around 300 by fiscal year 2010. Toshiba already had software development bases in both China and India.

Toshiba America Consumer Products announced its plans to launch marketing initiatives to support the company's HD DVD and REGZA brands. *The Sopranos* TV show star Michael Imperioli will appear in HD DVD print ads and REGZA and HD DVD TV commercials. Toshiba's REGZA premium LCD TV line offered eight different screen sizes. A major objective of the campaign was to share the "REGZA difference." The other HD DVD campaign ads would spotlight key player attributes. In 2010, Toshiba announced the launch of its Toshiba

Regza GL LCD glasses-free 3D television, to be released in December 2010.

Sony Corp. Tokyo-based Sony wields one of the most powerful brand names in the industry. In 2005 televisions, VCRs, stereos, and other consumer electronics accounted for more than two-thirds of the company's revenues, which totaled US$77.2 billion in 2010. Sony reported having 167,900 employees. More than 80 percent of its 225 designers were based in Japan.

Sony was listed among the world's 25 most innovative companies in the third annual special report by *Business Week.* The company ranked 10th, moving up from 13th in previous listings, due in part to the development of software for use in online game consoles. the Boston Consulting Group consulted nearly 2,500 executives worldwide to vote for the companies worthy of listing.

Sony announced its plans to introduce its first HD radio products in July 2007. The hot product summer launch would allow Sony to join the growing group of companies striving to make the next generation of radio technology a standard feature in audio products. HD radio, in the form of digital radio broadcasting, allows radio stations to deliver digital musical content in addition to their analog signals. In excess of 1,200 radio stations had adopted the technology.

According to *Business Week,* Sony's U.S. chiefs were becoming more confident in their ability to reject products created in Japan that wouldn't work for their market. They rejected a Walkman that was considered to be too small to be a worthy alternative to Apple's iPod. Furthermore, products designed or improved in the United States were believed to be having a positive impact on Sony's sales.

Mitsubishi Electric Corp. Mitsubishi was established in 1921 from the electrical machinery division of Mitsubishi Shipbuilding's Kobe shipyard. Mitsubishi's diverse output includes televisions and VCRs, as well as satellites, cell phones, fax machines, semiconductors, medical equipment, and security equipment. Electronic devices were responsible for 4.3 percent of Mitsubishi revenue in 2004, and home appliances for 22.8 percent. Mitsubishi Electric Corporation's sales totaled US$32.6 billion in 2007, and the company employed more than 102,800 workers.

Sanyo Electric Company Ltd. Sanyo was established in 1947 and is headquartered in Osaka, Japan. Revenues for 2010 were US$20.4 billion. The company employed about 90,600 people.

In March 2007, Sanyo announced a major change in its leadership ranks. Executive Officer Seiichiro Sano was set to replace Toshimasa Iue as president, putting an end to the founding family's leadership of Sanyo's management. It was the first time a member of the founding family would not hold either the chairman or president position. The announcement followed Sanyo chairwoman Tomoyo Nonaka's resignation. The resignation was in response to conflict over whether or not to launch a thorough investigation into an accounting scandal at the company.

Sharp Corp. Also headquartered in Osaka, Sharp originated in 1912. In the early 2000s, consumer audio/visual products accounted for 20 percent of total revenues. Sharp has a significant presence in international markets; the Asian market represented 70 percent of Sharp's sales in 2001. In 2010 Sharp experienced an increase in sales, to US$33.6 billion, up from US$21.4 billion in 2004, and the company employed 64,500 people. In 2007, Sharp took a controlling stake in the Pioneer Corporation and in June 2009 agreed to form a joint venture with them in the optical sector.

Pioneer Corp. Pioneer was established in 1947 in Tokyo as a successor to a loudspeaker manufacturing company. Unlike some of its more diversified competitors, the firm produces household audio and video equipment almost exclusively. Pioneer's innovations in laser optical hardware and software in the 1980s made the firm a leader in consumer and industrial audiovisual equipment. In 2007 the company posted sales of US$9.4 billion, an increase from the US$6.6 billion in 2004, and had a workforce of more than 37,600 employees. In February 2009, Pioneer announced its intention to cease manufacturing television sets by spring 2010.

Matsushita Electric Industrial Company Ltd. Matsushita was founded in 1918 and is headquartered in Osaka, Japan. A top maker of consumer electronics, the firm produces products under the brand names of Panasonic, Technics, Quasar, and National. Its principal operating subsidiary in this industry is the Matsushita Communication Industrial Company Ltd., which was established in 1958 and is headquartered in Yokohama, Japan. In the mid-1990s Matsushita began manufacturing many of its products abroad to take advantage of lower labor costs. In fiscal 2010 the company posted sales in excess of US$79.38 billion. As of March 2010, the company employed 384,586 people globally.

In April 2007, Matsushita announced that it had started manufacturing liquid crystal display TVs in Malaysia in order to meet a growing demand in the region. The company's local subsidiary, Panasonic AVC

Networks Kuala Lumpur Malaysia Sdn. Bhd., said it officially started producing the Viera series LCD TVs at its plant in Shah Alam, located near Kuala Lumpur. Panasonic AVC Managing Director Akihiko Hayase claimed that global demand for LCD TVs had reached 51 million sets and was expected to rise to 100 million sets by 2010.

Another April 2007 announcement revealed that Matsushita and CMS Magnetics Corp. had reached a settlement in a lawsuit Matsushita had brought against CMS related to its use of patented technologies regarding DVD discs. Matsushita will receive patent royalty from CMC to pay for damages and use of proprietary technologies.

Business Week Online discussed Matsushita's practice of using the same basic technology platform of microprocessors and software in Panasonic TVs, DVD recorders, and navigation systems. Director of Platform Development Satoru Fujikawa was reportedly responsible for the plan to design consumer electronics capable of connecting with each other.

MAJOR COUNTRIES IN THE INDUSTRY

The U.S. Bureau of Labor Statistics projected declines in all 32 occupations in the industry between 1992 and 2005. Most of these occupations were projected to suffer double-digit declines, with 13 of the 32 occupations projected to have declines of 30 percent or greater. However, trade liberalizations of the mid-1990s—brought about by the North American Free Trade Agreement (NAFTA) and the Uruguay Round of the General Agreement on Tariffs and Trade (GATT)—were expected to stimulate growth of the industry in general. In 2003, the United States imported US$5.2 billion of household audio and video equipment, increasing US$5.2 billion over a five-year period. U.S. exports declined US$485 million over the same period to a low of US$5.2 billion in 2003. As the decade-ending global recession continued to impact the industry, sales were primarily in the cheaper imported-product sector rather than in the unionized industrial countries. Prices could be kept lower in the developing countries where there were few (or ineffective) labor unions monitoring wages, working hours, or working conditions. Imports continued to be on the rise as of 2010.

Japan was the world's leading producer and exporter of household audio and video equipment throughout the 1990s. However, its dominance was challenged during the 1980s and 1990s by rapidly expanding production in South Korea, China, Singapore, Hong Kong, Malaysia, and Taiwan. Nevertheless, Japan remained a major exporter of audio and video equipment. Companies used

strategic partnerships to strengthen their positions in the face of increased competition worldwide. As of early 2005, Hitachi and Matsushita had agreed to cooperate in the plasma display business; Sharp Corporation agreed to buy Fujitsu's LCD business and related patents; and Sony has signed a cross-licensing pact with South Korea's Samsung Electronics Co. covering a range of digital technologies.

Japan's leading export position eroded in a number of key respects. With greater competition from other Asian countries such as South Korea, Singapore, China, and Malaysia, Japan's stronghold on world exports diminished. Therefore, control of the audio and video equipment market in the 1990s became more evenly distributed among Asian countries with developing economies. However, the successful production of household audio and video equipment in these Asian countries resulted in part from investment by Japanese firms, many of which had extensive overseas operations.

Mexico, backed by Japanese and U.S. manufacturers seeking a lower-wage labor market, emerged as a leading force in the industry. Mexico became the top exporter of TVs in 1994 and retained this position through 2001. Because of its participation in NAFTA and its proximity to the United States, the leading market for audio/video products, Mexico became an advantageous place to manufacture television sets. Most of Mexican production, however, was based on investment by Japanese, South Korean, and U.S. firms. In this sense, Mexican production of audio/video equipment was an extension of trade between the United States and Asia.

BIBLIOGRAPHY

Alpeyev, Pavel. "Hitachi to Cut 11 percent of Disk Jobs: Action will Also Shutter Factories in Japan and Mexico." *International Herald Tribune,* 23 March 2007.

Archer, Bob. "CE Pro Consumers, Manufacturers Increase Focus on Good-Looking Products," CE Pro, 11 May 2007. Available from http://www.cepro.com.

"Audio Products in France, Germany, UK, US." *Euromonitor,* August 2004. Available from www.majormarketprofiles.com.

Edwards, Cliff, and Kenji Hall. "Remade in the USA: Sony's Comeback May Ride on Its Yankee Know-How." *Business Week,* 7 May 2007.

"Fierce Global Competition in the Flat Panel Television Market Is Leading Major Japanese Electronics Makers to Seek Partners for Advanced Technologies and Lower Costs." *Asia Africa Intelligence Wire,* 7 February 2005.

Hall, Kenji. "Matsushita's Platform for Success." *Business Week Online,* 29 March 2007. Available from www.businessweek.com.

"Hoover's Company Capsules." *Hoover's Online,* 2007. Available from www.hoovers.com.

"Household Penetration of CE Products Soars in 2005." *Business Wire,* 17 May 2005.

Magiera, Marcy. "Rental Finishes Flat." *Video Business,* 3 January 2005.

"Matsushita Begins Production of LCD TVs in Malaysia." *Kyodo News International,* 5 April 2007.

"Matsushita, Taiwan Optical Maker Settle Patent Violation Suit." *Kyodo News International,* 2 April 2007.

Nordwall, Eric. "Sony to Introduce HD Radio Devices." *USA Today,* 29 May 2007.

"Pioneer Hires AIS for Digital Needs." *Marketing,* 28 February 2007.

"Research and Markets Assesses Plasma TV Market." *Wireless News,* 1 May 2005.

Sanchanta, Mariko. "Hitachi Shuts Mexican Plant Amid Revamp of Hard-Disc Unit." *The Financial Times,* 23 March 2007.

"Sanyo Approves Iue's Resignation, to Have Sano as New President." *Kyodo News International,* 29 March 2007.

"Toshiba Sets Up Vietnamese R&D Center for Embedded Software." *AsiaPulse News,* 9 May 2007.

"Toshiba to Appeal EU Cartel Fine; Others May Follow Suit." *AsiaPulse News,* 25 January 2007.

"Toshiba's New Marketing Campaign to Feature *Sopranos* Star Michael Imperioli." *Wireless News,* 7 May 2007.

SIC 3640

ELECTRIC LIGHTING AND WIRING EQUIPMENT

NAICS CODE(S)

3351. Lighting and wiring equipment manufacturers supply electrical goods such as light bulbs, lighting fixtures, electrical outlets, switches, fuses, and similar devices, and hardware for commercial and residential electrical service.

INDUSTRY SNAPSHOT

The electric lighting and wiring equipment industry incorporates a wide variety of products and companies. It includes among its major players some of the largest diversified corporations in the world, and mergers and acquisitions are common. The various facets of this broad

Industry Leaders, 2010

	Revenue, in billions of U.S. dollars
General Electric	$156.78
Siemens AG	$112.23
Hitachi Ltd.	$102.70
Royal Philips Electronics N.V.	$ 33.22
Cooper Industries	$ 5.07

SOURCE: *Forbes,* "The Global 2000," April 21, 2010.

field constitute a multibillion-dollar industry. Due to the global nature of the industry, most manufacturers are able to stay competitive. Whenever one nation's economy suffers, thereby impacting sales, there are numerous customers in other parts of the world to counterbalance the lost revenue.

In a highly competitive industry, lighting and wiring equipment manufacturers move quickly to meet changing environmental and economic demands. Few revolutionary technological breakthroughs have occurred in recent years and, as a result, most companies' research and development (R&D) efforts were focused on increasing the energy efficiency of lighting fixtures and related electrical devices to accommodate the demand for environmentally sound, efficient products. However, lighting and wiring manufacturers continue to seek new markets, which has led them to address specialized needs such as highway, emergency, entertainment venue, and landscape lighting.

Closely tied to construction and renovation activity, growth in the lighting and wiring categories depends largely on general economic health, and thus the climate for building, in each country. While the incandescent bulb is still the mainstay product around the world, manufacturers are increasing offerings to the construction industry. In times of economic bounty, demand for specialized and customized products increases.

After a downturn during the recession of the early part of the century, the U.S. lighting industry was steadily increasing in the mid-2000s, largely due to new construction and the growing remodeling and renovation market sectors. In 2003, the lighting industry was up 5 percent, to more than US$5 billion. In the United States, lighting products were expected to account for around 30 percent of electrical distribution sales in 2005, reaching $26 billion. Worldwide, the market was valued at about US$12 billion in 2003, according to an analyst from Strategies Unlimited. Globally, the lighting market was expected to grow about 6.5 percent annually through 2014, according to a September 2010 report by the Freedonia Group. In the mid-2000s, China was the largest exporter to, and one of the largest importers from, the U.S. market. By 2004, China's market accounted for more than 80 percent of all U.S. lamp and lighting imports. Lamp imports, which totaled US$166 million in 2001 and US$409 million in 2002, increased another 8 percent in 2003. As the U.S. construction industry stalled during the recession at the close of the decade, sales within the U.S. sector slowed. However, China was expected to account for one-third of all new demands as their building boom is expected to continue through 2014.

ORGANIZATION AND STRUCTURE

Most of the leaders in production and sales of electric lighting and wiring equipment are divisions of major, diversified international corporations. Maximizing the potential financial impact of increased international trade through agreements such as the North American Free Trade Agreement (NAFTA) has proven to be a major springboard for many of these and smaller corporations. Increasingly, companies, especially in the United States, manufactured products overseas where labor is significantly cheaper, and imported them back into other markets for sale, a trend that caused imports to surge in the 1990s.

While lighting is an essential aspect of life in industrialized countries, production levels of the lighting industry are linked to the notoriously cyclical construction industry. During periods when relatively few houses and office buildings are being built, fewer lighting fixtures are sold. Conversely, when the construction industry is booming, sales of lighting fixtures are also strong. The 1980s saw a period of unparalleled real estate construction worldwide, with the downtowns and peripheries of large cities undergoing extensive expansion and refurbishment. In the early 1990s, construction inevitably slowed before a mild upturn in the mid-1990s. A decade later, construction would be back on the rise.

Production and sales of wiring were largely dependent on nonresidential building, of which there was substantial growth in the mid-1990s. However, fluctuations in that segment were far more dramatic (and common) than for residential construction, to which the lighting industry was closely linked. Non-current-carrying wiring devices, in particular, derived the vast majority of applications from nonresidential construction.

Environmental concerns continued to play a major role in the industry. Because most countries spend a substantial amount of electricity on lighting (close to one-quarter in the United States), the industry has seen pressure from the outside and from internal competition to develop more energy-efficient products. In 1997, the U.S. Environmental Protection Agency (EPA) initiated the voluntary Energy Star program, which encouraged manufacturers of electric lighting equipment to produce lighting that emits less carbon dioxide, sulfur oxide, and nitrogen oxide while simultaneously realizing cost-saving benefits.

According to Eufemio Cariaga, the California Energy Commission's enactment of its Title 24 revision helped to drive energy conservation demands. Title 24 established mandates related to new and remodeled residential and non-residential facilities, forcing them to comply with stricter energy-efficiency standards. These standards, plus customer demands for products that reduced energy costs, prompted manufacturers to create more "energy-efficient lighting solutions" and make them accessible for electrical contractors. These new products were capable of outstanding performance when retrofitting existing facilities or installing new ones. Special certifications, such as ASTM E283, a test method that measures air leakage through exterior windows, walls, and doors, offered one means of finding more energy-efficient products.

BACKGROUND AND DEVELOPMENT

Electric Lighting. The first electric light was invented in 1860 by English physicist Joseph W. Swan. He created a vacuum inside a glass bulb that allowed a small piece of carbonized paper to burn for a short time. However, it was difficult to maintain the perfect vacuum pressure required for steady, consistent burning. Nevertheless, Swan's work paved the way for Thomas Alva Edison, a young New Jersey scientist, to invent his electric light in 1879. In that year, both inventors developed a way to manufacture reliable electric light bulbs by putting the filament inside the bulb, pumping out the air, and then sealing it up. Early successes relied on platinum wires to conduct the electricity into the bulb, but subsequent experiments revealed that copper-plated nickel alloy was also suitable. That alloy is the material used in today's light bulbs.

Edison worked on electric lights for nearly his entire adult life. He was determined to develop a lamp in which the filament became incandescent—that is, producing a glowing white light resulting from the heat of the electric current going through it. Subsequently, he spent thousands of dollars experimenting with different combinations of metals and gases that would provide a long-lasting incandescence. On October 21, 1879, Edison's work paid off when he was able to get a piece of burnt cotton thread in a glass vacuum bulb to burn for more than 40 hours. The cotton was eventually replaced by charred bamboo, which in turn was replaced by tungsten, a metal with a very high melting point. Additional refinements included spraying hydrofluoric acid inside the bulb to create a frosting that diffused the light and reduced glare, and filling the bulb's vacuum with a bit of argon or nitrogen to prolong the life of the tungsten filament. Not incidentally, Edison also developed an entire system of electricity generation and distribution. Such a system, of course, needed to be installed in every city and town in order to deliver electric light to residences and businesses, and for public use.

Neon lights were invented in the late nineteenth century when scientists realized that electricity applied to both ends of a glass tube filled with neon gas would start to glow bright red. Mercury vapor used in the same way glows blue; helium, golden; and mercury in a yellow-tinted tube, green. Several gases combined yielded white. This technology was immediately adopted for advertising and signs.

In the 1930s, fluorescent lights were invented by coating the inside of a glass tube with a substance that reacted with mercury gas to glow white a hundred times more brightly than it would have without the coating. Subsequent developments, such as high-pressure gas lamps, were adapted for street lighting.

Wiring. Ancient civilizations probably made wire for jewelry and decorative purposes by rolling gold and other metals into flat strips and then twisting them. The process of making perfectly round wire in long strings by pulling metal through a tiny die by hand took root in Europe in the Middle Ages. By 1270 in France and 1465 in England, wire was a commodity that was manufactured in large quantities for domestic use and export.

Such early precursors set the stage for electrical uses, which required electrically conductive yet concealed wire to carry electrical service into homes and businesses and within devices powered by electricity. Wire was crucial to various manufacturing and telecommunications industries, so its quality was constantly monitored. The basic process of making wire has changed little since the 1940s. This involves heating a bar of metal to about 2,200 degrees Fahrenheit and rolling it into a thin rod. Very thin wire is made by a drawing block, powered by an electric motor, that pulls the rod through a die; the narrower the hole, the thinner the wire. The finest wires are drawn through numerous successive dies, each 5 to 20 percent narrower than the last. In between drawings the metal is briefly heated to keep it pliable. This process rapidly erodes the dies, which must be frequently replaced.

Wire is essential to the production of heating elements in household and commercial appliances, electric motors and generators, light bulbs, screens, vehicles, and stringed instruments. Wire made of copper and aluminum, which has low resistance to electricity, is required by the telecommunications industry. To prevent the loss or misconduction of electricity, those wires usually are coated with plastic, rubber, or waxy cotton fibers. Most current-conducting wire is made of a nickel and chromium alloy.

CURRENT CONDITIONS

The electric lighting and wiring equipment industry has seen steady growth since the 1990s. Competing manufacturers continue to produce high quality, reliable everyday lighting and bulbs, but they also look to niche markets to build customer bases. Specialized lighting for buildings such as laboratories, performance halls, restaurants, and 24-hour facilities is being improved constantly. Manufacturers are asking customers for input about these venues, and the results are mutually beneficial. In the public sector, improved highway lighting makes travel safer, and innovations in emergency lighting help to ensure safety in times of crisis. Considerable attention and research funding also have gone into improving automotive lighting. Residential housing is another area in which manufacturers are offering more choices for indoor and outdoor lighting, such as patio sconces and landscaping lights.

As of late 2004, the top five global lighting technologies were compact fluorescent, linear fluorescent, halogen, high-intensity discharge, and light-emitting diodes. Whether lighting solutions were needed to reduce energy costs, cover a large area, highlight a display, or deliver high brightness, each technology required a unique solution.

While the traditional incandescent light is still the bulb of choice, with 15 billion bulbs sold annually, the halogen bulb is slowly gaining in popularity. Although halogen bulbs are less desirable because they generate more heat than their incandescent counterparts, researchers hope to offer low-heat-producing halogen bulbs in the future. According to a Freedonia Group study, high-intensity-discharge (HID) and fluorescent lamps also were expected to see growth into 2007, largely due to increasing demand for energy-efficient products. In addition, industry analysts expected energy-efficient and long lasting light-emitting diodes (LEDs) to grow in use as production costs declined. According to *EDN,* by 2007 LED costs would drop 75 percent, bringing LEDs in line with fluorescents. As reported in *Harvard Business Review,* Sandia National Laboratories predicted that solid-state lighting could decrease global electricity consumption by 10 percent during 2005. The article stated that LEDs can "light an entire rural village with less energy than that used by a single conventional 100-watt lightbulb."

As environmental awareness grows, the electric lighting and wiring equipment industry has scrambled to meet rising consumer demand for energy-efficient products. Customers from the residential, commercial, and public sectors are becoming more aware of how costly energy consumption is becoming, both financially and environmentally. Manufacturers in the electric lighting and wiring industry are responding to these emerging realities with educational programs and new energy-efficient products. The variety of products continues to increase, boosting sales in what is perhaps the most competitive and quickly changing realm of the industry. In the 2000s came the expectation by some industry analysts that companies offering products that can be retrofitted to accommodate existing structures will be good sellers.

Halogen bulbs were gaining popularity in the residential sector of Europe. These cost-efficient lighting alternatives made it possible to focus light while providing energy efficiency and cost savings. The United Kingdom, Germany, and Sweden reportedly accounted for 40 percent of the households in the European Union and nearly 50 percent of electricity consumption. Halogen lights had filaments capable of reaching higher temperatures than ordinary bulbs and producing brighter light.

As lighting efficiency measures are passed in more and more countries, the industry has seen a decline in incandescent light bulbs for general lighting. Brazil and Venezuela began phasing out the bulbs in favor of more energy-efficient lighting alternatives in 2005. The European Union (EU), Switzerland, and Australia started to phase them out in 2009, and other nations are planning to phase them out by 2012. Moreover, by 2015, most of the developed countries and many developing countries are expected to no longer be using incandescent lighting.

New restrictions on incandescents will be in place in the United States by January 2014. In an effort to "test the waters," the state of California will become a test market in 2011, according to General Electric. California's energy commission has the authority to regulate consumer and business lighting products. As a result, consumers in California will begin to experience the phase-out of the 100-watt incandescent bulb in January 2011. Thereafter, 75-watt, 60-watt, and 40-watt incandescent bulbs will be phased out rapidly.

LED billboards are signs of modern high-tech times. These utilize light-emitting diodes to instantly change and display information and images. Billboard companies can sell the same space simultaneously, as it were, with complete efficency. The ability to have new ideas transmitted from billboards within a matter of hours is a clear benefit to advertisers. ClearChannel Outdoor's first "digital" billboard in the Cleveland market generated US$3.5 million from January to December 2006.

RESEARCH AND TECHNOLOGY

In the United States, a substantial fraction of all electricity is used for lighting. The search for efficiency is ongoing. Manufacturers are always looking for better ways to make longer-lasting, cooler lights. Producers of electrical lighting and wiring work closely with power generators to develop, market, and encourage consumer use of energy-saving devices. The benefit of such a strategy is a reduced—or at least stable—draw on electrical power for lighting.

In 1991, the U.S. Environmental Protection Agency introduced "Green Lights," a voluntary program to encourage U.S. companies to install energy-efficient lighting. The goal was to cut electrical use for lighting in half, saving about US$18.6 billion annually and resulting in a drop in pollutants put out by power plants. To supplement this program and further its ends, the EPA established its Energy Star program. Still going strong as of the mid-2000s, the program honors numerous organizations, companies, and schools every year for "outstanding contributions to reducing greenhouse gas emissions through energy efficiency." By 2005, in fact, more than 7,000 organizations had become Energy Star partners. The combination of these efforts with increased consumer concern (and demand) for efficient products has spurred producers of electric lighting to invest heavily in the research and development of such products.

Due to its efficiency, variety of design and color, lighting quality, longevity, and low cost, fluorescent lighting accounts for the majority of electric lighting installations worldwide. Fluorescent lamps, especially in combination with electronic ballasts, which stabilize the flow of current through an electrical load, are becoming an industry standard. Ballasts can interface with automation systems, reduce eyestrain and fatigue, be programmed to enable users to control the amount and direction of light, and generally reduce utility costs. They are also safer for the environment than fluorescent lighting, which is common in most commercial buildings. There were more than seven billion fluorescent lamps in use in 2001, most of which provided workplace lighting.

Lamp manufacturers continue to experiment with new materials and concepts. The xenon-discharge lamp, for instance, produces the artificial light considered most like sunlight. LEDs remain popular because they can be used in very small devices, do not use much power, and are long lasting. As LEDs increased in brightness and came down in price, LED technology continued to displace incandescent bulb-technology. Internationally, about 500 million lamps are discarded each year, according to the International Association of Lighting Management companies. Specialty lamps have been developed for television, industrial applications, photography, moviemaking, and other uses.

The dramatic increase in home Internet connections, along with the trend toward home offices, led to home wiring upgrades, which have generated a great deal of new business for manufacturers of non-current-carrying wiring devices. It also has led to an increased demand for lighting that is better for the eyes, which is a selling point for ballasts. Some companies addressed the computer-using public's desire for devices to enhance the use of computers. Philips, for example, introduced a product in 2000 that allows computer users to designate an area of the screen for high-resolution imaging. This enables them to watch streaming video or participate in Web conferencing while performing other, simple tasks such as document composition.

The category of related electrical components has seen the introduction of the ground fault circuit interrupter (GFCI). These devices shut off current to an outlet or an entire house when they detect moisture. The U.S. National Electrical Code now requires GFCIs in new construction and renovation, which virtually guarantees steady demand for the product.

Improvements to existing products generally are well received by buyers. General Electric's Reveal line of bulbs is sold in supermarkets and discount stores for the average consumer's use, but they offer the advantage of casting vivid light that is less yellow than other bulbs. In response to environmental concerns, GE also released its Ecolux XL T8 fluorescent lamps, which contain less mercury, thereby limiting potential spill-outs in landfills. These lamps also are designed to be up to 50 percent more energy efficient. In 2001, Allied Lighting Systems Co. worked with the California Department of Transportation to create better lighting for highway signs. The product that resulted from this collaboration produces the same amount of light but costs significantly less to operate and lasts four times longer than previously used products.

In 2007, Streamlight introduced its first application of high-intensity discharge (HID) xenon lamp technology. In *Product News,* Streamlight CEO Ray Sharrah explained that the new product combined the latest HID lamp technology with the company?s LiteBox series of lanterns. The result was a lamp with exceptional brightness (3350 lumens). The increased output represented a major advance for industrial professionals seeking an ultra-bright portable light capable of providing large-scale scene lighting and spot lighting. Applications included emergency lighting at a large oil refinery or other industrial facility.

Streamlight also introduced its Streamlight Stylus Pro LED, a brighter and more powerful version of the company's Stylus penlight. The new version, offering more than twice the previous output, also incorporated an internal polymer body liner and shockproof switch housing that allowed for optimal operation under the most extreme conditions combined with design features that ensured waterproof use.

Another 2007 product innovation announcement saw the advancement of glowing sheets of light that would someday replace less efficient incandescent and more expensive fluorescent bulbs. Organic LEDs could be placed on plastic with flexibility expanding application options. At the GE Global Research Center, researchers are working on ways to refine the product, including making them last longer. There are plans to have organic light-emitting diodes on the market by 2010.

INDUSTRY LEADERS

Royal Philips Electronics N.V. The largest manufacturer of light bulbs and related products in the world, Philips emerged from the rubble of World War Two's European manufacturing base to become one of the leading innovators of the industry. The company concentrated almost solely on consumer electronics and related products, shunning heavy industrial products such as engines. Philips was formed in 1891, only 12 years after Edison invented the incandescent light bulb. Gerard Philips, a Dutch engineer, was fortunate to have a father with money to invest and a younger brother, Anton, who had a flair for management. By the 1920s, Philips was making inroads in neighboring countries and the United States. Philips was an early competitor with GE in fine-tuning the incandescent light bulb with variations on filaments, inert gases, and other innovations.

In the 1950s, Philips rebuilt its Dutch plants and moved into manufacturing transistors, integrated circuits, television sets, and appliances. It was one of the first companies to introduce VCRs, audiocassette systems, and compact disc players. In the 1980s, Philips bought the lighting operations of the U.S. firm Westinghouse. It also began offering wiring solutions through its Philips-MECO division. Philips' 2009 sales were US$30.69 billion compared to US$38 billion in sales during 2004. Sales were highest in Europe and Africa, which accounted for US$16.7 billion, followed by the Asia Pacific, which had sales of US$10 billion in 2004. North American revenues were US$9.36 billion, followed by Latin America, which provided Philips with US$1.9 billion in sales. In addition, the market in China offered great opportunity for Philips, which expected sales there to top US$10 billion in 2005. Its sales in the lighting sector accounted for US$5.68 billion, or 13.1 percent of overall sales. Philips employed more than 115,900 people in more than 60 countries as of 2009.

General Electric Company. Another company that has dominated the light-manufacturing industry is General

Electric (GE). Based in Fairfield, Connecticut, GE is a direct descendent of Edison Electric Light Company, formed in 1879 by Thomas Edison. Business magnates of the day immediately recognized the value of Edison's inventions, and capital flowed in to finance expansion of the fledgling company. In 2010, *Forbes* ranked GE as the world's second largest company, based on a formula that took into account total sales, total assets, profits, and market share value.

In 1892, financier J.P. Morgan took over Edison Electric and combined it with other firms to form General Electric. True to form, Morgan immediately came up with a high-profile scheme to demonstrate to the world the benefits of electricity: an elevated electrical train at the Chicago World's Fair in 1893. GE also created the first corporate research facility, which developed the tungsten filament still used today in incandescent light bulbs. The X-ray was another of the lab's early triumphs. Developed in 1913, it was the initial entry in GE's foray into medical diagnostic equipment.

To accelerate demand for its power plants, GE inventors introduced a steady stream of electrical household appliances to an eager public. Toasters and irons were first introduced in 1905, followed by electric stoves, waffle irons, refrigerators, vacuum cleaners, and washing machines in the next decade. By the 1920s, GE's influence was so widespread that the U.S. government used antitrust legislation to force the company to divest itself of its power generating businesses. Subsequently, GE also was forced to make public its patent for light bulbs. In the 1980s, GE added entertainment and consumer credit services. Still, it continued to be an innovator in lighting, inventing a small but sturdy bulb for auto manufacturers that enabled them to redesign headlights. In 1989, the company bought Tungsram, a Hungarian lighting manufacturer; and in 1991, it added the light-bulb business of the European firm Thorn EMI.

GE's total revenues for 2009 were US$157 billion, according to its annual report. The company was forced to erase US$343 million in profits from 2001 through the first three quarters of 2006 due to improperly accounting of fluctuating interest rates. As Rob Varon reported in the *Connecticut Post,* GE consulted with the Securities and Exchange Commission about its accounting formulas for variable interests rates related to its financial lending business before announcing plans to restate earnings dating to 2001. In 2009, GE had a workforce of over 304,000.

Siemens AG. Siemens of Munich, Germany, is a major European player in the manufacturing of lighting equipment. Founded in 1847 when hobby scientist Werner Siemens became fascinated with telegraphy, the small

company got its first big break when it was hired to set up a telegraph system between Frankfurt and Berlin. Other government contracts soon followed and Siemens became a specialist in laying intercontinental and interoceanic cables, including cables from London to India.

When news of Edison's incandescent bulb reached Siemens, he immediately acquired a license to manufacture the bulbs. In the 1920s, Siemens added traffic lights to its repertoire and formed a European light bulb consortium with two other German companies, AEG and Auer.

Like its counterparts in the United States and the Netherlands, Siemens branched out to manufacture a variety of medical, industrial, computer, and telecommunications products after World War II. In 1993, Siemens acquired the Sylvania lamp company from GTE and merged it with Osram, Siemens' lighting manufacturing division. Total revenues for Siemens AG in 2004 were US$93.4 billion; Osram sales in 2004 were more than US$5.3 billion. Siemens AG sales in 2009 were US$101.4 billion with approximately 420,800 employees.

Aranee Jaiimsin reported that Siemens AG entered Thailand's switch and socket markets with a range of products at competitive prices. This followed Siemens AG's years of selling similar products to clients in Europe and the United States. During the launch at Architect Expo 2007, Siemens AG introduced two models under its Delta Azio series. Thailand's switch and socket market was expected to grow 10 percent from 2006 rates to 1.5 billion baht.

In April 2007, Jack Ewing discussed the departure of Siemens' CEO Klaus Kleinfeld and the impact of company scandals. Kleinfeld was credited with making Siemens AG more profitable. In 2006, Kleinfeld authorized expenditure of US$7.6 billion for acquisitions to strengthen core businesses and build Siemens' presence in emerging markets such as China and India. Unfortunately, there were also scandals related to misuse of funds and the possibility that Siemens AG had secretly financed a workers' organization to act as a counterweight to IG Metall, which negotiated for most of the company's workers in Germany.

Hitachi Ltd. Tokyo-based Hitachi Ltd. is one of the world's largest producers of various types of wire. Namihei Odaira, an engineer and dedicated tinkerer, formed Hitachi in 1920. In the 1930s, Hitachi became Japan's first manufacturer of light bulbs and vacuum tubes. The company lost many plants during World War II and nearly failed. However, it re-emerged during the reconstruction period of the 1950s. Hitachi regained its prominence in household appliances and electronics and was engaged in joint partnerships with several major U.S.

firms, including GE, RCA, and IBM. Total revenue for fiscal year 2004 was US$84.36 billion, an increase of 5 percent over 2003. Hitachi's High Functional Materials & Components sector, which included wiring products, earned more than US$14 billion. Overseas revenues increased 10 percent to US$53.7 billion, with Japan remaining the company's primary revenue source at US$30.6 billion. The rest of Asia provided US$13.1 billion in revenue, North America US$8.4 billion, Europe US$6.6 billion, and other areas of the world US$2.4 billion. Total revenue reported for 2010 were US$95.9 billion and 359,746 for sales and employees, respectively.

Cooper Industries. Another important player in the production of wire, lighting, and related products is Cooper Industries, based in Houston, Texas. In 1997 the company announced that it would sell its automotive products division to focus on its electrical products and tools and hardware divisions. The electrical products division, which makes fuses, electric wires and cables, and security lighting, contributed US$3.7 billion to the companyrsquo;s total US$4.46 billion in 2004 revenues, 9.9 percent more than Cooper earned in 2003. Cooper Lighting was responsible for 27 percent of annual revenues, Cooper Wiring Devices for 6 percent, and Cooper Menvier for 6 percent. Cooper Menvier was the companyrsquo;s overseas anchor for global market expansion, helping Cooper Industries branch into markets in Eastern Europe and the Middle East. Cooper reported sales of US$6.5 billion in 2008, and a workforce of over 31,200.

BIBLIOGRAPHY

Altman, Emlyn G. "Light Moves: A Lighting Expert Suggests Ways to Maintain the Integrity of Your Lighting Design." *Lodging Hospitality*, 1 January 2007.

"An Even Brighter Idea." *The Economist*, 23 September 2006.

Anderson, Eric. "Research with a Bright Future: GE Develops Flexible, Thin, Lightweight Sheets That Could Someday Replace Light Bulbs." *Times Union*, 23 June 2007.

Aujla, Simmi. "LED, a New Sign from Above: ClearChannel Tests Light-Emitting Diode Billboards in the Orlando Market." *Orlando Sentinel*, 27 June 2007.

Cariaga, Eufemio. "Necessity Drives Lighting Efficiency Innovations: Energy Costs and Mandated Efficiency Standards Combine to bring a Wealth of Energy-Efficiency Lighting Products into the Marketplace." *Electrical Contracting Products*, March 2006.

"Cooper Industries to Shutter Sarasota, Florida, WPI Plant." *Industrial Distribution*, 1 May 2007.

Costlow, Terry. "LED Outlook Brightens: More Applications Are Switching to Solid-State Lighting." *Design News*, 18 April 2005.

"Cree Announces Breakthrough 100-Lumen Xlamp LEDs Available in Volume Quantities." *PrimeZone*, 27 June 2007.

"Energy-Efficient Lighting and LightQuick Service Provide New Opportunities." *EC&M Electrical Constructions & Maintenance*, July 2001.

Ewing, Jack. "Siemens Boss Steps Down: Chief Executive Klaus Klienfeld Steered the German Electronics Firm to Unprecedented Profits." *Business Week*, 25 April 2007.

Funk, Dale. "Lamp Demand to Reach $5 Billion by 2007." *Electrical Wholesaling*, 1 April 2004.

"'Green' Economics in Relamping." *EC&M Electrical Constructions & Maintenance*, April 2000.

"Halogen Bulbs Light Up the Path to Energy Efficiency." *BLT Direct*, 7 June 2007.

"Hoover's Company Capsules." *Hoover's Online*, 2007. Available from www.hoovers.com.

Jaiimsin, Aranee. "Siemens Goes Head to Head with Market Leader." *Bangkok Post*, 7 May 2007.

"LED Penlight Measures 5.3 In. and Weighs 1.64 Oz." *Product News Network*, 26 June 2007.

"Lighting & Electrics: New Wiring Accessory Range." *What's New in Building*, 19 February 2007.

"The Lighting Report." *HFN*, 7 June 2004.

Meyer, Nancy. "A Brighter Perspective." *HFN*, 7 June 2004.

———. "A Matter of Increasing Imports." *HFN*, 7 June 2004.

Mocherniak, Terry. "Lighting Technologies Produce Energy Savings: Advanced Lighting Controls Can Accommodate Multiple Energy Management Strategies at the Same Time." *Energy & Power Management*, May 2006.

Papanier, Jordon. "LEDs: Rugged, Versatile Light Sources." *Control Engineering*, 1 August 2006.

"Philips China Expects over $10 Billion in Sales by 2005." *Emerging Markets Economy*, 10 September 2004.

"Rechargable Lantern Uses HID Xenon Lamp." *Product News Network*, 11 May 2007.

"Saving the Planet." *Electronics News*, 1 December 2006.

Varnon, Rob. "GE's 4Q Earnings Hit High: Company to Get Out of Plastics Business." *Connecticut Post*, 20 January 2007.

"Waking Up Lighting Sales." *Electrical Wholesaling*, March 2005. Available from http://www.ewweb.com.

SIC 3670

ELECTRONIC COMPONENTS

NAICS CODE(S)

3344. The global electronic components industry fabricates an extensive array of electronic devices used in the manufacture of finished electronic products. Examples of industry output include: printed circuit boards; electron tubes; electronic capacitors; electronic resistors; electronic connectors; electronic transformers; electronic coils; and electronic inductors.

Finished electronic goods, such as audio and video gear, are discussed in separate articles, as are semiconductors. (See

Connector Sales Worldwide, 2009

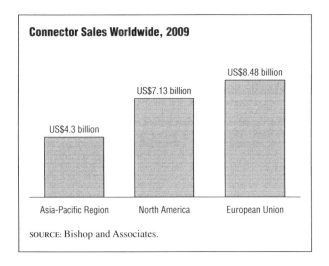

US$8.48 billion

US$7.13 billion

US$4.3 billion

Asia-Pacific Region   North America   European Union

SOURCE: Bishop and Associates.

also **Audio and Video Equipment, Computers, Semiconductors,** and **Telecommunications Equipment.**)

INDUSTRY SNAPSHOT

Electronic component manufacturing is characterized by intense competition among companies as well as countries. Most electronic components, which are the unassembled or partially assembled parts used in virtually any electronic device, are traded as commodities with slim profit margins for their makers.

Three chief divisions of industry output exist: printed circuit boards (PCBs), electron tubes, and passive components. By far the most ubiquitous and remunerative are PCBs and passive components; by value, passive components—a catch-all term that encompasses many distinct products—is the largest category. A finished electronic end product, such as a television, generally contains components from all categories, including numerous kinds of passive components. In the mid-2000s, the increased use of electronic devices, particularly digital electronics such as digital versatile disc (DVD) players, mobile phones, high-speed devices, and flat-screen televisions and computer monitors, fueled a dramatic upswing in demand for connectors, resistors, switches, and other passive components, and an accompanying upswing in materials prices.

Electronic components are the fundamental building blocks in every kind of electronic device or appliance. The demand for components is based on the varying demand for end-user products. Electronics' use of integrated circuits is increasing with each producthaving approximately 20 passive components. The electronic components global market was valued at close to US$169 billion in 2010.

For the first decade of the twenty-first century, the annual growth rate for the global electronic component market was about 7.1 percent. Worldwide printed wiring boards were expected to retain its domination of the electronic components market to exceed US$71 billion in the 2010s. This segment also expected to have the highest growth rate potential, with the connectors market expected to have the second highest growth rate.

The Asian-Pacific territory accounted for about 27.9 percent of the global electronics components market while offering the highest growth potential in the late 2000s. Europe was the second largest electronic components market with an estimated US$34.5 billion in 2007. Globally, the United States represented the largest market for connectors and switches.

According to the Global Sources' Seventh Annual Electronic Components Distributor Survey, 46 percent of mainland China electronics manufacturers preferred to source from mainland China distributors in 2007. The survey received 1,028 valid responses from managers working for electronics manufacturing companies in China. It showed participating manufacturers expected to increase their annual component purchases to an average of US$42 million in the late 2000s.

ORGANIZATION AND STRUCTURE

The electronic components industry is made up of original equipment manufacturers (OEMs), such as IBM and Hewlett-Packard, and contract manufacturers, with electronic distributors also playing a key role. When OEMs produced electronic components, it was typically for use in their own products, an arrangement known as captive production, and they did not derive any direct revenue from the components themselves. In the past, contract manufacturing operations began as printed circuit board assemblers. In the late 1990s, however, OEMs such as IBM and Hewlett-Packard were increasingly turning to contract manufacturers to manufacture either subsystems or complete electronic products. Thus, brand-name manufacturers might not be involved in the physical manufacturing of products bearing their names. According to *Venture Outsource*, the global electronics manufacturing services (EMS) market was expected to reach US$257 billion by 2012. EMS and Original Design Manufacture (ODM) were among the most rapidly growing industries in the electronics arena. Countries with low-cost production expenses—Asia-Pacific, Latin America, and Eastern Europe—have emerged as the leading outsourcing locations.

Distributors of electronic components also were jumping into the fray. As profit margins on component sales shrank, distributors attempted to drive profits through higher volume sales. These distributor-contractor manufacturers typically had three major advantages over those that were strictly contract manufacturers: (1) the distributorship provided a ready source of capital, hard to come by for many contract-only firms; (2) the distributorship's established supply channels provided an abundant supply of components, which many smaller contract manufacturers lacked; and (3) the distributorship provided an existing customer base. Three of the largest components distributors in the world were Great Neck, New York-based Avnet Inc., with US$16.23 billion in 2009 revenues; Arrow Electronics of Melville, New York, with US$14.7 billion in 2009 revenues; and Tyco Electronics of Berwyn, Pennsylvania, with a US$10.3 billion in 2009 revenues.

BACKGROUND AND DEVELOPMENT

Electron tubes in the form of gas-discharge tubes were invented in the late nineteenth century and vacuum tubes were developed a short while later. The cathode ray tube (CRT), used in televisions, was invented in 1897 by Karl Ferdinand Braun at the University of Strasbourg in France. Then in 1907, Boris Rosing, a Russian scientist, used a CRT to receive an experimental video signal to form a picture. He was able to display simple shapes onto a screen, which marked the first time that CRT technology was used for what is now television.

In the 1920s, the first widespread use of these tubes began in radios; vacuum tubes were later crucial to the development of television and early computers. In the 1940s and 1950s, solid-state technology—in which a signal passes through a solid instead of a vacuum— represented a substantial advance in technology. The 1960s, however, saw the invention of integrated circuits, which could do much of the same work as the comparatively bulky transistor. Solid-state technology lends itself to complex, low-power circuitry, such as that found in consumer radios. However, electron tubes remained useful in applications that required higher powers and frequencies because they were smaller, lighter, cheaper, and more reliable. Vacuum tube transmitters still did quite well against solid-state technology, particularly in commercial applications for television, radio, and microwave ovens.

The global electronic components industry in the mid-1990s experienced modest growth. OEMs began to outsource more functions to contract equipment manufacturers (CEMs), a move that allowed OEMs to lower cost, reduce time to market, and gain access to the latest technologies. Some companies added capacity to meet growing demand, while others divested unprofitable business lines to increase profits. Since many electronic component manufacturers did business on a worldwide basis, the Asian financial crisis of the mid-1990s affected the entire industry; in addition, electronic component production in Japan declined from ¥9.57 trillion in 1996 to ¥9.45 trillion in 1998.

Advances in technology boosted component demand in the late 1990s. For example, new computer microprocessors required higher density interconnect packaging, and the increased use of Ethernet switches for local area networks (LANs) required more passive and active fiber-optic components. Other growth stimulants were the new ultra-thin notebook computer design, which required new types of connectors, and the rise of high-speed digital signals that required new interconnect methods. Also important to the industry was a dramatic increase in the use of cellular phones.

Capacitors and resistors experienced solid growth in the late 1990s. Along with soaring cellular telephone sales, analysts credited the increased use of electronics in automobiles and new developments in computer technology for the upswing. However, of concern to many capacitor and resistor manufacturers was the rising price of palladium, a base metal used in many component parts. Many capacitor and resistor firms also found themselves struggling to keep up with surging demand in 2000.

One of the more significant trends in the electronic components manufacturing industry in the late 1990s was the outsourcing of production. In other words, OEMs hired other manufacturers who specialized in manufacturing to complete subsystems or even entire products, often more inexpensively than the OEMs could do it themselves. This "virtual manufacturing" allowed the original equipment maker to control costs and concentrate on core competencies. The largest customer of contract manufactured products was the computer hardware industry, followed by the communications and medical equipment industries.

After eight years of steady growth, the connectors sector of the electronic components industry saw sales fall dramatically in the early 2000s, due to an industry-led recession caused by the dot-com bubble burst, causing demand for Internet-related products in this industry to plummet. Other factors included an overall slowing of the U.S. economy, which eventually made its way to both Europe and Asia, after the terrorist attacks against the United States in September 2011.

In 2001, Korea displaced Japan as the world's leading producer of liquid crystal displays (LCDs). Korean

LCD manufacturers, led by Samsung Electronics Inc. and L.G. Philips LCD Co., secured a 41.5 percent share of the global LCD market, compared to the 39.5 percent share held by Japanese firms. By the end of 2007, LCD televisions had surpassed CRTs in worldwide sales. The following year, LCD television garnered 50 percent of the market share of the 200 million TVs that were expected to be shipped globally.

CURRENT CONDITIONS

The Cathode Ray Tube (CRT) demand fluctuated significantly in the first decade of the twenty-first century. In 2005, Sony announced it would stop production of CRT computer displays. The normal lifespan for CRT-based televisions and monitors is five to six years on average. As of the 2008 Consumer Electronics Show, most high-end CRT-based monitors were being replaced by rear-projection displays and liquid crystal display televisions and monitors. However, the demise of the CRT is much slower in the developing world. According to iSupply, production in units of CRTs was not surpassed by LCD production until the end of 2007, owing largely to CRT production at factories in China. In the United Kingdom, DSG (Dixons), the largest retailer of British-made electronics, reported that CRTs made up 80 to 90 percent of the volume of televisions sold at Christmas in 2004. A year later that figure had dropped to 15 to 20 percent, and by 2007, Dixons had ceased selling CRT televisions altogether.

Early in the twenty-first century, the LCD market had been faced with competition from developments such as the flat plasma display unveiled by Matsushita; the organic display developed by Kodak, which could process images 100 times faster than LCD or plasma screens while using considerably less energy; and CRT arrays, a less expensive alternative to plasma. However, by the mid-2000s, major manufacturers were putting US$10 billion into building 10 inch or more large capacity LCDs for flat-screen televisions.

According to *Venture Outsource*, OEM LCD televisions offered the largest dollar increase of any consumer electronics segment in 2010. After a 6.7 percent drop in 2009, the global consumer electronics market was expected to achieve a mild recovery in 2010, with revenue expanding by 1.6 percent, according to research firm iSuppli Corp. Worldwide consumer electronics OEM revenue was expected to rise to US$317.3 billion in 2010, up from US$312.3 billion in 2009.

The global connectors market experienced a modest recovery in 2002. According to the research firm Bishop & Associates, by 2003 the connector market was back up to an estimated US$25 billion, fueled largely by soaring demand for high-speed computer and other communication technologies. The market continued to shift during the mid-2000s, as prices stabilized and demand from all industries grew, especially in China. The United States market actually dropped by one percent, and companies were expanding operations to China and Malaysia to take advantage of the market. The industry saw its first year of significant growth in 2005, as new products and designs helped grow the market. However, in 2008, investment bank Deutsche Bank lowered the expectations for connector and distribution industries due to the decline in the euro and dollar exchange rate, higher borrowing costs, and a slowing macro-economic environment. As discretionary spending dropped due to the economic downturn, all areas of the electronic component market took a hit through 2010.

As with most sectors of the electronic components industry, capacitor and resistor sales dropped significantly in the early 2000s. As a result, the firms that had been scrambling to increase capacity suddenly found themselves burdened with excess inventory. Industry analysts forecasted a turnaround for the industry, basing predictions on anticipated growth in cell phone sales and increased U.S. defense spending, likely sparking demand for various communication devices, as well as on growth from the computer and digital electronic sectors. Even though the demand for electronic components took a dramatic plunge in 2008, the increased volume requirement of capacitors in industrial, medical, telecommunications, automotive, aerospace and defense markets is likely to propel sales to US$21.5 billion by 2015.

Sri Lanka was cited for being ripe for rapid development in the electronics industry. According to Bandula Sirimanna, Sri Lankan workers stood out among others as the best educated and most trainable in the South Asian Region. Young workers at the Tos Lanka Company Ltd. were considered to be proof positive. Tos Lanka was a wholly owned subsidiary of Toslec Co. based in Kyoto, Japan. It is one of the leading manufacturers and suppliers of electronic components to Matsushita Electronics, Hitachi Media, and many others. Workers were trained for periods ranging from three months to one year. Female workers were dominant in the workforce and applauded for their precision in following technical instructions to the letter.

INDUSTRY LEADERS

Capacitors and Resistors. The world's largest passive electronics suppliers in the world, including capacitors and resistors, in 2005 were Murata Manufacturing

Co. Ltd., headquartered in Kyoto, Japan; EPCOS of Munich, Germany; and Vishay Intertechnology Inc., based in Malvern, Pennsylvania. Other notable companies were AVX Corp. of Myrtle Beach, South Carolina; TDK Corp. of Tokyo, Japan; Kyocera Corp. of Kyoto, Japan; and Rohm Co. Ltd., also of Kyoto, Japan.

Connectors. In 2010, the world's largest connector manufacturers were Tyco Electronics, of Beryn, Pennsylvania, and Molex Inc., of Lisle, Illinois. Other notable companies were Amphenol Corp. of Wallingford, Connecticut, and Kyocera Corp. of Kyoto, Japan, as well as Delphi Connection Systems, FCI, and Yazaki. Consolidation was a major trend among the largest connector firms in the late 1990s. For example, Tyco International acquired AMP Inc., which had been the global leader in connector production in the mid-1990s, as well as the OEM arm of Thomas and Betts. In addition, Molex acquired the interconnect operations of Axsys Technologies Inc. Of the world's estimated 1,245 connector makers, the largest 100 firms accounted for 80.5 percent of the North American market, 88.8 percent of the European market, and 94.5 percent of the Japanese market. The leading markets for connectors continued to be computers and peripherals, followed by telecommunications, automotive, and industrial.

Liquid Crystal Displays (LCDs). In 2008, the largest manufacturers of LCDs, the leading alternative to cathode-ray tube displays, were Merck KGaA of Germany and Samsung Electronics Inc. and L.G. Philips LCD Co., both based in Korea. Other industry leaders, all based in Japan, included Sharp Corp.; Seiko Epson Corp.; Display Technologies Inc., a joint venture involving Japan's Toshiba Corp. and IBM; NEC Corp.; and Hitachi, Ltd.

MAJOR COUNTRIES IN
THE INDUSTRY

Asia. In the Asia-Pacific region in 2009, connector sales slipped from US$5 billion in 2008 to US$4.3 billion. Bishop & Associates reported that globally, connector sales dropped by 21.8 percent in 2009, thus ending six years of steady growth.

Japan. Japan is one of the most prominent electronic component industries globally and is home to the world's largest electronics manufacturers, including: Sony, Hitachi, Mitsubishi Electric, Panasonic, Sharp, Canon, Sanyo, Toshiba, Pioneer, Nikon, Nintendo, and Olympus, to name a few. Due to this concentration of high tech companies, Japan is the largest consumer electronics manufacturer in the world. Due to the stellar reputation of Japan's electronics, it dominates the electronic export

market. However, South Korea is rapidly gaining strength and Samsung Electronics boasted an operating profit more than two times larger than the combined profits of nine of Japan's largest consumer electronic companies.

North America. In North America, connector sales fell from US$9.4 billion in 2008 to US$7.13 billion in 2009. This was due to a slowdown in the telecommunications and data communications industry, which weakened demand. Recessionary economic conditions and the September 11, 2001, terrorist attacks against the United States also were blamed for the slowdown.

United States. In 2009, the electronic component industry in the United States was showing a steady uphill climb. Most noticeably in the sales of printed circuit boards and semiconductors. The global semiconductor industry was worth US$248 billion by 2010, with China accounting for US$63 billion of it. China, the United States, and Japan are the largest semiconductor producers in the world. The computer and office equipment industry is led by the United States, Japan, and Europe, with the United States representing an annual revenue of US$180 billion in that industry alone as of 2010. The United States is the leading market globally for communications equipment, which contributed approximately US$95 billion in 2006.

European Union. After significant growth in the European Union, the demand for electronic components declined, reaching a value of 56 billion Euros in 2008. The top four countries within the Union—Germany, Spain, Italy and France—accounted for 60 percent of the total. Thirty-four percent of the electronic components in Europe went to the computer industry, with 21 percent going to the telecommunications industry. Nineteen percent went to the automotive industry, with industrial (15 percent) and consumer appliances (10 percent) making up the balance. The value of the EU production of components in 2008 reached approximately 50 billion euros. Germany dominates production with a 35 percent share of the total output. Europe remained the second largest connector region of the global market in 2009, totaling US$8.48 billion.

One emerging European stronghold in the electronic components industry was Ireland, where more than 300 electronics companies employed more than 30,000 workers. According to the U.S. Department of State, the move by global technology leaders like Apple Computer, Dell Computer, and Gateway Inc. into Ireland in the late 1990s fostered the growth of the electronic components industry there. As a result, by 2000, the components market in Ireland was worth US$2.45 billion, more than half of which was produced locally. The recessionary economic conditions and reduced technology spending that plagued the North American market had also reached Europe by late 2000. As a result, connector sales in Europe dropped from US$8.07 billion in 2000 to US$7.22 billion in 2001.

Brazil. Brazil's forward-looking elected officials were creating an atmosphere that helped poise their country as a major player in the electronics industry. They have created high-tech centers in its world-class universities throughout Brazil and have been recruiting staff from some of the industries' leading universities and businesses worldwide. The results of this innovative thinking were paying big dividends by 2010. The country's first all-Brazilian semiconductor manufacturing facility began production. In addition, IBM selected Brazil as the location of its first new research facility in twelve years. Brazil accounts for nearly half of all IT spending in South America.

BIBLIOGRAPHY

"7th Annual Electronic Components Distributor Survey Reveals Shift in China Sourcing Preference to Domestic Suppliers." *PR Newswire,* 21 June 2007.

Connector Market Handbook 2010, World Connector Statistics; Bishop and Associates, 2010. Available from www.bishopinc.com.

Current Industry Trends, IPC Market Research, 2010. Available from www.ipc.org.

"Electronic Component Orders Take Small Dip in May." EMS Now, June 2007. Available from www.emsnow.com.

Pearne. "2006 Was Great — Worldwide! But What for 2007?" *CircuiTree,* April 2007.

Sirmanna, Bandula. "Electronic Industry On Path Towards Rapid Development." *The Sunday Times FT,* June 2007.

Sumitomo Precision Products Co. Ltd. "Japan's Sumitomo Precision Products Co. Ltd. Acquires Primaxx, Inc." 28 June 2007.

Trends and Observations; Venture Outsource, Global Industry Analysts, Inc. Available from www.ventureoutsource.com.

SIC 3621

MOTORS AND GENERATORS

NAICS CODE(S)

335312. The motors and generators industry manufactures electric motors and power generators for a diverse range of industrial applications, mostly as components for other manufacturers' finished products. Industry output includes motors and generators for trains, buses, and trucks.

INDUSTRY SNAPSHOT

Electric motors and generators provide much of the power for the world's industrial production. Typically, manufacturers purchase motors and generators for use in a wide range of products. The most widespread use of motors has been for integration into consumer and industrial appliances, including heating and air-conditioning systems, refrigerators, and cleaning equipment such as vacuum cleaners.

Household appliances were projected to be one of the fastest growing markets for motors approaching 2005. According to *Appliance Manufacturer,* volume was projected to exceed 61 million units in 2005, a significant increase from 19 million units in 2000. Especially in the United States, the automotive industry is another important market for manufacturers of motors, generators, and related parts. Automobile manufacturers use motors as components for accessories such as air conditioners and windshield wipers.

In late 2003, the U.S. Census Bureau reported that industry shipments were valued at US$8 billion. Fractional horsepower motors accounted for US$3 billion, followed by integral horsepower motors (US$1.3 billion), prime mover generator sets (US$2 billion), and electric motor generator sets (nearly US$929 million). According to the Freedonia Group, explosive growth is projected in the newer fuel cell sector, which is set to reach US$1.1 billion by 2008 and US$4.6 billion by 2013.

The motor and generator manufacturing industry was one of the key industries of the so-called second industrial revolution of the late nineteenth century. The pioneering and dominant countries for most of the industry's history have been the United States and Germany. In the post-World War II years, Japan joined these countries, becoming a leading producer and exporter. Most of the industry's largest firms were based in these three countries, and rank among the world's largest multinational companies. In fact, the industry is so highly concentrated that the 50 largest companies generate nearly 80 percent of the revenue in each of the segments.

In the United States, there is a combined revenue of nearly US$30 billion annually in the motor and generator, pump and compressor industry. Industrial and manufacturing companies drive the demand for products, and there are nearly 1,000 companies in this sector in the United States alone. Many of these are smaller companies that specialize in one or two specific areas, and they are more likely willing to adapt products for special needs. The industry is costly: the average annual revenue per employee is approximately US$330,000. Thirty-five percent of the industry revenue is from electrical motors and generators, with pumps another 35 percent and compressors 30 percent.

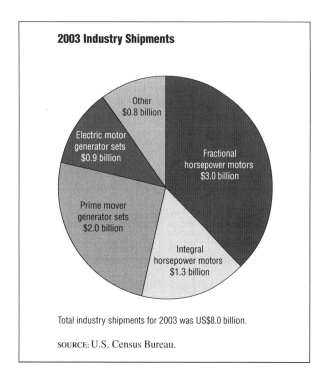

2003 Industry Shipments

Other $0.8 billion

Electric motor generator sets $0.9 billion

Fractional horsepower motors $3.0 billion

Prime mover generator sets $2.0 billion

Integral horsepower motors $1.3 billion

Total industry shipments for 2003 was US$8.0 billion.

SOURCE: U.S. Census Bureau.

Within the motor and generator industry, *fractional horsepower motors* (fractions of one horsepower) account for the majority of production followed by *integral* horsepower motors (multiples of one horsepower) and *prime mover* generators (powered by prime movers like diesel or steam engines). Nearly all motors and generators are sold to industrial users as sources of power or as emergency electrical solutions for consumers.

According to *Military & Aerospace Electronics,* the Frost & Sullivan firm issued an "Emerging Opportunities in the Russian and Ukrainian Electric Motors Markets" report that acknowledged challenges arising from using old and outdated equipment. Although Russian and Ukrainian manufacturers knew that this was a problem, most of them could not afford to replace their equipment. As a result, out of the necessity to buy new equipment with more efficiently running motors, the replacement cycle in those markets was expected to intensify in the immediate future.

As with other manufacturing industries, motor and generator production has been affected by environmental concerns. Specific issues facing this industry include energy efficiency, noise pollution, and the effects discarded motors have on the environment in landfills.

Power generators were expected to make profits as the second phase of the European Union's emissions trading scheme was anticipated. It imposed a limit on carbon dioxide emissions from industry and was set to run from 2008 to 2012. Electricity generators were expected to pass

on the cost of buying allowances to customers in liberalized electricity markets.

ORGANIZATION AND STRUCTURE

Standards of compatibility in the United States for the motors and generators industry were developed under the sponsorship of the National Electrical Manufacturers Association (NEMA). NEMA is a member of the American National Standards Institute (ANSI) Committee on Electrical Rotating Machinery. The committee serves as a forum to hear the views of motor and generator manufacturers and users, as well as other concerned parties. Upon establishing a consensus, ANSI publishes national standards. Other organizations in the United States have also developed standards for safety and performance. These organizations include the Institute of Electrical and Electronics Engineers (IEEE), Underwriters Laboratories Inc., the American Gear Manufacturers Association, the Edison Electric Institute, and the Hydraulic Institute. European manufacturers of motors and generators produce goods to the standards of the International Electrotechnical Commission (IEC).

The major competitors with U.S. firms in the domestic market in the 1990s were large internationally oriented firms, including the Toshiba Corporation, the Mitsubishi Electric Corporation, and Hitachi, Ltd. of Japan; Siemens AG of Germany; and Asea Brown Boveri AG of Switzerland.

International trade for the leading producers of electric motors and generators is marked by strong patterns of regional specialization. For Germany, the most important export market was the rest of Europe; for Japan, most exports went to Asia and North America; for the United States, the most important export markets were North American Free Trade Agreement (NAFTA) partners Canada and Mexico.

European manufacturers in the industry were served by the European Committee of Manufacturers of Electrical Machines and Power Electronics (CEMEP). The committee, founded in 1960 and headquartered in Paris, seeks to represent members regarding standards, policies, and legislation affecting the industry.

BACKGROUND AND DEVELOPMENT

Electric motors convert electricity into rotary mechanical energy, while generators do just the opposite. Technological advances have allowed the same machine to serve as both an electric motor and generator, with energy flowing in either direction. Generators have historically been most widely used in centralized power production facilities, although they are also used to generate electrical power in automobiles, ships, trains, and aircraft. The use of electric motors is more decentralized, ranging from home appliances to heavy industrial applications. Motors and generators are designated as either permanent magnet or electromagnetic, and typed as either alternating or direct current.

The electrical motors and generators industry originated in the 1880s, when firms arose in the United States to commercialize the inventions of Thomas Edison, Elihu Thomson, and George Westinghouse. The industry was one of the few in which the key inventors successfully commercialized their inventions and launched companies that became industry leaders. Compared with most manufacturing industries, these firms required greater numbers of technically trained employees. These employees were necessary not only for designing and producing commercially viable electrical machines, but also for marketing, installing, and maintaining them. Producers of electrical machinery also made large investments in research and development.

Because of the considerable expense of manufacturing electrical machinery, producers found it necessary to establish substantial lines of credit to buyers. The largest German firms established banks to facilitate sales of their machinery. Buyers also purchased electrical equipment with their own stocks and bonds, leading some producers of electrical machinery to establish holding companies. Firms in the industry thus became vertically integrated across a wide range of activities early in the sector's development.

In these early years, the Thomson-Houston company established the industry's most sophisticated domestic and international marketing organization. Thomson-Houston merged with Edison General Electric in 1892 to form the General Electric Company. The merger was facilitated by the firms' complementary product lines; Thomson-Houston was strong in arc lighting and alternating current, while Edison's strength lay in incandescent lamp lighting and direct current. In 1896 General Electric and Westinghouse formed a patent pool, a move that accelerated their dominance of the U.S. market.

General Electric and Westinghouse then entered into cooperative arrangements with the two large German producers in the industry, Siemens and Halske and Allgemeine Elektricitäats Gesellschaft (AEG). The four firms dominated the world market for electrical machinery by the early 1900s, a state of affairs that continued uninterrupted for several decades. The power of these companies was based not only on sales but also on direct investment. For example, in England, two-thirds of

electrical equipment manufactured in the mid-1910s was produced by subsidiaries of General Electric, Westinghouse, and Siemens. In terms of electrical machinery exports, Germany was the most successful of these countries prior to World War I. German companies were responsible for three times more exports than the United States and two-and-one-half times more than England. In the 1920s, General Electric purchased large shares of Siemens and AEG. Siemens and General Electric remained among the world's largest producers of electrical motors and generators into the 1990s.

One of the growth strategies of these firms was diversification into related products, including household appliances. Diversification into household appliances provided a direct outlet for parts (such as small electric motors) produced in increasing quantities by these firms. At the same time, appliances contributed to the growing demand for electrical power, which these firms also supplied via other equipment. In his book *Scale and Scope,* Alfred Chandler Jr. described General Electric's rapid diversification this way: "The number of GE's product lines rose from 10 in 1900 to 30 in 1910, to 85 in 1920, to 193 in 1930, and to 281 in 1940. By World War I, GE had developed one of the most diversified product lines of any industrial enterprise in the world. Nearly all these products were related to its electrical equipment base."

The fortunes of U.S. producers of motors and generators took a substantial turn for the worse after the mid-1970s. From 1972 to 1985, there was very little growth in real output and the industry was plagued with excess capacity. As measured by after-tax return on sales, profitability declined over these years. It was also during these years that the United States changed from a net exporter to a net importer of electric motors and generators. In 1976, exports accounted for 17 percent of industry shipments in the United States, while imports accounted for 7 percent of domestic use. By 1986 exports accounted for only 10 percent of shipments, but imports accounted for 18 percent of domestic use. In an effort to improve international competitiveness, leading U.S. producers looked to produce goods in regions that featured lower labor costs, building plants in Canada, Mexico, Brazil, and Singapore and entering into joint ventures in Taiwan and South Korea, among other countries.

World industry output increased from the early 1980s to the early 1990s. In a highly cyclical industry, sales of motors and generators slumped as a result of the economic recession of the early 1990s, but recovered steadily. It was not until the 1990s that conditions for

U.S. producers of motors and generators improved. This resulted in large part from generally improved business conditions in the United States, long the world's largest market for motors and generators.

The value of shipments in the U.S. motors and generators industry was US$12 billion in 2000, down 2 percent from 1999. Projections for the future are optimistic, however, and continued long-term growth is expected based on the demand for high-efficiency motors developed as a result of environmental and energy concerns. The sluggish economy of 2000 and 2001, made worse by the terrorist attacks on the United States on September 11, 2001, took a toll on the motor and generator industry, as it did on most industries. As the economy began to rally in 2002, however, rising consumer confidence helped many industries regain hope.

CURRENT CONDITIONS

A major worldwide trend in the motor and generator industry was the push for smaller, lighter, and more energy-efficient products. The rapid development of energy-efficient technologies triggered new demand. In *Air Conditioning, Heating, & Refrigeration,* the National Electrical Manufacturers Association stated that electric motors require ten to twenty-five times the amount of the purchase price in annual electricity costs. This demonstrated how important any degree of improved efficiency can be. New developments in the area of energy efficiency were among the most important for manufacturers in terms of maintaining profitability and market position.

As pointed out in *Design News,* in addition to creating smaller size motors or "micro motors," there was a tendency to provide more for less. Motors were in demand that delivered additional speed and torque while fitting into thinner, smaller, and lighter product designs.

After the devastating impact of hurricanes in 2004 and 2005, a law was passed requiring gas stations near storm-evacuation routes and major highways to be pre-wired for backup power generators by June 1, 2007. Fuel station owners who did not comply were subject to second-degree misdemeanor charges and a US$500 fine. The Department of Environmental Protection had sent letters to more than 1,000 gas stations in Florida informing owners of the law, and began surveying some stations for compliance.

Many of the southeastern U.S. supermarket chains had acquired full-power generators or promised to do so by the end of the 2007 hurricane season. The Publix supermarket chain announced plans to invest US$100 million in hurricane-related improvements and had 500-kilowatt stationary generators in 127 stores. The generators were also viewed as a possible loss prevention tool. The stores had previously loss a substantial amount of their inventory in power outages during hurricane seasons.

Because of sporadic energy shortages and energy prices that were prone to unexpected spikes, many industrial facilities were seeking ways to generate power on-site. While meeting the extensive energy needs of such facilities is possible with diesel-fired generators, interested companies encountered prohibitive regulatory obstacles, particularly with regard to air quality. In addition, increased consumer concern and demand for environmentally friendly products pushed research and development efforts in that direction to the point where a company's future success or failure in the motor and generator market was largely dependent upon it. Researchers were challenged by demands to create energy-efficient motors that were also affordable and durable. Electronic components and software represented areas of broadening research. For example, Ford Motor Company was working with the Environmental Protection Agency (EPA) on Ford's Clean Diesel Combustion program in an effort to offer low-emission diesel engines. The first phase of the program was complete in 2005.

One major trend in the motors segment was the development of hybrid engines that draw power from both gasoline and an electrical battery. Similarly, researchers were working toward creating reliable fuel cells for vehicles. These draw energy directly from fuel sources to create electricity to power the vehicle?s electric motor. In a fuel cell, energy comes from the chemical process, not through combustion. Fuel-cell technology, which obviates the need for the internal combustion engine, had the potential to substantially reduce dependence on foreign oil. Worldwide sales of hybrid cars produced by Toyota, the market leader, had reached 1 million by May 2007. By the summer of 2010, hybrid cars were being sold in over 70 countries or regions. The United States is the market leader with 1.6 million registered. The Toyota Prius is the vehicle leader with California having the largest number of hybrid vehicles.

The fuel cell market was expected to grow rapidly. While estimates of total sales in 2000 were US$218 million, projected sales for 2013 were US$4.6 billion. Some 2,800 systems were produced in 2003, and by early 2004 there were 7,000 systems in operation. *Fuel Cell Technology News* reported that the European Union had slated nearly US$3.5 billion for such projects into 2015.

Major universities, such as the California Institute of Technology, the University of Tokyo, and Technical University of Denmark made fuel cell technology application the focus of their research, as did industry leader Toshiba. According to a Freedonia Group study, the largest market for fuel cells in 2004 was electric power generation. By 2008, 50 percent of fuel cell demand was slated to come from grid support, cogeneration, and remote power supplies.

According to a Frost & Sullivan study, however, the large generator set market for on-site power generation, was not dead yet. In 2002, the market was valued at US$1.4 billion. By 2011, the market was projected to grow to US$1.9 billion.

RESEARCH AND TECHNOLOGY

From development in the late nineteenth century through the 1970s, the basic technology of electric motors and generators changed little. However, since the 1980s, significant advances have been seen in the development of new high-efficiency motors, miniature motors, insulating materials for electric motors' wire windings, and the use of superconducting materials.

Hybrid motors were receiving more attention and were gaining acceptance as a viable strategy for the future. Hybrid engines draw on two types of energy, gasoline and electrical batteries. In 2001 Ford Motor Company announced its agreement with the EPA to develop a hybrid engine using pressurized liquid in a hydraulic motor system in place of the electrical-motor component of the standard hybrid system. Ford expected to have a functioning prototype of its hybrid by 2010.

The U.S. Air Force had a prototype diesel-electric truck that was tentatively planned for commercial production in 2009. The advanced diesel-electric hybrid systems were a product of a cooperative venture by Volvo Powertrain North America and Mack Trucks. A major benefit was the motor's ability to efficiently launch the truck from a standstill and then function as a generator to convert the truck's inertia to alternating current.

Briggs & Stratton Marketing Manager Michael Betker described the benefits of new smaller, quieter home-use standby generators. Hybrid generators were also available that could work on propane tanks running like standbys but working like portable models.

The potential of fuel cells as energy for vehicles was being explored by researchers. In early 2002, for example, the U.S. Department of Energy announced that it would work with three auto manufacturers to produce viable hydrogen generators to supply fuel cell vehicles.

Fuel cells in the automotive industry had the potential to benefit automobile and parts manufacturers, consumers, and the environment. However, the applications of fuel cells go beyond the automotive industry. The National Aeronautics and Space Administration (NASA) was working to realize the potential of fuel cells for use in satellites, aircraft, space stations, and planetary bases in zero-gravity and micro-gravity environments. The Army National Automotive Center hoped to utilize fuel cells for auxiliary power aboard military battlefield vehicles.

High-efficiency motors were an important area of development for the industry. The development of high-efficiency motors was significant not only for the user's operating costs, but also for the energy requirements of the economy at large.

With variable-speed systems, designers were able to specify smaller, less-expensive motors while continuing to offer attractive prices to consumers. Aengus Murray explained in *Machine Design* that running motors at lower speeds resulted in energy savings due to reduced power requirements. Murray also pointed out that it was very important to efficiently use electricity and water in, for example, domestic washing machines. Efficient motor control was considered to be a key factor in meeting the demand for the minimum consumption of resources.

In the late 1980s, researchers discovered superconductive ceramic-like materials that were cheaper and more practical than previously known superconductive materials. Research was launched to investigate the use of these superconductive materials to construct electromagnets of unprecedented power. Some engineers estimated that these superconductive materials, which transmit electricity without resistance, could enable the production of electric motors that were half the size, lighter, and more efficient than conventional motors for a given level of horsepower. The general consensus within the industry was to make high-horsepower electric motors using high-temperature superconducting technology (HTS) ready for commercial use by 2000. Although the industry did not meet this goal, it seems to be within reach. In later years, two groups of engineers, one from the Siemens Research Center at Erlangen, Germany, and the other from Rockwell Automation in South Carolina, introduced motors with high-temperature superconducting technology, bringing the industry closer to the commercial use of this technology.

Toshiba Corp. of Japan announced its development of the world's smallest electromagnetic motor in 1992. It was considered too small and insufficiently powerful to have any commercial applications, but in 2001 Scottish engineer Rod MacGregor announced his matchstick-sized electric motor. Called the Nanomuscle, this motor had potential applications in computers, consumer electronics, office equipment, telecommunications equipment, movable automobile parts, and medical equipment. MacGregor claimed that the motor was five times more efficient than its existing counterparts. The toy company Hasbro planned to use the Nanomuscle in toy products released for the 2002 Christmas season. By 2004 Nanomuscle Inc. had offices in North America, Europe, and Asia. In a similar development, in 2001 Pennsylvania state engineers introduced an ultrasonic motor the size of a grain of rice. Its intended application is breaking down kidney stones.

Products such as General Electric's Power in a Box power generators offer energy efficiency and self-contained power. In 2001, two of these units were ready to go to a resort in California, where installation was scheduled for 2002. Expected to operate at 80 percent efficiency, these generators were intended to dramatically reduce the resort's electricity costs. The generators met strict emission guidelines, making them especially environmentally friendly.

INDUSTRY LEADERS

Toshiba Corporation. Tokyo-based Toshiba Corp. was one of the world's largest producers of electric machinery and electronic equipment. In addition to motors and generators, the firm is a top maker of portable computers and producer of computer peripherals, medical equipment, industrial machinery, home appliances, and semiconductors. Top executives are concerned about the possibility of being too diversified, however, and plans are being made to streamline operations by cutting less profitable product lines and reducing the workforce. The 2010 sales total was US$75.97 billion. The firm had entered into cooperative arrangements with other key producers in the industry, including Siemens AG of Germany and the General Electric Co. of the United States.

Mitsubishi Electric Corporation. Mitsubishi Electric Corp. is also headquartered in Tokyo. The firm was established in 1921 from the electrical machinery division of Mitsubishi Shipbuilding's Kobe shipyard. Of the US$32.6 billion in revenues the company generated in 2001, information systems accounted for 22.6 percent, electrical systems for 22.0 percent, home appliances for 17.7 percent, electronic devices for 17.2 percent, and automation equipment and other industrial products for 16.0 percent, with miscellaneous product lines comprising the balance. In 2007, revenues totaled US$32.6 billion.

In addition to motors and generators, Mitsubishi produces electronics, telecommunications products, industrial machinery, automotive electronics, and consumer appliances. The firm had an expansive worldwide network, with operations in more than 35 countries, and employed 102,835 people.

Hitachi Ltd. Hitachi was established in 1934 and is headquartered in Osaka, Japan. Its product lines include mainframes; semiconductors; elevators and escalators; industrial equipment; cable, audio, and video equipment; and consumer appliances. To stay competitive in the fast-paced technology market, Hitachi is focusing on developing its Internet-related and information technology products, which accounted for about one-third of total revenue. The firm has 1,000 subsidiaries and related companies worldwide. By 2010, Hitachi reported US$95.98 billion in sales, and a workforce of 359,746.

Meidensha Corporation. The Meidensha Corporation was established in 1897 and is headquartered in Tokyo. Meidensha's products fall into three categories: powertronics (utility plant construction and generators); mechatronics (factory automation machinery); and electronics (including information technology and communications products). Its primary customers are in the utility, construction, and transportation industries. In 2004, Meidensha's revenues reached US$1.7 billion with a net income of $22.1 million.

Fanuc Ltd. Fanuc Ltd. was established in 1956 and is headquartered in Yamanashi, Japan. A diversified manufacturer of factory automation and various industrial motors, Fanuc is the world leader (with more than 50 percent of the international market) in production of computer numerical controls (CNCs), which are used on machinery. Fanuc is also known for its robotics, a product line that accounts for about 45 percent of the company's annual sales. The firm has subsidiaries in the United States, Japan, and Europe, and was partly owned by Fujitsu. Revenue in fiscal year 2009 totaled US$3.02 billion, with a workforce of 4,872.

Siemens AG. Siemens AG, headquartered in Munich, is one of Germany's largest industrial firms, employing 420,800 people in more than 190 countries in 2009. The firm produces a wide array of electrical and electronics-related equipment and maintains a highly diversified range of manufacturing interests. Siemens rapidly expanded its overseas operations throughout the 1990s, with particular growth in China. Total revenue from all divisions in 2009 reached US$101.49 billion.

Mabuchi Motor Co. Ltd. The Chiba, Japan-based Mabuchi Motor Co. Ltd. was established in 1954. Compared with most other industry leaders, Mabuchi was a relatively specialized producer of small electric motors. In 2004, sales reached US$1.1 billion. Small electric motors accounted for 46 percent of the firm's revenues in 2000, while motor parts accounted for 23 percent. Mabuchi holds 70 percent of the global market for motors used to move car door mirrors, door locks, and air conditioning damper actuators.

ABB Ltd. ABB Ltd. of Zurich, Switzerland, was jointly owned by ABB AG of Switzerland and ABB AB of Sweden. These companies are participants in utilities, process industries, manufacturing, and oil and gas. Total 2009 revenues were US$31.8 billion with a workforce of 117,000. While the firm had been moving heavily into the Asia-Pacific region, its core business area was Europe.

General Electric Company. The General Electric Co. of Fairfield, Connecticut, is by far the largest U.S. company in the industry in terms of both sales and employment. A highly diversified company, GE produces household appliances, lighting, electric distribution and control equipment, generators, engines, turbines, nuclear reactors, medical equipment, and plastics. The 1990s witnessed substantial sales growth at GE. Sales increased from US$70 billion in 1995 to more than US$157 billion in 2009, with net sales of almost US$10.7 billion. GE employed 304,000 people worldwide. According to Euromonitor, GE captures the largest share of the U.S. market for motors and generators, with 25 percent.

Emerson Electric Company. The Emerson Electric Company of St. Louis, Missouri, is another major U.S. producer in the industry. Emerson operates 380 facilities globally. Emerson's sales in 2008 totaled US$24.8 billion with net income of US$2.4 billion. The firm has greatly expanded its foreign operations with a global presence in 150 countries and a workforce of over 140,700 employees. Sales abroad accounted for 40 percent of Emerson's 2000 revenues.

McDermott International Inc. McDermott International Inc., based in Houston, Texas, is a major U.S. player in the industry, with 27,800 employees and sales of US$4.1 billion in 2006. McDermott's sales totaled US$1.8 billion in 2000 and US$1.9 billion in 2004, a substantial decline from 1997, when sales were US$3.15 billion. As of 2004, McDermott International had 12,500 employees.

Other major industry players included Yaskawa Electric Corporation. Headquartered in Kitakyushu, Japan, the company produced mechanical-electronic products, including industrial robots, servomotors, generators, automated factory production systems, electrical industrial equipment, and motion controllers. In 2004 Yaskawa earned US$283.4 million in sales and employed 450 people. Baldor Electric Company, based in Fort Smith, Arkansas, designed, manufactured, and marketed electric drives, motors, and generators for industry. In 2005, Baldor ran 15 plants in the United States and one in Bristol, England. During 2004, sales went up more than 15 percent to US$648.2 million, and the company's net incomes rose 35.1 percent.

MAJOR COUNTRIES IN THE INDUSTRY

The leading countries in the motors and generators industry throughout the 1990s were the United States, Japan, and Germany. The United States and Germany have been dominant countries in the industry since its origins in the late nineteenth century, while France, Italy, the United Kingdom, and Spain have long been important secondary countries.

According to *Euromonitor,* the U.S. market was valued at US$8.3 billion in 2003, and was projected to increase 13.2 percent between 2004 and 2008, reaching US$10.1 billion by 2008. Fractional horsepower motors were the largest segment, with more than 35 percent of the market. Germany's market was valued at more than US$2.2 billion in 2002, and was forecast to reach US$2.3 billion in 2007. Multi-phase AC motors were the largest segment, and the biggest end user was the commercial appliance sector.

Fractional horsepower motors continued to be an important product for the U.S. industry, worth US$3.1 billion. The United States imported US$5.5 billion and exported US$3.2 billion in 2003, although the value of imports was half of the value of domestic products sold in the domestic market, as reported by the Office of Trade and Industry Information in 2005.

According to *Xinhua Economic News,* China produced 15,500,000 kilowatts of AC electric motors in April 2007. Output for the period of January to April reached 52,068,000 kilowatts, as stated by the National Bureau of Statistics. On the other hand, *China Business News* reported challenging times for small power generators. China shut down 101 generators in the January to April period of 2007. *China Business News* said Xinhua News Agency had reported plans of some regions to totally eliminate small thermal power generation capacity.

AsiaPulse News reported that new thermal power generators had begun commercial output and would boost the electricity reserve on South Korea's top resort island. The two 100,000-kilowatt-capacity thermal power generators that came online in May 2007 cost US$363.3 million to build. The extra power advanced Jeju's ongoing plan to build a new "international city" by 2011. The island was a popular attraction for tourists coming from the rest of Korea and neighboring countries such as China and Japan.

BIBLIOGRAPHY

ABB. "ABB to Supply Automation and Electrical Systems for Germany's Newest Coal-Fired Power Plant," 19 June 2007. Available from www.abb.com.

Allan, Roger. "MEMS: A New Power Source for Portables." *Electronic Design,* 17 March 2005.

Berg, Tom. "Heavy Hybrid Motors Smartly." *Construction Equipment,* 1 March 2007.

"China Shuts 101 Small Thermal Power Generators in the First Four Months of 2007." *China Business News,* 18 May 2007.

"China's Output of AC Electric Motors in April 2007." *Xinhua Economic News,* 10 June 2007.

"Generators Are Based on Field-Effect Transistor Technology." *Product News Network,* 4 June 2007.

Harvey, Fiona. "Generators to Cash in On New Emissions Trading." *The Financial Times,* 19 May 2007.

"Hoover's Company Capsules." *Hoover's Online,* 2007. Available from www.hoovers.com.

Johnson, Mark, ed. "FYI." *ABRN,* April 2005. Available from www.abrn.com.

Kaporech, Thomas. "Driving the Future." *Appliance Manufacturer,* September 2001.

"Large Generator Set Market on Comeback Trail." *Pipeline & Gas Journal,* April 2004.

Lazich, Robert S., ed. *Market Share Reporter.* Detroit: Thomson Gale, 2004.

"Motors and Generators." In *Current Industrial Reports.* Washington, D.C. U.S. Department of Commerce, 2002.

"Motors and Generators in France, Germany, UK, US." *Euromonitor,* August 2004.

"Motors Keep Machinery Humming." *Food & Drug Packaging,* February 2006.

"Micro Motors Deliver More." *Design News,* 25 September 2006.

Mraz, Stephen J. "Superconducting Research Spawns Superefficient Motor." *Machine Design,* 27 September 2001.

Murray, Aengus. "Appliance Motors Turn Green." *Machine Design,* 14 December 2006.

"New Generators to Keep Food Fresh After a Hurricane at More Than 100 Area Supermarkets." *South Florida Sun-Sentinel,* 1 June 2007.

"New Market Opportunities Emerge for Electric Motors in Russia and Ukraine." *Military & Aerospace Electronics,* November 2006.

"New Thermal Generators to Boost Jeju Island's Low Power Reserve." *AsiaPulse News,* 30 May 2007.

Nunes, Thais. "Generating New Horizons in Brazil," June 2006. Available from www.scania.com.

Shade, Norman. "Stationary Power Systems: Driving the Energy Industry." *Diesel Progress North American Edition,* June 2006.

Smith, Tammy. "Home-Use Generators Could Come in Handy." *Biloxi-Gulfport Sun Herald,* 1 June 2007.

Torres, McNelly. "Most Gas Stations Have Generators Ready to Go." *South Florida Sun-Sentinel,* 2 June 2007.

"Superconductor Start-Up." *Global Design News,* October 2001.

U.S. Census Bureau. "Motors and Generators," 12 January 2001. Available from www.census.gov.

"U.S. Fuel Cell Demand." *Batteries International,* April 2004.

Vidal, Steve. "Differentiating Between DC and AC Motors." *EC&M Electrical Construction & Maintenance,* 1 February 2007.

SIC 3861

PHOTOGRAPHIC EQUIPMENT AND SUPPLIES

NAICS CODE(S)

333315. Manufacturers of photographic equipment and supplies provide the world's cameras, film, developing and enlarging equipment, photographic chemicals and papers, and related supplies. Industry output includes both still and motion cameras, but not video cameras, which are discussed in **Audio and Video Equipment.**

INDUSTRY SNAPSHOT

The photographic equipment and supplies industry's products include five general categories: still picture equipment; motion picture equipment; photocopying and microfilming equipment; sensitized photographic film, plates, paper, and cloth; and prepared photographic chemicals.

In established markets, growth in the photographic goods industry was generally fueled by the introduction of new products using innovative technology, particularly digital cameras and one-time-use (OTU) disposable cameras. By 2003, digital cameras outsold traditional film cameras. As a result, the overall film sector began to weaken, although some consumers were returning to the use of film prints for digital images. Major industry players began to scale back their Advanced Photo System (APS) camera activities in favor of digital cameras, sales of which were expected to grow 13 percent in 2005 to 20.5 million, according to the Photo Marketing Association International

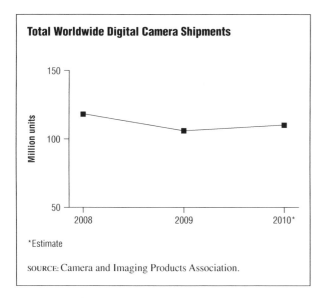

Total Worldwide Digital Camera Shipments

*Estimate

SOURCE: Camera and Imaging Products Association.

(PMAI). The fastest growing sector was digital cameras with four or more megapixels. Consequently, major companies in the industry began to focus less on combating digital technology and more on developing products for the organization and storage of digital images. Industry analysts expected the digital market to remain steady as the sector became saturated. However, the Japanese trade group Camera and Imagine Products Association (CIPA) in 2009 reported a projected decrease in digital cameras for 2010 as the market reached the saturation point. Overall sales dropped by 11.6 percent in 2009 to 105.9 million units over 2008. However, integrated-lens camera sales were projected to continue rising by as much as 3 percent, and sales of digital cameras with interchangeable lenses were expected to be 11.1 percent more than in 2009.

In 2004, OTU cameras peaked at 218 million units, with the expectation that sales would remain flat in 2005. Film sales declined to 438 million units in 2004, down 157 million, and a further decline to 315 million was anticipated in 2005. The majority continued to be 35mm film, with 66 percent, while APS trailed with 6 percent. Prints made from digital images increased a massive 71 percent over 2003 figures. Traditional camera sales remained in decline, with analog camera sales dropping 45 percent and 35mm cameras sales dropping 43 percent in 2004. Despite the continuing decrease in film sales, the market was not dead, and approximately 532 million rolls of film were expected to sell in 2005. However, in an article for *Gadget Lab* on May 14, 2008, Charlie Sorrel wrote that CIPA had stopped compiling sales figures for film cameras because so few were being sold in Japan that year. Only 529

35mm film cameras were produced in 2008 in Japan, which had been the top manufacturer of film cameras, leading to the claim that film was a niche rather than a mainstream product.

ORGANIZATION AND STRUCTURE

The majority of the photographic equipment industry's products were considered leisure or nonessential goods, which meant that industry sales were somewhat sensitive to reduced consumer spending during economic stagnation or recession. Nevertheless, the broad range of photographic products offered partially insulated the industry from fluctuations in consumer demand. Because it provided an essential service in most business and government offices, photocopying equipment sales were relatively independent of consumer spending levels. In the mid- to late 1990s, photocopying equipment accounted for roughly one-third of industry sales, and high-end photocopiers were particular lucrative products.

The industry has grown increasingly globalized as leading photographic equipment companies had worldwide research and development, manufacturing, marketing, and servicing divisions. Industry leaders operated through a worldwide network of affiliates and subsidiaries that were business offices and "transplants" (foreign manufacturing sites), providing access to both regional and national consumer markets as well as to local labor pools. International leaders in the industry comprised a complex, shifting network of affiliation and cooperation, combined with competition and rivalry.

The international distribution of industry products stood to benefit from the economic globalization reflected by political treaties like the mid-1990s General Agreement on Tariffs and Trade (GATT) and the North American Free Trade Agreement (NAFTA). In addition, national and local governments provided a variety of economic incentives to encourage industry firms to continue or establish operations and facilities within their areas of jurisdiction. For example, in 1993, the regional government of Castilla y Leon in Spain arranged a Pta850 million guaranteed loan through the Banco Bilbao Vizcaya Argentaria, the second-largest bank in Spain, to assist Valca, a local manufacturer of photographic equipment that faced severe financial difficulties. In 1994, the French government granted financial aid to Toshiba for the expansion of its photocopier and toner plant near Dieppe.

National and international courts had historically monitored trade, monopoly, and patent issues within the industry. For example, the Eastman Kodak Company was fined US$873 million for infringement of copyrights held by the Polaroid Corporation, and Honeywell won a US$96 million judgment against the Minolta Camera Company for copyright infringements involving autofocus cameras. In addition, the European Court of Justice upheld a complaint by European companies against unfair trade practices by Japanese photocopying equipment manufacturers, including Minolta. With the ratification of GATT, the United Nations established the World Trade Organization (WTO) in 1995 to govern global trade and trade policies. Shortly after its formation, the WTO began hearing complaints from the United States and Europe alleging that Japan's film market was unfairly restrictive. In 1998, however, the WTO found in favor of Japan.

BACKGROUND AND DEVELOPMENT

The photographic equipment and supply industry developed as a result of research and technology around the world. The precursor of the modern camera was the closet-sized *camera obscura* developed by tenth-century Islamic scientists. In the sixteenth century, Italian scientist Giambattista della Porta published his research on fitting the *camera obscura* with a lens to strengthen or enlarge the image projected. In 1727, German professor Johann Heinrich Schulze took an important step forward by permanently capturing the image produced by a *camera obscura* when he discovered that silver salts darkened when exposed to sunlight. As early as 1816, French amateur inventor Joseph Nicephore Niepce, building on his interest in lithography, obtained an image of Paris on paper treated with silver chloride. By 1827, Niepce had achieved the first permanent photographic image taken from nature, a view of his country estate. Niepce termed his discovery "heliography" (Greek for "sun writing").

In 1826, French scene-painter Louis Jacques Mande Daguerre, hoping to exploit photographic images in the creation of theatrical backdrops, began corresponding with Niepce about heliography. Working with copper plates coated with silver iodine, Daguerre discovered that a latent image exposed for the relatively short span of 30 minutes, could be developed by exposing it to mercury vapor. Ignoring the role played by Niepce, Daguerre marketed this discovery as the "daguerreotype," which proved to be a commercial sensation.

At the same time, English scientist William Henry Fox Talbot, attempting to capture a permanent photographic image on paper, created an early form of negatives (reversing black and white tones). Talbot's photograph of Lacock Abbey, Wiltshire, in 1835, is considered the first successful photograph made from a negative image to be taken from nature. Talbot subsequently developed a portable camera consisting of a wooden box fitted with a lens and partially lined with treated paper. By 1841, Talbot had perfected his discovery and patented it under the name of "talbotype." The daguerreotype was superseded as the most popular form of photography when English sculptor and inventor Frederick Scott Archer developed the use of glass plates treated with collodion in the early 1850s.

U.S. inventor George Eastman was responsible for mass-merchandising photography and amateur manual cameras. Experimenting in his mother's kitchen, Eastman was able to coat glass photographic plates with a gelatin emulsion containing silver chloride. The emulsion, once solidified, left a light-sensitive "dry plate" that was 60 times more sensitive than collodion-based plates, which freed the camera from the tripod. In 1881, Eastman founded the Eastman Dry Plate Company and rapidly introduced dry plates and several other advances in photography. The paper and gelatin photographic film packaged in a small cassette that Eastman patented in 1884 allowed a significant reduction of camera size. Five years later, Eastman marketed a celluloid film that was much tougher than his original paper and gelatin version. Adopting the international trade name "Kodak" in 1888, Eastman successfully marketed innovative folding, hand, and pocket cameras that made photography accessible to even the casual amateur.

In the late 1850s, Scottish physicist James Clerk Maxwell developed what became the standard method of color photography: the additive three-color process. Employing this process, U.S. inventor Frederic Eugene Ives first made color photography practical for professional photographers with his 1893 Photochromoscope camera. French inventors Auguste and Louis Lumière, in addition to developing cinematography, introduced the autochrome method, the first method of color photography accessible to amateurs. In 1912, German scientist Hans Fischer made a further breakthrough by proposing that color photography could be achieved chemically, rather than optically, through oxidation of chemicals in a multi-layered film. By mid-century, George Eastman, in collaboration with others, had developed the color film marketed as Kodachrome.

In 1947, Dr. Edwin Herbert Land, founder of the Polaroid Corporation, introduced the first "instant" film and camera. In 1959, the Haloid Company, which was quickly renamed the Xerox Corporation, introduced the first successful commercial photocopier, the 914 model.

During the 1980s and 1990s, Japan, the United States, and Germany led the world in production of photographic equipment and supplies, accounting for 80 percent of the global market. Japan and the United States held the largest share, while Germany remained a distant third. Japan led in exports of photographic equipment and supplies, with a 36 percent market share for equipment and a 24 percent market share supplies in 1995. The United States controlled 9 percent of the equipment export market and 13.9 percent of the supply export market. According to U.N. estimates, total industry trade in 1996 reached about US$30 billion, about the same as 1995, but up from US$24 billion in 1994.

International trade policies on photographic equipment and supplies came under increased scrutiny during the 1990s as the United States and the European Union both argued that Japan unfairly shielded its photographic equipment and supply market from outside competition. Spearheaded by Kodak, the United States and the European Union took their complaint before the WTO in 1996. Although the United States expected the WTO to agree with Kodak's allegations, the WTO ruled in January of 1998 that the Japanese government did not restrict film imports, specifically from Kodak. The United States announced in February of that year that it would not appeal the decision.

CURRENT CONDITIONS

The development of the digital camera was a major turning point in the global photographic equipment and supplies industry. At first, industry analysts speculated as to how the camera, with its limited ability to produce high-quality photographs, would fare. Technological advances that increased resolution coupled with declining prices to transform the digital camera from a personal computer accessory to a full-fledged rival to the standard 35-millimeter camera. Nearly one-third of U.S. households owned digital cameras in 2003, the first year that traditional film cameras were outsold. Analysts predicted that by the end of 2004 that percentage would be 42 percent, and by 2006 the global digital camera market would be worth US$9 billion, with nearly two-thirds of all cameras sold being digital.

As digital camera sales began to outpace 35mm camera sales early in the twenty-first century, new players entered the photographic equipment and supplies industry. Traditional companies like Eastman Kodak found themselves in competition with such firms as Sony Corp. In 2001 Sony held a 25 percent share of the global digital camera market, compared to 14 percent held by Kodak. A handful of major camera makers in Japan, including Konica Corp., Olympus Optical Co., and Minolta Co.,

stopped producing APS cameras. In addition, Nikon Corp. and Asahi Optical Co. both downsized APS production, putting those resources into digital technology. Conversely, despite the shrinking APS market, Fuji and Canon, two of the world's largest APS camera makers, both announced their intentions to launch new APS products during 2002.

The growth in the digital camera segment of the industry not only undercut sales of APS cameras, but also affected the film segment, which traditionally boasted high profit margins and provided consistent business for industry leaders like Kodak and Fuji. Because digital technology allowed for the storage of photographs on either a hard drive or a disk, film was unnecessary for digital camera users. In 2001 the 10 to 15 percent of all digital camera users who chose to print photographs had a wide range of high-quality paper options. According to the PMAI, however, the outlook for prints was positive in the mid-2000s. Women and young families, who comprised the typical users of traditional film cameras, were shifting to the digital market and were more likely to want prints of digital images. PMA predicted that long before the end of the decade, total prints produced would return to 2000 levels.

Digital camera sales declined worldwide in 2009, primarily due to the global economic crisis and reduced spending. Predictions for 2010 were for a rebound in sales. In 2009 total worldwide shipments were 106 million units, an 11.6 percent drop from 118 million shipped in 2008. A 3.8 percent increase to 110 million cameras was forecast for the industry in 2010 according to CIPA.

By 2004 the fastest-growing film processing sector was one-time-use disposable cameras (OTU). In contrast to the declines in other sectors, OTUs commanded more than 22 percent of film processing, a 3 percent increase over the prior year.

While Japan proved to be the largest digital camera market in 2001, many analysts expected China to claim that title by 2005. By 2009, China was continuing to close its gap in sales with Japan. China and Japan were predicted to hold a combined 60 percent of the market. The Asian digital camera market was expected to continue growing to more than 30 percent of the global market with shipments expected to reach 54.33 million in 2009, and revenue climbing to US$7.25 billion. Kodak and Fuji responded by announcing plans to manufacture their digital cameras in China at transplant operations. Kodak teamed up with Seagull, a Chinese camera maker, to jointly manufacture digital cameras in Shanghai, while Fuji forged a similar joint venture in Suzhou. The Chinese photocopier industry was also expected to grow at least 10 percent annually during the early 2000s, which resulted in the opening of related plants in China by Ricoh Co., Fuji, Xerox Co., and Canon.

RESEARCH AND TECHNOLOGY

Research and development (R&D) was the lifeblood of the photographic equipment and supply industry. In 1997 the Eastman Kodak Company invested US$1.04 billion (7 percent) of its US$14.5 billion in net sales in R&D, Fuji Photo Film Company invested about US$600 million (5.6 percent) of its US$10.6 billion in sales, and Xerox invested about US$1 billion (5 percent) of its US$18.1 billion in sales.

In the early 1990s, technological developments in the photocopier market included Ricoh's creation of a photocopying machine that turned the pages of a book as it was being photocopied and one that translated documents from English to Japanese as they were being reproduced. In addition, Mita Industrial Company announced a five-year joint venture with the University of Tokyo to develop photocopying machines that were self-repairing. Industry leaders responded to the need to install sophisticated anti-counterfeiting technology in color photocopiers.

In the 1990s, the most significant technological innovation within the photographic equipment and supplies industry was the advent of electronic imaging, which uses semiconductor sensors instead of film to record images and display them on television screens or computer monitors. Electronic imaging threatened to radically affect the sales of photographic equipment and supplies because the technology did not employ film, paper, or conventional photographic chemicals to produce an image. By the mid-1990s, the Eastman Kodak Company alone spent over US$1 billion in the development of this technology.

A broad technological trend for the industry was the modification of design, manufacturing, packaging, and waste disposal processes to create environmentally sound products. In 1988 the Polaroid Corporation set up a Toxic Waste and Use Reduction program that achieved company-wide waste reductions of 6 percent annually. In 1990 Canon Inc. began refurbishing used photocopying equipment as a form of recycling. In the early 1990s, various industry leaders reported significant reductions in photocopier ozone emissions and discontinued the use of chlorofluorocarbons (CFCs) in their manufacturing processes. At the same time, the Konica Corporation developed a minilab system using tablet form photo-chemicals that reduced levels of chemical effluent 50 percent. In 1993, the Ricoh Company developed a "peel off" toner system that allowed photocopying paper to be reused. The system earned the inaugural Queen's Award for Environmental

Achievement for Ricoh UK Products Ltd. In 1994, German photographic companies and the recycling organization Vereinigung für Werstoffrecycling set up a recycling system comprised of 800 sites to collect used retail packaging.

During the mid-1990s, photographic equipment and supply manufacturers also rolled out Advanced Photo System (APS) cameras and film. Although earlier attempts to supplant the 35mm format, such as Kodak's disk camera, had failed, manufacturers hoped the convenience and power of this camera would become popular. Using silver halide technology, APS cameras and film made it easier to take pictures and to develop them. According to manufacturers, APS offered the power of a 35mm camera with the simplicity of a point-and-shoot camera. In addition, APS technology was supposed to yield higher-quality pictures because magnetic codes on the film automatically adjusted the camera settings for factors such as lighting. Kodak, Canon, Nikon, Fuji, and Minolta jointly developed the APS format and introduced the product in the form of a disposable cameras to test the market. Although touted by manufacturers, retailers reported mixed responses to the product in 1997. Nonetheless, analysts predicted that APS would remain on the market for some time and that sales would grow to account for about 20 percent of all camera purchases and 7 percent of all film sales. However, the analysts failed to foresee the impact of digital technology on traditional 35mm cameras.

With the growing penetration of personal computers and the global popularity of the Internet, camera manufacturers in the late 1990s introduced digital cameras, which stored images on computerized camera's disk or hard drive memory. When attached to a computer, images could be downloaded for manipulation and printing. Digital cameras produced higher-quality images than most scanned photographs and allowed users to quickly take a photograph and place it in a report or e-mail message, or on a Web page. By the end of 2000, companies like Nikon and Olympus were selling digital cameras with a resolution of 2 million pixels for roughly US$500. Such cameras were able to compete with standard 35mm cameras because they were capable of producing high-quality 4x6 photographs. By 2004, 38 percent of digital cameras sold had resolution of 3 to 3.9 megapixels and 27 percent sold had 4 to 4.9 megapixels. Cameras with higher resolutions were sold to 28 percent of buyers. In 2004 the PMAI reported that the average price per megapixel was $82, down from $119 the previous year.

In 2006 FotoNation launched FotoNation Face Tracker for camera phones. The innovative approach identifies and locks onto human faces in a preview image and follows the subjects as they move around, making automatic adjustments. Face Tracker was also available for digital cameras.

Vimcro, a fabless semiconductor company that designed advanced mixed-signal multimedia products and solutions, introduced a PC camera processor VCO326 in 2006 to address the need for a next-generation PC camera that was compatible with a standard driver within the Microsoft Windows Vista operating system. The VCO 326 received Windows Hardware Quality Lab (WHQL) certification for Windows Vista.

WORKFORCE

In the early-to-mid-2000s, the international photographic equipment and supplies workforce continued to shrink. Kodak continued to streamline its workforce, eliminating 9,600 jobs in 2004. It shut offices and facilities in Brazil, Canada, Germany, Japan, and Spain, among other locations. Xerox eliminated about 10,000 jobs in the 1990s, including 200 jobs at a Canadian plant and 478 jobs at its French sales subsidiary. In 2004, the firm trimmed another 4.9 percent from its ranks. Although some companies, including Ricoh and Canon, added to their workforce during the late 1990s and early 2000s, most positions were for other operations such as manufacturing computer printers.

INDUSTRY LEADERS

Kodak. The largest producer of photographic film in the world, with 70 percent of sales in 2003, Eastman Kodak also produced photographic paper, cameras, motion picture films, microfilm paper, and X-ray film. Worldwide net sales totaled US$13.5 billion in 2004, up 5 percent from 2003. Sales related to digital and film imaging totaled more than $9 billion, $5.3 million of which were generated outside the United States. International sales accounted for more than half of annual revenues. In 2009, sales totaled US$7.9 billion, down from $13.3 billion in 2004. Kodak reported a workforce in 2009 of 20,250 people.

The Eastman Kodak Company was established in 1881 by George Eastman in Rochester, New York. The historic leader of the photographic equipment and supplies industry, Eastman Kodak in the early 1990s controlled 75 percent of the U.S. market and 50 percent of the international market for photographic film and paper. In the late 1990s Kodak began targeting new sectors of the population, including children, the elderly, and childless adults, and formed alliances with stores to offer Kodak film exclusively. Kodak Service and Support backed the sale of all Kodak products. This team includes more than 3,000 professionals in 120 countries. Kodak was named the Best Support Organization at the 2006 International Business Awards.

Due to increased competition on the domestic front from rivals like Fuji in the late 1990s, Kodak strove to expand its sales by tapping the potentially largest market in the world: China. Although per capita film use in China was just a half roll of film per year, Kodak planned to stimulated Chinese consumption by opening manufacturing plants there and accelerating marketing. In 1998 Kodak acquired three unprofitable Chinese manufacturers of photographic supplies and began modernizing them. By 2001, the firm had also launched more than 6,000 Kodak franchises in China, which had become the second-largest consumer film and paper market for Kodak.

Despite Kodak's success in China, sales continued to decline beginning in the late 1990s and continuing into the 2000s. Along with increased competition, the firm faced a shrinking film market. According to Goldman, Sachs and Co., global film use declined 5 percent in 2001, mainly due to the growing popularity of digital cameras. Although Kodak had added digital cameras to its product line, the company's 14 percent share of the global digital camera market was behind the 25 percent share held by Sony. Compounding the problem was the fact that digital cameras were simply a much less profitable business than film. The firm's EasyShare digital camera, launched in April of 2001, proved to be a best seller throughout the year and boosted Kodak's market share in that sector considerably. In order to stay competitive, Kodak was putting more and more money into digital equipment and technologies in the mid-2000s, with an accompanying reduction in its workforce. The company had 54,800 employees worldwide in 2004, compared to 62,300 the year before. By 2009, that number had been reduced by more than half to 20,250.

In a 2005 advertorial, Kodak addressed the industry dilemma as retailers who had invested in digital minilabs for their full-service photofinishing business had to choose between extending leases while hoping customers would return to making more traditional prints or exploring economical options. Kodak recommended that retailers consider its "Kodak Picture Maker," which offered an increase in return-on-investment and improved customer experience. The advertorial also claimed that households using traditional film captured approximately 240 images each year and made an average of 340 prints. Digital camera users shot more photos, capturing an average of 400 images annually, but chose to print significantly fewer of them.

In 2007 Kodak celebrated the second straight year of being recognized by an international panel of design experts when the new Kodak Easyshare V1003 digital camera earned a 2007 Red Dot Award for product design. The V1003 featured digital stabilization, a 2.5-

inch LCD screen, and a high ISO 1600 mode for shooting in low-light conditions. Experts evaluated 2,548 innovative products from companies in 43 countries. In Europe the red dot Award is one of the most highly regarded forms of recognition as an acknowledgement of quality, sophistication, and innovative design.

Also in 2007, six newspaper printers chose Kodak thermal digital solutions, ordering 11 thermal CTP devices and digital plates. The transition to the new equipment was trouble-free and allowed sharper reproduction of photographs than the equipment it replaced.

In the mid-2000s Kodak had developed a family of light management films used in a variety of applications that were initially used for the flat panel industry. In 2007 Rohm and Haas Company and Kodak entered into an agreement for the former to acquire Kodak's Light Management Films business, including rights to patents and trademarks, know-how, trade secrets, the business's portfolio of current and future products, and a license to additional intellectual property.

In April 2007, Kodak introduced an industry-first service for Kodak Gallery Premier members. The Kodak Picture Protection plan applied to all digital photos stored on the Kodak Gallery and protected prints and other gift items stored or purchased through the Kodak Gallery. If destroyed, members would receive a credit up to US$500 to recreate their items through the Kodak gallery. Kodak Gallery Premier members paid an annual subscription fee of US$24.99 for basic protection.

In a further effort to evolve from traditional film photography to digital photography, in 2009 Kodak announced that it would retire Kodachrome color film after 74 years as the film industry leader.

Fuji. The top photographic film and paper manufacturer in Japan, Fuji was Kodak's closest competitor globally in the mid-2000s. Fuji's Imaging Solutions division, which included film, digital cameras, photofinishing equipment and services, paper, and chemicals, accounted for 31.9 percent of the US$24.1 billion in revenues for 2004. The company had a presence in the Americas, Asia, Europe, and Australia, but the majority (52.2 percent) of Fuji's sales came from the Japanese market in 2004. The company reported revenues of US$33.89 billion in 2008 with a workforce of 76,358.

The Fuji Photo Film Company was established in 1934 by Mokichi Morita in Tokyo. The company's photographic products included photographic films and papers, motion picture films, still and instant cameras, camcorders, and photocopiers. In contrast to the company's steady growth in the early 1990s, sales remained stagnant in the late 1990s before falling 16 percent in

2001 to US$11.5 billion. In the late 1990s, Fuji remained Japan's leading film producer and controlled 70 percent of the country's general photo supply market. Worldwide, Fuji had a 37 percent market share. By 2001, the firm had secured a 30 percent share of the film market in China, compared to the 50 percent share held by Kodak.

Xerox. The Xerox Corporation, which was the pioneer in photocopying, was established in 1906 as the Haloid Company and adopted its present name in 1961. Corporate headquarters were in Norwalk, Connecticut in 2010. Xerox's photographic products included plain paper and color photocopying equipment. Xerox reported total revenues of US$18 billion in 2008. The company's international workforce fell from 99,000 in 1991 to 58,100 in 2004, but by 2010 the number of employees had grown to 133,200.

Over the years, the firm struggled to overcome sluggish sales and high costs. In the early 2000s, Xerox continued to develop and market digital color copiers and integrated copier and communications hardware, as well as printers, scanners, and software. International operations accounted for roughly 45 percent of annual revenues.

Canon. Canon Inc. was established in 1937 in Tokyo and laid the foundations for its role as a global exporter by selling "Kwanon" cameras to post-World War II U.S. occupation forces. The company's photographic products included single-lens reflex (SLR) cameras; compact cameras; camcorders; and full-color, office, and personal photocopiers. By the late 1990s, Canon led the world in camera and copier sales. Canon posted sales of US$33.3 billion in 2004. Printers and other peripheral devices for personal computers brought in approximately 40 percent of revenues, while copiers secured 30 percent. Cameras garnered less than 13 percent of sales. Efforts to increase the company's presence in Asia resulted in Canon securing a 25.1 percent share of the digital camera market in Malaysia by the end of 2001. That year, less than one-third of sales were attributed to domestic clients. By 2007, Canon had grown to become the top patent holder in industry technology, ranking third overall in the United States, with global revenues of US$34.47 billion in 2009 and a workforce of 166,980.

In March 2007, the Canon Medical Services division of Canon U.S.A. demonstrated its total digital imaging and workflow management solutions at the International Vision Expo East Show in New York City. The Eye Q Prime Imaging Systems' software linked retinal images from the Canon Non-Mydriatic camera with measurement devices like the tonometer and auto-ref keratometer.

The process enhanced opportunities for quick diagnosis by collecting patient information in one easy-to-use database.

In April 2007, Canon U.S.A. announced several hardware and software solutions designed to enhance the digital printing workflow experience for corporate users, print service providers, and production printers. Canon also introduced its imagePRESS C7000VP digital press and related imagePRESS workflow solutions at AIIM on Demand in Boston.

Ricoh. The Ricoh Company, Ltd., was established in 1936 as Riken Sensitized Paper Company in Tokyo. Ricoh's photographic products included cameras, video cameras, and photocopying equipment. As of the mid-2000s, the company boasted more than 400 subsidiaries around the world and ranked among the world's leading copier, fax machine, and camera manufacturers. Ricoh Corporation, Lanier Worldwide, and Savin were listed among the company's U.S.-based subsidiaries. To boost sales, the firm began to focus on laser printers and other networked imaging products in the early twenty-first century. In 2010 the company's revenues were US$12 billion, and Ricoh and its subsidiaries reported a workforce of 108,525 that year.

In 2007, for the third consecutive year, Ricoh was listed among the Corporate Knights Inc. of Canada's "Global 100" after Corporate Knights evaluated the sustainability of more than 1,800 major corporations in all business sectors based on research and analysis data provided by U.S.-based Innovest Strategic Value Advisors. Ricoh's aggressive environmental policy, as well as its long-term vision through 2050, were highly regarded.

Agfa-Gevaert NV. Agfa-Gevaert NV was established in 1964 by the merger of the Belgian partnership Agfa-Gevaert N.V. and the German partnership Agfa-Gevaert AG. From 1981 until 2002, it had been a wholly owned subsidiary of Bayer AG. As of 2010 the firm's headquarters were in Mortsel, Belgium. Its photographic products included photographic film, paper, chemicals, and machinery; photo-laboratory and minilab equipment; and photocopiers. The company's sales rose slowly in the 1990s, reaching US$4.9 billion in 2000, up from US$4 billion in 1991. By 2004, sales were US$5.13 billion, but by 2007, sales had dipped to US$4.39 billion. More than 80 percent of Agfa's sales came from exports. The company reported a workforce of 13,565.

Polaroid. The Polaroid Corporation, with headquarters in Concord, Massachusetts, as of 2008, was established in 1937 by Edwin Herbert Land. Polaroid's photographic products included hand-held instant cameras; instant cameras under license by Minolta; amateur and professional photographic films; film holders; film recorders; and photocopiers. Polaroid led the industry in instant image photographic equipment and supplies, which accounted for nearly 75 percent of sales. Due to waning demand for instant cameras and film, Polaroid's sales dropped in the late 1990s, eventually falling to US$752.7 million in 2003, compared to US$2.1 billion in 1997. In April 2005, Petters Group Worldwide acquired Polaroid for US$426 million. Following an FBI investigation of Petters, Polaroid filed for bankruptcy protection. In 2009, Patriarch Partners LLC won the assets of the company at auction.

MAJOR COUNTRIES IN THE INDUSTRY

As of the mid-2000s, the United States and Japan dominated the international photographic equipment and supplies industry. The U.S. photographic equipment market grew 11.2 percent to US$8.9 billion in 2003 when the nation's five largest companies accounted for 75 percent of the market. The digital camera sector proved to be the most successful. This sector surged 645 percent in value between 1996 and 2000 and was expected to reach a value of US$7.2 billion by 2008, which would represent half of the photographic market. To maintain market share in an intensely competitive market, manufacturers have continued to pour money into marketing endeavors, as well as research and development efforts designed to yield innovative product developments. *Euromonitor International* predicted that the U.S. photographic equipment industry would grow 35.7 percent to US$17.1 billion by 2005. This growth was expected to be fueled by growing digital camera sales.

In 2000, U.S. imports of photographic/imaging products declined by 3.6 percent to US$7.62 billion, while exports grew 15.3 percent to $4.86 billion, according to the Photo Marketing Association. In 1995 Japan led the world in photographic equipment and supply exports with 36.6 percent and 24 percent shares, respectively. In 1996, Japan's equipment exports totaled US$4.48 billion, and its supply exports were US$4.02 billion. As the world's leading camera producer, Japan focused on digital and compact models in the late 1990s and early 2000s.

China was expected to replace Japan as the largest digital camera market in the world by 2010. The country also was considered one of the most promising new markets for photocopiers, as well as other photographic equipment and supplies. The Polaroid, or "pola," has become a cult favorite among fans on the Internet, with an online forum that has more than 2,500 registered members from all over China.

Digital cameras dominated some European markets. In 2003 the total German market was valued at US$2 billion, with digital cameras accounting for a 40 percent share. In the United Kingdom, however, film was the largest market sector, accounting for 80 percent of sales.

BIBLIOGRAPHY

"About PMA." Photo Marketing Association International, 2004. Available from www.pma.org.

"Canon U.S.A. Showcases Its imagePRESS C7000VP and Digital Printing Workflow Solutions at 2007 AIIM On Demand in Boston." *Business Wire,* 17 April 2007.

"Canon U.S.A. Showcases Total Imaging and Workflow Management Systems for the Ophthalmic World at Vision Expo East." *Business Wire,* 23 March 2007.

"CIPA Issues 2009 Sales figures and 2010 Forecast." *Digital Photography Review,* 26 January 2010. Available from www.dpreview.com.

"Digital Camera Growth 'Exponential.'" *Africa News Service,* 11 May 2004.

Draper, Deborah J., ed. *Business Rankings Annual.* Detroit: Thomson Gale, 2004.

"FotoNation Announces Face Tracker for Better Cameraphone Pictures." *Digital Imaging Digest,* June 2006.

"Hoover's Company Capsules." *Hoover's Online,* 2007. Available from www.hoovers.com.

"Kodak Announces First-of-its Kind Picture Protection Plan to Replace Treasured Pictures." *Yahoo! Finance,* 16 April 2007. Available from biz.yahoo.com.

Lazich, Robert S., ed. *Market Share Reporter.* Detroit: Thomson Gale, 2004.

Minji, Yao. "The Magic of Polaroid—a Vanishing Image." *Shanghai Daily,* 3 April 2007.

"Photo Industry 2005 Review and Forecast." Photo Marketing Association International, 2005. Available from www.pma.org.

"Photographic Equipment in France, Germany, UK, US." *Euromonitor,* 2004. Available from www.euromonitor.com.

"PMA Launches Digital Outreach." *Association Management,* February 2004.

"PMA Processing Survey Through April 2004." Photo Marketing Association International, 12 July 2004.

"The Print Predicament." *Photo Marketing Magazine,* July 2005.

"Ricoh was Listed Again in 2007 in the '2007 Global 100 Most Sustainable Corporations in the World' for Three Consecutive Years." Ricoh Company Ltd., 14 February 2007. Available from www.ricoh.com.

"Rohm and Haas Company Agrees to Acquire Kodak's Light Management Films Business." *Yahoo! Finance,* 18 April 2007. Available from biz.yahoocom.

Shankland, Stephen. "Digital–camera Sales Set to Rebound in 2010," *Deep Tech,* 26 January 2010. Available from news.cnet.com.

"Six Newspaper Printers Migrate to Kodak Thermal Digital Solutions to Meet Quality and Deadline Demands in Competitive Market." *M2Presswire,* April 5, 2007. Available from www.outputlinks.com.

"Smile! Digital Camera Market in Asia Grows Strongly, Country by Country." *Research and Markets,* May 2005. Available from www.researchandmarkets.com.

Sorrel, Charlie. "Film Cameras Officially Dead in Japan." *Gadget Lab,* 14 May 2008. Available from www.wired.com.

Tarnowski, Joseph. "The Hybrid Theory." *Progressive Grocer,* 1 May 2004.

"Vimcro Launches PC Camera Multimedia Solution Certified for Windows Vista." *Wireless News,* 8 November 2006.

SIC 3674

SEMICONDUCTORS

NAICS CODE(S)

334413. The semiconductor industry consists of manufacturers of semiconductors and related solid-state devices. Industry products include semiconductor diodes and stacks (for example, rectifiers, integrated microcircuits, transistors, solar cells, and light-sensing and emitting semiconductor devices). Semiconductors are used in the manufacture of electronic goods that range from television sets and toys to computers and missiles. High-speed computer processor chips and computer memory chips rank among higher profile industry products. The manufacture of products that integrate semiconductors and the manufacture of machines used to produce semiconductors are not categorized as part of the semiconductor industry itself.

INDUSTRY SNAPSHOT

The semiconductor industry has traditionally been characterized by swift change, hefty capital investments, and high risk. It is highly consolidated, with just a handful of companies in a few countries supplying the majority of industry output. According to the Semiconductor Industry Association's (SIA) *2006 Annual Report,* the industry employed nearly 234,000 people in the United States. With an excess of US$43 billion in exports for 2005, the semiconductor industry was the leading U.S. exporter. More than 75 percent of U.S. chip industry sales, however, occurred outside the United States. The total global market climbed from US$213 billion in 2004 to US$260 in 2009. Semiconductors form the nucleus of the electronics industry. Their role is primary and vital. The contribution semiconductors make enables the generation of approximately US$1,200 billion in the electronics business, which in turn creates over US$5,000 billion in services—close to 10 percent of the global gross domestic product.

High technological requirements, massive capital investments related to research and production facilities, and entrenched market leaders generally discourage new entrants to the industry. However, leaps in technology in recent years made by the industry's market leaders opened the door to new manufacturers who specialized

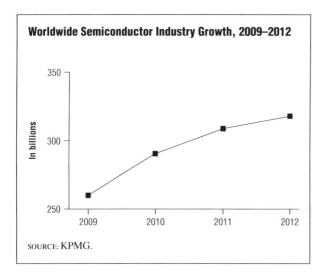

Worldwide Semiconductor Industry Growth, 2009–2012

In billions

350

300

250

2009   2010   2011   2012

SOURCE: KPMG.

According to *World Semiconductor Trade Statistics*, growth of 8.6 percent and 12.1 percent was expected for 2007 and 2008, respectively. The Asia-Pacific region was expected to be the largest regional market. The forecast anticipated a consistent, positive growth peaking in 2008. Although the semiconductor market did not show a pronounced cyclical pattern, it did reflect that some product groups maintained cycles similar to historical patterns. The industry performed better than anticipated in 2009 in spite of the economic downturn. According to the SIA, global sales of semiconductors reached US$226.3 billion in 2009, up from the US$219.7 billion predicted. The upturn was attributed to superior inventory management, new product launches, and strength in the consumer and PC markets toward the end of the year. The consumer and PC markets consumed 60 percent of the total semiconductors sales.

in commodity products and helped to satisfy increased customer demand.

On average, the semiconductor industry has enjoyed a growth rate of 17 percent per annum since 1959. In 1990, global sales hit a record US$50.5 billion. Five years later, sales had tripled to US$144.4 billion, and in 2000 sales reached US$204 billion. By 2004, after the sharp economic downturn in the early years of the decade, global sales topped US$200 billion for the first time since 2000. As reported in *CMR*, semiconductor sales for 2004 were US$227.24 billion. Of that total, 13 percent was earned by industry leader Intel. World semiconductor shipments were expected to continue rising into the late 2000s, as the rapid expansion of the telecommunications industry continued to create more demand for semiconductors for use in networking and wireless communications devices. The rapid increase in the use of digital technologies and the world's appetite for electronic devices made it certain that strong growth would continue to characterize the industry.

In 2009, the semiconductor market was strongest in the Asia Pacific region with 52 percent (excluding Japan), followed by Japan and the Americas with 17 percent each, and the balance from Europe. Japan retained its position as the global leader with a market value of US$8.2 billion, followed by Taiwan with US$7.7 billion, and North America with US$5.81 billion. Coming up close were Korea with US$4.61 billion and China with US$2.68 billion.

By 2005, according to Standard & Poor's *Semiconductor Industry Survey*, the 10 largest semiconductor companies continued to be established, dominant industry leaders. They were Intel, Samsung, Texas Instrument, Toshiba, STMicroelectronics, Infineon, Renesas, TSMC, Freescale, and NXP.

ORGANIZATION AND STRUCTURE

Semiconductor devices effectively act as the brains of the mechanisms that they control and coordinate. In essence, a semiconductor is a material that conducts electricity at room temperatures better than an insulator. When treated or "doped," a semiconductor (e.g., silicon) can be made to act as an insulator under some conditions and a conductor under others. Besides managing communication, financial, and information systems, semiconductors are found in automobiles, planes, tractors, toys, medical equipment, and other goods. The single largest market for semiconductors is the computer industry, which uses the chips primarily in the construction of personal computers and workstations. Other markets for semiconductors include both the rapidly growing consumer electronics industry and the automotive industry.

Categories of semiconductor devices include metal oxide semiconductor (MOS) memory (including DRAM); MOS micro (microprocessors and digital signal processors); and MOS logic, analog products, and discretes (devices that perform a single function affecting the flow of electrical current).

The MOS memory market declined in the mid-2000s, depressed in part by lowered prices for DRAM memory chips and uncertainty in the Asian economy. However, during the 2000s, memory sales recovered, thanks to the booming wireless market and the demand for flash devices used in consumer electronics applications. The DRAM market grew 61 percent during 2004, earning US$26.8 billion.

BACKGROUND AND DEVELOPMENT

The United States' Bell Laboratories invented the solid state transistor, the first semiconductor device, in 1948.

The device was an improvement over conventional vacuum tube mechanisms because it had no filament to burn, consumed less power, and was much smaller. Furthermore, transistor operation was dependent on the characteristics of the solid material rather than heat. In 1956 Bell Laboratory scientists William Shockley, John Bardeen, and Walter H. Brattain were awarded a Nobel Prize for their 1948 invention. That same year, Shockley left the company to form his own concern, Fairchild Semiconductor. Fairchild and Texas Instruments, also of the United States, simultaneously unveiled the integrated circuit (IC) in 1958 in a pivotal breakthrough that effectively combined the functions of several discrete devices into a single silicon wafer. Robert N. Noyce, the head of Fairchild during the development of the IC, left the company in 1968 to form Intel, which introduced the memory integrated circuit in 1971. That and other developments spawned a massive rise in consumption of semiconductors during the 1970s.

In addition to huge technological advances, declining prices boosted semiconductor use during the 1970s. Industry employment reflected this increased usage and surged from about 100,000 units in the early 1970s to about a quarter million by 1980. Despite a cyclical downturn in 1975, global semiconductor production grew at a rate of about 30 percent annually between 1976 and 1980. Although the United States still supplied nearly 70 percent of all semiconductors and had a near lock on the high-tech, high-margin segments of the industry, other countries were entering the marketplace. Most notably, Japan invested heavily in semiconductor technology and controlled 25 percent of the world market by the early 1980s.

The industry experienced a major production shift during the 1980s. Japan, buoyed by a government/industry consortium, targeted the fast-growing DRAM market and flooded the United States with inexpensive integrated circuits (ICs), quickly gaining market share. By blocking semiconductor imports and taking advantage of low export barriers into the United States, Japan succeeded in capturing 38 percent of the world IC market by 1990, even while chip production in Europe and other Asian nations increased. Meanwhile, U.S. IC market share dropped from 67 percent in 1980 to just 29 percent. Frustrated U.S. producers succeeded in securing a trade pact between the Japanese and U.S. governments requiring Japan to boost semiconductor imports. Japan failed to meet the terms by 1991, and a diluted version of the original agreement was negotiated.

Regardless of which countries produced the devices, semiconductor sales mushroomed during the 1980s, and

prices for commodity-like chips plummeted as competition proliferated and new manufacturing techniques were introduced. That price drop contributed to a rise in the number of applications for semiconductors in industries such as personal computers, telecommunications, consumer electronics, and automobiles. Sales also were boosted by advancements that vastly increased the power, reduced the size, and increased the flexibility of semiconductors and the devices into which they were incorporated. Consequently, annual worldwide semiconductor industry sales shot up from about US$20 billion in the early 1980s to nearly US$60 billion by the early 1990s.

In 1998 and 1999, the semiconductor industry had three major challenges: weak pricing and too much inventory, recession in the Asian economy, and the changing personal computer market. The oversupply was due to the industry's attempts to keep up with rapid growth in the personal computer market during the mid-1990s. Manufacturing was expanded to accommodate demand at the time, but when demand slowed, the large facilities were still producing goods. The Asian economy affects the U.S. economy because the two are interdependent in many ways; thus, the reduction in revenues from Asian buyers was a blow to the semiconductor industry. Finally, consumers were responsive to the influx of low-priced computers that offer many of the capabilities and performance features of higher-priced models.

CURRENT CONDITIONS

According to a report by KPMG, the industry was valued at US$260 billion worldwide by 2009. The market is expected to increase by 28.4 percent in 2010 to US$290.5 billion, and US$308.7 billion—a 6.3 percent increase—by 2011. The SIA predicts the industry to continue growth in 2012 to US$317.8 billion.

According to *Euromonitor,* the market in China was seeing explosive growth and was expected to increase 141 percent by 2007. By comparison, the U.S. market was expected to grow 65 percent, followed by France (39 percent), Japan (22 percent), the United Kingdom (19 percent), and Germany (9 percent). Integrated circuits were the biggest producer worldwide, with sales of US$184.6 billion projected for 2005, according to *World Semiconductor Trade Statistics.* The consumer semiconductor market was expected to double between 2004 and 2009, rising from US$14 billion to nearly US$30 billion during the five-year period, as reported in *Electronics News* in May 2005.

RESEARCH AND TECHNOLOGY

The semiconductor industry was distinguished from many other growth industries by its extreme emphasis on technology, an emphasis that served as a major entry barrier to potential competitors. Companies that concentrated on proprietary technology had to risk massive capital investments to drive the research and development machines that generate new semiconductor designs. Likewise, entities and nations that concentrated on the production or commodity side of the industry needed to invest heavily to develop sophisticated, complex manufacturing operations.

The race between Intel, Digital, and IBM to achieve gigahertz microprocessor unit (MPU) speeds dominated semiconductor technology news in the late 1990s. Intel, the leader in commercial production of microprocessor units (MPUs), coupled announcements of higher-speed processors with price cuts that made existing chips even more attractive to consumers. The Intel Pentium II processor was based on advanced fabrication technology that created circuits just 0.25 microns in width, the equivalent of packing 400 lines of circuitry into the size of a human hair. Although smaller companies, notably Cyrix Corporation and Advanced Micro Devices (AMD), possessed an increased market share as the new century approached, it remained difficult for them to mass-produce chips of comparable power.

Gallium arsenide (GaAs) emerged in the mid-1990s as a profitable technology, although it had been proffered as early as the 1980s as a synthetic alternative to silicon. GaAs proponents cite its advantages of high speed, superior temperature tolerance, and low power requirements. In addition, GaAs can emit light, making it useful in fiber optical communications systems. Because it is brittle and difficult to process, however, GaAs was slow to emerge as a viable technology. In the early 1990s, only 50 percent of the chips produced per batch were usable, compared to 70 percent or more for most silicon chips. As a result, GaAs chips typically cost five times more to produce than similar silicon circuits.

In 2003, U.S. companies invested US$14 billion in semiconductor research and development. Further, more than 30 percent of total revenues were invested in the future in some way, such as in research or education. This suggests a commitment on the part of industry leaders to stay competitive and build a strong foundation for the future of the industry. Leaders in other countries were also investing heavily in R&D. In 2004, *Solid State Technology* reported that South Korea would invest US$830 million into research and development over five years.

Trends in the industry include a push to make chips and transistors smaller, experimentation with new materials such as copper, and the emergence of new consumer goods such as chip cards. Chip cards can be used as debit or credit cards and to place calls at pay phones. As new applications are developed for chip cards, industry analysts expect their numbers and desirability to grow among increasingly technologically savvy consumers.

WORKFORCE

During the late 1990s and early 2000s, the number of firms and employees in the semiconductor industry increased. In 1998 the industry was comprised of 750 firms and 204,610 employees. However, by 2001 the number of firms had risen to 866 and the number of employees was 243,893. By 2003, according to the SIA, there were 226,000 workers in the U.S. industry. According to the SIA's *2006 Annual Report,* the industry employed nearly 234,000 people in the United States.

Trade organizations (such as SIA) and alliances have made safety a priority in the semiconductor industry, and as a result, it is among America's safest industries for workers. According to the U.S. Bureau of Labor Statistics, the semiconductor industry had one of the lowest rates of work-related injuries and illnesses in 1999, with only 2.2 cases per 100 full-time employees. By working with the Environmental Protection Agency, manufacturers have reduced the emissions to which workers are exposed, while at the same time taking steps toward protecting the environment.

INDUSTRY LEADERS

Intel Corporation. Intel was ranked as the number one semiconductor manufacturer worldwide in 2009 with sales of nearly US$35.13 billion. It continued its reign as the world's dominant producer of microprocessor chips, and arguably the best known enterprise in this field. Dell and Hewlett-Packard were among its largest clients, together representing 35 percent of sales. As of 2008, Intel reported having 83,500 employees.

Founded in 1968 by Robert N. Noyce, Gordon E. Moore, and Andrew S. Grove, Intel unveiled the first memory integrated circuit (IC) in 1971. The company also pioneered metal oxide semiconductor technology. In the 1970s and early 1980s, Intel was recognized as a major supplier of memory chips for mainframe computers and minicomputers, and it became the top producer of microcomputer integrated circuits in the mid-1980s.

Development of a series of advanced microcomputer chips helped Intel make its mark during the late 1980s and early 1990s. From 1981 onward, Intel processors drove IBM and IBM-compatible personal computers. Intel is known for its computer flash-memory chips, microcontrollers, networking products, and videoconferencing systems, but it probably is most closely associated with the processor technology that has so many PCs stamped with the words "Intel Inside." R&D efforts in this arena culminated in Intel's introduction of the Pentium—and later Pentium II and Pentium III—processors, high-performance microprocessors that incorporated reduced instruction set computer (RISC) technologies. Intel's sales and profits boomed during the 1990s, as shipments of the new Pentium chips increased. As of the mid-2000s, the majority of PCs contained Intel processors. In 2004, the company reported US$34.2 billion in revenue, an increase of almost 14 percent more than 2003. Revenues were earned largely in the Asia Pacific region, where the company earned US$4.4 billion, or 46 percent of sales. Remaining revenues were earned in the Americas (US$2.04 billion, or 21 percent), Europe (US$2.2 billion, or 24 percent), and in Japan (US$853 million, or 9 percent). Intel's workforce numbered 85,000 in 2004.

As smaller firms, such as Cyrix and AMD, increased penetration of the market, Intel's expansion policies grew more aggressive. Intel's spending on R&D during 2004 totaled close to US$4.8 billion, but with competitors' research and development departments contending for the equivalent of a processor "blue ribbon" award for high speed, Intel ceased to rely exclusively on the market growth provided by its own outstanding technology and turned to acquisition to strengthen its market presence.

In May 2007, three industry visionaries announced that they had entered into an agreement to create a new semiconductor company. Intel, STMicroelectronics, and Francisco Partners were planning to utilize key assets of companies with a combined annual revenue of US$3.6 billion. The focus of the new company was to supply flash memory solutions for a variety of consumer and industrial devices. Those products included cell phones, MP3 players, digital cameras, and computers. The new company will unite the established companies' efforts for key research and development, manufacturing, sales, and marketing. In addition to serving its customers, company goals include accelerating the move to future non-volatile memory technologies.

Samsung Electronics. South Korea's Samsung Electronics, part of the Samsung Group, was the fastest growing company in the semiconductor top ten in the early 1990s, due largely to its aggressive manufacture of commodity-like DRAM (dynamic random access memory) chips. It jumped to the number two position among industry leaders when ranked by semiconductor sales. Supported by the Korean government, Samsung invested heavily in the development of semiconductor manufacturing technology during the middle and late 1980s. By 1997 Samsung was shipping more than US$6 billion worth of semiconductors. However, because of the softening of the DRAM market, this figure actually was 7 percent less than the previous year's sales. Samsung was the number one manufacturer of DRAM, SRAM (static random access memory), and flash memory worldwide in 2003. That year, total sales reached US$54.3 billion. Fully two-thirds of Samsung's sales were from exports. In 2004 semiconductor sales for Samsung Electronics totaled US$15.8 billion, compared to US$10.4 billion in 2003. By 2008 its parent company's sales and net income, to which Samsung Electronics was a major contributor, were US$173.4 billion and US$10.7 billion, respectively. Samsung Electronics was a recognized leading producer of digital TVs, memory chips, cell phones, and TFT-LCDs.

Texas Instruments. Texas Instruments (TI) is among the world's oldest and largest manufacturers of semiconductors. In 2000, semiconductors represented fully 90 percent of its sales, or US$10.9 billion in 2004 and 4.5 percent of the global market, with total revenues of US$10.43 billion in 2009 and a workforce of 27,100 employees in 2010. Analog chips accounted for about 40 percent of the company's sales in 2006. TI easily earned its ranking as the world's leading supplier of analog chips. In spite of its dominance, TI Chief Executive Richard Templeton discussed plans with *Business Week* for increasing analog chip market share. Of TI's total sales, 75 percent originate outside the United States. TI's world leadership in digital signal processors (DSPs) is reflected in the fact that more than 50 percent of wireless phones worldwide contain Texas Instruments DSPs. These digital signal processors, which convert sound and light into digital signals, are used in a variety of programmable products, such as VCRs. Activity in this arena and explorations into digital light processor (DLP) technology did not supplant TI's earlier focus on chip production. The memory chip market, rendered unstable by heavy chip production on the part of Pacific Rim corporations, still was attractive to TI, which protected itself through a variety of joint ventures that relied on business partners to remarket TI-licensed technology.

Infineon Technologies AG. Infineon Technologies AG, based in Germany, was Europe's top chip maker and moved up to fourth place in 2004 with semiconductor sales of US$9.18 billion and 4 percent of the global market. The company's revenues increased nearly 25 percent from 2003, the largest portion of which were derived from memory chips. In 2009, Infineon had sales of just over US$4 billion with approximately 26,460 employees.

Renesas Technology Corp. Renasas Technology is an industry leader based in Toyko. It achieved consolidated revenue of JPY983 billion for fiscal year 2006, ending in March 2007. Renasas has a global network of manufacturing, design, and sales operations in approximately 20 countries with about 26,500 employees worldwide. The company was formed by a merger of Hitachi and Mitsubishi's non-DRAM chip assets into a new entity, which ranks as one of the world's top chip makers.

STMicroelectronics. STMicroelectronics is a Switzerland-based global leader in developing and delivering semiconductor solutions for a number of microelectronics applications. It provides a combination of silicon and system expertise, manufacturing strength, an intellectual property portfolio, and strategic partners that keeps the company at the forefront of chip technology. In 2009, STMicroelectronics' net revenues totaled US$8.46 billion, with net earnings of US$1.13 billion. In 2009, it had 51,560 employees worldwide.

STMicroelectronics focused on electronics companies in Japan and China in order to increase the proportion of revenue derived from domestic manufacturers in those countries. In 2006, the company's Japanese revenues grew by 31 percent. In 2007, STMicroelectronics ranked third in the Chinese semiconductor market (excluding microprocessors and DRAM memory) with about 40 percent of sales coming from local manufacturers. STMicroelectronics planned to operate plants in five cities across China. By May 2007, the company employed 4,000 people in greater China.

Toshiba. Holding 3.9 percent of global market, Toshiba also manufactured a variety of other products. From computers, cell phones, and X-ray machines to elevators, electric tubes, and railway transportation systems, the company's diverse offerings crossed industry lines. In 2009, Toshiba reported US$75.8 billion in revenues, and employed 166,000 people.

NEC Corporation. NEC dropped to ninth place, with 2.9 percent of the world semiconductor market share, in 2005. The company stayed in the top ten and remained a leader in the manufacture of computers, peripheral equipment, and network solutions. Founded in 1899,

NEC gained an international presence during the early 2000s, with 20 percent of its sales coming from outside Japan in 2001. With increased global use of all aspects of technology, NEC exported a large variety of computers. In the 1980s NEC partnered with Honeywell Information Systems and Groupe Bull of France to enhance penetration of the mainframe market. By 1997, attention was back on the desktop, and the company held a 49 percent stake in Packard Bell NEC Inc., the third largest U.S. PC manufacturer. Smaller, more limited applications of high technology and, in particular, semiconductor use, were included in NEC's purview; worldwide, NEC products included an array of electronic products ranging from cellular phones to highly sophisticated digital switching systems. During the 1980s NEC achieved respected status in the semiconductor industry by efficiently producing vast quantities of DRAM chips, a pursuit that in the 1990s became far less valuable with the entry of Samsung and other companies into the memory chip market. NEC's strong ASIC and microprocessor sales have helped insulate it from the steep declines in DRAM prices. In 2007, the company stated it had 25 subsidiaries worldwide, including NEC Electronics America and NEC Electronics (Europe) GmbH. In 2010, it reported revenue of US$42.8 billion, with 142,358 employees.

In May 2007, NEC Electronics announced the availability of system LSI chips. These were capable of enabling reception of global TV broadcasts on personal computers. TV broadcasts in the United States, Europe, and Japan were rapidly migrating from analog to digital formats, and the new chips helped upgrade and expand previously existing feature sets. They allowed PC OEMs to provide many flexible, state-of-the-art TV tuner solutions to customers, regardless of format.

Philips Semiconductors. Philips Semiconductors, now known as NXP Semiconductors, based in the Netherlands, was another of the world's largest suppliers of semiconductors. The company had 2.5 percent of the world market and US$5.69 billion in semiconductor revenue in 2004. As reported on the company's Web site, Philips Semiconductors ran 20 manufacturing facilities and delivered products to clients in 60 countries. Manufacturing facilities were located in the United States, the Asia Pacific region, and Europe. NXP saw revenues of more than US$5.44 billion in 2009 and had more than 28,000 employees.

Foundries. During the mid-2000s, foundries thrived as outsourcing of chip production increased. According to market research company IC Insights, revenues for semiconductor foundries grew 45 percent to US$16.7 billion in 2004. New to the list of top semiconductor companies as rated by *Electronic Business* was TSMC, a semiconductor foundry based in Taiwan. TSMC was the leading foundry with 2006 revenues of US$9.76 billion. Other strong foundries included UMC of Taiwan and SMIC of China. Foundries showed strong growth from 2001 and remained strong through 2005.

MAJOR COUNTRIES IN
THE INDUSTRY

As recently as 1990, the semiconductor industry consisted of just two countries of origin: the United States and Japan. By the end of the century, the European market had grown to the point that companies from two European nations occupied positions in the top tier of semiconductor producers. As of the mid-2000s, Japan had widened its lead as leader of the semiconductor capital equipment market, with a value of US$8.28 billion, as reported in *Solid State Technology* in May 2004. However, Taiwan was closing in on the global market, valued at US$7.76 billion, followed by North America with US$5.81 billion, Korea with US$4.61 billion, Europe with US$3.44 billion, and China with US$2.68 billion. The rest of the world accounted for US$4.49 billion of the global market valued at US$37.08 billion. Korea and China saw the largest growth in the industry, increasing market share by 45 percent and 132 percent respectively from 2003 to 2004.

In the face of industry globalization, the World Semiconductor Council (WSC) was formed in 1996 to enhance mutual understanding, address market access matters, promote cooperative industry activities, and expand international cooperation in the semiconductor sector into the twenty-first century.

The council was conceived during bilateral semiconductor trade negotiations between the United States and Japan, which, as leaders, saw the need to address the growing globalization of the industry. The WSC included the Semiconductor Industry Association (SIA), the Electronic Industries Association of Japan (EIAJ), the European Electronic Component Manufacturers Association (EECA), the Korea Semiconductor Industry Association (KSIA) and, as of 1998, the Taiwan Semiconductor Industry Association (TSIA).

BIBLIOGRAPHY

"Asian Equipment Markets Flex Muscles in 2004." *Solid State Technology* (May 2005).

Beucke, Dan, and Arik Hesseldahl. "Taking the Pulse at Texas Instruments: CEO Templeton Discusses the Company's Desire to Capture Even More of the Analog Chip Market and Hints at Future Involvement in Advanced Medical Devices." *Business Week Online,* 16 May 2007. Available from www.businessweek.com.

"Consumer Semi Market Set to Double, IDS Predicts." *Electronics News* (2 May 2005).

Draper, Deborah J., ed. *Business Rankings Annual.* Detroit: Thomson Gale, 2004.

"Foundries Thrive as More Chips Are Outsourced." *Purchasing* (19 May 2005). Available from www.purchasing.com.

"Hoover's Company Capsules." *Hoover's Online,* 2007. Available from www.hoovers.com.

"IBM, Chartered, Samsung, Infineon and Freescale Expand Technology Agreements." Seoul, South Korea: Samsung Group, 23 May 2007. Available from www.samsung.com.

"Intel, STMicroelectronics and Francisco Partners Establish a New Leader in Flash Memory." Santa Clara, Calif.: Intel Corp., 22 May 2007. Available from www.intel.com.

Lazich, Robert S., ed. *Market Share Reporter.* Detroit: Thomson Gale, 2004.

Lerner, Ivan. "Consumers Driving Semiconductors." *CMR* (18-24 April 2005).

Mello, Adrian. "The Top Semiconductor Companies." *Electronic Business* (May 2005).

"Memory Chip Makers Posted Double-Digit Growth in '04." *Purchasing* (19 May 2005).

"NEC Electronics Announces System LSI Chips that Enable Reception of Global Television Broadcasts on Personal Computers." Kawasaki, Japan: NEC Electronics Corp., 21 May 2007. Available from www.necel.com.

Ohr, Stephan, and Brian Fuller. "As It Seeks to Widen Margins, CEO Says Strong Growth of 31 Percent in 2004 Laid to Analog, DSP." *Electronic Engineering Times* (16 May 2005).

Semiconductor Industry Association. *Annual Report,* 2006. Available from www.sia-online.org.

Semiconductor Industry Outlook, August 2010. Available from www.zacks.com.

"Semiconductor Market Forecast." *World Semiconductor Trade Statistics* (28 October 2003).

"South Korea Plans to Invest Approximately $830 Million Over the Next Five Years in Semiconductor Research and Development." *Solid State Technology* (February 2004).

Starnes, Tom. "Rich Processor Variety Adds Up to 18 Percent Growth in 2004." *Electronic Design* (12 January 2004).

Taylor, Paul. "STMicro Looks to Japan, China for Growth." *The Financial Times* (14 May 2007).

"The Tech Dragon Stumbles; China's Upstarts Are Finding Life in the Big Leagues Tougher Than They Reckoned." *Business Week* (14 May 2007).

World Semiconductor Trade Statistics. *WSTS Semiconductor Market Forecast Autumn 2006,* 31 October 2006. Available from www.wsts.org.

SIC 3873

WATCHES AND CLOCKS

NAICS CODE(S)

334518. The global watch and clock industry comprises the manufacture of clocks, watches, watchcases, and clock and watch parts.

INDUSTRY SNAPSHOT

In 2009 the Federation of the Swiss Watch Industry (FHS) estimated in its report entitled "The Swiss and world watchmaking industry in 2008" that the number of timepieces produced worldwide was approximately 1.2 billion. The world's largest consumers of clock and watch materials were Hong Kong, the United States, Japan, Switzerland, and China. These countries, as reported by the FHS, accounted for more than 70 percent of global trade.

In 2007, retailers told *National Jeweler* that consumers still preferred white metal in mid-range luxury wristwatches.Sales for stainless steel watches within the US$1,500 to $9,999 price point jumped 22 percent from August 2005 to August 2006.This increase created a US$1.2 billion market.Luxury Goods Index (LGI) shared this data after tracking sales data for 6,800 retailers across the country.Gold watch sales in the same category decreased 30 percent to US$21.6 million and 18-karat watch sales dropped 7 percent to US$70.4 million.

William George Schuster reported that in spite of concerns about competition from cell phones and other high-tech products, watches continued to be popular choices for U.S. adults.A 2006 national survey by The Jeweler Consumer Opinion Council found that most survey respondents owned two or more watches.More than half of all survey respondents owned watches made of precious metals.

In August 2009, *Mail Online* rang in with the news about a research poll involving 1,500 people with results reflecting 82 percent of those people owned a cell phone and more than half of them used it as an alarm clock rather than utilizing an actual one. The Old Clock Shop owner Sasha Kent believed that younger generations were "straying away from the traditional alarms." Beth Hale shared this news and added insights about how Finnish scientists created the best of both worlds in 2008. Those scientists "designed a considerate alarm clock that monitors sleep pattern and picks the gentlest time to rouse the unsuspecting slumberer."

Many market experts claimed that the luxury watch market was stronger than ever before. For the 2007 Elite Traveler/Prince & Associates Summer Spending Survey, about 73 percent of respondents said they would spend approximately US$94,000 on luxury watches or fine jewelry. That was an increase of 50 percent more than the summer of 2005.

According to Michael Balfour, there was an important tie to the "Swiss Made" name appearing at six'o-clock on watch dials. Those words were symbols for "the remarkable fact that Switzerland has achieved something no other country has managed: it has branded itself in law." The Official Swiss Chronometer Inspectorate

(COSC) was considered to be an important support system "which certifies accuracy and excellence in both mechanical and quartz timekeeping."

The value of Swiss watch exports in 2006 increased 10.9 percent to about US$11 billion. According to FHS, wristwatches posted an increase of 27 percent by value and 34.7 percent by volume. There was an overall 11.6 percent increase in value terms for wristwatches. The 18-carat gold styles rose 7.6 percent and steel watches increased 10.3 percent. The strongest increase in exports was for gold-plated products and increased by 59.6 percent. The top export market destination was the U.S. with an increase of 6.1 percent to US$1.7 billion.

As of April 2007, luxury watch demand was expected to accelerate during the next six months. A Goldman Sachs survey found a record 89 percent of retailers anticipated sustained growth.Most respondents stated they expected strong demand for high-end watches. On the other hand, the low end was expected to stagnate while the mid-end stabilized.

World clock production has steadily decreased since 1997, when an estimated 440 million units were produced, according to figures published by JCWA. However, the market was beginning to pick back up in the mid-years of the first decade of the 2000s, albeit slowly, due to the changed purpose and use of household clocks. By 2003, production was at 360 million units, a 13 percent increase over 2002 totals. According to *HFN,* because most households have clocks in many locations, such as the microwave and VCR, clockmakers were challenged to create new demand for clocks as decorative items, including such technologies as sound chips.

According to the *Roanoke Times,* the manager of the clock division for Howard Miller said sales of grandfather clocks were "flat at best." Paul Hoffman hoped that sales of these clocks would increase as baby boomers aged and reflected on the legacies to leave for their children.

In August 2009, Bain & Company predicted cloudy days for the luxury goods watch segment. Its *Luxury Goods Worldwide Market* predicted "sales could shrink the market from its 2008 level. In addition to reduced shopper confidence, other significant variables demanded attention. "Luxury goods producers are also feeling the additional squeeze of intense pricing pressure and markdowns from retailers and higher-end department stores," concluded Bain Partner and Research Study Author Claudia D'Arpizio. It was believed jewelry and watches would perform slightly better than the other sectors," falling about 12 percent.

ORGANIZATION AND STRUCTURE

The international watch industry produces three major types of watches: quartz analog, digital, and mechanical.

Quartz analog watches represent the world's leading segment in the industry, accounting for the majority of the watches produced throughout the world. In the 1980s Switzerland's Swatch watch helped spark worldwide interest in inexpensive fashion quartz analog watches at a time when digital and mechanical movement watches overshadowed them. Consequently, the quartz analog watch became the industry leader even in the most prosperous developed countries, and producers of high-end mechanical watches such as Rolex started offering quartz analog watches.

Digital watches, which dramatically changed the dynamics of the watch industry in the 1970s, remained popular in the mid- to late 1990s but trailed quartz analog watches considerably in terms of sales. This market segment remained a steady one in the 1980s, registering modest annual upturns in production. However, because of the surge in production of, and demand for, quartz analog models, the digital watch annual market share dropped from about 50 percent in 1982 to less than 25 percent in the mid-1990s.

Production of mechanical-movement watches rebounded in the mid-1990s, after suffering declines because of competition from quartz and digital watches. While annual unit production has hovered around 100- to 135 million since the 1980s—when digital and quartz analog models swiped significant market share—mechanical-movement watches experienced renewed growth in the latter half of the 1990s. Swiss companies, long the industry leaders in the production of expensive watches, exported about 25.1 million watches in 2004 worth US$7.9 billion. A FHS report argued that the surge in exports indicated the recovery of the timepiece once thought obsolete. Industry analysts expect the high-end watch market will remain a viable one in the future.

BACKGROUND AND DEVELOPMENT

The clock first emerged as a marketable product in the sixteenth century, though weight-driven clocks had already been in existence for several centuries. In the sixteenth century, however, the popularity of timepieces increased with the introduction of watches in Germany and France. Primarily regarded as ornamental jewelry at the time, watches slowly took on greater functional importance.

Clock manufacturers dominated the industry for years, however. Though most models were expensive, heavy, and delicate, they were also regarded as significant investments and important family heirlooms. The Industrial Revolution spurred the development of less cumbersome clocks and the growth of watch manufacturing. By the latter part of the nineteenth century, pocket watches,

first produced in quantity by the American Waltham Watch Co., were popular possessions, and Switzerland had become established as a renowned center of watch and clock craftsmanship. The world's leading watch and clock maker in the 1990s was founded during this period as well. In 1881, K. Hattori & Co.—the company that eventually became Seiko Corporation—was established in Tokyo as an importer of clocks. By the early 1900s, the company was manufacturing wall and table clocks, pocket watches, and alarm clocks.

In 1918 the Shokosha Watch Research Laboratory, the precursor to Citizen Watch Co., was established in Japan. The organization manufactured its first pocket watch six years later and gradually emerged as one of Seiko's chief competitors. These two companies, as well as a few other Japanese manufacturers, battled for control of the Asian market. With the onset of World War II, however, they made no inroads into other markets until well after the conclusion of the war.

Industry giant Timex Enterprises, Inc., was founded in the United States in 1941 by two Norwegian refugees, who had fled their own country after the German invasion in 1940. They purchased the nearly bankrupt Waterbury Clock Co. in Connecticut and instituted a highly mechanized assembly process. The Timex watch became known as a dependable product, and the company quickly expanded despite its negligible presence in jewelry stores. Instead, Timex sold their watches through consumer outlets such as drugstores. By the 1960s, the company had established a distribution network of 250,000 outlets and posted sales exceeding US$70 million.

By the late 1960s, Timex was dominant in the U.S. market, though international competitors such as Seiko and Citizen sought to expand their international sales. Switzerland, however, continued to reign as the world's watch production leader based on its control of the luxury watch market. The Soviet Union had become a significant presence in the industry as well via exports of low-cost, low-quality products to developing countries.

In 1967 the electronic quartz wristwatch was announced by the Swiss Horological Electronic Center; a number of Swiss firms had pooled together millions of dollars in research money to develop the watch. Yet it was Seiko—still known at the time as K. Hattori—that marketed the first quartz wall clock and watch. Japanese watch manufacturers proved more proficient at adapting to the popularity of the quartz watches and the new digital technology that swept through the industry in the 1970s. Both Seiko and Citizen tallied huge gains in the vital U.S. market during this period, and Japan slipped past Switzerland as the industry leader in unit production. Embattled Swiss manufacturers and U.S. companies such as Timex belatedly turned their attention to the new technologies that were proving so profitable for their competitors in Japan and Hong Kong.

Inexpensive brands proliferated around the world in the 1980s, and Japan became entrenched as the world's leading manufacturer of watches. By 1989 worldwide watch production reached approximately 690 million units. Industry leader Seiko Corporation produced about 109 million of those units itself, in addition to another 32 million clocks.

In the mid- to late 1990s, mid-grade and high-end clock and watch sales benefited from rising disposable incomes in countries such as Japan, the United States, Germany, Italy, France, and the United Kingdom. On the other hand, low-price clocks and watches have benefited from income growth around the world and from fashion trends. These trends spurred new growth because of increased interest in watches that complement clothing, accounting for expanding sales of inexpensive fashionable watches such as those by Swatch. Consumers began buying more than one watch in order to have timepieces to complement both formal and casual attire.

During the late 1990s and the turn of the century, Hong Kong, Japan, and Germany traded places as the leading exporter of finished watches, with France making a surge in 2000, as reported by FHS. In 1998 Hong Kong controlled 9.1 percent of the export market based on value, followed by Japan with 6.5 percent, and Germany with 3.8 percent. In 1999 these three countries shared nearly identical percentages: 4.9 percent for Japan, 4.6 percent for Hong Kong, and 4.5 percent for Germany. In 2000 Germany claimed 5.1 percent with Japan and France sharing 3.3 percent each. Hong Kong's share of the global watch export market fell to 1.8 percent, behind the United Kingdom, which captured 2.5 percent of the export market.

Also in the late 1990s, clock and watchmakers experienced a period of acquisition and consolidation with the rise of multinational conglomerates such as Swatch Group and LVMH. Throughout the mid- to late 1990s and into the twenty-first century, the watch industry remained highly competitive, with manufacturers and retailers launching major television and print campaigns to promote products. Companies such as Swatch Group also began opening chic "mono-brand" stores to showcase popular brands. Consumer demand for luxury watches was especially high in the late 1990s, which benefited many Swiss manufacturers who specialize in that market. Michael Balfour reported in the *Financial Times* that at the Swatch Group alone, sales for luxury watches increased 30 percent in 2000.

In 2000 the world produced approximately 1.5 billion finished watches and movements worth close to US$12 billion, according to figures published by the FHS. The Japan Clock and Watch Association (JCWA) estimated that nearly 1.3 billion watches were produced worldwide in 2000. JCWA breaks down world watch production by type as follows: 908 million analog quartz watches (71 percent), 340 million digital quartz watches (27 percent), and 22 million mechanical watches (2 percent).

Of the total watch and components produced, finished watches accounted for 700 million units in 2000, according to FHS. The vast majority of finished watches, approximately 80 percent, were produced in China or Hong Kong. However, Switzerland, the leader in high-end luxury watches, led the industry based on sales, controlling over half the market with revenues of approximately US$6.3 billion.

CURRENT CONDITIONS

In Japan, which the JCWA estimated produced more than half the world's watches and movements in 2000, consumers showed a strong interest in expensive foreign watches and cell phones. In a March 2001 article in *Jewelers' Circular Keystone,* William George Shuster explained that many young Japanese consumers prefer small cell phones—with their date/time display functions—over traditional wristwatches. "A few Japanese watchmakers," Shuster wrote, "worry that something similar could develop in Europe or the United States (which has 97 million cell phone users vs. Japan's 50 million), though most still think the markets are too dissimilar for that to happen." Nevertheless, watches produced at the turn of the twenty-first century offered more high-tech features, such as built-in pagers and computer-download capabilities. Another emerging trend was the development of new marketing strategies in response to the increased popularity of Internet retailing, particularly online auctions.

The luxury watch market segment, focused on units priced at US$10,000 or more, continued to grow into the mid-years of the first decade of the 2000s. As *Brandweek* observed, this largely was because the estimated US$65 billion luxury goods market is relatively recession-proof. Tom Kuczynski reported in *National Jeweler* that fine watch sales in the United States generated about $3.8 billion in retail sales in 2004. While revenues were up, however, dollars earned were attributed to the number of consumers purchasing pricier merchandise. The number of watches sold fell by 4 percent.

In 2004 the Swiss watch industry produced 25.1 million units with a value of 10.2 billion Swiss francs (almost $US8 billion). Exports of mechanical watches rose 12.7 percent in 2004, compared to .7 percent for electronic watches. Most of the Swiss market's products were exported, with more than 99 percent going to Asia and Oceania, Europe, and the Americas. The United

States was the largest consumer, with 16.9 percent of Swiss exports valued at 1.87 billion Swiss francs (US$1.45 billion). Hong Kong was the fastest growing market for Swiss exports, with a 2004 increase of 15.6 percent.

In April 2007, substantial competition was coming from Internet sites selling watches that turned out to be counterfeits.Consumers were warned to be cautious of purchasing high-end goods from unauthorized dealers via the Internet.In March 2007, the Royal Canadian Mounted Police Federal Enforcement Section issued a search warrant linked to a three-year investigation of a Windsor, Ontario, Canada, businessman suspected of selling counterfeit watches. CBSA Windsor and Detroit's Integrated Customs Enforcement Agency offered assistance in the investigation.It was determined that watches valued more than US$1 million were sold.

While many industries were focusing on addressing issues related to "going green," some watch manufacturers offered new linked products. Seiko's "Think the Earth" watch retails for US$500 and contains a small globe rotating at the same speed as the Earth.Wearers will have the location and time displayed for where they are anywhere in the world. Some The of the proceeds are earmarked for environmentally friendly initiatives.

RESEARCH AND TECHNOLOGY

The watch and clock industry has been transformed several times during its history by technological advances. Timepieces that operated using electricity, quartz crystal vibrations, and atomic or molecular oscillations (atomic clock) all changed the manner of production of clocks and watches to some degree. Digital technology dramatically altered the fortunes of many watch manufacturers during the 1970s and 1980s.

As the watch manufacturing industry entered the twenty-first century, significant research advances continued to have an impact. Timex's Indiglo brand, which features an electroluminescent light powered by the watch's battery, proved vital to the company's efforts to recover from market losses of past years. In 1993 the Indiglo brand accounted for 40 percent of all units sold by the company. Timex believed that illumination would become a standard feature of watches just like water resistance, though some of Timex's competitors dispute this contention.

Proposals for more radical innovations, including watches with computing or communications functions, pagers, small electronic personal organizers, and similar devices, gained popularity in the late 1990s. However, industry observers cautioned that in the mid-1990s, prototype watches equipped with such communication capabilities were cumbersome units that could not be worn

comfortably. Such devices, in fact, may interest companies outside the watch industry more than they appeal to traditional watch companies. Telecommunications giants such as AT&T were active participants in this area of research in the mid-1990s.

In the late 1990s, companies also rolled out voice-controlled clocks and watches, such as Voice Clock, that allow users to change the time and activate and deactivate the alarm simply by uttering a command. Watchmakers also experimented with radio-controlled watches that could be programmed via radio signals to change when entering different time zones.

During the first decade of the 2000s, innovations included "eco-drive" watches, which ran by converting light into electrical energy using a rechargeable battery. Innovations in clocks included "wave clocks" or atomic clocks, which adjusted anywhere in a given geographical area based on electric waves that set the time automatically.

Dutch watchmaker Christian van der Klauuw introduced astronomically oriented watches called "the smallest planetarium in the world." The "Planetarium" watch features a heliocentric revolution of the planets of Mercury, Venus, Earth, Mars, Jupiter, and Saturn. It sells for US$23,700.

The Suunto US$199 T4 training watch has software capable of recommending customized workouts.After reviewing fitness aspects—such as height, weight, gender, maximum heart rate, and activity level—workout plans are recommended for improving status.Based on wearer performance, the program alternates high intensity periods with rest times.In addition, data is tracked in an accessible log. The watch also has "Training Effect" software designed to measure effort level on a scale of one to five and log it, too.

One of the Swedish boat Victory Challenge sponsors, Corum luxury watch company, debuted the Admiral's Cup Competition 48 Victory Challenge. It is an US$8,000 limited-edition diving watch that is water-resistant up to 300 meters or 990 feet. The Citizen Men's Promaster Professional Diver Watch offers a black urethane wristband along with a watch featuring date functionality plus water-resistance up to 990 feet. This watch was designed to be an attractive alternative for deep sea divers or folks just taking a shower.

Europe's Galileo in-orbit verification satellite carries two rubidium clocks. One of the clocks is operational while the other one is a spare. ESA and the European Commission operate Galileo as a joint initiative. When fully deployed, it will serve as the first civilian positioning system to offer global coverage.

Jun Ye of the University of Colorado at Boulder and researchers at the US National Institute of Standards and Technology created a strontium clock. It was reported to have the accuracy of the best caesium-ion clocks. The design process involved using laser beams creating light waves to trap atoms. Adjusting the laser's frequency resulted in ability to measure time. Ultimately, usage of strontium was expected to surpass caesium.

Watchshop trend watchers say U.S. watch sellers are predicting a "digital revolution." Citizen watches were extremely popular linked selections. The news grew out of a National Jeweler research project. The project was conducted to determine U.S. market trends for popular watches.Furthermore,Watchshop shared research results related comments made by Bob Bonaci. Bonaci was a Washington state boutique owner. His statements reflected a belief that the digital revolution was "killing" market. Generational distinctions tied in for preferences. Bonaci had observed older people preferred traditional designs with hands and many of them selected Citizen.

INDUSTRY LEADERS

Citizen Watch Co., Ltd. Japan's Citizen Watch Co. was the world's leading watch and clock manufacturer in 2003. While Citizen has branched out into several manufacturing areas over the years, most notably electronics, it remains primarily known for its watch business. Founded in 1918 and incorporated in 1930, the company sold its products only in Asia prior to World War II. It was battered by the economic devastation in postwar Japan but eventually returned to its former stature. By the late 1950s, it had resumed exporting watches to China, and in 1960 the company entered the American market, distributing watches manufactured by another firm, Bulova. By 1965, Citizen and K. Hattori & Co. (later known as Seiko) together accounted for approximately 80 percent of total watch production in Japan. Citizen's success at the time was due in part to its knack for developing new products, such as shock-resistant and water-resistant watches.

In 1968 Citizen opened its first international subsidiary, Citizen de Mexico. During the 1970s, Citizen diversified into several other business areas, although the watch-manufacturing arena remained its primary concern. Convinced that it would be unable to overtake K. Hattori as Japan's leading watch producer without a significant U.S. product, Citizen introduced its own watches in the mid-1970s. Both its quartz analog and digital product lines proved tremendously successful, and Citizen posted significant increases in market share in the late 1970s. During the 1980s and 1990s, the international watch industry grew increasingly crowded, but Citizen was able to maintain a sizable presence. Citizen was a leader in developing light-powered wristwatches and in 1995 introduced the Eco-Drive line that uses solar cell and thermal power technologies. In 1999 Citizen

began producing Aspec watches made of a highly durable stainless steel and titanium composite. Citizen also uses the Internet to allow consumers to design their own watches and reported approximately 40,000 orders were generated through this channel in the late 1990s and early years of the first decade of the 2000s.

In fiscal 2004, Citizen posted annual sales of US$3.5 billion, a 27.6 percent increase over 2003. Watches and clocks accounted for almost 34 percent of sales in 2004. Sales of wristwatches and clocks showed a 4.4 percent decline from 2003. Sales did increase in one market segment, however, that of radio-controlled watches, both in Japan and overseas. Citizen, a component of the Nikkei 25 Stock Average, employed approximately 17,987 people as of 2004, with watch, movement, and clock production concentrated in Japan. Additional production facilities operate in Hong Kong, China, and Korea, with some assembly work done in Germany.

Citizen launched major print and TV ad campaigns with an "unstoppable" theme. It featured young sports stars, including U.S. Figure Skating Champion Sasha Cohen.

Art of Time, formerly a Bulova Corporation, was reportedly doing well during a transitional period. Citizen acquired the grandfather clock manufacturer in January 2008 for US $250 million. Based on the ultimate quest to build its image as a multi-brand company, Art of Time would keep ticking along as a "separate organization."

Citizen also planned to expand its horizon with the "Eco-Drive" collection. That distinctive classification featured watches designed to never require batteries. The timepieces inventively functioned in any kind of light. Models included watches ranging from dress to sport to professional dive watches.

The Swatch Group Ltd. The Swatch Group (formerly Société Suisse de Microélectronique & d'Horlogerie, SMH) was the world's second leading producer of watches in 2003. The Swatch Group's roots date back to two major Swiss watchmakers of the 1930s: Allgemeine Schweizerische Uhrenindustrie AG (ASUAG) and Société Suisse pour l'Industrie Horlogère SA (SSIH). Fierce competition from Japanese watchmakers in the 1970s and early 1980s nearly forced both ASUAG and SSIH out of business. Hayek Engineering, led by Nicolas G. Hayek, conducted a study and recommended the merger of ASUAG and SSIH and the creation of a new low-cost, technologically advanced watch to target a youthful, brand-conscious market. In 1983 ASUAG and SSIH merged, creating SMH, with Hayek as CEO.

In 1998 SMH changed its name to the Swatch Group to reflect the strength of its Swatch brand. Following the Swiss watch industry trend of the late 1990s of acquisitions and consolidations forming large watch conglomerates, Swatch is composed of the following brands representing the full range of price and market segments: Blancpain, Endura, FlikFlak, Lanco, Longines, Omega, Rado, and Swatch, among others. The company's 2004 revenues were US$3.5 billion, a 13.6 percent growth exceeding 2003. The watch division accounts for about 70 percent of the Swatch Group's sales.

SMH captured a significant segment of the Asian market in the 1980s. Armed with the wildly popular Swatch brand—a thin plastic watch comprised of about only 50 parts—SMH dramatically increased its production capacity in the early 1990s and maintained this level throughout the decade. In 1997 SMH controlled 22 to 25 percent of the global market, according to the company's own figures.

Ultrathin watches featuring accurate timekeeping, innovative technology, and a sense of youthful individualism have been a hallmark of the Swatch brand. In 1979 a subsidiary of ASUAG launched the Kaliber 999, a gold watch just 0.98mm high, considerably thinner than the latest Japanese model that stood 2.5mm high. The Kaliber 99 eventually led to the development of the 3.9mm-high plastic Swatch watch, which could be easily mass-produced and offered a variety of colors. Throughout the remainder of the 1980s the marketing of the Swatch watch became increasingly personalized, as unisex watches became gender-specific, and traditional model number names were replaced by phrases such as "Don't be too late" and "Black Magic."

In 1991 Swatch integrated a pager into the Swatch the Beep wristwatch. In 1994 SMH introduced the Swatch Irony line of shockproof, water-resistant, and thicker watches made of steel and later of aluminum. The Swatch Access, which provides access to ski resorts around the world using microchip technology and a small antenna, debuted in 1995. Also in 1995, the light-powered Swatch Solar first appeared. Other popular models include the Swatch Chrono and the Swatch Beat, which feature Internet timekeeping. The Swatch Group has been named the official timekeeper for the Olympics through 2010.

Swatch announced its plans to buy and convert part of Shanghai's Peace Hotel into a retail showcase for its leading watch brands. Part of the six-story building would also be converted into retail space, artists' rooms and studios, restaurants, and leisure facilities.

Employing nearly 21,000 employees worldwide, Swatch is headquartered in Switzerland with plants in Europe, the United States, the Virgin Islands, and Asia Pacific. Swatch also operates about 500 retail outlets. In addition to finished watches, Swatch produces watch movements and components, as well as advanced technology

components for the telecommunications, electronic, and automotive industries.

Seiko Corporation. The world's leading producer of watches and clocks in the mid-1990s, Seiko, controlled by the Hattori family of Japan, fell behind the Swatch Group in the late 1990s. Watch brands under the Seiko umbrella include Pulsar, Lorus, Lassale, Alba, and Seiko. Founded in 1881, the company first produced wall clocks, the most popular timepiece of the period. In 1893 the company's manufacturing plant was moved to Taihei-cho, Tokyo. In the early 1900s, the company initiated its first export venture while also introducing its first wristwatch models.

In 1917 K. Hattori & Co., Ltd., became a public company. An earthquake destroyed its manufacturing facility in 1923, but the company persevered and eventually regained its former stature. By 1936 K. Hattori marketed 2.06 million of Japan's total clock and watch production of 3.54 million units. World War II interrupted the business, as the company's facilities were converted to produce military items. During the mid-1950s, however, the company resumed its position as a leader in the Japanese market. It also turned its attention to the lucrative U.S. market for the first time. In the late 1960s, K. Hattori offered the world's first quartz watch and quartz wall clock, and in 1973 it unveiled a digital watch with a liquid-crystal display. Over the next several years, the firm diversified, marketing a variety of new products under new brand names. The company name was changed to Seiko Corporation in 1990.

In the 1990s, Seiko manufactured a wide array of products, including batteries, personal computers, ophthalmic frames and lenses, jewelry, contact lenses, semiconductors, and printers. Watch sales, however, continued to lead its product line, accounting for 57 percent of Seiko's sales. The company sold its goods in more than 100 countries in the late 1990s and held approximately 30 percent of the medium- and high-quality watch market in the United States.

In 2001 Seiko Corp. became a holding company, and Seiko's watch business was spun off as a wholly owned subsidiary, Seiko Watch Corp. Seiko Watch handles design and marketing, and other Seiko subsidiaries, Seiko Epson Corp. and Seiko Instruments, Inc., are responsible for watch and movements production. Seiko Corp.'s sales for fiscal years 2005 were US$1.9 billion, a loss of 3.1 percent over 2004. Approximately 70 percent of sales come from watches and clocks. Tsutomu Mitome, former president and CEO of Seiko Corp. of America, was named the president of Seiko Watch.

Reporting for *Business Week Online,* Aili McConnon wrote that Seiko was shifting its focus to the mid-market where watches sold for between US$50 and US$1,000. New licenses were acquired including one from the estate of pop artist Andy Warhol enabling creation of its Andy Warhol Pop Art watches. The watches, popular among Japanese teens and young adults, sold for US$150 resulting in approximately 4,500 unit sales by the end of 2006. Seiko's strategy has also allowed it to expand distribution beyond mass-market outlets into specialty boutiques attracting a third of all watch dollars.

Timex Enterprises, Inc. Founded in 1854, Timex is the biggest watch manufacturer in the United States. Timex, which had long been known as a manufacturer that provided reliable, if unexciting, watch models at affordable prices, appeared to have recovered in the early 1990s from earlier marketing miscalculations. Slow to react to new digital technology in the 1970s, Timex saw its share of the U.S. consumer market drop. The drop in digital watch prices during the 1970s exacerbated this deterioration. By 1976 the price of a digital model was competitive with that of mechanical models— Timex's primary product. Timex continued to lose market share. Front-office turmoil and questionable marketing strategies also hurt the company. In the 1980s and 1990s, however, Timex turned to new brands and designs in an effort to shake its staid image.Its popular Ironman Triathlon digital sports watch, introduced in 1986, quickly became a bestseller. In 1992 Timex debuted the Indiglo night-light watch face, which would appear on more than 75 percent of Timex watches manufactured in the 1990s. In the mid- and late 1990s, Timex introduced high-tech watches that featured computer-download and pager technology, such as the Beepwear wrist pager.

Timex estimates it controls about a third of the U.S. watch market, according to William Schuster of *Jewelers' Circular Keystone*. Annual sales for the privately owned Timex, which employs 7,500 people, were estimated at US$800 million in 2003. Timex, the only U.S. watchmaker with production facilities in the United States, announced in June of 2001 the closing of its last domestic plant in Little Rock, Arkansas.

In April 2007, Timex announced plans to increase its business in India by setting up approximately 200 retail stores by the end of 2009. The majority of new locations will be placed in metropolitan areas.According to *The Press Trust of India*, Timex General Manager-Marketing Vikram Arora shared company plans to increase market share to 30 percent in the organized quartz watch segment.

India was a land of opportunity for Timex. As reported by watch shop U.K. Timex Group Chief Hans-Kristian Hoejsgaard as he shared the news with livemint.com in an exclusive interview, India's ranking as prime geography for growth placed it second only to

the U.S. for "biggest market" potential. The ultimate goal, he said, was to make Timex advance as "a more respected brand around the world."

MAJOR COUNTRIES IN THE INDUSTRY

Switzerland. After years of solid growth in the mid-1980s and early 1990s, the Swiss watch industry experienced a brief stagnant period in the mid-1990s. However, the late 1990s and the early years of the first decade of the twenty-first century were a period of tremendous success for the Swiss watch industry. Switzerland produced 25.1 million finished watches valued at about US$7.9 billion in 2004, an increase of 2.1 percent over 2003. This was the first year of growth in the number of units sold in 10 years, as reported by the FHS. Growth of the Swiss watch industry had been based on increased value, not production volume. The number of finished watches produced has steadily dropped since 1998, going from about 34 million in 1998 to 31 million in 2000, with a further reduction in volume through the early years of the first decade of the 2000s. In its 2000 annual report, the Federation of the Swiss Watch Industry (FHS) explained that the record performance of 2000 was due to "sustained demand in major markets, a weak Swiss franc against the dollar, and the 'millennium' effect, difficult to quantify but real none the less."

Switzerland, which exports about 95 percent of its watch output, dominates the world in exports of finished watches and has steadily increased its share into the twenty-first century. In 1998 Swiss manufacturers accounted for 74 percent of value of exports of finished watches, which increased to 80 percent in 1999 and 84 percent in 2000, according to FHS. In 2000 Swiss exports exceeded 10 billion Swiss francs for the first time (about US$6 billion), and by 2004, the export market was up to 11.11 billion Swiss francs (about US$8.63 billion). Switzerland exported approximately 34 percent of its watches to Europe in 2004. Asia and Oceania accounted for 44 percent of Swiss exports, North and South America combined accounted for 21 percent, and Africa for 1 percent. According to the FHS, total sales for 2008 were US$15.8 billion.

Historically regarded as the world's leading producer of luxury watches and clocks, the high quality of Swiss products enabled Swiss watchmakers to charge premium prices. As a result, the average 2000 export price of a Swiss watch was US$187, which the FHS estimated to be more than twice the average export price of watches from other countries. The quartz analog watch accounted for the largest segment of Swiss production, both in terms of volume and value, in 1997 through 2000, as reported by the FHS. During this same time, the total annual value of complicated mechanical watches—often prized as collector's pieces—accounted for an average of 47 percent of total Swiss production, while worldwide production volume hovered at a mere 8 to 9 percent. Quartz digital watches have consistently made up a minor portion of overall Swiss watch production. 25.9 million total units were produced in 2003, of which 22.8 million were quartz analog.

China. China, including Hong Kong, is the most important player in the industry based on volume. With the return of Hong Kong to Chinese rule in 1997, China became the global watch powerhouse, producing about 80 percent of the world's finished watches. China also exports a large portion of its output as the world's largest unit exporter. Dependent on quartz analog models, China shipped more than a quarter of its total watch and clock exports to the United States. In addition, China constitutes the largest import market for clocks and watches. Imports to Hong Kong alone were valued at US$4.6 billion in 2004, and China's imports were valued at US$1.1 billion.

Writing in *American Time,* Norma Buchanan reported that Hong Kong's 460 watch companies exported a total of US$5.6 billion in watches and clocks in 2000. Figures for the first half of 2001 showed exports down 4 percent, with exports to the United States—Hong Kong's leading export destination—down 7 percent, mainly due to the U.S. economic slowdown. In 2004, Hong Kong's watch exports were back on the rise, increasing 9 percent to $5.9 billion. China's export market was valued at $2.1 billion. Roughly 25 percent of Hong Kong's exports go to the United States.

Japan. Japan ranked third in the industry in terms of clock and watch exports. Led by Citizen and Seiko, Japan produced an estimated 731 million finished watches and movements in 2000, valued at about US$1.9 billion (216.7 billion yen), according to the Japanese Clock and Watch Association (JCWA). This total, which is almost entirely exported, represented approximately 58 percent of total world output of finished watches and movements, as estimated by JCWA. Total Japanese exports for 2004 were valued at US$1 billion, down 4 percent from 2003. Asia and North America represented the largest export destinations by volume.

In *Jewelers' Circular Keystone,* William Shuster reported that Japan's leading watchmakers saw sales and profits in their watches and clocks divisions decrease in the late 1990s. This occurred as a surplus of watches, and especially movements, resulting from several years of sustained high production volumes worldwide, increased competition from Swiss and Far East producers and as Japan's recession decreased regional sales.

Germany. Germany ranks among the world's largest producers, importers, and exporters. Although Germany led the world in clock production in the early 1990s, China and other countries with low-cost labor surpassed it by the mid-1990s. Michael Balfour of the *Financial Times* reported that sales of German watches, clocks, and clock movements amounted to approximately US$265 million in 2000. Watch and luxury goods conglomerates acquired several prominent German watchmakers. Most notably, the Richemont Group acquired A. Lange & Sohne, and the Swatch Group acquired Glashutter Uhrenbetrieb. Another leading German brand, Junghans, marked its 140th year of business in 2001.

BIBLIOGRAPHY

Adams, Ariel. "Louis Vuitton Ladies Tambour Diver Watch." 24 August 2009. Available from www.vialuxe.com.

Adams, Duncan. "Grandfather Clocks: Behind the Times? Today's More Informal Lifestyles and Home Design Trends Have Affected Sales." *Roanoke Times,* 29 April 2007.

Balfour, Michael. "Expansion into the Global Marketplace is the Watchword: Germany." *Financial Times,* 24 March 2001.

———. "Rules Tighten Around Coveted Mark of Quality Swiss Made: Switzerland May Soon Strengthen Its Already Strict Watch Manufacturing Laws, Writes Michael Balfour." *Financial Times,* 14 April 2007.

Bernard, Sharyn. "A Hands-On Decision." *HFN,* 16 February 2004.

———. "The Good Times Roll on in the Luxury Sector: In Spite of Continuing Brand Consolidation and the Declining Numbers of Leading Watch Companies, Family-Controlled Groups Are Flourishing." *Financial Times,* 25 March 2000.

Biever, Celeste. "The Tick, Tock of a Strontium Clock Gets Steadier." *New Scientist,* 9 December 2006.

Braverman, Beth. "Gold Down, Steel Up in Watch Sales." *National Jeweler,* 1 February 2007.

Buchanan, Norma. "The Elimination Game: Even Before the Calamity of Sept. 11 Put the U.S. in an Economic Tailspin, Many Hong Kong Watch Companies Were Duking it Out in a Fight to Survive." *American Time,* December 2001.

"Christiaan vander Klaauw's Astronomical Watches." 23 May 2007. Available from www.portlino.it.

Citizen Watch Co. *Overview of the Year Ended March 31, 2005,* 2005. Available from www.citizen.co.jp.

"Citizen Watch Co. Subsidiary Sells Art of Time." 25 August 2009. Available from www.watchshopuk.com.

"Counterfeit Watches Sold Over Internet Result in Charges." *CNW Group,* 2 April 2007.

De Burton, Simon. "Prestigious Properties Platinum: Simon de Burton Discovers Why This Precious Metal is Growing in Popularity." 14 April 2007.

"Digital revolution is 'dominating' the watch market." 25 August 2009. Available from www.watchshopuk.com.

ESA. "Hyper-Accurate Clocks — The Beating Heart of Galileo." 12 May 2007. Available from www.yubanet.com.

Federation of the Swiss Watch Industry. *Swiss Watch and Microtechnology Industry: A Profile.* 5 July 2000. Available from www.fhs.ch.

————. *Swiss Watchmaking Exports January-June 2001: Five Billion in Six Months,* 6 August 2001. Available from www.fhs.ch.

————. *The Swiss Watch Industry Today.* 5 July 2004. Available from www.fhs.ch.

————. *The Swiss and World Watchmaking Industry in 2004.* 2005. Available from www.fhs.ch.

Green, Barbara. "Swiss Watch Exports Fall, but Less Than Expected." *National Jeweler,* 1 May 2004.

Hale, Beth. "Time may be up for alarm clocks as half of us use mobiles to wake up instead." 25 August 2009. Available from www.dailymail.co.uk.

"Hoover's Company Capsules." *Hoover's Online,* 2007. Available from www.hoovers.com.

"India is priority market for Timex watches." 25 August 2009 Available from www.watchshopak.com.

Japan Clock and Watch Association. *The Japanese Watch and Clock Industry in 2000: An Outlook on its Global Operation,* 2000. Available from www.jcwa.or.jp.

————. *The Japanese Watch and Clock Industry in 2003: An Outlook on its Global Operation,* 2003. Available from www.jcwa.or.jp.

Japan External Trade Organization. "Timepieces." *Marketing Guidebook for Major Imported Products,* 2000. Available from www.jetro.go.jp.

Karimzadeh, Marc. "Focusing on Best Facets." *WWD,* 3 December 2001.

Lazich, Robert S., ed. *Market Share Reporter.* Detroit: Thomson Gale, 2004.

"Luxury goods spending set to fall in 2009." 25 August 2009. Available from www.watchshopuk.com.

McConnon, Aili. "At Timex and Seiko, the Clock is Ticking; These Companies and Other Makers of Non-Luxury Watches Are Scrambling to Rethink the Timepiece for the Cell-Phone Era." *Business Week Online,* 20 March 2007. Available from www.businessweek.com.

Murphy, Robert. "Swiss Watch Sales See Significant Gains." *WWD,* 22 March 2004.

O'Loughlin, Sandra. "Good Timing." *Brandweek,* 8 September 2003.

SEIKO Watch Corporation. "SEIKO launches a new global campaign to tell the SEIKO story." 2009.

Schuster, William George. "Watches Remain Vital to U.S. Consumers." *Jewelers Circular Keystone,* 1 January 2007.

Shaw, Kerry. "LVMH Sales Dropped 5% in October." *New York Times,* 12 November 2001. Available from www.nytimes.com.

————. "SCA's Mitome Will Head New Seiko Watch Corp." *Jewelers' Circular Keystone.* 23 March 2001.

"Survey: Super Rich Consumers Will Splurge on Jewelry, Watches." *Jewelers Circular Keystone,* 28 May 2007.

"Survey Sees Rise in Luxury Watch Demand." *WWD,* 13 April 2007.

"Swatch Group's Profits Fall 9.8%, Despite Rise in Sales, Earnings." *Jewelers' Circular Keystone.* 1 November 2001.

"Swiss Watch Exports Down 4.4 Percent in 2003." *Jewelers' Circular Keystone.* April 2004.

"Timex Ends 56 Years of Watchmaking in the U.S." *Jewelers' Circular Keystone,* 22 June 2001.

"'Value' and 'Style': The New Watchwords of Japan's Watchmakers." *Jewelers' Circular Keystone,* 1 March 2001.

Simonian, Haig. "Swatch to Spend Dollars 70m on Shanghai Showcase." *The Financial Times,* 20 April 2007.

"Timex Watches to Open 200 Retail Stores in India." *PTI—The Press Trust of India Ltd.,* 16 April 2007.

Vella, Mark. "Suunto's Sexy Sports Watch; This Stylish Timepiece Carries Through On Its Claim to Provide a Personalized Workout, But the Learning Curve is Steep." *Business Week Online,* 19 January 2007. Available from www.businessweek.com.

Zarcostas, John. "Swiss Watch Expert Hit Record Level in 2006." *WWD,* 6 February 2007.

ENTERTAINMENT AND RECREATION

———————— ▪ ————————

AMUSEMENT PARKS

NAICS CODE(S)

713110. Amusement parks operate a variety of entertainment attractions on one premises. Popular features include mechanical rides, electronic and conventional games, stage shows, refreshment stands, and picnic grounds. The industry includes such venues as theme parks, water parks, kiddie parks, and similar recreational facilities.

INDUSTRY SNAPSHOT

Visitors of all ages continue to enjoy the thrill of visiting amusements parks throughout the world. At times, however, substantial investments of time and money were required by the industry in order to keep the excitement going and roller coasters running during troubling economic times.

According to the International Association of Amusement Parks and Attractions (IAAPA), millions of dollars were being spent on new attractions scheduled to make their debut at U.S. sites during the summer of 2009. In excess of 300 million visitors were expected to pass through the gates of the United States' 400 amusement parks and attractions. Some of the excitement was linked to grand re-openings such as Freestyle Music Park in the Hard Rock Park space. In a 17,000 square foot kiddie area, visitors to "Kids in America" will find innovative new rides with distinctive song-linked themes. Italian ride manufacturer Zamperia was inspired by the music with the same titles as rides—namely "Get Off My Cloud"

"Fly Like an Eagle," "Wheels in the Sky," and "Life is a Highway."

Worldwide, attendance at theme parks was escalating, bringing worldwide revenues to more than US$20 billion, with a whopping 25 percent growth projected into 2008. Most parks continued to try to outdo each other with the development of new rides that technology was permitting to be higher and faster.

This growth was despite concerns in 2003—affecting the very dynamics of the amusement industry—about the U.S.-led war with Iraq and potential terrorist attacks. According to a 2002 *USA Today* poll, 10 percent of Americans rated amusement parks and sporting events as the most likely target for a terrorist attack, behind nuclear plants (14%), all places (15%), and large city downtowns (19%). By comparison, Americans were less concerned about terrorist attacks at airports (7%), reservoirs (7%), national monuments (6%), military installations (5%), and bridges/tunnels (5%).

In 2004, 328 million people around the world visited amusement parks. According to Pricewaterhouse-Coopers (PWC), visitors spent approximately US$20 billion, and that amount was expected to grow to US$24.7 billion by 2008. IAAPA Vice President of Communication Services Beth Robertson expected the amount to be even more because 100 new attractions opened or had been announced in 2005. Robertson acknowledged, however, that the energy crisis and currency rates would have an impact on actual results.

PWC also stated that as fewer people traveled from afar to visit so-called destination theme parks, such venues attempted to attract more local and regional visitors. This trend had a negative impact on per capita spending. Another trend saw local and regional parks trying to attract more overnight visitors, which had the effect of increasing per capita spending for those venues. In the mid-years of the first decade of the 2000s, the trend was away from roller coasters toward more family-oriented entertainment and enhanced amenities.

The practice of marketing amusement parks to religious groups was becoming more widespread. Great America estimated that 2,700 people came for its Sikh Youth Day. Although there were a lot of event planning details involved in carrying off these types of targeted events, it was believed to be well worth the effort. A national trend was gaining momentum for amusement parks to place on their calendar Praise Days, Muslim Unity Days, Jewish Heritage Days, and other faith-linked celebrations. They ranged from times where group members might be invited in while the park handled business as usual or days with special activities planned and food ordered just for them. Some parks considered the practice to be an outgrowth of JoyFest events featuring a lineup of Christian acts.

According to Sweden's *The Local,* it was Financial Times Deutschland's conclusion that German amusement parks were thriving amidst an otherwise struggling economy. Attendance figures for its largest park, Europa Park, showed record numbers. In 2008, Europa Park admitted 3.5 million visitors. A major contributing factor to the success was considered to be the addition of accommodations, such as hotels on site. Europa Park claimed it had 90 percent of a total 5,000 bed full rating. In addition, The Local claimed The Foundation for Future Studies concluded 62 of every 100 German families were amusement park visitors in the 2008-2009 year.

ORGANIZATION AND STRUCTURE

Amusement parks and their thrill rides were regulated in 42 of 50 states by 2005. According to Saferparks, a non-profit organization that follows safety issues in the amusement park industry, in the United States only 37 states were required to report ride-related injuries as of 2004. Of these, about half limited their reporting requirements to deaths or the most serious injuries. Alabama, Arizona, Kansas, Mississippi, Montana, Nevada, North Dakota, South Dakota, Tennessee, Utah, and Wyoming did not regulate amusement park rides at all.

Of the states that do require amusement parks to report safety data, Saferparks reports that this information is often difficult for consumers to obtain. Some states, such as Pennsylvania, prohibit the public from accessing such information. In other states, reporting requirements are not applied across the board. For example, in Florida—home to such leading destinations as Universal Studios and Disney World—those parks employing more than 1,000 people were exempt from

reporting requirements, even in the case of accident-related deaths. State investigators were not allowed to inspect rides or investigate accidents at such leading parks.

Amusement park safety was a global concern as of the mid-years of the first decade of the 2000s. By 2004, the European Union (EU) was in the process of developing a uniform amusement safety standard. According to the IAAPA, the EU was pursuing this "so that all rides located throughout its member countries will be built and maintained to the same exacting specifications. Once this process is complete, the code is expected to be designated as a universal standard that can be adopted by any nation in the world." In addition to the EU's efforts, the American Society for Testing and Materials' (ASTM) amusement ride standard was expanded during the first decade of the 2000s, with international input, and made available globally.

Cedar Fair gained both industry stature and debt with its purchase of five Paramount amusement parks for US $1.24 billion in 2006. It transcended from being the owner of highly successful Cedar Point to an internationally-recognized industry leader. By selling land near Canada's Wonderland Park, a suburban Toronto location, Cedar Fair gained US$50 million for 87 acres of land.

BACKGROUND AND DEVELOPMENT

The amusement park industry's roots date to medieval Europe. In approximately 1133 A.D., the monk Rahere, a former jester in the court of Henry I, held the first trade fair beginning on August 25, the day after Bartholomew's Day, and continuing for 10 days. For 500 years, traders from all over the world came to Bartholomew Fair to display and sell their wares. While designed for commercial purposes, the public came for strolling entertainers, the food, and the atmosphere. During the Elizabethan period, the fair slowly became an amusement with jugglers, puppet shows, freak shows, and dancers, among other performers. The last Bartholomew Fair was held in 1855, with unruly mobs, petty thieves, and unsavory characters.

In the late seventeenth and eighteenth centuries, pleasure gardens began to appear attached to taverns and inns on the outskirts of European cities. The pleasure gardens featured live entertainment, dancing, fireworks and even primitive amusement rides. By the late eighteenth century, the gardens featured fireworks, tightrope walkers and fees for admission. Political unrest in the eighteenth century forced many of these attractions to close. In the United States, by the late nineteenth century, electric trolley companies began building amusement parks at the end of the trolley line as a way to encourage patronage on the weekends when there were few riders. These facilities consisted of picnic areas, restaurants, dance halls, and a sprinkling of amusement rides. The parks quickly became successful and sprang up across the United States.

The golden era of amusement parks began with the 1893 World's Fair Columbian Exposition held in Chicago. During the Exposition, the Ferris wheel and the midway were introduced to the world, with a selection of rides and concessions. The midway was a huge success and dictated the design of amusement parks for the next six decades. In 1894, Paul Boynton opened his Water Chutes attraction on Chicago's South Side; the success of that attraction persuaded him to open a similar facility at the Coney Island resort in New York in 1895. Over the next three decades, Coney Island became the center of the industry, which grew tremendously as hundreds of new amusement parks opened around the world.

By 1919 there were more than 1,500 amusement parks in operation in the United States. A decade later, the country entered the Great Depression, and by 1935 the economic downturn had exacted a terrible toll on the fledgling industry. Only 400 parks survived, and they struggled to break even. The ones that did faced a new struggle, World War II, when many parks closed and others held off adding new attractions because of rationing.

After World War II, the amusement park industry enjoyed record attendance and revenues. A new concept, Kiddieland, was born to take advantage of the postwar baby boom and introduced a new generation to the fun that could be had at amusement parks. As the 1950s arrived, many outside factors all took their toll on urban amusement parks. The factors included television, desegregation, urban decay, and suburban growth.

By 1955 a new concept in amusement parks had begun at Disneyland in Anaheim, California, but many did not think Disneyland would survive without a midway. In place of the midway, Disneyland Park had five themed areas, which allowed guests to travel to different lands and different times: Main Street U.S.A., Adventureland, Frontierland, Fantasyland, and Tomorrowland. Within six months, more than 1 million visitors had been to Disneyland, followed by 4 million more visitors in 1956. The 50 millionth visitor passed through the turnstiles in July 1965. One of the primary attractions of the park, as Judith Adams observed in her book, *The American Amusement Park Industry: A History of Technology and Thrills,* is that it allows the visitor to be immersed in historical environments and fantasy worlds instead of observing them on TV. The Disneyland formula reflected the public's desire for both entertainment and escape.

Disneyland's success spawned a series of imitators. It was not until 1961, when Six Flags Over Texas opened, that another theme park would succeed. The 35-acre Six Flags Park had six areas with themes, each of them linked to a flag that had waved over Texas, including the flags of Spain, France, Mexico, the Republic of Texas, the Confederacy, and the United States. Unlike Disneyland, however, thrill rides were liberally sprinkled throughout each theme area. The Six Flags backers started a corporate park chain, Six Flags Inc., and built two new parks, Six Flags Over Georgia, near Atlanta, and Six Flags Over Mid-America, near St. Louis, Missouri. Unlike Disneyland, which required separate coupons for each attraction, admission to these parks allowed access to all the rides and attractions located there. Other theme parks were built across the United States in the 1970s and began spreading around the world in the 1980s. The amusement park remained an international favorite through the 1990s.

In 2005, the world's oldest operating amusement park was Bakken, north of Copenhagen, Denmark, which opened in 1583. Next was the Prater in Vienna, Austria, which opened in 1766. The Blackgang Chine Cliff Top Theme Park in Ventnor, United Kingdom, opened its gates in 1842. The Tivoli, also in Copenhagen, opened in 1843. The oldest operating amusement park in the United States, which also was among the oldest amusement parks in the world, was Lake Compounce Amusement Park in Bristol, Connecticut, which began operating in 1846. The only other U.S. park on the National Amusement Park Historical Association's list of the world's 10 oldest parks was Cedar Point in Sandusky, Ohio, which began operating in 1870.

There are several classic amusement park rides that had all but disappeared by the late 1990s. The most familiar of these are the carousel and the roller coaster. The carousel, also known as the merry-go-round, is a ride with seats most often in the form of horses that go up and down around a fixed center. The roller coaster is an elevated railway constructed with curves and inclines upon which cars roll. The world's oldest operating roller coaster began operating in 1912 at Luna Park, in Melbourne, Australia. The world's oldest existing roller coaster, the Leap-the-Dips coaster at Lakemont Park in Altoona, Pennsylvania, was built in 1902. In the late 1990s, efforts were begun to restore the ride and place it back into operation.

Other classic amusement park rides include: Auto Race, in which small electric cars travel along a wooden track; Caterpillar, similar to today's Himalaya Rides in which a train goes in a circle along an undulating track; Circle Swing, in which passengers ride in circles in gondolas suspended by cables from a structure overhead;

Fly-O-Plane, in which passengers ride in airplane-shaped cars and try to flip the cars over; Flying Coaster, three-person cars that travel in a circle along a track; Flying Scooter, in which two-seater cars are suspended from a center arm with wings in the front of each car controlling the ride's motion; Fun House, a walk-through attraction with obstacles like revolving barrels; Noah's Ark, a walk-through attraction similar to the famous boat; Old Mills, also called the Tunnel of Love, in which boats travel down dimly lit passageways; Racing Derby, a high-speed carousel simulating a horse race; Tumble Bug, where riders sit in circular cars moving over an undulating track; Venetian Swing, with riders in passenger boats suspended from a large A-frame; and The Whip, in which cars travel along an oval-shaped course with a whipping effect.

As amusement parks added attractions in the late 1990s, ticket prices crept inexorably upward, as they had since the late 1950s. As Tim O'Brien wrote in *Amusement Business,* each time prices were raised, park officials thought they were as high as they could go. But as the popularity of the parks picked up steam in the 1970s and 1980s, all the parks raised their rates to previously unthinkable levels.

In the late 1990s, industry consolidation began to occur, as operators such as Premier Parks gobbled up smaller parks and family-run operations. As a result, theme parks became hot commodities, and acquisition prices for theme park properties rose to record levels. Late 1997 and early 1998 saw the largest deals to that time. The largest acquisition was the US$1.9 billion paid for the Six Flags Theme Parks chain by Premier Parks, a publicly owned theme park operator based in Oklahoma City, Oklahoma. Premier bought the chain from Time Warner and Boston Ventures, an investment firm. In late 1997, Cedar Fair L.P. made what was then the largest park deal in U.S. history, paying US$250 million for Knott's Berry Farm in Buena Park, California, which was eleventh on the list of North American parks ranked by attendance in 1997. By January of 2002, Cedar Fair owned and operated six amusement parks and five water parks, and they announced that the combined attendance for their 2001 season was a record 11.9 million people.

In August of 2001, theme and amusement park operators were concerned with the drops in attendance at many parks. Cedar Fair suffered a 4.5 percent drop in revenues compared to the prior year. Revenues at Disney were reported as stagnant, primarily because of falling attendance. Attendance at Universal Studios and other theme parks in California and Florida had also declined. Kathy Styponias, the senior entertainment analyst for Prudential Services, described this as the "dichotomy with the amusement park industry" in an interview with Edwin McDowell of *The New York Times.* This refers to the vulnerability of parks whose visitors come from at least 150 miles or more to visit. The terrorist attacks on September 11, 2001, hit the already lagging amusement and theme park industry hard, as people became hesitant to travel. Bruce Orwall of the *Wall Street Journal* reported in an article in early 2002 that Disney had been hit especially hard by the terrorist attacks, which resulted in a significant plunge in their attendance rates and caused Disney to cut 4,000 jobs in early 2002.

In its December 22, 2003, issue, *Amusement Business* reported that North America's leading 50 amusement parks suffered a 1.6 percent decline at the gate, as attendance fell nearly 2.8 million from 2002—the second consecutive year that attendance declined. Other sectors of the entertainment and recreation industry also suffered in 2003. For example, at 11.4 million attendees, the leading 15 U.S. water parks saw their numbers fall 26,066 from 2002 levels. The top 50 fairs suffered a decrease in visitors as well. At 43.2 million, attendance declined 1.6 percent from 2002. Carnivals at the top 50 fairs also experienced a decline, with attendance falling from 38.1 million in 2002 to 37.4 million.

Difficult times were not restrained by the geographic boundaries of North America. Severe Acute Respiratory Syndrome (SARS) affected the industry in Asia, although the impact was minimal. In Europe, the U.S.-led war with Iraq, hot weather, and economic factors contributed to a slight decline in attendance. Gate totals for the region's leading 10 parks fell to 40.2 million visitors in 2003, down from 41 million visitors the previous year.

CURRENT CONDITIONS

Instead of planning for and taking elaborate vacations, more families were spending quality times at amusement parks for "staycations." Upstate New York Seabreeze Amusement Park President Rob Norris claimed corporate outing booking reductions occurred while season pass sales increased by about 7, percent reflecting a trend to vacation closer to home.

In 2004, the world's amusement parks earned about US$20 billion in revenues according to research done by PricewaterhouseCoopers. Growth is expected to be more than 25 percent in the period up to 2008. The situation was looking good for the industry that had suffered difficult times during the early years of the first decade of the 2000s due to an economic recession, high unemployment, and a drop in consumer travel amidst concerns over terrorism. According to the IAAPA, in 2003, attendance at U.S. amusement parks and attractions was 322 million, down from 2002 levels of 324 million. That year, revenues totaled $10.2 billion, up from $9.9 billion in 2002 and $9.6 billion in 2001.

The 10 leading parks around the world, based on attendance during 2004 and as reported by *Forbes* were: the Magic Kingdom at Walt Disney World (Florida) with nearly 15.2 million visitors, Disneyland (California) with almost 13.4 million, Tokyo Disneyland with 13.2 million, Tokyo Disney Sea with 12.2 million, Disneyland Paris with 10.2 million, Universal Studios (Japan) with 9.9 million, Epcot at Walt Disney World with 9.4 million, Disney-MGM Studios at Walt Disney World with nearly 8.3 million, Lotte World (Seoul, South Korea) with 8 million, and Disney's Animal Kingdom at Disney World with about 7.8 million.

As fewer amusement park properties become available due to consolidation in the U.S. industry, operators must work harder to attract and retain attendees by adding new rides, new shows, and new experiences. These additions also are needed to keep visitors coming back to the parks. During the early years of the first decade of the 2000s, such additions had several broad themes. They added interactivity, allowing the audience to react and participate and riders to control factors such as speed and height; high-tech gadgets such as motion simulators, holograms, lasers, and virtual reality; education, such as vacations built around cooking or horticulture; and animals, as almost every theme park operator now has some type of animal attraction.

Although new attractions are important to industry players, by the mid-years of the first decade of the 2000s, amusement parks were not investing as heavily in magnificent roller coasters. Instead, they were focusing more on family-oriented rides and amenities like air-conditioned restrooms and better food. In its January 5, 2004, issue, *Amusement Business* reported that only 12 of the nearly 50 roller coasters announced across the globe could not be categorized as family-oriented rides. Commenting on the movement away from super rides, IAAPA Chairman John Collins said: "The coasters were the remedy for a great deal of the ills of the industry a decade ago. People wanted coasters, parks obliged, and the people came. Now, the masses of people don't necessarily want more coasters, but many operators keep throwing them out there and wonder why their gates don't increase."

In 2005 PricewaterhouseCoopers was predicting that improved economic conditions in the United States, as well as a weakening dollar, would be a benefit to parks in encouraging tourism. A new park in Hong Kong in 2005 and two others in Japan and South Korea (2008 openings) were also thought to be positive for the future earnings of the industry.

Cedar Fair Entertainment executives predicted that Starlight would be a bright, crowd-pleasing addition, launched during the summer of 2009. Starlight Experience was created as a "themed lighted walkway" on the Frontier Trail reflecting changing seasons. In addition, theme-linked floats and large Peanuts character replicas would be part of the scene. Scheduled to be an evening adventure, the Starlight Experience was set to start at twilight running through the evening from Memorial Day weekend to September 6, 2009. The word Starlight was also linked to an admission option. Registered guests at a Cedar Point property were eligible for the Starlight admission option. That option offered tickets for US$14.99 with a savings of US$15 per ticket.

Cedar Point expanded its Physics, Math, & Science Day into a five-day event called Math & Science Week. Invited participants included students and teachers from Indiana, Michigan, and Ohio schools. Featured partners included NASA's Glenn Research Center in Cleveland, the Detroit Science Center, and COSI in Columbus. In addition to popular attractions, days during the week focused on interactive experiences related to distinctive curriculums.

More and more amusement parks were jumping on the green nation band wagon. Timothy B. Wheeler described how internationally-acclaimed attractions such as Disney and Universal Studios had shown their green consciousness by confirming plans to reduce greenhouse gas emissions and hosting "Eco-fairs" featuring celebrities respectively. Regional attractions were going green by turning on LED lights, promoting recycling and utilizing used vegetable oils for rides.

INDUSTRY LEADERS

Walt Disney Company. In 2006, the world's largest theme park operator continued to be the Walt Disney Company. Although the company's media holdings generated the largest share of its total revenues, followed by its studio entertainment segment, parks and resorts earned the company US$9.93 billion of its total earnings for 2006. The company owned Walt Disney World Resort in Florida and Disneyland Park in California. It had a 51 percent interest in Disneyland Resort Paris and a 43 percent interest in Hong Kong Disneyland. In addition, Walt Disney earned royalties on Tokyo Disneyland Resort, which saw a 3.3 percent increase in attendance from April to September 2006, to 12 million. According to Oriental Land Company, the operator of Tokyo Disneyland and Tokyo DisneySea, the increase reflected the first rise on a six-month basis in three years. Walt Disney World Resort is North America's most visited tourist attraction and it features four acclaimed theme parks: The Magic Kingdom, Disney-MGM Studios,

Epcot, and Animal Kingdom. The resort also featured hotels, water parks, and golf courses. Walt Disney also acknowledged its connection to the residential community founded in 1994 known as Celebration, Florida.

Euro Disney was a sore spot for the Walt Disney Co. in mid-2004. Although Disneyland Paris and Disney Studios Park rated as Europe's leading tourist destinations, poor earnings and financial woes prompted a second restructuring that year, following an initial restructuring in the mid-1990s. Euro Disney was initially established as an independent enterprise, in which the Walt Disney Company had an ownership stake. However, new accounting rules forced the parent company to consolidate Euro Disney into its corporate structure in 2004, which was expected to impact Walt Disney in a number of ways, including stock investment and the provision of credit.

Disney Imagineer Stephen Silvestri was confronted with a creative challenge for the "Year of a Million Dreams" 15-month campaign. The company vowed to give away more than one million prizes. One popular prize was the opportunity to spend a night in Cinderella's castle. That Magic Kingdom icon did not have a Royal Suite when the campaign was launched so one had to be created for it. Silvestri and his team researched seventeenth century royal French life and tried to create artwork and furnishings representative of that time period. Modern complementary items such as shampoos and lotions were packaged in French glassware. To maintain an overall look appropriate for the Cinderella story-linked experience, technology such as a large TV was hidden from view and creatively stored for the lucky family to discover during their visit. The design evolved into a 650-square-foot suite with a bedchamber, bathroom, and parlor. The elevator was inspired by Cinderella's carriage. Two sets of three parlor windows revealed views of Fantasyland and Liberty Square.

Six Flags Inc. Six Flags was the second-largest theme park operator in the United States in 2006. It was formerly known as Premier Parks, an Oklahoma City company that began acquiring parks aggressively in 1996. Premier catapulted into the number two position from the number seven slot with its acquisition of the Six Flags Theme Parks chain in early 1998. Approximately 28 million visitors traveled to the company's 27 North American parks in 2006, providing the company with revenue of US$945,665. More than half of the company's sales were attributable to gate receipts, with the remainder coming from merchandise and food. Most of the company's parks operated under the Six Flags name. These included Six Flags Great America, Six Flags Over Texas, and Six Flags Magic Mountain. Most Six Flags parks featured water slides, thrill rides, and other forms of family-oriented entertainment. Six Flags enhanced its

popularity by licensing Warner Bros. characters such as the Looney Tunes, Batman, and Superman.

According to Six Flags, it is "the world's largest regional theme park company." Its strongest presence is in the United States, where the company operated 15 of the nation's largest theme parks. In fact, 98 percent of the U.S. population lived within an eight-hour drive of a Six Flags location during the mid-years of the first decade of the 2000s. In April 2004, Six Flags completed the sale of its European Division, which included locations in Belgium, France, and Germany, for approximately US$200 million. Six Flags' European operations formerly contributed about 20 percent of total revenue. Following the sale, Six Flags continued to operate international parks in Canada, Mexico, and Spain. In addition, the company also sold Six Flags Worlds of Adventure in Ohio for about US$145 million.

Due to a controversial Halloween 2006 promotion, Six Flags and the People for Ethical Treatment of Animals (PETA) had a confrontation. The promotion was "A Cockroach is Your Ticket to the Front of the Line" and called for visitors to eat a live Madagascar hissing cockroach. Their reward would be unlimited line-jumping privileges for the park's scariest rides. PETA was outraged that a corporation with animal theme parks would have this type of promotion. Six Flags official spokesperson Debbie Evans responded that "Cockroaches are insects. They are considered a delicacy in many parts of the world. They are a great source of protein." Some Six Flag parks offered the promotion stunt opportunity for one weekend while others made it available every weekend in October.

In 2007 Six Flags Great Adventure unveiled its "Wiggles World" theme area. This area was uniquely designed to allow young visitors to experience the setting of the popular children's entertainers in its name. Their recognition was high among two- to six-year-olds. The Wiggles have sold more than 22 million DVDs and videos plus more than 5 million albums worldwide. The Wiggles' popular TV show has been broadcast on Disney Channel's Playhouse Disney since 2002.

Anheuser-Busch Companies Inc. The world's largest brewer of beer was also in the theme park business. Its Busch Entertainment Corporation (BEC) subsidiary operated nine theme parks in five states. Those attractions included Busch Gardens Tampa and Busch Gardens Williamsburg in Florida and Virginia, respectively. In 2005, they earned revenues of about US$924 million for the parent company. BEC additionally owned three SeaWorld parks in California, Florida, and Texas. The Florida location was also the home of Discovery Cove where visitors could swim with dolphins and other marine life. The roster of other BEC attractions included Florida' Adventure Island and Virginia's Water Country USA.

Busch Gardens showed off its high-tech savvy with the launch of "BG Blast," billed as an "online community for teens by teens." It featured music download opportunities, commentary from teens across the country, and Busch Gardens promotions. The format also spotlighted teen hosts and chances for fans to serve as hosts.

A special partnership resulted in Sesame Street-themed attractions and characters appearing at Busch Gardens' park. Planned attractions included rides, special effects theatre, and live character shows. Sesame Street characters visiting the parks included Big Bird, Elmo, and the Count.

Universal. Operating three theme parks in the United States and one in Japan, Universal Parks and Resorts, a subsidiary of Universal Studios, earned approximately US$893 million in 2004. Part of Vivendi Universal until 2004, the theme parks were sold along with Vivendi''s other entertainment assets to NBC, a subsidiary of General Electric.

Universal followed Walt Disney World and Sea World in its move to drop trans-fat additives from food sold at its parks. This lengthy process involved changing hundreds of recipes in ways to ensure they were healthier but remained tasty. Related actions served as a blueprint for others in the industry in subsequent years.

Universal offers families the opportunity to experience island fun on the mainland. A getaway can include traveling through five islands packed with innovative rides and 3-D attractions centered around myths, children's stories, cartoon heroes and much more. Magical days and nights were destined to be in store after the launch of another "theme park within a theme park" in 2010. It was called "The Wizarding World of Harry Potter." The tie-in with a favorite fantasy bestseller character was destined to make the area a must-see attraction.

The Tussauds Group. Marie Tussaud started her famous waxworks museum in London in 1835 after 33 years of touring Britain with a collection inherited from wax modeler Phillippe Curtius. After opening several other museums and attractions throughout the years, the company was purchased by Pearson plc, the owner of the Chessington Zoo in England. In 1987, the zoo was remodeled into a theme park, starting the company's ventures into this market segment. In 1990 it acquired Alton Towers, another theme park. Tussauds was acquired by Charterhouse Development Capital in 1998, and went on to manage and operate the London Eye, the world's tallest observation wheel. By 2005, in addition to other entertainment holdings, Tussauds was operating four theme parks in the United Kingdom. The company's total 2004 revenues exceeded US$300 million.

In 2007, Tussauds was sold to Blackstone as part of the U.S. private-equity group's attempt to create a European

challenger for Disney. The deal meant Tussauds would become part of the Blackstone-controlled theme park operator Merlin Entertainments. Merlin already owned Alton Towers, Legoland, London Dungeon, the Sea Life aquarium chain, and many other European attractions.

MAJOR COUNTRIES IN THE INDUSTRY

United States. Valued by the IAAPA at US$10.8 billion in 2004, the theme park industry in the United States remained highly consolidated. The top five companies in the industry accounted for 97.5 percent of the total market, according to market research firm Euromonitor. The industry leaders operating in the United States were Walt Disney Company, Anheuser-Busch Companies, Six Flags Inc., Vivendi Universal (now NBC Vivendi), and Cedar Fair LP. The market was expected to grow by 14 percent into 2008.

Multi-generational destination parks were becoming innovative competitors for U.S. amusement parks. These parks offered diverse play experiences and outdoor physical fitness opportunities for groups ranging from toddlers to senior citizens. They might feature play structures for young children, skate ramps for teens, and wellness paths for active adults/seniors. The parks were becoming popular attractions for residents in local communities, as well as tourists reportedly traveling hundreds of miles.

Japan. In 2004, about 11 percent of visitors to Japan's various and numerous tourist attractions chose to visit a theme park. About 31 percent of the money spent on tourist attractions added to theme park revenues. New parks in nearby countries, however, were posing a competitive threat. In 2006 Tokyo Disney Resort saw an increase in attendance but Universal Studios Japan experienced a decrease in its attendance figures.

United Kingdom. In 2003 the United Kingdom's amusement parks had almost 50 million visitors. And when most Britons think amusement, they think Blackpool. Packed along 12 miles of seaside promenade, Blackpool in England offers visitors wax museums, amusement rides, and numerous other leisure activities. The country's biggest tourist attraction was Blackpool Pleasure Beach, founded in Blackpool in 1896. In 2004, this theme park hosted 6.2 million visitors and held about 14 percent of the total market. Other industry leaders included Tussauds Group Ltd. and Lego.

France. Theme parks in France had 35.4 million visitors in 2003, with Disneyland Paris accounting for 37 percent. Other industry leaders included Grevin et Compagnie SA (which was operating Parc Astérix north of

Paris), Futuroscope, and Nausicaa. Euromonitor expected industry growth of more than 23 percent between 2003 and 2005.

Asia. Heading into the mid-years of the first decade of the 2000s, Asia was experiencing the strongest growth within the amusement park industry, in terms of both visitors and parks. In fact, a 2003 report from Economics Research Associates indicated that North America's share of the global theme park industry would fall from 43 percent in 1990 to 32 percent in 2005. That year, Asia was expected to surpass the relatively mature North American market with a share of 35 percent. Europe was expected to hold 25 percent of the market, with the remainder attributed to other nations. At 8 percent, Asia was forecast to have the strongest annual growth rate of any country between 2005 and 2010. China, in particular, was poised for explosive growth, as the nation prepared to host the 2008 Olympics in Beijing. A PWC Global Entertainment and Media Outlook report predicted the attraction and amusement industry in Asia will grow faster than in any other region of the world. Asia was projected to generate average annual revenue increases of 5.7 percent for a total of US$8.1 billion in revenues by 2009. An improved global economy, plus the modernization and development of new rides, were key contributing factors.

BIBLIOGRAPHY

"Amusement Industry Expects Strong 2004 Season." Alexandria, Va.: International Association of Amusement Parks and Attractions, 21 May 2004. Available from www.iaapa.org.

"Amusement Parks Report Thrilling Scales Despite Crisis." *The Local,* 14 August 2009. Available from www.thelocal.de.

"Attendance at Tokyo Disney Resort Rises for 1st Time in 3 Years." *Jiji,* 2 October 2006.

Banay, Sophia. "World's Most Fun Amusement Parks 2005." *Forbes,* 2005. Available from www.forbes.com.

"Blackstone Pays Pounds 1bn to Take Over Tussauds." *The Independent,* 6 March 2007.

Bogues, Austin. "A Kid-Friendly Addition: Big Bird and the Sesame Street Crew Are Coming to Several Amusement Parks to Entertain Children." *Daily Press,* 2 September 2006.

Boyd, Christopher. "Universal Shoves Trans Fat Off Plate: Disney and SeaWorld Have Already Announced Efforts to Shift Toward Healthful Menus." *Orlando Sentinel,* 21 December 2006.

Cedar Fair Entertainment. "Cedar Point's Math and Science Week to Feature NASA, COSI-Columbus and the Detroit Science Center." 2009. Available from www.cedarpoint.com.

————. "Starlight Experience to Brighten Cedar Point's Frontier Trail." 2009. Available from www.cedarpoint.com.

"Economic Forecast Bright for Asian Attractions and Amusement Industry, Leading Experts Say." Alexandria, Va.: International Association of Amusement Parks and Attractions, 23 May 2006. Available from iaapa.org.

"For Your Information." Oklahoma City, Okla.: Six Flags Inc., 21 July 2004. Available from www.sixflags.com.

Hong Kong Disneyland. "The Hong Kong SAR Government and the Walt Disney Company Applaud the Legislative Council's Approval of the Hong Kong Disneyland Expansion Plan." 15 August 2009. Available from news-en.hongkongdisneyland.com.

"Hoover's Company Profiles." *Hoover's Online,* 2007. Available from www.hoovers.com.

International Association of Amusement Parks and Attractions. "U.S. Theme Parks Unveil New Attractions for 2009." 1 June 2009. Available from www.iaapa.org.

Johannes, Amy. "Pity the Roaches: Six Flags Dare Bugs PETA." *Promo,* 29 September 2006.

"Launchpad: Disney Takes Over Eurostar." *Travel Trade Gazette UK & Ireland,* 23 March 2007.

Mooradian, Don. "Industry Rides Out Rough '03." *Amusement Business,* 22 December 2003.

"Multi-generational Destination Parks Promote Fun and Fitness Among All Ages and Abilities." *Government Product News,* January 2007.

National Amusement Park Historical Association. *History of Amusement Parks.* Alexandria, Va.: NAPHA, 1997. Available from www.napha.org.

————. *Operating Classic Amusement Park Rides.* Mount Prospect, Ill.: NAPHA, 1997. Available from www.npha.org.

————. *World's Oldest Operating Amusement Parks.* Mount Prospect, Ill.: NAPHA, 1997. Available from www.npha.org.

Niedt, Bob. "Upstate New York amusement parks say business is good as families have fun on a budget." 27 July 2009.

Norris, Floyd. "Disney Gives Details of Plan to Aid European Parks." *The New York Times,* 1 July 2004.

O'Brien, Tim. "Admission Prices Continue to Rise." *Amusement Business,* 4 May 1998.

————. "Big Ticket Projects Scarce in 2004: Parks Focus on Family Rides, Amenities." *Amusement Business,* 5 January 2004.

Powers, Scott. "Details Fall Into Place at Disney: Designers Create a Suite Where Some Lucky Winners Stay as Part of the Year of a Million Dreams Campaign." *Orlando Sentinel,* 14 November 2006.

Reklaitis, Victor. "Busch Gardens Aims at Teenagers: a Web site Will Feature Comments, Music Downloads and Promotions for the Theme Park," 4 October 2006.

"Report: Injuries Rising at Amusement Parks." *CNN,* 24 August 2001. Available from www.cnn.com.

"Safety in the Amusement Industry: Serious Business Around the World." Alexandria, Va.: International Association of Amusement Parks and Attractions, 19 July 2004. Available from www.iaapa.org.

Samavati, Shaheen. "Sandusky based amusement park operator Cedar Fair sells land in Canada to pay down debt." 23 July 2009. Available from www.cleveland.com.

"Six Flags Closes Previously Announced Sales of European Division and Six Flags Worlds of Adventure." Oklahoma City, Okla.: Six Flags Inc., 13 April 2004. Available from www.sixflags.com.

State Regulation Governing Amusement Rides. Safer Parks, 20 July 2004. Available from www.saferparks.org.

"Theme Parks in Germany (US, UK, and France)." *Euromonitor,* October 2004. Available from www.euromonitor.com.

"Top 10 Amusement/Theme Park Chains Worldwide." *Amusement Business,* 22 December 2003.

Traiman, Steve. "ERA Research Eyes Park Biz in 2005." *Amusement Business,* 10 May 2004.

"Travel and Tourism in Japan: Executive Summary." *Euromonitor,* March 2005. Available from www.euromonitor.com.

"U.S. Amusement/Theme Parks & Attractions Industry— Attendance & Revenues." Alexandria, Va.: International Association of Amusement Parks and Attractions, 19 July 2004. Available from www.iaapa.org.

Universal. "Universal's Islands of Adventure: Live the Adventure of a Lifetime!" 15 August 2009. Available from www.Universalorlando.com.

"Video: Six Flags Great Adventure Unveils Wiggles World Based Off the Most Popular Children's Entertainers in the World, 'The Wiggles,' April 2 Six Flags Wild Safari Debuts the Exploration Station—a New, Interactive Adventure." *PR Newswire,* 3 April 2007.

Vo, Kim. "Marketing Fun to the Faithful: Amusement Parks, Teams Court Religious Groups." *San Jose Mercury News,* 6 August 2006.

Wheeler, Timothy B. "Amusement Parks Giving Green Rides." *Baltimore Sun,* 5 August 2009. Available from www.baltimoresun.com.

Zoltak, James. "Industry Execs Foresee Strong Business in '04: The Year Ahead." *Amusement Business,* 5 January 2004.

SIC 7993, 7999

GAMING AND GAMBLING ESTABLISHMENTS

NAICS CODE(S)

713120, 713990. Gambling organizations, which may include governments as well as for-profit companies, provide various means for betting or wagering money based on a chance of a winning outcome, usually in the form of a game. The most common gambling venues are lotteries, casinos, and the Internet. Certain industry firms also operate hotels and restaurants; see also the industry profiles entitled **Hotels and Lodging** and **Restaurants**.

INDUSTRY SNAPSHOT

The gambling industry includes government-run operations, such as state and national lotteries, as well as private operations such as casinos. The gambling industry continued to receive greater acceptance around the world, with most countries that had already legalized gambling

permitting more operations, and with many other countries considering its legalization in order to remain competitive. In 2004, the United Kingdom remained the leading country in betting, with revenues channeled through bookmakers and permitted—while taxed and overseen—by the British government. The year 2005 was bringing major changes to the regulations governing U.K. gambling. The United States remained the main source of gambling dollars, particularly in the growing online gambling segment.

In the 1990s and the first decade of the 2000s, casinos around the world started to shift to theme-oriented gaming houses. In part, this was an effort to attract families—a move anti-gambling activists deplore out of fears that children may become gamblers later in life. Companies such as Harrah's, Mirage, Sun International, and Circus Circus led in operating theme casinos throughout the world, combining gambling with other forms of entertainment. The theme format also helped differentiate one casino from another, because most were located in gambling districts and offered otherwise similar services. In addition, more casinos relied on slot machines for their revenues, because gamblers like their easy-to-use, low-wager format. By 2004, leading manufacturers of slot machines were reporting record earnings, benefiting from both so-called cashless machines, which were rapidly replacing traditional coin-operated slots, and from relaxed laws and increased machine placement in a handful of locations.

ORGANIZATION AND STRUCTURE

The gambling industry comprises five main categories: pari-mutuel betting at race tracks, off-track betting, bingo/keno, government lotteries, and casino gambling—all of which involve chance or have odds of winning. Pari-mutuel betting refers to a pool of bets for racing (mostly horse or dog) where bettors on the first three winners share the prize money, minus a cut for the racing operation. Pari-mutuels incurred income slippage in the late 1990s and the first decade of the 2000s because of competition from casinos and the Internet. Off-track betting is wagering by bettors who do not attend the race, but place bets through a booking agency instead. In bingo and keno, players cover the numbers on their playing cards, trying to cover five in a row and win prize money if they succeed. Government lotteries in their various kinds, including daily and weekly drawings, award monetary prizes for ticket holders who match a certain amount of numbers correctly, or otherwise purchase tickets that have the potential to result in winning, as in so-called instant lotteries. Casino gambling includes live games of chance, such as blackjack, poker, craps, and roulette, as well as machine-based betting, such as slot machines. Casino gambling accounts for the greatest share of revenues in most countries where it is legal. Casino games also give players the greatest odds of winning, while lotteries usually have the lowest odds.

Some casinos have changed drastically since their inception, moving from purely gaming houses to theme and fantasy parks and trying to cater to the family crowd. Casinos also may offer services such as child care or video arcades. Casino gambling districts and resorts are often combined with 24-hour shopping malls and visual attractions, like talking statues, erupting volcanoes, and mock ocean battles between pirate ships. Slot machines have been an increasingly popular addition to casinos. At one point, casinos devoted only around 30 percent of their space to slot machines, but by the mid- to late 1990s, they began to devote as much as 90 percent of their space to these money makers.

Although some businesses and political leaders view the gambling industry as an economic panacea, or at least as an economic benefactor, industry observers and religious organizations offer a far more grim account of the industry and its effects on economies and societies. Gambling advocates often portray casinos and other gambling operations as economic stimulants that create jobs and pump more money into local and national economies. Opponents point out that the jobs created are primarily low-skill, low-paying positions, such as money counters and janitors. Furthermore, detractors claim that simply building casinos in declining and blighted cities has failed to revitalize them, and competition among casinos usually erodes their profits, according to the *Economist*.

In addition, casinos, unlike other forms of gambling such as lotteries, require peripheral services that cities usually incur, including additional law enforcement and street cleaning expenses. Moreover, some critics argue that casinos also cause a variety of social problems, such as gambling addiction, mismanagement of personal finance, and deterioration of families, creating the need for additional social services such as counseling. The cost of a casino, in terms of the problems associated with one, brings a community nearly twice the expense compared to its benefits, claims Earl L. Grinols, a University of Illinois economist who estimates the annual U.S. national loss to be US$27.5 billion.

Numerous religions forbid gambling, including Hinduism, Buddhism, Islam, and some Christian denominations. Under Islamic law, gamblers must donate their winnings to the poor, and evidence given by gamblers is not acceptable in an Islamic court. Betting on horse racing has generally been an exception to this prohibition. Texts of Hinduism, such as the *Rig Veda,* ban and warn against gambling and several other sacred texts refer to it as a vice. Gamblers also cannot serve as legal witnesses under Hindu

law. Buddhism views gambling as a worldly distraction that leads believers astray. Finally, Protestant denominations, as well as Mormons and Jehovah's Witnesses, also oppose gambling, considering it a sinful recreation with harmful social and economic consequences. Other churches, such as the Catholic Church, have long supported bingo and gaming wheels at church functions, such as lawn fetes.

In 2005, gambling remained highly regulated in most countries in which it was legal, with participating governments earning large amounts of money from the industry. However, online gambling, which easily crosses borders, was proving more difficult to regulate. In the United States, providing online gaming remained illegal; however, the government was not taking action against foreign-based companies doing such business with Americans.

BACKGROUND AND DEVELOPMENT

Cultures throughout the ages have gambled through lotteries and other games of chance, and ancient texts and artifacts from many cultures all over the world refer to gambling and games of chance. For example, the ancient Romans gambled for entertainment, and medieval Europeans instituted gambling as a recreation for festivals. Gambling in China dates back about 4,000 years, and excavations at Ur, Crete, India, and Egypt (2000 to 1000 B.C.) showed signs of gambling in these cultures, because dice and gambling boards were found. Later in Europe, feudal rulers and merchants relied on gambling for revenues. During the sixteenth century, European governments became particularly interested in gambling for income, and many began to require licensing from the crown and established government monopolies over the industry. England, for example, would issue licenses for gambling operations in England and the country's colonies, and the government operated its own lotteries from 1709 until 1826, when it was banned.

In the eighteenth century, European aristocracy enjoyed gambling in the resorts of Europe, although European governments officially opposed gambling, and some countries outlawed it. With the rise of the middle-income merchant class, Europe began to establish permanent gambling venues throughout the continent, including Baden-Baden and Wiesbaden, Germany, and Baden, Austria. Moreover, the Casino de Monte Carlo became a model for casinos throughout Europe, which continued to spread through the nineteenth century.

The U.S. gambling and casino industry grew out of the westward migration of pioneers, who shunned the puritanical ways of some of the eastern cities and states. With few other forms of entertainment available, many of these U.S. settlers chose gambling as a key leisure activity. Between 1800 an 1840, towns along the Mississippi River became ports for riverboats transporting goods and people. The riverboats also became moving gambling parlors. Further west, in the mining camps and small towns, public, organized systems of gambling were evolving. Most of the gambling involved card games, such as Monte and Poker, but some wheel games existed.

As emerging U.S. cities in the Midwest, South, and West grew wealthier and more sophisticated, they sought acceptance from the East. In order to gain acceptance, they tried alleviating their problems, including gambling, since the East largely prohibited it. Many of these cities, therefore, outlawed gambling and arrested gamblers.

As U.S. cities began banning gambling in the mid-nineteenth century, Europe continued to embrace it. This especially was true of casino gambling, which was considered a more elegant form of gambling. Casino gambling differed from other forms, because it used large tables and machinery, such as roulette wheels. Esteemed vacation resorts and health spas, such as Baden-Baden and Bad Homburg, Germany, along with Nice, Cannes, and Monte Carlo on the French Riviera, soon offered casino gambling.

François Blanc, a former casino manager in Bad Homburg jailed for stock fraud, moved to Monaco in 1863 where he built and ran a casino—despite resistance and protestations from Prince Charles II. Blanc successfully transformed Monaco into a wealthy gambling resort, and is considered the founder of the modern casino. Later, Las Vegas casinos adopted his management theories and rules for customer relations.

Although interest and acceptance of casino gambling games, such as baccarat and roulette, grew rapidly in Europe, these games faced heightened resistance in the United States because of national scandals in the late nineteenth century affecting the country's lotteries and horse races. By 1910 the government outlawed most forms of gambling in the United States.

U.S. betting on horse races became legal again in the 1930s, but was subject to strict state laws and regulations. During the U.S. Prohibition, speakeasies were venues for various forms of illegal gambling, such as crap pits, poker and blackjack tables, and slot machines. In the 1940s and 1950s, Las Vegas became the country's gambling capital, using its gambling resorts to attract tourists. In 1946, Benjamin "Bugsy" Siegel, a notorious gangster, decided to bypass California's prohibition of gambling by opening a luxury hotel and casino (the Flamingo), in Las Vegas. Siegel's casino ushered in the highly influential trend, which the industry followed through the late 1990s, of large flamboyant hotel and casino operations. The Flamingo also offered free lodging and meals to keep gamblers playing as long as possible. Nevada monopolized the U.S. industry until 1976, when New Jersey opened up casinos in Atlantic City.

Although the gambling industry experienced exceptional growth in the early to mid-1990s, it began to slow down in the late 1990s, notably in the United States. Analysts attributed the industry's lower growth rates to less government involvement in the late 1990s, in contrast to a plethora of casino initiatives around the world early in the decade, when many economies worldwide underwent recessions. For example, after the U.S. industry's revenues rose by more than 10 percent annually throughout the first half of the decade, they grew by only 5 percent in 1997. The United Kingdom continued to lead the world in gambling revenues with US$65 billion in 1997, followed by the United States with US$49 billion. However, the United States possessed the largest casino industry, whereas much of the United Kingdom's gambling revenues came from its National Lottery. In 2002, casino interests were exploring the feasibility of opening casinos, similar to those in Nevada, in the United Kingdom. In 2002 the United Kingdom prohibited bookmakers from gambling on the national lottery, although bookmakers did accept bets on the Irish national lottery.

The global industry benefited from the rise of slot machine casinos and the addition of slot machines to other casinos in the 1990s. Slot machines contributed significantly to the industry's growth in the mid- to late 1990s, accounting for the majority of casino revenues in countries such as the United States and France. In addition, because they are easy to use, slot machines appeal to neophyte gamblers and gamblers with limited budgets, since gamblers typically wager with small-denomination coins.

As a result of the high demand, casinos around the world began to change their formats to emphasize slot machines and some even began to move away from posh theme-oriented casinos. In fact, many successful casinos of the late 1990s featured only slot machines. Furthermore, slot machine manufacturers began to enhance their products, making them more interactive and visually stimulating. Nevertheless, grand theme casinos continued to fare well and gambling companies continued to launch more of them in recent years.

Casinos also began to market their services to families in the mid- to late 1990s. They added family-oriented themes to their gaming houses, such as circus, carnival, ancient Egypt, and lost treasure themes, and started to provide other services to make casinos a viable option for family outings. These services included offering childcare for adults who wanted to gamble, as well as providing alternative activities for older children. The themes, furthermore, aided casino operators in distinguishing their gaming houses from those of other operators as competition increased.

Although analysts believed Asia had a strong market for gambling, many Asian countries still resisted gambling and casinos in the late 1990s. China, for example, remained adamant in its ban on gambling. Nonetheless, investors built the resort town Sanya, on Hainan Island. The island served as a place to entice visitors with gambling amenities. Japan officially opposed gambling as well, but the country did allow gambling to accompany pachinko, a popular game of chance that is roughly a cross between a slot machine and a pinball machine. Even Hong Kong, where annual bets totaled US$90 million in 1996 for horse racing, faced gambling restrictions when it returned to Chinese rule in 1997. In 2002, Hong Kong officials were considering legislation to tax Internet gambling profits and to safeguard Hong Kong's horse racing enterprises. In response, many Asians traveled to Australia and Macau, where gambling was legal.

CURRENT CONDITIONS

According to a 2004 Gallup study, approximately two-thirds of the U.S. adult population gambled in the previous year. Lotteries were the most popular choice, followed by casinos. While sports betting was the leading choice in the United Kingdom, it had grown more and more unpopular each year since 1989 in the United States.

In 2005, many countries were making the move to legalize gambling, and those that had already done so were imposing new regulations to allow for online gambling and providing licenses to new entities in the industry. The United Kingdom continued to be home to the two largest companies in the industry, betting companies Ladbrokes and William Hill. China's Macau region was readying itself to surpass Las Vegas in terms of revenues generated. Worldwide, gambling in 2004 was estimated to be worth in excess of US$243 billion.

By 2004, casinos were legal in 20 states, although Las Vegas and Atlantic City were still the market leaders. American Indian casinos in particular were growing exponentially, both in terms of location and in terms of the number of machines and tables per location. The largest centers of Indian casino locations were on opposite coasts, in California and New York.

Critics continued to attack the success of casinos as a means of revitalizing declining city centers, especially in the United States where some of the most ambitious programs were launched. Unlike Las Vegas, most other cities that allowed gambling failed to draw visitors for extended stays. Instead, customers largely patronized only the casinos in these cities, including Atlantic City, not the restaurants, hotels, and other businesses. Moreover, according to the

Economist, the money earned tends not to be additional money, but to be a share of the money that would have been spent on other industries in the area, as businesses discovered in Gary, Indiana. Along with the nation's economic upswing, the gaming industry was a rising star again. Las Vegas held the honor of being the most popular tourist spot in the country.

The global online gaming industry was growing rapidly by 2005. Having been established in the 1990s, this sector of the industry had not yet begun to be fully developed. Research by Christiansen Capital Advisors estimated that about US$8.2 billion was generated by online gaming in 2004, and predicted the value would rise to almost US$25 billion by 2010. About 50 percent of the online market is estimated to come from the United States, which was considered to be the result of the high degree of Internet use in the country as well as its level of discretionary income. As such income levels improve in other parts of the world, growth rates in Europe and Asia were expected to exceed those in the U.S. by 2009. Although online gambling remained illegal in many countries, including the United States, players appeared willing to participate.

In 2006, the tribal gaming revenues grew by more than 11 percent to US$25.07 billion at 387 U.S. reservation casinos. The tribal commission's Region V saw the largest percentage increase in revenue. It rose to US$2.1 billion in 2006 from US$1.7 billion in 2005. Region V states were Kansas, Oklahoma, and Texas.

RESEARCH AND TECHNOLOGY

The growth of Internet use and the development of effective online security systems from 1995 up through the latter part of the first decade of the 2000s prompted casino operators to establish online gambling sites. Although this part of the industry only began to take off in the late 1990s, analyst Sebastian Sinclair predicted that income by the end of 2002 could be as high as US$3 billion in worldwide revenues, according to *USA Today.* Internet gambling sites allow users to bet on sports events, participate in lotteries, and play virtual versions of casino games. Most of the online gambling operations are based in the Caribbean, where licenses are easy to acquire.

Online gambling operations have come under considerable attack because existing laws on gambling do not cover the specifics of the Internet in any straightforward way. U.S. law, for example, prohibits placing bets via interstate telephone lines; however, this law does not include wagering across international boundaries, such as those that exist on the Internet where gambling houses from all over the world can set up online casinos and lotteries. Consequently, U.S. senators began introducing bills that would ban online gambling and punish gamblers, although very few convictions were recorded in the early years of the first decade of the 2000s. Major casinos expressed mixed opinions; while some supported online gambling, others resisted, fearing it would reduce their profits. In 2002, Nevada gambling regulators rejected requests by the casino industry for Internet gambling approval.

Moreover, the United States started to prosecute offshore gambling operations that allowed U.S. citizens to place bets in violation of U.S. federal law in 1998. Despite the antagonism to online gambling, analysts believe this portion of the industry will continue to grow with or without government support. On the other hand, Australia and the United Kingdom supported online gambling and promised to help regulate it, making it inevitable that the United States will follow suit.

In the late 1990s, gambling equipment manufacturers also introduced slot machines with new technology. These slot machines included new features, such as more accurate calculation software and a nudge option, which allows players another chance at a jackpot. Equipment makers believe these features make slot machines more fun to play, and casino owners like them because of their power to draw both novice and returning customers.

In the late 1990s, Wells Fargo & Co. and Mr. Payroll Corp. developed a new kind of automatic teller machine (ATM) for casinos that recognizes the face of the user. The ATM, called Quest, dispenses cash and tickets without the use of an ATM card and is designed to expedite ATM use, allowing customers to quickly cash checks, receive cash advances, and withdraw money. The face-recognition technology is the same as that used in security systems of the Pentagon and other high-security places.

By 2005, gaming was being highly influenced by several new distribution channels. Online gambling was growing globally, particularly as the number of people with high-speed Internet access continued to grow. Interactive television and wireless telephone applications were also allowing for gaming to be done using those mediums.

In June 2009, The National Indian Gaming Commission shared research findings related to growth in gaming revenues. There was an increase of 2.3 percent related to US$26.7 billion in 2008 taken in by tribal casinos overall. The Commission also noted a consistent research result was for maximum growth in Oklahoma tribal areas.

INDUSTRY LEADERS

Hilton Group PLC (Ladbrokes). Hilton Group of the United Kingdom owns the rights to the Hilton hotel brand name around the world, with the exception of the United States. Ladbrokes is the company's betting and gaming division, and in 2005, it continued to be the world's biggest bookmaker. It was operating more than 2,300 betting shops in the United Kingdom, Ireland, and Belgium, as well as operating telephone betting ande-gaming sites available around the world in more than 13 languages. Through its various services, one could bet on horses, greyhounds, soccer, and other sports, and play poker and casino games. Gaming laws in the United Kingdom required that participants register as members 24 hours in advance of playing. Ladbrokes' telephone betting system claimed 125 million active members at the end of 2004, while e-gaming held an active membership base of 390 million people. With a worldwide employee count of more than 12,800, Ladbrokes earned revenues in 2004 approaching US$18 billion and had profits of more than US$480 million. The growth of online betting continued to increase each year. Prior to the Euro 2004 and the summer Olympics, the company invested millions of pounds into reworking the site architecture.

In 2007, Ladbrokes launched an online game based on the Grand National to encourage site visits before the event. Players were challenged to compete against three computer-controlled horses. It also encouraged players to spread the word to friends about the venue.

In 2007 Ladbrokes announced that it acquired Sponsio. Sponsio was its online betting partner in Sweden, Norway, Denmark and Finland. The Sponsia acquisition was targeted at strengthening Ladbrokes' position in the Nordic region, where per capita spending on gambling was considered to be among Europe's highest levels.

William Hill PLC. Founded in 1934, William Hill was the second-largest off-track betting organization in the United Kingdom in 2005. Processing an average of 859,000 betting slips each day from its more than 1,600 betting shops, telephone betting systems and e-gaming sites, the company was accepting bets on more than 25 sports as well as offering casino-style games. In 2004, the company had revenues of more than US$14.5 billion and employed more than 10,700 people. In May 2005 William Hill announced plans to acquire Stanley Leisure for $880 million, which will make it the United Kingdom's biggest bookmakers and allow the company to enter Northern Ireland and the Republic of Ireland where it previously did not have any betting shops. After that acquisition, the decision was made in 2006 to offer new voluntary benefits packages that will offer U.K. staff a range of discounts. The discounts included options for dental plans, restaurants and high-street retailers. They offered the flexibility to be used on a weekly basis.

Stanley Leisure PLC. In addition to owning more than 600 betting shops, Stanley Leisure was the United

Kingdom's largest operator of casinos with 41 casinos across the country. The company began in 1958 when it operated two betting shops in Belfast. The company moved into the English market in the 1970s growing through the acquisition of other betting shops and casinos. In 1979, Stanley Leisure moved its head office to Liverpool. Revenues for the year 2004 were about US$2.9 billion, during which time it employed almost 7,000 people.

MGM MIRAGE. MGM MIRAGE operates some of the most famous casino-resorts in the United States including the Las Vegas-based Bellagio, MGM Grand, The Mirage, Luxor, Excalibur, Circus Circus, and New York-New York. In total, the company had 19 operations in 2007 in Nevada, Michigan, Mississippi, and New Jersey. These properties also offered customers a choice from almost 27,000 rooms and suites for accommodation. In 2004, MGM MIRAGE reported revenues of US$4.24 billion of which about 75 percent came from its Las Vegas-based properties. More than US$2.22 billion was earned directly from gaming in the casinos, while the remainder was non-casino revenue consisting of money earned from room accommodations, food, entertainment, and retail services. In 2002 MGM MIRAGE was the most active casino in the United States in terms of exploring profitable possibilities on the Internet, and by 2004 it acquired the Mandalay Resort Group for US$4.8 billion. In 2005, the company was working on the development of another 4,000-room casino-resort in Las Vegas and the MGM Grand Detroit hotel-casino complex. In addition, it had formed strategic alliances with several U.K. companies in anticipation of gambling reforms there, and had also established a joint-venture agreement to build a hotel-casino resort in Macau.

Since 2000, MGM MIRAGE has reported its diversity performance. The company's Diversity Initiative transcended race and gender to include "comprehensive global perspective into our diversity matrix." In 2006, minority employees totaled more than half of the workforce at 56.2 percent. MGM MIRAGE had also been successful in broadening the base of minority, women and disadvantaged enterprises with which it works. Through its employee-funded Voice Foundation and corporate philanthropy, the company increased by 16 percent its grants provided to nonprofits serving diverse communities and organizations. Since its 2002 launch, the foundation had awarded more that US$17 million in employee donations to charities and places where MGM MIRAGE does business.

Harrah's Entertainment Inc. In 2005, United States-based Harrah's Entertainment Inc. owned or managed more than 40 casinos in the United States, Australia, and New Zealand, mainly under the brands of Harrah's, Caesars, Bally's and Horseshoe. Harrah's roster of companies also included owned and operated casinos in Canada,

England, Egypt, and South Africa. In the United States, Harrah's owned casinos in thirteen states, including Nevada, Arizona, Illinois, Indiana, Mississippi, Louisiana, Missouri, New Jersey, North Carolina, and Washington. Harrah's also published annual surveys on the gambling and casino industry. One of the comeback business stories for Harrah's was its New Orleans casino, long a troubled franchise. Harrah's Entertainment Inc. had done well financially with out-of-the-mainstream sites in Council Bluffs, Iowa, and Maricopa, Arizona. By 2004, combined sales from its operations were US$4.55 billion of which US$4.08 billion came directly from casino operations. In 2005, the company acquired Caesars Entertainment, formerly Park Place Entertainment, in a more than US$9 billion dollar deal. In 2006, Harrah's was acquired by two private-equity firms for US$27.8 billion. Las Vegas was reportedly the only U.S. region to post a positive cash flow for the company in 2006.

Beefed up security efforts helped Harrah's reduce its fraudulent and injury claims. On-site cameras showed what really happened when guests claimed to have suffered damage to their vehicles on company lots or when valet parking was utilized. According to Roberto Ceniceros, writing in April 2007 for *Business Insurance,* Harrah's Director of Claim Management for its Risk Management Department Roger Davis said his company closed approximately 8,000 general liability claims each year and approximately 40 percent related to valet accounts.

Casino representatives gained visible support from hundreds of others when contract talks did not go smoothly. Casino dealers and slot machine technicians obtained United Auto Workers (UAW) representation. Consequently, large groups of AFSCME members showed support for workers seeking their first UAW contract in negotiations that went on for 18 months. Harrah's Entertainment was of course not thrilled about workers from New Jersey, New York, Delaware and Pennsylvania picketing on the boardwalk.

Sociedade de Jogos de Macau. Casino tycoon Stanley Ho enjoyed a monopoly on gambling on the island nation of Macau until a few years after the Portuguese colony was handed back to Chinese rule. In 2002, the government allowed others into the market. However, Ho's license was extended for 20 years. The 12 casinos earned revenues of US$3.7 billion in 2003.

The Rank Group PLC. In 2004, gaming operations earned London-based The Rank Group more than US$1.6 billion in revenue. About 31 percent of its revenues came from its 120 bingo clubs operating under the Mecca Bingo name. With 4.6 million members in 2005, the company was second in bingo gaming to Gala Group. A further 21 percent of Rank's gaming revenues came from its Grovenor Casinos business, which operated 36 casinos under both the Grovenor and Hard Rock brands. The casino business had 1.2 million members. About 47 percent of the company's gaming revenues came from its Blue Square division, which operated Internet and telephone betting services. The remainder of the gaming revenue was derived from 35,000 amusement machines operating in various venues. The company sold its machine segment in 2004. Rank also provides a range of manufacturing, distribution, and related services for the motion picture and media industries.

Trump Entertainment Resorts Inc. Trump Entertainment Resorts (formerly Trump Hotels & Casino Resorts Inc.) filed for Chapter 11 bankruptcy protection in November 2004 after accumulating US$1.8 billion in debt. The company reorganized, reduced its debt and reissued its stock, emerging from bankruptcy protection in May 2005. This was the third time the company had been through bankruptcy, failing to turn a profit in ten years. Chairman Donald Trump's share was reduced from about 53 percent to about 29 percent after the reorganization. The company owns Trump Plaza Hotel and Casino, Trump's Marina, Trump Indiana Casino, and Trump Taj Mahal in Atlantic City, New Jersey. In 2004, revenues were US$1.5 billion of which about US$1.25 billion was from gaming. Net losses were US$37.3 million.

According to Suzette Parmley, writing for *The Philadelphia Inquirer/McClatchy-Tribune Regional News,* after emerging from the bankruptcy, Trump Entertainment was about US$1.4 billion in debt. Industry insiders said the company was receiving more profitable proposals from private-equity firms than other casino operators. Morgan Stanley was expected to cut its losses related to its 20 percent ownership of Trump Entertainment.

Mashantucket Pequot Gaming Enterprises, Inc. (Foxwoods). Of the casinos run by Native American tribes in the United States, the largest is the Foxwoods Resort and Casino, operated by the Mashantucket Pequot tribe in Connecticut, who were considered the wealthiest tribe in the U.S. In fact, in 2005, Foxwoods was the largest casino resort in the world. Mashantucket Pequot Gaming Enterprises, Inc., the tribe's corporate entity, owns the casino, which is estimated to garner sales of roughly US$1 billion each year. By 2005, the tribe owned six casinos, three hotels, and 25 restaurants in Connecticut.

Gala Group Limited. In the United Kingdom, Gala means bingo. In 2005, the company was operating 166 bingo clubs across the country that were accommodating 33 million admissions each year. In addition to bingo, the company was also operating 32 casinos in the U.K., the Isle of Man and Gibraltar, as well as 93,000

gambling machines in multiple locations. Players must become members, and Gala boasted more than 5 million bingo members and 1.2 million casino members in 2004. Between 1998 and 2000, the company grew significantly through acquisitions, including Ritz Clubs (17 bingo clubs), Jarglen Clubs (10 bingo clubs), Riva Clubs (27 bingo clubs), and 27 Ladbrokes casinos from the Hilton Group. Revenues for the company during 2004 were almost US$960 million. The company sold its high-end casino, Maxim's, located in London, in early 2005.

Gala Group acquired Reuben Page Ltd. consisting of 44 betting shops. Other 2007 acquisitions included 23 betting shop outlets from C.L. Jennings Ltd., 24 outlets from Joe Jennings Ltd. and 30 outlets from Paul Dean Ltd.

With its announcement of 200 job losses in November 2008, it became apparent Gala Coral Group felt the necessity to cut back on business. A smoking ban was believed to be a contributing factor to decisions resulting in closing 13 bingo halls and four casinos plus eliminating Section 21 gaming machines. Plans were under consideration by the summer of 2009 to close six of 156 clubs and terminate 180 jobs. By 2011, an additional 40 to 50 clubs could potentially be sold.

PartyGaming Plc. Online gambling was growing rapidly. As a means to provide gambling globally and with most countries lacking any regulation for this sector of the industry, people from countries where gambling was illegal could participate. PartyGaming was operating the world's most successful online poker operation. Founded in 1997, the firm is based in Gibraltar, a British overseas self-governing territory and a tax haven. Its quartet of founders included Ruth Parasol, an operator of pornographic chat lines and web sites, and her husband, Russell DeLeon. Those founders together own more than half of PartyGaming. The company began its PartyPoker.com web site in 2001. In 2006, the company had revenues of about US$1,104 billion and 1,200 employees.

MAJOR COUNTRIES IN THE INDUSTRY

United Kingdom. The United Kingdom has the largest market for gambling in terms of annual revenues, with a strong national lottery. From 2002 to 2003, the amount staked on gambling totaled approximately US$113 billion, according to the Gaming Board for Great Britain. By March 2004, there were 131 casinos open in the country with 24 in London alone, the largest number held by a capital city anywhere in the world. Industry casino staff totaled about 13,000 and they handled about 11.9 million visits to casinos. At the same time, there were about 695 commercial bingo clubs, with about 18,500 employed to handle this sector's 3 million members. An additional 22,000 people found employment handling the 250,000 gaming machines operating at a variety of sites and establishments. Ticket sales for lottery sales were about US$225 million, which resulted in revenues of approximately US$115 million for various causes.

The United Kingdom's industry had suffered from inconsistent and out-of-date laws and regulations covering gambling. However, in April 2005, a new gambling act was established. As part of the act, a Gambling Commission, which was to be independent of the government, was to be set up beginning in the autumn of 2005. It will have the power to license gambling operators, while local authorities will license individual establishments. Under the new regulations, casinos can stay open 24 hours per day, there will not be a membership requirement, advertising will be allowed, age checks would be compulsory for gambling web sites operating from the United Kingdom, and it would become a criminal offence to encourage or cause a child to gamble.

Several U.K. bookmakers were successful in their efforts to obtain licenses in Italy after the liberalization of that country's large gambling industry. They included Ladbrokes and Gala Coral. which won 142 and 403 licenses respectively. As reported by John O'Doherty, these new licenses allow Ladbroke to open up 142 new outlets for horse-racing betting and general sports betting.

The United States. According to a 2003 survey conducted by Harrah's, 53.4 million Americans over the age of 21 had gambled at a casino. That was 26 percent of the adult population who made an average of 5.8 trips to a casino betting shop. It had reached US$72.87 billion in the United States in 2003, making the U.S. industry the world's second largest. Commercial casinos accounted for about 30 percent of the industry's revenues, while lotteries took 27 percent, casinos on Native American reservations 23 percent, pari-mutuels 5 percent, charitable games and bingo 3 percent, and card rooms and legal bookmaking took the remaining percent. The United States houses some of the biggest gambling and casino cities in the world with Las Vegas and Atlantic City.

Las Vegas controlled the largest share of the U.S. industry, accounting for 26 percent of the industry's revenues in 2003. Atlantic City ranked second with 15 percent of the revenues. Atlantic City's revenues grew at a faster rate than those of Las Vegas in the mid- to late 1990s, as the city vied with Las Vegas to be the country's leading gambling city. By 2003, Atlantic City hotels were maxing occupancy rates, with other establishments being planned and built. But as of the mid-years of the first decade of the 2000s, Las Vegas was still on top. It

had moved away from the lackluster family-oriented entertainment of roller coasters and amusement parks, and back to its once-again wildly successful gambling and casino roots. In addition to the steady stream of people relocating to the area, the city was the nation's biggest tourist draw in 2003, with a reported US$32.8 billion in revenue, $6.1 billion of which was related to the gaming industry that year.

Casinogamblingweb.com shared updates about Representative Barney Frank's efforts to promote changes related to the Unlawful Internet Gambling Enforcement Act. Substantial Support was provided by New York and California.

The struggling U.S. economy had a severe impact on one of the world's major vacation destinations. All along the Las Vegas Strip, casinos were experiencing profit losses. As a result, major corporations were changing how they do business. Modifications included reducing hotel room rates, discounting popular show tickets and issuing casino credits. Las Vegas Sands Chairman and CEO Sheldon Adelson revealed plans resulting in projected savings of US$500 million annually. Furthermore, in the *Daily Mail,* writer Sarah Gordon shared insights related to Adelson's reluctance "to make further cuts at the expense of morale among his employees."

Rick Alm, in a May 9, 2007, *Kansas City Star* article, reported that based on American Gaming Association data, "one in four U.S. adults visited a casino in 2006." This made commercial casino profits soar to a record US$32.4 billion. The list of U.S. gambling market leaders was led by Las Vegas, Atlantic City, and Chicago with profits of US$6.7 billion, US$5.2 billion and US$2.6 billion respectively. Commercial casinos employed approximately 366,197 people and contributed US$5.2 billion in gambling taxes to state and local governments.

France. Napoleon laid the foundation for the gambling industry in France in 1806, when he established state-controlled lotteries to raise tax revenues. Although France's casinos once emphasized elegant gambling facilities with upscale gaming, dining, and lodging services, in the late 1990s France began to model establishments on the style of Las Vegas casinos, catering to its largest customer segment: middle-aged suburban wives spending about US$16 a day on slot machines. Casinos are allowed to be set up in towns on the sea, and in 2004 there were about 182 such operations. In 2003, gaming was valued at about US$21 million in France.

There were two major players in the industry. Groupe Partouche SA held about 27 percent of the market through its operations of about 45 casinos in France. The company also had casinos in Switzerland, Morocco, Belgium, Spain, and Tunisia. In 2004, Partouche had revenues of about US$550 million. The other leader in the industry in France was SHCD, a company created in 2004 through the merger of casino assets held by the Barriere-Deseigne family, Accor Casinos, and Colony Capital of the U.S. After the merger, the group operated 37 casinos and had gross revenues of approximately US$1.1 billion.

Online gambling was very popular with the French. Nielsen/NetRatings announced that in February 2005, 22 percent of those who were online spent more than one hour gambling. That was estimated to be about three times the amount of time than that being spent by Britains. Interestingly, the laws in France only allowed for state-managed, land-based gambling. But in 2005, there were indications that France was going to legalize online gambling.

Canada. Canada's gambling industry also ranks among the world's leaders, as a multi-billion dollar industry that serves 45 million visitors a year. In 2005, a team of researchers working for the Law Commission of Canada valued the industry at about US$11 billion. About 59 percent of the country's population earning less than about US$16,600 dollars per year gambled in 2001, while of those earning more than about US66,000, 77 percent gambled. In 2001, it was estimated that the average household spent almost $215 per month on government lotteries alone.

In 2002, Statistics Canada figures showed that about 42,000 people were employed in the industry across the country, with 55 percent being women. To compare, non-gambling businesses averaged 46 percent women.

In May 2007, the Fair Air Association of Canada shared survey results for a study on the impact of banning smoking in 121 bingo halls owned by the Loto-Quebec network. Nearly half of the 85 bingo halls responding to the survey claimed they had a drop of 20 to 30 percent in the number of bingo players. The drop in attendance resulted in decreased income from 20 to 30 percent for 47 percent of the bingo sites. Consequentially, revenues were reduced from 30 to 50 percent.

South Africa. South Africa embraced the gambling industry in the mid-1990s, although the country allowed gambling under apartheid in the reservations for black South Africans. Casino operator Sun International built Sun City in Bophuthatswana during this period, and owned 17 casinos in South Africa before gambling was legalized throughout the country. The country's mid-1990s legislation paved the way for the licensing of 40 new casinos and a national lottery. Even though the majority of the country's citizens possessed very little disposable income, the South African government figured its rising number of tourists would patronize its casinos. For the year ended March 2005, gross gambling revenue for the country was approximately US$1.5 billion, with

casinos accounting for 83.8 percent, betting a further 15.6 percent, and bingo and other forms the remaining 0.6 percent.

China. Macau, the former Portuguese colony returned to Chinese rule in 1999, has developed a vibrant gaming industry. Revenues in the country's 17 casinos were valued at US$5 billion, making it almost equal to Las Vegas. Industry analysts projected that it would surpass Las Vegas in 2005. In 2002, the 40-year monopoly held by Sociedade de Turismo e Diversoes (STDM) was ended by the government, and three new gaming licenses were granted to Sociedade de Jogos de Macau (SJM), Galaxy Casino, and Wynn Resorts. SJM is the newly-formed subsidiary of STDM that holds the new 18-year gaming concession. In 2004, plans were announced for a joint venture casino held equally between SJM and MGM MIRAGE. Gambling remained illegal on mainland China, although it was a significant part of the culture. Most gamblers in Macau came from the mainland. Macau predicted that approximately 35 million visitors would come to the region by 2010.

Macau' success in the industry has prompted other Asian countries to follow into the gaming business. Singapore reversed its ban on casinos and gave permission for the building of two casino resorts. These were expected to be in place by 2009. The Philippines, Malaysia, South Korea, and Cambodia were also operating casinos, making the total value of the Asian market about US$20 billion. Japan and Thailand were expected to enter the industry by 2010.

In 2007, Ladbrokes announced that it had invested in a joint venture with Magainfo. Magainfo is a Hong Kong-based technology company. The main purpose of the joint venture was to develop products for the Chinese betting market.

On May 12, 2007, James Packer's Crown Macau casino opened. It was the first six-star casino to open in Macau. Serving as the casino empire's launching pad, it planned to target ultra-wealthy Chinese gamblers.

BIBLIOGRAPHY

Alm, Rick. "Casino Revenue a Record: The $32.4 Billion Generated in 2006 Was An Increase of 6.8% Over the Previous Year. *Kansas City Star,* 9 May 2007.

———. "Tribal Casinos Rake It In: The Growth in 2006 Gambling Revenues Outpaces Increase at Commercial Sites, With Bingo Leading the Gains in Oklahoma." *Kansas City Star,* 6 June 2007.

Berns, Dave. "Numbers Confirm 2001 Was Poor Year for State's Casinos." *Las Vegas Review-Journal,* 13 February 2002.

"Bet and Board in the New South Africa." *Economist,* 5 August 1995, 43.

"Bookie Beefs Up Benefits." *Employee Benefits,* 10 February 2006.

Brumback, Nancy. "Here She Is, Atlantic City." *Restaurant Business,* 1 October 2003.

Brumley Bryan. "Venetian Reveals Option to Back Out of Macau." The Associated Press, 13 March 2001.

Ceniceros, Roberto. "Casino Cameras Lower Odds on Fraud; Security Surveillance Network Also Effective in Combating Bogus Claims." *Business Insurance,* 30 April 2007.

"Conference Analysis." *High Yield Report,* 24 May 2004.

DeFoe, Jeannine. "Harrah's Shares Rise." *Bloomberg News,* 8 March 2002.

———. "MGM Mirage Ventures into Internet" *Bloomberg News,* 13 February 2001.

Eckl-Dorna, Wilfried. "A Jackpot or a Risky Bet?" *Fortune,* 26 July 2004.

"Eyes Down as Gala Coral Mulls Bingo Hall Closures." *Business Times,* 15 June 2009. Available from www.business.timesonline.co.uk.

"The French Out Bet the British in Online Gambling." *Casino City Times,* 20 April 2005. Available from www.casinocitytimes.com.

"Gala Coral Group Acquires 44 Shops From Reuben Page Ltd." Gala Coral, 8 June 2007. Available from www.galacoral.co.uk.

"Gambling: An Update." *The Daily,* 22 April 2003. Available from www.statcan.ca.

Gambling Cultures: Studies in History and Interpretation. New York: Routledge, 1996.

"Gambling Law Changes on the Way." *SAPA (South African Press Association),* 18 April 2002.

"Gaming Revenue." *American Gaming Association,* 2004. Available from www.americangaming.org.

Gordon, Sarah. "Las Vegas Hotels go Budget as Casinos Post Huge Losses." *The Daily Mail,* 31 July 2009. Available from www.dailymail.co.uk.

"Harrah's Survey '04 Election Year Edition: Profile of the American Casino Gambler." 2004. Available from www.harrahs.com.

"Hoover's Company Capsules." *Hoover's Online,* 2007. Available from www.hoovers.com.

"Hundreds March Against Harrah's Entertainment." Pressofatlanticcity, 30 July 2009. Available from www.pressofatlanticcity.com.

"In Brief: Ladbrokes Launches Grand National Game." *New Media Age,* 5 April 2007.

"Internet Gambling Estimates." 2004. Christiansen Capital Advisors, April 2005. Available from www.cca-i.com.

Knightly, Arnold M. "Atlantic City Weighs on Harrah's." *Las Vegas Review-Journal,* 9 May 2007.

"Ladbrokes Secures Two New Overseas Development Partners." *Leisure Report,* March 2007.

"Ladbrokes to Launch Fantasy Footie Website." *Precision Marketing,* 18 June 2004.

Lazich, Robert S., ed. *Market Share Reporter.* Detroit: Thomson Gale, 2004.

"Maintain a Poker Face as You Read This Item." *Adweek,* 19 April 2004.

"Major Crisis for Charity Organizations—A Year Into the Smoking Ban in Bingo Halls, Non-Profit Organizations (NPOs) Fear for Services to the Vulnerable and Needy." *CNW Group,* 30 May 2007.

"MGM MIRAGE Champions Diversity Evolution." *PR Newswire,* 24 May 2007.

Montlake, Simon. "Asia Lays Bet on Casino Gambling." *BBC News,* 20 April 2005. Available from news.bbc.co.uk.

Murdoch, Scott. "Packer's Macau Casino Chases Ultra-Rich." *Australasian Business Intelligence,* 13 May 2007.

"National Gambling Statistics: National Gambling Board, 2004/2005 Fiscal Year." 2005. Available from www.ngb.org.za.

Nguyen, Chris T. "Casinos Display Golden Touch." *Monterey County Herald,* 7 July 2004.

"NIGC: Tribal gaming revenues grew by 2.3 percent." Indianz.com, 3 June 2009. Available from www.indianz.com.

"Non-casino Firm Seen As Trump Buyer: Gaming Companies Could Be in the Running, But Private-Equity Suitors Were Seen As Having the Cash Needed to Play the Game." *Philadelphia Inquirer,* 19 May 2007.

O'Leary, Christopher. "US Company News." *High Yield Report,* 19 July 2004.

Palmeri, Christopher, and Laura Cohn. "Ready to Bet Big on Britain." *Business Week,* 23 February 2004.

"Park Place Move Awaited." *Leisure Report,* November 2003.

"Rep. Mattei From New York Joins Frank Online Gambling Bill." 1 August 2009. Available from www.casinogambling.com.

"Report of the Gaming Board for Great Britain 2003-04." Greyhound Board of Great Britain, 25 June 2004. Available from www.gbgb.org.uk.

Rosenthal, Franz. *Gambling in Islam.* Leiden: Brill, 1975.

"Rush of New Casinos Lifts Number of Visitors 19%; International Traveler." *International Herald Tribune,* 23 May 2007.

Savvass, Antony. "Ladbrokes Gears Up for e-Bet Spree." *Computer Weekly,* 25 May 2004.

Stein, Joel. "The Strip Is Back!" *Time,* 26 March 2004.

Stovall, Sam. "Lady Luck Smiles on Investors." *Business Week Online,* 23 June 2004. Available from www.businessweek.com.

"Update on the Macau Gaming Industry and the Opportunities for U.S. Companies to Supply Gaming-related Equipment and Services." Industry Canada, 1 March 2005. Available from www.strategis.ic.gc.ca.

"Vegas-Style Gambling Here." *Birmingham Post,* 27 March 2002.

"William Hill PLC." *AB UK,* June 2004.

Wong, Gillian. "Asia's Casino Business to Take Off Following Singapore Liberalization." Goldsea Asian American Daily, 22 June 2005. Available from www.goldsea.com.

SIC 7011

HOTELS AND OTHER LODGING PLACES

NAICS CODE(S)

721110. The hotel industry provides short-term lodging and related amenities to business and recreational travelers. Common formats include hotels, motels, and vacation resorts that integrate lodging with recreation. Many industry firms also host conferences and events.

INDUSTRY SNAPSHOT

Fear of having empty wallets and purses can result in less reservations and empty rooms. That is the reality many hotel operators were experiencing by the summer of 2009. As a result, there was an abundance of hotel deals available in travel hot spots. Writing for *The Baltimore Sun* on August 9, 2009, Tom Parsons revealed there were some exciting Orlando promotions offering "free consecutive nights" at family-free hotels. Parsons also pointed out some Las Vegas sites offered "free consecutive nights" plus show tickets and other amenities for a few dollars more than normal room rates.

The international lodging industry is a vital part of the travel and tourism trade and is one of the largest economic forces in the world. Accounting for 11 percent of the world's economic output and more than 250 million jobs, the hotel industry is the third-largest foreign currency earner.

The industry is dominated by hotel chains, especially in the United States and Europe, although Asia saw a supply increase of 10 percent in 2003, the largest rise worldwide. Most of the world's largest hotel chains are based in the United States. Attempting to expand their customer base, hotel chains, led by Holiday Inn, turned to segmentation. This approach involved offering various types of lodging facilities based on size, service, and space. Another trend was the adoption of computer technology. Although the hotel industry once failed to fully comprehend the benefits of computerized operations, in recent years hotel companies have turned to technology to standardize operations, communicate among properties and the home office, and create more efficient and cost-effective operations. Centralized reservation systems have become critical to any large lodging chain.

According to a 2004 MKG Consulting survey, the world's top ten hotel groups handled three-quarters of the global hotel market, which totaled approximately 4.6 million rooms. About 70 percent of these hotels were located in Europe and North America, according to the International Hotel Association.

The hotel industry continues to rely on both business and leisure travelers. Since the 1980s, business travel has been the leading money-maker for hotels, providing nearly two-thirds of all sales. The robust business segment of the industry also gave rise to extended-stay hotels in the late 1990s that specifically targeted business travelers. Nonetheless, leisure travel increased during this period as well. In part, this shift resulted from changing demographics, especially in the United States, and from rising disposable incomes around the world as part of the global economic recovery.

Each year, the hotel industry has increased its marketing dollars for campaigns to attract more business and leisure travelers. A PKF Hospitality Research study reported that there was an additional 6.1 percent in marketing spending in 2004. Nevertheless, travelers still left their destinations dissatisfied with the level of service received and their overall experience. It was a challenge for hospitality companies to get beyond creative campaigns and amazing promises to actually provide the quality of service that would generate return visits and positive word of mouth.

Hotel Interactive pointed out that, from a management perspective, resort hotels were a unique form of lodging. Their multiple offerings, such as several restaurants and shops, made them more complex to operate than typical hotels. They were also frequently established in remote locations. Consequently, there were often challenges for managers to overcome. Those potential challenges included supply deliveries, utilities, transportation, and weather. According to a PKF Hospitality Research study, room revenues at 53.7 percent comprised just over half of the total revenues at a sample size of 199 resorts averaging 366 rooms in 2005.

In March 2007, Lodging Econometrics, which describes itself as a "full service real estate firm emphasizing hotel brokerage, management and consulting," announced the compilation and publication of the first comprehensive "Lodging Development Pipeline" with forecast for new hotel openings through 2009 and beyond for every country in Europe. The resource reported that there were 513 construction projects being actively pursued by developers, including 93,669 rooms throughout Europe. Approximately 59 percent of the total, or 302 projects having 52,580 rooms, were already under construction. Another 74 projects with 13,380 rooms were scheduled to start construction in the next 12 months. An additional 137 projects with 26,989 rooms were in various stages of early planning.

According to provider of hotel Internet marketing services TravelCLICK's 2006 fourth quarter and consolidated full-year eTRAK results, the hotel industry maintains steady growth while consumers continue to shop for their hotels online and book electronically. The Internet was believed to have accounted for 38.3 percent of 2006 brand hotel bookings. That estimate reflected a 20.2 percent growth rate compared to 2005.

Like other countries throughout the world, the hotel industry in India was impacted by economic challenges. Unfortunately, the industry also felt adverse effects after November 2008 terrorist attacks on hotels. The number for foreign tourist arrivals did not see an increase until June 2009.

ORGANIZATION AND STRUCTURE

The major types of hotels found throughout the world are full-service, economy, resort, all-suites, conference center, and convention hotels. A full-service hotel generally provides a wide variety of facilities and amenities, such as food and beverage outlets, meeting rooms, and recreational activities. These types of hotels can be further classified as basic, upscale, or luxury. A basic property offers minimal expected services. Upscale hotels, such as the facilities operated by Hilton Hotels Corp. or ITT Sheraton Corp., have additional services and higher quality facilities, while luxury hotels, such as the Four Seasons and Ritz-Carlton, offer top-of-the-line service for a premium price.

Economy properties, such as Days Inn and La Quinta, provide comfortable rooms at low rates, but lack additional services. This type of hotel can be divided into two general groups: limited service and hard budget. Limited service hotels offer little or no food and beverage service and have marginal meeting facilities. Meanwhile, hard budget hotels, such as industry leader Motel 6, provide Spartan accommodations at inexpensive prices.

Although relatively new, all-suite facilities have continued to report high occupancy rates. With 20 percent more space than a conventional hotel room, a suite is separated into a living area and a bedroom. These hotels have targeted both business travelers and weekend vacationers. A second type of all-suite property is the growing category of extended- and long-stay properties. Catering to guests who stay five days or longer, the extended-stay suite provides a full kitchen. Many properties offer a fitness center, executive work area, and grocery shopping services as well. Resort hotels provide recreational facilities and entertainment and many are located in close proximity to established vacation spots.

Conference centers and convention hotels are often used by companies for specialized training classes. A conference center may offer a complete package of guest accommodations, meals, full-service meeting rooms and staff. Some conference centers are operated by major corporations, while others are part of universities or operated by private companies. Convention hotels serve large groups such as trade shows, corporate annual meetings and major conferences for organizations of all kinds including professional and volunteer groups. The properties provide facilities and services geared to meet the specialized needs of large groups. These hotels typically have hundreds of guest rooms and a substantial amount of flexible meeting space.

The hotel industry—especially in the United States—has experienced substantial structural changes as a result of hotel segmentation and the consolidation of companies. As the industry tries to anticipate customer needs—whether the customer is a business traveler or budget-minded vacationer—hoteliers have divided lodging facilities along the line of price, service, and space. With U.S. companies leading international expansion, the usage of segmentation has spread to areas outside North America.

Lodging companies have found that segmentation has added to their growth. Since hoteliers have had little control over increasing demand, they instead have expanded their customer base by providing all levels of lodging managed by one parent company. Segmentation also has allowed companies to leverage corporate resources such as management experience, access to capital markets, and back-office operations.

Participation in the Industry. Participation in the lodging industry has taken various forms. Companies may choose to own, manage, or franchise properties, and some combine all three. Franchising has been one of the most common ways for companies to expand internationally. Using a franchise agreement, the local hotel owner pays an initial fee and monthly royalty fees in exchange for the use of the chain name, logo, reservation system, and national advertising campaign. Franchised hotels can be found in nearly every country. Franchising has allowed companies to maintain their basic brand images while offering lodging services that fit the specific needs and desires of the local company.

Strategic alliances in the hospitality industry are a type of joint venture intended for a specific geographic region. For example, when Radisson Hotels International became interested in moving into international markets, the company allied itself with Mövenpick in Switzerland and Germany and opened a series of Mövenpick-Radisson hotels. In a strategic alliance, each partner brings its strongest assets to the venture. Usually, the U.S. partner will offer an internationally recognized brand name, a technologically advanced reservation system, and management expertise. The local partner contributes an understanding of local operations and labor, and authority to negotiate contracts with government suppliers.

International Investment in the United States. International hotel owners and operators have expanded into the United States through direct investment in well-known U.S. hotels. This investment and acquisition strategy is used because the U.S. lodging industry is an extremely competitive market already full of well-established and commonly known brand-name hotels. Given this level of development, a substantial investment would be necessary for a new company to successfully enter the U.S. market with a new product line. One example of such foreign investment was the 1990 acquisition of Motel 6 by the French firm Accor SA.

BACKGROUND AND DEVELOPMENT

Until the development of commerce and the standardization of a compact medium of financial exchange, the hotel remained a scant one-room inn, nothing more than an extra room sold to an infrequent traveler. By the present era, the advent of money suddenly expanded the trading radius of the ancient world and brought about significant growth of travel.

The Industrial Revolution (1760–1840) spurred the creation of the English inn. Located along coach trails, inns provided modest accommodations and food for stagecoach passengers. As roadways were built into the countryside, the famed English cottage was established. The first U.S. hotels were similar to their English counterparts and could be found on stagecoach trails and in seaport towns. These included inns of approved London style and were residences, some with additions built on. At their best, they were like an average well-kept home, but not much bigger.

As the United States expanded westward, the railroad created new population centers and new hotels, grand in size and service. When stock companies began to finance hotel construction, the industry moved from a small-time operation to big business, similar to the development of the railroads and industrial plants.

The first of the large-scale hotels built by a stock company was the City Hotel of New York, which was established in 1794. Compared to a colonial inn, this 73-room facility was enormous. During the years prior to the Civil War, U.S. hotels were built in established cities and boom towns. Some of these facilities were both elegant and expensive. Those who could not afford such extravagance were left to rooming houses, but scores of people were drawn to these first-class establishments. Some even took up residence in these facilities. Public areas of hotels—such as the lobby and the bar room—became popular social settings and meeting places. The hotel also was host to numerous balls and banquets and became a focal point for political and business activities.

The 1920s brought a boom in hotel construction in the United States. With occupancy rates reaching 85 percent in 1920, companies expanded properties and constructed hundreds of new and larger facilities. The industry came to a screeching halt with the onset of the Great Depression. In the 1930s nearly 80 percent of all hotel companies were forced into foreclosure or receivership. With all travel stymied, the average hotel occupancy rate hovered at 50 percent. While it forced many hoteliers out of business, the Depression gave some lucky buyers new properties at rock-bottom prices. It was during this time that the future industry giants ITT Sheraton Corp. and Hilton Hotels Corp. first purchased many of their hotels.

The onset of World War II revived the U.S. hotel industry as the national occupancy rate soared to nearly 90 percent. Although most cities needed additional lodging facilities, few were built because financing, materials, and labor were diverted to the war effort.

The motel, or motor hotel, developed as a direct result of the explosive growth of the auto industry and the expansion of highway systems following the war. The first motels were simple, single-story structures, usually with 20 rooms or less. Located on inexpensive land on the edge of town, motels usually were managed by resident owners and had few paid employees.

During the 1950s, the motel business was still in its infancy and had few industry standards. Lacking brand identity, patrons had no guide to judge the quality, comfort, and price of motels. Travelers often examined the accommodations prior to payment (a custom still practiced in Europe). But the motel market changed dramatically at the hands of Tennessee resident Kemmon Wilson.

Wilson, already a successful Memphis home builder, became irritated with the inconsistent quality and fluctuating prices of lodging accommodations during the course of a family vacation. Wilson decided that with the growing love of the automobile and the open road, the U.S. family needed and would welcome inexpensive, efficient motels. By the time he returned from his vacation, Wilson had calculated the minimum size of a hotel room and called a friend who was a draftsman to work the dimensions into a hotel. The first Holiday Inn—named after a Bing Crosby feature film of the same name—was thus built in Memphis in August 1952. It included a restaurant, a gift shop, and a swimming pool. In addition, each room was equipped with an air conditioner and a television. When Wilson wanted to expand his operations, the first efforts involved contacting fellow home builders. When only three decided to join him in the hotel business, Wilson turned to franchising the product. The facilities were an instant hit and in five years Holiday Inn became a public company.

Accor founders Gerard Pelisson and Paul Dubrule had similar ideas in France. In 1967, they decided to build moderately priced U.S.-style hotels along the highway. The first to break into this market in Europe, Pelisson and Dubrule met with immediate success, and by 1973 they formed Sphere SA, a holding company for a new hotel chain called Ibis. Accor was also the first to tap into the European hotel market of budget-conscious consumers.

Since the 1950s the hotel industry, led by the United States, has experienced cycles of growth and decline, and each upturn has brought a new type of hotel into the market. The budget motel arrived in the late 1960s and flourished during the boom of the early 1970s. These properties offered accommodations at prices substantially lower than the established rates of existing full-service motels. Companies also began to expand their chains through franchising during this time, following the example first set by Holiday Inn.

The combination of readily available financing and aggressive companies selling franchises led to an influx of hotels managed by inexperienced owners and situated in poor locations. Combined with inflation, rising construction costs and interest rates, and the energy crisis, the hotel industry fell again in the late 1970s until all-suite hotels arrived in the 1980s with new construction.

In the late 1990s, the industry's assets, principally in the form of land, buildings, and furnishings, amounted to around US$170 trillion. Until the economy slowdown in 2000-2001 and the September 11 attacks, the global industry's sales in the mid- to late 1990s indicated its full recovery from the recession that hampered the world market in the early 1990s during the Iraq crisis. During the mid- to late 1990s, occupancy levels and revenues reached record highs throughout the world, particularly in Europe and the United States.

After the global recession in the early 1990s, many countries recovered in the mid-1990s and continued to prosper going into the late 1990s. The economic turnaround, the emergence of new markets, and the balancing of hotel supply and demand all played a decisive role in the industry's success in the mid- to late 1990s. During this period, hotels around the world reported record revenues and occupancy rates. The United States, for example, saw its hotel industry revenues grow by 4 percent from 1995 to 1996, reaching a record US$75.4 billion, according to the American Hotel and Motel Association. Furthermore, occupancy levels soared in Europe with London reporting more than 85 percent, Rome 83 percent, Zurich 79 percent, Amsterdam 78 percent, and Edinburgh 76 percent. Simultaneously, the Middle East experienced the most significant increase in visitor arrivals worldwide. With ongoing peace talks between countries in the region, a number of new hotels cropped up, especially in Jordan, where the price of hotel rooms rose by 11.5 percent in 1996.

The hotel industry consolidated in the mid- to late 1990s. In the first half of 1997 alone, the United States reported mergers and acquisitions worth US$4.1 billion, twice as much as reported in the first half of 1996. Marriott International made one of the largest acquisitions, purchasing Renaissance Hotel and its holdings such as Renaissance and Ramada International for US$1 billion. Extended Stay America also bought Studio Plus hotels for US$290 million.

Large hotel chains, especially those in the United States, began seeking new markets in the late 1990s as their domestic markets verged on saturation. Companies such as Sheraton relied on their brand names to fuel their international expansions, setting up hotels in large cities and branching out into smaller cities after successfully establishing themselves. Smaller operations opted to place their hotels in strategic locations after careful planning to ensure sufficient demand. In the late 1990s, the top five international emerging hotel markets included Chile, Cuba, India, Poland, and Saudi Arabia, according to *Hotel & Motel Management.*

In Asia, Japan's domestic hotel operations continued to lose the struggle against foreign-owned chains such as Park Hyatt Tokyo, Westin Tokyo, and Four Seasons Hotel Tokyo. Both domestic and international customers prefer these hotels to Japan's domestic hotels, according to a *Nikkei Weekly* report. Additional hoteliers, including Ritz-Carlton Hotel, planned to tap into Japan's market in the late 1990s and early years of the first decade of the 2000s.

Though luxury hotels led the industry in Asia in the 1980s, moderate-priced hotels forged ahead of them in the 1990s. Heightened travel between Asian countries by middle-income travelers sparked demand for these hotels, according to *Lodging Hospitality.* Despite the success of mid-priced hotels, luxury hotels flourished in Indonesia and the Philippines by combining social and business functions with lodging services.

China's hoteliers, however, concentrated on expanding their business accommodations by developing business suites. South Korea's hotel industry confronted serious challenges in the late 1990s. The country's devalued currency, which reduced domestic purchasing power, coupled impeded investment and new hotel construction, even though the country has a paucity of hotel rooms. Korea has only 118 hotel rooms per 10,000 tourist arrivals, in contrast to the United States, which boasts of 683 rooms per 10,000 arrivals. Nonetheless, South Korea experienced increased growth in its tourist traffic, which circulated about US$5.6 billion through the country's economy.

Throughout Asia, hotels witnessed the improvement of infrastructure, the growth of new business opportunities, and the possibility of international expansion. Nonetheless, because some markets neared saturation points and faced labor problems, the trade journal *Hotels* predicted accelerated consolidation would take place in these areas. The number of resorts and conference centers in Asia was forecast to grow from the late 1990s through 2010.

The health of the international hotel industry continues to depend largely on the strength and stability of national economies, as the number of travelers, whether business or pleasure, increases with economic growth and prosperity, as well as a perception that travel is safe. In 2001, deflated by a recession that had started the previous year, the industry was hit with the slowdown in bookings attributed to the terrorist attacks of September 11, 2001, against the United States, leading to a significant stoppage in the worldwide building of new hotels, according to the *Financial Times.* The attacks were blamed for the loss of up to 500,000 jobs worldwide, some of which were regained as bookings for some hotels began to return to normal demand levels, according to industry analyst Plasencia Group Inc. Significantly, the slowest chains to recover have been the luxury hotels such as Four Seasons and the resorts run by Club Med. Industry analyst firm PwC expected a 59.4 percent hotel occupancy rate in the United States in December 2002, compared to 60.3 percent in 2001 and 63.7 per cent in 2000.

Hotel industry sales grew to approximately US$295 billion in 1999, a significant increase from 1996 figures of US$250 billion. The world hotel industry recorded a strong growth rate in the late 1990s through 2000 as well. However, the terrorist attacks on September 11, 2001, coupled with an existing downturn in U.S. travel because of recessionary economic conditions, left the industry reeling and undercut normal profits. The hardest hit U.S. cities were Boston, Seattle, and San Francisco, the latter of which saw its room occupancy rates drop 24 percent in one year, according to the *Financial Times.*

CURRENT CONDITIONS

Quick to rebound was New York City, where room occupancy rates returned to 69 percent as of December 2001, compared to 77 percent in December 2000, according to the *Financial Times.* However, various acts of terrorism around the globe continued to cause the industry to hold its collective breath, since a single incident such as planes crashing into the World Trade Center has had a corrosive effect on tourism. As of February 2002, Smith Travel Research, the industry's data tracking company, reported that U.S. hotel occupancy rates were 45.4 percent, down from 48.3 percent the previous year.

After three bad years, beginning with the 2000 economic downturn and solidified by the 2001 terrorist attacks, the hotel industry was set for an upswing in 2004 and 2005. Around the world, occupancy rates increased. According to Deloitte Touche Tohmatsu, increases for the year ended January 2005 were 6.9 percent in the Asia/Pacific region, 10.5 percent in Central and South America, 6.7 percent in the Middle East

and Africa, 3.5 percent in North America, and 3.2 percent in Europe. Revenues per available room were also up significantly: 19.1 percent in Asia/Pacific, 25.8 percent in Central and South America, 29.4 percent in the Middle East and Africa, 8 percent in North America, and 11.6 percent in Europe. Several cities around the world showed signs of a remarkable upswing. Beijing, recovering from the effect of the SARS virus, had an increase in occupancy exceeding 33 percent. Hong Kong and Singapore also showed increases of more than 18 percent. However, areas in Asia affected by the tsunami of December 2004 were seeing few tourists by June 2005.

The extended-stay segment of the industry continued expanding to meet the needs of the influx of business travelers. Extended-stay hotels cater to businesses by offering rates and amenities targeted to meet corporate budgets and needs. According to *Market Share Reporter,* the extended-stay segment of the market was projected to rise to 294,361 rooms in 2007 from 2002's count of 229,852.

Faced with external and internal challenges, Marriott reported that its profits dropped 76 percent in 2009 and remained cautious about future projections. The greatest related factors were cited as being "weaker travel demand and the restructuring" of Marriott. Restructuring costs were largely attributed to severance costs and exit costs related to timeshares.

RESEARCH AND TECHNOLOGY

With a growing global market and increased customer needs, communication between individual hotels, the corporate office, travel agencies, and airlines became necessary. The computer remains one of the most important operational tools in the hotel industry, improving both efficiencies and guest services. Most hotels have automated front-office functions such as reservations, and many have considered adding applications like yield management (maximizing occupancy or revenues at any given time) and integrating their point-of-sale and restaurant computer systems. In addition, hotels have begun using the Internet to market their services and to allow customers to make reservations and obtain information.

Technological growth has been especially evident in the area of reservation systems, the backbone of any international lodging operation. The development of worldwide central reservations systems (CRS) has created a global network in which a guest can make a reservation for a hotel room from anywhere in the world. In addition, such a system can be used for targeted marketing and yield management, the science of last-room availability. Hotels can instantly access guests' history and preferences to efficiently accommodate them. The key to success, however, has been to link hotel systems with airline systems. Because of this connection, some industry observers contend that independent properties without access to a global reservations system will be seriously threatened by chain operators.

Technological advances have also been used to increase security at hotel facilities around the world. Of all the new security devices available, the card key locking system has become the most commonly used product in all segments of the hotel industry. Continued advances in card technology have led to the creation of the smart card, a credit card with a computer chip that contains information such as a traveler's personal data, medical history, and credit card numbers. Proponents argue that at some point in the future these cards may be used for transactions with a wide range of institutions associated with the travel industry, including airlines, hotels, and car rental agencies. Although relatively new, the smart card has already been used in Europe. Other security methodologies under examination by the hotel industry center around biometrics, the technology of recognizing a person by some physical characteristic, such as a fingerprint. This type of security device already has been used in some controlled areas of hotels, especially in casinos, but remains quite expensive to implement.

Launched in 2003, Marriott's "At Your Service" system was designed to keep track of a guest's preferences, from room service food to the type of in-room amenities to room location. As of late spring 2004, the service only worked within stays at the same property, but Marriott planned to have such guest preference information accessible by the staff at any Marriott location.

WORKFORCE

The hotel industry ranks among the world's largest employers, accounting for 11 million jobs worldwide or 5 percent of the world's travel and tourism workforce. North and South America represent about 40 percent of these workers, with 4 million. In Europe the figure has jumped as high as 1 in 10 tourism jobs. Industry employment was expected to nearly triple from 1990 to 2005, according to the Brussels-based World Travel and Tourism Council, an outlook that makes travel and tourism and the affiliated hotel industry among the most promising of international job markets.

When the question was "How Long is the Road?" there were some interesting answers about the journey from bellboy to general manager. The question was posed and answers analyzed by 4hoteliers.com. Data reflected insights gained from 60 people working in numerous countries with distinctive backgrounds. It takes only 14.75 years, on average, in North America for the shortest length of time. At the other end of the

spectrum, Asia had an average of 16.5 years. The area of specialization had an impact on how fast employees moved from entry level to the executive suite. It took the shortest time (14.8 years) for people who started as management trainees. The second shortest time (15.3 years) was for people who came through the rooms division. Survey findings reflected that a clear majority of general managers started their careers in the food and beverage division. Throughout the world, general managers tended to earn respect. They frequently moved on to other important roles such as CEOs and COOs.

According to Bill Marriott, immigration laws could have a tremendous impact on hotel jobs. If laws were passed to deport illegal immigrants, there would be problems finding people to replace them. Marriott predicted that inflation would result from related efforts.

Some analysts have predicted future jobs in the hotel industry will be concentrated in low-level service areas since management has continued to remain lean. Opportunities for employment in the hotel industry in Europe remained more promising than in the United States and some other regions. Because of a relatively small number of people in the 16-to-24-year-old bracket, traditionally a leading source of entry-level service workers, the United States faced a shortage of hotel employees during the late 1990s. "We've tapped virtually all the available resources," John Gay of the American Hotel & Lodging Association admitted to *RCI Timeshare Business* magazine. "The only answer is foreign workers." According to the Hotel & Restaurant Employees International Union, about 18 percent of some 17.7 million employees working in the United States in 2001 were foreign nationals in the hospitality industry, many of whom were hired through broker services abroad that assist with travel, proper documentation, and other necessary paperwork.

INDUSTRY LEADERS

InterContinental Hotels Group PLC (formerly Six Continents, formerly Bass Hotels & Resorts). The world's largest hotel company with approximately 556,000 rooms, Intercontinental Hotels is also the most global, operating in almost 100 countries. Intercontinental is the owner of such well-known brands as Holiday Inn, Crowne Plaza Hotels & Resorts, and Intercontinental, running more than 3,600 leased, managed, owned and franchised properties. About 1,500 limited-service locations operate as part of the Holiday Inn Express brand. In 2005, the company reported revenues of US$3.29 billion, and employed 21,986 people.

In 2007, building on its distinction as the "Official Hotel of Major League Baseball," Holiday Inn announced confirming National Baseball Hall of Famer Cal Ripken, Jr., to participate in the brand's successful

"Look Again" integrated marketing campaign. A Scarborough Research national study found that more than 6 in 10 Holiday Inn guests (approximately 13.5 million guests) are self-identified Major League baseball fans. In addition, those fans who go to games comprised approximately one quarter or 24 percent of Holiday Inn guests and accounted for more traffic to the chain's hotels than attendees of any other sport. Ripken joins the roster of professional athletes, including NASCAR drivers Jeff Burton and Scott Wimmer, championing the Holiday Inn brand. The "Look Again" campaign takes a humorous look at life on the road for today's business travelers. The primary target of the campaign is what has been identified as the "modern everyday hero," a blended attitudinal segment that spans Generation X and Baby Boomers.

The launching of IHG Agency Awards was another exciting 2007 InterContinental Hotels Group announcement. The purpose of this new awards program was to recognize teams and individuals known to provide the hotel industry with the highest levels of value, innovation, and support throughout the past year. Award categories included Agency Account Manager/Director of the Year, Conference and Incentive Agency of the Year, Agency Booking Team of the Year, and overall Agency of the Year. Winners' prizes included a brand new Vauxhall car and a luxury vacation at the InterContinental Carlton Cannes. Holiday Inn had maintained a two-year sponsorship of the Vauxhall's VX Racing Team in the British Touring Car Championship.

Tracing its roots back to an English brewery company started in 1777 that purchased a small chain of hotels in 1987, the company's real growth in the industry came with its purchase of Holiday Inn International in 1988 and the remainder of the North American business in 1990. During the late 1990s and through 2002, its Holiday Inn chain was the single largest hotel brand in the world. With Holiday Inn worldwide headquarters based in Atlanta, Georgia, approximately 83 percent of the company's hotels were located in the United States. The Holiday Inn chain began with the creation of a single hotel in 1952. Crowne Plaza hotels were launched in 1994, aimed at an upscale market. Mid-scale hotels were sold off in 1997, but the company maintained its brands through franchising agreements. Pan Am Airlines founded Intercontinental Hotels in 1946. The hotel chain acquired the company in 1998. South Pacific Hotels was acquired in 2000, strengthening the firm's position in Southeast Asia. That same year, the company sold off its brewery business to focus on the hospitality trade, changing the name of Bass Hotels & Resorts (BHR) to Six Continents Hotels in 2001 to reflect the corporation's growing worldwide presence. The company continued to expand globally. In 2001 it acquired the

U.K. chain Posthouse and the Intercontinental Hotel in Hong Kong. Further brands were added in the middle of the decade: Candlewood Suites and Staybridge Suites, extended-stay hotels mostly in the United States, and Hotel Indigo.

Cendant Corporation (formerly Hospitality Franchise Systems Inc.). A giant in the real estate brokerage business through its ownership of the Century 21 and Coldwell Banker brands, as well as being the world's largest car renter with its Avis and Budget brands, Cendant was also the second largest hotel franchisor by the end of 2004. It had 520,860 rooms across 6,396 properties. In addition, the company had the lion's share of timeshare condominiums.

Revenues for the entire company were US$19.79 billion in 2004, of which 15 percent was related to the company's hospitality services division. About 2 percent of total revenue was from the lodging franchise business, with Cendant operating eight brands in this sector: Wingate Inn (138 properties; 12,934 rooms); Ramada (1,005 properties; 119,991 rooms); Howard Johnson (466; 44,923); AmeriHost (107; 7,451); Days Inn (1,872; 153,701); Travelodge (527; 40,476); Super 8 Motel (2,076; 125,844); and Knights Inn (205; 15,540). In 2004, the company issued master franchises in China and Russia.

From the timeshare sector was 3 percent of Cendant's total revenues in 2004. The company's One Resort Condominiums International subsidiary provided more than 3 million subscribers with access to more than 3,900 resorts in 100 countries. In 2004, 10 timeshare resorts were added in China. Vacation rental properties accounted for a further 1 percent of revenues. Providing global marketing services to approximately 42,000 independent owners of villas, cottages, bungalows, apartments, and caravans in vacation parks, this business sector was active in 22 countries.

Hilton Hotels. With one of the most recognizable names in the hotel industry, Hilton Hotels Corporation operates primarily in the United States, where its Waldorf Astoria Hotel in New York is world famous. United Kingdom-based Hilton Group plc owns the rights to the Hilton name outside of the United States. The two companies operate under a strategic alliance whereby they share sales and marketing functions, loyalty programs, and a central reservation system. In 2004, the U.S.-based group posted revenues of US$3.68 billion and employed 70,000 people, while the U.K.-based group reported revenues of approximately US$5 billion from its hotel division.

Together, the two companies provided customers with a choice of 2,800 hotels and 490,000 rooms in 80 countries in 2006, operating under the Hilton, Hampton

Inn, Homewood Suites, and Scandic brands. The U.S.-based group was also operating Hilton Grand Vacation Club, a vacation ownership business. Other affiliated brands included Doubletree and Embassy Suites Hotels. The companies had a team of about 150,000 members worldwide. In October 2004, terrorists bombed the Taba Hilton in Egypt near the Israeli border killing 31 members of the staff and guests.

The company's Conrad brand was named in honor of its founder, Conrad N. Hilton. In 2006, that brand included 19 world-class luxury hotels or resorts. They operated in the United States, England, Ireland, Belgium, Egypt, Turkey, Indonesia, Hong Kong, Singapore, Thailand, Australia and Uruguay. Plans for new Conrad Hotels, both in major U.S. cities and resort destinations around the world, are in various stages of development.

In January 2006, Hilton announced plans to introduce a new luxury hotel line called "The Waldorf-Astoria Collection." The collection was launched with its world-renowned hotel and three world-class luxury resorts that will be newly managed by Hilton. Those three properties were Grand Wailea Resort Hotel & Spa on the island of Maui in Hawaii, the Arizona Biltmore Resort and Spa in Phoenix, and La Quinta Resort in California. Criteria for the exclusive designation will include architectural significance, unique decorative items and original artwork, historic or landmark status, and a reputation for product and service excellence.

In September 2006 Hilton announced it had become "founding corporate partner" of the Hispanic Hotel Owners Association (HHOA). Hilton received the exclusive sponsorship designation by providing initial funds required for the association's formation and preliminary development. The formation of HHOA was a direct result of Hilton's minority franchise development outreach "Hospitality 101" seminar. This seminar was piloted by Hilton and has become a "best practice" in minority franchise development outreach across the industry. It focuses on teaching minority entrepreneurs the basics of hotel development. In addition to HHOA, Hilton enthusiastically continues to support the National Black Hotel Owners and Developers and the Asian American Hotel Owners Association.

In August 2009 Blackstone Group was considering plans for potentially breaking up its Hilton Hotels. The private equity firm purchased Hilton for US$26 billion in 2007. Possible related actions included selling some of its properties to competitors.

Marriott International Inc. What started in 1927 as a root beer stand in Washington, D.C., turned into a chain of 2,800 lodging properties across the United States and 67 other countries by 2007. By the end of 2006, it had approximately 151,000 employees. Marriott

thrived by operating utilizing many different brands, several of which incorporate the Marriott name in them. However, one of its most famous brand names stands alone: The Ritz-Carlton, with luxury hotels and resorts around the world. In October 1993 Marriott Corp. was divided into two companies: Host Marriott Corporation, which owns real estate and operates airport concessions; and Marriott International, the lodging business. By 2004 Marriott had about 255,000 rooms, with revenues of more than US$10 billion. In 2004, Marriott controlled 17 percent of all branded full-service hotel rooms in the United States. In fiscal year 2006, Marriott International reported sales from continuing operations of US$12.2 billion.

While other hoteliers have moved into the gaming industry, Maryland and Washington, D.C.-based Marriott has focused on continued segmentation and international expansion. Its product line includes Marriott, JW Marriott, The Ritz-Carlton, Renaissance, Residence Inn, Courtyard, TownePlace Suites, Fairfield Inn, SpringHill Suites, Bulgari, Ramada International Marriott Ownership Resorts (vacation time-sharing), and Marriott Golf, which operates golf facilities. By converting existing properties and developing new hotels, Marriott's international expansion has included the establishment of full-service properties in the Pacific Rim, Europe, Latin America, and the Caribbean.

Marriott International is also a 2006 U.S. Environmental Protection Agency Energy Star Partner. Further evidence of environmental consciousness was found in its long-term strategic plans. In March 2007, the company reported being on track to reduce its greenhouse gas emissions by nearly one-fifth during the 10-year period from 2000 to 2010. This industry-leading effort is part of a comprehensive effort to reduce Marriott's environmental footprint and save energy costs. In April 2007 all of its 2,800 hotels helped to celebrate Environmental Awareness Month. The company planned to launch a pilot program at 30 hotels to measure, standardize, and expand recycling company-wide. It was estimated that more than 96 percent of Marriott hotels around the world actively recycle. Each hotel in the Marriott system has a designated energy and environmental ambassador who helps the property maintain standards and finds new ways to improve the environment.

According to *DiversityInc* magazine, for the fourth consecutive year, Marriott was ranked among the "Top 50 Companies for Diversity" as the highest in the lodging industry. Marriott also placed number four in the "Top 10 Companies for People with Disabilities" category. A total of 317 companies completed the survey. Additional noteworthy recognition in 2007 included several special distinctions for the company. They included being named as one of the "Top 10 Companies for Executive Women" by the National Association for Female Executives, "Top 50 Corporations for Supplier Diversity" by *Hispanic Trends* magazine, and "Top 50 Places to Work" for African-American women by *Essence* magazine.

PFK Hospitality Research discovered that the Caribbean hotel industry was experiencing trouble in paradise. Market conditions earned low ratings and were expected to continue their strong impact on profit declines through 2010. The tracking period was 2007-2008 for the 2009 edition of Caribbean Trends in the Hotel Industry. It was a common response for managers to focus on implementing more cost reductions. Going green was a practical, money-saving alternative due to higher utility and insurance costs for Caribbean hotel properties compared to their U.S. counterparts.

Accor. Paris-based Accor SA is the largest European hotel operator and among the top five in the world. Accor has a presence in nearly every international hotel market, operating 4,000 hotels with more than 475,000 rooms in 100 countries by 2007. The company owns hotels in all price ranges, but the majority of its holdings include moderate and low-price hotels. Brand names include Novotel, Sofitel, Mercure, Ibis, Red Roof Inn, Motel Six, Motel Formula 1, Suitehotel, and Etap Hotel. Accor employed 160,000 workers in 2007.

Accor offers valued services to corporate clients and public institutions. An estimated 21 million people in 35 countries benefit from Accor Services products including meal and food vouchers, people care plus incentive and loyalty programs.

Opening its first Novotel hotel in Lisse, France in 1967, Accor was soon one of the first lodging companies to have segmented service. Although Accor owned about 50 percent of its hotels in the late 1990s, in order to maintain tight control on its operations, by 2005 it owned 21 percent of its properties, franchised or managed another 37 percent, and leased space at the remaining 42 percent. In June 2005, the company added its 4,000th hotel with the addition of a Novotel in Madrid, Spain.

In keeping with its global development strategy aimed at opening 200,000 new hotel rooms by 2010, of which 60 percent would be in emerging markets, Accor signed into partnerships that promote major expansion in India. This expansion plan covered the full spectrum of India's hotel market. It included budget Formule 1 hotels, economy Ibis hotels, mid-market Novotel hotels, and upper-upscale Sofitel properties. In addition, Accor is discussing opportunities with leading Indian business groups for a variety of developments including the launch of the Mercure brand in India. Accor is present in India through its Services business.

Accor Services is a global leader in the field of employee benefit, incentive, and loyalty programs. It opened its Indian subsidiary in 1997 and introduced two of its major products: Ticket Restaurant meal vouchers and Ticket Compliments gift vouchers, used by more than 180,000 Indian company employees.

Club Meditérranée SA is most commonly known to many as Club Med. This French company pioneered the all-inclusive resort, featuring deluxe accommodations and a full schedule of sports, entertainment, and activities for guests. The club gained a reputation among North Americans as a young singles resort, but by 2002 analysts said the old formula of games and communal meals at high prices was a turnoff to vacationers. As a result, the company vowed to make significant changes in approach and in marketing. Nearly 60 percent of its visitors came from Europe. The company has tried to enlarge its markets to include couples, families with children, and business meeting attendees. After two years of losses, Club Med reported sales of about US$1.9 billion for 2004. That year, Accor became the company's primary shareholder, jumping out of its main corporate concerns to expand in the leisure/pleasure hotel market. In 2005, sales were again reported as being about US$1.9 billion.

MAJOR COUNTRIES IN THE INDUSTRY

United States. The United States remains the hotel industry's international giant, routinely posting the highest amount of international tourism revenue. Tourism was the country's third-largest industry, behind automotive and food stores. However, although valued at US$70.4 billion by Euromonitor in 2003, growth in the hotel industry had been flat, posting only a 0.5 percent increase over the previous year. Pre-tax profits for the industry were US$12.8 billion, according to research done by Smith Travel Research. To compare, in 1999 the industry had pulled in US$22.0 billion in pretax profits, according to the American Hotel & Motel Association (AH&MA). But in 2003, the industry was still feeling the effects caused by the September 11th terrorist attacks. The small hotel sector (fewer than 75 rooms) did grow by more than 10 percent between 2002 and 2003. By 2008, the entire spectrum of hotel sizes was expected to grow by 21 percent, but almost three quarters of the revenue was to come from the small hotel sector.

Leading destinations in the United States included Florida, Southern California, and New York. Top U.S. markets for hotel expansion in recent years have included Las Vegas, Nevada; Orlando, Florida; and San Antonio, Texas. Hotel developers also have watched the surge in legalized gambling in the United States with great interest, a development that could benefit the hotel industry tremendously. In the early years of the first decade of the 2000s, the average room rate stood at US$85.00, a fairly hefty increase from 1996 when the average room rate was US$69.66, according to Smith Travel Research. However, by 2004 this had declined to US$82.52. Of the total number of U.S. hotel guests, vacationers account for 23 percent, business travelers for 30 percent, conference and meeting attendees for 26 percent, and other travelers for the remaining 20 percent.

Hotels in New Orleans struggled to rebuild after the devastating impact of Hurricane Katrina. Some of the damage they incurred included shattered windows and flooding. Many of the hotels, however, reopened by year-end 2005. Hotel supply continues to increase due to completion of renovations of damaged rooms. Many of the demand generators lagged behind, such as completion of renovations on tourist attractions. Thus, the tourist crowds and major conventions were not returning to New Orleans quickly. By 2009 the forecast looked a lot more positive and area industry leaders predicted a long lasting turnaround.

Beth Kormanik, editor of the Hotel Interactive Web site's online publication, the Daily E-News, shared insights in an August 5, 2009, article about a mutually beneficial partnership between a long-established convention center and new hotel. The Earle Brown Heritage Center has an interesting legacy back to 1929. Its namesake was a sheriff and Minnesota Highway Patrol Founder. Brown originally built the home and farm that evolved into the full-service conference site featuring 10 interconnected barns. Approximately 500 events and 160,000 people visit the center annually. On April 25, 2009, Embassy Suites Minneapolis-Brooklyn Center opened its doors. It was a much needed hotel venue companion that will ultimately have an enclosed connecting walkway. Nestled in a prime North Minneapolis suburban community, the hotel helped provide convention participants and other travelers with a viable alternative to accommodations downtown.

France. Hotel industry giant Accor makes its home base in France, but small, independent hotels account for about 50 percent of its market value. France's hotel and lodging industry was valued by Euromonitor at about US$17.6 billion in 2003, and was expected to rapidly increase by more than 17 percent. After Accor, three other companies hold small, but significant market shares: Best Western International, Intercontinental Hotels, and Group Taittinger. In 2005, Paris was vying to be the host city for the Olympic Games in 2012, viewed to potentially benefit many hoteliers in the city.

Morgan Stanley, the Wall Street firm that owns in excess of 80 hotels worldwide, announced plans to purchase two hotels in France in 2007. One hotel was

identified as the Hilton Charles de Gaulle near Paris. Morgan Stanley sought to benefit from increased travel to Europe and hotel companies's efforts to sell properties but continue to profit from managing them.

United Kingdom. As in France, the small hotel dominated the U.K. market in 2003. More than 80 percent of the hotel and lodging market's value of US$10.6 billion was attributed by Euromonitor to hotels of 50 rooms or less. In 2005, there were about 22,000 hotels and guesthouses registered, plus an additional 16,000 bed and breakfast establishments. Of the large players in the market, Granada plc was the largest, capturing a 9 percent market share. Other leaders included Whitbread, Thistle Hotels, and Hilton Group. The U.K. industry, like others, was greatly affected by the terrorist attacks in the United States on September 11, 2001. By 2004, however, occupancy rates had increased to levels last seen in the late 1990s.

Tiffany Phillips, writing for Self-Catering-Breaks News, a Web site self-described as "the international properties' free ads Web Site," reported there was a price war going on between UK "mid-range" hotels. The major focus was winning over a recession-impacted, reduced-in-size group of travelers. Big names involved in the price war included Travelodge, Express by Holiday Inn, and Premier Inn. Related citings included Travelodge room rate comparisons to Express without stating they did not provide breakfast. InterContinental Holiday Inn hotel owners' responses included a PR stunt where coaches were sent to Birmingham and London Travelodge hotels offering breakfast. Premier Inn launched an ad campaign with plays on words challenging travelers to think differently about its competitors. For example, "It's time to take a holiday from Holiday Inn."

China. In 1978, China was the 48th ranked nation in the world for tourism. Its doors had been closed to most foreigners for so long that when the government did make it easier to enter the country, it took some time for the tourists to come. But come they did. In 2002, China was the fifth-ranked tourist destination, playing host to 33 million visitors. A short time later, according to Deloitte Touche Tohmatsu, in the first eight months of 2004, 71 million overseas visitors came to China. Many foreign hoteliers have added China to their expansion plans. At the end of 2004, Intercontinental Group had 44 hotels in greater China, plus an additional 53 management agreements signed or under negotiation. As of March 2005, Accor had more than 5,550 rooms in 20 hotels, providing employment for almost 8,300 people.

BIBLIOGRAPHY

Accor. "Accor Takes a Major Step in its Expansion in India," 27 November 2006. Available from www.accor.com.

"Accor to Help Reposition Club Med." *Hotels,* July 2004.

Adams, Bruce. "On the Rise." *Hotel & Motel Management*, 3 May 2004.

"All New Orleans Needs Are Travelers," 5 March 2007. Available from www.4hoteliers.com.

Brudney, David M. "Mood of Hotel Investors and Operators is Euphoric," 24 April 2007. Available from www.4hoteliers.com.

"Cal Ripken, Jr. Teams Up with Holiday Inn," 29 March 2007. Available from www.ihgplc.com.

Draper, Deborah J., ed. *Business Rankings Annual*. Detroit: Thomson Gale, 2004.

Deloitte Touche Tohmatsu and Smith Travel Research. *Global Lodging Review* (2 March 2005) 2:6. Available from hotelbenchmark.com.

"First Ever Development Pipeline and Three Year Hotel European Openings Reveals Robust Development Through Decade's End." *Hotel Interactive*, 5 March 2007. Available from www.hotelinteractive.com.

Fitch, Stephane. "Soft Pillows and Sharp Elbows." *Forbes*, 10 May 2004.

"HHC Extends World's Greatest Hotel Name to Create Luxury Brand Line," 17 January 2006. Available from http://phx.corporate-ir.net.

"Hilton Hotels Corporation Becomes Founding Corporate Partner of Hispanic Hotel Owners Association (HHOA)," 22 September 2006. Available from http://phx.corporate-ir.net.

"Hoover's Company Capsules." *Hoover's Online*, 2006. Available from www.hoovers.com.

"Hotel companies climb after economic news." Associated Press, 7 August 2009.

"Hotels in France, Germany, UK, US." *Euromonitor*, October 2004. Available from www.majormarketprofiles.com.

"IHG Launches Travel Agency Awards." Intercontinental Hotels Group, 3 April 2007. Available from www.ihgplc.com.

Kormanik, Beth. "When a Site Chooses You: Hoteliers constantly strive to find good locations, but what if the site selects you?" *Hotel Interactive*, 5 August 2009. Available from www.hotelinteractive.com..

Lazich, Robert S., ed. *Market Share Reporter*. Detroit: Thomson Gale, 2004.

Mandelbaum, Robert. "Resort Hotels—Wanted: Eaters, Golfers, and Shoppers." *Hotel Interactive*, 26 June 2006. Available from hotelinteractive.com.

"Marriott International profits fall 76%." *The Business Journals*, 18 July 2009. Available from www.bizjournals.com

"Marriott On Track to Reduce Greenhouse Gases by 1 Million Tons Over 10 Years—2000 to 2010." Marriott International, 22 March 2007. Available from marriott.com.

"Marriott Ranks Highest in Lodging Industry for Diversity." Marriott International, 21 March 2007. Available from www.marriott.com.

Parsons, Tom. "Hotels Roll Out Deals to Get Their Fill." *Baltimore Sun*, 9 August 2009. Available from www.baltimoresun.com.

Phillips, Tiffany. "UK Hotels Jump into Price War." 10 August 2009. Available from www.self-catering-breaks.com.

McArthur, Stacey. "The New Workforce." *RCI Timeshare Business*, November/December 2001.

"Caribbean Hotel Profits Hit Hard by Economic Recession." *PR Newswire*, 10 August 2009. Available from news.prnewswire.com.

"Ranking of Hotel Groups 2004." *Hotel Online*, 2004. Available from www.hotel-online.com.

Sandler, Kathy. "Blackstone Prepares To Break Up Hilton Hotels Group-Report." *Wall Street Journal*, 9 August 2009. Available from online.wsj.com.

Tandon, Shubhra. "Vacant rooms hit hotels' profits." *The Hindu Business Line*, 10 August 2009. Available from www.thehindubusinessline.com.

Veller, Tatiana. "Bellboy to General Manager—How Long Is the Road?" 27 April 2007. Available from www.4hoteliers.com.

Wang, Terry. "Beyond the Wall: China Reveals Its Hidden Tourism Potential." *Executive Report*, January 2005. Available from www.deloitte.com.

Weinstein, Jeff. "April 2004 Market Performance." *Hotels*, July 2004.

———. "Radical Thinking?" *Hotels*, July 2004.

"Worldwide Online Bookings Up 8 Percent." *TravelCLICK*, 20 April 2007.

Young, Fara. "Perfecting the 180." *Hotel Interactive*, 10 March 2006. Available from www.hotelinteractive.com.

Yu, Hui-yong. "Morgan Stanley Plans to Buy 10 European Hilton, Person Says." *Bloomberg News*, 26 April 2007. Available from www.bloomberg.com.

SIC 7812, 7822

MOTION PICTURE VIDEO PRODUCTION AND DISTRIBUTION

NAICS CODE(S)

512110, 512120. The motion picture production and distribution industry, which is commonly known as the movie industry, records, publishes, and distributes motion pictures worldwide, primarily to theaters and broadcasters. A strong secondary market exists for the transfer of films to videotape or DVDs at the end of the theatrical run, when they may be sold or rented directly to consumers. In some cases, the films bypass theaters and are marketed immediately to consumers. The industry also produces movies exclusively for television viewing (see **Video Tape Rental and Retail**).

INDUSTRY SNAPSHOT

In the early twenty-first century, the movie industry was becoming global. For example, in mid-2004 *The New York Times* reported that international ticket sales accounted for about 60 percent of worldwide box office receipts, up from 40 percent in 2002. In 2003 member companies of the Motion Picture Association of America (MPAA) reported total global revenues of US$41.2 billion, with 40 percent coming from international sales. As the industry became more international, casting actors with international appeal became more important to success at the box office.

In the early 2000s, economic conditions were favorable for the motion picture industries of many industrialized countries, such as the United States, France, Germany, the United Kingdom, and Japan. Box-office receipts and attendance reached some new highs, especially in 2001 as much of the world was in the midst of a recession that caused increased demand for less expensive entertainment that was close to home after the September 11, 2001, terrorist attacks against the United States. Several countries released record-breaking blockbusters.

By the mid-2000s, DVDs represented a growing revenue pool for moviemakers. Citing data from Adams Media Research, *The Economist* indicated that DVD rentals and sales made up about 40 percent of movie studio revenues by 2003, up from 1 percent in 1997. In the United States alone, consumers spent US$22.5 billion on videocassettes and DVDs combined in 2003. Some analysts argued that relying on DVD sales increased the vulnerability of the industry to the growing problem of piracy, which had wreaked havoc on the music industry. In mid-2004, the MPAA reported that the motion picture industry had lost US$3.5 billion because of piracy.

BACKGROUND AND DEVELOPMENT

The U.S. film industry began in 1889 when Thomas Edison invented the kinetoscope, a primitive version of the movie projector. In 1896, Edison used his Vitascope projection device to show the world's first movie in New York City. Technological advances in the 1920s synchronized a movie's sound with its picture, enhancing the cinema experience and opening the door to many possibilities. Hollywood, California, soon became the world's capital of movie production and the home of the blockbuster, the kind of film in which large amounts of money are invested in production and marketing in the hope of reaping huge profits. In 1915, D.W. Griffith produced *Birth of a Nation* with US$110,000. The 158-minute U.S. Civil War epic took in more than US$50 million at the box office. Griffith also helped put Hollywood on the map by spending the winter of 1910 in Los Angeles with his cast and crew.

Before World War I, France and Italy all but owned the world's movie market, but after the war Hollywood emerged as the industry powerhouse, a position it held for the rest of the century. Hollywood was full of business-smart immigrants who were intent on making a mark in their new homeland. When Adolph Zukor acquired Paramount Pictures in early 1910, he merged it with his own production company. Carl Laemmle started Universal Film, and William Fox created Twentieth Century-Fox in 1912. Marcus Loew purchased

Metro Pictures from Louis B. Mayer, and merged the two companies with Goldwin Pictures to create Metro-Goldwyn-Mayer. The four Warner Brothers started making movies in 1912. These companies dominated films by 1919, much to the consternation of Charlie Chaplin, Mary Pickford, Douglas Fairbanks, and David Griffith, who had founded the sixth major studio, United Artists. These firms competed fiercely against each other during the 1930s. However, in the 1940s, the industry experienced even better times, producing military propaganda and home-front melodramas before and during World War II, and the upbeat postwar U.S. mood to portray after the war. However, the popularity of television in the 1950s shook Hollywood until the mid-1960s, when movie makers assumed a meaningful role in producing television shows, and the blockbuster production movie created a new era of US$10 million movie advertising budgets that helped to draw world audiences.

In the mid- to late 1990s, the movie industries in countries worldwide began to privatize, shifting from being dependent on government and becoming market dependent, which allowed them to compete effectively with the U.S. industry. The growth of international demand for movies was supported by the worldwide expansion of large multi-screen theaters (multiplexes) that allowed theaters to screen many movies at once.

From 1997 to 2002, U.S. movies like *Pearl Harbor* earned more abroad than at home, partially because of weakened cinema industries around the world and partially because of better release schedules in other countries than in the United States. For example, the action-adventure movies *Collateral Damage*, *Hart's War*, and *John Q* were released around the same time in the United States in 2002, competing head-to-head for an audience. However, international distributors had more control of release dates for their movies and could leave several weeks between each opening, allowing audiences in those countries to develop an appetite for a certain genre again.

CURRENT CONDITIONS

Although many entertainment sources vied for consumer attention by the mid-2000s, home theaters in general and DVDs in particular provided competition for traditional movie theatres. As DVD player prices fell below the US$30 mark for some units and the number of available titles continued to explode, the number of DVD-equipped households continued to rise. By the end of 2004 more than 70 million U.S. households and 171 households internationally had a DVD. In China, about 42 million households had DVDs. According to Adams Media Research, in 2003 DVD rentals and sales accounted for approximately 40 percent of revenues for movie studios, for a 1 percent increase over 1997. Time Warner's 2004 annual report indicated that growth in its film entertainment division was driven by the sales of DVDs.

Although DVDs created lucrative profits for moviemakers, reliance on the medium made the industry vulnerable to the growing problem of piracy, which had decimated profits in the music industry. By the mid-2000s, the proliferation of DVD recorders made it easier and faster than ever to pirate copies of movies, especially in Asia, where illegal copies of popular movies that were made with video recorders in theaters or from advance preview releases were available everywhere from street corners to five-star hotels for less than US$1. The rising number of broadband Internet connections also made illegal movie downloads easier for computer users.

According to MPAA figures, by 2004 piracy was costing the motion picture worldwide about US$3.5 billion. Veronika Kwan-Rubinek, international distribution president for Warner Brothers Pictures, reported that in 2003, losses from piracy totaled US$275 million in Russia, US$120 million in the United Kingdom, and US$100 million in Germany. The movie industry was responding to piracy with film trailers to remind the viewing public that piracy is a criminal act.

The movie industry's globalization continued into the mid-2000s. By mid-2004, international ticket sales represented about 60 percent of worldwide box office receipts, up from 40 percent in 2002. In 2003, the MPAA's member companies reported total global revenues of US$41.2 billion, with US$16.6 billion coming from international sales. However, studios seemed to emphasize total box office revenues rather than the number of people who purchased tickets. A study of budgets, distribution, and genre by SNL Kagan, "Economics of Motion Pictures," found that "the most expensive films posted the largest revenues and average net profit."

Some blockbuster films, like the *Lord of the Rings* and *Harry Potter* series, doubled their U.S. box office returns with strong international showings, making actors with international appeal increasingly important. In the July 5, 2004, issue of *The New York Times*, Stephen Moore, president of international film and home entertainment at Twentieth Century Fox, said that "Hiring international talent is a movie-making law." In this environment, international actors who formerly played supporting or villainous roles in U.S. films suddenly were elevated to star status, as in the case of Japanese actor Ken Watanabe in *The Last Samurai*.

Film locations were important for the industry as well as for tourism and the local economy. For example, *Australia*, which debuted in the 2008 holiday season, was expected to encourage travel to the continent Down Under, and Tourism Australia created promotional ads. In the United States, government leaders and citizens in states like Michigan rolled out the red carpet for filmmakers in the hopes of stimulating the economy and creating jobs as well as encouraging tourism.

Movies based on best-selling books for all ages were highly successful. For example, in November 2008, advanced marketing of *Twilight* to teenage girls and women resulted in approximately US$70.5 million taken in at the box office over the movie's opening weekend. The independent film cost US$37 million to produce and had been rejected by Paramount's MTV Films.

RESEARCH AND TECHNOLOGY

While film remains important in motion picture production, digital technology and computer-generated imaging was the wave of the future, according to the U.S. Department of Labor. Expensive editing changes, such as scene set-ups, can be digitally manipulated inexpensively. Scenery can be digitally altered instantaneously if a director finds a location unsatisfactory. Even actors can be created digitally. Some of the most significant developments were being made by independent filmmakers, with savings in total production costs helping make these small companies competitive with mega-studios.

The digital studio business was growing between 25 and 30 percent per year. Computers and digital technology revolutionized filmmaking in the 1990s, leaving industry carpenters, decorators, and electricians at risk of losing their jobs to computers that can synthesize large scenes and create images of live action. Furthermore, computer technology has cut expenses from movie production. Because a top actor can demand more than 18 percent of a movie's gross box office receipts, some studios were developing virtual actors, much the same way dinosaurs were digitized for *Jurassic Park*. Between 2005 and 2010, extensive use of computer-derived human images were expected to replace movie extras. This technique was used for the HBO mini-series *John Adams*, which also used digitized buildings and backgrounds.

U.S. companies such as Silicon Graphics, IBM, Microsoft, and Autodesk, and Canadian firms Soft-Image and Discreet Logic were leading digital technology firms. Special effects company Industrial Light and Magic employed 400 digital specialists, and Sony's Imageworks, founded in the early 1990s, employed 100 digital artists. Disney continued to be a digital technology with its world-class animation division. Other specialists included Boss Film Studios and Digital Domain. In mid-1994, Twentieth Century-Fox announced that it would spend US$100 million on a computerized animation studio in Arizona. High tech computer firms in California's Silicon Valley joined forces with Hollywood to develop this technology for filmmaking, earning the Santa Monica area the nickname *Silwood*.

In addition, movie producers began to rely on high-bandwidth connections to facilitate filmmaking in the late 1990s. Some studios started to use the technology to increase communication and efficiency in spite of the considerable investment because movie studios required high-speed connections to transmit images.

Digital technology was predicted to also transform distribution, bringing film into theaters via satellite or fiber optic cable, according to the U.S. Department of Labor. In the late 2000s, many theaters being built had the capability to receive films through use of the new distribution technology. Major studios and independent companies welcomed such advances as a means to cut distribution costs. In addition, five major studios were expected to spend approximately US$70,000 per screen to help convert theaters to allow digital projection by paying "virtual print fees" between US$800 and US$1,000 for each film per screen.

The industry continued to fight the distribution of software that allowed DVD movies to be copied. Real Networks, of Seattle, Washington, was sued by six major U.S. movie studios for distributing software that permitted the illegal copying of copyrighted films, allowing sizeable illegal film libraries. The industry also was challenged by an increasing number of movies being available on legal web sites. For example, Hulu, which was created by NBC Universal and News Corp., provided easy access to an abundance of titles, and the YouTube Screening Room added four new releases to its list of available films every two weeks.

INDUSTRY LEADERS

Time Warner Inc. Warner Brothers was founded in the 1920s by brothers Harry, Albert, Jack, and Sam Warner and produced the first talking feature film, *The Jazz Singer,* in 1927. One of Hollywood's largest movie studios, Warner was known for such classics as *Casablanca* and *Rebel Without a Cause.* Following a decline in the 1950s and 1960s, the studio was acquired by Kinney National Service Corporation and was renamed Warner Communications in 1971. In the 1980s the company reported a decline in earnings and was the target of a takeover attempt by Rupert Murdoch, but Warner rebounded, becoming one of the most stable studios in the movie industry. In 1989, Time Inc. merged with Warner Communications to form Time Warner Inc, the world's largest publishing and entertainment company, with film accounting for 25 percent of revenues. In 1991, the company sold a 12.5 percent interest in its cable television, cable programming, and film operations to two Japanese companies. The same year, Time Warner entered into a long-range agreement with the Dutch-owned Regency International Pictures, the French pay-TV company Canal Plus, and the German

production and distribution firm Scriba & Deyhle. The three companies agreed to provide Time Warner with US$600 million to produce at least 20 movies for international distribution. Time Warner increased its control of the entertainment world by acquiring Turner Broadcasting in the mid-1990s, which owned New Line Cinema.

In 2000, Time Warner merged with AOL creating an industry giant with US$160 billion in its wallet. Nevertheless, total profits of the combined venture were disappointing as AOL advertising sales sagged, but AOL Time Warner achieved instant financial success with the production of blockbuster movies. The powerful Internet presence of America Online boosted Warner Bros. and its affiliate New Line Cinema to number-one box office respectability over Walt Disney in 2001. With ten number one films at the box office right after opening, Warner accounted for 22 percent of all movie studio profits for 2001. Leading the charge for the studio were the *Harry Potter and the Sorcerer's Stone* and *The Lord of the Rings: The Fellowship of the Ring,* productions which continued to amass tremendous profits in 2002 as tickets went on sale at international theaters.

By 2004, AOL Time Warner had changed its name to Time Warner Inc., with America Online Inc. operating as a separate subsidiary. That year, Warner Bros. Pictures released 22 motion pictures, including *Harry Potter and the Prisoner of Azkaban* and *Million Dollar Baby,* which won the Academy Award for Best Picture. The division distributed films in 125 countries, and had international releases of 18 English-language films and 23 local-language films that it had acquired or produced. New Line, which produced and distributed independent films, released 14 movies during 2004. New Line also continued to receive significant revenue from its video distribution, especially from *The Lord of the Rings: The Return of the King.* Warner Home Video Inc. distributed the vast library of film products from the company's other subsidiaries. At the end of 2004, the library contained more than 6,600 motion picture titles, 40,000 television titles, and 14,000 animation titles. Time Warner's filmed entertainment segment produced US$11.85 billion in revenues in 2004, representing 26 percent of the total company revenue, which was primarily a result of the sale of DVDs. By 2007, Time Warner reported sales of US$46.5 billion and 86,400 employees.

The Walt Disney Company. Brought to life in 1923 when Walt Disney and his brother Roy started a film studio in Hollywood, the Walt Disney Company established a reputation as the preeminent producer of animated films in the world. The Walt Disney Company has diversified into several other business areas over the years, including theme parks, hotels, and cruise ships; cable television; publishing; and merchandising. While the Walt Disney Company has enjoyed a long and generally successful life, the company's film business suffered in the 1970s as revenues from films dropped from more than 50 percent of company revenues in 1971 to only 20 percent in 1979. In 1980, the company's leadership changed, and in 1984 the Bass family of Texas bought a controlling interest in the company. Michael Eisner, formerly of Paramount, was installed as the company's new CEO. Eisner and Frank Wells, a former Warner Brothers executive, were credited with Disney's reemergence as a major presence in the film industry during the 1980s. In 1993, Disney acquired Miramax, a privately held independent producer. Miramax, which was founded in 1980, was a top producer of movies made outside the traditional Hollywood studio system. In late 1994, Disney announced the creation of a Miramax subsidiary to promote French films in the United States. Buena Vista Pictures Distribution, Disney's releasing company, was the largest film studio subsidiary in the United States. Disney also owns Touchstone Pictures, a prominent U.S. movie distributor.

In 1991, Disney entered into a feature film agreement with computer animations studio, Pixar. Owned 51 percent by the co-founder and CEO of Apple Computers, Steve Jobs, Pixar produced six full-length animated films released by Walt Disney, including *Toy Story* (1995), *A Bug's Life* (1998), *Toy Story 2* (1999), *Monsters Inc.* (2000), *Finding Nemo* (2003), and *The Incredibles* (2004). All of the movies did extremely well domestically and internationally, with several beating box office records held at the time of their release. Pixar received 15 Academy Awards for its films. The final film under the Pixar/Disney agreement is expected to be released in 2006, after which Pixar's relationship with Disney for any new titles will end.

By February 2002 Disney had lost not only its undisputed title of number one studio that it had held since 1995, but also its reputation as the leader in animated films, possibly as a result of entering business areas traditionally outside the studio's traditional strength. For example, *Pearl Harbor* was an expected blockbuster, but ticket sales were well below expectations. Disney stock dropped 26 percent from 2001 to 2002 and Disney Chairman Peter Schneider was replaced by Richard Cook. Cook was a former Disneyland park employee, who had the task of helping the company regain its number one status from DreamWorks with the production of a first rate animation film of *Fantasia* quality.

In 2004, the Studio Entertainment division of the Walt Disney Company accounted for US$8.71 billion of the company's total revenues of US$30.75 billion, representing a 19 percent increase over 2003. However, revenues from worldwide theatrical film distribution were

down US$215 million, with movies like *Arthur, The Alamo,* and the animated feature *Home on the Range* reporting weak box office numbers. The gain in overall revenues came from higher DVD sales, with such DVD releases as *Pirates of the Caribbean* and *Finding Nemo.*

As of September 30, 2004, Disney had released 832 full-length live-action features, primarily in color; 69 full-length animated color features; approximately 540 cartoon shorts; and 53 live action shorts under the Walt Disney Pictures, Touchstone Pictures, Hollywood Pictures, Miramax, and Dimension banners. During 2005, Disney was expecting to distribute 37 feature films.

In July 2005, Disney announced that it had reached an agreement with the founders of Miramax, Bob and Harvey Weinstein, who would leave the company in September 2005, with Disney retaining the Miramax name and the Weinsteins taking the Dimension name. The Weinsteins had been responsible for such films as *Pulp Fiction* (1994), *Chicago* (2002), and *The Aviator* (2004), with the subsidiary winning 53 Academy Awards, including three for best picture.

In 2008, Disney continued to be a popular source for family films, such as *High School Musical: Senior Year.* Disney's real world figures for 2007 were US$35.5 billion with 137,000 employees.

Viacom Inc. Viacom was formed in 1970 by the Canadian Broadcasting Corporation (CBC) after the U.S. Federal Communications Commission (FCC) ruled that networks could not own cable systems and television stations in the same market. After a hostile takeover attempt by Carl Icahn in 1986, and a six-month bidding war with movie theater chain Sumner Redstone's National Amusements, Redstone purchased 83 percent of Viacom for US$3.4 billion. In 1994, Viacom acquired Blockbuster Entertainment Corporation, an international home video and music retailer. In the late 1990s, Blockbuster Entertainment had reigned as the king of the video rental industry in the United States, with about 25 percent of the domestic market. Blockbuster operated more than 5,300 video stores in the United States and throughout the world. Nonetheless, Viacom considered selling Blockbuster in the late 1990s, anticipating a decline for the video rental industry.

Also in 1994, under Redstone's guidance, Viacom won its bid to purchase Paramount, a much larger company, for an estimated US$10 billion after a fierce battle with TV Shopping Network, a hostile bidder. While the price Viacom paid for Paramount was high, Viacom was encouraged by a successful summer season in 1994 as Paramount recorded a company record US$413 million in box office receipts. Paramount ranked third among movie studios in 1996 with a 13 percent market share, and in 1997, Viacom's sales rose 9 percent to US$13.2 billion. By 2002, Viacom was bolstered by a revitalized Blockbuster, and the publishing, video, and entertainment conglomerate announced 2001 revenues of US$23.2 billion, a 16 percent increase. Total earnings for 2007 were US$13.4 billion with 13,100 employees.

In 2004, 18 percent of Viacom's revenues of US$25.26 billion came from its Entertainment division, which included the company's motion picture production and distribution businesses. The Entertainment division also included publisher Simon & Schuster, Paramount theme parks, Famous Players movie theaters, and Famous music, which was involved in music publishing. That year, Paramount released 16 movies, including *Collateral,* starring Tom Cruise. In addition, the company earned revenue through DVD sales and license fees for television broadcast of films in its library. Revenue from feature film exploitation earned the company an additional US$2.21 billion. With its ownership of Paramount, one of the original major motion picture film studios, Viacom was one of the world's leading film producers and distributors in 2005. It owned a library of more than 1,100 titles, including the highest grossing movie to that time, *Titanic,* as well as *Forrest Gump* and the franchises for *Star Trek, The Godfather,* and *Indiana Jones.* In 2005, Viacom was expecting to release 15 feature films. In addition, in June 2005, the company announced plans to spin off its holdings into two separate, publicly traded companies: a new Viacom (of which the company's film production and distribution would be a part) and CBS Corporation.

In 2008, *The Canadian Press* reported that Paramount would distribute Marvel Entertainment movies linked to some of its most popular characters, including *Iron Man 2, Thor, The First Avenger: Captain America,* and *The Avengers.*

The News Corporation Limited. One of the world's most extensive media empires, News Corporation had holdings on four continents and in all of the major English-speaking communications centers. The Australian company was founded in 1923 by Sir Keith Murdoch, and was taken over by his son Rupert in 1952 when the elder Murdoch died. The younger Murdoch expanded the existing newspaper holdings, adding magazines, radio, and television. In 1985, News Corporation made a move into the motion picture industry with the purchase of the Twentieth Century Fox film company for US$575 million. Twentieth Century Fox had formed as the result of a 1935 merger between Fox Film Corporation, an independent producer, and Twentieth Century Pictures.

The company's Fox Filmed Entertainment business was one of the world's largest distributors and producers of motion pictures in 2004 under its Twentieth Century

Fox, Fox 2000, Fox Searchlight Pictures, and Twentieth Century Fox Animation subsidiaries. In 2004, the company produced and/or distributed such films as *Master and Commander* and *The Day After Tomorrow.* At that time, filmed entertainment accounted for about US$5.4 billion of the company's total revenues of approximately US$22 billion. Figures by June 2008 had soared to US$32.9 billion.

Sony Corporation. Founded in 1946, Sony has long been recognized as a leader in consumer electronics, but did not move into entertainment until the 1970s when it introduced the Betamax videocassette recorder, beginning the mass market for home video. Sony later purchased Tri-Star Pictures and Columbia Pictures Entertainment Inc., which served notice to the rest of the film entertainment industry that a significant new competitor had emerged. Columbia Pictures had been founded in the 1920s as a small, independent film producer. Columbia was the first studio to reduce production costs by filming movie scenes out of sequence, and was also the first to move into television production. In 1982 Coca-Cola Co. purchased Columbia Pictures and later combined it with Tri-Star Pictures, which had been founded in 1982 as a joint venture between Columbia Pictures, Home Box Office, and CBS, to form Columbia Pictures Entertainment. Sony purchased Tri-Star and Columbia Pictures in 1989, acquired the Guber-Peters Entertainment Company as part of the transaction. Sony earned US$50.7 billion in 1997 from its various businesses, the majority of which were outside the movie industry, and its movie studios held an 11 percent market share in 1996.

In April 2005 a consortium of investors, including Sony, purchased Metro Goldwyn Mayer, keeping the company privately held. As part of the deal, Sony Pictures Entertainment maintained the distribution of MGM's library of 4,000 films and 10,400 television episodes and was expected to co-finance film productions with MGM. With 2004 sales of US$1.72 billion, MGM remained an important industry player. However, the company was not without its challenges, having reported net losses of US$161.8 million in 2003, and US$29.2 million in 2004. MGM hits in the early 2000s had included *Hannibal* and *Legally Blonde.* The venerable studio also had a film library of studio hits, such as the James Bond sequels.

For 2005, Sony Corporation's subsidiary, Sony Pictures Entertainment (SPE), which had operations in 67 countries, earned the company about 10.7 percent of its total revenue of approximately US$66.6 billion. The company distributed films under the banners of Columbia, TriStar, Sony Pictures, and Revolution Studios. By 2007, overall Sony sales were reported as US$89 billion with 163,000 employees.

NBC Universal Inc. NBC Universal was created in 2004 through the combination of NBC and Vivendi Universal Entertainment, the entertainment assets of media and telecommunications giant, Vivendi Universal. The new company was 80 percent owned by General Electric and 20 percent by Vivendi Universal. In 2004, NBC Universal released such films as *The Bourne Supremacy* and *Ray* through its Universal Studios company, and sales were approximately $US13 billion. The company also earns revenues from its catalog of more than 4,000 titles.

Vivendi CEO Jean-Marie Messier spearheaded a 2000 merger with Seagram that combined a media empire with a movie and TV studio, recording studio, and theme park empire. According to *USA Today,* Vivendi purchased Seagram for US$34 billion, or US$77.35 per share. Upon completion of the deal, the French-run Vivendi Universal assumed the status of a major player in Hollywood. By the end of the 2001, Vivendi Universal reported a 9 percent growth in revenues as a string of movie hits offset some faltering in its music division, according to *Financial Times.* Vivendi Universal posted 2001 profits of US$25.3 billion 2001 with its Universal Studios division producing audience pleasers like *Jurassic Park 3* and *The Mummy Returns.* By 2003, Vivendi Universal had sold its movie studio, theme parks, and TV interests to NBC to pay down debt. Vivendi continued to concentrate on telecommunications and on its Universal Music division.

Universal Studios began as Music Corporation of America, or MCA, in 1924 as an entertainment booking company. In addition to representing bands, the company began to buy talent agencies and contracts of individual entertainer. In the 1950s MCA moved into the area of television production, which provided jobs for MCA's clients. By the late 1950s MCA earned revenues from over 45 percent of all network evening programs. In the 1970s and early 1980s the company became a successful producer of major motion picture with *Jaws* and *The Deer Hunter.* The late 1980s, however, were less successful, and the company began to lower production costs. Under the foreign ownership of Matsushita Electric Industrial Co., entertainment profits only amounted to an average 2.7 percent over five years in 1994. In 1995, Seagram Co. acquired 80 percent of MCA and later changed its name to Universal Studios, which had a strong year in 1995 with *Apollo 13* and *Casper.* The company continued to control 8 percent of the market in 1996 despite a lack of blockbusters. By 2007, Vivendi reported US$15.4 billion.

MAJOR COUNTRIES IN THE INDUSTRY

The United States. Following record box office receipts in the early 2000s, the U.S. motion picture industry experienced ongoing success moving into the mid-2000s. In 2003, box office receipts totaled US$9.5 billion, down less than 1 percent from 2002 and the second highest level in industry history. Theater admissions were down 4 percent in 2003, to about 1.6 billion. Nevertheless, this was still impressive considering the competition movie theaters faced from video games, television, VCRs, DVD players, the Internet, cable television, and satellite TV. The top five companies in the United States were Sony, Walt Disney, Time Warner, General Electric, and The News Corporation, which together accounted for about 64 percent of the market in 2003. That year, 495 films were produced in the United States., up from 467 the year before according to *Euromonitor.*

Although 2003 theater admissions were down 4 percent from 2002, attendance of almost 1.6 billion was still very impressive. In a March 23, 2004 news release, Motion Picture Association of America (MPAA) CEO Jack Valenti remarked: "Remember, in order to find any range of admissions that compared to 2003, you have to go back 48 years, to 1955, before television and cable." Valenti acknowledged that movie theaters faced heightened competition from an explosive video game market as well as television sets in 108 million homes, VCRs in 98 million homes, and DVD players in 47 million homes, computers in 67 million homes, Internet connections in 62 million homes, cable television in 74 million homes, and satellite TV in 20 million homes.

The success of mergers, such as AOL Time Warner and Vivendi Universal, created a "golden age" of prosperity for Hollywood during the early 2000s, similar to the 1930s and 1940s. However, it faced the alarming reality that increasing numbers of people were turning to video games and other forms of home entertainment over the cinema, which resulted in an increase in the sale of DVDs from their libraries of films as a result.

A major employer, the motion picture production and distribution industry oversaw about 287,000 wage and salary jobs in U.S. studios by 2000. According to the U.S. Labor Department, jobs included directing, scriptwriting, casting, acting, editing, film processing, motion picture and videotape reproduction, and equipment and wardrobe rental. Other businesses, such as catering, security, and hairdressing, also provided vital services to studios.

An evolution of "a vertically integrated, full-service motion picture production and distribution company targeting the growing entertainment interest" of the growing Latino population in the United States, according to *Market Watch.* For example, Maya Entertainment was "the first Latino owned and operated, production, distribution, and exhibition entity in the U.S. to focus specifically on bringing culturally relevant entertainment to the over 45 million Latinos living in the U.S. responsible for purchasing 297 million box office tickets" in summer 2008. The company's list of titles included critically-acclaimed *How the Garcia Girls Spent Their Summer,* with scene-stealing performances from Elizabeth Rena.

India. The film industry in India dates back to 1896 when a pioneering cinematography company from France called the Lumière Brothers' Cinematographe filmed six silent films in the country. Prior to the nineteenth century, the first films made by an Indian filmmaker, Harishchandra Sakharam Bhatvadekar, were two short, entertaining documentaries on wrestling and monkeys. In 1913 *King Harishchandra,* created by filmmaker Dhundiraj Govind Phalke, was the first full-length silent movie made entirely in India. Eighteen years later, the Imperial Film Company of India released a full-length feature with sound called *Alam Ara.*

Indian feature films typically are about three-hour long musicals with the actors lip-synching and dancing at various points in the movie, and may be stylized remakes of Hollywood films. With the country having many languages, the film industry is regionalized by language. Mumbai (formerly Bombay) is the largest region, and has become known as Bollywood due to the large number of movies made there. Indian films were becoming more popular in Western countries. In 2004 the English-language films *Bride and Prejudice* and *Vanity Fair* were Indian-produced films that were popular worldwide.

In 2004 the industry in India was valued at about US$1.3 billion, and the country continued to be the world's largest producer of films, turning out about 1,000 each year. However, the industry was noted for accompanying criminal activity. According to *Business Week,* loan sharks and gangsters bankrolled more than half of the country's movies, charging 40 percent interest, because banks considered lending money for movies to be risky. In the late 1990s, the industry faced widespread corruption as angry gangsters began killing movie industry affiliates. Much of India's more than US$1 billion film industry took in profits that were never recorded as a result of various illegal activities, including usury. Films were produced far less expensively in India than in Hollywood. A movie with a US$2 million budget would be considered a high-budget film.

In 2008 the highly-successful director Steven Spielberg provided Hollywood and Bollywood with a golden opportunity when he convinced Indian billionaire Anil Ambani to financially support the reopening of Spielberg's studio, according to *The Guardian.* In addition, the *Economic Times* reported that Walt Disney (India) had announced plans to produce four live-action films,

including director Bharat Bala's *The 19th Step,* in India. Disney had previously collaborated with Yashraj Films and was expected to continue to do so for some other animation projects.

Hong Kong. In the 1980s, Hong Kong was third largest film exporter in the world, producing about 300 films per year. However, in 2004 64 movies were made locally. The industry was greatly affected by the availability of inexpensive, pirated copies of DVDs and videos, an issue affecting local as well as popular foreign films. According to PricewaterhouseCoopers, up to 98 percent of films in mainland China were pirated copies. In addition, although Hong Kong was returned to Chinese rule by the British in 1997, by 2003 films made in Hong Kong continued to be considered "foreign," making them subject to Chinese import restrictions.

France. The Commission Nationale du Film was formed in 1996 to promote French films and filming in France by moviemakers from other countries. French studios upgraded their equipment throughout the 1990s to attract more outside movie producers, especially U.S. moviemakers. France also continued building multiplex theaters, opening 233 screens in 1996 alone.

Based on ticket revenues, France boasted one of Europe's most productive film industries in the early 2000s. With government subsidies making profits almost inevitable, and government-imposed regulations to keep films from Hollywood overshadowing national films, France was second in the world with 184 million tickets sold. *Amelie,* a Miramax film directed by Jean-Pierre Jeunet, was France's leading artistic success and box office moneymaker, selling 8 million tickets. The sequel *La Verité si je mens? 2 (Would I Lie to You? 2),* was nearly as successful with 7.8 million tickets.

The French industry began to make a stand against Hollywood domination in the late 1990s, churning out 150 movies in the first 10 months of 1996. In 2001, Hollywood movies accounted for only about half of all movie receipts, in part because the blockbuster films *Harry Potter and the Sorcerer's Stone* and *Lord of the Rings: Fellowship of the Ring* were released in November and December, respectively, meaning they would be audited for 2002 box office receipts. Therefore, in 2001 *Shrek* was Hollywood's top money maker in France with 3.9 million tickets sold. Many U.S. films, including *Cast Away,* starring Tom Hanks, and *A.I.,* directed by Steven Spielberg, played to basically empty theaters in France.

France's film production industry was valued at about US$1.4 billion in 2003, about 73 percent of which were entirely French-produced films. Leading industry players included Gaumont, TF1, Canal+, and Pathé. According to

Euromonitor, films produced entirely in France were expected to account for the majority of the French market leading up to 2008.

Germany. Like other countries worldwide, a spate of multiplex theaters were built in Germany in the mid- to late 1990s, fueling some of the industry's sales. Analysts were concerned that without more restraint, multiplex theaters could flood the market and undercut the industry's growth. Nevertheless, Germany's movie ticket sales showed a 15 percent increase from 2000 to 2001, grossing US$109 million as of October 2001. According to *Euromonitor,* more than 100 films were produced or co-produced by German film production companies in 2003. In 2003 Germany's theaters faced a number of difficulties, including sour economic conditions and rising competition from DVDs. That year, box office figures fell 11.5 percent to US$1.1 billion, according to *Variety.* Germany's 1,831 theaters had 4,868 screens and reported 149 million admissions in 2003. The market leader in the country was X-Filme Creative Pool which produced the film *Good Bye Lenin.*

Japan. Although Japan's motion picture industry suffered from declining theater attendance in the early 1990s, the industry's fortune changed in 1997, when attendance shot up 17.7 percent to 140.7 million moviegoers. Japan's *Princess Mononoke* was the best-selling blockbuster in the country's history, leading the industry's comeback and garnering US$142 million at the box office. In addition, multiplex theaters contributed to the resurgence of the industry as did the economic prosperity of the country. Japan had 1,884 screens in the late 1990s and over 2,825 by 2004. In 2004, box office revenues had grown to about US$2 billion. About 60 percent of the leading movies were foreign, although the number one film at the box office that year was a Japanese animated film titled *Howl's Moving Castle,* followed by the U.S. film *The Last Samurai.* Although movies from the United States had long been popular in Japan, in the late 2000s movies from South Korea were increasingly popular. In 2004, 29 films were released from that country, although they did not dominate in terms of box office receipts.

Mexico. Approximately 400 million people around the world spoke Spanish in the late 2000s, making Spanish-speaking nations the largest single-language market in the world and offering great potential to international firms. Mexico was considered the only Latin American country with a true film industry, although it was just emerging in 2000. Mexico's film industry hoped to revive its previous "golden age" of the 1940s and 1950s, when it had produced 15 percent of the world market for movies, many of which were slapstick comedies. After World War II, the country released many big-screen romantic classics until the nationalization of the film and television industry in 1975. In the early 1990s, Mexico's recession stifled its film industry, and only 29 movies were produced. However, as Mexico's economy recovered, its movie industry also began to grow, and ticket sales were increasing by the late 1990s. Theatergoers in Mexico City, for example, bought 46.8 million tickets in 1999 compared to 28 million in 1995. While only eight movies were made in 1998, around 25 were filmed by Mexican filmmakers in 2000. Two of the top ticket sellers by Mexican filmmakers were the 1999 production of the comedic *Sexo, Pudor y Lagrimas* (*Sex, Shame, and Tears*) and the earthy 2002 film *Amores Perros* (*Love's a Bitch*), winner of the Critics' Week first prize at Cannes 2000.

Spain. The cinema remained as popular in Spain in 2002 as it had been in the late 1990s. Spain had one of Europe's largest markets for movies and seemed to have weathered the national increase in the price of tickets in 2001, despite having once had nearly the lowest ticket prices worldwide. After experiencing financing problems in the 1990s, the native Spanish film industry was strong in 2001 as *The Others* earned revenues of US$24 million, and the comedy *Torrente 2* brought in US$21 million. Increased sales of around 140 million tickets led to an estimated 10 percent increase in 2001 box office profits. Another boost to the Spanish film industry in 2001 was the fact that local audiences provided a much more lukewarm reception to Hollywood films than they had in the late 1990s.

By 2003, Spain continued to have some of the lowest ticket prices in Europe, but the country's movie market was cooling off. According to *Variety,* admissions fell from a record 146.8 million in 2001 to 140.7 million in 2002 and 137.5 million in 2003. Explosive growth in the number of movie screens, which skyrocketed 137 percent from 1993 to 2003, also had slowed by 2003 as the market reached a saturation point. In 2003, the country had 1,194 theaters with 4,253 screens, and about 458 movie releases, led by *Mortadelo & Filemon: The Big Adventure,* resulted in total box office sales of about US$770 million.

Canada. In 1996, the combined revenues of Canada's film and television production industries totaled US$2.7 billion. The Canadian government played an instrumental role in the country's movie industry, by awarding grants and tax incentives to film investors to advance the industry. Sheila Copps, Canadian Heritage Minister, promised to change Canadian film policy to help increase the number of Canadian movies shown on Canadian screens. However, even though Canada has been able to produce a good number of movies per year, few Canadians actually watch them. In the late 1990s, about 3 percent of the country's total screen time was devoted to Canadian movies. In 2001, with an upswing in the building of megaplex theaters in Canada, Statistics Canada reported that the nation's movie attendance was its highest per capita in decades. However, smaller theaters were closing in large numbers as their quality of screen, sound, and ambiance failed to match the attraction of the giant theater complexes. In contrast to declining movie profits from the mid-1990s until 1999, in 2001 the movie industry announced record profits of US$8.4 million and record ticket sales of US$1.49 billion, according to *Film Journal* magazine. In 2003, *Variety* reported that Canada's 529 movie releases resulted in sales of US$714 million.

Great Britain. In 2003, film production in the United Kingdom was valued at approximately US$2 billion by *Euromonitor,* with Time Warner having the largest market share at 30 percent. Although dominated by U.S.-based industry giants, 109 films were produced in the United Kingdom or had U.K. financial involvement in 2003. Theatre admission in 2003 was 167.3 million, down from 2002 levels of 176 million. British feature films released that year earned about US$14.5 million, while co-productions with other countries had box office grosses of more than US$234 million. The most successful co-production that year was the film *Love Actually.* The British moving-going public viewed some 422 movie releases, including the leading *Lord of the Rings: Return of the King,* which grossed more than US$105 million in the United Kingdom. That strong performance followed a period of general prosperity during the early 2000s when Britain's box office sales were estimated at around 152 million tickets in 2001, easily topping the 143 million box office receipts collected in 2000.

Many of the most successful films in Britain during the early 2000s were either based in England or were about English subjects, but were financed or produced by Hollywood studios. One popular film in England, *Captain Corelli's Mandolin,* starring Nicholas Cage, fared poorly in the U.S. market. U.S. smash hits based in England, such as *Harry Potter and the Sorcerer's Stone* and *Bridget Jones's Diary,* were successes overseas as well. *Harry Potter* earned US$63 million and *Bridget Jones's Diary,* which had been considerably less expensive to produce, took in US$61 million.

British studios have been particularly attractive to international film producers because of their low costs. Historical dramas with authentic backdrops were in demand, as well as English-speaking actors and film crews. The British are well known for their quality stage construction and technicians and were developing a reputation for their special effects work. In 1992, the British Film Commission used its state-financed resources

to attract foreign investment. The Conservative government pledged to provide over US$130 million of national lottery money and put it into the production and distribution of British films from 1995 to 2000. In the late 1990s, the government began to restructure the industry to make it stable and ensure its success with the Film Policy Review by Department of Culture, Media, and Sport.

Italy. Once as receptive to Hollywood films as Germany, in 2001 Italian filmmakers hoped that the earnings of Italian pictures signified a more receptive local market for Italian films. Among the highest audience-drawing films of 2001 were Aldo, Giovanni & Giacomo's *Ask Me If I'm Happy* and Gabriele Muccino's *The Last Kiss.* Nonetheless, U.S. films such as the successful *Bridget Jones's Diary* continued to outpace Italian films overall, although not as noticeably as in the past. Hollywood movies earned 60 percent of all Italian revenues, and Italian films had an 18 percent share of that market.

By 2003, multiplex theaters represented only one-third of Italy's cinema screens, according to *Variety.* Although this was low in comparison to other European countries, Italy's multiplexes brought in half of the country's movie sales. Italy's 2,298 theaters had 3,628 screens in 2003 with 109.3 million admissions, supported by the top film, *Harry Potter and the Chamber of Secrets,* and produced box office sales of US$766.5 million.

Egypt. In 1923, Egypt started producing silent films, and patterned its first large production facility, Studio Misr, after Hollywood in 1935. In the 1940s and 1950s, Egypt's film industry was known as *Hollywood on the Nile,* when it produced more than 100 films per year. However, by 1994 the number of films produced in Cairo dropped significantly to 22. The dismal outlook for the 1990s was the result of a combination of heavy taxes, censorship, satellite dishes, and video piracy. There were approximately 36 fees and taxes placed on the industry, with assessments going to everyone from the Minister of Finance to the Police Benevolent Society. The state's censor office placed all films through a synopsis, final script, and release approval, often resulting in substantial revision of the original script. The Ministry of Tourism often charged high fees to use great ancient sites, such as the Great Pyramids. Efforts to revive the country's cinema continued in the late 1990s. In 2001, U.S. movies earned US$2.7 million, roughly consistent with earnings of US$2.9 million in 1998, the highest profits ever recorded in Egypt.

BIBLIOGRAPHY

Andrews, Nigel. "Bullets over Bollywood." *Financial Times,* 22 November 1997, WFT1.

Bentsen, Cheryl. "Don't Call It Bollywood." *CIO,* 1 December 2000. Available from www.cio.com.

Brown, Amanda. "What has Happened to the Once Prolific Hollywood of the East?" *Asian Broadcaster,* April 2003. Available from www.pwchk.com.

Brown, Hannah. "Comedy to Shatter the Glass Ceiling." *The Jerusalem Post,* 15 September 2008. Available from www.jpost.com.

Chmielewski, Dawn C. "Hollywood Studios Sue to Stop Distribution of DVD Copying Software." *The Los Angeles Times,* 30 September 2008. Available from www.latimes.com.

———. "Major Studios in Deal to Convert to Digital Movie Projection." *The Los Angeles Times,* 2 October 2008. Available from www.latimes.com.

Chipman, Kim. "Disney Studio Promotes Cook to Head Its Namesake Film Studio." *Bloomberg News,* 15 February 2002.

"(Canada's) Cinemas Paying for Overcapacity." *The Record* (Kitchener–Waterloo), 2 February 2002.

Clark, Jayne. "Australia Gears Up for an 'Australia' Boom." *USA Today,* 21 November 2008.

Coyle, Jake. "10 Films You Just Can't Watch on the Smallest of Screens." *The Detroit Free Press,* 22 November 2008.

Dawtrey, Adam. "United Kingdom: Blighty Distribs Feeling New 'Passion' for Indie Pics." *Variety,* 10 May 2004.

De Pablos, Emiliano. "Spain: Dire TV Situation Forces Distribs to Renegotiate Pic Pacts." *Variety,* 10 May 2004.

———. "Spain: Screen Slowdown Hits B.O." *Variety,* 21 June 2004.

"Film Industry in Hong Kong," May 2005. Available from www.info.gov.hk.

"Films to Generate $35 Million into Local Economy." *Business Update,* 30 January 2009. Available from www.businessupdate.com.

Fineman, Josh. "New Line's 'John Q' May Top Four Other Films." *Bloomberg News,* 15 February 2002.

"Focus on Movie Box Office Hides Fact Fewer People Buying Tickets." *The Canadian Press,* 19 September 2008. Available from canadianpress.google.com.

"Glut of Indie Movies Weighs Down Market." *Vancouver Sun,* 16 September 2008. Available from www.canada.com.

Gross, Neil, et al. "The Entertainment Glut." *Business Week,* 16 February 1998.

Groves, Don. "Mideast Finds Film Oasis." *Daily Variety,* 21 November 2001.

Hasden, Don. "A Sign of America's Changing Tastes." *Chattanooga Times/Chattanooga Free Press,* 11 February 2002.

———. "International Actors a Passport to Profitability." *The New York Times,* 5 July 2004.

"Homegrown Pix Gain in Europe." *Variety,* 6 January 2002.

James, Alison. "France: Territory Overheats Under Release Overload, as Ancillary Markets Cool Off." *Variety,* 10 May 2004.

"Japanese Film Industry." *Japan Economic Monthly,* May 2005. Available from www.jetro.com.

Kelly, Brendan. "Canada: Quebec Pics Still on a Winning Streak, While DVD and TV Improve." *Variety,* 10 May 2004.

Kilday, Gregg. "ShoWest: Biz Strong but Antipiracy Battle Continues." *The Hollywood Reporter,* March 23, 2004. Available from www.hollywoodreporter.com.

Kingsley, Simon. "Germany: Teutonic B.O. Hit by Economy and Piracy." *Variety,* 21 June 2004.

Kingsley, Simon, and Ed Meza. "Germany: Smaller Distribs See Opportunity in Wake of Big 2003 Losses." *Variety,* 10 May 2004.

"Major Market Profiles: Film Production in USA (Germany, UK, and France)." *Euromonitor,* October 2004. Available from www.euromonitor.com.

"Maya Entertainment Makes Waves in Hollywood." *MarketWatch,* 2 October 2008. Available from www.marketwatch.com.

"MGM Reports Record Earnings." *Agence France Presse,* 6 February 2002.

"Reversal of Fortune: The Need to Forge a New Strategy for Canadian Productions." Canadian Film and Television Production Association, February 2005. Available from www.cftpa.ca.

"Romancing the Disc; The Movie Business." *The Economist,* 7 February 2004.

Schwarzacher, Lukas. "Japan: Losses and Consolidation Spur Local Pic Focus." *Variety,* 10 May 2004.

"Valenti Reports 2003 Box Office as Second Highest in History at ShoWest." Motion Picture Association of America Inc., 23 March 2004. Available from www.mpaa.org.

Verrier, Richard. "'Twilight' Leaves Its Box-Office Mark." *The Los Angeles Times,* 24 November 2008. Available from www.latimes.com.

"Viacom's Paramount to Distribute Marvel, Movies Including *Iron Man 2* and *Thor.*" *The Canadian Press,* 2 October 2008. Available from canadianpress.google.com.

Vivarelli, Nick. "Italy: Lack of Screens Curbs Exhibits." *Variety,* 21 June 2004.

Vivienne, Walt, and David Lieberman. "Vivendi Confirms Seagram Purchase: French Firm Now Powerful Player in Entertainment." *USA Today,* 20 June 2000.

"Walt Disney Co. Goes Solo in India." *Economic Times,* 3 October 2008. Available from economictimes.indiatimes.com.

Watling, John D. "Amores Perros Spearheads New Age of Mexican Cinema." *Business Mexico,* 1 August 2000.

Waxman, Sharon. "I Love You, Now Go Away; Egypt's Relationship With the West Is a Case Study In Contradictions." *The Washington Post,* 17 December 2001.

SIC 7941

SPORTS CLUBS AND PROMOTERS

NAICS CODE(S)

711211. Firms in the sports clubs and promoters industry operate professional athletic teams and clubs worldwide. Examples of sports clubs include franchises for soccer, which is known in many parts of the world as football, basketball, baseball, American football, hockey, and rugby. The sports industry also encompasses sporting event promoters and players' agents.

INDUSTRY SNAPSHOT

At the close of World War II, increasingly sophisticated means of public communication created a sports audience that previously had been loyal but difficult to address as a unit. As television introduced a huge audience to the visual impact and drama of sports, franchise owners, athletes, and promoters quickly considered the resulting fan accessibility as an extremely lucrative source of revenue. Suddenly, sports became not just business, but big business. The fact that the U.S. sports business was intertwined with every aspect of the economy, from media and apparel to food and advertising, added to its explosive growth, but also added to the industry overhead.

Sports became a means to an end as an important component of a total entertainment package, capable of bringing in fans and generating revenue. As sports revenues increased, players' unions became an entity to be reckoned with. The business of sport produced sophisticated player/player and agent/owner negotiations; added importance to venues, including stadium construction; and introduced potential franchise owners to the concept of high-stakes profit and loss, as well as wheeling and dealing. This, in turn, changed the games themselves as the attempt to bring in more fans to an event inspired the need to appeal to the general public, not just sports fans.

In the late 2000s sports franchises were affected by plunging stock market values. Profit from the Manchester United soccer team's US$101 million sponsorship deal with AIG was doubtful. In the National Hockey League (NHL), Maple Leaf Sports and Entertainment CEO Richard Peddie vowed to delay retirement due to "getting clobbered." Peddie acknowledged that companies were cutting discretionary spending to lower costs and increase earnings. Sports fans could spend US$250 in May 2008 for tickets, parking, food, and souvenirs for a father and son to attend a sporting event, and many fans were deciding to watch sports at home. In the National Basketball Association (NBA), the ability of fans to pay US$2,000 for courtside seats came into question.

The NBA laid off 80 employees, or 9 percent of its workforce, in 2008. The Miami Heat promoted season ticket sales with prizes for early purchases, including US$5,000 to help pay property taxes and US$4,000 for utility bills. National Football League (NFL) teams, including the Dallas Cowboys, the New York Giants, and the New York Jets were using personal seat license fees (PSLs), which allowed fans to purchase season tickets for several years, to finance new stadiums scheduled to open in 2009 and 2010. While sales were initially strong, fans were becoming anxious about costs, suffering from "buyer's remorse." Sports teams had been successful getting corporations to pay naming rights, with some

corporations paying millions of dollars to have their names linked to stadiums. However, some later went through mergers or bankruptcies, such as the Wachovia takeover by Wells Fargo, resulting in Philadelphia's Wachovia Center facing its fourth name change in 12 years. However, multi-year broadcast and sponsorship rights helped all leagues.

Female fans were a growing percentage of sports viewers even for events that were traditionally male-oriented, such as the Super Bowl football championship. Consequently, leading advertising agencies and marketing firms had begun to consider sports as an important venue to reach female consumers. According to research completed by the NFL, 45 percent of fans in 2008 were women, and approximately 35 percent of them were avid fans. Dove and other beauty products were advertised during the Super Bowl to reach women.

The Detroit Shock of the Women's National Basketball Association (WNBA) was evolving "from Champions to role models" as gender bias began to disappear and young fans could have female sports heroes. "This isn't a women-supporting-women thing anymore. I think we're touching a lot more people now," Shock forward Taj McWilliams-Franklin stated.

ORGANIZATION AND STRUCTURE

The sports industry includes a wide range of establishments that are involved in one of several aspects of the presentation of sporting events. Team owners may be individuals or companies that own sports clubs, although in the United States the NFL forbade outright corporate ownership. Promoters include global entities, such as the Federation Internationale de Football Association and the International Olympic Committee, and regional or national sports organizations, commercial promoters, and organized groups of players.

Athletes approached or were approached by sports clubs directly until around 1990 when most professional athletes were represented by agents or managers who negotiated on their behalf with clubs, sponsors, and event promoters. The establishment and ongoing maintenance of sports franchises involved similar negotiations with advertisers/sponsors, broadcasters, host cities, and merchandisers. Each of these participants tried to forge deals in their own best interests, which inevitably created conflicts. Negotiations between agents for athletes and teams were often contentious, reflecting the desire of both sides to receive as much of the money as possible from ticket sales, television rights, advertising, and merchandising rights. Conflict often escalated to arbitration, and occasionally litigation. In some sports, player strikes occurred, adding financial losses associated with fan dissatisfaction to the obvious tally for legal advice and lost revenues. In the United States, a baseball players' strike from 1994 to 1995 had an outright cost to team owners of more than US$1 billion, and the fallout from fan dissatisfaction continued through the end of the century.

The competitive structure of the late twentieth century sports industry varied by region and country. While the sports leagues in the United States typically shared revenues in some way, professional leagues in Europe, South America, and elsewhere were generally operating under a survival-of-the-fittest mentality.

In the United States, revenue sharing within organized sports leagues allowed small-market teams to compete on equal or nearly equal footing with wealthy teams in major metropolitan areas. Each league established a company to sell merchandising rights, sharing profits equally among league members, regardless of individual team contribution to the total sales. Revenue sharing extended to the lucrative national television rights without which many smaller teams would disappear. However, the disparities in local television and stadium revenues worked at a disadvantage for teams in some small markets who had less money to spend and, thus, less voice in league-wide negotiations. This was particularly evident when affluent organizations signed players to multimillion dollar contracts. The escalating salary benchmarks placed huge pressure on small and middle-market teams. Revenue sharing lessened the discrepancy between have and have-not clubs, and in fact did much to ameliorate a situation that otherwise could have resulted in several franchises going out of business.

Elsewhere in the world, the situation was dramatically different. Competitive clubs in many nations could not afford to field a team with star players. Without revenue sharing, rich teams secured the lion's share of high-priced talent, increasing the value of their ticket sales and television rights, while poorer teams stumbled toward financial ruin.

Lacking the sheer bulk associated with the U.S. sports industry, international sports organizations were forced into increased reliance on outside entities to remain viable. Private investment initially had been seen as a disadvantage as many teams in all sports "lived off" wealthy owners or their companies, but in the early 1990s the practice became increasingly necessary. In Spain, where soccer was a national obsession, only one or two clubs in the early 1990s reported sizable profits. Olympique Marseille, the French champion club recorded a loss of more than US$3 million in 1991, while smaller clubs lost division placement solely because of their debts. In Brazil, heavy private investment was necessary to ensure funding necessary to sign suitable players. However, by the late 1990s, the "Americanization" of global sports had begun. In 2002 the Florentina professional soccer team was struggling to

find enough cash to operate another season, and the collapse of the Argentine economy threatened the existence of all but the wealthiest of soccer teams. Even these teams debated "selling" their best players for operating capital paid in dollars, not devalued Argentine pesos.

Soccer led the way in the increased commercialization of sports originating outside the United States. In Europe, broad deregulation of the television industry opened competition for television broadcast rights, which provided the revenue for player salary increases. The German Soccer Association experimented with the notion of pay-per-view events in 1996, and in South America Pepsi Cola bought heavily into the Argentine Soccer Federation. These and similar events combined to create a system for international soccer that was increasingly patterned after the heavily marketed, heavily endorsed U.S. sports industry. At the same time, rugby, although dependent on amateur talent, went through many of the trials and tribulations of soccer. In Wales, where rugby had been viewed as much a religion as a national sport for a century, aggressive marketing and outside investment was nevertheless necessary to save a struggling national team from oblivion. Where rugged men still stained from work in the mines used to be the only persons allowed on the playing field, suddenly female mascots waved new logos, and small children paraded the Welsh dragon for TV cameras. British Gas joined such high profile investors as Schweppes, South Wales Electricity, Heineken, and Volkswagen in sponsorship of the game, and the Welsh Rugby Union relaxed its emphasis on amateurism to allow top players to be compensated financially.

BACKGROUND AND DEVELOPMENT

During the 1960s and early 1970s, professional and amateur sports were popular but were not financial juggernauts. Television contracts for broadcast rights to a sporting event were modest and relatively few, and the sports industry relied almost exclusively on ticket sales. While the dependence on ticket sales gradually decreased, they remained a significant source of revenue for the sports industry, fueled in the late 1990s by the sale of enclosed private boxes and corporate suites.

Steady public enthusiasm for sporting events, combined with the technology of television, increased the profile of the industry. Other companies with products and services to sell gradually recognized that sporting events offered significant advertising possibilities, and sponsorship of sporting events, including advertising during sports broadcasts, became increasingly commonplace. Industries that were prevented by law or by convention from advertising on television and in certain other media, such as tobacco and liquor products, looked to athletic event sponsorship as a method of circumventing the regulations to advertise their products. The most obvious example was the sponsorship of large signs inside stadiums, courts, or arenas bearing the brand name of a vendor, such as a tobacco company, whose advertising was restricted. These ads were then seen in the background on the walls during television coverage of the game.

Sponsorship eventually became standard practice for many companies, and extended to sponsorship of individual players, items of clothing, tarpaulins, lists of statistics, leagues, events or series of events, sports news broadcasts, and entire ballparks. In 1998 it was not unusual to hear a play-by-play broadcaster with a comment similar to, "That home run places [player name] on the [company name] all-time list of home run hitters." Machinery and equipment frequently in public view bore multiple advertising logos. Signage in 1998 ballparks and arenas flourished the way it had 60 years earlier, when poster boards were used as the sole vehicle for sports advertising. In fact, many ballparks and stadiums carried the name of corporate sponsors, causing some newspapers to threaten to leave out the corporate name, and causing fans to grumble about the greed of the sponsors in erasing the traditional names of the stadiums they had come to love.

The post World War II advent of television evolved quickly into a force capable of driving the entire sports market. Although sports had existed throughout recorded history, television spread many sports to broader audiences than ever before, extending across national and cultural borders. Basketball, relatively unknown in France, blossomed when French television began to broadcast U.S. games. Soccer, long outside the mainstream of U.S. sports, was common on U.S. playgrounds in 1998. While sports of all sorts initially functioned as a boon to a fledgling television industry, it was not long until the relationship reversed itself. By the 1960s the purveyors of various sporting events came to realize that advertising dollars, associated with an expanding viewer audience, also could be channeled easily into direct support of sports franchises.

As a result of the infusion of television dollars, the cash value of sports franchises exploded. Franchise values grew exponentially, especially in the United States, where owners were quick to utilize the new source of revenue. In 1983, US$43 million was a record price for a baseball team and by 1993, it was US$173 million. Three years later, in 1996, the New York Yankees were valued at US$241 million. In 1988, an NBA expansion team cost US$32.5 million, but by 1994 it cost US$125 million. In 1996, the NFL's Dallas Cowboys carried a price tag of US$320 million. The Boston Red Sox baseball team went to a consortium of bidders in 2002 who made a

US$700 million offer, which was more than double the previous highest price ever paid for a baseball club—US$323 million for the Cleveland Indians in 2000.

Individual team values rose worldwide throughout the 1990s and into the 2000s despite a drop in team profits. In the United States, where such things were regularly documented, it was apparent that as team revenues increased, cost of player salaries increased even faster. The effective impact on operating income was to reduce it by as much as 35 percent for the average team. In spite of this, the actual value of each franchise increased at a pace that matched the revenue stream.

Escalating player salaries and increased overall operating costs may have placed a huge burden on the sports industry in the final years of the twentieth century, but they did little to dampen the enthusiasm of potential investors. As major corporations began to endorse professional sports organizations worldwide, the phenomenon of corporate and private investment approached a zenith in the United States.

Television. Television remained a huge source of income for the sports industry, but some networks like Fox Sports have reported staggering losses as advertising revenues and viewer numbers were far lower than anticipated in 2000s. In 2002, the News Corporation elected to write off its football, baseball, and NASCAR TV contracts as bad investments, and some analysts were predicting that future TV contracts would decline or stay roughly equal for some time, not escalate.

Although early attempts at satellite broadcasting had some failures, by the 1990s technology for direct broadcast satellites (DBS) ushered in an age of better, smaller, and less expensive satellite dishes. Fans willing to pay for a satellite dish receiver had a much wider array of sports programming choices than were available with other television programming. Satellite television leaders such as DirecTV and BSkyB featured a multitude of sporting events and actively pursued a variety of sports contracts, resulting in an additional windfall for professional sports in terms of increased exposure as well as increased revenue. Sports, especially leagues with a smaller fan base than other major professional sports, were expected to enjoy a proportionately greater boost from satellite TV arrangements. However, the potential for conflict with more conventional broadcasting arrangements caused some observers to reserve opinion regarding the long term impact.

Merchandising and Sponsorship. The single aspect of late twentieth century and early twenty-first century sports that most obviously differed from prior decades was the exponential increase in sports marketing and merchandising. When Nike announced a US$18 million unilateral marketing agreement with the Dallas Cowboys in 1995, proponents of revenue sharing were appeased by a subsequent agreement for US$200 million made with the NFL as a whole. The Nike logo, which was seen everywhere in the 1990s, came to symbolize the proliferation of similar licensing and marketing agreements. Between 1988 and 1993, spending by U.S. and Canadian corporations to sponsor all sporting events increased 15 percent per year, reaching US$2.4 billion dollars as league-licensed merchandise sales soared. NBA-licensed goods, which had garnered less than US$200 million in retail sales in 1986, pulled in nearly US$3 billion in 1993. In 1973, Rich Products spent US$1.5 million for a 25-year license to place its name on the Buffalo Bills' new football stadium. A little more than 20 years later, it cost MCI US$4.4 million a year over 10 years for a total of US$44 million to have naming rights for a new Washington, D.C., arena.

The revenue potential of merchandising contracts was evident in the case of the NBA's Portland Trail Blazers, which earned US$2.2 million in the 1994–1995 season, through the sale of suites, signage, parking, and concessions. The following year, the team moved into a new arena, which offered a greater opportunity to exploit the same revenue sources, with these "venue revenues" promptly increasing to US$15.2 million for the season. In addition, the New England Patriots earned millions via merchandising deals after winning the Super Bowl in 2002. The Patriots had lined up media properties that they controlled with an Internet web site, merchandise shops, and TV and radio shows, according to the *Providence Journal–Bulletin.*

With such large amounts of revenue streaming into league coffers around the world, the relationships between team owners and athletes and their agents were tested. This was particularly true in the United States, where both National Hockey League and Major League Baseball seasons were disrupted by player strikes in the mid-1990s. Even umpires have gone on strike for higher pay. Fan anger at these events was particularly pronounced during the baseball strike, which was marked by unusually insensitive player and owner attitudes. The profound fan disgust for players and owners, combined with rising ticket costs, produced significant variations in game attendance in subsequent seasons, and continued to impact franchise operation in the twenty-first century.

Salary Cap. Team payrolls in the United States jumped substantially in the mid- to late 1990s, and owners of the four major leagues turned to the salary cap as a substitute for self-restraint. The NBA had successfully utilized the cap as part of its effort to revitalize the league when it was losing money. Players and agents fought the institution

of any such cap, while other observers argued that the cap was not reliable. Some teams spent as much or more time and money circumventing the cap than they did trying to fit their payrolls into it. Similarly, after the first full season of the NFL's salary cap, one observer described it as a disaster, creating "a refugee class of unwanted, highly paid veteran talent." Many talked about the cap's elimination as part of the scheduled 1999 contract talks, but proponents argued that it remained necessary. The difficulty in measuring the overall impact of a salary cap increased the level of debate. For example, while basketball's salary cap was regarded as a contribution to the success of the NBA, that success occurred at a time that all-star players such as Larry Bird, Michael Jordan, Magic Johnson, and Isaiah Thomas flourished. In 2002, the Denver Nuggets, with a losing record, guaranteed years of future struggling by trading their high scorers, Nick Van Exel and Raef LaFrentz in an effort to eliminate about US$100 million in contracts and hire less expensive and arguably inferior players as well as to trim an inflated salaried roster, according to general manager Kiki Vandeweghe.

Stadiums. In 2002, jaws of fans dropped when the city of Jacksonville and boosters offered its professional football team, the Jaguars, some cosmetic improvements to Alltel Stadium worth US$33 million, to be completed by 2005. Construction of new playing venues came to be regarded by many professional sports clubs as an absolute precursor to successful operation. However, legions of investigative reporters have called owners to task for demanding that cities either build them a new stadium or say goodbye to the team. Modern stadiums were touted as a panacea that would restore flagging attendance, entice reluctant athletes to sign contracts, and even revitalize entire metropolitan downtown areas. With all the hyperbole, new stadium construction, with an emphasis on luxury boxes that sold for more than US$100,000 a season, entertainment centers, and club-controlled parking, dramatically boosted so-called "venue revenue," at least in the short term. Even the construction period itself was utilized as a fundraiser. Naming rights, signage, and various services were sold to the highest bidder. Nevertheless, amid the frenzy of stadium construction in the United States and other parts of the world in the late 1990s and early 2000s, several issues remained open to question, including the best way to fund stadium construction; how to control construction costs; how long the impact of a new venue would last in a given market; and how much was lost as ballparks, integral to the history of the sport they served, were met by the wrecking ball.

The prophecy that new stadiums were essential to profitability became self-fulfilling when franchises attempted to raise revenue dollars in old stadiums by the same methods used in new ones. In judging the economic viability of various franchises, many senior sports executives insisted that stadium revenue was essential. Analysts recommended that teams should expect to receive at least 50 percent of revenues from stadium concessions, 100 percent of stadium advertising revenue, and 50 percent of parking revenues. When added to the enormous ticket revenue attached to the sale of luxury boxes and suites, the significance of total stadium revenues became increasingly apparent.

In some cases, the surge in new stadium construction had a significant effect on an entire sport. For example, the NHL, with clubs in Canada and the United States, credited its success in attracting fans partially to the opening of nine new arenas within three years. Major league baseball owners, in the midst of widespread stadium construction in the late 1990s, obviously hoped that new ballparks would offset the negativism spawned by the player and umpire strikes earlier in the decade. When minor league teams introduced their marketing efforts they typically paid liberal attention to whatever park, stadium, or arena construction was being built for their franchise.

Professional sports clubs rarely attempted to finance construction or substantial renovation of stadiums out of their own pockets, choosing instead to take one of two approaches. Some clubs targeted private placement funding that normally demanded substantial owner investment, relatively high interest charges, the presale of luxury suites and skyboxes, and even the licensing of the right to buy suite tickets to bring in the needed money. The result of the combined corporate oversight, implied by private placement funding, resulted in stadiums being completed closer to original budget estimates than other stadiums. The second approach was to seek taxpayer dollars from local or state governments, and teams often added a threat to move from the host city. The emotional blackmail represented by the specter of a beloved team's possible departure led many cities to sink large amounts of money into the renovation of old facilities or the construction of new ones. Some of these cities hoped that at the very least they would receive a return on public investment in terms of new tax revenues or spin-off economic activity. Others expected new sports arenas to revitalize dying city centers. Regardless of the approach, the phenomenon of full or partial public funding for stadiums grew steadily at the end of the twentieth century. By 2002 the St. Louis Cardinals baseball team was trying to convince the city to build a stadium that opponents argued could cost US$1 billion over 30 years at a time when many public improvement projects lacked funding.

The unpopular public funding that would benefit the millionaire owners of sports franchises caused governments to become increasingly creative as they identified public revenue sources. Taxes on hotels, restaurants, and rental cars were more palatable to the public because the burden was not heavy for local citizens. Similarly, taxes on gaming, cigarettes, and liquor (so-called "sin" taxes) arguably were voluntary. In most cases, would-be stadium builders did not rely on a single source of revenue, but on a combination of sources.

Control of actual stadium construction costs had practical and political aspects. When construction estimates repeatedly proved unreliable, fundraising became more difficult. Labor problems and unforeseen construction issues repeatedly played havoc with targeted dollars. Some analysts blamed the tendency of stadium builders to seek a location near water, such as lakes or rivers, causing drainage problems and similar challenges. The removal of existing antique infrastructure in urban locations, or simple land acquisition costs, proved to be another complication as bidders and landholders vied with each other to record profits. Banks balked at implied risks when asked to underwrite owner contributions. Detroit Tigers baseball franchise owner Mike Ilitch was unable to persuade local banks to take a chance on his solvency and was forced to turn to Japanese interests to complete the franchise's portion of funding for stadium construction. In 2001, the Florida Marlins baseball team was stunned when its request for a stadium, or long-term tax break, was denied, which had the potential to cause the team's liquidation during the 2000s.

A consequence of rising cost estimates was the fear that revenue increments might not be indefinite. Oriole Park at Camden Yards in Baltimore, which was one of the premier new baseball stadiums in the 2000s, continued to attract large crowds after its construction, but New Comiskey Park in Chicago did not have a similar impact. While the difference may have been stadium design and community demographics, other factors were likely at work. Small businesses driven out of downtown areas by new stadium construction contradicted the theory that new sports venues would revitalize city centers. Cities beset by cost overruns watched in vain for returns on initial investments. In Cleveland, a group-loan program made loans of US$28 million to projects related to stadium construction, but in spite of sellouts at Jacobs Field, the businessmen expected to write off the US$28 million.

As cities and team owners built new stadiums, the disposition of the abandoned facilities became the issue. Many old stadiums held sentimental history for serious fans who opposed the use of the wrecking ball. For example, in Detroit, fans ringed the unused Tiger Stadium, but the highly publicized "hugs," had no impact on demolition decisions. However, many fans admitted that they were also expressing overall dissatisfaction with the direction of the sport.

The need for new stadium construction was not limited to the United States, and taxpayers worldwide were involved in the construction of sports venues. In communities throughout Europe, arena operating costs were often subsidized.

Insurance Costs. A unexpected additional expense for sports franchise owners was the dramatic increase in premiums for insuring athletes who had been hired at exorbitant salaries. Because athletes were paid the full amount of their contracts, even if they were injured or otherwise lost their ability to play, insurance underwriters became uneasy about long-term contracts, which was reflected in higher premiums. The insurance issue was exacerbated in the 2000s when the Baltimore Orioles filed a US$27 million total disability claim following Albert Belle's departure from the team following a career ending hip injury in 2001.

CURRENT CONDITIONS

Television remained a major component of the industry during the mid-2000s, despite wildly inflated rates for television rights and lowered ratings for most sports. Football, the industry's cash cow at US$77 million per team, was a notable exception. In fact, the sport benefited from a US$2 billion DirecTV satellite deal finalized by the NFL. In 2003, nearly 16 million households watched each televised game. Baseball's bottom line revenue also stood to jump an estimated US$500 million due to televised games if the major leagues agreed to sport product logos from corporate sponsors on player uniforms.

As of 2004, the top 50 highest paid athletes in the world had a combined income of US$1.1 billion, 40 percent of which was from product endorsements. Three-fourths of these athletes played team sports as opposed to individual sports. Despite the appearance of a football player in the number three spot, football salary caps kept player compensation in line with the overall revenue of the teams. At the top of the list of highest paid athletes was golfer Tiger Woods, followed by race car driver Michael Schumaker, football player Peyton Manning, basketball player Michael Jordan, basketball player Shaquille O'Neal, basketball player Kevin Garnett, tennis player Andre Agassi, soccer player David Beckham, baseball player Alex Rodriguez, and basketball player Kobe Bryant.

In North America in 2004, *Forbes* reported that the National Football League had US$5.3 billion in revenues compared to US$4.3 billion for Major League Baseball, US$2.9 billion for the National Basketball Association, and US$2.2 billion for the National Hockey League. In Europe, the top 25 soccer teams earned a combined total of US$4.2 billion in revenues.

In the United States a bill was introduced in Congress in 2004 that would benefit franchise owners. Originally intended to manage a dispute with the European Union (EU) over trade, the bill had many other items tacked on, including a provision for owners to write off the total values of their franchises over 15 years. Franchise values, which were approximately US$41 billion, were expected to gain US$2 billion after the bill passed. The bill was expected to become a law before the end of the year.

The impact of economic struggles in the United States in the fall of 2008 was expected to be small, yet noticeable. The price of tickets to sporting events had been rising since the 1990s. By the late 2000s, fans found the cost of tickets, parking, food, and souvenirs for the average family increasingly prohibitive, causing many to argue that sports venues were pricing themselves out of the reach of the common consumer, forcing club dependency on corporations and the wealthy. In 2002 the St. Louis Rams were tenth among all NFL teams with an average ticket price of US$53.52.

Team incomes varied based on "a sliding equation that includes tickets, luxury suites, national and local broadcasting, sponsorship, advertising, concessions, parking and licensing." The NBA laid off some employees and the league closed its office in Los Angeles, California, although NBA Commissioner David Stern claimed that revenue was on target in spite of expected challenges in 2009 and 2010. Stern had recommended that NBA owners attempt to lock in long-term TV contracts with regional sports networks, some of which were partially controlled by team owners.

According to Nandan Kamath, a sports lawyer and director of Go Sports, a Bangalore-based sports career management firm, India had "a large sports-watching population" with "the potential to build one of the largest sports industries in the world." He further explained that, "The major sources of revenue for tournaments are broadcast rights, sponsorships, merchandising and ticket revenues. Each of these is premised on eyeballs and engagement." Future success for the sports industry in India would be dependent on the growth of sports being played in the country.

INDUSTRY LEADERS

The professional sports franchises of the United States dominated the international sports industry. Global broadcasts of U.S. sporting events had combined with the marketing and merchandising savvy of promoters to lead the National Hockey League (NHL), Major League Baseball (MLB), National Football League (NFL), and National Basketball Association (NBA) to create business valued in the mega millions. However, the number-one ranked team in terms of both value and fan base was the United Kingdom's soccer franchise, Manchester United.

Baseball. The top five franchises in Major League Baseball in 2004 ranked by value were the New York Yankees (US$950 million), the Boston Red Sox (US$563 million), the New York Mets (US$505 million), the Los Angeles Dodgers (US$424 million), and the Seattle Mariners (US$415 million). Baseball did not have a salary cap in the late 2000s, and being good was not always good enough to be at the top of the standings, according to David Hale.

On October 1, 2008, Major League Baseball announced a milestone achievement when the National League set a new record for single-season average attendance. In addition, seven teams all set all-time franchise records for home attendance during the 2008 regular season. Total attendance for the 2008 Major League Baseball regular season was 78,614,880. That figure was the second highest overall single-season total in baseball history. The 2007 overall attendance of 79,503 ranks as the record high for Major League Baseball.

New York Yankees Partnership. The most winning team in U.S. history, the New York Yankees had established a brand reputation that was internationally famous. With 2004 earnings of about US$315 million, the privately held company was owned by George Steinbrenner and his partners. Steinbrenner also owned the New Jersey Nets and 60 percent of the Yankee Entertainment & Sports television channel. Alex Rodriguez of the Yankees had a ten year, US$252 million contract, making him the highest paid baseball player in the world and the highest in the history of the sport.

Yamiuri Giants. Baseball remained Japan''s favorite sport, and the Yamiuri Giants were the oldest and most popular team. Formed in 1934 by the Yamiuri Newspapers, the Tokyo-based team has been the home of many national sports heroes, including Oh Sadaharu whose record surpassed that of the United States's Babe Ruth and Hank Aaron.

Football. According to *Forbes,* the top five franchises in the National Football League in 2004, ranked by value were the Washington Redskins (US$1.1 billion), the Dallas Cowboys (US$923 million), the Houston Texans (US$905 million), the New England Patriots (US$861 million), and the Philadelphia Eagles (US$833 million). The average team value increased 17 percent to US$733 million from 2003 to 2004. The eight top teams in the league owned their stadiums, which allowed them to earn sponsorship and advertising revenue. Between 1993 and 2003, 20 stadiums were built or completely redone exclusively for the use of NFL teams. David Hale considered

the NFL "the poster child for how a professional sports league should be run."

Washington Football Inc. Founded in Boston in 1932 and moved to Washington, D.C., in 1937, the Washington Redskins was the richest sports franchise in the United States, breaking the US$1 billion value mark. The team played at FedEx Field in Landover, Maryland, just outside Washington, D.C. The privately held company had earnings of US$245 million in 2004.

Basketball. The top five franchises in the National Basketball Association in 2004 ranked by value were the Los Angeles Lakers (US$510 million), New York Knicks (US$494 million), Dallas Mavericks (US$374 million), Houston Rockets (US$369 million), and the Chicago Bulls (US$368 million). As in other sports, the leaders own their venues and earn significant revenue from sponsorships and advertising.

The NBA had formed alliances with 27 marketing and promotional partners to support NBA Europe Live 2008, a four-game series that was presented by EA Sports in Europe in October 2008. The 2008 tour, which was considered "vital to NBA growth beyond the U.S.," had its highest level of support in terms of marketing dollars and partners. More than 60 licensed partners in Europe, the Middle East, and Africa distributed NBA merchandise to more than 16,000 retail locations. During the 2008 tour, the EA Sports NBA Live Tour 09 videogame was launched.

The Los Angeles Lakers Inc. In 2004, The Los Angeles Lakers reported revenues of US$170 million, matching the earnings of the New York Knicks. The Lakers franchise, began in Minneapolis in 1947 and moved to Los Angeles in 1960. Kobe Bryant, the tenth highest paid athlete in the world, was playing for the Lakers in 2004 when his earnings were US$26.1 million.

Soccer. On a worldwide basis, the most popular sport remained soccer. Although not immediately popular as a professional sport in the United States, it was the country's fastest growing sport. The number-one ranked team by value of any type of sport in the world was the Manchester United soccer team in Manchester, England. Manchester United was valued in 2004 by *Forbes* at US$1.25 billion. The top 10 soccer teams on the *Forbes* list of richest soccer teams were Real Madrid in Spain (US$920 million), AC Milan (US$893 million) and Juventus in Italy (US$837 million), Bayern Munich in Germany (US$627 million), Arsenal in the United Kingdom (US$613 million), Internazionale in Italy (US$608 million), Chelsea (US$449 million), Liverpool (US$441 million), and Newcastle United (US$391 million) in the United Kingdom.

Manchester United PLC. The most popular team in the world in terms of fan base remained Manchester United of the United Kingdom. With a global fan base of 75 million people, the team's owner has been able to establish strong commercial partnerships with several major companies, including Nike and telecommunications company Vodafone. A four-year deal with Vodafone beginning in 2003 was worth more than US$60 million. In the first year of its 13-year contract with Nike, "Man U" added more than US$6 million to its revenues. In addition, the company launched soccer schools in Disneyland Paris and in Hong Kong, taking advantage of the strong fan base in those two areas. The company also has a licensed partner who opened two One United Cafes in Mainland China. In 2004, revenues for the company approached US$300 million, earned through ticket sales as well as through its ownership of retail outlets, hotels, catering services, sponsorship deals, and partnerships with finance-related companies that offer its customers credit cards, mortgages, loans, and car insurance. In 2005, U.S. businessman Malcolm Glazer obtained control of 98 percent of the company, over the protests of fans who feared Glazer's use of debt for the takeover would mean increased ticket prices for them.

The former member of Manchester United and Madrid Real teams before moving to Los Angeles to play for the Galaxy, David Beckham was arguably the sport's most famous player worldwide. He had become a household name following his appearance on the cover of *Vanity Fair,* through his association with the popular movie, *Bend it Like Beckham,* and his marriage to Spice Girl Posh Spice. In 2004, Beckham earned about US$32 million, earning more from endorsements than any other soccer player. He was ranked eighth on the *Forbes* 2005 list of the highest paid athletes.

Ice Hockey. In the 2004-2005 season, the 30 rinks of the National Hockey League in North America were empty. The players were locked out by the owners after the players went on strike and neither side would negotiate a compromise. *Forbes* reported that 17 teams had lost money the previous season, with the total loss for the league reaching US$96 million. The league was demanding a salary pay cap per team of US$31 million, down from US$41 million the previous year, but the players refused it.

The top five hockey teams in terms of value in 2004 were the New York Rangers (US$282 million), Toronto Maple Leafs (US$280 million), Philadelphia Flyers (US$264 million), Dallas Stars (US$259 million), and Detroit Red Wings (US$248 million).

Francis X. Donnelly shared his vision of "the cup's magic power" evident when the Detroit Red Wings won hockey's most coveted award—the Stanley Cup. Even in regions where differences were normally a constant, sports championships provided a way to bring everyone together. As fan Don Schroeder of Detroit suburb Pontiac said, "We're all happy about the same thing. We're the champs." Donnelly said psychologists acknowledged the positive impact a major sports title can have on a community. "Any successful team has the opportunity to bring a community together in ways that would not be possible under normal circumstances," observed Peter Roby, the former director of the Center for the Study of Sport in Society in Boston.

Promoters and Agents. Although the relative maturity of the U.S. sports industry essentially compelled leading promoters and agents to be located in the United States, promoters and agents serve the industry worldwide.

IMG (formerly International Management Group), a Cleveland-based marketing and management company for athletes, as well as performing artists, writers, fashion models, and broadcasters, was founded by Mark McCormack in the early 1960s when he took on golfer Arnold Palmer as a client. With 2,200 employees around the globe, the company's estimated revenues in 2003 were US$1.2 billion. In 2005, the company managed the number-one ranked athlete in terms of earnings in the world, Tiger Woods, who *Forbes* had reported to have 2004 earnings of US$80.3 million. Investment firm Forstmann Little & Co. purchased IMG for US$750 million in 2004.

SFX Sports Group Inc. counted tennis players Andre Agassi and Andy Roddick and golf professional Greg Norman among its clients in 2005. The company was the management representative for more than 500 professional athletes and had ten offices in the United States with branches in Europe and Australia. In 2004, the company was opening offices in Buenos Aires and Moscow, and had formed an alliance with Globo Media Group to explore opportunities in India. The company was a subsidiary of Clear Channel Entertainment, a producer and promoter of live entertainment.

The Interpublic Group of Companies operated a sports and entertainment group that includes several subsidiaries with offices in more than 100 countries. One of these subsidiaries, Octagon, employed more than 1,000 people in 60 offices around the world. The congolomerate represented such athletes as tennis star Anna Kournikova. In 2003, revenues for the sports and entertainment segment of Interpublic were US$428 million. By 2007, the company reported having 43,000 employees.

MAJOR COUNTRIES IN THE INDUSTRY

The interest in global sports is especially apparent during the Olympic Games. Although designed to promote amateur sport, the Olympics have become big business. In 2000, of the 3.9 billion people who had access to a television around the world, 3.7 billion could tune in to watch the Olympics in Sydney, and broadcasting rights were valued at US$1.32 billion. Winning a gold medal can mean millions of dollars in endorsements for U.S. athletes, and the dollar figures have been increasing for athletes in other countries as markets open. Advertising is also big business during the Olympics, according to a Hill & Knowlton study that was conducted by Commetric regarding coverage received by 36 major Olympic sponsors and partners in thousands of articles for two years before the 2008 Summer Olympic Games in Beijing, China, as well as during the Olympics. Visa, McDonald's, Coca-Cola, and adidas were the top four advertisers/sponsors.

While no other country approached U.S. dominance in terms of the total revenue generated by sports, professional leagues in Japan, Canada, and many areas of Europe and South America brought in substantial amounts of money as well. In the mid-2000s, the rate at which the international sports industry expanded in terms of the number of sports and leagues that were established each year showed no sign of slackening. Commercialization through the use of each game venue for as much profit as possible was appealing worldwide, despite an growing audience for the great variety of sports broadcasts on television.

Some export of sports was expected from areas strongest in the industry. Games that had been established in Canada and the United States became popular around the world, generating new professional leagues. Professional baseball and basketball leagues were common in many countries by the late 1990s. Although the quality of play was not equal to that in North America, the talent pool continued to improve. For example, beginning in the late 1990s, Japanese baseball teams provided their U.S. counterparts with outstanding players, and the Seattle Mariners' Ichiro Suzuki was named Most Valuable Player in 2001. In addition, in 2002 the San Francisco Giants signed top-rated Japanese star, Tsuyoshi Shinjo, even though he was 30 years old, an age when many U.S. baseball players considered retiring from the sport. Even American football, once eschewed in other countries, caught on outside the United States, if only as a curiosity, as U.S. teams played exhibition games on world tours. More significantly, in 1998 the NFL Europe League, which evolved from the NFL-sponsored World League

of American Football, fielded professional teams in Holland, Scotland, Germany, Spain, and Great Britain.

The interchange and expansion of professional sports was not limited to North American export. The Federation Internationale de Football Association took soccer's World Cup tournament to the United States in 1994 in an effort not only to turn a profit, but also to stir U.S. interest in a sport that already was wildly popular worldwide. By 1998 the viability of soccer in the United States had been established. Multiple major and minor professional leagues were publicized and reported good attendance, and the success of amateur soccer in schools and on playgrounds offered continued promise to professional soccer. Soccer also became popular in Africa.

The successful Japanese soccer league, the "J-League," was Japan's first professional sports league that was run as an independent business. The J-League took advantage of unexploited regional loyalty by naming teams after cities rather than businesses, as was the standard practice for other Japanese sports. By the end of the first season of play, more than 4 million Japanese had been to a professional soccer game. The following year, attendance climbed to 5.5 million, and almost all games were sold out two days after tickets became available. Not to be outdone, Japanese baseball also became more and more part of a global enterprise. Professional baseball in Japan, as in the United States, endured considerable loss of appeal when challenged by the popularity of soccer in the late 1990s, but there were signs suggesting a resurgence. As athletes began to resist the harsh discipline and poor playing conditions that had long been associated with Japanese baseball, player dissatisfaction brought a colorful style of play to the game. Even if the most rebellious of its players were sent to the United States, conservative cultural traditions had begun to give way by the late 1990s and early 2000s. The future of Japanese baseball continued to be positive as principles were updated and competition remained active.

All sports reflected the influence of the driven industry that twentieth century professional sports had become. Baseball and soccer were the most "American" in style and marketing. In England and Wales, amateur rugby reported a loss of fans, money, and appeal, but as management shifted to resemble that of professional sports, it experienced a dramatically renewed popularity. Manipulation of fan attitude through skillful marketing illustrated the lucrative potential of professional sports that came with the tradeoffs and sacrifice of traditions. The reality of aggressive marketing of games to non-fans in the early twenty-first century was combined with the treatment of the sport as part of a larger entertainment package.

BIBLIOGRAPHY

Aznoff, Dan. "Baseball Star Coverage Harder to Come By." *National Underwriter,* 29 0ctober 2001.

"The Best-Paid Athletes." *Forbes Online,* 24 June 2004. Available from www.forbes.com.

Blum, Ronald. "Sport Franchises Hit by Recession." *AZ Central,* 19 September 2008. Available from www.azcentral.com.

"The Business of Basketball." *Forbes Online,* 6 February 2004. Available from www.forbes.com.

Curran, Tom E. "Patriots Hit the Jackpot on Field and in the Wallet." *Providence Journal-Bulletin* (Providence, RI), 26 February 2002.

Donnelly, Frank X. "The Cup's Magic Power." *The Detroit News,* 6 June 2008.

Dukcevich, Davide. "The Business of Baseball." *Forbes Online,* 23 April 2003. Available from www.forbes.com.

Ferzoco, George. "A Suspicion of Bribery (Canadian Soccer Association)." *Maclean's,* 17 August 1987.

Feschuk, Dave. "Market Fall Imperils Sports Franchises." *Toronto Star,* 17 September 2008. Available from www.thestar.com.

Ganey, Terry. "Few Speak Against Ballpark." *St. Louis Post-Dispatch,* 7 March 2002.

Gerstner, Joanne C. "Shock Making Leap from Champions to Role Models." *The Detroit News,* 7 October 2008.

Hale, David. "Baseball Has Risen from Lockout's Ashes.' Available from www.macon.com.

Janoff, Barry. "NBA Takes Europe By Storm." 2 October 2008. Available from www.brandweek.com.

Jessell, Harry A. "Sports on the Rocks." *Broadcasting & Cable,* 3 November 2003.

Lapper, Richard. "Playing for Survival." *Financial Times* (London), 19 January 2002.

Kamath, Nandan. "The Law Should Protect Investments in Sport." *The Hindu Business Line,* 18 September 2008. Available from www.hindubusinessline.com.

Livingstone, Seth. "MLB Fortunes Turn On Pitching." *USA Today,* 27 June 2008.

Lowery, Tom. "The NFL Machine." *Business Week,* 27 January 2003.

McCarthy, Michael. "Marketers After Their Pitches With More Females Tuning In." *USA Today,* 17 September 2008.

———. "Sports Also Paying a Price Amid Struggling Economy". *USA Today,* 17–19 October 2008.

"National League, Seven Clubs Set All-Time Attendance Records." October 2008. Available from www.mlb.com.

Ozanian, Michael K. "Football Feifdoms." *Forbes,* 3 September 2004. Available from www.forbes.com.

———. "Ice Capades." *Forbes,* 29 November 2004. Available from www.forbes.com.

"The Richest Soccer Teams." *Forbes Online,* 24 March 2004. Available from www.forbes.com.

Ringolsby, Tracy. "Players Association All in Favor of Some Kinds of Revenue Gaps." *Chicago Sun-Times,* 17 February 2002.

Ryan, Thomas J. "Major Leagues Debate Corporate Logos on Uniforms." *Sporting Goods Business,* May 2004.

Sandomir, Richard. "The Media Business." *The New York Times,* 14 December 2002.

Sharkey, Peter. "Italian Crisis Spells Cash Warning." *The Evening Standard* (London), 14 January 2002.

Thomas, Jim. "Rams Are Raising the Price of Tickets." *St. Louis Post-Dispatch,* 20 February 2002.

Vaillancourt, Meg, et al. "Red Sox Sale." *The Boston Globe,* 21 December 2001.

Washkuch, Frank. "Olympic Ties Earn Brands Good Press." *PR Week,* 30 September 2008.

Wilson, Duff. "Bill Would Raise Franchise Value of Sports Teams." *The New York Times,* 2 August 2004.

SIC 3940

TOYS AND SPORTING GOODS

NAICS CODE(S)

33992, 33993. Manufacturers in this industry produce toys, dolls and doll clothing, stuffed toys, children's vehicles (see also SIC 3751, **Bicycles**), games (see also SIC 5731, **Video Games**), and sporting and athletic equipment. Excluded from this industry segment is athletic apparel (see SIC 5091, **Sporting and Recreation Goods**), athletic footwear (see SIC 5139, **Footwear, Athletic**), small arms (see SIC 3484, **Small Arms**), and small arms ammunition (see SIC 3482, **Small Arms Ammunition**).

INDUSTRY SNAPSHOT

According to the International Council of Toy Industries (ICTI), in 2003 sales of traditional toys around the world was US$59.4 billion. While the toy market always had an international flavor—the creations of German toy makers delighted U.S. children in the nineteenth century—by the 1990s the industry had become truly global. This continued to be the case in the mid-2000s. Giant toy makers, such as the Mattel Inc. in the United States, Lego in Denmark, and Nintendo in Japan, generated much, if not most, of their revenues overseas. Indeed, parents in Moscow sometimes spent a month's wages to buy their daughters Mattel's Barbie, which was the most popular doll in the world with US$1.5 billion annual revenues worldwide.

Like the toy business, the sporting goods manufacturing segment is also global in nature. At the 2002 World Sports Forum in Lausanne, Switzerland, Margaret Mager, president of research at Goldman Sachs, and Andrew Gorgemans, secretary general of the World Federation of Sporting Goods Industry, indicated that the world sports market was worth US$92 billion, with the United States and the European Union accounting for 50 and 38 percent of sales, respectively. However, these markets were maturing and the interest for sports in the United States was actually declining. New growth was expected to come from Asia and other developing markets in the mid-2000s. Around the world, several brand names dominate the industry, including Nike, Reebok, and adidas-Salomon that account for one-fifth of the market. Sporting goods manufacturers have also come under criticism for several issues, especially involving the use of child labor.

The majority of manufacturing facilities for both industries are in China, although these are primarily third-party manufacturers doing contract work for companies from other countries as so-called outsourcing. By 2005, according to the ICTI, 75 percent of the world's toys were being produced in China.

In 2005, concerns of consumers, workers, environmental groups, and human rights organizations included the use of PVC and chemicals in toy manufacturing, packaging and electronic waste, the effects of electromagnetic interference, working conditions in factories, the use of child labor, and sales and marketing practices aimed at children. From a business-to-business perspective, the industry faced the ongoing problem of toy counterfeiting.

According to the Associated Press, toys were typically thought to be "recession-proof as parents are likely to cut back on themselves before their children." According to Needham & Co. analyst Sean McGowan, toys are traditionally low on the list for spending cuts in tough times. In 2008, there was a lot of concern about how much people facing severe economic challenges would be willing to spend on toys, which led to innovative promotional efforts, including classic toys, nostalgic toys, and cross-promotional efforts.

Approximately 45 million toys were recalled in 2007, leading to the passage of the U.S. Consumer Product Safety Improvement Act, which was "designed to overhaul the nation's product safety watchdog agency." Nevertheless, toxic chemicals were expected to still be found in toys through 2009 when all of the protections of the Act will be enforced, especially for choking hazards for children under the age of three.

ORGANIZATION AND STRUCTURE

Toys. While the largest market for toys continued to be the United States in the late 2000s, by far the largest source for toys was China. In 2004, according to the *China Plastics and Rubber Journal,* China's more than 6,000 toy manufacturers were producing 70 percent of the world's toys. However, approximately two-thirds of the toys produced used designs and raw materials supplied by other countries, and a large share of the revenues

come from contract manufacturing, or outsourcing, for large toy companies and license holders.

The four large companies that dominated the global toy manufacturing scene were Mattel, LEGO, Bandai, and Hasbro, with Bandai and Mattel having a marketing alliance. However, the industry overall was very fragmented and regionally based rather than global. In addition, many toys were produced on behalf of license holders, including Disney, Warner Brothers, and McDonalds.

According to business researchers from INSEAD, about 95 percent of toys were sold via retail outlets and few manufacturers sold directly to the final consumer. However, by 2005 there were an increasing number of partnerships between manufacturers and fast-food chains, cinemas, and direct-sellers, including Avon. In addition to traditional retailers, an increasing number of sales were being made through new Internet-based companies.

Since the early 1980s, U.S. law has enforced standards for small parts, breakability, paint, and other points of safety in children's toys. The standards have been effective in reducing deaths and injury, but children under three playing with the toys of their older siblings still caused major safety concerns. According to the Consumer Product Safety Commission (CSPC), 143,000 children were treated each year in hospital emergency rooms because of toy-related injuries.

Although manufacturers are regulated by the governments of the countries in which they operate, the toy industry has faced growing demands for increased global regulations from consumers, labor and human rights groups, environmentalists, and trade associations. The New York-based International Council of Toy Industries (ICTI) is made up of toy associations from Australia, Austria, Brazil, Canada, China, Chinese Taipei, Denmark, France, Germany, Hong Kong, Hungary, Italy, Japan, Mexico, Russia, Spain, Sweden, the United Kingdom, and the United States. The ICTI promotes not only ethical and safe working practices, but also establishes toy safety standards and attempts to reduce or eliminate trade barriers. ICTI member companies and their suppliers must not use forced or underage labor and must provide a safe working environment for all employees. In 2004, the Council established a committee to draft a voluntary code for advertising aimed at children, which followed guidelines set by the U.S. Better Business Bureau.

Sporting Goods. The sporting goods segment includes a wide scope of businesses and products. While there are numerous participants in the segment, specific sectors are dominated by a few large companies. For example, Callaway is the world's leading supplier of metal golf clubs, including the "Big Bertha." Nike and adidas-Salomon are among the most recognizable names in the world, especially for athletic footwear and apparel. However, they have moved into the sports equipment segment and their brands are licensed on many related products, making them industry leaders in the equipment arena as well.

BACKGROUND AND DEVELOPMENT

Toys. The first toy was probably made around the time the first child was born. The children of ancient Egypt played with balls, tops, and pull-along animals, and kites were first flown in China around 200 B.C. Germany, however, generally has been considered the pioneer in toy making as an industry. By the end of the eighteenth century, one German toy firm, Bestelmeier of Nuremberg, was issuing a catalog with more than 1,200 entries. At the beginning of the twentieth century, toy making was one of Germany's most important industries, and one-fourth of the toys produced there were exported to the United States.

Because of the reliance on European toy makers, the industry in the United States developed slowly. However, at the beginning of World War I shipments from Germany were halted, which gave a strong boost to U.S. toy makers. Imports from Germany resumed after the war, but the U.S. Congress had installed high tariffs on imported goods, protecting U.S. manufacturers. By 1939, about 95 percent of all U.S. toys were manufactured domestically, compared to 50 percent in 1914. The toy industry in the United Kingdom followed a pattern similar to the United States with an initial heavy reliance on Germany, and strong growth in the first decades of the twentieth century. The Japanese toy industry initially had a reputation for shoddy workmanship and cheap toys made by inexpensive labor that flooded European markets. As in many other industries, however, Japan eventually gained a reputation for fine products.

In the postwar period, toys based on the American Wild West were popular in Europe and North America, and construction toys, pioneered by the Danish firm LEGO, also captured kids' imaginations. Television contributed to the spread of toy culture, fueling the mass merchandising of toys that were considered requisites by the children of mainstream households. Two of the most successful toys in history were Barbie and G.I. Joe, which were introduced in 1959 by Mattel and in 1964 by Hasbro, respectively, bringing those companies to the forefront of the industry. By 2002 Hasbro had decided to increase marketing for these perennial favorites and family games like Monopoly, eschewing the sometimes lucrative but often boom-or-bust toy fads that had created uneven economic times for the company.

By the mid-1990s, the world's two largest markets, the United States and Japan, showed signs of maturity, while Southeast Asia had the fastest growth. European markets were strengthened by the video game craze, which appeared in Europe after it had in the United States. In the United States, sales of so-called traditional toys, which excludes video games, rose only 1.6 percent in 1993, but video game volume jumped 18 percent. The traditional toy market did get a boost in 1994 from the popular Mighty Morphin Power Rangers, even though some parents thought both the toys and the TV show on which they were based were excessively violent. Concerns about violence in U.S. society and its causes also forced Toys "R" Us and other retailers to stop selling several realistic toy guns. However, in 2002, the Toy Industry Association (TIA) had gathered research from university professors that challenged a link between violence and such toys, and the debate was sure to continue or increase well into the 2000s. In 2001, robots were the toys of choice for youngsters in Japan, Europe, and the United States.

Gendered Toys. Throughout much of the history of toys, a significant gender gap has existed in toy offerings. While boys in the 1990s could look forward to action figures, radio-controlled cars, boats, planes, sports toys, and construction sets, girls' playthings were ostensibly limited to dolls and their accessories. Critics said that the industry had not attempted to offer imaginative toys for girls, and that its marketing remained geared to the Barbie mentality. Industry executives, however, blamed societal norms and a conservative streak in many mothers, who purchased 75 percent of all toys in the United States. Statistics showed that parents were more generous with sons than daughters when they buy toys. They also noted that girls tended to mature faster than boys, generally starting to ask for items like clothes and music CDs as gifts rather than toys during their preteen years.

In Japan, however, a non-doll toy that appealed to girls was the electronic organizer. The petite digital assistants featured not only appointment calendars and phone directories, but also fortune-telling and computer-animated virtual pets. The primary market for the digital assistants was girls in the fourth and fifth grades.

U.S. Trends. The difficult times following September 11, 2001, terrorist acts against the United States took a relatively small toll on the toy industry, but did soften sales enough during the holiday season to result in belt tightening measures nationwide. In 2002 Toys "R" Us shut 64 stores and eliminated 1,900 jobs. In 2001, Zany Brainy and FAO Schwarz were in dire financial straits. Zany Brainy especially suffered after a merger with top rival Noodle Kidoodle combined with a lack of standout toys to draw buyers into their stores. In 2001 highflying competitor The Right Start acquired Zany Brainy and FAO Schwarz, creating a single company called FAO Inc. that featured three divisions: The Right Start, Zany Brainy, and FAO Schwarz. However, by 2003 FAO Inc. had filed for bankruptcy and closed stores in its Zany Brainy division in the midst of a cutthroat industry climate. In addition, in early 2004 KB Toys announced plans to close one-third of its stores in the wake of its bankruptcy filing.

Consolidation was rampant among toy makers in the 1980s and 1990s. For example, Mattel purchased Fisher-Price and Hot Wheels, and the more broadly based Hasbro owned Playskool, Kenner, Milton Bradley, and Parker Brothers. Nevertheless, smaller companies were still able to succeed in the business, provided they could come up with a product that sold well. Cash requirements for start-up were relatively low, since manufacturing could be outsourced. Foreign-made products dominated many sectors, including the vast majority of the doll and stuffed toy segment in the 1990s. Large U.S. toymakers not only produced overseas, but also vigorously expanded their marketing efforts abroad. For example, in 1993 Mattel set up an independent sales and marketing organization in Scandinavia to boost growth and replaced its distribution plan with Swedish toy maker Brio.

The U.S. toy industry typically relies as much on instinct and gut feeling as market research, although executives from Hasbro and other executives indicated that there would be renewed marketing on tried-and-true family toys with less emphasis on fads that could end up unsold in warehouses. About 5,000 to 6,000 new toys are introduced annually, but only about 20 percent remain on store shelves by the following Christmas. A few dolls have perennial appeal, such as G.I. Joe, which was introduced in the early 1960s. About 30 years later, around 250 million G.I. Joe action figures had been sold, along with 115 million vehicles. Industry analysts credited successful brand extensions, such as melding G.I. Joe with Street Fighter II video game characters, for the brand's longevity.

Educational Toys. Educational toys, which once accounted for only about 20 percent of the overall U.S. toy market, began gaining popularity in the late twentieth century. Part of that strength came from computer-based toys, with names like "Little Smart Alphabet Desk" and "Talking Whiz Kid Genius." Toy makers and retailers liked educational toys since their profit margins were 50 percent compared to about 30 percent for conventional toys. However, labeling a toy as "educational" can reduce its appeal to children who have learned to think of "educational" toys as being less

enjoyable than conventional ones. Therefore, educational toys were more likely to be advertised in parenting magazines than during cartoons or children's programming. Curiously, in Japan, which is perceived as being more educationally rigorous than the United States, educational toys only held between 7 and 10 percent of the market in the early 1990s, although their share steadily increased.

Multicultural Offerings. In the early 1990s, the number and quality of dolls that reflected the ethnic diversity of Americans increased significantly. According to one manufacturer, black and Hispanic consumers accounted for about one-sixth of total toy purchases in 1991, and many were eager to give their children dolls that projected a positive self-image. Because African-American, Hispanic, and Asian children were projected to represent 41 percent of all U.S. children in 2010, versus 32 percent in 1994, manufacturers were marketing dolls with realistic features, such as authentic-looking hair, and making them with better materials. They also made dolls modeled on black historical figures. The big toy companies increased their advertising budgets for black versions of best-selling dolls like Barbie and Thumbelina, and were able to boost their sales significantly. In the 2000s, the successful Baby June dolls that were created by entrepreneur Selina Yoon with Asian features.

Maru, the star attraction of a new line of dolls designed by a marketing expert to "celebrate the ethnic and cultural diversity characterized by today's youth," was even given a birthday party at The Children's Museum in Manhattan. *The People's Court* TV Judge Marilyn Millian participated in the grand launch party of Maru. Doll Designer Dianna Effner and Maru and Friends were acknowledged as excellent role models for young Latinas. Maru has friends and a book, *Forever Friends,* that tells the story of this young Hispanic girl who moves to the United States copes with a new life and new friends is also available.

Japan. In 1992, Mattel decided to market the same Barbie doll in Tokyo that it sold in Chicago, resulting in a watershed event for Japanese society as well as the toy industry. Until that time, the Barbie dolls sold in Japan had a decidedly innocent, school-girlish look that supposedly was more in tune with local tastes. However, they made little headway against the Jennie and Licca dolls made by Takara, which held 90 percent of the market. Mattel decided that as Japanese pop idols became more adventurous and even risque, the Japanese market was ready for the Ferrari-driving, hipper Barbie adored by Western children.

In the 1990s, the largest player in the Asian market was unquestionably Japan, which represented about 85 percent of the continent's total 1992 volume. It was also the second largest toy market in the world, which attracted the attention of foreign toy makers and marketers. In the 1990s, Toys "R" Us opened several stores in Japan. The company's stunning variety and low prices had begun to change the buying habits of the Japanese consumer, which in turn affected the Japanese toy industry. The convoluted distribution system and the close relationships between manufacturers and retailers began to break down, and Japanese toy makers could not afford to ignore the buying muscle of Toys "R" Us, which bypasses wholesalers and reduced costs by purchasing directly from the manufacturer. The country's large department stores, as well as the big toy chains, such as Chiyoda's Hello Mac and Marutomi's Ban Ban, responded by offering deep discounts on toys, even during the Christmas season.

An industry fact of life is that new toys eventually become old. For many years, Pokemon toys were best sellers for Japan's Tomy Co., but that market collapsed at Christmas in 2001, forcing Tomy to pay a dividend only half that of the 2000 dividend. The news was welcomed by other Japanese toymakers, such as Takara Co. and Bandai Co., that moved relentlessly to secure market share in 2002.

Europe. Germany, France, the United Kingdom, and Italy accounted for about 70 percent of the overall European market in 1992, while all of Eastern Europe represented less than 7 percent. In general, European firms continued to make traditional toys as opposed to the short-lived "fashion" toys that required expensive publicity. Between 80 to 90 percent of European toy companies were small concerns with less than 20 full time employees. European output was highly fragmented, spread out over a vast number of products. With the exception of the Danish manufacturer LEGO, Europe had no multinationals equal to the United States' Mattel or Japan's Nintendo. Firms also tended to be concentrated within certain regions, such as Bavaria and Baden-Wurtemberg, Germany; Lombardy, Italy; Jura and Rhone-Alpes (Ain), France; and Barcelona and Alicante provinces in Spain. Each country also tended to specialize in a certain product line, including plastic toys, model trains, and paper toys in Germany; dolls and board games in Italy; die-cast and mechanical toys, board games, and stuffed toys in France; and metal and plastic miniatures, as well as table and board games, in the United Kingdom.

The emergence of international retailer Toys "R" Us accelerated the consolidation trend in the European toy industry. With Toys "R" Us taking a greater share of the retail market, fewer people were responsible for purchasing decisions. In addition, the company often dealt with the more professional, international manufacturers that may not have previously been major factors in local markets. Toys "R" Us also contributed to an increase in overall demand. When the company tried to open its first store in Germany, it was greeted with a partial boycott by German toy manufacturers who ridiculed the idea of a toy superstore. Toys "R" Us persisted and became Germany's largest toy retailer in 1991. The company has been given credit for reviving the German toy market, which was largely stagnant during the 1980s. Similarly, Toys "R" Us took 15 percent of the U.K. market within two years of opening its first store there, but the country's total toy sales still grew 7 percent in 1991.

The news from Europe for Toys "R" Us was less than encouraging in the 2000s as the giant U.S. chain decided it had over-expanded in international locales such as Germany and the United Kingdom. The result was a decision in 2002 to close at least two dozen of the nearly 500 international stores that were reporting losses.

Sporting Goods. The history of any sport was intimately related to the history of its equipment. For example, the first golf balls were made from wood, but in the early seventeenth century balls made out of boiled feathers that could be hit further were introduced. In the nineteenth century, gutta-percha balls, which were made from the evaporated milky juice of various trees, were much less expensive to produce, making golf more affordable and therefore more appealing. The first balls made from rubber were introduced in the twentieth century. The impact of these balls, which were easier to hit and gave the player a sense of power, was revolutionary, drawing whole new classes of players, including women, into the game.

The sporting goods industry has often been propelled by such technological advances, but its growth in the twentieth century also was due to the increase in leisure time, the increase of professional sports, and the influence of television. Sports like American football became so integral to the fabric of U.S. culture that it was hard to believe that they were once the sole preserve of prep school boys at elite colleges. There was also a general trend of sports moving from West to East as golf, baseball, and soccer became as popular in Japan as in any Western country, if not more so.

Although the sports manufacturing industry includes numerous small players, some segments have historically been dominated by a few companies. For example, Prince and Wilson held 70 percent of the U.S. tennis racquet market in the mid-1990s, and the top six tennis racquet manufacturers combined held 98 percent of the market. The top firms in the industry were often parts of conglomerates that engaged in a variety of business activities. Wilson Sporting Goods, for example, which offered a broad range of sporting goods equipment, was owned by the Amer Group, a Finnish company that also made paper envelopes and textbooks, among other products.

After a decade of strong growth, the U.S. sports equipment industry slowed in the early 1990s because of the recession and, for some sports, the wrong weather. Toward the end of 1992, however, as the economy began to pick up, sales rebounded. In 1993, shipments rose about 4 percent, nearly the same increase as in 1992. European and Japanese demand for sporting goods in the early 1990s continued to be suppressed by the weakness in those economies.

Performance among the industry's numerous segments varies significantly as a sport's popularity waxes or wanes depending on demographics, economics, marketing, and simple fads. For example, during the 1990s in-line skating remained a standout as skate sales in the United States rose from US$53 million in 1990 to US$243 million in 1993. In-line skating also appeared to have good prospects in Europe. Revenue from tennis goods, on the other hand, was notably down in the United States with sales of racquets dropping from US$170 million in 1983 to US$111 million in 1993. Industry observers attributed the decline to fewer baby boomers at peak tennis-playing age (tennis was primarily played by those under 25); shifting tastes (some said tennis's image was too highbrow); and poor marketing by the industry. Nevertheless, in world markets much depended on the quality of the stars: tennis sales took off in France in the mid-1980s because of the popularity of Yannick Noah. By the early 1990s, the French passion for tennis had cooled, only to be rekindled in Germany on the strength of stars Boris Becker and Steffi Graf.

The golf segment has done well as technologically improved products have been introduced and the increase in golfers among the aging baby boomers. Demand for golf clubs helped to sustain the Japanese sporting goods industry during a recession, although much of the increased demand was for U.S. products, including those made by Callaway. Fitness equipment was another sector where changing demographics had improved performance. For example, U.S. sales grew at a compound annual rate of 14 percent between 1988 and 1993. Increasing attention to health boosted the popularity of some products while others faded.

Europe. Demand for sporting goods grew in Europe throughout the 1980s, albeit at different rates for different countries, as general economic prosperity and increased emphasis on fitness combined to boost sales. The economic slowdown of the early 1990s, however, cooled the growth in these markets. Skiing was the favorite sport in Alpine regions, such as Northern Italy and Switzerland, while in the United Kingdom golf was the largest market, with sales of approximately US$115

million a year. The European sporting goods industry was characterized by numerous small to medium size companies, but as in the toy industry there was a move toward consolidation.

Asia. Because of changing lifestyles and government efforts to alleviate persistent trade surpluses, the Japanese population began working less and playing more in the early 1990s. Japanese consumers were devoting more time to pursuing traditional sports, such as golf, as well as relatively new ones, including soccer. Japan's first professional soccer league, the J League, was a huge marketing success story that generated US$4.8 billion in its first year of play, 1993, according to one analyst's estimate. While most of that activity was not due to sales of soccer balls alone, the long-term trend of more free time was expected to increase sporting goods volume. In China, the founding of The Highsun Sport City in Guangzhou is most emblematic of the tremendous upsurge in sporting goods sales and popularity. The privately-owned Highsun Enterprises Group is set up in the style of a U.S. shopping mall with 7,000 square meters of floor space and shops dedicated to Chinese products as well as international best sellers, including Andi, YY-Yonex, Dunlop, adidas, Nike, K-Swiss, Umbro, Kappa, and Fila.

Latin America. The restoration of democracy to many Latin American governments was accompanied by improved economic conditions that augmented consumers's spending power. Moreover, the trend toward increased trade was also a significant factor, as Argentina, Brazil, and Chile sharply reduced trade barriers for imports. While Latin Americans were always passionate about soccer, they also began to play typically U.S. sports like basketball and in-line skating, where U.S. companies held an edge. They were also eager to join health clubs, which helped increase fitness equipment sales. Brazil held the largest market among producers of fishing equipment with roughly 20 percent of the population—some 30 million people—taking part. Nonetheless, the general economic slowdown in the early 2000s had not led to signs of a financial comeback in South America by 2002. For example, Italian sportswear maker Fila attributed part of its overall poor sales performance in 2001 to slumping South American sales. The company posted a loss of US$46.8 million for the fourth quarter and the annual loss was US$144.8 million.

CURRENT CONDITIONS

Toys. The world market for traditional toys (excluding video games) in 2003 was US$59.4 billion, according to the ICTI. The United States held 41 percent of the market, Europe had a 30 percent market share, Asia and Oceania had 29 percent, and Africa held only 1 percent. According to a report from The NPD Group Inc., a Port Washington, New York-based research firm, toy industry sales in 2004 in the United States totaled US$20.1 billion, down 3 percent from 2003 figures, which themselves were down 2.9 percent over 2002 levels. However, growth was reported for electronic educational toys. Sales of action figures and building sets continued to decline, but had slowed. Much of the decline was attributed to the closure of many toy retailers and increased competition for other product categories, including consumer electronics and video games.

Although by the mid-2000s a few companies dominated the toy manufacturing industry, most toys were still being manufactured by small, regionally based companies, mostly in China, Hong Kong, and Taiwan. According to the *China Plastics and Rubber Journal,* in 2004, 50 percent of the toys sold in the United States and Europe were made in China. Grave consequences resulted for U.S. towns that had depended on toy production as the toy industry continued to outsource manufacturing to China. In 2004, the town of Bryan, Ohio, was still feeling the effects of a decision by Ohio Art Co. to shift the production of its famous Etch-A-Sketch to Shenzhen, China, several years earlier. In addition to job loss, the move also hurt the city's already suffering tax base, which had been impacted by a declining U.S. manufacturing sector. A similar move occurred at Chicago-based Radio Flyer Inc. in April 2004. The 87-year-old firm announced a decision to lay off half of its 90-person workforce and transfer the manufacture of its metal wagons to China, where its scooters and tricycles were already being made.

In 2005, several trends were greatly impacting the toy manufacturing industry. Consolidation among retailers was having an immense effect on where manufacturers could sell their products as well as on their profit margins. For example, in 2004 Wal-Mart and Target stores in the United States accounted for an increasing share of the retail toy market, with 25 percent and 12 percent, respectively, and the profit margins of manufacturers decreased as these retailers engaged in pricing wars. In March 2005, the second largest U.S. toy retailer, Toys "R" Us, which had held a 16 percent share of the market in 2004, was privatized by an investment group. This caused some concern among manufacturers as Toys "R" Us historically carried a much broader range of toys than other outlets and was always willing to market new toys.

As a result of this increasing retail consolidation, a second trend continued to affect the industry. Toy manufacturers continued to look for alternative distribution sources for their toys in 2004, frequently including partnerships with other types of retailers, including food outlets and drug retailers, as well as home furnishing and home improvement stores and sports stadiums.

According to the U.S.-based Toy Industry Association Inc. (TIA) ,age compression and its associated "Kids Getting Older Younger" theory (KGOY) has altered the marketing patterns of toy makers. Children are becoming more technologically sophisticated each year, increasing their use of non-traditional toys, such as electronic toys and games, at an increasingly younger age. Associated with this trend is a shortened life-cycle for products, as technological advances are fueled by the need to remain competitive and vie for the attention of the young consumer.

Sales of toys introduced prior to 1990 represented only 3 percent of 2003 sales according to The NPD Group. However, this apparently was changing as nostalgic toys began to make a comeback. For example, 2003 NPD figures showed toy sales related to *The Hulk* movie were US$156 million, followed by Care Bears (US$136 million), Disney Princess (US$81 million), Strawberry Shortcake (US$60 million), Ninja Turtles (US$58 million), Polly Pocket (US$56 million), Transformers (US$50 million), and My Scene Barbie (US$43 million). According to the TIA, the Smurfs were expected to make a comeback in the mid-2000s.

In France, a surprisingly successful voodoo doll was made in President Nicholas Sarkozy's likeness and sold with needles and a voodoo curse instruction book. Sarkozy lost the lawsuit he filed against the manufacturer, with the court saying, "This unauthorized representation of Nicholas Sarkozy's image does not degrade his human dignity and cannot be considered as a personal attack."

Toys that were tied in to movies, TV shows, and comic books were extremely successful in 2008. For example, *Kit: A Tree House of My Own* was linked to the "American Girl" movie and allowed girls to build a project on their computers. A 1.3 mega pixel digital camera was being sold at Target in connection with the *Hello Kitty* series. In addition, Holiday Barbie faced competition with Graduation Dolls tied in to *High School Musical 3.* However, both dolls were made by Mattel.

Sporting Goods. Like the toy industry, the majority of the manufacturing of sports equipment (about 65 percent) was completed in China, although the primary marketplace was the United States. Globally, the sports manufacturing industry was heavily dependent on trade, with approximately one-third of the world market involving the international flow of goods. Typically, low cost items were produced in the Far East, where lower wages offered a pricing advantage. Higher value goods were produced primarily in developed countries and Taiwan.

The sporting goods market in the United States has grown every year since 1985, until an economic slowdown and the terrorist attacks against the United States on September 11, 2001, led to losses in many sectors. Because disposable income, especially in the United States, also was expected to continue growing by 2003, the outlook for the sporting goods industry remained healthy. In addition, baby boomers continued and increased their participation in recreational activities, unlike past generations. However, this trend also marked a reduction in the market for high-impact, strenuous activities, and a marked increase in activities such as golf and exercise using low-impact equipment with built-in monitors. Many exercise machines were sold through "infomercials" broadcast on the ultimate non-exercise recreational equipment, the television.

In its *2004 SGMA International State of the Industry Report,* the Sporting Goods Manufacturers Association (SGMA) reported that U.S. manufacturers shipped US$49.8 billion worth of merchandise in 2003, down 0.5 percent from 2002. A slight increase of 1.3 percent was expected in 2004, as consumers continued to buy sale items, average sales prices decreased, and there was a glut of retail capacity. Summarizing the sporting goods retail climate as the industry headed into the mid-2000s, the SGMA said, "The excess of sporting goods retail space continues to plague the industry. The excess results in severe price competition, mergers and acquisitions, and a threat of bankruptcy for many companies."

Amid these conditions, the industry experienced a high level of consolidation in 2003. Noteworthy examples included the merger of retailers The Sports Authority and Gart Sports, and the purchase of Worth Inc. by Rawlings. In addition, Spalding sold its Top-Flite and Hogan golf lines to Callaway and its team sports division to Russell Athletic. Other examples included Technica's purchase of Rollerblade, and Brunswick Corp.'s acquisition of Navman NZ Ltd. and Land 'N' Sea.

The SGMA also noted that manufacturers were shifting or outsourcing production to nations where production costs were lower. In addition, leading retailers were increasing their private label brands, which further pressured brand name sporting goods retailers. Combined with declining levels of team sports production, which various industry players were trying to counteract with promotional campaigns, a challenging environment faced the industry moving into the late 2000s.

Low labor costs have resulted in increased outsourcing, but when some children in developed nations are playing a game on the soccer field, others in India may have already experienced a big loss. For instance, Gurmet

Kumar was the subject of "HBO's Real Sports" as an example of too many Indian youths forced into the tedious, underpaid work of stitching together soccer balls to survive. Ironically, some of those youths stitch together panels imprinted with the claim that the product is "child labor free." Soccer balls are only one of many consumer goods being made by child labor in developing countries.

RESEARCH AND TECHNOLOGY

The rapid introduction of computer technology by retailers allowed many of the largest stores to reduce inventories, as they received goods "just-in-time" to make the sale. This greatly reduced inventory costs but a major drawback in the toy sector was the lack of backup stock when a toy became an instant hit, so the retailer often could not satisfy demand. Moreover, the store was not always able to quickly get more products from the manufacturer who might need three months or longer to make and ship the goods. This proved a boon to toy collectors, who made a business out of predicting which products would become discontinued or unavailable, and therefore more valuable as collectibles.

Research and development (R&D) played a vital role in the sporting goods market. Consumers were often driven to purchase new equipment because of the real or perceived advantages of products incorporating new technology. While the relative sales strength of golfing equipment over fishing gear reflected several factors, new technology was an important element. The introduction of oversized woods was a boon for makers like Callaway, but there were few technological advances in fishing gear.

Additionally, innovative entrepreneurs sometimes created substantially new sports through their products. In the mid-1970s, NordicTrack ushered in a new generation of exercise equipment with its cross-country ski systems based on a mechanical flywheel. In the mid-1990s, however, as its patents ran out and competing flywheel designs became available, NordicTrack introduced an electronic flywheel design that protected its market and boosted sales. The new design allowed the user to regulate resistance force and simulate snow conditions more easily.

The traditional wooden tennis racket stayed pretty much the same until the 1960s, when manufacturers began to redesign it in an effort to improve performance and ease of play. The introduction of durable metal and fiber-reinforced-composite rackets was followed by oversized and wide-faced models. By the 2000s, manufacturers had introduced finely balanced rackets with shock- and vibration-dampening handles and string bed patterns that provided improved accuracy. One manufacturer, Inova Inc., used computer software to design a racquet called the Handler, which was supposed to eradicate tennis elbow.

Perhaps the most famous example of a sport created through new technology was the development of in-line skating by Scott Olson. The 19-year-old minor league ice hockey goaltender found a pair of roller skates with the wheels arranged in a single row in 1980. Although they felt clumsy when Olson tried them, they gave him the sense of skating on ice. Olson located the manufacturer, who had stopped making the line, and bought the existing stock. Eventually, he began putting blades on good skate boots and sold them out of his house. In 1983, he bought the existing patents and started the company that eventually became Rollerblade, which became a generic term for in-line skates. Designers have continued to improve the skates Olson first developed. The number one cause of skating-related injuries was the inability of skaters to slow down. In 1994, Rollerblade introduced active braking technology (ABT) to reduce these injuries. The new design used a built-in brake lever and ankle cuff to engage the break pad when a skater's breaking foot was extended. Rollerblade, which had lost market share to upstart competitors producing less expensive skates, was hoping that new technology would restore luster to its product line.

INDUSTRY LEADERS

Toys.

Mattel, Inc. Founded in 1945 in a garage workshop in Southern California, Mattel had been the world's largest toy maker off and on since the end of the 1960s. The company reported sales of US$6 billion in 2007 with 31,000 employees.

Dollhouse furniture was Mattel's first toy offering, but its most famous product, the Barbie doll, was an immediate success when it was introduced in 1959. The following year, Mattel began selling Chatty Cathy, the first talking doll, which was another hit. The company went public that year, and continued to enjoy strong results and popular products throughout the 1960s. Mattel aggressively diversified with worldwide acquisitions, but the early 1970s brought hard times and disrepute. The company's chief financial officer was caught recording cancelled orders as sales, and eventually Mattel reported a big loss, leading to an investigation by the U.S. Securities and Exchange Commission. While the company recovered in the late 1970s, the 1980s was another period of poor performance. Many of Mattel's acquisitions proved unprofitable, and a slump in video game sales drove it out of that sector. In 1984 the company teetered on the verge of bankruptcy.

A new president, John Amerman, began turning the company around in 1987. He closed 40 percent of the company's operations and slashed headquarters staff. Perhaps most importantly, he focused on the company's core products, including the Barbie doll. The Barbie line was expanded to 90 different dolls with around 250 accessories. Between 1987 and 1992, sales of Barbie products more than doubled to over US$1 billion. Three brands accounted for half of Mattel sales: Barbie products, toys and other items based on licensed Disney characters, and die-cast cars sold under the name Hot Wheels. Mattel also continued to acquire companies, including the 1994 purchase of Kransco, which made Frisbees and Hula Hoops.

Amerman, who had been head of the overseas division, continued to strengthen the company's international operations. For example, the company bought the major New York-based toymaker for infants and toddlers, Fisher-Price, in 1993 with the conviction that it could expand the company's strong product line overseas, where Fisher-Price had relatively few sales. By 2004, the international market accounted for 42 percent of Mattel's sales. The company's main manufacturing facilities were in China, Indonesia, Thailand, Malaysia, and Mexico, but it also has many third-party manufacturers in the United States, Europe, Mexico, Asia, and Australia.

Mattel's US$3.8 billion buyout of The Learning Company in 1998 was disastrous, and the company was sold two years later to the Gores Technology Group. In 2001, mass closings of Kmart stores resulted in a glut of Mattel products. Still the world's largest toy company in 2004, Mattel was seeking to reduce its dependence on the likes of Toys 'R' Us, Target, and Wal-Mart, which accounted for a total of about 46 percent of sales by engaging in direct-to-consumer sales through its own catalog as well as via online sales.

In 2008, Mattel offered an expensive version of the popular Elmo doll for the Christmas season. "Elmo Live," which was capable of more movement than ever before, was sold for approximately US$60. According to Nicholas Casey, it is "able to cross its legs, flap its arms and fluidly mimic the famous television Muppet." Casey also contrasted the new sticker price with the traditional US$50 toy-pricing limit that was generally considered high. Although there were other expensive toys making their debut in 2008, some retailers were promoting "low cost toys to lure customers," Casey stated.

Hasbro, Inc. The company famous for G.I. Joe, Play Doh, and Tonka, as well as some of the world's most recognizable board games, including Scrabble and Monopoly, Hasbro had 2007 sales of almost US$4 billion. The company employed nearly 6,000 workers, significantly fewer employees than its leading rival, Mattel.

Hasbro traces its origins to a small U.S. textile business begun by the Hassenfeld brothers in 1923. Using cloth leftovers, the company began by making pencil-box covers, and extended their business to pencils, school supplies, and ultimately toys. In 1952, the company introduced Mr. Potato Head, the first toy to be advertised on TV, which continued to generate high-margin sales in the 1990s. In 1954, Hasbro became an important licensee for Disney characters. By 1960, Hasbro was one of the largest toy companies in the United States. In 1964, the company released the G.I. Joe action figure, which was an immediate hit that quickly represented two-thirds of the company's sales.

Hasbro went public in 1968, although most of the stock remained in the hands of the Hassenfeld family. Ill-conceived product introductions, discontinuance of G.I. Joe in 1975 (partly induced by higher plastic costs), and family squabbling hurt profitability in the 1970s. In the 1980s, however, the company fought back with the reintroduction of G.I. Joe in 1982, and the introduction of the highly popular Transformer line in 1984. It also began to acquire other toy companies, taking over Milton Bradley in 1984, Coleco Industries in 1989, and Tonka in 1991, including the Kenner and Parker Brothers lines. Hasbro also purchased Galoob, once ranked number three among U.S. toy makers with its popular Micro Machines, licensed vehicles, and Star Wars film trilogy tie-ins, as well as Pound Puppies.

In 1994, Hasbro vied with Mattel for the title of the United States' biggest toy company. Hasbro was the more diversified of the two, with no individual toy or game representing more than 5 percent of sales. The company expanded into Asia with the purchase of Japan-based Nomura Toys and Palmyra, a Southeast Asian toy distribution firm. Both companies were expected to become distribution channels for Hasbro's move into Asia. Hasbro also began to sell electronic versions of some of its most popular games, including Monopoly. By 1998, Hasbro ranked number two among U.S. toy manufacturers, behind its long-time rival Mattel, which had unsuccessfully attempted to buy Hasbro in 1996.

Hasbro and Universal had announced plans to produce a *Monopoly* movie. While toy companies typically pay film companies for licensing rights to make products that tie in with a movie, Hasbro planned to license "the rights to the name, characters and themes of its board games to Universal, which pays for the production and gets the box office receipts." Universal would also receive revenues from tie-ins and any related rebates. Hasbro Chief Executive Officer Brian Goldner was credited for "the collaboration" providing a distinctive way to promote one of Hasbro's core brands.

Bandai Co. Ltd. The world's third largest toy manufacturer, Japan-based Bandai was founded in 1950 with the production of celluloid toys, metallic cars, and rubber swimming rings. The U.S. arm of the company was established in 1978, and most global expansion occurred in the 1980s. In 1993, the Power Rangers series of action toys were a huge hit in the United States, and the Tamagotchi virtual pet quickly followed in 1996. By 1997, the Tamagotchi was so successful that the company was unable to keep up with demand and had to issue a public apology to consumers. Bandai was more diversified than Mattel and Hasbro, producing apparel, animated film production, candy, and video games. By 2007, the company's sales had reached an estimated US$7.1 billion.

The LEGO Group. Lego was the maker of Lego System bricks, a construction toy that in the early 1990s could be found in 80 percent and 70 percent of households with children in Europe and the United States, respectively. The company traces its origins to the decision of Ole Kirk Christiansen in 1932 to extend his carpentry business by making a line of hand-carved, wooden toys. He created the name "LEGO" from a contraction of two Danish words, *leg godt*, meaning "play well." The LEGO System dates from 1954, when the company decided to design a toy that could be enjoyed by boys and girls, span a wide age range, include a large number of components, and have compatible pieces that could be added to parts already purchased. After several years of trying to come up with the right product that fit these criteria, in 1958 the company created the now-famous LEGO brick, with studs on top and tubes underneath. The child could place the bricks together in any configuration, as proven by 1,060 combinations for only three eight-studded bricks.

The toy was an immediate success, and the company's facilities in the village of Billund, Denmark, were flooded with orders from around Europe. By 1960 the company had stopped making all other toys to concentrate exclusively on the small plastic bricks.

In the United States, the toy was initially licensed in 1961 to the Samsonite Corporation, which thought the plastic toy would blend with its plastic and retailing businesses. Although Samsonite did well with the toy, it never recreated the success LEGO enjoyed in Europe and in 1973 the company gave up its license. LEGO immediately established a U.S. sales company and through heavy advertising and promotion increased volume ten times within two years. By 1994, Lego held the leading position in the construction toy market in the United States, which continued through 2005. The company's headquarters remains in Billund, Denmark.

During the 1990s the firm introduced new lines geared to different themes, including town, space, castle, and pirates, and in the 2000s began to market tie-ins with movies, such as the *Harry Potter* series, with each brick compatible with the components of all other product lines. In addition to toys, LEGO had four theme parks in Denmark, California, England, and Germany. In 2004, LEGO's total sales declined to approximately US$1.36 billion, a drop of 6 percent, which was the worst pre-tax loss in the company's history. As a result of its losses, this privately owned company sold its non-core lines, including its theme parks, and decreased its 8,000 strong workforce in 30 countries.

Sporting Goods.

adidas-Salomon AG. Second in the world in terms of sales of athletic footwear, German-based adidas entered the sports equipment market with its merger with Salomon, the French golf and ski equipment manufacturer. The new company became a leader in high-tech sports equipment. The company was also noted for producing such brands as Maxfli and TaylorMade golf equipment, Mavic cycle components, and Cliche skateboard equipment. By the end of 2006, the company employed about 25,000 people and had sales of approximately US$13.3 billion.

Amer Sports Corporation. Finland-based Amer Sports was one of the world's leading sports equipment manufacturers, but was perhaps most famous for its Wilson-branded volleyball that starred opposite Tom Hanks in the movie *Cast Away*. By 2005, it had become of one the top two suppliers in all its selected sports areas, including racquet sports, golf, team sports, winter sports, sports instruments, and fitness. In addition to its Wilson brand, Amer also manufactures the internationally recognized Atomic, Suunto, and Precor brands. By the end of 2006, the company reported 6,533 employees with sales of approximately US$2.4 billion.

Brunswick Corp. Brunswick was a leading U.S.-based manufacturer of recreation and leisure products. Founded in 1845 to make billiard tables, it had become the world leader in its product categories of pleasure boats, marine engines, fitness equipment, bowling equipment, and billiards tables. Sporting goods represented about 19 percent of the firm's 2004 sales of US$5.23 billion, with marine engines and pleasure boats accounting for the remainder. Total sales for 2007 were US$5.7 billion with 29,920 employees.

Nike. The world's leading seller of athletic footwear and apparel, Nike was also a leading supplier of sports equipment, including Bauer/Nike branded hockey equipment. Of the company's US$12.25 billion in sales in 2004, about US$751 million came from the worldwide sale of sports equipment. Total sales for 2008 were US$18.6 billion, and the company had 32,500 employees.

Callaway Golf Company. Callaway's Big Bertha line made it the largest maker of metal golf woods in the

world. During the early 1990s, Callaway grew astonishingly fast, with revenues doubling and net income tripling each year. In the 2000s Callaway and IBM collaborated to create a means for serious golfers to record swing characteristics and improve individual scores. By 2003, the company was the leading player in the golf market. That year, it acquired the Ben Hogan, Strata, and Top-Flite golf brands from Spalding Holdings, which had declared bankruptcy. However, gross profits continued to decline and by 2007 reported US$1.1 billion and 3,000 employees.

Russell Corporation. Founded in 1902 as a producer of sporting apparel, Russell Corporation continued that tradition in 2005, but was also famous for its sports equipment brands, most notably Spalding, which is a leading producer and marketer of basketballs, footballs, volleyballs and soccer balls under the Spalding brand name and softballs under the Dudley brand. In 2004, Russell recorded sales of almost US$1.3 billion, with just under half of this coming from equipment sales.

Mizuno. Japan's largest sporting goods manufacturer was founded in 1906. The company's 2004 sales reached US$1.33 billion, with approximately 80 percent of that going to the Japanese marketplace. However, the company was showing increases in its non-domestic sales in 2004, with more than 5 percent going to the U.S. market and 10 percent going to the European market. For 2006, Mizuno reported US$6 billion in sales.

MAJOR COUNTRIES IN THE INDUSTRY

Toys. China had the greatest number of toy manufacturers in 2005, accounting for 75 percent of world toy production. However, approximately two-thirds of the toys produced used designs and raw materials supplied by other countries, and a large share of the revenues came from contract manufacturing for large toy companies and license holders. The world's biggest marketplace continued to be the United States, followed by Europe and Asia.

According to the U.S. Census Bureau's International Trade Administration, total exports of toys, games, and dolls from the United States were US$835 million in 2002, down from US$867 million in 2001 and US$1 billion in 2000. During the early 2000s, some analysts predicted that the strongest export growth regions would be in developing regions and countries like Latin America, the former Soviet states, India, and China. U.S. manufacturers were concerned that China, which had been accused of not enforcing foreign intellectual property rights, would allow products to be copied without permission, which could limit U.S. exports to that country, even though its economy is growing rapidly.

Sporting Goods. In 2005 China was the leading manufacturer of sports equipment, accounting for about 65 percent of all goods produced, but the primary marketplace was the United States. The industry continued to depend on trade, with about one-third of the world market involving imports and exports. Typically, low cost items were produced in the Far East, where lower wages offered a pricing advantage. High value goods were produced primarily in developed countries and Taiwan. Labor is the key factor in the manufacture of such products as baseballs and fishing equipment, which are more likely to be produced in less developed countries where labor costs are lower. Often U.S. manufacturers outsource production, contracting the manufacture of such labor-intensive goods abroad.

In 2003, the Sporting Goods Manufacturers Association (SGMA) reported that U.S. exports were valued at US$1.84 billion, which followed a decline of 7.2 percent in 2002, and was attributed to a more positive economic climate in much of Europe and Canada than in the United States. In addition, the U.S. dollar was weak against the euro, yen, and Canadian dollar. The largest export increase was in tennis racquets (176.7 percent), while the largest decrease was in basketballs (51.6 percent). The SGMA further reported that total sporting goods imports totaled US$9.38 billion in 2003, up 4.1 percent from the previous year. Sports equipment was a leading category at US$4.13 billion, which was an increase of 8.2 percent from 2002. Leading exporters of sports equipment to the United States in 2003 were Mainland China (56 percent), Taiwan (9.3 percent), Canada (4.8 percent), Mexico (4.2 percent), and South Korea (2.5 percent).

BIBLIOGRAPHY

"2004 A Year In Review: The Growth, Challenges & Opportunities of the Toy Industry." *Toy Industry Association Inc. Annual Report.* Available from www.toy-tia.org.

Casey, Nicholas. "Mattel Gambles on Pricey Elmo for Holidays," *Tucson Citizen,* 10 October 2008. Available from www.tucsoncitizen.com

Coleman-Lochner, Lauren. "Diversity in Toys," *Indianapolis Star,* 13 March 2002.

———. "Toys "R" Us Plans Cutbacks," *The Record* (New Jersey), 29 January 2002.

Cummins, H.J. "A '90s baby boom," *Star Tribune* (Minneapolis, MN), 22 May 2001.

Earley, Mark. "Stolen Childhood: How Your Kid's Soccer Ball is Made." *The Christian Post,* 1 November 2008. Available from www.christian post.com.

Elkin, Toby. "PlayGloom," *Advertising Age,* 4 February 2002.

Fasig, Lisa B. "Coming of Age—It's a Brand New Game for Hasbro," *The Providence Journal-Bulletin,* 17 February 2002.

"Fila Fourth-Quarter Loss Widens as Sales Decline." *Bloomberg News,* 28 February 2002.

Frasier, Lady Antonia. *A History of Toys.* New York: Delacorte Press, 1966.

Fun Facts. Port Washington, N.Y.: The NPD Group, Inc., 2004. Available from www.npd.com.

Gill, Ronnie. "Robots Lead March of Season's Toys," *Newsday* (New York, NY), 9 December 2001.

Hallett, Vicky, and Marc Silver. "Toyland Tuneup." *U.S. News & World Report,* 23 February 2004.

"Hoover's Company Capsules." *Hoover's Online,* 2008. Available from www.hoovers.com.

"Industry Statistics." *Toy Manufacturers of America.* Available from www.toy-tma.com.

International Council of Toy Industries. *The Traditional Toy Market in the World in 2003 (Without Video Games),* ND. Available from www.toy-icti.org.

"Japan's Tomy Expects Group Loss on Waning Pokemon Sales." *Asia Pulse,* 6 February 2002.

Kahn, Joseph. "An Ohio Town Is Hard Hit as Leading Industry Moves to China." *The New York Times,* 7 December 2003.

Kepos, Paula, ed. *International Directory of Company Histories.* Detroit: St. James Press, 2005.

Kiley, Erin. "Parents Moving to Box Stores, Internet for Toys." *Business Record* (Des Moines), 1 March 2004.

"Overseas Adventure for U.S. Toys." *Business Week,* 3 November 2002.

Peers, Alexandra. "Barbie Boom Going Bust." *Forbes,* 30 January 2002.

Pereira, Joseph. "Hasbro to Take its Games to the Movies." *The Wall Street Journal,* 1 July 2008. Available from www.online.wsj.com.

"Sarkozy Voodoo Dolls Here to Stay," 1 November 2008 Available from www.msnbc.msn.com.

"There's a New Doll in Town." *Market Watch,* 22 October 2008. Available from www.marketwatch.com.

Today's Sporting Goods Industry: The 2004 Report. Sporting Goods Manufacturers Association: Orlando, Fla., 11 January 2004. Available from www.sgma.com.

"Toy Industry Upbeat on 2001." *Consumer Electronics,* 11 February 2002.

"Toy Trends are Cited by ShopKo." *MMR,* 17 November 2003.

U.S. Department of Commerce. *Annual Survey of Manufactures.* Washington: 2005.

U.S. Sporting Goods Exports Resume Growth. Sporting Goods Manufacturers Association: North Palm Beach, Fla., 20 February 2004. Available from www.sgma.com.

U.S. Sporting Goods Imports Continue Growth. Sporting Goods Manufacturers Association: North Palm Beach, Fla., 8 March 2004. Available from www.sgma.com.

"Wagon Maker to Close Chicago Plant." *The New York Times,* 1 April 2004.

Whipps, Heather. "Voodoo Dolls, Zombies and France's President." MSNBC, 24 October 2008. Available from www.msnbc.msn.com.

World Federation of the Sporting Goods Industry. *Newsletters,* 2004. Available from www.wfsgi.org.

———. *Official International Handbook 2003.* Available from www.wfsgi.org.

SIC 7841

VIDEO TAPE RENTAL AND RETAIL

NAICS CODE(S)

532230. The global video industry includes outlets that rent and sell video tapes, DVDs (digital video discs), and related items to the general public. See also **Motion Picture Production and Distribution**.

INDUSTRY SNAPSHOT

The global video rental industry looked as if its best performance days were behind it by 2005. Although revenue figures for home video entertainment were on the rise and sales of DVDs had been growing far more rapidly than the declines in VHS sales, rental revenues were continuing to fall. Piracy issues, competition from video-on-demand, and the trend of consumers to buy DVDs and then trade them in, were all having a strong affect on the industry.

Beginning in 1999 with the creation of Internet-based Netflix, the video rental and retail industry joined the ranks of other industries finding success with e-commerce. By 2005 Netflix boasted 40 million DVDs and 3 million subscribers. Other upstart companies, such as California-based QwikFliks, hoped to cash in on the enormous and growing online DVD rental business, as did Video Island and other companies in the United Kingdom. Even brick-and-mortar players, including international behemoth Blockbuster, jumped into the world of online DVD rentals; Blockbuster launched its offering in 2004, first to the U.K. market and then to the U.S. market. Discount giant Wal-Mart also was a player in this niche, and in 2003 it surpassed Blockbuster for the first time in terms of video sales. Due to reduced overhead fees, such operations could keep a far greater selection of titles than a traditional store could even dream about.

The industry saw competition arise from some leaders in other sectors. Amazon.com started offering Unbox Video Downloads. This option made it possible to rent or buy movies and TV programs as downloads instead of ordering them on DVD.

CinemaNow and Movielink were among the Web sites offering downloaded movies and RV shows to rent or buy. CinemaNow movies could be burned to a DVD for making permanent copies.

Internet Wire claimed that DVDs continue "to be a standard and popular preference in the marketplace for simple and high-quality means of viewing and storing digital media content." There was, however, growing demand for high definition technology resulting in opportunities in a variety of industry segments. Doors were opening for companies linked to providing streaming video and high quality downloads.

Although used DVD sales had gained momentum that major studios and rent retailers found to be unnerving, they were easily accessible through major movie rental chains. Blockbuster sold used DVDs in stores while taking a public stance against the product, Erik Gruenwedel claimed Movie Gallery and Hollywood Video collaborated with operation Homefront to donate "three used DVD movies for purchases of two used US \$14 .99 used DVD's purchased for "DVD's for the Troops" promotion.

An industry's "boom" could add up to more employees gloom, according to Marias's Halkas. Self-service Kiosks utilization frequently translated into job elimination. Kiosks were believed to be "nearly 30 percent of the U.S. market in 2010." It was expected that Blockbuster's decision to add Kiosks and close stores would impact because, as Halkas pointed out, each store had about 10 employees.

ORGANIZATION AND STRUCTURE

Operations that rent and sell videos and DVDs largely include two groups: exclusive video rental shops or video specialty shops (VSS) such as Blockbuster Video and Hollywood Video and video rental departments of supermarkets and general retailers such as Target and Wal-Mart Stores Inc. Supermarkets have found the video business to be especially lucrative as a convenience offering to shoppers who would otherwise need to stop at a separate store to obtain videos. However, given the increasingly competitive market, some supermarkets and general retailers have turned to video rental chains to run their video rental services. First-run movies usually come to video about six months after their initial releases or after a six-month window, whereas they come to pay-per-view service after another one-to-three-month window and to cable movie channels after an additional three-to-five-month window. Video rental operations usually pay between US\$50 and US\$80 for each first-run video cassette for rental use and between US\$10 and US\$15 for sell-through use.

In addition to offering videos and DVDs, rental and retail shops also may provide video games and CD-ROMs for rent. Many national VSS chains have diversified in this manner, and competitive in-store services have followed this pattern in order to keep up. Larger VSS chains may rent VCRs and/or DVD players as well. Besides their rental items, these outlets also often sell a host of concessions such as candy, microwave popcorn, and soda, as well as new and used video cassettes. In addition, many in-store video outlets also sell new and used video cassettes.

Depending on the laws and rating systems of various countries, VSS chains and in-store shops may cater to specific crowds. In the United States, some VSS operations court the adult crowd by providing an X-rated section, although many larger companies such as Blockbuster and Hollywood Entertainment have averted potential problems by eliminating adult sections or not introducing them in the first place. Small, independent U.S. video shops often concentrate on or exclusively offer art and foreign films. Furthermore, a number of in-store shops only target the family crowd, not wanting to offend the sensibilities of shoppers who might object to R-rated fare. However, in countries such as Germany, video specialty stores offer the whole gamut of movies from pornography to children's movies.

A number of movie video distributors provide videos to rental and retail stores. While many stores rely on several distributors, some video operations began to consolidate their accounts in the late 1990s. For example, U.S.-based Kroger Co. announced in 1997 that it would pare its distributors down to just one and began taking bids to see which distributor would win its contract. In addition, Blockbuster bypassed distributors altogether and began to buy directly from movie studios in 1996.

In 2000 the studios and major video chains adopted what is known as the rental revenue-sharing business model. The goal was to get customers to move from VHS to DVD. Prior to the agreement, video stores were paying an average of US$40 per video to purchase videos that they could then rent out to recoup their costs. Under the new agreement, the major chains were given the movies on a consignment basis, with the two sharing any rental revenue received. The studios received 60 percent of the revenues, and the video chains received the remaining 40 percent. Eventually, the used videos were sold for between US$5 and US$15 and the revenues split evenly between studio and chain. Once consumers started accepting DVD over VHS, the studios began to decrease the number of videos entered into the revenue-sharing scheme, and began to offer discounts to wholesalers and retailers to encourage consumers to purchase DVDs.

In 2002, however, independent video retailers filed lawsuits against Blockbuster and other video giants claiming that the revenue-sharing model used by Blockbuster and the major studios constituted unfair competition, a charge Blockbuster's attorneys denied. Undeniably, however, Blockbuster's ability to purchase huge quantities of new releases gave the chain a leverage few rivals could compete with since a tape that costs Blockbuster US$10 could cost a rival six times that amount because of Blockbuster's agreements to share revenues with studios. In

addition to the bankruptcies of numerous small stores, a small number of national chains have gone bankrupt or have seen their demise predicted by industry analysts.

The Video Software Dealers Association (VSDA) serves the U.S. video rental industry. With headquarters in Encino, California, the VSDA promotes home video rental through conventions, newsletters, education, and industry reports. The VSDA also provides members with screening videos and retailing handbooks to help them market new releases and remain competitive. The VSDA's accomplishments include lobbying for and helping bring about the adoption of state and federal antipiracy laws, as well as the maintenance of competitive pay-per-view windows. The International Video Federation (IVF) serves the European industry, providing support for video rental and retail operations and statistics on the industry.

Outside of the United States, the video industry operates in an environment that includes some similarities to the U.S. system, as well as some important and impactful differences. Similar is the fact that movies are released using a sequential distribution plan for economies of scale. However, in some countries and trading blocs, home video retailers are required to obtain a license to purchase then rent videos. Studios often charge home video retailers more for a video that is to be used for rental purposes then they do for one that is going to be sold to the consumer. This two-tiered pricing has increased the competition faced by video rental stores in such markets as the United Kingdom, Ireland, Spain, and Italy, who must compete with mass merchandisers.

BACKGROUND AND DEVELOPMENT

The video cassette recorder (VCR) appeared on the market in 1975, as the first step in the development of the video rental and retail industry. New entertainment services also emerged around this time including cable television that fueled the popularity and usefulness of the VCR because the VCR allowed users to tape TV movies and television shows. Shortly after the introduction of the VCR, movie studios released video cassettes of classic movies to add to their revenues. The advent of the VCR/videotape movie combination presented consumers with more entertainment options. They no longer had to rely on the schedules of movie theaters or premium cable channels to see movies. Instead, they could see them any time they wanted by purchasing movies on video cassette, known in the trade as sell-through videos. However, sell-through videos carry a financial burden because few consumers can afford to pay US$10 to US$25 for each movie they want to see.

In 1977, George Atkinson of Los Angeles bought 50 VHS and 50 Betamax movies, and placed an advertisement in a local paper saying that they could be rented for US$10 per day. He established a rental store, but was soon facing threats of a lawsuit by the film production industry. However, U.S. copyright law allowed for the rental of videos, so soon Mr. Atkinson had 600 franchised stores in operation. He passed away in 2005 with the claim to the moniker "the inventor of video rental." Video rental and retail shops emerged to serve people who wanted the convenience of home video without the expense of purchasing sell-through video cassettes, in addition to those consumers willing to purchase their own copies. Video rental grew quickly, since, after an initial US$150 to US$500 investment for a VCR, people could rent a cassette for a lower price than an individual ordinarily would pay for movie theater admission. Video rental especially filled the family entertainment niche where consumers needed tickets for the entire family, which cost a total of US$20 to US$30, in contrast to a US$3 expenditure to rent a video. By 1985, the U.S. industry alone took in revenues of US$3.5 billion, which grew to US$9.8 billion by 1990, according to the Video Software Dealers Association.

A new laser disc format called the digital video disc (DVD) emerged in the late 1990s as an increasingly popular replacement for the video cassette: DVDs can store between 4.5 and 17.0 gigabytes of data, which translates to between 135 and 540 minutes of playing time. Besides offering a higher capacity and better audio and video qualities, DVDs also have interactive capabilities, allowing users to witness multiple angle shots of a single scene, to read sets of multiple subtitles, and to move to favorite parts of movies by pressing a button. DVD player prices started at about US$500 in the mid-1990s.

Depending on the maturity of the industries, and on domestic economic conditions, the video rental and retail industries of various countries and regions experienced different results in the late 1990s. After a period of strong growth through 1994, video rental and sell-through revenues dropped in 1995 in the United States, the industry's largest and most mature market, but began rebounding strongly in 1998. Following the 1995 drop in revenue, the U.S. industry became alarmed and took extra measures to increase its revenue. The following year, sales rose to US$16.0 billion and climbed 3 percent to US$16.6 billion in 1997. Research by the Video Store group found that consumers spent US$2.6 billion on both VHS and DVD videos during the first quarter of 2002 alone, a significant increase of nearly 7 percent from the US$2.4 billion spent during the same quarter in 2001. Movie distributors tried to shorten windows to increase revenues from video sales in the late 1990s, especially for movies that performed below expectation at the box office.

Asia's economic crisis of the late 1990s affected its video rental and retail industry as consumers became less willing to spend money on non-essential items. Because of the region's growing inflation and unemployment, consumers in countries such as South Korea, Indonesia, and Thailand drastically cut their video rentals and purchases in late 1997 through mid-1998. For example, Thailand reported a 30 percent drop in video sales in mid-1998. Nonetheless, Japan's industry remained the bright spot in Asia as video rentals increased in the late 1990s because of hit movies such as *Princess Mononoke*, *Independence Day*, and *Lost World*.

The European Union's video industry posted moderate growth in the mid- to late 1990s as strong growth in some countries compensated for stagnation and declines in others. While video purchases rose in the European Union, rentals continued to fall, so that purchases surpassed rentals as the industry's leading source of revenues in the mid-1990s. The European Union bought an average of approximately 220 million videos in the mid-1990s, valued at about US$3.7 billion. The EU's total market was worth an estimated US$6.4 billion in 1996, when video rentals accounted for only US$2.7 billion. The EU's VCR penetration stood at about 64 percent during this period and 27,000 video rental and 56,000 retail stores operated in EU countries.

With a drop in sales in 1995 and the emergence of competitive alternatives to video rentals and sales, video rental and retail stores began seeking ways of maintaining and increasing their customer traffic. Supermarkets with video shops have tried to offer "dinner and movie" specials to keep their video departments thriving, according Dan Alaimo in *Supermarket News*. Stores have provided promotions giving customers movie rental discounts with the purchase of deli items and prepared entrees. With such promotional campaigns underway, some video stores considered large-scale alliances with restaurants. Blockbuster launched a promotional campaign with Planters Nuts, and Hollywood Entertainment teamed up with Domino's Pizza to offer free movies with pizza purchases.

Other modes of home entertainment continue to compete with the video rental industry. Alternative forms of home entertainment such as digital television, pay-per-view, and direct-broadcast satellite remained a challenging force for video stores in the late 1990s. Although these alternatives provided some advantages over video rental—including higher resolution for digital television and some greater conveniences such as not having to return videos for pay-per-view and direct broadcast movies—video industry proponents point out that they also cost substantially more and sacrifice features such as being able to pause and rewind movies. Furthermore, these alternatives have a much more limited selection than video stores. Nonetheless, an A.C.

Nielson survey conducted in the United States indicated that only 35.8 percent of the participants with direct satellite systems rented a video during the three-month sampling period, even though 95 percent of them owned a VCR. Moreover, 73 percent of the participants reported that they rented fewer videos after installing direct satellite systems.

Inadequate international copyright protection is a perennial problem plaguing the industry. Pirated video cassettes make up a large part of some markets in Latin America, and piracy also undercuts the video rental industries in East Asia, the Middle East, and Eastern Europe (though the practice, of course, also occurs in the United States and Western Europe). The Chinese government officially banned piracy. Fines, however, are low for video counterfeiters and the financial rewards have been worth the risk for the unscrupulous. Such copyright infractions have strained relationships between video producers and distributors and government agencies of various countries. In the late 1990s, the video industry continued to lose a large amount of revenues to piracy. For example, the U.S. industry annually lost about US$250 million to worldwide video piracy, according to the Motion Picture Association of America (MPAA), and Europe lost about US$275 million, according to Federation Against Copyright Theft (FACT). Consequently, agencies and associations such as the MPAA, the VSDA, and FACT increased their efforts to combat and prevent video piracy.

At the end of 2001 the video and DVD rental industry found itself among the few industries to substantially benefit, particularly in the United States, from the terrorist attacks against the United States. In late 2001, more families opted for entertainment they could enjoy at home, according to some industry observers, and revenues for the industry surged. Also helping to bolster sales was a weak North American economy, which prompted consumers to look for less expensive entertainment options.

Lower DVD prices have coincided with increased sales and market competition for customers. To respond to customer demand, many video stores have emptied their old tape sections to offer new movie releases and popular classics on DVD. Blockbuster, for example, replaced approximately 25 percent of all tapes with DVD discs in 2001, enticing customers to make the changeover with US$99 offers for DVD players and even free DVD players to those who purchased a US$199 DVD rental card.

CURRENT CONDITIONS

According to *The Hollywood Reporter*, the video rental and retail industry in the United States boasted almost US$26 billion in revenue for 2004, $16 billion of which

was for DVDs. By the end of 2004, more than 70 million U.S. households, 42 million Chinese households, and 171 households in other countries had DVDs. Citing data from Adams Media Research, *The Economist* revealed that DVD rentals and sales made up some 40 percent of movie studio revenues by 2003, up from 1 percent in 1997. In its 2004 annual report, Time Warner reported that the largest driver behind its growth in the filmed entertainment segment was the sale of DVDs from its library of film titles. The industry move to DVD allowed Internet companies such as Netflix to thrive; because DVDs are smaller and more lightweight than video cassettes, they were comparatively more affordable to mail. Waiting time was becoming increasingly less of an issue as well. By 2005, Netflix had 35 distribution centers handling its 40 million DVDs, allowing for 24-hour delivery in most markets. Seeing the competition's success, Blockbuster entered the online market in 2004 in both its U.S. and U.K. markets.

Sales and rentals of VHS-format movies continued their downward spiral, dropping by 50 percent in 2004. However, the overall increase in revenues for the sales and rental market of all video formats was not only due to the acceptance of the DVD format, but of the desire for consumers to own movies in this format. The rental market, when analyzed independently of sales, was actually on the decline. Adams Media Research had found that rentals of both DVD and VHS had dropped by 11 percent from US$9.8 billion in 2003 to about US$8.8 billion in 2004. Industry analysts were projecting that as other options become more widely used, the rental market will decline 4 to 5 percent annually. A possible monkey wrench in the phenomenal growth of both traditional and online stores could prove to be the growing popularity and availability of video-on-demand (VOD), a service that allows viewers to choose movies from home to view instantly. According to PricewaterhouseCoopers, the VOD market will encompass 20 million households by 2007. However, the VSDA projected that the VOD market would not be a major factor until 2008, when revenues were expected to hit US$2.5 billion.

According to *The Hollywood Reporter*, the trading of DVDs was also expected to aid in the decline of the rental market. Consumers were buying DVDs and then trading them in for cash or credit. The advantage to store owners was the ability to resell DVDs without having to share the profit with film studios. This trend took off in 2004, with estimates on the value of this type of selling being about US$1 billion.

Netflix initiated the strategy of not charging its customers late fees. For a flat fee, consumers could keep a video as long as desired. The other major video chains followed suit, reducing or eliminating late fees. However, such fees had accounted for as much as 10 percent of the fees earned by studios and about 15 percent of revenues earned by Blockbuster. Several studios responded to these trends by discounting the price of its DVDs to both wholesalers and retailers. As a result, the cost of buying a new DVD dropped to between US$10 and US$17 dollars, with many selling for less than US$5 in bargain bins. This pricing strategy served to further encourage the number of DVDs purchased rather than rented. Discounters, such as Wal-Mart and Target, began to outpace the video chain giants in terms of sales of DVDs. In addition, the studios were more aggressively promoting video-on-demand. Where once video renters received movies first after box-office release, the playing field was expected to become more even, with cable television companies being offered the chance to be the first to show movies after their box-office runs.

However, this buying trend was also showing signs of a decline. In 2004, the average number of DVDs purchased per year per household dropped from 10 in 2003 to 8. High-definition DVDs were launched in 2005, a move many hoped would help to revitalize the industry. Franchised films made the most money for the industry in 2004. *Shrek 2* led the video rental and sales market, with about US$458 million in revenue of which about US$44 million was from rentals. *The Lord of the Rings* trilogy also earned significant money for the industry, with sales and rentals of US$415 million.

According to Kagan Research, although the home video market was expected to grow to a value of US$33.8 billion by 2009, the amount of revenues from rentals was expected to continue to decline, reaching US$6.3 million in 2009. With this trend will come the continued consolidation of the industry. A July 2005 report in *The Hollywood Reporter* even commented on the struggle facing the VSDA, as the number of independent rental stores declines.

RESEARCH AND TECHNOLOGY

To track industry performance and consumer habits, the VSDA introduced VidTrac to the U.S. industry in January of 1996. The point-of-sale service collects data from a large sample of video rental operations throughout the country. More than 4,500 stores participate in VidTrac with nine of the most successful rental chains among them. The VSDA tabulates and circulates the data each week, offering statistics and projections for the video rental community. The tabulations are made available on the VSDA Web site. In 2002, *Variety* charged that the statistics may be off by 20 to 40 percent and demanded more accurate figures.

Internet rental pioneer Netflix developed software to offer recommendations for other movies based on past rental activity. This ability offers the best of both worlds, because customers received a personalized service that also had the advantage of being automated.

In 2005, two technologies were expected to have great influence on the video industry. The first was the introduction of high-definition DVDs. This new system will provide consumers with surround sound and three-dimensional-like pictures. With the ability to hold six-times more data than conventional DVDs, studios will not have to spend so much time compressing data to fit, and will be able to add more marketing-related information. Consumers will be required to buy new players in order to take advantage of this new viewing format.

The second technology affecting the industry is the availability of video-on-demand (VOD). In 2003, according to the VSDA, about 12.5 million U.S. households already had access to VOD, with 25 percent having access to the Internet through high-speed broadband. With VOD, consumers can access movies and television programs when they want via their cable, satellite or Internet service.

INDUSTRY LEADERS

Blockbuster Inc. Headquartered in Fort Lauderdale, Florida, Blockbuster Entertainment Group led the global video rental and retail industry in 2005, after beginning operations with a single store in 1985. After watching its revenues fall a whopping 20 percent in 1997, Blockbuster devised a strategy of providing good service and value to the greatest number of customers. Stripping from shelves the games and little-rented titles to make room for more copies of blockbuster movie releases, Blockbuster immediately won accolades for improved customer service and the availability of desirable hit titles. A subsidiary of Viacom Inc. from 1994, Blockbuster divested in 2004 to become an independently trade public company. At the end of 2004, Blockbuster had more than 9,100 stores in 25 countries, and revenues of US$6.1 billion. Revenues from outside of the United States made up 30.5 percent of all sales. The company was a franchisor of its stores, with 1,095 franchised operations in the U.S. and 734 in other countries.

To compete with the success of Internet-based video rental companies, Blockbuster launched its own online subscriptions service in May 2004 in the United Kingdom and in August 2004 in the United States. By the end of 2006, Blockbuster had more than 2 million subscribers and the company added 700,000 new subscribers by the end of the year after its November 1 launch of "Total Access."

Blockbuster executed product launch and Presidents' Day-linked promotions targeting Netflix subscribers and offering them in-store benefits usually available exclusively for Blockbuster "Total Access" members. Netflix members were allowed to bring in their tear-off address flaps from rental envelopes and receive a free movie rental in exchange for every flap submitted at Blockbuster stores. Netflix members were required to sign up for a free Blockbuster account during their visit.

In the first quarter of 2007, Blockbuster gained more online subscribers than Netflix. It added 800,000 online subscribers for a total of three million. For the entire year, the company made a substantial investment in promotional efforts adding up to approximately US$170 million. By 2008, Blockbuster reported sales of US$5.3 billion and 58,561 employees.

Blockbuster was taking a more aggressive strategic approach reflecting "a proactive agenda with plans for expansion," NACS online stated the *Wall Street Journal* had reported. Plans for establishing up to 10,000 DVD rental kiosks by the middle of 2010. Another option involved showing "pre-released, lower budget films."

Movie Gallery Inc. Movie Gallery grew its video chain in the United States by concentrating on rural and secondary markets. In early 2005, the company had about 2,500 retail stores located in small towns and suburban areas of cities. Revenues for 2007 were US$2.5 million. The company reported having 36,500 employees in 2007. Movie Gallery operated more than 4,600 stores in the U.S. and Canada under brands of Movie Gallery, Hollywood Video, and Game Crazy.

In January 2005, the company acquired Hollywood Entertainment. Based in Wilsonville, Oregon, Hollywood Entertainment Corp. grew quickly in the mid-1990s to become the second-largest U.S. national video rental chain. Hollywood Video claimed in 2002 that it was opening one new store every day. From a single store in 1988, Hollywood operated 1,006 stores in the U.S., eschewing the international competition that Blockbuster had embraced. Hollywood Entertainment was begun by husband-and-wife entrepreneurs Mark and Holly Wattles and expanded through a series of acquisitions. The firm's profits in the early 2000s were hurt by its previous US$90 million purchase of online video merchant Reel.com, an acquisition widely criticized as extravagant. Eventually, Amazon.com took over the site, but Hollywood continued to provide content. The company had US$1.78 billion in sales in 2004. Amanda Barber noted that Hollywood Video's EVP and COO Tim Winner said stressing common goals related to delivering exceptional experiences helped address issues related to mergers, acquisitions and staff retention. This observation acknowledged that Movie Gallery with an initial strong small town market had

successfully acquired and with grown with Hollywood Video focused on urban markets.

According to Bob Geiger, Hollywood Video implemented a new strategy related to space utilization. It set the goal of subleasing one-third of the space at its 2,200 stores. The plan called for attracting smaller retailers willing to open stores within stores at Hollywood Video locations. Geiger also reported that Hollywood Video had placed video DVD rental kiosks in some Minneapolis area Club Foods stores.

Movie Gallery also acquired St. Paul, Minnesota-based Video Update in 2002. Video Update had unexpectedly declared bankruptcy in 2000. The chain continued to do business in January 2002, despite cutting loose some 110 stores to streamline operations. That year, Video Update came under fierce criticism for its payment of huge salaries to its top executives, even as the company demanded Chapter 11 protection. In 2000, the chain had swelled to 586 units after purchasing the Moovies Inc. chain of stores.

Movie Gallery partnered with Major League Baseball (MLB) Properties for a promotion providing fans with a chance to attend game four of the 2007 World Series. The promotion automatically entered customers who rented or bought MLB-licensed games at any Movie Gallery, Hollywood Video or Game Crazy (another Movie Gallery subsidiary) store into the sweepstakes that ended on April 29. The grand prize was a trip for two to the World Series and the first prize was four tickets to an MLB park of their choice. The promotion was supported with online and in store materials. Movie Gallery had a three-year partnership with the MLB. It also partnered with sports trading card producer Topps Co. and inserted free game rental or US$5 coupon toward the purchase of a 2007 MLB-licensed game in select packages of baseball cards.

After six consecutive months of sales decline for Game Crazy stores, Movie Gallery decided to close more than 200 stores located in Hollywood Video sites. The move was not expected to impact movie rental stores.

Netflix Inc. The early 2000s saw a rise in e-commerce, and the video rental industry was no exception. Begun in 1999, Netflix offered access to thousands of DVD titles available for rental. By 2002, Netflix had emerged as the reigning king of online DVD rentals. For one fee (between US$9.99 and US$17.99 monthly in 2005), customers could go online to rent a pre-specified number of movies and keep them as long as they pleased, with no late fees. The DVDs arrive via the U.S. post office and are returned the same way, postage paid. In January 2002, Netflix boasted that it had 500,000 subscribers, and by the 2005 that number had swelled to more than 3 million. Subscription numbers were continuing to grow.

By May 2007 subscriptions had grown to nearly 7 million. Netflix reported 2004 revenues of US$506.2 million, an increase of more than 200 percent more than 2003 levels. For 2008 revenues reached nearly US$1.4 billion. Netflix had 1,644 employees.

Joseph Rose shared information about how observant Netflix changed its way of doing business. In 2001 company executives discovered that the San Francisco area led the U.S in subscriber growth. San Jose, California, however, was the only shipping and receiving site then. After realizing that next-day delivery was its major selling point, Netflix opened 11 more centers in 2003.

Netflix's "Instant Movie Watching" feature makes it possible for Internet users to watch movies. Streaming videos permitted viewers to immediately watch movies in real time. It did, however, prevent them from downloading the movies. According to Liane Cassavoy, all Netflix subscriptions would include the service allowing each subscriber a certain number of Internet viewing hours corresponding to the monthly fee on their account.

Netflix employees enjoyed the ability to take as much vacation time as they wanted. After an employee argued that since daily hours were not tracked vacation time should not be either, the vacation non-policy was considered and implemented. It was estimated that most employees average about 25 to 30 vacation days per year. They were encouraged to schedule vacation time within the rhythm of their jobs and make sure work was completed efficiently.

According to Yuval Rosenberg, Netflix CEO Reed Hastings set goals for 50 percent annual profit growth for the next few years. Hastings confidence in part was impacted by Netflix's stock ending its long slide and soaring more than 50 percent since August 2006.

When a team of fierce competitors unites to earn major competition prize of US $1 million great things are bound to happen. For its US $1 million challenge contest, Netflix claimed there were "more than 40,000 teams from 186 countries." The contest was launched in 2006 and the first set of winners was announced in September 2009. Suggestions from competitors had already been implemented resulting in substantial improvements. The winning team members previously competed against each other before uniting to achieve their goals. They are software and electrical engineers plus statisticians and machine learning researchers. The nations they represented included Austria, Canada, Israel and the United States. The major focus of the challenge was "to improve upon the company's ability to accurately predict Netflix members' tastes by 10 percent."

Tsutaya. Tsutaya began operations in 1983. By 2005, the company operated more than 1,155 stores and had more than 18 million members in Japan. The company held a 31.5 percent market share in Japan in 2003. The company is part of Culture Convenience Club Co. Ltd. that had revenues of approximately US$1.7 billion in 2004. In 2006 projections were made for Tsutaya to have 1.8 billion bacht in sales. In Thailand in March 2006, there were 251 outlets nationwide with 30 being company-owned and the others franchises. By the end of 2011, that number was expected to increase to 900. According to Barung Ammatcjarpemrot Tsutaya (Thailand) CEO Wanchai Phlaphongphanich was confident both household membership and sales figures would continue to soar.

MAJOR COUNTRIES IN THE INDUSTRY

United States. The United States led the world in revenues from video tape rentals and sales and housed the world's top video rental chains, such as Blockbuster and Hollywood Video, owned by Movie Gallery. The VSDA reported that these three video store chains held 50 percent of the U.S. market for rentals in 2003. The number of video stores had been on the decline since 1990's high of 31,000; by 2003 there were 24,300 video rental specialty stores. Most of this decline has been attributed to consolidation and the rise of the video mega-shops. However, in 2003, about half of all stores were still single-store operations, and an additional 4,100 other retailers (mainly pharmacies and supermarkets) were also renting videos. Blockbuster was surpassed in terms of video sales for the first time in 2003; Sam's Club had more in revenues from this source than did Blockbuster.

U.S. video rental operations have achieved their success in part because of the 90 percent VCR penetration into U.S. households and 53 percent DVD penetration in 2003. However, DVD sales and rentals were dominating the market. Of the US$22.2 million spent on video sales and rentals in 2003, 16 million was spent on DVDs—a 40 percent increase over 2002 levels. Video sales and rentals was also contributing significantly to the bottom lines of the major film studios in the U.S., with home video accounting for about 60 percent of all revenues received from filmed entertainment.

United Kingdom. In the mid- to late 1990s, the United Kingdom led Europe in revenues from video rentals and purchases, and while there was a slight dip in 2000 and 2001, annual revenues jumped here in 2002 thanks to strong interest in DVD format videos and the release of the Harry Potter video. With videos priced at US$16.75 apiece in the United Kingdom, video sales make up about 63 percent of the U.K. industry's revenues. Since VCR penetration remains on par with the United States, the U.K. industry accounts for about one-third of the European Union's video rentals and sales. In

December 2001, following the September 11 terrorist attacks against the United States, the UK's largest home-based store franchise, HMV Media, reported a return to strong video sales and rentals. In a January 2004 report, the British Video Association estimated that video retail market in all formats was up 29.7 percent from 2003 to around 199 million units. While VHS sales dropped by 19 percent to 60 million, DVD sales increased 75 percent, making up for any decline.

Germany. Europe's second largest video rental and retail market is Germany, which has about 6,000 video stores. Germany's video rental industry slumped in the late 1990s, experiencing its slowest year in 1997 since 1993. Because of stagnation in German consumers' disposable incomes, the country recorded an 11 percent drop in video rentals in 1997. The industry's total revenues for rentals and purchases fell to US$878 million that year. In 2001 Germany continued to experience a continuation of its recession, according to *Fortune International* magazine, but nonetheless video store sales and rentals were US$1.04 billion, a 22 percent gain over 2000.

Japan. In the late 1990s through 2002, many Japanese citizens, especially those who worked in service industry-related jobs, suffered through hard economic times. Until 2001 video and DVD rental stores reported the same downturn in the industry that was seen in the United States during the late 1990s. However, the downturn ended in 2001 in Japan as customers in increasing numbers began staying at home and turning to movie rentals, which typically cost one-third to one-quarter the price of a US$20 cinema seat ticket. Japan's industry also grew during this period, led by *Princess Mononoke*, the country's most popular video rental of all time, which had been released in 1997. The leading Japanese video store is Tsutaya, a franchise operation owned by the Culture Convenience Club Company; Tsutaya also owns stores in Thailand.

BIBLIOGRAPHY

Ammatcjarpemrot, Barung. "Movies Are Both a Way of Life and Making a Living for Tsutaya CEO." *Bangkok Post,* 6 March 2006.

Barber, Amanda. "Cultural Focus: Many View a Corporate Acquistion As the End of an Era." *American Executive,* February 2007.

Behar, Richard. "Bejing's Phony War on Fakes." *Fortune,* 30 October 2000.

"Blockbuster Crafts Expansion Plan." NACS Online, 5 October 2009. Available from www.nacsonline.com.

"Blockbuster Tempts Netflix Customers." *The Online Reporter,* 17 February 2007. Available from http://www.onlinereporter.com/article.php?article_id=8837.

Cassavoy, Liane. "New Ways to Watch Movies on Your PC." *PC World,* May 2007.

Desjardins, Doug. "Blockbuster Looks Ahead After Viacom Spinoff." *DSN Retailing Today,* 19 July 2004.

———. "Hollywood Video Looks to Chart a Private Course." *DSN Retailing Today,* 19 April 2004.

"Digital Media Stocks; Trends and Opportunities in DVD, Streaming Video, Anti Piracy Technology and High Definition; Digital Media Stocks Internap (INAP), Netflix, Infosmart, (OTCBB: IFSG) and USA Video Interactive (OTCBB: USVO) Offer Global Perspectives on Current and Future Trends as Digital Media Industry Participants." *Internet Wire,* 20 April 2007.

Draper, Deborah J., ed. *Business Rankings Annual.* Detroit: Thomson Gale, 2004.

"DVD Boosts Germany's Video Industry to Record Highs." *Deutsche Presse-Agentur,* 3 March 2002.

"DVD Player Sales Take Off." *Reuters,* January 2002.

"Future Bleak for Video Rental Market." *Europe Intelligence Wire,* 23 July 2004.

Geiger, Bob. "Struggling Chains in Minneapolis Take Small Approach." *Finance and Commerce Daily Newspaper,* 3 May 2007.

Gruenwedel, Erik. "Movie Gallery, Hollywood Video give 20,000 DVDs to U.S. Troops." *Home Media Magazine,* 6 October 2009. Available from www.homemediamagazine.com.

Halkias, Maria. "Blockbuster's Growth Costly: Video Rental Chain Adds Online Subscribers." *Dallas Morning News,* 3 May 2007.

———. "Self-service Kiosks boom." *The Inquirer* (Philadelphia), 6 October 2009. Available from www.philly.com.

Harvey, Fiona. "The Smash Hit." *New Media Age,* 26 February 2004.

"Helen Mirren Calls on Public to Reject Piracy as Video Sales Grow by 30 Per Cent." British Video Association (news), 7 January 2004. Available from www.bva.org.uk.

"Hoover's Company Capsules." *Hoover's Online,* 2007. Available from www.hoovers.com.

Huffstutter, P.J. "Yahoo's Search for Profits Leads to Pornography." *Los Angeles Times,* 11 April 2001.

Johannes, Amy. "Blockbuster Incents Netflix Customers with Free Rentals." *Pronto,* 13 December 2006.

Kapner, Fred. "HMV Media Puts U.S, Jitters Aside." *Financial Times* (London), 8 December 2001.

Lazich, Robert S., ed. *Market Share Reporter.* Detroit: Thomson Gale, 2004.

McCartney, Jim. "A Dream Unravels: Video Update." *St. Paul Pioneer Press,* 25 February 2001.

"Movie Gallery Launches World Series Sweepstakes." *Promo,* 28 March 2007.

Mullaney, Timothy J., and Tom Lowry. "Netflix: Moving Into Slo-Mo?" *Business Week,* 2 August 2004.

Muller, Henry. "Shadows Over Germany Globalization and a Business Downturn are Forcing Europe's Biggest Economy to Reinvent Itself." *Fortune International,* 23 July 2001.

"Netflix Awards $1 Million Netflix Prize and Announces Second $1 Million Challenge." Netflix, 21 September 2009. Available from netflixmediaroom.com.

"Netflix, Blockbuster Compete for Supremacy with New DVD Services." *Pittsburgh Post-Gazette,* 28 January 2007.

"Netflix Has a Simple Vacation Policy; Take As Much As You Want." *Work-Life Newsbrief,* May 2007.

Ranii, David. "Blockbuster: Like Gangbusters." *The News &
    Observer* (Raleigh, NC), 27 December 2001.

"Record-Breaking First Quarter DVD Rental Revenue Surpasses
    Entire Year 2000." *PR Newswire,* 23 April 2002.

Rose, Joseph. "Netflix Rips, Slides, Stuffs to Success." *Orian, 24
    May 2007.

Rosenberg, Yuval. "What's Next for Netflix?" *Fortune,*
    11 December 2006.

Sporich, Brett. "2004 home video wrap." *The Hollywood
    Reporter,* 19 January 2002. Available from
    www.hollywoodreporter.com.

———. "Research: DVD Rentals Spin Faster." *The Hollywood
    Reporter,* 24 April 2002.

"Tiny QwikFliks Seeks to Carve Out Piece of Netflix's DVD
    Action." *Los Angeles Business Journal,* 5 April 2004.

Twist, Jo. "What High-Definition Will Do to DVDs." BBC
    News, 31 January 2005. Available from www.bbc.co.uk.

Video Software Dealers Association. "2004 Annual Report on
    the Home Entertainment Industry," 2004. Available from
    www.vsda.org.

"Video Software Dealers Association." *DSN Retailing Today,*
    21 July 2003.

"Video Store Trade Association Mourns Passing of 'Inventor' of
    Video Rental." Video Software Dealers Association (Press
    Release), 7 March 2005. Available from www.idealnk.org.

"Yahoo! Reports Fourth Quarter, Year End 2001 Financial
    Results." *Business Wire,* 16 January 2002.

Yoskowitz, Andre. "Movie Gallery Set to close over 200 game
    crazy stores." 3 October 2009. Available from
    www.afterdawn.com.

FINANCE, INSURANCE, AND REAL ESTATE

BANKING AND INSURANCE

NAICS CODE(S)

5221, 5222, 524. Banks and insurance companies constitute a major component of the broad global financial industry. The banking segment is comprised of commercial banks, savings banks, international banks, credit unions, mortgage bankers, loan brokers, and trust companies. Insurance encompasses life, casualty, property, surety, pension funds, and health policy brokerages and agents. Some banks derive all or a significant share of their revenues from credit card accounts (see **Credit and Debit Card Issuers**).

INDUSTRY SNAPSHOT

The finance and insurance industries experienced growing deregulation, globalization, and consolidation. As countries throughout the world, including industrial leaders such as Japan, the United States, Germany, and France, liberalized their finance systems, banks and insurance brokers pursued foreign markets and began to integrate their services. In addition, banks and insurers continued consolidating to achieve cost-effective economies of scale and scope, as well as to increase product offerings to customers. Rankings of the world's largest financial service firms were repeatedly reshuffled as mergers created new industry giants and economic woes forced the giants to fall. Consequently, there were landmark bailouts for major industry leaders, such as AIG.

The banking industry suffered unprecedented challenges in 2008. Efforts to survive included variations to some traditional products and services. JPMorgan Chase offered business customers up to US$250 when they transferred funds from other banks. Sun Trust made a US$100 donation to charity after customers opened a new checking account and were approved for and used a Visa debit card. Several large banks were considering selling assets and consolidating to remain in business. "When the industry is hurting, the natural thing to do is look inward and say 'What do we have?' and 'What should we have?'," acknowledged Silver Lane Advisors Managing Partner Elizabeth Nesvold of the New York City-based investment bank.

ORGANIZATION AND STRUCTURE

Bank Structure. Commercial banks are usually classified in three categories: unit, branch, and group. Some nation's banks are characterized by only one type, but most have all three. Unit banking exists when a single-office institution provides banking services. Historically, this was the most common form of banking in the United States. The presence of unit banking is often a result of tradition, law, vested interests, and the ability of this type of organization to meet the demands of local banking customers. When communities are homogeneous and are dominated by small businesses and farming, unit banking works well. Unit banking becomes less practical as a nation becomes increasingly industrialized and culturally diverse, as well as expanding geographically. This is especially evident as large geographical areas become economically interdependent. In industrial societies, populations are highly mobile, placing increased importance on the convenience provided by multiple bank locations. The need for large institutions is even stronger among businesses, which engage in transactions on a national or international scale and thus require complex services to support such activities as issuing stock, acquiring other businesses, or financing a new business venture. As a result, branch banking has become the norm in the world's major economies.

Branch banking exists when a single banking firm conducts operations at multiple sites. Branches are wholly owned and usually controlled by one headquarters. The level of service may vary between branches of the same bank, as some small satellite offices may not offer the full line of services available at major branches or headquarters.

One of banking's essential functions is to facilitate the transfer of funds. As the use of checks, credit cards, debit cards, electronic transfers, and other non-currency payment accelerates among the world's populations, this function becomes increasingly important.

The second major function of banks is to serve as a financial depository for customers' liquid assets. This service provides an efficient and highly secure means of storing wealth for accumulation or future use. Banks generally hold a fixed proportion of their customers' aggregate deposits in reserve in order to have funds available on demand. The remainder of deposited funds is channeled into various operations of the bank, notably as credit to other customers.

Credit for customers, including a variety of loans and credit accounts, has traditionally made banking lucrative. By charging the borrower interest fees in excess of what they pay back to the depositor, banks earn revenue by serving as the intermediary. Lending is very important to all nations' economies because it enables communities to finance agricultural, commercial, and industrial activities. This type of credit-infused growth is called indirect or "roundabout" production. Direct production refers to consumer goods secured by the direct application of labor to land or natural wealth. Most countries regulate their banking systems exclusively on the national level. The United States, however, regulates its banking system on national and regional levels.

Commercial banks also serve a variety of functions specific to business transactions. They can issue commercial letters of credit, sometimes called lines of credit, which are written statements guaranteeing that a bank will loan a customer a specified range of money. Banks issue letters of credit when a seller is unwilling to release his or her products and wait for payment to arrive in the mail. A letter of credit makes a loose financial arrangement binding and businesslike. When a bank issues a letter of credit, the buyer and seller are each protected. The credit of the bank is substituted for the credit of the buyer, which is designed to reassure the seller. A great deal of international trade is financed in this manner, which frees the flow of commerce among nations. As foreign trade and travel increase throughout the world, so do the services of international commercial banks.

Commercial banks also provide trust services to customers worldwide. Individuals who have accumulated estates, even of moderate size, provide for the distribution of assets prior to death by writing wills and securing bank trust departments to act as executors. In many cases, bank trust departments are responsible for investing and caring for the funds within an estate. They also distribute the proceeds as established by trust agreements.

The oldest service provided by commercial banks is the safekeeping of valuables. Banks have vaults that are nearly impossible for non-authorized people to enter and that have established records of safety. In most cases, the protection of valuables falls into two areas or departments within a bank: safe deposit boxes and safekeeping. Customers can rent safe deposit boxes from banks, which gives them control of their valuables, such as securities, deeds, insurance policies, at all times the bank is open. The bank simply provides the vault, the box, and the other facilities necessary for a safe deposit box. Most importantly, the bank controls access to the vault and guarantees that the customer who rented the box is the only one permitted access.

Safekeeping differs from safe deposit box services because the bank assumes custody of the valuables and acts as an agent for the customer, which is often a corporation. Items accepted for safekeeping differ considerably, but the service usually covers securities like stocks and bonds. In most commercial banking situations, the safekeeping department holds securities that a customer has pledged as collateral for a loan or has turned over to a trust department as part of an estate.

Commercial bank trust departments provide many additional services to corporations. In some cases they administer pension and profit-sharing plans for companies. They also serve as trustees for bonds and as transfer agents and registrars for corporations. In some cases, commercial bank trust departments administer sinking funds and perform other duties associated with the issuance and redemption of stocks and bonds.

Throughout the late twentieth and early twenty-first centuries, commercial banks engaged in brokerage services, buying and selling securities for customers. This diversification has encouraged banks to form joint ventures with full-service brokerages to provide complete advising and investment services. In many countries, the authority of commercial banks to provide brokerage services is prohibited. Governments justify this prohibition on the belief that excessive bank credit based on speculation can lead to bank failures and economic disarray. International banking authorities are not completely successful in controlling banking stability because of the lack of well-defined jurisdictions from one nation to another, but national authorities within many large industrial countries elaborately control banking practices. These controls are designed to prevent banks from failing and to safeguard the country's financial system if they do.

In the United States, the Glass-Steagall Act of 1933 formally separated banking from securities and prevented banks from establishing securities affiliates. However, by the late 1990s this separation was eroding quickly. The Gramm-Leach-Bliley Act of 1999 officially repealed Glass-Steagall, leaving U.S. banks free to diversify into new areas, such as securities and insurance. The Interstate Banking and Branching Efficiency Act of 1994 opened new commercial bank growth opportunities and created incentives for mergers. The Japanese banking industry experienced similar deregulation in the late 1990s. The merger and acquisition of financial services surged in the United States and Japan in the 2000s. Unlike the United States and Japan, Europe has a long history of offering many services under one company, and banks continued to combine banking, insurance, and securities operations in the 2000s.

Insurance Structure. With increased competition from banks, all sectors of the insurance industry have changed the way they operate and the kinds of policies they offer. Nonetheless, in their most basic form, insurance companies collect payments or premiums from policyholders; invest the premiums; return some of the investment to policyholders through dividends, annuities, or policy payments; and provide reimbursement for qualifying events, such as death, disability, loss of property, or medical treatment, depending on the type of insurance. Insurers obtain their money for investment from policy reserves, liability for unearned premiums and deposited funds, and separate account liabilities. Policy reserves comprise the money companies put away for making future policy payments.

For insurers to profit, they must accurately balance the money kept in loss reserves for paying policy claims and the money invested. If a company reserves too much money for losses, it will lose potential investment growth and may have to raise its rates to be profitable. However, if a company reserves too little for losses, it will look more profitable, but runs the risk of not having funds available should it suddenly have to pay an unexpected number of claims. To achieve this accurate balance, companies must estimate the value of future claims as precisely as possible, including real economic growth, inflation, and interest rates, as well as the likelihood of claims arising at a particular time.

The two kinds of ownership that exist in the insurance segment are companies owned by stockholders, known as stock insurance, and companies owned by policyholders, known as mutual insurance. For stock insurance, companies issue stock as shares of their ownership. Mutual insurance companies use capital called "policyholders' surplus." The property and casualty sector of the industry bears the risk of future losses, which it

shares with policyholders. Major property/casualty policies include homeowner's, auto, and theft, among others, as well as workers' compensation.

The life insurance sector has evolved from making payment only when policyholders die to offering a wide selection of policies for savings, taxes, retirement, and estate planning. Life insurance products include:

- Whole life policies, which require premiums to be paid throughout the life of the policy, includes a cash value that can be accessed by the policyholder, and provides a payment at death and;

- Universal life policies, which offers flexible death benefits and premium payments and has a cash value with a rate of return similar to that of money market accounts;

- Variable life policies, which have flexible premiums and death benefits, and offer a full-scale investment component of mutual and money market funds providing a cash value that can be accessed by the policyholder;

- Term life insurance, which provides a guaranteed death benefit and premium for the length of the term (e.g., five or ten years) after which the policy can be renewed annually for an increasing premium;

- Group life insurance, which is usually purchased by an employer to provide death benefit coverage for employees and is typically a renewable one-year term policy;

- Annuities, which can be either fixed or variable, are insurance contracts providing tax-deferred value and supplemental retirement income that can make numerous payments to the policyholder beginning either immediately or at a future date.

BACKGROUND AND DEVELOPMENT

In the West, the modern banking industry developed in northern Italy in conjunction with long-distance trade in the fourteenth century. The primary activities of early banks was exchanging and transferring money rather than holding deposits and lending money because the Catholic Church prohibited usury, which at the time was considered any lending of money for interest. These early banks consisted of pawnbroker-like operations that provided small loans to farmers and artisans, and sent papal taxes from various regions in Christian Europe to Rome.

As commercial trade spread throughout Europe, trade centers adopted these banking techniques. In the fifteenth century, Lyons, France, replaced Geneva, Switzerland, as the leading financial center, and Bruges, Belgium, lost its key trade position to Antwerp, Belgium. Bankers in Antwerp developed bank endorsement and discounting in the sixteenth century, facilitating the negotiation and transfer of money. When these bankers moved to Amsterdam, Holland, the state established the Amsterdamsche Wisselbank, a public deposit and clearing bank that proved highly successful. Innovative banks allowed Amsterdam to remain a powerful financial center through the early eighteenth century.

Public banks opened along European trade routes during the medieval period and gradually acquired the characteristics associated with their contemporary banks. The prohibition against usury diminished and banks began providing loans for governments as lending became a key activity by the eighteenth century. Banks also offered services to the public, including savings accounts, loans guaranteed by collateral, and check-like paper documents and credit receipts. In the eighteenth century, banks like the Neapolitan Public Bank and Sweden's Bank of Stockholm introduced paper money.

In the United States, the Continental Congress established the first chartered bank in North America. Based in Philadelphia, the bank supported the credit of the budding country and issued paper money that could be converted into gold and silver, and other banks quickly followed. By the beginning of the nineteenth century, more than 30 commercial banks operated in the country, including the First Bank of the United States.

Banks began to play a decisive role in the Japanese economy around 1882 when the Bank of Japan was founded as the country's central bank. From its inception through the early 1970s, the Bank of Japan helped Japanese industries grow by supporting city banks, regional banks, and other operations that lent money to industries. In 1973, as inflation was soaring, the Bank of Japan took on the additional responsibility of maintaining the yen's stability.

As banks, insurance companies, and some brokerage houses merged in the mid-1990s, they formed diversified companies that offered banking, securities, and insurance services. Banks have completed mergers and acquisitions for decades with European banks leading the way in diversified acquisitions, such as Deutsche Bank's 10 percent purchase of insurance company. The French refer to this merging of banks and insurers as "bancassurance," but the term has not been accepted worldwide as of the late 2000s. In 1998, in anticipation of industry deregulation that would allow banks to offer insurance services, Citicorp, a leading U.S. bank, announced plans to merge with insurance giant, Travelers Group Inc., creating the first such integrated service in the United States. Reforms of the financial services industry in Japan resulted in companies offering a wide array of services as the lines blurred between banks and insurance companies.

Traditional consolidation in the banking industry continued as well. For example, U.S.-based Chase Manhattan Corp. acquired Chemical Banking Corp. in 1996.

In Japan, two of the country's largest banks—Mitsubishi Bank Ltd. and Bank of Tokyo Ltd.— merged in 1996 to become the world's largest financial institution at the time with assets of more than US$700 billion and annual revenues of US$46.4 billion.

Expansion into international markets became more feasible in the late 1990s due to the increased deregulation that took place on a global scale. At the end of the Uruguay Round of Multilateral Trade Negotiations, which resulted in the 1994 General Agreement on Tariffs and Trade (GATT), financial services negotiations had remained incomplete. Participating countries made commitments to open their markets to outside nations, but felt that the negotiations were not satisfactory. The 1994 agreement allowed reciprocity-based exemptions for most-favored-nation treatment wherein countries could offer trade benefits to whatever countries they chose to make special offers. In 1995, the World Trade Organization (WTO) sponsored another round of talks, producing the Interim Agreement of 1995. For the Interim Agreement, 29 members of the WTO intensified their commitments, while three members opted for most-favored-nation reciprocity. Discussions resumed in 1997, and 102 WTO members pledged to make their financial services markets more accessible by March 1999. The new commitments reduced or eliminated restrictions on foreign ownership of local financial operations and on expansion of existing operations. Moreover, the agreement offered all signing members the same trade benefits available to any other country, eliminating most-favored-nation treatment. WTO members account for 95 percent of the world's financial services market.

For the 29 members of the Organization for Economic Cooperation Development (OECD), which account for 95 percent of the global insurance market, insurance providers posted premiums worth US$2.05 trillion in 1995, up 9 percent from 1994. Life and non-life insurance each represented about 50 percent of the total premiums. The United States led the world with US$758 billion in premiums for 37 percent of the market, followed by the European Union with US$635 billion, or 31 percent, and Japan with US$471 billion, or 23.3 percent, according to the OECD. In the United States, US$1,167 per capita was spent on property and casualty insurance in 1996, followed by Japan with US$714 per capita and Western Europe with US$621 per capita. In contrast, China's premiums per capita stood at only US$3. However, emerging markets in Eastern Europe, South America, and Southeast Asia reported the highest growth rates in the 1990s as demand for insurance increased. The *National Underwriter Property & Casualty-Risk & Benefits Management* magazine reported that these markets were anticipated to account for 50 percent of the world's insurance sales by 2025.

The financial services industry of the late 1990s was characterized by increasing globalization and diversification as banks expanded their geographic reach and their selection of services to include categories such as annuities, mutual funds, insurance, and capital market products. In the U.S. market alone, between 1997 and 2001, securities firms completed more than 400 mergers and acquisitions, the average value of which reached US$2.5 billion in 2000, according to *Business Week.* In the late 1990s one of the most noteworthy deals was the merger of Travelers Group and Citicorp to form Citigroup, the second largest financial services firm at the time. In its quest to further diversify its services, in 2000 Citigroup paid US$30.8 billion for Associates First Capital Corp., the leading consumer lender in the United States. To extend its global reach, Citigroup strengthened its position in South America in 2001 when it paid US$12.82 billion for Grupo Financiero Banamex, one of Mexico's leading banks.

Like Travelers Group and Citicorp, many firms within the United States first took advantage of deregulation on a domestic level. In early 2001, Chase Manhattan and investment banker J.P. Morgan merged in a US$36.5 billion deal that created JP Morgan Chase. In Europe, banks and insurance providers also began capitalizing on U.S. deregulation because moving into the U.S. market was simplified. For example, Credit Suisse, one of Switzerland's largest banks, added Donaldson, Lufkin, and Jenrette and First Boston to its holdings. In addition, Swiss bank, UBS AG, acquired Paine Webber, and Dutch insurer, ING Group, acquired the financial services operations of Aetna Inc. and ReliaStar Financial.

The merger of the Industrial Bank of Japan, Fuji Bank, and Dai-Ichi Kangyo Bank that created Mizuho displaced Germany's Deutsche Bank as the world's largest bank in terms of assets in 2000. Deutsche Bank slipped behind Citigroup as well that year. Mizuho reported assets of US$1.2 trillion, Citigroup had assets of US$902.2 billion, and Deutsche Bank had assets of US$874.7 billion. In 2000 the world's thousand largest banks secured US$317 billion in profits, a slight increase over 1999 profits of US$310 billion. The United States and the European Union accounted for about 74 percent of the US$118.1 billion total profits of the top 25 banks, while Japanese banks continued to struggle with non-performing loans.

Consolidation among Japanese banks continued in 2001, including the merger of Sakura Bank and Sumitomo Bank to form Sumitomo Mitsui Banking Corp.; the joining of Bank of Tokyo-Mitsubishi, Nippon Trust Bank, and Mitsubishi Trust to create Mitsubishi Tokyo Financial Group Inc.; and the merger of Sanwa Bank, Tokai Bank, and Toyo Trust and Banking Co. into UFJ

Holdings Inc. When the dust had settled, the number of banks in Japan had fallen from 20 to 9 in 1996. According to *AsiaPulse News,* the consolidation was part of an effort by the Japanese banking industry to improve profitability by streamlining operations. Saddled with massive numbers of nonperforming loans, major banks in Japan were under mounting pressure to cut costs and increased efforts to slash the number of their branches. In fiscal year 2000, Sumitomo Mitsui closed 75 branches, while UFJ shut 13 branches and planned to shut more than 100 additional offices and lay off 5,280 workers by the end of 2005. Japanese banks planned to reduce their combined workforce by approximately 25,000 employees.

Although weakening economies in the United States and Europe helped slow the pace of consolidation by the end of 2001, major deals continued to materialize. American International Group Inc. paid US$23 billion for American General Corp., creating the largest insurance deal in industry history to that time. In addition, Germany's leading insurer, Allianz AG, acquired the 80 percent of Dresdner Bank that it did not already own.

In June 2003, the United States Agency for International Development announced plans to provide US$10 million over four years for the development of the Indian insurance sector. Bearing Point was awarded the contract to implement this program of technical assistance with the Insurance Regulatory and Development Authority (IRDA). This U.S. assistance was expected to help the IRDA build its institutional capacity in the areas of solvency and market conduct supervision, promote an enabling policy as well as a regulatory and institutional environment for the development of the health insurance system, develop key professions associated with the insurance sector, and develop comprehensive databases on insurance.

Although China's insurance industry was small compared to many other countries, it experienced rapid growth in 2003. Life premiums came in at US$36 billion, up 32 percent from 2002. Property premiums increased to US$10.4 billion. According to the China Insurance Regulatory Commission, the severe acute respiratory syndrome (SARS) outbreak in 2003 mildly disrupted insurance sales in some regions of China, but "served to catalyze a surge in demand for insurance coverage."

According to Karl-Heinz Goedeckemeyer, an independent financial analyst from Frankfurt, Germany, international consolidation would continue, while size would become increasingly important as a strategic factor. Banks were expected to continue targeting specific customers, products, or regions.

CURRENT CONDITIONS

The Banker reported that the world's top one thousand banks in 2004 had aggregate pre-tax profits of US$417.4 billion dollars, up 65 percent over 2003. Growth was attributed to improved economic conditions, led by the United States, followed by Japan and most of the European Union. However, Germany's banks showed a net aggregate loss of US$306 million as that country's economy was slow to recover. Total industry-wide assets grew more than 19 percent, reaching US$52.39 trillion.

While the world's major economies had improved, they experienced slow growth during 2004, but the economies of developing countries reported very strong growth. This growth was positive for those in the financial services industry, but some countries were also showing record-levels of debt and bankruptcies. In 2004, in the United States and the United Kingdom, personal bankruptcies remained at historically high levels and consumer debt levels were very high. As a result, banks were seeking ways to manage their credit risks, including using a third party to insure them against defaults.

While consolidation through mergers and acquisitions slowed during 2002, they increased through the late 2000s. Deloitte Touche Tohmatsu credited the increase to the need for banks to add to their product offerings as well as broaden their coverage in international markets. In 2004, Bank of America added 6 million customers when it acquired FleetBoston Financial. The Royal Bank of Scotland acquired Charter One Financial of the United States, and Spain's Santander Central Hispano purchased Abbey National of the United Kingdom in 2004. In 2005, UFJ Holdings of Japan created the world's largest bank when it merged with Mitsubishi Tokyo. In addition, the world's largest banks began to actively pursue interests in Asia as CitiGroup purchased KorAm and HSBC showed interest in a Chinese bank.

Deloitte's research also showed that bank customers were growing increasingly dissatisfied. In the United States, banks were retaining an average of only 50 percent of their customers. Many banks had begun to realize they had lost a valuable form of marketing when they moved customers out of the branches in favor of using ATMs, and were looking at ways to bring customers back inside branches to market other services to them directly. Customer perceptions were also affected by the transfer of some bank services to low-cost providers in other countries. Some that had moved call centers were experiencing problems with customer service, while others who had transferred technology out of the United States were concerned with data integrity and security.

The financial service industry had also come under increasing regulatory pressure, with the cost of compliance bearing down heavily on many companies. The *Basel II Capital Accord* required banks to set aside enough capital to cover any risks. The *Sarbanes-Oxley Act* in the United States put the burden on CEOs and directors to certify that their control systems are adequate. In addition, the London, England-based International Accounting Standards Board set new standards that were adopted by many European banks in 2005.

The insurance industry had to cope with regulatory issues related to alleged improper activities. For example, Marsh & McLelland and AON were under investigation for "bid-rigging" by getting insurance providers to submit deliberately high bids to give consumers the idea that they were getting competitive quotes. High-bidding providers would then be "given" the next client. Some companies also came under scrutiny for providing loss mitigation insurance products to clients, who then transferred losses off their balance sheets.

Mother Nature took a toll on the insurance industry in 2004, which was the most costly year on record for the insurance business. That year, four hurricanes hit the Florida coast, bringing with them the most significant single catastrophic event in U.S. history, with an estimated US$21 billion in insured losses. This was considerably more than the estimates for the economic impact from the tsunami that hit 10 countries and killed more than 200,000 people in south Asia in December 2004. Unlike Florida, much of the loss of life and property from the tsunami was uninsured, resulting in industry estimates of the cost to insurers reaching between US$5 billion and US$10 billion.

RESEARCH AND TECHNOLOGY

Banks have employed computers and other sophisticated forms of technology to speed the check-clearing process, reduce personnel and expenses, and improve the accuracy of record keeping. As computers began to handle the work that previously had been done manually by many employees, most tasks began to be accomplished electronically, requiring little paperwork. As a result, world economists predicted that commercial banking was headed toward a "checkless banking society" in which the electronic transfer of funds would eliminate the need for bank checks and all the work they entail. In the late 1980s and early 1990s, members of the banking community began to experiment with a system that used debit cards that were somewhat similar to credit cards. Use of a debit card in financial transactions, such as purchases, activated computers in banks worldwide and automatically transferred funds from the purchaser's account to the seller's account. The forerunners of the debit system were automatic teller machines (ATMs) that were subsequently installed in most banks as well as many retail establishments worldwide. ATMs allowed customers to withdraw cash, make deposits and loan payments, and transfer funds between depositors' savings and checking accounts without having to set foot in a bank branch.

Banks throughout the international banking community scrambled to take advantage of customers' needs for new import and export products and services, especially services for mid-sized corporations. In the early 2000s, mid-sized companies were looking to commercial banks for solutions to their global business challenges. Evidence of a trend to "one-stop shopping" was banks helping companies structure their financing; arrange for shipping, handling, and insurance; track the movement of goods; and provide data on sales and receivables. The concept that one bank should be able to meet all of a company's international financial services needs was relatively new in 2004. Many banks had found that by packaging international services under one umbrella, they could offer a competitive, value-added product. For example, French banking giant Credit Lyonnais provided a range of services to foreign companies doing business in France, including financing, site location, identifying suitable joint-venture partners, and providing legal and tax advice. Credit Lyonnais also offered a full complement of standard cash-management and corporate banking services.

In the early 2000s, the concept of the corporate bank gained favor among large companies. A corporate bank confines it activities within a single, multinational company without involving the public, unlike a commercial bank. Many corporate banks were the primary holding companies for major corporations, making it ideal for the global economy as trade barriers fell and national financial markets opened to monetary transfers, borrowing, and investment. Corporate banking functions include conducting intercompany banking, handling financial transactions, and managing corporate liabilities within the financial community.

Updated ATMs in the late 2000s allowed customers the benefit of quickly recorded deposits that were given service linked names, such as "deposit image," and "deposit friendly." The new ATMs could scan checks and count cash, eliminating the need for deposit slips and envelopes as well as courier trips to pick up deposit paperwork. They were environmentally friendly, and although the initial cost was high, over the long term they were expected to save money.

Technology in Commercial Banking. Many experts believed that future success of global banking was based on an understanding of the business advantages possible through new technology. Throughout the international community, there was a growing demand for immediate

information, and most banks had instituted programs that provided online access to cash management and trade related services. However, international banks still had room to grow in the area of integrated information and services. For example, customers could gather information in a basic foreign exchange/cash management package that allowed them to access accounts and make transfers and payments in various currencies. In contrast, trade packages allowed customers to open letters of credit, make collections, and manage open accounts. Banks in the early 2000s developed technology that combined the two packages to manage international trade and treasury in a single system. The result was expected to be improved efficiency for banks and greater convenience for the customers.

Despite its shortcomings, many local and regional banks used available technology to enter the global market. Technology enabled small banks to compete in the once-inaccessible world of international banking. By establishing direct links to corresponding banks in other countries and rounding out the international trade services they offered customers, small banks were able to offer services to compete with the major money centers worldwide. This competition was possible because the cost of technology dropped each year, allowing even the smallest competitors to gain access to these systems.

Many regional banks profited from the emergence of new global markets at the end of the twentieth century. Banks in the southeastern United States, for example, benefited from increased growth and trade in South America, Central America, and the Caribbean Basin. Likewise, U.S. banks along the borders with Canada and Mexico expected increased trade with those countries resulting from the North American Free Trade Agreement (NAFTA).

In the buyer's market of the early 2000s, many analysts believed that the most successful banks would be those that were sensitive to their corporate customers' international needs. For most banks, this meant developing a good international correspondent network, topnotch technology, attentiveness to customer requests, and flexibility in adjusting quickly to a rapidly changing global marketplace.

By the mid-2000s, banks around the world had instituted online banking services, allowing customers to conduct banking activities via the Internet at any time. Internet transactions allowed banks to provide more cost- and time-efficient services to more customers, since online transactions typically involved less time and expense than their traditional brick-and-mortar counterparts. The Internet enabled customers to apply for loans, find account information, transfer funds, and make payments from a personal computer at their convenience.

In addition, digital technology allowed for electronic money as a new kind of currency. Rather than instilling value in paper and coins, ways were created to store value in a digital format represented by a string of numbers. Electronic money permitted users to easily trace their transactions and spending because computers would automatically balance accounts and provide instantaneous financial statements and reports. Furthermore, electronic money was replaceable if lost because the owner was able to cancel the digits representing the money lost and replace them with new digits.

INDUSTRY LEADERS

Banking and Finance.

Citigroup. Citigroup was the result of the 1998 merger of Citicorp and Travelers Group Insurance and forged a new level of vertical integration in the U.S. finance industry. The Travelers Group included the investment bank and bond trader Salomon Brothers and the Smith Barney brokerage firm. The Travelers Group also owned consumer loan provider Commercial Credit and mutual fund broker Primerica Financial Services. In May 2004, Citigroup announced plans to set up a life insurance joint venture in China. The new personal foreign exchange deposit product market-lined account was the first product launched by Citibank at its Beijing and Shanghai branches after the bank began offering related services in China on March 25, 2004. The product required a minimal investment of US$25,000. In 2005, Citigroup sold Traveler's Life & Annuity, including almost all of its international insurance business, to MetLife.

U.S.-based Citigroup was listed as the largest global company by *Fortune* on its 2005 list of the 2,000 largest global companies. However, Citigroup continued to compete with Mizuho of Japan for the title of the world's largest financial services enterprise on other listings, depending on the criteria used. With more than 200 million customer accounts in 2005, this diversified financial services company was operating in more than 100 countries, offering customers banking, insurance, lending, investment services, asset management, and credit cards. Truly global, the company reported 148,000 employees in the United States and an additional 146,000 employees internationally. Citigroup had assets of US$1.48 trillion, total deposits of US$562 billion, and net income of more than US$17 billion. However, by late 2008, Citigroup was part of the bailout provided to many U.S. financial institutions under Troubled Assets Relief Program (TARP) of the U.S. Department of the Treasury.

Mizuho Holdings Inc. Mizuho Holdings was created in September 2000 by the merger of Industrial Bank of Japan, Fuji Bank, and Dai-Ichi Kangyo Bank. After the merger, Mizuho reduced its number of domestic branches from 560 to 444, and its overseas branches from 49 to 41. In 2002 Mizuho operations were divided into Mizuho Bank as a consumer bank and Mizuho Corporate Bank. In May 2004 Mizuho announced plans to reorganize its wholesale operations to better meet customer needs, including consolidating 26 wholesale banking departments into 16 that were each focused on a particular industrial sector like electrical machinery, automobiles, and general contractors. In addition, Mizuho Trust and Banking Co. was the first in the industry to handle intellectual property rights by overseeing the software copyright owned by a Nippon Life Insurance Co. subsidiary. The company announced cost-cutting measures, including the elimination of more than 7,300 jobs by 2006. With assets of US$1.3 trillion, Mizuho was the second largest financial services provider in the world in 2004. Mizuho held US$733.5 billion in deposits and had net income of almost US$3.9 billion.

Crédit Agricole Groupe. With its acquisition of Crédit Lyonnaise in 2003, Credit Agricole joined the ranks of the giant of banking. France's largest bank, the organization was made up of 2,629 local banks serving 21 million customers in 2004. In addition, it operated in 66 countries. Its total assets in 2003 were US$1.09 trillion, with net income of more than US$3 billion.

JPMorgan Chase. JPMorgan Chase was created in July 2004 when the company, which was the second largest bank in the United States in terms of assets, merged with Bank One Corporation, which was the sixth largest bank in the United States. The company had assets of US$1.1 trillion at the end of 2004, and provided investment banking, financial services for consumers and businesses, financial transaction processing, asset and wealth management, and private equity in more than 50 countries.

HSBC Group. Named after its founding member, The Hong Kong and Shanghai Banking Corporation Limited, HSBC was created in 1865 to finance the growing trade between China and Europe. By 2005, HSBC was based in London, and was one of the world's largest banking and financial services providers. The organization had almost 10,000 offices in 77 countries in Europe, the Asia/Pacific region, the Americas, Africa, and the Middle East.

Royal Bank of Scotland Group plc. With a history dating to 1727, the Royal Bank of Scotland (RBS) had grown through a series of big-name acquisitions. In 1988, it entered the U.S. market with the acquisition of Citizens Bank of Rhode Island. In 2000, RBS acquired NatWest in what was the biggest takeover in British history to that time. In 2004 RBS expanded in the United States when it acquired Mellon Bank and Charter One. RBS also has a strong place in the motor insurance industry, having created Direct Line in 1985.

The company's insurance segment became the second largest provider in the United Kingdom upon its acquisition of Churchill. RBS ended 2004 with total assets of US$1.06 trillion and net income of about US$8.7 billion.

Bank of America. In 2005, the U.S.'s third largest bank had more branches in more states than any other bank. In addition to its 5,889 banking centers, the company also had offices in 35 countries covering Asia, Europe, and the Americas. Bank of America was also the leading issuer of debit cards in the United States with nearly 17 million cards issued and was the leading online bank with about 12 million active online customers and 6 million bill-payment customers. At the end of 2004, the bank had assets of US$1.11 trillion, with total deposits of US$618.6 billion, and net income of US$14.1 billion, making it the world's fifth most-profitable company. In 2004, the company acquired FleetBoston Financial, adding 6 million customers.

According to Reuters, in November 2008, Bank of America announced it would assume US$16.6 billion of debt and guarantees of Countrywide Financial Corp., which it had acquired in July. Before being acquired by Bank of America, Countrywide had been the largest U.S. mortgage lender.

Deutsche Bank. Once the world's largest bank, Deutsche Bank was in third place after global consolidation in the late 1990s and early 2000s created industry behemoths, and by 2004 it was ranked sixth in terms of assets. Deutsche Bank operated two divisions: Private Clients and Asset Management, and Corporate and Investment Banking. A planned merger with domestic competitor Dresdner Bank fell through in 2000, prompting a management shakeup. Sluggish retail banking operations resulted in a series of cost-cutting measures, including the elimination of jobs in the early 2000s when employment fell from 98,000 in 2000 to 65,400 by 2004. In early 2005, the company was criticized for its plans to reduce its domestic workforce by laying off an additional 6,400 employees. The company's domestic retail banking unit was suffering from low returns, which it attributed to competition from non-profit financial institutions. In 2004 Deutsche Bank's total assets were reported at approximately US$1.1 trillion, deposits were US$413.6 billion, and net income was US$3.1 billion. The firm employed 65,400 workers in 74 countries.

Mitsubishi Tokyo Financial Group Inc. Mitsubishi Tokyo Financial Group was created in April 2001 when Mitsubishi Trust and Banking merged with Bank of Tokyo-Mitsubishi, the leader in the global finance and insurance industry in 1996. Services included commercial, investment, foreign exchange, investment management, load production, real estate management, retail, securities banking services, and specialized trust serves in more than 40 countries. Mitsubishi Tokyo Financial owned approximately two-thirds of UnionBanCal, the parent company of United Bank of California. With 2001 sales of US$20.4 billion, Mitsubishi Tokyo Financial Group was one of the world's largest banks. The company reported 57,500 employees in 2003.

BNP Paribas. France's BNP Paribas was one of the largest banks in Europe and also had a large international presence in Asia and the United States. The company handles corporate and investment banking, retail banking, and asset management, with a global presence in 85 countries. The company operates BancWest (Bank of the West and First Hawaiian Bank) in the Western United States, Banque Internationale pour le Commerce et l'Industrie (BICI) in French-speaking Africa, as well as having operations in Morocco, Tunisia, Algeria, Madagascar, the Comoro Islands, the Middle East, and the Near East. Total assets for BNP Paribas reached US$1.13 trillion in 2004, with customer deposits of approximately US$411 billion, and net income of US$5.8 billion.

Insurance.

American International Group, Inc. (AIG). AIG was the world's leading insurance company and one of the top financial services providers, operating in more than 130 countries. The company offered property/casualty insurance, life insurance, retirement planning, and asset management services. In 2004, AIG was investigated by the Securities and Exchange Commission for allegedly helping a client hide underperforming loans. The company was then accused of failing to adequately inform its investors about the SEC and Justice Department probes. AIG paid an SEC-imposed fine of US$10 million without admitting any guilt. In 2003, AIG reported net income of US$9.3 billion, and had delayed filing its annual report for 2004 pending a reevaluation of its financials.

The U.S. government agreed to give AIG US$123 billion in the fall of 2008. In November 2008, additional financial assistance included US$40 billion from a US$700 billion financial bailout for financial institutions. AIG also was granted a reduction of a US$85 billion loan to US$60 billion and a US$37.8 billion loan was substituted for a US$52 billion aid package.

Allianz AG. Allianz, based in Munich, Germany, was founded in 1890 as a personal accident, fire, and transport insurance provider. Most of the company's income was earned outside Germany. In July 2001, after acquiring the 80 percent of German bank Dresdner it did not own, Allianz moved into the number four spot among the world's largest financial services firms. The firm also held a stake in Deutsche Bank. By 2005, the company had 60 million customers in more than 70 countries and was providing property and casualty insurance, life and health insurance, asset management, and banking services. Allianz posted revenues of more than US$121 billion and profits of US$8.6 billion in 2004.

ING Groep N.V. Formed in 1991 from the merger of Nationale-Nederlanden and NMB Postbank Groep, Internationale Nederlanden Group changed its name to ING. The company grew through acquisitions, the first major of which occurred in 1995 when it acquired Barings Bank, making ING a well-known name worldwide almost overnight. In 1997 it acquired Belgian Bank Brussels Lambert, U.S. insurer Equitable of Iowa, and U.S. investment bank Furman Selz. In 1999 it acquired German merchant bank, BHF-Bank. The acquisition of ReliaStar and Aetna Financial doubled its U.S. presence and made the company the largest insurer in South America and the second largest insurer in the Asia/Pacific region. ING earned 22 percent of its profits from each of its American and European insurance segments, 10 percent from its Asian insurance segment, 25 percent from wholesale banking, 15 percent from retail banking, and 6 percent from direct retail banker ING Direct in 2005. ING had total assets of approximately US$1.08 trillion in 2004 and net income of US$7.5 billion.

The Dutch Government pledged to buy "non-voting preferred shares and appoint two representatives to the board of ING" according to ING CEO Michel Tilmant, who explained that the government would "have a say in ING's executive compensation and get a share of profit."

Nippon Life Insurance Company. One of the world's largest insurance companies and the largest in Japan, Nippon Life Insurance Company experienced difficulty during the early 2000s when its sales and profits plunged. By 2004, the company had been actively changing its management and had reported an increase in its core operating profit. However, it continued to experience declines in income from insurance and reinsurance premiums. Nippon Life offered life insurance and annuities, and following deregulation of the Japanese insurance industry, it provided property and casualty insurance as well as financial planning services. With more than 20 branches throughout North America, Europe, and the Pacific Rim, Nippon was an international insurance provider. Its major focus for overseas activities was providing coverage to Japanese companies and citizens abroad. In March 2004 Nippon announced the expansion of its alliance with Marsh & McLennan Companies, which was involved in risk and asset management worldwide. It roughly doubled its investment in Marsh & McLennan to US$217 million. After sales dropped in Japan, Nippon announced plans to expand its presence in other Asian countries, hoping to increase its global market share. The company also planned to raise the reserves that it had set aside against a rise in the mortality rate along with other

internal reserves around 380 billion yen to more than 1.3 trillion yen for fiscal year 2003.

AXA. Founded in 1816 as Mutuelles Unies, the company acquired the Drouot group in 1982 and became France's largest insurance company. Mutuelle Unies changed its name to AXA in 1984. Based in Paris, France, AXA offered the whole gamut of insurance products, including life insurance, property/casualty insurance, and reinsurance, as well as financial services and real estate investment. AXA had offices in Western Europe, North America and the Asia/Pacific region. International subsidiaries included AXA Financial, previously known as the Equitable Companies, which owned Alliance Capital Management. In May 2004, AXA Financial announced that stockholders of The MONY Group had voted to approve a US$1.5 million merger with the company, which was considered an opportunity to add scale to the company. In 2004 AXA earned approximately US$90 billion in revenues, 65 percent of which came from the life insurance segment, 25 percent from property and casualty, 5 percent from international insurance, 4 percent from asset management, and 1 percent from other financial services.

MAJOR COUNTRIES IN THE INDUSTRY

Japan. Japanese banks had reported a net loss in 1996, but by 1997 operating profits outweighed bad debts and marginal profits were reported by city banks, including Bank of Tokyo-Mitsubishi, Fuji, Dai-Ichi Kangyo, and Daiwa. In addition, Japan's trust banks, including Mitsui, Mitsubishi, Sumitomo, Yasuda, Nippon, Toyo, and Chuo, posted combined net profits of US$23.8 billion, according to *Banker*. In 1998 Japanese banks ranked among the world's least profitable and were becoming increasingly cautious about lending to avoid risky loans. The government proposed a US$250 billion bailout to rescue the banking industry, and the worst of the industry's troubles appeared to be over. However, nonperforming loans continued to cause problems in the early 2000s.

The Japanese Ministry of Finance had reduced its role in the overall administration of the finance and insurance industry with the beginning of deregulation in March 1998. Deregulation, known as "the Big Bang," allowed holding companies to operate in Japan and enabled banks to offer investment and insurance products. In addition, greater investor protection was provided.

Asia Pulse Businesswire reported that Japan's major banking groups and regional lenders recorded a remarkable rebound of market capitalization in fiscal 2003. Many regional banks, however, were lagging behind in their recoveries. By 2003, the commercial banking industry in Japan was valued at US$7.6 trillion by *Euromonitor,* with four banks dominating the industry: Mizuho Banks, Mitsui Sumitomo Bank, Tokyo Mitsubishi Group, and UFJ. In 2005, the world's largest bank, Mitsubishi, was in the process of purchasing Japan's fourth largest bank, UFJ Holdings. Assets of the combined company were US$1.8 trillion. Analysts at Deloitte Touche Tohmatsu believed that the acquisition had set the stage for further consolidations in the banking industry.

The United States. The United States was a world leader in the banking and insurance industry and was home to the world's most profitable banking and insurance companies. Significant mergers in the mid-1990s gave the United States a greater global presence, following the trends of banks and insurance brokers in Japan and Europe. The repeal of the *Glass-Steagall Act* in 1999 allowed U.S. banks to continue to grow and resulted in the creation of such behemoths as Citigroup and JPMorgan Chase.

The commercial banking industry was valued by *Euromonitor* at US$6.5 trillion in 2004, with the five largest players, Citigroup, Bank of America, JPMorgan Chase, Wells Fargo, and Wachovia, accounting for about 55 percent of the market. The highly-fragmented retail banking market was valued at about US$1.24 trillion, with the top five players, including Citigroup, Bank of America, JPMorgan Chase, Wells Fargo, and Bank One, accounting for about 35 percent of the market, with the rest going to a large number of small regional banks. Both sectors were expected to grow more than 10 percent by 2008. However, U.S. banks were facing a serious problem retaining customers, and Deloitte Touche Tohmatsu research showed that only 26 percent of customers would recommend their bank to others.

The U.S. government agreed to bailout the banking industry in late 2008 under provisions of the Troubled Asset Relief Program (TARP). While the Treasury Department and banking regulators predicted that up to 1,000 publicly held institutions saddled with nonperforming loans would apply for bailout money, many were concerned that healthy banks would also apply.

The U.S. life insurance industry was valued at US$128.6 billion in 2008, while property insurance was valued at US$324.5 billion and healthcare insurance was at US$65.5 billion. Growth in all sectors was expected to approach or exceed 10 percent by 2008. Property insurance remained concentrated among the top five companies of State Farm, Allstate, American International, Nationwide, and St. Paul Travelers, with automobile insurance being the largest part of that market. In the life insurance sector, 88.1 percent of the market was covered by Prudential, Metropolitan, New York Life, Northwestern Mutual, and John Hancock Financial. The healthcare market remained highly fragmented, with the largest companies, including CIGNA, UnitedHealthcare, Kaiser, AFLAC, and Aetna, holding less than 36 percent of the market.

On November 19, 2008, *The New York Times* reported that the health insurance industry had consented to a special agreement to ensure coverage for all Americans. Many individuals could not afford insurance, and the trend was to not purchase insurance until being diagnosed with an illness. Consequently, pre-existing health conditions would not be a consideration for health care.

Germany. In the mid-1990s, German banks established a large new bond market, making it a strong source of international investment. They also developed a significant global presence by acquiring U.S. and U.K. investment firms. In 1996, 3,551 banks operated in Germany, giving it the world's densest bank concentration. However, to become more competitive, German banks consolidated. Between 1990 and 1996, large banks absorbed more than 1,000 small banks.

Germany's banking and financial systems were restructured in the late 1990s and early 2000s, similar to those around the world. Two of Germany's largest banks, Bayerische Hypo-Bank and Bayerische Vereinsbank, announced they would merge in 1997. At the same time, Deutsche Bank bought a 5.2 percent share of Bayerische Vereinsbank. Allianz, the country's leading insurance company, owned 22 percent each of Bayerische Vereinsbank and Germany's second largest bank, Dresdner Bank. In 2001 Allianz acquired Dresdner Bank, creating a new German powerhouse.

In pursuit of new clients, German banks also turned to Eastern Europe, especially in Poland, the Czech Republic, and Hungary, as well as in Slovakia, Slovenia, and the Baltic states as well. Deutsche Bank opened branches in Eastern Europe to establish its presence there, while Commerzbank acquired local banks. Although German banks initially offered standard commercial services in Eastern Europe, they added investment banking services once they had established a strong customer base.

In 2003 the statutory health system provided 80 percent of Germany's healthcare premiums, which were valued at US$106 billion. However, the market for other forms of insurance was open to private companies. Allianz remained not only a worldwide leader, but was also a domestic leader in the life and property insurance lines.

Germany had the European Union's largest banking community, with commercial banking valued at US$3.97 trillion and retail banking valued at US$4.05 trillion. Deutsche Postbank, spun off from Deutsche Post in 2004, was the market leader in both segments. However,

Deutsche Bank was the leading banking group and had a strong international presence. Dresdner Bank and Commerzbank were also significant players in the industry.

The United Kingdom. The United Kingdom not only represented one of the world's largest finance and insurance markets, but was also one of the most profitable. U.K. banks recovered from losses incurred from failed lending ventures, posting enormous profits in the mid-1990s. The five leading U.K. banks at the time were Abbey National, Barclays, Lloyds, TSB, Midland, and NatWest, which generated a combined US$13.1 billion in profits in 1996. The banks turned to consumer-oriented business to achieve their turnaround, focusing on savings accounts, credit cards, and car loans, which compensated for the dwindling profit margins of corporate banking services. Banks in the United Kingdom also began to convert from mutually-owned operations to stockholder-owned diversified financial services. In 2000, the Bank of Scotland acquired NatWest. The leading U.K. bank, HSBC Holdings, paid US$63 million for an 8 percent stake in Bank of Shanghai in 2002, becoming the first foreign commercial bank to own a portion of a bank in mainland China in more than half a century. According to *Europe,* the purchase was the result of China's entrance into the World Trade Organization. The acquisition "is expected to lead to more alliances between overseas banks and insurers in the run-up to full liberalization of the country's financial services in 2006." Domestically, commercial banking was valued by *Euromonitor* at about US$624 billion, while retail banking was valued at about US$2.7 trillion. Barclays held the highest share of both markets, with more than 18 percent of each.

France. France was one of the leading nations in the industry boasting headquarters for top bank BNP Paribas and leading insurer AXA, both of which were major global players outside the domestic market. In 2003, French commercial banking was valued at US$2.5 trillion, while retail banking was worth US$2.3 trillion. Domestically, Crédit Agricole was the market leader in the retail sector, while BNP Paribas was the leader on the commercial side.

French banks and insurers followed the international trend of consolidation. Insurance giants AXA and UAP merged to become AXA–UAP, one of the top financial service providers in the world in 1996. AXA–UAP eventually changed its name back to AXA, and in 2003, remained the market leader in all insurance sectors. French banks were restructured after some experienced losses early in the deregulation process. Some banks, such as Credit Foncier de France and Suez, experienced great losses when they rushed into the property market right before it crashed. France's state-owned Credit Lyonnais was on the verge of bankruptcy in the early 1990s due to

overly ambitious expansion and continued to flounder in the mid-1990s, reporting US$17 worth of bad loans while also dealing with loan fraud. Restructuring was slow, however, and critics blamed the government's heavy-handed management for the delays. Consequently, bank profits in France, which came primarily from international markets, slumped according to *Euromoney.* The French government appointed a commission to find solutions for some of the industry's problems.

By 2000 most of the country's banks, including Credit Lyonnais, had been privatized. However, scandal continued to permeate the French banking industry. In 2001 Credit Lyonnais remained under investigation for its dealings with Executive Life, a U.S.-based insurer that the French bank had helped rescue from collapse in the early 1990s.

China. According to *China View,* the Beijing Central Business District (CBD) was expected to grow substantially by 2010. Plans called for 50 international financial companies to be included in the Beijing CBD, resulting in the district's significance gaining leadership stature in the international financial community.

BIBLIOGRAPHY
"2005 Global Banking Industry Outlook." Deloitte Touche Tohmatsu, January 2005. Available from www.deloitte.com.

Aversa, Jeannine. "Government Provides New Aid to AIG." Associated Press, 10 November 2008. Available from ap.google.com.

AXA. "AXA Financial Announces That MONY Stockholders Approve $1.5 Billion Merger," 18 May 2004. Available from www.axaonline.com.

Baker-Self, Terry, Beata Ghavimi, and Matthew Dickie. "Top 1000 World Banks." *Banker,* 2 July 2004. Available from www.thebanker.com.

Barnard, Bruce. "HSBC, the London-Based International Bank, Paid $63 Million for 8 Percent of the Bank of Shanghai." *Europe,* February 2002.

"Briefing—Asia Insurance—May 19, 2004." *Asia Pulse Businesswire,* 19 May 2004.

"Business in Asia Today—March 26, 2004." *PR Newswire,* 26 March 2004.

Calvey, Mark. "Citigroup' Government Rescue Signals Depth of Banking Woes." *St. Louis Business Journal,*26 November 2008.

Chu, Kathy. "Banks Give More Generous Perks for New Deposits." *USA Today,* 9 November 2008.

"Citibank Launches New Personal Forex Product in China." *Asia Pulse Businesswire,* 20 May 2004.

"Citigroup Plans Life Insurance JV in China." *Asia Intelligence Wire,* 20 May 2004.

Cooper, Louise. "Deutsche Bank Faces Critics at Home." *BBC News,* 17 March 2005. Available from www.bbc.co.uk.

"Dutch Government Hands ING Groep $19 bn Rescue Pack." *The Australian News,* 21 October 2008. Available from www.theaustralian.news.com.au.

Ellis, David. "Banks: Everything Must Go." *CNNMoney.com,* 3 July 2008. Available from money.cnn.com.

"The Fortune Global 500." *Fortune,* 2005. Available from www.pathfinder.com.

"From Emerging Market to Global Business Hub." *Xinhua News,* 7 August 2008. Available from www.chinaview.cn.

"Industry Outlook 2001: Banking and Securities." *Business Week,* 8 January 2001. Available from www.businessweek.com.

"Insurance Market Outlook." Deloitte Touche Tohmatsu, February 2005. Available from www.deloitte.com.

"Japan's Mizuho Corporate Bank to Revamp Wholesale Operations" *Asia Pulse Businesswire,* 20 May 2004.

"Major Market Profiles." *Euromonitor,* October 2004. Available from www.euromonitor.com.

"Nippon Life, 2 Other Insurers to Boost FY03 Internal Reserves." *Asia Pulse Businesswire,* 14 May 2004.

Nishio, Natsuo. "Japan Sector Outlook: Most Banks to Report Profit Recovery." *Dow Jones Newswires,* 17 May 2004.

Pasternak, Sean B. "Canadian Banks Don't Need Rescue, Toronto-Dominion's Clark Says," 24 November 2008. Available from www.bloomberg.com.

Pear, Robert. "Health Insurers Offer to Accept All Applicants, on Condition." *The New York Times,* 14 November 2008. Available at www.nytimes.com.

"Profile: Japan's Banking Industry." *Asia Pulse Businesswire,* 13 May 2004.

"Profile: Japan's Banking Industry." *AsiaPulse News,* 16 May 2001.

"Pushing Limits in Europe." *Investment Dealers' Digest,* 7 January 2002.

Simms, James. "Japan FSA Issues Operations Improvement Order to Deutsche Bank." *Dow Jones Business News,* 20 May 2004.

"The State of the Industry 2005." *CrossCurrents,* Winter 2005. Available from www.ey.com.

Teichova, Alice, Ginette Kurgan-van Hentenryk, and Dieter Ziegler. *Banking, Trade, and Industry: Europe, America, and Asia from the Thirteenth to the Twentieth Centuries.* Cambridge, UK: Cambridge University Press, 1997.

"Update 2—Bank of America Assumes $16.6 bln Countrywide Debt." Reuters UK Business and Finance, 10 November 2008. Available from www.reuters.com.

"U.S. Economic Slowdown Drives Merger Rumors." *Banker,* July 2001.

Williamston, Elizabeth. "Rescue Cash Lures Thousands of Banks." *The Wall Street Journal,* 3 November 2008. Available from online.wsj.com.

Yung, Katherine. "High-Tech ATMs Give Images, Fast Credit." *The Detroit Free Press,* 8 June 2008.

SIC 6221

COMMODITY AND FUTURES TRADING

NAICS CODE(S)

523130. Commodity trading firms buy and sell commodity contracts on either a spot or future basis for themselves or on behalf of others. They are members, or are associated with members, of recognized commodity exchanges. This discussion also includes a review of commodity exchanges.

INDUSTRY SNAPSHOT

In 1972, 18 million futures and options contracts were traded worldwide. In just the first six months of 2010, this volume had reached 5.7 billion contracts, according to figures compiled by the Futures Industry Association (FIA), the industry's trade association. Fueling the phenomenal growth of the futures industry in the early 2000s was the surge in interest rate and equity index trading activity. Financial trading as a whole grew 75.3 percent in 2001, with equity index trading up 117.9 percent and interest rate trading up 44 percent. Non-financial trading, however, dropped 4.5 percent, due to lagging agricultural commodity and non-precious metal trading.

The once commonly used term "commodity trading" continued to be used in the early twenty-first century but was being replaced by "futures trading." The terms were used interchangeably when contracts were made on foreign currencies and government securities as well as on tangible or storable products. "Futures trading" became more widely used after 1981 when the Chicago Mercantile Exchange (CME), the largest futures exchange in the United States, introduced trading in eurodollar futures. CME was the first exchange to call for settlement in cash rather than by delivery of the underlying physical commodity.

Futures and options on futures are classified by categories, including interest rates, equity indices, agricultural commodities, energy products, foreign currency/index, precious metals, and non-precious metals. Commodities and futures are known as "derivative instruments" because they are dependent upon underlying cash markets for their identities. The two economic functions they serve are transferring risk—or hedging—and price discovery. The U.S. Commodity Futures Trading Commission (CFTC) defines hedging as "taking a position in the futures market opposite to a position held in the cash market to minimize the risk of financial loss from an adverse price change." Price discovery is the market's free negotiation of prices based on supply and demand.

By 2010, there had been considerable consolidation among formerly independent exchanges. Korea Exchange remained the largest global futures and options exchange in terms of contract volume. CME Group, which includes both Chicago Board of Trade (CBOT) and Nymex, was second largest, followed by Eurex, which includes ISE. Fourth was NYSE Euronext, and fifth was the National Stock Exchange of India. Many of the largest exchanges had converted to for-profit status, called demutualization, by this time, as a means of increasing efficiency and cutting costs.

One major topic for the industry in the wake of the global recession of 2007 to 2009 was dealing with higher levels of regulation. In the U.S., the Dodd-Frank financial reform bill passed into law in 2010. It contains 848 pages of legislation. Especially intended to bring oversight to the market for over-the-counter derivatives, which are traded apart from the established exchanges, some have alleged the law goes too far and will create new problems. Richard Levick of *Forbes* raises the question of whether the financial incentives for whistleblowers that the law creates might lead employees to bypass their own company's internal enforcement mechanisms. Such effects of the reform on the industry remain to be seen. The legislation is very complex and many of the enforcement details have yet to be worked out. Understanding and adjusting to the new laws will be an ongoing process.

ORGANIZATION AND STRUCTURE

Futures exchanges, industry members, and federal regulators share responsibilities for commodities and futures trading. They work together worldwide to protect the interests of all futures market participants.

U.S. Regulators. The Commodity Futures Trading Commission (CFTC), which is based in Washington, D.C., and has offices in Chicago, Kansas City, Los Angeles, Minneapolis, and New York City, is the federal agency responsible for the regulation of the U.S. futures markets. Created in 1974 by Congress, the CFTC has a threefold mission: to ensure fair practice and honest dealing in futures trading; to permit accurate price discovery; and to provide for efficient hedging through competitive, manipulation-free markets. The president of the United States, with the advice and consent of the U.S. Senate, appoints commissioners to fill vacancies on the five-person commission. Each commissioner serves a staggered five-year term. The CFTC had a budget of US$168.8 million in fiscal 2010 with approximately 650 employees to oversee 13 commodity exchanges in the United States. For fiscal 2011, the commission requested an increase to US$216 million and 745 employees.

In 1998, the CFTC approved rules that would facilitate the merger of the Coffee, Sugar & Cocoa Exchange and the New York Cotton Exchange. The new entity was controlled by a holding company that was called the Board of Trade of the City of New York. The merger was completed in June 2004.

The National Futures Association (NFA) is the industry-wide, self-regulatory organization for the futures industry. Authorized by Congress in 1982, the NFA was created in response to a proposed futures transaction tax. Rather than institute the tax, Congress decided that an industry-funded, self-regulatory organization would serve as an effective, efficient, and equitable way to share the regulatory costs between the futures industry and public participants.

The NFA's four main areas of responsibility are registration, compliance, arbitration, and education. The NFA had accepted responsibility for screening and registering firms and individuals who conduct business in the futures industry, including futures commission merchants (FCMs); commodity pool operators (CPOs); commodity trading advisors (CTAs); introducing brokers (IBs), who were previously known as agents of FCMs; associated persons (APs), who are associated with a firm and included firm principals and sales personnel; floor brokers; and floor traders. The NFA developed an arbitration program for the resolution of customer disputes between NFA members. The NFA also monitors the financial and sales practices of its members. In 2009, the NFA employed 291 employees and had total unrestricted revenues of US$35.7 million. The NFA was completely self-financed by membership dues and fees as well as from assessments paid by NFA members and futures market users.

Another key organization in the futures industry, the FIA, based in Washington, D.C., is the industry's trade association, with representatives from all segments of the marketplace, including the largest brokerage firms, and domestic and international futures exchanges, banks, law and accounting firms, insurance companies, and pension and mutual funds, as well as other market users.

International Regulators. Regulatory bodies monitor the industry worldwide. The principal regulatory agency in Australia is the Australian Securities Commission, based in Sydney. Brazil's leading regulatory body is Comissao de Valores Mobiliarios (Brazilian Security Exchange Commission), and Canada maintains the Office of the Superintendent of Financial Institutions. Europe is heavily involved in commodity trading, and the primary regulatory agencies are the Commission des Operations de Bourse and the Conseil du Marché à Terme in France; the Bundesaufsichtsamt für das Kreditwesen in Germany; the Comision Nacional del Mercado de Valores in Spain; the Department of Trade and Industry (DTI) and the Securities and Investments Board in England. Leading Pacific Rim regulatory agencies include the Securities and Futures Commission of Hong Kong, the Ministry of Finance and the Ministry of International Trade and Industry (MITI) in Japan, the Commodities Trading Commission in Malaysia, and the Monetary Authority of Singapore.

In July 1997, the CFTC established the Office of International Affairs to enable the commission to respond quickly to market crises that could have global implications. On October 31, 1997, regulators from 16 countries issued an agreement on certain basic principles of regulation in futures and options markets, covering contract design, market surveillance, and information sharing that would protect U.S. markets from events in foreign markets. They would also level the international regulatory playing field for markets and commodities professions.

The Nature of Commodity Trading. Futures exchanges do not set prices but are free markets where the forces that influence prices, including supply and demand, currency exchange rates, inflation rates, and weather, are brought together in an open auction atmosphere. As the marketplace assimilates the information that becomes available during the trading day, the fair market value or price agreed upon by buyers and sellers is determined.

The open-outcry auction market, which was first used in the nineteenth century, continued to be used in the early 2000s in the United States because it was considered to be the most efficient method to quickly assimilate market information and translate that information into a fair market price. Offers are made to buy or sell by open competitive outcry so any exchange member in the pit or ring can accept the offer. Once members agree on prices, they are recorded and disseminated instantly via state-of-the-art telecommunications equipment to market participants and interested observers worldwide. Electronic platforms had supplanted open-outcry at most leading European exchanges by the early 2000s. In the United States, the percentage of volume handled by electronic systems such as Globex rather than by open outcry has increased steadily since 2000. By 2008 Globex trades accounted for more than 90 percent of volume on CME Group exchanges.

Floor brokers and floor traders in the pit or ring communicate by open outcry and standardized hand signals to confirm their verbal communications. The position of a trader's or broker's hand informs another trader or broker whether he is buying or selling. When a trader or broker faces the palm of his hand toward himself, he is indicating that he is buying, or "wants." When a trader or broker faces the palm of hand outward, he is indicating that he is selling, or "does not want." When the trader or broker holds his arm and the fingers of his hand in a horizontal position, he is indicating the price at which he wants to buy or sell. These hand signals also are used to communicate the quantity or number of contracts that the trader or broker wants to buy or sell. Once a trade has been made, the price is posted immediately and constitutes "the market" until another trade is made at the same or different price, which may be as soon as the next second.

BACKGROUND AND DEVELOPMENT

The history of modern futures trading dates back to the early nineteenth century. As Chicago's importance as a grain market grew, so did problems with supply and demand, transportation, and storage. The natural outgrowth was a centralized marketplace where buyers and sellers could meet to "exchange commodities," which was the forerunner to the commodities exchange.

The Board of Trade of the City of Chicago (CBOT) was formed in 1848 by 82 merchants as a centralized marketplace that used "cash forward contracts" to allow buyers and sellers of agricultural commodities to specify delivery of a particular commodity at a predetermined price and date. However, cash forward contracts lacked standardization, especially in relation to quantity and delivery time. In 1865, the CBOT formalized grain trading with "standardized agreements" that became known as "futures contracts." The only variable was the price, which was determined through an auction-like, open outcry system on the trading floor of CBOT.

The two groups of market participants who were attracted by this standardization were producers and users of the commodity and speculators. The producers and users of the commodity wanted to protect, or hedge, themselves and their crops from uncertain price movements. Speculators, on the other hand, bought or sold contracts based on their perception of where the price might be in the future. If they looked for prices to rise, they would buy, and if they were correct and the market rallied, the speculators would sell and take their profit. Likewise, if they predicted lower prices in the future, they would sell, and if they were correct and the market dropped, they would buy at the lower price and take their profit. In *Speculating in Futures,* the CBOT defined hedgers as individuals who use futures markets to protect their cash position against the risk of unfavorable or adverse price movement. The role of the speculator is to provide risk capital, while the goal is to profit by accurately forecasting future price movement.

The popularity of futures trading increased in popularity during the late nineteenth century and early twentieth century. However, it did not make huge gains until the early 1970s after the introduction of the first financial futures and interest rates futures contracts that were designed to meet the demands of a changing world economy. The world economy at that time was characterized by frequent changes in interest rates, sharp increases in government debt, and heightened financial interdependence among the nations of the world.

Under the Bretton Woods Agreement, which took effect in 1946, countries within the International Monetary Fund (IMF) agreed that their currencies would have fixed parities in terms of both gold and dollars. Milton Friedman, an expert on Bretton Woods, indicated that a public futures market was unnecessary under the terms of the Bretton Woods Agreement for fixed exchange rates because exchange rates were traded in narrow ranges that limited interest. However, that all changed on August 15, 1971, when the Bretton Woods system ended.

The Chicago Mercantile Exchange (CME) was credited as the pioneer of financial futures when the CME's International Monetary Market (IMM) introduced trading in several foreign currency futures contracts in May 1972. These markets included the British pound sterling, the Canadian dollar, the West German mark, the Italian lira, the Japanese yen, the Mexican peso, and the Swiss franc. However, futures trading in the Italian lira was delisted, but the French franc and the Dutch guilder were added.

The CBOT entered the financial futures and interest rate futures arena in October 1975 when it introduced futures trading in Government National Mortgage Association certificates. Growth in this category had been partially attributed to not only the traditional hedgers and speculators who were expected to trade in this market, but also to a new breed of market participants that included banks, bond dealers, insurance companies, and pension funds.

In the 1980s, stock index futures were introduced. Leading the way was the Kansas City Board of Trade, which introduced trading in 1982 in the Value Line Stock Index. The New York Futures Exchange and the CME quickly introduced futures trading in the New York Stock Exchange Composite Index and the Standard & Poor's 500 stock index, respectively. Also in 1982, the Commodity Futures Trading Commission (CFTC) designated the first contract markets for options on futures contracts. Unlike the underlying futures contract, an option gives the buyer the right, but not the obligation, to buy or sell a specified quantity of a commodity at a specific price within a certain time, regardless of the commodity's market price.

Substantial growth in financial futures contracts on non-U.S. futures exchanges also occurred in the 1980s, led by the London International Financial Futures Exchange in the United Kingdom, the Marché à Terme International de France in Paris, the Singapore International Monetary Exchange in Singapore, and the Tokyo Stock Exchange in Japan.

Another factor that contributed to the growth of this industry and others was the increasing popularity of "managed account programs" or "managed account trading," in which an investor gives full trading authority to a professional money manager who has the time, resources, and expertise to monitor several futures markets simultaneously. According to the CFTC's *Vision and Strategies for the Future* strategic plan, money managed in U.S.-registered commodity pools increased from approximately US$675 million to almost US$26 billion from 1980 to the end of 1996.

On April 30, 1987, CBOT became the first domestic exchange to offer "night trading," providing price discovery and hedging for businesses worldwide when the Chicago markets traditionally are not open. Night trading was designed to help the CBOT regain its competitive edge and position as the largest and leading futures exchange worldwide. In September 1987, the CME entered a long-term agreement with Reuters Holdings PLC to create an after hours, global electronic automated transaction system for trading of futures and options on futures. That system, which began operation in June 1992, became known as GLOBEX. After 18 months of intense negotiations and the realization that it would be cost prohibitive for the industry to maintain two after hours systems, the CBOT decided to join the CME in GLOBEX.

The New York Mercantile Exchange unveiled NYMEX ACCESS, its electronic trading system on June 24, 1993. Developed in cooperation with AT&T, NYMEX ACCESS was designed to permit "screen-based" trading in the exchange's energy contracts and platinum during nontraditional, non-pit trading hours.

The next April, the CBOT announced that it had decided to withdraw from the GLOBEX joint venture. The CBOT proceeded with PROJECT A, an alternative vehicle for listing its financial futures and options on futures during off hours in what is defined as "non-pit trading hours." PROJECT A would enable CBOT members as well as public customers access to those CBOT financial contracts.

In 1997, the CFTC implemented "fast-track" processing procedures to speed approval of new contracts. In June of that year, the CFTC approved streamlined procedures for allocation of customer orders that were bunched for execution by Commodity Trading Advisors (CTAs). This relieved Futures Commission Merchants (FCMs) regarding the capital treatment of short options positions. The CFTC also streamlined many of its reporting and disclosure requirements, allowed FCMs to deliver confirmations and account statements solely by electronic media, and authorized CTAs and commodity pool operations (CPOs) to file their disclosure documents with the commission electronically. The CFTC also approved 51 applications for new futures and options contracts, including contracts based on inflation-indexed debt instruments issued by the U.S. Treasury.

Chicago's two futures exchanges agreed to combine their clearing operations in March 1988. Their goal was to provide industry standards, while reducing costs and increasing efficiencies. They also planned to ensure the ability of the exchanges to compete in a rapidly changing marketplace.

In April 1998 the CFTC announced a pilot program that would enable agricultural trade options, which are off-exchange options offered to a commercial producer or commodity user. Trade options on many agricultural commodities had not been allowed for more than 60 years, and the CFTC reviewed its ban in response to the growing need for risk management tools in the agricultural community. The pilot program required entities that solicited and offered those options to register with the CFTC as agricultural trade option merchants (ATOMs). The pilot program continued operating in the early 2000s.

Scandals and Market Improprieties. While the commodity trading industry was thriving into the mid-1990s, the industry had not enjoyed a wholly unblemished record. Scandals and market improprieties marked the late twentieth century. The New York Mercantile Exchange (NYMEX) declared a default in its May Maine potato contract in May 1976, and potato futures were no longer listed for trading at the NYMEX. In November 1977, the CFTC declared a market emergency in the December coffee "C" contract on the New York Coffee, Sugar & Cocoa Exchange, although the contract remained active. The CFTC prohibited further trading in the wheat contract at the CBOT in March 1979 even though the futures contract continued to be traded.

Silver. The largest scandal occurred in 1979 as the Hunt family of Texas purchased large quantities of silver as a hedge against inflation during a "bull," or rising, stock market, causing a dramatic rise in the price of silver. In 1973, the price was US$3 per ounce. It had reached US$6 per ounce in early 1979, but the Hunt's "pyramid" purchases of silver that year caused the price of silver to reach more than US$35 per ounce by the end of 1979 before jumping to more than US$50 per ounce in a month. The silver market then took a nose dive, losing more than 30 percent of its value in only a week. It continued to drop through the end of March 1980, stabilizing at US$10.80 per ounce, for a drop of 78.5 percent. The Hunts were unable to meet the US$100 million margin call, and the "Hunt silver bubble" burst.

Another factor in the rapid decline of silver prices was an unprecedented ruling by the CBOT and the Commodity Exchange (COMEX) whereby any new buy orders in the silver futures market were refused. Only buy orders already in the brokers' hands could be executed if and when the market hit those prices, and the only way for that to happen would be for prices to fall to lower levels. However, the marketplaces continued to accept new sell orders.

An investigation into the rapid rise and decline of silver prices by the CFTC, the Federal Reserve Board, and the Securities and Exchange Commission (SEC) did not reprimand the exchanges for their intervention. The CFTC concluded, however, that Nelson Bunker Hunt, William Herbert Hunt, and other individuals and firms had attempted to manipulate silver prices in 1979 and 1980.

CBOT and CME Investigations. In 1988 and 1989, the U.S. Attorney General and the Federal Bureau of Investigation launched a full-scale investigation into

trading practices on Chicago's two largest futures exchanges, CBOT and CME, following customer complaints of alleged abuses in trading practices, according to John J. Merrick, Jr., in *Financial Futures Markets: Structure, Pricing & Practice.* The exchanges were charged with several transgressions, including

- prearranged trading, defined by the CFTC as trading between brokers in accordance with an expressed or implied agreement or understanding;

- accommodation trading, defined by the CFTC as noncompetitive trading entered into by a trader, usually to assist another with illegal trades;

- frontrunning, defined by the CFTC as taking a futures or option position based upon non-public information regarding an impending transaction by another person in the same or related future or option;

- bucketing, defined by the CFTC as directly or indirectly taking the opposite side of a customer's order into the broker's own account or into an account in which the broker has an interest, without open and competitive execution of the order on an exchange;

- wash trading, the practice of entering into, or purporting to enter into, transactions to give the appearance that purchases and sales have been made, without resulting in a change in the trader's market position;

- curb trading—also known as kerb trading—the practice of trading by telephone or other means that takes place after the official market has closed;

- cuffing, defined by Merrick as "delaying the filling of customer orders to benefit another member."

As the investigation unfolded, specific traders were indicted, trials took place, and some guilty verdicts were returned. The exchanges pledged to do a better job of self-regulation in the future.

Barings PLC. In 1995, one of Great Britain's most revered merchant banks, the 233-year-old Barings PLC, collapsed dramatically over the weekend of February 24. The bank's collapse was allegedly caused by a 28-year-old employee who made unauthorized purchases of futures on the Nikkei stock average listed on the Singapore International Monetary Exchange (SIMEX) and Nikkei 225 futures listed on the Osaka Securities Exchange (OSE). Rather than taking a loss when the market fell, he continued his purchases, hoping that future profits would offset those early losses. The resulting loss of US$1 billion was more than the bank's assets. The Bank of England tried to organize a bailout, but other U.K. banks remained unconvinced that they should recapitalize because the full extent of the losses was unknown. London's High Court granted approval for Dutch financial firm ING Group to take over Barings in March 1995 for a symbolic one pound (US$1.65). ING Group agreed to continue to use the Barings name.

Sumitomo Corporation. In the summer of 1996, the venerable Sumitomo Corporation of Tokyo, Japan, announced that it had lost at least US$1.8 billion following alleged unauthorized trading in copper and copper derivatives on the London Metal Exchange (LME) by Sumitomo's former chief trader, Yasuo Hamanaka. Following the announcement, the copper market immediately plummeted 25 percent, with copper prices ultimately plunging from US$2,800 per metric ton to US$1,860 per metric ton before settling out at US$2,045 a ton. Closing Sumitomo's positions cost another US$800,000, and Sumitomo also agreed to pay a US$150 million fine. The company's losses from Hamanaka's trades totaled a staggering US$2.6 billion.

Hamanaka had been called "Mr. Five Percent" by other copper traders because Sumitomo traded roughly 500,000 metric tons of copper annually, representing five percent of total world demand of about 10 million metric tons. Hamanaka was accused of manipulating the price of copper in 1995 and 1996 by buying up significant amounts of copper futures on the London Metals Exchange, as well as acquiring a dominant position in the physical supply of copper stock. This caused an artificial spike in copper prices, including on the U.S. cash and futures markets. The Sumitomo trader then allegedly liquidated the company's large portfolio of futures contracts and LME warrants at the higher prices. In February 1997 Hamanaka pleaded guilty to fraud and forgery charges. The former copper trader was ultimately sentenced by a Tokyo court to eight years in prison for defrauding Sumitomo's subsidiary in Hong Kong of US$770 million by ordering remittances on fake transactions and forging the signatures of his superiors on funds transfer authorizations.

Tokyo General. Tokyo General, a firm primarily engaged in trading commodity futures, was accused of mismanaging customer funds and failing to meet a margin payment to the Tokyo Commodity Exchange in January 2004. According to *Futures Industry Magazine*, Tokyo General's trading activities were stopped by the Exchange, which also liquidated the firm's positions. The final government investigation report had not been completed when Tokyo General failed in 2004, but it appeared that customer funds were mingled with the firm's capital and spent on investments by the company's owner and former chairman, Katsumi Iida. Tokyo General's collapse resulted in stricter segregation of customer funds, more frequent inspections, and tougher capital gains requirements. Government officials, exchange representatives, and industry groups united to update and amend the Commodity Exchange Act, which was scheduled to take effect in April 2005.

Demutualization. Demutualization—the process of converting to for-profit status, which typically includes completing an initial public offering—was the largest item on the agenda of commodity and futures exchange operations in the late 1990s. For example, in April 1999, the London International Financial Futures and Options Exchange (LIFFE) made the decision to demutualize after increased competition from fully electronic competitors began to whittle away its market share. The conversion to for-profit status proved highly beneficial, as LIFFE was able to streamline operations and cut costs over the next two years. Euronext, itself a merger of stock and futures exchanges in France, Belgium, and Holland, acquired LIFFE in 2001.

In Asia, the Hong Kong Futures Exchange completed its demutualization, as well as a merger with the Hong Kong Stock Exchange, in the late 1990s. The futures exchange in Singapore also merged with the stock exchange there, creating SGX in 1999; the newly merged entity completed its initial public offering the following year.

In the United States, both CBOT and CME began preparing themselves for initial public offerings by reducing expenses and laying off employees. After reporting losses for two consecutive years, CBOT and CME both returned to profitability in 2001. While this was due in large part to the unstable U.S. financial market, which prompted increased investment in futures and options, the cost cutting measures undertaken by both exchanges were also instrumental in the turnaround. In November 2000, CME took two key steps toward demutualization by offering shares to its members and shifting to a holding company structure. Consolidation appeared likely throughout the remainder of the decade, according to some analysts, as exchanges like CME and CBOT would be looking for ways to continue cutting costs and boosting profitability once their public offerings were conducted.

Technology. Increased use of technology was another issue facing commodity and security exchange operations in the late 1990s. The CBOT and the CME wanted to move beyond open outcry trading to increase the speed of order entries and reduce trading costs by using computerized trading systems. In January 1998 the CBOT replaced its evening trading session with the PROJECT A computerized trading system, hoping to move closer to its objective of an entirely paperless trading floor. In August 2000 CBOT replaced PROJECT A with the Alliance/CBOT/Eurex (a/c/e) electronic trading system. Despite the new technology, open outcry continued to be the primary trading method for CBOT traders. The CME used the Globex2 electronic trading system, which accounted for roughly 20 percent of CME's total trading volume in 2001. As with the CBOT, the traditional open outcry continued to account for most CME transactions. While systems like GLOBEX and PROJECT A were once incompatible, which forced traders to use separate terminals for each exchange, cross-platform compatibility had largely been achieved by the early 2000s. The CME reported an average monthly record of 1.6 million contracts per day in April 2004 on GLOBEX, up 62 percent over the same period in 2003.

The impetus for increased use of technology was competition from non-U.S. exchanges, particularly the success of Germany's Deutsche Terminboerse (DTB), an all-electronic exchange. In 1997, DTB's volume increased 47.8 percent, although some of that growth was attributed to the merger of DTB and the Swiss Stock Exchange to form Eurex. Other moves toward electronic trading also occurred in the late 1990s. The Sydney Futures Exchange closed its open outcry trading floor, France's Marché à Terme International de France launched electronic trading, and LIFFE began allowing all-day electronic trading alongside its traditional open outcry trading system. By 2000, Eurex held the number one position among futures exchanges, with 289 million contracts trading hands. According to Jim Kharouf in *Futures Industry,* "the exchange's growth has highlighted one of the biggest advantages of electronic trading—its members do not need to be physically present in a single location. Eurex has created network hubs in market centers in other parts of the world to link its members to the exchange through dedicated lines." In the first quarter of 2004, Eurex's volume increased 9.3 percent to 289.6 million and set a monthly volume record that March. Eurex's EuroBund topped the list of futures contracts with volume over 62.1 million, although in the first quarter of 2004, its trading dropped 5.7 percent over the first quarter of 2003.

Deregulation. Debates over the deregulation of the U.S. futures market had been a key industry issue throughout the 1990s, and it remained a topic of debate into the 2000s. In 1998, the Commodities Future Trading Commission (CFTC) began to consider allowing block trades on the futures exchanges, similar to those on the stock market. Allowing block trades would simplify business and cut costs for big brokerage firms and institutional money managers, but floor brokers did not like the proposal because they would miss the chance to bid on a piece of those large transactions occurring on the exchange floors. The CFTC raised the issue in order to address the concerns of big investors and to make futures more vibrant when compared to the fast-growing over-

the-counter derivatives market. In early 2000, the CFTC granted permission to the Cantor Exchange, a joint venture between the New York Board of Trade and eSpeed, for block trading of U.S. Treasury futures.

Another regulatory issue centered on single stock futures, which were not traded in the United States as of early 2002. The global market for single stock futures, which are contracts for shares in a single company, grew from 2.2 million contracts in 2000 to 13.4 million in 2001. Ten exchanges offered single stock futures contracts that year, all of which were located outside the United States. Proponents of deregulation believed U.S. exchanges should be granted access to this booming market.

In 2004, *Futures Industry* reported that the volume of global futures and options trading contracts was approximately 8.9 billion. Of this total, 3.5 billion transactions were for futures, up 16.3 percent over 2003 levels, while the remaining 5.4 billion transactions for options trading had recorded a 4.6 percent increase over 2003 levels. In 2003, 105.4 million transactions trading foreign currencies were recorded, representing an increase of 35.4 percent over the previous year.

In May 2004, CME announced that combined open interest in the CME and CBOT contracts that were managed by the CME Clearing House had surpassed the 50 million contract mark for the first time. The CME also reported it moved approximately US$1.5 billion per day in settlement payments in the first quarter of 2004 and managed US$38.1 billion in collateral deposits in March 2004, which was the busiest trading month in the exchange's history to that time. The next month was the second consecutive month of record activity as average daily volume totaled 3.3 million contracts per day, up 44.4 percent over the previous year.

In the first two months of 2005, volumes in the United States increased almost 19 percent, reaching 514.1 million contracts, with the most growth being seen in the equity, foreign currency, and energy markets. The Chicago Mercantile Exchange was the fastest growing exchange in terms of volume at the start of 2005, with 147.5 million contracts. However, exchanges outside the United States reported that volumes were down in the first two months of 2005 over the same period in 2004, with an overall decline of 2 percent because of a 4.4 percent decline in options trading. However, this statistic is somewhat misleading as most of it could be attributed to ongoing low trading numbers at the Korea Exchange. The Eurex and Australian exchanges showed gains during the period.

While trading in agricultural commodities was on the rise in the United States in 2005, non-U.S. totals were down 19.7 percent. China's declines in soybean and rubber trading were the primary reasons for the overall global declines. However, several commodities were doing well, including the Tokyo Grain Exchange, which had become the leading coffee exchange, and the New York Board of Trade, which reported an increase of 47 percent in sugar trading volumes. Metals trading was down in almost all exchanges, with non-precious metals reporting a 12.6 percent decline in contracts and precious metals trading at 28.4 percent lower volumes.

The U.S. market's futures regulator granted approval to sell Swiss index futures to U.S. investors to Eurex, a European derivatives market owned by Deutsche Borse and the Swiss Exchange. "The U.S. is one of the Eurex's most important markets," according to Heike Eckerts, executive vice president of Eurex's U.S. activities. He continued, "The approval of additional products gives our U.S. participants new trading and diversification opportunities." Following the December 2007 acquisition of the International Securities Exchange, Eurex was considered one of the top two U.S. options markets.

The spike in oil in the first half of 2008 caused considerable damage to the global economy, including the commodities market. Tobias Levkovich, the chief equity strategist at Citigroup, offered the opinion that the increase in the commodities market in the early 2000s was a bubble that was ready to burst. The credit crunch resulted in an economic chain reaction that slowed industrial activity and weakened demand for commodities.

A drop in commodities prices did not necessarily mean a drop in the cost of foods. Some prices remained level, others rose, and some did fall. Food manufacturers handled higher overhead costs by not only raising retail prices, but also downsizing cereal boxes and snack food bags while maintaining prices. "As long as we're in this world of expensive oil and commodities, the prices that you're seeing now in the grocery shelves are not going away," said an economist with the U.S. Department of Agriculture. Violent food riots broke out in third world countries like Haiti and Senegal where the governments were struggling to feed their citizens in 2008. In addition, expensive animal feed challenged poultry producers. "From a consumer standpoint, more and more of these feed costs are going to be passed on and that means higher prices at the supermarket," explained Bill Roenigk, senior vice president of the National Chicken Council.

One commodity that was overlooked in the news was sugar. Prices had risen but remained lower than the commodity's historic highs and prices of other commodities. "Sugar is the only commodity that hasn't seen a runup in the past few quarters," said George Schultze, president of Schultze Asset Management. Demand for sugar was expected to be steady for traditional uses as well as for its use to solve environmental concerns. More sugar was projected to be needed to make ethanol. For example, more than 50 percent of cars being driven in Brazil,

the world's largest sugar producer, were using ethanol made from the country's abundant sugar crop. Although demand for sugar as a key food ingredient in the United States and Europe slowed dramatically, demand in developing countries like China and India was on the rise.

CURRENT CONDITIONS

In August 2008, the National Commodity and Derivative Exchange announced plans to begin futures trading in thermal coal in September 2008 to hedge the risk for price exposure. A second power exchange was being designed in a joint venture with the National Stock Exchange.

U.S. futures markets have seen an explosion in volume as electronic trading has grown in the twenty-first century. While the growth has generally been seen as positive within the industry, there have been noted drawbacks. A 2008 article in *Futures* magazine explored the pros and cons of the issue. Benefits were seen in the greater access that electronic trading has brought to investors. Persons who might have placed very infrequent trades in the past can become much more active participants in the market. The quick availability of information and news about futures markets has also played a role in this increased participation. The enhanced trading that results means that futures and option markets have much greater liquidity than in the past, so that contracts can be quickly and easily bought or sold at the going prices.

Among the negatives, the fast growth of electronic trading places considerable costs on institutions, which must keep up with the ever changing environment. For instance, such a premium has developed around speed of trade execution that some firms pay large sums to locate their computer servers near those of the exchanges. This shortens the distance that the electronic signals have to travel, which can be a significant trading advantage in the modern market. Traders with the means to invest in the cost of this can not only gain speed but can even bypass the need to work through a broker-dealer. Trading on electronic platforms has also increased the opportunities for large traders to move their activity away from established exchanges. This has been a particularly current issue in the world of stock trading, where "dark pools" of liquidity have developed in cyberspace, away from the open transparency of the exchanges. Growing electronic trading in the futures markets raises the possibility of the same thing happening. The possibility also exists of the speed and efficiency of the electronic market simply overwhelming the human brain's ability to process information. Loss of focus or even "analysis paralysis," in which a trader cannot make decisions due to an overload of available information, is a potential hazard. Allowing computers to make buy and sell decisions based on algorithms that humans program into them may become increasingly common in this environment. There is worry that this could lead to excessive volatility in futures markets. Such volatility was demonstrated in the U.S. stock market's "flash crash" of May 6, 2010. Prices tumbled hundreds of points and recovered, all in less than an hour. The role of algorithm trading in this debacle has not been fully understood, but regulators continue to work at coming to grips with such ramifications of technology change. Overall, regardless of the pros and cons, electronic markets are likely to continue to grow in the foreseeable future.

The "Great Recession" of 2007–2010 led to considerable turmoil within the futures industry. One of the recession's causes was widely thought to be subprime mortgage loans which were bundled together for sale to investors. Financial derivatives tied to the value of these loans were heavily traded in self-regulated, over-the-counter markets. The collapse of the bubble brought with it calls for greater regulation of such markets. In the summer of 2010 the passage of the Dodd-Frank Wall Street Reform and Consumer Protection Act was intended to deal with this issue. The Commodity Futures Trading Commission (CFTC) is playing a role in writing the new rules that the legislation calls for. While there has been concern within the industry about the cost of conforming to the new regulations, CFTC commissioner Bart Chilton was quoted as saying that the overhaul would not increase costs for those in the market pursuing legitimate hedging activities. This would include, for example, airlines using the futures market to protect themselves from changes in the price of jet fuel. Despite such assurances, the full scope of the overhaul will take time to play out, and the effects on the industry will be judged as they occur.

As relates to the physical side of commodities, in the summer of 2010, a drought in Russia led to increases in wheat prices, which raised the specter of a food crisis akin to that of 2008. Those involved in futures trading often come under fire in such situations for a perception that they are magnifying the problem. However, an August 2010 article in *New Statesman* argued that the wheat crop in most of the world was good, and that fact would likely prevent a repeat of the 2008 crisis.

WORKFORCE

Futures industry participants include futures brokerage firms, which are known as futures commission merchants (FCMs). FCMs are individuals, associations, partnerships, corporations, and trusts that solicit or accept orders for the purchase or sale of any commodity for future delivery, subject to the rules of an exchange. An FCM accepts payment from or extends credit to those whose

orders are accepted. By the end of 1997, 233 FCMs were registered with the NFA, down nearly 41 percent from the 393 FCMs registered in 1980, according to figures NFA provided the CFTC. Also at the end of 1997, there were 1,583 introducing brokers (IBs); 2,606 commodity trading advisors (CTAs); 1,351 commodity pool operators (CPOs); 9,299 floor brokers (FBs); 1,331 floor traders (FTs); and 45,950 associated persons (Aps). As of 2010, the number of member firms was 4,200 and associated persons had increased to 55,000.

The CFTC defines IBs as "a person (other than a person registered as an associated person of a futures commission merchant) who is engaged in soliciting or in accepting orders for the purchase or sale of any commodity for future delivery on an exchange who does not accept any money, securities, or property to margin, guarantee, or secure any trades or contracts that result therefrom." A CTA is "a person who, for pay, regularly engages in the business of advising others as to the value of commodity futures or options or the advisability of trading in commodity futures or options, or issues analyses or reports concerning commodity futures or options." A CPO is "a person engaged in a business similar to an investment trust or a syndicate and who solicits or accepts funds, securities, or property for the purpose of trading commodity futures contracts or commodity options. The commodity pool operator either itself makes trading decisions on behalf of the pool or engages a commodity trading advisor to do so. A floor trader, or local, is "a person with exchange trading privileges who executes his own trades by being personally present in the pit or ring for futures trading is a member of a futures exchange who trades for himself in the trading pit or ring." A floor broker is "a person with exchange trading privileges who, in any pit, ring, post, or other place provided by an exchange for the meeting of persons similarly engaged, executes for another person any orders for the purchase or sale of any commodity for future delivery."

According to the U.S. Bureau of Labor Statistics, employment of securities, commodities, and financial services sales agents is projected to grow 9 percent from 2008 to 2018, about as fast as the average for all occupations. Consolidation within the industry is expected to prevent faster growth. Competition for available jobs is expected to be stiff. Median annual earnings for these jobs were US$68,680 as of May 2008.

INDUSTRY LEADERS

Korea Exchange. The Korea Exchange (KRX) began in 2005 and combined the Korean Stock Exchange (KSE) and Korea Futures Exchange. As of June 2010, Korea Exchange was the leading derivatives exchange in the world, handling nearly 1.8 billion transactions for the first six months of the year. In 2001, the forerunner KSE had moved from fourth place to first place among the world's largest futures and options exchanges when its volume grew 300 percent from 213.49 million to 854.7 million contracts traded that year. In 2003, the KSE handled a total of 2.84 billion options contracts and a 62 million futures contracts.

Eurex. The third largest exchange was Eurex, with 1.5 billion contracts traded during the first six months of 2010, a 6 percent increase from the same period in 2009. Like other exchanges, Eurex had shown tremendous growth in trading in the 2000's. Eurex continued to lead the futures and options market for euro-dominated derivative instruments. Created in 1998 by the merger of DTB (Deutsche Terminbörse) and SOFFEX (Swiss Options and Financial Futures Exchange), Eurex is operated jointly by Deutsche Börse AG and SWX Swiss Exchange. An electronic trading platform, Eurex traders were connected to the system from more than 700 locations worldwide. Eurex US was launched in February 2004 as an all-electronic futures and options exchange.

CME Group. The CME Group, which includes the Chicago Board of Trade (CBOT) and Nymex, continued to be the largest U.S. futures exchange, and second largest in the world. Founded in 1898 as the Chicago Butter and Egg Board, the CME was formed in 1919, primarily to trade agricultural products. Although the CME continues to use open outcry, it is linked to an electronic trading platform. The first financial futures were created by the CME in 1972, and by 2004, the CME was the world's largest regulated foreign currency exchange, trading 51 million contracts.

In August 2008, the CME acquired its parent company NYMEX Holdings for a reported US$9.4 billion, with the major benefit considered to be the addition of global energy and precious metals products. Related moves were considered positive ways to solidify its dominance for interest rate, foreign exchange, stock index, agricultural futures, and options on futures. CME and NYMEX predicted a US$60 million cost savings as a result of the merger. CME was projected to be successful with the integration of "Mammoth" exchanges. In July 2007 CME Group was created after the US$11.9 billion merger of CME and CBOT. In the first six months of 2010 CME Group saw almost 1.6 billion contracts traded or cleared.

NYSE Euronext. Initially set up as a financial futures and options exchange, LIFFE's 1996 merger with the London Commodity Exchange added trading in such commodities as cocoa, coffee, white sugar, feed wheat, corn, milling wheat, and rapeseed, as well as potato futures. LIFFE

(Holdings) plc, the London International Financial Futures and Options Exchange, had been formed by the merger of the Amsterdam, Brussels, and Paris exchanges in 2000, and was purchased by Euronext in 2002. Euronext was bringing all its trading venues under a single platform, which it began to accomplish when the derivatives business of Eurnoext and LIFFE were combined to trade under one electronic platform. In 2003, the Brussels and Paris markets were added. In 2005, it was the world's fourth largest exchange. The New York Stock Exchange bought Euronext in 2007 for US$10 billion, creating the first trans-Atlantic exchange and global stock market. In 2007 NYSE Euronext reported sales of US$4.2 billion with 3,083 employees. In the first half of 2010 NYSE Euronext was the world's fourth largest derivatives exchange with over 1.2 billion contracts.

The Chicago Board of Trade. The Chicago Board of Trade (CBOT Holdings Inc.) was founded in 1848 to trade agricultural commodities, such as corn, wheat, and oats. Non-storable agricultural products were added and were quickly followed by gold and silver. In April 2005, CBOT was converted from a non-profit corporation into a for-profit one. In 2005 the company traded electronically as well as through open auctions in five categories: interest rate products, agricultural products, stock market indices, metals, and energy products. CBOT became part of CME Group in July 2007.

Brokers.

Refco Group Ltd. LLC. New York City-based Refco Group was one of the world's leading providers of execution and clearing services for derivatives trade on exchanges, as well as one of the world's largest independent derivative brokers. The company brokers futures trading as well as cash market products in 14 countries. In 2005, Refco had approximately 2,400 employees who managed the accounts of more than 200,000 global customers. During 2004, Refco provided the largest volume of customer transactions to the CME, processing 461 million derivatives contracts. Revenues from principal transactions, commissions, brokerage fees, interest, and asset management and advisory fees totaled US$1.87 billion in 2004. In June 2005, Refco announced plans to acquire the global brokerage operations of Chicago-based Cargill Investor Services. Refco filed for bankruptcy in December 2006 and went out of business.

ICAP plc. Based in London, ICAP was formed in 1999 from the merger of Garban and Intercapital plc. The world's largest interdealer broker, ICAP reported more than US$1 trillion of transaction volume per day, about half of which was done electronically. The company handled over-the-counter derivatives, fixed-income securities, money market products, energy, credit and equity derivatives, and foreign exchange. In fiscal 2009, the company's revenue figures were more than US$2.6 billion.

MAJOR COUNTRIES IN
THE INDUSTRY

The first commodities exchange was created in Japan in the eighteenth century. However, failure to modernize and make improvements in compliance and monitoring areas kept many global players out of the Japanese market. Japan's largest futures exchange, The Tokyo Commodity Exchange (Tocom), began to make changes in 2004, creating a clearinghouse and working with software engineers to provide electronic access to its products. The demise of one of the country's largest futures brokers, Tokyo General, occurred in 2004 after the government claimed it had fraudulent business practices.

As of 2000, 85 international futures exchanges were in operation. Japan operated 11; the United States operated eight; the United Kingdom operated four; Spain and Canada each operated three; and Germany, Holland, and Italy each operated two. China, which at one time boasted 40 exchanges, had only three in the early 2000s.

During the first half of 2004 Asian derivatives exchanges accounted for 37 percent of the world's trading volume, according to *Futures Industry*. The region was expected to become home to the majority of trading, with equity trading dominating. More commodity products were being introduced to the trading exchanges as the desire for more efficient pricing grew. Although cross-border trading in Asia remained low in 2005, it was expected to grow. Holding back the region from more rapid development was a fear of speculation caused by the financial crisis of the late 1990s. At that time, the Chinese government had severely curtailed futures trading in the wake of a trading scandal that had rocked the nation's economy. Nevertheless, China was considered by some industry experts to be a key growth market for futures trading after it was admitted to the World Trade Organization in the early 2000s. China continued to experience rapid commodity trading growth. Development was being delayed by the lack of a telecommunications and technology structure that could support trading on the same scale as in European and North American markets. Korea, the home of the world's largest futures and options exchange, was an exception.

Mitsui O.S.K. Lines Ltd. and Nippon Yusen K.K. experienced gains in Tokyo after the Baltic Dry Index, which measures shipping prices, rose. The Baltic Dry Index was considered to be "a benchmark" for the price of shipping bulk commodities. Bulk shipping accounted for to 88 percent of Nippon Yusen's operating profit in 2008.

The National Stock Exchange became the first exchange in India to receive regulatory approval, enabling it to launch FOREX derivatives trading in its home country. Trading in foreign exchanges in India had been severely limited and focused exclusively on banks and companies with foreign currency exposure. Indian commodity brokers reportedly advised customers to invest in soft commodities, such as cotton, sugar, and coffee, which were predicted to have good performance throughout 2008.

Despite a commodities futures industry that had languished for years and seen Korea become the regional leader, a June 2010 *Futures* magazine article made the case that Japan might be ready to begin recapturing its former glory through an industry renewal.

BIBLIOGRAPHY

Acworth, Will. "A New Day for Kofex" *Futures Industry*, May/June 2004. Available from www.futuresindustry.org.

Acworth, Will, and Mary Ann Burns. "The European Scene." *Futures Industry*, May/June 2004. Available from www.futuresindustry.org.

"After Metal & Crude, Soft Commodities Stoke Straight." *The Economic Times*, 22 August 2008.

Aldridge, Irene. "Lightning fast futures." *Futures*, July 2010.

"Annual Report." *ICAP*, 2009. Available from www.icap.com.

"Annual Report." *National Futures Association*, 2009. Available from www.nfa.futures.org.

Burghardt, Galen. "Off the Charts: Futures Volume Soars to Record Highs." *Futures Industry*, January/February 2002. Available from www.futuresindustry.org.

Clark, Aaron, and Asjylyn Loder. "Overhaul Won't Raise Legitimate Hedging Costs, Chilton Says." *Bloomberg*, 25 October 2010. Available from www.bloomberg.com.

Curran, Rob. "Charting the Breakdown in Commodities Stocks." *The Wall Street Journal*, 3 September 2008. Available from blogs.wsj.com/marketbeat.

DeGrandis, Megan. "First Quarter 2004 Volume Report" *Futures Industry*, May/June 2004. Available from www.futuresindustry.org.

Fulsher, Mitch. "Japan: The Big Bang, Finally." *Futures Industry*, May/June 2005. Available from www.futuresindustry.org.

Furukawa, Tsukasa. "Feud Looms as Hamanaka Trial Starts." *American Metals Market Online*, 19 February 1997. Available from www.amm.com.

"Gimme Some Sugar." *Smart Money*, July 2008.

"Global Futures and Options Volume Rose 8.9 Percent in 2004." Futures Industry Association Press Release, 31 March 2005. Available from www.futuresindustry.org.

Gorham, Michael, Susan Thomas, and Ajay Shah. "India: The Crouching Tiger." *Futures Industry*, May/June 2005. Available from www.futuresindustry.org.

Gramza, Daniel. "Electrification of Markets." *Futures Magazine Fall Special, Revolutions in Trading*, 2008.

Grede, Frederick. " Unlimited Opportunities in Asia's Emerging Derivatives Markets." *Outlook 05*, 2005. Available from www.futuresindustry.org.

Jacobs, Stevenson. "Commodities Slump Won't Mean Lower Food Prices." *San Francisco Chronicle,* 20 August 2008. Available from www.sfgate.com.

Jeffs, Luke. "Eurex Makes Swiss Step Into U.S.," 20 August 2008. Available from www.efinancial news.com.

Kharouf, Jim. "Trading Engines Evolve to Meet Trader Demands." *Futures Industry,* August/September 2001. Available from www.futuresindustry.org.

Kojima, Eiichi. "Clearing the Deck: The Tokyo General Default." *Futures Industry,* May/June 2004. Available from www.futuresindustry.org.

"KRX History." Korea Exchange, 4 November 2010. Available from eng.krx.co.kr.

Levick, Richard. "A Whole New Ballgame: Dodd-Frank's Whistleblower Provisions." *Forbes Communicators Blog,* 2 November 2010. Available from blogs.forbes.com.

McGregor, Megan. "Trading Volume: U.S. Exchanges Lead the Pack in First Two Months of 2005." *Futures Industry,* May/June 2005. Available from www.futuresindustry.org.

"NCDEX to Launch Coal Futures in Sept; Energy Exchange in Oct." *The Economic Times,* 20 August 2008. Available from economictimes.indiatimes.com.

"NSE to Start Forex Futures Trading from Aug 29." *The Times of India,* 21 August 2008.

"Occupational Outlook Handbook, Securities, Commodities, and Financial Services Sales Agents;" *U.S. Bureau of Labor Statistics,* 2010-2011. Available from www.bls.gov.

Pendley, Kevin. "Going Corporate: The Outlook for U.S. Futures Exchanges." *Futures Industry,* January/February 2002. Available from www.futuresindustry.org.

"President's Budget and Performance Plan." *Commodity Futures Trading Commission,* 2011. Available from www.cftc.gov.

Preston, Alex. "Lessons from the Wheat Crisis." *New Statesman,* August 2010.

"Refco Group, Ltd., LLC." *Bloomberg Businessweek Snapshot,* 4 November 2010. Available from investing.businessweek.com.

Schmerken, Ivy. "CME Seals the NYMEX Purchase, So Who's Next?" *Advanced Trading,* 20 August 2008. Available from www.advancedtrading.com.

Szala, Ginger. "Asian Volume Boom Missing Japan?." *Futures Magazine,* June 2010.

"Trading Volume Statistics." Futures Industry Association, 4 November 2010. Available from www.futuresindustry.org.

Ueno, Kiyori, and Tetsuya Komatsu. "Mitsui O.S.K., Nippon Yusen Lead Gains by Japanese Shippers." 14 August 2008. Available from www.bloomberg.com.

"Who We Are;" National Futures Association, 4 November 2010. Available from www.nfa.futures.org.

SIC 6099

CREDIT AND DEBIT CARD ISSUERS

NAICS CODE(S)

522320, 522220. Industry firms grant credit and debit accounts to businesses and individuals. Certain banks in this industry are also engaged in other aspects of commercial banking (see **Banking and Insurance**).

INDUSTRY SNAPSHOT

Visa, MasterCard, and American Express are the world's largest players in the financial card market, offering credit and debit cards to consumers around the world. Visa's market share of credit and debit card transactions worldwide was 68 percent as of 2008. MasterCard had the next largest share at 28 percent. The United States is the world's largest credit card market. Americans held almost 610 million credit cards in 2010 with an average per-household credit card debt of US$15,788.

Smart card technology continued to make inroads in most areas around the world, except in the United States. Most European countries were conforming to the international Europay/MasterCard/Visa standard for cards embedded with microchips rather than having a magnetic strip. The microchips allow the cards to be read internationally with increased privacy and security. In the late 2000s, contactless cards that transmit radio signals were beginning to be promoted in the smart card arena.

The number of credit cards issued in countries that had not previously encouraged their use increased in the early 2000s. This marked a "cultural shift" from debt being a disgrace to being acceptable. However, cards being handed out to "unsophisticated consumers" was a serious concern. The two biggest card issuers in Turkey, Yapi Kredi and Garants, for instance, had a branch in the Akmerkez shopping mall. In 2006, a law was passed to control the marketing of credit cards and limit the approval of credit applications with minimal credit checks. The number of credit cards in Turkey had risen from 10,000 in 1977 to more than 38 million cards in 2008. Consumers around the world were piling up debt that would take years to repay.

In Great Britain, companies were discouraging the formerly popular business lunch. Other trends included asking employees to turn in company credit cards or cut back on their use and thinking about how company money was being spent.

The results of the 2008 Consumer Action credit card survey indicated that four of the top 10 credit card companies (American Express, Bank of America, Capital One Financial Corp., and Citigroup) could be expected to raise interest rates based on market conditions, economic conditions, and business strategies, over which credit card users have no control. Customers could also expect to see interest rates increased and credit limits reduced through the practice of "universal default," which is based on a customer's payment record with other credit companies. Other factors considered by card issuers were perceived risk and account history.

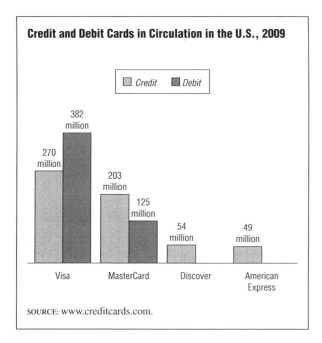

Credit and Debit Cards in Circulation in the U.S., 2009

Credit ▪ Debit

270 million
382 million
203 million
125 million
54 million
49 million

Visa MasterCard Discover American Express

SOURCE: www.creditcards.com.

In the United States, tighter regulations passed in the wake of the "Great Recession" of 2007 to 2009 that impacted card issuers' ability to solicit new customers. Visits by card issuers to college campuses had to be registered with the school and offering of incentive gifts was prohibited. Issuers were also required to provide information on such things as how long it takes to pay off balances with minimum payments. If encouraging more responsible issuance and use of debt was the purpose, the policies may have had an effect. In September 2010, U.S. credit card defaults fell to an 18-month low.

With such pullbacks in the U.S. market, issuers such as MasterCard are looking at emerging markets like China to provide future growth. China had some 207 million credit cards as of June 2010, four times the number in 2006. Chen Bin at MasterCard Advisors stated in the Wall Street Journal that China would likely have 800 to 900 million credit cards by 2020, because of fast economic growth and urbanization. This would place China ahead of the U.S. as the world's largest credit card market by number of cards.

ORGANIZATION AND STRUCTURE

The credit card industry consists of credit card associations, such as Visa and MasterCard, which provide an international brand name that is owned by their member issuers, as well as credit card issuers, such as Citicorp and MBNA Corp. Some credit card companies, such as American Express, issue their own cards. The industry includes four major kinds of issuers: banks, oil companies, retailers, and travel and entertainment companies.

In terms of revenues, bankcards have led the industry since their introduction. Banks and other financial institutions issue universal cards, which are valid at any participating business or institution. Retail and oil cards (sometimes referred to as charge cards) continued to be popular throughout the last half of the twentieth century. Retailers and oil companies traditionally provided cards that were only valid at affiliated stores or gas stations, but many of these cards were joint ventures with major credit card companies, namely Visa and MasterCard, and could be used anywhere. Like retail and oil cards, travel and entertainment cards were traditionally valid only at a limited number of places relating to travel and entertainment. Cards such as American Express, Diners Club, and Carte Blanche provide this kind of credit card.

The credit card business became an industry in its own right in the 1960s when it began to offer common services and share features. Governments began to pass legislation to cover the credit card industry at this time as issues of privacy and equal access to credit cards arose. In 1970, criminals began to intercept credit cards that were being sent unsolicited by credit card companies who were trying to increase the numbers of credit card holders. The criminals would run up large bills, which were then received by the original intended recipient. The Federal Trade Commission placed a moratorium on the mailings of unsolicited credit cards, and President Richard Nixon banned the practice completely. Although existing laws protected consumers from responsibility for the bills run up by the criminals, consumers had to go to court to prove their innocence, which took considerable time and money.

Some governments established a series of laws and regulations to protect consumers against possible credit-card-related problems. The United States passed the Fair Credit Billing Act of 1972, which required credit card issuers to allow a 60-day period for consumers to make written complaints about their bills, a 15-day period for credit card issuers to acknowledge these complaints, and a 60-day period for credit card issuers to investigate, correct, and explain their bills after receiving complaints. Congress revised this act in 1975 to add a provision for cardholders to receive their bills 14 days prior to the end of the billing period. Further legislation and rulings addressed other consumer complaints involving privacy, including credit card companies' sharing of personal information with state and federal agencies, as well as the sale of cardholder mailing lists to other companies.

The largest and most persistent problem the industry continues to face, however, has been fraud. Early kinds of credit card fraud resulted from stolen or lost credit cards. Later, some criminals developed methods for producing fraudulent credit cards, while others obtained credit card numbers through mail fraud and used them to make purchases over the telephone. Some merchants perpetuated credit card fraud by charging consumers for merchandise that they did not purchase. Credit card companies, along with state and federal governments, collaborated to prevent and contain the proliferation of credit card fraud. As a result, U.S. federal law imposes a 10-year prison sentence and a fine of US$10,000 for credit card fraud from US$1,000 to US$5,000.

Another legislative action related to the U.S. credit card industry took place in 2001. In the mid-1990s, the U.S. Department of Justice launched an investigation of some allegedly anti-competitive activities of MasterCard and Visa. The main issue, which was the practice of restricting banks that issued MasterCard or Visa from issuing rival cards such as American Express or Discover, eventually resulted in a formal lawsuit filed by the Justice Department in 1998. More than three years later, in October of 2001, a U.S. district judge ruled that MasterCard and Visa could no longer prevent member banks from issuing other cards.

In 2010 six states had joined the U.S. Department of Justice in filing an antitrust lawsuit against Visa, MasterCard, and American Express for policies that prevented merchants from promoting special offers to customers using a preferred card. Visa and MasterCard relented and changed those policies. The suit continued going forward against American Express.

Sources of Credit Card Revenues. Unlike retail and gas credit cards, which earn the issuer money through both finance charges and increased sales, universal cards issued by banks and other financial operations strive to make a profit mainly by enticing cardholders to use their credit lines. Consequently, credit card issuers implemented a number of measures to increase their profits, including raising the fee they charged merchants (typically 2 to 3 percent of a transaction). Issuers also marketed products like insurance, sold their cardholder lists, sold advertising space on their payment envelopes, and modified their methods of calculating interest.

Because many states had laws that placed caps on interest rates under usury laws, credit card issuers could not increase their basic finance charges. Instead, they changed the way interest was applied to the account. At first, credit card issuers charged interest on a cardholder's balance minus any payment made, but many banks later adopted an average daily balance method, charging interest on a daily basis from the time a charge was made unless the cardholder paid the balance in full by the due date.

Credit card issuers also started marketing other financial products along with their credit cards, including insurance and loans. In addition, they began offering cardholders cash advances on their credit cards through

a participating bank or an automatic teller machine (ATM). Many credit card issuers automatically charge interest on a daily balance basis for cash advances, whether paid in full by the due date or not. Since banks and other financial institutions provide a limited number of services, they also market a host of wares from other companies, such as tape recorders, watches, pens, cameras, radios, and collectibles. The credit card issuer receives a 15 percent commission on these sales. Credit card issuers use their remittance envelopes and statements to advertise these products.

Some credit card companies charge annual fees to increase their revenues, especially from cardholders who do not use their revolving credit. However, the industry has grown increasingly competitive as issuers have begun to offer credit cards with no annual fees to shore up their cardholder ranks. Such moves forced other issuers to waive their annual fees to retain their cardholders. In a 2008 survey by Aite Group, consumers ranked "no annual fee" as the most important factor in choosing to apply for a certain card. According to Consumer Reports, in the first three months of 2009, only 27 percent of card offers had an annual fee.

Since most standard credit cards charge interest rates well above those of other forms of consumer credit like loans, banks can easily borrow money at a comparatively low interest rate to extend credit lines to their cardholders, who must repay their charges at the much higher interest rate if they use their revolving credit. The combination of these methods provides credit card issuers with a means of garnering significant revenues and profits relative to other financial products.

BACKGROUND AND DEVELOPMENT

Although credit has been part of society for over 3,000 years, the credit card evolved after World War II from the social, political, and economic conditions in the United States, which continued to be the strongest proponent of the credit card industry through the 1990s and controlled the largest share of the world market. However, consumer credit had existed for millennia, with early references dating to about 1750 B.C. in the ancient Babylonian Code of Hammurabi, a set of laws established by the Babylonian ruler Hammurabi that referred to credit as debt.

The modern credit card developed from the combination of a number of credit options that had been available for much of the twentieth century. Diners Club, which was started in 1950, was the first such credit card company. It opened an office in Canada in 1953, becoming the first international credit card company. Other credit card companies soon began operations. In 1958, American Express and Carte Blanche joined the industry with the introduction of universal credit cards. These cards did not offer revolving credit, where cardholders had the option of making partial payment and rolling the rest of the debt over to the next month. Instead, they required complete payment at the end of each billing period. However, at the end of the 1950s and in the early 1960s, Bank of America and Chase Manhattan jumped into the fray, and the demand for revolving credit grew rapidly. In the late 1960s, Diners Club began to lose its position at the top of the credit card industry. By 1980, Citibank had purchased Diners Club and Carte Blanche.

Credit card companies began to expand within the United States and internationally during the 1970s. The country's leading credit cards, BankAmericard and Master-Charge, competed in Europe and Asia, forming franchise agreements with businesses and banks in these regions. Initially, MasterCharge led the industry at home and abroad, but the company was quickly surpassed by Bank-Americard. By 1972, BankAmericard International had 6.2 million cardholders; 15,000 bank affiliations; and 250,000 business agreements. Nonetheless, its presence in Europe remained weak, except for its Barclay Card in the United Kingdom. MasterCharge excelled in Europe, where it held a majority share of the market until negative feelings about the U.S. conflict in Vietnam subsided.

MasterCharge signed an agreement with EuroCard, the leading European credit card, which had affiliates in the United Kingdom, Germany, France, and Sweden. EuroCard functioned like a debit card, automatically withdrawing charges from its cardholders' accounts, with no revolving credit. By the mid-1970s, BankAmericard began to surpass MasterCharge, in part by changing its name to Visa, a word easily recognizable around the world and one that had an international feel. With the new name and identity, Visa successfully forged alliances with banks in leading credit card markets like France, Spain, and Israel. In 1980, MasterCharge also adopted a more global-sounding name, becoming MasterCard, and formed agreements similar to Visa with banks through-out the world.

By 1978, the popularity of credit cards was growing, along with U.S. consumer debt, as 52 million Americans carried at least two credit cards. Consumer debt continued to grow through the late 1990s. In 1969, U.S. credit card debt stood at US$2.7 billion, and by 1994, U.S. credit card debt had risen to US$74 billion, adjusted for inflation.

Despite the growth of the industry, credit card companies had trouble posting profits without economies of scale. In the 1980s, credit card issuers began to adapt to boost profits. Banks and lenders realized their profits would rise as consumers stopped paying off their entire balances. Therefore, credit card issuers started to increase their cardholders' credit lines to encourage additional use

that would result in large monthly expenses that many cardholders would prefer to repay over months or years. In addition, cards were offered to people who would be considered risky in less economically prosperous times. This was a successful strategy for the industry, and credit cards became the most profitable form of bank debt by the mid-1980s. Rising interest rates in the 1980s and through the 1990s allowed credit card issuers to continue earning large profits through the 1990s. Interest from revolving credit was the source of 90 percent of all bank revenues in the mid-1990s.

The credit card itself also evolved throughout the industry's history. It began as a charge-plate or charge coin in the retail industry, a paper card in the gasoline industry, and a paper book in the universal credit card industry. Eventually, credit card issuers, including banks, retailers, and gasoline companies, adopted a standard magnetically encoded plastic card. Furthermore, as credit card issuers sought more secure credit cards, some companies began to embed cardholder pictures on their cards, and merchants began matching the signature on the card to the signature on the sales receipt.

By the mid-1990s, credit card transactions accounted for about 17 percent of all purchases, compared to 11 percent in the early 1980s. Credit cards moved beyond being only for emergency and occasional use, and became a frequent form of payment, just like cash or checks. Cardholders used their credit lines for day-to-day products, such as food, gas, and clothing, in the late 1990s, instead of only for larger purchases, such as furniture and appliances. This trend was a result of several factors, including the proliferation of credit cards around the world, greater acceptance of credit cards at businesses and institutions worldwide, added security measures by the industry, and growth of shopping on the Internet. In 1997, the world's credit card purchases rose to over US$1.8 trillion.

To fuel continued growth, credit card companies used promotions like low introductory interest rates, no annual fees, and low-rate balance transfers to win new customers. Using the balance transfer option, cardholders could move their balance from a high interest rate card to a new, lower-rate one. In another promotion, credit card issuers instituted reward programs to encourage cardholder loyalty by offering discounts and free credit on a variety of products and services after reaching designated spending goals.

As technology allowed accurate credit statements and people led increasingly busy lives around the world, more people relied on credit cards to avoid miscalculations that could happen with cash and check transactions, as well as to avoid making additional trips to the bank or an ATM for cash. In the European Union, credit card use increased 18 percent per year in the late 1990s, with fastest expansion in Italy, the Netherlands, Switzerland, and Spain. The United Kingdom and France remained the European Union's overall leaders, accounting for about 30 percent of all credit card transactions, and Greece recorded the lowest use of credit cards within the European Union. Consumers in the European Union used credit cards about 23 times per year, in contrast to those in the United States, who used them about twice per week. Canadian consumers, on the other hand, tended to use credit cards the most, averaging four credit card transactions per week.

Visa remained the world's leading credit card association in the late 1990s, representing US$1.1 trillion in purchases worldwide in 1997 and controlling about 52 percent of the world market. In 1996, Visa became the first credit card to report total purchases of more than US$1 trillion. MasterCard held its position in 1997 as the world's number two credit card with US$602 billion in purchases, representing 30 percent of the market.

Credit card portfolio sales—the transfer of a credit card operation from one issuer to another—increased in the late 1990s. In 1997, portfolio sales rose to US$20.8 billion, up from US$7.1 billion in 1996. By mid-1998, several high-profile credit card portfolio sales were already underway, including Citicorp's acquisition of AT&T's credit card operations for US$14 billion. Altogether, 22 portfolio sales took place in 1997, up from 21 in 1996. The largest purchase was the acquisition of Advanta Corp.'s credit card unit by Fleet Financial Group for US$10.5 billion.

Despite the growth of the industry worldwide, credit card issuers faced declining profits in the mid- to late 1990s. For example, in 1996, profits slipped from 2.71 percent of total credit card revenues to 2.14 percent in the United States. However, credit card operations remained more profitable than other banking services, which yielded a return of only 1.86 percent on assets. Nevertheless, credit card issuers started to look for ways to increase their profits and urged legislators to review their caps on interest rates and fees.

The rise of credit card use led to increased consumer debt around the world, especially in the United States where during the mid- to late 1990s, consumer debt escalated to record highs. In addition, the American Bankers Association reported that credit card delinquencies had reached a new record high in 1996. As a result, bankruptcy became a widespread means for consumers to unload their growing debt in the United States, and the number of bankruptcies in the country soared. By early 1997, seriously delinquent credit card accounts amounted to US$4.07 billion, or 1.8 percent of all outstanding credit card debt in the United States.

Improved economic conditions in the late 1990s helped reduce the number of bankruptcies in the United States. As a result, credit card issuers reported growth in loan profits for the first time in five years, from 17.4 percent in 1998 to 17.9 percent in 1999. The following year, profits grew again, reaching 18.4 percent. The percentage of credit card profits from late fees and other charges increased 33 percent between 1995 and 1999, growing from 18 percent to 25 percent. In 2000, fees accounted for 28 percent of earnings, due in part to the lower interest rates credit card companies had to offer to remain competitive. To compensate for lower rates, credit card issuers began reducing or eliminating grace periods and raising fees for late payments for charges that exceeded credit limits. They also began peddling accessory services, such as minimum payment insurance, which guarantees the payment of a card holder's minimum balance in the event of a disability.

The number of consolidations increased in 2000 as large companies continued to purchase credit card portfolios from small card issuers. For example, MBNA bought the US$5.6 billion credit card portfolio of First Union Corp. in 2000. That same year, Citigroup purchased the US$47.38 billion portfolio of First Capital Corp. The total number of significant portfolio transactions in 2000 reached 36, compared to 21 in 1999 and 26 in 1998. The economic slowdown that had taken hold of North America in the early 2000s prompted large banks to slow their spending, resulting in a drop in the number of portfolio purchases to 25 in 2001. The largest deal of the year was Bank One Corp.'s purchase of the US$8 billion portfolio of Wachovia Corp. In 2002, Next Card Inc. began to consider selling its US$2 billion portfolio, and Providian Financial Corp. put roughly US$3 billion of its credit card assets up for sale.

In Asia, credit card use grew an average of 30 percent annually in the late 1990s, although China's potential market of nearly one billion cardholders remained largely untapped. According to *The Financial Times,* China had fewer than 15 million cards in circulation in the mid-1990s. Chinatrust, based in Taipei, became the first Taiwanese bank to enter the ranks of the world's 100 largest credit card issuers in 2001, after it issued 400 million cards and increased its domestic market share to 17.65 percent. According to the *Korea Herald,,* nearly 90 percent of the Asia-Pacific market for credit cards remained untapped.

In May 2004, The People's Bank of China and China Banking Regulatory Commission gave approval to American Express, Citibank, and HSBC to issue credit cards in China and ABN Amro and MasterCard created a partnership to issue credit cards. MBNA opened an office in Shanghai, and Morgan Stanley announced plans to begin issuing the Discover Card in China.

The credit card market in South America was also forecast to expand rapidly in the twenty-first century. South America, led by Brazil and Argentina, represented about US$20 billion per year in credit card purchases in the late 1990s, and the region had 13 million cards in circulation, divided evenly between Visa and Master-Card. However, economic turmoil in Argentina in 2001 slowed the potential of this growth market.

The world's three largest financial card companies—Visa, MasterCard, and American Express— continued to advance the use of debit, credit, and charge cards around the world. Countries once opposed to capitalism, such as China and Russia, were allowing foreign financial companies to enter the market and establish card systems. These three companies reported that their credit and debit card transaction volumes reached US$4.5 trillion in 2003, an increase of 15.4 percent over 2002 levels according to CardForum.

Card companies continued to enjoy increasing earnings, with the highest profit margins for the industry since 1992 reported in 2003. A slight drop in 2003 revenues from cardholder penalties, including late fees and overlimit fees, was attributed to lower debt levels. Regardless, these penalty charges earned card companies approximately US$7.7 billion.

The purchase of Bank One, which was the third-largest credit card issuer in the United States, by JP Morgan Chase in 2004 was significant for the industry. Bank One had been the sixth largest bank in the United States with more than 51 million cardholders as well as its other bank assets; combined with JP Morgan Chase, the third largest bank, the purchase created the second largest bank.

In the mid-2000s, merchants had begun to balk at the costs of accepting financial cards as payment. In 2004, Wal-Mart stopped accepting MasterCard debit cards because the card cost too much and accounted for only 1 percent of its sales. However, after several months of negotiations and a class-action lawsuit headed by Wal-Mart over the use of debit cards, Wal-Mart began to accept them again. The major credit card companies had required merchants to accept all their cards, including debit cards. Visa and MasterCard were accused of artificially inflating the transaction fees paid by retailers. Visa and MasterCard settled with Wal-Mart and the approximately five million other retailers who had joined the class action suit, with the card companies agreeing to pay US$3.05 billion in cash over 10 years. In addition, they agreed to stop requiring retailers to honor all their cards and to make distinguishing between credit and debit cards easier.

The United States continued to be the only major country that did not embrace smart card technology, partly because only one percent of total sales volume of credit cards with magnetic strips was attributed to fraud. However, data is easier to obtain from a magnetic strip than from a smart card chip, so technology experts predicted that fraud would increase in the United States where criminals will have the greatest pool of cards with magnetic strips.

The use of pre-paid gift cards had grown rapidly in North America. Deloitte Touche Tohmatsu reported that gift cards had generated about US$45 billion in sales in 2003. Many of these cards were issued directly by retailers, but general purpose cards from Visa, Master-Card, American Express, and Discover were also being issued with the advantage of being accepted at an extensive number of retailers.

CURRENT CONDITIONS

Consumers were becoming more selective and restrictive about spending in response to economic challenges in the late 2000s. Experian reported that in 2008 the average debt for Americans with credit was US$16,635, excluding mortgages. Between 2000 and 2008, total credit card debt showed a dramatic increase of more than 50 percent. This over-leveraging of consumers played a role in the severity of the recession and the overhang households were left with when the housing bubble burst. Consumer expert Faith Popcorn reported that 90 percent of respondents in a 2008 survey were considering a shift to a simpler lifestyle. Another survey revealed that having their finances under control and paying off their mortgages were better indications of success than having a large income or owning a luxury car. A 2010 survey by United Services Automobile Association (USAA) found that 90 percent of respondents planned to use cash for upcoming holiday shopping, while only 41 percent planned to pay with credit cards.

Further evidence of an anti-debt shift in the United States could be seen in the form of new regulations passed against credit card companies. These had the effect of tightening the supply of credit at the same time that demand for credit waned. This practice led to increased use of debit cards. A 2010 study by Global Industry Analysts projected that the number of debit cards in use worldwide would grow to 5.3 billion by the year 2015.

In October 2010 the PCI Security Standards Council released new payment card industry data security standards, set to take effect in 2011. Over 1,500 people from 600 organizations around the globe participated in the effort. The Version 2.0 standards were not a radical change, but they did include a stronger focus on managing cardholder data and prioritizing any vulnerabilities. A number of companies had expressed concern over credit card data security issues with attacks on lender systems happening more often.

RESEARCH AND TECHNOLOGY

The most prominent technological advancement affecting the credit card industry in the late 1990s was the introduction of the multipurpose smart card. In 1994, France created the smart card version of the credit/debit card, which featured a computer microchip instead of a magnetic strip to store financial data. The smart card functioned as both a credit card and a debit card. It also served as identification and fraud/misuse prevention was accomplished with built in encryption that scrambled codes and rendered the card virtually useless to criminals. In early 1998 French transportation services, including trains, buses, and subways, along with bars, restaurants, and stores located in transportation stations, accepted smart cards. The country launched the system simultaneously with the 1998 World Cup tournament in Marseilles.

Smart cards are also known as ePurses, or electronic wallets, and have been more readily accepted in some countries than others. Europeans were more likely to use a pre-paid debit card with smart card technology that requires a PIN number for purchases instead of using a credit card. The London Transport Company's Oyster card allows customers to pay bus and subway fares by purchasing prepaid tickets that are added to their card. Passengers pass the Oyster card over an electronic reader at the gate to the subway to gain entry to the system. London Transport had plans for the cards to be used for other purchases. However, experience in Germany has shown that such cards need to be multi-functional and provide the user with a benefit for their use, such as savings over the regular price of a good.

While standards for the smart card varied around the world, Visa, MasterCard, and Europay had developed a standard that was used in most European countries and was promoted by those countries to facilitate use of the card internationally. The United States and other countries, however, lagged behind French smart card technology four to six years. Smart cards were first introduced in the United States in 1999 when American Express launched its Blue Card. These failed to gain widespread acceptance in the United States by the early 2000s in spite of low interest rates offered for smart cards by Bank One and Providian Financial, among others.

Other key developments emerged in response to the rise of Internet-based commerce. To promote the use of credit cards as a means of online payment, Visa and MasterCard collaborated with Microsoft, IBM, and Netscape to develop a standard for secure online transactions called Secure Electronic Transaction (SET). SET verifies the parties participating in the transaction and provides digital certificates to credit card issuers, which transfer them to their cardholders. This security system also uses advanced encryption technology developed by the Massachusetts Institute of Technology, which establishes two unique "keys" for both cardholders and businesses, a public and a private one. The public key is published in an electronic directory, while the private key is kept secret. When sending a message, the public key encrypts the message, while the private key unscrambles it. This method prevents hackers from obtaining confidential information such as credit card numbers because even if they intercept the message, they cannot decode it without the proper private key.

In May 2004, MBF Cards (Malaysia) Sdn Bhd introduced the MBF Cards EMV Chip credit card, which had the ability to include more embedded data than other similar smart cards. MBF Cards President Al Alagappan said that the product offered safety and security in new ways. E-purse card technology was expected to be successful quickly in South Korea, where consumers liked to be among the first in the world to use the latest technology.

Security remained of high concern to consumers. In June 2005, approximately 200,000 records were stolen and the data of 40 million credit card accounts were compromised when computer hackers breached the system of credit card processing company CardSystems Solutions of Atlanta, Georgia, which handled all major credit cards. In 2003, a similar incident had occurred at Data Processors International of Nebraska, where the account numbers of 8 million credit cards were stolen. New encryption methods are tested continuously in an effort to secure data. However, the United States has been criticized for its privacy and data protection laws, which lag behind those of other developed countries. In Europe, for example, card holders in most countries are required to specifically opt-in to allowing their data to be share or stored. However, in the United States, the consumers are required to opt out. In addition, laws in Europe make it illegal for companies to share most financial information, which is contrary to common practice in the United States. In Sweden, security is taken very seriously, and credit card users are required to produce photo identification and a signature match.

In 2010 technology firm Dynamics, Inc. developed three products with the potential to reshape the way credit and debit cards are secured and used. Dynamic's "Redemption" card fits 70,000 electronic components onto a regular-sized card's magnetic stripe. Instead of a number, the card has five buttons. An activation code is entered on these each time the card is used. After each transaction, the memory is wiped clean until time for the next transaction. If stolen, the card is useless to thieves unless they know the activation code. Dynamic's founder and CEO Jeffrey Mullen said the feature could make the cards fraud-proof. Dynamic reached an agreement with Citibank to use the card and expected agreements with more big banks by the end of 2010. Dynamic's products also include one which can imbed multiple credit and debit accounts on a single card and one enabling cardholders to tell their card at the point-of-sale to pay using reward or loyalty points.

INDUSTRY LEADERS

Card Associations.

Visa. Visa began in 1958 as BankAmericard, which was Bank of America's credit card operation. Bank of America licensed its BankAmericard to other banks starting in the 1960s. In 1977, the credit card's name was changed to Visa on the basis of a strong national and international presence. Besides credit cards, Visa offers traveler's checks, smart cards, corporate and business cards, and Internet commerce systems.

In 2010, Visa International had the world's leading credit card and was the largest processor of financial transactions, with 1.8 billion Visa credit cards in circulation accepted in more than 200 countries and territories. Its processing network is capable of handling over 20,000 transactions per second. Visa, as a card association, does not actually issue credit cards. Visa reported US$5 trillion in total volume for fiscal 2010. Cash transactions accounted for about 38 percent of Visa business and purchases accounted for another 62 percent. Visa members also participate in the VisaNet payment system, which provides authorization, transaction processing, and settlement services for purchases from 24 million merchants worldwide. The company raised approximately US$17 billion in its initial public offering in 2008. Visa Inc. operates separately from Visa Europe, which is owned by its member financial institutions.

MasterCard International Inc. MasterCard International began as a private company in 1966 when a group of bankers decided to enter the credit card business. They initially called the venture Interbank Card Association, which issued MasterCharge cards. The association later was renamed MasterCard along with its credit card. With a declining market share, MasterCard began lobbying for acceptance in new kinds of businesses such as bus depots and hospitals.

Although it claimed to have more member enterprises and is accepted in more countries, MasterCard continued to be the number two credit card association based on the number of cardholders. With 966 million MasterCard credit and debit cards worldwide in 2009, MasterCard reported net revenue of US$5.1 billion. The MasterCard brand is one of the most widely recognized in the world, but

the company includes the Maestro brand, which is an online PIN-based debit card system used at ATMs. The company also operates the Cirrus ATM network and Mondex International chip-based smart card subsidiary.

The company's "MasterCard Working for Small Business" was a comprehensive global program providing small business with payment cards, online tools, and other resources that delivered financial control, data management, and analysis and reporting, as well as rewards and benefits. In May 2004, the program released its *MasterCard Procurement Opportunities Guide: An Entrepreneur's Guide to Selling to Governments and Corporations* at the Small Business Association Conference 2004. At that conference, the company released results of a *Small Business Economic and Spend Outlook Survey,* which reported that small businesses considered the management of expenses and finances as their most pressing concerns. The survey polled U.S. businesses with annual revenue between US$100,000 and US$10 million. The number of delegates and exhibitors doubled from 2003 for the MasterCard-sponsored the Cards Middle East conference in May 2004 in Dubai. New card technologies, such as online prepayment terminals, were decidedly appealing to conference attendees. Dubai Ports, Customs and Free Zone Corporation became the first government organization in the region to adopt the new MasterCard corporate purchasing card. The system's B2B transaction application replaced petty cash with a payment card that could be monitored online and reconciled to Oracle Financials software. MasterCard's award-winning "Priceless" advertising campaign, which was seen in 96 countries in 47 languages, expanded the company's global reach and scope. By 2007, the company's workforce had grown to 5,000 employees and earnings were reported at US$4.1 billion.

In 2008 the U.S. Treasury Department announced the impending launch of an innovative application of debit MasterCard through Comerica Bank called Direct Express. The program was established to encourage Social Security recipients without bank accounts to have their benefits loaded electronically onto a debit card. Major cost savings were projected for the federal government. Direct Express had been introduced in ten states as of June 2008.

In October 2010 MasterCard announced its "contactless" pay system, PayPass, which was being tested at the Galeries Lafayette department store in Berlin. Customers simply hold their cards in front of the terminal. The terminal reads the card and records the transaction, and a visual and audio signal lets the user know the process worked. Purchases of less than 25 euros do not even require a PIN or signature.

American Express Company. In the late 1990s, American Express reorganized itself to focus on its credit card and travel operations and spun off its stockbroker arm, Lehman Brothers. Berkshire Hathaway owned about 10 percent of American Express. Although the company originally did not provide revolving credit to its clients, the company launched a credit card called Optima in the mid-1990s that offered a revolving credit line. Besides its credit cards, American Express led the world in traveler's checks and published magazines, including *Food & Wine* and *Travel & Leisure*. The company offered online banking, mortgage, and brokerage services and had plans for global expansion. Nearly 80 percent of American Express's revenues were generated in the United States. American Express was a leading captive center (offshore shared service) operator and opened a customer service center in India. The company reported US$24.5 billion in revenue and 58,300 employees in 2009.

American Express is a global financial, travel, and network services company operating three segments. Travel Related Services included charge and credit cards, travelers' checks, and the world's largest travel agency. American Express Financial Advisors had more than 12,000 advisors offering financial planning, brokerage services, mutual funds, insurance, and other investment products. American Express Bank offered banking services to wealthy individuals, corporations, and retail customers outside the United States. American Express remained the world's third largest credit card, well behind Visa and MasterCard.

DiscoverFinancial Services Inc. Formerly part of the Sears, Roebuck and Co. financial services, Dean Witter, Discover became an independent company in 1993. Dean Witter launched the Discover card in the 1980s while part of Sears. In 1997, Dean Witter merged with Morgan Stanley to become Morgan Stanley Dean Witter. Discover reported more than 50 million cardholders, and the Discover/NOVUS Network was the largest proprietary credit card network in the United States with more than four million merchant and cash access locations. Like other major credit card companies, Discover offered prepaid stored value gift cards.

Discover launched distinctive advertising campaigns and promotional partnerships. The "It Pays to Discover" tag line was linked to TV ads highlighting unique rewards and industry innovations. Cashback Bonus award opportunities highlighted ways participating card members would accrue awards on every purchase and merchants who would double amounts. Another series featured "Discover 2GO Card," with a unique, compact shape housed in a protective case that easily attached to a key chain, belt, or money clip for maximum convenience. Discover partnerships include ESPN's College

Day. Discover acquired naming rights to a Discover Mills shopping center near Atlanta, Georgia that allowed Discover Card members to take advantage of special promotions, events, and offers.

Discover remained a large credit card issuer in the mid-2000s. The company was spun off from former parent Morgan Stanley in 2005. In 2009, Discover reported revenue of US$6.7 billion and 10,500 employees.

Diners Club. In 1949, when Frank McNamara left his billfold at home and could not pay his dinner tab, he began to conceive the idea for the Diners Club credit card. While lunching with his partner, Ralph Schneider, in February 1950, McNamara presented a cardboard card to pay for their meals, and the credit card industry that has continued into the twenty-first century was born.

Although stores and gas stations had issued credit exclusive to their services for years, the idea conceived by McNamara and Schneider offered consumers the ability to use their credit card wherever accepted, instead of only at a specific chain store or gas company. Diners Club became an intermediary between the credit grantors and the credit users. McNamara and Schneider believed that the primary users of Diners Club credit cards would be traveling salespeople who would charge their accommodations and meals while on the road. Because Diners Club did not charge a fee, many business travelers signed up immediately.

In its first month of business, Diners Club handled US$2,000 worth of credit, yielding income of seven percent, according to the monograph *The Credit Card Industry*. The company's business expanded quickly as McNamara and Schneider relied on the simple, inexpensive marketing technique of placing leaflets in nearby offices. Instead of performing a credit check on its members, McNamara and Schneider conducted interviews with them.

Because Diners Club required substantial credit and funds to operate, the company had to develop several methods to stretch funds as far as possible. For example, Alfred Bloomingdale came up with the idea, later known as "float," that gave the company more time to use its money before checks cleared. Diners Club would pay its New York bills with a Los Angeles bank account and its Los Angeles bills with its New York bank account, giving the company time between writing the checks and money being withdrawn from their accounts. Nevertheless, as check clearing procedures began to take less time, the value of this technique declined.

The company also coordinated the payments of their cardholders with their payment due dates for the businesses. Suppliers were paid 30 days after the charges accumulated through the month, while Diners Club cardholders would pay their charges at the end of the month. While the industry was in its infancy, almost all cardholders paid their bills in full on time, which prevented Diners Club from incurring additional finance problems.

However, the emerging industry encountered a number of difficulties. Due to the structure and arrangement of the industry during this period, Diners Club had to rely on the signatures on the receipts in order to determine who made the charges for billing purposes. Those signatures were not only often difficult to decipher, but also could vary from the cardholder's name since people would lend the card to friends. At the time, the company imposed no credit limit, but maintained a list of stolen or misused credit cards. The company hired private detectives to investigate deadbeat cardholders and confiscate their cards.

McNamara finally concluded that the credit card industry held no potential beyond business travelers and restaurants and sold his share of the company to Schneider and Alfred Bloomingdale. In 1951, Diners Club bought Bloomingdale's Dine & Sign credit card company, and Bloomingdale served as CEO until 1971. From 1952 to 1970, the company continued to turn a profit, securing credit first from small banks and then large ones. Diners Club had opened offices in most major U.S. cities by the late 1950s, and in 1953 it opened its first international office in Canada. In 1970, Continental Insurance Company acquired Diners Club.

JCB International Co. Ltd. Established in 1961, JCB (Japan Credit Bureau) launched a consumer credit card in the U.S. in 1993. JCB remained a leader in the Japanese credit card industry in 2010 with annual sales of US$67.9 billion. The company had 59.8 million cardholders, with its cards accepted by 12.3 million merchants in 190 countries and territories.

Card Issuers.
Citigroup Inc. Citicorp, the world's leading issuer of credit cards, became the world's largest financial services firm in 1998 when it merged with the Travelers Group to become Citigroup. By 2010, Citigroup offered MasterCard, Visa, and private label credit and charge cards, with 200 million customer accounts in more than 160 countries and jurisdictions. The company also offered Diners Club cards to affluent individuals and corporations. Private label cards included Sears and Home Depot. Internationally, Citigroup was the first foreign bank to issue credit cards in Russia and was the owner of the majority of Diners Club Europe. In 2009, the company reported a net loss of US$1.6 billion, but stated that its core businesses, known collectively as Citicorp, were profitable with US$14.8 billion in net income.

MBNA. Because of its affinity card marketing agreements with more than 5,000 professional, recreational, charitable, and other groups and organizations, MBNA, founded in 1982, was the world's largest independent credit card lender. The company also offered home equity financing, insurance premium financing, and professional practice financing. In 2005 MBNA had operations in the United States, where it held 13.1 percent of the market at the end of 2003; Canada; Ireland; Spain; Mexico; and the United Kingdom. MBNA held 15 percent of the U.K. credit card market in 2003 and was the first U.S. company to issue credit cards in Ireland. In 2006, MBNA was acquired by Bank of America.

JP Morgan Chase. In 2004 JP Morgan Chase bought the third largest credit card issuer, Bank One, which was also the sixth largest bank at the time. The resulting entity was the second largest financial services firm in the United States. In 2003, Bank One held 11.6 percent of the U.S. credit card market. At the end of 2004, JP Morgan Chase had 94 million cardholders, generating revenues of more than US$15 billion with operating income of US$1.68 billion. Customers charged more than US$282 billion worth of goods on Chase credit cards in 2004. In 2009, JP Morgan Chase reported more than 145 million cards in circulation. By 2010 JP Morgan Chase had over 200,000 employees operating in more than 60 countries and total assets of US$2 trillion.

MAJOR COUNTRIES IN THE INDUSTRY

The United States. Despite the economic downturn that gripped the nation between 2000 and 2002, credit card spending grew in the United States as consumers used their cards as a means for short-term loans through cash advances. The financial card industry also experienced an increase in the use of debit cards, with smart cards being increasingly accepted by consumers. Smart card technology, including anti-fraud devices and the ability to store personal information, was expected to eventually gain wide acceptance by retailers and replace traditional credit and debit cards.

As the United States encountered its second economic downturn of the twenty-first century in 2007, debt imbalances were clearly reaching unsustainable levels. The average credit card balance carried by U.S. households in 2001 had been US$8,562. In 2010, the figure was US$15,788. New legislation, as well as thriftier attitudes, led to a tightening of the consumer credit market and increased use of debit rather than credit cards. The U.S. credit card default rate hit 13.01 percent in April 2010. The 60-day delinquency rate was 4.27 percent. Those figures declined in later months, but as of June 2010, Americans still carried US$2.42 trillion in consumer debt. The United States continued to have the largest market for credit cards as well as the leading number of credit card issuers and cards in circulation. In 2009 there were a total of 576.4 million credit cards and 507 million debit cards in circulation. Visa led in both categories, with 270 million and 382 million credit and debit cards, respectively. Master-Card was second at 203 million and 125 million. Discover and American Express were third and fourth with 54 million and 49 million credit cards, respectively.

According to a U.S. Public Interest Research Groups survey, two-thirds of college students had at least one credit card, and collegians with student loans had an average debt of US$3,000. Exclusive agreements involving millions of dollars paid by card issuers to schools and alumni associations that allowed preferential treatment to market specific credit cards to students were being called into question. Director Robert D. Manning of The Center of Consumer Financial Services at the Rochester Institute of Technology claimed that 300 of the largest U.S. universities received more than US$1 billion per year for these marketing deals, and the New York attorney general was leading an investigation into the practice.

The United Kingdom. In the United Kingdom, many Londoners have begun to use smart cards to replace small change, travel passes, security cards, and even house keys. London Transport Company's Oyster cards had the largest number of smart card customers in the United Kingdom. By June 2010, over 34 million had been issued, and the uses for the cards were being extended to include paying for newspapers, grocery items, and parking, providing a new revenue source for London Transport.

The credit and charge card market was valued at US$216 billion by 2003. The United Kingdom's big banks and building societies were the largest providers of credit cards, with Barclays Bank and the Bank of Scotland being the leaders in the industry. Consumers used credit cards mostly on travel, which accounted for about 15 percent of all charges.

In the United Kingdom, minimal fraud was expected as the country moved from magnetic strips to the secure smart chip embedded in credit and debit cards. However, concern over the ease of identity theft remained.

MBNA, Europe's biggest credit card lender, began a two-year plan to provide contactless credit cards for its U.K. customers in 2010. By the end of 2011, over 5 million contactless-enabled credit cards are planned to be issued. In 2010, there were already some 10 million such cards in circulation from all lenders. By 2012, that figure could reach 25 million.

France. By 2003, the six leading credit and charge card companies in France were extremely competitive, accounting for about 72 percent of the market. Société

Général was the overall leader with almost 16 percent of the market. Average annual use of Visa cards was reported in 2010 to be higher in France than in any other European nation, at US$8,275.

Japan. In the early 2000s, Japan experienced a slowdown in its economy with incomes on the decline and fewer jobs and slowed consumer spending. However, of the spending that was occurring, more was being done using credit cards, resulting in an increase in their use. Between 2000 and 2003, credit card use in Japan increased 41 percent, reaching a value of approximately US$231 billion. With credit card fraud continuing to rise in Japan, customers had begun to embrace smart card technology, with smart card usage increasing 185 percent between 2000 and 2003. As of 2010, Japan was the fastest growing regional market for smart cards.

South Korea. In the late 1990s, credit card use in South Korea grew even as the country faced severe economic setbacks in the wake of the South Korean won's 1997 plunge in value. The country reported 35.7 million credit cards in circulation in late 1996, with annual credit card purchases of US$60.6 billion. Futhermore, the South Korean government's efforts to promote "credit card use as a weapon against the black economy" was successful, as credit card use in South Korea doubled annually between 1999 and 2002, and the South Korean market became the second largest in the world.

In 2003, banks in South Korea had experienced large declines in profits as a result of bad debts from credit cards and household charges. The most commonly used financial card was a deferred debit card, known locally as a "charge card," which was linked to a personal bank account. In an effort to boost spending, the government altered regulations on credit cards, giving consumers tax breaks for spending. However, by 2003 the country's credit card debt totaled 14 percent of its gross domestic product. In response to the "crash" in credit cards, the government provided a bailout package for debtors, and credit card companies cut back significantly on the limits allowed for cash advances. Despite this, Koreans remain heavy users of credit cards as of 2010, although credit card growth is expected to decline in the coming years.

BIBLIOGRAPHY
"About JCB." JCB International, 3 November 2010. Available from http://www.jcbusa.com.
"About Us." JP Morgan Chase & Co., 3 November 2010. Available from http://www.jpmorganchase.com.
"About Visa." Visa, 3 November 2010. Available from http://corporate.visa.com.
"Annual Report." American Express, 2009. Available from http://www.americanexpress.com.
"Annual Report." Citigroup, 2009. Available from http://www.citigroup.com.

"Annual Report." Discover, 2009. Available from http://investorrelations.discoverfinancial.com.

"Annual Report." JP Morgan Chase & Co., 2009. Available from http://www.jpmorganchase.com.

"Annual Report." MasterCard Worldwide, 2009. Available from http://investorrelations.MasterCardintl.com.

"Best Credit Card Perks, And Where they Are." CBS News, 9 August 2008. Available from http://www.cbsnews.com.

Birtwistle, Joanne, and Simon Binns. "Fee Worries Threaten Jobs, Lunches and Credit Cards," *Crain's Manchester Business,* 11 August 2008. Available from http://www.crainsmanchesterbusiness.co.uk.

Chu, Kathy. "Weigh Before You Pay: Debit or Credit?" *USA Today,* 1 August 2008.

Cicutti, Nic. "Banks Insist They Are Keeping Card Fraudsters at Bay." *The Scotsman,* 10 August 2008. Available from http://www.scotsman.com.

Clancy, Ray. "Millions of MBNA Credit Cards to Go Contactless." *Investment International,* 3 November 2010. Available from http://www.investmentinternational.com

"Debit Cards in Use Worldwide to Reach 5.3 Billion by 2015, According to a New Report by Global Industry Analysts, Inc." *PRWeb,* 3 November 2010. Available from http://www.prweb.com.

D'Innocenzio, Anne. "U.S. Credit Card Issuers Plan Debut of Smart Card." *The Detroit News,* 2 January 2001. Available from http://www.detnews.com.

Epstein, Jonathan D. "Watch Out: The Rate on Your Credit Card May Go Up." *The Buffalo News,* 10 August 2008. Available from http://www.buffalonews.com.

"Fitch: U.S. Credit Card Defaults Drop to 18-Month Low, DQs Hit 2-Year Low," *Yahoo! Finance,* 2 November 2010. Available from http://finance.yahoo.com.

Glader, Paul."Hyundai Capital Aims to Expand GE Venture in Korea." *Wall Street Journal,* 27 October 2010.

"Global Market for Smart Cards to Reach US$26.9 Billion by 2015, According to New Report by Global Industry Analysts, Inc." *PRWeb,* 28 October 2010.

"Korea: Asia's Most Exciting Credit Card Market." *Korea Herald,* 19 December 2001.

Landler, Mark. "Outside U.S., Credit Cards Tighten Grip." *The New York Times,* 10 August 2008. Available from http://www.nytimes.com.

Lee, Sam. "New Global Credit Card Security Standards Announced," *Creditnet,* 1 November 2010. Available from http://www.creditnet.com.

Machetta, Jessica "Attorney General sues Visa, MasterCard, American Express." *Missourinet,* 6 October 2010. Available from http://www.missourinet.com.

Mandell, Lewis. *The Credit Card Industry.* Boston, MA: Twayne Publishers, 1990.

Medoff, James L., and Andrew Harless. *The Indebted Society.* New York: Little, Brown and Company, 1996.

Miller, Pete. "Holiday shoppers turn to cash over credit," *e-wisdom.com,* 3 November 2010. Available from http://www.e-wisdom.com.

Olson, Thomas"Credit Card Strips Saved." *Pittsburgh Tribune-Review,* 3 November 2010. Available from http://www.pittsburghlive.com.

"Pros and Cons of New Debit Card." *Health Care Weekly Review,* 23 June 2008.

Palmer, Kimberly. "The End of Credit Card Consumerism." *US News & World Report,* 8 August 2008. Available from http://www.usnews.com.

Pugh, Tony. "College Students' Credit Card Debt Spurs Concern." *The Detroit Free Press,* 11 August 2008.

Read, Madlen. "JP Morgan: Credit Card Rules Could Mean Big Losses." *Business Week,* 5 August 2008. Available from http://www.businessweek.com.

Rocco, Matthew. "Credit Card Companies Facing Tighter Regulation on Campus," *The Sentinel* (Edison/Metuchen, NJ), 27 October 2010.

Rong, Frank. "AmEx's Pair Likely Discover's Gain," 11 August 2008. Available from http://seekingalpha.com.

Shawkey, Bruce. "Credit Cards: The Shape of Things to Come." *Credit Union Executive,* January–February 1998.

"Shopping Becomes Tap & Go." *MasterCard news release,* 27 October 2010. Available from http://www.MasterCard.com.

Stein, Ron. "Visa's Future: Credit—Yes; Cards—not Necessarily." *Globes: Israel's Business Arena,* 17 October 2010.

Woolsey, Ben, and Matt Schulz. "Credit Card Statistics, Industry Facts, Debt Statistics," *CreditCards.com,* 3 November 2010. Available from http://www.creditcards.com.

Yu, Rose. "MasterCard Sees Surge in China Credit-Card Use," *Wall Street Journal,* 10 September 2010.

SIC 6500

REAL ESTATE

NAICS CODE(S)

531. The real estate industry encompasses a broad range of businesses involved in the development, transfer, and management of real property. Major segments include developers, property managers, and real estate agents and brokers. For discussion of new building construction, see also **Construction, Residential Building** and **Construction, Nonresidential Building.**

INDUSTRY SNAPSHOT

Historically, real estate has been a cyclical industry in which property values often mirror the fluctuations and conditions of national and global economies. The U.S. economy suffered downturns in both the early 2000s and the late 2000s, and a similar lack of verve held back the real estate market in many other parts of the world, including Latin America and much of the European Union, hitting Germany particularly hard. Certain sectors of the industry performed well, however. In Europe, for example, retail-related real estate transactions flourished. In the wake of the 2001 recession, real estate continued to be the one bright spot in the U.S. economy, as historically low interest rates led to record home sales in 2002 and 2003. Investors were also lured to real estate in greater numbers, as the stock market continued to give

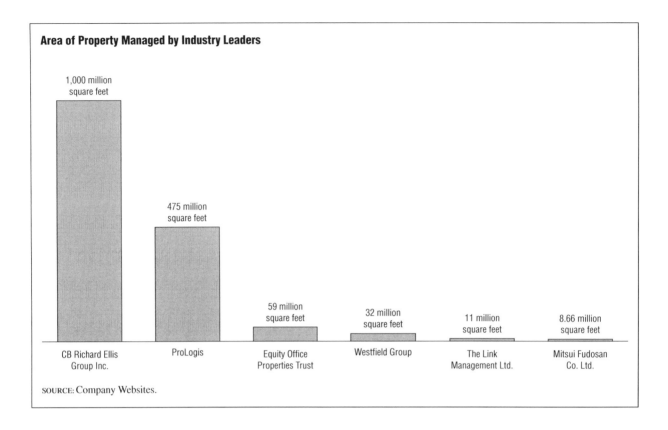

Area of Property Managed by Industry Leaders

SOURCE: Company Websites.

unimpressive returns throughout the early 2000s. The appearance of real estate investment trusts (REITs) in many markets showed their appeal to investors who could now purchase this type of investment through public exchanges. The real estate bubble began to collapse in 2006, especially in the residential sector. As of 2010 the industry had still not recovered, although the resulting recession had technically ended in 2009.

The commercial real estate industry became more of a global affair during the boom years of the late 1990s, and the interconnectedness of global capital markets has continued to strengthen. Commercial real estate suffered from falling rents and rising vacancy rates virtually worldwide during the early 2000s. Globalization, lowering of trade barriers, and the easier mobility of capital in the early 2000s also meant that more companies could compete directly for real estate assets. Increased competition tended to keep prices down. Globally, however, conditions in the real estate industry varied widely because of local conditions. By 2005, countries were again seeing gains in the industry. China, with the world's fastest-growing economy, was seeing a tightening of available real estate in many of its popular urban centers, particularly once it allowed foreign investment in many industries. Despite Germany's position as the slowest European country to recover from the economic downturn, the sheer size of its market continued to make it an attractive opportunity for many investors.

According to the National Association of Realtors, the commercial real estate market reached a record of US$306.8 billion in 2006, up from US$276 billion in 2005. The association predicted that the market would level off in 2007. Instead of simply leveling off, the industry was caught up in the economic downturn that began in the United States late that year. Credit markets froze, as seen in issues of new mortgage backed securities which declined from US$200 billion in 2007 to US$12 billion in the first six months of 2008. As the flow of money slowed to a trickle, the industry petitioned the government for help. Trade association representatives met with political leaders to request access to public credit facilities.

By 2010, the return of economic growth had begun to create new demand for office space. According to Bruce Mosler, co-chairman of Cushman & Wakefield Inc., the largest privately held property services company, the commercial market had bottomed and rents were expected to rise in 2011.

On the residential housing scene, recovery proved more difficult. According to the National Association of Realtors, existing home sales reached a ten-year low in July 2010, and in September, they remained at the third lowest level in a decade. Panelists at a Bloomberg Real Estate Briefing in November 2010 emphasized that significant job growth needed to return before the housing market could truly recover.

Industry support experts known as "stagers" had an impact on sales success stories. They were hired to come in and eliminate clutter plus add some distinctive touches in order to combat the sluggish real estate market.

ORGANIZATION AND STRUCTURE

Property available for individual or corporate ownership in free-market economies is valued primarily using two factors: the marketplace, which establishes demand, and location, which determines value. Typically, there is a high demand in large cities for office and residential space centrally located in prime work and commercial areas. However, the softening of the economy in the United States and much of the rest of the world in the early 2000s and the late 2000s led to slackening demand for such property, bringing rents and prices down.

Many factors influence demand: access to public transportation, highway, and rail networks or port facilities; income levels of inhabitants; property taxes; access to good schools; employment opportunities; and local economic incentives. While a property may be well located, it is still subject to fluctuations of local, national, and global economies. For example, when localities experience increased crime, non-responsive government, economic downturn, or civic mismanagement, then demand may abate, or property values may sink, and the local real estate industry may experience a corresponding downturn.

In markets where property is sold or leased by the government, corporations or individual investors work with government officials to effect the transaction. To serve foreign investors or corporations, development boards are established to work as liaisons with authorities. Several of the most aggressive direct investment agencies are the Netherlands Foreign Investment Agency, the Invest in Britain Bureau, and the Hong Kong Industrial Promotion Office. India, which has had a fast growing economy in the twenty-first century, only began allowing direct foreign investment in real estate in 2005. This change in regulations makes India a potentially hot growth spot for real estate investment. China, also a growing economy, began to privatize some land ownership in the 2000s. Almost half the direct foreign investment in China in the early 2000s was in real estate.

As the world's economies grow increasingly interconnected through international trade, many governments view locations that offer logistical advantages as increasingly important. These advantages include road and rail networks, as well as accessibility to seaports and airports. In the United States, many ports sold or leased port-owned property as office and industrial sites to raise funds to upgrade port facilities. Many airports and seaports designated free zones with complete facilities and warehouses through which goods could enter the country duty free for assemblage, packaging, and redistribution.

In the 2000s, security concerns added a whole new layer of complexity to the economics of real estate. The attacks on September 11, 2001, that destroyed the World Trade Center in New York brought a new awareness of vulnerability to the world's other impressive buildings. In the United States, the insurance industry redefined its risk coverage after the attacks on the World Trade Center and, in most cases, made coverage against terrorist acts a separate category, instead of including it under general risk. Coverage against terrorist attacks was generally not available or only at very high rates. This situation left open the possibility of uninsured buildings being destroyed, and lenders, such as banks, being left with no collateral. The issue of terrorism insurance needed to be resolved by the real estate, banking, and insurance industries, and by legislatures. This existing issue did not, however, slow the building of skyscrapers around the world. The world's tallest building at the time, Taipei 101, was completed in 2003 in Taipei, Taiwan. Taipei 101 was taller than the Petronas Towers in Kuala Lampur, Malaysia, completed in 1998. Taipei 101 did not hold the world's record for long, as the Burj Khalifa in Dubai took the record at 828 meters (2,717 feet) in January 2010. In October 2010, Kingdom Holding Company announced a plan to build a new world's tallest building in Jeddah, Saudi Arabia.

The spread of technology was changing the face of real estate, both residential and commercial. Buyers and potential buyers in technology-rich nations such as the United States were able to conduct independent research and comparison easily from their own homes. There was a wealth of information available on the Internet, enabling buyers to research communities, school districts, building and property costs, taxes, and any other real estate consideration. Homebuyers could even look online to find houses for sale, most with photos and some with video technology that offers a virtual tour.

BACKGROUND AND DEVELOPMENT

Agrarian societies are believed to be the first group to establish property rights. Ancient Greece, and later the Roman Empire, set laws that confirmed this absolute right of ownership. However, with the decline of the Roman Empire and the advent of the Middle Ages, much of European society fell into a period of feudalism wherein a landlord oversaw and owned vast quantities of land. Individuals or "vassals" worked this land on his behalf, paying rent in the form of farm products and labor in exchange for protection. With some notable exceptions, Europe's feudal systems were largely abandoned in the thirteenth century.

The concept of absolute freedom and the rights of the common man did not begin to develop in Europe until the late eighteenth century. No doubt, these ideas were developed through colonial expansionism, which revealed to the Europeans vast amounts of land previously unknown to them.

Development of real estate soared during the late nineteenth and early twentieth centuries, particularly in England and the northeast United States. Multistoried facilities for mass production of automobiles, textile products, and consumer goods were constructed. In turn, these industrial and commercial centers spurred the growth of towns and cities in surrounding regions.

Modern industrial development took on a different focus after World War II. Rapid postwar population growth, coupled with general economic recovery and expansion, spurred the development of both residential and commercial properties in many countries.

In most free-market economies, the 1950s was an era of entrepreneurship. Small companies spun off from larger corporations. Real estate developers seized such opportunities and, responding to the need to create more commercial and industrial facilities, began building on speculation.

A glut of vacancies resulted in the real estate downturn of the 1970s. Real estate values fell, and many small developers and brokers left the industry. Large local and national developers and brokerage firms bought out their smaller competition. However, the 1980s gave rise to a period of renewed global economic growth. Residential communities and office and industrial parks on large tracts of land were planned, developed, sold, and leased. Many sprung up around single industries; for example, the suburban area east of San Francisco known as the "Silicon Valley" largely resulted from commercial and residential development. Amenities that went beyond landscaping became the norm. They included day care, on-site restaurants, health clubs, hotels, travel services, and even heliports. The idea was to attract tenants and create value. Given that this period was often dubbed the "golden era" of real estate, developers spared no expense when it came to interior and exterior design. Some even included valued collections of art, crafts, and sculptures. Many developers built on speculation using state-of-the-art technologies and building materials, even where markets were not established. Despite warnings that markets were becoming overbuilt, the boom continued.

In the United States the economic crisis of 1987, dubbed the "cash crunch," brought the real estate development frenzy to a jarring stop. A sudden tightening of money by the U.S. Federal Reserve and changes in bank loan policies made financing unavailable for projects, particularly speculative ones. With too much product on the market, lessees began to shop for less expensive rent. Perhaps in desperation to attract business in a depressed market, some lessors even offered designated free-rent terms encompassing months, sometimes years. Buyers demanded lower prices. Commercial and residential property values dropped, particularly in markets that experienced the highest increases during the 1980s. As more and more firms declared bankruptcy or merged, groups such as the National Association of Industrial and Office Parks (NAIOP) saw their membership drop from about 7,000 in the late 1980s to less than 3,000 in the early 1990s.

Global recession continued to have an impact on the real estate industry during the last decades of the twentieth century. A wave of consolidations, mergers, and bankruptcies resulted in fewer, but larger, companies in the industry. Brokerage firms merged and, to combat diminished sales, became more heavily involved in property management. Likewise, developers also pared back their staffs, often concentrating on property and asset management. For example, Trammel Crow Company, the United States' biggest commercial-property developer in the 1980s, lost billions in the depressed market but survived by switching its main business to property management. In 2001 revenues were up again, reaching US$35.4 million and topping US$692 million in 2003. Another boon to the U.S. real estate industry came in 1992 through a repeal of the tax code of 1986. Real estate professionals were once again allowed to write off paper losses against other income. Many developers entered into joint ventures with outside sources of venture capital to develop property.

The real estate industry mirrored global economic conditions in the early 2000s in some sectors, particularly commercial property, with rising vacancy rates, falling rents, and lower demand than in the generally more prosperous years of the late 1990s. The industry remained flat in many places, as large corporations trimmed jobs and held down costs. But conditions were not uniform. Some areas of the world saw continued growth during the early 2000s, particularly in India and China. Their real estate markets were not necessarily in synch with other economic factors, yet the conditions in their real estate industries remained distinct from much of the rest of the world. In the United States, the residential housing market was particularly strong. Investors wary of poor stock market returns also increasingly turned to the real estate sector. Though returns on investment in real estate were not particularly high in the early 2000s, the real estate market was nevertheless favored by investors for its perceived stability.

In the United States, the consumer housing market remained very strong in the early 2000s, despite the generally poor economy and the loss of some 2.5 million jobs between 2001 and mid-2004. Sales of existing homes set a record in 2002, with 5.6 million houses changing hands. This record was bested in 2003, when 6.1 million existing homes were sold. Mortgage rates in the early 2000s were at their lowest point in 30 years, setting extremely favorable conditions for buyers. The retail property market in the United States, comprising non-office commercial space such as stores and malls, also did well in the early 2000s. In general, rents remained stable and vacancy rates rose only slowly. Institutional investors gravitated toward the retail real estate market because the sector was thought to hold up well against recession. Malls anchored with groceries were presumed to be particularly good investments, pushing their prices up. Some cities saw more investment in downtown areas, as private and public entities pushed for revival of neglected urban shopping areas.

The office property sector of the real estate industry suffered the most in the early 2000s. The overall office vacancy rate rose over the period, hitting 16.8 percent in 2003 in the United States. Rents, particularly in downtown offices, fell over the same period. Though there were indications of a strengthening economy by mid-2004, industry analysts expected that it would take a while before the effects hit the commercial real estate industry. Without strong job growth, and with increasing export of jobs overseas, the U.S. office real estate sector was anticipated to remain vulnerable.

These conditions were repeated in many countries around the world. Recession dragged down the real estate sector in many parts of Europe. Germany, France, the Netherlands, and Portugal did worse than some of their neighbors. Spain, Greece, and Britain showed stronger economic results in the early 2000s. In the poorer performing countries, the real estate sector in general sank, while in countries that did better, numbers for the real estate industry typically were flat. In Asia, local economies were volatile in the early 2000s. The outbreak of Severe Acute Respiratory Syndrome (SARS) in 2003 stalled economic growth and caused uncertainty about the future. The real estate sector across the Asia Pacific region was flat across 2003, but Asian economies were expected to pick up over the subsequent few years. China and India were both considered to be on the brink of a large upsurge in their real estate markets.

Most Latin American economies grew only slowly in the early 2000s. Vacancy rates in Mexico City office spaces rose to as much as 25 percent by 2004. Rents rose, while some 3.5 million square feet of office space was under construction by 2004. Vacancy rates in most South American metropolises were similarly above 20 percent, as many cities were already oversupplied with offices.

International investment in real estate in Africa remained limited over the early 2000s. Most countries allowed only domestic or inter-African investment in real estate. Johannesburg was a leading African real estate market, especially because ongoing challenges, such as high crime and HIV/AIDS, made real estate seem like a safer investment than some other options.

By 2005, the real estate industry was truly global in nature. Borders were becoming more transparent in terms of the transactions taking place. PriceWaterhouse Coopers was reporting that capital flow into the real estate market in the United States was valued at US$79 billion in the first half of 2004, compared to US$113 billion in all of 2003. Real estate investment trusts (REITs), which were started in the United States in the 1960s, had allowed for property assets to be traded on public exchanges. These proved so popular that their availability had spread throughout the world. In 2005, the Hong Kong Housing Authority was expected to launch the world's largest initial public offering (IPO) of a REIT to date. Markets were continuing to open up, particularly in India and China, whose economies were doing very well, and in Central and Eastern Europe.

In terms of real estate market size, the North American market was valued by Deloitte Touche Tohmatsu at US$1.6 trillion, representing 34 percent of the total market. Continental Europe held US$1.3 trillion or 27 percent, Southeast Asia held US$825 billion or 17 percent, Japan accounted for US$600 billion or 13 percent, the United Kingdom held US$361 billion or 8 percent, South America stood at US$50 billion or one percent, and Australia totaled US$38 billion or one percent.

In terms of specific regional or city markets, coastal locations were still preferred in the United States, with the Pacific region seeing the largest amount of growth. However, in terms of urban centers, Washington continued to have the highest investment and development prospects. London was considered the leading European city in terms of commercial space development and the city that had best fought back against the economic downturns of the early 2000s.

The greatest growth in the United States was happening in the industrial, apartment, and office sectors, whereas in Europe, most growth in the real estate industry was occurring in the retail sector. Shopping center transactions in continental Europe were valued at more than US$9 billion in 2004, reaching their highest level ever. In addition, the United Kingdom alone had retail transactions of US$8.4 billion. Outside the United Kingdom, Poland was the leading center for shopping-center investments. In Asia, 2004 saw the retail market in China opened to foreign investment. As a result, cities such as Beijing were experiencing shrinking supplies of retail space.

RISMedia discussed the evolution of "a shifting paradigm" for real estate business models. Some of the new models included MLM, annuity, residual, auctioneering, flat-fee, and no fee. Many brokers, however, were hanging onto traditional models. It typically took between 5 and 10 years for a new business model to establish a paradigm shift, but the timeline was becoming shorter.

CURRENT CONDITIONS

While the recession which struck the United States and many other developed nations so hard from 2007 to 2009 ended, recovery proved slow, a situation that had been keenly felt in the real estate market. U.S. residential real estate was hit particularly hard, as the failure of sub-prime housing loans was a key factor in the onset of the recession. By mid-2010, about the best that had been said was that the housing market had possibly passed its low point. Continuing slow economic growth and high unemployment rates could work against the market for an extended period.

Commercial real estate has had a difficult recovery as well, with values having fallen 20 percent to 30 percent from peak levels in some U.S. markets. This was leading to problems with existing loans. Over one-third of the US$270 billion in maturing commercial real estate loans in 2010 were expected to be "under water," meaning the unpaid balance is above the market price of the property. The National Real Estate Investor expects this proportion to rise to over one half by 2012. Among the few bright spots are premium or "trophy" properties in major cities, where in 2010, prices had recovered 23 percent from their 2009 lows.

Internationally, emerging markets continue to be the focus of attention, and large amounts of foreign direct investment in real estate is expected to flow to those places in the coming years. In the first two quarters of 2010, China's economy grew at 11.9 percent and 10.3 percent on an annualized basis. Other emerging markets included India and Brazil. Brazil is Latin America's largest economy and experienced an 8.8 percent annual economic growth rate in the second quarter of 2010. An article by David Lynn, Ph.D., head of investment strategy for ING Clarion Partners, characterized most of the money going into real estate in the emerging economies as "opportunistic" with regard to risk and rewards, but that in the coming years simple "value-added" strategies will become more common.

WORKFORCE

Real estate brokers and agents earn their living chiefly through commissions paid for selling or leasing a property. According to the U.S. Bureau of Labor Statistics, in 2008, there were about 517,800 real estate brokers and sales agents in the U.S. Some 59 percent were self-employed. Employment for the industry was expected to grow 14 percent from 2008 to 2018, faster than the average for all industries. U.S. population growth was expected to be a driver of the increase. Median annual earnings as of May 2008 were US$40,150 for salaried real estate sales agents and US$57,500 for salaried real estate brokers.

Real estate brokers and agents spend much of their time researching markets, inspecting properties, and working with both sellers and buyers. They first work with the owner of a property for sale to establish sales prices or rental rates and enter into an agreement that delineates how to market the property and the time frame of their agreement. Then, real estate agents coordinate the process of signing a lease or a sales agreement with the buyer. However, some buyers are uncomfortable with the biases brokers may present toward their own sales listings. To address this concern, a trend toward "buyers' brokers" has developed. A buyer's broker is paid to protect the buyer's interests rather than try to get the buyer to pay the highest amount possible (so the broker receives a higher commission). The broker tries to get the lowest price and best overall deal for the buyer and is paid a flat fee or a flat fee plus a percentage of the reduction in price of the house.

Brokers were making changes in their staff by hiring agents better equipped to handle the cyclical trends of the industry. In order to do this, some companies were searching for potential agents in other fields that require similar skills. Coldwell Banker Mid America had been successful in working with teachers and planned to target nurses next. Recruiting the right agents was considered to be challenging for mid-level managers. Approximately 80 percent of new agents did not last more than two years after obtaining their real estate license.

In contrast, land developers purchase real estate in its "raw" or undeveloped state. They may work with local authorities to purchase and assemble parcels of land. Next, they either further develop the land as a residential, commercial, or industrial project, or they sell these assembled parcels to developers whose goal is to sell them or lease them to the public at large. Financing schemes as well as approvals for development and marketing plans are usually complicated and require banks or private investors.

Managers oversee the business of owning real estate property. In 2008 there were some 304,100 property, real estate and community association managers in the U.S. These jobs were expected to grow about 8 percent from 2008 to 2018, about as fast as the average of other occupations. Median salary was US$46,130. These managers market vacant space; negotiate lease agreements; collect rents; and pay mortgages, taxes, insurance premiums, and other costs related to real estate. They are likewise responsible for hiring individuals or maintenance firms to keep the property in top shape and often interact with tenants, making sure their needs are met.

INDUSTRY LEADERS

Equity Office Properties Trust. With over 59 million square feet, 400 buildings and 4,000 resident businesses in the U.S., Equity Office Properties Trust continued as a leader in the real estate market in 2010. Equity operated in Los Angeles, San Francisco, San Diego, and New York, among other places. It acquired Beacon Properties in 1997. Equity Office Properties Trust was led by Tom August, whose role expanded from Chairman to President and CEO in 2010. During 2004 the organization disposed of almost all of its industrial properties.

The Link Management Ltd. At the start of 2005 The Hong Kong Housing Authority had delayed what had been described as the world's largest initial public offering (IPO) of an REIT. The Housing Authority was citing legal issues for the delay. The REIT will be formed from 2.85 million square feet of ground floor retail space in Hong Kong and 59,000 commercial parking spaces owned by the Housing Authority. The IPO was being valued at US$2.7 billion. With land scarce in Hong Kong, the REIT was expected to be very popular with investors. As of 2010, The Link was the largest real estate investment trust in Hong Kong, with 11 million square feet of retail facilities and 80,000 parking spaces.

ProLogis. Prologis was the largest REIT devoted to industrial distribution, with more than 475 million square feet of distribution facilities across North America, Europe, and Asia in 2010. Founded in 1993 as Security Capital Industrial Trust, in 1998, the company changed its name to reflect its growing global business. The company began its expansion in 1998, entering markets in the Netherlands and Mexico. In 2001, expansion continued into Asia with completed developments in Japan reaching a value of more than US$1 billion by 2004. That year, the company also made forays into China. ProLogis added 137 properties to its portfolio when it merged with Keystone Property Trust in 2004. In June 2005, the company announced plans to merge with Catellus Development, a leading U.S. property development company. In May 2007, ProLogis announced plans to develop a large distribution center in northeast Spain for a subsidiary of ARC International. Plans called for construction of the distribution center to feature sustainable design techniques to reduce its impact on the environment.

CB Richard Ellis Group Inc. CB Richard Ellis was a leading commercial real estate services firm in 2009, with 425 offices and 29,000 employees worldwide. Property sales for the year totaled US$40.5 billion and leasing revenues totaled US$56.7 billion. Begun as a small, San Francisco-based firm in 1906, CB Richard Ellis was a leading real estate firm in the western United States by the 1940s. By the 1970s, the company had expanded across the United States, expanding globally in the 1990s. Known as CB Commercial until its acquisition of Richard Ellis of London in 1998, the company also acquired Hillier Parker May & Rowden, one of the United Kingdom's leading property management companies. In 2003, CB Richard Ellis merged with competitor Insignia Financial Group, a dominant player in the New York market. San Francisco financier Richard Blum owned the controlling interest in the company.

In 2006, CB Richard Ellis made a total of US$224.6 billion in combined leasing and investment sales globally. That figure was up 33 percent from its US$150.4 billion in 2005 and nearly US$100 billion higher than its 2004 volume of US$127.4 billion. Some of the growth reflects full-year volume for Trammell Crow Company that CB Richard Ellis acquired in December 2006. Consequently, CB Richard Ellis retained the top spot on National Real Estate Investor's Annual Top Brokerage Survey for the fourth consecutive year. CB Richard Ellis reported revenues of nearly US$4.03 billion from its operations in nearly 35 countries.

Another major 2006 development involved CB Richard Ellis' representation of MetLife as the seller for "the largest commercial property sale in history" of Peter Cooper Village/Stuyvesant Town. That apartment complex was a 110-building complex located on the east side of Manhattan. It sold for US$5.4 billion to New York-based Tishman Speyer Properties and its partner Blackrock Realty.

In April 2007, CB Richard Ellis announced its acquisition of DGI Davis George. That acquisition was evidence of the company's strategic plan to strengthen its position in the UK industrial and logistics sector. It also advanced the company's goals to enhance its full-service capabilities.

In October 2010, *Newsweek* ranked CB Richard Ellis number 30 out of 500 companies appearing on its 2010 Green Rankings. The list measured the environmental performance of the largest publicly traded U.S. companies.

Westfield Group. Sydney, Australia-based Westfield Group is the world's largest owner, manager, developer, and leaser of shopping malls. In 2010, the company had investment interests in 119 shopping centers in the United States (55), Australia (44), New Zealand (12), and the United Kingdom (eight), valued at more than US$62 billion. Founded in the 1950s, Westfield expanded into the United States in 1977. At the end of 2009, Westfield had revenues of more than US$4 billion. The company also managed real estate assets for others.

Trizec Properties Inc. TrizecHahn was formed in 1996 through the merger of Horsham Corporation and Trizec Corporation and became a major player as the owner, manager, and developer of retail and office properties. In 2002, the company reorganized. It became the publicly traded real estate investment trust (REIT) called Trizec Properties Inc., a Chicago-based company. The company owned or managed 52 officer properties in North America, including a share of the Sears Tower in Chicago and full ownership of the infamous Watergate office building in Washington, D.C. Trizec Properties was the second-largest REIT in the U.S. market, with revenues of more than US$712 million in 2004. In 2006 Trizec was acquired by Brookfield Office Properties, which owned and managed premium properties in North America and Australia.

Mitsui Fudosan Co. Ltd. Japan's leading real estate services provider, Mitsui Fudosan reported more than US$17 billion in fiscal 2010 revenues. The company leased almost 4.5 million square meters of office and retail space, with a vacancy rate of 3.1 percent. Mitsui Fudosan Finance Co. Ltd. was a subsidiary of Tokyo-based Mitsui Real Estate Development Co. Ltd., which was a member of the Mitsui Group, a general trading company. Mitsui Real Estate was Japan's leading developer of office buildings, commercial properties, and housing. Capitalizing on Japan's land shortage, Mitsui specialized in high-rise complexes that made profitable use of premium space. Its Kasumigaseki Building in Toyko is cited as the country's first skyscraper. The company also owns hotels and offers real estate brokerage services. Mitsui Real Estate was founded in 1941 as the real estate division of Mitsui Gomei Kaisha, a central holding company of the Mitsui financial group. The company's steady growth continued throughout the 1970s, when it began international operations. By 1990, Mitsui Real Estate owned property in New York City, Honolulu, San Francisco, and Nepal, as well as 88 subsidiaries. Its U.S. subsidiary, Mitsui Real Estate Sales USA, sold in excess of US$1 billion worth of property in the United States between 2000 and 2003, much of it in California. The subsidiary was applauded for its acquisition and redevelopment of the renowned Halekulani Hotel in Waikiki, Hawaii.

MAJOR COUNTRIES IN THE INDUSTRY

The United States. The United States possesses one of the world's largest and most sophisticated real estate markets. The percentage of homeowners in the United States reached 68.6 percent by 2003, a record surpassing even the 1980s high of 65.8 percent.

The record low in interest rates in the early 2000s led many more people into homeownership, making the apartment rental market suffer. Investors focused instead on retail properties, formerly a neglected category. Malls and commercial strips became popular investment items. Across the United States, vacancy rates were on the decline over those of the early 2000s. By the beginning of 2005, rates in major downtown locations stood at 13.8 percent, while those in suburban locations had declined to 16.3 percent from their 17.1 percent level in 2004. The levels of construction of new office space remained low. CB Richard Ellis was also reporting that strong demands for shipping activities and a stabilizing manufacturing sector were the cause for low vacancy rates in the industrial sector of the real estate market. In the United States, the national rate stood at 10.1 percent by early 2005.

According to Real Capital Analytics, investment sales throughout the United States were US$317 billion in 2006. That amount reflected a 15 percent increase beyond 2005 sales volume of US$270 billion.

Robert Trussell analyzed the trend for real estate developers to be featured as TV stars. Although the real estate market was down, there were many cable TV shows featuring people trying to achieve their goals while working in the industry. Such new programs included "Bought & Sold" that premiered on HGTV in May 2007. It tracked real estate agents in Essex County, New Jersey. Established programs included "Flip This House," in its third season on A&E. It showcased the efforts of real estate developers in three cities. The shows tended to have an educational focus sharing dos and don'ts. The personalities frequently seemed larger than life and experienced dramatic developments.

A nationwide survey conducted by Housing Predictor.com revealed the Hottest 10 Buyers Markets in the United States were mainly located in the nation's southern half. The top spot was Albuquerque, New Mexico. It was projected to appreciate 9.1 percent by the end of 2007. Growth resulting in a population of almost a million people was attributed to substantial business growth including new movie studios and an airplane factory. Housing Predictor made its selections based on surveys conducted in 75 markets under construction from the more than 250 local housing markets forecast on its Web site.

As it turned out, much of this twenty-first century growth turned out to be a bubble. A classic speculative frenzy developed around easy credit, especially in the residential market, in which it was assumed prices would continue to increase indefinitely. This led to real estate loans being made to people with questionable ability to repay the loans. As these loans began to fail and housing prices began to decline, the fallout helped push the entire economy into recession in late 2007. While the recession ended in 2009, the real estate market continued to experience the doldrums in 2010. Accoring to Moody's, in August 2010, more than one in four commercial sales involved distressed properties, and U.S. commercial property prices fell to their lowest level since June 2002.

China. China continued to be home to the world's fastest growing major economy in 2010, with annualized GDP growth rates of 11.9 percent and 10.3 percent during the first two quarters of the year. Foreign investors hurried to get on board. The real estate market was hot in Shanghai, which saw the building of several new skyscrapers. Prices for all categories of real estate, from residential to commercial, rose sharply in Shanghai in the early 2000s, leading to fears that speculators were fueling a pricing bubble that would soon burst. China's central government enacted rules to curb real estate speculation, including increasing the amount of required down payment. Shanghai's neighboring provinces, Jiangsu and Zhejiang, also saw a lot of new industrial development and foreign investment, and real estate there was expected to follow a similar upward pattern.

In 2004, there were about 25,000 real estate brokerage agencies in China, with total employment of about 200,000 agents. However, many did not hold the proper license. The property management sector was a huge employer, giving jobs to more than two million people in the country. Until 1999, the home resale market was almost non-existent in China; people stayed in their homes. However, the government began to encourage the sale of old homes in favor of new, bigger ones. Approximately 59 percent of Chinese people in urban areas owned their homes in 2004, with the average household of two to four people having about 538 to 861 square feet of space. Most houses were being financed using personal savings, although the use of bank loans and government funding for financing was on the rise.

The luxury sector of the real estate industry saw particularly strong growth in China. Yet oversupply led some developers to simply abandon projects unfinished. The number of luxury apartments and villas grew by 35 percent over 2002. The Chinese government imposed a ban in 2003 on further sales of land for luxury housing.

China's Supreme People's Procuratorate focused its anti-graft campaign on officials taking bribes from real estate developers. Prosecuting departments investigated in excess of 9,000 cases of commercial corruption in 2006. One-third of those cases involved engineering projects and land sales.

In 2006, Chinese real estate developers invested US$251 billion in projects. In addition, the Chinese Academy of Social Sciences claimed input in residential housing projects was 1.9 percent higher than the figure in 2005. The related breakdown was as follows: 41.8 percent for developing ordinary residential housing projects, 3.6 percent for low-cost housing projects, and 7.3 percent for upmarket apartments and villas.

According to the A.T. Kearny Foreign Direct Investment (FDI) Confidence Index, a survey of business executives around the world, China was rated as the best market for foreign direct investment in 2010.

Europe. As they entered the twenty-first century, European countries tried to assert their national identity in an ever-increasing global market. Often, by grouping like-industries together in industrial and office parks, governments created a business synergy that helped establish national reputation in key, domestic industries.

A number of U.S. firms established operations in the European Union's increasingly unified markets. Many of these real estate firms engaged in myriad development projects such as major office complexes; retail (shopping) centers; and especially resort and recreational developments including hotels, second homes, golf and ski resorts, retirement housing, and other recreational venues. In some cases, U.S. brokers and developers were sponsored by European corporations seeking to expand or develop real estate projects.

Typically, firms operating in the global real estate industry found European development a lengthy process because of more restrictive planning controls. Foreign-based development companies frequently engaged in joint ventures with other European developers, local governments, or corporate tenants. Most developers in Europe, however, were merchant builders that developed projects only after investors secured permission. U.S. firms were often sought for European projects; the experience in leasing, master planning, gaining approvals, and creating mixed-use developments these firms possessed made them comfortable working a project from ground zero, thereby building an added-value product.

Developing distribution patterns throughout the European Union (EU) to create a pan-European market changed land-use patterns across Europe. Signatories agreed to work in concert to create an EU marketplace that was conducive to economies of scale. Thus, member nations worked independently and jointly to enhance transportation networks and create centralized warehouses. Corporations consolidated their manufacturing operations (and sometimes physical plants) to serve new distribution systems.

France passed legislation allowing real estate investment trusts in 2003, and Germany and United Kingdom were expected to do the same. New job growth and low interest rates across Europe were also expected to help boost the real estate industry in the middle 2000s.

In the industrial sector, demand continued for space near major transportation lines. New construction increased in France, Italy, and Spain over the early 2000s but was almost nil in Germany and Belgium. The entrance of more Eastern European countries into the European Union in 2005 was expected to improve infrastructure. This development would in turn heat demand for good industrial property. Eastern Europe was considered a top growth area, while in other parts of Europe, growth in this sector was expected to be slight or stable.

The recession that hit U.S. real estate markets so hard also hit Europe, where prices declined in the late 2000s. In November 2010, Liam Bailey, head of residential research at Knight Frank, noted that prices had just begun to return to sustainable levels, adding that "potential risks to future growth are many and varied."

Germany. Europe's largest economy, Germany was one of the worst hit by the economic downturns in Europe, with the country coming slowly out of a mild recession that hit in 2003. That year, the commercial real estate and property management market was valued at about US$8.4 billion, with office space holding 55 percent of the market. The leading companies in the industry captured a larger share of the market; Bayerische Hypo- und Vereinsbank, Deutsche Sparkassen Leasing, and Viterra increased their combined market share to 38 percent in 2003, up from 31 percent in 2002, according to Euromonitor. In the downturn of the late 2000s, Germany's economy performed better than some other E.U. nations such as Greece, which had to be bailed out of sovereign debt problems. As of 2010, Germany ranked as the fifth best market for foreign direct investment in A.T. Kearny's FDI Confidence Index, highest of any European country.

The United Kingdom. Of Europe's large economies, the United Kingdom had the most success at managing the economic turmoil of the early 2000s. *Euromonitor* had valued the commercial real estate and property management markets at about US$13.1 billion, with retail accounting for 50 percent of the market. PriceWaterhouse Coopers had acknowledged that retail was the top performing sector heading into 2005, but a weakening retail environment was expected to affect this sector. The industry remained highly fragmented, with the top four players (Land Securities, MEPC plc, Slough Estates,

and British Land Company plc) taking only a total of 22 percent of the income from this sector. The U.K. real estate market was hit along with the rest of the developed world by the late 2000s recession, but the U.K. still ranked as the tenth best market for foreign direct investment in 2010, according to the A.T. Kearny index, trailing only Germany and Poland among the European nations.

India. Many industry insiders considered India to be a land of emerging potential. *Little India* reported that international funds invested some US$2.5 billion in Indian real estate. Approximately 24 domestic funds had raised another US$3.5 billion for similar investments. Indian policy changes in 2005 offered encouragement for investors by allowing foreign investment of up to 100 percent in construction development projects with fast-track approvals. *Little India* claimed the major attraction was potential investment returns of 25 percent and more in Indian projects that might be hard to find in the United States and Western Europe. As of 2010, the A.T. Kearny index ranked India as the world's third best market for foreign direct investment.

Financial Express reported on a new competitive tactic that was gaining popularity in India. Domestic real estate developers were outsourcing construction and design assignments to foreign companies through joint ventures. This so-called "USP" would reportedly "bring in the latest technology and international expertise in design, construction, safety, speed and efficiency." It afforded excellent opportunities for domestic developers to establish meaningful partnerships with foreign engineering and infrastructure majors.

BIBLIOGRAPHY
"About Us." Equity Office, 5 November 2010. Available from http://www.equityoffice.com.
"About Us." The Link Management, 5 November 2010. Available from http://www.thelinkmanagement.com.
"About Us." Prologis, 5 November 2010. Available from http://www.prologis.com.
"About Westfield Group." Westfield Group, 5 November 2010. Available from http://www.westfield.com.
"Business Activity 2009." CB Richard Ellis Group, 5 November 2010. Available from http://www.cbre.com.
"China's Anti-Graft Body Targets Real Estate Corruption." 27 April 2007. Available from http://www.china.org.cn/english/MATERIAL/209127.htm.
"Chinese Real Estate Developers Pump US$251 Bln into Projects." *ANTARA*, 3 May 2007. Available from http://www.antara.co.id.
"Corporate Overview." Brookfield Office Properties, 5 November 2010. Available from http://www.brookfieldproperties.com.
"Fact Book." *Mitsui Fudosan Group*, 31 March 2010. Available from http://www.mitsuifudosan.co.jp.
Hedgpeth, Dana. "Commercial Real Estate Industry Seeks U.S. Aid." *The Washington Post*, 23 December 2008.

"Hottest 10 Buyers Real Estate Markets Announced." *WebWire,* 3 May 2007. Available from http://www.webwire.com.

Howley, Kathleen M. "U.S. Housing Recovery Hinges on Employment, Executives Say." *Bloomberg Businessweek,* 4 November 2010. Available from http://www.businessweek.com.

———. "U.S. Commercial Real Estate Rents to Rise in 2011, Cushman's Mosler Says." *Bloomberg,* 4 November 2010. Available from http://www.bloomberg.com.

Knight, Oliver. "European Real Estate Recovery Gathering Pace." *IPIN Live,* 2 November 2010. Available from http://www.ipinglobal.com.

Lynn, David J. "Sharp Increase in Foreign Direct Investment Expected in Emerging Markets." *NuWire Investor,* 2 November 2010. Available from http://www.nuwireinvestor.com.

"Newsweek Ranks CB Richard Ellis Group Inc. Number 30 Among Top 500 Greenest U.S. Companies." *CB Richard Ellis news release,* 20 October 2010. Available from http://www.cbre.com.

"ProLogis to Develop Distribution Center in Spain for ARC International—International Tableware Distributor Will Occupy 516,000 Feet in Zaragoza—New Warehouse Facility Will Feature Environmentally Advanced Design." *PR Newswire,* 3 May 2007.

"Property Giant Snaps Up Industrial Services Specialist." *Daily Post,* 25 April 2007.

"Real Estate Auction Wave Led by Pacific Auction Exchange." *Business Wire,* 3 May 2007. Available from http://home.businesswire.com.

"The Real Estate Industry, Though Volatile, Offers Riches to Those Who Know Where to Look." Philadelphia: The Wharton School of the University of Pennsylvania, 2 May 2007. Available from http://knowledge.wharton.upenn.edu.

"Realogy Corporation Named to the Fortune 500 as the No. 1 Company in the Real Estate Industry." *Realogy,* 19 April 2007. Available from http://www.realogy.com.

"Riding the Deal Wave to New Heights." *National Real Estate Investor,* 12 April 2007.

Snell, Robert. "Stagers Help Put Best Face on Slow-Moving Homes." *Detroit News,* 29 May 2007.

Soni, Varun. "Outsourcing Construction, Realty Companies' New USP." *The Financial Express,* 23 May 2007. Available from http://www.financialexpress.com.

Trussell, Robert. "Real Estate Without Work." *Detroit Free Press,* 13 May 2007.

U.S. Bureau of Labor Statistics. "Occupational Outlook Handbook, Property, Real Estate, and Community Association Managers," 2010-2011. Available from http://www.bls.gov.

U.S. Bureau of Labor Statistics. "Occupational Outlook Handbook, Real Estate Brokers and Sales Agents," 2010-2011. Available from http://www.bls.gov.

"U.S. Investors Bullish on Indian Real Estate." *Little India,* April 2007.

"What the Real Estate Industry Fears Most." *RISMedia,* 4 May 2007. Available from http://www.rismedia.com.

Wong, Vanessa. "Commercial Real Estate's Uneven Rebound." *Bloomberg Businessweek,* 4 November 2010. Available from http://www.businessweek.com.

"World's Tallest Tower for Jeddah." *The Straits Times,* 21 October 2010.

FOOD, BEVERAGES, AND TOBACCO

SIC 2082, 2084, 2085

ALCOHOLIC BEVERAGES

NAICS CODE(S)

312120, 312130, 312140. Three major segments constitute the global alcoholic beverage trade: breweries, which manufacture beers and ales; wineries, which produce wines and brandies; and distilleries, which produce various liquors and blended alcoholic drinks. For discussion of nonalcoholic beverages, see **Soft Drinks and Bottled Water.**

INDUSTRY SNAPSHOT

Alcoholic beverages have long been a part of cultures throughout the world. They are important consumer products and are heavily advertised and marketed. There are literally tens of thousands of brands of alcoholic beverages. Global consumption of alcoholic beverages increased steadily through the late 1990s and the early years of the first decade of the 2000s, reaching about 195 billion liters by 2003. According to Green Facts, by 2009 approximately 2 billion people across the globe consume some form of alcohol. Worldwide, adults consume an average of 5 liters of beer, wine, or spirits annually. Average consumption is highest in Europe, followed by the Americas and Africa.

Dana Flavelle, business correspondent for the *Toronto Star,* reported on June 10, 2008, that beer remained consistently Canada's number one beverage of choice, but wine continued to grow at a faster pace. Data from Statistics Canada further revealed that Canadians drank more than US$18 billion worth of alcoholic beverages in 2006, which was an increase of

4.9 percent over 2001. That amount was equivalent to US$667 for every person in excess of age 15 or an increase of US$22 per person. According to Green Facts, in 2010, alcohol consumption was largely determined by location and availability. In several European countries and Africa, beer was the drink of choice. However, in wine-producing countries, wine was the heavy favorite. In Eastern Europe and Asia, spirits were preferred.

According to Emma Schwartz of *U.S. News & World Report* on October 8, 2007, the effects of heavy drinking are worse for young people because the brain does not fully develop until they are in their mid-20s. Consequences are both short and long term. Alcohol-related incidents continue to be the leading cause of death among teens, including car accidents at 38 percent, homicide at 32 percent, and suicides at 6 percent. In addition, research findings showed that teens with histories of starting to drink before age 15 were four times as likely to eventually become alcoholics as those who waited until they were 21 years old. Those who started drinking at a young age were more likely to also have additional substance abuse problems. Some other health issues directly linked to alcohol consumption included an increase in some types of cancer, particularly lip, tongue, throat, liver, and breast cancers.

An article published on June 25, 2008, in *The Observer* pointed out that since Canadian baby boomers were more concerned about their longevity, they were being more conscious about the alcohol they chose to drink. After careful consideration, it was determined that "alcohol is alcohol." That was true whether it came in the form of beer, liquor, wine, or a cooler. It was also true that less did not always mean better because calories and sweeteners were frequently added to the equation.

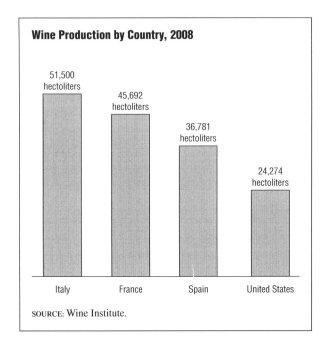

Wine Production by Country, 2008

51,500 hectoliters — Italy
45,692 hectoliters — France
36,781 hectoliters — Spain
24,274 hectoliters — United States

SOURCE: Wine Institute.

Far from an innocent past time, alcohol consumption can have dramatic long-term results. Overall there is a casual connection between alcohol consumption and more than 60 types of disease and injury. Alcohol consumption worldwide was on the rise in the early years of the twenty-first century, with the majority of the increase in developing countries that have little experience with prevention, control, or treatment. According to the World Health Organization, alcohol causes 2.5 million deaths (3.8 percent of all deaths) and 69.4 million (4.5 percent) of disability-adjusted life years worldwide. Accidental injuries alone account for about 2.5 million.

Beer. Beer dominated the alcoholic beverage industry, with about 157.8 billion liters consumed worldwide in 2005. Production of beer throughout the world increased from 1.395 billion hectoliters (36.85 billion gallons) in 2000 to some 1.468 billion hectoliters (38.78 billion gallons) in 2003. In the early years of the 2000s, there were 56 major beer markets in the world, and the average global per capita consumption of beer was 5.6 gallons. The country with the highest per capita consumption was the Czech Republic with 45.3 gallons, followed by Ireland, Germany, Slovenia, and Austria. Although the United States had traditionally been the largest beer market by volume, vigorous growth in China spurred both production and sales in that country, which became the world's top beer producer in 2002 and was the largest and most rapidly expanding market as of 2004.

Although Asia suffered economic downturns, beer consumption typically remained stable through the 1990s. The demand in Asia accelerated in the early years of the first decade of the 2000s, especially in China. The outlook at that time was positive as well for Latin America's beer market due to factors including fast population growth, increase in the beer-drinking age group, and regional weather conditions conducive to drinking beer. Consumption in Eastern European countries, particularly Russia, also rose in the early years of the twenty-first century's first decade, prompting major brewing companies to step up investment in those regions.

According to Australian Broadcasting Company News, the Australian National Health and Medical Research Council planned to lower its recommendation on the top limit for safe drinking to four standard drinks. Prime Minister Kevin Rudd responded to an opposition attack calling for him to state his position by accusing the opposition of being "in cahoots" with Australian distillers.

Wall Street Journal correspondent Nancy Keates reported on June 14, 2008, that some restaurants were replacing 16-ounce pint glasses with 14-ounce glasses. The Damon's Grill restaurant chain switched glass sizes in 2006 without reducing prices. The glass shape distorted the beer drinker's perception of how much beer they had been served. Jeff Alstrom, *Beer Advocate* magazine founder, called it the "Less for More" phenomenon. Alstrom urged users of his www.beeradvocate.com web site to "raise a fist and refuse to pay" when served a skimpy pint.

Wine. In 2002, wine comprised 13 percent by volume of the global alcoholic beverage market. Although exports were the mainstays of wine markets in most countries, there was a growing trend in the international wine industry toward a more global, market-oriented strategy. Countries were recognizing the need to work with each other to solve problems in regard to the reduction of trade barriers in the wine market. Western Europe, with its long history of old-world wines, was no longer setting the standard in the wine trade. Branded varietals (grape types) from other parts of the world, including Australia and California, played a bigger role in the international wine market, although they accounted for only 5 to 7 percent of global exports and were responsible for just one-seventh of the world's wine production.

In 2004, according to the U.S. Department of Agriculture (USDA), the countries with the largest vineyard acreage and highest levels of wine production in the world were Spain, France, and Italy. Europe accounted for more than 50 percent of global consumption. The top five countries in the world for wine consumption were France, Italy, the United States, Germany, and Spain. Luxembourg was the leader in per capita wine consumption, followed by France, Italy, Portugal, and Croatia, with the United States ranked thirty-fourth. In 2000, wine sales in the United States totaled US$19 billion, compared to US$6.2 billion in 1980. In 2004, U.S. wine sales reached a record volume of 278 million cases and imports grew by 4.4 percent, totaling 72 million cases.

Liquor. Economic downturns in high-growth markets caused problems for the global distilled spirits industry. Large multinational organizations countered these downturns by establishing premium brand groups that ultimately accounted for increased growth in international markets. They targeted other brands more narrowly, using a local or regional approach. In the early years of the first decade of the twenty-first century, white spirits made up approximately 42 percent of the market for branded distilled spirits, local spirits accounted for 28 percent, and whiskey came in at 18 percent. Together, liquors made up 10 percent of the alcoholic beverages industry. China, Russia, and India were the largest spirits markets in 2002. By 2005, spirit sales, along with most alcohol sales, appeared to be more nationally specific. Local commercial spirit producers dominated in emerging regions, but were geographically fragmented due to the ongoing popularity of traditional national specialties. Thus, in the Asia-Pacific region, Jinro produced *soju* for its vast South Korean market, Sang Som manufactured Sura Khao for Thailand, and San Miguel had taken over the Filipino gin market. Similarly, the leading Latin American companies were Cia Muller de Bebidas and Egnarrafamento Pitu Ltda, who created the popular *cachaca* in Brazil.

Branded beverages made up approximately 71 percent of U.S. distilled spirits exports in the early years of the first decade of the 2000s. Whiskey made up 59 percent; rum, 7 percent; and liquors and cordials, 3 percent. Vodka and gin were at the low end with 1.3 percent and 0.4 percent, respectively. The largest U.S. export market for whiskey was Japan, while the biggest U.S. export markets for distilled spirits overall were Japan, Germany, and Australia.

ORGANIZATION AND STRUCTURE

Beer. Beer is made from a "mash" of fermented barley, malt, and rice or corn. It is naturally cloudy from sediment in the brews, but most commercial beers are clarified through filtration systems. U.S. brewers frequently use additives to stabilize foam and to maintain freshness, while European brewers use these additives less often. Almost all bottled and canned beer is pasteurized in the container to make sure that any remaining yeast does not continue to ferment. Draft beer, served from large kegs in taverns, bars, and other outlets, is not pasteurized and must be refrigerated to prevent spoilage.

In the early years of the twenty-first century, lager, which is a pale, medium-hop-flavored beer, was the most popular beer produced in the United States. It averaged 3.3 to 3.4 percent alcohol by weight and was highly carbonated. While many lagers were also produced in Europe, heavier, dark beers, such as stout, porter, and malt liquor, held a higher percentage of beers production.

There are many different types of commercial beer, including pilsner, lager, ale, stout, light, malt liquor, dry, ice-brewed, bottled draft, and nonalcoholic. Stout, a very dark and almost syrup-like beer, was popular in Europe, particularly in the United Kingdom and Ireland. Porter is a sweet malt brew with a high alcohol content of 6 to 7 percent. Malt liquor is beer made mostly from malt with a high level of fermentable sugars. Light beers have reduced calories and are made by either reducing the amount of grain or by adding an enzyme to reduce the starch content of the beer. In the United States, the market is further segmented by price and quality. U.S. beers are categorized as super premium, premium, and popular-priced.

Microbreweries and brewpubs in the United States had annual double-digit increases throughout most of the 1990s. By the early years of the first decade of the 2000s, "craft" beer was the country's fastest growing segment of the alcoholic beverage industry. According to a study by the *American Journal of Sociology,* the surging popularity of "craft brewing" was in part due to consumer reaction against established industrial brewers' lack of attention to new consumer preferences for more variety of flavor, color, freshness, foam, and other qualities of beer. In particular, 1997 was a banner year for the U.S. microbrewery industry, as the number of U.S. breweries surpassed those in Germany for the first time in at least 200 years. Germany operated 1,234 breweries in 1997 compared to 1,273 in the United States, and by the middle of 1999 there were 1,414 U.S. breweries, compared to just 43 in 1983. In 2004, the craft beer segment posted its second consecutive year with higher growth than imports.

However, at the end of the 1990s, a number of microbreweries experienced declines as a result of rapid over-expansion, although firms that tended to focus on regional sales reported better results. Acquisitions, mergers, and shutdowns were more common, but new microbrewery firms continued to open throughout the United States and showed significant growth. In 2009, the Association of Brewers reported 456 microbreweries, 64 regional specialty breweries, and 962 brewpubs in the United States.

Wine. Usually made from fermented grape juice, most wines are classified as red, white, or rose, as well as dry, medium, or sweet. Wine categories include vintage wines, table wines, sparkling wines, and fortified wines.

Europe traditionally dominated the international wine business, although increasing competition from quality vineyards in Australia, California, and Chile was changing this market. French wines continued to be considered world leaders in quality. Important French wine-growing regions include Bordeaux, Burgundy, Champagne, the Rhône valley, Alsace, the Midi, and Provence. German wine producers are known mainly for producing light, fruity white wines. The best German wines are said to be made from the Riesling grape in three areas: the Rhine River (Rheingau, Rheinhesse, and Rheinpfalz), the Nahe Valley, and the Mosel/Saar/Ruwer valleys.

Italy was the world's second leading wine producing nation by volume in 2003-04, just behind France. About two-thirds of Italian wines are classified as table wines. The most popular wines, from northern Italy, are Barolo, Asti Spumante, and vermouth from Piedmont; Chianti from Tuscany; and Soave, Valpolicella, and Bardolino from Veneto. The sparkling, sweet red Lambrusco comes from central Italy. While not considered a world leader in quality, Italian viticultural standards and vinification methods were reportedly improving. Italy's quality seal is known as the Denominazione d'Origine Controllata (DOC).

Spain is known for its sherry, a fortified wine produced in the southern part of the country. Vineyards in northeast Spain produce Rioja, the country's leading table wine. There are a wide variety of Portuguese wines, from the popular light, slightly sparkling pink wines, including Mateus and Lancers, to the "granddaddy" of fortified dessert wines, port. Madeira, a Portuguese archipelago, produces dessert wines of the same name.

In the early years of the first decade of the 2000s, over 90 percent of U.S. wine was produced in California. Once considered an inferior wine-producing region, California became a world leader in the last half of the twentieth century. In the 1950s, a few fine California wines were recognized in the United States. By the 1980s, some California wines had gained worldwide recognition, albeit grudgingly. The number of premium California wineries exploded in the 1970s and 1980s, reaching more than 600 by the mid-1980s. Early in the first decade of the 2000s, California produced a large quantity of good commercial wines, as well as some very high quality vintage wines. While French wines are usually named by the region, town, or vineyard where they are produced, California wines are most often named for the principal grape variety in the wine. A small amount of U.S. wine also comes from New York's Finger Lakes region, south of Lake Ontario. There are other wine producers scattered around the

United States, but none of them have challenged the popularity of California wines.

The global wine industry consists of two parts: the high volume, heavily marketed commercial segment, which was dominated by large, multinational conglomerates in the early years of the first decade of the 2000s, and the lower volume, high-quality vintage wine business, which was dominated by small vintners with long histories. The high-quality wine trade has a rich culture, which includes exclusive trading houses, wine critics and writers, auctions of rare vintages, and high prices for individual wines. The commercial segment produces lower quality wines, but in the 1970s and 1980s helped expand the appeal of wine to a wider global audience. In the mid-1990s, however, wine consumption stabilized and even fell in some established markets, leading many observers to consider the market mature in such traditional areas as North America and Europe.

Liquor. The distilled spirits business includes two major groups: clear "white goods," such as gin, vodka, rum, and tequila, and "brown goods" (whiskey), such as bourbon, scotch whisky, or straight whiskey. Younger drinkers tended to prefer lighter drinks, creating small increases in white goods sales in the early 1990s, while sales of brown goods fell sharply. In the United States, consumption of distilled spirits rose 4.1 percent in 2004, the seventh consecutive year of growth. Bacardi Rum, Smirnoff Vodka, and Seagram's Gin, which are all white goods, were among the five top selling brands in the mid- to late 1990s.

The leading white goods are gin, rum, vodka, and tequila. Gin, made from a mixture of grains, is flavored with juniper berries and has a slightly blue cast. It was first made in Holland in the seventeenth century and spread quickly throughout Europe. Gin is considered to be an English liquor and has been very popular in England since the early eighteenth century. Since it was cheap and widely available, gin became known as "blue ruin" for those who overindulged. English-style gin is very dry compared with Holland or Geneva gin, which is heavy-bodied and strongly flavored with a malty taste.

Tequila is made from the fermented and distilled sap of agave plants. It originated in Mexico, which remained a major producer at the beginning of the 2010s. Tequila is double-distilled to increase potency and purity. While tequila has been typically considered as a party drink for young adults, some manufacturers were promoting premium tequilas made from 100 percent agave juice (less expensive brands contain as little as 51 percent agave). Premium brands included El Tosoro, distributed by Jim Beam, and Patron, distributed by Seagram. In the mid- to late 1990s, the largest tequila producer, Diageo's Jose

Cuervo SA, stepped up marketing of its premium brand, Cuervo 1800.

Vodka is traditionally associated with Russia and Poland, where its production and use are widespread. Vodka is practically tasteless and is made from grain, sugar beets, potatoes, or other starchy foods. Vodka is widely traded in the world market, with major producers including the United States, Russia, Sweden, and Finland.

Whiskey is distilled from a fermented mash of grains. This mash may contain barley, oats, corn, wheat, or rye. Straight whiskeys are made from at least 51 percent of a single grain and are aged in new, charred white oak barrels for at least two years. Light whiskeys are typically made from corn. Blended whiskey is a blend of straight and light whiskeys and may have as many as 50 ingredients. Bourbon whiskey, which is almost exclusively a U.S. product, must have at least 51 percent corn in the mash. U.S. exports of Kentucky bourbon and its close relation, Tennessee whiskey, more than tripled from 1985 to 1990, to 11 million gallons.

Scotch whisky is made from corn and barley and is processed in continuous stills. Distillers combine up to 40 true malt whiskeys with grain whiskeys to create the individual flavor of their brands. Scotch whisky is sold in 190 countries, and 4 of the top 10 spirits in the world in the early years of the first decade of the 2000s were scotch whiskies. During those years, the biggest exporter of spirits was the United Kingdom, with annual exports of 60 million cases, 90 percent of which were Scotch. The world's largest spirits manufacturer, Diageo, which was created in 1997 following the merger of Guinness PLC and Grand Metropolitan PLC, is based in the United Kingdom. Irish whiskey, a cousin to Scotch, is made with barley dried in a closed kiln and is distilled three times, unlike all other whiskeys, which are distilled no more than twice.

Other major segments in the alcoholic beverage market are the cordials and liqueur category and ready-to-drink cocktails. Originating in Europe, cordials and liqueurs are prepared by mixing spirits with flavorings. The cordial category includes schnapps, liqueurs, cremes, and brandies.

BACKGROUND AND DEVELOPMENT

Beer. Beer making has been part of society and commerce almost from the beginning of civilization. A Mesopotamian tablet from 7000 B.C. includes a recipe for beer, described as the "wine of the grain." The town of Pilsen (now in the Czech Republic) produced the first pilsner beer in 1292. Pilsner Urquell, a major brand, traces its roots back to that thirteenth century brew.

Germany, famous for high quality brews, claims one of the world's oldest breweries—Brauerei Beck.

Germany's first brewing guild was formed in Bremen in 1489, and Beck was founded 64 years later, in 1553. In the early twenty-first century, all German beers continued to be brewed to standards of what is called the world's first consumer protection act: the *Reinheitsgebot* purity law of 1516, which calls for the use of only water, barley, hops, and yeast in brewing beer.

Wine. Cultivation of grapes for winemaking began several thousand years ago. The ancient Egyptians made wine, and the early Greeks exported it on a considerable scale. Vineyards were a major part of the Roman Empire's economy and were extended into France, Germany, and England as the Empire expanded. From about 1200, monasteries throughout Europe became centers for winemaking. During the nineteenth century, European vineyards were devastated by several diseases and pest infestations. The plant louse *phylloxera* was particularly debilitating, destroying European vines by attacking their roots. The European wine industry was saved by the grafting of European vine species onto immune U.S. rootstock.

Winemaking came to the United States with the colonists when California's earliest vineyards were planted by Franciscan monks in 1769. Commercial wine operations began operating in the 1830s with the efforts of Frenchman Jean Louis Vignes from Bordeaux, France. His vineyard was located in what subsequently became downtown Los Angeles. The U.S. wine industry was devastated when Prohibition went into effect in 1921 but revived after the Volstead Act was repealed in 1933.

Taxation and Abuse. Alcoholic beverage industries in all countries deal with similar issues, including high taxation, growing regulation, legal challenges, and the specter of alcohol abuse. Taxation is a critical issue because governments around the world are partial to heavily taxing all forms of alcohol, both to raise revenue and to discourage consumption. Taxes on alcoholic beverages are particularly effective, since high-volume consumers tend to buy the same amount of alcoholic beverages no matter how high the taxes. The Nordic countries have some of the highest taxes on alcohol in the world, partly to discourage high alcohol consumption rates. Many other European countries also have high rates of taxation. The United States has historically had lower alcohol taxes than many other Western countries. However, U.S. taxes on alcoholic beverages were raised sharply in 1991. At that time, the federal excise tax on beer was doubled to US$18 per barrel, the equivalent of 16 cents to 32 cents per six-pack of 12-ounce bottles or cans.

Producers of alcoholic beverages in many countries have also come under fire about alcohol abuse, underage drinking, and drunk driving. Alcohol abuse has had devastating health and social consequences in almost every country. For example, between 40 and 50 percent of all traffic accidents in the United States are reportedly alcohol related. Alcohol abuse also reduces productivity in the workplace and causes family stress. In the United States, the National Institute of Alcohol Abuse and Alcoholism estimated the entire cost of alcohol abuse at nearly US$140 billion annually.

Sentiment grew for harsher punishments for drunk drivers in the United States in the late 1990s. In March 1998, the U.S. Senate passed an amendment to federal highway legislation requiring states to toughen drunken driving laws. Senators voted 62 to 32 to pressure states to reduce the legal blood alcohol level to 0.08 percent from 0.10 in most states. Under the bill, states that did not adopt the legislation by 2001 would lose 5 percent of their federal highway construction money, with the annual loss increased to 10 percent the following year. The same measure would have applied to states that did not ban open alcohol containers from cars and trucks by 2002. As of 1998, 22 states allowed passengers to hold drinks, and in five states a person was allowed to drink while driving. However, the amendment was opposed by beer, wine, and liquor manufacturers as well as by the American Beverage Institute, which represents restaurants and retailers that sell alcohol. Due to opposition to the measure in the House of Representatives, the amendment was deleted from the final highway bill, which passed in May 1998. However, some of these proposed changes later became law.

By 2009, alcohol abuse had been on the rise in spite of global economic downturns. In countries such as Ireland, the United Kingdom, and Denmark, binge drinking was common. Binge drinking refers to drinking heavily over a short period of time. It is common to consume four or more liters of beer or seven pints of beer in an evening. The intention seems to be simply to get drunk. Ireland's consumption of alcohol had doubled from 7 liters in 1970 to 14.5 liters by 2001 according to the World Health Organization. In comparison, alcohol consumption in France declined from 20.4 liters in 1970 to 13 liters in 2004. Alcoholism was reportedly rampant in the Commonwealth of Independent States (CIS) and Eastern Europe during the 1990s. During the communist era, widespread alcohol abuse was linked to the failing economic system and lack of personal freedom. However, after the collapse of the communist system, alcoholism appeared to increase rather than decrease. In 1995, Poland's minister of health said that Poland's annual per capita consumption of alcohol was 11 liters of pure alcohol, which was nearly double the 1987 rates. In Western countries, per capita consumption of 2 liters of pure alcohol was considered high. Ironically, improving economic conditions in Poland were blamed for making alcohol more affordable.

In Russia and Ukraine, alcoholism was also rampant. Per capita consumption in those countries soared from 4.4 liters in the mid-1960s to a staggering 15 liters by 1985. A major public anti-alcohol campaign by former Soviet leader Mikhail Gorbachev in the late 1980s was a notable failure. In the late 1990s, the Russian government banned television advertising of liquor, but the rate of consumption continued to rise. Per capita annual consumption of neat spirits (a straight shot of any spirit taken in a single swallow without accompaniment) in Russia grew from 5.3 liters to 8.3 liters between 2000 and 2001, and by 2004 about 2.2 million Russians were reported to have alcohol-related problems. In Hungary, which also had an annual per capita consumption rate above 10 liters, it was estimated that 8.1 percent of all citizens were alcoholics.

In Western Europe, regulation and public pressure were successful in curbing some of the adverse effects of alcohol consumption. For example, extremely strict drunk driving laws in Norway and Sweden greatly reduced highway deaths caused by drunk drivers. In the United States, Mothers Against Drunk Drivers (MADD) was effective in lobbying for tougher state laws that punish drunk drivers.

CURRENT CONDITIONS

Beer. The beer industry is a global market with several multinational breweries and thousands of smaller producers worldwide. In excess of 133 billion liters (35 billion gallons) are sold annually. In 2006, total beer revenues reached US$294.5 billion. By the mid to late 2000s, sales in North America and Western Europe had declined or at least remained stagnant, due in part to a combination of continued maturation of the market and intensified competition from wine and spirits.

As of 2002, the Czech Republic had the highest per capita beer consumption rate in the world, almost twice as much as the United States. The Czech Republic produced 18 million hectoliters annually, with exports of 1.5 million hectoliters. Czech breweries had suffered losses of approximately US$28 million at the end of the twentieth century mainly because of overcapacity. Poor management also plagued some companies. However, the Czech beer industry was predicted to be increasingly competitive in the twenty-first century with the help of investment and management expertise from abroad. At the beginning of the twenty-first century, the country was the sixth largest market for beer in Europe.

In 2001, the *German Embassy Newspaper Online* reported that the average German was drinking less beer, and the industry was suffering as a result. Per capita consumption, once 156 liters in the 1970s, had fallen to roughly 126 liters in 2001 for a 20 percent decline. By

2003, consumption had dropped to 120 liters. Over-production plagued the 1,270 German breweries that produced more than 5,000 different brands with beer suppliers producing 30 percent more beer than demand required. Declining sales meant that small companies, which had historically dominated the industry, were finding it increasingly difficult to remain competitive. Between 2002 and 2003, Dutch brewer Heineken and Belgian brewer Interbrew took over 18 percent of German production, and analysts forecast more mergers and closures in the near future. According to Steve Zwick in the August 11, 2003, edition of *Time Europe,* a Credit Suisse First Boston analyst predicted that a handful of global companies would control 70 percent of German production by 2010. Factors contributing to the decreasing rates of beer drinking included consumer preference for wine and soft drinks, the blood alcohol limit for drivers being lowered to 0.05 percent, young consumers associating beer with the older generation, and beer being seen as unhealthy. However, microbreweries offering beer mixed with various flavorings and fruit juices were reporting increasing numbers of young beer drinkers.

Beer sales in Japan decreased after 1997, and with no signs of an economic recovery, the future looked dim for the country's beer industry. However, *The Economist* reported that Japan's low-malt beer (*happoshu*) was making strides as the only sector of the beer market showing growth. Production of low-malt beer in Japan started in the late 1990s. Brewers recognized that they could charge less for low-malt brews because the government taxed beer in accordance to its malt content. Prices for low-malt beer were two-thirds less than for regular beer, which resulted in bargain-hunting consumers beginning to stockpile beer. In 2000, low-malt beverages accounted for one-fifth of Japanese beer sales. Kirin continued to be the top selling beer brand in Japan, and it dominated the low-malt market as well. However, rival Asahi was catching up to Kirin. In 1994, Asahi owned only one-fourth of the beer market, with half of all beer sales in Japan going to Kirin. That changed, however, with the worldwide success of Asahi's Super Dry brand, which became the third best- selling beer in the world. In 2000, Kirin held 38 percent of the beer market, with Asahi right behind it at 36 percent. Asahi's low-malt Honnama beer, released in February 2001, helped the company overtake Kirin as Japan's top beer maker in 2001. With sales of low-malt beer remaining brisk through the early years of the first decade of the 2000s, Asahi introduced another *happoshu* beer in 2005, with plans to ship 3 million cases in the first month alone.

The Latin American beer market continued to grow. In 2002, Venezuela topped the list with the highest per capita beer consumption in the region (an average of 21.8 gallons). By 2003, the two largest beer markets in

Latin America were Brazil and Argentina, which reported average annual growth of 5 percent. When AmBev, the Brazilian company that virtually controlled the Latin American beer market (with a 64 percent market share in Brazil, 77 percent in Argentina, 94 percent in Paraguay, and 99 percent in Uruguay and Bolivia), merged with Belgian company Interbrew in 2004, analysts predicted that the move would greatly improve exports for AmBev brands outside of Latin America.

According to the Beer Institute, the U.S. beer industry grew steadily after 1996. More than 3,500 brands were on the market by 2002, which was twice the number in the early 1990s. Production reached about 6.2 billion gallons in 2003. According to a 2010 report by the Brewers Association, U.S. beer sales overall were down 2.2 percent in 2009, and imported beer sales were down 9.8 percent for a loss of 2.8 million barrels. There were a total of 1,595 U.S. breweries in 2009, the highest since before Prohibition. Total U.S. beer sales had continued to decline in the first half of 2010, dropping 2.7 percent.

Beer firms in the United States continued to embrace the import sector and entered into agreements to become U.S. distributors of international brands. Of the top 13 U.S. malt beverage producers, six were either import firms or U.S. affiliates of beer suppliers based outside the United States. Licensing agreements, direct exports, and foreign investment all played a role in the continuing trend of U.S. beer producers expanding their foreign markets. The U.S. beer industry exported to almost 100 countries worldwide. In 2003, the most U.S. beer by gallons was exported to Mexico, followed by Hong Kong and Canada. U.S. beer exports to Japan, which ranked third in 2001, dropped 33.8 percent between 2002 and 2003. Beer imports to the United States were led in 2003 by Mexico, the Netherlands, Canada, and Ireland.

Wine. France has long been the world leader in wine consumption per capita with the exception of Vatican City State. As of 2008, Vatican City had a population of 932 with a consumption rate of 65.67 liters per capita. France, with a population of 60.87 million, had a consumption rate of 53.22 liters per capita, for a 2.5 percent decrease over 2004. In 2008, Italy took over the number one spot in terms of wine production with a 16.8 percent increase over 2004. Italy produced 51,500 hectoliters in 2008, followed by France at 45,692 hectoliters, Spain with 36,781 hectoliters, and the United States at 24,274 hectoliters. A total of 283,898 hectoliters was produced in 2008, which was a 2.8 percent reduction from 2004 figures. The volume of French wine exports, which accounted for about 25 percent of national production, dropped by almost 10 percent in 2003 according to the

Guardian. Domestic sales also declined that year by about 5 percent. The change in domestic consumption was blamed on shifting demographics, as well as on stricter enforcement of drunk-driving laws.

Exports, however, were being devastated by market-savvy winemakers from such disparate places as California, Chile, and Australia, which became known as the "New World" producers. These vintners marketed heavily in North America, Northern Europe, and Asia, where consumption of wine, especially offerings under US$15 per bottle, continued to rise. They discovered that the typical wine consumer wanted lighter, lower-priced wines instead of a heavy, expensive Bordeaux that needed time to mature. Of the 10 biggest winemakers in the world in 2000, only one company—Castel Freres—was French, and it ranked fifth. The top spot went to E&J Gallo Winery in the United States, with sales that year of US$1.5 billion. In 2000, French wine exports fell in value to US$4.6 billion, a 5.4 percent drop. The country's U.S. market share decreased from 7 to 5 percent after 1998. In contrast, Australia reported that its U.S. market share jumped to 3 percent, with sales having tripled since 1995.

In the early years of the first decade of the 2000s, increasing mergers and takeovers in the beverage industry also adversely affected the French wine market. In October 2000, Australia's Foster's Group purchased Napa Valley, California's Beringer Blass Wine Estates for US$1.9 billion. In February 2001, Australia's Southcorp purchased winemaker Rosemount for US$725 million. Among other factors, the deeper pockets of these newly merged firms bolstered their marketing efforts, making it difficult for small French vintners to compete. For example, Gallo's 2000 marketing budget in England was US$2.5 million, more than double the amount the entire Bordeaux region spent on advertising and promotions. The marketing tactics used by many New World vintners proved particularly savvy. Several California wineries were tourist destinations that boasted such amenities as art galleries, cooking demonstrations, and lavish tasting rooms, while many French chateaux vineyards were not open to the public. Australia has used celebrities to attract attention to its brands. Foster's Beringer signed Australian golfer Greg Norman to create Greg Norman Estates wines. In addition, actor Jackie Chan was a mascot for Australia's Lindemans wines in the Asian market.

The Earth Times reported that French wine makers were responding to both dried up market sales and government attempts to solve industry problems with legislation. Table wines have been the least regulated of all classifications. In spite of creative opportunities to promote freedom of expression, common related practices reflected that it was even producing table wine in France had become a challenge.

French winemakers face other disadvantages as well. The weather in Burgundy and Bordeaux is unpredictable, which can lead to variations in vintages. However, the steady climates of wine production regions in the United States, Australia, and Chile allow regular harvesting and consistency in product. French wine labels display the geographic origin of the wine instead of the grape type (varietal), which makes French wines difficult to distinguish for the average wine consumer. In contrast, American and Australian wine labels boast brand names that are easy to remember and clearly indicate the varietal, whether it is Pinot Noir, Merlot, or Cabernet Sauvignon.

Anthony Rose, a reporter for *The Independent* (London), in June 2008 described a "boom in biodynamic viticulture" due to taste for wines free from pesticides. As a result, more organic bottles began to appear on supermarket shelves. Susan McCraith, Master of Wine and wine buyer with ethicalwine.com, is a strong supporter of biodynamic wines. McCraith believes the discussion needs to go beyond organics that gained certification to "support people making a genuine environmental effort to reduce sprays, use organic fertilizers, and experiment with biodynamics." Experts debated whether it was better to have separate sections for organic wines or have them share shelf space with traditional wines. For the largest organic offering, wine drinkers turned to specialty stores, such as Whole Foods Market and Planet Organics.

Celebrity endorsement has had an impact on purchases of wine drinkers. Associated Press reporter Michelle Locke reported that several celebrities, including Olympic figure skater Peggy Fleming, golfer Greg Norman, and rocker Mick Fleetwood. In partnership with her retired dermatologist husband, Greg Jenkins, Fleming opened Fleming-Jenkins Vineyards & Winery. The winery's labels reflect Fleming's skating background symbolically. According to Locke, Nielsen figures from a 2007 grocery store sales report that sales of celebrity wines were up 19 percent from 2006, equivalent to US$42 million of total wine sales.

In 2008, U.S. wine exports passed the US$1 billion mark for the first time with more than US$1.008 billion, an increase of 6 percent from 2007. Ninety percent of the U.S. wine exports were from California according to the Wine Institute in San Francisco. That figure constituted nearly 130 million gallons (55 million) cases of wine. While the United States is the fourth leading wine producer in the world, the country has only a 6 percent share of the global wine market, leaving room to grow. Nearly 50 percent of U.S. wine exports were shipped to the European Union in 2008, accounting for US$486 million in sales. Following the European Union for U.S. wine export were Canada, with US$260 million;

Japan, with US$61 million; Hong Kong, with US$26 million; and Mexico, with US$23 million.

Liquor. According to *Beverage Industry,* the distilled spirits market continued to thrive at the beginning of the twenty-first century due to several trends, including new flavored spirits and high-end offerings. For instance, although Scotch sales were generally lower in 2000, the high-end single malt sector recorded a 7.6 percent rise in consumption. This lead gave way to a number of new single malt Scotch products, including a 15-year-old Glenmorangle from Brown-Forman Beverages Worldwide. The Scotch market posted significant gains by 2004, when U.K. exports of malt whisky alone rose 15 percent, totaling more than 55 million bottles. U.K. exports of all Scotch whiskies reached 953 million bottles that year. The United States remained the most valuable export market for Scotch, while emerging markets in Brazil, Russia, Turkey, and especially China offered substantial opportunities for export growth in this segment.

The overall U.S. whiskey segment reported a decline, but that did not stop high-end bourbons from selling well. Handcrafted straight whiskies, such as Evan Williams Single Barrel 1991 Vintage and Russell's Reserve from Wild Turkey, became popular.

A number of high-end gins, new cognacs, premium Irish whiskies, and boutique tequilas debuted in the United States, hoping to cash in on the upscale trend, along with upscale vodkas. Import Stolichnaya posted an increase in sales of 11.3 percent. In 2001, Allied Domecq Spirits USA acquired the distribution and import rights for the vodka maker. France's high-end Grey Goose vodka had a sales increase of 175 percent in 2000. The company introduced an orange-flavored vodka called Grey Goose L'Orange. Smirnoff, the best selling vodka in the United States, joined the trend for flavored vokdas with the introduction of Smirnoff Orange Twist and Raspberry Twist.

According to *Alcohol Atlas of India* in 2008, alcohol production in India has steadily increased. The country was expected to triple its production by 2007-2008 to 2,300 million litres. Overall consumption remained low, although patterns of alcohol consumption vary throughout India, with a much higher proportion of alcohol consumption reported in Punjab, Andhra, Pradesh, Goa, and Northeastern states.

RESEARCH AND TECHNOLOGY

A *First* magazine article on June 30, 2008, reported on research indicating that white wine shared health benefits previously only attributed to red wine. Studies at Monash University in Australia revealed that white wine contained smaller and more easily absorbed antioxidants than red wine. A report from a university at Buffalo, New York, claimed the antioxidant quercetin in white wine repairs and maintains lung tissue, increasing lung capacity.

INDUSTRY LEADERS

Anheuser-Busch. Located in St. Louis, Missouri, Anheuser-Busch was the largest brewer in the world and the biggest beer producer in the United States throughout the first decade of the 2000s. The company produced more than 30 beer brands, including Budweiser, Busch, Bud Light, and Michelob. The company also produced the specialty brands ZiegenBock Amber, Red Wolf Lager, and the nonalcoholic brew, O'Doul's. In addition, Anheuser-Busch operated popular theme parks and water parks, including Busch Gardens and SeaWorld, and held a 50 percent interest in Mexico's Grupo Modelo. The firm's outlook in China, where it established local production of Budweiser and invested some US$1.2 billion in the early years of the twenty-first century, was favorable. Main competitors included Miller Brewing, Adolph Coors, and Heineken. Total revenues topped US$16.7 billion in 2007 when the company reported 30,849 employees.

According to TNS Media Intelligence, Anheuser-Busch was among the 50 largest advertisers in the United States, spending about U.S. $475 million per year. In an article on June 14, 2008, analyzing Budweiser's marketing as "America's Beer" strategy, *The Economic Times* pointed out Budweiser's efforts would be compromised if it was taken over by Belgium's InBev. The article reported that Web sites were calling for the public to apply pressure to keep the company out of InBev's hands. Those protests were unsuccessful, however, and InBev completed its acquisition of Anheuser-Busch in November 2008.

AB InBev. When Belgian giant Interbrew acquired Brazil's Companhia de Bebidas das Americas in March 2004, it created the world's largest brewer by volume. The new company, InBev, controlled 14 percent of the global beer market. InBev also owned Canadian Labatt Brewing Company and the German Brauerei Beck & Co. Its leading brands were Beck's; Bass; Stella Artois, the number seven international lager brand worldwide in 2000; Hoegaarden, Labatt Blue, Leffe, and Rolling Rock. U.S. sales of InBev's popular Bass Ale overtook sales in the United Kingdom. To gain regulatory approval for its 2000 acquisition of Bass Brewers, which was criticized by some rivals in the U.K. beer industry as anti-competitive, the company sold Carling, the United Kingdom's top standard lager, to brewer Coors. InBev posted total sales in 2004 of US$8.8 billion, up 20.7 percent from the previous year.

In November 2008, InBev completed its bid to take over Anheuser-Busch for US$52 billion. This firmly established InBev as the world's largest brewer. The merger created a yearly sales revenue of more than US$36.8 billion.

SABMiller plc. When South Africa Breweries (SAB) acquired Miller Brewing Company in July 2002, the new company, SABMiller, became one of the largest brewers in the world. SABMiller controlled 98 percent of the South African beer market in 2003, and its Castle Lager brand was the continent's best seller. SABMiller produced other local brands as well, including Hansa Pilsener and Ohlssons. With operations in 40 countries, SABMiller began to expand into Europe, acquiring Dojlidy Brewer in Poland in 2003. The company had plans to expand its market in Russia as well. In 2009, SAB-Miller employed more than 70,000 workers and reported revenues of US$18.7 billion.

Heineken N.V. Headquartered in The Netherlands, Heineken annually brewed 111.9 million hectoliters of beer as of 2006. The company boasted operations in more than 40 breweries in 39 countries worldwide and sold beer in more than 170 countries. Heineken was Europe's number one brand and the number two imported beer in the United States behind Grupo Modelo's Corona. Other globally marketed brands included Murphy's, sold in more than 65 countries, and Amstel, Europe's number two brand. Heineken's other international brands were Asia's Tiger, Italy's Moretti, and Argentina's Quilmes. Heineken reported total sales of US$15.6 billion with 65,648 employees in 2006. Major competitors were Interbrew, Guinness/UDV, and AB InBev.

Heineken is committed to make a substantial investment in upgrading the breweries in Mons-en-Barcuel (in northern France), Sehiltigheim (Alsace), and Marseille through 2011. Another major move included the sale of the non-branded beer business of Saint Omer brewery. The sale was expected to include the loss of 126 jobs in Alsace and 62 in Mons-en-Barceul by the end of 2010.

Asahi Breweries Ltd. Asahi ranks as Japan's number one beer maker, with total beer sales slightly over those of rival Kirin. The success of its Super Dry brand, along with the 2001 introduction of a low malt offering, Asahi Honnama, helped the brewer retain its top spot. Asahi had operations in Europe and the United States and boasted distribution and production arrangements with Miller Brewing, Molson, and Bass Brewers. Kirin was Asahi's major competition, along with Sapporo Breweries and Suntory. Asahi, which diversified into the food,

pharmaceuticals, real estate, soft drinks, wine, and whiskey industries, posted total sales in 2006 of US$12 billion with 15,280 employees.

Reuters correspondents Taiga Uranaka and Ritsuko Shimizu reported on June 13, 2008, that Asahi trailed Kirin in profits during 2007 as a result of group revenue and related profits. Asahi and its Japanese rivals continued to struggle with global mega-brewers for customers as well as increasingly costly raw materials and major beer market consolidation. Asahi also was being pressured by rising prices for barley, malt, and other materials. In January 2009, Asahi acquired 19 percent of Tsintao Brewery from Anheuser-Busch for US$667 million. In addition, in 2009, Asahi purchased the Australian beverages unit of Cadbury Schweppes.

Kirin Brewery Company, Limited. Tokyo-based Kirin has long been the market share leader in Japan, holding as much as 60 percent. By 2002, however, the company lost its lead to archrival Asahi Breweries. Kirin realized a 14.7 percent growth in sales from 2002 to 2003, with total sales of US$10.8 billion. In 2006, Kirin reported sales of US$14 billion and 23,232 employees. Kirin's best known beers were Ichiban Shibori, Kirin Lager, and Kirin Tanrei, the top low malt beer in Japan. The company had distribution deals with Anheuser-Busch, among others, and invested in the Lion Nathan brewery in Australia. Top competitors to Kirin, in addition to Asahi, were Sapporo Breweries and Suntory.

Diageo plc. Diageo, the world's leading producer of alcoholic drinks, was formed in 1997 when brewing giant Guinness merged with Grand Metropolitan. In 2000 the company continued to pursue aggressive growth, acquiring spirits manufacturer Joseph E. Seagram & Sons, known for such popular brands as Crown Royal, Chivas Regal, and Glenlivet. By 2003, the London-based Diageo controlled 21 percent of the U.S. spirits market, and analysts predicted that its share could reach 25 percent before 2010. Through its Guinness/UDV unit, Diageo produced Guinness Stout, Harp Lager, and Kilkenny Irish beer. Diageo also produced Johnnie Walker scotch, Tanqueray gin, and Smirnoff vodka. The company pushed hard to air liquor advertisements on U.S. television, which had not been allowed since 1946. In 2009, Diageo reported total sales of US$16.879 billion with 20,000 employees.

Scottish & Newcastle plc. Founded in 1749, Scottish & Newcastle was the largest beer producer in the United Kingdom and Europe. Its top brands included Courage, John Smith's, Kornenbourg, McEwan's, Newcastle, and Theakston's. It also produced licensed beers. In 1999, Scottish & Newcastle Retail acquired a chain of pubs, restaurants, and lodges that sold its brands. Most of these establishments were sold by the end of 2001, placing the company in a highly favorable position as consolidation accelerated in Europe. In 2000, Scottish & Newcastle announced partnerships with two leading European beer companies, Danone in France and Sociedade Central de Cervejas in Portugal. In 2002, Scottish & Newcastle's acquisition of Finland's leading beverage company, Hartwell, opened additional markets in Russia, Ukraine, Kazakhstan, Lithuania, Latvia, and Estonia. Further expansion occurred in 2004 when Scottish & Newcastle acquired a 19.5 percent interest in Chinese brewer Changqing Brewery Company. Along with Heineken, major competitors included Interbrew and Guinness/UDV. In 2008, the company's assets were split between Heineken and Carlsberg. The company name was only used for the leased pub division, Scottish & Newcastle Pub Company.

Carlsberg A/S. Carlsberg Breweries, a 60 percent owned subsidiary of Denmark-based Carlsberg A/S, was the fourth largest beer producer by volume worldwide. The firm was Denmark's top brewer, but 90 percent of production was sold in some 150 countries. Brands included Carlsberg and Tuborg, as well as many regional beers. In 2001, Carlsberg and Orkla of Norway, which owned 40 percent of Carlsberg Breweries, combined their beer operations and planned to expand further into Asia and Europe. At the time, major competition for Carlsberg came from Heineken, Anheuser-Busch, and Scottish & Newcastle. In addition to its brewing operations, Carlsberg operated the Carlsberg Research Center, which included 80 beer-brewing laboratories. In 2004 the company bought out Swedish firm Orkla's 40 percent interest in Carlsberg Breweries and Holsten-Brauerei, a German brewery. Carlsberg reported total sales in 2009 of US$10.94 billion with over 43,000 employees.

Sapporo Holdings Ltd. Sapporo ranked third in Japan in both the beer and wine markets. Beer brands included the premium brew Yebisu, the Black Label flagship offering, and Brau, a low malt brew. Sapporo also had success with The Winter's Tale, the first limited run, seasonal brew in the Japanese beer market. The company also had a distribution agreement with Guinness to sell its beer in Japan. Wine holdings included the Ureshii and Uogashi brands, as well as the Okayama and Katsunuma wineries. Other businesses included ownership of more than 200 beer halls and eating establishments. Sapporo's main competition came from the top two beer producers in Japan, Asahi and Kirin, as well as from Suntory. In 2004, Sapporo posted sales of US$4.8 billion.

For beer drinkers seeking an out-of-this-world brew, Sapporo launched a new taste sensation in November 2008. It brewed the world's first "space beer" in collaboration with scientists from Japan's Okayama University. It claimed an extra special ingredient of barley grown in the Russian unit of the International Space Station in 2006. None of the beer was sold on the market, but was offered in a lottery system at US$119.74 per six pack.

E. & J. Gallo Winery. Gallo is one of the biggest wine producers worldwide. Along with making approximately 30 percent of the wine consumed in the United States, Gallo is also the top wine exporter in the United States. While the company has made much of its fortune on inexpensive brands, such as Thunderbird, Carlo Rossi, and Gallo, it has also had success in the premium wine market with Gossamer Bay and Turning Leaf brands. Owned by the Gallo family, the winery holds more than 3,000 acres in Sonoma County, California. The vintner also manufactures its own bottles and labels. In addition, Gallo imports and sells Ecco Domani, an Italian wine, and is a top brandy producer. Major competitors include the Robert Mondavi, Beringer Blass, and Constellation brands. Gallo enjoyed a 50 percent growth in sales in 2004, boosting revenues that year to an estimated US$3 billion. In 2006, the company reported sales of US$2.7 billion and 4,600 employees.

On September 14, 2007, E. & J. Gallo Winery announced that beginning in January 2008, it would launch a limited release of three new wines under the "Martha Stewart Vintage" label in Atlanta, Boston, Charlotte, Denver, Phoenix, and Portland.

On September 24, 2007, the company announced the launch of "Consumer Vinsights," which it described as "a new research resource based on actual consumer behavior targeting unique usage occasions that highlight how consumers incorporate wine into their daily lives and the increased and varied occasions at which they consume wine." Steve Sprinkle, vice president of the winery's sales, added, "Through these observations, we can learn many things about consumers that impact their purchasing decisions at the point of sale." The data collection process involved conducting more than 10,000 proprietary surveys to demonstrate how consumer motivation and attitudes about wine change depending on how they plan to use it.

MAJOR COUNTRIES IN THE INDUSTRY

The United States. Long the world's beer industry leader, the United States slipped behind China in terms of production in 2002. In 2003 the United States produced an estimated 6.2 billion gallons of beer, according to *Modern Brewery Age* on December 8, 2003. Exports went to more than 100 countries worldwide. In 2001, Mexico was the largest importer of beer in terms of gallons from the United States. Hong Kong was the second-largest importer, followed by Canada and Japan.

Microbreweries and craft breweries continued to report particularly strong performances. The Association of Brewers reported growth in this segment of 3.4 percent in 2003 and 7 percent in 2004. Total annual retail sales for the U.S. craft beer industry in 2004 exceeded US$3.7 billion. Although beer remained the most popular alcoholic beverage in the United States in the early years of the first decade of the 2000s, growth in this market slowed substantially. As consumption of wine increased, and as the spirits industry invested heavily in advertising, beer's share of U.S. alcoholic drinks sales fell 3 percent between 1995 and 2003. In response to tepid growth in domestic beer consumption, major brewers announced significant increases in promotions in 2003 and 2004.

In 2000, the United States was ranked as the fourth largest wine producer worldwide in terms of vineyard area, with 880,880 acres. Some analysts predicted that the country's wine exports, valued at US$548 million in 2001, would increase to US$914 million by 2005. Domestic consumption was also poised for growth. Jacob Gaffney, in the February 5, 2001, edition of *Wine Spectator* reported that a study by Vinexpo indicated that by 2005 the average U.S. wine drinker would consume an average of approximately three more bottles of wine annually than in 2001, reaching about 17 bottles per year, compared to an average of 14 bottles consumed in 2001. Not only had volume increased, but U.S. consumers were buying more expensive wines as well. By the year ending in March 2005 dollar sales of wines had increased 7 percent over the previous year. According to industry analyst Jon Fredrikson, the United States was poised to become the largest wine consuming country in the world by 2010, although it was not expected to rank among the leaders in per capita consumption.

Twenty-three states passed "social host" laws targeting adults for allowing underage drinking in their homes. Some form of civil liability laws are on the books in 33 states. An important related statistic is that two-thirds of teens in the United States get their alcoholic beverages from adults.

China. China was the fastest growing beer market in the world by 2004, with beer production increasing 25 percent annually through the 1990s. In 2002 it surpassed the United States in beer output, producing a total of 239 hectoliters. By 2004, beer production had reached 29.1 million metric tons, a 15.2 percent increase from the previous year. As of 2004, China was the second largest global market for beer, with total sales rising 85.99 percent

since 1996. Significant potential existed for further growth through 2010, since per capita consumption of about 5 gallons per year remained relatively low but was expected to rise with improving income levels. Analysts considered it likely that China's beer market would be the largest in the world by 2010. China's entry into the World Trade Organization spurred the country to improve quality and develop new products in the alcoholic beverage industry to attract overseas customers. The beer sector was the strongest in the Chinese alcoholic beverage industry. According to *Global Sources*, by 2001 the country had approximately 530 breweries. Two-thirds of the segment was made up of small-scale enterprises with yearly output of less than 50,000 tons each. The top two Chinese beer brands were Beijing-based Yanjing and Tsingtao, based in Shandong. In 2000, Yanjing's total output was valued at US$550 million, while Tsingtao was ahead with US$716 million. By 2002, China's fragmented market had attracted the interest of big international players like Anheuser-Busch, which that year increased its shares in Tsingtao from 4.5 to 27 percent. In 2004, Anheuser-Busch went on to acquire Harbin, one of the three most popular brands in China, for US$757 million. The same year, Scottish & Newcastle purchased a 19.5 percent interest in Chongqing Breweries. Analysts expected continued rapid consolidation in the sector through the remainder of the decade.

Chinese wine-making traditions go back more than 2,000 years, and in 2001 China had approximately 300 winemakers. Eighty percent of the country's wine output was from the Shandong, Beijing, Hebei, Anhui, Henan, and Tianjing regions. China has exported its wine to more than 10 countries, including the United States, Japan, Germany, Belgium, Australia, Russia, Malaysia and Korea. One of the largest wine exporters has been Tonghua Grape Wine Stock Co. Ltd., which specializes in wine made from grapes grown in Jilin Province's Changbai Mountain. Wine output from China was expected to reach 500,000 tons by 2005. China's liquor market, however, had experienced a decline at the end of the 1990s. In 2000, the country produced 5.02 million tons of liquor, 14 percent less than the previous year's output. Whiskey also rose in popularity in China, which imported only about US$1.9 million of scotch in 1999, but more than US$47.8 million in 2004.

Japan. While Japan had a growing liquor market for much of the 1980s, consumption rates leveled off or declined in the 1990s as the Japanese economy went into recession. That recession continued throughout the 1990s, leading to decreased demand for liquor. One of the most popular liquors was bourbon, consumption of which grew at a 50 percent annual clip in the late 1980s before leveling off or declining in the early to mid-1990s. Most alcohol consumption in Japan has historically been on-premise, either in bars or restaurants. As on-premise consumption rates fell in the early to mid-1990s, however, beverage alcohol marketers began to promote at-home consumption. Another popular liquor was a traditional product, *shochu*. Consumption of this liquor, which has an alcohol content ranging from 36 to 25 percent compared with 40 percent for most spirits, grew steadily from 1995 to 2001 and remained on the rise through the early 2000s. Once thought of as a drink for the working classes, *shochu* benefited from savvy packaging and marketing campaigns, and has emerged as a top choice for sophisticated drinkers in Japan's trendy nightclubs.

Japan was also a major beer market. *Happoshu*, a low malt beverage that has a similar taste and appearance to regular beer but is taxed at a lower rate, continued to outsell traditional beer in the first part of 2002. *Reuters Business* in April 2002 reported that shipments of traditional beer decreased by 14.7 percent in March of 2002 compared to 2001. Beer shipments totaled 333,199 kilolitres, declining for the twenty-fourth month in a row, while *Happoshu* shipments rose for the seventieth month in a row. However, a possible tax increase was expected to eliminate *Happoshu*'s advantage over traditional beer. The overall beer sector showed decreasing shipments, declining by 3.1 percent in March 2002 and by 8 percent in 2003. The sluggish beer market and stiff competition in the *Happoshu* market resulted in only slight profit margins.

As a result of many Japanese companies screening employees for metabolic syndrome as part of their medical check-ups, Japanese beer companies in spring 2008 anticipated an increase in demand for sugar-free, low-malt beer. Kirin launched its sugar-free *Happoshu*, Kirin Zero, in February 2008. Kirin Zero gained popularity with a reduced alcohol content of 3 percent and a lighter taste. The company's annual sales plan for Kirin Zero was revised to 6 million cases, or 1.5 times the original figure.

Russia. Russians remained the world leaders in consumption of alcohol and at the beginning of the twenty-first century were consuming 16 quarts of pure alcohol annually. Despite the country's economic turmoil, Russia remained the world's largest vodka market in the twenty-first century. However, according to Scott Petersen in the *Christian Science Monitor* on June 13, 2001, sales of vodka decreased, and production was down 9 percent in 2000. That year, production of alcohol was responsible for US$3.2 billion in revenue, more than 5 percent of the state's total income. In August 2000, Russian president Vladimir Putin signed into law a new system of excise stamps to help the alcohol industry stem the tide of increased bootlegging, which had comprised between 40 and 70 percent of the

country's alcohol market. However, confusion over the new regulations resulted in the shutdown of a number of the country's legal vodka producers and, ironically, ensured a golden opportunity for the nation's bootleggers. In 2002, Russia re-instituted its government monopoly on the manufacture of leading vodka brands, including Stolichnaya and Moskovskaya. Alcohol imports were also restricted to create fair trading conditions.

Vodka remained the dominant alcoholic drink in Russia, accounting for about 70 percent of domestic sales. However, new products began to play a larger role in the market. According to *World Food Moscow 2002*, Russian production of beer in 2000 increased by 20 percent over 1999, and by the end of 2001, the Russian beer market was worth approximately US$5 billion per year, with annual production between 3.5 and 3.7 billion liters. Beer was appealing increasingly to the under-30 market, according to a BBC report, and showed prospects for vigorous growth through the early 2000s. Beer consumption grew by more than 10 percent annually between 1996 and 2001, and rose by 11.4 percent in 2002. Vodka's dominance among Russian alcoholic beverage consumers was challenged by a new nonalcoholic beer called Baltika No. 0, which debuted in 2001. It was advertised as a health-conscious alternative to vodka and became especially popular as Russians became more aware of the dangers of alcoholism. In 2000, there were 34,000 deaths from alcohol poisoning, an increase of 13.7 percent over 1999. The mortality rate worsened in 2002, exceeding 40,000. Analysts attributed 40 percent of those deaths to illegally manufactured spirits.

BIBLIOGRAPHY

"Alcohol Production Increasing in India." *The Economic Times*, 2 May 2008.

Anderlini, Jamil. "Beer Run on China." *Asia Times*, 22 March 2005.

"Asahhi To Release '3rd Category Beer' Wednesday." *Kyodo News*, 19 April 2005. Available from www.beverageworld.com.

Brandes, Richard. "Stateways Identifies the Fastest-Growing Brands of Wines and Spirits in the Beverage Alcohol Industry." Adams Beverage Group, 2005. Available from www.beveragenet.net.

"Brewers Association Reports Craft Beer Production Grows 7 Percent," 2 February March 2005. Available from www.beertown.org.

"Budweiser Could Pay the Price for Being 'America's Beer'." *The Economic Times*, 14 June 2008.

"Cheers! New Research Reveals White Wine is As Healthy As Red." *First*, 30 June 2008.

"China's Beer Market: Still Room for Investment." *Food Production Daily*, 8 June 2004. Available from www.foodproductiondaily.com.

Chura, Hillary, and Kate MacArthur. "Leveling the Playing Field: Diageo Bucks Convention, Markets Spirits Like Soda." *Advertising Age,* 13 October 2003.

Ciolett, Jeff. "A New Global Giant Is Born." *Beverage World,* 15 March 2004.

Cline, Harry. "U.S.Expected to be No.1 Wine Market." *Western Farm Press,* 12 February 2005. Available from westernfarmpress.com/.

"Convergence Starts to Show in Beer Markets." *Beverage Daily,* 12 January 2005. Available from www.beveragedaily.com.

Echikson, William. "Wine War." *BusinessWeek Online,* 3 September 2001. Available from www.businessweek.com.

"Exposing the Alcohol Illusion." *The Observer,* 25 June 2008.

Flavelle, Dana. "Beer Sales Are Flat But Wine Sparkling." *The Toronto Star,* 10 June 2008. Available from www.thestar.com.

"French Wine Makers Resurrect the Lowly Table Wine." *Earth Times,* 12 June 2008. Available from www.earthtimes.org.

Gaffney, Jacob. "U.S. Wine Consumption to Increase Into 2005, Report Shows." *Wine Spectator,* 5 February 2001. Available from www.winespectator.com.

"Global Beer: Consolidation Continues." *Beverage World,* 15 February 2004. Available from www.beverageworld.com.

Heineken International. "Heineken Announces Reorganization and Invests in Breweries in France," 30 May 2008. Available from www.heinekeninternational.com.

Henley, Jon. "France's Wine Industry in Decline." *Guardian,* 24 February 2004. Available from www.guardian.co.uk.

"Here's to Shochu." *Trends in Japan,* 24 September 2003. Available from www.web-japan.org.

Ueno, Teruaki, Miral Fahmy, and Jerry Norton. "Japan Brewing Beer That's Out of This World," 28 May 2008. Available from www.uk.reuters.com.

"Japan's Tubby Tipplers Drink a Toast to No-Sugar Beers." *Mainichi Daily News,* 31 May 2008.

"Japanese Beer Shipments Slump Again in March" *Reuters Business,* 10 April 2002. Available from biz.yahoo.com.

Keates, Nancy. "Beer Drinkers Getting Shortchanged." *Detroit Free Press,* 14 June 2008.

Locke, Michelle. "Viniculture is Where It's at For Growing Number of VIPS." *Detroit Free Press,* 14 June 2008.

Leonard, Christopher. "Little Chance to Stop Anheuser Busch Bid." *Detroit Free Press,* 13 June 2008, sec. E.

"Malt Whiskey Exports Soar in Solid Year for Scotch." The Scotch Whisky Association, 22 March 2005. Available from http://www.scotch-whisky.org.uk/swa/CCC_FirstPage.jsp.

McGraw-Hill, Department of Commerce, and International Trade Administration. *U.S. Industry and Trade Outlook 2000.* New York: McGraw-Hill, 2000.

Nigro, Diana. "United States Ranks as the World's Fourth-Largest Wine Producer" *Wine Spectator,* 11 April 2002. Available from www.winespectator.com.

Peterson, Scott. "In the Land of Vodka, A Boom in Alcohol-Free Beer." *The Christian Science Monitor,* 13 June 2001. Available from www.csmonitor.com.

Phillips, Kevin. "China's Beer Market Anything But Fragile." *Beverage Daily,* 6 April 2004. Available from www.beveragedaily.com.

"Proposed Transaction Between SAB and Phillip Morris Regarding Miller." SAB Press Release, 30 May 2002. Available from http://www.sab.co.za/pdfs/millerPress.pdf.

Rodgers, Emma. "Gov't Pressured to Reveal Position on Beer, Wine Tax." 16 June 2008. Available from www.abc.net.au.

Rose, Anthony. "Wine: Natural Selection." *The Independent,* 14 June 2008. Available from www.independent.co.uk.

"Russia: Drunkenness a Killer as State Moves to Impose Spirit Monopoly." Channel One TV, Moscow, 3 May 2003. Available from www.cdi.org.

"Russian Vodka Faces Flood of Beer." BBC News, 20 June 2002. Available from news.bbc.co.uk.

"Scientific Facts on Alcohol." Green Facts: Digests, 10 May 2009. Available from www.greenfacts.org.

Schwartz, Emma. "A Host of Trouble." *U.S. News & World Report,* 8 October 2007.

"The Structure of the Beverage Alcohol Industry." *International Center for Alcohol Policies,* March 2006. Available from www.icap.org.

———. "A Threat to Teen Brains." *U.S. News & World Report,* 8 October 2007.

U.S. Department of Agriculture, Foreign Agricultural Service. "2003 Wine Production Lowest in 10 Years." *Gain Report: European Union: Wine,* 11 October 2003. Available from www.fas.usda.gov.

U.S. Department of Commerce, Bureau of the Census. "U.S. Beer Exports," January 2003. Available from www.beerinstitute.org.

Uranaka, Taiga, and Ritsuko Shimizu. "Asahi Targets Y200 bln Overseas Revenue." Reuters, 13 June 2008. Available from www.reuters.com.

"What's Tasteless but Very Expensive (Vodka)." *Wall Street Journal,* 2 April 1998: B1.

"Wine Prices Rebounding." *Wine Business Insider,* 18 April 2005. Available from www.winebusiness.com.

Wiseman, Paul, and William M. Welch. "Senate Votes to Lower Drunken Driving Limit." *USA Today,* 5 March 1998: 11A.

"World Beer Production 2000–2003." *Modern Brewery Age,* 8 December 2003.

World Food Moscow 2002. Available from www.ite-exhibitions.com.

World/Global Alcohol/Drink Consumption 2009. Finfacts Ireland Reports. Available from www.finfacts.ie.

World Wine Consumption by Country and Production, Wine Institute, 2009. Available from www.wineinstitute.org.

Zwick, Steve. "German Beer Goes Flat." *Time Europe,* 11 August 2003.

SIC 2043

CEREAL PRODUCTS

NAICS CODE(S)

311230. Cereal makers around the world manufacture hot and cold breakfast foods and related products from milling and processing various grains.

INDUSTRY SNAPSHOT

First formulated as a "health food" by Americans, ready-to-eat (RTE) cereals have grown into a multibillion-dollar global business. According to an AC Nielsen study, 95 percent of U.S. households purchase ready-to-eat cereals. *Progressive Grocer* reported in 2007 that there are more than 250 types of breakfast cereals and U.S. consumers purchase almost 3 million packages annually.

Kellogg Company, a pioneer in the business, has historically led the industry and remained the number one U.S. breakfast cereal company in 2006 with 33.1 percent of the market and sales of US$1.89 billion. Close behind was General Mills, which garnered US$1.68 billion and held 26.6 percent of the market. Kraft Inc., which owns the Post and Nabisco labels, came in third with US$806.7 million, and Quaker fell to fifth place with US$374.9 million, behind private label brands, which in 2003 had held only 10 percent of the market. In 2006, private label brands slid into the number four spot with US$536.8 million in sales and a 12.9 percent market share. Other branded cereal manufacturers held smaller shares of the global market. Of the top five, only Kellogg and private label brands showed an increase in sales from the previous year, and even these were minimal.

However, after years of flat performance of ready-to-eat (RTE) cereals in the late 1990s and early years of the first decade of the 2000s, (according to research firm Mintel International, sales of RTE cereals grew only 1 percent annually between 1998 and 2003, when the market was valued at about US$9 billion) sales finally started to pick up in the middle of the first decade of the 2000s, due in part to the efforts of the industry to address Americans' increasing health concerns. With more products containing whole grain and less sugar, the industry was hoping to see a revival in the late years of the decade.

Cereal products offer taste profiles that appeal to a wide variety of consumers of all ages in many different markets. Their convenience makes them a frequent choice in time-pressured households, a significant fact as the middle class grows in Asia and South America. RTE cereals also have a positive nutritional image, and some cereals can contribute to the type of low fat, high fiber diet recommended by medical authorities throughout the world. Global growth prospects for the RTE cereal market were further enhanced by the successful conclusion of the Uruguay Round of the General Agreement on Tariffs and Trade (GATT) and the signing of the North American Free Trade Agreement (NAFTA) in 1994. Growing political stability and economic development in major markets around the world have also helped the cereal industry.

For the most part, English-speaking countries are the high volume consumers of RTE cereals. For example, cereal consumption in non-English markets in the mid-1990s was about 25 percent of English-speaking markets. In the early years of the first decade of the 2000s, Middle Eastern markets were just emerging, with Saudi Arabians consuming over 5,000 metric tons annually, over half of which was supplied by U.S. cereal producers. Per capita consumption of RTE cereal in France was just 1.8 pounds in the mid-1990s, while per capita consumption in England was 13.3 pounds. This led Kellogg and other cereal manufacturers to invest heavily in raising consumption in continental Europe. With an educated population and modern grocery distribution system, the European market held significant growth potential as its citizens moved away from traditional breakfasts. Latin America also held promise. Mexico represented the world's third largest breakfast cereal market in dollar terms in 2003. In Chile, where RTE cereals were one of the fastest growing grocery products, imports soared almost 50 percent from 1996 to 1998.

BACKGROUND AND DEVELOPMENT

RTE cereals were first developed in the United States in the late nineteenth century. These cereals—in the form of flakes, puffs, shreds, biscuits, and granules—were the first packaged convenience food, a category that exploded in popularity in the twentieth century.

RTE cereals were an outgrowth of the U.S. vegetarian/health foods movement of the nineteenth century. These cereals developed from a succession of new food products, which included graham crackers, invented in 1829 by Sylvester Graham; Granula (later Grape Nuts), developed by James Jackson of the Jackson Sanitarium; and Shredded Wheat, invented by Henry Perky in 1893.

Battle Creek, Michigan, was the center of the RTE cereal industry from the late 1800s throughout the twentieth century. The Eastern Health Reform Institute was founded in Battle Creek by the Seventh Day Adventist Church in 1866. The institute, later renamed the Battle Creek sanitarium, came under the leadership of John H. Kellogg in 1876. Kellogg, a physician, surgeon, and inventor, advocated the use of cereal grain foods that he had developed. Kellogg was joined at the sanitarium by his brother, W. K. Kellogg. A patient at the sanitarium, Charles W. Post, was inspired to found the Postum Cereal Company in Battle Creek in 1897. The company sold Postum, a hot cereal beverage, and Grape-Nuts cereal. The Postum Cereal Company became General Foods Corp. in 1929. General Foods by the early years of the first decade of the 2000s was part of Kraft Foods Inc., which continued to produce Post cereals. W. K. Kellogg left his brother John and the sanitarium in 1906 to form the Kellogg Company, also based in Battle Creek. The RTE cereal industry soon grew and helped create a burgeoning market for other packaged foods as well.

General Mills began as the Washburn Crosby Company, entering the RTE cereal market in the 1920s. Its Wheaties cereal was developed in 1924. Crispy Corn Kix joined the General Mills lineup in 1937, and Cheerioats (subsequently Cheerios) became the first RTE oat cereal in 1941. The Quaker Oats Company, another important cereal producer, was founded in 1873 as the North Star Oatmeal Mill in Cedar Rapids, Iowa. North Star reorganized with other companies to form the Quaker Oats Company in 1901.

During the 1940s, U.S. cereal makers improved their methods of puffing cereal products. During the first decade of the twentieth century, the puffing process was accomplished by shooting grains from cannons. Characteristically, the cereal industry incorporated this into advertising, with one cereal boasting that it was "shot from guns."

In the twentieth century, RTE cereals were introduced to other English-speaking countries, largely by the Kellogg Company. Domestic competitors developed in these new markets and made incremental progress in taking market share from Kellogg. However, they still had a long way to go. Kellogg had an early start in the world market by entering Canada in the 1910s, Australia in the 1920s, the United Kingdom in the 1930s, and South Africa in the 1940s. In the 1950s, Kellogg entered its first non-English speaking market, Mexico, as well as many other countries in the following three decades.

While RTE cereals began as health foods, in the 1950s the industry developed high-calorie, pre-sweetened cereals aimed at the children's market. Later developments included Total, a highly enriched vitamin cereal, which was developed in 1961. The RTE cereal business was subject to various nutritional fads in the 1980s and 1990s, as specific "healthy" ingredients became known, promoted, and then controversial. For example, the RTE cereal industry latched onto oat bran in the 1980s, which was touted as a way to reduce cholesterol. Products specifically labeled "oat bran" sold at a US$34.9 million rate in the United States in 1987, jumped to US$105.2 million in 1988, and peaked at US$328.2 million in 1989. Scientific studies then emerged challenging the ability of oat bran to lower cholesterol levels, leading to the demise of many oat bran products. However, a good number of the oat-based cereals introduced in this era survived. Also, research in the mid-1990s confirmed the positive health benefits of oat bran, which helped spur sales of oat-based products once again. As the RTE cereal market experienced flat or near-flat growth in the early years of the first decade of the 2000s, Kellogg and others

increased promotion of more portable breakfasts, such as cereal bars and RTE cereal/milk combinations.

Heavy promotion was a characteristic of the RTE cereal industry since its beginning. Advertising, premiums, coupons, rebates, and buy-one-get-one-free deals were all used to promote RTE cereals. In fact, of the US$3.26 cost of a box of Honey Nut cereal in the mid-1990s, just 39 cents reflected the cost of the cereal; 97 cents went to its marketing and advertising.

At the beginning of the twenty-first century, the cereal market was characterized by pricing and marketing wars in the United States, sluggish growth in established markets such as North America and the United Kingdom, and strong sales growth in low per-capita consumption markets such as continental Europe.

In the spring of 1996, Kraft Foods initiated an industry price war when it instituted a 20 percent price cut in its Post brand cereal line. Post experienced a significant gain in volume through August 1996, when other industry players responded with similar price cuts. The price cuts seriously damaged the industry's profits in 1996, and only partial recovery in profits was achieved in 1997.

Ironically, despite the lower prices, volume did not increase markedly. As a result, total U.S. dollar sales of RTE cereals dropped to about US$7.2 billion in 1997, from as high as US$8.5 billion a year earlier, according to a report in the *Wall Street Journal*. The 2001 sales volume increased only slightly to US$7.4 billion. Even with cereal prices falling, consumers switched to lower-priced bagged cereals or more "portable" breakfast foods, such as cereal bars and bagels.

Minneapolis-based General Mills' move in 2000 to merge with cross-town rival Pillsbury allowed it to double international operations and move the new company to the third slot in North American food sales and fifth in worldwide food sales. A 10-year joint venture with Nestle to form Cereal Partners Worldwide (CPW) steadily increased its non-North American RTE market share through the 1990s—to a 6 percent growth in 2001—in a market still dominated by Kellogg. For its part, Kellogg had introduced several successful new line extensions, including Smart Start in early 1998 and runaway hit Special K Red Berries in 2000.

Chicago-based Quaker Oats in the late 1990s successfully introduced a line of low-priced bagged, rather than boxed, cereal. In 1997 the company enjoyed dramatic volume and share gains from the bagged cereal line. While most of the volume gains in the line were said to come from gaining new outlets for the product line and from new products in the line, growth also came from established products and accounts. The bagged cereal product line grew faster than the industry average through the late 1990s, but Quaker saw 2000 sales drop 5 percent, the first negative year since its 1997 introduction of bagged cereal. Quaker Oats was acquired late in 2001 by snack food giant Pepsico. Quaker's 2000 sales were US$5 billion, including US$690 million of Quaker's RTE cereal share. Its RTE sales were down 5 percent from 1999. Quaker held the top slot in the hot cereal market at US$515 million, which was a 6 percent increase. The acquisition also brought Pepsico the top-selling sports beverage brand worldwide, Gatorade, as well as a larger market share of Quaker's healthier snacks.

Nutraceuticals. The development in the 1990s of "nutraceuticals," or foods that go beyond the "low-fat, low-sodium" profiles and are marketed as being able to prevent specific diseases, was a continuation of the industry's venture into providing healthier products. Some cereal products were ideally suited to this trend since grains, their primary ingredient, have been found to have several health-enhancing properties.

Kellogg maintained a functional foods division in order to develop and market new nutraceutical products. In early 1998 Kellogg expanded its Healthy Choice cereal line, licensed from ConAgra Inc., by converting two existing brands, Low-Fat Granola and Mueslix, to the Healthy Choice label. The move was said to be an attempt to conserve marketing dollars and rejuvenate the brands, which had seen sharp sales declines. Kellogg already had three Healthy Choice cereals and discontinued one of them, golden Multi-Grain Flakes, as part of the reorganization.

All major cereal producers took advantage of the U.S. Food and Drug Administration's (FDA) 1997 approval of limited health claims for oat bran. Quaker had enriched many of its products with a soluble, oat-based fat substitute, which, in addition to oatmeal's well-known ability to lower total cholesterol, replaced fat content. In early 1998, the FDA ruled that more breakfast cereals and dietary supplements could claim to reduce the risk of heart disease. Products containing soluble fiber from psyllium seed husks could claim to reduce heart disease risks, the FDA ruled, if they are consumed as part of a diet low in saturated fat and cholesterol. Kellogg's Bran Buds cereal contained soluble fiber from psyllium husks, which are cultivated mostly in India.

However, the Center for Science in the Public Interest (CSPI), a nutrition-focused consumer group, said the FDA's action simply encouraged a cereal marketing fad and failed to underscore the underlying dietary habits, such as eating fresh fruits and vegetables, that collectively produced the touted health benefits.

Nutrition expert Molly Kimball shared insights about types of fiber and cereal options. Kimball stated

soluble fiber was present in many types of food. Although Cheerios were high on many lists for being cholesterol-lowering cereal, other good options were cited such as Quaker Oat Bran and All-Bran Bran Buds. Eating fiber in a variety of foods was a viable alternative to taking statins or supplements with side effects.

Private Label Challenge. Private label products, also known as store brands, have long been a part of the RTE cereal market. They gained share in the early 1990s as many consumers in North America and Europe responded to a global recession by increasing their purchases of less costly cereal products.

The quality and packaging of private label RTE cereals improved markedly in the 1980s and early 1990s. As a result, private label cereals gained new appeal. In the United States, both the Malt-O-Meal Company and Kraft made high-quality RTE cereals under the brand name of major retailers. In Europe, and especially the United Kingdom, where private labels are known as stores' "own labels," the private label challenge was even more of a threat, as powerful retailers such as J. Sainsbury in the United Kingdom were successful in promoting and stocking their own brands.

While this trend was less prevalent in the United States, one U.S. chain, Save-A-Lot, a unit of the major Minneapolis-based food distributor Supervalu Inc., was successful in specializing in private label brands. While branded products continued to account for about 80 percent of supermarket sales in the United States, at Save-A-Lot, 85 percent of sales came from private label items.

Some major brand manufacturers began using legal weapons against private label products in the 1990s. In Europe, Irish grocery chain Dunnes Stores launched a private label brand, Crispy Rice Pops, in the fall of 1994. Kellogg sued Dunnes, charging an infringement of its registered trademarks, which include Pop!, Pop, and Pops. Kellogg was particularly sensitive about the Irish market since per-capita consumption there was three times higher than in continental Europe.

Not all the major brands were at war with private label products, however. In addition to making its own brands in Europe, CPW was quietly manufacturing private label products for major European supermarket chains.

Ultimately, the appeal of private label cereals was limited since it depended on the marketing and promotion activity of national brands to create an identity for the category. Also, improving economic conditions usually lessened private labels' appeal. In the mid to late 1990s, when they cut prices, major manufacturers reduced the price difference between their products and private label products.

What's in a brand name? Is a store brand just as good as a more expensive national one? More and more grocery store shoppers are answering "Yes" to those questions. Although they still want tasty foods, economic challenges make it essential to spend their dollars wisely. Private Label Manufacturers Association shared The Nielsen Company data reflecting growth in store brands purchases exceeding 10 percent in 2008 for US $83.3 billion. An average amount for savings linked to purchasing store brand cereals was 30 percent.

Shoppers seeking quality products for less money are wise to choose store brands for basic grocery and household items. Private Label Manufacturers Association research findings showed that this was true even in an era of enhanced coupon clipping and price promotions for national brands. During a six-week time period, the study focused on prices for 42 basic grocery and household items found in most supermarkets. Results showed that the study helped shoppers gain savings of an excess of 20 percent. Survey administration called for it to be repeated weekly from April 18 through May 23, 2009.

CURRENT CONDITIONS

At the start of the twenty-first century, following trends in consumer health consciousness and widespread alarms over obesity, brands labeled "organic" and cereal brands containing healthier ingredients saw increasingly strong sales in the industry. Private label brands and organic brands saw the biggest growth, while traditional companies such as Kellogg and General Mills struggled to find ways to adapt to Americans' changing preferences. To capture a share of the organic sector, General Mills launched four new organic cereals through its Cascadian Farms brand. Kellogg entered the segment with its acquisition of Kashi in 2000 and subsequently introduced Kashi Apple Pie Pillows and Kashi Good Friends Cinna-Raisin Crunch. In 2003, organic brands accounted for about US$55 million of the total RTE cereal market and the organic brand cereal market reached about US$250 million in sales.

Nature's Path, which marketed 60 kinds of breakfast cereal, was the leading organic brand, generating sales of about US$82.2 million in 2006. This figure showed a significant increase from 2001, when sales totaled only US$20 million. Two of its brands, Nature's Path and EnviroKidz, together were the top-selling USDA Organic-certified breakfast cereal in U.S. natural food supermarkets. In 2002 the company also added flaxseed to its Hemp Plus Granola. Flaxseed is another health ingredient found in RTE cereals and advertised as a good source of omega-3 fatty acids, which promotes cardiac health.

Alarming rates of obesity in children and adults, which increases the risks of heart disease, diabetes, cancer, and many other illnesses, raised concern throughout the world and impacted the industry. Diets high in simple carbohydrates, sugar, fat, and salt, including several breakfast cereal brands, were implicated in the trend toward excessive weight gain. A British consumer group in 2004 found that 9 out of 28 cereals marketed to children contained 40 percent sugar, and 18 brands were high in salt. To combat the rise in obesity, health officials and consumer advocates began pressuring food manufacturers to reduce calories in their products.

In response, several breakfast cereal companies announced changes to their children's brands. In 2004, Kellogg introduced versions of Frosted Flakes and Froot Loops containing one-third less sugar. In 2005 the company introduced Tiger Power, a whole-grain kids' product, and Smart Start Healthy Heart, aimed at adults, touting it as "the only nationally distributed cereal with ingredients that can help lower blood pressure and cholesterol." General Mills cut the sugar content in Trix, Cinnamon Toast Crunch, and Cocoa Puffs by 75 percent. The company also announced that it would increase the whole grain content of selected children's brands.

Advertising of sugary foods to children, too, came under attack. In the United States, where 15 percent of children ages 6 to 19 and 10 percent of those ages 2 to 5 are obese, future legislation allowing broad regulation of advertising to children via television, the Internet, and other media was a distinct possibility. The food industry opposed government regulation and argued that companies should be allowed to regulate themselves. Kraft, for instance, "now only runs commercials featuring healthy foods such as sugar-free drinks . . . and whole-grain products," according to a *Boston Globe* report. At the same time, industry leaders touted cereal as a wise choice for weight and health conscious consumers. Kellogg introduced its "Kellogg's Special K 2-Week Challenge" diet, which claimed that participants could lose up to 6 pounds while following dietary guidelines that included meals with Special K. Kellogg also cited studies showing that "children who eat breakfast—and cereal in particular—have a lower body mass index (a measure of fatness). Cereal eaters also have lower fat and cholesterol intakes compared to people who don't eat cereal."

In France, public anti-obesity campaigns stressing the importance of eating a healthy breakfast contributed to substantial growth in sales of RTE cereals. According to NutraIngredients.com, a daily online news service published by Decision News Media, a business-to-business publisher supplying news to the desktops of decision-makers in the science, cosmetic and food industries, the French market for healthy breakfast cereals grew by 20.4

percent from 2003 to 2004. Ironically, however, the greatest growth was in chocolate brands aimed at children, which rose by 35.7 percent. The market for all children's sugary brands grew by more than 50 percent,

Andrée Picard, public health reporter for *The Globe and Mail,*a Toronto-based newspaper, shared background information about how the Canadian government adopted mandatory fortification policy. White flour was on the list of impacted products. The program that other companies have adapted was credited with reducing neutral tube defects including spina bifida by more than half. Although acknowledging the benefits of folic acid really was already in products, this concern gained significance due to a movement to double folic acid levels added to foods in order to have a greater impact on birth defect reduction. Too much of a good thing was not considered good any more. A common problem linked to that was it became more difficult to detect Vitamin B12 deficiency linked to anemia.

Diversification. General Mills began a marketing trend in 2001 with CD-ROM giveaways in boxes of several of its most popular brands. Partnering with toymaker Hasbro and similar companies, the company experienced dramatic growth, in part because the games are full versions of well-known classics, not demos. Following Kellogg's success with its Special K Red Berries, General Mills launched two kinds of Berry Burst Cheerios—strawberry and "Triple Berry," which featured strawberries, blueberries, and raspberries.

In 2001 General Mills broke new promotional ground by opening its own retail store in the Mall of America in Minneapolis, Minnesota, which, as of the early years of the first decade of the 2000s, annually attracted 43 million international customers. The store provides play areas and gives customers the opportunity to see how cereals are manufactured. General Mills is hoping that the store will boost awareness of its brands and expand its customer base.

General Mills was not the only cereal producer seeking to grow and diversify. Following its 1999 acquisition of Worthington Foods Inc., a leading producer of meat alternatives, Kellogg acquired Illinois-based Keebler Foods in March 2001 for US$4.5 billion. The move strengthened Kellogg's position in the cookie and cracker market and provided a larger presence on U.S. supermarket shelves by inheriting Keebler's strong brand recognition.

In 2002 the company entered a global relationship with Disney, creating cereals tied to Disney movie releases such as *Finding Nemo, Lilo and Stitch,* and *The Incredibles.* Kellogg also boosted its health-conscious profile, announcing its Healthy Beginnings Health Check program in 2005, which provides consumers at participating stores with free health screening and information.

Wheaties brand plans called for it to go where no cereal had gone before by spending a large chunk of its budget to appeal to men. Wheaties Fuel will be marketed to men. General Mills worked with a panel of male athletes for both nutritional and flavor input. The decision was made to eliminate folic acid from the cereal recipe and add Vitamin E. While folic acid was often deficient in women's diets, Vitamin E represented a challenge for men. In an article published in *The New York Times,* General Mills Marketing Manager David Clark explained, "Men don't use their wives' razors or deodorants; why would they be eating their cereal?" Approximately 60 percent of Wheaties eaters were classified as men.

According to Andrew Adam Newman, General Mills had mixed results for its brand extensions. Wheaties past efforts did not go well. Wheaties Energy Crunch was only available for three years. Honey Frosted Wheaties and Wheaties Raisin Bran were discontinued after seven years.

RESEARCH AND TECHNOLOGY

The beginning of the twenty-first century saw diminishing profits in the RTE cereal market. Furthermore, price cuts and the willingness of the public to buy generic private label brands led to a difficult road in new product introduction. Kellogg's 1998 introduction of its Ensemble line of cholesterol-fighting foods failed after only a year. Its Breakfast Mates cereal/milk combinations struggled early on. General Mills and Kellogg invested heavily in research and development. Eye-catching nuggets, quick-to-market seasonal products, and advances in packaging led to the goal of cereal brand identification.

A study published in the *Canadian Journal of Public Health* revealed that some cereals and other products contain between 90 to 377 per cent more folic acid than listed on the product label. The average was for products to have 50 percent more than was reported. The principal research author and Director of Clinical of Dietetics at the Hospital for Sick Children led the first team to conduct that type of research in Canada. The research team tested 92 "most commonly purchased folic-acid-fortified foods" including ready-to-eat cereals.

Charmed. In 1975, General Mills first changed the contents of its Lucky Charms cereal, long advertised with four kinds of solid-colored candied marshmallows called "marbits." The addition of "blue diamonds" led to a 31 percent increase in sales. Later additions of purple horseshoes and red balloons led to similar increases, which, according to General Mills' former chairman and chief executive Bruce Atwater, resulted in permanent gains in sales.

Food engineers tackled difficult technical manufacturing and production issues, such as producing swirled rather than solid-colored marbits. Such small-sized marbits could not be baked but must be extruded, or squeezed out, through small dies. Multiple colors must be co-extruded at the same rates to achieve the desired design effect, and small dots or faces are even more technically challenging, requiring changes in consistency and micro-precision flow rates.

The ability to change the cereal's composition frequently allowed General Mills to capitalize on current events, such as the Olympics; seasonal changes such as snowmen or mittens; and even Millennium Fever, when many manufacturers introduced number two shapes to go along with their O-shaped cereal. A new manufacturing process developed by J. Rettenmaier, which can create either high or low-absorbent food fibers, is expected to be useful in keeping breakfast cereals crisp after the addition of milk. In addition, because vitamins, minerals, and other nutraceutical substances can have unpalatable tastes and textures, the trend toward fortification of cereals has led manufacturers to explore new ways of enhancing flavor in such products.

WORKFORCE

According to U.S. Census Bureau statistics, about 13,447 people were employed in the breakfast cereal segment of the nation's grain-based foods industry in 2005. Average annual wages were US$48,861. With North American growth in RTE essentially flat from about 1996 to about 2004, employers were expected to keep layoffs to a minimum through attrition and retirement and anticipated growth in international markets.

INDUSTRY LEADERS

Kellogg. Founded in 1906, the Kellogg Company has long been the world's market leader in ready-to-eat (RTE) cereals. Kellogg had total sales of almost US$11 billion in 2006, up 7.2 percent from the previous year. Though approximately 80 percent of sales came from RTE cereal in the late 1990s, by the mid-years of the first decade of the 2000s the company was relying increasingly on its snack foods category to generate revenues. Kellogg's share of the U.S. breakfast cereal market fell to around 30 percent in 2000 but recovered the following year and reached about 33 percent in 2003, just ahead of General Mills. Kellogg produces an extensive line of grain-based convenience foods, including toaster pastries, frozen waffles, cereal bars, and bagels; and in 2001 it acquired Keebler Foods, a leading cookie and cracker producer. In 1997 the company opened the

W. K. Kellogg Institute for Food and Nutrition Research (WKKI) in Battle Creek, Michigan. This facility brought together Kellogg research and development (R&D) people from 23 nations to generate products for launch in multiple markets.

Kellogg's international RTE cereal volume decreased in 1998 by 2 percent but rebounded in 1999 by 3 percent. Kellogg has seen strong growth in the Asia-Pacific region, particularly in Korea. Growth was also reported in Spain, Venezuela, and Latin America. In 2003 Kellogg saw net sales growth of 3 percent (adjusted for currency conversion) in Europe. The company reported a 1 percent gain in market share for RTE cereals in Britain and a 2.4 percent gain in France. As of 2004, Kellogg had manufacturing facilities in 19 countries and marketed to more than 180 countries worldwide.

Kellogg was the first U.S. company to venture into the international RTE cereal market when it began distributing its products in Canada in 1914. The first Kellogg plant in the United Kingdom opened in 1938, and Kellogg moved onto the European continent in the 1950s. In 1999 the company held 37 percent of the world's RTE cereal market (down from 42 percent in 1994 and 39 percent in 1997). That global share included 31 percent in North America, 40 percent in Europe, 43 percent in the Asia Pacific region, and 60 percent in Latin America. The value of RTE imports in 1998 reached US$5.4 million, with Kellogg and Quaker the primary importers. Kellogg owned the two leading global cereal brands: Kellogg's Corn Flakes and Kellogg's Frosted Flakes. In 1997, it opened a new plant in Thailand, streamlined its European cereal infrastructure, and purchased cereal businesses in Ecuador and Brazil.

Kellogg CEO and President A. D. David Mackay claimed sales had soared from US $6.5 billion to US $13 billion during a tough seven-year span, according to Freddy Hunt. Furthermore, Hunt stated, Mackay "attributed the success to Kellogg's brand affordability and variety." In addition, Mackay revealed plans to consolidate global marketing and advertising efforts by having commercials that could be used throughout the world rather than in one of a few countries. Hunt also wrote about plans to add fiber to ready-to-eat cereals, including 80 percent of Kellogg's products, by 2010.

General Mills. As of 2004, General Mills was Kellogg's closest competitor. It took over the number one spot in the North American market from perennial rival Kellogg in 1999, capturing a 32 percent share of the cereal market compared with 31 percent for Kellogg. Though its market share held steady, however, General Mills slipped back to number two after Kellogg gained a 33 percent share in 2003. General Mills' consumer foods division included familiar brands such as Wheaties, Chex, Cheerios, Gold Medal Flour, Betty Crocker mixes, Hamburger Helper, and Yoplait and Columbo yogurts. General Mills' 2006 sales were US$11.6 billion, up 3.5 percent from 2005. July 2000 saw the acquisition of its cross-town rival Pillsbury for US$10 billion. Pillsbury's parent company, European giant Diageo, acquired one-third of General Mills. The deal made General Mills the third largest food company in the United States and the fifth largest worldwide, and brought a stronger international presence to the General Mills mix. The largest gains in the acquisition might prove to be distribution and supply chain efficiencies and new international markets for General Mills. This deal followed only three years after the General Mills acquisition of Ralcorp Holdings Inc., including Chex cereals and Chex Mix snacks.

In the midst of a troubled California economy, General Mills decided to build upon its success by moving to new warehouse and distribution space in Stocktown. The community was strategically located in central Northern California. That geography was a significant factor for site selection, revealed Don Little Real Estate Group President and CEO Don Little. Furthermore, Reed Fujii, writing for The Stockton Record, concluded General Mills was outstanding among San Joaquin County's major employers.

Wheelchair Racer and 2008 Paralympics Summer Games Competitor Josh Cassidy earned a coveted spot on Cheerios boxes. This achievement involved more than just Cassidy's smiling face being shown in a special place. There were 16 Olympic and Paralympics athletes chosen for the honor. An additional recognition and support component involved entering bar codes on line in athletes' names so they can earn additional donations up to US $25,000.

Kraft. Kraft Foods and Kraft Foods International, previously units of Philip Morris Companies but spun off in 2007, together comprise the second largest food company in the world and the largest in the United States. Post brands include Shredded Wheat, Grape Nuts, Honey Bunches of Oats, Blueberry Morning, Alpha-Bits, Waffle Crisp, and Great Grains. In 2005 Kraft announced its "Post Healthy Classics 3-Step Plan," a weight-loss program featuring singer Naomi Judd. The company claimed that the program, which advocated daily servings of Post Grape Nuts, Raisin Bran, or Shredded Wheat, could help people lose an average of 10 pounds. Also that year, the company announced the debut of several products, including cereal, under the South Beach Diet brand, associated with the popular diet of the same name. Kraft markets its products in 155 countries, and total sales in 2006 equaled US$34.5

billion. Seven of Kraft's brands (Jacobs, Kraft, Milka, Nabisco, Oscar Mayer, Philadelphia, and Post) bring in annual revenues of US$1 billion; more than 50 other brands net US$100 million per year.

Largely due to the fact that food is linked to the necessity to eat, companies involved in the cereal industry were experiencing growth in 2009 and projecting more for the future. In fact, Kellogg reported 13 percent growth in the second quarter exceeding market projections.

Quaker. Quaker Oats Co., which merged with PepsiCo in 2001, was an early in the first decade of the 2000s active player in several world RTE cereal markets. Its leading brand, Cap'n Crunch, was the top-selling pre-sweetened children's brand in the United States in 2004. Within the much smaller hot cereal segment, Quaker held over 60 percent of the U.S. market in 2001 and remained the leader in 2004. In addition to cereal products, Quaker Oats produced several other food products, including pasta (Pasta Roni), rice (Rice-A-Roni), and side dishes (Near East).

With its new "Go humans go" theme in early 2009, Quaker embarked on a new advertising and marketing campaign with the focus on a "super grain." This marks the first time the company would speak with a unified tone reflecting confidence in its brand identity. Chief Marketing Officer Annie Young-Scrivner explained that this campaign also marked the first time the company would speak about its products reflecting a unified portfolio.

BIBLIOGRAPHY
Analysis: Cereal Makers Hoping to Sweeten Market with Healthy Options." *Marketing Week,* 6 July 2006.

"Breakfast Foods—Ready-to-Eat Cereal: Industry Overview." *Progressive Grocer,* 15 November 2006.

Cash, Rona. "Store Brands: Smart Shopping or Waste of Money." 4 August 2009. Available from blogs.ajc.com.

"Cereal Bars Lead the Way to Healthy Sales." *Candy Business,* November-December 2006.

Food and Agricultural Organization. "Production of Cereals and Share in World." *Statistical Yearbook, 2004.* Available from www.fao.org.

Fujii, Reed. "General Mills Leases Huge Space Near Airport." 30 July 2009. Available from www.recordnet.com.

"General Mills Revealed Plans to Promote the AD Council's Coalition for Healthy Children Message of Nutritional Balance, Portion Control and Physical Activity." *The Food Institute Report,* 12 February 2007.

Gregory, Helen. "They're Rising and Shining." *Grocer,* 20 January 2007.

"Health Driving French Cereal Market." *Nutraingredients.com,* 7 December 2004. Available from www.nutraingredients.com.

"Hoover's Company Capsules." *Hoover's Online,* 2009. Available from www.hoovers.com.

Howell, Debbie. "Wellness-marketed Cereals Fatten Profits; Ready-to-Eat Bars also Boost Bottom Line." *DNS Retailing Today,* 22 March 2004.

Hunt, Freddy. "Kellogg CEO glad to be in food business." 17 July 2009. Available from www.milve.com.

Kimball, Molly. "Increase your fiber with bran cereals and legumes so you can avoid side effects of statins and supplements." 17 July 2009. Available from www.nola.com.

Kirsche, Michelle L. "Healthy Cereal Choices for Breakfast." *Drug Store News,* 25 October 2004.

"Kraft Foods Q2 Profit Rises 11%; Lifts FY09 Earnings-Outlook-Update." 4 August 2009. Available from www.rttnnews.com.

Langlois, Denis. "Cassidy a Cereal Box Sports Star." 4 August 2009. Available from www.Owensoundsuntimes.com.

Lempert, Phil. "Super Bowl: The New Snap, Crackle, and Pop of Product Diversity in the Cereal Aisle Seem to be Working." *Progressive Grocer,* 1 March 2007.

Mishra, Raja. "Push Grows to Limit Food Ads to Children." *Boston Globe,* 18 April 2005.

Newman, Andrew Adam. "For Those Who Want Their Cereal Extra Manly." *New York Times,* 23 July 2009. Available from www.nytimes.com.

Picard, André. "Labels on Fortified foods are wildly inaccurate." *Globe and Mail* (Toronto), 27 July 2009. Available from www.theglobeandmail.com.

Private Label Manufacturers Association. "Market Basket Analysis Shows Savings Continue for Consumers Buying Store Brands." *PR Newswire,* 13 July 2009. Available from news.prnewswire.com.

"Ready-to-Eat Cereal." *Progressive Grocer,* 1 July 2006.

Roberts, William Jr. "A Soggy Cereal Market." *Prepared Foods,* August 2004.

U.S. Census Bureau. *2002 Economic Census Industry Series Reports, Manufacturing.* Available from www.census.gov.

Wade, Marcia A. "Double-Duty Dietary Fibers." *Prepared Foods,* 1 April 2005. Available from www.preparedfoods.com.

"Watchdog Names Worst 'Obesity' Cereals." *Times* (London, England), 31 March 2004. Available from www.timesonline.co.uk.

White-Sax, Barbara. "Industry Seeks to Tie Cereal to Healthy Trends." *Drug Store News,* 5 March 2007.

SIC 2095

COFFEE, ROASTED

NAICS CODE(S)

311920. Firms in the world's coffee industry roast, grind, and package coffee beans for retail and commercial sale. Coffee producers may also manufacture specialty coffees and instant coffees in various forms. For additional details on the growing of coffee beans, see **Agricultural Production—Crops.**

INDUSTRY SNAPSHOT

Coffee is the second most widely traded commodity in the world. The global coffee industry experienced a flavorful past with significant growth. In the early years of the first decade of the 2000s, oversupply and waning demand contributed to market conditions that, according to the *New York Times,* plunged the industry into the most serious crisis in its history. However, in 2004, coffee was the number one agricultural export for 12 countries around the world, and was the world's seventh-largest legal agricultural export in 2005.

At the beginning of the twenty-first century, the total global coffee retail trade was valued at US$33 billion. Global exports, according to an *Observer* report, were US$10 to US$12 billion per year in the 1990s, and retail sales of coffee contributed some US$30 billion to the world economy. By 2003, however, coffee consumption was growing much more slowly than production. While production grew by about 3 percent, reaching 115 million bags in 2002 and 117.32 million bags in 2007, demand grew by only about 1 percent. However, in developing countries, the demand for coffee continued to increase and was projected to grow to 1.9 million tons by 2010, which is an annual growth rate of 1.3 percent. As of the mid-2000s, *The New York Times* reported that green coffee prices were at their lowest point since the early 1970s, and real prices were the lowest in 100 years when adjusted for inflation. The value of world coffee exports plummeted to only US$4.8 billion. Small and medium-sized producers were the hardest hit, and the economies of many coffee-exporting nations were all but destroyed. Taking advantage of extremely deflated prices, roasters and distributors were able to reap hefty profits, with retail sales of coffee worldwide rising to more than US$70 billion in 2002. Niche marketing to consumers of gourmet coffees also enabled large companies to increase prices while keeping costs low.

Prices of the industry's raw material, green coffee beans, are highly volatile and influence the industry's financial performance. In general, when green coffee prices are high, coffee growing is profitable, and, conversely, when prices are low, coffee roasters profit instead. (Relatively few coffee enterprises in the world integrate growing and roasting operations.) Due to the fluctuation of coffee prices, the demand for coffee is projected to decrease by 1 percent annually throughout North America. Developed countries were expected to continue to account for the largest chunk of the world coffee consumption. Their share of consumption was projected to be approximately 72 percent (5 million tons or 83 million bags) in 2010. Europe's demand for coffee is projected to increase by 0.4 percent annually to 3.1 million tons (51 million bags) in 2010. The EC (European Community) is expected to account for 2.2 million tons

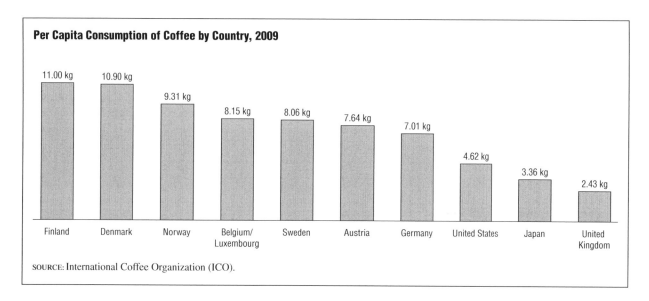

Per Capita Consumption of Coffee by Country, 2009

SOURCE: International Coffee Organization (ICO).

(36 million bags), or 68 percent of the total European consumption.

Around 2000, four multinational companies accounted for the bulk of coffee sales, but the industry was characterized by intense competition. The global in-home coffee market was controlled by Nestlé SA, with 22 percent, and Kraft Foods (formerly Philip Morris, which continued to retain part ownership), with 14 percent. Sara Lee Coffee & Tea Worldwide accounted for 6 percent, edging out Proctor and Gamble, which captured 5 percent. More than one-third of market share was controlled not by a single large company but by small, specialized coffee roasters.

In a June 2008 article in *The Economic Times*, Nidhi Nath Srinivas pointed out that there had been "intense investor excitement" in international coffee markets. Since the start of 2008, robusta futures rose to their highest point in more than 12 years and were the leaders of the agri-commodities market. This reflected an increase in global demand for robusta. Arabica futures had also soared to decade-high levels. Consequently, coffee prices were increased and passed on to consumers by roasters.

ORGANIZATION AND STRUCTURE

Coffee Species. Two species of coffee historically have made up the vast majority of the world's commercial coffee: *Coffea arabica* and *Coffea robusta*. The output of the two main species is divided further by commercial classification due to varying processing methods, altitudes of growth, bean size, bean density, and age, all of which impact flavor. The London-based International Coffee Organization categorizes the varieties as Colombian milds (which make up 15 percent of the world's coffee production), other milds (25 percent of world production), Brazilian and other arabicas (35 percent), and robustas (25 percent).

While arabica beans continued to command the largest market share through the 1990s and the first years of the 2000s, the demand for robusta beans has been increasing following the introduction of commercially-produced soluble coffee, which is better known as instant coffee. The robusta bean's ascendance was fueled by its higher yield of soluble extracts than arabicas during the processing for instant coffee, as well as being less expensive. According to Richard L. Lucier in *The International Political Economy of Coffee*, robustas rose from only 8 percent of world production in the late 1940s to nearly triple that in the 1970s. In the same period, soluble coffee's share of the world market went from almost zero to about 25 percent.

Developments in Roasting Equipment. As the popularity of roasted coffee spread throughout the world, the methods of roasting beans changed. Europeans first roasted beans at home in their ovens. In the nineteenth century, equipment was developed that enabled people to roast larger quantities of coffee. The introduction of this equipment spurred the commercialization of coffee roasting.

Three main types of roasting equipment are used in commercial production. A batch roaster roasts beans in approximately 15 to 18 minutes, depending on the types of beans, by tumbling them in a drum that is blown with hot air. The beans are then cooled on a tray and mechanically stirred. Batch roasters can accommodate amounts ranging from less than a pound to more than 500 pounds of beans, and some batch roasters can run continuously. A fluid bed roaster roasts beans in 6 to 12 minutes. It operates much like a hot air popcorn popper, blowing air from the bottom of a stationary cylinder containing beans. Continuous roasters, first developed in the United States in 1940 by Jabez Burns, roast beans in about three minutes. Made of long cylinders with six-inch-wide compartments, continuous roasters turn like corkscrews. As the cylinder turns, the beans pass into different compartments that heat and then cool the beans. Continuous roasters can roast from 500 to 10,000 pounds of coffee per hour. Unlike other types of roasters, continuous roasters are most often monitored and controlled by computers.

Roasting Process. Despite the differences in roasting equipment, each process obtains similar results. When green coffee beans are roasted, a series of chemical changes alters their weight, appearance, and taste. The International Coffee Organization estimated that 1.19 pounds of green coffee beans go into a pound of roast coffee. Sugars, oils, proteins, and minerals develop and change within the beans as they are subjected to heat. Coffee beans absorb heat relatively uniformly, and during the last few minutes of a roast, the beans make a popping noise as they enlarge and unfold. The popping noise indicates that the production stage known as the development of the roast is taking place.

Because the changes in the beans occur quickly, the roastmaster (the person in charge of roasting the coffee beans) must keep a careful eye on the batch to achieve the desired flavor in the beans. The roastmaster's goal is to roast the coffee beans to a color consistent from the inside to the outside of the bean as well as throughout the batch. In large commercial operations, computers determine when to end the roast using photometric reflectance instruments that measure the color of the roast as it relates to the temperature of the beans. There are myriad degrees of roast, but they can be simplified into four categories: light, medium, dark, and very dark. Each variation has a distinct flavor.

Blended Coffee. Blended coffee has long dominated the global roasted coffee market. Because different types of coffees contain varying amounts of taste, aroma, and body, coffee is often blended to create a unique product. Beans can be blended before they are roasted if they are of similar variety, but blending can also take place after the roasting process if the beans in question require different roasting criteria. Coffees are blended to suit different tastes. For example, in Japan, mild coffees, such as those from Peru, are most popular, while in Germany, coffee drinkers are more likely to prefer full-bodied blends, such as those from Honduras.

Although large commercial roasters blend coffee beans to achieve a consistently flavored drink, specialty coffee roasters blend coffee beans to make uniquely flavored coffee. Some coffees are sold as varietals—coffee beans from a particular country of origin that have been roasted alone. However, blended coffee has usually been marketed without mention of the types of coffee beans contained within the blend. Many coffee blends are sold by emphasizing company brand names, rather than coffee species or country of origin.

Instant Coffee. Instant coffee is the extracted form of roasted, ground coffee. It is made by blending and roasting beans in the same way as regular coffee, although the end product is generally of a coarser quality. The ground coffee is then fed into industrial percolators, which have hot water pumped into them to make a concentrated coffee extract. The coffee's coarser grind keeps excessive pressure from developing in the percolator's hydraulic system.

Once the solubles have been extracted, they are dried into a powder by spray or freeze-drying. Although spray-drying was the most common form of drying instant coffee in the 1990s, freeze-drying, which had become commercially sustainable in Europe and the United States in the 1960s, was associated with higher quality instant coffee because freeze-dried coffees retain more of their aroma. The dried powder that is the final product is packaged in glass jars or plug-closure metal containers with foil liners. Since the process of making instant coffee takes away some of the flavor and aroma of the coffee, instant coffee's aroma is often enhanced with collections from coffee grinders, percolator vents, or concentrated percolate.

Instant coffee sales are greatest in countries with little history of coffee drinking. In the United Kingdom, Japan, and Australia, all of which are predominantly tea-drinking countries, instant coffee accounts for a much higher percentage of total coffee consumption than in countries where regular coffee drinking has had a long history. Despite the ongoing perception that instant coffee was a product of lesser quality than regular ground-roasted coffee, instant coffee experienced gains in the 1990s due to consumer demand for convenience and the addition of specialty coffees to the instant coffee market in Europe.

Decaffeinated Coffee. Decaffeinated coffee first became commercially available around 1900 in Europe. Most coffee is decaffeinated while it is green. In green form, arabica coffees contain about 1 percent caffeine by weight, while robusta coffees contain twice that amount. To decaffeinate coffee, green coffee beans are moistened, which moves the caffeine to the surface of the beans. Solvents are then used to wash the caffeine from the beans' surfaces. After the decaffeination process, the green beans are dried to their original moisture content before roasting.

Before the 1980s, man-made solvents removed caffeine from the beans. In the 1980s, however, natural solvents were made commercially available to remove the caffeine. Some natural solvents used for decaffeination include water, carbon dioxide, fats and oils, and ethyl acetate. Although caffeine has a slightly bitter taste, its removal from the coffee bean has little effect on the strength of the coffee's taste. A coffee's strength is dependent more on the degree of roast and the ratio of water to coffee in the brewing process than on caffeine.

Packaging. Packaging is of paramount importance to the roasted coffee industry because coffee is highly perishable. After coffee is roasted it begins to oxidize or grow stale. Roasted coffee first loses its aroma and then its flavorful oils and fats. In addition, roasted and ground coffee quickly can become contaminated through the absorption of other foods, flavors, or odors. Although specialty coffee is often sold in wax-lined paper bags with wire ties, most coffee retailers use airtight containers to package their coffee. Vacuum-packed metal cans were the most popular packing method until the late 1970s, according to the Specialty Coffee Association of America. By the 1990s, however, vacuum packages, called one-way valve bags, and brick packs had become popular as well.

One-way valve bags allow producers to package coffee immediately after it is roasted or ground. This ability is important because after coffee is roasted or ground, it releases carbon dioxide. As a result, roasters commonly had to let coffee sit for 1 to 30 hours, depending on the roast or grind, before packaging. The one-way valve bags are made of many layers of polyethylene and aluminum foil and include a valve that allows carbon dioxide to escape without letting oxygen enter. Other coffee packages include polyethylene or nylon film pouches that have been flushed with nitrogen, glass jars, and plastic-lined paper cartons.

Major Trade Agreements. Since the 1989 failure of the International Coffee Agreement (an agreement of the 72-nation International Coffee Organization cartel that had set coffee prices since 1962), the roasted coffee industry has been subject to market forces. Without the support of the cartel, green coffee prices plunged more than 45 percent in 1989 and consuming countries built up a surplus of green coffee. As a result, the artificially high profit margins that had supported the coffee-producing nations shifted to benefit the coffee-roasting companies. Retail prices of coffee did not drop as precipitously as green coffee prices after the failure of the cartel but increased rapidly in 1994 in the wake of a frost that battered the all-important Brazilian coffee crop.

By the mid-1990s, coffee manufacturers' high profits were in jeopardy. The 1993 organization of 28 producing nations that formed into the Association of Coffee Producing Countries (ACPC) devised a supply quota scheme

to withhold about 20 percent of exportable coffee from the market in an attempt to raise coffee prices, and efforts continued toward negotiating a new International Coffee Agreement. By 1995, however, the United States had withdrawn from the negotiations, citing a preference for free trade of coffee.

When coffee was traded freely after the demise of the International Coffee Agreement, coffee prices fell and importing countries built up stocks of green coffee. When the producing countries retained some of their stocks, importing countries were forced to draw down their stocks. This strategy, however, did not result in higher prices for green coffee, but caused production to soar while demand lagged. By early 2002, green coffee prices (adjusted for inflation) reached their lowest level in 100 years.

In 1994 a new version of the General Agreement on Tariffs and Trade (GATT) resulted from the Uruguay Round discussions of 1986 to 1994. Under the agreement, participating nations cannot introduce any new export subsidies, and U.S. and EU subsidies are subject to restrictions. GATT called for the reduction and elimination of tariffs designed to impede and control foreign competition in favor of domestic businesses. All participating countries agreed to cut tariffs by 33 percent, and the United States, the European Union, Canada, and Japan decided to remove most of the tariffs inhibiting trade among themselves. GATT also established a formal organization for the implementation of systematic global trade policies, the World Trade Organization.

Coffee Crisis. Early in the first decade of the 2000s, the lifting of quotas had contributed to significant oversupply, especially of lower-quality robusta. Brazil, for example, doubled robusta production in the 1990s. At the same time, Vietnam increased robusta production from 84,000 tons in 1990 to 950,000 tons in 2000, making it the second largest producer in the world. To maintain profitability, some big roasters reconfigured their blends with larger amounts of less expensive robusta beans and smaller proportions of higher quality arabica beans. This step, according to Marcelo Vieira of Brazil's specialty coffee association, created an inferior product and contributed to further decline in demand.

While a small number of producers with access to capital were able to grow and process higher quality blends for the expanding niche market of specialty coffees, most producers faced significant losses. From 1992 to 2002, coffee revenues in Colombia, which had been the second leading coffee producer before being overtaken by Vietnam, dropped by 50 percent. According to the U.S. Agency for International Development (USAID), the situation, which was exacerbated by serious droughts in many parts of Latin America, led to coffee export losses of about US$1 billion in 2000 and 2001. Conditions were so alarming by 2003 that some analysts recommended radical measures. The charity organization Oxfam, for example, called for the destruction of 5 million bags of low quality coffee in warehouses, believing that it would boost market prices by 20 percent. Others believed that stimulating more demand was the most important response to diminishing sales.

The U.S. Agency for International Development (USAID) defines itself as an independent federal government agency that gives foreign assistance and humanitarian aid to countries recovering from disaster, trying to escape poverty, or attempting democratic reforms, with input from the U.S. State Department on foreign policy objectives. In response to the alarming conditions that prevailed in 2003, USAID initiated two major programs in Central America and Colombia to assist the coffee industries there. The agency established an alliance with Green Mountain coffee to help small and medium-size producers to grow, process, and market high-quality coffees for export. In 2002, USAID signed a Quality Coffee Agreement with Costa Rica, El Salvador, Guatemala, Honduras, Nicaragua, the Dominican Republic, and Panama that promoted similar goals. USAID has also instituted several programs in Africa to help improve coffee quality and provide access to markets. In 2003, the government of Tanzania passed legislation allowing direct exports, which enabled coffee growers to begin selling directly to foreign buyers.

According to the International Coffee Organization (ICO), the supply imbalance began to improve by 2004, when total crop production fell to 112.67 million bags. Production of arabicas fell to an estimated 62.86 million bags, compared to 80.36 million bags the previous year. Robustas showed a smaller decline, falling from 39.08 million bags in 2003 to 38.52 million bags in 2004. Total exports in the first part of 2004 fell by about 9.7 percent from the corresponding period in 2003. The ICO expected further production cutbacks in 2005 and 2006 to an estimated total of 106 million bags. As a result of smaller harvests, opening stocks in exporting countries in 2004 were the lowest in more than 10 years. A further positive development was the announcement in 2005 that the United States would accede to the 2001 International Coffee Agreement and would rejoin the International Coffee Organization. With export volumes increasing in 2004 and 2005, ICO analysts were cautiously optimistic that the industry had begun to recover.

Coffee Associations. The International Coffee Organization (ICO) includes such major exporters and importers around the world as Brazil, Vietnam, Ecuador, and Colombia. Established in 1963, the ICO administers the International Coffee Agreement and coordinates diplomacy in world coffee trade. In addition, the ICO publishes information and statistics on the industry and leads campaigns to promote coffee consumption.

The Specialty Coffee Association of America (SCAA) serves specialty and gourmet coffee roasters, as well as retailers, producers, exporters, importers, green coffee brokers, and manufacturers of coffee-related equipment and other products. The SCAA strives to advance the specialty coffee industry through the development and circulation of information that fosters coffee excellence within the trade.

Mission Grounds Gourmet Coffee is a nonprofit organization dedicated to helping needy children throughout the world. The main focus is to help orphans and children in Atlanta as well as impoverished children both in other inner city U.S. neighborhoods and Third World countries. In June 2008, Mission Grounds established a partnership with Kroger, one of the largest grocery retailers in the United States, to carry Mission Grounds Gourmet Coffee in all of its southeastern U.S. stores. All proceeds from coffee sales were set to go directly to the Children's Restoration Network to provide backpacks and school supplies for children in homeless shelters. The goal is to help up to 3,000 homeless children.

Fair Trade-Certified Beans. Beginning in the 1990s and continuing into the twenty-first century, coffee beans began to be certified in a new manner, based not on flavor or aroma, but on human rights and environmental concerns. Starting first in Europe and then moving to North America and Japan, a fair trade consumer movement led to coffee labeling based on certain criteria, namely that coffee importers pay at least US$1.26 per pound for green coffee. The fair trade certification program assists "marginalized" coffee growers, which are typically family-run farms, cooperatives, and plantation workers, by ensuring that they are paid fairly rather than allowing middlemen to absorb overly large shares of profits, leaving the producer at times with barely enough to cover production costs.

The Fairtrade Labeling Organizations International (FLO), established in 1997, was the umbrella organization that oversaw worldwide fair trade labeling programs for products such as coffee. Coffee retailers paid the FLO (or one of its regional affiliates) a licensing fee that allowed them to label their products with the fair trade seal. The consumer, who has been educated to look for this seal, is willing to pay a higher price for the coffee at a retail outlet, knowing that the coffee producer is being paid fairly and that in many cases the producer uses sustainable agricultural practices. In 2000, Starbucks, the leading gourmet coffee retailer in the United States, agreed to become the nation's first coffee retailer to sell fair-trade-certified beans in more than 2,000 of its outlets after activists and consumer groups threatened a large scale protest. Other companies in North America followed suit, including Sara Lee Coffee & Tea, Green Mountain Coffee Roasters, Tully's, Mountain View Coffee Co. in Canada, and many other regional and independent roasters and importers. According to TransFair USA, the U.S. member of FLO, Fair Trade coffee is also served in the European Parliament and in Toyota and Warner Brothers Europe's corporate headquarters. *The New York Times* reported in 2003 that since 2000, approximately 140 coffee companies in the United States were offering fair-trade blends in some 10,000 outlets throughout the country. Sabrina Vigilante, marketing coordinator for the Rainforest Alliance, expected the niche for fair trade coffee to double in 2004. A 2005 study done in Belgium, however, concluded that consumers' buying habits are not consistent with their attitudes towards ethical products. An average 46 percent of European consumers claimed to be willing to pay considerably more for products deemed "ethical," including fair-trade products such as coffee. However, the study found that the majority were unwilling to pay the actually price premium of 27 percent for fair trade coffee.

BACKGROUND AND DEVELOPMENT

Coffee has been used for multiple purposes and in many forms—from medicinal potions to food and wine—beginning as early as 800 A.D. *Caffea arabica* is believed to have been first cultivated in Ethiopia, where it grows wild, and first roasted in present-day Yemen on the Arabian Peninsula. By the late Middle Ages, coffee had become a staple beverage in the Mediterranean region's Islamic cultures, which eschewed alcoholic beverages, although alcoholic coffee drinks existed. Coffee was thus known in the period as "the wine of the Arabs."

During the seventeenth century, coffee consumption spread throughout Europe. As early as 1570, coffee was traded in Venice, and over the next 150 years its consumption gradually spread to most of continental Europe's urban and cultural centers. By the mid-eighteenth century, European colonists and merchants traded coffee in Africa (where both species were indigenous), North America, and South America, and Dutch colonists began cultivating coffee beans in what was later called Indonesia, notably on the island of Java, leading to another of coffee's nicknames. In the late eighteenth century, coffee gained popularity in British colonial North America as an alternative to tea when militant colonists rebelled against a British tea tax through boycotts and such incidents as the Boston Tea Party.

Gourmet Coffees and Emerging Markets. Although consumption of regular coffee stagnated in the late 1980s and early 1990s, the trend toward increased consumption of gourmet coffee was a worldwide phenomenon. In the United States, sales of gourmet coffee quadrupled between 1986 and 1997, and by the latter part of the decade, gourmet coffee accounted for about 30 percent of market sales. The bulk of specialty coffee sales in the United States came through specialty coffee retail stores. Starbucks Coffee Co. and Caribou Coffee were two of the leading specialty coffee roasters/retailers in the United States in 1998, with a spate of smaller coffee roasters and cafés across the country.

Instant Coffee. Instant coffee was developed in 1899 by a Japanese chemist and used by members of an Arctic expedition, according to C. F. Marshall's *The World Coffee Trade.* In the 1980s, instant coffee accounted for one-fifth of the world coffee market, and instant coffee was the fastest growing segment of some roasted coffee markets.

Considered inferior by some continental European consumers, instant coffee nonetheless enjoyed healthy sales growth throughout Europe in the mid-1990s and gained ground in prime roast and ground coffee markets, such as Germany, France, and Italy, where despite instant coffee's small market penetration, high coffee consumption rates translated into sizable sales volume for instant coffee. Furthermore, Eastern European countries, such as Poland and Russia, represented increasingly important markets for instant coffee. Russia, for example, consumed more instant coffee than France and Germany combined in 1996. Instant coffee was also increasingly popular in China, where coffee sales grew 90 percent between 1998 and 2003. Nestlé was the most popular brand, accounting for 46 percent of retail coffee sales in 2002.

Profit Margins. Profit margins for regular coffee sales at leading companies narrowed in the 1980s. Some analysts predicted that the belated entry of some of the largest coffee processing companies into the specialty coffee market would reverse this trend since specialty coffee typically garnered higher margins. Nevertheless, after the collapse of the 1989 International Coffee Agreement, coffee roasters' profits remained tied to the fluctuating green coffee market. In 1995 the market experienced price hikes after frost devastated Brazil's coffee crop.

Europe's coffee roasters also faced shrinking profit margins in the mid-1990s as retailers slashed prices in new marketing schemes to increase their store-wide sales. Coffee price wars, especially in Germany and France, led to retail prices that fell below the open market price paid by coffee companies. Small roasters and cafés were hit particularly hard.

The Role of the International Coffee Organization. The International Coffee Organization (ICO) aggressively marketed coffee in China and Russia with its generic coffee promotions. The organization devoted its entire advertising fund of US$3.8 million to these two largely tea-drinking countries in 1997. As a result of promotions, coffee imports increased in Russia in the 1990s, rising from 1.08 million 60-pound bags in 1991 to 2.44 million bags in 1995. The ICO also subsidized marketing efforts in Japan to build up that country's coffee market.

CURRENT CONDITIONS

Coffee Consumption. Over 53 countries worldwide make up the coffee growing industry, and all of them lie along the equator between the Tropic of Cancer and Capricorn. Over the last several decades of the twentieth century, coffee consumption trends varied greatly from country to country and economy to economy. Countries that import their coffee (as opposed to those that produce it domestically) consumed almost three-fourths of the world's coffee in 2000, a pattern that remained relatively unchanged through 2008. The United States remained the largest consumer of coffee, drinking 400 million cups of coffee per day, or the equivalent to 146 billion cups of coffee annually. Coffee represents 75 percent of all caffeine consumes in the United States. Consumption in developing countries, however, including Russia and China, increased by 4.05 percent annually, causing analysts to predict that these markets will demonstrate the best potential for growing coffee sales through the early years of the twenty-first century.

In terms of per capita consumption, ICO statistics showed that Finland led the world in 2009, consuming 11 kilograms (kg) per year. Denmark came next with just under 11 kg, just ahead of Norway with 9.31 kg. Belgium and Luxembourg consumed 8.15 kg, Sweden consumed 8.06 kg, and Austria's consumption was 7.64 kg. Germany's per capita consumption was 7.01 kg. Per capita consumption in the United States was 4.62 kg, while it reached only 2.43 kg in the United Kingdom. U.S. consumers favored roast and ground coffees, while those in the United Kingdom preferred soluble (instant) coffee. Japanese per capita coffee consumption in 2009 was 3.36 kg.

Throughout the 1990s and into the twenty-first century, the popularity of high quality, specialty coffee continued to grow, especially in the mature markets of the United States and the European Union, which together consumed an estimated 64 percent of the world's coffee. The fastest growing markets in the roasted coffee industry, however, were countries relatively new to coffee drinking, such as the Eastern European countries

of the Czech Republic, Hungary, Latvia, Lithuania, and Slovenia, where coffee consumption generally increased throughout the late 1990s and into the twenty-first century, according to the ICO. Consumption had also steadily increased in Australia, Puerto Rico, and Taiwan.

Types of Coffee Drinkers. In a study of 95 markets and regions worldwide, Nestlé SA developed a profile of coffee drinkers as "Sophisticated," those who drink one or more cups daily; "Intermediary," those who drink somewhere between one cup per day to one cup per week; and "Starting," those who consume only one cup a week or less. The vast majority (57 percent) of people labeled themselves as starters, while sophisticated drinkers made up about 17 percent of the population. Nevertheless, as expected, the sophisticated group consumed the majority of the world's coffee at 65 percent, while intermediate drinkers accounted for 29 percent.

Starbucks CEO Howard Schultz announced the company's plans to license 150 new coffee shops in Germany, Great Britain, and France. Schultz said the international business was helping counteract the weak market in the United States. The European coffee-drinking culture is different than the United States, with Europeans choosing to sit and enjoy their coffee on site, while Americans typically get their coffee to go.

Green Coffee Prices. According to a September 2010 news report, coffee prices had reached a 13-year high which was expected to trickle down to the individual purchaser. The increased bean costs quickly caused bulk carriers to raise their prices to offset the rise in expenses. The partial cause of the depressed coffee trade was dry weather threatening crops in South America, particularly in Brazil, which was one of the top exporters. Rumors that Vietnam and Brazil were talking about hoarding their stocks at a time when U.S. stockpiles were at a 10-year low, also had an impact on pricing. Individual cups of coffee either had or were expected to increase by as much as 44 percent if all these factors continued. The International Coffee Organization (ICO) reported that the average annual per pound price for green coffee rose from nearly US$0.86 cents in 1999 to just under US$0.46 cents in 2001. However, in October 2010, the price had jumped to just over US$1.61. World coffee production flourished in the 1990s due to exceptionally warm and dry climates in key coffee-growing regions, causing the world's coffee supplies to further increase, while consumption remained essentially flat, particularly in the European Union and the United States.

Gourmet Coffee. Kraft Food's coffee sales dropped almost 20 percent after 1996 as coffee drinkers preferred going out to a coffeehouse, café, or a restaurant for a gourmet cup of coffee. Much of the surge in interest in gourmet coffee was fueled by Starbucks, which opened a new market in the United States. According to Matthew Flemm in an April 2001 article for *Crain's New York Business,* sales in the United States for regular Colombian coffee stagnated while demand for Guatemalan Antigua, Kona, Mountain, and other premium coffees and blends flourished as consumers grew more sophisticated in their tastes. Premium and flavored coffees could be readily purchased at fast food chains and delis. The trend for gourmet coffee and the increasingly consolidated coffee processing industry favored small, independent roasters. Such regional roasters often specialize in unique blends customized to local tastes along with a high level of customer service and are adept at providing a constantly changing array of flavors that consumers seek.

Soluble Coffee. Soluble, or instant, coffee continued to be popular in many regions of the world, especially Japan, the Philippines, and Chile, where nearly 100 percent of coffee consumed is instant. Other countries where soluble coffee consumption accounted for more than 90 percent of total coffee consumption are China (97 percent), Korea (97 percent), South Africa (94 percent), Australia (93 percent), the United Kingdom (92 percent), Russia (92 percent), and Thailand (91 percent), according to Nestlé SA. Countries with the lowest percentage of instant coffee consumption were Italy (4 percent), Sweden (9 percent), and Brazil (9 percent). In the early twenty-first century, the world consumed approximately 196 billion cups of soluble coffee compared to 355 billion cups of roast and ground coffees. Nestlé dominated the soluble market, controlling 59 percent, followed by Philip Morris (subsequently Kraft Foods) with 13 percent, and Proctor and Gamble with 3 percent. According to Nestlé, world sales of soluble coffee rose by 35 percent between 1993 and 2003.

In Russia, more than 100 brands of Brazilian soluble coffee are sold, according to the *Tea & Coffee Trade Journal.* Brazil's soluble coffee exports totaled US$200 million in 2001, and the country continued to seek new markets for soluble coffee through the early years of the first decade of the 2000s. Under a new agreement with the European Union, the *Tea & Coffee Trade Journal* reported that the European Union would likely allow Brazilian imports to make up a quota of 87.4 percent of its total imports of instant coffee from around the world starting in 2002.

RESEARCH AND TECHNOLOGY

Research study findings from a team led by Han-Seouk Seo of Seoul National University revealed insights about coffee aroma. This study is the first effort to elucidate the effects of coffee bean aroma on the sleep deprivation-induced stress in the rat's brain. Comparisons were made between groups of rats who were stressed and sleep-deprived with those who were not. While attempting to "unravel the molecular effects" of the smell of coffee on the brain, discoveries were made. Coffee-sniffing sleep-deprived rats showed different levels of activity in 17 genes in the brain. Furthermore, levels of some brain proteins also changed in ways that potentially had a calming effect on stress or had an anti-oxidant function. The correlation to humans still remains to be seen. Complete report results were published in the 25 June 2008 issue of the *Journal of Agriculture and Food Chemistry.*

Siamak Bidel, one of Finland's National Public Health Institute researchers, said his findings show excessive amounts of coffee might check adult-onset diabetes. Coffee drinking also appeared to reduce the risk for overweight people and those who drank a lot of alcohol to get Type-Two diabetes. It remained to be determined which of the hundreds of chemicals contained in coffee affect diabetes. In Finland, approximately half a million people have adult-onset diabetes. Bidel's research was part of his doctoral thesis about the link between coffee and diabetes in Helsinki. A total of approximately 60,000 participants participated in five surveys.

Studies were mixed on the health benefits and/or risks from drinking coffee. In some tests, coffee drinking has been linked closely with various cancers, but it also had not been determined if it was the coffee itself or a chemical within the coffee that caused the problem. Different methods or preparation seem to also play a part in beneficial and harmful effects of coffee consumption. Some studies suggest that coffee consumption can reduce the risk of being affected by Alzheimer's disease, Parkinson's disease, and heart disease. However, coffee consumption can lead to iron deficiency anemia in mothers and infants. Caffeinated coffee may aggravate such preexisting conditions as migraine headaches, arrhythmias, and gastroesophageal reflux disease.

INDUSTRY LEADERS

Nestlé SA. Created from the 1905 merger of two competing condensed milk companies, Nestlé SA of Vevey, Switzerland, is the world's largest consumer packaged goods company in the world and the market leader in coffee production. Nestlé entered the coffee market in 1938 with Nescafé, a soluble coffee powder and the company's first non-dairy product, after the Brazilian Coffee Institute asked if Nestlé could make "coffee cubes" to help Brazil deal with its large coffee surplus. The company originally intended to produce Nescafé in Brazil, but the number of administrative barriers in that country convinced Nestlé to begin production in Switzerland instead. By 1991, Nescafé was sold in more than 100 countries.

Nestlé brought ground roast coffee to its product line when it bought the third-largest U.S. coffee firm, Hills Brothers Inc., in 1985. By the start of the twenty-first century, Nestlé was a diverse and multinational company, with more than 500 factories operating in over 86 countries worldwide. Increased productivity following upgrades of many of its facilities in the early 1990s led to an expanded presence in a number of countries. The company also opened a production facility in China in 1991. Developments of note at these facilities included the company's 1992 announcement that its French facility would not participate in the four-week holiday Europeans normally take in August. In 1999, Nestlé divested its Hills Brothers, MJB, and Chase & Sanborn roast and ground coffee brands in the United States to concentrate on promoting a new premium line of Nescafé products that were introduced on the West Coast.

Through the early years of the first decade of the 2000s, Nestlé continued to dominate the world's instant coffee market. The company posted beverage (excluding water) revenues of CHF21.79 billion (about US$18.3 billion) in 2004, with soluble coffee accounting for CHF8.079 billion (US$6.78 billion) in sales. According to company statistics, sales of Nescafé alone rose 40 percent from 1993 to 2003. The company's chief markets are the United States, France, Germany, Brazil, the United Kingdom, Italy, and Japan. In 2004 Nestlé relaunched its Nescafé premium coffees throughout Europe and successfully relaunched Nescafé Cappuccino. The company claimed that 3,000 cups of its coffee are consumed every second. Nestlé's soluble coffee brands—its most popular coffee—include Nescafé, Taster's Choice, Ricoré, and Ricoffy; its roast and ground coffee brands are Nespresso, Bonka, Zogas, and Loumidis. In 2009, the company had a total revenue of US$107.987 billion with 283,000 employees.

In a June 23, 2008, article in *Business Standard,* Vishal Chhabria concluded that new product launches had worked well for Nestlé India. It launched a new instant mild coffee appropriately called Nestlé Mild. The product was also introduced in sachet form. Chhabria said small and low-priced packs helped to drive consumption by increasing affordability and convenience.

Kraft Foods Inc. Philip Morris, one of the world's largest cigarette manufacturers, spun off Kraft Foods, one of the world's largest coffee producers, in June 2001, while retaining 84 percent ownership. Philip Morris first entered the coffee market when it purchased the world's largest coffee roaster, General Foods Corporation, in 1985.

Although General Foods had distributed Sanka brand coffee since 1927, it did not begin roasting coffee until 1928. That year, the company, known at the time as the Postum Company, acquired Maxwell House Coffee, a company that had started in 1892. The company continued to enlarge its coffee business, purchasing the Sanka Coffee Corporation in 1932, developing instant coffee for the U.S. Army in 1941, and acquiring French coffee roaster Établessements Pierre Lemonnier SA in 1961.

When Philip Morris acquired Kraft Inc. in 1988, the cigarette maker merged Kraft with General Foods. This 1989 merger created the world's second largest food company, Kraft General Foods Inc. The two segments were later integrated further as Kraft Foods Inc. In 1990, Philip Morris bought Kraft Jacobs Suchard (KJS), a Swiss coffee and chocolate manufacturer and Europe's largest coffee roaster. KJS controlled 30 percent of Germany's large roasted coffee market. Since 1998, Kraft has marketed and sold Starbucks brand coffee to retail grocery stores in the United States under a licensing agreement with the coffee chain giant.

In 2000 Kraft Foods International reported strong volume growth in emerging markets in Central and Eastern Europe, as well as in the mature markets of Sweden, Austria, Italy, and the United Kingdom. Volume in the Chinese market increased with the re-launch of Maxwell House coffee mix. The company held the top spot in the 2000 coffee market based on volume in France, Germany, and Sweden. Worldwide, Kraft Foods was the top brand in the roast and ground coffee market in 2000, controlling 15 percent of the market. In the total in-home coffee market, Kraft Foods captured 14 percent of the market, trailing Nestlé. In 2003, Kraft was the leading coffee company in seven European countries as well as South Korea.

Kraft posted net revenues in 2004 of more than US$32 billion. Its international beverage division sold approximately 94 billion cups of coffee annually, or about 257 million cups of coffee daily. As of 2004, Kraft Foods' coffee brands in the United States included General Foods International Coffees, Gevalia, Maxim, Maxwell House, Sanka, Starbucks (under a licensing agreement), and Yuban. Its international brands included Carte Noire, Gevalia, Grand' Mère, Kaffee HAG, Jacobs Krönung, Jacobs Milea, Jacobs Monarch, Jacques Vabre, Saimaza, Kenco, and Maxwell House, among others. In 2009, Kraft posted revenues of more than US$40.4 billion and reported 96,000 employees.

Sara Lee/DE. Sara Lee/DE, formerly Sara Lee Coffee & Tea Worldwide and a business segment of Sara Lee, sells to both the retail and the foodservice sectors around the world. In 2000 the company completed the acquisition of the Chock Full o' Nuts coffee brand, which had annual sales of US$350 million. Sara Lee also purchased the Hills Brothers, MJB, and Chase & Sanborn roast and ground coffee brands from Nestlé USA Inc., a business that generated about US$280 million in annual revenues. The company holds the top position in coffee sales in Brazil and several European countries, and its Superior Coffee is the leader in the U.S. foodservice market. Following the acquisition of Hills Brothers, the company had the third best selling coffee in the U.S. retail sector. Sara Lee's European coffee brand is Douwe Egberts, and its South American brands are Caboclo, Cafe do Ponto, and Pilao. Its SENSEO coffee pod system, sold throughout Europe and in the United States, brews single servings of frothy-style coffee. The company reported net sales totaling US$12.88 billion in 2009 with 33,000 employees.

The Procter & Gamble Company. The Procter & Gamble Company started in 1837 as a manufacturer of candles and soap. With the acquisition of the Folger Coffee Company in the 1960s, Procter & Gamble applied its aggressive and extensive marketing and advertising strategies to its new brand to make it one of the world's most popular coffees. By 2002, Folgers had overtaken Maxwell House as the top U.S. coffee brand. According to company statistics, Americans drink 85 million cups of Folgers coffee each day. Procter & Gamble posted total corporate sales of US$78.9 billion in 2010. In 2010, the company reported 127,000 employees working in 80 countries worldwide.

J.M. Smuckers announced plans to buy Folgers from Proctor & Gamble in a U.S. $2.95 billion all-stock deal. Folgers would become the tenth number one brand in the Smucker's stable. With the deal, Smuckers would nearly double its size.

MAJOR COUNTRIES IN THE INDUSTRY

World coffee production is estimated between 110 and 120 million bags per year, with coffee shops making up the fastest growing industry within the restaurant business, with a 7 percent annual growth rate. Over 53 countries grow coffee around the world, all of which are on or along the equator between the Tropic of Cancer and Capricorn, so, with the exception of Hawaii and Puerto Rico, no coffee is actually grown within the United States or its territories. An acre of coffee trees can produce up to 10,000 pounds of coffee cherries, or approximately 2,000 pounds of beans after they are hulled and milled.

Brazil. For two centuries, Brazil has been the world's leading producer and exporter of coffee. As of the early

years of the 2000s, the country accounted for about a third of global coffee production each year. Exports in 2004-05 totaled 27.2 million 60-kilo bags, up from 24.8 million bags in the previous year. Hit by the overproduction crisis of the late 1990s and early 2000s, Brazil aggressively promoted domestic consumption, resulting in a doubling of the country's internal market. By the early 2000s, more than half of Brazil's coffee crop was consumed domestically. Brazil also took steps to boost consumption in foreign markets. To increase coffee consumption in China, for example, the Brazilian Ministry of Agriculture in 2002 began a program establishing Chinese coffee chains based on the Starbucks model. By 2008, Nidi Nath Srinivas, in a June 22, 2008, *The Economic Times* article, claimed that Brazil had noticeably increased its coffee intake while consumer tastes matured and incomes rose. In 2010, it was projected that Brazil would produce 1.339 million tons, a noticeable decrease from its average production of 2.103 million tons.

Colombia. Traditionally the second largest coffee exporter, Colombia slipped to third place in the early years of the first decade of the 2000s behind Vietnam. In the mid-1970s, coffee comprised 50 percent of Colombia's legal export market. By the 1990s, this figure had plummeted to only 7 percent. With domestic consumption at only about half the world's per capita average, the Colombian coffee industry was particularly hard hit by the collapse of the export market. Starting in 2003, the industry launched several initiatives to increase coffee drinking in Colombia in hopes of raising domestic consumption from 1.4 to 2.8 million bags per year. In 2004-05, Colombia exported 10.66 million bags of coffee, barely above the 10.63 million bags exported the previous year. Colombia was projected to produce 747 million tons in 2010.

Vietnam. A relative newcomer to the world coffee market, Vietnam dramatically boosted production through the 1990s and by the early years of the first decade of the 2000s had overtaken Colombia as the second ranked coffee exporting nation. In 2001, Vietnam's coffee output reached a record high of 900,000 tons. In response to oversupply problems, however, Vietnam cut production to only 700,000 tons by 2003. At the same time, it shifted production to higher-value arabica beans. In 2003-04, Vietnam had overseas sales of 12.5 million bags, and in 2004-05, the country increased exports to 14.4 million bags. Coffee production projections for 2010 in Vietnam were 561 million tons.

According a June 22, 2008, article in *The Economic Times,* Nidi Nath Srinivas, reported that coffee had become an important way to protect personal wealth by 2008. Wealthier Vietnamese who could afford to hold coffee within the country, as opposed to selling it, found coffee took on a "quasi-currency status."

The United States. Although coffee consumption had declined significantly in the United States from 3.1 cups per day in 1962 to 1.6 cups per day in 1996, coffee consumption rebounded to 3.3 cups per day in 2000, while the size of the cup increased over time to an average nine ounces. According to a *Nation's Restaurant News* report of the National Coffee Association's (NCA) annual survey, coffee consumption hit an all-time high in the United States in 2000 when 79 percent of adults, or 161 million people, indicated that they drank coffee. Approximately 54 percent consumed coffee on a regular basis, while 25 percent were occasional drinkers. NCA also found that about 18 percent of coffee drinkers consumed gourmet coffee on a daily basis. *DSN Retailing Today* reported that in the United States, retail coffee sales reached US$18.5 billion in 2000. The U.S. market remained flat in 2003, however, with a slight decline in volume sales offset by an increase in coffee prices. In 2009, according to the ICO, Americans consumed an average of 4 kilograms of coffee annually per capita, or about 400 million cups a day.

Gourmet coffees were increasing in popularity at the beginning of the 2010s. For approximately US$15, River Maiden Artisan Coffee customers can sip one of the world's finest coffees. Customers at the Vancouver, Washington, site reportedly believe the high price for Panama Esmeralda Especial Reserva is worth it.

The United Kingdom. The U.K. coffee market was dominated by instant coffee, which accounted for nearly 90 percent of consumption in the early years of the first decade of the 2000s. Nestlé held a 57.9 percent market share in the instant coffee market in 1994. While ground coffee has traditionally been a very weak seller in the United Kingdom, the 1990s saw a strong increase in ground coffee sales. Between 1992 and 1996, ground coffee consumption rose by 53 percent. In 1997 the United Kingdom consumed US$154 million worth of ground coffee and US$1.2 billion worth of instant coffee, according to estimates by *Market Intelligence.*

At the start of the twenty-first century, Britons consumed more coffee (generally soluble coffee) than tea outside the home with consumption at 0.5 kg of coffee per person annually, substantially less than many other European countries. Sweden, for example, consumes almost 9 kg per person each year, according to BBC News. While the number of coffee bars continued to increase steadily, with eight times more coffee bars in Scotland alone in 2000 than in the mid-1990s, there was still considerable room for market penetration. The BBC News reported that in 2000, there was real estate space

available for 1,500 coffee houses across the United Kingdom, but with less than half of the sites in use, "it is felt there is a long way to go before the U.K. sees a coffee house on every corner, like some continental countries."

In June 2008, Polly Vernon wrote in *The Observer* about her coffee habit while working in the United Kingdom. Vernon reported that more than 8 million fair trade hot drinks were consumed each day. It was further acknowledged that fair trade made up only 5 percent of the U.K. coffee market and 20 percent of the market for roast and ground coffees. Approximately 294 fair trade coffee products were available in British shops and supermarkets, as well as on Virgin Trains and Ryanair.

Japan. Although coffee consumption was almost nonexistent in Japan as late as the 1950s, by 2000 the country became the third largest importer of coffee behind the United States and Germany. In 2004, imports reached 7.1 million bags of coffee, while per capita consumption totaled 3.36 kilograms. Japan's fondness for coffee arose out of increased "Westernization" of consumer trends, an overall increase in living standards, the popularity of instant (soluble) coffee, the increased accessibility of coffee makers for home use, and the emergence of chic coffee bars as places for young people to socialize. While consumption of coffee outside the home accounted for approximately 20 percent of consumption, in-home consumption was the largest and fastest growing coffee trend, with soluble coffee leading the segment. More than half of Japanese coffee consumption occurred in the home, and as regular coffee sales increased this was expected to rise. Another popular form of coffee in Japan was canned, ready-to-drink (RTD) coffee, both hot and cold, which made up about one-third of the Japanese coffee market.

China. Chinese interest in Western culture has increased interest in coffee drinking in that country, which is regarded by some analysts as a potential gold mine of untapped customers. As in many countries with a history of tea drinking, instant coffee was the most popular type of coffee sold in China. Since the mid-1980s, the coffee market in China has nearly doubled every two years, and analysts projected that volume sales will grow by 70 percent between 2003 and 2008.

Although prospects for growth in China were appealing, coffee sales made up a minuscule portion of the country's total drinks market at the beginning of the first decade of the 2000s. According to various estimates, mainland China consumed annually about 1,500 cups of tea per capita, compared to only 1.2 cups of coffee per capita. Consumption of roast ground coffee in China was so low that it was difficult to measure. Nestlé's Nescafé brand led the Chinese coffee market in the early 1990s, ahead of Kraft's Maxwell House brand. Coffee shops, Internet cafés, and fast food restaurants accounted for most coffee sales. China's trade policies also have impeded the availability of coffee. The country established a 40 percent tariff for unroasted coffee imports and a 60 percent tariff for roasted coffee. Since China became a member of the World Trade Organization, many expected the market to further open.

BIBLIOGRAPHY

"Brazil to Establish Coffee Chain Stores in China." *Peoples Daily,* 5 July 2002. Available from www.china.org.cn.

Chhabria, Vishal. "Nourishing Gains." *Business Standard,* 23 June 2008. Available from www.business-standard.com.

"Coffee House Market Bubbling." BBC News, 1 September 2000. Available from news.bbc.co.uk.

Colihan, Kelley. "Coffee's Aroma Stirs the Brain." WebMD, 13 June 2008. Available from www.webmd.com.

Ensor, James. "Eastern Europe—A Tough, But Strategic, Nut to Crack." *Grocer,* 16 November 1996: 52.

Flamm, Matthew. "Roaster Redux." *Crain's New York Business,* 9–15 April 2001: 17-18.

Harris, Brian. "Coffee Market Perking Up, but Growers Still Smarting and Cautious." *The Miami Herald,* 22 November 2004.

Hornblower, Margot. "Wake Up and Smell the Protest." *Time,* 17 April 2000: 58.

International Coffee Organization. "Coffee Market Report," 2009. Available from www.ico.org.

———. "ICO Indicator Prices Monthly and Annual Averages 1999 to 2002," February 2002. Available from www.ico.org.

———. "Press Release: International Coffee Agreement, New Initiatives," 1 October 2001. Available from www.ico.org.

Kirschbaum, Erik. "Starbucks Says International Growth to Cushion U.S. Weakness." Reuters U.K., 16 June 2008. Available from www.uk.reuters.com.

Kraft Foods. *2009 Annual Report.* Available from www.kraft.com.

"Kroger to Sell Mission Grounds Coffee at Metro Atlanta Stores." MissionGrounds.com, 18 June 2008. Available from www.prnewschannel.com

Larkin, Stephanie. "Coffee Consumption Around the World." *Food,* 4 May 2008. Available from goarticles.com.

Luxner, Larry. "Brimming with Optimism." *Tea & Coffee Trade Journal,* 20 January 2002: 51-5.

Madeley, John. "Coffee Price Rise Is Just a Hill of Beans." *Observer,* 4 April 2004. Available from www.ico.org.

Nestlé SA. "Coffee at Nestlé: A Presentation by Olle B. Tegstam, Head of Coffee & Beverages Strategic Business Unit," 25 October 2001. Available from www.ir.Nestle.com.

———. *2009 Annual Report.* Available from www.Nestle.com.

Philip Morris Companies Inc. *2009 Annual Report.* Available from www.philipmorris.com.

Ruggless, Ron. "Better Latte than Ever: Coffee Players Perked Up Over Sales." *Nation's Restaurant News,* 12 February 2001.

Sara Lee/DE. *Annual Report, 2009.* Available from www.saralee-de.com.

Smith, Tony. "Difficult Times for Coffee Industry as Demand Falls." *New York Times,* 25 November 2003.

"Smuckers Bids for Folgers." *Detroit Free Press,* 5 June 2008.

Sorby, Kristina. "Coffee Market Trends." Background paper to "Toward More Sustainable Coffee." World Bank Agricultural Technology Note 30, June 2002. Available from lnweb18.worldbank.org.

Srinivas, Nidhi Nath. "Smell the Coffee." *The Economic Times,* 22 June 2008.

Tetzler, Christy. "$15 for a Cup of Coffee?" 16 June 2008. Available from www.9news.com..

United Nations. "Medium-Term Prospects for Agricultural Commodities." Food and Agricultural Organization, Economic & Social Development Department. Available from www.fao.org.

U.S. Agency for International Development. "USAID's Response to the Global Coffee Crisis." Available from www.usaid.gov.

U.S. Department of Agriculture. Foreign Agricultural Service. "Coffee Update," December 2001. Available from www.fas.usda.gov.

———. *Tropical Products: World Markets and Trade,* June 2003. Available from www.fas.usda.gov.

Vernon, Polly. "I've Spent How Much on Coffee?" *The Observer,* 22 June 2008.

Worldwide Coffee Statistics; Coffee-Statistics.Com. Available from www.coffee-statistics.com.

SIC 2070

FATS AND OILS

NAICS CODE(S)

311225. Industry firms extract and process a variety of fats and oils, mostly for use in human foods and animal feed. Major production categories include cottonseed oils, soybean oils, other vegetable oils, animal fats and oils, and margarine, shortening, and related products. (Production of butter, however, is not included under this topic.)

INDUSTRY SNAPSHOT

In the middle years of the twenty-first century's first decade, global supplies of fats and oils were sufficient to meet steadily increasing world demand. According to analysis of the Food and Agricultural Organization (FAO) of the United Nations, production of oil-bearing crops increased by 4 percent worldwide in 2005. World consumption of oilseeds rose steadily through the 1990s, reaching 347 million metric tons (mmt) in 2004. Of this total, about 288 million metric tons (mmt) were expected to be crushed for oil or oilmeal.

Growing demand in developing countries was expected to account for more than 60 percent of this increase. Soy and palm oil consumption was expected to increase the most, while use of sunflower seed oil was likely to decrease. Use of non-edible oils was also expected to rise, most notably for the production of biodiesel fuels.

Global trade in oilseeds and oilseed products experienced astronomical growth in the late twentieth century, due largely to expanded production of soybeans. Trade in oilseeds, cakes, and meals increased almost 900 percent from 1964 to 2004, while the global market for vegetable oils during the same period grew by a stunning 1,800 percent. While trade slowed in 2004, it picked up again in 2005. Most of the increase, according to the UN's Food and Agricultural Organization (FAO), could be attributed to palm oil, with trade in soybean and rapeseed oils also increasing. The market for sunflower seed and ground seed oils, however, diminished. Although the United States and the European Union have historically led world production, much of the industry's recent expansion came from developing markets in Asia. India, Indonesia, and Malaysia, in particular, are expected to continue to lead worldwide market expansion, both in terms of production and consumption. By the late 1990s, Malaysia had already become the world's largest edible oil producer because of its prodigious output of palm oil. By 2005, the world's seven top exporters of oils and fats accounted for 82 percent of global import needs, and the FAO expected this concentration to continue.

Consumers worldwide continued to shift from high-cholesterol animal and marine oils to lower-cholesterol vegetable oils. While vegetable oil output increased 60 percent from 1970 to 1980, animal and marine oil production only grew by 9 percent and actually started to decline in the 1990s. In addition, consumers also began to bypass oils high in saturated fat, such as tropical oils, and choose those with low levels of saturated fat, like olive and canola oil. Consumers' desire to have low fat and low cholesterol alternatives for their diets was a major motivator in research efforts. Americans, in particular, wanted to reduce the fat in their diets without sacrificing taste or texture. Consumers also wanted to avoid eating trans fats, often used to cook French fries, chips, and other popular snack foods, and also used in the production of baked goods such as cookies and muffins. Manufacturers responded by announcing changes in their ingredient lists. Frito Lay, for example, announced in 2005 that it was the first U.S. company to completely eliminate trans fats from its major snack brands.

ORGANIZATION AND STRUCTURE

Most fat and oil products (more than 60%) of this industry are produced and consumed domestically. Although many nonfood uses for fats and oils have been discovered, the vast majority (about 80%) of the industry's production in the mid-years of the first decade of

the 2000s was still for human or animal consumption. In the United States, for example, salad and cooking oils accounted for 50 percent of all vegetable oil production. Another 40 percent is used in baking or frying, and almost 10 percent is used to produce margarine. Notwithstanding the negative health connotations associated with consumption of fats and oils, these substances constitute one of the three primary nutrients. Also, because fats carry more than twice as much energy as the other two groups, proteins and carbohydrates, they have been characterized as "nature's storehouse of energy." (A gram of fat contains nine calories compared to four calories per gram in carbohydrates and proteins.) In many cultures, the consumption of rich fatty foods is considered a sign of affluence. Not surprisingly, per-capita consumption of edible fats and oils in developed countries outstripped that of developing nations by a three-to-one margin. In developing countries, according to the U.S. Department of Agriculture (USDA), for every 1 percent increase in income, consumers will spend an additional 0.55 percent on fats and an additional 0.4 percent on oils. By the early years of the first decade of the 2000s, per capita consumption of edible fats and oils in both developed and developing countries was on the rise. The FAO projected that world consumption of oils and fats would grow by 2.8 percent annually in developing countries (compared to 1.8 percent growth in developed countries) through 2010. Developing countries were expected to capture 62 percent of the market during that period, up from a 60 percent share in 2004.

Industry output can be classified according to its sources (animal or vegetable), its products (mealcake, fat, or oil), and its uses (food or nonfood). Fat and oil meal cakes can be consumed as fodder by animals or used as fertilizer. Cottonseed oil, soybean oil, and vegetable oil mills produce oil for purposes other than human consumption such as animal feed. Oil from these mills only constitutes about 1.3 percent of the world's total fats and oils output. Other businesses produce animal and fish mealcake, greases, and fats. The mealcake can be used as fodder or in manufacturing but not as food for humans. Crude animal fats and vegetable oils are processed for human consumption by manufacturers and include shortenings, table oils, margarines, and other edible fats and oils. Production is subject to the vagaries of the seasons, the weather, and demand.

The markets for cottonseed oil, soybean oil, and vegetable oil mills are driven by the highly volatile demand for animal feed. Since livestock producers have a wide variety of feedstock from which to choose, they are very sensitive to price. By extension, demand for oil cakes and meals is also driven by the amount and variety of demand for meats. The primary factors driving demand for edible fats and oils are price, consumer health concerns, product innovation, and international trade regulations. Heavy outlays for advertising and promotion of the top branded edible fats and oils also characterize this industry segment. These concerns have influenced the evolution of large consumer products companies that have the financial wherewithal to compete effectively.

There are three basic steps in the production of fats and oils: growing, processing, and refining. Some companies only process and refine oil, while others are vertically integrated and perform all three tasks. Although most modern processors use solvents to remove oil from seeds, they are nonetheless referred to in the literature as "crushers," in reference to the historical pressing method. Refiners, who process vegetable oil or crude animal fats, use techniques such as bleaching, filtering, deodorizing, and/or hydrogenating to extract oil. Many companies in this industry group are subsidiaries or divisions of major consumer products conglomerates.

There was destined to be a 5 to 15 percent increase in the cost of processed food products, according to an August 2009 article published by *The Economic Times.* It was noted that prices had been rising for key ingredients including edible oils and wheat flour. Sharp increases in processed food products pricing, however, would undoubtedly result in consumers purchasing less of the items. Pickwick Hygienic Products General Manager Madhav Damle additionally admitted the wafer biscuit company had increased prices for some products in August 2009, a mere two months after raising prices for same items.

Healthy eating chef, author, columnist, and consultant Steve Petusevsky, formerly director of Creative Food Development for Whole Foods Market, the nation's largest natural/organic retail market chain, wrote that there were more than 100 types of oils available, making cooking options "confusing and even daunting." Some terms such as "light" were not used correctly to give potential users a completely accurate picture. Furthermore, during travels, Petusevsky discovered rules for using extra virgin olive oil differed from actual practices of cooks in the Mediterranean. Uncommon oils highly suggested for being worth trying included nut and tea oils.

Nonfood oils. Cottonseed oil mills. This industry segment includes companies that manufacture cottonseed oil, cake, meal, and linters, or process purchased cottonseed oil into forms other than edible cooking oils. In 2004 global cottonseed cake output stood at 26.4 million metric tons (mmt). Production in the United States reached 1.8 mmt in 1994, but declined steadily through the late 1990s and early years of the first decade of the 2000s.

Until the early nineteenth century, unplanted cottonseed was considered a health hazard because it

contained the poisonous pigment gossypol. But after 1833, when the first successful cottonseed oil mill was launched, the southern United States soon became the industry's largest producer and consumer. Cottonseed was a leading product in the global fats and oils industry, but production fell steadily in the late twentieth century. In the early 1990s, rapeseed supplanted cottonseed as the second most produced oil cake in the world. Cottonseed cake constitutes the majority of this industry segment's production. It is usually used as a high-protein supplement to livestock and poultry feed. Virtually all crude cottonseed oil is refined into salad or cooking oil, but low grades of the substance are sometimes used in the manufacture of lubricants, paint, and soap. Linters—short cotton fibers extracted from cottonseeds before they are crushed—are used to make sterile absorbent cotton and in the manufacture of paper, film, explosives, plastics, and rayon.

Soybean oil mills. This portion of the industry includes manufacturers that produce soybean oil, cake, meal, and soybean protein isolates and concentrates or process purchased soybean oil into something other than edible cooking oils. Throughout most of the twentieth century, soybean meal and oil constituted the most important segment of the fats and oils industry. The soybean originated in Asia, where it was used for many centuries as a high-protein diet staple. It was developed commercially in the United States, where it was first planted in the early nineteenth century. The legume languished as a horticultural oddity until the introduction of three new Japanese varieties in the early twentieth century. The development of an oil-deodorizing process in the early 1930s and the rising demand for edible oil during World War II promoted the use of soybean oil in margarine, shortening, salad oil, mayonnaise, and other food products (however, such food uses are not considered part of this segment).

Soybean cake (crush) and meal are the main output of this industry segment. Global production of soybean meal grew from 116.48 million metric tons (mmt) in 2001 to approximately 137 mmt in 2005. Soybean cake output rose from 146.91 mmt to 174.29 mmt during the same period. U.S. production of soy cake remained relatively stable through the early years of the 2000s' first decade, reaching about 45 mmt in 2005. U.S. production of soybean meal, which reached 35.73 mmt in 2001 but fell to 32.95 mmt in 2004, grew to approximately 36 mmt in 2005. The oil cake is used primarily as an animal feed, but the development of isolated soy proteins has the potential to open up a vast consumer market as a high-protein supplement to the human diet. These products, which are essentially flavorless yet consist of 90 percent protein, can be used as dietary supplements or as replacements for dairy products and eggs. They are also used as emulsifiers and binders in meat products, as well as meat and milk substitutes. The very small percentage of crude soybean oil that is not processed into food is used in chemical products, mainly in the resins and plastics industries.

Other vegetable oil mills. This industry segment comprises companies that manufacture vegetable oils, cake, and meal (with the exception of corn, cottonseed, and soybean) or process such vegetable oils into forms other than edible cooking oils. This industry segment produces the meals and inedible oils of sunflower seeds, peanuts (sometimes called "groundnuts"), linseeds, rapeseeds (canola), coconuts (or copra), and palm. World production of oil cake, according to FAO statistics, topped 250.1 mmt in 2004. Oilseed cake and meal production in the United States fluctuated substantially in the 1990s, reaching 811.8 mmt in 1993 and falling to 160.1 mmt in 2000. Output for 2001 was projected at 260.9 mmt. Production of oilseed crush was projected at 48.7 mmt for 2005, with meal production expected to reach 37.6 mmt. Like soybeans and cottonseeds, the meals of these oilseeds are also used for livestock feed and fertilizer.

While the vast majority of these seeds' oils are refined for human consumption (see below), there are notable exceptions that fall into this industry category. Virtually all linseed oil, for example, is used in the production of resins, plastics, paint, and varnish. Rapeseed oil that contains high levels of erucic acid (a known carcinogen) is used in steel and iron production. Coconut, olive, and palm oils are used in the manufacture of soap, paint, varnish, and fatty acids.

Animal fats and oils. This industry segment includes companies that produce animal oils (including fish oil and other marine animal oils) and fish and animal meal, together with those rendering inedible stearin, grease, and tallow from animal fat, bones, and meat scraps. At just 3.93 mmt of global annual production, fish and animal meals constituted only about 7 percent of the world's total meal output. The primary products of this industry segment are high protein sources of feed for fisheries and livestock. Tallow (rendered cattle fat) is marketed as both an edible and inedible product. The inedible product is derived from inedible slaughterhouse and locker plant byproducts, from fat trimmings collected from retail butchers and institutions, and from dead or condemned animals. It is used mostly in the production of animal feed, fatty acids, and soap.

Oils from fish and marine animals fall into three general categories: fish liver oils, fish body oils, and other marine animal oils. Cod liver oil is a well known example of the first type of oil. Fish body oils, known in the industry as menhaden, are used in the production of

paint, linoleum, leather, and other products. They are also used in the production of margarine in Europe and Canada. Fish meal, another by-product of fish processing, constitutes a small but growing proportion of the market for livestock feedstuffs.

Edible oils. Often referred to as edible fats and oils, this is the most important category in the fats and oils industry. It constitutes 98 percent of all fats and oils produced worldwide and 59 percent of the industry group as a whole. This category encompasses the refined products of edible fats and oils, namely, shortening, salad and cooking oils, and margarine. These products may be made from soybean oil, cottonseed oil, sunflower seed oil, peanut oil, rapeseed (canola) oil, coconut oil, palm oil, or olive oil, as well as animal and marine oils and fats. Some of the products are sold in bulk to food service institutions and food manufacturers, and some quantities are sold on the consumer market.

The manufacturing of shortening, cooking oils, and margarine requires full or partial hydrogenation of refined vegetable oil. This process helps prevent rancidity and converts some fats from liquid to semi-solid or solid forms for particular food uses. Although soybean oil is the most widely hydrogenated oil, cottonseed, corn, sunflower, and other oils or fats also undergo the process. Notwithstanding its widespread use, hydrogenation came under fire in the early 1990s when medical research linked use of hydrogenated oils (especially margarine) to increased incidence of heart attack.

Vegetable oils. Global production of vegetable oils and fats exceeded 100.5 mmt in 2004 and was projected to rise. Vegetable oils, including soybean, sunflower seed, peanut, cottonseed, rapeseed, and olive oils, constitute the most important segment of this category, contributing over half of the edible oil production in the mid-years of the first decade of the 2000s. Soybean oil, which is used on its own and in combination with others to make a variety of products, continued to dominate this category. Production of edible soybean oil totaled 30 mmt in 2004, or more than one-fourth of all edible fats and oils. Growth of both production and consumption of soybean oil lagged the industry overall for the last third of the twentieth century. The net result of this trend was that soybean oil's contribution to total oil production declined from 35 percent in 1970 to 30 percent in 1985 and 21 percent in 1997. Other oils clearly made inroads into its share during this period.

Perhaps the most aggressive growth in the industry was enjoyed by palm oil. From the late 1980s to 1997, production increased 70 percent, accounting for 19 percent of the global output and catapulting the product to rank second only to soybean oil. By 2004, production exceeded 31 mmt, and further growth was expected. The primary force driving this rapid expansion was the burgeoning demand in the huge, and as yet largely untapped, markets of Asia. In addition, palm yields a high percentage of oil per hectare, roughly 10 times the yield of soybeans, and requires only low production and refining costs. Malaysia and Indonesia are the largest producers and exporters of palm oil.

Rapeseed (canola) oil, which grew at an average of 10.5 percent annually in the 1980s, was another challenger to soy oil's traditional dominance. The seed's low levels of saturated fats appealed to consumer health concerns, with consumption growing fastest in North America and northern Europe. Through the early years of the first decade of the 2000s, canola oil ranked third in global production of major vegetable oils, with outputs reaching a 16 mmt in 2005.

Sunflower seed oil was another high-potential commodity, especially popular in Europe. While its growth rate, at 4.7 percent per year in the 1980s and less than 1 percent in the 1990s, was far below that of canola and palm, sunflower seed oil was the fourth highest produced oil in the world in 2005, with a projected 8.78 mmt.

Olive oil enjoyed rising popularity in the early years of the first decade of the 2000s as well. Although production levels constituted only 2.5 percent of global edible fats and oils, they increased by over 50 percent to 2.5 mmt in 1997 alone as consumers around the world discovered its low levels of saturated fat and its unique flavor. By 2004, global production exceeded 3 mt for the first time in history. The vast majority came from the European Union, with an output of almost 2.5 mt. Spain produced about 1.4 mt, while Greece produced almost 370,000 tons.

Margarine. Many combinations of the edible animal and vegetable fats and oils discussed above are used to manufacture margarine (also known as oleomargarine), a key product of this industry. It was invented in 1869 by a French chemist named H. Mége-Mouriés, at the behest of Napoleon III. After initial resistance to the product—especially and predictably from dairy interests—margarine production expanded rapidly in Europe, North America, and eventually to most of the world. Consumer protection concerns prompted most countries to require that the fat content of margarine be at least 80 percent and that water not exceed 16 percent by weight. Rising health concerns about dietary fat gave rise to a growing array of low and no-fat "margarines" that were subsequently more correctly classified as "table spreads." U.S. production of margarine fell from 2.69 million pounds in 1991 to 2.39 million pounds in 2000. Domestic consumption also fell. In 1999, per capita consumption was 10.6 pounds; by 2003, this figure had fallen to 8.3 pounds.

Concerns about health problems related to *trans* fatty acids, which occur in partially hydrogenated fats such as margarine, may have contributed to this decline. Starting in 2006, food manufacturers were to be required by the U.S. Food and Drug Administration (FDA) to label *trans* fat content separately from other fat content on product nutrition labels. Manufacturers began to research and develop alternative types of margarines with reduced levels of trans fats, or with no trans fats at all. There was general consensus that the manufacture of low fat products would continue to grow, given consumer demand and cost savings (since the new products were expected to contain more water).

Shortening. Baking and frying fats (also called shortening) include both unmixed hydrogenated vegetable oils and compounds of hydrogenated vegetable oils with animal fats such as lard or tallow. In 2003, world production of margarine and shortening together totaled 13.1 mmt. That year, world exports of hydrogenated vegetable oils totaled 1.8 mmt.

BACKGROUND AND DEVELOPMENT

Fats and oils from animal and vegetable sources have been a primary source of energy for humans and animals since prehistoric times. Many ancient cultures also discovered nonfood uses for the substances; for example, in lamps. The Egyptians used oils and greases as lubricants, and the Greeks made soap from tallow and oil. While the Chinese developed a three-step pressing process that highly resembled modern oilseed crushing, many civilizations used a simple mortar and pestle to extract oil from seeds and fruits. The availability of certain fats and oils has greatly influenced the development of regional food ways. For example, Asian soybeans are used in the production of tofu and soymilk, and olive oil is a staple of Mediterranean cuisine.

However, it was not until the late eighteenth and early nineteenth centuries that insight into the chemical composition of oilseeds—and the invention of the hydraulic press—led to the commercial production of fats and oils. Most of the early discoveries were made in Europe. In 1779, Swedish chemist C. W. Scheele isolated glycerol from olive oil, and Michel-Eugéne Chevreul of France expanded on that work in the early 1800s. Later that century, the development of the hydrogenation process—which transformed liquid oils into solids—was a cornerstone of the modern vegetable oil and shortening industry. The expansion of the chemical industry after World War I led to the discovery of many new applications for fats and fatty acids, which in turn bolstered the market for fats, oils, and oilseed meals.

World trade in oilseeds and their products grew to become an important segment of the global agricultural industry, comprising 10 percent of total agricultural trade by the 1970s. Vertical and horizontal integration through mergers and acquisitions, typical of many modern industries, have resulted in a highly globalized fats, oils, and oil cake market. Most of the leading companies have affiliates around the world and are often part of a larger consumer products company. Although the industry in general is highly automated and centralized, some segments (for example, olive oil) are characterized by small production facilities.

Global production of oil meal between 1992 and 1998 rose by about 21 percent to 156.2 mmt, according to the USDA's Economic Research Service (ERS). The ERS estimated that the worldwide output of edible oil reached 75.5 mmt in 1998, up 23 percent from 61.3 mmt in 1992. Cross-border trade of oil meal totaled an estimated 52.1 mmt in 1998, up from 42.4 mmt in 1992, according to the ERS. Meanwhile, the ERS estimated that international edible oil trade grew to 30.6 mmt in 1998, up from about 22.0 mmt in 1992.

Through the early years of the first decade of the 2000s, the oil meal segment continued expanding, reaching 175.7 mmt in 2005. Global oil meal trade also climbed. According to FAO statistics, global exports of oilseed cake and meals was more than US$23.4 billion in 2003, while trade in edible oils reached about US$3 billion. FAO analysts expected consumption of fats and oils to expand most rapidly in newly industrialized countries. Demand for oil meals was expected to grow steadily through the first decade of the 2000s. Global consumption increased about 22 to 24 percent from 1992 to 1998 and was expected to continue to grow, according to the ERS.

World production of major oilseed crops, according to USDA figures, grew from 314.23 million metric tons (mmt) in 2001 to a projected 382.79 mmt in 2005. The largest crop by far was soybeans, at 219.23 mmt in 2005, followed by rapeseed (45.55 mmt), cottonseed (45.12 mmt), peanut (33.44 mmt), and palm kernel (8.74 mmt). Expansion was expected to accelerate. Most of this increase was expected to come from developing countries, especially in South America and Asia. Significant growth in oil production was also expected in China and India, where improvements in extraction facilities had increased output of oils.

In 2005, global oil cake (crush) production was broken down as follows: soybean cake, 174.29 mmt; rapeseed (canola) cake, 40.72 mmt; cottonseed cake, 32.46 mmt; sunflower seed cake, 21.73 mmt; groundnut (peanut) cake, 15.82 mmt; and palm kernel cake, 8.64 mmt. World production of soybean oil reached 32.09 mmt, just ahead of palm oil, at 31.13 mmt. However, combined palm oil production—including palm kernel oil output of 3.76 mmt—exceeded that of soybean oil.

Rapeseed oil totaled 15.6 mmt, while ground nutoil was 5.03 mmt and cottonseed oil was 4.69 mmt.

Since 1980, palm oil production and consumption have increased dramatically to make this the world's second largest vegetable oil segment. In addition, palm oil was the most traded oil, reaching 22.68 mmt in 2001. Global exports of palm oil topped 20.8 mmt in 2003, while exports of palm kernel oil were 1.6 mmt. That year, the world exported more than 10 mmt of soybean oil.

Asia since the late 1990s has increased its own production capacities for fats and oils, necessitating fewer imports. By the early years of the first decade of the 2000s, however, substantial growth in Asian economies boosted both demand production. The FAO estimated that Southeast Asia would remain a primary importer of oilseed meals throughout the mid-years of the decade.

CURRENT CONDITIONS

One of the significant issues in the mid-years first decade of the twenty-first century regarding fats and oils was health concerns. In response to these concerns, many restaurants in the United States became "trans-fat free," including Kentucky Fried Chicken, Wendy's, Ruby Tuesday, California Pizza Kitchen, and Taco Bell. McDonald's had vowed to replace its trans-fat cooking oils in 2002, but it was not until 2007 that the company found a substitute that would retain the desired flavor and texture of its French fries. Some changes were taking place in Europe as well. European president of McDonald's Denis Hennequin stated that a new cooking oil (a mixture of rapeseed and sunflower) with lower trans fat levels will be used in the McDonald's outlets beginning in 2008. According to *Oils & Fats International,* despite the rally against trans fats in the United States, many fast food places that do continue to use trans fat oils have not lost business. Trans oils are so common in Americans' diets, in fact, that the average individual consumes 4.7 pounds a year. According to ERS data, Amercians' intake of fats and oils has increased 63 percent since 1970.

Despite the questionable health status of the actual products, the fats and oils industry remained healthy in the United States in the mid-years of the first decade of the 2000s. According to the USDA, agricultural exports were expected to reach an all-time high in the latter part of the decade. Two-thirds of the increase was attributed to the grain and oilseed sectors. One of the trends responsible for the rise in oilseed exports was a slower production growth rate of oilseed in South America.

Another notable trend mid-decade was the use of oils to produce biodiesel fuel. Biodiesel, an alternative fuel that is derived from fats and is biodegradable and non-toxic, can be used in standard diesel engines with little or no modification. Europe is the largest producer of bio-diesel fuel, with an output in 2005 estimated at between 2.4 and 2.6 million tons. According to private sector estimates cited by the FAO, between 10 and 15 percent of EU vegetable oil production in 2005 was destined for biodiesel. *Energy Bulletin* reported that biodiesel processing consumed nearly 50 percent of EU rapeseed oil production in 2005. The ERS estimates this level at about 30 percent. Though biodiesel is seen as an affordable means of reducing world dependence on petroleum, it is not without its critics, who charge that it is unethical to use food products to run machines.

Environmental Leader, "The Executive's Daily Green Briefing," shared news reported in the *New Zealand Herald* featuring a consumer protest response action taken by Cadbury New Zealand. The company decided to curtail its usage of palm oil in dairy milk chocolate products. Originally, palm oil usage was instituted as a cost-saving measure. The response, however, led Cadbury to become aware of environmentalist views about palm oil production damaging rain forests. According to Mongaby.com, joint efforts of Cadbury and "Green groups" to develop palm oil production environmental standards were being called into question as well as other industry practices.

Concern about the high amount of trans fat in foods led to government regulation. In Canada, for example, mandatory labeling and other government efforts resulted in severe reductions in the amount of trans—fat usage or its elimination. According to an article posted on bclocalnews.com, high levels of trans fat were evident contributors to the heart disease related deaths of approximately 3,000 Canadians each year. Health Canada still claims some foods' tests results indicate high trans—fat content. Croissants in some cases had up to 43 percent trans fat. It was also difficult to gauge how much trans fat was in restaurant food where labels were not used. Furthermore, it was noted in the aforementioned article that "industrially produced trans fat give snacks and bakery products flavor, texture and freshness—and they are cheap to produce."

WORKFORCE

The majority of this manufacturing industry's employees are engaged in direct production. Others oversee finances, participate in management, and market the products. In general, the fats and oils industry is highly automated; labor costs for operations in the United States and Europe account for less than 20 percent of total costs. But in developing countries, where labor is far less expensive than technology, employment levels are higher. Vertical and horizontal integration throughout the global industry have also helped to raise productivity. These factors, combined with a modest growth rate in the industry overall, contributed to a generally shrinking rate of employment.

RESEARCH AND TECHNOLOGY

The fats and oils industry is research intensive. Most research and development expenditures focus on the development of new consumer products such as fat replacements. Biodiesel, an automotive fuel derived from vegetable oils and animal fats, had the potential to increase the nonfood aspect of animal and vegetable oil consumption. Most biodiesel progress was made in the United States, where a major processing plant was built in the 1990s. In 2003, the U.S. Department of Energy funded a joint research program with Cargill, a leading fats and oils company, to evolve technologies for developing chemicals and alternative fuels from oils. Environmental concerns also stimulated new waste-reducing initiatives, both in terms of production and packaging. In addition, fat and oil producers also researched ways of reducing the fat and cholesterol content of their edible oils in the middle to late 1990s in response to consumer demands, especially in the European Union and the United States. One notable product to reach the market was Procter & Gamble's Olestra, a controversial fat substitute introduced in the United States in 1996. The product, used initially in snack foods, is an engineered fat that cannot be digested like conventional fats and thus has no nutritional or caloric value. However, its passage through the digestive tract actually depletes certain beneficial substances such as vitamins, and consumption of Olestra can trigger digestive problems.

INDUSTRY LEADERS

Unilever. World leader Unilever, a British/Dutch conglomerate, was a major oilseed processor at the beginning of the twentieth century. In 1885, the company was founded in the United Kingdom by William Hesketh Lever to manufacture soap. It ventured into oilseed crushing in the early 1900s and began producing edible vegetable oils and margarines shortly thereafter. The company maintained its leading position in the industry and the food market in general through vertical integration, aggressive globalization (it had overseas operations as early as 1900), and many acquisitions. The company spent over US$5 billion on acquisitions in the late 1980s. In 1993, Unilever acquired olive oil manufacturer Bertolli from Italy's Fisvi for about US$90 million. The purchase added US$150 million in annual olive oil sales and 8.5 percent of that market to Unilever's existing 14 percent share. In the late 1990s, Unilever's oil products—margarine and olive oil—held some of the highest market shares in the industry worldwide. In 2000, Unilever became one of the world's top three food companies when it acquired Bestfoods (which included the brands Hellmann's and Skippy). As of the middle years of the first decade of the 2000s, Unilever owned the following brands, among others: Ben & Jerry's, Lipton, Bird's Eye, and Slim-Fast. The long-term goal, however, was to reduce the number of brands from 1,600 to about 400 in order to streamline the company and ensure efficiency and manageability. The company's overall sales totaled US$54.4 billion in 2006.

Bruce Horovitz, money and marketing reporter for *USA Today,* said there was a big change in store for some of Unilever's most popular brands. The company planned to change the recipes for its soft spread brands by eliminating partially hydrogenated oils. Those artificial trans fats had been present in "I Can't Believe It's Not Butter," "Shedd's Spread Country Crock" and other brands. According to the U.S. Food and Drug Administration, foods containing less than 0.5 grams of trans fat per serving can have a label of "0 grams of trans fat." Unilever's new recipes were set to include "a mixture of palm oil and interesterified fat or plant oil."

Archer Daniels Midland (ADM). Activities of the Archer Daniels Midland Company (ADM) are concentrated in the United States, Europe, South America, and, more recently, Asia. Founded in 1903, the firm earned a spot among top fat and oil producers by maintaining a focus on agriculture and investing in research, especially studies of textured soy protein. ADM manufactures oil from soybeans, sunflowers, canola, corn, and other oilseeds for home use and for further processing into margarine. As of 2004, two-thirds of Archer Daniels Midland's revenues came from oilseed products (especially soybean and peanut), including vegetable oils, animal feed, and emulsifiers. ADM generated revenues of US$70 billion for the fiscal year ending 30 June 2008. ADM has approximately 27,000 employees with more than 230 processing plants serving markets in more than 60 countries.

In May 2009, Archer Daniels Midland Company Chairman and CEO, Patricia Woertz, announced the introduction of "ADM Cares," which she described as an innovative program focusing on social investment via three areas: "strong roots," "strong communities," and "strong bonds." Woertz linked the three areas to basic human needs for growth. "Whether we are helping to make sure certain farm families stay safe, promoting education in ADMhometowns or protecting environmentally sensitive habitats, ADM will seek out partnerships and programs that help ensure the responsible, sustainable development of agriculture," Woertz stated.

ConAgra. Another U.S. company, ConAgra, ranked among the world's largest manufacturers of oilseed products in the mid-years of the first decade of the 2000s. ConAgra is also one of the largest food service manufacturers in the United States, providing poultry, French

fries, and dough-based products for the food service industry. Some of its brands include Banquet, Chef Boyardee, Egg Beaters, Healthy Choice, Hunt's, Jiffy, Orville Redenbacher's, PAM, Slim Jim, and Van Camp's. With total sales of more than US$14.5 billion in 2004, agricultural processing was a minority segment of the conglomerate's activities, which focused on production of prepared foods by the middle of the decade. ConAgra generated US$11.5 billion in sales in 2006 and had 33,000 employees.

Bunge Limited. Founded in 1818, Bunge became the world's leading oilseed processing company in 2003 with its acquisition of Cereol. The largest player in South America since the 1990s, the company further expanded its capacity in 2004 with the acquisition of a major crushing facility in Ukraine. Its placement near key transport facilities was expected to boost sales in Asian markets. Bunge is also the world's top seller of bottled vegetable oils, as well as Europe's primary producer of soybean meal. Bunge entered into a partnership with DuPont to create Solae, a top producer of soy protein products. Bunge is also a leading producer of canola seed, sunflower seed, wheat and corn. In 2008 Bunge reported total sales of more than US$52.6 billion and employed 24,787 workers.

MAJOR COUNTRIES IN THE INDUSTRY

The United States. The United States has historically led the global fats, oils, and oil cake industry, due primarily to its dominance in the largest oilseed category, soybeans. In 2003, the United States produced more than 40 percent of the world's total soybean crop and accounted for almost half of world soybean exports. Though production decreased in 2004, production in 2005 totaled 19.5 billion pounds. Other production that year included corn oil at 2.4 billion pounds, cottonseed oil at 983 million pounds, and peanut oil at 160 million pounds. The United States also ranked among the leading traders of fats and oils.

China. Ranking second in production in 2003 and the world's major market for oils and oilseed products, China was expected to boost total oilseed production from about 50.8 mmt in 2004 to 58.5 mmt in 2005. Demand for vegetable oils and oilmeal increased dramatically in China in the late 1990s and early years of the first decade of the 2000s. Consumption of edible oils grew by an unprecedented 60 percent between 1999 and 2000, while consumption of oil meal rose by 40 percent. Production of total oilcakes and meals reached 28.5 mmt in 2003. Soybean cake output rose impressively from 18.9 mmt in 2001 to a projected 29 mmt in 2005, while soy oil production was expected to total 5.17 mmt. By

2004 China's consumption was thought to account for almost 20 percent of world usage in this market. In 2004, imports of soybeans were estimated at 22 mmt (33 percent of world trade), and imports of vegetable oils were about 5 mmt (14 percent of world trade).

Brazil. Brazil was among several developing countries that emerged as competitors in the global oils and fats industry. Production continued to climb, reaching 23.8 mmt in 2003 and making Brazil the third-ranking country in total oil cake and meal output. Of this total, soybean cake accounted for 22.45 mmt and soybean oil production was 5.5 mmt. In 2004, production of oil cakes and meal exceeded 40.5 mmt.

Argentina. Argentina, which ranked sixth worldwide in 1998, rose to fourth place in 2003 after expanding its soybean production by 132.3 percent. Argentina's output of oil cake and meal grew further from 20.7 mmt in 2003 to 27.0 mmt in 2004. Exports of oilseed cake and meal, which increased 117.1 percent from 1996 to 2002, exceeded 19.8 mmt in 2003. Argentina is also a major producer of sunflower seeds and oil.

The European Union. Tied with China for total production in the late 1990s, the European Union (EU) slipped to fifth place in 2003. Production of oil cakes and meals that year exceeded 19.8 mmt, and production of vegetable oils and fats reached 10.6 mmt. FAO statistics place EU oil cake production for 2004 at 12.1 mmt. The EU's fat and oil industry grew slowly in the mid- to late 1990s as a result of its internal production quotas that limit the amount each country can produce. Nonetheless, the EU remained one of the leading producers of oil meal and edible oil, with prospects for significant growth after 2004, when former eastern-bloc countries became members. The entry of Poland, which joined the EU in May 2004, was expected to result in significant increases in rapeseed acreage and production. According to *FWN Financial News*, Poland's rapeseed harvest was expected to reflect growth by about 40 percent in 2005, while rapeseed meal production would increase about 23 percent. Rapeseed was the dominant oilseed crop by far in Europe, with production in 2005 projected at 14.65 mmt, followed by sunflower seed (3.7 mmt). The European Union also remained the world's leading producer of olive oil.

India. India's oil cake production surpassed 16.9 mmt in 2004, as the country ranked sixth in this segment. India also produced 6 mmt of edible oil in the same year. While India exported no edible oil, the country remained a major exporter of oil meal in the late 1990s with 4.1 mmt in 1998. In 2001 a variety of factors (the weakening

rupee against the U.S. dollar, declining world oil meal prices, and bumper crops) resulted in a substantial increase (almost 39% over 2000 totals) in oil meal exports for India. This boon to exports was much needed after sharp declines between 1998 and 2000 that came from the weakening Asian economy during that time.

Business Standard shared insights about India's vegetable oil status in observations from the Solvent Extractor's Association of India (SEA). Vegetable oil importation saw an increase of 4 percent in July 2009. Standouts during the edible oil year, spanning from September to October, were the palm group of oils with a share of 75 per cent.

Malaysia. In the early years of the first decade of the 2000s, Malaysia remained by far the world's leading producer of palm kernel oil. The country accounted for more than 52.8 percent of world production and, with Indonesia, for approximately 90 percent of world trade. From 2002 to 2003, Malaysia's production of palm oil grew 12.1 percent, reaching 13.1 mmt, while production of crude palm kernel oil, a non-edible product, grew by 11.6 percent to reach 1.64 mmt. In 2005 palm oil output reached 14.75 mmt. The country's burgeoning demand for soap and detergent was expected to increase consumption of crude palm kernel oil by 10 to 15 percent in 2004. Exports also increased. Total exports of palm oil, palm kernel oil and cake, oleochemicals, and finished products grew by 14.2 percent in 2003, totaling 16.78 mmt. In 2005 Malaysia exported 12.9 mmt of palm oil alone.

BIBLIOGRAPHY
Athale, Gouri Agley. "Processed foods to be costlier," 19 August 2009. Available from economic times.indiatimes.com.

Buckley, John. "Supply Hopes Pinned on Rebound in Soya." *Oils & Fats International*, September 2004.

"Bunge Moves East with Ukraine Venture." *Food Navigator Europe*, 18 March 2004. Available from www.foodnavigator.com.

Canadian Department of Agriculture and Agri-Food Canada. *Market Analysis: Overview: World Oilseed Sector and Canadian Marketing Opportunities*, 2 April 2004. Available from www.agr.gc.ca.

"Cottonseed Meal Comes Full Circle." *Southeast Farm Press*, 13 March 2007.

Food and Agriculture Organization of the United Nations. *FAOSTAT*, 2 April 2007. Available from www.fao.org.

Frumkin, Paul. "Trans Fat Future Revolves Around Alternative Oil Outlook." *Nation's Restaurant News*, 26 February 2007.

"Hoover's Company Capsules." *Hoover's Online*, 2009. Available from www.hoovers.com.

Horovitz, Bruce. "Unilever gets all the trans fat out of its margarines." Available from www.usatoday.com.

"India's veg oil import rises by 4 percent in July." 13 August 2009. Available from www.business-standard.com.

Lim, Serena. "Transforming the Food Industry." *Oil & Fats International*, 2 January 2007.

Low, Benjamin. "Biodiesel Boom Raises Ethical Issues." *Energy Bulletin,* 7 March 2005. Available from www.energybulletin.net.

McDonald's Set to be Trans Fat-Free." *The Food Institute Report,* 5 February 2007.

Peksa, Vlad, and Eszter Dargo. "Outlook for Edibles Oils Market." *Oils & Fats International,* May 2006.

Petusevsky, Steve. "The Essentials of Cooking Oils." 19 August 2009. Available from tampabay.com.

"Poland's Rapeseed Crop to Rise 40 Percent." *FWN Financial News,* 5 April 2004.

"Protests Push Cadbury to Drop Palm Oil from Milk Chocolate." 18 August 2009. Available from www.environmentalleader.com.

"Record Olive Oil Production." *Oils and Fats International,* January 2005. Available from www.oilsandfatsinternational.com.

"The skinny on trans-fats." 5 August 2009. Available from www.bclocalnews.com.

U.S. Department of Agriculture. "Crop Projection Update," 8 April 2004. Available from www.usda.gov.

———. *Oilseeds: World Markets and Trade,* April 2005. Available from www.usda.gov.

U.S. Department of Agriculture, Economic Research Service. *Oil Crops Outlook,* 11 April 2005. Available from www.ers.usda.gov.

"U.S. Food Consumption Up 16 Percent Since 1970." *Amber Waves,* November 2005.

"World Business News: U.S. Agricultural Exports Booming." *Farmers Guardian,* 16 March 2007.

SIC 2041

FLOUR AND OTHER GRAIN MILL PRODUCTS

NAICS CODE(S)

311211. Manufacturers in this industry mill flour or meal from various raw grains, excluding rice. The products of flour mills may be sold plain or in the form of prepared mixes or dough for specific purposes.

INDUSTRY SNAPSHOT

For the flour market (the primary end use of wheat), fluctuating wheat production imposes the most critical global ramifications. As of the mid-2000s, more than 60 percent of the world's wheat supply was converted to flour for making breads, biscuits, cakes, and other dough products. On a consumer level, flour and grain products constitute a substantial part of the world's staple diet, because they are basic ingredients of practically every meal consumed by the world's 6.8 billion people. Fluctuating wheat production statistics largely portend the amount of food consumption and, in many parts of the world, the

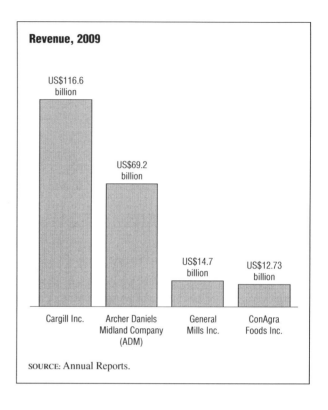

Revenue, 2009

US$116.6 billion — Cargill Inc.
US$69.2 billion — Archer Daniels Midland Company (ADM)
US$14.7 billion — General Mills Inc.
US$12.73 billion — ConAgra Foods Inc.

SOURCE: Annual Reports.

availability of food supply. The USDA estimates that the 2010 U.S. winter wheat crop totaled 1.458 billion bushels. In 2009, there were 960 million bushels of hard red winter wheat, 283 million bushels of soft red winter wheat, and 215 million bushels white winter wheat. The average yield is 45.9 bushels per acre. The volume of flour and its products consumed has declined in recent years, as more Americans reduced carbohydrates in their diet. Despite this, wheat is still one of the most valuable crops, and the US is the fourth-largest wheat producer in the world. Sixty pounds of wheat produces 60 pounds of whole wheat flour which can then be turned into 90 loaves of whole wheat bread. Sixty pounds of wheat can also be turned into 42 pounds of white flour, 42 loaves of white bread, 42 pounds of pasta, 45 boxes of wheat flake cereal, or 210 servings of spaghetti.

A key factor affecting companies' survival in the flour industry is the ability to compete within the ever-changing condition of wheat production and consumption worldwide. Companies must maintain the structural and financial stability to weather fluctuations in national currencies, weather-induced wheat shortages, and socio-economic realities that figure so prominently in the industry. Many companies struggling to reinforce their market foothold attempt to expand their flour-based operations by acquiring new products, diversifying current products, or tapping new investment sources. Insufficient knowledge of consumer tastes and failure to take a long-term approach invariably lead to costly lessons for some companies, particularly those attempting to penetrate foreign flour markets.

ORGANIZATION AND STRUCTURE

The flow of wheat from field to table relies on a multitude of factors. The quality of a bountiful wheat crop ripe for the flour market industry depends on mild weather that lacks the extremes of cold or heat, rain or drought, wind, snow, or hail. Flour's various end uses derive from the milling process. In some parts of the world, even as recently as the early 2000s, homemakers or local village millers still ground flour by crushing wheat between two stones or pounding wheat with a mortar and pestle. However, most modern mills employ sophisticated high-tech rollers, sifters, and purifiers for cleansing, grinding, separating, and blending wheat. Because individual flour mills normally grind only one wheat class prior to milling, several wheat varieties may be blended and tested. Hard wheats are primarily used for breads and rolls; soft wheats are used in sweet goods, crackers, and prepared mixes; and durum wheat is used in pasta noodles.

Two factors have largely determined flour utilization patterns: national food preferences (and the lifestyle changes in diet) and flour availability. Although wheat flour is the most popular, any grain can be converted to flour. Part of the universal appeal of wheat flour is that wheat cultivation adapts to a wide variety of climatic conditions. The global acceptance of wheat flour as a food staple resulted from its nutritional qualities. Wheat contains a unique protein called gluten. Mixed with water, gluten forms elastic dough capable of expanding to several times its original volume during baking. The smaller amount of gluten protein contained in rye flour produces better dark rye breads, or if blended with wheat flour, produces finer-textured light rye breads. Oat flour, the most nutritious flour, and oat meals are primarily used in breakfast food and granola-type products, while barley flour can be found in baby foods and malted milks. In some countries, large quantities of barley flour are used for bread making. Sorghum and millet flours are popular in India, Central America, and Ethiopia in the making of flat bread, tortillas, and pancakes. A small percentage of rice is converted to flour for use in baby foods and sauces. Buckwheat flour is often used in pancakes. Soybean technology has introduced soya flour and grits, which contain 50 percent protein and are adaptable to a variety of bakery products such as cereals, meat products, and soup mixes. Less appealing characteristics of soybean flour result from the multiplication of bacteria, especially during processing with steam and moisture. An excessively high bacterial count causes emission of off-odors and undesirable flavors. There has been continued research aimed to eliminate these adverse side effects.

All flour products must meet certain nutritional and cleanliness standards promulgated by various government agencies such as the U.S. Food and Drug Administration (FDA). The amount and type of additives, carbohydrates, protein, and other nutrients included in flour products derive from required nutritional and safety standards. By law, bread labeled "whole wheat" must be made from 100 percent whole wheat flour. U.S. legislation requiring truth-in-nutrition labeling mandates all food products to be labeled with a list of nutritional contents. The average composition of white flour includes 73.6 percent nitrogen-free extract and 13.5 percent water or other moisture. Millers can ill afford substandard products caused by too much or too little moisture, flour, or sugar, so most dough batches, under government controls, contain very small amounts of potassium bromate and other ingredients to enhance dough baking or other preservation qualities. Likewise, the differences between bleached and unbleached flour also affect color and baking quality: bleached flour adds to baking quality and color values while unbleached flour performs better for cookies, pie crusts, and crackers. Despite numerous changes in flour composition and uses, the U.S. public's preference for white flour for bread remains undiminished—probably a carry-over from past eras when white bread symbolized a status befitting royalty.

Because grains are harvested close to the ground, sanitation factors largely determine the survival of flour mills. The Food and Drug Administration regulates sanitation controls for the United States' milling industry by defining levels for unavoidable, naturally occurring food defects considered non-hazardous to human health. High levels of flour bacteria are normally exterminated through numerous milling processes. It has been argued that the cleansing effectiveness of modern machinery not only removes all the bran and germ but also removes the part of the traditional bread flavor as well. On the other hand, some reports cite popular raw cookie dough as a contamination source because of the persistence of live microbes, apparently unaffected by milling heating or baking processes.

The primary structural change by the early 2000s was the worldwide shift of control over wheat and flour production and purchasing decisions from governmental agencies to private enterprises. In 1990, about 80 percent of these decisions where made by governments; in 1998, private millers and grain traders made 70 percent of such decisions. Latin America, in particular, underwent a very dramatic shift of this kind in just a few years. In most cases, privatization led to increased wheat consumption, quality-consciousness, and competition.

Major Uses of Flour. In the mid-2000s, the heaviest volume users were commercial bakers who used more than 72 percent of the U.S. flour supply to make breads and cakes. Professional bakers buy flour by grades of refinement, while individual consumers purchase straight flour and convenience mixes. Typically, 100 pounds of wheat yield an average of 72 pounds of white flour, or depending on the variety, 100 pounds of wheat flour. Besides bread, flour is essential in the production of rolls and sweet goods (such as pastries, doughnuts, cakes, and cookies); tortillas, which account for one-fourth of the corn flour market, alongside corn chips and other snack foods; and pasta and noodles, for which the enrichment value ranks the highest of wheat flour-based products.

Perhaps the greatest impetus to guilt-free use of pre-packaged foods was the 1920 introduction of biscuit mix, which promised a convenient, tasty product by following a few simple steps. As popularity of mixes increased, flour mills began producing large unit volume mixes, which expanded commercial bakers' application of mixes for all types of products such as doughnuts, pastries, pie shells, cakes, and different breads. After a while, the lustrous period of mixes plummeted because flour marketers believed consumers lacked the time and interest in tradi-tional home baking. A Pillsbury official reiterated the potential of the flour mix market by reminding manage-ment that modern bakers are mostly mothers who crave convenience and easy-to-use products that are capable of producing homemade bread. The evidence was sufficiently convincing for Pillsbury to energize flour marketing and spark sales of bread machines and bread mixes by 1994. In the 1990s, 47 percent of volume baking mix users were homemakers with children aged 6 to 11.

BACKGROUND AND DEVELOPMENT

Perhaps more than any other food, wheat has survived consumer fickleness and food fads throughout the ages. In the 2000s, wheat continued to hold its 10,000-year-old status as the staff of life. Anthropologists have ascribed the cultivation and storing of wheat as a pivotal factor in stabilizing habitation patterns. This stability soon stimu-lated experimentation in expanding wheat as a food sup-ply. Nomadic tribes discovered that using wheat as a food source increased their chances of survival. Archeological finds along the Nile River documented Egyptians applying various techniques of wheat harvesting and using the leavening process in bread making around 2600 B.C. The Romans improved the milling process and are acknowledged as the first people to make white bread. Bread became so important that it gained symbolic sig-nificance in some religions. As wheat and bread developed into more lucrative commodities, questions about the more unseemly aspects of bread consumption also arose. During the eighteenth century, for example, controversy erupted regarding the use of new versus old (aged) wheat preferred by French bakers. While the profit factors of new

wheat appealed to traders, the public believed that new wheat caused diarrhea, pernicious gas, and possibly epidemic diseases. According to twentieth-century investigations, contaminated bread—allegedly a cause of psychosis—contributed to witchcraft persecution, which was prevalent during the eighteenth century in Europe.

One of the oldest types of wheat known is bulgur wheat, and the earliest means used to separate the parts of the wheat kernel involved rubbing the grain between the hands. Other methods included having hoofed animals walk over grains that had been spread on hard ground, and winnowing, a process in which grains were tossed in the air so that the chaff would blow away (removing the individual grains from the rest of the plant was necessary before milling could take place).

Grain milling practices were developed to separate the kernel components and make flour. The first types of milling procedures involved the use of rubbing stones, mortar and pestles, or querns. Querns were devices made from two stacked, disk-shaped stones. Wheat grains were poured into the quern through a hole in the top stone. As the two stones turned against each other with a rotary motion, the abrasive movement separated the parts of the wheat kernels and ground the endosperm into flour. The flour was then discharged between the stones.

The first continuous system for milling wheat into flour was developed during the last part of the eighteenth century by an American, Oliver Evans. Evans' mill design used steam technology and employed conveyors and bucket elevators to move the grain through a multi-phase milling process. Further advances in milling technology occurred during the nineteenth century. In 1865, Edmund La Croix developed a middlings purifier that separated the granular endosperm from the bran so that it could be reground to produce a better grade of flour. During the 1870s, the first roller mills were constructed in the United States.

Roller mills possessed several advantages: they elim-inated the need to dress millstones; they were able to produce flour through a more gradual extraction process, which enabled millers to yield a larger percentage of better grade flour; and the greater efficiency of these mills made the construction of larger mills more feasible.

During the middle of the twentieth century, funda-mental changes occurred in the primary location of mills. Prior to the 1950s, the cost of shipping wheat and the cost of shipping flour were approximately equal, and mills were frequently built close to wheat fields. During the early 1960s, the cost of shipping grain decreased following the introduction of hopper rail cars. At the same time, costs surrounding sanitation requirements increased the price of shipping flour. As a result, mills were constructed closer to end markets rather than near the wheat fields.

Granular flour, a product made with particles of a uniform size with carefully controlled amounts of atomized moisture to reduce clumping, was introduced during the 1960s. Although granular flour was more expensive than regular flour, it offered several advantages: it produced less dust, was easier to pour, did not require sifting, and dispersed in cold liquids.

During the 1970s, sales of household flour declined as developed societies moved away from home baking, and homemakers demonstrated a preference for the convenience and consistency of prepared mixes. More women were joining the work force and shortcuts were necessary to provide healthy home cooked meals for their families. In addition, many mixes were less expensive than individual ingredients. Baking from "scratch" ceased to be an activity of necessity and was relegated to hobby status. Demographic information revealed that households with higher incomes were more likely to use flour than lower income households. Declines in flour use by households were partially offset by increases of flour sales to commercial bakers. Also during this period, the flour and grain mill industry was adversely affected when a nutrition-conscious population denounced starchy breads and tantalizing sugar products. Others rejected the reduced quality of commercial bakery products because of overuse of additives.

Acquisition activity and globalization continued to transform the industry, particularly as such activity was concentrated in emerging markets in Asia, Eastern Europe, and South America. China's transition from an agrarian economy to an industrial one posed opportunities for major international corporations such as U.S.-based Cargill Inc. and Archer Daniels Midland to make substantial inroads into that country. Middle Eastern countries continued to modernize their milling operations, allowing for the region's growing global presence within the industry. Qatar's flour milling industry, for example, realized the effects of a healthy economy and improved technology and computer mechanization. As a consequence, grain-based food consumption in Qatar increased about 10 to 15 percent annually in the late 1990s.

In the 2000s, not all developing countries were greeting increased internationalization with open arms, however. Zambia, for instance, countered what it viewed as unfair foreign competition with a ban on flour imports in 2002. Indonesia, amid massive deregulation of its economy, maintained a flour consumption rate that was roughly a quarter that of the United States, which presented a significant market for potential growth to

foreign corporations. As the market itself became privatized, the government implemented substantial tariffs on wheat flour to stave off foreign competition that could overpower domestic producers.

Such protective actions were not limited to developing nations. In the United States, the federal government took action against what it saw as harmfully high imports of wheat gluten.

Another issue of increasing prominence within the industry was health consciousness and quality control. Consumer demand for a nutritionally positive product dramatically altered the dynamics of the industry. As individual millers and companies assumed control of production and purchasing activities from governments, the focus shifted from the high quantity, low price demand that prevailed under governmental authority to the increased competition among industry players to offer consumers a high quality product at affordable prices. As a result, many companies invested substantial sums in research aimed at improving quality control. Grain quality included an assessment of the physical characteristics of grain such as weight and moisture content, cleanliness and phytosanitary conditions (such as presence of weed seeds or pests), and an assessment of the intrinsic nutritional characteristics such as protein and gluten content. Reportedly less than a third of the world market demands these high wheat standards, but these markets include higher income groups that prefer protein, wholesome white bread, corn sweeteners, and tofu. Purchasing decisions may be affected by other factors, particularly price, but USDA studies found that grain importers most often base purchases on intrinsic characteristics. Purchases by state trading agencies in developing countries reportedly reflect less attention to quality and more to price. In the wake of world trade liberalizations such as the General Agreement on Tariffs and Trade (GATT), U.S. exporters may need to treat each market individually, dealing with importers' preferences almost on a retail basis.

CURRENT CONDITIONS

Although the United States produces only 10 percent of the world wheat, it is consistently the world's leading wheat exporter. Over the last decade, U.S. wheat exports have exceeded 30 million metric tons twice. They peaked in 2007-2008 when they reached a high of 34 mmt, comprising 30 percent of the world wheat exports. One reason U.S. wheat exports grew over the other exporting countries during the 2007-2008 season was its larger than normal stocks, which then fell by four million metric tons. Another import factor during that time was that the U.S. dollar depreciated by about 25 percent. The dollar's fall in value reduced the price for U.S. wheat compared to that produced by other countries. Thus, the U.S. exports that season were boosted and the exports of other major wheat producers were lowered. By 2009, the United States, Canada, Australia, the European Union, the former Soviet Union (including Russia, Ukraine, and Kazakhstan), and Argentina accounted for about 90 percent of the world's wheat exports.

In the years before 2005-2006, world wheat trade peaked in 1987-1989 at 11.5 million metric tons, when China and the Soviet Union were importing vast amounts. However, after that exporting boon and up until the 2005-2006 season, imports by Eastern Europe, the former Soviet Union, and China were much lower, and world wheat trade did not match that same level despite significant growth in imports by developing countries. In 2005-2006, world wheat exports reached 114 million metric tons. By the next year, total wheat trade increased modestly, but in 2007-2008, wheat trade stagnated due to high prices and a sloping economy.

The demand for wheat has increased to meet the need for staple food products in countries such as Sub-Saharan Africa (Nigeria, Sudan, and Kenya) and North Africa (Egypt, Algeria, and Morocco); South-East Asia (Indonesia, Philippines, and Vietnam); and Latin America (Brazil and Mexico). At the same time, some major importers from North Africa and the Middle East increased wheat imports when adverse weather lowered their supplies.

According to the U.S. Department of Agriculture, per capita consumption of flour in the U.S. by 2007 was estimated at 137.5 pounds, up three pounds from 2006. The highest per capita consumption figure since 141 pounds in 2001. One trend affecting domestic flour sales by the mid-2000s was the growing popularity of low-carbohydrate diets. Per capita consumption of flour in the United States decreased by seven pounds per year between 2001 and 2003, due largely to the influence of low-carbohydrate diets. This trend particularly affected bread and pasta manufacturers. In response, companies were introducing low-carbohydrate versions of these products in which some portion of refined flour was replaced by a higher-protein ingredient, such as whole wheat flour, wheat germ, or soy protein.

RESEARCH AND TECHNOLOGY

In the mid-2000s, new flours and ingredients continued as research priorities for the flour and grain industry. Milo grain, a sturdy, nutritious variety of sorghum cultivated for about 30 percent less cost, was being studied as a wheat flour substitute for pancake mixes. The wet and dry milling process for milo offered tremendous potential as a top-quality wheat flour steeped in vitamins and minerals. Without the grittiness and bitter taste of whole grain, the palatability of milo grain products could

possibly convert almost 40 percent of the population to whole grain products. By making whole grain flour more easily extruded, ConAgra planned to stimulate this virgin market with the introduction in schools of ultra fine whole grain flour mixes for making pizza crust, griddle mix, buttermilk muffins, and a host of other products. Genetic engineering and unconventional use of baker's yeast may possibly lead to wheat that produces a superior baking flour with more nutrients.

A United Nations report in 2004 blamed "alarming" deficits in IQs, productivity, and health across entire countries on the lack of simple nutrients, such as folic acid, niacin, and iron. Folic acid, a natural component of wheat and whole wheat products that is mostly lost in the milling process, is an essential vitamin that aids metabolic processes and produces red blood cells. The United States has, since 1998, required that food companies must add folic acid to most enriched bread, corn meal, flour, pasta, and rice products. Given folic acid's potential to protect the health of newborns, doctors strongly advocate women begin a regimen of folic acid-induced products and supplements at least three months prior to the time they conceive. It has been shown to reduce a certain group of birth defects called neural tube defects, which result in conditions like spina bifida. Studies published in 2009 suggest that folic acid may also play a role in preventing some forms of heart defects and in preventing premature births. Flour is also routinely enriched in other western countries, but nutrients are not added to flour in developing countries, where grain is most often processed in small mills. However, to prevent vitamin deficiencies, which contribute to mental impairment, birth defects, and other debilitating conditions, the United Nations has urged that developing countries follow the U.S. policy and start to increase their production of enriched foods such as flour.

Genetic selection and genetic engineering made up an area of concentration for researchers in the mid-2000s. It has been found that protein content and overall quality of corn meal and other products can be enhanced by these means. In addition, debranning techniques, by which bran layers are stripped from the endosperm and hydrated before the milling process, came into play in the late 1990s. This technique allows for greater, more accurate control of finished flour moisture, which in turn improves bread quality and baking quality. A process to separate gluten and starch from wheat flour using ethanol instead of water may reduce waste treatment costs associated with the conventional process.

New Equipment. Extreme precision in moisture management plays a key role in increasing cost-efficiency in grain milling. Excessively high or low moisture content signals a problem for the flour industry. Moisture content affects insect growth if moisture is below 14 percent and mold accumulation if it is higher than 14.5 percent. Wheat arrives at the mill with different moisture levels; therefore, without manual adjustment of moisture, mills have difficulty maintaining flour finish moisture of 14 percent. The Buhler Group has created a moisture control unit (MYFC) and water proportioning unit (MOZF) to create an ideal symbiosis. The moisture control unit continuously monitors the moisture of the grain and computes the exact volume of water needed for obtaining the required final moisture content.

INDUSTRY LEADERS

Archer Daniels Midland Company (ADM). Started as the Archer-Daniels Linseed Company in 1903, the Archer Daniels Midland Company spent its first two decades purchasing oil processing companies in the Midwestern United States. In 1930, the Commander-Larabee Company, a major flour miller, was purchased. By the company's fiftieth anniversary in 1952, Archer Daniels Midland was manufacturing over 200 standard products and had extended its operations overseas. ADM, whose grain milling division produced flour for bread, cakes, pasta, tortillas, and various ingredients for the baking industry, generated revenues of US$69.2 billion in 2009, with wheat and other milled products accounting for about 12 percent of the total. Approximately 33 percent of ADM's revenues came from outside the United States, and the company had food processing plants in Africa, Asia, Australia, Canada, Europe, South America, and the United States. ADM's reputation was tarnished in the 1990s by a federal investigation and subsequent lawsuits stemming from price-fixing allegations relating to high-fructose corn syrup. In 1997, ADM was fined US$100 million, the largest antitrust fine in U.S. history at that time. In 2004, the company agreed to pay US$400 million in damages to Coca-Cola, Pepsi Cola, and other food manufacturers that had brought claims against ADM. By 2010, ADM was enjoying a revised reputation in the food industry. *Fortune* magazine named it "Most Admired" company in the food industry for the second year in a row.

General Mills Inc. For more than 60 years, General Mills survived as an independent corporation by relying on its flour milling and breakfast cereals. Although incorporated in 1928, the company's origins date back to 1866, when Cadwallader Washburn opened a flour mill in Minnesota. His business, which soon became the Washburn Crosby Company, competed with local miller C. A. Pillsbury. In 1928, General Mills was formed, employing 5,800 workers and generating sales of US$123 million. Its strongest products at the time were Gold Medal Flour, Softasilk Cake Flour, and Wheaties, a then recently introduced ready-to-eat cereal. Also in 1928, Betty Crocker's name was introduced in connection with General Mills'

consumer goods. Although the company through the years bought and sold such diverse entities as Eddie Bauer, Talbot's, and the Red Lobster and Olive Garden chains, by the late 1990s, General Mills again focused on food products as evidenced by its decision in 2001 to double its size by purchasing Pillsbury from Diageo. General Mills also produced its own flour, which it sold to bakeries. In 2009, sales continued their steady climb, reaching US$14.7 billion.

Cargill Inc. One of the largest U.S. privately held multi-national corporations, Cargill Inc. was one of the largest grain and commodities players in the world and a long-time leader in the U.S. flour milling industry. William Wallace Cargill began his grain business in 1865 in Iowa. The business grew as it followed the expansion of the railroad in the period after the U.S. Civil War. During the Great Depression, Cargill invested heavily in the storage and transportation of grain, secure in the knowledge that a recovering economy would find Cargill reaping the benefits. By 1940, 60 percent of Cargill's business involved foreign markets. In 1955, the company opened a Swiss subsidiary to sell grain in Europe, and in the early 1960s, Cargill began its move into communist countries. In the 1990s, Cargill stepped up its foreign ventures, resuming trade with post-apartheid South Africa and expanding its Asian and Eastern European operations. Total revenues were US$107.9 billion in 2010.

ConAgra Foods Inc. ConAgra maintaieds a strong presence in nearly all areas of the U.S. food processing industry. Conceived in 1919 when a collection of mills consolidated to form Consolidated Mills Inc., the company steadily diversified and grew to become a national food powerhouse. In 1971, Consolidated Mills changed its name to ConAgra Inc. It grew consistently through the 1990s, by which time it had diversified heavily within the food industry and expanded into a global outfit, with over 25,000 employees in 32 countries. By the mid-2000s, ConAgra was one of the largest food service manufacturers in the United States, providing poultry, French fries, and dough-based products for the food service industry. In 2009, ConAgra's total revenues were US$12.73 billion. Only a small segment of this was attributed to agricultural processing, however, as the company's focus shifted to prepared foods in the late 1990s. ConAgra's top brands, such as Chef Boyardee, Banquet, Chun King, Healthy Choice, Hunt's, Peter Pan, Parkay, and Van Camp's, generated approximately US$100 million in sales each year.

BIBLIOGRAPHY
"Business Outlook: Flour Mill Product Manufacturing." *Food Magazine,* 24 February 2005.

ADM Named Most Admired Food Production Company, March 2010. Available at http://www.adm.com.

California Wheat Commission, March 2008. Available from http://www.worldgrain.com.

China's Corn Output Reaches Record High." *Asia Pulse,* 14 March 2007.

"Hoover's Company Capsules." *Hoover's Online,* 2007. Available from http://www.hoovers.com.

"Opening Up New Markets for UK Wheat." *Farmers Guardian,* 20 March 2007.

Ramachandran, Arjun. "Flour Mill Product Manufacturing." *Food Magazine,* 1 February 2006.

Schlachter, Barry. "Giving Bread a Boost: New Additives Are Touted as a Way to Help Lower Bad Cholesterol, Aid Health." *Fort Worth Star-Telegram,* 4 April 2007.

U.S. Department of Agriculture. *U.S. and World Wheat Trade, 2009.* Available from http://www.ers.usda.gov.

———. *Grain: World Markets and Trade,* March 2007. Available from http://www.fas.usda.gov.

———. *World Wheat, Flour, and Products Trade,* 9 March 2007. Available from http://www.fas.usda.gov.

SIC 2086

SOFT DRINKS AND BOTTLED WATER

NAICS CODE(S)

312111. Producers in this industry supply the world's sodas, bottled waters, and other prepared non-alcoholic beverages. (See also **Alcoholic Beverages.**)

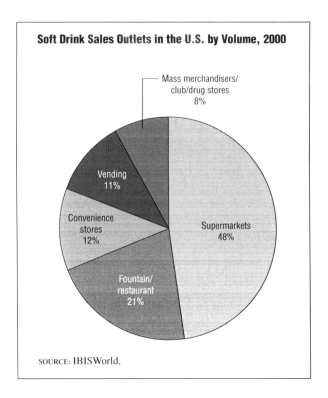

Soft Drink Sales Outlets in the U.S. by Volume, 2000

Mass merchandisers/club/drug stores 8%

Vending 11%

Convenience stores 12%

Supermarkets 48%

Fountain/restaurant 21%

SOURCE: IBISWorld.

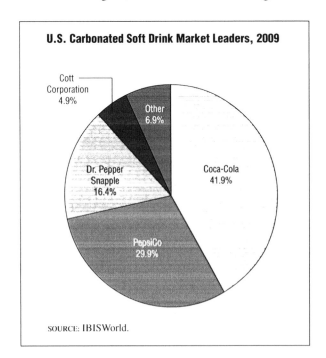

U.S. Carbonated Soft Drink Market Leaders, 2009

Cott Corporation 4.9%

Other 6.9%

Dr. Pepper Snapple 16.4%

Coca-Cola 41.9%

PepsiCo 29.9%

SOURCE: IBISWorld.

INDUSTRY SNAPSHOT

The global soft drinks industry is almost exclusively a marketing phenomenon. The actual product is a comparatively simple blend of water, sweeteners, flavors, and other additives. The industry's genius lies in convincing billions of consumers to drink soft drinks instead of plain water or other beverages. Through its vast annual investments in advertising and marketing, the industry has enjoyed some of the highest brand recognition in the world along with spectacular sales. In 2009, the U.S. soft drink market slipped 2.1 percent to nearly 9.4 billion cases in 2009, representing the fifth consecutive year of steady decline. Causes for the drop include the growing popularity of alternatives, such as bottled water and flavored waters. The two big industry leaders, Coca-Cola and Pepsi, both showed declines in 2009 of 4 percent and 5.5 percent, respectively. Dr Pepper Snapple, however, posted a gain of 4.8 percent in 2009 after dropping 1.3 percent in 2008. The company counts the growth of *Crush,* which had a 377 percent increase in cases sold. The rise in bottled water consumption over that of soda and the global recession contributed to the changes in the liquid refreshment industry. U.S. consumption of carbonated soft drinks in 2009 fell to 736 eight-ounce servings, which was down from the per capita consumption peak in 1998 of 864 eight-ounce servings. However, even with the drop in U.S. consumption, the country continued to boast the highest world consumption of soft drinks.

Global soft drinks consumption reached 327 billion liters in 2003, a 5.7 percent increase from the previous year, with the global soft drink industry being valued at US$393 billion in 2002. While soft drinks are enjoyed in virtually every nation on earth, most of the major markets, including North America, Europe, and Japan, were considered mature, meaning that per capita consumption was expected to rise slowly, if at all. For example, in Europe only about 2.5 billion gallons of soft drinks were consumed annually, according to Britvic, a leading soft drinks manufacturer in the United Kingdom and Europe. As a result, throughout the 1990s and into the first decade of the twenty-first century, soft drink manufacturers moved aggressively into developing but highly populated areas, such as the alliance of 11 former Soviet Republic countries that made up the Commonwealth of Independent States (CIS), as well as Eastern Europe, China, and India. The industry was projected to grow by about 5 percent through the early 2000s, with the largest increase expected to come from Asia.

The U.S. soft drinks industry in 2009 was dominated by the Coca-Cola Company and PepsiCo Inc. Coca-Cola held a 47 percent share of the global carbonated soft drinks (CSD) market in 2000. By 2009, Coca-Cola controlled about 41.9 percent of the CSD market. PepsiCo ranked second, with about 11 percent of the global market in 2002 and 29.9 percent of the U.S. market in 2009. Dr Pepper Snapple, the third largest soft drink company, captured 16.4 percent of the U.S. market in 2009. Cott Corporation, the world's largest producer of store-brand carbonated soft drinks, claimed 2 percent of the global market and 4.9 percent of the U.S. market in 2009. While the local brands of most countries captured a significant share of their markets, few could match the manufacturing, marketing, and distribution prowess of Coca-Cola and, in some markets, Pepsi, which does business in international markets as Pepsi-Cola International(PCI).

Some industry analysts believe the traditional concept of equating soft drinks primarily with carbonated beverages, particularly colas, must be revised to reflect the growing popularity of other ready-to-drink (RTD) beverages, such as teas, coffees, herbal beverages, juices, and sports and energy drinks. When viewed in this broader sense, another group of soft drink competitors emerges, most notably Proctor & Gamble in the United States, Danone in France, Nestle Beverages in Switzerland, and Unilever in England. The latter company estimated its share of the total nonalcoholic (RTD) beverage market in 2000 at about 19 percent. As of 2004, Coca-Cola-trademarked RTD beverages accounted for 1.3 billion of the 50 billion beverage servings of all kinds consumed around the world each day.

ORGANIZATION AND STRUCTURE

Soft drink manufacturing is remarkably similar worldwide. Soft drink companies manufacture and sell beverage syrups and bases to bottling operations, a growing proportion of which are owned by the soft drink manufacturers themselves. The bottling operations add sweeteners and carbonated water to produce the final product and distribute it, usually in specific territories assigned by the soft drink manufacturers.

Global soft drink manufacturers usually develop local bottling operations in the countries in which they operate. They license bottlers to sell their products or buy local bottlers outright. While they might import ingredients, bottling is done locally. By the early years of the first decade of the 2000s, PepsiCo and Coca-Cola had company-owned franchised bottling plants in more than 120 countries that produced their respective brands. Some soft drinks, including mineral waters like Perrier, have distinct qualities that cannot be reproduced in local markets and are exported in bottled form to foreign markets.

In the bottling operation, incoming water is cleaned and clarified. Carbon dioxide gas, which provides effervescence, is supplied to bottlers either in solid form (dry ice) or under pressure in liquid form. To create a finished product, the flavoring syrup is diluted with water and then cooled, carbonated, and bottled. The bottling process is highly automated, as is the washing of returnable bottles.

In the United States and elsewhere, major soft drink manufacturers like Coca-Cola (CCE) and PepsiCo (PCI) have acquired many independent bottlers and consolidated them into single enterprises. CCE, for example, was the world's largest soft drink bottler in 2009 with over 92,800 employees worldwide and more than 3,300 different beverages offered in more than 200 countries. According to the company's annual report, CCE's net operating revenues in 2009 reached approximately US$30.9 billion. Pepsi bottling operations accounted for 52 percent of PCI's soft drink products in the United States. The same trend was evident in the company's overseas market, particularly in Latin America, where PCI was active in integrating various bottling operations.

Cultural Differences. Soft drink consumption varies widely by region and by culture. As a result, consumption does not necessarily coincide closely with population or economic development. For example, combined sales of Coca-Cola Co. products in Germany, Great Britain, Spain, Italy, France, and the Benelux countries (Belgium, the Netherlands, and Luxembourg), which are some of the most highly developed economies in the world, were matched by sales in Mexico and Brazil, despite their developing economies.

Soft drinks are available around the world in two forms: packaged and fountain service, where soft drinks are dispensed into cups. While packaged products account for the majority of soft drink volume in most countries, fountain sales had the most rapid growth in the early to mid-1990s as soft drink manufacturers aggressively sought additional outlets for their products. In the United States, Coca-Cola dominated the fountain business, with 65 percent of the market at the beginning of the first decade of the 2000s, compared to 25 percent for Pepsi and 10 percent for Cadbury Schweppes.

Packaging and Vending. Most packaged soft drinks come in glass or plastic bottles and aluminum, steel, or plastic cans. While the majority of packaged soft drinks were sold in multi-packs in stores, a large proportion was sold from vending machines, which began in the early twentieth century as ice coolers. In the early years of the first decade of the 2000s, refrigerated vending machines dispensed soft drinks in cups, cans, or bottles.

The worldwide growth in vending continued throughout the first decade of the 2000s in nations with rising living standards and receding inflation levels. The high inflation rates in many countries were one of the main barriers to international vending because of the speed in which vending prices could become obsolete. However, as inflation came under control in most countries in the mid- to late 1990s, vending operations began to grow rapidly.

Impact of Private Labels. While branded products are the heart of the soft drink industry, private label soft drink products (also referred to as "store brands" or "own labels"), sold exclusively by individual retailers like supermarkets, hold a significant share of many of the world's markets. As supermarkets and general merchandisers have grown in size and influence around the world, they have become more aggressive in marketing their brands, including soft drinks.

Although consumers usually prefer advertised brands to private label products, they look for bargains in their selections. During recessions, sales of private label soft drinks tend to increase. Major brands respond by lowering their prices to compete with private labels, but profits decrease.

Nonetheless, private label products present strong competition for soft drink manufacturers. Most supermarkets, particularly in Europe, carry an extensive array of private label products. Private label soft drink products were a hot trend in the mid-1990s, largely because of the spectacular success of Toronto, Canada-based

Cott Corp. Cott adopted a strategy of offering top-notch quality for its private label products, mostly colas. Using syrup from Royal Crown Co., Cott packaged its private label brands in eye-catching packages and sold them for 25 percent less than Coke and Pepsi. More importantly, Cott developed close relationships with some of the most powerful food and general merchandise retailers in the world, such as J. Sainsbury in Great Britain and Wal-Mart in the United States. As a result, Cott gained prized shelf space in stores, often in the premium eye-level positions.

In the United Kingdom, the J. Sainsbury chain introduced Sainsbury Classic Cola in April 1994, which was supplied by Cott, with spectacular results. The Classic brand accounted for 75 percent of Sainsbury cola sales just a few months later, causing Pepsi's share of Sainsbury soft drink sales to drop from 21 to 10 percent and Coke's share to decrease from 44 percent to 9 percent.

While branded products continued to account for about 80 percent of supermarket sales in the United States, at Save-A-Lot, a unit of Minneapolis-based food distributor SUPERVALU Inc., 85 percent of the chain's sales derived from private label items. The successful, fast-growing chain, which specialized in private label brands, had opened more than 1,000 stores in 37 states by 2004. By the early years of the first decade of the 2000s, Save-A-Lot had produced a net profit margin of about 2 percent of sales, nearly double the supermarket industry average of just over 1.1 percent. In the soft drink category, the chain marketed Bubba Cola instead of Coke, and Dr Pop as a replacement for Dr Pepper, as well as other brands.

International Challenges. The nearly universal demand for soft drinks requires companies to use creative strategies to supply customers under sometimes very difficult circumstances, such as in war-torn areas. For example, the soft drink bottler and distributor Postobon (known formally as Gaseosas Posada Tobon SA) thrived in Colombia even in the midst of a civil war in the late 1990s. With headquarters in Medellin, Colombia, Postobon had 33 bottling plants. It was able to operate in "hot" areas of the country by skillfully handling charged situations involving two guerrilla armies and local authorities. The frequent kidnapping of businessmen was another major problem in Colombia. To minimize this risk, the sites and timings of monthly Postobon meetings were frequently changed. In addition, so as not to appear to be taking sides, managers never visited local army bases to circumvent the destruction of bottling plants by guerrilla forces.

BACKGROUND AND DEVELOPMENT

The term soft drink was coined to distinguish flavored drinks from hard liquor. Soft drinks are nonalcoholic beverages, carbonated or un-carbonated, containing a natural or artificial sweetening agent, natural or artificial flavors, and other ingredients. Coffee, tea, milk, cocoa, and undiluted fruit and vegetable juices are not usually classified as soft drinks. Soft drinks were originally designed to substitute for liquor in an effort to reduce alcohol consumption.

Soft drinks first appeared in seventeenth-century Europe as a mixture of water and lemon juice sweetened with honey. In 1676, the Paris-based Compagnie de Limonadiers was founded and granted a monopoly by the French monarchy. Company vendors dispensed cups of lemonade from tank packs on their backs. The first carbonated beverages, which also debuted in Europe, were inspired by the popularity of effervescent water from natural springs, which were widely thought to have medicinal value.

Joseph Priestley, called the father of the soft drinks industry by some, experimented with carbon dioxide gas from brewery fermenting vats. In 1772, he invented a small carbonating apparatus in London that pumped carbon dioxide into water. Mineral salts and flavors were later added as the appeal of soft drinks spread.

In 1886, John Pemberton, an Atlanta, Georgia, pharmacist, invented Coca-Cola, the first cola drink. In the nineteenth century, soft drinks were only sold in outlets that could provide fountain service, but when bottling machinery was invented in the 1890s in the United States, soft drinks could be distributed to other retail outlets. By the beginning of the twentieth century, sales of Coca-Cola were booming throughout the United States as a network of bottlers developed. This type of distribution system then began to be used by other manufacturers and in other countries.

The consumption of soft drinks continued to expand worldwide throughout the twentieth century, as rising disposable incomes in industrialized countries allowed more consumers the luxury of drinking beverages other than water. During the 1960s, low-calorie soft drinks using artificial sweeteners became popular with consumers concerned about the excess calories in sugar. These diet soft drinks were first sweetened with cyclamates (later banned after being deemed carcinogenic), then saccharine, and finally aspartame (NutraSweet), a more natural-tasting artificial sweetener. During this time, Gatorade, a sports soft drink designed to replace fluids lost during exercise, was developed at the University of Florida. It quickly gained popularity, and attracted competitors in the late 1980s and early 1990s. In the early 1990s, so-called New Age beverages, such as ready-to-drink teas and coffees, trendy fruit juice combinations, and flavored waters, became popular in the United States and soon were gaining ground in other countries.

While markets with high per capita consumption of soft drinks like the United States, Mexico, and Canada produced the highest sales volume for soft drink manufacturers, in the late 1990s manufacturers were working to develop franchises in low per capita consumption markets. Many of these markets, such as Eastern Europe, Russia, and China, had been closed to competition for decades but invited expansion from soft drink manufacturers as their economies became liberalized. India and Vietnam were liberalizing their economies in the mid- to late 1990s as well, and soft drink makers moved quickly to take advantage of the situation. South Africa, long closed to Western investment during apartheid, was reopened in the mid-1990s and attracted high profile soft drink investors.

With growing international trade and falling trade barriers, very few countries remained closed to the largest multinational beverage companies in the mid-1990s. For example, by the early years of the first decade of the 2000s, Coca-Cola did business in almost every country in the world.

CURRENT CONDITIONS

The United States Department of Agriculture (USDA) reported that more than US$393 billion worth of soft drinks were produced worldwide. The largest soft drink markets were the United States, Japan, Mexico, Germany, China, and Brazil. The United States also ranked first in per capita consumption, with Americans consuming an average of just over 52 carbonated soft drinks per year in 2003. The next leading consumer was Germany, with about 8 percent of the market by volume at the beginning of the 2000s. The largest market segment in 2001, according to the USDA, was carbonated beverages, with sales of US$193 billion. Fruit and vegetable drinks ranked second, with sales of about US$6.9 billion each. However, by 2004, bottled water overtook juices as the second largest market segment, with sales of US$9.2 billion.

The United States also controlled global soft drinks sales, with two U.S.-based companies, Coca-Cola and PepsiCo, dominating this increasingly concentrated industry. Coca-Cola, which posted total revenues of US$21.96 billion in 2004, controlled about 25 percent of the global soft drink industry, according to the USDA. PepsiCo controlled about 11 percent, with worldwide beverage sales of US$7.6 billion in 2003. The third largest soft drinks manufacturer, Cadbury Schweppes, reported sales of $US12.9 billion (including snack foods) in 2004.

However, significant growth in the United States and other mature markets was not expected, especially in the carbonated soft drink (CSD) market. Global sales growth of CSDs reached only 0.8 percent in the United States in 2002, and analysts predicted that the strongest performances through the early 2000s would come from the industry's non-carbonated segment. The Asian and South American markets were expected to show the largest growth, outpacing North America, Europe, Africa, and Oceania (countries and territories in the Pacific Ocean). Mid-range growth was expected for the Middle East. Both PepsiCo and Coca-Cola expected a similar overall growth rate.

Moving Away from Traditional Colas. In the soft drinks industry, the consumer trend in the first decade of the 2000s was toward increasing health awareness, with declining demand for traditional colas. Although Coca-Cola and Pepsi-Cola remained the top carbonated sodas in 2004, each dropped in popularity between 1998 and the early 2000s, when consumers began demanding healthier beverages, or those perceived as healthier, such as diet colas, fortified fruit juices, bottled waters, sports, energy drinks, and iced teas. Diet colas posted strong growth in 2000 in the United States. Diet Pepsi posted the biggest overall gain with a 4 percent growth in terms of volume, and Diet Coke claimed the third spot in terms of volume with a 2.5 percent increase.

Unlike the carbonated soft drink market, the non-carbonated beverage market, which was the fastest-growing segment of the industry, was fragmented at the onset of the twenty-first century, with several key players and products vying for market share. The multinationals responded to growing popularity in this segment through acquisitions and new product launches. Coca-Cola acquired Nestea iced teas and Minute Maid fruit juices brands and introduced Dasani bottled water. Pepsico also grew through a combination of acquisitions that included a merger with Quaker Oats Company, as well as the introduction of new products. PepsiCo's brand portfolio in 2004 included Tropicana fruit juices, SoBe new age beverages, Gatorade sports drinks, Frappucino coffee drinks, Lipton iced teas, and Aquafina bottled water, in addition to its core group of colas.

Large multinational companies dominated large portions of nearly every segment of the non-carbonates market, which included sports and energy drinks, bottled water, and fruit juices and fruit drinks. However, in a few instances, such as the energy drinks market, smaller companies led the larger ones.

Sports drinks also developed into a major international soft drink category. Sports drinks are consumed to replenish fluids, minerals, and energy lost during exercise. Leatherhead Food RA reported that sport and energy drinks were valued at US$7.45 billion with a market volume of 5 billion liters in 2000. A press release from beverage industry analysts at Canadean estimated a 6 percent average annual growth rate through 2005 for this segment, with global sales projected at the time to exceed 10 billion liters by 2004. PepsiCo's Gatorade dominated the overall sports and energy drink market, producing nearly one-third of the global volume, according to Canadean. However, in the energy drinks sector, Red Bull GmbH, a private Austrian company founded in 1987, controlled 60 to 70 percent of the global energy drinks market, which introduced more than 30 new brands in 2001.

Morgan Stanley research analyst Bill Pecoriello tracked the consistency of soft-drink industry trends, which were for small gains or losses or stagnant. Coke and the Dr Pepper Snapple Group, which was spun off by Cadbury Schweppes in April 2008, experienced small losses, while Pepsi reported small gains, and private labels were flat. Although sales of Pepsi's Gatorade softened, G2 and Tiger turned out to be good brand extensions for the company.

Chatsmore Catholic High School Acting Head Ann Ward announced in the spring of 2008 that Red Bull was banned from her school grounds in Worthing, West Sussex, United Kingdom, following observations that students' conduct changed when they drank Red Bull. The energy drink contains 80mg of caffeine per can, which is equivalent to the amount of caffeine in a cup of coffee. According to BBC News, Red Bull's manufacturer said the drink was suitable for people of the same age as those able to drink coffee or other caffeinated beverages.

Bottled water has long been a major category in certain parts of the world. Europeans, for example, drink bottled water instead of tap water. While slower to begin drinking bottled water than the Europeans, U.S. consumers took to bottled water in a big way in the late 1990s, including both bulk still water and so-called refreshment water beverages, which were usually carbonated. In the United States, bottled water sales grew significantly in the late 1990s to US$5.7 billion in 2000, and by 2004 it was the second in sales behind carbonated soft drinks in the United States, with sales worth almost US$9.2 billion. Canadean expected bottled water to take the number one spot by 2010, citing that the U.S. market for bottled water was growing 16 percent annually.

The top-selling bottled water company in 2004 was Nestle Waters North America, accounting for about 30 percent of sales. PepsiCo's Aquafina, the leading bottled water brand, captured 11.3 percent of the market, while Coca-Cola's Dasani took a 10 percent share. Several innovations in the bottled water segment were introduced in the early years of the first decade of the 2000s, including new flavored waters and vitamin-enhanced products. Others focused on specific health claims. In 2004, for example, Eon Beverage Group, Inc., launched Eon, a "structured water", with claims that the product provided cellular absorption and improved the body's oxygenation. Zaqua!, a micro-structured water from Advanced H2O, boasted an adjusted pH level to help with digestion and with the elimination of waste products from the body.

An *International Herald Tribune* article on June 17, 2008, analyzed the reasons tap water was gaining on bottled water in popularity. The yearly tab for drinking the 64 ounces of water daily in bottles could reach thousands of dollars. U.S consumers reportedly spent US$16.8 billion on bottled water in 2007. An article in *Beverage Digest* reported that U.S. consumers had spent US$16.8 billion on bottled water in 2007. Concerns about the economy and environment were making tap water preferential for those choosing to drink water. People began to use water bottles that could be refilled safely to their tote bags and brief cases. The Tappening Project launched a campaign in November 2007 to promote drinking U.S. tap water as a clean, safe and more eco-friendly option. More than 200,000 reusable hard plastic and stainless steel bottles had been sold through the end of the first decade of the twenty-first century.

The trend to move away from drinking bottled water had not reached Australia by spring 2008, however. Tony Gentile, the chief executive of the Australian Beverages Council, claimed there was no consumer backlash. In spite of inexpensive, good-tasting water that was bottled and sold elsewhere, Australians continued to enjoy bottled varieties. "It's a free society and people can choose what they want to drink," Gentile stated. However, residents of the small town of Bundanoon, New South Wales, voted to outlaw bottled water in response to a push from a bottling company with desires to siphon off thousands of gallons of water from the local aquifer.

In the mid-1980s, when the Snapple Beverage Company introduced the first ready-to-drink (RTD) iced tea, that category began to grow dramatically. By 1994 there were 122 different tea labels in the United States alone, including offerings from Snapple, Coca-Cola, Nestlé Refreshments, Pepsi-Lipton, Tropicana Fruit Teas, and Celestial Seasonings (herbal teas). In 2001 the top-selling RTD tea in the United States was PepsiCo's Lipton Brisk, but by 2004 relative newcomer AriZona Iced Tea had overtaken the number one spot from Brisk. With impressive sales growth of 45 percent that year and revenues of more than US$147 million, AriZona took 23.3 percent of the market compared to second place rival Snapple with 14.5 percent. Lipton Brisk ranked third, with 13.5 percent of the RTD tea market.

National and Private Label Challenges. In 2000 private labels captured nearly 14 percent of carbonated soft drink (CSD) volume in the United States and approximately 7 percent of sales. According to the March 21, 2005, edition of *Business Week,* the U.S. market for private label goods had stabilized in 2004 at about 16 percent. Private labels also proved increasingly popular in Europe, where they accounted for 13 percent of volume in the soft drinks market in 1999. National brands claimed 53 percent of the market, compared to 34 percent for multinational brands. With European retailers devoting more shelf space to private labels, global brands suffered. For example, their share of European bottled water sales declined from 53 percent in 1997 to 40 percent in 2004. Nestle's sales of Perrier and Vittel in Europe fell by 8.4 percent between 2002 and 2004. Rapid growth of discount retailers, such as Aldi Group in Germany and Leader Price in France, which almost exclusively stock private labels, was expected to drive further growth in private label soft drink sales.

Private labels also performed well in the bottled water market. With US$325 million in sales in 2004, private label bulk bottled water ranked second only to PepsiCo's Aquafina. "Consumers drink bottled water for its perceived purity and healthfulness," according to Kitty Kevin, writing "Water Log, 2004" in *Beverage Industry,* adding that "Private label is reaping the benefits."

At the beginning of the 2000s, while the multinational soft drink companies were not as effective in selling universal, one-size-fits-all products in markets where consumers favored regional flavors and brand images, national brands surpassed the multinationals in growth. For example, in the Czech Republic, Poland, Romania, and Russia, national brands dominated the soft drink market with 75 to 80 percent in terms of volume. In Eastern Europe, multinationals saw volume growth of about 25 percent between 1995 and 2000, while national brands grew by 33 percent. Non-carbonated drinks and bottled water were the primary products in this segment.

National brands were more adept at forging partnerships with retail and supermarket chains. They could also produce beverages at a significantly reduced cost of up to 14 percent lower compared to a multinational cola, as estimated by Canadean.

Bottling Operations. Coke's relationship with its bottlers both helped the company and hurt it, with many claiming that Coke used its bottlers to make its own profits look better. During the mid-1980s and throughout the 1990s, Coke began to spin off its bottling operations, which were typically capital-intensive, retaining ownership of less than 50 percent. In doing so, according to Betsy McKay in the January 23, 2001, edition of the *Wall Street Journal Online,* Coke was able "to wipe capital-intensive assets and billions of dollars in debt off its books. But it also saddled its bottlers with huge debts." The system allowed Coke to raise the price of its concentrate, the syrup sold to the bottlers, who then added the water and packaging, even if the bottlers were unable to raise prices at the consumer level. Admittedly, Coke would subsidize the marketing efforts of the bottlers, but McKay went on to say that "this funding often didn't make up for the concentrate price increase."

Coke, responding to complaints from the bottlers, made a commitment in 2001 to alter how it calculated concentrate prices and advertising funds, at least with its largest bottler, Coca-Cola Enterprises Inc. (CCE). The bottlers' struggle eventually had a negative impact on Coke. Coke reported US$155 million in income from its bottlers in 1997, but by 2000 that had dropped dramatically to a US$280 million loss as CCE reported sales of US$14.8 billion, with net income of US$233 million in 2000. Meanwhile, Pepsi's largest bottler, Pepsi Bottling Group (PBG), posted revenues of nearly US$8 billion in 2000, with net income of US$229 million.

Twenty-First Century Challenges. By the early years of the first decade of the 2000s, physicians had begun to recognize obesity as a significant public health threat throughout both the developed world and developing countries. Although many factors are involved in the development of obesity, one significant contributor is the consumption of high-calorie foods and drinks. It was expected that public health officials would increasingly target soft drinks in anti-obesity campaigns. In Coca-Cola's annual report, obesity was listed first among the key challenges facing the company throughout the decade. Industry leaders planned to respond to this challenge by contributing to fitness campaigns and by continuing to offer a wide range of consumer choices, including diet soft drinks, juice-based drinks, energy

drinks, and water. PepsiCo, for example, announced in 2004 the launch of Pepsi Edge, described in a company news release as a "full-flavored cola with 50 percent less sugar, carbohydrates, and calories than regular colas."

In addition to the consumption of sugar-sweetened soft drinks being closely associated with obesity, studies have shown a connection between type 2 diabetes, dental cavities, and low nutrient levels. Regular sodas use high-fructose corn syrup (HFCS), which has come under attack from the health industry as a leading cause of childhood obesity. Artificial sweeteners continued to be controversial. Other ingredients of concern in sodas are caffeine, which is linked to anxiety and insomnia, and sodium benzoate, which has a potential link to DNA damage and hyperactivity.

The quality and availability of water, the primary ingredient in soft drinks and bottled waters, was also expected to affect the industry as droughts, pollution, and climate change threatened global water supplies. According to Coca-Cola's 2003 annual report, this limited resource faced "unprecedented challenges from over-exploitation, increasing pollution, and poor management." In 2004, for example, Coca-Cola halted production at its Plachimada, India, plant because of government pressure about the company's use of scarce groundwater. India claimed that Coca-Cola's water use during a period without rain contributed to the loss of needed farmland and depleted the region's water table.

INDUSTRY LEADERS

The Coca-Cola Company. The Coca-Cola Company has been a virtually unstoppable marketing machine for more than 40 years. Not only is it the leading soft drink company in the world, but according to a 2003 *Business Week* special report entitled "The Top 10 Brands," it is also the number one global brand. Coca-Cola's dominance of the international market had its roots in World War II, when the company underwent a vast expansion to supply U.S. soldiers in Europe and Asia with soft drinks. By 2007, Coca-Cola had grown to include more than 400 brands manufactured and sold in 200 countries—virtually every nation on earth—with sales reported at US$29 billion. More than half of the company's revenue is generated in developing markets.

Through the mid-1950s, the company sold one product, Coca-Cola, in one or two bottle styles. However, it quickly became a marketing giant with product and packaging diversity. Coca-Cola introduced the Fanta line of soft drinks in 1960, which grew to become the fourth best-selling brand in the world. Sprite, launched in 1961, became a leading lemon-lime carbonated beverage.

In 1963, Coca-Cola created the first successful diet soft drink, Tab. In 1982, the company launched Diet Coke, the first-ever extension of the Coca-Cola trademark. Although Diet Coke diminished Tab sales, it quickly became the most successful new soft drink entry in the twentieth century, becoming the world's best selling low-calorie soft drink in just two years. Diet Coke was one of the first diet soft drinks to use the NutraSweet brand of aspartame, which eventually replaced saccharine as a sugar substitute in most bottled and canned diet soft drinks.

Even Coca-Cola's mistakes turned out well. On April 23, 1985, the company stunned soft drink consumers worldwide by changing the hallowed, secret Coke formula. While the new taste was widely preferred in blind taste tests, a huge consumer backlash forced Coca-Cola to bring back the original product within three months as Coca-Cola Classic, retaining the new version as Coke or Coke II. Sales of the combined brand hardly missed a beat.

In the late 1990s, the Coca-Cola Company continued to expand through acquisitions. For example, in 1996 Coca-Cola essentially bought out an unusual franchise agreement it had with a major competitor, Cadbury Schweppes. The two companies agreed to end their 10-year-old joint venture in the United Kingdom, called Coca-Cola and Schweppes Beverages Ltd. (CCSB). CCSB had been created in 1986 as a franchisee to produce, distribute, and sell the two companies' brands in what was then considered an undeveloped market. The plan was for each company to take charge of marketing its own brands, while CCSB acted as a franchisee to produce, distribute, and sell them. However, in subsequent years, the partnership was strained as both firms put more focus on their own products.

In June 1996, Coca-Cola and Cadbury Schweppes agreed to sell their CCSB stakes to Coca-Cola Enterprises (CCE) Atlanta, Coke's major bottling partner worldwide. As a result, CCE, which was 44 percent owned by the Coca-Cola Company, became the key bottler in a strong market. Meanwhile, Coca-Cola regained control over much of the marketing of its brands, while Cadbury Schweppes took £620 million (about US$1 billion) away from the deal. Cadbury Schweppes intended to make acquisitions in the confectionery industry with the proceeds.

Coca-Cola continued its acquisition strategy in 1997 when it agreed in late December to purchase the Orangina brand from France's Pernod Ricard SA for FFr5 billion (US$840.5 million). The deal included all Orangina brands and four bottling and concentrate plants. The transaction gave Coca-Cola control of about 58 percent of the French soft drink market, up from about 50 percent. That large market share prompted some to speculate that the deal could be challenged by France's Competition Council.

Coca-Cola's sales distribution demonstrates the vital importance of the globalization of the soft drink industry. By 2003, more than 70 percent of Coca-Cola's sales came from global markets outside the United States. When developing new markets, Coke, like archrival Pepsi, usually created strong identities for their famous brands. However, in some countries, a different approach was necessary. For example, after being absent from the market in India for over 15 years, Coca-Cola purchased the Thums Up brand from an Indian bottler in 1993. Coca-Cola became India's biggest manufacturer of soft drinks, with 45 soft drink plants and 20 water plants in 2001.

Thums Up began in 1977, when Coca-Cola left India after a new government there ordered the company to reduce its stake in its Indian unit and reveal its secret formula. As a result, Coca-Cola bottlers were left without a product to sell. One bottler formulated Thums Up and packaged it in Coke bottles. After Coca-Cola returned to India in 1993 with the purchase of Thums Up and other brands from the Parle Group, the company aggressively merchandised Coke brands. However, resistance from bottlers combined with consumer indifference prompted the company to change course and put more advertising and marketing support behind Thums Up. With the combined strength of Coke brands, Thums Up, and other products, Coca-Cola held about 52 percent of the Indian market as of 1999, compared to 46 percent for Pepsi.

In 1997, the Coca-Cola Company's long-time leader, CEO Roberto Goizueta, died. Goizueta, who had assumed leadership of the company in 1981, was credited with vastly improving the firm's profitability and global profile. Not surprisingly, the new chairman of Coca-Cola, M. Douglas Ivester, pledged no major shifts in the company's successful business strategy. However, in December 1999, Ivester abruptly quit amid difficulties within the company, as well as in the global marketplace. The Asian market crisis, collapsing economies in Russia and Brazil, and strong challenges by PepsiCo for market share, resulted in Coke's earnings falling two straight years under Ivester's leadership. Coca-Cola was also plagued with other problems. In the spring of 1999, 2,200 African-American employees charged Coca-Cola with race discrimination, resulting in a US$192.5 million settlement in November 2000. In the summer of 1999 Belgian schoolchildren became sick after drinking Coke, which turned out to contain contaminated carbon dioxide. Then a fungicide was found in cans of Coke shipped from France. The contamination problems turned out to be relatively minor, although Ivester was faulted for not acting quickly to explain the situation and calm jittery European consumers. In November 1999, Coca-Cola announced a price increase of its concentrate (the syrup purchased by its bottlers), further adding to tensions between the company and its bottlers.

Douglas N. Daft assumed the task of solving the problems left by Ivester. Through internal restructuring, acquisitions, and strengthened partnerships, Daft hoped to turn Coca-Cola around, promising a 15 percent or better gain in earnings per share, as had occurred during Coca-Cola's peak period of global expansion during the 1980s, and predicting overall volume growth of 6 to 7 percent. In 2000, Coca-Cola cut roughly 20 percent of its 29,000 employees, removed or reassigned nearly 94 percent of its top management, and attempted to buy Quaker Oats. However, Coca-Cola's board rejected the Quaker acquisition and Quaker, with its top-selling sports drink Gatorade, later merged with PepsiCo.

In March 2001, the company announced a joint venture with Proctor & Gamble Co. to better position its Minute Maid juices, but the deal was called off in September. However, Coca-Cola completed two key acquisitions in 2001 with the purchase of Mad River Traders (specialty iced teas, lemonades, and juice cocktails) and Odwalla Inc. (fruit and vegetable drinks, spring water, nutritional bars, and organic milk sold in health stores). Coca-Cola's expansion of its joint venture with Nestle S.A. was continued in 2001. The Coca-Cola and Nestle Refreshments (CCNR) venture was renamed Beverage Partners Worldwide (BPW). BPW, headquartered in Zurich, Switzerland, planned to operate in 40 countries, up from 24 countries under the initial CCNR venture. BPW was expected to compete against Unilever's Lipton brands in the much-coveted ready-to-drink (RTD) coffee and tea market.

Daft also oversaw changes on the advertising front. While predecessor Ivester discouraged movie deals, Daft invested $US150 million in 2001 to co-market Warner Brothers' blockbuster Harry Potter movie. Coca-Cola also made a "one-time" marketing investment of US$300 million in 2001. Coca-Cola's bottlers felt the new ads did little to boost sales, which had declined in the United States since the mid-1990s. Following the period of decline, Coca-Cola's U.S. volume sales growth was 3.9 percent per year, while PepsiCo saw annual growth of 4.5 percent. Nevertheless, despite near stagnant growth in the United States, Coca-Cola managed to continue its dominance of the U.S. market. A report by *Beverage Digest* showed Coca-Cola had a 44 percent market share in the United States in 2000, unchanged from the previous year. PepsiCo's market share was 31 percent, also unchanged from 1999. Coca-Cola sold 5

of the top 10 carbonated soft drinks (CSDs) in the United States in 2000, with Coke Classic as the market leader. In 2000, Coke's unit case volume in the worldwide soft drinks market grew only 4 percent, much lower than Daft's projections, with only 1 percent growth in the North American market. In 2002, in hopes of boosting sales, Coca-Cola introduced Vanilla Coke, their first new flavor in 17 years, since the introduction of Cherry Coke in 1995.

In 2003, Coca-Cola began to sell Vanilla Coke and diet Vanilla Coke in more than 50 countries and introduced various Sprite brand extension products in Belgium, Italy, Australia, and Hong Kong. In addition, it launched several new products in the United States, including the soft drinks Sprite Remix and Barq's Floatz. Other new products were Minute Maid Premium Heart Wise, an orange juice containing cholesterol-lowering plant sterols; Minute Maid Limeade; and a milk-based product called Swerve. The company also launched a natural juice-flavored soft drink, Nativa, in Argentina and extended the Kuat line in Brazil. Dasani, Coca-Cola's bottled water brand, was introduced in Ghana and Kenya. Coca-Cola also bought several brands and trademarks in 2003, including Cosmos in the Philippines, Multivita in Poland, Neverfail Springwater in Australia, Chaudfontaine in Belgium, and Valpre in South Africa.

Coca-Cola also took steps in 2003 to streamline operations, eliminating 3,700 jobs. The following year, several new products were launched, including Zu, a ready-to-drink canned coffee with ginseng that debuted in Thailand, and Aqua Shot, a flavored water with vitamins introduced in New Zealand. New flavors for existing brands also proliferated, including Sprite Icy Mint in China, Fanta Citrell in Germany, and Fanta Naranja Chamoy in Mexico. In 2005 the company introduced Coca-Cola Zero, a zero-calorie cola, in the United States. Coca-Cola reported total revenues in 2004 of US$21.96 billion, up 4.4 percent from 2003. Japan remained the company's most profitable market, while China represented the potential for highest future growth. As of the first quarter of 2005, Coca-Cola's sales in North America and Europe were relatively flat, while sales were up 28 percent in Africa, 12 percent in Latin America, and 8 percent in Asia. Coca-Cola Hellenic, the second largest bottler of Coke beverages, reported its steepest decline in Bloomberg records history in 2008. Consumer spending worldwide was impacted by soaring food and fuel prices.

PepsiCo Inc. Pepsi-Cola is the beverage division of PepsiCo Inc., which also owns Frito-Lay snacks, Quaker, and Gatorade, as well as other businesses. Pepsi soft drinks, including Pepsi, Diet Pepsi, Slice, Mountain Dew, and

Mug Root Beer, held about 32 percent of the U.S. soft drink market as of 2004.

Pepsi-Cola was created in 1898 in New Bern, North Carolina, by druggist Caleb D. Bradham, who claimed it cured dyspepsia (indigestion). The Pepsi-Cola Co. grew throughout the twentieth century and in 1963 acquired Frito-Lay, the largest U.S. snack foods company. The company changed its name to PepsiCo Inc. and later acquired restaurant chains, including Pizza Hut (1977), Taco Bell (1978), and Kentucky Fried Chicken (1986), later known as KFC. The restaurant holdings were divested in 1997.

By the late 1990s, Pepsi-Cola North America (PCNA), a division of PepsiCo, manufactured and sold soft drink concentrate to company-owned and independent bottlers operating facilities in the United States and Canada. The division also provided fountain beverage syrups to restaurants. Pepsi-Cola International (PCI), later renamed PepsiCo Beverages International (PBI), controlled the company's international soft drink operations. Through PCI, Pepsi-Cola products were sold in over 150 countries and territories and held about 18 percent of the international soft drink market. PCI owned the rights to produce and sell Seven-Up brands internationally, while U.S. Seven-Up operations were owned by Cadbury Schweppes.

Pepsi-Cola International (PCI), the second-largest international marketer of soft drinks, faced severe financial problems in the late 1990s. PCI lost US$846 million in 1996 and another US$50 million in 1997. However, PepsiCo vowed to challenge Coca-Cola overseas by having PCI concentrate on less developed markets rather than those in countries where Coca-Cola was entrenched, such as Venezuela. By the early years of the first decade of the 2000s, this strategy was proving to be successful. Despite an economic slump in Latin America and a boycott of U.S. brands in the Middle East, PepsiCo Beverages International (PBI), as the division later became known, increased its volume by 5 percent from 2001 to 2002, with revenue growth of 1 percent and an increase of operating profits of 23 percent. The strong numbers posted showed that PBI's attention to large emerging markets paid off. Volume growth in China, India, Turkey, Israel, Burma, and Russia remained at double digits well into the mid-2000s.

PepsiCo dramatically changed its corporate structure in 1997 to more effectively compete in the soft drink business. In October, the company spun off its restaurant operations to shareholders as a new publicly traded company called Tricon Global Restaurants Inc. The idea was to make the new PepsiCo more attractive to investors since they would be able to see more clearly the results from the company's higher margin beverage and snack

businesses after they were separated from the low margin restaurant business. However, 1997 profits at PepsiCo's beverage unit were squeezed by a combination of "cut-throat" soft-drink pricing, flat sales for the flagship Pepsi brand, and heavy investment in the beverage business. Pepsi executives characterized 1997 as extremely tough year for Pepsi-Cola North America and a significant disappointment.

In the late 1990s, Pepsi was investing heavily in the fountain segment of the soft drink business, trying to attack Coca-Cola's dominance of that category. Coca-Cola's fountain business worldwide was three times that of Pepsi's. One of PepsiCo's strategies was to sue Coca-Cola in May 1998, charging that Coca-Cola was violating U.S. antitrust laws by attempting to "freeze" Pepsi out of the business of selling soft drinks in restaurants and movie theaters served by independent food distributors. The charges were that Coca-Cola threatened distributors with losing their Coke business if they offered Pepsi products. Coca-Cola, denying the charges, countered that its contracts, which specified that Coke distributors not sell rival products, were not illegal. Some observers were puzzled by the suit, noting that Pepsi also had such exclusive contracts with its fountain customers.

In 1998, PepsiCo acquired Tropicana, which as of 2001 was the world's leading juice brand. Pepsi One was launched in 1998 as a one-calorie cola designed for health-conscious men. In March 1999, PepsiCo spun off its Pepsi Bottling Group unit as PepsiCo began to focus on its soft drink products and its snack food operations. PepsiCo also unveiled its new "The Joy of Cola" advertising slogan, ending the reign of the "Generation Next" campaign. The following year, PepsiCo also resurrected its "Pepsi Challenge" campaign from the early 1980s. In 1999, Steven S. Reinemund was named president of PepsiCo. The Pepsi Center opened October 1, 1999, as the new home of the NBA Denver Nuggets and NHL's Colorado Avalanche.

At the beginning of the twenty-first century, PepsiCo's core brands of Pepsi, Mountain Dew, and Slice comprised approximately 25 percent of company sales, with more than 60 percent of sales generated by the company's salty snacks division. Although still the number two soft drink maker in the world, PepsiCo made moves to significantly challenge its strongest competitor, Coca-Cola. In August 2001, PepsiCo purchased Quaker Oats for roughly US$14 billion to form the world's fifth largest food and beverage company. The move added the extremely popular Gatorade, an isotonic sports drink, to PepsiCo's beverage line. In 2005, PepsiCo surpassed

Coca-Cola Company in market value for the first time in 112 years.

PepsiCo has been lauded for successfully appealing to a younger audience with products beyond traditional colas. As a prime example, in 2001 it launched Code Red, a cherry-flavored version of the popular Mountain Dew, using a unique marketing approach. The brand was heavily advertised during the X Games and on the Mountain Dew Web site. In addition, 4,000 free bottles were sent out in advance of the product being available in stores. After its first 11 weeks of distribution, Hillary Chura, in the August 27, 2001, edition of *Advertising Age,* reported that ACNielsen named it the fifth-largest-selling 20-ounce soft drink. In 2004, PepsiCo launched the Gatorade Endurance Hydration Formula, a sports drink tailored for the needs of high-endurance athletes, and Pepsi Edge, a full-flavored cola with half the sugar, carbohydrates, and calories of regular cola.

By 2001, PepsiCo had transformed itself and seemed on the verge of winning the cola war with archrival Coca-Cola, at least in terms of investor confidence. According to the April 2, 2001, issue of *Fortune,* "From 1997 to 1999, Pepsi gave itself a makeover—a very Coke-like makeover—by spinning off its fast-food restaurant business and some of its bottling operations. By the early years of the first decade of the 2000s, Pepsi, like Coke, owned less than 50 percent of its bottlers, which means that this low-margin, capital-intensive business isn't consolidated in Pepsi's financials." Pepsi also shrewdly began expanding its offering of non-carbonated soft drinks (CSDs), a market that became the fastest selling at the turn of the century.

In 2003 PepsiCo combined its primary North American beverage brands into a new organization, PepsiCo Beverages North American (PBNA). In 2009 PepsiCo reported revenue of US$44.3 billion (including snack foods) with 203,000 employees globally in 2010. Net sales outside the United States accounted for about 34 percent of PepsiCo beverage sales. The company's largest foreign markets were Mexico, Great Britain, and Canada.

Pepsi-Cola sponsored a "Four Weeks for Father!" campaign to celebrating fathers and father figure roles in the African-American community. Student artists submitted drawings through a partnership with Howard University. On June 12, 2008, *Rolling Out* announced graduating senior Nia Lindsey as the winner of the competition. Her designs were featured on the Web site and throughout the booklet. Other celebration-linked activities included the www.pepsigreatfathers.com essay contest opportunity to spotlight fathers and win $500. Pepsi also partnered with the National Fatherhood Initiative

focused on promoting relationships with responsible and committed fathers.

Jerry Gleeson described how the Pepsi Portfolio was changing to include more non-carbonated products. Bottled water, juices, and teas gained popularity. In 2008, the product mix was 30 percent non-carbonated and 70 percent carbonated. Future plans included increasing sales of fountain and vending machine drinks, as well as promoting 20-ounce bottles beyond grocery stores and large retailers.

Dr Pepper Snapple Group. The Dr Pepper Snapple Group, formerly known as Cadbury Schweppes PLC, was the number three global soft drink producer in 2010. In 2006-2007, the British soft drink and candy manufacturer acquired a large stable of soft drink companies and brands, including Dr Pepper/Seven-Up Companies Inc., which was purchased outright in late 1994. In addition to Dr Pepper and Seven-Up (United States only), Cadbury Schweppes soft drink brands in 2009 included Canada Dry, Hawaiian Punch, Mott's, Clamato, Schweppes, Crush, Hires, Nehi, Welch's, Orangina, Snapple, Nantucket Nectars, A&W, Yoo-Hoo, Squirt, and Sunkist.

Prior to the Cadbury purchase, the Dr Pepper Co. had been made a private company in 1984 in a leveraged buyout. Dr Pepper later absorbed the U.S. operations of The Seven-Up Company. In August 1993, Cadbury Schweppes purchased 12.2 million Dr Pepper shares from Prudential for US$231.3 million, increasing its stake in Dr Pepper/Seven-Up to about 26 percent. At the time, industry analysts speculated that Cadbury could help Dr Pepper expand into international markets after a full buyout, a prediction that came true a little over a year later.

With the Dr Pepper buyout, Cadbury Schweppes held 17 percent of the U.S. market by combining its own 3.5 percent share with Dr Pepper/Seven-Up's 11.5 percent share and a 2 percent share from A&W Brands, which Cadbury had purchased earlier. Cadbury Schweppes controlled about half of the U.S. non-cola business and had a platform for further expansion in international markets.

In early 1998, Cadbury Schweppes bolstered the distribution of its soft drinks by purchasing, along with investment firm Carlyle Group LP, two Midwest U.S. bottlers for US$724 million. The two bottlers—Beverage America Inc. in Holland, Michigan, and Select Beverages Inc. in Darien, Illinois—were combined in a separate company called American Bottling Company. Cadbury's management was operating American Bottling although its stake was only 40 percent. The deal was made to address Cadbury Schweppes' relative lack of strength in bottling in the United States compared with Coca-Cola and Pepsi. Plans called for the new bottling company to acquire smaller bottlers and eventually become a public company.

Cadbury acquired RC Cola in September 2000 as part of its $1.45 billion acquisition of the Snapple Beverage Group from Triarc. In 2001, Cadbury sold its international RC Cola business to Cott Corp., keeping its RC Cola business in the United States, Mexico, Canada, and Puerto Rico, allowing the company to focus its efforts in North America, continental Europe, and Australia. Late in 2001, Cadbury acquired France's Pernod-Ricard's soft drinks business, including Orangina and Pampryl fruit juice brands that are sold in continental Europe, North America, and Australia. In 2002, the company acquired Nantucket Nectars in the United States and Squirt in Mexico.

In 2003, Cadbury announced a business restructuring that included an amalgamation of its North American beverage businesses. In 2008, the company demerged its Cadbury Schweppes to form Dr Pepper Snapple. Beverage sales, led by Dr Pepper, had total sales of more than US$5.53 billion in 2009.

Cott Corp. Riding its private label successes of the mid- to late 1990s, Cott, once a small family business, increased its revenues from about US$65 million in 1991 to US$665 million in 1994 and more than US$1 billion in 1997. By 2003 the company accounted for 4.7 percent of the global market. Cott's original "premium" private label product was President's Choice Cola, which was sold in Ontario's Loblaw supermarket chain. Cott captured 50 percent of all cola volume in Loblaw stores and 30 percent of cola volume throughout the province after expanding to nearly every supermarket chain in Ontario. Cott also supplied the Wal-Mart chain.

In 1991, Cott began purchasing Royal Crown (RC) concentrate from the RC Columbus, Georgia, facility to use in its private label colas. The high quality of the cola, along with improvements in packaging, not only helped Cott find success but also dramatically increased the image of private labels. As private label soft drink products caught on, they grabbed large market shares at supermarkets in major markets in the mid-1990s, including 30 percent in Great Britain, 27 percent in Switzerland, 22 percent in Canada, 17 percent in France, and 9 percent in the United States.

However, by the late 1990s, Cott's star had fallen somewhat, and the company put itself up for sale in October 1997. Cott was struggling with weak sales and earnings as well as reduced profit margins due to a

protracted price war with branded soft drink companies in the mid- to late 1990s. As a result, private-label bottlers like Cott were forced to make additional price cuts. Cott also tried to move into private label foods, but after disappointing results, made plans to sell the business. Cott also incurred a high debt load while building a bottling network in the United States. All of these factors hurt the company, although its market share in the United States continued to climb at the expense of smaller, private label soft drink manufacturers. In early 1998, Cott took itself off the market, saying that the offers it received were not sufficient. At the same time, it was searching for a new CEO.

In mid-1998, Cott named Frank E. Weise president and CEO. Along with a new management team, Weise began a program of internal renovation with the goal of focusing the company on its core business, namely the premium private label business in Canada, the United States, and the United Kingdom. During the late 1990s and into the early years of the first decade of the 2000s, Cott took the first step in its restructuring process by divesting its non-soft drink interests, including its pet food subsidiary, frozen food division, and U.S. PET bottling operations. In 2000, Cott acquired Concord Beverage, a regional private label producer in the northeastern United States, strengthening its 56 percent market share of the private label carbonated soft drink industry in the United States. With the acquisition, Cott added A&P, Acme, Pathmark, and others to its customer base that already included Wal-Mart, Kmart, and Safeway.

In a significant revitalization move, Cott purchased RC Cola's international business and its concentrate supply contracts from Cadbury Schweppes in 2001. The move gave Cott ownership of the formula used in its retailer brand colas as well as increased presence in 60 countries outside North America, including Israel and the Philippines. In 2001, Cott formed Northeast Retailer Brands (NRB) with independent bottler Polar Beverages of Massachusetts. NRB gave Cott additional leverage in the Northeast, where its sales had not matched those of other regions. In the meantime, Cott also looked internally to address quality, plant utilization, and customer service issues.

Cott initially posted losses in the late 1990s as its restructuring efforts were being implemented. However, by the end of 2001, Cott, which had become the fourth largest soft drink company in the United States and the world's largest retailer brand soft drink supplier, reported eight consecutive quarters of profitable results. Sales rose steadily through the early years of the first decade of the 2000s, from US$990 million in 2000 to US$1.19 billion in 2002 and US$1.4 billion in 2003. Total sales grew by

16.1 percent in 2004 to exceed US$1.6 billion, and by 2009 revenue figures reached US$1.77 billion. Cott's work force was slightly less than 3,000.

AriZona Iced Tea. Introduced in 1992, AriZona Iced Tea reported remarkable success competing against ready-to-drink (RTD) teas from established brands like Lipton and Nestea. A small, family-owned company founded in 1971, Ferolito, Vultaggio & Sons established itself as a distributor of beer products in New York City. By 1986, the company had introduced its first product, Midnight Dragon Malt Liquor. This was followed by Crazy Horse Malt Liquor, which in 1992 sold more than 1 million cases. In 1992, the company entered the RTD iced tea market with AriZona Iced Tea. As with Crazy Horse, the product was distinguished by innovative and award-winning packaging, using twenty-four-ounce single serve containers with the bright hues and graphics of the U.S. Southwest culture.

By the end of 1993, AriZona had sold more than 10 million cases and was selected as one of *Fortune* magazine's top products of the year. In 2002, Ferolito & Vultaggio signed with Celestial Seasonings and Allied Domecq to respectively produce and market Celestial Seasonings RTD teas and juices and Kalhua Iced Coffee. By 2004, the AriZona brand included seven flavored teas, seven juice drinks, two coladas, four flavored diet teas, a carbonated soft drink, and a line of Rx Herbal Tonics. By 2004, AriZona was the top-selling brand in the United States.

AriZona Beverages joined with Saladworks in 2008 to sign a multi-year beverage agreement, making some of the most popular AriZona brands available at Saladworks locations. Consumers would be able to enjoy Lemon Tea, Green Tea, Peach Tea, Pomegranate Green Tea, Arnold Palmer Half & Half, and various energy drinks along with their salads.

MAJOR COUNTRIES IN THE INDUSTRY

The United States. At the end of the twenty-first century, the U.S. soft drink industry was the largest in the world both in terms of sales and consumption. However, growth remained relatively sluggish. Carbonated drink sales grew by only 0.7 percent in 2004, up about 72.5 million cases from 2003. Per capita consumption, however, fell for the sixth consecutive year, reaching 53.7 gallons in 2004. Diet soft drinks accounted for most of the category's growth as consumers sought healthier, low-calorie drinks. In 2009, Coca-Cola controlled more than 50 percent of the global market, followed by PepsiCo with 32 percent. Dr Pepper/Seven Up, the third largest branded soft

drink company in the United States, reported 2.4 percent volume growth in 2004, for the first increase in market share in several years as Dr Pepper surpassed 7-Up as a top 10 brand. Cott enjoyed a 17.5 percent volume increase.

The fastest growing category by volume in the United States was bottled water, which grew 8.6 percent in 2004, exceeding 6.8 billion gallons. Bottled water became the second leading beverage among U.S. consumers behind carbonated soft drinks. The U.S. bottled water market was valued at almost US$9.2 billion in 2004. The largest bottled water category was non-carbonated bottled water (6.4 billion gallons and 94.2 percent of volume in 2004). The leading U.S. bottled water company in 2009 was Nestle Waters North America (NWNA), with more than US$3.8 billion in wholesale revenues. In 2008, Coca-Cola's Dasani was in second place with US$2.9 billion in revenue. PepsiCo's Aquafina was the third leading brand, with revenues reaching US$2.8 billion. The market for flavored bottled water was expected to see rapid expansion with the introduction of several new brands. According to *Beverage Marketing*, this segment was expected to report sales of more than US$800 million by 2009.

While bottled water dominated sales of non-carbonated soft drinks, the outlook for fruit beverages also appeared favorable, particularly for shelf-stable juices. Single-serve products, which drove growth in this segment, benefited from several innovations in the early years of the first decade of the 2000s, including low calorie and low carbohydrate products and juice drinks enhanced with vitamins and other nutrients.

Supermarkets were the largest outlet for sales of soft drinks in the United States, accounting for 48 percent of total volume in 2000, followed by fountain/restaurant sales at 21 percent, convenience stores at 12 percent, vending at 11 percent, and mass merchandisers/club/drug stores at 8 percent.

Mexico. In the early years of the first decade of the twenty-first century, Mexico was the world's number two soft drink market. Mexico's more than 90 million people annually consumed an estimated 560 eight-ounce servings of soft drinks per capita, lagging just slightly behind U.S. levels. In 2001, according to a report by the Market Research Centre and the Canadian Trade Commissioner Service, sales of carbonated drinks in Mexico grew 5 percent to reach almost US$15 billion. As with other North American markets, Mexico began to see significant growth in sales of juices and bottled water in the remainder of the 2000s. As of 2003, bottled water accounted for about 45 percent of nonalcoholic beverage sales in Mexico.

According to InfoLatina S.A. de C.V., by 2001 there were about 43 soft drink companies in Mexico. However, 70 percent of sales came from eight of those companies, with Coke and Pepsi as the major players. As of 2001, Mexico's soft drinks market was dominated by Coca-Cola's approximately 70 to 75 percent market share, while PespsiCo controlled about 20 percent of the market. Figures varied as both Coke and Pepsi battled fiercely for market share in a country where each franchise usually allowed one company to control a given geographical region. As a result, there was often a lack of competition to keeps prices in check, and advertising became a crucial means of gaining market share.

According to Coca-Cola, the company employed more than 86,000 people in Mexico as of 2004. Operations included 15 bottlers, 78 bottling plants, and 465 supply centers. PepsiCo considered Mexico its second most important market outside the United States, and in early 2002 announced a goal to invest more than $1.2 billion in Mexico by 2006, according to FWN Select. One key strategy was obtaining the contract to supply soft drinks to the country's largest cinema chain, Cinemex, which had previously been supplied by Coca-Cola. PepsiCo's Mexican sales accounted for over US$4 billion annually.

By early in the first decade of the 2000s, PepsiCo's principal bottlers in Mexico were Grupo Embotelladoras Unidas, Grupo Embotellador Bret, and Pepsi-Gemex, S.A. de C.V., which was PepsiCo's second largest bottler outside the United States. Fomento Economico Mexicano SA (Femsa), owned Mexico's largest Coke franchise, in Monterrey. In 2001, Arca became Coke's second largest bottler in Mexico as a result of the merger of Procor and Arma.

On January 1, 2002, the Mexican government approved a 20 percent tax on soft drink manufacturers who use fructose sweeteners in an effort to stimulate the domestic sugar industry. According to *Futures World News,* some soft drink producers had voluntarily switched to sugar-only formulas, while others, like Coca-Cola, did not expect the tax to cause a price increase or negatively impact sales.

The Middle East. Shifting political trends in the Middle East were changing the soft drinks market. For example, the Coca-Cola Company for years had been unable to do business in Saudi Arabia because of an Arab boycott stemming from Coke's operations in Israel. As a result, PCI (Pepsico) was able to build Saudi Arabia into its third largest foreign market in the mid-1990s, trailing only Mexico and Canada.

By March 1998, however, Coca-Cola claimed that it was outselling PepsiCo in the Middle East and North Africa, although the claim was disputed by PepsiCo. Coca-Cola's aggressive and expensive campaign there appeared to be working, and the company contended that its collective market share for the region was 38 percent compared with Pepsi's 36 percent. While Coca-Cola admitted that Pepsi continued to be the clear leader in Saudi Arabia and other Persian Gulf countries, Coca-Cola said its leadership in countries like Israel and Egypt, combined with strong market share gains in other Arab countries, gave it regional supremacy. PepsiCo, however, claimed that its market share in the area was 46 percent, with Coke holding just 38 percent.

During the late 1990s, Coca-Cola made several key moves to increase its Middle East position. In 1998, Ramallah-based National Beverage Co. became the sole Palestinian Coca-Cola franchise, and Coca-Cola planned to further invest in the bottling plant in 2000. In 1999, Coca-Cola opened a US$20 million bottling plant in Riyadh where it controlled 30 percent of the soft drinks market. In 2000 Coca-Cola relocated its Middle East and North Africa division from Britain to Bahrain to further strengthen its local presence and to act in accordance with the company motto to "Think local, act local." At the time, Coca-Cola claimed a 45 percent market share in the region, which comprised 15 countries with 55 plants.

With the outbreak of the Al-Aksa Intifada in the Palestinian Territories in the fall of 2000, Coca-Cola faced an increasingly difficult market in the Middle East and in the West Bank in particular. A boycott of U.S. products sparked by the Intifada contributed to Coca-Cola's 7 percent loss in the Middle East and North Africa, according to the company's 2000 annual report.

BIBLIOGRAPHY
All Change: Strategic Outlook for the Soft Drinks Industry in 2010,
    7 February 2001. Available from www.industrysearch.com.au.
"Americans Dominate World of Soft Drinks." Leatherhead Food
    RA, September 2001. Available from
    www.foodlineweb.co.uk.
"The Big Brands Go Begging in Europe." *Business Week,*
    21 March 2005. Available from www.businessweek.com.
Bolling, Chris. "Globalization of the Soft Drink Industry."
    Agricultural Outlook. Economic Research Service, United
    States Department of Agriculture, December, 2002. Available
    from www.ers.usda.gov/.
"Bottled Water Strengthens Position as No. 2 Beverage."
    Beverage Marketing, 25 April 2005. Available from http://
    www.beveragemarketing.com.

Cadbury Schweppes PLC. *2004 Annual Report,* March 2001. Available from www.cadburyschweppes.com.

Chura, Hillary. "Pepsi-Cola's Code Red is White Hot; Mountain Dew Extension Taps Trends, Flies Off Shelves." *Advertising Age,* 27 August 2001.

Coca-Cola Company. *2004 Annual Report.* Available from www.coca-cola.com.

"Coke Halts Production at Indian Plant," 14 March 2004. Available from www.just-drinks.com/.

"Coke Winning Mexican Cola War: Analyst." InfoLatina S.A. de C.V., 26 June 2001.

Deogun, Nikhil, and Jonathan Karp. "For Coke in India, Thums Up Is the Real Thing." *Wall Street Journal,* 29 April 1998, B1.

"Feeling Thirsty, The Thirsty Reach for Tap Water." *International Herald Tribune,* 17 June 2008.

The Fruit Juice and Soft Drink Market in Mexico. Market Research Centre and the Canadian Trade Commissioner Service, July 2003. Available from http://atn-riae.agr.ca/.

Gleeson, Jerry. "Pepsi Bottling Sees International Push, More Non-carbonated Drinks." 29 May 2008. Available from lottud.com.

"Global Soft Drinks Growing by 5 Percent a Year." *The Beverage Network,* November 2002. Available from www.bevnet.com.

Gutschi, Monica. "D. J. PepsiCo Reiterates to Invest $1.2B in Mexico Over 6 Years." *FWN Select,* 4 February 2002.

"Increasing Soft Drink Sales Drive New Launches." *AP-Foodtechnology,* 23 July 2004. Available from www.foodtechnology.com.

Kevin, Kitty. "Water Log, 2004." *Beverage Industry,* 2004. Available from www.bevindustry.com.

Lee, Julian. "Bottled Water Fad Springs a Leak." *The Sydney Morning Herald,* 3 May 2008.

"Local Players in a Multinational Landscape." Canadean press release, January 2001. Available from www.canadean.com.

Mallory, Maria. "Pop Goes the Pepsi Generation; A Struggling Pepsi-Cola Offers Cautionary Tale in Brand Stewardship." *U.S. News & World Report,* 16 June 1997, 48.

McKay, Betsy. "Coca-Cola: The Real Thing Can Be Hard to Measure." *Wall Street Journal Online,* 23 January 2002. Available from www.wsj.com.

———. "Guess Who's Winning the Cola Wars?" *Fortune,* 2 April 2001.

"New Flavored Water Brands Flooding the Market." *Beverage Marketing,* 10 February 2005. Available from http://www.beveragemarketing.com.

"Pepsi Plans to Up Market Share in Mexico." InfoLatina S.A. de C.V., 3 September 2001.

Petrakis, Maria. "Coca-Cola HBC Plunges After Cutting Annual Forecasts," 13 June 2008. Available from Bloomberg.com.

Phillips, Bob. "Fruit Beverages: Sweet Revenge." *Progressive Grocer,* 1 April 2005. Available from www.progressivegrocer.com.

Prince, Greg W. "Cott Corp. Acquires Concord, Expanding Private Label Lead." *Beverage World,* 15 November 2000.

———. "Steep to Conquer: Whether it's Creating the Best-selling Tea or Most Successful Beverage Alliance, Pepsi and Lipton Prove It's all About Patience and Good Ingredients." *Beverage World,* 15 October 2001.

———. "Cott Dances with Bear: Private Label Leader Teams with Polar." *Beverage World,* 15 December 2001.

———. "Good Stuff: Private Label's Premium Image is What has Store Brands Maintaining Their Shelf Space." *Beverage World,* 15 October 2001.

"Repairing the Coke Machine." *Business Week,* 19 March 2001.

"RO and Pepsi Present the Father' Day Takeover." *Rolling Out,* 12 June 2008.

"Saladworks Inks Deal with Arizona Iced Tea," 22 May 2008. Available from www.fastcasual.com.

"School Bans Red Bull From Grounds," 6 June 2008. Available from news.bbc.co.uk.

"Shaking Up the Coke Bottle." *Business Week,* 3 December 2001.

Sicher, John, ed. "Special Report: Top 10 U.S. CDC Companies and Brands for 2003." *Beverage Digest,* 5 March 2004. Available from http://www.beverage-digest.com/pdf/top-10_2004.pdf.

"Soft Drink Facts." American Beverage Association, 2004. Available from www.ameribev.org.

"Soft Drink Markets in 174 Countries Worldwide Documented in Massive Five-Volume Report from Beverage Marketing Corporation." Beverage Marketing Corporation News Release, 15 June 2001. Available from www.beveragemarketing.com.

"Soft Drinks: A Fluid Picture." TGI Global News, February 2004. Available from www.tgisurveys.com/.

"Solid Growth Expected In Mexico's Soft Drink Market." InfoLatina S.A. de C.V., 24 August 2001.

"Sports and Energy Sector to Remain High Value." Canadean press release, January 2002. Available from www.canadean.com.

Squires, Sally. "Soft Drinks, Hard Facts." *Washington Post,* 27 February 2001.

Steinriede, Kent. "Enrico Battles Back: Pepsi's International Efforts Will Focus on Developing Markets." *Beverage Industry,* December 1996, p. 11.

Tarpley, Natasha A. "What Really Happened at Coke: Doug Ivester Was a Demon for Information." *Fortune,* 10 January 2000.

———. "Crunch Time for Coke: His Company is Overflowing with Trouble." *Fortune,* 19 July 1999.

Theodore, Sarah. "RTD Coffee, Tea Create a Buzz." *Beverage Industry,* 2004. Available from www.bevindustry.com.

"The Top 10 Brands." *Business Week,* 2003. Available from www.businessweek.com/.

"U.S. Beverage Sales Threatened by Rising Water." Canadean press release, January 2002. Available from www.canadean.com.

"U.S. Soft Drink Sales Up Slightly in 2004." *Beverage Marketing,* 14 March 2005. Available from http://www.beveragemarketing.com.

Warner, Melanie. "Coke Finds Its Bright Spots in Faraway Places.rdquo; *New York Times,* 20 April 2005.

"Water, Water, Everywhere." *American Demographics,* 1 October 2001.

SIC 2100

TOBACCO PRODUCTS

NAICS CODE(S)

3122. The tobacco industry produces the world's cigarettes, cigars, smoking and chewing tobacco, snuff, and reconstituted tobacco. Certain industry firms are also involved in the industrial processing side of the business, which includes stemming and re-drying tobacco.

INDUSTRY SNAPSHOT

The tobacco products industry in the early twenty-first century was one of contrasts. In many Western countries consumption was falling, as it had done through the 1990s. The United States, for instance, was characterized by a particularly vocal and effective antismoking movement that helped bring down smoking rates and lobbied for increasing restrictions on smoking in public. Tobacco companies in the United States also faced a growing number of lawsuits brought on behalf of smokers and victims of secondhand smoke who had become seriously ill or died. In addition, state and federal legislative proposals threatened to further restrict the industry. For example, the Master Settlement Agreement, signed on November 16, 1998, by various state attorneys general and leading U.S. cigarette makers, included the stipulation that cigarette makers pay US$206 billion to U.S. states over a 25-year period to reimburse costs associated with treating illnesses related to smoking. Analysts predicted that the settlement would increase the cost of cigarettes and thus contribute to a decrease in cigarette smoking throughout early twenty-first century. The U.S. Department of Agriculture (USDA) reported that cigarette consumption in the United States had fallen 7.5 percent between 1998 and 2000 as a result of increased prices, increased understanding of health risks, and bans on smoking in public places.

In Asia and Eastern Europe, however, cigarette sales increased as income levels rose (with U.S.-made cigarettes becoming very popular). In China, for example, the per capita consumption rose an estimated 250 percent between the early 1970s and late 1990s. Global cigarette consumption, which accounted for about 90 percent of all tobacco use, was fairly flat throughout the 1990s, tending to increase at a rate of 1 or 2 percent per year. The divergent attitudes toward smoking between the East and the West had a profound impact on the major cigarette manufacturers. With markets in North America and Western Europe sluggish, the big multinational tobacco companies, including Philip Morris, R.J. Reynolds, Japan Tobacco, and British American Tobacco (BAT), aggressively pursued sales in emerging markets like Russia.

Although a Russian economic downturn in 1998 allowed domestic brands to gain ground on more expensive imports, improved economic conditions there in 2000 boded well for the industry leaders, which by then were pursuing development of domestic

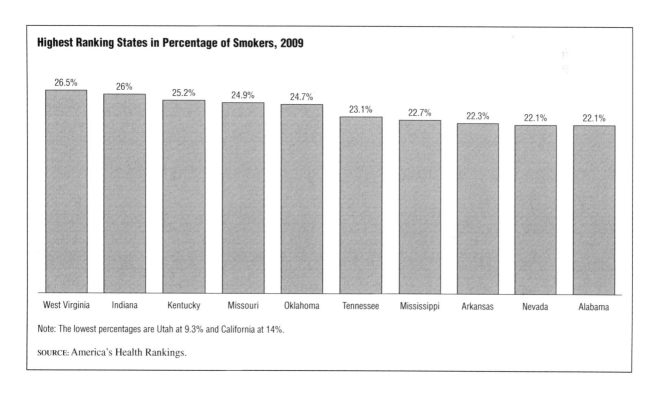

Highest Ranking States in Percentage of Smokers, 2009

West Virginia 26.5%   Indiana 26%   Kentucky 25.2%   Missouri 24.9%   Oklahoma 24.7%   Tennessee 23.1%   Mississippi 22.7%   Arkansas 22.3%   Nevada 22.1%   Alabama 22.1%

Note: The lowest percentages are Utah at 9.3% and California at 14%.

SOURCE: America's Health Rankings.

manufacturing facilities. An excise tax on cigarettes passed by the Russian Duma (parliament) in 2003 was not expected to diminish sales, which according to *Pravda* were worth about US$15 billion annually. The large tobacco companies seemed to be using their same old advertising strategies to encourage smoking among the Russian people. The target audience for this advertising was women and adolescents, and both categories continued steady growth. While there were laws and taxes regarding smoking in the West and in Europe, there were no such laws in place in Russia. Bans on public smoking were nearly nationwide in the United States and were growing in popularity in European countries as well, but no such bans existed in Russia.

In a January 10, 2010, article for CiggyFree.com, Debra Birkholz wrote that Gregory Feifer of Radio Free Europe had commented on the effects of a growing tobacco industry in Russia, which had no laws against smoking in public. Feifer indicated lower taxes, coupled with a mind-set that smoking was a sign of independence, would lead to continued growth in Russia at a time when the tobacco industry in the West was losing ground.

During the late 1990s, a growing number of people, especially in the United States, turned to products other than cigarettes, notably cigars and smokeless (chewing) tobacco. There was growing concern among public health officials at the possible misapprehension that cigars and smokeless tobacco were not health risks. Of concern as well was the rise in cigarette smoking among children and teenagers. Legislation emerged related to the targeting of teens in cigarette advertising, and several countries put laws in place that prevented tobacco companies from marketing their products to children under the age of 18.

Given the numerous uncertainties of the tobacco industry's future, few companies were eager to enter the business, thus limiting competition to those already in place. Many industry leaders pursued consolidation aggressively in an effort to broaden international reach, which further reduced the number of large cigarette manufacturers. At the beginning of the twenty-first century, Philip Morris, BAT, and Japan Tobacco accounted for 40 percent of the global tobacco industry. At the same time, however, the profit potential in cigarette manufacturing remained considerable. As famed investor Warren Buffett was quoted in Bryan Burrough's *Barbarians at the Gate: The Fall of RFR Nabisco*: "I'll tell you why I like the cigarette business. It costs a penny to make. Sell it for a dollar. It's addictive. And there's fantastic brand loyalty."

In the United States, the American Heart Association has estimated that 24.8 million men (approximately 23.1 percent) and 21.1 million women (18.3 percent) smoked as of 2008. Broken into demographic categories, 23.5 percent of white men and 20.6 percent of white women smoked; 25.6 percent of African-American men and 17.8 percent of African-American women smoked; 20.7 and 10.7 percent of Hispanic men and women smoked, respectively. In other key demographic groups in the United States, 9.9 percent of adults in the Asian community, 24.3 percent of adult Native Americans and Alaska Natives smoked.

The statistics for underage smoking include a staggering 80,000 to 100,000 kids who start smoking every day worldwide. Approximately one-fourth of the children in the western Pacific region will die from smoking according to the World Health Organization (WHO). The WHO has estimated that about one-third of the world population over the age of 15 smokes tobacco. In 2004 there were about 1.3 billion tobacco users, and by 2025, this number was expected to rise to 1.7 billion.

Tobacco is grown in at least 100 countries, with international sales estimated at over US$330 billion at the end of the first decade of the twenty-first century. The leading brand of cigarettes worldwide was Philip Morris's Marlboro.

ORGANIZATION AND STRUCTURE

Stemming and Re-drying. In the United States and other countries, tobacco processors purchase tobacco leaf from farmers and prepare the plant for manufacture through stemming and re-drying. Universal Corporation, Standard Commercial, and DIMON Inc. are the three companies that control most of this business, and all have large operations in important tobacco growing regions of the world. In 2009, Universal remained the largest of the global leaf tobacco dealers, with sales of US$2.54 billion. Second-ranked DIMON, was the result of a 1994 merger between former rivals Dibrell Brothers Inc. and Monk-Austin Inc. The merger created the world's second largest leaf tobacco dealer behind Universal. DIMON posted sales of US$835.3 million in 2004, and the next year merged with Standard Commercial, which had reported 2004 sales totaling US$780 million. That merger created Alliance One, which reported revenues of US$2.3 billion in 2010.

Large tobacco processors either purchase the farmers' tobacco at auction, a practice common in the United States, or buy tobacco directly from a farmer. In some overseas markets where firms have contracted to buy a farmer's entire crop, such as Zambia, companies often provide financial and technical assistance to support the grower and ensure the quality of the tobacco. In the United States, most processors purchase tobacco at auction to fulfill specific orders from the major domestic and overseas cigarette producers. In many cases, the processors' relationships with cigarette producers extend over many years.

After purchase, tobacco is processed to meet the specific needs of the cigarette manufacturer, whose representatives are frequently at the processor's facilities to monitor the work on a company's particular order. At the factory, tobacco is reclassified according to grade; blended to meet customer requirements regarding color, body, and chemistry; and threshed to remove the stem from the leaf (although some tobacco is processed in whole leaf form). Processed tobacco is then dried again to remove excess moisture so it stored for long periods. The processors generally do not manufacture cigarettes or other consumer tobacco products.

Asia. The tobacco industry in Asia has been dominated by national monopolies or near monopolies like the China National Tobacco Corporation, the Thailand Tobacco Monopoly, and the Korea Tobacco and Ginseng Corporation. China is the largest producer and consumer of cigarettes worldwide, manufacturing about 1.6 trillion cigarettes annually. In 1994, the Japanese government partially privatized its tobacco monopoly in a stock offering that received a notably poor reception from the investment community. Japan Tobacco International Inc. continued to control most of the market, although the share of imported cigarettes sold in the country rose after trade rules for the product were liberalized in 1985. By 2002, leading multinational firms had secured roughly 20 percent of the Japanese market, while Japan Tobacco maintained a 75 percent share. Tobacco production in India, the second largest country in terms of tobacco production and the third largest in terms of consumption, is regulated by the Indian Tobacco Board, which sets output levels and manages unsold stocks.

Europe. The role of government in the tobacco industry tends to be more varied and less prominent in Western Europe than elsewhere. Italy and Portugal have state-owned tobacco monopolies that control the manufacture and retail sales of tobacco products. The former monopolies of Seita in France and Tabacaler in Spain were privatized in the late 1990s. Those two companies eventually merged to form Altadis, one of the largest cigarette makers in the world and maker of the famous Gauloises brand. Tobacco companies are also privately owned in the United Kingdom, Germany, Belgium, Greece, and Ireland. In the United Kingdom, Imperial Tobacco is the top cigarette manufacturer, followed by Gallaher Group. The two companies control about 80 percent of the

U.K. tobacco industry. Philip Morris, Reemtsma, and BAT are influential forces in the German market.

Even in countries with state-run monopolies, however, the big firms have gained substantial market share through licensing and export maneuvering. In France, for example, Philip Morris, Rothmans, and R.J. Reynolds secured 35 percent of the market before Seita was privatized. Philip Morris doubled its sales between 1984 and 1994 in Europe, and its Marlboro brand became the industry leader, even though it often cost twice as much as products of the state monopolies.

The collapse of the Soviet Union and other communist regimes opened the markets of Eastern Europe to Western firms. Smokers in the former Soviet bloc consumed about 700 billion cigarettes in 1993, about 40 percent more than the 500 billion smoked in the United States. In Russia alone, according to *Pravda*, 50 percent of boys, 25 percent of girls, and 74 percent of young men were regular smokers, and sales of tobacco products reached US$15 billion each year. Recognizing this demand, Western multinationals feverishly bought production facilities in Russia and its former satellites. Philip Morris, for example, invested in Hungary, Lithuania, Russia, and Kazakhstan, with its biggest investment coming in Tabak, the former state tobacco monopoly of Czechoslovakia. Altogether, Philip Morris invested almost US$1 billion in the region, which was growing at more than 5 percent per year between 1989 and 1993. By 2000, total foreign investment in the Russian tobacco industry had exceeded US$2 billion, making tobacco one of Russia's most successful industries. International firms held more than 65 percent of the cigarette production market there.

United States. The tobacco products industry in the United States is entirely in private hands, although the government's price support program for tobacco did help stabilize leaf prices through the mid-1990s. Such price supports ended under a 1996 reform of U.S. farm subsidies. The top producers as of 2008 were Philip Morris USA, with almost 50 percent of the market; Altria Group; Reynolds American; and R.J. Reynolds Tobacco. Large multinationals, such as Philip Morris, that have a strong presence abroad have made the United States the world's biggest cigarette exporter. Exports reached a high of 250 billion cigarettes in 1996, but by 2000 that number had fallen to roughly 150 billion due to weakened demand, as well as the increasing numbers of operations set up by U.S. manufacturers in other nations. Export volume continued to decline through the early 2000s, falling from 127.4 billion pieces in 2002 to 121.4 billion in 2003. Exports declined more slowly in 2004, reaching 121 billion pieces. Until the late 1990s, the United States had also been the leading exporter of tobacco leaf. By 2000, however, Brazil had begun exporting larger leaf volumes.

Latin America. The second largest market in the Western Hemisphere is Brazil, which produced 154 billion cigarettes in 1992. The industry was dominated by British American Tobacco (BAT), which carried about 83 percent of the market. An export tax levied by the Brazilian government in 1999 in an effort to prevent the importation of Brazilian cigarettes previously exported to Paraguay undercut production levels in 1999 to 144 billion. Production in 2000 was about 104 billion pieces. Although manufacturing increased to 106.6 billion pieces in 2002, levels fell to 96.7 billion pieces in 2003 and even further in 2004. The cigarette industry in Mexico, which is controlled by two manufacturers—PM Mexico, with 54.8 percent of the market, and Cigarrera La Moderna, with about 45 percent of the market—produced about 56.3 billion cigarettes in 2000. Both production and consumption of cigarettes in Mexico leveled off in the late 1990s due to price increases and growing health concerns. In 1995, for example, per capita cigarette consumption in Mexico was 856, but by 2000 that number had dropped to 712. Export volume, however, grew from 6.5 billion pieces to 10 billion pieces, and the USDA reported Mexican cigarette exports at 20 billion pieces per year between 2000 and 2004.

In Argentina, cigarette output reached approximately 40 billion units in 2000. Masalin Particulares, owned by Philip Morris, controlled 59.4 percent of the market in 2001, with the remainder going to Nobleza Piccardo, a British American Tobacco (BAT) company. With domestic consumption declining from 1,976 cigarettes per capita in 1980 to 1,418 cigarettes per capita in 2000, Argentina's tobacco industry looked to international markets to remain profitable. Exports of cigarettes rose from 724 million in 1990 to 2.4 billion in 1995 and 2.5 billion by 2000. According to USDA figures, exports held steady through 2004 at 2.4 billion pieces.

Canada. The Canadian market is dominated by Imperial, RBH, and RJR-MacDonald, all of which are subsidiaries of large multinational tobacco companies. Imperial controlled 70.1 percent of the market in 2000 and 69.5 percent in 2001. Rothmans, Benson & Hedges, which held 35.5 percent of the Canadian market in 1980, reported that its share decreased steadily through the 1990s. It ranked second in 2001, with 16.4 percent of the market. Cigarette consumption was reduced by 31 percent between 1982 and 1991 in Canada because of major price hikes and increased awareness of the health risks associated with smoking. While cigarette exports rose rapidly in the early 1990s, most of the increase reflected tax avoidance schemes. Officials estimated that 80 percent of all foreign shipments found their way back to Canada. In 2001, domestic cigarette sales exceeded 42 billion pieces.

Africa. By the early 2000s, cigarette production had remained relatively low in Africa. South Africa was the biggest producer on the continent in 1990, with an output of 41 billion units. Consumption was also high, reaching about 34 percent of the adult population by 1995. The anti-apartheid government that came to power in 1993, however, launched aggressive anti-smoking measures that helped reduce the number of smokers 20 percent by 1997. Because of economic sanctions against the apartheid government in the 1980s, the South African tobacco industry faced little international competition until the early 1990s. Rothmans International, had been formed in 1995 with the merger of Rembrandt and Richemont tobacco companies. British American Tobacco (BAT) manufactures its own brands in South Africa, and Philip Morris granted Rembrandt exclusive rights to manufacture its Marlboro brand.

In addition, Zimbabwe and Zambia are two important leaf-producing countries in Africa. Zimbabwe was the world's third-largest exporter by the early 2000s. BAT and Philip Morris were facing allegations that they had targeted under-age smokers in Nigeria in an effort to increase sales in developing countries as their sales continued to decline in the West. In an effort to recruit young smokers, attorneys for Kano, Nigeria's largest state, argued that the tobacco companies gave away free cigarettes and sponsored sporting events and pop concerts. As of 2010, Kano and two other Nigerian states were seeking damages of US$38 billion.

BACKGROUND AND DEVELOPMENT

In 1492, Rodrigo de Jerez, one of Columbus's crewmen, noted that the natives of Cuba ignited dried tobacco leaves and inhaled the smoke. De Jerez tried it himself and thus became Europe's first confirmed smoker. Back in Spain, however, his neighbors, terrified by the smoke that poured from his mouth, thought the devil had possessed him. He was imprisoned by the Inquisition.

Tobacco usage has often generated such controversy. King James I of seventeenth-century England despised smoking, wrote a "Counterblast to Tobacco" and beheaded Sir Walter Raleigh, the man who first imported tobacco to Europe. However, King James I was also the first in power to extract substantial revenue from tobacco import duties.

Paper-wrapped cigarettes were supposedly developed in the sixteenth century by the beggars of Seville, Spain, who rolled discarded cigar butts in scraps of paper. Factory production of cigarettes in quantity began in the nineteenth century. In 1881, a patent was issued for a cigarette-rolling machine capable of making 120,000 pieces a day. By 1900, there were over 160 brands available in the United States.

Despite the large number of brands, however, 9 out of every 10 cigarettes purchased in the United States was produced by the American Tobacco trust, run by the ruthless James Buchanan Duke. After decimating his competition in the United States, Duke turned to Great Britain in 1900 and prepared to invade that market with a price-slashing strategy that he hoped would allow him to dominate the market. Preparing for Duke's arrival, local producers banded together to form Imperial Tobacco. A battle ensued for the British market. After about a year, Imperial announced it would counterattack by turning to the United States—the primary territory of American Tobacco—with its own brands. Duke decided to negotiate a settlement, which neatly divided the global market. His company got the U.S. territory, while Imperial took Great Britain, and a new company, BAT Mfg. Ltd., was created to promote smoking and produce cigarettes in the rest of the world. The cartel lasted for a decade until 1911, when the U.S. Supreme Court broke up Duke's trust into a new "big four": American Tobacco, R.J. Reynolds, Lorillard, and Liggett & Meyers.

One legacy of the Duke trust and subsequent breakup is that a single brand may be produced by different multinationals in different countries. For example, British American Tobacco (BAT) owns Benson & Hedges in most markets, but in the United States, Philip Morris holds the trademark, and in Britain it belongs to American Brands' subsidiary, Gallaher. Another example is Kent, which is owned by Lorillard in the United States but by BAT in international markets.

In 1913, Richard J. Reynolds developed what came to be known as the American cigarette—a blend of flue-cured and burley tobacco mixed with a small amount of Turkish product. It became immediately popular in the United States. In the late 1920s, a machine was developed that combined several cigarette-making procedures into one process. The machine made the package, packed the cigarettes, and affixed the revenue stamps, thus decreasing the cost of cigarette packaging to less than 1 cent per 1,000 units.

Filter-tipped cigarettes were developed in Western Europe in the 1950s and began to gain popularity just as health considerations concerning smoking first came to light. Cigarette sales in the United States peaked in 1965 at 529 billion, an average of more than half a

pack for every citizen over the age of 18. Thereafter, as a result of the report of the U.S. Surgeon General on the dangers of smoking, consumption fell. In the 1970s, cigarette commercials were banned on U.S. radio and television and legislation was passed that required that all cigarette packages and advertising to include health warnings. U.S. consumption levels dropped consistently throughout the 1980s, and recognition of the dangers to health that smoking presents spread throughout the world, particularly in Canada and Western Europe. In many countries, however, cigarette use rose during the 1980s and 1990s.

By the mid-1990s the United States, Germany, China, and Japan were the four top producers of cigarettes worldwide. China continued to be the world's leading producer and consumer of tobacco products. India, despite its size, was only the fifth-largest producer in the mid-1990s. However, in India the *bidi* (tobacco wrapped in a temburni leaf) was also extremely popular, which put India in second place for per capita tobacco consumption worldwide according to the World Health Organization (WHO). The cigarette market in Asia, home to 60 percent of the world's population, continued to boom throughout the decade. While many Asian countries launched antismoking campaigns, and several, like China, banned tobacco advertising, the attitude toward cigarette smoking remained one of indulgence or even tacit approval. A brand of cigarette remained a status indicator, with U.S. and other western brands regarded as the most prestigious. In Vietnam the cigarette of choice was BAT's 555, in Thailand it was Dunhill, and in China Marlboro was favored. Many of the inroads made by Western companies in the 1990s were attributable to market-opening measures instituted by Asian governments that lifted trade barriers to imports.

Cigarette smoking remained primarily a male pursuit in Asia in the 1990s. WHO estimated in 1996 that 44 percent of men in Southeast Asia smoked compared to 4 percent of women, while in India, 40 percent of men and 3 percent of women smoked. This demographic breakdown was in contrast to the fairly equal division by gender in many industrialized countries, such as New Zealand and the United States. Nevertheless, by the late 1990s young women in Asia were smoking in increasing numbers, although overall the percentage was below 10 percent.

As health concerns about smoking grew, consumption in Western Europe remained flat. In Eastern Europe, however, smokers were less aware of the health risks and there was no government control protecting citizens from those risks. As Michael Herron of the

American Cancer Society told the *Los Angeles Times*, Russia was regarded as being more than three decades behind the United States in terms of social and medical awareness of smoking's risks. For major manufacturers, these markets presented new opportunities for sales and investment. In Eastern Europe, the prevalence of female smoking also was much higher than in other regions of the world. In the Russian Federation, for example, the World Health Organization estimated that 67 percent of men and 30 percent of women smoked.

In the United States, legislation was introduced in 1994 to allow federal recovery of Medicare and Medicaid costs associated with tobacco-related illnesses. This proposal was based on legislation with similar objectives in several states. By 1998, courtroom and legislative battles were becoming daily fare for U.S. tobacco manufacturers. Juries awarded damages in the millions of dollars to survivors of smokers who had died of lung cancer, notably the Rose Cipollone (later overturned) and Milton Horowitz cases. Executives of the large cigarette companies were brought to testify before Congress about whether they had knowingly sold a hazardous drug, particularly targeting children and teenagers. The famous "Joe Camel" cartoon character, which antismoking advocates claimed was intended to draw children to smoking, vanished from advertisements for Camel cigarettes. At least 39 states filed lawsuits against tobacco companies asking that damages be awarded and devoted to the healthcare costs caused by smoking. However, despite a prohibition on advertising tobacco on U.S. television, tobacco marketers successfully employed other media, including billboards, magazines, and large signs displayed at gas stations and convenience stores. All such practices caused controversy.

In 1998, the U.S. Congress carried on a heated debate about the "tobacco bill," sponsored by Arizona Senator John McCain, which proposed to raise cigarette prices by US$1.10 over a five-year period and impose a host of restrictions on the marketing of tobacco. A key component of the bill, which was at the center of the controversy, was whether there should be a cap of US$8 billion per year on damages awarded in lawsuits against tobacco companies. The companies claimed that even this amount could drive them to bankruptcy, while antismoking advocates such as former U.S. surgeon general C. Everett Koop and former Food and Drug Administration head David Kessler found it unacceptable that damage awards against the tobacco companies would be limited. The *Washington Post* estimated that as of May 1998, tobacco companies had spent US$25 million in advertising to defeat the tobacco bill. In June 1998 the legislation died in the Senate, owing to the

tobacco lobby's pressure on senators according to some observers.

Faced with this legal barrage, the once-solid front presented by the tobacco companies began to crumble—but only slightly. Liggett, which had been the defendant in the Cippolone suit, admitted that smoking can cause cancer (an argument still not publicly accepted by most other companies) and volunteered to release secret industry documents that showed tobacco companies had long been aware of the health risks of cigarettes and also had encouraged marketing to under-age smokers. In June 1998 these documents came back to haunt cigarette manufacturers, when Brown & Williamson was found guilty of conspiracy charges tied to the lung cancer death of a long-term smoker. The documents served as a strong factor in the award of the first punitive damages against a tobacco company.

Despite protracted legal wrangling in the 1990s, which eventually resulted in hundreds of billions of dollars in settlements being paid to the U.S. government, U.S. tobacco makers remained highly profitable during the decade. The industry was also heartened by several developments stemming from the mid-1990s. The boom in exports to Asia and Eastern Europe gave the industry a big lift, as did the initial defeat of proposals by the Clinton administration to levy heavy taxes on cigarettes. By the late 1990s, however, legal battles facing the U.S. tobacco manufacturers had escalated, and the percentage of adult smokers continued to drop. Public opinion of the companies plummeted as records indicating their early awareness of health risks and their alleged targeting of underage smokers became public. Nevertheless, as of 1996, the Centers for Disease Control estimated that 47 million adults continued to smoke cigarettes, resulting in over 430,000 deaths per year and direct and indirect health costs of over US$100 billion. In light of the hostility they faced at home, U.S. companies began to increase their efforts to sell their products in developing nations.

Legal battles in the United States eventually resulted in the Master Settlement Agreement, signed on November 16, 1998, by the majority of U.S. states and the top U.S. cigarette makers. The agreement required cigarette manufacturers to pay US$206 billion to U.S. states over 245 years to offset treatment costs associated with smoking-related illnesses. In addition, the firms agreed to spend US$1.5 billion in a 10-year antismoking campaign, US$250 million on efforts to curb smoking by youths, and US$5.15 billion in a 12-year program to compensate tobacco farmers for the reduced tobacco sales likely to result from the agreement. Between 1998 and 2000, cigarette use in the United States fell by 7.5 percent, according to the U.S. Department of

Agriculture, and analysts pointed to a cigarette price increase of 45 cents per pack, which took effect when the Master Settlement agreement was passed, as a major cause.

U.S. cigarette smokers faced another price hike in January 2000 when a federal excise tax on cigarettes was increased from 24 cents to 34 cents per pack. Although the tax was officially levied on manufacturers, most of the cost was eventually added to the retail price of cigarettes. The excise tax was increased another 5 cents per pack in January of 2002. According to the Centers for Disease Control, the average smoker paid US$250 in cigarette taxes in 2000 based on estimates that 22.7 percent of U.S. citizens over the age of 16 were smokers. According to the USDA, U.S. tobacco usage, particularly cigarette smoking, was expected to continue to drop between 1 and 3 percent annually.

While cigarettes were being pummeled by the media and the medical establishment in the United States, the little-noticed cigar industry gained new aficionados and even a certain cachet. From 1989 to 1993, annual sales rose from 88 million to 109 million, an increase of almost 25 percent. About two-thirds of cigars sold in the United States were imported. In recognition of the estimated 8 million cigar smokers in the United States, cigar clubs, cigar dinners, and special events grew increasingly commonplace in the 1990s. Cuban cigars, illegal in the United States, nonetheless maintained their stature in the 1990s with up to 5 million being smuggled into the United States each year at prices of up to US$30 each. By the late 1990s, however, some industry observers thought that the popularity of cigars had peaked.

The sales of smokeless tobacco, chiefly moist snuff, also rose in the United States during the 1990s, although cigarettes still accounted for 95 percent of tobacco product sales. Leading brands included Copenhagen and Skoal and were made by the United States Tobacco Company. Restrictions on smoking in public places helped the industry, which also benefited from effective advertising promotion.

Consolidation intensified in the tobacco industry throughout the late 1990s, allowing the largest players to grow even larger. In 1999, British American Tobacco (BAT), the world's second-largest tobacco company, acquired 58 percent of Canadian tobacco giant Imasco (parent company of Imperial Tobacco of Canada). The C$10.7 billion deal marked one of the largest acquisitions in Canadian business history. That year, BAT also purchased Rothmans International, which held a 7.75 percent share of the U.K. market, from Compagnie Financiere Richemont AG in 1999. The deal allowed

BAT to increase its global market share to 15.4 percent, gaining ground on rival Philip Morris, which held a 17 percent share. Also in the late 1990s, Japan Tobacco, the third largest tobacco manufacturer in the world, paid US$8 billion for the international operations of R.J. Reynolds, which were renamed JT International.

CURRENT CONDITIONS

Consolidation continued in the industry when Imperial Tobacco Group, the top-ranking cigarette manufacturer in Britain, purchased German tobacco company Reemtsma to become the world's fourth largest tobacco firm in 2002. The next year British American Tobacco acquired Ente Tabacchii Italiani, making BAT the number two player in Italy, which was the second largest tobacco market in the European Union. In 2004, Reynolds merged with Brown & Williamson Tobacco to form Reynolds American Incorporated. Philip Morris expanded in 2005 with acquisitions of Indonesian cigarette manufacturer PT HM Sampoerna Tbk and Colombian cigarette company Coltabaco.

In addition to government regulation of cigarettes, the tobacco industry continued to face other regulatory challenges. In 2003, member states of the World Health Organization unanimously adopted the WHO Framework Convention on Tobacco Control, the world's first public health treaty. Aiming to reduce tobacco-related deaths worldwide, the treaty required countries to restrict tobacco advertising, sponsorship, and promotion; improve labeling of tobacco products; and enforce tighter laws against tobacco smuggling. The treaty also addressed measures to protect consumers against second-hand smoke. In addition, WHO members called for health professionals themselves to quit smoking. The treaty was signed by approximately 170 nations, including the United States. As of 2010, approximately 5.4 million deaths annually were directly caused by tobacco. That number was projected to increase to 6.5 million people by 2015 and to 8.3 million by 2030.

The European Union voted in 2002 to ban tobacco advertising in print media and on the Internet, as well as at international sports venues by 2005. This regulation complemented an earlier ban on cigarette ads on television in the European Union. In addition, the European Union began talks in 2004 aimed at phasing out agricultural subsidies paid to tobacco farmers.

In Asia, where cigarette advertising on television and in magazines was already banned, tobacco companies were able to make use of alternative outlets to sell their products. In China, tobacco companies sponsor sporting events, plaster their brand names on billboards and public transportation, and license their names to clothiers and shoe manufacturers. Philip Morris sells Western-style clothing, while R.J. Reynolds sponsors an annual tennis tournament in Beijing. Much of the advertising in Asia is directed at young women with beautiful models pictured smoking in scenes of Western-style luxury. Some U.S. companies play up their roots, as in the Philippines, where Winston brand cigarettes are touted as "The Taste of the U.S.A."

Tobacco packaging is also an area that continues to face scrutiny from regulators. For example, the European Union passed legislation in February of 2001 requiring health warnings to cover 30 percent of the front and 40 percent of the back of all packs of cigarettes. Warnings were required to include graphic pictures of the negative health effects of smoking. In addition, labels were no longer allowed to include such descriptions as "light" or "mild."

In August 2008, Hongyun Group and Honghe Group announced plans to merge, forming the world's fourth-largest cigarette producer in terms of volume. The new company would operate as Hongyun Honghe Tobacco Group Company Ltd. with headquarters in Yunnan and the northwestern Xinjiang region for its production facilities. The 2007 revenues for the Hongyan group and Honghe Group were US$4.2 billion and US$2.3 billion respectively. According to the *Business Herald*, companies in the Yunnan province in southwestern China produced 4.6 million cases (50,000 cigarettes per case) of cigarettes in 2007.

In the *American Chronicle* on September 2, 2008, Bobby Ramakant reported that in accordance with the Cigarettes and Other tobacco Products (Prohibition of Advertisement and Regulation of Trade and Commerce, Production, Supply, and Distribution) Act of 2003 the Indian Ministry of Health and Welfare announced the beginning of a tobacco warning program as of November 30, 2008. All tobacco products would have to include approved pictorial warnings along with the message "Tobacco Kills/Smoking Kills." In addition, graphics of diseased lungs would be printing on cigarette *bidi* and *gutka* packaging, covering 40 percent of the surface area of the packet.

In August 2008, Tobacco One announced an agreement for an exclusive distribution with Consejo Nacional Del Transporter of Mexico City. The taxi union body will assist Tobacco One with publicity in more than 120,000 taxi cabs throughout Mexico. The program involves a voluntary participation program for drivers who exclusively offer Rojo's brand cigarettes for sale to potentially millions of customers each week.

RESEARCH AND TECHNOLOGY

Since people in many countries have become less tolerant of secondhand smoke, tobacco companies are eager to find ways to eliminate it or at least reduce its impact, which has led to the search for a "smokeless" cigarette. R.J. Reynolds has been a leader in this research, having introduced a smokeless Premier brand in 1989, but the cigarette never made it out of test markets and wound up costing the firm as much as US$800 million. Test audiences complained that the product had no taste in addition to having a foul smell.

Also in 2008 Philip Morris introduced Next, a no-nicotine cigarette created through a high-pressure carbon dioxide process. However, this product had higher levels of tar than many standard cigarettes and failed to attract consumers. It was withdrawn from the market. Five years later, Reynolds announced that it was testing a new and substantially different version of the smokeless cigarette, named Eclipse. Reynolds claimed that by using a special charcoal tip, the cigarette did not burn tobacco at all. The company said that the new product eliminated most secondhand smoke and reduced the amount of tar and carcinogenic compounds inhaled by the smoker. A study by the Massachusetts Department of Public Health, however, concluded that Eclipse produced as many or even more toxins, as well as higher levels of carbon monoxide than two ultralight brands. Reynolds also announced in 1994 the development of a new cigarette that the company said reduced the stale smell of smoke. The company claimed that the cigarette had smoother flavor, "with a proprietary paper technology that masks and changes the odor" of cigarette smoke.

In the late 1990s Philip Morris introduced its version of a smokeless cigarette, Accord. It included a US$40 kit containing a kazoo-shaped cigarette holder, a battery-operated lighter, and a carton of Accord cigarettes. The lighter contained a microchip that was activated when the user puffed on the cigarette in the holder. The process sent a burst of heat to the cigarette, giving the smoker one hit but producing no actual smoke. The company claimed that Accord produced 83 percent fewer toxins than regular cigarettes.

On the ArizonaCentral.com Web site, Ken Alltucker reported that there was a surprising link between tobacco and cancer. Rather than causing it, some scientists in Arizona believed that tobacco plants might provide a means to develop personalized cancer vaccine as well as treatments for other diseases. The vaccine was tested in an early-stage clinical trial with findings showing an immune response for 70 percent of non-Hodgkin's lymphoma patients without harmful side-effects. The vaccine is created from a patient's diseased cells. While it will not prevent non-Hodgkin's lymphoma, the vaccine is programmed to attack that person's cancer. Bayer spent approximately US $15 million on a facility in Germany where it will grow the tobacco plants to make personalized vaccines for lymphoma patients.

Advances in Tobacco Growing. The major tobacco companies have become significantly involved in plant genetics and biotechnology. For many years the tobacco plant was the experimental plant of choice for researchers, leaving scientists with more knowledge about tobacco than any other plant in existence. *Nicotiana tobacum* became the scientific standard because it is easy to grow and easy to use to construct hybrids and crosses. The tobacco industry was successful in fighting plant diseases in large part because disease-resistant varieties of tobacco can be bred so easily.

Industry critics contend that the best known example of the industry's use of biotechnology was the development of Y-1—the high-nicotine tobacco plant FDA commissioner David Kessler cited in 1994 as an effort to manipulate nicotine levels and thereby further addict smokers. In 1998, the manufacturer of Y-1, DNA Plant Technology, pleaded guilty to illegally transporting their product to Brown & Williamson, leading to suspicion that the company had "spiked" its products with high nicotine levels. However, researchers also believed that the tobacco plant could be genetically engineered to make products like anticancer agents, human vaccines, antibodies for therapeutic uses, enzymes that go into laundry detergents, and even food additives. In the early years of the twenty-first century, tobacco companies have engaged in research to lower the content of nitrosamine, the most potent of the carcinogens found in tobacco.

The *American Journal of Public Health* published findings of Mayo Clinic/Stanford University research startling findings of Mayo Clinic and Stanford University research. Tobacco companies suppressed their own internal research finding significant levels of Polonium-210 in tobacco. In a Harvard School of Public Health press release on July 16, 2008, Dr. Howard Koh indicated that tobacco industry deception has been ongoing. "For decades, the tobacco industry has carefully manipulated menthol content not only to lure youth but also to lock in lifelong adult customers," Koh said. The FDA gained limited authority for tobacco when federal legislation referred to as passed the U.S. House of Representatives. The so-called "Marlboro Protection Act" was supported by Philip Morris. The bill did not demand removal of toxic gases like cyanide or radioactive substances like plutonium or uranium. In 2008, Philip Morris International split from Philip Morris

America, which put the company's products and marketing outside U.S. regulation.

INDUSTRY LEADERS

Philip Morris. Philip Morris is a relative newcomer to the ranks of leading international cigarette producers. After the breakup of the American Tobacco trust in 1911, a few splinter companies not associated with any of the "big four" eventually came together under the name Philip Morris. Although the company was a relatively small player in the early 1930s, by 1960 it was a major firm and ranked sixth among the tobacco companies. The Philip Morris International division, originally known as Philip Morris Overseas, was established in 1955, and was selling products in over 160 countries worldwide by 2010.

In 1985, the company restructured, creating the Philip Morris Companies Inc. holding company that became the parent company of Philip Morris Incorporated. Philip Morris Companies Inc. was renamed Altria Group Inc. in 2003. Philip Morris assumed its preeminent position in the 1990s on the strength of several business decisions made during the 1960s and 1970s. The company was the first to anticipate the potential for overseas tobacco sales. In addition, the company's Marlboro Man advertising campaign became one of the most successful in the world. These factors played well off each other, and Marlboro became one of the industry's best-selling brands. Some cite Marlboro's popularity as the primary reason for the leading position of the United States in world cigarette exports in the mid-1990s.

As the health risks associated with smoking became more profound in the public's mind, the company sought diversification, most notably in the foods sector. It paid US$5.8 billion for General Foods in 1985 and US$12.9 billion for Kraft in 1988. Other company holdings included Miller Brewing Co. and Kraft Jacobs Suchard, a Swiss maker of coffee and chocolate. By 1993, non-tobacco businesses made up more than half of Philip Morris's sales.

On April 2, 1993, which came to be known in the industry as "Marlboro Friday," Philip Morris cut the price of its leading brand by 20 percent in order to regain market share that had been lost to discount brands and Reynolds' Camel brands. While many investors questioned the staying power of all consumer brand names, the price cut was a clear success for Marlboro. It quickly regained eight points of market share, bringing it back to the 30 percent level.

In 1994 there was much discussion about a plan to segregate non-tobacco operations to protect shareholders from the negative impact of lawsuits and an unfavorable regulatory climate. The proposal was ultimately defeated, however. Disappointed institutional investors were wooed instead with a 20 percent increase in the dividend and a share buyback program. Some industry analysts noted that despite all the furor over the future of smoking, the fact remained that the tobacco business, especially the international segment, had proven to be far more profitable than food operations in the early 1990s.

As of 2007, Philip Morris continued to control almost half of the U.S. tobacco market and 15.6 percent of the global tobacco market, bolstered by the world-leading Marlboro brand. The company also continued to pursue acquisitions through the early 2000s, buying a 40 percent stake in Indonesian cigarette manufacturer PT HM Sampoerna Tbk for approximately US$5.2 billion in 2005. That same year, Philip Morris paid US$299.6 million for a 96.65 percent share in Coltabaco, the largest cigarette manufacturer in Colombia. Altria, Philip Morris's parent company, reported that its tobacco segment had net domestic revenues of US$17.5 billion and net international sales of US$39.5 billion in 2004. Altria spun off Philip Morris in March 2008. In 2007, the company reported annual revenues of US$10.847 billion with over 75,500 employees.

In August 2008 Philip Morris International had to withdraw sponsorship and promotion of a concert in a developing country for the second time after receiving international criticism for cigarette marketing appealing to children. The company withdrew from a reunion concert in the Philippines for the Filipino band Eraserheads scheduled for August 3, 2008. A month earlier, Alicia Keys had requested that Phillip Morris withdraw its sponsorship of her concert in Jakarta, Indonesia.

British American Tobacco PLC. According to an agreement between American Tobacco and Imperial Tobacco of Britain in 1902, British American Tobacco (BAT) was given full rein to produce and market cigarettes anywhere outside the United States and Britain. By the latter part of the twentieth century, some 80 percent of the company's assets were located outside Britain. Its products were sold in some 180 countries and duty-free markets, and it owned the leading brand in over 30 markets with brands that included Dunhill, Kent, Lucky Strike, and Pall Mall. The company continued as a prime player in major tobacco markets like Brazil and Germany, but its attempt to establish itself in the British market during the early 1980s proved unsuccessful. It owned the Brown & Williamson Company, the third largest U.S. tobacco firm. Under a settlement with the U.S. Federal Trade Commission at the end of 1994, it took over most of American Tobacco, the fourth-largest tobacco company in the United States.

The takeover was a change in direction for BAT, which had spent much of the 1970s and 1980s diversifying

outside the tobacco industry, becoming a major player in insurance, retailing, and paper products. After a hostile takeover bid from Sir James Goldsmith in 1989, however, the company sold or spun off all of its retail and paper operations. In 1990, after California insurance regulators blocked Goldsmith's attempt to force BAT, by then known as BAT Industries, to sell its Farmers Insurance subsidiary to AXA-Midi of France, Goldsmith called off the takeover. In the mid-1990s, BAT Industries carried on diversified activities, notably mortgage lending and insurance sales. It eventually spun off its tobacco interests as British American Tobacco PLC (BAT), which acquired Switzerland-based Rothmans International in 1999.

As of 2008, BAT remained the world's second-largest cigarette maker, behind Philip Morris International. The company sold 685 billion cigarettes and reported US$22.395 million in 2009 with 50,000 employees in 2010. In 2004, BAT's former U.S. unit, Brown & Williamson, merged with J.R. Reynolds Tobacco.

Japan Tobacco Inc. In the 1850s, British and U.S. imports gave the Japanese their first exposure to cigarettes. In 1883, Iwatani, a trading company, began production of Tengu, Japan's first popular domestic brand. Murai Brothers initiated production of Sunrise cigarettes a few years later. The firm also imported Hero cigarettes from the United States. The Japanese government joined other governments in considering cigarettes as a source of revenue, and Japan instituted taxes on the product in 1888. In 1898, a bureau was established within the Ministry of Finance to administer a government tobacco monopoly. In 1905, the government's salt monopoly was also brought under its jurisdiction.

When the Allies restructured the Japanese economy in 1949, they reorganized the bureau as the Japan Tobacco and Salt Public Corporation. While still wholly owned by the government, the company conducted its tobacco business on a commercial basis. In 1985 the company was restructured as Japan Tobacco International Inc., but the newly issued shares continued to be held entirely by the Japanese government.

In 1994, as part of a program to privatize government assets, the company was listed on the Tokyo Stock Exchange with the objective of selling one-third of its equity to private investors. The move was a failure by most accounts as the shares were poorly received by the investment community. Some critics charged that the government had mishandled the offering, while others cited the fundamental financial uncertainties surrounding the company. Tobacco sales had risen just 0.7 percent in 1993 and the long-term picture was clouded by the shrinking adult population and increasing awareness of the health risks associated with consumption of their staple product. In addition, foreign competitors had penetrated the domestic market during the early 1990s (by 1994, foreign cigarettes had taken 18 percent of the market). Whatever profits the company was making appeared to come from cost-cutting, not new demand. Moreover, even with partial privatization, the company remained burdened by government-directed obligations, such as the requirement that it buy 50 percent of its raw tobacco from Japanese farmers at three times the world price. The company's efforts at diversification into agribusiness, beverages, pharmaceuticals, real estate, and health-club operations accounted for only 12 percent of revenue by the mid-1990s.

Remaining under majority control of the Japanese government, Japan Tobacco saw its domestic market share slip from 80 percent in the 1990s to just over 70 percent by 2003 due to increased competition from global rivals and to a decrease in domestic consumption from about 27 percent to about 24 percent of the adult population. The firm acquired the international operations of RJR Nabisco in 1999, gaining access to such brands as Camel, Winston, and Salem, sold through its newly named global unit, JT International. Total sales for Japan Tobacco, which had become the world's third-largest tobacco company, surpassed US$55.56 billion in 2005 with 31,476 employees. After losing its license to sell Philip Morris's Marlboro brand in April 2005, Japan Tobacco continued to seek increased international sales in such promising markets as Russia (which was the fourth-largest cigarette market in 2003) and in Turkey. Japan Tobacco bought Britain's Gallfer Group for about US$15 billion in 2007.

Reynolds American Inc. The second-largest U.S. tobacco company, R.J. Reynolds merged with third place Brown & Williamson in 2004 to create Reynolds American Inc. The new company included four operating subsidiaries: R.J. Reynolds Tobacco Company; Santa Fe Natural Tobacco Company, Inc.; Lane Limited; and R.J. Reynolds Global Products. The origins of Reynolds American date to 1874, when Richard Joshua Reynolds began growing tobacco in Winston, North Carolina. In 1890, the J. R. Reynolds Company issued its first shares, but Reynolds still owned 90 percent of the firm. After manufacturing only chewing tobacco for 20 years, the company introduced its first smoking tobacco brand in 1895. Reynolds, who needed capital to expand his operations, reluctantly turned to industry czar James Buchanan Duke for help. By 1900, two-thirds of the company Reynolds had founded was in the hands of Duke, although Reynolds was allowed to keep much of his independence.

After the U.S. Supreme Court broke up Duke's tobacco trust in 1911, R.J. Reynolds became the smallest of the "big four" spin-offs. Within 12 years, however, the

success of its Camel brand (the famous "I'd walk a mile for a Camel" campaign dates from 1919) and its innovative marketing techniques (like selling cigarettes by the carton) helped it surge past American Tobacco to become the industry's profit leader in the 1920s. In the 1950s, the company introduced the Winston and Salem brands, which made tremendous profits. This period, however, was also marked by the first critical attacks on the industry for the potential health risks of its products.

In the 1960s, the company diversified into food and other product areas, buying such companies as Chun King and Sea-Land Industries, followed by the 1970 purchase of Aminoil and later purchases of Del Monte and Heublein. R.J. Reynolds' major non-tobacco purchase was Nabisco in 1985, which increased the company's revenues from non-tobacco business to 40 percent. At the same time, however, management sold a number of its unrelated subsidiaries, including Aminoil.

In 1988 Reynolds became the focus of one of the great dramas of U.S. business history. Company President F. Ross Johnson proposed a massive leveraged buyout (using company assets as collateral for the huge loans needed to buy the stock of shareholders) in which he and other company executives would become the principal owners. Some of Reynolds' directors did not like Johnson or his plan, and they opened the bidding to other proposals. After much suspense and intrigue, the eventual winner was Kohlberg Kravis Roberts & Co. (KKR), whose bid was actually lower than that made by Johnson's group.

KKR immediately began to cut costs and sell assets, including Del Monte and parts of Nabisco, to pay off the enormous debt. In 1991 the company once again went public, although KKR continued to hold the majority of shares. In the mid-1990s, the price cut that Philip Morris announced on Marlboro Friday cut Reynolds' share of the U.S. cigarette market. The company's cigarette business, however, continued to benefit from sharp increases in overseas exports and ownership of foreign subsidiaries.

In 1997, RJR Nabisco Holdings Corp., R.J. Reynolds' parent, had revenues of over US$17 billion, equally divided between its tobacco and food operations. RJR Nabisco spun off R.J. Reynolds in 1999. Earlier that year, RJR Nabisco had also sold its international tobacco operations to Japan Tobacco. In 2002, Reynolds acquired Santa Fe Natural Tobacco Co. for US$340 million.

The company's 2004 merger with Brown & Williamson added Kool and Lucky Strike to Reynolds American's major brands, which included Camel and Salem. According to a press release from BAT, which owns 42 percent of Reynolds American, Reynolds could expect annual sales of about US$8.4 billion. In 2008 the company posted sales of approximately US$9 billion and reported 7,300 employees.

In 2006, Reynolds American ventured into the smokeless-tobacco industry by acquiring Conwood, the second-largest smokeless tobacco company in the United States. Conwood produces moist and dry snuff, loose leaf, plug, and twist chewing tobaccos.

R.J. Reynolds Tobacco Co. and its parent company, Reynolds American Inc., announced plans to completely analyze its business and eliminate jobs deemed to be nonessential or not relevant to company plans. Employees were told that they could volunteer to have jobs eliminated, with those whose jobs were targeted for elimination being eligible for early retirement or severance packages. Furthermore, company spokesperson Maura Payne said the process was part of preparation for several factors potentially impacting the business' future. They included potential increases in cigarette taxes and additional states or municipalities instituting public smoking bans resulting in depressed sales.

MAJOR COUNTRIES IN THE INDUSTRY

China. In 2003, China had about 250 million smokers representing one-third of the world total, according to CNN. The country produced more than twice as many cigarettes as the world's next largest producer, the United States. By 2003, annual sales of cigarettes in China generated about US$16 billion. Cigarette consumption in China, according to the USDA, was 1.777 trillion pieces in 2004.

The smoking industry has had a huge health impact on China as well. By 2010, 1.2 million people (2,000 people per day) in China died annually from smoking-related illnesses. Up to 2.5 million people were projected to die annually in China by 2025 if the trend in the 2010s for increasing tobacco use continues according to *Beijing Daily Messenger.*

Tobacco was introduced in China as early as the seventeenth century and was often mixed with opium for pipe smoking, but it was James Duke and his cohorts at BAT who created the booming market for cigarettes early in the twentieth century. Duke's people proselytized smoking across China. The company blanketed the country with advertising. In Ying-kvou, Manchuria, for instance, BAT was responsible for 2,000 large paper placards and 200 large wooden and iron signboards. The resulting demand was supplied from four factories employing some 13,000 Chinese workers. Annual consumption grew from 1.2 billion cigarettes in 1902 to 25 billion in 1920. By that time, BAT was earning about one-third of its worldwide profits from China. When World War II ended the company's involvement in the

country, the smoking habits they had induced became well entrenched in Chinese society.

China invested in its cigarette facilities throughout the 1980s and greatly expanded capacity. Production output increased 2.8 percent in 1992 to 1.6 trillion units, following a similar rise in the prior year. These increases were held in check by a production cap instituted in 1991. Some 500 brands of cigarettes were produced by 147 factories and marketed regionally. The production facilities themselves were operated by semi-independent companies organized by province, but they all fell under the control of the state monopoly. Most Chinese cigarettes consisted of flue-cured tobacco, with the highest quality leaf coming from the Yunnan province in the south. In 1993, blended cigarettes represented less than 10 percent of production, but their popularity was rising.

China aggressively developed markets throughout Southeast Asia, Eastern Europe, and the Commonwealth of Independent States in the 1990s. At the same time, the Chinese cigarette market remained difficult for international competitors to infiltrate, although imports increased somewhat in the 1990s, a development that most observers attributed to the rising income of its citizens. Countries like the United States continued to fight to bring down the barriers to foreign cigarettes, which had been exclusively sold in foreign currency shops. Only multinationals that had organized joint ventures with a domestic factory were allowed to produce in China. It was difficult, however, to determine true market share when the bulk of China's imports arrived via Hong Kong. Before Hong Kong's 1997 return to Chinese control, cigarettes exported to China often returned to Hong Kong through illegal channels to avoid Hong Kong's high taxes.

In anticipation of China's entrance into the World Trade Organization in the early twenty-first century, the State Tobacco Monopoly Administration and the China National Tobacco Corp. created the China Tobacco Import and Export Group in August 2000. According Brandy Fisher in the January 2002 issue of *Tobacco Reporter,* the group was formed to "adapt to the trend of building transnational enterprise groups in the international tobacco circle, to beef up the strength of China's tobacco import and export and its competitiveness, and to improve the management of tobacco import and export." By 2002, the new group had forged alliances with Philip Morris, BAT, and Japan Tobacco. As of early 2004, however, it remained unclear to what extent China would open its tobacco market to international competition.

The United States. In the United States, four companies virtually control the cigarette market: Philip Morris, Reynolds American, Lorriland, and Liggett. Consumption fell as much as 2 percent annually in the 1990s, attributed to aggressive antismoking campaigns, increased awareness of smoking's dangers, higher prices, and increased taxes. In 1999 alone, U.S. cigarette consumption dropped 6.5 percent to 435 billion pieces. In addition, U.S. cigarette production fell from a high of 755 billion pieces in 1996 to 595 billion pieces in 2000. By 2003 the figures were even lower. According to the USDA, U.S. cigarette consumption dropped by almost 100 billion pieces between 1993 and 2003, with a 4 percent drop in 2003. In 2004, U.S. consumption totaled 402 billion cigarettes. Per capita consumption among adults in 2003 averaged 1,903 pieces, while the rate for ages 16 through 18 was 1,833.

In 1997, the United States exported tobacco products valued at almost US$5 billion dollars to foreign nations. The 10 leading importers of U.S. tobacco products were Japan (US$1.6 billion), Belgium (US$1.1 billion), Russia (US$234 million), Saudi Arabia (US$206 million), Lebanon (US$179 million), South Korea (US$154 million), Turkey (US$137 million), Cyprus (US$127 million), Hong Kong (US$89 million), and Singapore (US$81 million). In turn, U.S. imports of tobacco products (excluding smuggled cigar products) totaled almost US$500 million in 1997. The Dominican Republic (US$232 million), Honduras (US$76 million), Nicaragua (US$31 million), Canada (US$27 million), the United Kingdom (US$16 million), Jamaica (US$12 million), Japan (US$11 million), the Netherlands (US$11 million), and Spain (US$10.6 million) were the top 10 countries for U.S. imports of tobacco products. Although the United States remained the largest tobacco importer and exporter in the world, both volume and revenues of cigarette exports fell in the early 2000s. Volume dropped 5 percent in 2003, with export earnings valued at US$1.4 billion. The largest markets for U.S. cigarettes in 2003 were Japan, Saudi Arabia, Israel, Lebanon, Iran, and the European Union.

The health impacts of smoking have not been lost on the United States even though statistically smoking as fallen flat due to anti-smoking legislation. Over 443,000 people (over 18 percent of all deaths) die because of smoking-related illnesses annually in the United States. Second-hand smoke accounts for approximately 50,000 of those deaths. The Centers for Disease Control reported that the states with the most smoking-related deaths were Kentucky, West Virginia, Nevada, Mississippi, Oklahoma, Tennessee, Arkansas, Alabama, Indiana, and Missouri. The CDC reported that the states with the lowest numbers of smoking-related deaths were Utah and Hawaii.

Japan. While Japan's domestic demand in the early 1990s was sluggish, exports of Japanese cigarettes rose during that period. Although cigarette consumption in

Japan remained extremely high (more than 50 percent of adult men and 14 percent of adult women), tax hikes and economic turbulence contributed to a 2.3 percent drop in consumption to 324.5 billion cigarettes in 2001. The USDA estimated a further decline to 278.885 billion cigarettes for 2004. The leading producer within Japan in 2004 was Japan Tobacco, which held a 75 percent market share. The company's Mild Seven brand, which was the second-best selling cigarette in the world, held a 34 percent share of the domestic market. In Japan, smoking was the leading cause of death and was responsible for 20 percent of all cancers.

Germany. In Germany, cigarette production in the early 1990s totaled 222 billion pieces a year. Official statistics put domestic sales at 153 billion cigarettes per year, although industry followers noted that about 10 billion cigarettes were smuggled into the country each year. Some Germans also used "cigarette rolls," a specially designed device that enables the smoker to produce his own cigarette, which was devised to skirt the high tax rates of packaged brands. Historically, some 75 percent of all German cigarette exports went to other EU member nations, but in the early years of the 2000s Germany developed export markets in Eastern Europe, the Commonwealth of Independent States (former Soviet states), and the Middle East.

Philip Morris dominated the German cigarette market with a 37 percent share in 2001, while Reemtsma and BAT each controlled about 22 percent and Japan Tobacco had gained a 3.6 percent share. Germany was one of the strongest cigarette markets in Western Europe through the mid-1990s, since roughly 30 percent of its adult citizens smoked. However, increased regulations and growing awareness of health concerns resulted in a drop in sales from 145 billion cigarettes in 1999 to 139.6 billion cigarettes in 2000 and 127 billion cigarettes in 2004. By 2010, about 140,000 deaths in Germany were attributed directly to tobacco-related illnesses. Approximately one in three German adults smoked regularly as of 2010.

BIBLIOGRAPHY
Alliance One 2010 Annual Report. Available from www.phx.corporate-ir.net.
Alltucker, Ken. "A New Weapon to Fight Cancer-Tobacco Plants." ArizonaCentral.com, 22 August 2008. Available from www.azcentral.com.
BAT Annual Report, 2004. Available from www.bat.com.
Birkholz, Debra; *Weak Tobacco Laws in Russia Increase Risk to Women and Children.* Available from www.ciggyfree.com.
"China Mulls Cigarette Ad Ban." CNN News, 17 November 2003. Available from edition.cnn.com.
Connolly, Ceci. "Tobacco Bill Faces Snags in House." *Washington Post,* 24 May 1998.

"EU Adopts Tobacco Ad Ban." BBC News World Edition, 2 December 2002. Available from news.bbc.co.uk.

"EU Eyes Ending Tobacco Subsidies." BBC News World Edition, 22 March 2004. Available from news.bbc.co.uk.

Fisher, Brandy. "Friends From Afar." *Tobacco Reporter,* January 2002. Available from www.tobaccoreporter.com.

———. "Powerhouse." *Tobacco Reporter,* January 2002. Available from www.tobaccoreporter.com.

Frankel, Glenn. "Big Tobacco's Global Reach." *Washington Post,* 18 November 1996.

———. "U.S. Aided Cigarette Firms In Conquests Across Asia." *Washington Post,* 17 November 1996.

Frankel, Glenn, and Steven Mufson. "Vast China Market Key to Smoking Disputes." *Washington Post,* 20 November 1996.

Harvard School of Public Health. "Tobacco Industry Systematically Manipulated Cigarette Menthol Content to Recruit New Smokers Among Adolescents and Young Adults." Press release, 16 July 2008. Available from www.hsph.harvard.edu.

Lewis, Jay. "A Firm Market." *Tobacco Reporter,* April 2001. Available from www.tobaccoreporter.com.

Muggli, Monique E., Jon O. Ebbert, Channing Robertson, and Richard D. Hurt. "Waking a Sleeping Giant: The Tobacco Industry's Response to the Polonium-210 Issue." *American Journal of Public Health,* 16 July 2008. Available from ajph.aphapublications.org/.

Parker-Pope, Tara. "'Safer' Cigarettes: A History." *Nova,* Public Broadcasting Service, 2 October 2001. Available from www.pubs.org.

Philip Morris International Annual Report, 2004. Available from www.altria.com.

"Philip Morris International Forced to Drop Another Concert Sponsorship; Philippines Health Department Applauded for Taking Action." *Market Watch,* 29 August 2008. Available from www.marketwatch.com.

Ramakant, Bobby. "Pictorial Warnings on Tobacco Products in India." *American Chronicle,* 2 September 2008. Available from www.americanchronicle.com..

Reynolds American Annual Report, 2004. Available from www.reynoldsamerican.com.

Ridgway, Laurence. "Merging in the Millennium." *World Tobacco,* January 2000.

Rupert, James, and Glenn Frankel. "In Ex-Soviet Markets, U.S. Brands Took on Role of Capitalist Liberator." *Washington Post,* 19 November 1996.

"Russia is One of the Tobacco Most Smoking Countries." *Pravda,* 8 June 2001. Available from English.pravda.ru.

Schultz, Stacey. "Breathing Easy." *U.S. News & World Report,* 23 June 2003.

Shafey, Omar, Suzanne Dolwick, and G. Emmanuel Guindon, eds. *Tobacco Control Country Profiles 2003.* American Cancer Society. Available from www.globalink.org.

"Tobacco Companies Hide Hazard." *Baxter Bulletin,* 26 August 2008. Available from www.baxterbulletin.com.

Tobacco Institute of Japan. *Tabako Hambai Jisseki [Cigarette Sales],* 21 April 1997. Available from jin.jcic.or.jp.

"Tobacco One, Inc. Obtains Agreement to Sell and Promote Its New 'ROJO's' Brand Cigarette Within Mexico's Vast Taxi Network." *Business Wire,* 20 August 2008. Available from www.businesswire.com.

Tuinstra, Taco. "Saturation." *Tobacco Reporter,* October 2001. Available from www.tobaccoreporter.com.

U.S. Centers for Disease Control and Prevention. *Targeting Tobacco Use,* Atlanta, Georgia, 1998. Available from www.cdc.gov.

U.S. Department of Agriculture. Economic Research Service. "Tobacco Outlook-Summary," April 2004. Available from usda.mannlib.cornell.edu.

U.S. Department of Agriculture, Foreign Agricultural Service. *Tobacco: World Markets and Trade,* September 2004. Available from www.fas.usda.gov.

U.S. Department of Agriculture. *Trends in the Cigarette Industry After the Master Settlement Agreement,* October 2001. Available from www.ers.usda.gov.

U.S. Department of Commerce. *Annual Survey of Manufactures.* Washington, DC: Annual.

World Health Organization. "An International Treaty for Tobacco Control," 12 August 2003. Available from www.who.int.

———. "The Tobacco Epidemic: A Global Public Health Emergency." *Tobacco Alert,* April 1996. Available from www.who.int.

FURNITURE

———————————■———————————

FURNITURE, HOUSEHOLD

NAICS CODE(S)

3371. This industry's participants manufacture all types of furniture for household use. Their products range from all-wood furniture and cabinetry to upholstered pieces and mattresses. For coverage of office furniture, see **Furniture, Office.**

INDUSTRY SNAPSHOT

The production and sale of household furniture is a large, highly competitive business in which thousands of different companies worldwide participate. Once largely confined by national boundaries, household furniture has become a multibillion-dollar import and export business. Although dominated on all continents by a handful of growing corporations aiming at the mass market, the furniture market still has room for craftsmen and small companies. The majority of these small operations produce furniture within their native countries for two important reasons. First, they are unable to compete with the resources and distribution channels of larger companies. Second, they are better equipped to meet the needs of buyers looking for customized furniture and one-of-a-kind pieces, mostly who look to small, local operations to meet these needs. While industry dynamics make it unlikely that these small competitors will ever grow as large as the conglomerates, the furniture industry still invites growth for companies developing products that fill niche markets. The key is finding the correct blend of price, function, and appealing style, and supporting the product line with an efficient and extensive distribution system.

Household furniture, along with other home decor elements, is part of an industry that rises and falls with the state of the economy. As a general rule, manufacturers of household furnishings enjoy greater demand for their goods when employment and consumer confidence are high and interest rates are low. While there are exceptions (most notably retailers like Heilig-Meyers and Levitz Furniture, both of which filed for Chapter 11 bankruptcy restructuring during the economic boom of 2000), furniture manufacturers' success is closely related to the economy as a whole.

While many online retailers have made an impact on their industries, this is not the case with furniture. As of the mid-years of the first decade of the twenty-first century, the presence of online retailers had had little effect on the industry, and consequently the failure of some high-profile online furniture retailers (such as living.com and furniture.com) did not weaken the industry. A new approach to selling furniture online was tested by both Ethan Allan and Pottery Barn. This approach, called "clicks and mortar," was proving to be a promising alternative to straight e-commerce. A clicks and mortar retailer is one that has both online ordering capabilities and traditional stores. More important than online retailers was the trend toward manufacturers entering the retail market directly. Rather than producing goods for wholesale to retailers, more manufacturers began introducing their products to consumers under new brand names.

Although all European countries host a domestic furniture industry, Germany, Italy, Belgium, Denmark, and Sweden possess the most competitive and the most highly developed industries. The vast majority of

Europe's 65,000 furniture companies are small. Some countries such as Italy and Spain tend to specialize and customize their furniture, while others gravitate toward the mass market. This affects the number of companies operating in each country. For example, in the early years of the first decade of the 2000s, many of the 12,000 furniture makers in Spain tended to be artisans who made limited numbers of pieces to order for customers. Germany, in contrast, took a larger mass manufacturing approach, with fewer companies yet much higher production volumes.

Furniture manufacturing in the United States largely resembles the global industry in that it is made up of hundreds of small companies. As with most countries, furniture manufacturing is centered near the nation's wood supply—more than one-third of furniture manufacturers are located in North Carolina. While the industry in the first decade of the 2000s supported hundreds of competitors, the top 25 U.S. manufacturers accounted for almost half of all furniture produced in the country. This was attributed to these manufacturers' domination of U.S. retail distribution channels.

Asia was a rapidly expanding manufacturing center, with dominant manufacturing countries such as China, Taiwan, Malaysia, and Indonesia, which led in worldwide furniture exports. Taiwan was one of the most successful producers both on the Asian continent and as an exporter to the West. By the early years of the decade, China had become the largest furniture exporter in the world.

ORGANIZATION AND STRUCTURE

The home furniture industry is loosely structured. A company with a superior product can usually reach the market successfully, even if it has to bypass the traditional manufacturer-to-retail distribution chain dominated by the large conglomerates. Furniture companies in the United States can be part of conglomerates like Furniture Brands International, owner of Broyhill and Thomasville. They may also be large private companies like Klaussner or be one of the hundreds of smaller companies employing under 100 people.

European furniture manufacturers were usually much smaller with less sophisticated channels of distribution. Only a handful of European companies such as IKEA of Sweden and Natuzzi of Italy were considered international companies because of their success in exporting to the United States. As a consolidated European market emerged, the larger companies became more important because they were able to mass produce popular pieces. At the outset of the twenty-first century, European customers enjoyed a wide variety of designs. Imports from the United States and Asia were relatively

small, as European customers saw little need to buy foreign when the designs they liked were readily available to them from Continental manufacturers.

Most Asian manufacturers were even smaller than those found in Europe. For example, there were more than 12,000 manufacturers of wooden furniture in Japan. Almost 80 percent of these companies had fewer than 30 employees. Organized as handmade artisans, these companies were slow to produce pieces and were in danger of being replaced by imports from other Asian countries such as Taiwan. While individual Asian companies might be small, their collective economic power, when organized by their governments, was growing.

From about the mid-1990s, the liberalization of world trade, via such agreements as the North American Free Trade Agreement (NAFTA) and the General Agreement on Tariffs and Trade (GATT), contributed to rapid growth in the world furniture market. NAFTA phased out tariffs on most goods between Canada, Mexico, and the United States, but established initial trade quotas to protect markets from price dumping while the agreement was being implemented. Most of the safeguard tariffs and quotas expired in 2004, with the remainder eliminated by 2005, creating virtually unrestricted trade between these countries. NAFTA appeared to have benefited Canada's furniture market; between 1992 and 2000, Canada's furniture exports increased by 405 percent. In 2003, Canada's total furniture exports, including residential, office, and institutional products, were worth US$6.9 billion. More than 90 percent of Canadian furniture exports went to the United States.

The 148-nation GATT, which reduces and eliminates tariffs that protect domestic industries, also affected the furniture trade. All participating countries, as members of the World Trade Organization, agreed to cut back tariffs by 33 percent, and the United States, the European Union, Canada, and Japan pledged to remove most of the tariffs inhibiting trade between them. China—already one of the top 10 furniture exporters in the mid-1990s—was able to greatly expand overseas furniture sales as it prepared for membership in the WTO, which it joined in 2001. In 2000, China's furniture exports exceeded US$3.5 billion, and the industry employed more than 3 million people.

BACKGROUND AND DEVELOPMENT

The technology of making household furniture was simple for generations—wood and other natural materials were pegged or nailed together to make objects on which people could sit, sleep, or eat. In the sixteenth and seventeenth centuries, artisans realized that hard wooden seats would feel better if they were covered with upholstery stuffed with animal hair or wool. By the twentieth century, people began to think that furniture could do double duty—a couch could turn into a bed, and a chair could recline.

Automation of manufacturing had not been a tremendous force in the furniture industry. Robot-controlled saws were able to turn out wooden chair arms consistently. However, there was no machine that could tie a chair spring tighter or faster than a skilled person, robots did not have a fashion eye to check for the proper lineup of floral patterns on a sleeper sofa, and there was as yet no mechanical substitute for the beauty an artisan can add to a hand-inlaid table.

Twenty-First Century Trends. In the early years of the first decade of the 2000s, the global furniture outlook was positive, especially with increasing demand for computer furniture at home, according to national trade associations and industry analysts. Previously, major furniture-producing countries such as the United States, Germany, France, and Italy experienced slightly falling revenues and production levels. Consumer demand for new styles resulted in a rise in imports from Asian manufacturers. These styles included rustic features, simple lines, carved wood, Asian embellishments, and mixed media, such as combining wood with marble or bamboo. Manufacturers in many of the leading countries enjoyed growth at the end of the 1990s, as economies flourished, disposable incomes rose, unemployment levels remained low, and international trade became easier. When these factors were adversely affected by the terrorist attacks on the United States on September 11, 2001, the household furniture industry, like most others, slowed. As the economy began to rally again, however, business analysts projected that most industries would benefit. In fact, the value of the U.S. furniture market increased 2.7 percent in 2002.

The furniture industry continued to be increasingly price-driven. Without established criteria of quality, retailers often marketed furniture solely on its price, giving rise to a proliferation of highly competitive discount furniture stores. Manufacturers' efforts to differentiate their products had failed thus far, strengthening the position of the price-competitive discount furniture brokers.

U.S. demand for wood furniture changed the international dynamics of the industry by increasing imports. As of 2005, about 54 percent of all wood furniture sold in the United States was imported, and nearly one-quarter of this came from China, which increased its exports of wood furniture 1,630 percent from 1995 to 2005.

Upholstered furniture was less impacted by the increase in importing because so much upholstered furniture was ordered with a degree of customization in fabric, style, accessories such as pillows, or any combination of these elements. Customization requires close contact with customers, which explains why this segment of the industry continued to be dominated by domestic manufacturers.

Major Challenges.

Obtaining Raw Materials. There was growing concern that wood—the raw material in most home furniture—may become scarce within the first few decades of the twenty-first century as a result of the failure to renew trees cut from forests. Wood supply was rated almost as important as government regulations in a mid-1990s survey of the major concerns of the largest furniture companies' chief executive officers. The potential problem gained importance in the minds of executives. The report showed that 63 percent of those surveyed had come to think the issue was more important than in the previous year. With increasing pressure from environmentalists and consumers, the industry began to move toward use of certified wood, which is harvested from sustainably managed forests.

Government Regulations. Increasing concern about health problems associated with the industry's use of volatile organic compounds (VOCs) in its finishing processes led to government regulations in the United States. Furniture manufacturing uses a tremendous amount of chemicals, primarily solvents to clean the raw material, and a chemical finish to coat the furniture before final shipment to retailers. Upholstered furniture can also contain numerous VOCs, including formaldehyde. In 1995, the U.S. Environmental Protection Agency created the National Emission Standards for Hazardous Air Pollutants (NESHAP) to control emissions from the manufacture of wood furniture.

International Trade. Many traditional leaders in the furniture industry in the early years of the first decade of the 2000s faced increasing competition from Asia. China in particular captured significant market share. In 2004, it shipped more upholstered furniture (mostly leather) to the United States than did Italy, which had prior to that year dominated in this segment. China's world shipments of all types of wood furniture increased 1,630 percent from 1995 to 2005. During that same period, its exports of wood furniture to the United States grew by a stunning 7,418 percent. Vietnam, Malaysia, and Thailand also increased world exports of wood furniture by substantial amounts. The influx of furniture from China led U.S. manufacturers to push for anti-dumping policies. In 2004, the U.S. Department of Commerce imposed duties ranging from 10.92 percent to 198.08 percent on wood bedroom furniture imports from China, the largest U.S. anti-dumping action to date against that country. In 2005, the tariffs were reduced by about 2 percent. At the same time, Chinese companies began to outsource more of their production to cheaper suppliers such as Vietnam.

Bypassing Traditional Retailers. One of the most heated issues between furniture manufacturers and retailers was whether customers should be allowed to shop for their furniture directly from the manufacturer or through a wholesaler. Traditionally, furniture shoppers bought from their local furniture stores. As is common in retail trade, these stores set prices sometimes as much as 100 percent over the price they paid the manufacturer or distributor. In the late 1990s, some U.S. furniture manufacturers—particularly those based in North Carolina—opened their own discount operations. Shoppers in faraway states could go to their retailers, find furniture they liked, and copy down the name of the manufacturer and model number. They then would order the same furniture directly from the manufacturer, paying the manufacturer's price and the cost of shipping; customers realized a savings of hundreds of dollars off the cost of buying retail by shopping this way.

CURRENT CONDITIONS

The state of the industry in the United States and Canada was not particularly good in 2007, whereas China's industry statistics were on what seemed to be a perpetual rise. In the United States, the housing boom of the early years of the first decade of the 2000s that fueled furniture sales had ended, and imports from China had increased substantially, causing many furniture companies to shut down. According to the CEO of Robb and Stucky, "A huge shift from American furniture to imported Chinese furniture has caused prices to drop and thrown the whole industry into a state of flux." Other factors contributing to the downward trend in the furniture industry were the fact that people were spending more money on electronics such as big-screen televisions and less on furniture. The housing slowdown affected the industry because people spend six to eight times as much money on furniture in a year when they move, according to *The Tampa Tribune,* and people had stopped moving as much as they had earlier in the decade. These downtrends for retailers and manufacturers, however, were expected to be advantageous for the consumer, who saw drastic reductions in furniture prices as businesses attempted to compete.

Other than China, two other countries that were becoming influential as the industry headed into the late years of the first decade of the 2000s were Vietnam and Malaysia. Vietnam's furniture exports, though smaller in value than China's at US$3.7 billion in 2005, increased 171.4 percent that year, and furniture ranked fifth in

overall export revenues for the nation, behind crude oil, footwear, garments, and seafood. The Vietnamese government worked to increase foreign investment in the furniture industry, and as a result, furniture outsourcing also increased. In Malaysia, the value of furniture exports totaled US$1.97 billion in 2006. Rubberwood was the main source of materials for Malaysian furniture production, and experts were recommending an increase in hardware furniture production in order to remain competitive in the international market.

RESEARCH AND TECHNOLOGY

In the middle years of the first decade of the 2000s, wood was still the product of choice for tables and chairs; upholstered sofas were still the most popular; and plastic seating was just a fad that came and went quickly during the 1970s. Turn of the millennium innovations in home furniture were items designed for entertainment rooms. A few U.S. companies created easy chairs with built-in stereo speakers to enhance the "surround-sound" effect when the user is watching a video. Adjustable beds, once associated with the elderly market, received high-tech overhauls and were poised to appeal to a broader range of consumers.

Virtual reality—the most interesting technological advancement in buying home furniture—was mostly used as an arcade attraction for teenagers, but it presented a way people in the future might buy their furniture. As envisioned in 2004, buyers using virtual reality would be able to walk into a furniture store armed with the dimensions of their living room, a carpet swatch, and a paint chip so that the furniture store manager can match colors. Once a facsimile of the living room is entered into the computer, the customer may don a virtual reality helmet and step on a computer-controlled floor so he or she can experience "walking" around the living room with the new furniture in place.

WORKFORCE

While virtually every country in the world makes furniture, it is not a huge industry for employment. Neither were its positions typically well paid. Manufacturing jobs were subject to decline as technology advances mechanized many of the mass production functions. In niche markets, however, artisans' skills, such as carpentry, specialty finishes, hand-painting, and inlaying wood, were less vulnerable to replacement by machinery.

The same was true for most of Europe, where roughly 90 percent of the continent's 65,000 furniture manufacturers had fewer than 20 employees. Only nine German companies had more than 1,000 employees each. The number of furniture manufacturers in each country had little to do with the number of people they employed. There were more than 12,000 furniture manufacturers in Spain and only 1,500 companies in Germany. However, Germany had a much larger industry, including a sizable export surplus, which it shipped to other European countries.

With regard to the Asian industry, Japan had more than 12,000 furniture manufacturers, around 80 percent of which had fewer than 30 employees. Indeed, more than half of Japan's 6,000 furniture manufacturers had three or fewer employees. Research reports on the Japanese furniture industry predicted that many of these small companies would disappear, as Japanese consumers succumbed to the lure of mass-produced furniture imported from Taiwan. In Asia, wages ranged from more than US$11 per hour in Japan to US$0.10 per hour in Vietnam.

INDUSTRY LEADERS

IKEA International A/S. IKEA International of Sweden was unusual in the global furniture industry in that it operated its own retail store chain. These stores were self-serve; the sales people did not follow prospects around from suite to suite. IKEA worked to produce and deliver quality furniture at affordable prices. It created its own designs, which were then manufactured by more than 1,300 suppliers in more than 50 countries. IKEA, which also sold its products by mail order and the Internet, operated more than 231 stores in 24 countries, and employed 127,800 people worldwide. For financial year 2008, the company posted sales of US$21.1 billion.

IKEA's popular catalog has more than 200 million copies published in 52 editions and 27 languages. In addition to being a shopper's guide, it is considered to be a collector's item.

Leggett and Platt Inc. Leggett and Platt Inc. led in production of bedding components such as box springs, mattress innersprings, and seating components. Based in Carthage, Missouri, Leggett and Platt also manufactured finished products, including recliners and beds, with its Wallhugger and ADJUSTA-MAGIC brands. More than 70 percent of the company's sales were derived from its finished products and parts for household and commercial furnishings. In 2008, Leggett and Platt, had 20,000 employee-partners worldwide.

Furniture Brands International Inc. Furniture Brands International Inc., of St. Louis, Missouri, with its Broyhill Furniture Industries, Lane Co., and Thomasville Furniture Industries subsidiaries, became the leading U.S. residential furniture manufacturer in 2001 after the breakup of industry giants Masco Home Furnishings and Interco. Furniture Brands International produced wood and upholstered living room, bedroom, and dining room furniture. Its Broyhill subsidiary offered moderately priced domestic pieces, while Thomasville and Lane offered higher-end furnishings. In 2008, the company posted sales of more than US$1.74 billion and employed 8,100 workers.

La-Z-Boy Incorporated. Founded in 1928, La-Z-Boy Chair Company of Monroe, Michigan, a U.S. manufacturer that operated its own retail stores, specialized in recliners. La-Z-Boy was the dominant manufacturer of upholstered furniture in the United States and continued to be the largest producer of recliners in the world. La-Z-Boy also offered wood furniture, and by acquiring smaller furniture makers, it came to be able to offer consumers high-end furnishings. The company's sales rose steadily in the 1990s, surpassing the US$1 billion mark in 1997 and reaching US$2.2 billion in 2001. Earnings for the 2009 fiscal year were US$1.2 billion. The company had about 7,730 employees.

La-Z-Boy President and CEO Kurt L. Darrow experienced "a distinct priviledge" and was saluted for all efforts and achievements. Darrow returned to Adrian College, his alma mater, where his commencement address was given to the 2009 graduating class. Adrian President Dr. Jeffrey R. Docking described the address as "thought provoking and inspirational."

Ashley Furniture Industries Inc. Founded in 1945, Ashley Furniture Industries was a leading U.S. manufacturer and exporter of home furniture. The company produced and sold upholstered, leather, and hardwood items, as well as bedding. In addition to manufacturing, the company ran Ashley Furniture HomeStores, 300 independently owned stores that carried Ashley products exclusively. Those stores were established in the United States, Canada, and overseas. Sales in 2007 reached approximately US$3.4 billion, representing a 27.5 percent increase from the previous year, and the company employed approximately 17,000 people.

Klaussner Furniture Industries Inc. Klaussner Furniture Industries Inc. of Asheville, North Carolina, was one of the largest privately owned furniture companies in the world in the middle years of the first decade of the 2000s. Klaussner's core products included upholstered wood sofas, leather furniture, recliners, and occasional furniture. It restructured its manufacturing facilities in North Carolina, California and Iowa, giving them the capability to be resources as service centers. In addition to its Distinctions and Klaussner, the company licensed the Sealy and Dick Idol brands.

Natuzzi S.p.A. Natuzzi of Italy was one of the more successful exporters of high-quality leather furniture to the United States. In fact, it was the world's top maker of residential leather furniture and had a presence in 140 countries. Natuzzi operated 15 factories in Italy, with about 90 percent of production for export. Half of the company's sales, which in 2003 topped US$967 million, came from North and South America. In 2005, however, the company saw declining sales of its branded upholstered furniture, prompting a restructuring plan that included cutting about 1,320 jobs. Sales in 2005 totaled US$793.5 million, with 7,847 employees. By 2008, the company had sales of US $938.8 million with 7,569 employees.

MAJOR COUNTRIES IN THE INDUSTRY

The United States. The U.S. household furniture market was worth approximately US$71.6 billion in 2003. The strongest demand for household furniture came from the metropolitan areas of New York City, Chicago, Los Angeles, and Washington, D.C. In 2002 upholstered furniture accounted for the largest portion of sales, 45.7 percent. Demand also grew for newer kinds of furniture, including entertainment furniture to house or store home theater components, stereo equipment, and other home electronic goods.

U.S. household furniture exports, which began to accelerate in the mid-1990s, were valued in excess of US$22 billion in 2000. Strengthened by NAFTA, Canada and Mexico became significant exporters to the United States with US$2.5 billion and US$645 million worth of furniture, respectively, in 2000. NAFTA countries were also the largest importers of U.S. furniture, with the biggest market, Canada, accounting for 49 percent of all U.S. furniture shipments in 2004. Mexico ranked second, followed by China. These figures changed quickly in 2005, when imports from China burgeoned.

RTE Business reported that U.S. Federal Reserve Chairman Ben Bernanke concluded the U.S. recession had ended in September 2009. Bernanke, however, also shared a cautionary observation predicting only a "modest recovery." A related retail sales report supported Bernanke's views. There was projected strength for virtually all sectors excluding furniture. This factor solidified belief that "household spending was probably mending".

China. From the 1980s into the early years of the first decade of the 2000s, China rapidly expanded its wood furniture industry. By 2000 it had become one of the world's major producers, with a total turnover in 2002 of US$19.88 billion. About one-fourth of its output was sold overseas to major export markets such as the United States, the European Union, and Japan. The value of all Chinese furniture exports in 2002 rose 30 percent from the previous year, totaling US$5.42 billion; this figure increased in 2003 to US$7.33 billion. China led the world in furniture exports and was also the biggest exporter of furniture to the United States, which accounted for 52 percent of China's furniture shipments in 2004. U.S. imports of wooden bedroom furniture alone from China reached almost US$1.2 billion in 2003. By that year, according to some analysts, China manufactured 40 percent of all furniture sold in the United States.

In the mid-years of the first decade of the 2000s, the furniture industry in China continued to grow. In 2005 the nation experienced a 27.4 percent increase in furniture sales over the previous year, churning out 333.9 million pieces, and sales of furniture in the first quarter of 2006 were 31.7 percent higher than they had been in the first quarter of 2005. The export value of furniture in China in 2005 reached US$13.7 billion, representing a growth rate of almost 33 percent.

China's growing economy also contributed to increased demand for furniture, and major international companies competed for a greater share of the Chinese market. Ethan Allen opened a store in Tianjin and partnered with Markor Furniture International, a leading Chinese manufacturer, to develop a chain of Ethan Allen retail stores throughout the country. IKEA also established a presence in China.

The overall furniture market in China was expected to remain promising, as rising incomes—averaging increases of 10 percent per year—stimulated increased demand for household furniture and other goods. China's hosting of the Olympic Games in 2008 was expected to give a significant boost to furniture sales.

Japan. In the 1990s and into the early years of the first decade of the 2000s, Japan produced around US$20 billion in household furniture annually. After recession struck the Japanese economy in 1991, the furniture industry remained unstable into the beginning of the twenty-first century, though by the early years of the first decade of the 2000s, Japanese manufacturers hoped to start capturing a bigger share of the export market. In 2002 Japan imported about 377 billion yen worth of furniture, while exports were valued at only 53 billion yen, approximately US$450 million. Analysts pointed to the fact that Japanese furniture is designed for Japanese tastes. It is also relatively expensive. Most Japanese furniture is handmade by small furniture companies that stand little chance of significantly increasing capacity. Some major Japanese companies, however, began to focus on export markets, especially in the United States, Britain, China, South Korea, Australia, and countries in Southeast Asia.

European Union. The European Union's furniture industry, valued by the European Commission at 82 billion euros, approximately US$99.6 billion, in 2004, produced about half of the world's furniture that year and employed approximately 1 million people. Germany, the largest furniture maker in the European Union, accounted for 27 percent of total production. Italy followed with 21.6 percent, while France and Italy accounted for 13.5 percent and 10.4 percent of production, respectively. World exports of EU furniture were valued at 10.2 billion euros (about US$12.7 billion) in 2002 and fell slightly to 9.6 billion euros (US$12 billion) in 2003. Imports grew steadily in value from 7.1 billion euros in 2000 (US$8.8 billion) to 8.2 billion euros (US$10.2 billion) in 2003. Germany faced some challenges in the early to mid-1990s, as it struggled to bring the former East German states into the fold of prosperity enjoyed by the states of former West Germany. By 1998, however, disposable income increased by 2.5 percent, leading to a 2.2 percent increase in domestic furniture consumption. In 2002 the German furniture market was worth about US$30.4 billion.

Italy was the second largest producer of furniture in the world in the early years of the first decade of the 2000s, with 35,000 companies employing about 230,000 people. Italy was also the leading furniture exporter, shipping about 45 percent of its total production, which accounted for 17 percent of the global market. Between 2002 and 2003, however, the Italian furniture industry saw production value decline by 4.1 percent, due mostly to a sharp decline in exports, which fell by 5.1 percent, while imports climbed by 8.5 percent. Italy's share of wood furniture exports to the United States fell from 16.6 percent in 2000 to only 11.9 percent in 2003. In 2004, for the first time, Italy lagged behind China in exports of leather upholstered furniture to the United States.

French furniture was made by about 773 companies in the early years of the first decade of the 2000s. More than 90 percent of these businesses employed fewer than 100 people, and about half of wood furniture companies employed fewer than 50. While most of its production stayed inside the country, France also imported more millions of dollars worth of furniture each year, notably from Italy. In 2003, declining domestic demand contributed to a 6.1 percent drop in the value of the French furniture market.

The vast majority of EU countries saw negative growth in their furniture markets in 2003, due largely to flat demand and a fall in exports to their traditional markets. Nevertheless, sales to countries outside the EU increased by 4 percent in value in 2003, though exports to the United States, which represented 25 percent of exports, declined by 4 percent in volume and 15 percent in value. Imports, however, rose substantially, led by China with a 45 percent volume increase.

Canada. Canada's furniture industry grew significantly through the 1990s, with household furniture accounting for about 38.5 percent of production. In 2000, Canada was the world's fourth largest furniture exporter; by 2003 it had risen to second place, with exports of US$6.9 billion. Some 96 percent of its furniture exports in 2003 went to the United States; Canada also remained a leading importer of U.S. furniture. Furniture sales in Canada grew more than any other retail sector in 2003, rising 11.6 percent in 2002 and 6.5 percent in 2003.

Approaching the late years of the first decade of the 2000s, Canada was feeling the effects of increased imports. According to the Canadian Furniture Industry, in 2007 Canada saw an increase in both Chinese and American imports of home furnishings, whereas Canadian exports were on the decline. The Canadian Furniture Industry estimated the furniture industry was worth about US$5.2 billion that year. Joe Malko, president of Winnipeg-based Furniture West, told *Business Edge* that the reason for the decline in the industry was the amount of imports coming from the United States and Asia. Malko said, "It's mainly from China, although other countries in Asia are becoming furniture manufacturers and exporting product as well. But China has been the giant." One of the ways by which Canadian furniture manufacturers were dealing with the situation was through the creation of the program Connections West. According to *Business Edge,* "The move will help the independent dealer work with the manufacturers to produce unique products with innovative designs that are appropriate for their markets."

BIBLIOGRAPHY

"China Furniture Market Report, 2006-2007." *China Research,* December 2006.

Colbert, Catherine. "Natuzzi Company Description." *Hoover's Online,* 2009. Available from www.hoovers.com.

———. "La-Z-Boy Incorporated Company Description." 2009. Available from www.hoovers.com.

"Employment and Wages in the American Furniture Industry," 2004. Available from www.globalwood.org.

"Exports Climb 10 Percent in 2004." *Furniture Today,* 7 April 2005. Available from www.furnituretoday.com.

Foreign Agricultural Service/USDA Office of Global Analysis. *Wood Product Update,* March 2007. Available from www.fas.usda.gov.

Gunin, Joan. "Leather Sources Ready to Fire Global Shots." *Furniture Today,* 13 April 2005. Available from www.furnituretoday.com.

"IKEA. "Facts & Figures." 2009. Available from www.Ikea.com.

"In 2006, China's Furniture Industry Continued to Keep a Higher Growth Rate and the Export Value Amounted to USD 4.042 Billion in the First Quarter of 2006." *Business Wire*, 30 January 2007.

"Japanese Makers Have High Hopes for IFFT 2003," 20 April 2004. Available from www.cens.com.

Kirgan, Linnea. "Ashley Furniture Company Description." 2009. Available from www.hoovers.com.

Klaussner. "About Klaussner Furniture." 2009 Available from www.klaussner.com.

LaZBoy. "LaZBoy CEO Awarded Honorary Doctorate." 4 May 2009. Available from la-z-boy.com.

"Made in Italy." Italian Ministry of Foreign Affairs. Available from www.esteri.it.

Leggett & Platt. "Leggett & Platt Announces 2008 Results." 2009. Available from phx.corporate.ir.

McLeod, Lashonda. "The Canadian Furniture Industry Presents Opportunities for U.S. Hardwoods." *AgExporter*, January 2004.

"Natuzzi Announces Second Quarter 2009 Earnings Call." *PR Insider*, 15 September 2009. Available from www.pr-insider.com.

Normington, Mick. "N.C. Furniture Exports Up, China a Possible Target Market." *Business Journal*, 19 April 2004.

"Overview: EU Furniture Industry." European Union, 2006. Available from ec.europa.eu.

Pierce, Rachel. "Furniture Brands International Company Description." 2009. Available from www.hoovers.com.

"Real Household Furniture Spending in U.S. Forecast to Grow by 23.8 Percent." *Furniture World*, 6 May 2005. Available from www.furninfo.com.

"The Residential Furniture Industry in Canada," 2004. Available from strategis.ic.gc.ca.

"Review—Far East: Thai Challenge." *Cabinet Maker*, 13 April 2007.

RTE Business. "US Recession Probably Over Fed Chief. 15 September 2009. Available from www.rte.ie.

Sasso, Michael. "Housing Slump Hits Furniture Stores Hard." *The Tampa Tribune*, 4 April 2007.

Severs, Laura. " Furniture Industry Builds Creative Strategies: China's Market Growth Prompts Industry Rethink." *Business Edge*, 12 January 2007.

"UK Market for Upholstered Furniture." *Global Wood*, 27 September 2006. Available from www.globalwood.org.

U.S. Industry and Trade Outlook. New York: McGraw-Hill and U.S. Department of Commerce, 2000.

"U.S. to Slap Tariffs on Chinese Furniture." *China Daily*, 20 June 2004. Available from www.chinadaily.com.cn.

"Vietnam Now Malaysian Furniture Industry's Biggest Competitor." *Thanh Nien News*, 15 December 2006.

"Vietnam Rising in the Global Furniture Market." *Business in Asia*, 2006. Available from www.business-in-asia.com.

Xu, Meiqi, et al. "China's Wood Furniture Industry." *Asian Timber*, September-October 2003.

"Zero Tariff Won't Harm Furniture Sector." *China Daily*, 19 November 2004. Available from www.chinadaily.com.cn.

SIC 2520

FURNITURE, OFFICE

NAICS CODE(S)

3372. This industry classification covers manufacturers of office furniture, including desks, conference tables, chairs, credenzas, bookcases, portable partitions, and other equipment used in both traditional office settings and the emerging home office environment.

INDUSTRY SNAPSHOT

Highly dependent upon a broad range of socioeconomic factors and general business practices, the global office furniture industry sustained itself during difficult economic times. The industry was concentrated in the United States, which produces the majority of office furniture and also imports billions of dollars in office furniture every year. Changing dynamics in the workplace, as companies in all fields of business activity rearrange their organizational and operational structures, have resulted in new challenges in the industry. For example, many large corporations were forced to downsize in the sliding economy of the first decade of the 2000s, reducing demand for new furniture. Small and mid-sized companies, however, fared better and continued to buy office furniture. To keep costs down, more companies opted to purchase ready-to-assemble (RTA) or refurbished furniture. Although measuring the volume of refurbished furniture is difficult, the Business and Institutional Furniture Manufacturer's Association (BIFMA) cited estimates at 8 to 10 percent of new furniture sales. Increased sales of low cost and RTA furniture affect distribution channels, as this type of furniture is sold through office superstores, discount stores, and warehouse clubs rather than through specialty office furniture stores.

Another key factor affecting the office furniture market is the price of steel, the primary raw material used in production of desks, office tables, cabinets, and chairs. After beginning to recover from a shaky market between 2000 and 2003, U.S. office furniture companies were faced with a sudden spike in steel prices in early 2004 that threatened newly reestablished profit margins. At the same time, increasing competition from lower-cost suppliers in developing countries was beginning to play a larger role in the market—a trend that analysts expected would continue through the first decade of the twenty-first century.

As the corporate world followed a trend toward cutting costs in the 1990s and early in the first decade of the 2000s, offices were reorganized to adapt to the smaller spaces in which workers operate. Most notably, exclusive—and often divided—offices gave way to more communal cubicles. Furthermore, many companies altered their internal business dynamics. Rather than the hierarchical, individual-based productivity methods and office configurations that were the rule since the massive proliferation of white-collar jobs earlier in the twentieth century, companies fostered team-based, highly communicative business structures. As a result, the emphasis in the office furniture industry shifted from elaborate and opulent design methods to efficient, "egalitarian" furniture that more readily reflects the need for active and frequent intercommunication in the workplace.

The massive proliferation and rapid development of office technology also had a dramatic effect on the office furniture industry. Companies within the industry had to adjust their design and manufacturing processes to efficiently accommodate new technology, while remaining abreast of rapidly emerging office technology. Overall, this shift resulted in an industry-wide focus on office furniture that is flexible and adjustable, so businesses can avoid having to purchase new furniture as technology is developed with different components and configurations. Furniture that allows the greatest degree of support and facility and that has reconfiguration and multipurpose capabilities is expected to continue as the dominant industry trend in the twenty-first century.

While the heaviest concentration of the office furniture industry's business is in the United States, nearly one-fourth of that in the state of Michigan, rapidly expanding markets all over the world are expected to broaden the industry significantly. Because small, domestic companies constitute the vast majority of industry participants, especially outside the United States, markets in Eastern Europe, Latin America, and the Pacific Rim region were expected to foster significant industry growth within those regions.

The U.S. office furniture industry saw record sales of US$13.3 billion in 2000, but the next four years were disappointing, as shaky economic conditions cooled demand. According to a report published in *Forbes*, office furniture shipments declined by 39.3 percent between late 2000 and late 2003. Sales reached about US$8.47 billion in 2003, a decline of 4.7 percent from the previous year. By 2004, however, signs were more favorable for the industry, with sales picking up 5.4 percent that year to reach US$8.93 billion. While much of the world's trade depends on imports and exports, office furniture tends to be manufactured and sold close to home.

Industry insights were abundant in an excerpt from a Research and Markets (a Dubline online international market research firm) "Furniture Manufacturing" report. It was rated as "an essential report" and highlighted by PR-inside.com in 2009. The U.S. furniture manufacturing industry was estimated to be worth approximately US $65 billion in sales for about 20,000 companies. Typically, companies have one plant producing less than US $150 million in revenue. Several sectors are highly concentrated with metal office furniture being notable among them. Overall, the industry tends to be fragmented. Thus, "the largest 50 companies hold less than 40 percent of the market" Sales volume for home and office furniture are linked to "level of home sales" and "health of U.S. economy" respectively. It is typical for manufacturers to choose a specialty of either the US $40 billion household furniture market or US $25 billion office furniture market. In addition to industry giants, many small companies achieved success in the marketplace. They did so by producing "specialty items or high-quality workmanship that can sell for a premium price."

ORGANIZATION AND STRUCTURE

While many industries are dominated by a handful of manufacturers, such is not the case in the global office furniture industry. Thousands of companies make office furniture, with varying degrees of specialization, and the general consensus within the industry was that any company able to deliver quality products had a healthy chance at profitability. In the United States, however, a handful of corporations manage to generate nearly half of the office furniture market. Still, there are few barriers to keep competitors from attacking its position in the marketplace. In both Europe and Asia, there are few large companies, though some of the largest U.S.-based companies maintain a strong presence in these regions.

The largest companies sell their products through a network of representatives, wholesalers, and retailers. Depending on a company's size and distribution strategy, it may opt to bypass these middlemen and market its products directly to customers. Such cases, while not uncommon, constitute a relatively small share of the industry's distribution channels.

The type of office furniture designs and the accompanying sales often vary depending on the country of origin. In the United States, there has always been a high priority placed on worker privacy. Company managers traditionally marked the occupation of an office (and its location) as an indication of seniority and authority. From the 1950s through the 1970s, authority was represented by an office in the corner of a building with windows and aesthetically pleasing and extravagant office furniture. The 1990s witnessed a rapid shift in this dynamic within the workplace. The downsizing of the office led to a new category of office furniture, called "systems furniture," which is usually comprised of a portable wall with electrical outlets, a desk surface, and a matching chair.

In Asia, portable walls are rare, as privacy is generally considered unnecessary to work performance. Desks and workers are arranged side by side in large open areas and supervisors frequently sit at elevated desks overseeing the workers. In Europe, this same custom of open space prevails with a similar emphasis on teamwork. Individual desks are often replaced with large, communal desks shared by teams of workers endeavoring to solve the same problem. The partitions so popular with office designers in the United States are rare. In some parts of Europe, laws and employee contracts specify that employees must be able to look up from their work and see sunlight. Varying work customs such as these are part of the reason why office furniture is a regional industry that does not accommodate intercontinental exchange of products. Companies wanting to export must be absolutely sure they have a superior product, as thousands of domestic manufacturers are ready to meet any unfulfilled customer needs.

As markets expand globally, the industry has seen a push for international standardization of certain product specifications that will allow for simpler trade considerations. The International Organization for Standardization (ISO) instituted two new voluntary standards that began to influence the industry and were expected eventually to make way for increased international trade of office furniture. ISO 9000 standardizes quality assurance guidelines, while ISO 14000 regulates environmental aspects. These will most notably affect office furniture made from wood products. By 2005, most of the companies that adopted these standards were larger corporations. These corporations were far more likely to engage in international trade.

BACKGROUND AND DEVELOPMENT

The office furniture industry is relatively new. Manufacturing of office furniture started in earnest in the early twentieth century when the service industry emerged—following the inventions of the telephone, electric power, and the typewriter—and more people began working at desks. White collar and service jobs proliferated in the golden years of corporate growth between the world wars and in the 1950s. In those days, office furniture manufacturers selling through retailers delivered tens of millions of desks, tables, chairs, file cabinets, and bookcases—everything to make the tasks of corporate employees easier. New sales were generated in large part due to the shift in the U.S. economy from a manufacturing to a service emphasis, a change that boosted the fortunes of the office furniture industry. When the information age dawned in the early 1980s, the massive influx of information processors into the workplace further expanded the office furniture industry.

The office furniture industry began to change in the late 1980s, when the *Fortune* 1000 businesses—the companies that had staffed up so dramatically during the previous 80 years—began to trim their labor forces in pursuit of lower operating costs. The effect on purchases of office furniture was devastating, as the elimination of employee positions caused a substantial decline in demand for new office furniture. The office furniture industry was hit hard by this first wave of mass corporate layoffs, which was followed by a related worldwide recession that slowed spending by corporations that were trying to maintain their employee ranks. By 1991 sales had actually declined by 8 percent compared to 1990, the first sales drop in two decades.

In the 1990s, the industry recovered steadily from the recession as the changing dynamics of the workplace, increased demand for facilitation of evolving office technology needs, and the growing trend toward home offices created challenging and competitive new areas in which the industry competes. A surge in start-up companies also increased demand. By 2000, U.S. sales of office furniture soared to a record US$13.3 billion.

In the early years of the first decade of the 2000s, an estimated 41 million Americans performed work to some degree in their homes. Increased computer efficiency and Internet availability allowed many people to engage in a diverse number of business-related activities in their homes, be it connection to a central office at which they were employed, the operation of a personal business enterprise, or the maintenance of a stock portfolio. Almost all of these home offices have desks, chairs, and filing cabinets—the same sort of equipment the office furniture industry supplies to the *Fortune* 1000. Instead of selling desks in bulk to a single corporate client, the industry sells an increasing number of desks to individuals. Office furniture for home offices is less industrial in look and feel, and people buying furniture for home offices look for designs and colors that fit their homes and individual tastes. With this diversification of the industry's customer base has come a greater emphasis on competitiveness in the area of customer service practices.

The home office market has seen great penetration by the ready-to-assemble (RTA) segment of the office furniture industry. While old-style office furniture retailers delivered full-sized desks to the workplace, RTA manufacturers sell customers furniture in cardboard boxes. The customers follow the directions to build their own desks and bookcases. The desks may not be as attractive as the solid cherry executive model the corporate CEO has, but they are much less expensive and portable.

In the first few years of the twenty-first century, the U.S. office furniture industry suffered setbacks as the economy took a pronounced downturn. Between 2000 and 2003, office furniture shipments fell by almost 40 percent. Total exports of non-wood office furniture, which had reached US$551 million in 2000, declined to only US$318 million in 2003. During this period, large corporations—which account for the majority of office furniture sales—cut back their spending. Facing sharp declines in profits, office furniture companies were forced to cut their workforces and scale back some product lines.

Not until 2004 did the situation begin to improve, as office construction showed signs of growth and economic recovery fueled demand for new furniture or replacements of worn items. However, a sudden rise in the price of steel in early 2004 threatened this recovery. One steel manufacturer raised its prices to commercial customers by 8.5 percent, and the price of steel in some grades jumped more than 30 percent. As a result, major office furniture companies such as Steelcase, which had anticipated healthy profits for the first time in four years but then had to lower its forecasted first-quarter earnings, announced that they would raise prices on their products. This move led to concern that consumers would seek lower prices elsewhere. With steel prices remaining high into 2005, the availability and price of wood, which accounts for approximately 25 percent of production of office furniture, also continued to affect the industry. There was growing concern that forests worldwide were being depleted at a rate far outpacing their renewal, and environmental concerns stemming from this issue contributed to higher demand for products made from certified lumber—wood harvested from sustainable-managed forests.

CURRENT CONDITIONS

The U.S. office furniture industry had recovered somewhat by 2005, when total market value of shipments reached US$10.0 billion, and 2006 saw another slight improvement to US$10.9 billion. These figures were still far from the record production of $13.3 billion seen in 2000, but experts predicted 7 to 8 percent annual increases in 2007 and 2008, slowing to a 4 to 5 percent growth rate thereafter. Twenty-seven percent of the office furniture sold in the United States in 2005 was wood. Systems furniture accounted for the largest share at 28.8 percent. Other items, the growth of which outpaced the overall office furniture industry, included tables (up 31.2 percent), seating (up 12.7 percent), and desks (up 11.8 percent). Storage furniture was the fastest growing segment of the industry, having increased more than 50 percent between 1995 and 2005. Filing cabinets, on the other hand, grew by only 3.2 percent during that time, due in part to the transition from paper to electronic files. California remained the largest consumer of office

furniture in the United States and was responsible for US$1.2 billion of the total market in 2005, followed by Texas (US$755 million), New York (US$635 million), and Florida (US$592 million). Together these four states accounted for more than 30 percent of the entire U.S. office furniture industry in 2005.

U.S. furniture export figures also improved as the industry moved toward the late years of the first decade of the 2000s. After experiencing steady drops from 2001 to 2004, the value of furniture exports increased to US$438 million in 2005, up from US$347 million in 2004, and rose again to US$492 million in 2006. A majority of office furniture exports went to Canada. Likewise, Canada provided about 45 percent of the United States' office furniture imports. China was the second largest importer of office furniture to the United States at that time, although by 2006 China had overtaken Canada's number one spot. Other countries that exported large volumes of office furniture to the United States in 2006 included Taiwan and Mexico. U.S. imports of office furniture, totaling about US$2.5 billion in 2005, remained much higher than exports.

The upturn in the office furniture industry was not as pronounced in Europe, where factors that were affecting growth in the United States, such as white-collar employment, new office construction, and corporate profitability, were not as prominent. Of the European markets, the United Kingdom showed the most positive trends.

Rapid economic growth in China remained a significant factor in the international office furniture market in the mid-years of the first decade of the 2000s. Commercial booms in major Chinese cities resulted in strong demand for new or upgraded office spaces and furniture. With import tariffs eliminated at the beginning of 2005, analysts expected that China would substantially increase its consumption of office furniture from foreign suppliers, whose products are often considered superior to locally produced goods. At the same time, China was increasing its global exports of office furniture. By 2005, more U.S. office furniture came from China than any other country; shipments from China totaled US$1.05 billion in 2005 and almost $700 million in the first half of 2006 alone.

The retreat to more functional, less expensive systems in this mature product market resulted in the disappearance—by merger and acquisition—of many smaller companies that could no longer compete in some market niches due to the relatively small breadth of their product lines. Many of the larger corporations, on the other hand, acquired these smaller, more specialized companies in order to enter their market fields. Like many other industries, it is generally less expensive for larger companies to acquire smaller companies with existing products than it is for the larger companies to launch new product lines of their own.

At the same time, smaller companies offering unique or better-made products sustain a healthy profit. Small companies with the capital to carry out effective marketing and distribution strategies can still compete against the larger conglomerates. This is particularly true in the European and Asian markets where large companies are more rare than they are in the United States.

First impressions are important for offices, too. That is why what people see upon entering a site is so important. With those thoughts in mind, Executive Desk Company is attempting to expand throughout the United States from its San Diego base during challenging economic times. It is a hard-sell time for large ticket items including high end office furniture. "Reception desks are, without a doubt, one of the most important pieces of office furniture every company should make the proper investment in," Executive Desk Company managing partner Todd Trieu claimed. People seeking European style desks and matching accessories purchase products "characterized" by sophistication, structural integrity, and quality real wood veneers from Executive Desk Company.

Flexibility. Quickly developing office technology has created demands for furniture that is designed with flexibility and durability to facilitate changing work configurations, varying computer systems, and use of other office equipment. Concurrently, the demand for lightweight design has modified production, as manufacturers engage in the assembly of adjustable, multi-level workstations.

Functionality. To further accommodate technological progress and the shift of office dynamics from an isolated, hierarchical structure to a more cooperative, team-based model, office furniture designers have shifted their focus. Primary consideration is now given to companies' specific organizational structure and interaction needs. The trend for businesses is toward functional, efficient, and inviting office atmospheres that foster productivity and cooperation, rather than extravagance. Ergonomics continues to be a concern for employees and employers, so comfort features and injury prevention are popular selling points.

RESEARCH AND TECHNOLOGY

"Ergonomic" is a word that furniture manufacturers were barely familiar with in 1990. Since then, many companies have tried to incorporate the concept into their designs and advertising. The word ergonomic has become a catchall phrase meaning furniture specifically designed for a person's physical well-being. A primary concern of designers is

the avoidance of contributing to repetitive strain injuries (RSI) that result from a worker's repetition of acts from the same position over a significant period of time. A common RSI among office workers is carpal tunnel syndrome. Furniture without the proper consideration given to ergonomic design can aggravate or help cause RSIs. Chairs reflecting these concerns should have the right amount of back support, encourage good posture, and not have too much padding in front, as blood circulation to the worker's legs may be cut off. Examples of ergonomic designs that account for this and other concerns include fold-down typing keyboard drawers in desks at the correct height so typists reach neither too high nor too low, adjustable desk portions of systems furniture to fit the height of different people, and furniture pieces that accommodate the disabled.

Although industry negotiations probably eliminated any long-term problems with regulations governing the use of chemicals in the workplace, many companies are continuing their own research on how to make furniture using fewer and safer chemicals. Their motivation is to reduce the cost of processing and reduce the danger to employees. In addition, BIFMA International has worked with regulatory bodies such as the U.S. Environmental Protection Agency (EPA) to coordinate efforts to maintain a clean-air environment in corporate and home offices. This would in turn reduce worker compensation claims and threats of employee lawsuits over dangerous workplaces.

Engineered wood has gained considerable favor among manufacturers and customers for its attractive look and its machinability. Companies worried about the long-term world supply of wood suitable for manufacturing, however, are constantly researching new materials. The systems furniture used in many office settings in the 1990s was often made of plastic or another composite. Even manufacturers long skilled in using wood were experimenting with substituting wood laminates that would make their products look like wood. Another material that made inroads in the office furniture market is vinyl. Vinyl's efficient and diverse design capabilities make it a favorable material for manufacturers striving to meet the market demand for ergonomic design and functionality. Furthermore, its flexible aesthetic capabilities allow it to resemble many different surfaces, including wood. Another option is the use of recycled materials. Steelcase and Herman Miller are among the companies that produce furniture using such materials.

Radia Amari, writing for the *Denver Business Journal* in March 2009, described how nontraditional office "furniture" could advance efforts to create and sustain a healthy workplace. The Walkstation encourages employees to be more productive while they work. Stepping along on the station can lead to weight loss and enhanced energy. It incorporates a treadmill resulting in a shared resource for employees inclined to be sedimentary vs. active. When compared to "a full-scale workout" after work, Amari wrote that studies showed that walking on the station for five minutes approximately seven times daily was more effective. Amari described a Kaiser Permanente Colorado pilot project focused on its call center employees and effects of the Walkstation. Study design calls for 32 weeks with 20 volunteers working with the Walkstation for two hours during eight-hour shifts.

Office furniture shoppers don't want to just imagine what their work environments will look like, they want to experience it. That insight was shared by Office Furnishing Interior Solutions (OFIS) executives, according to Al Bawaba, a Mideast news Web site, and has led "one of the UAE's leading office furnishings and interior solutions, providers" to make plans and implement them related to the trend. A "state-of-the-art showroom" with more than 30,000 square feet featuring "contemporary furniture and interior solutions for modern work environments" opened its doors in Dubai. In addition to static displays, the OFIS showroom has interactive display areas. In those settings, shoppers are encouraged to test all products. "We want our customers to come into our showroom and be able to visualize themselves at the work station of their choice," explained OFIS corporate parent Easa Saleh Al Gurg Group Business Manager Jagan K. Another distinctive design feature is the OFIS showroom, which has the first built-in auditorium for a store in Dubai. The room is "fully functional" spotlighting "various designs in seating."

OFIS offers "The Cube" from Bosse, an "all-inclusive office" functioning as "modular space system." The distinctive system has its own independent "lighting, air conditioning and electrical system" making it a welcome addition for any "open space."

WORKFORCE

The office furniture workforce is relatively small. Only a handful of companies have more than a thousand employees. In the United States, it is estimated that less than a half million people manufacture both office and household furniture.

Most European and Asian office furniture manufacturers are much smaller than U.S. corporations. The average German furniture company (both office and household furniture) has 125 employees. Only a few German furniture manufacturers have more than 1,000 employees. The employment figures in Asia are even smaller. Japan, the office furniture industry leader, has only a few companies employing more than a few hundred workers.

INDUSTRY LEADERS

Steelcase. Steelcase of Grand Rapids, Michigan, remained the world's largest office furniture manufacturer, with sales exceeding US$2.8 billion in 2006, a 9.8 increase from the previous year. The company's brands include Leap, Pathways, and Turnstone. Steelcase distributes its products, which include all manner of office furniture, through more than 800 dealers in 120 countries. Steelcase is an innovator and global leader in the field of systems furniture and offers services such as workspace planning. The company employed 13,000 people in 2006.

HNI Corporation. Tied with Haworth as the number-two office furniture company in the United States, HNI manufactures desks and chairs, filing cabinets, shelving, modular systems, and similar products. Its subsidiaries include Allsteel, Gunlocke, Hearth & Home Technologies, Maxon Furniture, and Hearth & Home, which makes fireplaces. Sales in 2006 reached US$2.6 billion, on the strength of 14,200 "members."

When explaining its corporate culture centered around "members" versus employees, HNI stressed the significance of "Rapid Continuous Improvement." Consequentially, all members are encouraged to share what makes them special.

Understanding end users is something HNI believes can help it grow and expand. This heightened level of research goes beyond looking at initial sales experiences to consider what happens later. Considerations include "overall experience" as well as installation and delivery. Another unique aspect of this approach involves extended time frame, potentially continuing years after initial product purchase. HNI maintains its competitive edge by "using information gained to drive changes" for processes.

Haworth. Haworth, which made a name for itself when it invented pre-wired partitions for cubicles, continued to grow because of acquisitions that expanded its operations (which included distribution in more than 120 countries) and its product lines. Sales in 2008 reached US$1.6 billion. Among its brands were Berlin, if, PLACES, and X99. Haworth is privately held by the Haworth family and employs 7,500 people.

In the summer of 2009, Haworth proudly shared the news that it had been the recipient of some "prestigious design association" awards. Those awards were the International Interior Design Association's Titan Award and the American Society of Interior Designers' Patron's Prize. The Titan Award acknowledged "outstanding service" plus "commitment...based on shared values." The Patron's Prize was accompanied by a statement celebrating that

"Haworth's new headquarters and showrooms represent not only the evolution of sustainable design, but also illustrate the company's commitment to practice what they preach to their clients."

At the World's Trade Fair NeoCon 2009, showcasing the latest trends and innovations for office environments, Haworth stood out with its introduction of four new products and several product enhancements. As a result, Haworth was a Best of NeoCon winner, earning three silvers and one gold. The Compose desking product was an exceptional new addition to the scene featuring "a specific focus on benching" and the ability to function in a superior manner when "arranged in a variety of applications." Compose acquired a silver for its Desking Benching Enhancements for Furniture Systems.

Haworth announced its plans to idle its Calgary, Canada, plant and bring about 500 jobs to Holland, Michigan, according to the *Grand Rapids Press*. It was a sign of consolidation for the office furniture industry. The move was linked to "a steep industry slowdown" and tax breaks adding up to US$224 million from the Michigan Economic Growth Authority.

U.S. office furniture production was approximately US$11.2 billion in 2008. Shipments dropped by nearly 29 percent in 2009. That meant they added up to US$8 billion, as the *Grand Rapids Press* reported that the Business and Institutional Furniture Manufacturer's Association had revealed.

Herman Miller Inc. With US$1.6 billion in 2009 fiscal year sales and around 6,300 employees, Herman Miller of Zeeland, Michigan, was a leading U.S. manufacturer of office furniture. The company manufactures in the United States, the United Kingdom, and Japan, and ships its products around the world to subsidiary sales companies. However, exports comprise a relatively small portion of total sales; more than 80 percent of its sales in the early years of the first decade of the 2000s were in the United States. Like Steelcase, Herman Miller is one of the leading manufacturers of systems furniture. Herman Miller has developed a line of furniture especially for start-up companies; the furniture is marketed as affordable and reliable.

From a field of approximately 100 nominations, Herman Miller was selected as the "Green Champion." Nominees reflected diversity in a variety of industries. When considering granting the award to Herman Miller, *Business Review West Michigan* was impressed by "Perfect Vision" goals. Those goals "include 100 percent reduction of VOC emissions to air, hazardous waste and solid waste to landfills by 2020."

Office furniture industry analyst Michael Dunlap forecasted that the hard-hit industry had perhaps "hit bottom and is starting a long, slow recovery," according to the *Grand Rapids Press*. The improving plight of Herman Miller was considered to be a positive sign of better days ahead. After acknowledging the company was "facing tough market dynamics," Herman Miller CEO Brian Walker stated, "But we've been here before and we have a long-term strategy that we are confident is guiding us in the right direction."

MAJOR COUNTRIES IN THE INDUSTRY

With an estimated one-third of world production, the United States dominated the global industry in office furniture manufacturing. Canada was the largest export market, accounting for about 50 percent of U.S. foreign sales.

The United States also was a major importer of office furniture, and during the 1990s imports quadrupled. In 2000, the total value of U.S. imports was more than US$2 billion, an increase of about 18 percent; of this, about US$1.7 billion was for non-wood office furniture. Imports fell slightly in 2001 but rose in each of the next two years. In 2004, imports were valued at US$2.4 billion. Canada, the largest supplier, contributed about 45 percent of U.S. imports, down from about 60 percent in the late 1990s. China was the second leading supplier, followed by Taiwan, Mexico, and Italy. In 2005, China overtook the number one position as top exporter of office furniture to the United States, followed by Taiwan, Canada, and Mexico.

European furniture production rose by 6.6 percent in 2000, and sales of office furniture in Europe rose by 6 percent. In 2001 the European furniture market was worth about 82 billion euros (US$98.9 billion). Office furniture, the third-leading category after upholstered and kitchen furniture, accounted for 11.7 percent. Germany, Italy, France, and the United Kingdom are the leading manufacturers of office furniture in Europe, and most of their output remains on the continent. Some of the trends shaping the U.S. market are also shaping the European market, most notably the high demand for furniture that will accommodate changing technology in the workplace. European buyers are also concerned with flexibility and multi-functionality.

In Asia, thousands of small companies supply the needs of both domestic markets and regional trading partners along the Asia-Pacific Rim. Japan accounts for the largest share of Asian manufacturers.

BIBLIOGRAPHY

Amari, Radia. "Some nontraditional office 'furniture' can be beneficial." 3 April 2009. Available from denver.bizjournals.com.

Barile, Gina. "Profile of Quebec's Furniture Manufacturing Industry." U.S. Commercial Services, 2006. Available from commercecan.ic.gc.ca.

Berdon, Caroline. "On the Move: The Office Furniture Industry Is in a Much Better Place Than It Was Two Years Ago, But Growth Worldwide Is Uneven." *Office Products International,* February 2006.

Coleman, Katie. "Steelcase's Strategy for an Environmentally Sound, Profitable Business." *Wood & Wood Products,* February 2007.

"The Demand for Office Furniture in the United States." *Global Wood,* 1 November 2006. Available from www.globalwood.org.

Flaherty, Michael. "Steel Prices Pinching U.S. Office Furniture 2004." *Forbes,* 3 March 2004.

Gold, Robert. "Outlook Improves for Office Furniture Industry." *Holland Sentinel* (Michigan), 5 May 2004.

Grand Rapids Press. "Analysts sees Possible Beginning of Office Furniture Recovery in Herman Miller's Latest Quarter." 2009. Available from blog.mlive.com.

Grand Rapids Press. "Haworth is latest of office furniture industry consolidations; this round benefits Holland with 500 jobs." 18 August 2009. Available from www.mlive.com.

Haworth. "Haworth's New & Enhanced Product Introductions." 15 June 2009. Available from www.haworth.com.

———. "Haworth Receives Prestigious Design Association Awards." Summer 2009. Available from www.haworth.com.

Herman Miller. "Herman Miller, Inc., Named Green Champion by Business Review West Michigan." 3 September 2009. Available from www.hermanmiller.com.

HNI Corporation. "Member Culture." 2009. Available from www.hnicorp.com.

"Hoover's Company Capsules." *Hoover's Online,* 2007. Available from www.hoovers.com.

Koeing, Karen M. "Office Furniture Industry Takes Action." *Wood & Wood Products,* October 2006.

Miel, Rhoda. "Office Furniture Makers Cautiously Comfortable." *Plastics News,* 8 January 2007.

"Office Furniture Industry Performance and Projections." *Deseret News,* 14 May 2006.

"Office Furniture Shopping Becoming More Experiential." 2009. Available from www.albawa.com.

Phillips, Tom. "Sitting Pretty: All Rise Please for the Office Furniture Industry!" *Office Products International,* November 2006.

Research and Markets. "Research and Markets: An Essential Report on Furniture Manufacturing." PR-Inside, 31 August 2009. Available from www.pr-inside.com.

"Steelcase, Maker of Office Furniture, Will Cut 600 Jobs." *New York Times,* 29 March 2005.

"The U.S. Office Furniture Market." The Business and Institutional Manufacturers Association, 14 February 2007. Available from www.bifma.com.

U.S. Department of Commerce, International Trade Administration. "Office Furniture Export and Import Statistics, 1996—2005." Available from www.ita.doc.gov.

GLASS, PLASTICS, AND RUBBER PRODUCTS

GLASS CONTAINERS AND GLASSWARE

NAICS CODE(S)

3272. This industry classification is divided into two principal groups: manufacturers who use techniques of blowing or pressing to shape glass into containers and manufacturers who produce glass that is used for ornamental purposes. The use of glass for containers lends itself to a range of activities from commercial packaging and bottling to home canning. Glass containers may be cosmetic jars, fruit jars, jugs for packing, medicine bottles, wine bottles, milk bottles, vials, or water bottles. Ornamental glass includes art glassware, glass ashtrays, barware, bowls, candlesticks, centerpieces, glass chimneys for lamps, Christmas tree ornaments made from glass, glass and glass ceramic frying pans, glassware, goblets, glass lampshades, lantern globes, stemware, tableware, and vases.

INDUSTRY SNAPSHOT

The case studies of some glass industry stand-out companies had the potential to inspire professionals in many different fields with a shared commitment to sustaining traditions, exploring product innovation, addressing environmental issues and solidifying a profitable future. For example, Majan Glass has achieved both commercial and industrial success from its Oman base. Established in 1995, the company grew from humble beginnings to become the largest manufacturer of glass bottles in the Middle East. By 2009, it had 172 employees. This status was achieved after overcoming major losses in early years. Some of them were due to challenges from plastics and difficulties experienced when establishing plants on foreign soil. As a testament to its achievements and success, Majan was awarded the "Omani Quality Mark." "We believe that our success can be attributed to the commitment of our employees who are motivated by a need for excellence and constantly strive for quality performance. The award is an encouragement for us to put in sustained effort across various fields," Majan Chairman Ali Sultan acknowledged. The Mark sets apart products in terms of quality and aims to protect consumers against fraud as well.

During the middle of the first decade of the 2000s, glass products experienced uneven demand, and at times delivered disappointing returns to their makers. Glass containers, which constitute the larger of the industry's two segments, face intense competition from both aluminum and plastics, especially polyethylene terephthalate (PET), a material commonly used for plastic drink containers. This is especially so in the food products and beverage sector, which accounts for the largest glass container production numbers in many markets. Nonetheless, glass retains marketing strength as an attractive material, and glass packaging is seen by many consumers as having a high-quality image. Glass enjoys numerous regional niche strongholds that make it still an attractive growth prospect for producers and investors willing to weather difficult times. Also, strides made by plastics in the container market could be counteracted by increasing concerns regarding toxic emissions and waste in the manufacturing and recycling of these materials, especially since glass manufacturing overall has a better environmental track record.

In mature markets such as the United States and Western Europe, glass sales in certain categories have been flat or declining. Coupled with falling prices, these trends have made glass manufacture unprofitable for some companies and given rise to consolidation, particularly in Europe. However, most of the world's emerging economies are potentially strong growth markets for glass containers in the longer term. Within more mature markets, various niches, such as premium beverage bottles, and efficient, consolidated producers, will also continue to obtain favorable results.

In societies concerned about ecology, the stability of the glass industry is bolstered by the fact that glass never wears out, is 100 percent recyclable, and can be recycled forever. With the exception of recyclable aluminum beverage containers, no other packaging material has experienced as rapid a growth in recycling as glass. Recycling glass saves from 25 to 32 percent of the energy required to make glass. Most of today's bottles and jars contain at least 25 percent recycled glass, and the Texas Agricultural Extension Service reports that many plants have increased the amount of recycled glass, known as cullet, in their products to 40 percent or more.

With an eye toward the future while staying in tune with a strong heritage, the glass industry was moving ahead with innovative plans. A notable example incorporated many distinctive aspects to create the blueprints for the biggest float glass plant in the Gulf. Obeikan Glass is building a fully integrated state-of-the-art float glass plant in Yaribu, Saudi Arabia. Production plans call for it to ultimately produce approximately 800 tons per day. The plant's creation serves as a model for effective collaborations that unite companies from different countries and implement efforts related to maintaining a reduced ecological footprint. "Fives Stein, a French company, eagerly accepted the opportunity to incorporate its on-line coatings capabilities. Plant designers addressed issues related to meeting international emissions standards for the site, scheduled to open its doors in April 2010. It will reportedly be the biggest float glass plant in the Gulf."

ORGANIZATION AND STRUCTURE

Glass is part of the packaging market known as rigid packaging. Other rigid packaging materials include rigid metal, such as aluminum and tin-plated steel, plastic, and composite or multi-material containers. According to research compiled by First Boston Corporation, the rigid container market in 1960 was made up of 66.7 percent metal cans and 32.6 percent glass containers. By 1993, glass accounted for only 18 percent of the market, metal's share had fallen to 60 percent, and the plastic category had

grown to 22 percent. Although the use of plastic gained favor in the 1970s, noticeably in the soft drinks market, glass remains a competitive packaging material because it is recyclable and contributes to marketing appeal.

To deal with the impact of plastic bottles and cans on the glass packaging industry, manufacturers have sought a variety of new packaging ideas. Although the standard wine bottle size is 750 milliliters, the industry designed a 500-milliliter bottle for special-occasion use. This allowed manufacturers to capitalize on the smaller bottle's appeal to consumers who consider the larger size wasteful. Long neck, commemorative, proprietary shape, and new-age market bottles are expected to shore up glass's share of the soft drink market and ultimately account for as much as 25 percent of all glass soft drink bottles. According to the Society of Glass and Ceramic Decoration, unusual glass packaging and decorating effects do much to advance various marketing efforts. Unique bottle design creates a demand among vendors who use glass packaging to enhance their product image, as well as among collectors who capitalize on the incremental value associated with limited edition bottles and containers.

As long ago as 1990, at the Conference on Glass Problems held at The Ohio State University, it was predicted that the need for glass would remain high due to the beer market, and that the soft drink market also would remain a solid one for glass—especially for those products sold in vending machines and convenience stores. In the face of pressure from plastic in food packaging and, to a lesser degree, in the soft drink market, the major opportunity for glass industry growth was seen in expansion of the glass container market. The corollary to this prediction was container manufacturers' need to improve productivity, quality, and the cost of the average glass container.

In 1997, emphasis was placed on the need to reduce contaminants in recycled glass. Contaminants causing most concern include aluminum caps, steel lids, lead bottle collars and light bulb filaments, ceramics, stones and dirt, plate or window glass, heat-resistant glass, and lead-based glass. Mixing of glass colors is discouraged, because most glass-container customers will not tolerate variances in glass color. Because specific colors of glass admit light to different degrees, container glass always is produced in one of three colors. Sixty-four percent of glass containers are flint (clear), 23 percent are amber, and the remaining 13 percent are green. In an attempt to improve the quality of recycled glass, the Glass Packaging Institute (GPI) launched "Glass Container Recycling: Today and Tomorrow," described as an outreach effort targeting public and private sector haulers, cullet processors, state agencies, and local recycling officials.

BACKGROUND AND DEVELOPMENT

Glassmaking originated 5,000 years ago in the Middle East. To make glass, common sand, which contains silica, is mixed with ashes from trees (potash) or marine plants (soda). The mixture then is "fired," using intense heat (a minimum of 1,000 degrees Fahrenheit) until it melts. The resulting "molten blob" of glass can be blown, cut, and colored, according to how it is to be used. Glass was common in a number of ancient civilizations. Blown glasses and bottles have been used in Syria and Italy since the first century B.C.

In the seventeenth century, the technique of adding lead oxide to molten glass was discovered. In addition to making the crystal more brilliant and durable, the lead made the glass softer and easier to work. From the time the process was discovered, the beautiful products made of lead crystal have been regarded as a symbol of luxury.

The eighteenth century saw the expansion of both the glass and wine industries. As vintners proved they were learning how to make wine that aged, glassmakers discovered a new market: making bottles for long-term wine storage. Additionally, tabletop art was coming into vogue, and glassmakers began producing decorative glasses and decanters. Consumers in Georgian England (1714 to 1830) were adamant that a wine glass "be more than a mere receptacle for liquid." Pre-Georgian glasses are recognizable today by their simplicity and heaviness, but in 1746, a tax was levied on glass weight. Thus prompted, manufacturers began to produce lighter glassware with a more delicate form. Georgian wineglasses are characterized as having a foot, a stem, and a bowl that may be blown as a unit with the stem.

Following the Georgian era, the glass industry boomed, given a significant boost in 1780 when English glass houses set up shops in Ireland to take advantage of a newly established tax-free trading status in that country. Nineteenth-century developments furthering the industry's progress included the invention of the Mason jar in 1859 (enabling fruits and vegetables to be preserved) and the invention of the Owens automatic bottle machine in 1903 (leading to high-speed production of bottles and jars of uniform height, weight, and capacity). As a result of these innovations, labor-intensive glass blowing relinquished its place as the major method of glass production.

The processes of "press-and-blow" and "blow-and-blow" were discovered between 1850 and 1890. The blow-and-blow process employed an inverted blank mold in order to gain a larger opening to receive the charge of glass. In the same period, it was discovered that the finish of the bottle needed to be constructed first and that two molds, a neck ring and a tip, were required.

According to the U.S. Census Bureau, glass container production reached 248.5 million gross in 2002, up from 240.5 million gross in 2001. Of this total, glass beer bottles comprised the largest segment, at 52.9 percent. Food containers were the next largest category (19.8 percent), followed by general beverage bottles (8.9 percent), ready-to-drink alcoholic coolers and cocktail containers (5.8 percent), wine bottles (5.1 percent), other containers (4.4 percent), and liquor bottles (3.2 percent).

In 2003, the U.S. Census Bureau reported that total glass container production fell to 245.4 million gross. This downward trend continued through mid-2004, as production for the first six months of the year reached 123.7 million gross, compared to 126.5 million gross at the same time in 2003.

In August 2002, *Glass* reported that western European glass production reached 18.2 million tons in 2000 (the most recent data available), up from 15.3 million tons in 1990. Germany had the largest share of total production, with 23.4 percent, followed by France (20.1 percent), Italy (17.8 percent), Spain (10.8 percent), and the United Kingdom (9.4 percent).

By early 2003, the U.S. glass container industry remained heavily consolidated. In its January 31, 2003 issue, *Packaging Strategies* revealed that Owens-Illinois controlled 44 percent of the nation's market, followed by Saint Gobain Containers (31 percent), and Consumers Packaging/Anchor (19 percent). The remaining industry players accounted for a mere 6 percent of the market. As further evidence of industry consolidation, by 2001 there were 54 manufacturing plants in the United States, compared to 121 in 1983.

Anyone seeking more insights about the origins of glass making in the United States can find them at the Sandwich Glass Museum in Cape Cod's oldest town. Operated by the Sandwich Historical Society, the site recalls legacy of The Boston & Sandwich Glass Co. which was a major industry force from 1825 to 1888. Until competition made it too hard to compete with pricing challenges, the company carried on with more than 500 employees. Their legacy can be celebrated by viewing diverse beautiful glass creations and collectibles.

Glass versus Plastic. During the early years of the first decade of the 2000s, polyethylene terephthalate (PET) containers continued to have a significant effect on the global glass container market. The leading glass container companies also established plastics packaging businesses. The many performance advantages of plastic packaging continue to undermine glass as the material of choice, especially in the food and beverage packaging sectors.

CeramicsIndustry.com, reporting data from The Freedonia Group, indicated that in the early years of the first decade of the 2000s, baby food maker Gerber announced plans to replace most of its glass jars with plastic. The company based its decision on market research that showed consumer preference levels of almost 70 percent for baby food in plastic containers. Miller Brewing Company, seeking to give consumers a flexible packaging choice, began marketing its Miller Lite, Miller Genuine Draft, and Icehouse brands in plastic bottles in March 2000. However, glass still stands tall as the material of choice for the packaging of beer.

Many consumers in the developed world see glass containers as prestigious and associate the packaging with higher value. Therefore, companies will tend to use glass for new product introductions and for upscale products, such as specialty beers. However, research has shown that consumers in the developing world see aluminum packaging as being more attractive and of higher quality than glass.

Glass has a number of advantages over other packaging materials. Unlike plastic, glass containers are easy to sort (by color) for recycling and can be repeatedly recycled to make new containers. Using cullet, or recycled glass, results in more efficient and cleaner production. Glass containers are reusable, retain carbonation for longer periods and can be irradiated for use in sterilized applications. On the downside, glass containers have a risk of breakage; have higher weight and therefore higher shipping costs; often require an opener; and vary in how well they can be resealed.

Legislation. Forced deposit laws lead the list of issues facing the glass packaging industry because glass surcharges—bottle deposits—are thought to hurt sales and discourage packagers and retailers from using glass packaging. Advanced disposal fees (ADFs) offer another challenge. ADFs are applied to containers whose recycling rate is less than 50 percent. As recently as 1994 the glass industry's recycling rate was just 37 percent, imposition of ADFs has had its effect on industry development. Although in theory intended to encourage manufacturers to work more diligently to raise recycling rates, there has been an expressed concern that the fees are a detriment to sales, penalizing manufacturers despite their recycling efforts. ADFs enjoy international popularity, and, according to EcoRecycle Victoria (Australia), they tend to be low enough to minimize any impact on purchasing patterns. In the United States, Florida was the first state to impose an ADF, but then allowed it to lapse. California substituted a one cent ADF on packaged beverages as an alternative to container deposit legislation.

Labor. It is estimated that labor accounts for 35 percent of total cost for glass, compared with 13 percent for plastic and 9 percent for cans. These relatively high labor costs are offset by the fact that direct materials only account for 28 percent of the cost for glass, compared with 60 percent for plastic and over 75 percent for aluminum.

Another issue facing the glass industry is revealed by an efficiency measure known as "percent pack." Only 85 to 90 percent of the raw materials melted to make glass convert to a marketable product; the remainder becomes recycled glass. It is unusual for an industry to put so much labor and energy into producing a product, only to discard 10 to 15 percent of it once it is manufactured. A need for quality control is implied by this degree of waste, and there is an increasing focus on efforts to monitor glass composition, glass temperatures, and the forming process, the ultimate goal being production of quality glass containers at least 95 percent of the time.

Cost Reduction. Attempts to reduce glass production costs have led to what is termed "lightweighting," which allows for faster production of more glass containers, using less glass per container. A process known as "narrow-neck press-and-blow" has successfully trimmed glass weight by 10 to 15 percent versus the traditional blow-and-blow process. Other trends for reducing costs in the glass container industry include the usage of vision based and computer driven inspection systems for quality control; process control systems; just-in-time delivery to customers; and bulk palletization systems.

Controlling Oil and Grease in Glass Container Plants. Many glass container plants are faced with the need to upgrade wastewater treatment technology. Research has shown that the majority of oil or grease found in the outflow or effluent from a glass manufacturing plant emanates from three sources: soluble oils used in glass shearing, forming machine lubrication oils, and condensate from compressed air systems. In addition to being a major source of oil or grease, the soluble oils used in glass shearing combine with forming machine oils to create additional pollutants.

One solution to the direct and indirect discharge of industrial wastewater is known as zero process water. Zero discharge can be attained through diligent control of water input into the cullet quench system, use of cullet quench water as batch wetting water, and/or installation of an evaporator for disposal of excess wastewater. The first approach, diligent control of water input, has been successful on a limited basis, most notably in smaller glass container plants. Difficulties tend to arise in larger, more complex plants. The second approach, use of cullet quench water as a batch wetting water, is considered to be viable, having been practiced successfully for approximately 15 years. The downside, however, is that the amount of wastewater for disposal is limited to the amount of batch wetting water utilized, which often is less than the amount of wastewater available. The third approach, the installation of an evaporator, is considered to be the ideal means to control wastewater problems. However, as the operating cost for evaporation was approximately US$60 per thousand gallons, this solution may only be cost effective for small discharges.

Modification of existing systems may be the most economical remedy for plants with discharges that only slightly exceed regulatory standards. One modification calls for review of the design and operation of the cullet quench re-circulation system and oil separator. If not included in the original design and installation, inclusion of a cooling tower circuit within the cullet quench system is recommended. Cullet quench systems already installed need to be checked for biological growths that degrade the efficient removal of oil or grease and pose a potential health hazard from Legionnaire's disease.

CURRENT CONDITIONS

U.S. production of glass containers totaled 247.2 million gross in 2006. Of that total, about 58 percent went to beer bottles. The remainder was used as containers for food (16 percent), beverages (8 percent), wine (5 percent), liquor and ready-to-drink cocktails (5 percent), and other products (4 percent). Retail sales of glassware in the United States reached $1.3 billion in 2005, with most (62 percent) sold through mass merchants and clubs. Specialty stores accounted for 30 percent of sales, whereas department stores and other stores were responsible for only 4 percent each.

U.S. imports of glass remained fairly steady at about US$1.1 billion annually throughout the first decade of the 2000s, according to the U.S. Department of Commerce. However, changes occurred regarding the countries from which the imports came. China, which more than quadrupled its percentage of exports to the United States from 9 percent in 1996 to 36 percent in 2005, was the number-one glass exporter to the United States, followed by Austria (8 percent), Poland (8 percent), France (7 percent), and Ireland (6 percent). U.S. export amounts of glassware were much lower than imports but increased from 2001 to 2006. Most U.S. glassware export products went to France and China (US$1.8 million each), Germany (US$1.7 billion), and Japan and Italy (US$1.1 billion each).

Looking ahead to the late 2000s, glass container manufacturers looked to premium, "new age" beverages like natural juice drinks and teas to drive growth. Industry growth also depended on the continued popularity of so-called "malternatives"—premixed flavored alcoholic beverages (FAB), such as Bacardi Silver, Smirnoff Ice, and Skyy Blue. *Packaging Strategies* reported that an estimated 8 percent of industry capacity was devoted to the FAB sector in 2003. However, rather than increase existing capacity to satisfy demand, many U.S. manufacturers looked to imports from foreign plants.

All India Glass Manufacturers' Federation spokesman Arun Kumar acknowledged it was a major challenge to find an effective solution for the impact counterfeit drug usage was having on glass container manufacturers. Kumar admitted it was problematic to solve the problem in a way that assisted packaging and pharmaceutical companies with stopping improper distribution of counterfeit drugs after bottles had been picked up, incorrectly washed and improperly reused for drugs. Related practices were hurting reputable companies in both industries in addition to individuals. The glass industry felt it was essential to have a "traceability system" on glass bottles. It was believed counterfeits were depleting approximately 15 percent of glass industry revenues.

RESEARCH AND TECHNOLOGY

By the mid-years of the first decade of the 2000s, manufacturers were employing a variety of cutting-edge techniques to set glass containers apart from rival forms of packaging. These approaches included expensive acid etching to frost glass, the use of colors that are sprayed and baked onto glass, organic inks that enable manufacturers to spray labels directly onto glass containers, applied ceramic labeling, as well as embossed labels and plastic "shrink sleeves." Some of these techniques involved the use of computer-aided design (CAD) software, especially when it was necessary to design oddly-shaped bottles.

As Kate Bertrand summarized in the June 2004 issue of *Food & Drug Packaging*, because of "sophisticated decorating technologies and tools such as computer modeling, glass packaging is reinventing itself once again. For food and beverage packagers, the result will be packages that not only stand up to high-speed bottling and high-speed distribution but also catch the consumer's eye at the point of purchase."

In her well-researched feature for ancestrymagazine. com, Roseann Reinemuth Hogan, Ph.D shared insights about glass ornaments as part of the overall focus on "unwrapping the glitz of Christmas." Family collection glass ornaments could possibly have originated in about the 1870s. The first imported glass ornaments and silver glass orbs (kugels) were manufactured in Lausha, Germany. Due to their cost and perceived value, it was considered to be a sign of high status to own the kugels. In the later years of the 1870s, kugels were sent to the United States and put up for sale at the Five and Dime. By the 1920s, after Czech-made ornaments had brought down cost for German designs, domestic production of ornaments helped meet growing demand issues. The 1930s saw glass ornaments for holiday trees become an established trend that has grown into a popular and widely-celebrated tradition.

Recycling. Prior to the 1980s, manufacturers made decisions regarding packaging preferences using two criteria: cost and consumer convenience. Environmental impact and recycling, two buzzwords of the 1990s, were not key considerations. Ironically, manufacturers discovered that one way to lower packaging costs was to reduce the materials required to produce the package, improving the industry's impact on the environment in the process. Reductions that lower manufacturing costs by as little as one-tenth of one cent can result in millions of dollars worth of savings. Over a 10-year period, the material weight of a 16-ounce glass bottle has been reduced by 30 percent. In the 1990s, glass containers were 44 percent lighter than those manufactured 20 years prior. This reduction in materials also meant that less packaging made its way to already-overcrowded landfills.

Every glass bottle and jar manufactured by the 1990s was 100 percent recyclable. According to the Washington, D.C.-based Glass Packaging Institute (GPI), glass recycling reduces the costs of landfill dumping and saves over a ton of natural resources for every ton of glass recycled. Similarly, use of 50 percent recycled glass can reduce mining waste by as much as 75 percent. Glass containers account for 1.6 percent of materials that end up in municipal solid waste systems. Overall, glass materials account for 5.5 percent of all solid waste, compared with 5.1 percent for aluminum, 4.8 percent for steel, 41 percent for plastic, and 43.6 percent for paper. According to the GPI, in 1998 Americans recycled about 13 million glass jars and bottles each day, and the average American was able to save six pounds of glass in one month. However, the Container Recyclying Institute reported in 2005 that U.S. consumers disposed of 131 billion plastic, glass and aluminum beverage containers in 2004 rather than recycling them, up from127 billion in 2003 and 60 percent higher than 1990. Reasons cited were lack of incentive to recycle and lack of opportunity.

For glass manufacturers, recycling extends furnace life and reduces energy costs. Every one percent of cullet used results in a one-half of one percent drop in energy costs. Manufacturers use as much as 70 percent cullet in some glass mixtures.

Consumer Preferences. Glass is popular among consumers for bottled water—known as the hydro segment of rigid packaging—but glass has many other consumer uses. In 1994 a qualitative research study was conducted by Glenn Bauer and Associates for Ogilvy, Adams, Rinehart and the Glass Packaging Institute (GPI). Titled

"Consumer Attitudes Regarding Glass Packaging," this study was designed to help the GPI promote glass packaging by ascertaining consumer preferences toward glass, plastic, and metal packaging materials. The study demonstrated that recycling is a major concern for consumers and does influence their buying decisions. To glass's disadvantage, however, another noteworthy item was that consumers with young children indicated a preference for products that are packaged using unbreakable materials.

Study participants felt that factors such as price, brand name, and ingredients were more important than the material used to package the product. If all of these key factors were equal, only then would packaging material influence a purchase decision. Participants perceived both foods and beverages packaged in glass to be sanitary, fresh, pure, truer tasting, natural, and honest. They pointed out that the contents of glass packages are completely visible, that glass packages are re-sealable, and that glass is puncture and tamper resistant. They voiced a preference for buying pasta sauce and salsas in glass containers because glass enabled them to determine the "richness" and "chunkiness" of these particular foods. Similarly, they preferred to buy mushrooms in glass containers rather than cans that preclude visual examination of the product.

The study indicated an overall preference for purchasing single-serve size beverages in glass, with the possible exception of single-serve size bottled water. The safety and lightness associated with plastic made it the more practical choice for indoor/outdoor recreational use. Indeed, in the 1990s, major U.S. soft drink companies such as the Coca-Cola Company and PepsiCo, and their affiliated bottlers, moved away from glass in favor of plastic bottles. Elsewhere in the world, however, the same soft drink brands are still found in glass bottles. For example, according to a Donaldson, Lufkin & Jenrette Securities report, in Asia glass bottles occupy a 40 percent share of the soft drink market, considerably higher than the world average. In the U.S. consumer study, participants agreed they preferred beer in glass bottles to metal cans. A similar preference is found in Europe. Beer in plastic bottles was not even considered a viable choice. However, it is interesting to note that breweries began using plastic bottles during the early years of the first decade of the 2000s. Overall, plastic packaging evoked feelings of convenience, safety, and durability. The advantages of metal packaging included long shelf life and ease of storage. However, foods and beverages in metal packaging were considered to be low quality, processed, unresealable, and susceptible to contamination when the package was dented.

In March of 2004, *Packaging International* reported on research conducted by Glasspac, the promotional division of the British Glass Manufacturers' Confederation.

Based on a survey of 1,000 consumers, Glasspac found that glass was the overwhelming choice for food and beverage packaging in the United Kingdom. More than 80 percent of respondents indicated that glass eclipsed plastic in terms of its attractiveness. In addition, 74 percent perceived glass as being more natural than other packaging. Finally, almost 70 percent indicated that glass conveyed an image of quality.

The Society of Glass and Ceramic Decoration emphasized that glass packaging greatly enhanced a consumer's perception of a product. Non-commodity brands, including alcoholic beverages, iced teas, and sparkling waters, seeking a quality image can benefit from a glass container's appearance. Glassware manufacturers find that container decoration adds to a quality image and can be a crucial selling point for products packaged in glass. This emphasis on decoration and the flexibility of glass in that regard was echoed by the GPI in a Web page devoted to current trends in consumer habits. According to the GPI, visibility has surpassed labeling as a means to increase the consumer appeal of upscale foods and beverages: "From soup to spirits, marketers are matching glass with minimal labels to showcase premier products."

In a November 1, 2005, article, "Unwrapping the Glitz of Christmas" on www.ancestrymagazine.com, Roseann Reinemuth Hogan noted that putting forth effort to make sure that ornaments are stored correctly could result in having them to cherish with future generations. It was felt to be significant for families "to think about shifting from the old cardboard box that stores the ornaments in the attic to acid free archival boxes in heat-controlled environments so we can preserve these treasures for future generations."

Glass Use in Hazardous Waste Disposal. A US$1.3 billion U.S. Department of Energy plant was opened in South Carolina to test the feasibility of encasing radioactive material in glass. The initial plan was for the South Carolina facility to stabilize nuclear wastes by encasing them in "logs" of strong glass, which in turn are wrapped in steel cylinders that measure 10 feet high and two feet across. Each steel cylinder has the capacity to hold 165 gallons of waste. If experiments such as these prove successful, glass soon may play a significant role in the disposal of a variety of highly hazardous materials.

INDUSTRY LEADERS

Owens-Illinois, Inc. Headquartered in Toledo, Ohio, Owens-Illinois (O-I) is the largest producer of glass containers in the world. In 2009, the company's second quarter net sales reached US$1.8 billion. That reflected the impact of ongoing global recession as reflected by glass shipments being down 12 percent year-over-year. Its

employees serve general line distributors in the food, beverage, beer, drug, chemical, wine, and liquor industries, among others. O-I also manufactures plastic containers such as prescription bottles and plastic closures. The firm's customers include Procter & Gamble, Anheuser-Busch, and H.J. Heinz.

Compagnie de Saint-Gobain. Saint-Gobain, a French company, operates in many countries and is the third largest glass producer worldwide. Saint-Gobain produces billions of glass jars, bottles, and flasks annually and also supplied the glass for the Louvre pyramid. Sales in 2008 reached US$60.673 million with approximately 206,000 employees.

Lancaster Colony Corporation. Lancaster is an eclectic U.S. company that makes a wide variety of products including salad dressings, potpourri, candles, and automotive accessories. Its offerings in the glass sector include floral containers marketed directly to the wholesale florist industry under the brand name Brody; glassware brands Indiana Glass and Colony; and industrial glass and lighting components made under the name Lancaster Glass. In 2009, sales reached US$1.1 billion. Based in Columbus, Ohio, the company employed 3,200 workers in 2006. Specialty foods was the company's largest and fastest growing business division.

The company profile on Lancaster Colony's corporate Web site reflects an interesting history. It was formed from a distinctive combination of small glass and related housewares manufacturers in 1961. In 1963, the company launched a shareholders' reward strategy where they were paid in dividends. The company has maintained that practice. After going public in 1969, Lancaster Colony bought T. Marzetti Company the same year for its entry into the specialty foods business.

Gerresheimer Glas AG. Although Gerresheimer's most important market is the pharmaceuticals industry, its various specialty systems continue to grow. Formerly a subsidiary of Owens-Illinois, the firm held roughly 35 percent of the German glass container market in the early years of the first decade of the 2000s and was bought by the investment firm The Blackstone Group in 2004. In 2002, sales reached US$576.6 million, and the company employed 5,500 workers. New designs have bolstered sales of bottles for premium-brand products and liquors, and Gerresheimer further enhanced this segment of its operation by acquiring a 60 percent interest in the Belgian glass manufacturer Nouvelles Verreries de Momignies S.A., which produces high quality glass packaging for cosmetic products. In early 1997, Gerresheimer sought growth in international markets by acquiring the remaining 49 percent interest in its U.S.-based Kimble

Glass Inc. joint venture with Owens-Illinois. By 2009, Gerresheimer reported worldwide sales of US $1.06 billion with 10,000 employees working around the world in 40 locations.

BIBLIOGRAPHY

"Beer, 'Malternatives' Continue to Help Drive Glass Bottle Demand." *Packaging Strategies,* 31 January 2003.

Bertrand, Kate. "Glass Technologies Break the Mold: Glass Molding and Decorating Techniques Yield a Premium Look for Foods and Beverages." *Food & Drug Packaging,* June 2004.

"Building the biggest float glass plant in the Gulf." 2009. Available from www.glassonweb.com.

Burrows, Stephen J. "European Glass Markets and the Minerals Supplier's Viewpoint: The EU Is the World's Largest Glass Market In Terms of Production and Consumption." *Food & Drug Packaging,* June 2004.

Business Rankings Annual. Farmington Hills, Michigan: Gale Group, 2004.

"Container Demand Grows, but Sizes Shrink." *Beverage Industry,* April 2004.

Gerresheimer. "Gerresheimer Expands in the Global Pharmaceutical Plastic Business." 22 September 2009. Available from www.gerresheimer.com.

"Glass Has Class, Say Consumers." *Packaging Today International,* March 2004.

"Glassware." *Imports/Exports: 2001-2005.* 15 June 2007. Available from www.intracen.org.

Halperin, Alex. "Greener Pastures in Tech." *Business Week Online,* 13 April 2006. Available from http://www.business week.com/investor/content/apr2006/pi20060413_693178. htm.

Hogan, Roseann Reinemuth. "Unwrapping the Glitz of Christmas." 1November 2005. Available from www.ancestrymagazine.com.

"Hoover's Company Capsules." *Hoover's Online,* 2007. Available from www.hoovers.com.

"Institute Wants to Reverse Container Trend." *Waste News,* 17 January 2005.

Lazich, Robert S., ed. *Market Share Reporter.* Farmington Hills, Michigan: Gale Group, 2004.

"Majan Glass Company bestowed with Omani Quality Mark." 29 September 2009. Available from www.menafn.com.

"New Coatings for Container Glass." 15 June 2007. Available from wwww.glasstec-online.com

"New Wine Bottle Plant to be Built in US." *Glass International,* 25 June 2007.

O'Connor, Carla Webb. "Tabled Growth." *HFN The Weekly Newspaper for the Home Furnishing Network,* 11 September 2006.

"O-I Looks to the Future." *Glass International,* January-February 2007.

O-I. "O-I Reports Second Quarter 2009 Results." 29 July 2009. Available from www.o-i.com.

Ramana, K V. "Counterfeit drugs are killing bottle manufacturers." 30 September 2009. Available from www.dnaindia.com.

"Successful Year for International Container Glass Manufacturers." 15 June 2007. Available from wwww. glasstec-online.com.

Ullmann, Norbert. "Domestic Glassware Continues to Fight its Battles." *Glass,* August 2006.

"Understand the Glass Container Manufacturing Industry in the U.S. and its Foreign Trade." *Business Wire,* 17 January 2007.

U.S. Census Bureau. "Glass Containers: 2006." *Current Industrial Reports.* June 2007. Available from www.census.gov.

Webb, Carla. "Ruling Glass: The Glassware Segment Continued to Grow, as Manufacturers Benefited from Improvements in Design and Quality." *HFN The Weekly Newspaper for the Home Furnishing Network,* 12 September 2005.

Woodward, Nancy, and Richard Woodward. "Cape Cod—Massachusetts." Available from www.courant.com.

Zisko, Allison. "Baking in the Dough." *HFN The Weekly Newspaper for the Home Furnishing Network,* 31 July 2006.

———. "Commerce Department: U.S. Glass Imports Steady." *HFN The Weekly Newspaper for the Home Furnishing Network,* 25 September 2006.

SIC 2821

PLASTICS MATERIALS AND RESINS

NAICS CODE(S)

325211. Global plastics makers manufacture various synthetic resins and plastics that other industries process into sheets, rods, film, and other products. Related industries include plastic products, synthetic rubber, and man-made fibers.

INDUSTRY SNAPSHOT

Synthetic plastics were pioneered in Europe and the United States during the late nineteenth century and were produced commercially by the early 1900s. The industry expanded rapidly with the development of improved plastic materials. The United States assumed global industry dominance following World War II and continued to lead the production of plastics in the early 2000s. However, its share of the global market fell after the 1950s as manufacturers in both industrialized and developing nations boosted output. Plastics output is traditionally about equal to domestic consumption. Plastics and resins constituted a significant portion of the patents issued in the overall chemical industry.

World plastic production ballooned from 63.5 million metric tons in 1982 to more than 150 million in 1998. Although growth has been uneven across regions and years, the industry's long-term outlook remains decidedly positive, especially in emerging economies, as plastics are increasingly substituted for other materials in applications ranging from transportation and construction to packaging and consumer products. Japan, Western Europe, and the

United States continued to lead output at the beginning of the 2000s, but low-cost producers of commodity plastics in developing regions amassed a rising share of world production by 2005, especially as economic growth accelerated in China.

One leading issue across national boundaries was environmental pollution, which sparked a wave of legislation and other initiatives to reduce toxic wastes resulting from plastics production as well as to control the amount of plastic consumed and disposed. These concerns motivated—and in some cases required—industry participants to recycle plastic and develop less toxic and biodegradable plastics. Among the primary targets was PVC, used extensively in the construction industry as well as in packaging. Though environmental campaigns resulted in several companies agreeing to eliminate PVCs from their products, U.S. output of PVCs actually increased in 2004 by 8.8 percent, reaching a total of 16 billion pounds.

ORGANIZATION AND STRUCTURE

Plastics are giant polymers—long-chain molecules that contain thousands of repeating molecular units. Although some plastics are made from natural materials such as wax or cellulose, most are synthesized from petrochemicals or other organic substances. Because synthesized materials can be manipulated into an infinite variety of grades and types, they are important alternatives to natural materials in numerous applications.

Products. Plastics manufacturing involves a three-step process: (1) synthesizing the polymer, usually from petrochemicals or coal-related processes (i.e., coal gasification); (2) compounding, which integrated additives; and (3) shaping, an activity not included in this industry classification. The physical properties of plastic can be altered at different stages of the production process, but the most versatile stage is during compounding. For example, additives, such as colorants, flame retardants, heat or light stabilizers, or lubricants may be added to the resin to achieve desired characteristics. The end result of the compounding process is resin, usually in the form of pellets, flakes, granules, powder, or liquid.

Plasticizers, the most common additives used to alter plastic resins, increase a resin's flexibility and are often used to make polyvinyl chloride (PVC) resins that can be utilized in construction products. Impact modifiers are additives that boosted a plastic's resistance to stress. Likewise, antioxidants retard the oxidation and breakdown of plastics, and heat-stabilizing additives help resins maintain their physical structure during processing. Light stabilizers filter out radiation that can cause a plastic to deteriorate as a result of exposure to sunlight and flame-retardants enable resins to resist combustion. Colorants

are another major additive used in the compounding process. Aside from additives, fillers or reinforcement such as glass fibers, particulate materials, and hollow glass spheres can also be added during compounding. Another option is to combine polymers to create a polymer blend or alloy.

Thermoplastics and thermosets are the two main classes of plastics. Thermoplastics account for the bulk of industry output. They solidify by cooling and are repeatedly remelted to form new shapes. The major thermoplastic resins are: polyethylene (PE), used primarily to create packaging; PVC, commonly consumed in the manufacture of pipes, siding, gutters, windows, and other goods utilized in construction; polypropylene (PP), used to create fiber and filaments, molded consumer products, and packaging; and polystyrene, which is formed into disposable packaging, furniture finishings, and miscellaneous consumer products. Other thermoplastics segments include polyamide resins, styrene-butadiene, and some polyesters.

According to *U.S. Thermoplastic Elastomers,* new analysis from Frost & Sullivan revealed that this market generated revenues of US$1.29 billion in 2003, and was likely to reach US$1.72 billion in 2010.

Thermosets are a smaller, more mature, and less dynamic division of the plastics industry. In contrast to thermoplastics, thermosets harden by chemical reaction and cannot be melted and shaped after they are created. Typical thermosets include phenolics, which make adhesives, insulation, laminates, and other related goods; urea-formaldehyde resins, commonly used in the production of plywood and particle board; epoxies, often used as metal coatings in packaging and construction; and polyesters, used to create plastics reinforced with glass fiber and other materials.

Plastics resins span four major commercial divisions: commodity, intermediate, engineered, and advanced. Commodity resins, which represent the bulk of industry production, are low-tech plastics available in standardized formulas from many companies throughout the world. Intermediate resins are generally considered more advanced and somewhat specialized in comparison to commodity resins. Likewise, engineering resins exhibit more advanced performance characteristics and are produced on a smaller scale than commodity and intermediate resins. Finally, advanced resins are those most capable of withstanding impact and high heat, carrying loads, and resisting attacks by chemicals and solvents.

ASTM International's D20.95 subcommittee on recycled plastics is leading the way for potential change in the plastics industry resin identification coding practices. ASTM members cast a ballot related to preferences for 18 items. The items included modifying the definition of PET and adding classifications for polyactic acid polycarbonante and linear low density polyethylene. Several more ballots will no doubt take place before coding changes are made in 15 months or more Mike Verespei reported industry insiders had revealed. Major considerations included adding recycling numbers 8-11 and providing detailed composition of materials used for resins related to code 7.

Competition and Markets. Partly because of technological requirements, the global plastics industry is dominated by major industrial powers. As a whole, North America, Japan, and Western Europe accounted for more than 80 percent of the industry output and around 60 percent of plastics use in the 1990s, though by 2005 growth in developing Asian markets' plastics industries outpaced that in North America and Europe. The output of plastics was roughly equal to domestic consumption in most nations, although industrialized countries tended to be net exporters. The United States, Japan, and Germany together consumed and produced slightly more than 50 percent of this output in the 1990s; the remainder of the market was widely distributed. Aside from technical expertise related to the production process, manufacturers in those countries benefited from immediate access to most of the companies that purchased and processed plastics and resins.

In general, commodity resins have been manufactured by large, integrated companies in industrialized regions, although a rising share of production occurs in emerging economies such as those of Southeast Asia. Intermediate, engineered, and advanced resins are more likely to be manufactured (and consumed) in developed nations, sometimes by smaller manufacturers with expertise in this niche. Industry profitability in each nation is closely linked with both global plastics prices and domestic economic performance; when other industries, such as construction and motor vehicles, are growing and consuming plastic products, prices and profits are usually high. Likewise, when demand slows, profits often plunge. Packaging is the largest market for plastics and resins, followed by building and construction products such as roofing materials and geotextiles. Other major markets include motor vehicles, electronic devices, furniture, housewares, and medical products.

BACKGROUND AND DEVELOPMENT

Crude forms of natural plastic have been used since at least the 1740s. The first known use of plastic was in present-day Malaysia; it was later imitated by European and North American manufacturers in the mid-nineteenth century. Malayan natives were observed in 1843 molding a plastic made from gutta percha, or gum elastic, into knife handles and other articles. "Parkesine," the first synthetic plastic, was invented in 1862 by Alexander Parkes, an Englishman. John Hyatt, a U.S. printer, recognized the important plasticizing effect in the Parkesine production process. He renamed the substance celluloid in 1870, giving birth to synthetic plastics applications. Despite its flammability, celluloid was used to make carriage and automobile windshields and motion picture film.

Dr. Leo Hendrik Baekland, a Belgian-American, invented the world's first moldable plastic material in 1909. Baekland's thermosetting phenolformaldehyde resin provided a tremendous impetus for other inventors, who began to develop molding techniques and add resins to paints and varnishes. Baekland's resin, later called "Bakelite," was also used in the electrical industry to make some of the first molded, synthetic plastic components. This led to a colorless resin, urea-formaldehyde, which was invented in 1918. Plastics research and development began to proliferate in the 1920s and 1930s.

German chemist Hermann Staudinger's polymer research spawned an outburst of scientific investigation that resulted in numerous breakthroughs. The Germans took the lead in the creation of many new thermosetting resins; however, researchers in the United States and several European nations made significant contributions in the area of plastic molding and extrusion machines and later in the advancement of thermoplastics. During World War II the plastics industry expanded explosively as warring nations scurried to develop new and better materials for war machines. Industry shipments continued to rise during the 1950s and 1960s, and the United States surpassed its war-torn European peers. As demand for all types of consumer, commercial, and institutional products soared, plastics producers scrambled to keep pace with expanding markets. The United States dominated, supplying well over 50 percent of global plastics output.

Pivotal breakthroughs in chemical technology and production techniques continued to open vast new markets during the 1970s and 1980s. Most importantly, producers in other industries began to realize the advantages of substituting plastics for more expensive, less versatile natural materials. A variety of factors, such as excess capacity and high petroleum costs, contributed to brief periods of slow production or stagnant profits in most regions. In general, however, industry participants in Europe, Japan, and the United States benefited from numerous influences. For example, new additives and plastic alloys contributed to demand growth by opening entirely new markets for resins.

As many segments of the industry matured and grew competitive, falling prices allowed plastics to penetrate a number of metal, glass, and wood markets. Automobile and truck manufacturers, seeking plastics' advantages of low cost and physical versatility, became a vital market for resins during the 1980s. Likewise, makers of electronic equipment, appliances, and other consumer products significantly increased their use of various resins in the same period. Packaging markets grew as well. Disposable items, such as microwavable food and beverage containers, gained in popularity. As evidence of that trend, the global portion of plastics-based packaging materials soared from 13.2 percent in 1985 to 36 percent in 1993.

Another important industry dynamic during the 1970s and 1980s was the entrance into the plastics industry of a number of developing nations, particularly in Latin America and the Pacific Rim. While developed nations still accounted for more than 80 percent of world output, plastics production in Africa and the Middle East skyrocketed to approximately 2 million metric tons (an increase of more than 400 percent) between 1982 and 1993. During the same period, Latin American plastic shipments jumped more than 100 percent, to about 4.8 million tons. Although traditional plastics-producing nations surrendered a portion of the global market share, they still enjoyed solid gains. Plastic output in North America swelled nearly 70 percent, while output in Western Europe leapt 45 percent. Japan realized similar increases.

In the wake of the late 1990s Asian financial crisis, plastics manufacturers considered new locations for their expansions in 1997 and 1998. Some plastics manufacturers from Japan, Germany, and the United States turned to Mexico and elsewhere in Latin America for their new facilities. Mexico provided an appealing venue for plastics production, in part because of its low labor costs and participation in the North American Free Trade Agreement, which would make trade advantageous between Mexico and the United States and Canada.

Even though Europe, Japan, and North America already consume 60 percent of all polyethylene, their use will continue to grow as their share of the market declines. Analysts attribute the growth in demand to increased global reliance on convenience products including plastics films, containers, and bottles. In South America and Eastern Europe alone, use of plastic bottles made from polyethylene terephthalate (PET) resin—notably soft drink bottles—rose by approximately 20 percent annually in the late 1990s.

In the packaging market, plastics manufacturers began to capitalize on the growing bag-in-the-box trend. Throughout the world, especially in North America and Europe, producers of soft-drink syrup, milk, wine, oil, and other products for institutions responded favorably to the plastic bag stored inside a cardboard box for easily dispensed liquids.

World plastics and resins output continued to rise through the late 1990s and early 2000s. During this period plastic was the most widely used material in the world, making it the material with the most product volume. Although some industrialized nations suffered a profit downturn spurred by overcapacity earlier in the decade, profits started to rise by the middle of the decade. In the mid-1990s, the plastics industry took advantage of limited supply and robust demand and obtained strong prices for plastic products. Asia drove the market with its expanding use of plastics, and by the mid-2000s the region was a greater producer and exporter of plastics, reversing its role as an importer. Escalating demand in the Asian market, especially China, prompted substantial expansion of petrochemical output in the Middle East. According to a *Forbes* report, synthetic resin production in the region from 2010 to 2015 is likely to be 33 percent higher than output in 2004. In addition, an *Asia Intelligence Wire* revealed that BASF forecast global plastics demand to grow 5 percent per year until 2015, due to rising standards of living, especially in Asia.

In 2003 and 2004, the European plastics industry encouraged visitors to click visit its Aquaplastics Web site. For every click, an arrangement was made to donate US10 cents to help WaterAid deliver clean water and sanitation to people in Madagascar and Malawi.

In May 2004, the General Assembly of the Association of Plastics Manufacturers in Europe voted to change its statutes and officially establish a new pan-European plastics association to be named PlasticsEurope. It represents plastics raw materials manufacturers and handles issues that affect plastics in general, as well as product-specific issues through a series of work groups.

CURRENT CONDITIONS

The increased demand for plastics in China was having an effect on the industry in the mid-2000s. China's per capita consumption of plastics was around 48 pounds in 2006, compared to 11 pounds in India and 300 pounds in the United States, according to *Plastics News*. Overall demand for plastics in China grew 10 percent in 2006, and the huge rise in the use of recycled plastic was affecting the production of virgin resin. In 2006, some 5.8 million tons of all kinds of recycled or scrap polymers were imported into China, according to David Jiang of Sinodata in Beijing. China's capacity for plastics production was also increasing. In 2006 this increase totaled 7.5 million tons a year, and the government's five-year plan set a goal of adding 10.5 million tons of capacity annually by 2010. The increase in capacity was reflected in the figures for China's exports of finished plastic goods, which grew from less than 4.4 billion pounds in 1995 to almost 19.8 billion pounds in 2006.

Heading into the late 2000s, another trend was the increased demand for plastic packaging as opposed to paper. According to the Freedonia Group, growth in demand for plastic packaging will outpace that of paper packaging by a 10:1 margin through 2010. Demand for plastic packaging was predicted to increase 2.9 percent a year compared to a 0.3 percent annual increase in paper packaging demand. Freedonia cited the reasons for the growth in the demand for plastic packaging as cost and performance advantages over paper. Segments of the market that were expected to see the most rapid growth included soy and other nondairy beverages, pet food, frozen food, fruit beverages, and detergent.

Recycling continued to be a major issue facing the industry in the mid-2000s. As plastic consumption has expanded, so have efforts in developed nations to reduce related environmental hazards. Environmentalists hoped that the recycling of plastics would become more common in both developed and developing nations. Technology was not a barrier; rather, problems with collection (i.e., separation of plastic wastes by resin type and cleaning the plastics) and the comparatively low cost of making new resins hampered recycling growth. In the mid-1990s biodegradable plastics started to look like a viable alternative to recycling; however, they were not cost effective. Depending on the resin type, biodegradable plastics cost between 2 and 15 times more than conventional plastics.

In the United States, initiatives at the local, state, and federal levels succeeded in increasing recycling of common consumer plastics, such as those used to make milk jugs and soft drink bottles. According to the American Chemistry Council, in 2005 U.S. consumers recycled a record 2.1 billion pounds of plastic bottles, an increase of 187 million pounds from 2004. However, efforts were hindered by many problems, including the high cost of recycled resin. Legislation was bolder in several European nations. For example, Germany and other countries enacted ordinances requiring recycling of transport packaging, and some even required 100 percent. Nonetheless, recycled plastics could not compete with new plastics even by the latter part of the decade, forcing major plastics producers to jettison their recycling operations or otherwise exit the recycling side of the business. Still, other companies inaugurated new recycling businesses even as others withdrew.

WORKFORCE

In the mid-2000s, the United States employed about 638,000 people in the plastics product manufacturing industry, 60 percent of whom were production workers. The average hourly salary for production workers in the industry in the United States was US$11.53 an hour in 2004.

RESEARCH AND TECHNOLOGY

Producers of plastics and resins rely heavily on research and development (R&D) to create potential markets for their products and to increase market share. Aside from creating better resins and plastics, research expenditures have also been applied to the reduction of pollutants emitted during the production process, recyclability, and improvement of manufacturing productivity. The bulk of R&D expenditures at the beginning of the 2000s was shouldered by Japan, North America, and Western Europe, which rely on technology to compete not only with each other, but with low-cost producers in emerging regions. In general, Japan spent the largest share of its gross domestic product on R&D, followed by Germany, the United States, and several Western European countries.

The majority of R&D in the early to mid-2000s centered on the creation of better polymers, resins, and additives. Producers successfully developed plastics that were stronger, lighter, more durable, easier to process, and cheaper to manufacture. Most major producers in developed regions were pursuing breakthroughs in areas such as conductivity and increased tensile strength in hopes of developing plastics to replace metals and other costly materials for appliance and automotive manufacturing. Specialty plastics are also necessary for markets such as the medical industry and the military.

On the environmental front, low styrene emission products received a great deal of attention because they were able to limit volatile organic compound (VOC) emissions during production. New resins were introduced that could be used to manufacture products such as carpet padding and packaging foams that emitted little, if any, chlorofluorocarbons (CFCs). New biodegradable plastics, including weak-link and bacterial polymers, also offered growth opportunities. Although the production cost of most biodegradable plastics was prohibitive when they were first introduced, costs were expected to fall as technology was refined. In 1997, DuPont and Bayer launched biodegradable plastics that could be molded easily and formed into blister packs, waste bags, and other plastic products. But because plant-based plastics have poor heat resistance, they are poorly suited for molding into larger rigid shapes useful in other industries. In 2005, the Fujitsu and Toray companies announced a joint venture that had developed a new plant-based plastic that blends polyactic acid with a non-crystalline plastic to improve heat-resistance and moldability. According to a Toray Industries report, the new substance is the first environmentally friendly plastic suitable for large-size plastic housing for laptop computers. Additional uses were also being explored.

Researchers have also looked for more efficient methods of recycling plastics, since separating different types of plastic can take a considerable amount of time and precision. To address this challenge, improved plastic testers have been developed to simplify the process. Identification devices, called the Tribopen and the Portasort, provide recyclers with a means of sorting plastics efficiently. Tribopen determines the type of plastic by reading its static electricity and is designed for recycling companies that specialize in only a few kinds of plastic, while the Portasort uses infrared spectroscope to identify the kinds of plastic and can be used to determine a more diverse mix of plastics.

The National Association of PET Container Resources (NAPCOR) APR and the PET Resin Association (PETRA) issued the recycling report. For the sixth consecutive year, PET bottle recycling increased in 2008. An amount exceeding 1.45 billion pounds meant PET recycling rate was 27 percent. Mike Verespei claimed that percentage was highest rate since 1997 and reported on related dynamics. Verespei concluded that "strong PET recycling numbers mask several similar troubling trend." The increase for 2008 was lower than the one for 2007which were 55 million pounds and 124 million pounds respectively. An increase for PET recycling rate was contrasted with drop in PET resin production. Export markets, especially China, utilized higher percentages of the PET collected in U.S. than domestic PET recyclers. There was a decrease in the amount U.S. PET recyclers purchased from domestic sources. The corresponding rates for 2007 and 2008 were 641 million pounds and 615 million pounds respectively.

INDUSTRY LEADERS

BASF Aktiengesellschaft. German-based BASF AG is the world's largest chemical company, edging out other top companies such as DuPont and Bayer AG. Although BASF was incorporated in 1952, its history dates back to the early 1860s. The company was formerly part of the mammoth German cartel IG Farben, which dominated the world chemical industry during the 1930s (see also **Industrial Organic Chemicals.**) The company rebounded after the war to become one of the world's major plastics and chemical producers.

BASF reported total sales of US$69.4 billion in 2006, up from US$51.5 billion in 2004 and a 37.2 percent increase from 2005. Above-average growth in its plastics segment was a major factor in the company's strong performance. Other segments included consumer products, dyes, oil and gas, and chemicals. The European market accounts for 60 percent of BASF's revenues. In all, BASF has more than 150 major manufacturing facilities and does business worldwide. In 2006 the firm employed 80,954 people. The company sold its fiber unit in 2003 to focus on core chemical operations. In

2006 the company purchased the chemicals division of Engelhard, which it renamed BASF Catalysts.

In June 2004 *Asia Intelligence Wire* announced Nizhnekamskneftekhim, a Russian petrochemicals plant, talked with BASF about expanding cooperative efforts. Working committees will evaluate relevant projects including setting up production of acrylic dispersions for building materials at the Russian company. In the same news item, it was revealed that BASF is interested in North America because the petrochemicals sector in North America and Western Europe was exhibiting a downward trend. In mid-2004, BASF also announced a new license deal with Bayer to make polyether polyols using Bayer's Impact technology. The technology specifies a process for polyalkoxylation that uses double metal cynanide as catalyst. BASF planned to cut its ABS product line from 15,000 grades to 10 because the material "has increasingly developed from a specialty into a standard product," according to a news report.

Bayer AG. Top-ranked competitor to BASF, Bayer AG is best known for its aspirin, but the company's production includes a wide variety of chemical-based goods. Bayer, like BASF, was spun off from IG Farben after World War II. Bayer competed closely with BASF throughout the 1990s and posted revenues of US$32.4 billion in 2006 with 93,700 employees. The company's diverse portfolio includes basic and fine chemicals, plastic colorants and inorganic pigments, and specialty chemicals for the paper and textile industries. Among the other industries served by Bayer Chemicals are wood, metal, leather, paints, plastics, energy, and electronics. It maintains operations in 50 countries worldwide. In 2005 Bayer spun off its separate chemicals subgroup, completely converting the subgroup into a publicly traded company operating under the new name of Lanxess. In June 2004, *Asia Intelligence Wire* issued several reports about Bayer Chemicals' takeover of production for all the biocidal formulations based on thiabendazole and dibromodicyanobutane that it acquired from Ondeo Nalco at the end of 2002. Bayer invested some US$500,000 in the expansion of production facilities in Wellford, South Carolina, to service the global market. Another important acquisition included the US$20 billion purchase of pharmaceuticals giant Schering in 2006.

The Dow Chemical Company. The largest chemical company in the United States and the second-largest in the world, Dow Chemical is a leading manufacturer of engineering plastics, polyurethanes, and polyethylene resins for packaging, fibers, and films. The company includes six operating segments: Performance Plastics, Performance Chemicals, Agricultural Sciences, Plastics, Chemicals, and its smallest division, Hydrocarbons and Energy. In 2006 Dow had 165 manufacturing facilities in 37 countries and employed almost 43,000 people. Total sales in 2006 reached a record US$49.1 billion. Much of this growth was due to price increases, which grew by an average 24 percent in this segment between 2003 and 2004, while volume grew by an average of only 5 percent. Sales grew 32 percent for polyethylene, 34 percent for polypropylene, and 44 percent for polystyrene. In 2007 the company made more than 3,000 products.

Eastman Chemical Company. Eastman Chemical Company was separated in the 1980s from the Eastman Kodak Company, which traced its roots back to the late 1800s. Eastman Kodak was a pioneer in the global plastics industry and was credited with a number of innovations and improvements. In 2006, Eastman Chemical generated sales of about US$7.4 billion and employed a workforce of 12,000. The company manufactures a broad line of plastics materials for industrial customers specializing in high-performance plastics and related chemical products. The company's Performance Polymers division is the world's largest manufacturer of polyethlene terephthalate (PET). PET is used in packaging for food and pharmaceutical products. In May 2004 the U.S. International Trade Commission ruled that there is a reasonable indication that the U.S. domestic PET industry is being damaged by subsidized imports from Indonesia, India, Thailand, and Taiwan. The investigation was launched after complaints by DAK Americas, Nan Ya Plastics, Wellman, and Voridian. In 2006 Simon Moorhouse of Chemical Market Associates Inc. predicted in *Plastics News* that PET demand would grow faster than capacity through 2011. The journal estimated demand would grow an average of 7.2 percent annually, whereas capacity would increase only 4.5 percent per year.

MAJOR COUNTRIES IN THE INDUSTRY

United States. The United States was the leading producer of plastics materials and resins in the mid-2000s, and production and sales continued to grow. The economic slump after 2001 contributed to relatively flat volumes and sales through 2003, but according to data posted by the American Plastics Council, output of resins increased by 8.1 percent in 2004, reaching 115.1 billion pounds, while sales and captive use grew by 6.9 percent, the highest rate of growth since 1996. The United States accounted for more than 50 percent of global production and consumption following World War II, but its dominance waned as Western European and Japanese competitors gained a foothold during the mid- to late 1990s. The United States continues to trade as a net exporter. Among other advantages, producers in the United States benefit from extensive experience in the field, a strong technology

base, and immediate access to the largest plastics market in the world.

In 2003 the U.S. plastics materials and resins market grew by 2.9 percent to reach almost US$53 billion. About 83.3 percent of value sales were attributed to thermoplastics (polyethylene and polypropylene products). Resin production grew 6.4 percent in 2004. In 2006 the U.S. plastic resins industry rebounded from the effects of major hurricanes on the Gulf Coast in 2005, registering a 3.1 percent increase from 2005. According to the American Chemistry Council, U.S. plastics and resin production reached 113.2 billion pounds in 2006, and total sales grew 2.2 percent to 113 billion pounds.

In 2004 the United States exported US$3.7 billion worth of polyethylenes and nearly US$1.1 billion of amino resins, phenolics, and polyurethanes. Mexico was the primary destination for polyethylenes (US$936.9 million), followed by Canada, Belgium, and China. In 2006 U.S. exports of plastic resins increased 13.3 percent to a record $32.5 billion. Imports also increased in 2006, up 8.2 percent to $18.8 billion, another record.

Japan. At the beginning of the 2000s Japan ranked second in the industry with about 15 percent of global production. Most plastics in Japan, as in other industrialized nations, are produced as side businesses by large, diversified chemical and petroleum concerns. Japan enjoyed steady output gains during the 1980s as domestic demand for plastics surged. Japan's broader recession in the 1990s was intensified for the plastics industry by proliferating competition from low-cost producers in South Korea, Taiwan, and China. Although production fell in the early 1990s, it rebounded in the mid-1990s. Increased domestic consumption and exports fueled the recovery. In the long term, Japanese producers sought to take advantage of increased regional demand for high-margin, high-performance resins and materials; some have also opted to transfer production of low-margin products to lower-wage economies.

Japan remains a major trading partner with the United States in the plastics materials and resins market. In 2004, Japan exported US$254.7 million of PVCs to the United States, making it the second-largest supplier behind Canada. Japan also ranked second in exports to the United States of polypropylenes and other olefins. Japan was the third-leading supplier of amino resins, phenolics, and polyurethanes, as well as polyamides.

Germany. With approximately 10 percent of the global plastics market in the early 2000s, Germany was the industry's third-largest producer, with sales totaling US$58 billion in 2000. An industry pioneer, Germany continued to play a prominent technological role, investing heavily in research and development. Nevertheless, Germany's plastic materials and resins market shrank by

4.7 percent between 2002 and 2003, reaching an output of 13.9 million tons. Other technical plastics remained the largest market for plastics materials and resins, and industry analysts expected this sector to grow by about 1.9 percent through 2008. Other European countries were the primary market by far for Germany's plastic materials and resins sales, with Europe accounting for about 70 percent of exports and 80 percent of imports by volume. Euromonitor expected the German plastic materials and resins market to grow in volume by 6.3 percent by 2008.

The expansion of the construction industry in Germany was partly responsible for the upswing in the European plastics industry in 2006. Along with growth in France and a revitalized Eastern Europe, demand in Germany helped increase the plastics construction sector by approximately 2.8 percent in 2006. The overall plastics industry in Europe grew 3.9 percent that year, according to *Plastics News*.

BIBLIOGRAPHY
American Chemistry Council. "ACC Released December 2006 Resin Production and Sales Stats." 28 February 2007. Available from www.americanchemistry.com.

———. "Plastic Bottle Recycling Reaches Record High of More Than 2 Billion Pounds Annually." 5 February 2007. Available from www.americanchemistry.com.

———. "U.S. Plastic Resins Industry Rebounds in 2006." 5 April 2007. Available from www.americanchemistry.com.

Clayton, Mark. "Popular Plastic in Crosshairs." *Christian Science Monitor*, 17 March 2005.

Esposito, Frank. "Materials Briefs." *Plastics News*, 9 April 2007.

"Fujitsu and Toray Develop World's First Environmentally-Friendly Large-Size Plastic Housing for Notebook PCs." Toray Industries, Inc., 18 January 2005. Available from www.toray.com/.

Higgs, Richard. "Europe's Processors Expect More Growth." *Plastics News*, 15 January 2007.

"Hoover's Company Capsules." *Hoover's Online*, 2007. Available from www.hoovers.com.

International Trade Association (ITA). *Trends Tables: Plastics Materials and Resins (SIC 2821)*. U.S. Census Bureau, 2005. Available from www.tse.export.gov.

Martin, Mitchell. "The World Tilts Toward China." *Forbes*, 5 April 2004. Available from www.forbest.com.

Sun, Nina Ying. "Foreign Firms Plan for Growth." *Plastics News*, 2 April 2007.

"Plastic Materials and Resins in Germany." *Euromonitor Reports*, 2004. Available from www.euronomitor.com.

"Plastic Materials and Resins in the USA." *Euromonitor International*, October 2004. Available from www.euromonitor.com.

Spaulding, Mark. "Plastics Demand Outpaces Paper 10:1." *Converting*, 1 February 2007.

"Thermoplastic Elastomers—Is It Still a Specialty Market?" 2005. Available from www.chemicals.frost.com.

"U.S. Plastic Resins Growth Surges in 2004." American Plastics Council, 10 March 2005. Available from www.apcnews media.com.

Verespei, Mike. "Change planned for resin identification codes include categories for PC, PLA." *Plastic News*, 26 October 2009. Available from plasticnews.com.

———. "Higher U.S. PET Recycling numbers mask some problems." 23 October 2009 Available from plastics news.com.

———. "Target and CVS launch incentives to discourage plastic bags." *Plastic News*, 19 October 2009. Available from plastic news.com.

SIC 3000

RUBBER PRODUCTS, FABRICATED

NAICS CODE(S)

326. Fabricated rubber products include a diverse assortment of goods made from both natural and synthetic rubber. Important product categories include rubber belts and hoses, rubberized fabrics, rubber gaskets and seals, rubber tubing, and mechanical rubber components.

Tires, which account for roughly 50 percent of the world's rubber output, are discussed specifically under **Tires and Inner Tubes.**

INDUSTRY SNAPSHOT

Fabricated rubber products are often used as intermediaries for products in other industries: more than 80 percent of the industry's output is channeled into other products, including motor vehicle parts, sports equipment, and a wide variety of other applications. Expected to increase 4 percent annually to 26.5 million metric tons in 2011, the world tire and rubber market would see primary gains in the automotive sector as well as a rebounding global economy. In 2010, the United States, China, and Japan dominated the global market in terms of rubber consumption and were projected to continue to do so, collectively accounting for more than half the global market in 2011. China led in worldwide rubber consumption following a decade-long surge in terms of automotive production and industrial goods manufacturing. In the late 2000s, the world's top rubber manufacturers were Bridgestone, Michelin, and Goodyear. By that time, U.S. rubber plants were looking at ways to reduce emissions of cancer-causing 1,3-butadiene, among other air pollution toxicants.

By product type, world rubber consumption has changed little since the mid-1980s. The industry is now characterized as quite mature, with intense competition and enormous sales, but relatively low profits. Immediately following the conclusion of World War II, the United States held more than 50 percent of the world's rubber market share. During the mid-twentieth century, Japan, Western Europe, and the Soviet Union joined the United States as leading producers of rubber goods. Since the 1980s, a chief industry trend has been increased production by emerging industrial powers in Latin America and Asia. Some industry analysts contended that long-term growth in rubber products shipments would mirror gains in global economic growth, with demand for non-tire applications increasing most quickly. In fact, non-tire rubber was expected to outpace tire rubber consumption through 2012. This demand was generated through rising industrialization in developing countries and stabilized opportunities in the automotive, industrial, construction, and consumer products markets. Synthetic rubber was expected toregister slightly slower growth than the demand for natural rubber through 2013.

ORGANIZATION AND STRUCTURE

Rubber products are manufactured with both natural and synthetic materials. Natural rubber is a yellowish, elastic substance tapped from various tropical plants, particularly the renowned rubber tree. Synthetic rubber usually starts out as petroleum or coke (a distillate of coal) and is created through a process of polymerization whereby molecules are rearranged to resemble long chains. The resulting substance is a tacky, soft thermoplastic (a substance that can be re-melted and manipulated) that resembles natural rubber. Most synthetic rubber is produced in equatorial regions in Asia, Africa, and South America. Much of that output is shipped to developed nations for the manufacture of tires and other goods. Natural rubber is more commonly manufactured in the United States, Japan, Europe, and the Commonwealth of Independent States (CIS).

Natural rubber offers a narrow range of grades and characteristics in comparison to synthetic rubber, but it proffers superior attributes important to the manufacture of many products. Natural rubber is strong, sticky, resilient, and fatigue-resistant, and it has outstanding tensile strength. Those traits are necessary in products that require low heat build-up, tear resistance, and the ability to withstand repeated flexing. A common example of such an application is that of tire sidewalls. Natural rubber also is desirable as latex for dipped rubber products such as condoms and surgical gloves. A chief disadvantage of natural rubber in comparison to synthetic rubber is poor resistance to oxygen, oil, and other natural elements.

The four primary stages of the manufacturing process for dry rubber goods are preparing the raw rubber, compounding, shaping, and vulcanizing. Compounding entails mixing rubber and chemicals to create different types and grades of rubber, and synthetic rubber and natural rubber are often combined during this stage of the manufacturing process. Rubber characteristics can be modified during this production step with additives and processing agents such as accelerators, antioxidants, flame retardants, and stabilizers. The goal is to produce rubber materials with the traits needed for specific applications. During the shaping and vulcanization processes, the rubber is formed and treated with heat and chemicals to contribute properties such as resilience and elasticity. The end product typically cannot be re-melted and formed.

Chief benefits of rubber products, as opposed to goods produced from other natural and man-made materials, include poor electrical conductivity; the ability to flex and regain an original shape; low production costs; and, particularly in the case of synthetic rubber, resistance to corrosion and breakdown caused by exposure to fluids and gases. Those characteristics have made rubber a desirable substance in demanding applications such as automobile tires and account for rubber's reputation as an ideal substitute for wood, ceramics, metals, and fibers. In addition to tires, the largest rubber production category, other major rubber product segments include vehicle parts such as hoses and belts; wire and cable covering; clothing and footwear; construction materials such as roofing products and geo-textiles; consumer items; and latex goods such as gloves and adhesives.

Competitive Structure. The rubber products industry is a mature one. New products play an important role, but producers compete largely on price. Factors such as high productivity, control of raw material resources, diverse markets, and economies of scale are thus crucial to a company's success or failure in the industry. The industry is highly consolidated and market leaders are entrenched. Many of them are integrated, with vast holdings of rubber plantations in developing nations. They are also heavily dependent on exports and invest extensively in foreign manufacturing operations. Major barriers to entry for new competitors, particularly in the tire segment, include massive start-up costs and technological expertise.

Regulations. The rubber products industry is heavily impacted by both national and international regulations. In addition to tariff and trade restrictions that typify most commodity-like industries, environmental regulations were increasingly impacting producers in the 1990s. Rubber's longevity, combined with problems related to toxicity of manufacturing processes, have forced the industry to comply with pollution-related initiatives designed to blunt the impact of rubber manufacturing on the environment. Manufacturers have increasingly been forced to help find—and pay for—solutions. On the production side, proliferating national legislation in the mid-1990s in some countries sought to reduce toxic emissions of nitrosamines and other substances. Nitrosamines, a suspected human carcinogen, are released during the compounding, forming, and vulcanization process. Regulations designed to control emissions of such manufacturing by-products have in some cases resulted in higher manufacturing costs and reduced competitiveness of producers in developed regions. In 2007, the U.S. Department of Transportation enacted the Energy Independence and Security Act. This included a requirement that the National Highway Traffic and Safety Administration develop a national tire fuel efficiency consumer information program to educate consumers about the effect of tires on fuel efficiency, safety, and durability. Up to that point, there were 240 million passenger cars and light trucks in the U.S., and they consumed about 135 billion gallons of fuel annually. This bill is designed to reduce this energy consumption which in turn will reduce the greenhouse gas emissions and improve air quality. This study will also inform consumers about rolling resistance of replacement tires which may influence safety performance of vehicles on the highways.

BACKGROUND AND DEVELOPMENT

The rubber products industry dates back to at least the fifteenth century, when European explorers witnessed natives in the New World using latex to make bouncing balls, bottles, waterproof apparel, syringes, and other items. What was later called rubber first came to Europe in 1521, when Aztecs transported from Mexico played a game using a rubber ball in front of the Spanish royal court. In the early 1700s, rubber products made by Native Americans aroused the interest of the European scientific and professional community. In the 1750s, for example, Parisian architects discovered that rubbing the substance on pencil marks would erase them—hence the name "rubber." By the late eighteenth century and early nineteenth century, rubber was utilized in a number of applications.

One of the first manufacturers of rubber goods on record, a rubber band maker, was founded in 1803 near Paris. In 1811, J.N. Reithoffer opened another rubber goods factory in Vienna. During the mid-1830s, a recognizable rubber products industry emerged in Europe, North America, and a few other regions. The fledgling industry developed an international flavor as well. Rubber grown in the Amazon, for example, was made into rubber shoes in Brazil and exported for sale in the northeastern United States.

Boosting industry growth during the period was several major technological advances. American Edward M. Chaffe invented a rubber milling and rolling machine in 1836. Nicknamed "The Monster," the machine

weighed 30 tons. More importantly, American Charles Goodyear discovered the vulcanization process in 1839. That breakthrough eliminated many of rubber's drawbacks—most notably, susceptibility to temperature changes—and made the substance a desirable ingredient in the production of a broad new range of goods.

During the mid-nineteenth century, vulcanized rubber was used in industrializing nations to make toys, dipped products, clothing, and other goods. A pivotal event in the industry's development, though, was Germany's introduction in the 1880s of the automobile, which used rubber tires. During the early 1900s, mass automobile production was pioneered in the United States, spawning what would soon become a massive rubber tire industry. By the late 1930s, automobile tires were consuming the lion's share of global rubber output, and the United States had assumed the global rubber products industry lead. Global production of rubber goods exploded during and after World War II, as reflected by a rise in rubber consumption from 1.25 million metric tons in 1940 to 2.59 million by 1950. By 1960, rubber goods manufacturers were devouring about nine million metric tons of rubber annually.

Concurrent with and contributing to huge gains in rubber output during the mid-twentieth century was the introduction and popularization of synthetic rubber. Although scientists had made advances related to synthetic rubber, it was not until 1910 that Russian chemist S.V. Lebedev polymerized butadiene to produce the first commercially viable synthetic rubber. Germany and Russia were producing synthetic rubber commercially by the 1930s. Other nations joined them during World War II, as global output of synthetic rubber products lurched from about 10,000 tons in 1935 to more than one million tons by 1944. Synthetic rubber output even surpassed natural rubber production for a few years in the early 1940s due to the war. Nevertheless, superior natural rubber products continued to dominate the market through the 1950s and 1960s.

Major scientific advancements quickly boosted synthetic rubber's share of the market, however. German chemists Karl Ziegler and Giulio Natta discovered a polymerization process that created synthetic rubber virtually identical in molecular structure to natural rubber. In addition, new additives, processing, and molding techniques were pioneered. Synthetic rubber output ballooned during the 1960s from about 2 million metric tons in 1960 to roughly six million by the early 1960s. By the 1970s, rubber goods producers were consuming around 9 million metric tons of synthetic rubber annually, as well as about 4 million tons of natural rubber.

Industry growth was driven primarily by the global explosion of the car and truck industries. Between 1950 and 1980, annual worldwide tire production vaulted from 133 million to about 657 million. The evolution of synthetics allowed manufacturers in industrialized nations to displace equatorial countries as the leading suppliers of rubber.

Growth of the rubber goods industry slowed considerably in the mid-1970s for several reasons. Importantly, the huge postwar economic boom, highlighted by the growth of the automobile industry in North America and Europe, had come to an end. Other factors that squelched gains in rubber goods output included rising energy prices, which heightened the cost of synthetic rubber; a global trend toward smaller cars and, therefore, smaller tires; and the development of long-lasting radial tires that diminished the tire-replacement market. The mature industry registered only modest production gains during the 1980s. Total global rubber output increased from 12 to 13 million metric tons in 1980 to about 15 million metric tons by 1990. Much of the growth that did take place was the result of increased demand by rubber products manufacturers for natural rubber rather than synthetic rubber.

In addition to increased use of natural rubber in relation to synthetic rubber, another rubber products industry trend during the 1980s and 1990s was greater production of non-tire rubber goods. While consumption by rubber goods producers of both natural rubber and synthetic rubber for the manufacture of tires in the United States, Japan, and Germany rose 14 percent—to nearly 3 million metric tons—during that period, growth in the non-tire market was significantly higher. During the same period, rubber consumption for non-tire goods in those countries jumped more than 30 percent, to about 2.4 million tons. While tires still accounted for about 50 percent of industry output in the mid-1990s, that share was expected to fall. Major product segments driving non-tire industry expansion included automotive belts, hoses, gaskets, and moldings; adhesives, padding, belting, wire sheathing, and other industrial items; toys, door moldings, sporting equipment and other consumer goods; and construction products like roofing, sealants, and exterior moldings.

While output of rubber products in developed nations slowed or stagnated, production in developing regions surged during the 1990s and continued in the 2000s. Bolstered by low production costs, loose regulatory environments, and access to growing markets, among other advantages, manufacturers in emerging industrial regions advanced greatly in comparison to their Western and Japanese peers. Areas realizing the greatest market share gains included South America and Asia, particularly the countries of Brazil, Mexico, China, and South Korea. Many industry analysts expect an even greater reshuffling among world producers as China takes on a more preeminent role in the world trade community. As developing nations vied for world rubber product market share, producers in developed nations scrambled to increase competitiveness and open new markets for rubber goods.

A potentially serious threat to the rubber products industry, and what has been characterized as an open secret within the industry, is the biological threat posed by a pest in the major Southeast Asia producers. The South China Sea-area plantations, which are the source for about 90 percent of the world's natural rubber, are the product of a genetic clone derived from plants in the Amazon more than 100 years ago. Unfortunately, a fungal pestilence that rendered cultivation of rubber in that region nearly impossible has found its way to Southeast Asia. While some industry insiders remain confident in the ability of synthetic rubber technology to make up for a decrease in natural rubber production, this potentially dramatic threat could have drastic consequences on a variety of industries. Many products, analysts note, have no potential substitute for natural rubber.

Advances in technology are looked upon as a vital area of development for rubber product manufacturers. Much of this technology, however, inherently limits the growth of sales volume. For instance, one of the primary concerns of manufacturers is greater durability of products, especially in the tire market. Because technological innovations are one of the prime selling points in this mature industry, the search for durability must be a major focus for producers who want to attract customers. For example, because tires generally do not perform properly after they are six years old, the feasibility of tire expiration dates was being considered. By early 2004, in fact, the National Highway Traffic Safety Administration was conducting multi-year studies on the correlation between tire durability and tire age, in order to determine if lab trials could accurately mimic tire aging and performance. In March 2010, the Unites States Department of Transportation signed into effect the Tire Fuel Efficiency Consumer Information Program. This regulation is designed to be provided to the consumers at the point of purchase and is to encourage them to purchase better performing replacement tires. This was issued in connection to the Energy Independence and Security Act of 2007.

Another concern is the use of recycled rubber in new products. According to the Rubber Manufacturers Association, by the mid-2000s, about three-fourths of scrap tires were used annually for end use markets, of which the highest growing segment was civil engineering applications. The forecast was for annual growth in this area to increase exponentially, from 20 to 50 percent. Sales of industrial rubber products were forecast to grow 5 percent annually to more than US$16 billion by 2008, according to a report published by the Freedonia Group. Some current uses for recycled rubber are alternative fuel sources for industries, cushioning material in children's playgrounds, mulch for play areas, raincoats, boots, athletic shoes, and even clothing and accessories.

CURRENT CONDITIONS

According to a study by the Freedonia Group, rubber used for non-tire products will outpace the demand for automobile tires by 2011. This expanding field will include ethylene-propylene, nitrile, and polychloroprene, which are used to make hoses, belts, gaskets, and weather-stripping. High performance tires will keep the demand for tire rubber growing as the popularity of performance tires grows. Such types use more rubber than radial tires, and also have a shorter lifespan, thus creating a demand for quicker replacement.

The Asia/Pacific region led the pack in rubber consumption, accounting for 57 percent of all global rubber demand in 2008. This trend is expected to continue through 2013. China, the largest national rubber market, was expected to continue growing in terms or rubber consumption and was expected to account for almost one-third of the global market by 2013. The Japanese market will continue to see a decline along with North America and Western Europe. Primarily the downturn is based on a slumping economy and an automotive industry on the decline due to the global economy. However, total worldwide use of natural and synthetic rubber is expected to continue a 4 to 4.3 percent increase annually, to 27.9 million metric tons in 2013.

RESEARCH AND TECHNOLOGY

The rubber products industry is heavily impacted by technological changes that contribute to the production of materials that are less expensive and feature desirable properties (such as mold ability, strength, and flexibility). The greatest focus is given to the modification of existing polymers rather than on the development of new ones. The battle to utilize new technology to gain a competitive edge was particularly in evidence in the tire industry in the 1990s. Midway through the decade, manufacturers in that segment hoped to create tire products that would reduce rolling resistance, improve vehicle handling in harsh weather, and improve tire function after air loss. Significant advances had already been made in these and other performance areas since the late 1980s. By the mid-1990s, tire warranties had increased from 20,000 to 30,000 miles, on average, to as high as 80,000 miles. Other advances included models that reduced hydroplaning and non-pneumatic spare tires that were puncture-proof and weighed 20 percent less than conventional pneumatic mini-spares.

Consumers are becoming increasingly aware of the sheer volume of tires and other rubber products that must be disposed of every year. Not surprisingly, rubber manufacturers are feeling pressure from the public and environmental groups to address the need to dispose of used rubber responsibly. Researchers are tackling issues of recycling and long-term deterioration in hopes of curbing the growing problem. As researchers learn more about different kinds of rubber and their production, they also are better able to protect employees from potentially carcinogenic emissions.

The product development process also accelerated during the early and mid-1990s through increased use of computer-aided design (CAD) systems. CAD allowed both tire and non-tire rubber products to be modeled and tested quickly by computer. Other notable areas of research in the 1990s related to reducing environmental hazards resulting from the production and disposal of rubber goods. In the early 1990s alone, new strategies for making use of old tires had resulted in a huge climb in the percentage of scrap tires reclaimed for other uses. In the United States, the largest tire-consuming nation in the world, that percentage jumped from less than 10 percent in 1990 to nearly 60 percent in 1996. New uses included paving materials, alternative fuel, outdoor furniture, children's playground padding, adhesives, molding, toys, cushions and artificial reefs.

Many rubber products manufacturers are looking to the chemistry field as a source of development, concentrating on the mixing process of their rubber supplies. Realizing that inefficiencies and missteps in this stage of the process can greatly exacerbate problems and add to costs later in the production process, manufacturers are working to perfect mix-design systems. One solution involves the increased reliability of temperature control within the mixer. Another innovation is a process called surface modification, in which scrap rubber reacts with gases, producing an irreversible chemical change, the result of which then bonds with other materials. This process is used primarily in the production of sealants.

In 2003, research in New Zealand found that scrap tires were a potential source of carbon for water treatment. When tires go through pyrolysis, activated carbon is produced, an element used to purify drinking water. If the use of this form of carbon was proven successful, such use of scrap tires would reduce the need to use up natural resources such as wood and coal in order to manufacture the carbon.

WORKFORCE

The rubber products industry workforce is primarily employed by large, multinational companies in developed nations. Partly because of the strong labor union presence, workers in the industry are well paid in comparison to most other industries. Workers in some European nations, particularly Germany, received higher salaries than their U.S. counterparts. The 1,200 U.S. firms that manufacture fabricated rubber products, not including tires, employed about 90,000 people.

Most growth in the rubber products workforce in the 2000s was occurring in such emerging industrial powers as South Korea, China, and Brazil. While wages in those nations have improved somewhat in recent years, they remain quite low compared with those of traditional powers. Compensation in less developed rubber-producing regions—such as Malaysia, Indonesia, and Thailand—remained low as well. Wages for workers in those nations, which typically export most of their rubber and manufacture few products, ranged from about US$35 to US$150 per month. This state of affairs provided emerging nations with an important competitive advantage over companies in the United States, Japan, and Western Europe.

INDUSTRY LEADERS

Bridgestone Corp. Headquartered in Japan, Bridgestone was ousted in 2008 as the world's largest tire manufacturer by Michelin. Tires account for fully 80 percent of the company's annual revenues, which totaled US$29.7 billion in 2007. The company was founded in 1931 as a general rubber products firm and became the leading Japanese tire producer during the mid-twentieth century. In addition to tires, it produced construction materials, bicycle tires, conveyor belts, hydraulic hoses, marine fenders, rubber tracks, and even golf balls, to name just a few of its diversified products. The company bolted to global leadership with the 1988 acquisition of Firestone, the U.S. tire leader. Bridgestone started out making rubber-soled footwear for Firestone's family clothing business. Tires were added in 1923 and, with Ford Motor Company as a major customer, Firestone became one of the big three tire makers in Akron, Ohio, which was dubbed the "Rubber Capital" of the world. In 2006, Bridgestone acquired Bandag, Inc., a leading truck tire retreader with over 900 franchised dealers worldwide. The Bridgestone company opened factories in Indonesia, Singapore, and Thailand during the 1950s before expanding throughout the world in the 1960s, 1970s, and 1980s. By 2007, the firm employed 133,750 people.

Bridgestone came under fire in 2001 when a widespread tire recall was initiated after the discovery that Ford Explorers were outfitted with faulty tires. Litigation mounted, and the fiasco ended Bridgestone's 95 year relationship with Ford. By 2003, the company was back in control, and 2003 revenues rose more than 13 percent over 2002 levels. However, Bridgestone voluntarily recalled nearly 300,000 Steeltex tires in 2004 as a result of a class action lawsuit alleging design defects.

Compagnie Generale des Establissements Michelin. As of the last quarter of 2008, Michelin moved into the position of the world's largest tire manufacturer with plants in France, Germany, the United States, the United Kingdom, Canada, Brazil, Thailand, and Italy. Michelin made approximately 36,000 products, including tires for cars, aircraft, and motorcycles. Besides the Michelin brand, the company also owned BF Goodrich, Uniroyal, Kleber in Europe, and Warrior in China. The company revenues in 2009 totaled US$20.78 billion with 109,190 employees.

Goodyear Tire & Rubber Co. Goodyear Tire & Rubber Co. was the third largest tire manufacturer in the world. It is named after the inventor of the vulcanization process, and was founded in 1898 by Frank A. Sieberling. The company produced a wide range of rubber products, including belts, hoses, and other rubber products, for the transportation industry and for various industrial and consumer markets in addition to its core tire business. The company also sold Dunlop tires. Goodyear led the industry in international expansion before World War II and is credited with major innovations related to all-weather tires. It became the global tire industry leader during the mid-1990s, largely as a result of its strength in the expanding North American economy. Goodyear assumed significant debt in 1986 as part of an effort to avert takeover attempts by foreign suitors. Indeed, the merger and acquisition binge of the late 1980s made Goodyear and the Cooper Tire & Rubber Co. the only major domestically owned tire manufacturers in the United States by the early 1990s. Goodyear was aligned with Sumitomo Rubber Industries of Japan. The company generated sales of US$19.6 billion in 2007 and employed about 71,000 workers in plants worldwide. In 2008, The Goodyear Tire & Rubber Company received the honor of being recognized as one of America's most respected companies by the Reputation Institute and *Forbes* magazine.

Continental AG. Germany's Continental AG captured U.S. tire giant General Tire in 1987, dramatically expanding its scope to the world's fourth largest tire manufacturer. Continental's 2009 revenues totaled US$18.2 billion, of which the vast majority was derived from Europe. In addition to the Continental brand, the company sold Uniroyal and General tires. As of 2009, it had 134,430 employees.

MAJOR COUNTRIES IN THE INDUSTRY

The United States. The United States maintained its long-time position as the largest supplier of rubber products in the world throughout the 2000s. The U.S. rubber goods industry was started in 1833 when the Roxbury India Rubber Company opened a rubber shoe factory in Connecticut. The nation assumed an early global lead when, in the early 1900s, it became the first nation to mass-produce automobiles. Although European nations challenged U.S. dominance during World War II, the United States emerged as the dominant global supplier of rubber products. The United States supplied more than 50 percent of global rubber products demand in the late 1940s. Although the country continued to lead production, its share of the global market steadily declined to less than 25 percent by the 1990s. In 1990, manufacturing operations located in the United States accounted for 28 percent and 16 percent of international car tire and truck tire output, respectively.

In 2009, the United States shipped more than 259 million tires with an expected increase of 3 percent in 2010, and an even larger increase predicted for 2011. U.S. producers were churning out about US$21.3 billion worth of other rubber goods. There are more than 1,225 firms, more than a third of which are in the Midwest, manufacturing fabricated rubber products, and another 139 making tires and inner tubes. Major trade areas included the NAFTA region (Mexico and Canada) and Western Europe. The fastest-growing trade region for U.S. rubber products manufacturers was Latin America. Although its leadership in the industry was acknowledged, U.S. global market share was difficult to precisely determine for several reasons. The United States commonly exports rubber goods that are subsequently imported back into the country on cars. Moreover, U.S. manufacturers were active in joint ventures and had investments in rubber companies throughout the world. Importantly, the 1980s and early 1990s were marked by heavy foreign investment that placed control of major North American producers in the hands of European and Japanese competitors.

Russia. Russia is another major producer of rubber products, and was an early leader in the production of synthetic rubber and related products, accounting for the bulk of world output during the early 1900s. Although it was eventually surpassed by the United States, the former Soviet Union continued to boost production. During the 1980s, in fact, the Soviets increased synthetic rubber output from about 2 million metric tons to about 2.4 million metric tons, surpassing production in the United States. The rubber was used primarily to supply growing rubber products industries, many of which were military-related, throughout Russia and the Eastern Bloc. Total Soviet output of tires, for example, surged from 32.7 million in 1980 to about 51.4 million by 1990. Soviet output of synthetic rubber and related products plunged

following the disintegration of the Soviet Union and the entire Eastern Bloc in 1991, however. In 2000, total tire production in Russia was more than 28 million units. Sales to individuals increased compared to 1999 figures, but commercial sales decreased, for a net increase in total sales of only 0.5 percent from 1999. In 2009, the sales for tire production in Russia took a sizable decline from the same period in 2008, in some instances a 50 percent decline.

Japan. Japan achieved its position as a world leader in the rubber products industry by developing the biggest automobile industry in the world. Over half the rubber, by weight, in Japan was consumed by tire producers in the 1990s. As car production surged, Japanese tire output jumped from about 111 million units annually in 1980 to 150 million by 1990. Output of other vehicle-related products—gaskets, belts, and hoses—rose similarly. Japan displaced France in the early 1980s as the leading exporter of rubber goods. Growth of Japan's rubber goods sector slowed in the early 1990s, partly because of a domestic economic slowdown. Japanese producers also were plagued by increased competition from low-cost competitors in neighboring nations such as China and South Korea. To combat the threat, Japanese companies in the mid-1990s increasingly turned to investments and the establishment of links with companies in South Korea and Taiwan, among other areas. In 2002, Japan produced some 168 million tires and 41 million in the first quarter of 2003, with the value of exports increasing from US$2.9 billion in 2001 to US$5 billion in 2005. Four of the top 10 tire manufacturers in the world were based in Japan. They were Bridgestone (first), Sumitomo Rubber Industries (fifth), Yokohama Rubber Co. Ltd. (seventh), and Toyo Tire & Rubber Co. Ltd. (ninth). In addition, Bridgestone was the top producer of non-tire rubber products throughout the 2000s.

Europe. The other major players in the rubber industry are Germany and France, which both helped to pioneer the synthetic rubber and related goods industries during the early twentieth century. Synthetic rubber output in both countries was roughly equal throughout the middle of the century. West Germany, however, buoyed by its giant automobile industry, gained on France during the 1980s and 1990s. Both countries registered significant increases in rubber goods exports. German and French rubber products industries invested heavily in U.S. companies during the late 1980s. Although German and French rubber product manufacturers chafe under environmental and labor restrictions, both countries will likely retain leadership roles in the industry in the long term. Germany's growth, however, outpaced France's at the turn of the millennium. Germany's total output in

2002 was more than 69.3 million tires compared to France's 60.9 million. In 2005, Germany and France werethe third and fourth largest exporters of tires in 2005, with US$3.7 billion and US$3.1 billion in sales, respectively.

Emerging Nations. Among the fastest-growing national competitors at the dawn of the new millennium were China, Brazil, South Korea, Indonesia, and Malaysia. Although these nations played relatively small roles in the rubber products industry during the mid-twentieth century, they benefited during the 1980s and early 1990s from strong domestic demand and hefty export gains. Low production costs and protected domestic markets were key advantages. Combined tire shipments in those three countries ballooned more than 90 percent between 1980 and 1990, to about 90 million units. Simultaneously, production of synthetic rubber rose to more than one million metric tons by the late 1990s. Indonesia's non-tire rubber industry grew significantly in the mid to late 1990s, specializing in rubber fabricated for sports shoes, latex gloves, hoses, belts, seals, and sports equipment. South Korea has become a major contender in the tire market since the late 1990s. Its production of 70 million units represented an increase of almost seven percent over 1999. This volume, combined with the high growth rate, suggests that South Korea may not be considered merely an emerging market for long. China, which had tire output of 160 million in 2002, earned approximately US$4 billion in the tire market in 2003, which amounted to about 5 percent of the world's total. In 2007, China surpassed the United States to become the world's leading rubber consumer. Imports of synthetic rubber in the first four months of 2007 reached 484,000 tons, 14.7 percent more than the same period the previous year, and were valued at US$930 million.

BIBLIOGRAPHY
"China Imports More Synthetic Rubber at Higher Prices." Xinhua Economic News Service, 18 June 2007. Available from http://www6.lexisnexis.com.

"Hoover's Company Capsules." *Hoover's Online,* 2007. Available from http://www.hoovers.com.

"Indian Rubber Futures Set Global Benchmark." *Rubber World,* Spring 2007.

Meyer, Bruce. "Globalization: U.S. Industry's Top Hurdle." *Rubber & Plastics News,* 5 February 2007.

"Niche Business Is One Route to Success in Rubber." *European Rubber Journal,* 1 May 2007.

"Slight Increase Seen for Tire Shipments." *Rubber World,* April 2007.

"World Rubber Consumption Continues to Increase." *Rubber World,* May 2007.

SIC 3011

TIRES AND INNER TUBES

NAICS CODE(S)

326211. Known in Great Britain as "tyres," this industry's output includes tires and inner tubes for all types of vehicles, aircraft, bicycles, motorcycles, and farm equipment.

INDUSTRY SNAPSHOT

The U.S. tire manufacturing industry consisted of about 100 companies with combined annual revenue of close to US$15 billion annually as of 2010. In the late 2000s, the combined global tire and rubber industry was valued at US$70 billion. A mature industry, growth rates in most regions continued to be relatively small, with little possibility of a projected dramatic increase. Most large tire makers experienced a surge in sales in the mid-2000s due to the robust economies of North America, Europe, and Asia, and as the global economy improved from the beginning of the decade. However, the global economic downturn that began in 2007 impacted the tire manufacturing industries as well.

In the late 2000s, the industry was dominated by a cosmopolitan array of seven multinational corporations—one headquartered in France, one in the United States, three in Japan, one in Germany, and one in Italy. Although the industry's top four companies shared more than 75 percent of worldwide sales in 2009, manufacturing of tires—a long-established commodity—is characterized by intense competition, most of which takes place in the realm of product development and innovation, though not always to the benefit of sales figures. A spate of mergers in the late 1980s and early 1990s presaged an intense examination of capacity, employment levels, and productivity. The top players in the global tire industry, as in the automobile industry to which it is closely allied, purchased or moved production facilities in order to reduce labor costs, take advantage of currency fluctuations, and circumvent trade limitations. Dominant concerns of these leaders included reduction of acquisition-related debt and overhead, retention and augmentation of market share, and recycling of waste tires.

Many industry observers have pointed to the strategic alliance between Goodyear and Sumitomo Rubber, which allowed Goodyear to make Dunlop tires in North America and Europe and Sumitomo to make Goodyear tires in Japan, as the precursor to another industry reshuffling mirroring, albeit on a smaller scale, the consolidation of the late 1980s. The second-tier firms—those falling just below the "Big Three" of Bridgestone, Michelin, and Goodyear in sales—are likely to get squeezed between their larger multinational competitors and the smaller regional and niche market firms. Some analysts believe that alliances with the Big Three will be necessary for survival in the twenty-first century.

ORGANIZATION AND STRUCTURE

Tire sales are divided between the original equipment and replacement markets. Original equipment sales are made directly to auto manufacturers and comprise less than one third of the total market. Unit sales of replacement tires total over two-thirds of worldwide sales. During periods of economic growth, when new automobile sales typically surge, original equipment tire sales sometimes keep pace with sales of replacement tires. For example, global original equipment tire sales grew 4 percent in 2000, roughly the same rate as replacement tire sales growth that year, due to the highly favorable economic conditions that fueled record levels of automobile production.

The original equipment manufacturer (OEM) market offers both benefits and drawbacks. OEM sales can increase a tire maker's market share at a minimum advertising and distribution cost. Moreover, since car owners tend to replace original tires with the same brand, it follows that more OEM sales mean more replacement sales. Competition in this business segment is intense and automakers often use their buying power and marketplace clout to negotiate ever-lower margins on OEM sales.

The replacement market has proven more stable and profitable. Whether consumers purchase new cars or not, they need to replace worn tires. Tire makers also garner significantly higher profit margins on retail replacement sales. Ironically, the industry's development of longer-lasting radial tires has stunted this segment's growth. Some analysts predict that the private-label segment of this market is the key to future sales, but they caution that this shift may "cannibalize" premium brands or dilute their image.

BACKGROUND AND DEVELOPMENT

The history of the tire industry is intimately connected to the development of rubber, since virtually all tires were made from natural rubber until World War II. Early European explorers noted that indigenous peoples used the gum from certain trees for a variety of purposes, from constructing toy balls to waterproofing garments. Known initially as "caoutchouc," rubber earned its common name for its capacity to rub out pencil marks. In early nineteenth century Britain, Charles Macintosh and Thomas Hancock developed elementary processing techniques for the manufacture of rubberized rainwear that came to be known as "mackintoshes."

Rubber remained an unreliable substance, however. It was sticky and smelly, and subject to vast changes in consistency when temperatures changed. In 1839, U.S. inventor Charles Goodyear combined rubber, lead, and sulfur in the presence of extreme heat to create what he called "vulcanized" rubber. Although he himself did not benefit from the discovery, Goodyear's process formed the foundation of the global tire industry.

Most early tires were made of solid rubber. British engineer Robert William Thomson has been credited with the concept of a pneumatic, or air-filled, carriage tire, but his 1845 patent was not applied commercially for nearly half a century. Scottish veterinarian John Boyd Dunlop developed and patented pneumatic bicycle tires in 1888. His invention featured an inner canvas tube with a valve for inflation and an outer shell of vulcanized rubber, all mounted on a solid wooden rim. Detachable pneumatics were developed almost concurrently in Britain and France in the 1890s. In 1895, the Michelin brothers, André and Edouard, patented the world's first pneumatic auto tire. Virtually all the world's major tire producers were launched by the turn of the century. Although most early tires were designed for bicycles, the tire industry was soon intertwined with the automobile industry, which added a new and seemingly insatiable outlet in the early twentieth century.

Whereas rubber tree cultivation is limited strictly to equatorial regions with annual rainfall of 100 inches (2,500 millimeters) or more, global centers of natural rubber production are located in Southeast Asia (especially in nations on the South China Sea such as Malaysia) and West Africa (such as Liberia and Nigeria). Until the 1940s, all the world's rubber originated from these regions. Chemists and engineers struggled for decades to create a viable synthetic rubber and thereby reduce reliance on natural resources. The first synthetic rubber was developed in Germany during World War I. When Asian sources of rubber (which had supplied over 95 percent of U.S. tire manufacturers' needs) were cut off during World War II, U.S. tire manufacturers hurriedly collaborated with government chemists to develop man-made alternatives. Although these butadiene/styrene combinations were expensive and largely abandoned at the war's end, experimentation continued. Low-temperature polymerization, or "redox" (for reduction and oxidation), produced a more uniform product and was perfected in Germany after the war.

After a sharp decline in the immediate postwar era, use of synthetic rubber equaled, then surpassed, natural rubber to become the preferred tire material. By the early 1990s, the two materials were used about equally in tire production. Although the development of synthetic rubber has reduced the industry's dependence on natural sources, it has tied manufacturers' fortunes to the petroleum industry.

Other innovations in tire production and design took place during the twentieth century as well. France's Michelin pioneered tubeless tires in 1930, treads in 1934, and low-profile tires in 1937. The company revolutionized the European (and later the world) tire industry with the 1946 patent of radial tire design. Before radials, tires were constructed with ply casings of fabric or steel cords arranged "on the bias" at 25 to 40-degree angles to the direction of travel, hence the name "bias ply." Michelin's design, launched in 1949 as the "X-tire," featured cords arranged perpendicular to the direction of travel. Considerably more durable than their predecessors, radials also handled better and helped lower fuel consumption. In spite of U.S. and British tire makers' reluctance to foot the expensive bill for conversion from bias to radial construction, over 95 percent of all tires featured this superior structure by the late 1970s.

The tire industry of the 1980s and 1990s was characterized by consolidation and competition. In 1985, fourteen companies shared three-fourths of the global market. After a series of mergers in the late 1980s, only six companies split that same 75 percent market share, and Goodyear, Michelin, and Bridgestone controlled over half the industry. A confluence of forces spurred this globalization of the world tire market. In the late 1980s, as the world's leading tire makers registered record earnings, they sought ways to put the influx of cash to work. Acquiring companies sought increased penetration of original equipment markets, greater private brand business, more comprehensive product lines, and the benefits of global economies of scale. The marked devaluation of the U.S. dollar during this period, along with the weakness of some leading U.S. manufacturers, facilitated the revolution.

With European economic and monetary union imminent in the late 1990s, major players, like Germany's Continental, shifted their capacity and workforce to less costly nations in Eastern Europe, in part because of the price advantages, but also out of recognition of the growth potential in that emerging region. While Japan, Western Europe, and North America remained the dominant regions in the global tire industry, producing a combined 75 percent of the world's car and truck tires, the largest growth regions in the late 1990s were the Asia-Pacific markets, where booming industry, increased proliferation of automobiles, and poorly maintained roads led to greater demand for tires. Overall, world tire sales reached 975 million units in 1997, 275 million new tires and 700 million replacement tires.

Strong economies in Western Europe, Asia, and the United States boosted automobile production levels to record highs in 2000. As a result, worldwide tire production and sales also soared. Light vehicle tire sales grew four percent to more than one billion units, while commercial vehicle sales climbed to more than 100 million units. When economic conditions began to weaken in 2001, car production began to wane. As a result, light vehicles tire sales fell two percent and commercial vehicle tire sales dropped more than 10 percent.

Between 1995 and 2000, global replacement tire sales growth averaged roughly four percent. A massive tire recall by Bridgestone, related to accidents involving Ford Explorers fitted with Bridgestone tires, helped to offset the impact of the deteriorating economy in 2001 by fueling demand for replacement tires, particularly in North America. As a result, global replacement tire sales that year remained level with the previous year. The North American tire industry was among the hardest hit by the recession in 2001. Original equipment shipments fell from 321 million units to 303 million units, reflecting a nearly 6 percent decrease.

In 2010, the Rubber Manufacturers Association (RMA) reported that U.S. tire shipments were projected to reach 282 million units, up nearly eight percent from 2009's 260 million units. This was primarily due to a 38 percent increase in the original equipment sector for passenger tires and a 5 percent increase in replacement. The increase in tire shipments was a positive sign that the economy was rising from the severe economic downturn of the late 2000s and was coupled with the recent turnaround of the auto manufacturer's industry.

China remained a key growth market for tire makers in the late 2000s. This was consistent with previously established trends. For example, according to *AsiaPulse News,* "Foreign tyre manufacturers are expanding their investments in China with the rapid expansion of the country's automobile market and rising demand for car tyres and high-performance tyres following China's entry into the World Trade Organization." For example, France-based Michelin and China-based Shanghai Tire Co. created a joint tire production venture in Shanghai. Japan's Yokohama Rubber, which held a three percent share of the Chinese tire market, forged a joint tire production operation in Hangzhou with Hangzhou Rubber Group in January of 2002.

In December 2003, *European Rubber Journal* indicated that the global tire market increased 3.1 percent in 2002, with a significant share of the rise attributed to Chinese companies. According to the publication, much of this growth came at the expense of the world's "Big Three" tire producers. Of the world's leading 75 tire makers, 16 were Chinese concerns, with combined revenues of nearly

US$3.3 billion. This follows a decade-long surge in terms of automobile production and industrial goods manufacturing. China overtook Japan as the second largest rubber products producer in the last part of the 1990s, and moved into first place in terms of leading consumer of rubber worldwide.

CURRENT CONDITIONS

According to a World Tire Industry Report, by 2007, the global tire industry was worth US$130 billion and directly employed over 600,000, with several million more employed indirectly. According to *Business Week,* the top three tire manufacturers—Michelin, Bridgestone, and Goodyear—held about 75 percent of the global tire market. Replacement was the largest segment of the market, accounting for 70 percent of tires sold and 75 percent of revenue in 2006. Although growing economies in such countries as India and China were expected to fuel the tire industry, players faced some significant challenges in the late 2000s, the most significant of which were rising energy and raw material costs.

In the United States, tire production increased from US$12.7 billion in 2002 to nearly US$15 billion in 2009. Imports of tires also increased dramatically, from US$4.4 billion in 2001 to US$8.3 billion in 2005. Other major importers were Germany, Great Britain, Ireland, and France.

According to a study by Industry Week, the real growth in the United States came from average price per tire, which increased from US$59 in 1999 to US$76 in 2005. Mintel attributed the increase in price to a variety of factors, including the increasing number of SUVs, light trucks, and luxury vehicles on the road. According to the report, "If the market is to see more rapid growth, suppliers and retailers must persuade consumers that a higher-performance tire is a safer tire." It was expected that the cost per tire would increase by as much as 6.5 percent by the end of 2010 due to a number of factors, including a rise in the cost of natural rubber production due to a lag behind the soaring demand. Weather extremes and aging rubber-producing trees in southeastern Asia were expected to reduce natural rubber production to 10.25 million metric tons (mmt) in 2010, while the natural rubber consumption was projected to be 10.31 mmt. By 2011, the projected demand would be 11.26 mmt, a significant expansion over the 11 expected production. According to an analysis by Goldman Sachs Group, this would be the result of a projected 16.4 percent rise in global automotive production in 2010 and an 8.5 percent increase in 2011.

One such tire was the "run-flat" tire. After decades of experimentation, Bridgestone, Goodyear, and Michelin began to introduce these tires, which allow drivers to continue driving at normal speeds after losing part or all of their air pressure. Run-flat tires make use of improved rubber mix-design technology that allows scrap rubber to react with gases to produce a chemical change, the result of which can bond with other materials and fill punctures in tires. Automobile manufacturers had eagerly awaited this innovation, which promised to do away with roadside tire changes and the ever-present heavy spare tire, thereby increasing fuel efficiency. However, the high cost of the air pressure sensors needed to make use of the new tire technology remained a deterrent, as did concerns over the heavy weight of run-flat tires, which compromised fuel efficiency. By the mid-2000s, though, manufacturers were forced to invest heavily in this type of technology to maintain market share. Although overall product development was geared toward longer-lasting tires, which inherently delimits future sales, in this technology-driven market, durability was one of the premier selling points for customers. In addition to the safety feature, the fact that the run-flat tire eliminated the need for a spare tire or jack appealed to consumers. By the mid-2000s, manufacturers were installing run-flat tires as standard features in luxury vehicles; growth was seen in the family car market as well. According to *MSN Autos,* the new regulations put forth in the National Highway Transportation Agency's Transportation Recall Enhancement, Accountability and Documentation (TREAD) Act, which, among other measures, required low pressure warning systems for all 2004 and later vehicles, was expected to help spur the growth of run-flat tires, and "in a few years, accidents due to tire blowouts should become a thing of the past" as run-flat tires become standard in all vehicles.

RESEARCH AND TECHNOLOGY

Intense competition drove heavy investments in research and development in the early 1990s. New tire designs proved vital to higher profit margins and improved market share. Technological research and development targeted lightness, safety, comfort, fuel economy, and durability. In particular, companies have focused on developing wet weather tires and "run-flat" tire technology.

Michelin continued to be a leader in product and process innovation. In 1991, the company launched the XH-4, a radial that offered 60 percent longer wear than most other tires on the market. The company introduced a new "green" tire in 1992. Its reduced rolling resistance promised up to 4 percent better fuel efficiency, and therefore less air pollution, than standard tires. That same year, the company helped promote tire recycling by paving a U.S. highway with "rubberized asphalt." In terms of process, Michelin's automated, secretive "C3M" process combined several stages of tire building and required only 10 percent of the floor space of existing plants, thereby holding the potential to dramatically reduce two of tire manufacturers' biggest costs: payroll and physical plant expenses. In response, Goodyear introduced its own production technology innovation in the form of its Integrated Manufacturing Precision Assembly Cellular Technology (IMPACT), which aims to diminish inventory levels and reduce cycle times.

In 1999, Goodyear began giving an air pressure sensor system free to anyone who purchased a set of Eagle Aquasteel run-flat tires. The following year, Michelin unveiled its PAX tire/wheel system, a more fuel efficient run-flat tire system. Eventually, Goodyear and Michelin created a joint venture to promote more widespread acceptance of run-flat tires. The two tire makers agreed to use Michelin's PAX system as its main product line.

Closely related to run-flat tires were tire pressure monitoring systems, which notified drivers when tires lost air pressure. In April 2003, *European Rubber Journal* indicated that five years of research had led to the development of a number of direct and indirect pressure sensing systems. The former provided drivers with absolute pressure readings, while the latter used tire diameter measurements to determine if a loss in pressure was occurring. The article explained that while there was no consensus on which system was the best, manufacturers like Ford Motor Co. had received negative customer feedback regarding direct systems. U.S. government requirements—namely the National Highway Traffic Safety Administration's enforcement of the Transportation Recall Enhancement, Accountability, and Documentation (TREAD) Act—were expected to spur U.S. growth in tire pressure management systems.

Advances in technology are looked upon as a vital area of development for tire manufacturers. Much of this technology, however, inherently limits the growth of sales volume. For instance, one of the primary concerns of manufacturers is greater durability of products, especially in the tire market. Because technological innovations are one of the prime selling points in this mature industry, the search for durability must be a major focus for producers who want to attract customers. For example, because tires generally do not perform properly after they are six years old, the feasibility of tire expiration dates was being considered. By early 2004, in fact, the National Highway Traffic Safety Administration was conducting multi-year studies on the correlation between tire durability and tire age, in order to determine if lab trials could accurately mimic tire aging and performance. In March 2010, the United States Department of Transportation signed into effect the Tire Fuel Efficiency Consumer Information Program, issued in connection with the Energy Independence and Security Act of 2007. This regulation was designed to be provided to the consumers

at the point of purchase and was to encourage them to purchase better performing replacement tires.

Growing concern over the adverse environmental impact of scrap tires pushed the issue of reuse (in retreads, for example), recycling, and ultimate disposal of tires to the forefront of the industry's environmental agenda. According to the Rubber Manufacturers Association, by the mid-2000s, about three-fourths of scrap tires were used annually for end use markets, of which the highest growing segment was civil engineering applications. The forecast was for annual growth in this area to increase exponentially, from 20 to 50 percent. Sales of industrial rubber products were forecast to grow five percent annually to more than US$16 billion by 2008, according to a report published by the Freedonia Group. Some current uses for recycled rubber are alternative fuel sources for industries, cushioning material in children's playgrounds, mulch for play areas, raincoats, boots, athletic shoes, and even clothing and accessories. In the early 2000s, Goodyear began reexamining the potential of urethane tires, which were fully recyclable, as well as not susceptible to flats or blowouts, because the tires use no air. Urethane had been tested by tire makers as early as the 1950s, but nothing commercially viable ever emerged.

WORKFORCE

Globalization and consolidation trends combined to herald both massive job cuts and radically changed labor-management relations. After the acquisition spree of the late 1980s, leading tire companies seeking economies of scale and increased productivity eliminated redundant plants and many of the workers in them. The Big Three—Michelin, Goodyear, and Bridgestone—reduced their combined employment levels by an average of more than 10 percent from 1990 to 1993. Goodyear made the biggest cuts during that period, cutting its employment numbers by 12.4 percent. All the leaders embraced popular new management techniques emphasizing lean production, reliance on teams, and total quality management.

Adjusting to the leaner tire industry of the 1990s was particularly difficult for members of the U.S. United Rubber Workers (URW), who had used pattern bargaining to negotiate contracts with U.S. tire companies since 1946. After Goodyear came to a relatively generous 1994 agreement with the group, the Rubber Workers expected their competitors with U.S. operations and subsidiaries to follow suit. Instead, other tire makers balked. Led by Michelin, which had studiously avoided organized labor before 1990, a number of manufacturers, including Sumitomo, Yokohama, Bridgestone, and Pirelli, objected to the union's demands. Some local unions made concessions, but eight percent of the URW's membership went on strike. Early in 1995, Bridgestone hired 2,000 replacement workers. Some analysts hailed the end of pattern bargaining, noting that lower wage costs could allow manufacturers to increase capital and research budgets. Union supporters decried Bridgestone's decision, however.

Workforce reductions continued into the early 2000s as Goodyear trimmed nearly 10 percent of its staff in 2001. That year, Michelin revealed its intent to downsize its North American employment base by seven percent. Some industry leaders, such as Tokyo-based Bridgestone Corp., continued to struggle into 2004. However, there were signs of brighter times on the road ahead as some industry leaders announced plans to expand operations. For example, by 2006, some 350 new jobs were expected to result from the establishment of a new U.S. factory by Japan's Toyo Tire & Rubber Co. Another 30 jobs would likely stem from expanded capacity at Cooper Tire & Rubber in Findlay, Ohio. Most of the growth in the workforce is expected to be in the developing countries where more of the major producers are moving or expanding operations to take advantage of cheaper wages and a less demanding economy.

INDUSTRY LEADERS

In the late 2000s, seven multinational companies—Michelin, Bridgestone, Goodyear, Continental, Pirelli, Sumitomo, and Yokohama—accounted for almost 80 percent of the world's tire output. The top tier of companies consisted of the Big Three: Michelin, Bridgestone, and Goodyear. Together, these three companies produced approximately half of the world's tires.

Bridgestone. Despite its status as one of the world's leading tire producers in 2000, sales at Tokyo, Japan-based Bridgestone Corporation fell 14.1 percent in 2000 to US$17.32 billion, and earnings dropped 82.1 percent to US$155 million that year. Blamed for the poor performance was the widely publicized recall of 6.5 million Firestone tires, many of which were used on Ford Explorers. Several accidents involving Explorer sport utility vehicles had revealed defects in the Firestone tires in 2000. The resulting recall cost Bridgestone roughly US$350 million and its long-standing partnership with Ford Motor Company. The firm also found itself targeted in several lawsuits initiated by parties who had been injured while driving on the tires. By 2007, Bridgestone's revenues totaled US$29.7 billion. At this time, the company employed 133,750 workers.

Bridgestone founder Shojiro Ishibashi originally established his rubber company to manufacture footwear in 1931. During the years before World War II, Bridgestone's growth was based on the expansion of Japan's

military and automotive sectors. The company expanded throughout Asia in the postwar era, then into Europe in the 1970s. Growth came primarily through acquisition in the 1980s. The most notable example of this was the 1988 purchase of Firestone Tire & Rubber Company. A period of wholesale restructuring and reinvestment followed, during which the Firestone operations suffered a loss. That retrenchment paid dividends in the late 1990s. In 2006, Bridgestone acquired Bandag, Inc., a leading truck tire retreader with over 900 franchised dealers worldwide. The Bridgestone company opened factories in Indonesia, Singapore, and Thailand during the 1950s before expanding throughout the world in the 1960s, 1970s, and 1980s.

Michelin. France's Compagnie Générale des Établissements Michelin is the world's leading tire producer in the late 2000s, with sales of US$20.78 billion in 2009, up from US$14.8 billion in 2000. Michelin was also a leading producer of inner tubes. Although the majority of the company's sales were made in Europe and the Americas, Michelin spent much of the late 1990s working to increase its market share in Asia. As a result, sales in China grew 57 percent in 1999. With business in approximately 170 countries and about 76 manufacturing plants, Michelin maintained a payroll of 109,190 employees.

Originally founded in 1830 as a sugar manufacturer, Michelin soon diversified into rubber products. Production of pneumatic tires began after the Michelin brothers, André and Edouard, took charge of the company in the 1880s. The brothers established a tradition of innovation that was carried on by succeeding generations at the family-controlled company. Its most notable breakthrough was the radial tire, developed secretly during the German occupation of France during World War II. Michelin advanced from the second place rank among global tire manufacturers to number one in 1990 through its acquisition of the Uniroyal-Goodrich Tire Company in the United States. The company continued to be led by descendants of the Michelin family into the late 2000s.

Goodyear. The Goodyear Tire & Rubber Co. ranked third among the world's tire manufacturers in 2007, with US$19.6 billion in sales. The firm recorded a US$203.6 million loss in 2001—its first annual loss in nine years—due to increasingly expensive raw materials, a weakening global economy, and unfavorable exchange rates. To cut costs, Goodyear pared down inventory, divested peripheral operations, and trimmed its workforce by 10,000 positions. By 2007, employees numbered 71,000. Goodyear formed an alliance with Japan's Sumitomo Rubber Industries during the early 2000s and planned to increase production levels in China.

Frank A. Seiberling founded the company, named for the originator of vulcanized rubber, in 1898 to manufacture bicycle and carriage tires. The company began production of automobile tires in 1901 and grew quickly on the strength of contracts with the Ford Motor Company. Although it was not the world's first tire producer, it became the world's largest in 1916. Instead of acquiring its North American competitors in the late 1980s, Goodyear borrowed heavily to invest in a stock buy-back after a hostile takeover attempt in 1987. Goodyear relinquished its claim to the top spot in the international tire industry in 1990, but maintained its rank as one of only two publicly traded U.S. tire companies. A turnaround engineered by CEO Stanley Gault resulted in a massive expansion program geared toward recapturing Goodyear's status as the industry's first-ranked player. The company emphasized innovative new products, attacked the replacement market with new vigor, shored up distribution through mass retailers, and expanded into the emerging markets of Latin America and Asia. However, nearly two-thirds of the company's sales were still focused in North America.

Continental. Ranked fourth among the world's tire manufacturers, with 2009 sales of US$18.2 billion, Germany's Continental AG was a premier company in the European market, generating a substantial share of its sales in the region. The company was formed in 1871 by a consortium of financiers and industrialists to manufacture a general line of rubber products, including fabrics, footwear, toys, and tires. The company became the first in Germany to produce pneumatic bicycle tires in the 1890s, and expanded into automotive tires by the turn of the century. Acquisitions within Germany helped promote Continental to the forefront of its home country's tire industry by 1929, but the company continued to lag behind its rivals in terms of international expansion. The German pre-war build-up helped boost Continental's operations, and the company participated in the development of synthetic rubber, but the postwar era brought stagnation and uncertainty. The vigorous expansion of the German car industry, however, brought equally rapid growth to Continental. A major acquisition spree begun in 1979 culminated in the 1987 purchase of General Tire, the United States' fifth largest tire producer, for US$650 million. Continental repulsed a takeover attempt by Italy's Pirelli in 1991, but speculation that the company was vulnerable to further unfriendly merger attempts continued in the early 1990s. However, the firm remained independent into the late 2000s, and in 2009, it employed 134,430 workers.

Pirelli. Pirelli & C. SpA, based in Milan, Italy, was also an industry leader, generating sales of US$6.26 billion in

2009. Pirelli is one of the most diversified of the world leaders in tire manufacturing. Second to energy cables, tires were responsible for roughly 45 percent of sales.

The company was established by Giovanni Battista Pirelli in 1872 to manufacture a variety of rubber products. The company's product line eventually included bicycle and car tires. Pirelli gained a reputation as a producer of high-performance racing tires in the 1920s. The company expanded organically, establishing its own operations throughout Europe and beyond in the 1960s and 1970s. Acquisitions, including the 1988 purchase of the United States' Armstrong Tire Co., fueled growth during the 1980s. Ill-conceived battles for control of Firestone in the late 1980s and Continental in the early 1990s did not come to fruition. Some critics charged that these attempts only distracted management from concentrating on competition in the global market. Analysts estimated that the Continental attempt alone cost Pirelli US$300 million. Pirelli divested some extraneous businesses in the mid-1990s to concentrate on its core interests in cables and tires. As of 2009, Pirelli employed 29,570 people.

Sumitomo. With 2010 revenues of US$10.57 billion and 72,030 employees in 115 countries around the world, Japan's Sumitomo Rubber Industries, Ltd. was another major tire producer. Tires account for roughly 71 percent of the firm's total revenues. Sumitomo also makes industrial products, marine products, and sports equipment.

The firm is an affiliate of the Sumitomo *keiretsu,* one of Japan's largest conglomerates. By the time Sumitomo Rubber was formed in 1917, its parent had already bought into Dunlop Japan, a subsidiary of Britain's Dunlop. In 1963, the Sumitomo group purchased a controlling interest in Dunlop Japan, combined it with its existing rubber interests, and renamed the venture Sumitomo Rubber Industries. Reasoning that its cheaper textile radials would maintain their market share, Dunlop had eschewed the European radial revolution of the 1960s, and the company had a difficult time catching up when it realized its mistake. Sumitomo used Dunlop as a stepping stone to greater global influence in the mid-1980s when it acquired a 98 percent interest in the latter's ailing European operations for US$240 million. The "white knight" merger and subsequent rationalization of both companies' operations helped each survive the cutthroat competition of the late 1980s and early 1990s. In 1999, Sumitomo sold the right to manufacture Dunlop tires in North America and Europe to Goodyear in exchange for the right to manufacture Goodyear tires in Japan.

Yokohama. Another Japanese manufacturer, the Yokohama Rubber Co., Ltd. had sales of more than US$10.57 billion in 2006 with 14,617 employees. Tires accounted for roughly 70 percent of total revenues. Yokohama also makes aviation components and industrial rubber products. Operations outside Japan span the remainder of Asia, Europe, and North America.

Established in 1917, Yokohama specialized in the manufacture of cord tires. Its reputation for innovation enabled it to become the supplier to top Japanese car manufacturers Nissan and Toyota. In the post-World War II era, the company expanded into aircraft tires, high-performance racing tires, truck and bus tires, and radials. Yokohama was relatively late to establish overseas operations: the company did not have a significant international presence until the late 1960s and early 1970s. The firm followed the global pattern of consolidation—albeit on a much smaller scale than the "Big Three"—when it joined Toyo Tyre and Rubber Co. and Continental in the cooperative construction of a radial truck and bus tire plant in the United States in 1988. The following year, Yokohama acquired Mohawk Rubber Co., Ltd., a U.S. tire manufacturer, for US$150 million and instituted a capital investment plan.

MAJOR COUNTRIES IN THE INDUSTRY

In the January 2003 issue of *European Rubber Journal,* University of Akron (Ohio) economics professor Dennis Byrne indicated that, as the mid-2000s approached, North America would increase its global share of tire production from 2000 levels of 31.2 percent. In 2003, North America held a 46.6 percent share of the global tire and rubber market. Annual growth of 1.8 percent was expected for total tire shipments in the United States through 2010. In the United States, more than 259 million tires were shipped in 2009, with an expected increase through 2011.

Eastern Europe's share of the world market amounted to 15.2 percent in 2003. In June 2004, *European Rubber Journal* indicated that a pending tire disposal surcharge in France led to a surge in tire replacement sales during the early months of 2004. In all, Europe saw passenger tire sales rise 5.6 percent during the first quarter of the year (41.2 million units), while 4x4 tires increased 12.2 percent (1.4 million units), light truck tires rose 9.6 percent (3 million units), and heavy duty truck tires were up 7.3 percent (2.3 million units). Germany and France were the third and fourth largest exporters of tires in 2005, with US$3.7 billion and US$3.1 billion in sales, respectively.

Japan, the global automobile industry leader, held its place as the number-one exporter of tires throughout the early to mid-2000s, with value of exports increasing from

US$2.9 billion in 2001 to US$5 billion in 2005. Japan was home to four of the world's leading tire manufacturers, including Bridgestone Corp., Sumitomo Rubber Industries Ltd., Yokohama Rubber Co. Ltd., and Toyo Tire & Rubber Co. Ltd. In 2003, the Asia-Pacific region as whole held about 34.5 percent of the worldwide rubber and tire market.

North America, Western Europe, and Japan together accounted for roughly 75 percent of world tire production in recent years. However, the most promising markets for the international tire industry were in Asia and the emerging market of Latin America. Asia, which had a 34 percent world market share in 2003, was expected to increase its market share at an annual rate of 5 percent into the late 2000s. South Korea had become a major contender in the tire market since the late 1990s. Its production of 70 million units represented an increase of almost 7 percent over 1999. China, which had tire output of 160 million in 2002, earned approximately US$4 billion in the tire market in 2003, which amounted to about 5 percent of the world's total. In 2007, China surpassed the United States to become the world's leading rubber consumer. Imports of synthetic rubber in the first four months of 2007 reached 484,000 tons, 14.7 percent more than the same period the previous year, and were valued at US$930 million. South America, despite a lack of large investments by major tire companies, also showed significant growth potential.

BIBLIOGRAPHY

2010 Tire Shipments Report; Rubber Manufacturers Association. Available from http://www.rma.org.

Davis, Bruce. "China's Tyre Companies Start to Show." *European Rubber Journal*, December 2003.

"ERJ Newsbriefs." *European Rubber Journal*, 1 April 2004.

"Hoover's Company Capsules." *Hoover's Online*, 2007. Available from http://www.hoovers.com.

Natural Rubber Costs Pump Up US Tire Costs; *Industry Week*, October 2010. Available from http://www.industryweek.com

"Potholes Ahead for Global Tire Makers." *Business Week*, 31 March 2006.

Raleigh, Patrick. "French Tyre Sales Surge, Rest of Europe Grows Too." *European Rubber Journal*, 1 June 2004.

"RMA Ranks States on Tire Recycling Efforts." *Recycling Today*, February 2007.

Robinson, Aaron. "The Skinny of Run Flat Tires." 15 June 2007. Available from http://www.mobiloil.com.

Rubber Manufacturers Association. "Little Growth Predicted for 2007 Tire Shipments." 13 March 2007. Available from http://www.rma.org.

"Rubber Tyres." *Imports/Exports: 2001-2005*. 15 June 2007. Available from http://www.intracen.org.

"Run-Flat Tires: A New Standard Rising." MSN, 15 June 2007. Available from http://autos.msn.com/.

Shaw, David. "Runflat Technology Is Top Priority: Many Observers Predict Buoyant Future for Extended Mobility Tyres." *European Rubber Journal,* April 2003.

———. "UK Remains Good for Tyre Sales." *European Rubber Journal,* 1 April 2004.

"Slight Increase Seen for Tire Shipments." *Rubber World,* April 2007.

"Top 75 Global Tyre Producers 2002-2003." *European Rubber Journal,* December 2003.

White, Liz. "China Has Most Growth Potential for Carbon Black." *European Rubber Journal,* January 2003.

World Tire Industry Report; November, 2010. Available from http://www.worldtirereport.com.

INDUSTRIAL MACHINERY AND EQUIPMENT

---■---

ELEVATORS AND MOVING STAIRWAYS

NAICS CODE(S)

333921. The vertical transportation industry includes the manufacturers of passenger and freight elevators, automobile lifts, dumbwaiters, and escalators. Elevators, as referenced here, are better known in Europe as "lifts" and are used to move passengers and equipment from level to level. They do not include farm elevators (primarily grain storage devices) or aerial work platforms (included under construction machinery and equipment).

INDUSTRY SNAPSHOT

According to *Buildings,* "elevators, escalators, and moving sidewalks are the building industry's equivalent to trains, planes, and automobiles." Although the industry experienced a brief expansion in the latter part of the twentieth century, the beginning of the twenty-first century brought the dual pressures of a downturn in construction and a simultaneous increase in the number of elevator manufacturers worldwide. Greater emphasis was placed on service companies. Large elevator manufacturers swallowed smaller corporations, making the industry increasingly global in nature. The industry subsequently consolidated into just a few major players by the mid- to late years of the first decade of the 2000s. Otis Elevator Company, later part of United Technologies, founded the elevator industry and was first in the

industry for decades. In fact, it wasn't until well into the first decade of the 2000s that its leadership position was threatened by competitor Schindler Lifts. In 2005, other major worldwide players included KONE of Finland and ThyssenKrupp of Germany, as well as Mitsubishi and Hitachi of Japan.

The state of the elevator industry depends entirely on the health of the construction industry. Although service is an increasingly important aspect of the vertical transportation market, the manufacture of new elevators is dependent on the creation of the new buildings that require them. In the first decade of the 2000s, the economic emergence of China and other Asian countries shifted the construction industry's focus from Europe and the United States to the rapidly growing construction markets in developing nations along the Pacific Rim. Developing technology included the implementation of multidirectional cabs, high-technology elevator-passenger interfaces, higher speed transportation, and optimal reliability, bringing with it an emphasis on greater environmental friendliness.

ORGANIZATION AND STRUCTURE

Once elevators were technologically able to service large buildings, two distinct categories of elevator construction emerged: electric elevators designed to be used exclusively in high-rise buildings and hydraulic elevators capable of accommodating low-rise buildings of five stories or less.

Hydraulic elevators are relatively slow with a maximum speed of 150 feet per minute (ft/min) or 46 meters per minute (m/min), which is not a disadvantage as long as a building has very few floors. Hydraulic elevators are seen as ideal for smaller buildings because they do not need overhead hoisting machinery. Generally, the elevator sits atop a piston that moves inside a cylinder that is sunk in the ground at a depth equal to the maximum height to which the elevator will rise. So-called hole-less hydraulic elevators rely on power that is transferred via a sliding plunger on the side of the elevator.

Electric elevators fall into one of two categories: gearless traction elevators and geared traction elevators. Gearless traction elevators are quite fast and regularly travel at 400 to 2000 ft/min (120 to 610 m/min). They are powered by large slow-speed motors and are generally installed in high-rise buildings with more than 10 stories. Geared traction elevators travel at a slower rate of speed—a maximum of 450 ft/min (140 m/min)—but can carry up to 30,000 pounds (13,500 kilograms) and have many industrial applications.

It is a given in the elevator industry that passengers often must wait for an elevator car to arrive. Escalators, on the other hand, offer a mode of vertical transportation that is continuously accessible. Depending on design, the "moving stairways" that make up escalators can transport up to 4,500 passengers per hour on a series of steps running in a continuous chain up an incline. Most escalators service floors separated by a 20-foot (6 meter) slope, although 100-foot (30 meter) escalators also are in use. All escalators are powered by alternating current electric motors and move at about 100 ft/min (30 m/min).

Other Modes of Vertical Transportation. A third, relatively small part of the vertical transportation industry is a dumbwaiter. Dumbwaiters are used exclusively as material-handling systems (they do not accommodate passengers) and are widely used for such applications as moving books between floors in libraries or transporting food and medical supplies in hospitals. Dumbwaiters are always operated from outside the system, never from inside a cab. Dumbwaiters are limited to nine square feet of platform area and must be of a height no more than four feet. Any system larger than this is classified as an elevator and is therefore subject to more stringent safety requirements.

Regulatory Agencies. In the United States, the agency that regulates elevator and escalator safety, operation, and design is the American National Standards Institute (ANSI). ANSI is an organization of industrial and consumer groups and pertinent government personnel. Under their aegis, on-site safety inspections of elevators, dumbwaiters, and escalators are made by state and local inspectors.

BACKGROUND AND DEVELOPMENT

The elevator of the twenty-first century operates on many of the same basic principles first perfected by Elisha Graves

Otis back in 1854. An elevator is basically either an open platform or a closed cab powered by a unit that moves it up and down an enclosed shaft through various combinations of pulleys, cables, counterweights, and gears.

While the concept of an elevator-like device able to move heavy loads vertically was investigated by the ancient Greeks (the Greek mathematician Archimedes invented a type of elevator in 230 B.C.), such an apparatus of vertical transportation had limited application well into the Industrial Revolution because of seemingly unsolvable safety problems, especially the fact that there was no way known to stop a falling elevator. If the lifting cable or rope used in the operation of an elevator broke, the results were disastrous for the elevator, its passengers, and any freight on board. Demand, however, overrode safety concerns in certain situations. The advent of the Industrial Revolution saw elevator use increase in industrialized countries, especially in the United States and Great Britain. By the 1840s, patents had been granted for steam and hydraulic elevators. Nevertheless, the safety question cast a pall on elevators' general acceptance and thus stifled technological development. New buildings remained more or less "stunted," because the practical height of a building was inextricably tied to the ability to vertically move people and freight to the upper floors. Until this could be accomplished quickly and safely, the multi-story buildings and skyscrapers that are the hallmarks of modern urban architecture had to wait.

Vertical transportation embarked on its "golden age" in 1853 after Elisha G. Otis, a 43-year-old mechanic from Albany, New York, dramatically demonstrated an elevator safety device of his own invention. First unveiled at the Crystal Palace Exposition in New York City, the device had been constructed by Otis in a Yonkers, New York factory. Otis's safety innovation consisted of a pair of spring-loaded "dogs," which, if the elevator's lifting cable broke, would engage cogs mounted along the elevator shaft rails, thus halting the uncontrolled fall of the elevator. *Scientific American* called the device an "excellent" and "much admired" invention. Buoyed by the exciting reception, Otis and his son began in earnest to manufacture "safety elevators." In 1857 Otis installed the first commercial passenger elevator in a department store in New York City. This steam-powered elevator rose through the building's five stories in just under one minute, carrying passengers effortlessly to the top floor and conveying the Otis Elevator Company with seemingly comparable ease to an undisputed position as leader of the vertical transportation industry.

Once Otis had shown the way, advances in elevator technology paralleled the increasing demand for higher buildings and skyscrapers. Elevators became faster, safer, and more capable of carrying heavier loads, and the steam elevators of the nineteenth century gave way to the electric and hydraulic elevators of the twentieth. Otis Elevator Company introduced the first escalator at the 1900 Paris Exposition, but development of this alternate approach to vertical travel did not begin in earnest until the 1920s. Prior to 1950, escalator use was generally restricted to stores and transportation terminals, such as airports. After the middle of the century, however, they became increasingly popular features in schools, offices, public buildings, and other buildings where large numbers of people had to be moved among a relatively low number of floors.

In the 1980s the vertical transportation industry saw stability in Europe and a boom in Asia, but began to level off in the United States. The world market expanded in the latter part of the 1980s at a rate of roughly 15 percent a year, and by 1989 sales topped US$17 billion annually. This figure, however, included the influx of revenue sources based on maintenance and modernization, which by 1990 would account for 40 percent of industry revenue. In 1990, Otis, Schindler Holding Ltd., and KONE Corporation held approximately 50 percent of the market, in part through policies of expansion and acquisition.

In 1990 the United States was feeling the beginnings of a recession, and elevator sales dropped by 5 to 20 percent in certain domestic markets. In the five years immediately prior to the onset of the recession, the U.S. market had already leveled off to an annual growth rate of about 2 percent. Dramatically higher growth in other market segments did much to offset this otherwise alarming trend. In Europe, the elevator market grew at a rate of about 10 percent a year, while portions of the expanding Asian market displayed growth rates as high as 40 percent. In consequence, many companies, including industry leader Otis, turned their attention to the more lucrative effort. To further compensate for the slowdown in the U.S. market, savvy industry leaders were ready with modernization and service contracts to make up for the decline in new installations in the early 1990s.

By 1996, even allowing for the explosion of the Asian consumer market, annual worldwide demand for elevators and escalators dropped from 90,000 units in 1991 to 70,000 units—a fall of more than 22 percent. Although traditionally conservative, the elevator industry was suddenly forced into the same survival techniques used in more competitive industries as individual corporations cut costs and downsized. Smaller manufacturers and service groups were absorbed into larger corporations, which depended on increased research and development capabilities and greater global presence for survival.

By the end of the twentieth century, major elevator manufacturers, such as Otis Elevator Company and Schindler Elevator Corporation, had conducted extensive

restructuring and implemented cost-cutting measures. Otis cut more than 1,000 jobs in 1998 in order to strengthen its financial position in the wake of the Asian economic crisis of the late 1990s. The European economy faced uncertainty as the euro began its phase-in during 1999. Elevator companies and the building industry experienced significant slowdowns until the Euro began to stabilize late in 2001. Global companies (the European market accounted for more than 77 percent of Otis's sales in 2000) were impacted heavily by the fluctuation.

The recession of the early 1990s encouraged the elevator industry to concentrate on service contracts rather than new sales. In 1991 services accounted for just US$600 million of industry revenue. Four years later, in 1995, KONE gleaned more than 61 percent of its revenues from various service contracts and modernization efforts, and in 1997, Dover reported a similar 60 to 40 revenue split. Companies worldwide emphasized renovation and redesign of previously installed units, especially of control systems. In the United States, the passage of federal legislation aimed at making public and private facilities more accessible to persons with disabilities provided considerable impetus for the elevator industry to focus on service and modernization. Service became such an important segment of the industry that new equipment was often under-priced, and companies depended on profits generated by service contracts. By 1996, estimates showed that over the first 20 years in the life span of an average elevator, total maintenance costs would equal the original purchase price. The Japanese also embraced the concept of service as a lucrative adjunct to the elevator industry. In 1997 Hitachi introduced the high-technology Hitachi Elevator Remote and Intelligent Observation System (HERIOS), a remote maintenance system targeted particularly at providing optimal reliability, comfort, and security for elevator users, particularly the aged.

Expansion of operations through acquisition was an accepted means of coping with localized business slowdowns as early as the late 1980s and early 1990s. After the fall of the Berlin Wall in 1989, Eastern Europe presented a burgeoning market for business, including the elevator industry. Otis Elevator Company promptly used its European Transcontinental Operations subsidiary to acquire 60 percent of Berliner Aufzugs und Fahrtreppenbau, quickly establishing operations in East Germany. In 1993 Otis opened a joint venture with the Shcherbinka Lift Factory in Shcherbinka, Russia. The initial production goal for Otis's Russian venture was just 1,200 units annually, a tenth of the capacity of Otis' newly acquired Belarus facility. This goal was kept low in part because the lure of 260,000 grossly outdated units installed across Russia presented a huge potential market for service and modernization. With only KONE

Corporation of Finland as a major competitor for this market (the approximately 5,000 KONE units installed in the Commonwealth of Independent States represented 99 percent of all Russian elevator imports), Otis continued to press forward.

In 1997 Otis looked toward the south and purchased more than 80 percent of Rade Koncar-Inzinjering Vertikalnog Transporta. This Croatian firm had offices in Croatia, Bosnia, and Macedonia, thus providing Otis with a grip on the Balkans, which were rebuilding after years of civil war. While Otis Elevator Company stood as the leading competitor in the emerging markets of Poland, Slovakia, Hungary, the Czech Republic, and the Ukraine, Schindler made overtures in the Middle East. In 1996 Schindler concluded negotiations to purchase a major interest in Nehustan, Israel's primary elevator company.

Even as high technology and acquisition alternately spurred and propped up the market in Europe and the United States, rapid economic changes in Asia brought construction upsurges that opened vast opportunities for newly successful elevator manufacturers. South Korea's focus on technology reached its elevator market, and Dongyang Elevator Company began in 1997 to tout "smart" elevators whose multifunctional capacities were reminiscent of some of the recent Schindler and Otis innovations. Hyundai Elevator Company turned to high speed as a niche, and LG Industrial Systems devoted an entire presentation room to its variety of elevator products.

In April 2000, Mitsubishi and Schindler entered into a cooperative agreement in which the two would supply each other with major components for elevators and escalators. Mitsubishi reported that the two companies negotiated for business cooperation on a global scale in an attempt to maintain the top positions in the world market and to expand further.

A major source for much-needed industry vitality came from various technological and design innovations, sparked both by the earnest effort of companies trying to remain competitive and by the zeal of emerging new firms. As late as 1987, U.S. Elevator was touting conservatism as the main reason it could pump profit into parent Cubic Corporation. Ten years later, giants such as Schindler and KONE depended on high technology displays and environmental friendliness to differentiate their businesses. In fiction, the voice-activated turbo lifts of Gene Roddenberry's *Star Trek* gave the more earthbound a sense of the possible future of the vertical transportation industry, and by the end of the twentieth century, multidirectional elevator passage became a reality. In 1996 Otis introduced Odyssey, whose "cabs" could carry passengers from their offices in 1000-foot office buildings to

parking lots outside. Schindler Elevator Corporation, through its "Miconic," the previous year taught elevator passengers to communicate with an intelligent operating center and use keypads and displays to identify "assigned" elevators that would stop automatically at designated floors. In the late 1990s, KONE introduced the machine-room-less elevator, MonoSpace. The machine-room-less elevators boasted faster speeds and required less space, according to KONE.

Perhaps the most significant technological advances were born not from the elevator industry itself but from the communications industry and the Internet, which enabled fast communication between elevator manufacturers and customers. In 1999, Otis launched its e-business strategy, which included online display, ordering, and customer service features. Thyssen developed its site in an effort to assist in communications, particularly relating to its 500,000 exclusive maintenance contracts.

Already braced for a U.S. economic recession, United Technologies (Otis Elevator Company's parent company) announced Otis was recession-resistant after extensive restructuring and strong sales outside the United States. Early in 2002, elevator companies were reporting modest growth, despite the recession in the United States, as the Asian and European economies stabilized.

Although the service element of any industry tends to be recession-proof, renovation and modernization of existing machinery was ultimately regarded as a finite market. However, the service industry was a double-edged sword, as elevator service was increasingly provided by private companies specializing in service and not by the original manufacturer. This in turn led to increasing competition for the service fees and a downturn in some service revenues. In October 2004, Schindler Elevator announced an innovation in the service area called "Schindler FieldLink." This handheld device was the latest addition to the company's service programs, the Schindler Elevator Network for Service Excellence (SENSE). The FieldLink combined dispatching, parts ordering, manuals, troubleshooting, and cell phone capabilities into a single unit for service technicians to carry.

However lucrative modernization and service appeared to be, some industry analysts contended that the future still depended on new construction. In the middle of the first decade of the 2000s, the National Association of Elevator Contractors pointed out that in addition to industry consolidation, changes in business models—including the emphasis on Internet business and e-commerce—made the industry small. To compete in the global society, a company had to be well known and well respected.

Indeed, globalization made for creative partnerships in the elevator industry. In December 2001, KONE of Finland and Toshiba of Japan entered into an agreement that provided for the exchange of shares and the extension of Toshiba's license to market KONE's MonoSpace machine-room-less elevators. KONE acquired a 20 percent share in Toshiba's Elevator and Building Systems Corporation, and Toshiba got a 5 percent shareholding in the KONE Corporation. KONE granted Toshiba exclusive rights to manufacture the MonoSpace in China, a rapidly growing elevator market.

Although a worldwide increase in demand was not predicted, Mitsubishi Electric estimated China's market would expand most rapidly. In 2001 Mitsubishi reported the demand for new elevator installations was 30,000. This was expected to increase due to the strong demand for public infrastructure and housing and the special demand stemming from the Beijing Olympics.

CURRENT CONDITIONS

Enhancements and innovation in service and technology were important toward gaining a competitive edge during the late years of the first decade of the 2000s. Of a global market approaching US$40 billion, new sales accounted for 40 percent of revenues, with the remaining 60 percent coming from system maintenance and modernization. Maintenance and updating were important sectors of the industry due to the fact that more than one-third of the world's elevators were more than 20 years old. Examples of such modernization projects late in the late decade included KONE's updating of 23 escalators at O'Hare International Aiport and the modernization of the escalator system in Moscone Center in San Francisco, both of which won Project of the Year awards from *Elevator World*. Industry leaders and smaller companies worked to gain market share in these areas. United Technologies Corp. (UTC) acquired security software systems maker Lenel Systems International Inc., as reported by Avital Hahn in *Investment Dealers' Digest*. By doing so, UTC hoped to adapt Lenel's traditional security systems and create central systems that monitor building entry, computer access, and elevator use through ID cards. Schindler's FieldLink system, the ability to monitor elevator systems remotely via the Internet, and other system innovations were used to help manufacturers gain and retain market share. All companies in the industry were moving toward quieter, more environmentally friendly equipment, and other industry leaders were following KONE's example and offering machine-room-less elevator systems, which required far less space.

Global market expansion continued to provide companies with sources of revenue growth. Almost half of new elevator sales were sold in the Asia-Pacific area,

according to KONE Corporation. China and Russia were important areas in the elevator industry, with increasing opportunity for imports and new construction. Increasing imports meant increased competition among the industry's major manufacturers. In April 2005, KONE announced it was embarking on another joint venture with Toshiba Elevator and Building Systems Corporation (TELC) to build escalators in China. KONE planned to own 70 percent of the company, which would run both companies' existing manufacturing facilities in Kunshan and Shenyang. In the same month, KONE also announced a joint venture with Russian elevator company Karacharovo Mechanical Factory (KMZ). Together, KONE and KMZ hold more than a 35 percent market share of the new elevator market in Russia.

RESEARCH AND TECHNOLOGY

Leading industry players relied on research and development in efforts to increase market share. Japanese elevator manufacturers concentrated on the development of faster elevators. Conversely, the focus of the Western world was on state-of-the art control systems. Increasingly, Otis, Schindler, KONE, and other manufacturers moved away from the traditional electromechanical methods of running elevators and replaced them with microelectronic control systems and artificial intelligence capable of ensuring the most efficient and convenient use of installed elevator cars or cabs. In 1997 the environmentally friendly nature of this new technology was apparent, and Otis was selected as the elevator vendor supplying New York City's first "green" office tower, the Conde Nast building. Here, Otis was asked to install what would be the first U.S. example of high-speed elevators utilizing AC (alternating current) variable frequency drive systems. In this case, the importance of the chosen drive system was its low energy consumption and clean operation, not its speed.

Another innovation employed to make elevators more environmentally friendly was the use of soy-based hydraulic fluid in one of the United States' national symbols, the Statue of Liberty. Since November 2002, the Statue of Liberty's elevator has been running on this biodegradable fluid, which replaced petroleum-based mineral oil. Manufactured by Agri-Lube Inc. in Ohio, the soy-based oil was created by the ARS National Center for Agricultural Utilization Research in Peoria, Illinois, based on the National Park Service's request for "a hydraulic elevator fluid that would readily biodegrade in the environment, come from a renewable resource, be produced by an economical and nonpolluting process, and meet industrial safety and performance standards."

Japan's Mitsubishi held the certificate for the world's fastest passenger elevator, which reached speeds of 2,500 feet per minute. Installed in the 70-story Yokohama Landmark Tower, the elevator hurtled from the second floor to the sixty-ninth floor in 40 seconds. Hitachi Ltd. made similar claims about an elevator model of its own. This emphasis on speed was a calculated gamble on the part of the Japanese manufacturers, but they noted that elevators that broke speed records gained media attention and were strong selling points to the designers and owners of newer and higher buildings, who would use the speedy elevators to attract tenants.

Otis, Schindler, KONE, and other Western elevator manufacturers resisted the elevator speed derby for numerous reasons. They reasoned that unless buildings increased considerably in size, there was little genuine need for faster elevators. Because of the time it takes an elevator to accelerate and decelerate, in most skyscrapers elevators reached maximum speed for duration of only five seconds. Similarly, in nearly all cases, the extra time for a slower elevator to travel added only a few seconds to the trip from ground level to the upper stories of a building. When the elevator in question made numerous stops on the trip, the importance of speed decreased. The comparative example applied by engineers was that of a "bullet train" installed on a milk run, stopping for each town.

The high cost of super-speed elevators was another deterrent, at least from a Western perspective. The US$3 million to US$5 million price tag was approximately 20 percent higher than the price of comparable slower-speed units. The Japanese justified their strategy in constructing the pricey equipment by the fact that this ongoing research and development was a necessary investment in a future filled with 150-story buildings. This rationale did not appeal strongly enough to either Otis or Schindler to cause them to throw development energy into the direction of sheer speed.

To companies outside of Japan, elevator control systems were the key to future technology. The computer intelligence behind sophisticated "fuzzy logic" control systems took multiple factors into account in the course of elevator system operation. While traditional systems dispatched elevators according to which could reach a given floor most quickly, new high-tech elevator control systems examined multiple factors, not just speed and timing. Decisions were made based on real and perceived demand, the number of people in each car, passenger convenience and inconvenience, the number of times a waiting passenger depressed a button, and the relative proximity of the elevator to the desired floor. An ideal time spent waiting for an elevator was perceived to be about 20 seconds, although 30 seconds was considered an acceptable average. Developers believed that the longest a passenger should ever have to wait for an elevator under any circumstances was 90 seconds. With these relatively aggressive targets in mind, proponents of the new

intelligent systems contended that "fuzzy logic" would reduce waiting time by up to 15 percent.

Another microelectronic control system under development was neural networking, a system wherein an elevator "learns from its mistakes." If, for instance, there was high demand for elevators at a certain time (such as lunch time or quitting time) on an upper floor, the elevator anticipated demand by recording usage patterns. The elevators subsequently "learned" to park themselves on the appropriate floors at the appropriate times instead of automatically awaiting calls at the lobby floor. Other technological innovations under development called for numerous elevator cars to circulate around a continuous shaft resembling a Ferris wheel. Research was also undertaken on linear motors that would propel elevators via a magnetic field, thus doing away with lift cables.

Otis led in researching elevator systems equipped with linear induction motors through its Nippon Otis Company, a Japanese joint venture. Unlike linear motors proposed for the future, the current units included lifting cables and needed special facilities for hydraulic pumps or a rooftop hoisting gear. The linear motor rode with the counterweights in back of the elevator cab and moved up and down the hoistway in opposition to the elevator. Elevators with linear induction motors had fewer moving parts than conventional elevators. Other benefits included lower construction, installation, and maintenance costs, and greater reliability. Because of code restrictions, linear motor elevators were not in operation in the United States in the 1990s. A growing market for this system was envisioned in Japan, however, because of different building codes and architectural preferences.

Otis and Schindler were not alone in the introduction of new technology to the industry. In early 1998 KONE announced a new drive system that eliminated the need for the familiar machine room that historically occupied the space above each elevator shaft. The new system used 40 percent less energy than hydraulic systems and was suitable for installation in newly constructed buildings or could be retrofitted into existing buildings. In response to an increase in building size, Hitachi also introduced an intelligent elevator supervisory-control system. In 1997 press releases, Hitachi representatives spoke of a "genetic algorithm" simulating "biological evolution," and using the resultant artificial intelligence to deploy elevators efficiently. That year, Hitachi extended its technology inwardly as well, announcing technical improvements in the design and production environments. Even the small producer Alimak brought a kind of innovation to the industry. Developed originally to meet the requirements of construction, the "rack and pinion" system perfected by Alimak found uses wherever simplicity and strength were desirable.

In 2004 ThyssenKrupp announced its ISIS elevator system, in development for three years. A machine-room-less elevator, ISIS saved an average of 60 square feet of space per elevator in buildings because it was space-efficient and contained completely within the elevator shaft. In addition, the ISIS was quieter than other elevators because it used DuPont Kevlar's synthetic rope instead of steel rope. By mid-2004, all leaders in the industry offered elevator solutions that did not require machine rooms.

INDUSTRY LEADERS

Industry leaders in Europe were facing challenges associated with the increased cost of raw materials such as oil and steel, rising labor prices in some markets, such as North America, and increased price competition. This was reflected by marginal revenue increases from 2003 to 2004. Industry leaders remained profitable but did so because of innovation in service offerings, new technology, increased sales in new markets, or a combination of these factors, which helped to offset rising costs associated with labor and materials.

By 2009, the old guard manufacturers—Otis, Schindler, and KONE—were still on top, although they ceded market share to counterparts in Japan (notably Hitachi and Mitsubishi) and elsewhere. As the giants struggled for world market share, the stubborn health of a variety of smaller international firms saw multiple small companies divide what was less than half the total market.

Otis Elevator Company. The number one company in the industry, Otis Elevator Company, based in Farmington, Connecticut, is a wholly owned subsidiary of the United Technologies Corporation (UTC), and was responsible for generating 24 percent of UTC revenues and 33 percent of UTC operating profits in the mid-years of the first decade of the 2000s. Otis held close to 28 percent of the world market for new elevator and escalator equipment in 2005. Many of Otis's elevator designs were particularly suited for high-speed passenger operations in high-rise buildings, and Otis elevators were installed in eleven of the world's twenty tallest buildings, according to an Otis Fact Sheet from March 2005. Otis was also involved in the maintenance and modernization of pre-existing vertical transportation systems and manufactured horizontal transportation systems such as moving sidewalks and shuttle systems. In 2005, Otis's global presence extended to manufacturing facilities in Europe and Asia as well as the Americas. In the middle of the decade, Otis boasted 61,000 employees, 52,000 outside the United States, and 2 million elevators and escalators in use worldwide. Company revenues in 2009 were US$12.9 billion, with foreign revenue accounting for a major part of that total. The company had 64,000 employees.

One of the company's innovations was its NextStep escalator, a machine-room-less system built for commercial and public use. Otis advertised the system as environmentally friendly, as it does not require lubricant and includes the added safety feature of the Guarded step, which removes the gap between moving risers and the escalator panels. By investing more than US$115 million in engineering and research and development during 2004, Otis sought to keep its place as the industry leader.Additional Otis products offer transport around the world. Those innovative products can be found in diverse places such as the Eiffel Tower and the Sidney Opera House.

It was definitely noteworthy that Otis became the first United Technologies Corp. unit to earn LEED (Leadership in Energy and Environmental Design) recognition. LEED is a globally recognized green building certification system created by the U.S. Green Building Council, a 501(c)(3) non-profit group dedicated to providing to everyone the framework for green building design, construction, operation and maintenance, with emphasis on energy savings, water efficiency, carbon dioxide emission reduction, and indoor environmental quality, within a generation. Otis rose to the top by earning four credits for pioneering initiatives in water conservation, green building education and green housekeeping. In addition, its TEDA Center "also earned all five LEED Water Efficiency credits for reducing potable water consumption and maximizing water efficiency."

XiziOtis, an Otis Elevator joint venture, contracted with highly-ranked real estate developer Long for Properties to take commercial and residential business projects to new heights in four China cities. Products cited to be included in the orders were machine roomless Gen2 systems plus "other energy-efficient gearless systems featuring permanent-magnet machines and Regen drive technology," The Otis commitment to moving efficiently in a greener-conscious world earned special recognition from the U.S. Green Building Council. Its TEDA Center office building helped Otis earn Gold-level Leadership in Energy and Environmental Design (LEED) Status.

Otis's parent company, United Technologies Corp., logged US$58.7 billion in sales in 2008 and employed 223,100 people. In early 2005, United Technologies Company purchased Lenel, a security software firm, with whom it planned to develop all-in-one systems that would monitor building, elevator, and network access and activity. By 2009, Otis accounted for approximately 20 percent of United Technologies's sales and employed 64,000 people. It also reportedly provided products and services in more than 200 countries and territories. The company maintained 1.6 million elevators and escalators worldwide.

Schindler Holding Ltd. Schindler Holding Ltd., the second largest company in the industry, began in 1874 in Lucerne, Switzerland, as a precision engineering firm. Solidly established as part of the Swiss economy a hundred years later, in the 1980s Schindler acquired several other firms involved in the vertical transportation industry. Many of these acquisitions were relatively small operations, but in 1989 Schindler acquired the entire escalator and elevator business of the Westinghouse Electric Corporation, the assets of Westinghouse's former Canadian operations. By the middle of the first decade of the 2000s, Schindler had a market presence in more than 100 countries, with 250 locations in North America alone. The company also realized a 12.8 percent increase in the number of unit orders for new installations during 2004. In 2006 Schindler Elevator purchased HAR Elevator Services and MCM Elevator, both in Canada, and Omni Lifts in Texas. Schindler reported overall sales of US$6.7 billion in 2006 with 40,385 employees. Sales in the elevator and escalator business rose 4.4 percent in 2004, reaching US$5.38 billion.

The first half of 2009 was a productive time for The Schindler Group. It experienced growth in both operating profit and profit with increases of 13 and 2 percent respectively compared to 2008 same period. The company, however, still reported being impacted by global economic and foreign exchange challenges.

As evidence of its commitment to elevate communities by helping to lift them above unfortunate circumstances, Schindler was very generous to projects benefiting children of Sichuan province. In a region hit by an earthquake in May 2008, every donation helps assist the population there. Schindler generously donated approximately US$1 million for earthquake relief and reconstruction. Funds will help build Schindler Daguan Village Kindergarten and Schindler Lixin Central Primary School. Another special effort involved establishing the "Schindler Scholarship for the Wenchuan Earthquake." The scholarship's focus is "to help talented pupils, whose education was interrupted by the earthquake."

KONE. The KONE Corporation was founded in Finland in 1920. In the 1980s it began to actively acquire smaller companies involved in the vertical transportation industry, and by 1998 KONE was firmly established on five separate continents: Europe, Asia, North and South America, and Africa. Europe clearly remained its biggest market. At the turn of the twenty-first century, KONE easily held its position as one of the three leading manufacturers of elevators worldwide. Offering an extensive variety of products and services, from planning and traffic analysis to post-installation maintenance, KONE elevators were in evidence in industrial and commercial

buildings, as well as in office buildings, hotels, and hospitals. By 2007 the company had installed about half a million elevators and escalators worldwide. In addition, KONE held service contracts for approximately 570,000 units and installed around 30,000 new elevators and escalators every year. Major agreements in the first decade of the 2000s included the company's joint ventures with China and Russia, as well as a contract to build 26 elevators reaching 97 floors for the new Trump Tower in Chicago.

KONE orders rose 10 percent in Europe (more strongly in eastern Europe), the Middle East, and Africa. In North America, order levels remained unchanged, as they were in the Asia Pacific. KONE reported 2006 net sales of US$7.1 billion. Most sales revenue came from Europe, the Middle East, and Africa, followed by the Americas and Asia Pacific. KONE expected improvement in revenue growth through improved operations in the United States, restructuring, better management of major projects, and new plants in China and the Czech Republic, with streamlined processes leading toward increases. KONE employed 33,000 people and operated 800 service centers in 50 countries in 2009. Its service base consists of approximately 650,000 elevators and escalators plus more than 270,000 automatic building doors.

KONE received a prestigious contract to modernize all of the elevators and escalators at the Los Angeles International Airport (LAX). It has been estimated 59 million people per year use LAX. "Besides serving the United States' second largest city, LAX is the western gateway for many foreign visitors. It is important that they can travel throughout the airport complex, from arrival to departure, with ease," said KONE EVP and Area director for the Americas Vance Tang. KONE plans to use "energy-saving products" for the project, scheduled for completion by July 2011.

Hitachi, Ltd. Japan's Hitachi, Ltd. was formed in 1910. Over the years it became engaged in the manufacturing of a wide variety of consumer and industrial products, including power systems, electronic and communication devices, industrial machinery, and chemical products. The company's primary territory for elevator sales in the 1990s was Asia and the Pacific Rim. Underscoring this fact, in 1996 Hitachi established three joint venture companies in China's Canton province: Hitachi Elevator (Guangzhou) Co., Ltd.; Hitachi Escalator (Guangzhou) Co., Ltd.; and Guangzhou Guangri Elevator Co., Ltd. These three new ventures were in addition to Shanghai Yungtay Engineering Co., Ltd., which had been established in 1995; Beijing Hitachi Elevator Service Co., Ltd.; and Hainan Hitachi Elevator Co., Ltd. In 2000, Hitachi reorganized all elevator and escalator businesses, pulling them in under Hitachi Ltd.'s new Building Systems Group. The business was reorganized again, and elevator systems became part of Hitachi's Power & Industrial Systems Division. Hitachi Ltd. reported 2009 revenues of $100.8 billion for the entire company with 361,796 employees. Hitachi expected its domestic and Asian business to remain healthy, but due to cost of raw materials and declining market conditions, it expected global growth to slow.

Hitachi proudly announced the delivery of 46 elevators to the Bank of China headquarters building. Approximately 30 of the elevators were the "latest-model inverter-controlled high speed elevators." The Bank of China headquarters was built in recognition of the 50th anniversary of the founding of the People's Republic of China. Its design features included entrance jambs of passenger elevators with "mirror-finished stainless steel and a cage with double-laminate glass on the inside," setting it apart from other structures.

Hitachi shared the news about its Siam-Hitachi Elevator, Co., Ltd., and the new Suvarnabhumi International Airport. The elevator company is Hitachi's elevator and escalator sales and manufacturing entity for the Southeast Asian region. It agreed to provide 95 moving sidewalks for the airport set to be built by the New Bangkok International Airport Company Limited.

Mitsubishi Electric Corp. Mitsubishi Electric Corp. was established in Japan in 1921. It manufactures a wide variety of electronic, heavy machinery, and industrial products. Its principal subsidiary in the elevator and escalator industry is Mitsubishi Elevator Co., based in Cypress, California. In the late 1990s, Mitsubishi's achievements included the world's fastest elevator and perhaps the world's most graceful escalator. In 1997 Mitsubishi married escalators to the spiral staircase, resulting in spiral escalators capable of adding their curves to modern building design. The company reported 2006 revenue figures at US$31.7 billion. The company's U.S. branch employed 3,700 people and accounted for US$2.2 billion that year.

ThyssenKrupp AG. In 1999, Germany's merger of Thyssen AG and Fried.Krupp AG Hoesch-Krupp created ThyssenKrupp. In the first decade of the 2000s, the company was one of the world's largest steel producers. Thyssen's elevator segment, named Thyssen Elevator AG, reported income of US$480 million in 2004, up almost $19 million from 2003. The most significant increases were realized in Europe and Latin America. Thyssen-Krupp as a whole reported 2006 income of US$50.6 billion, representing a growth rate of 4.5 percent from the previous year. ThyssenKrupp attributed its growth in profits to ongoing strengthening of its service business.

Thyssen's elevators are used in such well-known buildings as the Sydney Opera House, London's City Hall, and New York's Time Warner Center. In 2007 the firm employed 187,984 workers.

The global recession was taking its toll on ThyssenKrupp's business. This acknowledgement was made in the company's third-quarter report, according to ElevatorWorld.com. On the technology side, it was reported that business "remained relatively robust" for three areas. Those areas were elevators, escalators, and plants technology.

BIBLIOGRAPHY

Brugh, Scott. "Moscone Center EcoMod." Elevator World, January 2005.

Calderone, Melissa A., and Martha Harbison. "FYI: Space Elevators." Popular Science, August 2006.

"Daily Update." Elevator World, 2006. Available from www.elevator-world.com.

Daniels, Nancy. "Company Profile Hitachi Ltd." 2009. Available from www.hoovers.com.

Dorsch, Jeff. "Company Profile - KONE." 2009. Available from www.hoovers.com.

———. "Company Profile - United Technologies Corp." 2009. Available from www.hoovers.com.

"Elevators and Escalators Take Center Stage at National Building Museum." Buildings, June 2003.

Hahn, Avital Louria. "M&A Transforms The World of Security." Investment Dealers' Digest, 4 April 2005.

Hitachi. "46 Elevators Delivered to Bank of China's Headquarters in Beijing." 2009. Available from www.hitachi.co.jp.

———. "95 Moving Sidewalks for Thailand Suvarnabhumi International Airport." Available from www.hitachi.co.jp.

Hitachi Ltd. "Hitachi Announces Consolidated Financial Results for the Third Quarter of Fiscal 2004," 2 February 2005. Available from www.hitachi.com.

KONE. "About KONE." 15 June 2007. Available from www.kone.com.

———. "KONE to modernize elevators and escalators at the Los Angeles International Airport." 8 July 2009. Available from www.Kone.com.

"KONE Corporation to Establish Joint Venture in China." Nordic Business Report, 20 April 2005.

"KONE Corporation to Establish Joint Venture in Russia." Nordic Business Report, 19 April 2005.

Lindquist, Kelley. "O'Hare International Airport." Elevator World, January 2006.

Mitsubishi Electric. Annual Report, 2006. Available from www.mitsubishielectric.com.

"Mitsubishi Electric Corporate Overview." 15 June 2007. Available from www.mitsubishielectric.com.

NAEC. "About NAEC." National Association of Elevator Contractors, 2006. Available from www.naec.org.

"New Home of the Mets Taps Energy-Efficient Otis Elevators." Energy Resource, 15 May 2007.

Otis "About Otis." 15 June 2007. Available from www.otis.com.

———. "Leading developer selects energy-efficient Otis products for projects across China." 7 July 2009. Available from www.otis.worldwide.com.

————. "Otis Elevator Company recognized for leadership in environmental sustainability." 10 June 2009. Available from www.otisworldwide.com.

Otis Elevator Co. Otis Fact Sheet. Farmington, CT: March 2005. Available from www.otis.com.

Parthymuller, Peter. "Company Profile ThyssenKrupp" 2009. Available from www.hoovers.com.

————. "Company Profile Thyssen Elevator AG" 2009. Available from www.hoovers.com.

"Schindler Elevator Rolls Out FieldLink Service Handheld." Wireless News, 8 October 2004.

Schindler Holding Ltd. Annual Report, 2006. Available from www.schindler.com.

————. "Schindler: Sustantially Improved Results." 28 February 2005. Available from www.schindler.com.

Schindler Management Ltd. "A good performance in a difficult environment." 18 August 2009. Available from www.schindler.com.

"Statue of Liberty Goes Green with Soy." Resource: Engineering & Technology for a Sustainable World, December 2004.

"System Eliminates Pushbuttons and Calculates Passenger Patterns." Environmental Design & Construction, April 2007. ThyssenKrupp AG. Annual Report, 2006. Available from www.thyssenkrupp.com.

Thyssen Krupp. "ThyssenKrupp Elevator Rises to Challenge." 2009. Available from www.thyssenkruppelevator.com.

"ThyssenKrupp Introduces World's Most Technologically Advanced Elevator." PR Newswire, 17 February 2004. "ThyssenKrupp Fiscal Third Quarter." 19 August 2009. Available from www.elevator-world.com.

"United Technologies Corporation: Company Profile." Datamonitor, 17 November 2004.

SIC 3510

ENGINES AND TURBINES

NAICS CODE(S)

333611. The turbine segment of this industry manufactures turbines powered by steam, hydraulic, gas, wind, and solar energy sources, along with complete steam, gas, and hydraulic turbine generator set units, commonly known as turbogenerators. In the engine segment, the industry includes companies that produce gasoline, diesel, semi-diesel, and other internal combustion engines (ICEs) for such uses as on-site power generation; powering construction equipment; and marine applications, among others. Aircraft and automotive engines are discussed elsewhere; see also **Aircraft Manufacturing** and **Motor Vehicle Parts and Accessories.**

INDUSTRY SNAPSHOT

The most important application of turbines, and to some degree diesel and other ICEs, is to produce electricity for power consumption. There are relatively few manufacturers of turbines and turbo-generators for this purpose worldwide because production requires large amounts of capital. As a result, leading firms in the industry, such as General Electric, Volvo, Siemens, and Caterpillar, are part of the world's largest multinational corporations, many of which are highly diversified across industry lines.

While other energy sources, particularly nuclear, were declining by the mid-2000s, "green" turbines and engines powered by wind and solar energy were coming to the forefront. In 2003, the worldwide wind power industry was valued at approximately US$8 billion and expected to supply a fifth of the global energy needed by 2030, and the solar power industry was valued at US$5 billion. In the United States, renewable energy sources were less than 10 percent of the industry, but were expected to grow throughout the decade.

In September 2008, the U.S. Environmental Protection Agency (EPA) announced new emissions rules on small engines (25 horsepower or less). Gregory Lamb explained that there was a need for a transmission from two- to four- spoke engines. These standards will reduce hydrocarbon and nitrogen oxide emissions 35 percent. In addition, the EPA estimated that by 2030 reductions would result in significant health benefits. Predictions also called for fewer work and school days lost due to pollution-related illnesses.

The EPA launched new standards to be phased in according to engine type starting in 2010. It was estimated that there will be a resulting annual decrease of 600,000 tons of smog-forming volatile organic compounds and 150,000 tons of smog-forming oxides of nitrogen when the standards were fully implemented. The EPA estimated that gasoline engines were responsible for approximately 15 percent of U.S. hydrocarbon pollution. These engines are major contributors to urban ozone and predominately used in the summer. It was estimated that more than 50 million pieces of lawn and garden equipment are being used throughout the United States.

The EPA's 1–3 Tier Standards were to be phased into operation throughout the U.S. by 2008. In 2004, the EPA signed into effect the final ruling introducing Tier 4 emission standards, to be phased in from 2008 to 2015. The new level of standards require that emissions of PM and NOx be further reduced from the previous levels by 90 percent. This can be achieved through the use of control technologies, including advanced exhaust gas after-treatment—similar to those required in the 2007–2010 standards for highway engines.

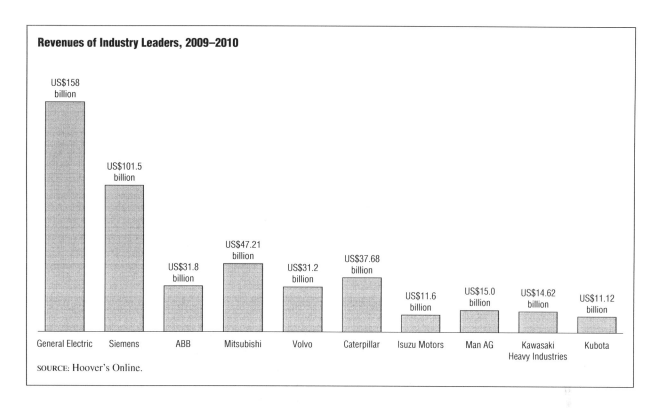

Revenues of Industry Leaders, 2009–2010

SOURCE: Hoover's Online.

ORGANIZATION AND STRUCTURE

Most turbines and turbo-generators are made to order, custom-designed to accommodate the specific requirements of a power plant. Equipment is produced in specialized factories that are generally erected and assembled at the power plant sites. While turbines have relatively few parts, their production tolerances—the allowable variations from their original production and assembly specifications—are exacting.

Trade Structure. One of the important distinctions between the United States and both Japan and Europe is the decentralized nature of electricity production in the United States. In Japan and Europe, power equipment manufacturers, architects, construction firms, utilities managers, and governments typically develop projects on a partnership basis. The U.S. Department of Commerce has argued that whatever the merits might be for the domestic operations of U.S. firms, the situation puts them at a decided disadvantage in penetrating the more mediated Japanese and European markets.

The arrangement is coordinated under the International Electrical Association (IEA), an export cartel formed in the 1920s by producers of power generation equipment. The U.S. Justice Department compelled U.S. producers to withdraw from the IEA in the 1930s. Japanese producers were admitted as special members of the IEA in the 1960s. Not surprisingly, the IEA includes European and Japanese manufacturers of power-generating equipment exclusively. The U.S. Department of Commerce contends that the IEA's system of price setting and market allocation has given European and Japanese producers a significant competitive advantage in the markets of the developed countries.

In an effort to improve their competitiveness, U.S. manufacturers have focused on increasing sales to developing countries and on entering into joint ventures with Japanese and European firms. At the same time, U.S. manufacturers have focused research and development efforts on:

- smaller plants;

- combined-cycle gas and steam turbines;

- pumped-storage hydroelectric systems;

- high-temperature gas turbines, especially their materials and coatings; and

- cogeneration, which harnesses the excess heat or steam produced in industrial processes to make more energy available for consumption at a commercial or industrial site.

Continuing deregulation of U.S. electric utilities in the early 2000s prompted U.S. producers to seek markets overseas, particularly in China and elsewhere in Asia. The European Union (E.U.) market was a difficult one for U.S. producers to penetrate because Europe's nationalized electric utilities most often favor European producers. However, deregulation of electricity markets in some E.U. countries could provide an opportunity for U.S. turbine producers to further develop small combined-cycle or cogeneration facilities. The best market prospects for U.S. producers in the decade were in Germany, Italy, Spain, and the United Kingdom.

Turbine Trade Groups. Several large trade organizations serve the turbine industry. The International Gas Turbine Institute (IGTI) of the American Society of Mechanical Engineers is based in Atlanta, Georgia, and publishes the *Global Gas Turbine News.* The Paris-based International Conference on Large High Voltage Electric Systems was founded in 1921, and publishes the bimonthly *Electra* in English and French. Other associations serving the industry include the European Commission of Manufacturers of Electrical Installation Equipment and the European Committee of Manufacturers of Electrical Machines and Power Electronics, both headquartered in Paris. The latter organization seeks to promote members' interests in accordance with trade agreements associated with the E.U.

Engine Trade Groups. The European Committee of Associations of Manufacturers of Internal Combustion Engines was founded in 1963 and is based in Zoetermeer, the Netherlands. The organization was established to represent the interests of European diesel engine producers in Europe's then emerging collective market. The engine industry is also served by the International Council on Combustion Engines, founded in 1951 and based in Paris. The organization promotes the advancement of technical knowledge regarding internal combustion engines in various ways, including publishing a number of technical papers as part of its biennial *Congress Proceedings.*

BACKGROUND AND DEVELOPMENT

Turbines convert fluid motion into rotary motion, which is harnessed to perform a wide range of work, most notably the production of electricity. The principal types of turbines are defined by the energy source driving their blades. The most important in terms of market share are steam, water, and gas. Turbines generally consist of a number of blades or fins attached to a rotor so the rotor spins as steam, water, or gas is forced past the blades or fins. Steam turbines may be powered by fossil fuels or nuclear energy. Water turbines are most widely used in hydroelectric dams. According to figures published by the U.S. Energy Information Administration (EIA), for all countries of the world in 1995, petroleum-based sources accounted for 61.8 percent of electricity produced, nuclear-fueled steam for 16.6 percent, and renewable sources (mostly hydroelectric) for 21.2 percent. The EIA predicted that by 2015 fossil fuels will expand to 67.8 percent of world electricity generation, while nuclear fuel will decline to 10.6 percent and renewable energy sources will remain largely unchanged at 21.5 percent. Natural gas will be the fastest-growing fossil fuel source for electrical power generation.

The majority of electrical power is produced by steam turbines from heat generated by fossil fuels or nuclear power. Steam turbines have the capacity to generate a large amount of electrical power in a small space—more than 1.3 million kilowatts from a single rotor. The first steam turbines that had successful commercial application were developed by American William Avery in the 1830s. About 50 steam turbines of Avery's design were used in sawmills and cotton gins. Although as efficient as piston-driven steam engines in converting fuel to mechanical power, these early steam turbines gradually fell out of use due to their noise and frequent need for repair.

By the early twentieth century, generators driven by steam turbines were the most important producers of electricity in the world. Economies of scale were important in steam turbines, leading to increasingly larger units. By the 1940s, single-turbine units were capable of producing 100,000 kilowatts. Large steam turbines also were important as ship engines. The *Lusitania,* a British ship later made famous when it was torpedoed and sank during World War I, and its twin the *Mauritania,* launched in 1906, were driven by fossil-fueled steam turbines generating 68,000 horsepower. Nuclear-fueled military ships in the 1990s were also driven by steam turbines.

Although generally not classified as such, gas turbines are a form of internal combustion engine, with a turbine rather than a piston being driven by a controlled explosion. Gas turbines have an advantage over piston internal combustion engines in that they are able to create more power in less space. Gas turbines consist of a compressor, a combustion chamber, and the turbine itself. Industrial gas turbines are used to drive power generators, pumps, or propellers.

Gas turbines played an increasingly important role in generating power in medium-size plants and, in the early 2000s, in some of the world's largest new power plants. Since water for steam turbines requires several hours to heat, gas turbines provide a compact means to meet the demands of peak-hour production with low initial cost. Gas-fired plants accounted for only 8 percent of U.S. electricity capacity in the mid-1980s, but by the beginning of 2000 that figure had increased to nearly 22 percent. Gas turbine-generator manufacturers in the early 2000s included AEG-Kanis, Asea Brown Boveri, General Electric, Mitsubishi, Siemens, and Thomassen. (By 2000, one major turbine manufacturer, Westinghouse Electric Corporation, had been acquired by Germany's Siemens AG.)

The use of gas turbines for producing electrical power expanded with the development of gas/steam turbine-generators, also known as combined cycle or combined-heat-and-power (CHP) systems. These systems make use of the heat generated by gas turbines to provide heat for steam turbines with substantially greater efficiency than pure gas turbines. Combined cycle power is viable because exhaust gases from gas turbines are relatively clean and hot, ranging from 750 to 1,000 degrees Fahrenheit. Combined cycle power plants became increasingly viable following the oil crises of the 1970s and in the face of opposition to nuclear-fueled power production; this format had gained wider acceptance by 2000. Combined cycle plants are relatively environmentally friendly, emitting no ash and little air pollution.

By the year 2000, combined cycle power plants represented most of the market volume for power generation equipment in the United States. Gas turbine combined cycle plants had achieved 55 percent efficiency levels, with the prospects of reaching 60 percent thermal efficiency later in the early 2000s.

In terms of the number of steam turbines produced in 1990, the leading countries were Austria with 1,337, France with 823, the Commonwealth of Independent States (CIS) with 428, Germany with 426, and Japan with 406. In terms of share of world exports by U.S. dollar value, the leading countries in 1992 were Japan with 25.8 percent, Germany with 19.5 percent, the United States with 15.9 percent, England with 6.5 percent, and France/Monaco with 6.3 percent. The total value of world exports was US$2.1 billion in 1992. Among the Organization for Economic Cooperation and Development (OECD) countries in 1999, the largest producers of nuclear-fueled steam electricity were the United States with 777,885 gig watt hours, France with 394,244, Japan with 316,616, Germany with 170,004, and England with 96,281.

Hydraulic turbine production in 1990 was led by France with 3,763, the Czech Republic with 112, Romania with 41, and Japan with 28. The CIS was also a significant producer in 1990 in terms of kilowatt capacity. Among OECD countries, in 1999 the largest producers of hydroelectricity were the United States with 318,619 gig watt hours, Japan with 95,577, France with 77,082, Italy with 51,777, and Germany with 23,402.

Ranked by total world gas turbine exports, the leading countries in 1992 were the United States with 25.4 percent, Britain with 18.2 percent, Canada with 12.3 percent, Germany with 6.9 percent, and Japan with 6.8 percent. That year, the total value of world exports was US$3.5 billion.

Among makers of nonautomotive diesel engines as of 1991, the top countries were India with 1.6 million, Japan with 1.1 million, Germany with 228,132, and the United States with 184,245. In terms of the number of other nonautomotive internal combustion engines produced, the leading countries in 1992 were the United

States with 18.2 million, Japan with 5.9 million, Romania with 110,000, Poland with 105,000, and Germany with 36,000.

Export market share for miscellaneous internal combustion engines in the early 1990s was divided among Japan with 19.5 percent, the United States with 16.7 percent, Germany with 16.4 percent, France/Monaco with 8.9 percent, and Britain with 7.3 percent. Total value of world exports was US$40 billion in 1992.

Water turbines are essentially updated, efficient versions of waterwheels, which were used for millennia. The first commercially successful water turbine design was developed by Frenchman Benoit Fourneyron (1802–1867) in the 1820s. More than 100 such turbines were eventually installed worldwide. These turbines were, however, costly to construct, physically unstable, and difficult to control for speed of rotation. They were eventually supplanted by the designs, developed in the 1830s, of American James Francis. Francis-type turbines remained one of the key turbine types used in contemporary applications. Water turbines were in widespread use by the mid-nineteenth century, primarily in powering saw and textile mills, though they were soon supplanted in these applications by steam engines.

The first use of water turbines to generate electricity on a commercial basis came in 1882, when a 12.5 kilowatt station in Wisconsin provided power to light two paper mills. The use of hydroelectric power grew rapidly thereafter, with the first 100,000-kilowatt installations built in the 1930s. From the 1940s to the early 1970s, a large number of small hydroelectric stations, most with less than 1,000 kilowatt capacity, were shut down due to their relatively high cost. Meanwhile, from the 1950s to the late 1980s, the production capacity of typical water turbine generators doubled, from 150,000 to 300,000 kilowatts, with the largest of modern units capable of producing 750,000 kilowatts.

Economic viability of hydroelectric production was determined not only by direct costs of energy production, but also by the costs of acquiring land and constructing reservoirs. The latter costs typically accounted for about half of the initial outlay for a project. In the Pacific Northwest and Rocky Mountain regions of the United States, hydroelectric power enjoyed a cost advantage over electricity produced by fossil fuels, partly because of the combined function of hydroelectric facilities, which also served to control floods and store water for municipal water systems and rural irrigation.

The one key problem with water turbines was the inability to store large amounts of electricity. Another was that water turbines generally were much less efficient during off-peak production times, such as at night or on weekends. This problem was addressed by pumping water into a second, high-level reservoir during off hours for use during peak hours. This was accomplished by using reversible turbines, which served as pumps during off hours, and reversible generators, which served as electrical motors to drive turbines operating in reverse. In 2001, there were approximately 18,000 megawatts of this type of generating capacity, called "pumped storage" hydroelectric capacity, in the United States.

The vast majority of hydroelectric facilities are situated on rivers, but hydropower stations driven by tidal flows are also feasible along ocean coasts with high tides. A 240,000-kilowatt capacity plant with 24 water turbines operated on the Brittany coast in France, while the Commonwealth of Independent States built a similar plant on its eastern coast.

The largest producers of hydroelectric power were the United States, Russia, Brazil, and Canada. In Brazil, 92 percent of generating capacity was supplied by hydropower in 1997. In 2001, hydroelectric stations provided at least 10 percent of the electricity in the United States. However, the potential for increasing this share was limited, since about three-fourths of the potential capacity for hydroelectric production in the contiguous United States had been tapped. In fact, seven states— Washington, California, Oregon, New York, Tennessee, South Carolina, and Virginia—represented about 64 percent of all U.S. hydroelectric capacity in the late 1990s. Much untapped potential, however, remained in Alaska, northern Canada, the former Soviet Union, and parts of Africa, South America, and the Himalayan region. China also was aggressively developing its hydroelectric resources, but proposed hydroelectric stations in Malaysia and India were abandoned in the late 1990s because of protests by environmental groups. Canada projected a one-third increase in its hydroelectric capacity by 2020, with the lion's share expected to be added after 2010. Plans for large-scale hydro dams in Canada largely have been abandoned; future projects in Canada will be limited to 500 megawatts.

One major issue affecting hydroelectric power in the early 2000s in the United States was the expiration of operating licenses for many of the country's hydroelectric stations. According to the Federal Energy Regulatory Commission, more than 35 hydro operating licenses were scheduled to expire in the 1990s, while an additional 69 operating licenses were scheduled to expire in 2000 and 2001. The greatest amount of authorized generating capacity up for relicensing was expected to occur in 2007. All told, the Energy Information Administration reported that the expiring licenses between 1995 and 2010 accounted for more than 24 gigawatts of generating capacity, or just about half of current non-federal hydro capacity.

A continuing issue for the hydroelectric industry in the United States was fish kills, particularly salmon and steelhead trout. These fish attempt to swim upstream, from the sea to the river, while spawning. However, when a hydroelectric station is along their path, the fish can get caught in the turbine blades. This is particularly problematic in Washington's Columbia River Basin in the Pacific Northwest. Salmon and steelhead runs there declined from rates of 11 to 16 million fish a year in pre-Colonial times to 2 million or fewer fish in the late 1990s.

Wind-powered generators offer an increasingly viable alternative power source. Windpower often is cited as the fastest-growing form of renewable energy, enjoying a 28 percent increase in worldwide capacity in 2000. Single, giant windmills capable of providing electricity to several thousand homes were operating in 2001 in some areas of the United States. As the cost of other sources of energy keeps escalating and the resources being depleted, wind-powered energy is continuing to grow in popularity.According to the Global Wind Energy Council (GWEC), wind could meet 12 percent of global power needs by 2020, and up to 22 percent by 2030.In a report dated October 2010, the GWEC and Greenpeace International affirm that wind power could play a significant role in satisfying the world's increasing power demand, while at the same time achieving significant greenhouse emission reductions.The 1,000 gig watt of wind power capacity projected to be installed by 2020 would save as much as 1.5 billion tons of CO_2 annually.

With the 1996 bankruptcy of the U.S. manufacturer Kenetech, Denmark, became the world's largest producer of wind turbines, accounting for 60 percent of the market, according to the Danish Wind Turbine Manufacturers Association. Denmark has a wind power capacity of 750 megawatts, or 5 percent of Denmark's electricity. Vestas of Denmark was the world's largest windmill constructor, with 21 percent of global market share. However, as the surge to get in on the industry grows, so does the competition. As of 2009, Vestas market share had decreased from 28 percent in 2007 to 12.5 percent. In late 2008, Vestas expanded their production in both Colorado and Oregon, and in October 2010, announced plans to close factories in Scandinavia which resulted in the loss of 3,000 jobs.

Since the mid-1980s, the cost of producing electricity with windmills has dropped more than fourfold, bringing wind power on a par with power produced using oil, coal, and natural gas. However, windmills had the disadvantages of being noisy and dangerous to birds. When properly situated, however, it is possible to mitigate these problems.

In 1992, the U.S. Department of Energy and the Electric Power Research Institute (EPRI) implemented a program to increase the commercial viability of wind power turbines by evaluating advanced turbines developed by U.S. electric companies. The first was a 6-megawatt facility in Fort Davis, Texas, which used 12 550-kilowatt wind turbines, while the second, with 11 550-kilowatt turbines, began operating in Searsburg, Vermont, in 1997. Three 750-kilowatt wind turbines were installed in Algona, Texas, prior to 2000, while other wind turbine projects were on tap for Nebraska, Texas, Oklahoma, New York, Wisconsin, and Alaska.

Market conditions in the United States and many industrialized nations moved from decent in the mid-1990s, when they were limited in part by overcapacity and by conservation and efficiency gains, to vibrant at the turn of the century. Demand in Asia, particularly China and India, offered significant growth opportunities. The power generation market, especially the gas turbine sector, enjoyed a growth pattern described as an "elongated bubble." Turbine shipments enjoyed a period of robust growth in the mid- to late 1990s, which continued through 2001, with North America constituting a hotbed for both gas turbines and internal combustion engines.

An anticipated return to the slow growth of earlier decades did not materialize. Nevertheless, industry experts doubted that growth could continue at the healthy pace of the period from 1995 to 2001. According to a Fredonia Group study, world turbine demand was expected to continue to increase through the early 2000s, thanks to strong demand for new and upgraded generating capacity in both developed and developing countries. Competition for these markets has been fierce as large Western turbine manufacturers faced stiff competition from turbine producers in Eastern Europe, China, and Russia. Consequently, many producers heavily discounted prices of their older turbine technologies. From 1998 to 2001, the United States led a surge in turbine orders created by capacity expansion and the upgrading of turbines necessary for combined cycle power plants. In addition, privatization and deregulation of electric power generating systems, along with the realities of power shortages and high electricity costs, ensured that U.S. orders of large turbine units will continue to increase, although somewhat more slowly than before.

The global picture for diesel, dual-fuel, and natural gas ICEs remained favorable, reflecting buyers' growing concerns about power quality and availability and the economic losses involved in power outages (most of these shipments constitute additions to diesel or other fuel-powered standby service). Additionally, concerns about energy shortages promoted purchases of diesel and natural gas engines for both standby and continuous service.

Relatively strong demand for turbines in the few years before 2000 prompted turbine producers around

the world to rush turbines to the market before all potential problems were identified, according to a report from *The Wall Street Journal Europe*. New turbines from U.S.-based General Electric Co. and Europe's GEC-Alsthom had to be temporarily shut down because the bolts inside cracked. In addition, Siemens AG's new turbine, adapted from ring burner jet engine technology, experienced excessive vibrations, while Asea Brown Boveri's turbines had portions of their heatshields come loose during operation.

As of the late 1990s, 429 nuclear reactors were in operation globally, producing more than 345 billion watts (or gigawatts) of electricity, generating about 7 percent of the world's electricity. As of 2001, 30 nuclear reactors were under construction, primarily in developing and industrialized Asia. Combined, these were expected to produce an additional 22 gigawatts. However, the industry continued to be hindered by the safety and environmental problems of nuclear power plants, as demonstrated by the 1979 accident at the Three Mile Island plant in Middletown, Pennsylvania, and by the 1986 disaster at Chernobyl in Ukraine, Soviet Union. No new U.S. nuclear plants were built in the last quarter of the twentieth century, and three reactors were closed down prematurely in the late 1990s, reducing the number of operating reactors in the United States to 104 as of 2001. Thus, nuclear never generated more than 20 percent of U.S. electricity, whereas in 2001, France produced 78 percent of its electricity via fission reactors; Belgium, 62 percent; and Lithuania, 82 percent. These three were the world's leaders in domestic nuclear power generation. However, U.S. energy suppliers were beginning to plan new nuclear power plants in Michigan and Florida in mid-2008.

According to the International Energy Agency, though France is a world leader in nuclear power, design flaws and public complaints about costs and unreliable service have nearly brought its construction of reactors to a halt. With the exception of two new reactors added in the late 1990s, no further French nuclear capacity has been announced, and in Italy, all nuclear reactors were shut down. Authorities in Sweden debated over a timetable to do the same and the Swedish government eventually voted to retire two of the country's 12 operating units, one in 1998 and one in 2001. Construction of reactors was also halted in Germany, and Finland canceled plans for the construction of what would have been its only nuclear reactor.

Not surprisingly, opportunities for growth in the nuclear power industry in the late 1990s and beyond were limited to areas outside Western Europe and North America. At the end of 1996, 18 nuclear units were under construction in developing Asia. Countries in developing and industrialized Asia with operating nuclear plants at the turn of the century included China, Taiwan, India, Pakistan, and South Korea, with units scheduled to become operational in North Korea in 2020. In industrialized Asia, Japan's nuclear capacity was expected to increase by 11 units to a total of 12.5 gig watts. In the late 2000s, Iran and Japan had nuclear power plants going online.

Denis Gregory shared the story of how communities and families were split about the decision whether to support wind turbine's future in Australia. While some property owners agreed to allow turbines on their farms, others vehemently opposed related plans. Those on the opposing side believed that high turbines would dramatically impact their lifestyles, landscapes and land values. Some charges included that the turbines killed birds, operated inefficiently and did not store the power they generated. The related issues reportedly divided many families. John McGrath felt betrayed by family members who agreed to have turbines placed on their farms before consulting him. Furthermore, McGrath revealed that his mother was "dead against these things and her brother, my uncle, has been promoting them."

CURRENT CONDITIONS

By 2004, the gas turbine market was worth $67 billion and projected to increase 7 percent per year through 2007 to reach the $77 billion mark. The strong growth, however, could not equal the gains of the 1998 to 2001 period. In 2001, global gas turbine orders increased 55 percent in terms of capacity and 13 percent in terms of number of units. Specifically, capacity increased 41,390 megawatts to 117,240 megawatts, and the number of units increased from 1,203 to 1,357. According to *Diesel and Gas Turbine Worldwide,* North America is still the most popular destination of these turbines, accounting for 67 percent of the total 1,357 units ordered. In the combined output ranges of 30 to 180 megawatts, North America received 76 percent of these turbines. South America saw an increase of 204 percent in large gas turbines to be located there, rising from 21 units in 2000 to 64 units in 2001. However, orders for Western Europe declined nearly 32 percent. In a report by *PRLog*, thermal energy is still the most dominant energy source globally for electricity.In 2000, the cumulative installed capacity was at 2.5 million megawatts.According to the report, that number was expected to reach 3.7 million megawatts by 2009, representing a combined annual growth rate of 3.9 percent. It was predicted that the trend will continue with a total of 5 million megawatts by 2020.

As with turbines, orders for diesel, dual-fuel, and natural gas ICEs (also known as reciprocating engines) increased substantially in 2001, with units ordered up 68

percent to 10,795 and total output up 39 percent to 16,263 megawatts. Major growth continues in North America, with orders increasing 66 percent to 5,051 units. Western Europe's orders increased significantly as well, up 47 percent to 826 units. There also was a healthy increase of 111 percent in combined order activity throughout the Middle East, the Far East, and Central Asia. South America posted an astounding 126 percent increase in the number of orders—from 146 units to 330 units.

A number of nuclear reactors in operation in the United States faced possible shutdowns for technical and economic reasons. This early retirement trend was expected to continue to 2020, eliminating 25 percent of the generating capacity that existed at the beginning of the twenty-first century. Other countries with more economical options for power generation also were expected to begin letting their nuclear capacity lapse, according to the Energy Information Administration. Experts forecast world nuclear generation capacity of 172 gigawatts in 2020, a more than 50 percent decline from a peak of 367 gigawatts. In Western Europe, only Turkey and France project increases in nuclear capacity by 2020; eight other European countries expect their total nuclear capacity to decrease because of reactor retirements.

As of the mid-2000s, wind and solar power generation was on the rise. In 2003, the worldwide wind power industry was valued at approximately US$8 billion and was expected to hit US$16 billion by 2007. GE Energy had 13 percent of the wind turbine market share worldwide in 2003. The solar power industry was valued at US$5 billion that year, of which the United States had US$700 million of the market share. As of 2003, most of the solar energy power generation market came for photovoltaic panels.

By 2004, wind power was the fastest growing segment in the energy generation industry, with annual 20 percent increases predicted through 2008. The world's main wind energy markets were, in order of estimated megawatt production, Germany, the United States, Denmark, Spain, India, the Netherlands, Italy, the United Kingdom, China, and Sweden. According to the European Wind Energy Association, wind capacity nearly doubled in 2001, with the largest percentage increases for Germany and Spain. Germany was the fastest-growing market for wind generation in Western Europe, while India was second to Germany in terms of capacity. Denmark, with 20 percent of its energy wind-generated in 2003, expected large gains in wind capacity by the early 2000s, as did the United Kingdom. In addition, Greece had the potential to develop an estimated 100 megawatts of wind capacity in a few years. Before 2000, 13 wind farms had been constructed in the Greek Islands with a combined capacity of 22 megawatts. In Italy, 120 megawatts of wind capacity were planned, and Finland planned 100 megawatts of wind capacity by 2005. General Electric acquired its wind turbine segment from Enron in 2002, and by the following year was the second largest company in wind power worldwide.

YLE News reported that the Finnish government had announced plans to build several wind power plants that would generate approximately 2,000 megawatts of wind power by 2020. An important directive for the plan was to develop wind parks in key catchment areas along the coast and near the sea. This proposal was a part of government's climate and energy strategy.

Solar energy markets also were beginning to see a surge in the 2000s. Industry leader G.E., for example, acquired AstroPower Inc., the largest solar equipment company in the United States, in 2004 for US$15 million. Unlike wind power generation, however, solar technology has been a stagnant technology, with little advancement in more than 30 years, making it somewhat of a new technology with high cost and relatively low success. Photovoltaic panels, the leading product of solar energy conversion, were successful at converting only 15 percent of solar energy to useable power. In addition, installation of photovoltaic panels costs two to four times more than installation of a mid-sized wind turbine.

RESEARCH AND TECHNOLOGY

The industry has sought to implement cogeneration systems, which maximize the energy derived from a source fuel by harnessing both mechanical and thermal energy to serve various needs. The use of cogeneration systems grew rapidly in the last few decades of the twentieth century. Cogeneration is used in a number of applications outside traditional electric power utility plants, including paper production and oil refining. Paper mills use steam to cook and dry paper pulp. This steam is then captured by turbines that drive generators to fulfill the electrical requirements of the mill. Similarly, oil refineries used steam heat to break down crude oil into its refined components. Electrical power was then generated from the steam to drive refinery pumps. Cogeneration systems fueled by natural gas were particularly promising on both cost and environmental grounds.

The U.S. Office of Technology Assessment stated that gas turbine cogeneration systems used 25 percent less fuel energy than oil- or coal-fueled cogeneration systems and produced far less pollution. Natural gas also was widely available and low in cost compared to other fuels. The U.S. National Energy Technology Center (NETL) of the U.S. Department of Energy runs clean-energy research programs, including the Strategic Center for Natural Gas High Efficiency Engines and Turbines

(HEET). A goal of the HEET program is to develop coal-fueled, ultra-high efficiency, zero emissions power modules for visionary twenty-first century applications. HEET currently funds a Clean Energy System (CES) project that involves a zero-emission rocket engine used on NASA's space shuttles. Ongoing programs at CES in the early 2000s initially tested the gas generator at a 10 megawatt output level.

General Electric has demonstrated the feasibility of using biomass fuel—gas derived from wood chips and other organic material—to drive gas-turbine electric generating systems. Previously, natural gas, heating oil, and gasified coal were the only viable fuels for gas turbines. General Electric speculated that electricity generated from biomass fuel would be cost competitive with fossil fuels, since the expensive pollution-abatement equipment required in order to use the fossil fuels was not necessary. The firm acknowledged that gas-turbine power generation plants using biomass fuels would be small, in the 15 to 50 megawatt range. General Electric's research in biomass fuels was part of its overall effort to make gas turbines the predominant method of generating electricity.

Research and development in the production of diesel engines focused on minimizing noxious emissions and improving fuel efficiency, resulting in substantial improvements in the few decades before 2000. The U.K. firm Ricardo Consulting Engineers has experimented with the viability of recycling diesel engine exhaust (exhaust gas recirculation and catalytic cleaning had been more thoroughly developed for gasoline ICEs). In response to the U.S. Clean Air Act's diesel emission requirements, the Japanese firm Nippon Shokubai Co. Ltd. entered into a joint venture with the German firm Degussa AG to produce a catalyst that cleaned diesel exhaust.

In 1992, Volvo Truck of Sweden announced the development of the world's first turbocharger-supercharger diesel truck engine, which operated the supercharger up to 1,650 rpm and the turbocharger above 1,500 rpm. The hybrid design enabled the engine to produce low levels of pollutants at all engine speeds. Saab-Scania of Sweden introduced the first mass-produced turbo-supercharger diesel engine in 1994. That same year, Japan's Hino Motors Ltd. announced the development of a diesel engine with record fuel efficiency that was up to 10 percent greater than the next most efficient diesel engines. Hino's engine featured graphite-containing cast-iron pistons and a redesigned turbocharger. In 1993, Hino introduced a diesel-electric hybrid engine, which used a multifunction electric generator-motor to reduce pollution.

Diesel emissions also could be slightly reduced by the use of vegetable oil fuels, such as those derived from rapeseed. The Federal Environment Office of Germany released a report in 1993 indicating that rapeseed oil fuel could reduce greenhouse gas emissions 0.5 to 0.7 percent. Since the German government hoped to reduce emissions 25 percent by 2005, the office advocated research and development in new engine designs rather than in the use of biodiesel fuels. Nonetheless, the commercialization of biodiesel fuels in Europe was expected to continue.

In addition, the industry continued to explore alternatives to ICEs, such as fuel cells, gas turbines, and electric motors. ICEs' thermal efficiency is poor—they use only 15 percent of the energy in a gallon of gasoline or diesel fuel. Diesel engines, it was hoped, would ultimately reach 45 percent thermal efficiency. Some industry observers, however, were skeptical that any viable alternatives would arise to replace ICEs on a large scale before the middle of the new century.

In the late 1990s, scientists were exploring the idea of using jet and rocket engines—specifically axial compression ram engines—for power generation with operational efficiencies of 52 percent, according to *Mechanical Engineering Power*. Because the engine was compact, it was perceived as perfect for developing countries. It was also projected to be ideal for use in distributed generation, when small power plants are located closer to a center of population than central-station baseload generating plants that were common. The fuel in an axial compression ram engine burns cleaner than in a gas turbine, and the engine is capable of burning natural gas, biogas, No. 2 diesel, and hydrogen, among other fuels. The engine has two main components: the ramjet engine and a synchronous generator that connects to the engines and locks it into a speed. Full production of the engines was expected to begin in 1999.

While wind power generation continued to be more expensive than non-renewable sources in the mid-2000s, new turbine designs were in development. The Wind Turbine Co. of Washington was continuing more than a decade of research and development (R&D) on a two-blade downwind turbine, to replace the typical three-blade wind-facing turbine. If viable, the new turbines would shave 25 percent off the cost of construction, bringing the cost of wind technology in line with non-renewable sources. Another potential development in renewable energy was in cascading closed loop cycle (CCLC) technology. CCLC, which was in the process of being patented in 2004, allowed for generation of power from the waste heat produced by most industries. San Antonio-based GCK Technology developed a Gorlov helical turbine in 2005 that was designed to provide inexhaustible energy from the flowing water of ocean and tidal currents, rivers, small dams, hydro power dams, and industrial plant discharges.

ASME International Gas Turbine Institute Chair Reza S. Abhari discussed the "need to improve the efficiency of turbomachinery components." Abhari viewed this as being essential in order to reduce carbon dioxide emission from aircraft engines. The outcome was expected to possibly involve sequestration and storage of carbon dioxide.

ChangeWave's survey of the alternative energy industry indicated that solar power had "experienced the most rapid growth" from August 2007 to August 2008. Employees of 196 alternative energy sectors completed the survey. Solar power was expected to continue at a rapid rate of growth through 2010.

Hydrogen Engine Center (HEC) announced progress in its efforts to have HEC's power generation systems provide clean power utilizing the hydrogen-based-byproduct fuel that was produced by Startech Environmental Corp. During the week of September 1, 2008, the OXX Power power generation system at Startech's demonstration facilities was commissioned by HEC. This made it possible to observe how the Startech-Hec system worked to produce clean power. HEC projected that it will be possible to reach levels ranging from 5 KW to 1 MW depending on the size of the unit and type of fuel being used.

INDUSTRY LEADERS

General Electric. General Electric (G.E.) is the market leader in the design, manufacture, and servicing of turbines and generators, whether gas, steam, or hydroelectric. G.E.'s gas turbines for marine and industrial applications began with the company's highly successful jet engine programs. G.E.'s Energy division, formerly the Power Systems (GEPS) division, based in Atlanta, Georgia, made the turbines. One of GE's biggest divisions, it was ranked number one among engine/turbine manufacturers, with customers in 119 countries. GE Energy also provides nuclear fuels and services. G.E.'s Italian manufacturing affiliate, Nuovo Pignone, produces turbines and related equipment.General Electric reported revenue of US$158 billion in 2009, with a collective workforce of 304,000 in all its branches worldwide.

Siemens. Siemens AG, headquartered in Munich, Germany, was ranked second in the industry and was one of Germany's largest industrial concerns. Siemens, like G.E., was a large and powerful multinational company with many divisions. Total 2009 revenue from all divisions was nearly US$101.5 billion. Siemens acquired Westinghouse's fossil fuel power plant business in 1998, cementing its position as the market's number two supplier worldwide, with more than 90 percent of its orders coming from outside Germany. By 2001, Siemens had merged its nuclear and hydroelectric power generation activities into two joint ventures in which the company held minority stakes. Both new companies were number one worldwide in power generation sales for nuclear and hydroelectric. After streamlining its operations, Siemens reported 420,800 employees in over 190 countries worldwide.

ABB. Third-ranked ABB Group, headquartered in Baden, Switzerland, is 50 percent-owned by holding company ABB Brown Boveri Ltd. The other 50 percent of the ABB Group is held by Sweden-based Asea AB. The ABB Group is composed of 1,300 companies in over 100 countries worldwide that are involved in the production of equipment for power generation, transmission, and distribution. The largest firm in the ABB Group is Asea Brown Boveri AG, based in Mannheim, Germany. An ABB company developed the first commercially successful gas turbine, which was used for oil refining. In the 1990s, the firm developed a gas turbine designed to compete directly with highly successful units produced by GE since 1989. However, in 2001 ABB divested its share of ABB Alstom Power to Alstom of France, finalizing the sale of its nuclear activities and completing its exit from the large-scale power generation field. The company launched a new business to focus on small scale alternative energy solutions, including wind power, combined heat and power plants, microturbines, and fuel cells. ABB was a leading wind turbine generator supplier. More than 8,000 ABB generators, from a single unit to large windparks, operate worldwide. The company reported US$31.8 billion in 2009 revenue with 117,000 employees.

Mitsubishi. Mitsubishi Heavy Industries Ltd. (MHI), headquartered in Tokyo and ranked fourth in the turbines and engines industry, was established in 1917. Its power systems division is the gas and turbine maker of Mitsubishi, a highly diversified company that also produces automobiles, consumer electronics, planes, ships, farm machinery, and air-conditioning units. MHI reaped its share of growing worldwide demand for gas turbines in the late 1990s and early 2000s. The company received orders for gas turbine combined cycle thermal power plants from Mexico, the United States, Azerbaijan, and Taiwan, and secured an order for a geothermal plant in Kenya. The total value of new orders for the power systems division in 2001 was US$5.9 billion. Total sales in 2007 reached nearly US$38.1 billion, all but 10 percent of which came from within Japan. By 2008 the company had 63,500 employees.

Volvo AB. Volvo AB, the largest industrial firm in Scandinavia and fifth-ranked in the industry, is headquartered in Göteborg, Sweden. In all of its commercial areas—marine and industrial power systems, construction

equipment, trucks, buses, and aeronautics—its global presence is significant. Volvo Penta is the company division that produces its marine and industrial engines, with production facilities in the European Union, the United States, and Brazil. In the late 1990s, Volvo Penta's expanded product range, especially in new marine diesel engines, helped maintain strong sales. In 1997, marine and industrial engines accounted for 7.9 percent of Volvo AB's SEK183.6 billion in sales. In 2001, Penta reported an increase of 50 percent in industrial engine orders. Penta's net sales that year totaled SEK7.4 billion, and operating income reached a record SEK658 million. Total 2009 revenues were US$31.2 billion with 90,210 employees.

Caterpillar. Based in Peoria, Illinois, Caterpillar Inc. is a legendary U.S. company with total 2010 sales of US$37.68 billion and 93,813 employees. In the early 2000s, robust demand worldwide for electric power generation resulted in higher sales in North America, the Asia-Pacific region, and Europe, which helped offset Caterpillar's lower sales in South America. The firm's engines were used in semi-trailer trucks, locomotives, and construction machinery. In 1997, Caterpillar announced its intention to acquire Perkins Engines of the United Kingdom, a manufacturer of small and medium diesel engines, which posted sales of US$1.1 billion in 1996. The sale price was US$1.33 billion in cash. Caterpillar said the combination of the two companies created the world's largest full-line producer of reciprocating and turbine engines.

Isuzu Motors Ltd. Established in 1937, Tokyo-based Isuzu Motors Ltd. produced cars, light trucks, trucks, and diesel engines, especially in cooperation with U.S.-based General Motors (G.M.). Engine parts and components accounted for US$3.9 billion of the company's sales in 1997. In the late 1990s, Isuzu set up a manufacturing base for its small diesel engines in Poland. In early 2001, Isuzu aimed to become the world's leading producer of diesel engines, with a production volume targeted at 1.8 million units by 2005. In July 2000, the joint venture between Isuzu and G.M. began production of diesel engines for G.M. full-size pickup trucks. The company reported 2010 revenues of US$11.6 billion and 7,571 employees.

Man AG. Headquartered in Munich, Germany, Man AG (also known as the Man Group) produced both turbines and diesel engines. With more than 77,000 employees worldwide, Man also produced commercial vehicles and components, printing presses, and other industrial equipment. The diesel engine subsidiary continues to profit from the shipbuilding market and from growth in power plants. In 2001, the company secured growth of 25 to 28 percent in its Diesel Engines division, having purchased the English manufacturer MBD Ltd. from Alstom in 2000. Turbo engine sales by Man's Industrial Equipment and Facilities division grew by 53 percent, due in part to Man's acquisition of Sulzer Turbomaschinen in 2001. The Industrial Equipment and Facilities division, as a whole, recorded growth of 3 to 5 percent. Due to the extremely high level of orders on hand at the beginning of 2001, Man Group's sales that year increased 11 percent to € 16.2 billion. In 2009 total revenues were US$15.9 billion and they had a workforce of 47,740 employees.

Kawasaki Heavy Industries Ltd. Kawasaki Heavy Industries Ltd., headquartered in Kobe, Japan, was established in 1896 as a shipbuilder. Kawasaki focused on four fields of business: aircraft and jet engines; motorcycles and other general-purpose vehicles; rolling stock; and systems engineering/services, which covered power generation and distribution (e.g., industrial equipment including gas turbines, boilers, robots, medical equipment, and construction machinery). In 2001, while orders for industrial equipment, including turbines and engines, rose 16 percent to ¥412.9 billion, sales declined 17.5 percent to ¥327.7 billion. Major orders included a cogeneration combined cycle power plant from Mexico and power generation equipment for Chubu Electric Power Co.'s Hekinan, Japan, thermal plant. In 2010 their revenue reached US$14.62 billion and they had approximately 30,000 employees.

Kubota Corporation. Like Kawasaki, Kubota Corporation, headquartered in Osaka, Japan, was established in the 1890s. The company is renowned for its machinery's agricultural applications—namely tractors. Kubota has grown to become an international leader in three product groups: internal combustion engines and machinery, industrial products and engineering, and building materials and housing. Sales in all three product areas were affected by the economic downturn in the Far East during the late 1990s and early 2000s, although sales in the industrial products and engineering sector proved to be the healthiest. By 2010 company revenues were US$11.12 billion, and it reported approximately 24,000 employees. Kubota operates subsidiaries or affiliates in more than 130 countries.

MAJOR COUNTRIES IN THE INDUSTRY

Global turbine production in the mid-2000s was led by the United States, followed by the United Kingdom, France, Germany, Denmark, Switzerland, Japan, and Italy. The import/export business in world turbines accounted for roughly 40 percent of global output in foreign trade annually. Although the largest producers were also the largest exporters, the large domestic demand for turbines in the United States resulted in the United Kingdom becoming the largest net exporter in turbine products. The U.K. trade surplus in turbines was $US2.7 billion in 2002, followed by Denmark with $US 1.8 billion, with mostly wind turbines, and the United States at $US1.6 billion. Other countries with positive trade balances of more than $US100 million in 2002 were Canada, Russia, Sweden, and Switzerland.

As a sign of energy-option-consideration times, plans involving building four giant wind turbines near the Peak District National Park in the United Kingdom were debated before being approved. In July 2008, Planning Inspector Robin Brooks took five main issues into consideration, including "the impact of turbines on the character and appearance of the landscape on tourism." Ultimately, Brooks concluded there would not be "unacceptable harm" to the character and appearance of the national park, but they would contribute renewable energy generation goals.

Frank Dohman told the inside story about potentials for high-tech wind turbines thanks to Quiet Revolution. Quiet Revolution is an innovative company located in Great Britain. Founded in 2005, the company showed its potential in 2007 when its first model, the QR5 was installed on several rooftops in England, including high-rise buildings. RWE, the German energy major company, bought a small stake in Quiet Revolution after it started to show promise. Future prospects call for utilizing RWE's investment to replace the carbon-fiber material with less expensive materials to make the turbines.

BIBLIOGRAPHY

Abhari, Reza S. "The Link Between Climate Change and Turbomachines." *Global Gas Turbine News,* May 2008.

———. "View from the Chair." *Global Turbine News,* August 2008.

"Added Operational Flexibility Would Boost Combined-Cycle Profits." *Power Engineering,* September 2003.

Carton, Paul. "Solar Energy Is Up—But Wind Power Is Also Surging," 16 September 2008. Available from www.seekingalpha.com.

Dohman, Frank. "A Big Future for Tiny Wind Turbines?" 2 September 2008. Available from www.businessweek.com.

"Energy Statistics of OECD Countries: 1998–1999." Washington, D.C.: Organization for Economic Cooperation and Development, 2001.

"Engine Order Survey: Engine Orders Go Through the Roof." *Diesel & Gas Turbine Worldwide,* 2001. Available from www.dieselpub.com.

"Engine Suppliers Face Ownership Overhaul." *Flight International,* 19 July 2005.

"Environmental Defense Fund Welcomes EPA Standards for Nonroad Gas Engines," 4 September 2008. Available from www.MarketWatch.com.

Ernst, Steve. "New Design May Lower Costs to Run Wind Turbines." *Sacramento Business Journal,* 12 September 2003.

"Free Flowing." *International Water Power & Dam Construction,* May 2005.

"Global Gas Turbine Market Analysis to 2020. " *PRLog,* July 2010.Available from www.prlog.org.

"Global Wind Turbine Market to Grow Apace." *Modern Power Systems,* February 2003.

Gregory, Denis. "Wind Turbines Have Farmers Spinning Out." 31 August 2008. Available from www.smh.com.au.

Hester, Edward D. "The Global Marketplace for Turbines." *The Freedonia Group,* July 2004.

"Hoover's Company Capsules." *Hoover's Online,* 2008. Available from www.hoovers.com.

"Hydrogen Engine Center Announces Commissioning of Hydrogen Power Generation System of Startech Environmental Corp," 17 September 2008. Available from TradingMarkets.com.

Hydropower: Partnership with the Environment. Washington: U.S. Department of Energy Hydropower Program, June 2001.

"IGTI Creates Industrial Gas Turbine Technology Award." *Global Gas Turbine News,* August 2008.

"International Trade Statistics." 2004. Available from www.wto.org.

"Isuzu Motors Limited Annual Report," 2010. Available from www.isuzu.co.jp.

Lamb, Gregory M. "Cleaning Up An Engine's Act." *The Christian Science Monitor,* 16 September 2008.

"Nonroad Diesel Engines," Emission Standards United States. Available from www.dieselnet.com.

Perin, Monica. "New Electricity Technology Gathers Steam." *Houston Business Journal,* 30 April 2004.

Rubner, Justin. "GE Energy Entering Solar Biz." *Atlanta Business Chronicle,* 2 April 2004.

———. "GE Power Rides Wind Energy." *Atlanta Business Chronicle,* 7 November 2003.

Smith, Douglas J. "Gas Turbines Breaking Through the Barriers to Higher Reliability." *Power Engineering,* May 2003.

Walsh, Angela. "Breaking News: Green Light for Wind Turbines." 17 September 2008. Available from www.derbyshiretimes.co.uk.

"Wind Power." *The Oil and Gas Journal,* 3 February 2003.

"Wind Power Latest News" Global Wind Energy Council, 12 October 2010. Available from www.gwec.net.

"Wind Turbines, Photovoltaics Winners in Distribution Market." *Energy User News,* May 2004.

"Wind Turbines to Propel Renewable Energy in Finland," 14 September 2008. Available from www.yle.fi.

SIC 3523

MACHINERY AND EQUIPMENT, AGRICULTURAL

NAICS CODE(S)

333111. The farm machinery industry manufactures a wide variety of products for planting, maintaining, and harvesting crops, as well as for performing other agricultural activities. Common kinds of farm equipment include tractors, combines, sprayers, planters, and harvesters.

INDUSTRY SNAPSHOT

Despite difficulty in the early 2000s, the agricultural machinery and equipment industry rebounded during the middle part of the decade. U.S. sales of two-wheel drive tractors increased 7 percent from 2003 to 2004, and four-wheel drive tractor sales increased more than 100 percent. Self-propelled combines also surged in demand, with a 75 percent increase in sales from 2003 to 2004, followed by an 18.1 percent increase in sales from first quarter 2004 to 2005, as reported in the Association of Equipment Manufacturers' (AEM) March 2005 Flash Report. In its *State of the Ag Industry* report, the AEM found that the factors most influencing new equipment sales projections were farm debt and credit availability, grain exports, and beef and hog prices.

Agricultural equipment sales also increased in developing markets. South Africa showed growth of 118 units, or 35.8 percent in tractor sales, according to the SA Agricultural Machinery Association. Combine harvester sales in June 2004 were almost double those of June 2003, rising from 15 units to 29, and baler sales showed a small increase (three units) over the previous year as well. The Association expected tractor sales in South Africa would continue to increase. Indian tractor manufacturer Mahindra & Mahindra Ltd. (M&M) sold 15,066 tractors during the first quarter of 2004, compared to 10,049 for the same period a year earlier. The company has sold more than $100 million of equipment to the United States, and was working in late 2004 on a joint venture with Jiangling Tractor Company in China.

In the mid- to late 2000s, several new innovations in agricultural machinery were joining the market. Tier III engines, tractor auto-steering capabilities, and site-specific GPS application equipment were just a few of the technologies to watch. Such developments were aimed at improving the markets of industrialized economies. Agricultural machinery was a mature industry and primarily a replacement market, since sales depended mostly on replacement equipment and parts. The trend toward farm consolidation in developed countries hastened this transformation. Agricultural equipment manufacturers continued to discover new markets, particularly in developing countries such as Uruguay, Paraguay, Brazil, and Argentina. The United States exported US$405.1 million of farm equipment to South America in 2004, an increase of 43 percent from 2003, according to the AEM. Exports to Australia/Oceania reached US$673 million, a 64 percent increase.

China serves as Vietnam's major source of agricultural production machinery by supplying more than 60 percent of the related products. In addition, the Vietnam Engine and Agricultural Machinery Corporation revealed a large amount of "components used to produce machinery locally are also Chinese imports." Approximately 20 Chinese business operating in Vietnam made components priced approximately 25 percent of local cost. An estimate of approximately 550,000 agricultural production machines in use throughout Vietnam was given by *Viet Nam News*. Common types of machines included ploughs, threshing machines and electric generators.

Science–related trends impacting tractors included building them to be "more environmental friendly and emission compliant." All farm equipment was being designed to have an increased amount of "fail-safe" aspects mixed in with design features. GPS was being used more and more for tractors and other machinery. In spreading and spraying applications, it achieved more exact results thanks to "pinpoint accuracy."

ORGANIZATION AND STRUCTURE

Product Share. Although the agricultural machinery industry claims myriad products, the production of tractors and combines has accounted for the largest portion of the farm machinery and equipment market for many years. The scale of economy required to produce tractors and combines helped a few large multinational companies, referred to as full-line companies, dominate world markets. Nevertheless, more specialized products associated with the industry enabled many smaller companies to compete and profit as well.

The farm machinery industry serves large, medium, and small farms. Large farms prevail in the United States, Canada, Australia, Brazil, Argentina, and to an increasing extent in Europe. These operations require larger, more expensive machines and thus are capital intensive. The high cost of producing such machinery has effectively restricted participation in world markets to large multinational companies, many headquartered in the United States. Medium-sized farms, found mainly in Europe and supplied by European firms, diminished in number during the 1990s. During the 1980s, Japanese producers penetrated the medium-sized farm market and serviced the small-scale farm market in developed nations as well. Certain developing nations also produced machinery for small farms.

Differences in tractor size help describe how farms' needs vary according to the size of operations. According to the U.S. Department of Commerce, two-wheel drive tractors under 40 horsepower were built mostly in Japan, where farms are generally small. In the late 1990s, Japan's market for small tractors was 3.5 times the size of the

market for small tractors in the United States. Two-wheel drive tractors between 40 and 100 horsepower were supplied by Japan and Europe. Europe's high share of medium-sized farms made European demand for such tractors three times that of the United States. Finally, two-wheel drive tractors with horsepower above 100 were mostly produced in the United States, where farms are typically large, though since the mid-1980s Japanese and European firms competed in this market as well.

Distribution. Franchised dealers, who specialize mainly in one manufacturer's products, sell the majority of the world's farm machinery and equipment. Dealers may distribute more than one manufacturer's products if those products do not directly compete. Manufacturers generally support dealers by financing inventories, training staff, and advertising. Demand for farm machinery fluctuates seasonally, and farm machinery has a long life span. For example, tractors sold in the United States could last nineteen years. In the past, manufacturers were obliged to maintain large inventories of whole parts and replacement parts to meet supply demands with short notice. As the industry moved toward a build-to-order approach to manufacturing, however, dealers began consolidating inventories to sell to larger areas while servicing customers through closer satellite offices. The service end of this industry became increasingly important in the 1990s.

Major Trade Agreements. As the industry entered the twenty-first century, product standardization and international trade became paramount issues. Europe's economic unification spurred firms to seek cross-national standards that would allow them to compete throughout the common market. In addition, the General Agreement on Tariffs and Trade (GATT) signed in 1994 pledged a gradual reduction of trade barriers among participating countries, thereby leveling the competitive playing field for certain products in some markets. Among its other stipulations, the 1994 GATT eliminated farm machinery tariffs between the United States, the European Union, Japan, Canada, and other industrialized nations. The World Trade Organization (WTO), which was created on January 1, 1995, replaced the GATT as the formal institutional mechanism for regulating international commerce, but carried on GATT rules in expanded and revised form. As of 2005, some 148 nations belonged to the WTO.

In addition, the North American Free Trade Agreement (NAFTA) promised to gradually eliminate tariffs and other trade barriers among the North American countries. Signed in 1994, NAFTA ultimately phased out tariffs on farm equipment. In its implementation, NAFTA initially established trade quotas to prevent price dumping and other disruptive trade practices. The majority of protective tariffs and quotas expired in 2004, with the rest eliminated by 2005.

Agricultural Manufacturers of Canada reported on changing times for the Farm Improvement and Marketing Cooperative Loans Act (FIMCLA). Canadian Prime Minister Stephen Harper announced plans for act offering and estimated US $1 billion in loans through 2014. The focus of FIMCLA is to "finance farm improvements and fund the processing, distribution and marketing of farm products." Farmer assistance has offered "up to 80 percent financing to a maximum of US $250,000 for financing new or used assets."

BACKGROUND AND DEVELOPMENT

In most cases, working farmers were not responsible for the innovation and design of modern farm machinery. Most of the development of new farm equipment came from designs by various tradesmen, according to historian Reynold M. Wik in *Agricultural History*. Wik noted that some of the inventors of the plow, including John Deere, were blacksmiths, as were the inventors of the thresher, John and Hiram Pitt. One inventor of a reaper was a draftsman, and other inventors included machinists and practical engineers. Less surprising, Wik also found that most mechanical innovations came from the largest societies, with fewer contributions coming from inventors in less-developed regions.

One of the most significant innovations in modern farming was the gasoline-powered tractor. In the late nineteenth and early twentieth centuries, power for farm machines was transferred from steam traction engines to gasoline traction engines. John Froelich built one of the first machines with a gasoline traction engine in 1892. This machine became a forerunner to the John Deere tractor line. In 1907 C.W. Hart and C.H. Parr, two Iowans who had started the first tractor manufacturing business in 1906, coined the word tractor to refer to the gasoline traction engine.

Another important innovation in farm mechanization was the combine, a machine that harvests and threshes grain in one operation. Generally credited to Hiram Moore and J. Hascall of Kalamazoo, Michigan, the 1836 invention of the horse-drawn combine met with little demand until it was introduced to California's San Joaquin Valley in 1854. It took nearly 50 more years until other regions of the United States used the combine. According to Wik, the California valley's dry weather was particularly conducive to use of the first combines since the sun could cure the wheat, an impossibility in the damper grain-growing areas of the United States. After many improvements, including gasoline-powered engines, combines became one of the most important pieces of farm machinery in the world. Today combines harvest most of the commercially produced grain in the world.

The rate of farm mechanization varied greatly throughout the world. In general, the most industrialized nations possessed the highest levels of automation, although the developing world likewise had a long history in some types of agricultural mechanization. More than 3,000 years ago, the Chinese used cattle to ease the burden on human workers, and over 2,000 years ago, water power was first used in China and Mesopotamia, while wind power was used in the Mediterranean. These ancient innovations, however, did not spur farm mechanization in developing countries to the same extent as in the United States, Europe, and Japan.

Even in the United States, Europe, and Japan, however, many years separated the introduction and widespread use of some types of farm machinery. Reaper-binders, for example, were introduced in the United States in the mid-nineteenth century but did not become a substantial part of the European market for another 40 years or of the Japanese market for 100 years, according to Graham Donaldson, a contributor to the second International Conference on Agricultural Mechanization in Developing Countries. Donaldson concluded that farm size, nonagricultural demand for labor, and capital costs helped explain differing rates of farm mechanization.

Some observers posit that use of agricultural machinery is central to industrialization. A United Nations study entitled *Report of the Expert Group Meeting on Agricultural Machinery Industry in Developing Countries* found that the "agricultural machinery industry should have a very special place in a developing country since it diffuses technology throughout the countryside and involves a large sector of the working population in its activities." By the 1990s, many developing nations successfully initiated local production of farm machinery or entered into joint ventures with some of the industry's leading multinational firms. Farm equipment from Brazil, India, South Korea, Eastern Europe, Romania, and the Commonwealth of Independent States began reaching the United States and other export markets.

Since small farms were more prevalent in developing nations, the high cost of machinery impeded the sustained success of some initiatives within those countries. The United Nations publication, *Transnational Corporations in the Agricultural Machinery and Equipment Industry,* noted that the oligopolistic nature of the industry produced some global machinery-component standards that favored large-scale farming methods, to the disadvantage of small-scale farms. Consequently, new products specifically designed to be convenient and affordable to small-scale farmers unaided by government subsidies did not originate from large international manufacturers but from small, independent local manufacturers in developed and some developing countries.

The 1980s and early 1990s were marked by consolidations and acquisitions within the industry. The most significant changes in the industry occurred in the shuffling of the largest companies' stock. J.I. Case bought International Harvester, regained profitability, and was spun off by Tenneco Inc. Ford bought New Holland and then sold that stock to N.H. Geotech n.v., a Netherlands holding company owned by Fiat S.p.A. Deutz bought Allis Chalmers, and White merged with Avco New Idea. In 1994, AGCO acquired Massey Ferguson.

After a disastrous performance in the 1980s because of economic recessions and farm consolidations, the agricultural machinery industry came back in the mid-1990s with strong demand and healthy sales around the world. Major crop producers such as the United States, the European Union, and Canada continued to require new farm equipment. Further, South America became the fastest-growing market for agricultural equipment, with demand increasing by 15 percent in 1995.

In response to farmer demands in mature markets, the industry moved toward build-to-order equipment that fit farmers' specific needs during the 1990s. For example, French farms demanded environmentally friendly equipment that would increase productivity while reducing the emission of pollutants. This was happening in an industry once driven by the production of new technology that dealers convinced farmers they needed. However, due to economic difficulties in the 1980s, farmers became more cautious shoppers. Manufacturer and dealer inventories mounted and stalled by the 1990s. In order to avoid excess future inventories, manufacturers developed build-to-order systems and lean manufacturing plants modeled after the Japanese automobile industry.

Strong agricultural industries in the United States and the European Union, plus expanding markets in South America, helped fuel robust sales in the mid-1990s. Sales then dropped off toward the end of the decade. Trade liberalization agreements GATT and NAFTA were expected to further stimulate the industry and to allow established manufacturers greater access to other markets. In 1995 the United States, Germany, Italy, and the United Kingdom led the world in farm equipment exports, while imports were greatest in the United States, France, Canada, and Germany. Some significant acquisitions and sales within the industry shuffled the positions of the top producers in the mid-1990s, but industry dominance by large multinational corporations continued.

In the mid-1990s, many of the major farm machinery manufacturers planned to increase their presence abroad. For example, U.S. companies such as AGCO and Deere & Co. targeted South America and Europe as focal markets for the next century. These companies hoped to expand sales by acquiring producers and forming alliances with manufacturers in targeted countries. European producers turned to the United States and South America with similar tactics to achieve growth.

The *Financial Times* reported global sales of farm machinery totaling US$43.4 billion in 1996, more than twice 1991's US$21.3 billion. Western Europe continued to dominate the industry, led by Italy, Germany, France, and the United Kingdom, and posted sales of US$16.2 billion in 1996. North America ranked second with US$11.9 billion in revenues, followed by Eastern Europe with US$6 billion, Asia with US$5.0 billion, South and Central America with US$2.4 billion, Africa with US$800,000, and Oceania with US$1.1 billion.

By 1999, according to the Food and Agriculture Organization (FAO), low-income countries used just 11.0 percent of the world's agricultural tractors, with the least-developed countries using only 0.4 percent of the global count of farm tractors. In contrast, an estimated 18 percent of the world's farm tractors were used in the United States alone. Usage rates for harvesters and threshers were similar: just 0.3 percent in 1999 for the least-developed countries and 1 percent for the low-income countries—equivalent to the percentage used in the United States. Even more striking contrasts appeared in usage rates for milking machines worldwide (excluding counts for Mexico, Canada, and the United States and selected other countries): only 2 percent of milking machines tallied by FAO were used in the low-income countries while less than 0.02 percent were used in the least-developed countries. In contrast, Europe used nearly 78 percent of the milking machines counted. The difference between developed and developing nations in terms of mechanization in the agricultural sector was thus stark. Intra-regional differences also were pronounced.

In Africa, 527,621 farm tractors were in use in 1999, though only 160,795 of these were in sub-Saharan Africa. Similarly, of the 38,295 harvesters and threshers used in all of Africa that year, just 5,002 were in the sub-Saharan region. One example of an international initiative aimed at fostering development in this part of the world is the African Growth and Opportunity Act (AGOA), signed into law in the United States by President Bill Clinton in May 2000 as Title 1 of the U.S. Trade and Development Act of 2000. AGOA was designed to improve the trade climate between the United States and sub-Saharan African countries by reducing tariffs and rewarding African nations found to be practicing "good governance." In the year 2000, exports of agricultural machinery from the United States to sub-Saharan African countries were facilitated by AGOA and totaled US$68.5 million, contributing to the modernization of the agricultural infrastructure in this most-impoverished region of the world. By April 2005, 38 African countries were eligible to trade under AGOA.

Crop surpluses in wheat, corn, and soybeans led to significant drops in commodity prices and challenges for farmers in many developed countries, including reductions in the amount of funds available for purchasing agricultural machinery and equipment. The result was increased consolidation of farms into larger enterprises, the continued growth of multinational agribusinesses, and a trend toward the production and use of larger and more technologically advanced agricultural machines and equipment. In 1999, nearly 1.2 million agricultural tractors were sold for export around the world, with developed countries selling more than 1 million of these and developing countries exporting only about 145,000. According to *U.S. Industry and Trade Outlook 2000,* most farm machinery buyers were either leading food producers like Archer Daniels Midland or smaller providers of specialized crop production and maintenance services such as planting, fertilizing, and harvesting.

In the early 2000s, greater effort was directed toward encouraging the production and distribution in developing countries of a wider range of farm machinery and equipment suitable for small farmers as well as larger agricultural enterprises. A February 2000 United Nations Food and Agriculture Organization (FAO) report recommended greater public-private cooperation to promote and facilitate agricultural mechanization in the developing world. As L.J. Clarke, Chief of FAO's Agricultural Engineering Branch of the Agricultural Support Systems Division in Rome, noted in this report, for importers, distributors and small retail outlets to develop successful businesses, they need "a stable market in which to sell products, access to foreign exchange at undistorted rates, foreign contacts, removal of unfair competition from the state, access to business and marketing development assistance, access to credit for business and cash flow development." Clarke also observed that to produce farm machinery and equipment in developing countries, manufacturers must be able to purchase raw materials at stable prices on a regular basis and build and maintain relationships with international business allies.

Technological improvements in the marketing of agricultural machinery and equipment were also flourishing. In December 2001 two major farm machinery online traders—the United Kingdom's Farmec Limited, and *The Ag Dealer,* based in Canada and the northern United States—joined together to create one of the largest databases of farm machinery available for sale in the world. This initiative made the more than 800 Canadian and North American dealers registered in *The Ag Dealer* database dually accessible through Farmec. Farmec would thus be able to offer more than 28,000 machines advertised in *The Ag Dealer* to its European clientele directly through the Farmec Web site. Other online databases for specialized farm machinery and equipment were similarly attempting to capitalize on newly emerging electronic trading opportunities to increase sales around the world.

EMI's Flash Reports indicated that, in number of units sold, U.S. sales of under-40 HP, two-wheel drive tractors were strongest compared with all other categories of U.S. tractors. Totals increased 8.4 percent from January 2001 to January 2002, and were up again from June 2003 to June 2004. Retail sales of farm tractors in the United States increased by about 9.0 percent each year during 2000 and 2001. In January 2002, EMI forecast a decrease of 3.3 percent for U.S. farm tractor sales for the calendar year 2002. By mid-2004, the market had risen 8 percent over 2003 levels. Similarly, while U.S self-propelled combine sales increased 4.0 percent in 2000 and nearly 13.0 percent in 2001, sales of combines increased a whopping 75 percent between June 2003 and June 2004. And in 2003, global farm machinery and equipment sales exceeded $10 billion for the first time, according to *The 2004-2005 Outlook for the Farm Machinery and Equipment Market.*

Among other major agricultural machinery and equipment producers in the developed world, France was the European industry leader in the early 2000s. France's market for agricultural machinery in 2002 was US$4 billion, nearly a third of which came from tractor sales and another 30 percent from combine harvesters, with a decline forecast into 2007. The German market for agricultural machinery in 2002 was the next largest among the Europeans at US$3.2 billion, with growth forecast into 2007. In Germany, tractor sales accounted for 50 percent of the market. In the United Kingdom, agricultural machinery sales plummeted in the early 2000s.

U.S. exports of agricultural machinery increased for the third straight year from $4.8 billion in 2003 to almost $5.7 billion in 2004. This increase of almost 19 percent was the result of growth in exports to all regions, according to the Association of Equipment Manufacturers (AEM), with the largest percentage increases reflected in exports to Australia (64 percent growth, to $673 million) and South America (43 percent growth, $401.5 million). As measured by dollar amount, Europe ($1.7 billion) and Canada ($1.6 billion) purchased the most agricultural machinery from the United States during 2004. Other regions importing U.S. farm equipment included Central America ($642 million), Asia ($486 million), and Africa, ($179 million).

The market abroad showed growth as well. The United Kingdom showed a 2.4 percent increase in agricultural tractor registrations from 2003 to 2004, according to the Agricultural Engineers' Association (AEA). It was the United Kingdom's highest new tractor registration number since 1997. Performance declined somewhat over the second half of the year, and a similar downturn was expected during early 2005.

Factors influencing the North American market for farm equipment in 2005 included modest increases in interest rates, cash receipts, and net farm income. Planted acreage was expected to remain about the same, Equipment prices for new and used equipment increased from 2004 and remained a significant factor in the number of units sold. Of all sectors, the higher-horsepower (HP) machines were expected to sell at the most robust levels in the United States in the mid-2000s as U.S. farms continued to expand in size and shrink in number. The projected growth in sales through 2005 reflected a trend toward purchases of larger, more expensive machines rather than significant increases in numbers of machines purchased.

CURRENT CONDITIONS

Total shipments of farm equipment in the United States reached US$19.1 billion in 2005, up 6 percent from US$8 billion in 2004, according to the U.S. Census Bureau. Also, a study by the Association of Equipment Manufacturers in 2007 found that the U.S. agricultural equipment industry generates more than$82 billion in economic activity and is responsible for nearly 250,000 jobs in all 50 states.

Germany and the United States took turns as the number-one exporter of farm machinery throughout mid- to late 2000s. In 2005, Germany exported US$6.2 billion worth of products and the United States, US$5.5 billion. Japan was the third largest exporter of tractors, whereas Italy was the number-three exporter of other farm machinery. Regarding imports, the United States remained the largest importer of farm machinery in a trend that had lasted several years. Although the United States imported about same amount of farm machinery as it exported, the number/value of tractors imported increased more substantially (from US$1.6 billion in 2001 to US$3.4 billion in 2005) than that of other farm machinery (from US$1.1 billion in 2001 to US$2.1 billion in 2005). Other major importers of tractors were France, Canada, and Spain, and the largest importers of other farm machinery besides the United States were France and Germany.

Although not one of the top five importers or exporters of farm machinery in the late 2000s, China's market for such products was expected to increase as its economy grew. Annual sales of agricultural equipment by large manufacturers was up 25 percent in 2006, and the number of Western-style farms was increasing. According to a 2007 article in *Farmers Guardian,* "Whatever the outcome on this vast country's drive for more food, a massive demand for mechanization on the land looms ahead."

The farm machinery and equipment industry was expected to continue modest growth into the latter 2000s, according to Global Insight. Slight declines were expected following 2006. The broader global construction and farm machinery and heavy trucks sector was forecast to reach a collective value of $135.9 billion by 2008, a projected increase of 24.3 percent from 2003, according to a Datamonitor report.

Giltrap made a major acquisition linking it to Bucktons Engineering. Bucktons spreaders were popular New Zealand design variations. They featured a low center of gravity for safer slope usage. Carrying on a two-decade-plus legacy of dependable performance, Giltrap acquired manufacturing rights for Bucktons Spreaders.

Tractor sales experienced a dramatic drop in September 2009 compared to the same 2008 period. For 2008 and 2009, there were 840 and 480 tractors sold respectively. South African Agricultural Machinery Association pointed out that the last four months in 2008 were rated as "exceptional." Combine sales from September 2008 compared to September 2009 were 25 and 3, respectively.

How do you deal with a small tractor market that has been struggling since 2007? For Montana McCormick and Kukje Machinery Co. and Branson Tractors, the answer was in part to form special joint ventures and agreements. The companies united to form "a joint venture to market tractors in North America." Montana Vice President of Sales and Marketing Roger Kretchmer forecasted that "the access agreement could lead to a single line of Kukje tractors bearing the Montana name by mid-2010."

INDUSTRY LEADERS

Caterpillar. Caterpillar Inc. of Peoria, Illinois, was one of the farm machinery industry leaders. The company was also the world's number-one manufacturer of earth-moving machinery. The firm has plants worldwide and sells its equipment in 3,500 locations in 180 countries. With almost 95,000 employees in 2006, Caterpillar raked in US$41.5 billion in sales, a 14.2 percent increase from 2005.

Deere and Company. Deere & Company, also based in Illinois, was the global industry leader from 1963 until the November 1999 merger of Case Corp. with New Holland N.V. In the years following the merger, CNH Global NV surpassed Deere and became the world leader in manufacturing agricultural tractors and combines. The two companies continued to vie for the industry leader position in the late 2000s. Deere & Company was originally founded by John Deere in 1837 and for more than a century and a half led the world market with its trademark sales of green and yellow farm equipment. The company's original product was a self-scouring plow, built to turn over the tough soil of the Midwestern United States. Deere first began to manufacture overseas in 1956 when it acquired a controlling interest in the Mannheim, Germany-based Heinrich Lanz Company, a producer of farm machinery since 1859. In the mid-1990s, Deere began to profit from its restructuring efforts.

Employment, which peaked in the early 1980s at 68,000, was reduced to 34,400 by 1997, when the company produced goods in nine countries and sold farm machinery and equipment in 160 countries. In 2000, Deere experienced an average sales growth of just 3.3 percent but took 33.6 percent of the US$11 billion market for agricultural machinery in the United States. In its 2001 annual report, Deere noted that it had adapted to new farming practices aimed at controlling soil erosion and reducing production costs by designing and selling new forms of planters, drills, and tillage equipment. The company also developed a holistic approach to agricultural management that included advanced technology and global satellite positioning. By 2004, according to the company's annual report, Deere & Company net equipment sales were up 32 percent to $17.67 billion, and by 2006, Deere employed 47,400 people. Total sales for 2006 reached US$22.1 billion. Due to sales goals in Europe and expansion into foreign markets such as South America, India, and China, Deere & Co. expected continued growth. By October 2008, Deere had approximately 56,700 employees.

John Deere researched and introduced an innovative tractor lighting application. Innovative lighting packages were designed to complement the newest tractor models. The packages provide realiable assistance for those seeking "greater nighttime visibility" plus wider fields of vision. In addition, Deere engineers designed HID lighting system incorporating smaller housing and remote-mounted ballast, according to John Deere Product Line Marketing Manager Chad Hogan. By ordering lights at time of purchase, it was often easier to include them than add utilizing kit later, Hogan believed.

In October 2009, Deere announced it had reached an agreement with the United Auto Workers plus continued the tradition of doing so without stopping work maintained for the past 20 years.

Randi Alles shared an insider's view of a local success story starring Reynolds John Deere dealership. The Muncie operation's sales Representative Craig Black predicted that 2009 would be an exceptionally good year. Keys to the business' success were specialized business practices and competitive buyers, according to Black. A competitive challenge related to John Deere's restrictions allowing dealership to only have eight tractors at a time plus requiring those be sold before additional ones could be ordered. This practice was maintained even when there was a volume of tractor orders.

CNH Global. CNH Global NV of Amsterdam, formed by the merger of Case and New Holland, was the number-one producer of farm machinery in the world in the late 2000s when Deere & Company was not. With plants in 14 countries and 11,500 dealers around the world, CNH was the market leader in Western Europe for agricultural equipment. In 2004, the company's growth was fueled by better-than-expected growth in combine sales of 43 percent in North America, 17 percent in Western Europe, and 34 percent in the rest of the world. Sales in 2006 totaled US$12.9 billion, about 60 percent of which came from farm equipment. At that time, CNH Global employed approximately 25,300 people.

The Case Corporation was founded as J.I. Case Threshing Machine Co. of Wisconsin in 1842, its original products being threshing machines. New Holland n.v. originated in 1895 as the New Holland Machine Company, a specialized farmstead engine maker. The first automatic hay baler, requiring only one operator instead of three, was one of New Holland's significant innovations before World War II. In 1947 New Holland became a division of the Sperry Corporation. After combining operations with part of Ford Motor Company, Ford New Holland Inc. was the world's third largest agricultural machinery manufacturer by 1987. New Holland n.v. was formed in 1991 when Ford sold its Ford New Holland Inc. stock to N.H. Geotech n.v., a Netherlands holding company owned by Fiat S.p.A. The intricacy of these mergers and acquisitions illustrates the degree to which multinational corporations set on capturing ever larger shares of the global market now dominate the industry.

AGCO Corporation. In 2006, AGCO Corp. was the third largest company in the agricultural machinery and equipment industry. AGCO was headquartered in Duluth, Georgia, and sold 17 brand names, including Massey Ferguson, Gleaner, and Fendt, in more than 140 countries. Massey Ferguson, reported by AGCO as the world's most widely sold brand of tractor, is one of

AGCO's brands. By taking over Caterpillar's production and marketing of tractors in early 2002, AGCO was positioned to occupy an even larger share of the world tractor market. AGCO reported 2008 net sales of US$8.4 billion. The company had more than 2,800 independent dealer and distributors throughout the world.

Claas Gruppe. Germany's leading farm machinery manufacturer is Claas Gruppe, which also ranks among the top manufacturers worldwide. Founded in 1913 in Clarholz, Westphalia, by brothers August and Franz Claas, Claas was a pioneering producer of agricultural machinery from its inception. Claas' achievements include the development of the European combine harvester in 1930, the manufacturing of the first pick-up baler in 1936, construction of the first self-propelled combine harvester in 1953, and contributions to the development of AGROCOM, a satellite-based agricultural information system. The company also launched a joint venture with Caterpillar to distribute its combine harvesters in North America. In 2004, Claas Gruppe earned $1.9 billion in net sales, a 28.9 percent increase over 2003. Of sales, 76.8 percent were earned in Germany, with the remainder due to exports.

Kubota Corp. One of the top Japanese manufacturers is Kubota Corp. Founded by Gonshiro Kubota in 1890 as a manufacturer of cast iron water pipe under the name Ohide Imono, the company first entered the agricultural machinery industry in 1922 as a producer of kerosene engines. By 1950 Kubota also produced horizontal diesel engines, and it made its first tractors a decade later. Four-wheel drive tractors followed in 1971. Kubota's strength is in lower horse-powered tractors that serve smaller farms. The company specializes in niche farm equipment markets, and the United States has been its largest overseas market. Kubota Tractor Corp. continued to enjoy success and opened new manufacturing facilities in the United States during 2004 and 2005. These included the company's fifth facility in Georgia. In 2006, Kubota's sales reached US$8.9 billion with 23,049 employees. Kubota Tractor Corp. (KTC), a subsidiary of Kubota formed in 1972, markets and distributes Kubota agricultural machinery in the United States and is the leading marketer and distributor of under-40 horsepower tractors in the nation.

BIBLIOGRAPHY
"2004 Mid-Year State of the Ag Industry Outlook." *Association of Equipment Manufacturers,* 2004. Available from www.aem.org.

"AEM Projects 2007 Equipment Sales." *Feedstuffs,* 6 November 2006.

"Agricultural Machinery (excluding Tractors)." *Imports/Exports: 2001-2005.* 15 June 2007. Available from www.intracen.org.

"Agricultural Machinery in France, Germany, UK, US." *Euromonitor,* August 2004. Available from www.majormarketprofiles.com.

Agricultural Manufacturers of Canada. "Canada updates FIMCLA." 2009. Available from www.a-m-c.ca.

Alles, Randi,. "John Deere Success in 2009." 22 October 2009. Available from www.newslinkindian.com.

"The appliance of science to farm machinery." 2009. Available from www.corkman.ie.

Association of Equipment Manufacturers. "AEM Releases Annual 'Outlook' for 2005 Farm Machinery Sales." 6 April 2005. Available from www.aem.org.

———. "Canadian Ag Flash Reports: September 2009 Flash Report Canada unit Retail Sales." 9 October 2009. Available from www.aem.org.

———. "New Study Details Contributions of U.S. Agricultural Equipment Industry to American Economy," 2 March 2007. Available from www.aem.org.

———. "U.S. Ag Flash Reports: September 2009. Flash Report U.S. Unit Retail Sales." 9 October 2009. Available from www.aem.org.

"China dominates Viet Nam farm machinery market." 26 September 2009. Available from vietnamnews.vnagency.com.vn.

Crummett, Dan. "Small Tractor Market In Upheaval." 21 October 2009. Available from indianaprarie.

Daley, Will. "Deere Reaches Labor Accord for 9,500 Union Employees (Update 3)." 1 October 2009. Available from www.bloomberg.com.

Draper, Deborah J., ed. *Business Rankings Annual.* Detroit: Thomson Gale, 2004.

"Equipment Sales Flat." *Farm Industry News,* 17 November 2006.

"Exports of Farm Equipment Increase 19 Percent in 2004." *Association of Equipment Manufacturers,* 21 February 2005. Available from www.aem.org.

"Farm Machinery and Equipment Manufacturing." *U.S. Industry Quarterly Review: Machinery and Equipment.* Global Insight, December 2004.

"Feed Sector Faces Further Rationalisation in Bid for Survival." *Dairy Farmer,* 11 March 2004.

"FGBusiness: China Prepares for Biggest Agricultural Reorganisation Ever." *Farmers Guardian,* 4 May 2007.

"From the Top." *Apply,* 1 May 2004.

Global Construction & Farm Machinery & Heavy Trucks: Industry Profile. Datamonitor, May 2004. Available from www.datamonitor.com.

Grooms, Lynn. "Tools of the Trade: Dependence on New Agricultural Equipment in the United States." *Apply,* 1 December 2006.

"Hoover's Company Capsules." *Hoover's Online,* 2007. Available from www.hoovers.com.

"International Trade Statistics." 2003. Available from www.wto.org.

Johnson, Andrea. "Engineers improve tractor lighting for night field work." 21 October 2009. Available from www.theprairiesstar.com.

Lazich, Robert S., ed. *Market Share Reporter.* Detroit: Thomson Gale, 2004.

Pretorius, Leon. South African Agricultural Machinery Association: September 2009; Tractor, Combine Harvester and Bailer Sales.

Robertson, Don. "Sales of Heavy Agricultural Equipment Rockets." *Africa News Service,* 12 July 2004.

Robinson, Elton. "Tractor Controlled with Radio Remote." *Southeast Farm Press,* 23 May 2007.

Saunders, Mark. "Giltrap unveils new sprayers." 23 October 2009. Available from www.weeklytimesnow.com.

"South America." *Implement & Tractor,* July/August 2003.

"Tractor Giant Agco Puts Faith in Innovation to Push Expansion." *Europe Intelligence Wire,* 7 March 2005.

"Tractors." *Imports/Exports: 2001-2005.* 15 June 2007. Available from www.intracen.org.

"U.S. Ag Flash Report." *Association of Equipment Manufacturers,* 14 July 2004.

"U.S. Agricultural Equipment Industry." *Agri Marketing,* May 2007.

U.S. Census Bureau. "Farm Machinery and Lawn and Garden Equipment: 2005." *Current Industrial Reports.* June 2006. Available from www.census.gov.

SIC 3560

MACHINERY AND EQUIPMENT, GENERAL INDUSTRIAL

NAICS CODE(S)

3332. The general industrial machinery and equipment industry comprises at least four major categories of products: 1) pumps for liquids; 2) fans, filters, and gas pumps; 3) mechanical handling and packaging equipment; and 4) ball and roller bearings. Lesser categories include speed changers, drives, and gears; industrial process furnaces and ovens; and mechanical power transmission equipment. Other segments include other types of parts and machines. For information on specialized industrial machinery, see **Machinery, Refrigeration and Service Industry.**

INDUSTRY SNAPSHOT

The products in this industry, and consequently the leaders in this industry, cover a broad range of machines and parts and are applied diversely. Therefore, the industry's fortunes are closely tied to the general health of world industrial production. Those fortunes equally provide an indicator of the level of a country's or region's industrial development. Mature industrialized countries—Germany, Japan, the United States, Italy, France, and the United Kingdom—continue to dominate world production and exports. Emerging countries such as South Korea, China, India, and Brazil have also become important producers

and consumers of general industrial machinery and were forecast to fuel much of the industry's continued growth.

China, Taiwan, and India held the top three exporter positions for both pumps machinery and packing machinery in the mid-2000s. According to the Freedonia Group, bearings were expected to experience 4.5 percent annual growth in the United States into 2010, 6.4 percent annual growth in Canada and Mexico, 4.8 percent in Western Europe, and 7.8 percent in Asia and the Pacific Rim. The Freedonia Group also predicts the demand for the fluid-handling pump will rise 6.5 percent annually through 2014. The prediction is for the pace of these gains to be realized primarily in the more industrialized nations as the global economy rebounds.

BACKGROUND AND DEVELOPMENT

The use of mass production technologies enabled U.S. manufacturers to master the world market for industrial machinery in the early twentieth century. In the years before World War I, leading U.S. producers rapidly expanded production and marketing facilities, establishing factories both domestically and abroad. In 1914 there were about 20 U.S. machinery firms operating two or more plants in Europe.

Alfred D. Chandler Jr., in his book, *Scale and Scope,* described the situation of U.S. industrial machinery producers in this period. U.S. machinery producers dominated the European market, thanks to economies of scale and product-specific sales organizations for marketing and distribution. This was despite the fact that patents did not fully or even partially protect many of the machines. Few European companies could produce machines superior to those of the United States at similarly modest prices, as well as offer the necessary ancillary services of marketing, demonstration, installation, after-sales repair and service, and consumer credit. Manufacturers of industrial machines continued to expand overseas facilities until the Great Depression.

As with many other U.S. industries in the early 1900s, in the non-electrical machinery and equipment industry there was a wave of mergers. These mergers were not so-called horizontal mergers—mergers involving a combination of directly competing firms. Rather, the mergers were based on the establishment of complementary product lines. Thus, the diversification strategies of U.S. firms had them staying within closely related product lines. The Ingersoll-Rand Company, for example, produced pumps, compressors, and engines, all of which were used for mining operations. Early in the twentieth century, Worthington Pump was the largest U.S. producer of pumps, making a wide range of steam and gasoline-pumping equipment, as well as compressors,

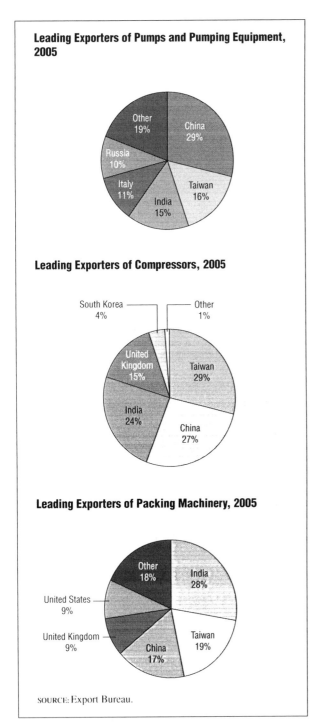

Leading Exporters of Pumps and Pumping Equipment, 2005

Other 19%
China 29%
Russia 10%
Italy 11%
India 15%
Taiwan 16%

Leading Exporters of Compressors, 2005

South Korea 4%
Other 1%
United Kingdom 15%
Taiwan 29%
India 24%
China 27%

Leading Exporters of Packing Machinery, 2005

Other 18%
India 28%
United States 9%
United Kingdom 9%
China 17%
Taiwan 19%

SOURCE: Export Bureau.

particularly competitive, with extensive international marketing operations and credit and repair services. They also were among the world's largest, with average employment ranging from 3,500 to 5,000 by World War I. Indeed, some German producers of industrial machinery employed more than 15,000 workers at this time.

German manufacturers grew primarily by investing retained earnings. Thus, they were less beholden to banks than German firms in the chemical, metal- making, and electrical machinery industries. Nor had they, like many firms in other industries, made extensive overseas investments before World War II. Thus, they suffered less from the burden of reparations after the war. Given the nature of heavy industrial machinery and equipment, competition took place largely on the basis of performance and service, rather than price. As a consequence, the cartels notable in many other German industries did not play an important role in the industrial machinery industry.

German industrial machinery companies were generally more widely diversified across industry lines than their U.S. counterparts. Maschinenbau-Anstalt Humboldt was established in the 1850s as a machine shop serving one of Germany's leading mining firms. From this starting point, the firm diversified into other material-handling machinery; locomotives and railroad cars; and air-moving and cooling machinery used in mines, breweries, and slaughterhouses. By World War I, Maschinenbau-Anstalt had diversified—by reverse integration—into the production of steel-making machinery and equipment. The firm claimed that this strategy reduced the manufacturing costs of any given product while still offering diversification.

The German firm Borsig provided another example of the broad diversification strategies of leading German producers of industrial machinery and equipment. Borsig began as one of Germany's pioneering locomotive producers. The firm then undertook the production of steam engines and boilers, pumps and pump lines for oil production, and turbines, compressors, and cooling machinery. Allis-Chalmers of Milwaukee, Wisconsin was the only large U.S. producer of industrial machinery that was as widely diversified as the leading German firms. Allis-Chalmers had strong ties to Germany. Indeed, the merger by which it was created was financed by one of Germany's largest banks.

The leading German industrial machinery firms included Hannoversche Maschinenbau AG, Berliner Maschinenbau AG, Maschinenfabrik-Augsburg-Nurnberg, and Gebruder Koerting AG. As distinct from their U.S. and British counterparts, these were heavily involved in the production of locomotives. In Britain locomotives were produced by the major railroad companies. In the

generators, and meters. In the 1920s Worthington combined these products into systems for transferring water and heat, and later into cooling and air conditioning systems.

From the early twentieth century on, Germany rose to challenge U.S. dominance of the industry, becoming the leading European producer of industrial machinery. German producers of heavy industrial machinery were

United States, they were produced by a handful of large, relatively specialized manufacturers.

The development of packaging machinery was closely tied to the rapid growth of branded, packaged products in the late nineteenth century. Packaging became more important and more mechanized as both mass marketing and mass production, with their tendency to expand capacity, developed. Producers developed their own marketing operations, rather than relying on traditional wholesale merchants, and began to transform the economy.

Important innovations were made in the production and packaging of cigarettes and food products. Among the important innovations was James Duke's cigarette packaging machinery, developed as a response to the cigarette-making machines marketed in the 1880s. Grain processors took a similar route, leading to the establishment of companies like Quaker Oats Company, General Mills Inc., and Pillsbury Company. As with the cigarette industry, the development of branded packages rose in response to the dramatic increase of output made possible by the era's new rolling mills. In both cases, packaging became an integral part of the production process. That is, the new firms took over the wholesalers' traditional task of subdividing bulk goods into quantities suitable for retail purchase. In addition, unlike wholesalers, these firms advertised and sold products across the entire United States rather than to certain regional or local markets.

Another important innovation in packaging machinery was the automatic canning line, developed in 1883. This innovation led to the formation of such U.S. food-packaging firms as Borden, Campbell Soup Company, Libby, McNeill and Libby, Del Monte, and Heinz Company, as well as the American Can Company and the Continental Can Company.

The British were generally unable to compete with U.S. and German producers with respect to industrial machinery in the twentieth century. However, the British had a great deal of success in the production of branded packaged products. The largest of the British producers in the industry was Lever Brothers, a soap company. The firm followed the example of U.S. producers and invested heavily overseas. By World War I, Lever Brothers had built plants in Australia, Canada, the United States, and Japan, as well as in seven European countries. The British also used mass-production packaging machinery for cigarettes and food products, although they were late in taking up automatic canning machinery—allowing U.S. canning firms to dominate. Also in contrast with the U.S. firms, British packaging firms generally remained family-owned and operated between the world wars, leaving them with fewer financial resources and less sophisticated

structures of management. There also were relatively fewer mergers among packaging firms in Britain than in the United States, leaving British firms less diversified across product lines than U.S. firms.

Pumps and Compressors. Business in pumps and compressors was positive in the mid- to late 1990s, with the global market growing about 5 percent annually. Gains in the emerging economies of Asia and South America fueled this growth, as did demand in North America, which also grew about 5 percent annually. Because of the use of compressors in higher-value applications and more mature markets, the global compressor market was expected to grow faster than the pump market. With prices rising in the mid to late 1990s for metal and other raw materials, pump prices rose slightly during this period. In 1998, pump-for-liquids exports from the world's top 25 exporters totaled US$18.2 billion. As reported in *Purchasing,* demand for fluid-handling pumps was forecast to increase by almost 6 percent through 2008, according to a study by the Freedonia Group. Growth was primarily expected from less-developed markets, such as China, where annual growth was projected to be as high as 10 percent per year for the next five years. This offset less than average gains expected from established markets such as the United States, Japan, and Western Europe.

It was observed that air compressor design was closely linked to efficiency and reliability. An inefficient or failed compressed-air system had the capacity to waste production time and negatively impact customer relationships. Efficient compressors were able to play key roles in success for shops.

Bearings. The demand for bearings was stronger than for pumps and compressors. The global market expanded by roughly 8 percent annually through 2000. Growth in Central and South America was the highest, followed by Asia and Africa. Growth in demand for bearings in North America was less, but still strong, at about 5 percent. However, by 1999, North American market growth had fallen to below 2 percent, thanks largely to Asian economic upheavals beginning in 1997. Many bearings suppliers suffered from a lack of demand from original equipment manufacturers supplying to Asia. This caused a chain reaction. With production down in many areas, manufacturing equipment was not used as much, and machine parts, including bearings, did not wear as quickly.

Nevertheless, by 1998, ball and roller bearing exports for the top 25 producing countries had risen to more than US$11.1 billion. To sustain their margins and market share, manufacturers worked on developing bearings created from plastics, ceramics, and composites, among other materials, in an attempt to make bearings ever lighter and more resistant to heat.

Miniature ball bearings fit the needs where a design envelope may be small without overriding performance requirements. Due to advances in bearing technology, design engineers have been able to derive more than ever before from bearing selection.

Tied to the uncertain automotive market, the North American market for bearings experienced a corresponding slump in the early 2000s. The U.S. market was expected to grow about 2 to 3 percent annually as of 2003. By comparison, the Freedonia Group forecast 6.5 percent growth for the global market into 2005. This would bring the worldwide bearings total to US$42 billion. The North American packaging machinery industry was expected to see a rise as well, particularly in the six markets that make up more than 80 percent of this segment: foods, beverages, personal care, durables, chemicals, and converters.

Packaging Machinery. The packaging industry benefited from increasing demand for packaging equipment in China, especially from China's food-packing industry. In the mid- to late 1990s, the need for grain packaging equipment soared in the country, which helped drive production and trade in this segment. In 1998, global exports of mechanical handling equipment by the world's 25 top producing countries stood at US$27.7 billion. However, in the late 1990s, packaging equipment production fell in some leading countries, such as the United States. Still, throughout the world, manufacturers continued to produce more efficient machinery as packaging plants consistently sought greater productivity. According to a report by Freedonia, packaging machinery in China will grow at a rate of 8.7 percent annually through 2014, driven primarily through packaged food and beverages, drugs, and personal care products. It is predicted that the largest segment will continue to be filling and form/fill/seal equipment.

By 2003, U.S. shipments of packaging machinery climbed to US$4.88 billion, according to *Packaging Digest.* The amount of machinery exported by the United States grew more significantly, increasing by 33.1 percent during 2003 to US$952 million. The United States was the largest producer of packaging machinery, earning US$4.9 billion in shipments during 2003, followed by Japan with $4.1 billion. Germany, Italy, and China all earned more than US$1 billion in the industry as well. Shipments of new packaging machinery neared US$5.5 billion in 2004, thanks in part to demand for variable speed drives in the North American market. The packaging machinery market in the United Kingdom was forecast to grow by about 9 percent between 2004 and 2008, according to *Packaging Magazine.* Global demand

for packaging machinery was expected to rise 5 percent each year through 2008 to US$31 billion, according to the same source. Most gains were expected in developing areas of Latin America and the Asian Pacific, where industrial output and consumption were on the rise.

The Packaging Machinery Manufacturers Institute reported that, based on U.S. Census estimates, there was strong growth in packaging machinery exports. From January through November 2006, U.S. exports increased 7 percent compared to 2005 for a total of US$783 million.

The global demand for packaging machinery was forecast to increase by 4.9 percent per year through 2010, reaching more than US$33 billion. Labeling and coding equipment was expected to experience the strongest gains. Expectations also called for the food industry to remain by far the largest single market for packaging equipment by accounting for more than two-fifths of all product demand in 2010.

Material Handling. Manufacturers were realizing increased volume in new business and expansion systems during 2004, as reported by the Material Handling Industry of America (MHIA). A study by the Freedonia Group suggested healthy increases in this segment's growth through 2008, increasing by 4.3 percent per year. Demand was attributed to technological innovations that led to greater efficiency, easier operations, and automation. Automated storage and retrieval systems comprised the largest category of automated equipment. The market for convention equipment, including trucks and lifts, was expected to reach US$14.4 billion by 2008. Trucks and lifts remained the largest category of the material-handling sector and were also expected to see the largest gains.

CURRENT CONDITIONS

The global general industrial machinery and equipment trade expanded moderately into the 2000s. Taiwan, China, India, the United States, and Turkey led the industry in exports during 2004 and early 2005. The leading importers of industrial machinery during the first decade of the twenty-first century were India, China, Pakistan, Bangladesh, and the United Kingdom, as reported by the Bureau of Export Administration. A report published by research group Datamonitor in May 2004 projected the global market for industrial machinery would reach a value of US$303.1 billion, a 17.3 percent growth from 2003 value of US$258.5 billion. The largest segments of this category include elevators, pumps, and compressors. U.S. revenues attributed to industrial machinery during 2004 neared US$40 billion, as reported by the U.S. Industry Quarterly Review. Analysts at Global Insight predicted that industry revenues would continue to rise through the end of 2008, reaching US$50 billion.

International trade agreements such as the General Agreement on Tariffs and Trade (GATT) and the North American Free Trade Agreement (NAFTA) reduced or eliminated trade barriers. GATT, for example, brought about a 40 percent reduction of tariffs on industrial products, including machinery and equipment, imported by developed countries. GATT also fostered a 37 percent reduction in the volume of products imported from developed countries, according to the World Trade Organization (WTO). The agreement calls for the GATT tariff reductions to be fully implemented by 2005. NAFTA facilitated a similar gradual reduction of trade barriers in North America; this reduction of barriers was scheduled for full implementation in 2002. In 2004, India, Taiwan, China, the United States, and the United Kingdom were the top five exporters of packing and packaging machinery. That same year, China, India, Taiwan, Russia, and Italy were the top five exporters of pumps machinery.

In general, the need for companies to comply with expanding energy conservation policies and stricter conservation laws throughout the world led to a greater need for energy-efficient drives and speed changers. Because of the high costs of replacing malfunctioning drives and speed changers, more companies opted to have them rebuilt, creating a robust rebuilt market for these products. Customers were also concerned with energy conservation for industrial pumps, for which 85 percent of associated costs were attributed to energy consumption, according to *Purchasing*.

INDUSTRY LEADERS

Ingersoll-Rand. Ingersoll-Rand Company, located in Woodcliff Lake, New Jersey, reported total 2003 sales of US$9.9 billion, a 10 percent growth over 2002 levels. The company comprises three main divisions: construction machinery and equipment, industrial machinery and equipment, and components such as bearings. The Industrial Solutions division handles the industrial machinery and equipment industry segment. Sales for the division were more than US$9.3 billion in 2004. The company's leading brands are Blaw-Knox, Bobcat, Club Car, Fafnir, Steelcraft, Thermo King, Torrington, and Worthington. About half of the company's manufacturing plants are located outside of the United States, and roughly 40 percent of its revenues are derived from exports. In 2007, Ingersoll-Rand announced that it would investigate selling or spinning off its construction business, a move that could affect approximately 14 percent of its workforce in Davie County of North Carolina. The decision was linked to an announcement

that Bobcat might be targeted for sale or spinoff. The divisions under consideration accounted for approximately US$2.6 billion in revenue in 2006. In 2009, the company boasted sales of US$13 billion with over 60,000 employees.

SKF. Aktiebolegat SKF led the world in roller bearing production. The company produces a fifth or more of the world's roller bearings annually. Founded in 1907, the company includes three divisions: bearings and seals, tools, and special steels. Based in Göteborg, Sweden, SKF's bearing and seal division primarily serves the automotive and machinery industries. In the late 1990s, SKF had manufacturing plants at 80 locations in 20 countries. The company began to expand into new product areas with the acquisition of Russell T. Gilman Inc., one of the leading producers of spindles for machine tools in the United States. The company enjoyed the 5 percent growth in sales common in the industry during this time, with bearings typically accounting for 80 to 90 percent of total sales. In 2004 sales were up 18.7 percent to US$6.7 billion, and SKF's net income rose 59 percent from 2003 to reach US$447.4 million in 2004. In June 2007, SKF announced its plans to build a Greenfield factory in India for the manufacturing of large-size bearings. SKF had started a factory for large-size bearings in China, and observed a growing need for ball bearings in India due to its two-wheeler industry. SKF had 41,000 employees worldwide plus manufacturing operations at 100 locations and sales companies in 70 countries in 2009, and had a revenue of US$8.04 billion.

Ebara. The Ebara Corporation was established in 1920 and is headquartered in Tokyo. The firm is one of the world's leading producers of industrial pumps, fans, and compressors, along with industrial systems that make use of these products. Pumps, fans, and compressors accounted for 34 percent of the company's total sales in the late 1990s. The company had six overseas subsidiaries, four in the United States and one each in Italy and the Netherlands. Although the company's exports have been small, Ebara planned to stake out other markets, especially in Asia. In 2010, Ebara's sales were almost US$5.22 million and the firm employed over 15,500 workers.

Sumitomo. Sumitomo Heavy Industries Ltd. (SHI) was established by a merger in 1969 and is based in Tokyo. In the late 1990s, SHI's mass production machinery division remained its strongest, with steady sales and profit growth. That division accounted for about 70 percent of the company's profits during that period. At that time, Sumitomo had 14 overseas subsidiaries: five in the United States, three in Canada, two each in the United Kingdom and Germany, and one each in Mexico and Singapore. SHI's sales totaled US$3.67 billion in 2008. Sumitomo employed more than 14,400 people. Sumitomo and Nisshin Steel announced plans to set up a joint venture to make steel tubes for automobiles in India. On June 28, 2007, Sumitomo announced that it had acquired Primaxx, a leading high technology manufacturer of microelectrical-mechanical systems (MEMS) etch-release equipment.

NSK. Headquartered in Tokyo, NSK Ltd. was established in 1916. The firm is Japan's largest manufacturer of bearings. In 2003, bearings accounted for 65 percent of NSK's revenues. Automobile, aircraft, and train manufacturers use NSK bearings in their products. In the late 1990s, NSK had 17 plants in Japan and 20 overseas in Asia, Europe, and the Americas. NSK had net sales of US$7.7 billion in 2004, up from US$4.9 billion in 2004, and employed more than 25,000 workers. In 2007, NSK announced that it had developed tapered roller bearings and cylindrical roller bearings incorporating new pin-type cages that have up to six times the strength of conventional cages against the effects of shock loads.

Daikin. Daikin Industries Ltd. was established in 1934 and is headquartered in Osaka, Japan. It is Japan's largest producer of air-conditioning equipment, which comprises 80 percent of sales, and industrial refrigeration equipment. In the 1990s, the company had subsidiaries in Belgium, Australia, Singapore, Hong Kong, the United States, and Thailand. In 2007 Daikin's sales were US$10.86 billion. In 2007, Daikin announced its plans to sell 4.9 million units worldwide in fiscal year 2008. By fiscal year 2010, it intended to catch up with the global leader Carrier Corp.

Toyota Industries Corp. The company that is perhaps Japan's best known, best-selling automaker is also a manufacturer of industrial machinery. Toyota's consolidated sales in 2009 were approximately US$16.3 billion with a workforce of over 39,500.

MAJOR COUNTRIES IN THE INDUSTRY.

Overview of Top Producers. The United States was the highest producer, making 36 percent of machinery products worldwide, and the world's leading revenue generator, earning 35.7 percent of the global market. Europe was responsible for 29 percent of world machinery production. Other key exporters in 2005 included Italy with 5 percent of export orders, the United Kingdom with 4 percent, South Korea with 4 percent, Australia with 3 percent, and Russia with 3 percent.

Export Segments. For pumps and pumping equipment, the top five leading exporters in 2005 were China, with 29 percent of export orders; Taiwan, with 16 percent; India, with 15 percent; Italy, with 11 percent; and Russia, with 10 percent.

The top five exporting countries for compressors in 2005 were Taiwan, with 29 percent of exports; China, with 27 percent; India, with 24 percent; the United Kingdom, with 15 percent; and South Korea, with 4 percent.

In 2005, the top five exporters of packing machinery, also known as mechanical handling equipment, included India, at 28 percent of export orders; Taiwan, with 19 percent; China, with 17 percent; the United Kingdom, with 9 percent; and the United States, with 9 percent.

BIBLIOGRAPHY

"Japanese Firms Nisshin Steel, Sumitomo Corp to Set Up India Auto Parts JV." 18 June 2007. Available fromwww.abcmoney.co.uk.

"Aggregated Trade Statistics: International Trade Center, United Nations Conference on Trade and Development/World Trade Organization" February 2002. Available from http://www.intracen.org.

Annual Survey of Manufactures. Washington, D.C.: U.S. Census Bureau, February 2002.

"Bearings & Seals: Bearing Cages Steeled Against Shock Loads." *What's New in industry* (31 March 2007).

"Driving Forces for Change." *Packaging Today* (April 2007).

Ebara Corporation Annual Report 2010. Available 30 November 2010 from www.ebara.co.jp.

Global Industrial Machinery Industry Profile. Datamonitor, May 2004. Available from http://www.datamonitor.com.

"Hoover's Company Capsules." *Hoover's Online*, 2007. Available from http://www.hoovers.com.

Industrial Components: Freedonia Group. Available November 30, 2010, from www.freedoniagroup.com.

"International Trade Statistics." 2003. Available 30 November 2010 from http://www.wto.org.

"Japan's Daikin to Crank Up Global Air Conditioner Output." *AsiaPulse News* (8 May 2007).

"Liquid Handling Pumps Eliminate Refill Cycles." *Laboratory Equipment* (March 2007).

"Machinery Demand Rising Worldwide." *Packaging Digest* (March 2005).

"Machinery Global Industry Trade Statistics." Export Bureau, 27 April, 2005. Available from http://www.exportbureau.com.

"Material Handling Equipment and Systems Demand to Reach $20.4 Billion by 2008." *Material Handling Management* (January 2005).

Murphy, Elena Epatko. "Mixed Automotive Demand Slows Recovery." *Purchasing* (6 February 2003).

"New High-Tech Features Help Buyers Cut Total Costs." *Purchasing* (21 October 2004).

"Packaging Machinery Growth Predicted Globally: Global Growth in Packaging Machinery Will Rise Nearly 5 Percent

Per Year Through 2010." Available from www.fredonia group.com.

"Packing Machinery Trade Statistics." Export Bureau, 24 July 2004. Available from http://www.exportbureau.com.

"PMMI Study Shows Strong Spending Trends for 2004." *Feedstuffs* (7 June 2004).

"Pumps Machinery Trade Statistics." Export Bureau, 24 July 2004. Available from http://www.exportbureau.com.

Rasche, Michael J. "Floundering Global and Domestic Markets Frustrate U.S. Bearings Market." *Motor & Control News,* February 2002. Available from http://www.motorcontrol.com.

"Roller Pumps Withstand Harsh Chemical Exposure." *Product News Network* (4 January 2007).

"SKF to Set Up New Plant in India." 8 June 2007. Available from http:/machinist.in/index.

Snyder, Daniel R. "Getting Your Bearings Straight: Machinery Designers Want Smaller, Faster and Quieter Motion." *Product Design & Development* (February 2007).

Sullivan, Ed. "Pressed for Profitability: Without the Proper Compressor Technology, Shops Face Premature Failures, High Maintenance Costs, Additional Compressor Unit Purchases and Exorbitant Downtime." *Automotive Body Repair News* (April 2007).

Sumitomo. "Sumitomo Takes Stake in Canadian Metals Company." Reuters U.K., 15 June 2007. Available 30 November 2010 from http://uk.reuters.com

"Swedish Seals and Bearings Manufacturer SKF to Invest SEK250m in New Ball Bearings Plant in India." *Nordic Business Report* (26 April 2007).

"UK Machinery Outlook." *Packaging Magazine* (April 2004).

"U.S. Packaging Machinery Exports on the Rise." *Motion System Design* (May 2007).

SIC 3580

MACHINERY, REFRIGERATION, AND SERVICE INDUSTRY

NAICS CODE(S)

3334. The five major segments of the refrigeration and service machinery manufacturing industry are vending machines; commercial laundry equipment; heating and cooling equipment; service station pumps and grease guns; and miscellaneous service machinery, such as floor-cleaning machines and commercial dishwashers and cooking equipment

INDUSTRY SNAPSHOT

After the down years of the early 2000s, the global service machine and refrigeration industry enjoyed generally strong growth worldwide. This uptick was fueled by the rapid emergence of several formerly underdeveloped economies into the technological and consumer economy

mainstream, led by China's seemingly insatiable product demand. In 2003, the United States alone exported US$376 million in heating ventilation, air conditioning, and refrigeration (HVAC/R) equipment to China, and China exported 14.8 million units that same year. Sean Zhang reported in *Appliance* that industry experts expected 60 percent of China's 2005 air conditioner sales would be exported. Total U.S. exports in that category during 2003 were just over $7.1 billion. By comparison, U.S. imports showed steady and significant growth over the five-year period beginning in 1998, when U.S. imports were valued at US$2.89 billion, and ending in 2003, when imports were almost US$5.3 billion. World demand for commercial refrigeration equipment was expected to grow through 2008 at about 5.8 percent per year, reaching US$25.8 billion, according to The Freedonia Group.

Freedonia also reported that U.S. demand for heating ventilation and air conditioning (HVAC) equipment was expected to reach US$12 billion by 2007, fueled by increased construction and the growing replacement market. *Euromonitor* projected U.S. HVAC growth of 26 percent. In Europe, the market in France was expected to grow 10 percent, followed by 15 percent growth in Germany and the United Kingdom. Refrigeration and freezing equipment were the largest sectors for Germany and the United Kingdom, and air conditioners were the largest segment in France and the United States. Environmental and cost reduction concerns led to a new generation of increasingly efficient and sophisticated heating, refrigeration, laundry, and gas-pumping technologies.

In October 2008, *MarketWatch* reported that about 70 percent of the approximately 56 million vending machines in operation around the world dispensed liquid products like soft drinks. Coca Cola had 7 million vending machines worldwide. In Japan, US$137 per capita is spend annually on vending machine products.

ORGANIZATION AND STRUCTURE

Refrigeration, Air Conditioning, and Heating. The global heating ventilation, air conditioning and refrigeration (HVAC/R) equipment industry manufactured machines in several product categories in the early 2000s. The largest of these were self-contained, mechanically refrigerated, heat transfer equipment; unitary air conditioners; compressors and compressor units; commercial refrigerators and equipment; room air conditioners and dehumidifiers; and warm-air furnaces, humidifiers, and electric comfort heating equipment; as well as parts and accessories. Miscellaneous industry products included electric heat pumps, furnaces, refrigerated display cases, soda fountains, beer dispensers, and snowmaking machinery.

The HVAC/R industry had historically grown 2 to 3 percent a year. In the United States, which is one of the world's largest HVAC/R equipment markets, the motor vehicle and building construction industries were the primary end users of HVAC/R industry equipment. New home building was a primary factor in unitary air conditioner sales, which accounted for 50 percent of sector demand by 1999. Because of global agreements to phase out environmentally harmful coolants, the retrofit, or upgrade, of older heating and cooling systems was a significant end use for industry products by early 2000. As the result of these environmental policies, a new industry sector to develop energy-efficient "green building" technology had emerged in the early twenty-first century. Common industrial uses of refrigeration equipment in 2000 included food distribution, storage and preparation, and, in the chemical industry, the manufacture of petrochemicals, liquefaction of gases, separation of chemicals, and process control. Heating systems, refrigeration equipment, and air conditioners, manufactured by industry firms, supply the world's office buildings, hospitals, schools, restaurants, supermarkets, hotels, and other nonresidential large-capacity environments that require climate control.

Unlike household air conditioners, commercial and industrial heating and ventilation systems are often customized to match the widely varying needs of each customer's building/installation, from warehouses and stores to high-rises and sports stadiums. Industry firms are motivated by the need to create the most efficient heating and cooling systems possible and to balance that goal with the need for "real-world" functionality. During the final decades of the twentieth century, industry revenues were directly affected by commercial construction activity, including new office buildings or malls, environmental laws governing refrigerant use and recycling, and the willingness of customers to purchase new units rather than maintain old ones.

Vending Machines. According to the National Automatic Merchandising Association (NAMA), vending sales grew from a US$2.5 billion industry in 1960 to a US$38.7 billion industry in 2000. By 2005, annual vending machine revenues were still hovering in that range. When first introduced to consumer markets, automated vending machines were relatively uncomplicated mechanical devices, from which products (mostly food items in prepackaged servings) were purchased when a coin was inserted in a slot. These machines evolved into complex electromechanical hybrids capable of dispensing an extremely diverse range of products and equipped to accomplish a financial transaction with paper bills, tokens, prepaid debit cards, and even credit cards. Although traditionally associated with simple coin-operated beverage, snack, newspaper, and cigarette machines, during the 1990s the vending machine industry's global marketing strategy addressed increased consumer leisure time for shopping and a dwindling interest in home cooking. In the early 2000s, economic uncertainty and labor scarcity forced corporations to replace full-scale food service operations with vending machines. In the two largest vending machine markets, Japan and the United States, automatic merchandising machines comprised more than two-thirds of the vending machine manufacturing market by the late 1980s. In the early 2000s there were more than 5.5 million vending machines operating in Japan, 1 for every 20 people, responsible for about US$56 billion in sales.

Vending machines traditionally were fashioned from formed sheet metal and metal and plastic parts. Small electric motors and generators drove their product-dispensing mechanism and managed payment validation/acceptance (i.e., verifying the type of currency inserted based on properties like weight, size, or magnetic qualities). In the late 1990s, the industry trend was for electronic machines containing microprocessors and modems capable of keeping a machine's supplier updated on sales or notified of low product supplies. Such machines were expensive, however, and mechanical or simpler electronic vending machines remained common, particularly for beverages. In 2001 technological advances enable vending machine orders and payment via cell phone, which provided a reduction of mechanical malfunctions for vending coin collection. By 2004, the vending of cash had emerged as emerging as a trend in vending machine sales. *The Kiplinger Report* predicted that revenues would increase to US$70 million by 2010. *Kiplinger* also claimed that vending would be transformed by wireless-activated payments, with customers spending more than $100 using cashless transactions. Customers who used debit or credit cards preferred these machines and were willing to spend more when using them. A pilot program in the United States at Regal Cinemas showed vending sales increased 139 percent over one year, with credit or debit card transactions accounting for more than 30 percent of total transactions, according to *Screen Digest.*

The most common industry practice was to sell vending machines directly to product manufacturers, such as soda beverage bottlers, or to third-party vending machine distributors, who installed and maintained them. By 2001, some of the more active global vending machine manufacturers included Germany's NSM AG and CWS Deutschland GmbH; the United States' Cubic Corp., IMI Cornelius Inc., Rowe International Inc., and National Vendors; the United Kingdom's Enodis PLC; and Japan's Glory Ltd. and Sanden Corporation.

Commercial Laundry Equipment. The commercial laundry equipment manufacturing industry could be divided into three broad categories: commercial laundry equipment and laundry presses, dry-cleaning equipment and clothing presses, and miscellaneous commercial laundry equipment and parts. Within these product categories, however, a wide range of machines was manufactured, including washers; ironers; laundry presses; drying tumblers; garment manufacturers' presses; extractors; feather cleaning and sterilizing machines; and equipment to clean, dry, and nap rugs. These generally were big machines, accommodating loads exceeding 22 pounds, and were used by a variety of institutional clients, including hospitals, restaurants, hotels, government institutions (such as prisons), and of course commercial laundering businesses.

In the mid-1990s, it was not unusual for industry firms to produce approximately 50,000 machines annually. Representative firms in the industry included Wanderer-Werke, MEIKO Maschinenbau GmbH and Co., and Alfred Kaercher in Germany; Dowding and Mills PLC in the United Kingdom; Mexicana de Maquinaria in Mexico; Fukui Machinery in Japan; and White Consolidated Industries, Whirlpool Corp., Bissell, Inc., Pellerin Milnor, and Staber Industries in the United States. In the sizable U.S. industry, the commercial laundry equipment business was estimated to be only one one-hundredth of the size of the U.S. residential laundry equipment business.

Measuring and Dispensing Pumps. The global measuring and dispensing pump industry primarily manufactures pumps for dispensing gasoline at filling stations. These units usually have several pumps that are capable of pumping ten gallons per minute or more and are often computerized with digital readouts indicating the amount of gas pumped. They usually offer consumers the ability to purchase fuel directly at the pump using a credit or debit card. As early as the late 1980s, computerized gasoline dispensing pumps in the United States, which was one of the world's largest exporters of measuring and dispensing pumps, accounted for 42 percent of industry shipments. Other industry products include pump parts and attachments, non-computing and other measuring and dispensing pumps, miscellaneous measuring and dispensing pumps, lubricating oil pumps and barrel pumps, and grease guns.

The leading producers of liquid pumps in the 1990s were Germany, China, and the United States. Representative international firms in the segment in the late 1990s included Penn Process Technologies, Jesco Products, and Alfred Conhagen Inc. (United States); Dresser Canada (Canada); Magdeburger Armaturen Maw (Germany); Tatsuno Corporation (Japan); and Capacitores Componentes de Mexico (Mexico). Additional participants

engaged in the manufacture of measuring and dispensing pumps include Veeder Root Brasil Comercio e Industria (Brazil); Molson Companies, Tokheim, and Gasboy (Canada); Intent SA (Spain); Gilbarco (United States); Scheidt and Bachmann GmbH (Germany); and General Electric Company PLC and Enodis PLC (United Kingdom). These businesses also owned commercial laundry equipment firms in the United States, an increasingly commonplace industry trend in the measuring and dispensing pump industry.

Miscellaneous Service Machines Industry. Miscellaneous service machines made up the second largest industry segment in the late 1990s and encompassed a wide variety of products. The first product group was commercial cooking and food-warming equipment, including ovens, broilers, microwaves, deep-fat fryers, griddles, toasters, coffee urns, steam pressure cookers, and steam tables. The second group was commercial and industrial vacuum cleaners, including portable and central system vacuums and associated parts. The third group was service industry machines and parts, including such products as non-household water heaters; industrial and household water softeners; commercial and industrial floor and carpet cleaning equipment, including sanding, scrubbing, waxing, and polishing machines; commercial dishwashers; sewer pipe and drain cleaning equipment; high-pressure cleaning and blasting machinery; motor vehicle washing equipment; sewage treatment equipment; and trash and garbage compactors. End users of this segment's products ranged from sewer system construction companies, electrical repair shops, and government institutions to hotels, transportation and warehouse firms, and schools.

Industry sales were heavily dependent on the economic health of end users, who were restaurants and other food-preparation facilities, commercial cleaning firms, and certain consumer segments of the world economy. In the late 1990s, the wide range of firms participating in one of the industry's largest markets, the United States, indicated the sheer diversity of products included in this composite segment of the service machine industry. These included vacuum cleaner maker Hoover North America, water treatment supplier Culligan International, cooking equipment maker Frymaster Corp., and car wash equipment producer Hanna Car Wash International. Firms in Illinois, Ohio, and California dominated the U.S. industry.

A number of industry firms were exclusively engaged in the manufacture of such service machines in the late 1990s, including Xerox Do Brasil (Brazil); Bunn-O-Matic Corporation (Canada); Osorno Produktions für Autowaschtechnik (Germany); Chiyoda Manufacturing (Japan); and Hermetik (Mexico). Several other industry firms had diversified into other businesses from sheet metal work to the manufacturing of precision instruments, but the lion's share of their sales came from manufacturing miscellaneous service industry machines. These included Garland Commercial Ranges (Canada), Japan Organo Company (Japan), and Amano Partners USA (United States).

BACKGROUND AND DEVELOPMENT

Vending Machines. Gum and penny candy vending machines were introduced on elevated train platforms in New York City in 1888, cigarette machines were introduced in 1926, and the first soft drink machines appeared in 1937. Long production shifts in factories during World War II greatly spurred the development of the vending machine industry, which responded to the need for a convenient dispenser of hot coffee by placing coffee vending machines on factory floors. After the war, the global reach of the vending machine industry was significantly extended when major U.S. beverage producers like Coca-Cola and Pepsi began to penetrate overseas markets aggressively. Because retail space in Japan was limited, the vending machine became a major factor in the growth of the Japanese product distribution system by the 1960s. Microprocessor-controlled vending machines appeared on the U.S. market in 1992. By the late 1990s, vending machines were being used to sell a myriad of goods, including liquor, train tickets, toys, beef, fishing bait, power tools, business cards, women's clothing, and jewelry.

In the late 1990s, the world's largest vending machine markets were the United States, Japan, and Europe, with roughly 1,000 different types and models of vending machines available. In 1995 the number of vending machines in operation in the United States climbed past 6.4 million, one for every 50 people, compared to an estimated 5.5 million machines with 2.6 million for beverages in Japan in 1997, one for every 23 people. By 1997 the value of goods sold in vending machines in Japan had grown to US$55 billion, up 2 percent from 1996, while the U.S. market reported sales of US$28 billion. The European Union had about 5 million vending machines in operation, about 1 for every 75 people, in the late 1990s.

U.S. vending machines have historically been placed as private independent merchandising outlets inside offices, factories, and public spaces. Conversely, Japanese vending machines, more than half of which sell beverages, are primarily located on public sidewalks and are often used as point-of-sale merchandizing outlets to evade Japan's high labor costs. By 2001, the food and beverage vending market in Japan offered excellent

opportunities for international beverage machine manufacturers because of the Japanese consumer's openness to new food and beverage product mixes, merchandised through innovative vending technologies.

Between 1987 and 1997, sales through vending machines in Japan almost doubled, and innovative uses for vending machines continued to be tried. By the 1990s, however, Japan's often quite elaborate vending machines were consuming almost 4 percent of all electricity consumed on the island nation, leading the government to mandate that the electricity consumption of canned beverage vending machines be reduced by 20 percent by 1997. When the Japanese vending equipment industry met this goal, a further 15 percent electricity reduction by 2002 was called for at that time.

Between 1995 and 1998, the approximately 105 automatic vending machine makers in the United States reported an estimated increase in revenues of almost 10 percent, from US$940 million to US$1 billion. In 1999 worldwide industry sales rose to US$36 billion from US$34.8 billion in 1998, a gain of about 5 percent. By 2005, sales remained stable, but they were expected to more than double by 2010, largely due to cashless vending and new machines capable of accepting debit or credit cards. U.S. firms were among the leaders worldwide in implementing new high-tech vending machines that greatly improved the variety and quantity of goods sold, the serviceability of vending machines, and the accuracy of the vending operators' sales and inventory data. As early as 1993, one U.S. industry executive said that the maturing international vending machine market had begun to become "very hot." For the first time, many U.S. firms made a commitment to aggressively penetrate the world's growing vending machine markets. The growth of vending markets in some of the more urbanized regions of the Middle East, especially Saudi Arabia, and Latin America, including Venezuela and Argentina, substantially surpassed growth in other international markets. For example, Thailand was the only country in Southeast Asia to have vending machines up to 1998.

The vending segments's typically high-margin products, hot and cold cup beverages, remained strong in 1999. In the United Kingdom, beverage sold in vending machines increased in the mid- and late 1990s; canned cold drinks dominated, with dollar sales increasing 8.3 percent to US$15.7 billion, or 42.9 percent of total industry volume in 1999. Packaged confections and snacks held second place, with a 10.8 percent gain to US$7.2 billion.

Perhaps the biggest challenge facing European vending machine makers in the late 1990s was the European Monetary Union, which began to phase in the euro (also known as the European currency unit, or ECU) in 1999.

By 2002, national currencies in participating countries were eliminated. The euro was expected to put a strain on vending machine manufacturers, who estimated spending more than 10 percent of their annual budgets to rebuild equipment to accommodate the euro. The controllers and coin validators on all existing machines had to be reprogrammed for the euro and the machines had to be tested for reliability. Europe's vending machine operators, rather than the manufacturers, bore the brunt of the cost of retrofitting existing machines to the euro.

Laundry and Dishwashing Machinery. In the eighteenth century, laundry had been established as a viable small-business enterprise that was typically operated by individuals and dependent on individual manual labor. The development of its auxiliary industry, the manufacture of laundering machinery, was made possible when the first patent for a clothes-washing device was awarded to Nathaniel Briggs in 1797. Over the next 50 years, more than 200 patents were granted for washing machines. The dry-cleaning process was invented between 1825 and 1845 when it was accidentally discovered that a volatile liquid like camphene cleaned soiled clothes without using water. In 1863 Hamilton E. Smith patented a reciprocating washing device that reversed the motion of the revolving drum in the washing machine, turning the clothes over inside the drum and splashing them in soapy water. The first wooden-tub washing machine was introduced in 1900. A commercial laundry industry began to emerge as the development of washing and drying technology eventually evolved to electrical machines, and the spin-dry washing machine was introduced by 1924. The first electrically driven domestic dishwashers began to appear in Europe in 1929, and in the late 1970s the first computer-controlled washing machines, tumbling dryers, and "sensor-touch" dishwashers appeared on the market.

In 1993 a European commission began awarding "Eco-Labels" to manufacturers of environmentally-friendly laundry machines, reflecting the growing worldwide concern for energy savings and the impact of chemicals and detergents on the environment. A European Union initiative that went into effect in 1995 set safety standards for machinery sold in the common market and compelled many commercial laundry equipment makers to re-evaluate their products. To gain the "CE mark" of approval, firms were required to identify and reduce potential design and operational hazards in machines, as well as maintain technical construction files on each product built.

Firms in the United States, Asia, and Europe dominated the worldwide commercial laundry equipment industry in the late 1990s. Exports accounted for approximately 12 percent of all revenues for the U.S. commercial laundry equipment industry in 1996. Industry activities in East Asia reflected that region's rapid growth as a center

manufacturing service industry machines. South Korea's Daewoo Electronics Company invested heavily in the construction of washing machine plants in the mid-1990s and began exporting washing machines to Russia, while the South Korean firm LG Electronics exported 50,000 of its washing machines to Taiwan's Taistar in 1995. In 1994 Japan's Sanyo Electric announced plans to assemble and sell washing machines in mainland China.

Gas Pumps. The invention of the gas meter is credited to Samuel Clegg in 1815, but the gas pump in gas service stations had to wait for the development of the gasoline engine and the automobile. Following the worldwide adoption of the centrifugal pump by about 1850, John Tokheim, the founder of U.S.-based Tokheim Corporation, invented the first underground gasoline tank in 1898. By 1906 gasoline measuring pumps for the automobile were developed, followed by the first electrically operated pumps and computerized gas pumps with digital displays and automated payment features.

Leading world exporters of gas pumps included the United States, Japan, Germany, Italy, and France. In 1996, nearly 10 percent of U.S. industry shipments were exported, and in 1998, the United States had one of the world's largest pump manufacturing industries with about 70 companies generating revenues of US$1.33 billion.

In 2000 U.S. manufacturers pursued a domestic market consisting of roughly 200,000 service stations. Amoco's 3,000 service stations alone were estimated to spend at least US$12 million annually on equipment. Pump makers historically focused on large firms at the expense of small or independently run companies as a result of the dominance of the large U.S. gasoline and oil producers, like Amoco and Shell.

The world's less developed nations represented a major opportunity for industry firms in the late 1990s. China, for example, with five times the population of the United States, had only 5,500 service stations in the mid-1990s, which was less than 3 percent of the U.S. total. Large international measuring and dispensing pump makers continued to produce sophisticated digital pumps for developed markets and simple non-computerized gas pumps for developing markets. In 1993 Tokheim Corporation, one of the world's largest international manufacturers of measuring and dispensing pumps, reported increased sales in its Latin America and Asian markets. The company announced a US$72 million contract to supply pump equipment to Shell Europe and was pursuing a similar arrangement with Shell International.

Refrigeration, Air Conditioning, and Heating. The fundamental principle of modern refrigeration was that volatile liquids, such as ethyl ether, absorb heat when evaporated, which was discovered by William Cullen in 1748. Nonetheless, the refrigerator did not begin to replace the icebox until 1918.

Growth in world trade involving food products that require refrigeration also had a positive impact on equipment demand in the 1990s. In 1998 it was estimated that the HVAC/R equipment industry of the Pacific Rim countries was growing faster than the region's gross domestic product. As a newly prosperous global consumer class dined out more, restaurants multiplied, fueling the need for commercial refrigeration equipment. As office, store, and warehouse construction grew, so did the need for bigger and more efficient heating, ventilation, and cooling machines. By 2002 industry analysts lauded industry growth due to widespread chain grocery "superstores" requiring extensive refrigeration cases. The world's heating and refrigeration industry was also increasingly intermeshed, with international joint ventures, acquisitions, and partnerships flourishing, particularly in Asia's emerging economies, such as China. Between 1987 and 1997, exports of U.S. heating, ventilation, and air conditioning equipment doubled, and international sales accounted for as much as 35 percent of revenues for many U.S. firms by the late 1990s.

In 1902, Willis Carrier devised the first air conditioner, which was installed in a New York printing plant. Chlorofluorocarbons (CFCs), which were later found to be damaging to the environment, were introduced in the 1930s as a substitute for the flammable coolants used in earlier air conditioners. In 1939 Carrier developed the first air conditioning system for high-rise buildings, and by the end of World War II the air conditioner was in widespread use. The United Nations' Montreal Protocol of 1987 mandated the phase-out of (CFCs) in the 1990s, and many individual countries, such as the United States with the Clean Air Act Amendments, instituted their own restrictions. However, factory and office building owners seemed to be in no hurry to meet the deadlines. Of the 80,000 centrifugal and screw chillers that used CFCs in the United States in 1992, roughly 76 percent still needed CFCs to operate in January 1997. In the United States there was an installed base of HVAC/R equipment valued at more than US$137 billion in the late 1990s. In addition, it was estimated that in 1993 one-fifth of all U.S. heating systems were at least 20 years old and that 15 percent of all central cooling units were at least 10 years old. Moreover, in 1996 there were 130 million motor vehicle air conditioners and 5 million commercial refrigeration systems that still ran on CFCs. By 1998 about 20,000 CFC-based chillers had been converted or replaced in the United States. Clearly, at the beginning of the twenty-first century, industry firms around the globe could look forward to a bountiful

market supplying heating and cooling replacements and upgrades.

Heating equipment manufacturing became a mature industry in the 1700s. The first cast iron stove was manufactured in the American colonies before the American Revolution, and by 1744 Benjamin Franklin had invented a stove using movable ventilating doors to control temperature. Since then, the development of improved heating sources, insulating and construction materials, and temperature control have greatly improved the efficiency and sensitivity of equipment, making more innovative and productive commercial applications possible.

In 1996 the United Nations reported that world exports of industrial heating and cooling equipment reached US$36.4 billion, an increase of less than 1 percent from 1995. The United States led this segment with exports of US$5.9 billion, followed by Japan (US$5.4 billion), Germany (US$4.8 billion), Italy (US$4.8 billion), and France (US$2.6 billion). Leading importers that year included the United States (US$3.3 billion), Germany (US$2.4 billion), South Korea (US$2.2 billion), Canada (US$1.8 billion), France (US$1.8 billion), and China (US$1.7 billion).

The heating ventilation, air conditioning, and refrigeration (HVAC/R) equipment industry is extremely cyclical in nature because demand for its products depends on the health of end-use industries that are themselves notorious for wild swings in demand. The industry benefited from a robust year in housing starts in 1998, with 1.54 million units purchased. Housing, industrial, and commercial construction in developing warm-weather countries, as well as Eastern Europe, drove demand in 1998. Sales in Vietnam grew 18 percent each year, the Indian subcontinent 15 percent, Central Europe 10 percent, and Latin America nearly 8 percent. In the refrigeration sector, an aging population patronizing restaurants and an increasing demand for fresh and frozen food items shipped via refrigerated truck was anticipated to boost sales.

In addition to keeping up with environmental mandates for equipment requiring less harmful refrigerants, other challenges faced by industry firms in 2000 included international performance standards for all heating, ventilation, and air conditioning products so international firms could reduce the number of machine types and specifications worldwide. In the United States, industry firms faced the effects of the increasing deregulation of the U.S. energy utilities industry with uncertainty.

In the United States, HVAC/R equipment market, shipments of chillers doubled between 1987 and 1997. In the late 1990s about 97 U.S. industry firms set all-time sales records, including the shipping of 5.25 million central heating units in 1996. In 1997, 5.36 million central air conditioners and air conditioner source pumps were shipped along with 14,239 reciprocating liquid chiller packages that were used for comfort cooling in commercial, institutional, and government buildings.

By 2000 the worldwide HVAC/R equipment industry was benefiting from a favorable global economy and the new technology brought about by international agreements to reduce the use of greenhouse gas coolants. Many industry firms relied increasingly on international trade for profits. The rapid rise of a global middle class in countries that had been underdeveloped a generation earlier, many of which were in warm regions of the world, was opening up vast new markets for residential, commercial, and industrial air conditioning and cooling products. In addition, significant transportation costs and region-specific products were international trade factors driving companies to open plants worldwide and establish patterns of e-commerce.

CURRENT CONDITIONS

Vending Machines. In 2002, U.S. colleges had the highest vending sales of any other market segment, and more hospitals were adding machines than any other market segment. Beverages accounted for the majority of sales, at 48 percent, followed by snacks with 22 percent. According to *The Kiplinger Report,* vending machine revenues were expected to rise to US$70 billion by 2010.

In the mid-2000s, the fastest-growing trend in the segment was for vending machines that only accepted credit or debit cards, with sales authorized locally via wireless technology. Industry leaders expected this trend to reduce theft and vandalism, since there would be no cash in the machines. According to North County Vending, which was one of the largest vending companies in the United States, machines that had been retrofitted with card-only capabilities were no longer subject to vandalism and theft.

In January 2008, Convendium launched the Vendi vending machine that allowed shoppers to pay for convenience goods using eft-pos, credit cards, or by texting a code using a Vodafone mobile phone. The appropriate amount is deducted from a pre-paid balance or is added to a monthly statement. The "txt-to-pay" system was developed by the technology company Fronde.

Refrigeration, Air Conditioning, and Heating. According to a Freedonia Group study, HVAC demand was expected to rise more than 2 percent annually through 2007, reaching a value of US$12 billion. In addition to construction, the replacement market was expected to contribute to the growth of this sector. Reports from the Air-Conditioning and Refrigeration Institute were optimistic following a study that found that heat pump shipments had risen 11 percent from 2003 to 2004, and central air conditioner shipments were up 6 percent over the same period. Shipments of air source heat pumps and unitary air conditioners passed 7 million units for the first time in 2004 an increase of 9 percent over 2003. Furnace shipments were up 7 percent as well, with more than 3.5 million units of gas furnaces shipped. Canada reported improvements for heater sales and residential furnaces in 2004, but declines for commercial and residential air conditioning shipments.

Miscellaneous Service Machines Industry. More than 1,000 firms competed in the U.S. miscellaneous service machines industry. More U.S. companies were active in this segment than in the U.S. vending, commercial laundry, gas pump, and HVAC/R equipment industries combined. Several diversified international producers of service machines were significant contributors to the industry, including Xerox do Brasil (Brazil), Schmalbach-Lubeca AG (Germany), Fonderie Sime (Italy), and Ebara Corporation (Japan).

RESEARCH AND TECHNOLOGY

Vending Machines. Despite the somewhat prosaic image of the vending machine, the self-operating, or "robotic," nature of such equipment allows creative technical innovation. The world's vending machine industry had accepted advances in technology and innovative product merchandising that continued to revolutionize the segment in the late 1990s. A growing range of products was dispensed by vending machines from toys, plastic laminates for driver's licenses, cut flowers and picture frames, sandwiches, and greeting cards to pills (in hospitals), videocassettes and compact discs, cigars, frozen beef (in Japan), travel tickets, salads, and even beer and alcohol (in Canada and Asian countries).

The introduction of microprocessors and electronic controllers inside vending machines led to the development of features that improved marketability, such as elaborate multimedia displays and the capacity of some machines to perform a self-inventory of product supply or a self-diagnosis of mechanical functions. Vending machines could even transmit information about product supply and machine conditions to a computer at the vending service company via a modem inside the machine, using either the Internet or proprietary electronic data interchange to communicate the data. Route servers for vending machine operations increasingly used handheld computers that allowed them to visit only machines they knew to be low in product or in need of repair. The machines could also transmit their highly detailed sales and self-diagnostic data into the service person's computer so it could be analyzed, graphed, and sent back to the office.

Vending service firms traditionally had to adjust thermostat controls in temperature-variable machines by hand, but self-adjusting vending machines were designed in the mid- and late 1990s that reacted to changes in their surroundings. Some machines were programmed to stop selling products when temperatures reached a predetermined level. Other innovations in the 1990s included vending machines that were equipped to process credit cards, greet potential buyers with computerized welcome and thank-you messages, and use laser scanning beams to identify up to 4,000 different coin types accurately. Machines that protected against vandalism, handled 36 separate columns of beverage cans or preparing 96 different beverage combinations, and verified driver's licenses to prevent underage teens from buying tobacco or alcohol were also introduced. In addition, Vending and food service companies were adding Vending Miser to their product lines. When installed on existing refrigerated vending machines, Vending Miser decreases a machine's energy use and makes it environmentally friendly.

In 2008, Patriot Energy announced the worldwide launch of a vending machine solution that would provide just-in-time inventory control and monitor activity to prevent unauthorized activity by remote surveillance. Projected sales for the new vending machine add-ons were US$33,500 for 100,000 units, with monthly recurring revenues of up to US$2.5 million.

Commercial Laundry Equipment. In May 1994 the U.S. Department of Energy issued updated energy efficiency standards for appliances, including commercial washers and dryers, and planned to announce more stringent standards by 1999. These guidelines required some industry firms to upgrade product lines to improve machine performance. Beginning around 1991, innovations in the external design of commercial laundry machines, as well as their internal functions, began to result in substantial changes. In 1993 Staber Industries of the United States began to market a top-loading, horizontal-axis washing machine similar in basic design to European washers. U.S. manufacturers hoped to capitalize on increasing concern for environmental issues by marketing the European top-loading design that used less water and detergent, breaking the attachment of U.S. consumers to front-loading, vertical axis machines. Innovations in washer technology included 18-pound wash load capacities; no clutch transmission or brake mechanisms; and improved washing processes that actively pumped detergent fluids into the laundry fibers, rather than relying passively on the motion of the clothes during the wash cycle.

According to *Consumer Reports*, Energy Star ratings did not consistently indicate the greatest energy or money savings based on their testing. Some differences were attributed by federal officials to testing methods using different technology.

Gasoline Pumps. In the late 1990s, worldwide research and development in the pump sector centered on modifications inspired by environmental concerns as well as technological advances for payment, display, and automation features. The United States was a forerunner in legislation to reduce the amount of gasoline fumes released during vehicle fueling. Some states passed more stringent laws than the federal government, requiring the installation of vapor recovery features in fuel pump products that could recover up to 95 percent of escaping gas fumes.

Gas pumps with digital readouts and automatic card payment features became common in many developed economies in the late 1990s. Other innovations geared to urban markets included electronic sensors that shut off a pump when a gas tank reached capacity or a customer drove off without removing the nozzle from the gas tank. New pump designs also offered efficient electronic configurations that substantially reduced the number of connections, boards, and cables used to construct and operate pumps.

Refrigeration, Air Conditioning, and Heating. Technical advances in heating and refrigeration equipment in the late 1990s centered on improving the performance, quality, and efficiency of machines and developing technologies that used refrigerants that were not harmful to the environment and conformed to indoor air quality guidelines issued by urbanized countries. Global consensus to protect the environment led to more efficient refrigerant recycling and recovery components, and alternative, non-chlorine-based refrigerant technologies. The first widespread substitute refrigerant for CFC was hydrochlorofluorocarbon or HCFC. However, it was scheduled to be phased out by 2020 along with other freon-type refrigerants. Alternatives were sought, from natural gas, steam, and low-pressure refrigerants, such as Du Pont's SUVA 123, to ammonia, lithium bromide/water, and ammonia/water-based refrigerants. In the late 1990s, radical innovations to heating and cooling systems were introduced. Ground-source or geothermal heat pumps (GSHP) exchange heat with the earth itself rather than the external air by using a loop of underground pipes, thus avoiding the greenhouse issue altogether. Another approach was to design fully closed or zero-emission chillers that, while using CFC-type refrigerants, allow none to escape into the atmosphere. At the rate CFC chillers were being replaced in the late 1990s, they were not expected to be eliminated in the United States until 2010, according to the American Refrigeration Institute.

By the late 1990s, industry firms were so successful at improving the efficiency of heating and cooling products that engineers only had system control designs left to improve. A new generation of electronic controls offered tighter tolerance ranges than ever before, ensuring greater efficiency by creating machines that ran closer to their ideal performance set points. Other control innovations included self-contained diagnostic features that guided repair people to the malfunctioning part or ran periodic self-checks, alerting repair people at remote locations via computer if a problem arose. Controls could notify the user when the machine needed cleaning or the air filter should be changed.

Other research focused on reducing equipment noise levels in condensing units to conform to noise pollution regulations and adopting scroll compressor technology to replace traditional reciprocating methods in refrigeration condensers, improving energy efficiency. One innovative approach was a thermal energy storage (TES) system, which was a chiller that only operated at night when electricity rates are lowest. It stored the cooling it generated in the form of ice, cold water, or other material. When cool air was required during the day, the system retrieved the cool energy it had stored the night before.

Industry firms in the 1990s also employed less complex designs for air conditioners, effectively reducing the number of parts and the amount of maintenance needed. Improved designs also included double-wall construction in air conditioners, advanced heat pumps, air conditioners with improved seasonal energy efficiency ratings (SEER), and heaters with enhanced heating season performance factors (HSPF). Industry product engineers increasingly relied on engineering software tools such as computer-aided design (CAD), which enabled them to design increasingly accurate virtual components and systems on their computers that were capable of simulating the actual performance of a real product without the cost of manufacturing a prototype.

Miscellaneous Service Machines. Developments in the miscellaneous service machine segment in the 1990s included increased energy efficiency, improved ease of use, and products that were environmentally sensitive. Improvements in design also enabled manufacturers to create products for highly specific applications by incorporating sensors, automation, and computerized, or "smart," features, creating increased functionality and productivity. Innovations were sometimes rooted in consumer applications, such as commercial scanning ovens that "read" coded cooking instructions and commercial kitchen appliances that reached high temperatures in short periods of time. Traditional institutional end users also benefited from such advances as carbon dioxide steam cookers that could cook, pasteurize, sterilize, and cool with a temperature accuracy of

plus or minus 0.5 degrees as well as jet steam ovens that used high-intensity vertical air flow to evenly brown foods in high-yield food preparation environments.

WORKFORCE

Vending Machines. Some of the industry firms with the largest number of employees in the late 1990s included Germany's Effem GmbH (1,375 workers); Japan's Glory Ltd. (1,800), Nippon Signal (1,939), and Sanden Corp. (2,608); and Holland's Philips Machinefabrieken Nederland (2,000). The largest U.S. vending equipment makers, IMI Cornelius and Rowe International, employed 1,500 and 1,200 employees, respectively, in 1997. Total employment in the U.S. vending machine industry in 1998 was estimated at 7,000, with annual average wages of US$20,000 in the mid-1990s for the 73 percent of that number who were production workers.

Commercial Laundry Equipment. Large international employers in the commercial laundry equipment segment of the industry in the late 1990s included China's Guangdong Jiangmen Washing Machine Factory (1,062 workers), India's HMP Engineers Ltd. (650), Hong Kong's Process Automation (Holdings) Ltd. (700), and Germany's Bosch-Siemens Hausgeraete GmbH (27,625).

In 1998 the United States was the world's largest commercial laundry equipment manufacturer, employing an estimated 5,000 workers. Firms in Florida, Kentucky, and Louisiana accounted for 45 percent of the segment's U.S. employment. The typical U.S. establishment employed 67 workers with an average annual wage for production employees of US$22,174. The largest U.S. employers in this segment in 1996 were Pellerin Milnor (900 workers), Cissell Manufacturing (400), and Unimac Company (400).

Service Station Pumps. In 1997, the largest employers in worldwide pump manufacturing were Japan's Kawamoto Pump Manufacturing, South Korea's Lee Chun Electric Manufacturing, Mexico's Capacitores Componentes de Mexico, and Switzerland's ABB Turbo Systems. In 1998 the U.S. industry was the largest worldwide for this segment, employing an estimated 6,400 workers. A typical industry establishment employed 79 workers and paid production employees US$30,216 annually. The largest U.S. employers in this segment in 1996 were Graco Inc. (2,100 workers), Wayne (900), and Tokheim Corp. (1,900).

Refrigeration, Air Conditioning, and Heating. The United States claims the world's largest HVAC/R equipment industry, with an estimated 208,250 employees, 75 percent of whom were on the production line earning an average of US$15.62 an hour in 2000. The average establishment in the U.S. HVAC/R equipment industry employed 141 workers and paid its production workers about US$32,490 a year. Assemblers, fabricators, and miscellaneous hand workers constituted the largest single occupational category in the U.S. industry segment.

Outside the United States, large industry employers included France's Unite Hermetique; the United Kingdom's York International Ltd. and Halma PLC; China's Chunlan Group Corp. and Baocheng General Electronics; Japan's Daikin Industries and Hitachi Air Conditioning Refrigeration Co.; and Germany's Wolf GmbH, Gebrueder Trox, and Viessmann GmbH.

Miscellaneous Service Machines. In the late 1990s, many of the largest employers manufacturing miscellaneous service industry machinery were U.S. firms. In the mid-1990s a typical U.S. establishment employed 38 workers and paid production employees US$23,065 per year, and by 1998, the segment employed about 44,200 workers. The largest U.S. employers in this industry sector in 1996 were Welbilt Corp., Hoover North America, Ionics Inc., and Tennant Co. Major employers worldwide included two German firms, Kloeckner-Humboldt-Deautz and Schmalbach-Lubeca, the United Kingdom's Sapalux, Japan's Ebara Corporation, and Brazil's Xerox do Brasil.

INDUSTRY LEADERS

Panasonic Corp. Matsushita Electric Industrial Company's participation in the world service machines industry, particularly air conditioners, was rooted in its largest business division, communication and industrial equipment. In 2008, Matsushita reported combined sales from its 650-plus companies throughout the world at US$92 billion with approximately 328,645 employees. Through its world-leading consumer electronics products, Matsushita had been at the forefront of the high-tech home electronics revolution of the 1970s and 1980s, marketing video equipment, digital videodiscs, flat-panel televisions, personal digital assistants, miniature VCRs, and notebook computers. The company was most well-known for its Panasonic brand.

To consolidate its market position and ensure corporate stability in its core industries, Matsushita invested heavily in refurbishing factories and vowed to raise its international sales from 45 to 50 percent of its total revenues, spearheaded by sales offices in Eastern Europe and Central and Southeast Asia. Matsushita remained a highly diversified company in 2002, with major interests in electronic components, home appliances, audio equipment, batteries, and kitchen appliances, along with a wide range of other products, from industrial robots and fax machines to pagers, copiers, and bicycles.

In September 2008, the company had announced plans to stop using the Japanese brand name of "National," changing it to "Panasonic." On October 1, 2008, *Business Week* reported that the name change was complete and that the company's ticker on the New York Stock Exchange was changed to "PC" from "MC." In addition, the company planned to launch a marketing campaign called "Hello Panasonic" in order to boost its market share. The complete changeover was expected to be accomplished by March 2010.

Mitsubishi. In addition to its role as one of the world's largest air conditioning system manufacturers, Mitsubishi Heavy Industries, reporting US$22.4 billion in annual sales for 2004, was a significant multinational manufacturer of aircraft and industrial machinery and equipment. As one of Asia's largest multinationals, and part of Japan's Mitsubishi conglomerate of affiliated companies, or *keiretsu,* the company was well positioned to exploit the rapidly growing industrial and infrastructure development in countries like Malaysia, Thailand, and mainland China.

Mitsubishi Electric Corporation, whose origins were linked to a shipping firm founded in 1870, had five primary sectors: energy and electric (power generation plants, monitoring systems and escalators), appliances (air conditioning systems, projection TVs and monitors), information and communication systems (automotive multimedia systems, satellites and networking equipment); industrial automation systems (logic controllers, circuit breakers and robotics) and electronic devices (semiconductors and interposers). Approximately three-quarters of company sales came from Japan.

Together, Mitsubishi's machinery and construction divisions accounted for 40 percent of 2004 sales. The company expanded air conditioner production at its Asian plants and marketed a new line of ceiling-mounted air conditioners. In 1996 the company's machinery interests, through which it participated in the services industry machines market, accounted for 18 percent of its total sales. Like other Japanese companies, including Matsushita, Mitsubishi suffered from the protracted Japanese recession of the 1990s.

United Technologies. United Technologies (UT) was founded in 1934. Between 1980 and 1990 Carrier expanded its European business 800 percent, claiming 23 percent of the U.K. air conditioning market alone, and estimated its ventures in Thailand, Indonesia, and Malaysia would triple by the beginning of the twenty-first century. The six major industries UT participated in by the late 1990s were aircraft engine manufacture, helicopters, elevators and escalators, heating and air conditioning systems, aerospace and industrial systems, and motor vehicles and car bodies, spread over 183 countries. In an attempt to free itself from its dependency on defense contracts, UT began a policy of acquisitions and diversification in the 1980s that stressed the development of low-profile partnerships with foreign companies in such countries as Vietnam, Russia, and China. For example, Carrier successfully entered a number of foreign markets by establishing joint ventures in which local companies maintained management control in exchange for a Carrier product platform that helped penetrate local air conditioner markets. In 1992 it bought a controlling interest in China's Tianjin Uni-Air Conditioning Co.

By the late 1990s, UT's Carrier division accounted for 24 percent of total sales and, in addition to air conditioners, operated in the building controls and larger refrigeration, heating, and ventilation industries. In 2007, Carrier's revenues were $14.6 billion. Carrier had almost 43,000 employees around the world and in the late 2000s was the number one heating and air-conditioning company worldwide, reporting US$54.7 billion in 2007 sales.

Carrier Commercial Refrigeration (CCR), a subsidiary of Carrier Corporation, was a major food-service equipment manufacturer, manufacturing equipment necessary for commercial refrigeration, beverages, and desserts. CCR's customers have included fast food restaurants (McDonald's, Burger King, and Wendy's), breweries, convenience stores, soft-drink bottlers and grocery store operators. CCR's divisions include Beverage-Air (refrigerated coolers and display cases), Taylor (dispensers for soft-serve ice cream, milk shakes, and frozen yogurt) and International Cold Storage (walk-in coolers). For 2007, CCR reported an estimated US$453.4 billion in sales and 4,282 employees.

American Standard. The merger of American Standard America, Crane Plumbing Holding Corp., and Eljer Holding Corp. formed American Standard Brands. Trane, a subsidiary of American Standard and the world's largest supplier of heating, ventilation, and air conditioning comfort systems for the building management industry, accounted for 60 percent of American's sales in the mid-1990s, about the time it unveiled a commercial air conditioner that did not use CFC coolants. American Standard/Trane concentrated on building its international presence in the Pacific Rim and Europe. With 89 manufacturing plants in 27 countries, almost one-half of Trane's sales in 1995 were from outside the United States. Its two primary service industry machinery business sectors were applied systems (custom-engineered air conditioners for commercial use) and unitary systems (factory-assembled central air conditioning systems).

In 2004 American Standard reported sales of US$9.5 billion, an 11 percent increase over 2003. The company claimed that it was increasing its range of products and focusing on high quality, value, and customer service, promising "a broader portfolio brand, a more comprehensive set of product lines, enhanced distribution opportunities, cost benefits and greater scale in relevant markets."

MAJOR COUNTRIES IN THE INDUSTRY

In 2000 the United States, Japan, Germany, and Italy were the leading exporters of heating and cooling equipment worldwide. Other major exporters included France, the United Kingdom, Hong Kong, Denmark, Sweden, and the Netherlands. The United States, Germany, Hong Kong, and China were the leading importers. By the mid-2000s, China had joined the ranks of leading world exporters as well. Developing nations were expected to see the greatest opportunity as improved standards of living stimulate demand. A flourishing construction industry in China was expected to increase the value of China's commercial air conditioner market to nearly US$2.4 billion by 2005, with demand in major cities growing 70 to 80 percent annually, as reported by *Appliance.*

The United States. The United States, a leader in the global industry, exported more than US$2.5 billion worth of refrigeration and heating equipment in 1996. In the late 1990s, the country was a leading exporter of non-household refrigeration equipment and parts, heating and cooling equipment, air conditioning machinery, and pumps for gases worldwide. In 1999, more than 2,000 U.S. industry firms generated US$34.1 billion in revenues and employed about 179,000 workers. The largest segment in sales continued to be refrigeration and heating equipment, which accounted for 72 percent of industry shipments. According to *Euromonitor,* that segment was expected to grow 26 percent to US$37 billion by 2007.

By 2001, Tokheim Corporation claimed roughly one-third of the U.S. pump market and approximately one-sixth of the total world market, with subsidiaries in the Netherlands, Britain, Germany, South Africa, and Canada. For the fiscal year ending June 30, 2008, USA Technologies reported revenues of more than US$16.1 million.

Japan. In the mid-1990s, Japan was the second largest exporter of heating and cooling equipment worldwide, accounting for 15 percent of all equipment exports. It ranked high in exports of gasoline pumps, air conditioning machinery, heating and cooling equipment, non-household refrigeration equipment, and refrigeration equipment parts. Between 1988 and 1992, Japan's share of total global market exports for heating, refrigeration, and cooling equipment averaged 15 percent, but the country reported much larger global market shares in two other industry sectors. Although gas pump exports were flat in the early 1990s, Japan captured a consistent 22.5 percent market share. Air conditioner exports grew from 23 percent in 1989 to almost 29 percent in 1992, with Matsushita Electric and Mitsubishi Heavy Industries being the most successful companies.

Japanese firms in the industry have served as the model for quality control, improved productivity, and just-in-time inventory control, which have been adopted by international service industry machine manufacturers, from American Standard to Lennox Industries and United Technologies. After the 1989 meltdown of the Japanese stock market, a stagnant economy engulfed Japan in the late 1990s, including its heating and refrigeration industry. By the mid-2000s, the Japanese market had matured, showing improvement from slow growth between 1998 and 2003, although it was expected to show below average gains through 2008.

According to the Japan Soft Drink Association, Japan has about 2.8 million vending machines that sell Japanese stew, flowers, books, magazines, and underwear, as well as defibrillators for people trying to save heart attack victims. Beverage machines may dispense hot or cold drinks. Revenues of some vending machines benefit pediatric cancer patients or the homeless.

Germany. Germany ranks among the top five exporters in heating and cooling equipment, service station pumps, air conditioning machinery, and non-household refrigeration equipment and parts. It has been the market leader in imports of non-household refrigeration equipment and parts. Despite a general decline in the German air conditioning market in the early 1990s, roughly 2,600 firms were still active in the industry in 1999 and accounted for DM11.5 billion, with sales of German air conditioning units beginning to rebound.

German vending machines accounted for one-half of the approximately 5 million vending machines in operation in the European Union in the late 1990s, most of which sold cigarettes. German vending machine manufacturers and importers reported 1996 sales of US$305 million, and Germany's vending machines accounted for roughly US$9 billion in sales in 1997. Between 1996 and 1997, German vending equipment industry firms reported an increase in revenues of about 5 percent, and their business was expected to grow 9 to 12 percent per year through the end of the twentieth century.

The collapse of the Soviet Union in the early 1990s created enormous potential for German heating and refrigeration firms in Eastern Europe, as well as in the Russian Federation. Although monetary instability, changing tax laws, and a deeply uncertain business and political climate made conducting business in Russia difficult, German heating and refrigeration manufacturers successfully sold large systems to Russian hotels, hospitals, and other buildings. Investments to modernize Eastern Germany, along with rigid and costly labor policies, not only created a drag on the German economy, but also stifled economic growth in the 1990s. The adoption of a single European Union currency, however, was expected to streamline international trade within the common market as well as benefit Germany's heating and refrigeration industry. According to *Euromonitor,* this market segment was expected to grow 15 percent by 2007.

BIBLIOGRAPHY

"American Standard America, Crane Plumbing and Eljer Complete Merger, Creating a Leading North American Bath and Plumbing Company." 3 June 2008. Available from www.americanstandard-us.com.

"Cashless Machine Spurs Concessions Spend." *Screen Digest,* February 2005.

"Consumers 'In a Hurry' Ideal Market for USA Technologies' e-Port(R) Cashless Vending Solutions." *PR Newswire,* 2 March 2005.

Fukada, TaKahiro. "Anything, Any Time, Anywhere." 23 September 2008. Available from japantimes.co.jp.

Hall, John R. "What Does the Future Hold?" *Air Conditioning, Heating & Refrigeration News,* 3 May 2004.

Hendry, Simon. "Payments by Texting Prove a Hit at Convendium Vending Machines," 18 September 2008. Available from www.nzherald.co.nz.

"Hoover's Company Capsules." *Hoover's Online,* 2008. Available from www.hoovers.com.

"Industrial Air Conditioning, Refrigeration and Heating Machinery in France, Germany, UK, US." *Euromonitor,* August 2004. Available from www.majormarketprofiles.com.

"Leading Trade Publication Cites Cashless Vending as New Competitive Weapon." *PR Newswire,* 11 March 2004.

"MTI Reports That the Heat Treating Industry Generated Sales of $72.8m in September 2003." *Furnaces International,* January–February 2004.

"Nigerian Industries Convert to Ozone-friendly Technologies." 26 September 2008. Available from www.thisdayonline.com.

"Occupational Outlook Handbook, 2002–2003." *US Department of Labor,* 2001.

"Patriot Energy's Subsidiary, TelTeck to Marketing Vending Machine Solution." *MarketWatch,* 1 October 2008. Available from www.marketwatch.com.

"Reports: Energy Star Ratings Not So Accurate." Available from www.printthis.clickability.com.

"Schools to Drop Snack Food." *Baltic Times,*25 September 2008. Available from www.baltictimes.com.

Siegel, James J. "January A/C Shipments Rise 6 Percent." *Air Conditioning, Heating & Refrigeration News,* 15 March 2004.

———. "Study Predicts Rise in Equipment Demand." *Air Conditioning, Heating* & *Refrigeration News,* 15 March 2004.

"South Africa: Eyeing Australia for Greater Growth." *Business Day* (Johannesburg), 8 September 2008. Available from allafrica.com.

"Study: Vending Machine Demand to Rise." *Beverage World,* 15 April 2004.

Sutton, William G. "Looking to the Future Through China's Eye." *Appliance Manufacturer,* June 2004.

Turpin, Joanna R. "Manufacturers Come Off Record Year." *Air Conditioning, Heating* & *Refrigeration News,* 28 March 2005.

"U.S. Vending Machine Demand to Reach $1.6 Billion." *Candy Industry,* March 2003.

"USA Technologies Inc. Reports Revenue Growth for Fiscal Year," 26 September 2008. Available from www.amonline.com.

"Vending Machine Company Completes Installation of Card-Only Accepting Machines." *Cardline,* 11 July 2004.

"Vending Volume Up 20 Percent on Average." *Food Service Director,* 15 August 2002.

"World Commercial Refrigeration Demand to Grow Through 2008." *Appliance,* March 2005.

Zhang, Sean. "China Refrigeration 2004." *Appliance,* July 2004.

SIC 3579

OFFICE MACHINES

NAICS CODE(S)

333313. The global office machine industry supplies numerous devices used in office settings. Major product classes include word processing equipment (except computers), typewriters, adding machines and calculators, postage meters, envelope sealers and openers, other mail-handling machines, and simple mechanical devices such as staplers and paper cutters. Two important categories of office machines excluded from the following discussion are computers and photocopiers, which are treated separately under **Computers** and **Photographic Equipment and Supplies,** respectively.

INDUSTRY SNAPSHOT

Overall growth in the office machines industry remained stagnant through the 2000s, due primarily to the effect of technological developments outside the industry, as well as the slumping global economy. Just as photocopying rapidly supplanted mimeograph duplicating, computers have largely supplanted typewriters and word processors due to increased demand in the business community for Internet and network connectivity. Furthermore, recent years have witnessed massive growth in the market for multifunction office machines, which typically contain facsimile, printing, photocopying, and scanning capabilities in a single unit, which is then connected to the computer network. Such multifunctional equipment

had the lion's share of the U.S. market, with 68 percent, a figure that was projected to reach 74 percent by 2007, according to *Euromonitor.* From the point of view of office machines manufacturers, however, technological transformations are only problematic if the manufacturer is unable to diversify into the newer products.

The quick migration to such newer technologies has been most pronounced in leading markets such as the United States and Japan, while other nations still rely more heavily on older forms of office machines. According to *Euromonitor,* France was projected to have 39 percent industry growth into 2007, while Germany was expected to have 9 percent growth and the United Kingdom, 5 percent growth. The Asia Pacific region was another area expected to realize growth. According to the World Trade Organization (WTO), office and telecom equipment accounted for one-third to two-thirds of total exports in 2004 for five Asian economies, contributing significantly to the area's success.

According to *Office Products International,* consolidation was key for industry players to remain competitive throughout the 2000s. The high rate of acquisition activity that has characterized the office machines industry for years continues to make the industry's boundaries relatively ambiguous. Manufacturers of office machines and related parts and accessories typically are highly diversified firms with operations in a variety of industries. In particular, electronics and computer manufacturers tend to be among the leading producers of office machines, especially word processors and typewriters, the most prominent products in the industry. In most cases, general office machines accounted for a small portion of such firms' revenues.

ORGANIZATION AND STRUCTURE

In spite of slow growth overall, markets for typewriters remain strong in some countries, including India, Indonesia, China, Brazil, and Germany. The major suppliers of office machines in these regions, as well as in more mature markets such as Japan, the United States, and the European Union (EU), are primarily large, highly diversified international corporations involved in everything from camera production to superconductor technology to personal pagers to business consulting. In addition to these industry giants, smaller, more specialized domestic firms maintain a healthy position in localized and niche markets. Most of the major players conduct the bulk of their business through large retail dealerships like Staples and Office Depot, though many supplement this business with outlet establishments and mail-order services. Due in large part to the generally flat or declining demand for typewriters and word processors, many industry players have focused attention on customer

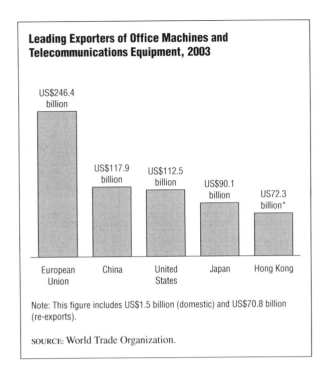

Leading Exporters of Office Machines and Telecommunications Equipment, 2003

US$246.4 billion — European Union
US$117.9 billion — China
US$112.5 billion — United States
US$90.1 billion — Japan
US72.3 billion* — Hong Kong

Note: This figure includes US$1.5 billion (domestic) and US$70.8 billion (re-exports).

SOURCE: World Trade Organization.

service operations, which have become one of the primary selling points in a market that has seen its research and development investments re-appropriated to rival industries such as personal-computer manufacturers.

Two associations served the industry in Europe. The European Association of Manufacturers of Business Machines and Data Processing Equipment (EUROBIT) was established in 1974 in Frankfurt, Germany, and represented nearly all of the region's manufacturers of business machines. The European Federation of Importers of Business Equipment (FEIM), headquartered in DeMeern, the Netherlands, was established in 1965.

BACKGROUND AND DEVELOPMENT

The development of the typewriter was one of the most important and influential events in the office machines industry, as well as in the general business climate. The typewriter transformed the organization of offices in both public and private sectors, and was instrumental in adding to the number of office occupations, as well as the number of female secretaries, in the United States and Europe during the late nineteenth century. Moreover, typewriters played an important role in the development of other office machines. As typewriters facilitated the reorganization and systematization of the office climate and data records, typewriter manufacturers expanded operations to include data-processing equipment and other office appliances. Because research and development efforts were already geared toward office systems and needs, and

because production methods were already in place to enable such diversification, these manufacturers used the massive profits derived from typewriter sales to manufacture this new equipment. In addition, these companies had already established a client base in the office products market and could easily offer new products to companies and individuals who took a liking to their typewriters.

During the late nineteenth century, there were approximately 20 significant typewriter-related innovations that preceded the commercialization of the typewriter in the 1870s. Most of these developments originated in the United States, with the remainder in Europe. Working intensively between 1867 and 1873, Christopher Latham Sholes of Wisconsin developed the first commercially successful typewriter. Sholes's typewriter was manufactured by E. Remington and Sons of Ilion, New York, a producer of weaponry that had grown rapidly during the United States Civil War years. Seeking to diversify its production after the war, Remington sold several hundred typewriters during the first year of production, with prices ranging from US$25 to US$50.

A number of other firms began producing typewriters in the 1870s and 1880s, and many of them featured technical innovations. Most of the features associated with modern manual typewriters were available in the 1890s, including upper and lower case letters, a space bar, and "front-strike" technology, which enabled a typist to see what was being typed. The industry experienced rapid growth soon after its origins, and in 1886 a total of 50,000 typewriters were sold in the United States. In 1888, the Remington Standard Typewriter Company produced 18,000 typewriters and was still unable to keep up with demand.

A U.S. government survey estimated that there were 30 firms employing 1,735 workers in the U.S. typewriter industry during these early years. The rapid growth of the industry was predicated on manufacturers' development of a service and marketing apparatus to accommodate the complexity and relatively high cost (up to US$100 by 1890) of typewriters. The largest firms in the industry in 1905 were Remington (which became Remington Rand in the 1920s), Underwood, Royal, and L.C. Smith (which became Smith Corona in the 1920s).

In addition to typewriters, other important products for the industry were developed in the late nineteenth century. These included carbon paper for typewriters—patented in 1872—and mimeograph paper and machines, commercialized shortly thereafter by the A.B. Dick Company. Until the development of electrostatic copying by RCA in the 1950s and xerographic copying by the Xerox Corporation in the 1960s, carbon paper and mimeographs were the primary means of duplicating forms. Furthermore, the first commercial dictating machine was produced in 1888 by the Columbia Graphophone Company, which later evolved into the Dictaphone Corporation.

In the first half of the twentieth century, U.S. manufacturers dominated world trade, particularly in Asia and Latin America. The United States and Canada made up the world's largest market for office equipment, followed by Europe. Sales of office machines to Europe accounted for 30 to 45 percent of U.S. output. During these years of rapid growth, U.S. manufacturers established overseas distribution and production facilities. This growth was indicated by U.S. employment in the office machines industry, which by that time included the production of calculating machines and cash registers. In 1925, the industry had 69,000 employees in the United States. Employment subsequently rose to 78,000 in 1927 and 90,000 in 1930. Sales of leading manufacturers stagnated during the Great Depression, but rebounded dramatically upon the United States' entry into World War II. From 1940 to 1941, Remington Rand's sales increased from US$49 million to US$77 million, IBM's from US$46 million to US$63 million, Underwood's from US$26 million to US$37 million, Royal's from US$19 million to US$24 million, Smith Corona's from US$11 million to US$15 million, and Pitney Bowes' from US$4 million to US$6 million.

The development of the office machines industry followed a similar path in Europe, with smaller firms operating in Britain, Italy, France, and the Scandinavian countries. The country most like the United States in terms of firm size, research, and new product development was Germany. The largest German firm at the time was Brunsviga Maschinenwerke, which was established in the late nineteenth century and developed a diversified product line and a sales and service network throughout Germany.

The growing market for typewriters and other office machines in the post-World War II years was in part the result of the rapidly growing service sector. Between 1920 and 1970, the share of service sector employees in the United States doubled, from 30 percent to 60 percent. From 1940 to 1950, the number of clerical workers in the United States increased from 4.9 million to 7.2 million, and the number of factory workers producing office machines increased from 24,000 to 40,000. The growing use of the electric typewriter, with a typing stroke powered by an electrical motor, was an important change during these years. Although initially commercialized in the 1920s, the sales of electric typewriters did not take off until the postwar years, outstripping the sales of manual computers by the mid-1960s. IBM (International Business Machines) introduced its first electric typewriters in the 1930s and became one of the top

sellers of typewriters after the war. Combined with its earlier developments in data processing equipment, IBM's entry into typewriter production facilitated its evolution into the world's largest producer of computers.

IBM divided its domestic and foreign operations by establishing the IBM World Trade Corporation in 1949. IBM World Trade established sales and production facilities in 58 countries in Europe, Asia, and Latin America, as well as its own research and development facilities in the United States. These specialized facilities enabled the firm to accommodate the requirements of individual foreign markets, including the development of machinery for Asian alphabets. In 1949, IBM World Trade's sales were only US$6.3 million. By 1956, sales had increased to US$158 million, compared to US$734 million for the domestic firm. In 1944, IBM developed the Mark I—a large electromechanical computer—in cooperation with Howard Aiken at Harvard University. IBM began production of computers for business in 1955. These first generation computers were large, featuring vacuum-tube electronics and employing punched cards as a recording medium.

In 1948, Remington Rand was second only to IBM in terms of assets and employment and provided another example of the direct connection between the production of mechanical office machinery and the production of computers. Remington Rand evolved from being the first firm to produce typewriters on a commercial basis to becoming, after World War II and a name change to Sperry Rand, the first firm to produce computers on a commercial basis. Its breakthrough computer was the UNIVAC I, which was first used in 1951 by the U.S. Bureau of the Census. The UNIVAC I calculated on a purely electronic rather than electromechanical basis, and featured internally stored programs and extensive use of peripherals, including magnetic tape readers and high-speed printers. Sales of the UNIVAC I peaked in 1955. Olivetti of Italy was another large firm that made the transition from production of typewriters to production of computers and was the second largest firm in the industry in the early 1990s by volume of sales.

Network Ltd. pioneered the bilingual typewriter, introducing its Hindu-English typewriter in 1986, and went on to market five other types of bilingual electronic typewriters. Indonesia imported 191,457 typewriters in 1991—23 percent from Japan, 11 percent from Taiwan, and 7 percent from China. The Shanghai Electric Meter Factory of China entered into a joint venture with the NEC Corporation of Japan in 1992 to increase production of its advanced multilingual typewriter. Shanghai's typewriter noiselessly printed in seven languages and could also send facsimiles.

Word processors evolved from automatic type-writers, also called autotypists, which were developed in the mid-1930s. The autotypist made use of a punched paper tape to store information for form letters. The first true word processor was IBM's Magnetic Tape/Selectric Typewriter, produced in 1964. This version of the Selectric was a high-speed typewriter that made use of magnetic tape for storage and retrieval. By the early 1970s, minicomputers were being used for word processing. One of the key changes in word processing equipment at that time was the use of visual displays. This was facilitated by the development and commercialization of the personal computer by Apple in the late 1970s and by IBM in the early 1980s. The development of the personal computer provided space for the rapid growth of word processing. At the same time, personal computer innovations were incorporated into more specialized typewriter-based personal word processors, which led to the development of hybrid units that combined features of typewriters and personal computers.

The value of world exports of office machines and office machinery parts and accessories decreased slightly in 1996, totaling US$95.8 billion compared to US$97.8 billion in 1995. The market for personal word processors grew at a rate of 21 percent per year in the early 1990s. World production of typewriters, on the other hand, declined from 7.7 million to 5.1 million units over the same years. In the mid-1990s, between 750,000 and 800,000 electronic typewriters were sold annually in the United States. This was down from a high of 1.4 million units sold annually between 1986 and 1988, and a direct reflection of the growing use of personal computers and word processors.

Japan, once the largest standalone word processor market, saw a significant decrease in the production of word processors. According to Teikoku Databank America, the integration of the standalone word processor's functionality with the personal computer is the main reason for this decline. In 2000, heavyweight home appliance manufacturers—including Fujitsu Ltd., Matsushita Electric Industrial Co. Ltd., and NEC Corporation—all eliminated the word processor from product offerings. South Korea also recognized the decline of the typewriter, with a number of the country's firms discontinuing electronic typewriter lines. In the late 1990s, Samsung Electronics Company Ltd. was the only South Korean exporter of electronic typewriters.

CURRENT CONDITIONS

Datamonitor forecast that the global market would increase an additional 38.4 percent by 2008, reaching $445 billion. The United States held 40.2 percent of the world market, the Asia Pacific region held 23.6 percent,

Europe held 20.1 percent, and the rest of the world comprised the remaining 16.1 percent of the global market. According to the Information Technology Industry Council, the number of typewriters shipped in the United States fell significantly in the early 2000s; still, in 2002 Americans purchased 434,000 word processors and electronic typewriters, according to the Consumer Electronics Association, as reported in 2004 by *Technology Review.* The advantages of such relatively obsolete equipment cited in the article were freedom from virus invasion and/or corruption of disk drives, and the better performance of typewriters in envelope printing.

Pitney Bowes continued to be the leader in production of postage meters and mailing systems. The company went from manufacturing low-level technologies such as electronic meters in the 1970s to digital meters in the 1990s. In 2001 the company presented its sophisticated network architecture that allowed two-way communication between users and postal facilities. Pitney Bowes Chairman and CEO Michael J. Critelli also noted that, in the wake of the anthrax-tainted mail that surfaced in the United States in 2001, the use of metered mail could help companies easily identify the origin of a package or envelope. Firms could thereby teach employees how to distinguish a professional mailing from one that could be suspicious.

Other market concerns included the search by corporations for specialized markets upon which they could capitalize, such as the development of office machines specifically designed for the disabled, and the struggle to manufacture products whose production methods and functionality are deemed environmentally sound. In Europe, governmental bodies and industry regulatory boards continue work on the development of clear, concise standardization of product and legal guidelines to facilitate trade.

Japan's decreased demand for office machines impacted the growth of China's exports to that country. Growth totaled a mere 8.5 percent in 2006, compared to 15.8 percent in 2005.

RESEARCH AND TECHNOLOGY

Electronic typewriters were first produced in 1978, when the Exxon Corporation introduced its QYX model. Electronic typewriters were distinct from electric typewriters in that mechanical elements—springs, belts, levers, and motors—were replaced with computer chips and circuit-board-mounted components. This enabled electronic typewriters to be less expensive in terms of both initial and maintenance costs. IBM and other manufacturers followed Exxon into the electronic typewriter market, and by the mid-1980s there were 25 electronic typewriter producers in the United States, Europe, and Japan.

Sales of electronic typewriters peaked in the mid-1980s but declined thereafter as personal computers made wider inroads into the market. As the computer industry has developed at astonishing rates, electronic typewriters have lost their footing in the competition for office systems. However, manufacturers of electronic typewriters continue to augment models with increased processing power, incorporating techniques from the computer industry as far as they can be implemented into the lower-technology platform of typewriters. Among the areas of improvement in electronic typewriters are memory and display power.

Significant improvements have also been made in personal word processors. These units featured disk drives, large memories and displays, and built-in word processing programs. Some of the newest models had spreadsheet programs and others were DOS-compatible and could run commonly-used spreadsheet programs such as LOTUS 1-2-3. Most personal word processors made use of impact daisywheel printing, which limited font types and sizes. However, the most sophisticated units featured ink jet printing, enabling higher resolution and printing speed.

The classification of these products as electronic typewriters, personal word processors, or personal computers was ambiguous in some cases. This ambiguity was not merely academic, for it played a central role in a trade dispute between U.S. and foreign producers. In 1990, the U.S. Department of Commerce ruled in favor of Smith Corona of Connecticut against Panasonic, Canon, Sharp, and Brother of Japan, as well as Olivetti of Italy, when it held that typewriters with pop-up visual displays and disk drives were not personal computers. This distinction was important because typewriters were subject to price-dumping penalties whereas personal computers were not. Smith Corona sought to further its case by filing a complaint with the Department of Commerce arguing that typewriters with detached keyboards should also not be classified as personal computers.

Other office machine products have registered improvements and innovation as well. The standard time clock that allows an employee to punch a time card when a work shift begins or ends is still in use in many industries. However, a number of sophisticated employee time-tracking systems have also been developed as company needs have evolved into the twenty-first century. Some employ data collection terminals that use employee badges, along with time and attendance software. Others have replaced time cards with "hand punching," which uses biometric technology for error-free verification of an employee's identity. It is likely that the demand for sophisticated labor management solutions will increase. According to Kronos Incorporated, only one-third of firms in the United States employing more than 100 workers have completely automated time and attendance processes.

Flexographic labeling machines have been developed that add a variety of features and options to businesses involved in extensive labeling. These machines are able to laminate, delaminate, color, and cut labels to the characteristics specified by the user. In addition, many are capable of producing self-adhesive labels.

INDUSTRY LEADERS

ACCO Brands Corp. ACCO Brands has a strong heritage in the office machines industry. The company grew out of a partnership between rival industry leaders General Binding Corp. (GBC) and Fortune Brands. ACCO makes many popular products. These include Swingline staplers, Kensington computer accessories, and Day-Timer personal organizers. ACCO products have been sold to office and computer products wholesalers, retailers, and mail-order companies throughout the world. The product distribution reached out to more than 100 countries. In May 2007, ACCO Brands Canada announced that it had enabled its Kensington computer products group to operate separately. The products had previously been sold as part of the ACCO family of products. Subsequent review resulted in the decision that Kensington was not an office products vendor. ACCO reported a 2009 revenue of US$1.27 billion and had a workforce of 6,000 people.

GBC was a market leader in the production of laminating and binding business equipment. The company also made paper shredders, commercial laminators, and bulletin and marker boards. GBC, Ibico, Shredmaster, and Quartet are some of the company's brand names. The firm served customers via a global network of 16 manufacturing plants and more than 20 distribution centers in more than 115 countries. Sales for 2004 totaled US$712.3 million, US$14.4 million or 2.1 percent more than the year before. Net sales were US$191.2 million. Of 2004 revenue, approximately US$85 million was attributed to shredder sales, which remained one of the fastest growing categories of office equipment. The increasing number of shredders sold was attributed to cautionary advice to consumers regarding identity theft, and competitors for shredder business included Fortune Brands and Fellowes Inc. In April 2005, GBC announced plans to merge with Fortune Brands' office products groups to form a new company, ACCO Brands Corp. General Binding would own 34 percent of the new company.

Brother Industries Ltd. Headquartered in Nagoya, Japan, and incorporated in 1934, Brother was the market leader in a variety of office machine products including typewriters, standalone word processors, and electronic labeling machines. Consolidated net sales for 2004 were US$4.2 billion, an 18 percent increase over 2003. The company employed more than 17,000 people worldwide.

Brother International Corporation of Bridgewater, New Jersey, was founded in 1954. It produced portable electronic typewriters and personal word processors for the American market as well as various business products, home appliances, and industrial products. Brother Industries faced revenue hits during 2005 in response to malfunctions with some of its printers, but sales were still up 2.2 percent due to strong demand in the European market.

In December 2006, Brother announced its plans to open a new sales facility in the city of Mumbai, India. Brother International (India) Pte. Ltd. was designated as the operational base for the company's sales activities in India. The market for Brother's flagship products was expected to increase along with the rapidly growing business climate in India.

In March 2007, Brother received the first-ever patent granted under the Accelerated Examination Program by the U.S. Patent and Trademark Office. The program was launched in August 2006. In September 2006, Brother applied for the patent, which represents a technological advance in its printer ink cartridge gauge. Based on its success, Brother planned to use the Accelerated Examination Program for important future inventions.

Casio Inc. The U.S. subsidiary to the Japanese firm Casio Computer, Casio Inc. offers a variety of products including watches, handheld computers, digital cameras, and calculators. Casio Computer's sales for 2004 were US$5 billion, a 34 percent increase over 2002. The company reported revenues of US$7.4 billion in 2008 with 13,200 employees. Casio sells to both the business and consumer markets.

Kronos Inc. Founded in 1977, Kronos was first a manufacturer of traditional time clock products. During the mid-2000s, Kronos produced data collection systems to manage automatically posted employee attendance data. The firm's ShopTrac system tracks labor hours and factory production. In 2004, Kronos posted sales of US$451 million, with a one-year sales growth of more than 13 percent. The company had 3,000 employees throughout the world.

In March 2007, Kronos agreed to a US$1.8 billion buyout of the company by private equity firms. The transaction was expected to close in the third quarter of 2007 after obtaining shareholder approval.

Kronos introduced a Strategic Sourcing Service to assist organizations with local sourcing dynamics. One impressive application case study featured Burgerville, a 39-restaurant chain in the U.S. Pacific Northwest. Kronos' service identified locations with sourcing issues and drivers behind the recruitment challenges. It was applauded for helping to provide a steady stream of qualified applicants.

Pitney Bowes Inc. Pitney Bowes was the world leader in the production of postage meters, with market share of approximately 60 percent worldwide and 80 percent in the United States, according to a 2004 report by Datamonitor. It also offered online postage services, shipping and weighing systems, and shipping management software. The firm's fax and copier division, Pitney Bowes Office Systems, is now a separate public company under the name Imagistics International. Sales grew 8.3 percent in 2004 to approximately US$4.9 billion. That year, the company's employment stood at more than 35,000. The company's top competitors include Neopost, Moore Corporation, and Francotyp-Postalia, as well as a host of national and local firms specializing in similar business areas. During the mid-2000s, Pitney Bowes focused on enhancing mail services to retain its competitive edge, offering all-in-one solutions that combined the utilities of software programs and paper handling. In 2009, the company reported revenues of US$5.6 billion and approximately 36,150 employees serving more than 2 million businesses through direct and dealer operations.

In May 2007, Pitney Bowes announced that the latest releases of its CODE-1 Plus and Finalist address cleansing software had received U.S. Postal Service CASS certification for the upcoming Cycle L requirements. Those requirements were scheduled for implementation on August 1, 2007. CASS solutions were components of Group 1 Software's Address Quality Hub platform designed to help mailers address the impact of upcoming postal rates plus CASS Cycle L requirements designed to reduce mail that was undeliverable as addressed.

Site managers from Pitney Bowes worked closely with clients to reevaluate their mailstream operations in anticipation of postal rate industry increases and changes in practices. They conducted webinars, such as "The Changing Postal Environment," to share money-saving insights. The company also launched a special Web site at www.pb.com featuring additional advice and downloadable reference materials.

Pitney Bowes prepared for a new CEO to take the reins on May 14, 2007, during its annual shareholders meeting. The company's CEO and Chairman Michael Critelli had assumed the leadership position during a period of long-anticipated postal reform in the United

States and Europe. Critelli had also served as co-chairman of the Mailing Industry Taskforce and had advised Congress on postal reform. Murray Martin, who joined Pitney Bowes after its acquisition of Dicta-phone, was considered to be a very competent successor. Martin was credited with encouraging the company to move beyond institutional customers and reach out to other mail-intensive areas such as the consumer market.

Pitney Bowes restated its commitment to growth strategies believed to be suitable for the company's commitment to expansion in the fastest-growing segments of the global mailstream. These included growing company cash flow, increasing value for customers, improving operating efficiency, solidifying performance of its core mailing business, expanding internationally, and focusing on high-performance mailstream areas. Pitney Bowes' expansion in the software area was evident by its acquisition of MapInfo, a move that allowed for an increased presence in location intelligence.

MAJOR COUNTRIES IN THE INDUSTRY

According to the World Trade Organization, the leading exporters of office machines and telecommunications equipment in 2003 were the European Union, China, the United States, Japan, and Hong Kong. The European Union had exports valued at US$246.4 billion, with 26.4 percent of world market share. China's exports reached US$117.9 billion, accounting for 12.6 percent, and the United States had exports worth US$112.5 billion, with a 12.1 percent share. Japan had exports with a value of US$90.1 billion, and a 9.7 percent share of the world market. Finally, Hong Kong showed domestic exports valued at US$1.5 billion, and re-exports valued at US$70.8 billion.

The top five leading importers of office machines and telecom equipment in 2003 were the European Union, the United States, China, Hong Kong, and Japan. The EU's imports in 2003 were valued at US$302.9 billion, 31.9 percent of the world market.

The United States had imports valued at US$180.5 billion, a 19 percent share. China imported US$96.3 billion worth of office and telecom equipment, taking 10.1 percent, and Hong Kong claimed US$77.4 billion in imports, retaining US$6.6 billion. Share percentage statistics were not available for Hong Kong. Japan imported US$54.5 billion and claimed 5.7 percent of the market in 2003.

BIBLIOGRAPHY

"Brother Downgrades Profits Outlook." *Printing World* (17 February 2005).

"Brother International Corp. Establishes Sales Facility in India," 20 December 2006. Available from www.brother.com.

"Brother Receives the First Patent Granted Under USPTO's Accelerated Examination Program," 16 March 2007. Available from www.brother.com.

Cullen, Scott. "Featured Product: Paper Shredders." *OfficeSolutions* (November/December 2006).

Del Nibletto, Paolo. "Kensington to Operate Independently." *IT Business* (9 May 2007).

"Global Office Services & Supplies." *Datamonitor,* May 2004. Available from www.datamonitor.com.

"Hoover's Company Capsules," *Hoover's Online*, 2007. Available from www.hoovers.com.

Lazich, Robert S., ed. *Market Share Reporter.* Detroit: Thomson Gale, 2004.

Murphy, H. Lee. "Shredder Sales Jump." *Crain's Chicago Business* (28 February 2005).

"Office Equipment in France, Germany, UK, US." *Euromonitor,* August 2004. Available from www.majormarketprofiles.com.

Scigliano, Eric. "Technologies that Refuse to Die." *Technology Review* (February 2004).

Troy, Mike. "After Several Years of Trying to Divest Its Office Products Groups, Fortune Brand Will Merge Its Office Products Business with the Operations of General Binding." *DSN Retailing Today* (11 April 2005).

"World Trade Growth to Slow Down This Year." *Businessline* (15 April 2005).

World Trade Organization. "International Trade Statistics." Geneva, Switzerland. 2003. Available from www.wto.org.

Yan, Dai. "China May Become Japan's Largest Trade Partner," 11 April 2007. Available from www.chinadaily.com.

INFORMATION MEDIA AND TELECOMMUNICATIONS

---■---

SIC 2731

BOOK PUBLISHING

NAICS CODE(S)

511130. The international book publishing industry includes publishers of mass-market, trade, academic, reference, electronic books (e-book), and specialty books. For discussion of other print publishing trades, see also **Newspaper Publishing, Periodical Publishing,** and **Printing, Commercial.**

INDUSTRY SNAPSHOT

Global spending on books was US$85.3 billion in 2000. In the United States alone the average consumer spent US$103.60 annually on books in 2007. The U.S. Census Bureau predicted that this figure would rise to US$117.45 by 2012. The international book publishing industry faced significant challenges throughout the first decade of the twenty-first century. World demand for books, which had once topped US$80 billion, dropped significantly in 2002. Numerous factors in 2001 and 2002, especially the terrorist attacks against the United States on September 11, 2001, had combined to throw the industry into one of its worst downward spirals ever, threatening independent booksellers in particular and causing layoffs at Amazon.com, as well as at the large independent chains. In response, some publishers, notably German giant Bertelsmann AG, owner of U.S.-based imprint Random House, engaged in unprecedented slashing of costs, including employee layoffs across all sectors, such as dictionaries and travel books, as well as high-ranking Ballantine executive editor Peter Borland and

nonfiction editor Jeremie-Ruby Strauss. The company's actions, along with its unwillingness to provide the business press with exact information, led to fears that defensive strategies and cost slashing had replaced aggressive marketing as the strategy for book industry survival in the 2000s.

In contrast to Random House, however, two other prestigious book publishers questioned Bertelsmann's budget and staff cuts, arguing that an aggressive but more positive strategy was needed in spite of two soft budget years. The two publishing houses that planned "business as usual" for the immediate future were the Penguin Putnam division of Pearson, the world's second-largest book publisher, and the prestigious HarperCollins book division of News Corporation. Following the publication of the Penguin Putnam and HarperCollins strategies, a Bertelsmann-Random House spokesman told *Publishers Weekly* that he defended what appear to be the industry's most all-encompassing budget slashes in the face of hard economic accounting realities since 2000, in general, and September 11, 2001, in particular.

Although book sales began to improve slightly by late 2001 as consumers returned to the stores for Christmas shopping, profits remained elusive for many industry players as sales growth was tepid through 2003. The situation did not appear significantly brighter until 2004 when the global economy improved and book sales picked up in several major markets. Weekly sales in the United Kingdom in May 2004, for example, rose 11.1 percent over revenues for the corresponding period in 2003. Industry members were guardedly optimistic that a leaner, better-managed book business might indeed rebound, but admitted the need to contain rising production costs and attract a wider customer base in order to boost growth and profits.

579

With the worst of the slump apparently over in 2004, analysts at Veronis Suhler Stevenson (VSS) predicted that sales of consumer books in the United States would increase about 1.9 percent through 2008. The United States led all nations in book shipments, with a value of US$19.53 billion in 2003, but only five conglomerates publish 80 percent of U.S. trade books, according to former Pantheon book executive Andri Schiffrin, author of *The Business of Books: How International Conglomerates Took Over Publishing and Changed the Way We Read*. However, citing a

significantly worse than anticipated economy in 2009, VSS revised their industry forecast to reflect the slump. With the increase of digital media, traditional book publishing along with all other print publishing industries were expected to be impacted. The communications industry is growing, but it is growing more towards electronic forms of entertainment, news, and education. According to a 2010 report from VSS, the communications sector approached US$1 trillion in spending in 2009, which was up from US$63 billion in 1975.

In the early 2000s, the increasingly interlinked world economy, along with an increasingly educated and affluent global book-buying public, suggested that the international book publishing industry could look forward to steady, if unspectacular, growth in the remainder of the decade in spite of predictions of the demise of the book as a medium. The global adoption of U.S.-style intellectual property and copyright principles; the solidification of English as the language of world commerce; and the opportunities offered by new electronic formats, including the Internet; and distribution channels, such as online booksellers, gave the world's book publishers cause for some optimism. Major challenges included:

- controlling enormous advances for new titles (which could be US$5 to $10 million or more for sought-after writers and up to the US$8 million that was paid to celebrity politician Hilary Clinton, US$9 million to former British Prime Minister Tony Blair, US$1.25 million to former Alaska Governor Sarah Palin; and the leading US$15 million to former U.S. President Bill Clinton;

- acquiring and protecting rights to foreign editions and fighting textbook piracy in Asia;

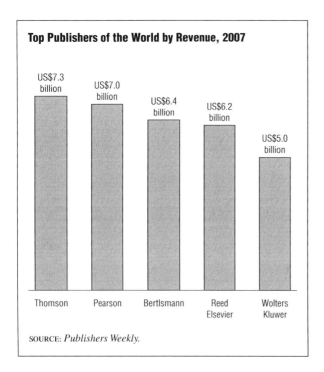

Top Publishers of the World by Revenue, 2007

SOURCE: *Publishers Weekly.*

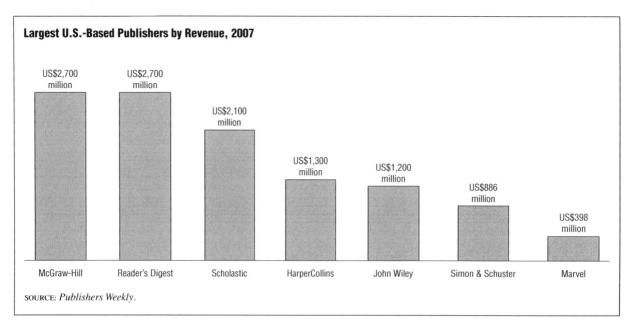

Largest U.S.-Based Publishers by Revenue, 2007

SOURCE: *Publishers Weekly.*

- rising book prices;

- escalating paper costs;

- managing excessively large print runs;

- rising return rates from booksellers; and

- escalating costs associated with development of electronic books.

However, big expenses can produce big profits if customers can be lured into stores by blockbuster books and celebrity writers like John Grisham and Stephen King. As a result of 2001 releases of movies based on J.K. Rowling's *Harry Potter* books and J.R.R. Tolkien's *The Lord of the Rings* trilogy, stores did big business globally, including boxed books sets by each author. Houghton Mifflin tallied sales of US$4.5 million for *The Lord of the Rings* in 2001, a tenfold sales increase over 2000 sales for that title. Even before the release of the sixth Potter book, *Harry Potter and the Half-Blood Prince,* in July 2005, Rowling's total sales had reached 250 million copies. In 2007, the seventh and final book of the series was released and broke records as the fastest growing book of all time. It sold a record 11 million copies the first day of sales in the United States and the United Kingdom. The Potter books became a global enterprise worth US$15 billion with the books translated into 65 languages by the end of the first decade of the 2000s. Always looking for extraordinary receipts from tie-ins of best-selling books with hot-draw films, Viacom Inc. merged Simon & Schuster books with its film division in 2002, hoping for more cinema successes based on Simon & Schuster books like *A Beautiful Mind,* by Sylvia Nasar.

According to data released by the Association of American Publishers in 2009, sales were down 1.8 percent overall to US$23.9 billion. However, adult hardcover sales increased 6.9 percent from the slump reported in 2008. Estimated net sales for 2009 were reported for adult hardbound books at US$2.6 billion, but adult paperbound books fell 5.2 percent to US$2.2 billion, children's hardbound books were at US$1.7 billion, children's paperbound were at US$1.5 billion, mass market paperbacks decreased from 2008 to US$1 billion, religious book sales dropped to US$659 million, and higher education text books reached US$4.3 billion. Audio books were rapidly becoming a large sector of the publishing industry as well. Nevertheless, in 2009, audio book sales dropped 12.9 percent to US$192 million from the previous year. Sales of e-books in 2009 overtook audio books with sales at US$313 million, a 176.6 percent increase from 2008.

ORGANIZATION AND STRUCTURE

The publishing industry deals in content development and marketing more than in formatting the content on pages, which often is done by independent typesetters or compositors, or in physical manufacturing of books, which may be outsourced to independent printers and binders. The

book publishing process begins with an idea proposed either by a querying author, an agent, or the publisher itself. Once a concept is proposed, the publisher performs a market analysis to determine whether other books in the market cover the book's subject matter, and then reshapes or rejects the book's concept accordingly.

After the publisher has determined that a book's projected sales minus anticipated production costs can generate a profit, which is sometimes highly uncertain, a final decision is made to proceed with the project, and the development or acquisition of the book's content is secured through a cash advance to the author or some other form of book contract. As the author completes the actual writing or rewriting of the book, or responds to the editor's changes, the publisher's design and marketing staffs determine the book's type specifications, size, artwork, cover design, and marketing/distribution strategy. When the content of the book reaches its final form, the book is sent to a typesetter or is composed in-house. The typesetter may produce camera-ready copy (a high-resolution, formatted print copy of the entire book), film, or a digital file for the printer, who then creates plates of all the pages for use in a printing press. Plates also may be engraved by a specialty firm rather than the printer. After a book's pages come off the press, they are bound and the cover is attached. The finished books are usually shipped back to the publisher's warehouse for distribution.

International Publishing Structure. About 10,000 book publishers in 180 countries constituted the international book publishing industry at the beginning of the first decade of the 2000s. The five major categories for this industry are trade books; textbooks; technical, scientific, and professional (TSP) books; mass-market paperback books; and all others.

The issue of copyright, which is the legal protection accorded to an author for his or her intellectual product, grew in importance as the book industry became more global in the 1980s and 1990s. The global book industry was governed by various conventions regulating the protection of book copyrights in the world market. The Universal Copyright Convention of 1952 requires that each signatory nation provide foreign works with the same copyright protection given to books published within its own borders. Similar copyright protection agreements observed by various countries worldwide include the Berne Convention of 1886 and the Buenos Aires Convention of 1910.

In the 1990s, an increasing number of book publishers began to focus on selling book rights to foreign producers rather than assuming the risks associated with selling their books directly in foreign markets. The sale of book rights, which was a principal activity of the world's largest annual book fair in Frankfurt, became a more important source of publishers' revenues in some regions of the world than book sales. For example, foreign rights alone for the most popular novels published in the United States can earn their authors US$10 million and more. In the mid-1990s, the United States was the recipient of US$300 to US$500 million in annual royalties from foreign publishers for the sale of rights and translations to U.S. works, a figure that some analysts had expected to increase 100 percent by the beginning of the 2000s. As the 1990s progressed, resolving "electronic rights" disputes, which arose when an author's material was used in new non-book formats, such as the Internet, also became an increasingly crucial issue. In 2001 the U.S. Supreme Court determined that publishers, such as *The New York Times,* must pay royalties to freelance authors whose works were published in electronic databases without written permission in the form of a contract.

The factors affecting the characteristics of the world's book market were complex and varied, including the number and budgets of public libraries, government support, political instability, birth rates, education, living standards, labor costs, cultural traditions, and the availability of leisure time. The structure of the industry in every region of the world is based largely on these factors. The terrorist attacks against the United States on September 11, 2001, quickly had a direct impact on book publishing worldwide. In Germany, the 2001 Frankfurt Book Fair was poorly attended. In India, an already somewhat depressed economic climate declined further, especially in tourist books, which were a staple of success when tourists felt safe traveling the world. Coffee table book sales also plummeted at Indian publishing houses. Overall, Indian publishers looked for about a 10 percent drop in 2001 sales over 2000 when all receipts were counted. According to *Business Line* textbook sales remained the only booming sector for those publishers.

North America. While the United States's book publishing industry was the world leader, Canada and Mexico were also significant book producers. Canadian publishing's small size compared to that of the United States was a reflection of the dominance of U.S. publishing, not representative of meager demand for books. In 1997 Canada was the biggest importer of U.S. books worldwide (US$775 million in shipments), accounting for 4 of every 10 U.S. books exported.

The Canadian book publishing industry has been languishing since the 1990s and endured an anemic 1 percent annual growth rate between 1990 and 1995 (one-tenth that of U.S. publishers). Book sales in 2001 reached C$1.13 billion, but the lack of a national sales data analysis service in Canada made it impossible to determine the breakdown of sales figures. However, analysts indicated that most purchases were of U.S. titles. At the beginning of the twenty-first century, Canada's largest publishers were Tele-Direct (Publication) Inc., Harlequin Enterprises, Readers Digest Association, and

Thomson Canada Ltd., as well as textbook publishers McGraw-Hill Ryerson and Prentice-Hall Canada.

In 2001, the struggling Chapters bookstores, which had been previously restructured in 1995 from the merger of Cole' and W.H. Smith bookstores, and the more solidly entrenched Indigo Books and Music merged. The mergers branch of the Canadian government's Competition Bureau asked Indigo to sell 23 Chapters bookstores, but Indigo received no offers for the properties. As a result, in 2002 Indigo was given a mandatory code of conduct limiting what it could and could not do with the Chapters chain stores. Indigo was expected to close many of the troubled stores. The limitations were intended to help Canada's independent booksellers and publishers during increasingly difficult times as the large chains continued to dominate the book sales industry.

In April 2010, The Canadian Booksellers Association (CBA) urged the federal government to amend the laws that restrict importation of books from foreign publishers into Canada. Members of the CBA stated that the limit of "parallel importation" are "no longer commercially reasonable and should be repealed." Under the guidelines, Canadian booksellers must buy directly from Canadian-owned distributors or the Canadian arms of multinational publishing houses. Booksellers can only circumvent this regulation if the titles are not available from Canadian sources or are priced at more than 10 percent of the U.S. price. The CBA reasoned that if distributors are allowed to buy en masse from the U.S. publishing houses, there would be no need for the existence of Canadian publishers. This could also force Canadian-owned publishers to lower prices to compete with the competition.

Mexico's book market, centered largely in Mexico City, was the world's largest Spanish-language book market in the late 1990s, with 15,505 titles published in 1997. However, while the volume of consumer books increased 6 percent between 2001 and 2002, sales began to fall due to an economic recession and declining interest in reading. According to *Euromonitor,* although Mexico has a 91 percent literacy rate, Mexicans read an average of only one or two books per year, and the country had only 500 bookstores for a population of 100 million. To help stimulate book publishing, the Mexican government had provided financial support for publishing and had resisted efforts to impose a tax on books. Most government support, which accounted for 60 percent of publishing production, was for textbooks in basic education programs.

The peso crisis of 1994 had a devastating effect on Mexico's economy, and its book publishing industry was still returning to pre-crisis levels in 1997. Following the crisis, book imports dropped 50 percent in 1995, while book exports rose to US$98 million. Spurred by the North American Free Trade Agreement (NAFTA), U.S. book exports to Mexico in 1997 rose to US$58.2 million, up from US$40.8 million only four years earlier. In the early 2000s Mexico remained the fifth largest market for U.S. book exports and was worth US$66.1 million in 2004. In 2007, that number had declined to US$32.38 million, slightly behind Colombia at US$36.27 million.

By 2001, the peso had rebounded strongly. In 2002 the rising demand for Latin American books also extended to Mexico's relatively prosperous book industry. While the 2001 Frankfurt Book Fair was a disappointment, a Mexican book fair exceeded all expectations as worldwide industry representatives flocked to the fifteenth annual Feria Internacional de Libros (International Book Fair) in Guadalajara, Mexico. According to *Publishers Weekly,* the Mexican fair attracted a record high of 386,620 participants, including 13,500 from the book industry, with an extremely high librarian attendance. There were 1,258 publishing houses from 32 countries represented at the Feria Internacional de Libros.

Europe. The European book market was well developed but fragmented and had historically experienced steady, moderate growth. Despite its size and tradition, it was strongly influenced by trends in the United States. Most European publishers were moderate in size, but unlike their U.S. counterparts they handled both the publishing and printing of their titles. More than 90 percent of all printers in Europe were associated with a publishing firm. Most of Europe's publishing companies were diversified beyond book publishing, reflecting the European book industry's evolution from magazine publishing. Moreover, Europe's largest publishing companies were often involved in a range of other media such as television, film, or newspaper publishing.

Although Europe's population was roughly the same as that of the United States, it published as much as five times as many titles annually. Between 1982 and 1991 alone, production and sales of books in Europe doubled, with the United Kingdom and Spain reporting the greatest growth in production between 1976 and 1986, with 68 percent and 50 percent, respectively. While British, French, and German publishers were the largest in Europe, significant book publishers came from elsewhere in Europe.

In the 1990s the number of mergers and acquisitions in Europe's book industry increased, and European publishers continued to pursue opportunities for international expansion, particularly in the United States, where British, Dutch, French, and German publishers historically had a strong market presence. Norway's book industry enjoyed great growth in the late 1990s, but Sweden's, Finland's, and Denmark's were stable at best. The so-called Retail Price Maintenance systems of France, the Netherlands, and Germany, which forbids discounts on the cover price of books, came under pressure in the late 1990s, but the

European Commission declared in 2000 that a modified agreement between publishers and booksellers did not violate European Union rules governing competition.

Following the collapse of the Iron Curtain in 1990, a number of Eastern European publishing houses were privatized, demand for German- and English-language books intensified, and book prices skyrocketed (as much as 300 percent in Hungary, for example). Among the problems affecting the publishing industries of Hungary, the Czech Republic, and Poland in the late 1990s were the inability of publishers to afford the cost of purchasing book rights, an inadequate book distribution system, and high book prices. Despite these obstacles, German-based Bertelsmann AG successfully opened book clubs in Hungary, the Czech Republic, and Poland in the early 1990s.

In 1998 Poland's 1,700 book publishers produced between 12,500 and 20,000 individual titles, with shipments valued at less than US$250 million. Thirty imprints commanded roughly 80 percent of all sales. After a flurry of book selling following the fall of the Soviet empire (where a Stephen King book could easily sell 300,000 copies) in the late 1990s, the Polish book industry had settled into a much slower but still quite profitable growth phase, reflecting the health of the Polish economy. Despite some inroads by foreign publishers, two Communist-era firms held 40 to 50 percent of the total book market. Government-run WSIP (School and Pedagogical Publishers) was the largest Polish book publisher in 1998, with sales of US$51.5 million, and privately owned PWN (Polish Scientific Publishers) generated sales of US$50 million with 350 new titles per year.

In a report released by the Federation of European Publishers (FEP), in June 2010, the total annual revenue of the book publishers of the European Union and the European Economic Association (EEA) was approximately 23.75 billion euros in 2008, which showed a decrease over 2007. Germany represented the largest market, followed by the United Kingdom, France, Spain, and Italy. Approximately 510,000 titles were introduced in 2008, which was an increase of 4 percent from 2008. The countries reporting the largest production figures were the United Kingdom (120,947), Germany (83,381), Spain (42,592), France (38,354), and Italy (36,409). According to the FEP report, 135,000 people were employed full time in book publishing in Europe in 2008.

Russia. Although the fall of the centrally planned Soviet economy in 1990 was expected to result in a more productive and profitable private book industry for Russia in the long term, by the late 1990s and beginning of the twenty-first century, the Russian book market continued to be dogged by high inflation rates, systemic bribery, a wildly unstructured distribution system, underworld involvement in the book printing industry, and even murder. The greatest problem affecting Russian book publishing in the 1990s, however, was illegal printing, which accounted for 90 percent of all foreign books translated into Russian and could be traced in part to a stunted perception of copyright law that had been in effect only since 1990. Moreover, in the late 1990s Russia continued to lack established authors, Western-style bookstores (Moscow claimed only 30 shops in all), and effective public relations. For these reasons, in 1994 Germany-based Bertelsmann postponed plans to develop schoolbook publishing and printing projects in Russia.

Despite these difficulties, Russian publishers produced at least 440 million books in 1995, and in 1996 Russia boasted one of the world's three highest book-spending rates as a percentage of total leisure and education spending. After the Russian government eliminated the value-added tax and profit tax on books in 1996, production soared to 70,332 new titles in 2001, which was the highest number in the country's history. The notoriety of success in Russia's publishing had its price, however, as in 1997 when two executives of a Russian textbook publisher were found murdered. In 2002, there were approximately 54 Russian publishing houses issuing more than 100 new titles each while 43 publishing houses issued more than 1 million copies each. The top five publishing houses were AST, Eksmo Press, Drofa, Prosveshcheniye, and Olma Press. Only Prosveshchenie was state-owned, and the state share of the Russian book market had been reduced to 12.6 percent. At the 2010 Russian Book Fair, Irina Shishova, foreign rights director of Eksmo Press, predicted that by 2014, digital sales would represent 25 percent of the annual book revenue. Eksmo had reported US$215 million in annual revenue prior to the global economic crisis that began in late 2007, but by the end of the first decade of the 2000s that figure had dropped to US$200 million annually. Eksmo's publishing market included approximately 1,000 titles per month.

South America. For years South America was just a footnote in the publishing industry, but that was no longer the case in the early twenty-first century. Latin America was expected to be the fastest growing economic region for book sales in the world, with growth projected to reach 9.1 percent annually, "as governments make a concerted effort to promote education and literacy," according to *The Write News* on June 6, 2001. More than half a million different Spanish-language book titles, including those from Spain and Spanish North America, were printed in 1997. Spanish textbooks, in particular, had found world demand. The growing market for Spanish and bilingual books in the United States, worth US$350 million in 2003, promised a good outlook for Spanish and Latin American publishers. Random House, for example, imports about 120 titles each year from Spain and South America. Knopf's Vintage

Espanol imprint announced in 2005 that it would double its output of titles by 2010. Its *Memorias de mis putas tristes* (*Memories of My Melancholy Whores*) by Colombian Nobel Laureate Gabriel Garcia Marquez, which was published in 2004, sold 120,000 hard covers and paperbacks.

Brazil, the largest South American book market and eighth largest in the world in terms of volume in 2004, produced 45,111 new titles in 2000 and generated US$1.87 billion in revenues. Its largest market was textbooks, which accounted for 80 percent of volume and value sales in 2002. Major publishers included Editora Atica, Editora Scipione, Ediouro, and Editora Campus. Consumer books fared relatively poorly in Brazil, which had lower readership levels than other South American countries. Book sales were also affected by the scarcity of bookstores with 89 percent of municipalities having only one bookstore.

In the 1980s and early 1990s many South American countries were plagued by unstable currency exchange rates, and the U.S. dollar became the standard currency for the region's book trade. For the majority of South American countries, high book prices led to low print runs, which were rarely over 3,000, and inadequate copyright protection resulted in book piracy and illegal copying. In the mid-1990s, however, South American economies began to rebound, and the region's book industries enjoyed strong growth. Following a period in which the Spanish book market became increasingly European in focus, the South American book industry began to look to the United States for its book trade. In the 1990s Colombia and Chile joined Argentina and Mexico as major regional producers in the Latin American market. In an effort to promote a cooperative, regional approach for the South American book market, South American book publishing nations formed the Salon Internacional del Libro Latinoamericano.

In 2008 the Fordham University Graduate School of Business Administration reported that 99,566 new titles were produced in Latin America in 2006, representing an 8 percent growth over the previous year. Of those new books, 57,847 were published in Spanish and 39,627 were in Portuguese, with the remainder in other languages. An additional 76,768 Spanish titles were produced in Spain. Latin American exports in the book publishing industry in 2006 reached US$15.4 million, with U.S.$1.43 million in imports. In 2007, the book exports from Latin America to the United States included US$32.38 million from Mexico, US$36.27 million from Colombia, US$6.97 from Peru, and US$5.88 million from Brazil. The religious books segment from Colombia was the largest category, with US$20.69 million, followed by textbooks from Columbia at US$6.5 million, and professional and scholarly books from Mexico at US$5.8 million.

Asia and the Pacific. The *PricewaterhouseCoopers Global Entertainment and Media Outlook* for 2001–2005 reported that Asia and the Pacific market was expected to grow at a 3.6 percent annual rate. Growth was hindered by slowing Japanese economy, as well as a slumping global economy, the threatened lowering of the Japanese yen against the dollar, and an antiquated distribution system that required modernization.

With 60 percent of the world's population and half of its total gross national product, Asia constituted an increasingly important segment of the global book industry in the late 1990s. Japan, the region's book publishing giant, surpassed all other Asian and Pacific Rim countries with roughly 5,000 book publishers in the mid-1990s, led by three firms: Kodansha Ltd. Publishers, Gakken Company Ltd., and Nihon Keizai Shimbun Inc. China, Australia, New Zealand, and South Korea, along with other countries in the region had significant numbers of publishers as well. Japan and China together imported US$184 million of U.S. books in 1996 for 10 percent of U.S. book exports and exported US $358 million of books. Other Asian nations imported US$129 million from U.S. publishers and exported US$130 million worth of books to the United States in 1996.

The Asian book market began to mature in the early 1990s after a period of exceptional growth in which regional book sales doubled annually. With demand abating, the market was expected to be characterized by an increasing number of competitive products. Pirating, however, continued to be a nagging issue for foreign publishers in the Asian market. The efforts of many Asian countries to invest in education signaled the development of an increasingly important textbook market for international publishers, and in the mid-1990s international textbook producers viewed the local-language educational book market in Asian countries, such as South Korea and Taiwan, as a source of significant future revenue. The Asian debt and currency crisis of late 1997 and 1998 had a severe effect on book industry sales, however, and some publishers feared that some Asian publishing houses would cancel book contracts and book pirating might increase.

The fastest growing book market in the world in the early 2000s was China, where 190,000 titles were printed in 2003 and sales reached about US$5.6 billion, despite the fact that the average price for a general interest book was only about US$2.40. By 2009, textbooks accounted for between 50 and 60 percent of all book purchases in China, and about 6 percent of books sold were translations, with U.S. titles comprising almost 50 percent of foreign titles. Despite its apparent potential, the Chinese book publishing industry posed significant problems for both domestic and foreign investors. For example, despite the presence of about 30,000 private publishers

in the country in 2004, private publishing remained technically illegal. Only the country's 577 state-owned presses were operating within the law, but printing and distribution were open to private and foreign investment. This situation resulted in what *New York Times* writer Mike Meyer described on March 13, 2005, as an "openly illegal" but generally tolerated system in which private publishers were able to obtain the necessary documentation to publish their titles. Technically, the Chinese government was the sole issuer of International Standard Book Numbers (ISBNs), which a title must have before it can be published. The only choice for private investors, therefore, was to deal with black-market operations known as "culture houses" or "booksellers" which would, for fees ranging from US$1,250 to US$2,500, secure the required ISBNs and arrange for some aspects of production and marketing. While some analysts expected state control of publishing to be abolished, it was uncertain that this would occur.

Another huge concern for foreign investors was copyright violation. Piracy of intellectual property, according to Meyer, remained rampant in China, but infringement cases were increasingly being pressed and won. Although Chinese publishers had begun to pay authors advances against royalties, piracy made it difficult to gather reliable sales figures. Publishers in the United States, according to Meyer, say that they receive an average of only US$2,500 per title for Chinese publication rights.

As the Chinese government relaxed some of its control on book content, publishers bought a dizzying array of foreign titles, from religious books to business how-to books. The all-time best-selling work in translation was *Who Moved My Cheese?* which officially sold 2 million copies. Other top-selling titles included *The Da Vinci Code, Monica's Story,* and the Atkins diet books.

In the 1980s British publishing magnate Robert Maxwell had established an ill-fated publishing office in Beijing, and in 1995 Simon & Schuster had opened an office there as well, with plans for offices in Shanghai or Canton in 1998. By the late 1980s, the Chinese publishing group Sino United Publishing (SUP) of Hong Kong began to abandon its traditional focus on Communist propaganda books for more profitable fare, including entertainment, computers, home decorating, self-help, reference books, and CD-ROMs. Led by China's oldest and largest publisher, Commercial Press, SUP consisted primarily of about 30 Hong Kong publishers left over from the Communist takeover in 1949. By the late 1990s, SUP had begun teaming with Taiwan's publishing industry, which was valued at about US$2 billion. They offered marketing services to publishers from the United States, Great Britain, and the Pacific Rim, and published titles in Hong Kong that were still officially banned in mainland China.

However, with Hong Kong's return to Chinese jurisdiction, some of its more liberal policies were reversed. By 1997, SUP was posting revenues of US$205 million.

In January 2003, Annie Wang described the challenges faced by Chinese writers in *Time Asia Magazine,* saying that "success outside China does not always translate into success on the mainland." China's publishing houses publish approximately 180,000 titles each year, over half of which are textbooks. The concern was for a titles' potential market.

In July 2004 *Publishers Weekly* took a close look at suppliers from Hong Kong/China and Singapore. Asia Pacific Offset experienced tremendous growth in 2003. President Andrew Clarke noted constant demand for reprints and felt this was evidence of the persistent and ongoing need for just-in-time inventory. Colorcraft was challenged in 2003 by cancellations from U.S. clients who feared contracting Sudden Acute Respiratory Syndrome (SARS), while others made decisions linked to the Iraq conflict. Addressing these and related issues led the company to be more innovative and customer-oriented. Everbest Managing Director Ken Chung said his company's growth was a by-product of the global economy. Chung credited the strength of the European and Australian currencies as a major influence on success. The company's business in the United States, handled mainly through agents, remained steady although the currency there was weak. In 2009, the country's top publisher was Higher Education Press (HEP) with 2.56 percent of the market share. HEP releases more than 2,000 new titles annually and sells over 121 million units. They had US$343 million in revenue in 2009.

Publishers Weekly also announced in July 2004 that the Harvard Business School Press had signed a three-year exclusive publishing deal with the Beijing-based Commercial Press to publish Harvard Business School Press titles in Chinese. Commercial Press was entitled to publish up to 150 Harvard Business School titles during the course of the deal.

The China Book International Program, launched in 2004, gained a boost from international market activities. The State Council Information Office and General Administration of Press and Publication program's mission was to "make China known to different nations fully and truly." Since 2005, it had provided financial support for 108 publishing houses in 27 countries with 645 book projects, which totaled 893 books published and distributed in 16 different languages. In the September 9, 2008, publication of *Living Art,* State Council Information Office Director Wu Wei concluded that, "Chinese books have not gained enough attention from the mainstream publishing houses and readers in the West." Wu hoped China would "seize this opportunity to expand both domestically and globally" in terms of its publishing industry. The trend for growing interest for Chinese-specific themes and stories in international markets was expected to continue after the Beijing Olympics. Following the removal of the ban on purchasing Christian books in China, that genre began to grow, and by 2009 there were eight Christian publishing companies in the country. In 2002, only 36 of the more than 60,000 books published in China were Christian. In addition, there was only one Christian bookstore in Shanghai, and it carried approximately 60 titles in 2002. By 2009, that store carried more than 600 Christian titles.

In India, 12 independent women publishing companies changed the publishing industry with presses launched from 1994 to 2004. They published everything from children''s books and feminist studies to critically acclaimed fiction and non-fiction. The women were inspired to leave secure jobs in mainstream journalism although failure was predicted by many observers. The women made amazing advances and huge contributions to the "intellectual, social, cultural and political life of the country," in the words of Ritu Menon in the September 7, 2008, issue of *The Hindu.*

According to Graham Beattie in an article in *The New Zealand Herald* on August 30, 2008, New Zealand had a perceived female-dominated boutique publishing industry. Christine Cole-Cathey, of Cape Cathey, had been an industry leader in New Zealand for almost 35 years by 2008. Her career had changed direction when, as a freelance editor for Reeds, she encountered the manuscript for *Behind the Tattooed Face* by Heretaunga Pat Baker. After Reeds turned it down, Cole-Cathey decided to open her own business and publish the book. Film rights were sold when the book was in its sixth edition.

The Middle East. Among the region's largest book publishers in the mid-1990s were Israel's Steimatzky Ltd. and Yediot Ahronot Ltd., and Saudi Arabia's Modokhil Group. Israel exported US$18.8 million in books in 1992 and was the region's largest book exporter, while Saudi Arabia was the Middle East's largest book importing nation, with US$82.8 million in import value. Behind Israel in 2002 were Egypt and Lebanon with 20 publishers each, and Jordan and Saudi Arabia with 10 each.

Industry expectations for the Middle East were marginally good in the early years of the twenty-first century, as *The PricewaterhouseCoopers Global Entertainment and Media Outlook* anticipated 2.8 percent growth through 2005. There had been renewed interest in many Middle East topics due to world tensions that had resulted in higher sales of regional specialty books. Israel led all Middle Eastern countries in the book publishing industry by 2009 with roughly 1,500 book publishers who produced just over 7,000 titles.

Africa. Africa's book publishing industry traditionally has been dwarfed by those of other continents. The good news is that growth estimated at 2.8 percent through 2005 was estimated by *The PricewaterhouseCoopers Global Entertainment and Media Outlook.* While a number of African countries maintained modest book publishing industries, many African states had fewer than five operating publishing houses at the beginning of the 2000s. African countries with the largest number of book publishers included South Africa (100 firms), Nigeria (65), Zimbabwe (50), Ghana (40), and Tanzania (27). In 1992 Africa's leading book-importing countries were South Africa (US$90 million in value), the Ivory Coast (US$40 million), and Morocco (US$27 million). According to the Cape Sector Fact Sheet, more than 60 percent of the South African publishing sector's revenue was generated in the Western Cape. Natural history and tourism-related publishing were projected to grow.

African publishers in the early 2000s were seeking more opportunities to export titles. However, as Cynthia Sithole of Zimbabwe Book Publishers Association pointed out, book trade across borders within Africa was stymied by pricing issues, foreign currency problems, and country-specific curriculum requirements in the textbook sector. She called for such measures as the development of an African Book Marketing Trust to stimulate regional trade, the utilization of Internet marketing, and the creation of licensing and co-publishing agreements.

Gordon Graham reported in *The Book & The Computer/Global Exchange* on December 15, 2003, that Book Aid International (BAI) was utilizing book surpluses to make an impact on education in Africa. The company's warehouse did not take special orders by title but did try to fill specific requests for help on subjects from schools and libraries in African countries. BAI initially confronted acceptance problems involving both the British government and the publishing industry. Graham pointed out that questions remained, including how to move from the idea that books donated today would have to be purchased in the future. Graham asserted that while the publishing industry in a developing country was growing, "it is better that surplus books from book-rich countries should be donated instead of being pulped."

In September 2008 Random House South Africa and Struik Publishing announced merger plans. The new company, called Random House Struik, would be 50.1 percent owned by New Holland Publishing SA with the balance held by the Random House Group. Half of the company's output was projected to be books written in both English and Afrikaans. The merger was expected to create a stronger platform for moving into digital publishing and gaining access to new audiences worldwide.

BACKGROUND AND DEVELOPMENT

The first important publishing house was opened by Louis Elzevir in Holland and published its first book in 1583. Publishing houses subsequently began to appear in cities across Europe and in the United States. As book publishing developed, specialization became commonplace, and a number of publishers concentrated on sheet music or map publishing. In the twentieth century this house specialization took the form of the division of subject matter and content. In the 1930s and 1940s paperbound, pocket-sized books, which were first introduced by Simon & Schuster, became enormously popular. Public acceptance of paperbacks increased the overall market for books and made it necessary for publishers to adopt high-volume, low-cost production methods.

The 1950s marked a period of tremendous financial and artistic growth for the book publishing industry. In the 1960s, however, a trend developed in the United States wherein firms were bought and consolidated with other companies. Many publishing houses either acquired one another or joined forces with communications conglomerates. As a result, the consolidation of power in the United States pared down the number of big publishers controlling the industry to only a few. By the 1970s and 1980s Europe's book industry had begun to follow the U.S. mass market-driven model, and bestseller lists began to appear in European papers.

When the North American Free Trade Agreement (NAFTA) was signed, the industry expected significant growth in the U.S. book trade between Mexico and other Latin American markets in the late 1990s and into the 2000s. Similarly, the Uruguay Round of the General Agreement on Tariffs and Trade (GATT) produced enhanced protection for international copyrights, which was expected to lead to larger markets for international publishers in Asia, the Middle East, and Eastern Europe. Meanwhile, in Latin America, Africa, and Asia, publishers had reached widely differing degrees of business and technical sophistication. Typical problems facing book publishers in these regions included book piracy, low literacy rates, inflation, censorship, technological limitations, and high production costs.

As publishers worldwide continued to produce more titles than the market demanded, average print runs declined. Print runs of 5,000 copies for contemporary fiction in Germany and of 2,000 to 5,000 in the United States became the rule. In addition, publishers' shares of book cover prices fell to between 20 and 30 percent in the United States in the mid-1990s.

The acquisition of Random House by German megafirm Bertelsmann AG in 1998 seemed to single-handedly wrest English-language publishing away from U.S. publishers, and by 1998 only two of the biggest U.S. book publishers—AOL Time Warner and William Morrow—were still domestically owned. However, Bertelsmann's willingness to fork over US$1.8 billion for the "Cadillac of publishing" attested to the continuing size and attractiveness of the U.S. market in the global book-buying scene.

CURRENT CONDITIONS

In 2007, there were several acquisitions and divestments that dramatically impacted the international publishing marketplace, especially for the top publishers, including Thomson (US$7.3 billion), Pearson ($US7 billion), Bertlsmann (US$6.4 billion), Reed Elsevier (US$6.2 billion), and Wolters Kluwer (US$5 billion).

As a result of a softer economy for books and other causes, the book industry was reassessing long-term profit anticipations, noted industry expert James DePonte, a partner in PricewaterhouseCoopers' Entertainment & Media practice. According to DePonte, "Books are divided into three market segments: consumer, education, and professional and technical. The consumer segment is the biggest, and the recession is clearly leading some people to reduce their discretionary spending."

The PricewaterhouseCoopers Global Entertainment and Media Outlook (PwC) estimated that global spending on books would grow at a 4.2 percent compound annual rate, rising from US$85.3 billion in 2000 to US$104.6 billion in 2005. Book sales in the United States were projected to increase from about US$34.2 billion in 2004 to US$40.5 billion in 2009, although other analysts predicted much lower growth in keeping with inflation and the slumping global economy. Sales of e-reader devices were steadily increasing. Asia surged to the forefront in that market, with 800,000 e-readers in China as of 2009. In 2010, that number had grown to 3 million. China was expected to surpass the United States in e-reader sales by 2015.

Publishers Weekly on September 13, 2010 reported that the U.S. Commerce Department data for the first half of 2010 indicated a drop in U.S. book exports of 0.8 percent to US$911.1 million. Mexico reported the largest increase (21.6 percent) due to a demand for professional books. Although Canada remained the primary destination for U.S. books, with imports worth US$423.1 million, exports to China increased by 13.8 percent to reach US$11.1 million. Predictably, exports to China increased by a substantial margin (13.8 percent), India (15.6 percent), and Brazil (16.4 percent). The United Kingdom posted the largest decline (down 11.1 percent).

Although exports of publications slipped in the first half of 2010, the book import segment rose 7 percent to US$842.7 million. China's imports to the United States increased 16.4 percent to slightly more than US$343 million. U.K. imports rose 19.3 percent to US$112.4 million, making the United Kingdom the second largest source of books, edging out Canada, which fell 11.9 percent to US$104.7 million.

A growing trend in 2005 was proprietary publishing, which industry leaders found attractive because proprietary titles are nonreturnable and relatively inexpensive to produce. Proprietary publishing produces books intended to be sold exclusively by a particular retailer. Examples include John Wiley & Sons' 2004 title, *Wi-Fi for Dummies,* produced for communications firm Intel U.K.; and Health Communications Inc.'s *Chicken Soup for the University of Michigan Soul,* produced for the University of Michigan as a fundraiser. Among companies planning to expand into proprietary publishing were HarperCollins, which budgeted US$10 million in 2005 for proprietary titles, and Simon & Schuster. Some insiders, however, treated this trend with skepticism, claiming that it could devalue books and degrade successful brands.

Dean Rader, an associate professor of English at the University of San Francisco wrote in the *San Francisco Chronicle,* in September 2008 that "The Earthworks initiative is an award-winning series of poetry collections by contemporary American Indian writers." Of special note was the location of the publisher, Salt Publishing, in Cambridge, England. The series had experienced "combined success and invisibility" linked to the plight of U.S. poetry in general and the sub-category of U.S. native American poetry specifically. Overall, poetry is not a popular genre among most readers or publishers. Consequently, it is often passed over by key groups, including book reviewers and book clubs. Earthworks features poetry that has contemporary themes written "by some of the field's heaviest hitters." As of September 2008, there were 18 books in the series, several of which had earned awards. Rader also felt they were earning another distinction that involved "augmenting the cannon of American letters."

Liz Gunnison described in *Conde Nast* on December 9, 2008, how Scholastic hoped to solve the mystery of how to publish a widely popular book series like Harry Potter novels again with the introduction of *The 39 Clues.* The 10-book series made its appearance with initial publication of *The Maze of Bones* in September 2008. The new publication was not just another children's literature series, but was multi-dimensional with a treasure hunt plot linked to an online component that offered an opportunity for kids to compete for US $100,000 in prizes.

In August 2008, Random House's decision to cancel publication of the *The Jewel of Medina* was the subject of debate. The romance novel, written by American Sherry Jones, told the story of the Prophet Muhammad and his wife, Aisha. Although incidents like death threats had accompanied the 1988 publication of Salman Rushdie's book, *The Satanic Verses,* Random House felt that Jones's love story was still worth telling. In May 2008, however, University of Texas Islamic history Professor Denise Spellberg called the publisher to warn them about a "national security issue." Spellberg had read a review copy and rated it "ugly" and "stupid." It was the professor's opinion that the book's publication would be in poor taste. "You can't play with a sacred history and turn it into soft core pornography," Spellberg concluded. Random House subsequently consulted with "credible and unrelated sources," who advised that the book's publication might offend some Muslims and incite violent acts "by a small, radical segment." However, following the 2008 publication of the book by Beaufort Books, it has been published in five countries with plans to debut it in several more by the end of 2010.

Taschen Books responded to concerns to link plans for art books to issues related to growing popularity of unknown artists with the *Basic Art* series. This series evolved over two decades to move beyond an initial line up of old and modern masters. For US$9.99 each, Taschen offered 96-page introductions for such artists as Francis Bacon. The company also offered a "movement" series. A volume published in 2010 titled *Trespass. A History of Uncommissioned Urban Art,* was filled with public art in the form of graffiti. Additional evolving categories for Taschen and other art book publishers included survey volumes, monographs, and catalogs, as well as deluxe and limited editions.

Many publishers were exploring new markets, including the sale of their contemporary titles in non-traditional retail stores. For example, Phaidon's catalog for the New Museum's Elizabeth Peyton exhibition will be featured by Banana Republic in its major markets.

RESEARCH AND TECHNOLOGY

Since the 1980s, the evolution of computer technology has had a significant impact on the international book publishing industry, from book editing and manuscript preparation to book production, distribution, and marketing. By the late 1990s, the Internet and the larger digital revolution were transforming the very nature of the industry, inevitably leading some to predict the demise of the book as a medium.

Technology for digitally ordering, printing, and binding books on demand outside the traditional book shipping process represents one aspect of the publishing technology revolution of the 1980s and 1990s. The use of computerized text editing and word processing software programs by authors and editors for the preparation

of book manuscripts also became standard practice in the publishing industries of many developed nations. The use of computers for storing authors' manuscripts and editors' changes, which otherwise would be exchanged via paper, offered publishers increased savings in storage and shipping costs and a more efficient means of creating backup copies of manuscripts. Desktop publishing computer systems for manipulating text and images enabled publishers to reduce typesetting and production costs, streamline book reprinting and inventory control procedures, and shorten book production schedules. By 1998, it had become possible for the development of a book from writing to final printing to be conducted digitally, making it possible for publishers, typesetters, and printers to transmit a book's data files almost instantaneously. PUBNET, a computerized book-ordering network made up of roughly 65 U.S. publishers and 2,400 bookstores, enabled publishers to gain detailed book sales summaries direct from booksellers, thereby improving their marketing and distribution decision making.

The emergence of "electronic book" (e-book) technology in the world's developed nations represented another way in which the global publishing industry was reinventing itself in the 1990s. The trend began in the United States with the conversion to paperless online reference products, such as computerized databases on CD-ROM disks that were capable of storing the equivalent of 250,000 pages each. Companies then began marketing e-books on CD-ROMs or computer diskettes that consumers could read using computers or handheld devices. Such e-books offered a less expensive and less bulky format that could potentially enable readers to have immediate, around-the-clock access to a wide variety of titles, as well as increased search capabilities. In the early 1990s, 700 U.S. companies providing data packaged in electronic formats formed a national Electronic Publishing Group to advance the interests of that segment of the U.S. publishing industry. By the end of the decade every major book publisher had an "interactive" book initiative of some kind. For example, John Wiley launched an online service to enable readers to access the journals they subscribed to via the Internet.

Digital technology also made it possible for publishers to offer customers customized books whose precise content they could select from a wide range of choices and then unite in a combination of their choosing. These flexible books could then be printed at book outlets or downloaded from the publisher's Web site. Beginning in 1996 publishers had the ability to scale print runs to meet exact, limited demand. It became no more expensive to print 25 copies than 25,000, offering publishers the hope that they could eliminate one of their most punishing and wasteful costs by eliminating the expense of shipping too many books to booksellers and then reclaiming them when booksellers returned the unsold copies.

By the late 1990s scores of large and small book publishers, especially in the United States, were using the World Wide Web to establish an online presence, initially for book promotions or to offer "reader community" sites. However, Web sites also have been used in growing numbers to push direct book sales, create interactive collaborative literary projects, and drum up potential authors.

In the 2000s, publishers only half-jokingly referred to electronic publishing as "Gutenberg's Revenge," alluding to the high costs and lower-than-anticipated revenues associated with the development that drove a number of e-publishers, such as Audiohighway.com, Bookface.com, Booktech, and Contentville.com, to join the rash of Web-related closings when the dot-com bubble burst. Even the highly heralded Netlibrary reported financial problems in 2001, and downsizings led to staff cuts at Questia, Xlibris, iUniverse, ebrary, DigitalOwl, and Intertrust. Overall, electronic publishers laid off about 2,000 workers in 2001, and all indications were that the electronic book publishing industry was here to stay. Analysts predict that the sector will become profitable once publishers cut overhead, reduce staff size, and forge ahead with viable business plans. Major cost factors were associated with maintaining a Web presence in 2001. Web losses for Random House were US$790 million, US$444 million of which came from e-commerce. Nonetheless, the creation of so-called "books on demand" promised to continue to gain momentum in the 2000s, adding revenues to reduce the high costs associated with Web maintenance.

In 2004 and 2005, the Internet search engine Google created controversy with the introduction of the Google Print for Library program, which created searchable digital archives of books from participating libraries at four universities and the New York Public Library. Publishers challenged the legality of the program, arguing that it violated copyrights and would potentially cut into publishers' sales. Google officials, however, responded that the company made material viewable only with appropriate permissions. As more digital options become available, more titles will become available to readers who probably would not buy the actual book. The innovations in technology were expected to lead to conflict between the formats.

INDUSTRY LEADERS

The international book publishing industry boasts a number of giant publishers. German multi-media giant Bertelsmann AG posted total sales of US$21 billion in 2009 and was the largest English and German language publisher in the world with some of the largest divisions in the industry, including Random House (the world's largest trade book publisher) and Gruner & Jahr (the largest magazine publisher in Europe). Other major German publishers included Heyne, which was perhaps the largest paperback publisher;

the sci-tech house Springer-Verlag; and Georg von Holtzbrinck Publishing. Between 1985 and 1998 Holtzbrinck channeled US$300 million into the U.S. book industry, acquiring such prominent U.S. publishing houses as Farrar, Straus & Giroux, Henry Holt, and St. Martin's Press.

The French publishing industry was rocked at the beginning of the twenty-first century when the country's largest publisher of the 1990s, the venerable Havas Publications Edition, was bought by Vivendi in 1998. The deal resulted in the creation of Vivendi Universal Publishing (VUP) in 2000. The new company pursued an aggressive acquisition strategy, including U.S. publisher Houghton Mifflin for US$2.2 billion in 2001, which made Vivendi Universal the third largest publisher in the world and the second largest education publisher. However, massive debt dogged the company, and Vivendi, deciding to concentrate on strengthening its other media divisions, sold its publishing assets to Lagardere Group in 2002. Lagardere received authorization from the European Commission to retain 40 percent of VUP's publishing assets in 2004, while the remaining group, taking the name Editis, was bought by Wendel Investissement later that year. Editis reported net revenues of 717.4 million euros (US$1.04 billion) in 2007, which made it the second-largest publishing group in France. Among other leading French publishers were Hachette Livre, which produced a broad range of general books, business titles, and reference books, and Gallimard, which published about 750 new titles annually. Heavy debt forced Hachette to merge with French defense industry titan Matra in 1992 to form Matra-Hachette, and in the late 1990s the company bought school publisher Hatier. Hachette Livre reported that it distributed 10,000 new titles and sold 140 million reference books each year.

In Great Britain, book publishing was dominated by two companies. London-based Pearson plc, which owned the Penguin Group (including the Penguin, Putnam, and Viking imprints), was the world's top education publisher through its Pearson Education unit, which owned the imprints Pearson Scott Foresman, Pearson Addison Wesley, and Pearson Prentice Hall. In 2005, Pearson purchased AGS Publishing, creating Pearson AGS Globe, which produced materials for special needs education, for US$270 million. Sales for the Penguin Group, which published such top-selling authors as Tom Clancy and Patricia Cornwell, topped US$9.04 billion in 2009.

Reed Elsevier, a joint venture between the Netherlands-based Elsevier N.V. and U.K.-based Reed International PLC, was a leading publisher of educational books through its Harcourt Education division. The company reported total revenues in 2009 of US$8.46 billion. In 1996, the four largest trade publishing groups in the Netherlands accounted for 50 to 70 percent of the US$480 million Dutch market, which generated 12,000 new titles per year. Among its leading publishers in the late 1990s were Meulenhoff; trade house Veen; and Veen's parent, Wolters Kluwer. A planned merger between Wolters Kluwer and Britain's Reed Elsevier to create an US$8 billion professional and scientific megahouse (challenged only by the Thomson Corporation), was called off in 1998 when the European Commission raised antitrust objections.

In the United States, the largest publisher throughout the first decade of the 2000s was Bertelsmann-owned Random House. Although Random House struggled with declining profits in 2002 and 2003, largely because of the weak dollar against the stronger euro, the company's performance improved considerably in 2004, when operating profits rose 22 percent. Random House posted sales in 2009 of US$2.348 billion and carried 17.5 percent of the book publishing market in the United States. Pearson-owned Penguin Group, which made about two-thirds of its sales in the United States, experienced a drop in operating profits of 24 percent in 2004, due primarily to the weak dollar. Nevertheless, the firm reported a 40 percent increase in titles that made *The New York Times* bestseller list, including million-copy selling *Eats, Shoots & Leaves*. Pearson carried 11.3 percent of the 2009 U.S. book publishing sector. The Hachette Book Group was the second largest book publisher worldwide, with 130 books on the *The New York Times* bestseller list in 2009. McGraw-Hill, a leading textbook publisher, posted 2009 revenues of US$5.95 billion.

MAJOR COUNTRIES IN THE INDUSTRY

United States. In April 2008 *Publishers Weekly* reported that the largest U.S.-based publishers for 2007 were McGraw-Hill (US$2.7 billion), Reader's Digest (US$2.7 billion), Scholastic (US$2.1 billion), HarperCollins (US$1.3 billion), John Wiley (US$1.2 billion), Simon & Schuster (US$886 million), and Marvel (US $398 million).

Three major U.S. publishing houses were sold to non-U.S. conglomerates between 1996 and mid-1998, but U.S. publishers also grabbed a steadily growing share of foreign book markets. In 1998, Bertelsmann shocked the world publishing industry by buying Random House, the world's largest English-language general trade book publisher, from Advance Publications for US$1.4 billion. The acquisition made Bertelsmann the largest English-language publisher globally.

In the early years of the twenty-first century the book publishing industry in the United States remained the world's largest. However, rising costs since 1997, when the nation's book industry netted US$20 billion, had failed to excite the large conglomerates that dominated the trade.

By September 2010 the Association of American Publishers reported slumping sales with a 21 percent decline compared to the same time in 2009, which was at US$23.86 billion. However, overall sales were up 3.8 percent for the year, with growth coming from the e-book category, which was up 188 percent (US$313.2 million) in 2010. The only other category on the rise in 2010 was in the higher education publishing sector, which reported an increase in sales of 10.6 percent for 2010.

Perhaps no area of publishing had changed quite as much as the publishing houses connected with miscellaneous colleges and universities, particularly in the United States. The major college houses in terms of sales, longevity, and annual books published included Cornell University Press, Harvard University Press, and Indiana University Press. These presses survive on business acumen, not university subsidies. As a result, they continued to publish not only scholarly titles by academics, but also more popular books calculated to reach a wider audience and to earn reviews in major publications. In 2002 these presses also signed publishing deals with ebrary.com, enabling consumers to access and retrieve on-demand, full-text copies of books on their respective lists, including some titles no longer available in print editions.

Harvard University Press, created in 1913, listed more than 2,800 titles in print, including some that had won such prestigious awards as the Pulitzer Prize, National Book Award, Bancroft Prize, and National Book Critics Circle Award. Cornell University Press, established in 1869, was one of the oldest U.S. university presses in continuing existence and operated with an all-faculty review board. Indiana University Press, although only in existence since 1950, had become the tenth largest university press in the country. It had published the work of first-class scholars and authors, including Umberto Eco, Henry Glassie, Langston Hughes, Alfred Kinsey, and Scott Russell Sanders. In contrast to these successful university presses, many other university presses were in a beleaguered financial state as many university libraries cut their budgets to the bone and acquired fewer titles in the first decade of the 2000s. In 2001, for example, Northwestern University Press incurred a loss of US$877,000 on revenues of US$1.54 million. It was typical of university presses struggling to find a blockbuster best seller to balance traditionally low sales for scholarly books and import books of ideas. By 2004, however, several university presses had succeeded in boosting output by capturing key niche markets, such as Arabic language titles. In 2004, university press output had reached a record high of 14,848 new titles and editions, with 55 percent of the increase coming from history, biography, and law books.

Unauthorized publication of books on the Internet was a growing problem, as Stephanie Meyers discovered when she postponed publication of the last novel in her vampire series, *Midnight Sun.* When the unfinished manuscript for the young adult romance appeared on the World Wide Web, Meyers said "the writing is messy and flawed and full of mistakes" The publisher for the rest of her books, Little, Brown, did not have a contract to publish *Midnight Sun.* Meyers's fans signed an online petition at petitionsite.com in support of the author.

Japan. Reflecting the moribund Japanese economy of the 1990s and 2000s, Japan's book industry suffered, especially in such areas as comic books and paperbacks, but translations of U.S. titles remained profitable. The Japanese book market was dominated by about 10 large family-owned firms that controlled the country's two large book distributors, and thus 80 percent of the Japanese book distribution market. As in Europe, the Japanese book industry as a whole evolved from the magazine industry, and many of Japan's publishers continued to publish magazines along with books. Dai Nippon Printing Company Ltd. diversified with the production of promotional materials, direct mail pieces, business forms, CD-ROMs, catalogs, smart cards, and packaging for consumer products. Many of Japan's major book publishers were privately managed, and the top 120 publishers controlled 50 percent of the nation's book sales volume, a trend toward consolidation that continued through the mid-1990s.

In 2003, Japanese publishers admitted that losses had plagued the nation's industry for the sixth year in a row, according to the Research Institute for Publications and *Publishers Weekly.* Sales in Japan for 2001 dropped 3 percent from 2000, leading to wide bookstore closings despite publishing successes such as a 10 million Japanese print run of the Harry Potter books. The closings were partially responsible for high book returns, which were said to be around 40 percent. Many in the industry put the blame on consumer preferences for video games and movies.

Despite low sales, however, book use was up at libraries, reaching about 500 million books borrowed a year in 2003. Output of new titles was also up, rising 13.3 percent in April 2002. The Japanese government had joined publishers in various efforts to promote reading, including a law passed in 2001 to fund school libraries' purchase of books, and the establishment of multipartisan federation to improve the reading climate for the general public.

The market for electronic books opened opportunities for the Japanese book publishing industry. Daiki Naito reported that the Sharp Corporation Web site for the Zaurus personal digital assistant allowed visitors to download pictures and data. More than 50 books could be stored on a data card roughly the size of a postage stamp. In 2007, Sharp announced plans to discontinue production of the Zaurus PDA line, even though the demand was still strong.

In June 2004, in Arts Weekly/Japan, Suvendrini Kakuchi discussed the phenomenal difference a new novel was making in the conservative Japanese publishing world. Natsuo Kirino's *Out* was about a husband killer and psychopath gangsters. In 2003, it was nominated for best novel in the prestigious 2004 Edgar Allen Poe Awards. According to Kakuchi, *Yomiuri Shimburn* editor Kenichi Sato pointed out that "Kirino's style was a far cry from the past where Japanese writers, like Nobel prize winner Yasunari Kawabata and the country's best post-war novelist Yukio Mishima, gained international limelight for writing hauntingly elegant prose depicting the uniqueness of Japanese culture and portraying women as innocent beauties devoted to men." In New York bookstores, *Out* had become a favorite, but was displayed in the mystery section, rather than Japanese section.

Germany. In 2002, Bertelsmann-Random House's decision to cut costs dramatically at all its publishing houses caused alarm and protest throughout the book publishing industry. Bertelsmann announced worldwide Random House sales of approximately US$1.85 billion for the fiscal year ending June 30, 2001. The Bertelsmann-Random House merger gave the German publisher ownership of 43 percent of the U.S. book market, with U.S. firms claiming only 30 percent. The two largest categories of books in Germany were specialist/scientific books (39 percent of market value) and general literature including fiction (53 percent of total market value). The leading categories in terms of volume sales were language and literature (22.3 percent) and the social sciences (21.5 percent). Valued at US$22 billion, Bertelsmann AG of Germany was, with Time Warner and Disney, one of the world's largest media concerns at the beginning of the twenty-first century, with books generating about 31 percent of its total sales.

In Germany, even with a global economic crisis impacting virtually every sector, the book market continued to grow. Between 2006 and 2008 the production of books reached between 94,000 and 96,000. In 2007, the market increased 3.4 percent, and by 2008, Germany posted an increase of 0.4 percent for US$13 billion.

United Kingdom. In the 2000s the publishing success of Harry Potter author J.K. Rowling gained global attention. While the book industry languished elsewhere, during the January–September 2001 reporting period, British book exports were US$1.25 billion, only slightly less than the US$1.27 billion for the United States, although the British industry was only one-fifth of U.S. book operations, according to *Publishers Weekly.* The United Kingdom has traditionally been a major center of operations for the European continent's publishing giants, and in the 1990s through

2010, it remained an important entry point for U.S. publishers seeking to establish themselves in Europe. Once insulated from U.S. book industry trends, the British book industry increasingly mirrored U.S. publishing practices by the late 1990s. Such U.S. imports as the author book tour, online book ordering, and the book superstore, not to mention the dominance of U.S. titles on British publishers' lists, all attested to the influence of U.S. publishers on Great Britain's market. Britain had been second only to Canada as the largest importer of books from the United States in 2003 (US$274.6 million in value) and was the largest exporter of books into the U.S. market (US$288 million). However, in the first half of 2004, U.K. exports to the United States dropped 11.6 percent, placing it third behind China and Canada.

Doreen Carvajal reported in *The New York Times* on June 16, 2008, that Amazon had disabled its "buy now with 1 click" icon on its British Web site for hundreds of books published by Hachette Livre's British unit. Customers were then required to interact with third-party sellers of new or used books and had to pay for shipping. Some bloggers organized letter-writing campaigns that accused Amazon of transforming itself into "the bully of the publishing industry." In markets where Amazon had a commanding position, negotiations were frequently considered to be intense. Hachette also had its titles dropped from promotions with other titles in the genre suggested instead. When small publishers in the United States had their "buy now" buttons disabled, it was believed to be linked to decisions about not working with BookSurge, which was owned by Amazon. BookSurge offered print-on-demand services and reportedly demanded a discount of as much as 52 percent on the retail price.

France. During the 2000s, book publishing in France differed from the book industry elsewhere. For example, between 50 and 60 percent of all 2002 children's book sales stemmed from the sale of comic books, such as "Asterix," which was a classic in France. In 2000, total sales of books in France, including book club sales, were US$2.5 billion, according to *Publishers Weekly* in August 2001. Book and publishing sales grew 3.2 percent in volume and 2.9 percent in value between 1998 and 2002, according to *Euromonitor*. Consumer books account for most sales in France, with school and library purchases playing a much smaller role in the market.

BIBLIOGRAPHY

Asada, Tomiji. "Sales of Books, Mags Down for 5 Straight Years." *Japan Economic Newswire*, 25 February 2002.

Association of American Publishers, Industry Statistics 2009. Available from www.publishers.org.

Baker, John F. "A Buoyant Mood in London." *Publishers Weekly*, 18 February 2002.

Baker, John F., and Nathalie Atkinson. "Canada: Reaching Out." *Publishers Weekly*, 13 June 2005.

Beattie, Graham. "Size Matters in Boutique Publishing," 30 August 2008. Available from nzherald.co.nz.

"Book Consumption Declines in the U.S." *Graphic Arts Monthly*, August 2004.

"Book Exports Up 7.8 percent in Six-Month Period." *Publishers Weekly*, 13 September 2004.

Book Industry Trends. New York: Book Industry Study Group, 2005.

"Books and Publishing in Mexico." April 2003. Available from www.euromonitor.com.

"Books Without Buyers." *Publishers Weekly*, 30 May 2005.

"Bowker: Titles up 19 percent in 2003." *Publishers Weekly*, 31 May 2004.

Bowman, Becky. "Northwestern U. Press' Woes Typical of Smaller Publishers." *Daily Northwestern*, 25 February 2002.

Carvajal, Doreen. "Small Publishers Feel Power of Amazon's 'Buy' Button." *New York Times*, 16 June 2008. Available from nytimes.com.

"CBA Demands Changes to Parallel Importation Laws." *Quill & Quire*, 30 April 2010. Available from www.quillandquire.com.

"Cultural Industries in the Latin American Economy: Current Status and Outlook in the Context of Globalization." Organization for American States, Office of Cultural Affairs, Washington, D.C., 2005. Available from www.oas.org.

Danford, Natalie. "How Do You Say 'Growing Pains' in Spanish?" *Publishers Weekly*, 17 January 2005.

"European Book Publishing Statistics." Federation of European Publishers. Available from www.fep-fee.be.

Fischer, Ernst. "A Land of Readers: The Book Market in Germany." Goethe-Institut, August, 2009. Available from www.goethe.de.

Graham, Gordon. "Promoting Reading in Africa." *The Book & The Computer/Global Exchange*, 15 December 2003. Available from www.honco.net.

Greco, Albert. *Book Industry in Latin America: 2008–2020*. Cerlalc, 6 August, 2008. Available from www.cerlalc.org.

Gunnison, Liz. "Recreating Harry Potter's Spell." *Conde Nast*, 9 September 2008. Available from www.portfolio.com.

"Harvard Press Inks Deal with Commercial Press." *Publishers Weekly*, 1 July 2004.

"Industry Sales Post Modest '07 Gains." *Publishers Weekly*, 7 April 2008.

Kakuchi, Suvendrini. "Mystery Novel Gives Women a New Voice." *Arts Weekly/Japan*, 8 June 2004. Available from www.ipsnews.net/.

Khanna, Lalitha. "Books Shelved?" *Business Line*, 14 January 2002.

Kirkpatrick, David D. "Random House Cutting Sharply, Stirring Talk In Book Trade." *The New York Times*, 22 January 2002.

Livingston, Gillian. "Indigo Takes Control of 23 Chapters/ Indigo Stores After No Buyers Found." *Canadian Press Newswire*, 8 January 2002.

Liyong, Zhu. "Publishers Cater for Worldwide Demand." *China Daily*, 5 September 2008. Available from www.chinadaily.com.cn.

———. "Spread the Word." *China Daily*, 9 September 2008. Available from cblog.chinadaily.com.cn/.

Lottman, Herbert R. "French Sales Top US$2 billion." *Publishers Weekly,* 6 August 2001.

Maysuradze, Yury, and Boris Esenkin. "The Russian Book Market Rebounds." *The Book* & *The Computer/Global Exchange,* 12 November 2003. Available from www.honco.net.

Menon, Ritu. "Making a Difference." *The Hindu,* 7 September 2008. Available from www.thehindu.com.

Meyer, Mike. "Letter from Beijing: The World's Biggest Book Market." *New York Times,* 13 March 2005.

Milliot, Jim. "B&N, Borders Report Strong Holiday Gains." *Publishers Weekly,* 14 January 2002.

———. "Exclusively Yours." *Publishers Weekly,* 20 June 2005.

———. "Google Draws Fire, Creates Book Page." *Publishers Weekly,* 30 May 2005.

———. "Profits Improve at Random." *Publishers Weekly,* 21 March 2005.

———. "Publishing's Top Guns." *Publishers Weekly,* 14 July 2008.

———. "Random House Results Skewed by Currency Changes." *Publishers Weekly,* 5 April 2004.

———. "Trends: More Evidence of Softness." *Publishers Weekly,* 30 May 2005.

Milliot, Jim, and Calvin Reid. "Reality Check: Despite Setbacks in 2001, the Groundwork for the Success of E-publishing Has Been Laid." *Publishers Weekly,* 7 January 2002.

Morales, Ed. "Mexico Fair Draws Spanish Publishers from Around the World." *Publishers Weekly,* 10 December 2001.

Naito, Daiki. "Ailing Publishing Industry Turning to e-books for Salvation." *Kyodo News,* 19 March 2002. Available from www.japantimes.co.jp.

Paddock, Polly. "The Year in Publishing." *Charlotte Observer* (North Carolina), 3 January 2002.

Picchi, Aimee. "Viacom Merges Simon & Schuster with Film Group." *Bloomberg News,* 31 January 2002.

Picklyk, Douglas. "By the Book." *Canadian Printer,* December 2001.

PricewaterhouseCoopers Global Entertainment and Media Outlook, 2004. Available from www.pwcglobal.com.

Rader, Dean. "British Publisher Touts American Indian Poets." *San Francisco Chronicle,* 7 September 2008. Available from SFGate.com.

"Random Error." *Washington Post,* 22 August 2008. Available from www.washingtonpost.com.

"Random House South Africa and Struik Publishing Merge to Create Leading Force in South African Publishing." Random House press release, 2 September 2008. Available from www.pressatrandom.co.uk.

Raugust, Karen. "Licensing Watch: Europe." *Publishers Weekly,* 5 May 2001.

"Russian Book Market Revs Up; " *Publishers Weekly,* 13 September 2010. Available from www.publishersweekly.com.

Schiffrin, Andre. *The Business of Books: How International Conglomerates Took Over Publishing and Changed the Way We Read.* Brooklyn, NY: Verso, 2000.

Sithold, Cynthia. "The Movement of Books Across Borders— Current Challenges." *Proceedings of the Indaba 2003.* Zimbabwe International Book Fair. Available from www.zibf.org.zw.

Trachtenberg, Jeffrey A., and Emily Steel. "Vampire Novel Is Put on Hold." *The Wall Street Journal,* 3 September 2008.

"U.S. Book Production Reaches New High of 195,000 Titles in 2004; Fiction Soars." *Business Wire,* 24 May 2005. Available from www.thefreelibrary.com.

"U.S. Book Sales for 2001 Posted by Association of American Publishers." Available from www.publishers.org.

"VSS Study Projects Slow Consumer Book Growth." *Publishers Weekly,* 2 August 2004.

Wang, Annie. "A New Chapter: Chinese Writers Are Discovering That Books Have Become a Tricky Business." *Time Asia Magazine,* 27 January 2003.

Zeitchik, Steven, and Jim Milliot. "Comeback Kid? Amazon Revival Could Shake up Industry." *Publishers Weekly,* 11 April 2005.

"Zeroing In On Some Savvy Suppliers." *Publishers Weekly,* 1 July 2004.

SIC 4841

CABLE AND OTHER PAY-TELEVISION SERVICES

NAICS CODE(S)

513210. Participants in the global subscription television industry deliver live and recorded programming, most often via cable lines or satellite transmission, to businesses and consumers. Carriers may provide closed circuit television services, direct-broadcast satellite (DBS) or direct-to-home (DTH) satellite services, multi-channel multipoint distribution systems (MMDS) services, and satellite master antenna systems (SMATV) services. Certain firms in the industry also participate heavily in other telecommunications services; see also **Telecommunications Services** later in this chapter for

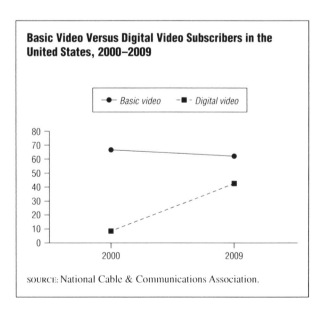

Basic Video Versus Digital Video Subscribers in the United States, 2000–2009

SOURCE: National Cable & Communications Association.

more detailed treatment of those activities. Television networks are not included in this discussion.

INDUSTRY SNAPSHOT

Although the industry's two main segments, cable and satellite, have coexisted for some time, some industry observers foretell the ultimate ascendance of one over the other. Predicting which one might prevail in this struggle depends on the observer: cable companies claim their broadband digital format far exceeds the interactive abilities of satellite, yet satellite proponents have a much easier time implementing mass-audience systems and claim to offer impressive interactive capabilities in their own right. To date, cable is winning the battle in terms of subscriber counts, and cable systems' ongoing technology investments is equipping them to quickly deploy digital services on a large scale in most places. Even Microsoft's Bill Gates has been hedging his bets: while pumping billions into cable, Microsoft also has sizable interests in low-orbit satellite systems that promise to extend the satellite medium into all corners of the global telecommunications field.

In reality, cable television tends to be strongest in parts of the world where satellite is weakest, usually where cable installations were begun in the 1970s and early 1980s, and satellite services lead in markets in which cable infrastructure is lacking. Such an arrangement is unlikely to change anytime soon, even as the respective systems upgrade to digital services. Microwave-based MMDS systems, on the other hand, have thus far only attracted small followings and few expect them to gain a mass viewership on the scale of the other two formats.

According to the National Cable & Communications Association 2010 statistics, the number of basic video customers in the United Stations dropped from 66.6 million in 2000 to 62.1 million in 2009; a decline of over 4 million. In the same time, digital video customers increased from 8.5 million in 2000 to 42.6 million in 2009; a dramatic increase of over 34 million. As of 2010, millions of people had already switched from cable to satellite TV, and the trend was continuing. Satellite dishes were popping up all over the world.

The following are just a few of the differences between cable and satellite TV:

- Price: On average, basic cable will cost between US$40 and US$50 per month, with additional charges for any add-ons or for digital programming. With satellite, the average price for basic service, which generally includes digital channels, is between US$30 and US$40.

- Choice: Generally, the choices in cable TV programming are more limited than satellite TV channels, or the cost is more to get the same number of channels available to Satellite users. Cable TV

providers are also behind in the number of high-definition channels being offered.

- Outages: According to studies and statistics provided by all the cable and satellite providers, cable TV providers nationwide experienced 3 to 5 percent outages, while satellite TV providers only experienced 1 percent.

- Customer Service: For the past five years, the top satellite TV providers were ranked higher than the top cable companies by JD Powers and Associates.

- Local Programming: Although in previous years, the consumer could not get local programming through satellite, this is generally no longer the case. By 2005, the higher level satellite television providers offered options throughout most of the nation for local programming.

The outlook for pay television remains positive. Changes in consumer preferences for video-on-demand and enhanced viewing capabilities have allowed the pay-TV industry to make huge inroads into traditional broadcast markets. Increased disposable income in countries such as China and India with their huge potential markets will also be of benefit to the industry. Countries continue to deregulate industries, allowing companies to pursue foreign investment, although many countries continue to top such investment levels at 49 percent.

In a November 2010 article published by *Cable Spotlight*, ABI Research, a leading provider of in-depth analysis and quantitative forecasting of trends in global connectivity and other emerging technologies, published the results of the study, "Pay-TV Subscriptions: Cable, IPTV (NewsAlert), Satellite, Digital Terrestrial," as part of its ongoing study on TV and Video Research Service. According to the ABI Research Pay-TV market data reports, the net subscriber addition in the global Pay-TV market has seen an increase of two percent in the third quarter of 2010 over that in the second quarter 2010. The report also highlighted the increase in seven world regions including the Western European market of France, Spain and Italy; Eastern Europe; Asia-Pacific; North America; Latin America; Middle East; and Africa.

The ABI Pay-TV market database includes key subscribers in the video platforms, which is satellite, cable, and telco TV, the global subscriber market share, as well as the Pay-TV subscriptions by the service providers or operators. The entry of new television platforms such as digital terrestrial TV and online video, are not encouraging the subscribers to invest in Pay-TV market, hence the slow subscriber growth especially in areas like Western Europe and North America, which are high penetration areas, meanwhile traditional cable TV and Pay-TV are expected to remain strong in Eastern Europe and Latin American areas.

In many markets the industry's fastest-growing segments are satellite services and the rapidly increasing digital television market. Indeed, the two formats are increasingly offered in conjunction by leading-edge firms. Satellite service enables operators to establish broad geographic presence rapidly in a relatively non-intrusive way compared to cable or microwave infrastructure, a significant benefit when local laws or terrains restrict the laying of cable. These services also often boast a mix of programming different from that of cable or other alternatives. Aggressive deployment and marketing efforts by such leaders as DIRECTV and some of the Sky Broadcasting ventures have also contributed to the medium's growth. The digital side entices subscribers with higher technical quality in programming and, particularly with digital cable, the potential for interactive services such as Internet browsing and home shopping.

Mark Fleischmann reported that TV providers and satellite service companies scored the lowest of any industry in the 2007 American Consumer Satisfaction Index. The industries combined score on the index was only 62. That ranking reflected a one-point increase from 2006. Compared to 2002, however, the ranking was actually down by one point. According to Fleischmann, University of Michigan Professor Claes Fornell said "monopoly-like pricing" was one contributing factor to the poor score. Basic cable rates rose 5 percent in 2006.

Major cable companies were testing and seriously considering new options for including advertising with their programming. In a special California market test, Cox and Walt Disney planned to offer prime-time TV shows and college football games on demand in which Cox had disabled the fast-forward option to zoom past ads. This deal did not impact Cox's digital video recorder service. Time Warner Cable was considering adding targeted advertising based on what subscribers' watched.

ORGANIZATION AND STRUCTURE

As opposed to terrestrial broadcast methods used by traditional network channels, which may be received essentially by anyone within a certain geographic range, subscription television services employ three methods to transmit controlled-access, high-quality signals: cable, microwave, and satellite. First, coaxial or fiber-optic cables may be directly wired between subscribers and distribution points. Subscriber lines are fed signals by a local "headend," or distribution facility; a network of one or more headends serving a geographic region forms a cable system.

All of the world's major cable operators run more than one system, and thus they are sometimes referred to as multiple-system operators (MSOs). Second, services may use a multi-channel, multipoint distribution system (MMDS) to carry signals from a television studio to a microwave transmitter, which then relays them to rooftop receivers. This method is also known as wireless cable. Third, subscription services may offer satellite transmission in which a broadcaster uplinks a signal to a transponder on

a satellite, which retransmits either to home dishes (known as DBS or DTH service) or to a satellite master dish (SMATV). Companies offering satellite services may own the satellites used to transmit their signals, but more often they lease space from a third-party satellite vendor.

A separate and increasingly important technological difference is whether services are analog or digital. While both transmit signals via electromagnetic waves, digital services first encode the pictures and sound as binary information, much like computer data, that is then decoded by the receiving television set. Thus, digital signals minimize deterioration during transmission and enable more powerful technical manipulation and embellishment of the programming information. Digital programming may be disseminated through any of the three transmission methods, as well as through terrestrial broadcast, but requires equipment capable of processing digital data at both the sending and receiving ends. Digital technology is in some cases less expensive for operators as well; estimates place the operating cost of digital satellite channels at one-third of that for their analog counterparts. Many analysts say that analog will be history nearly everywhere in the world by 2010.

In addition to their competing technologies, pay-television services differ in pricing and programming options. Most of the world's subscription services involve some form of flat fee, typically monthly, to obtain the most basic level of service. Many operators also offer premium or elective services for additional fees, and some provide programming on a transaction basis known as pay-per-view (PPV) television. Pricing for comparable services in different parts of the world varies widely, as do programming choices. PPV services can be distributed in analog or digital formats via any of the three transmission methods.

Pay-per-view (PPV) services represent a small but expanding world niche. These services typically offer high-profile programming, such as recent movies and live sporting events, on a transaction basis. *Broadcasting & Cable*, a U.S. journal for the trade, reported that at the close of the century viable PPV markets were established only in France, Germany, Hong Kong, Italy, Japan, the Netherlands, and the United States. Test runs were underway in other nations, however.

The industry's structure varies by region and by country. In Western Europe, for instance, several countries possess similar technological infrastructures, but language and regulatory differences make for highly divergent programming. These countries' telephone carriers, many of which until recently were state owned, provide the bulk of cable television services. However, in an era of deregulation and privatization, they are beginning to face challenges from other vendors. The reverse has been true in the United States, where phone companies and cable operators were traditionally separate and only recently have phone services begun to explore cable services. Similarly, parts of

Europe and Asia, such as the United Kingdom and Japan, possess limited infrastructure for cable services, and thus satellite and MMDS services predominate. In such places as the United States and Germany, extensive cable networking exists and, as a result, cable is considerably more common than other forms. Meanwhile, cultural norms, socioeconomic conditions, and the quality and breadth of local terrestrial broadcasts help fashion pay-television demand in particular countries and regions; it may not be taken for granted that programming and delivery methods popular in one well-established market will be popular elsewhere.

According to an August 2010 report in *the Wall Street Journal*, the subscription television industry—including cable, satellite and telecommunications companies—suffered its first drop in total subscribers in the second quarter, according to research firm SNL Kagan. The firm cited the weak U.S. economy as the main culprit for the decline, along with the after effects of the government-mandated transition to a digital broadcast spectrum. The stumble comes at a fragile time for the TV business as it navigates the transition to digital media. New options for online video entertainment are proliferating, offering consumers a potentially cheaper alternative to the traditional pay-TV offering of bundled channels. While there is little evidence that consumers are making the switch, the risk of them doing so is rising as more over-the-top television services, which allow users to access the Internet through their TV sets, become available.

The entire industry lost 216,000 customers in the second quarter of 2010, compared with a gain of 378,000 the same time a year earlier. Cable suffered its worst quarterly video loss to date, losing 711,000 subscribers, with six of the eight U.S. operators reporting their worst quarterly video losses. Satellite companies, such as DirecTV and DISH Network Corp., managed to add 81,000 TV subscribers, while telecommunications companies, like Verizon Communications Inc. and AT&T Inc., gained 414,000 customers.

While cable has been losing shares in the video market for some time, major cable operators such as Comcast Corp. and Time Warner Cable Inc. have managed to continue boosting their revenue through price increases and added services. The cable operators also have taken market shares in the broadband Internet service segment, a key growth engine for the industry that could help it thrive in the age of digital media.

Subscription television carriers are often different from, although they may be linked to, the enterprises that actually produce television programming. Much of the content originates in various networks, known to the end user as channels, which provide brand names such as CNN or HBO under which to market their programming. The carriers then pay the networks fees based on the number of subscribers to each network's programming.

Carriers also may arrange with local broadcast channels and community organizations to deliver local programming to subscribers. However, major operators often hold sizable production facilities as well, and may produce some channels' content. An interesting development in 2002 was the decision of three U.S. baseball teams—the Minneapolis Twins, the Baltimore Orioles, and the New York Yankees—to create their own cable presence. The Yankees have a cable presence on the Yankees Entertainment & Sports Network (YES), and all other major league teams are at least in discussion stages to follow suit.

New media competitors are snapping up video-content rights and making in-roads onto living-room TV sets and other screens. Hulu LLC, a joint-venture among General Electric Co. unit NBC Universal, Walt Disney Co. and News Corp., owner of The Wall Street Journal, launched a subscription service costing under $10 a month that provides access to a large library of premium TV and movie content. The offering allows consumers to stream video on Apple Inc. mobile devices, as well as on TV sets through devices such as Sony Corp.'s game console, the PlayStation 3.

In a 2010 release by Reuters, the Seattle-based online retailer, Amazon.com, Inc. has approached media companies including Time Warner Inc, CBS Corp and Viacom Inc, with a proposal for a subscription service that gives users unlimited access to some television shows and movies over the internet. Amazon's website already features a range of TV shows and movies in its video-on-demand section that are generally available for sale individually from $1.99. However, an Amazon subscription service would likely be similar to Netflix's online streaming service which works in tandem with its DVD rental business. Like Netflix, most of the TV shows and movies available for streaming would be older because the media companies are wary of devaluing their content. *The Wall Street Journal* also reported that in at least one version of Amazon's proposal, subscriptions could be bundled with its existing Amazon Prime service immediately, giving the service a large number of built-in subscribers.

Hollywood studios and media companies are vying to boost their online businesses, in part to stem online piracy of their content and also because of the higher margins they receive on digital sales. At the same time, studios have reacted with some unease to the shift in distribution of movies and TV shows to the Web, given that they have lucrative deals with cable providers to air that content.

Apple Inc. is expected to unveil the latest version of its Apple TV product. The new service is expected to offer TV shows for rent at 99 cents each. Bloomberg said the new service will feature Netflix's online service. Google

Inc. has also been eyeing a TV or movie subscription service for its YouTube website. It has had ongoing conversations with several studios as well. In 2009, online sales and streaming of movies amounted to US$300 million in the United States, and US$340 million for TV shows, according to Adams Media Research. NBC Universal, News Corp's Fox Broadcasting and Walt Disney Co's ABC network have collaborated to offer online streaming of shows at Hulu.com, but one of the fastest areas of digital distribution of Hollywood content has been Netflix's online streaming service.

BACKGROUND AND DEVELOPMENT

Pay television's potential has aroused the attention—and the pocketbooks—of some high-profile investors from outside the industry. Widely seen as a strong vote of confidence in the industry, Microsoft Corporation's 1997 US$1 billion investment in the U.S. cable carrier Comcast signaled that there would be high stakes in the integrated information-entertainment services contest. More dramatically, in 1998 the long-distance telephone powerhouse AT&T Corporation agreed to purchase Tele-Communications Inc. (TCI), the United States' largest cable operator. The move positioned AT&T, which also had a strong Internet service franchise, to provide integrated cable, local phone, long distance, and Internet access services through TCI's infrastructure.

In spite of all the business failures, mergers, and general uncertainties, where even a giant power such as AOL Time Warner has seen its stock plummet 30 percent almost overnight, the cable readiness of developed countries speeds ahead full steam. In 2002, the United States had cable readiness in 97 percent of all TV markets, for example. According to the Cable Center history site, 60 percent of all households, about 64 million, subscribed to cable in 2002.

In Canada, some of the largest providers of cable services have seen their profits sink as a result of intense competition between cable companies. Videotron, both the third largest cable-TV provider in Canada and a Quebecor Inc. company, lost 71,000 of its 1.5 million customers from January 2001 to April 2002; losses amounted to about US$25 million, according to *Bloomberg News.* Videotron's competition comes from direct-to-home satellite services such as Bell ExpressVu (owned by BCE Inc.) and Star Choice (owned by Shaw Communications Inc.).

The rising costs of operating cable have been passed on, in part, to subscribers. Cable television fees jumped 7.5 percent across the United States from 2000 to 2001, according to an April 2002 news release by the Federal Communications Commission.

According to an April 2002 *Hollywood Reporter* article, the stagnant U.S. economy in 2001, mimicked by similar slow economies in other parts of the world in 2002, was expected to keep cable from becoming attractive to investors until 2003 or 2004. In the first three months of 2002, cable stocks lost almost a quarter of their value. Even the giants like Charter Communications and Comcast said growth in digital cable holdings had slowed significantly, according to the *Hollywood Reporter.*

While the times haven't been consistently harsh for all the industry's participants, many have not met expectations of their investors and a few have alienated their customers with rising costs and slow headway toward implementing the radically improved technologies some have promised. As a result of these and other strains on profitability and cash flow, worldwide merger and acquisition activities were brisk in the latter half of the 1990s through the early 2000s.

Part of the upheaval in the subscription television industry is a by-product of international telecommunications trade reforms negotiated under the General Agreement on Trade in Services (GATS) through the World Trade Organization. These negotiations concluded in 1997, and the telecommunications agreement entered into force beginning in 1998, though individual nations have different compliance schedules. In many leading countries, deregulation initiatives preceded the agreement, which liberalizes trade by reducing entry barriers and reining in monopolies. Television is not covered by the agreement, but in many parts of the world subscription television services have been linked with telephone companies that have needed to undergo myriad changes to prepare for the new competitive environment. These moves were the culmination of more than a decade of telecommunications regulatory changes that sought to demonopolize national industries and spark competition. Despite these advances, however, in many world markets, notably for cable services, de facto monopolies persist and consumers have few alternatives to their regional operator.

From the mid-1990s on, the price of cable TV rose twice as much as the Consumer Price Index, to an average cost of US$50 per month per subscriber in 2004, according to *Forbes.* Considering this, it was no surprise that the top two satellite companies in the country lured nearly 2 million subscribers away from cable in 2003. Even HBO lost subscribers in 2003. According to *Broadcasting & Cable,* networks needed to replace up to 60 percent of their subscribers to stay even.

CURRENT CONDITIONS

By 2004, 54 percent of the money being spent on filmed entertainment worldwide was being spent via pay-TV service rather than through video purchases or in cinemas, which had 33 percent and 13 percent, respectively. According to *Screen Digest*, the amount being spent on pay-TV for this purpose has increased by 4 percent since 1996. Both video and cinema had shown declines during this period.

On a global basis, the market for pay-TV services continues to expand, with markets continuing to grow in countries such as India and China as technology becomes more widely available and governments deregulate the industry. At a corporate level, mergers continue to dominate, and these large companies are positioned to provide the necessary equity for expansion in many underserved areas. However, the face of competition is changing as non-traditional players, such as telecommunication companies, enter the market offering bundled packages of video-on-demand, Internet service and telephone services to their customers.

In the United States, after the AT&T coup by Comcast, coupled with the rising star of satellite services, other cable providers began to decline, some up to 28 percent. Still, the cable market was stable, at least for outside advertisers. Upfront advertising revenues hit US$6 billion in 2004, an increase of about 16 percent. Digital cable providers raked in between US$50 billion and US$100 billion of the upfront total.

Many analysts expected that interactive digital capabilities such as video-on-demand (VOD) would play a greater role in future industry growth. Worldwide revenue for VOD alone was valued at US$4.4 billion in 2004, with projections for growth to US$11.5 billion by 2010. History has shown that people are willing to pay for individual preferences and premium services when such items meet an individual need or desire, and one major challenge beyond the mid-2000s was to fill a multitude of niches all at once.

Lessons from digital terrestrial television (DTT) have proved that many consumers are looking for a second delivery channel into the home for TV in order to support multiple TV sets. The current limited ability of WiFi networks to carry video around the home will also act as a key driver for IPTV to act as a complementary platform, not a substitute platform, in a significant number of cases—at least in the short term. DTT will play a competing and complementary role. DTT is a true broadcast technology and is much quicker, simpler and cheaper to roll out than TV over broadband. In some cases, therefore, DTT will impact negatively on IPTV growth. DTT platforms are offering a lot of free-to-air content, with just a one-time charge for the set-top box. This means some consumers will allocate spend on DTT in preference to IPTV (or other pay TV platforms) when they first go digital. However, in the longer term, DTT will help to stimulate overall uptake of digital TV; and where DTT providers start to add paid-for elements, IPTV will then be able to compete

on a more even footing. Additionally, in some cases DTT will provide a valuable platform for telcos that are launching hybrid DTT/VoD strategies.

IPTV growth will be modest over the forecast period. IPTV penetration of the broadband customer base will vary between markets, but within our forecast five-year growth period (up to the end of 2009) we are cautious in our overall view of IPTV and VoD growth. Lessons from operators who have had services running for over a year prove there are still a number of technical, competitive and cultural (brand awareness) barriers to overcome. VoD will be a key strategy in some markets. In some markets incumbents and competing telcos will choose to include a strong focus on VoD in their strategies.

Deloitte Touche Tohmatsu was predicting that digital terrestrial television (DTTV)—whereby broadcast frequencies are used by telecommunications companies to get more bandwith and deliver increased entertainment services—would begin to take market from satellite and particularly cable television suppliers. The technology is seen as an inexpensive method by which consumers could obtain more channels.

By June 2007, AT&T was showing that it might have a dramatic impact on the TV-service battle. Kathryn Balint reported that the company's U-verse service was part of US$6.5 billion "effort to create a hybrid network of fast fiber-optic cable and conventional copper wires to deliver TV programming to homes." An estimated 400,000 U.S. households bought their TV service from telephone companies. AT&T announced plans to offer its U-verse service to 18 million California homes plus 12 other states by the end of 2007. The service claimed to provide quality service at cheaper rates than cable or satellite TV.

Balint also reported that AT&T and Verizon were the first major U.S. telephone companies to use Internet protocol TV technology capable of transmitting only the channel selected by the customer. The same copper wires utilized to transmit telephone calls were used to transmit video to customers' homes.

In a May 2010 press release, the American Consumer Satisfaction Index states that customer satisfaction with cable and satellite TV rose to its highest level in 10 years, up 5 percent to 66, with nearly all companies registering improvements. ACSI measures the relatively newer fiber-optic providers for the first time, and both Verizon's FiOS and AT&T's U-verse led the way with scores of 73 and 72, respectively. Satellite TV still led over traditional cable, with DISH Network soaring 11 percent to 71 to overtake rival DIRECTV for the first time since 2005. DIRECTV fell 4 percent to 68 as aggressive pricing promotions by DISH—coupled with a price increase by DIRECTV—had the two satellite TV providers moving in opposite directions.

All four of the largest cable providers showed some improvement. Charter Communications made the biggest leap, gaining 18 percent to 60. Although this was not enough to pull Charter out of last place, the company was statistically tied with Comcast and Time Warner Cable, both up 3 percent to 61. Cox Communications gained 2 percent to 67 to lead all traditional cable companies for a seventh straight year.

In November 2010, Motorola released the results of a new global survey today as part of the company's ongoing Media Engagement Barometer (MEB). One of the high-level findings was that consumers across the world prefer paid subscription TV services to free, over-the-air content. According to the press release, "while free-to-air services are available to 67 percent of global viewers, compared to 57 percent for paid-for services, the most preferred TV services are subscription only." In other words, content is king.

The Motorola survey found that 86 percent of Americans pay for TV services. (The NPD Group pegged the number at 81 percent 2008.) Even with regular industry discussion on how TV is evolving, the subscription service model is still holding strong.

According to the survey, respondents in the US are watching the most video content:

- Americans are watching an average of 21 hours of video content a week, the most globally

- 86 percent of Americans pay for TV services

- Only 6 percent of US respondents are using Video/TV services on the internet

- 39 percent watch mostly scheduled/live TV

US viewers are adopting internet enabled devices quicker than 3D TV.

- 59 percent of US respondents own an HDTV; 17 percent plan to buy one in the next 18 months

- 20 percent own an Internet enabled TV set; 15 percent plan to buy one in the next 18 months

- 25 percent currently own a smartphone; 18 percent plan to own one in the next 18 months

- Only 4 percent of US respondents own a 3D TV; only 11 percent plan to get this technology in the next 18 months

Americans are looking to TV providers to deliver Social TV experience.

- 32 percent of Americans have used social networks, chat or email to have a conversation about a TV show they are watching

- 46 percent of Americans use these channels to frequently converse while watching video content

- 13 percent of Americans would pay extra for a Video/TV service that integrates internet capabilities (e.g. chat on screen with social network contacts)

- 15 percent of Americans would pay extra for a Video/TV service that integrates with their laptop or tablet

- 37 percent of Americans would change TV provider to one that offered access to social networks, chat, and email while watching live TV of video

INDUSTRY LEADERS

Comcast Cable Communications Inc. Comcast is the number one cable company in the United States. Comcast was number three until its acquisition of AT&T Cable in 2002 for US$72 billion. By 2005, Comcast had 24 million cable customers and more than 12 subscribers to its digital cable services. Revenues for 2005 were reported to be approximately US$21 billion. There were about 62,000 employees in 2005.

In 2004, the company began offering video-on-demand service, allowing customers to select from more than 3,000 programs. The company continues to expand its holdings, owning about 17 percent of Time Warner Cable, with which it joined forces with in January 2005 in order to purchase the cable assets of the U.S.'s fifth largest cable provider, Adelphia Communications. Comcast also has significant holdings in networks (including E! Entertainment Television, Style Network, G4, The Golf Channel, and Versus), distribution (ThePlatform), and related businesses.

On December 1, 2009, CNBC reported that a tentative agreement had been reached between Comcast and GE. The deal was formally announced on December 3, 2009. Under the agreement, NBC Universal would be 51 percent owned by Comcast and 49 percent by GE. Comcast is to pay US$6.5 billion cash to GE. Comcast will also contribute US$7.5 billion in programming including regional sports networks and cable channels such as Golf Channel and E! Entertainment Television. GE plans to use some of the funds, US$5.8 billion, to buy out Vivendi's 20 percent minority stake in NBC Universal. After the transaction completes, Comcast will reserve the right to buy out GE's share at certain times. GE will also reserve the right to force the sale of their stake within the first seven years. As of August 2010, Comcast's proposed acquisition of a majority stake in NBC Universal is pending government approval.

Xfinity is the name for the re-branded triple play services in Comcast's largest markets, which include the company's digital cable, cable Internet access, and cable telephone services. Smaller markets currently will retain the Comcast branding for all services until they have been upgraded to full digital services. According to Comcast, the name Xfinity stands for infinite content choices and cross-platform features. A major push involving the new Xfinity branding took place during the 2010 Winter Olympic Games coverage on NBC, which was in the early stages of a merger with Comcast. The company proposed adding more HD channels, foreign language programming, video on demand content (especially with the end of analog cable by 2012), and more programming on its Fancast.com video portal. Additionally, the company is likely to push faster Internet bandwidth along with DOCSIS 3.0 cable modem service where available under the new branding.

In 2002, AT&T's cable and broadband digital services were inextricably linked. The company intended to bring broadband to all areas where it had cable during the 2000s. However, in the spring of 2002 AT&T and Comcast were in negotiations for AT&T to sell its cable interests to Comcast, as AT&T president David Dorman dismissed cable as unprofitable to the company's core business. The move was hailed by shareholders, concerned about cash-rich AT&T's plunge in stock values in 2001 and early 2002, who saw the cable sale as a way to unload debt.

The story of AT&T's cable expansion began in 1998 with one of the most important mergers in business history. Despite its stature as the largest U.S. cable company in terms of subscribers, in 1998 Tele-Communications Inc. (TCI) faced debt and costly infrastructure expenses that challenged its profitability. However, significant relief came from AT&T's US$48.3 billion acquisition of TCI. The all-stock purchase integrated TCI into a new AT&T unit named AT&T Consumer Services. Some of TCI's side ventures and affiliates were not folded into AT&T. TCI appealed to AT&T because it had networking in place to potentially access 33 million U.S. households—about a third of all households—compared to AT&T's existing long-distance subscriber base of 66 million.

Still then nominally the United States' largest cable operator with 14.1 million subscribers under its management in 1998, TCI had embarked on a program of fiscal tightening and market focusing that was expected to leave it a close second to Time Warner's combined cable holdings. These moves were prompted in large part by a bitter fiscal 1996 that saw burgeoning debt coinciding with declining subscriber counts and revenues. TCI hoped to improve efficiency and make its vast holdings more manageable through selective downsizing. In 1997 it concluded a couple of agreements with Time Warner that improved each company's customer clustering and placed more subscribers under Time Warner's management.

Much like the history of AT&T itself, the history of AT&T's U-verse starts with an acquisition. It all began when SBC Communications Inc. announced it would buy AT&T in January 2005, and the acquisition was finalized in June of that year. Even though SBC was the purchaser, the company

decided to brand themselves with the much more universally known AT&T. It was a changing of the guard at AT&T, not just in personnel and corporate structure. "The New AT&T" was launched in June 2007, with CEO and chairman Randall Stephenson announcing that wireless services would be the focal point of what was in essence a re-launch. U-verse was also part of this announcement. This was attempt to update the company, rolling out more Internet-based services and going away from the traditional land-line telephone service, which began drastically declining in numbers.

AT&T U-verse is a VDSL (or very-high-vibrate digital subscriber line) service that brings telephone, Internet, and television services to its subscribers through a fiber-to-the-node communications network. AT&T has continued to improve upon U-verse, and has continued to add services—some for free to its customers—in the three years it has been in operation. AT&T U-verse is a VDSL service offered by AT&T in various parts of the United States. It provides broadband internet access, TV, and phone through a fiber-to-the-node communications network. As of December, 2009, U-verse Internet had 2 million customers (up 100 percent in last year). U-verse is available to 20 million units in 22 states.

A New York state judge's ruling that Comcast could move the NFL Network from basic digital cable platforms to more expensive digital sports tier was viewed by Allan Kreda as a possible signal of a new era for pay TV for sports. The ruling was being appealed by the league. It would make the NFL Network only available for Comcast customers willing to pay an extra US$15 per month to see eight games per year. If Comcast turned out to be victorious in this legal battle, rival cable operators such as Time Warner Cable were expected to seek the same rights.

Time Warner Cable Inc. Time Warner Cable (TWC) Inc., once the nation's largest cable company but now second following Comcast after Comcast acquired AT&T. TWC had approximately 14.6 million subscribers, including more than 7.3 million digital video customers in 2006. It had 2006 revenues of approximately US$11.8 billion. Owned 84 percent by the world's leading media company, Time Warner, with the remainder held by Comcast, this cable company manages an empire that includes a number of distinct corporate entities and joint ventures with other companies. TWC teamed up with Comcast in 2006 to buy Adelphia Communications. Time Warner also owns a number of high-profile cable networks carried by many pay-television services throughout the world, including Cinemax, CNN, and HBO, the United States' most popular premium channel.

Time Warner CEO Richard Parsons discussed the possibility of Time Warner diminishing its ownership in TWC as the cable company continued to buy up more systems. Time Warner had spun off 16 percent of its cable services division as part of its plan to create publicly equity that could be used to finance purchases.

DIRECTV Group. With approximately 15 million subscribers in the U.S. and about 4.1 million customers through its DIRECTV Latin America segment in 2006. It had US$14.7 billion in revenue in the Americas in 2006, DIRECTV was a leader among satellite services. Formerly Hughes Electronic, the company changed names in 2004 when it decided to concentrate its efforts on its direct-to-home satellite business. The company is also a leading satellite television provider in Latin America, where its 2004 subscriber based amounted to 1.6 million people. In 2002, the company completed its divestiture of its operations in Japan. In August 2004, DIRECTV also sold its 80.4 percent interest in the satellite operator PanAmSat, one of the world's largest private satellite systems, through which it sold satellite time to other services.

DIRECTV announced plans to add up to 1,000 Denver-area jobs at the company's operations hub in Centennial, Colorado. In a news release, the president of DIRECTV's Sales and Service John Suryani stated that the expanded center would be at the core of everything the company offers it 16 million subscribers nationwide as well as future customers.

The Disney Channel gave DIRECTV exclusive rights to broadcast the premiere HD version of High School Musical 2. DIRECTV announced it would air the movie in HD a few days after its standard-definition premiere set for August 17 on the Disney Channel.

DIRECTV also announced a series of agreements for HD channels set for fall 2007 roll out. They included deals to launch HD broadcasts feeds of the Discovery Channel, TLC, Animal Planet, and the Science Channel in September. Other September plans involved launching three new HD movie channels: Starz Edge, Starz Comedy, and Starz Kids & Family plus Starz's east- and west-coast HD feeds. DIRECTV's plans for the busy month of September also included launching a new 24-hour The History Channel HD network and A & E HD.

British Sky Broadcasting Group Plc. Launched in 1989, Sky Digital had reached one million homes in the United Kingdom by 1990. That year, the company merged with British Satellite Broadcasting to form British Sky Broadcasting. By 2006, the company was in more than 16 million homes with offerings of more than 400 channels, and had earnings of more than US$7.5 billion.

British Sky Broadcasting and Virgin were involved in a legal battle. In April 2007, Virgin launched the legal proceedings linked to the cost for access to some of British Sky Broadcasting's channels. British Sky Broadcasting's decision to pull access in March 2007 prevented Virgin viewers from seeing popular rated programs including "Lost" and "24." "Sky is dominant in the UK pay TV market and has engaged in a strategy to stifle competion by using its dominance against Virgin Media," Virgin claimed in a statement. British Sky Broadcasting, however, fared well in spite of the controversy. It added 51,000 customers, almost double the 27,400 forecast by City analysts, in the first quarter of 2007.

The News Corporation Ltd. Few companies are as intricately embroiled in the television industry as Rupert Murdoch's News Corporation of Australia, which has interests in numerous world subscription television services in addition to its vast international holdings of broadcast television, media production, and newspaper concerns. The company, which obtains an estimated 70 percent of its revenues from the United States, owned a 35 percent stake in British Sky Broadcasting Group PLC in 2004, the United Kingdom's largest pay-television service with 14.3 million subscribers. News Corporation also controls Australia's Foxtel cable service and Sky Latin America. Its subsidiary Fox Broadcasting owned 34 percent of DIRECTV in 2004. That year, the company earned approximately US$1.8 billion from its direct broadcast satellite television operations.

The firm was one of the leading backers of a Japan Sky Broadcasting Co. venture slated to come online in 1998, but in early 1998 the resources were merged instead with PerfecTV Corporation, Japan's top digital satellite company, to form Japan Digital Broadcasting Services Inc. With an 11.38 percent stake, News Corporation was one of the venture's five principal shareholders. PerfecTV had 570,000 subscribers entering the merger, and the enhanced offerings of the new service, called SkyPerfecTV, were expected to draw up to a million subscribers by the end of 1998. Also in Asia is News Corporation's Star TV, a free satellite-based service reaching more than 62 million Asian households largely through cable retransmissions. News Corporation planned to phase in subscription-based versions of Star TV in several national markets, including China, India, Indonesia, and Japan. Meanwhile, the company also held a majority interest in American Sky Broadcasting Co., a troubled U.S. start-up that sought to merge with an established satellite partner in 1997; after a fallout with EchoStar, Murdoch's company agreed to merge operations with Primestar in 1998, subject to approval by the U.S. Federal Communications Commission.

In December 2001 News Corp. announced an agreement to bring a cable television with Mandarin-language programming to south China. In 2001 News Corp. posted a loss of US$606 million for the second quarter, compared to a smaller US$23 million loss in 2000. The entire Murdoch empire struggled mightily in 2001, although its sheer size and its entrepreneurial business moves into China showed the company retained considerable vigor in spite of severe setbacks. By 2003, the company's revenues stood at US$20.1 billion.

Canal+ Group. In 2004, Canal+ Group remained one of Europe's largest pay-TV providers. It owns 49 percent (the maximum allowed by the French government), of France's Canal Plus, which was ranked as the world's largest PPV service, claiming 4.9 million subscribers scattered across Europe and parts of Africa. In addition, it owned 66 percent of CanalSatellite, a digital pay-TV service with 3 million subscribers in France as of January 2005. In turn, Canal+ Group is owned by media and telecommunications giant, Vivendi.

MAJOR COUNTRIES IN THE INDUSTRY

The technical quality of on-air TV advanced recently with the adoption of broadcast digital TV or DTV. By 2010 about half of the world's major countries had converted to digital broadcasting. The first country to make a complete switch to digital over-the-air (terrestrial) broadcasting was Luxembourg, in 2006. Shortly thereafter, the Netherlands made the switch. Finland, Andorra, Sweden and Switzerland followed in 2007.

In June 2009, all major broadcast stations in the United States switched to DTV. Some lower power TV stations were allowed to stay with the much older NTSC analog standard for a period of time. Some countries don't plan a complete analog-to-digital transition until around 2020.

Europe. In Western Europe, cable was still more prominent than satellite in all but four countries in 2004: Italy, Greece, Spain, and the United Kingdom. Approximately US$25 billion was spent on pay television services, with *Screen Digest* predicting the amount would reach almost US$32 billion by 2006, when pay TV market penetration was expected to reach 50 percent. *International Marketing Reports* was predicting that the fastest growing sectors in European pay TV would be in broadband and video-on-demand (VOD). In terms of market size, the United Kingdom was expected to remain the largest, with the United Kingdom, France, Spain, and Scandanavia being the strongest markets by 2008.

United Kingdom. Although in 2003, cable and satellite television serviced reached a combined 9.4 million U.K. homes, satellite service dominated the market, accounting for 76 percent of these homes. The market remained highly concentrated, with only four companies accounting for 90 percent of marketshare and with the British Sky Broadcasting Group PLC (BSkyB) servicing 58 percent according to Euromonitor statistics. Its 7 million subscriptions include pay-per-view and monthly customers. BSkyB and other pay-television services compete with the thoroughly entrenched and popular British Broadcasting Corporation (BBC) for market share, although they do carry BBC programming. The BBC's mostly terrestrial broadcasts are supported by a strong transmission infrastructure that ensures high-quality television reception in the majority of the country, reducing technical performance as a selling point for subscription services in the United Kingdom. However, by 2003 28.7 percent of British homes had a satellite dish and 8.7 percent were cable subscribers. Euromonitor was forecasting the market to grow by 11.4 percent by 2008, with the satellite sector continuing to dominate the pay-TV market.

Germany. Of Germany's 35 million households, 31.9 million had cable or satellite television service. Euromonitor expected this number to grow by 11.2 percent by 2008, with cable leading with a 60.3 percent market share.

In the 1990s, Deutsche Telekom's far-reaching cable empire dominated the German pay-television market, the largest in Europe. At one time, the company had 17 million subscribers, controlling approximately 90 percent of Germany's pay-television market. The DT monopoly controlled all of the nation's cable television market officially until 1997. In 1999, the subsidiary Kabel Deutschland GmbH was formed to managed DT's cable operations separately, while the market opened up. In 2003, the company was purchased by a consortium of financial investors, including Goldman Sachs. By the end of 2004, Kabel Deutschland had 9.7 million subscribers.

France. Like its German neighbor, the pay-TV industry in France continued to be dominated by cable services in 2003, but the gap was rapidly closing with satellite expected to overtake cable by 2008. In 2003, 52 percent of the 7.3 million houses with pay-TV service had cable. Euromonitor was predicting that satellite would surpass cable reaching a 55 percent market share by 2008. The total number of households with pay-TV service was expected to increase to 9.9 million.

Like other European countries, the market in France remained quite concentrated, with four companies (TF1, Canal+, France Télécom and Suez) controlling 73 percent of the market. Canal+ Group remained the leading provider of both services, covering 30 percent of the households.

Asia. Though less developed than Europe and North America, Asia is home to the world's largest potential regional market for pay-television services. Until the 1997 financial crisis in Asia, pay-television companies had been furiously expanding services in burgeoning Asian economies such as Indonesia, Malaysia, and Thailand, because of their growth potential. Given that Southeast Asia's short-term purchasing power diminished through currency devaluations, however, a number of firms from inside and outside the region began reevaluating their Asian expansion strategies. But by 2004, changes in the competitive environment and regulatory arenas were resulting in extensive improvements in the pay-TV industry in the region. The market was valued at US$18.6 billion that year. The number of multi-channel subscribers had reached more than 192 million, representing a market penetration of 34 percent.

Japan. The regional leader in 2004 in terms of industry-related revenue, Japan's cable and satellite television market was valued at US$5.9 billion by year end. The country expanded the availability of digital cable, but penetration was growing slowly, reaching only 320,000 by 2004. The top two leading pay-TV providers were J-COM Broadband (with 2004 revenues of US$1.49 billion) and Sky Perfect Communications (US$720 million).

China. With its large population base and increasing amounts of disposable income, China had emerged as a significant player in the world's cable and satellite television industry by 2004. Of Asia's 192 million multi-channel subscribers, 105 million were located in China, generating industry-wide revenue of US$3.5 billion.

The pace of growth in terms of digital cable subscriptions slowed due to government regulations, but by 2004 China still remained a leading regional market for this technology. However, during that year, the Chinese government ended the monopoly held by China Digital TV Media, issuing licenses to four other companies. New regulations also allow foreign firms to own up to 49 percent of joint ventures producing programming.

By 2005, the cable industry in China remained highly fragmented, with most provinces and cities operating their own cable system. However, with increased competition and more openness to foreign investment, consolidation of the industry was expected.

Latin America and the Caribbean. In Latin America, as in many places in the world, the pay-television landscape varies widely by locality. Argentina has one of South America's largest market penetration rates, with 47 percent of television households receiving pay services (5 million subscribers), but Brazil is considered a much larger growth market because its infrastructure is comparatively underdeveloped and it has a much larger population—more than four times that of Argentina. Only 5 percent of Brazilian households with televisions are equipped to receive cable (1.5 million subscribers), and television-per-household penetration is relatively low. In response, the Brazilian government has been selling cable and wireless franchises to a number of eager domestic and foreign contenders. Brazil's pay-television market is approaching 12 million subscribers in 2002. By 2005, DIRECTV offered more channels and covered more areas than any other direct-to-home service in the region.

According to Colin Bennett, Canitec, Mexico's cable industry association, stated that it expected the country's cable firms to have approximately 150,000 voice subscribers by the end of 2007. In order for cable firms to offer related services they were required to secure interconnection agreements with telecos.

United States. By January 2005, there were almost 110 million television households in the United States, and cable was active in more than 73 million of them. According to Kagan Research, the industry had annual revenue of US$57.6 billion in 2004 provided by 8,875 cable systems and an estimated 390 national cable networks. But competition for viewers continued to be hot; the National Cable & Telecommunications Association (NCTA) was reporting that one out of four subscribers obtained multi-channel programming from a company other than their local cable company. Digital Broadcast Satellite (DBS) was providing the heaviest competition to cable, offering in excess of 150 channels to its customers. The number of DBS subscribers had increased more than 14 percent in the year to reach almost 24 million subscribers by September 2004. The United States's largest satellite provider, DIRECTV, was only second in terms of the number of pay-TV customers to Comcast, the United States's largest cable company. However, Euromonitor was predicting that by 2008, cable would still dominate the pay-TV sector, while industry-wide revenues were forecast to reach US$69.8 billion.

The U.S. industry remains concentrated, with the top five cable and satellite companies (Comcast, Cox Communications, Time Warner, Charter Communications and Adelphia) controlling more than 71 percent of the market in 2003. However, the number of industry leaders is due to get smaller. In 2002, Adelphia declared bankruptcy and it 2004 the company's founder, John Rigas and his son, former company CFO Timothy Rigas, were found guilty of fraud. In April 2005, Adelphia agreed to sell its U.S. assets to Time Warner and Comcast.

In its efforts to remain competitive, particularly against satellite providers, the cable industry had spent almost US$95 billion between 1996 and 2005 in order to upgrade its service to fiber optic technology. This technology is necessary for the provision of digital cable and video-on-demand services as well as the Internet and telephone services offered by most cable companies in the United States.

Stephen H. Wildstrom discussed implications of implementation of new Federal Communications Commission (FCC) rules on July 1, 2007. They required cable companies to split the functions of cable boxes. The first function of authentication, coordinated via a Cablecard, involved telling cable companies who subscribers are and what cable channels they could receive. The second function of cable tuning focused on decoding signals. This function would be opened up to many companies who make set-up boxes or might have that function build into equipment. Equipment such as TV sets, game consoles, and computers already existed and devices with capabilities were anticipated. Related concerns included cost and complexity plus limitations of the program options current Cablecards provided.

The FCC announced plans to cut off analog TV signals in February 2009. Consequently, broadcasters will be prohibited from sending programming via an analog signal. Viewers without digital TV, digital cable or a satellite package will be prevented from watching basic network programming with basic antennas. This restricts access to ABC, CBS, NBC, and Fox with "rabbit ears" antennas. Restrictions also include not being able to view some cable channels as CNN unless a digital set-top box is used. In addition to this information and related observations, Kimberly S. Johnson reported that Comcast had already started pushing customers toward subscribing to more expensive packages for cable services. Comcast removed MSNBC, CSPAN2, and the TV Guide Channel in some markets resulting in customers calling in to inquire about what happened and order upgrades.

Legislation was under consideration that would protect consumers and open up the market. It eliminated the need for companies seeking to provide TV service to negotiate town-by-town franchise agreements. It also included a provision for companies to provide "four-hour appointment window" and give customers US$25 credit if it was missed.

BIBLIOGRAPHY

"2004 Year-End Industry Overview." National Cable & Telecommunications Association, 2005. Available from http://www.ncta.com.

"AT&T President David Dorman: What's Next for What's Left of AT&T?" *Newhouse News Service,* 12 February 2002.

Atkinson, Claire. "Upfront Wraps." *Advertising Age,* 28 June 2004.

Balint, Kathryn. "AT&T Gets Bundled Up for TV-Service Battle." 4 June 2007. Available from http://signonsandiego.printthis.clickability.com

Brister, Kathy. "Cable Fees Increase on Average 7.5 Percent Nationally." *Atlanta Journal and Constitution,* 5 April 2002.

Brown, David. "European Pay-TV Forecasts: Pay-TV data forecasts to 2008." International Marketing Reports Ltd., June 2003. Available from http://www.imr-info.com.

Burgi, Michael. "Fighting to Be Heard." *Brandweek,* 3 May 2004.

"Cable and Satellite TV Services in France, Germany, UK, US." *Euromonitor,* October 2004. Available from http://www.euromonitor.com.

Bennett, Colin. "Canitec: Cable Firms Set for 150,000 Voice Users by Year-End - Mexico." 5 June 2007. Available from http:www.bnamericas.com.

Cassidy, Padraic. "EchoStar Wagers Startups to Close DIRECTV Deal." *Daily Deal,* 4 April 2002.

"Consumer Protections Are Cable Bill Victory." 7 June 2007. Available from http://www.suntimes.com.

"DIRECTV Continues Rollout of HD Channels." 23 May 2007. Available from http://losangeles.bizjournals.com.

"DIRECTV to Add 1,000 Jobs in Colorado." 7 June 2007. Available from http://news.moneycentral.msn.com.

Draper, Deborah J., ed. *Business Rankings Annual.* Detroit: Thomson Gale, 2004.

EchoStar's Planned $26.8 Billion Merger with DIRECTV." *Business Week Online,* 28 December 2001. Available from http://www.businessweek.com/bwdaily/dnflash/dec2001/nf20011228_7933.htm

Emling, Shelley. "Vivendi Shakes Up Media Industry: French Company Ready to Battle AOL Time Warner." *Atlanta Journal and Constitution,* 20 January 2002.

Fagan, Mary. "C&W Halves Capital Outlay." *Sunday Telegraph* (London), 24 February 2002.

Fleischmann, Mark. "Consumers to Cable: You Stink." 4 June 2007. Available from http://www.hometheatermag.com.

"France's Biggest Cable TV Groups Up for Sale." *Financial Times* (London), 3 April 2002.

Fritz, Ben. "Report: VOD Demand Is Skyrocketing." *Daily Variety,* 8 June 2004.

Gray, Campbell. "Late Starter? Japan's Pay TV Market." *Media Week,* 1 February 2002.

Greek, Dinah. "DTI May Cap Sky's Horizon." *Computer Active,* 17 May 2007.

Higgins, John M. "Premium Networks Take a Hit." *Broadcasting & Cable,* 9 February 2004.

"Hoover's Company Capsules." *Hoover's Online,* 2007. Available from http://www.hoovers.com.

Johnson, Kimberly S. "Comcast Tuning in to Future." 5 June 2007. Available from http://www.denverpost.com.

Keefe, Bob. "Cable Giants Look Beyond TV." 13 May 2007. Available from http://statesman.printthis.clickability.com.

Kreda, Allan. "Will NFL Fans Get Sacked by Cable Companies?" 16 May 2007. Available from http:/www.bloggingstocks.com.

Lazich, Robert S., ed. *Market Share Reporter.* Detroit: Thomson Gale, 2004.

Lewis, Katherine Reynolds. "Comast Vows More Fast Web, Digital Video with AT&T Cable Unit." *Bloomberg News,* 29 March 2001.

Luehrs, Bill. "A 'One Size Does Not Fit All' Future." *CED,* 15 December 2003.

Make, Jonathan. "Adelphia Hires Banks to Help Sell Cable-Television Assets." *Bloomberg News,* 5 April 2002.

———. "Hughes' DirectTV to Add More Subscribers Than Forecast." *Bloomberg News,* 21 March 2002.

Mathieson, Clive. "Deutsche Telekom Faces Credit Setback." *Times (London),* 20 March 2002.

Mouawad, Jad. "TV Losses Mount." *Television Digest,* 18 February 2002.

"News Corp.'s Star TV Gets Ready to Shine in China." *Media Week,* 29 March 2002.

Pomerantz, Dorothy. "The Other Cable Guys." *Forbes,* 7 June 2004.

Screen Digest, 2005. Available from http://www.screendigest.com.

Szalai, Georg. "Cable Market Picture Darkens: Experts Don't See Recovery on Horizon for Beleaguered Sector." *Hollywood Reporter,* 4 April 2002.

"Tech Innovations, Competition to Drive Pay TV in Asia: MPA." IndianTelevision.com, 20 January 2005. Available from http://www.indiatelevision.com.

"Time Warner Sees Possible Separation of Cable." *Reuters,* 7 June 2007.

Tomesco, Frederic. "Quebecor Cable Unit Losing Subscribers at Faster Pace." *Bloomberg News,* 4 April 2002.

Waters, Richard. "A Media Giant (AOL Time Warner) Finds the Future Less Rosy." *Financial Times* (London), 28 March 2002.

"The Week: City News — Subscriber Boost for BSkyB." Campaign, 11 May 2007.

Wildstrom, Stephen H. "Unchained from the Cable Box." 06 June 2007. Available from http://www.businessweek.com.

GREETING CARDS

NAICS CODE(S)

511191. The greeting card industry designs and publishes greeting cards for all occasions. In addition to paper cards, the industry has adapted to Internet demand and makes available many lines of cards intended for electronic transmission. These cards are published for mass sale and exclude hand-painted cards and other one-of-a-kind cards made by crafts people for individual sale.

INDUSTRY SNAPSHOT

Throughout the centuries, people have exchanged messages of goodwill, good wishes, condolence, and love. It was only during the twentieth century, however, that these messages were formalized into "greeting cards," and only in the very recent past that electronic cards became an immensely popular way to communicate. In 2006 the Greeting Card Association (GCA) reported that Americans purchase approximately 7 billion cards annually, generating almost US$7.5 billion in sales. The U.S. Postal Service delivers millions of these communications daily. Christmas is the number one holiday and accounts for about 60 percent of sales of holiday cards. Valentine's Day, which inspired the sale of about 180 million greeting cards in 2006, is second. After that comes sales for Mother's Day, Easter, and Father's Day. Birthday cards account for 60 percent of everyday cards, followed by anniversary, get well, friendship, and sympathy.

The audience for cards is quite clear. Females purchase 80 percent of all cards in general and 85 percent of all Valentines. The industry promotes and endorses special and personal occasions that keep the cards flowing, including "days" for secretaries, bosses, and grandparents. In fact, these personal occasion and "just because" cards hold a majority of the market, even ahead of Christmas. Nearly 87 percent of all card sales fall under the categories of birthday (60 percent of category sales), anniversary, get well, friendship/encouragement, and sympathy. One of the most frequent senders of cards is the U.S. White House, which sends birthday cards from the current president to citizens older than age 80, to newlyweds, and others for approved special occasions.

In short, what was a US$2.9 billion dollar industry in 1988 in the United States grew into an industry with sales of US$5.5 billion in 1997. This steady, though measured, growth came to a halt at the turn of the century, however. Falling revenues in 2000, 2001, and 2002 for the major players in the card industry, such as Hallmark Inc. and American Greetings, demonstrated that buyers tend to

purchase more cards in times of prosperity and economic good news. The volatile dot-com e-card business collapse in 2000 also taught the industry that major losses could be incurred in spite of frequent and repeated customer visits at the "free" card sites. By October of 2001, industry analysts stressed that the September 11, 2001, terrorist acts had thrown the greeting card market into further freefall, and although the industry tried to fight back with new lines of patriotic cards, industry-wide losses were expected through 2003. Although unit sales have picked up slightly since then, revenues have remained flat.

According to U.S. government figures, about US$117.8 million worth of U.S. cards were exported in 2004, primarily to Canada, Mexico, Australia, the United Kingdom, and Germany. This was substantially lower than the US$137.2 million exported in 2003 and far below a high of US$152.9 million in 1997. Though the value of U.S. greeting card exports to Canada and Mexico declined from 2003 to 2004, these countries remained the primary destinations for U.S. cards, importing US$90.8 million and US$15.9 million, respectively, in 2004. By contrast, sales to Australia increased in value from only US$1.1 million in 2003 to US$2.0 million in 2004.

Card prices range from US$0.50 to US$10. The impact of deep discounting stores helped cut the average price per card to just under US$1 by 2003. In a typical year, a person is likely to receive 20 cards, 8 of them birthday cards. U.S. households purchase about 35 cards annually, and about 90 percent of all households send at least one card annually. The GCA publisher member companies account for 90 percent of the industry market share, including independent greeting card publishers, although the top two industry giants, Hallmark and American Greetings, dominate with market shares of 50 percent and 35 percent, respectively.

Since 1988, the GCA has sponsored the LOUIE awards. The international competition with 50 plus categories was held annually for publishers of greeting cards. The six primary judging criteria include "Imagination, Impact, Artistry, Harmony, Sendability and Value."

ORGANIZATION AND STRUCTURE

Not that many years ago, one out of every two greeting cards was sold in card shops. In the 1990s that ratio changed to one in three. The change was caused by the growing number of greeting cards sold through mass retailers. Hallmark Cards Inc. was affected most by this shift, and was forced to close some of its card shops and shift its attention to distribution through third-party retail outlets. American Greetings Corporation and Gibson Greetings Inc. were less affected by this shift as they had traditionally turned to retailers for the distribution of their products. In fact, according to an August 1992 article in *Industry Week,* American

Greetings employed the only in-house, full-time sales promotion department in the industry geared to the development of chain-specific promotions and retail traffic.

Industry analysts point to what they call Hallmark's over-reliance on its own retail stores for distribution as one reason the company lost market share in the early 1990s. Representing about 42 percent of the market in 1994, Hallmark had claimed 45 percent only five years earlier.

As the marketplace became more diverse, vendors continued to seek new ways of meeting the needs of their customers and increasing sales. Alternative or non-occasion cards were the fastest-growing segment in the greeting card industry. Other significant areas of growth were the senior and Hispanic markets. Environmentalism was another topical issue, the importance of which had not escaped the greeting card industry.

Between 1989 and 1995, employment in the greeting card industry stabilized between 21,000 and 23,000 employees. The industry tends to employ people with creative arts backgrounds, from graphic designers and writers to photographers and printers. Also, the work of many notable writers throughout the years—including Ogden Nash, Charles Dickens, Walt Whitman, Emily Dickinson, Mark Twain, Elizabeth Barrett Browning, and Norman Vincent Peale—has been used in greeting cards. Helen Steiner Rice, who wrote verses for Gibson Greetings (now part of American Greetings), was "discovered" in the 1960s when one of her poems, "The Priceless Gift of Christmas," was read on the Lawrence Welk Show. Greeting cards with her verses were soon in great demand. In 2002, Hallmark started a line of cards under the imprint of famed author and poet Maya Angelou known as the Maya Angelou Life Mosaic line. The majority of cards, though, are produced entirely (written, designed and printed) by employees of the card companies.

According to *VFW Magazine,* Hallmark has successfully reintroduced its Veterans Day card line originally tested in 1985 and 1999. Popularity is credited to an outpouring of patriotism since the September 11, 2001, terrorist attacks. There were 24 cards in this line available during 2003, including specific cards for Air Force, Army, Coast Guard, Marine Corps, and Navy veterans. Patriotic card lines available throughout the year include congratulations on joining the armed forces, sympathy, and appreciation cards.

BACKGROUND AND DEVELOPMENT

While people have traditionally communicated with each other through permanent or written form, greeting cards as a means of communicating were a relatively new phenomenon, having appeared about a century and a half ago. Historians credit the development of the first Christmas card to Englishman Sir Henry Cole, in 1846. In *The Romance of Greeting Cards,* Ernest Dudley Chase wrote that Cole suggested to Joseph Calcutt Horsley, a Royal Academy artist, that he create a custom Christmas greeting for friends to exchange. Horsley designed such a piece bearing the wish, "A Merry Christmas and a Happy New Year to You," along with a space for the sender to sign. One thousand copies of the card were lithographed, printed, and colored by hand. In the United States, Louis Prang, an exile from the German revolution of 1848, settled in Boston where he started a small lithographic business. In 1866, he perfected a process of multicolor printing and called his printed pieces "Chromos." The expense of this printing process (sometimes involving up to 20 colors) meant that the prices of U.S. cards were higher than those produced overseas. Prang began producing Christmas cards in 1874, first placing the cards on the English market and later selling them in the United States. However, lower-priced German imports eventually hurt his business and by 1890, he had given it up. While foreign distributors (most notably German) were early players in the greeting card industry, by the early 1900s, U.S. producers were poised for market dominance.

The impetus for the development of greeting cards seemed to be the advent of the postage system and the "penny postcard." These early greetings were the forerunner of today's greeting cards and, in fact, Joyce Clyde Hall, the founder of Hallmark, began his career by selling these postcards out of shoe boxes from his room at the YMCA.

By the early 1910s, these postcards proliferated. In the United States, Detroit Publishing offered more than 60,000 different cards. In England, the majority were produced by Raphael Tuck and Sons. However, with the onset of World War I, postcard imports from Europe ceased, and the United States soon became the leader in this industry—a position it still held almost a century later in the 1990s.

Early cards focused primarily on Christmas and Valentine's Day. However, the offerings expanded as new holidays were introduced. In 1919, Joyce Clyde Hall recognized the need for cards to commemorate more than holidays and introduced "friendship cards."

In 1921 Hall found himself faced with a legal challenge. Hall had been provided with a poem was used in a Christmas card. Later, the original author asserted that Hall had no right to use the poem. To settle the matter, Hall offered the writer US$500 in cash for the verse. The poem, "A Friend's Greeting," was written by Edgar A. Guest (1881–1959) and turned out to be a best-seller for many years.

By 1939 greeting cards were an US$80 million industry, and by the 1950s the greeting card industry was producing about 5 billion cards annually. The industry grew to US$4 billion in the 1990s. Until 2001, conventional industry belief said that even slow economic times had little impact on the performance of this industry. However, falling sales in the final quarter of 2001 for Hallmark and other brands caused a reevaluation of this truism.

Contributing to the success of the greeting card industry was the continued success of non-occasion cards, with messages such as "Sorry you're feeling blue," or "I shouldn't have said what I said." The baby boom generation was credited with the strong sales of these items. Sales of greeting cards in the late 1980s and early 1990s indicated a return to more traditional values according to many greeting card vendors. However, as sales of newspapers plunged in the late 1990s and early years of the first decade of the 2000s, and educators and analysts alike wrung hands over the growing segment of young adult non-readers, the greeting card industry found itself supplementing its traditional cards with warm and fuzzy verses with snappy sight gags and one-line quips, many of them bawdy or even insulting to the reader.

Outside the United States, the greeting card industry has grown more rapidly. Most notable among other countries, India has a burgeoning card market. *The Hindu* reported there have been big changes in the India greeting card market since Archies, now operating online like its Western counterparts, came on the scene in 1980. The late 1980s and early 1990s represented a boom time, prompting sales to grow. The ITC Group entered this market with its Expressions brand featuring 784 new designs for Christmas and the New Year available through approximately 12,000 retail outlets in 700 cities. Christmas through New Year is viewed as the most important card season, with nearly 20 percent of sales for the entire year occurring during the period. English language daily Indian newspaper *The Hindu* also revealed that the greeting card industry contributes significant sums to relief organizations such as Helpage India and UNICEF. Along with innovative ideas hot in metro areas, industry companies also believe in a "small town market" of customers seeking generic floral patterns and restricted humor.

E-cards were also on the rise. Compared to the way video sales complemented movie theaters, online cards were seen as a positive force in the industry and a driver for printed card sales. Ed Fruchtenbaum, president of American Greeting Cards, said in a 1997 interview with CNN that the electronic card segment would benefit the traditional sector because of the element of "reciprocity." When a card is received, the person is "likely to respond in e-mail fashion, or you could respond with the traditional greeting cards. So just the way I think videos have prompted people going to movie theaters, I think the whole electronic area will actually prompt more traditional greeting card sending."

The Greeting Card Association (GCA) offered words of caution for people who receive e-cards. Such individuals are subject to being part of e-card scams. By being eager to hear from unidentified family and friends, it is highly possible to literally click into trouble, including a virus or "malicious software" capable of causing severe damage to computers. The Association warned that senders are identified by name or e-mail address in legitimate card mailings. In addition, legitimate e-card companies provide a method for downloading cards directly from their sites.

Furthermore, the GCA reported on a sociological study by Dr. Barry Wellman, professor of sociology at the University of Toronto, and Dr. Keith Hampton, professor of Urban Studies and Planning at the Massachusetts Institute of Technology. The two-year study of a residential Toronto suburb wired with high speed Internet access resulted in the following findings: "The Internet naturally promotes communication, and of course communication is what relationships are about—and an increased number of relationships is good news for the traditional greeting card market."

Online card centers logged millions of hits per week in the late 1990s. According to Blue Mountain Arts General Manager Bob Gall, the company's site registered more than 10 million hits per day in 1996, and the company estimated 225 million hits per day in 1997. According to Derek Hoffman, who runs Electronic Postcards' site, electronic cards are inexpensive and practical. "Costs involved for postcard sites are in setting the site up, [and] in designing the cards." Not all online offerings were free. Sites such as Hallmark's Connections offer both free cards and cards for purchase by credit card. Americangreetings.com started off as a free site but then initiated a membership fee. In the early years of the first decade of the 2000s, it had more than 2 million subscribers and also generated sales from advertising. Users can send greeting cards via e-mail plus create and print hard copies.

Many free Internet card sites were paid for by revenues generated via advertising banners. While approximately one-third (37 percent) of U.S. households paid for Internet access at the end of 1998 (although that access was higher given school, library, and work access), this figure was estimated to be 58 percent by 2003, according to Inteco (Industrial Techno-Economic Services P. Ltd.), an international industrial consulting firm. Thus, far more people are likely to purchase a store-bought card than fire off an Internet greeting card. This trend was impacted by fears related to computer viruses. About 100,000 outlets offer consumers cards in the United States, according to the GCA. Nonetheless, Internet family news sites such as Myfamily.com send automatic reminders to friends and family each time a member's birthday rolls around, allowing other members to send a greeting in just a few clicks.

Industry analysts estimate that there were approximately 2,000 greeting card manufacturers in the industry in 2002, a far cry from the mere 100 in business in 1941 when the GCA was founded. Through the years, three major companies continued to dominate the market. Known as the "Big Three," Hallmark Cards, American Greetings, and Gibson Greetings (now owned by American Greetings) captured 85 percent of the U.S. market in the mid-1990s and had sizable presence in a number of other countries. Smaller companies had a difficult time competing against these giants and were frequently acquired or merged with another small company. In the 1990s, overall industry growth was a stable but uninspiring 2 percent annually. In subsequent years, however, the major card companies would have cheered for even slow growth.

Twenty-First Century Trends. Distribution patterns began to expand from card and gift shops to include drugstores, supermarkets, and discount stores. This change was attributed to increasing consumer demand for convenience and one-stop shopping. The demographics of the industry also began to change. While women had traditionally been the primary purchasers of greeting cards, representing about 90 percent of the market, the industry was attempting to reach beyond this market to attract younger customers and male customers. By 2005 mass retail stores were the fastest growing retail distribution channel for U.S. greeting cards, particularly for major companies. Smaller independent card makers, on the other hand, saw better sales growth through specialty stores or the Internet.

By 2001 many Internet card companies instituted an annual charge for unlimited cards, a decision which quickly resulted in a significant drop in access by those who wanted something for nothing. According to New York-based market research company Jupiter Media Metrix, visits to sites maintained by American Greetings (the most-accessed Internet provider of e-cards with an Internet presence at Americangreetings.com, Bluemountain.com and Egreetings.com) dropped 10 percent in December 2001 to 22.9 million (compared to 25.5 million in November 2001), ordinarily the biggest card-sending period. Furthermore, sites with free greeting cards and no subscription fees saw a good portion of that lost traffic come to them. For example, visits to Yahoo! Greetings and Hallmark.com increased 70 and 74 percent, respectively, from November to December 2001. Some of the smaller online greeting card companies, such as California-based Getacard.com, announced that they were available for sale in the early years of the first decade of the 2000s.

On the other hand, some small card manufacturers saw the opportunity to capture important niche markets. Several start-up companies aimed to attract customers from ethnic groups, women, religious denominations, or other markets not well-served by leading card makers. Lyrics2go, for instance, offered greetings influenced by hip-hop culture; it also incorporated new technology that made its cards play 10 seconds of music when they were opened. Founder Ron Williams explained in a *USA Today* article that he wanted to create cards that "speak the way that I speak." Still a tiny part of the greeting card market in 2005, small independent companies were selling primarily through the Internet.

While e-cards continued to affect greeting card sales, the growing popularity of text-messaging was seen as a further threat to revenues. As an industry executive told *Asia Times* about the market in India, "The main reason why mobile phone users are adapting to the messaging culture is cost. A simple paper greeting card is 10 times the price of an SMS [short messaging service] message. The cost and speed of the service are turning people away from the plain old greeting cards."

In an article about the 36th SIGGRAPH, an annual international conference on computer graphics and interactive techniques, Janet McCaughney shared e-cards statistics provided by the industry majors. Since launching its e-cards in 1996, American Greetings has grown its base to 3.9 million e-card subscribers. Subsequent to its e-card kick off in 1998, Hallmark estimates, "One e-card is sent for every 20 paper cards bought and distributed to family and friends."

The greeting card industry in the United Kingdom generated about 1 billion pounds (about US$1.7 billion) annually in the early years of the first decade of the 2000s. More than 2 billion cards are sent there each year, making per capita sales the highest in the world by volume. The average U.K. consumer spends 20 pounds (US$34.75) each year on greeting cards, and in turn receives 55 cards annually.

CURRENT CONDITIONS

Despite the competition from the Internet and other electronic media, the paper greeting card industry was alive and well in the latter mid-years of the first decade of the 2000s. According to the Bureau of Economic Analysis, Americans spent US$11.5 billion on cards in the first three quarters of 2006, a figure that does not include Christmas card sales for the year. In 2007 the GCA reported that 90 percent of American households purchase at least one card per year, and on average, each family purchases 30 cards a year.

The latter mid-years of the first decade of the 2000s saw the two major U.S. greeting card companies taking steps to remain competitive and innovative. In 2007 Hallmark added two new lines of cards. The "New Relationship" line, targeted to Valentine's Day buyers, addressed things other than romantic love and included more cards with a humorous message. The "Journey" line of cards addressed illnesses and situations that had been ignored by greeting card companies in the past, including cancer and eating disorders. Other unique situations for which one could offer thoughts, support, and condolences were quitting smoking, miscarriages, caring for aging parents, loved ones in the military, and traumatic loss. The 176-card line could be purchased initially only at Hallmark Gold Crown stores.

The most successful product launch made by Hallmark in 2006 was its line of sound cards. The line covers birthday, anniversary, friendship, and "thinking of you." Each card includes a sound clip that plays 15 to 45 seconds of music when the card is opened. Some examples of songs used in the cards included "Wonderful World" by Louis Armstrong and "All Star" by Smash Mouth.

Marking its 100th anniversary in 2007, American Greetings launched a US$100 million merchandising program called "Winning at Cards," featuring hundreds of new cards that the company hoped were more relevant to their main buyers—women. Three new lines were introduced, known as "Share a Laugh" (humor), "Share your Style" (trends), and "Lift Your Spirit" (inspirational). The company also planned to sell non-card merchandise such as jewelry and envelope seals, placed next to the greeting card sections of stores.

American Greetings' fastest growing segment in 2007 was AG Interactive, which that year had 3.4 million paid subscribers on five Web sites: americangreetings.com, BlueMountain.com, Egreetings.com, and newcomers BloomByAg.com and HatterChatter.com. In addition to electronic greeting cards, the division offered products for instant messaging and mobile platforms. Sales for AG Interactive alone in 2006 totaled $89.6 million.

In a "Statement on Environmental Responsibility," adopted by the GCA Board of Directors on 27 September 2008, a pledge was made to be environmentally responsible related to both production and business operations. This pledge included an enhanced awareness of material selection and manufacturing dynamics plus waste reduction.

Cardstore.com provided visible evidence of its commitment to the environment by going green. It made the decision to use 100 percent post-consumer waste paper. In addition, Cardstore.com strives to reduce its usage of hazardous chemicals linked to printing ink.

INDUSTRY LEADERS

Hallmark Cards Inc. Hallmark's slogan, "When you care enough to send the very best," was created in 1954 from the writings of C.E. Goodman, a former Hallmark sales vice president. It had been identified several times through independent research as one of the most believed advertising slogans in the United States. Accompanied by the company's five-point crown logo, the slogan had become a familiar trademark for a well-established company.

By the late 1990s, the privately owned Hallmark held 42 percent of the U.S. greeting card market. This figure remained steady since 1994, as the company outpaced American Greetings' market share. Hallmark published 20,700 cards in more than 30 languages in approximately 100 countries, making it the undisputed leader in the greeting card market. The company's market share declined in the early years of the first decade of the 2000s, owing to what some analysts believe was an over-reliance on its own retail stores for distribution, rather than distributing cards through drugstores and other outlets as the other major players do.

Hallmark's lines of cards included the humorous Shoe Box Greetings, its traditional Hallmark Crown, and the newer Windows (recordable greetings). In addition, Hallmark operated a separate division, Ambassador Cards, that was by itself the number three card maker in the United States. Hallmark also was a leading producer of gift wrap, Christmas ornaments, wedding products, and related gift items. Hallmark also owned crayon manufacturer Crayola and offered electronic greeting cards and flowers through its Web site. Hallmark products were showcased by 41,500 places just in the United States alone plus 3,400 Hallmark Gold Crown stores. The company's brand was also a popular attraction for Hallmark Hall of Fame TV movies and the acclaimed Hallmark Channel. In addition, exclusive celebrity-spotlight CDs were sold in stores along with the original movies. In 2008, the company published approximately 65,000 products in more than 30 languages distributed in 100 countries around the world. Hallmark Cards had 2008 consolidated revenues of US$4.3 billion.

Hallmark was founded in 1910 by Joyce Clyde Hall in a room at the Kansas City YMCA where the 18-year-old entrepreneur sold picture postcards from two shoe boxes. Joined by his brother Rollie in 1911, Hall added greeting cards to the line in 1912 and opened Hall Brothers, a store selling postcards, gifts, books, and stationery. The store was destroyed by fire in 1915, but the Halls persevered. Obtaining a loan, they purchased an engraving company and were able to produce their first original greeting cards in time for the Christmas season. A third brother, William, joined the company in 1920. By 1922 the Hall brothers had salespeople in all 48 states and employed 120 people. Prior to 1936, greeting cards had been kept under counters or in drawers. That year, the Hall brothers patented the "Eye-Vision" display case and sold it to retailers across the country.

Hallmark grew rapidly after World War II, opening its first retail store in 1950 and broadcasting the first "Hallmark Hall of Fame" in 1951. The company's name was changed to Hallmark Cards in 1954 and overseas sales were implemented in 1957. Joyce Hall died at the age of 91 in 1982; his son Donald J. Hall became chairman of the company the following year. Personally approving every new card produced by Hallmark until he was in his late seventies, Joyce Hall played a pivotal role in the company until his death.

Eventually, Hallmark built a network of card shops, which became its primary means of distribution. Of the 10,000 shops, 216 were company owned; the remainder were owned and run by independent operators. Hallmark's Kansas City headquarters occupied more than 2 million square feet. The facility was adjacent to the Crown Center, an 85-acre redevelopment project on the southern edge of downtown Kansas City. Launched in 1968, the Crown Center intended to rejuvenate the area surrounding the Hallmark headquarters.

By the late 1990s, Hallmark concentrated its production in Kansas cities—Lawrence, Leavenworth, and Topeka—and in Kansas City, Missouri. Distribution centers in Connecticut, Missouri, California, and New York handled the shipping of cards to more than 100 countries. Hallmark employees numbered more than 12,000, and in 1996 the company posted sales of US$3.6 billion. Sales sagged in 2001, as the worldwide economy slumped.

Introduced in 1994, the Hallmark Gold Crown Card was the first consumer reward program in the greeting card industry. It is one of the largest loyalty programs in the United States, with more than 13 million active members.

In the May 29, 2004, issue of *The New Zealand Herald*, journalist Colin Taylor applauded Hallmark for its transformation "from a big industrial ugly duckling into a sleek and downsized corporate swan" by implementing "just in time warehousing." Turnaround for the new system is 24 hours, and the need for massive inventory is eliminated by gathering information, placing orders, and sending out items immediately to customers. This new business model allows for stock stored in Australia to also be sold in New Zealand. As a result, approximately 2,000 more products are available than were previously stored in New Zealand.

Hallmark commissioned a national survey to tap into the thoughts of dear old mom. The Opinion Research Corporation's CARAVAN Omnibus Survey (CORC) was a telephone-centered study. Its sample dynamics included 319 mothers in the continental United States 18 years of age or older. The study's time frame was July 9–13 and 16–20, 2009. Results showed 8 out of 10 moms seek encouragement from other moms to deal with "challenges of motherhood." Survey results also showed mothers had a

need to encourage their children during difficult times or major transitions. One of these times was definitely back-to-school season. Consequently, Hallmark launched a new series of targeted cards just for mothers called "Edge of motherhood." The series cards were especially designed to encourage moms and kids, by focusing on "everyday moments" in exceptional ways.

The Detroit News journalist Neal Rubin shared insights about the New Haven, Michigan-based contenders for a Hallmark contest. Finalist Jackie Wright submitted a photo of her daughter, Jaelyn, stepping out for "a pretend trip to Target." In addition to bragging rights, the ultimate nationwide contest winner whose card sold the most copies would win a designer's prize of US$2,500. Wright was in competition with four other Michigan amateur card designers and others.

MARVEL Comics and Hallmark have united to bring more excitement wherever cards are sold. Popular characters will be featured on gift cards and stationary. Some of them appear in conjunction with new movie premieres such as those for *Iron Man 2* and *Captain America*. Other tie-ins will include those with animated titles such as *Wolverine* and *X-Men*.

In a July 31, 2009, blog post on www.branding strategyinsider.com, "Qaid," a former Hallmark brand management leader, reflected on the success of "brand insistence advertising that spotlighted the highly recognizable Hallmark crown logo and white space on the back of cards. When "the Hallmark brand insistence message" appeared in publications, it was well received by readers and industry leaders. As a result, feedback was positive overall and requests came in to take out clean-looking ads in other magazines not originally in the marketing mix.

American Greetings. The number two position in the greeting card industry belonged to Cleveland-based American Greetings Corp. In addition to greeting cards, which made up almost 60 percent of its sales in the middle of the first decade of the 2000s, American Greetings manufactured and sold gift items, gift wrap, and party supplies. Cards were marketed through drug stores, supermarkets, and large retail stores. In 2008, American Greetings had annual revenue of US$1.7 billion. Its major brands are American Greetings, Carlton Cards, Gibson, Recycled Paper Greetings and Papyrus. Additional paper products include DesignWare party goods, Plus Mark gift wrap, and DateWorks calendars. Popular character brands are also created and licensed through the company's American Greetings Properties group.

In 2000, the company faced widespread criticism and even ridicule in the media after announcing massive layoffs and losses just 30 days after predicting it would achieve massive growth in coming months and years. Instead, American Greetings saw its market value bottom out in a single day, falling from US$1.3 billion to US$746 million. The losses led to layoffs of 1,500, and shares of American Greeting stock fell from US$45 to US$11 at the end of 2001.

More than 125,000 retail outlets worldwide sell American Greetings products. The company also has a major share in mass market and grocery retailers—the fastest growing channels for greeting cards.

American Greetings has wholly owned subsidiaries in the United Kingdom, Canada, Australia, New Zealand, France, and Mexico. It owns 80 percent of S.A. Greeting in South Africa and has licensees in 70 other countries.

One of American Greetings' most successful years was 1995, when it jettisoned the unprofitable Carlton Cards division, its major U.K. brand, and purchased a major card publisher in South Africa. In 1996, American Greetings acquired John Sands, the top card publisher in Australia and New Zealand, and made an abortive effort to acquire its rival, Gibson, a goal it eventually would reach three years later.

American Greetings traces its beginnings back to 1906, when Jacob Sapirstein (the family later changed its name to Stone) began a card wholesaling business in his Cleveland home, eventually selling postcards from a horse-drawn wagon. His three young sons—Irving, Morrie, and Harry—eventually joined the business and, by 1932, Jacob was producing his own cards.

The company name of American Greetings Publishers was introduced in 1940, and the company went public in 1952. In 1967, Holly Hobbie, named after the artist who created her, was the first licensed character introduced through American Greetings subsidiary Those Characters from Cleveland, Inc. (TCFC). Holly Hobbie was followed by Ziggy in 1972 and the Care Bears in 1982—the same year American Greetings first made the *Fortune* 500 list. Jacob died in 1987, and Morrey Weiss (Irving's son-in-law) became CEO of the company. Irving was still serving as "founder-chairman" in 1998, at the age of 89. American Greetings had offices and production facilities in Canada, France, Ireland, Mexico, England, and the United States, and controlled about 35 percent of the greeting card industry in 1997.

In 1997 the company set its sights on purchasing the number three greeting cards giant, Gibson Greetings Inc., which posted 1997 sales of US$397.2 million, a 2 percent growth from 1996 figures. Gibson had struggled in the mid-1990s, posting losses of US$28.6 million in 1994 and US$46.5 million in 1995. Initially, the firm fended off American Greetings' takeover attempts, believing it could turn itself around. By late 1999, though, the struggling company had been fully acquired by American Greetings.

In 2001, American Greetings posted US$113.8 million in losses on US$2.5 billion in sales. That year, the firm announced its intent to compete intensely in the Internet greeting card arena, purchasing Bluemountain. com for US$35 million. This was perhaps a bargain, in that Bluemountain.com was sold to Excite@Home for US$1 billion in 1999, the booming days of dot-com profits. By 2005, American Greetings led in the online greetings segment through its AG Interactive division, which operated americangreetings.com, BlueMountain. com, BlueMountainCards.co.uk, Egreetings.com, and MIDIRingTones.com. AG Interactive reported more than 2 million paying subscribers in 2005.

In 2004, americangreetings.com announced a special campaign offering Mother's Day Cards featuring art by Alzheimer's patients. The artwork was paired with encouraging, inspirational messages. They were sponsored by Janssen Pharmaceutica Products L.P., makers of REMINYL. That medication is prescribed for treatment of mild to moderate Alzheimer's disease. The art was provided by the Alvin A. Dubin Alzheimer's Center.

American Greetings launched an innovative partner for its ever-popular cards. It is "the first-ever music and sound envelopes." Each time the flap is opened card recipients will hear music or sounds linked to celebrations and special occasions. The selected music and sounds include The Romantics' "What I like About You," the song "Happy Birthday," or cheering crowds. The cost per card is US $3.49.

American Greetings has done its part to make sure hot summer releases do not only apply to books and movies. The card industry leader has introduced some new lines and "fun formats" in time for summer reading and entertainment. One new notable line salutes the legacy of classic comedy and punch lines by accenting carefully selected words with sound effects. Another line expands on the innovative special music and sound envelopes with some kid-focused products.

BIBLIOGRAPHY

Bynum, Aaron H. "MARVEL + Hallmark Team on New Properties." 17 July 2009. Available from www. animutioninsider.net.

"Can't Say It? Post It!" *The Hindu,* 5 June 2004.

Carter, Julie. "Hallmark with Cards." *VFW Magazine,* November 2003.

Cirillo, Frank and Meghan Olmstead. "American Greetings," May 2009. Available from www.corporate.americangreetings.com.

Desjardins, Doug. "Greeting Cards Get Innovative for 2007." *Drug Store News,* 11 December 2006.

"Does White Space Increase Advertising Effectiveness?" 31 July 2009. Available from www.brandingstrategyinsider.com.

"Everyone's Buying Cards Again." *MMR,* 20 February 2006.

"The Facts About Greeting Cards." Greeting Card Association, 2006. Available from http://greetingcard.org.

Flynn, Susan Keen. "From the Mailbox to the Inbox." *Inside Business,* February 2007.

Grant, Lorrie. "Little Guys Take on Greeting Card Giants." *USA Today,* 16 June 2005.

Greeting Card Association. "Facts and Figures: Interesting Facts About Greeting Card Industry." 2009. Available from www.greetingcardassociation.com.

———. "How to Recognize and Avoid E-Card Scams." 2009. Available from www.greetingcard.org.

———. "LOUIE Awards." 2009. Available from www.greetingcard.org.

———. "Statement on Environmental Responsibility." 27 September 2008. Available from www. greetingcard.org.

"Greetings and Sales-utations." *Gifts & Decorative Accessories,* 1 April 2007.

"Hallmark Breaks New Ground." *Chain Drug Review,* 5 March 2007.

Hallmark Corporation. "National Survey Shows Moms Look to Each Other for Encouragement: New Hallmark Cards Offer Encouragement for Everyday Mom Moments." 27 July 2009. Available from corporate.hallmark.com.

"Holiday Cards and Photo Cards Retailer Cardstore.com Goes Green." 17 July 2009. Available from www.messagemeg.com.

"Hoover's Company Capsules." *Hoover's Online* 2009. Available from www.hoovers.com.

McConnaughey, Janet. "Future tech on show at 36th SIGGRAPH." 3 August 2009. Available from www.google.com.

"Net a Viable Venue for Cards." *MMR,* 20 February 2006.

"New Twists Enliven Greeting Cards Arena." *Chain Drug Review,* 5 February 2007.

Rubin, Neal. "The Hallmark moment for a New Haven mom." 30 July 2009. Available from apps.detnews.com.

Taylor, Colin. "Slimming Works for Card Giant." *The New Zealand Herald,* 29 May 2004.

"There's More to Love in the Card Aisle This Summer." 22 July 2009. Available from www.entrepreneur.com.

"Top 25 Export Destinations for Greeting Cards." U.S. Department of Commerce, 2005. Available from www.ita.doc.gov.

SIC 7375

INFORMATION RETRIEVAL SERVICES

NAICS CODE(S)

514191. Information retrieval services supply textual, numeric, and graphic data, usually in the form of searchable databases, to their customers electronically via CD-ROM and online services. See **Internet Services** for Internet-only access services and **Information Technology Services** for other services related to information technology.

INDUSTRY SNAPSHOT

Information retrieval services make information easier to access, understand, and use. Individuals can quickly explore archives of material that might otherwise take hours or days to search and locate using traditional cataloging systems with a simple mouse click or by typing a few words on a keyboard. In addition, information services allow people and organizations to provide and access remote data, update information regularly, communicate efficiently, and complete transactions with customers and service providers worldwide, reducing consumption of paper, among other benefits.

Commercial information retrieval services emerged in the 1970s, but were not recognized as an industry for more than a decade. However, during the mid-1980s the segment experienced exponential growth as the result of technological advances related to personal computers, computer networks, modems, and improved data storage devices. Nevertheless, the growth of the Internet in the mid-1990s resulted in a number of changes in the information retrieval industry. Media Web sites, including those for radio and television news, newspapers, and periodicals, drove a number of small information retrieval services such as NewsNet out of business by the late 1990s. In addition, information retrieval services began to consolidate and change corporate owners, including the sale of such industry leaders as Lexis-Nexis and Dialog. By the mid-2000s, the industry faced further consolidation, but demand remained strong and the outlook was positive for information retrieval services with large aggregate databases and strong name recognition like Dow Jones News/Retrieval and Lexis-Nexis. In addition, specific information niches were targeted for services by expanding markets. Industry players competed in an environment characterized by leaner library budgets. However, information providers benefited from the fact that libraries were purchasing greater shares of electronic versus print content.

By the second half of the 2000s databases were being consolidated, or linked, so a search for information could begin at one point of access. Federated, or meta-searches, in which technology allowed users to search across multiple databases simultaneously were used increasingly. In addition, popular Internet search engines like Google were expected to join with premium databases.

Most information providers were also expanding on their abilities to provide users with data in real time. This was being demanded more, particularly by corporate users. The financial industry, including online brokerages, were also providing an increasing amount of real time data to their clients.

ORGANIZATION AND STRUCTURE

The information retrieval industry encompasses a variety of organizations offering a wide range of services, stemming from the fact that the industry, which was just beginning to mature in the 2000s, is influenced by rapid changes in technology, ease of entry, and an almost infinite array of unfilled market niches. Companies or individuals that can fill or create a need in the market using existing technology can profit, often with only a minor capital investment. Creativity, knowledge of a market need, and technological expertise are the greatest requirements, and industry participants could be large online services with millions of customers to individual entrepreneurs who compile and sell information to a small base of customers. Despite this diversity, a handful of large online service providers accumulate the bulk of industry revenues.

Types of Information. Most information service offerings can be categorized as either business/research or personal. Business/research information retrieval services primarily offer numeric and bibliographic data that includes technical and topical information. Most companies that supply information services compile data from primary sources and reconfigure it for electronic accessibility. Firms that generate proprietary data, such as mutual fund performance or electronic training manuals, are usually classified in their respective industries. Companies may offer abstracts and text from periodicals, books, and journals, or financial and trade data, press releases, news updates, and historical company/industry information. Some companies repackage unwieldy, publicly available government data into an easily accessible, understandable electronic format.

The largest business/research segments provide legal and investment data as well as marketing, scientific, and library information services. The remainder of the sector serves a variety of niche markets, many of which are managed by nonprofit organizations. For instance, services can be tailored specifically to one industry or profession, such as chemical, healthcare, civil engineering, agricultural, banking, insurance, or food service. Major players on the business side of the industry 2005 included North American firms Thomson, Dun Bradstreet, Bloomberg L.P., ProQuest, and Dow Jones. Major players outside of North America included Reuters (the United Kingdom), Wolters Kluwer (the Netherlands), and Deutsche Presse-Agentur (Germany).

Electronic information services targeting the consumer market also provide current news and financial information. In addition, they typically offer features like electronic shopping, recreational bulletin boards and other interpersonal communication domains, weather and sports data, encyclopedias, games, travel information, and home and garden advice. In comparison to business information services, most personal systems are inexpensive, primarily because of the number of users in the market. For instance, many consumer-oriented online services allow

subscribers unlimited access for less than US$20 per month. In contrast, the rate for many business-oriented information databases can exceed several thousand dollars per month.

According to the Gale Directory of Databases, which provides a listing of 14,250 databases worldwide, about 3,075 databases, or 24 percent, were business-oriented, while 2,340 databases, or 18 percent were available for the science, technology, and engineering industries, and 1,578 databases, or 12 percent, were general information. Other databases included law, health/life sciences, humanities, social sciences, multidisciplinary academic, and news. In 2002, Gale alone maintained more than 600 databases.

Media. The primary means of delivering electronic information services are online systems and CD-ROM, which are used along with magnetic diskette, magnetic tape, and audiotext. Consumers access online systems with a modem, which allows a computer to send and receive information, usually by calling a local telephone number to access a central data bank. In addition to the central data bank, most online service providers supply access to other services and data sources, including communications networks like bulletin boards that enable users to communicate with each other. The service provider may charge the customer a flat monthly rate for unlimited access or charges may be based on the length of time the database is used, the amount of information that accessed and printed, or the type of information accessed. In the 2000s, Lexis-Nexis began offering a service to the general public that enabled a potential customer to purchase a single article for a small fee.

One advantage of online systems the availability of up-to-the-minute information that is required by many users. Database managers are able to continually update information related to stock quotes and other financial data, legal rulings and court proceedings, sporting events, world news, and many other subjects. Online systems also allow access to massive amounts of information that would be difficult or impossible for customers to maintain in-house. The most popular online services offer a conglomeration of individual databases, communication services, and products that can be searched simultaneously. The disadvantage of online services from the late 1990s through the 2000s was high cost. Expenses related to collecting timely information, accessing phone lines, and supporting sophisticated data storage and networking equipment can require immense overhead. Customers who access large amounts of tax and legal information, for example, may pay tens of thousands of dollars per month in online charges.

In contrast to online services, CD-ROM products allow customers to store and retrieve information on their own computers using photo-optical technology. Data providers can store hundreds of thousands of pages of data on a single CD that customers can search for specific information. CD-ROM products offer the advantage of relatively low cost in comparison to online systems. The cost of a CD-ROM product can range from under US$80 for the equivalent of an entire set of encyclopedias or as high as several thousand dollars for an annual subscription to some business CD-ROM services.

CD-ROMs also allows users to more easily retrieve photographs and animated images. Additionally, customers may have unlimited access to information at a fixed price, although some CD vendors incorporate system locks that limit the amount of information that can be retrieved and, like the online model, sell additional increments of information for extra fees. One disadvantage of CD-ROM products is the lack of timely data because disks are often delivered monthly or quarterly, making information less current than what is available online.

Floppy disk and magnetic tape systems are similar to CD-ROM retrieval devices but have limited storage capacity, cost, and portability. Audiotext services allow customers to access voice-transmitted information, such as sports scores, via a fee-based telephone number like the 900 area code in the United States. The consumer is charged between US$0.50 and US$5 per minute for a call.

BACKGROUND AND DEVELOPMENT

The information retrieval services industry began in the United States during the post-World War II information age. The advent of computers following this period allowed the distribution of large amounts of data to scientists, engineers, businesses, and government agencies. U.S. government investments in information technologies in the 1950s and 1960s were supplemented by increased private sector spending on research and higher education. The net result of research and development efforts was that scientists and researchers were able to create, store, and quickly access large amounts of data electronically.

The purpose of the first retrieval systems was only to store and print information, mostly for scientific and technical endeavors. As the number and size of the databases grew, systems engineers began to focus on search capabilities that could filter out unnecessary data. Eventually, users were able to type commands into a computer that would search for information containing specific keywords or phrases that would be displayed on the computer screen. The first computerized bibliographic database systems were the result of the U.S. government's need for efficient applications of research dollars and an effort to eliminate duplicate analyses. Some of the more popular databases developed in this period were

MEDLINE, NASA/RECON, and ERIC. The U.S. government also subsidized nonprofit efforts, such as the American Chemical Society's chemical abstracts database.

In the 1960s and 1970s, in addition to supporting nonprofit services, investments were made by first the United States and then by Western European governments to initiate many of the private information retrieval services that dominated the market in the 1980s and early 1990s. For instance, Dialog, a U.S. online information service, began from a venture between the U.S. National Aeronautics and Space Administration (NASA) and U.S.-based Lockheed Corporation that was called Project RECON. Another dominant force in the industry was ORBIT Information Technologies, which was the result of U.S.-based System Development Corporation's work with the U.S. National Library of Medicine. In addition, U.S. industry giant Mead Data Central, which became the Lexis-Nexis Group, was started with seed money provided by U.S. Air Force projects.

Federal governments in the United States, Western Europe, and Japan played pivotal roles in developing telecommunications networks that made online services possible. Networks like Tymnet and Telnet, which essentially provided affordable online access for database users through local telephone lines, were developed through efforts in the U.S. Department of Defense (DOD). Called ARPAnet, in 1969 the DOD created a network to connect their many computers across the country. In the early 1980s, ARPAnet was connected to an expanding number of other networks, and the resulting network became known as the Internet. By 2000 the Internet was accessed by 200 million users all over the world. As more efficient telecommunications networks were developed and computer technology advanced in the late 1960s and 1970s, a significant commercial market for electronic information services began to emerge. Companies and libraries increasingly relied on technical and electronic legal and scientific information to provide a competitive edge in the marketplace and to make their research efforts more efficient. In addition, business productivity was increased for consumers who accessed information electronically.

As electronic markets began to grow, many publishing houses began to experiment with electronic publishing as a means to distribute information. In the United States, H.W. Wilson and Company began delivering documents online through WILSONLINE. McGraw-Hill and other periodical publishers began offering their publications online as well. One of the preeminent commercial uses of electronic information was for legal research. Lexis, a legal database that Mead began offering in 1973, averaged 43 percent annual growth throughout the 1970s and 1980s.

By the end of the 1970s the emerging information retrieval services industry was establishing itself in many sectors of government, academia, and industry, although technical limitations kept costs extremely high. In addition, most systems were complicated and could not be used effectively without professional research skills. For example, a database might use a highly structured query language that users had to learn in order to take advantage of its powerful features. As a result, estimated industry revenues were still well under US$500 million by 1980.

Technological breakthroughs in personal computers and data storage devices fueled rapid industry growth beginning in the mid-1980s. At the same time that microcomputers were becoming smaller and faster, users were becoming accustomed to working with modems, computer networks, and other communications technology that allowed large numbers of people to gain access to collections of data. For the first time, information providers were able to expand their services to the end user—the person who actually used the information—rather than professional researchers.

As end users became the target market for information services, industry participants began to emphasize user-friendly system interfaces that allowed easier data searching and access. Those firms were also quick to take advantage of new data retrieval technologies, such as online services that gradually increased modem communication speeds from 1,200 bits per second (bps), to 2,400 bps, and to 4,800 bps in the late 1980s, leading the way for modem speeds that rose considerably faster in the 1990s and 2000s. As technology advanced, computer equipment prices and online charges began to decrease quickly, which opened the massive small business and home information markets. The commercial manufacture and distribution of high-tech storage devices such as CD-ROM drives also strengthened the industry. As consumers became comfortable with information services and began to realize their benefit, more users began accessing greater amounts of data.

As new markets emerged, information service companies began to expand their offerings, and huge numbers of competitors entered the field. Online information "supermarkets" like Dialog evolved where users could access hundreds of specialized databases covering thousands of publications. Information "boutiques" that offered simultaneous online access to multiple databases and services for one particular industry or profession also emerged and individual niche services flourished. Between 1987 and 1992, the number of electronic databases available internationally leapt from 3,369 to over 9,000. By 1990 worldwide industry revenues had jumped to approximately US$10 billion.

Information retrieval service companies continued to post solid sales gains averaging about 15 percent annually during the early 1990s, despite a worldwide economic slowdown. The number of people subscribing to online services skyrocketed to nearly 8 million in 1993 after falling about 20 percent annually in 1991 and 1992. Business and professional services continued to account for about 95 percent of all online sales, but consumer services posted the greatest annual gains, with 27 percent in 1993. Fast-growing online markets during the early 1990s included consumers of medical, legal, and investment information. Online services continued to account for the bulk of industry receipts, with about 70 percent of the market during the early 1990s.

A more notable contribution to worldwide gains than online services was the CD-ROM market. Following their commercial introduction in 1985, CD-ROM services grew slowly. The high cost of CD-ROM systems led to limited use, primarily in libraries, institutions, and large corporations during the late 1980s. Between 1985 and 1990 the price of CD-ROM disk drives plummeted 50 percent to around US$1,000 and the average cost of a CD-ROM with information fell from about US$1,000 to US$400. By 1993 the average cost of a CD-ROM drive and disk had declined to a more marketable US$400 and US$75, respectively, putting the technology within easy grasp of small businesses and even individual consumers. The result was that the number of CD-ROM drives installed globally ballooned from less than 1 million in the early 1990s to 6 million by 1993. By 1994 more than 20 million CD-ROM drives were in use worldwide.

In the late 1990s the information retrieval service industry began to adapt to the business environment of the period. Companies in the industry began expanding their services and increasing their assets to win over more customers. *Library Journal* predicted that many online information retrieval services would survive after redefining themselves and identifying their place in the information market. Large international companies with substantial collections, numerous services, and many global customers were expected to have the best chances of succeeding, while small companies offering articles from a limited number of newspapers targeting the general consumer were projected to encounter the most severe challenges.

Because of the changing market for information retrieval services, the industry experienced a consolidation spree at the end of the decade. In December of 1997, Market Analysis and Information Database PLC (M.A.I.D.) bought Knight-Ridder Information, Inc., and laid off 25 percent of its staff. M.A.I.D. renamed the company Dialog Corporation, and subsequently sold it to The Thomson Corporation. NewsNet and UMI/Data Times also changed hands in 1997. Throughout the decade many of the leading information retrieval services were bought and sold, including Dialog, DataStar, Information Access Company, Lexis-Nexis, Westlaw, ORBIT, and BRS.

Consolidations and sales within the information retrieval services industry were the result of the increasing competition from the Internet's World Wide Web. The web allows users to access sources like *The New York Times* or *The Wall Street Journal* directly without having to go through an intermediary like Lexis-Nexis and having to pay information retrieval service fees, although newspapers and magazines may charge fees of their own for searching and retrieving information from their site archives. NewsNet, for example, discontinued its full-text information retrieval service in August 1997 in part because it could no longer generate revenues to sustain itself with competition from Internet news sites.

Small information retrieval services, such as News-Net, could not provide a marketable service by simply offering press releases and a limited amount of newspaper and magazine articles, because most newspapers and magazines offered searchable Web sites of their own and companies such as the Associated Press made press releases available. Data Times also had the same fate as NewsNet. In 1996, after UMI Company purchased Data Times, an online information retrieval service with full-text regional newspaper articles, to expand its presence in the business and corporate market, the company terminated the Data Times service in late 1997.

Companies like UMI, which later became a brand of Proquest, realized the difficulties of entering new markets as they tried to expand their market presence. Instead of developing products for the corporate market segment, UMI reached an agreement with Dow Jones to blend its core product, ProQuest, which had an academic, public, and school library focus, with Dow Jones News/Retrieval, which had a business and corporate focus. The agreement allowed each company to focus on core businesses while gaining access to peripheral markets.

CD-ROM-based information retrieval services reported its fastest growth rates in the late 1990s, while the growth of online-based services cooled, partly because of the Internet. By the late 1990s the average cost of a CD-ROM drive fell below US$200 and the average cost of a CD-ROM product had slipped under US$25, although business databases remained in the thousands of dollars. Consequently, CD-ROM drives had become standard equipment in most personal computers sold in North America, Japan, and Western Europe by late 1994, fueling a proliferation of CD-ROM information services for business markets although general consumers were the leading CD-ROM service customers. In 1992, 65 percent of all electronic databases worldwide were available online, while CD-ROMs accounted for only 15 percent of the market. By 1997 the figures had shifted to 49 percent and 30 percent, respectively. Nevertheless, online information services retained a competitive advantage over CD-ROM versions, particularly for timeliness.

The information retrieval industry continued to grow rapidly in the late 1990s as evidenced by the number and type of databases. Between 1994 and 1997 the number of database products and services rose from 8,778 to 10,338, while the number of database vendors rose from 1,691 to 2,115. However, the rise in the number of databases fails to reflect the huge rise in the amount of information supplied by the database segment of the information services industry. The total number of electronic database records in the world shot up from 2 billion to 11 billion between 1987 and 1997, primarily because of improved data storage technology as well as data transmission and retrieval speed. However, just before and after the U.S. Supreme Court decided the Tasini case against *The New York Times* in 2001, hundreds of thousands of articles that were written by independent contractors or might have been written by freelance writers were pulled from host sites.

Industry participants based in North America have the benefit of immediate access to the largest, most-saturated computer and information technology market in the world. Only a few Western European nations come close to matching U.S. computer use, and the United States continued to increase its lead. In 1998, for example, computer penetration exceeded 40 percent in the United States, compared to about 35 percent in many Western European nations. However, Western Europe was investing heavily in information technologies and some nations were gaining on the United States. In fact, by late 2002 *Nua Internet Surveys* estimated that the United States ranked third among the world's 605.6 million Internet users, at 182.7 million. Europe was the world leader with 190.9 million users, followed by the Asia/Pacific region (187.2 million users).

CURRENT CONDITIONS

By 2005, the convergence from print to electronic information delivery was continuing as a corporations, especially those in the financial sector, sought data provided in real time. Thomson, for example, had 98 percent of its financial products available electronically and reported a 1 to 2 percent growth in revenues from electronic products.

The shift to providing data electronically was also evident at the world's libraries large purchases of the information retrieval industries services and products. About 30 years after the introduction of services like LexisNexis and Dialog, libraries were purchasing greater shares of their holdings in electronic formats. This critical shift was changing the very dynamics of how libraries operated. According to *Online,* virtually all library services have been affected by technology, from cataloging, circulation, and document delivery to interlibrary loans, the reference desk, and staff training. In addition, the widespread acceptance of the Internet by consumers as well as businesses accelerated the rate at which technology affected libraries. Patrons, librarians, publishers, and vendors had to adapt as technology changed the way people used libraries with a decrease in the use of books and the reference desk and an increase in remote access of library services via the Internet.

The use of popular Internet search engines was a hot topic within the information retrieval industry during the mid-2000s. Everyone from students to learned professionals relied on the search engines of Google and Yahoo! to meet their research needs. By 2004 Google was used for approximately 290 million searches every day, providing a wider, higher quality range of results, which was a concern within the information retrieval industry. However, in January 2004, Thomson/Gale President Allen Paschal predicted that alliances would be made as search engines entered "the traditional space of the premium and proprietary database providers. They will expand by integrating premium, relevant content in the initial search instead of just linking to Web sites." In 2003, Thomson/Gale formed a partnership with Google in which the search engine's technology could be used within Gale's databases to perform image searches. In addition, Microsoft Office 2003 incorporated a functionality that provided users with the ability to search for business information from within the software interface, as opposed to requiring the user to perform a separate search.

These trends reflected the changing needs of researchers and casual information seekers, who desired one simple point of access for searching. For example, an increase was reported in federated or meta-searching, which allowed users to search simultaneously in multiple databases for information. In one respect, this made searching within premium databases similar to searching on the web. In 2004, MuseGlobal Inc. unveiled MuseSeek, a consumer-oriented meta-search tool designed for incorporation into other software applications. MuseSeek allowed users to select different information sources via a simple checkbox interface and then perform standard keyword-type searches across those sources.

According to *Information Today,* advances in meta-search technology, such as extensible markup language (XML), were removing obstacles between stored information, making access readily available, and giving users results with improved accuracy. Other benefits addressed by Factiva President and CEO Clare Hart included "unlocking content stores, revealing previously unknown information, and linking it to related information stored both within an organization and in other places, such as the Web or commercial information services. Organizations that put these technologies to use as part of their information strategy will gain competitive advantage."

The ability to fill a void for news and business information on corporate intranets and help companies gain a competitive advantage became increasingly important. For example, LexisNexis introduced several products during the early 2000s, including LexisNexis Intranet Publisher and LexisNexis Web Publisher, that allowed companies to integrate their proprietary corporate content with relevant outside resources.

In 2005, the information retrieval services industry was experiencing consolidation. While smooth product integration and too much focus on the financial aspect of mergers were of concern to some customers within the library market, other customers considered consolidation to be positive because new and better products sometimes resulted. Nonetheless, information retrieval companies were pressed to deliver maximum value to end users as they addressed the reality of lean library budgets. However, some observers indicated that in a climate of reduced resources, providers of e-books and online databases would benefit from increased sales resulting from increased sales of electronic products, in lieu of comparatively more expensive printed resources.

In August 2008, Francine Fialkoff opened Library Journal's "Corner Office" and turned the spotlight on Gale leaders. Gale announced plans to introduce "Global Issues in Context," as an electronic reference with no print equivalent. "This is going to be all electronic, (with) feeds from newspapers all over the world, getting different perspectives, not just the United States," explained Gale President Patrick Sommers. According to Gale Executive Vice-President John Barnes, the new product would engage users as Gale began to think about products from a user perspective.

The Internet. The Internet continued to pose a formidable challenge to the industry in 2005. The mass appeal and subsequent growth of the Internet had shaken the information retrieval services industry had made earlier forms of information retrieval services obsolete, including those that targeted a general audience with general news. With 200 million people on the Internet worldwide in 2000, publishers realized a strong potential for expanding their readership, which resulted in the Internet becoming a source of news and information worldwide, especially in the United States, Western Europe, and Japan, which were the leading countries for information retrieval services. Consequently information retrieval vendors increasingly have included an Internet presence in their business strategies as existing customers preferred the ease of accessing data through web browsers instead of emulation or proprietary programs, and as potential new customers were attracted to the Internet. By 2008, RoadRunner.com estimated that there were 47.5 million users on the Internet in the United States alone, and that at least 165 countries were connected to the Internet.

Although the Internet contains a plethora of business, government, and news documents, it lacks the structure of information retrieval services. In contrast to commercial online services with paid subscribers, the Internet is unregulated and uncontrolled. An individual on a personal computer or workstation can tap into the Internet and access tens of thousands of addresses, sites, and services with interactive texts, images, videos, and sounds. However, an individual typically cannot simultaneously search multiple newspapers and periodicals without some kind of information retrieval service fee. Consequently, information retrieval services remained competitive by bundling an extensive collection of news and information sources for businesses, libraries, and professional researchers to use, searching according to their needs. Nevertheless, the Internet cut into the usefulness of information retrieval services for general users who may want to search only one or two sources at a time, so information retrieval services turned to the Internet for their own growth and development. Services like Dow Jones News/Retrieval, Lexis-Nexis, and Dialog offered Internet-based subscriptions to their services, which are available only by subscription, as with their non-Internet services.

The Future. Industry growth is expected to be driven by ongoing technological improvements in data storage, communications, and data processing. Increased computer literacy, particularly in developed nations with relatively low computer penetration, the trend in the United States and Western Europe toward telecommuting and home businesses, and the development of international data and communication standards are projected to encourage industry expansion. As the cost of technology continues to fall and demand for information grows, the variety of services are predicted to increase in response to new market niches. As the volume of available information grows, demand is expected to increase for value-added service providers that can locate, access, and organize information in such a way that makes it usable to consumers. Private citizens may challenge the legality of storage of personal information. By 2002 the only apparent changes that had been put in place by large database providers were legal disclaimers and offers to provide individuals information on their own database particulars at a reduced rate, similar to the way a credit bureau provided individuals with information about particular public records.

According to a 2003 report from IDC Research, the worldwide volume of Internet traffic was expected to double every year between 2002 and 2007, when users will share a mass of daily information some 64,000 times greater than the contents of the Library of Congress. By 2007, businesses are expected to represent 40 percent of all Internet users, while consumers will account for the majority.

RESEARCH AND TECHNOLOGY

Two of the most important technological factors for the information retrieval services industry were storage capacity and retrieval speed. Storage capacity was being enhanced in the form of CD-ROMs, which were being designed to store increasing bytes of data and to deliver that information at greater speeds. At the same time, advances in magnetic storage devices offered the potential of similar storage capacity with much faster information retrieval speeds. Increases in online retrieval speeds were being accomplished through more efficient, high-speed modems.

Telecommunications services began offering Internet users alternative lines, such as T1 and ISDN lines. T1 lines can transfer data at 1.5 million bps, more than 25 times the speed of state-of-the-art consumer modems via telephone lines at 56,000 bps. T1 connections were used mostly by businesses and organizations with large computer networks or special high-volume requirements. T1s also were used to connect some of the Internet's backbone computers. ISDN (integrated services digital network) lines, another high-end technology, could transfer data at a maximum speed of 128,000 bps. Other potential high-speed transmission technologies included satellite and coaxial cable connections.

Other technologies augmenting industry expansion in the late 1990s and 2000s were related to interactive multimedia, or the integration of audio, video, text, and images into a user-controlled environment. For example, scanners were introduced that could inexpensively convert photographs into high-quality images accessible online or through CD-ROM. Likewise, inexpensive production and editing systems allowed individuals and companies to generate digital videos at continually dropping prices, opening new markets for CD-ROM products. Among the most sensational and promising developments was virtual reality, allowing users to access and enter artificial three-dimensional worlds through online services, CD-ROM devices, or other information retrieval systems. Information retrieved by the customer could be combined with touch-sensitive gloves and head-mounted displays to create 3-D environments for a multitude of purposes.

University of Michigan researchers developed the American Customer Satisfaction Index (ACSI) to measure business performance with customer expectations using a 100-point rating scale. Private research firm, For See Results, reported that Google was the most user-friendly major portal and search engine. However, the firm also found that "People are starting to go directly to the Web site or use bookmarks if they know what they're looking for, rather than using a portal." Nonetheless, Google had the potential to remain a valuable resource that could remain relevant for those without background knowledge of their search subject.

INDUSTRY LEADERS

The Thomson Corporation. In 2005, The Thomson Corporation of Canada was providing information in law, accounting, higher education, tax, healthcare, scientific research, general reference, finance, and corporate e-learning and assessment to customers in approximately 130 countries. The company employed about 40,000 people in 45 countries in 2004. Thomson was organized into four main groups. The Legal & Regulatory division accounted for 42 percent of Thomson's US$8.1 billion in sales, followed by Learning (27 percent), Financial (21 percent), and Scientific & Healthcare (10 percent). Subscription-based products accounted for 65 percent of company revenues, and 82 percent of revenues came from North American. About 66 percent of sales were from electronic products, software, and services. By 2004 Thomson had sold most of its print media interests, including about 130 newspapers and its ownership interest in Bell Globemedia, to concentrate on electronic resources. Thomson's growth was through a series of strategic acquisitions. Between 2002 and 2004, the company acquired 114 companies, including Elite Information Group, a provider of practice management software to law firms, and Information Holdings Inc, a provider of intellectual property and regulatory information. The company also sold some subsidiaries, including Thomson Media group, a provider of mostly print-based information on banking, financial services, and their related technology services.

The Thomson Corporation also owned Dialog Corporation, which offered online company, industry, business, and international news. Dialog's main platform services included Dialog, Dialog Profound, Dialog DataStar, Dialog NewsEdge, and Dialog Intelliscope, which had accessed about 1.4 billion documents in 2004. Dialog formed a strategic partnership in 2002 with Gale, another professional information source owned by The Thomson Corporation, to build information sources for academics, libraries, and businesses, which had been Dialog's strength. The first joint ventures were to be targeted toward libraries. Gale's strengths include being an information provider to libraries, academic researchers, and corporate users.

Dialog was started in 1972 by Dr. Roger K. Summit, who envisioned the possibilities of information retrieval in such fields as medicine, law, and business using computers and online technology. By 2002 North Carolina-based Dialog was accessed in more than 100 countries, according to *Internet Wire.* In mid-2004, the company offered more than 900 databases to its subscribers, who performed approximately 700,000 searches and viewed more than 17 million document pages each month.

The McGraw-Hill Companies Inc. The world's largest producer of textbooks, McGraw-Hill is also an industry leader within the information services industry. In addition to publishing more than 9,000 books and such titles as *Business Week* and *Aviation Week & Space Technology,* and owning Standard & Poor's, McGraw-Hill provides information retrieval services to the government, businesses, schools, and the general public. In 2004, the company had 17,000 employees and sales reached US$5.25 billion, which was up almost 9 percent from 2003.

According to McGraw-Hill Companies President Harold McGraw, media companies had to become technology companies that were capable of efficient delivery of new services appealing to a generation of readers who spent minimal time with printed pages. In the early 2000s, McGraw's flagship publication, *Business Week,* launched Business Exchange, its biggest digital investment. Business Exchange allows editors and users to create and then follow content all around the World Wide Web for topics "meaningful to them," making it possible to create niche publications.

Thomson Reuters. Thomson Reuters was founded in London, England, in 1851. In 1999, a marriage of convenience and mutual profit was arranged between the business information divisions of Reuters and New York-based Dow Jones. Dow Jones & Company, Inc., headquartered in New York, was the publisher of leading business-oriented newspapers, including *The Wall Street Journal* and *Barron's.* Dow Jones was ranked among the industry leaders for its Dow Jones News/Retrieval Service, which provided access to more than 3,600 publications from all over the world. Following the merger, the joint venture tried to keep both names in its corporate title as Dow Jones Reuters Business Interactive LLC, but dropped the unwieldy handle in favor of the new brand name Factiva. By 2004, Factiva was the world's leading supplier of global news and information to corporate end users, and was ranked second in revenue in the archival business news and information marketplace. The company offered exclusive third-party access to Dow Jones and Reuters Newswires, *The Wall Street Journal,* as well as an additional 9,000 global sources. By 2003, sales totaled US$245 million, which was up 1.6 percent from 2002.

Although Thomson Reuters was best known as the world's largest news agency, in 2005 about 90 percent of company revenues were from the supply of information to about 330,000 professionals in the equities, fixed income, foreign exchange, money, commodities, and energy financial services markets. By 2005 the company operated in 91 countries with an employee count of 14,500. The company was able to provide real-time data on 5.5 million financial records, maintained data on 35,000 global companies, and provided financial data from more than 300 exchanges and over-the-counter (OTC) markets. The company owned 62 percent of the world's largest electronic securities broker, Instinet, through which it also offered access to a wealth of financial information used by traders.

In April 2008, Thomson Corp. bought the Reuters Group for approximately US $15.8 billion, resulting in a second quarter loss of 54 percent because related moves cut into profits. The company provides financial data and business news to diverse markets, including legal, financial services, tax and accounting, scientific, healthcare, and media markets. Thomson Reuters Corporation and Thomson Reuters PLC share ownership of Thomson Reuters in a complex duel listed company structure. Thomson Reuters reported 2007 earnings of US$7.3 billion and 50,000 employees.

Bloomberg L.P. Based in New York, privately held Bloomberg posted sales of US$3.5 billion in 2004 as one of the world's top information retrieval services. Bloomberg provided investors and universities with about 170,000 proprietary terminals that featured up-to-date business news, analysis, and market information. In addition, Bloomberg operated national wire services for the TV, radio, and newspaper industries and published magazines. The company had 8,000 employees in 2004 and revenues of about US$3.5 billion. In 2001 company founder Michael Bloomberg was elected the 108th mayor of New York City.

In September 2008, Bloomberg expanded its news operation into the Persian Gulf region when it opened The Bloomberg Jerusalem Bureau. The expansion is expected to impact the Ramat Gan Bloomberg Bureau.

Reed Elsevier Group plc. One of the world's leading medical, legal, education, and business information providers, London, England-based Reed Elsevier earned about 31 percent of its 2004 revenues from electronic information products. Its LexisNexis subsidiary earned 61 percent of its revenue electronically, while its Elsevier subsidiary earned 43 percent from electronic sources. In 2003, the

company combined its businesses with Amsterdam-based Reed Elsevier NV to form Reed Elsevier Group as a joint venture. Each parent company retained their separate legal form and trade on separate exchanges, although they have combined operations. In February 2005, Reed Elsevier reported total revenues of approximately US$9 billion, which included 55 percent that was earned in North America, 18 percent in the United Kingdom, 10 percent in the Netherlands, 11 percent in the rest of Europe, and the remainder from the rest of the world. Reed Elsevier sold its education holdings in 2007.

Reed Elsevier's LexisNexis division provided about 27 percent of its parent company's total revenues for fiscal 2005. Based in Ohio, Lexis-Nexis catered to the legal, news, and business markets, and in 2004 provided full-text documents from law journals and selected periodicals from 16,000 database sources. In 1997, Lexis-Nexis reported US$715 million in sales and employed 6,700 people. By 2005, sales totaled about US$2.5 billion, and the company employed 12,900 workers.

Wolters Kluwer nv. Amsterdam-based Wolters Kluwer was a leading provider of health, tax, accounting, corporate, financial, education, and legal and regulatory information, ranking first or second in more than 80 percent of its markets in 2004. With offices in more than 25 countries, Wolters Kluwer employed 18,393 people and reported revenues of about US$4 billion in 2004. The company has operations in more than 25 countries, primarily in Europe and North America.

Wolters Kluwer NV announced in 2008 that it was in exclusive talks to buy Waltham, Massachusetts-based Up To Date, which provided diagnosis and treatment information via the Internet to about 320,000 doctors and medical workers in 130 countries. Up to Date was expected to generate US $80 million revenue in 2008.

ProQuest Company. The ProQuest Company was formed in 2001 from Bell & Howell Company's two information access businesses, Bell & Howell Information and Learning and Bell & Howell Publishing Services. The company was one of the world's leading providers of information to the academic, automotive, and power equipment markets. Through its ProQuest Information and Learning segment, the company offered an electronic database of periodicals, dissertations, and newspapers under licensing agreements with more than 9,000 publishers worldwide. ProQuest also was a leading archivist of journals and newspapers on microfilm and CD-ROM and produced scanners that allow businesses to convert documents to electronic formats. The Proquest Business Solutions segment of the company was the world leader in information products for the automotive products markets and provided information to the power equipment and power sports markets, allowing automotive dealers to access technical documentation electronically. In addition, Proquest collected and distributed statistics on dealer performance.

In 2003 and 2004 the company expanded through acquisitions, including the purchase of Copley Publishing Group, Reading A-Z, Axiom Press, Serials Solutions, SIRS Publishing, and Entigo Inc. In 2007, ProQuest sales were US$110.5 million with 1,555 employees. As of 2008, ProQuest provided access and navigation of more than 125 billion digital pages of scholarly data as well as to about 16,000 periodicals, 7,000 newspapers, 150,000 out-of-print books, 550 research collections, and more than 15 million proprietary abstracts. Access was by subscriptions held by most academic libraries around the world. The company operated two divisions: UMI (formerly University Microfilms International) and Chadwyck-Healey.

In 2008, Google announced plans to partner with ProQuest and Heritage to archive newspaper stores in their originally published formats rather than in text versions. The articles would include original photos and advertisements. A major goal of the project was to include newspapers from small town weeklies to large national dailies.

MAJOR COUNTRIES IN THE INDUSTRY

In the late 1990s and 2000s industry growth occurred in Eastern Europe, South America, and particularly the Pacific Rim. Businesses in those regions were expected to demand increasing amounts of business, legal, and financial information about the United States and other developed markets. Expansion of information services in the Pacific Rim was anticipated as high levels of investment in communications infrastructure were apparent in the region. For example, South Korea and Singapore were investing in national fiber-optic networks that would eventually permit the rapid transfer of data on computer networks.

The United States. The United States initiated the information retrieval industry in the 1970s and continued to lead it in the mid-2000s. The electronic information services market was valued by *Euromonitor* at US$61.4 billion in 2003, up 6 percent over 2002. The five largest companies in the industry in the United States were Reed Elsevier, Dun & Bradstreet, Dow Jones, Reuters, and Thomson, which controlled just under 40 percent of the market. *Euromonitor* predicted 62.5 percent growth between 2003 and 2008.

In 2003, figures from Leichtman Research Group indicated that the United States would continue to be a key information retrieval services market through the early years of the twenty-first century. Leichtman

estimated that high-speed Internet users, which numbered 14.7 million in 2002, would surpass narrowband subscribers in 2005 and mushroom to 49 million by 2007.

Among the leading proprietary subscription online services geared for the consumer market in the late 1990s were CompuServe Corporation, Prodigy Services Inc., and America Online, Inc. (AOL). All three were U.S.-based services that catered to individual interests like shopping and hobbies. They originated as closed networks offering a variety of magazines, news services, and member discussion bulletin boards, but as the Internet's popularity surged in the mid-1990s, they began offering Internet access in addition to their own information content. America Online bought CompuServe in 1997 and made it a subsidiary. CompuServe, with a focus on business information, brought in US$841.9 million in 1997. Prodigy's 1997 sales totaled only US$225 million and America Online reported US$1.6 billion in revenues. Prodigy had fewer than 1 million subscribers in 1998, while America Online had about 13.5 million, including 2.5 million from CompuServe. America Online also had services in Europe, as did CompuServe before the acquisition.

In 2002, Prodigy Communications, a subsidiary of SBC Communications, continued to serve more than 3 million subscribers and 1.3 million DSL Internet customers. In the 2000s AOL experienced highs and lows following a merger with Time Warner in January 2000. In January 2000 the AOL stock price was US$72.62, and on April 12, 2002, it plunged to US$20.10 a share, less than the cost of a month's dial-up service for a customer. In April 2002, AOL's debt level was US$23 billion, according to *Business Week.*

Western Europe. The information retrieval services industry in Western Europe has faced challenges, including language and cultural barriers, as well as a restrictive regulatory environment that is not present in the United States. Nevertheless, several key European players had joined North American information service providers by the late 1990s, including Reuters in England, VNU in the Netherlands, and French Minitel online service. Reuters and VNU garner a large portion of their revenues from sales in the United States. The leading European producers and consumers of electronic information were the United Kingdom, France, and Germany, where telecommunications services offered ISDN connections that augmented the demand for not only information retrieval services, but also the Internet.

Research from Datamonitor indicated that the number of high-speed Internet users in Europe was expected to increase from about 10 million in 2002 to more than 41 million in 2006. By that time, Germany would have the most broadband subscribers, followed by the United Kingdom and France. Along with this increase, consumers in Western Europe were expected to spend more on paid electronic content, with spending reaching US$3.4 billion annually by 2006, or US$76 per user.

The United Kingdom was the leader in Europe for the use of electronic information services, with a market valued at US$12.3 billion in 2003, 86 percent of which was for online services. Reuters led the market with a 25.5 percent market share, but Thomson, Reed Elsevier, and Bloomberg were also major players. Financial service companies were the biggest users of the industry.

Although Germany was a much smaller market than the United Kingdom, the former's market was growing strongly according to *Euromonitor*. With a value of approximately US$1.8 billion in 2003, Deutsche Presse-Agentur (DPA) was beating its rivals for market share with 9 percent of the market. Of the remaining top four companies in 2003, only Reuters was foreign. Other industry players were FIZ Karlsruhe GmbH, Verlagsgruppe Georg von Holtzbrinck GmbH, and Verband der Vereine Creditreform eV. The financial industry was the country's biggest user of electronic information.

In 2003, Reuters led the market in France, where electronic information service sales accounted for about US$3.3 billion. Dun & Bradstreet and France Télécom were other industry leaders.

Germany's Bertelsmann AG, which had a partnership agreement with America Online, operated one of Europe's largest consumer online services and took over CompuServe's European service after it was acquired by America Online.

Japan. Japan was the third-largest market for information retrieval services, although the country lagged well behind the United States and several Western European nations in the amount of information services it provided. However, increasing computer literacy in Japan was projected to continue to increase market share. By 2003, 54.5 percent of the Japanese population (or 80 percent of all Japanese households) was online, along with about 79 percent of Japanese businesses. Nearly 30 percent of Internet users had access to high-speed connections.

In 2003, the Japanese electronic information services market was valued at about US$5.6 billion, of which commercial, online-access services made up about 62 percent. Japan was home to a number of high-powered databases of science, engineering, and economic information of interest to U.S. companies and institutions. Japan also enjoyed a leading edge in a few specific emerging information service technologies, such as those related to car navigation systems. Japan's information retrieval industry had suffered a setback during the mid-1990s

when corporate users reduced their investments in information technology and services. In addition, the Japanese industry lost a share of its customers to open Internet databases, but these factors combined to make the industry in Japan much more competitive.

BIBLIOGRAPHY

"AsiaBizTech: Over 50 Percent of Japanese Population Online." *Nua Internet Surveys*, 12 March 2003. Available from www.nua.ie/surveys.

"Bloomberg News Expands in the Middle East with Jerusalem Bureau." *Market Watch*, 11 September 2008. Available from MarketWatch.com.

Corbin, Kenneth. "Study: Google Tops in e-Business Satisfaction." *IT Management*, 19 August 2008. Available from InternetNews.com.

"Datamonitor: Broadband Adoption on the Up in Europe." *Nua Internet Surveys*, 20 March 2003. Available from www.nua.ie/surveys.

"Dialog And Gale In Alliance To Build New Library Services." *Internet Wire*, 1 April, 2002.

"Dow Jones, Reuters to Combine Interactive Services." *Bloomberg News*, 17 May 1999.

Duffy, Caroline A. "Online Evolution." *PC Week*, 16 January 1995.

Fialkoff, Francine. "Corner Office: Gale's Sommers & Barnes." *Library Journal*, 15 August 2008.

Gale Directory of Databases. Detroit: Gale Group, 2004.

"Getting Your Facts Straight." *New Media Age*, 1 November 2001.

Hajime, Kuwata. "Japan's Information Service Industry: Supporting Downsizing & Network Introduction Keys to the Future." *Japan 21st*, March 1996.

"How Many Online?" *Nua Internet Surveys*, September 2002. Available from www.nua.ie/surveys.

"IDC Research: Worldwide Net Traffic to Rise." *Nua Internet Surveys*, 3 March 2003. Available from www.nua.ie/surveys.

Jarvis, Steve. "Sum of the Parts: Fast-growing Industry Delivers Data to New Markets, Piece by Piece." *Marketing News*, 21 January 2002.

Konieczko, Jill. "The Next Evolutionary Step for Corporate Intranets and Internets: Tools that Integrate Relevant, Continually Updated External Content." *KMWorld*, January 2003.

"Leichtman Research: More High-Speed Net Subscribers in US." *Nua Internet Surveys*, 2 April 2003. Available from www.nua.ie/surveys.

"Major Market Profiles: Electronic Information Services in France (Germany, Japan, UK, USA)." *Euromonitor*, October 2004. Available from www.euromonitor.com.

"MuseGlobal, Inc. Announced the Release of MuseSeek, a New Consumer-Oriented Version of Its Metasearching Technology." *Online*, January–February 2004.

Patrick, Aaron. "Wolters in Talks to Buy Up To Date." *The Wall Street Journal*, 3 September 2008. Available from online.wsj.com.

Picchi, Aimee. "McGraw-Hill Has Fourth Quarter Loss on Expenses for Job Cuts?" *Bloomberg News*, 29 January 2002.

Plosker, George R. "The Information Industry Revolution: Implications for Librarians." *Online*, November-December 2003.

Tenopir, Carol. "E-resources in Tough Times." *Library Journal*, 1 June 2004, 42.

———. "Will Online Vendors Survive?" *Library Journal*, 1 February 1998, 35.

"Thomson Reuters Reports Lower Profit on Costs of a Merger."
The New York Times, 13 August 2008. Available from
nytimes.com.

"What's Ahead for 2004?" *Information Today,* January 2004, p. 1.

"Will AOL and Yahoo Trade Places?" *Business Week Online,*
11 April 2002. Available from www.businessweek.com.

SIC 4822

INTERNET SERVICES

NAICS CODE(S)

518111. The Internet services industry includes
Internet service providers (ISPs), backbone network operators, World Wide Web navigation services, Internet
security services, and Internet or electronic commerce
(e-commerce) providers. Internet service providers may
also offer Internet hosting and programming services, e-
mail and messaging services, and Web site design services. Companies that use the Internet to promote sales,
such as automobile manufacturers allowing customers to
price cars online, are not considered part of the industry.
(See also **Information Technology Services** and **Packaged Software**.)

INDUSTRY SNAPSHOT

The Internet has been the fastest-growing communications technology in history, according to the U.S.
Department of Commerce. Radio was available for 38
years before gaining 50 million listeners, and television
was available for 13 years before gaining that many viewers. However, the Internet reached the 50-million-user
mark in only four years. By the end of 1997, more than
102 million people were using the Internet. By the end of
2003, there were 700 million Internet users worldwide.
This number was expected to reach 945 million by the
end of 2004 and exceed 1 billion by 2007.

The growth in Internet users is occurring in tandem
with an increase in the number of Web sites. Domain
name registrations for Web sites carrying the ".com"
extension increased 23 percent between 2002 and 2003,

Worldwide Usage of Internet Browsers, October 2010

Internet Explorer	48%
Firefox	30%
Chrome	13%
Safari	8%
Opera	1%

SOURCE: W3 Counter.

---

while Web sites carrying the ".net" extensions jumped 20
percent from the first half of 2003.

By 2009, with the developments of broadband Internet and connected TVs, the convergence between Internet and TVs gradually came into being. Internet-enabled
TVs not only allowed users to watch TV programs but
also served as a medium for multimedia interactive services. Telecom and cable TV operators began providing
TV networking applications via their closed networks,
while consumer electronics manufacturers also sought to
tap into the market.

Change was happening within the U.S. Internet
population on many levels. The average age of Internet
users rose simultaneously with that of the general population, for example, while racial and ethnic characteristics were more closely mirroring those in the offline
population. In 2010, 221 million people in the United
States were online, or about 71 percent of the total
population. Their numbers were projected to continue
to grow, reaching 250 million by 2014, or more than 77
percent of the population.

Internet users are on the go, and they are taking the
Internet with them. Thanks to the plethora of mobile
devices available, the personal computer (PC) is on its
way to being at least a secondary point of access. Nevertheless, form follows function, and consumers were looking to the Internet first to facilitate communication, then
for news and information, and by 2010 to entertain.
They will adopt the devices that best suit their personal
need for communication and information, whether it is a
laptop, netbook, smartphone, or e-reader.

Marketers knew they were navigating a dynamic
digital landscape by 2010, and the results of some demographic shifts taking place at the end of the first decade
of the twenty-first century were expected to become more
evident by 2015. Internet users will be older, and many
will have lower levels of education and annual income.
However, they will be more diverse racially and ethnically
and expect marketing messages to appeal to them.

There is no question that the Internet has become a
mainstream medium. In 2009, the U.S. Internet population grew to nearly 200 million users, or 65 percent of
the total population. By 2013, 221 million people are
expected to be online, or nearly 70 percent of the population. The U.S. Internet Users report analyzes trends
that continue to drive online population growth and
usage. The demographics of the U.S. Internet population
are evolving to reflect the offline population. More
women are coming online and so are more users age 35
and older. Daily Internet usage among nearly all demographic groups is climbing. Average time spent online by
adults in the United States shot up to 14 hours per week
in 2008, compared with 11 hours in 2007. Nearly

two-thirds of adults claim they go online every day, and most are on for more than one hour. A 2010 survey conducted by the Pew Research Center reports the percentage of American adults who use the Internet went from 15 percent in 1995 to nearly 80 percent in 2010, for an increase of 64 percent.

Businesses have been quick to take advantage of the Internet's potential and are realizing significant business cost savings and competitive advantages. The Internet is a driving force behind globalization and electronic commerce, as well as for communication and collaboration within and between companies. In 1997 an estimated US$40 billion in global business was transacted over the Internet. By the end of 2004, global business-to-business (B2B) was expected to bring in US$2.7 trillion, according to *eMarketer,* with the United States accounting for about US$1 trillion of that total. Although 70 percent of companies had attempted online purchasing by early 2003, about 90 percent of their spending continued to occur offline according to *eMarketer.* A survey conducted by *Information Strategy* revealed that 98 percent of the businesses that responded had some sort of presence on the Internet and almost half of those had sites offering interactive communication with customers. About 15 percent of those companies actually conducted business over the Internet, although most marketed services rather than physical products.

According to Frost & Sullivan, businesses are being compelled to cut costs and enhance worker productivity, causing them to increasingly evaluate the use of collaborative tools like Web conferencing for connecting dispersed teams and remote employees. Frost & Sullivan's research identifies industry drivers and restraints, competitive landscape, revenues and revenue forecasts, market shares and key trends, within the global Web conferencing services market. Businesses with a connection between the public Internet and their own internal network or Web site for company business realize the need to conduct an Information Security Gap Analysis on a regular basis. Standards for these analyses have been developed by the International Organization for Standardization (ISO), the Information Systems Audit and Control Association (ISACA), and the National Institute of Standards and Technology (NIST). They are a good starting point when developing a plan. Moreover, a Security Gap Analysis should be developed as part of a comprehensive business security or continuity plan to define an Information Security Gap Analysis, looks at possible pitfalls, and provides a step-by-step implementation plan.

Figures from Nielsen NetRatings for March 2005 showed that 451.5 million people worldwide had access to the Internet from a home computer. Users visited an average of 62 unique domain names that month, viewing about 1,148 total Web pages. In addition, people spent approximately 26 hours and 55 minutes on their computers, with average Web surfing sessions of 51 minutes and 11 seconds. Individual Web pages were viewed for an average of about 44 seconds.

James Cicconi, a top lobbyist for AT&T, said the industry would be using the entire capacity of the Internet by 2010, and lobbied against legislation that would prevent ISPs from adding surcharges for heavy use. According to Richard N. Clarke of AT&T, providing unlimited Internet use could cost as much as US$416 a month. The views expressed by Cicconi and Clarke indicated the need for ISPs to closely monitor the use of the Internet by their customers. Meanwhile, Internet use continued to grow at a steady 35 to 50 percent per year according to research studies by the University of Minnesota and Cisco Systems.

ORGANIZATION AND STRUCTURE

Internet Service Providers (ISPs). Internet service providers allow users to connect to the World Wide Web. Companies from several major industries, including local and national telecommunications companies, software developers, and cable television companies, provide businesses and individuals with access to the Internet. Those who did not offer their own services have pursued joint ventures to do so. Speed has become as important as easy access in the late 2000s.

The Internet may be accessed in several ways, including dedicated lines and dial-up telephone line access. Dedicated lines include T1 and T3 lines (fiber optic lines to an ISP) and others lines, such as digital subscriber lines (DSL). Dial-up lines include the Integrated Service Digital Network (ISDN) and phone lines with use of a modem.

A "dedicated line" means that a data transmission line is used only for Internet access and is always open rather than dialing into the Internet each time a user or company wants access. Dedicated, or permanent, lines provide much greater speed and greater bandwidth (the amount of data that can be transmitted at one time over the connection) than dial-up access. Dial-up access is available on an individual or network basis and runs more slowly than dedicated lines. However, for individuals and some small companies, dial-up access to the Internet is sufficient. The number of simultaneous users who need access and the type of tasks they perform are considerations when determining the type of access required. For example, some users may need to send and receive large graphics or data files regularly, and a slow connection would impede their productivity.

Internet service providers (ISPs) supply a network connection that allows users to access the Internet and allow people and corporations to sponsor Web sites.

Customers either dial in or use a dedicated line to the ISP, which in turn is linked to "national ISP" systems. Many ISPs purchase their access from network operators or national providers that do not serve the general public.

Network Operators. Some companies made a mark in the industry by selling fiber-optic networks and bandwidth to telecommunications and Internet access providers. One such company was Qwest Communications, which provided national fiber-optic services to major telecommunications companies like WorldCom, Sprint, and GTE.

In order to provide easy access to the Internet for educational and nonprofit institutions, the Federal Communications Commission (FCC) announced in 1997 that it would offer free wireless access at 300 megahertz (MHz) of the radio spectrum for short-distance connections. These connections had the potential to bring the Internet to schools, hospitals, libraries, and other institutions for which access costs were prohibitive.

Security. Security is one of the primary concerns for businesses pursuing commercial ventures on the Internet. While most companies want to take advantage of this exploding market, they are concerned about public access to private files and competitive information. Such information has become the primary corporate intelligence target. Therefore, security services have become a growing market in the Internet services industry. Security services include consulting and security system design, as well as the installation of firewalls (software security structure) and virtual private networks.

Consulting services might include design and maintenance of corporate security policies, network security design, and site audits. Consultants also provide comprehensive external audit services. These audits include evaluating firewalls, detecting "back doors" on internal networks, and validating security tools. Other consulting services are host penetration testing and evaluation of internal compliance with corporate security policies.

Firewalls are installed in computer networks to protect internal hosts from unauthorized external access. A firewall is placed between a corporation's private network and public Internet access, monitoring access to the corporate network and its authorized users. Regular as well as suspicious activity can be monitored and reported to network administrators when necessary. The virtual private network (VPN) is another tool used to enhance network security, which has started replacing wide-area networks in many corporations. This type of network offers secure connections over the Internet and can connect branch offices, remote users, business partners, and clients on one network.

"TRUSTe," a global initiative dedicated to the issue of Internet security, was launched in 1997 by the Electronic Frontier Foundation and CommerceNet, an Internet commerce industry organization. TRUSTe was created to instill confidence in the electronic exchange of information by dispensing green "trustmarks," or seals of approval, to Web sites following set privacy guidelines. TRUSTe was initially aimed at the general consumer, but was slated to move into Internet commerce security.

In a November 2009 article from Internetnews.com, IBM's X-Force security research and response team unveiled its top security trends for enterprise customers. X-Force researchers predicted a resurgence in what it called "old school" attacks by 2010 with so-called worm attacks becoming more common and the Trojan viruses continuing to serve as the staple of the cyber threat community. IBM also predicted that an increase in denial-of-service attacks as "attack services" mature through organized cyber crime rings based in the United States and abroad.

In addition, antivirus software vendor Symantec issued its own list of the Top 13 security trends to look for by 2010. The top five included: (1) Antivirus software is not enough; (2) Social engineering will be the primary attack vector; (3) Rogue security software vendors will escalate their efforts; (4) Social networking third-party apps will fraud targets; (5) Windows 7 will come in the crosshairs of attackers. A report released in 2010 by the Anti-Phishing Working Group (APWG) found that fake anti-malware and security software programs soared more than 585 percent in the first half of 2009 alone. In 2007, more than 3.6 million people lost more than US$3.2 billion to malicious phishing scams. Not surprisingly, companies were expecting more sophisticated hacking tactics and an even stronger emphasis on social engineering to spread malware and execute elaborate phishing scams. Pirated software can be expected to drive insecurity in more dramatic and dynamic ways. Because users of pirated software are afraid to download updates, they and their PCs will be exposed to even more security risks because their applications have not been updated with protective patches. As a result, IBM said that users of pirated software will become the new "Typhoid Marys" of the global computing community. IBM is looking for social networks to provide authors of social engineering schemes with new avenues for creative compromises. As the decade of the 2010s begins, criminal organizations can be expected to increase the frequency and sophistication of their attacks on different social networking sites, particularly against so-called high-value individuals who have registered on Facebook or LinkedIn. IBM expects cyber crooks will use these sites in creative, new ways that will accelerate compromises and identity theft, especially as new commercial applications increase the disclosure of valuable personal information on these sites. However, the researchers expect the wireless world to remain relatively secure. Even as smartphones continue to become more capable, serious attacks against these devices will remain far and few between in 2010, according to reports, simply because PCs remain a much more valuable target for criminals.

E-commerce. One of the most fundamental shifts in the way companies conducted business during the late 1990s and early 2000s arose from increased online product ordering. This type of business is referred to as e-business (electronic business), e-commerce (electronic commerce), or I-commerce (Internet commerce). This shift represented a change in business strategy as much as in technology. IBM was among the first companies that attempted to profit from the opportunity to provide corporate customers with e-commerce hardware, software, and services.

Established Internet companies, such as browser giant Netscape Communications Corporation, also shifted service offerings to take advantage of opportunities in electronic commerce. Netscape was positioning its own Web site as an "Internet tollbooth for each transaction to pass through on its way to accessing services deployed on top of enterprise software from Netscape," according to Dana Gardner in the June 1, 1998 edition of *Info World*.

In September 1995, eBay was founded in Pierre Omidyar's San Jose living room. From the start it was meant to be a marketplace for the sale of goods and services for individuals, but it has become the industry's model for e-commerce. eBay has built an online person-to-person trading community on the Internet, using the World Wide Web. In July 2002, in a move that helped millions of Internet users buy and sell online, eBay Inc., the world's online marketplace, announced that it would acquire PayPal, Inc., the global payments platform.

Multichannel ecommerce (also called eCommerce, e-commerce, or electronic commerce) consists of selling products or services through third-party retail partners. Multichannel ecommerce can be differentiated from traditional retail distribution partnerships in that the manufacturer usually maintains a single product management system that electronically feeds into multiple partners. These partners can be a comparison shopping engine like Google Product Search, a search engine like Bing Marketplace, an online marketplace like Amazon, or online shopping malls like Yatego. Between 2005 and 2010, multichannel distribution became a significant part of the overall ecommerce universe. The key factor in the development of multichannel ecommerce has been the advent of online marketplaces, which aggregate product and inventory information from multiple merchants to display on their own sites, either in a branded or a non-branded fashion. Companies like Amazon, eBay, Buy.com, Shop.com, and Overstock all allow online merchants to synchronize product information to their product and inventory databases and generally receive a commission for goods sold through their marketplaces. According to Amazon.com, up to 40 percent of its revenue is derived through the sales of third-party goods through its Merchants and Amazon Associates programs.

The 3rd Quarter 2010 Retail E-Commerce Sales Report released in November 2010 by the U.S. Census Bureau stated that the estimated U.S. retail e-commerce sales for the third quarter of 2010, adjusted for seasonal variation, but not for price changes, was US$41.5 billion, an increase of 4 percent from the second quarter of 2010. Total retail sales for the third quarter of 2010 were estimated at US$978.7 billion, an increase of 0.8 percent from the second quarter of 2010.

E-mail and Messaging Services. One of the primary attractions of the Internet is e-mail and messaging. Most companies and services providing Internet access to consumers also offer one or more e-mail addresses for each account opened, which allows subscribers to communicate with anyone who has access to the Internet. In the late 1990s and early 2000s, corporate e-mail and messaging were important software markets, and products were all-inclusive systems for internal corporate communication as well as outside e-mail. The industry's leading vendors in e-mail and messaging included IBM-owned Lotus Development Corp. (Lotus Notes and cc:Mail), Microsoft (Microsoft Outlook and Entourage), and Novell (GroupWise).

The advent of social media has dramatically altered, and many say, enhanced connectivity and communications. Facebook is a privately owned social network service. As of July 2010 Facebook had more than 500 million active users. Quantcast estimated that Facebook has 135.1 million monthly unique U.S.-based visitors. A January 2009 *Compete.com* study ranked Facebook as the most used social network by worldwide monthly active users, followed by MySpace. In 2010 there were hundreds of social media sites offering everything from blogs to dating Web sites. Some of the most visited social networking/media sites at the end of the first decade of the twenty-first century included Facebook, MySpace, youtube.com, twitter.com, and LinkedIn. Communication tools, such as Constant Contact and Vertical Response, have made interacting with friends, customers, and potential customers a relatively easy and inexpensive way for nonprofit and for profit businesses to stay in touch with each other.

Web Site Hosting, Design, and Programming. Many companies specialize in Web hosting, Web site design, and programming services. Web hosting services provide server or network space to companies or individuals who want to post a Web site on the Internet. This type of service is often included among the service offerings of larger Internet service providers, sometimes as part of a package that customers receive when they sign up for Internet access. For example, an access provider might make a certain amount of server disk space available to each customer who purchases a service contract. Customers can then design and post their Web site on the Internet using that ISP's network resources.

In addition, ISPs often offer design services, although that segment of the industry is served largely by small, specialized firms or independent contractors. Much like the early software industry, start-up costs for Web site design businesses are relatively inexpensive with great revenue potential. Companies needing a Web site design might outsource overall Web site management to a company specializing in Web site design services, or they might hire their own Webmaster, who designs, programs, and maintains the company's site. Since Web sites range from small public relations tools to interactive commercial businesses, companies have to analyze their specific needs and resources before deciding how to design, post, and maintain their Web sites.

Web site designers are often called upon to perform the functions of several professionals, such as graphic artists, software programmers, and network administrators. Web sites need to be aesthetically pleasing so they appeal to Internet "surfers" and bring visitors back to their site. If a site is even slightly complex and requires tasks such as database access and manipulation or e-commerce, more extensive programming than the Internet's standard publishing language of hypertext markup language (HTML) is needed. Maintaining the Web site and ensuring that its host network runs smoothly can be additional responsibilities. Therefore many companies offering comprehensive Web services hire specialized personnel for each step.

In 2010, *HostingReview.com* listed the top 10 Web hosting providers as iPage, FatCow, justhost.com, ixwebhosting, HostPapa, bluehost, myhosting, GoDaddy, 1&1, and Yahoo! in that order. Each provides easy-to-navigate and utilize domain and Web site set ups with a variety of resources and templates that make Web hosting and design accessible to non-tech users.

Industry Regulation. The Internet consists of several thousand independent networks, each with its own administrative authorities. However, the general direction of the Internet is organized by the Internet Society, a voluntary membership organization whose stated purpose is to "promote global information exchange through Internet technology." Another authority, the Internet Network Information Center (InterNIC), is responsible for the registration of all computers and networks connected to the Internet, as well as for special consulting services to the member networks. The InterNIC is made up of several commercial organizations and operates under an agreement with the National Science Foundation.

However, the Internet Society and InterNIC do not regulate ongoing daily functions of the Internet, which is left to each network's administrators. These individual networks make rules and regulations for the use of their proprietary data networks and network services. Some networks prohibit commercial data traffic, while others prevent unsecured local and remote data traffic. Nevertheless, the Internet is free of restrictions on its use, despite recurring legislative initiatives in various parts of the world to limit or tax its use. Exceptions are in countries whose governments frown on the unregulated flow of information, such as China, where Internet users may not have the same privileges as their neighbors in South Korea.

Continuing regulation was keenly debated during the late 1990s and early 2000s. Domain name registration, which involves paying a fee to reserve a unique Web address, such as "hanknuwer.com," has continued to be a hot issue. Such registration is necessary because e-mail and Web page access is routed through standard Internet-wide name servers that link a textual address, like "hnuwer@ hanknuwer.com," with a coded numeric location of the proper host computer, such as an ISP's server. Thus, domain names are user-friendly names that serve as a front-end alias for the string of numbers and periods that represent an Internet server's technical address. A given Internet server may be host to hundreds of domain names and thousands of e-mail addresses. The Accredited Registrar Directory keeps listings of domain name registrars that record domain names.

In an effort to regulate domain name registration, the U.S. government reviewed a proposal to establish a nonprofit agency run by Internet users and technical experts to oversee regulation of domain name assignment and registration. The plan was not fully detailed, however. It allowed domain registries and top-level domains (TLDs), such as ".com," ".edu," ".gov," and ".org," to be created, but attempted to impose U.S. government mandates for global standards. In June 1998, the Clinton administration announced that the United States was no longer pursuing control over management of Internet addresses. On June 6, 1998, Amy Harmon reported in *The New York Times* that an international nonprofit organization would assume global control of Internet domain names for everyone from major corporations to individuals who wanted to establish Web sites. It would also be given the authority to establish "top-level domains," that indicate the type of Web site, such as ".web," and would mediate disputes between companies or individuals seeking the same Web site domain. The shift in control of domain names was considered to be a continuation of the move to self-government of the Internet.

Encryption has been another subject of much proposed legislation. U.S. government agencies wanted access to encrypted files for law enforcement purposes, but were meeting resistance due to citizens' concerns about protecting their privacy. Privacy advocates feared that the technology used by law enforcement officials also could serve as a mechanism for increased encroachment on the free exchange of ideas, data, and information over the Internet.

Encryption was also being examined by European Union Commissioner Martin Bangemann, who proposed the development of an international charter to deal with the issue. In the United States, a Federal Information Processing Standard (FIPS) was adopted for the Advanced Encryption Standard FIPS-197. This standard identified "a FIPS-approved symmetric encryption algorithm that could be used by U.S. government organizations (and others) to protect sensitive information," according to the National Institute of Standards and Technology (NIST), an agency of the U.S. Department of Commerce's Technology Administration.

In 2010, the Obama administration proposed a stepped-up approach to policing Internet privacy that called for new laws and the creation of a new position to oversee the effort. The strategy was expected to be unveiled in a report from the U.S. Commerce Department. As of 2010, no comprehensive U.S. law protected consumer privacy online. Internet privacy issues generally were policed by the FTC, which could take action only if a privacy-violating action is deemed "deceptive" or "unfair."

BACKGROUND AND DEVELOPMENT

The Internet is a result of a U.S. government project conducted during the 1970s by the Department of Defense Advanced Research Projects Agency (ARPA). This project, known as the ARPANET, was designed to be a wide-area network (WAN) service for computer communications. Standard networking protocol, a communications protocol for exchanging data between computers on a network, was developed in 1973 and 1974. This protocol became known as TCP/IP or the "IP suite" of protocols. TCP/IP enabled ARPANET computers to communicate regardless of the operating system or hardware in use. Other such protocols, termed "heterogeneous," include UNIX, an operating system developed during the same period, which became almost synonymous with TCP/IP. Due to its low cost, UNIX soon spread to educational institutions around the United States. Multi-user systems like UNIX soon became the most popular method of accessing computer network communications.

Once information processing (IP) protocols were in place, much of the software and services that make up the Internet appeared. The basic services for remote connectivity,

file transfer, and electronic mail (e-mail) began appearing in the mid- to late 1970s. The Usenet news system appeared in 1981, Gopher made its debut in 1982, and the revolutionary World Wide Web appeared in 1989. By 1990, ARPANET was connected to many other networks, and its role as the Internet network backbone was taken over by the NSFNET, which was funded by the National Science Foundation. Networking companies and organizations providing data connections to Internet hosts continued providing easy global network access.

In the late 1990s and early 2000s, the Internet consisted of thousands of computer networks that utilized a common set of protocols to establish worldwide communications. Users accessed the Internet through individual networks at educational and commercial institutions, via commercial Internet access providers, and through other organizations. Each individual network was controlled by a different organization; was a different size; and used a range of network technologies, operating systems, and hardware. However, all were united by common communications protocols and services.

Regulatory mandates will continue to drive organizations to comply with security standards to avoid fines. However, IBM security researchers warned that many business customers, especially those that only focus on the minimum requirements for passing an audit, will discover that the regulations are a guideline and will be blindsided in the long run.

CURRENT CONDITIONS

By 2002, when many "dot-coms" were failing and filing for bankruptcy, analysts became increasingly realistic about the Internet. In the fourth quarter of 2001, domain name registrations dropped for the first time, partly because speculators, who had chosen domain names with plans to sell them, later opted not to renew their registrations when they failed to find buyers. While online activity per person dropped 10 percent from 2000 to 2002, it continued to command a reasonably high average of 83 minutes each day. By mid-2004, conditions were improving along with the overall U.S. economy.

A record US $18.5 billion had been spent for holiday shopping online in 2003, according to combined data from Nielsen NetRatings, Harris Interactive, and Goldman Sachs. This represented a 35 percent increase from 2002 levels of US$13.7 billion. According to figures released for March 2005 by Nielsen NetRatings, there were more than 451 million home-based Internet users worldwide, 299 million of whom visited an average of 1,148 Web pages each month. Nielsen excluded government, education, and pornographic sites from its ratings figures.

In 2005, security continued to be the central focus of the Internet services industry. IBM's Global Business

Security Index Report reported that in 2004, the number of known viruses had increased 25 percent over 2003 levels, reaching 112,438. In 2002, 0.5 percent of all e-mails scanned contained a virus, but by 2004, that figure had increased to 6.9 percent. In addition, IBM reported that 73 percent of all e-mail was unsolicited "spam."

Security measures to protect users from "phishing," a scheme to trick people into revealing personal financial and identity data, including credit card, bank account, and social security numbers, by luring them to a fraudulent Web site, resulted in U.S. banks and credit card companies spending US$1.2 billion in 2003. IBM reported that the number of phishing e-mails increased 5,000 percent in 2004. An example of phishing is an e-mail message that appears to be from a legitimate financial company requesting that the recipient verify account data. In order to appear legitimate, such e-mails sometimes include actual stolen logos and information from the real company. However, the attacks are often initiated by organized crime groups in faraway locales, such as Russia or South Korea.

As of November 2010, a total of 124,837,774 domain names were registered and active reports *DomainTools.com*. Of those, 155,886 were new and 126,937 were transferred.

According to the FBI, in 2010 the most common Internet scams were letters of credit fraud; non-delivery of merchandise; credit card fraud; investment fraud; business fraud and Nigerian letter, or "419" fraud.

The number of U.S. households with Internet access was expected to reach 89 million by 2007, an increase of 33 percent from 2002. That growth stimulated the Internet's recovery from the dot-com collapse of the early 2000s. Online holiday sales in 2003 reached a record US$18.5 billion, which prompted projections of 200 million Americans spending US$120 billion online in 2004, according to *InternetWeek*.

In the mid-2000s, ISPs benefited from increasing use of high-speed and broadband Internet connections, which provided a means to transmit large files and to receive streaming audio and video feeds. E-commerce worldwide was supported by broadband connections, especially in the United States and the European Union, which in turn created new job opportunities. In 2002, there were 14.4 million high-speed Internet subscribers, up 6.4 million from 2001. Leichtman Research predicted that high-speed subscribers would surpass "narrowband" subscribers in 2005, and would reach 49 million by the end of 2007. The number of high-speed subscribers in Europe was expected to reach 41 million in 2006, with the most subscribers in Germany and the United Kingdom. The leading means of access was expected to be DSL, except in the Netherlands, where more subscribers

were expected to make their Internet connections using cable modems.

The primary use of the Internet was expected to move increasingly from e-commerce to communications, following a trend that had begun in the early 2000s. For example, Voice over Internet Protocol (VoIP) allowed low-cost long distance voice communication and videoconferencing over the Internet. The VoIP market was projected to increase from US$46 million in 2001 to more than US$36 billion by 2008. According to Atari founder Nolan Bushnell in a June 10, 2003, article in *Business Week Online*, "the distinction between talking on the phone and watching movies and playing games will become blurred" as varied media combine over the Internet.

Competition in the African Internet market had intensified when the Pan-African ISP Africa Online introduced a pay-as-you-go package called Infinet Flex. Africa Online's goal was to increase its revenues from bundled Internet products. Group head of marketing Salma Mazrui reported that market research indicated a significant market for pay-as-you-go packages. In 2007 Africa Online was shifting its marketing from dial-up to offer an increased number of wireless products through Infinet Flex.

A survey conducted by the Pew Research Center in 2010 reported that adoption of broadband Internet access had slowed dramatically over the previous year. Two-thirds of American adults (66 percent) had a broadband internet connection at home by 2010, which is only slightly more than the 63 percent with a high-speed home connection in 2009. Most demographic groups experienced flat-to-modest broadband adoption growth during 2010. The notable exception to this trend was among African Americans, who experienced 22 percent year-over-year broadband adoption growth. In 2009, 65 percent of whites and 46 percent of African Americans were broadband users. In 2010, 67 percent of whites and 56 percent of African Americans are broadband users.

By a 53 percent to 41 percent margin, Americans said they did not believe that the spread of affordable broadband should be a major government priority. Contrary to what some might suspect, non-Internet users were less likely than current users to say the government should place a high priority on the spread of high-speed connections. This report is based on the findings of a daily tracking survey on Americans' use of the Internet. The results in this report were based on data from telephone interviews conducted by Princeton Survey Research Associates International between April 29, and May 30, 2010, among a sample of 2,252 adults ages 18 and older.

RESEARCH AND TECHNOLOGY

Programming languages have been very important to Internet development, although they generally are related specifically to the software development and programming industries. Examples of Internet languages in high use are the industry standard HTML (Hypertext Markup Language) and more extensive languages, such as Java, Perl, and CGI. Although the lines often blur, HTML differs from other languages in that it is primarily a system of tags for various document attributes and structures, such as fonts, colors, and image placement, while the other programming languages offer more powerful development tools to create entire processes. For example, a developer could write a program to validate a user's password. The end-product of HTML programming is an encoded, tagged document, and the output of the more sophisticated languages is a process-oriented script or program. HTML is the only requisite for producing pages on the World Wide Web, but other programming languages are used for all but the most basic Web pages. Additional languages first developed for mainframe or PC applications, such as C++ and Visual Basic, are also used to build Web sites.

HTML was the first and best-known Internet language. Its simplicity, however, meant that to complete complex tasks like database manipulation on the Internet, more complex languages like Java and Perl had to be developed and used in conjunction with HTML. Proponents of HTML responded by adding such technologies as Dynamic HTML, cascading style sheets, and tags that allowed additional functionality. However, many developers continued to look for a standard that offered some of the same options that higher-level programming languages did, especially for site automation and interoperability. One such effort was an adaptation of SGML (Standard Generalized Markup Language) called the XML (Extensible Markup Language). HTML is also an application of SGML principles, but is much simpler than XML, which was designed to foster the creation of other markup languages. XML defines a document's structure rather than simply its display format and allows users to define their own tags.

PHP: Hypertext Preprocessor is a widely used, general-purpose scripting language designed to produce dynamic web pages. PHP code is embedded into the HTML source document and interpreted by a Web server with a PHP processor module, which then generates the Web page. PHP code is processed by an interpreter application in command-line mode performing desired operating system operations and producing program output on its standard output channel. It may also function as a graphics application. PHP is available as a processor for most servers and as a stand-alone interpreter on most operating systems and computing platforms. PHP has been in continuous development since it was originally created by Rasmus Lerdorf in 1995.

Another area of research in Web site development was personalization, which can act as the equivalent of a store's salespeople, sizing up customers and making recommendations. Although the supporting technology could be expensive to design and implement, personalization was becoming a valuable marketing tool. The software performs tasks like collaborative filtering, which links user preferences to databases containing user input. Such software was costly to develop, however, with a price range between US$15,000 and US$50,000. Some companies were specializing in personalization software development, offering services on a contract basis so site developers could contain costs.

INDUSTRY LEADERS

Internet Service Providers (ISPs)/Infrastructure Enterprises.
America Online. America Online, which is better known as AOL, was the world's leading Internet services provider in 2005, with 34 million members in 12 countries. Its parent, Time Warner, was the leading media company in the world. AOL was the first company to offer instant messaging and was the first service designed specifically for broadband customers. Founded in 1985, its customers were sending 450 million e-mails and 1.5 billion instant messages everyday by 2005. Its subsidiaries included ISPs Netscape and CompuServe, MapQuest, and AIM (AOL Instant Messenger). The company had partnered with Wal-Mart Stores Inc. to offer a co-branded AOL/Wal-Mart dial-up service that was a version of CompuServe. In December 2009, Time Warner spun AOL off into a publicly traded company, ending their eight-year relationship.

In 2004, AOL reported subscriber and advertising fee revenues of more than US$8.6 million, with US$934 million in net operating income. The number of subscribers had been declining, a trend that was expected to continue due to the maturation of its market for dial-up service and the migration of customers to high-speed broadband or lower cost dial-up services. By 2007, AOL reported more than 100 million users with online access provided to more than 8.5 million subscribers. Its 2009 reported revenue was US$3.257 billion.

Approximately 84 percent of 1,000 British Internet users surveyed in an AOL study on privacy and advertisements claimed that they would not release income and personal information online, although 89 percent would give that same kind of information to AOL. "Our research identified a gap between what people say and what they do when it comes to protecting sensitive information online," said AOL Chief Privacy Officer Jules Polonetsky. Results of the survey also indicated that increased awareness of potential privacy violations did not translate to increased concern.

According to Stephen Ellis in the August 19, 2008, edition of *Australian IT* an AOL study about user's attitudes about advertisements included questions about privacy. Approximately 84 percent of the consumers claimed they would not give income details online, but 89 percent responded later in the survey that they were willing to give AOL that information. "Our research identified a gap between what people say and what they do when it comes to protecting sensitive information online," said AOL Chief Privacy Officer Jules Polonetsky. In addition, the survey showed that the more people understood about nature and risks of online privacy violations, the less they were concerned about them. Polonetsky went on to say that "Personalizing content and delivering relevant advertising online will only succeed for consumers and for advertisers if it is done in a trustworthy and transparent manner."

Microsoft Network. One of seven product segments of Microsoft, Microsoft Network (MSN) provides worldwide personal communications services, including e-mail and instant messaging, and information services, such as search products and information and purchasing portals. The company derives its revenues from providing Internet-related access, software subscriptions, e-mail services, bill payment services, and radio from subscribers and advertisers. According to studies by Nielson Net Ratings and comScore Media Metrix, MSN Web sites are visited by more than 350 million users every month. MSN Hotmail is one of the world's largest e-mail services, with more than 187 million accounts, and MSN Messenger is one of the world's largest instant messaging services with more than 135 million accounts.

By 2004, MSN was earning more than US$1 billion in revenues from advertising and reporting a 40 percent growth over the 2003, as overall revenue grew 13 percent to US$2.22 billion. The company was not expecting the growth trend to continue in 2005 as projected declines in the number of subscribers to its narrowband service would offset any gains made in advertising and premium Web services.

In 2006, Microsoft repackaged online content, e-mail instant messaging, and other digital community services as part of Windows Live. MSN reported more than 460 million users each month through more than 40 country-specific sites by 2008.

Earthlink. Founded in 1994 with only 10 modems, Earthlink became one of the largest ISPs in the United States. By 1995, the company had formed an alliance with UUNET Technologies that allowed Earthlink to offer dial-up access in 98 cities across the United States. Earthlink's 1999 merger with MindSpring made it the second largest ISP in the country. An alliance with Apple Computers in 2000 made Earthlink the official ISP for Apple systems. In 2004, the company reported revenues

of US$1.38 billion and a positive net income for the first time in several years. In January 2005, Earthlink entered a joint venture agreement with Korea's leading mobile communications company to market wireless voice and data services in the United States. By 2007, the company reported revenues of US$1.22 billion and 998 employees. By 2010, their reported workforce had been reduced to just under 600 employees.

Earthlink was considering focusing on dial-up access to add more subscribers by acquiring the dial-up customers of other ISPs, such as AOL. The idea was to create economies of scale with an existing customer base and reduce costs while generating profits that could be used to expand.

MCI Inc. MCI Inc., formerly Worldcom, was a leading player in the Internet industry, operating one of the world's fastest and largest IP networks under parent company Verizon. In 2004, the company reported US$20.7 billion in revenues, about 23 percent of which came from large global corporate and government customers with complex communication systems, 44 percent from domestic U.S. customers, and the remainder from international and wholesale markets. However, MCI reported net losses in all three sectors, for a total loss of US$3.2 billion in 2004.

MCI's Internet roots date to 1997, when it acquired MFS Communications for US$12 billion. The deal included the Internet infrastructure of UUNET Technologies Inc., which MFS had recently acquired. Once based in Fairfax, Virginia, UUNET had been founded in May of 1987. It went public in 1995 and merged in 1996 with MFS Communications. After its acquisition by Worldcom, UUNET became the world's largest ISP. UUNET focused exclusively on offering businesses and online service providers access to the Internet. UUNET developed one of the largest systems of Internet networks in the world. UUNET owned and operated national networks in the United States, Canada, the United Kingdom, Germany, Belgium, the Netherlands, and Luxembourg. It also had extensive partnerships in Europe and the Asia/Pacific region. UUNET's strengths included direct fiber-optic connections between Europe, North America, and Asia. In addition, satellite services were available for remote areas that lacked other connections. UUNET also offered products and services like Internet access, Web site development, wholesale network access, and Internet security. In the early 2000s, UUNET recorded the highest Internet backbone access speed level of 10 Gbps OC-192c to that time. In 2002, most of the UUNET services were offered under the WorldCom name.

WorldCom was established in 1983 as Long Distance Discount Services (LDDS). LDDS began by leasing a wide-area telecommunications service (WATS) line and resold time to other businesses. Over the years,

LDDS was capitalized through the acquisition of other businesses, such as Telephone Management Corp. in 1988, National Telecommunications in 1991, and IDB WorldCom in 1994. In 1995, LDDS acquired WilTel Network Services and changed its name to WorldCom. That year, the company hired Michael Jordan as its spokesperson. In 1996, WorldCom acquired UUNET Technologies, MFS, and BLT Technologies, successfully becoming an ISP. In early 1998, WorldCom took control of CompuServe and America Online's network units as part of an agreement in which AOL acquired CompuServe's consumer business. That year, the company formed its first international partnership, teaming with MCI and Spain's Telefonica to expand the company's reach in Europe and Latin America.

WorldCom became a telecommunications giant following its 1998 acquisition of MCI Communications Corp., which was contested on antitrust grounds by industry participants. The company provided local and international telecommunications services, such as voice, data, and paging services, and Internet access. In addition, it provided services over its own network that included fiber-optic cables around several major cities and between the United States and the United Kingdom, as well as a joint project with Cable & Wireless PLC involving the sale of MCI's Internet backbone business. The company leased and resold excess network capacity and services to other phone companies, businesses, and government agencies. WorldCom's Internet services focused on offering network access through integrated and dedicated lines.

In 2000, the company was reorganized into two divisions: MCI Group and WorldCom Group. The former division concentrated on the consumer market, including dial-up Internet services, while WorldCom managed networking, data, and Internet operations. In 2002, WorldCom filed for Chapter 11 bankruptcy protection amid charges of accounting fraud and an investigation by the U.S. Securities and Exchange Commission (SEC). By April of 2004, the company had installed new executive leadership, reorganized as MCI Inc., relocated its headquarters to Ashburn, Virginia, and paid several billion dollars to settle matters with the SEC. In 2006, Verizon acquired MCI.

Navigation Services. By October 2010, new Web browsers appeared, including Firefox, Google Chrome, Safari, Opera, Mobile Browser, and Bing. Browser usage statistics vary significantly in different geographic regions globally. In South Korea, the most used browser is Internet Explorer, with 95 percent usage, because of a law requiring active-x be used in financial transactions. This law was removed in June 2010. In Germany, Firefox is the most popular browser, with 60 percent usage. In Ukraine the leading browser is Opera, with 35 percent

share. Worldwide use for browsers on Wikimedia was reported as 48 percent using Internet Explorer, 30 percent using Firefox, 13 percent using Google Chrome, and 8 percent using Safari.

Yahoo! Inc. Yahoo! was created in 1994 by Stanford University graduate students David Filo and Jerry Yang. In 1995, Yahoo! and publisher Ziff-Davis launched an online and print magazine titled *Yahoo! Internet Life*. When Yahoo! went public in 1996, it was one of the first and most successful initial public offerings in the Internet services industry. Yahoo! expanded further through strategic alliances and partnerships, including Netscape. Yahoo! and Netscape created a topic-based navigation service to be used on the Netscape Communicator browser. However, Yahoo! acted with excessive confidence in the chaotic economy of the late 1990s and early 2000s and for a time stumbled badly with losses, debts, and payroll commitments.

Yahoo! Inc. was one of the first navigation services on the Internet. Unlike many of its competitors that relied on computer programs, Yahoo! used human effort to organize its search engine. In 2005, it continued to be the most widely used Internet search engine in the world, reaching 345 million unique users in 25 countries and providing service in 13 languages. Revenues in 2004 were approximately US$3.6 billion, with recorded net income of almost US$840 million. Eighty-eight percent of the company's revenue was derived from advertising. The fee paid by advertisers was based on the number of times an image or text appeared on a page for a viewer. In addition, fees were received for consumer and business listings, including those related to job markets, auto sales, and real estate sales. Transaction revenue was being received from sales made from Yahoo!'s travel and shopping portals. The remaining 12 percent of revenue was coming from the provision of Internet broadband and dial-up services.

In 2001 and 2002, under newly appointed Chief Executive Terry Semel, Yahoo! assured its niche as the most consulted network on the Internet when it purchased the popular employment service HotJobs, while simultaneously, and somewhat ironically, slashing its payroll through layoffs. In 2002, Yahoo! moved toward increased profitability when it offered users not only its free search engine, but also a method to purchase hard-to-locate articles for a fee. In 2005, Yahoo! announced that it had entered an alliance with Verizon to deliver co-branded broadband service. By 2007, Yahoo! reported sales of $7 billion and 14,300 employees. In 2008, Microsoft rejected Yahoo!'s unsolicited buyout offer.

Bing. Bing (formerly Live Search, Windows Live Search, and MSN Search) is a Web search engine created by Microsoft. Bing was unveiled by Microsoft in May 2009. Notable differences from other sites included the listing of search suggestions as queries that are entered, along with a list of related searches (called "Explorer pane") based on semantic technology from Powerset that Microsoft had purchased in 2008. In July 2009, Microsoft and Yahoo! announced a deal in which Bing would power Yahoo! Search.

Google. The name of the search engine Google is derived from "googol," the number 1 followed by 100 zeros, and the company site refers to the symbolism of the term as it tries to organize the seemingly infinite universe called the Internet. Google's origins go back to 1996 when Stanford University graduate students Larry Page and Sergey Brin created a method to search what they called the "back links" to a given Web site. Their first search engine was called BackRub. In 1998, with investments from friends, family, and Sun Microsystems co-founder Andy Bechtolsheim, Page and Brin began Google. A year later, armed with sufficient venture capital, the founders left their humble leased space and opened a headquarters in Mountain View, California. Managing to lure AOL/Netscape as the first of many clients, Google became an overnight financial success in 1999. In 2000 the company reported 18 million user hits a day and was proclaimed by many as the most efficient search engine on the Internet. In 2002 the company made another giant gain when it enticed EarthLink, Inc., the number three U.S. Internet service provider, to use the Google search engine instead of its former search engine, Overture.

By mid-2004, Google had become the largest search engine in the world, with nearly 82 million users every month. More than 50 percent of Google's users were located outside of the United States. The site offered results in 35 different languages and was ranked as the top search engine in Australia, France, Germany, Italy, the Netherlands, Spain, Switzerland, and the United Kingdom. In 2004, the company had sales of almost US$3.2 billion, an increase of more than 117 percent over the previous year, with net income of US$399 million. Although the company initially derived its earnings from license fees for the use of its search engine on other Web sites, by 2004, the bulk of its revenue came from the sale of advertising. In 2002, Google's advertising fees began to be based on the number of times a user clicked on an advertiser's text message when it appeared on a search screen. For 2009, Google reported sales of US$23.65 billion and 23,331 employees.

In April of 2004, Google announced its initial public offering (IPO) in an auction format, which generated a great deal of publicity. The auction process, which began on August 13, 2004, was criticized by some observers. For example, in the August 15, 2004, issue of the *Boston Globe,* columnist Steven Syre called the auction an "unnecessarily complicated, confusing process," marked by "an emphasis on secrecy when transparency should have been the standard." However, the IPO was expected to raise as much as US$3 billion for Google.

Google Chrome was able to provide a lot of data about consumers, but security issues about privacy had the potential to reduce the expected profits. Web strategy expert Google Chrome had the potential to provide extraordinary information about online consumers. Behavioral targeting for Internet users continued to be controversial. In July 2008, the U.S. House and Senate conducted hearings about online privacy. In August 2008, members of the House Committee on Energy and Commerce sent letters to 33 Internet and cable companies requesting details about their privacy practices.

Telecommunications. Telecommunications companies have been able to establish a strong foothold in the Internet services industry. The two industries are highly interrelated, and telecommunications companies are among those in the best technological position to take advantage of the opportunities available in the Internet marketplace. AT&T is an international telecommunications company that has expanded to include significant Internet services offerings. Many local and regional telecommunications companies offer similar services.

AT&T. AT&T was formed in 1899 when its name was changed from National Bell Telephone. The company held a virtual monopoly on the telecommunications market until 1968, when the FCC stripped AT&T of its telephone equipment monopoly and allowed specialized carriers like MCI access to the phone network, creating room for competition in long distance services. Another government suit led to the 1984 settlement that spun off seven "Baby Bells," leaving AT&T with long distance services and Western Electric. In a renewed focus on communications, AT&T divested NCR, Lucent Technologies, and AT&T Capital Corp. during the 1990s. In 1996 the company began offering Internet access through promotional deals with Excite, Infoseek, and Lycos to offer WorldNet services on their search engines. A pending deal with Yahoo! would allow users to purchase AT&T services from Yahoo! sites. Nevertheless, AT&T's most substantial transaction was its 1998 acquisition of Tele-Communications, Inc. (TCI), the United States' largest cable television service. In the Internet service industry, TCI had been developing its infrastructure to test Internet access bundled with its cable television service. AT&T already had a flourishing Internet service but lacked infrastructure for such bundling due to the limited speed and bandwidth over telephone lines.

Top-ranked long distance telephone service provider AT&T has made its presence known on the Internet primarily through its consumer-oriented WorldNet Internet access service. However, the company was also looking to gain market share as an ISP for businesses with AT&T WorldNet Business Services, including Internet dial-up or dedicated access over its backbone network. The company also offered virtual private networks and managed network services, data network services, and web site hosting though its AT&T Easy World Wide Web service. AT&T's 1997 revenues were US$51.3 billion. Revenues reached US$52.6 billion in 2001, but were down to US$30.5 billion in 2004. By that year, the company had divested its cable television services in order to focus on the business services market. In early 2005, the company had agreed to be acquired by SBC Communications.

In 2010, the survey company TopTenReviews listed the top 10 ISPs as a result of their market survey. Earth-Link was rated number 1 by consumers, followed by AOL, Comcast, MSN, NetZero, Verizon, AT&T, Juno, Qwest, and ISP.com.

A January 2010, article by Nielsen NetRatings reported that the telecommunications industry, the fourth largest industry to advertise online, was the fastest growing industry year-over-year in online advertising, increasing six percentage points in share of impressions. The wireless service segment led in online advertising with 52 percent of all telecommunications impressions in December 2004. The ISP/broadband segment came in second with 18 percent during the same time, while the local/long distance segment took 15 percent of impressions in December 2004. The share of advertising for these industry segments remained relatively the same as compared to 2003.

MAJOR COUNTRIES IN THE INDUSTRY

The Internet has been marked by astounding growth. In 2002, there were 533 million users. Growth was expected continue, reaching 945 million users worldwide in 2004 and exceed 1 billion users by 2007. During the early 2000s, there were nearly 278 million Internet users in the United States and 32 million in Canada. The industry was dominated by the United States, with Europe and the Asia-Pacific region playing lesser roles. According to *Latin Trade*, in March 2004, the investment firm Morgan Stanley indicated that in Japan and North America, 60 percent of the population would be using the Internet by 2005. In Europe, penetration was expected to reach 46 percent, while use among Latin Americans was forecast to be only 13 percent.

Business Week reported that the United States was home to many of the world's leading Web sites in 2004 domestically and abroad. For example, Google reached 36.7 percent of all European Internet users, followed by MSN (35.7 percent), Microsoft.com (33.3 percent), eBay

(20.7 percent), and Yahoo! (19.7 percent). In sixth place was France' Wanadoo (13.2 percent), followed by Italy's Tiscali (10.1 percent) and Spain's Lycos Europe (9.8 percent). Other leaders in the European market included U.S.-based Amazon.com (9.6 percent) and Germany's T-Online (9.3 percent).

In spite of U.S. domination, in the early 2000s there was a substantial market for international expansion in countries with lucrative markets in Latin America, Asia, and Eastern Europe. All had completed the first stages of technological advancement and were led by government officials who realized the importance of advanced communications to sustain national economies in the so-called information age.

The most sought after market was China, which planned to privatize many state-owned utilities. Although the Chinese government presented many roadblocks for potential ISPs, the market continued to appeal to investors. There were 12 million Chinese users in 2000, but that number had reached 80 million by mid-2004. By 2006, Piper Jaffray forecasts published in *Business Week* indicated that 153 million Chinese citizens would be online, surpassing the United States. Such figures led Yahoo! to introduce a Chinese search engine called Yisou in June of 2004, on the heels of competitor Google, which had purchased an interest in a Chinese search engine called Baidu.

In an interview with *China Daily*, Nokia President and Chief Executive Officer Olli Pekka Kallasvuo acknowledged that "many industries here are converging, or even sometimes colliding." Nokia was working hard to expand beyond just being the world's largest mobile phone maker. As a part of that mission, and in response Apple's and Google's inroads in the China market, Nokia launched an online platform called Ovi, reflecting the company's desire to become an Internet company. Kallasvuo described Ovi as being "a brand with a wide service offering" and distinctive "scope."

Nate Anderson wrote in *ars Technica* in July 2010 that only two ISPs in China provide service for 20 percent of Internet users worldwide. China Telecom has 55 million subscribers, and China Unicom has slightly more than 40 million subscribers. The other ISPs serve mature markets, including third place NTT in Japan, with 17 million subscribers. Rounding out the top 10 in 2010 were U.S.-based Comcast with 17 million;, U.S.-based AT&T with 14 million; Germany's Deutsche Telekom with 12 million; Time Warner Cable and Verizon of the United States with 9 million and 8 million, respectively; France Telecom with 7 million; and KT with 6 million.

BIBLIOGRAPHY
"Africa Online Ups Stakes in Internet Services with New Package." *IT News Africa*, 3 September 2008. Available from www.itnewsafrica.com/?p=1015.

"Aging Internet Slows Down." *Daily Telegraph* (Sydney), 30 March 2002.

Clifford, Stephanie. "Will Google's Chrome Help or Hurt Advertisers?" *The New York Times,* 3 September 2008.

"Datamonitor: Broadband Adoption on the Up in Europe." *Nua Internet Surveys,* 20 March 2003. Available from www.nua.ie/surveys.

"E-commerce Takes Off; To Come." *The Economist* (US), 15 May 2004.

Ellis, Stephen. "Net Users Lower Guard Too Easily." *Australian IT,* 19 August 2008. Available from www.australianit.news.com.au/story/0,24897,24202907-5013640,00.html.

"eMarketer: Worldwide B2B Revenues to Pass One Trillion." *Nua Internet Surveys,* 1 April 2003. Available from www.nua.ie/surveys.

Fisher, Dennis. "Worms Wreak Havoc on the Net in '03." *eWeek,* 3 April 2003.

Gardner, Dana. "Netscape Pulls It Together." *Info World,* 1 June 1998.

"Global Internet Index: Average Usage." Nielsen NetRatings, March 2005. Available from www.nielsen-netratings.com.

"Global Usage, March 2004." *ClickZ,* 3 May 2004. Available from www.clickz.com.

Goldberg, Steven T. "Numbers Do Lie." *Kiplinger's Personal Finance Magazine,* April 2002.

Grech, Herman. "Software Piracy Drops, But Is Still High." *The Times* (Malta), 14 August 2004.

Green, Heather. "China's Great March Online." *Business Week,* 12 July 2004.

Hafner, Katie. "Living the Broadband Life." *The New York Times,* 15 July 2004.

Harmon, Amy. "U.S., in Shift, Drops Its Effort to Manage Internet Addresses." *The New York Times,* 6 June 1998.

"IBM Global Business Security Index Report." IBM, 9 February 2005. Available from www-1.ibm.com.

"The Internet Has Enormous Impact on 'Offline' Spending." *The Online Reporter,* 13 September 2003.

Internet Market Research. Available from www.marketresearch.com.

Internet Usage. Available from www.marketresearch.com.

Keizer, Gregg. "Online Retailers Tally Record Holiday Sales." *Information Week,* 7 January 2004. Available from www.informationweek.com.

Kharif, Olga. "The Net: Now, Folks Can't Live Without It." *Business Week Online,* 10 June 2003. Available from www.businessweek.com.

Lardner, James. "Yahoo! Rising." *U.S. News & World Report,* 18 May 1998.

"Leichtman Research: More High-Speed Net Subscribers in U.S." *Nua Internet Surveys,* 2 April 2003. Available from www.nua.ie/surveys.

Marsan, Carolyn Duffy. "Domain Name Registrations Drop." *Network World,* 28 January 2002.

Morrison, Scott. "EarthLink Bets on Dial-Up." *The Wall Street Journal,* 20 August 2008.

"The Nearly World Wide Web." *Latin Trade,* March 2004.

"Net Gains in the Marketspace." *Information Strategy,* June 1997.

Pew Research Center. *Pew Internet and American Life Project* . Available from www.pewinternet.org.

Reinhardt, Robert, and Robert D. Hof. "Europe Hits the E-Mall. U.S. Companies Dominate as Web Sales Explode Across the Continent." *Business Week,* 12 July 2004.

Roberts, Paul. "Security: The Year Ahead." *InfoWorld,* 5 January 2004.

"Sector Shake-Up Forces Nokia to Change Tack," 2 September 2008. Available from chinadaily.com.cn.

"TNT Trends: Technology Predictions 2005." Deloitte Touche Tohmatsu, January 2005. Available from www.deloitte.com.

Web Hosting Overview. Hosting Review Web site. Available from hosting-review.com.

Wildstrom, Stephen H. "Traffic Growth Isn't Using Up the Internet." *Business Week,* 3 September 2008.

SIC 2711

NEWSPAPER PUBLISHING

NAICS CODE(S)

511110. Firms in the newspaper industry develop, publish, and market newspapers, and many, although not all, perform their own printing as well. In the first decade of the twenty-first century, some print journalism outlets were expected to merge with other media such as cable television news, Internet news, text television, and telefax newspaper, as part of the trend toward media convergence according to industry analysts. A few global operations had converged this way by the end of 2010. See also **Periodical Publishing**.

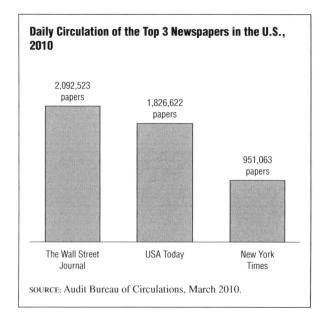

Daily Circulation of the Top 3 Newspapers in the U.S., 2010

2,092,523 papers — The Wall Street Journal

1,826,622 papers — USA Today

951,063 papers — New York Times

SOURCE: Audit Bureau of Circulations, March 2010.

INDUSTRY SNAPSHOT

From the late 1990s through the first years of the twenty-first century, the newspaper industries in most mature markets such as Japan, the United States, and the European Union continued to experience declines in newspaper sales and advertising revenues. These industries all tried to capture younger readers in hopes of keeping them as life-long newspaper subscribers. Art Valjakka, editor in chief of *Turun Sanomat* in Finland, argued that conservative journalists would have to become multimedia proficient, as newspapers continued to converge with other media, such as cable television news, telefax newspaper, and Internet news on demand. In 2001, the World Association of Newspapers argued that all online newspaper access by readers needed to be counted to get a truer picture of the industry's health. As the Internet presence continued to grow, more print copies of newspapers declined as people seek immediate news on demand. In addition, most handheld devices, such as mobile phones and palm-size PCs, offered news on demand applications. To stay viable in the news industry, corporations were forced to join the electronic revolution.

Industry analysts worry about the financial health of print journalism, which is particularly threatened in wealthier nations where citizens have diminished reading skills and appreciation. In addition, the industry traditionally is subject to a slump in sales during recessions. In 2002, newspapers from London to Los Angeles admitted to experiencing the worst overall business slump since the early 1980s, according to *The Guardian* of London, which starkly stated that many citizens have forsaken newspapers to retrieve their news from the Internet, television, or radio. Some U.K. papers, such as *The Mirror,* point to 1946 as the last year in memory that sales had been so abysmal. By 2010, according to a survey conducted jointly by *Internet & American Life Project* and *Project for Excellence in Journalism,* "An overwhelming majority of Americans (92 percent) use multiple platforms to get their daily news."

Newsroom conditions had been no less gloomy in the United States, particularly after the terrorist attacks on September 11, 2001, led to a nationwide pulling of ads by the travel industry. In January 2002, the Washington Post Co., publishing home to *The Washington Post,* posted dismal fourth-quarter earnings for 2001 that were about 50 percent of fourth-quarter earnings in 2000. Because of investments and revenue declines of 14 percent in 2001, *The Washington Post*'s 2000 fourth-quarter income was US$37.7 million, for US$3.98 a share, compared to 2001 fourth-quarter earnings of US$14.5 million and US$1.53 a share. Overall, the picture was brighter for the full 2001 fiscal year as the company listed earnings of US$229.6 million, compared to US$136.5 million in 2000. As reported in *The Washington Post,* the company's revenue was flat at US$2.4 billion,

and operating revenues were 35 percent lower in 2001 than in 2000. In 2002, the *Post* noted that 2001 ad revenue at *The Wall Street Journal* had slipped 38 percent, and the *Philadelphia Inquirer* had a 14 percent advertising slump from 2000 levels.

As U.S. papers faltered economically, newspapers in Asia and South America saw their circulation and shares of advertising funds generally rise. By 2008, Asia published 74 percent of the world's top 100 dailies, 62 of which were published in India, China, and Japan. The largest newspaper market in the world was China, with a paid circulation of 107 million copies daily. India came second, with 99 million copies sold daily, followed by Japan (68 million), the United States (51 million, down from 2004's 55.6 million), and Germany (21 million). Although China led in total circulation, its main paper, *The People's Daily,* ranked eighth in the world in circulation, with three million copies sold worldwide.

Despite growth in some Asian markets, the newspaper industry in Korea had faced increasing challenges in 2004. According to data from the Korean Society for Journalism and Communication Studies, the country's nine largest newspapers experienced a 4.4 percent decrease in revenues in 2004, contributing to a 17 percent decline since 2002. Only four papers remained profitable. Aggressive competition from other papers, particularly the free dailies that had sprung up since Metro International launched *Metro* in Seoul in 2002, cut into circulation, as had competition from online and other news sources. According to the Korea Press Foundation, the subscription rate declined nearly 29 percent between 1996 and 2006. According to the report, there were 213 papers sold per 1,000 people; in comparison, the United Kingdom boasted 303 papers sold per 1,000 people.

To the surprise of some business insiders, the global newspaper industry reported a slight circulation gain in 2004, not only among developing markets but also in mature markets. The World Association of Newspapers (WAN) announced a 2.1 percent rise in global sales and a 5.4 percent increase in advertising revenue. Timothy Balding, former WAN Director General for Global Affairs and former CEO, described this growth as "extraordinarily positive" and noted that "it has been a very long time since we saw such a revival in so many mature markets." He attributed this success to new products, improved formats, new editorial approaches, and improvements in distribution and marketing. Furthermore, Balding added, advertising revenues had risen substantially, saying, "Despite the competitive challenges in the advertising market, newspapers have more than held their own, and their revenues are strongly on the increase again."

Jim Chisolm, a strategist at WAN's 2005 conference, suggested that new digital media will "accelerate the newspaper's renaissance" through such options as text messaging to announce breaking news, participatory activities like opinion polls and contests, and video feeds. Some of these strategies were used during the tsunami disaster in South Asia in late 2004, when text messaging services were sending information to readers more quickly than print or online services.

Throughout the world, newspapers, especially in more developed nations such as the United States and the United Kingdom, were forming partnerships with schools. In the 2000s, virtually all English-speaking publishers realized a need to counteract the long-developing trend toward declining newspaper readership, and reading in general among young adults, according to researchers such as Clark, Martire & Bartolomeo of Englewood Cliffs, New Jersey. Predictions were that readership would continue to decline in future generations unless some action was taken; only 40 percent of young adults in the U.S. read. Elsewhere in the world, the readership of young adults was quite high, as Singapore, for example, counted 92 percent of young adults as readers, and Canada counted 82 percent.

Bill Clark reminded his *Columbia Tribune* readers about some shocking observations made by others. Phillip Meyer predicted that the final printed newspaper would be delivered in 2043 in his book, *The Vanishing Newspaper*. In *The New Yorker* magazine article entitled "Out of Print," Eric Alterman acknowledged that "Only 19 percent of Americans between 18 and 34 even look at a daily paper; the average age of the American newspaper reader is 55 and climbing." Clark concluded that small-market papers would keep the industry going on beyond Meyer's expectations, saying that small-market papers "are the nerve centers of their communities." Newspapers were also fighting for their survival in small town America, but they continued to play key roles, such as allowing local advertisers to promote businesses.

ORGANIZATION AND STRUCTURE

In the first years of the 2000s, the newspaper industry continued to undergo a transition that began in the 1980s. Technological advances and greater competition from other media contributed to the newspaper industry's transformation. Technology both helped and hindered the industry by creating more efficient printing and production equipment, as well as by creating more alternatives, including cable television, satellite television, and the Internet. With the proliferation of alternative media, subscription circulation had peaked throughout much of the world by the 1980s. For example, Australia's newspaper consumption reached its apex in 1956, the United Kingdom's in 1957, the United States' in 1971, and Japan's in 1981. India, China, and other developing countries, on the other hand, comprised some of the

world's major growing newspaper markets in the 1990s and 2000s.

Some newspapers in small markets are distributed weekly, while large marketing areas have at least one daily newspaper available, including a feature-rich Sunday newspaper. For a time, many cities in the United States had two or more competing newspapers providing news. However, as female readers joined the workforce in increasing numbers, and so-called white-collar workers wanted their news delivered in the morning, many evening papers, which were sometimes owned by the same company producing the morning edition, folded.

The production of newspapers has always been controversial because editorial writers frequently clamor for environmental reforms, even though the newspaper industry itself is a threat to global forests. Publishers have largely begged off from the environmental consequences of publishing, complaining that the cost of newsprint already threatens the newspaper industry. By 2001, only a small number of companies produced newsprint, and publishers were jittery about the very real possibility that newsprint costs would escalate further. From the 1990s through the early 2000s, newspapers came under fire from environmentalists for hypocrisy and poor environmental practices when industry lobbyists pleaded with Congress to ease restrictions regarding the recycling of newsprint. Other environmentalists have berated the publishing industry for its use of contaminants in inks that are classified as pollutants.

Many newspapers in the United States, Canada, and Europe, and increasingly in other industrialized countries, are owned by large media conglomerates such as Dow Jones & Company Inc., Gannett, CanWest Global Communications Corp., Knight Ridder, News Corp., and Thomson International.

CanWest Global Communications Corp. (CanWest) is an excellent case study example of a modern newspaper company. Canada's largest media conglomerate with coast-to-coast assets, including newspapers, television and radio stations, multimedia production facilities, and Internet publishing operations, the company owns all or part of TV stations in Australia, Ireland, and New Zealand. It also owns a film production and distribution company and had plans to launch a book publishing division.

In addition, political parties and religious organizations also own and operate newspapers. Because of the costs involved in producing newspapers, many rely on subsidies from other businesses and institutions that buy newspapers to disseminate and influence information. Nevertheless, many small, independent newspapers continued to exist worldwide.

American City Business Journals (ACBJ), which was known for its specialized business journals, had become one of the largest publishers of metropolitan business newspapers in the United States. It served more than 4 million readers in 41 metropolitan areas. ACBJ also ran *Bizjournals*, the online version of the newspapers, and operated sporting news publications, such as *The Sporting News*, and its radio subsidiary, *Sporting News Radio*, the leading publisher of NASCAR magazines.

The World Newspaper Industry noted that newspaper costs could be sorted into five basic categories: newsprint, production, advertising sales, circulation and distribution, and administration. Labor costs were included in these categories and made up 50 percent of all newspapers' costs. Because of the high and escalating costs of newsprint, newspaper publishers implemented more efficient ways to reduce waste and began using lighter paper. Nevertheless, newsprint prices have risen throughout the world since the 1970s and were predicted to skyrocket as consolidations of newsprint manufacturers led to lessened choice supply and fewer newsprint suppliers.

Technological advances in the 1980s and 1990s, such as the adoption of computers, modems, and more efficient printing systems, reduced some of the industry's production costs during this period. Production costs were divided into prepress, printing, and building. Pre-press costs included news writing expenses, as well as expenses for page composition, photoengraving, and platemaking. Pre-press costs accounted for nearly 50 percent of all production expenses. Printing costs included production supplies and utilities needed for printing, while building costs included the operation and maintenance of the newspaper facilities.

Circulation expenses accounted for 75 percent of all circulation revenues for large newspapers and roughly 15 percent of overall newspaper costs. This part of the industry is the most labor intensive because workers must move the time-sensitive newspapers from the factories to the customers on a tight schedule. Distribution costs for large newspapers were higher than those for small papers because large papers were delivered to a wider geographical area and had to negotiate congested traffic and contend with maintenance of the delivery vehicle.

Censorship. In certain countries, such as Burma (run by the military junta called the State Peace and Development Council) and Nigeria, governments imposed direct censorship of the media including newspapers, according to the U.S. State Department, which viewed such heavy-handed censoring as an abuse of human rights. More commonly, in countries such as Egypt and Saudi Arabia, the censorship was less severe but still a repressive factor for journalists and the public alike. Censoring governments dictated what constitutes acceptable material for publication and often oversaw the news content even

before it was published. Other countries may have censored the media indirectly by establishing instructions and warnings that delineated the boundaries that journalists must respect. The World Association of Newspapers considered the killing of journalists to be the ultimate form of censorship.

The range of censorship varied from highly regulated newspaper industries in countries such as China or Burma to the staunchly defended free press in the United States and Canada. However, even free press nations adhered to forms of voluntary "self-censorship" in times of war, crisis, or other situations, in spite of objections by some journalists who proclaimed the public right to know all so that informed decisions could be made. At the request of the government or a member of the royal family, newspapers could be censored. For example, in Afghanistan in 2007 and 2008, there was a deal struck between the British media and the Ministry of Defense in the United Kingdom to keep secret Prince Harry's location on the frontline in Afghanistan. Major Japanese papers also excluded the Prime Minister Tanaka/Lockheed scandal from their pages because of possible negative repercussions. In addition, the press in the United Kingdom did not cover the Falkland War in 1982 at the government's request. Furthermore, the U.S. military allows limited press access to certain war zones for journalist and soldier safety and military secrecy.

Newspapers served two markets: readers and advertisers. Advertisers exerted influence, either small or great, depending upon the publication, because the industry generates far more revenue from advertising than it does from subscriptions.

Therefore, advertisers could exert a kind of censorship over a newspaper, and the practice occurred around the world. Advertisers increasingly placed pressure on newspapers to preview their content prior to publication as a clause in their contract with publishers, and publishers in the 2000s had tried to exert some control by publishing advertising guidelines and restrictions. Some advertisers asked for preferential placement of ads near favorable news copy, a practice that all journalism associations condemn as unethical, although it occasionally occurs. Furthermore, companies had dropped their advertisements from publications over content issues. Tandy Corp., for example, removed its advertisements from the *Arizona Republic* after the paper published a less-than-flattering editorial cartoon about Texas A&M student deaths in a collapsed bonfire in 1999; the ads were pulled at the request of a Texas A&M alumni.

Industry Associations. The World Association of Newspapers (WAN), formerly the International Federation of Newspaper Publishers, began in 1948. Its members are on five continents and include 78 newspaper publisher associations from more than 122 countries, as well 10 global news agencies and 10 regional press organizations. Overall, the WAN had 18,000 member publications on its roster. The association defended freedom of the press, aided the development and expansion of the industry, and encouraged cooperation between its members. WAN is a member of the International Freedom of Expression Exchange, a network of non-governmental organizations whose main objective is to monitor free speech violations globally. In 2009, WAN president Gavin O'Reilly announced plans to merge WAN with the Germany-based IFRA, with more than 3,000 members throughout 70 countries.

Immediately after the 2008 Summer Olympics, WAN announced plans to continue "a major campaign calling on the Chinese government to honour the promise of reform" made at time games were awarded to their country. WAN accused the Chinese government of failing to fulfill its pledges. In addition, the association claimed there were acts reflecting increased repression of free expression and press freedom. There were reportedly more than 30 journalists and in excess of 50 cyber reporters imprisoned in China in addition to total control of the country's media by authorities. WAN concluded that "authorities must allow for freedom of expression both among journalists and ordinary citizens."

The Newspaper Association of America (NAA), a U.S. nonprofit organization, had a membership of nearly 2,000 newspapers that represented nearly 90 percent of the daily circulation in the country and a wide range of nondaily U.S. newspapers. NAA also has many Canadian and international members. The NAA mission statement said the organization sought the advancement of the newspaper industry in the United States and around the world. The merger of seven associations on June 1, 1992, resulted in creation of NAA. Those associations were the American Newspaper Association, the Newspaper Advertising Bureau, the Association of Newspaper Classified Advertising Managers, the International Circulation Managers Association, the International Newspapers Advertising and Marketing Executives, the Newspaper Advertising Co-op Network, and the Newspaper Research Council. In 2002, NAA listed six the specific areas of priority as marketing, public policy, diversity, industry development, newspaper operations, and readership.

The National Newspaper Publishers Association (NNPA), which was also known as Black Press of America, was a federation of more than 200 African-American U.S. community newspapers. Since World War II, it had also served as the industry's news service. In 2000, NNPA launched NNPA Media Services, a print and Web advertising-placement and press release distribution service. In 2001, in association with the NNPA Foundation, NNPA

started building the BlackPressUSA Network to serve as its nation's premier network of local African-American news and information portals. The Network was anchored by BlackPressUSA.com, the national Web portal for the Black Press of America. They have a combined readership or 15 million.

BACKGROUND AND DEVELOPMENT

China started one of the earliest news collection and dissemination networks in the world during the Han dynasty between 206 B.C. and 219 A.D. During this period, the imperial court created a message system for garnering news on occurrences and events around the empire. The system was analogous to the postal system of the Middle Ages in Europe, when the Holy Roman Empire had its agents draft articles on events in the various regions and sent them along specified routes. During the Tang dynasty from 618 to 907 A.D., China had a formal publication called the *Ti Pao,* translated as *Official Newspaper.* This handwritten publication included information collected along China's message routes. The imperial court produced its own newspapers. Later, the *Ti Pao* reached many intellectual groups in China and larger segments of society.

China began producing newspapers with some of the standard technology and materials that continued to be used centuries later: ink, paper, moving letters, and moveable type. China used these materials long before the appearance of any European newspaper, but there were no public, scheduled newspapers until Europeans started their own in China during the nineteenth century. Rome also had an early predecessor of the newspaper, called the *Acta Diuna,* or *Daily Events,* which the government circulated from 131 B.C. to 14 A.D.

The modern newspaper industry grew out of the European invention of the printing press, which was perfected in the middle of the fifteenth century. With Johan Gutenberg's invention of movable type, European publishers could mass produce and circulate texts quickly. This technology has benefited not only the newspaper industry but also other publishing industries. Moreover, it has been attributed to the growth of nationalism, industrialism, and widespread literacy. Early publications included the Bible and various encyclopedias.

With the establishment of postal routes and the evolution of greater printing capacities in the early 1600s, Europe's newspaper industry began to grow quickly, bolstered by demand to know developments in the religious wars of the period. Articles from newspapers of the seventeenth century indicate that they covered a wide expanse of Europe on a daily basis and that they had consistent contact with their readers, according to *The Newspaper: An International History.*

By the mid-1660s, forebears of the twenty-first century newspaper industry began in England. The *Oxford Gazette* gained government approval in 1665 and later moved to London, where the name was changed to the *London Gazette. The Daily Courant,* the first daily newspaper, reached the market in the early eighteenth century. Benjamin Franklin launched the first paper without government sanction in American colonies during the 1720s. Franklin's *Pennsylvania Gazette* was one of the first commercially successful newspapers, according to The World Newspaper Industry.

The technological developments of the nineteenth century greatly boosted the prosperity of the newspaper industry. The linograph and rotary press increased the speed of newspaper production. In addition, new communications technology, including the telegraph, telephone, and wire services like Reuters, aided the collection and dissemination of news worldwide. Typewriters also enhanced the writing of newspaper articles, while wood pulp reduced the cost of producing newspapers. Finally, the railroad in Europe and the United States improved the circulation of newspapers.

In the late nineteenth century and early twentieth century, journalism became more opinionated and press barons like William Randolph Hearst and Joseph Pulitzer began molding the news to fit their views. A sensational, muckraking style of journalism, called "yellow journalism," became popular in the United States during the late nineteenth century. During this period, competition grew fierce as newspapers fought for readers by relying on sensational stories to win new customers. Given rising literacy and leisure time in the early 1900s, newspaper industries in established markets achieved record revenues and profits, which continued to grow until World War I. After 1918, however, radio began competing with newspapers, capturing a share of their advertising revenues. Later in the century, television emerged as a broadcast medium and reduced advertising in newspapers even further. By the late 1950s, circulation began to decline already in some of the world's largest markets, including the United Kingdom.

The 1980s. By the 1980s, the newspaper industry around much of the world had peaked. Greater competition from television, along with new technology, such as the Video Cassette Recorder (VCR), captured a larger share of consumers' entertainment spending. During this period, newspapers in the world's major markets began to undergo significant changes to remain a viable news medium. As they struggled to return to profitability, large media conglomerates acquired some of the world's largest newspapers. Newspaper monopolies increased during this period as well,

as only one paper served a region or a segment of a country's readership.

Lifestyle changes around the world also worked against the newspaper industry in the 1980s. Automobile ownership and dependence continued to grow, and fewer people read newspapers while in transit or bought newspapers from hawkers on the street. In addition, a gradual migration from downtown areas to suburbs during this period, especially in North America, further eroded the circulation of large city papers. Furthermore, the increase of dual income and single-person households in the 1980s meant there seemed to be less time for reading newspapers.

The U.S. newspaper industry led the Western world in circulation during this period. Because of its expansive geography, the United States housed more daily newspapers serving regional markets than other countries, with a total of 1,688 in the mid-1980s. This was in contrast to 125 in Japan, 93 in the United Kingdom, and 91 in France. Daily circulation in the United States stood at 63.08 million and Sunday circulation at 57.6 million in 1985. *The Wall Street Journal* led the country's papers in circulation and profitability during the 1980s with about two million subscribers at mid-decade. During the 1980s, Gannett launched what would become the country's second largest newspaper, *USA Today,* which like *The Wall Street Journal* was a satellite-transmitted paper, meaning that it could be simultaneously printed at regional centers for rapid and efficient national distribution. *USA Today* also developed the circulation tactic of bulk distributions to college populations, hotel guests, and other targeted audiences, substantially elevating its total daily circulation figures. Although U.S. per capita newspaper consumption ranked below that of Scandinavia, the United Kingdom, and Japan, the country's use of newsprint per capita was the highest in the world, because U.S. papers were generally larger than their counterparts elsewhere.

The United States also dominated the newspaper industry in terms of influence, setting the daily news agenda around the world. U.S. newspapers provided a significant number of the news stories to the United Press International (UPI) and Associated Press (AP) news wires, which disseminated much of the news around the world for both print and electronic media such as radio and television.

Nonetheless, the competition among regional newspapers began to decline in the 1980s, not only in the United States but also around the world. Single newspapers monopolized markets around the country when their leading competitors folded or merged. In many cases, advertising demand and advertiser preference for the leading newspaper led to the demise of multi-newspaper markets. In addition, joint-operating agreements (JOAs) became prevalent as newspapers found they could no longer compete with each other. Instead, under the Newspaper Preservation Act of 1971, they merged their advertising, circulation, and management personnel, while remaining editorially distinct. In 1984, 7 of the top 10 newspapers in the United States were monopolies owned by large newspaper and media conglomerates.

The United Kingdom's newspaper industry ranked high among the world leaders in the 1980s. Some of the world's largest newspapers in terms of circulation were in the United Kingdom. London's daily newspapers, for example, had a combined circulation of more than 14 million in 1986. By the 1980s, these papers had long served as national newspapers and, consequently, the country's regional papers remained small. Technology continued to change the U.K. industry during the 1980s. Newspapers had to adapt to commercial radio, television, satellites, and videotext. During this period, landmark U.K. papers like the *Times* and *Daily Express* lost money, and media conglomerates began to acquire them, not for profits but instead for enhancing their images and increasing their influence.

By the mid-1980s, Germany's newspaper industry took on characteristics of both its U.S. and U.K. counterparts. Germany's geographic size made establishing a national newspaper difficult and expensive, as did its division into 11 states. Hamburg and Frankfurt were the country's largest cities before the reunification of East and West Germany, and these cities housed the country's largest newspapers. Hamburg's *Bild Zeitung* was the country's largest daily paper with 5.9 million subscribers, followed by *Anzeiger* with 1.7 million. Axel Springer controlled 29 percent of the market at the time and owned the *Bild Zeitung,* as well as *Die Welt,* a paper created in 1946 by the British government and modeled after the *Times.* The strength of the newspaper industry during this period was due in part to the government's limit on television advertising, which made newspapers the leading source of advertising.

The French newspaper industry, unlike some of its Western counterparts, continued to be regulated by the government in the mid-1980s. The government controlled France's press agency, Agence France Presse, and guaranteed newsprint to all newspapers at the same price as well as unbiased, equal distribution. The Parisian daily newspapers faced dwindling circulation in the 1980s. While the 13 Parisian dailies had a combined circulation of 3.8 million in 1980, they had a circulation of only 2.5 million by 1986. Furthermore, the circulation of the country's provincial papers fell to 7.5 million in 1980, down from 9 million in 1946. Hersant led the French newspaper industry with 22 provincial papers. Like newspaper industries in other industrialized countries, France's became more monopolistic with a trend toward one daily paper per market. By 1985, France had only 10 Parisian newspapers and 75 provincial titles. In addition, per capita consumption continued to fall during the 1980s.

Japan's modern newspaper industry began in 1945 during the reconstruction under the leadership of U.S. General Douglas McArthur. In 1947, Japan's newspapers started operating as a free press. By 1985, Japan's largest paper, *Yomiuri Shimbun,* reported a circulation of 5.4 million, followed by *Asahi Shimbun* with 3.8 million. Not only were these papers Japan's largest, but they also were the largest in the world. With its dense population and high literacy rate, Japan was the world's second largest market for newspapers, trailing only the Soviet Union while remaining ahead of the United States. Following the collapse of the Soviet Union, Japan became the global frontrunner.

CURRENT CONDITIONS

Outlook and Trends. Because of shrinking domestic markets since the 1980s in most developed countries, newspaper publishers had expanded their focus to include international markets. For example, *The Wall Street Journal* increased its operations abroad, while *The New York Times* expanded its global presence via joint operations with newspapers in other markets. In May 2004, The Washington Post Co. announced the acquisition of *El Tiempo Latino,* a leading Spanish-language weekly newspaper in the greater Washington, D.C., area. The publication was eventually named the "Best Hispanic Weekly in the United States" by The National Association of Hispanic Publications.

With competition from other news media, especially television, radio, and the Internet, newspaper circulation declined throughout the 1990s and 2000s for some of the world's largest newspapers, particularly in the United States. According to the Audit Bureau of Circulations, as of March 2010, the top-selling newspaper in the U.S., was *The Wall Street Journal,* with a circulation of 2,092,523 daily, up 0.5 percent from 2009, making it the only newspaper in the U.S. to show growth in terms of readership. The second largest-selling paper in the United States was *USA Today,* with a circulation of 1,826,622 daily, a decline of 13.8 percent. Most other major papers, however, experienced steep circulation declines. The *New York Times* was third with a circulation of 951,063, down 8.47 percent from 2009. Nationally, newspaper circulation had declined 8.7 percent in 2010 from the previous year.

Analysts projected that lower circulation numbers would likely affect advertising revenues. National advertising, which grew 8.1 percent to US$7.8 billion in 2003, was the fastest growing newspaper advertising segment, but its continued robust growth looked uncertain in 2005. The *New York Times* announced in March 2010, that 2009 was the "worst year the newspaper business has had in decades." According to the report, advertising revenue fell 27.4 percent or more than US$10 billion from 2008—which was, at the time, the newspaper industry's worst year since the Depression. Advertising revenue reached its peak in 2005. From 2005 to 2009, ad revenue declined 44.2 percent, from more than US$49.2 billion to less than US$27.6 billion in 2009.

Robert Andrews revealed an alternate trend that was emerging where a senior newspaper writer was becoming a blog writer. The Telegraph.co.uk's "Three Line Whip" columnist Jonathan Isaby left to join Conservative Home. The independent blog was credited with doing "a good job of rallying the Tory party in the last couple of years."

The Tabloid Revolution. A significant trend in the early 2000s was the growing popularity of tabloids. In particular, these small-sized papers attracted the younger market for which every newspaper was competing. A key player in this segment was Metro International, publishers of 56 *Metro* daily papers in 18 countries in 15 languages across the world. Aimed specifically at readers in their twenties and thirties, the free tabloid-sized dailies are distributed at college campuses and at busy commuter areas, such as subway stations. By 2009, they were reaching more than 17 million readers per day and more than 37 million readers per week. With the papers being free to the consumer, all revenue is generated via advertising. The company reported in 2010 that advertising revenues had increased a compound annual rate of 41 percent since the first edition appeared in 1995. According to the company, *Metro* content includes leading local, national, and international stories, produced in a "standardized and accessible format and design, which enables commuters to read the newspaper during a typical journey time of less than 20 minutes. *Metro*'s editorial content is also free from bias and focuses on giving readers the news they need at the time they read, rather than comment or views." The popularity of *Metro* led to the introduction of similar free tabloids and affected sales of established newspapers in many markets, including Korea.

In response to market research indicating that young readers prefer a small format, several leading papers, including the London *Times* and *Independent,* converted to tabloid size. Indeed, according to a *Kansas City Star* article by Steve Johnson, newspaper designers believe that many, if not most, major U.S. papers will convert to tabloid by 2010. Although this move would appeal to readers, who have demonstrated a decided preference for small-sized papers, the question of advertising revenues could remain tricky. "Advertisers would have to be

persuaded that a full-page tabloid ad is worth as much as a full-page broadsheet ad," wrote Johnson, adding that this matter was "proving no easy challenge in the U.K."

In the meantime, several papers in the United States had already experimented with tabloid-sized editions. In 2002, the *Chicago Tribune* launched a *RedEye* edition, aimed at young commuters; the Chicago *Sun-Times* responded with *Red Streak.* In 2003, the *Washington Post* introduced *Express,* a commuter newspaper of 20 to 24 pages, designed to be read during a 15-minute commute. Tribune Publishing announced that it would produce *amNewYork,* another paper aimed at young urban commuters. In 2004, Meximerica Media announced plans to publish *Rumbo,* a tabloid with a target audience of Hispanic men and women under age 45.

Uncertain Ad Revenues. Newspapers' share of aggregate advertising spending shrank in many developed countries during the late 1990s and early 2000s. In 1995, it stood at only 22.4 percent in the United States. In 1996, television surpassed newspapers for the leading share of advertising funds after lagging for 50 years. Even before the September 11, 2001, terrorist attacks against the United States caused advertisers to scale back dollars previously targeted for newspaper display ads, the non-profit Newspaper Association of America said that advertising expenditures for the second quarter of 2001 had dropped to US$11.1 billion, or 8.4 percent. The situation then began to improve, with the global newspaper industry reporting a 2 percent increase in advertising revenues in 2003 and a 5.3 percent rise in 2004, for the largest increase in five years. Newspapers' share of the global advertising market peaked in 2005. By 2009, advertising had continued to decline, falling 44.2 percent from its peak in 2005. In spite of the steady decline, newspapers remained the second largest advertising medium in the world after television. Broadcast advertising followed the steady decline in the last half of the decade as well. However, the decline was projected to be about half as steep as that of newspapers. According to a 2010 report released by ZenithOptimedia, all advertising spending was expected to fall by 8.7 percent in 2010.

Developing countries remained the bright spot for the industry as circulation and advertising spending continued to rise. The International Federation of Newspaper Publishers reported that circulation in countries like Malaysia, Brazil, and India rose dramatically in the mid-1990s in contrast to declines in Japan, the United States, and the European Union. Furthermore, advertising revenues in developing countries shot up 30 percent during this period.

There was an important link between declines in revenues and declines in classified advertising. Until around

2003, newspaper classified ads functioned as major "community bulletin board" and were a valued information resource. The successful introduction and reception of Internet web sites, including Craigslist, Cars.com, and Monster.com, resulted in formidable competition for classified ads. Classified ads had once increased profits for many newspapers. Publications' own Internet sites were also contributing to newspapers' struggles, causing them to compete with their online versions. In 2009, classified ad revenue fell by 38.1 percent. Since 2000, classified ad revenue had fallen by more than two-thirds.

According to a publishing industry market review for 2008, it was crucial for newspapers to maintain advertising revenues while increasing readership. Newspapers were affected by the attrition created when subscribers died and there were no new readers to take their places. Newspapers were also affected by the evolution of other alternatives, such as satellite and cable television, satellite radio, and the Internet, which resulted in less time for newspaper reading and a decline in sales. Newspaper publishers recognized the need to increase their online presence.

Global Circulation and Trade. India's newspaper industry was one of the most prominent expanding newspaper industries in the world. India's newspaper count grew from just 300 in 1947, the year the country gained independence from British colonial rule, to 2,000 in the mid-1990s, when India became the world's leader in quantity of daily newspapers. About 70 of India's papers had circulation of more than 100,000, and newspapers reached approximately 22 percent of the country's prodigious population. Newspapers controlled 66 percent of the country's advertising dollars in the mid-1990s, and India's papers ranked among the least expensive in the world, roughly US$0.06 a paper. In 2009, the country's total circulation was reported at just over 143 million, the second largest in the world.

The Germans are among the world's most news-hungry population. In Europe, the United Kingdom and Germany have about four dailies sold for every ten people. As in the United Kingdom, the most popular title in Germany is a tabloid; Germany's *Bild,* formerly *Bild Zeitung,* had a circulation of 3.8 million by 2005. Germany's newspaper circulation grew from the early 1990s to the mid-1990s, largely as a result of the country's reunification. During this same period, Spain reported growth of 14 percent, Israel reported 18 percent, and Turkey reported 22 percent, albeit from very low levels. Emerging economies in Asia, South America, and Australia also reported some of the best growth in the industry.

Journalist Safety and Press Freedom. By 2001, journalists had experienced more dangerous conditions than they had in the late 1990s. In 1997, 26 journalists from 14 countries were killed while gathering and reporting

news, down from 46 killed worldwide in 1996. In 1999, that figure jumped to 70 journalists killed. In 2001, about 60 journalists and media workers lost their lives on the job, as Latin America, in particular, became a deadly place to report the news. Other journalists were under siege from arrests and threats of arrest in South Africa, Nigeria, and other countries. In 2002, the abduction and murder of *Wall Street Journal* reporter Daniel Pearl called world attention to the dangers reporters face from zealots, human predators, warlords, and war-zone conditions. The third most deadly year for journalists since 1812 was 2006, with a total of 110 lives lost; the majority of these occurred as a result of the wars in Afghanistan and in Iraq.

The Internet. The Internet increased competition with newspapers, allowing companies not affiliated with the industry to publish news and information on the world wide web. Newspapers responded by quickly launching online versions of their papers in order to capture media-savvy online consumers and advertisers, who understood the attraction of Internet consumers. For example, some companies created employment Web sites, which absorbed a share of the employment classified ads newspapers received, while others provided news headlines and information on their sites.

By the mid-1990s, roughly 500 U.S. and European newspapers had set up online versions of their papers. The U.S. newspapers led the foray into online publishing, ahead of other media in the United States and other newspapers around the world. About 78 South American papers and 28 in Japan also had Internet versions by 1996. In addition to enabling them to compete in their local markets, the Internet also provided newspaper publishers with a means of reaching the entire world, thus increasing their readership and advertising. To compete with non-newspaper news sites online, publishers formed alliances with various Web sites to provide news and information. Tribune Company, for example, teamed up with America Online to offer *Digital City,* which offered news and entertainment information on six metropolitan areas.

Despite these efforts by newspaper publishers, some industry observers contend that newspapers and broadcast television would still lose a significant share of their audiences to computer-based services. As a result, nearly all major newspapers were studying ways to strengthen and preserve their position in the twenty-first century. In 2002, with media convergence a reality, some industry analysts worried that traditional ethics and standards associated with newspapers during the mid-to-late twentieth century would fall by the wayside as newspapers lost their identity and combined functions with the online press, television cable news, and news-on-demand suppliers. Regional dailies were competing online more with titles that were not previously seen as competition.

Karen Love, National Newspaper Publishers Association vice-chairman, pointed out many Black-owned newspapers were moving to an Internet economy. In 2008, the *San Antonio Informer* decided to "shut down its printing press and instead has decided to put all its eggs in the basket of the Internet economy." Love also stated that a Pew Research Center study found 43 percent of newspaper editors thought that "Web technology offers the potential for greater-than-ever journalism and will be the savior of what we once thought of as newspaper newsrooms."

RESEARCH AND TECHNOLOGY

As environmental regulations increased worldwide from the 1980s through the early 2000s, so did the number of regulations impacting print trade in general. Although this included newspapers, the latter lobbied hard for exemptions. The regulation of waste disposal meant that newspapers had to keep close tabs on what went down the drain, from photography chemicals to printing ink. These regulations meant changing operations, from implementing recycling programs to more drastic changes. More drastic measures included wholesale changes in press technology to shift away from the use of oil-based inks. In the United States, for example, the Resource Conservation and Recovery Act specified the manner in which items designated as hazardous wastes were to be handled and covered substances used by the newspaper publishing industry. In the mid-1990s, some industry analysts reported that fines by the U.S. government had increased fivefold during this period.

Furthermore, increased environmental concerns regarding recycling of newsprint gave rise to proposals mandating greater use of recycled paper. For example, by 2007, over 73 percent of the old newspapers in the United States had been recovered and recycled. In 1989, U.S. newspapers contained 10 percent recycled paper. However, environmental groups tried to push for legislation requiring newspapers with circulation greater than 200,000 to use paper products containing no less than 35 percent recycled material. Proponents argued that municipalities could realize savings of US$1.5 billion per year in waste disposal costs. Trade groups, particularly the National Newspaper Association, protested, saying that these types of mandates would lead to much higher capital expenditures for small newspapers, even if they already used recycled paper. As of 2007, the average amount of recycled fiber in newsprint in U.S. papers was more than 30 percent.

Emerging newspaper technology in the late 1990s included the digital press, digital prepress, keyless inking, shaftless presses, and keyless offset presses. The digital press, however, remained unsuitable for newspaper printing in the late 1990s, although publishers could use digital prepress data to preset their conventional presses. Keyless inking technology, on the other hand, alleviated some of the labor from presetting, while shaftless printers increased flexibility and efficiency. Keyless inking systems eliminated manual adjustments by presetting ink levels before the press began, reducing waste from test printing and improving consistency. Sales of keyless offset printers rose throughout the world during this period as one of the leading new printing technologies. In 1955, Swiss manufacturer Wifag introduced the shaftless printer, which featured individually motorized moving components and a gearless transmission that reduced waste and labor. The growth of shaftless presses in Europe encouraged their growth in the United States, which began manufacturing and buying them in the late 1990s.

In the mid-1990s, newspapers also took advantage of on-screen typesetting via computers, which enabled publishers to increase the efficiency of the typesetting process. On-screen typesetting eliminated the need for skilled workers to create and design newspaper pages. Instead, workers were able to create pages easily with the aid of computer software. During this period, the newspaper industry also began to use digital cameras that allowed users to capture images on a disk or the camera's hard drive and transfer them to a computer for adjustment and manipulation. Digital cameras reduced the time needed to process photographs and decreased costs spent on newspaper photographs, by eliminating film and dark room expenses.

INDUSTRY LEADERS

News Corp. The News Corporation Limited, owned by twenty-first century media mogul Rupert Murdoch, was one of the leading newspaper conglomerates in the early 2000s and was the top publisher in the world of English-language newspapers. Its publications included *The New York Post, The Times* (London), and the *Australian,* as well as magazines such as *TV Guide* and book publisher Harper-Collins. The company's other media holdings included television stations as well as cable and satellite operations in the United States, South America, and Australia, and movie studio Twentieth Century Fox.

News Corp. suffered a substantial decline in ad revenues in 2001 along with the rest of the industry, posting a drop of 16 percent in second quarter operating revenue. Overall, only the Australian newspaper holdings seemed able to avoid being battered as it reported an increase in advertising and circulation. While growth remained strongest in Australia through 2004, News Corp. succeeded in boosting its U.K. circulation across all its newspaper titles in 2004, resulting in a 7 percent growth in advertising revenues. In 2007, News Corp. reached an agreement to purchase Dow Jones, the publishers of *The Wall Street Journal,* for approximately US$5.6 billion. In addition, the corporation started a business news channel from the Fox News network—Fox Business Network. In 2009, News Corp. created NewsCore, a news wire service designed to provide breaking news stories globally to all of its journalistic outlets. Operating income for News Corp.'s newspapers segment rose from US$686 million in 2003 to US$831 million in 2004. For 2009, the company reported sales of US$30.423 billion and 64,000 employees. More than 75 percent of News Corp.'s sales were from its U.S. holdings. Murdoch's family controls about 30 percent of the company with Rupert Murdoch keeping tight control of the company.

Gannett Company, Inc. Gannett Company, Inc., which was also a global newspaper and media power, had become the leading newspaper publisher in the United States in terms of distribution. However, the same is not true of its prestige, as critics condemn its flagship *USA Today* daily with pejorative names such as "McPaper." As of 2004, Gannett's 100 U.S. daily papers claimed a paid circulation of just under 8 million. Since 1997, *USA Today* moved from being the country's second largest newspaper, with a circulation of 1.6 million, to the number one paper in the early 2000s, with a circulation of about 2.3 million. As of March 2010, *USA Today* boasted a circulation of 1.8 million daily.

Nonetheless, not even the giant Virginia-based chain could completely overcome the advertising woes gripping nearly all U.S. newspapers in the early 2000s. While managing to report a small revenue gain in 2001, Gannett Co. reported a significant advertising revenue loss in the final three months of 2001. The company blamed much of the loss on the September 11, 2001, terrorist attacks against the United States, as travel ads shrank in all chain dailies. When the bottom line was revealed in 2002, Gannett posted earnings of US$831.2 million on revenue of US$6.3 billion. This was significantly lower than the 2001 Gannett figures of US$1.7 billion on revenue of US$6.2 billion. However, earnings improved in 2003, when the company posted operating revenues of US$6.7 billion. The following year, sales rose to US$7.3 billion, resulting in net earnings of US$1.3 billion. Gannett posted earnings of US$5.6 billion in 2009 with approximately 49,675 employees.

In addition to *USA Today,* Gannett also owns Newsquest. It is one of the United Kingdom's largest newspaper groups with more than 30 titles, including 17 newspapers. Gannett's Internet presence includes more than 60 Web sites.

Asahi Shimbun. Asahi Shimbun Publishing Company produced the world's second largest newspaper in circulation, *Asahi Shimbun.* In 1996, *Asahi Shimbun's* circulation stood at 12.6 million, but after years of falling ad revenue, intense competition from rival newspapers, and declining readership, its circulation dropped to about 12

million in 2004. The company claimed 14,400 employees in 2005.

Knight Ridder. Knight Ridder remained a major force in the global newspaper industry and the second most dominant player in the U.S. industry. The company was formed by the 1974 merger of Knight Newspapers Inc. and Ridder Publications Inc. In the United States, Knight Ridder ranked second as a chain, behind Gannett, with papers such as *The Detroit Free Press, Miami Herald,* and *Philadelphia Inquirer.* Overall, the company published 31 daily newspapers in 28 markets around the United States with its print and online versions. Knight Ridder reported daily circulation of 9 million and Sunday circulation of 12 million in 2004. The company restructured itself to focus on its core operation, the newspaper business, in the late 1990s by shedding non-newspaper holdings such as its cable interests. Furthermore, Knight Ridder bought a number of new papers during this period, including the *Fort Worth Star-Telegram,* the *Kansas City Star,* and the *Times Leader of Pennsylvania.*

The Miami-based company's sales edged up three percent in 1997 to US$2.87 billion. However, in 2002, as flagship newspapers in Detroit and Philadelphia continued to lose subscribers and revenue, the company posted substantial losses. Non-advertising and non-circulation revenue plunged 41 percent from December 2000 to US$8.9 million in the final quarter of 2001, according to the company. Meanwhile, non-advertising and non-circulation revenue for 2001 fell 25 percent from 2000 postings to US$133.4 million. By 2004, earnings had begun to improve. In its May 2004 statistical report, Knight Ridder reported total advertising revenue was up 2.9 percent for May and up two percent year to date. Total sales for 2004 reached US$3 billion. In 2006, the McClatchy Company purchased Knight Ridder and immediately sold several of its papers to the MediaNews Group for US$6.5 billion in cash, stock, and debt. This gave McClatchy Group 32 daily newspapers in 29 markets with a circulation totaling 3.3 million. As a pioneer in online news, the company operated several Web sites. It also owned stakes in an advertising company and newsprint mill.

Axel Springer. Axel Springer Verlag AG produced *Bild,* Germany's leading newspaper, as well as *Die Welt,* and numerous other papers. As a media conglomerate, Axel Springer also has magazine, book, radio, television, and information holdings. The company, with interests in 36 countries, owned a stake in 30 publishing companies throughout Europe with more than 230 newspapers and magazines, as well as 80 online sites. It also has holdings in television and radio stations. Berlin-based Axel Springer's sales totaled US$2.86 billion in 1996, about 7 percent above its 1995 sales. However, difficult times in the media industry put Axel Springer under media scrutiny in 2002 as newspaper ad revenues plummeted and its falling stock shares reflected financial losses. In 2002, the media giant informed stockholders it was paying no profits after a year of falling revenues and poor advertising performance. Axel Springer reported a welcome 5 percent revenue increase in 2003, bringing total sales to US$3 billion and boosting net income 155 percent over the previous year. For 2009, Axel Springer reported income of US$3.67 billion and 10,740 employees. In 2010, Axel Springer extended an offer to a prominent French real estate Web site operator, seloger.com, for US$635.7 million. This caused the shares to rise significantly, and the offer was increased by one million dollars after the shareholders rejected the deal.

MAJOR COUNTRIES IN THE INDUSTRY

In 2010, there were over 12,297 different daily newspaper titles published worldwide.

China. In 2006, China was the largest audience for daily newspapers, with 96.6 million daily copies sold through its more than 2,200 different newspapers. In 2010, China led the world in terms of largest number of daily papers among the world's top 100, with 25. Although its primary newspaper was *The People's Daily,* a national edition with a circulation of three to four million in 2009 and the official paper of the Communist Party, it was second in circulation to the *Shanghai Daily.* As of 2003, China's newspaper industry, which included 2,100 papers, reported an increase in advertising revenues of 29 percent in 2004, more than twice the growth for the previous year. Between 2001 and 2006, ad revenues grew by 128 percent.

India. In 2006, India followed China in terms of audience for daily newspapers, with 78.7 million newspapers sold daily. In 2010, India had the largest list of paid subscription newspapers with 2,500.

Japan. Japan, which led the global newspaper industry in the late 1990s and early 2000s, slipped to third place in 2004 in terms of total circulation (70.4 million), but continued to produce the world's top-selling paper, *Yomiuiri Shimbun,* which sold more than 14 million copies daily. However, by 2010, Japan had regained the top spot for a newspaper with the largest circulation with *Yomiuiri Shimbun,* selling 10.02 million papers daily. Among industrialized countries, Japan remained one of the few with circulation growth in the late 1990s. Japan held six of the world's highest circulating newspapers, and circulation remained well above its closest competitor, the United States.

United States. In 2010 in the United States, more than 71 percent of adults, or 165.6 million people, read a newspaper either in print or online each week, according to a study by the Scarborough Research Group. The study found that newspapers continue to attract highly educated and affluent consumers. In terms of advertising, newspapers are still a good investment. Even as circulation continued to decline to 2010, Scarborough Research and Nielsen Online showed nearly 100 million adults still read a printed newspaper every day and newspaper Web sites averaged more than 74 million unique visitors a month during the first quarter of 2010.

Consolidation continued to affect the U.S. newspaper industry, with Lee Enterprises' purchase of Pulitzer in 2005 for US$1.46 billion, making Lee the fourth largest owner of dailies in the United States with 53 daily newspapers in 23 states, with more than 300 weekly papers, classified, and specialty publications. Lee had previously owned 44 community newspapers, including the *Quad-City Times* of Iowa. The deal added US$440 million to Lee's 2004 revenues. In 2009, their revenue reached US$842,030 with over 10,700 employees.

According to a 2009 Consumer Expenditure Survey, the print newspaper suffered a decade-long slide from 1999 to 2008 with the nominal amount per consumer per year decreasing by 38 percent from US$97 to less than US$61. While at the same time, the amount spent by American consumers to access information through the World Wide Web nearly quadrupled, from US$49 annually in 1999, to US$222 in 2008. In 2002, the U.S Department of Labor predicted stagnating employment for news analysts, reporters, and correspondents through 2010, as more evening newspapers closed and more cities had only one local newspaper covering events. Other jobs were expected to be lost due to papers merging and consolidating, according to Department of Labor forecasts. The overall prognosis for reporters was both good and bad. Traditional U.S. papers were expected to have circulation fall, expenses increase as computer-assisted reporting and other costs run up, and advertising revenue declines, unless the industry could stem the loss of advertising to other media.

Europe. Europe also had one of the world's strongest markets for newspapers in the late 1990s, although, like other mature markets, most countries in Europe experienced declining circulation in 2001 and 2002. Germany led Europe and was fifth in the world in terms of daily circulation (21.5 million) in 2005. Nevertheless, this figure represented a 2.5 percent decline over circulation for the prior year. After Germany's reunification in the early 1990s, publishers there produced 406 newspapers in 1995, up from 356 in 1990. As of 2006, that figure had dropped to 305 local, regional and national papers. Germany also dominated newspaper and periodical trade in the mid-1990s with exports of US$982.4 million, imports of US$318.5 million, and a trade balance of US$663.9 million, the largest in the world.

The U.K. industry was the second largest market in Europe with circulation of 20 million and 103 papers in 1995. The United Kingdom also was a major newspaper and periodical trader, with exports of US$600 million and imports of US$149.2 million. However, the boom in U.K papers had disappeared by January 2002 as national morning newspaper sales plunged from 13.1 million in December 2000 to 12.9 million in December of 2001. *The Guardian* of London said that newspaper sales were at their lowest levels in two decades, both in the region and countrywide, with a 2010 average daily circulation of 283,063, behind the *Daily Telegraph* (842,912 daily in 2009) and *The Times* (692,581 daily in 2005). Perhaps an unwitting comment on national values and character was that the United Kingdom's best-selling newspaper was *The Sun,* Rupert Murdoch's racy tabloid, with daily sales of 3.14 million.

The U.K. newspaper industry weathered some changes in the early 2000s, as circulation fell 11.41 percent between 2000 and 2004, and traditional circulation bases shifted. Stephen Glover of the *Spectator* attributed this growth to the papers' new tabloid format—a move he considered "downmarket" but profitable. Other papers experienced substantial drops in circulations between the mid-1990s and 2004. The *Sun* dropped from 4 million to just over 3 million by 2010, while the *Daily Mirror* declined almost 33 percent. On the other hand, sales of the *Daily Star* grew more than 15 percent during this same period. *The Guardian,* which according to Glover lost some readers to the *Independent,* planned to adopt a smaller format in 2006. The *Financial Times* lost a substantial number of U.K. subscribers but posted circulation gains overseas. Nevertheless, the loss of ad revenues combined with increased production costs eroded the paper's profits.

A digital version of Associated Newspapers *Metro,* launched in August 2008, illustrated some key themes of a newspaper revolution for the United Kingdom. *Metro* was a widely distributed free publication with a large readership. The decision to launch an online version represented a major issue publishers faced about whether to focus on expanding audiences or on steady flows of revenue.

Although Europe in general had a highly ranked newspaper market, circulation varied greatly from country to country. Italy, for example, had one of the lowest circulation rates in the industrialized world. According to a 2004 AP report, only 1 in 10 Italians, compared to one in three Japanese, buys a newspaper. Free tabloids accounted for about one million of Italy's total newspaper circulation of seven million, and the number continued to grow. Nevertheless, Italy was one of eight E.U. nations that reported an increase in paid circulation (0.19 percent) in 2004. Austria, Belgium, Estonia, Finland, Portugal, and Spain also posted increases, with Poland leading in circulation growth

(15.21 percent). Liechtenstein led in paid subscriptions for daily newspapers, with 714 adult readers per 1000.

BIBLIOGRAPHY

Andrews, Robert. "Print Publishing Jobs in Choppy Waters," 6 August 2008. Available from http://www.paidcontent.co.uk.

"Axel Springer Verlag Posts Loss for 2000." *Die Welt,* 21 February 2002.

Baron, Ed. "Lessons from Abroad." *Presstime,* November 2001.

Benson, Lee. "Newspapers' Cash Cow Being Slaughtered." *Deseret News,* 6 August 2008.

Clark, Bill. "Small-Town America Relies on Its Printed Newspaper." *Columbia Tribune,* 1 August 2008. Available from http://www. columbiatribune.com.

de Kretser, Leela. "US Reporters Have Nothing to Celebrate." *Herald Sun,* 5 August 2008.

Dunnet, Peter J. S. *The World Newspaper* Industry, London: Croom Helm, 1988.

"Facts About Newspaper Recycling." Newspaper Association of America, 6 June 2007. Available from http://www.naa.org.

Greenslade, Roy. "An Annus Horribilis." *The Guardian,* 17 December 2001.

Love, Karen. "Minority Media Ownership in the Internet Economy." *The Michigan Chronicle,* 6 August 2008.

Perez-Pena, Richard. "It's Official: 2009 Was Worst Year for the Newspaper Business in Decades" *New York Times,* 24 March 2010. Available from http://http://mediadecoder.blogs.

Rosenberg, Jim, and Lucia Moses. "The Newsprint Crisis Has Receded for Now." *Editor and Publisher,* 6 August 2001.

Saba, Jennifer. "Text Messaging May Be Way to Reach Young Readers." *Editor & Publisher,* 27 May 2004. Available from http://www.mediainfo.com.

Sigmund, Jeff. "Newspapers Reach Nearly Three-In-Four Adult Consumers With Buying Power Every Week. "Newspaper Association of America, 20 October 2010. Available from http://www.naa.org.

Smith, Anthony. *Goodbye, Gutenberg: The Newspaper Revolution of the 1980's,* New York: Oxford University Press, 1980.

———. *The Newspaper: An International History,* London: Thames and Hudson, 1978.

Vanacore, Andrew. US Newspaper Circulation Down by 8.7 Percent." Associated Press, 26 August 2010. Available from http://www.breitbart.com.

Veitch, Skrevet av Martin. "Metro Newspaper Goes Free and 'e' to Web." 4 August 2008. Available from http://news.idg.no/cw/art.cfm?id=8F0A6A71-17A4-0F78-31805552A40D8CB1

WAN. "WAN Campaign for Press Freedom in China." 26 August 2008. Available from http://www.wan-press.org.

SIC 7372

PACKAGED SOFTWARE

NAICS CODE(S)

511210. The packaged software industry designs, develops, and publishes computer software programs for retail and wholesale distribution. Although some programs

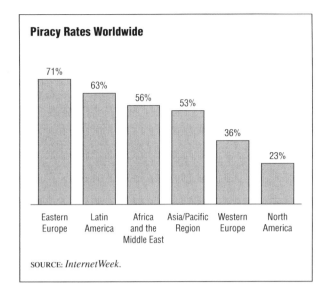

Piracy Rates Worldwide

- Eastern Europe: 71%
- Latin America: 63%
- Africa and the Middle East: 56%
- Asia/Pacific Region: 53%
- Western Europe: 36%
- North America: 23%

SOURCE: *InternetWeek.*

are marketed for specialized or technical end uses and some programs may be distributed electronically rather than in actual packages, these products are known as packaged or off-the-shelf software, in contrast to custom programs that are written for a specific customer. Important industry products include operating system software, system utilities, and application tools and solutions. For custom programming business and related computer services, see also **Information Technology Services.**

INDUSTRY SNAPSHOT

Prepackaged software falls into two main categories: either application software or system infrastructure software, the latter of which includes operating system software, system utilities, and program compilers. Though plagued with two global economic downturns in the 2000s, the industry has experienced continued growth, with global software spending expected to reach US$232 billion for 2010 according to IT research firm Gartner.

Three markets—the United States, Western Europe, and Japan—accounted for roughly 90 percent of global sales, but as they matured, more rapid growth was expected to come from emerging markets in Asia, especially China. The volatility of the packaged software industry typically encourages competition and provides more choices for consumers by forcing software makers to create better products at a lower cost. Software development is often outsourced to India, which has an educated, English-speaking labor force that remains low cost compared to that in other countries in the early twenty-first century.

Piracy remained a major issue in the 2000s. Piracy cost software producers billions of dollars in lost revenues as unethical consumers make copies of programs for friends and unscrupulous companies mass-produce illegal

copies. The Software Publishers Association estimated that half of all business applications installed in the late 1990s had been pirated. In mid-2004, software piracy remained a concern to the industry, with 2003 industry losses reported to be US$29 billion, according to research from the Business Software Alliance (BSA) and the research firm IDC that was cited in *InternetWeek.* In 2009, the Software and Information Industry Association (SIIA) reported removing 90,000 websites involved in piracy, a record. SIIA also reported bringing a record number of lawsuits against sellers of pirated software. Altogether they reported removing US$75 million of illegal products from the market.

Another important trend is toward what is known as "cloud" computing. This involves software being hosted on remote computers rather than the user's own computer or network. The user accesses the software through the Internet using a PC or other device such as a mobile phone or Apple iPad. In November 2010, the National Institute of Standards (NIST), the U.S. government's standards organization, announced a plan to develop new standards and guidance for cloud computing. In *InformationWeek,* NIST director Patrick Gallagher said the purpose of the standards would be to help create structure in what is currently "kind of a free-for-all."

In the case of enterprise software, cloud computing has given users the power to go out and adopt software they like rather than accept what is installed on their PC or network by their firm's IT department. The ability to access software from mobile devices as easily as from a desktop computer is an important part of the trend and often involves relatively low subscription fees rather than large, one-time purchases. ABI Research projects that such low-cost mobile cloud software will grow into a US$5.2 billion industry by 2015, encompassing 240 million customers.

ORGANIZATION AND STRUCTURE

Prepackaged software is divided between system infrastructure software and application software. System software, which manages computer resources and organizes data, can be further divided into three main areas: operating system software, which controls the operations of a computer; system utilities, which manage system resources and data; and program compilers, which act as interpreters of programming languages. Operating systems help the various components of a computer—disk drive, a monitor or monitors, and keyboard—work as a unit. The best-known operating system (OS), the Microsoft Disk Operating System (MS-DOS), was produced by U.S. software giant Microsoft Corporation and was ubiquitous on IBM-compatible personal computers (PCs) until the mid-1990s when it was eclipsed by Microsoft's Windows OS. Another popular, and free, operating system is Linux, a Unix-related system created by Linus Torvalds and his colleagues. Another powerful Unix-related system with an easier interface than Linux is the Mac OS sold by Apple, which combines the power and stability of UNIX with customizable tools for programmers, graphic designers, and other creative occupations.

Application software can be divided into application tools and application solutions. Application tools are software packages that enable access, manipulation, and retrieval of data, including programming applications that are used to develop other software programs. Application solutions are software packages that perform specific functions, such as word processing and accounting.

The consumer software market experienced particularly rapid growth during the late 1990s, and remains a major purchase area that includes educational products ("edutainment"), computer games, and home management software, such as budgeting and tax preparation programs. The edutainment segment of this market has been projected to grow rapidly as universities compete for students choosing distance education options.

Various international organizations and agreements were made because of disparities in international copyright and licensing laws and standards in developing, implementing, and maintaining software. These organizations and agreements provided some standardization in the industry and decreased fraud and piracy. In 1987, the Joint Technical Committee 1 (JTC1) was created by the International Organization of Standardization (ISO) and the International Electrotechnical Commission (IEC). It was created to develop standards for information technology. SC7, a subcommittee of JTC1 with 19 countries as voting members, was also created. Its main objective was to develop and adapt standards to improve software engineering processes and commercial transactions, with particular focus on quality assurance standards (internationally accepted practices used in the development of software), life cycle processes (the procurement, creation, operation, and maintenance of software in contracts), and software processes.

One of the main issues addressed by regulatory agencies is software piracy. The 1974 Trade Act of the United States as amended by the Special 301 provisions of the 1988 Omnibus Trade and Competitiveness Act allowed United States Trade Representatives (USTR) to investigate infringements of intellectual property rights worldwide. Countries that did not provide adequate protection of intellectual property rights were placed on a priority list and faced possible trade sanctions and restrictions. Countries that did not meet all the requirements to be placed on priority status could be placed on the priority watch list or on the lesser watch list. However,

to improve the progress of intellectual property rights agreements, "out-of-cycle" reviews and "immediate-action-plans" were implemented to give countries more opportunities to be removed from the priority lists in the mid-1990s. Countries such as Taiwan, Thailand, and Hungary benefited almost immediately from these measures. Furthermore, the United States eased export restrictions on selected software and cryptographic equipment used for electronic banking and money transactions.

Other countries have also taken steps to curb software piracy. In 1993, the European Union developed measures of its own to protect intellectual property rights, including the Directive on the Legal Protection of Computer Programs. Under this directive, computer programs were protected for the life of the programmer and an additional 50 years, just as with literary works. However, only six European Union member nations and three nonmember nations implemented this directive into their national laws. In Asia, China joined the Berne Convention, an international organization designed to protect the intellectual property rights of any of its members, much like the Universal Copyright Convention (UCC). Taiwan signed a bilateral copyright agreement in 1992.

Encryption was also the basis for much proposed legislation. Government agencies had wanted access to any encrypted files for law enforcement purposes before lifting export restrictions. However, they had met resistance over privacy concerns. In May 1998, *The New York Times* reported that proposed U.S. legislation (the E-Privacy Act) attempted to balance the reasonable need for law enforcement access with protections from government abuses and the invasion of privacy. While the E-Privacy Act was the closest the two sides had come to reaching agreement, debate continued over whether it adequately addressed concerns on both sides.

Despite the efforts of regulators and industry, the market for pirated software has continued to thrive. Large scale criminal organizations have gotten in on the act, including Mexican cartels which employ software pirating as a profitable sideline to drug smuggling. The single largest pirated software bust happened in China in July 2007. In an assembly and shipping warehouse was found US$2 billion worth of pirated Microsoft products in eleven different languages. Products from this operation were found in 36 different countries.

BACKGROUND AND DEVELOPMENT

The prepackaged software industry originated following a 1969 U.S. Justice Department decision that forced IBM to sell software for its mainframe computers separately from the hardware. IBM had included basic software on the computer with additional software typically developed in-house. The 1969 decision allowed individual entrepreneurs finally to compete with IBM. Small software companies sprang up, usually to offer a single program or utility, while most mainframe software was licensed rather than sold.

For the most part, the rise of the prepackaged software industry was a direct result of the appetite for software for personal computers (PCs). PC sales got off the ground late in the 1970s as computer enthusiasts bought computers made by Apple, Tandy, Atari, and Commodore. Software publishers, such as Microsoft, were formed to write programming languages for these computers that were sold at retail outlets. By the end of 1979, Microsoft had already sold one million copies of its BASIC programming language. Spreadsheets and other applications began to appear as well, all of which were created by relatively unknown companies. Pre-packaged software was something of a cottage industry, with programs written by individuals in their spare time. Because software program creation required virtually no equipment, people who wrote software programs risked only their time, but could earn between US$200,000 and US$1 million if their program was successful, as perhaps one percent were. Electronic computer manufacturers, particularly Apple, encouraged these companies because software helped to sell hardware. VisiCalc, the first spreadsheet for microcomputers, was successfully introduced in 1979 and sold many Apple computers. It also raised public awareness of PCs in general. The Apple FORTRAN programming language was introduced in March 1980 and led to the creation of additional software, especially for technical and educational applications.

IBM introduced its personal computer in 1981. Other hardware manufacturers, with the notable exception of fiercely independent Apple, began to make hardware that was compatible with the IBM system, providing standardization for the industry. Microsoft won the contract to supply IBM with its MS-DOS operating system, which resulted in most IBM-compatible computers using Microsoft's product. Such standardization benefited consumers because application software, which is usually customized to a particular operating system, could run on all manufacturer's computers with minimal modification. Standardization also helped software marketing because third-party applications were clearly delineated for use on specific systems. However, standardization also had the disadvantage of creating monopoly status for the authors of a standard OS, such as Microsoft.

IBM's prestige helped change the image of the PC in the mainframe-dominated business world from that of a toy to that of a valuable tool, and sales of software rose accordingly. In 1980, 300,000 people owned microcomputers, and by 1983 that number had increased nearly

ten-fold. All those owners were potential software purchasers. By the end of 1983, 500,000 copies of MS-DOS had been sold, bringing Microsoft's annual sales to US$69 million. Other software firms, such as Lotus Development Corporation, gained momentum as well. Lotus introduced the 1-2-3 software spreadsheet program in 1983, which was an immediate success, with some businesses buying computer hardware just so they could utilize the Lotus software.

By 1983, over 21,000 PC software packages were available. Packaged software generated about US$2.7 billion in retail sales a year as early as 1981, and the industry grew at a steady 50 percent per year. Given this tremendous growth, the prepackaged software industry and PCs began to attract a great deal of attention from the press and investors, and a number of successful software companies went public. Ninety software firms raised more than US$188 million in venture capital in 1983, and 20 firms went public. With computer hardware no longer as profitable as it had been, many investors transferred investment capital to software companies.

Businesses, even large corporations, found that writing custom programs in-house was not cost or time effective. As a result, demand for pre-packaged software increased as corporations sought those programs. By 1984, packaged software sales reached US$10 billion and software companies that had been tiny entities only a few years earlier were reporting huge sales.

Sales of PC software were growing much faster than any other segment of the industry. Companies that had focused on software for mainframe computers bought PC software firms, and firms that had specialized in PC systems began to sell application software. As competition rapidly intensified and prices for software fell among similar programs, starting a software publishing firm required substantial financial backing.

New marketing tactics and price wars also made it increasingly difficult to start small software firms. In the 1990s, large software vendors began to offer some products either for free or at costs far below market value. For example, in 1993, Computer Associates, the world's third-largest software vendor, released the first million copies of a new accounting package, *Simple Money,* at no cost. Other companies followed a similar strategy to gain market dominance and then make sales in upgrades and ancillary products. Furthermore, software companies, such as Microsoft, Lotus, and Novell, in conjunction with Borland, began selling various applications together as "suites." These suites usually included a word processing program, a spreadsheet application, and a presentation package at a significant discount from individual prices. Other incentives included special introductory prices and low upgrade prices when users owned previous versions or competitors' programs.

However, profit margins fell as software companies lowered prices, causing many companies to merge. Discount packages from Microsoft were firmly in place in the 2000s at college and university bookstores, assuring the company of steady lifelong customers.

In 1997 alone, the worldwide software market was estimated to have grown 15 percent to US$122 billion. Analysts predicted that the industry would continue to grow through the late 1990s and into the 2000s at 12 to 15 percent. According to the International Data Corporation (IDC), software price pressures were offset by several factors, such as globalization of businesses, anticipated year 2000 (Y2K) compliance problems, and the availability of improved software solutions. To raise profits, companies cut costs by sharing research and development costs and integrating businesses, which was expected to result in more mergers between software publishers.

An ongoing saga in the 1990s involved antitrust probes into Microsoft, owned by Bill Gates, and other computer companies that had allegedly participated in questionable business practices. In 1994, the U.S. Justice Department investigated Microsoft's licensing practices for MS-DOS. Although a lawsuit was avoided, Microsoft agreed to start selling its operating systems to personal computer makers based on the number purchased, rather than on the number of processors sold. Microsoft came into the legal limelight again in 1995 when three online services, CompuServe, America Online, and Prodigy, urged Microsoft not to bundle its own online service with Windows 95. The online services called on Congress to hasten an antitrust probe into the matter. Windows ultimately was allowed to release its online service, and the market remained competitive. However, in May of 1998, the U.S. government and 20 states filed suit against Microsoft, accusing the company of "unfairly trying to maintain its monopoly in personal computer software and to extend that monopoly into the new markets of Internet software and commerce," according to *The New York Times.* The suit was based on Microsoft's integration and bundling of its web browser, Internet Explorer, into its latest release of Windows. Although shipment of Windows 98 would not be delayed, the suit asked that Microsoft loosen contracts with PC makers to facilitate software modification and ease use of competitors' browsers. This trend was not limited to the software industry. In May 1998, the Federal Trade Commission announced that it was considering a suit against microprocessor giant Intel Corporation for "abusing its position as the monopoly manufacturer of microprocessor chips" and bullying computer manufacturers. The prevalence of Microsoft's Windows OS running on Intel processors gave rise to the term "Wintel" to describe the technological hegemony of the two companies.

In 2001, the government settled its case with Microsoft, and the company appealed the judgment to the U.S. Supreme Court, which refused to hear the case. An appeals court had disagreed with a lower court decision that would have forced Microsoft to divide its operations into two entities but found that the giant company had violated antitrust laws. The court finding in 2002 resulted in lawsuits against Microsoft by AOL Time Warner and its Netscape Communications Corp. that claimed Microsoft had used unfair trade practices to boost its Explorer browser. In March 2002, Sun Microsystems pursued a US$1 billion lawsuit against Microsoft, accusing the company of using anti-competitive practices against Sun's Java platform when Microsoft removed the Java program from Windows XP. In 2002, nine states pursued litigation against Microsoft.

One of the biggest concerns in the software industry was the year 2000 (Y2K) issue, which ultimately proved to be more hype than fact. During the 1960s and 1970s, memory was costly and programmers saved money by storing dates in systems and software with only the last two digits of the year. For example, 1975 became "75." However, as the millennium approached, programmers and the public feared that computers would read 2000 as 1900 ("00"), causing potentially catastrophic system failures. While the problem was not limited to software, the industry assumed a large portion of the problem. All companies worldwide were facing the same deadline, so all were competing for the same resources to fix the problem—namely, programmers to isolate the problems and fix old codes and testing personnel. Some software companies cashed in on the problem by manufacturing and marketing software designed to help companies plan and monitor Y2K testing projects. New software updated years to be read as four digits, but the Y2K problem turned out to be no problem at all, and computers smoothly made the adjustment to 2000.

The global software industry had revenues of more than US$200 billion in 2003, with the United States dominating the market, purchasing 53 percent of the world's software. Western Europe purchased 29 percent and the Asia/Pacific region purchased 15 percent. However, emerging countries were expected to outpace purchasing in developed countries. The United States was the supplier of more than 80 percent of the world's products. Of the top 20 software suppliers that year, only four were not American.

The software industry suffered during the early 2000s in the wake of the dot-com bust and an economic recession. In its 2003 Software 500 ranking, *Software Magazine* reported that difficulties continued as the mid-2000s approached. Combined sales of both software and services for the listed companies totaled US$289.7

billion, down from US$301.8 billion the previous year. About 46 percent of the 500 firms reported a decline in revenues compared to 34 percent in the publication's 2002 ranking.

While the industry had started 2004 on solid ground, the second quarter was not as promising. Amidst project cancellations and delays, analysts revised their estimates for industry growth. For example, Gartner adjusted its projection for revenue growth in 2004 from 5 to 3 percent. Heading into 2005, analysts were optimistic about the industry's performance with predictions that 2005 would be a strong year as companies continued hiring more workers, began to purchase software again, and resumed IT projects that had been tabled during the recession.

According to the July 15, 2004, issue of *Business Week,* uncertainty about economic recovery within the corporate sector was one factor for the slowdown in activity. However, the software industry faced other challenges, including the number of industry players. As companies scaled back on the number of software vendors from which they purchased applications and services and the amount of investment capital began to be stretched, mergers and acquisitions became more commonplace. Gartner indicated that up to one-half of all software companies could disappear by 2006, leaving the market open for industry giants like Oracle and Microsoft. Niche market participants were being bought up by larger companies that were trying to increase their offerings to customers. In turn, customers sought to reduce contract costs by buying in volume from one supplier.

As the software industry's market matured, there has been a tendency toward standardization, particularly of infrastructure technology. As a result, many vendors have merged in order to gain economies of scale.

Security was at the forefront of the software industry during the mid-2000s. Companies and home computer users alike were plagued by viruses and other security breaches. Some industry players were prompted to call 2003 the "Year of the Worm," in reference to a particularly malicious form of computer virus that caused widespread problems and cost companies a great deal of money. Notable worm outbreaks involved the SQL Slammer worm, as well as Code Red.F, Lovgate, and Deloder. In the first quarter of 2003, Internet Security Systems Inc. reported that Internet security attacks and incidents had increased 84 percent from the last quarter of 2002.

As experts prepared for more threats in 2004 and beyond, efforts were made to bolster security. For example, Microsoft continually worked to identify and patch vulnerabilities in its products. Companies also increased efforts to protect their IT infrastructures, from individual

computers to networks, by purchasing security software. Gartner reported that security software sales rose 9.6 percent in 2003, reaching US$5.62 billion.

In addition to security software, in December 2003, *Software Magazine* noted that systems integration applications were replacing e-business-related programs and services. Gartner expected systems integration application market to increase more than 10 percent in 2004, reaching US$9.4 billion. The research firm also predicted strong growth for engineering and design software, which was expected to grow to US$10.7 billion in 2004, up 11.7 percent from 2003.

In mid-2004, software piracy remained a concern to the industry. Citing research from the Business Software Alliance (BSA) and research firm IDC, *InternetWeek* reported that piracy cost the industry about US$29 billion in 2003. Peer-to-peer file sharing networks, which was used mostly for trading music online, was a risk as consumers began to use high-speed Internet connections. Piracy rates were the highest in Eastern Europe (71 percent), Latin America (63 percent), Africa and the Middle East (56 percent), and the Asia/Pacific region (53 percent). They were also considerable in Europe (36 percent) and North America (23 percent). However, market value was a variable to consider as losses in North America were US$7.2 billion, while losses in Latin America were US$1.3 billion, even though the region's piracy rate was much higher than in North America.

Stealing software had continued because of the high cost and easy access of software. Bundling of software and hardware was common with the first PCs, and consumers came to expect to pay for one and not the other. As computer companies discontinued the practice of bundling software with its hardware, stealing software became routine, and users were motivated to copy it from friends. Because the corporate market continued to pay high prices for software, individuals buying software for home use were not expected to see low prices.

Offshoring software development was also a rising trend in 2004, especially to India, which had low labor costs and a large pool of skilled labor. Although the result has been an increase in wages in India, this was not expected to affect the region's cost advantage for at least 20 years. The United States continued to dominate India's offshore services, where labor laws allow it. However, offshoring is not allowed by many Western European governments.

CURRENT CONDITIONS

The application service provider (ASP) model, often referred to as cloud computing, in which companies and individuals buy software as a hosted service rather than buy and install applications locally, continued to impact the industry in 2010. *Business Week* reported that up to half of all corporate software purchases would soon be purchased under a contract, and software was expected to be "rented" on a per-use, monthly, or annual basis. Companies were also looking at software from the standpoint of how much value it could bring to them and were not willing to get rid of existing applications.

The launch of the beta version of Internet browser Rockmelt in November 2010 was hailed as an important development in cloud computing. Rockmelt is backed by Marc Andreesen, the founder of Netscape. Unlike traditional browsers that exist on the user's local computer, the user logs in to Rockmelt, so a user can access it on any computer or device connected to the Internet and have access to a personalized browsing experience complete with favorites and social networking friends. Rockmelt was designed to leverage the popular social networking phenomenon by synching with sites such as Facebook and Twitter through Application Programming Interfaces (APIs).

The April 2010 launch of the Apple iPad tablet computer was also a potential watershed development. The iPad sold 300,000 units in its first day, and Apple delayed the international launch of the product to try to keep up with the domestic demand. This success spawned competitors to begin developing their own similar devices. Software on the iPad is entirely in the form of "apps" which are purchased through an online store and downloaded to the device so they can then, in most cases, be used without being connected to the Internet. Traditional packaged software is completely done away with. Whether competing devices, once they arrive, use the same model remains to be seen. One competing device, the JooJoo tablet, reportedly runs only Web-based apps. Market research firm IDC projected that in 2011, 15 million media-centric tablet computers could be sold. By 2015, ABI Research expected annual sales to reach 57 million.

The U.S. economy continues to grapple with the issue of outsourcing. There have been concerns in the U.S. software industry, in particular, of outsourcing of jobs to India. On a November 2010 trip to India, U.S. President Barack Obama addressed these by saying that open economic relations between the two nations could be a win-win and that India was a creator of jobs in the U.S. rather than a destroyer.

RESEARCH AND TECHNOLOGY

As businesses and individuals looked at computers and software to increase efficiency and communication, research and development has played a major role in the prepackaged software. Software makers began to develop emerging markets, such as software agents, middleware, groupware, multimedia software, enterprise resource planning (ERP) software, and Internet software.

Software agents are artificial intelligences that perform specific, repeating, predictable tasks for a computer user or another software application, such as maintaining an electronic calendar, locating information, or monitoring network and computer performance and informing an administrator should there be a problem. Ongoing development was expected to increase the sophistication and proliferation of software agents. As client/server technology continued to escalate, along with budding open computer systems and electronic communication, businesses began to seek software solutions to create computer networks and link platforms and software. These solutions would mediate and translate unrelated systems, allowing them to share information in a common format and making the differences between systems imperceptible to their users and programmers. According to the International Data Corp. (IDC), "Business enterprises will increasingly deploy large-scale distributed applications, but will depend on an industry that spares business applications developers from the burden of dealing with each network technology's idiosyncrasies." Increased reliance on middleware, which consists of programs that reconcile communications between end-use applications and network operating systems, was expected to provide a growing niche in the business software market.

Groupware, another offshoot from the proliferation of client/server technology, allowed groups of people to share information and communicate electronically. A similar application that increased corporate efficiency was enterprise resource planning (ERP) software. ERP software was customized to help companies manage complete business, manufacturing, and communication functions within one system. Leaders in the industry included SAP AG, Oracle Corporation, Baan, and PeopleSoft.

One of the hottest growth areas for software developers was the Internet and the accompanying rush to create personal and corporate web pages. Other strong Internet markets were browser and application building tools, including PERL, CGI, C++, VB, ASP, and DHTML. Internet programming language was a decidedly competitive market with high growth potential. The industry standard was the hypertext mark-up language (HTML), but other languages had to be used in conjunction with it for Web sites to perform complex tasks. In the late 1990s, Java programming language from Sun Microsystems was the target of much controversy for its slow loading and running speed on the desktop. When Microsoft developed a Windows-only version of Java, Sun sued Microsoft and won an injunction that prevented Microsoft's use of the Java logo. Nevertheless, many in the industry encouraged Sun to make Java more available to promote growth in the Windows market and gain leadership as a provider of Internet programming language.

In 2002, as losses mounted, software companies worked to return to profitability by focusing on the storage of networking software to increase their share of corporate dollars. Nearly all the technology frontrunners and many of the small independent companies began to write software that allowed all firms, even if their computers were incompatible with other computers, to efficiently access data from storage providers. However, the result of intense data-storing competition was that some competitors were crushed.

In the mid-2000s, "brain fitness" software programs experienced increased popularity with the aging baby boomer generation. Studies of brain functions showed that ongoing stimulation from new ideas and regular mental exercise increased brain fitness. Programs like *mPower Cognitive Fitness System* from DaKim, *Mindfit* from Cognifit, and *Brain Fitness Program* from Posit Science helped people suffering dementia and memory loss. A study done by the *New England Journal of Medicine* showed that people who regularly completed brain stimulation tasks lowered their risk of dementia 63 percent.

Considerable resources continued to be devoted to battling software piracy in 2010. Microsoft remained a leader in this, with 10 of its own crime labs and an estimated US$200 million annual budget devoted to anti-piracy technology. The security devices being deployed included holographic imagery and a special strand of thread embedded in authenticity stickers. Microsoft's labs can also analyze software CDs and compare them to a global database of known CD pressing machine patterns to determine where a particular CD was made. Despite such safeguards, counterfeiters adapt, and it remains a battle for software firms to keep up with them.

WORKFORCE

The need for labor for the software industry was on the rise in 2005, but the trend to send work offshore was raising some flags in several countries. For example, in mid-2005, IBM was proceeding with its plans to lay off 13,000 workers in Europe and the United States, while adding 14,000 workers in India. Governments worldwide were carefully watching this trend which was causing increased unemployment in their countries.

According to the U.S. Bureau of Labor Statistics, computer software engineers and programmers accounted for about 1.3 million jobs in the U.S. in 2008. Employment for these positions is expected to grow by 21 percent between 2008 and 2018, faster than the average of other jobs. The number of computer programmers is actually expected to decline, but the growth of computer software engineers to work with Internet and mobile technologies is expected to more than offset. Median annual earnings of this group were US$85,430 in May 2008.

INDUSTRY LEADERS

Microsoft. Bill Gates started Microsoft in 1975 after he dropped out of Harvard at age 19 and founded "Microsoft" with friend Paul Allen in a hotel room in Albuquerque, New Mexico. In 1979, Gates moved Microsoft to his hometown, Bellevue, Washington, where he developed software that enabled users to write programs for personal computers. In 1980, Microsoft beat strong competitor Digital Research to write operating system software for IBM's new PC. For less than US$100,000, Gates and Allen bought the rights to the existing QDOS, which stood for "quick and dirty operating system," from Tim Paterson of Seattle Computer Products; they renamed the software MS-DOS.

MS-DOS was an instant success and eventually became the standard OS for all IBM and IBM-compatible PCs. Microsoft continued to develop software for other companies, including Apple and Radio Shack. Paul Allen left Microsoft in 1983, but continued to own approximately 10 percent of Microsoft stock and to sit on the company's board of directors. Gates continued to move Microsoft in new directions, introducing Windows in the mid-1980s. By 1986, he had taken the company public, retaining 45 percent of its shares. In 1993, Microsoft introduced Windows NT client/server software, keeping pace with increasing use of the network operating system (NOS). In the late 1990s, Windows NT5, which was renamed Windows 2000, and Unix were fighting to be the dominant corporate system architecture. In 2001, when Windows XP was introduced, InfoWorld reported that the OS failed to perform as well as Windows 2000, which it had replaced. Microsoft CEO Steve Ballmer promised that the next Windows operating system would be simpler and unified, addressing long-standing deficiencies in storage. The next version of Windows was originally nicknamed "Longhorn," but was launched as Windows XP in 2005.

During the 1990s and into the early 2000s, antitrust suits were brought against Microsoft by the U.S. Department of Justice as well as several others, including the European Commission. In 1995, the company agreed to alter marketing tactics to settle an antitrust investigation and cancelled plans to acquire Intuit, the owner of the successful Quicken financial software package. In 1998, Microsoft was targeted in a lawsuit alleging that the company abused its "near monopoly" by bundling its web browser, Microsoft Explorer, with its Windows operating system. In spring 2002, the revised settlement between Microsoft and the federal government stopped Microsoft from promoting Windows Media Player and the Explorer browser over those of competitors like AOL Time Warner. The government required the Windows operating system to allow its competitors' software to also launch if that was a customer's preference. In 2004, the European Commission assessed Microsoft a US$655 million fine after it found that the company had abused its monopoly position. In addition, the company was told that it had to offer a version of Windows that did not include its own media player so other industry players could compete in the market.

Security remained an important issue with Microsoft. In 2008, Microsoft launched Equipt, "an all-in-one security and productivity software subscription service for consumers." Equipt is a single package combining Microsoft Office Home and Student 2007 and including Word, Excel, PowerPoint, and OneNote as well as OneCare Security Suite.

In 2009, Microsoft launched the latest version of its flagship operating system, Windows 7. In fiscal 2010, Microsoft's revenue reached US$62.5 billion, with net income of US$18.8 billion. It had offices in over 100 countries and had begun offering cloud-based services such as Web App versions of its Word, Excel, Powerpoint, and OneNote products.

While Bill Gates has turned over day-to-day management of the company to Chief Executive Officer Steve Ballmer, Gates was called "the foremost applied economist of the second half of the 20th century" by Steve Lohr, who gave credit to Gates and Microsoft for shaping the way people think about the behavior of twenty-first century technology markets. Microsoft had been described as being "a master practitioner of network effects and more" and had been identified as an expert in attracting consumers and software developers to technology. As the number of users of technology increased, the number of available products also increased. However, as the Internet has gained popularity, Microsoft struggled to catch up to Google, which had become the Internet leader the way Microsoft led the PC segment.

International Business Machines Corporation. Charles Flint created Calculating-Tabulating-Recording (CTR) in 1910 by merging his two companies, International Time Recording Company and Computing Scale Company, with a third company called the Tabulation Machine Company, which had been started by Herman Hallerith. In 1914, Flint hired Thomas Watson as the general manager of CTR. Watson would later become president of the company. Watson created a powerful business sales force that became known for its superior customer service and devoted most of the company's resources to the tabulator division. Under his leadership, the company quickly expanded in sales and size, moving into Europe, Asia, and Latin America. In 1924, CTR became known as International Business Machines, focusing on large tabulations machines. By 1949, it had operations in 58

countries and created IBM World Trade Corporation, which enjoyed the same dominance in foreign markets as it did in the United States.

The rise of PC software firms such as Microsoft cut into IBM's industry dominance in the 1970s and 1980s. In 1995, IBM purchased Lotus Development Corporation, which had been the seventh largest software publisher, for US$3.5 billion and began major restructuring efforts. A plan was implemented that allowed one contract and one discount to cover multinationals wherever they did business, making it easier for multinational companies to do business with IBM and break down barriers between countries. In an effort to unify its global operations, the company shifted power from managers who oversaw the operations of an entire country to managers of 14 industry sectors. IBM had continued to expand its software division through the acquisition of key products. By June 2005, it had acquired identity resolution software developer SRD, enterprise data integration software Ascential Software, open source application infrastructure software Gluecode Software, application relocation software Meiosys, and asset management software Isogon.

In 2009, IBM reported revenues of US$95.8 billion and net income of US$13.4 billion, with 399,409 employees worldwide.

Fujitsu Ltd. In 1935, Fuji Electric Co., Ltd., created Fujitsu to build telephone equipment. In 1954, it entered the data processing arena with the development of Japan's first computer, which was called the FACOM 100. To ensure the success of its new computer industry, Japan's Ministry of International Trade and Industry (MITI) put up trade barriers. Japan also sponsored the development of new computers through a public utility created in the 1950s called National Telephone and Telegraph that created a guaranteed market for Japanese-made computers. In the 1960s, MITI helped fund and direct Fujitsu's creation of mainframe systems. Despite these efforts, however, Fujitsu computers continued to lag technologically far behind those of IBM. In 1972, Fujitsu invested in the Amdahl Corporation, which was owned by the primary creator of IBM's extremely successful 360 series computers, and in 1997, it completed the acquisition when it bought the remaining 55 percent of Amdahl. This investment gave Fujitsu the technological knowledge it needed and put the company on a par with IBM.

In 2002, the company's finances faltered. Fujitsu announced that it planned to lay off as many as 4,000 employees after reporting a US$2.9 billion loss in fiscal 2002. The company planned to close shops in more than 400 locations around the globe. By 2004, the company reported revenues of US$45.1 billion, up more than

17 percent from 2003. For fiscal 2010, the company reported revenues of US$58 billion and some 173,000 employees. It was the largest IT services firm in Japan and third-largest in the world.

Oracle. Programmers Lawrence Ellison and Robert Miner teamed together in 1977 to start a new software firm. Ellison had been a vice president of systems development at Omex Corporation and met Miner at Ampex Corporation where Miner was his supervisor. Both had extensive experience creating customized database programs for government agencies, and they picked up a lapsed US$50,000 contract to build a database for the Central Intelligence Agency (CIA). They pooled their money; rented office space in Belmont, California; and started Oracle. In 1978, they created the Oracle RDBMS (relational database management system), which was the world's first such system to use SQL. By 1982, the company became profitable with US$2.5 million in revenues.

As the world's largest enterprise software company, Oracle grew stronger in January 2005 when it acquired competitor PeopleSoft for US$10.3 billion after a hard-fought takeover battle. It was the largest merger in the software industry to that date. Oracle was a provider of Information Architecture, offering databases designed for large-scale computing; application software, including that designed to aid the management of customer relationships, corporate performance, finances, human capital, procurement, projects, and the supply chain; and middleware products. The merger with PeopleSoft boosted the company's total employee count to more than 50,000 and its application customer count to 23,000.

Oracle's strength was the ability of its product to run across multi-platform computer environments, share data with other software packages, and use structured query language (SQL). SQL was an industry-standard created by IBM that enabled access to various databases and provided information about the data using a common language. The company's principle business activities included the development and marketing of an integrated suite of computer software products used for database management, computer-aided systems engineering, applications development and decision support, as well as families of software products used for financial, human resource, and manufacturing applications (ERP software). Through its subsidiaries, Oracle marketed its products along with related consulting, educational, support, and systems integration services.

In April 2009, Oracle acquired hardware and software firm Sun Microsystems, claiming that the move made Oracle the only provider of a "complete technology stack in which every layer is integrated to work together as a single system." In fiscal 2010, the firm reported

revenues of US$26.8 billion, up 15 percent from 2009. The firm counted more than 370,000 customers in over 145 countries.

CA Technologies. CA Technologies was founded in 1976 as an agreement between Charles Wang and Switzerland's Computer Associates to sell the company's software in the United States. Wang and four employees began by selling CA-SORT, a file organizer for IBM storage systems. By 1980, Wang was successful enough to buy out his Swiss partners. CA continued to acquire existing software products and in 1989, became the first independent software company to reach US$1 billion in sales. By the 1990s, CA was marketing software for mainframe utilities, microcomputers, and mainframe databases. Acquired products included spreadsheet software from Sorcim in 1984, accounting software from BPI in 1987, and data security software. CA also acquired companies such as Applied Data Research from Ameritech in 1988; Pansophic Systems, a developer of applications for IBM AS/400 machines, in 1991; rival Legent, in 1995; and Cheyenne Software, a network management expert, in 1996.

CA is known for its acquisition of struggling software companies that it then vigorously downsizes. In the mid-1990s, Computer Associates acquired ASK Group, a software group that makes database and manufacturing management software, which helped the company penetrate the client/server market. In 2005, the company continued its acquisition strategy, despite several years of poor financial results.

Among the world's leading management software companies in 2010, New York-based CA Technologies was providing software and services that dealt with storage, security, operations, product lifecycle, and service management. Market research firm IDC reported that CA was the world leader in asset management software sales with a global market share of 12.7 percent. By 2008, revenues had reached US$4.3 billion. In 2010, CA Technologies reported 13,200 employees, of whom some 5,600 were engineers. For fiscal 2009, the company again reported approximately US$4.3 billion in revenue.

SAP AG. Founded in 1972, German software giant SAP AG was the world's third largest independent software supplier in 2005 and was the largest provider of inter-enterprise software products that allow businesses to collaborate. In 2007, the company reported sales of about US$15 billion. In 2010, SAP reported 52,921 employees and over 105,000 customers in more than 120 countries. Total revenue for fiscal 2009 was US$14.7 billion

The company produced midrange and high-end applications suites and dominated the global client/server arena. SAP gained dominance in the marketplace by offering software modules for business areas, such as accounting, manufacturing, and human resources that were highly integrated with each other. It gave companies a single solution to tracking business operations instead of combining a hodgepodge of disparate systems. Two of SAP's main product lines were R/2 software for mainframes and R/3 software for client/server systems. SAP also was credited as a founder of enterprise resource planning, known in the information technology (IT) industry as ERP, which was one of the hottest industry trends of the late 1990s. ERP software helped corporate technology professionals automate manufacturing processes, organize accounting books, and streamline departments like human resources, in addition to a variety of other functions related to the corporate trend toward reengineering for optimal cost efficiency.

Novell, Inc. Novell was founded in 1980 as a manufacturer of personal computers. The company was on the verge of dissolving when it was rejuvenated by Raymond Noorda, an electronics engineer, who purchased 33 percent of the company after seeing its software. Noorda then propelled the company into the network-computing arena. Novell was the leading network software company, principally through its NetWare product line, and was the industry's tenth-largest software provider in 1996, with software sales of US$1.2 billion. Major competition for Novell came from IBM-owned Lotus Notes, which competed against Novell's corporate information management and e-mail systems GroupWise and Manage-Wise, as well as Microsoft's Windows NT OS, which was competition for Novell's NetWare. After an unsuccessful attempt to compete with Microsoft in the desktop suite market by acquiring WordPerfect Corporation for a short time before selling it to Canada's Corel Corporation, Novell continued to seek new business in the mid- to late 1990s.

Massachusetts-based Novell offered infrastructure software and services in 43 countries in 2005. The company was one of the hardest hit in the software industry in 2001 and began restructuring in 2002 by cutting one-fifth of its workforce. For 2001, Novell's revenues were US$1.04 billion, down from US$1.16 billion in 2000. In 2001, the company also reported an unprecedented loss of US$272.9 million, compared to its slim profit margin of US$49.5 million in 2000. In 2003, Novell continued to struggle as revenues fell 2.5 percent to US$1.1 billion, and the company reported a US$161.9 million net loss. The figures were looking better by 2004, when revenues increased slightly to US$1.17 billion, and net income was positive once again at US$57.2 million. However, in 2009, the company continued to face financial challenges, reporting a net loss of US$212.7 million, the third straight year of a net loss.

MAJOR COUNTRIES IN THE INDUSTRY

China. Although China was barely in the computer software industry in 1990, by 2003, the country had emerged as a small, but confident and vigorous, player in the software industry. Valued at about US$7.2 billion in 2000, software sales in China had reached about US$19.3 billion by 2003 according to the China Software Industry Association. In 2000, China was home to 8,582 software companies that marketed approximately 18,000 products. Of those companies, the top four (IBM, Microsoft, Oracle, and Sybase) received only 19 percent of total industry sales. China's growth rate exceeded 30 percent annually in the early to mid-2000s and had been hard to ignore. The PC business market for software was expected to grow 215 percent between 2003 and 2008. The business software portion of the market was valued at US$2.4 billion in 2003. Applications software was the largest segment of this sector, accounting for more than 50 percent of market value. The Chinese government had attempted to eliminate piracy in the industry after China was admitted to the World Trade Organization.

Growth continued at an explosive pace, bolstered by the development of systems integration software. Outsourcing of software production was also helping the industry. China had become the largest external manufacturing base for Japan in the late 2000s.

France. Software developed in France was created primarily for the aeronautics, finance, defense, and manufacturing industries, but 70 percent of the packaged software used was being imported primarily from the United States. PC software sales in the early 2000s had slowed in France as they had in many countries, but by 2003, the market was again reporting growth. France's domestic packaged software market had been valued at US$7.6 billion in 2002 by the U.S. & Foreign Commercial Service. French software companies posted sales of US$28.5 billion, making it Europe's leading nation in the industry. By 2003, PC business software sales grew to a value of more than US$2.5 billion, up more than 14 percent over 2002 levels, and the sale of word processing packages made up the largest component of this at more than 34 percent. Industry leader, Microsoft, dominated this market sector, taking in over 60 percent of all PC business software-related sales.

According to Syntec informatique, the software industry association of France, the French software industry continued growing in 2004 as the software package tool sector showed 3 percent growth and the software application sector reported 1 percent growth. Growth during 2005 was about 5 percent. More than 30,000 people were employed in the industry.

In 2008, it was reported that seven leading national software firms had been acquired by foreign companies in the prior year, marking a turning point for the industry in France. As a result, revenues of the top 100 software firms in France fell some 13.2 percent. Bernard-Louis Roques, a General Partner with Truffle Capital, noted that French software firms would need to "internationalize" to remain viable in the face of competitive challenges from India, China, and the United States.

Germany. In 2003, the U.S. Commercial Service found that Germany was the second leading software market worldwide, although the United Kingdom was very close in terms of market size. Valued at US$18.75 billion, the software market in Germany had shown slight declines in the early 2000s due to the country's economic slowdown. However, the market grew about four percent in 2004. Leading this growth trend was an increased demand for security software.

The German market remained highly fragmented, with the top 25 companies controlling about 40 percent of the software market, although the industry was experiencing consolidation. The vast majority of products were imported from the United States and sold through German-based subsidiaries. Of the total software market, networking software sales were about US$1.6 billion in 2003, PC business software sales were US$2.2 billion, and multimedia software sales were about US$1.6 billion. Productivity products, including Internet browsers and e-mail software, were the primary areas of growth in the PC business software sector, while software for commercial used dominated sales in the multimedia sector.

By late 2003, Germany's Federal Ministry of Education and Research had entered into a 30-person venture with China's Ministry of Science to form the Sino-German Joint Software Institute. According to *IPR Strategic Business Information Database,* the inter-governmental venture was created to create high-end software applications, including "operational systems and middleware for a parallel processing next-generation central processing unit, software for mobile communications and multimedia mobile applications, and a common platform for software interface and management."

In November 2010, German software firm SAP was sued by Oracle for US$2.3 billion for allegedly downloading Oracle materials without permission. SAP admitted to the wrongdoing in its now-defunct division TomorrowNow, but disputed the size of damages Oracle was seeking. The case was taking place in California.

Japan. In 1996, with a total software market valued at US$14 billion, Japan held 13 percent of the worldwide market. According to *Business Week,* Japan fell behind in the 1980s by "clinging to proprietary systems" when the market was calling for open standards. Overall computer penetration rates in Japan continued to trail U.S. rates in the 1990s. However, the number of personal computers in Japan increased eight to nine million units per year during the late 1990s as Japanese companies slowly began to use PCs and client/server architecture.

In 2003, the PC business software market in Japan was valued at US$7.7 billion. Although 2003 was a period of low economic activity in Japan, the software industry reported growth of more than 10 percent. During 2003, IBM became the market leader in Japan in this sector, followed by Microsoft, Novell, and Adobe. Pre-packaged business software had taken an increased share of the Japanese market as businesses found the costs of customized packages too high. Growth in the pre-packaged market was expected to be almost 45 percent between 2003 and 2008, according to Euromonitor.

The United States. In spite of growing competition from around the world, the United States continued to be the world leader in the packaged software industry in 2004. The Software & Information Industry Association (SIIA) valued the total software market in the United States at US$103.1 billion that year. More than 905,000 people were working at 23,311 software establishments in the country, with the largest concentration of companies in California.

The PC business software market was valued by Euromonitor at about US$9 billion in 2003, which was a modest increase of 3.6 percent over 2002 figures. In this sector, the five companies that dominated the market were IBM, Microsoft, Novell, Adobe, and Corel. Industry growth was expected to continue to be good; market value reached about US$11.3 billion by 2008.

The media software market in the United States was made up primarily of media development tools and software plug-ins, which combined for sales of US$7.1 billion in 2003. This industry sector remained fragmented, with the five industry leaders (Microsoft, Macromedia, Adobe Systems, Avid Technologies, and Real Networks) taking only about one-quarter of the market. Sales were about US$7.2 billion in 2008 for this sector.

Networking software, which is comprised of network operating systems and groupware, grew 4 percent from 2002 to 2003, reaching a market value of US$4.1 billion. The four companies that controlled about 85 percent of the networking software market were Microsoft, Novell, IBM, and Oracle.

According to the Software Publishers Association, the largest export market for the U.S. software industry was expected to continue be Western Europe, which was home to a sizable technology base.

In its 2010 Software Benchmarking Industry Report, the SIIA reported that the U.S. software industry was coming out of the late 2000s recession "stronger than ever." Revenue of the firms surveyed grew an average of some 15 percent in 2009, and nearly 75 percent of companies expected further growth in 2010.

BIBLIOGRAPHY

"About IBM." International Business Machines, 9 November 2010. Available from http://www.ibm.com.

"About Novell." Novell, 9 November 2010. Available from http://www.novell.com.

"About Oracle." Oracle, 9 November 2010. Available from http://www.oracle.com.

"About SAP." SAP, 9 November 2010. Available from http://www.sap.com.

"About Us." CA Technologies, 9 November 2010. Available from http://www.ca.com.

Allen, Danny. "Apple's Rivals Scramble to Match the iPad." *ComputerWorld,* 21 April 2010. Available from http://www.computerworld.com.au.

Baliga, Harish. "India is Obsessed with SAP Based Custom Software Application—What Happened to Packaged Software? Where is the Indian Software Talent?" 6 July 2008. Available from http://www.indiadaily.com.

Bonasia, J. "Software Programs Feed Need for Brain Exercise," 3 July 2008. Available from http://www. investors.com.

"CA Corporate Fact Sheet." CA Technologies, March 2010. Available from http://www.ca.com.

"China: Beijing Records Record US$120M in Software Exports." *IPR Strategic Business Information Database,* 4 January 2004.

"China: China and Germany to Jointly Develop Software Industry." *IPR Strategic Business Information Database,* 21 October 2003.

"China: Chinese Sales of Software and System Integration Products to Hit 25.3 Billion." *IPR Strategic Business Information Database,* 1 February 2004.

"China—Software Sector Growing, but Faces Challenges." *Information Week,* 12 February 2002.

"Customers Turn to Oracle to Address Performance Management and Business Intelligence Needs," 16 July 2008. Available from http://www.earthtimes.org.

Dannen, Chris. "The Great Mobile Cloud Disruption." *MIT Technology Review,* 8 November 2010.

Desmond, John P. "2004 Software 500: Growth Came in Segments." *Software Magazine,* October 2004. Available from http://www.softwaremag.com.

———. "Infrastructure, Security, Services Sectors Fared Better in a Down Year for the Software 500." *Software Magazine,* December 2003. Available from http://www.softwaremag.com.

"Enhanced Tracking Software, IntelliTrack Version 7.0," 7 July 2008. Available from http://www.datacollectiononline.com.

Fisher, Dennis. "Worms Wreak Havoc on the Net in '03." *eWeek,* 3 April 2003.

Fontana, John. "Microsoft VP Confirms Windows 7 Ship Date: January 2010." *PC World,* 7 July 2008. Available from http://www. pcworld.idg.com.au.

"Fujitsu at a Glance." Fujitsu, 8 November 2010. Available from http://www.fujitsu.com.

"Gartner Predicts 2010." *Gartner Special Report,* January 2010. Available from http://www.gartner.com.

Hickey, Andrew R. "Rockmelt Looks To Liquefy Browser Rivals With Cloud Computing, Social Networking." *CRN,* 8 November 2010. Available from http://www.crn.com.

Hoover, J. Nicholas. "2004 NIST To Develop Cloud Roadmap." *InformationWeek,* 8 November 2010. Available from http://www.informationweek.com.

"India, Creator of US Jobs." *The Economic Times,* 8 November 2010. Available from http://economictimes.indiatimes.com.

Kerstetter, Jim. "Finally, Oracle Nails PeopleSoft." *Business Week Online,* 13 December 2004. Available from http://www.businessweek.com/technology/content/dec2004/tc20041213_8884_tc024.htm

———. "Suddenly, a Mushy Software Market; Corporations Aren't Buying Because of Rising Costs or Concerns About the Economy." *Business Week Online,* 15 July 2004. Available from http://www.businessweek.com.

Lohr, Steve. "Cutting Here, but Hiring Over There." *The New York Times,* 24 June 2005. Available from http://www.nytimes.net.

———. "Google, Zen Master of the Market." *My Times,* 7 July 2008. Available from http://www.mytimes.com.

Lohr, Steve, and Joel Brinkley. "Antitrust Talks Founder on Microsoft's 'Desktop.'" *The New York Times,* 18 May 1998.

Matsutani, Minoru, and Michelle Kessler. "Fujitsu to Cut as Many as 4,000 Jobs." *Bloomberg News,* 8 March 2002.

Meller, Paul. "EU Competition Chair Advocates Open Standards." *Network World,* 10 June 2008. Available from http://www. networkworld.com.

"Microsoft Investor Relations." Microsoft, 9 November 2010. Available from http://www.microsoft.com.

"More Than One-Third of Software is Pirated." *InternetWeek,* 7 July 2004.

Nichols, Shaun. "Microsoft Touts Office Subscription Plan," 3 July 2008. Available from http://www.vnu.co.uk.

"Oracle-SAP legal fight pulls in HP." *San Francisco Chronicle,* 7 November 2010. Available from http://www.sfgate.com.

Roques, Bernard-Louis. "Truffle 100 France," *Truffle Insiders,* May 2008. Available from http://www.truffle.com.

Rosenberg, Steven. "Stealing is Still Stealing." *Press Telegram,* 5 July 2008. Available from http://www.presstelegram.com.

"SIIA Anti Privacy." Software & Information Industry Association 2010. Available from http://www.siia.net.

"Software: Pay-As-You-Go Is Up and Running." *Business Week,* 12 January 2004.

Sondag, Jennifer. "SAP Sees Sales Increasing 15 Percent." *Bloomberg News,* 23 January 2002.

Stape, Andrea L. "Data Storage Firm EMC Notes Loss of $70 Million in Fourth Quarter." *Bloomberg News,* 29 January 2002.

Swartz, Jon, and Michelle Kessler. "Microsoft Predicts Tough Year." *Bloomberg News,* 11 March 2002.

U.S. Bureau of Labor Statistics. "Occupational Outlook Handbook, Computer Software Engineers and Computer Programmers;" 2010-2011. Available from http://www.bls.gov.

"US Software Market To Grow;" *Newsy Stocks,* 25 June 2010. Available from newsystocks.com.

Vance, Ashlee. "Chasing Pirates: Inside Microsoft's War Room." *New York Times,* 6 November 2010.

von Wedel, Xenia. "Korea in Major Push for Software Leadership." Sys-Con Media, 8 November 2010. Available from http://www.sys-con.com.

PERIODICAL PUBLISHING

NAICS CODE(S)

511120. Periodical publishers develop, publish, and market all kinds of magazines and journals, and may or may not perform their own printing. Publishers also may or may not have electronic web versions of the issue currently on the stands. See also **Newspaper Publishing** and **Printing, Commercial.**

INDUSTRY SNAPSHOT

The international periodicals industry is a major source of information and entertainment and serves as a vital advertising medium for other industries. The world's most popular kinds of periodicals are news, sports, lifestyle, outdoor, and computer magazines. From the late 1990s through the early 2000s, the periodical publishing industry grew around the world with modest advances in mature markets, such as Europe and the United States, and more marked growth in developing markets, such as Asia and South America. After the terrorist attacks against the United States on September 11, 2001 (9/11), the industry suffered slowed sales, massive returns of single-copy issues, and, at some publishing houses, employee layoffs.

Quickly following 9/11 came the anthrax-related deaths of postal workers, leading consumers to throw away unread direct-mail solicitations they received and causing even industry leaders such as *Reader's Digest* to put direct mailings temporarily on hold. Nevertheless, a handful of magazines, such as *People,* sold well. Moreover, while the sales of men's magazines in general dropped dramatically in sales and women's magazines had mixed sales, some publications actually gained ad pages. These included outdoor magazines, because consumers chose a vicarious experience through printed media while homebound.

A study by the Graphic Arts Marketing Information Service, titled "Magazines in the 2000–2010 Era," estimated industry growth to be constant at around five percent. It concluded that classes of magazines would have different experiences. For example, weekly news magazines and trade publications were expected to have moderate declines in sales due to online competition in terms of price and the immediacy of news being delivered.

New launches of periodicals are always risky, with about 50 percent folding within 12 months, according to University of Mississippi journalism professor and director of the Magazine Innovation Center, Samir Husni, who kept track of all launches in his annual *Samir Husni's Guide to New Consumer Magazines.* New magazine titles

released in late 2001 and 2002 were on particularly shaky ground, given shrinking ad sales and loss of direct mail effectiveness in the short run. In recent years, the most stunning magazine launch in terms of public recognition and overall success has been Oprah Winfrey's *O,* which had a circulation of 2.5 million in 2010. In 2002, Winfrey announced plans to launch a South African edition of her magazine, although by the end of 2010, that magazine had not yet been launched.

Publishers neared saturation levels in mature markets, with all sorts of periodicals covering a plethora of topics, and some of them looked to new markets for expansion through acquisitions or mergers with foreign producers, joint ventures for new products, or the licensing of periodical titles to foreign companies for local language editions. In the early 2000s, the United States was second to Europe in the production of periodicals, putting out more than one-third of the number of titles published in Europe. In 2002, the United States distributed approximately 10,493 periodicals, generating annual advertising revenues in excess of US$17 billion. By 2008, even as the economy was on a rollercoaster of ups and downs, according to the *National Director of Magazines,* there were over 20,500 titles within the United States.

Mygazines was a magazine-sharing Web site created under the name John Smith. The site provided digitized magazine issues from around the world that had been scanned in their entirety. Many of the magazines available on the site were placed there without their publisher's consent. The Periodical Publishers Association was urging its members to send letters of protest about perceived violation of intellectual property rights. Smith argued that *Mygazines* would "increase current revenue, halt and reverse advertising revenue lost to the Internet, and overcome the lack of the ability for magazines to stay current." It was set up like Youtube, where a registered member uploaded a PDF file of his or her publication, or compiled his or her own publication out of articles from different publications. Within the first month of launch, *Mygazines* had 5,000 registered members without having done marketing. By the second month, there were over 130,000 registered members with over 1 million visits.

ORGANIZATION AND STRUCTURE

The classification "periodicals" encompassed a variety of publications, including business news magazines; statistical reports; comic books; fashion, women's, and home magazines; erotic material; religious periodicals; regional or "city" magazines; literary, travel, and general interest magazines; specialized business and professional periodicals; and a host of other periodicals such as newspaper magazines and supplements, and club and association newsletters.

For magazine publishers in developed countries in Europe, Asia, and the Americas, revenues were derived from two primary sources: sales to customers through subscriptions or the newsstand, and income from advertising space sold to companies advertising in the magazine. In purely economic terms, a magazine's editorial content—its stories and images—can be seen as a vehicle for matching information or entertainment to an identifiable target audience that was willing to pay for it. Once this readership was identified, advertisers seeking to reach that group of consumers supplemented the publisher's circulation sales revenues by paying for the opportunity to market their goods through the magazine's ad pages. In the United States, the amount of revenue a typical publisher derived from advertising versus sales of subscriptions and single copies was almost equal. In the world's less-developed media markets, however, where the number of potential advertisers was limited, magazine publishers relied on sales to readers for a greater proportion of their revenue.

The International Federation of the Periodical Press (FIPP) was the only organization of magazine publishers with members from countries around the world. Founded in France in 1925, FIPP served as a platform for the exchange of ideas and for the freedom, integrity, and development of the world's periodical industry. In 2010, FIPP reported more than 800 members in 68 countries, representing more than 560 publishing companies and 213 associate companies. FIPP represents more than 6,000 member magazine titles including most all of the worldwide leading magazine brands. With headquarters in London, FIPP's membership represented magazine titles in the United Kingdom, the United States, France, the Netherlands, Japan, and South Korea.

Global Contrasts. The characteristics of the world's periodical markets varied widely. While magazines in the United States came and went in substantial numbers every year, magazine markets like those of the United Kingdom were comparatively stable, with loyal readerships for specific titles. Similarly, while two-thirds of all new magazines in the United States were quarterly or bimonthly publications, the vast majority of mainland China's magazines were published monthly.

Other aspects of the periodical publishing industry varied widely around the world. According to a report by the Pew Project for Excellence in Journalism, the number of ad pages in the U.S. had been declining in the last half of the 2000s. They experienced a dramatic drop in 2009 to 34,795 in U.S. magazines, a 9.4 percent decline from 2008. Ad revenue fell 3.9 percent to US\$4 billion. *U.S. News & World Report* was hit the hardest with 81 percent fewer advertising pages in 2009. This was largely reflective of its change from a weekly magazine to a monthly

one. Six of the nation's leading magazines were studied; collectively, they saw a 25.6 percent ad revenue decrease from 2008. Moreover, while subscriptions accounted for 90 percent of the sales of many consumer magazines in the United States, less than 10 percent of consumer magazine sales were subscription-based in the United Kingdom and even less in Asia. This rate was indicative of the emphasis on newsstand sales throughout Europe. There were several reasons for the meager subscription totals in Asia and Europe. Postage rates in most Asian and European nations are substantially higher than in the United States, making subscriptions sales a much costlier proposition for European and Asian publishers, as well as for outside publishers looking to enter those markets. In addition, while U.S. publishers maintained exhaustive mailing lists or rented them from other publishers, many other countries in the world had far less advanced customer lists or had strict privacy laws regarding periodical sales via the mail.

Furthermore, population size influenced the periodical publishing industry around the world. Given the United Kingdom's small population, for instance, British publishers were generally forced to use much smaller print runs than U.S. publishers. Per-copy production costs for most British magazines were consequently much higher, and British publishers did not share the luxury of U.S. publishers to accumulate production cost deficits in anticipation of future sales. Similarly, while U.S. publishers in the early 2000s continued to seek ways to reduce the print costs of periodical titles, publishers in Japan continued to produce magazines that required the use of varying paper grades and printing techniques within a single issue. In unstable markets such as Russia, rampant piracy of printed material led to huge losses through outright theft or illegal duplication, while limited freedom of the press in markets such as China and Singapore placed editorial constraints on periodical publishers. Other factors, such as copyright law, postal efficiency, inflation rates, and sophistication of printing technology, all varied from region to region, making generalizations about the global periodicals market difficult. Because magazines were judged in far more subtle and subjective ways than other products—with the success of any given magazine resting heavily on matters of style, cultural expectation, and taste—the global periodicals industry in the 2000s was still far from real standardization.

Magazine publishers were constantly challenged by postal rate increases and benefited from unique services such as RR Donnelley's DistributionOptimizer Service. Use of the service, which allowed the company to place bundled periodicals from different titles onto the same pallet, resulted in improved delivery times, lower postage rates, and more predictable mail costs.

North America. The United States, Canada, and Mexico comprised one of the world's largest periodical markets, with the United States leading with 10,493 titles in 2002. Mexico's magazine publishing sector, with about 1,500 titles, surpassed the approximately 1,400 titles from Canada, in part owing to the implementation of the North American Free Trade Agreement (NAFTA) in the mid- to late 1990s that stirred increased international activity in Mexico's periodicals market.

Europe. The European magazine market was both saturated and segmented. There was little demand for new magazine titles, and existing titles could not easily be extended from one market to another. While the U.S. periodicals market was fluid and did not present significant barriers to entry, the sheer diversity of the European market, with 20 languages in 24 countries, represented a major obstacle to foreign entry. Nonetheless, magazines remained a significant medium for advertisers in Europe in contrast to other parts of the world, accounting for about 25 percent of all advertising expenditures. In North America, magazines represented 14 percent of the total advertising expenditures, and in Asia, 7 percent. Much of the international placement of magazines was targeted toward large airport traffic areas, such as Philadelphia, New York, and Washington, D.C. That was also true of outlet store placements that had the best sales in U.S. communities, with large ethnic groups or large numbers of international travelers represented.

In 1995, Europe was the largest exporter of periodicals in the world, accounting for no less than 62.8 percent of the total value of global periodical exports, including books and newspapers, and 50.3 percent of global imports. Nonetheless, Europe controlled a smaller portion of the world's publishing industry than it did in the mid-1980s when it held 75 percent of the export market. The leading European periodical-producing nations from the mid-1990s through the 2000s were Germany, France, the United Kingdom, Italy, the Netherlands, Belgium, Spain, Austria, and Switzerland. The European Magazine Publishers Federation (Federation Europeenne d'Editeurs de Periodiques, or FEEP) was the representative trade association of the European periodical press. It represented 7,000 publishers of 40,000 magazine titles with annual 2001 sales of US$40 billion. A 2000 survey of publishers in Poland, Hungary, the Czech Republic, Estonia, Latvia, Slovakia, Slovenia, and Lithuania found that nearly 20 percent of all print publishers also had online editions.

In the mid- to late 1990s, U.S. and British magazine imports were also increasingly in demand in Eastern European countries. *Playboy* successfully launched Czech, Polish, and Hungarian editions in the 1990s, while *Business Week* and *Scientific American* introduced local-language editions in Hungary, *Reader's Digest* began a

Hungarian-language edition in 1991 and planned a Czech edition, and *Okay America* was introduced in Poland. As former Soviet-bloc countries joined the European Union in 2004, enjoying improved economic conditions, analysts expected to see increased competition in the region's traditionally fragmented industry, with likelihood of accelerated consolidation.

Russian Federation. In 1995, Russia exported US$61.9 million worth of magazines, periodicals, and books, up more than 300 percent from US$14.6 million in 1994. *Reader's Digest*'s introduction of a Russian-language edition in 1991 illustrated the growing number of international publishers testing the market in the former USSR. In the mid-1990s, however, Russia's publishing industry remained plagued by piracy, inflation, and economic and political uncertaint,y. By 2002, Russia had made great inroads in the area of copyright and respect for artistic rights of composition. While Germany and other nations had a financially rough 2001, ad sales in Russia in 2001 were the best since 1997, and the magazine industry's 2001 revenues were 43 percent higher than in 2000. Taking advantage of what its president and COO called the "great growth opportunities" in the Russian market, European media giant SanomaWSOY announced its planned acquisition in 2005 of Independent Media, the Russian Federation's leading magazine publisher.

South America. South America's leading exporters included Colombia, Chile, Argentina, and Brazil. While Colombia's and Brazil's international sales fluctuated throughout the 1990s, Chile's and Argentina's grew steadily from less than US$10 million (including newspapers and magazines) in 1991 to more than US$56.6 and US$33.2 million respectively in 1995. However, dire circumstances developed in the late 1990s, with magazine circulation in Argentina alone dropping 50 percent between 1998 and 2004. In 2001, Argentina had 1,118 international titles and 1,007 domestic titles, but by 2002, this number had plummeted to 398 and 692, respectively. Although this climate made South America a risky location for international publishers seeking success in the local magazine market, some international companies made Latin American purchases in 2001, including Thomson Legal & Regulatory, which bought *La Ley*, Argentina's biggest publisher of legal periodicals. Thomson also bought into Brazil publishing with the purchase of *Sintese*, Brazil's highest circulation electronics publication in 2000. Thomson's worldwide revenues in 2000 were US$2.6 billion.

Brazil's largest magazine publishers were sizable companies, such as Grupo Abril, the largest magazine publisher in Latin America; Bloch Editores; and Correio Brasiliense. Similarly, leading periodical publishers in

Colombia, including Cano Isaza Y Cia and Legislacion Economica Ltda, were often diversified companies with interests in other areas of manufacturing such as stationery and newspapers. Venezuela's magazine publishing industry was anchored in Caracas, where firms primarily focused on magazines, such as Editorial Primavera CA, competed for the magazine market against companies like Editora Noti-Globos CA, which primarily published newspapers, and Grabados Nacionales CA, which was a book publisher and commercial printer. Similarly, Argentina's Editorial Atlántida SA and La Ley SA Editora e Impresora were major magazine publishers involved in their country's book publishing, printing, and, in the case of La Ley, newspaper publishing industries.

Asia and Oceania. In addition to repercussions from the terrorist attacks against the United States on September 11, 2001, which quickly and adversely affected ad sales in Asia, the market for Chinese-language magazines became far more competitive as Taiwan and mainland China became associated with the World Trade Organization (WTO). Taiwan had about 6,000 magazines in 2001, but most analysts believed that the potential market for readers was untapped as only about 10 percent were found in stores, with the remainder being subscription only. Three thousand of those magazines were launched after 1996 in Taiwan. Magazine publishing in Asia and Oceania consisted of several highly individualized markets dominated by Australia, Singapore, China (including Hong Kong), and Japan. In 1995, Australia ranked among the leading ten importers of periodicals in the world with imports valued at US$158.1 million. The leading magazine publishers in Australia were Australian Consolidated Press, which published its own titles as well as magazines licensed by foreign publishers, and Rupert Murdoch's The News Corporation Limited which suffered global financial reversals in 2001. More than 75 percent of the corporation's sales were from its U.S. businesses. As of 2010, Murdoch's family controlled approximately 30 percent of the company.

Mainland China's magazine market has grown substantially in the early twenty-first century. Advertising in Chinese magazines, while still small relative to U.S. magazines, began to increase throughout the 1990s as more Western magazines entered the market. In fact, by 1997, China ranked eighth for advertising dollars spent on magazines with US$6.7 billion. Family, health, and education titles succeeded in China's market because many consumers were reported to prefer magazines that promoted common good and culture. The number of consumer magazines in China rose from 1,000 in 1978 to about 9,500 titles in 2008. Of those titles, over 5,000 of them were for natural sciences and engineering technology.

Hong Kong returned to Chinese control in 1997, merging one of the world's top ten exporters with one of the world's significant importers. Hong Kong's crowded magazine industry served a population of only six million. An abundance of advertising revenue resulted in an unusually high number of coexisting titles in the mid-1990s. As a result, major U.S. and European magazine publishers, including the U.S. firms AOL Time Warner Inc. and Hearst Corporation and the French publisher Hachette Filipacchi Medias, published Hong Kong editions of their own titles or magazines that originated in Hong Kong. While Hong Kong was geographically small, it carried disproportionate weight in the global periodicals market.

Singapore's magazine industry was significantly influenced by the censorship imposed by its government. The country's market, therefore, remained small and restricted, and men's lifestyle, business, and fashion magazines, introduced by Western publishers, had not been successful. Its leading magazine companies included Singapore National Printers Ltd. and Toppan Printing Co. (Singapore) Pte. Ltd.

South Korea remained a significant trader of periodicals in the late 1990s and early 2000s, where the level of demand for foreign periodicals in the country, which was reflected in the value of magazines and newspapers imported, exceeded that of Thailand, Malaysia, and even Hong Kong. Licensed magazines from multinational publishers constituted a large segment of the market with strong interest in titles such as *Reader's Digest, GEO, Elle, Marie Claire,* and *Enfants.*

In 2002, Asian magazines continued to struggle. One of the larger corporations, Next Media, with holdings in Hong Kong and Taiwan, cut nearly 200 jobs, or 10 percent, of its workforce after stock prices fell in 2002. The layoffs saved the company about US$5 million. Even so, in the early 2000s, analysts expected the most rapid growth for magazines to occur in the Asia-Pacific region, with China and India being the primary contributors to the increase. For the region as a whole, growth of 2.4 percent annually was predicted between 2004 and 2008, reaching about US$11.9 billion. Advertising revenues for magazines were expected to grow about 2.7 percent per year. Japan and Australia, the region's leading publishers with 75 percent of total media revenue, were projected to increase advertising revenue 1.2 percent and 4.4 percent, respectively, in 2005. Even larger ad revenue growth of 6.6 percent was expected in India.

BACKGROUND AND DEVELOPMENT

The history of periodicals began with the insertion of book notices in European news books published in the early seventeenth century. By the middle of that century, publishers began to include critical comments in the notices. In the meantime, digests and abstract journals made their first appearances. These periodicals provided information on books, authors, and important scientific and philosophical matters of the day. The *Journal Des Scavans,* first published in Paris on January 5, 1665, is recognized as the parent of the modern periodical manufacturing industry.

Periodicals offering opinion, news, and entertainment proliferated. In the early eighteenth century, journals of political thought and a broad range of other interests appeared. The first American periodicals were *American Magazine* and *General Magazine,* both of which started in 1741 only to fail less than a year later. While numerous early magazines failed, about 100 magazines and journals had been established in the United States by 1825. By 1850, the total number of magazine titles in circulation had risen to 600. During this period, *Harper's New Monthly Magazine* was launched. This heavily illustrated periodical paved the way for a new era of magazine publishing. Imitators proliferated, and the industry continued to grow.

In the early twentieth century a number of periodicals that continued to endure were founded around the world. Only in the 1950s did a threat to the industry finally present itself as television stole both customers and advertisers. The periodical publishing industry proved to be resilient, however, and continued to enjoy steady growth around the world from the 1960s through the 1980s.

In mature markets, such as Europe and the United States, magazine publishing grew at a moderate pace from the mid-1990s through 2001, led by heightened interest in specialty magazines, lifestyle magazines, and those with computer and technology themes. In developing markets, the industry expanded at a more rapid pace when countries became more open to magazine imports, as incomes and leisure time rose, and as wider segments of these populations achieved higher levels of education.

Magazine publishers around the world continued to grapple with problems associated with the availability and cost of paper. In the face of deforestation worldwide and criticism from governments and environmental organizations, publishers sought new ways to overcome these problems. The Internet offered the most prominent and most successful alternative to traditional print periodicals in the early 2000s. Publishers launched numerous magazines and academic journals, first on proprietary services such as CompuServe and America Online, and later on the Internet. Academic journals, in particular, enjoyed the cost efficiency of the Internet for making their articles quickly available to their readership. Besides offering an alternative to paper periodicals, the Internet also became a popular topic for magazine titles, spawning numerous magazines such as *Wired,* that were devoted to it.

Many of the established U.S. and European periodical publishers have turned to overseas markets in order to increase their circulation and advertising revenues. As growth in their domestic markets continued to slow, these publishers tried to take advantage of the burgeoning markets abroad. By forming joint ventures with local publishers and by licensing their periodicals, these publishers made their foray into Asian and South American markets in the mid- to late 1990s. For example, U.S. Hearst Publications teamed with local publishers to offer *Harper's Bazaar* in South Korea and Russia, and Italy's R.C.S. Rizzoli joined forces with Germany's Burda Verlag GmbH to exploit the Asian magazine market. In order to reap local advertising dollars, some publishers also offered special editions or spin-off titles of their periodicals abroad. *Readers's Digest,* for example, launched several international projects based on the model of Reiman Publications, which it purchased in 2002. These new magazines were circulation-driven and featured reader-contributed editorial content. Among *Reader's Digest*'s new titles were *Our Canada* in Canada and *Sabor di Casa* (Taste of Home) in Brazil. *Scientific American,* which derives more than 85 percent of its international revenues from circulation, had 15 international editions as of 2010, read in more than 30 countries by more than 5.3 million people.

Furthermore, companies in the industry continued to consolidate in the late twentieth century, and the trend was expected to continue for some time. The United Kingdom's United News & Media PLC merged with MAI PLC, becoming a magazine publishing colossus with an arsenal of 200 magazines. The second largest U.K. publisher, EMAP, also expanded its empire by acquiring CLT Multi Media, a Luxembourg publisher. Reed Elsevier, the largest U.K. publisher, considered a merger that would have made it the largest periodical publisher in the world. However, the deal with Dutch Wolters Kluwer fell through because of regulatory objections by the European Commission and the United States. Nonetheless, Reed Elsevier acquired Matthew Bender, a publisher of legal books and periodicals, for US$1.6 billion later in 1998 as part of the company's effort to reposition itself as an information and technology publisher. In addition, Japanese Softbank Corporation, a major publisher in the country, acquired U.S. Ziff Davis, known for its business and computer magazines. Finally, Primedia purchased 29 periodicals, including *Cowles Enthusiast Media* and *Cowles Business Media,* from McClatchy Newspapers Inc. As of 2003, Primedia was the leading publisher of special interest periodicals in the United States.

The global periodicals industry in the 1990s was affected in several ways by continually increasing sophistication. These impacts included less expensive yet more advanced means of magazine production, such as the widespread use of desktop publishing software and computer systems for in-house publication, an increased focus on opportunities offered by multi-media and information-distribution technologies for publishers, and the emergence of more specialized periodical niches and submarkets geared to highly specific reader tastes and interests.

Electronic versions of magazines became more commonly available. By the mid-to-late 1990s, many major U.S. magazines, including *Fortune, Time, People,* and *U.S. News and World Report,* as well as international magazines such as Germany's *Der Spiegel,* were available in electronic editions. These versions enabled readers with a personal computer and Internet access to download articles and images, listen to "sound files," send e-mail to editors, search back issues, and renew their subscriptions. In the mid-1990s, The Electronic Newsstand Inc. began providing periodical publishers in the United States with an online presence, the Global Computer and Information Network. By 1997, more than 90,000 U.S. and Canadian magazines and journals made themselves available on the Internet, with many more in the 2000s. Other nontraditional, "paperless" media, explored by magazine publishers in developed nations, included cable television outlets and interactive multimedia "digital magazines" on CD-ROM.

CURRENT CONDITIONS

A shaky economic period after the September 11, 2001, terrorist attacks against the United States resulted in slow growth for magazine publishing, but stronger economic conditions by 2004 boded well for the industry. Analysts at Pricewaterhouse Coopers (PwC) predicted global spending on magazines to rise from US$80.7 billion in 2003 to about US$93.4 billion in 2008. However, with the economy taking a significant downturn by the mid-2000s, that figure fluctuated up and down dramatically, and by 2010 it was significantly down. In fact, PwC predicted that there would be 3.8 percent annually compounded growth rate in terms of entertainment and media spending through 2014, to reach US$517 billion. However, due to the dramatic rise in electronic media applications, newspaper and consumer magazine publishing would be lower in 2014 than it was in 2009. Consumer behavior is what drives the ever-changing media landscape, with the upsurge in Internet entertainment and news consumption, the rising popularity of mobility devices, and the willingness of the consumer to pay for immediate and convenient delivery of information to personal electronic devices, print periodicals will continue the downward spiral for the foreseeable future.

Periodical publishers worldwide sought new ways to increase their profits in response to a decline in the growth rate of advertising revenue and heated competition with other periodicals and various media outlets such as cable and satellite television. To improve overall profitability, some U.S. publishers explored staff layoffs, salary freezes, reductions in employee benefits, more

efficient mailing procedures, alternative transportation modes, lighter grades of paper, and increased use of subscriber database information. They also increasingly looked to nontraditional revenue sources. Some publishers sold subscriber information to other companies, while others marketed nonprint products and services geared to their readers' interests and lifestyles. Another challenge facing the industry in the late 2000s was the tendency for some advertisers to pull out at the last minute and not commit to future pages.

According to the Study of Public Place Engagement conducted by McPheters & Company, 57 percent of all magazine reading was done away from home. The survey was conducted by McPheters, with support from Conde Nast, Time Inc., Reader's Digest Co., Source Interlink, Hachette Filipacchi Media U.S., and Magazine Publishers of America. Conde Nast Senior Vice President Scott McDonald acknowledged that reading in public places "is one of the key ways that readers engage with magazine brands." According to an article by Joanna Pettas in *Folio,* more than one-third of study participants claimed that they preferred to read in public places, such as doctors' offices, barber and beauty shops, car dealerships, and airline clubs, and more than two-thirds reported that they looked for their favorite magazines in public places. However, more than half of the respondents to the survey indicated that they try new magazines when they are found in public places.

Starting with the October 30, 2008, issue, *Rolling Stone* scaled its issue down to the standard size of most magazines. As the magazine celebrated 41 years of publication in 2008, it had set itself apart from others on the newsstand for decades. "All you're getting from that large size is nostalgia," claimed publication founder, publisher, and editor Jann Wenner. Richard Perez-Pena, in an article in *The New York Times,* acknowledged that "nostalgia" was a powerful marketing tool, even for a magazine that included a youthful demographic. The magazine not only changed its size but also began to use glossy paper and perfect bound design.

Another interesting development was with the October 2008 issue of *Esquire,* which was the first magazine to embed revolutionary digital technology into a mass produced print product by incorporating electronic paper. This achievement was possible due to collaboration with E Ink Corporation, which was exclusive to the magazine through 2009. The potential for growth for print media using new technology was large.

INDUSTRY LEADERS

Hachette Filipacchi Medias (HFM). In the magazine shakeout of 2001 and 2002, the media empire that ascended to the top financially in the wake of AOL

Time Warner's mounting economic crises was the French firm Hachette Filipacchi Medias (HFM), a major figure in international magazine sales. In 2002, Crain Communications announced that HFM had become the world's largest periodical publisher. With annual sales in excess of one billion copies from periodicals such as *Elle, Premiere, Paris Match, Woman's Day, Road and Track,* and *Car and Driver,* the company not only survived the worst year in recent magazine sales, but thrived. Hachette Filipacchi Medias reported annual revenues in 2009 of about US$2.34 billion. In 2010, the company reported that it published about 38 French magazines, 107 international magazines, and six daily French newspapers in addition to its interests in multimedia, Internet, and printing industries. Chairman and CEO Gerald de Roquemaurel and Editor-in-Chief Jean-Louis Ginibre ran the company. French media and industrial conglomerate Lagardere bought the remaining one-third of HFM in 2000. Crain also reported that Roquemaurel had added to the HFM empire's stable of titles with Japanese *Jujingaho,* and a 42 percent interest in *Marie Claire* in 2001. In 2009, HFM sold several magazines to the Bonnier Group, including *American Photo, Flying, Boating, Popular Photography,* and *Sound and Vision.*

Reed Elsevier NV. Like Hachette Filipacchi Medias, the English-Dutch empire of Reed Elsevier not only made it through 2001's general magazine collapse, but it also prospered. In 2001, Reed Elsevier, known for its acclaimed scientific journals, announced a 20 percent increase in its profits for the year. The company benefited from its 2001 acquisition of Harcourt General Inc. for US$5.65 billion. The media group encountered some losses, most notably with the U.S.-based Cahners group, but by cutting staff and taking other cost-cutting measures, Reed Elsevier minimized damage. In 2007, it reached an agreement to sell Harcourt to the Houghton Mifflin Riverdeep Group for US$4 billion in cash and stocks. In April 2010, Reed Elsevier announced plans to sell 21 U.S. magazines and 23 additional trade magazines would cease publication by the end of the decade. The closures were necessitated mostly by the weak economy that created an advertising slump. Net income for 2009 was US$8.46 billion. In 2007, it had 32,000 employees.

Time Warner. Time Warner Inc., formerly AOL Time Warner, was the largest publishing and entertainment company in the world in 2004. Without question, its four major weekly titles made Time Inc. the global king of news and sports publishing. In 1997, it led all U.S. periodical publishers in share of total advertising dollars (21 percent) and revenues of US$24.62 billion, of which publishing accounted for 17 percent. Formed through the merger of Time Inc. and Warner Communications in 1989, Time Warner published such high circulation periodicals as *Fortune, Money, Entertainment Weekly, Sports Illustrated, People, Life,* and *Time.* The company did not shy away from international markets. Time Warner explored more than 20 joint ventures or other arrangements with European and Asian media companies, acquiring, among others, U.K. giant IPC Group Limited. The merger of AOL with Time Warner in 2001 did not pay off for Time Warner, however, due to AOL subscription stagnation and other growth barriers.

Nonetheless, in 2004, the AOL Time Warner properties remained among the most competitive in publishing globally. With 150 magazines worldwide, its Time Inc. brand launched nine major magazines from 1992 to 2002. The company also owned 49 percent of *Essence,* a magazine targeting African-American women. In addition, Time managed the publication operations of American Express and owned the United Kingdom's top magazine publisher, IPC Group Limited, with a collection of approximately 80 titles, including *Marie Claire.* Total sales in 2009 surpassed US$25.8 billion with 31,000 employees.

The Reader's Digest Association, Inc. The world's most popular magazine dates back to 1922, when DeWitt and Lila Wallace published 5,000 copies of their first issue for US 25 cents. In addition to its familiar monthly general interest magazine, Reader's Digest Association, Inc., annually publishes several million books in more than 20 countries, and in the 1990s maintained operations in 50 cities around the world. The company's flagship publication, *Reader's Digest,* had a worldwide readership of 85 million in 2004, with sales reaching US$2.38 billion. That year, the company implemented a major restructuring plan that included regional consolidations, elimination of some non-profitable activities, and reduction of staff. In August 2009, the company filed for bankruptcy, emerging in February 2010 owned by its lenders.

In the early years of the twenty-first century, *Reader's Digest* reinvented itself editorially, adding strong health-related cover lines as a way to continue the publication's broad-based appeal. The Association also published thriving consumer special interest periodicals and special interest magazines that included *Selecciones, The Family Handyman, American Woodworker, New Choices, Moneywise,* and *Benchmark.*

Axel Springer. Axel Springer Verlag AG, based in Berlin, is one of Germany's leading publishers and a key player in several media. Axel Springer owns more than 230 newspapers such as *Die Welt* and *Bild.* In addition, the publisher also controls radio, television, and online operations and a share of America Online's German service.

The family of the founder owns 55 percent of the firm. In 2002, at the end of February, Axel Springer reported reduced revenue and declining advertising sales, as well as losses in other areas of the media empire. That year, the company was struggling to find backers and was refinancing to continue some operations. In addition, it told stockholders that no dividend would be paid, according to the *Los Angeles Times.* Sales improved in 2004, growing 7.2 percent to reach US$3.2 billion.

Simon Thiel reported that Axel Springer had posted an increase in sales of approximately US$2.1 billion during the first six months of 2008. Contributing factors included expanded Internet business, acquisitions that added titles from outside Germany, and the purchase of stakes in foreign TV companies. Axel Springer's goal was to become less dependent on the German economy and the traditional newspaper business. In 2009, the revenue was US$3.64 billion with 10,740 employees.

Hearst. Although traditionally associated with newspaper publishing, the Hearst Corporation entered the magazine business early in its history, launching *Motor* magazine in 1903 and purchasing *Cosmopolitan* in 1905 and *Good Housekeeping* in 1911. As it gradually sold some of its newspapers in the 1950s, it continued to expand its magazine empire, adding such titles as *Popular Mechanics, Redbook,* and *Esquire,* between 1950 and 1990. As of 2009, the company owned nearly 200 magazines around the world. Hearst reported total sales of about US$4.1 billion in 2003. The company expanded its presence internationally by acquiring and forming alliances with local newspapers and magazines. In 2002, the company disclosed that falling ad revenues had rocked its profit structure. In an attempt to stop the decline, Hearst handed pink skips to 8.5 percent of its workforce.

MAJOR COUNTRIES IN THE INDUSTRY

United States. In 2002, total U.S. business and consumer periodicals amounted to about 10,493 titles, according to FIPP. Of this number, slightly more than half were consumer publications and half were business titles. Revenues from advertising continued to rise through 2001, when the September 11 terrorist attacks against the United States marked a decline in ad spending that contributed to sluggish growth for the magazine industry. In addition, implementation of the National Do Not Call Registry in 2003 restricted a favored marketing strategy for publishers. Nevertheless, advertising revenues for consumer magazines began to improve in 2003, and by 2004, they had grown 11.5 percent over the previous year. However, according to a report by the Pew Project for Excellence in Journalism, the number of ad pages in the U.S. began steadily declining in the last half of the 2000s, with a dramatic 9.4 percent decline from 2008 to 2009, for total revenue of about US$4 billion.

Some of the declines in U.S. magazine advertising were voluntary, such as when the tobacco industry agreed to remove ads from youth-oriented magazines under pressure from the *Journal of the American Medical Association.* The largest markets for U.S. publishers in the early 2000s were women's magazines, news magazines, business magazines, and general audience periodicals. The country's leading periodicals included *TV Guide, Good Housekeeping, Family Circle, People, Sports Illustrated, Time,* and *Reader's Digest.*

The U.S. periodical publishing industry has remained vital despite increased competition from television, catalogs, and direct mail for the critical advertising dollar, along with fierce maneuvering to secure a profitable share of the maturing subscription and newsstand circulation market. In the late 1990s and early 2000s, periodical publishers began to explore new segments of the country's population, giving rise to lavish lifestyle magazines, such as *More,* that targeted affluent baby boomers and ethnic magazines that targeted ethnic groups, with titles such as *Latina, Black Enterprise,* and *Inside Asian America.*

In 2001, one of the magazines to suffer massive stock declines and layoffs in its magazine division was the venerable *Playboy.* Hurt by general declines of ad sales and the decision to add hard-core, pay-per-view options (although not under the *Playboy* name) in 2001, some stockholders unloaded their holdings. *Playboy* continued its claim as the top men's magazine, with more than three million readers.

In summer 2003, the San Francisco-based Public Library of Science made an announcement that shook the academic publishing world when it offered a business model based on charging contributors US$1,500 to publish their papers in their journal. The *online publishing news* claimed the library's actions were in response to "steeply rising subscription cost of the most prestigious—and generally highly profitable'research journals."

CBC News analyzed the impact the U.S. economy's problems were starting to have on periodical publishing as newsstand sales of U.S. magazines fell 6.3 percent in the first half of 2008. The Audit Bureau of Circulations concluded that consumers cutting back on non-essential spending due to rising gas and food costs hurt sales of most magazines. Even *Cosmopolitan* reported that sales fell 6 percent to 1.75 million, which was counter to its usual status as the top-selling magazine on the newsstand. Newsstand prices generated substantial revenue because their prices are higher than the prices for subscriptions. Many magazines increase their efforts to get reader subscriptions when there is an economic downturn.

Germany. Until Germany's periodical industry suffered reversals in the 2000s, it had been Europe's most profitable and, in terms of the number of magazines, biggest player. Magazines were taken far more seriously as a cultural source of ideas in Germany than in many other countries, and only Japan produced a wider range of periodicals. In 2010, the German magazine industry was dominated by the "Big Four:" ad sales-beleaguered Axel Springer Verlag, Germany's largest publisher, which had a revenue of US$3.6 billion; Bauer Media Group (US$2.48 billion); Gruner + Jahr AG, a subsidiary of the mammoth international publisher Bertelsmann AG and the largest European printing and publishing firm; and Burda GmbH, with 30 magazines and more than US$1 billion in revenues.

While Heinrich Bauer Verlag published mass circulation periodicals, Gruner + Jahr produced Germany's largest news-oriented magazine, *Der Spiegel,* and the flashy general interest magazine *Stern.* Axel Springer published a highly regarded automobile magazine and shared titles with other major players, such as AOL Time Warner. Burda GmbH was best known as the German version of *Forbes.* Other major German publishers were Gong-Verlag GmbH, Frankfurter Allgemeiner Zeitung GmbH, Verlag das Beste GmbH, and Weltbild Verlag GmbH.

France. During the 1980s and early 1990s, the French magazine market was aggressively targeted by foreign publishers, primarily Germany's Big Four. These international investments succeeded because of the country's outmoded distribution procedures and chaotic advertising rates, and because France's periodicals industry had failed to keep up with readers' tastes. Consequently, German publishers grabbed sizable shares of France's magazine market. France came back strongly in the 2000s, while some German companies faltered due to severe ad sales drops. The dominant player in France's magazine industry during the 2000s was Hachette Filipacchi Medias (HFM), the world's largest periodical publisher. The company boasted annual sales exceeding 1 billion magazines. FIPP claimed HFM's CEO Lagardere was eager to buy more magazines throughout the world, especially in the United States.

In 2004, only *Paris Match,* posted a circulation gain among weekly magazines in France, when readership grew to 4,380,000. By 2010, however, circulation had declined to 1,360,000.

United Kingdom. In the 1990s and early 2000s, fashion magazines performed well when advertising volume increased substantially, climbing to its highest level since 1990. Home decorating magazines also became popular during this period. Interest in car and bike magazines also was revived in the late 1990s. The leading British consumer title, *What's On TV,* sold 1.58 million copies per week in 2004, primarily through newsstand sales, which in the United Kingdom accounts for 92 percent of all consumer magazine sales. Thanks to Reed Elsevier's dominance in educational and scientific titles, as well as its U.S. entertainment industry trade magazine *Variety,* the United Kingdom managed not only to get through the difficult industry times in the 2000s, but also managed to thrive. Nonetheless, to achieve profits, Reed Elsevier continued to publish titles with considerably fewer editorial employees than at U.S. periodical houses. In 2001 and 2002, the lean staffs became even leaner as Reed trimmed 1,000 jobs, or 2.6 percent of its workforce, according to *Bloomberg News.* By 2007, Reed had a staff of 32,000 and by 2009, it announced intentions to sell off most of its North American trade magazines such as *Publishers Weekly* and *Broadcasting and Cable.* However, it would retain *Variety.*

Some publishers elected to pour money into their magazines to keep quality and readers in anticipation of a return to normal ad sales. Conde Nast, for example, announced that in spite of dwindling ad sales for the British *GQ,* it planned to add 20 pages to each issue and hire celebrities to pen regular columns. In 2002, Conde Nast bought Ideas Publishing Group, which produced publications targeted at Spanish speakers, and renamed it Conde Nast Americas.

Netherlands. Major magazine publishing firms in the Netherlands included Verenigde Nederlandse Uitgeversbedrijven BV, Roto Smeets De Boer NV, Hollandse Dagbladcombinatie BV, Sythoff Pers BV, and the English-Dutch partnership of Reed Elsevier PLC, Elsevier NV. Elsevier was the publisher of more than 1,000 scientific and other journals. While Reed Elsevier weathered the 2001 downturn better than most publishers, in late February 2002 it folded its relatively new title, *Electronic Business Asia,* because the monthly publication that was devoted to the microchip trade had about one-fifth of 2000 advertising and about one-third the sales income of 2000.

Canada. Canada houses about 1,400 domestic magazines. However, with scarce advertising revenues, only about half of them turned a profit. The Canadian Magazine Publishers Association reported that almost 80 percent of the magazines on newsstands came from outside Canada, with the majority coming from the United States.

In the mid-1990s, the Canadian government responded to Canadian magazine publishers' fears by taking steps to protect its domestic periodicals industry from encroaching U.S. publishers (a Canadian edition of *Sports Illustrated,* for example, had been introduced in 1993). Although such arrangements had long been in place, legislation was passed that required all prospective Canadian editions of foreign magazines to first gain the approval of the Canadian government. The law was the latest development in a long-standing battle between Canadian and U.S. magazine publishers for market share. This struggle had previously spurred the abolishment of the tax deduction for businesses that advertised in non-Canadian publications and contributed to legislation that required that periodicals sold in Canada pass strict Canadian ownership and content requirements. Finally, in 1997, the World Trade Organization (WTO) ordered Canada to liberalize its protectionist magazine policy when U.S. complaints persisted. In particular, the WTO objected to Canada's 80 percent excise tax on advertising in Canadian editions or split-run editions of non-Canadian magazines. In 1999, the government greatly softened restrictions on U.S. magazines that allowed Canadian advertisers to purchase ad space.

In 2002, as magazine ad sales in general were very soft in Canada, U.S.-based *People* magazine began exploring ways to more aggressively target Canadian advertisers, incurring the displeasure of the Canadian Magazine Publishers Association (CMPA). Hoping to jumpstart Canadian magazine sales, the CMPA joined forces with the Ministry of Tourism, Culture and Recreation to maintain the MagOmania web site, with a goal of putting all Canadian magazines in easy reach of potential readers or advertisers. In 2002, the CMPA continued to work on its National Circulation and Promotion Program (NCPP), a US$5.6 million campaign to ignite reader loyalties for Canadian magazines. The battle was hard to win for the industry. As if the industry did not have enough challenges, in 2002 the Canada Post Corporation (CPC) increased magazine postage, on average, 6.5 percent in April 2002, 4 percent in January 2003, and 6 percent in January 2004.

MacLean Hunter Ltd. of Toronto was the largest Canadian periodicals publisher. The newsweekly *MacLean's* remained the company's flagship publication in the 1990s, but MacLean Hunter continued to be primarily a business trade publisher. Other major Canadian periodical publishers included CCH Canadian Limited, Key Publishers Company Ltd., and Hebdos Telemedia. The media corporation Rogers Communications, Canada's largest, published 70 consumer and trade magazines and ran cable and wireless services. While it had some losses in 2001, its revenue of US$652 million for the year was 6.7 percent higher than 2000 revenue. The company's total sales for 2009 surpassed US$11.359 billion. Canadian magazine sales were expected to grow about 2.1 percent between 2004 and 2008, with ad revenues increasing 4.3 percent annually.

Japan. The Japanese periodicals market remains one of the world's largest. Most of the country's magazine sales come from newsstands because of low subscription levels. Comic book periodicals accounted for 25 percent of all magazine sales in Japan, and the comic magazine *Weekly Shonen Jump,* which sold more than 7 million copies weekly throughout Japan in the mid-1990s, became "the

best-selling product in the history of U.S. comic publishing" when it was introduced to the U.S. market in 2003, according to *Anime Insider* managing editor Robert Bricken, as quoted in a *Time* interview. The launch boosted revenues for publisher Shueisha, which had seen circulation for *Weekly Shonen Jump* decline to only 3.4 million. In the period between 2008 and 2009, the periodical rose in circulation. However, the next closest competitors dropped during that same period. Because of the crowded field of magazines, there was little room for new foreign entrants without the financial resources to absorb short-term losses. The giant Kodansha Ltd. Publishers led the Japanese periodical publishing industry. Other firms in Japan's competitive magazine industry included Asahi Shimbun Publishing Co. Ltd., Shueisha Publishing Inc., and Gakken Co. Ltd. Newspaper publisher Nihon Keizai Shimbun Inc. also maintained a significant presence in the industry via its Nikkei Business Publications Inc. subsidiary.

China. China's booming economy in the early 2000s prompted analysts to predict strong growth in consumer and business-to-business magazines, according to BPA Worldwide. While magazines' share of advertising in China had remained relatively small, it had grown about 33 percent annually since the mid-1980s and was expected to reach US$381 million in 2005. China had reformed its policies on media industry investment to allow greater access to capital, a move that insiders considered likely to spur the development of new publications. As of 2009, China had more than 9,000 magazine licenses, about 1,400 of which were publications produced by the Communist Party or other political institutions. There are 134 national magazines with at least 250,000 subscribers. Analysts expected to see increased consolidation in China's magazine publishing industry through the early 2000s. At the same time, increased competition was seen as a factor that would result in the adoption of best business practices. The Chinese magazine industry's readiness to adopt digital technology had allowed it to cut distribution costs significantly. China's magazine industry was still considered to be in its infancy in terms of business practices. There was a lack of conclusive circulation measurement, which led to exaggerated circulation and revenue figures throughout the industry. To gain new advertisers, due to this practice, businesses could only judge effectiveness from the selling point. This pushed publishers to spend more money on distribution channels rather than improving content and design.

India. Industry analysts have touted India as a huge market since the country agreed in 2004 to allow foreign investors to obtain full ownership of periodicals there. Magazines on technological subjects showed particular potential. International publishing services company

IDG established a subsidiary in India in 2004 and introduced a new magazine, *OutSourcing World,* with a circulation of 30,000. In the works in 2005 was IDG's *CIO India,* an Indian version of the global magazine *CIO.* Also in 2005, both *Business Week* and *Forbes* announced plans to develop Indian editions.

India was inundated by Western magazines that began arriving on newsstands in 2007. They included Indian versions of *Vogue, Rolling Stone, OK!, Hello, Maxim, FHM, Golf Digest,* and *People.* The new Indian editions were targeted at a "new class of nouveau riche Indians" created when the economy soared and two-income families became the norm in some upper-income urban areas. The magazines were written, photographed, edited, and designed almost completely in India, but were published in English with content completely different from their U.S. or British counterparts. For example, the July 2008 Vogue issue featured a cover story about Bollywood debutante Asin Thottum Kal.

There are more than 300 million literate individuals in India who reportedly read no publications. In trying to reach this untapped market, publishers targeted the metros and India's 15 largest population centers. Only three of the most read magazines in India are in English, with the rest published in Hindi or other regional languages. However, the English magazines collect the largest percentage of advertising dollars throughout the country. The International Federation of the Periodical Press predicted that magazine advertising in India would grow 20 percent to US$302 million in 2008. As of 2009, the industry reported revenues of US$335 million, an increase of 7.2 percent. There was an expected annual growth rate to 2013 of 6 to 10 percent.

BIBLIOGRAPHY
2009 Japanese Manga Magazine Circulation Numbers; 18 January, 2010. Available from http://www.animenews network.com.

"Book Sales." *Bloomberg News,* 24 January 2002.

"Esquire Becomes First Magazine to Merge Digital Technology with Printed Pages." *Market Watch,* 22 July 2008. Available from http://www. marketwatch.com.

Fraher, John. "European Stocks Rise, Led by Media, Auto Shares." *Bloomberg News,* 25 February 2002.

Gallagher, Rachael. "Mygazines Creator Defends May Sharing Website." *Press Gazette,* 5 August 2008. Available from http://www. pressgazette.co.uk.

Global Entertainment and Media Outlook 2010-2014. PricewaterhouseCoopers, 2010. Available from http://www. pwc.com.

Ovide, Shira. "Massive Outlay of Ads No Longer in Vogue." *The Wall Street Journal,* 11 August 2008. Available from http://online.wsj.com.

Patterson, Alan. "Reed Elsevier Closing Hong Kong Magazine on Advertising Slump." *Bloomberg News,* 25 February 2002.

Perez-Pena, Richard. "Rolling Stone Switching to Smaller Size." *New York Times,* 14 August 2008.

Pettas, Joanna. "Study: 57 Percent of All Magazine Reading Done Outside the Home." *Folio,* 11 August 2008. Available from http://www.foliomag.com.

Picchi, Aimee. "Martha Stewart 4th-Quarter Profit Falls As Ads Slip." *Bloomberg News,* 20 February 2002.

————. "Reader's Digest 2nd-Qtr Net Drops on Slower Ad Sales." *Bloomberg News,* 24 January 2002.

Puente, Maria. "The High Cost of Celeb-Baby Fever." *USA Today,* 4 August 2008.

"Seventeen Magazine and WNBA Partner for Exclusive Sports Survey for Teen Girls." *Market Watch,* 7 August 2008. Available from http://www.marketwatch.com.

Thiel, Simon. "Axel Springer Says First-Half Operating Profit Rose." *Bloomberg News,* 22 July 2008. Available from http://www.bloom berg.com.

Timmons, Heather. "In India, Magazines That Translate Well." *The New York Times,* 14 July 2008. Available from http://www.nytimes.com.

SIC 2750

PRINTING, COMMERCIAL

NAICS CODE(S)

32311. Printing companies engage in lithographic, gravure, or other commercial printing. The industry likewise performs offset and photo-offset printing and photolithographing.

INDUSTRY SNAPSHOT

The years between 1980 and the middle of the first decade of the 2000s were a period of digital revolution for the world's multibillion-dollar printing industry. Forced by nontraditional media, notably CD-ROMs and Internet publishing, to assimilate technology or fold their shops, printers had to find their place in a new era of information delivery. They were hungrier than ever for the benefits of new technology to keep printing competitive by decreasing production costs and improving the quality and timeliness of their services. Other challenges included the industry's habitually fierce competition, the fluctuating cost of paper products, and competition from television and radio for advertiser dollars. In 2002 the latest technology push was for printers to develop so-called remote printing capabilities for documents and photographs through Internet printing, such as the PrintMe Network system. PrintMe Networks allowed professional-level printing to PrintMe printers from wireless and cable-free devices such as personal computers, two-way pagers, and mobile phones, as well as dial-up devices such as fax machines. Other industry-wide developments in the first decade of the 2000s included plateless press technology and highly evolved computer-integrated manufacturing in the printing process.

Many of the largest commercial printers responded to these marketplace realities through diversification into information services, redefining their role as providing communication solutions rather than just printed products. By the late 1990s, some printers had begun to offer services as diverse as database management and information warehousing. These firms were well placed to do this work for several reasons. Their business had always dealt with the packaging of information; producing CD-ROMs, for instance, could be seen as merely a change in medium. Some companies, such as R.R. Donnelley, garnered experience with such media through supplying manuals for the computer software industry. Others, such as Cadmus Journal Services, found a niche providing Web publishing for their clients in addition to traditional printing.

As traditional printing companies continued to go out of business, nearly all major companies accepted integrated media as crucial to their existence, realizing that they must offer such services by 2010. In addition to print and video capabilities, by 2005 large printers offered services related to database management, image vending, electronic and technology-related equipment sales, and multimedia sales presentations.

Electronic file transfer forced many printers to become savvy about digital networking requirements, and some even found a profit center in marketing their networking expertise to their clients' in-house needs. The impact of electronic file transfer, direct-to-plate technologies, and digital printing was an ongoing vector of industry change. Due to the high costs of printing and specialized equipment, many newspapers and magazines "outsourced" the printing of publications to printing firms that served as outside contractors.

Writing for the *Rochester Democrat and Chronicle*, Matthew Daneman reported on the commercial printing industry challenges that mirrored what was happening as companies were struggling to generate "financial black ink." From major companies to smaller ones, the struggle to keep commercial printing industry-linked businesses was a daunting one. Daneman pointed out that major companies with thousands of employees made billions per year selling equipment to printers, but an analysis showed that the printing industry was severely impacted by the recession of late 2008 and into 2009. It was concluded that key industry players—such as Kodak and Xerox—were facing major challenges from others.

ORGANIZATION AND STRUCTURE

The three largest commercial printing firms in the Western Hemisphere—R.R. Donnelley & Sons of the United States,

Quebecor Printing Inc. of Canada, and Carvajal S.A. of Colombia—accounted for approximately 10 percent of industry sales through the 1990s. At the other end, 58,000 plants competed for 82 percent of the market. A similar structure was found at the national level: 80 percent of U.S. printers had annual sales of less than US$2 million in the early 1990s. Most firms in the industry were small; the 40,000 U.S. commercial printers had an average size of 20 employees. In Japan, 80 percent of printing companies employed fewer than 10 workers in the early 1990s. Although average profits were better for larger firms, the profit leaders in the smaller size categories tended to be more profitable than those in the larger categories. Efficiency and marketing penetration were other important factors influencing profitability.

Short-run printing—two- or three-color and process color printing in runs of fewer than 5,000—accounted for an estimated 26 percent (US$20.1 billion) of the copying and commercial printing market in the United States. Analysts noted that shorter printer runs with smaller signatures and heavy reliance on bindery technology to produce customized publications for narrowly targeted markets was an increasing trend in the U.S. market. Conversely, European printers favored all-at-once printing practices to save time and labor and eliminate the need for special binder operations.

Various regions specialized in certain segments of the printing industry. For example, Brazil emerged as the packaging center of South America, while areas with low production costs, such as Mexico, attracted labor-intensive operations in the areas of bookbinding and other post-press sectors of the printing industry.

Literacy and disposable income were limiting factors in any region's print industry as well. While the United States and Canada produced an average of US$305 worth of printed materials per person in the 1990s, less than US$2.50 per person was produced in Asia outside of Japan. Fifteen percent of the world's population accounted for consumption of more than 80 percent of the world's printed products, according to some industry analysts.

Other factors made it difficult for printers in developing countries to produce high-quality print products and thus compete globally. A consistent supply of materials, such as paper and ink, was vital, but in China, for instance, most printing materials were available only through domestic suppliers (although high-quality paper was sometimes imported for special projects). Careful handling and protection from moisture also was required, necessitating a level of sophistication often lacking in less developed facilities. However, some countries, such as Thailand, succeeded in achieving high printing standards at prices that were a fraction of those in the United States. In a similar manner, the printing industries of other regions, such as the Middle East—which utilized European and Indian equipment and expertise—began to develop businesses that were competitive with long-established printers in the United States and Europe. Investors noted this trend in the industry.

BACKGROUND AND DEVELOPMENT

The commercial printing industry originated with the introduction of handbills and broadsides used to publicize goods for sale or auction, cultural events, and other public notices. Commercial printers were also hired to print currency, stamps, and government documents. Often the same firms became publishers of almanacs, Bibles, and other books. It was not uncommon for publishing firms to diversify into commercial printing, and a single publishing house that supplied newspaper, periodical, book, and commercial printing often dominated developing regions.

Printing in general is one of the world's oldest industries. Woodcuts of illustrations were in use by the ancient Egyptians, Babylonians, and Chinese. However, textual matter was not printed until the eighth century A.D. Approximately 300 years later, innovators in China and Korea experimented with moveable type made from various materials including wood, clay, bronze, and iron; however, their efforts were impeded by the complex characters of their written languages.

Aided by the simple Roman phonetic alphabet, Johannes Gutenberg developed a revolutionary method of printing in the mid-fifteenth century called letterpress. Letterpress and the Bible, traditionally held to be the first book printed by Gutenberg, were responsible for the global spread of printing. In Thailand, for example, the first printers were seventeenth-century missionaries. Letterpress endured for years as the dominant printing process, and it continued to be prized by purists for its clear printing of type. It also offered other advantages, such as the ability to change a line of type without having to create an entirely new plate. Letterpress was eventually displaced by offset lithography for short and medium runs and gravure printing for long runs.

Hand-engraved etchings of illustrations in copper plates, called intaglio, were used to illustrate books. Banknotes were printed using the same practice. Widespread forgery in Great Britain resulted, for in the early nineteenth century there existed thousands of engravers skilled enough to print credible forgeries. Nevertheless, intaglio remained unmatched for security printing due to several unique properties. Since the image areas were engraved into the surface of the plate, the resulting print, made under very high pressure, was three-dimensional. Tonal variation was also unique, created through variations in the width and length of lines. The gravure process that later developed was different, employing millions of minute cells filled to varying depths with ink. Besides hand-etched images, security engravings often included complex, machine-generated patterns whose precision could not be matched by any craftsman. Fluorescent fibers or inks were also used in the quest to make banknotes and stock certificates ever more difficult to duplicate.

With the development of lithography by Aloys Senefelder in 1797, images could be printed from a flat rather than engraved surface. Ira S. Rubel, a U.S. printer, discovered by accident in 1904 that the image from a lithographic plate would still print after being first transferred, or offset, to a rubber cylinder. Plates could last indefinitely in this process. This durability, coupled with the process's economy, print quality, and ability to print on many textures, made lithography tremendously popular.

Joseph Nicéphore Niepce, who four years earlier had made the first permanent photograph, produced the first photogravure plate in 1826. This process requires an image to be transferred onto a plate coated with a light-sensitive material, then etched into it with a solvent. Thus, it was not practical for commercial printing until the end of the nineteenth century, when Czech artist Karl Klic developed the predecessor to modern rotogravure printing using light to etch an image onto a metal cylinder. In the 1990s, gravure accounted for one-fifth of the commercial printing market, as did flexography, a method of printing with flexible rubber or plastic plates.

Within printing and publishing, the US$20 billion per-year U.S. book segment experienced approximately 3 percent annual growth through the 1990s, although industry profits dropped sharply in 2001, particularly after the September 11, 2001, terrorist attacks against the United States. Leading companies continued to fall under the control of such giant conglomerates as Random House, Simon & Schuster, Bantam Doubleday Dell, HarperCollins, and Pearson. As with many other segments of the printing industry, increasing amounts of business were shipped to Asian manufacturers, which became more attractive as they improved quality in four-color printing for the children's book market. U.S. textbook printers, however, were optimistic that new adoptions in 2005 would boost demand. As a result of the federal No Child Left Behind legislation, state-specific versions of textbooks were needed across the country, creating high overall demand but smaller individual press runs. (For more information on book publishing trends, see also **Book Publishing.**)

In the newspaper segment, annual revenue growth of more than 5 percent seemed to signal an optimistic turnaround for newspapers in the late 1990s, bringing the industry to more than US$50 billion annually. However, several factors, including loss of advertising revenues in the aftermath of the September 11, 2001, attacks, a decline in paid subscriptions, and increasing competition from television and Internet news sources, led to uncertain conditions for the industry through the first decade of the 2000s. Due to the high costs of printing and specialized equipment, many newspapers and magazines "outsourced" the printing of publications to printing firms that served as outside contractors. (See also **Newspaper Publishing.**)

The emergence of newly independent nations of the former Soviet Union created a new market for currency, security printing, directory printing, and other types of commercial printing in the late 1990s and early years of the first decade of the 2000s. Although export figures to these developing markets had not increased substantially by 2000, analysts predicted a boom in export printing for the United States as these foreign markets stabilized.

One of the challenges shared by printers in the United States and abroad was a shortage of skilled labor. In a 1998 study by the Printing Industries of America (PIA), half of the firms surveyed had a significant problem in finding qualified people to hire. A quarter of those surveyed even had trouble finding entry-level help—an effect of the United States's low 5 percent unemployment rate in the late 1990s as the economy added an average of 3 million new jobs a year. Because all pre-press production of publication layout was computerized as the standard practice in North America, Europe, and other high-technology countries (and would be the standard everywhere by 2010), the U.S. Department of Labor reported that the industry expected to add people to the workforce with specialized training or knowledge in electronics, mathematics, and computers.

In 2006, *Graphic Arts Monthly* reported that pay increases for workers in the printing industry are not as high as those of general business occupations. The average pay increase for printing industry employees was 2.9 percent in 2005, the same as it was in 2001 through 2004.

Digital equipment and other technological advances helped the printing industry to increase its productivity in the 1990s. Digital image manipulation and graphic design tools were supplemented by color creation, film making, and typesetting programs that placed increased control of the printing process in the hands of clients, graphic designers, and printers.

Economic recession in the early years of the first decade of the 2000s hit the commercial printing industry hard. In the United States, a sharp drop in print advertising after the September 11, 2001, terrorist attacks contributed to declining revenues for commercial printers, and more than 2,000 printing shops closed between 2001 and 2002—substantially more than the yearly average of 700. Annual sales revenues for printing companies remained flat through 2002 and 2003 at about US$156.7 billion. By the end of 2004, however, analysts were predicting welcome growth of about 4 percent

through mid-2006. For the first three quarters of 2004, total print shipments rose 4 percent. Ink on paper shipments grew by 3.5 percent, while digital printing increased by 5.9 percent and value-added products and services grew 4.9 percent. Further growth was projected for 2005, largely due to direct-mail advertising, which was expected to increase by up to 3.5 percent. The labels, wrappers, packaging, and related printing segment was poised to grow by 2 percent. The segment likely to sustain slowest growth was periodicals and magazines, expected to increase by only 1 percent.

In the mid-years of the first decade of the 2000s, the United States had between 37,000 and 44,000 commercial printing shops and was the world's largest printing consumer and exporter, with exports valued by the U.S. Department of Commerce at US$1.45 billion. Imports in 2004 reached US$1.43 billion. Canada remained the primary destination for U.S. commercial printing exports (US$430.8 million), followed by Mexico (US$248.7 million), the United Kingdom (US$148.9 million), Netherlands (US$76 million), and Japan (US$59 million). Canada was also the leading source of U.S. imports in 2004 (US$758.7 million), but Mexico slipped to third place behind China, which supplied commercial printing imports to the United States worth US$186.5 million.

Compliance with environmental regulations—which varies dramatically around the world—posed a significant challenge to the printing industry. In the early years of the first decade of the 2000s, nearly all major companies had one or more environmental experts on the payroll to use for consulting purposes and to field media questions. Due to the potentially hazardous chemicals used or created during the printing processes, the industry had come under scrutiny from environmental agencies and citizen groups. Wastewater discharges from printing establishments, for instance, had long come under sharp criticism. In addition, there were concerns regarding the industry's use of vast amounts of natural resources in the production of newspapers, catalogs, direct mail items, and countless other products. Industry participants hoped that increased use of recycled materials would blunt some of this criticism. Another trend in printing—using digital presses that entirely forego the need for film or plates—lessened the use of harsh chemicals in the industry as a whole as these cutting-edge presses were adopted. (The bulk of dangerous chemicals in the industry were used in the platemaking and film process.) During the early twenty-first century, digital press technology had grown from infancy to adolescence as the number of full color digital presses increased significantly worldwide.

CURRENT CONDITIONS

Approaching the late years of the first decade of the 2000s, the Internet continued to have a significant impact on the printing industry. According to *Graphic Arts Monthly*, "...the

Internet is rapidly and dramatically changing the print landscape...New concepts such as Wikipedia, RSS feeds and Web communities (like MySpace and Facebook) are changing how people get information and how they relate to each other, giving consumers more control over when and where they view content—and make purchases." Regardless, the North American print industry showed sustained growth, driven by a healthy economy and expanding advertising and promotion spending. Total U.S. printing shipments in 2006 were US$170.3 billion, up about 3 percent from 2005. The strongest growth was in toner and digital printing, followed by printers' ancillary services.

Print Week agreed that digital printing would be the area of strongest growth in the future. Frank Romano of the Rochester Institute of Technology told the journal, "The printing press of the future will be totally digital. Toner and ink-jet technologies are advancing rapidly, and will be poised to replace some gravure, flexo and litho presses by 2015." Another report by *Print Week* claimed that 13.5 percent of all print would be digital by 2008, and subsequent years would show meteoric growth. Demand for digital printing was also growing in Europe, though not as quickly as some expected. *Ink World* estimated Europe's growth rate in digital at 10 percent annually. Part of the reason for the slower than expected growth was printers' reluctance to invest in the equipment needed for full-scale digital operations.

Printing on demand was also a major trend nearing the late years of the first decade of the 2000s. With printing on demand, printers can print from one to a few hundred books at time, based on demand, rather than running thousands of copies of a book, with the risk that not all the copies would sell. In 2006, U.S.-based On Demand Books revealed a printer that could produce an entire book in seven minutes; the same year, Hewlett-Packard announced an on-demand partnership with Amazon. Indeed, a report in *Print Week* predicted the on-demand market would quadruple by 2012, and printers were set to capitalize on this rapidly growing market.

Heading into the late years of the first decade of the 2000s, other challenges for the printing industry included rising costs of materials used in the printing process, such as petroleum, plastic substrates, and adhesive petroleum. As materials costs rose, printers were pressured to not only keep up but to cut production costs. According to a 2006 report published in *Printing World,* the market for printed magazines would shrink to 40 percent of current values by 2016. Thus, "printers will have to slash production costs by 50 percent if they are to remain attractive to the publishing industry." This was a challenge for the printing industry, considering the rising costs of materials. Some solutions provided by the report included using recycled paper and becoming more "electronic." *Print Week* presented a similar

picture, stating that printers in the United States and United Kingdom will have to reduce production costs by 30 percent by 2011 to remain competitive. Competition from the low-cost labor countries of Eastern Europe, Latin America, and especially China, posed a significant threat. China's print sector was expected to grow by 195 percent, from 11.1 billion pounds to almost 33 billion pounds, by 2010.

RESEARCH AND TECHNOLOGY

Evolving technologies were pivotal in the development of the commercial printing industry. Industry observers estimated that printers in the United States alone invested more than US$2 billion in new technology annually to remain competitive. The development of high-quality copying machines spurred printers to adopt more sophisticated printing presses equipped with innovations in color capacity, automation, and press speeds.

Although digital technologies opened up tremendous possibilities for printers, incompatibility among various proprietary systems remained a problem, particularly in the area of data communications since digitized pictures occupied a great deal of computer memory. Realizing that a lack of standards was affecting their own sales, computer manufacturers promoted an international standard for page description, such as the one already in existence for textual data. The page description language PostScript, developed in the mid-1980s by former Xerox programmers, helped meet these needs to a degree. Another format from Adobe Systems Inc., portable document format (PDF), received much attention. Although it was popular on the Web, PDF's prospects looked less promising for the printing trade.

A 2004 Graphic Arts Marketing Information Service (GAMIS) study revealed that the digital printing process will continue to attract the bulk of R&D. Another finding was that paper grades for conventional printing processes need to be more uniform and consistent.

The flat screen display industry represented a potentially promising new market for printing companies in the early years of the first decade of the 2000s. Dai Nippon (also known as DNP), a leading commercial printer headquartered in Tokyo was among major companies developing new organic light-emitting diode (OLED) printing processes.

In August 2009, WhatTheyThink, an online media organization of the printing and publishing industry providing market analysis, industry news and an industry blog via three Web sites, announced the availability of *Printing Continues to Go Green: An Updated What They Think Primer on Environmental Sustainability in the Commercial Printing Industry.* The report provides a detailed analysis of green printing initiatives in the U.S. and their link to the commercial printing industry. In the report,

What They Think June 2009 survey results showed 33 percent of all respondents in the industry reported that the top green practice U.S. commercial printers implemented was to "identify itself in marketing and sales materials and promotions an environmentally sensitive business." At a time when people are cutting back on their printing projects in hopes of saving the environment, the report researcher encouraged commercial printers to make it clear "how environmentally sustainable we can be as an industry."

INDUSTRY LEADERS

Dai Nippon Printing. The world's largest printer, Dai Nippon Printing Co. Ltd. (DNP) was founded in Tokyo in 1876. First known as Shueisha, the company took the name Dai Nippon in 1935. Dai Nippon was Japan's first modern printing company. The company diversified considerably from its original business of printing newspapers and invested heavily in developing new printing technologies. DNP became an innovator in printing such specialized applications as packaging and identification cards. DNP also produces direct mail pieces, books, magazines, business forms, and packaging for consumer products, as well as printing for electronics applications. In 2008 the company's revenues were US$16.3 billion and it had more than 38,600 employees.

In 2003 DNP entered into a partnership with Poet Software, forming a strategic alliance relationship to provide e-catalog content and outsourcing services in Japan. Around this time, DNP had thirty-three Japanese and eight overseas plants. In June 2004 DNP announced that it would implement new technology to create holograms, which will allow viewers to see images from different perspectives by moving the hologram around. Research papers providing such images would be able to clearly share results with readers. In July 2004, DNP announced the transfer of technologies to Taiwan's Sintek and Quanta Display Corp. *Asia Intelligence Wire* also claimed DNP was the world's second largest manufacturer of color filters, and that it was attempting to focus on boosting its presence in Taiwan through cooperative efforts.

Printing opportunities expanded for DNP in a dramatic way when it achieved its certification to manufacture UnionPay brand credit cards, debit cards and pre-pay cards. It has distinguished itself by now being able to manufacture all six major global payment brands including Visa, Mastercard, JCB, American Express and Diners.

Toppan Printing. Ever-expanding Toppan Printing Co. Ltd. was DNP's chief rival since it was formed in 1900 to meet Japan's increased demand for printing. Securities, books, and business forms were originally the core of the company's business, although it was successful in diversifying into electronic circuits, business forms, packaging,

and information and marketing services, among other areas. It became the first Japanese printer to establish production facilities in Hong Kong (1962) and the United States (1979). In 2006 Toppan had year-end sales of US$13.1 billion and 35,954 employees. *Asia Intelligence Wire* reported that Toppan saw a smooth run in its fifth-generation color-filter plant in Taiwan and was stepping up construction of its sixth-generation plant. The source also said Sony and Toppan had created a CD-like disk with a 25 GB capacity, consisting mainly of paper. Toppan has operations throughout Asia, Australia, Europe, and North America. In 2005 the company acquired DuPont Photomasks, which manufactures materials used in a variety of electronics applications. Toppan's new hologram printing was introduced in 2005 and targeted at credit card companies and manufacturers of gift cards. By 2008, sales were reported to be approximately US$16.8 billion and the company had 38,570 employees.

R.R. Donnelley & Sons. Chicago-based R.R. Donnelley & Sons was the leading printer in the United States and the second largest in the world, putting out well-known newspapers and magazines, books, catalogs, and advertising materials. For 2008, R.R. Donnelley reported its sales in millions as US$11,581 and claimed there were almost 60,000 employees working throughout the world. The company traced its origins to the educational, religious, and historical publishing and printing firm of Church, Goodman, and Donnelley, which Richard Robert Donnelley joined in 1864. It was incorporated as the Lakeside Publishing and Printing Company in 1870. After several name changes, it became known as R.R. Donnelley & Sons Company in 1882. The company was first publicly traded in 1956. Catalogs (such as the Sears catalog) historically accounted for most of the company's business, though it also was known for printing mass-market books, magazines, telephone directories, computer software documentation, and religious books.

R.R. Donnelley aggressively expanded into digital media and database marketing services in the 1990s. The company had operations in Asia, South America, and Europe, and 50,000 employees. In 2004, the company bought printer Moore Wallace, a leader in forms and labels, making it the largest commercial printer in the United States.

The company announced several major initiatives in 2005, including the acquisition of the Astron Group, a provider of document business process outsourcing. In addition, Donnelley entered an agreement with Creative Printing Services Inc. to create what a Donnelley statement described as a "joint strategy to provide diversity sourcing options to customers in the print industry." Also in 2005, Donnelley's Primedia Technologies division launched Pipeline, an online project-tracking system. The company posted 2006 sales of $9.3 billion.

In 2009, R. R. Donnelley announced an extra special certification had been gained again. The Occupational Safety and Health Adminstration{OSHA}recertified the Roanoke, Virgina production facility for Voluntary Protection Program{VPP}Star Status. This level of certification was the highest awarded by the administration. Consideration for it requires a successful completion of a comprehensive on-site evaluation and confirmation that the facility's injury and illness rates are below the industry average. Other Donnelley facilities also achieved VPP status. Donnelley Group President Daniel Knotts noted, however, it is especially challenging to get recertified because "continuous improvement is integral to the evaluation."

MAJOR COUNTRIES IN THE INDUSTRY

In the first decade of the 2000s, the United States, Japan, and Canada led the world's commercial printing industry, which by sales volume is concentrated in leading industrial countries and in high-population metropolitan areas such as New York, Tokyo, and Montreal. Thus, while a minority of countries account for the lion's share of the printing market, nearly every region of the globe is involved in the industry to some degree. The Graphic Arts Intelligence Network (GAIN), a European printing consultancy group, claimed in its "2009 European Printing Industry Report" that printing was the United States's largest manufacturing industry in terms of establishments. In 2003 there were more than 44,000 printing plants providing 1.1 million jobs and producing approximately US$157 billion in printed products and services. The global consultancy Strategis Communications, headquartered in Brussels, Belgium, ranked Canada's commercial printing industry as the fourth largest manufacturing employer, with more than 84,000 employees working in 5,834 establishments.

Commercial printing shipments were down in volume by U.S.$4.6 billion for the first half of 2009 compared to same time frame for 2008. What They Think's Economic and Research Center Director Dr. Webb attributed some the losses to the postal service summer discount for large mailers that was launched July 1, 2009. Related dynamics and other significant issues are discussed in the center's *The North American Monthly Printing Shipments Report.*

A profile of Hong Kong's printing industry, issued by the Hong Kong Trade Development Council (TDC), characterized it as "famous for quality, quick delivery, competitive pricing, and ability to cope with short-notice printing jobs." The report also noted Hong Kong's industry made substantial advanced machinery investments resulting in production capacity expansion and improved quality standards. In 2002 the United States was Hong Kong's largest market for printed matter,

adding up to 39 percent of the total. Filmless printing was considered to be the industry's development trend.

In Mexico, commercial printing grew significantly through the 1990s and the early part of the first decade of the2000s as manufacturing activities increased, especially among "maquiladoras," shops near the U.S. border where finished goods are assembled for export to the United States. This manufacturing creates demand for printed matter, such as instruction manuals for the products being assembled. In 2000, about 45 percent of Mexico's 11,383 printing shops were formally associated with maquiladoras. This segment exported US$423 million worth of products in 2000, but this figure does not represent the entire value of production, since many items—including price tags and retail inserts for products—do not have a stated export value. In addition, maquiladora plants also print a wide range of books and magazines for U.S. consumption, including *Newsweek, Reader's Digest,* and Scholastic children's books. In the middle of the first decade of the 2000s, Mexico was one of the principal trading partners with the United States in commercial printing. It was the second-largest destination for U.S. printed goods, and the third-largest source of U.S. print imports, in 2004.

Brazil, the largest economy in South America, led the way in commercial printing in the early years of the first decade of the 2000s, with Argentina, Venezuela, and Chile also boasting competitive industries. Printing companies in these countries have benefited from reduced import duties and the machinery leasing policies of U.S. suppliers, for whom the Latin American market is increasingly important. According to *PrintCom Brasil,* Publisher Kai Hagenbush, the Brazilian Association of the Printing Industry, estimated that the sector invested US$63 billion in modernizing machinery during the past decade. It accounted for 3.3 percent of the country's GNP in 2000. Commercial printing was believed to have accounted for approximately 13 percent of the Brazilian print and media sector's sales. *Ink World* magazine indicated that there is a tremendous move toward globalization due to printers expanding their operations into Mexico because of the North American Free Trade Agreeememt between Mexico, Canada, and the United States. Industry insiders evaluated the market as being one where big companies were swallowing up smaller ones. Overall, Latin America was viewed as being in a "slowdown mode" impacted by the United States' economic status.

Among the Pacific Rim countries, Japan has felt increased pressure from the printing industries of Hong Kong, Singapore, Brunei, Taiwan, and South Korea. Australia and New Zealand also had healthy printing industries. According to the April 2004 issue of *IBISWorld,* from 2002 to 2003 the Australian printing industry had turnover of $5.5 billion, employing 32,926 workers in 2,500 enterprises.

Commercial printing in the United Kingdom was felt to mirror U.S. developments, with a similar level of technological advancement. Whitworth, Gilmore and Andrews Consulting (WGA), a global risk management consulting firm, estimated that the U.K. sector consisted of approximately 7,870 commercial printers, trade shops, implants, and newspapers. In the early years of the first decade of the 2000s, about 2,000 jobs were created in the printing industry via major new facilities in northern England. Polestar, Europe's largest independent printing company, opened a 110 million pound (US$193.2 million) gravure plant in Sheffield that started production in March 2005. Prinovis, a joint venture among Bertelsmann-owned Arvato Print, Gruner + Jahr, and Axel Springer, was scheduled to open with 400 employees in Liverpool in mid-2006. In 2005, U.K. newspaper company Associated Newspapers, which had built up one of the largest newspaper printing facilities in the world with global press manufacturer Koenig and Bauer (KBA), announced a US$140.4 million deal with Italian printing company Cerutti to develop a printing plant in Didcot, Oxfordshire, which would begin production in 2008. The company cited Cerutti's new satellite cylinder technology as the primary reason for the deal.

BIBLIOGRAPHY

"A Decade in Print: How Data and Digital Have Changed our Industry Since 1997." *Print Week,* 1 February 2007.

"Adding to the Talent Pool." *Dotprint,* 29 June 2005. Available from www.dotprint.com.

Brown, Andrew. "International Printing: Going Global." *Print Solutions,* May 2005. Available from www.printsolutionsmag.com.

"The Current State of Green Printing, New Report." 14 August 2009. Available from whattheythink.com.

Curwen, Ginger. "Wait Till Next Year: A Lackluster Market in 2004 Has Manufacturers Looking Ahead to the Promise of Better Times in 2005." *Publishers Weekly,* 11 October 2004.

Daneman, Matthew. "Commercial print industry feels head winds." *RocNow,* 17 August 2009. Available from rocnow.com.

"Digital Printing Technology Report: Digital's Future." *Print Week,* 13 July 2006.

"DNP Acquires China UnionPay Brand Card Manfacturing Certification: Response to Expansion into Asian Market of High Function Smart Cards." 6 July 2009. Available from www.dnp.co.jp.

Esler, Bill. "Technology Tremors." *Graphic Arts Monthly,* 1 October 2006.

"Green Scene." *American Printer,* 1 April 2007.

Haughey, James. "Print Prospects Brighten for 2004." *Graphic Arts Monthly,* December 2003.

James, Bruce. "This Is Truly Print's Future." *Graphic Arts Monthly,* 1 January 2007.

"June 2009 U.S. Commercial Printing Shipments Down 12 %." 7 August. Available from whattheythink.com.

"Mail Group Stuns Industry to Abandoning KBA for Cerutti." *Dotprint,* 29 June 2005. Available from www.dotprint.com.

Makin, Michael, Chuck Miotke, Peter Tobin, and Steve Johnson. "Outlook 07: Ok to Run." *Graphic Arts Monthly,* 1 January 2007.

Mason, Dennis E. "Global Report: Asia: China and Printing." *Printing News,* 25 September 2006.

Milmo, Sean. "Ink and Equipment Manufacturers See Good Opportunities in Digital Market." *Ink World,* July 2006.

RR Donnelley. "About Us." 2009. Available from www.rrdonelley.com.

——— "RR Donnelley Printing Operation Recertified for OHSA's VPP Star Status." 25 June2009. Available from www.rrdonnelley.com.

"Technically Speaking: Comment—Competing Globally Takes Productive Technology and a Range of Services." *Print Week,* 31 August 2006.

"Technology Report: Digital Books to your Door." *Print Week,* 18 January 2007.

"Toppan Printing, Tokyo, Expects to Generate First-Year Sales of US$9.2 Million for Its Newly Developed Holograms." *Graphic Arts Monthly,* May 2005.

"U.K. Summary." TrendWatch Graphic Arts Reports, 2004. Available from www.trendwatchgraphiccarts.com.

U.S. Department of Commerce. "U.S. Commercial Printing Export and Import Statistics." May 2005. Available from www. ita.doc.gov.

Whitcher, Joann. "Market Outlook: Not Picture Perfect: Key Numbers Are Up, but Print's Performance Is Still a Far Cry from the Pre-2001 Levels." *Graphic Arts Monthly,* December 2004.

SIC 4832

RADIO BROADCASTING STATIONS

NAICS CODE(S)

515112. Radio broadcasters transmit radio programs to the public. Included in the discussion are radio networks and companies that provide pay-radio services.

INDUSTRY SNAPSHOT

Radio broadcasting began as a stable industry controlled in most parts of the world by national and regional governments. Before the collapse of the Soviet Union and other Communist nations, those governments exercised complete state control over the airwaves. In Western Europe, state-owned or state-chartered corporations broadcast a limited amount of programming—much of it educational in nature—and commercial channels were almost nonexistent. Japan had a strong radio market, but the rest of Asia remained relatively undeveloped. In the United States, commercial stations dominated the market, but the industry was fragmented due to complex government regulations limiting the number of radio stations that could be owned by one company.

By the mid-1990s, however, rapid technological and political change had completely altered the rules of the global broadcasting industry. In former communist nations, fledgling commercial radio stations challenged state-run corporations, which struggled to change with the times. In Europe, commercial radio stations competed with state-sponsored broadcasters such as the British Broadcasting Corporation (BBC). In the United States, new ownership rules led to a major structural change in the radio industry, and options for mass communications and information technology continued to grow.

By the twenty-first century, technological advances made it possible for music lovers to get commercial-free music anywhere in the world. Online radio programming via the Internet, subscription-based satellite radio, and radio-on-demand services were just a few of the innovations coming to prominence, as traditional radio was seeing an increased slump in listeners. However, radio broadcasting was still strong. According to a study from Arbitron, about 228 million listeners over the age of 11 listened to traditional radio once a week or more.

ORGANIZATION AND STRUCTURE

One of the unifying features of broadcasting around the world is government regulation. Radio broadcasting is less than 100 years old and developed during a century of growing government control over industry. Airwaves are viewed in most countries as a scarce public resource. As such, nearly every radio market in the world has been tightly regulated or directly controlled from its inception by the government.

In Europe, public service broadcasting was the only game in town for many decades, as monolithic state-run institutions provided the programs they thought would educate and entertain. In communist countries, the state was the network, and radio existed to legitimize the government and inform people of its activities.

In the United States, commercial radio had dominated the airwaves for many years, although National Public Radio—a non-profit organization partially funded by the government—provided an alternative in many markets. However, the FCC tightly controlled many aspects of the radio business and was responsible for licensing radio stations and approving their ownership.

Some of those structures crumbled and others changed dramatically in the 1980s and 1990s. As communist governments collapsed in the USSR and Eastern Europe, private ownership of radio stations began to take hold. In Western Europe, more licenses for commercial radio stations were granted, providing competition for traditional state-owned radio stations. In Asia, new stations sprang up, and satellite broadcasts of radio signals became a reality. In the United States, new ownership

structures substantially changed the business, as media conglomerates looked for ways to expand the advertising potential of their new holdings.

Artem Zagorodnov took an information-packed look at Russia's radio industry. As Radio Moscow, an international radio broadcasting debut was made in 1929. Ten years later Radio Moscow was speaking out in English, French, German, Italian, and Arabic. History recorded that both Mussolini and Hitler personally ordered the blocking of Radio Moscow. In 1991, it became known as "Voice of Russia." Content is a key part of the longevity. Mike Giblin from the United Kingdom a 40-year listener, saw a trend for less politics and more lifestyle information. The Voice of Russia head Andrei Bistritsky claimed "Content-more than ever-has to be adjusted to fit local demand." Bistritsky revealed there were plans to develop Internet broadcasting but refused to declare what budget total added up to be. A need, however, was expressed for at least three times more funding than currently available.

Large radio networks supplied the content for many radio stations, whether they were government-operated or privately owned. In this arrangement, a network produces programming such as news, music, or commentary, which is then broadcast by a large number of individual stations. The British Broadcasting Corporation is an example of a government-run network, and ABC Radio in the United States is an example of a private network.

Except for certain high-power operations, most AM radio stations regularly reach only a limited geographical area. As a result, there are literally thousands of individual stations in large countries such as the United States. Those AM stations that could reach distant households gave certain "jocks" (such as Tom Shannon of Buffalo, New York; Walter (Salty) Brine of Providence, Rhode Island; and Ed Dickinson of northern California) a semi-celebrity status.

In keeping with May 2009 certified tariff established by the Copyright Board of Canada, a mandate requested multi-channel subscription satellite radio services to make monthly payments for broadcasting Canadian music. In September 2009, the Canadian Press announced that XM Canada had agreed for the satellite radio company to pay Canadian musicians and songwriters' royalties. Groups affected included the Society of Composers, Authors and Music Publishers of Canada. Legal Action had been eminent from many groups seeking money.

If listeners tune in to a station critical of the president and discover that it has been closed down, it may not be for the reason they think. That was the case in Cameroon where Communications Minister Issa Tchiroma Bakary explained that expressions of dissatisfaction were accepted and many critical stations "continue to operate under the government's policy of "administrative tolerance even though they have not paid their" broadcast license deposit. Those stations were allowed to broadcast even when critical of Cameroon President Paul Biya because existence was established unlike stations who just started broadcasting on open frequencies. The closed station was owned by George Gilbert Baongla who started broadcasting without permission after closing down *Le Dementi* newspaper in 2008 providing similar content. Bakary revealed there were plans to close additional "pirate stations" as part of plans to "clean up" Cameroon's media landscape.

BACKGROUND AND DEVELOPMENT

Before World War I, inventors Guglielmo Marconi, Lee DeForest, Reginald Aubrey Fessenden, and Edwin Armstrong devised the technology needed to broadcast radio signals, but a wartime ban on nonmilitary broadcasting delayed the advent of radio broadcasts until the ban was lifted after the war ended in 1919.

The first AM radio station in the United States, KDKA in Pittsburgh, began operating in 1919. By 1922, there were 570 licensed AM stations in the United States. Commercial networks soon emerged to broadcast programs and advertising on different stations simultaneously. National Broadcasting Company (NBC) was founded in 1926 to operate two networks for its parent company, the Radio Corporation of America (RCA). Columbia Broadcasting Systems (CBS), a major competitor, established a network of 16 stations by 1928.

Radio broadcasting soon caught on in Europe and other regions with the capacity to support commercial or state-sponsored broadcasting. The British Broadcasting Corporation (BBC) was formed in 1922 as a private company and in 1927 was chartered by Parliament as the sole provider of British radio broadcasting. Although it operated under charter from the Crown, it was free of government oversight and functioned as an independent entity. Other European governments set up similar monopolies, though some were subject to more government control.

Frequency modulation (FM) radio, invented by Edwin Howard Armstrong in 1933, developed commercially in the 1940s. In the United States, FM was used as an alternative to AM and featured "highbrow" programs such as in-depth news analysis and classical music. FM receivers were more expensive than AM radios, and because of the higher radio frequencies that FM utilizes, coverage areas were severely limited. As a result, FM was slow to catch on in the 1960s and early 1970s despite its static-free sound quality. Then the cost of FM receivers dropped, and in the mid to late 1970s and 1980s, FM flourished as rock-and-roll stations proliferated in the United States.

In the Soviet Union, radio and television broadcasting was exclusively a propaganda arm of the government until the late 1980s when Communist party and state control over the media eased. In July 1990, Chairman Mikhail Gorbachev ordered major changes in the state-run broadcasting monopoly, allowing radio outlets to operate independently of political organizations and provide objective coverage of news events. The complete collapse of the communist government continued this trend, although restrictions on radio broadcasting remain.

In the 1980s and 1990s many Eastern European radio stations bloomed as governments eased their heavy grip on the airwaves. Major companies such as France's Europe Developpement and CLT Multi-Media of Luxembourg, along with many local firms, invested in commercial radio properties in Eastern Europe. In the 1990s, the Czech Republic, Slovakia, and Poland led the move to open radio licensing for foreign and domestic firms.

At the same time, there was some globalization of the radio industry, as countries loosened ownership rules for broadcast mediums. For example, in 1995 the U.S. Federal Communications Commission (FCC) relaxed its rules on foreign ownership of radio stations, which was expected to bring a number of well-heeled international investors into the U.S. market. Growing satellite transmission of radio programs has made it much easier to distribute programming across national borders.

In 1996, the FCC also eased its restrictions on the number of radio stations one company could own. That led to a frenzied market for radio stations, as major media conglomerates rushed to buy large numbers of stations with the idea of creating vast networks across the country. Radio emerged as perhaps the hottest media market in the United States, and prices paid for stations shot up dramatically. From the beginning of 1996 to early 1998, more than 25 percent of the nation's 10,000 stations changed hands.

Digital production and transmission of radio gained a foothold in the mid-1980s, with some ventures, such as Star Radio in Asia, taking advantage of the new technology by distributing radio via satellite. In the United States, talk radio gained in popularity as personalities like Rush Limbaugh used the medium to rally supporters of a particular political viewpoint, and "shock radio" hosts such as Howard Stern became popular using a format pioneered by still-active and intentionally obnoxious Joey Reynolds, later on the WOR Radio Network. Other formats, such as all-sports, took off as well, and a very few local sports broadcast stars (such as Jack Brickhouse of Chicago, Bob Uecker of Milwaukee, and Phil Rizzuto in New York) garnered a national following for their excellence and/or humor. Listeners with a strong bent for public affairs programming opted for National Public Radio (NPR), becoming fans of morning host Bob Edwards and shows such as *All Things Considered*. However, by 2002 some

NPR listeners had begun expressing concern as their beloved "public" radio began welcoming corporate sponsors with increasingly wider arms.

In the 1990s, radio broadcasting stations faced more challenges than ever before, as the options for mass communications and information technology continued to grow. Traditional music and news formats were still popular, but there was also strong growth in "talk radio," which features hosts commenting on issues and taking calls from listeners. This format is particularly popular in the United States. The number of wild and crazy morning duos such as Bob and Tom, stars of an Indianapolis-based syndicated show, seems to ever expand, as stuck-in-traffic commuters look for chuckles with their weather, news, and road reports. In the 2000s, as radio stations in local markets compete for ad dollars and listeners, it is not unusual for a station to alter its format radically, abandoning one audience for another. In 2002 the undisputed ruler of the radio waves, in terms of station ownership, was Clear Channel Communications Inc., of San Antonio, Texas. Nevertheless, even this operation could not turn a profit in 2001 as ad sales slumped. That year, Clear Channel self-reported a net loss of US$1.14 billion on revenue of US$7.97 billion. By comparison, in 2000 Clear Channel recorded a profit of US$248.8 million on US$5.35 billion in revenue, according to the *San Antonio Express-News*.

Radio Europe. In the 1980s and 1990s, mainstream "Top 40" radio stations in the United States fragmented into niche formats that reached more segmented parts of the population. The same process was taking place in Europe early in the twenty-first century as radio stations proliferated in markets that were once tightly regulated. As of 2005, however, European radio was still dominated by either state-run mainstream stations, such as BBC Radio One FM, or Top 40 commercial stations.

Consolidation. Massive changes in the U.S. radio market were under way in the mid-to-late 1990s. The most significant change was that the FCC loosened its radio ownership regulations governing duopoly arrangements. Under the revised rules, a single party could own or control both an AM and an FM duopoly in individual markets. A duopoly is defined as two AM and/or two FM radio stations, up to four in total, in the same market. That change led to the consolidation of U.S. radio station ownership by large media groups, which were trying to benefit by reducing promotional costs and boosting the number of total listeners to attract advertisers. As a result, the fragmented U.S. radio industry became highly consolidated over a very short period.

For example, CBS Radio quickly became the nation's largest radio station group with a series of major acquisitions. In April 1997, Chancellor Broadcasting Co., which operated one of the nation's largest radio station groups, merged with Evergreen Media Corp., also a leading station owner. The merger included Evergreen's purchase of 10 Viacom radio stations and the sale of two stations to ABC Radio in order to meet FCC regulations. In March 1998, Jacor Communications Inc., another large radio station group, closed plans to acquire Chancellor Broadcasting and Talk Radio Network Inc.

The hot market for U.S. radio stations continued. In early 1998, the U.S. Justice Department approved two big radio mergers. CBS Corp.'s US$1.6 billion acquisition of American Radio Systems Corp. was okayed on the condition that the companies sell seven radio stations. Capstar Broadcasting Partners, based in Austin, Texas, saw its US$2.1 billion buyout of SFX Broadcasting Inc., based in New York, cleared as well, on condition that the combined companies sell 11 stations.

In March 1998, according to the *Wall Street Journal,* the run-up in radio station prices weeded out all but the biggest and most determined buyers. It also provided "hybrid media companies," publishing businesses with broadcast holdings, the opportunity to cash out their radio side at a substantial profit.

A joint agreement was formed between the Malaysian National News Agency and China Radio International to share in production and exchange of programming. Plans called for operations to be coordinated in Bahasa, Malaysia.

Format Changes. As station ownership structures changed, so did program formats. For example, talk radio was fast becoming the dominant format in the United States' AM radio market in the late 1990s. Using this format, large stations reportedly generated profits of 25 to 35 percent. For example, WLS-AM, based in Chicago, was broadcasting Rush Limbaugh and Dr. Laura Schlessinger, the nation's two most popular syndicated talk show hosts, as of early 2002. The lure of radio was great even for established television celebrities. In May 2002, author and political commentator Bill O'Reilly, host of the Fox cable television show *The O'Reilly Factor,* began taking his views to the radio waves on his show *The Radio Factor With Bill O'Reilly.*

One problem with talk radio, however, was demographics. In 1998, the biggest audience for talk radio—50 to 60 percent of the estimated 100 million weekly listeners—included people 55 years old and older. However, 99 percent of the audience for U.S. FM album-oriented rock stations was younger than 55, and one-third were between the ages of 12 and 24.

Advertisers, looking for free-spending younger listeners, noted this trend. In 1993, 5 of the top 10 U.S. radio stations based on advertising revenue were AM stations. The top FM station was in fifth place. By 1997, however, only 3 of the top 10 stations were on AM, while FM stations held the number two and three spots.

In 2002, the job market for disc jockeys (DJs) worsened because of station preference for voicetracking, requiring DJs to tape their shows in advance for multiple markets. Corporations that owned a string of radio stations could thus have a single DJ on multiple stations—a half dozen or more at a time. Even the most popular DJs who do voicetracking make a fraction at each station of what the going rate would be for one DJ at one station.

Pay-for-Play. In 1998, some U.S. radio stations began considering a controversial policy of trading air time for cash payments from record companies, similar to the infomercials shown on some television stations or the advertising inserts in magazines. Under the "pay-for-play" concept, record companies would promote their artists by paying radio stations to broadcast programs such as one-hour country music showcases or even individual songs. The record label would disclose its sponsorship on the air.

In 1997 the CBS Radio network began promoting this idea to country music producers. EMI Group's Capitol Nashville record label, which records Garth Brooks among others, was said to be backing the idea of paying radio station groups as much as US$1 million an hour for prime time programming featuring its artists. Jacor Communications, which had 192 radio outlets including 19 country stations in 1997, reportedly was working on market partnerships and distribution plans with record labels.

However, some critics charged that such commercial arrangements were inherently unethical and might alienate listeners. They also argued that taking programming decisions out of the hands of radio stations would prompt stations to play less popular music just for commercial reasons, leading to drops in their ratings.

The 2000s saw a return of dozens of allegations that some station employees accepted under-the-table money in exchange for preferential playing of newly recorded songs. In 2002 Mary Catherine Sneed, an executive with Radio One Inc., the best known African-American music station, alleged that "payola"—the word comes from combining pay and Victrola—practices and kickbacks were about to destroy listener confidence in the industry. Radio rules require stations to disclose if payments were received in exchange for playing an artist's music.

CURRENT CONDITIONS

By the mid-2000s, as traditional radio was seeing an increased and lengthy slump in listeners—14 percent from 1994 to 2004—radio-on-demand, subscription-based satellite radio, and Internet radio programming were just a few of the innovations coming to prominence. Critics of traditional radio complained about incessant advertising and repetitive playlists, among other factors, and this discontent turned their ears, and money, to the newer offerings.

Similar to video-on-demand (VOD) technology for television programming, radio-on-demand was taking off by 2003. Unlike VOD, however, the listener could pick programs on the spur of the moment, rather than being forced to choose programs in advance. The technology allowed the listener to hear programs of his or her choice at any time via the Internet. The BBC Radio Player radio-on-demand service in the United Kingdom logged 1.5 million requests each week.

For listeners who just wanted an alternative to traditional radio, several other new technologies were rising to prominence. For instance, satellite radio, operated on a subscription basis, offered radio channels of digital compact-disc quality music across the United States, primarily to car and truck radios. In addition, the channels were commercial-free. Leaders in this segment were seeing their annual valuations balloon more than 300 percent. There were a reported 2 million subscribers to satellite radio in 2004.

There were approximately 7 million people who tuned in to online radio at the beginning of the century, but by 2004 that number had climbed to 19 million and was continuing to grow by about 43 percent each year.

The Radio Heritage Foundation took time to salute "several shining examples of radio broadcasting dedication in the face of extreme danger." Dangerous times occurred when an earthquake radiated through Pago Pago, American Samoa. Even though it became clear their lives were at risk, some DJs gripped their mikes tight and held on to the airwaves while pleading for others to seek safer havens. World Radio TV handbook reported that five stations remained on the air in American Samoa. In independent Samoa, an additional DJ kept working while the earthquake continued its path of destruction in the islands.

RESEARCH AND TECHNOLOGY

One technology affecting radio was the World Wide Web, which gave radio stations the opportunity to broadcast on the Internet. U.S. radio companies were taking different approaches to Internet technology in the late 1990s and early 2000s. In November 1997, the CBS Radio network forbade its company-owned radio stations from simultaneously broadcasting on the Internet. CBS Radio wanted to prevent World Wide Web "netcasts" from cannibalizing its broadcast network audience. Non-company-owned radio stations that were part of the CBS Radio network were allowed to continue offering netcasts via the Web.

However, in April of 1998, ABC Radio selected the Real Broadcast Network to broadcast its ABC-owned radio stations and ABC Radio Networks programming in "RealAudio," a hosting and promotional agreement that gave Internet users access to ABC Radio programming. ABC and RealNetworks planned to extend the reach of RealAudio programming to ABC affiliate stations nationwide. RealNetworks Inc., based in Seattle, is a specialist in the "streaming media" market. In the early 2000s, Internet sites were useful for listeners of National Public Radio and nearly all commercial stations as a place where interviews could be accessed easily for downloading and later listening. According to BRS Media, the number of radio webcasters in 2001 was 4,600, about 25 percent of which were webcasting live online.

One of the most important technological changes in broadcasting is digital transmission of radio signals, which has enhanced quality and led to changes in the way programs are produced and distributed. Broadcasters use computers for scheduling radio time via the "radio-in-a-box" method. A Digital Audio System allows radio stations to select programming through use of satellite dishes. Music libraries can be formatted on a computer to play without the presence of a DJ during programming hours.

Satellite radio is yet another new radio concept. The idea is to develop a subscription-based satellite radio system to deliver commercial-absent channels of digital compact-disc quality music across the United States, primarily to car and truck radios. Pay radio programming is designed for broadcast on satellites over a proposed new radio band, the "S-band," with a range of up to 35,000 km.

In 2007, it was estimated that fewer than half a million Americans used HD radio. The technology had earned praises for its digital format, resulting in better sound quality on both AM and FM bands. HD radio also lets AM stations offer two audio signals instead of one. FM stations deliver three or four sound streams. Expensive radio sets, however, had impacted extent of usage. Wal-Mart Stores's launch for a 2007 promotion to sell HD-compatible car radios for about US$190 in nearly 2,000 of its stores was expected to dramatically impact HD radio sales and usage.

In a "Newsmakers" interview, WNIN-PBS9 Executive Vice President and Chief Operating Officer Vincent Curren discussed views about industry's future with Courier & Press Editor Mizell Stewart III. Curren believed that the advancing of technology meant there were "more ways to serve listeners and viewers." Nevertheless Curren expressed sentiments reflecting belief it was best to be practical when faced with both advantages and disadvantages of being not-for-profit in "a very challenging time." "I think at the end of the day, we have to go back to fundamentals and say we are about journalism, we are about education and we are about culture," Curren admitted.

INDUSTRY LEADERS

XM Satellite Radio Holdings Inc. Of the companies included in *Fortune* magazine's 2005 list of the 2000

largest global companies, only two from the radio industry made the ranking—and both provided satellite radio services in the United Stated. XM Satellite Radio was founded in 1992 and was granted a satellite radio license in the U.S. in 1997. By 2004, it had more than 150 channels serving 3.77 million subscribers. In April 2005, the company announced plans to work with America Online (AOL) to create a new online radio service. The combination was expected to produce the world's largest digital radio network. XM's 2004 revenues of US$244.4 million represented a 166 percent increase over 2003 figures; however, the firm continued to show increasing net loss figures year over year.

Sirius Satellite Radio Inc. The second radio industry company on *Fortune*'s list was Sirius Satellite Radio. By 2006, Sirius had 135 channels: 70 channels offering commercial-free music and more than 65 channels of sports, talk, news, weather, traffic, and entertainment. It also offered sports content from the National Football League and NASCAR. In 2006, Sirius had more than 6 million subscribers, with an increasing number of subscribers coming from auto dealers offering the radio systems as options in their cars. Subscriptions could also be purchased for Internet-based radio. With an employee base of only 614 people for 2006, the company reported revenue of US$637.2 billion in 2006, an increase of more than 163 percent over the previous year. Sirius established alliances with several carmakers including AUDI, BMW, and Ford. Alliances were also established with Best Buy and Sears. The company had entered into a joint venture agreement with the Canadian Broadcasting Corporation to offer satellite radio service in Canada, and was in discussions to offer similar services in Mexico and the Caribbean.

In 2007 Sirius agreed to acquire its rival XM Satellite Radio. That US$13 billion merger would create a satellite radio monopoly. While critics opposed the merger and urged antitrust regulators to reject it, officials of the two companies claimed they would still face tough competition. Sources for that competition were viewed by some as being many different types of rivals including HD-radio stations. Not everyone shared this point of view. Analyst Jimmy Schaeffer of the research firm Carmel Group surmised that HD radio was not major competition for XM and Sirius. HD radio had a half-million listeners while XM and Sirius had about 15 million subscribers.

Clear Channel Communications Inc. Clear Channel was the largest radio company in the United States. In 2006 it owned, operated, programmed, or sold airtime for nearly 1,200 radio stations. It also had equity interests in about 240 international radio stations. Countries tuned into its frequencies included Australia, New Zealand, and Mexico.

With other interests in outdoor advertising and live entertainment, Clear Channel's 2006 sales was US$7.1 billion. Clear Channel owns a 90 percent stake in one of the world's largest outdoor advertising companies, Clear Channel Outdoor Holdings. Clear Channel also owns or manages about 50 TV stations and sells spot advertising for more than 3,300 radio and TV stations through Katz Media. In 2005 the company employed 31,800 people. Clear Channel agreed to be taken private by an investment group led by Thomas H. Lee Partners and Bain Capital.

Clear Channel was perhaps the biggest winner after the 1996 industry deregulation, having begun with a mere 42 stations. Even though its numbers indicated control of only about 10 percent of the U.S. market, Clear Channel was seen by many as the big, bad corporate behemoth come to run radio into the ground with homogenization of content and incessant advertising. Others hailed the company as a hero, rescuing doomed stations from bankruptcy. After paying a US$1.75 million fine for airing a particularly obscene show of controversial shock-jock Howard Stern, Clear Channel dropped his show completely, citing a lack of desire to promote indecent programming.

In 2006 Clear Channel's Format Lab was unveiled for creative applications. It united a virtual community of more than 200 programmers and production professionals developing fresh and unconventional radio and online content.

In March 2007 Clear Channel announced activation of its plans to add music programming from 10 stations to mSpot's radio services. Furthermore, mSpot planned to start distribution in April 2007 of live broadcasts from about 100 Clear Channel stations. Clear Channel agreed to provide Contemporary Hits Radio (CHR) and urban programming from five of its most popular terrestrial stations. Those stations were cited as leaders in these formats for the New York, Los Angeles, Chicago, and Miami markets. Innovative programming availability also included Spanish-language content from four Latin channels and a high-energy playlist of Hip-Hop hits that were all created by Clear Channel Radio's Format Lab and available commercial-free.

On May 12, 2008, Clear Channel conceded to a takeover by Bain Capital and THL Partners for US $17.9 billion. By allowing the two private equity firms to takeover, Clear Channel ended an almost two year battle to take the company private.

Another March 2007 Clear Channel announcement revealed that *Institutional Investor* had ranked it as the most shareholder-friendly company in the radio and TV broadcasting sector for the second consecutive year. In addition, Clear Channel CFO Randall Mays was included in *Institutional Investor*'s top CFO's list. The surveys appeared in the magazine's February and March 2007 issues.

ABC Radio Networks Inc. ABC Radio Networks is owned by Walt Disney Corp.'s television and radio broadcasting division. ABC, however, announced plans to sell ABC Radio Network to Citadel Broadcasting. The network distributes programming to approximately 4,600 affiliate radio stations throughout the United States. ABC Radio Networks' diverse offerings included five full-service line networks, Paul Harvey News & Comment, ESPN Radio Network, long-form programming, ABC News, sports, and daily and weekly features. It also distributed music and entertainment shows, including family-friendly pop music from Radio Disney. The company provided sound effects and other production materials used by radio stations to create promotional spots and lead-ins.

Capital Radio PLC. Capital Radio was the dominant U.K. commercial radio broadcaster in 2005. It held 21 analog and 58 digital licenses. Its main operations were the two London ILR stations, Capital FM, which was number one in London, and Capital Gold. The FM service was pop and dance music-based; the AM Gold service broadcasts hits from the '50s, '60s, and '70s. Total revenues for 2003 were US$192.2 million.

In 1996, Capital Radio bid for an FM band license in Yorkshire, England, as part of its national expansion plans. That initiative continued in 1997 when Capital Radio purchased competitor Virgin Radio for US$106 million. The deal, which was expected to further Capital's digital audio broadcasting plans, also included the transfer of Virgin's US$35.7 million debt to Capital.

In 2001 and 2002, Capital Radio encountered the same setbacks in ad sales that faced other media due to the tepid post-September 11, 2001 business climate. In March of 2002, Capital Radio posted a 7 percent decline in revenue for the six months prior to March 31, 2002. By 2004, sales had increased 12.2 percent over the previous year, reaching more than US$215 million, with net income of US$10.6 million. In September 2004, the company announced its plans to merge with GWR Group, which owned 30 stations and generated US$235 million in revenues in 2004.

CBS RADIO Inc. CBS RADIO, formerly known as Infinity Broadcasting, is counted among the United States' leading radio broadcasters. It owned and operated 170 radio stations in about 40 major markets nationwide. CBS RADIO stations offer a variety of programming from talk and sports to diverse music styles. Its operating strategy called for regional clusters sharing back office functions such as ad sales and marketing. The company also manages radio syndicator Westwood One and produces news, sports, and entertainment shows for more than 5,000 affiliate stations. CBS RADIO is a subsidiary of broadcasting giant CBS Corporation.

CBS RADIO is an innovator with insight as evidenced by the ability "to make aggressive moves to converge new and traditional media." Key methods include HD radio and pod casting. There are approximately 200 CBS RADIO audio streams available on line. Many sports franchises have chosen CBS RADIO. They include teams belonging to the MLB, NFL, and NBA. CBS RADIO maintains a "long-standing alliance" linking it to Westwood One. Westwood One handles sales and affiliate relations. In addition, it provides significant programming segments and special events coverage. Options include news, sports, music, Olympic coverage and music awards show features. CBS RADIO owns the CBS Radio Network.

In 2007, veteran radio host and TV personality Don Imus was dropped initially by MSNBC and then by CBS. Imus called the Rutgers University women's basketball team "nappy-headed 'hos'." The National Association of Black Journalists, followed soon by the National Association of Hispanic Journalists, expressed their disgust with Imus. Civil rights activist Al Sharpton called for Imus to be taken off the air. Those protests led to a two-week suspension of Imus' show. Major advertisers started pulling their ads. The companies doing so included industry leaders such as GlaxoSmithKline, General Motors, Proctor & Gamble, Staples, and American Express. After that, MSNBC pulled Imus permanently. Bruce Gordon, a CBS board member and former NAACP president, then publicly called for Imus' dismissal. In response, CBS finally let him go. The decisions related to Imus's actions were considered to be related to economics more than ethics in a time when more minorities and women had taken seats at boardroom tables.

Cox Radio Inc. Cox Radio is one of the nation's largest radio broadcasters, with 80 stations in 18 markets. Those markets include Atlanta, San Antonio, and Tampa. Through Cox Radio Syndication the company produces programs and distributes them to more than 200 affiliate stations through a partnership with Jones Radio Network. Cox Radio Interactive creates Web sites for its stations and sells advertising on those sites. Cox Enterprises controls 95 percent of the company through its 65 percent equity holding.

Rogers Media. Rogers Media is a division of Rogers Communications, a Toronto, Ontario-based telecommunications conglomerate. Rogers has major interests in cable TV, cellular phones, radio and TV broadcasting, telecommunications, publishing, and video stores. In 2005 Rogers Broadcasting held 43 AM and FM radio licenses across Canada, several of which are clustered in major Canadian cities such as Toronto. Rogers reported 2004 revenues of US$4.7 billion.

MAJOR COUNTRIES IN THE INDUSTRY

Canada. Coming out of a downturn in the 1980s and early 1990s, the Canadian radio industry entered 2000 on an upswing. By 2003, air time sales by private broadcasters had increased by 8.4 percent to a value of almost US$1 billion and the industry produced the highest profits in its history. FM stations held 75 percent of the market and their market share was expected to increase.

The Canadian Broadcasting Corporation (CBC), through its CBC/Radio Canada segment, provides national radio stations operating in English, French, and eight aboriginal languages. The stations include CBC Radio One and CBC Radio Two in English, CBC Radio Three, Premiere Chaine and Espace Musique in French. Public funds provide the majority of CBC's operating budget, with additional revenue coming in through advertising and subscription fees. CBC has helped to develop Canadian talent in the entertainment business, with its content being more than 90 percent Canadian. Its music, drama, and documentary programs are highly regarded.

Canadian broadcasting is regulated by the Canadian Radio-Television and Telecommunications Corp. (CRTC), which licenses networks and private stations and specifies required percentages of Canadian content in programming.

China. With its large population, it is not surprising that China should have the second largest radio market in the world. In 2004, there were more than 500 local stations in the country, all government controlled. Nearly half of China' population listened to the radio each week, with listeners near the capital tuning in for more than 14 hours per week.

France. In 1989, the Socialist government of France formed the Conseil Superieur de l'Audiovisuel (CSA), or Supreme Audiovisual Council, to supervise radio and television broadcasting. In radio, two government agencies, France Culture and France Musique, produce the bulk of cultural programs. Radio France, a unit of the Conseil, operates six national radio networks: France-Inter, network A (entertainment and news); Network B (educational); France-Culture, network D (culture and public affairs); France-Musique, network E (music); Regional stations, network F; and France Info (24-hour news). Private radio stations also exist. According to *Euromonitor*, the market was valued at US$1.68 billion in 2003, and was expected to grow to US$2.06 billion by 2008.

Germany. Only public corporations were permitted to broadcast in Germany until the mid-1980s, when a new system allowed commercial stations on the air for the first time. However, by 2003, public broadcasters still dominated the industry, holding 57.1 percent of market share, with the top three being Westdeutscher Rundfunk (WDR), Norddeutscher Rundfunk (NDR), and Sudwestrundfunk (SWR). The share held between public and private broadcasters was not expected to change up to 2008. Licensing of broadcasters is handled by the Federal Ministry of Post and Telecommunications, while television and radio owners pay annual fees to support public broadcasting. As in England, German public broadcasters are relatively free to establish their own broadcasting policies, though more so in television than radio. Nine different public corporations offer regional radio and TV programs. In Germany, there were 64.4 million radio listeners each day in 2003.

Italy. While all broadcasting in Italy was once the province of Radiotelevisione Italiana (RAI), private firms have emerged as major competitors. RAI is still a major player in the radio market, however, providing three radio services on national networks in AM and FM. The first, a national program, offers a balanced output; the second is essentially entertainment; and the third is educational. In addition, there is substantial regional output. RAI devotes 70 percent of its radio output to light entertainment, 16 percent to news and information, 4 percent to cultural programs, and 1 percent to youth and educational programs. RAI's revenues come from a government-determined proportion drawn from the sales of radio and television receiving licenses, and advertising.

Japan. The radio market in Japan is more developed than in other Asian countries. Japanese radio broadcasting was begun in 1925 by Japan Broadcasting Corporation (Nippon Hoso Kyokai, or NHK), a public corporation financed by license fees paid by TV and radio users. NHK broadcasts radio and television programs with no commercial interruptions. In 2005, NHK operated three radio networks: two AM and one FM. One of the AM networks was exclusively devoted to educational programs. The FM network service mainly presented cultural and local music programs. NHK had 173 medium wave transmitters for the First Radio network, 141 for the Second, and 474 for the VHF-FM network. NHK also broadcast overseas programs in many different languages on its short wave service, Radio Japan. In the early 2000s, there were about 300 commercial radio stations in Japan.

The United Kingdom. British television and radio broadcasting has traditionally been dominated by the British Broadcasting Corporation (BBC), which in 2003 had a 45 percent market share. The BBC gets its operating budget from license fees paid by television users. In 2004, the BBC had 10 national radio networks, including five digital stations added in 2002. More than

40 BBC local radio stations serve England and the Channel Islands, and regional and community radio stations cater to Scotland, Wales, and Northern Ireland. A number of private radio stations also have been established, including a new talk radio network. The total market was expected to grow to US$3.2 billion by 2008.

GCap Media was the leading commercial radio operator in the United Kingdom, with about 120 stations reaching more than 15 million listeners or more than 30 percent of the national audience. That includes 55 analog stations and almost 100 digital stations. GCap also operates several radio networks, including Choice FM, Core, The One Network, and Xfm. It also owns more than 60 percent of the Digital One commercial digital radio multiplex and it has a 50 percent stake in Wildstar Records. The record company was a joint venture with Telstar Records.

The United States. By 2003, the radio market in the United States was valued at US$22 billion, according to figures compiled by *Euromonitor*, and was expected to grow to US$29.8 billion by 2008. Local advertising accounted for 78.2 percent of the industry's revenues. At this time, the country's top five radio companies (Viacom, Cumulus Media, Clear Channel, Cox Radio, and Entercom Communications) accounted for 34.2 percent of the market, indicating the highly fragmented nature of the industry in this country. Most U.S. commercial stations specialized in a single type of output, such as popular music, classical music, news, sports, or tourist information. While AM radio stations once specialized in music programs, by the late 1990s FM stations had taken over most of that market. AM stations in the United States have moved toward talk and news formats.

Non-commercial radio in the United States is primarily National Public Radio (NPR), which receives funding from the federal government, foundations, and other sources. NPR produces a variety of news, information, and music programs, which are distributed to affiliated stations around the country, most of them on FM. The local stations are owned and operated primarily by non-profit groups and universities. Funding for the local stations comes from grants and listeners' donations.

Learn more about Wisconsin radio broadcasting by tuning in on line. The broadcasting history is rich in the state of Wisconsin. That wealth, however, did not extend to The Wisconsin Museum of Broadcasting supporters' budget. Wisconsin Broadcasters Association Foundation President and CEO John Lambs described how everyone came to agree on a creative alternative. During a planning session, it was suggested to do things in the most modern way and go online. Broadcasting in Wisconsin had its origin with an experimental Beloit College station launched in

1908. Additional historical reflections are shared via clips in the museum section called "Broadcasters Attic."

Challenging economic times have created additional challenges for radio broadcasters and others attempting to restructure businesses. U.S. Federal Communication Commission rules restrict ownership of media in markets as foreign ownership guidelines. When debts continue to climb and loan payment deadlines are missed, companies seeking to restructure have much more to think about now. Something Mike Spector and Sarah Mcbride described as "another unintended consequence of the credit boom" was resulting in lenders taking over businesses they never intended to actually run.

BIBLIOGRAPHY

"America Listens to ABC." ABC Radio Networks 2004. Available from www.abcradio.com.

Bernama To Exchange Radio TV Programmes With CRI." 11 October 2009. Available from www.bernama.com.

The Canadian Press. "Satellite Radio Company XM Canada reaches royalty payment agreement." 15 September 2009.

CBS RADIO. "About Us: Corporate Profile." 11 October 2009. Available from www.cbsradio.com.

Citadel Media Networks. "About Citadel Media." Available from abcradionetworks.com.

"Clear Channel Accepts Smaller Takeover Bid." 14 May 2008. Available from dealbook.blogs.nytimes.com.

"Clear Channel Communications Lands Premier Spot on Institutional Investor's Top Corporate Rankings." San Antonio, Tex.: Clear Channel Communications, 14 March 2007. Available form www.clearchannel.com.

"Clear Channel Radio Adds Music Channels to mSpot Radio." *Business Wire,* 27 March 2007.

Cox Radio. "Our Company." 2009. Available from coxradio.com.

"Does New Technology Mean the End of Old Technology?" *Innovation Analysis Bulleting,* 3 October 2004. Available from www.statcan.ca.

Draper, Deborah J., ed. *Business Rankings Annual.* Detroit: Thomson Gale, 2004.

Fonda, Daren. "The Revolution in Radio." *Time,* 19 April 2004.

Grillo, Jean Bergantini. "Rebound for Radio in '04." *Broadcasting* & *Cable,* 5 January 2004.

Harris, Ron. "A Downpour." STLtoday.com 15 April 2007. Available from www.stltoday.com.

"HD Radio Pumps Up Volume." *Boston Globe,* 2 April 2007.

"Hoover's Company Capsules." *Hoover's Online,* 2007. Available from www. hoovers.com.

Johnson, Jackie. "Wisconsin Museum of Broadcasting goes on line." Wisconsin Radio Network, 9 October 2009. Available from www.wrn.com.

Lazich, Robert S., ed. *Market Share Reporter.* Detroit: Thomson Gale, 2004.

Lorek, L.A. "Clear Channel CEO Pledges Corporate Changes, Says Company not Radio Monolith." *Knight Ridder/Tribune Business News,* 26 July 2004.

Mullaman, Jeremy. "Weak Signal for Radio." *Crain's Chicago Business,* 31 May 2004.

"Nielsen Media Research." *Mediaweek,* 28 June 2004.

Poling, Travis E. "Clear Channel Tallies $1.14 Billion Loss." *San Antonio Express-News,* 27 February 2002.

"Radio Broadcasting in France, Germany, UK, US." *Euromonitor,* August 2004. Available from www.majormarketprofiles.com.

"Radio One Reports Preliminary 4Q Results." *Wireless News,* 22 March 2007.

"Radio Today: How America Listens to Radio, 2005 Edition." Arbitron, December 2004. Available from www.arbitron.com.

"Rajar Shows 1 Percent Boost for Commercial." *Campaign,* 14 May 2004.

"Samoan Radio Survives Tsunami-Brave Broadcasters Defy Danger." 8 October 2009. Available from pacific.scoop.co.nz.

Sirius Satellite Radio. "Corporate Overview." Available from www.sirius.com.

Spector, Mike, and Sarah Mcbride. "Media Rules Complicate Restructurings." *The Wall Street Journal,* 18 September 2009. Available from online. wsj.com.

Stewart, Mizell III. "Public broadcasting adapts in changing world." *Evansville Courier* & *Press,* 11 October 2009. Available from www.courierpress.com.

Zagorodnov, Artem. "Russia Now: The changing face of the radio industry." Available from www.telegraph.co.uk.

SIC 3660

TELECOMMUNICATIONS EQUIPMENT

NAICS CODE(S)

517. Telecommunications hardware manufacturers build multiple components to sustain the world's communications systems. Serving both commercial and residential users, examples of industry products include transmission and switching equipment, telephones, and related devices for facilitating and managing voice and data communications. For information regarding providers of communication services using such equipment, see **Telecommunications Services**.

Leaders in the Telecommunications Equipment Industry, 2009

	Revenue, in billions of U.S. dollars
Siemens	$101.5
NEC	$42.78
Alcatel-Lucent	$20.07
Motorola	$22.04
Nortel Networks	$ 4.50

SOURCE: Company Websites.

Facts and Figures about the Internet

- The number of Internet users has doubled between 2005 and 2010.
- In 2010, the number of Internet users will surpass the two billion mark, of which 1.2 billion will be in developing countries.
- A number of countries, including Estonia, Finland and Spain have declared access to the Internet as a legal right for citizens.
- With more than 420 million Internet users, China is the largest Internet market in the world.
- While 71% of the population in developed countries is online, only 21% of the population in developing countries is online. By the end of 2010, Internet user penetration in Africa will reach 9.6%, far behind both the world average (30%) and the developing country average (21%).

SOURCE: International Telecommunication Union.

INDUSTRY SNAPSHOT

The outlook for the telecommunications industry remained positive worldwide through the first decade of the twenty-first century. Demand for telecommunications equipment continued to register healthy gains as mobile cellular subscriptions reached 5.3 billion at the end of 2010. Ninety percent of the world had access to mobile networks, including 80 percent of the population living in rural areas. Having access to fixed, or landline, phone service was no longer sufficient for a large portion of the world population. At the end of the first decade of the 2000s, 940 million people in both industrialized and developing nations subscribed to 3G services. By 2010, 143 nations offered 3G technology compared to 95 countries in 2007. Global telecommunication revenues reached US$2.1 trillion in 2004, according to the TIA, and were expected to reach $2 trillion worldwide by 2007. The network equipment market was expected to reach $16.4 billion in 2005, followed by 7 percent annual growth through 2007.

In mature markets, manufacturers emphasized emerging technology like wireless and networking equipment because of the robust demand for the Internet and computer networks, while the focus in developing markets was on basic telephone technology like phones, answering machines, and switching equipment. Consequently, telecommunications equipment companies expected the industry to experience increasingly strong growth by 2010. The wireless communications segment was the fastest growing in the industry during the mid-2000s. Internet protocol (IP) applications and systems were a major growth area, with 70 percent annual increases in traffic. Revenue for IP applications like web conferencing also rose quickly, and Internet equipment was expected to grow more than 7 percent annually through 2007, according to the TIA. By the end 2010, the number of Internet users was expected to surpass the 2 billion mark, 1.2 billion of which will come from developing markets.

The telecommunications industry was led by a few major companies. The top 10 companies in the industry, which controlled slightly less than three-quarters of the global market, were concentrated in North America, Western Europe, and Japan. These regions have historically been the major markets due to extensive telephone communication systems developed to meet the expanding needs of business. Although new technologies and markets were changing the industry, the same companies remained the industry leaders for decades, some for more than a century. Participants in the telecommunications equipment industry previously had been confined to domestic markets. However, international trade in the industry was expanding rapidly. Most leading companies derived at least 30 percent of their revenues from foreign sales. The industry was also characterized by high research and development expenditures that were more easily absorbed by huge corporations and conglomerates. By the mid-2000s, the industry was experiencing a high number of mergers and acquisitions, and this trend was expected to continue for the foreseeable future.

Infonetics Research reported an increase in sales of equipment to service providers to US$139 billion for 2007, which represented a 13 percent increase over the previous year. Total equipment sales were predicted to reach US$174 billion by 2011. These increases would be reflected in areas, such as China and India, where large companies had a minimal presence, producing switches, routers, and Internet Protocol Television (IPTV) gear. As of 2010, China had 420 million Internet users, making it the largest market in the world.

ORGANIZATION AND STRUCTURE

The equipment market consists of network equipment, which is used by telephone service operators, and customer premises equipment. Network equipment includes switching and transmission equipment. Switching equipment includes central office switches, switchboards, packet switches, mobile telephone switching offices, microwave switches, and data communication switches. Unlike other switching equipment, data communication switches are increasingly used on private premises to facilitate data transmission within computer networks. Transmission equipment includes multiplexing equipment to transmit multiple signals over a single communications line, repeaters to strengthen signals over long distances, and line-conditioning equipment.

Customer premises equipment, also called terminal equipment, is privately owned or leased equipment attached to the telecommunications network. It includes private branch exchange (PBX) equipment to switch multiple lines on private premises; telephones; key telephone systems to handle multiple lines, but fewer lines than PBXs; fax machines; modems to convert between analog and digital signals in order to connect computers to telephone networks; telephone answering machines and voice mail systems; and video communications equipment. Technological innovations that enable switching between wireless fidelity (WiFI) and wireless systems, as well as Internet protocol-based systems, were also emerging during the mid-2000s.

Leading telecom equipment companies manufacture central exchange office switching and PBX equipment and offer products in most other equipment categories. Many small companies manufacture customer premises equipment, but not for the commercial market. Some further specialize in certain types of terminal equipment, such as fax machines or modems. Dozens of new companies also compete in the growing market for data communications equipment, especially in the United States, where the industry is primarily an outgrowth of the country's strong computer industry.

BACKGROUND AND DEVELOPMENT

The precursor to modern telecommunications, the telegraph was based on the invention in 1880 of the voltaic pile, a device used to convert chemical energy into continuous electric current, and the invention of electromagnetic detectors in 1836–37 by William Cooke and Charles Wheatstone in Great Britain and by Samuel Morse in the United States. Telegraph systems involved the interruption of, or change in, the polarity of direct current (DC) signaling to convey coded information over cables. The basic telegraph apparatus was the telegraph key, a switch for making and breaking a circuit to create pulses of information in Morse code. Early manufacturers of telegraph equipment usually manufactured other electric equipment as well. As the industry developed in the latter half of the nineteenth century, specialized manufacturers emerged.

In 1876 Alexander Graham Bell patented the telephone in the United States. He developed both variable resistance and magneto-induction devices. While the former was superior, the latter was more reliable at first and hence was the first commercialized version. Initial outdoor transmissions used telegraph lines. Some early telephone equipment companies had been manufacturing telegraph equipment and diversified, while the rest were entirely new companies, created to satisfy the huge new market. As telephone networks spread in the twentieth century they largely replaced telegraph systems, and telegraph equipment became an insignificant part of the industry.

Various advances in telephone equipment have been made over the years. The first coin-operated telephones were introduced in 1889 and AT&T patented the first automatic dial systems in 1891. In 1912, the introduction of the vacuum-tube repeater improved signals carried over long distances. Long-distance service was further enhanced with the invention of the diode and the refinement of the triode, audion, and hard valve lamps between 1904 and 1915. By 1960, rotary switching systems began to be replaced by crossbar switching, an electro-mechanical system that used sets of magnets on vertical and horizontal bars. The first electronic, as opposed to electro-mechanical, switching equipment was introduced in the United States in 1965. This equipment accelerated automatic switching and permitted a significant increase in the volume of telephone traffic. Large scale integrated circuits improved in the 1970s to the point of allowing the development of digital switching, which replaced electronic analog switching in central offices.

Before 1970, the telecommunications equipment industry consisted of a small number of companies, many of which approached monopolies, in each country to supply their respective domestic markets. The market consisted primarily of public telecommunications operators, which, as government monopolies, procured equipment through bids but tended to favor one or two suppliers through close relationships. The objectives were to achieve common equipment specifications and stability of supply. Government telecommunications administrators protected the equipment industry and true free market competition was not fostered. In this sense, the telecommunications industry resembled the structure of the defense industry. Pockets of international competition existed, however. Equipment companies from industrialized countries expanded and competed in developing countries where indigenous telecommunications manufacturers were either nonexistent or lacking in needed technology.

Historically, telephones and other customer premises equipment were sold exclusively to telephone operators rather than directly to the customers. Telephone companies in turn leased this equipment to subscribers. Customer premises equipment was considered part of the same network system and compatibility had to be maintained. It also was feared that third-party equipment might somehow damage the network. Regulations in many countries actually prohibited customers from connecting equipment to telephone lines that was not provided or authorized by the telephone company. For example, the use of non-AT&T equipment in the United States was not allowed until 1968, and in Germany, customers were not permitted to purchase telephones privately and connect them to the official telephone network until as late as 1990. The adoption of industry-wide standards for customer premises equipment and deregulation of the telephone equipment industry in various countries allowed customers to choose and buy their own equipment. Consequently, equipment manufacturers began to market directly to customers, selling equipment through retail stores. This also opened a new market for consumer electronics manufacturers that had not been part of the telecommunications industry.

Customer premises equipment is manufactured both by traditional telecommunications equipment companies, which continue to produce network equipment, and by numerous consumer electronics manufacturers. Low-end customer premises equipment (e.g., telephones, answering machines, and fax machines) has become more of a commodity and is increasingly manufactured in the emerging economies of Asia, where it can be produced less expensively due to lower labor costs.

In 1996, the global telecommunications equipment market rose to between US$180 to $195 billion. However, the top manufacturers accounted for US$140 billion, or roughly 71 percent, of worldwide telecommunications equipment sales, according to Northern Telecom Ltd. By-product, cable, and wire accounted for 11 percent of sales, transmission devices for 14 percent, consumer equipment for 15 percent, switching equipment for 17 percent, data communication equipment for 20 percent, and wireless technology for 23 percent. Telecommunications equipment imports totaled US$60.7 billion in 1995, according to the International Telecommunication Union. Western Europe accounted for 33 percent of these imports, followed by Asia with 28 percent, and North America with 22 percent.

The industry's collective revenues jumped to about US$1 trillion by 2002. Deregulation, new markets, new technology, and trade liberalization were making the telecommunications equipment industry more competitive, international, and dynamic. Deregulation and privatization of national telephone carrier monopolies worldwide have been changing the market for telecommunication equipment suppliers. Market forces have compelled telephone companies to purchase high quality and cost-effective equipment in order to offer competitive services. Existing regulatory restrictions on equipment manufacturers also were being lifted. Global network equipment sales totaled about US$72 billion in 2002. Analysts expected growth of approximately 2 percent for 2004, as the U.S. and world economies rebounded after a dismal period during the early 2000s. Optical networking equipment was reporting growth in the mid-2000s after several consecutive years of decline.

Trade accords, such as the North American Free Trade Agreement (NAFTA) and the General Agreement on Tariffs and Trade (GATT), led to the Information Technology Agreement (ITA). After a few years of negotiation, many of the world's economically powerful and not-so-powerful countries signed the ITA, which pledged willingness to eliminate tariffs on specified information technology (IT) products, including computer software, hardware, and peripherals; telecommunications equipment; analytical

instruments; semiconductor manufacturing equipment; and semiconductors. By 2002, about 95 percent of World Trade Organization member countries had signed the ITA. Nations that signed the Information Technology Agreement as of mid-2001 were Albania, Georgia, New Zealand, Australia, Austria, Norway, Bulgaria, Belgium, Iceland, Oman, Canada, Denmark, India, Panama, Costa Rica, Finland, Indonesia, the Philippines, Croatia, France, Israel, Poland, Cyprus, Germany, Japan, Romania, Czech Republic, Greece, Jordan, Singapore, El Salvador, Ireland, Korea, Slovak Republic, Estonia, Italy, Kyrgyz Republic, Slovenia, Taiwan, Luxembourg, Latvia, Switzerland, the Netherlands, Liechtenstein, Portugal, Lithuania, Thailand, Spain, Macau, Turkey, Sweden, Malaysia, the United States, the United Kingdom, and Mauritius.

Under GATT, the ITA led to further industry expansion by opening the industry's major markets around the world to international competition. Although the agreement directly affected telecommunications service providers, manufacturers have seen indirect benefits because increased competition spurred telephone companies to purchase equipment for the new telephone networks and to upgrade equipment more often to stay competitive.

Customer Premises Equipment. Because of maturing markets and technological advances, the customer premises equipment (CPE) segment of the industry experienced heightened competition and lower prices in the latter half of the 1990s. Manufacturers outsourced production of lower-end CPE products to low-wage economies such as those in Asia. Much of the new growth in this segment resulted from innovative products like video-conferencing equipment. Cordless phones were the fastest growing category in the fixed-line telephone segment. The market for fax machines and modems was also booming, but standard handset phone demand experienced slower growth because of its high penetration level.

Since most customer premises equipment is largely standardized, companies were addressing issues of standardizing public network equipment, including synchronous digital hierarchy/synchronous optical network transmission (SONET) and asynchronous transfer mode (ATM) switching. As equipment conforming to these standards created new markets, many small companies took advantage of the new standards to enter the industry. Public telephone operators, however, were slow to adopt these standards.

Customer premises data communications equipment drove the industry in the 1990s. This segment enjoyed strong growth throughout the decade, and continued growth was expected in the twenty-first century. This segment includes modems, fax machines, and computer networking and Internetworking equipment, which is used by companies as they establish larger and more complex computer networks. This growing market was being exploited by established telecommunications equipment companies, computer and computer peripheral manufacturers, and new specialized companies, such as Cisco Systems and Bay Networks, which were among the fastest growing companies in the telecommunications equipment industry.

The convergence of telecommunications technology with that of the computer industry contributed to the growth of the customer premises data communications equipment market. This included computer local area network (LAN) adapter cards, switches, routers, and bridges. The introduction of asynchronous transfer mode switching (ATM) to LAN products allowed LAN manufacturers to enter telecommunications companies' markets. LAN equipment manufacturers were taking a growing share of the public network infrastructure market, if not directly, then through resellers. Therefore, traditional telecommunications equipment companies were beginning to face competition from computer hardware companies. Unaffected by the recession, the LAN market continued to grow rapidly through the 1990s. This also spurred growth in the PBX and key system (KTS) markets, where manufacturers had developed equipment to be part of communications networks instead of being independent. The U.S. Department of Commerce predicted that the Pacific Rim countries, Eastern Europe, and South America would make up the leading PBX and KTS markets in the early twenty-first century.

Wireless Telecommunications Equipment. Because global wireless saturation was only 1 percent in 1997, this segment of the industry expected explosive growth as new spectrum and digital technologies became more available, more wireless service providers entered the market, prices declined, and mass appeal of wireless telecommunication increased. However, the lack of universal wireless standards had the potential to slow the growth of the industry and hurt wireless equipment trade in the United States, Europe, and Japan, which had adopted different standards. Excluding the United States, 50 percent of the world's wireless systems used the European GSM/DSC 1800 (Global Systems for Mobile Communications) standard in 1997. Japan also controlled a large percentage of the market with its PHS (Personal Handyphone Service) standard, but the United States continued to promote its CDMA (Code Division Multiple Access) standard, which was gaining global popularity.

Worldwide demand for wireless telecommunications equipment increased dramatically, and almost every country had at least one cellular telephone service by 2002. The number of cellular telephone subscribers continued to rise around the world in the mid-2000s. The United States was the leader, followed by Japan, the United Kingdom, China, and Italy. Analysts expected that companies would continue to license cellular systems, leading to added growth for global wireless equipment makers. Each new license benefited manufacturers because it required building a new cellular system and resulted in greater demand for user handsets.

CURRENT CONDITIONS

As reported by the International Telecommunication Union, the Chinese market was booming in the telecommunications industry by 2010. Growth in Japan was expected to be 23 percent, followed by South Korea (36 percent) and Australia (68 percent). In Europe, the market in France was projected to increase 65 percent, with an increase of 12 percent in the United Kingdom. The U.S. market, valued at US$785 billion in 2004, was expected to grow 9.5 percent annually, reaching US$1.1 trillion by 2008. Rapidly growing segments of the industry included voice over Internet protocol (VoIP), WiFi (wireless fidelity) and streaming media, fiber optics innovations, dense wavelength division multiplexing (DWDM), and wavelength-division multiplexing (WDM).

According to a Yankee Group study, by 2007 infrastructure equipment costs would have a corresponding decline, to less than 7 percent of revenue. *Euromonitor* predicted that mobile phones would remain the largest industry sector in China, Japan, South Korea, France, and Germany into 2007. So-called smart phones, mobile handheld converged devices, reported some of the largest growth in this sector in 2003, with 181 percent growth over 2002, according to *2.5G–3G*.

By the end of 2010, there were 2 billion Internet users worldwide, compared to 20 million a decade earlier. As a result, Internet service providers and telephone companies realized that they had to invest in more digital switching and new products, such as wavelength division multiplexing (WDM) equipment, to reduce network congestion.

Because traditional equipment for voice communication had saturated markets in the developed economies of Western Europe, the United States, and Japan, manufacturers anticipated that the strongest growth in these regions would come from data communication equipment. With the explosive popularity of the Internet and related activities, such as e-mail, text messaging, e-commerce, and telecommuting, telecom equipment producers planned to focus on this expanding market by providing modems, fax machines, computer networking equipment, and other kinds of data communications equipment.

The mobile cellular growth boom had started to slow by 2010 due to reaching the saturation point in most of the developed world. By 2010, there was an average of approximately 116 subscriptions per 100 inhabitants. However, in developing nations the growth remained strong, up 73 percent in 2010 from 53 percent in 2005. India and China were expected to add over 300 million mobile subscriptions in 2010. Africa had a 41 percent saturation rate in 2010 compared to 76 percent globally, and that sector was looking for growth.

In developed markets, such as Western Europe and the United States, telephone companies had completed almost all digitalization projects begun in the 1970s. Consequently, telecommunications equipment investments had been shifting from switching and transmission equipment to software and service enhancements. In contrast, developing countries represented a growing market as the process of industrialization led to investments in telecommunications infrastructure, including central office switching and transmission equipment. This enabled leading telecommunications equipment companies to maintain steady growth in sales of switching and transmission equipment through exports, despite maturing domestic markets.

Among the developing markets, Asia represented the fastest growing market, especially China. South American countries also constituted strong markets for growth in telecommunications production and trade. As South American countries moved toward telephone penetration levels achieved in developed nations (see **Telecommunications Services**), they were becoming one of the most important markets for telecommunication equipment. Internet and wireless technology were expected to grow quickly in Asia and Latin America.

RESEARCH AND TECHNOLOGY

The telecommunications industry invests heavily in research and development (R&D) to develop new equipment and standards that will lead to more reliable, cost-effective services that offer more features. Spending on R&D averages 12 percent of revenues for leading telecommunication equipment companies. On the high end, some companies spend close to 20 percent.

The conversion of central office switches from analog to digital, a worldwide telecommunications industry process that began in the 1970s and continued into the 2000s, allowed central switches to be controlled by computers. This created new possibilities for software development to provide more sophisticated services. In 2005, Infonetics Research reported that Internet Protocol (IP) PBX systems were experiencing intense growth of more than 50 percent between 2003 and 2004.

The telecommunications industry was also gradually replacing copper wire with fiber-optic cable, which has better transmission quality over long distances, greater transmission capacity (bandwidth), higher security, and greater energy efficiency. To take advantage of the wider bandwidth, equipment was developed to provide concurrent transmission of voice, data, and video signals, based on the synchronous optical network (SONET) standard. SONET, a set of interfaces for fiber-optic transmission devised in 1988, utilizes fiber optic's wider bandwidth, but is also compatible with copper wire-based systems.

Data transmission capabilities were the focus of R&D efforts at the beginning of the 2010s. Increased speeds and bandwidth were in demand for transmitting computer data and were necessary for the transmission of video images for purposes like video conferencing. New switching technologies were developed to address these needs, including frame relay, switched multi-megabit data service (SMDS), and asynchronous transfer mode (ATM). SMDS was popular in the United States because it was designed to be compatible with the existing network. Frame relay offered low-cost data-switching capabilities, but had fewer features than SMDS or ATM. ATM had been expected to become the dominant broadband technology by the end of the 1990s, but R&D costs were high, so it was expected to take longer. In the meantime, new techniques in data compression were being developed to handle the needs of video transmission.

A promising new piece of telecommunications equipment, the Internet telephone, immediately drew the attention of business Internet users and intrigued home Internet users. Internet telephony allows users to place calls via the Internet, bypassing the high costs of long-distance voice communication. In terms of equipment, service providers required flexible Internet gateway servers that could accommodate both large and small numbers of users. On the users' side, a special Internet telephone was needed. Voice over Internet Protocol (VoIP) was expected to be a major growth factor in the industry through the 2010s. Growth was expected to be somewhat limited by quality and reliability issues, as well as lower than expected cost savings.

The Digital Subscriber Line (DSL), which was a big improvement over the standard, slow analog modem connection, enabled a customer to tap into the regional telephone network to link a dedicated line with a central office point of presence (POP) account and connect to the Internet. The best DSL modems were up to 125 times faster than a 56.6K analog modem. Broadband connections were starting to outnumber dial-up accounts in many countries in 2005 as costs declined, according to Deloitte's Media and Telecommunications Group.

By the mid-2000s, mobile phones were no longer getting smaller. Instead, manufacturers were developing converged products that could handle many different capabilities, including color displays, cameras, Internet browsers, and WiFi without increasing the handset size by developing converged chips that integrated functions in the architecture itself. Such third-generation (3G) devices were in development by Motorola, Intel, and Texas Instruments, as well as other companies in throughout the 2000s.

INDUSTRY LEADERS

Siemens AG. In 1997 Siemens was the world's leading electrical and electronic equipment manufacturer. Telecommunications equipment represented about a third of its business. Siemens' telecommunications products included digital telephone switching systems, communications network software, cellular telephones and base station equipment, broadband network adapter equipment for multimedia transmission, asynchronous transfer mode switches, and telephone handsets. Siemens was the world market leader in PBXs with a 10 percent market share in the mid-1990s. By 2009, the company's total sales from all divisions was US$101.5 billion, with a collective workforce in all divisions of 420,801 throughout 190 countries.

Although Siemens diversified into many areas of electrical, electronic, computer, and semiconductor equipment, the company originated as a telecommunications equipment manufacturer. It was founded in 1847 in Berlin as Siemens and Halske to produce telegraph equipment. Shortly after the invention of the telephone, Siemens patented an improved version and began producing equipment. In the 1920s, Siemens established a joint venture subsidiary in Japan called Fuji Electric, which became the parent company of Fujitsu. The latter eventually became Japan's second largest telecommunications company. In 1988, Siemens acquired IBM's Rolm System subsidiary, the third largest supplier of PBX telephone switching equipment in North America.

By 2004, Siemens planned to market its own line of phones based on the Universal Mobile Telecommunications System standard. In 2002 and 2003, it had purchased Motorola-made phones with fast Internet capabilities, as well as Motorola handset chips, and marketed them under the Siemens brand. Siemens also controlled 13 percent of the US$2.3 billion spent in 2001 by global service providers for DSL equipment, according to the March 25, 2002, issue of *Fiber Optics News.*

Los Angeles billionaire and buy-out specialist Alec Gores, owner of the Gores Group private equity firm, bought a 51 percent majority interest in Siemens telecom equipment unit called Siemens Enterprise Communications. The unit made telephone handsets, switching equipment and software for business customers. Gores looked at the competition as providing an opportunity for additional acquisitions, making them market leaders.

Alcatel-Lucent. Alcatel NV was the world's leading manufacturer of telecommunications equipment from 1990 to 1996, when Siemens took that lead. However, as spending by global service providers on DSL equipment for 2001 rose to US$2.3 billion, Alcatel was the world leader with 37.8 percent. In 2004, the company shipped 19.6 million parts, a 24 percent increase over 2003. Alcatel also launched an IP-based broadband access platform, the Intelligent Services Access Manager, in 2004 to help service providers offer "100 percent Triple Play" services to all of its customers at the same time, either from the central office or from remote terminals. Alcatel had sales of US$20.07 billion in 2009, with more than 77,100 employees.

A pioneer in telecommunications equipment, Alcatel was founded in France in 1879. In the early 1970s, it was acquired by Compagnie Générale d'Electricité (GCE), a state-owned engineering and electrical equipment conglomerate, which was subsequently privatized in 1986. GCE expanded its telecommunications equipment business with the acquisition of Thomson-Brandt's telecommunications operations in 1983 and a majority stake in the European telephone equipment business of United States-based ITT Corp. in 1986. ITT's operations were merged with Alcatel's to form the new subsidiary of Alcatel NV, headquartered in Belgium. Upon incorporation in the Netherlands the company became the second largest telecommunications equipment company in the world. In 1990, parent company GCE changed its name to Alcatel Alsthom Compagnie Générale d'Electricité, often referred to as Alcatel Alsthom, to reflect its two major subsidiaries.

Om Malik reminded readers of his technology blog on July 29, 2008, that "the merger of Alcatel and Lucent was driven primarily by the lack of market control by equipment vendors." Some small companies were put out of business as a result of the trend for carrier consolidation.

AT&T had long been the world's leading manufacturer of telecommunications equipment, but the top position to Alcatel in 1990. Subsequently, AT&T started to focus more on telecommunications services than on telecommunications equipment, spinning off its telecommunications equipment development operations as Lucent Technologies in April 1996. Lucent was then the United States's second-largest and the world's fourth-largest producer of telecommunications equipment. In 2004 Lucent reported a 6.8 percent increase in sales to US$9 billion and acquired 100 percent of Telica, a provider of VoIP switching equipment. Wireless revenues accounted for more than US$4 billion of Lucent's revenues, voice networking for US$1.3 billion, data and network management for US$933 million, optical networking for $715 million, and the remaining revenue derived from other products and services.

Alcatel-Lucent struggled with falling profits and increased competition for its core business of network management for telecommunication companies. In an effort to diversify, the company took on a project for the U.K. Highway's Agency to update the communication systems on highways in Great Britain as a way to manage traffic flow. Alcatel-Lucent planned to diversify in other areas as well, but the future was uncertain. In 2007, the company reported revenues of US$26.2 billion with 76,410 employees.

Motorola Inc. The Galvin Manufacturing Company, started in 1928, named its first commercially successful car radio under the brand name of Motorola, which is a blend of "motor" and "victrola." The company officially changed its name to Motorola Inc. in 1947, the same year the first Motorola television was introduced. The Motorola TV became so popular that within months of its introduction, the company was the fourth largest television seller in the nation. The company expanded its operations in the 1960s, establishing facilities in Mexico and Japan. The cellular remote telephone system was developed by AT&T's Bell Laboratories in the early 1970s. Motorola assisted in the design and testing of the phones and supplied much of the transmission-switching equipment. In 1989 the company introduced the world's smallest portable telephone and by 1997 had generated annual sales of more than US$29.7 billion as the second-largest producer of analog cellular phones and the third-largest producer of digital cellular phones.

However, by the 2000s, Motorola appeared to be in a freefall. The company had failed to recognize that its Iridium satellite phone had a limited market, and the venture left the company with debts that took years to overcome. The company contained costs with extensive layoffs that in turn destroyed its reputation as a stable and secure place to work. In October 2001, Ed Breen was hired as president and COO. Breen raised Motorola's cellular phone market share from 12 to 18 percent from 2000 to 2002, according to Arik Hesseldahl in the January 31, 2002, edition of *Forbes*. A struggling Motorola rose to second in the market, behind Nokia's 37 percent share. Motorola reported an annual revenue of US$22.04 in 2009, a sharp decline from the US$31.32 billion in total sales in 2004. Hesseldahl noted that Motorola's wireless sales began to increase in China in the 2000s, "landing $1.4 billion in infrastructure contracts, and [the company] has become that country's dominant handset supplier." In 2004, China accounted for 9 percent of Motorola's sales, behind Europe (19 percent) and the United States (47 percent). In 2010, Motorola had a workforce of nearly 60,000 employees.

NEC Corporation. Better known in the fields of computers and semiconductors, NEC is Japan's leading telecommunications equipment manufacturer. Communications systems and equipment accounted for US$14.9 billion, or 37 percent, of its total US$39.9 billion in 1997 revenues. This included digital switching equipment, fiber-optic radio transmission systems, space electronics, mobile communications systems, and customer premises equipment. By 2010, NEC reported US$42.78 billion in sales and 142,358 employees. NEC's largest single client has been Nippon Telegraph and Telephone Public Corp. (NTT), one of the largest telephone companies in the world. NEC also exports its telecommunications equipment.

Originally named the Nippon Electric Company, NEC was founded in 1898 as a joint venture between Japanese investors and Bell subsidiary Western Electric Company, then the leading telecommunications equipment company in the United States. Western Electric sold its stake in NEC in 1925 to U.S.-based ITT Corp., which held shares in NEC until 1978. NEC started out importing equipment from Western Electric and General Electric, but soon began producing its own telephone sets as the Japanese government expanded the country's telephone systems. Although there were some competitors in Japan, NEC had a near monopoly in the telephone equipment market early in the twentieth century. After NTT was formed in 1952, NEC became one of its four major suppliers, and NTT accounted for more than 50 percent of NEC's sales in the 1950s and 1960s. Communications equipment, with the addition of radio and television broadcasting equipment, remained NEC's major business until the 1960s, when the company diversified into computers and other electronics.

Nortel Networks. Nortel Networks was formed from the 1998 merger of Canada's Northern Telecom with California-located Bay Networks. It is the leading company with telecommunications equipment accounting for most of its revenue, which was approximately US$4.5 billion in 2009, significantly down from the US$10.9 billion reported in 2007. The global economic crisis severely impacted Nortel. In 2009, they filed for protection from their U.S. creditors under the Chapter 11 bankruptcy code, in Canada under the Companies' Creditors Arrangement Act, and in the United Kingdom under the Insolvency Act. They became the first major technology company to file for protection during the economic downturn. The company's products include network switching equipment, telephone sets, wireless systems, multimedia communication systems, transmission wire and cable, broadband networks, and network applications, accounting for every kind of equipment required for Internet use. The United States is its largest market. A pioneer in digital switches, Nortel's predecessor, Northern Telecom, held close to one-third of the U.S. digital switch market at the time of the merger. Nortel Networks Corp. decided to keep its base of operations in Toronto.

Northern Telecom was a partially owned subsidiary of BCE Inc., the holding company of Canada's leading telephone company, Bell Canada. It was established by Bell Canada as its manufacturing arm in 1895 under the name Northern Electric and Manufacturing Company Ltd. In 1914, it merged with Imperial Wire and Cable and took the name Northern Electric Company Ltd. Since AT&T owned part of Bell Canada, AT&T's manufacturing subsidiary, Western Electric, owned part of Northern Electric. Northern Electric primarily manufactured products designed by Western Electric until Bell Canada began to buy out Western Electric's shares in Northern Electric in 1957, with the remaining shares going to Bell Canada in 1964. Northern Electric established its own research and development unit, Northern Electric Laboratories, in 1958, which became the Bell-Northern Research Ltd. subsidiary in 1971. Bell Canada sold shares of Northern Electric to the public in 1973, retaining slightly more than 50 percent. In 1976 the company changed its name to Northern Telecom Ltd. and made the critically shrewd business decision to make an equipment changeover to digital switches.

Other Industry Leaders. Other industry leaders included Nokia, the number one supplier of mobile phones, responsible for 33.9 percent of global shipments in the fourth quarter of 2004. Although not as large as industry leader Siemens, Cisco Systems was acknowledged to be the most powerful in the telecom equipment sector, based on name recognition, price, product performance, product quality and reliability, and service and support. Cisco earned $40.04 billion in revenue in 2010. China-based Huawai was considered to be a developing market leader, although id had not established a significant presence in North America.

MAJOR COUNTRIES IN THE INDUSTRY

The United States. As the largest telecommunications equipment market, the United States has led the telecommunications industry in sales and exports, although Japan earns comparable revenues, and both suffered similar losses during the global economic slump of 2001. In 1999, the U.S. market for telecommunications equipment was valued at more than $3.9 billion and continued rising through 2002, when it reached $7.6 billion before dropping to $5.3 billion in 2003. The future of the U.S. market was dependent on its ability to export its products to developing countries, which posed a challenge. In 2003, the United States exported $112.5 billion of office

machines and telecom equipment according to the World Trade Organization (WTO), and imports were valued at $180.5 billion.

Japan. In the 2000s, Japanese telecommunications companies like NEC were reporting falling profits with no recovery in sight. In a November 2001 economic report, the Japan Research Institute said, "It is the fate of developed nations to be caught up with by newly industrialized nations, and, if anything, the true reason for the rapid contraction of Japan's manufacturing base is its failure to change a high cost structure and inflexible industrial and employment systems, and its slowness to foster new industries and to respond to the IT revolution." In 2002, large Japanese companies seemed to take the criticism to heart. The *International Herald Tribune* on March 15, 2002, Ken Belson reported that Fujitsu, NEC, and other large industry concerns attempted to turn Japan's poor economic climate around during the first years of the 2000s by taking advantage of an abundant resource—its inventors. In 2003, the WTO reported that total exports of office machines and telecom equipment for Japan were slightly more than US$90 billion and imports totaled US$54.5 billion.

China. In 2004, the power in the Asian telecom market appeared to be shifting to China. Chinese companies and vendors were winning major contracts, making deals with Western partners, and gaining new accounts by offering low prices. Huawei, a Chinese equipment vendor, was fourth in world market share among manufacturers of DSL equipment. The company was close behind industry leaders Alcatel and Siemens, according to Synergy Research Group (SRG). By January 2005, Huawei shocked even its Asian rivals by winning a contract to expand CAT Telecom's CMDA network, beating industry leader Motorola, as well as Ericsson and Thailand's Advanced Info Service (AIS). Huawei was also a partner with British Telecom and other European companies during the mid-2000s, earning contracts with its combination of quality equipment and low pricing. China imported $96.2 billion of office machines and telecom equipment in 2003, and exports were valued $117.9 billion.

ZTE was also growing quickly in the Chinese market, gaining market share. ZTE Corporation was considering the use of direct-marketing to sell low-cost handsets in India using its own brand name. The company, China's largest telecom provider, was expected to increase handset production from 30 to 50 million from 2007 to 2008. More than 15 million of the expected production was planned to be sold in India, up from 10 million in 2007. However, there were no immediate plans to begin manufacturing handsets in India.

Huawei Technologies planned to increase its presence in Europe to take advantage of its struggling Western rivals, especially Alcatel-Lucent and the Nokia-Siemens joint venture.

India. Small and medium-sized telecommunications companies with up to 999 employees in India were on track to spend more than US$64 billion in 2008 on telecom equipment and services, reflecting an increase of approximately 7 percent over the previous year. Those companies were expected to adopt unified communications in the late 2000s to integrate multiple communications, which would streamline the distribution of information and allow employees in remote locations to collaborate with their colleagues elsewhere. Integrated communications included mobile voice, e-mail, instant messaging, and facsimile (fax) transmissions.

Germany. Germany, which is one of the world's largest markets, is the largest telecom equipment maker in Europe. Its telecommunications equipment industry grew faster than any other in Europe in the 1990s and early 2000s, and was valued at US$6.62 billion in 2003. Part of the country's growth stemmed from its goal to finish converting remaining analog equipment to digital equipment, which required large expenditures for new equipment. Equipment revenues peaked in 2002 at US$9.6 billion, but like the rest of Europe, the German market decreased significantly between 2002 and 2003. The early years of the 2000s were challenging for German companies like Siemens, which were caught in the general downturn that affected mobile network businesses worldwide. Exports of office machines and telecom equipment for the European Union totaled US$246.4 billion, and imports totaled US$302.8 billion, according to the WTO in 2004.

Germany ranked as the world's second largest exporter of telecommunications equipment, exporting US$8.5 billion of telecommunications equipment in 1997. Germany also led in exports of switching equipment. The leading company in the German industry was Siemens. Alcatel NV's German subsidiary Alcatel Sel AG also contributed significantly to the industry.

France. The French telecommunication equipment industry was worth approximately US$5.3 billion in 2003 and one of the world's largest markets for the industry. Revenues peaked in 2002, and like the United Kingdom, some decline was reported in the middle of the first decade of the twenty-first century. Nevertheless, innovations in wireless and data helped to keep the country's market strong. The leading company was Alcatel Cit, the France-based subsidiary of Alcatel NV.

The United Kingdom. The United Kingdom was Europe's third largest market for telecommunications equipment in 2003, according to *Euromonitor* in August 2004. In 1997, the U.K. market for telecommunications equipment was valued at more than US$2.6 billion and continued rising to a high of US$3.68 billion in 2002 before decreasing to US$3 billion in 2003. Some recovery of the market was expected due to demand for mobile networks and broadband access, prompting British Telecom and Cable & Wireless to expand and upgrade telephone systems.

NB Data research found that telecom equipment used by 56 percent of U.K. businesses was more than three years old. The study also found that productivity would be increased through the use of cordless handsets because moving around would increase user flexibility as well as efficiency. The data did not account for the use of desktop applications by a contact center agent when handling customer support. There were no written rules for customer call centers to use when dealing with consumers, but outdated equipment was likely to reduce productivity and increase the cost of doing business.

BIBLIOGRAPHY

"2003 Worldwide Mobile Phone Shipments Up 29.7 Percent in Fourth Quarter and 23.3 Percent for the Year, According to IDC." *2.5G–3G,* February 2004.

"2004: A Good Year for Mobile Phone Shipments, Especially in the Fourth Quarter." *Wireless News,* 1 February 2005.

Abboud, Leila. "Alcatel-Lucent Shifts Direction to Offset Slow Growth." *The Wall Street Journal,* 28 July 2008. Available from online.wsj.com.

"Alcatel Leads Siemens, Lucent in DSL Market." *Fiber Optics News,* 25 March 2002.

"AMI Partners: Telecom Spending Among India SMBs Set to Cross US$64B in 2008." *Business Wire,* 11 August 2008. Available from www.businesswire.com.

Belson, Ken. "Japan Firms Are Cashing in on Patent Caches." *International Herald Tribune,* 15 March 2002.

"Broadband Equipment Market Grows Over 25 Percent." *The Online Reporter,* 29 May 2004.

Buergin, Rainer. "German Rebound Not Assured." *Bloomberg News,* 10 April 2002.

"Business Telecommunications Equipment in Australia, China, France, Germany, Japan, South Korea, UK, US." *Euromonitor,* August 2004. Available from www.majormarketprofiles.com.

Campbell, Susan J. "Research Shows Telecom Equipment Plays a Key Role in Success of Contact Center," 11 August 2008. Available from ip-pbx.tmcnet.com.

"Carriers Say Cisco is Tops in Telecom Equipment Market." *Networks Update,* April 2005.

Davis, Jessica. "Everything but the Kitchen Sink." *Electronic Business,* May 2004.

Donahue, Patrick. "German Stocks Rise." *Bloomberg News,* 17 April 2002.

Harbert, Tam. "A Thaw in Telecom's Nuclear Winter." *Electronic Business,* January 2004.

Hesseldahl, Arik. "Galvin's Semiconductor Slump." *Forbes,* 31 January 2002.

"Japan's NEC to Restructure System Chip Production." *Asia Pulse,* 2 April 2002.

Japan Research Institute, 2002. Available from www.jri.co.jp.

Kalambakal, Jupiter. "Canadian Telecom Equipment Maker Nortel Rolls Out Wireless for Algerian Railway Lines." 19 July 2008. Available from www.allheadlinenews.com.

Long, Geoff. "Power Shift." *Telecom Asia,* March 2005.

Malik, Om. "Alcatel-Lucent: Sign of an Industry-Wide Malaise," 29 July 2008. Available from gigaom.com.

Marsan, Carolyn Duffy. "Domain Name Registrations Drop." *Network World,* 28 January 2002.

"Optical Set for Small Rebound." *Telecom Asia,* October 2003.

Palmeri, Christopher. "Gores' Siemens Buy: One Big Bet." *Business Week,* 29 July 2008. Available from www.business week.com.

Parker, Andrew, and Sundeep Tucker. "Huawei Vows Aggressive European Push." *Financial Times,* 10 August 2008. Available from www.ft.com.

Sasi, Anil. "ZTE to Ramp Up Presence in Indian Telecom Market." *The Hindu Business Line,* 16 July 2008. Available from www.thehindubusinessline.com.

Shukla, Anuradha. "Report: Falling Components Costs to Drive 40-Gbit/s Adoption." Technology Marketing Corporation (TMC), 11 August 2008. Available from www.tmcnet.com.

"Telecom Recovery?" *Optoelectronics Report,* 15 April 2004.

"Telecom Trends." *Australian Banking & Finance,* 15 February 2005.

"The World in 2010, The Rise of 3G." Telecommunications Development Bureau, International Telecommunications Union. Available from www.itu.int.

World Trade Organization. "International Trade Statistics." Geneva, Switzerland: 2003. Available from www.wto.org.

"The World's Online Populations," 2002. Available from www.cyberatlas.internet.com.

"Worldwide IP PBX Market Catches Fire." *TelecomWeb News Digest,* 7 March 2005.

"Yankee Group: Wireless Equipment Vendors Face Challenging Market." *Wireless News,* 30 June 2004.

SIC 4810

TELECOMMUNICATIONS SERVICES

NAICS CODE(S)

517. The rapidly changing field of telecommunications services includes local, long distance, and international telephone services, as well as cellular and other mobile phone and paging services. A number of industry firms also transmit cable television services and offer Internet access (see **Cable and Other Pay-Television Services** and **Internet Services**). In addition, many telecoms have historical ties to communications equipment manufacturing (see **Telecommunications Equipment**).

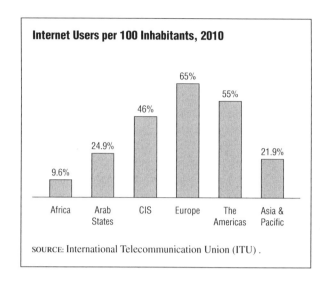

Internet Users per 100 Inhabitants, 2010

Africa	9.6%
Arab States	24.9%
CIS	46%
Europe	65%
The Americas	55%
Asia & Pacific	21.9%

SOURCE: International Telecommunication Union (ITU) .

Telephone Users Worldwide, 2003

	Total lines	Percent of population
Europe	767 million	96.28%
Africa	71 million	8.65%
Asia	1 billion	28.52%
Oceania	30 million	94.85%
North and South America	567 million lines	66.62%

SOURCE: International Telecommunication Union (ITU).

INDUSTRY SNAPSHOT

According to the International Telecommunication Union (ITU), the widespread availability of telephone and other telecommunications services in the United States is significant, especially considering that one-third of the world's population has never made a telephone call. In 2003, there were approximately 2.5 billion people served by telephones for an average of 40.32 telephone lines for every 100 people. However, a review KMI Corp.'s cybermaps of existing and planned fiber-optics installation reveals that the one-third statistic will become outdated in an astonishingly short time, particularly since many humanitarian groups are raising funds to get cell phones into underserved areas in Africa, Asia, and South America.

In 1993, fixed, or land, lines outnumbered cell phones 12 to 1. However, by 2002 the number of cell phones outnumbered fixed telephone lines, and those margins continued to increase through the first decade of the 2000s. Mobile phone use is the highest in developing counties, especially China and India, according to the ITU. Mobile phone sales in the United States continued to grow, although most owners of mobile phones use them for text messages, music, and even as GPS (global positioning) devices.

By the end of 2009, the ITU reported fixed telephone use of 17.8 percent per 100 inhabitants, mobile cellular use of 67 percent, fixed broadband subscriptions at 7.1 percent, and Internet use at 9.5 percent. The ITU estimated 1.21 billion global landlines were in use at the end of 2009, down from 1.27 billion at the end of 2008. In the United States, the Federal Communications Commission (FCC) reported that 114 million households had wired landlines at the end of 2009. However, landline subscriptions continued to decrease as more and more consumers relied on their mobile phones as their primary phone lines and began to use Voice Over Internet Protocol (VoIP), including Skype for international long distance calls.

Mobile cellular phones have been the most rapidly adopted technology in history. By 2009 they had become the most popular and widespread personal technology worldwide, with an estimated 4.6 billion subscriptions globally by the end of the year. Mobile broadband subscriptions overtook fixed broadband subscribers in 2008, highlighting the huge potential for the mobile Internet.

In 2009, more than a quarter of the world's population was using the Internet. That year, 1.9 billion people had access to a computer at home, while three-quarters of households globally had a TV and only one-third had a computer. With prices for computer and Internet technology continuing to decline, and the ongoing convergence of devices for multitasking, that gap was expected to narrow.

By the end of 2010, observers estimated that there would 5.3 billion mobile cellular subscriptions worldwide, including 940 million subscriptions to 3G services. Access to mobile networks was available to 90 percent of the world population and 80 percent of the population living in rural areas at the end of the first decade of the twenty-first century. People were moving rapidly from 2G to 3G platforms in both developed and developing countries. In 2010, 143 countries were offering 3G services commercially, compared to 95 in 2007. A number of countries, including Sweden, Norway, Ukraine, and the United States, had started to offer services at even higher broadband speeds, moving to next generation (4G) wireless platforms.

According to the ITU, investment in the telecommunications infrastructure was more than US$200 billion in 2000. By 2003 it had reached approximately US$215 billion, and the industry generated estimated revenues of US$1.3 trillion. National telephone service represented 33 percent of the world's telecommunications service revenues, while international service accounted for 5 percent and mobile service for 30 percent.

The leading trends in the telephone services industry included privatization of state-owned monopolies, the introduction of telephone service markets to overseas competition, and deregulation. Other trends were the continuing rapid growth of the wireless telephone service segment; the

expansion of telephone services in developing countries; and international alliances, joint ventures, and investments. Many trends stemmed from the World Trade Organization's 1997 telecommunications agreement between its member countries that established policies for opening key markets to international participation and increased competition.

The World Trade Organization (WTO) reported that as of November 2010, a total of 108 members had made commitments to facilitate trade in telecommunications services, including the establishment of new telecoms companies, foreign direct investment in existing companies, and cross-border transmission of telecoms services. Ninety-nine of the 108 members had committed to extend competition in basic telecommunications, such as fixed and mobile telephony, real-time data transmission, and the sale of leased-circuit capacity. In addition, 82 WTO members had committed to the regulatory principles spelled out in the "Reference Paper," a blueprint for sector reform that largely reflects so-called best practices in telecoms regulation.

According to the WTO, telecommunications are included in the services negotiations that began in January 2000. In the Doha Round of negotiations at the close of the first decade of the twenty-first century, additional market openings in telecommunications, as well as the binding of recent reforms, such as a commitment not to increase a rate of duty beyond an agreed level, were the objectives of many of the negotiating requests made by WTO members. As of July 2008, 39 governments had made offers to improve their existing commitments or to commit for the first time in the telecommunications sector.

A new sector-specific negotiating mechanism was mandated by the trade ministers at the Hong Kong Ministerial Conference in December 2005. Negotiating objectives outlined by WTO members in the chairman's note to the Trade Negotiations Committee included:

- achieving broad coverage in a technology-neutral manner and significant commitments in all modes of supply;

- working with least-developed countries and developing countries to find ways to encourage new and improved offers and to provide technical assistance to support this process;

- reducing or eliminating exclusive rights; economic needs tests, such as a test using economic criteria to decide whether the entry into the market of a new foreign firm is warranted; restrictions on the types of legal entity permitted; and limitations on foreign equity;

- commitment to all provisions of the telecommunications Reference Paper; and

- the elimination of exemptions to most-favored nation (MFN) treatment, such as non-discrimination.

Plurilateral negotiations followed, with progress reported regularly to the Special Session of the Council for Trade in Services.

Although many companies struggled to gain market share in the 2000s, giant conglomerate Verizon prospered, and the Competitive Local Exchange Carrier (CLEC) was introduced. CLECs are telephone companies that compete for customers with the existing Incumbent Local Exchange Carrier (ILEC), including well-known telecommunications companies like Sprint. A typical CLEC was US LEC, a voice, data, and Internet telecommunications carrier that did business in the U.S. Southeast and mid-Atlantic. According to the FCC, CLEC lines increased more than 9 percent over a three-year period in the early 2000s. Wireless telephones, mobile Web browsing, camera phones, and phones as MP3 players augmented the worldwide growth in the telecom services market. This growth was expected to continue as wireless data services and mobile e-commerce technologies became increasingly common.

In November 2010, in Dakar, Senegal, the Global Symposium for Regulators (GSR) defined Best Practice Guidelines that were predicted to stimulate the roll-out of the next wave of information and communication (ICT) networks, particularly for broadband access. The GSR welcomed 437 participants from 81 countries who arrived at a shared vision and understanding of the complex challenges facing ICT regulators in the converged markets.

The Best Practice Guidelines encourage regulatory frameworks that foster innovation, investment, and affordable access to broadband and other services in the global market through a set of core principles to be adopted by regulators, who can adapt them to local market conditions. The Guidelines underscore the importance of a clear and transparent regulatory process, including the adoption and enforceability of rules governing service provision, the principle of a technology-neutral approach, and the benefits of competitive network and service provision. They also call on regulators to embrace forward-looking rules that are subject to regular review, in order to ensure the removal of any regulatory barriers to competition and innovation that might emerge.

The Best Practice Guidelines concede that "a new ladder of regulation may now be required" to achieve the right balance between service and infrastructure competition. This includes ensuring equal and non-discriminatory access to networks and the lifting of potential bottlenecks that could prevent users from enjoying the full benefits of a digital environment that is increasingly driven by speed, access, and affordability, regardless of the location of network providers and users. "Our goal is to encourage the development of progressive and enlightened regulatory frameworks that foster innovation, investment and affordable access—particularly in the area of broadband, which

represents the next big leap forward in ICT services and applications," said Dr Hamadoun Touré, ITU Secretary-General. "The best practices adopted at this meeting will help regulators stimulate ICT deployment and deliver real benefits to consumers, through lower prices and innovative new services."

In March 2010, the FCC reported that the telephone subscriber penetration rate in the United States had reached 96 percent, an increase of 0.4 percent over March 2009, and the highest reported rate since the CPS began collecting this data in November 1983. The telephone penetration rate for households with annual income of less than $15,000 was at or below 92.8 percent, while the rate for households with annual income of more than $50,000 was at least 98 percent. Among the states, the penetration rates ranged from a low of 91 percent to a high of 98.8 percent. Penetration rates ranged from 93.8 percent for households headed by a person under 25 to at least 96.1 percent for households headed by a person over 55. Households with one person had a penetration rate of 94.2 percent, compared to a rate of 96.8 percent for households with four or five persons. The penetration rate for unemployed adults was 95.4 percent, while the rate for employed adults was 96.9 percent.

ORGANIZATION AND STRUCTURE

Companies that provide telephone communication services to the public through their own communication networks, as opposed to companies that lease networks, are called public telecommunication operators, telephone carriers, or telephone companies. For fixed-line telephone service, users are connected to a switched network of cables through individual mainlines. Radiotelephone service providers also operate communications networks, but instead of telephone cables, radio broadcast towers and sometimes satellite communications stations comprise their networks. Fixed-line telephone services may also use satellites for global transmission.

Telephone communication services traditionally have been provided by a single monopoly in each country, often a state-owned enterprise or government agency. In the latter case, national telephone services are often provided by the same organization that provides postal and telegraph services because telephone communications have historically been considered a public service utility requiring government involvement to ensure widespread distribution and compatibility of service and equipment. Even in countries with more than one telephone company, the industry tends to be heavily regulated, and competition may be restricted. The significant involvement of national governments in the telephone industry has created a national market structure, although the industry provides international service. Bilateral treaties have governed costs sharing for the transmission of international phone calls.

In some countries, different categories of service may be provided by the same company, or the industry may be regulated so companies may only offer certain services, including local calls, domestic long distance, international long distance, local mobile telephone communications, national mobile communications, and specialized services like leased lines. Certain sectors of the industry may be open to competition while others may be handled by a single monopoly. In general, mobile communications tend to be the most open to competition, while local telephone service has less competition.

Mobile communication services, which use radio frequencies for transmission, include cellular telephones, paging, personal communications services (PCS), specialized mobile radio, satellite communications, and data services. Paging services, which use inexpensive, simple technology, account for the greatest number of mobile communication subscribers, whereas cellular telephone service generates the most revenues. Cellular telephone service, which was developed in the 1960s and introduced in the 1980s, differs from traditional radiotelephone services by using a network of low-power transceivers, each covering its own area, or cell, covering between 2 and 10 miles. Mobile telephone services are provided by the major public telecommunication operators as well as by small, specialized companies.

In the 1990s, the structure of the worldwide telecommunications industry began a rapid transformation. In industrialized and developing countries, some categories of telephone services began to be privatized, deregulated, and opened for competition. The countries with the most open competition as of 1998 were the United Kingdom, the United States, Japan, Sweden, Finland, and New Zealand. Despite the easing of restrictions, telephone communication remained one of the most regulated industries in the world.

The International Telecommunication Union (ITU) is a division of the United Nations, serving as an international regulatory body for the global telecommunications services industry. The union fosters collaboration among its government and private sector members for the establishment of consistent rates and service standards and allocates radio frequencies, among other activities. The ITU also strives to bring telecommunications services to developing countries by monitoring the progress of telephone service development in these countries and promoting increased international involvement.

In February 1997, the World Trade Organization (WTO) announced that after several years of negotiations, its 72 member countries had reached an agreement to open all markets to foreign competition and establish regulations to promote and ensure the fair trade of telecommunications services trade. The participating countries represented about 90 percent of the world's overall telecommunications market. Known as the Information Technology Agreement (ITA), it would take effect in February 1998, although WTO member countries had varied schedules for implementation of the policies. The WTO expected this agreement would result in lowered prices, improved service, advanced technology, and increased investment. The accord included provisions for voice telephony, data transmission, facsimile transmission, privately leased circuit services, satellite communications, and mobile communications. According to the U.S. Department of Commerce, the ITA would eliminate tariffs on approximately 95 percent of specified information technology (IT) products, including analytical instruments; computer software, hardware, and peripherals; telecommunications equipment; semiconductor manufacturing equipment; and semiconductors.

The countries that agreed to the terms of the ITA as of July 2001 were Albania, Georgia, New Zealand, Australia, Austria, Norway, Bulgaria, Belgium, Iceland, Oman, Canada, Denmark, India, Panama, Costa Rica, Finland, Indonesia, Philippines, Croatia, France, Israel, Poland, Cyprus, Germany, Japan, Romania, Czech Republic, Greece, Jordan, Singapore, El Salvador, Ireland, Korea, Slovak Republic, Estonia, Italy, Kyrgyz Republic, Slovenia, Taiwan, Luxembourg, Latvia, Switzerland, the Netherlands, Liechtenstein, Portugal, Lithuania, Thailand, Spain, Macau, Turkey, Sweden, Malaysia, the United States, the United Kingdom, and Mauritius.

BACKGROUND AND DEVELOPMENT

Commercial telephone service was introduced in the northeast United States in 1877, one year after Alexander Graham Bell invented the telephone. The first systems were direct lines between pairs of subscribers. In 1878 the first telephone exchanges, which switched calls and lines, were established in towns and cities throughout the United States and permitted multiple subscribers to call each other. However, competing private companies provided separate, incompatible telephone systems.

The technology of telephone service spread rapidly throughout the world shortly after its development. Canada opened its first telephone exchange in the 1877. The first telephone exchange in England was opened in London in 1879. In Switzerland the first private telephone exchange was established in 1880, and telephone exchanges were established in Australia in 1880 and Brazil in 1881. France's first telephone exchange was established in Reims in 1887, while Japanese public telephone service was introduced in 1890.

The development of metallic circuits reduced interference enough to permit the introduction of long distance service in the United States beginning in 1881 with a connection between Boston, Massachusetts, and Providence, Rhode Island. In 1884, the introduction of hard-drawn copper wire to replace galvanized iron wire resulted in decreased attenuation over telephone lines, allowing lines to be introduced between Boston and New York. The first international call was made between the United Kingdom and France in 1891. The invention of the automatic switchgear in 1889 permitted connection without the use of human operators, although the widespread installation of automated switching at central exchanges did not occur until the twentieth century. Long distance service was enhanced with the invention of the diode and the refinements of the audion to the triode, and then hard-valve lamps between 1904 and 1915.

In the United States, Bell Telephone Company, founded by Alexander Graham Bell and his financial backers, was able to dominate the fledgling industry because it held the patents to the technology. When the patents expired and competition emerged, Bell was ahead of the rest with its established telephone networks. Although the industry remained in the control of private concerns for all but one year, 1917–1918, Bell acquired small competitors and established a virtual monopoly. Bell Telephone was renamed American Telephone and Telegraph (AT&T) in 1899.

In most of the world, telephone systems were government-owned. In Great Britain in 1896, the British Post Office, which had taken over telegraph services in 1869, took over trunk (long distance) service and in 1912 took over all telephone services. In Germany, the government held a monopoly from the beginning. The German Empire's first postmaster introduced the telephone to Germany and put it under the control of the Bundespost, the state postal authority. In France, telephone service was originally handled by private businesses, but soon was taken over by the government. Three private phone companies licensed by the government merged in 1883 to form the Société Générale des Téléphones, which was nationalized in 1889. The development of the French phone system subsequently lagged behind that of other countries due to bureaucracy. One of the problems was that municipalities wishing to establish a telephone system had to provide funding for the system in advance and were reimbursed by the national telephone systems later, based on the income it received from the local subscribers.

In 1878, the Swiss government announced that it would assume control of telephone systems and that telephone network providers had to be licensed by the states. The government began installing exchanges in 1881. In 1886, the government bought the only private system after which all telephone services were run by the postal and telegraph authority, the Schweizerische Post-, Telefon- und Telegrafen-Betriebe (PTT), a part of the Switzerland Ministry of Energy, Transportation, and Communications. In Switzerland the government monopoly's service was efficient but not heavily used.

In Japan the government approved a state-run telephone system that came under the Ministry of Communications in 1899. In 1952, state-owned Nippon Telegraph and Telephone Public Corp. was formed.

Telephone service did not become popular as quickly in other countries as it did in the United States. This was partly due to inferior service and equipment quality resulting from artificially low rates set by the government. Outside the United States, early telephone facilities were efficient and widely used only in Scandinavia. By 1900, 1 in every 60 people in the United States had a telephone, in Switzerland 1 in 129, in Sweden 1 in 155, in Germany 1 in 397, in France 1 in 1,216, in Italy 1 in 2,629, and in Russia 1 in 6,988.

During most of the twentieth century, telephone service remained monopolies or were under government control worldwide. The breakup of monopolies occurred first during the mid-1980s in the three biggest telephone markets, the United States, the United Kingdom, and Japan. In the United States, AT&T's monopoly was broken up in 1984 with the spin-off of regional Bell operating companies (RBOCs) and the exclusion of the parent company from offering local telephone services. Also in 1984, British Telecommunications was privatized and the first competitor was issued a license to operate in the United Kingdom. In Japan, the state-owned telephone company was privatized and reincorporated as Nippon Telegraph and Telephone Public Corp. (NTT) in 1985. Three new telephone companies were formed that year and won approval to compete with NTT. As these former monopolies became more profitable than their state-owned counterparts, other countries were encouraged to follow their example in the 1990s.

Trends. A wave of telecommunications service privatization hit the industry in the mid-1990s, following a trend that began in the United States and the United Kingdom in the 1980s. Most of the world's largest companies, including NTT, Deutsche Telekom, and France Télécom, were restructured to make themselves competitive in the world of publicly traded, diversified global telecoms. These changes allowed telecommunications companies to take advantage of new technology and operate more efficiently to meet the growing demand for improved quality of service and lower long distance rates. Deregulation also permitted telephone companies to form strategic partnerships with other companies and share expertise and innovative technology.

Since competition can lead to lower rates and better quality, which in turn can stimulate increased revenues and use of telephone services, some telecoms have welcomed heightened competition. However, others have feared a rapid loss of market share and have stepped up anti-competitive practices, at least unofficially. In 1990, only Japan, the United Kingdom, and the United States permitted competition in basic telecommunications services. By 1995, eight more countries had opened their markets to competition, and by the end of 1998, the International Telecommunication Union (ITU) expected more than 18 additional countries to follow this trend. The countries of the European Union were scheduled to open their telecommunications markets to competition in 1998, although some changes took place sooner.

In the local telephone services market, not only was competition expected among local exchange carriers, but also from cellular/personal communication services providers and traditional long distance companies entering local markets. Telephone carriers were also entering into competition with other industries, most commonly cable television system operators and Internet service providers. Cable operators were beginning to offer voice and interactive video services through cable networks, and telephone companies were expanding their services to include video.

According to the ITU, the volume of telephone traffic rose approximately 12 percent annually through 2000, when telecommunications service users placed an estimated 35.8 billion calls. Greater penetration of telecommunications services and greater efficiency were expected to drive continuing increases. Analysts predicted that the price of telecommunications services would drop worldwide due to further development of efficient technology and competition.

Internationalization and Global Alliances. The industry also was becoming more international as a result of global deregulation and privatization. Well-established privatized telecommunications services, especially in the United Kingdom and the United States, started to either offer telephone services directly in international markets or to form joint ventures with phone companies throughout the world. For example, British Telecommunications and MCI Communications Corporation formed a joint venture called Concert that offered a single worldwide service to multinational corporations. Concert, in turn, established strategic agreements with Norwegian Telecom, Tele Danmark, and Telecom Finland. MCI also had an alliance with the Canadian long distance company Stentor, as well as a joint venture in Mexico, before being acquired in January 2006 by Verizon. Mexico's telephone market was scheduled to open to competition in 1998, and U.S. long distance companies had started forming alliances with Mexican companies. AT&T, meanwhile, formed the WorldPartners alliance to expand its international influence. AT&T owned 50 percent of the

WorldPartners joint venture, Kokusai Denshin Denwa of Japan owned 30 percent, and Singapore Telecom owned 20 percent. WorldPartners comprised an association of telecoms from around the world, including Bezeq (Israel), KDD (Japan), Hong Kong Telecom, PT Indosat (Indonesia), and Telecom Malaysia. AT&T also planned to form a joint venture consortium called Unisource with KPN of the Netherlands, Telia of Sweden, PTT of Switzerland, and Telefonica of Spain.

Deutsche Telekom, France Télécom, and Sprint teamed up to create Global One, which began in 1996 with sales offices in more than 60 countries. Unisource N.V. came about through the equal partnership of four of the Netherlands' telephone service companies and operated in 16 European countries with AT&T as a cooperative partner.

Telecommunications Service in Developing Economies. In early 1998 the world's telecommunications services still could not provide even basic telephone service to meet global demand. As of 1996, 42 million people around the world were on waiting lists for telephone service. In Cambodia, for example, there were only 0.07 telephones per 100 people, and 25 percent of the ITU's members, including China and India, which were the world's most populous countries, had teledensities (the number of phones per 100 people) below 1.0. Although the telecommunications service industry continued to post increasing revenues and profits, it had not penetrated areas of Africa and Asia that desperately need telephone service for emergencies as well as for business and personal use. Once telephone service penetrates these areas, the ITU predicted that teledensity would grow slowly nonetheless, taking about 50 years to climb from 1 telephone per 100 people to 50 telephone lines per 100 people. Wireless satellite networks and multinational telecommunications operations had the potential to accelerate the growth of supply and access to telephone and information services.

In Africa, there was a dramatic broadband divide, with very few fixed broadband subscribers or mobile broadband subscriptions and substantial differences within regions. In Africa, penetration rates were predicted to reach an estimated 41 percent at the end of 2010, compared to 76 percent globally, creating a significant potential for growth. Although subscriptions are increasing, a penetration rate of less than 1 percent illustrates the challenges that persist in increasing access to high-speed, high-capacity Internet access in the region.

Asia, the Pacific region, and Europe had the greatest numbers of mobile broadband subscriptions. Asia and the Pacific, including Japan and the Republic of Korea, account for 70 percent of broadband subscribers. Emerging Asian economies, including China, Indonesia, Malaysia, the Philippines, Singapore, and Taiwan, continued to achieve significant expansion as these countries continued to invest hundreds of billions of dollars in telecommunications infrastructure. Because of the high cost, telephone companies had formed joint ventures and alliances with companies and governments from developed countries.

Wireless Telecommunications Services. The wireless telecommunications segment was one of the fastest growing segments in the industry, expanding at an quickened pace throughout the 1990s. However, growth slowed significantly in the early 2000s because of overproduction. Cellular phone and paging services were the principal segments. Cellular services were forerunners in telecommunications service deregulation and liberalization because no universal service requirements existed and because cellular service afforded private companies strong growth potential.

Cellular phone service has the technical capacity to provide service to virtually anyone at any location via satellite networks. Consequently, if companies can provide these services at an affordable cost to users in developing countries with low teledensity, such as Africa and Asia, they could experience considerable rapid growth and help relieve the shortage of communications and information services that plagues these regions.

Satellite-based wireless services are inherently geared toward international service in that they transcend national boundaries as one network may have the potential to provide worldwide service. The two main kinds of satellite networks are fixed satellite services (FSS) and mobile satellite services (MSS). FSS can provide point-to-point and point-to-multipoint service to permanent locations and can transmit telephone, video, and data signals from satellites to terrestrial receivers or earth stations. MSS serves the mobile communications market by connecting users to a base telephone network. Companies like Qualcomm and American Mobile Satellite Company began providing these services in the United States in the 1980s. In addition, the Iridium consortium had planned to begin operating its network of 66 low-earth-orbiting satellites by September 1998, providing voice, data, fax, and paging service worldwide. To realize the network's potential, Iridium began seeking approval of national governments to operate its services in their countries. Other satellite-based wireless networks in the late 1990s included GlobalStar, an international joint project by Loral, QUALCOMM, AirTouch France Télécom, Alcatel, and Hyundai, among others, and Teledesic, Microsoft, and AT&T Wireless Services.

CURRENT CONDITIONS

According to the ITU, there were 2.5 billion people with telephone service worldwide in 2003, an average of 40.32 per 100, although that figure varied widely depending on location. Europe, with 767 million total telephone lines,

had the highest average, with 96.28 per 100 people. Africa, on the other hand, had the lowest average, with 71 million total telephone lines, which represented an average of 8.65 per 100 people. While Asia had the highest total number of telephone lines, with 1 billion, or 40 percent, of the worldwide total, it also had the second lowest average, with 28.52 per 100 people. Conversely, Oceania had the fewest total lines, with 30 million, and the second highest average, with 94.85 per 100 people. North and South America had 567 million lines for an average of 66.62 per 100 people.

There were around 57 million fewer fixed telephone lines at the end of 2009 than there were at the end of 2006. The ITU reported that 75 percent of households worldwide have television sets, but only 25 percent have access to the Internet. While close to two-thirds of people in the developed world have access to the Internet, four-fifths of people in the developing world do not. The ITU noted, however, that most of the Internet growth is taking place in the developing world, which accounted for 600 million of the 777 million new Internet users worldwide between the end of 2005 and the end of 2009.

By 2010, several major factors were creating changes in the telecommunications sector, including a shift in business and commercial telephones to Voice over Internet Protocol (VoIP) services, a shift in residential and personal use from wired services to wireless, intense competition between cable and wired services providers, steady increases in Internet usage for communications of all types, and wireless technologies, including more advanced smartphones, wider availability of 3G services, and 4G services that were being introduced.

The number of Internet users doubled between 2005 and 2010. In 2010, the number of Internet users surpassed the 2 billion mark, of which 1.2 billion were in developing countries. A number of countries, including Estonia, Finland, and Spain, have declared access to the Internet as a legal right for citizens. With more than 420 million Internet users, China was the largest Internet market in the world. While 71 percent of the population in developed countries was online, only 21 percent of the population in developing countries was online.

Africa continued to have the fewest users, with 9.6 percent per 100 inhabitants, followed by Asia and the Pacific, 21.9 percent; the Arab States, 24.9 percent; CIS, 46 percent; Europe, 65 percent; and the Americas, 55 percent. The world average for Internet use is 30 percent, while developing countries account for 21 percent.

While in developing countries 72.4 percent of households have a TV, only 22.5 percent have a computer and only 15.8 percent have Internet access (compared to 98 percent, 71 percent and 65.6 percent respectively in developed countries). At the end of 2010, half a billion households worldwide (29.5 percent) will have access to the Internet. In some countries, including the Republic of Korea, the Netherlands, and Sweden, more than 80 percent of households have Internet access, almost all of them through a broadband connection. The number of people having access to the Internet at home has increased from 1.4 billion in 2009 to almost 1.6 billion in 2010.

Increased competition between fixed and mobile service providers, a maturation of markets in developed countries, and a large and growing potential market in developing countries like China and India combined to persuade many companies to globalize and improve their domestic positions through mergers and acquisitions as well as through marketing and operational alliances.

There has been strong growth in fixed (wired) broadband subscriptions in both developed and developing countries. At the end of 2010, fixed (wired) broadband subscriptions were expected to reach an estimated 555 million people worldwide for 8 percent penetration, up from 471 million (6.9 percent penetration) in 2009.

Trends. Growth for major companies in the industry was based on service bundling. Bundled offerings could include any combination of local, long-distance, wireless, or Internet services, depending on the company and plan. However, the trend was challenged in 2003 by online phone services as phone calls made over the Internet were rising in popularity.

According to Vince Vittore and Glenn Bischoff in the October 27, 2003, edition of *Telephony,* trade liberalization, deregulations, and new technology was projected to drive growth in the telecommunications service industry through the 2000s. Trade regions, such as North America, the European Union, and Japan, along with East Asian countries, such as South Korea, Taiwan, and Malaysia, were expected to stimulate the international expansion of the most competitive firms. In addition, analysts expected new technology to fuel greater demand. Telecoms had been using optical transmission and switching technologies; asynchronous transfer mode (ATM), integrated service digital network (ISDN) and T-1 lines for data communication; and satellite-based communication networks beginning in the mid-1990s.

However, despite the trends of many countries to privatize their telecommunications services and split them into smaller companies, the opposite occurred in the United States. Although the Bell/AT&T monopoly resulted in one large long distance service and a number of regional Bell operations, over time the various "Baby Bells" began to merge back into large-scale companies. For example, Bell Atlantic merged with NYNEX in 1997, becoming the country's second largest telecom, which then merged with GTE to form the powerhouse

Verizon. By 1998 SBC Communications had acquired Pacific Telesis and Ameritech to form the largest local service carrier. Analysts argue that for telecoms to maintain fixed costs for infrastructure, which is important for survival, they would have to achieve economies of scale.

Internationalization and Global Alliances. In March 2002 delegates from 152 countries went to Turkey for a global development telecommunications conference, where they signed the Istanbul Declaration and Action Plan. The plan was a call to action by private and government sectors to bring telecommunications technology to developing nations between 2003 and 2006. The conference also considered financing and innovative forms of cooperation, according to the ITU.

From 2005 to 2010, the total number of fixed broadband subscribers grew more than threefold, from about 150 million in 2004 to almost 500 million by the end of 2009. In Africa, there was only one fixed broadband subscriber for every 1,000 people, while in Europe there were 200 subscribers per 1,000 people. In 2008, China overtook the United States as the largest fixed broadband market in the world. At the end of 2008, China's fixed broadband penetration was 6.2 subscribers per 100 inhabitants, the highest of any low or lower-middle-income economy in Asia.

In a 2008 report, the ITU indicated that the price for fixed broadband access remained prohibitively high in most developing countries, effectively limiting access to the Information Society. The relative price for information and communication (ICT) services was highest in Africa, which had the lowest income levels. In Africa, the cost for ICT services represented 41 percent of the region's monthly average income. In contrast, Europe, with the highest income levels, has the lowest relative prices for telecom services.

On May 26, 2010, the ITU held the World Telecommunication Development Conference where new commitments were announced to build at least three "momentum connect" schools and communities in each of three Sub-Saharan countries. Delegates at the conference reviewed legal, policy and regulatory measures to stimulate school connectivity, such as utilizing funding for public works, adding requirements to connect schools into 3G licenses, or initiatives using Universal Service Funds. Participants also explored how connected schools could be used as platforms to provide ICT services to other groups in the community, including women, persons with disabilities, and indigenous persons.

ICT Ministers and senior officials from several countries around the world gathered to share experiences and best practices and forge common approaches during a round table session dedicated to ITU's flagship initiative,

"Connect a School, Connect a Community." The initiative had been launched in 2009 by ITU Secretary-General Hamadoun Touré with United Nations Secretary-General Ban Ki-moon and Mr. Al Basheer. The objective was not only to expand access to broadband connectivity, but also particularly to launch innovative applications in areas such as health, education, and commerce to help stimulate progress towards achieving the UN Millennium Development Goals.

Following an open "call for partners" by Mr. Sami Al Basheer Al Morshid, Director of the ITU Telecommunication Development Bureau, the government of France announced that it would provide 500,000 euros in matching funding. Portugal announced that it would provide laptops and related project support for one school in each of 10 interested countries through its eSchool International program. Industry partners Microsoft and Intel announced their intention to provide laptops, computer lab solutions, and software licenses for courseware.

As part of the Connect a School, Connect a Community initiative, ITU has identified and compiled best practices on policies, regulation, low cost computing devices and practical experiences in connecting schools, including establishing school-based community ICT centers.

Telecommunications Service in Developing Economies. By the end of 2008, there were more Internet users in the developing world than in the developed world. Between 2005 and the end of 2009 fixed broadband penetration rates in the developing world almost tripled, and mobile broadband penetration rates grew more than tenfold, according to the ITU.

The developing world's share of fixed (wired) broadband subscriptions was growing steadily, and by the end of 2010, the developing world accounted for an estimated 45 percent of global subscriptions (up from 42 percent in 2005). Despite these promising trends, penetration levels in developing countries remained low at the end of the first decade of the twenty-first century, with 4.4 subscriptions per 100 people compared to 24.6 per 100 in developed countries.

More than 1.6 billion of the 1.9 billion new cellular telephone lines were in developing countries, compared to fewer than 300 million in the developed world, according to the ITU. In many developing countries more than half of rural households had a mobile phone by the end of the first decade of the twenty-first century. In China and India, which are the two most populous nations in the world, over 90 percent of villages were connected to mobile telephones.

Mobile cellular growth was slowing worldwide by 2010. In developed countries, the mobile market was reaching saturation levels with on average 116 subscriptions per 100 inhabitants at the end of 2010 and a marginal growth of 1.6 percent from 2009 to 2010. At the same time, the developing world was increasing its share of mobile subscriptions from 53 percent of total mobile subscriptions at the end of 2005 to 73 percent by the end of 2010.

In the developing world, mobile cellular penetration rates were expected to reach 68 percent by the end of 2010, particularly in the Asia-Pacific region. India and China alone were expected to add over 300 million mobile subscriptions in 2010.

Wireless Telecommunications Services. In spite of setbacks in the early 2000s, the wireless telecommunications segment experienced robust growth through 2005 as a result of customer appreciation of innovations such as color, camera insertion, and global Internet access for games, business, and personal use.

The wireless services segment was experiencing the most growth during the mid-2000s, due in part to the next generation of young people who had grown up preferring digital, online, and wireless technologies. Some industry analysts considered "wireless substitution" as the greatest threat to traditional landlines. A 2004 study from TRBI and Research Now! reported that 10 percent of wireless customers between 16 and 35 years old did not use fixed phone lines. Among respondents from France, 19 percent reported having never used a fixed line phone. The Yankee Group reported that 40 percent of the overall market in Europe was wireless.

One of the trends for wireless customers was a preference for pre-paid calling plans over flat rate subscriptions. Add-on services and innovations like color displays, cameras, and Internet access were causing the wireless phone segment to grow in the mid-2000s. Alexander Resources reported that so-called infotainment services, such as SMS (short message service) messaging, data and finance management tools, and news and sports services, were expected to grow from US$1.5 billion in 2004 to US$7.2 billion by 2008. According to Baskerville, by 2009 users of pre-paid services were projected to command 59 percent of the total wireless market. In addition, the research firm IDC indicated that SMS messaging was set to explode in popularity, with growth from 2.4 billion messages in 2002 to a projected 31 billion by 2007. The increase in use was expected to push the value of SMS to US$2 billion.

The total number of SMS sent globally tripled between 2007 and 2010, from an estimated 1.8 trillion to a staggering 6.1 trillion, which translates to close to 200,000 text messages being sent every second. Assuming an average cost of US$0.07 per SMS, in 2010 SMS traffic generated an estimated US$812,000 every minute (or around US$14,000 every second). In 2009, SMS revenue accounted for 12 percent of China's largest mobile operator's total revenue. The Philippines and the United States accounted for a combined 35 percent of all SMS sent in 2009.

Cell phone service has prompted tens of millions of consumers to cancel their landlines completely, eating into traditional revenue streams at AT&T and Verizon, among others. Meanwhile, wireless access to the Internet was threatening traditional DSL broadband providers.

RESEARCH AND TECHNOLOGY

Although integrated service/equipment companies continued, even with major divestments like AT&T's spin-off of its equipment arm as Lucent Technologies, most new technology in telephone communications was developed by the equipment industry (see **Telecommunications Equipment**), which served as the supplier of the telecommunications industry. The telephone service industry then developed ways to commercialize those innovations to provide improved services. Some telephone service operators spent nothing on research and development, merely adopting technology developed by others. Whether innovations in equipment technology were used in new services was dependent not only on the commercial viability of the technology, but also on the adoption of industry-wide standards and a favorable regulatory environment.

The adoption of integrated circuits, computers, and software in the switching operations of telephone service companies has led to greater capacity, lower costs, improved quality, and enhanced features in telephone services. For the full utilization of integrated circuits and computerized capabilities, the telephone central switching facilities and lines must be updated to digital from the traditional analog equipment. Telephone systems worldwide were being converted from analog to digital, and customers with providers still using analog were becoming increasingly impatient for updates.

Not only do equipment innovations enhance telephone service, but new types of equipment also can take better advantage of the services. More types of equipment were being connected to public switched telecommunications networks, such as fax machines, computers, and mobile telephone base transceivers. The integration of telephone services with computer technology has led to the introduction of videoconferencing services.

Low-cost laser and fiber-optics had greatly expanded the carrying capacity and bandwidth of information links. Optical fiber is a thin glass filament that transmits information as pulses of light. Light pulses are not affected by random radiation in the environment as electrical pulses are and can travel much farther than electrical signals without attenuation, so that higher sound quality is maintained without the use of repeater

devices. In addition, fiber-optic cable has the advantage of increased security, because it does not generate electromagnetic radiation that can be detected. Public telecommunication operators around the world were in the process of installing fiber-optic cable, often in place of copper wire, which is expected for business customers in many countries and for most residential customers in a few countries.

In the early twenty-first century, advances in mobile telephone services have included the ability to transmit at higher frequencies and the splitting of cells into smaller areas to increase the level of radio frequency re-use. Cellular services, which at first were only analog, became increasingly digital, providing greater capacity through a more efficient use of the radio-wave spectrum. Digital cellular networks were most pervasive in Europe, and the United States was also making the transition from analog to digital. Subscribers were able to use cellular phones outside a basic service area because of alliances among cellular service providers. Wireless communications systems based on networks of low earth-orbiting satellites were also being developed.

A new telecommunications technology standard developed in the 1980s that began replacing standard telephone lines in the 1990s was the integrated service digital network (ISDN). ISDN allows the transmission of voice, video, and data simultaneously over a single digital communications line. It uses out-of-band signaling, which sends control information over a separate channel, and transmits data at 128 kilobits (kbps) per second. However, inconsistent costs, combined with faster telephones lines, resulted in mixed success for ISDN in the mid-1990s. T-1 lines, on the other hand, have much larger bandwidth and can transmit data as fast as 1.54 megabytes per second (Mbps), but high prices hindered their initial popularity. Asymmetric digital subscriber lines (ADSL), another telephone line alternative, can reach speeds of 6 to 8 Mbps.

In the first decade of the twenty-first century, wireless providers began to develop third generation (3G) wireless access. Before 3G, which improves Internet access with high-speed data transmissions, cellular phones provided limited text-based information. Connected to a house or business by antenna, 3G wireless becomes the equivalent of line systems. By 2005, 3G wireless access had been launched with great success in Italy and Britain, with Italy reporting more than 2.5 million subscribers by the end of 2004.

With the rapidly increasing high-bandwidth content and applications on the Internet, there was a growing demand for higher-speed connections. For example, at the minimum broadband speed of 256 kbps, downloading a high-quality movie takes almost 1.5 days, compared to 5 minutes at a connection speed of 100 Mbps.

Fixed (wired) broadband prices dropped by 42 percent between 2008 and 2009, but there were huge differences among countries when it comes to the affordability of broadband. In 2009, an entry-level fixed (wired) broadband connection cost an average of 190 PPP$ per month in developing countries, compared to only 28 PPP$ per month in developed countries. This had significant implications for the uptake of ICT services, which was much higher for lower-cost mobile cellular than for the higher-priced fixed broadband.

Telecommunications, which, by definition, encompasses not only the traditional areas of local and long-distance telephone service, but also advanced technology-based services, including wireless communications, the Internet, fiber-optics, and satellites. Telecom is also deeply intertwined with entertainment of all types, including cable TV systems, since cable companies were aggressively marketing local exchange service and high-speed Internet access. The relationship between the telecom and cable sectors had become even more complex as telcos began to sell TV via Internet protocol (IP) services, competing directly with cable for consumers' entertainment dollars.

The mobile sector of the telecommunications industry grew from approximately 10 million subscribers in 2002 to 220 million subscribers by 2007, according to the "India-Telecoms Market Trends & Forecasts" report from Research and Markets. Despite projections for regulatory reform failure by early 2008, the mobile industry was continuing to progress steadily.

WORKFORCE

Telephone carriers are unusual among companies of similar size in that they employ almost their entire workforce in local markets. Although the telephone communications industry remained a significant source of domestic employment in many countries, its share had continued to decline. The falling number of jobs in the industry was the result of companies seeking greater efficiency, more automation, and increased outsourcing. Therefore, while employment in the telephone communications industry was declining, employment within a broad range of industries providing telecommunication-related services remained strong. The nature of the workforce was also changing as the adoption of computer technology by telephone service providers required employees with new skills.

In 2003 the U.S. Department of Labor reported that there were about 1.08 million hourly and salaried jobs in the U.S. telecommunications industry. About one-half were employed in wired communications and 20 percent in wireless. The average salary was US$49,420.

The telecommunications industry provided about 1 million hourly and salaried jobs in 2008. Wired telecommunications carriers accounted for about 666,100 of these jobs in 2008, while 202,700 were in wireless telecommunications carriers. Telecommunications jobs are found in almost every part of the country, but most employees work in cities that have large concentrations of industrial and business establishments. Although the telecommunications industry employs workers in many different occupations, 52 percent of all workers are employed in either installation, maintenance, and repair occupations or work in office and administrative support positions. Telecommunications remains one of the major providers of employment in the world, with nearly 1 million employees in the United States alone.

INDUSTRY LEADERS

China Mobile (Hong Kong) Limited. Listed in 1997 on the New York and Hong Kong stock exchanges, by 2005 China Mobile was the world's largest mobile phone company on a subscriber basis, serving 214 million customers. With 2004 revenues of almost US$25 billion, the company reported more than 88,000 employees. China Mobile Limited was formed as the result of the reforming and restructuring of China's telecommunication industry in preparation for entry into the World Trade Organization. Its parent company, China Mobile Communications, remained government owned, but British telecom giant Vodafone owned slightly more than 2 percent of the shares. The two companies had a strategic alliance and shared management, technical, and operational expertise, research, and new product and service introductions.

With more than 450 million customers, as of 2008 it is the largest wireless network operator in the world in terms of subscribers (ahead of China Unicom at home and surpassing U.K.-based wireless giant Vodafone Group on the global stage). China Mobile Communications operates primarily through its publicly-listed operating subsidiary China Mobile Limited which provides wireless services under the GoTone and M-Zone brands in 31 regions of mainland China. In addition to mobile voice and data services in China, it offers international roaming access through agreements with network operators worldwide. The company is controlled by China's Ministry of Information Industry. The company reported over 138,000 employees.

Vodafone Group Plc. The number two ranked wireless phone provider in the world was the United Kingdom' Vodafone. Founded in 1984 as a paging company, the company became independent from its parent, Racal Electronics, in 1991. Vodafone merged with U.S.-based AirTouch Communications in 1999, forming the basis for Verizon Wireless, which became the largest mobile phone provider at the time. At the end of 2004, service was provided to approximately 151.8 million customers in continental Europe, the United Kingdom, the United States, and the Far East. The company employed 60,000 people.

Vodafone Group and other companies in a consortium won Qatar's second fixed line telephony license, which ended the monopoly of state-run Qatar Telecom. The Vodafone consortium announced plans to launch wireline and WiMax-based services. Vodafone Qatar planned to launch mobile services beginning in March 2009.

In a report issued by Vodafone Group March 2010, the company had 341 million private and corporate mobile customers. Their business structure is divided into three regions, to reflect their focus on emerging markets: Europe, Africa, Central Europe; Asia Pacific; and the Middle East.

Verizon Communications. The growth of Verizon Communications has seemed particularly impressive compared to the declining fortunes of its U.S. rivals. The company posted revenues of US93.5 billion in 2007. It serves nearly 69 million customers nationwide and by 2008, Verizon employed more than 228,600 people

Verizon was the result of the Bell Atlantic Corp. merger with NYNEX Corp., which was quickly followed by a merger with the GTE Corp. that resulted in the name change to Verizon. Bell was once a leading regional phone provider, and Verizon maintained that segment while also becoming a giant provider of long distance, wireless services, and Internet services. In February 2005, the company announced plans to acquire MCI, which had been formed after accounting fraud resulted in long distance provider WorldCom filing the largest bankruptcy in history at the time. Verizon estimated the acquisition would add US$7 billion in revenue and savings. Verizon Wireless was a market leader in the United States.

On September 12, 2008, Verizon filed a proposal with the U.S. Federal Communications Commission to help reform the United States' outdated inter-carrier compensation system. Verizon sought to ensure the viability of rural telecommunications infrastructures by providing carriers with a predictable and reliable source of support.

On May 13, 2009, Verizon announced it was selling all of its wireline assets in Arizona, Idaho, Illinois, Indiana, Michigan, Nevada, North Carolina, Ohio, Oregon, South Carolina, Washington, West Virginia, and Wisconsin, as well as some assets in California, to Frontier Communications. That transfer took place on July 1, 2010.

Nippon Telegraph and Telephone Corp. (NTT). Nippon Telegraph and Telephone Corp. (NTT) is the world's number one telecommunications service company, with 2004 revenues of US$105.67 billion, divided among telephone services, including subscriber lines and cellular telephone services and telecommunications equipment. Other services include pagers, digital data exchange, integrated service digital network (ISDN) and F-net, leased circuit services, data communication facility services, and telegraph services. NTT also does a small amount of business selling terminal equipment.

NTT was incorporated as a publicly traded company in 1985 to replace state-owned telecommunications monopoly Nippon Telegraph and Telephone Public Corporation (NTTPC). Although NTT enjoyed a monopoly of Japan's telephone service market, in 1999 the company reorganized, splitting into separate companies, including two regional services and a long distance service provider. The company also owned 63.5 percent of Japan's leading mobile phone company, NTT DoCoMo. In 2004, NTT employed more than 205,000 people. In 2005, the company announced that it would end its pager service in 2007 because the number of customers had decreased to 290,000 from a high in 1996 of 6.49 million. By 2008, the company had approximately 54 million fixed-line customers and 51 million wireless subscribers.

The NTT Web site reported that as of the first quarter of 2010, there were 195,000 employees with 5,650 recruitments taking place. The reported revenue for 2009 was US$106.2 billion, with a projection of US$1.46 billion for the first quarter of 2011.

AT&T Corporation. One of the leading long distance companies in the United States, AT&T became one of the largest U.S. telecommunications companies following its acquisition by SBC Communications.

AT&T was founded in 1877 as the Bell Telephone Company by telephone inventor Alexander Graham Bell and his financial sponsors, and changed its name to American Telephone and Telegraph (AT&T) in 1899. AT&T was the parent company of affiliated regional Bell operating companies, and in the early twentieth century aggressively acquired many smaller competitors. The Graham Act of 1921 exempted telecommunications from the Sherman Antitrust Act, enabling AT&T to maintain its monopoly. In 1982 a Justice Department suit led to a 1984 settlement that required AT&T to divest its regional Bell operating companies and stop offering local telephone service. However, U.S. telecom deregulation in the 1990s reinstated AT&T's ability to carry local service. By 1997, the company had restructured, focusing on three core areas of business: international telephone service, wireless communications service, and Internet access. In 2000, the company was further restructured into a group of separate, publicly held companies: AT&T, AT&T Wireless, and AT&T Broadband. In 2002, AT&T Broadband merged with Comcast.

By 2010, AT&T continued to be the largest communications holding company in the world in terms of revenue. Operating globally under the AT&T brand the company offers one of the world's most advanced and powerful global backbone networks, carrying 18.7 petabytes of data traffic on an average business day to nearly every continent and country, with up to 99.999 percent reliability.

The company states they are the nation's fastest mobile broadband network, serving millions of customers and enabling them to travel and communicate seamlessly with the best worldwide wireless coverage, and offering the most phones that work in the most countries, voice coverage in more than 220 countries, data roaming in 200 countries, and 3G in more than 125 countries. More than 17.46 million total broadband connections are supported by AT&T, which is the nation's largest provider of broadband.

AT&T manages the nation's largest Wi-Fi network, with more than 23,000 AT&T Wi-Fi Hot Spots in the United States, and access to more than 125,000 Hot Spots around the globe. One of the world's largest providers of IP-based communications services for businesses, with an extensive portfolio of Virtual Private Network (VPN), Voice Over Internet Protocol (VoIP) and other offerings that are all backed by innovative security and customer support capabilities.

Deutsche Telekom AG. As the world's third largest and Europe's number one telecommunications service, as well as Germany's top fixed phone line provider, Deutsche Telekom AG (DT) reported more than US$78 billion in revenues for 2004. More than one-third of the company's revenues were generated outside of Germany in the 64 other countries in which it does business, including the United States, under the T-Mobile name. With 247,000 employees worldwide, the company had facilities supporting 57.2 million line telephone connections, 77.4 million mobile telephone subscriptions, and 6.1 million DSL customers in 2004. The company also provided paging, interactive videotext, telex, cable television connections, and equipment for television and radio broadcasting and videoconferencing.

Deutsche Telekom was named Deutsche Bundespost Telecom until January 1995, having been established as a state-owned company in 1989 when Germany's posts and telecommunications organization, Deutsche Bundespost, was split into three separate entities for postal, bank postal, and telecommunications services. DT remained under the indirect control of the Ministry of Posts and Telecommunications during the 1990s.

The company struggled to adapt to the industry's newly competitive environment in the late 1990s. Some of its practices, which severely penalized customers for leaving its service, drew the ire of European Union (EU) competition regulators, who considered the German behemoth to be flaunting its anti-competitive tactics. However, figures released by Deutsche Telekom in 2001 and 2002 showed that the company had regained customers. In April 2002, Deutsche Telekom's mobile communications companies and shareholdings boasted 66.9 million subscribers. The company's shareholdings reflected a global presence, with DT involvement outside Germany in the United States, the United Kingdom, the Czech Republic, and Croatia.

DT announced restructuring plans to reduce its domestic workforce and boost profits to survive rising competition and falling prices in Germany. Forced layoffs were unusual in Germany but were expected to be considered if workers did not approve concessions. Plans included consolidating DT's 63 German call centers into 24 locations, which would affect 8,000 workers. In 2005, Deutsche Telekom launched a program to eliminate 32,000 domestic positions by 2008.

BT Group PLC. The British Telecommunications Corporation was established in 1981 as a state-owned company, which moved telecommunications services out of the post office. The company was privatized and incorporated as British Telecommunications PLC in 1984, although the government retained a 48.6 percent stake in the company until 1991. In 2002, British Telecommunications PLC (BT) was a wholly owned subsidiary of the holding company, BT Group. British Telecommunications boasted more than 28 million exchange lines in the United Kingdom in April 2002. According to the *Bloomberg News* in April 2002, the BT Group's biggest problem in the 2000s was that it lacked the growth potential of rivals France Télécom and Deutsche Telekom.

BT Group was the number one telecommunications company in the United Kingdom with 29 million lines in 2004, 1 million business customers, and 19 million consumer customers. Total 2009 revenues were more than US$34 billion, and the company employed over 128,000 people as of March 2010.

France Télécom SA. France Télécom was established as a state-owned corporation in 1991, replacing the government agency Direction Générale des Postes et des Télécommunications (DGT). The company lost its monopoly in some areas of telecommunications in 1993, when competing value-added network providers were allowed to operate in accordance with the European Union's Open Network Provision. In 2004, the French government owned about 56 percent of the company.

The company reported 2009 revenues of approximately US$62.84 billion, with 192.7 million customers in 220 countries and territories. In addition to traditional phone service, France Télécom also provided audiovisual, mobile, cable television, Internet, and terminal telecommunications equipment and software. Its U.K.-based Orange wireless division had 50 million subscribers in 16 countries.

Telefónica S.A. In the mid-2000s, Telefónica offered fixed and cellular services to over 100 million customers in 13 countries in Spanish and Portuguese-speaking markets. In 2004, the company agreed to buy the Latin American assets of the U.S.-based BellSouth, making it the leading mobile operator in the region. In March 2005, Telefónica continued acquiring companies, moving away from its niche market, with a 51 percent stake in Czech phone company, Cesky Telecom, which was being privatized by the Czech government.

MAJOR COUNTRIES IN THE INDUSTRY

The United States. *Euromonitor International* reported in 2003 that the U.S. market for telephone services was valued at US$199.3 billion, a decrease of 1.5 percent from 2002. The long distance market was estimated to account for 48.8 percent of that market. The cellular and wireless market was valued at US$5.2 billion in 2003.

The telephone communications industry in the United States was comprised of a national and international long distance market, as well as a local and regional market. This legal division of the U.S. industry was the result of the 1984 breakup of the AT&T monopoly. The 22 local Bell operating companies were reorganized into six regional Bell operating companies, each with its own geographic area of service. These are Bell Atlantic (which acquired NYNEX in 1997) in the Northeast and mid-Atlantic states; Ameritech (acquired by SBC Communications in 1998) in the Midwest; BellSouth in the Southeast; SBC Communications, which operates under Southwestern Bell and Pacific Bell (and acquired Pacific Telesis) in the West and Southwest; and US West in the West. These regional companies hold monopolies on local telephone service and also tend to dominate local toll and long distance service within their regions.

When the U.S. Congress passed the Telecommunications Act of 1996, which was expected to open local markets for competition and permit local telephone companies, national long distance companies, and cable television providers to compete in the same markets. In addition, the act allowed U.S. companies to court international customers and encourage international telecommunications services to enter the U.S. market. As a result

of the act, telecommunications providers began to bundle services to include not only local and long distance service, but also wireless, cable, and Internet access. The legislation also prompted large-scale mergers.

By 2005, the traditional telephone, or wireline, sector in the United States was facing immense competition from cable and wireless companies. Voice over Internet Protocol (VoIP) was allowing these companies to provide customers with a bundled package of telecom services, including voice, data, and video. However, in 2004, the Federal Communications Commission (FCC) ruled that those companies that had been providing local service (known as incumbent local exchange carriers or ILECs) at the time of the 1996 Act, would not have to lease their new fiber lines to competitors. The 2005 announcement of plans for SBC Communications to acquire AT&T, Verizon to acquire MCI, and the merger of wireless providers Sprint and Nextel, indicated that the industry would continue to restructure in the face of increasing domestic and international competition.

China. As of 2004, China was adding approximately 62 million mobile subscribers per year, much more than the next highest country, the United States, which was adding 15 million subscribers annually. China had the second highest number of active phone lines in the world with 22 million, compared to the U.S. with 32 million lines. China was expected to take the lead in the early 2010s. It was also expected that Chinese companies in the industry would begin to expand beyond their borders. Analysts at The Insight Research Corporation predicted that the growth occurring in China would propel the telecommunications industry in the Asia/Pacific region to overtake North America by 2007 in revenues due primarily to the large size of the underserved population. In 2003, the four state-owned telecommunications companies (China Unicom, China Mobile, China Telecom Corp., and China Netcom) had a combined 98.4 percent market share.

In 2008 companies who wished to provide telecommunications services in China would pay US$146 million, which was half of what they had to pay in the past, although they would continue to be allowed to own up to "49 percent of phone-and-Web-service companies, and to 50 percent of providers of so-called valued-added services," according to the Chinese Ministry of Industry and Information Technology.

Japan. Japan's telephone services were divided between domestic and international. The privatization of Japan's telecommunications services in 1985 resulted in the creation of Nippon Telegraph and Telephone Public Corp. (NTT) for national domestic In 1985 three new independent telephone companies were established and won approval to compete with NTT: Daini-Denden, Nippon Telecom, and Teleway Japan. NTT and Kokusai Denshin Denwa (KDD) continued to dominate their respective markets.

In 2007, the industry was excited about the release of NTT DoCoMo's hand-held mobile phone with a speech synthesizer that could detect mouth movements. This phone would allow the caller to merely mouth words to be heard by the person on the other end, doing away with an annoyance that has made mobile phone users unpopular in airports and restaurants. The news also was welcomed because sales of cell phones had been dropping at a steady rate of 2.4 percent per year since January 2001, according to Gartner Japan Ltd. In 2002 NTT DoCoMo was facing increasing competition from international telecommunications giant KDDI (under the brand of AU Corp.), which was formed in the 1990s by the merger of former rivals DDI, IDO, KDD, and Tu-ka. In 2005, Deloitte Touche Tohmatsu analysts predicted that consolidation and price wars would continue in Japan.

In 2003, *Euromonitor* research showed the Japanese market for fixed line telephone services with a value of US$57.8 billion, and reported that the cellular market had a value of US$88.7 billion. Local calls accounted for 51 percent of the value of the fixed line sector. NTT accounted for a substantial share of the market, with 79 percent. By 2008, the market for fixed line services was expected to fall 22 percent.

Germany. The German market for telecommunications services dropped 14.1 percent between 2002 and 2003, while the German cellular market grew 9.8 percent, with 75 percent of the population having some type of mobile phone. The cellular market was dominated by four companies: T-Mobile Deutsche Telekom, Mannesmann Mobilfunk, E-Plus Mobilfunk, and Viag Interkom.

The ITU ranked Germany as the third largest telephone service market in 1995, with about US$48 billion in sales. Germany had 53.8 telephone lines per 100 people and 11.6 cellular subscribers per 100 people in 1996, according to the ITU. Deutsche Telekom held a monopoly for years on basic telephone services, including local and international switched networks, but beginning in 1989, mobile telephone service, paging, videotext services, and some satellite communications systems were open to competition. Moreover, as part of the European Union's telecommunications service agreement, Deutsche Telekom began privatizing its operations in 1998.

The United Kingdom. The United Kingdom was considered the most deregulated telecommunications market in the world for its size because it allowed competition on the local, national, and international levels. Following the

1984 privatization of BT Group, there was a period of a duopoly between BT and Mercury Communications Ltd. that lasted until 1991. In the early 1990s, an increasing number of small competitors entered the market, including cable television operators and foreign telecommunications companies. The mobile communications market opened to competition in 1985.

In 2003, the market in the United Kingdom reported a decline of 7.1 percent over 2002 values, reaching US$46 billion. However, the cellular market grew 7.7 percent, reaching a subscriber base of 52.6 million users by 2003, and was expected to reach 62.8 million by 2008.

France. The telecommunications market in France was valued at US$35 billion in 2003, but the growth of fixed line services in France was expected to continue to decline due to the introduction of cable, mobile, and VoIP technologies. The number of landlines decreased 1.7 percent in 2003 as businesses and other multiple-line users began to use to mobile phones. The cellular market in France was expected to grow from 40.9 million in 2003 to 48.4 million in 2008. State-owned France Télécom dominated both the fixed line (63.1 percent market share) and cellular markets (50.2 percent).

BIBLIOGRAPHY

"The 2005 Telecommunications Industry Review: An Anthology of Market Facts and Forecasts." The Insight Research Corporation, February 2005. Available from www.insight-corp.com.

Adegoke, Yinka. "10 Percent of European Youth Never Use Fixed Phone Lines." *New Media Age,* 12 February 2004.

———. "Pay-as-You-Go Mobile Users to Outnumber Subscribers." *New Media Age,* 25 February 2004.

"AT&T Looks to Disconnect from Traditional Phone Service Market." *Wireless News,* 22 July 2004.

Baburajan, Rajani. "Report: Technology Fuels Telecom Equipment Market Growth." Satellite Spotlight 15 September 2008. Available from satellite.tmcnet.com.

Baker, Stephen, and Heather Green. "Big Bang!" *Business Week,* 21 June 2004.

"Cablecos Threaten Telcos; Time Warner Cable Tests Digital 'Phone'." *The Online Reporter,* 23 August 2003. Available from www.theonlinereporter.com.

"Cell Phone Revenues May Surpass Land Lines in Europe." *The Online Reporter,* 28 February 2004. Available from www. theonlinereporter.com.

Cellular Telecommunications and Internet Association (CTIA). Web site, 2002. Available from www.ctia.org.

Cimilluca, Dana. "SBC Communications to Eliminate 8,000 Jobs This Year." *Bloomberg News,* 18 April 2002.

———. "Telephone-Cell Phones Expected to Exceed Fixed Lines in 2002." *EFE News Service,* 8 February 2002.

Dillon, Nancy. "Dialing for a Deal: AT&T Wireless, Cingular Seen in Merger Talks." *New York Daily News,* 16 April 2002.

Draper, Deborah J., ed. *Business Rankings Annual.* Detroit: Thomson Gale, 2004.

"Escalating Demand for Wireless Services to Drive Telecom Services Market, According to a New Report by Global

Industry Analysts." PRWeb, 10 September 2008. Available from www.prweb.com/.

Esterl, Mike. "Deutsche Telekom, Union Clash." *The Wall Street Journal,* 12 September 2008. Available from online.wsj.com/.

Fish, David. "Verizon Submits Plan to Reform Intercarrier Compensation System," Verizon Web site, 12 September 2008. Available from newscenter.verizon.com.

Fuller, Meghan. "CLEC Build Strategy Changes Focus." *Lightwave,* August 2003.

Hall, Ben, and Andrew Parker. " France Télécom Turns Its Attention to Africa." *Telecoms,* 16 September 2008.

"Hoover's Company Capsules." *Hoover's Online,* 2008. Available from www.hoovers.com.

International Telecommunication Union. Web site, 2010. Available from www.itu.int.

"International Trade Statistics." World Trade Organization, 2010. Available from www.wto.org.

KMI Corp. Web site, 2002. Available from kmicorp.com.

Krapf, Eric. "Progress Report." *Business Communications Review,* July 2003.

Lagesse, David. "Who Needs Phone Lines?" *U.S. News & World Report,* 11 August 2003.

Lanman, Scott. "Siemens to Resell Motorola Phones, Buy Motorola Chips." *Bloomberg News,* 15 April 2002.

Liu, John. "China Halves Requirements for Foreign Phone, Web Investments." *Bloomberg,* 16 September 2008. Available from www.bloomberg.com.

"Major Market Profiles (short profiles): Executive Summaries." *Euromonitor International,* 2004. Available from www.euro monitor.com.

"Mexico's Mobile Sector Neck and Neck with Fixed-Line Business." *Latin America Telecom,* September 2003.

"Mobile Infotainment Services to Reach $7.2b in '08." *The Online Reporter,* 10 January 2004. Available from www.online reporter.com.

"Mobile Lines Overtakes Fixed in Delhi." *India Telecom,* July 2003.

"More Than 11 Million Cellular Lines in Argentina by Year-End." *Latin America Telecom,* June 2004.

Morrison, Diane See. "States of Play." *New Media Age,* 15 April 2004.

Nikkei BP, 2010. Available from www.nikkeibp.com.hk.

"NTT Staying Big in Japan." *Business Wire,* 13 September 2008. Available from www.businesswire.com.

Ovum Reports Web site, 2002. Available from www.ovumkc.com.

"Reconnected to Growth: Global Telecommunications Industry Index 2005." Deloitte Touche Tohmatsu, 2005. Available from www.deloitte.com.

Research-and-Markets. "India Continues to Be One of the Fastest Growing Major Telecom Markets in the World." *Earth Times,* 16 September 2008. Available from www.earth times.org.

"Trend of Consumers Switching from Wireline to Wireless-Only Phone Service to Intensify in 2004." *The Mobile Internet* (Boston, MA), December 2003.

"UK Stocks Advance." *Bloomberg News,* 5 April 2002.

Vittore, Vince, and Glenn Bischoff. "Bundling Strategy Provides Soft Landing." *Telephony,* 27 October 2003.

"Vodafone Wins Qatar's Second Fixed-Line License." 15 September 2008. Available from www.hatiftelecom.com/ news/Qatar.html.

Wearden, Graeme. "NT DoCoMo Hits 20 Million Subscribers." *Net UK News,* 5 March 2001. Available from www.news. zdnet.co.uk.

SIC 4833

TELEVISION BROADCASTING STATIONS

NAICS CODE(S)

515120. The television broadcasting stations industry is comprised of companies that broadcast television programs to the public, including commercial, religious, educational, and other television stations. The industry also includes organizations that primarily provide television broadcasting services as well as and produce programs. (See also SIC 4841, **Cable and Other Pay Television Services.**)

INDUSTRY SNAPSHOT

In the early twenty-first century, television broadcasting stations faced more challenges than ever as the number of options for mass communications and information technology grew exponentially. Cable television was followed by satellite broadcasting and the Internet, which became threats to, and possible partners with, traditional broadcast stations. While it was unlikely that broadcast networks, with their strong ability to provide mass audiences for advertisers, would soon be eliminated, newer types of media were anticipated to take a growing share of listener and viewer time from broadcast stations.

The world's television market was valued at US$130.7 billion in 2003, and was predicted to increase to US$178 billion by 2008. After three years of slowed growth, the television industry was showing signs of recovery in 2004, with the United States anticipated to show the most progress at a compound annual growth rate of 7.5 percent. Canada followed, with a projected growth rate of 6.1 percent, Latin America with 6.1 percent, Asia with 5.5 percent, and the EMEA (Europe, the Middle East, and Africa) with 4.3 percent. As of 2004, more than three-fourths of advertising revenues were spent on television, and the numbers continued to rise into the late 2000s.

In fall 2008 TV network programming executives worldwide sought suitable content for digital channels that were to be launched by networks beginning in January 2009. Australian networks were discussing "feel good" rather than dramatic programming. In the United States, the fall 2008 TV season introduced innovative shows such as *Life on Mars* and *My Own Worst Enemy* that were thought to be representative of future programming. Verne Gay of *Newsday* described them as "superficially peculiar but hardly unfamiliar" as they were reminiscent of early programs, such as *The Twilight Zone*.

ORGANIZATION AND STRUCTURE

One of the unifying features of broadcasting around the world was government regulation. Television, which was introduced in the mid- to late 1940s, matured during a half-century of growing government control over industry when airwaves were considered a scarce public resource in most countries. As such, nearly every television market in the world was tightly regulated or directly controlled by the government from its inception. With its high public profile, television broadcasting in many countries was often the focus of controversy over violence, sexual content, and cultural content. In the United States, TV programs were frequently the focus of boycotts by various groups, and the U.S. Senate passed a bill in 1995 requiring that new televisions contain "violence-blocking" circuitry.

The controversies surrounding television reveal that it became a major cultural force in the world economy that was changing rapidly. New technology and political changes drove major modifications in the regulatory and business climate for broadcast stations and networks around the world in the mid- to late 1990s. In Europe, public service broadcasting was the only game in town for many decades, as monolithic state-run institutions provided the programs they thought would educate and entertain. In Communist countries the state was the network, with television existing to legitimize the government and inform people of its activities. In the United States, three huge commercial networks provided the programs people could watch, based on rating systems. In all cases, choices for viewers were limited. However, by 1995 most of these broadcast monopolies or oligopolies had either disappeared or were in decline.

From the end of World War II to the 1980s, most European countries had two or three state-owned television channels paid for by taxes or license fees. However, in the 1980s and early 1990s, almost every western European country deregulated its broadcast system, adding commercial channels to the mix. Political change spurred this trend, as did the advent of new cable and satellite channels. In 1980 there were about 40 television channels in France, West Germany, Italy, the Netherlands, Belgium, Luxemburg, Ireland, the United Kingdom, Denmark, Greece, Spain, Portugal, Finland, Sweden, and Austria. By 1994 there were 150 European channels, more than 50 of which

were provided via satellite. In 2001, 95 percent of homes in the European Union had TV, spending an average of 3.5 hours a day watching programming.

The development of digital terrestrial and satellite TV transmission, as opposed to traditional analog transmission, increased the number of channels even more. Astra 1E, the first dedicated digital satellite in Europe, began operating on January 1, 1995. In 1996 Italian pay-TV group Telepiu launched three digital channels, and French pay-TV operator Canal Plus launched 20 digital channels. In the United Kingdom, which was seen as the world leader in digital terrestrial television broadcasting ,the government expected all technical, political, and commercial criteria for digital TV to be in place by early 1998.

BACKGROUND AND DEVELOPMENT

The world's first regular television service was established in England by the British Broadcasting Corporation (BBC) in 1936. The BBC launched its second TV channel, BBC2, in 1964. Over the years, BBC programs were acclaimed for their dramatic quality. The BBC's television monopoly ended in 1954 when the British Parliament established the Independent Television Authority (ITV), which grew into a consortium of 15 regional television companies, each operating a single channel within an assigned area. The organization later became the Independent Broadcast Authority (IBA) when radio was added to its charter. IBA television companies produced many of their own programs and generated revenue through the sale of commercial airtime.

The first television networks in the United States were NBC, CBS, ABC, and DuMont, which began as divisions of major radio networks and television and radio manufacturers. While DuMont's network failed in the 1950s, the other three dominated television broadcasting in the United States almost unchallenged until the 1980s, when cable television and a new network, Fox Broadcasting, began to seriously challenge them for viewing time.

In the Soviet Union, television broadcasting was exclusively a propaganda arm of the government until the late 1980s, when Communist party and state control over the media was relaxed. In July 1990 General Secretary of the Communist Party and President of the USSR Mikhail Gorbachev ordered major changes in the state-run broadcasting monopoly that allowed television outlets to be run independently of political organizations and provide objective coverage of news events. Following the collapse of the Communist government this trend continued, although restrictions on television broadcasts remained. In January 2002 many journalists and Russian citizens were angered when TV6, the last independent television station, which was owned by outspoken Russian media mogul Boris Berezovsky, was pulled off the air during a musical broadcast. The station had consistently been critical of Russian President Vladimir Putin. The government offered station employees a deal to stay on the air if they would cut all ties with Berezovsky that they ultimately rejected. The government did keep the station on the air as TV-S until economic conditions and management struggles forced them to shut it in June 2003.

The financial difficulties of the three big U.S. networks in 2001–2002 were present across the entire television broadcasting industry. Instead of ad sales soaring as they had in times of plenty, the ad sales of the "big three" television networks—CBS, NBC, and Capital Cities/ABC Inc.—plummeted in the early 2000s. The Broadcast Cable Financial Management Association, which tracked TV revenues, said the three networks had a combined 10 percent loss in revenues, which represented the worst performance by an industry that consistently had reported profits in spite of poor quality programming. Revenue for the three big networks from ad dollars dropped from US$11.4 billion in 2000 to US$10.2 billion in 2001. In addition, the Federal Communications Commission (FCC) regulations that kept conglomerates from swallowing up air space were disappearing quickly. All indications in the early twenty-first century were that television networks were going to form huge conglomerates, similar to those found in other media industries.

Until the mid-1970s, television broadcasting was a stable industry. With few exceptions, broadcasts stayed neatly within national boundaries. The Soviet Union and other Communist nations exercised complete state control over their airwaves. In Western Europe, state-owned or state-chartered corporations broadcast a limited amount of programming, much of which was educational, while commercial channels were almost nonexistent. Japan had a strong television market, but the rest of Asia remained relatively undeveloped. In the United States, the big three television networks reached a mass audience of consumers, all with apparently similar tastes. U.S. television networks were prohibited by law from producing their own prime time shows and typically distributed other companies' entertainment products.

In less than three decades, the industry had changed considerably. By the late 1990s and 2000s, rapid technological and political change had completely changed the rules of the global broadcasting industry. In former Communist nations, fledgling commercial television stations challenged state-run corporations, which struggled to change with the times. In Europe, commercial television, whether distributed by broadcast, cable, or satellite, competed with state-sponsored broadcasters like the British Broadcasting Corporation (BBC). In the United States, the big three networks reported a drop in audience share from 90 percent to about 60 percent in 1995, and

to 50 percent by early 1998 as cable companies and direct satellite transmission gradually took the audience that networks once took for granted.

By the mid-1990s, Fox Broadcasting Co. had become a legitimate fourth network in the United States. Fox quickly gained a growing share of the network television market with its strategy to target young viewers. In February 1998, Fox finished ahead of ABC in a critical "sweeps" month, which TV networks in the United States used to set future advertising rates. In 1995, the Disney Company had purchased ABC, which declined steadily for the next three years, affecting the network's prime time lineups and other shows, including news programming. Fox's strength in 1998 came from its hit series, such as *Ally McBeal* and *Party of Five*. In 2001, as viewers abandoned the series and, even worse, as Fox's backing of NASCAR, pro football, and pro baseball proved disastrous, the fourth network struggled to attract advertisers to keep its flagship station from weakening further.

In 1994, the FCC had begun to allow networks to produce their own primetime programs, for themselves as well as for competing networks, and the trend continued to grow. Simultaneously, companies formerly devoted to programming, such as Time Warner and Paramount Communications, launched television networks, guaranteeing outlets for their productions. A federal appeals court in the District of Columbia ruled in 2002 that there should be no restrictions on the number of stations a media outlet could own. The ruling also allowed ownership of multiple cable and network stations by one entity in the same market. The court decision appeared to allow conglomerate ownership of TV stations, and resulting in the management of U.S. television programming by a few giant companies, such as Disney, AOL Time Warner, Viacom, News Corp., and General Electric.

The growing globalization of the broadcast TV industry was also evident in the late 1990s through the early 2000s. For example, in 1995 the FCC relaxation of rules on foreign ownership of television stations was expected to bring a number of well-heeled foreign investors into the U.S. market. Beginning in the 1980s, cable television companies became major rivals to broadcast television networks. Cable bypassed traditional broadcast networks by beaming TV signals off satellites to local transmission companies, where the signals were received and re-transmitted to area customers via coaxial cable. Growing satellite transmission of television programs made it much easier to distribute programming across national borders. Rupert Murdoch's News Corp. made headlines with its satellite broadcasting systems, British Sky Broadcasting Ltd. and Hong Kong-based Satellite Television for the Asian Region (STAR television). While Star was unprofitable as of 1995, it was transmitting in different languages and dialects to 3 billion people in Asia. India opened its market to private broadcasters, largely in response to the success of Star in that country. Star was also responsible for the Chinese ban on the use of home satellite receivers, which the aging Communist regime feared would have "destabilizing" effects.

The United States was one of the first major industrial nations to be "wired." By 1994 about 66 percent of U.S. households with televisions were hooked up to at least basic cable service, with 61 million cable subscribers. In 2001 cable penetration in all U.S. households had reached 81 percent. However, in 2001 the Hispanic population had a relatively low penetration of 63 percent, with 64 million connected to cable or satellite TV, according to Nielsen Media Research and *Broadcasting and Cable*. In other countries, cable penetration varied widely. As of 1994 cable penetration was 3.8 percent in the United Kingdom, 5 percent in Mexico, and 5.6 percent in France. In contrast, by 1994, cable penetration had reached 55 percent in Denmark, 42.3 percent in Germany, 34.8 percent in Spain, and 20.3 percent in Japan.

Direct-to-home (DTH), which used satellite transmission of programming to reach a growing number of subscribers, and cable broadcasts competed increasingly with broadcast television stations worldwide. This competition and the growing concentration and globalization of the television industry continued to overtake the broadcast television market, particularly as countries relaxed ownership rules for broadcast media.

The erosion of broadcast television's market share was the most pronounced in the United States. Ratings for the three biggest broadcast TV networks fell steadily during the 1990s to 50 percent of the total audience in 1998, while the number of cable and DTH viewers continued to grow. In 1998, the major U.S. networks began a negative marketing battle against cable TV, alleging that cable airtime was less valuable than network airtime since cable attracted viewers that had less buying power than network viewer. In general, the networks claimed that U.S. cable viewers were less affluent and less educated than the U.S. population as a whole.

Cable TV executives argued that the networks' attack was based on "desperation." Indeed, advertising spending on cable in the United States climbed steadily in the 1990s, and in 1998 was expected to top US$9 billion, a 15 percent increase over 1997, when spending was US$7.9 billion. U.S. broadcast TV continued to lead the market, with revenue for 1998 expected to reach US$13 billion for commercial time on the big four networks of ABC, CBS, Fox, and NBC, representing a 5.2 percent increase from 1997. However, the gap between network and cable in the United States appeared to be closing. Paul Kagan Associates, a market research firm,

predicted that by 2005 advertisers would be spending US$18.9 billion for commercial time on network TV in the United States and US$14.5 billion on cable.

One area in which U.S. cable TV companies were particularly successful in the 1990s and early 2000s was children's television, which was traditionally dominated by the big networks' Saturday morning cartoon lineup. By the late 1990s and 2000s, however, many U.S. networks had reduced their children's programming, overwhelmed by cable channels such as Nickelodeon and The Cartoon Network. Those cable channels were also very popular exports and were licensed in stations in many countries outside the United States.

In the mid-1990s and especially in the early 2000s, the growing alternatives to network television in the United States convinced the FCC to relax many of its restrictions on television station content and ownership. One of the most significant moves was the May 1993 repeal of a rule preventing the networks from producing and owning their own prime time programs. In November 1995, the remaining rules that had prevented the networks from syndicating shows on their prime time schedule expired. This change meant the networks could own rerun rights to the prime time shows they carried, a very profitable part of television production. The end of these rules, together known as "fin-syn," allowed the networks to become production companies rather than simply programming outlets.

U.S. station ownership rules also changed in the 1990s. In 1996, the FCC eliminated the 12-station ownership cap, expanded allowable station group audience reach from a 25 percent limit to at least 30 percent of total U.S. households, and allowed ownership of more than one television station in markets with "effective" competition. In 2002 a federal court ruled that this new ruling remained too restrictive and allowed conglomerates like AOL Time Warner to purchase multiple stations and provide cable TV.

When the 1996 regulations went into effect, a bidding war broke out for broadcast properties in the United States. Strong bidding by potential acquirers drove prices up to historic levels as large media companies attempted to expand their asset base. In 1998 that hot market continued. In March, Pulitzer Publishing put its TV and radio holdings up for sale. The company's nine network-affiliated TV stations and five radio stations were expected to be sold for more than US$1 billion. Of Pulitzer's nine TV stations, five were affiliated with NBC and two each with CBS and ABC.

Regulatory changes had the additional effect of pushing NBC, ABC, and CBS quickly into the production business. All of the networks produced some shows for the 1994–1995 season, and Capital Cities/ABC went formed its own studio to produce programming in partnership with the new entertainment company Dream-Works SKG, which included Steven Spielberg.

Prior to the change in syndication rules, the big four U.S. networks' principal source of syndication revenues was in international sales. CBS, for example, covered production deficits on several programs with international sales in the early 1990s. However, the United States was not the only exporter of television programming. Mexico's Televisa and Brazil's TV Globo exported popular soap operas, called "telenovelas," to many countries.

In the late 1990s, U.S. action adventure and drama series continued to sell well in international markets, particularly Germany and the United Kingdom. For example, *The X-Files* was one of the top shows in Germany and one of the few U.S. series to broadcast in prime time, appearing on Germany's ProSieben channel.

Non-U.S. broadcasters, particularly in Germany, were also developing co-financing and co-production deals with U.S. studios rather than paying the very high prices the studios were demanding for the right to broadcast their shows. For example, a joint-production deal between MCA and leading German broadcaster RTL gave RTL access to U.S. programming, and provided additional revenue from licensing the programming in other regions.

While the major networks were happy to be producing their own shows, traditional television production houses feared losing outlets for their programs if the networks moved most of their production in-house. That fear resulted in the founding of the Warner Brothers (WB) Network and the United Paramount Network (UPN) in the United States. WB had 50 affiliates, and UPN had 96 as of early 1995, and each claimed to reach about 80 percent of U.S. viewers. However, 18 percent of Warner's viewers received the network via cable providers. NBC, ABC, and CBS, in turn, were concerned that Warner and Paramount would choose to take hit shows they had been producing for the big three networks and put them on their own networks.

By the early 2000s, change was imminent for network television. Networks already were contending with higher production costs than cable, and in 2003 their audience was down 8 percent among adults up to age 49. Most viewers were lost to cable and satellite providers, which had double digit gains in the early 2000s that were expected to continue, although more slowly, into 2008.

Few twenty-first century television viewers under the age of 50 are able to recall when Walter Cronkite and Huntley-Brinkley dominated the evening newscasts. Even in 1982, 72 percent of Americans tuned in nightly for the network newscasts. However, by 1994 that figure had dropped to 60 percent, and by 2000, it had dropped to 30 percent. After the terrorist attacks against the

United States on September 21, 2001, only 17 percent of viewers preferred the network news to cable outlets such as CNN when it came to getting hard news. Although 17 percent was considered a large audience, the over-50 age group that still liked a nightly news fix was not the megabucks-spending audience that advertising agencies wanted for their free-spending clients.

The large U.S. networks managed to hold on to a mass audience even as their share of the market dwindled. However, traditional U.S. broadcast TV was experiencing major changes, including the addition of Fox to the "big three," making them "big four." by the mid-1990s. In addition, two of the major U.S. networks were purchased by larger companies, which would not have been possible under the old FCC regulations. In 1995, the Walt Disney Company acquired Capital Cities/ABC for US$19 billion in stock and cash and Westinghouse Electric acquired CBS Inc. for US$81 a share, or US$5.4 billion, in cash. The Disney/Capital Cities deal combined a top-flight programming producer with a well-managed broadcasting operation, while the Westinghouse/CBS merger created a broadcasting giant that included 15 television and 39 radio stations. The Disney acquisition was expected to have international implications as well. Both Disney and ABC had interests in overseas programming, cable, and broadcast operations that the merged companies were expected to expand. Additional consolidation in the U.S. television broadcasting industry had been projected for the late 1990s.

CURRENT CONDITIONS

By 2003, the world's television market was worth US$130.7 billion. Analysts at PricewaterhouseCoopers projected that to increase to US$178 billion by 2008. The industry was experiencing an upswing following three years of slow growth. The United States was predicted to be the beneficiary of most of this growth with a compound annual growth rate of 7.5 percent, followed by Canada and Latin America (6.1 percent each), Asia (5.5 percent), and the EMEA (4.3 percent). The large populations and relatively low market penetration of India and China made those countries major sources for projected growth for Asia, especially with the fastest economic expansion in the world. Non-Chinese television broadcasters were not allowed into the market, however. Some, such as MTV, were required to syndicate shows to Chinese broadcasters as opposed to having a branded channel.

Three-fifths of the top 10 shows in the U.S. were reality shows in 2004, occupying 18 network programming hours. The change was expected to affect other markets because reality shows are not likely candidates for future use as reruns in syndication, unlike regular scripted programming. Therefore, the producers only come up with money for the networks on the front end. In addition, reality shows typically do not have the longevity of popular scripted programs, a large percentage of which are comedies. Only 19 comedies were picked up by the networks in 2004, a decrease from previous years. By 2005, networks were reporting poor economic recovery provided by such shows when they went to syndication. In addition, programming schedules were rapidly changing, with shows airing multiple times during a week as well as year-round

In addition, the increased use of digital video recorders (DVR), along with other factors, negatively affected advertising revenue. Networks began to investigate other streams of income, including video-on-demand (VOD) services, and considered restructuring how advertising could be purchased, moving away from traditional annual bulk advertising sales in late spring. Product placement in TV programs was an example of innovative advertising that was beginning to augment and replace traditional commercial advertising. The average time for commercial placement in TV programming was about 18 minutes per hour, but some shows had up to 22 minutes of commercials per hour.

One example of creative product placement occurred during an episode of the ABC comedy show *Samantha Who?* when one of the title characters' best friends mentioned she wanted to go to see *Australia* rather than simply saying she wanted to go to the movies. Later in the same episode, there was a scene in a movie theatre with a scene from *Australia* on the screen. The episode first aired a couple of days before the aforementioned movie's opening day.

Lifetime, the Sci-Fi Channel, and the Hallmark Channel were three TV cable networks taking over the original TV movie genre that had been pioneered by ABC, CBS, and NBC beginning in the mid-1970s. Lifetime was especially known for making a few excellent movies with big stars. The cable networks were either owners or partners for repeat airings of made-for-TV movies in the late 2000s.

RESEARCH AND TECHNOLOGY

Throughout the first decade of the twenty-first century as the technological revolution continued, competition among traditional broadcasters was expected to continue. For example, in the mid-1990s, telephone companies began to distribute entertainment products over existing phone lines. In the United States, cable companies and phone companies developed plans to supply on-demand movies and other programming, with full "VCR control," allowing customers to select programming from boxes on their TV sets. In addition, interactive TV was proposed to take sporting events, game shows, and other traditionally passive TV fare to a new level.

However, by the twenty-first century, many of these bold changes either had yet to materialize or existed only in small pockets of the country. For example, interactive television systems were abandoned as a result of the astronomical costs to install them combined with modest customer interest.

One of the most important technological changes in broadcasting in the late 1990s and early 2000s was digital transmission of television signals, which was expected to enhance quality and lead to changes in TV production and distribution. Digital transmission produced a much higher quality television picture than analog transmission and could be used in both terrestrial and satellite TV transmissions. Digital broadcasts required separate frequencies from traditional analog broadcasts and required different equipment on the receiving end.

Most countries planned to allow some existing channels to broadcast their programs in both analog and digital format on different frequencies. The analog signal would eventually be phased out, after a 10- or 15-year period, allowing consumers the time to buy new receivers. As of 1998, those receivers were extremely expensive, but by 2002, that price had dropped somewhat as consumer demand grew. By 2007, a deadline of February 17, 2009, was set for all TV transmissions to be digital.

New digital sets were expected to be quite different than their analog counterparts. For example when Mitsubishi Consumer Electronics America Inc. introduced its first digital television in 1988, it came in two parts: a projector-screen for viewing and a receiver for picking up and translating the digital signals into images. The receiver contained the electronic hardware of the set, similar to a personal computer. This system would allow consumers to upgrade to new digital TV technology without purchasing a new projector screen.

By 2001 digital television was admired by some for its cinema-like screen with outstanding resolution and magnificent Dolby surround sound, and U.S. sales of digital TVs and products jumped to US$2.6 billion. Nevertheless, many cable operators in 2002 still could not bring their customers the service, and the price of digital TVs was between 3 and 50 times more expensive than traditional analog sets. However, prices began to come down, and at least 8 million digital TV sets were expected to be sold by 2005. The major TV networks and broadcasters proposed a different digital TV standard based solely on high definition television (HDTV). While HDTV offered extremely sharp pictures, the sets were extremely large and initially priced at about US$10,000.

Some blending of the two formats was expected, such as the efforts of ABC and Fox in the United States who adopted digital broadcast formats friendly to Microsoft's digital strategy. The compact operating system was called Windows CE and was modified from Microsoft's initial venture into interactive TV with cable and tele-phone companies that was abandoned due to its high cost. In 2002 Microsoft, Maxi, and Sony were moving quickly toward the final design and release of splashy digital home entertainment hubs.

The United States mandated a switch to digital TV that meant that "free commercial broadcast networks would not be available for viewing any more on analog TV sets with only rabbit ears or antennas on roof tops." U.S. President George W. Bush had signed the legislation that ordered all television programs to be broadcast only on with a digital signal beginning on February 17, 2009. Between 15 and 20 million U.S. households received over-the-air programming in 2008, which resulted in an information campaign created by the broadcasting industry and various government agencies educate Americans of the change to digital. The National Association of Broadcasters outlined options of cable or satellite broadcasting or buying a new TV with a built-in digital tuner. The U.S. government offered a US$1.5 billion converter box program as an alternative, and distributed US$40 coupons toward the purchase of a converter for those with older sets.

TV programmers were criticized for "duping viewers more than ever with heavily promoted shows dropped just weeks after they first air," according to Marcus Casey. Networks became notorious for making scheduling changes that caused viewers to search for favorite shows. Although the Internet and mobile devices were making inroads for viewing television programs, TV continued to dominate as the medium of choice for viewers. The aver-age time spend watching television was 142 hours and 29 minutes per month, or 8 hours and 18 minutes per day, according to *Broadcasting & Cable.*

Direct broadcast from satellite (DBS) television (also called DTH, or direct-to-home) emerged in the early to mid-1990s, first in Europe and then in the United States. Direct broadcast differed from cable TV in that consum-ers purchased small satellite dishes to receive the trans-mission, bypassing the cable companies' coaxial cable systems. Using high-powered satellites and the latest digital video compression technology, DBS made a suc-cessful entry to the U.S. market as DirecTV, which created a major challenge to the traditional cable tele-vision industry. DirecTV was reported to be one of the factors that fueled a mid-1990s trend to merge U.S. cable TV operations. In 2002 a company called DigiVision boasted that it provided direct broadcast services in every ZIP code in the continental United States.

In the DirecTV system, more than 150 CD, audio, and laserdisc video quality digital channels were received by a relatively inexpensive, compact 18-inch satellite dish and receiver/decoder. The capital cost of DirecTV per U.S. television household was about US$7.00, compared

to more than the US$700 per subscriber capital cost to wire households for cable TV. From June to December 1994, DirecTV signed up more than 350,000 subscrib-ers, with millions more projected through the end of the twentieth century. The U.S. cable television industry recognized the threat from DBS, which some cable com-panies called the "Deathstar," and planned to spend aggressively in digital video compression and fiber optic cable to improve reception and increase channel capacity. By the late 1990s, DBS growth had hit a plateau, and cable successfully held its market share in most of the United States.

Outside Europe and the United States, interest in direct broadcast continued in 2004. In India, China, Taiwan, and the Philippines, potential local and multi-national investors were said to be forming partnerships to set up systems that would reach Asia's newly prosperous middle class viewers.

INDUSTRY LEADERS

Viacom Inc. (CBS Inc. and UPN Networks). As one of the world's largest media companies, Viacom has inter-ests in a variety of media, including movie production, television and radio broadcasting, and the Internet. The company the company owned the CBS and UPN broad-cast stations and television networks, which included production and syndication services.

Founded in 1927, New York-based CBS operated a national U.S. television network of 20 company-owned stations and more than 200 independent affiliates, as well as a radio network of company-owned stations and affili-ates. In 1995, CBS was purchased by Westinghouse Corp. for US$5.4 billion and the new company was named Westinghouse/CBS. However, after Westing-house sold most of its other assets, the company was re-named CBS Inc. in 1997.

In 1994 and 1995, CBS was battered by the collapse of an agreement to purchase QVC Networks, the loss of NFL football rights to Fox Broadcasting, the defection of several major affiliates to Fox, and low ratings for its prime time schedule, which resulted in a drop to third place behind NBC and ABC in U.S. ratings. CBS made up some ground and in 1998 moved to number two, ahead of ABC. In addition, CBS outbid NBC for rights to broadcast NFL football games that resumed in 1998. In 1996 CBS purchased Infinity Broadcasting Co., which had major holdings in TV and radio broadcasting. In 1999 the media story of the year was the Viacom pur-chase of CBS for nearly US$35 billion in stock, creating what CNN called a US$80 billion giant. In 2002, CBS acquired UPN, and both remained under Viacom con-trol. Viacom owned 39 broadcast television stations in 2004 and had reached the 39 percent market reach allowed by FCC rules. CBS reported US$11.8 billion in revenue in 2004, a 7.7 percent improvement over 2003 figures.

General Electric Co. (NBC). One of the world's largest corporations, Connecticut-based General Electric Co. was the owner of the National Broadcasting Company Inc. (NBC). NBC owned U.S. television stations in many major markets, including New York City, Chicago, Los Angeles, and Washington, D.C., and like the other U.S. networks, had a large stable of affiliate stations. NBC had branched out into other markets with the acquisition of Superchannel, a general programming channel in Europe, and the development of Asian NBC (a financial channel) and CNBC (a U.S. cable channel specializing in financial news and talk television). In 1998 NBC faced the loss of the top-rated *Seinfeld* show, as well as the loss of its NFL broadcast rights when it was outbid by CBS. In 1997 NBC pledged to invest US$225 million into its MSNBC Internet venture with Microsoft over five years. In October 2001 GE's NBC division continued a commitment to reach the large Hispanic audience worldwide when it paid US$2.7 billion to purchase Telemundo Communications Group Inc., the number two U.S. Spanish-language TV broadcast company with ten TV stations in metropolitan areas such as New York, Los Angeles, and Chicago.

NBC faltered in ad sales in 2001, as did MSNBC News, which never challenged CNN for ad revenue dollars. In January 2002, MSNBC had only half the audience of CNN and its other competitor, the Fox News Channel, which briefly overtook CNN in the ratings in January. In contrast, NBC had much to boast about in 2002 as critics raved about the quality of the Salt Lake City Winter Olympics coverage. NBC recorded a US$75 million profit from the Olympics, selling US$740 million in advertising, which was a turnaround after a year of slowed ad sales connected to sports at Murdoch's Fox Network, in particular.

In 2004, NBC and Vivendi Universal Entertainment combined to form NBC Universal, which was 80 percent owned by General Electric and 20 percent owned by Vivendi. The company accounted for 8.5 percent of its parents' 2004 revenues of US$151.3 billion.

Walt Disney Company (ABC Television Network). The primary broadcasting assets of this U.S.-based, second largest media company are the ABC television network, the ABC television station groups, radio station and network operations, and majority ownership of the ESPN cable station. In 2002, ABC's financial picture was dismal as its prime-time audience numbers had fallen 23 percent from 2001 levels. Worse, it embarrassed itself and its longtime news commentator Ted Koppel when it tried to shore up ratings in 2002 by publicly dumping

Koppel's *Nightline* for David Letterman. That move blew up when Letterman refused to jump networks and leave CBS.

The News Corporation Ltd. (Fox Broadcasting). The News Corporation Ltd. is based in Australia and owned by controlling chairman and chief executive Rupert Murdoch. It vastly expanded its TV holdings in the late 1980s and early 1990s, making it one of the world's largest media conglomerates. News Corp. made a successful entry into the U.S. market through its Fox Broadcasting Network, and in 1993 the company acquired 63 percent of Star Television.

In 2002, Murdoch's empire was not on solid ground after banking on some of the world's formerly lucrative sports events (Major League Baseball, the National Football League, and NASCAR) and losing more than US$1 billion in the last half of 2001. In addition to the slump in sports viewing, viewers grew tired of former hit shows *Ally McBeal* and *The X-Files* that year. In early 2002, however, Fox News caught and passed its arch rival CNN in the news rating war, although it did not hold the lead for long. In the 2000s News Corp. also aggressively acquired properties, including Chris-Craft Industries Inc. for US$5.4 billion.

By 2004, News Corp. was earning more than US$5 billion from its television sector. The company owned 35 U.S. television stations through Fox Television, strategically holding duopolies, or two stations in one large market, in 9 of the 20 major U.S. markets. In Asia, the company's Star Network expanded into Hong Kong and Singapore.

RTL Group SA. Luxembourg was home to Europe's largest television company, Compagnie Luxembourgeoise de Telediffusion SA (CLT). In 2000, the company merged with FreemantleMedia, formerly known as Pearson Television, to form RTL. In 2005, RTL reported operating 31 television channels in ten countries and 170 million daily viewers. The company employed more than 8,000 people and generated US$7.4 billion in 2006 revenues.

MAJOR COUNTRIES IN THE INDUSTRY

Australia. The first two Australian commercial TV licenses were awarded in Sydney and Melbourne in 1955, and by 2002, commercial television stations were well established. By 2005, there were 52 licensed commercial television stations in Australia. Commercial providers were allowed to transmit digitally in 2001. The two public networks that received government funding were the Australian Broadcasting Corporation (ABC), providing Australian content, and the Special Broadcasting Service (SBC), providing multi-cultural programming. The commercial industry was valued at US$2.5 billion in 2002.

Canada. Canada was the first country in the world to use geostationary satellites for television broadcasting. In 2005, the publicly owned Canadian Broadcasting Corporation (CBC) continued to provide two national networks for radio and television, one in English and one in French. A second national network, the privately owned CTV, also operated in the 1990s. Other private television networks served limited areas, such as Global TV in Ontario. Cable and satellite connections provided Canadians access to U.S. television networks. Canadian broadcasting was regulated by the Canadian Radio-Television and Telecommunications Corp. (CRTC), which licensed networks and private stations and specified percentages of Canadian content in programming.

Two direct-to-home (DTH) satellite services were launched in Canada in 1996: ExpressVu, backed by a Canadian consortium that included telecommunications giant BCE Inc., and Power DirecTV, a joint venture of Montreal-based Power Corp. and U.S.-based DirecTV. Five more Canadian DTH pay-per-view programming services were also licensed. DTH was considered to be competition for Canadian cable companies. Not surprisingly, the loss of Canadian television broadcast stations mirrored losses by those in the United States as sales of ads dropped.

The European Union. New digital cable and satellite services were in place in Europe by the end of 1995, bringing more channels to a marketplace that had had a very small number. According to some observers, it was unlikely that cable television in Europe would ever reach the penetration and usage that it had in the United States because cable operators had to compete with new technology such as direct transmission satellites, a much less costly system to install in viewers' homes.

One of the key issues in European television was local content. During their startup phase, many new European stations filled their broadcast time with imported and dubbed U.S. programming, largely because it was about ten times less expensive than original European production. However, a European Union directive required broadcasters to air European-produced programming at least 50 percent of the time. While considerable controversy surrounded this issue, for well-established European channels it was fast becoming irrelevant in the mid to late 1990s. As their audience and revenues grew, European commercial channels found that viewers preferred local productions, which the stations were better able to afford.

France. In 1989 the Socialist government of France formed the Conseil Superieur de l'Audiovisuel (CSA), or Supreme Audiovisual Council, to supervise radio and television broadcasting. France had two main public networks, Antenne 2 and France Regions 3, as well as four private stations. The formerly state-run Television Française was privatized in 1987. Canal Plus was the country's first private channel, launched in 1984. Cable broadcasting began in 1987 but was very slow to catch on, with Paris being the only area with a significant number of subscribers. Cable had a low penetration and had been affected by slow construction levels and low "sign-on rates," which translated to 1.3 million of France's 21.6 million TV homes subscribing to cable by 1996. As a result, there was a great deal of interest in satellite digital TV in France in the late 1990s, with two large companies, Canal Plus and TPS, launching digital satellite services. By 2005, the CSA continued to tightly control television content.

In 2003, *Euromonitor* reported that private television represented 52.8 percent of the market in France, with TF1 remaining the dominant channel with a 31.5 percent share. Valued at US$8.6 billion in 2003, the total market was expected to reach US$11.8 billion by 2008. The average TV viewer in France spent 3 hours and 33 minutes watching television in 2003.

Germany. Only public corporations were permitted to broadcast in Germany until the mid-1980s, when a new system allowed commercial stations to be licensed for the first time. The Federal Ministry of Post and Telecommunications handled licensing of broadcasters, while television and radio owners paid annual fees to support public broadcasting. As in the English system, German public broadcasters were relatively free to establish their own broadcasting policies, although that was more likely for television than radio. Nine different public corporations offered regional radio and TV programs in Germany. In the early 1990s, the regional TV channels combined to produce one evening television program on Channel 1 (ARD). A second national public station was Channel 2 (ZDF). A third channel, ARDIII, broadcast along regional lines. Regionally-based state regulatory units, called *Medienanstalten,* controlled television licenses. Representatives from regional governments, communities, and institutions controlled these 15 units. In addition to public television, as of 1996, Germany had several commercial channels, including ProSieben, RTL, RTL2, and SAT1, and several cable and local channels. German broadcasters introduced digital transmission in the late 1990s and early 2000s. Public broadcasters ARD and ZDF launched a four-channel digital TV system in 1997. Public broadcasters have faced increasing competition from private, commercial television companies, with RTL Group leading with a market share of 29.8 percent in 2003. However, public broadcaster ARD remained the largest of its kind in Germany, as well as one of the largest in the world.

In 2001 and 2002, Germany television companies faced economic challenges similar to the German publishing industry. In February 2002 ProSieben listed a 27 percent plunge in annual surplus and a drop in pre-tax profit of 50 percent. ProSieben lost additional money in association with other media outlets, such as the Kirch media group. However, in 2003, the television market had grown 8.4 percent from 2002 to US$10.17 billion, with continued growth to US$11.88 billion by 2008.

Italy. While all broadcasting in Italy was once the province of Radiotelevisione Italiana (RAI), private channels emerged as major competitors. RAI broadcast on three channels: RAI 1, 2, and 3. Private channels included Canale 5, Italia 1, and Rete 4. In the mid-1990s, Canale 5 held the highest audience share of the terrestrial networks, with about 20 percent, followed closely by RAI 1 with slightly less than 20 percent. Satellite channels, such as RTL2 and VIVA, were introduced in the mid-1990s. A digital satellite package, DStv, had 40 to 50 channels on the air as of early 1997. However, the service had to compete with dominant terrestrial broadcasters who had a strong lock on the market in the late 1990s. In 2001, while many of the world's television companies were in freefall, Italy's largest company, MediaSet, and its three commercial channels managed to post "slightly" better ad sales revenues than it had reported in 2000.

Spain. Spanish broadcasting was regulated by Radiotelevision Española (RTVE), a government organization. Public television was transmitted on two channels, TVE1 and TVE2, with TVE1 reaching the majority of the country's population. A group of regional public stations was also in operation. Well over a third of Spain's households with televisions were wired for cable in the mid-1990s. Three private networks operated in Spain in 2000: Antena 2, Telecinco, and CanalPlus, a cable channel. In 2000, government-owned Telemadrid was privatized by the local Madrid government, according to *Bloomberg News.*

The United Kingdom. The BBC and the Independent Broadcasting Authority (IBA) traditionally dominated British television. However, the Broadcasting Act of 1990 reorganized independent broadcasting by reassigning the TV regulatory responsibilities of the IBA to a new group called the Independent Television Commission (ITC). The ITC was put in charge of licensing and regulating all non-BBC television services, including Channel 4 and Channel 5, as well as cable and satellite services. The BBC continued to expand to operate several channels, including BBC One (broad range of programming); BBC Two (comedy and cultural interest); BBC Three (aimed at young adult market); BBC Four (most intellectually and culturally enriched channel); CBBC (children); CBeebies (pre-schoolers); BBC News 24; BBC Parliament; and BBCi (interactive television available to digital television

subscribers). The BBC broadcast around the world in 40 languages and offered a worldwide service in English 24 hours a day. The BBC and ITC were public bodies licensed by the government, but the government rarely interfered with their day-to-day management. The BBC controlled 30 percent of the market in 2003 and 37 percent of the audience share.

As in other European countries, new cable and satellite channels emerged to challenge the dominance of traditional English broadcasters. In 2001, particularly during the fourth quarter, the United Kingdom's ad sales slipped drastically for many television broadcast companies. ITV reported its advertising sales were down 12 percent from 2000. In March 2002 the British giant Granada, a major production studio known for its independent investigative features for Bill Kurtis on A&E in conjunction with *The New York Times,* eliminated 1,430 staff jobs, while a competitor, Carlton, laid off 400 employees. Granada lost US$187 million in revenue for the full year ending September 2001. Advertising revenues for 2002 were down 2.6 percent early in the year. Total market value grew a nominal 0.3 percent in 2003 to reach US$11.7 billion.

Asia. In 1993 Rupert Murdoch's News Corp. bought control of Star TV, which helped the industry focus on Asia as one of the world's hot growth markets. Asia was expected to be home to two-thirds of the world's population by 2005, at which time it would be served by 2,000 terrestrial and satellite-delivered channels serving 400 million homes.

Star TV initially aired a large proportion of non-Asian produced programming, a strategy that was not expected to be viable in the long term. For example, TVB International Ltd., a successful Hong Kong broadcaster, competed effectively with Star by tailoring its programs for the many different ethnic and linguistic groups in its audience. While there was significant demand for western programming, Asian viewers, like those in other regions of the world, preferred quality programming that reflected their own culture. In addition, foreign content was disturbing to many Asian governments, especially in China and Singapore, who feared that it would destabilize their regimes. However, Star TV was very successful in penetrating Taiwan and India. In response to the success of Star, India's state-owned television network, Doordarshan, launched five satellite channels in 1993 to compete with Star. Unlike India's traditional broadcast channels, time slots on the new satellite channels were sold to independent producers and television companies.

As in Europe, the maturation of the Asian market, resulted in the expectation for local producers to have more resources to make higher quality programs, a trend that had the potential to hurt U.S. TV programming exports. Nevertheless, the vast expansion of channels brought about by cable and satellite services was expected to help U.S. producers maintain a prominent position in overseas markets.

China. China, which as of 1997 still had a minuscule private broadcast industry, was changing in the mid-1990s. Some local Chinese public television stations dramatically changed the content of their broadcasts from propaganda to programs that produced profits for the station. For example, the Shanghai Bureau of Radio and Television gained the right to import entertainment shows without central government review and was broadcasting many western programs.

The Chinese market, with its entrepreneur development and huge population, had enormous potential. China was expected to have 263.5 million households with televisions by 2005. Several commercial television stations were developing plans to introduce services to China. The re-acquisition of Hong Kong by China in 1997 had influenced the Chinese TV industry, without a clash between the government and TV program powers-that-be. Hong Kong was the center of Asia's broadcasting industry prior to the takeover, and was home to two broadcast stations, a major cable operation, and six satellite networks, including News Corp.'s Star TV, NBC Asia, and Turner International Asia Pacific.

In 2001 companies like Murdoch's entered the Chinese market by generally avoiding controversy and giving the government the official right to ban foreign intrusion but not exercising that power. A number of Chinese entrepreneurs and Murdoch's Star TV combined resources to offer Phoenix Television to about 45 million households in 2001 according to *The Los Angeles Times.* However, the general economic slowdown in Asia at the end of 2001 and beginning of 2002 severely hurt China's television interests. In 2002 Television Broadcasts Ltd. carried out a wage freeze on salaries in an attempt to avoid mass firings of employees after 2001 ad sales plunged.

Japan. Radio and television were developed earlier in Japan than in other Asian countries. Japanese radio broadcasting was begun in 1925 by Japan Broadcasting Corporation (Nippon Hoso Kyokai, or NHK), a public corporation financed by license fees paid by television set owners. As of the mid-1990s, NHK broadcast on radio and television with no commercial interruptions. NHK made its first television broadcast in 1952, and in 1953 it began to broadcast overseas programs, such as *Radio Japan,* in many different languages. Private commercial broadcasting began in 1952 and gained widespread popularity, with five private networks in operation in the mid-1990s: Nippon TV, Tokyo Broadcasting System, TV Asahi, Fuji TV, and TV Tokyo. Japan had 34.6 million homes with televisions in the mid-1990s and direct satellite and cable television were in 20 percent of those

households. As of 1996, Japan continued to account for more than half of all TV advertising expenditures in Asia.

In March 2002, as the Japanese economy sagged, it threatened the revenues of four of Japan's biggest TV broadcast groups that had logged record profits in 2001. However, Nippon Television Network Corp., Tokyo Broadcasting System Inc., Fuji Television Network Inc., and Asahi Broadcasting Corp. all recorded better than average annual revenue increases in the spring of 2002.

New Zealand. A state-run broadcasting company inaugurated television service in New Zealand in 1960. Beginning in 1988, TV broadcasts were controlled by Television New Zealand Ltd. (TVNZ), a government-owned company. Television deregulation in 1989 removed restrictions on foreign and cross-media ownership in New Zealand, allowing for true commercial competition. Television New Zealand operated TV One and TV2, which dominated the market as of the late 1990s. However, TV3, which was the only privately owned, national commercial network in New Zealand, was reported growing market share. Regional TV stations were licensed to provide selected local program services. Multichannel TV, such as cable and direct broadcast, was not a major factor in New Zealand. TVNZ reported that advertising sales and revenues were down in 2001 along with a drop in market share from 83 to 61 percent for the decade ending in 2001.

The United States. The United States had about 1,200 commercial television stations, about half of which were UHF stations, with the other half being VHF stations. There also were about 370 public TV stations. As of March 2002, 258 TV stations provided customers with digital broadcasting and another 650 had informed the FCC that they would launch digital service within the next year after overcoming problems with financing, zoning laws, and other miscellaneous complications that kept them from complying by the May 1, 2002 deadline. At the end of 2003, the total market was valued at US$42.4 billion, and was expected to reach US$56.3 billion by 2008 according to *Euromonitor.* Network television accounted for the largest share of total revenues with 53.7 percent, and the four leading networks were ABC, CBS, NBC and Fox. NBC was by far the largest network, capturing 35.4 percent of 2003's market.

Jobs in television broadcasting were always competitive, but became more difficult even for TV veterans to obtain. Network executives began to be overwhelmed with hundreds of resumes and tapes for a single job opening as thousands of positions were lost in the 2000s due to cost-cutting and consolidations. News anchor and reporting jobs in small and mid-sized markets were under scrutiny as network executives increasingly complained that such markets were over-saturated with news coverage. Just as the trend to have only one newspaper in a city since the 1980s, it was unlikely that three or four competing stations would offer news programming in the 2000s. In 2002, stations in St. Louis, Missouri; Kingsport, Tennessee; and Bristol, Virginia, ordered their news anchors to sign off for the last time and replaced news with other programming.

The writer's strike that ran from early November 2007 to mid-February 2008 quickly affected the TV industry. Late night talk shows and regular programming were replaced by reruns as soon as the strike began. Everyone involved with the production of any kind of television programming stopped everything they did for TV shows. Many, like Tina Fey of NBC's hit show *30 Rock,* not only stopped writing, but also gave up other tasks and joined the picket lines in support of the writers. More than 12,000 Writers Guild movie and TV writers participated in the three and a half month long strike according to *The New York Times.* They sought a "large increase in pay for movies and TV shows released on DVD and bigger share of revenue." In the meantime, many favorite shows were left with a limited number of new episodes available for broadcast. When the strike ended, not all shows that had been on the air in November were likely to continue. New shows were especially challenged to survive the strike and retain their audiences.

In 2008, the Coalition for Local TV joined with more than 150 local TV stations with demands for the FCC to develop ways to allow small community TV stations to complete the conversion to full power. Such a conversion would enable the stations to continue broadcasting after the switch to digital. The stations were located primarily in African American and Hispanic communities where viewers typically did not have converter boxes or cable TV.

Reality TV programming is either "must see" or "wasted air time," depending on demographics. The hosts of five popular reality programs were nominated in an Emmy Awards category that had been created for them in 2008. According to Jeff Probst, host of *Survivor,* in a *TV Guide* interview, "I think all of us sense there is a certain bit of skepticism—like really? I think it is important to establish early that we're in on the joke that we don't take ourselves seriously."

BIBLIOGRAPHY
Adalian, Josef. "Primetime." *Variety,* 1 December 2003.

Adler, Shawn. "Television Feeling Immediate Effects of Writer's Strike." Available from www.mtv.com.

Albiniak, Paige. "Networks Adapt to Changing Times." *The Boston Herald,* 24 May 2004.

"Asian Media." *Campaign,* 21 May 2004.

"Australia Now: Broadcasting.' Australian Government, Department of Foreign Affairs and Trade, 2005. Available from www.dfat.gov.au.

Bachman, Katy. "Local Sweeps Races Tight." *Mediaweek,* 31 May 2004.

Baker, Jim. "Olympics Golden with Viewers." *The Boston Herald,* 26 February 2002.

Berg, Christian. "Digital TV's Picture-perfect Outlook is Obscured." *The Morning Call* (Allentown, PA), 27 January 2002.

"Broadcast Rights for WWF, Baseball Push Headline Media into Q3 Loss." *Canadian Press Newswire,* 26 July 2001.

Carman, John. "Goliaths of TV Likely to Get Fatter: Ruling Good for Giant Firms—but Viewers May Suffer." *The San Francisco Chronicler,* 21 February 2002.

Casey, Marcus. "Television Networks Axe Shows for Ad Dollars," 10 October 2008. Available from www.news.com.au.

Chipman, Kim. "Owner of CBS Network Reports 4th-Quarter Loss." *The Record* (Bergen County, NJ), 14 February 2002.

Cieply, Michael. "Writers Begin Strike as Talks Break Off." *The New York Times,* 5 November 2007. Available from www.nytimes.com.

Draper, Deborah J., ed. *Business Rankings Annual.* Detroit: Thomson Gale, 2004.

Edelstein, Rob. "The Emmys Get Real!" *TV Guide,* 15 September 2008.

Eggerton, John. "Study: TV Usage At All-Time High." *Broadcasting & Cable,* November 24, 2008.

"Fewer Ads, Smaller Crowds Pummel Disney." *The Record* (Bergen County, NJ), 9 November 2001.

Furman, Phyllis. "MSNBC Comes Up Short vs. the Competition." *Daily News* (NY), 31 January 2002.

Gay, Verne. "TV's Dynamic Trio: 'Fringe,' 'Life on Mars,' 'Enemy'." 12 October 2008. Available from www.newsday.com.

"Global Entertainment and Media Outlook: 2004–2008 (Industry Previews)." PricewaterhouseCoopers, 2004. Available from www.pwc.com.

Hiestand, Jesse. "Scripps Boosts Q1 Forecasts as TV Ad Sales Rise." *The Hollywood Reporter,* 13 March 2002.

Higgins, John M. "Media's Pink Slip Blues." *Broadcasting and Cable,* 28 January 2002.

"Hoover's Company Capsules." *Hoover's Online,* 2008. Available from www.hoovers.com.

Jack, Andrew. "Last Privately Owned Russian TV Station Taken off Air." *Financial Times* (London), 23 January 2002.

"Japan's 4 Large TV Broadcasters Log Record Group Profits." *Jiji Press Ticker Service,* 28 May 2001.

Kohl, Christian. "European TV Giant Posts US$2 Billion Loss." *Daily Variety,* 5 March 2002.

Laugesen, Ruth. "Broadcast Blues." *The Sunday Star-Times* (Auckland), 24 February 2002.

Lazich, Robert S., ed. *Market Share Reporter.* Detroit: Thomson Gale, 2004.

"Local TV Stations Call for Fair Access for Community, Minority Voices on Cable." *MarketWatch,* 10 October 2008. Available from www.marketwatch.com.

"Local TV Stations Call for Fair Access for Community, Minority Voices on Cable." *MarketWatch,* 10 October 2008. Available from www.marketwatch.com.

Loving, Gary. "TV Movies Migrate to Cable, Abandon Networks." *USA Today,* 17 October 2008.

McConnell, Bill. "Over 650 Stations Want Waivers." *Broadcasting and Cable,* 11 March 2002.

McIntyre, Paul. "Networks Chase the Feel–Good Factor." *Sydney Morning Herald,* 2 October 2008. Available from business.smh.com.au.

"More Product Placements Showing Up in TV Programs." 14 October 2008. Available from www.bworldonline.com.

Pennington, Gail. "Is There Room for Network News? And That's The Way It…Used To Be." *St. Louis Post-Dispatch,* 27 January 2002.

"ProSieben Suffers Profit Drop." *Financial Times Deutschland,* 28 May 2001.

Romano, Allison. "Checking the Census." *Broadcasting and Cable,* 1 October 2001.

Schmuckler, Eric. "Facing Reality." *Mediaweek,* 31 May 2004.

Stephen, Curtis. "Are You Ready? The Switch to Digital Television" *The Crisis,* Winter 2008.

Tilles, Daniel. "Granada Posts Fiscal Full-Year Loss on Ad Sales Fall." *Bloomberg News,* 28 November 2001.

Tessler, Joelle. "FCC Investigating TV Networks, Military Analysts." *Arizona Star,* 8 October 2008. Available from www.azstarnet.com.

Trigoboff, Dan. "Live at 11? Maybe Not for Long; As Profit Pressure Mounts, Some Experts Consider Local Newscasts to be Endangered." *Broadcasting and Cable,* 11 February 2002.

"TV Broadcasting in France, Germany, UK, US." *Euromonitor,* August 2004. Available from www.majormarketprofiles.com.

Wilkofsky Gruen Associates Inc. "Global Entertainment and Media Outlook: 2002–2006." PriceWaterhouseCoopers, May 2002. Available from www.pwc.com.

Wong, Kenneth. "TVB to Freeze Wages." *Bloomberg News,* 6 December 2001.

MEDICAL EQUIPMENT AND SERVICES

———————————■———————————

HOSPITALS

NAICS CODE(S)

622. Hospitals provide diagnostic services, extensive medical treatment that includes surgical services, and other medical services, as well as continuous nursing services. These establishments have an organized medical staff, inpatient beds, equipment, and facilities to provide complete health care for patients. Specialized group industries include general medical and surgical hospitals; psychiatric hospitals; and specialty hospitals for alcoholism rehabilitation, children, cancer, orthopedics, chronic diseases, and drug addiction.

INDUSTRY SNAPSHOT

The world hospital industry consists of an estimated 100,000 hospitals. While the world's hospitals differ considerably in structure, organization, and services, as well as in purpose and mission, they share the goal of fulfilling curative, preventive, and educational health needs around the world. Health centers and clinics are considered to be hospitals. In many parts of the world, however, the hospital industry generally adheres to World Health Organization (WHO) standards that distinguish hospitals as permanent facilities staffed by at least one physician offering inpatient services or nursing care. In the United States, hospitals are operated by government agencies, not-for-profit organizations, and for-profit corporations.

The quality and extent of hospital care typically correlates favorably with the percentage of a country's gross domestic product (GDP) expended for health care. According to WHO, expenditures for health care increased from 3 percent of the global GDP in 1948 to 14 percent in 2004. In less affluent countries, the number of available hospital beds varies greatly depending on national factors other than GDP, such as demographics and the type of government. A 2009 study by the Center for Healthcare Research & Transformation reported that the U.S. spends more on health care than any other country as a percentage of GDP. The U.S. spending figure of 15.2 percent of GDP was 33 percent higher than the second place nation of Switzerland.

In the United States, the overall cost of health care escalated rapidly beginning in the 1970s, reaching more than US$2.3 trillion in 2008, an average of US$7,681 per person. Continued high inflation in health spending was confirmed by data from the U.S. Department of Health & Human Services, which showed that health care spending rose 4.4 percent in 2008, after rising 6.0 percent in 2007. Health care spending was projected to increase an average of 6.1 percent per year from 2009 to 2019. Spending on hospital services was expected to reach US$761 billion in 2009 and grow at 6.1 percent per year through 2019. Spending on physician and clinical services was projected to grow 5.4 percent per year for the same period. A March 2008 report from the American Hospital Association stated that U.S. hospitals employed more than 5 million people and were the second largest private sector employer behind restaurants. It further reported that a third of U.S. hospitals lose money on operations.

ORGANIZATION AND STRUCTURE

Hospitals are generally distinguished by their sponsorship or ownership by organizations that are described as

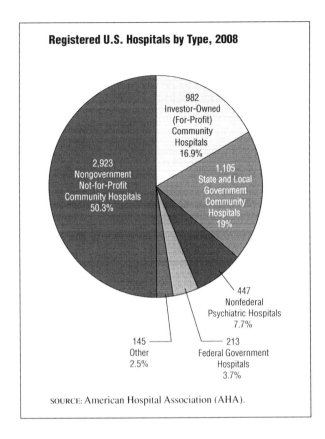

Registered U.S. Hospitals by Type, 2008

982 Investor-Owned (For-Profit) Community Hospitals 16.9%

2,923 Nongovernment Not-for-Profit Community Hospitals 50.3%

1,105 State and Local Government Community Hospitals 19%

447 Nonfederal Psychiatric Hospitals 7.7%

145 Other 2.5%

213 Federal Government Hospitals 3.7%

SOURCE: American Hospital Association (AHA).

voluntary and non-profit; government-owned or public; and for-profit, private, or proprietary. In the United States, the number of hospitals had fallen steadily since 1980, with the percentage of hospitals operated by for-profit corporations escalating in the 1990s. According to the American Hospital Association (AHA), there were 5,815 hospitals in the United States in 2008, providing a total of more than 951,000 staffed beds. Of these hospitals, 982 were investor-owned, for-profit community hospitals.

Since the early 1990s, rather than wait for changes mandated by legislation or other adverse situations, most hospitals have restructured to implement effective, cost-cutting measures. According to a survey by the AHA, which was the primary U.S. hospital advocate, participation in health networks was a potentially viable way to restructure for nearly 11 percent of the nation's community hospitals. Health networks were described as a group of hospitals, physicians, insurers, or community agencies working together to deliver a broad spectrum of health services that were designed to eliminate duplication of services and create improved integration of care among community providers. Networks also operated as proprietary hospitals that were owned by individual or groups of physicians or that were owned and controlled by corporate investors. Hospitals were also teaming up with physicians in various types of

integrated arrangements, such as physician-hospital organizations (PHOs), independent practice associations (IPAs), management services organizations, medical foundations, and hospital owned or joint hospital/physician owned group practices. The less formal arrangement offered by physician-hospital networks allowed hospitals and physicians increased flexibility because of lowered legal structures.

In the early 1990s, a drop in hospital inpatient activity was buffered by an increase in ambulatory outpatient services, such as hospices, home health care, and psychiatric services that were arranged through joint venture or other contractual agreements. Treatments and procedures routinely requiring an inpatient stay in the early 1980s were performed as outpatient procedures at a much lower cost by the early 1990s. Facilities like those at Duke University in the United States realized as much as US$60,000 savings per patient by shifting some treatments to outpatient clinics. For example, bone marrow transplants, one of several treatments traditionally requiring long-term inpatient care, appeared adaptable to outpatient treatment. Medical experts had some doubts as to whether outpatient services adequately filled the gap in health care or created more critical treatment gaps. For example, in cases involving outpatient treatment of chronically ill cancer patients, the issue was whether hospitals would have immediate access to patient information in case of an emergency inpatient admission.

Community Hospitals. In the United States in 2008, of the 5,815 registered hospitals, 5,010 were community hospitals. Of these, 2,923 were operated by non-government, not-for-profit organizations, 982 were investor owned (for-profit), and 1,105 were run by state or local governments, according to the AHA. Community hospitals were open to the public and often bore the brunt of economic defaults, primarily because they typically served as the only "refuge for the poor and ill." From the 1980s through the 1990s, there was an ongoing decline in the number of community hospitals in the United States. In 1980, there were 3,547 hospitals operated by not-for-profit organizations. Taking 1993 as an example, 34 hospitals closed, approximately 18 merged, and others were absorbed by various structures. More than one-half the community hospital closures occurred in large, urban hospitals with an average of 200 to 300 beds, which contributed to a loss of 99,000 hospital beds over 10 years. New facilities and re-openings may have partially offset the hospital reductions, but a decrease in substitutions compensated for the losses of rural hospitals.

The Community Health Network was named the "Most Wired" in the United States in the 2008 Most Wired Survey and Benchmarking Study released in the

July 2008 issue of *Hospitals* & *Health Networks* magazine. The use of technology was reported as the reason for improved outcomes in patient satisfaction and other quality measures.

District Hospitals. Hospitals, particularly in rural areas of developing countries, operated under the umbrella of district health systems that included local health centers that were capable of delivering a variety of curative, preventive, and educational health services. A typical rural health district in Africa served about 160,000 inhabitants with approximately 140 beds, 3 physicians, and 10 peripheral health units, admitting about 4,000 patients annually. Few of these health centers maintained laboratory, X-ray, or surgical facilities. In terms of primary care, health centers or stations were designated as initial referral points for hospital admission. Consequently, direct access to hospitals was limited in favor of service at the local health center. The proximity of local health centers permitted quicker access to health care and eased the burden on hospital resources. However, the lure of hospital technology frequently led patients to bypass local health centers and go directly to hospitals. A study of one underutilized Vietnamese district health center indicated that 68 percent of hospital referrals were primarily because doctors gave hospital consultations without any price differential. Under these circumstances, health centers suffered from the hospital's competition for resources, and hospitals became overloaded with primary care work.

Religious Hospitals. Non-governmental, voluntary, non-profit hospitals included facilities owned or sponsored by religious and other nonsecular groups. In 2008, there were 620 Catholic community hospitals in the United States, providing 122,475 beds and 649,336 full-time-equivalent staff. A survey of international health services in the early 1990s showed that Catholic hospitals provided services in 58 countries, with the highest number in Latin America, the Commonwealth of Independent States, and Africa. In many countries, religious and governmental organizations shared almost equivalent hospital sponsorship. In Kenya, for example, about 25 percent of the facilities—equivalent to 7,000 hospital beds—were sponsored by religious organizations. Perhaps more than most hospital sponsors, religious organizations had historically maintained an ecumenical presence when providing primary medical care through hospitals, long-term care facilities, or funding health service networks in the most remote areas of the world. International health intervention by voluntary organizations was probably vastly understated because of meager funding and minimal, if any, publicity. Other factors contributing to the anonymity of these organizational services may have been the lack of central service provider registries and the assumption of sponsorship by larger organizations or governments in some instances.

Government Hospitals. Government-sponsored hospitals were characterized as facilities controlled by various levels of national, provincial or state, local county, or municipal governments. A large proportion of foreign hospitals was government owned, with hospital use determined by governmental structure. For a militarily controlled government, more hospital beds would be reserved for military personnel. Until 1949, China's hospitals were primarily sponsored by missionary organizations. The number of public hospitals grew rapidly as China's society opened, from some 9,000 in 1978 to more than 14,000 in 2009. Private hospitals made their appearance in 1984, and in 2009, there were 5,736 of them. In the United States in 2008, state and local governments sponsored 1,105 hospitals and the federal government sponsored 213 hospitals, according to the American Hospital Association. Government hospital sponsorship included a range of hospitals for illnesses such as psychiatric diseases, tuberculosis and other respiratory diseases, chronic diseases, mental retardation, alcohol and chemical dependency, and other long-term care needs. Federally sponsored U.S. hospitals provided care for members of the armed services, veterans, and Native Americans. The Veterans Health Administration (VHA) was the largest federal hospital sponsor, with 153 medical centers as of 2010, plus numerous clinics and other facilities providing health care to more than 5.5 million veterans annually. Overall, in the United States, 1,318 hospitals were operated by a government entity in 2008, as opposed to 2,562 in 1980.

Federal hospitals in the United States have received their share of accusations of management excesses. The VHA hospitals' prominence in treating spinal cord injuries, stress disorders, prosthetics, and substance abuse was often tainted by allegations of pork barrel budgets and facility under-utilization. The annual US$47 billion budget in 2010 served about 5.5 million unique patients. Veteran empathy runs high, so increasing VHA budgets met little, if any, opposition from the general public. The slightest hint of hospital closure or contracting of services to private providers results in loud protest from veterans' groups and from politicians, particularly those representing regions in which VA complexes serve as the major employer for hundreds of community residents. Veterans' groups like the American Legion believe that the need for enhanced productivity and accountability will ultimately change the structure of VA hospitals.

For-Profit Hospitals. A rapidly growing number of U.S. hospitals had come under private ownership in the early twenty-first century, increasing to 1,399 in 2002 compared to 942 in 1980. While there was disagreement that U.S. hospital care faced excessive commercialization, most analysts concurred that commercialized health care was a permanent fixture. Some reformers believed that privatization would better provide quality health services, promote hospital productivity, and increase cost containment. For-profit hospitals took advantage of structures like investor-owned chain hospitals, health maintenance organizations (HMOs), preferred provider organizations (PPOs), and exclusive provider organizations (EPOs), or a combination of several structures. Commercial chains would buy out financially strapped hospitals and, in some instances, develop new hospital systems. The most frequent justification for conversion to private markets centered on the potential for augmented financial stability. Another significant reason was greater efficiency and productivity of medical services, although some observers believed the latter was not proven despite growing evidence supporting commercialization. An analysis by the Congressional Budget Office (CBO) revealed that care provided through insurers or group model HMOs cost 15 percent less than other plans, with an overall national savings potential of 10 percent if the entire population enrolled in HMOs. However, in light of the turbulence of U.S. health systems, health analysts expressed some doubt as to whether privatization unequivocally represented the best solution to health reform.

The rise of investor-owned, for-profit hospitals and specialty clinics tended to further dissipate limited sources for community hospital revenue. Profit motives accounted for the development of chain-managed resources, largely because available Medicare reimbursements confirmed profits for investors. Several high-tech procedures, such as the treatment of end-stage renal disease that was formerly administered by hospitals, began to be administered by for-profit clinics. The investment appeal of dialysis clinics was partially because the service is Medicare-reimbursable.

Psychiatric Hospitals. The psychiatric hospital market reflected some of the strongest growth from the mid-1980s to the mid-1990s. In contrast to other segments of the hospital industry, the number of psychiatric hospitals in the United States increased from 584 to 737 between 1986 and 1993, accompanied by an increase of 191,000 admissions. Higher psychiatric admissions may not have necessarily denoted progress, but the positive elements of these higher admissions became evident in view of shorter hospital stays, which dropped from 106 days in 1983 to 52 days in 1993. These trends also reflected significant modifications of

psychiatric treatment, such as improved pharmacological therapy, outpatient treatment for chronic mental illnesses, and the closure of many large state-run mental hospitals in favor of expanded outpatient treatment services. By 2007, the U.S. Census Bureau reported a decrease to 569 psychiatric and substance-abuse hospitals.

Specialized Hospitals. The number of specialized hospitals providing a range of inpatient services for all age groups, including those sponsored by government, voluntary organizations, and for-profit chains, grew from 30 in 1993 to 532 in 2002. In the mid-1990s, services of long-term care and specialized hospitals expanded to include facilities for AIDS patients. A handful of hospitals also specialized in treating patients with tuberculosis and other chronic conditions. Research findings and technological advances offered dramatic improvements in the quality of life for patients with spinal cord, head, and other trauma injuries.

BACKGROUND AND DEVELOPMENT

The medieval Christian period probably reflects the first formal hospital structure. The bishops of the Catholic Church were instructed by the Council of Nicea in 325 A.D. to found a hospital in every cathedral city in Christendom.

As Europe's Renaissance spurred scientific and social experimentation, hospital development reaped the benefits, including improved hygienic conditions, nursing services, and other patient care refinements. The admission of paying patients and the development of specialty maternity hospitals, among other improvements, meant that hospitals had become permanently integrated into their communities. The first hospital in the western hemisphere was built in Santo Domingo about 1503.

Under the auspices of religious authority, hospitals were a symbol of refuge for the sick and poor. This image of hospitals continued well into the nineteenth and twentieth centuries, when doctors at Massachusetts General Hospital were not allowed to charge their patients for care, a rule that lasted as late as 1908. Physicians treated people who could afford medical care in their own homes. The burden of patient care costs shifted hospital control and expenses to joint management between religious and civil authorities.

The discovery of ether as an anesthetic was a major turning point in the history of hospitals. W.T.G. Morton, a Georgia dentist, first used ether during a hospital surgical procedure in 1846. Another physician, Crawford Long, claimed to have used ether for surgery as early as 1842, but did not immediately publish his findings. The use of anesthetics greatly decreased the public's fear of hospitals and led to a sharp increase in the number of surgical procedures performed. Likewise, the development of sulfa drugs in the 1930s and penicillin in the 1940s decreased the infection mortality rate associated with surgery and contributed to a positive public image for hospitals.

CURRENT CONDITIONS

According to the World Health Organization (WHO), global per capita expenditure on health care was US$802 in 2007, up from US$481 in 2000. There was great disparity among different nations. The per capita figure for high income nations was US$4,405 in 2007, up from US$2,657 in 2000. For low income nations, per capita spending was a mere US$27 in 2007, up from US$14 in 2000.

In the U.S., where per capita spending was highest at US$7,285 in 2007 and US$4,703 in 2000, the AHA reported that over 35 million people were admitted to hospitals each year. Nearly 118 million were treated in Emergency Departments (EDs). Over four million babies were delivered and 481 million outpatients provided with care. Taking account of hospital purchases of other industries' goods and services, hospitals were said to support one in every ten U.S. jobs and US$1.9 trillion in economic activity.

Indeed, during the 2000s, the hospital industry proved to be something of a mainstay during difficult economic times. For example, in 2001, the industry achieved 2.3 percent annual growth, despite a recession that negatively impacted scores of other U.S. industry sectors.

Patient satisfaction was a key performance indicator within the health care industry. U.S. physicians received high marks from most patients who required an overnight stay in the hospital, according to a 2004 Press Ganey Associated survey of 300,000 patients at 1,326 hospitals. The survey also reported that patients' overall satisfaction was 91 out of 100 possible points. The majority of respondents to the survey gave their physicians a top rating of very good. The courtesy and friendliness of the nursing and physician staff also ranked very high, as did the skill of the nursing staff.

During the 2000s, the U.S. hospital industry experienced a major construction boom. Construction began to increase in 2001, even as the rest of the nation endured difficult economic times. In 2002, the AHA reported that 19 new acute care hospitals were opened in 2002, representing the first increase since 1975. In fact, from 1975 to 2002, acute care hospitals had decreased 16.5 percent, according to *Modern Healthcare*. Bruce Crowther, president and CEO of Northwest Community Hospital in Illinois, stated in 2010 that the past decade

had been the biggest hospital construction boom in the U.S. in 50 years.

Although some industry players were concerned about creating excess capacity, a number of strong trends were supporting the industry's growth initiatives. With the aging of the baby boomer generation and high growth in the suburbs came the expectation of increased business for hospitals, which spurred health care systems nationwide to initiate construction. Growth was also encouraged by low interest rates, improved Medicare reimbursements, and the desire of health care professionals to offer patients state-of-the-art technology.

A February 2004 Turner Construction Co. survey of 200 health care industry executives showed that almost 70 percent of respondents expected their organizations would pursue a significant capital expansion project by 2007. Bank of America Securities *Kiplinger Business Forecasts* reported that 60 percent of non-profit rural hospitals and 85 percent of urban non-profit hospitals had plans to expand or upgrade their facilities in the early to mid-2000s.

Also in the 2000s, the issue of medical malpractice liability reached crisis levels in some parts of the United States. In states with no financial limits to malpractice claims, hospitals and physicians shouldered the burden of skyrocketing medical malpractice insurance rates. In some cases, policies were in the six-figure range, making the cost of practicing medicine very high.

These conditions prompted a mass exodus from some medical specialties. For example, in Illinois, some obstetrician/gynecologists either opted to stop providing obstetric care or left to practice in nearby states like Wisconsin, where malpractice insurance cost significantly less because reforms limited liability claims. This same phenomenon affected other high risk specialties, such as emergency medicine and neurosurgery. In rural areas where a limited number of specialists served a large geographic area, the physician shortage had dire consequences for area residents, causing reduced hours or complete department shutdowns.

Expenditures. Expenditures for health care surpassed US$2.3 trillion in 2008 and were projected to reach US$2.6 trillion for 2010 and to continue to grow at an annual rate of 6.1 percent through 2019, based on the accelerating increase in spending for prescription drugs, increase in provider costs, inability of insurers to negotiate discounts in prices, and increase in income growth.

Political pressure to deal with accelerating costs, as well as a lack of health insurance coverage for many Americans, resulted in a major legislative overhaul being passed by the U.S. Congress and signed into law by the president in 2010. The changes are complex and take effect over a period of years, but among the major changes will be a mandate for individuals to purchase health insurance, as well as spending controls on Medicare. Further complicating the picture, Republican control of the House of Representatives after the 2010 elections had many in the party calling for the reform's repeal. However, hospitals and other industry stakeholders continue to plan on the new requirements taking effect.

Revenue Sources. In most countries, hospital revenues were generated primarily from government assistance or subsidies, third-party payers such as insurers, and self-paying patient fees. The AHA defined gross patient revenue as the amount a hospital would receive if all patients paid full "retail" charges. While this revenue was not an evaluation factor of a hospital's financial position, such revenues reflected the use of services across broad patient categories. For most hospitals, the era of liberal government revenues or subsidies had vanished. Fewer hospitals expected the windfall budget increases of the past and instead calculated using cost of living increases or other factors.

Several countries, including Canada, ensured equitable health care for all citizens by maintaining public health insurance that is provincially managed and financed by taxes. The insurance covered all residents and was the sole payer for hospital and physician care. Patients could freely choose their doctors and hospitals and incurred no out-of-pocket expenses. Many Americans considered this ideal, but the Health Insurance Association revealed that the behind-the-scenes workings of the Canadian system might indicate otherwise. For instance, patients in need of surgery generally had to endure long waiting periods. Coupled with the lack of private hospitals, many Canadians traveled to the United States for needed surgeries. Open health care access gave the appearance of equitable health care, but was considered by some to have contributed to waste due to the lack of controls.

Britain and France provided high-quality health care to all citizens through a national social security system, which in France covered all hospital and maternity expenses and about 80 percent of all other medical, pharmaceutical, and dental bills. In Britain, the National Health Service was supplemented by private medical insurance and hospitals, many of which were small facilities with fewer than 100 beds.

RESEARCH AND TECHNOLOGY

The benefits of advanced medical technology were well documented. However, for most hospitals, state-of-the-

art technology also strained the budget. The biggest problem was maintaining the latest high-tech equipment because obsolescence invariably followed each model. Expanded applications of laser technology accounted for progressive treatment in areas such as ophthalmology, plastic surgery, and general surgery. However, what is state-of-the-art one day may be superseded quickly by an improved version on the market the next day.

A compelling economic factor for hospitals in emergent countries was the application of increasingly rigid standards in the selection of equipment. Few developing countries created or manufactured their own technology. Due to their low economic standing, they could not afford to be lured by high-tech equipment that often led to a "technology trap" in which equipment remained unopened due to environmental conditions or lack of funds to train staff and buy maintenance parts. One study estimated overuse and inappropriate use of technology ranging from 30 to 70 percent in some locations. To ease the burden of equipment acquisition and maintenance, many hospitals maintained national and regional inventories for stockpiling equipment and spare parts. Obsolete equipment from hospitals in industrialized countries often became coveted advanced technology for developing countries.

In 2004, the federal budget for medical research in the United States was US$28.7 billion, an amount that had doubled since 1998. One study estimated that five percent annual inflation in health care costs was due to developments in medical science and technology, especially advances in genetic research that promoted the cure and control of debilitating and fatal diseases such as cystic fibrosis, multiple sclerosis, and AIDS. The Director General of the International Hospital Federation explained that biogenetic research offered potential treatment for 4,000 untreatable diseases. Patient and donor selection procedures for using some of these genetic advances introduced several ethical and practical dilemmas that had potential to cause hospitals costly litigation.

From the 1990s into the 2000s, almost every aspect of hospital management and treatment was affected by computer technology. Affordable prices and proven advantages had converted most hospital procedures to computerized functions. In many hospitals, patient records, which were once bulky and frequently illegible, were computerized and could be retrieved in seconds in a more comprehensible format.

However, although a number of medical centers had implemented electronic medical records systems (EMRS) over the years, most patient records continued to be stored on paper at a single location, according to *The Journal of the American Medical Association.* Paper records can result in crucial patient information like medical conditions, drug allergies, and electrocardiograms being inaccessible and illegible in an emergency as well as in a routine medical setting. At the beginning of the twenty-first century, the ethical, legal, and technical aspects of EMRS were being debated by physicians and hospital administrators; by the mid-2000s, a growing number of health systems were implementing EMRS technology; and by the late 2000s, concerns about health care costs and a desire to improve quality provided strong impetus to use EMRS. The global market for EMRS technology was projected to grow from US$4.4 billion in 2009 to US$10 billion in 2015.

By mid-2004, use of the Internet had resulted in significant savings for hospitals as improved operations managed materials. By automating and simplifying product selection, order placement, and contract management, employees were able to focus on meaningful endeavors. Automated systems also helped reduce errors, increase the number of transactions per employee, and shorten delivery and receiving times. In July 2004, *Hospital Materials Management* reported that 9 of the 31 hospitals using San Jose, California-based Neoforma's materials management system realized savings of US$500,000 or more by switching to Neoforma, with the remainder saving US$100,000. About 70 percent of the reported savings were expected to recur annually. In addition to Neoforma, the Global Healthcare Exchange (GHX) of Westminster, Colorado, was a leading player in health care e-commerce. The company claimed to have cut over US$1 billion in supply chain costs out of the health care industry between 2006 and 2010. It planned to cut US$5 billion more by 2015.

While many hospitals had basic Web sites that offered only basic information about the facility and its services, many began to realize the need for a more sophisticated Internet strategy. Some hospital Web sites had become interactive experiences for patients and doctors. Patients can log on to view and pay their medical bills, as well as track charges to their insurance providers. Some hospitals allow physicians to view clinical summaries online and sign their own transcribed reports electronically. They also have online access to a picture archiving and communications system that lets them view diagnostic images.

Another pressing issue for the hospital industry was related to waste disposal. In 2001, the American Hospital Association (AHA) launched the second phase of its Hospitals for a Healthy Environment (H2E) campaign to reduce the amount of chemical and hazardous waste

generated by AHA member hospitals. The overall goals of the campaign included the reduction of hazardous waste (and overall waste) 33 percent by 2005 and 50 percent by 2010. The WHO had taken up the cause and in 1999 released the first worldwide comprehensive guide on waste disposal, *Safe Management Wastes from Health-Care Activities.* Aimed at hospital management, policy makers, public health professionals, and others, it detailed the importance of waste minimization, recycling, disposal options, handling, and training in regard to chemicals, syringes, vaccine waste, radioactive waste, incineration, and more.

WORKFORCE

The U.S. Bureau of Labor Statistics reported that the health care sector would generate 3.2 million new jobs between 2008 and 2018, more than any other sector of the U.S. economy, largely because the elderly population was expected to grow rapidly as the "baby boom" generation begins entering old age. While hospitals make up a small percentage of health care establishments, about one percent, they employ some 35 percent of health care workers. Seventy-two percent of hospital workers worked in establishments with over 1,000 workers. In the aggregate, hospitals employed some 5.7 million people in 2008, and this was expected to grow 10.1 percent by 2018, slower than the expected growth of health care overall. With hospitals seeking to deliver services more efficiently, care continues to shift to outpatient care as much as practicable.

In 2010, the shortage of hospital workers, particularly nurses, continued to increase based on a number of factors. Employment options for health care professionals expanded in the early twenty-first century, and salaries for some professions were significantly higher outside hospitals. For example, chain drug stores and superstores were able to lure pharmacists with much higher wages than hospitals offered. The labor shortage manifested a vicious cycle of stressors, especially for registered nurses, who often had to work under significant pressure to pick up the slack from job vacancies.

Observers became concerned about the extra-long hours nurses and nursing assistants were working in the nation's hospitals. Amid continued staffing shortages, many facilities permitted or even mandated that their nursing staff work more than 12 hours per day. According to the *New York Times,* a report issued by the National Academy of Sciences' Institute of Medicine stated that "Long work hours pose one of the most serious threats to patient safety, because fatigue slows reaction time, decreases energy, diminishes attention to detail, and otherwise contributes to errors." The report recommended that patient safety could be served if the staff limited its work hours to no more than 60 hours per week, and 12 hours or less of any 24-hour period.

The aging labor force was another contributing factor to the nursing shortage. For example, in 2000, the average age for a registered nurse was 43.3 years. By 2010 the majority of nurses was expected to be 50 to 60 years old, and the workforce was projected to decrease as nurses began to retire. By 2020, when baby boomers will be in their late sixties and seventies and require more health care than ever, the number of working registered nurses was expected to plummet to almost 20 percent below the number needed.

Hospitals were trying a variety of creative strategies to attract new employees, such as signing bonuses, comprehensive employee benefits, flexible schedules, and tuition reimbursement. Hospitals had also tried to increase salaries. Nevertheless, changing the work structure, improving the workplace environment, and discovering new pools of potential employees were some of the long-term goals that were expected to continue to challenge the hospital industry.

Earnings in hospitals varied widely, since different positions can require greatly different levels of education and training. On average, nonsupervisory hospital workers earned US$23.99 per hour in 2008. This was higher than the average for all private industries.

INDUSTRY LEADERS

HCA Inc. With 163 hospitals and 105 outpatient surgery centers in 2010, Hospital Corporation of America (HCA) had facilities in 20 U.S. states and in London, England. Based in Nashville, Tennessee, HCA cut expenses and reduced operations in response to increased costs and declines in reimbursement rates. The company faced fraud charges regarding over-billing and suffered through investigations and lawsuits. In 2003, revenues totaled US$21.8 billion, with a one-year sales growth of 10.5 percent, while net income rose almost 60 percent to US$1.3 billion. HCA Inc. employed about 242,000 people in 2003, up from 174,000 in 2001. HCA underwent a leveraged buyout in 2006 and was no longer publicly traded. By 2009, the company reported revenue of US$30.1 billion.

Ascension Health. The Ascension Health network of hospitals was established in 1999 when the Sisters of St. Joseph Health System and the Daughters of Charity National Health System merged. Headquartered in St. Louis, Ascension was the biggest not-for-profit health care system in the United States and third largest overall. Facilities included Roman Catholic general acute-care hospitals, long-term health care centers, and rehabilitation hospitals and psychiatric hospitals. In addition, Ascension operated hospitals under joint venture agreements, mostly in the Northeast, Midwest, and South United States. Altogether, Ascension operated more than 500 facilities in 20 U.S. states and the District of Columbia. Ascension's governing board had several clergy members, but a non-clergy CEO headed the firm as of 2010. The network delivered US$1.1 billion worth of unpaid charity care in 2009 and had more than 113,000 associates.

Catholic Health Initiatives. The Catholic Health Initiatives was a not-for-profit health network formed by the consolidation of four Roman Catholic health care systems: Sisters of Charity of Nazareth Health Care System of Bardstown, Kentucky; Catholic Health Corporation of Omaha, Nebraska; Sisters of Charity Health Care Systems of Cincinnati; and Franciscan Health System of Aston, Pennsylvania. Headquartered in Denver, Colorado, Catholic Health Initiatives' facilities included 73 hospitals; 40 assisted-living, long-term care, and residential facilities; and two community-based health organizations. In fiscal 2010, revenues totaled approximately US$9 billion, and the organization provided some US$590 million in charity care and community benefit.

Tenet Healthcare Corp. Although Tenet Healthcare was one of the United States' largest hospital chains, decreased Medicare funding had caused it to shut its medical practice management business and sell some other facilities to reduce costs. In 2005, the chain included 74 acute-care hospitals in 13 states after selling 12 of its hospitals and closing two others. In addition, the company sold the one foreign hospital it held in Madrid, Spain, in 2004. Tenet's subsidiaries included operations in HMOs, clinics, outpatient surgery centers, and home health care programs. Following reorganization, revenues in 2004 were US$9.9 billion, down from more than US$13.2 billion in 2003. The number of employees dropped from close to 110,000 in 2003 to 75,743 in 2004. In 2010 Tenet employed approximately 57,000 people. Net operating revenues for 2009 were US$9 billion.

General Healthcare Group Ltd. The leading private health care provider in the United Kingdom, General Healthcare had operated about 57 acute-care hospitals through its BMI Healthcare division. The company also had operated hospitals on behalf of the National Health Service (NHS). In 2010, it reported 9,200 employees.

MAJOR COUNTRIES IN
THE INDUSTRY

United States. Hawaii Health Systems Corp. announced layoffs, an end to physician recruitment, and limited on-call services at its network of public hospitals in response to a US$62 million deficit. However, reductions had to be approved by the state legislature, which created a joint task force to investigate the situation. The Hawaii Health System, which is the fourth largest public hospital system in the United States, is responsible for 14 public hospitals that employ 4,200 with 800 affiliated doctors, generating approximately US$65 million.

Several hospitals in Metropolitan Detroit, Michigan, also reported declines in 2007. The number of unpaid medical bills, combined with decreases in investment income, had a strong impact on hospital profits during a slowdown in the economy. "When the economy goes down, everybody feels it, including hospitals," said Dean Smith, a public health professor at the University of Michigan. The three largest hospital systems in the Detroit area were Oakwood Health, the Detroit Medical Center, and Henry Ford Health System, all of which reported decreased gains in 2007. Much of the drop was due to a 42 percent increase in bad debt and unpaid bills.

In California, 1,002 cases of serious medical harm were reported between July 2007 and May 2008 in conjunction with a state law that required disclosure of substantial injuries to patients. Injuries included severe bedsores and foreign objects like surgical equipment being left in patient's bodies. In addition, in many cases, wrong procedures were performed, and doctors operated on the wrong part of the body or on the wrong person. California reported fewer emergency rooms per capita than any other state.

The sea change confronting the industry in 2010 was the coming implementation, in stages, of the new health care reforms. Even this was uncertain, since Republicans, energized by victories in the 2010 elections, began calls for the reform's repeal. At the state level, governors and commissioners were working on the structure of state exchanges where residents would shop for insurance starting in 2014. How such details of the law would be worked out remains uncertain.

United Kingdom. The United Kingdom's National Health Service (NHS) was based on a system of health care services funded by the public and organized through public trusts. All British citizens and residents had access to health care with some services requiring modest fees. The United Kingdom also had a number of private hospitals not affiliated with the NHS.

According to World Health Organization (WHO) data released in 2010, health expenditures in the United Kingdom were US$3,867 per capita in 2007, up from US$1,769 in 2000.

In July 2004, the NHS reported that it had increased the number of doctors and nurses it employed in order to reduce waiting times for patients and take a more proactive approach to treatment. In 2000, the NHS announced that it planned to add 2,000 general practitioners to its ranks by 2004, but exceeded the target and added 2,660. By adding about 10,000 nurses in late 2003 and early 2004, the NHS was well on its way to meeting a goal to add 25,000 nurses by 2008. The NHS planned to add 1,000 oncologists by 2006 and had surpassed previously established targets for cardiologists and cardiothoracic surgeons by early 2004.

News Wales reported that the U.K. Health Minister Edwina Hart announced an investment of 100 million pounds was being made in new hospital buildings and equipment in honor of the NHS's 60th anniversary. Plans included a new 128-bed hospital in Mountain Ash, with a 16-chair dentistry facility providing NHS treatment for up to 10,000 people. In addition, new Mountain Ash and Aberdare primary care centers would be built, as well as other new and renovated medical centers.

Spain. Spain's strong economy, political stability, and low unemployment rate had contributed to significant improvements in the country's health care system, according to *Modern Healthcare International.* Spain's primary care infrastructure was well organized and offered medical care to all 41 million of Spain's population free of direct charge. Roughly 90 percent of Spain's health care budget was financed by general taxes. This monetary amount funded 750 public hospitals, insured most of the country's 40 million people, and provided medical education. Revenues from social security funded the rest of the system. Spain has a large quantity of physicians, with 4.1 per 1,000 patients. By contrast, there were 3.1 physicians per 1,000 patients in the United States and three physicians per 1,000 patients within the European Union. Most doctors worked approximately 24 hours per week in the public health care system, and earned less than US$50,000 annually. Many supplemented their income by also working in private practices.

Spain also had a robust private health care system. Approximately 6 million residents had private insurance, and another 4 million purchased supplemental coverage from private insurers. The country had 142 privately owned hospitals. According to WHO data, Spain's per capita health care spending was US$2,712 in 2007, up from US$1,036 in 2000. About 28.7 percent of the total expenditure on health was private.

Canada. In the early 1990s, many hospitals in Canada merged, were downsized, or shut due to cutbacks, according to *Modern Healthcare International.*. The number of Canadian hospital beds had suffered a significant decline. In 1991, there were 1,128 public hospitals and 175,376 beds, and by 1999, there were only 877 public hospitals with 122,006 beds. Hospitals were the most expensive part of Canada's health care system and accounted for approximately 33 percent of the total health care budget. Because hospitals were receiving reduced public funds, Canada was moving toward privatization in ways that did not violate the country's laws governing health care institutions funded by public monies. Some hospitals were turning their lobbies into shopping areas, while others were establishing food franchises on their campuses. Others were looking into e-health services on the Internet where patients could have a diagnostic test performed in their own country, but have it read by a Canadian doctor for a fee. According to the WHO, health expenditures in Canada were US$4,409 in 2007, having risen from US$2,082 in 2000. About 30.1 percent of the total spent on health care was private.

China. In 2010, the WHO reported that health expenditures in China were US$108 in 2007, up from US$43 in 2000. About 55.3 percent of the total health care expenditures came from private funds in 2007, down from 61.3 percent in 2000. By the end of the twentieth century, China had 311,000 hospitals, clinics, health care centers, disease prevention agencies, research institutes, and medical schools, compared to 314,100 in 1998, according to the country's Ministry of Health. In 1999, the number of workers in the health care system numbered 5.57 million, an increase of approximately 35,000 from 1998. There were 239 hospital beds, 167 physicians, and 102 nurses per 100,000 residents. About 80 percent of the health budget was allocated to major urban hospitals. However, 69 percent of the total population in China lived in rural areas, and growth of basic health care services for these citizens had been slow due to the lack of investment. Approximately 50 million Chinese citizens were hospitalized in 1999, and clinics and hospitals served about 2.08 billion patients. In 2010, China began a public hospital reform project in 16 cities to promote funding of public hospitals and training of medical staff.

France. The WHO's 2005 analysis of health care systems in the major countries of the world ranked France as having the best system, followed by Italy, Spain,

Oman, Austria, and Japan. *The Irish Times* reported that France had eliminated waiting time by adding over-capacity to its health care system. The country's number of acute-care beds was higher than the European average, and rates for bed occupancy were approximately 75 percent. France's social security system, which was established in the 1940s, funded the health care system. Social insurance was compulsory in France and covered nearly 100 percent of the population. France's hospitals are public as well as private. Hospital physicians' salaries range from FFr295,000 to FFr535,000. Doctors could offer private practice services in public hospitals for up to 20 percent of their work week. The WHO reported that health expenditures in France were US$4,627 in 2007, having risen from US$2,256 in 2000. About 21 percent of the total spent on health care was from private funds.

Because the French work week had decreased from 39 to 35 hours beginning in 2002, public hospitals were expected to create 45,000 new jobs by 2005. Beginning in June 2000, the French government gave public hospitals over US$4.1 billion to create jobs and improve working conditions and salaries for nurses. The country's 1,300 private hospitals and clinics, concerned that many nurses would leave to work in public hospitals, considered this unfair competition. As a result, they had requested the government pay them with some FFr6 billion in funds.

BIBLIOGRAPHY
"100 Million for Welsh Hospitals," 2 July 2008. Available from GoHolidays.net News Wales.

"About Ascension Health." Ascension Health, 11 November 2010. Available from http://www.ascensionhealth.org.

"About GHX." GHX, 11 November 2010. Available from http://www.ghx.com.

"About Us," General Healthcare Group, 11 November 2010. Available from http://www.generalhealthcare.co.uk.

"About VA," U.S. Department of Veterans Affairs, 11 November 2010. Available from http://www.va.gov.

Annual Survey of Hospitals. Chicago: American Hospital Association, 2005.

"Career Guide to Industries: Healthcare." U.S. Department of Labor, Bureau of Labor Statistics, 2010-2011. Available from http://www.bls.gov.

Catholic Health Initiatives. Available from http://www.catholic healthinit.org.

"China builds 5,000 more public hospitals in 30 years: ministry," *People's Daily* Online, 10 November 2010. Available from english.people.com.cn.

"Corporate Profile," HCA Healthcare, 11 November 2010. Available from http://www.hcahealthcare.com.

Crowther, Bruce. "Inside Healthcare: Reasons behind hospital building boom." *Chicago Tribune Local: Arlington Heights,* 3 November 2010. Available from triblocal.com.

DePledge, Derrick. "With $62M Deficit, Hospitals to Cut Jobs." *Honolulu Advertiser,* 1 July 2008. Available from http://www.honoluluadvertiser.com.

DeWidt, Lynda. "Community Has Been Named Nation's Most Wired Hospital Network." *Indianapolis Star,* 16 July 2008. Available from Indystar.com.

"Fast Facts." Catholic Health Association of the United States, 11 November 2010. Available from http://www.chausa.org.

"Fast Facts on U.S. Hospitals." *Hospital Statistics.* Chicago: American Hospital Association, 2008.

"Health Care Spending by Country, State and Payer." *Center for Healthcare Research & Transformation,* 14 December 2009. Available from http://www.chrt.org.

Hospitals Closing Doors to Patients. *Independent Television News Limited,* 1 July 2008.

Johnson, Avery, and Peter Loftus. "Health-Care Industry Still Braces for Change." *Wall Street Journal,* 4 November 2010.

"Medical Liability Crisis Affects Communities' Access to Care." Chicago: American Hospital Association. 28 April 2003. Available from http://www.aha.org.

"National Health Expenditure Data." U.S. Department of Health & Human Services, 11 November 2010. Available from http://www.cms.gov.

"Patients Rank Physicians High in Satisfaction Survey." *Modern Healthcare,* 29 March 2004.

Rau, Jordan. "Serious Patient Errors at California Hospitals Disclosed in State Filings." *The Los Angeles Times,* 30 June 2008.

Rogers, Christina. "Poor Economy Hits Hospitals." *The Detroit News,* 12 June 2008.

Wallace, Natasha. "Hospitals Choked with Admissions." *The Age* (Melbourne, Australia), 1 July 2008. Available from http://www.theage.com.au..

World Health Statistics 2010. Geneva, Switzerland: The World Health Organization, 2010. Available from http://www.who.int.

"Worldwide Electronic Medical Records (EMR) Market To Be US$9,957 Million By 2015." *Medical News Today,* 11 November 2010. Available from http://www.medicalnewstoday.com.

SIC 3851

OPHTHALMIC GOODS

NAICS CODE(S)

339115. Optical goods manufacturers produce a variety of corrective eyewear, implants, and eye-care supplies. Common examples of industry output include eyeglasses, spectacles, contact lenses, sunglasses, and lens cleaning solutions.

INDUSTRY SNAPSHOT

The global optical goods industry was characterized by steady net demand for most of its products and frequent upgrades to the materials and technologies used in production. Vision impairment occurred at fairly predictable rates in human populations. Residents of affluent countries were more likely to seek corrective lenses or surgeries when compared to people who lived in developing countries. In the United States, macular degeneration, a condition in which part of the retina becomes scarred, was the number one cause of eyesight loss. The number of macular degeneration cases was expected to double during the next 25 years. Two important factors led industry experts to predict increased demand for ophthalmic goods and services in the future: the continual rise of diagnosed cases of diabetes and the aging of the baby boomer generation.

Demand for particular products within the world's optical goods markets was not always even, however. Both eyeglasses and contacts were subject to fashion trends and enhancements in comfort or other features that rendered older eyewear less appealing to some consumers. For example, in the United States and Western Europe there was a pronounced trend toward disposable contacts, which were considered more comfortable, convenient, and sometimes cheaper than longer-lasting rigid lenses. In most markets, eyeglasses changed substantially so that newer models were lighter weight, thinner, more durable, and more varied in frame styles.

Other industry products were subject to greater fluctuations. Sunglasses, in particular, faced more volatile demand because they are not as essential to vision as corrective lenses. Also, the underlying technology in most sunglasses was much less sophisticated than that of prescription eyewear. Thus, the low-end sunglasses trade was a commodity market.

In order to increase sales for their spectacles and sunglasses, designers sought to make their creations stand out in special ways. Some stuck with innovative applications of their own logo. Others, however, tapped into house motifs to gain new customers from the ranks of people who wanted to show off their brand loyalty. Instead of choosing to wear easily-distinguishable Christian Dior glasses, a fashionable consumer might select glasses with Tom Ford's discreet metal T set flush to the temple. The 2007 Coach collection included glasses designed to complement popular handbags. Eyewear designer Alain Mikli used shapes, colors, and distinctive materials to establish brand recognition for his line.

Solutions used to clean contact lenses could be easily interchanged among different brands and, in some cases, different formulations. Coinciding with the rise of disposable lenses, the trend in Europe and the United States was toward multipurpose solutions that perform all necessary sanitizing actions on lenses rather than using separate solutions for each task.

The ophthalmic goods industry was thoroughly internationalized, particularly among the developed nations. World market leaders in various product categories included France, Italy, Switzerland, and the United States. In the mid-2000s nearly 100 million people wore contact lenses, and an estimated 1.5 billion people wore corrective lenses in 2005. As documented in Ellisor's *2004 Annual Report,* by 2025 almost one-third of the world's total population will be over the age of 45, most of whom will need corrective lenses as a natural result of aging. The best growth was being realized in the markets for plastic, polycarbonate, and high-index lenses.

The spectacles market experienced a short-term increase in sales with an estimated 8.9 million units in 2006. That reflected an increase of 4 percent from March 2005 to March 2006. Prescribed spectacle lenses and frames continued to be the most popular, accounting for 90 percent of total market share value.

Beyond traditional sales outlets, eye glass wearers were faced with a sometimes controversial alternative choice. Several online contact lenses suppliers were prepared to sell the product without checking to see whether consumers had valid prescriptions. This was the major finding when *Optician* conducted a mystery shopping exercise in 2007. There were 65 calls made to an assortment of online suppliers. The caller expressed an interest in ordering daily disposable lenses based on details read during the conversation. A small number of companies agreed to do this and four orders for contact lenses were made and completed to double check that no valid prescription was required during any phase of the ordering process. Companies willing to do this were located in both the United States and the United Kingdom.

ORGANIZATION AND STRUCTURE

The ophthalmic goods industry was a labor-intensive industry populated by numerous smaller, specialized companies churning out everything from sunglasses and safety goggles to shooting glasses and lorgnettes. In 1989, 68 percent of U.S. companies in this industry had fewer than 20 employees. In Canada, the figure was closer to 75 percent. While these smaller companies were engaged exclusively in the production of ophthalmic goods, industry giants such as Bausch & Lomb typically manufactured a wider array of goods including medicines, dental products, and optical goods.

The labor-intensive nature of the ophthalmic goods industry attracted countries with large pools of low-wage labor such as China and Taiwan. By 1992 East Asia had become a leading supplier of low-end sunglasses and

vanity glasses, accounting for 32.8 percent of total ophthalmic goods imported by the United States—just a few points shy of the 35.3 percent share held by the European Union. The European Union—besides being a major producer of glasses and contact lenses—dominated the market for designer frames. Japan was another leading producer of ophthalmic goods, and was the world's largest exporter of optical equipment throughout the 1990s. Other leading exporters included, in descending order, the United States, Italy, Germany, France, and China.

Products manufactured by the ophthalmic goods industry ranged from low-cost nonprescription sunglasses to highly sophisticated prescription contact lenses. Some products could be purchased from street vendors; others were only available from qualified optometrists and ophthalmologists. Frames and sunglasses accounted for the bulk of world production of ophthalmic goods. Sunglasses, in particular, attracted a broad spectrum of users and were available in both prescription and nonprescription forms. Technically, sunglasses were supposed to block a portion of sunlight from entering the eyes and protect them from ultraviolet (UV) radiation, which can damage the lens and the retina. The amount of protection sunglasses actually afford depends on the color and the depth of the tint. In practice, however, many sunglasses were little more than fashion accessories, affording little or no protection to the eyes. Growing consumer awareness prompted competition among high-end sunglasses manufacturers to produce more effective UV protection and resulted in the introduction of a new labeling system on some sunglasses telling consumers what percentage of ultraviolet light was blocked. Other types of glasses popular among prescription users included photochromic glasses; these contained tinted lenses that became darker in bright sunlight and lighter in a dark room.

Beginning in the 1980s, manufacturers of ophthalmic goods sought to broaden the market by encouraging consumers to treat eyewear both as medical devices and jewelry. Industry advertising heavily promoted both sunglasses and prescription glasses as fashion accessories. Ads such as Bausch & Lomb's "Take a good look" for its line of Ray-Ban sunglasses and L.A. Eyeworks' "A face is like a work of art. It deserves a great frame." spurred new growth in the market. People who might once have owned only one pair of glasses now needed a different pair for every occasion. Discount vendors sprang up in North America, Japan, and Europe offering consumers a huge variety of frames from which to choose. Growth in this area was substantial throughout the 1980s, with an estimated five out of six vision-impaired Americans still preferring eyeglasses to contact lenses.

In spite of the fact that contact lenses were much less commonly used worldwide than glasses, they were a tremendous source of revenue for the ophthalmic goods industry and a primary source of income for companies such as Bausch & Lomb, Allergan, and CIBA-Vision. Much of the value of contact lenses was derived from the need to replace them more frequently than glasses and from secondary products such as cleaning solutions. The U.S. market for contact lenses was estimated at US$2 billion in 1994, with an estimated 25 million contact lens wearers—76 percent of whom used soft lenses. Though effective in correcting most common vision problems such as myopia (near-sightedness) and hyperopia (far-sightedness), contact lenses had yet to supplant standard eyeglasses. As Ilene Springer pointed out in *Cosmopolitan,* "only about 50 percent of would-be wearers do well the first time lens meets eye. 'Dry eyes,' allergies, unusually shaped corneas, recurring infections, and hypersensitivity can make fittings difficult, sometimes impossible, almost always expensive." Once fitted, contact lenses—even extended-wear lenses—require regular maintenance and periodic replacement. Daily-wear soft lenses—the most popular—could be damaged easily and did not provide as clear vision as glasses or the less popular hard contact lenses. Although providing better vision and capable of correcting even severe astigmatism, hard contacts tended to irritate the eyes and popped out easily. More sophisticated lenses, such as extended-wear rigid gas-permeable lenses, solved many of these problems but were too expensive to attract a large market. Despite their limitations, contact lenses, particularly disposables, remained a high-growth item entering the late 1990s.

Other products manufactured by the ophthalmic goods industry included safety, industrial, and underwater goggles or glasses made of special shatterproof, impact-resistant materials such as polycarbonate and tinted yellow, vermilion, or orange for enhanced visibility.

BACKGROUND AND DEVELOPMENT

Eye problems have been a common cause of human disability since time immemorial. When all secondary causes—such as infectious disease and malnutrition—are removed, the most common eye problems are errors in refraction that are usually caused by defective genes. While humans have attempted to cure these problems for millennia, the development of devices to correct or enhance vision is fairly recent. No one knows exactly when or where eyeglasses were developed, however, Roger Bacon—a thirteenth century English scholastic philosopher—is sometimes credited with their invention. Whatever the case, spectacles had become quite common among the wealthy by the fifteenth century; and by the nineteenth century, advances in optics technology and

the introduction of large-scale manufacturing spread them among the general population in Europe and America. Although early spectacles consisted of little more than a pair of crude magnifying lenses in a wire frame, scientific advances in the nineteenth century spurred not only the development of more sophisticated lenses but increasing sophistication in ophthalmologic diagnosis. By the end of the nineteenth century, lenses were being customized to correct the particular problems of individual wearers and the rise of the modern ophthalmic industry had begun. Early innovators included John Jacob Bausch who, together with Henry Lomb, ran a small American company that imported European optical goods. Bausch invented Vulcanite (a hard rubber) eyeglass frames, which were more durable than the wire and metal frames of the day. Fitting the new frames with lenses from Europe, Bausch and Lomb quickly became leaders in the young American ophthalmic goods industry.

More sophisticated testing techniques and rising populations helped assure the industry's continuous growth through the first half of the twentieth century. While eyeglasses were the most important single product, contact lenses were already coming into popular use in the late 1930s. These early contact lenses were known as scleral lenses. Covering almost the entire surface of the eye, they interfered with the movement of tears over the eyeball and had to be used in conjunction with an artificial tear solution. The inconvenience and discomfort of these early lenses proved unattractive to consumers and even as late as the 1960s, companies such as Bausch & Lomb saw no advantage in entering the contact lens market.

In the late 1940s, another type of contact lenses—corneal lenses—was introduced. These covered a smaller portion of the eye surface and floated on the eye's own layer of tears. Originally made of hard plastic, they had to be removed and sterilized daily. By the 1950s, these lenses had been refined enough to make them a genuine alternative to conventional corrective eyewear—despite their high cost and the discomfort they caused. At the same time eye examinations were becoming more common in developed nations, resulting in higher demand for corrective eyewear. These factors led to unprecedented growth in production and sales in the ophthalmic goods industry during the 1960s.

By 1960 annual sales of contact lenses had reached US$60 million in the United States, and hundreds of small companies jumped into the market. At about US$200 a pair, however, they were priced too high for the average consumer. More than half of those who tried them found them uncomfortable and reverted back to conventional corrective eyewear. Nevertheless, the development of this new market created enormous excitement, leading to a flurry of false advertising complaints and acrimonious patent disputes.

Meanwhile, as the contact lens market endured its growing pains, sales of conventional frames and lenses skyrocketed. Much of this growth was attributed to the overall buoyancy of the world economy, rising disposable incomes, and most importantly, to the increasing numbers of people undergoing complete eye examinations—a trend begun in the 1950s and fostered by the postwar introduction of national health plans throughout the industrialized world. In the United States, the number of corrective lens wearers grew by 30 percent between 1955 and 1965. Sales of ophthalmic goods were also facilitated by new product developments such as a new bifocal lens without a visible line separating each half of the lens; and lightweight, shatterproof plastic lenses.

Sunglasses also enjoyed record growth in the 1960s, with sales nearly tripling between 1960 and 1966. No longer just a practical device to protect the eyes from the summer sun, sunglasses became a year-round fashion accessory—especially in the huge youth market. Dominated by companies such as Bausch & Lomb, whose Ray-Ban sunglasses (first introduced to the public in 1936) were *de riguer* for the truly fashionable, the sunglasses market became one of the most lucrative in the ophthalmic goods industry by the end of the decade.

However, the most notable development of the 1960s—the invention of soft contact lenses—did not make its impact felt until 1972. Made from a thin, soft plastic invented in 1960 by two Czechoslovakian scientists, soft contact lenses were flexible, water absorbent, and highly gas-permeable. Because this permeability allowed sufficient oxygen to reach the cornea soft contact lenses could be worn comfortably for longer periods of time than the hard hydrophobic lenses then in use. In 1966 Bausch & Lomb acquired the exclusive rights to market and manufacture this new lens material, and by 1971 had received U.S. Food and Drug Administration (FDA) approval to sell its soft contact lenses. Although expensive, the new lenses were an immediate success, generating enough sales to vault the company into the Fortune 500 and make it the world's leading manufacturer of contact lenses—a position it still held in the 1990s.

Rapid expansion of the ophthalmic goods market continued through the 1970s, encouraged by the introduction of the new soft contact lenses and continuing population growth. At the same time, competition intensified as countries such as Japan entered the market delivering high volumes of low-cost, high-quality frames, lenses, and sunglasses. Sunglasses were such a lucrative business that hundreds of companies around the world jumped into the market attaching the names of well-known fashion designers to products and furthering the establishment of sunglasses as a fashion accessory. So successful was this strategy that conventional frames soon had "designers" as well, and the range of styles proliferated. As competition heated up, pricing strategies became of paramount importance and many companies began moving from labor-intensive manufacturing operations to low-cost offshore locations.

In the 1980s, sales in the ophthalmic goods industry continued to climb at a prodigious rate. Despite a disappointing slump in sales of sunglasses in the early part of the decade, they quickly regained their market thanks to the popularity of films like *Top Gun* and *Risky Business,* in which well-known actor Tom Cruise was featured wearing sunglasses. Retail sales of sunglasses in the United States increased by 100 percent from 1980 to 1990 and similar increases were seen in other developed countries.

The real story of the 1980s was the rising popularity of contact lenses. Falling prices and advances in soft lens technology fueled explosive growth in this category. While consumer options were limited to hard lenses vs. soft at the beginning of the decade, by 1988 they could select from a wide assortment of standard and specialty contacts, including extended wear lenses, dirt-resistant lenses, more comfortable hard lenses, color-changing lenses, and bifocal lenses. The year 1988 also saw initial test marketing of disposable lenses that eliminated cleaning altogether. The number of wearers—21 million in the United States in 1988—was more than twice what it had been a decade earlier. In the space of only five years, companies such as Bausch & Lomb saw sales more than double from US$584 million in 1984 to more than US$1.2 billion in 1989.

According to Tony Montini, senior vice president of purchasing and merchandising at U.S. pharmaceutical chain Reliable Drug Stores, the ophthalmic goods market was one of the most volatile categories of the 1980s. Quoted in *Chain Drug Review,* he argued that the market had become so overheated that once it reached a certain level it could no longer sustain the kinds of increases it had been enjoying. From 1988 to 1995, increases in the number of contact lens wearers in the United States started to taper off, settling at around 25 million in 1992. At the same time, new product introductions waned and competition within the industry began to focus more on encouraging existing users and wearers of eyeglasses to switch to the new disposable lenses—a category whose steady replacement rate made it look like the product of the future. In addition, medical risks associated with extended-wear lenses were expected to boost demand for disposable lenses.

Stagnant growth in the market and intense competition led to some bizarre strategies. For instance, in 1994 Bausch & Lomb was marketing the exact same contact lens in four different ways—as "daily wear," "planned replacement," extended-wear disposables, and one-day disposables. The lenses were priced at US$70, US$15, US$8, and US$3, respectively, but the only difference between the lenses was in cost and use—not material. The company's justification for the price differences was that it hoped to lure people away from eyeglasses by making the more-convenient disposables affordable.

As countries emerged from the recession in 1993, growth in the ophthalmic goods industry showed few signs of picking up where it left off in 1989. From an average annual growth rate of 10 percent through 1989, it had fallen below 2 percent in 1991 and remained between 2 and 3 percent for the next few years. Forecasts for the remainder of the decade put growth at about 3 percent annually. Faced with a glut of sunglasses manufacturers and a mature, low-margin contact lens market, industry leaders diversified into other lines of health products and placed increased emphasis on various contact lens care products. In the contact lens market hopes remained that emerging demand for disposable and colored/tinted contact lenses would provide a new growth area. Also on the horizon was an anticipated increase in the demand for multifocal lenses generated by the rapidly rising number of older people living in developed nations. Perhaps the best news was for U.S. manufacturers, whose dominance of the contact lens market was expected to continue thanks to U.S. advances in contact lenses and polycarbonate and high-index plastic lens materials.

In the eyeglass lens market, increased demand for the new lighter and thinner polycarbonate and high-index plastic lenses was expected to help fuel new growth. Demand for scratch-resistant and ultraviolet-resistant lens coatings—heavily promoted by opticians—was also expected to rise. Additionally, pending FDA requirements that all general-purpose and cosmetic-use sunglasses block 99 percent of certain levels of ultraviolet radiation were expected to have a significant impact on the ophthalmic market—possibly weeding out the current surfeit of manufacturers and stimulating new demand.

CURRENT CONDITIONS

The value of ophthalmic goods imported into the U.S. in 2008 equaled approximately 50 percent of U.S. production, according to the "Ophthalmic Goods Manufacturing Industry in the U.S. and its International Trade" report. The Opthalmic Goods industry had an export rate of approximately 30 percent of U.S. production. Findings also reflected a consistent "large dependency on personal consumption" severely impacted by "recessionary effects."

Shipment values for the ophthalmic goods industry totaled US$4.25 billion in 2002. At US$1.89 billion,

contact lenses were by far the largest product category, followed by other ophthalmic goods and prescription ground eyeglass lenses (US$1.22 billion), ophthalmic plastics focal lenses (US$576.01 million), ophthalmic glass focal lenses (US$65.8 million), and ophthalmic fronts and temples (US$42.36 million).

The United States was the world's largest market for optical goods and is also a major producer. In 2003, the size of the U.S. market for ophthalmic goods was approximately US$25.6 billion, up more than US$2 billion from 2002. The United States exported more than US$1 billion. Exports increased every year since the late 1990s, growing 6.8 percent and 8.5 percent in 2000 and 2001, respectively. With the exception of a 1.1 percent decline in 2001, U.S. imports also have increased every year since the late 1990s. In 2002, imports totaled US$2.0 billion, up from US$1.9 billion in 2001.

According to U.S. Census Bureau data released in August 2004, the U.S. ophthalmic goods industry consisted of 559 establishments (488 companies) in 2002, down from 573 in 1997. Nearly 31 percent of industry establishments employed 20 people or more. However, small firms were dominant, with nearly 44 percent of establishments employing 1 to 4 employees.

By the end of 2003, *Ophthalmology Times* estimated the number of consumers wearing contacts lenses at 100 million, or around 5 percent of all who use corrective lenses. Due to ongoing improvements in convenience and comfort, significant growth was expected for the contact lens market during the late 2000s. Midway through the decade, market share for products such as one-day disposable lenses was growing by double-digit rates. Also gaining market share in Asia and Europe were progressive contact lenses, which replaced bifocals and trifocals.

By 2007 glasses were being widely worn as popular fashion accessories. Many people had "wardrobes of glasses" to carry them from day to late night. Instead of small and metal frames, colorful and larger alternatives were in again. Marisa Fox noted that many people were influenced by red glasses worn by the TV hit show title character called Ugly Betty. Others chose plastic frames, glasses with thick temples, or some with decorative accents. Costs for a single pair could range from US$49 to US$800 and beyond.

Making the decision to get amber colored contacts to look like characters in the movie Twilight could be one with long-lasting impact, according to Michigan Optometrists. Many teens are acquiring the lenses without getting prescriptions. Decorative lenses are classified as a medical devise and regulated by the U.S. Food and Drug Administration, but they are constantly marketed and sold directly to consumers through a variety of stores and outlets. When contacts are not properly fitted and distributed by professionals, users risk severe eye problems and vision damage. Related factors may be not obtaining correct wearing and cleaning instructions. The Michigan Optometric Association, in its "tips for decorative contact wearers" cautioned users to be aware that wearing the products may impair night vision and they should never be shared with others.

RESEARCH AND TECHNOLOGY

Research and development in ophthalmic goods continued to make strides in the development of new lens materials for both eyeglasses and contact lenses. Plastic lenses—first introduced for eyeglasses in the 1960s—became extraordinarily light, strong, and impact-resistant by the 1990s. New compounds such as high-index plastics and polycarbonate lens materials were developed in the United States. These materials were shatterproof, yet light and affordable. However, because glass and C-39 plastic were easier to work with and less likely to be damaged in manufacturing processes than polycarbonates, the market was limited to sports, industrial applications, and children's eyeglasses. In the early 1990s, development of new computer-controlled molding injection processes overcame these problems and put polycarbonates on equal footing with the more commonly used glass and C-39 plastic. Eventually, polycarbonates were expected to replace existing materials altogether.

One of the most prominent developments in the contact lens field was aspheric lenses. Because they were flatter than conventional spherical lenses, they afforded more comfort and better vision. New polymer blends enabled the development of a lens material that lets oxygen pass through 25 times better than existing contact lenses. Several research groups were also working on producing lenses made of siloxane, a silicone-oxygen compound that produces strong, flexible films.

Research studies involving young subjects have shown children in elementary school can handle their contacts properly without any increase in complications. In fact, 8- to 11-year olds tended to be more responsible users when compared to most teenagers. Modern advances made contacts more comfortable and easier to keep clean. Consequently, eye experts were more willing to prescribe contacts for young people.

Clinical research, conducted among contact lens wearers, demonstrated that daily-wear silicone hydrogel contact lenses can improve comfort significantly versus hydrogel lenses in most surroundings. The research also revealed that newer, second-generation silicone hydrogels made from senofilcon A and galyficon A significantly reduced the frequency of commonly reported ocular surface symptoms. Those symptoms included dryness and discomfort in adverse environments and during visually demanding tasks such as night driving and reading. The study population included nearly 500 contact lens wearers between the ages of 18 to 40. The study's primary purpose was to measure the proportion of daily-wear hydrogel contact lens wearers who wear lenses in challenging environments and during visually demanding tasks, and to evaluate their resulting comfort in those situations. Study findings were published in the April 2007 issue of *Optometry and Vision Science.*

University of Washington scientists worked on developing sunglasses that changed color with the touch of a button. They used smart plastics that change when an electric current flows through them. A watch battery activated the protypes that were capable of changing from dark to light blue in seconds. Other scientists reported developments such as lenses to help color-blind people distinguish red from green, cosmetic lenses, ultraviolet-resistant lenses, and lenses chemically treated to darken in the center as light intensifies—basically sunglasses.

The Eyecare Trust claimed good photochromic lenses, capable of darkening upon exposure to sunlight, blocked out 100 percent of the most harmful sun rays 100 percent of the time. The transitions caused adapting to changes from light to dark in a matter of seconds. Researchers at James Robinson, working with University of Leeds scientists, developed a single dye for photochromic lenses. It had two peaks of absorbency allowing the traditional grey or brown of sunglasses to be experienced by wearers.

University of Arizona and Georgia Institute of Technology scientists worked to eliminate traditional bifocals by developing eyeglasses that can automatically refocus. Prototype lenses utilize liquid-crystal material sandwiched between two flat sheets of glass. The transparent coating of indium-tin oxide functions in the manner of an electrode. The lenses' focal length was altered when researchers applied a voltage as low as 1.8V, changing the orientation of liquid crystals.

Perhaps the most notable development affecting the ophthalmic goods industry during the 1990s and 2000s has been the advances in laser eye surgery, in which surgeons used lasers to sculpt the cornea to focus light more precisely. The procedure was relatively noninvasive, did not require any significant recovery time, and had the potential to eliminate patients' need for glasses or contacts. However, the procedure was not foolproof and was not appropriate for all eye conditions. While this technology received a good deal of publicity during the mid-1990s, by the end of the decade it had failed to make any significant inroads into the vision correction market. This primarily was due to the large number of Americans who wore glasses or contact lenses. For example, there were some 140 million people in the market (as either contact-lens wearers or eyeglass wearers) in 1999, and yet only 1.5 percent were estimated to have had laser correction surgery.

Additional areas on which research focused included cleaning products (developing faster-working products), improved surgical instruments, and improving and creating pharmaceuticals. Researchers also worked diligently on improving drug delivery systems and devices. The reason was that 40 percent of eye diseases originate behind the eye where the retina attaches, but this is an extremely difficult area for medicine administration. In fact, despite the high percentage of diseases in this area, only 5 percent of pharmaceutical sales are for those diseases. Clearly, there is a dual incentive—profit and advances in eye care—to improve drug delivery to the back of the eye. As of 2002 Bausch & Lomb was running trials on a system known as Envision TD, which administers medication by way of a small implant.

Some of the most interesting new research into optical devices focused on so-called electronic glasses, which employed a camera, sensors, and display technology to aid vision. The devices, which were mostly experimental, were intended for people with severe sight loss for whom conventionally styled glasses or contacts are inadequate. As of the late 1990s these systems remained fairly obtrusive compared to conventional glasses because they require electronics to be worn near the forehead, but they represented a substantial improvement over larger, manual telescopic lenses or other existing technology to correct serious vision impairment.

A "serious cause of visual impairment" linked to contact lens wear identified as a major risk factor for cornea infections will be further investigated by a team of researchers at Case Western Reserve University School of Medicine. Eric Pearlman, Ph.D., professor and research director in the Department of Ophthalmology and Visual Sciences, and his talented team were granted US $1.57 million renewal grant reflecting ongoing support of the National Eye Institute (NEI) of the National Institutes of Health. Research will focus on bacterial keratis. Efforts were launched in 2008 with a grant for US $2.4 million from the National Eye Institute. "When one considers that 34 million people in the United States and about 140 people world wide wear contact lenses, even a low percentage of side effects translates into a large number of affected individuals," Pearlman said.

Denise Dador reported that approximately 25 percent of U.S. citizens were nearsighted. Dador then shared insights about how optometrists were conducting studies involving contact lenses worn only at night resulting in improved day time vision. Dr. Ron Davis explained cornea reshaping contacts had a distinctive design meaning they were "flat in the center and steeper on the sides."

Nighttime wearers woke up with temporarily corrected vision. When 300 youth participated in a study requiring regularly wearing reshaping lenses, those actually wearing the lenses maintained vision following the initial year of lens wearing. FDA approval has already been obtained for adults to wear the lenses. Data collection continues for the extension to be made to the youth market.

After acknowledging that amateur sports men claimed their skills improved while wearing contact lenses, Acuvue offered an alternative suggestion. The company pointed out that contact lenses provided "superior peripheral vision to glasses and do not fall off as one begins to sweat." In addition, another benefit was not misting or obstructing goggles and helmets. A poll by Ultralense, laser eye firm, found 64 percent of respondents did not wear dye correction although admittedly vision impacted performance. Olympic gold medalist Jonathan Edwards supported the laser eye firm's advice to have surgery.

The world famous Olsen twins, Mary-Kate and Ashley, will be offering a fresh take on vintage-inspired sunglasses via their luxury "The Row" label. While dashing around and trying to avoid photographers, the 23-year-olds have been spotted in some fashionable pairs. Their own designs will be sold at high-end department stores and range from US$325 to US$390. It was challenging for the experienced designers of jewelry and shoes to take on eyewear. "Designing eyewear was definitely more complicated than we thought, and of course, we wanted to be extremely hands-on," admitted Mary-Kate in a WWD.com interview according to *Daily News* staff writer Gina Salamone. *WWD* also reported planned styles included round shapes, classic metal aviator and vintage-inspired brow-line looks.

WORKFORCE

According to the U.S. Census Bureau, the ophthalmic goods industry employed 21,086 people in 2002, with a total payroll of US$845.6 million. Of the total number of employees, 67 percent were employed in production, with an average annual salary of US$33,903. Florida employed the most workers (3,038), followed by Colorado (2,827), New York (1,827), and Massachusetts (1,475). Most U.S. industry employees worked for companies with 20 employees or more. A total of 2,922 worked for companies with 20 to 49 employees, followed by firms with 50 to 99 employees (2,438 workers), 100 to 249 employees (3,860 workers), 250 to 499 employees (4,239), and 500 to 999 employees (3,250 workers).

INDUSTRY LEADERS

Bausch & Lomb. Rochester, New York-based Bausch & Lomb Inc. is one of the world's top ophthalmic goods companies. Its products can be found in more than 100 countries worldwide. Founded in 1853 by German immigrant John Jacob Bausch, the company had revenues of US$2.5 billion in 2007 and 13,000 employees. It was long known for its premium sunglasses, which included the Ray-Ban and Killer Loop brands. Ray-Ban had been sold to Luxottica Group S.p.A. by 2004. Bausch & Lomb has a strong line of contact lenses. The company also makes personal health care products (contact lens solutions), medical products (contact lenses), and pharmaceuticals (glaucoma treatments and over-the-counter eye drops). Its lens care line includes the trade names Boston, ReNu, and Sensitive Eyes.

Demand for surgical tools and instruments (such as for cataract, vitreoretinal, and refractive surgeries) continued to rise. Over the course of its history Bausch & Lomb made significant contributions to the advancement of optical and ophthalmic technology including the creation of Ray-Bans (originally developed in 1929 for the U.S. Army Air Corps), the Cinemascope lens, satellite and missile lens technology, and soft contact lenses. In the late 1990s, however, Bausch & Lomb was accused in the United States with marketing identical products under different brand names and unfairly charging higher prices for some; the dispute resulted in a US$1.7 million settlement. Bausch & has continued to expand its operations through acquisitions and increased its R&D funding.

In 2006 Bausch & Lomb stopped distribution of its ReNu MoistureLoc brand contact lens solution in the United States following the diagnosis of eye infections reported by users. The Food and Drug Administration released statistics showing 109 preliminary reports of rare fungal infection that may cause loss of vision had been received by the Centers for Disease Control and Prevention from 17 states.

In May 2007, Bausch & Lomb launched its "Through a Mother's Eyes" program to coincide with Mother's Day. The company partnered its PureVision Multi-Focal contact lenses brand with *MORE* magazine for a special contest. One grand prize winner would receive a year's supply of the product, a free eye exam, plus a beauty makeover from fashion expert and TV show host Finola Hughes.

On October 5, 2009, Bausch & Lomb acquired commercial assets for Italy's Tubilex Pharma S.p.A. Although it is a major source of branded generic products and over-the-counter medicines developed and marketed in Italy, Tubilux also coordinates distribution to approximately 30 additional countries. The deal allowed Tubilux to maintain its responsibilities for manufacturing operation and produce Bausch and Lomb products under a multi-year agreement. Consequently the Bausch and Lomb presence in Italy more than doubled. This fact was revealed by Carl van Zyl, head of Bausch & Lomb's Pharmaceuticals business for Europe, Middle East, and

Africa. Benefits of the agreement for Tubilux included ability to "strengthen its focus and presence in the ophthalmic pharmaceutical contract manufacturing sector, including ointments, gels, and eye drip formats," claimed Group Tubilux Chief Executive Officer Emidio Fedeli.

On September 28, 2009, Bausch & Lomb announced that CROMA had granted rights to several of the Bausch & Lomb subsidiaries. The rights enabled subsidiaries "to co-promote and sell bromfenac ophthalmic solution in Europe when it becomes available to the market." The aforementioned solution is designed for treatment of postoperative ocular inflammation and pain linked to cataract extraction procedures. CROMA is a well-established pan-European company. Geography in service regions related to the agreement included "all European member states plus Belarus, Croatia, Montenegro, Norway, Russia, Serbia, Switzerland, Turkey and Ukraine." In addition, "CORMA will market bromfenac together with Bausch & Lomb in Austria, France, Poland, Romania, and Spain."

Bausch & Lomb planned to change its worldwide contact lens manufacturing practices by substantial consolidation. Plans called for shifting the bulk of global lens production to Waterford, Ireland, and Rochester, New York, existing sites. Consequently Bausch & Lomb was consulting with Livingston, Scotland, employees before launching " a phased withdrawal" from site during 2010 and early 2011. The major product involved would be SofLens (R) daily disposable lens.

Allergan Inc. Allergan Inc., a leading producer of intraocular lenses and surgical products, lens care items, and pharmaceuticals, is also prominent in the ophthalmic goods industry. Allergan also produces skin care products. Its eye care products include medications for cataracts, glaucoma, and pink eye. The company plans to focus future research efforts on developing niche pharmaceuticals, such as those used for glaucoma treatment. Past pharmaceuticals have been successful, most notably Botox, manufactured by Allergan's skin care segment. Botox was initially used for muscle spasms but later became widely used to diminish the appearance of wrinkles.

Established in 1950, the company's first product was an antihistamine eye drop called Allergan. The company adopted the name of the eye drop and in 1960 moved into the nascent contact lens market, specializing at first in contact lens solutions and later manufacturing its own lenses. After watching sales leap from US$100 million in 1980 to over US$700 million in 1989, the company struggled through a difficult transition period in the early 1990s and sales fell off from US$897 million in 1992 to US$857 million in 1993. In 2004 sales were up to US$2.04 billion, a 15 percent increase from 2003. Net income for 2004 was $377 million, compared to a net loss the year before, with 69.1 percent of sales derived domestically in the United States. Eye care pharmaceuticals were responsible for $1.13 billion of net sales. The company spent $345 million on research and development. Allergan earns nearly one-third of its revenues from outside the United States and has operations in Europe, China, Latin America, and India. The company had 5,055 employees in 2005. For 2008, the company reported revenues of US$4.4 billion and 8,740 employees.

The U.S. Food and Drug Administration approved Allergan's ACUVAIL, a Ketorlactromethamine ophthalmic solution for treatment of past cataract surgery pain and inflammation. In its announcement release, some enlightening statistics were provided indicating "cataract surgery is the most frequently performed surgical procedure in the United States, with more than 3 million procedures performed each year."

Essilor. Based in France, Essilor International SA concentrates its research and sales efforts primarily on lenses for eyeglasses. Essilor maintains a presence in more than 100 countries, with 200 prescription laboratories. Worldwide the company employed 26,534 people in 2005 and recorded sales of nearly US$2.9 billion. Among Essilor's products were Varilux progressive lenses and Crizal lenses, which are anti-reflective and smudge-resistant. Essilor was also marketing progressive lenses, which replaced bifocals and trifocals.

In July 2009, Essilor revealed several transactions in Europe, North America and the Middle East had helped advance "external growth strategy." In roads were made into the Belgian market with acquisition of all outstanding De CEUYNCK shares. There was tremendous U.S. market growth with acquisition of four laboratories Barnet & Ramel Oprical, Apex Optical, ABBA Optical and Vision Pointe Optical. Essilor gained "a foothold in the Middle East" through a partnership establishing a 50/50 joint venture to operate Amico's prescription pharmacy in Dubai. Through this entity service is provided to several areas in the region including the United Arab Emirates and Kuwait.

Luxottica. Italy's Luxottica Group SpA heads up the world's largest eyewear business. Luxottica Retail is the holding company for eyeglass retailer Lenscrafters and the specialty sunglasses retailer Sunglass Hut International. In addition to carrying designs by top names such as Chanel and Giorgio Armani, Luxottica has in-house designers who created hundreds of new designs every year. Revenues in 2008 were nearly US$7.3 billion with 61,000 employees.

In April 2007, *India Business Insight* reported that Luxottica had expressed its desire to enter India either directly or via one of its subsidiaries. A related proposal had been sent to Ray-Ban Sun Optics India Ltd. requesting that company issue a no-objection certificate

for this purpose. Plans included distributing spectacle frames and sunglasses. In addition, Luxottica planned to establish a wholly owned subsidiary in India for entering into the wholesale cash-and-carry business in luxury and fashion brand eyewear other than the Ray-Ban brand.

Shoppers Stop India's superior premium department store chain, bestowed Luxottica India with its prestigious "Pinnacle Award" for "Best Eyewear Brand for 2009." The outstanding achievement was in part attributed to efforts of a team led by Akash Goyle and created for developing key accounts with department stores and optical chains.

Sola International. U.S.-based Sola International Inc. is another major lens maker. It competes directly with Essilor in the production of glass and plastic lenses. Plastic lenses account for the majority of Sola's annual sales. That is due in large part to the popularity of its Spectralite brand of lightweight polycarbonate lenses. In 2003, about half of the company's US$650 million sales came from outside North America. That year, Sola suffered a US$13.5 million net loss and employed 6,634 people. By 2006, Sola reported having more than 6,800 employees located in 28 countries serving 50 markets worldwide. Sola counted itself among the largest lens makers in the world and had manufactured more than one billion lenses.

Other Leaders. Several large, diversified corporations also play significant roles in the industry. Among them are Johnson & Johnson (J&J), whose Acuvue brand and other disposable contacts make it the world's largest disposable lens producer. The US$47.3 billion-a-year J&J also manufactures numerous personal and medical products that fall outside the scope of the optical goods industry. Switzerland's Novartis AG is another important competitor. Formed through the merger of Ciba-Geigy AG and Sandoz Ltd., Novartis is a US$28.2 billion pharmaceutical, nutrition, and life science conglomerate. Its principal eye products are produced through CIBA Vision and Novartis Ophthalmics.

CIBA Vision led the way with innovative advertising and marketing campaigns. It aggressively went after its goal of creating 500,000 new contact lens wearers in 2007. A study conducted by Opinion Research for CIBA Vision found that contact lens wearers spent three times as more in practice than spectacle wearers. CIBA Vision launched a Focus Dailies consumer campaign to raise awareness among 16- to 24-year-olds about the benefits of daily disposable contact lenses. The advertorials were designed to spotlight pop singer Rachel Stevens and stress the all-day comfort of Focus Dailies. CIBA Vision had reportedly achieved success with a London multimedia advertising campaign for its daily disposable contact lens brand Focus Dailies with AquaComfort.

BIBLIOGRAPHY

Allergan. "Allergan Receives FDA Approval for ACUVAIL Ophthalmic Solution for the Treatment on Pain and Inflamation following Cataract Surgery." 23 July 2009. Available from agn.client.shareholder.com.

Bausch & Lomb. "Bausch & Lomb Acquires the Commercial Assets of Italian Ophthalmic Pharmaceuticals Company Tubilex." 5 October 2009. Available from www.bausch.com.

———. "Bausch & Lomb Proposes to Consolidate Contact Lens Manufacturing." 4 September 2009. Available from www.bausch.com.

WWD "Bausch & Lomb Subsidiaries and CROMA will Co-Promote Bromfenac Ophthalmic Solution in Europe." 28 September 2009. Available from www.bausch.com.

"Bausch & Lomb and MORE Magazine Partner to Honor Moms Across the Country." *Business Wire*, 9 May 2007.

Burns, Martin. "Contact lenses 'can help sports performance'." 28 September 2009. Available from contactlenses.co.uk.

"Case Western Awarded $1.57M for Corneal Infection Research." 8 October 2009. Available from www.medicalnewstoday.com.

"CIBA Targets London with Multimedia Lens Campaign." *Optician*, 27 October 2006.

"Contact Lenses Solution Controversy." *World Entertainment News Network*, 12 April 2006.

Dador, Denise. "Perfect vision without contact lenses?" 5 October 2009. Available from www.abclocal.go.com.

Essilor. "Essilor Forges New Strategic Partnership Around the World." 7 July 2009. Available from www.essilor.com.

"Far-sighted Researchers Envision Autofocus Eyeglasses." *EDN*, 27 April 2006.

Fox, Marisa. "Focus on Frames; Glasses Are No Longer for Vision Correction Alone. Here Are Some Eye-Catching Options." *Business Week*, 26 February 2007.

Gaston, Janice. "An Eye for Latest Trends: Fashion in Eyeglasses Always Changing, with Boundless Styles, Colors, Materials." *Winston-Salem Journal*, 23 February 2007.

"Hoover's Company Capsules." *Hoover's Online,* 2007. Available from www.hoovers.com.

Kleinman, Rebecca. "Signs of the Times; Sunglasses Branding Is Appealing to the Fashion Insider." 24 July 2006.

Laurent, Lionel. "Eyeglasses for the Poor." 22 September 2009. Available from www.forbes.com.

"Luxottica India, the Best Eyewear Brand for 2009." Available from www.luxottica.com.

Michigan Optometrists Association. "Michigan Optometrists Warn: Halloween Eye Accessories May Permanently Damage Eyes." 14 October 2009. Available from www.prlog.org.

Mindbranch. "Ophthalmic Goods Manufacturing Industry in the U.S. and its International Trade [Q3 2009 Edition]." Available from www.mindbranch.com.

"New Year, New Focus." *Optician*, 15 December 2006.

"Newer Silcone Hydrogel Contact Lenses Offer Significantly Improved Comfort Over Hydrogel Lenses in Adverse Environments, Clinical Study Shows." 25 April 2007.

"News." *Optician*, 6 April 2007.

"Pop Star Has Eyes for CIBA Campaign." *Optician*, 9 March 2007.

Powell, Cheryl. "First Contact—Lenses Making Advances: More Preteens Wearing Lenses as Advances Make Them More Comfortable and Easier to Clean." *Akron Beacon Journal*, 27 March 2007.

"Ray-Ban Sun Optics Issues NOC to Luxottica." *India Business Insight*, 27 April 2007.

Salamone, Gina. "Mary-Kate and Ashley Olsen get shady with a new line of sunglasses." 14 October 2009. Available from www.mydailynews.com.

Scerra, Chet. "Contact Lens Market Sees Growth." *Ophthalmology Times*, 15 December 2003.

"Slipping Through the Net." *Optician*, 10 November 2006.

"Spectacles." *Optician*, 25 August 2006.

United Nations, Statistics Division. *International Trade Statistics Yearbook.* New York, 2004.

U.S. Census Bureau. *2002 Economic Census,* August 2004. Available from www.census.gov.

U.S. Department of Commerce, Bureau of the Census, International Trade Administration. *NAICS 339115: Ophthalmic Goods,* 3 September 2004. Available from www.ita.doc.gov.

Winder, Rob. "Sunlight Express: Photochromic Lenses Can Turn Prescription Glasses into Sunglasses in a Flash, and Lenses are More Sensitive Than Ever." *Chemistry and Industry*, 19 June 2006.

SIC 3841

SURGICAL AND MEDICAL EQUIPMENT

NAICS CODE(S)

339112. The world's surgical and medical equipment industry manufactures medical, surgical, ophthalmic, and veterinary instruments and apparatus. Representative products include syringes, clamps, hypodermic and suture needles, stethoscopes, laparoscopic devices, catheters and drains, and blood pressure monitoring devices. The industry also includes more high-tech instruments, such as implantable devices, remote monitoring and dosing products, and micro-sized biomonitors and drug-delivery systems.

INDUSTRY SNAPSHOT

In first decade of the twenty-first century, aging populations, the trend toward home healthcare, and a growing interest in delivering products and services utilizing the Internet contributed to a steadily growing market for surgical and medical instruments and apparatus. As the baby boom generation reached retirement age, the growing needs in the sector grew as well. Growth was expected to rise steadily at around 4.6 percent per year through

2010. Valued at US$57.6 billion in the early years of the first decade of the 2000s, the global medical industry is one of the world's fastest growing industries, at least 10 percent of the global Gross Domestic Product of developed nations. In the United States alone, the medical industry comprises more than 750,000 physicians and over 5,200 hospitals, not to mention untold numbers of clinics and private medical offices. With over 3.8 million inpatient visits and 20 million outpatients visits daily, the medical industry is big business. The U.S. medical and surgical device market alone was expected to grow at a compound annual rate of about 8 percent through the remainder of the decade, driven largely by devices for non-invasive surgical procedures, especially in the realm of interventional cardiology, according to research from global growth consulting firm Frost & Sullivan. Giant leaps in technology encouraged the growth of the medical manufacturing market, particularly in the implantable medical devices segment, which was expected to grow annually through 2014 at a rate of 8.3 percent. Among those items expected to grow substantially are spinal implants, cardiac stents and orthobiologics.

Other high growth segments included patient monitoring equipment, retail diagnostics, blood pressure monitoring equipment, and minimally invasive surgical equipment. Laparoscopic handheld instruments alone were expected to generate more than US$235 million of revenue by 2009, as reported in *Medical Device Technology* in mid-2004. One of the industry's applications that is expected to grow the most significantly is in the area of nanotechnology. According to a 2010 report by the *Freedonia Group,* nanotechnology is expected to grow 17.1 percent annually through 2014. The fasted growing applications for nanotech medicine will be in cancer treatment and studies as well a the central nervous system disorders.

Surgical and medical instrument manufacturing was fiercely competitive in the mid-years of the first decade of the 2000s. The fact that highly-specialized surgical tools could be invented, produced, and distributed by small high-technology firms allowed manufacturers with relatively small gross sales to have significant impact on certain segments of markets belonging to industry giants. Toward the close of the twentieth century, a way to meet this competition was to grow, amalgamate, and diversify. As high technology assumed a greater place in medicine and various living organisms were incorporated into treatment formats, the concept of biotechnology as an industry segment grew in importance (see also **Biotechnology**).

By the turn of the twenty-first century, fewer major manufacturers concentrated specifically on certain types of equipment, or on pharmaceuticals, or on treatment of a certain disease. Instead they diversified, sometimes through acquisition, to broaden their presence in the biotechnical industry. By embracing biotechnology, companies like Baxter, long dominant as an international supplier of medical and surgical devices, suddenly were in competition with megaliths like Johnson & Johnson and Roche, four times Baxter's size. Medtronic's 2001 acquisition of insulin pump leader MiniMed and Medical Research Group furthered its entry into the chronic disease management market. Tyco International, a conglomerate of high-technology instrumentation businesses, expanded into the health care market, swallowing high-profile firms United States Surgical in 1999 and C.R. Bard in late 2001.

The advent of managed care—with attendant pressures to hold down the cost of medical treatment—added further incentive to innovators in the industry, while in some cases limiting their profits. Less invasive surgeries such as laparoscopy, cardiac balloon angioplasty, and laser surgery, while posing manufacturing challenges, permitted less invasive surgical techniques and subsequent cost savings in actual patient care (i.e., shorter hospital stays implying lower labor costs, fewer patient complications, quicker recuperations).

Compared to 16 percent in 1980, more than 85 percent of surgical procedures in the U.S. were performed without an overnight stay by 2008. Casa Grande Regional Medical Center staff claimed access to smaller, more portable instruments plus the technology that made it possible were major reasons for the trends success.

The explosive growth of the Internet, and in particular e-commerce, found most major medical device manufacturers scrambling to enhance their online presence with streamlined electronic business transactions, supply chain management, and even remote monitoring of implanted devices through dedicated Internet channels.

ORGANIZATION AND STRUCTURE

Inspired in part by increasing emphasis on ISO 9000 standards in all segments of industry, regulatory bodies of several countries set and restructured guidelines for medical manufacture. The use of quality marks, as well as European (CE) certification marks on medical devices continued to be a stumbling block as regulatory officials, device manufacturers, and private certification and testing firms strove to find consensus on what value quality marks add to a product, and whether consumers can be misled by a mark that merely indicates a base requirement for marketing in a particular country, rather than value-added testing. Various government promotion of standardization of safety and quality regulations helped to stabilize the industry, and the same regulations served to ease trade barriers.

The European Community Council formally adopted the Medical Device Directive as a regulatory initiative on

June 14, 1993, with implementation beginning January 1, 1995. The European Free Trade Association (EFTA) followed suit, actively enforcing the directive. Any products imported or manufactured in affected European countries were required to be tested and certified at the direction of European Union-accredited "Notified Bodies." Now it was necessary to meet just a single set of standards. This eliminated the unpleasant marketing/manufacturing decisions of the past, when manufacturers either could limit their exports, manufacture variations on a single product in an attempt to satisfy each member nation, or create equipment that could match 12 separate standards simultaneously.

A variety of trade agreements devised in the last decade of the century had effect, direct and indirect, on the global market for surgical and medical equipment. The North American Free Trade Agreement (NAFTA)—signed in 1994 by the United States, Mexico, and Canada—eliminated tariffs between the three nations. Prior to NAFTA, Canada and Mexico already were the second and fourth largest importers of U.S. surgical and medical instruments, and the United States received its third largest supply of medical and surgical instrument imports from Mexico. With the implementation of NAFTA, the three countries were in ideal positions to increase their respective export market positions with their North American neighbors, especially since imports into North America from other countries were still subject to tariffs that, in some instances, were as high as 50 percent. The effect of NAFTA was still being felt in 2002, as the export market for medical laboratory equipment alone in Canada reached US$2.75 billion and was confidently expected to continue slow, steady growth (5 percent per annum) through the mid-years of the first decade of the 2000s. The U.S. territory of Puerto Rico benefited even more directly from NAFTA, due to the Section 936 preferences of the U.S. Internal Revenue Code. This section of the Code exempted Puerto Rican investments from corporate taxation, and therefore allowed substantial tax breaks for U.S. companies that located operations in Puerto Rico.

The Uruguay Round of the General Agreement on Trade and Tariffs (GATT)—signed in 1994—included an agreement to remove inter-country tariffs on medical equipment and drugs among the world's leading seven market economies, better known as the G-7: Canada, France, Germany, Italy, Japan, the United Kingdom, and the United States. Removal of these tariffs was expected to save manufacturers of medical devices and equipment millions of dollars per year. In late 1994, this initiative was supplemented by the Medical Technologies Agreement, a segment of the overall U.S.-Japan Economic Framework, a structure that facilitated U.S.-Japan bilateral trade negotiations. This agreement was intended to ease U.S. manufacturer penetration of the Japanese

public sector market for medical services and equipment, and it saw fruition almost immediately upon adoption. The agreement called for periodic reviews of related commerce, and the initial review, conducted less than a year after implementation, showed U.S. manufacturers holding 43 percent of foreign market share and 18 percent of the total Japanese market for medical equipment. As promising as these figures were, by the end of the decade the Health Industry Manufacturers Association reported that when all medically related products were included in the assessment, Japan's total expenditure for foreign-produced equipment was approximately 3 percent of its national health care budget.

Lowering tariffs to speed the acquisition of vital health care products had practical implementation worldwide. In 1998, India expedited the modernization and expansion of national health facilities by instituting government directives permitting state-run hospitals and related public institutions to import approximately US$250 million worth of medical equipment duty free. In spite of the Asian financial crisis of the late 1990s, during the mid-years of the first decade of the 2000s the Indian medical equipment and supplies market was growing at a rate of 10 to 15 percent annually.

Needs to pool medical knowledge and supplies were addressed by the Global Harmonization Task Force, convened in the 1990s and attended by representatives from Canada, the European Union, Japan, and the United States. The task force's mission was to develop a standard set of quality guidelines for internationally acceptable medical devices. They imposed guidelines for joint reviews of new products and encouraged an information exchange intended to result in a single quality inspection recognized by all major global markets.

The U.S. Food and Drug Administration (FDA) held the sometimes lauded, sometimes deplored distinction of being the world's strictest and most arduous reviewer with the lengthiest approval process for the medical device industry. Certainly FDA approval processes were a source of woe for many U.S. manufacturers of medical and surgical instruments. In the late 1990s, it was not unusual for FDA approved U.S. manufacturers, although holding a competitive edge in certain export markets, to lose that edge when new products were caught in the lengthy FDA application process, and foreign competitors thus were given time to overtake them. There was a certain amount of frustration within the U.S. market, as well, as surgical products readily available in Europe waited on the FDA for acceptance and distribution in the United States.

This lengthy FDA review of medical devices was based on one of two procedures. If the product was not similar to another FDA-approved product already on the market, a manufacturer was required to submit a

Premarket Application (PMA) to the FDA. The information included in the PMA was intended to establish product safety as well as therapeutic or diagnostic benefit, all of which had to be demonstrated through intensive animal and human testing. On the other hand, if the new device was generally the same as one already marketed and sold, the manufacturer needed only to file under a procedure known as the FDA 510(k) pre-market notification. Historically, neither procedure was assured of fast approval. Faced by the fact that more and more U.S. companies exported manufacturing as they sought more immediately profitable European markets, the FDA in the late 1990s attempted to improve its performance. In 1998 the FDA received 65 PMA submissions, down slightly from 1997, and review time of those submissions increased to 290 days from 207 in 1997. The average time for approval still was problematic—over a year and a half—but the 16.6 month figure in 1997 was down from 25.9 months in 1996, and a number of applications were approved in less than six months. The 510(k) clearance was even more promising, taking only a little over three months (97 days), a 9 percent improvement over performance a year earlier. Even more significant, the FDA could point to two consecutive years (1996 and 1997) completed with zero backlog of 510(k) clearances. The 1997 passage of the FDA Modernization Act sought to streamline the FDA's reviews by allowing reduced filing requirements for relatively simple devices, and allowing third-party review of some others.

The FDA's involvement in medical manufacture was not limited to pre-market situations. In 1990 the U.S. Congress passed the Safe Medical Device Act in an effort to broaden the regulation of safety standards for medical devices. From 1990 onward, all U.S. health care facilities were required to report serious injuries and deaths resulting from the use of medical devices—both to the FDA and to the manufacturer of the product—and to make the information available to the media. The act also provided for civil penalties for violation of the new regulation, more intense post-market surveillance, and a requirement that more data be provided on 510(k) applications. Four years later, the FDA was involved in the revision of the Good Manufacturing Practice Standards. This revision included a design control process similar to the International Organization for Standardization's quality control standard ISO 9001. Compliance with the labeling, packaging, and product performance guidelines of this ISO-like standard became critical for U.S. manufacturers trying to market abroad. In the year 2000, the FDA also established guidelines for reprocessing devices labeled "disposable" or "one use only" by the original manufacturer. Reprocessors must follow strict guidelines and seek approval for all devices cleaned, sterilized, or reconditioned.

BACKGROUND AND DEVELOPMENT

The development and rise of the medical equipment industry relied on the emergence of medical science technology. When instruments of a lower technology grade, (e.g., stethoscopes, surgical clamps, hypodermic needles and syringes, and surgical knives) were critical for the general practice of medicine and surgery around the world, there was intense global competition among manufacturers in their production. The competition forced down prices for these products, at the same time engendering a continuous struggle for position within the international marketplace. Then price, which translates into profit, tended to guide further market expansion, and international trade of lower-technology items typically gave way to pressure to permit the manufacture and distribution of their higher-technology counterparts.

Manufacturers with the financial and engineering resources to capitalize on technological innovations grew internationally. Particularly those products that resulted in lowered labor costs (often by reducing patient hospital stays), or that allowed patients to be cared for in environments less costly than full-scale hospital facilities, were the products in greatest demand. As an example, consider the advent of surgical staplers in the mid-1960s. By the 1980s, a full complement of stainless steel and absorbable synthetic staples that dissolve in the body had been designed. Since staplers closed incisions and wounds faster than sutures, they allowed less blood loss and tissue damage and encouraged faster post-operative recovery time. Although four times as expensive as suturing, the speed and convenience of stapling coupled with cost savings during the period of patient recovery make it an increasingly lucrative product in the industry. Once a product like the stapler was introduced, the door was opened to further innovation. In 1978, United States Surgical Corp. (USSC), one of the world leaders in development and sales of surgical staplers, made several design changes, including a disposable skin stapler that eliminated lengthy cleaning and sterilization procedures necessitated by rival stainless steel staplers. Two years later, this concept was extended, again by USSC, to include a disposable internal stapler.

The balloon, or transluminal, angioplasty catheter—an instrument used to forge through plaque-clogged or narrow arteries as an alternative to heart bypass surgery—became increasingly popular during the 1980s and continued to be used on a widespread basis through the 1990s. This device utilized a balloon guide wire attached to a very thin catheter, and was inserted into a patient's arm or leg. The wire was fed through the arterial system until it reached a clogged area, where the balloon was inflated, widening the arterial passageway by pressing the plaque against the arterial wall. Hundreds of thousands of angioplasties were performed globally on a fairly routine basis. However, because angioplasty did not remove the plaque that caused the blockage, it was not unusual for patients to experience further arterial clogging. In the mid-1990s, manufacturers developed atherectomy instruments that used tiny blades to cut through and remove plaque, but, by the end of the decade, medical focus seemed to be on angioplasty. Instead of performing atherectomy, doctors tended to give angioplasties followed by vascular stenting—the insertion of mechanical dilators designed to hold open areas from which obstructions had been removed. More traditional bypass surgery was beginning to be performed by surgeons manipulating robotic arms and tiny laparoscopes. Although the US FDA still considers such computer-assisted bypass surgery experimental, the potential for less invasive surgery accurate to micrometers continues to drive development and demand for such devices.

The introduction of laparoscopic surgery was an undisputed milestone for surgical and medical instrument manufacturers—and for the entire medical community worldwide. Laparoscopy involved the use of trocars or surgical tubes inserted into tiny slits in the skin as entry points for specialized instruments. The long slender optical instrument called a laparoscope housed a miniature video camera. Directing this camera allowed surgeons to explore within the human body with minimal patient trauma. Laparoscopy changed the practice of surgery, allowing surgeons to perform such high-volume procedures as gall bladder and kidney removals, hysterectomies, appendectomies, hernia removals, and cancer stagings, all with far less invasive methods than had previously been used. Before laparoscopy, performance of these procedures automatically mandated lengthy hospital stays and long recuperation periods for patients. With the advent of laparoscopy, many procedures could be performed in hospital outpatient departments or ambulatory surgery centers. Not only was patient trauma reduced and recovery eased, but costs associated with each procedure and the associated patient stay were dramatically reduced also. It is not an exaggeration to say that laparoscopy changed the face of surgery delivery systems worldwide, although, at the same time, it should be noted that the early implementation of laparoscopy was closely tied to the ability of an institution to train doctors in its use.

The desire to find less invasive means of performing surgery prevailed throughout the 1990s. No particular aspect of surgery was exempt. Moreover, ease of use was equally important. In 1998, a "catarex probe" was introduced by Optex. This device, with a whirling blade and accompanying vacuum, required less surgical expertise in the excision of cataracts. That same year, Sulzer Osypka

GmbH (a German component of the Swiss Sulzer Medica, Ltd.) presented a means of repairing certain heart defects with no surgery at all. By introducing two tiny "umbrellas" over a "rail" comprised of a wire catheter, surgeons were able to use the same catheter to screw the umbrellas in place, repairing holes in the atria of the affected heart. To the minimal patient trauma associated with the first use of the device was added the knowledge that a similar catheter could be used to effect unlimited repositioning of the umbrellas, if future adjustment was necessary.

A rising trend in the 1990s was the sale and utilization of used or refurbished medical equipment as a means of containing costs. The United States took over the majority of this market in the mid-1990s. Canada, China, central Europe, Latin America, and Russia were destinations for reconditioned equipment as well. Especially in those nations where health care budgets were extremely tight, refurbished equipment could more easily be obtained and allowed them to provide current technological advances at a fraction of the original purchase costs. The refurbished medical device market accounts for only a small fraction of the instrument business. Few medical entrepreneurs can afford to weather the high costs of multiple difficult chemical cleaning processes and FDA approval, to say nothing of convincing the surgeon or hospital to purchase used equipment. If being resold or reused in the United States, refurbished devices are subject to U.S. Food and Drug Administration regulations requiring pre-market approval or pre-market clearance before reuse. These rules came following reports of patients harmed by contaminated instruments that had not been sufficiently reprocessed.

The Internet began to revolutionize the medical device market. Late 1999 saw the introduction of the first wireless Internet-based heart monitoring system. The Mayo Clinic and University of California at San Francisco are anticipating clinical trials data from patients on the web. Teleradiology, a new field involving imaging via the internet, allow physicians across the globe to view and mark up medical images in real time.

CURRENT CONDITIONS

As the world industry leader, the United States consumed 40 percent of global output and accounted for about 50 percent of production of medical devices. After the United States, Western Europe and Japan were the next biggest world markets. During the mid-years of the first decade of the 2000s, the industry was on solid footing, bolstered by continued spending on research and development (R & D) initiatives that ensured success well into the future. Worldwide, the market for medical and surgical devices was valued at approximately US$140 billion in 2002, according to a 2003 report from the research firm Frost & Sullivan. Other estimates valued the industry at US$165 billion, down from US$169 billion in 2001. As reported by Research and Markets, growth was expected to continue at about 5 percent annually through the mid to late years of the first decade of the 2000s.

The market for orthopedic equipment specifically was valued at $20 billion worldwide, more than half of which was manufactured in the United States. The market grew 13 to 15 percent annually during the middle of the first decade of the 2000s. Rapid growth was expected to continue for the medical device market overall, due to an aging population, longer life spans, higher rates of obesity and injury, growth in emerging markets, and direct-to-consumer marketing, as reported by Jim Lorincz in *Tooling and Production.*

Cardiac surgical devices were another lucrative category during the first decade of the twenty-first century. According to a November 2010 article on the PR Newswire, the cardiovascular surgical devices used in operating rooms represented an estimated US$31 billion in 2010. Based on estimates from Standard & Poor's, this sector of the medical device industry was expected to experience 8.7 percent annual growth through 2015, to an expected US$48 billion. Despite the efforts to significantly boost the interventional cardiac procedures, traditional cardiac surgical devices are expected to expand faster, mainly due to the growth of the cardioprosthetic devices such as ventricular assist devices. This category was worth approximately US$7 billion in 2010 and is expected to increase at a 10.9 percent annual rate to reach US$12 billion by 2015.

A December 2003 report from the Centers for Medicare and Medicaid Services (CMS) revealed that some 80 percent of industry players fell into the category of small or emerging companies during the early years of the first decade of the 2000s, with annual sales below US$100 million. While contributing only 10 percent of industry sales, these small companies spent 28 percent of all research and development dollars. To fund these efforts, small firms depended heavily on funding from venture capitalists. After peaking at more than US$2.5 billion in 2000, venture capital funding decreased during the early years of the decade. However, in its November 1, 2003, issue, *Venture Capital Journal* noted that funding for medical device market increased 54 percent in the second quarter of 2003 alone, signifying a potential comeback. Heading into the middle of the decade, some analysts also predicted an uptick in merger and acquisition activity, as established players sought new technologies and devices for their product lineups.

RESEARCH AND TECHNOLOGY

Most major manufacturers of surgical and medical instruments—and medical products in general—spend more on research and development than other industries. This was especially true of U.S. manufacturers. By the end of the century, in companies that also pursued biotechnical remedies, R&D expenditure often ran as high as US$101,000 per employee.

The global rise in conservative, cost-conscious views about health care sparked criticism of large capital investments in R&D, at least in the United States. Germany and Japan continued to emphasize technology, and with socialized health care in both countries, this led to speculation that critical resources in those countries possibly were shared more effectively than they were in the United States. At least it could be said that technology and innovation were encouraged in these markets, and that their governments were not left with the economic problem of paying the price of treatment for those without insurance coverage.

In the United Kingdom in the late 1990s, emphasis was placed on research funded in a variety of ways: public, private, charitable, or combinations of these. This research was intended to be "mission-oriented;" that is to say, focused on a particular goal that could be identified as being of benefit to the population. This focus may have given rise to the high degree of public support for research in that country. Canada, too, in 1998 anticipated a plan that would double federal funding of university-based medical research. This is not to say that the United States lacked incentive to continue the aggressive medical research begun earlier in the decade—only that the reporting of this research occasionally was received differently by the public it served. In fact, at the beginning of 1998, a glance back at the preceding medical year demonstrated an impressive depth of exploration into a huge variety of surgical and medical issues.

One of the more promising developments in international research and development efforts was the introduction of the Standard for the Exchange of Product (STEP) model data. Initiated in the early 1990s, STEP represented yet another effort to standardize manufacturing procedures and subject product development, from manufacturing to post-marketing surveillance, to state-of-the-art computer-aided manufacturing (CAM) procedures. The improved documentation and communication implied by STEP usage created a single product data exchange standard by which manufacturers were able to select vendors whose tools were compatible with their own computer-aided design (CAD) software.

Nanotechnology is beginning to emerge from the medical research laboratory and see significant commercial applications. Micro-sized devices, commonly known as Microelectromechanical Systems, or MEMS, are currently used in such common applications as ink-jet printer heads and automobile airbag inflation systems. Their use as implantable medical devices promises a new frontier in disease management and treatment. Medical devices that circulate freely in the bloodstream searching out cancerous cells or clogged arteries are currently being developed in Biomedical Engineering Centers in several U.S. universities. Researchers at The Ohio State University have manufactured particles in the realm of 1 micron and foresee their use as drug delivery systems for controlling metastatic cancers.

Writing for *Scientific American Magazine,* Larry Greenemeier shared the news about exciting prospects for nanotubes. Researchers project they may be able to repair injured and worn-out cartilage with assistance of nanotubes. They forsee being able to insert microscopic carbon nanotubes into injured joints. This surgery alternative encourages new stronger cartilage cells to grow. According to findings reported in the *Journal of Biomedical Materials Research Part A,* researchers successfully grew cartilage around carbon nanotubes inside a lab. In September 2008, the researchers plan to implant carbon nanotubes in sheep joints to test the technique outside the lab for the first time. The research team consists of Brown University Associate Engineering Professor Thomas Webster, Brown researcher Dongwoo Khang and Grace Park. Park was one of Webster's former Ph.D. students and a Becton, Dickson and Company research scientist.

In an effort to enhance public awareness of nanotechnologies, The European Commission announced its plans to host a related consultation. European Health Commissioner Androulia Vassiliou said it was a regulatory challenge to ensure society experiences benefits while protecting health, safety and environment in areas related to nanotechnologies. Related regulation covered many fields including chemicals, foods, cosmetics and medicine. Projections called for the nanotechnologies world market to span between US$750 billion and US$2,000 billion until 2015. It was also estimated that up to 10 million nanotechnologies-related jobs could be created by 2014.

Telemedicine has also moved toward commercial adoption. In 2000, the FDA approved for marketing a device that allows patients to provide simple medical information such as blood pressure, temperature, and heart rate through a phone or data line. The American Telemedicine Association and providers of home health care services promote the use of telemedicine to patients unable to travel long distances to health facilities. Other applications appearing on the horizon for telemedicine include remote dosing and monitoring of insulin for diabetes patients, and high-risk pregnancy monitoring.

According to Dan Engel, regional sales manager for Polycom, telemedicine made excellent usage of technology capable of linking professionals plus 'extending the reach of healthcare." The key to its distinctive support for achieving medical goals was that telemedicine transported data rather than individual people. Applications for healthcare education included video conferencing, making it possible to have quality training opportunities on site or at remote locations throughout the world.

The Medical Journal of Australia reported that a study involving staff at a large metropolitan hospital and small district hospital resulted in mixed findings for telemedicine applications. The study's co-author, Professor Johanna Westbrook from the University of Sydney, said telemedicine worked best when moderate trauma patients were involved but additional stress occurred for medical specialists. Inquiries found that specialists sometimes felt stressed due to feeling like they were in the room with patients but not having "any power to take action."

WORKFORCE

The medical and surgical equipment workforce is highly diversified, ranging from mechanical and electrical engineers to high-tech manufacturing technicians, and an increasing number of software developers. With the emergence of Internet-based monitoring devices, the number of Web application programmers and information technology employees is expected to increase. This counters the general downward economic trend in 2002 that forecast information technology careers would remain flat.

INDUSTRY LEADERS

GE Healthcare. With US$16.6 billion in 2006 sales, GE Healthcare offered a broad range of products and services worldwide. With roots tracing back to 1900, GE Healthcare is a major segment of General Electric and includes subsidiaries GE Healthcare Technologies and GE Healthcare Bio-Sciences. The company's main focus, medical imaging, began with X-ray technology, and continued with products in Computed and Positron Emission Tomography (CAT and PET scanners), Magnetic Resonance Imaging (MRI), and, more recently, full digital scanning. GE also produces a wide variety of clinical information systems, patient monitoring systems, and other medical information technology products. GE Healthcare employed more than 46,000 people in more than 100 countries in the Americas, Europe, and Asia.

BioOptics World reported that GE Healthcare announced availability of a complete package of molecular imaging tools. "From imaging agents to future imaging technologies, GE Healthcare provides the industry's most comprehensive portfolio of clinically-relevant offerings," stated Gene Saragnese, vice president of GE Healthcare's molecular imaging and CT business. The "portfolio" includes single photon emission computed tomography (SPECT), imaging applications, positron emission tomography/computed tomography MotionFree technologies plus pre-clinical and radiopharmaceutical offerings that were showcased during the Society of Nuclear Medicine annual meeting in June 2008. GE Healthcare also revealed plans related to launching two software packages for its 4-slice SPECT/CT, the Infinia Hawkeye 4. Volumetrix Suite was designed to enhance image clarity plus aid in more precise disease detection and localization. Earlier in 2008, GE Healthcare announced expansion of its partnership with Fraunhofer Institut fur Toxikologie und Experimentelle Medizin. The partnership would explore molecular imaging and its application to the development of novel cancer therapeutics.

Johnson & Johnson. Johnson & Johnson, known the world over for such highly visible brand names as Band-Aid, Tylenol, and Motrin, as well as popular pharmaceuticals such as Hismanal and Ortho-Novum contraceptive products, also was a dominant presence in the field of surgical instruments. In 1941 the number of Johnson-produced surgical products was sufficient for the formation of a separate division, which, in 1949, became known as Ethicon, Incorporated. In 1992, Ethicon subdivided further to form two companies, Ethicon Incorporated and Ethicon Endo-Surgery. The surgical firm produced a variety of endoscopic procedure products and mechanical (non-suture) wound closure implements, including the Palmaz-Schatz Balloon Expandable Stent and the Ultracision Harmonic Scalpel. In 1997 the parent company's purchase of California-based Biopsys Medical added to the Johnson portfolio a surgical device enabling minimally invasive breast cancer diagnostic procedures. Johnson & Johnson's sales reached US$61.9 billion in 2009 with a workforce of 118,700 employees.

In December of 2004, Johnson & Johnson announced it had agreed to purchase fellow industry leader Guidant for $25.4 billion in cash and stock. The merger was the third largest of 2004 and the largest in industry history. By adding Guidant to its ranks, Johnson & Johnson strengthened its portfolio of medical devices, which would grow to consist of 42 percent pharmaceuticals, 41 percent medical devices and diagnostics, and 17 percent consumer products. The company's best growth was realized in the Asia-Pacific and Africa, where sales increased almost 20 percent. This, and previous acquisitions of Cordis and DePuy, helped solidify Johnson & Johnson's position as a market leader.

With 2004 sales of US$3.7 billion, Guidant was the established leader in the cardiovascular market, producing stents, angioplasty and other balloon catheters, and defibrillator and pacemaker systems. With significant revenues coming from its stent and angioplasty products, Guidant acquired the Intermedics Corporation, a pacemaker manufacturer, in 1999. In mid-2000, Guidant announced the U.S. availability of its first implantable

pacemaker/defibrillator. Guidant's history dates from a 1994 spinoff of pharmaceutical giant Eli Lilly. By 2004, the company marketed its products in 100 countries, but mainly in the United States, Japan, and Europe. In April 2006, after a bidding war between Johnson & Johnson and Boston Scientific Group, Guidant accepted a US$27.2 billion offer from Boston Scientific Group and made the move. According to *Fortune* magazine, this was the "second worst deal ever" and asserted that BSG paid too much for Guidant.

Baxter International Inc. Of firms dedicated to high technology medical manufacture, Baxter International was clearly a world leader, exporting some 120,000 different products to more than 100 nations. Noted Baxter products included heart surgery equipment, home dialysis systems, various blood and circulatory treatments, heart valves, and a variety of minimally invasive surgical devices. Baxter's research into animal/human organ transplant encouraged addition to its line of surgical devices. Although medical and surgical instruments occupied only a portion of its total sales, all Baxter products were the top or second place sellers in 85 percent of their respective industries. At the close of the century, Baxter, based in Deerfield, Illinois, was aggressively expanding its foreign market, which made up over 50 percent of its total sales. By 1998 Baxter operated 50 manufacturing plants outside of the United States, including facilities in North and South America, Europe, Australia, Asia, and the Pacific Rim. Sales reached US$12.56 billion in 2009 with 48,500 employees.

Baxter International was founded in 1931 to distribute intravenous solutions manufactured by one of its founders, Dr. Donald Baxter. Another founder, Dr. Ralph Falk, took over the company in 1935, and by 1939 introduced a sterilized vacuum-type blood collection device capable of storing blood for three weeks. Expanding rapidly, in 1951 Baxter went public to facilitate its acquisition of other companies. Exponential growth, highlighted by the takeover of five other firms, saw Baxter's sales total US$1 billion in 1978. Less than 10 years later (1985), Baxter purchased American Hospital Supply, thereby becoming the largest hospital supply company in the world. Their policy of using acquisition to expand continued as the twenty-first century approached. Early in 1998, Baxter formed an agreement with the prestigious Cleveland Clinic Foundation, granting Baxter exclusive rights to the cardiovascular products developed by the foundation's Lerner Research Institute in return for Baxter's funding of the institute. Later the same year, Baxter acquired a portion of Ohmeda Medical Systems, a pharmaceutical products corporation that had enjoyed recent visibility because its equipment was featured in the popular *E.R.* television series. The company owns facilities in the United States and Canada as well as in Europe, Latin America, and Asia.

Baxter International has not been without controversy. In 2001, dialysis machines were malfunctioning resulting in several deaths directly attributed to the machines. In 2008, the company was responsible for supplying doses of tainted heparin, and in 2009 lethal doses of H5N2 avian flu virus were delivered to laboratories throughout Europe, mixed with seasonal flu vaccines.

Roche Diagnostics. In 1998, Swiss-based Roche merged with Germany's Boehringer Mannheim to form the Roche Group. Internationally dominant in the pharmaceutical industry, the addition of the Boehringer Mannheim family of companies to the Roche affiliation gave the giant conglomerate significant presence in the medical and surgical equipment industry. Boehringer Mannheim, in the years prior to the merger, had ranked fourth in international medical and surgical equipment sales, grossing US$1.4 billion annually. Boehringer Mannheim saw the merger as an opportunity to increase its R&D budget to include many new surgical applications and enhance its existing product offering—and increase its already formidable industry presence. As of the middle of the first decade of the 2000s, Roche Diagnostics was the world's foremost provider of in-vitro diagnostics. In addition, the company offered a wide variety of medical testing products and services. With 81,500 employees, the division held 20 percent of the world market for diagnostics, and was responsible for 23.7 percent of the Roche Group's total sales, which totaled US$49 billion in 2009. Significant gains in 2004 revenue were reported from Iberia/Latin America (14 percent increase in sales) and the Asia-Pacific region (13 percent), particularly in China, India, Korea, and Taiwan.

Siemens Medical Systems. A division of German multinational Siemens AG, Siemens Medical focuses on four primary device specialty areas: oncology, cardiology, neurology, and molecular diagnostics. With its parent company's history in electronics, its non-invasive surgical products and systems make it a major competitor of GE Medical. Siemens Medical is also know for its groundbreaking Lithostar lithotripsy system for non-surgical treatment of kidney stones and its huge variety of patient monitoring devices—including telemetry devices, pulse oximeters, and other diagnostic tools.

Siemens went clinical with The ARTISTE Solution in three cancer centers. Patients experienced the benefits of professionals working with the linear accelerator engineered especially for Adaptive Radiation Therapy at MAASTRO Clinic in the Netherlands; German Center in Heidelberg, Germany; and Baton Rouge General's Pennington Cancer Center in Louisiana.

Becton, Dickinson and Company. Becton, Dickinson and Company celebrated its 100th anniversary in 1997. Its BD logo is ubiquitous in hospitals around the globe. Its three major divisions, BD Biosciences (Clontech, Discovery Labware, Immunocytometry Systems, and Pharmingen); BD Diagnostics (Diagnostic Systems, Healthcare Consulting, and Preanalytical Systems); and BD Medical, fueled the company's US$7.1 billion in 2009 sales. The company's emphasis on global presence and global medical technology had been apparent from its 1897 founding, when Maxwell Becton and Farleigh Dickinson shook hands while on a sales trip and proceeded to import and sell fever thermometers and syringes purchased in England and France. By 1998, Becton Dickinson operated in more than 40 countries and had expanded its manufacturing operations to include a significant presence in the rapidly growing markets of India and China. Although over 50 percent of its sales were in overseas markets, Becton Dickinson held over half of the U.S. hypodermic needle and syringe market, and was the nation's leading supplier of intravenous catheters. Spurred by AIDS-related sensitivity to handling of blood and blood products, Becton Dickinson patented a variety of safety devices in the late 1990s, including Safety-Lock syringes, Hemogard blood tube closure systems and the InterLink needleless injection system.

Freelance health and medical writer Charlotte LoBuono reported that Becton Dickinson acquired Cytopedia in May 2008. Cytopedia is the cytometry shop known for its inFlux cell sorter. Both companies have complementary platforms. With inFlux, Becton Dickson can reach into emerging markets that have been out of reach for its FACAria II. This includes sorting larger cells with potential stem-cell research, drug discovery and marine biology applications.

Medtronic Inc. Minneapolis based Medtronic was established in 1949 as a modest medical equipment repair shop, and quickly specialized in cardiac research. Medtronic is the world's largest maker of implantable biomedical devices. Because of its focus on cardiovascular disease, Medtronic also produced a wide variety of catheters and other minimally invasive instruments used in cardiac surgery. Reaping sales of US$14.59 billion in 2009, the company has grown markedly since the 1990s. Medtronic sells its products in more than 120 countries, and employs a global workforce of 41,000.

Johanna Bennett shared insights about Medtronic. In June 2008, the company's chief executive unveiled a five-year plan focused on speeding up profit growth. Central to the plan were smaller parts of the business with growth potential and cutting costs. Medtronic plans to focus more on overseas markets. It announced plans to reduce the cost of goods sold by US$1 billion and cut its workforce by 1,100 jobs. By 2013, the company was projected to generate US$20 billion to US$22 billion a year. Medtronic's "cornerstone" is pacemakers and defibrillators. These devices generated 37 percent of the company's sales.

Boston Scientific Corporation. Dr. Joachim Burhenne, who pioneered the field of minimally invasive medical/surgical procedures, was the major inspiring force behind Boston Scientific Corporation, along with co-founder John Abele, who began Medi-tech in the late 1960s. The firm's steerable catheters won it acceptance in surgical circles.

Boston produces a wide variety of catheters, endoscopes, and laparoscopes used in applications ranging from vascular surgery and cardiovascular surgery to urology, gastrointestinal procedures, and pulmonology. Its 1998 acquisition of Schneider from Pfizer Medical Inc. allowed Boston to expand into Schneider's key markets: brachytherapy, aneurysmal disease, and stent products. Boston's flagship products include the NIR coronary stent and the Maverick balloon dilation catheter. A major U.S. exporter, the company reported sales of US$8.5 billion in 2008, with a workforce of 28,600 employees.

Stryker Corp. Kalamazoo, Michigan-based Stryker Corporation transformed itself into a top medical device manufacturer with its 1998 acquisition of Howmedica from Pfizer Inc. for US$1.6 billion. Primarily known for its manufacture of surgical instruments, Stryker added Howmedica's line of orthopedic implants and bone and tissue repair devices to its product line. Sales reached US$6.7 billion in 2008 with nearly 17,000 employees.

Covidien. Formerly known as Tyco Healthcare, Covidien has broken away from the Tyco family. It was spun off as part of the conglomerate's break-up. Covidien had sales of US$10.4 billion in 2008 with 41,800 employees as of 2010. It provides a wide array of generics, pharmaceuticals and health care supplies to businesses around the world. It maintains operations in approximately 60 countries.

MAJOR COUNTRIES IN THE INDUSTRY

United States. In 1998 the emerging biotechnology industry—which embraced a large number of corporations also specializing in medical and surgical device manufacture—was growing at a rate of 11 percent a year. Medical device sales rose at 7 percent a year during the same period. By the end of the twentieth century, U.S. manufacturers controlled between 40 and 50 percent of the US$169 billion medical device world market, although Japan was a strong presence, and both established and emerging Northern European firms were making serious technological gains. The decline of economic recessions in Europe and Japan meant increased spending on U.S. exports such as stethoscopes, needles and syringes, ophthalmic instruments, and sphygmomanometers. Use of laparoscopy, internal stapling, and other less invasive

surgical procedures was on the rise globally. U.S. global dominance in the medical supply industry did decrease slightly as the year 2000 approached, dropping to a 40 percent share of the market by the late 1990s.

The United States held a strong position in the surgical and medical instrument industry throughout the 1990s and into the first decade of the 2000s, with some areas showing particularly strong growth during the middle of the decade. Sales of patient monitoring equipment were expected to reach $8.7 billion in 2005. Telemetry was the fastest growing segment of that market, with 24.2 percent growth between 2002 and 2005, though a slowdown was expected later in the decade. External defibrillators (16.2 percent growth) and glucose self-monitoring equipment (13.1 percent), and sleep apnea monitoring equipment (16.8 percent) were other areas of high growth in the mid-decade years. The retail diagnostic market was expected to surpass $540 million, rising 8.5 percent annually from 2002 to 2009, as reported in *Medical Device Technology*, based on data from Frost & Sullivan.

Driven by devices for non-invasive surgical procedures in general, and interventional cardiac devices in particular, the U.S. medical and surgical device market was expected to grow at a compound annual rate of about 8 percent through 2005. The U.S. market was valued at US$57.6 billion in 2002 by Frost & Sullivan. Other category leaders included reconstructive implants for orthopedic surgery, as well as biologic and spinal devices, and those related to the administration and delivery of medication.

According to GenomeWeb News, the Food and Drug Administration wanted to spend US$100 million to improve the agency's medical and drug programs. They would include more aggressive safety surveillance of adverse events linked to medical products. This would include device identifiers that can help them track devices, facilitate recalls and support inventory management.

Europe. Europeans saw a 5 percent growth in EU member countries' biomedical markets in the late 1990s. The effect of the Euro currency, rolled out in January 2002 and supplanting all but three European currencies, was yet to be seen. Though mature, Europe's market for medical products still accounted for more than 30 percent of the global medical equipment and supplies market. The market was valued at US$31.1 billion in 2005, and was expected to grow $6.1 billion from 2005 through 2010. Disposable medical supplies were expected to perform well, with the greatest growth rates for high-tech devices expected in angioplasty catheters. Smith & Nephew, a leading medical device company based in the United Kingdom, is expected to compete fiercely with U.S. firms Guidant and Boston Scientific, among others.

China. According to a 2009 study by the *Export Bureau*, China was responsible for significantly more of the world's import and export activity for medical and surgical supplies than any other nation. In 2010, the over 2,000 medical equipment companies in China covered over 22 percent of the exports and 8 percent of the import market. The Chinese market for medical equipment and supplies was worth $7 billion in 2002, making it the world's third largest. Growing at a faster rate than Western markets, the market increased 10 percent in 2000 alone. *Datamonitor* predicted that the market would more than double by 2007. Most medical device manufacturing in China encompasses low-technology supplies, and no Chinese companies have a major worldwide medical presence. The government cracked down on black markets in China in 2000, primarily affecting sales of pharmaceuticals, but also sales of illegal medical devices.

According to the U.S. Department of Commerce, China imported approximately one-third of its medical devices from the United States by the early years of the first decade of the 2000s. Excluding Hong Kong, U.S. medical device exports to China increased from US$204 million in 1999 to US$350 million in 2002. Exports reached US$228 million during the first half of 2003. Compared to the same period a year before, this represented a strong increase of 48.6 percent. When U.S. exports to Hong Kong are factored in, the value of the Chinese market is even greater. From 1999 to 2002, U.S. exports to Hong Kong climbed from $215 million to $274 million, with exports for the first six months of 2003 going up 17 percent from the same period in 2002. According to *The Market for Medical Devices & Equipment in Brazil, Russia, India & China*, China's revenues from medical equipment could surpass Germany by 2009, Japan by 2015, and the United States by 2039.

In April 2004 Assistant Secretary of Commerce Linda M. Conlin led a trade mission to Beijing and Chengdu, China, in an effort to promote medical device trade. A document outlining the mission explained that exploding demand boded well for U.S. medical supply exporters, despite the challenges small and medium-sized companies would face to comply with trade rules and establish a viable market presence.

Japan. With the world's third largest economy, Japan has continually maintained a huge trade surplus. However, its strength in the medical equipment industry was not great enough to completely offset that of either the United States or Germany. In fact, in 2003, Japan held only 13 percent of the worldwide market for general medical equipment. The Japanese government's Ministry of Health and Welfare (MHW) tried to shore up industry revenues through various subsidies, while at the same time positioning regulatory stumbling blocks in the paths

of U.S. (and other) firms exporting to Japan. The erosion of the Japanese market by foreign suppliers continued throughout the 1990s, but the nation's pursuit of high technology combined with government support of private business to ensure that by the end of the 1990s, some 200 Japanese companies had entered the world biotechnical and medical equipment markets. In 2002, the Japanese market for medical and equipment supplies was worth $23.7 billion, 35.5 percent more than five years before. This was expected to rise significantly by 2007 to $37.6 billion, as reported in a 2003 edition of *Datamonitor*.

BIBLIOGRAPHY

"2004 Annual Report." Baxter International, 2005.

"2004 Annual Report." Johnson & Johnson, 2005. Available from www.jnj.com.

Bennett, Johanna. "Medtronic on the Mend." *Weekly Trader*, 17 June 2008.

Cardiovascular Surgical Devices: The Global Market. *Health Care Industry Market Update.* 5 December 2003. Available from www.cms.gov.

Centers for Medicare and Medicaid Services. *Reportlinker through PR Newswire.* 9 November 2010. Available from www.thefreelibrary.com.

"Commission Launches Public Dialogue on Nanotechnologies." 18 June 2008. Available from cordis.europa.eu.

Engel, Dan. "Telemedicine — The Next Level of Service." 12 June 2008. Available from wwwcomputingsa.co.za.

"Exporter & Importer Statistics 2010." Available from www.exportbureau.com.

Ferrari, Mauro, and Jun Liu. "The Engineered Course of Treatment." *Mechanical Engineering*, December 2001, 44-47.

Frost & Sullivan. *Medical Devices.* 24 September 2004. Available from www.healthcare.frost.com.

"GE Healthcare Boasts Complete Package of Molecular Imaging Tools." 17 June 2008. Available from bioopticsworld.com.

"GE Healthcare Fact Sheet." General Electric Corporation, 2005. Available from www.gehealthcare.com.

Greenemeier, Larry. "Nanotech to Regrow Cartilage and Soothe Aching Knees." 16June 2008.

"HHS, White House Aim to Add US$275M to FDA's 2009 Budget." 10 June 2008. Available from http://www.genome web.com/.

Herman, William A. "Health Technology is Coming Home." *FDA Consumer*, May 2001, 36.

"Hoover's Company Capsules." *Hoover's Online*, 2008. Available from www.hoovers.com.

"How to Invest in Cardiac Surgical Devices." *Venture Capital Journal*, 1 November 2003.

"The Ins and Outs of Outpatient Surgery." *Arizona City News*, 17 June 2008.

"J&J Cordis/Guidant $25.4 Billion Merger to Control Stent Market." *Caribbean Business*, 23 December 2004.

LoBuono, Charlotte. "Becton, Dickinson Acquires Cytopeia in Effort to Reach New Cell-Based Markets." 23 May 2008. Available from www.cba-news.com.

Lorincz, Jim. "Rx for Healthy Manufacturers." *Tooling and Production*, June 2005. Available from www.toolingand production.com.

"Medical Industry Overview." Available from www.themedica.com.

Mraz, Stephen. "MEMS and Medicine." *Machine Design,* 13 September 2001, 61-64.

"Research and Markets: Global Medical Device and Equipment Market Expected to Grow Steadily by Around 4.6 Percent Over Next Five Years." *M2 Presswire,* 24 May 2005.

"Research and Markets: Real Growth Potential in Market for Medical Devices & Equipment in Brazil, Russia, India & China." *Business Wire,* 18 January 2005.

"Siemens Next Generation Technology May Bring New Hope to Cancer Patients." 17 June 2008. Available from www.innovations-report.de.

"Telemedicine Causing Stress and Benefits: Study." 16 June 2008. Available from www.abc.net.au.

U.S. Department of Commerce. "Mission Statement, Medical Device Trade Mission to China, April 19-23." 2004. Available from www.trade.gov.

"US Market Update." *Medical Device Technology.* July/August 2004. Available from www.medicaldevicesonline.com.

METALS MANUFACTURING

———————— ■ ————————

HAND TOOLS AND HARDWARE

NAICS CODE(S)

332212, 332213, 332510. The hand tool industry manufactures tools for metalworking, woodworking, and general maintenance. Among the many tools produced by companies in this category are axes, drill bits, blow torches, c-clamps, hammers, hand clamps, handsaws, glass cutters, chisels, files, spades, can openers, garden hand tools, hay forks, machetes, screwdrivers, hatchets, jewelers' hand tools, mallets, saw blades, wrenches, trowels, and yardsticks.

INDUSTRY SNAPSHOT

Despite its low profile and mature markets, the hand tools and hardware industry has been one of the most consistently successful industries in the world. Less susceptible to recessions and economic fluctuations than many other industries, toolmakers achieved steady growth throughout the 1990s. However, the economic climate of the 2000s challenged the industry, leading to plant closures and layoffs. By 2003, for example, Snap-on Inc. had closed two of its four manufacturing plants, which had both been in operation for more than 65 years. The outlook for the industry appeared brighter heading into the next decade. As economic conditions began to improve, so did the demand for hand tools, prompting leaders like Stanley Black & Decker to increase hiring.

Following two successful decades, Stanley Works remained the industry leader during the mid- to late 2000s. This leadership position was built from the mid-1980s to the late 1990s, when the company saw its sales more than double. In 2010, Stanley Works merged with another industry leader, Black & Decker, to further their leadership in the industry. Other leading tool manufacturers included Snap-on Inc., Cooper Tools Inc., and Blount International Inc. The industry's key customers include carpenters, mechanics, jewelers, farmers, and innumerable do-it-yourselfers. Even when recessions caused slowdowns in the construction or industrial equipment industries, hand tools and hardware manufacturers continued to perform well due to increased demand by consumers who wanted to save money by making repairs or undertaking projects themselves. In the United States alone, the power and hand tool demand is forecast to increase 3.3 percent annually through 2012, reaching US$14.5 billion. As the economy slowly emerges from a recession, the construction industry is expected to recover by 2012, thus creating a demand from the professional sector. Up to that point, the continued interest in do-it-yourself projects will sustain the demand for tools.

While many of its products are considered low-tech, the industry itself is highly automated and employs state-of-the-art materials and technologies in its factories. Research has focused on improving the quality, durability, and usability of many different tools. Foreign innovations are eagerly adopted and efforts continually are made to improve the precision of tools and to customize them to suit the traditions and preferences of different markets. Beginning midway through the 1990s and continuing into the late 2000s, technological advances included ergonomically advantageous tools designed to prevent injuries related to tool use and "smart" tools that can perform tasks more precisely than their conventional counterparts.

ORGANIZATION AND STRUCTURE

Hand and Edge Tools. The hand and edge tool industry manufactures basic hand tools and implements for domestic use and for professional mechanics and carpenters. Being held in the hand and powered by the person using them distinguishes hand tools from power tools and machine tools.

The long tradition of hand tool manufacturing in most countries means that different countries or regions have developed tools that often look and work quite differently from those used elsewhere. While European and North American tools are generally very similar, differences do exist. The French, for example, prefer levels shaped liked elongated trapezoids. Central Europeans use pliers to pull out bent nails, so they do not need hammers with claws. The differences between Western and Asian tools, however, are much more marked. Japan's well-established tool industry produces tools whose details and overall design are often quite different from anything in use in North America and Europe, as seen, for example, in the traditional Japanese block plane. While most Japanese tools are produced using sophisticated industrial processes, many traditional forms remain. Many of these tools are well received in other countries, where their quality, versatility, and efficiency attract professional carpenters and mechanics as well as amateur woodworkers.

According to figures compiled by the United Nations, Germany is the world's leading exporter of precision tools (including hand tools, power tools, tools for machine tools, grinding tools, molds, and measuring instruments), followed by Japan, the United States, Italy, the United Kingdom, Switzerland, Sweden, and China. Taiwan is also a leading exporter of low-cost base-metal hand tools such as pliers and wrenches. Other prominent manufacturers of basic tools and implements can be found in Israel, Turkey, Malaysia, and Australia.

As in many other industries, the resources required for investments in automation and other production technologies increasingly have pushed the industry toward greater consolidation. Economies of scale, increased efficiency, and precision are as important in this industry as in any other. The evolution of global trading patterns and increasing competition from low-wage producers has made it essential that production costs be kept to a minimum— something that could only be achieved by increasing automation in factories. Only in Japan, where the tradition of handcrafted tools has been strong, have artisans and small producers been able to hold onto their market niche.

Saw Blades and Handsaws. The products manufactured by saw blade and handsaw manufacturers come in all varieties and styles. What all saws have in common is a serrated edge or a perimeter with a series of sharp, usually V-shaped teeth, each of which removes a small piece from the material being cut. Wood saws are designed to cut with or across the grain of the wood. Ripsaws, also designed to cut with the grain, have teeth that work like chisels, chipping out pieces of wood. Crosscut saws are designed to cut cleanly through wood fibers, while backsaws feature numerous, tiny teeth for use in joinery work, where a clean cut is desirable. Dovetail saws are similar to backsaws, but are smaller and used for very fine cuts. Other saws such as compass, keyhole, and coping saws are designed to cut curves. The most common metal-cutting handsaw is the hacksaw. Circular saw blades are used in power saws for cutting lumber and boards to size. Chain saws consist of a continuous toothed chain and are used to cut down trees and cut logs. Other types of saw blades include tree-pruning saws and flooring saws.

As with hand tools, the style and design of saw blades and handsaws differs around the world. Asian—particularly Japanese—saws feature some unique innovations. The main difference between Japanese and Western saws is that Japanese saws are designed to cut when pulled, allowing them to be very thin and light. Less force is required to use these saws and their harder teeth keep them sharper longer. Their main disadvantage is they can be broken easily if handled carelessly. The double-edged Ryoba saw, which combines a ripping-tooth pattern on one side with a cross-cut tooth pattern on the other, proves especially popular because it cuts on both the pull stroke and the push stroke. First imported to the United States by Stanley Works, double-toothed saws grew so popular that the company eventually began making them, too.

Japan is also one of the leading exporters of saw blades, shipping about 15 percent of total production to overseas markets. Fifty-five percent of Japanese exports go to Southeast Asia and another 27 percent to North America. Japanese analysts expected to increase their shipments to Southeast Asia as countries in the region developed their own lumber industries.

BACKGROUND AND DEVELOPMENT

Hand tools and saws are as old as humankind itself; their development not only marked the beginning of human technology but also launched humanity on a journey that is still ongoing. While wood, bones, and antlers were all shaped into specialized implements, the fundamental element throughout this period was stone. Stone provided the hard edge necessary to shape other materials and to process plants and animals for eating. The three most important properties that stones and minerals required for use as tools were hardness, brittleness, and homogeneity. These properties ensured that the stone was strong enough to be a useful tool, while still being easy to chip or fracture into the desired shape. Early humans proved remarkably adept at finding and exploiting stones with these properties—flint, quartz, and obsidian were among the most widely used.

As humans moved from stone to metals, tools became increasingly diverse, efficient, and specialized. Individuals no longer fashioned tools for their personal use; instead, skilled craftsmen and artisans took over the task. Metalworkers hand-forged the cutters and blades, while woodworkers carved and attached the handles. For thousands of years, tool making remained a specialized, cottage industry. Some independent toolmakers sold their wares at markets and fairs, while others produced tools directly for those who could afford to hire them.

With the rise of mass production and advanced metalworking processes during the Industrial Revolution, the modern tool and saw industries began to take shape. In the pre-industrial United States, production was centered in the New England region, as this was where the largest markets and greatest numbers of skilled craftsmen could be found. Later, as the need for skilled craftsmen declined with the onset of industrialization, the industry spread to other areas.

The impact of industrialization turned tool and saw making into a highly sophisticated, assembly-line process that quickly wiped out the traditional art of tool making. Only in countries such as Japan, where ancient traditions remained a compelling value, did individual artisans continue to use the old skills.

Following World War II, the hand tool and saw blade industries enjoyed almost continuous high growth. Expanding economies, growing populations, rising incomes, and intensive construction activity provided these industries with a steady stream of customers. Even the recessions of the early 1980s and 1990s failed to put a significant damper on the prosperity of companies in these industries. Stanley Works, for example, one of the world's oldest and biggest manufacturers of hand tools and handsaws, doubled sales between 1985 and 1990 and continued to increase its sales through the early 1990s. In Japan, growth of these industries was temporarily stalled by slowdowns in construction and manufacturing caused by the rapid rise of the yen in 1985 and 1986. However, the industries quickly recovered and by the end of the decade were posting record sales.

The 1980s and 1990s were also a time of consolidation and increasing integration. Stanley Works, for example, acquired four tool companies in 1986 alone, one of which was based in Taiwan. These acquisitions boosted Stanley's existing position in the hand tools market and also provided it with complementary product lines such as high-end mechanic's tools and industrial implements. Vermont American Corporation, a major manufacturer of hand tools, handsaws, and drill accessories, was bought by a joint venture that included St. Louis-based Emerson

Electric Company and an investment bank owned by Sears, Roebuck and Company—whose line of Craftsman tools competed head-to-head with Stanley's products in the consumer tools business.

Despite an economic downturn, the hand tool industry suffered less damage than other sectors during the 2000s. However, it did not emerge completely unscathed. The economic slowdown had caused spending cutbacks within the corporate sector and high levels of unemployment, which had a negative impact on hand tool purchases. According to U.S. Census Bureau data released in January 2003, shipment values for hand and edge tool manufacturing fell from US$7.4 billion in 2000 to US$6.9 billion in 2001. Likewise, shipment values also fell for saw blade and handsaw manufacturers, dropping from US$1.6 billion to US$1.5 billion during the same period. By the end of the decade, unemployment rates were still at record highs and the construction industry had all but stalled. As the recession began to end, *Industry News* predicted that by 2012, the construction business would be in full recovery and demand would be on the rise.

As proof of the industry's difficult times, in 2003 Stanley Works eliminated 1,000 jobs and shut down two of its plants in an effort to trim costs. From 2001 to mid-2003, Wisconsin-based Snap-on Inc. in Kenosah cut 1,200 jobs throughout the world, citing heightened competition and depressed industrial economies in both Europe and North America. In July of 2003, the company announced that it would shed another 560 jobs by 2004, in conjunction with tool factory closures in Mount Carmel, Illinois, and Kenosha. In operation since 1937 and 1929, respectively, the two plants represented half of Snap-on's manufacturing facilities.

Heading into the late 2000s, the hand tool industry also was challenged by pressure from retail behemoths such as Wal-Mart, Home Depot, and Lowe's. An article in the October 22, 2003, issue of the *Wall Street Journal*, appropriately titled "Feeling the Squeeze," explained: "Unlike even just a decade ago, these huge retailers have clout to squeeze suppliers and replace their products with private label in-house brands. As the tool makers respond by rushing to move production to cheaper markets, they risk jeopardizing the quality of the products, the only advantage they have over the private-label offerings."

In March of 2004, Manufacturing.net provided a detailed look at conditions within the hand tool industry. Citing data from the Port Angeles, Washington-based research firm Thinking Cap Solutions Inc., it demonstrated that average product prices for hand and edge tools fell almost 0.7 percent from September 2002 to September 2003, while average prices for handsaws and saw blades increased a modest 1.5 percent. At the same time, direct manufacturing costs for these categories were on the rise, increasing 0.2 percent and nearly 0.9 percent, respectively. Manufacturing.net also reported that from December 2002 to December 2003, U.S. end markets for these categories were either stagnant or declining. For hand and edge tools, growth amounted 0.1 percent, while growth in the handsaws and saw blades category actually fell 0.1 percent. On the bright side for manufacturers, mechanics' hand tools and handsaws were expected to garner higher prices in 2004, rising between 1.7 and 1.9 percent.

A study by the Freedonia Group published in 2005 found that while the introduction of lighter, more powerful electric tools will aid the U.S. tool market, demand for hand tools would decrease due to increased imports and reduced tool expenditures from the construction industry, resulting in an overall rise in tool demand of 3.8 percent per year through 2009. The report further stated that the trend toward consolidation among retailers would negatively affect prices.

According to a report by *PRLog*, in spite of a decline in the new housing market and construction industry, there will continue to be a shift toward the power tool market in the private sector. Spurred on by the new lighter, cordless, more user-friendly power tools, the home repair sector is predicted to continue to grow throughout 2016. Power tools are forecast to outpace their more durable hand tool counterparts.

Ergonomic tools remained popular during the late 2000s. Demand for this hand tool category has been strong because of consumer and company interest in preventing injuries. Ergonomic tools do not cause as much strain and fatigue as conventional tools because they are designed to better fit the human hand and to better suit arm and hand motions. This is a concern of professionals as well as do-it-yourselfers and has driven research into improved materials and design.

CURRENT CONDITIONS

U.S. shipments of hand tools and saw blades reached US$7.4 billion in 2005, up from US$7 billion the previous year. In the last quarter of 2004 alone, 3.9 million hammers were sold in the United States for a retail value of US$45.9 million. Traditional claw-style hammers comprised 82.8 percent of sales.

By 2006, the U.S. tool industry was feeling the effects of certain trade practices. According to Stan Modic of *Tooling & Production*, "Machine tool exports . . . are stymied because of the Commerce and State Departments' inability to expedite export licensing. What's worse, Washington continues to pass free trade agreements with emerging nations without fully exploring the impact on U.S. competitiveness." Forty-seven percent of U.S. machine

tool production in the first quarter of 2006 was exported; 10 percent went to China, the leading consumer of machine tools. China bought US$12.9 billion in machine tools in 2005, as compared to about half that (US$6.2 billion) in the United States. The Association for Manufacturing Technology reported that U.S. market share in China has decreased by about 38 percent since 1996, due mostly to export controls and government inefficiency in processing licenses.

Indeed, according to figures from the International Trade Administration, the number of U.S. exports of hand and machine tools increased only slightly between 2001 and 2005, from US$2.4 billion to US$2.9 billion. On the other hand, U.S. imports in this category shot up from US$3.3 billion in 2001 to US$4.6 billion in 2005. Likewise, Chinese imports of hand and machine tools increased almost four-fold from US$370 million in 2001 to US$1.4 billion in 2005. As of 2005, the United States was the largest importer of hand and machine tools, followed by Germany, Canada, China, and France. The largest exporter was Germany, followed closely by China. Spots three through five went to the United States, Japan, and Taiwan, respectively.

Experts looked to the future of the hand tool industry with optimism. According to the Bharat Book Bureau, power and hand tool demand in the United States will rise more than 3 percent annually through 2011. Growth of power tools was expected to outpace that of traditional hand tools, due in part to increased consumer interest and improved technology and usability of such lightweight cordless tools as saws, sanders, polishers, and grinders. Also, although professional users were responsible for about two-thirds of overall tool demand in 2006, growth in consumer tool demand was expected to grow faster due to the ongoing popularity of do-it-yourself activities and hobbyists and the trade-up by consumers to feature-laden, light cordless power tools.

RESEARCH AND TECHNOLOGY

Hand and Edge Tools. Given the nature of the products it manufactures, a major research issue in the hand and edge tools industry is the development of durable, high-quality, low-cost materials—especially for consumer tools. Items such as garden spades, rakes, and pruning tools need to be lightweight, strong, easy to clean, and rustproof. For example, in the 1990s many companies began using plastic materials not only for handles, but also for blades and tines.

Other research has focused on means of maintaining competitive, low-cost production while meeting the requirements of stringent new U.S. anti-pollution laws. Stanley Works, for instance, adapted an advanced chrome-plating process known as "sputtering" to finish tape-measure cases. Its previous system had produced millions of gallons of contaminated water that the company had been forced to clean up. The new process, on the other hand, used no water, cost the same as the previous method, and provided a stronger, more durable coating.

Automated production technologies were eagerly adopted by hand and edge tool manufacturers. For the big U.S., Japanese, and European companies that could afford them, computer-controlled production lines were the key to competing with the low-cost Southeast Asian producers that invaded established markets during the 1980s and 1990s. Computer-aided design also facilitated the production of more efficient and more precise tools. Reliable precision tools were extremely important to professional mechanics and carpenters, and brand-name manufacturers spared no expense in ensuring that their products were as accurate as possible. Stanley, for example, used laser scanners to check the markings on its tape measures to guarantee accuracy.

As part of the industry's ongoing effort to produce more ergonomic tools, Bettcher Industries Inc. introduced its Airshirz pneumatic scissors in the late 1990s. Specifically created for the poultry industry and designed to fit comfortably in the palm of the hand, these scissors are powered by air pressure, not human muscle. This greatly reduces the amount of gripping force needed to operate the scissors.

Besides ergonomic tools, manufacturers concentrated on producing other new tool technologies called "smart" tools in the late 1990s. Using laser and computer technology, smart tools perform tasks more quickly and accurately than conventional tools. One such smart tool is the laser level, which has a graphic display and a sensor that can be calibrated electronically. By 2004 laser technology had become very affordable, and was driving sales within the hand tool industry. Indeed, consumers were able to buy laser levels from stores such as Wal-Mart for under US$50. In its December 15, 2003, issue, *DSN Retailing Today* reported that laser-guided tools were "the hottest thing," with strong growth expected.

Another technological advancement in the hand tool category was the Weight Forward hammer from Rockford, Illinois-based Estwing. By shifting the center of gravity, the tool's design helped to reduce user fatigue, while at the same time maximizing its striking power. The hammer was especially popular in the United Kingdom. In *Contract Flooring Journal,* Estwing distributor the Rollins Group reported that it had sold 10,000 of the hammers from fall 2003 to summer 2004 alone. In 2004, the Weight Forward hammer won an Industrial Design Excellence Award (IDEA) from *Business Week* and the Industrial Designers Society of America.

Saw Blades and Handsaws. According to Naohide Morikawa, managing director of the Japanese Industrial Saw and Knife Association, the quality of saw blades directly affects the productivity and production costs of mechanical processing and woodwork. Consequently, the precision and performance of cutting tools had to match that of other modern precision technologies. Automated, labor-saving, and unmanned operations were equally important in saw blade and handsaw production. With a significant portion of production focused on manufacturing cutting tools for use in modern machining processes, it is essential that saw makers be able to provide cutting tools with long service life, high working and feeding speeds, and extra-high precision.

Advances in materials technology also meant that the number and variety of materials requiring processing was also increasing rapidly. This, in turn, compelled the saw blade and handsaw industry to fund research on the development of new cutting materials suitable for new applications. To compete with advances in laser technology that threatened to reduce the need for industrial saw blades in metal and plastics cutting, Japanese, German, and U.S. manufacturers all concentrated their research and development efforts on advanced design and manufacturing technology.

Even for basic handsaws, investigation of new materials and designs was no less common, particularly for high-end, professional-use products. Accuracy, durability, and flexibility were seen as increasingly important. Moreover, the demand for cutting tools thin enough and precise enough to minimize material waste is growing as builders and manufacturers seek ways to reduce waste.

INDUSTRY LEADERS
Hand Tools.

Stanley Works. In March 2010, Stanley Works marched with Black & Decker to become Stanley Black & Decker. No hand tool manufacturer is as ubiquitous as Connecticut-based Stanley Black & Decker (SB&D), which leads the hand tool industry with over 17,600 employees and 2007 sales of US$4.48 billion. In July of 2005, the company announced its largest acquisition since its inception in 1843 with its agreement to purchase the Paris-based Facom Tools for $485 million. With roughly 30 percent of the company's sales already originating overseas, the Facom deal would bring that total to 40 percent. The company also bought National Manufacturing for $170 million.

Although SB&D competes with many other much larger companies, such as the Illinois Tool Works and Cooper Industries Corporation, none of them comes close to matching Stanley's share of the hand tools market. The company's familiar yellow and black tools dominate the hardware aisles in stores throughout North America and represent the top-selling brand in the United States.

Unlike other companies in the tool industry, SB&D manufactures just about every kind of tool imaginable. Its major product lines are consumer tools (carpenter's tools, tool boxes, and masonry tools); industrial tools (hand tools, electronic diagnostic tools, and cabinets); engineered tools (pneumatic nailers, staplers, and office products); hardware (hinges, hasps, brackets, and bolts); and specialty hardware (residential door systems, power-operated gates, and garage-door openers).

With manufacturing and distribution centers in more than 30 countries around the world, Stanley is truly a global business. Its plants operate in Germany, Canada, France, Poland, Taiwan, and Thailand. The company's subsidiaries include Best Lock Corp., Blick plc, Frisco Bay Industries Ltd., and ZAG Industries Ltd. Some of the internationally known brand names attached to Stanley's products include Bostitch, Goldblatt, Husky, MAC Tools, and Monarch.

One of the oldest tool-making companies in the world, Stanley Works was born in a converted War of 1812-era armory in New Britain, Connecticut, in 1843. There, Frederick T. Stanley installed New Britain's first steam engine and began producing bolts and house trimmings. In 1852 he and his brother got together with five friends to form Stanley Works. The business expanded rapidly during the U.S. Civil War and afterwards when westward migration stimulated a growing market for hardware and tools.

By the end of the nineteenth century, Stanley was the leading producer of hand tools in the United States and was poised to expand even more rapidly in the twentieth century. By 1914 the company had established operations in Canada and made numerous domestic acquisitions. In 1926 it set up shop in Germany, and in 1929 formed an electric tool division.

In the post-Great Depression years, Stanley geared up for war production in the 1940s and later launched a massive expansion program that continued into the 1990s. By staying within its product line, Stanley was able to effectively manage its growth and maintain its reputation for quality. Dozens of companies fell into Stanley's orbit during this period, including Berry Industries (garage doors, 1965), Ackley Manufacturing and Sales (hydraulic tools, 1972), Mac Tools (1980), and National Hand Tool Corporation (1986). During the 1980s, Stanley acquired some 21 companies, which, by 1990, were responsible for about half of the company's total revenues.

In Western Europe, Stanley owns Atro Industriale, an Italian tool-making company. Stanley also established a strong presence in Israel with the purchase of ZAG Industries in 1998. In addition, anticipating that future growth would depend on a strong presence in the fast-growing Pacific Rim market, Stanley launched an aggressive bid to capture market share by establishing high-tech plants in Taiwan, Thailand, and Australia. Its acquisitions of Dallas-based National Hand Tool Corporation and Chiro Tool Manufacturing Corporation of Taiwan were motivated in large part by the factories both companies operated in Taiwan.

In the late 1990s, Stanley underwent a significant restructuring process to remain competitive. Former General Electric CEO, John M. Trani, took over the helm at Stanley at the end of 1996 and began making his trademark cost-cutting changes. Stanley consolidated its 123 operations and manufacturing plants into just 70 facilities and laid off 4,500 employees, or 25 percent of its workforce. Stanley planned to spend more on research and development and hoped the restructuring would free funds for its R&D budget. Stanley also announced it would divest itself of some of its concerns in order to focus on its core products—tools.

Snap-on Inc. Another leading maker of hand tools is Snap-on Inc. of Kenosha, Wisconsin. Formerly known as Snap-on Tools Corporation, the company changed its name to Snap-on Inc. in the mid-1990s. Specializing in automotive hand and power tools and tool storage products for professional mechanics, Snap-on Inc. posted US$2.5 billion in 2006 revenues. From 2001 to mid-2003, Snap-on eliminated 1,200 jobs worldwide in the face of heightened competition and depressed industrial economies in both Europe and North America. In July of 2003, after shutting down two of its four manufacturing facilities, the company announced that it would shed another 560 jobs.

Snap-on's 12,400 employees—down from 14,000 in 2001—produce a wide range of specialized tools including wrenches, wheel balancing and alignment equipment, sockets, aircraft tools, chisels, punches, pliers, screwdrivers, hammers, pneumatic impact wrenches and chisels as well as power-assisted equipment and electronic diagnostic equipment.

Incorporated as Snap-on Wrench Company in 1920, Snap-on Inc. was born as the result of an innovative idea—interchangeable wrench handles and sockets. Unable to persuade his employer to take his idea seriously, Joe Johnson and co-worker William Seidemann made a sample set of five handles and ten sockets. Two Wisconsin salesmen, Stanton Palmer and Newton Tarble, sold over 500 orders and set up their own distributing business demonstrating tool sets at customer sites. In 1921 they bought out the Snap-on Wrench Company and Palmer became president.

In 1930 the company reincorporated as Snap-on Tools, Incorporated, and in 1931 opened its first foreign subsidiary (Canada). During World War II, to meet widespread civilian shortages, Snap-on salesmen began carrying tools in their trucks and vans. The concept has remained Snap-on's trademark. Red and white Snap-on Tools vans loaded with high-quality tools traveled to garages and gas stations throughout North America. High quality, dependability, and, above all, service made Snap-on Tools North America's leading supplier of hand tools to professional mechanics in the 1990s and early 2000s.

Snap-on Inc., like Stanley Works, expanded rapidly during the postwar period. Unlike its competitor, however, Snap-on did not focus on acquiring other manufacturers. Instead, it relied on expanding its dealerships, establishing franchises, and providing mechanics with a reliable source of up-to-date tools, training, and service. Dealers called on customers once a week, demonstrating new products and delivering new tools. In addition, Snap-on offered its customers interest-free credit and eventually built up its own financial services operation.

Snap-on Inc.'s growth closely paralleled that of its rival, Stanley Works. From 1985 to 2001, Snap-on's sales nearly quadrupled, climbing from US$540 million to more than US$2 billion. The company earned a reputation for quality when it became the sole supplier of tools to NASA for its space shuttles. In 1992 the company established Snap-on Tools Japan and in 1994 changed its name to Snap-on Inc. to reflect its movement away from its traditional core business of tools. Today, Snap-on tools are available in 150 countries.

Other Leaders. Also prominent in the North American hand tools market was Cooper Tools Inc., a subsidiary of Cooper Industries. Cooper Industries employs 31,200 people worldwide and recorded 2008 sales of US$6.5 billion. Elsewhere in the world, leading companies in this category have included Kuang Yuang Industrial Company of Taiwan, Vargus of Israel, and Finetools SDN BHD of Malaysia.

Saw Blades and Handsaws.

Black & Decker. Among the leading companies are those with a strong line of power tools such as Black & Decker Corporation of the United States and Makita Corporation of Japan. The world's largest power tool maker, Black & Decker is also a leading maker of saw blades. The company's Maryland-based subsidiary Black & Decker Corporation Accessories and Fastenings handles production of saw blades and drill bits for use in the company's tools. On March 12, 2010, the corporation merged with Stanley Works to become Stanly Black & Decker. Besides the Black & Decker name, the company also owns the DeWalt brand of hand tools. Overall,

Black & Decker posted sales of US$6.09 billion in 2008. After eliminating 900 jobs and closing two plants in January 2004, the company reported a 61 percent hike in second quarter earnings. In July 2004, Black & Decker announced that it would acquire Pentair Inc.'s tool unit in a deal worth US$775 million. Pentair manufactured the well-known line of Porter-Cable and Delta power tools. Black & Decker also purchased Vector Products in 2006 for US$160 million. Among Black & Decker's largest customers are Home Depot and Lowe's, two popular do-it-yourself superstores which, in 2008, together boasted a workforce of 27,000.

Blount International, Inc. Another large company operating in this sector is Blount International, Inc., a major manufacturer of chainsaws. Blount employed 3,100 people in 2009, down from 5,000 in 2001, and reported sales of US$502.4 million. The company also manufactures timber harvesting equipment and industrial tractors.

Robert Bosch Tool Corp. Based in Mount Prospect, Illinois, the Robert Bosch Tool Corp. was created with the merger of Vermont American Corp. and S-B Power Tool Co. It subsequently acquired the North American tool operations from its parent, Robert Bosch. The company ranks among the leading manufacturers of saw blades and handsaws, and manufactures such well-known brands as Bosch, Dremel, Skil, and Vermont American. In addition to power tools, handsaws, and saw blades, the company manufactures Gilmour lawn and garden tools. In 2008 the company employed approximately 4,000 workers and reported sales of US$1 billion.

MAJOR COUNTRIES IN THE INDUSTRY

United States. There were more than 1,000 firms in the hand and power tool market by the mid-2000s, with the top six firms accounting for 55 percent of 2004 sales. With major tool producers such as Stanley Works and Snap-on Inc. based in the United States, the country stands out as the single leading producer and market for hand tools. Still, the U.S. continues to be the largest importer of hand tools in the world.

European Union. The European Union maintains a strong global presence in the hand tool industry with Germany as a leading exporter of tools. Although Germany is a significant importer (second behind the United States worldwide), the country exported about twice as much as it imported in the mid-2000s, controlling roughly 20 percent of the export market.

Asia. In Asia, Taiwan has emerged as a competitor with Japan and China, which have traditionally dominated this industry. Taiwan has become a major exporter of hand tools and hardware. In 2002, its base of mainly small manufacturing firms produced US$295 million worth of power tools alone, mainly on the low end of the quality spectrum. With this in mind, Taiwan relies on imports to satisfy demand for higher-quality power tools among a growing do-it-yourself market, as well as customers in the remodeling and decorating industries. According to a report from *STAT-USA,* Japan supplied 44 percent of Taiwan's imports, followed by Germany (24 percent) and the United States (8 percent). The power tool market in Taiwan was valued at US$41 million in 2002, down 31 percent from the previous year due to weak economic conditions. By 2005 Taiwan was exporting US$1.6 billion worth of hand and machine tools.

China was set to make a significant impact on the world economy by causing a spike in steel prices. This, in turn, was expected to impact the hand tool market. The nation's burgeoning economic growth spurred a flurry of construction projects in addition to its preparations for the 2008 Olympics. In fact, in the mid-2000s China was the world's leading consumer of scrap steel products. Although its industrial production increased 25 percent from March 2003 to March 2004, the nation was relying on its own steel to support domestic growth instead of exporting to other nations. In the April 2004 issue of *Do-It-Yourself Retailing,* House-Hassen Merchandising Vice President Allen Winn indicated that retailers would likely increase nail prices by 40 percent. Taking a broader view, he said: "Anything that's got steel in it is going to go through the roof."

BIBLIOGRAPHY

Arditi, Lynn. "Hand-Tool Maker's Subsidiary to Expand." *The Providence Journal* (RI), 19 February 2004.

"Black & Decker Buys Pentair." *Home Channel News,* 9 August 2004.

"China to be No. 1 in Tools." *Appliance Design* (August 2005).

Content, Thomas. "Kenosha, Wis.-Based Snap-On Tools to Eliminate 560 Jobs by 2004." *The Milwaukee Journal Sentinel,* 22 July 2003.

"Feeling the Squeeze." *The Wall Street Journal,* 22 October 2003.

HardwareB2B. *Taiwan Registers Increase in Hand Tool Exports for 2000.* Asia TradeMart.com, 1 March 2001. Available from http://www.hardwareb2b.com.

"Hoover's Company Capsules." *Hoover's Online,* 2007. Available from www.hoovers.com.

Howell, Debbie. "Laser-Guided Tools." *DSN Retailing Today* (15 December 2003).

"Lighter Hammer Reduces Fatigue." *Contract Flooring Journal* (June 2004).

Loftus, Peter. "Black & Decker's Profit Jumps: Deal Is Set for Pentair Tool Unit." *The Wall Street Journal,* 20 July 2004.

Nussbaum, Bruce. "Winners 2004: The Best Product Designs of the Year." *Business Week* (5 July 2004).

Modic, Stan. "Sitting Between a Rock and a Hard Place." *Tooling & Production* (May 2007).

"Power and Hand Tools Industry Forecasts to 2011 and 2016." Bharat Book Bureau, 2007. Available from www.bharatbook.com.

Power and Hand Tool Industry News: Professional Power Tool Guide, 14 January 2009. Available from http://professional-power-tool-guide.com.

"Power Tools." *STAT-USA Market Research Reports* (2 June 2003).

"Price Hikes Expected for Some Industries, but Not All." *Manufacturing.Net,* 1 March 2004. Available from www.manufacturing.net/.

"Stanley Adds to Tool Box." *Knight-Ridder Tribune Business News* (19 July 2005).

"Steel Shortage Could Hit Industry Hard." *Do-It-Yourself Retailing* (April 2004).

"Study Gauges Power Tool Demand." *Home Channel News Newsfax* (23 May 2005).

"Tools for Use in the Hand or in Machines." *Imports/Exports: 2001-2005* (15 June 2007). Available from www.intracen.org.

U.S. Census Bureau. "Statistics for Industries and Industry Groups: 2004." *Annual Survey of Manufacturers* (December 2005). Available from www.census.gov.

U.S. Department of Commerce. Bureau of the Census, International Trade Administration. "U.S. Industry Sector Data." 1 August 2004. Available from www.census.gov.

"Who Is Buying That?(Hammer Sales)." *Home Channel News* (7 March 2005).

SIC 3320

IRON AND STEEL FOUNDRIES

NAICS CODE(S)

331511. Iron and steel foundries manufacture malleable, ductile, investment,and gray iron castings. These establishments generally operate on a job or order basis, manufacturing castings for sale to others or for interplant transfer.

INDUSTRY SNAPSHOT

Foundries are factories that produce metal castings. The foundry industry is a highly fragmented yet essential element of the modern global economy. Metal castings are required in numerous machinery applications, including automobiles, aircraft, and other transportation equipment. According to the North American Die Casting Association, castings are used in 90 percent of all finished manufactured products. Beginning in the late 1990s and continuing into the 2000s, however, castings of iron and steel faced continued competition from aluminum, zinc, various alloys, and plastics. As a result, the more traditional iron and steel castings lost market share, and demand for some has been stagnant. Nevertheless, the U.S. Geological Survey estimated that U.S. iron and steel

Users of Metal Castings by Industry, 2008

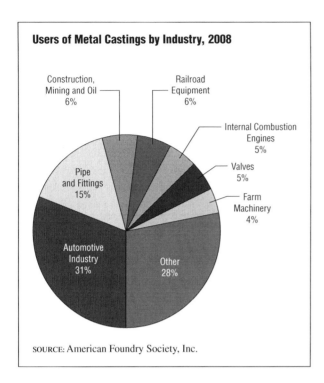

SOURCE: American Foundry Society, Inc.

industry and ferrous foundries produced goods worth US$117 billion in 2008.

Metal casting production remains fragmented due to several influences. In a minority of cases—about 13 percent in the United States—metals are cast directly by manufacturers of end products rather than by specialized foundries. The independent foundries are often highly specialized and serve specific niches, such as automotive brake and power train components or turbine equipment for power plants. Ongoing consolidation has greatly reduced the number of ferrous foundries in operation, but it has not given rise to any major producers that can be said to dominate the industry, either on a global level or on a national level in leading countries.

As of 2008, due primarily to the auto and transportation industries steep slump, the iron and steel industry took a significant hit in terms of production demand and revenue from sales. Pig iron and raw steel foundries had a combined production capability of 113 million tons. Foundries in Indiana accounted for 25 percent of raw steel production, followed by Ohio at 14 percent, Pennsylvania at 6 percent, and Michigan at 5 percent. Approximately 564 iron foundries and 239 steel foundries were operating in the U.S. in 2008.

ORGANIZATION AND STRUCTURE

Most of theworld's metal castings are ferrous, which means they ultimately derive from iron ore, as is the case with all types of iron and steel. The casting process involves forming metal shapes or structures by pouring

molten metal, in this case iron or steel, into molds or dies. Most molds are made of sand, which is able to withstand high temperatures, but wax and other materials may be used. Wax is used in a form of metal casting known as investment casting. When a die is used, the process is often called die casting. Die casting differs from other methods in that metal shapes are actively pressed in dies using force, whereas other forms of casting allow the metal cast to passively take the shape of a mold. The various production techniques offer different advantages of strength, precision, and cost effectiveness for the casting of different source metals.

The industry is heavily engaged in manufacturing pipes, pipe fittings, and numerous mechanical components. However, other segments of the industry are growing in response to changing market demands. For example, the automotive industry switched most engine components to aluminum in response to consumer demands for lighter, more fuel-efficient cars. While this move has hurt some gray and ductile iron foundries, it has also forced them to find alternative markets.

The automotive and aerospace industries were historically large customers of gray and ductile iron foundries. So large was the demand that each of the Big Three U.S. automakers owned several foundries of their own. In the 1980s and 1990s these industries were beset in some places with production slumps and requirements for new materials. Although the automotive industry and their suppliers enjoyed a brief period of increased demand in the late 1990s, by 2001, the industries faced a recession. Consumer demand changed, decreasing the iron portion of the automotive casting business. Likewise, in the mid- to late 1980s and early 1990s, the poor financial performance of both the U.S. automotive and aerospace industries forced closings of many self-contained foundries. Outsourcing the casting business was a cheaper alternative than underutilizing plant and labor capacities.

In the European Union (EU), most foundries are small businesses employing fewer than 50 people. However, as more companies automate molding lines, three work shifts are needed to meet required efficiencies, thus creating a change in the European industry toward larger foundries. Due to the need to reduce costs, many foundries have been taken over by large groups, thereby cutting out the middleman and controlling a wide range of casting technologies.

In July 2008, the United Steelworkers signed an agreement to merge with the United Kingdom and Ireland-based union, Unite, to form a new global union entity called Workers Uniting. This new union had a membership of three million members.

BACKGROUND AND DEVELOPMENT

For at least 5,000 years, humans have been casting metals. Metallurgy began in the Bronze Age, when humans started extracting ores and forming them through melting or hammering. The Iron Age began in Europe around 1100 B.C. Only through contact with Europe did the Americas enter the Iron Age.

Even though iron is the fourth most abundant element and makes up more than five percent of the earth's crust, cast iron did not come into commercial use until 1700 when a mechanic named Abraham Darby and some Dutch workmen established a brass foundry in Bristol, England. It was there that he and his men started experimenting with iron as a replacement for brass. This presented technical problems, as brass and iron are completely different pouring mediums in terms of reaction with sand and solidification patterns. Darby received little cooperation from his workers, and the project met with little success. Darby's luck changed when an eager boy working in his shop, John Thomas, said that he thought he "saw where they had missed it." The two worked all through that night and into the next morning before successfully casting a complete iron pot. For proprietary reasons, Darby and Thomas entered into an agreement in which the boy was to remain his servant to keep the secret.

Malleable iron was patented in Europe by Samuel Lucas in 1804. However, he was not the first to develop the alloy. A Frenchman named Reaumur described the process in 1722. In 1630, Englishman David Ramsey was granted a royal patent. In its infancy, malleable iron was difficult to attain, due to necessary chemical controls and the lack of equipment to monitor the chemistry. Unfortunately, when a bad batch of malleable iron was made, it was totally useless because it was too brittle and therefore unmachinable. Despite this, its popularity was unparalleled because it offered the fluidity of cast iron and the ductility of steel. In Europe, malleable iron was used for cutlery, pulley blocks, harness hardware, and railroad rails. In 1831, Seth Boyden received a U.S. patent, signed by President Andrew Jackson, after winning a silver medal in 1828 for his castings displayed at the Fourth Annual Exhibition of the Franklin Institute of the State of Pennsylvania.

The mass production of inexpensive steel became possible after the introduction of the Bessemer process, named after its inventor, British metallurgist Sir Henry Bessemer. Bessemer reasoned that carbon in molten pig iron unites readily with oxygen, so a strong blast of air through molten pig iron should convert the pig iron into steel by reducing its carbon content. In 1856, Bessemer created a converter, a large pear-shaped receptacle with holes at the bottom to allow injection of compressed air. He then filled the converter with molten pig iron, blew compressed air through the molten metal, and found that the iron was cleared of carbon and silicon in a few

minutes. Moreover, instead of freezing up from the blast of cold air, the metal grew hotter. One shortfall of the Bessemer process was that it did not remove phosphorus from the pig iron, which makes steel excessively brittle. Thus the process could only be used on phosphorus-free ores which are relatively scarce and costly. In 1876, Welshman Sidney Gilchrist Thomas discovered that adding limestone to the converter draws the phosphorus into a slag which floats to the top of the converter and can then be skimmed off, resulting in phosphorus-free steel. This crucial discovery meant that vast stores of iron ore from around the world could be used to make pig iron for the converters, which in turn led to skyrocketing production of cheap steel in Europe and the United States. Steel magnate Andrew Carnegie's genius for lowering production costs would drive prices as low as US$14 per ton by the end of the nineteenth century. This drop in cost was followed by an equally dramatic increase in quality as steel replaced iron rails, which had an average life of two years. The new steel rails had a lifespan of 10 years and could bear railcar weights of up to 70 tons as opposed the eight tons. Carnegie was quick to recognize the importance chemistry in steelmaking, which was one of the keys to his success as a steel manufacturer.

Ductile iron was not discovered until after World War II. Laboratorymetallurgists at International Nickel Company noticed that the addition of a higher content of magnesium than normally required for gray iron produced a structurally different material. Upon observation at a microscopic level, the graphite particles had taken on a spheroidal shape, thus coining the name "nodular iron" in the United States and "spheroidal graphite cast iron" in Great Britain. The recognition of nodular iron's mechanical strength, while providing more ductility than other metals in its class, provided it with its more commonly accepted name, ductile iron. Since its release to the marketplace in 1949, it has gained acceptance as an important engineering material and replaced many of the previous applications formerly reserved for steels and other irons. In the engineering materials community, the discovery of ductile iron is one of the greatest in the twentieth century.

The U.S. metal casting industry was wounded severely in the 1980s. During the 1970s, the industry was overwhelmed with back orders that exceeded annual capacity. This produced a seller's market, which was reflected in pricing strategies and profit margins. However, shipment volume was the key issue during the 1970s, not quality or price. During the 1980s, foreign competitors emerged who could sell better quality castings at lower prices and provide on-time delivery. When the economy entered recessionary times, consumers turned to overseas suppliers, leaving domestic producers behind. U.S. foundries were operating at no more than 50 percent capacity by the mid-1980s.

By the mid-1990s, U.S. iron foundries had lost nearly 60 percent of the tonnage shipped compared to levels in 1978. Gray iron suffered a huge decline between 1978 and 1982, from approximately 18.5 million tons to 9.5 million tons. Between 1982 and 1990, gray iron shipments continued to decrease. Ductile iron, however, has shown slight growth in shipments since 1982, continuing a trend started in 1966. The growth of ductile iron is largely due to its increasing recognition as a better alternative, economically and structurally, to gray and malleable irons.

The foundry industry experienced largely stagnant demand in the mid- to late 1990s and a recession late in 2000 and 2001. After declines in previous years, some manufacturers viewed the stagnant years as a relatively healthy period. In the United States, annual production of ferrous castings hovered at the 13 million ton level between 1994 and 1997. In 1997, these iron and steel castings were valued at approximately US$18 billion. By 2000, the value of all U.S. castings shipments, including aluminum and other nonferrous metals, was expected to reach US$33 billion on a volume of 16.3 million tons, representing a 10 percent increase in value and a four percent rise in volume from 1997 levels.

However, production fell short of projections. In 2000, U.S. foundries shipped 14 million tons worth of iron and steel castings, the lowest shipping year since 1992, with sales of US$28 million. Projections for 2001 were even more grim, and foundries braced themselves for an economic slowdown, particularly in the automotive industry.

CURRENT CONDITIONS

Although the United States experienced a decrease in light vehicle production in 2006, metal casting shipments rose more than 1.5 percent over 2005 to 14.6 million tons. Sales of metal castings were estimated at US$35 billion for 2006 and forecasted to increase to US$44 billion by 2016, although aluminum was expected to experience a faster rate of growth than steel or iron, according to *Modern Casting*. In 2008, more than 12.6 million tons of castings in the United States were valued at more than US$31.5 billion. The United States is the world's second largest metal casting producer, coming in behind China, followed by Japan, Russia, Germany, and India. More than 90 percent of all manufactured goods and capital equipment are created by using castings in their manufacturing process.

According to the American Foundry Society, Inc., the automotive industry is the largest users of castings, with 31 percent of the total as of 2008. Pipe and fittings utilize 15 percent, while construction, mining, and oil field equipment take 6 percent. The rest is used to make internal combustion engines, railroad equipment, valves, and farm machinery. All sectors of the United States military heavily rely on metal castings for tank, truck, jet engine and other vital components, as well as weaponry and ammunitions.

Based on first quarter sales and production in 2009, total metal casting shipments were expected to fall by over 2.3 million during the remainder of the year. Iron castings were expected to decline annually and reach a low of 806,000 tons in 2012, as the average weight of gray iron per light vehicle is expected to drop to 140 lbs. Shipments of steel castings for autos were also expected to decrease at a rate of about seven percent annually. Other end-use segments of the market were predicted to see similar drops in gray iron and steel shipments while aluminum and ductile iron increase. Some of the trends that were affecting the industry in the late 2000s in the United States included a decrease in housing starts, an increase in imports, and replacement by plastic and aluminum.

As the United States moved into the late 2000s, conventional iron and steel castings continued to encounter rising competition from lighter and more highly engineered materials, particularly aluminum and alloys, as well as from manufacturing alternatives to metal casting. This has been especially true in end markets like the automotive industry, in order to decrease vehicle weights to improve fuel efficiency to comply with federal fuel economy regulations. The U.S. government mandated in 1977 that fuel economy for new U.S. cars must average 27.5 miles per gallon. In order to comply, automakers needed to produce lighter cars. The impact on the steel industry was tremendous. In 1980, the average U.S. car contained 600 pounds of cast iron. Two decades later, it contained only 325 pounds, and by 2005, it averaged 220 pounds, according to the American Foundry Society. In 2009, light vehicle ductile iron castings dropped to 175 pounds. In 2007, commercial vehicle makers accounted for 80 percent of the castings market. By 2009, shipments of aluminum castings were expected to grow by 50 percent.

Some of the newer materials are more expensive than steel and iron, and some industry experts believe that by revising specifications for steel and iron castings, they may achieve similar weight reductions that manufacturers seek when using alternative metals. In addition, ferrous metal castings enjoy a strength advantage over aluminum. In very lightweight conditions, aluminum components may require reinforcement, while iron or steel counterparts of similar specification do not. In a few cases, manufacturers have returned to iron castings after disappointing results with aluminum's price and performance. Nonetheless, barring a major technological breakthrough, most observers expect aluminum—along with plastics and engineered materials—to continue to wrest market share from iron and steel castings well into the 2000s.

Much of the cast steel market that remains faces fierce global competition, particularly in the gray iron municipal castings and diesel components markets. In particular, the foundry industry faces growing competition from the booming market in China and India. Imports of Chinese gray iron castings in the United States alone grew by 45 percent in a mere three years, from US$85 million in 2000 to US$123 million in 2003. In the United Kingdom, however, *Furnaces International* reported that more than 80 percent of foundries were reporting positive outlooks in the mid-2000s, particularly in Scotland. Worldwide metal casting shipments were expected to rise to 105.5 million tons by 2016.

Foundries in the United States use and recycle 100 million tons of sand every year. It is continuously recycled until it loses its properties. Approximately six percent of the sand used in the casting process cannot be recycled for foundry use and is then shipped for reuse in brick and concrete production. Scrap metal is remelted and the residual pollutants create significant problems. While nearly all foundries reuse scrap metals, using 15 to 20 million tons of recycled scrap metal annually, economics force the foundries to use more original materials. Energy costs rose significantly in the mid-2000s, impacting both the melting processes and transportation costs. Many foundries purchased more original pig iron for use in production as a result. Furthermore, because foundries required cleaner scrap metal than steel mills, scrap which is free of paint and other contaminants, the prices for foundry scrap are generally higher than mill scrap.

RESEARCH AND TECHNOLOGY

In the mid-1990s, English automaker Lotus Group and SinterCast of Sweden were codeveloping a production process for compacted graphite iron (CGI) for automotive uses. CGI's benefits are that it combines the benefits of gray iron's ease of machining, casting, and thermal characteristics with ductile iron's toughness and strength. SinterCast's process, which calculates the amount of reagent needed in CGI before pouring the iron into the mold, was used earlier in 1993 by Fagor Ederlan of Spain and RH Sheppard of Hanover, Pennsylvania. In another codevelopment during 1993, Tennant Metallurgical of England and Globe Metallurgical of Ohio created Tenbloc, an in-mold inoculation product. Tenbloc represented a new method of pressing and sintering that bonds

the inoculating particles. The blocks have proven to be effective in inoculating gray and ductile iron castings.

Another material, austempered ductile iron (ADI), gained acceptance throughout the world due to its lower weight when compared to steel and higher mechanical properties when compared to conventional ductile iron. Previously impossible applications were possible with ADI, and designers around the world learned how to use it. National standards have been available since 1992 in the United States and Japan. Other countries, such as the United Kingdom, Germany, Canada, and Sweden, submitted standard proposals in 1992.

Electro Steel Castings Ltd. of India gained more customers for its ductile iron pipes. The pipes exhibited better mechanical stability than regular cast iron pipe. The lighter weight translated into lower transport costs and greater longevity (150 years), which made up for the five to 10 percent higher cost of ductile iron. The pipes have been accepted by municipalities, corporations, water supply boards, and public health departments and are manufactured in India with local raw materials. Approximately 10,000 metric tons were exported overseas in 1992, and shipments of 30,000 metric tons were expected in the following years. Other countries planning to use ductile iron pipes for water supply systems include Turkey and the Czech Republic. The winner of these contracts, Pont-a-Mousson of France, beat competition from U.S., Japan, German, Czech, Italian, and Austrian firms in 1992.

Evaporative pattern casting (also known as lost foam) gained popularity around the world. This type of casting process uses a pattern made from unbonded sand that will evaporate when the molten metal is poured into the mold. Many foundries in the United States, Japan, and Europe embraced the process by the 1990s. A study in 1997 found that evaporative pattern casting processes accounted for approximately 140,000 tons of aluminum casting in the United States alone, and forecast that by 2010, the process would account for 29 percent of the aluminum and 14 percent of the ferrous casting markets.

Favorable activities were taking place in the iron foundry industry, especially with ductile iron. The U.S. government was interested in the replacement of many forged steel components with cast ductile iron. Particularly, the U.S. Navy was researching the increased lethality of ductile iron projectiles over those made from steel. Other contractors were looking for less expensive alternatives to using forged steel components where the mechanical properties of ductile iron can suffice (generally in lower stress applications). However, more research and development was needed for this material because other lighter weight materials were replacing ductile iron in lower stress applications. Ductile iron's low production price tag is enticing and is one of its larger benefits.

Cast thermal analysis, also called numerical modeling/simulation, is a way to improve quality and productivity in the foundry through pattern design optimization. The cost-saving benefits of using numerical modeling are substantial, especially with respect to time and material waste. Computer technology displaces the standard "pour and pray" method of metal casting by helping the engineer optimize the casting design.

For the foundry industry as a whole, the advent of rapid prototypingtechnology was perhaps one of the most exciting advancements of the 1990s. Rapid prototyping is a computer-integrated method of accelerating the step between the designing and manufacturing of a part. Under normal circumstances, a foundry would take weeks to construct a pattern, and core boxes if necessary, from an original design. With rapid prototyping, this process can take only days, possibly only hours, to create a limited production pattern. The competitive edge this technology offered was substantial, especially considering the accuracy it lent to the price-quoting process.

In 2003, industry leader Intermet produced a new ductile iron called machineable austempered ductile iron (MADI), which was solidly in the middle of available materials in terms of strength. MADI, which was resistant to cracks and subsequent deformation, was designed for easy machineability. For the first time, both improved mechanical properties and improved machinability were optimized.

In May 2005, an article in *Foundry Management & Technology* announced Ashland Casting Solution's Exactherm technology provided a solution to the problem of casting thin-walled metal sections. Exactherm, which began development in the late 1990s, would allow metal casters the ability to custom tailor the thermal properties of a mold or core to meet specific casting section needs and make possible the casting of thin-wall metal sections.

WORKFORCE

Casting production requires a large workforce of employees with varying skills and educational levels. Most foundries—approximately 58 percent—are small businesses, employing fewer than 100 people, whereas the larger firms are global leaders in the industry.

Although the workforce shrank in the late 2000s due to decreased product demand and increasing automation, the industry still frequently experiences a shortage of technical, management, and supervisory personnel. Technical personnel are particularly difficult to recruit because engineers are drawn to other technical industries. Disparities between union and non-union shops also played a significant role in wages. The industry has continually tried to recruit new employees by offering opportunities to high school graduates and on-the-job training for more skilled positions. As of 2009, the metal casting industry employed 200,000 within the United States.

In the U.K. foundry industry, one-fourth of workers are injured on the job and subsequently kept out of work for three days or more, an average more than double that of the general manufacturing industry average. Accordingly, safety initiatives were begun in 2003 to eliminate one-third of injuries and improve employee health over five years.

INDUSTRY LEADERS

Important trends among foundry companies have been offering integrated services to customers and broadening the revenue base from reliance on individual technologies and single end markets. Sluggish or declining ferrous castings business in a number of segments during parts of the 1980s and early 1990s taught competitive foundries not to depend on one industry, such as the auto or aerospace industries, for all sales. Consequently, many leading companies have branched out to offer a wider mix of castings, including both ferrous and nonferrous, to a broader range of customers. Others, capitalizing on the strong trend in the auto industry toward the use of fewer integrated suppliers instead of many small component producers, sought to expand their offerings to include more assembled components and integrate several steps of the production chain for their clients.

Intermet. Intermet Corporation ranked as one of the world's largest independent foundries. With 2003 sales of US$731 million—low for an industry leader—Intermet's major customers were Ford and Delphi, with 11 percent of sales each, and DaimlerChrysler with 10 percent. More than 80 percent of Intermet's sales were from the North American market. The company produced gray and ductile iron castings, along with aluminum ones, primarily for the automotive industry. Its customers included some 20 top automakers, including the largest in the United States and Germany. In the mid-1990s, Intermet Corporation launched a joint venture with Comalco Limited of Australia to extend its iron making expertise to aluminum. Intermet built a pilot plant in Lewisport, Kentucky, banking on two prevalent trends in the automotive industry: outsourcing and aluminum components. The replacement of iron engine blocks with aluminum was expected to continue to accelerate into the twenty-first century, and the company's development of aluminum castings positioned it to capitalize on the transition. By 2004, due to the rising cost for scrap metal, the company's cost of ferrous scrap rose from US$160 a ton in 2003 to US$395 by August 2004. This created a need to seek protection under Chapter 11. Throughout 2005, Intermet closed several facilities and renegotiated metal surcharges and secured new loans to emerge from bankruptcy in November 2005. In 2009, Intermet had just over 2,300 employees. The falling economy had impacted Intermet largely due to its tight affiliation the auto industry. The demand for auto parts is mostly driven by new car sales, and that industry took a major downturn by the mid-2000s. Intermet and its subsidiaries filed for Chapter 11 relief from creditors in 2008. In 2009, the company was ordered to liquidate its assets.

Doncasters Group Limited. Doncasters was an important force in the U.K. foundry industry. With GE Aircraft Engines, Rolls-Royce, and Boeing among its major customers, its strength historically was in serving the aerospace industry, which accounted for 60 percent of revenues until its 1998 acquisition of Triplex Lloyd plc, another important U.K. metal caster. Both companies had extensive business with firms in other European countries. Triplex diversified Doncasters' business by adding more automotive and power plant components to the casting mix. The strategic buyout was seen as the method by which Doncasters could insulate itself from downturns in the aerospace sector. However, in the mid- to late 1990s, the aerospace business in Europe was recovering, and Doncasters was benefiting. Doncasters demonstrated how the foundry business could be profitable in the 1990s by achieving profit margins consistently in the 10 percent range. The purchase of Triplex Lloyd, which was larger than Doncasters in terms of annual revenues, added some US$328 million to Doncasters' US$217 million in 1997 revenues. However, the company planned to sell off Triplex's automotive division, which would subtract nearly US$100 million from Triplex's 1997 revenues. In 2008, the group revenue was approximately US$1 billion. The company was later acquired by Royal Bank Private Equity. Doncasters operated from sites in the United Kingdom, Europe, United States, China, and Mexico. As of 2010, the company employed approximately 5,000 people around the world.

Precision Castparts Corp. With sales of US$5.49 billion for fiscal year 2010, Precision Castparts specializes in investment castings primarily for aerospace customers, notably Pratt & Whitney, Rolls-Royce, and General Electric. However, like Doncasters, it has moved toward diversifying its casting and other businesses. The company grew rapidly in the 1990s through a string of acquisitions. In 1997, it acquired seven companies, and as a result, its sales nearly doubled between 1996 and 1998. The company reported steadily increasing sales between 1996 and 2001. Precision was hit hard by slowdowns in the aircraft industry during the early 1990s, which saw its sales plummet from US$583 million in 1992 to US$420 million in 1994. In 1993, the company barely turned a profit. The turnaround began in 1995, as both sales and profits, along with its stock price, began an upswing. By 1998, the company recorded a 6.5 percent net profit margin, ahead of its 10-year average of 5.9 percent annually. In 2001, Precision Castparts's sales grew by 39 percent, up to US$2.3 billion, with more than 80 percent of its sales in the United States. In 2010, the aerospace market accounted for 54 percent of PCC's revenue, a decrease of 17 percent from 2009. Precision Castparts had approximately 18,100 employees in 2010.

BIBLIOGRAPHY

American Foundry Society. "Imports Continue to Rise." 15 June 2007. Available from http://www.afsinc.org.

"Castings." *Investors Chronicle,* 25 May 2007.

Castings for Industry. "How the Foundry Industry Has Changed." 15 June 2007. Available from http://www. castingsforindustry.com.

"Foundries Exceed Their Expectations." *Furnaces International,* September-October 2003.

Foundry Industry Recycling Starts Today (FIRST). "Industry Overview." 15 June 2007. Available from http:// www.foundryrecycling.org.

"Hoover's Company Capsules." *Hoover's Online,* 2007. Available from http://www.hoovers.com.

Imberman, Woodruff. "Meeting and Beating the Imported Competition." *Foundry Management & Technology,* March 2005.

"Iron and Steel." *Mineral Commodity Summaries.* U.S. Geological Survey, January 2007. Available from http://www.usgs.gov.

Kirgin, Kenneth H. "A Study of End-Use Markets Shows an Expansion in Casting Shipments for 2004 with Considerable Gains in Aluminum and Steel." *Modern Casting,* 2004. Available from http://www.moderncasting.com.

———. "U.S. Casting Sales to Maintain Course with 3.7 Percent Rise." *Modern Casting,* January 2007.

"Meeting and Beating the Imported Competition." *Foundry Management & Technology.* March 2005.

North American Die Casting Association. "Die Casting Industry." 15 June 2007. Available from www.diecasting.org.

"Outside the Sand Box." *Foundry Management & Technology,* May 2005.

"PCC Delivers Strong Sales and Income in First Quarter Fiscal 2005." *Modern Casting,* 14 July 2004.

Precision Castparts Corp. *2010 Annual Report to Shareholders.* Available from http://www.precast.com.

"U.S. Demonstrates Steady, Sustained Growth." *Foundry Trade Journal,* April 2007.

SIC 3310

STEEL MILLS

NAICS CODE(S)

331111. Steelmakers operate blast or electric furnaces to create raw iron and steel. The same manufacturer may produce any number of intermediate or finished steel products from crude steel. Examples of industry output include hot-rolled steel products; cold-rolled steel products; iron

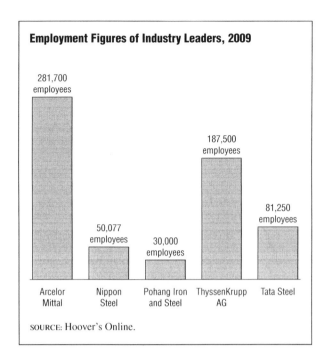

Employment Figures of Industry Leaders, 2009

281,700 employees — Arcelor Mittal
50,077 employees — Nippon Steel
30,000 employees — Pohang Iron and Steel
187,500 employees — ThyssenKrupp AG
81,250 employees — Tata Steel

SOURCE: Hoover's Online.

and steel bars; steel ingots; stainless steel; iron and steel forgings; steel wire and nails; and steel pipes and tubes.

Companies that produce steel castings are discussed separately under **Iron and Steel Foundries,** and those that process nonferrous ores into metals are covered under **Metals, Primary Smelting and Refining of Nonferrous Metals.**

INDUSTRY SNAPSHOT

In 2009, the world's steel market reached 1,219.7 million metric tons (mmt) of crude steel according to the World Steel Association. By 2010, China, Japan, and the United States were among the top five steel producers worldwide. In a November 2010 report, the world steel market had reached 118 mmt in October alone. China's crude steel production had fallen slightly from the same time a year before. It was reported at 50.3 mmt for October 2010—a 3.8 percent decrease. However, elsewhere in Asia the steel production rates were climbing. In Japan, October 2010's production was 9.5 mmt (an 8 percent increase over the previous year), and South Korea's production was at 5.2 percent (an 11.4 percent increase) over October 2009. The World Steel Association released a report in April 2010, forecasting world steel use to increase by 10.7 percent to 1,241 mmt in 2010, after contracting by 6.7 percent in 2009. It this figure holds, the world steel demand in 2010 will exceed the 2007 levels prior to the global economic crisis. The forecast calls for the steel demand to reach 1,306 mmt in 2011—an historical high in the steel industry.

ORGANIZATION AND STRUCTURE

Steel is manufactured using iron ore, coke, and limestone. Typically, the coke (a high-grade coal distillate) is used as fuel to heat a blast furnace. The coke emits carbon monoxide as it burns, as does the limestone. The ore melts, creating a molten iron and carbon mixture. A basic oxygen furnace (BOF) is used to supply super-heated air, which removes impurities and converts the molten iron into steel. The steel is usually cast into ingots, which are later formed into standard shapes, usually billets, slabs, or blooms. A more advanced production technique, "continuous casting," bypasses ingots. These slabs, billets, and blooms are processed at mills into rails, rolls, plates, tubes, bars, or other more marketable products. Those units are used by automobile companies, for example, to create parts or body panels for vehicles.

This conventional steelmaking technique is referred to as integrated manufacturing because it integrates all aspects of the process, including melting the iron ore. In the 1990s, an increasing number of steelmakers, particularly in the United States and other highly developed nations, were utilizing minimills. Minimill producers, or non-integrated steel manufacturers, start with scrap iron or steel, rather than iron ore. They use electric arc furnaces (EAFs), rather than blast and basic-oxygen furnaces (BOFs), to continuously cast blooms and billets. Most minimills produce a limited number of finished products, such as rods and bars used in light construction, but some non-integrated manufacturers also produce plates, sheets, pipes, and other steel goods.

Many integrated steel mills can produce millions of tons of steel annually, while minimills typically churn out between 100,000 and 500,000 tons. However, minimills may generate as much as 10 times more profit per ton of steel produced. A primary advantage of minimills is that they do not have to be located near supplies of iron ore. Instead, they are commonly constructed near primary customers, significantly reducing shipping costs. That advantage, when combined with high-tech manufacturing techniques such as use of EAFs, allows non-integrated producers in industrialized nations to compete aggressively with low-cost importers for domestic market share.

Regardless of their production techniques, most steel companies manufacture a category of steel called carbon steel. Carbon steels account for roughly 90 percent of global output. They contain relatively few alloying additives and their high degree of malleability makes them ideal for general purpose uses such as automobile bodies, structural steel for buildings, and shipbuilding. The remainder of industry output is categorized in one of four segments: alloy, stainless, tool, and high-strength low alloy (HSLA). Alloy steels, the second largest industry product segment by output volume, contain various alloying materials such as vanadium, silicon, manganese, and copper. They offer characteristics such as corrosion resistance, high electrical or heat conductivity, and greater strength, qualities that make alloy steel useful for a variety of applications ranging from tools and electrical components to machine parts and armor.

Stainless steel, the third largest product group, includes chromium/nickel alloy steels that resist corrosion and may be stronger or more heat resistant than lower-grade steels. Large markets include aerospace, medical device, and plumbing-related industries. Tool steels, the fourth industry segment, integrate molybdenum, tungsten, or other elements to produce ultra-hard alloys commonly used in tool and metalworking industries. Similarly, HSLA steels, the most recent family of steel products, use relatively small amounts of alloying materials, but are specially processed for hardness and light weight. Such steels are popular in applications where strength and weight factors are crucial, such as freight cars. In general, newly industrialized nations are more likely to focus solely on the production of low-tech carbon steel, while established Western and Japanese manufacturers are more likely to compete in alloy, stainless, tool, and HSLA steel markets.

Competitive Structure. Because of high start-up costs and slow-growth markets, the steel industry is a difficult one to enter. In traditional steel-manufacturing regions, such as western Europe, the Russian Federation, the United States, and Japan, industries are highly consolidated with only a few manufacturers controlling the lion's share of the market in their respective countries. In general, new entrants to the industry are minimill producers, which incur start-up costs about one-quarter as great as those required to open an integrated facility.

Entry barriers are generally lower in emerging nations, where steel demand rose in the 1980s and early 1990s. Nevertheless, most newcomers were fully integrated and had to secure hefty sources of capital to build steel mills. Other obstacles have varied by country. In some nations, such as South Korea, access to the industry has traditionally been limited by the national government. Likewise, Brazil's steel industry was effectively controlled by the government until the early 1990s, when privatization occurred. In other regions, such as Eastern Europe and China, hurdles have included the lack of a dependable distribution and supply infrastructure.

On an international level, the steel industry is characterized by fierce competition, not only among individual producers but also among different nations. In fact, the industry has traditionally been heavily influenced by government control for reasons related primarily to defense and economic stability. In addition, because

carbon steel is essentially a commodity, companies compete primarily on price. To help their producers compete internationally, governments in virtually all steelmaking nations support domestic producers through measures such as subsidies or restrictions on imports. By subsidizing steel exported to international markets a government can help its producers establish a presence and boost market share. Governments can help those companies maintain dominance of their domestic market by instituting tariffs or stringent quality controls on imported material.

Barron's reported that steel mills planned additional price increases by September 2008. Steel mill owners were increasingly pessimistic about the possibility of passing along any increases in the fourth quarter of 2008. Widely reported declines in ferrous scrap pricing, along with increasing slumps in demand, were causing a reduced outlook for distributors as they determined pricing. As a result, those mills aware of demand expectations were reducing service center inventory.

Agreements and Standards. Widespread government support of domestic steel producers has contributed to an environment conducive to trade wars that featured dumping practices (selling steel below cost), sanctions, and retaliatory import restrictions and tariffs. To reduce friction and enhance free markets, several countries had entered agreements with other nations to help ensure free trade and/or regional cooperation. For example, the North American Free Trade Agreement (NAFTA) reduced trade barriers between the United States, Canada, and Mexico. Several European countries had also pursued agreements or acquiesced to regional regulatory bodies in an effort to drop trade barriers and to cooperate against export threats from other regions. The European Commission, for example, worked to enhance free steel trade on the continent, among other objectives. Similarly, European Union (E.U.) members signed bilateral consensus agreements (BCAs) in the late 1980s that eliminated regional tariffs, subsidies, and other government supports.

In the mid-1990s several nations continued to seek a multilateral steel agreement (MSA) that would effectively put all steelmaking nations on a level playing field. International MSA negotiations failed in 1992, but several nations continued to pursue the effort. The United States was a strong proponent of the MSA because it had battled anticompetitive foreign trade practices for several years in an effort to revive its ailing steel industry. In addition to various tariffs and restraints, the United States, like several other nations, had diminished the effects of other nations' dumping practices by turning to the International Trade Commission (ITC). The ITC has the power to assess dumping penalties and to restrict specific trade initiatives that it deems unfair.

One final major regulatory influence is national environmental law. Japan and other industrialized nations must comply with environmental laws that designate the amount and type of pollutants that may be released during the manufacturing process, among other guidelines. Steel producers in the United States, for example, invested a combined sum of more than US$100 million annually in pollution control devices for their factories. Environmental legislation was even more costly in certain Western European nations. In contrast, manufacturers in less industrialized nations benefited from comparatively weak domestic regulations or slipshod enforcement.

The dominant international steel industry standard in the mid-1990s was ISO 9000, a set of quality standards created for various industries by the International Standardization Organization (ISO). The goal of ISO 9000 is to provide a quality certification program that will ensure that members can meet specific quality standards. Certification was considered a relatively expensive and difficult endeavor in the mid-1990s, but ISO 9000 was gradually being adopted by steel producers throughout the world, particularly in the most industrialized nations. Accreditation or certification was carried out by regional bodies such as the Dutch Council for Certification, the British Studies Intelligeneer (BSI), and Underwriter's Laboratories of the United States.

BACKGROUND AND DEVELOPMENT

Steelmaking dates back to fourteenth-century Europe, but mass-production methods were not developed until the mid-nineteenth century in Great Britain. Simple forges were originally used to heat iron ore and charcoal in a box for several days. Furnaces gradually increased in size, and steelmakers eventually learned to force air over the molten iron to speed the heating process. Sir Henry Bessemer, a British inventor, is credited with developing the Bessemer Furnace in 1855. It was the first device to refine molten iron with blasts of oxygen. The invention languished until bulk production of oxygen began later in the century.

Demand for steel surged with the onset of the Industrial Revolution in Great Britain. As the Industrial Revolution spread to other European nations and the United States in the late nineteenth century, global steel production soared. The open-hearth furnace was developed, which allowed producers to use scrap iron and produce higher-grade steel. Factors spurring industry growth during the early 1900s included new automobile markets, steel-framed construction, and industrialization in Japan and the Russian Federation. Massive demand

for steel during World War II spurred giant increases in production capacity and steelmaking technology.

Shortly after World War II, the basic oxygen furnace was developed in Austria. It eventually replaced open-hearth technology, although the latter remained dominant until the 1970s. BOFs forced pure oxygen into the molten iron mixture, allowing furnaces to create a unit of steel in less than one-quarter the time required by open-hearth furnaces. Another pivotal development was the use of electric arc furnaces (EAFs) to manufacture carbon steel, which was a departure from their original use to only produce stainless and other types of steel. Other important technological breakthroughs during and after World War II related to the use of alloy additives, a development that initiated a new generation of high-performance steel products.

In 1950, following the giant production surge of the 1940s, global steel producers turned out about 190 million metric tons annually. War-ravaged European, Russian, and Japanese industries were rebuilding during this time, so the United States dominated the sector. In the early 1950s the United States produced nearly 60 percent of global steel output. It continued to lead production throughout the 1960s and into the 1970s as well, although other regions achieved steady gains. Japan's steel output soared from 5 million metric tons in 1950 to 23 million in 1960, and then to a whopping 93 million by 1970. Similarly, the European production amounted to 32 million tons in 1950, 72 million in 1960, and more than 150 million tons in the early 1970s, although some of that gain was attributable to the integration of Great Britain.

Perhaps the most impressive postwar recovery occurred in the former Soviet Union, where steel output rocketed from 27 million tons in 1950 to a staggering 116 million tons in 1970. In 1974 the Soviet Union overtook the United States as the leading producer of steel. Soviet supremacy in the global steel industry marked the end of the dominance of United States and Western European manufacturers. This shift in industry dynamics actually started in the late 1960s when steel demand in Western nations leveled off. Factors in the early 1970s, including concern about the availability of oil and recessionary conditions, exacerbated the trend. At the same time, steel substitutes, such as plastics and aluminum, rapidly supplanted steel in many applications, including those in the automobile industry. Industry participants also claimed that regulations related to labor practices and pollution control constrained productivity and competitiveness.

Steel output in most industrialized Western nations peaked in the 1970s before dwindling, or even stagnating, throughout the 1980s. Total global steel output hovered around 800 million tons during those two decades, but the share of the market served by the seven largest steel-producing western nations plummeted from 54 percent to just 37 percent. Even Japan's steel output waned after the early 1970s, despite a common perception in Western nations that Japan's steel industry was robust. Between the early 1970s and 1990 the total tonnage of steel manufactured by the United States, the European Economic Community (EEC), and Japan slipped from about 420 million tons to about 325 million. Meanwhile, the former Soviet Union continued to stretch its lead, increasing output to a peak of 163 million tons in 1988.

More notable than advances in the Soviet Union and some Eastern Bloc countries during the 1970s and 1980s was the rise of steel industries in several Third World and newly industrialized countries. Production in Latin America, for instance, shot up from 19 million tons in 1975 to about 30 million tons in 1980. Overall, steel production in emerging countries grew from less than 75 million tons annually in the 1970s to about 175 million tons annually by the late 1980s. The strongest of the new contenders included South Korea, Brazil, and China. However, numerous countries chipped away at the aggregate global steel market, including nations in the Middle East, Asia, South America, and Africa. Besides labor and regulatory advantages, those producers typically benefited from newer production facilities in comparison to their more industrialized counterparts, as well as better access to regions where steel demand was increasing.

Steelmaking industries in Western Europe and the United States staggered as developing nations infringed on both the domestic and the ever-growing export markets. The percentage of total steel exported had shot up from 10 percent in 1950 to more than 25 percent by the late 1980s. Battered producers scrambled to sustain profitability and many of them eventually folded or merged with their domestic peers. Throughout the 1980s, many of the world's largest steel companies took drastic actions to reinvent themselves and revive their competitiveness. They automated factories, slashed payrolls as much as 50 percent or more, integrated new technology, and focused on developing high-performance steels that could compete with proliferating synthetic and aluminum substitutes. By the late 1980s the efforts began to show tangible results.

Critical to the revival of steel industries in the United States, Europe, and even Japan in the late 1980s and early 1990s, were new steel manufacturing technologies, particularly minimills and continuous casting. Minimills sprang up in the United States during the 1960s and by the late 1970s had begun to compete with large steel producers. Their great efficiency and technological superiority were highlighted during periods of industry turbulence such as the latter part of the 1980s. By the early 1990s, minimills accounted for more than 35 percent of all steel output in the United States. The share of U.S. steel made with continuous casting jumped from 15 percent to 85 percent by the early 1990s, mimicking Japan's steel sector. European producers eventually followed the lead of their North American and Japanese counterparts.

Despite temporary setbacks brought on by a fiscal crisis in 1997, Asia remained the world's premier steel-producing center, supplying more than 35 percent of the world's crude steel in 2000 alone. China, Japan, and South Korea dominated the industry, and together they manufactured one-third of the steel produced worldwide. China's booming economy surged on, scarcely affected by the crisis. However, production and consumption began to drop sharply in Japan and South Korea in late 1998. One result of the Asian crisis was to draw attention to the advantages of consolidation. In October 2000 the region's two main competitors and the largest steel firms in the world, Nippon Steel and POSCO, announced a strategic alliance. NKK Corp and Kawasaki Steel also announced merger plans. Analysts at the Nomura Securities Company forecast that by 2005 Japan's steel trade would be controlled by two groups, Nippon Steel and NKK-Kawasaki.

After languishing in the early and mid-1990s, Europe's steel industry, in the east and in the west, began to recover in the latter part of the decade. Demand in places such as Germany, which was Western Europe's largest producer, rose as key markets like the auto industry increased business. Consolidation of the European Union's steel industry was well underway by mid-2001 when five companies were responsible for about 60 percent of output, up from 23 percent in 1993. Eastern Europe, while showing important gains, continued to perform unevenly as its economies grappled with the free-market transition. Poland's steel production, for example, experienced healthy increases in the mid-1990s, but plunged 11.5 percent between 1998 and 1999. In 2000, with growth from 8.8 to 10.5 million metric tons, the country finally seemed to be heading toward a recovery. Steel production in the leading Eastern European nations of Poland, the Czech Republic, Slovakia, and Romania, grew more than 11.5 percent from 1999 to 2000, reaching 25.2 million metric tons. Among the former Soviet states, Russia performed the best in 2000, finally emerging from the slump it suffered after the breakup of the Soviet Union in 1991. In 2000 Russia surpassed 1993 levels for the first time, reaching 59.1 million metric tons, an increase of 14.7 percent from 1999. The Ukraine also continued a strong performance with a 31.4 million metric ton output in 2000 that was 14 percent higher than 1999 figures. Despite the apparently strong showing by the Commonwealth of Independent States (CIS), questions remained concerning the ability of their relatively old facilities to compete in the world market.

North America, on the other hand, remained a strong steel market in 2000, driven by a strong U.S. economy. Overall, North American steel output reached 128.9 million metric tons, three-quarters of which was produced by the United States. That was slightly off the record-setting 130.1 million metric tons produced in North America in 1997. Consumption of steel in North America during 2000 also reached historic highs. In fact, supply fell short of demand during 2000 for some steel products in the United States. The United States led all other nations in steel imports in 1999 with 32.7 million metric tons, which equaled nearly one-third of the steel the country actually produced. In spite of general agreement throughout the U.S. industry that there was a pressing need for widespread consolidation, no companies seemed willing to take the plunge. A joint statement by U.S. Steel and Nucor, which were the largest integrated producer and the largest minimill producer, respectively, in support of ending government subsidies to steel facilities that were unable to compete on the open market in quality or price was seen as a first sign that the industry was embracing consolidation. Nevertheless, there was concern that the longer the inevitable was postponed, the more precarious U.S. industry's position would be in the world market. The United States had long produced far less steel than it consumed, with estimates of the extra steel needed ranging from 15 to 28 million tons. At least in the beginning, consolidation and plant closings would serve foreign steelmakers, as well as the U.S. industry.

Combining resources was seen not only as a means of giving steelmakers access to the capital needed to invest in new technologies, it was also a way of trimming facilities and firms that were not performing with maximum efficiency and reducing competition that kept profit margins razor thin. Between 1990 and 1998, the global steel industry experienced mergers worth about US$66 billion, a pittance compared to industries such as petroleum refining. The trend continued to pick up speed in the 2000s. Significant mergers in both Europe and Asia were planned or already under review by regulatory agencies by late 2001. Determined to downsize its steel industry, Asia pressed ahead with strategic alliances, mergers, and joint ventures. Although the need for consolidation in the bloated U.S. market was acknowledged almost universally, at the beginning of 2002 no significant steps toward it had been taken.

The rise of e-commerce in the late 1990s ushered a minor revolution into the usually conservative steel business. In the mid-1990s, private, web-based steel exchanges, such as Metal Suppliers, MetalSite, Metal Network Exchange Services (MNSX), and eSteel, were founded. Each functioned differently, with some allowing producers to auction their steel to the highest bidder, others acting as online forums where buyers and sellers could hammer out terms, and still others giving sellers the ability to post quantities and prices. The sites charged a transaction fee, but by the early 2000s large steelmakers began taking control of online distribution and foregoing fees. Bethlehem Steel, Bermingham Steel, Nucor Corp., and Weirton made plans to set up private exchanges on their company Web sites. The private exchanges were not left entirely out of the picture. The most enterprising continued to sell their expertise to steel companies as Internet consultants.

Despite rising output and increasing sales, world steel prices fell steadily between 1999 and 2001 at an annual rate of 2.7 percent, according to CRU International, a metals consulting company. It was a trend that could not continue. "Ultimately," a CRU report stated, "prices must bear some relationship to costs." Beginning in 2002, however, steel prices began to rise again. According to *Fortune*, U.S. hot-rolled steel, for example, rose from US$260 per ton in June 2003 to US$410 per ton by April 2004. U.S. steel in 2002 was protected by tariffs that were lifted a year and a half later, and in 2003 U.S. steel production was about 101 million metric tons. By 2004, the world steel capacity was nearly 1.2 billion metric tons and expected to increase to more than 1.3 billion per year in 2006.

At the close of 2003, Japan was leading the world in steel packaging recycling with 86 percent, followed by South Africa with 63 percent according to *European Report*. More steel was being recycled in Europe than ever before, with about 60 percent of total steel packaging being recycled. Belgium recycled the most steel packaging with 93 percent, and Portugal recycled the least with 28 percent. Australia's total was 59 percent, and the United States recycled 43 percent.

CURRENT CONDITIONS

Demand was also rising in the 2000s, particularly from the booming Chinese market. According to the International Iron and Steel Institute, China's steel demand was up to about 282 million metric tons in 2004, an increase of 11 percent over 2003, and was expected to rise another 10.7 percent in 2005. By 2010, China's steel use had increased to 579 mmts and was predicted to reach 595 mmts in 2011. The cost of steel production was also rising, particularly in the United States, despite the lifting of the 2002 tariffs. According to *Automotive News*, steel prices increased as much as 50 percent from December

2003 to June 2004. Prices of steel were subject to change between the time of agreement and the time of shipment. Scrap steel alone was priced at about US$310 per ton in early 2004. The automotive industry was also a major consumer of hot-rolled steel; General Motors alone required 24,000 tons of steel per day.

Minimills, which produce steel products from recycled materials rather than raw ores, continue to deliver better fiscal results than integrated mills, which create steel from raw minerals. This stems in part from minimills' use of scrap metals, which has prices that tend to fluctuate favorably with crude steel prices so that when steel prices are down, minimills do not pay high prices for their raw materials.

United Steelworkers Union (USW) members protested the closing of Weyerhaeuser Corporation's OSB 2000 mill in 2008. The mill, located in northern Saskatchewan, was an integral part of a small community's economic future and was the last operating Weyerhaeuser mill in the Canadian province. USW Local 1-184 President Paul Halen vehemently expressed his concerns in a letter to Phil Dennet, vice president of Strand Technologies for Weyerhaeuser. Halen acknowledged that there was deterioration in market conditions but did not believe that it was cause to close the mill completely. The USW, representing more than 280,000 laborers in every sector of the economy, was Canada's most diverse union. In 2010, the United Steel Workers union had 1.2 million active and retired union members globally.

Due to the inclusion of major wage and benefit increases, the United Steelworkers believed a new standard for the industry was set with a tentative four-year contract reached within U.S. Steel. The proposed settlement, which covered 16,000 steelworkers at 12 plants, provides bonus and enhanced benefit programs for active employees and retirees as well as reduced health care premiums for retirees. The contract was set to replace a five-year pact due to expire September 1, 2008.

RESEARCH AND TECHNOLOGY

Research and technology played a heightened role in the global steel industry going into the mid-1990s. Scientific advances were vital to developed nations in their efforts to maintain market share in the face of challenges from low-cost foreign competitors. Improvements in minimill production, for instance, were essential to producers in Western Europe, Japan, and North America. A major drawback of minimills before the late 1980s was their inability to efficiently produce sheet and strip steel. However, SMS Chloemann-Sieman AG (or SMS Concast) of Germany developed a "thin-slab" casting technique that allowed minimills to continuously cast steel in thicknesses of less than two inches. This important development, combined

with emerging strip-casting technology, has allowed minimills to compete in the last bastion of the integrated mills, sheet and strip steel, which is preferred by many industries (such as the automobile sector) because it is easier to process.

Nucor Corp.'s Crawfordsville, Indiana, plant was the first minimill to integrate large scale thin-slab casting. The plant began turning out sheet steel in 1989 under the watchful eye of the worldwide steel industry. Other important thin-slab minimill operations began shortly thereafter in Germany and Italy. The initial success of those operations resulted in plans for similar thin-slab minimills in the mid-1990s. Nucor, for example, opened a plant in 1992 that was capable of thin-slab casting of about 1 million tons of steel annually. It subsequently announced plans to double that capacity by year-end 1994. Luna ECR (Endless Casting Rolling), introduced at an Italian mill by Danielli in 2000, was a technique that could process 500,000 tons of bar. Danielli was working on refining the process to make it economical for specialty steels such as stainless steel.

Related advances included efforts to develop both thin-slab and thin-strip minimill processes that reduce finished steel contaminants inherent in the production of steel from scrap. Researchers hoped that advances in this area would allow minimills to compete with integrated mills in automobile and other major industries that require high-grade flat steel. Notable techniques being developed or implemented in the mid-1990s that promised to increase the quality and efficiency of thin casting included: in-line strip production (ISP), which was being pioneered in Italy; integrated compact mill (ICM) innovations under development by Voest-Alpine of Austria; and the Tippins-Samsung Process (TSP).

Computers promised to bring down costs and pollution while improving the quality of steel produced. In the mid-1990s, Usinor in France introduced SACHEM, a computer software program that runs blast furnaces. The program continuously monitors and processes thousands of factors in the furnaces, including temperature, water pressure, and oxygen supply. Not only did SACHEM produce better steel, it also extended the life of the furnaces more than a third, decreased the generation of greenhouse gases, and reduced costs US$1.55 per ton. The European Union was pleased with the results of SACHEM and looked to introduce more efficient technologies.

In addition to production-related advances, research and technology efforts produced better grades of steel in the mid-1990s. Carbon steel continued to comprise the vast majority of industry output. However, alloy, stainless, tool, and HSLA steels offered higher profit margins and better opportunities for growth, especially for industrialized nations. Steelmakers tried to protect existing markets by offering low-weight, high-strength, malleable, corrosion-resistant steels that were better than existing plastics or aluminum. Other industry observers have pointed to innovations such as high-performance steel coatings made with synthetic materials as keys to future industry growth. Such steel coating actually registered marked sales gains in the mid-1990s on the strength of potentially vast markets such as the roofing industry. Proponents contended that coated steel roofing systems installed in the mid-1990s could last 40 years with minimal maintenance.

In the mid-2000s, research in Japan's Steel Research Center was focused on eliminating "creep," which is the natural change in the makeup and structure of metal over time, particularly when it is subjected to pressure or heat. A type of steel was being manufactured that was able to withstand such deformation, making the steel product last considerably longer. The new steel was fortified with carbonitride nanoparticles, which filled in the gaps between steel molecules in order to hold them in place and form stronger bonds. The technology was in the early stages by late 2003, as the new steel still had to prove its flexibility and corrosion resistance.

INDUSTRY LEADERS

Arcelor Mittal. With annual output of 45 million metric tons and 2009 sales of US$65.11 billion, Arcelor was the undisputed steel champion. Formed by a three-way merger between Arbed of Luxembourg, Usinor or France, and Aceralia of Spain, Arcelor was based in Luxembourg.

The 1997 acquisition of Aristrain, a medium-sized European steelmaker, vaulted Luxembourg's Arbed SA from seventh largest to the world's third largest steel company by volume. Its combined holdings manufactured some 24.1 million metric tons of crude steel in 2000. Although it had a diverse product line, the company was heavily involved in supplying Europe's auto industry with steel.

France's Usinor SA was the sixth-ranked steel manufacturer with 2000 output of 21 million metric tons. The company was created in 1988 by the merger of French steel giants Usinor and Sacilor, both of which had been government-owned since the early 1980s when the French industry was in crisis. As a private company, Sacilor dated back to the eighteenth century, and Usinor was formed from a 1948 merger of two French steel companies. By the early 1980s the two were the pillars of the French steel industry in terms of production, but they faced high debt and poor market conditions. The French government intervened and acquired both companies. The subsequent merger, combined with later acquisitions, resulted in a company that produced more

than 90 percent of France's steel in the early 1990s. The company produced its steel primarily through integrated mills. Usinor-Sacilor remained government-owned until 1995, when it re-privatized, and it was renamed Usinor SA in 1997. The company extended its global reach during the early and mid-1990s by investing heavily in European and overseas steelmaking operations. It also entered into numerous joint ventures with other companies to develop new steelmaking technologies.

The family-owned and run Netherlands-based Mittal Steel was created in late 2004 with the merger of the public company Ispat International (70 percent owned by the Mittal family) and the Antilles-based LNM Holdings (100 percent owned by the Mittals). The combined company became of the world's largest steel companies, producing 42.8 million metric tons in 2004. Some of the company's leading clients included Ford Motor, General Motors, Maytag, and Whirlpool. The company's 2004 sales totaled more than $22 billion while net income stood at $4.7 billion.

Plans were announced in August 2008 for Arcelor Mittal to spend US $1.6 billion to build steelworks that would address Brazil"s supply demands. Arcelor Mittal was expected to nearly double its Brazilian output of long carbon steel used to make machines and construct buildings to approximately 6.5 million metric tons a year by mid-2011. The company stated that its production of wire rod, bars, rebars, and structural sections "recognizes the important growth potential of the domestic market" in Brazil.

Arcelor Mittal announced plans to build a US$600 million steel mill in Mexico and buy a U.S. coking coal plant, according to the *Economic Times* in August 2008. The plant in Mexico was expected to supply the Mexican government's plan to upgrade infrastructure and build more housing. However, also in 2008, Arcelor Mittal announced it planned to close several plants including Bethlehem Steel and LTV Steel.

With the acquisition of International Steel Group, world steel leader Mittal Steel Company N.V. formed subsidiary Mittal Steel USA and surpassed the United States Steel Corporation in 2004 to become the top U.S. steel mill. Mittal merged ISG's operations with those of its North American subsidiary, Ispat Inland. Arcelor Mittal reported 2009 sales of US$65.11 billion with 281,700 employees.

Nippon Steel Corporation. Japan's Nippon Steel has shown solid growth to arrive at its status as the world's second largest steel producer. Its annual crude steel output is approximately 35 million tons. The company rose to prominence during the post-World War II industrial boom in Japan. By the early 1990s, Nippon was producing well over US$20 billion worth of steel from eight different iron and steel making plants. Nippon produces its steel primarily through integrated mills. During the late 1980s and early 1990s the company cut costs and overhead in an attempt to remain competitive in the increasingly crowded steel export market. Lackluster performance forced the company to step up those efforts in the early 1990s. The company has also attempted to reduce the share of its sales dependent on steel because it has numerous nonsteel subsidiaries, but as of 2000 steel continued to account for nearly three-quarters of its annual revenues. By the mid-2000s, Nippon was promoting its energy and engineering sectors most heavily. The company posted sales of US$36.5 billion in 2007 with 50,077 employees in 2009.

Nippon Steel stepped up its plan in 2005, for recycling waste plastic into coke by 30 percent. To that end, they invested over US$38 million to install equipment at two of its main facilities. In 2006, Nippon Steel and Mitsubishi Heavy Industries merged forces to create a high tensile strength steel that was used for the hulls of container ships. In 2006, Nippon Steel announced a pilot program to process waste food into ethanol.

Pohang Iron and Steel Co., Ltd. Producing approximately 31 million tons of crude steel per year in 2003, POSCO of South Korea reported US$31.9 billion in revenues in 2009, with nearly 30,000 employees. POSCO enjoyed a rapid ascent to the front ranks of international steel producers. The company was formed in 1968 with the help of the South Korean government. In late 2000, under pressure from the United States, POSCO was fully privatized when the Korea Development Bank sold the government's last 7 percent share in the company. At the same time, the Korean government announced it was doing away with restrictions on foreign ownership in POSCO. The company's production facilities were among the most technologically advanced and efficient in the world. POSCO had ventures in the United States, China, and elsewhere. By 2003, in fact, POSCO was exporting approximately 2.5 million tons of steel to China and was planning to invest well over US$1 billion in China operations by 2006. It formed a strategic venture with Japan's Nippon Steel in 2000. In 2006, they completed construction of their sixth continuous galvanizing line, which places them in the number two position as producer of sheet steel. In 2007, Warren Buffett's Berkshire Hathaway company purchased a stake of 4 percent in POSCO.

ThyssenKrupp AG. Another product of a late 1990s merger, ThyssenKrupp was formed by the merger of Thyssen AG and Friedrich Krupp AG, both leaders in Germany's steel industry. Thyssen was founded in 1891.

It supplied the German war machine during both world wars, although output was severely curtailed following World War II. The company posted a steady recovery, however, and its steel output peaked in 1974 at about 17 million tons. As the German steel industry slumped during the late 1970s and 1980s, Thyssen diversified into other industries. The company announced a 21 percent decline in net profits for the second quarter of 2008. ThyssenKrupp experienced a drop in net income due to high stainless steel prices during the prior year, and their steel division was hurt by high-raw material costs, pre-operating expenses for new steel mills, and restructuring expenses. By 2009, Thyssen was reporting annual sales of US$34.5 billion. ThyssenKrupp AG had 2009 sales of nearly US$53.7 billion and a workforce of nearly 187,500 employees.

Corus Group plc. The Corus Group originated from British Steel's acquisition of the Dutch firm Koninklijke Hoogovens. British Steel had grown out of the 1967 privatization of the British steel industry, during which 14 U.K. firms merged. With nearly US$17.9 billion in 2004 sales, Corus produced a variety of steel products, which it sells in large part to the auto and construction industries. Most of Corus' sales were made to nations of the European Union. In 2006, Corus agreed to Tata Steel's takeover bid. Tata Steel was the largest steelmaker in the world, producing more than 100 million tons annually. After a bidding war with Brazilian steelmaker CSN, Tata acquired Corus for US$11.3 billion in 2007.

Corus realized US$600 million in internal performance improvements that were generated through various projects. Each of Corus' main divisions were impacted by company initiatives for ongoing improvements. In addition, Corus recorded a liquid steel production of 20.3 million tons for 2008 compared to 18.8 million in 2006. Deliveries were reported at 23.1 million tons for 2008 against 21.6 million tons in 2006. In 2010, Tata Steel realized a revenue of over US$21.58 billion and had over 81,250 employees.

MAJOR COUNTRIES IN THE INDUSTRY

China. Advances by China's steel industry during the 1980s and 1990s catapulted it to the forefront of the steel industry. In the early 1950s China produced only 2 million metric tons of steel annually. With help from the Soviet Union, it increased capacity to about 19 million tons by 1960. After the Soviet Union withdrew in 1960, output plummeted and recovery was slow. By the late 1970s, in fact, China's annual production of steel was less than 25 million tons. Output increased to 40 million tons in 1983, however, as China launched a concerted effort to increase capacity. The government-controlled industry produced 60 million tons of steel by 1989. Output surged to 80 million tons in 1992 and then 89 million tons a year later. By 1996, China surpassed the United States and Japan in annual production when it reached 101.2 million metric tons. In 2000 it reached 127.2 million metric tons and by 2004, China produced more than 270 million tons, up 22.5 percent from 2003. Steel prices were reporting corresponding increases, rising from 30 to 50 percent from the end of 2003 to the middle of 2004 alone. There was a 24 percent decline in steel imports by China in 2004 while Chinese steel exports doubled to more than 17 million metric tons. The Chinese demand for steel was expected to grow exponentially for the foreseeable future, and production was expected to reach 340 million tons by 2006, representing 30 percent of total world steel production.

In 2009, China's steel production reached 567.8 million metric tons, to make it the industry leader by a long shot. According to the World Steel Association, China's steel use in 2010 is predicted to increase by 6.7 percent to 579 mmt, after an exciting increase of 24.8 percent in 2009. The 2011 forecast for China steel use is expected to slow to 2.8 percent bringing it to 595 mmt. China will account for 45.5 percent of the world apparent steel use, compared to 48.4 percent in 2009.

China's steel industry is also much less advanced than those of the leading industrial powers. During the 1980s, in fact, much of the steel-making equipment that China purchased was used equipment from Japan, the United States, and western Europe. With easy access to raw materials and inexpensive labor, but little scrap metal, much of China's manufacturing capacity in the early 1990s was attributable to large, integrated, and sometimes antiquated plants that relied on huge numbers of workers. China's largest steel plant, Anshan, employed 220,000 workers in 1990, while the entire Japanese steel industry employed fewer workers. In the late 1980s and early 1990s, however, the country began to invest in more advanced facilities that incorporated BOF and continuous casting technology. Observers also noted that while China had been a rising star in global steel, most of the growth resulted from internal demand. China exported only 6 percent of its steel output in 1994, but China's steelmakers increased their share of the international market in later years. Although the Chinese industry remained considerably more fragmented than those of other leading countries, in the late-1990s China successfully took the first steps to rationalize its sprawling steel industry. Between 1997 and 2000, China's leading firm, Shanghai Baosteel, jumped from nineteenth place in world rankings to tenth.

Japan. With approximately 7.17 percent of global production in 2009, Japan had slipped to the number three spot in world steel production. Prior to World War II, Japan's steel industry had been among the world's largest. After the war, however, national steel output plummeted to only 5 million metric tons. Japan gradually rebuilt its industrial base, boosting production to 23 million tons by 1960 and to more than 90 million tons by 1970. Industry output and employment peaked during the early 1970s at about 120 million tons annually and 350,000 workers, respectively. Like other industrialized nations, Japan's steel output gradually shrank, reaching a low of 97 million tons in 1983, in the wake of dormant market growth and increased competition from industrializing nations. Japan's domestic demand remained flat in 1998 and 1999, only picking up in 2000 when Japanese steel consumption jumped from 68.9 million metric tons to 76.1 million metric tons. In 2009, Japan steel production reached 87.5 million metric tons, a sizable decline from the 120.2 mmt it produced in 2007.

Unlike steel producers in the United States and Europe, Japanese manufacturers benefited from several factors in the 1980s. Massive growth in the domestic production of automobiles and other consumer and industrial goods pushed Japanese steel production upward to around 100 million tons and even surged as high as 110 million tons in 1990. Although Japan fared much better than its industrialized peers during the 1980s, it still suffered from outside competitive pressures and waning domestic demand. By the late 1980s Japanese steelmakers had clearly lost much of their productivity advantage and regional competition proliferated. Steel imports rose, but still accounted for only 7 percent of domestic steel consumption by the early 1990s. At the same time, however, a steadily rising yen hurt export demand and the nation's economy slumped into an ugly recession, leaving domestic steelmakers battered.

Japanese steel output reached 101.6 million metric tons in 1995 and 104.5 million metric tons in 1997, just before the Asian financial crisis hit. By 1999 output had decreased to 94.2 million metric tons. Ailing producers continued scrambling to sustain profitability. Since the mid-1980s, in fact, most companies had embarked on streamlining programs that included consolidation of blast-furnace operations, installation of new equipment, and reductions in labor costs as industry employment in Japan fell from 459,000 in 1970 to less than 200,000 in 1999. Cost-cutting efforts continued in the early 1990s as some companies cut into management ranks, reduced production capacity, and stepped up efforts to update mill technology. Looking ahead to the late 1990s, many Japanese steel producers sought joint ventures or invested in production facilities in China, Thailand, and other countries. In the early 2000s, Japanese companies were taking bold steps toward consolidation. Nippon Steel forged a strategic alliance with its competitor POSCO.

In early 2001 NKK Corp. and Kawasaki Steel Corp., Japan's second and third largest steel makers, respectively, announced a merger that would form the largest steel producer in Japan.

United States. The United States was relegated to fourth place in terms of industry production following China's mid-1990s ascent. U.S. steel shipments slipped to under 80 million tons in 1991, but a strong manufacturing sector contributed to a rise in output in 1994 and 1995 to roughly 90 million tons. Indeed, the mid-1990s marked a period of tremendous success for U.S. steelmakers, whose shipments peaked in 1997 at 98.5 million metric tons. Production dropped again in 1998 and 1999, falling as low as 97.4 million metric tons. The U.S. industry reached 98.9 million metric tons in 2004, up from 93.7 million metric tons in 2003. By 2009, U.S. steel production had declined to 58.1 mmt, or 4.7 percent of the world's total, pushing the U.S. to fifth place.

The United States dominated global steel production until the early 1970s. Output plummeted, however, from about 120 million tons in 1970 to a discouraging low of 67 million tons in 1982. Inefficient and outdated, U.S. steelmakers embarked on a period of painful restructuring. The workforce was slashed from 521,000 in 1970 to 204,000 in 1990, and 151,000 in 2000. Long-established methods and practices were re-examined as well.

While restructuring was an important element of the U.S. steel recovery, the minimill revolution was also vital to the industry's reversal of fortune. By the early 1990s, highly efficient minimills were producing about 35 percent of U.S.-made steel. Minimill production continued strongly into the 2000s. TXI Chaparral Steel spent $400 million on a minimill in Petersberg, Virginia, and Ipsco and Steel Dynamics each built new facilities. Nucor completed a plant in Cofield, North Carolina, and planned another one in Crawfordsville, Indiana. In fact, Nucor's expansion pushed it past long-time U.S. industry leader U.S. Steel. The importance of the minimill sector to the U.S. steel resurgence was supported by industry statistics. Between 1986 and 1991, for example, U.S. minimills enjoyed sales growth of 66 percent, while integrated producers gained only 1 percent. During the same period, employment at minimills jumped 19 percent while employment at integrated facilities dropped 30 percent. Most importantly, U.S. minimills showed an average profit of US$32 per ton during the late 1980s and early 1990s, while integrated producers gleaned only US$3 per ton. Armed with such minimill productivity, domestic producers were able to effectively buffet growing threats from low-cost, loosely regulated foreign producers. The U.S. steel industry had hoped to maintain its lead in the conversion to minimill production. It was also

expected to focus on the development of high-tech, high-margin steel products intended to open new markets and allow steel to compete with synthetic and metal substitutes.

The Russian Federation. While China's rise during the late 1980s and early 1990s in the international steel industry was rapid, it was not as dramatic as the decline of the Russian steel industry. Russia remained the fourth largest steel producer in the world in 1997. For most of the 1990s, the country was the world's fourth largest manufacturer of steel, but its annual results were shrinking steadily. In 1999 Germany surpassed Russia in production. By the end of the twentieth century, however, Russia staged a stirring turnaround, putting out 51.5 million metric tons, and in 2000 the figure rose again to 59.1 million metric tons. By 2004, Russian production of crude steel stood at 65.6 million metric tons, up from 61.5 million metric tons the previous year. In 2009, Russian steel production had fallen to 59.9 mmts, or 4.9 percent of the world's total.

The downturn in output in the Russian Federation and the other members of the Commonwealth of Independent States (CIS) was the result of a number of factors. A deteriorating industrial infrastructure, skyrocketing energy prices, stifling taxes, weak defense-related demand, and plummeting consumer-related demand all contributed to the country's woes. The Russian government turned to privatization and outside financing to update its production facilities, but the Russian Federation's steel output had not recovered by the late 1990s. Nonetheless, in 2001 Russia and the Ukraine had a combined 56 million tons of excess production capacity, a discrepancy that resulted in Russia selling steel to developed nations at prices sometimes lower than the cost of production, according to some U.S. firms. Some argued that treaties guaranteeing U.S. purchases of Russian steel should be replaced with aid to develop Russia's domestic steel market.

Germany. Germany slipped from fifth to seventh in world steel production in 2009, with its 32.7 million metric tons exceeded by South Korea with 48.6 million metric tons. While levels decreased to 40.5 million metric tons in 2002, output was about 44.8 million metric tons by 2003. Germany's steel output peaked in the 1970s at about 60 million tons. Shipments slid to about 40 million tons by the late 1980s. The East German steel sector, stifled for decades by a government-controlled economy, languished. By the late 1980s its steel output had fallen to about 5 million tons annually. In 1991, following reunification, Germany's steel output was about 43 million tons, although the East continued to lag behind. The German steel industry, although technologically advanced, endured extremely high labor costs and chafed under government regulations designed to protect the environment and address other issues. Critics of such regulatory measures contend that the country's competitiveness in relation to other steelmakers declined in the late 1980s and early 1990s as a result of such legislation. Output dwindled going into the mid-1990s, but a surge in prices buoyed profits for many German producers. As in Japan, some German manufacturers were engaged in a period of reorganization in the mid-1990s as they laid off workers, increased automation, and worked to reclaim the former East German steel sector.

BIBLIOGRAPHY

"Arcelor Mittal Spends $1.6B to Expand in Brazil." *Canadian Press,* 7 August 2008. Available from canadianpress.google.com.

"Arcelor Mittal to Build $600-m Steel Mill in Mexico." *The India Times,* 5 August 2008. Available from economictimes.indiatimes.com.

Bagsarian, Tom. "Beyond Steelmaking." *New Steel,* 1 May 2001.

———. "E-commerce: The Growth of Private Company Exchanges.' *New Steel,* 1 March 2001.

———. "Faster Heats, Fewer Impurities." *New Steel,* 1 April 2001.

———. "Nucor, Ipsco Lead Spending." *New Steel,* 1 September 2000.

———. "The Recovery Accelerates." *Iron Age New Steel,* 1 January 2000.

———. "Strip Casting Gets Serious." *New Steel,* 1 December 2001.

Berry, Bryan. "Restructuring Steel." *New Steel,* 1 August 2001.

Bright Outlook for Steel Industry in 2005-2006 Forecast at OECD/IISI Conference, Organization for Economic Co-operation and Development, 17 January 2005. Available from www.oecd.org.

"Business: Welding Bells: A European Steel Merger." *Economist,* 24 February 2001.

Chang, Peter. "POSCO Doubling Output of Automotive Steel." *Automotive News,* 31 March 2003.

Chappell, Lindsay. "Scrap Steel Prices See Hefty Decline." *Automotive News,* 5 April 2004.

Cheng, Allen T. "Gearing Up for Battle." *Asiaweek,* 22 December 2000.

Connolly, Allison. "Lower Stainless Steel Prices Hurt Thyssen Krupp Results." 14 August 2008.

Cordes, Renee. "Europe's Steelmakers Get Lean and Green." *Business Week,* 19 February 2001.

Crude Steel Production, Global Steel Production, 19 November 2010. Available from www.almatis.com.

Draper, Deborah J., ed. *Business Rankings Annual.* Detroit: Thomson Gale, 2004.

"EU/OECD." *European Report,* 6 March 2004.

Furakawa, Tsukasa. "Japanese Steelmakers Map Long-Range Strategies." *American Metal Market International Steel Supplement,* 3 October 2000.

Garvey, Robert A. "Getting Serious About Consolidation." *Iron Age New Steel,* 1 February 2001.

———. "How E-commerce Will Add Value." *New Steel,* 1 November 2000.

Graham-Rowe, Duncan. "How Not to Give Steel the Creeps." *New Scientist,* 19 July 2003.

"Healthy Appetite: As Long as Development Economies Need Steel, the Hunger for Scrap Will Continue." *Recycling Today,* January 2005.

Hogan, William T. *Minimills and Integrated Mills: A Comparison of Steelmaking in the United States,* Lexington, MA: Lexington Books, 1987.

———. *Steel in the United States: Restructuring to Compete.* Lexington, MA: Lexington Books, 1984.

"Hoover's Company Capsules." *Hoover's Online,* 2008. Available from www.hoovers.com.

"International Trade Statistics." World Trade Organization, 2003. Available from www.wto.org.

Kolkata. "Corus Delivers $600 mn of Internal Performance Improvements." *Buisness Standard,* 12 August 2008. Available from www. business-standard.com.

Kosdrosky, Terry. "Suppliers Get Deals to Cushion Rising Steel Prices." *Automotive News,* 28 June 2004.

Marsh, Peter. "Arbed Hopes the World Will Prove Its Oyster." *Financial Times,* 29 March 2000.

"Posco Completes Privatization." *New Steel,* 1 November 2000.

"Posco Looks Beyond the Boom in China to Entrench Position." *Australasian Business Intelligence,* 20 November 2003.

"Prime Time for E-commerce." *New Steel,* 1 August 2000.

Rawson, Randy. "Steel Yourself." *Heating/Piping/Air Conditioning Engineering,* April 2004.

"Recycling." *European Report,* 19 November 2003.

Richard, Bob, and Luke Folta. "Steel Demands Outlook Less Than Riveting." *Barron's,* 14 August 2008. Available from online.barrons.com.

Ritt, Adam. "Endless Casting and Rolling of Bar." *New Steel,* 1 November 2000.

———. "Reversing a Legacy of Poor Returns." *New Steel,* 1 January 2001.

"Semi-Fabricated Steel in France, Germany, UK, US." *Euromonitor,* August 2004. Available from www.majormarketprofiles.com.

Serwer, Andy. "This Is Not Your Father's Steel Bubble." *Fortune,* 26 January 2004.

Sherefkin, Robert. "Steel Crisis Drives Supplier to Chapter 11." *Automotive News,* 29 March 2004.

"Specialty Imports Break Record in 2000." *New Steel,* 1 April 2001.

"Stainless: Fewer Players, Faster Growth than Carbon." *New Steel,* 1 December 2001.

"The Table Is Set." *New Steel,* 1 May 2001.

United Steelworkers. *Who We Are.* Available from www.usw.org.

"US Steel Labor Contract Includes Significant Increases Report," 14 August 2008. Available from www.steelguru.com.

"Usinor, Arbed, Aceralia to Form World's No. 1 Steelmaker." *New Steel,* 1 March 2001.

Wilhelm, Paul J. "Consolidation Will Be Selective and Global." *New Steel,* 1 December 2001.

"Will Euro, Asian Mergers Force U.S. Mills to Act?" *Purchasing,* 3 May 2001.

World Steel in Figures: 2005. International Iron and Steel Institute, 2005. Available from www.worldsteel.org.

"World: Steel Output Slows In October 2000." *Metal Bulletin,* 23 November 2000.

"World Steel Production Increases but US Output Slips, IISI Data Shows." *American Metal Market,* 21 June 2005.

World Steel Short Range Outlook, World Steel Association, 20
   April 2010. Available from www.worldsteel.org.
Yamaguchi, Yuzo. "Blast Threatens Japan Auto Output."
   Automotive News, 8 September 2003.

SIC 3410

METAL CANS

NAICS CODE(S)

332431. This industry consists of companies that manufacture metal cans, metal shipping barrels, drums, kegs, and pails, typically from purchased materials.

INDUSTRY SNAPSHOT

The world metal can industry, which is a major component of the US$345.93 billion global packaging industry, represented a growing multibillion-dollar market in the early and mid-2000s. In 2003, the U.S. market alone was valued at more than US$13 billion. According to the Aluminum Association, Inc., there were 100.5 billion cans produced in the United States in 2004. Industry firms produced billions of aluminum cans, who were forced by intense competition, threats from new packaging technologies, and the enormous costs of metal can manufacturing to develop new can designs and improved manufacturing processes while looking to overseas markets for new sources of revenue.

Most metal cans manufactured in the United States were for soft drinks, producing more than 57 billion cans in 2004. Production of beer cans was nearly 28.8 billion units. Beverage cans held the highest rate of recycling as well, with 51.5 billion cans recycled in 2004.

The growing popularity of premium beverage packaging solutions by glass and plastic beverage packaging producers was fueled by the explosion of microbreweries and boutique beverage brands. Although these were more expensive than cans, they offered beverage makers a way to differentiate their products with consumers. For instance, the so-called aluminum "bottle can" that was introduced to the U.S. market in 2004 allowed the containers to be filled on pre-existing glass bottling lines. Can makers emphasized the low cost and superior graphics of metal cans and pressed harder to develop ways to make the "one style fits all" metal can stand out on store shelves. In less developed economies where beverages sit longer on store shelves and refrigeration is less reliable, can industry firms were confident of their prospects for protecting market share.

By 2004 several developments were expected to help the metal can industry grow, particularly in the area of packaging, which was driven by the market and consumer preferences. Differentiation in packaging's "look" did more to boost the industry than anything else. For example, pop-top cans have more than half the shelf space in some markets. Unusually shaped (square, barrel, kettle), embossed, and other standout cans have been appearing on shelves worldwide for some time and are expected to increase in abundance. Some companies were experimenting with the viability of manufacturing resealable cans. According to *Brand Packaging*, companies were reporting enormous upswings in revenue by offering their products in differentiated cans.

ORGANIZATION AND STRUCTURE

Historically, can making has been a mature, slow-growth, capital-intensive business that relied on economies of scale and high-volume production efficiencies to profit from the fraction of revenue not spent on purchasing materials, installing new equipment, product marketing, equipment maintenance, labor, depreciation, and taxes. In contrast to cyclical industries like automobile manufacturing, can making is relatively resistant to boom-and-bust cycles in the economy. Sales of soft drinks, beer, and certain canned food staples often increase during economic downturns as consumers switch from up-market, glass-packaged products to low-cost canned goods.

The metal can industry has been difficult for new entrants to break into because of the enormous capital outlay required to establish high-tech production facilities and distribution networks. For instance, in the late 1990s a modern beverage manufacturing line in Europe cost at least US$32 million to install. In industrialized nations like the United States, France, and Germany, the can industry has been dominated by a relatively small number of firms. In the overall European market, metal can making is relatively concentrated and has traditionally been divided between large firms that manufacture standardized, mass-produced can products like beverage and food cans and small to medium firms that specialize in customized cans with irregular shapes or unique label designs.

The price of materials was the controlling factor in the cost of manufacturing cans. Can makers negotiate supply contracts with metal producers like Alcoa that are heavily reliant on can industry purchases for their sales. To reduce transportation costs, can makers often build their plants near or in their primary customers. In the United States, the metal can industry has been characterized by periodic flurries of plant openings and closings as industry firms responded to changing demographics and conditions in the canned products industry while attempting to discourage canners from establishing facilities for the manufacture of their own cans. Historically, major can buyers have not purchased their cans from a single manufacturer but have signed contracts with one of the major can makers, dividing remaining purchases among the smaller producers. Because canned product firms usually require that their can orders be filled according to uniform specifications, the large can makers have been forced to sell their can line technology to smaller competitors handling the remainder of the customer's order. In the U.S. packaging industry, the ratio of customers to suppliers was seven to one in the mid-1990s.

The expansion of can manufacturing internationally has been affected by the supply of raw materials, such as finished metal plate. In less developed nations can makers may be forced to absorb prohibitive duties and shipping costs to import needed materials and may be aided by lack of water resources, which prevents packaging competitors in the bottling industry from maintaining essential bottle washing plants. Because shipping costs for metal cans are generally high, direct international trade in the metal can industry has been centered on business between contiguous markets such as the United States and Canada.

Intense price competition, overcapacity in the face of diminishing demand, loss of market share to new packaging methods, and the vagaries of consumer taste in packaged goods are among the perennial hurdles confronted by industry firms. To fortify themselves against such threats, can makers looked to overseas markets in developing countries and to diversification in rival packaging markets or entirely new industries through mergers and acquisitions or other means. However, for all the difficulties inherent in can manufacturing, the U.S. metal can industry, which is the world's largest, generally has outpaced U.S. manufacturing in new product and facilities investment, productivity, and wages.

The products of the larger metal container industry can be divided into two broad categories: metal cans and metal barrels, drums, and pails. The three major product groups are aluminum cans; steel cans and tinware products; and steel shipping barrels and drums larger than 12 gallons. The remaining 5 percent of industry output is divided among miscellaneous metal cans, 1- to 12-gallon steel pails, and other metal barrel types.

BACKGROUND AND DEVELOPMENT

The invention of canning for food storage and preservation is usually credited to Frenchman Nicolas Appert, who in 1795 began experimenting with food preservation techniques in response to a call by the French government for the development of a method for preserving food for transport over long distances. Appert discovered that by sealing food tightly in containers covered with wire and sealing wax and then boiling them to destroy

contaminating organisms, a wide range of foods could be preserved for extended periods. Using the prize money awarded to him by Napoleon Bonaparte, Appert established the world's first commercial cannery in Massy, France, in 1812.

Working from Appert's experiments, Englishman Peter Durand was awarded a patent for a cylindrical, tin-coated iron can capable of preserving foods without metal corrosion in 1810, and three years later two Englishmen founded a food processing plant for canned meats, vegetables, and soups for the British navy and army. The first U.S. cannery was established in 1820, where shortly before the U.S. Civil War, the can production process was shortened by adding calcium chloride to the water in which cans were boiled. Annual production by the emerging U.S. can industry grew from 5 million cans before the Civil War to 30 million after 1865, continuing to increase when mechanization and factory methods of manufacture were adopted by the nation's can producers in 1870.

As scientific understanding of the principles of food preservation improved at the end of the nineteenth century, the quality of the food canned by industry firms greatly increased as mass production was transforming canned goods into a common household item. In 1900 sanitary metal food can methods were invented, and can makers were able to market cans with folded airtight double seams that were manufactured at greatly improved speeds.

Mergers among industry participants created several conglomerates in the early twentieth century. In 1901, American Can was formed in the United States through the merger of 123 of the nation's 175 can manufacturers, and held 90 percent of the industry's market share. In 1912, a forerunner of can-making giant Toyo Seikan Kaisha began operation in Japan with can line equipment purchased from American Can, and in 1919 the Netherlands' Royal Packaging Industries Van Leer began manufacturing steel drums. Two years later, Britain's metal can leader, Metal Box PLC, was formed through the merger of four British can makers, creating Allied Tin Box Makers Ltd. (renamed Metal Box and Printing Industries a year later). Metal Box's early market dominance was quickly threatened by the adoption by British firms of the U.S. roll form of can manufacture in which the metal can blank is shaped into a cylindrical form by being fed against a deflecting plate, allowing Metal Box's competitors to turn out more than 200 cans a minute.

Intrigued by the British adoption of the new can making technologies, American Can attempted to acquire Metal Box and Printing Industries in the 1920s, forcing the latter to enter into an agreement with American's competitor, Continental Can (established in

1913), giving Metal Box exclusive British rights to Continental's technology and solidifying its market position. Metal Box acquired American's British subsidiary British Can and standardized can production and business operations at all its plants, forming subsidiaries and partnerships in France, the Netherlands, South Africa, India, and Belgium. After buying failing British can makers during the Depression, Metal Box was manufacturing 335 million cans a year by 1937. After World War II, can making speed catapulted to thousands of cans per minute. The invention of the aseptic method in which high temperatures and rapid cooking times are used to separately sterilize the metal can and its contents, allowed products that do not retain their nutrients or flavor well under traditional canning methods to be packaged in metal cans. The enormous growth of the beverage can industry in the 1960s was made possible in part by emphasizing the advantages that cans offered over bottles. Cans were disposable, required no deposit, were easier to stack, chilled more quickly, did not break, and took up less space in the refrigerator. When the pull-off or "poptop" tab eliminated the need for beverage can openers in 1963, the metal beverage can began to eclipse the bottle as the favored beverage packaging medium.

Aluminum cans, which initially were introduced in the meat, fish, motor oil, and frozen fruit juice markets, began to make serious inroads into the steel-dominated beverage can market when Reynolds Aluminum developed a method for making aluminum cans that used two pieces rather than three—a top or lid, a single-piece body, and bottom manufactured from can sheet using the single blow of a draw press. This manufacturing innovation uniquely suited to the malleable properties of aluminum, and by the mid-1960s a standard 12-ounce aluminum beer and beverage can began to gain a foothold in the U.S. market. Thereafter, the three-piece steel beverage can began a gradual slide in market share as sales of the two-piece aluminum can rose to 20 billion cans in the late 1970s, 40 billion in the early 1980s, and 100 billion by the late 1990s. Between 1977 and 1997 aluminum can production in North America quintupled.

The collapse of the Soviet Union in the early 1990s drew a number of international can makers to Eastern Europe despite the region's shortage of investment capital, absence of developed solid waste and recycling facilities, weak infrastructure, and severe capital shortages. In the mid-1990s, Continental Can Europe formed Continental Can Polska, and through its German subsidiary Schmalbach-Lubeca constructed a two-piece aluminum can plant for the Polish market. Through its French subsidiary Ferembal, the company acquired Obalex, the Czech Republic's second largest food can manufacturer. In 1997 Continental Can Europe merged the food can making operations of German can maker Schmalbach-

Lubeca and French can maker Pechiney to form Hexacan. The first beverage can plants began to sprout up in Russia in the late 1990s.

In 1996, the global can market was projected to expand 20 percent by 1999. While the European market grew an average of 6 percent per year through the 1990s and in 2000, the United States made up the majority of the metal can market. In 2000, 114 billion of approximately 210 billion metal cans were used in North America, with more than 100 billion used in the United States. Asia used 40 billion and Europe used more than 35 billion, while the South American market consumed 14 billion cans and the African market used 7 billion.

In January 2002, the European market promised even further growth when Denmark ended its 20-year ban on the use of steel and aluminum drink cans in conjunction with the establishment of steep recycling rates. The lifting of the ban was expected to result in the consumption of an additional 300 to 400 million canned beverages annually, adding to the 35 billion units already consumed in the European market annually.

CURRENT CONDITIONS

The worldwide metal can industry became increasingly international in the 2000s. Although business arrangements between foreign can producers go back to at least the 1920s, the global can industry continued to be characterized by a growing trend toward joint ventures, partnerships, licensing agreements, and mergers and acquisitions.

Slow growth continued in the early 2000s as energy costs associated with producing metal packaging skyrocketed. Price wars among U.S. metal container manufacturers, the ongoing battle between aluminum and steel for market share, challenges from glass and plastic container products, and the effect of "sin" taxes on beer were also factors affecting the health of the U.S. and global can industry. By the mid-2000s, with the enormous change in the consumer packaging industry, metal can production was experiencing an upswing.

In the mid-2000s, approximately 37 billion steel cans were manufactured by U.S. firms, the vast majority of which were used for food canning (99 percent steel) and general packaging (99 percent steel). Steel continued to lose ground to aluminum in its traditional product categories, such as food canning, where aluminum's share of the total food can segment rose from 8 percent to 9 percent. At the same time, steel's approximate US$3 to US$4 per thousand price advantage over aluminum along with new production techniques that neutralized some of the inherent superiority of aluminum as a canning metal enabled steel to reenter the beverage can market, increasing its share to 8 percent.

The recycling of metal cans continued to be a successful venture for the U.S. packaging industry. Created in the 1960s from environmental concerns, can recycling became critical in the U.S. metal can industry's production process. By using recycled aluminum rather than primary aluminum to make new cans, industry firms were able to save 95 percent on the energy costs of manufacturing cans from raw materials. By 1997, two-thirds of all U.S. beverage cans were recycled. In 2004, 51.3 percent of all U.S. aluminum cans, equaling about 1.51 billion pounds, were recycled.

In August 2008, Can Manufacturers Botswana (Pty) Ltd., a subsidiary of the Botswana Development Corporation Limited, became the first food can company in Botswana. The company, located in Lobaste, Botswana, was established in response to a 2002 feasibility study by the BDC that found unmet demands for food cans in the South African Development Community (SADC). Can Manufacturers Botswana was opened to develop markets for local farmers through fruit and vegetable canning companies.

In 2008, the controversy over the use of the chemical bisphenol A to manufacture plastic bottles, was expected to benefit the metal can industry. The Canadian government was the first to announce plans to prohibit the import, sale, and advertising for plastic bottles containing bisphenol A, which is used to make a hard, clear plastic known as polycarbonate. The chemical is also found in epoxy resins in the protective lining of metal food and beverage cans, and the industry was conducting research to find a replacement. On October 23, 2008, the Natural Resources Defense Council petitioned the U.S. Food and Drug Administration to ban bisphenol A's use in all food packaging or as a food additive.

RESEARCH AND TECHNOLOGY

One major goal of can industry research has been to reduce the amount of metal contained in each can, reducing the cost of metal purchases. Material content accounts for between 70 and 80 percent of the cost of a metal can, and a millimeter reduction in the thickness of can walls results in enormous cumulative cost savings for can manufacturers. Therefore, since 1975 the amount of steel in steel cans has been reduced about one-third, and by the mid-1990s the walls of steel drink cans had been made 33 percent thinner than aluminum can walls, with a 13 percent reduction in thickness since 1991.

Industry firms have traditionally looked for material reductions by using thinner gauge feedstock and by reducing the amount of metal wasted in the seams that join the can's parts. The amount of metal used in the aluminum can end alone, for example, can account for as much as one-third of the can's total weight, and the ongoing

adoption of the "202-type" can end in the mid-1990s resulted from the development of "spin flow" machinery that could make can ends thinner and smaller without any commensurate loss in sturdiness. The development of new methods for can "necking" methods, whereby the upper end of the can is compressed or stretched to fit a smaller can top, enabled industry firms to reduce material costs and eliminate stages in the can manufacturing process while offering a more stackable can.

New can designs in the 1990s included the "composite can," which was a mix of metal and paper and offered a 30 percent reduction in weight with a 10 percent reduction in material cost over metal cans, as well as increased savings for shipping and handling. The composite can was used in Europe primarily for dry foods, and began to be used by U.S. can makers for products like fruit juice, refrigerated dough, and instant coffee. In the mid-1990s, the British steel can industry also began marketing an "ultimate can," which offered a 30 percent weight reduction over traditional metal cans with the added benefit of not requiring new can line equipment during manufacture. Finally, "Ferrolite," a polymer-coated steel-based material developed by CarnaudMetalbox in the 1990s, offered improved corrosion resistance and a novel appearance and texture. In 1993, British Steel Tinplate began marketing baby food containers made from Ferrolite, and in 1995 CarnaudMetalbox began producing Ferrolite-based ends for aerosol cans.

Increasing can thinness combined with manufacturing processes to strengthen the stiffness of the can metal. These techniques included metallurgical alloying, new hardening processes, physical deformation methods like fluting, and improved techniques for joining the can's parts. In some processed food cans, for example, a method of folding the can's base seam underneath, rather than up, the side of the can, offered improved performance. The traditional advantages of aluminum over steel in can manufacture began to disappear as lighter, more flexible steel cans were developed that were virtually indistinguishable from aluminum cans while offering steel's strength and impact resistance.

Improved convenience and appearance were other major goals of industry research. Innovations in can "closure" features reflected the industry's attempt to solidify market share by making cans and metal containers less difficult to open and providing greater product differentiation. Such "easy-opening" ends traditionally focused on aluminum beverage cans, but in the 1990s steel food containers also began to appear with such enhancements, including the ring-pull feature. In the mid-1990s, CarnaudMetalbox began marketing the Quantum can, with an easy-opening end for premium food products like pasta sauces. In the United States,

Ball Corporation introduced a large-aperture Touch Top can feature that eliminated the traditional "stay-on" tab opener altogether by offering an integrated opening and pouring design. A nondetachable push-button can end known as Ecotop was also marketed in Europe in the 1990s that required one-third less energy to manufacture than traditional "stay-on" tabs, left no sharp edges, and provided a feature that allowed consumers to know when tampering had occurred. In 1998, Reynolds Metals received a patent for its Large Opening End, a pouring aperture 37 percent larger that traditional cans that enabled consumers to quaff beverages in greater volume without jeopardizing the structural strength of the can's seal.

The adoption of improved coatings for the interior and exterior of the can also enabled industry firms to reduce the reaction of the metal to the can's contents and provide more options for the can's aesthetic appearance, respectively. The burnished, highly reflective surface of cans developed in the 1990s allowed canned product manufacturers to create boldly innovative designs rivaling those previously possible only with paper-based labels. Between 1975 and the mid-1990s the amount of coating used in the manufacture of metal cans had been reduced 25 percent. These innovations were more than mere window-dressing. Glass and plastic bottle makers offered beverage producers greater opportunities to differentiate their products on store shelves, making it difficult for the uniform metal can to challenge the unique brand identities of alternative packaging. Despite the added cost for consumers who purchased premium beverage packaging products, their sales ate away at metal cans' market share throughout the late 1990s. Even Coke's durable plastic contour Classic Coke bottle was finding its way into vending machines that had once been the indisputable province of the metal can.

By the late 1990s the U.S. soft drink industry was consuming almost 5 billion 20-ounce plastic bottles per year, and some industry experts were proclaiming the demise of beverage cans in North America. In response, Crown Cork and Seal created a metal can for Heineken beer that was shaped and tinted like a brimming beer glass, and Budweiser worked on an embossed metal can with a "silky" feel to attract choosy, image-conscious beer drinkers. While contour metal cans required expensive retooling on the assembly line, the embossing process involved much less capital expenditure and seemed to offer can makers a way to way to ward off plastic and glass for the lucrative beverage packaging dollar.

Other developments included new can shapes and sizes, reclosable lids, and flashier graphics. The adoption of continuous casting techniques and computerized manufacturing and quality control methods also greatly improved the productivity of the can making process by reducing scrap and improving the ratio of rejected to acceptable cans. By using 70 different statistical quality control techniques, for example, Reynolds Metals of the United States reduced the number of unacceptable cans sent to customers by 42 percent in 1984. Other industry technology trends included line machines with increased can-per-minute production rates and the development of can materials that posed a decreased threat to the environment. For example, Japan's Toyo Lightweight Ultimate Can reduced much of the waste associated with metal can manufacturing processes.

An Ipsos research study on easy-open (EZO) ends focused on the impact of brand, size, shape, lid, and price on consumer purchases. "Not only do consumers indicate a clear preference for EZO ends in this category, but they back that preference with a willingness to spend more money for the convenience," said Silgan Containers Director of Marketing Carolyn Takata. Metal cans for fruit were preferred by 43 percent of consumers based on appearance and flexibility, offering contrast through shape and color on store shelves. "According to independent research, 68 percent of buying decisions are made at point-of-purchase," Takata explained. "Most of the time, your packaging statement is going to determine whether or not your product stays on the shelf or ends up in the shopping cart." Furthermore, major technological advances made shaped can production cost-effective and efficient for aluminum as well as steel. Product launches advanced sales through "product differentiation and enhanced functionality."

WORKFORCE

In the industry's early years, can making was performed by solitary craftsmen who formed each can individually by bending the body piece around a cylindrical mold and soldering the seams and end piece. After food was forced through the open end, the can maker soldered the top end to the can and began the process again, for an average of ten finished cans per day. As automation made production rates of 200 cans per minute possible, the artisan was replaced by line operators responsible for overseeing the production process and maintaining the machinery on the line.

In the early twentieth century, wages and labor conditions were poor in the first truly mass production can plants. In the United Kingdom the Trade Boards Act forced tin can manufacturers to improve industry pay scales and factory conditions. While automation drastically reduced the number of workers needed to make a can, industry expansion led to higher employment. For example, in 1939 (when *Fortune* magazine observed that "it is almost impossible to be fired from American Can") the largest U.S. producer, American Can, employed 22,000 workers but more than twice that by the early 1960s.

Employment in the international metal can industry began to decline as a result of increasing international competition, further improvements in can line automation, and loss of market share to other packaging. Between 1982 and 1990, for example, U.S. employment declined from 50,000 to 35,000, while employment in the United Kingdom was halved from 24,377 in 1981 to 12,384 in 1990. Declines in many of the major U.S. can industry employment categories, from machine forming operators and tenders to executives and managers, were expected to range from 33 to 40 percent between the mid-1990s and 2005.

INDUSTRY LEADERS

Crown Holdings Inc. Crown Cork and Seal (CC&S) was incorporated in 1927 and was one of the first U.S. can makers to explore the international packaging market, forming the Crown Cork International Corporation in 1928 as a holding company for its container and closure subsidiaries in foreign markets. In 1936 it entered the can making business through acquisition, but after suffering financial losses in its domestic operations in the late 1950s, the firm refocused on international markets in overseas container and aerosol can operations. CC&S won "pioneer rights" to develop new can and closure operations from governments seeking to develop their manufacturing sectors. This gave the company the opportunity to operate profitable can plants with aging machinery that would have rendered it uncompetitive in the free market. Through its policy of establishing overseas operations only with foreign nationals and equipping them with outdated can machinery, CC&S was able to cut startup costs at the same time that it developed a network of quasi-independent subsidiaries around the world.

In the 1970s and 1980s, the company's international activities included acquisitions of a British container closure plant, a German aluminum closures facility, and a Swiss packager as well as new or expanded plants in Canada, Ireland, Scotland, and Brazil. In the 1990s, CC&S teamed up with the Saudi Arabian can making firm Ahmad Hamad Algosaibi and Brothers to build beverage can plants in Jordan, Saudi Arabia, and the United Arab Emirates. It also partnered with a multi-party Asian group to construct a can plant in Vietnam. By the mid-1990s, CC&S's 20-year growth rate exceeded that of all other U.S. can manufacturers.

In 1996 CC&S bought French can making giant CarnaudMetalbox (CMB), making CC&S the world's largest producer of packaging containers. Along with

Pechiney, CMB had dominated the European can market, and in addition to its extensive European operations that accounted for 55 percent of its total sales, CMB had maintained a strong presence in Asia. In the 1990s, CMB was a prime player in the European can industry's attempts to develop environmentally friendly manufacturing methods that would, for example, reduce the effluent its can plants released during production. In 1991 CMB had established an aerosol can plant on the border of Germany and Poland and in 1992 purchased Hungary's leading food can and closure producer. A year later CMB acquired a majority share of GWS Metallipakkus to assume the assets of Finland's GW Sohlberg, positioning it to develop export markets in Eastern Europe, the Baltic States, and the Russian Federation. In 1995 CMB moved into the Chinese market when it opened a can making plant in Guangzhou.

In 1996 can production at the newly enlarged CC&S was halted at eight plants by strikes over union contracts. CC&S also sold its paint and oblong can business to B-WAY Corporation and acquired the Polish packaging firm Fabryka Opakowan Blaszanyck in 1996, reporting sales of more than US$8.3 billion. In 1996 CC&S opened its fourth plant in mainland China, and in 1997 bought 96 percent of Golden Aluminum, the one-time can making operation of Coors Brewery. In 1997 CC&S operated 247 plants in 49 countries. By 2000 CC&S had garnered 20 percent of the world's beverage can market and produced one-third of the food cans sold in North America and Europe. The company reported revenues of nearly US$7.7 billion in 2007 with 21,800 employees.

Pechiney. The French government is the majority shareholder of Pechiney, which originated as a chemical and aluminum producer in the nineteenth century and had no involvement in the packaging industry. Before it acquired American National Can (ANC) in the late 1980s, had no involvement in the packaging industry. Following its nationalization in 1982, the company's North American operations were restructured under the name Pechiney Corporation. It embarked on a string of mergers and acquisitions that culminated in 1988 with the purchase of American National Can (ANC), the largest soft drink and beer can maker in the world. The acquisition doubled Pechiney's assets virtually overnight and allowed the company to strike a balance between its consumer-based and raw materials-based interests. By the mid-1990s, Pechiney had become the world's largest packaging company with operations in over 20 countries and diversified interests in aluminum, turbines, and international trade, as well as nuclear fuel and heavy carbon manufacturing.

Pechiney's major can market activities in the 1990s included the formation of a joint venture with a Chinese firm for the operation of an aluminum beer and soft drink can plant in Zhaiqing City, a joint venture with a Japanese firm to enter the Asian food can market, and the purchase of a majority stake in Czech-based Strojobal that manufactured metal cans as well as plastic and aluminum products. In 1997 Pechiney's "Food Europe" food can operations were merged with the food can operations of German powerhouse Schmalbach-Lubeca to form a new European food can giant, Hexacan that was large enough to challenge Crown/CarnaudMetalbox for leadership of Europe's food can industry. In 1997 Pechiney maintained 300 industrial and sales facilities in 60 countries, with almost two-thirds of its can production occurring outside France.

Packaging accounted for 33 percent of Pechiney's total sales in the early 2000s. Although centered on American National Can with about 35 plants in ten countries, Pechiney's can making operations included a European metal food can division that manufactured lids and cans from aluminum and tinplate among other products, and a North American food plastic division that produced flexible packaging for food, health care, and industrial markets). The European market accounted for 59 percent of Pechiney's packaging sales, while North America made up 33 percent. Pechiney increased its share of the global beverage can market by relying on the development of new can designs, sale of uncompetitive facilities, strategic partnerships with its international clients, and judicious exploitation of potential markets in developing economies. The Beverage Cans Americas division was the leading North American manufacturer of aluminum beverage cans and ends in 1995, and Beverage Cans Europe was the leading European manufacturer of aluminum and steel beverage cans and ends. These two divisions accounted for 56 percent of Pechiney's packaging sector sales. In 2001 Pechiney's earnings fell 26 percent, but the firm's packaging operations recorded a sharp increase of 36 percent. By 2002, the company reported revenues of US$12.5 billion.

Pechiney, which also operated aluminum smelting plants, attempted a three-way merger with Alcan and Algroup in 2000. However, the merger was blocked by competition regulators, and the companies subsequently merged slowly. Alcan acquired Algroup in 2000, and in 2004 Alcan acquired Pechiney for US$4.7 billion.

In 2002, the company announced the consolidation of its shareholdings in smelters to take advantage of increasing opportunities in the fragmented specialist packaging sector. Early in 2002, Pechiney considered purchasing German metals group VAW and further expanding its food packaging sector by strengthening

relationships with customers like Kraft Foods, Nestle, and L'Oreal. The firm also deliberated the construction of a large smelter in Australia or South Africa to be operational by 2005.

Toyo Seikan Kaisha. Founded in 1933 as the successor of a Japanese can company whose canning technology had been acquired from American Can and Continental Can, Toyo Seikan Kaisha (TSK) survived World War II to become the dominant can manufacturer in Japan during the country's postwar economic renaissance. Like many Japanese corporations, TSK was restructured after World War II. In the 1950s the company joined an affiliation of other Japanese can makers that was known as the Toyo Seikan Group. The group began exploring the international can market, initially through export sales and then through product licensing and joint ventures in Indonesia, South Korea, Singapore, Thailand, and Nigeria.

By the 1990s, the Toyo Seikan Group consisted of 25 subsidiaries and affiliates; maintained technical agreements with such Western firms as Metal Closures, Continental Group, and Owens-Illinois; and had licensing arrangements with 25 companies in 13 countries. Almost three-quarters of the containers it manufactured were sold directly to the Japanese beverage industry, with the remaining container sales devoted to food, household, and general container products.

TSK introduced the Toyo Ultimate Lightweight Can (TULC), an attempt to slow Japan's conversion to aluminum cans by offering a lightweight, nonrusting, two-piece steel can for the beverage market. By 1996 TULC controlled 7 percent of the Japanese market, fueled by Coca-Cola and Lipton's adoption of the can in the Japanese market. Between 1996 and 1997, production of TSK's environmentally friendly TULC can grew 80 percent. With TULC's domestic success assured, in the late 1990s TSK targeted overseas can markets, primarily the food products sector, and eventually the beer and soft drink markets as well. The company reported 2004 revenues of US$6.3 billion. Beverage containers accounted for approximately 70 percent of sales.

Ball Corporation. Until the mid-1940s, the Ball Corporation of Indiana was essentially a manufacturer of bottles and jars, which it had marketed since it began operations in 1880. Can production contracts with such major beverage firms as Anheuser-Busch, Pepsi, and Coca-Cola, Ball carved out a small but profitable niche in the two-piece can market, which it developed into a solid 11 percent share of the U.S. beverage can market by 1990. In the 1980s and 1990s, Ball claimed a major piece of the world beverage can market when it acquired Continental Can's European packaging business in 1990. In the 1990s, Ball also expanded operations in Asia, introduced new can designs, and ceased production of the tin-and-aluminum bi-metal can.

In 1995 Ball entered the exploding PET/plastic container business and combined its glass container business into a newly formed company, Ball-Foster Glass Container. In 1996 it sold 42 percent of the company to its partner, the French materials megacompany Saint-Gobain Group. In 1996 Ball announced plans to build a PET plant in Iowa and a joint venture aluminum plant in Thailand as well as the sale of its aerosol can making business. In 1997 Ball joined the global can industry's move into the newly liberalized Chinese market by acquiring M.C. Packaging of Hong Kong, which made it the leading supplier of beverage cans to China. In 2000 the company reported sales had remained steady at US$3.7 billion. Losses totaled US$101.2 million in the wake of uncertainty in the U.S. stock market and increasing energy costs, which affected production. By 2004, the company reported an increase in revenues to US$5.44 billion, up 9.3 percent from 2003. The company reported revenues of US$7.5 billion in 2007 with 15,500 employees.

Rexam. Rexam had launched a revolutionary 360 degree embossing technique in 2007, and announced the creation of a unique can for Olvi's FIZZ Cooler cider in August 2008. The technique had become popular with drink companies in diverse categories. Olvi selected a "golf ball" design to create a distinctive look for their cans resulting in increased shelf life and visual stimulation. "As a brand, FIZZ Cooler is positioned as a refreshing and cool drink, and we believe that the golf ball embossing design reflects the image well," said Juha Wathen, Product Group Manager for FIZZ Cooler. The can also included Rexam's Illustration Impact to print photo-like images on cans and demonstrated the company's focus to provide value-added products. For 2006, Rexam reported sales of US$7.3 billion.

Silgan Containers. Silgan Containers, a subsidiary of Silgan Holdings, was the largest manufacturer of metal food containers in North America. Silgan had a 50 percent share of the U.S. market by volume in 2007, with net sales of US$1.68 billion. Silgan Its claimed that quality support, service, technology, low-cost producer position, strategically-located geographic locations, and extensive consumer research was "the cornerstone of its strong customer relationships."

MAJOR COUNTRIES IN THE INDUSTRY

Asia. The industrializing nations of Asia offered new markets to internationally minded can producers. In 1994, CC&S announced a joint venture to erect an aluminum can plant with an annual capacity of 400

million cans near Hanoi, Vietnam. France's CarnaudMetalbox began building a similar plant near Saigon and a new plant in Guangzhou, China. China's soft drink consumption reached more than 7 billion liters annually by 2000. China's first beverage can plant had opened in 1996, the same year that CC&S had opened its fourth Chinese plant and Ball Corporation had opened a new plant in Thailand. Although Asia's growth potential was promising through the mid-1990s, the continent suffered a financial crisis in 1998, and some beverage manufacturers had to close their factories. Can manufacturers were adversely affected by the closures, but Shanghai United Can Manufacturing Co. predicted that momentum would return in the early 2000s, due to rapid growth of the Chinese beverage market. In 2000, Japan's largest food and beverage packaging company, Toyo Seikan, had stabilized and increased its workforce with profits increasing from just over US$43 million in 1999 to more than US$240 million as the Japanese yen stabilized. In contrast, India continued to remain a largely undeveloped market in the mid-2000s despite its vast population and the exploratory moves of some world can makers. By 2003, metal accounted for more than 10 percent of Asia's containers and packaging market, which had reached US$91.69 billion.

Asia provided 75 percent of the world's tin. Indonesia was the world's largest tin exporter but had announced plans to cap production. The country's problems with tin from illegal mines being dumped on the market depressed prices and resulted in government requiring export permits. High prices motivated talks about resuming tin mining in Thailand.

Japan. Japanese can makers had historically relied on the U.S. can industry for industry production trends and technologies. Because of the unique characteristics of the Japanese beverage and food market, however, Japanese can makers have adapted Western ideas and equipment to meet the hugely diverse and specialized niches of Japan's food and beverage sector. More than 93 percent of the metal cans produced by the Japanese can industry in the mid-1990s was used for beverages, with 7 percent devoted to food products.

While the Japanese market for beverage and food cans dropped dramatically in the late 1990s, reaching a 20-year low in 1999, growth resumed by 2000. The Japanese began importing fewer cans in the 1990s, and by 2001 imported only 300 million empty cans, down 25 percent from 2000. However, the country imported 390 million canned foods and beverages in 2000 and 2001. The food and beverage export business was stagnant during that time, and Japan exported 300 million filled cans in 2000 and 2001. By 2003, the mature containers and packaging market in Japan reached

US$48.58 billion, reflecting a 0.2 percent compound annual growth rate in the previous five years. Metal packaging represented about 10 percent of that market.

Just as the United States introduced its can technology into the postwar Japanese economy of the 1940s and 1950s, Japan began selling its adaptations and improvements on U.S. can making equipment to Western customers in the 1970s and 1980s. The three firms that had benefited the most from the postwar transfer of U.S. technology were Toyo Seikan Kaisha, Daiwa Can, and Hokkai Can, which emerged as the leaders of the Japanese can industry. By the mid-1980s, Toyo Seikan commanded 55 percent of the domestic can market, Daiwa held 28 percent, and Hokkai claimed 11 percent.

In 1971 the first impact-extruding, two-piece aluminum can lines were introduced in Japan. Later, Daiwa, Japan's leading welded tin plate can maker, began producing the first drawn, wall-ironed steel and aluminum cans. By the mid-1980s, the number of drawing/wall ironing can lines in Japan had grown to 40 with a total capacity of 9.5 billion cans per year that was underutilized. By 1973, the three-piece steel can had been introduced for beer but became the standard in the soda vending machine market, which accounts for 60 percent of Japan's total beverage can sales. As in the United States, however, the two-piece can eventually replaced the three-piece can in Japan's beer and soda markets, reaching 5 billion cans per year in 1983. Aluminum cans began to replace steel cans in the 1970s when the country's aluminum companies opened their own aluminum can making plants to shift the industry away from steel. The two metals battled for market share until the early 1980s when Japanese demand for canned beverages stabilized.

Japan's depressed economy in the 1990s and early 2000s affected the sales of firms in the larger Japanese packaging industry, and the biggest Japanese packaging firms were hard pressed to increase sales 5 percent per year in the mid-1990s. Roughly 40 billion metal cans were consumed in Japan in 1996. The majority (54 percent) of steel cans were used for noncarbonated drinks, including canned coffee and oolong tea. The Japanese can industry produced 34 billion cans in 1993, of which 7.8 billion were noncarbonated beverage cans, the largest single segment of food and beverage cans, accounting for 52 percent of the market. The 2.9 billion carbonated beverage cans claimed 18 percent of the market, 2.7 billion food cans held 18 percent of the market, and 1.6 billion beer cans captured the remaining 11 percent. The market for food cans was declining in the 1990s, especially in the marine products segment that included tuna and sardine cans. Cans for some food products, such as spaghetti meat sauce and soup, were the lone growth sectors.

The Japanese can industry remained one of the world's most innovative, high-quality, and diversified sectors, reflecting the readiness with which Japan's comparatively affluent consumers embraced new product packages and often expensive designs. In the beer segment, there were more than 147 different formats, ranging in size from 135 centiliters to 3 liters. Japanese can manufacturers continued their relationship with the United States, importing more aluminum cans from that country in 1995 than they produced domestically.

About 16 billion aluminum cans, one-third of which were produced by Mitsubishi Materials, were consumed in Japan in 1997. Because Japan's metal can industry had the best reputation for quality in the world, metal cans had high prices, which resulted in inexpensive imported cans claiming an increase to 10 percent of total can consumption in 1995. However, inferior quality of the imported cans led to a consumer backlash in the late 1990s.

At the beginning of 1997, Japan's beverage can making industry included 49 aluminum beverage can lines (or plants) and 28 steel can lines. Japanese can industry firms were at the forefront of international can producers that capitalized on mainland China's relaxed trade policies in the late 1990s. In 1997 other representative Japanese can makers included Showa Aluminum Can Corporation and Takeuchi Press Industries Co. Ltd.

The European Union. In the late 1980s, the five largest European can makers dominated the production of beverage cans. In the 1990s the trend was toward even greater concentration as cooperation agreements, mergers and acquisitions, and joint ventures became common in the largest segment of the European metal can market. Sales growth in the large European packaging industry, which included nonmetal flexible packaging, recovered from a slump in the early 1990s to a brisk 20 percent pace in 1994 and 1995. Total 1995 sales for the average European packaging company, including metal cans, were 35 percent higher than 1991 at US$9.5 billion. Conditions in Europe's small can making segment, with 20 to 200 employees, were more chaotic in the 1990s, however. For these firms, profitability depended on the ability to maintain manufacturing flexibility to meet the unique design requirements of their generally low-volume customer.

In the late 1990s, U.S. firms such as U.S. Can; Crown, Cork & Seal (CC&S); and Continental Can had a much more aggressive role in Europe's metal can market. In 1996, for example, CC&S bought Carnaud-Metalbox, U.S. Can took over CC&S's aerosol can operations, and Continental Can Europe began eyeing the potentially profitable Russian beverage can market. However, in 1997 Sweden's PLM, the fourth largest beverage packager in Europe, beat everyone to the punch by building the first beverage can plant in Russia.

In 2002, however, CC&S scaled back its European and African interests and closed three European plants in Belgium, Denmark, and Hungary as well as four U.S. plants to streamline its operations. At the same time, the company implemented a salaried workforce reduction in its remaining plants, which cut approximately 100 jobs. In early 2002, CC&S sold its 15 percent share in South Africa's Crown Nampak to Nampak Ltd. for US$275 million.

By the mid-2000s, Europe reported a steady decrease in consumption of non-paper packaging materials, and in 2003 the segment accounted for only 23.3 percent of the market value share. Can shipments in Europe declined from 40 billion in 2002 to 38 billion in 2003.

The United Kingdom. In 1992 the United Kingdom consumed 63 percent (7.2 billion tons) of Europe's beverage can aluminum, ahead of Italy (15 percent) and Sweden (8 percent). Between 1981 and 1990, the number of firms in the U.K. canning industry had declined from 52 to 30, reflecting the effects of increased competition that favored efficiency and rationalization of resources industry-wide. By 1997, Britain's total packaging industry, including cans, had sales of more than 10 billion British pounds, led by industry leaders like Linpac UK and Specialty Packaging (UK) Plc. In 2003, sales of empty cans increased 2 percent over 2002 reaching 7.7 billion cans.

The emergence of less expensive plastic packaging represented an increased threat to British metal can makers, with the greatest growth occurring in the use of plastics like PET in beverage, household, and automotive goods. As a result of the ongoing emphasis on recycling and environmental programs like "Save-a-Can," more than 1 billion cans were recycled annually in the United Kingdom in the mid-1990s, and roughly 70 percent of all metal cans produced by U.K. can makers were eventually recycled.

Germany. Dominated by century-old packaging producer Schmalbach-Lubeca, Germany's metal can industry lost market share to PET bottles throughout the 1990s, and the share of cola can packaging alone was expected to drop from 25 to 15 percent between 1995 and 2006. German conglomerate VIAG, however, enjoyed substantial sales growth, and in 1996 it increased it ownership stake in Schmalbach-Lubeca, the second largest beverage can producer in Europe, to 61.4 percent. In 1997 Schmalbach-Lubeca and France's Pechiney merged their food can operations to compete with the effects of the Crown/CarnaudMetalbox merger. New legislation on non-returnable packaging had an exceptionally negative effect on can volumes in the mid-2000s, with the total

number of cans shipped in Europe overall in 2003 reported at 38 billion, compared to 40 billion in 2002.

France. France's metal can industry, like much of Europe's, was concentrated among a few large firms, the largest of which were Pechiney, CarnaudMetalbox, and Saint-Gobain. European packaging firms as a whole enjoyed higher sales and greater international sales than non-European packaging companies. Because France's largest can makers were major international producers, the French market represented a comparatively small part of their total revenues—25 percent of total sales for Saint-Gobain and CarnaudMetalbox and 10 percent for Pechiney. At the same time, the central role of France's food manufacturing sector in the country's economy has meant that the major French can makers faced little real competition from foreign manufacturers for the food canning market. In the mid-1990s, representative firms in the French can making industry included Application des Gaz, Safet Embamet, and Ferembal, while foreign can makers with operations in the French market included Van Leer (the Netherlands), along with CC&S and Continental Can (the United States). In 1996 U.S. market giant CC&S and France's perennial packaging leader CarnaudMetalbox joined forces to become the world's largest maker of packaging products for consumer goods.

The French packaging industry felt the effects of a national push for environmental waste regulation throughout the 1990s. Legislation enacted in the mid-1990s required that within 10 years 75 percent of all household packaging used in France be recycled. Although the regulations placed the obligation to recycle on firms selling packaged goods rather than on packaging and canning firms, the latter were expected to emphasize packaging methods that conformed to the new spirit of environmental friendliness.

In the early 1990s, the 3,000 establishments that made up France's packaging industry, including metal can manufacturers, generated revenues of about US$20 billion and employed 120,000 workers. The recession of the early 1990s led to declines in some metal can segments, such as cooked food cans, which declined 6 percent in 1992 and 5 percent in 1993. However, improved conditions in France's food manufacturing sector, which accounted for 78 percent of all metal packaging, resulted in increases in food can production during the mid-1990s. Beverage cans continued to do well, but threats from rival packaging materials and battles to defend market share were expected to result in ongoing overcapacity in the French metal can and overall packaging industries. The lingering effects of the recession were expected to lead to least-cost decision making by industry leaders as consumers were expected to also prefer low-priced canned goods.

Latin America. In the late 1990s and early 2000s, Latin America emerged as a promising market for world can makers because of rising consumer incomes and high soft drink consumption. In 2000, South Americans consumed approximately 14 billion canned beverages. Chile's first beverage can plant opened in 1995, and in 1997 CC&S and American National Can announced plans to build plants in Colombia and Brazil. In 1997, Brazil's aluminum can market was growing more rapidly than that of any other nation. In 1996, Grupo FEMSA, the largest producer of two-piece aluminum cans in Mexico, opened a world-class can making "megaplant" in Toluca, Mexico, with an annual capacity of 1.8 billion units.

The United States. The top 33 firms in the U.S. metal can industry generated total sales of US$36.1 billion and employed about 80,000 workers in the mid-2000s. The leading 35 firms in the small U.S. metal barrel and drum segment of the industry produced roughly US$1 billion in total sales and employed 6,800 workers. A typical U.S. metal can manufacturer in 1994 employed 86 production workers, which was more than twice the U.S. manufacturing average, and 15 nonproduction employees. Shipments had an average value of US$38 million, which was almost four times the U.S. average across all industries. Over one-half of the raw materials traditionally used by industry firms for manufacturing cans came from blast furnaces, steel mills, and aluminum rolling or drawing plants. The sectors of the U.S. economy purchasing the highest proportion of cans in the 1980s were malt beverage producers (24 percent), canned soft drink producers (21 percent), canned fruit and vegetable producers (12 percent), and other metal can makers (7 percent). The remaining one-third of the U.S. metal can industry's production was divided among producers of paint, coffee, pet food, frozen fruit juices, drugs, and a variety of other goods.

The largest U.S. producers of metal cans in the mid-2000s were Crown Cork and Seal, American National Can Co. (a subsidiary of Pechiney Packaging of France), Ball Corporation, Reynolds Metals Co. Can Division, and U.S. Can Corporation. The leading U.S. metal barrel and drum producers in 2004 were Imacc Corporation, Hoover Group, and Myers Container Corporation.

Aluminum remained the chosen metal for the majority of the cans produced by U.S. industry firms in the mid-2000s because of its flexibility, light weight, and corrosion-resistant properties. Aluminum cans thoroughly dominated the beer and carbonated beverage segments with 99 percent and 96 percent of the market, respectively. Steel cans, which accounted for 62 percent of the European and U.S. food and beverage packaging market in 1987, made up 45 percent of the market in 2000. Although shipments of aluminum beverage cans were projected to increase more than 5 percent between 1993 and 1994, reaching 100 billion cans, they remained stagnant through 1997. Between 1994 and 2000, the European and U.S. can market, including food and beverage, and non-food products like paint cans, grew 6 percent annually, while the total food and beverage packaging industry grew only about 1 percent per year. In 2000, the containers and packaging industry used more than 20 percent of the 22 billion pounds of aluminum produced worldwide, ranking second to the transportation industry. The periodic discounting of soft drink products to boost sales combined with slowed growth in plant capacity as a result of the expense of converting from steel can manufacture to aluminum and uncertainty over metal prices and the strength of future soft drink demand somewhat depressed the industry's outlook in the mid-2000s. The U.S. metal can industry generated US$13 billion in shipments in 2003.

Alcoa Inc. estimated that an increase of approximately 9 percent in demand for aluminum in 2008 would require about the opening of 80 additional smelters with 400,000 metric ton capacity each. The company expected demand to double by 2020.

BIBLIOGRAPHY
The Aluminum Association Inc. "Aluminum Beverage Can Recycling Rate Rising," 20 May 2005. Available from www.aluminum.org.

"Aluminum 'Bottle Can' Caters to Active Beer Drinkers." *Brand Packaging,* January 2004.

"Asia-Pacific-Containers & Packaging." *Datamonitor Industry Market Research,* 1 November 2004.

Can Manufacturers Institute, 2005. Available from www.cancentral.com.

"Canada to Ban Bisphenol A in Baby Bottles, U.S. Urged to Follow." *Silgan,* 23 October 2008. Available from www.silgan.com.

The Canmaker. West Sussex: Sayers Publishing, 2005. Available from www.canmaker.com.

"Can Makers UK Market Report 2004," 2005. Available from www.canmakers.co.uk.

"China-Containers & Packaging." *Datamonitor Industry Market Research,* 1 November 2004.

"Container Demand Spans All Categories." *Beverage Industry,* April 2005.

"Easy-Open Ends Preferred Over Sanitary Ends." *Packaging Digest,* 22 October 2008. Available from www.packagingdigest.com.

Furukawa, Tsukasa. "Aluminum Can Demand Expected to Climb Slightly in Japan in 2001." *Industry,* 28 February 2001.

"Global-Containers & Packaging." *Datamonitor Industry Market Research,* 1 November 2004.

"Global-Metal & Glass Containers." *Datamonitor Industry Market Research,* 1 November 2004.

"Hoover's Company Capsules." *Hoover's Online,* 2008. Available from www.hoovers.com.

"International Trade Statistics." World Trade Organization, 2005. Available from www.wto.org.

"Japan-Containers & Packaging." *Datamonitor Industry Market Research,* 1 November 2004.

Kaplan, Andrew. "Can Happen." *Beverage World,* 15 February 2004.

Kgwagaripane, Kgomotso. "Can Manufacturers Botswana Officially Opened." *Sunday Standard,* 27 August 2008. Available form www.sundaystandard.info.

Makely, William. "It's No Longer Your Mom's Food Can." *Brand Packaging,* February–March 2004.

"Metal Can, Box and Other Metal Container (Light Gauge) Manufacturing." *Valuation Resources,* 2004. Available from www.ibisworld.com.

Murdoch, Julian. "Tin: How to Play the Bounce." *Seeking Alpha,* 28 August 2008. Available from www.seekingalpha.com.

Park, Jill. "Crown to Increase Tinplate Food Can Prices." *Packaging News,* 23 October 2008. Available from www.packagingnews.co.uk.

"Rexam's 360 Degree Embossing Creates a Unique Can for FIZZ Cooler," 12 August 2008. Available from www.rexam.com.

"Siligan Containers Launches Shaped Can Making Capability Under Sculptured Metal Brand Name." Siligan Containers, 23 October 2008. Available from www.siligancontainers.com.

"U.S. Can: Company Profile." U.S. Can, 2005. Available from www.uscanco.com.

"US Can Recycling Figures Released." *Aluminum International Today,* May–June 2003.

SIC 3441

METAL, FABRICATED STRUCTURAL

NAICS CODE(S)

332312. The structural metal industry manufactures iron and steel structures off-site, for use in buildings, bridges, transmission towers, and ships, among other applications. Although some industry firms are diversified, the bulk of the industry's output is produced from purchased metals.

INDUSTRY SNAPSHOT

For statistical purposes, fabricated structural metal products are divided into five major categories: structural metal for buildings; structural metal for bridges; fabricated structural metal for ships, boats, and barges; other fabricated structural metal, and unspecified fabricated structural metal. Accounting for 55 to 65 percent of industry shipments, fabricated structural metal for buildings is by far the most important product, and the one most susceptible to downturns in the construction industry. During the building boom of the 1990s and early 2000s, the fabricated structural shipments were valued at over US$18 billion annually, and at the end of the 2000s, the value of shipments reached about US$30 billion.

Fabricated structural metal faces increasing competition from other primary construction materials, such as concrete and composites. Moreover, because the industry does little research and development of its own, it is dependent on R&D in other industries for technological advances. Unfortunately, many related technological advances had an adverse effect on the industry, further decreasing the need for fabricated structural metal. Facing similar problems, the steel industry embarked on a number of ambitious research projects aimed at developing higher-quality steels that could compete more effectively. It was expected that successful development and marketing of these products would benefit the fabricated structural metal industry.

Some of the industry's products are carports, bridge sections, greenhouses, silos, utility buildings, and radio towers. In 2003, the U.S. segment of the industry as a whole, including a small segment devoted to metal plate work, generated in excess of US$29.85 billion in revenue and employed nearly 162,000 people. According to *Valuation Resources,* less than five percent of the industry is due to exports or imports. Volume growth was about 2 percent per year through 2010, with annual price increases of 2 to 3 percent.

ORGANIZATION AND STRUCTURE

At first glance, the fabricated structural metal industry in the 1990s resembled an offshoot of the steel industry. Many integrated and nonintegrated steel companies, such as fast-growing Nucor Corporation, had sizable fabricated structural metal operations. Construction companies, bridge manufacturers, and heavy industry companies, were also sometimes shareholders or owners of metal fabricating companies. Nevertheless, fabricated structural metal was a distinct industry. Fabricated structural metal companies did not manufacture metal; they constructed structural metal forms from a diverse array of finished metal products such as sheets, bars, and tubes. These products included barge sections, boat sections, expansion joints, floor jacks, floor posts, dam gates, highway bridge sections, radio and television tower sections, and fabricated structural steel. In turn, fabricated structural metal products were assembled to form building frameworks, ships, bridges, transmission towers, and oilrigs.

Like the steel industry, the fabricated structural metal industry represented one of the cornerstones of the industrial era. Massive pieces of iron and steel were hammered, welded, and cut into structural shapes for use in the construction of buildings, bridges, and ships. Workers, clad in safety gear and helmets, forced the metal into the desired forms amid a shower of sparks and metal particles. Huge cranes and forklifts loaded the finished products onto trucks and railcars for delivery. Accidents were frequent and employee turnover was high. Largely bypassed by the technological revolution of the past few decades, the fabricated structural metal

Employment Figures, 2009

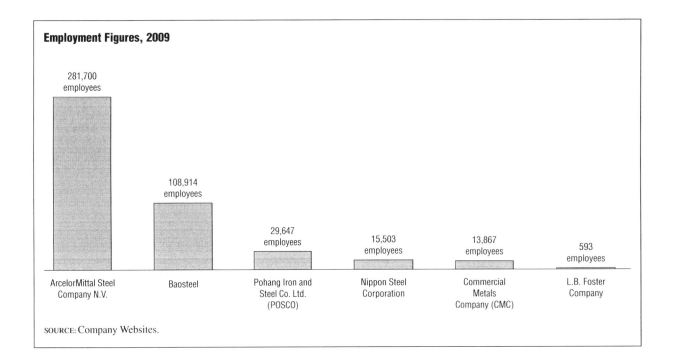

281,700 employees — ArcelorMittal Steel Company N.V.

108,914 employees — Baosteel

29,647 employees — Pohang Iron and Steel Co. Ltd. (POSCO)

15,503 employees — Nippon Steel Corporation

13,867 employees — Commercial Metals Company (CMC)

593 employees — L.B. Foster Company

SOURCE: Company Websites.

industry, like many other traditional industries, was eclipsed by the newer, cleaner, technology-intensive industries of the late twentieth century. Most major steel makers also own some fabricated product facilities, while smaller manufacturers in this section buy from the producer and transform the product through a discrete operation.

The fabricated structural metal industry depends heavily on the construction industry. Commercial and industrial buildings absorbed up to 65 percent of shipments, making the industry highly susceptible to recessions and accompanying declines in new construction. Other important construction markets for fabricated structural metals were public buildings, churches, hospitals, oil drilling rigs, and high-rise apartment buildings. In the United States, federal funding of highway projects was expected to support demand for structural steel, used in bridge and tunnel reconstruction and roadwork, through the mid- to late 2000s. With most major infrastructure already in place in developed nations, there was little room for growth in fabricated metal output. Output remained relatively flat through the 1980s and early 1990s, despite the mid-1980s boom in construction of office buildings and apartment buildings. Capacity utilization rates wavered between 80 and 85 percent, despite efforts at downsizing and capacity reduction.

With most of their output going to the construction industry, fabricated structural metal manufacturers, in effect, served as contractors on construction projects. As a result, the industry was highly dispersed and

international trade, in fabricated structural metal products, was relatively low in comparison with other industries. U.S. exports in 2000 reached about US$750 million, with imports valued at only US$475 million. The size and weight of some structural metal make it an unwieldy and unprofitable export over long distances, particularly when it competes with lower-cost local production.

A major factor in productivity growth has been the use of computer technology in the production process. Computer-assisted design and manufacturing eliminates manual drafting in the design process, thereby reducing labor costs and resulting in higher product quality and less product rework. In addition, computer numerical control (CNC) machine tools reduce labor requirements at the same time as they increase the need for skilled labor, while new microprocessor controls, like automatic welding, have enhanced productivity. The use of electronic data interchange (EDI) between producers and customers has increased industry demand for workers with great levels of computer and numerical literacy.

Small establishments (fewer than 20 workers) accounted for more than 90 percent of the fabricated structural metal industry's total plants—although in most countries, they produced only 10 to 20 percent of total shipments. In the United States, the top 75 companies (out of 677) recorded more than two-thirds of all sales and employed more than half the workforce. In countries such as Japan and South Korea, where giant industrial groups, such as Nippon Steel, Mitsui, Mitsubishi Corp., Sumitomo, and Pohang Iron and Steel Co. Ltd.

(POSCO) dominated all areas of private industry, the discrepancy was even greater. Massive industrial conglomerates were also the norm in Europe. In Canada, establishments with fewer than 20 employees represented about two-thirds of all establishments, yet produced only about 15 percent of shipments. Establishments with more than 200 employees made up only 2 percent of the total but accounted for 20 percent of shipments.

BACKGROUND AND DEVELOPMENT

Fabricated structural metal is a key element of modern industrial civilization. Hidden in the shadow of the mammoth world steel industry, the fabricated structural metal industry plays a central role in modern architecture and shipbuilding. The skyscrapers that house twentieth-century businesses and workers were erected around a framework of fabricated structural metal. The huge suspension bridges that soar across rivers and inland seas are assembled from fabricated structural metal components. The ships, oil tankers, and aircraft carriers that ply the oceans all depend on fabricated structural metal to keep them afloat. If concrete, glass, and sheet metal form the skin of modern structures, then fabricated structural metal is the skeleton.

The importance of metal is no accident. The development of the ability to work with metal parallels the development of human society—so much so, that the names of metals are commonly used by historians to label different eras of human civilization. The earliest metal to gain widespread use was copper. Soft and malleable, copper was hammered into simple tools, cooking utensils, jewelry, and other items. Later, when it was discovered that metals could be altered by fire, people began to experiment with different combinations of metals, creating entirely new substances with radically different qualities. Combining tin and copper, for example, produced bronze, a metal much stronger and more durable than that of either of the original metals. Bronze was used for weapons, body armor, tools, utensils, sculptures, and other items. It was also the first metal to be used for structural purposes. Between 292 and 280 B.C., the citizens of the Greek island of Rhodes erected a bronze statue of the sun god Helios beside the city harbor. Too large to be cast in a mold, the statue was built of bronze plates hammered into shape by an army of artisans and assembled on a frame of stone and iron. One of the seven wonders of the ancient world, the statue stood at least 36 meters (120 feet) tall. A raised base of white marble about seven meters (21 feet) high pushed the huge statue even further into the sky. Known as the Colossus of Rhodes, the statue collapsed during an earthquake 60 years later.

By the time the Colossus of Rhodes was built, people had already learned to smelt and forge iron. This powerful new metal quickly began replacing bronze as the preferred metal for weapons and tools. By about 100 B.C., iron was also beginning to see use as a semi-structural material. During the Roman period, advances in smelting technology led to the first appearance of steel, which was stronger, lighter, and more flexible than iron. However, because steel was expensive and difficult to produce, it was used almost solely for swords and similar weapons until the nineteenth century.

Although iron was sometimes used as a building material during ancient Roman times, the most significant developments in the use of metal, for structural purposes, did not take place until the Industrial Revolution. During this period, structural use of iron and steel began in earnest. Railroads were built throughout Europe and North America. Ships began to be assembled from fabricated structural iron and steel. New bridges and highways linked the busy industrial cities. In addition, new buildings were being erected everywhere. The demand for fabricated structural metal seemed inexhaustible, and the industry grew rapidly. One of the best-known examples of the use of fabricated structural metal in the nineteenth century is the Eiffel Tower. With no surface covering of concrete, glass, or steel sheet to conceal its framework, the rivets, bolts, and beams that make up this massive structure are clearly visible.

From the late nineteenth century until the years following World War II, the U.S. fabricated structural metal industry was the largest in the world, supplying the insatiable needs of a huge, rapidly growing country. Thousands of buildings, bridges, and ships had to be built. Much of the infrastructure, commonplace in the mid-1990s in the United States, was erected at this time, spurring exponential growth in the iron, steel, and metal fabricating industries. Similar rapid growth was seen in the Soviet Union under Joseph Stalin, as the country focused all its energy on becoming a leading industrial power.

After World War II, both Europe and Japan rebuilt their industries from the ground up, installing newer, more efficient technologies, and often operating their industries with the help of government subsidies and closed markets. Later, other newly industrialized countries such as China, Brazil, and South Korea, built their own industries, and combining efficiency with low wages, not only pushed U.S. fabricated metal out of their national markets, but were even able to compete in the United States itself. Generally, foreign producers entered into joint ventures with local partners or established their own plants to service the local market.

During the 1970s and 1980s, the fabricated structural metal industry struggled to cope with recessions, declining demand, and increased competition. Unlike the steel industry, which faced similar problems, the fabricated structural metal industry showed no signs of reinvigorating itself with new technologies and value-added production. In the United States, annual growth rates during this period averaged less than twp percent a year, and employment fell steadily, declining from 103,500 in 1982 to 67,000 in 1994. The story was much the same in Canada and Europe. Only in the fast-growing, newly industrializing countries of East Asia and South America did the industry experience considerable growth. By the mid-1980s, the U.S. industry was aggressively touting its products in these emerging markets and, by the 1990s, it had begun to achieve significant export gains.

In the mid-1990s, Japanese producers benefited from vast infusions of public funds aimed at jump-starting the faltering economy and replacing Japan's badly outdated public infrastructure. In the 1990s, dozens of massive public construction projects were underway or being planned. For example, a new international airport—the New Kansai International Airport—was built in Osaka Bay. This huge undertaking involved the construction of an artificial island several kilometers out to sea; a multi-part railway, car, and service bridge to connect it to the mainland; and, of course, the airport itself. Another big project completed during this period was a bridge between the main island of Honshu and the island of Shikoku. Other major activities included construction of the world's largest suspension bridge near Kobe, and a tunnel linking Honshu with the northern island of Hokkaido. Although U.S. and other foreign companies competed fiercely for a share of the Japanese largesse, most of the contracts went to Japanese companies. However, as Japan's economy lost footing in the mid-1990s and was battered by the region's 1997 financial crisis, such public spending slowed considerably.

China, Taiwan, and other parts of Asia showed steady growth due to their fast-growing economies; cities such as Taipei experienced an explosion of construction activity, which in turn helped fuel growth in the local fabricated structural metal industry. China produced nearly 49.2 million tons of semi finished and finished steel products in 2006—30.6 million tons more than it imported—according to the Iron and Steel Statistics Bureau (ISSB). Meanwhile, in the countries hardest hit by the late 1990s financial crisis, including Indonesia, Thailand, and South Korea, growth was expected to subside temporarily as those economies recovered from debt and a shortage of capital.

The recession of the early 1990s hit the fabricated structural metal industry particularly hard in North America. The recession-induced decline in construction of office buildings, commercial structures, manufacturing facilities, and apartment buildings, largely contributed to the slowdown in U.S. fabricated structural metal output. Industry

employment dropped by some 6.9 percent, from a high of 1.45 million in 1989 to approximately 1.44 million in 1991. By September 2010, the industry employed just over 1.3 million workers. Production capacity was also decreasing as U.S. fabricated metal manufacturers engaged in extensive restructuring and downsizing, or shut down plants altogether. However, by the late 1990s, new life was breathed into the fabricated structural metal industry by construction firms who responded to general economic health, in the United States and Western Europe, and increased demand for all types of construction in developing regions since the early 1990s. This surge in building has revitalized the demand for structural metals, which was expected to continue until the notoriously cyclical construction industry began to decline. In addition, residential construction surged in 1998, with housing starts exceeding 1.5 million.

Many of the problems facing the fabricated structural metal industry in the 1990s were not easily remedied. Downsizing and restructuring companies in this sector utilized all diversification, and other strategies, but nothing could be done about the most fundamental problem—the mature, postindustrial societies of Europe, North America, and Japan no longer needed the quantities of fabricated structural metal they once had. As a result, the focus of the industry seemed destined to shift to the developing world, whose growing economies still required vast amounts of steel, structural metal, and other primary products. However, the U.S. fastener sector thrived in the late 1990s, competing globally, improving production efficiency and quality with cutting-edge technology.

Worldwide imports of prefabricated metal materials increased 62 percent between 1997 and 1998. Canada was the largest importer ($181 million with a growth of 57 percent), followed by Mexico ($24 million with a growth of 28 percent), and Japan ($10 million with a growth of over 1,000 percent). During this period, U.S. steel shipments (primarily to Canada, Mexico, and Venezuela, in descending order of volume) fell 17 percent after an increase of 23 percent, from 1996 to 1997. Plant closings and diminishing production line capacity caused the decline in exports from the United States, which addressed global competition by developing new residential housing products to replace traditional lumber products. Other technological developments of the late 1990s included corrosion-resistant products for autos and appliances.

As it emerged from the recession of the early 1990s, the fabricated structural metal industry began to show signs of fatigue. Dependent on the construction industry for some 95 percent of its output, the industry suffered from both cyclical construction activity and decreasing market share. Advances in technology and the development of new building materials steadily eroded the demand for structural metal products, stifling both output and prices. Despite these factors, however, the continued growth in the construction industry during the mid- to late 1990s helped the fabricated structural metal industry maintain its footing. In 1997, the value of U.S. shipments of fabricated structural metal products was US$16.11 billion. By 2000, that figure had risen to US$18.85 billion. The cost of materials increased from US$9.96 billion to US$10.13 billion over the same period, and employment grew from 92,471 to 98,960 workers by 2000.

In both Canada and the United States, capital investments in new and used equipment were well below manufacturing industry averages. Moreover, with prices edging downward in both countries, there was little incentive for manufacturers to upgrade existing facilities. Price erosion and sliding demand were even more pronounced in this market, due to increasing competition from concrete for use in bridge construction. On the positive side, industry analysts expected that more than half the new bridges and bridge repairs, contracted for by the U.S. government, would primarily utilize steel materials, and infrastructure upgrade projects in the United States were expected to rise in the late 1990s and early 2000s. The U.S. Department of Commerce reported that over one third of American bridges were in need of repair or replacement.

Environmental and production cost concerns were one possible source of decreasing revenue. The increased use of construction materials that incorporated recyclable waste materials, like engineered wood, flat glass, and concrete, highlighted the lack of significant research and development breakthroughs in this metals industry and was a trend that was likely to negatively affect the industry's prevalence. Also affecting profits was the economic turmoil in Asia. As Asian currencies become more devalued, industry analysts in more developed regions feared a massive influx of cheaper Asian metals into their markets, which forced firms in developed regions to lower their prices to maintain competitiveness but delimited profits for the industry as a whole.

In light of these factors, the industry followed the broad trend of globalization which was at a low level in 2003. Many major industry players, seeking to maintain profitability in mature markets like Europe and North America, bought up their smaller competitors and consolidated their regional markets. Concurrently, many firms moved production to areas, especially Asia, where labor and materials were less expensive, environmental and regulatory standards were far less stringent, and demand for fabricated structural metals promised the greatest future growth. That, along with the falling value of the U.S. dollar abroad helped to create a negative turn throughout most of the 2000s.

To protect the U.S. steel industry, the United States imposed steel tariffs of up to 30 percent on foreign imports in 2002, heavily penalizing China, Japan, Germany, Taiwan, and South Korea, while exempting most poor nations, as well as Mexico and Canada. European Commission officials estimated that the tariffs affected some four million tons of European steel exported to the United States, diverting an additional 16 million tons of excess steel to Europe from other countries that could no longer trade with the United States. As a result, there was a sharp increase in domestic steel prices during the early 2000s.

There was another major cost to an already suffering U.S. manufacturing sector heading into the mid-2000s. Because the tariffs did not cover finished products but only the steel itself, manufacturers found themselves hit with a double whammy: higher priced steel being the only available option, coupled with cheaper finished products available overseas. Amid these conditions, many companies went out of business entirely. Although the tariffs were lifted by 2004, the expected lowering of prices did not immediately follow.

Leading North American producers sought to diversify their holdings by investing in other industries. Many North American and European companies also looked to Eastern Europe and Asia for new growth opportunities, while Japanese companies increasingly focused their attention on Southeast Asia. Joint ventures, partnerships, and acquisitions of overseas companies were frequently pursued. More concerned with protecting their industry than dominating it, many companies worked together to establish new markets and build new plants.

One way in which the industry was adapting in the mid-2000s was in the increase of firms with design-build capabilities. Dubbed "engineer-to-order" fabricated structural metal manufacturers, such companies were able to remain not only competitive but viable by providing custom manufacturing. The ETO Institute was a new association serving such companies across industry lines.

CURRENT CONDITIONS

By 2007, the steel industry had bounced back from the slump it experienced earlier in the decade, thanks to an improving worldwide economy. A surge in mergers and acquisitions also helped the industry. World crude steel output hit a record of 1.24 billion metric tons in 2006, 8.8 percent more than in 2005, according to the International Iron and Steel Institute (IISI). Asia accounted for 54 percent of this total, with China the leading country in the region. The top countries importing steel to the United States in 2006 were Canada (5.7 million tons), the European Union (5.3 million tons), and China (4.9 million tons). Imports from China to the United States increased a whopping 115 percent between 2005 and

2006, whereas countries holding spots four through six saw significant increases as well: Republic of Korea (59 percent), Turkey (109 percent), and Taiwan (210 percent). Imports from Russia also increased (133 percent). In fact, of the top 10 countries that supplied the United States with steel, only Mexico saw a decrease. However, Mexico's own consumption of steel was increasing at a rate of about six percent annually.

By 2009, virtually all markets associated with fabricated structural metals were impacted by the global recession. The one notable exception was China. It did slow initially, but then accelerated its growth during 2009 due to a very successful stimulus offering and an easing of their strict monetary policy. By the second half of 2009, Asia in general (apart from Japan) saw the market begin to recover. Australia, which was one of the last countries to enter the recession, was also one of the first countries out of the recession. In Europe, the steel markets were greatly impacted by the recession. They faced a fall off in terms of demand, coupled with high levels of inventory.

In 2009, revenue for the fabricated structural metals industry in the United States reached US$28.9 billion, of which gross profit was 26.79 percent. Imports were valued at US$2.6 billion from 76 countries. The industry also exported US$1.1 billion worth of products to 164 countries. In adding import value and subtracting export value from the total industry shipment value, the total domestic demand for fabricated structural metals in 2009 was worth US$30.4 billion. U.S. exports went mainly to Canada, Mexico, Algeria, Jamaica, and the United Kingdom.

RESEARCH AND TECHNOLOGY

As an industry primarily devoted to fabricating products, as opposed to creating them, the fabricated structural metal industry traditionally had not invested significantly in research and development. Technological advances in this sector were generally spin-offs from advances in related industries (particularly the steel industry), as well as the heavy machinery and equipment industries. Welding techniques, for example, changed regularly as a result of technological developments. Some of the more sophisticated welding techniques in use included: arc welding, achieved by high temperatures generated by an electric arc; and resistance welding, wherein the flow of electricity between two metals creates resistance and fuses them together. By the 1990s, more advanced welding equipment began to be used. Employing lasers, sound waves, or electron beams to cut or fuse metal, these new systems helped increase the precision and speed of fabrication processes.

Early skyscrapers, such as the Empire State Building in New York, contained twice as much steel per square foot as modern skyscrapers. Chicago's Sears Tower, if constructed today, would require 35 percent less steel

than it now contains, according to scientists. Because the use of lighter materials such as concrete and composite materials helped reduce construction costs, not to mention the greater strength of modern steel, fabricated structural metal was used less and less frequently over time. To combat this steady erosion of one of its most vital markets, the steel industry began to invest considerable funds in developing new technologies and processes that would increase the usefulness of its products. The steel industry had already begun revamping itself in the 1980s with "minimills" utilizing scrap metal and new high-value-added steels. In the 1990s, an industry trade group, the American Institute of Steel Construction (AISC), began funding research expected to help steel increase its share of the apartment building market. One of the main focuses of this research was shallow, vibration-resistant, preassembled, metal-deck framing systems that required no interior beams for spans up to 30 feet.

According to AISC president Roger Ferch, the structural steel industry has been working to maintain its position in the construction market and move it towards sustainability for decades by cutting its carbon footprint by nearly 47 percent since 1990. It has reduced its energy consumption by 67 percent since 1980. It has reduced its greenhouse gas emissions by 45 percent since 1975. In addition, according to the Environmental Protection Agency (EPA), the fabricated structural metal industry has become recognized as one of the best performing U.S. manufacturing industries.

Other research concentrated on production of high-tensile steel, able to endure a very high working stress while still being suitable for fabrication by flame-cutting and arc welding. Ideal for use in building construction, the successful development and marketing of these steels was likely to directly benefit the fabricated structural metal industry. Steel and fabricated metal manufacturers also encouraged the use of steel in single-family homes. Steel frames were promoted as more durable, more flexible, and easier to replace or upgrade than conventional wooden frames. In Florida, a developer built log cabins made of hollow tubular steel logs. Sturdy enough to withstand the worst Florida hurricanes, these houses also provided twice the insulation value of conventional building materials. As if to prove the point, some builders even built their own homes entirely from steel. Samuel Tenenbaum, vice-president of Chatham Steel Corporation, erected a home that made use of structural-steel beams and joists; it featured wide-open interior spaces with exposed steel beams, catwalks, railings, and grates. In all, 20 tons of steel were used in the construction of Tenenbaum's unique home.

Bridge manufacturers were also actively working on new systems, targeted at the growing short-span bridge repair and replacement market. Many of these utilized fabricated structural metal components in unique modular and pre-assembled systems, designed to enable rapid replacement of entire bridges or portions of bridges. An "All-Welded Steel Truss Bridge" was developed by the Ohio Bridge Corporation as an economical alternative to concrete beam and slab bridges. Among the advantages of this bridge were fast, easy installation; much higher load limit, lighter dead load; and easy replacement and repair of damaged sections. Other systems included modular steel bridge superstructures and customized bridges in prefab form.

WORKFORCE

Employees of the fabricated structural metal industry work in a factory environment where they cut, shape, and join metal parts for use in commercial and industrial buildings, bridges, ship sections, transmission towers, railroad car racks, and offshore drilling platforms. Much of this work requires heavy manual labor and, despite increased factory automation, the fabricated structural metal industry—like other traditional industries—remains relatively labor-intensive. Output per worker is much lower than the manufacturing average. For example, in 2002, the value of shipments produced by the 105,579 U.S. workers employed in this category was only about US$19.2 billion; considerably less per worker than in most other major industries. Employers in this industry required an estimated 62 percent more production worker hours than did all manufacturing to produce an additional US$1 in value-added sales. Average capital expenditures were less than half the manufacturing average—another indication of this industry's high level of labor intensity.

Workers in this field consist primarily of iron workers, welders, and cutters. Ironworkers assemble the frameworks of bridges, buildings, and other structures. Their work demands a great deal of physical labor as it usually involves lifting and positioning steel beams and other metal items with derricks and cranes. Welders join metals together using various processes such as electric arc welding, gas welding, resistance welding, and laser welding. Cutters use similar techniques to separate or cut preformed metal into new shapes or sizes for later assembly.

Workers in this industry face significantly higher health and safety risks than workers in other industries. Workplace accidents and injuries are nearly double the rate for all manufacturing (24.1 per 100 in 1989 versus 13.1 per 100). Overall, accident rates in the fabricated structural metal industry ranked 12th highest among some 370 individual manufacturing industries—an improvement from 1980 when its injury and illness rate ranked fifth highest in manufacturing. More than half the injuries occurring in the fabricated structural metal

industry were the result of overexertion (usually from lifting heavy objects) or of being struck by a falling or moving object. The leading positions affected were welders and cutters, accounting for more than one-fifth of the industry's total injuries. Hard work, high risks, and relatively low wages made the fabricated structural metal industry unattractive to many workers. Average hourly wages in the United States stood at US$21.22 in 2010.

Employment levels in this industry also declined steadily through the 1980s and 1990s, falling sharply during the 1990s recession; modest productivity growth was due to decreasing worker hours, as output per worker grew 13 percent between 1992 and 1999. By 2006, there were 73,000 structural iron and steel workers in the United States. One cause for the downward employment plunge in the industry was due to more advanced technologies in the automation of parts of the process. However, as the automation caused a drop in the labor end of the job market, according to a report from the Precision Metalforming Association, it was projected that the demand for sales personnel, industrial production managers, and cost estimators would increase.

INDUSTRY LEADERS

With nearly 700 companies in the United States alone devoting all or part of their operations to the production of fabricated structural metal products, industry market share is widely dispersed. Moreover, many integrated steel manufacturers, such as U.S. Steel Corp. (USX), Bethlehem Steel Corp., and Nucor Corporation, all derived substantial revenues from fabricated structural metal products. Inclusion of fabricated structural metal units within broader corporations was even more common overseas, where mammoth industrial conglomerates, such as Mitsubishi Heavy Industries, Nippon Steel, POSCO, and Friedrich Krupp, operated in a diverse array of industries. Industrial groups such as these manufactured everything from steel and fabricated structural metal to heavy machinery and entire steel production plants.

This depth of integration, so common in Asia, is less prevalent in North America and Europe. While leading U.S. steelmakers often have some interests in the fabricated structural metal industry, none—with the exception of Nucor Corporation—play a significant role. Independent fabricators dominated the industry. Because establishments involved in the fabrication of structural metal products were often diversified companies with numerous divisions operating in different industries, their rankings within the industry varied according to the criteria selected.

By the late 2000s, three notable companies were Commercial Metals Company, L.B. Foster Company, and Butler Manufacturing Company. Commercial Metals Company (CMC) reported 2009 revenues of US$6.8 billion, a 35 percent decline over 2008—the worst down cycle it had experienced in over 30 years. The company employed 13,867 people. Begun in 1915, CMC operated in well over 100 locations worldwide, which included 30 steel fabrication plants and 34 secondary metals-processing plants that process scrap metal. CMC's fabrication capacity is approximately one million tons. L.B. Foster Company, which served the railroad, mass transit, and highway industries, reported US$381.9 million in 2009 sales with 593 employees.

The top steel producer in the world in 2009 was ArcelorMittal Steel Company N.V. of the Netherlands. The company was formed in 2004 when Ispat International (70 percent owned by the Mittal family) bought LNM Holdings (wholly owned by the Mittal family) for US$13.3 billion. The combined company produced more than 77 million metric tons of steel in 2009 but consistently produced over 100 million metric tons per year. The company's 2009 revenue stood at US$65.11 billion. Mittal employed 281,700 people in 2009. In 2006, Mittal announced plans to buy rival Arcelor for about US$34 billion to create Arcelor Mittal. Arcelor SA of Luxembourg was a combination of France's Usinor, Luxembourg's Arbed, and Spain's Aceralia. With its acquisition by Mittal, it became become part of a steel company that was two times larger than its closest rival, China's Baosteel Group.

Based in Shanghai, state-owned Baosteel saw its revenue reach US$21.7 billion in 2009 with 108,914 employees. Japan's Nippon Steel Corporation was considered to be the world's most profitable steel company in the world, with 2007 sales of US$36.4 billion. It employed 50,000 people who worked in fields as diverse as steel production, construction, electronics, and communications. In South Korea, Pohang Iron and Steel Co. Ltd. (POSCO), the country's largest steelmaker, accounted for virtually all domestic production of iron and steel products, generating 36.9 trillion Korean Won in 2009 revenues, with 29,647 employees. Pohang Iron and Steel was also the third largest producer of steel worldwide.

BIBLIOGRAPHY

Commercial Metals Company, 2009 Annual Report. Available from http://phx.corporate-ir.net.

"Fabricated Structural Metal Manufacturing Industry in the U.S. and its Foreign Trade (1996-2008)." Supplier Relations US, May 2007. Available from http://www.mindbranch.com.

"Fabricated Structural Metal Manufacturing Industry in the U.S. and its Foreign Trade (2010)." Supplier Relations US, September 2010. Available from http://www.marketresearch.com.

"Hoover's Company Capsules." *Hoover's Online,* 2007. Available from http://www.hoovers.com.

Kinch, Diana. "Latin America Traders Eyeing Buoyant 2007." *American Metal Market,* 8 January 2007.

L.B. Foster 2009 Annual Report. Available from http://phx.corporate-ir.net.

"Mexico's Steel Consumption Seen Soaring." *Purchasing,* 18 January 2007.

Moll, Markus. "The Glimmer of Stainless." *Recycling Today,* April 2007.

Price, Phillip. "China's Steel Exports Rocket in 06." *American Metal Market,* 31 January 2007.

Sandoval, Dan. "Bulking Up: Merger and Acquisition Activity Is Helping to Create a Stronger Global Steel Industry." *Recycling Today,* April 2007.

"Steel Output Increases 9% Percent in 2006 to New High." *Purchasing,* 15 February 2007.

Stundza, Tom. "Heavy Steel Market Is Busy." *Purchasing,* 14 June 2007.

SIC 3330

METALS, PRIMARY NONFERROUS

NAICS CODE(S)

331. The nonferrous metals industry fabricates basic metal products made from crude ores other than iron or steel. This industry is termed "primary" to distinguish it from "secondary" producers that remanufacture metals from scrap. Major industry products, in descending order of annual global production by weight, are aluminum, copper, lead, and zinc.

INDUSTRY SNAPSHOT

Primary nonferrous metals, which constitute the vast majority of nonferrous metal production, experience markedly different demand and profitability depending on the type of metal, world production capacity, and the health of specific end-use markets. Therefore, while an individual metal smelting and refining company may produce several kinds of nonferrous metals, each may be subject to unique market conditions, which makes generalizations about all nonferrous metals difficult. Aluminum and copper were the two major segments of the industry.

In the price-sensitive metals business, supply and demand economics often closely dictate the industry's fortunes. Industry analysts frequently gauge market conditions in terms of global capacity, production, and demand. The ideal condition, from the perspective of a producer, is when capacity barely exceeds production, and production lags somewhat behind demand. Such a combination ensures that unused capacity is not going to waste, and prices will stay strong because buyers have fewer options and producers are not desperate to rid themselves of excess inventory. From the standpoint of a buyer, oversupply and low prices usually are favored. The commodity nature of most segments of metal production requires that producers be watchful of not expanding production too rapidly so that prices are driven downward.

The market for aluminum, which is the industry's largest product segment, has continued to experience robust demand in the 2000s. World production of aluminum stood at more than 22.5 million metric tons (mmt) in 2004. According to the Aluminum Association, the transportation sector is the heaviest consumer of aluminum, at 7.5 billion pounds annually. Although the automobile and aerospace markets continued to be heavy users of aluminum, those markets were leveling out by the mid-2000s. Instead, demand for aluminum was rising in the commercial and industrial transportation sectors. North America was by far the largest aluminum-producing region, followed by Europe and Asia. Worldwide aluminum production was increasing rapidly, but demand was increasing more rapidly, and shortages were projected to continue through at least 2006.

Primary copper, the industry's second largest product by value, has not fared as well as aluminum. Copper prices were particularly volatile between the mid-1990s and the mid-2000s because of excess supply due to overproduction. Even though demand increased and production declined, by 2002 supply still exceeded demand, although the gap was closing. These conditions were expected to lead to unpredictable copper prices, despite healthy demand in U.S. and European construction and electrical equipment markets as well as China's booming economy and subsequent increased copper demand. The Americas, Asia, and Europe were the world's top three major copper producing regions.

In October 2008, CRU Group predicted that the economic downturn would hurt demand for metals and result in sharp price drops. However, prices were expected to recover and CRU projected dramatic demand recovery leading to a tremendous boom. The group also anticipated seeing "some interesting and unexpected consolidation deals" in the late 2000s.

ORGANIZATION AND STRUCTURE

Aluminum. Aluminum, a lightweight, silvery metal, is the most plentiful metallic element in the earth's crust. The metal is desirable because of its numerous unique physical characteristics. Significantly, aluminum weighs less than one-third as much as an equal volume of steel. Besides its high strength-to-weight ratio, aluminum resists corrosion, becoming covered with a tough, protective layer of aluminum oxide when exposed to air. Additional properties, such as high conductivity and ease of recycling, make it useful for a multitude of applications from transportation and long-distance power transmission to construction and food and beverage packaging.

Aluminum, while abundant, is difficult to extract in pure form. It is a naturally occurring silicate (a compound containing silicon, oxygen, and other elements) and is often mixed with other minerals like sodium and potassium. Aluminum is extracted from an ore called bauxite through the Bayer process, which is a more expensive procedure than the method used to extract iron, copper, and other common metals. The most common refining technique is the Hall-Heroult process that entails dissolving alumina (aluminum oxide) in fused cryolite (a naturally occurring fluoride), and decomposing it through electrolysis to a molten metal.

The United States was the largest manufacturer of aluminum in the late 1990s, accounting for approximately 25 percent of global output. Other major aluminumproducing nations in 1999 included the Russian Federation (15 percent of global output), Canada (10 percent), Australia (6.3 percent), and Brazil (6.2 percent). Major consumers of aluminum in 1992, in descending order of consumption by weight, were the United States, Japan, the Commonwealth of Independent States (CIS), Germany, and China.

Copper. Copper, a reddish metal, is the 25th most abundant metallic element. Marketable characteristics include malleability, resistance to corrosion, and beauty. In addition, copper is second to silver in conductivity, making it useful in the production of electrical wire and cables. It is also commonly used to make money, cooking utensils, pipes, and architectural ornaments, among other goods. Finally, copper is often mixed with zinc to make brass, or with tin to create bronze. Unlike aluminum, copper is relatively easy to extract and is often found in pure form. Ore containing copper is crushed, washed, melted in a furnace, concentrated and purified before it is cast into shapes for milling into finished products.

Most copper is mined in developing nations and processed into intermediate and final products in developed countries. However, the United States is both a major producer and consumer of copper, and while it is second in mined copper production by weight to Chile, it is the largest producer of refined copper. In 1999 aggregate refined copper production worldwide reached 14.1 million metric tons. Major copper-producing nations in 1999 included Chile, the United States, Japan, China, and the Russian Federation. Leading consumers of refined copper, in descending order of consumption by weight, were the United States, Japan, Germany, and China, which accounted for roughly 50 percent of the global copper market.

Zinc. Zinc, the twenty-fourth most common element in the earth's crust and the third largest nonferrous metal industry product, is a bluish-white metal. Zinc is typically extracted from ore through a distillation process that uses an electric furnace to boil the zinc. Another technique involves leaching the zinc from the ore with sulfuric acid. Although it is brittle, it becomes malleable at temperatures of 120 to 150 degrees Celsius. When exposed to air, the surface of the metal forms a hard film that resists further oxidation. Zinc is soluble in alcohol, acids, and alkalis. Zinc's properties make it ideal for use as a protective coating for other metals. Its primary end use is to make galvanized steel, and it is also used as an alloying agent, particularly with copper to make brass. Zinc is used in other goods, including pigments, rubber tires, and wood preservatives.

Global zinc production in 1999 was approximately 8.3 million metric tons, up 19.7 percent from a worldwide output of 6.9 million metric tons in 1990. Major nations involved in zinc production included China (20.1 percent of global output by weight), Canada (9.4 percent), Spain (4.5 percent), Australia (3.9 percent), and Mexico, Belgium, Finland, and the Russian Federation (each with between 2 and 3 percent). The United States is certainly the largest consumer of zinc, accounting for about 15 percent of global consumption in 1992. Zinc is also used in Japan, Germany, Italy, and France that represented approximately 40 percent of the world market. In 1998, zinc import demand was greatest in the United States (1.1 billion mmt); Germany (531 mmt); Belgium (337 mmt) and Italy and France (241 mmt each).

Lead. Lead, the fourth most commonly processed nonferrous metal, is the thirty-sixth most often-occurring metallic element and is widely distributed throughout the world. It is malleable, dense, toxic, and a poor conductor of electricity. In addition, it is has relatively low tensile strength. Lead is most commonly used to make batteries, but is also utilized sheath electric cables, to line pipes and tanks, and in X-ray apparatus. It had been used in the manufacture of paints and pigments until it was found to cause severe health problems. Lead is typically extracted from ore through one of two processes similar to those used to make steel or copper. Important by-products of lead-making processes include silver, gold, and zinc.

Global production of lead in 1999 reached 5.69 mmt. Some of the richest lead deposits in the world were in the western United States, although those veins had been significantly depleted by the 1990s. Other high-quality, high-volume lead reserves were found in Australia, Canada, Mexico, Peru, and Serbia. The United States has been the world's largest producer of refined lead, accounting for one-fourth of global output in 1999. Other major producers included China, with 16.6 percent of global production, followed by the United Kingdom, Canada, Mexico, Germany, and Italy, each of which produced 4 to 6 percent of total output. Nations importing the most lead in 1998, in descending order,

were the United Kingdom, United States, Germany, Malaysia, and Korea.

Other Nonferrous Metals. Metals produced in small amounts in the industry include nickel, tin, molybdenum, magnesium, and titanium, as well as minor metals, such as antimony, bismuth, cadmium, indium, mercury, and cobalt. About 850,000 metric tons of nickel were manufactured in the early 1990s. Nickel was used mostly as an alloying agent to make stainless and specialty steels. Major producers included the Russian Federation, Canada, and Japan. The United States and Japan were the largest consumers of nickel, accounting for about 30 percent of the world market. In the early 1990s approximately 400 million pounds of tin was produced on an annual basis. Most tin is produced in South America, Asia, and Australia, and about one-fifth of all tin is consumed by the United States. It is used for various industrial processes, including the production of common alloys such as bronze and solder. Molybdenum is used mostly as an alloy in steel because it is strong and withstands high temperatures. It is produced and consumed primarily in the United States and Canada.

The United States is also the largest producer of magnesium. Magnesium is used chiefly as an alloying metal, often with copper and aluminum, for applications that require lightweight and high tensile strength. Titanium is an extremely high-performance metal used primarily for aerospace and defense-related purposes. Major titanium-producing nations include the Russian Federation, Japan, and the United States.

BACKGROUND AND DEVELOPMENT

Copper is believed to be the first metal used to make useful articles. It was probably discovered around 8000 B.C. in "the cradle of civilization" near the Tigris and Euphrates rivers in modern-day Iraq. Copper deposits in Egypt are known to have been mined as early as 5000 B.C., and the metal was discovered and used in ancient civilizations in Greece, Asia Minor, China, and southeastern Europe as well as by Native Americans. Lead and tin were also used by ancient civilizations. Tin has been found in ancient Egyptian tombs, while lead was utilized by the Romans to make pipes for carrying water. For more than 2,000 years white lead (lead carbonate) has been used as a white pigment. Several other nonferrous metals have been known for centuries as well, though they were not produced on a commercial scale.

The Industrial Revolution, which started in Europe and spread to North America during the eighteenth and nineteenth centuries, created massive demand for all types of refined metals. As new methods of mining, refining, and processing metals were developed, production soared. Advanced systems that used furnaces and chemicals to extract copper from ore were invented, and new lead and tin refining processes were developed. White lead, for instance, had long been made using the Dutch process, whereby lead gratings and acetic acid were wrapped in bark and placed in earthenware pots to ferment. That lengthy process was eventually replaced by refining systems that integrated blast furnaces, electrolysis, and other technologies advanced during the eighteenth century.

Unlike copper, other major nonferrous metals like tin and lead were not discovered until the eighteenth and nineteenth centuries and were not produced commercially until the Industrial Revolution. Zinc, for example, was not recognized as a separate element until 1746 by German chemist Andreas Sigismund Marggraf, and nickel was identified in 1751 by Swedish chemist Baron Axel Frederic Cronstedt. Subsequently, another Swedish chemist, Karl Wilhelm Scheele, identified molybdenum. In 1791 British clergyman William Gregor discovered titanium. However, most of these elements were not isolated or applied commercially until the late nineteenth or early twentieth century.

Aluminum was representative of the route to commercial success experienced by metals discovered in the eighteenth and nineteenth centuries. Aluminum was first isolated in 1825 by Danish chemist Hans Christian Oersted. However, 50 years passed before the first practical method for producing aluminum was developed by two scientists working independently on opposite sides of the Atlantic Ocean. During the late 1880s, American Charles Martin Hall and France's Paul Heroult simultaneously discovered the same process for the aluminum industry on their respective continents. Although the aluminum commercialization process mimicked that of other major metals, its success in the marketplace far surpassed that of its nonferrous cousins.

Production of all commercially viable nonferrous metals surged during the early 1900s. Metal demand for construction, transportation, communication, and consumer industries soared. Product demand and metal refining technology advanced significantly during World War I and World War II. Although technology and production capacity were significantly advanced during the latter war, by the end of the conflict the metal-producing infrastructure in most regions had been effectively quashed. The exception was the United States, which assumed a dominant role in both ferrous and nonferrous metal categories during the 1950s and 1960s. Importantly, Japan and the Russian Federation joined the United States and several European countries as industrializing nations.

Throughout the 1950s and into the early 1970s the United States was the leading producer in major metal categories, except zinc and nickel. Although statistics varied by category, the general trend was increased global consumption. In addition, metal industries emerged in

other nations that reduced the market share controlled by the United States and a few other leading nations. Japan and western European nations rebounded, becoming strong competitors in aluminum, copper, lead, and other metal categories. Other significant producers also emerged during this period. The Soviet Union and some Eastern Bloc countries developed vast production capacity, nearing and even surpassing U.S. output in important segments such as aluminum and copper. At the same time, several developing countries, including Chile, Mexico, Peru, Zambia, South Korea, and India, tapped rich natural resources to become major global suppliers of specific metals.

The early 1970s marked the beginning of a shift in the overall metal industry. For a variety of reasons, ranging from energy prices to environmental and labor laws, competition among the United States, western Europe, and Japan waned. The net effect was that metal output in those regions generally stagnated or dropped during the 1970s and 1980s. Meanwhile, the Soviet Union and several other nations had boosted production. This trend was evidenced most conspicuously by U.S. metal production statistics. U.S. aluminum output, for instance, jumped from 1.46 mmt in 1954 to a peak of 4.9 mmt in 1974. Between 1975 and 1993, however, U.S. shipments fluctuated between about 4 mmt and 5 mmt as world aluminum output surged from 12 to 19 mmt. Similarly, U.S. copper production grew from 1.1 mmt in 1961 to 1.7 mmt in 1973. Between 1974 and 1993, however, U.S. output hovered between 900,000 and 1.5 mmt as total global copper production rose about 25 percent because of the impact of countries like Chile and Indonesia.

By the 1980s, the global metal industry had become much more geographically diversified. Metal demand overall continued to rise during the 1980s, largely attributable to rising consumption in industrializing regions based in the Pacific Rim and Latin America. Long-industrialized nations, faced with slowing economic growth rates beginning in the 1970s, worked to sustain profitability through improved productivity and new products. For example, some market segments, such as specialized zinc coatings and high-performance alloys, offered hefty profit opportunities. Similarly, the demand for aluminum by the beverage and food industry swelled.

An important industry influence in the late 1980s and early 1990s was the decline and collapse of the Soviet Union. Metal output in the Russian Federation and the former Eastern Bloc plunged because of the political turmoil in those regions, but these nations dumped stockpiles and excess output of some metals onto the market. Most ceded Soviet market share was indirectly absorbed by rising metal-producing powers like China and India.

Metal industry performance during the early and mid-1990s varied by product segment. Aggregate aluminum output stabilized in the early 1990s after growing from about 15.4 mmt in 1986 to more than 19 mmt by 1990. Excess production capacity dogged competitors in many regions during the 1990s. The excess was caused in part by economic malaise in some industrialized regions. The Russian Federation, which maintained more than 80 percent of the aluminum-producing capacity of the former Soviet Union and was still the second largest aluminum manufacturer in the world, augmented the over-supply problem. As consumption in the Commonwealth of Independent States (CIS) plummeted, the Russian Federation dumped excess supply into world markets, contributing to weak prices and a glut of aluminum and other metals. Supply and demand dynamics, according to some industry analysts, were finally calming again by 1994, although most producers continued to suffer.

In the mid-1990s, North America was by far the largest aluminum-producing region, as Canada and the United States combined for about 30 percent of global output. Production in North America had been relatively stable for several years, with increases occurring solely in Canada. Aluminum output was rising most quickly in Australia, South America, and Asia. Most notably, Brazil's aluminum output had jumped from about 500,000 metric tons in the mid-1980s to about 1.2 million metric tons by 1992. During the same period, China increased its annual aluminum shipments from 400,000 tons to about 1 million metric tons. Similar gains were reported by Australia and India, the fourth and tenth biggest suppliers, respectively. In the long-term, aluminum consumption and production was predicted to rise 5 percent or more annually in developing regions, and more slowly in developed nations.

Copper industry dynamics mirrored those of the aluminum sector during the late 1980s and early 1990s. Aggregate production of refined copper jumped from 9.8 mmt to about 10.9 mmt. Much of the increase in demand came from China and a few other emerging industrial powers. The United States and Canada produced about 25 percent of all copper in the early 1990s, making North America the leading copper-producing region. As with aluminum, the regions with the greatest copper production gains were in the Pacific Rim and Latin America. Between 1986 and 1992, production in Chile and China rose 30 percent and 50 percent, respectively, accounting for 17 percent of global shipments. Meanwhile, output in the Commonwealth of Independent States (CIS) slipped from 1.3 million tons to 875,000, representing a drop of more than 30 percent. Long-term demand growth was projected at 2 to 3 percent annually during the mid- and late 1990s. Modest

growth expectations were attributed partially to a global shift from copper wire to fiber-optic cables.

Zinc output, spurred primarily by growing use as a steel coating in the vehicle and construction industries, grew steadily during the 1980s and early 1990s to about 7.5 mmt. Led by Canada, North America was the largest zinc-producing region, accounting for about 30 percent of total output. The CIS followed closely, although zinc shipments from that region slipped roughly 20 percent between 1990 and 1993 to less than 800,000 tons. Major zinc-producing nations that increased output during the late 1980s and early 1990s included Canada, Mexico, the United States, Italy, China, Australia, and Peru. Zinc prices were suppressed in the early 1990s, but recovering automotive and construction markets ignited a rally in 1994. The long-term outlook for global zinc appeared to be positive in the mid-1990s, with small increases in demand expected in both developing and industrialized regions.

Global lead production remained level from the early 1980s through the early 1990s at approximately 5.5 mmt, although prices were suppressed by industry overcapacity and generally weak demand. About 30 percent of all lead was manufactured and used in North America. The United States, the largest industry participant, increased its output from about 931,000 tons in 1986 to about 1.18 million tons in 1992. The only other countries achieving notable gains in lead production were Australia, China, and Peru. The biggest industry loser was the CIS. The long-term outlook for the lead industry was regarded by some observers as poor in the mid-1990s, as analysts pointed to likely reductions in the use of lead because of its toxicity and the emergence of increasingly popular lead substitutes.

Other industry trends evident by 2002 included declines in aerospace manufacturing that resulted in decreased demand for copper and aluminum. Demand for commercial airplanes dropped following the terrorist attacks against the United States on September 11, 2001. For 2001, Boeing reported a 45 percent drop in orders, and Airbus Industrie reported a 30 percent decrease in orders. Titanium producers, in general, were battered during the early 1990s by the end of the Cold War and an economic slump in industrialized nations. As core aerospace markets sagged, there was a glut in the titanium market that resulted in falling prices. Producers in the CIS, the United States, and Japan, which had traditionally dominated the titanium market, suffered as a result. Titanium demand and prices were expected to recover gradually as industrial and civilian aerospace markets improved, but CIS stockpiles were depleted. Other countries, including the United Kingdom and China, were also working to boost market share in the mid-1990s.

Although titanium revenue sagged in the early 1990s, molybdenum prices increased 30 to 60 percent depending on the region and product type in 1994. The growth was driven by surging international steel production and increased use of molybdenum as an alloying material. The long-term outlook for molybdenum was generally positive going into the mid-1990s, with North American producers expected to benefit the most.

While aluminum producers in the 1990s were cautious as they added capacity, copper production has often veered wildly off track of market demand, and consequently prices remained in a rut. Aluminum producers gained discipline after they experienced sporadic depressed prices in the 1980s and late 1990s, and some announced expansion plans in the late 1990. In 1993 U.S. aluminum manufacturers agreed to limit production to shore up flagging aluminum prices. Their strategy worked, and by the late 1990s leading producers like Alcoa were idling as much as 450,000 metric tons of their capacity for a total of more than a million metric tons idle industry-wide to preserve strong prices. By 1998, global aluminum supply exceeded demand by about 600,000 tons, due in part to a fall in demand precipitated by the mid-1990s Asian financial crisis. In 2000, the United States led in global aluminum demand, importing 2.2 mmt, representing 7.4 percent of global supply, followed closely by the European Union, with 2.1 mmt, or 7.2 percent. Canada led in world exports in 2000, shipping 1.36 mmt, or 4.7 percent of the global total, followed by Australia with exports of 900,000 mmt, or 3.1 percent, and Russia with exports of 770,000 mmt, or 2.7 percent of world supply. Industry analysts predicted a gradual decline in aluminum market surpluses as U.S. demand was expected to increase while world supply diminished.

Other metal segments mirrored the performance of the aluminum and copper industries. Producers of nickel, for example, were stymied during the early 1990s by overcapacity, generally weak demand, and low prices. Nickel output in the West declined while production in Japan, China, Colombia, and a few other nations climbed slowly. Long-term prospects for nickel were positive going into the mid-1990s, however, with demand expected to rise gradually throughout the late 1990s. By 1997 and 1998 consumption in the West had rebounded a solid 5 to 6 percent. While nickel markets like aerospace were projected to continue to flourish through the end of the century, some observers expected a cyclical decline in steel demand to eat into world nickel demand by 1999.

Similar forecasts were made for the tin industry in the 1990s. After surging during the late 1980s, global tin consumption slumped during the early 1990s. Tin

continued to lose market share to aluminum and other metals among Western nations, but demand was expected to increase slowly in developing regions throughout the 1990s and early 2000s.

Among other nonferrous segments, lead continued to disappoint producers with low prices. While lead use in Europe and North America exceeded demand, China had exported a large quantity of low-cost lead that had driven prices downward. Slack demand for batteries added to concerns in the lead industry because it was one of the primary uses for lead. Lead use in other applications had declined precipitously because of its toxicity to people and the environment.

In contrast, zinc was an industry success entering the late 1990s. North America and Europe were expected to consume about 6.5 mmt of zinc in 1998, a slight increase from 1997, but with considerably stronger unit prices. Used in such products as galvanized steel, automotive parts, and construction materials, slow and steady demand for zinc had exceeded output in the late 1990s.

CURRENT CONDITIONS

The market for aluminum, the industry's largest product segment, had continued to experience robust demand in the 2000s. Although worldwide aluminum production increased 6.1 percent in 2003, with levels expected to increase another 4.1 percent in 2004 and 4.8 percent in 2005, consumption was expected to grow even faster. Anticipated consumption levels were 13.4 percent higher for 2005 than 2003. Shortages were predicted, as supply was not projected to keep up with increased demand. China was the only country increasing demand exponentially, and by 2004 the country was consuming nearly one-fifth of worldwide aluminum production. There were projected shortages of 400,000 tons for 2004 and 1 million tons in 2005, according to *Aluminum International Today.* Prices were expected to remain high well into the middle of the decade.

Demand for aluminum was expected to continue in many industry sectors. European use of aluminum was increasing in the automotive industry faster than in the United States. Projections through 2010 for automotive use of aluminum in Europe was estimated at 25 pounds of aluminum per vehicle, compared to only 14 pounds in the United States.

Copper prices continued to be unpredictable due to a continuing imbalance in supply and demand, but in the early 2000s, the gap was beginning to narrow. For example, in 2002 there was a 105,000 ton surplus, as compared to the previous year's 536,000 ton surplus. These conditions were expected to lead to continued low copper prices, despite an increase that began in 2003, largely due to escalating demand for copper in the booming Asian markets. China especially increased consumption, which increased 26 percent between 2002 and 2003. Copper demand, especially in China, reached all-time highs in 2004 and 2005, resulting in dramatically higher copper prices.

RESEARCH AND TECHNOLOGY

The three main areas of research and technology affecting the nonferrous metals industry were new applications for metals that broaden potential markets; new production technologies that improve manufacturing productivity or create better metal products; and advances that reduce environmental hazards related to manufacturing processes. The first directly impacts all metal manufacturing countries, while the latter two are important to developed nations, which routinely compete against less-regulated, low-cost manufacturers in developing regions.

The aluminum segment continued to be impacted by environmental regulations in industrialized nations in the mid-1990s. Increasing pressure to reduce sulfur dioxide emissions in North America and Europe boosted operating costs in those areas. Japan was a minor presence in the aluminum industry at only 20 million tons produced annually in 1992. Because aluminum production consumes large amounts of energy, companies in many of those nations were building production facilities in areas with few environmental restrictions or large sources of power from coal alternatives, such as natural gas or hydropower. The net result was that European and North American producers that were dependent on coal-generated electricity began to lose their competitive edge and were forced to invest heavily in pollution-reduction technologies or expand foreign production. Another factor that hurt developed nations, particularly in North America, was a reduction in demand from the high-profit aerospace industry as a corollary of the end of the Cold War.

Alloy-related technological breakthroughs also broadened the aluminum market. Metal matrix composites (MMCs)—alloys that integrate aluminum to achieve a combination of strength and lightness—were being used for a broad range of applications in vehicle industries. Finally, technological advances in recycling technology have made aluminum manufacturing as much as 95 percent more energy efficient than extracting the metal from bauxite.

Like aluminum producers, copper manufacturers were also impacted by technology, although sometimes negatively. Copper wire, for instance, steadily lost market share to advanced fiber-optic cable for communications applications in the early 1990s. Copper producers, however, had also benefited from the general proliferation of electronic devices, many of which also utilized less-expensive copper wiring, although they were often connected by fiber-optic cables. Growing demand for such

applications helped industry participants offset losses in pipe markets, where plastic was used as a copper substitute, and losses to aluminum, which was replacing copper in car radiators, for example. Similarly, the zinc segment benefited from growing demand in the automobile and construction industries, which coated an increasingly large portion of steel products with zinc in the 1980s and early 1990s. Integral to that growth market was electrogalvanizing, a relatively new process used to coat and protect steel.

In the mid-1990s, lead producers in many nations continued to battle environmental regulations designed to curb pollution and faced increased competition from high-performance lead substitutes in the mid-1990s. Lead manufacturers were attempting to create new markets in an effort to replace diminishing traditional ones, the most promising of which was the lead battery market. The battery market showed solid long-term promise in transportation applications, partially because of pressures to reduce vehicle emissions. In addition, Argentina, the United States, Sweden, Belgium, and Canada were exploring the use of lead as a containment medium for high-level radioactive waste. In addition, a new lead compound called diayldithiocarbamate had been developed, and proponents said it could not only double the life of asphalt but also added only 5 percent to its cost. New uses for lead were also being pioneered in the field of magneto-hydrodynamics, an advanced electricity-generating technique being advanced primarily in Israel.

INDUSTRY LEADERS

Aluminum Company of America. Known to many as Alcoa, the Aluminum Company of America has long been the leader of the nonferrous metals industry through its dominant share of the world's aluminum production. The U.S.-based Alcoa was founded in 1888 by two Americans—Charles Martin Hall, who was the co-inventor of the Hall-Heroult process used to extract aluminum from bauxite, and Alfred Hunt. During the twentieth century Alcoa evolved into a multibillion-dollar corporation and became the leader in the aluminum industry, specializing in flat-rolled aluminum sheets used in beverage cans that it continued to dominate in the late 2000s.

Entering the mid-1990s, Alcoa was active in three business segments: the production of bauxite, alumina, and alumina-related chemicals; aluminum processing, including the production and sale of basic aluminum-cast, flat-rolled, and engineered products; and the manufacture of nonaluminum metal products, including gold, magnesium, and steel and titanium forgings. In 1996 and 1997 Alcoa took over state-run aluminum holdings in Italy and Spain. In 1998 Alcoa bought the United States' third-largest aluminum firm, Alumax Inc., which further secured its status as the world's pre-eminent aluminum company. The combined company had a smelting capacity of 3.2 mmt, which was nearly double its nearest competitor. A few years later, Alcoa formed an alliance with China's Aluminum Corporation.

In 2000, Alcoa acquired Reynolds Metals, then the United States' second largest aluminum manufacturer and the world's third largest primary aluminum producer. Best known in the United States for its Reynolds Wrap aluminum foil, Reynolds was highly diversified in all stages of aluminum production and marketing, from bauxite mining to refining to finished goods for the consumer, construction, and automotive sectors. Reynolds began in 1919 as a manufacturer of foil for cigarette packaging, expanding during World War II and the postwar U.S. economic and population boom. Reynolds emphasized global expansion during the mid-twentieth century, and by 1980 had more than 100 operations in 20 countries. It maintained global operations, including in Europe, Russia, India, and China.

Alcoa operated approximately 350 facilities in about 38 countries worldwide. The company had 2007 sales of nearly US$30.2 billion. With 107,000 workers that year, Alcoa also was one of the largest employers in the industry worldwide.

Rio Tinto Alcan. Rio Tinto Alcan (Alcan) has traditionally been one of Canada's most profitable conglomerates and a major force throughout the world. Although Alcan competed with Alcoa for the top position in the global aluminum industry, the company began when Alcoa spun it off as a subsidiary, Aluminum Limited, in 1928. The division continued to act as Alcoa's foreign subsidiary for 20 years, with operations throughout the world. Alcan eventually became completely independent. Revenue and profit growth was brisk in the late 1980s but slipped during the early 1990s in the wake of global overcapacity and weak prices. By the early 1990s the company was mining bauxite in seven countries and processing aluminum in 19 countries. The fully integrated producer was a leading global supplier of fabricated aluminum products, including foil, beverage can sheet aluminum, rod, cable, extruded aluminum, and various construction products in the mid-1990s.

In 2000, Alcan acquired the Swiss firm Alusuisse-Lonza, later renamed Algroup, which was at the time the sixth-largest contender in the international nonferrous industry, as ranked by primary aluminum output. Like Alcoa, Alusuisse was formed in 1888, shortly after the discovery of the Hall-Heroult process. In 2001, the Zurich-based Algroup was one of Switzerland's largest corporations, with 23,000 employees in 18 countries. Alusuisse primary materials; Alusuisse fabricated products; Lawson Mardon food flexible and

tobacco packaging; and Wheaton pharmaceutical and cosmetics packaging comprised Algroup's four divisions.

In 2004, Alcan acquired French competitor Pechiney and in early 2005, the company spun off its aluminum-rolled products unit with the newly formed Novelis, a public company. In 2006, Alcan earned US$23.6 billion in revenue. In 2007, Rio Tinto purchased Alcan for US$38 billion, which some criticized as being too expensive. Rio Tinto Chief Financial Officer Guy Elliot expressed the belief that by 2010, "we'll have a much higher rate of synergies."

In the late 2000s, as its rivals idled refineries due to high production costs, Rio Tinto announced plans to build and expand plants to add 2.6 million tons of aluminum capacity. The company was studying the use of hydropower and other technologies to survive at a time when competitors were closing due to the rapidly increasing cost of energy.

Nippon Light Metal Company. Nippon Light Metal Company of Tokyo posted 2004 revenues of nearly US$5.04 billion, a 17.5 percent increase over 2003. The company's net income had skyrocketed, however, to US$109.1 million, an increase of more than 83 percent over 2003. A leading producer of ladders, bridges, fuel tanks, and other fabricated aluminum products, Nippon employed 12,598 people in locations from Asia to North America. Its fabricated products and building materials units contributed more than two-thirds of sales. A joint venture with Mitsubishi allowed Nippon to produce aluminum sheet for automotive applications.

RUSAL. Russian leader RUSAL was high on the list of world's top aluminum producers. It was created in 2000 from various parts of the old Soviet stat apparatus. RUSAL reportedly produces approximately 4 million tons of aluminum, 11 million tons of alumina, and 6 million tons of bauxite. The company has packaging and foil operations as well as a network of smelters. In 2007, RUSAL merged with Russian aluminum producer Sual and Glencore's alumina unit.

Other Leaders. Numerous other companies hold noteworthy shares of the nonferrous metals markets, including copper and diversified producers Asarco Inc., Freeport McMoRan Copper and Gold, Olin Corp., Grupo Mexico SA de CV, Phelps Dodge, Noranda Aluminum Holding Corp., and Southern Copper Corp. A subsidiary of Grupo Mexico filed a bankruptcy reorganization plan seeking to regain their control of copper producer Asarco in which Americas Mining Corp. would make up to US$2.7 billion in cash available. The offer included a US$440 million guarantee that creditor claims would be paid along with payment of liabilities relating to asbestos and environmental claims.

MAJOR COUNTRIES IN THE INDUSTRY

The United States. While countries with metal-producing powers like Germany and the United Kingdom significantly increased production capacity during World War II, by the end of the conflict the United States was the only major industrialized power with its metal-manufacturing infrastructure intact. The United States became a world leader in nonferrous metals following World War II as U.S. producers benefited from foreign and domestic demand growth during the 1950s and 1960s, accounting for more than 30 percent of global production of some metals. The United States held its lead of the industry into the late 1990s, supplying roughly 20 percent of total global metal demand and dominating several major industry segments. For example, it shipped less than 1.5 million metric tons of aluminum in the early 1950s, but by the early 1970s, that number had risen to about 4.5 million.

The United States' share of world metal production deteriorated rapidly in the early 1970s. Although industry segments differed, the United States generally suffered from a lack of competitiveness and a slowdown in domestic demand. U.S. output of refined copper, for example, declined from about 2 mmt in 1973 to less than 1.5 mmt in the late 1980s. Aluminum output stagnated as well, despite a huge rise in new applications in packaging and construction industries, among others. The United States's share of world output and consumption continued to decline through the 1980s. By the early 1990s it was producing about 20 percent of the world's output of copper, aluminum, and lead, and about 6 percent of all zinc. The United States also was the largest metal consumer, typically consuming more metal than it produced.

Going into the mid-1990s, U.S. nonferrous producers benefited from a cyclical upswing in demand for most metals. However, prices generally were suppressed by global manufacturing overcapacity. Long-term aluminum demand from the important high-profit aerospace industry had slowed dramatically by 2002. Similarly, the giant packaging segment, which represented 28 percent of U.S. aluminum consumption in 1993, had matured and was expected to offer little growth. Industry participants were heartened, however, by the expectation of continued increases in aluminum use in the transportation and construction markets. Some industry analysts in the early 1990s anticipated long-term declines in lead output that could be supplanted by slow but steady growth in copper demand. Entering the mid-1990s, the United States was expected to continue to play a leading role in high-tech, high-profit alloy and specialty metal markets, areas where it enjoyed important

advantages over low-cost commodity-metal manufacturers in emerging nations. In 1996 the United States exported more than US$5 billion worth of aluminum and copper, and was the largest importer of aluminum, at US$4.95 billion in 1996, as well as a major consumer of most other nonferrous metals.

The U.S. market for aluminum reached 5.5 million metric tons in 2003, a decrease of 0.2 percent from 2002. The market was expected to grow 6.7 percent to 6.1 mmt in 2008.

Canada. Canada's nonferrous metal industry was the third largest in the mid-1990s. The country was a major exporter of metals to the United States and was heavily influenced by that market. In 1993, for example, Canada exported roughly 30 percent of its aluminum to its southern neighbor. Canada exported much of its metal to other countries as well, particularly the Netherlands. The country also was a major player in the global copper and lead industries, and was second only to the CIS in the manufacture of slab zinc and refined nickel. Most of Canada's nickel and zinc was exported to the United States, which produced less than 10 percent as much nickel and about 50 percent as much zinc as Canada. Canadian producers were projected to reap long-term benefits from healthy reserves of natural resources in major metal categories, as well as access to the giant U.S. metal market.

The Russian Federation. The business dynamics in the Commonwealth of Independent States were significantly different than those in North America throughout the 1990s. The Soviet Union had aggressively expanded its metal production capacity entering the mid-1980s, which established it as the second largest world manufacturer of aluminum and a key supplier of copper, zinc, lead, and other metals. The Soviet Union continued to boost capacity through much of the 1980s, largely to support its massive military machine. For example, the country produced about 2.4 mmt of aluminum annually during the 1980s, nearly 90 percent of which was used by the military and aerospace industry. Aluminum consumption peaked in the late 1980s at around 3 mmt, before plummeting to just 500,000 metric tons by 1997. Likewise, copper shipments fell from more than 1 billion metric tons in 1987 to less than 900,000 metric tons in 1990. Output of aluminum, lead, zinc, and other metals mirrored the decline of aluminum.

The breakdown of the Soviet metal industry was hastened by the disintegration of the country's long-established political establishment in 1991. Production volumes of most metal types plunged as the region spiraled into industrial decay. Metal manufacturers reeled under drastic reductions in demand from core military and aerospace industries at the same time that global metal prices, especially for aluminum, were in turmoil. The CIS attempted to raise cash in the early 1990s by dumping ferrous and nonferrous metals into export markets. European and North American countries, among others, tried to stem the tide with import quotas on CIS-produced metals. Other setbacks for CIS producers included huge jumps in energy prices, which had been a major productivity influence in metal manufacturing, and a deteriorating internal industrial infrastructure. Prospects for the CIS metal industry were dismal in the late 1990s, and little recovery was expected before the early 2000s.

China. China was among the fastest growing of the leading metal-producing nations in the 1990s. The country's vast supply of natural resources, combined with its rapidly developing industrial infrastructure, made it a potential contender for future global metal industry leadership. China's output of aluminum, for example, surged from about 400,000 metric tons annually in the mid-1980s to approximately 2.8 mmt by 1999. During the 1990s, China's copper production jumped 116 percent, from 561 mmt in 1990 to 1.21 mmt in 1999. China also was the leading global producer of tin. Gross national product (GNP) gains of more than 10 percent annually during the early 1990s boded well for the country's long-term metal industry expansion, although growth had slowed to a more moderate 9 percent, which was three times U.S. growth, in the late 1990s. By 2003, China was rapidly expanding its presence in the global aluminum market, importing 600,000 tons of aluminum scrap annually and exporting millions of pounds of extrusions. Between 1999 and 2002, Chinese exports of aluminum extrusions increased from 9 to 80 million pounds annually. By 2004, China's aluminum production reached 3.37 mmt. As of October 2008, SABC News confirmed that the Chinese economy was slowing, although growth was ongoing.

Other Countries. With the exception of North America and the CIS, the nonferrous metals industry remained relatively fragmented. Specific market segments typically were led by a few countries that were not necessarily considered developed nations. National output was primarily determined by available raw materials, along with the level of domestic consumption, which accounted for the influence of Japan and Western Europe in the industry. Japan's access to locally mined materials was essentially non-existent. However, it was second only to the United States in copper consumption in the early 1990s, and had created the third largest copper-refining industry in the world. Germany was not a leader in the mining of bauxite (for making aluminum) and copper, but

produced about 634 mmt of primary aluminum in 1999 and about 696,000 mmt of copper. Despite a dearth of raw materials, Norway was a leading producer of primary aluminum with about 800 mmt of output.

Despite their technological and manufacturing prowess, the competitiveness of developed nations was generally reduced by dependence on outside sources of raw materials, except in the United States and Canada. In addition, producers in developed nations were constrained by labor and environmental restrictions that were significantly stronger than those in developing regions. As a result, several emerging industrial nations had been able to tap large or high-quality natural resources to assume leading roles in specific industry segments. For instance, in the 1990s Chilean manufacturers accounted for nearly 20 percent of all mined copper in 1999, making it one of the world's ten leading metal-producers. Chile also aggressively expanded output capacity in the mid-1990s through the development of new mines. Brazil was the world's fifth largest manufacturer of refined aluminum. African metals investor interests had soared in the mid- to late 2000s, driven by increases in metals prices and demand from Asia, including China and India.

BIBLIOGRAPHY

"Alcan Sees Europe Outpacing US." *American Metal Market,* 11 August 2003.

"Aluminum Castings." *Aluminum International Today,* May–June 2004.

"Aluminum in France, Germany, UK, US." *Euromonitor,* August 2004. Available from www.majormarketprofiles.com.

"Aluminum Prices Strong Until 2005." *Aluminum International Today,* May–June 2004.

"Awaiting Its Surge." *Recycling Today,* November 2003.

Bresnick, Julie. "PD Expects Copper Use to Grow in China, US." *American Metal Market,* 29 April 2004.

Brooks, David. "Still a Waiting Game for Aluminum Extruders." *American Metal Market,* 12 March 2003.

"The Bull May Tire Soon." *Purchasing,* 2 June 2005.

Chambers, Matt. "Rio Tinto Stands by Its Alcan Acquisition." *The Australian,* 28 August 2008.

"China Economy Starts to Slow Down," 23 October 2008. Available from www.sabcnews.com.

China's Primary Aluminum Production, International Aluminum Institute. 20 June 2005. Available from www.world-aluminium.org.

Cole, Kevin. "Metal's Future Remain Murky." *Fabricator,* 29 January 2004. Available from www.thefabricator.com.

Delaney, Rob. "Rio Tinto Says 2.6 Million Tons of New Aluminum Capacity Likely." *Bloomberg News,* 9 September 2008. Available from www.bloomberg.com.

Dunn, Brian. "New Dawn on Horizon for Nonferrous Metals." *American Metal Market,* 21 January 2002.

"FACE Call for Immediate Abolition of 6 Percent EU Duty." *Aluminum International Today,* May–June 2004.

"Grupo Mexico Files Asarco Reorganization Plan." *Yahoo! Finance,* 27 August 2008. Available from www.finance.yahoo.com.

"Gulf States: Local Aluminum Production to Double by 2010."
    IPR Strategic Business Information Database, 16 December
    2003.

"International Trade Statistics." World Trade Organization,
    2003. Available from www.wto.org.

"Investors May Depart." *Purchasing,* 2 June 2005.

"Keeping Pace with Demand." *Aluminum International Today,*
    May–June 2004.

"Next Metals Boom May Outshine the Last? CRU," 23 October
    2008. Available from www.reuters.com.

Norris, Robert. "Trial Likely in ALCOA Health Benefits Case;
    Retirees Fill Federal Courtroom for Hearing." *The Daily
    Times,* 28 August 2008. Available from
    www.thedailytimes.com.

Pisculli, Alysson. "Economic Cooling Has Copper Set to Fly
    South." *American Metal Market,* 11 June 2003.

———. "Refined Copper Surplus Shrinks as Usage Rises,
    Output Declines." *American Metal Market,* 12 February
    2003.

Primary Aluminum Production, International Aluminum Institut,
    20 June 2005. Available from www.world-aluminium.org.

Taylor, Brian. "The Right Price." *Recycling Today,* January 2004.

"U.S. Primary Aluminum Production." *American Metal Market
    Online,* 2004. Available from www.amm.com.

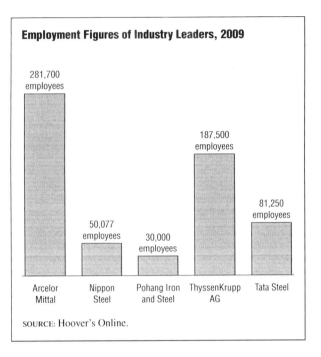

Employment Figures of Industry Leaders, 2009

SOURCE: Hoover's Online.

SIC 3310

STEEL MILLS

NAICS CODE(S)

331111. Steelmakers operate blast or electric furnaces to create raw iron and steel. The same manufacturer may produce any number of intermediate or finished steel products from crude steel. Examples of industry output include hot-rolled steel products; cold-rolled steel products; iron and steel bars; steel ingots; stainless steel; iron and steel forgings; steel wire and nails; and steel pipes and tubes.

Companies that produce steel castings are discussed separately under **Iron and Steel Foundries,** and those that process nonferrous ores into metals are covered under **Metals, Primary Smelting and Refining of Nonferrous Metals.**

INDUSTRY SNAPSHOT

In 2009, the world's steel market reached 1,219.7 million metric tons (mmt) of crude steel according to the World Steel Association. By 2010, China, Japan, and the United States were among the top five steel producers worldwide. In a November 2010 report, the world steel market had reached 118 mmt in October alone. China's crude steel production had fallen slightly from the same time a year before. It was reported at 50.3 mmt for October 2010—a 3.8 percent decrease. However, elsewhere in

Asia the steel production rates were climbing. In Japan, October 2010's production was 9.5 mmt (an 8 percent increase over the previous year), and South Korea's production was at 5.2 percent (an 11.4 percent increase) over October 2009. The World Steel Association released a report in April 2010, forecasting world steel use to increase by 10.7 percent to 1,241 mmt in 2010, after contracting by 6.7 percent in 2009. It this figure holds, the world steel demand in 2010 will exceed the 2007 levels prior to the global economic crisis. The forecast calls for the steel demand to reach 1,306 mmt in 2011— an historical high in the steel industry.

ORGANIZATION AND STRUCTURE

Steel is manufactured using iron ore, coke, and limestone. Typically, the coke (a high-grade coal distillate) is used as fuel to heat a blast furnace. The coke emits carbon monoxide as it burns, as does the limestone. The ore melts, creating a molten iron and carbon mixture. A basic oxygen furnace (BOF) is used to supply super-heated air, which removes impurities and converts the molten iron into steel. The steel is usually cast into ingots, which are later formed into standard shapes, usually billets, slabs, or blooms. A more advanced production technique, "continuous casting," bypasses ingots. These slabs, billets, and blooms are processed at mills into rails, rolls, plates, tubes, bars, or other more marketable products. Those units are used by automobile companies, for example, to create parts or body panels for vehicles.

This conventional steelmaking technique is referred to as integrated manufacturing because it integrates all aspects of the process, including melting the iron ore. In the 1990s, an increasing number of steelmakers, particularly in the United States and other highly developed nations, were utilizing minimills. Minimill producers, or non-integrated steel manufacturers, start with scrap iron or steel, rather than iron ore. They use electric arc furnaces (EAFs), rather than blast and basic-oxygen furnaces (BOFs), to continuously cast blooms and billets. Most minimills produce a limited number of finished products, such as rods and bars used in light construction, but some non-integrated manufacturers also produce plates, sheets, pipes, and other steel goods.

Many integrated steel mills can produce millions of tons of steel annually, while minimills typically churn out between 100,000 and 500,000 tons. However, minimills may generate as much as 10 times more profit per ton of steel produced. A primary advantage of minimills is that they do not have to be located near supplies of iron ore. Instead, they are commonly constructed near primary customers, significantly reducing shipping costs. That advantage, when combined with high-tech manufacturing techniques such as use of EAFs, allows non-integrated producers in industrialized nations to compete aggressively with low-cost importers for domestic market share.

Regardless of their production techniques, most steel companies manufacture a category of steel called carbon steel. Carbon steels account for roughly 90 percent of global output. They contain relatively few alloying additives and their high degree of malleability makes them ideal for general purpose uses such as automobile bodies, structural steel for buildings, and shipbuilding. The remainder of industry output is categorized in one of four segments: alloy, stainless, tool, and high-strength low alloy (HSLA). Alloy steels, the second largest industry product segment by output volume, contain various alloying materials such as vanadium, silicon, manganese, and copper. They offer characteristics such as corrosion resistance, high electrical or heat conductivity, and greater strength, qualities that make alloy steel useful for a variety of applications ranging from tools and electrical components to machine parts and armor.

Stainless steel, the third largest product group, includes chromium/nickel alloy steels that resist corrosion and may be stronger or more heat resistant than lower-grade steels. Large markets include aerospace, medical device, and plumbing-related industries. Tool steels, the fourth industry segment, integrate molybdenum, tungsten, or other elements to produce ultra-hard alloys commonly used in tool and metalworking industries. Similarly, HSLA steels, the most recent family of steel products, use relatively small amounts of alloying materials, but are specially processed for hardness and light weight. Such steels are popular in applications where

strength and weight factors are crucial, such as freight cars. In general, newly industrialized nations are more likely to focus solely on the production of low-tech carbon steel, while established Western and Japanese manufacturers are more likely to compete in alloy, stainless, tool, and HSLA steel markets.

Competitive Structure. Because of high start-up costs and slow-growth markets, the steel industry is a difficult one to enter. In traditional steel-manufacturing regions, such as western Europe, the Russian Federation, the United States, and Japan, industries are highly consolidated with only a few manufacturers controlling the lion's share of the market in their respective countries. In general, new entrants to the industry are minimill producers, which incur start-up costs about one-quarter as great as those required to open an integrated facility.

Entry barriers are generally lower in emerging nations, where steel demand rose in the 1980s and early 1990s. Nevertheless, most newcomers were fully integrated and had to secure hefty sources of capital to build steel mills. Other obstacles have varied by country. In some nations, such as South Korea, access to the industry has traditionally been limited by the national government. Likewise, Brazil's steel industry was effectively controlled by the government until the early 1990s, when privatization occurred. In other regions, such as Eastern Europe and China, hurdles have included the lack of a dependable distribution and supply infrastructure.

On an international level, the steel industry is characterized by fierce competition, not only among individual producers but also among different nations. In fact, the industry has traditionally been heavily influenced by government control for reasons related primarily to defense and economic stability. In addition, because carbon steel is essentially a commodity, companies compete primarily on price. To help their producers compete internationally, governments in virtually all steelmaking nations support domestic producers through measures such as subsidies or restrictions on imports. By subsidizing steel exported to international markets a government can help its producers establish a presence and boost market share. Governments can help those companies maintain dominance of their domestic market by instituting tariffs or stringent quality controls on imported material.

Barron's reported that steel mills planned additional price increases by September 2008. Steel mill owners were increasingly pessimistic about the possibility of passing along any increases in the fourth quarter of 2008. Widely reported declines in ferrous scrap pricing, along with increasing slumps in demand, were causing a reduced outlook for distributors as they determined pricing. As a result, those mills aware of demand expectations were reducing service center inventory.

Agreements and Standards. Widespread government support of domestic steel producers has contributed to an environment conducive to trade wars that featured dumping practices (selling steel below cost), sanctions, and retaliatory import restrictions and tariffs. To reduce friction and enhance free markets, several countries had entered agreements with other nations to help ensure free trade and/or regional cooperation. For example, the North American Free Trade Agreement (NAFTA) reduced trade barriers between the United States, Canada, and Mexico. Several European countries had also pursued agreements or acquiesced to regional regulatory bodies in an effort to drop trade barriers and to cooperate against export threats from other regions. The European Commission, for example, worked to enhance free steel trade on the continent, among other objectives. Similarly, European Union (E.U.) members signed bilateral consensus agreements (BCAs) in the late 1980s that eliminated regional tariffs, subsidies, and other government supports.

In the mid-1990s several nations continued to seek a multilateral steel agreement (MSA) that would effectively put all steelmaking nations on a level playing field. International MSA negotiations failed in 1992, but several nations continued to pursue the effort. The United States was a strong proponent of the MSA because it had battled anticompetitive foreign trade practices for several years in an effort to revive its ailing steel industry. In addition to various tariffs and restraints, the United States, like several other nations, had diminished the effects of other nations' dumping practices by turning to the International Trade Commission (ITC). The ITC has the power to assess dumping penalties and to restrict specific trade initiatives that it deems unfair.

One final major regulatory influence is national environmental law. Japan and other industrialized nations must comply with environmental laws that designate the amount and type of pollutants that may be released during the manufacturing process, among other guidelines. Steel producers in the United States, for example, invested a combined sum of more than US$100 million annually in pollution control devices for their factories. Environmental legislation was even more costly in certain Western European nations. In contrast, manufacturers in less industrialized nations benefited from comparatively weak domestic regulations or slipshod enforcement.

The dominant international steel industry standard in the mid-1990s was ISO 9000, a set of quality standards created for various industries by the International Standardization Organization (ISO). The goal of ISO 9000 is to provide a quality certification program that will ensure that members can meet specific quality standards. Certification was considered a relatively expensive and difficult endeavor in the mid-1990s, but ISO 9000 was gradually being adopted by steel producers throughout the world, particularly in the most industrialized nations. Accreditation or certification was carried out by regional bodies such as the Dutch Council for Certification, the British Studies Intelligeneer (BSI), and Underwriter's Laboratories of the United States.

BACKGROUND AND DEVELOPMENT

Steelmaking dates back to fourteenth-century Europe, but mass-production methods were not developed until the mid-nineteenth century in Great Britain. Simple forges were originally used to heat iron ore and charcoal in a box for several days. Furnaces gradually increased in size, and steelmakers eventually learned to force air over the molten iron to speed the heating process. Sir Henry Bessemer, a British inventor, is credited with developing the Bessemer Furnace in 1855. It was the first device to refine molten iron with blasts of oxygen. The invention languished until bulk production of oxygen began later in the century.

Demand for steel surged with the onset of the Industrial Revolution in Great Britain. As the Industrial Revolution spread to other European nations and the United States in the late eighteenth century, global steel production soared. The open-hearth furnace was developed, which allowed producers to use scrap iron and produce higher-grade steel. Factors spurring industry growth during the early 1900s included new automobile markets, steel-framed construction, and industrialization in Japan and the Russian Federation. Massive demand for steel during World War II spurred giant increases in production capacity and steelmaking technology.

Shortly after World War II, the basic oxygen furnace was developed in Austria. It eventually replaced open-hearth technology, although the latter remained dominant until the 1970s. BOFs forced pure oxygen into the molten iron mixture, allowing furnaces to create a unit of steel in less than one-quarter the time required by open-hearth furnaces. Another pivotal development was the use of electric arc furnaces (EAFs) to manufacture carbon steel, which was a departure from their original use to only produce stainless and other types of steel. Other important technological breakthroughs during and after World War II related to the use of alloy additives, a development that initiated a new generation of high-performance steel products.

In 1950, following the giant production surge of the 1940s, global steel producers turned out about 190 million metric tons annually. War-ravaged European,

Russian, and Japanese industries were rebuilding during this time, so the United States dominated the sector. In the early 1950s the United States produced nearly 60 percent of global steel output. It continued to lead production throughout the 1960s and into the 1970s as well, although other regions achieved steady gains. Japan's steel output soared from 5 million metric tons in 1950 to 23 million in 1960, and then to a whopping 93 million by 1970. Similarly, the European production amounted to 32 million tons in 1950, 72 million in 1960, and more than 150 million tons in the early 1970s, although some of that gain was attributable to the integration of Great Britain.

Perhaps the most impressive postwar recovery occurred in the former Soviet Union, where steel output rocketed from 27 million tons in 1950 to a staggering 116 million tons in 1970. In 1974 the Soviet Union overtook the United States as the leading producer of steel. Soviet supremacy in the global steel industry marked the end of the dominance of United States and Western European manufacturers. This shift in industry dynamics actually started in the late 1960s when steel demand in Western nations leveled off. Factors in the early 1970s, including concern about the availability of oil and recessionary conditions, exacerbated the trend. At the same time, steel substitutes, such as plastics and aluminum, rapidly supplanted steel in many applications, including those in the automobile industry. Industry participants also claimed that regulations related to labor practices and pollution control constrained productivity and competitiveness.

Steel output in most industrialized Western nations peaked in the 1970s before dwindling, or even stagnating, throughout the 1980s. Total global steel output hovered around 800 million tons during those two decades, but the share of the market served by the seven largest steel-producing western nations plummeted from 54 percent to just 37 percent. Even Japan's steel output waned after the early 1970s, despite a common perception in Western nations that Japan's steel industry was robust. Between the early 1970s and 1990 the total tonnage of steel manufactured by the United States, the European Economic Community (EEC), and Japan slipped from about 420 million tons to about 325 million. Meanwhile, the former Soviet Union continued to stretch its lead, increasing output to a peak of 163 million tons in 1988.

More notable than advances in the Soviet Union and some Eastern Bloc countries during the 1970s and 1980s was the rise of steel industries in several third world and newly industrialized countries. Production in Latin America, for instance, shot up from 19 million tons in 1975 to about 30 million tons in 1980. Overall, steel production in emerging countries grew from less than 75 million tons annually in the 1970s to about 175 million tons annually by the late 1980s. The strongest of the new contenders included South Korea, Brazil, and China. However, numerous countries chipped away at the aggregate global steel market, including nations in the Middle East, Asia, South America, and Africa. Besides labor and regulatory advantages, those producers typically benefited from newer production facilities in comparison to their more industrialized counterparts, as well as better access to regions where steel demand was increasing.

Steelmaking industries in Western Europe and the United States staggered as developing nations infringed on both the domestic and the ever-growing export markets. The percentage of total steel exported had shot up from 10 percent in 1950 to more than 25 percent by the late 1980s. Battered producers scrambled to sustain profitability and many of them eventually folded or merged with their domestic peers. Throughout the 1980s, many of the world's largest steel companies took drastic actions to reinvent themselves and revive their competitiveness. They automated factories, slashed payrolls as much as 50 percent or more, integrated new technology, and focused on developing high-performance steels that could compete with proliferating synthetic and aluminum substitutes. By the late 1980s the efforts began to show tangible results.

Critical to the revival of steel industries in the United States, Europe, and even Japan in the late 1980s and early 1990s, were new steel manufacturing technologies, particularly minimills and continuous casting. Minimills sprang up in the United States during the 1960s and by the late 1970s had begun to compete with large steel producers. Their great efficiency and technological superiority were highlighted during periods of industry turbulence such as the latter part of the 1980s. By the early 1990s, minimills accounted for more than 35 percent of all steel output in the United States. The share of U.S. steel made with continuous casting jumped from 15 percent to 85 percent by the early 1990s, mimicking Japan's steel sector. European producers eventually followed the lead of their North American and Japanese counterparts.

Despite temporary setbacks brought on by a fiscal crisis in 1997, Asia remained the world's premier steel-producing center, supplying more than 35 percent of the world's crude steel in 2000 alone. China, Japan, and South Korea dominated the industry, and together they manufactured one-third of the steel produced worldwide. China's booming economy surged on, scarcely affected by the crisis. However, production and consumption began to drop sharply in Japan and South Korea in late 1998. One result of the Asian crisis was to draw attention to the advantages of consolidation. In October 2000 the region's two main competitors and the largest steel firms in the world, Nippon Steel and POSCO, announced a strategic alliance. NKK Corp and Kawasaki Steel also announced merger plans. Analysts at the Nomura Securities Company forecast that by 2005 Japan's steel trade would be controlled by two groups, Nippon Steel and NKK-Kawasaki.

After languishing in the early and mid-1990s, Europe's steel industry, in the east and in the west, began to recover in the latter part of the decade. Demand in places such as Germany, which was Western Europe's largest producer, rose as key markets like the auto industry increased business. Consolidation of the European Union's steel industry was well underway by mid-2001 when five companies were responsible for about 60 percent of output, up from 23 percent in 1993. Eastern Europe, while showing important gains, continued to perform unevenly as its economies grappled with the free-market transition. Poland's steel production, for example, experienced healthy increases in the mid-1990s, but plunged 11.5 percent between 1998 and 1999. In 2000, with growth from 8.8 to 10.5 million metric tons, the country finally seemed to be heading toward a recovery. Steel production in the leading Eastern European nations of Poland, the Czech Republic, Slovakia, and Romania, grew more than 11.5 percent from 1999 to 2000, reaching 25.2 million metric tons. Among the former Soviet states, Russia performed the best in 2000, finally emerging from the slump it suffered after the breakup of the Soviet Union in 1991. In 2000 Russia surpassed 1993 levels for the first time, reaching 59.1 million metric tons, an increase of 14.7 percent from 1999. Ukraine also continued a strong performance with a 31.4 million metric ton output in 2000 that was 14 percent higher than 1999 figures. Despite the apparently strong showing by the Commonwealth of Independent States (CIS), questions remained concerning the ability of their relatively old facilities to compete in the world market.

North America, on the other hand, remained a strong steel market in 2000, driven by a strong U.S. economy. Overall, North American steel output reached 128.9 million metric tons, three-quarters of which was produced by the United States. That was slightly off the record-setting 130.1 million metric tons produced in North America in 1997. Consumption of steel in North America during 2000 also reached historic highs. In fact, supply fell short of demand during 2000 for some steel products in the United States. The United States led all other nations in steel imports in 1999 with 32.7 million metric tons, which equaled nearly one-third of the steel the country actually produced. In spite of general agreement throughout the U.S. industry that there was a pressing need for widespread

consolidation, no companies seemed willing to take the plunge. A joint statement by U.S. Steel and Nucor, which were the largest integrated producer and the largest min-imill producer, respectively, in support of ending government subsidies to steel facilities that were unable to compete on the open market in quality or price was seen as a first sign that the industry was embracing consolidation. Nevertheless, there was concern that the longer the inevitable was postponed, the more precarious U.S. industry's position would be in the world market. The United States had long produced far less steel than it consumed, with estimates of the extra steel needed ranging from 15 to 28 million tons. At least in the beginning, consolidation and plant closings would serve foreign steelmakers, as well as the U.S. industry.

Combining resources was seen not only as a means of giving steelmakers access to the capital needed to invest in new technologies, it was also a way of trimming facilities and firms that were not performing with maximum efficiency and reducing competition that kept profit margins razor thin. Between 1990 and 1998, the global steel industry experienced mergers worth about US$66 billion, a pittance compared to industries such as petroleum refining. The trend continued to pick up speed in the 2000s. Significant mergers in both Europe and Asia were planned or already under review by regulatory agencies by late 2001. Determined to downsize its steel industry, Asia pressed ahead with strategic alliances, mergers, and joint ventures. Although the need for consolidation in the bloated U.S. market was acknowledged almost universally, at the beginning of 2002 no significant steps toward it had been taken.

The rise of e-commerce in the late 1990s ushered a minor revolution into the usually conservative steel business. In the mid-1990s, private, web-based steel exchanges, such as Metal Suppliers, MetalSite, Metal Network Exchange Services (MNSX), and eSteel, were founded. Each functioned differently, with some allowing producers to auction their steel to the highest bidder, others acting as online forums where buyers and sellers could hammer out terms, and still others giving sellers the ability to post quantities and prices. The sites charged a transaction fee, but by the early 2000s large steelmakers began taking control of online distribution and foregoing fees. Bethlehem Steel, Bermingham Steel, Nucor Corp., and Weirton made plans to set up private exchanges on their company web sites. The private exchanges were not left entirely out of the picture. The most enterprising continued to sell their expertise to steel companies as Internet consultants.

Despite rising output and increasing sales, world steel prices fell steadily between 1999 and 2001 at an annual rate of 2.7 percent, according to CRU International, a metals consulting company. It was a trend that could not continue. "Ultimately," a CRU report stated, "prices must bear some relationship to costs." Beginning in 2002, however, steel prices began to rise again. According to *Fortune,* U.S. hot-rolled steel, for example, rose from US$260 per ton in June 2003 to US$410 per ton by April 2004. U.S. steel in 2002 was protected by tariffs that were lifted a year and a half later, and in 2003 U.S. steel production was about 101 million metric tons. By 2004, the world steel capacity was nearly 1.2 billion metric tons and expected to increase to more than 1.3 billion per year in 2006.

At the close of 2003, Japan was leading the world in steel packaging recycling with 86 percent, followed by South Africa with 63 percent according to *European Report.* More steel was being recycled in Europe than ever before, with about 60 percent of total steel packaging being recycled. Belgium recycled the most steel packaging with 93 percent, and Portugal recycled the least with 28 percent. Australia's total was 59 percent, and the United States recycled 43 percent.

CURRENT CONDITIONS

Demand was also rising in the 2000s, particularly from the booming Chinese market. According to the International Iron and Steel Institute, China's steel demand was up to about 282 million metric tons in 2004, an increase of 11 percent over 2003, and was expected to rise another 10.7 percent in 2005. By 2010, China's steel use had increased to 579 mmts and was predicted to reach 595 mmts in 2011. The cost of steel production was also rising, particularly in the United States, despite the lifting of the 2002 tariffs. According to *Automotive News,* steel prices increased as much as 50 percent from December 2003 to June 2004. Prices of steel were subject to change between the time of agreement and the time of shipment. Scrap steel alone was priced at about US$310 per ton in early 2004. The automotive industry was also a major consumer of hot-rolled steel; General Motors alone required 24,000 tons of steel per day.

Minimills, which produce steel products from recycled materials rather than raw ores, continue to deliver better fiscal results than integrated mills, which create steel from raw minerals. This stems in part from minimills' use of scrap metals, which has prices that tend to fluctuate favorably with crude steel prices so that when steel prices are down, minimills do not pay high prices for their raw materials.

United Steelworkers Union (USW) members protested the closing of Weyerhaeuser Corporation's OSB 2000 mill in 2008. The mill, located in northern Saskatchewan, was an integral part of a small community's economic future and was the last operating Weyerhaeuser mill in the Canadian province. USW Local 1-184

President Paul Halen vehemently expressed his concerns in a letter to Phil Dennet, vice president of Strand Technologies for Weyerhaeuser. Halen acknowledged that there was deterioration in market conditions but did not believe that it was cause to close the mill completely. The USW, representing more than 280,000 laborers in every sector of the economy, was Canada's most diverse union. In 2010, the United Steel Workers union had 1.2 million active and retired union members globally.

Due to the inclusion of major wage and benefit increases, the United Steelworkers believed a new standard for the industry was set with a tentative four-year contract reached within U.S. Steel. The proposed settlement, which covered 16,000 steelworkers at 12 plants, provides bonus and enhanced benefit programs for active employees and retirees as well as reduced health care premiums for retirees. The contract was set to replace a five-year pact due to expire September 1, 2008.

RESEARCH AND TECHNOLOGY

Research and technology played a heightened role in the global steel industry going into the mid-1990s. Scientific advances were vital to developed nations in their efforts to maintain market share in the face of challenges from low-cost foreign competitors. Improvements in minimill production, for instance, were essential to producers in Western Europe, Japan, and North America. A major drawback of minimills before the late 1980s was their inability to efficiently produce sheet and strip steel. However, SMS Chloemann-Sieman AG (or SMS Concast) of Germany developed a "thin-slab" casting technique that allowed minimills to continuously cast steel in thicknesses of less than two inches. This important development, combined with emerging strip-casting technology, has allowed minimills to compete in the last bastion of the integrated mills, sheet and strip steel, which is preferred by many industries (such as the automobile sector) because it is easier to process.

Nucor Corp.'s Crawfordsville, Indiana, plant was the first minimill to integrate large scale thin-slab casting. The plant began turning out sheet steel in 1989 under the watchful eye of the worldwide steel industry. Other important thin-slab minimill operations began shortly thereafter in Germany and Italy. The initial success of those operations resulted in plans for similar thin-slab minimills in the mid-1990s. Nucor, for example, opened a plant in 1992 that was capable of thin-slab casting of about 1 million tons of steel annually. It subsequently announced plans to double that capacity by year-end 1994. Luna ECR (Endless Casting Rolling), introduced at an Italian mill by Danielli in 2000, was a technique that could process 500,000 tons of bar. Danielli was working on refining the process to make it economical for specialty steels such as stainless steel.

Related advances included efforts to develop both thin-slab and thin-strip minimill processes that reduce finished steel contaminants inherent in the production of steel from scrap. Researchers hoped that advances in this area would allow minimills to compete with integrated mills in automobile and other major industries that require high-grade flat steel. Notable techniques being developed or implemented in the mid-1990s that promised to increase the quality and efficiency of thin casting included: in-line strip production (ISP), which was being pioneered in Italy; integrated compact mill (ICM) innovations under development by Voest-Alpine of Austria; and the Tippins-Samsung Process (TSP).

Computers promised to bring down costs and pollution while improving the quality of steel produced. In the mid-1990s, Usinor in France introduced SACHEM, a computer software program that runs blast furnaces. The program continuously monitors and processes thousands of factors in the furnaces, including temperature, water pressure, and oxygen supply. Not only did SACHEM produce better steel, it also extended the life of the furnaces more than a third, decreased the generation of greenhouse gases, and reduced costs US$1.55 per ton. The European Union was pleased with the results of SACHEM and looked to introduce more efficient technologies.

In addition to production-related advances, research and technology efforts produced better grades of steel in the mid-1990s. Carbon steel continued to comprise the vast majority of industry output. However, alloy, stainless, tool, and HSLA steels offered higher profit margins and better opportunities for growth, especially for industrialized nations. Steelmakers tried to protect existing markets by offering low-weight, high-strength, malleable, corrosion-resistant steels that were better than existing plastics or aluminum. Other industry observers have pointed to innovations such as high-performance steel coatings made with synthetic materials as keys to future industry growth. Such steel coating actually registered marked sales gains in the mid-1990s on the strength of potentially vast markets such as the roofing industry. Proponents contended that coated steel roofing systems installed in the mid-1990s could last 40 years with minimal maintenance.

In the mid-2000s, research in Japan's Steel Research Center was focused on eliminating "creep," which is the natural change in the makeup and structure of metal over time, particularly when it is subjected to pressure or heat. A type of steel was being manufactured that was able to withstand such deformation, making the steel product last considerably longer. The new steel was fortified with carbonitride nanoparticles, which filled in the gaps

between steel molecules in order to hold them in place and form stronger bonds. The technology was in the early stages by late 2003, as the new steel still had to prove its flexibility and corrosion resistance.

INDUSTRY LEADERS

Arcelor Mittal. With annual output of 45 million metric tons and 2009 sales of US$65.11 billion, Arcelor was the undisputed steel champion. Formed by a three-way merger between Arbed of Luxembourg, Usinor or France, and Aceralia of Spain, Arcelor was based in Luxembourg.

The 1997 acquisition of Aristrain, a medium-sized European steelmaker, vaulted Luxembourg's Arbed SA from seventh largest to the world's third largest steel company by volume. Its combined holdings manufactured some 24.1 million metric tons of crude steel in 2000. Although it had a diverse product line, the company was heavily involved in supplying Europe's auto industry with steel.

France's Usinor SA was the sixth-ranked steel manufacturer with 2000 output of 21 million metric tons. The company was created in 1988 by the merger of French steel giants Usinor and Sacilor, both of which had been government-owned since the early 1980s when the French industry was in crisis. As a private company, Sacilor dated back to the eighteenth century, and Usinor was formed from a 1948 merger of two French steel companies. By the early 1980s the two were the pillars of the French steel industry in terms of production, but they faced high debt and poor market conditions. The French government intervened and acquired both companies. The subsequent merger, combined with later acquisitions, resulted in a company that produced more than 90 percent of France's steel in the early 1990s. The company produced its steel primarily through integrated mills. Usinor-Sacilor remained government-owned until 1995, when it re-privatized, and it was renamed Usinor SA in 1997. The company extended its global reach during the early and mid-1990s by investing heavily in European and overseas steelmaking operations. It also entered into numerous joint ventures with other companies to develop new steelmaking technologies.

The family-owned and run Netherlands-based Mittal Steel was created in late 2004 with the merger of the public company Ispat International (70 percent owned by the Mittal family) and the Antilles-based LNM Holdings (100 percent owned by the Mittals). The combined company became of the world's largest steel companies, producing 42.8 million metric tons in 2004. Some of the company's leading clients included Ford Motor, General Motors, Maytag, and Whirlpool. The company's 2004 sales totaled more than $22 billion while net income stood at $4.7 billion.

Plans were announced in August 2008 for Arcelor Mittal to spend US $1.6 billion to build steelworks that would address Brazil's supply demands. Arcelor Mittal was expected to nearly double its Brazilian output of long carbon steel used to make machines and construct buildings to approximately 6.5 million metric tons a year by mid-2011. The company stated that its production of wire rod, bars, rebars and structural sections "recognizes the important growth potential of the domestic market" in Brazil.

Arcelor Mittal announced plans to build a US$600 million steel mill in Mexico and buy a U.S. coking coal plant, according to the *Economic Times* in August 2008. The plant in Mexico was expected to supply the Mexican government's plan to upgrade infrastructure and build more housing. However, also in 2008, Arcelor Mittal announced it planned to close several plants including Bethlehem Steel and LTV Steel.

With the acquisition of International Steel Group, world steel leader Mittal Steel Company N.V. formed subsidiary Mittal Steel USA and surpassed the United States Steel Corporation in 2004 to become the top U.S. steel mill. Mittal merged ISG's operations with those of its North American subsidiary, Ispat Inland. Arcelor Mittal reported 2009 sales of US$65.11 billion with 281,700 employees.

Nippon Steel Corporation. Japan's Nippon Steel has shown solid growth to arrive at its status as the world's second largest steel producer. Its annual crude steel output is approximately 35 million tons. The company rose to prominence during the post-World War II industrial boom in Japan. By the early 1990s, Nippon was producing well over US$20 billion worth of steel from eight different iron and steel making plants. Nippon produces its steel primarily through integrated mills. During the late 1980s and early 1990s the company cut costs and overhead in an attempt to remain competitive in the increasingly crowded steel export market. Lackluster performance forced the company to step up those efforts in the early 1990s. The company has also attempted to reduce the share of its sales dependent on steel because it has numerous nonsteel subsidiaries, but as of 2000 steel continued to account for nearly three-quarters of its annual revenues. By the mid-2000s, Nippon was promoting its energy and engineering sectors most heavily. The company posted sales of US$36.5 billion in 2007 with 50,077 employees in 2009.

Nippon Steel stepped up its plan in 2005, for recycling waste plastic into coke by 30 percent. To that end, they invested over US$38 million to install equipment at two of its main facilities. In 2006, Nippon Steel and Mitsubishi Heavy Industries merged forces to create a high tensile strength steel that was used for the hulls of container ships. In 2006, Nippon Steel announced a pilot program to process waste food into ethanol.

Pohang Iron and Steel Co., Ltd. Producing approximately 31 million tons of crude steel per year in 2003, POSCO of South Korea reported US$31.9 billion in revenues in 2009, with nearly 30,000 employees. POSCO enjoyed a rapid ascent to the front ranks of international steel producers. The company was formed in 1968 with the help of the South Korean government. In late 2000, under pressure from the United States, POSCO was fully privatized when the Korea Development Bank sold the government's last 7 percent share in the company. At the same time, the Korean government announced it was doing away with restrictions on foreign ownership in POSCO. The company's production facilities were among the most technologically advanced and efficient in the world. POSCO had ventures in the United States, China, and elsewhere. By 2003, in fact, POSCO was exporting approximately 2.5 million tons of steel to China and was planning to invest well over US$1 billion in China operations by 2006. It formed a strategic venture with Japan's Nippon Steel in 2000. In 2006, they completed construction of their sixth continuous galvanizing line, which places them in the number two position as producer of sheet steel. In 2007, Warren Buffett's Berkshire Hathaway company purchased a stake of 4 percent in POSCO.

ThyssenKrupp AG. Another product of a late 1990s merger, ThyssenKrupp was formed by the merger of Thyssen AG and Friedrich Krupp AG, both leaders in Germany's steel industry. Thyssen was founded in 1891. It supplied the German war machine during both world wars, although output was severely curtailed following World War II. The company posted a steady recovery, however, and its steel output peaked in 1974 at about 17 million tons. As the German steel industry slumped during the late 1970s and 1980s, Thyssen diversified into other industries. The company announced a 21 percent decline in net profits for the second quarter of 2008. ThyssenKrupp experienced a drop in net income due to high stainless steel prices during the prior year, and their steel division was hurt by high-raw material costs, pre-operating expenses for new steel mills, and restructuring expenses. By 2009, Thyssen was reporting annual sales of US$34.5 billion. ThyssenKrupp AG had 2009 sales of nearly US$53.7 billion and a workforce of nearly 187,500 employees.

Corus Group plc. The Corus Group originated from British Steel's acquisition of the Dutch firm Koninklijke Hoogovens. British Steel had grown out of the 1967 privatization of the British steel industry, during which 14 U.K. firms merged. With nearly US$17.9 billion in 2004 sales, Corus produced a variety of steel products, which it sells in large part to the auto and construction industries. Most of Corus' sales were made to nations of the European Union. In 2006, Corus agreed to Tata Steel's takeover bid. Tata Steel was the largest steelmaker in the world, producing more than 100 million tons annually. After a bidding war with Brazilian steelmaker CSN, Tata acquired Corus for US$11.3 billion in 2007.

Corus realized US$600 million in internal performance improvements that were generated through various projects. Each of Corus' main divisions were impacted by company initiatives for ongoing improvements. In addition, Corus recorded a liquid steel production of 20.3 million tons for 2008 compared to 18.8 million in 2006. Deliveries were reported at 23.1 million tons for 2008 against 21.6 million tons in 2006. In 2010, Tata Steel realized a revenue of more than US$21.58 billion and had more than 81,250 employees.

MAJOR COUNTRIES IN THE INDUSTRY

China. Advances by China's steel industry during the 1980s and 1990s catapulted it to the forefront of the steel industry. In the early 1950s China produced only 2 million metric tons of steel annually. With help from the Soviet Union, it increased capacity to about 19 million tons by 1960. After the Soviet Union withdrew in 1960, output plummeted and recovery was slow. By the late 1970s, in fact, China's annual production of steel was less than 25 million tons. Output increased to 40 million tons in 1983, however, as China launched a concerted effort to increase capacity. The government-controlled industry produced 60 million tons of steel by 1989. Output surged to 80 million tons in 1992 and then 89 million tons a year later. By 1996, China surpassed the United States and Japan in annual production when it reached 101.2 million metric tons. In 2000 it reached 127.2 million metric tons and by 2004, China produced more than 270 million tons, up 22.5 percent from 2003. Steel prices were reporting corresponding increases, rising from 30 to 50 percent from the end of 2003 to the middle of 2004 alone. There was a 24 percent decline in steel imports by China in 2004 while Chinese steel exports doubled to more than 17 million metric tons. The Chinese demand for steel was expected to grow exponentially for the foreseeable future, and production was expected to reach 340 million tons by 2006, representing 30 percent of total world steel production.

In 2009, China's steel production reached 567.8 million metric tons, to make it the industry leader by a long shot. According to the World Steel Association, China's steel use in 2010 is predicted to increase by 6.7

percent to 579 mmt, after an exciting increase of 24.8 percent in 2009. The 2011 forecast for China steel use is expected to slow to 2.8 percent bringing it to 595 mmt. China will account for 45.5 percent of the world apparent steel use, compared to 48.4 percent in 2009.

China's steel industry is also much less advanced than those of the leading industrial powers. During the 1980s, in fact, much of the steel-making equipment that China purchased was used equipment from Japan, the United States, and Western Europe. With easy access to raw materials and inexpensive labor, but little scrap metal, much of China's manufacturing capacity in the early 1990s was Attributable to large, integrated, and sometimes antiquated plants that relied on huge numbers of workers. China's largest steel plant, Anshan, employed 220,000 workers in 1990, while the entire Japanese steel industry employed fewer workers. In the late 1980s and early 1990s, however, the country began to invest in more advanced facilities that incorporated BOF and continuous casting technology. Observers also noted that while China had been a rising star in global steel, most of the growth resulted from internal demand. China exported only 6 percent of its steel output in 1994, but China's steelmakers increased their share of the international market in later years. Although the Chinese industry remained considerably more fragmented than those of other leading countries, in the late-1990s China successfully took the first steps to rationalize its sprawling steel industry. Between 1997 and 2000, China's leading firm, Shanghai Baosteel, jumped from nineteenth place in world rankings to tenth.

Japan. With approximately 7.17 percent of global production in 2009, Japan had slipped to the number three spot in world steel production. Prior to World War II, Japan's steel industry had been among the world's largest. After the war, however, national steel output plummeted to only 5 million metric tons. Japan gradually rebuilt its industrial base, boosting production to 23 million tons by 1960 and to more than 90 million tons by 1970. Industry output and employment peaked during the early 1970s at about 120 million tons annually and 350,000 workers, respectively. Like other industrialized nations, Japan's steel output gradually shrank, reaching a low of 97 million tons in 1983, in the wake of dormant market growth and increased competition from industrializing nations. Japan's domestic demand remained flat in 1998 and 1999, only picking up in 2000 when Japanese steel consumption jumped from 68.9 million metric tons to 76.1 million metric tons. In 2009, Japan steel production reached 87.5 million metric tons, a sizable decline from the 120.2 mmt it produced in 2007.

Unlike steel producers in the United States and Europe, Japanese manufacturers benefited from several factors in the 1980s. Massive growth in the domestic production of automobiles and other consumer and industrial goods pushed Japanese steel production upward to around 100 million tons and even surged as high as 110 million tons in 1990. Although Japan fared much better than its industrialized peers during the 1980s, it still suffered from outside competitive pressures and waning domestic demand. By the late 1980s Japanese steelmakers had clearly lost much of their productivity advantage and regional competition proliferated. Steel imports rose, but still accounted for only 7 percent of domestic steel consumption by the early 1990s. At the same time, however, a steadily rising yen hurt export demand and the nation's economy slumped into an ugly recession, leaving domestic steelmakers battered.

Japanese steel output reached 101.6 million metric tons in 1995 and 104.5 million metric tons in 1997, just before the Asian financial crisis hit. By 1999 output had decreased to 94.2 million metric tons. Ailing producers continued scrambling to sustain profitability. Since the mid-1980s, in fact, most companies had embarked on streamlining programs that included consolidation of blast-furnace operations, installation of new equipment, and reductions in labor costs as industry employment in Japan fell from 459,000 in 1970 to less than 200,000 in 1999. Cost-cutting efforts continued in the early 1990s as some companies cut into management ranks, reduced production capacity, and stepped up efforts to update mill technology. Looking ahead to the late 1990s, many Japanese steel producers sought joint ventures or invested in production facilities in China, Thailand, and other countries. In the early 2000s, Japanese companies were taking bold steps toward consolidation. Nippon Steel forged a strategic alliance with its competitor POSCO. In early 2001 NKK Corp. and Kawasaki Steel Corp., Japan's second and third largest steel makers, respectively, announced a merger that would form the largest steel producer in Japan.

United States. The United States was relegated to fourth place in terms of industry production following China's mid-1990s ascent. U.S. steel shipments slipped to under 80 million tons in 1991, but a strong manufacturing sector contributed to a rise in output in 1994 and 1995 to roughly 90 million tons. Indeed, the mid-1990s marked a period of tremendous success for U.S. steelmakers, whose shipments peaked in 1997 at 98.5 million metric tons. Production dropped again in 1998 and 1999, falling as low as 97.4 million metric tons. The U.S. industry reached 98.9 million metric tons in 2004, up from 93.7 million metric tons in 2003. By 2009, U.S. steel production had declined to 58.1 mmt, or 4.7 percent of the world's total, pushing the U.S. to fifth place.

The United States dominated global steel production until the early 1970s. Output plummeted, however, from about 120 million tons in 1970 to a discouraging low of 67 million tons in 1982. Inefficient and outdated, U.S. steelmakers embarked on a period of painful restructuring. The workforce was slashed from 521,000 in 1970 to 204,000 in 1990, and 151,000 in 2000. Long-established methods and practices were re-examined as well.

While restructuring was an important element of the U.S. steel recovery, the minimill revolution was also vital to the industry's reversal of fortune. By the early 1990s, highly efficient minimills were producing about 35 percent of U.S.-made steel. Minimill production continued strongly into the 2000s. TXI Chaparral Steel spent $400 million on a minimill in Petersberg, Virginia, and Ipsco and Steel Dynamics each built new facilities. Nucor completed a plant in Cofield, North Carolina, and planned another one in Crawfordsville, Indiana. In fact, Nucor's expansion pushed it past long-time U.S. industry leader U.S. Steel. The importance of the minimill sector to the U.S. steel resurgence was supported by industry statistics. Between 1986 and 1991, for example, U.S. minimills enjoyed sales growth of 66 percent, while integrated producers gained only 1 percent. During the same period, employment at minimills jumped 19 percent while employment at integrated facilities dropped 30 percent. Most importantly, U.S. minimills showed an average profit of US$32 per ton during the late 1980s and early 1990s, while integrated producers gleaned only US$3 per ton. Armed with such minimill productivity, domestic producers were able to effectively buffet growing threats from low-cost, loosely regulated foreign producers. The U.S. steel industry had hoped to maintain its lead in the conversion to minimill production. It was also expected to focus on the development of high-tech, high-margin steel products intended to open new markets and allow steel to compete with synthetic and metal substitutes.

The Russian Federation. While China's rise during the late 1980s and early 1990s in the international steel industry was rapid, it was not as dramatic as the decline of the Russian steel industry. Russia remained the fourth largest steel producer in the world in 1997. For most of the 1990s, the country was the world's fourth largest manufacturer of steel, but its annual results were shrinking steadily. In 1999 Germany surpassed Russia in production. By the end of the twentieth century, however, Russia staged a stirring turnaround, putting out 51.5 million metric tons, and in 2000 the figure rose again to 59.1 million metric tons. By 2004, Russian production of crude steel stood at 65.6 million metric tons, up from 61.5 million metric tons the previous year. In 2009,

Russian steel production had fallen to 59.9 mmts, or 4.9 percent of the world's total.

The downturn in output in the Russian Federation and the other members of the Commonwealth of Independent States (CIS) was the result of a number of factors. A deteriorating industrial infrastructure, skyrocketing energy prices, stifling taxes, weak defense-related demand, and plummeting consumer-related demand all contributed to the country's woes. The Russian government turned to privatization and outside financing to update its production facilities, but the Russian Federation's steel output had not recovered by the late 1990s. Nonetheless, in 2001 Russia and the Ukraine had a combined 56 million tons of excess production capacity, a discrepancy that resulted in Russia selling steel to developed nations at prices sometimes lower than the cost of production, according to some U.S. firms. Some argued that treaties guaranteeing U.S. purchases of Russian steel should be replaced with aid to develop Russia's domestic steel market.

Germany. Germany slipped from fifth to seventh in world steel production in 2009, with its 32.7 million metric tons exceeded by South Korea with 48.6 million metric tons. While levels decreased to 40.5 million metric tons in 2002, output was about 44.8 million metric tons by 2003. Germany's steel output peaked in the 1970s at about 60 million tons. Shipments slid to about 40 million tons by the late 1980s. The East German steel sector, stifled for decades by a government-controlled economy, languished. By the late 1980s its steel output had fallen to about 5 million tons annually. In 1991, following reunification, Germany's steel output was about 43 million tons, although the East continued to lag behind. The German steel industry, although technologically advanced, endured extremely high labor costs and chafed under government regulations designed to protect the environment and address other issues. Critics of such regulatory measures contend that the country's competitiveness in relation to other steelmakers declined in the late 1980s and early 1990s as a result of such legislation. Output dwindled going into the mid-1990s, but a surge in prices buoyed profits for many German producers. As in Japan, some German manufacturers were engaged in a period of reorganization in the mid-1990s as they laid off workers, increased automation, and worked to reclaim the former East German steel sector.

BIBLIOGRAPHY

"Arcelor Mittal Spends $1.6B to Expand in Brazil." *Canadian Press,* 7 August 2008. Available from canadianpress.google.com.

"Arcelor Mittal to Build $600-m Steel Mill in Mexico." *India Times,* 5 August 2008. Available from economictimes. indiatimes.com.

Bagsarian, Tom. "Beyond Steelmaking." *New Steel,* 1 May 2001.

———. "E-commerce: The Growth of Private Company Exchanges." *New Steel,* 1 March 2001.

———. "Faster Heats, Fewer Impurities." *New Steel,* 1 April 2001.

———. "Nucor, Ipsco Lead Spending." *New Steel,* 1 September 2000.

———. "The Recovery Accelerates." *Iron Age New Steel,* 1 January 2000.

———. "Strip Casting Gets Serious." *New Steel,* 1 December 2001.

Berry, Bryan. "Restructuring Steel." *New Steel,* 1 August 2001.

Bright Outlook for Steel Industry in 2005-2006 Forecast at OECD/IISI Conference, Organization for Economic Co-operation and Development, 17 January 2005. Available from www.oecd.org.

"Business: Welding Bells: A European Steel Merger." *Economist,* 24 February 2001.

Chang, Peter. "POSCO Doubling Output of Automotive Steel." *Automotive News,* 31 March 2003.

Chappell, Lindsay. "Scrap Steel Prices See Hefty Decline." *Automotive News,* 5 April 2004.

Cheng, Allen T. "Gearing Up for Battle." *Asiaweek,* 22 December 2000.

Connolly, Allison. "Lower Stainless Steel Prices Hurt Thyssen Krupp Results." 14 August 2008.

Cordes, Renee. "Europe's Steelmakers Get Lean and Green." *Business Week,* 19 February 2001.

Crude Steel Production, Global Steel Production, 19 November 2010. Available from www.almatis.com.

Draper, Deborah J., ed. *Business Rankings Annual.* Detroit: Thomson Gale, 2004.

"EU/OECD." *European Report,* 6 March 2004.

Furakawa, Tsukasa. "Japanese Steelmakers Map Long-Range Strategies." *American Metal Market International Steel Supplement,* 3 October 2000.

Garvey, Robert A. "Getting Serious About Consolidation." *Iron Age New Steel,* 1 February 2001.

———. "How E-commerce Will Add Value." *New Steel,* 1 November 2000.

Graham-Rowe, Duncan. "How Not to Give Steel the Creeps." *New Scientist,* 19 July 2003.

"Healthy Appetite: As Long as Development Economies Need Steel, the Hunger for Scrap Will Continue." *Recycling Today,* January 2005.

Hogan, William T. *Minimills and Integrated Mills: A Comparison of Steelmaking in the United States,* Lexington, MA: Lexington Books, 1987.

———. *Steel in the United States: Restructuring to Compete.* Lexington, MA: Lexington Books, 1984.

"Hoover's Company Capsules." *Hoover's Online,* 2008. Available from www.hoovers.com.

"International Trade Statistics." World Trade Organization, 2003. Available from www. wto.org.

Kolkata. "Corus Delivers $600 mn of Internal Performance Improvements." *Buisness Standard,* 12 August 2008. Available from www.business-standard.com.

Kosdrosky, Terry. "Suppliers Get Deals to Cushion Rising Steel Prices." *Automotive News,* 28 June 2004.

Marsh, Peter. "Arbed Hopes the World Will Prove Its Oyster." *Financial Times,* 29 March 2000.

"Posco Completes Privatization." *New Steel,* 1 November 2000.

"Posco Looks Beyond the Boom in China to Entrench Position." *Australasian Business Intelligence,* 20 November 2003.

"Prime Time for E-commerce." *New Steel,* 1 August 2000.

Rawson, Randy. "Steel Yourself." *Heating/Piping/Air Conditioning Engineering,* April 2004.

"Recycling." *European Report,* 19 November 2003.

Richard, Bob, and Luke Folta. "Steel Demands Outlook Less Than Riveting." *Barron's,* 14 August 2008. Available from online.barrons.com.

Ritt, Adam. "Endless Casting and Rolling of Bar." *New Steel,* 1 November 2000.

———. "Reversing a Legacy of Poor Returns." *New Steel,* 1 January 2001.

"Semi-Fabricated Steel in France, Germany, UK, US." *Euromonitor,* August 2004. Available from www.majormarketprofiles.com.

Serwer, Andy. "This Is Not Your Father's Steel Bubble." *Fortune,* 26 January 2004.

Sherefkin, Robert. "Steel Crisis Drives Supplier to Chapter 11." *Automotive News,* 29 March 2004.

"Specialty Imports Break Record in 2000." *New Steel,* 1 April 2001.

"Stainless: Fewer Players, Faster Growth than Carbon." *New Steel,* 1 December 2001.

"The Table Is Set." *New Steel,* 1 May 2001.

United Steelworkers. *Who We Are.* Available from www.usw.org.

"US Steel Labor Contract Includes Significant Increases Report," 14 August 2008. Available from www.steelguru.com.

"Usinor, Arbed, Aceralia to Form World's No. 1 Steelmaker." *New Steel,* 1 March 2001.

Wilhelm, Paul J. "Consolidation Will Be Selective and Global." *New Steel,* 1 December 2001.

"Will Euro, Asian Mergers Force U.S. Mills to Act?" *Purchasing,* 3 May 2001.

World Steel in Figures: 2005. International Iron and Steel Institute, 2005. Available from www.worldsteel.org.

"World: Steel Output Slows In October 2000." *Metal Bulletin,* 23 November 2000.

"World Steel Production Increases but US Output Slips, IISI Data Shows." *American Metal Market,* 21 June 2005.

World Steel Short Range Outlook, World Steel Association, 20 April 2010. Available from www.worldsteel.org.

Yamaguchi, Yuzo. "Blast Threatens Japan Auto Output." *Automotive News,* 8 September 2003.

MINING

---◼---

MINING, COAL

NAICS CODE(S)

2121. Coal mining companies extract lignite, brown coal, subbituminous coal, bituminous coal, or anthracite from the earth through surface or underground mining techniques. Industry firms may also administer mining operations and off-site preparation plants (also known as cleaning plants and washeries). The industry, particularly in North America, increasingly has touted its reclamation efforts to return soil and landscape to usable condition after all higher grade coal has been mined.

INDUSTRY SNAPSHOT

The global coal industry mines roughly 5 billion tons of material annually. Total recoverable reserves were estimated in the early 2000s at 1.083 trillion tons. Based on the consumption levels through the 2000s, industry analysts estimate that the current coal reserves might last another 119 years. About 60 percent of recoverable reserves were located in three regions: the United States (25 percent), the Russian Federation (23 percent), and China (12 percent). Another 29 percent was found in Australia, India, Germany, and South Africa.

Despite challenges in some applications and in some areas of the world by other energy sources like oil and natural gas, coal regained its worldwide reputation as a lower-cost primary fuel at the beginning of the twenty-first century. Global coal consumption through 2025 was expected to grow at a rate of about 1.5 percent a year, according to the U.S. Energy Information Administration (EIA). Areas of growth include Japan and developing Asian countries where coal has always been regarded as an important source of heat and energy. The United States, where the George W. Bush administration touted coal as an inexpensive answer to the country's costly energy demands, is another growth area. On the other hand, the EIA predicted a drop in use among European and former Soviet Union countries.

Coal has a primary role in supporting global development and alleviating poverty, as well as being a crucial part of the supply chain to meet the world's growing energy needs. As of 2010, coal supplied 27 percent of primary energy and 41 percent of electricity generation. Coal use is predicted to rise more than 50 percent by 2030, with developing countries creating 97 percent of the increase.

India and China were responsible for 36 percent of global coal consumption in 1999, and these two countries alone were expected to account for 67 percent of the increase in demand for coal through 2025. Other countries expected to increase coal consumption markedly by 2020 included South Korea and Taiwan. The anticipated increase in coal consumption led to some optimism on the part of Australian experts, who expected that the 2002 estimates of 3.7 billion metric tons annual consumption could substantially increase to 4.2 billion metric tons by 2010, according to Dudley White in the *Bloomberg News* on January 22, 2002.

Most of the coal mined worldwide in 2004 was used to produce electric power, but other major coal applications included those related to iron and steel production, as well as its use in various process industries like cement and textiles. Coal also remained an important source of home heat in many parts of the world.

Early in the twentieth century, North America and Europe were the two leading coal-producing regions.

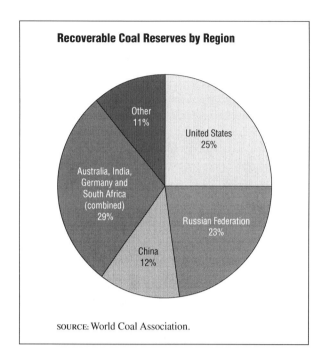

Recoverable Coal Reserves by Region

United States
25%

Other
11%

Australia, India, Germany and South Africa (combined)
29%

China
12%

Russian Federation
23%

SOURCE: World Coal Association.

During the mid-twentieth century, however, production volume shifted to Asia, Australia, and South Africa. By the 1990s North American and Western European mining companies represented only an estimated 35 percent of industry output. Although coal deposits are distributed widely across the world, three regions control about 60 percent of coal reserves: the United States, the Russian Federation, and China. Other top coal-producing countries include Australia, India, Germany, and South Africa.

The coal industry near the end of the twentieth century was generally characterized by weak prices, increasing environmental controls, and labor strife, which were especially prevalent in developed nations. Industry success in the most developed regions was also blunted by increasing foreign competition, stagnant demand growth, and taxes on energy consumption. Producers in North America and Western Europe countered by raising productivity, increasing low-cost surface mining, consolidating, and taking advantage of new environmental technologies. Meanwhile, mining companies near economic growth regions like the Pacific Rim enjoyed significant market expansion and a relatively lenient regulatory climate. Guarded optimism in the industry by 2002 also came from expectations that coal needs in Japan through 2010 could result in more favorable contracts for long-term suppliers.

CNNMoney.com reported that international demand for coal was driving prices for the commodity to "near-record" levels. Calyon Securities analyst Gordon Howard said coal shares had more potential for growth and expected them to climb through 2009. The price of coal used in steel production reflected the high demand for the product. Steam coal, used for producing electricity in boilers, was expected to gain even more as utilities renewed their annual contracts with customers.

Rich Duprey reported that the future outlook for coal was bright throughout the world. Coal was linked to 40 percent of the world's energy needs. India counted on coal for almost 70 percent of its energy supply. China needed coal for 78 percent of its energy supply, which translated to demand for one-quarter of the world's coal consumption.

ORGANIZATION AND STRUCTURE

Coal Types. The five grades of mined coal are brown, lignite, sub-bituminous, bituminous, and anthracite. Each category differs in moisture content, volatile matter, and amount of fixed carbon. As a result, each is distinguished by such factors such energy produced per unit of weight and the amount of pollutants released during burning.

Brown. Brown coal has an extremely high moisture content, sometimes as great as 60 percent or more. The material is relatively easy to mine and to ignite. However, it only produces around 6 million British thermal units (Btu) per ton, the lowest of all the coal grades. In addition, brown coal is difficult to store because it disintegrates when it is exposed to air and occasionally spontaneously combusts. It also has a high sulfur content, which makes it a major pollutant. Brown coal is most heavily mined in Central and Eastern Europe, although the largest reserves in the world are located in Victoria, Australia.

Lignite. Lignite is similar to brown coal in that it is a brownish-black mineral with a high moisture content, containing about 30 percent to 40 percent water. It also deteriorates rapidly in air, has a high sulfur content, and is liable to spontaneously combust. Therefore lignite is used mainly to generate electricity in power plants that are located near mines. It was also used in the early 2000s as a substitute for wood in many Third World countries. In contrast to brown coal, lignite may generate 9 to 17 million Btu per ton. The largest lignite deposits in the world are found in the United States and Canada. Lignite is also mined extensively in Europe and the Commonwealth of Independent States (CIS).

Sub-bituminous. Sub-bituminous coal is composed of 75 percent to 85 percent carbon and only 15 percent to 25 percent moisture. It produces 16 to 24 million Btu per ton and is used mainly to generate electricity. Its high moisture content and other negative properties make it less desirable than higher coal grades for most applications. Significantly, however, sub-bituminous coal contains little sulfur, and in some regions of the world, it is relatively easy to extract using low-cost surface mining techniques. As a result, consumption of this material proliferated in many regions of the world during the late twentieth century.

Bituminous. Bituminous, or soft, coal is the most common coal and is used in a range of applications. It has a deep, dull black appearance. Bituminous coal is composed of 80 percent to 90 percent carbon and about 10 percent to 20 percent moisture, One ton of bituminous coal typically generates 19 to 30 million Btu. The material has a relatively low sulfur content, which enables it to burn more cleanly than lower grades of coal. Because of its properties, bituminous coal is the principal steam coal used for generating electricity. It is also the primary cooking coal used in the steel-making process. The CIS, the United States, China, South Africa, India, and Australia are the leading producers of bituminous coal.

The huge bituminous coal segment can be further categorized as low-, medium-, and high-volatile coal according to its moisture content and heating capacity. Low- and medium-volatility grade bituminous coal typically generates between 18 and 29 million Btu per ton. High-volatile coal, in contrast, usually produces 26 to 30 million Btu per ton. A ton of bituminous coal, assuming an average 22 million Btu, produces about the same amount of energy as one cord of hardwood; 22,000 cubic feet of natural gas; or 160 gallons of fuel oil.

Anthracite. Anthracite, the highest grade coal, is mined in low quantities in only a few countries. In the United States, most of this high-grade coal has been extracted and exhausted for manufacturing purposes. The material burns with a hot, clean flame and contains only 3 percent moisture when it is mined. It also burns more slowly and uniformly than bituminous coal, which makes it excellent blast furnace material for the steel-making process.

Mining Techniques.

Surface Mining. The two principal coal mining techniques are surface and underground. Surface mining is usually practiced on relatively flat ground in situations where the desired coal is located less than 200 feet from the earth's surface. At mines where the coal is located on steep inclines, however, material may be excavated from open pits that can reach depths of several hundred feet. To get to the coal, miners must first remove the overburden, or strata, that covers the coal bed. Between 1 and 30 cubic yards of strata must be excavated for each ton of coal recovered. Dragline excavators, power shovels, bulldozers, front-end loaders, scrapers, and other heavy pieces of equipment are used to move the strata and extract the coal. Manpower is more likely to be used in less developed nations, while coal mining in developed nations is highly automated.

The two common methods of surface mining are strip and auger. At strip mines, large drills bore holes in the strata. Explosives are then placed in the holes and detonated. Power shovels or draglines operating at surface level move the broken strata, while power shovels dig up the exposed coal and load it onto trucks. The strata and coal are removed in long strips, with the debris from the newest strip being dumped onto an adjacent strip from which the coal has already been recovered. Auger mining consists of boring a series of holes that are 2 to 5 feet in diameter. These holes are bored parallel to one another to depths of 300 or more feet. They are bored so that they are placed horizontal to a seam of coal that has already been exposed by an outcropping or by strip mining methods. No blasting takes place, and the overburden is left intact. The coal is removed and loaded into waiting trucks. Auger mining is frequently used in open-pit mines where the strata is too thick to economically remove via strip methods.

The key advantages of surface mining are the low cost and high extraction rate. Surface mining is typically much more productive than traditional underground mining and can cost less than half as much per ton of coal produced. Mining companies are typically able to remove about 90 percent of the coal at surface mines, while underground mines permit only 50 percent to 80 percent extraction, depending on the mining methods used.

Underground Mining. Underground mining methods are typically used to extract coal that lies 200 to 1000 feet below the earth's surface, although some mines extend as deep as 2,000 feet. Underground mines consist of a series of parallel and interconnecting tunnels from which the coal is cut and removed with special machinery. The process is complex and sometimes dangerous. The mine must be adequately ventilated to protect miners from dust and explosive methane gas that is released by the coal. In addition, careful ground control must be practiced to prevent the roof of the mine from collapsing on workers and equipment.

Three types of coal extraction methods are used in underground operations. Drift mines feature a level tunnel that leads into the mine, while slope mines have an inclined tunnel, and shaft mines feature a vertical tunnel. The primary methods of extracting coal from all of these mines are room-and-pillar, longwall, and shortwall. Room-and-pillar mining is often the least efficient method, typically recovering only about 50 percent of the coal. Some room-and-pillar mines, however, can achieve a much greater recovery percentage. Longwall and shortwall mining practices, in comparison, enable miners to extract up to 80 percent of the usable coal.

In a room-and-pillar operation, coal is mined in a series of rooms cut into the coal bed. Pillars of un-mined coal are left intact to support the mine roof as miners advance through the coal seam. Sometimes the coal in the pillars can be extracted later in the retreat phase of operation. The two basic types of room-and-pillar mining are conventional and continuous. Conventional mining consists of a series of operations that involve cutting and breaking up the coal, blasting the bed, and then removing the shattered coal. Continuous mining, on the other hand, uses a machine that digs and loads coal in one operation without blasting. About 90 percent of room-and-pillar coal was extracted using continuous mining in the early 1990s.

Longwall mines use huge machines with cutting heads. The heads are pulled back and forth across a block of coal up to about 600 feet long. Coal is sheared and plowed into slices that are removed by a conveyor. Movable roof supports allow mined-out areas to cave in behind the advancing machine. Shortwall mining is similar to longwall operations, but the continuous mining machine shears smaller blocks of coal that are usually less than 150 feet long.

Processing. Members of the coal mining industry have to secure large quantities of material to be profitable. A relatively small fraction of mined material, often 20 percent or less, contains usable coal. That material is usually hauled from the mine to processing plants, where it is crushed, sized, cleaned, and washed. Refuse, ash, and pyritic sulfur are removed in the cleansing process to make the coal easier to transport and to increase its heating value. About 28 percent of the raw coal that makes it to the plant is removed as waste. After it is processed, different types of coal are often blended to produce uniform grades of commercial material. Blending may also occur at the point of use.

End Uses. Two divisions of coal output are steam and metallurgical. Steam coal, which consumes the vast majority of industry output, is most often used to power electric utilities. Metallurgical, or cooking, coal is used for industrial applications, particularly iron and steel production. Although they are classified as part of the same industry, steam and metallurgical coal differ in their reserve base, production facilities, distribution channels, and marketing requirements. Other major uses for coal include glass making, cement production, and other industrial uses.

BACKGROUND AND DEVELOPMENT

Coal is not a true mineral, but rather an organic compound formed from the remains of living organic material

deposited on the earth's surface 250 to 400 million years ago. The Chinese are believed to be the first to have used coal on a large scale, in about 1000 B.C. The Romans are also believed to have burned the material. The first written history of coal mining dates back to 1200 A.D., when metalworkers in Europe were observed using it. Widespread use of coal did not occur in Europe until the fifteenth and sixteenth centuries, but by the fourteenth century smog conditions were observed where large amounts of coal were being burned. Advancements that significantly promoted the use of coal during the eighteenth century included Abraham Darby's use of coal instead of charcoal in blast furnaces and forges and the coal-burning steam engine perfected by James Watt.

The advent of the steam locomotive in the mid- and late nineteenth century ignited a huge expansion of the coal industry. The development of this new distribution channel in conjunction with the start of the Industrial Revolution, resulted in massive industry growth. Between 1865 and 1905 global coal output ballooned from 182 million tons to 928 million tons as coal displaced wood as the world's primary industrial energy source. The United Kingdom led world coal production throughout the nineteenth century but was surpassed by the United States in 1900. By 1935 world output stood at 1.18 billion tons, about 250 million tons of which was mined in the United States.

Growth in the use of coal as an energy source and as an important part of iron and steel production continued at a moderate pace during much of the mid-twentieth century in most industrialized countries. By 1958, for instance, annual demand for coal in the United States stood at about 400 million tons. By the 1950s, however, massive growth in demand in previously undeveloped regions such as the former Soviet Union and China pushed annual global consumption past 2.5 billion tons. The Soviet Union, in fact, had surpassed the United States as the top coal-producing nation in the late 1950s, although the United States later regained its lead.

Demand for coal continued to increase during the 1960s and 1970s, despite the increasing popularity of alternative energy sources, such as petroleum, natural gas, and hydro-power. However, by the 1980s coal's share of the world energy market had declined from about 60 percent in 1950 to roughly 30 percent. Analysts predicted a resurgence in the popularity of coal during the oil crises of the late 1970s and early 1980. However, oil prices eventually dropped and coal demand grew only moderately from 1980 through 2001. Under the administration of President George W. Bush, the federal government once again became a proponent of large-scale coal use as a power source, attempting to quell vehement environmental protests with assurances that the administration was solidly behind development of cleaner coal-burning technologies.

Proliferation of Surface Mining. Coal was first taken directly from exposed ledges and outcroppings. When this meager supply was consumed, miners began to scratch beneath the earth's crust by utilizing surface, or opencut, mining methods. After easily accessible surface coal was extracted and the strata became too thick to remove, companies were forced to mine for coal using costly underground operations. Underground mines, however, could not safely access coal that was close to the earth's surface because the risk of mine collapses was too great. For this reason, much of the coal that lay just beneath the earth's surface, but under thick strata, remained inaccessible throughout the nineteenth and early twentieth centuries.

In the 1960s and 1970s, improved earth-moving equipment catapulted the surface, or strip, mining industry to center stage in some major coal-producing regions. New tools allowed miners to remove overburden more than 200 feet thick. Massive power shovels, many taller than a 12-story building, were developed that could remove up to 115 cubic yards of debris in a single scoop, and new earth-hauling trucks were capable of handling equivalent capacities. Coal companies found that new surface mining techniques were often less expensive and more efficient than even the best underground mining technology. Surface mining grew in popularity as a result. Surface mining accounted for only 35 percent of total U.S. coal production in 1965, but by the late 1970s auger and strip mining operations accounted for 60 percent of industry output.

Industry Development in the 1980s and 1990s. During the 1970s and 1980s industrialized nations reduced their emphasis on coal as an energy source, primarily for reasons related to pollution caused by mining and burning coal. Mining companies throughout Western Europe and the United States were stung by narrow restrictions governing coal mining processes and limits on permissible pollution levels during the burning process. Battles between management and labor unions further disrupted companies in developed countries. In contrast, many developing nations in Asia and South America greatly increased coal output and consumption as producers in those regions took advantage of comparatively lax environmental regulations and low labor costs.

During the 1980s, coal companies in the United States made great strides in productivity by integrating advanced mining technology, slashing workforces, and boosting surface mining. European producers also worked to improve productivity, although their gains were typically meager compared to the United States. The end result was a decline in output in many industrialized nations (with the exception of the United States and Canada) and significant global market share gains by producers in developing regions.

Annual world coal production hovered under the 5 billion-ton mark during the late 1980s and early 1990s. Coal output in developed nations stagnated or decreased during the global economic downturn of the early 1990s. During that time, sales of coal to energy producers slumped, as did demand for high-quality cooking coal for steelmaking. Low prices also dogged competitors. Hardest hit were state-run coal producers in the Soviet Union and Eastern Bloc nations. These countries had been suffering production declines since the late 1980s. When the Soviet Union finally dissolved in 1991, the coal industry in the region further deteriorated.

In contrast, coal production in many developing regions continued to surge during the late 1980s and early 1990s. Coal production in India, for example, jumped about 18 percent between 1986 and 1990 to 200 million metric tons and continued to increase into the early 1990s. Several countries near the burgeoning Pacific Rim enjoyed significant output gains. Australia, for instance, increased coal production 20 percent between 1986 and 1990. By the early 1990s, about half of its 250 million tons of annual production was exported, which made Australia the world's largest coal exporter. Developing nations posting solid output gains included China, Venezuela, Colombia, Zimbabwe, and Pakistan.

CURRENT CONDITIONS

The global coal industry was stronger from the late 1990s through 2010 than it had been in the 1980s and early 1990s. Some industry observers believed that it would continue to see robust growth well into the twenty-first century in terms of actual tonnage of coal mined and consumed rather than in its share of the total energy market. According to the EIA, world trade in coal was expected to increase from 656 million metric tons (mmt) in 2001 to 919 mmt in 2025.

Much of the optimism reported by *Bloomberg News* and other economic sources was due to expectations that Asian imports of coal suitable for conversion to electricity would reach more than 200 million tons by 2010. Other fuels, such as natural gas and oil, were projected to continue to replace coal in North America and Europe, but the anticipated expansion of the global economy, especially in Asia and the Pacific Rim, was expected to increase the demand for coal in these areas where environmental concerns continued to carry less weight than the need for affordable and plentiful energy. The booming economy pushed coal prices from US\$40 per metric ton in 2004 to US\$53 in 2005, according to Morgan Stanley figures published in *Bloomberg News* in an article on January 5, 2005. Increased exports from Indonesia and Australia, however, were expected to lower prices in 2006 to an average of US$46 per ton. By 2008 the cost per ton of coal had reached US$55.

Regionally, the conditions through the early 2000s were more varied. In North America, production was high but low prices and excess production capacity made coal mining less attractive to major companies. Some diversified energy companies, such as Atlantic Richfield, sold their coal mining operations altogether, and mining companies like Cyprus Amax sold some mines in an attempt to maintain profitability.

In Western Europe production was down. Great Britain's coal industry had shrunk considerably in the mid-1990s, and it passed back into private ownership in 1994. Although the U.K. coal industry has improved efficiency since then, with total production estimated at between 21 and 29 million tons in 2010 and projected to be between 15 and 21 million tons in 2016, it faced stiff international price competition. Furthermore, because most U.K. coal is high-sulfur, emissions control costs are expected to remain a significant factor limiting profitability. Meanwhile, the evolution of the European Union toward a single economy forced member countries like Germany and Spain to begin cutting back subsidies to their mining industries, creating great opposition from powerful unions. A German restructuring plan announced in 2003 called for production drops through 2012.

Coal production in Eastern Europe and the former Soviet Union continued to decline. Poland, Russia, and other countries struggled to create market economies, but their coal industry especially suffered. In Poland, Russia, and the Ukraine, the government closed a number of mines in order to stem economic losses. Thousands of miners lost their jobs, and in Russia miners went for months without pay. In Poland, in particular, environmentalists and world geologists alike became alarmed by the emissions pumped into the atmosphere by coal-burning electric plants. Responding to a continued drop in demand, Poland in 2003 announced that by 2020 it would close 12 of its 35 coal mines. The country persisted with comprehensive restructuring plans after joining the European Union in 2004, announcing a 2 billion euro aid package intended to streamline coal operations and further reduce production capacities.

In Asia and the Pacific Rim, which includes four of the world's leading coal producing countries—China, Indonesia, Australia, and India—prospects were much brighter, despite the financial crisis that struck some countries in the region in the late 1990s.

RESEARCH AND TECHNOLOGY

The three primary fronts for technological advancements in the coal industry in the early 2000s were improvements in, and the implementation of, mining techniques that reduce the cost of extracting coal and therefore expand the base of economically recoverable reserves; breakthroughs related to reducing pollutants that result from burning coal; and new uses for coal to broaden markets and potential applications. The latter two were of greatest importance.

Although coal operations became safer and there was far less waste of coal resources, as technology and machinery improve, there was a down side from a labor perspective: the coal industry in the United States and other developed nations continued to reduce its numbers of workers. In 2000, some 80,000 people were employed in the U.S. coal industry, nearly 10 times fewer than the number employed 80 years earlier.

The ruling of a Georgia court that a Dynergy coal plant had to limit the amount of carbon dioxide it releases was expected to potentially influence permits issued for all new coal-fired power plants in the United States. Yochanan Zakai of Co-op America called for a "moratorium on coal" calling it "the dirtiest of all fossil fuels—it creates more pollution than oil, natural gas and gasoline when burned." Zakai said more than 150 new coal plants were proposed by U.S. utilities since 2000. An opinion Research Corporation poll found 75 percent of respondents would support a five-year moratorium on new coal plants. Zakai claimed activist and consumer responses resulted in 58 coal plants being cancelled, abandoned, or put on hold.

According to Bree Freeman in the July 3, 2008, issue of the *Mining Journal* BP's Statistical Review of World Energy findings show coal continues to be the fastest growing fuel. Global consumption was rising by 4.5 percent, exceeding the 10 year average. Freeman noted that rapid industrialization in China and India had resulted in Chinese coal consumption rising by 7.9 percent. Although that was the weakest growth since 2002, it still totaled more than two-thirds of global growth.

Cleaner Burning. One breakthrough related to cleaner coal burning was the use of fluidized bed combustors. These mechanisms permit power plants to burn high-sulfur and low-quality coal cleanly and with only minimal sacrifice in efficiency. This technology allowed utility plants in some industrialized nations to continue burning coal in spite of more stringent regulations. Other sulfur-reduction techniques under examination use biotechnology. For example, one system under development incorporated genetically engineered bacteria that subsists on a diet of sulfur.

New Applications. Efforts to find new uses for coal in the twenty-first century included research into finely ground coal and oil or coal and water mixtures that could be substitutes for oil at power plants(some plants in the United States were already using this technique in the late 1990s). Researchers also experimented with mixtures of coal and methanol or natural gas. Other promising technologies centered on the use of synthetic fuels, or synfuels, created through the conversion of coal into other fuels and by-products. The primary advantage of the conversion process was that it eliminates the need for costly rail transportation of base coal material. In addition, several significant by-products can be recovered during the conversion process. The by-product methanol, for example, has the potential to become an important source of automobile fuel in the twenty-first century.

The two most popular synfuel processes under development beginning in the 1990s were coal gasification and liquefaction. These techniques were used to convert coal into a variety of clean-burning gases, solids, and liquids. Using these processes, one ton of coal could be converted into the equivalent of 20 to 125 gallons of liquid fuel, 15,000 cubic feet of high-Btu gas, or 75,000 cubic feet of low-Btu gas. Coal liquefaction plants were in operation in South Africa and Spain and under development elsewhere in the late 1990s. The creation of many other by-products was also possible. Some observers contended that the technology could potentially allow coal producers to reclaim energy market share absorbed by the petroleum industry.

INDUSTRY LEADERS

Many of the world's leading commercial coal mining enterprises were part of huge diversified mining companies, unlike state-run operations like China's. Moreover, the remaining large state-run coal operations experienced severe production declines in the late 1990s and in most cases were in the process of being privatized.

Rio Tinto. Rio Tinto, a British and Australian company, involved in gemstone (see **SIC 1499**), industrial mineral, and metal mining (see **SIC 1000**), as well as coal mining, is the world's largest mining company with worldwide mining operations. In 1997 coal was one of its least profitable divisions, accounting for one-seventh of revenue but only 5 percent of profit. Nevertheless, the company announced plans to double its output in the United States from 41 million tons to 85 million tons by 2005 and to expand Australian and Indonesian production from 39 million tons to 48 million tons. The company was also involved in large joint projects with Amcoal and Glencore in Colombian coal fields. A planned open cast coal mine at the Gokwe North energy plant in Zimbabwe, however, which was expected to supply about a third of the country's energy needs, failed to gain adequate government support and was not built. In

2003, Rio Tinto posted net earnings of US$1.5 billion, of which US$157 million was attributed to coal and uranium. Prices for Rio Tinto's coal exports rose sharply in 2004 after China drastically reduced its export levels to divert more coal to domestic consumption. In 2008 and 2009, the company divested three major assets for approximately US$3 billion. In 2009, Rio Tinto sold the Corumba iron ore mine and the Jacobs Ranch coal mine, along with an aluminum smelter plant in China and the company's potash operations for an additional US$2.5 billion. Total revenues in 2009 were US$44.03 billion, with coal accounting for about 20 percent of sales. By 2007, Rio Tinto had 35,000 employees.

Peabody Energy. Peabody Energy Corporation is the largest private-sector coal producer in the world. In the early 1990s British-owned Hanson PLC had acquired Peabody Holding Company Inc. but later spun it off as part of the Energy Group, which was in turn purchased by Texas Utilities in 1998. Part of that transaction included Lehman Merchant Banking Partners becoming owners of Peabody Energy Corporation and its subsidiary Peabody Coal. Restructuring resulted in significant improvements for the company. By 2004, Peabody Energy reported that sales by volume had doubled and that productivity and market share had tripled. In addition, it claimed a 74 percent improvement in its safety record, as well as a 47 percent reduction in production costs per ton. In 2004, Peabody operated 29 underground and surface mines in the United States and three in Australia. The company also owned a 25.5 percent share in the Paso Diablo Mine in Venezuela. Peabody employed 7,900 people worldwide and controlled 9.5 billion tons of reserves, which was more than any other company. In 2003 Peabody produced a total of 203.2 million tons of coal, which generated US$2.8 billion in revenues; a record 106.5 million tons came from the Powder River Basin operations in Wyoming, with the top facility—North Antelope Rochelle Mine—producing 80.1 million tons. Total output rose to 227.2 million tons in 2004, resulting in revenues of US$3.6 billion. In 2006, Peabody sold over 247 million tons. By 2008, Peabody had revenues of US$6.59 billion with 9,200 employees. The company's coal accounted for about 10 percent of the electricity generated in the United States and almost 3 percent worldwide. More than 90 percent of Peabody's sales are to U.S. customers.

Peabody Energy commissioned its El Segundo coal mine to serve Southwest Utilities, with plans to produce 6 million tons of coal per year at this site. El Segundo is also set to supply Tuscan Electric Power Co.'s Springville Generating Station through a long-term contract ending in 2020. In addition, the company signed a 19-year agreement with Arizona Public Service Co. to supply

65 million tons of coal to the Cholla Generating Station near Joseph City, Arizona.

Arch Coal. Arch Coal Inc., created by the 1997 merger of Ashland Coal and Arch Minerals, became the second-largest coal producer in the United States in 2000 and was one of the largest producers globally. A series of major acquisitions through the late 1990s and early 2000s dramatically boosted the company's output and reserves. In 1998 it acquired the Black Thunder, Coal Creek, and Thundercloud mines in Wyoming's Powder River Basin. In 2004, Arch acquired Triton's North Rochelle mine and combined its operations with those of the neighboring Black Thunder, creating the leading mine in the region. In 2005, Arch reported that the Black Thunder mine produced 5,000 pounds of coal every second of every day, 365 days per year.

In 2004 Arch Coal, which mines only low-sulfur coal, contributed about 13 percent of the U.S. coal supply. It operated 21 mines in the western United States and central Appalachia, which produced more than 125 million tons of coal annually. The company also owned proven reserves of 3.7 billion tons. Arch Coal posted revenues in 2008 of US$2.98 billion, an increase from the previous year, with 4,030 employees.

MAJOR COUNTRIES IN THE INDUSTRY

China. With plentiful coal reserves, China was the leading producer of coal in the late 1990s. In 1996 it produced a total of 1.376 billion tons of coal. Its coal exports grew substantially in 1996 as well, reaching about 30 million tons, making China the sixth-leading exporter of coal. Those figures dropped substantially in the late 1990s and 2000 as China made strides toward regulation, greater efficiency, and reduced costs. Between 1998 and 2001 China reportedly closed 400,000 unproductive mines resulting in production dropping from 1.05 billion tons in 1999 to about 950 million tons in 2000. China also became less resistant to overtures from the international business community interested in tapping into the nation's vast coal reserves. In spite of such drops, as of 2007 China continued to be the world leader in both coal production and consumption. That year China produced over 2.8 billion tons of coal (nearly 39.8 percent) of all coal produced worldwide.

Strong economic growth in China in the early 2000s increased demand for coal, which was used primarily for the generation of electricity, but was also used in the industrial sector. According to *Petroleum Economist*, China's use of coal for electricity was expected to balloon from 5.9 quadrillion Btu in 1999 to 17 quadrillion Btu in 2020. Production lags in the early 2000s, however, caused concern about China's ability to meet skyrocketing domestic demand. The *Asia Times* reported on January 5, 2003, that more than 70 percent of the country's electric power was generated by coal. However, an estimated 3 million ton coal supply shortage caused blackouts in power grid zones throughout the country. In late 2003 China ordered producers to boost output to guarantee supplies for power plants. The country also invested in several major energy projects aimed at easing reliance on coal for the production of electricity. The Three Gorges Dam began generating electricity in 2003, and was expected to be able to supply 5 percent of China's total electricity demand by 2010. The West-East Gas Pipeline Project, scheduled to open in 2005, was projected to substantially increase the country's access to natural gas resources. According to the EIA, demand for coal in China's electricity sector will decline by 44 percent by 2025. Non-electricity sectors, on the other hand, which accounted for 58 percent of demand in 2001, were projected to consume a much greater share of China's coal through the early 2000s. The country's first coal liquefaction plant, for example, which converts coal into petroleum products required to meet domestic transportation needs, started operations in 2007, processing up to 5.5 mmt annually.

In spite of improvements, China's coal industry lagged far behind that of more developed nations in the early 2000s. Safety remained a significant concern, with Chinese mines, particularly the small, illegally run operations, being the most dangerous in the world. In a 10-month period in 2001, the government closed 11,882 small mines because of alleged safety violations, during which time China reported 2,378 coal mining-related deaths. Fatalities continued to escalate, and in 2003 alone, according to a CNN report, explosions and other mine accidents claimed 6,702 lives. The BBC reported between 5,000 and 6,000 coal mining fatalities in China in 2004, and in 2005 the single worst mine disaster since 1949 claimed 210 lives at the Sunjiawan mine near Fuxin. In 2004 China produced only 35 percent of the world's coal, but was responsible for 80 percent of coal mining fatalities worldwide. The country's decision in 2003 to boost coal production to meet burgeoning domestic demand caused concern about the potential for even higher casualties in coming years. In 2004, according to the *Asia Times*, China planned to appropriate about US$265 million for safety improvements in its coal mines.

The biggest market for coal from China was Asia, which accounted for 65 percent of the global consumption as of 2010, with China consuming a significant percentage. China, the United States, India, Japan, and South Africa, which are the five largest coal users, accounted for 82 percent of total global use. However, transportation in China was a major problem. The highest quality deposits were in the northern part of the country, far from the major population centers and ports. Coal already used half of the country's railroad capacity and supply did not meet demand. An estimated 11 percent of the world's coal reserves were buried in China, including some of the highest quality coal reserves in the world. In the long term, easy access to burgeoning Pacific Rim economies bodes well for China's coal industry.

The United States. The availability of low-cost coal, which in 2010 accounted for 50 percent of electric power generated in the United States, significantly reduced energy costs for U.S. businesses. According to the EIA, U.S. coal production has averaged more than 1 billion tons of coal annually for the past 15 years. Demand, however, grew by 2.7 percent (reaching 1.12 billion tons in 2008) in the electricity sector and by 1.6 percent in other sectors. Through the late 1990s and early 2000s production from the Appalachian and interior regions declined, while production in western regions increased. Between 1997 and 2002, U.S. coal exports decreased, the number of U.S. mines dropped by 19 percent, and the number of mine workers dropped by 6 percent. According to the National Mining Association, however, the U.S. Energy Information Administration projected a rise in U.S. coal consumption from 1.12 billion tons in 2008 to 1.57 billion tons in 2025. It also projected that the percentage of electricity generated from coal would rise to 52 percent by 2025. A 2001 U.S. National Energy Policy (NEP) report from 2001, however, admitted that the nation was saddled with too many older coal-burning plants that were not fuel-efficient or equipped with scrubbing equipment to reduce health-threatening emissions.

In the mid-1990s, the United States was the second-largest world producer of coal, with about 959 million tons of mined coal of all grades. In 1997 production continued to grow, up 2.3 percent over 1996, despite the decline in prices that had persisted for a decade. Demand for low-sulfur and lower-ash residue coal from the western states, particularly Wyoming Powder River Basin coal, increased due to its low cost and its ability to meet the sulfur emission requirements of the Clean Air Act of 1990. Demand for Appalachian region coal (with the exception of West Virginia coal) lessened because of its higher sulfur content. Some major companies, especially those with interests in the oil industry like Amoco, Exxon, Shell, and Atlantic Richfield, began to divest their coal operations in the mid- and late 1990s. By 2002, U.S. production had increased slightly to 975 million tons of coal, mainly bituminous and lignite.

In 2001 the George W. Bush administration, under fire from environmental groups that objected to mounting piles of coal ash residue and air pollution, promised tax credits and a US$2 billion commitment over the next decade for cleaner coal technology to reduce sulfur

dioxide and nitrogen oxide. However, President Bush also pledged to strengthen the industry and preserve jobs. In 2004, the Mine Safety and Health Administration proposed changes to safety and environmental regulations intended to cut industry costs, but union officials and health workers argued that such measures would weaken environmental and safety regulations. Also in 2004, federal agencies attempted to streamline the permit process for new mines, issuing permits for 14 mountain-top-removal mines in West Virginia, up from only three approved in 2002. A federal judge, however, ordered that 11 of these permits be revoked until more information was available about potential environmental damage from this type of strip mining, which uses high explosives to remove the tops of mountains. According to a federal report released in 2003, rubble from mountaintop-removal mining has buried or damaged 1,200 miles of streams since 1990.

Halimah Abdullah reported in 2008 for McClatchy Newspapers that Mine Safety and Health Administration agency spokesman Matthew Faraci indicated that several new safety rules were established, as well as additional pending regulations. Requirements related to stronger seals in mines to help prevent explosions were approved in 2008. U.S. House of Representatives Democrats claimed that the Bush administration had failed "to work aggressively to keep miners safe on the job."

There were 600 coal generating facilities in the United States as of 2010 and 1,100 manufacturing facilities using coal, according to the EIA. Coal accounted for 32 percent of total U.S. energy production and 23 percent of the total energy consumption. The United States had nearly 262 billion tons of recoverable coal reserves, or 235 years' worth if consumption remained at the 2010 rate. Within the United States, the coal mining industry employed nearly 134,000 people as of 2010.

Russia. Countries that were part of the former Soviet Union that became the Russian Federation were at one time the world's leading producers of coal. In the years following the breakup of the Soviet Union, however, production declined dramatically as the newly independent countries adjusted to the new situation and, in some cases, shifted toward market economies. As of the early 2000s coal still made up about a quarter of the Russian Federation's energy supply.

Russian coal production in 1997 totaled 244 million tons, slightly more than half the 415 million tons produced before the breakup of the Soviet Union, and 4.8 percent less than 1996 production. At the beginning of 1998 Russian coal miners were owed US$27.5 million in back wages and had not been paid for seven months. In November 1997 the government abolished Rosugol, the corporation set up in 1992 to run the coal industry on a commercial basis, and returned the industry to direct government control. The World Bank reported that the Russian coal industry had increased productivity by 77 percent between 1994 and 1999.

By 2002, however, state funding amounted to only 10 percent of mining operations, with private owners taking up the slack. By 2003, according to *CoalTrans* in September/October 2003, Russian coal mining was dominated by three primary players: Siberian Coal Energetic Company, EurasHolding, and Severstal. With an investment of about US$1 billion for the construction and upgrades of facilities, private owners increased productivity to a monthly output of 103.4 tons per miner by 2003. Exports also rose, from 14 million tons in 1999 to a record 42 million tons in 2000. In 2004, Russian government sources reported total coal production of about 308.6 million short tons. In 2008, Russia's coal production had increased to 347 million short tons. Russia's coal consumption also rose in the early 2000s, perpetuating a trend that was expected to continue as the country aimed to reduce its use of domestic oil and natural gas in order to maximize exports of these commodities. Russia as of 2005 ranked fifth in the world for coal production.

CoalTrans went on to report that Russia had sufficient coal reserves to enable it to double production through the early 2000s. However, transportation remained a problem. The average distance between a coal mine and a seaport in Russia was 4,050 kilometers (km), making freight costs a significant issue. Investment in handling facilities at ports in the Russian Far East was expected to increase the country's export capacity.

In June 2008, Russia's technical watch dog announced plans to launch a month-long inspection of safety standards at Siberian coal mines following the death of more than 150 miners over 16 months. Rostekhnadzor planned to invite diverse government and scientific bodies to inspect mines in the Kemerovo region, which has been called the "coal mining heartland" of Russia. The country has been ranked as the world's fifth-largest coal miner and third-largest exporter.

Germany. Germany's coal industry, which experienced tremendous changes in the late 1990s, provides insight into the overall Western European coal mining environment. Throughout the twentieth century Germany was a leading coal producer, but output had fallen since the late 1950s, as it had in many other Western European nations, and other forms of energy had become popular. German coal companies, like those in the United States and Western Europe, had also come under increasing pressure from labor groups and environmental legislation, resulting in a 65 percent drop in output between

1960 and the early 1990s. During the same period, the German coal industry workforce plummeted from more than 450,000 to just over 100,000. Coal industries in other Western European nations similarly suffered. Output in Belgium, for example, fell 40 percent during the 1980s, while production in France declined 20 percent, and the United Kingdom posted a sharp 63 percent drop. In 2006, Germany was still the leader in brown coal production at 194.4 mt.

The German government tried to help domestic coal producers in the Ruhr coal basin with hefty subsidies during the mid-1990s. As a result German coal, priced at about four times the average cost of coal on world markets, became some of the most expensive in the world. However, as the European Union continued to work toward becoming a single economy, Germany, along with other EU member countries, was forced to begin reducing its subsidies. The government's first plan called for a reduction of subsidies from about DM9 billion (about US$5 billion) in 1997 to DM3.8 billion by the year 2005. However, strikes and demonstrations by miners and their supporters forced a compromise that would reduce subsidies to just DM5.5 billion by 2005. In 2003, a policy arrangement among government, industry, and workers agreed to maintain a long-term core mining industry, which could be ensured by downsizing production from 26 million tons in 2005 to 16 million tons by 2012. The mining workforce would be reduced correspondingly to 20,000 people by 2012. In 2003 Germany announced that between 2006 and 2012, some 17 billion euros in aid would be earmarked for the German coal industry.

To shore up the industry the German coal producers merged and created a company called Deutsche Steinkohle, which produced all but 5 percent of Germany's coal at some 15 coal mines. German coal production fell from 540.7 million short tons in 1989 to 230.9 million short tons in 2002. It was, however, the world's fourth largest consumer of coal, importing 43 million short tons in 2002.

India. Next to China, India was expected by 2020 to be the world's leading consumer of coal as an electricity source, unless the price of coal unexpectedly increased due to favorable contracts given to suppliers by such importing nations as Japan. India consumed 359 million short tons of coal in 2000 and was expected to increase demand to 430 million short tons in 2010 according to the EIA. In 2004, coal supplied more than 50 percent of India's energy needs, and 70 percent of coal consumption was used to generate electricity. Since India was a major coal producer and ranked third in the world in 2007 with 529 millions of short tons, it was able to meet most of its domestic demand without significantly increasing imports.

Australia. Due to expectations of profits from growing Asian markets, Australia became the world's leading coal exporter by the early 2000s. Major acquisitions by a small number of multinational coal companies, including Anglo and Glencore, as well as improvements in rail freight service to major coal ports, contributed to record exports exceeding 200 million tons in 2002. Some Australian coal industry experts anticipated that coal exports could increase to 230 million tons by 2010. According to the EIA, about 90.5 billion short tons of coal reserves were in Australia. About 75 percent of its total production is exported each year, mostly to Asian markets, accounting for 28 percent of the global market in coal. Nearly 85 percent of Australia's electricity production was supplied by coal. By 2007, Australia was the world's fourth leading coal producer with production of 428 millions of short tons.

BIBLIOGRAPHY
Abdullah, Halimah. "Little Progress Has Been Made in Mine Safety." McLatchy Newspapers, 19 June 2008. Available from www.mcclatchy.com.

"About Arch Coal." Arch Coal Company, 2005. Available from www.archcoal.com.

"Arch Company Profile." *Hoover's Online,* 2005. Available from www.hoovers.com.

"China Coal Mine Blast Kills 28." CNN, 3 March 2004. Available from edition.cnn.com.

"China Shuts Down 11,882 Small Coal Mines in 10 Months." *People's Daily,* 17 November 2001. Available from www.english.peopledaily.com.

"Coal Prices to Fall 13 Percent in 2006, Morgan Stanley Says." *Bloomberg News,* 5 January 2005. Available from www.bloomberg.com

Coal Statistics, *World Coal Association.* Available from www.worldcoal.org.

Drew, Christopher, and Richard A. Oppel, Jr. "Mines to Mountaintops: Rewriting Coal Policy." *New York Times,* 9 August 2004.

Duprey, Rich. "Is Coal a 4- Letter Word?" *The Motley Fool,* 3 July 2008. Available from www.fool.com.

"Facts about Coal." National Mining Association. Available from www.nma.org.

Freeman, Bree. "Comment: Coal Boom Spurs Equipment Demand." *Mining Journal,* 3 July 2008. Available from www.miningjournal.com.

Ivanov, Andrei, and Judith Perera. "Labor: Unpaid Russian Miners Driven to Desperate Deeds." *Interpress Service,* 6 February 1998.

Nuwer, Hank. "The Coal Truth." *Indianapolis Monthly,* June 2001.

"Over a Third of Polish Mines to Go by 2020." *CoalTrans,* May/June 2003. Available from www.coaltransinternational.com.

Paxton, Robin. "Russia to Inspect Safety at Siberian Coal Mines." Reuters, 20 June 2008. Available from UK.reuters.com.

"Peabody Coal Mine to Supply Southwestern Utilities." *The Business Journals,* 25 June 2008. Available from www.bizjournals.com.

Peabody Energy Annual Report, 2004. Available from www.peabodyenergy.com.

"Poland Plans to Grant Two Billion Euros to Coal Industry." *EUBusiness,* 2 June 2004. Available from www.eubusiness.com.

Project Profile: Russia Coal and Forestry Sector Guarantees Project. Sustainable Energy & Economy Network. Available from www.seen.org.

Rio Tinto Annual Report, 2004. Available from www.riotinto.com.

"Rio Tinto in Zimbabwe." Mbendi Business Reference, 2004. Available from www.mbendi.co.za.

"Rio Tinto Sees Sharp Rise in Thermal Coal Price." Reuters, 8 March 2004. Available from www.biz.yahoo.com.

"Russia Gets Its Act Together." *CoalTrans,* September/October 2003. Available from www.coaltransinternational.com.

Scott. "Byrd Moves to Preserve Coal Mine Safety Funds." *The Charleston Gazette,* 27 June 2008. Available from www.wvgazette.com..

"Spotlight: Coal Demand." *CNNMoney.com,* 27 June 2008. Available from money.cnn.com.

UK Coal Production Outlook: 2004–16. Department of Trade and Industry, London, England. March 2004. Available from www.dti.gov.uk.

United Nations. "United Nations Economic and Social Council, Economic Commission for Europe, ad hoc Group of Experts on Coal in Sustainable Development." *Report,* 14 November 2003. Available from www.unece.org.

U.S. Department of Energy, Energy Information Administration. *Country Profiles,* 2004 Available from www.eia.doe.gov.

———. *International Energy Outlook 2004,* January 2004. Available from www.eia.doe.gov.

White, Dudley. "World Coal Demand May Rise 14 Percent by 2010." *Bloomberg News,* 22 January 2002.

"World Coal: Sluggish Demand Growth, But It's Still Growth." *Petroleum Economics,* 10 September 2001.

Ye, Miao. "The Human Cost of Coal." *Asia Times,* 15 January 2003. Available from www.atimes.com.

"Oppose Mountaintop Removal." Green America, Come Together Web site, 19 October 2007. Available from www.greenamerica.org.

SIC 1499

MINING, GEMSTONE

NAICS CODE(S)

212319. The global gemstone industry is engaged in mining, developing mines, and exploring for gemstones such as diamond, emerald, ruby, sapphire, amethyst, aquamarine, and others.

INDUSTRY SNAPSHOT

The gemstone mining industry comprises two distinct segments: diamond mining and the mining of all other kinds of gemstones, such as ruby and emerald, referred to collectively as colored gemstones. The diamond industry is highly structured and characterized by large corporations and highly mechanized mining operations. Although sub-Saharan Africa dominated diamond mining through the twentieth century, by the first years of the twenty-first century its total output was surpassed by the combined production of Canada, Australia, Brazil, China, and Russia. The colored gemstone industry is highly fragmented and characterized by small organizations and a great variety of mining operations with little mechanization. Significant deposits were being worked on all continents except Antarctica. According to MBendi Research in 2002, the global diamond market had increased more than 250 percent since the late 1970s. Global diamond production reached 150 million carats in 2003, of which 80.9 million carats was gem quality. Australia ranked first in total diamond output, while Botswana ranked first in gem diamond production and value.

The global gemstone power shift that occurred between 2002 and 2006, was largely due to the discovery of the Diavik mine in Canada, which thrust Canada into the role of a major player in the diamond industry by more than doubling Canadian diamond production. De Beers predicted that Canada will continue to play a major role in the diamond industry as more major firms continued to expand their mining operations. Russia has also nearly doubled its diamond production during the last half of the first decade of the 2000s. Russia has jumped from US$1.5 billion to US$2.3 billion since 2005. Global diamond production grew to US$13.1 billion in 2006, a 56 percent increase over US$7.4 billion in 2002.

In terms of dollar value, the most important market for gemstones is the manufacture of jewelry. In terms of volume of production, however, the industrial use of diamonds dominates the gemstone industry. The demand for gem-quality stones fluctuates with the economy, although in the case of diamonds the price is maintained at a high level by the mechanisms of the diamond cartel led by De Beers. The price for some kinds of colored gemstones, such as rubies, is also affected by the availability of the gems.

One of the major problems facing the industry in the first decade of the twenty-first century was security. Diamond theft and illegal smuggling were practices that particularly plagued emerging countries. Export totals of Pakistani precious and semi-precious stones, for example, fell from US$3.76 million in 1991-1992 to US$2.17 million in 2000-2001, and the *Pakistan Newswire* on March 9, 2002, suggested that smuggling may have contributed to this decline. Mining operations in Colombia and adjacent lands worried about safety issues due to the presence of gang-like drug cartels. In addition, in many diamond-rich areas of Africa, militant groups have seized control of diamond operations and used the proceeds to finance armed insurrections.

According to Violet Cho in the June 25, 2008, edition of *The Irrawaddy,* environmental activists said the mining for jade and gems in northern Burma was ldquo;indiscriminate" and was destroying the ecology and the ecosystem in the region. Forest clearing being done by mining enterprises reportedly caused floods and landslides in the Hpakan and Mogok mining centers. Mogok was credited as being the ruby capital of the world. It was also the location where at least 11 people died in floods and landslides prompted night of torrential rain. According to Naw La, a researcher with the Kachin Developmental Network Group, the destruction of forests above Hpaken and Mogok removed a natural barrier preventing flooding and landslides. Naw La also accused the mining companies of damaging the Hpakan's river ecosystem. The Uru was negatively impacted by dumping soil into it.

ORGANIZATION AND STRUCTURE

The gemstone mining industry is both widely dispersed and highly diverse. Gem mining operations are scattered unevenly throughout the world, on all the continents except Antarctica. Many of the most famous and most valuable deposits are found in the poorest and most inaccessible regions. Members of the industry include some of the largest and most powerful corporations in the world, as well as individual "treasure hunters," both legitimate and illegitimate.

The products of this industry are also quite diverse. The island country of Sri Lanka, one of the most important centers of the industry, produces 55 different kinds of precious gems, yet there are many varieties that are not found there. Gems are generally divided into diamonds and colored gemstones in the retail trade, as well as throughout the industry. The diamond mining industry is highly developed and tightly structured, while the production of other gemstones is chaotic and in many places quite primitive.

Not including organic substances such as pearl and amber, which are sometimes classified with them, gemstones are defined as natural crystalline minerals that are rare, hard, chemically resistant, and beautiful. For thousands of years, they have been the objects of exploration, speculation, and arduous labor, as well as the subject of myth, legend, story, and song. In modern times some gemstones, particularly diamonds, have proven to be very valuable in industrial applications. The chemical composition of gemstones is in most cases the same as other, non-gemstone minerals. For example, diamond is chemically the same as graphite, and ruby and sapphire are chemically the same as corundum, a mineral that is used as a cutting and polishing material. The difference between gems and other minerals is the size and regularity of the crystal structure. Gems were formed millions of years ago when the necessary conditions of heat and pressure enabled the formation of very large crystals. Growing knowledge of the conditions in which gems were formed has enabled much more scientific exploration for gem deposits in the nineteenth and twentieth centuries than was possible in previous centuries.

Diamond. Diamond is the premier gemstone. It is the hardest substance found in nature, 140 times harder than the next hardest gem, which has made diamond an indispensable material in many industrial applications. Diamond powder is used to grind and polish other very hard substances in many industries. Fragments of various sizes are embedded in saw blades and drill bits for uses from dentistry to drilling oil wells. Because of its resistance to extremes of heat and cold, thin slices of diamond are used as tiny windows in space probes. Wire is drawn through a hole drilled in a diamond when the diameter of the finished wire must be precise and highly consistent, as in the filaments for light bulbs.

Gem-quality diamond is the most valuable mined substance and the most sought after gemstone. The value of an uncut, or "rough," diamond is determined by its size, color, and clarity. Most diamonds are yellowish, but the more nearly colorless stones are more valuable. The more rare colored diamonds—blue, pink, green, purple, brown, yellow, and black, called "fancy"—are often extremely valuable. Diamonds frequently have internal flaws, such as enclosed minerals that lower their value. Most diamonds are small and are fractions of a carat (a carat equals 0.2 grams), but occasionally very large gems are found and if they have good quality otherwise, they are extremely valuable. The largest ever found, the Cullinan diamond, weighed 3,106 carats, about 1.4 pounds.

Africa was the historic leader in global diamond production through the twentieth century, producing half the world's supply. By 2004, MBendi Research reported that the continent had produced more than 75 percent of world diamond value to date, worth an estimated US$158 billion. However, by 2002, total output (including both industrial and gem-quality diamonds) from five non-African countries (Australia, Russia, Canada, Brazil, and China) exceeded that of Africa. Nevertheless, with 12 of the 19 leading diamond producing countries on that continent, Africa remained a significant supplier. Botswana ranked first in production of gem-quality diamonds, followed by Australia, Russia, Congo (Kinshasa), Angola, South Africa, Canada, and Namibia. Brazil and China also ranked among the top 10, but the vast majority of their output was industrial quality diamonds.

In 2005, Angola announced that its national mining company Endiama would double its diamond output in 2006. In the 1990s, when the country was engulfed in civil war, Angola produced between 3 and 5 million carats per year. After military conflict ceased, diamond production increased to about 6.5 million carats in the early 2000s. If the country reaches its target of 12 million carats per year, it will become Africa's third largest diamond producer. The Angolan government claimed that adherence to the Kimberly Process has rid the industry of corruption, but some analysts have expressed concern about continued human rights violations and other illegal practices, such as smuggling.

Colored Gemstones. There are about 200 varieties of colored gemstones, but only a much smaller number are of great importance in the gemstone mining industry. The others are either very rare or not suitable for producing jewelry. The best-known and most valuable gems are ruby, sapphire, and emerald. Other important gems are amethyst, aquamarine, zircon, topaz, opal, ametrine, and tourmaline.

Australia accounts for 95 percent of global opal production for more than US$1 billion. The price for opals can reach more than US$30,000 per carat. The industry was considered to be highly fragmented with no major leaders due to no large discoveries during the past decade. For example, Opal Horizon of Australia has concentrated on mining in the opal-rich region of Western Queensland, claiming a success rate of four discoveries over an 18-month period. Opal Horizon was determined to become an industry leader with innovative exploration techniques.

Ruby. Ruby is generally the most valuable of the colored gemstones. The name comes from the Latin word for red, and the color varies from a fiery vermilion to a violet red. If the color is very light, the gem is called a pink sapphire. As with most gems, the more even in color and the more transparent the stone is, the more valuable it is. Large rubies, more than five carats, are very rare, and a large ruby that is of top quality may command a higher price than a diamond of the same size and quality. The most important sources for ruby are Myanmar (formerly Burma), Thailand, Sri Lanka, and Tanzania, as well as other countries.

Sapphire. Sapphire is chemically the same as ruby, with the difference being simply in the color. There are pink, violet, yellow, green, and colorless varieties of sapphire, but if the stone is simply called sapphire, it is understood to be blue. The most prized color is a pure cornflower blue. When indistinctly colored sapphires are heat-treated at high temperatures, they turn a bright blue permanently. A very desirable characteristic of some sapphires, as well as some rubies and other gems, is the presence of rutile needles within the crystal that reflect light in such a way that it looks like there is a six-pointed star inside the gem. Another arrangement of rutile needles in the crystal make it reflect light like a cat's eye. The most significant deposits of sapphires are in Australia, Myanmar, Sri Lanka, and Thailand. Sapphires have been discovered in Montana, where several mines have been developed.

Emerald. The word emerald comes from a Greek word meaning green stone, and the color of this gem is so distinctive and characteristic that it is simply called "emerald green." Like large rubies, fine emeralds exceeding two carats in weight are among the most highly valued gems and may bring a higher price even than diamonds. Only the finest emeralds are transparent. Often they are clouded with various inclusions, which are not considered faults but rather a sign of the authenticity of the stone. Unlike rubies, sapphires, and many other gemstones, emeralds are almost always mined directly from the rock in which they were formed, rather than being found in gem gravels created by erosion. This situation exists because they are less durable than these other gems and do not survive the process of erosion and transport. The most important emerald mines as of 2004 were in Colombia, with other sources being Brazil, Zimbabwe, Russia, and Pakistan.

Aquamarine and Beryl. Aquamarine and beryl are gemstones that have the same chemical composition as emerald but are different colors. Aquamarine is blue or light greenish blue, the darker blue being considered more desirable. Lower quality stones can be heat-treated to change them to the desired darker color, but too much heat can discolor them. The largest aquamarine of gem quality, found in Brazil, weighed 243 pounds and was cut into many stones with a total weight of over 100,000 carats. Beryl is found in a variety of other colors as well as green and blue. Heliodor is a light yellow-green beryl, morganite is pink, and gosheite is colorless. The most important deposits of aquamarine are found in Brazil, but aquamarine and other forms of beryl are found in Australia, China, the United States, and a number of other countries.

Amethyst, Citrine, and Ametrine. Amethyst, citrine, and ametrine are three gem varieties of quartz. The color of amethyst ranges from purple through violet to almost pink, sometimes in bands in the same stone. The name means "not drunken" because it was thought that the gem would protect the wearer from getting drunk. Amethyst is the most valuable form of quartz. Citrine varies from a pale yellow to a brownish yellow. Most commercial citrine is actually heat-treated poor quality amethyst or smoky quartz. Natural citrine is usually pale yellow. Ametrine is a striped quartz variety that is half amethyst and half citrine. Sources of these gems include Bolivia, Brazil, Sri Lanka, the United States, Madagascar, and Namibia, as well as a number of other countries.

Mining Methods. There are two general types of gemstone deposits. When the gems are found in the rock in which they were originally formed, known as the host rock, it is called a primary deposit. Often, however, the host rock eroded away long ago, and the gemstones were carried, usually by water, to a new location. Because gemstones are harder and generally denser than other rock, they survive the erosion forces better and are deposited on the bed of a stream or on a beach, resulting in what is known as a placer deposit. These accumulations of stones are then often, but not always, buried as a result of subsequent erosion. In earlier times most finds of gemstones were of placer deposits. Sometimes the original sources were then located.

Mining of placer deposits is generally simpler than mining a primary deposit. If the deposit is at the surface, mining consists of sorting the gravel to find the gemstones. If the gem-bearing gravel is buried, then a pit must be dug, perhaps 30 feet deep or more, and the gravel is hauled to the surface for sorting. In Sri Lanka, for example, almost all mining was done in this way in the 2000s, just as it has been for centuries. Varying degrees of mechanization have been introduced in some places, ranging from gasoline-powered pumps for removing the water from the pits to using bulldozers to uncover the buried gem-bearing gravel. Diamonds, rubies, sapphires, aquamarines, and beryl are a few of the kinds of gems that are mined in this way.

Although placer deposits usually have a higher proportion of gem-quality stones than primary deposits, prospectors always prefer to find the source of the gems, especially in modern times. Primary deposits typically lend themselves to more modern, efficient mining techniques. Modern gemstone mines of primary deposits are in fact similar to other kinds of mines. Depending on the depth at which the gem-bearing rock is found, surface or underground mining methods may be used. Surface mining is usually practiced on relatively flat ground in situations where the desired material is located less than 200 feet from the earth's surface. At mines where the gems are located on steep inclines, however, material may be excavated from open pits that can reach depths of several hundred feet. Dragline excavators, power shovels, bulldozers, front-end loaders, scrapers, and other heavy pieces of equipment are used to move the overburden and then the ore. The ore is then processed to recover the gem material. Primary deposits of diamonds are often mined this way.

Underground mines consist of a series of parallel and interconnecting tunnels from which the ore is cut and removed with special machinery. The process is complex and sometimes dangerous. The mine must be adequately ventilated to protect miners from dust and provide adequate air underground. In addition, careful ground control must be practiced to prevent the roof of the mine from collapsing on workers and equipment. In some areas where underground methods are used, safety is not highly regarded and accidental deaths are common. Emeralds and diamonds are often mined using underground mining techniques.

Whenever large-scale, mechanized mining is practiced, whether surface or underground, large quantities of ore must be processed to recover the relatively small yield of gemstones. Large diamond mines, such as those in southern Africa and Australia, extract huge quantities of ore that must be partially crushed. The crushed material is then sorted by some means to separate the diamonds. One separation method depends on diamond's resistance to water so water will not cling to it. Crushed ore is mixed with water and then spread on a greased surface. The diamonds settle onto the surface and, because they are not wet, stick to the grease, while the wet ore washes off the surface of the gem. A more sophisticated technique relies on diamond's fluorescence, which enables the gem to give off light when bombarded with X-rays. A stream of crushed ore falls down a column past stations that emit X-rays causing the diamonds to flash. An electric eye records the flash and releases a short blast of air that blows the diamond into a separate chute. In many cases, however, final sorting of the ore is done by hand, under tight security.

The host rock of diamonds is usually a rock called kimberlite, named after the area in South Africa in which it was first discovered. The Argyle deposit in Australia, however, is of lamproite. The diamonds were formed 90 to 190 miles below the surface, in the upper mantle, where temperatures and pressures are extremely high. At some point an eruption occurred, bringing the molten rock carrying the diamonds to the surface and forming a volcano. Through the centuries the volcanic cone eroded, sometimes carrying diamonds downstream to form placer deposits.

BACKGROUND AND DEVELOPMENT

Humans have valued gems from the earliest days of recorded history. The earliest written evidence of emeralds being mined comes from Egypt as early as 2000 B.C. These mines, later called Cleopatra's Mines, were rediscovered in 1818. Legend has it that King Solomon sent for gems to impress the Queen of Sheba in biblical times,

and the earliest recorded trading of diamonds took place in India and Borneo more than 2,000 years ago. The Spanish conquerors of the Americas found the indigenous population of Mexico trading emeralds that were mined in the area that later was called Colombia. Eventually the Spanish found the mines and worked them using slave labor.

India was Europe's first source of diamonds, which came via the Middle East and Venice until the Portuguese established a monopoly on the trade by going around Africa in the sixteenth century. In the seventeenth century the Dutch edged out the Portuguese in the Asian trade, and later the British began to exert their influence on India. In the eighteenth century, however, Europe was flooded with diamonds from a new source, Brazil. Prices fell and the trade with India was destroyed. For a century Brazil had an effective monopoly on diamonds, but this situation ended in 1870 when large deposits were discovered in South Africa.

The Modern Diamond Industry. Like those in Brazil, the first mines worked in South Africa were of secondary deposits in the Orange and Vall Rivers. Between 1867 and 1870, thousands of prospectors searched these rivers. Then, in 1870 diamonds were found on the plains between the two rivers. It was soon realized that these new deposits were not placer deposits but were actually the original source of the diamonds. No matter how deep the miners dug, they still found diamonds. This meant that mechanized methods could be effectively utilized.

The resulting impact on the diamond trade was enormous. While Brazil was producing about a quarter of a million carats per year, by 1871 South African production had reached that level. The following year its output surged to more than a million carats, and by 1880 it was at 3 million. Actual mechanized methods had not been established because the mines were located hundreds of miles by oxcart from any port and because the claims were all very small at 35 feet square each. In 1879 a railroad to the coast was completed, which halved the cost of bringing in machines. The miners also discovered that as they got deeper and deeper the tiny side-by-side mines were not workable.

In the mid-1870s a young man from England named Cecil Rhodes became involved in diamond mining through his brother. He began buying the small claims in one mine, De Beers, quickly gaining controlling interest in this mine and, within a few years, in several others. Soon his company, De Beers Consolidated Mines Ltd., controlled 90 percent of the world's diamond production. In 1887 he entered the Cape Colony Parliament, and in 1890, at the age of 37, he became the colony's prime minister. He died in 1902.

Cecil Rhodes had established the guiding principle of the diamond industry: diamonds are a luxury item, and the supply must be matched with the demand by centrally controlling the entire process from mining to supplying the cutters. In 1914 the first diamond cartel was established. The companies involved were all legally independent but agreed to work together to control the industry. World War I interrupted this experiment, but in 1920 a new cartel was created, including a company whose purpose was to buy up the production of mines outside South Africa.

For more than 70 years, the diamond industry followed Cecil Rhodes's principle, creating an industry that has been much more stable than other commodity industries, such as coal mining. De Beers Consolidated Mines and its sister company De Beers Centenary do not have a monopoly on diamond production, but they do have a huge share, and they do affect the supply when necessary by limiting their own production. The other major component of control is the Diamond Trading Company (DTC; formerly the Central Selling Organization), which is the division of the De Beers organization responsible for selling rough diamonds to cutters.

Through the DTC, De Beers enters into contracts with the major diamond producers stipulating that it will buy a set amount of their production and limiting what they can do with the rest. The DTC in turn sells the rough diamonds in limited amounts to a limited number (160) of diamond cutters in batches that the cutter has to accept or reject as a whole. The sales occur 10 times a year. If De Beers determines that the supply must be limited to keep both the market and the price stable, it has sufficient financial resources to allow it simply not to sell all that it bought. The biggest difficulty for the company is a large independent supplier that will not sell through the Central Selling Organization (CSO).

Through the late 1990s, the global diamond industry experienced an unusual amount of uncertainty. Production was still growing, and prices, at least for the better-quality gems, were still high, but the hold of the diamond cartel led by De Beers was seriously challenged. The Argyle Diamond Mines joint venture did not renew its contract with the CSO in 1996 and sold its production, primarily low-end and small diamonds, on the open market.

Russia also did not renew its contract when it expired at the end of 1995. After intense and protracted negotiations, Russian President Boris Yeltsin signed a decree late in 1997 authorizing an agreement between De Beers and Almazy Rossii-Sakha (Alrosa), Russia's largest diamond producer and only authorized exporter of uncut diamonds. The agreement stipulated that Russia would sell at least US$550 million of diamonds to De Beers per year but not more than 26 percent of its total output. It was also agreed that Alrosa would be allowed to sell some of its high-quality stones within Russia to encourage the development of the local diamond-cutting industry and could sell the rest of its production as it saw fit. The agreement was for only three years instead of the usual five. The challenge from Russia was not limited to this agreement. Alrosa entered into development joint ventures in Angola and Namibia, right in De Beers's backyard. De Beers in turn entered into a joint project with another Russian mining company to develop a diamond mine near Arkhangelsk.

De Beers took the steps it felt necessary to keep the industry stable. It decreased the amount of diamonds it sold to the cutting industry in late 1997 and early 1998. Sales from the CSO in the second half of 1997 dropped to 1994 levels, and sales in 1998 fell to about US$3.5 billion from US$4.64 billion the prior year. The strategy and a prosperous global economy in general brought prices back up in 2000 to a record US$5.67 billion. However, as the economy fell in 2001, De Beers's reported a drop in sales to US$4.45 billion, well below expected sales of US$4.8 billion.

CURRENT CONDITIONS

By the end of the 2000s, the global diamond industry was on a stronger footing. After weak demand through 2002, when Sudden Acute Respiratory Syndrom (SARS) and political unrest in the Middle East exerted a negative effect on the world economy, diamond jewelry sales grew in 2003, with especially strong demand in the United States, India, China, Britain, and Japan. The DTC raised its rough diamond prices three times during 2003. Full year sales by the DTC, according to De Beers company data, grew 7 percent in 2003, reaching US$5.52 billion. In response to positive economic projections through 2004, the DTC raised rough diamond prices 3 percent in early 2004. In 2009 the domestic production of industrial diamonds reached approximately 260n carats, with the United States as one of the world's leading markets.

The United States was responsible for more than 50 percent of world diamond sales according to the BBC. The U.S. market for unset gem diamonds reached an estimated US$10.5 billion in 2002, according to the U.S. Geological Survey, and the United States was expected to dominate global consumption through the year 2010. In 2004, the United States accounted for more than 35 percent of global demand for gem-quality diamonds, with imports estimated at about US$12.9 billion. Huge growth in Chinese demand, however, was expected to fuel substantial diamond sales in Asia through the early 2000s. Sales of diamond jewelry in China reached US$1.2 billion in 2003, which made it the largest diamond market in Asia, and demand was expected to double by 2013, with some analysts predicting that by 2010 China would the world leader in diamond consumption.

On the production side, the industry was strong. Mines in Botswana, already a leader in production, were increasing their output, and Russia expected to improve its facilities with the help of foreign investment. Bakwanga Mining (Miba), the largest mining company in Democratic Republic of the Congo, announced in 2004 that it planned to increase production and attract new investors. It expected to produce 8.5 million carats in 2005. The opening of the Ekati mine in Canada in 1998 paved the way for Canada to become a major global supplier. In 2003, the mine produced 5.57 million carats. Canada's Diavik mine, which opened in 2003, produced 3.8 million carats that year and was expected to reach annual production of 6 to 8 million carats. The Snap Lake mine, which was Canada's first completely underground diamond mine, was scheduled to begin operations in 2006. In 2003, Canada accounted for approximately 15 percent of world diamond mining. By 2006, Canada accounted for just over 11.45 percent of the world diamond mining.

By the early years of the first decade of the 2000s the "conflict diamonds" problem had become so severe in Africa that the United Nations took action. Conflict diamonds are diamonds that come from areas where armed groups fighting against the legitimately established government use diamonds to fund their armed insurgence. Conflict diamonds have financed insurrections in Sierra Leone, Liberia, Democratic Republic of Congo, and Central African Republic, as well as Angola. In 2000 the United Nations unanimously adopted a resolution recognizing the role of conflict diamonds in prolonging brutal conflicts by guerrilla movements in some African countries. The U.N. mandated a system of international certification for rough diamond shipments, known as the Kimberly Process Certification Scheme (KPCS), which would prevent conflict diamonds from entering legitimate markets. The Kimberly Process was implemented in 2002. A BBC report in March 2004, however, indicated that the protocol, which relies on voluntary compliance by governments that have signed it, had not been effective in preventing sales of conflict diamonds. In 2004, the U.S. military claimed that Al Qaeda was using conflict diamonds to pay for arms.

Meanwhile, the colored gemstone industry outlook appeared to be improving as governments in developing countries around the world took steps to open their economies to outside investment. New deposits of gemstones were being developed in many locations, particularly in Brazil, Myanmar, and Tanzania. Global production of non-diamond gemstones, according to the U.S. Geological Survey (USGS), exceeded US$2 billion in 2003.

According to Ed Merriman in the August 7, 2008, edition of the *Baker City Herald,* Brian Bolin, who had come to Baker City, Oregon, in search of gold, instead discovered "some pretty little rocks" that turned out to be opals. At first disappointed that his find was not gold, Bolin learned he had discovered the second highest selling gem in the world. The find changed Bolin's fortune from being a homeless man living in a Arizona barn to one with brighter prospects after answering his father's request to come to Baker City. Bolin decided to go public before the 2008 Miners Jubilee celebration in Baker City. Bolin believed discovering a frequently under-appreciated or recognized gem was even more exciting than finding gold. Value ranged from 50 cents for a common boulder opal to US $100 to US$500 per carat for some more colorful opals and up to US $5,000 per carat for rare opals that could be cut like diamonds. Bolin has continued to find opals in the region since his original discovery on August 20, 2007. He predicted that another three claims would be added to the seven that were already filed. Opportunities for creating distinctive jewelry were being explored as well. Bolin hoped that going public with his story would encourage others to search for other gems as an alternative to getting caught up in or frustrated by the gold rush.

The All Kachin Students and Youth Union (AKSYU) called for the boycott of Olympic souvenirs and jewelry made from Burmese jade in 2008. Approximately 90 percent of jadeite on sale in China comes from Burmese mines. According to Marwaan Macan-Markar on August 7, 2008, in an article for IPS News, the mines had "deplorable work conditions." Other industry linked problems included an HIV/AIDS epidemic and environmental destruction. Macan-Markar continued that thousands of people had been affected by the loss of their land due to expansion of mines, deaths in pit collapses, and company vigilantism. Furthermore, child labor and extortion had been linked to jade.

INDUSTRY LEADERS

Diamonds.

De Beers. Founded in the 1870s by Cecil Rhodes, De Beers, whose corporate headquarters are in Johannesburg, South Africa, remained the largest diamond mining company in the world as of 2010. The De Beers Group owned mines in South Africa and partnered with governments in Botswana, Namibia, and Tanzania to operate mines in those countries. In 2000 it initiated operations in Canada. In 2001, De Beers was acquired by DBI consortium. Production in 2004 accounted for more than 40 percent of the global gem diamond market by value, and the company's Diamond Trading Company handled about 60 percent of rough diamond sales. De Beers is involved in all aspects of the diamond business, including mining, exploration, sorting, and marketing, as well as advertising and promotion.

In 2002, De Beers reported that 2001 sales fell from a high of US$5.67 billion in 2000 to US$4.45 billion in 2001. De Beers blamed the September 11, 2001, terrorist attacks against the United States and the ensuing recession for the bulk of the 2001 slack sales. The company had launched major initiatives in 1999 and 2000 to address challenges related to market volatility. Its "As is—Plus" campaign was aimed to increase efficiencies throughout its businesses and its "Supplier of Choice" program outlined new marketing and sales strategies to drive consumer demand. Additionally, to strengthen its brand recognition De Beers renamed its Central Selling Organization as the Diamond Trading Company, along with a new logo—the Forevermark.

In 2004, De Beers Kimberly Mines reached a record production of 2 million carats, which was almost twice the output for the previous year and the highest production since 1914. The company's mines in South Africa produced 13.7 million carats in 2004, while operations in Botswana and Namibia contributed 47 million carats. In 2009 De Beers reported an 8 percent growth in diamond sales from 2003, bringing their annual revenue to US$6.8 billion.

In August 2008 Brendan Ryan reported that the disagreement between African Diamonds and DeBeers related to the proposed AK 6 diamond mine located in Botswana had intensified. The dispute centered around diamonds sold linked to a marketing agreement with the government of Botswana that was due for renewal in 2010. A former DeBeers executive attributed the problem to a failure to replace production it was so busy marketing. The Botswana government, however, took a harder line on marketing. DeBeers had reportedly rebelled by claiming the AK6 was not viable due to future power supply concerns.

Rio Tinto. Rio Tinto, the world's largest mining company, was a comparative newcomer to the diamond business. Rio Tinto's strategy is to build global demand for smaller gems. In the late 1990s it acquired a 60 percent interest in Australia's Argyle Diamond Mine, assuming complete ownership in 2002. Through Argyle, the world's largest diamond mine, Rio Tinto accounted for about 25 percent of world diamond production as of 2004. Rio Tinto also owns a 60 percent interest in Canada's Diavik mine. In 2002 the company established Rio Tinto Diamonds as the marketing division of its diamond business. In addition to its operations in Australia and Canada, the company has diamond interests in Zimbabwe and diamond sales offices in Belgium and India. In 2009, the company reported sales of US$44.036 billion with 35,000 employees.

Colored Gemstones. Unlike the large companies that led the diamond sector of the industry, the colored gemstone sector in the early years of the twenty-first century continued to be conducted by much smaller enterprises. Independent, individual miners generate a significant portion of colored gemstone production, although in the late 1990s some consolidation began to occur. In 1998, Chivor Emerald, a Canadian company operating in Colombia, was bought by AZCO Mining Inc., which had previously focused on copper mining. Another leading producer was Minerales y Metales del Oriente, which operated the Anahi mine in Bolivia, which was reportedly the world's leading source of amethyst. GTN Resources Ltd., formerly the Great Northern Mining Corporation NL, owned rights to explore and mine some of the richest sapphire fields in Australia. A collapse in the sapphire market in 2002, however, caused the company to suspend all mining operations, while drawing revenues from its sapphire reserves. GTN Resources announced plans in 2003 to merge with ZBB Energy Corporation.

MAJOR COUNTRIES IN THE INDUSTRY

Diamond Mining.

South Africa. Although South Africa ranked only fifth in diamond production in 2004 according to the U.S. Geological Survey (USGS), in many ways it still dominated the industry. De Beers Consolidated Mines, along with its sister company De Beers Centenary, was the largest diamond mining company in the world, with numerous mines in South Africa and large interests in many other companies and mines in other countries. South Africa was also the birthplace of the modern diamond industry. India and Brazil had each dominated the diamond trade in turn in earlier centuries, but with the discovery and exploitation of the primary deposits of diamonds in kimberlite pipes and the subsequent introduction of large-scale mechanization, production in South Africa multiplied many times over, and the industry was changed forever.

In 2005, South Africa proposed legislation that would tax exports of rough diamonds. The aim of the bill was to restrict the flow of rough diamonds into foreign cutting and manufacturing facilities, in effect forcing De Beers to sell most of its South African diamonds within the country and thus help to strengthen South Africa's economy.

Africa was frequently overlooked as an alternative for potential gem investors although it had earned acclaims as an outstanding source, along with India. Investors chose to focus on traditional Global Emerging Market countries of Russia, China, India, and the resurgent Latin America. The mining of tanzanite and emeralds had been successful Africa, and areas around Mount Kilimanjaro reported increases in the production levels of rare blue tanzanite gemstones.

Australia. Diamonds have been found in Australia since 1851, but it was not until the 1980s that the country was in a position to be an industry leader. In 2003, Australia ranked first in total production and second in production of gem and near-gem quality diamonds. The vast majority of Australian diamonds came from the Argyle Diamond Mines Joint Venture in the Kimberly region of Western Australia. This mine produced 40.9 million carats in 1993, representing 37 percent of global output. Production declined to 30.9 million carats in 2003, representing about 25 percent of world production. The Argyle deposit, a lamproite pipe rather than a kimberlite pipe, was the richest in the world, yielding nearly 7 carats of diamond per ton, but most of the production was "cheap gem" and industrial grade. Although Argyle produced some spectacular pink diamonds, only about 5 percent of its output was considered gem quality.

Although the opal is Australia's national gemstone, there were still many unknown factors about the industry. Opal Horizon Limited announced plans in 2008 to undertake explorations in western Queensland. The company had US $1.5 million in the bank but it was difficult to place a value on it because there was not a steady resource base or revenue stream. In *The Australian* on July 23, 2008, Wise-Owl.com research analyst Sven Restel said that "Opal mining is relatively in expensive and good stones can bring high margins, although revenue can be lumpy."

Botswana. Botswana was the world's leading producer of gem-quality diamonds in 2006, generating 22.5 million carats, according to USGS estimates. Diamonds accounted for three-quarters of Botswana's exports, one-third of its gross domestic product, and one-half of government revenue. In 2006, Botswana's US$3.3 billion diamond industry represented 27.3 percent of the world's total. Debswana, a company owned jointly by the government of Botswana and De Beers of South Africa, accounted for virtually all of this production and was the world's leading diamond company by value. One of its mines, Jwaneng, is widely believed to be the richest in the world, and another, Orapa, is one of the lowest in cost, making the future promising as the potential for further growth is there.

Russia. According to the USGS, Russia had become the second-highest producer of diamonds by 2006, with US$2.3 billion in the market. However, *Pravda* in December 2004, Russian output in 2003 reached 33 billion carats, making Russia the world's leading diamond producer. The information was made public only after Russia was scheduled to chair the Kimberly Process, which required that the country's diamond statistics be declassified for the first time

under Soviet rule. *Pravda* also reported that Russia ranked second in world diamond exports.

Russia's diamond deposits are located in Siberia, where mining conditions are very difficult. Winter temperatures average -40 degrees Fahrenheit and can get as low as -90 degrees Fahrenheit. Even summer brings little relief in terms of climate. The deposits are found in an area of permafrost where the ground thaws to a depth of only a few inches, and the warmer weather brings out hordes of mosquitoes. Nevertheless, the former Soviet Union had invested heavily in developing mines because they were an important source of foreign trade. Russia continued to exploit this resource, although this industry suffered somewhat along with the rest of the country, in the transition to a market economy after the collapse of the Soviet Union. Russian diamond mining companies also entered into agreements with Angola and Namibia to develop diamond operations in those countries. In 2002, the USGS noted that Russia's mining operations had reached a saturation point and new sources of diamonds needed to be discovered to maintain diamond output.

Colored Gemstone Mining.

Sri Lanka. Sri Lanka (formerly Ceylon) is an island country located off India's southeastern shore, and for centuries has been very important in the colored gemstone trade. As home to the second-highest variety of gemstones in the world after Brazil, Sri Lanka was a major producer in the early 2000s of sapphires and many other gems, including alexandrite, spinel, topaz, garnet, and beryl. It was also developing a competitive diamond-cutting industry. The government continued to resist offers from mining companies to introduce large-scale mechanized mining at its placer deposits, and the sites of many of Sri Lanka's primary deposits were unknown. Production declined somewhat in the mid-1990s, and the government proposed to develop the gem-cutting industry to make up for the decline, especially relationships with gemstone producers in Tanzania. In 2000, gemstones and jewelry were Sri Lanka's third-highest source of export revenues. In addition, gemstone sales remained an important part of Sri Lanka's tourist industry in the early 2000s. Tourists find the gems available for purchase in museums, the best hotels, and even on street corners from hawkers.

A research study found that illicit small arms sales in Sri Lanka were not only supporting crime, but also illegal economic activities in the gemstone mining industry. The police have seized 13,000 illegal small arms since 1998, according to the National Commission Against Proliferation of Illicit Small Arms. The Commission recommended tighter controls on military and police stock-piles.

Myanmar. Myanmar (formerly Burma) for centuries has been the world's leading source for fine rubies and quality jade, but it isolated itself from the gem-trading world when a military-backed socialist government took over in 1963. By the late 1980s, upon the resignation of longtime president Ne Win, the military had assumed a more dominant position, and Burma, renamed Myanmar, grew further isolated from international relations. In 1992, however, a major new deposit was discovered at Mong Hsu, and in 1995 the government decided to open its doors once again to the gem trade. A new gem-trading market was opened in Yangon, the capital, and foreign investors were encouraged to participate in gem-cutting and jewelry-making enterprises. As of 2001, however, only Myanmar citizens were allowed to mine gems in the tightly controlled nation.

Although the government was promoting its fine jade to attract tourism and commerce, by 2001 the country still had to overcome its long history of bloodshed and enslavement. Myanmar's efforts to increase its gemstone business, however, suffered a setback in 2003 when U.S. President George W. Bush signed the "Tom Lantos Block Burmese JADE Act of 2008," banning gem imports from Myanmar for one year unless the country instituted democratic reforms. Myanmar reportedly had been evading earlier sanctions by laundering stones in other countries and exporting them to the United States. The ban did not apply to Burmese jadeite or rubies imported for personal use, or to Burmese jadeite or rubies already in the United States.

Analysts predicted that the U.S. action would have a huge impact on the global gemstone business. Nevertheless, Myanmar's promotion of official gem emporiums, which attracted private buyers, helped to boost production and sales. According to government sources, Myanmar increased production of jade tenfold between 1995 and 2003, with an output exceeding 10,000 tons. In 2004, Myanmar reported gemstone exports of about US$60 million.

Colombia. Colombian emeralds were mined directly from primary deposits in very mountainous country. Both mechanized strip-mining and underground shaft and tunnel methods are used, and thousands of *guaqueros* (treasure hunters) sort through the scrap ore seeking emeralds that were overlooked. Others resort to less legal methods such as digging their own tunnels into the soft shale at night, a very dangerous process. In late 2001 Central Colombia's governing body, Boyaca, promised tax breaks and other incentives to mining interests willing to start or increase mining operations for emeralds and other gemstones.

Colombia was by far the leading source for emeralds in the early 2000s. The mining districts of Muzo and Chivor still dominated production, as they had under the Spanish conquistadors. The area was periodically disturbed by what the local inhabitants called the "emerald wars," which were fought for control of the rich deposits after Colombia privatized land and mining rights in 1973. One of these emerald wars occurred in the 1980s, involving the Medellin drug cartel. In the 1990s the situation became more stabilized, although the 1998 arrest of Victor Carranza Nino, owner of Colombia's largest emerald mining operation, caused the industry to falter. Carranza Nino's release in March 2002 fueled hope that the emerald industry would rebound in the early years of the twenty-first century. In 2004, the Colombian government was investigating the possibility of using new technology to certify the origin of its emerald exports to discourage trade in smuggled gems.

As reported by Helen Murphy in *The Miami Herald* on June 30, 2008, undisclosed materials were used to disguise natural flaws in Colombia's emeralds. "Emeralds all over the world are treated, but the fact that it's happening in Colombia, where the finest stones come from, is the problem," explained Gemological Institute of America Director of Identification Service Shane McClure. Colombia was credited with being the source of approximately half of the world's US$280 million annual emerald trade with other leading producers including Brazil, Zambia, and Afghanistan. The Colombian Government and National Emerald Federation announced plans to open a laboratory where buyers could test stones and have them certified. The two entities also planned to have joint publicity campaigns promoting goals to triple sales to as much as US$425 million by 2013 increasing from approximately US$140 million in 2007.

Brazil. Brazil, which had the greatest variety of gemstones on the planet, was also the world's leading emerald producer in the early years of the first decade of the 2000s, according to the International Colored Gemstone Association. The southeastern state of Minas Gerais ("general mines") was the site of a number of new discoveries in the early and mid-1990s, including emerald, tourmaline, and sapphire. Good quantities of aquamarine had also been mined in Brazil in the mid-1990s. A new government took office in 1995 and instituted more liberal economic policies, fostering outside investment in exploration and mine development.

In the 2000s a trend among Brazilian mining companies was to collaborate with international corporations seeking shared gemstone profits. In 2002, for example, the Brazil-based gemstone-cutting firm Stone World contracted with U.S.-based Seahawk Minerals to develop funds for additional mining operations.

BIBLIOGRAPHY
"Angola to Double Diamond Production in 2006." *Afrol News,* 14 March 2005. Available from http://www.afrol.com.

Australian Department of Mineral Resources. *Mineral Resources, New South Wales,* 2002–03. Available from www.minerals.nsw.gov.au.

Blamey, Chris. "One Company, 50 Million Carats of Sapphire a Year." *World Gem Mining Update,* 2002. Available from www.gemstone.org

Boreham, Tim. "$6 Millions to Widen Opal Miner's Horizons." *Criterion,* 9 July 2008.

"Boyaca Seeks Mining Investment—Boyaca." *Business News Americas,* 5 December 2001.

Canadian Department of Natural Resources. "Canada: A Diamond-Producing Nation." Available from www.nrcan-rncan.gc.ca.

Cho, Violet. "Gems Mining Destroying Environment, Activists Say." *The Irrawaddy,* 25 June 2008. Available from www.irrawaddy.org.

"Commerce: Export of Gems and Jewelry Rose." *Pakistan Newswire,* 9 March 2002.

"Conflict Diamonds 'Still on Sale.'" BBC News, 30 March 2004. Available from newsvote.bbc.co.uk.

"Congo Firm Miba to Increase Diamond Production." *National Jeweler,* 9 March 2004. Available from www.national-jeweler.com.

Coughlin, Donald G. "Sri Lanka: A Gemstone Buyer's Dream." *Gemology Canada,* 2002. Available from www.cigem.ca.

De Beers Group. "Company Profile." Available from www.debeersgroup.com.

Debswana. "Company Profile, 2004." Available from www.debswana.com.

Diamond Mining. Environmental Literacy Council. Available from www.enviroliteracy.org.

Diamond World News Service. "America to Ban Myanmar Rubies." 6 August 2008. Available from www.diamondworld.net.

"Diamonds Fuel CAR Conflicts." BBC News, 31 October 2002. Available from news.bbc.co.uk.

Eliezri, I.Z. "The 1995 ICA World Gemstone Mining Report." *International Colored Gemstone Association,* 1996. Available from www.gemstone.org.

"Emerald Czar Released from Jail." *Professional Jeweler,* March 2002. Available from www.professionaljeweler.com.

Federman, David. "The War of the Rubies." *Modern Jeweler,* 2002. Available from gemstone.org.

Global Diamond Production Statistics. Available from www.duke.edu.

"The Golden Land of Myanmar," 2002. Available from www.myanmar.com.

Gooding, Ken. "Survey—African Mining: Botswana, Diamonds: A Country's Best Friend." *Financial Times,* 15 September 1997.

———. "Survey—African Mining: Namibia as the Deposits Diminish." *Financial Times,* 15 September 1997.

Griffiths, Dylan. "DeBeers Diamond Sales May Rebound after 22 Percent Fall." *Bloomberg News,* 15 February 2002.

Hinde, Chris. "DeBeers Diamond Sales May Rebound after 22 Percent Fall." *Mining Magazine,* March 2002.

ICA World Gemstone Mining Update. Available from www.cigem.ca.

Ivanov, Andrei, and Judith Perera. "Commodities: Russian Diamond Giant Challenges De Beers." *Interpress Service,* 12 April 1998.

Katz, Sheryl. "China's Jewelry Sales Could Double by 2013." *Diamondnet News,* 4 April 2004. Available from www.diamonds.net.

———. "U.S. Military Official Affirms Al-Qaida/Blood Diamonds Link." *Diamondnet News,* 4 April 2004. Available fromwww.diamonds.net.

Khaing, Thet. "Emporiums Boost Publicity and Sales of Gems." *Myanmar Times,* 10–16 May 2004. Available from www.myanmar.gov.mm.

Macan-Markar, Marwaan. "Avoid 'Blood Jade' Olympic Souvenirs." IPS News, 7 August 2008. Available from www.ipsnews.net/.

Mbendi Research. "Africa: Mining—Diamond Mining Overview," 2002. Available from www.mbendi.co.za.

———. "World: Mining—Diamond Mining—Overview," 2002. Available from www.mbendi.co.za.

Merriman, Ed. "Striking It Rich-Without Gold." *Baker City Herald* (Oregon), 7 August 2008.

Muller, Emma. "De Beers Between Devil and the Deep Blue Sea." *Business Day* (Johannesburg, South Africa), 18 March 2005. Available from allafrica.com.

Murphy Helen, "Colombia's Emerald Reputation at Risk of Losing Luster." *Miami Herald,* 30 June 2008. Available from www.miamiherald.com.

"Opal Miner Starts Exploration to Widen Its Horizons." *The Australian, Wealth Supplement,* 23 July 2008. Available from www.wise-owl.com/images/user/2008_07_23_Aust_Supp.pdf.

Reich, Eugenie Samuel. "Tracing Emeralds' Origins Could Foil Smugglers." *New Scientist,* 17 January 2004.

Rio Tinto Company Profile, 2004. Available from www.riotinto.com.

"Russia Conquers the Diamond Market with Striking Export Volumes." *Pravda,* 23 December 2004. Available from English.pravda.ru.

"Russia: Malyshevskoe Rudoupravlenie Resumed Production of Emeralds." *Inzhenernaya Gazeta,* 1996.

Ryan, Brendan. "High Noon for DeBeers in Botswana." MiningMx, 7 August 2008 Available from www.miningmx.com.

Schumann, Walter. *Gemstones of the World.* New York: Sterling Publishing Company Inc., 1997.

"Sri Lanka Illicit Small Arms Threat to Business: Survey." Lanka Business Online, 28 June 2008. Available from www.lankabusinessonline.com.

"Stone World, Seahawk Sign Sales Pact—Brazil." *Business News Americas,* 30 January 2002.

United Nations General Assembly. *Resolution on Conflict Diamonds,* 21 March 2001. Available from www.un.org.

"U.S. Bans Products from Myanmar." *Professional Jeweler Magazine,* September 2003. Available from www.professionaljeweler.com.

U.S. Geological Survey. "Gemstone Statistics and Information; 2010 Report." Available from minerals.usgs.gov.

——— "Industrial Diamonds Statistics and Information; 2010 Report." Available from minerals.usgs.gov .

———. *Mineral Commodity Summaries,* January 2004. Available from minerals.usgs.gov.

World Diamond Council. Overview and Statistics. Available from www.worlddiamondcouncil.com.

Yingqing, Fu. "Israel Interested in Local Diamond Market." *Shanghai Star,* 1 July 2004. Available from app1.chinadaily.com.cn.

SIC 1000

MINING, METAL

NAICS CODE(S)

212. Metal mining firms explore the earth for numerous metallic minerals (ores), construct mines, and extract the ores for processing. Notable examples of metal ores mined throughout the world are: aluminum, copper, gold, iron, lead, manganese, nickel, silver, tin, and zinc.

After the materials are extracted from the earth, many industry firms also perform separation or other basic processing on ores, but the manufacture of finished or intermediate metal products, such as through smelting or refining, is not considered part of the mining industry. For discussion of the numerous forms of metal production, see also **Metals Manufacturing.**

INDUSTRY SNAPSHOT

The metal mining industry is truly international in scope with various countries around the world having a prominent presence in one or more metal mining sectors. While the largest countries, including China, Canada, the United States, Russia, India, and Brazil, typically have been able to parlay their vast natural resources into significant economic roles in mining segments, smaller countries have been important players as well, including Peru, Mexico, Australia, South Africa, and Chile, to name a few.

However, China's role in the industry has been particularly notable; its dynamic and growing economy has a huge impact on the mining industry. Backed up by a string of national policies regarding the mining industry, Chinese non-ferrous metals (metals that do not contain iron) enterprises gradually resumed overall industrial profitability. By the mid-2000s, it had emerged as a world leader in both production and consumption of mined metals. In 2009, a good developing pace took place in the nonferrous metal industry: recovery in production, rise in price, increase in investment, and huge growth in exports. China was the global leader in zinc and iron ore production, as well as a major source of copper, gold, and lead. It also led the world in copper and zinc consumption, while its consumption of iron ore, lead, and gold substantially increased world demand for these metals.

Ferrous metals are the most abundant of all commercial metals; alloys of iron and steel continue to cover a broad range of structural applications. Iron ore is readily available, about five percent of the earth's crust, and is easy to convert to a useful form. Iron is obtained by fusing the ore to drive off oxygen, sulfur, and other impurities. The ore is melted in a furnace in direct contact with the fuel using limestone as a flux. The

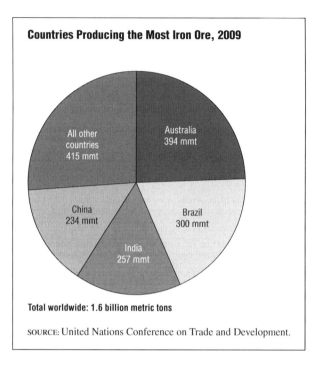

Countries Producing the Most Iron Ore, 2009

All other countries 415 mmt
Australia 394 mmt
China 234 mmt
Brazil 300 mmt
India 257 mmt

Total worldwide: 1.6 billion metric tons

SOURCE: United Nations Conference on Trade and Development.

limestone combines with impurities and forms a slag, which is easily removed. Nonferrous metals are specified for structural applications requiring reduced weight, higher strength, nonmagnetic properties, higher melting points, or resistance to chemical and atmospheric corrosion. They are also specified for electrical and electronic applications. Nonferrous metals include: aluminum, brass, copper, titanium, lead, nickel, and zinc.

According to the U.S. Geological Survey, total worldwide mine copper production was estimated at 15.8 million metric tons (mmt) in 2009, and worldwide production of iron ore dropped by 6.2 percent to 1.59 billion tons. Production levels for other industry metals in 2009 included gold (82.1 million troy ounces), nickel (1.37 million metric tons), silver (710 million ounces), zinc (11.1 mmt), and aluminum (53.6 tmt). In mid-2010, the sloping United States economy continued to limit the domestic metals demand with only the manufacturing sector generating much of a boost to metals consumption. However, robust manufacturing activity in China and other emerging economies could underpin global metals demand in the near future. The metals price leading index growth rate sank further into negative territory by mid-2010, suggesting further price declines in some metals into 2011.

Although metal mining is one of the oldest industries, during the early to mid-2000s it was still characterized by a vigorous search for new sources of unmined ores, new mining technologies, and new markets for ores. By 2000, worldwide exploration spending for new precious metal mines was US$2.7 billion. Environmental activists, however, continued to condemn the mining industry because certain mining activities can and do destroy natural habitats and pollute the ground. Even though the demand for metals has been on a steady increase, by 2009 there was a steep decline in exploration spending among the Top 40 mining companies by market capitalization. The cost of machinery, studies, trained employees and new safety standards, have elevated the cost of all forms of mining.

ORGANIZATION AND STRUCTURE

Mining methods vary depending on the mineral, its location, and the ratio of extraction costs to the mineral's revenue potential. The three major types of mining methods are surface, alluvial, and underground mining.

Surface mining includes open-pit bench mining and open-pit strip mining, as well as mountain-top removal mining. All involve the extraction of massive deposits that are housed at or near the earth's surface. This method can be used in almost any kind of terrain. Touted by supporters as cost-effective, efficient, and safer than underground mining, critics decry the environmental impact of such methods as they dramatically change the landscape.

Alluvial mining is employed to find minerals that are mixed with silt, sand, gravel, and other materials commonly found in the vicinity of creeks, rivers, and lakes, while underground mining is used to locate and harvest minerals buried deep beneath the earth's surface. Although underground mining practices reduce the impact on the surface environment and allow operations to proceed in inclement weather, this method is more hazardous to workers, requires more equipment, and is not always ideal for extracting some deposits. Also, production costs of other methods are much higher than those incurred by underground mining operations.

BACKGROUND AND DEVELOPMENT

The modern-style metal mining industry began in the nineteenth century, although metal ores had been mined for several centuries before that time. Dating clear back to biblical times, humans mined flint and stone to create tools and weapons. Iron, copper, tin, and gold had all been mined with varying degrees of success and effectiveness. The earliest known mine on archaeological record is the "Lion Cave" mine in Swaziland.

The Industrial Revolution, however, transformed the economies of developed countries and introduced iron, coal, and limestone as strategically important minerals. The growth of industry increased the demand for coal and iron to build and operate practical steam-powered machinery, while breakthroughs in the 1850s enabled inexpensive production of large amounts of steel.

The discovery of gold in California in 1848 proved to be an important factor in the settlement of the western United States. The discovery of significant deposits of silver, gold, and copper made the United States a world leader in metal mining by the beginning of the twentieth century. At the same time that prospectors were fanning out across the United States in search of gold, major discoveries of other metals were made around the world.

Moreover, researchers during the last century found new uses for industrial metals. Advanced economies such as those in Europe and North America increasingly relied on industrial metal mining. While these regions led the world in mining production and the broader metal industry, by the mid-1900s, a number of other industrializing nations, notably the Soviet Union and China, emerged as important metal mining centers.

Mining Safety. Mining has long been one of the world's most dangerous industries. While the majority of mining injuries and deaths have historically taken place in coal mines—nearly 3,200 men died in coal mine accidents in the United States in 1907 alone—a significant number of workers have been injured or killed in metal mining operations as well. Even in the mid-1970s, after a number of laws and regulations were enacted, about 8,300 disabling injuries were reported per year in metal and nonmetal mines (not including coal mines) in the United States. In countries with less stringent safety laws, accidents are more common. In 1995, 100 workers were killed in one gold mine accident in South Africa. In 2005, 209 miners were killed in an explosion accident in Liaoning province in China, just three months after an accident in Shaanxi province killed 166 miners. Rock falls, haulage accidents, methane explosions, mishaps with machinery, fires, cave ins and suffocation has all caused loss of life.

The first federal mine safety legislation in the United States, which was the principal mining nation in the world at the time, was primarily concerned with coal mining. In 1891, Congress passed the first federal statute concerning mines and their safety. This marked the beginning of what was to be an increasingly comprehensive federal legislation regulating mining activities. This new law was relatively modest legislation that applied only to mines in U.S. territories, and, among other things, established minimum ventilation requirements at underground coal mines and prohibited companies from hiring children younger than 12. The Organic Act of 1910, which created the U.S. Bureau of Mines as a new regulating agency under the Department of the Interior, was passed in reaction to a series of horrible coal mine accidents which claimed the lives of over 2,000 people annually. Other legislation in the first half of the twentieth century was also passed, but most of these laws had little real power. In 1952, however, the Federal Coal Mine Safety Act was passed. Under this act, safety regulations were made mandatory and inspectors were given added powers. Two other bills, the Coal Mine Health and Safety Act of 1969 and the Federal Metal and Non-metallic Mine Safety Act of 1966, became the primary safety codes for all mining in the United States. In 1973, the Mining Enforcement and Safety Administration (MESA) was created to oversee the U.S. industry.

Next, Congress passed the Federal Mine Safety and Health Act of 1977 (Mine Act) The Mine Act amended the 1969 Coal Act in a number of ways, and consolidated all federal health and safety regulations of the mining industry under a single statute. The Mine Act strengthened and expanded the rights of miners, while enhancing the protection of miners from retaliation for exercising such rights. Mining fatalities dropped sharply under the Mine Act from 272 in 1977 to 86 in 2000. The Mine Act also transferred responsibility for carrying out its mandates from the Department of the Interior to the Department of Labor, and named the new agency the Mine Safety and Health Administration (MSHA). Additionally, the Mine Act established the independent Federal Mine Safety and Health Review Commission to provide for independent review of the majority of MSHA's enforcement actions.

In 2006, Congress passed the Mine Improvement and New Emergency Response Act (MINER Act). The MINER Act amended the Mine Act to require, among other safety regulations, mine-specific emergency response plans in underground coal mines. It also added new regulations regarding mine rescue teams and sealing of abandoned areas, required prompt notification of mine accidents, and enhanced civil penalties.

As the world was celebrating the rescue of 33 trapped miners in Chile, anxious relatives awaited word on 11 miners still trapped in China after an explosion that killed 26 miners on October 12, 2010. According to the Chinese work safety administration, the blast at the Pingyu Coal and Electric Co. Ltd. occurred as workers were drilling a hole to release pressure from a gas buildup, in order to decrease the risk of explosions. Another gas explosion in the same mine killed 23 workers in 2008. In the wake of the Chilean rescue, the media called for a review of safety policies in mines around the world. China urged this as well, because its mining industry is the most dangerous in the world. China celebrated its own stunning mine rescue earlier in 2010, when 115 miners were pulled from a flooded mine in the northern province of Shanxi after more than a week

underground. The miners survived by eating sawdust, tree bark, paper, and even coal. Some strapped themselves to the walls of the shafts with their belts to avoid drowning while they slept.

CURRENT CONDITIONS

The status of the metal mining industry continued to vary at the start of the new millennium. Factors such as world demand, privatization, environmental concerns and regulations, economic conditions in producer countries, labor relations, and trade agreements all affected the metal mining industry and its various segments. The mining industry was also dependent on the strength and economic trends of many industries including those related to appliances, autos, beverages, and computers. The industry's outlook, however, remained strong due to consumer reliance on, and demand for, many products and services that depend on mining activities. In fact, according to the Office of Industrial Technologies, in the early 2000s, nearly 47,000 pounds of materials had to be mined for each person living in the United States in order to maintain their standard of living.

Some of the potential challenges for the mining industry include the threat of governments trying to hike taxes on the mining companies, a shortage of skilled workers and even the volatility in the price of the metal itself. There was a highly publicized political battle in Australia early in 2010 in which the government tried to significantly increase taxes on the mining companies, before the effort was scaled back significantly. Some executives predict that similar challenges could face the mining industry again as governments around the world look for new sources of revenue and notice that mining companies are faring better at a time of historically high metals prices.

The mining industry began to consolidate during the early 2000s, especially in the precious metals mining sector. Australia-based BHP Ltd. acquired United Kingdom-based mining firm Billiton PLC in 2001, forming BHP Billiton Limited. Newport Mining Corporation secured its leading position among gold mining companies when it purchased Battle Mountain Gold in 2001 and acquired Normandy Mining of Australia and Canada-based Franco-Nevada Corp. the following year.

Iron Ore. According to the U.S. Geological Survey's Mineral Commodity Summaries, world production of iron ore reached an estimated 1.6 billion tons in 2009, a 6.2 percent decrease from the previous year. Iron ore consumption in China has been the key factor on which the expansion of the international iron ore industry depended. China led the world in iron ore production until 2009. Australia led production with an estimated total of 394 mmt. It was followed by Brazil (300 mmt), India (257 mmt), and China (234 mmt). Iron ore is typically used for manufacturing various types of steel, magnets, auto parts, biochemical and metallurgical applications, paints and inks, cosmetics, and plastics and polishing compounds.

Aluminum. Aluminum is the second most abundant metallic element in the Earth's crust after silicon, yet it is a comparatively new industrial metal that has been produced in commercial quantities for just over a century. It weighs about one–third as much as steel or copper; is malleable, ductile, easily machined and cast, and it has excellent corrosion resistance and durability. Measured either in quantity or value, aluminum's use exceeds that of any other metal except iron and is important in virtually all segments of the world economy. The global aluminum industry reported total revenue of $50.2 billion in 2009, representing a compound annual growth rate (CAGR) of 2.1 percent for the period spanning 2005–2009.

Copper. World copper production reached an estimated 15.8 million metric tons in 2009. The top producer by far remained Chile, with an estimated total of 5.33 mmt. Peru replaced the United States, ranking second in copper production at 1.27 mmt in 2009. While the U.S. dropped to 1.19 mmt in 2009. Copper is one of the key commodities driving civilization and is a vital component in every electronic product and the global electrical infrastructure. Visiongain's analysis concluded that global value of the copper would reach $127bn in 2010.

Copper is a vital material which is inextricably linked to economic development. As emerging economies grow, demand for copper will increase, strengthening the market for this vital commodity. There will be growth in the copper industry due to items such as wiring, cabling, utensils, household products, electrical appliances and construction projects including buildings and electrical transmission and distribution (T&D) networks. As the global copper market adapts to regional shifts on the demand and supply side, the future of the industry will look very different that it has in previous years. The 2011 price forecast was about $7,900/ton.

Silver and Gold. The vast majority of silver produced is as a byproduct of other metal mining, such as copper, lead, and zinc. Silver production increased steadily in the late 1990s and early 2000s, as did consumption, thanks in part to growth in the sales of home computers and cellular phones. With world demand remaining high, the deficit between silver production and supply remained substantial at approximately 700 tons. The use of silver in photographic processing declined significantly between 1999

and 2006 as sales of digital cameras, which do not use film, rose dramatically. The global gold market generated total revenues of $73.5 billion in 2009, representing a compound annual growth rate (CAGR) of 20.1 percent for the period spanning 2005-2009.

The major countries involved in silver mining are Mexico, Peru, and Australia. Silver has been used for thousands of years as ornaments and utensils, for trade, and as the basis for many monetary systems. Of all the metals, pure silver has the whitest color, the highest optical reflectivity, and the highest thermal and electrical conductivity. Also, silver halides are photosensitive. Owing to the above properties, silver has many industrial applications such as in mirrors, electrical and electronic products, and photography, which is the largest single end use of silver. Silver's catalytic properties make it ideal for use as a catalyst in oxidation reactions; for example, the production of formaldehyde from methanol and air by means of silver screens or crystallites containing a minimum 99.95 weight–percent silver. According to the 2009 U.S. Geological Survey, the worldwide production of silver was 710 million ounces.

Gold prices, which remained low at the turn of the twenty-first century, rose during the early 2000s in response to the U.S.-led war in Iraq and concerns about global terrorism. The strength of the U.S. dollar in the late 1990s caused demand for gold to weaken and forced many firms to consolidate and pare back operations. By 2009, China emerged as the largest gold producer in the world with an estimated 310 mmt. Australia was the second largest gold producer. South Africa had dominated the global rankings for nearly a century, but by 2009, it had slipped to fourth place. Consumption of gold grew steadily in the 1990s as the world economy expanded. The world jewelry industry is by far the largest consumer of gold; the metal is also used in electronics and dentistry.

Lead and Zinc. Lead consumption has declined dramatically since the 1970s, in part because of environmental and health regulations designed to address concerns about some of the metal's properties. However, the abandonment of lead as an anti-knocking additive to gasoline and the development of replacement materials for batteries (which at one time accounted for 80 percent of U.S. lead demand) were regarded as more important factors in lead's fall in popularity. Lead production levels remained fairly unchanged from 1997 to 2000 and were much lower than copper, gold, and iron ore.

Zinc production, meanwhile, showed continued recovery from fifteen-year lows reached in 1996. Weak prices and high stock levels prompted some restructuring in the industry in the late 1990s, with some smaller and less efficient mines suspending operations or closing permanently while other companies upgraded facilities to enhance efficiency. Prices improved in 2003 and 2004, coupled with strong demand from China. Zinc output reached 11.1 mmt in 2009. Zinc is an important component in the manufacture of galvanized metal, brass, and other zinc-based alloys. In the mid-2000s, about 48 percent of zinc was used in construction industries and 23 percent in the automotive industry. China was the largest producer, followed by Australia and Peru.

Titanium, an important strategic metal, has many advantages, such as high specific strength, corrosion resistance, biocompatibility, and non-magnetism. Global consumption of titanium products is mainly concentrated in countries and regions like the United States, Europe, China, and Japan. In developed countries and regions such as the United States, Europe, and Japan, titanium is mainly applied in the aviation and aerospace field, making up about 60 percent; in China, it is mainly used in sectors including chemical, pharmaceutical, and metallurgy industries, covering around 70 percent. From the perspective of titanium industry supply and demand, the global production of upstream and downstream products such as titanium sponge and the processing of titanium mill products features higher regional concentration, and only the United States, Japan, Russia, and China have the complete industry chain from titanium sponge to the processing of titanium mill products. In 2009, the apparent consumption of titanium all over the world experienced a year-on-year drop of 32 percent, which resulted in a big fall in the output of titanium sponge and titanium mill products of the world's major titanium producers, of which China alone witnessed a decline of 17.8 percent.

INDUSTRY LEADERS

U.S. Companies. The United States is the home of many major metal mining companies. Leading gold and silver mining companies located in the United States included Newmont Mining Corporation, which became the leading gold miner in the world with its 2002 purchases of Battle Mountain Gold Co., Normandy Mining, and Franco-Nevada Corp. It posted revenues of US$5.53 billion in 2007 and employed 15,000 people. The company produced approximately six million ounces of gold each year as well as copper, silver, and zinc. Cliffs Natural Resources (formerly Cleveland-Cliffs) focused on iron ore and coal and produced approximately 23 million tons of iron ore pellets each year. To remain competitive with China and other foreign producers, Cliffs expanded globally and diversified into mining other minerals. Its sales in 2009 totaled US$2.3 billion, and the company employed approximately 4,000 workers. Freeport-McMoRan acquired Phelps Dodge Corp. in 2007,

becoming one of the world's leading producers of gold. It led the world in low-cost copper production. The company, which also mined gold, silver, and other minerals, posted sales in 2008 of US$17.9 billion with nearly 30,000 employees. Freeport-McMoRan Copper & Gold Inc. planned to defer some output at its Grasberg mine (the world's second largest mine) in Indonesia. Citing safety reasons, Freeport expected to forego the mining of about 130 million pounds of copper through 2014.

BHP Billiton. BHP Ltd., a steel company, acquired the United Kingdom-based mining concern Billiton PLC in 2001 to form BHP Billiton Ltd. and BHP Billiton Plc. The two firms had separate headquarters in Australia and England, were operated as a single business unit, and together were known as BHP Billiton. BHP was the world's largest mining company. The company mined copper, lead, zinc, iron, diamonds, coal, and manganese and had steel and petroleum operations. Total sales in 2009 were US$191.1 billion. BHP Billiton Ltd. said production from its Escondida in Chile, the world's biggest copper mine, would drop as much as 10 percent in 2011 because of current lower ore grades.

Anglo American. The Anglo American Corporation, based in London, was one of the world's largest mining companies, with major operations in gold, platinum, and diamond production. Its 2003 merger between Anglo-Gold and Ashanti Goldfields created the second-largest gold mining company in the world, AngloGold Ashanti, which produced about seven million ounces annually. Anglo American was also part owner of Anglo American Platinum, the leading platinum producer in the world. Anglo also produced various metals, coal, forest products, and industrial minerals. In 2001, it increased its stake in De Beers, the well-known diamond concern, and in 2002, it acquired the Disputada (Minera Sur Andes) copper operations in Chile, placing Anglo American among the world's top five copper producers. In 2003, the company's revenues from platinum fell 12 percent from the previous year, reaching only US$205 million. Gold earnings fell from US$205 million in 2002 to US$167 million in 2003. Earnings from base metals, however, including copper and zinc, rose from a mere US$69 million in 2002 to US$206 million in 2003. Anglo American reported a record operating profit of $45.7 billion in 2009.

Rio Tinto Group. Rio Tinto was one of the largest metal mining companies in the world in the mid-2000s. Rio Tinto mined primarily for aluminum, iron, and gold; about 20 percent of its sales came from coal. The company had dual headquarters in Australia and the United Kingdom; the Australian side was known as Rio Tinto

Limited and the U.K. entity was called Rio Tinto PLC. In 2009, Rio Tinto posted net earnings of US$5.34 billion. Rio Tinto employed more than 36,000 people worldwide. The company's major mines were located in Australia, North America, New Zealand, and Europe.

Codelco. Corporacion Nacional del Cobre de Chile (Codelco), the state-run mining company of Chile, was the world's largest producer of copper. Codelco also owned the world's largest copper reserves, amounting to 17 percent of known copper deposits. The company mined about 1.70 mmt of copper in 2009, 16 percent higher than in 2008. Nearly 17 percent of Chile's exports stemmed from Codelco's mining operations. Its business also accounted for nearly 3 percent of the region's gross domestic product. Codelco also produced small amounts of gold and silver which was residue from electro refining of copper. It reported revenue of $14.3 billion in 2008.

Teck Cominco Limited. Cominco was purchased by gold mining company Teck in 2001. The newly merged company mined gold, zinc, metallurgical coal, and copper, and had global exploration ventures. The majority of the firm's operations were held in Canada, the United States, Chili, and Peru. Company sales reached US$18.8 billion in 2009, of which most derived from zinc mining and refining.

MAJOR COUNTRIES IN THE INDUSTRY

United States. Some members of the metal mining industry in the United States remained among the largest and most influential in the world. Armed with large reserves of many metal minerals within its own borders, the United States had long been an important player, although at any given time some industry segments had performed better than others. According to the U.S. Department of Energy's Industrial Technologies Program, mined products contributed almost five percent of the U.S. gross domestic product by 2009, and mining operations directly employed more than 350,000 people.

In 2009, the United States' total raw, nonfuel mineral mining production industry was worth US$57.1 billion, representing a 20 percent decline from 2008. Gold was the one notable exception to the decline in metal prices. It reached an all time high of $1,215.21 per troy ounce in late 2009. Iron ore was among the largest to decline and decreased by nearly 50 percent in production quantity according to the USGS Mineral Commodities Report for 2010.

Thousands of products having various chemical composition, forms, and sizes are made of iron and steel by casting, forging, and rolling processes. Iron and steel comprise about 95 percent of all the tonnage of metal produced annually in the United States and the world. On the average, iron and steel are by far the least expensive of the world's metals. In some applications, such as steel framing for large buildings, no other materials are suitable, because of strength requirements.

China. Chinese steel demand is strong due to the ongoing processes of industrialization and urbanization, but the pace of growth will slow. Instead of focusing on raising capacity, the industry should be eliminating outdated production facilities and addressing the problem of weak pricing power in iron ore negotiation, according to the 2010 China Metals Report from BMI. The steel industry's performance in the first half of 2010 was very strong and proved many pessimists wrong, but BMI warned that over-optimism among Chinese steelmakers could be their downfall, with a distinct risk of market saturation and mounting stockpiles if output growth rates are not curtailed. The first half of 2010 saw Chinese crude steel output grow 25.4 percent year-on-year (y-o-y) to 213.87mn tons. Flat steel production in the same period amounted to 79.7mn tons, while long production totaled 103.8mn tons.

Latin America. The countries of Latin America have deep reserves of metal mineral deposits, and in the 1990s, the region was the recipient of much investment by large international mining companies. This influx coincided with, reforms of mining and investment laws throughout Latin America and a move toward privatization in some countries. Chile remains one of the world's largest producers of copper, projecting that its copper production would be up 14.4 percent in 2010 and would average US$3.29/pound in 2011.

In the mid-2000s, Mexico remained a leading producer of several mineral commodities, including lead, copper, gold, and zinc, and was the world's largest producer of silver. By 2008, over 10 million ounces of silver had been produced in Mexico. In 2006, mining and metallurgical export production accounted for US$8.1 billion. Mexico's output remains one of the world's highest.

Canada. By 2008, Canada's mining and mineral processing industry accounted for US$55.3 billion—about 8.7 percent—of the country's gross domestic product and employed over 400,000 people. According to the Mining Association of Canada, the mining industry had the highest level of productivity growth compared to the country's other industrial industries. Overall, Canada exported US$46.6 billion in minerals and metals in 2003, accounting for more than 13 percent of its total exports and making it the world's largest exporter of metals. Canada is a leading miner of potash, uranium, nickel, titanium and zinc, aluminum, cobalt, gold, copper, and lead.

Africa. Africa has deposits of 60 different metal and mineral products including gold, diamonds, uranium, manganese, chromium, nickel, bauxite, and cobalt. Exploration efforts were strong in gold and diamonds, and countries including Mozambique, Nigeria, and Madagascar were being explored for base metal and industrial mineral deposits. The African mining industry was centered in southern Africa (South Africa, Ghana, Zimbabwe, Tanzania, and Zambia), and exploration and development projects were underway in virtually every part of the continent. According to Mbendi Information Services, nearly 30 percent of the earth's mineral reserves are found in Africa.

One of the world's largest minerals producers, South Africa mined significant amounts of vanadium, titanium, aluminum, copper, chromium, nickel, iron, lead, and zinc. The country's gold mining operations, after a 30-year decline in production from 1970 to 2000, began an upward trend in 2002. Three major new mines opened in 2002 and 2003, increasing production by about 30 tons per year.

Europe and Central Asia. Western Europe's mining industry diminished in importance in the late 1990s. Countries increasingly relied on imports from Africa, Australia, North America, and South America. As the European Union finalized its transition to a single economy in the early 2000s, various member countries moved to privatize state-owned mineral enterprises. Exploration was carried on for base metals and gold in Ireland, Spain, Portugal, Sweden, Finland, Romania, and Turkey. Germany and Poland were major coal producers.

Mineral production in the former Soviet Union was dominated by Russia, Kazakhstan, and the Ukraine in the early 2000s. Russia was the sixth-largest copper producer in 2005, Russian mining enterprises accounted for 19 percent of the industrial production and employed 1,071,000 people, or 9.3 percent of the industrial labor force. Russia appears to have no clear strategy of developing its mineral resources. It is intensively extracting its reserves, which could lead to the depletion of the majority of these reserves before 2020. Russia ranked among the leading world producer of aluminum, coal, cobalt, copper, gold, iron ore, nickel, steel, and tin.

Middle East. Primarily known as a supplier of crude petroleum, the Middle East was far less involved in the world metal mining industry. Turkey and Iran ranked as the region's leading producers of metal minerals, while Israel, Jordan, and Saudi Arabia also had significant stakes in one or more production areas.

Asia and Pacific Rim. Metal mining and processing establishments in this region, which includes China, Indonesia, India, and Australia, were key producers in the international industry. Through the mid-2000s, the region experienced the greatest increase in demand for metals as its economies experienced rapid growth. Australia, besides being home to some of the world's largest mining companies, was among the top producers of copper, gold, iron, silver, and zinc.

In 1997, China announced its decision to accelerate its plans, begun in the early 1990s, to reform state-owned industries. The plans called for converting large- and mid-sized enterprises into independent corporations in order to promote globalization. The government continued this conversion into the new millennium. By early 2000, China was the world's leading producer of iron; in 2010, China was the largest tin producing country in the world, exporting about 60 percent of its total tin output. In 2004, it was also the top producer of zinc, as well as a major source of copper, gold, aluminum, and lead. Consumption in China also increased significantly; by 2003, the country led the world in consumption of copper and zinc and had also substantially increased demand for other metals, including iron ore and lead.

BIBLIOGRAPHY

Anglo American Annual Report, 2009. Available from http://www.angloamerican.com.

Australia Mining Report Q3 2010. Business Monitor International, Published: June 2010.

BHP Billiton Annual Report, 2009. Available from http://www.bhpbilliton.com.

China Metals Report Q3 2010. Business Monitor International, Published: June 2010.

Cliffs Natural Resources Annual Report, 2009. Available from http://www.cliffsnaturalresources.com.

Codelco 2009 Annual Report. Available from http://www.codelco.cl.

Commodity Online. Available from http://www.commodityonline.com, October 2010.

(The) Copper Market Analysis, Financials and Forecasting 2010-2020 By: Visiongain, Published: September 2010.

Department of the Interior, U.S. Geological Survey. *Mineral Commodity Summaries,* 3 April 2007. Available from http://www.minerals.usgs.gov.

Global and China Titanium Industry Report, 2009-2010, Research In China, Published: August 2010.

"Hoover's Company Capsules." *Hoover's Online,* 2007. Available from http://www.hoovers.com.

Metals and Mining: Global Industry Overview, 2010. Available from http://www.reportlinker.com, 2010.

Rio Tinto Annual Review, 2009. Available from http://www.riotinto.com.

Sykora, Allen "Taxes, Labor Shortages, Price Volatility among possible challenges for Mining Industry." *Kitco News,* Oct. 22, 2010. Available from http://www.dailyfutures.com/metals.

Teck Cominco Limited Annual Report, 2009. Available from http://www.teck.com.

PAPER AND ALLIED PRODUCTS

------■------

PAPER MILLS

NAICS CODE(S)

322121. Paper mills manufacture paper from wood pulp, wastepaper, and other fiber or chemical pulp. Many of the firms in this industry also produce converted paper products. Integrated pulping and papermaking operations are considered in this discussion when they have a sizable presence in papermaking. See also **Paperboard Mills, Paperboard Containers and Boxes,** and **Pulp Mills.**

INDUSTRY SNAPSHOT

Papermaking has been a global industry for centuries. After paper was invented in China in the second century, the craft of papermaking slowly spread throughout the world. The mechanization of papermaking in the nineteenth century spurred a near-simultaneous development of paper businesses in all major industrial economies. Paper mills and pulp mills are considered separate industries, but the two are, in reality, directly connected. A majority of the world's paper is produced at mills integrated with pulp production at the same site and is used for packaging and printing.

Countries with large forest resources, such as the United States and Canada, as well as in Scandinavia, dominate the paper industry since most virgin paper is produced close to its primary raw material—trees. However, recycled fiber plays an increasingly large role in paper production, and many countries, especially Germany, Japan, and South Korea, base the majority of their paper manufacturing industries on recycled paper.

While growth rates in industrialized countries have not been spectacular, developing nations have made strong gains in the per capita use of paper. As of the mid-2000s, the United States was by far the world's largest manufacturer and consumer of pulp, paper, and paperboard. According to the Environmental Paper Network, the average U.S. citizen consumes more than 700 pounds of paper annually—the world's highest per capita. As the Forest Products Association of Canada reported in 2005, paper demand has doubled since 1985 and is forecast to double again between 2005 and 2010. Overall annual consumption rates are expected to increase about 3.2 percent by 2015, with consumption rising about 2.5 percent annually in developed countries and 5.5 percent in developing nations.

Jeff Landin, president of the Neenah-based Wisconsin Paper Council, tried to explain the lower projected increase for the U.S. paper industry when he was a guest columnist for *The Green Bay Press-Gazette.* He presented an insider's analysis of the impact that the closing of four Wisconsin paper mills between August 2007 and August 2008 had on the state. The four reasons he cited were decreased demand for several kinds of paper, dramatically increased production costs, global competition, and the shift away from local ownership due to industry consolidation.

ORGANIZATION AND STRUCTURE

Most paper machinery, equipment, and chemical suppliers sell their products worldwide. Although some countries possess more sophisticated equipment than others do, the process of industrial papermaking is largely the same throughout the world.

Financial Structure. The paper industry is among the world's most capital-intensive manufacturing industries

851

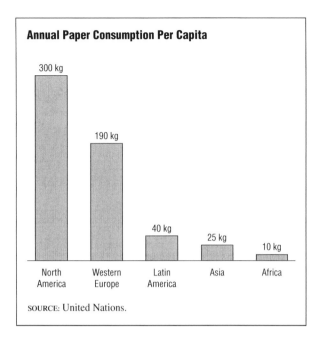

Annual Paper Consumption Per Capita

300 kg — North America
190 kg — Western Europe
40 kg — Latin America
25 kg — Asia
10 kg — Africa

SOURCE: United Nations.

oversupply, its prices tend to fall, and when demand exceeds supply, prices typically rise. For paper manufacturers, higher prices usually signal higher profits. The industry's health can be predicted by the health of magazine and catalog ad sales because declining ad sales translate to fewer printed pages and depressed coated stock prices.

BACKGROUND AND DEVELOPMENT

The invention of paper is generally credited to Ts'ai Lun, a member of the Chinese imperial court, around 105 A.D. Ts'ai Lun's paper was made from mulberry and other barks, fish nets, hemp, and rags. The fibers separated from this pulp were passed through a screen, formed into a web, and dried. This handmade process continued to be used for centuries. The Ancient Egyptians also used a substance made of mashed papyrus reeds to make paper for writing purposes. The word "paper" is derived from papyrus. The Ancient Greeks wrote on the dried leather skins of animals.

Papermaking arrived in Japan in the seventh century. The process of making paper began to spread into Europe during the twelfth century when Muslim settlers built paper mills in Spain. These mills typically used rags to make paper. With the advent of book printing in Europe in the middle of the fifteenth century, the use of paper began to grow rapidly. By 1690 papermaking had spread to the American colonies, when William Rittenhouse established the first U.S. paper mill near Philadelphia.

In 1798, a Frenchman named Louis-Nicolas Robert invented a machine to produce paper in a continuous process, instead of the handmade process that used vats and molds. In the early 1800s, two English papermakers, Henry and Sealy Fourdrinier, purchased patents for the machine. After modification, the Fourdrinier's machine became very popular in England and spread to other countries. This machine, in effect, had turned papermaking from a handmade process into an industry. The name "Fourdrinier" continues to be used to describe certain paper machines.

Recycled rag fibers from clothing had been used almost exclusively to make paper until the end of the 1860s, when straw fibers began to be used. Straw was quickly replaced by the use of groundwood and chemical pulp, both of which were in use in Europe and North America by the early 1870s. Another revolutionary event in the manufacture of paper occurred in the middle of the nineteenth century as wood pulp became the preferred component for making paper. At the time, it was in plentiful supply and was inexpensive.

The size and speed of paper machines increased rapidly between 1850 and the beginning of World War

because it requires nearly continuous investment in plants, equipment, and maintenance. Due to the vast amount of money required to build and maintain paper mills, large companies dominate production of papermaking worldwide. To maximize their returns, these firms purchase enormous, high-speed machines to achieve economies of scale by producing paper at the lowest possible unit cost. Since many grades of paper are widely exported, making them subject to international standards, most large paper mills throughout the world must remain technologically up-to-date. Technological advances have helped paper mills to simultaneously improve quality and drive down production costs.

The volatility of the pulp and paper business cycle was illustrated by changes in the global price of market pulp from 1994 to 1997. In 1994, the price of pulp increased 75 percent in one year due to increased demand and limited supply. However, the price of pulp began falling in late 1996, and six months later the price had dropped nearly 50 percent due to reduced purchases by customers and increased capacity by suppliers. In May 2002, after years of depressed prices, the paper industry was optimistic when the Canadian government announced that increased demand and shrinking inventories boded well for the industry in coming years. Nonetheless, that same month International Paper Company laid off some of its mill workers, saying the demand for coated papers failed to meet inventoried stock.

General economic expansion and capacity rates in individual countries are the two main factors that have affected the financial performance of paper companies worldwide. As with most commodities, when paper is in

I. After World War I, the paper industry worldwide began producing more paper containers and packaging, increasing its use of corrugated medium and linerboard to make shipping boxes, and producing a host of new products such as tissues and sanitary napkins. During World War II, paper and paperboard were vital materials for the armed forces of both the Allied and the Axis powers, which used paper packaging to ship and store military supplies. Paper drives became common during the war years, marking one of the earliest efforts to recycle paper.

After World War II, the global paper industry developed more scientific approaches to forestry and papermaking. Europe rapidly re-industrialized after the war, and up-to-date paper mills were built. By 1945, there were as many as 14,000 different paper products produced worldwide. That number continued to expand as new uses were found for paper, such as milk cartons and drinking cups. Many industry growth trends were centered on the use of disposable paper products.

For centuries, papermaking had been considered an art practiced by experts who used instinct and intuition in manufacturing. A shift in papermaking from art to science occurred during the 1950s and 1960s as wider and faster paper machines were invented, which helped to greatly increase the supply of paper and board throughout the world. By the early 1970s, the paper industry faced worldwide challenges from environmental groups that questioned waste product emissions into the air and water. New rules concerning clean air and water forced paper businesses in most industrialized countries to install expensive new air and water treatment systems.

In the 1970s Europe forged ahead in the production of alkaline paper and recycled paper, which mills in North America did not begin manufacturing until the late 1980s. In the 1980s and early 1990s there was extensive modernization in paper industries throughout the world as high-speed equipment and extensive automation brought papermaking quality and efficiency to new highs.

The forestry practices of Canadian pulp and paper companies, particularly clearcutting, began to be attacked by environmental groups such as Greenpeace in the early 1990s, and a sophisticated media campaign against Canadian producers continued through much of the 1990s. These efforts also spawned a well-organized European campaign to boycott purchases of Canadian market pulp. The Canadian industry mounted a strong defense of its forestry practices. In Europe, many paper mills converted to totally chlorine-free (TCF) bleaching systems to comply with public pressure to remove all chlorine-based chemicals from the papermaking process.

The global paper industry suffered from a negative public image through much of the 1990s. Despite industry participants' contentions that they promoted sustainable forestry by replanting land that had been logged, used a high proportion of recycled fiber, attempted to rapidly phase out the use of elemental chlorine from bleaching sequences, and met stringent wastewater requirements, many environmental groups and citizens considered the industry to be detrimental to the earth. Unaccustomed to such spirited public debate, paper companies in many countries were slow to present their cases to the public. However, with their continued use of forest resources challenged, many companies eventually responded either individually or through their trade organizations, presenting positive, factual information about forestry and papermaking through the news media, advertising, public relations, and other outlets.

While recycled paper had always been a major source of raw material for the paper industry, public pressure in many countries caused European and North American paper companies to expand their use of recycled paper. With limited supplies of wood, Europe traditionally had a high rate of recycling where many countries recycled more than 50 percent of their annual paper production. Japan, which was also short on virgin fiber, typically recycled more than 50 percent of its paper production. Other Asian countries with strong paper industries, such as Taiwan and South Korea, also depended to a great extent on recycled paper for much of their paper and paperboard production.

However, with its abundant supplies of wood, North American countries historically recycled at a much lower rate than those in Europe or in Japan. For example, the U.S. paper industry's recycling rate hovered just above 25 percent in the late 1980s. In the late 1980s, a perceived landfill crisis developed in the United States, causing increased public pressure to expand recycling. Consequently, in 1989 the U.S. paper industry set a goal to recycle 40 percent of the paper it produced by 1995. That goal was reached two years early, and the industry set even loftier goals.

Throughout the early 1990s, the Canadian and U.S. paper industries quickly improved their recycling capacities. Canadian mills, many of which produced newsprint for the U.S. market, had to comply with the laws of many U.S. states that mandated certain levels of recycled fiber in newspapers published within their boundaries. U.S. mills had to comply with federal guidelines for the purchase of recycled paper, which quickly became a de facto standard for many other purchasers of paper, both public and private.

Much of the credit for expanded recycling in Europe was given to strict German recycling laws that other European countries began to adopt. These laws required manufacturers of industrial and consumer products, such as packaging suppliers, to make provisions for collecting and recycling their products, including setting up recycling centers. Such a system was the reverse of that in the United States and Canada, where collection of wastepaper was handled voluntarily by businesses or by municipalities.

However, while environmental concerns about controlling pulp and paper emissions appeared to be abating, the availability of fiber—primarily raw wood from tree harvesting—emerged as an obstacle for the global paper industry. In the late 1990s, European and North American paper producers were confronted with sustained opposition to tree harvesting from environmental groups and harvesting restrictions imposed by government agencies. In the northwestern United States, tree harvesting on federal lands virtually came to a halt due to legal challenges in the early 1990s. Production resumed by the mid-1990s, but at a greatly reduced rate. The pace of "removals" of trees from federal lands continued at a low level into the early 2000s. Stricter control of harvesting practices on federal land in western Canada was expected to raise the cost of timber operations in that region as well.

Electronic display and storage of information presented another major challenge to the global paper industry. Many experts predicted that paper would become obsolete as computers became commonplace in homes and offices in the industrialized nations during the 1980s. However, by the 1990s it became apparent that the advent of computers and fax machines would have the opposite effect on the paper industry. These electronic devices encouraged users to use even more paper for printing than before. Nonetheless, due to the increasing sophistication and decreasing prices of computers, they were being used more often to replace paper for the storage and transfer of certain kinds of information. Some predicted this would eventually curtail the growth of paper usage. Others argued that since computers had vastly expanded the amount of information that could be stored, even the printing of a small percentage of this information would keep paper usage growing, albeit at a moderate pace.

In the 1990s many publishers who had traditionally used only paper-based publishing developed electronic products, such as e-books. Eager to preserve their market position as information providers, media giants such as *The Financial Times* of London and the German magazine *Der Spiegel,* moved into television. Many major U.S. newspapers produced online versions of their publications for households and offices with personal computers. Most of these new electronic media complemented traditional magazines and newspapers, serving to duplicate or extend information already available in print.

The major development in the paper industry in the 1990s was the rapid growth of paper manufacturing in

developing regions such as Asia Pacific and South America. These regions, with extensive timber resources, saw major growth in papermaking capacity. Companies such as Asia Pacific Resources International (APRIL) and Asia Pacific Pulp and Paper in Asia, and VCP and Aracruz in South America, opened several large new pulp and paper mills, dramatically expanding papermaking capacity in these regions.

Much of the new capacity was targeted for domestic consumption, since Asian economies especially were growing at double-digit rates for much of the 1990s. This growth, however, was threatened by the financial crisis affecting much of Asia in 1997 and 1998. Despite the economic difficulties, growth in Asian papermaking capacity in Asia was expected to outpace growth in established economies like North America and Europe at the beginning of the twenty-first century.

However, some of the Asian projects faced delays or cancellation due to the economic crisis in the region in 1997. The Asian paper market, which had been the fastest growing in the world for much of the 1990s, faced turmoil as the crisis stalled that region's fast-growing pulp and paper industry in 1998. Several paper companies faced significant financial challenges. As the currencies of major Asian pulp and paper producers, such as Indonesia, fell dramatically against the U.S. dollar, the financial impact on local companies was severe. Larger mills with modern equipment, recently purchased with U.S. dollars, struggled to recoup their investment. High debt loads by these companies made the financial problems even worse.

As the rate of economic growth slowed in Asia in 1997 and 1998, there was considerable speculation that the ownership structure of the Asian pulp and paper industry would change markedly as companies from outside the region—perhaps from North America and Europe—tried to buy Asian pulp and paper producers at what had quickly become bargain prices. For example, in late 1997 Procter & Gamble Co. obtained a controlling share of Sangyong Paper Co., believed to be the first large takeover of a South Korean company by a foreign firm.

However, in the 1990s consumption of paper increased rapidly in areas like China and Southeast Asia. Further consumption growth was expected in the region through the early 2000s, as the rapid increase in international trade boosted demand for packaging materials. The European Union (EU) experienced sustained growth, fueling a turnaround in its severely depressed paper industry.

In the United States, pricing and profits were greatly improved. In 1995 the average price for all grades of paper and paperboard soared 41 percent on top of an 8 percent increase in 1994. However, the high price levels did not hold. Much of the increase in prices was attributed to customers stocking paper in inventory in anticipation of further price increases. When customers had sufficient inventories, they made substantial cuts on new purchases and used the paper already in their inventory. This caused prices to drop sharply in late 1996 and early 1997, as well as in 2001 and 2002.

In the late 1990s, there was significant international trade in paper and paperboard, dominated by linerboard and coated paper. Worldwide trade in paper began to expand following the conclusion of the Uruguay Round Agreement of the General Agreement on Tariffs and Trade (GATT) in 1994. The revised GATT included a "zero for zero" provision for paper, in which all tariffs on paper in industrialized countries would be phased out over a ten-year period ending in 2005. Canadian and U.S. negotiators were unsuccessful in their attempts to reduce the phase-out period to five years. Furthermore, the North American Free Trade Agreement (NAFTA) between the United States, Canada, and Mexico expanded trade between Mexico and its northern neighbors who already had established free trade in paper. However, the 40 percent devaluation of the Mexican peso in late 1994 temporarily halted the rapid growth of U.S. shipments of paper to Mexico, although those numbers increased somewhat in 1997.

The more free economic climate between the United States and Canada also encouraged more investment in U.S. paper manufacturing facilities by Canadian companies. For example, in 1997 Montreal-based St. Laurent Paperboard acquired a West Point, Virginia, mill from Chesapeake Corp. of Richmond, Virginia. In 1997 and 1998, the structure of the Canadian paper industry changed considerably, partly in response to the new economic climate. In 1997, Canada's two largest paper companies, Abitibi-Price and Stone-Consolidated, merged to form the leading newsprint producer in the world, Abitibi-Consolidated, Inc. Most of the assets of another large Canadian company, Repap Enterprises, were sold in 1997 after the firm encountered severe financial problems. In early 1998, MacMillan Bloedel Ltd. of Vancouver began a major restructuring that included selling, exiting, or spinning off some businesses, closing unprofitable facilities, and downsizing 21 percent of its workforce of 13,000 employees. The company was expected to sell or spin off its groundwood paper business and to expand and possibly separate its Montgomery, Alabama-based packaging business.

CURRENT CONDITIONS

While the global paper industry remained strong throughout the 2000s, it faced several major challenges, including environmental and recycling concerns, an impending fiber shortage, and competition from alternative media. Advances in pulping and bleaching technologies helped reduce mill emissions of toxic substances, and in the early 2000s

mills in North America and Europe appeared to be ready to comply with new environmental regulations without serious damage to their profitability.

The global paper industry is highly competitive and is sustained by a modern, efficient manufacturing base as well as strong markets. Growth in established markets was expected to be modest, remaining at or slightly above the growth rate of gross domestic product (GDP), but some fear it could decline before there is annual growth again.

While North America and Europe were traditionally the leading paper producers in the world, new paper mills were more likely to be built in Asia than anywhere else early in the twenty-first centuryBoth India and China are expected to be key players in the paper industry growth over the next several years. Many top paper companies from around the world invested in expansion projects in China. Finland-based UPM, for example, invested US$470 million in a fine-paper production facility in Changshu in the early 2000s, upgrading its production capacity to 800,000 tonnes. In 2005, Singapore-based Asia Pulp & Paper and Daio Paper Corporation of Japan announced a joint venture in China worth US$30.2 million to produce a range of tissue products, industrial paper, packaging materials, and other paper.

Consumption of paper in the early 2000s tended to mirror living standards. Nations with high standards of living consumed the most paper. For example, per capita consumption was about 190 kg annually in Western Europe and more than 300 kg in North America. By contrast, average per capita consumption in the developing world reached only 17.5 kg, far below the 30 kg to 40 kg per capita considered necessary to meet minimum standards for communications and literacy. According to U.N. data, the average rate of paper consumption in Latin America was about 40 kg per capita, in Asia, this figure was approximately 25 kg, and per capita paper use in Africa was less than 10 kg per capita. Nevertheless, total paper and cardboard consumption in Asia surpassed that of Europe, and was projected to increase 3.5 to 5.5 percent annually through 2010.

In June 2004, Michael Ducey wrote in *Graphic Arts Monthly* that an increase in prices could be expected by most paper companies for lightweight coated machine-finished paper as well as economy No. 3 coated rolls. Variable included weight, finish, and brightness, as well as mills covering increased drying, transportation, and benefits costs. It was widely held that paper companies were instituting the increase early so that customers would not be shocked when buying increased in the summer.

Graphic Arts Monthly also reported that global demand for graphic papers was strong. During the first quarter of 2004, demand for all grades of printing and writing papers increased 2.3 percent. Mill inventories had dropped, while exports soared and production grew more slowly.

Technological advances, including the Internet, electronic documents storage, electronic books, microfilm, and microfiche, have played a part in the reduction of paper documents and their storage. Several major studies of electronic media in the late 1990s concluded that paper risked no imminent danger of being replaced by its electronic competitors. The studies reported that electronic media would not affect most grades of paper until about 2010, when some negative impact might be felt. The studies also indicated that some trends, such as continually decreasing newspaper circulation, was expected to have some effect on consumption of certain grades of paper before 2010. The long-term survival of paper media in the twenty-first century appeared to depend on several key questions, including whether or not advertisers would use electronic versions that made it easier for readers to avoid advertising messages and whether or not people would read from a screen for extended periods.

Simon Binns reported that family–owned SAICA, which is based in Zargoza, announced it would build a GBP250 million (US$499.68 million) paper mill at Partington Wharfside in Trafford. The facility is planned to be "the base for the world's most advanced recycled paper mill." SAICA decided on Trafford because of its location near highways and the Manchester Ship Canal. It is also well-situated to the great quantities of recovered paper throughout the north of England.

Deputy Minister Khu urged the members of the Vietnam Paper Association to operate their mills at capacity and to develop tangible plans to meet projected market demands, especially for academic needs. At the time, the paper mills in Vietnam were meeting only 60 percent of market demand for printed and writing papers.

WORKFORCE

The level of employment in technically advanced papermaking countries, such as Canada, Germany, Japan, and the United States, had declined slowly but steadily in the late 1990s and throughout the 2000s, despite regular increases in papermaking capacity. Increased automation was cited as the main reason for the declining labor figures. Employment in the sector has declined steadily with an annual compound rate of 2 percent

In most countries, paper industry employees were unionized and received wages that exceeded those of workers in other industries. Strong labor unions in countries like Germany, Canada, and Sweden exerted a powerful influence on the operation of their paper mills. However, in the United States many nonunion mills had opened in the 1970s and 1980s, including mills constructed by companies that had unionized mills in other

locations. The wages and benefits provided by nonunion U.S. mills were generally comparable to unionized mills.

Following World War II, paper mills worldwide were highly labor intensive and employed relatively low-skilled workers in production jobs. However, as paper mill automation became prevalent in every major papermaking country except China in the 1970s and 1980s, workers began to need technical skills to understand and direct the computerized operations of paper machines. In Europe, most paper mill workers had earned advanced degrees following high school in order to qualify for production work, while in the United States many paper companies increasingly hired recent college graduates who held bachelor's degrees and postgraduate degrees in paper science. About 10 U.S. universities had pulp and paper programs.

INDUSTRY LEADERS

International Paper. In 2008, U.S.-based International Paper Company (IP) reported annual sales of US$22.3 billion. With headquarters in Memphis, Tennessee, IP was the largest global paper company in production and sales, except in areas such as newsprint, where it was second to Abitibi-Consolidated. IP was the top producer of bleached board for milk and food packaging and uncoated freesheet paper. Other IP products included stationery, art papers, and many other grades of paper. Paper and packaging products accounted for more than 50 percent of annual sales. IP operated facilities in 31 countries. In the 1980s and 1990s, IP made many acquisitions worldwide, expanding its presence as a global producer of paper and paper products. Those acquisitions included Hammermill Paper (United States), Aussedat Rey (France), Zanders (Germany), Kwidzynie (Poland), and Carter Holt Harvey in New Zealand.

In 1996, IP acquired Federal Paper Board, which had operations in the United States and the United Kingdom, for US$3.5 billion. In 1998, the company acquired Weston Paper & Manufacturing Co. in Terre Haute, Indiana, for US$232 million. Weston's single corrugating medium mill and 11 corrugated container plants were added to IP's roster of five containerboard mills and 23 box plants in the United States. Internationally, IP had two additional mills and 20 container plants. In 2000, IP acquired Champion International Corporation. In 2003, IP sought approval to use its captive insurer to reinsure its group life benefits. In July 2004, *PR Newswire* reported that IP would be integrating Box USA's 24 industrial packaging converting facilities and containerboard mill into its industrial packaging business, which was comprised of 11 paper mills and 77 converting facilities worldwide. IP had operations in more than 40 countries and sold products in more than 120 nations with a workforce of over 51,500 employees.

Abitibi-Consolidated, Inc. Abitibi-Consolidated, according to *Associated Press* reports, slipped past International Paper to become the industry's number one world leading newsprint and uncoated groundwood manufacturing firm, following mergers and acquisitions from 1997 through 2000. Formerly known as Abitibi-Price Inc., Abitibi-Consolidated was created through a merger of Abitibi-Price with Stone-Consolidated Corp. The new company acquired Donohue Inc. in a multi-billion-dollar deal. As often occurs with industrial mergers, older, redundant equipment and mills were shut down following the mergers, which also led to the layoffs or early retirements of company workers. Abititi-Consolidated owns or is a partner in 30 paper mills, 20 sawmills, 4 remanufacturing facilities, and 1 engineered wood facility throughout Canada, the United Kingdom, the United States, South Korea, China, and Thailand. According to company information, it also is the global leader in recycling newspapers and North America's fifth leading lumber producer. Abititi-Consolidated does business in more than 70 countries. Its Pan-Asia Paper joint venture with Norske Skog (Norway) is the largest newsprint company in Asia. In 2007, Bowater and Abitibi-Consolidated merged, creating the third largest pulp and paper company in North America, and the eighth largest in the world. In 2005 the company posted sales of US$5.342 billion, with a workforce of 17,000 employees.

Georgia-Pacific. Atlanta-based Georgia-Pacific Corporation (G-P) was the world's largest producer of tissue products and the second largest U.S. producer of forest products as of 2004. It manufactured containerboard and packaging, communications papers, market pulp, and tissue at 81 facilities in the United States and one in Canada as of 1996. G-P was the second largest U.S. producer of containerboard. In 2001, G-P reported that it produced and sold more than 300,000 tons of kraft paper bags. The company also produced plywood, oriented strand board and other wood panels, lumber, gypsum wallboard, chemicals, and other products at 153 facilities in the United States and 7 in Canada. It is a well-known producer of quality office supply paper. In 2001 and 2002, stock prices dropped in the middle of a nationwide recession and rumors that G-P was considering filing for Chapter 11 bankruptcy reorganization as a result of threatened and filed asbestos lawsuits. CEO Pete Correll went public to discount the rumors and to affirm his belief in the company's future. Nonetheless, faced with plunging stock prices, G-P sold about half of its white paper assets to Domtar in 2000. Correll also told stockholders in January 2001 that 2000 had been one of the worst years the industry has ever had due to a weak demand for paper and other pulp products. Total bleached and paper sales in 2000 were US$9 billion. G-P sold 60 percent of its Unisource Worldwide distribution segment in 2002. In 2004, the company sold its building products distribution business and non-integrated pulp operations, which

cut its debt almost US$2 billion. That year, total sales reached US$19.6 billion. In December, 2005, G-P finalized a deal with Koch Industries to be bought for US$21 billion, and was removed from the Stock Exchange. Operating under Koch Industries, in 2008, Georgia-Pacific had 50,000 employees at more than 300 locations in both North and South America and in Europe.

UPM-Kymmene. UPM-Kymmene of Helsinki, Finland, was Europe's biggest forest industry group and one of the world's largest paper manufacturers. The company was formed in 1996 by the merger of Kymmene Corp. with Repola Ltd., the latter of which operated two subsidiaries, United Paper Mills (UPM) Ltd. and Rauma Oy. UPM-Kymmene's main markets were in Great Britain, Finland, Germany, and France. UPM-Kymmene's forest product business is conducted by seven divisions: magazine papers, newsprint, fine papers, packaging materials, sawmilling, special products, and plywood. In 2002, the company addressed lowered prices for paper and predicted that a turnaround was beginning to occur in certain global economies.

In 1997, UPM-Kymmene had announced an agreement with Singapore-based APRIL to exchange 30 percent of their respective fine paper operations in a non-cash transaction. The deal would involve the creation of two new companies owned by the two parent companies. Also in 1997, UPM-Kymmene purchased the Blandin Paper Co., a coated paper producer in Grand Rapids, Minnesota, from parent company Fletcher Challenge Canada. Furthermore, in 2002 UPM-Kymmene acquired G. Haindische Papierfabriken KGaA, a German paper producer, for US$2.4 million. That acquisition had reportedly made UPM-Kymmene the world's largest producer of magazine papers. In July 2004, the company announced that it was launching a feasibility study at its Blandin paper mill. In 2008, UPM announced that, in an effort to cut costs, it would lay off thousands of employees and two of its main mills would be closed. This was the largest layoff Finland had ever seen. In 2009, UPM-Kymmene's forest industry operations, including paper, reported 23,210 employees and posted sales of US$10.2 billion.

Stora Enso Oyj. With roots dating back to the thirteenth century, Swedish-based Stora Enso Oyj claimed to be the world's oldest company. In 1288, according to Stora's company history, Bishop Peter received one-eighth of Kopparberg Mountain in a mining charter.

Stora was one of the world's largest forest-products companies during the late 1990s, a position that was strengthened in 1998 by its merger with Enso Oy of Finland, which had been created in 1996 through the merger of Enso-Gutzeit and Veitsiluoto. Prior to the merger with Enso Oy, Stora had acquired China's largest fine coated paper producer, Suzhou Papyrus Paper, also in 1998, to tap into its annual capacity of 120,000 tonnes. In 2001, Stora Enso acquired a minority 26.5 percent share of stock of SPB Beteiligungsverwaltung GmbH of Austria, making its Stora Enso Timber Oy Ltd. a wholly owned subsidiary of Stora Enso, according to company financial reports.

Stora produces large amounts of pulp, printing paper, packaging paper, and board and fine papers, and operates mostly in Europe. Its pulp and paper operations are split into four divisions: Stora Cell, which manufactures pulp; Stora Feldmuhle, which manufactures newsprint, uncoated and coated magazine paper, carbonless paper, and fax paper; Stora Billerud, which produces liquid packaging board, regular packaging board, corrugating materials, kraft paper, bag paper, and plastic sacks; and Stora Papyrus, which manufactures coated and uncoated fine papers, colored papers, security papers, and label papers. Amid a depressed global sales market for all timber products, company sales were reported at approximately US$13.4 billion in 2001, with a net income of US$918 million. Sales rose to US$11.85 billion in 2009, with a workforce of over 28,700.

Svenska Cellulosa Aktiebolaget SCA. Svenska Cellulosa Aktiebolaget SCA is a European market leader in tissue products, packaging materials, and forest products. SCA's tissue products include consumer products, such as toilet paper and kitchen rolls, as well as those intended for industrial and institutional users, such as wipes and washroom systems. As of 2004, SCA Hygiene Paper was the largest tissue supplier in Europe. Another division produced fluff pulp for products such as disposable diapers. SCA Packaging was Europe's leading manufacturer of corrugated board packaging in the late 1990s. The division also produced containerboard, including both kraftliner and testliner. SCA's forest and timber division managed and developed SCA's forest product division and supplied the group's Swedish plants with virgin wood fiber for the production of paper, packaging, and hygiene products.

In 2004, approximately one-half of Svenska Cellulosa's annual sales came from tissue products, packaging accounted for another 30 percent, and publication paper accounted for 8 percent of sales. The company has mills in Sweden, the United Kingdom, and Austria. Between 2001 and 2002, the company acquired significant mill holdings from CartoInvest, Encore Paper Co., and Georgia-Pacific Corp. in an attempt to boost market share, according to *Bloomberg News*. In 2001, Svenska Cellulosa reported that its strategy of increasing tissue-making properties led to profits for five straight years. *Bloomberg News* reported that in 2002, the company's stock had risen a whopping 43 percent while revenue shares in forest products fell from 32 percent to 16 percent. The company posted sales of US$14.29 billion in 2009, and a workforce of approximately 45,000.

Nippon Paper Group, Inc. Nippon Paper Group, formerly Nippon Unipac Holding, is the largest paper-making company in Japan. The company was formed from the merger of Daishowa Paper Manufacturing Co. and Nippon Paper Industries in 2002. Nippon Paper Group controls about 40 percent of the Japanese paper market and operates 17 mills in Japan. It also has overseas facilities in Australia, Canada, Chile, New Zealand, Finland, Russia, South Africa, and the United States. The company's principal markets include newsprint, non-coated printing paper, slightly coated printing papers, coated printing papers, and communications paper. It also markets a range of specialty printing papers, including 100,000 metric tonnes of heat-sensitive and electrostatic papers. In addition, the company produced chemicals, processed papers, functional film products, and housing materials. Other Nippon Paper business operations served specialized markets, such as landscape gardening, greenery, and lumber.

Nippon Unipac was seriously harmed by falling advertising prices in the international magazine sector at the end of 2001. Nippon Unipac disclosed that group-operating profit for the six months ending September 30 were US$163.5 million, which represented a 48 percent drop from the combined group operating profit for the same period in 2000. The softened market was blamed on fewer ad sales for periodicals, and a drop in technical brochures and booklets ordered by electronics companies.

In 2002, the company participated in its thirteenth international reforestation purchase when it bought a significant interest in WAPRES, a subsidiary of Australia's Marubeni Corp. In 2006 the company reported sales of US$9.9 billion.

Oji Paper. Oji Paper Co. Ltd., Tokyo, is the second-largest paper company in Japan. It was created through the merger of the Oji Paper Company and Kanzaki Paper Manufacturing Company. That company, called the New Oji Paper Co., merged with Honshu Paper Co. Ltd. in 1996, and was subsequently renamed Oji Paper Co. Its main product areas are printing and writing papers (about 71 percent of sales); tissue, miscellaneous papers, and market pulp (14 percent); converted products (9 percent); packaging paper (5 percent); and real estate and other products (1 percent). Oji Paper was adversely affected by plunging paper sales in 2001, whih resulted in production cuts for of specialty paper production and loss of jobs for 150 employees in 2002. In July 2004, Oji Paper purchased five of two SmartView Paper Web Inspection Systems and three SmartView Winder Advisor Systems for paper machines at its Yonago, Japan mill from the Cognex Corporation, according to *Business Wire*. Sales in 2007 reached US$15.67 billion.

MAJOR COUNTRIES IN THE INDUSTRY

United States. In 2004, the United States was the largest producer and consumer of paper industry products, according to the Food and Agricultural Organization of the United Nations (FAO). The industry faced stagnating conditions from 2000 through 2002. In 2000, U.S. production figures for paper and paperboard production dropped 2.9 percent to 85 mmt. With additional losses due to the ad sales slump in the magazine industry combined with reduced printing runs for brochures and instruction booklets in the electronics industry, 2001 figures had dropped an additional 7.9 percent over 2000. The industry had continued to hope for a rebound in late 2002 or 2003. Perhaps the area most seriously hurt in 2002 was New England, where the bankruptcy of the German-owned American Tissue Inc. of New Hampshire put 860 laborers out of work. In Maine, workers routinely were asked to take unpaid leaves.

By 2004, overall conditions had begun to show slight improvement. The Global production in the pulp and paper sector is expected to increase on 77 percent from 1995 to 2020.Industrialized nations with 20 percent of the world's population—like the United States—consume 87 percent of the world's printing and writing papers.

Joel Dresang and Thomas Content reported in the *Journal Sentinel* that "The U.S. Department of Energy said it provide up to $30 million for the $84 million biorefinery proposed at the Flambeau River Papers mill in Park Falls" (Wisconsin), continuing, "... the federal grant will accelerate the start-up of a refinery for renewable sulfur-free diesel fuel made from forest byproducts." Flambeau River Biofuels President Bob Byrne agreed that the paper mill and the proposed biodiesel plant would work well together.

The Central Arbitration Committee ruled that the Unite Members' claim was admissible. It dealt with requests for a ruling on collective bargaining at the Kamns Mill. It is the hygiene paper manufacturing section of the Leicester Paper Company. The outcome was very noteworthy considering Unite Team Leader and national officer Perry Ellis acknowledged that organizing had been going on for many years under "very hostile circumstances," Ellis anticipated better working environment would evolve at Kamns Mill in Leicester in the future. In 2001, there were 114,670 employees within the paper mill industry in the U.S.

Japan. Japan was the third largest producer of paper and paperboard throughout the 2000s, and was also one of the world's largest consumers of such products. Japan was the largest wood importer in the world, with nearly all of its paper was made from imported wood or recycled paper. However, the Japanese paper industry struggled throughout much of the 1990s due to the stagnant Japanese economy. With the economy in a slow recovery, paper and board

production inched upward during the late 1990s. In the 2000s, very little timber for paper was cut in Japan itself because of recovery and sustained replanting costs, according to the FAO. During the early 2000s, hundreds of antiquated sawmills were being shut down as they were unable to match the production and efficiency of newer sawmills. According to Japan's Ministry of Economy, Trade and Industry, paper and paperboard production was 31.8 mmt in 2000 and 30.6 mmt in 2002. Newsprint production rose slightly, from 3.4 mmt to 3.5 mmt.

Large Japanese producers had expanded their ownership of plantations overseas. Oji Paper invested in Australia, while Nippon Paper Industries Co. Ltd. planted hardwood trees in Chile. In 2001, Japan's paper industry encountered difficult times as ad sales dropped, as did orders for electronics instruction manuals. Although the drop from 2000 to 2001 was only 1 percent, a much larger figure was expected in 2002 as Oji Paper Co. and other firms reduced total paper production.

In an attempt to recover from sluggish sales and low paper prices, Mitsubishi Paper Mills planned to cut its workforce and shut down the Tokyo-based Nakagawa Mill. Mitsubishi Paper Mills also announced that it had formed a joint venture with Kodak to sell photographic products in Japan. In addition, Hokuetsu Paper Mills, a major producer of white boxboard, decided to use chlorine dioxide rather than the traditional chlorine gas to produce bleached pulp, resulting in improved wastewater color.

China. China's paper industry grew steadily in the mid-1990s as economic reforms instituted by the Chinese government took effect. However, by 2002 government-mandated birth control regulations had begun to shrink paper and board demand. In particular, the extremely low female population had resulted in a greatly diminished demand for sanitary napkins paper, as well as baby-related products.

In 2002, much of China's paper industry stagnated. The country closed numerous paper mills and laid off many workers, which resulted in an urban unemployment rate of 3.6 percent in December 2001. However, demand for paper and paper goods increased after 2002. In 2003, consumption of paper and paperboard reached 48 mmt, or 16 percent of world consumption. As of 2004, there were more than 3,500 facilities producing paper and paper products in China, with a total capacity of 43 mmt each year. A net importer of paper products, China imported 17 mmt in 2002. To boost domestic production by 5.5 mmt of wood pulp by 2010, the Chinese government is encouraging private investment and joint ventures with foreign investors, and the China Paper Association projected demand to increase to 70 mmt by 2010.

Canada. With its vast forest area of 4.2 million square kilometers, Canada was one of the world's leading producers of forest products, market pulp, and newsprint. Canada exported most of the paper and paperboard it produced. In the late 1990s, the Canadian paper industry underwent a major reorganization, as many firms spun off different units, purchased other companies, and sold assets. In 2001, Canada suffered a slump in paper production, falling 2.2 percent from 2000 figures. By 2003 conditions had improved, and paper industry profits reaching US$1.2 billion in 2004. Nonetheless, by 2005 the industry expected a decline due to sluggish demand for newsprint in North America and increased costs. The Conference Board of Canada projected that 2005 profits would drop about US$500 million, for a total of about US$700 million. In 2006 the industry expected cost increases to level off, leading to projected profits of about US$1.3 billion.

Germany. The 1990s were difficult for the German paper industry, which struggled with a recession as well as the integration of relatively inefficient paper mills in the repatriated East Germany. Companies deemed it to be financially expedient to simply close many of those mills. Large Finnish companies bought some German companies in the mid-1990s, a trend that continued into the early twenty-first century. In 2001, Germany's largest paper producer, Haindl'sche Papierfabriken KgaA, was acquired by UPM-Kymmene of Finland and Norske Skog of Norway for US$2.6 billion dollars. Meanwhile, upgrades contributed to improvements in capacity. A joint project between Rhein Paper and Voith, which started in July 2002, produced 737 mmt of paper in one day, which set a record manufacturing speed. A new kraft pulp mill began production in Stendal in 2004, which was expected to produce 552,000 mmt of market pulp a year. That mill is projected to play a major part in boosting the German paper industry. In 2009, the global economic recession impacted the German pulp and paper industry by creating a significant fall in production and revenues.According to the German Pulp and Paper Association the industry-wide revenues dropped 16 percent over 2008, to US$16.5 billion.

Finland. With a relatively small population of 5.1 million, Finland possesses substantial forest resources and has developed a strong export-oriented economy, based largely on forest products, machinery, and engineering. Well over one-half of Finnish paper and paperboard production was in high-grade printing and writing papers. As of 2005, it exported the vast majority of the paper and paperboard it produced and accounted for as much as 15 percent of world paper and paperboard trade. UPM-Kymmene of Finland became a major market player in 2002 as it completed the buyout of a large German company, Haindl'sche Papierfabriken KgaA, in conjunction with Norwegian firm Norske Skog.

Industry production in Finland increased almost 5 percent in 2000, according to government statistics. Production in 2000 was higher in most categories than during the 1990s. In 2000, paper and paperboard production increased to a record 13.5 million tons, up 560,000 tons from 1999, according to the Finnish government's web site.

A major dispute between union and management in 2005, however, threatened those gains. Over 24,000 paper mill workers were locked out of their factories on May 15, 2005, following demands that employers no longer use temporary workers, keep factories running during some holiday periods, and abandon proposed limits on benefits. As of mid-June 2005, the strike had lasted four weeks and shut down mills owned by UPM-Kymmene and Stora Enso Oyj. According to an AP report, the strike had cost the Finnish forest products industry a staggering amount per day in lost production. The strike lasted until July 1 before a deal could be hammered out.

Sweden. Two-thirds of Sweden is woodlands, which contributes to its status as one of the world's leading producers of forest and paper products. In the late 1990s, its total forest resources covered 290,000 square kilometers; 240,000 square kilometers were zoned as commercial forests. Sweden's 8.7 million citizens also consumed a substantial amount of paper and paperboard. Swedish paper and paperboard producers focus on lower grades of paper, such as newsprint, corrugating materials, and paperboard. In 2002, the Swedish industry was hurt by declining ad pages in periodicals, as industry giant (number two in sales nationally) Stora Enso Oyj reported a drop in earnings of 21 percent for the fourth quarter of 2001. Sweden closed 14 paper mills between 1980 and 2001, but capacity steadily improved, reaching 11.2 mmt manufactured at 48 mills in 2001. Sweden's production that year reached 10.5 mmt, of which 8.7 mmt was exported.

BIBLIOGRAPHY
"Abitibi–Consolidated Reports Improving Results in the First Quarter—Higher Newsprint Prices and Lower Overall Costs Help Mitigate C$ Strength." *PR Newswire,* 23 April 2004.

Binns, Simon. "GBP250m Paper Mill to Bring 200 New Jobs to Trafford." *Crain's Manchester Business,* 14 July 2008.

"Cognex Receives Record Order from Leading Japanese Paper Maufacturer." *Business Wire,* 2 July 2004.

"Deputy Minister Tells Paper Industry to Meet School Needs," 16 July 2008. Available: from http//english.vietnamnet.vn/biz/2008/07/793894/.

Doyle, Dara. "SCA to Buy Catoinvest." *Bloomberg News,* 19 February 2002.

Dresang, Joel, and Thomas Content. "Biofuels Plan Wins Grant: Refinery Proposed at Flambeau River Papers." *Milwaukee Journal-Sentinel,* 14 July 2008. Available from www.jsonline.com.

Ducey, Michael J. "Paper Rides the Inflation Wave: Price Increases for Most Grades of Coated Groundwood Paper are Hitting

Printing Plants for the First Time in Nearly a Decade." *Graphic Arts Monthly,* 21 June 2004.

"Facts About the Paper Industry, Global Warming and the Environment." *The Daily Green,* 10 February 2007. Available from www.thedaily green.com.

Finland's Paper Industry Sees a Silver Lining; All Business; September 2005. Available from www.allbusiness.com.

"Finnish, Norwegian Paper Companies Complete Acquisition of German Rival." *Agence France Presse,* 30 November 2001.

"Finnish Paper Industry Shutdown in Fourth Week." Associated Press, 6 June 2005. Available from news.moneycentral.msn.com.

"From Reeds, Paper Got Its Start." *Chapel Hill Herald,* 10 February 2002.

"The Future of Paper . . . From Cyberspace to Fibrespace." Forest Products Association of Canada, 2004. Available from www.cppa.org.

"Germany's Pulp and Paper Industry Suffered Plunge in Turnover in 2009." *Forest Expert,* 10 June 2010. Available from www. forestexpert.com.

"Haindl Renames." *Printing World,* 4 March 2002.

"International Paper Completes Acquisition of Box USA, A Leading Corrugated Packing Company." *PR Newswire,* 2 July 2004.

Kline, James E. *Paper and Paperboard: Manufacturing and Converting Fundamentals.* San Francisco: Miller Freeman, 1982.

"Labor Department Approves Swedish Company's Employee-Benefits Captive." *BestWire Services,* 7 July 2004.

Landin, Jeff. "Guest Column: Paper Mills' Struggles Affect Everyone." *Green Bay Press Gazette,* 21 August 2008. Available from www.greenbay pressgazette.com.

"Oji Paper Sees FY Net Loss 21 Bln Yen vs 6.5 Bln Profit." *AFX News Limited,* 25 January 2002.

"Oji Paper to Halt Western-Style/Special Paper Output in 3 Facilities." *AFX News Limited,* 12 February 2002.

"Positioning Canada in China's Paper Chase." *Asia Pacific Bulletin,* 27 February 2004. Available from www.asiapacific business.ca.

"Production of Paper and Paperboard in Japan." Japan Paper Association, 2005. Available from www.jpa.gr.jp.

"Pulp and Paper Europe." *Chemical Business Newsbase,* 15 August 2001.

"Pulp and Paper Markets Showed Improvement in 2004." *Paper Age,* 25 January 2005. Available from www.paperage.com.

"UPM-Kymmene Corporation Launches Feasibility Study at Paper Mill in the US." *Nordic Business Report,* 1 July 2004.

Unite Gains Recognition at Kamns Paper Mill, Leicester. 18 July 2008. Available from www.prnewswire.co.uk.

Yoshizaki, Miho. "Nippon Paper Falls." *Bloomberg News,* 5 June 2000.

SIC 2650

PAPERBOARD CONTAINERS AND BOXES

NAICS CODE(S)

32221. Sometimes known as the converted paperboard industry, these manufacturers produce packaging often from purchased paperboard (see **Paperboard Mills**). Major segments include folding boxes, set-up (or rigid) boxes, corrugated boxes, fiber cans and tubes, and food containers.

INDUSTRY SNAPSHOT

Paperboard container and box makers provide the global economy with packaging and foodservice products for commercial and consumer applications for every industry. The primary application for paperboard containers and boxes is packaging. Boxes can be bright, visually attractive, and informational if they contain individual products, such as those used for cereal boxes. They also can be sturdy, such as corrugated containers that are used to send various products like cereal boxes to consumers or sellers to keep the cereal boxes undamaged en route to supermarket shelves. According to *Paper, Film & Foil Converter* magazine, the challenge for manufacturers in the 2000s will be how to satisfy their customers' need for "lower costs; quicker turnaround; lower quantity minimums; warehousing of packaging; and faster delivery."

Until the 1970s and Earth Day awareness programming, paper and paperboard packaging was a largely non-controversial, almost ignored, aspect of a worldwide product distribution system. However, as concern over landfills, solid waste, and recycling mounted, packaging was singled out as a major source of waste. Pressure grew in Europe and North America to eliminate or recycle packaging. In Germany, legislation was passed that required packaging producers to collect and recycle their products. Paperboard packaging was banned from landfills in much of the United States.

To comply with such regulations, packaging producers agreed to use more recycled paper and paperboard in their products. In addition, many industrial countries began to collect used packaging for recycling. Packaging producers defended their products, explaining that packaging was vital for the maintenance of public health and economic well-being. They maintained that rather than adding to the solid waste stream, packaging reduced it by protecting against damage and spoilage.

Producers claimed that competition with suppliers centered around packaging materials usually spurred suppliers to find ways of using less packaging, since that reduced the cost of their products to end users. Packaging represented an average of 7 percent of the cost of goods sold, so the competition provided an automatic "source reduction" without the need for governmental regulation. The industry's reliance on single-use containers in food and beverage packaging helped improve public health by eliminating at least one possible method of disease transmission. According to packaging producers, these benefits meant that packaging could have reduced negative effects on the environment while continuing a prominent role in the global economy.

On a global scale, the category of corrugated paperboard boxes has been the largest component of the converted paper and board products industry. By the beginning of the 2000s, corrugated boxes were used to ship 90 percent of the goods manufactured throughout the world. Major industrial users of corrugated products included food and beverages, agricultural products, paper and fiber products, petroleum, petrochemical resins, plastics, and rubber products. In order to reduce costs, some manufacturers began to examine the use of reusable plastic containers for business-to-business shipments (such as automobile components). In general, however, corrugated box manufacturers had relatively little need to consider alternative shipping methods. Corrugated containers in the form of point-of-sale displays were increasingly used as an integrated transportation and marketing device.

Consumption of corrugated products tends to reflect the overall standard of living and economic activity in most countries. Highly developed countries with complex, consumer-oriented economies are typically heavy users of corrugated boxes. *Paper, Film & Foil Converter* magazine projected that demand for corrugated and paperboard boxes would climb 2.8 percent annually, reaching more than $35 billion in 2007, with corrugated and solid fiber boxes leading the industry.

In September 2008, International Paper Company announced plans to shut a paper machine that produced approximately 430,000 tons of containerboard annually for corrugated packaging. International Paper's Industrial Packaging division Senior Vice President Carol Roberts announced that severance and assistance would be provided to affected employees. Decisions like this were considered to be signs of the times.

ORGANIZATION AND STRUCTURE

Paperboard is the primary raw material to make corrugated boxes and folding paperboard boxes. Classifications of the various grades of paperboard are based on the types of boxes and packages they are used to make. Cartonboard is usually defined as board of various compositions and is used to make folding boxboard and set-up (or rigid) boxes; foodboard is defined as single or multi-ply paperboard and is used for food and liquid packaging; and corrugated is typically defined as board for containers, consisting of two or more linerboard grades separated by corrugated medium (fluting) glued to the liners.

Corrugated Paper Boxes. In the early 2000s, a large share of the global corrugated box market was integrated. The containerboard (linerboard facing and corrugated fluting) used to make corrugated boxes was never sold on the open market. Instead, the product was shipped directly from containerboard mills to corrugated box plants within the same organization. In the United States, 80 percent of corrugated box production was integrated, and 20 percent produced by independent box plants. The European market was more fragmented with many small independent boxmakers, but a steady trend of consolidation began in the 1990s, with production expected to be under the control of fewer companies in the twenty-first century.

Shipments of corrugated and solid fiber boxes mirrored the demand for products that were shipped to market in box containers. When worldwide industrial activity increases, so do box shipments. When industrial activity increased in most of the major economies worldwide in the early to mid-1990s, corrugated container producers around the world struggled to keep up demand. For example, there was a 6 percent increase in demand for corrugated and solid fiber boxes in 1994. As the economy in the 2000s showed signs of weakening and then definite areas of collapse, the packaging industry's profits reflected a decrease of commercial opportunities as well.

Many weights, various degrees of thickness, and combinations of liners and corrugating medium are used to make different types of corrugated board because there are thousands of different applications for corrugated boxes. The corrugating process begins when flat corrugating medium board is softened with heat and moisture. The board is sent into a set of corrugating rolls that form the board into curved "flutes." The flute tips on one side of the medium are then coated with adhesive, and a separate, single faced piece of linerboard is laid onto the fluted medium to produce a "single face" web. This sheet of corrugating material is sent to the "double backer," where adhesive is applied to the other side of the flutes, and then back liner is applied to form "combined corrugated board." This combined corrugated board is cut into individual "blanks" on a trimmer-cutter and is sent to a printer-scorer-slotter to be converted into flat boxes. The flat boxes are shipped to the end user, who opens and glues the box prior to use. Corrugated containers are generally delivered by truck because of the large number of customers and a traditionally common demand for timely service. Shipping costs are a relatively high percentage of total costs due to the dispersion of customers and the fact that boxes are high-bulk, low-density, and low-value products. As a result, box plants tend to be located close to customers to reduce shipping costs.

Corrugating materials can be made from a wide variety of materials. The outside linerboard is usually a mix of virgin softwood pulp, virgin hardwood pulp, and/or recycled paper and board. The inner corrugating medium is typically made of virgin hardwood pulp and/or recycled paper and paperboard. In the pulping process, most pulp used as a corrugating medium is not fully "cooked" in the digesting process since it is beneficial to keep some of the lignin in the pulp (see **Pulp Mills**). This lignin, which acts as glue, helps give the corrugating medium added stiffness.

Recycling. Corrugated boxes have been recycled into new containers for years. However, events in the latter part of the twentieth century put increased emphasis on recycling of old corrugated containers (OCC), which accounted for the majority of all paper products recycled around the world from the late 1990s through the early 2000s.

Customers typically expect their suppliers to sell them products made from unbleached kraft linerboard to meet minimum standards of 80 percent sulfate, or kraft pulp, which is derived from previously unused wood chips. Production cost of unbleached kraft linerboard can be lowered if recycled fibers are used. The total production of recycled linerboard in 2000 was 3.9 million tons, a decline of approximately 5 percent from the 4.1 million tons of recycled linerboard produced in 1999.

In the mid-1980s minute amounts of dioxin were discovered in pulp mill bleach plant effluent in Europe and the United States. Until that time, a standard procedure in the industry had been to bleach paper and paperboard. However, once the dioxin was discovered, the procedure became controversial and manufacturers began to produce a majority of corrugated boxes in their natural brown color, which eliminated the need to bleach them white. Since a majority of boxes were not made from bleached paperboard, the environmental concern confronting paper and paperboard boxes was largely negated. Nonetheless, bleaching remained a controversial topic in the global marketplace in the mid-1990s as a growing percentage of corrugated boxes continued to be shipped with a bleached, white, outside liner of paperboard.

Environmental concern spread to the disposal of used corrugated boxes. Once collected, these boxes were found to be easily recycled and were biodegradable in landfills. Worldwide, between 60 and 80 percent of OCC was recovered for recycling into new boxes or other paperboard products in the late 1990s.

Responsibility for the collection of OCC differs around the world. For example, Germany's strict recycling laws require box producers to recycle make arrangements for accepting back from consumers every package they produced. This often involves creating recycling centers funded by the manufacturer. In the United States, the consumer of corrugated containers is responsible for recycling. Few U.S. laws require consumers of corrugated products, such as supermarkets, to recycle, but most have done so because OCC is a valuable commodity.

Many sources have claimed that more companies are using recycled paperboard for the first time and are pleasantly surprised by its quality and appearance. A survey of packaged goods manufacturers conducted the 100 Percent Recycled Paperboard Alliance found that the frozen food categorywas "the most positive industry sector overall." The study was completed in 220 telephone interviews with packaging, technical, and purchasing professionals at 143 U.S. companies in the dry and frozen/refrigerated foods, pharmaceutical, toothpaste, pet supply, soap, and office supply industries.

From the late 1980s through the mid-2000s, the amount of recycled paper and paperboard used to produce linerboard and corrugating medium increased sharply in many countries. A wide variety of recycled materials could be used to make these products. While many paperboard mills preferred to use OCC, they could also use newsprint, office waste paper, and other grades of recycled paper. Many firms began to use lower-cost recycled paper when the price of OCC in many markets reached record highs in 1994, jumping in one year from approximately US$50 per ton to more than US$200 per ton in the United States. However, in 1996, a glut of OCC on the market caused prices to fall, and many producers returned to their preferred source—OCC. This situation continued in 1997, although the price of OCC increased nearly 25 percent, reaching US$76.50 per ton by the end of the year. As of 1997, OCC accounted for more than 60 percent of all scrap paper recovered in the United States and was a major portion of recycling efforts in other industrialized countries as well.

Paperboard Packaging magazine estimated that almost 4,800 communities had paperboard recycling programs. Such efforts had resulted in recovering 40 percent of all paper, and that percentage was expected to grow. In *Official Board Markets,* 100 Percent Recycled Paperboard Alliance Executive Director Lynn Harrelson believed key contributing factors were progress in "generating conversions from other substrates, reaching out and capturing business in various industry segments, entering new market segments, and adding new licenses to the 100 percent recycled paperboard symbol."

With the issue of waste remaining a significant concern in the late 1990s, corrugated box manufacturers looked for efficient ways to recycle wax-coated corrugated boxes that were used for shipping moist products, such as produce and fish. Wax board was not accepted for recycling by paper mills because even a very small quantity would reduce the quality of packaging papers. In 1990, the largest Scandinavian paper recycler, Returpapper AB, began research on how to recycle wax board. Several other paper companies and wax companies joined the research project and produced a practical solution to the problem that involved modifying waxes prior to application on the box with a saturated fatty acid and a stabilizing nonionic surfactant. When the newly treated OCC was recycled, a hot dispersion process added alkali and removed the wax with redesigned pulp washing equipment that could then be incinerated.

In the United States, two developments in 1998 promised to help combat the problem of wax boxes in recycling systems. A new marketing program, developed by several industry associations, promoted voluntary guidelines for identifying waxed corrugated boxes so they could be removed from the recycling process. The boxes would be marked on the top inside label with the word "wax" in three languages. On another front, two companies, Thermo Black Clawson and Inland Paperboard and Packaging, jointly developed a new process that could eliminate wax in the re-pulping process. The new process was called Xtrax and was on the market as of early 1998.

The pulp made from OCC needs little cleaning and does not require bleaching. Unlike many grades of recycled paper, fiber strength and other important physical properties are not lost during the recycling of OCC. However, there is a limit to how many times fibers can be recycled. For example, Asian corrugated boxes had been recycled many times due to chronic virgin fiber shortages in those countries. As a result, their products tended to be weaker and less resistant to water than U.S. corrugated boxes. The fiber quality of Asian OCC was so low that many U.S. recycling mills excluded it from their processes.

Since corrugated containers are considered to be a commodity, competition in corrugated boxes is centered on price. In addition, international trade in finished boxes was expected to remain low. However, one of the two main raw materials in corrugated boxes—linerboard—was a major export product for paper- and board-producing countries. Many box producers were fully integrated, producing the raw materials for boxes aa well as the boxes themselves. In addition, many box producers owned operations in other countries or were part of joint ventures in several countries. As a result, leaders in the converted products industry tended to be the same as the leaders in the paperboard industry (see **Paperboard Mills**).

The majority of corrugated products have been used to package non-durable goods, such as general merchandise and food products. Consequently, the percentage of corrugated products used for non-durable goods typically rises during recessions because the sale of expensive durable goods, such as furniture and appliances, goes down as consumers delay discretionary spending. In the 2000s, a Graphic Arts Marketing Information Service study found that manufacturers of boxes serving the non-durable foods industries could expect their customers to battle for shelf space regulated by fewer big chain stores. This would lead to a need for high-quality, eye-catching visuals on these product boxes in order to command greater market performance and sales results. "The trend in graphics is toward more specialty colors, more process color, and more sophisticated design," according to *Paper, Film & Foil Converter* magazine.

The Tiny Box Company, a British company that began making gift boxes from recycled paper in 2008, doubled its size after the two founders appeared on the *Dragon's Den* reality show on the BBC. They received financial support from British millionaires who agreed that their recycling idea had a future and invested in 40 percent of The Tiny Box Company. The company's boxes are made from 100 percent recycled boxboard, recycled gift boxes, and recycled Kraft paper or at least 80 percent consumer waste. The start-up served a niche market for recycled jewelry.

Fiber Cans, Tubes, and Drums. Fiber cans, tubes, and drums have comprised a medium-sized segment of the converted paper and paperboard industry. An important market within this category includes spiral and convoluted wound tubes and cores, which are used in such familiar products as paper towel rollers, in addition to numerous industrial purposes. The demand for tubes and cores is largely driven by industrial production. Major users of this segments products include textile products, synthetic fibers, paper mills, flexible packaging, film, carpeting, and construction. The pulp and paper industry, which used cores to wind its rolls of paper and board, was the single largest user of tubes and cores.

Fiber cans, which are called composite cans in the United States and board cans in Europe, have a paperboard "body" and a paper, metal, membrane, or plastic end closure. These products may also have a variety of liners. Many composite cans contained a high percentage of recycled fibers. They were used throughout the world to hold prepared food, pastries, frozen concentrate, snacks, nuts, and powdered foods and beverages.

Sonoco Products, in Hartsville, South Carolina, is one of the world's largest industrial and consumer packaging manufacturers. Sonoco (formerly the Southern Novelty Company) had been in business since 1899. By 2007, it reported US$4.4 billion in sales to customers worldwide and 18,600 employees. Sonoco's products include paper cores, cones, and tubes that it sold to the paper, film, and construction industries. The company's consumer packaging unit made composite cans (primarily with paperboard bodies and metal or plastic ends), many types of flexible and rigid packaging for food (made from either paper or plastic), chemicals, and personal care items. Sonoco also operates its own paperboard mills

Sanitary Food Containers. Another medium-sized segment of the converted paper and board industry, sanitary food containers include a variety of paper plates, cups, and other disposable paper food packaging. Demand for these products grew steadily in several major markets during the 1990s and early 2000s. Despite the public's desire to reduce use of disposable products for environmental reasons, the convenience of disposable paper products continued to appeal to a growing number of consumers worldwide.

Once known for products that were plain white, or that had minimal border decoration, the paper plate and cup market exploded with color, designs, and licensed characters. For example, in the mid-1990s the venerable Dixie Cup franchise, marketed by Fort James Corporation, broadened its line by marketing products that appealed to children, such as "Zoo Friends" and "Dino Friends" cups and plates, as well as products that featured Disney characters.

Aseptic packages, which are known as drink boxes in the United States, are considered a hybrid product, since they include layers of paperboard, metal, and plastic. They have become widely used around the world, displacing products that competed with this portion of the paperboard market, such as glass bottles and metal cans. The aseptic processing system, also known as ultra high temperature (UHT) processing, required a large portion of available food-grade paperboard at the beginning of the 2000s.

Aseptic processing was first used in the milk industry to produce products with long shelf life that did not require refrigeration. This process was particularly well suited to European households, which generally had limited space for refrigeration, unlike U.S. households. In the late 1990s, aseptically processed milk accounted for more than 75 percent of all milk sales in France. Conversely, aseptic milk sales in the United States were negligible. However, during the 1980s and early 1990s aseptic packaging for fruit juices and other drinks captured a healthy share of the U.S. market. While the only aseptic containers commonly available in the United States in the late 1990s were single-serving juice boxes and milk cartons, by 2004 aseptic packaging had been introduced for numerous food products, including soups and broths; soy, grain, and nut beverages; tomato sauces and purees; puddings and flavored milks; and liquid eggs.

Folding Paperboard Boxes. Folding paperboard boxes represented a very large part of the paper and paperboard market. A vast array of dry, liquid, and frozen food products, such as beverages, dry bakery goods, and cereals, was packaged in folding paperboard boxes, making the segment highly dependent on global consumer spending. One particularly important consumer in this segment has been the beverage industry, which packaged many of its bottled and canned products in a secondary package made from high-quality paperboard. Many other consumer products also were packaged in paperboard boxes, including small appliances, detergents, toys, and sporting goods.

The worldwide growth in sales of consumer products had expanded the market for folding paperboard boxes. For example, in the mid-1990s beer and soft drink bottlers began to use more multi-can "cases" to package their products. Since the 1980s, folding paperboard box converters, like corrugated box producers, had responded to demands of consumer products manufacturers for packaging with higher visual appeal. Better graphics were deemed to promote impulse purchases by consumers, making the carton a primary sales vehicle in a company's marketing efforts.

One of the major competitors for folding boxboard packages was flexible packaging, which was typically a combination of layers of plastic and/or metal film configured into pouch-like packages. This type of packaging was common outside the United States, where it has replaced many paperboard applications. Flexible packaging was popular for various reasons, including perceived environmental superiority and decreased packaging waste, as well as for cultural and economic reasons. France and India marketed motor oil in pouches with and without outer cartons. In the United Kingdom, the Kellogg Company produced breakfast cereal bags using high-quality graphics without an outer paperboard carton. The concept was slow to be accepted in the United States.

CURRENT CONDITIONS

In most countries, corrugated and folding boxes have been produced domestically with little international or regional trade in finished packaging products until the 2000s. Box-making industries usually consisted of small, independent box makers. However, as major paper companies in North America, Europe, and Asia grew, they began to vertically integrate by acquiring more box plants. Some branched out further by buying or building box plants in foreign markets. U.S. and European firms were particularly interested in markets in Asia and Eastern Europe, since they offered much higher growth potential than the largely mature markets of North America and Western Europe.

Corrugated Paper Boxes. Since the mid-1990s, a growing percentage of corrugated boxes were made using preprinted linerboard, with the rest of the box made from unbleached brown containerboard. In addition, to reduce costs and compete with alternative packaging, the industry in the early 2000s gradually began to shift to production of lighter weight boxes with increased strength. Improved containerboard quality enabled box makers to decrease the overall weight of their boxes, which not only reduced shipping costs, but also reduced the cost to the end user.

Shippers and packagers of food products, the largest market for corrugated products, were one of the highest growth markets for the corrugated packaging industry in the 2000s. Another potential growth area involved the manufacture of corrugated paperboard shipping pallets, which had traditionally been made of wood. Shipping pallets, which could hold multiple containers during transport, had ended up in landfills, and there was growing pressure to replace them industry-wide. Innovative processing technology not only made possible the manufacture of stronger corrugated pallets, but also proved to be a less expensive way to make recyclable pallets. However, corrugated pallets had the disadvantage of losing strength when they became wet.

The need for high-quality printing surfaces on the outside of boxes was a major trend in corrugated containers that emerged in the 2000s. At this time, the growing strength of large European hypermarkets and U.S. discount stores, wholesale clubs, and other mass merchandisers, meant that more shoppers were choosing products without assistance from salespeople. Frequently, the only method consumers had to learn about the product was to read what was on the retail box. Producers of consumer products began including more photographic images, detailed instructions, and bright colors on their product packages to make them competitive on store shelves. This led producers of linerboard to make more "preprint" linerboard, which involved printing the outer liner before it was shipped to box plants and was made into corrugated board. Typically, preprint was made with "process printing," a less-expensive process than the traditional lithographic labels that were previously used for photo reproduction on box exteriors.

In the 2000s, *Paper, Film & Foil Converter* published the results of a Graphic Arts Marketing Information Service (GAMIS) study indicating that flexography was the single most used manner of printing in the packaging field. In 2001, flexo printing had sales of approximately US$15 billion, and the GAMIS study projected that sales would reach between US$18 billion and US$22 billion by 2005. GAMIS predicted that flexo manufacturers would take an increased share of the folding-carton market from manufacturers that used older technology methods, such as sheet-fed offset printing and the gravure process. The study anticipated flexo technology improvements in specific areas, such as "gearless presses; faster plate processing; and the use of ultraviolet inks," according to *Paper, Film & Foil Converter* along with increasing

consumer requests for products requiring color digital presses. The study concluded that the vast majority of companies employing traditional offset-printing methods could remain competitive "by raising press performance; increasing speeds, and adding productivity features."

The food packaging industry was expected to continue to grow based on several successful ventures in the early 2000s. For example, Thung Hua Sinn Printing Network, which originally printed labels, shifted to successfully manufacture corrugated paper boxes. The company started a subsidiary called TPN Flexpak to manufacture flexible packaging. *Food & Drug Packaging* revealed Bake 'n Ship containers from Laminating Technologies that allowed bakers to bake, freeze, slice, ship, and display their products in one package. In April 2004, *Purchasing* reported that North America's corrugated box makers sought to increase prices between 8 and 10 percent. Box prices were expected to remain volatile.

Fiber Cans, Tubes, and Drums. By the early 2000s, manufacturers of fiber cans, tubes, and drums, like other converted product manufacturers, were being asked by customers and government regulatory agencies to make their products with more recycled paperboard and less virgin paperboard. This turned out to be a marketing advantage because many competing products were made from plastic, which in the 1990s was being recycled at a much lower rate worldwide than paper and paperboard. The paper industry was one of the major users of fiber tubes, since most paper and paperboard mills used high-density fiber cores to wind their paper and paperboard rolls, before it was cut into smaller rolls and shipped to converting operations. Long fiber cores were either cut at the mill, to match roll sizes, or shipped to the mill, precut by the core manufacturer.

As competition in the fiber can, tube, and drum market intensified in the 1990s, manufacturers sought new ways of increasing their competitive advantage. For example, Sonoco Products Co. entered into "single supplier" relationships with some paper companies for roll packaging materials and services as the only supplier. In turn, the paper companies received enhanced services and lower prices. One such agreement was with Weyerhaeuser Company of Federal Way, Washington. Under a three-year, US$25 million agreement, Sonoco provided a full array of cores, roll heads, plastic and metal end plugs, wax-laminated roll wrap, and services like core cutting and core reclamation for Weyerhaeuser paper mills in the United States.

The use of fiber drums, however, was down in several countries where many industrial users were slowly eliminating the use of disposable containers. The chemical industry, once a major user of drums, essentially replaced metal and fiber drums with portable chemical feed containers that were made mostly of plastic. These returnable containers were delivered to the customer and then returned to the manufacturer when empty.

Sanitary Food Containers. The market for paper cups, plates, and other disposable paper products grew in many countries as many families began to reduce time spent on housework and home meal preparation by using disposable paper products. The growth of take-out food operations, which frequently used paper plates to serve food, also helped spur consumption. Nevertheless, paper plates faced increased competition from molded plastic plates and cups that were grease resistant and, in many ways, offered superior strength. Extra-thick premium paper plates and cups that were treated with a plastic outer layer easily competed with their plastic rivals. Moreover, the perceived negative environmental aspects associated with styrofoam helped paper recapture some of the hot beverage cup market share that had been lost in the early 1980s. For example, coffeehouse operators like Starbucks served their products in paper cups.

Paperboard milk cartons also faced serious competition from plastic. However, paperboard milk cartons continued to compete effectively against plastic in small sizes, such as one- and two-liter or one- and two-quart packages. European milk producers helped mitigate some of the paperboard industry's revenue losses when they shifted to aseptic packaging for milk. Milk carton manufacturers aggressively developed additional uses for paperboard cartons, including containers for laundry detergents and fruit juices.

Folding Paperboard Boxes. The folding paperboard box industry was expected to continue growing in the 2000s, while improving delivery times and other services to counter formidable competition from alternative packaging, such as flexible pouches. Improved strength and lighter-weight folding boxboard were expected to improve the competitive position of folding paperboard boxes in the packaging industry. Manufacturers of folding paperboard boxes also expected a fundamental market share, because their product was recyclable and contained recycled fiber.

The cost of raw materials for folding paperboard boxes, which was low in the early 1990s, shot up in the mid-2000s. Much of the price increase was passed along to the consumer. Revenues from box production were constricted by low linerboard availability, high-priced solid bleached sulfate paperboard (SBS) and recycled paperboard, and customer resistance to skyrocketing prices that had to be passed to their own customer base.

However, toward the end of the 1990s prices for all grades of paperboard began falling sharply as customers started to use inventory they had stockpiled in anticipation of future price increases. This led paperboard mills to take downtime and lower prices in order to restore balance to the market. However, by mid-1997 the price of standard linerboard remained at US$310 per ton, 41 percent below its 1995 peak of US$525 per ton, resulting in the costs of finished boxes dropping as well. While prices remained relatively low through the early 2000s, analysts predicted significant improvement after 2003.

RESEARCH AND TECHNOLOGY

Box makers looked to the processes and equipment of the printing industry to meet the growing demand for four-color, high quality, folding paperboard boxes and many installed expensive printing presses to meet demand. In the mid-to-late 1990s some box makers consolidated six-color printing presses and web litho folding carton capability into production operations, a process that typically had required separate converting steps. Some box makers also installed new web flexo printing processes, a folding carton technology that produced higher quality printing. Folding box producers also were developing ways to make shorter production runs, since many customers were moving to just-in-time use of paperboard products.

Beginning in the 1990s technical advances led to the development of paperboard grades that run well on both high-speed printing and converting equipment, as well as on high-speed carton erecting, filling, and sealing lines. In the corrugated board segment, mills developed the ability to produce lighter weight liner and corrugating medium. Machinery manufacturers then developed machines that produced smaller, finer grades of flute, which have found a ready market, in many cases serving as a replacement for folding cartonboard. The development of small flute corrugated packaging had the potential to combine the traditionally separate corrugated and folding box industries since the product could be used in applications in both industries. Folding carton manufacturers in Europe and especially in the United States were quick to convert to the new small flute corrugating technology in the late 1990s.

Innovative technology became a competitive advantage to some packaging producers. For example, Riverwood Holding Inc. expanded markets based on a strategic decision to design and sell proprietary packaging machinery that used the manufacturer's paperboard for multiple packaging applications (mostly bottled and canned beverages). One of the primary benefits to Riverwood was that the packaging machines were able to "pull through" Riverwood's paperboard boxes. Riverwood installed and serviced the sophisticated machinery in the bottling and canning plants of its customers. The machinery was able to insert cans and bottles of different heights and diameters into a variety of packages, styles, and configurations. The packaging machinery also was very fast, operating at a rate of up to 3,000 cans per minute. In the late 1990s, Riverwood was reported to have control of about 50 percent of the U.S. beverage carrier market, and close to 15 percent of the non-U.S. beverage carrier market. Moreover, Riverwood had significant investments in multiple container plants in Europe.

A growing trend in the early 2000s was the concept of universal packaging to produce packages that can be easily used by people with different physical challenges. Duracell, for example, redesigned its paperboard packages for hearing aid batteries to make them easier for users to pick up. Burgopak USA announced plans to introduce a paperboard package for medications in late 2005 that was designed to store and dispense the product more safely than plastic containers. Corrugated box manufacturers had made improvements to their designs that allowed products to be packed and shipped more efficiently and to be opened easily. As the Baby Boomer generation aged, inevitably developing physical impairments, analysts predicted that ease of use would become an increasingly important aspect of paperboard container design. Some analysts also predicted that the aging population would spur demand for single-serving packaging, since this demographic shift would result in a larger number of single-person households.

Paperboard made of components other than 100 percent paper were also being explored. For example, in Corvallis, Oregon, Local Boyz Hawaiian Cafe responded to a campaign against Styrofoam that was led by local Oregon State University students. The students cited ASOSU Environmental Task Force representatives and others who went before the Corvallis city council seeking a ban on plastic foam containers in November 2007 and a possible ban on plastic shopping bags. The restaurant explored various options, settling on containers made of 40 percent sugarcane, 45 percent reed, and 15 percent straw that looked like paperboard, but were sturdy enough to hold up to hot carry-out meals. In addition, the preferred containers decomposed more readily in landfills.

Cartonboard packaging companies sought improved ways to complete the manufacture of boxes with less labor and more speed in the late 2000s. For example, Switzerland-based Bobst launched a "'next generation' of folder-gluers, die-cutters and hot foil stamping equipment... using common branding to make them 'coherent and easy for firms to understand.'"

INDUSTRY LEADERS

The United States. In addition to being an integrated producer of linerboard, kraft paper, and packaging, Union Camp was a major manufacturer of corrugated containers,

heavy-duty shipping sacks, and other packaging. The packaging group of Union Camp Corporation, based in Wayne, New Jersey, was the company's largest operating unit, accounting for 43 percent of sales in 1996. International Paper acquired Union Camp in 1999.

MeadWestvaco Corporation's consumer packaging business diversified its product line in the late 1990s with products like ovenware cartons that allowed the use of one package to ship and display frozen food, which could then be heated in a microwave or conventional oven. That efficiency helped reduce customer expenses up to 30 percent and packaging volume up to 40 percent. The company's unbleached packaging unit operated worldwide, including the Rigesa Ltda. unit in Brazil. In 1996, Rigesa upgraded its mill in Tres Barras to improve production of linerboard for corrugated containers. Other enhancements included opening a new container plant in Pacajus, Brazil, to serve a fast-growing export trade.

As of 2005, MeadWestvaco operated 34 consumer packaging plants, 14 packing systems facilities, and 4 corrugated container plants. After selling its paper business to Cerberus Capital Management in 2005 for US$2.3 billion, packaging operations, including folding cartons, corrugated boxes, and printed plastics, accounted for almost three-fourths of sales. The company reported US$6.9 billion in sales and 24,000 employees in 2007.

Canada. Norampac, Canada's largest paperboard manufacturer, had been jointly owned by Cascades Inc. and Domtar Inc. before becoming a division of Cascades Canada. The company was a leading producer of corrugated products in Canada. With annual sales exceeding US$1.1 billion, it operated 27 corrugated products plants and five folding carton plants in Canada, the United States, and France. The company was ranked as the third largest boxboard producer in North America.

In July 2008, Norampac management reluctantly announced plans to close its Toronto boxboard mill indefinitely. Company sources cited "high labour costs, growing fibre supply costs and rising energy costs" as the reasons for the closure that affected approximately 140 employees.

Brussels, Belgium-based SCA Packaging was Europe's second largest producer of containerboard paper used for manufacturing corrugated board. The company employs 24,100 people at more than 240 production units in approximately 30 countries.

Russia's largest corrugated box manufacturer, Naberezhnochelninsky KBK Mill in Tatarstan, produced about 220 million square meters of corrugated boxes in 2004. Close behind was ZAO Gotek, the fastest growing corrugated box manufacturer, with annual production of 200 million square meters.

Stora Enso Packaging opened its fourth corrugated board plant in Russia to produce offset-printed packs for the consumer goods market. The company's Executive Vice President for Industrial Packaging Veli-Jussi Potka reported that the plant would manufacture a range of products for the fast moving consumer goods market.

Zao Gotek, a corrugated packaging products manufacturer, designed transportation and consumer packaging with flexo multi-colored printing. Based in Zhelezogorsk, Russian Federation, the company offered an impressive variety of products, including four-flap boxes, articles with complicated configurations, large-sized containers, and corrugated board.

MAJOR COUNTRIES IN THE INDUSTRY

The United States. In the early 2000s, the United States was the leading packaging producing country in the world, as well as an importer of packaging from Canada and other nations. Most U.S. production was highly integrated and many of the large packaging producers were expanding globally, including Union Camp Corporation, which was acquired by International Paper in 1999, and MeadWestvaco Corporation.

The United States also was the world's largest producer and exporter of linerboard, the principal component of corrugated boxes. In 1996, exports represented about 15 percent of U.S. kraft liner production, which comprised about 50 percent of total kraft linerboard exports from the world's 10 major supplying nations.

U.S. corrugated material producers reported an increase in the total number of shipments from 1995 to 1996, as the long-term U.S. economic recovery continued. In 2000, however, total shipments decreased slightly from previous years. According to the Fibre Box Association's 1996 annual report, shipments by the corrugated industry were a record 377 billion square feet, which was a 1.4 percent increase over 1995. Seventy-five percent of U.S. corrugated shipments came from vertically integrated paper companies with containerboard mills. However, while the total volume increased in 1996, shipment values dropped 11.1 percent to US$20.8 billion from a record of US$23.4 billion in 1995. Decreasing prices for corrugated materials began in 1996 and 1997, resulting in a drop in the price of linerboard and corrugated medium and leading to price declines in finished corrugated products. However, as prices for linerboard and medium stabilized and began increasing in 1997, the value of corrugated shipments was expected to increase steadily after 2002 as the economy improved.

The U.S. folding paperboard box industry grew steadily in the early to mid-1990s from US$7.4 billion to US$8 billion from 1991 to 1993, and US$8.79 billion

in 1995, according to the U.S. Department of Commerce. In 1996, the U.S. folding carton industry consisted of 445 companies. However, 37 companies that each had sales of more than US$25 million accounted for 68 percent of industry shipments.

In 2004, business models in the United States began to be designed to eliminate non-value added activities and waste. The result was shortened lead time, increased deliveries, and increased orders for tiny boxes. North American manufacturers increasingly emulated their European counterparts by creating a mini-converting plant to make corrugated components in exact quantities on a just-in-time basis.

Continued growth in the food and beverages market was expected to boost U.S. sales of corrugated and paperboard boxes to more than US$35 billion by 2007. Corrugated and solid fiber boxes comprised 72 percent of shipments by value in 2002, with most of the remainder being folding boxes.

Canada. The Canadian government's statistics show the corrugated paper box and packaging industry in a pattern of steady growth from 1990 to 1998, averaging about 3.4 percent. However, significant volatility affected the market in the 1990s, with the general pulp and paper industry posting profits only in 1990, 1995, and 1996. Oversupply remained a problem, leading to a $5.1 million loss in 1998 for Canada's largest paperboard manufacturer, Norampac. By early 2000, though, analysts saw indications of recovery, with shipments of linerboard, corrugated medium, and boxboard in 1999 up substantially from 1998 levels. In 2002, Canadian shipments of value-added paper products, which included paperboard containers, reached $9.2 billion.

Canada's largest folding carton user was the food industry. The next largest market share was the tobacco industry, followed by the beverage industry. While manufacturers of competitive materials were reportedly growing in Canada, the biggest threat to the industry was said to be to the glass and metal industries, rather than the folding carton and set-up box industry.

The European Union. In the 2000s, Europe was recognized by the packaging industry as a leader in industry standards and volume. For example, the United Kingdom produced around 2 mmt of packaging each year, according to the Corrugated Packaging Association (CPA). The United Kingdom has approximately 24,000 square kilometers of commercial woods, with 88 mills serving the industry and a workforce of more than 18,000 workers. The total paper and board capacity is more than 7 mmt. Top companies by production totals are BPB Paperboard Ltd. and Iveresk.

On a global basis, Europe had become the second leading producer of corrugated boxes behind the United

States. According to the Finnish Forest Industries Federation, Western Europe produced 96 metric tons of paper and paperboard in 2004, with Germany accounting for 21 percent, Finland 15 percent, and Sweden 12 percent. Like other major industrialized regions, Europe's main end use market for corrugated boxes was the food product sector. Lesser users included the agriculture and beverage industries.

One of the major threats to the European corrugated industry, as elsewhere, was the use of returnable plastic crates. In the mid-1990s, as European manufacturers became concerned that once users had switched to plastic they would not reconsider using corrugated, they mounted a public relations campaign to emphasize the recycling capablities and environmental friendliness of corrugated packaging.

In the mid-1990s, the folding carton industries in some European countries had a 2 percent growth rate, while other countries reported no growth. European folding carton manufacturers were using improved corrugated materials that were lighter in weight but were sufficiently strong. As a result, converters could make the same number of boxes from less corrugated material. Folding carton sales in 2003 surpassed those in North America, making Europe the second-ranked market after Asia. According to *Euromonitor,* growth in folding carton sales in Europe and Asia was attributed primarily to increased demand from the cigarette industry.

In 2000, Germany reported a 3 percent growth rate, which was one of the industry's best worldwide. However, as the global economic slowdown began to affect the country late 2001 and early 2002, the industry expected unemployment to continue to rise before growth would turn around. In 2000, with board and paper production in excess of 18 mmt, Germany was Europe's production giant. In response to increased competition from other packaging materials, the German folding carton industry had invested in new production processes, increased speed and flexibility, and improved lamination and printing.

Paperboard Packaging estimated that they industry would continue to grow in Europe through 2007. Of all liners used, European consumption of lightweight liners was expected to rise to 16.2 percent by volume by the end of 2007. Growth in lightweight fluting was expected to outpace growth of lightweight linerboard. Western Europe consumed almost 20 mmt of 31 million square meters of waste-based containerboard in 2002, and consumption was projected to grow to about 21.5 mmt by 2007.

Chief Executive Tony Thorne of London-based multinational packaging company DS Smith considered the U.K.'s corrugated box market to be the weakest in Western Europe, followed by the Spanish corrugated box market. Reports were based on a drop in corrugated case material costs in Europe, as well as high energy and waste paper costs.

In September 2008, SCA Packaging announced a design competition among European manufacturers to create a complete packaging concept to sell chocolates and create "a unique shopping experience." The winning packaging concept would win up to US$3,000 and an internship at the SCA Packaging Innovation Centre in Brussels, Belgium. SCA was the second largest manufacturer of containerboard for corrugated board.

The Russian Federation. During the Soviet era, Russians paid little attention to product packaging. Beginning in the early 1990s, however, the paperboard packaging industry has reported explosive growth, aided by newly imported manufacturing machinery and technologies. However, demand for corrugated boxes in Russia has outpaced supply since at least 1995. According to a *Paperboard Packaging* feature, the food industry has been the biggest factor in the growth of paperboard packaging in Russia. Demand for corrugated board in Russia was expected to grow about 6.3 percent annually through 2015, but the corrugated box market was expected to be less consistent.

Asia-Pacific Region. Although the Asia-Pacific region's corrugated industry grappled with a regional economic crisis in 1997 and 1998, and again in 2001, it continued to be the fastest growing corrugated industry worldwide in terms of production and consumption. Japan's 473 paper and board mills have a capacity of almost 35 mmt with about 44,000 employees in 2002.

Asia's corrugated production outside Japan increased 9 percent from 1995 to 1996, and remained much higher than in mature markets like North America and Europe even when that rate slowed in the late 1990s. By 2005, Asia was expected to produce 36 percent of all corrugated materials in the world, with the bulk of production in China, Indonesia, Thailand, and India. Asia's share of global corrugated demand increased from 13 percent to 18 percent between 1990 and 1996, with the highest growth generated by Indonesia, the Philippines, China, Vietnam, Malaysia, and Thailand. By 2005, the region's share of global demand was expected to reach 25 percent.

Rapid growth in China led to a dramatic increase in imports of paper and paperboard from 9 to about 20 percent between 1979 and 2004. Forest-rich countries, including Brazil, Canada, and Indonesia, were expected to be the beneficiaries of China's growing appetite for imported fiber. Analysts E.J. Krause & Associates projected Chinese that demand for paper and paperboard products would reach 70 metric tons by 2010. Demand for containerboard and corrugated paper in China averaged 13.7 percent annual growth in 2005.

Asia was also a growing market for folding cartons. While established regions, such as North America, focused on source reduction, the Asia-Pacific region began to use more packaging as living standards rose and more packaging materials became available. Microwavable and oven-ready foods were significant contributors to the growth in folding carton consumption in Asia.

Japan reported that consumer packaging increased in volume nearly 5 percent between 1998 and 2002, making it Asia's largest segment of the industry. Japan was known for its design of compact and functional packaging. Flexible packaging, which is created primarily for the food industry, represented the most commonly used packaging in the country. Despite robust sales through the 1990s, Japan's packaging industry faced uncertain growth in the early 2000s, due to the country's faltering economy. At the same time, however, increased competition among companies across most manufacturing sectors boosted interest in folding cartons as a promotional tool and as a means of cutting distribution costs. As a result, production of folding cartons grew 5 percent in 2002 to reach almost 26 billion units.

In August 2008, Research and Markets added the "Paper and Paperboard Container Manufacturing in China" report to its list, focusing primarily on businesses engaged in converting paperboard. Paper, paperboard, and old corrugated containers are converted into paperboard containers that complement a wide range of products, including corrugated paperboard containers, folding or solid cartons made of other paper, paper sacks, paper bags, and file boxes. Industry manufacturers in China also purchase raw materials as well as protective and adhesive chemicals to create corrugated paperboard sheets and boxes.

BIBLIOGRAPHY

"100 Percent Recycled Paperboard: Sleeping Giant or Emerging Tiger?" *100 Percent Recycled Paperboard Alliance,* 2005. Available from www.rpa100.com.

2003–2004 Pulp & Paper Global Fact & Price Book. Available from www.paperloop.com.

Andel, Tom. "Design for Ability." *Paperboard Packaging,* 1 May 2005. Available from www.packaging-online.com.

Brooks, Josh. "UK Box Market is 'Weakest in West Europe,' says DS Smith." *Packaging News,* 3 September 2008. Available from packagingnews.co.uk.

———. "Dragons Invest 60,000 Pounds in Recycled Box Start-up." *Packaging News,* 2 September 2008. Available from www.packagingnews.co.uk.

"China Paper/China Forest 2005." E.J. Krause & Associates, Inc.: 2005. Available from www.ejkrause.com.

Conn, Peta. "Cartons Weather Competitive Packaging Storm." *Euromonitor International,* 3 November 2004. Available from www.euromonitor.com.

"Containerboard Production Improves: PPPC." *Official Board Markets,* 20 March 2004.

Donberg, Deborah. "Corrugated, Boxes Rebound." *Paper, Film & Foil Converter,* 1 June 2004.

———. "The Future of Package Printing." *Paper, Film & Foil Converter,* January 2002.

Ellis, Jane. "Box Firm Backed by Dragons Doubles in Size." *Packaging News,* 3 September 2008. Available from packagingnews.co.uk.

"Frozen Suppliers Like Recycled Paperboard." *Frozen Food Age,* January 2004.

Goldstein, Simeon. "Bobst Launches Machinery Range for Cartonboard Packaging." *Packaging News,* 10 June 2008. Available from www.packagingnews.co.uk.

Grishchenko, Gregory. "Russia Hungry for Corrugated." *Paperboard Packaging,* 1 May 2005. Available from www.packaging-online.com.

Higham, Robert. "Trending Toward Lightweight." *Paperboard Packaging,* September 2003. Available from www.packaging-online.com.

"ICV Boxes in Packaging Deal." *Buyouts,* 7 June 2004.

"International Paper to Shut Okla. Paper Machine." *CNN Money,* 9 September 2008. Available from cnnMoney.com.

Krizner, Tricia. "Shorter...Smaller...Faster." *Paperboard Packaging,* June 2003. Available from www.packaging-online.com.

Lee, Eddie. "Pulp Friction," 4 May 2004. Available from straitstimes.asia1.com.sg.

Murphy, Kate. "Thinking Outside the Can: A Fresh Look at Food in a Box." *The New York Times,* 14 March 2004.

Nax, Sanford. "Annual Review." *The Fresno Bee,* 19 March 2002.

Nezanski, Matt. "Months–Long Search for Eco–Containers Ends." *Gazette Times* (Corvallis, OR), 11 August 2008. Available from www.gazettetimes.com.

Norampac. "Norampac Closes its Toronto Boxboard Mill Indefinitely," 7 July 2008. Available from www.norampac.com.

"North America's Corrugated Box Makers Want Higher Prices." *Purchasing,* 1 April 2004.

"Packaging in Japan." *Euromonitor,* April 2003. Available from www.euromonitor.com.

"Paper and Paperboard Container Manufacturing in China Report Out Now." *MarketWatch,* 27 August 2008. Available from www.marketwatch.com.

"Paper Industry Statistics." Norcross, Ga: TAPPI, 2005. Available from www.tappi.org.

"Paperboard Packaging Holds the Things We Need." *Paperboard Packaging,* November 2003. Available from www.packaging-online.com.

"Recycled Paperboard Makes Strides." *Official Board Markets,* 27 September 2003.

Rohleder, Ken. "Boxes in Small Batches." *Paperboard Packaging,* May 2004. Available from www.packaging-online.com.

"SCA Packaging Launches Design Challenge." *MarketWatch,* 9 September 2008. Available from www.marketwatch.com.

Smook, Gary A. *Handbook of Pulp and Paper Terminology: A Guide to Industrial and Technological Usage.* Bellingham, Wash.: Angus Wilde, 1990.

Testin, Robert F., and Peter Vergano. *Packaging in America in the 1990s.* Herndon, Va.: Institute of Packaging Professionals, 1990.

Thesaurus of Pulp and Paper Terminology. Atlanta: Institute of Paper Science and Technology, 1991.

"Tray Goes from Baker's Ovens to Consumers' Tables." *Food & Drug Packaging,* April 2003.

"Trendsetting Manufacturer: TPN Flexpak Has Added a New
   Dimension to the Art and Business of Product Packaging by
   Applying a Complete Range of Systems." *Plastics & Rubber
   Asia,* April 2003.
"Zao Gotek." *BusinessWeek,* 25 September 2008.

SIC 2631

PAPERBOARD MILLS

NAICS CODE(S)

322130. The world's paperboard mills manufacture
paperboard, often known in lay terms as cardboard, for
various purposes using wood pulp and other fiber pulp.
Certain paperboard mills also manufacture converted
paperboard products. For discussion of converted paperboard as used in containers, see also **Paperboard Containers and Boxes.** A general treatment of paperboard's
source material, pulp, is given under **Pulp Mills,** and for
information about paper manufacturers, see also **Paper
Mills.**

INDUSTRY SNAPSHOT

Paperboard production is usually considered a part of the
paper industry. Paperboard is defined as any thick,
heavyweight paper product. The distinction between
paper and paperboard is based on product thickness.
While all sheets above 0.3 mm can be classified as paperboard, enough exceptions are applied in the trade to
make that definition hazy. For the most part, paperboard
is made in the same manner as paper.

In some countries, such as the United States, total
paperboard production is equal to or exceeds paper production. In other areas, such as Europe, paper production still
exceeds paperboard production by a wide margin. Statistics
for these two areas are frequently combined in reports.

Most paperboard is used to make materials for corrugated boxes, and the growth of the global paperboard
industry is directly linked to the use of paperboard boxes
(commonly called cardboard boxes). Prior to the acceptance of corrugated containers for shipping, wooden crates
and boxes were used.

Worldwide production capacity grew steadily after
the mid-1990s but began slowing in 2000 and continued
its decline through the end of the 2000s. Most paperboard is consumed in its country of origin, but paperboard also is a major export product for many countries.
U.S. paperboard producers manufacture the majority of
the paperboard consumed in the U.S. In 2010, there
were over 825 paperboard mills within the United States
alone. In a report published in 2006 by the United
Nations Food and Agriculture Association (FAO), the

world paper industry absorbs more than 40 percent of
all timber cut worldwide. In spite of the surge in digital
communication, paper production is expected to continue to increase by 2.2 percent annually from 330
million tons to 440 million tons by 2015.

ORGANIZATION AND STRUCTURE

Two grades of paperboard—corrugating medium and
linerboard—are used to make corrugated shipping containers. (Corrugating medium is called "fluting" in Europe and
other regions.) Those two grades, together known as containerboard, account for the majority of paperboard produced
around the world. A third grade—solid bleached sulfate
(SBS), also called solid bleached board (SBB)—is used to
make folding cartons, such as those used in retail stores. SBS
accounts for a large share of the remaining production.

One major distinction among paperboard grades is
their classification as folding or non-folding grades. Folding grades must be flexible enough that the surface will
not split or crack when the board is folded to make a box.

Most paperboard can be classified as follows:

- Boxboard: board of various compositions used to
  make folding boxboard and set-up or rigid boxes;

- Foodboard: single or multi-ply paperboard used for
  food and liquid packaging; or

- Containerboard: board for containers consisting of
  two or more linerboard grades separated by
  corrugating medium glued to the liners.

The classification of paperboard usually depends on
how it is used. Folding boxboard, for example, is made to
permit folding without breaking the surface, while at the
same time providing good surface finish and the ability to
be used in a wide variety of carton shapes. The bending
property is not as important in set-up boxes, which
instead require board that can be easily scored (depressed
or partially cut). For foodboard, special surface treatments are usually needed to provide water or grease
resistance. Similarly, liquid packaging grades usually
require an additional conversion process in which plastic
or foil lamination takes place to make the container
impermeable to air and water.

The U.S. Department of Labor's OSHA division
classifies the following as primarily shipping paperboard
or paperboard products: binders' board; bottle cap board;
boxboard; bogus bristols; cardboard; clipboard (paperboard); clay coated board; container board; folding box-
boards; leatherboard; liner board, kraft and jute; manila
lined board; matrix board; milk carton board; news-
board; paperboard mills, except building board mills;
paperboard, except building board; patent coated paperboard; pressboard; setup boxboard; shoe board; special

food board; stencil board; strawboard, except building board; tagboard; and wet machine board.

Packaging is the single largest application for paperboard in most countries. Some countries, such as the United States, tend to use more virgin materials to manufacture paperboard, while others, such as South Korea, use more recycled fiber in their production process. The use of recycled fiber in paperboard production is growing fast, however, particularly in the United States. Most recycled fiber is used in products in which the reclaimed pulp does not need to be cleaned. Cereal cartons, for example, are typically made from a product called combination boxboard, with two white outside layers suitable for printing covering a gray, recycled inner layer. Kraft softwood (made from coniferous trees such as pine) has been the preferred pulp for making paperboard because of its strength. Most paperboard is unbleached (brown), but bleached (white) grades are used where appearance is important, such as for retail packaging.

Corrugated containers are, by far, the dominant global means of packaging goods for shipment. Converting plants, located in every industrialized country, use corrugating medium and linerboard to make boxes. Typically, these converting plants are located in urban areas, close to container users. While there are a large number of independent box converters (also called boxmakers), many box-converting plants are owned by the same companies that manufacture the linerboard and medium.

The two main raw materials used to make corrugating medium are semichemical hardwood pulp and recycled pulp (typically old corrugated containers that have been used and discarded). Hardwood pulp is made from deciduous trees such as oak and maple. The pulp from these trees has short, inflexible fibers that help make the corrugating medium stiff. This, combined with their lower cost in comparison to softwood fibers (from coniferous trees such as pine), make them the fiber of choice for medium. The term semichemical designates that the pulp used to make medium is only partially "cooked" in the digester and is partially washed, so it retains much of the glue-like lignin that hold the fibers together in the wood. With the lignin and other wood by-products remaining in the corrugating medium, it is easier to form a rigid fluted shape with a corrugating machine.

Use of recycled pulp in boxboard varies by country. For example, Asian countries, which often lack resources for virgin pulp, use a high percentage of recycled pulp to make boxboard. The United States, on the other hand, has traditionally used mostly virgin pulp. However, that equation was changing rapidly. Semichemical medium's share of total U.S. medium production declined to about 59 percent in 1996, from 72 percent in 1992 and 79 percent in 1980. The share of recycled medium production grew

to 28 percent in 1992 and to 41 percent in 1996. In 2006, 53.4 percent of the paper used in the United States (or 53.3 million tons) was used for recycling. The U.S. paper industry has set a goal of recovering 55 percent of all the paper used by 2012. Paper products used in the packaging industry made up about 77 percent of packaging materials recycled with more than 24 million pounds recovered in 2005.

Medium, like other grades of paper and paperboard, is categorized by "basis weights." The higher the basis weight, the heavier the paper or board. National standards for medium differ, but typical basis weights are 22-, 26-, 33-, 36-, and 40-pound. The standard U.S. weight is 26-pound, which accounted for the majority of all production in the late 1990s and early 2000s.

Medium production is directly related to worldwide production of corrugated boxes, measured as "shipments." After several weak years in the early 1990s, corrugated box shipments accelerated rapidly in 1994, rising six to seven percent worldwide. This led to a worldwide shortage of containerboard, pushing prices to historic highs in 1994 and early 1995 and dramatically raising the price of finished boxes for end users. However, prices of containerboard began falling in late 1996 and through most of 1997 due to a glut of containerboard on the market. This occurred even though overall demand for boxes kept rising with the generally favorable world economic climate, leveling off in 1999.

Linerboard is made primarily from softwood fibers. These fibers produce a much stronger sheet of linerboard. Still, linerboard may contain significant percentages of hardwood pulp and recycled fiber. Again, a variety of national standards exist for which fibers may be used in linerboard. For example, Korean and Japanese linerboard contains a large percentage of recycled fiber, making their linerboard significantly weaker than virgin linerboard.

By contrast, U.S. linerboard can contain no more than 20 percent hardwood pulp or recycled fiber. The recycled fiber is usually made from recovered corrugated material. If U.S. linerboard contains more than 20 percent recycled material, it must be called "recycled linerboard." In fact, 100 percent recycled linerboard grew very fast in the United States beginning in the late 1980s and throughout the 1990s. For example, recycled linerboard production jumped 80 percent in one year, moving from 1.93 million short tons in 1995 to 3.79 million short tons in 1996. At the same time, production of unbleached virgin kraft linerboard dropped 8.8 percent, from 17.65 million short tons in 1995 to 16.11 million short tons in 1996. By 2001, recycled linerboard represented 17 percent of U.S. linerboard production.

One of the highest-quality linerboard grades is solid bleached sulfate (SBS), made from pulp that has at least

80 percent bleached virgin fiber. It is used in high-quality packaging applications, such as boxes that are displayed in retail stores. A major portion of global SBS production is coated with a clay solution to improve its surface for printing. This is particularly important since consumer products manufacturers often use four-color process printing on their products' packages. SBS is commonly used to make cigarette packages and is also used for many food product applications, such as milk carton stock. SBS is available in basis weights ranging from 40 to 100 pounds. Other significant applications for SBS include disposable cups and plates.

The biggest buyer of SBS in the late 1990s was the tobacco industry, estimated to account for 60 percent of total demand. However, this grade was losing share worldwide to both folding boxboard and unbleached linerboard as product manufacturers downgraded from more expensive SBS to unbleached board for frozen food and liquor cartons. Folding boxboard was the primary beneficiary of this trend. Some of the advantages of using SBS packaging is that is it user-friendly. The packaging is easy to handle and easy to open and close, such as with cereal packaging. It was also possible to cook in the packaging.

Bleached bristol is another major grade made from SBS pulp. This comparatively lightweight grade is used for paperback book covers, greeting cards, and telephone directory covers.

In 2003, a major trend was for paperboard mills to move operations previously off machine to on-machine operations. These operations include coating and converting. Bulab Holdings Chairman Katherine Buckman Davis explained that the most active sectors involved with this trend were lightweight coated, coated paper, and coated board. Motivating factors for advancing this trend were efforts to "increase manpower efficiencies, decrease the need for extra machinery, eliminate the logistical problems of moving and storing paper and board, and reduce the maintenance involved in conducting the various steps." McDermott Consulting Services' Ted McDermott pointed out that "a negative aspect of going on-line is the need to do the product development and try to match the sheet properties of off-line created processes. For extremely flat-surfaced papers or extremely high gloss coated papers, on-line processes cannot achieve the off-line quality level."

BACKGROUND AND DEVELOPMENT

In the United States, corrugated boxes were declared legal by the Federal Trade Commission, in the Pridham decision, for shipping in 1914. Prior to that, wooden crates were used. As new methods of production helped improve the strength and durability of corrugated containers, their use in the global economy increased dramatically. World War II spurred major developments in corrugated shipping containers, which were used to ship military supplies. These innovations usually improved water and temperature resistance.

The use of corrugated paperboard containers in the global economy accelerated after World War II, and in most countries exceeded growth in gross national product (GNP). Other paperboard containers were developed as well, such as disposable containers for food and beverages. The popularity of this type of paperboard packaging stimulated sales of solid bleached sulfate (SBS) board.

The global consumption of paperboard tends to mirror economic conditions in individual countries. For example, in the early 1990s, paperboard consumption stalled in North America, which was suffering from the effects of a mild recession. In Europe and Asia, however, paperboard consumption grew significantly until those economies went into recession in the early 1990s. In 1993, all the major economies were either in recession or very slow recovery. As a result, growth in paperboard production suffered. A unified global economic recovery in 1994 and 1995 pushed up demand for linerboard significantly in nearly all markets. By this time, paperboard growth again exceeded the growth rate of gross domestic product (GDP), ranging from three to seven percent in major producing countries in 1994.

That growth continued in 1995, fueling a boom in paperboard production. Worldwide capacity expansions in paperboard averaged four to five percent in 1996. However, this expansion proved to be too rapid, and prices for most grades of paperboard plunged in late 1996 and early 1997, recovering slightly toward the end of that year and dropping in 2000 and 2001 as a result of recession and the post-September 11, 2001, general economic slump.

Paperboard is an internationally traded commodity, and much of the growth in demand in the mid- to late 1990s came from Asia, which except for Japan was experiencing rapid growth. However, the financial crisis that hit the region in early 1997 dampened economic growth. As a result, projections for increased paperboard demand in that region were scaled down.

Paperboard is largely viewed as part of the overall paper products industry. By 2007, the paper (including paperboard) market size had a US$630.9 billion value which represented 320.3 million metric tons. Forty percent of that market was in the European Union. Approximately 50 percent of all produced paper is used for packaging.

One of the best growth prospects in paperboard consumption came from the rapid development of liquid packaging systems in the 1990s, including both carton-board containers and the larger-sized bag-in-box packs. Originally developed for milk and fruit juices, the packs were being used more for soups, purees, and pastes, particularly in Europe and Asia. According to ProCarton, cartonboard sales in Europe come to around eight billion Euros with 5.4 million tons consumed annually.

According to FAO data, non-printing paper and paperboard production in the United States reached 54.5 mmt (million metric tons) in 2001 and rose to 55.3 mmt in 2003. Exports that year accounted for 6.4 mmt worth US$4.3 billion, a slight increase from 6.2 mmt exported in 2001 and valued at US$4.2 billion. The operating rate for U.S. containerboard facilities stood at 97.5 percent in May 2004.

According to Japanese government figures, the world-wide paperboard industry had begun to see slow but steady improvement by 2003. Shipments of processed food products, including health drinks and snacks, con-tributed to the rise in containerboard demand, while growth in folding carton and whiteboard was also boosted by growth in food industry demand.

To satisfy booming demand for paperboard products, particularly corrugated cardboard in which to package goods for its growing export markets, China increased imports of recycled cardboard. Unexpected beneficiaries of this trend were U.S. municipalities that, in 2005, were selling waste cardboard to China for US$90 per ton. Combined imports of paper, paperboard, waste paper, market pulp, and converted products totaled 21.99 mmt in 2003, an increase of 17.3 percent from the previous year. Coated boxboard ranked second only to newsprint in import growth in 2003.

CURRENT CONDITIONS

According to the US Corrugated and Paperboard Boxes Industry, the demand for paperboard products was on the increase after the steady declines that were registered from 2004 to 2009. The reason for the gain was due in part to an increase in shipments of nondurable goods such as food and beverages. In addition, as producers seek to gain prominence for their products, they look for ways to heighten the visual appeal of packaging in an effort to beat the competition. The growing trend in Internet-based shopping also created a demand for addi-tional consumer packaging that can serve a dual function of transport and promotion—sort of a packaging bill-board. The demand was projected to increase 2.3 percent annually through 2014 to US$37.5 billion.

Recycling was an important issue in the paperboard industry heading into the late 2000s. The AF&PA reported that a record amount of paper consumed in the United States in 2006 was recycled. About 53.5 million tons of

paper, or 53.4 percent of the total amount consumed, was recycled. The association announced a goal of reaching a 55 percent recycling rate by 2012, partly by increasing the amount recovered from offices and schools. Canada also was increasing the amount of paper it recycled and used. In 2004, approximately 46 percent of the paper and paper-board used in Canada was recycled, and 4.9 million tons of paper was transformed into other products. About 54 per-cent of the recycled paper used to make other products came from Canada, with the rest mainly from the United States.

Demand for recycled paper also was on the rise. Thirty-two percent of the paper recycled in the United States in 2006 was exported, with 10 million tons going to China. According to the American Forest & Paper Association (AF&PA), growing demand in China for newsprint and packaging material was driving increased demand for imports of recyclable paper in that country. Other growing market segments for recycled paper included Americans who were intent on practicing social responsibility. Many printing companies were respond-ing by incorporating environmentally friendly practices into their production processes and increasing the amount of recycled paper used for printing. For example, in 2007, Scholastic Inc. (New York) announced that all 12 million copies of the U.S. edition of *Harry Potter and the Deathly Hallows* would be printed on 30 percent post-consumer waste (pcw) paper, and 65 percent of the 16,700 tons of paper used in the U.S. first printing will be FSC (Forest Stewardship Council) certified. This marked the largest purchase of FSC paper to be used in the printing of a single book title.

RESEARCH AND TECHNOLOGY

Because production of paperboard is very similar to that of paper, many research trends in paperboard are similar to those in paper mills. Some differences exist, however. One area of particular interest to paperboard manufac-turers is the use of "impulse drying" to make linerboard. The Department of Energy has supported the research and development by the Institute of Paper Science and Technology and Beloit Corp. in the United States to perfect the technology of impulse drying—where the moisture content of the paper is reduced by 38 percent as it enters the drying section of the process. This involves heating one or more rolls in the press section of the paperboard machine, drying the paperboard web so less drying is required later in the dryer stage of the process. Because less steam is needed to heat rolls in the dryer section, this innovation enabled paperboard man-ufacturers to reduce steam costs and speed up produc-tion. Theoretically, paperboard manufacturers could improve productivity by 50 to 80 percent. It is estimated that the operation of 65 impulse drying units in 2020 could save 13 trillion Btus of energy annually for the paper industry. This will then translate into annual reductions in emissions of 1.2 million tons of carbon dioxide, 0.24 million pounds of volatile organic compounds, and 13 million pounds of particulates.

Another area of interest is the use of "stratification" in making paperboard. Stratification requires a special headbox that can produce three or more layers of paperboard simultaneously from different fiber sources. In this way, a layer of recycled fiber, or some other lesser quality fiber source, could be sandwiched between layers of better quality fiber. With newer model headboxes, these layers can be extremely thin. Several European paperboard manufacturers have adopted this technique.

The construction of containerboard improved considerably in the 1990s, as paperboard mills developed new production processes. Mills were able to produce lighter-weight linerboard and corrugating medium that still performed well in boxmaking plants. As a result, machinery manufacturers developed machines that produced finer grades of fluting at box plants. The boxes produced through these processes were able, in many applications, to replace boxes made from folding cartonboard. In 2002, International Paper introduced a recyclable moisture barrier in its bulk boxes.

INDUSTRY LEADERS

Because many paper companies produce large quantities of both paper and paperboard, leaders in the paperboard industry tend to include many of the companies profiled under **Paper Mills**.

Of the top 10 global pulp and paper companies, several producers had extensive interests in paperboard production. The U.S.-based International Paper Company (IP) was the world's largest forest products company. In the early 2000s, the company owned 6.3 million acres of forested land in the United States, as well as 1.2 million in Brazil and smaller tracts in New Zealand and Russia. However, by 2007, it had sold much of its forested land, retaining about 500,000 acres in the United States and harvesting rights for about one million acres in Brazil and Russia. In 2009, the company posted total sales of US$23.4 billion, with paper and packaging accounting for about two-thirds of sales. That year, the company employed 56,100 people. The company merged with Weyerhaeuser's packaging business and in 2009 generated more than US$500 million in the industrial packaging sector. However, 2009's severe economic downturn required tough decisions in the company. There was a 20 percent lack of order downtime, which forced the company to close some of its containerboard and coated paperboard facilities in North America and Europe.

Atlanta-based Georgia-Pacific Corporation was one of the largest U.S. producers of containerboard and the world's largest producer of tissue products. Its major brands included Brawny, Quilted Northern, and Dixie. Sales in 2004 exceeded US$19.6 billion. In 2005, Koch Industries finalized the US$21 billion acquisition of GP. Koch Industries realized a revenue of US$100 billion in 2009 with 80,000 employees. UPM-Kymmene, Helsinki, Finland, Europe's largest forest industry group, operated a packaging materials division, though it concentrated more on the publishing papers market. Despite significant downturns in the industry, it realized a 7.719 billion Euro revenue in 2009 with over 23,000 employees. Swedish-based Stora Enso Oyj, another of the world's largest forest products companies, mainly produced paperboard for the European market. In 2009, the company reported total sales of 8.945 billion Euros and 28,700 employees.

U.S.-based Smurfit-Stone Container Enterprises was a leading producer of packing materials, with corrugated containers accounting for more than 50 percent of sales (US$7.4 billion) in 2007. Svenska Cellulosa Aktiebolaget produced paperboard through its SCA Packaging unit, which was Europe's leading manufacturer of corrugated board packaging in the mid-2000s. In 2009, the company realized US$16.8 billion in sales with 45,000 employees.

Caraustar Industries was ranked as a major manufacturer of recycled paperboard and converted paperboard products. It operated more than 100 facilities in the United States along with plants in Mexico and the United Kingdom. Caraustar manufactured products primarily from recovered fiber derived from recycled paperstock. It produced various grades of uncoated and clay-coated recycled paperboard both for internal consumption and customers in four principal markets. The economic decline forced Caraustar to file for Chapter 11 protection in 2009 due to a US$99 million loss in 2008 and a US$4.4 million loss in 2009.

Tokyo-based Oji Paper Co. Ltd., Japan's second-biggest paper company, produced a large amount of paperboard, though its main focus was on paper grades. Oji realized a revenue of US$16.3 billion in 2007 with 20,056 employees.

The UPM Changshu paper mill is the largest producer of uncoated paper in China. Two thirds of the mill's production is sold to the Chinese market, with the remaining exported to the Asia Pacific region.

MAJOR COUNTRIES IN THE INDUSTRY

United States. U.S. paperboard producers ship the vast majority of paperboard consumed in the United States and have a strong position in the international market. Linerboard is one of the strongest export products for the U.S. pulp and paper industry. U.S. linerboard mills, mostly in the southern part of the country, are considered the low-cost producers throughout the world.

According to the U.S. Census Bureau, in 2002, employment in the industry amounted to about 158,600 employees. Due to technology advances, the employment numbers declined through 2010. Most paperboard jobs are located in Wisconsin, Georgia, and Alabama.

The drop in sales of non-durable packaging materials—caused by a combination of recession and post-September 11, 2001, shrinkage in consumer purchases—seemed to level off by the end of 2001. However, by 2002, some mid-sized companies were showing the strain of prolonged economic losses. After a disastrous 2000 loss of US$33 million, Idaho-based Potlatch Corp. saw conditions worsen even more in 2001. Even larger companies, such as International Paper, began mass layoffs in February 2002 as the effects of poor fourth quarter 2001 revenues became clear. The giant Smurfit Corp. of Chicago resorted to shutting machines and increasing downtime in its containerboard mills throughout 2001 and early 2002. Caraustar Industries filed for Chapter 11 protection at the end of the 2000s.

Industry capacity declined by 200,000 tpy in June 2001, when International Paper Co. closed its bleached board mill in Moss Point, Mississippi. It was the first permanent shutdown of a bleached board machine in more than 25 years. At that time, no new bleached board machine had been constructed since 1995.

In the mid-2000s, the United States was the world's leading paper and paperboard manufacturer, producing 83.4 million tons, or 23.2 percent of the world total, in 2004. According to the USDA Forest Service, production of paper and paperboard would grow slowly through 2050, while per capita consumption will increase at a faster pace.

Japan. In the mid-2000s, Japan was the world's third-largest paper and paperboard producer. Nevertheless, the industry had seen declines as the Japanese economy began slipping in the early 2000s. After showing slight production growth in the paper and paperboard industry of 1.2 percent in 1999, Japanese production dropped 3.5 percent from 2000 to 2001. The production for the year (including paper) equaled 30.73 million tons, as holiday sales and information technology business demonstrated corresponding drop-offs, according to the Japan Paper Association (JPA). About 2.6 percent of the decline was in cardboard used in shipping computers and appliances to home consumers, according to the JPA.

Total paperboard production in 2005 was 12.0 mmt, of which the greatest part (9.3 mmt) was containerboard. Folding carton production reached 1.8 mmt, while production of other paperboard totaled 850,000 mt. Most of Japan's production serves its domestic market. Paperboard exports peaked in 2000 at 448,000 tons, then started a steady decline, totaling only 185,000 tons in 2005. About 21.0 percent of exported paperboard was shipped to China in 2005. Taiwan received 12.2 percent, Hong Kong 11.6 percent, and the United States 10.1 percent, with the remainder going to other countries. Imports rose during this time, hitting a peak of 336,000 tons in 2004, and reaching 315,000 tons in 2005. The majority of imported paperboard (61.7 percent) came from the United States. Korea and Taiwan held the number two and three spots, respectively.

China. China, the world's second-largest manufacturer of paper and paperboard in the mid-2000s, had significant increases in demand as its economy expanded in the 1980s and 1990s. However, demand fell in 2002 due to demographic changes related to government-mandated regulations regarding the number of children one family could have. China produced around 49 million tons of paper and paperboard in 2005. In addition, annual production capacity was about 200 billion square meters.

In 2010, a giant paper mill consortium from China released itsplans to invest around US$1.1 billion to set up a vast 200,000ha forest plantation near current areas in mainland China that are affected by logging. This proposed project would be used as the source of raw material for paper and pulp mills.

Germany. Germany, the largest corrugated producer in Europe and fifth largest paper and paperboard producer in the world, manufactured 20.4 million tons of paper (excluding newsprint) and paperboard in 2005. With major operations in Germany and 16 other companies, Smurfit Kappa Group (Kappa Holdings) was one of the largest producers of packaging paper and board for business purposes, with a workforce numbering near 17,000 and more than US$8.58 billion in revenue in 2009. In 2001, the giant Kappa Packaging had greatly increased its company size after purchasing Swedish business rival AssiDomaen's corrugated and containerboard operations.

Canada. Canada's forest products industry focused primarily on the production and export of pulp, newsprint, and printing and writing papers. In the early 2000s, the country faced diminished export earnings in this sector due to global overproduction, which had lowered prices. In 2005, Canada produced 20.4 million tons of paper and paperboard. More than half its corrugated and folding boxboard production was exported, but the export value of case materials fell from US$737 million in 2000 to only US$498.3 million in 2003. Increased productivity in Canada's pulp and paper industry led to a reduction of about 13,000 jobs by 2002. In 2010, the Canadian government launched a US$100 million investment project for the Forest Industry Transformation (IFIT) program to help expand opportunities Canada's forestry industry.

South Korea. Since 2000, the industry news from Korea has mainly been bad. Company production capacity was only 73.6 percent in 2001, down 13.3 percentage points from 1995. South Korea imports more than 80 percent of the pulp it uses for making paper and paperboard. Almost 70 percent of the fiber used in South Korea to make paper and board comes from recycled paper and paperboard. This heavy reliance on recycled fiber means that South Korean paperboard tends to be weaker than paperboard made with more virgin fiber. Improvements in papermaking processes and high performance wet-strength agents are being used to improve the strength of South Korean paperboard.

Continuous capacity additions and the collapse of local and export paper markets in the fourth quarter of 1995 prompted significant downtime in South Korea's paperboard industry in 1996. According to one report, downtime ranged from 25 to 30 percent, and prices on key grades were discounted by as much as 25 percent. South Korean producers also suffered from the 1997 financial crisis, which severely tightened spending and inflated debt. As of 2002, Korea still faced overcapacity of 30 percent in the paper and paperboard sector. Total production in 2005 was 10.5 million tons.

BIBLIOGRAPHY

"AF&PA Shines Light on Recycling." *Official Board Markets*, 31 March 2007.

Decking, Noel. "Bleached Paperboard: SBS Mills Ramp Up Production, Backlogs." *Paperloop*, 2004. Available from http://www.paperloop.com.

Food and Agricultural Service of the United Nations. *FAOSTAT*, 15 April 2007. Available from http://www.fao.org.

"Hoover's Company Capsules." *Hoover's Online*, 2007. Available from http://www.hoovers.com.

"Linerboard Capacity Rises in 2006." *Official Board Markets*, 17 March 2007.

"Overview of the Recycling Industry." Paper Recycling Association, 2007. Available from http://www.pppc.org.

Paper Recycling Association, Canada, 2007. Available from http://www.pppc.org.

"Paperboard Mill Performance." *Official Board Markets*, 24 March 2007.

SIC 2611

PULP MILLS

NAICS CODE(S)

322110. Pulp mills manufacture pulp, the primary ingredient in paper, from wood or wastepaper (recycled fiber), although a small number of establishments use other materials for pulping, such as rags, cotton linters, and straw. Most major pulp operations are integrated with paper or paperboard production facilities. For additional information, see also **Paper Mills** and **Paperboard Mills.**

INDUSTRY SNAPSHOT

Pulp mills around the world produce a wide variety of pulps from wood fiber for making paper and paperboard. While the majority of pulp produced globally is chemical pulp, a substantial amount of pulp also is produced using the groundwood process. A growing number of mills make pulp from recycled paper. According to the Food and Agricultural Organization of the United Nations (FAO), total world production of wood pulp in 2003 exceeded 170.3 million metric tons (mmt). According to a report by *urgewald*, the pulp industry is projected to increase pulp production by more than 25 million metric tons annually through 2014. As production slows in the United States, an upsurge is expected in countries like Uruguay, Brazil, Indonesia, Australia, China, and Russia. The main reason for the industry swell is maturation of industrial tree plantations (or in Russia, forests).

In 2003, the United States led the world in wood pulp production with 53.1 mmt. Canada was second with 26.1 mmt. Other significant pulp-producing nations included Finland (11.9 mmt), Sweden (11.7 mmt), Japan (10.4 mmt), Brazil (8.8 mmt), Russia (6.6 mmt), and China (mmt).

Market pulp is a truly global commodity characterized by rapid price fluctuations in response to changes in capacity and demand. While market pulp is produced in about 25 countries, in the mid-2000s more than two-thirds of world production came from six northern countries: the United States, Canada, Sweden, Finland, Russia, and Norway. China was regarded as the fastest-growing producer of pulp. In addition, production numbers were rising in South America, most notably in Brazil and Chile. One major advantage South American mills enjoy is access to fast-growing pulpwood trees, such as eucalyptus and radiata pine species. These trees reach pulping maturity within seven years, compared to 30 years in some northern countries.

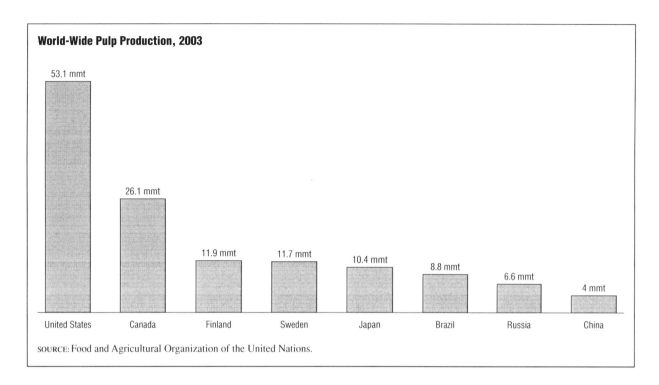

World-Wide Pulp Production, 2003

53.1 mmt — United States
26.1 mmt — Canada
11.9 mmt — Finland
11.7 mmt — Sweden
10.4 mmt — Japan
8.8 mmt — Brazil
6.6 mmt — Russia
4 mmt — China

SOURCE: Food and Agricultural Organization of the United Nations.

ORGANIZATION AND STRUCTURE

In most cases pulp mills need to be located near their raw materials—trees or wastepaper—to minimize transportation costs. Many of the leading world pulp producers such as the United States, Canada, Sweden, Finland, and Brazil have extensive forest reserves that are used, in part, for pulp production. Other leading pulp producers, such as Japan, possess limited forest resources but import logs and wood chips for pulp production.

While pulping and papermaking are very energy intensive, pulp and paper companies throughout the world are regarded as efficient energy users that gained their efficiency through producing their own electricity by burning many of their waste products, such as tree bark and spent chemicals from the pulping process. In some countries, pulp and paper mills generate over half of the energy required to run mills. Newer, large pulp and paper mills using chemical pulp are often completely self-sufficient in energy use. Nonetheless, environmental groups frequently criticize companies that supply wood to mills for endangering fish in small creeks by clear-cutting practices and the dragging of logs through these waterways. In addition, poor logging practices over as many as 80 years have brought attention to overlogging practices in the United States and other countries. Environmental groups oppose the practice of clear-cutting for several reasons, but with the spotlight on global warming, deforesting practices come under frequent attack.Forests have several positive effects on the environment: natural cooling, pollution filtration, and wildlife habitat.

Water is used in large quantities in pulp and paper manufacturing, and thus most mills are sited near lakes, rivers, or oceans. In decades past, waste water from the pulping process, or effluent, was released directly into receiving waters and caused substantial water pollution. Today, however, many pulp mills in countries whose governments adhere to sounder environmental practices reuse and/or clean process and waste water extensively before it is discharged. After water is reused within pulp and paper mills, it is sent to primary, secondary, and in some cases tertiary treatment plants.

More often than not, wood pulp is being replaced by recycled paper in new paper production. The percentage of fiber from trees, called virgin fiber, used in global paper and board production dropped from about 75 percent in 1970 to less than 62 percent in 1992, as more recycled pulp replaced wood fiber. By 1997 that percentage had dropped further, to 60 percent.

While the percentage of wood pulp in paper is expected to continue declining, it will likely remain the key ingredient in papermaking for years to come. Cellulose fibers can only be recycled about seven or eight times before they become so weak and short that they are washed out of the papermaking process. The overall use of wood pulp should grow, if only slightly, as the entire market for paper expands. Worldwide production of wood pulp was expected to rise by an average of 2 percent per year for the foreseeable future.

As of the mid-2000s, chemical pulp clearly remained the pulp of choice throughout the world. In 2003, chemical pulp production reached 124.4 mmt, representing approximately 73 percent of global pulp production. Mechanical pulp, at 34.8 mmt, accounted for about 17 percent of the total, while other pulp production was 18.6 mmt, or 10 percent.

While global consumption of pulp spiked higher and lower from year to year in the 1990s, the general trend has been toward higher consumption, particularly as rising incomes contribute to increased consumption of paper and packaging. In 1996 global pulp consumption was 172.9 mmt. The leading pulp-consuming region was North America, at 72.2 mmt, followed by Asia at 46.3 mmt, and Western Europe at 37.8 mmt. Other significant pulp-consuming regions were Latin America at 7.5 mmt and Eastern Europe (including Russia) at 5.65 mmt. While North America continued to lead in consumption of paper and paperboard, which are the chief end products of wood pulp, consumption in the region declined by 2.4 percent in 2000, with usage dropping by 2.3 percent in the United States and by 3.3 percent in Canada. The market for pulp was rosier in Europe, however, where paper and paperboard consumption rose steadily through the 1990s and into the early 2000s. The FAO projected that wood pulp consumption would also grow in Africa, where usage in 1994 was only 1.2 mmt. Consumption on that continent was expected to be 1.9 mmt in 2005, and nearly 2.08 mmt by 2010.

BACKGROUND AND DEVELOPMENT

Before the mid-nineteenth century, paper was made from rags or used paper. Rag collection for papermaking was an important part of the global economy at the time. However, as the global demand for paper increased, the demand for rags began to outstrip supply.

A major revolution in pulping occurred between 1851 and 1918, when wood pulp was invented, developed, and industrialized. This period saw the development and commercialization of all major wood pulping processes, including groundwood, soda, sulphite, and kraft (sulphate). Soda pulping was invented by Hugh Burgess and Charles Watt in England, and was patented in 1854 in the United States. Groundwood became established in the 1860s. Kraft pulping was invented in 1884 by German chemist Carl Dahl using sodium sulfate as the pulping agent. The pulp produced a strong brown paper, dubbed *kraft*, the German word for strong. Kraft pulping became the dominant method of pulp production in the twentieth century.

The science of pulping continued to develop along with the growth of papermaking. Among the decisive technological leaps in pulping was the invention of the chemical recovery boiler, in which spent pulping chemicals were burned for their fuel value. This process recovers the energy in the chemicals and some of the chemicals themselves, which can then be reused. Another key pulping development was the continuous digester, invented by the Swedish firm Kamyr AB, which replaced the slower batch digesting process at most pulp mills.

While wood pulp remains almost completely dominant in the global production of papermaking fiber, there has been renewed interest in using agricultural fibers such as kenaf, an African hibiscus, to produce paper. China and India already produce large amounts of pulp from agricultural fibers. Substances such as kenaf can be grown in areas of the world where trees are less plentiful and are viewed as more environmentally sustainable than wood pulp. Small-scale research on kenaf is underway in the United States, and there are currently several pulp mills using agricultural fibers throughout the world.

From a financial perspective, the 1990s and early 2000s were disastrous for most pulp mill operations, which suffered very low profits or incurred substantial losses due to free-falls in prices. This was largely due to a soft economy, further injured by fewer pages printed by media publications in the wake of the September 11, 2001, terrorist attacks on the United States. This collapse was exacerbated by stagnating demand and a huge oversupply of pulp.

In 1994, pulp mills worldwide went from gloom to gloating when the price for benchmark NBSK (northern bleached softwood kraft) rose an astonishing 75 percent and was headed even higher in 1995. However, in 1996 prices began falling again, and in 1997 many pulp producers worldwide were facing the prospects of very low profits or losses on their operations. By 1998, many Canadian pulp mills were again taking downtime to try to work off excess inventory and stabilize the price of market pulp.

Increased worldwide competition in pulp production remained a certainty. In 1996, Indonesia produced a record 2.64 mmt of pulp, and was by far the fastest-growing pulp-producing nation in the world. By 2000 its output had exceeded 3.6 mmt, and in 2003 the country produced just over 5.2 mmt. Virtually all new virgin pulp expansion projects in the late 1990s and early 2000s were in the Southern Hemisphere.

After an unprecedented expansion of pulping capacity in the late 1980s, the early 1990s saw demand falling, capacity rising, and prices plummeting. Market pulp prices reached a low for the 1990s of US$390 per ton for NBSK in the fourth quarter of 1993. By October 1994—with demand rising and capacity static—the price for NBSK had shot up to US$700 per ton and briefly touched US$1,000 per ton at the end of 1995. However, high prices and boom times in the global pulp industry are almost always followed by a price crash as new start-up operations, attracted by high profits, flood the world market with pulp.

That scenario played out in 1996 as lower demand, high inventories, and growing capacity produced another steep drop in pulp prices. By November 1996, prices for NBSK had dropped to about US$570 per ton. Prices continued to drift downward to about US$510 per ton at the end of March 1997. In the second quarter of 1997, however, prices began a gradual rise, and demand in most areas of the world began to increase. By November, the price of NBSK had reached about US$610 per ton.

World suppliers of chemical paper-grade market pulp delivered 31.7 mmt to their customers in 1997, breaking the previous record, which was set in 1995. Among major market pulp-consuming regions, the United States experienced the largest rise in percentage terms, up 13 percent in 1997, or almost 600,000 tons. In terms of volume, growth in Western Europe was the strongest in the world compared to 1996, up more than 800,000 tons, or 8 percent. Demand in Japan rose 2 percent, but deliveries to Africa and Asia (mostly Southeast Asia) declined 3 percent as new pulp mills in these regions began production, replacing market pulp from other countries. To satisfy the increased demand for market pulp in 1997, producers worldwide withdrew about 400,000 tons from inventory, which stood at about 2.9 mmt at the end of the year, enough to supply worldwide demand for 34 days.

Despite this good news, however, from 1998 through 2002, considerable uncertainty about the price trend for pulp plagued the industry worldwide. Asian buyers, who accounted for a large share of the demand for market pulp, contended with diminished purchasing power because of currency depreciations, while pulp sellers in North America and Europe, concerned about payments, slowed their shipments to Asia. This trend was expected to reduce prices for market pulp, at least in the short run. In the 2000s, the United States and Canada sparred about the price of Canada's pulp exports to the United States, as government aid to the Canadian industry made the price of imported pulp products lower than what U.S. producers charged.

While there were regional variations, bleached softwood kraft pulp was still the biggest grade of market pulp, accounting for about 45 percent of global market pulp production in the late 1990s. By 2004 most of the increase in pulp production was attributed to bleached softwood. According to the Market Pulp Association, bleached softwood capacity rose by 4.9 percent that year, while bleached hardwood capacity grew by only 1.5 percent. Recycled pulp remained a relatively small part of market pulp output (most recycled pulp was consumed by integrated pulp and paper mills). However, the amount of

recycled market pulp produced in North America grew rapidly in the mid-1990s. For example, in the United States the capacity to produce chemical grade market wood pulp grew by about 0.5 percent annually from 1998 through 2000, when capacity reached about 10.52 million short tons. Recovered paper-market pulp capacity in the United States, starting from a small base of 574,000 short tons in 1993, reached 1.76 million short tons in 1997.

The pulp industry finds itself in a volatile market. Indeed, stability has been hard to find. In a single day, the terrorist attacks of September 11, 2001, devastated many industries, which in turn had an immediate, deleterious effect on pulp prices. The promising rise in newsprint prices in the fourth quarter of 2000, in which global newsprint prices climbed to US$605 a ton, disappeared. This was a direct result of a drop in print ads and media pages, which resulted in newsprint prices falling to US$505 a ton.

Thus, the early 2000s marked continued harsh economic times for the pulp-mill industry. The world's largest producer, International Paper (IP), recorded 2001 fourth-quarter earnings of just US$58 million, not even half of 2000 fourth-quarter earnings. Annual 2001 sales for IP also faltered, with net earnings of US$214 million, well below comparable 2000 net earnings of US$969 million, according to *Printing World*. As a result, stable companies such as American Tissue, Kimberly-Clark, Voith Paper, IP, and many others found themselves forced to lay off employees in 2001 and 2002. IP dismissed more than 2,500 employees in 2000 alone. Not until 2003 did the situation significantly improve; that year, IP posted sales of US$25.2 billion and net earnings of US$302 million. The 2008 revenue had slipped to US$22.3 billion, with a workforce of approximately 51,500. In 2005 and 2006, IP sold off six million acres of forested land, along with several of its subsidiaries.

While North America, Europe, and Scandinavia have traditionally been the leading regions in pulp production, other regions have grown in importance—notably South America and Asia. In South America, Uruguay, Brazil, and Chile have greatly expanded their pulp production. In Brazil, eucalyptus trees grow to pulpable size nearly seven times faster than trees in the Nordic countries, giving Brazilian pulp mills a strong cost advantage in this area. Similar growth rates are recorded for Chile's radiata pine plantations, which are used for pulp wood as well as timber products. Several major pulp mills were built in Asia during the 1990s, making that region one of the strongest pulp growth areas. Strong economic growth rates in many Asian countries fueled demand for pulp and paper products, leading to the expansion. While Japan remained the dominant pulp producer in Asia, Indonesia was one of the region's fastest-growing producers of pulp, although much of it was cut illegally with the blessings of corrupt provincial officials. China has had several projects on the drawing board as well.

However, the Asian financial crisis that began in early 1997 and continued into the early 2000s had a major impact on that region's fast-growing pulp and paper industry. Several pulp and paper companies were facing dire financial problems. As the currencies of major Asian pulp and paper producing countries, such as Indonesia, fell dramatically against the U.S. dollar, the financial impact on Asian companies was severe. Larger mills with modern equipment purchased in U.S. dollars had trouble recouping their investment. High debt loads by these companies compounded their troubles.

While economic growth was expected to continue in Asia, the rate of growth was expected to slow significantly. There was considerable speculation that the ownership structure of the Asian pulp and paper industry would change markedly as companies from outside the region tried to buy Asian pulp and paper producers at what had quickly become bargain prices.

Indonesia—the focus of major pulping developments—was also embroiled in controversy in the late 1990s and 2000s following the toppling of its corrupt but stable military regime. While major new pulp mills were built at a very rapid pace with the promise of prosperity and jobs, allegations were raised by various environmental groups of illegal logging by pulp companies. Some observers feared that Indonesia's substantial forest resources would be devastated through aggressive harvesting by lumber producers and pulp manufacturers. According to a report from Friends of the Earth, cited in *El The Environmental Magazine*, the pulp and paper industry in Indonesdia "is destroying rainforest so quickly that it was predicted to run out of wood by 2007." In 1997 the country was also ravaged by extensive fires. The pulp industry in Indonesia produced the biggest debt default in emerging markets as Asia Pulp and Paper refused to continue repayment on its US$14 billion debt in 2001.

The European pulp industry was hit hard by the global recession in the early 1990s, with almost no new pulp mills being constructed. While that trend continued through much of the decade, many existing mills invested in new equipment and processes that helped incrementally to increase production. By the early 2000s the European pulp industry faced better conditions, with consumption growing at about 2.2 percent in Western Europe and 7.7 percent in Russia in 2004. This trend was expected to continue through 2005.

In North America, the development of recycling pulp mills dominated the news in the mid-1990s. Development of virgin pulp mills virtually ceased, while more

than 20 recycled pulp mill projects went forward. However, most of these mills were never built, and many of those that were built went bankrupt when pulp prices dropped sharply in late 1996 and early 1997. In general, these mills had difficulty competing on quality with virgin pulp while maintaining cost efficiency. Nevertheless, many pulp and paper companies producing virgin fiber added recycled fiber lines to their existing mills in the 1990s in order to develop combinations of virgin and recycled pulp. While this new recycled pulp was not sold on the open market, it still added to pulping capacity in the North American market. North American virgin pulp producers, as in Europe, also pursued a strategy of making capital investments in existing pulp mills to help improve productivity and boost production.

In South America, the 1980s saw several large pulp mills open, including the Aracruz pulp mill, with the production of 1 mmt per year. Although expansion was less pronounced in the early to mid-1990s, the pulp industry was expected to grow more rapidly in the early 2000s. Several new pulp mills were expected to begin operations between 2005 and 2007, boosting the region's production capacity by an additional 3.565 mmt of hardwood and 425,000 tons of softwood.

Brazil, the leading South American pulp producer through the 1990s and early 2000s, was expected to attract continued investment in its pulping industry. However, lower prices in 1997 meant that some pulp mills lost money and plans for new mills were put on hold. Despite these challenges, some Brazilian producers continued to invest in new capacity. In 2005, the new Veracel pulp mill in Eunápolis, Bahia was scheduled to begin operations. The joint venture between Stora Enso and Aracruz Celulose will be the world's largest single-line bleached eucalyptus pulp mill with an annual capacity of about 900,000 metric tons. As of 2003, Brazil accounted for 25 percent of world capacity for bleached hardwood market pulp. Aracruz, the largest producer in Brazil, controlled almost 50 percent of Brazilian capacity. However, with pulp mills and tree plantations comes controversy. In Brazil, the world's largest land-rights movement, the Movement of Landless Peasants, has repeatedly targeted pulp wood plantations as it fights for land rights. The movement says that the pulp industry in these regions will mean loss of jobs, increased poverty, and environmental destruction.

Chile entered the major leagues of pulping in the late 1980s and early 1990s, though controversy about the use of "ancient" Chilean forests has mounted. Many of Chile's pulp mills are financed by foreign companies, and much of the pulp is exported. The main market for Chilean pulp is Asia, which took about half the total in 1996, with the remainder going to Europe and elsewhere in South America. Overall, Chilean pulp production was up about 5 percent in 1997. That increase came after a 25 percent spurt in 1996, when volume jumped from 1.65 mmt to 2.06 mmt. From 1998 through the early 2000s, several major projects were underway that would increase Chilean pulp tonnage still further. In 2003, production exceeded 2.7 mmt; exports that year were 2.1 mmt.

Bleaching Controversy. From the mid-1980s into the 2000s, the most contentious environmental and regulatory issue in the global pulping industry was the use of chlorine and chlorine compounds in the pulp bleaching process. This controversy stemmed from the discovery in the mid-1980s of minute amounts of dioxin in pulp mill effluent. This by-product of the pulping process had not been previously discovered because older instrumentation was not sensitive enough to detect the minute amounts, which were in the parts-per-billion range.

While there was considerable scientific debate about whether minute amounts of dioxin affect human health, most pulp mills around the world dramatically reduced dioxin levels by either substituting chlorine dioxide for elemental chlorine in the bleaching process or by using no chlorine compounds at all. For example, in the United States pulp mills reduced dioxin discharges by 90 percent from 1985 to 1993, to less than three ounces for the entire U.S. pulp industry. By 1994, most of the world's market pulp mills were producing or planning to produce elemental chlorine-free (ECF) pulp using chlorine dioxide. In early 1998, the U.S. Environmental Protection Agency (EPA) issued its long-awaited Cluster Rule, which regulates air and water emissions of U.S. pulp and paper mills. As expected, the rule endorsed the use of ECF bleaching by pulp mills to meet strict water emission guidelines.

In Europe, a sustained campaign against the use of chlorine by environmental groups in the early 1990s led several European pulp mills to adopt totally chlorine-free (TCF) bleaching methods. One producer, Sweden's Sodra, aggressively marketed its TCF-bleached paper by attacking paper not made from TCF pulp. German pulp mills also converted to TCF. However, the fact that these pulp mills produced sulfite pulp instead of the more common sulfate process made it technologically easier for them to convert to TCF. It is much more costly to convert a sulfate pulp mill to TCF processes. Despite the pressure, many mills in Europe continued to produce ECF pulp. For example, Stora Billerud's Gruvon mill in central Sweden was a leader in the production of ECF pulp, but in 2001 the parent company focused on operations in other than its main enterprise.

In the United States, public pressure failed to materialize around the ECF/TCF issue. Most U.S. pulp mills used the sulfate process and most of those were committed to producing ECF pulp. Indeed, by the late 1990s the battle over ECF/TCF bleaching appeared to be over. In the United States, virtually all chemical pulp mills were expected to use ECF bleaching sequences, and production of ECF pulp was expanding rapidly worldwide. While ECF pulp was still produced by several European mills due to customer demand for the product, TCF's percentage of pulp production around the world was very small. Analysts expected this trend to continue, with new mills in Europe, South America, and Asia planning to incorporate ECF bleaching technology. *Reach for Unbleached* estimated that "with global annual growth forecast at 2.5 percent, the industry and its negative impacts could double by 2025."

After the ups and downs of the late 1990s, the pulp market began to see steadier growth. According to the Market Pulp Association, global demand for pulp rose faster than expected from 2001 to 2004, growing by 5.3 percent in 2004. Global production capacity grew by 2.8 percent that year.

CURRENT CONDITIONS

In 2007, prices in the pulp industry were expected to remain high due to increased exports to China and the declining value of the U.S. dollar. According to *Georgia Trend,* "the South is a high-cost producer of market pulp, as are Western Canada and Western Europe. These regions bear the brunt of any decline in global demand for market pulp and paper and are among the last to benefit from rising prices."

The latter part of the decade saw developments in biotechnology and engineering that would allow the "black liquor" by-product and residue of pulp mills to be "gasified" and converted to liquid fuels and chemicals. In essence, pulp mills would become bio-refineries. The American Forest & Paper Association (AF&PA) predicted that 10 percent of U.S. diesel fuel demand could be met through black-liquor/forest residue gasification. In addition, gasification is much more environmentally friendly than the traditional Tomlinson boiler used by most pulp mills and reduces emissions by 90 percent. Although more research and development was needed in the field to allow practical application of the idea on a widescale basis, some mills, including Chemrec in Sweden, were already putting gasification into practice.

RESEARCH AND TECHNOLOGY

With increasing regulatory attention focused on pulp mill emissions, research devoted to the "effluent-free" mill—also called the "closed mill"—increased sharply in the mid-to-late 1990s. In theory, the closed mill perfectly balances all of the inputs to and outputs from the pulping and papermaking process, so that the mill reuses, recycles, or cleans all its waste materials. Widely regarded as impossible just a decade ago, this prospect appears to be feasible, provided that current technology continues to develop and the cost of implementation decreases. Some pulp mills in Canada that use a combination of chemical and mechanical pulping have already "closed" the mill by producing zero effluent. Research continues on how to apply zero-effluent technology to traditional kraft pulping, a more difficult proposition. However, some have questioned the need for the effluent-free pulp mill, arguing that a mill producing effluent without negative effects on the environment would achieve the same end but without undue cost. Advocates of the total effect-free (TEF) mill say this type of mill is much more practical and would be achievable more quickly than the effluent-free mill.

In 2005, Integrated Paper Services Inc. announced a new automatic fiber analysis system, MorFi, which measures the size and shape of hardwood or softwood fibers in dilute pulp suspensions. A new stabilizer introduced in 2005, Clariant's Cartan RCF, reduces costs and improves whiteness during the pulp bleaching process.

The Center for Paper Business and Industry Studies claimed "significant and unpredictable pulp and paper price movements have led to a number of serious consequences for the pulp and paper industry, including excess capacity, unintended inventory build-up, and financial losses." According to the center, the economic vitality of the industry will be threatened by the unanticipated price movements. In addition, it claimed there was a need for literature offering "a clear explanation of market trends using a theoretical framework."

INDUSTRY LEADERS

Since pulp and paper production is largely integrated, the leaders in production of "captive pulp" are usually the same companies that lead in paper production. However, market pulp, even though it represents a minority of global pulp production, is a major international commodity. Some of the world's largest pulp and paper companies are also leaders in the production of market pulp. For example, the top four market pulp producers are all among the top global pulp and paper companies. However, some smaller companies specialize in market pulp and rank prominently on the list of top market pulp producers. These include Aracruz Celulose (the number one producer of bleached eucalyptus), Sodra, Celulosa Arauco (a major owner of forest plantations), and Rayonier (the premier supplier of high-performance specialty celluose fibers).

MAJOR COUNTRIES IN THE INDUSTRY

United States. The United States has a very large growing stock of pulpwood in several areas: the Pacific

Northwest, the Upper Midwest, the Northeast, and Southeast. Combined with an efficient manufacturing base, this makes the United States the lowest-cost producer of many grades of pulp.

The United States is the leader in world pulp production, with 53.1 mmt in 2003. It also exports substantial amounts of wood pulp (5.1 mmt in 2003). Despite producing and exporting large volumes of market pulp, the U.S. pulp and paper industry still imports a large amount of the commodity, largely because of its open trade with Canada. In 2003, pulp for paper imports totaled 6 mmt.

Consumption slowed in the early 2000s. From 1997 to 2002, the United States lost 72 paper mills and, in the combined paper, lumber, and pulp sectors, some 55,000 jobs over the same time period, according to American Forest and Paper Association figures.

As of 2010, there were 655 pulp mills operating in the United States. According to a March 2010 report from the American Forest and Paper Association, U.S. paper and paperboard capacity had declined 2.5 percent during 2009, to 93.9 mmts.The decline was not unexpected, however, as the world was struggling with a sluggish economy at the same time. Fourteen paper mills were also permanently closed in 2009, while several more were left sitting idle in response to the weak market conditions. The AF&PA predict that the industry will continue to decline 3.4 percent in 2010, and then remain stable through 2012.

Canada. From 1994 to 2002, some analysts questioned productivity in Canada's pulp mills, but environmental watchers argued that a lower level of productivity was to be expected as the nation reduced the effects of pulp-industry pollution. The push to clean up industry pollution has been a major goal of the Sustainable Forest Management Network, a non-profit research center under Canada's federal Networks of Centres of Excellence Program. Strict forest management controls have been in place since the 1990s. In this regard, the China Canada Cooperation Project in Cleaner Production was viewed as producing quite favorable results.

Canada produced 26.1 mmt of wood pulp in 2003, compared to about 25.7 mmt the previous year. Wood pulp exports in 2003 were 11.5 mmt. According to the Market Pulp Association, Canada was the largest market pulp supplier in 2004, contributing 18 percent of global capacity. In 2003 and 2004, Canada balanced declining shipments to Western Europe and Japan with increased sales to Asia, Africa, and North America. However, some in the industry expressed concerns in the mid-2000s as companies shut down mills and moved their manufacturing to South America, where, according to an article in

Northern Ontario Business, "wages are lower, the trees grow quicker and regulations are more lax."

China. China is second only to the United States in terms of paper and pulp production and consumption. China has more pulp mills than any other nation. However, many are very small, and many use agricultural fiber, such as straw and bamboo, instead of wood fiber. China's pulp and paper industry has been expanding rapidly since 1990, with 50 percent of the global expansion in production there. China's production has been in flux. Early production primarily used agricultural crops of rice and wheat in its pulp mills. However, as Chinese plants employ a more progressive technology, they increasingly use wood and recycled paper as their raw materials. In 2003 the country produced 14.3 mmt of pulp from non-wood fibers, but only 4 mmt of wood pulp. Pulp production of all kinds was expected to continue increasing and, at the same time, China has emerged as the most voracious user of pulp. Without high demand in China, for example, the global purchases of marketable pulp would have dropped 5 percent from 2000 to 2001, according to *Lloyd's.* Demand in China is expected to remain high; in addition, the country planned major expansions in domestic capacity, including APP, China's bleached hardwood kraft pulp mill on Hainan Island, which is expected to produce 1.0 mmt annually. While analysts predicted that this increase could slow hardwood pulp imports, they noted that softwood pulp imports would continue to rise. By 2005, consumption of paper per person had reached 45 kilograms, with total comsumption at 58 mmts. In 2007, China produced approximately 50 mmts annually, but predictions were that the number would increase to 70 mms by 2010.

In 2007, the Chinese government announced plans to close thousands of small-capacity straw-pulp mills across the nation in an effort to stem pollution.U.S. corporations increasingly looked to China for newsprint supplies during the early 2000s. For example, in 2002 Visonper International Company (USA) Ltd. announced its intention to invest US$125 million in an attempt to reap 500,000 tons of paper pulp in China for export.

Japan. Wood pulp production in Japan declined from 11.2 mmt in 1996 to only 10.4 mmt in 2003. From December 2001 to February 2002, the drop in the value of the yen led to higher prices for traditional Japanese imports such as beef and pulp. In turn, this led to fears among U.S. pulp suppliers that the devaluation of the yen could have adverse consequences for U.S. pulp companies, Weyerhaeuser spokesman Frank Mendizabel told *The New York Times.* Indeed, Japan's total wood pulp imports dropped from 3 mmt in 2000 to 2.6 mmt in

2001. This decline slowed thereafter, with imports reaching 2.5 mmt in 2002 and 2.4 mmt in 2003.

Sweden. Sweden's 46 pulp mills produced 11.7 mmt of wood pulp in 2003, showing a slight improvement over the 11.3 mmt of wood pulp produced the previous year. After a ten-year decline in pulp produced, Sweden's pulp inventory rose in 2001.

Finland. With 45 pulp mills, Finland was the third largest world producer of pulp in 2003, with 11.9 mmt of wood pulp. This represented a significant jump over its 9.68 mmt of pulp produced in 1996. In 2002, Russian and Finnish interests met to solidify future Finnish exports of Russian raw timber for pulp usage. The international decline in pulp prices in the 2000s hit Finland particularly hard. One of the larger companies, Stora Enso, had net profits of US$798 million in 2001, down 35.4 percent from 2000 profits, and the company elected to dissolve its pulp division. In the face of such challenges, Finland has invested significant resources in education related to the pulp and paper industry. Of 300 engineers who earned master?s degrees in pulp and paper studies in Europe in 2002, about 200 were Finnish.

Brazil. Toward the end of the twentieth century, a major trend in the pulp mill industry has been its restructuring through mergers and consolidations as smaller companies band together to make a collective input, according to *Bloomberg News.* For example, Votorantim Celulose e Papel SA bought a 12 percent stake in Aracruz Celulose SA, one of South America's most prominent producers, for US$370 million. In addition, takeovers worth more than US$1 billion occurred in Brazil during the early 2000s.

With 10.1 mmt of pulp production in 2005, Brazil is easily South America's largest pulp producer. Brazil employs 108,000 people in the pulp and paper industry. Output increased substantially in the early 2000s as miscellaneous pulp interests invested about US$6.6 billion by 2005 to modernize the industry and upgrade production and export facilities, according to the Brazilian Pulp and Paper Association (Bracelp). Wood pulp production rose from 5.9 mmt in 1995 to 7.4 mmt in 2002.

Chile. *World Rainforest Movement* shared findings in 2001 from TERRAM Foundation researcher and economist Consuelo Espinosa evaluating the impact of pulp production in Chile, where the industry was viewed as an ideal model for the region. However, according to Espinosa, the establishment of pulp mills there, while generating wealth for some, exacerbated poverty and destitution for local populations. Even so, plans proceeded in 2005 for expansion in pulp production. The Itata sawmill and wood pulp mill, near the city of Concepcion, was expected to produce 850,000 tons of pulp annually (50 percent pine and 50 percent eucalyptus). This capacity would bring the annual output of its owner, the Arauco Company, to about 3.1 metric tons of bleached and unbleached kraft pulp.

Russia. While the pulp industry stagnated or retreated elsewhere during the early 2000s, Russia's pulp tonnage increased, rising 7.4 percent from 2000 to 2001, according to *Food & Agriculture Report* and Russian State Statistics Committee reports. In 2000, according to FAO data, Russia produced 5.8 mmt of wood pulp. This figure rose to 6.1 mmt in 2001 and 6.5 mmt in 2001. Wood pulp production in 2003 was 6.6 mmt. In a special article for *The Russia Journal,* Natalya Pinyagina pointed out that the industry had "a lot ofpotential and should become a loco-motive to pull the whole forestry sector to a level that a great forest power deserves to have." She also said "the weak point" was not having enough processing facilities for low-grade timber throughout most of the country.

BIBLIOGRAPHY
American Forest and Paper Association Statistics. Available from www.afandpa.org.

"Banks, Pulp and People, A Primer on Upcoming International Pulp Projects; Pulp Mill Watch." Available from www.pulpmill watch.org.

Boswell, Clay. "Chipping into Success." *ICIS Chemical Business Americas* (5 March 2007).

"Chile: Tree Plantations and Pulp Production Generate Poverty and Destitution." *World Rainforest Movement Bulletin* (14 June 2004). Available from www.wrm.org.

"Forest Industry Biorefinery Could Provide Big Benefits, Compete on Cost with Coal-to-Liquids Diesel." *Diesel Fuel News* (15 January 2007).

Forestry Data: Pulp, Paper, and Paperboard. United Nations, Food and Agricultural Organization, 21 January 2005. Available from www.faostat.fao.org.

Humphreys, Jeffrey M. "2007 Industry Outlook." *Georgia Trend* (April 2007).

Louiseize, Kelly. "Americans Leaving Canada: It's a Bad Thing." *Northern Ontario Business* (July 2006).

"Market Pulp Prices Hit 10-Year High Fueled by Mill Closures, Asian Demand." *Pulp & Paper* (August 2006).

Motavalli, Jim. "The Paper Chase." *E/The Environmental Magazine* (May-June 2004). Available from www.emagazine.com.

"Overview of the Wood Pulp Industry." Market Pulp Association, 2005. Available from www.pppc.org.

"Pulp and Paper Manufacturing." European Commission, May 2006. Available from http://ec.europa.eu.

Pulp Projects by Country: Pulp Mill Watch. Available from www.pulpmillwatch.org.

Statement on Forest Products Markets in 2004 and Prospects for 2005. United Nations, UNECE Timber Committee and FAO European Forestry Commission, 8 October 2004. Available from www.unece.org.

PETROLEUM PRODUCTS

———————■———————

LUBRICATING OILS
AND GREASES

NAICS CODE(S)

324191. The world's lubricant industry refines, blends, and compounds oils and greases from purchased mineral, animal, and vegetable materials. (See also **Petroleum Refining.**)

INDUSTRY SNAPSHOT

Within the enormous worldwide oil industry, lubricants constitute a downstream specialty business that generates significant revenues and profits for producers. Most of the major oil companies are key players in the lubricants industry, but independent producers still hold a significant share of lubricant volume in many countries. The highest volume of lubricant consumers includes those in rubber manufacturing, transportation and equipment, passenger cars, chemical manufacturing, and railroads and aviation. Other industrial users of lubricants are those involved in primary metals such as aluminum, steel plants, and mining; the printing industry; fabricated metals; food processors; and pulp and paper manufacturing.

The vast majority of all lubricants are made from petroleum base stocks, but newer synthetic lubricants, which offer unusually long service life and enhance functionality, are becoming a larger presence on the global market. By the mid-years of the first decade of the 2000s, specialty companies such as Pennzoil, Quaker State, and Burmah Castrol were no longer separate entities but had been acquired by so-called "Big Oil" companies.

Two of the associations serving the lubricants industry are the Independent Lubricant Manufacturers Association (ILMA) and the National Lubricating Grease Institute (NLGI). ILMA manufacturing members are independent lubricant companies. These companies assume responsibility for producing more than 25 percent of all lubricants and 80 percent or more of the metalworking fluids and other specialty lubricant products sold in North America. Independent members are headquartered in other regions of the world. The NLGI had member companies in 26 countries. The member companies manufacture and market all types of lubricating grease. NGLI focuses on promoting technical advancement as well as new product innovations.

Product Variety. Lubricant manufacturers produce a wide variety of lubricant products, including consumer automotive products such as motor oil, brake fluid, and transmission oil. Other major product areas include commercial automotive, industrial metalworking fluids, general industrial and specialties, and marine lubricants. Within these categories there are hundreds of individual products, including cutting oils, lubricating greases and oils, hydraulic fluids, and rust-arresting compounds.

The primary ingredients in lubricants are base stock (a refined petroleum product) and additives, which impart special qualities to lubricants. Enhancements to base stocks and additives drive improvements in lubricant performance. Most technological improvements focus on creating lubricants that conserve energy and do a better job of controlling deposits. The largest category of base stocks is paraffinics, followed by napthenics and synthetics. Of these three, only synthetic base stocks are expected to grow rapidly—although they account for less than 10 percent of the global base stock market.

ORGANIZATION AND STRUCTURE

Automotive products were one of the major lubricants markets, accounting for well over 50 percent of the total lubricants market in many countries. Within this category, there were three main types of lubricants: crankcase oils (motor oil); transmission and axle lubricants; and fluids for the hydraulic torque converters and fluid couplings in automatic transmissions. Each category was further subdivided by viscosity, the degree of resistance to molecular flow. Automotive lubricants worked by cushioning adjacent metal pieces, oiling moving parts, and keeping dirt out of combustion chambers.

The motor oil market included two major subcategories—the DIY (do-it-yourself) market, for consumers who changed their own oil, and the DIFM (do-it-for-me) market, which included auto dealers, service stations, and the fast-growing quick oil change shops. One of the motor oil growth markets was in synthetics, which were more expensive and lasted much longer than conventional motor oils. Two major brands in this area were Castrol Syntec and Mobil 1. Globally, the trend by the mid-1990s was toward higher-margin synthetic and semi-synthetic oils, which were recommended by luxury car manufacturers such as Bayerische Motoren Werke AG (BMW) and Mercedes.

Changing Market. In the 1960s, the motor oil market in most countries was dominated by service stations that were operated by major gasoline marketers such as Shell and Mobil. However, the international oil crisis in the 1970s spurred the development of self-service gasoline outlets in many western countries, and more consumers began changing their own oil. This opened the door for new outlets to sell motor oil.

By the 1990s, motor oil sales had spread to many retail outlets throughout the world, including automotive chains, parts stores, supermarkets and hypermarkets, and general merchandise chains. This helped companies such as Pennzoil, Castrol, and Quaker State market their products directly to the consumer and take market share away from the major oil companies. For example, in the United States Pennzoil held the largest share of the DIY motor oil market in 1992 at 18.9 percent, followed by Castrol at 14.5 percent; Quaker State at 11.9 percent; and Texaco and Valvoline, both at 14 percent. In the mid-1990s, these companies were leaders in the global market, with Shell, Texaco, Castrol, Pennzoil, and Quaker State being the top five.

In the mid-1990s, motor oil producers were using increasingly sophisticated marketing efforts to bring their products to the attention of customers worldwide. For example, in 1994 Quaker State launched an extensive and expensive marketing program to promote its new synthetic oil, Quaker State 4X4, which was targeted at the growing sport utility vehicle market. Quaker State intended to regain some of the market share it lost in the 1980s and early 1990s in the United States and overseas markets.

While consumers who changed their own oil were a major market for lubricant manufacturers, they also created an environmental hazard. Many disposed of used oil by pouring it down household and storm drains. It was estimated that in the United States alone, the amount of improperly disposed motor oil each year was 10 times greater than the entire amount of oil spilled in the *Exxon Valdez* accident. Some lubricants manufacturers responded to this problem by collecting used oil and other lubricants and re-refining them for use as second-quality lubricants. For example, Quaker State operated a Specialty Environmental Services Unit, which collected and recycled used oil, antifreeze, filters and brake fluid, and other substances.

However, even this activity was controversial. In the United States, the Environmental Protection Agency (EPA) received protests from environmental groups and some oil industry groups in the early 1990s on its decision to classify used motor oil as a non-hazardous substance. The groups contended that since used oil could contain hazardous substances, it should be legally regarded as hazardous. Critics cited the fact that most used motor oil was burned as fuel, releasing toxic substances into the air, although they did acknowledge that burning was still better than consumers pouring used oil into sewer systems. Two manufacturers that marketed re-refined lubricating oils from recycled oil were Safety-Kleen and Evergreen Company, with annual capacities of 45 million and 10 million gallons respectively.

Other Markets. The industrial lubricants category was large and included a vast array of products, such as machine oils, cutting oils, natural and synthetic metal-working fluids, die-casting lubricants, industrial chemical cleaners, dry cleaning fluids, and deodorants. The purpose of these products was similar to that of automotive lubricants, but most had additional attributes, such as being able to prevent rust from high-temperature steams.

The marine market was small compared to the automotive category but included a wide range of products, from lubricants for supertankers to biodegradable two-stroke outboard motor oils. The United Kingdom-based Castrol, one of the leaders in this area, was particularly strong in Europe where it held the top position with a 17 percent market share.

Many lubricants from major companies were marketed through independent distributors. In Europe, distributors usually handled one brand exclusively, while U.S. distributors carried multiple brands of lubricants. Still, reduced margins and stiffer competition were spurring some European distributors to move into multi-line marketing. Large distributors, with their increased financial resources, generally covered broader geographic areas and handled more brands. They placed emphasis on bulk deliveries to commercial, industrial, and agricultural customers. More distributors were concentrating on selling bulk goods, leaving the "case goods" sales to large retail outlets. Some manufacturers purchased distributors in an attempt to vertically integrate their operations. For example, in 1994 Valvoline Inc. purchased six of its European distributors from the Fuchs Group, thereby greatly expanding its European distribution capabilities.

The Additive Market. Additives were a very important component in the manufacturing of lubricants since they provided lubricants with the special qualities expected by end users. For example, motor oil typically consisted of 80 percent base stock and 20 percent additives. Popular additives included detergents, dispersants, extreme pressure/anti-wear agents, viscosity index improvers, antioxidants, and corrosion inhibitors. About 80 percent of all additives were used in automotive lubricants, with other key additive-using categories being industrial engine lubricants, general industrial lubricants, and metalworking lubricants. Major additive suppliers included Ethyl Corp., Lubrizol Ltd., Paramins (a unit of Exxon Chemical), Oronite Additives (a unit of Chevron Chemical), and Royal Dutch/Shell's petroleum additives business. In 1996 these five entities controlled more than 80 percent of the US$6 billion worldwide lubricant additives market.

BACKGROUND AND DEVELOPMENT

At their most basic level, lubricants are substances inserted between two moving surfaces to reduce friction, which in turn reduces wear and extends the life of the surfaces. Lubricants also reduce the energy required to keep the surfaces in motion. If some contact occurs between the surfaces even after lubrication, the process is called boundary or thin-film lubrication. If the lubricant is thick enough to completely separate the two surfaces, the process is called fluid-film lubrication. In the latter case, the lubricant is kept under pressure to keep the surfaces separated. In another form of lubrication, hydrostatic lubrication, the pressure in the lubricant film is created by a pump. Other types of lubrication include hydrodynamic lubrication and solid lubricants. Lubricants can also dissipate generated heat, control corrosion, and remove sludge deposits in automobile engines. In some machine-tool operations, cooling is the main purpose of lubrication.

Lubricants made from animals and vegetables have been used for thousands of years, but beginning in the nineteenth century, mineral products began to replace them, particularly liquid and semi-liquid lubricants made from petroleum. There have been many ways of applying lubrication, including by hand, drop-feed, wick-feed, bath or splash, oil-mist, and force-feed (oil pump).

Following the development of oil drilling in the nineteenth century, petroleum products—including lubricants—became widely available. In the United States, production was dominated by the Standard Oil trust until its breakup in 1911. In the twentieth century, oil production and refining came to be dominated by the "Seven Sisters," five major U.S. oil companies that emerged from the Standard Oil trust, Royal Dutch/Shell (which had developed out of an Indonesian oil field discovery in 1885), and the Anglo-Persian Oil Company, formed after a 1908 oil find in Iran—formerly known as Persia. (Anglo-Persian later became known as British Petroleum.) The domination of the oil business by these giant companies was still evident in the 1990s, although many developing nations with large oil deposits had nationalized their oil industries by the latter half of the twentieth century. While these nationalized oil companies tended to dominate their local markets, many of these markets were opened at least partially to outside competition.

The largest lubricants market, automobile engines, changed in the 1990s as smaller, more powerful, and more efficient engines were developed. The size and speed of these engines generated very high temperatures, in some cases far higher than those at which conventional lubricating oils could still be effective. This quality encouraged development of more synthetic oils that burn very slowly at high temperatures while not leaving the residues of carbon or metallic ash that are deposited by ordinary oils.

Prices of lubricants depend on several factors, including the base oil stock, additives, and other processing costs. Within the industry the price of the benchmark West Texas Intermediate crude (regarded as an industry indicator of world oil prices) was rather volatile in the late 1990s and early years of the first decade of the 2000s. The average was US$14.40 in 1998, US$19.25 in 1999, US$30.30 in 2000, and US$25.92 in 2001. These numbers took a leap in 2006 when they went to around US$60 a barrel. These shifts make it difficult to create stability in the lubricating oils and grease industry because of its reliance on the price of oil on the global market. Fortunately, the major corporations have substantial reserves of oil that help them through fluctuations in price. This helps account for the fact that in the 1990s, mature lubricants markets such as the United States and the European Union (EU) remained relatively flat.

Toward the close of the twentieth century, some East Asian countries—such as China, India, and Indonesia—were emerging economies, and in many of these countries state-run oil companies controlled the lubricants markets. However, some East Asian countries such as India were opening up their markets. As a result of increasing East Asian growth prospects, development activity was brisk. Following the outbreak of the Asian financial crisis in the late 1990s, however, economic development slowed in general, and this included the lubricating oil and grease industry.

Meanwhile, major companies in the industry were increasingly turning to mergers and alliances to achieve cost savings and increase efficiencies. In early 1998, Pennzoil Company announced that it planned to spin off its downstream operations—including its lubricants and additives businesses—and merge them with Quaker State Corp. This deal brought together two of the biggest brand names in motor oil, which held a combined 35 percent of the U.S. market. A few years later, the company would be acquired by Royal Dutch Shell.

One concern of lubricant users is environmental regulation, which in many countries requires users to carefully monitor their use and disposal of lubricants. Many users were shifting the burden of compliance back to their suppliers and asking them to provide additional services, such as in-house protection and waste disposal programs. At the same time, lubricant manufacturers were being asked to develop formulations that could be used in new electronically controlled lubricant systems. These systems actually reduced lubricant usage since they applied lubricants in a more precise manner than traditional hydraulic control systems.

CURRENT CONDITIONS

In the mid-years of the first decade of the 2000s, there was a growing global trend toward the use of biodegradable lubricants. Biolubricants began being used in the mid-1990s. That segment was expected to remain small until more regulations were developed that mandated the use of biolubricants. One application of biolubricants is in the forest products industry. To harvest trees, heavy equipment that consumes large quantities of lubricants, such as hydraulic fluid and gear oil, is used. Traditional lubricants spewing from hose breaks or other spills could contaminate the forest and remain in the ground indefinitely, while biolubricants could break down in a short period.

Biolubricants are frequently based on vegetable oils, such as canola (rapeseed), soybean, and sunflower seed. For example, in 2007 Nano Chemical Systems Holdings Inc. (NanoChem) introduced a "nano-enhanced," green motor oil for automobiles that was nontoxic and biodegradable, thus eliminating the disposal issues. According to Lou Petrucci, VP of sales at NanoChem, "Disposing of used motor oil is a constant challenge for do-it-yourself consumers and, though it is never recommended, they will

dispose of it in a variety of ways including dumping it into their yard. With 100% biodegradable oil, this activity will no longer present an environmental concern."

The increased U.S. use of biolubricants was being legislated in the first decade of the 2000s. The USDA labels a product as "biobased" if 51 percent or more of the makeup is biomaterial. Executive Order 13134 and the 2002 Farm Bill both provided for increased purchase and use of bio-based materials by the government itself. The European Union also introduced a new environmental standard in 2005 with the enactment of Euro IV, which imposed tighter restrictions on harmful emissions such as carbon monoxide, hydrocarbons, and oxides of nitrogen. Total Lubricants, one of the world's leading oil and gas companies and the fifth largest lubricants producer, began developing, in cooperation with Idemitsu Kosan of Japan, a "new generation of lubricants" to comply with the standards, according to *ECN-European Chemical News*.

In an effort to promote a cleaner environment and help consumers choose environmentally friendly products, The Alberta Research Council conducted tests on biolubricant for chainsaw bars. The test were run for Greenland Corporation of Calgary, Canada.

The oil and grease industry, like most industries in the modern economy, continued to come under pressure from environmental groups. According to the National Petrochemical and Refiners Association, between 30 and 40 percent of petroleum-based lubricants sold in the United States were accidentally released into the environment in 2004.

INDUSTRY LEADERS

The leaders in the global lubricants industry varied by category but tended to include the same seven or eight very large global companies.

ExxonMobil Corp. In 2006, the largest oil company, ExxonMobil, operated 35,000 service stations in 100 countries and had 83,700 employees. About 16,000 gas stations were located in the United States. That year, ExxonMobil reported more than US$377.6 billion in revenues, breaking the record for U.S. annual corporate earnings for the second year in a row. It has 13.6 billion barrels of proved reserves. By 2008, the company reported earnings of US$477.36 billion and 79,900 employees. As evidence of its corporate social responsibility, Exxon and partners including ExxonMobil Foundation provided US$225 million in contributions worldwide. In recognition of its philanthropy, ExxonMobil was awarded the Institute of International Education's 2009 Opening Minds Corporate Leadership Award. The company's special efforts included working with math and science education initiatives.

Exxon was a highly diversified petroleum company that included lubricants among its many other businesses. The company was once called Standard Oil of New Jersey and marketed its products under the Esso brand. In 1972 the company changed its name to Exxon. Standard Oil of New Jersey was one of the major companies that emerged from the breakup of the famous Standard Oil Trust in 1911.

Fairfax, Virginia-based Mobil Corp. was a major producer of specialty and synthetic lubricants, marketing its products under such names as Mobil 1 and Mobilgrease. Mobil's new lubricant blending and packaging plants in Paulsboro, New Jersey, and Hong Kong were said to be low-cost producers of high-value lubricants. Mobil also was the largest exporter of lubricants to China, and in Europe, Mobil was the second-largest lubricants marketer. Mobil and state-owned Indian Oil Corp. formed a joint venture in 1994 to build a US$15 million lubricants plant in Haryana, India, to produce Mobil-brand lubricants for the Indian market.

In 1994 Mobil also created a new subsidiary, Mobil Lubricants Canada, to market and distribute automotive and industrial lubricants, including Mobil 1 motor oil. Mobil took Canadian distribution away from its previous distributor, Imperial. In early 1996, Mobil and British Petroleum entered into a joint venture that merged the two companies' European refining and marketing operations, including their lubricants businesses.

BP. This London-based firm remains one of the United Kingdom's largest companies and the world's second largest international oil company (behind ExxonMobil). Formed by the merging of Amoco and British Petroleum, BP reported 2008 revenues exceeding US$361 billion. BP employs approximately 92,000 people in 100 countries. With 22,600 service stations worldwide, of which more than half were located in the United States, the company had 18.1 billion barrels of proved reserves.

BP also acquired Atlantic Richfield Company (ARCO), as well as a stake in the Russian company TNK-BP. In 2000, BP acquired Burmah Castrol, one of the oldest oil companies in the United Kingdom. The company acquired the Castrol brand in 1966, and Castrol remained the heart of its lubricants business. Castrol has global sales coverage through operating companies in more than 50 countries. The promotion of the Castrol name had established the brand throughout the world as the leading independent oil, as opposed to major oil companies' own brands. Highly successful sponsorship in auto racing helped maintain Castrol's premium image in the marketplace during the 1990s when Castrol was producing more than 2,000 products, including automotive lubricants, synthetic lubricants, metal working oils,

hydraulic fluids, technical white oils, antifreeze, silicon brake fluids, marine lubricants, industrial and aviation gas turbine lubricants, and corrosion preventives.

Royal Dutch Shell. Formerly Royal Dutch/Shell Group, the world's third largest petroleum and natural gas company, Royal Dutch Shell was a Dutch/English partnership of two parent companies, Royal Dutch Petroleum and Shell Transport and Trading. The companies shared a 60/40 interest in three holding companies: the Shell Petroleum Company (United Kingdom), Shell Petroleum NV (the Netherlands), and Shell Oil Co. (United States). These companies were active in more then 100 countries. Depending on the business involved, group leadership alternated between the two parent companies, which maintained headquarters in The Hague and London. Royal Dutch Shell and Exxon joined forces in a worldwide petroleum additives joint venture in 1996. The company employs 102,000 people, operates 45,000 gas stations worldwide, and produces more than 3.2 barrels of gas and oil everyday. Revenues totaled US$458.4 billion in 2008.

Royal Dutch Shell acquired Pennzoil Quaker State in 2002. The following year, Pennzoil Quaker State was renamed SOPUS Products. Formed by the merger between Pennzoil and Quaker State, this company owned the top two motor oils and the top oil-changing service, Jiffy Lube. Pennzoil marketed its motor oil (in addition to Performax motor oils and lubricants, Wolf's Head lubricants, and other Pennzoil-brand lubricants) in more than 60 countries. The company's product line includes other brands of motor oils, Snap fuel additives and chemicals, Snap Fix-A-Flat tire inflator, Outlaw fuel additives, and Gumout cleaners.

Pennzoil products were first marketed by South Penn Oil of Oil City, Pennsylvania. South Penn was acquired by Zapata Petroleum in 1963, and the combined company was renamed Pennzoil. In 1985 Pennzoil won a US$10 billion judgment against Texaco as a result of its unsuccessful attempt to purchase Getty Oil. Pennzoil eventually settled with Texaco for US$3 billion in 1988. In late 1997 Pennzoil fended off a US$4.2 billion hostile takeover offer from Union Pacific Resources Group Inc. Six months later, Pennzoil announced a plan to spin off its downstream operations, including its lubricants and additives businesses, and merge them with Quaker State Corp., bringing together two of the biggest brand names in motor oil.

BIBLIOGRAPHY
"About Us." Independent Lubricant Manufacturers Association, 2005. Available from www.ilma.org.
"About Us." National Lubricating Grease Institute, 2008. Available from www.nlgi.com.

BP. "BP at a Glance." 2008. Available from www.bp.com.

"Biodegradable Lubricant Is Designed for Automobiles." *Product News Network,* 21 May 2007.

"Biolubricants Smooth Way to a Cleaner Environment." Available from www.azom.com.

Brice, Andy. "Smooth Operations." *ECN-European Chemical News,* 14 February 2005.

"ExxonMobil Honored for Commitment to Education and Social Responsibility." *Business Wire,* 24 September 2009. Available from www.businesswire.com.

Fischer, Margy. "Don't Stumble Over New Oils." *Farm Journal,* 2 November 2006.

"Hoover's Company Capsules." *Hoover's Online,* 2007. Available from www.hoovers.com.

"International Trade Statistics." World Trade Organization, 2005. Available from www.wto.org.

Lazich, Robert S., ed. *Market Share Reporter.* Detroit: Thomson Gale, 2004.

"National Statistics." *Petroleum Supply Monthly,* March 2007.

"Oil Nears $61 as Markets Tighten." *MEED Middle East Economic Digest,* 9 March 2007.

Pierce, Ira N. "Is Green Oil Ready to be Fast-Tracked to the Mainstream?" *Real Estate Weekly,* 6 December 2006.

"Shell at a Glance. About Shell." Shell, 2008. Available from www.shell.com.

U.S. Census Bureau. "Petroleum Lubricating Oil and Grease Manufacturing," 2005. Available from www.census.gov.

SIC 1311

PETROLEUM AND NATURAL GAS, CRUDE

NAICS CODE(S)

211111. Industry companies operate oil and gas field properties for the extraction of crude petroleum and natural gas. Key activities include exploration; drilling, completing, and equipping wells; operation of separators, emulsion breakers, desilting equipment, and field gathering lines for crude petroleum; and related preparation activities up to the point of shipment. (See also **Petroleum Refineries** and **Energy.**)

INDUSTRY SNAPSHOT

Crude oil and natural gas are the world's leading raw materials for energy. They are used in the production of motor vehicle fuel and in the generation of industrial power, heat, and electricity. According to the International Energy Agency, in 1995 oil accounted for 46.9 percent of the world's energy consumption, while natural gas accounted for 17.8 percent. By 2000, this balance had been reversed, and natural gas had increased to 22 percent of world energy consumption, while oil had

fallen to 39.8 percent. The Energy Information Administration (EIA) predicted that world energy use would grow 54 percent between 2001 and 2025, with oil remaining the primary source at about 39 percent. Natural gas, however, was expected to continue to be the fastest growing primary energy commodity. Concerns about the stability of future oil supplies, as well as increased research in hydrogen power, contributed to an effort to decrease reliance on oil, as did the popularity of natural gas as a more environmentally friendly source of energy than crude oil. Other benefits of natural gas include traditionally stable pricing and a high number of known untapped gas reserves.

As hydrocarbons, oil and gas are often considered to be part of the overall petroleum industry. These natural resources often are found in the same underground reservoirs and are also often produced by the same companies. Commercial production of oil and natural gas, however, usually comes from distinct oil and gas fields.

Crude oil is a liquid hydrocarbon mixture that may be characterized as "heavy" or "light," depending on its gravity, and as "sour" or "sweet," depending on the presence of sulfur impurities. Crude oil is refined to produce fuel (see **Petroleum Refining**) and lubricants (see **Lubricating Oils and Greases**). In its natural state, natural gas is a gaseous mixture of about 80 percent methane, 7 percent ethane, 6 percent propane, 3 percent pentane, 2.5 percent butane, and 1.5 percent isobutane. Natural gas is processed to produce commercial natural gas, which contains only methane and ethane. When natural gas condenses as it reaches the earth's surface, it is referred to as condensate. Natural gas may be liquefied to facilitate transportation. Crude oil, condensate, and natural gas liquids are collectively referred to as petroleum liquids.

World market prices for oil and gas commodities are determined by fluctuations in supply and demand, although some producing countries subsidize prices for domestic consumption. Levels of production are usually determined by market price, although quotas, especially for petroleum production, are used in some cases to prevent prices from falling and to prevent oil fields from becoming depleted too rapidly. The most significant international production quota system was voluntarily adopted by member countries of the Organization of Petroleum Exporting Countries (OPEC).

The United States was the leading market for oil and gas, consuming more than 25 percent of the petroleum and gas produced each year through the early 2000s. Although Japan was the world's second largest oil consumer until 2003, China surpassed Japan that year with petroleum consumption totaling 5.56 million barrels per day (b/d). According to the EIA, continued economic growth in China would stimulate demand for oil, reaching a projected 12.8 million b/d by 2025 and accounting for about 40 percent of world growth in demand. With consumption far surpassing demand, China's oil imports were projected to reach 9.4 million b/d by 2025.

In 2008, oil prices skyrocketed, and the resulting high prices of gasoline led to a drop in demand as consumers in developed countries decreased their use of gasoline. By late 2008, the market had adjusted, but the International Energy Agency predicted that oil would climb sharply again, settling near $120 per barrel by 2030.

ORGANIZATION AND STRUCTURE

The scope of the crude oil and gas industry is difficult to measure because it is an integral part of the broad petroleum industry. Many leading oil and gas extraction companies are vertically integrated petroleum companies that explore for and produce crude petroleum and natural gas from wells, refine petroleum, and process gas. They also transport oil and gas by pipeline and tanker and handle retail distribution and marketing of refined oil products, including gasoline and diesel fuel, at their own gas stations. The exploration and production side of the industry, including oil and gas extraction, is referred to as "upstream," while the refining and marketing side is referred to as "downstream." Some companies specialize in either upstream or downstream activities, but the largest companies in oil and gas extraction are integrated petroleum companies that do both.

In the early 2000s, the largest oil and gas companies in the world were state-owned companies in major petroleum-producing countries of the Middle East, Asia, Africa, and Latin America. These firms tended to be integrated petroleum companies with monopolies on domestic production. In some countries, however, domestic companies invited foreign companies with additional capital and expertise to participate in joint exploration and development of reserves in exchange for a share in production equity. State-owned companies of oil- or gas-producing countries, however, often preferred that foreign companies act as service contractors and retain control over their natural resources.

The best-known companies in the industry were the Western multinationals that had numerous subsidiaries worldwide in production as well as refined product distribution. These traditionally dominant companies were referred to as the "majors," both globally and within the U.S. industry, which was home to the largest number of international majors. "Independents" were other small companies that tended to operate at the domestic level and might specialize in areas of exploration and production.

Oil and gas production companies either own or lease the land from which they extract the natural resources, giving them ownership not only of the oil or gas that they produce but also the underground reserves. Industry participants sell oil to refiners, unless they are integrated companies with their own refineries, and gas to gas processors and utility companies. Nevertheless, the actual drilling and maintenance of oil and gas wells is often handled by third-party companies in the oil and gas services industry. Historically, these companies tended to be small, local, independent enterprises. By the late 1990s, however, industry consolidation had created a handful of major international service companies, the most notable of which were Halliburton Company, Schlumberger Limited, and Baker Hughes Incorporated. In fact, Halliburton grew even larger through a US$7.7 billion merger with Dresser Industries, Inc. in 1998, the same year that Baker Hughes acquired Western Atlas Inc. for US$5.5 billion.

Major natural gas-producing countries were not necessarily the same countries that led the world in oil production, partly because of the unique properties of natural gas, which must undergo a costly liquefaction process before shipping by tanker. Therefore, natural gas tended to be consumed domestically or sent to neighboring countries by pipelines rather than being exported globally. In the late 1990s, about 100 countries worldwide were commercially producing oil or gas, and the vast majority produced both. In addition, new exploration was bringing new countries into the industry constantly.

Oil-producing countries tend to be categorized by membership in OPEC. Along with Saudi Arabia, which is the largest producer and exporter of oil in the world, OPEC members in 2004 included Algeria, Indonesia, Iran, Kuwait, Libya, Nigeria, Qatar, the United Arab Emirates, and Venezuela. Iraq was also a member of OPEC, but in the wake of the U.S.-led invasion that began in 2003, the country was not operating under OPEC production ceilings. OPEC members adopt voluntary production quotas in order to maintain higher prices. OPEC's crude oil production in 1999 was 26.6 million b/d, accounting for 39.4 percent of the world's total, and OPEC countries accounted for about 61 percent of world oil exports. An even higher percentage of the world's known oil reserves were under OPEC control as of 1997 for 76.8 percent, or about 797.1 billion barrels, of the world total of 1.04 trillion barrels. However, by 2004, according to a *Boston Globe* report, OPEC's share of global oil exports had dropped to about 33 percent, largely because of increased production in Russia. OPEC deals only with oil production and not natural gas.

Outside OPEC, the leading countries in terms of proven crude oil reserves in early 2005 were Canada (178.8 billion barrels, including reserves in the country's oil sands), Russia (60 billion barrels), the United States

(21.89 billion barrels), China (18.25 billion barrels), Mexico (14.6 billion barrels), Norway (8.5 billion barrels), Kazakhstan (9 billion barrels), and Brazil (10.6 billion barrels). The leading countries in terms of proven natural gas reserves in 2005 were Russia (1,680 trillion cubic feet), Iran (940 trillion cubic feet), Qatar (910 trillion cubic feet), Saudi Arabia (235.5 trillion cubic feet), the United Arab Emirates (212.1 trillion cubic feet), the United States (189 trillion cubic feet), Algeria (160.5 trillion cubic feet), and Venezuela (151 trillion cubic feet).

In November 2008, *NIOC News* reported that the Iranian governor of OPEC considered the oil market to be "oversupplied" even though OPEC members had cut production in response to decreased demand in the fall of 2008.

BACKGROUND AND DEVELOPMENT

Crude oil has been known since ancient times in various parts of the world. In the Middle East, where mixtures of asphalt and petroleum known as bitumen oozed to the earth's surface, the substance was used as a sealant in building and road construction, as a medicinal ointment, and occasionally as a fuel for illumination. Natural gas was sometimes ignited to create eternal flames at temples.

It was not until the development of refining methods to produce the relatively clean and safe illuminant kerosene in the nineteenth century when, that oil extraction became an actual industry. Just when kerosene began to be replaced by electricity at the beginning of the twentieth century, the acceptance of the internal combustion engine created a new market for petroleum products, and demand skyrocketed throughout the twentieth century.

Although natural gas had occasionally been used along with oil as an illuminant starting in the nineteenth century, for much of the history of the petroleum industry it remained an unwanted by-product of oil drilling. Even in the early 2000s, natural gas from oil wells was often burned off. The emphasis on natural gas as a source of energy did not occur until the last quarter of the twentieth century. Until then, natural gas had been most commonly used to generate heat and electric power. The expanded use of natural gas was attributed primarily to changes in distribution beginning in the United States in the late 1940s when two former transcontinental oil pipelines were converted to natural gas pipelines.

Commercial oil extraction for the purpose of refining illuminants began independently in three parts of the world: first around Baku, Azerbaijan, when it was a part of czarist Russia, then in Galicia, a part of the Austro-Hungarian Empire, and shortly thereafter in Romania. The earliest commercial oil extraction ventures in the United States took place in northwestern Pennsylvania.

In both Baku and Galicia in the early nineteenth century, oil was extracted in hand-dug pits and hoisted to the surface in buckets, but in the United States commercial oil extraction began the practice of drilling for oil, which substantially increased output. The world's first oil well, managed by Edwin L. Drake and based on techniques for salt boring, struck oil in August 1859 in Titusville, Pennsylvania.

Large scale production and some degree of order and efficiency were brought to the global oil industry when a few large companies began to dominate production in different parts of the world. In most cases, however, the companies that began to control production had actually begun business in other aspects of the oil industry, such as refining or transportation, and vertical integration developed gradually. In the United States, Standard Oil began as a refining company, but came to hold a monopoly on the petroleum industry. A British shipping company, Shell Transport and Trading, which had entered the oil business by shipping Russian oil in 1891, entered the production field via exploration efforts in Borneo in 1895.

In the early years of the industry, a country with oil and gas reserves but lacking domestic firms capable of mining its resources often permitted foreign petroleum companies to do the work. These companies gathered the natural resources under lease, fee, royalty, and other monetary arrangements. The first major oil field concession from a foreign government was won by Englishman William Knox D'Arcy in Persia in 1901. His enterprise was incorporated in 1909 as the Anglo-Persian Oil Company, and changed its name in 1954 to British Petroleum (BP). It ranked as one of the world's leading multinational petroleum companies in the late 1990s.

Concerns about growing demand, oil shortages, and national security spurred foreign exploration by the major oil companies, producing major oil discoveries in Venezuela in the 1920s. By 1929, Venezuela had become the world's second largest producer after the United States, producing 137 million barrels annually. Venezuela's leading export market was the United States, accounting for up to 55 percent of its crude and refined oil exports. Protective U.S. tariffs introduced in 1932 caused Venezuela to shift its exports to Europe, where it overtook the United States as Europe's leading oil supplier. Venezuela remained the world's leading exporter of oil until 1970.

Shared production by the leading Western oil companies became the model in the Middle East, first seen in Iraq. In 1927, a well near Kirkuk produced an oil gusher, and production was shared by the major western oil companies based on a pre-World War I agreement that had set up an entity called the Turkish Petroleum Company (later named the Iraq Petroleum Company) covering the territory of most of the Arabic Middle East. Its owners included Anglo-Persian, Royal Dutch/Shell, and a consortium of U.S. companies.

Standard Oil of California (Socal, later named Chevron) began drilling in Bahrain in 1931. The company struck oil a year later, heralding the potential of the Persian Gulf area. Socal made major discoveries in Saudi Arabia in 1938, the same year a joint venture of Gulf Oil and Anglo-Persian discovered oil in Kuwait. Commercial oil production began in Kuwait in 1946, in Qatar in 1949, and in Abu Dhabi (part of the United Arab Emirates) in 1953.

To deal with rising production and falling prices globally, the major petroleum companies had made various attempts to reach market share agreements among themselves. The Achnacarry Agreement of 1928, which involved Royal Dutch/Shell, Anglo-Persian, Jersey Standard (Exxon), Standard Oil of Indiana, and Gulf, allocated quotas for each company in various world markets. They later agreed that a company's level of production could not surpass the demand of the market quotas unless the output was sold to another company member. Market factors, however, proved to be significant obstacles to the agreement. Many independent oil producers who were not part of the agreement made significant contributions to the market, and even the cooperating oil companies often competed with each other.

In the late 1930s the oil industry became increasingly politicized, in part because of growing nationalistic regulation. Several governments, especially in Europe, tried to set prices, impose import quotas, control trade through bilateral agreements, and force foreign companies to participate in national cartels. For example, the Mexican government confiscated all foreign oil company properties in 1938.

Countries with rich natural resources increasingly demanded a larger share of the profits in the 1940s and early 1950s. The financial relationship between foreign oil companies and the governments of the countries in which they operated changed fundamentally during this time. In 1943 a new government in Venezuela and foreign oil companies operating there reached an agreement to divide the profits of oil production evenly. Unprecedented prices were paid for oil concessions in the Arabian Peninsula between Saudi Arabia and Kuwait. Such developments quickly prompted other Middle Eastern governments to alter their existing agreements.

In the late 1950s discoveries were made in other countries, and new companies became involved in international exploration and production. A joint venture of Royal Dutch/Shell and BP discovered oil in Nigeria in 1956, while a French group of state-owned companies had similar success in Gabon. Oil was also discovered in Algeria in 1956 by another French-owned company, Régie Autonome des Petroles (RAP). The most significant oil discoveries of the period were in Libya, where the government leased 84 concessions to 17 foreign companies in 1957. By 1969 Libya's petroleum output exceeded that of Saudi Arabia, and was supplying 30 percent of Europe's oil.

The numerous independent oil companies that operated in Libya and elsewhere on single overseas concessions were not as constrained in their production as the major companies that had to balance production among the countries where they held concessions. As a result, production increased faster than demand, and prices and profits declined. In addition, the Soviet Union resumed exports of oil to the West in 1955 in response to sluggish domestic demand and excess inventory. The Soviet oil was priced lower than oil from other regions, forcing major international oil companies to respond. They lowered market prices by reducing the formerly unchanging official, or "posted," prices that were used by the countries in which they operated to calculate royalties. Alarmed by the resulting lower royalties, oil-rich nations took action.

In 1960, representatives of Saudi Arabia, Kuwait, Iraq, Iran, and Venezuela, which together accounted for 80 percent of the world's crude oil exports, formed OPEC to protect prices and regulate production. An agreement reached between OPEC countries and the major oil companies in 1971, known as the Tehran Agreement, marked a pivotal turning point in the industry's history. Under the Tehran Agreement, the OPEC nations were able to take the initiative to raise prices.

In the 1970s, demand caught up with supply. Excess capacity fell from 3 to 1.5 million b/d between 1970 and 1973, of which only 500,000 barrels were immediately available. By 1973, Saudi Arabia's share of world exports had risen to 21 percent. When the United States supported Israel in the October 1973 Arab–Israeli war, the Arab members of OPEC were entrenched as the world leaders in oil production and responded with a complete boycott of oil to the United States and selected other countries. OPEC also instituted monthly reductions of 5 percent in total production, a step that dramatically affected the global market. Crude oil prices rose from US$2.90 per barrel to US$11.65. Throughout the 1970s, the OPEC cartel instituted higher prices on oil that punished the economies of countries that had significant oil imports. Over time, however, OPEC's power was somewhat diminished.

Major oil discoveries in Alaska and the North Sea in the 1960s and 1970s had a significant impact on world production. A joint venture of Atlantic–Richfield (ARCO) and Exxon's Humble subsidiary made the largest discovery to that time in North America on Alaska's North Slope in Prudhoe Bay in 1967. The first major discoveries in the

North Sea were made on the Norwegian side in 1969 and the British side in 1970. Physical obstacles to recovering and transporting oil from these areas were considerable. North Sea oil did not reach a refinery until 1975, while Alaskan North Slope oil did not come to market until the Trans-Alaska Pipeline was completed in 1977.

During the early 1990s, the production of petroleum liquids remained steady. Worldwide demand continued to edge up despite the recession in the world's industrialized countries. Iraq's invasion of Kuwait in 1990 and the resulting Gulf War produced a temporary spike in the price of crude oil, after which prices remained relatively stable.

The mid- to late 1990s were a volatile period for the entire oil industry. Demand for oil and natural gas continued to increase until late 1997. Global oil consumption rose from 59.7 million b/d in 1985 to 69 million b/d in 1995, a 15.6 percent increase. Demand continued to accelerate in 1996 and 1997, when consumption increased 2.3 percent and 2.8 percent, respectively. The rapidly industrializing nations of East Asia were primarily responsible for this growth in demand. Ten of Asia's burgeoning economies accounted for more than 40 percent of demand growth from 1986 through 1996. The sudden onset of a financial crisis in East Asia in late 1997, however, threatened to dampen this trend significantly. The announcement in June 1998 that the Japanese economy was in recession presented an additional threat as Japan was the second largest consumer of oil worldwide.

In January of 1997, crude oil was selling for about US$20.50 per barrel. An increase in non-OPEC supplies, overproduction by OPEC members, and the return of Iraq's oil supplies to the world market resulted in a considerable downward trend for the price of oil that year. The threat of another war with Iraq in late 1997 resulted in a temporary price increase. During the winter of 1997–1998, a number of factors contributed to a sharp decline in crude oil prices. The most obvious was the financial crisis in Asia, which significantly curtailed demand in the region. Also of importance was the worldwide weather phenomenon known as El Niño, which resulted in warmer than normal winter weather for North America and Europe, cutting energy consumption. However, the continuing oil glut threatened long-term price decreases. By March 1998, the price of crude oil had fallen 55 percent to US$11.27 a barrel and eventually reached a low of US$10 per barrel.

To cope with deteriorating market conditions, many firms began forging alliances to share the costs of exploration and development. In November 1997, Russian natural gas giant Gazprom and Royal Dutch/Shell announced a worldwide strategic alliance a month after Gazprom took a 30 percent stake in a US$2 billion project to develop a

gas field in Iran led by French giant TOTAL S.A. Another alliance involving a Russian oil concern was announced in November 1997 when British Petroleum PLC agreed to take a 10 percent stake in AO Sidanco for US$571 million, as well as a 45 percent interest in Sidanco's massive eastern Siberian gas fields for an additional US$172 million.

Consolidation continued to play a pivotal role in the oil and natural gas industries in the late 1990s and early 2000s. The 1999 merger that formed Exxon Mobil resulted in US$4.6 billion in cost savings by 2001. Other major deals included the US$57 billion merger of British Petroleum and Amoco Corp. to form BP Amoco in 1998, as well as the US$26.8 billion stock purchase of Atlantic Richfield by BP Amoco, which became known as BP, in 2000. This made BP not only the world's leading private petroleum company, but it also resulted in economies of scale worth an estimated US$6 billion. In 2001, Chevron and Texaco joined forces to create ChevronTexaco Corp., the second largest oil company in the United States and the fourth largest in the world. The world's fifth largest integrated oil player was also the result of consolidation. Total Fina Elf was formed in 2000 when Total Fina, itself the result of a merger between France-based Total and Belgium's PetroFina in 1999, acquired Elf Aquitaine, also based in France. Total Fina Elf was renamed TOTAL S.A. in 2003

Despite the increasing size of the major companies, leading oil producers in Saudi Arabia and Russia continued to outpace them in terms of oil production. For example, Exxon Mobil's combined oil and gas production level was 4.3 million barrels of oil equivalent per day in 2000, compared to 8 million b/d of oil produced by the Saudi Arabian Oil Company. Saudi Arabia and Russia also led the world in oil exports with daily export rates of 7.6 and 4.7 million barrels, respectively. The two countries differed significantly, however, in production costs. Saudi Arabia had managed to refine its oil production processes to the extent that production costs per barrel remained under US$5.50 per barrel, while Russian production costs exceeded US$10 per barrel.

CURRENT CONDITIONS

Volatility in the oil industry continued into the twenty-first century. Political instability in Venezuela abruptly halted much of the country's oil exports in 2003, driving up prices. Civil unrest in Nigeria also contributed to price fluctuations. In addition, the U.S.-led war in Iraq left that country's oil production capacity uncertain. OPEC countries responded by adhering to strict production schedules. By 2004, worldwide demand for oil had reached its highest level in seven years, led primarily by the United States and China. After reaching a low of

US$10 per barrel in the late 1990s, oil prices surged to US$35 per barrel in 2004. OPEC responded by cutting its quotas 4 percent. Prices did not immediately rise in response, however, due to doubts about the enforceability of the quota and the increase in production from non-OPEC sources, especially Russia. Resumption of production in Iraq, which in 2004 was operating outside OPEC's production ceilings, was also expected to help mitigate the effects of the OPEC cuts. The EIA estimated that world oil prices would generally moderate after 2004 and then rise slowly through 2025.

Environmental issues have increasingly dogged the oil industry. Oil transportation practices had been called into question as a result of tanker and pipeline spills that resulted in devastating environmental consequences. Production was also increasingly restricted by environmental regulations. Oil companies, for instance, had been denied permits for offshore drilling in certain locations for environmental reasons. The late 1990s brought another regulatory threat to industry players in the form of the Kyoto Protocol on Climate Change that was adopted in December 1997 in Kyoto, Japan. The Protocol aimed to curb the emission of greenhouse gases that had resulted from the use of crude petroleum and natural gas, to levels well below those of 1990 by 2012. The European Union signed the Protocol in 1998, and despite opposition from the U.S. Republican Party, as well as public denouncement by U.S. President George W. Bush, the Protocol was finalized in November 2001. Many industry experts pointed out that the environmental impact of the Protocol would be somewhat compromised by the lack of U.S. participation.

Another critical issue was the amount of oil left to exploit. A *Christian Science Monitor* article reported that, by 2004, oil production had peaked for more than 50 oil-producing countries and that discovery of new oil sources, which had been declining for 40 years, had almost ceased. In 2002, world consumption was four times greater than the amount of newly discovered oil. With global demand projected to reach 119 million b/d in 2025, some analysts believed that world production had already peaked. Others calculated a decline in production by 2010, while more optimistic scenarios predicted that output would not level off until 2036. Improvements in drilling technology and exploitation of unconventional oil sources, such as Canada's oil sands and Rocky Mountain shale, could delay the decline, which analysts agreed was inevitable.

Concern about future supply caused increased competition among major oil importers for petroleum resources in Russia, the Caspian Sea region, West Africa, and Libya. China, where demand was expected to quadruple by 2030, proposed a pipeline from Angarsk, Russia, to the inland Chinese industrial city of Daqing. China also invested heavily in Africa, where in 2002 PetroChina signed a US$350 million refining deal with Algeria. The United States also increased its oil imports from Africa. In 2003, according to *The New York Times,* West African countries such as Angola, Nigeria, and Equatorial Guinea accounted for about 14 percent of U.S. oil imports and were expected to reach 20 percent within a short time. In late 2003 a US$3.7 billion underground pipeline began carrying crude oil 670 miles from Chad to Cameroon on the Atlantic coast. Chad's first share of royalties from the pipeline were expected to be about US$100 million. Royal Dutch/Shell signed a deal in 2004 with National Oil Corp of Libya giving Shell access to about US$1 billion worth of oil and natural gas in North Africa. Crude oil production in West Africa was expected to from 2.6 to 6.3 million b/d between 2002 and 2008. Angola, Nigeria, Chad, and Equatorial Guinea were anticipated to account for most of the increased output.

Despite skyrocketing demand for oil that was driven largely by China, where oil imports increased from less than 30 million tons in 1998 to nearly 70 million tons in 2000, growth in the energy industry was expected to come increasingly from natural gas, hydrogen, and renewable sources, such as solar and wind power. The *International Energy Outlook 2004* predicted that natural gas, which was considered more environmentally friendly than crude oil, would be the fastest-growing sector of the energy industry through 2025. World consumption of natural gas was expected to reach 151 trillion cubic feet in 2025, an increase of 67 over 2001. Natural gas consumption was expected to equal coal consumption by 2010 and to surpass coal by 12 percent by 2025. With a mature natural gas infrastructure in place, industrialized countries were expected to increase their use of natural gas to generate electricity from 20 to 30 percent during this period. The share of gas in the electricity sector in developing countries, on the other hand, was expected to grow only from 14 percent to 17 percent.

Canada's 21 oil reserves made the country second only to Saudi Arabia, which had 264 reserves. Oil sand production in Alberta Province made Canada the largest oil supplier to the United States. However, the Canadian government was taking environmental concerns into account when assessing oil production.

Concern in 2008 centered on the safety of drilling for oil and natural gas. Industry spokespersons confirmed the regulation and safety of the process. Another concern was the connection between the cost of petroleum and the cost of petroleum-based products. When the price of oil dropped in the late fall of 2008, gas prices dropped accordingly. However, the price of items like aspirin, diapers, toothpaste, golf balls, and plastic food storage bags did not follow suit. OPEC held a special meeting in September 2008 to discuss the oil market as it related to the global financial crisis. Hurricane damage to oil rigs in the Gulf of Mexico resulted in ongoing cuts in capacity up to 50 percent.

RESEARCH AND TECHNOLOGY

Throughout the history of the industry, technology aided oil and gas discovery, drilling methods, and production. The seismograph turned out to be one of the most important early innovations of the industry. Originally, only the rare seepage of actual oil, gas, or tar to the earth's surface indicated the possible presence of oil deposits. The seismograph, which was originally developed to record earthquakes, was first put to use in oil exploration in eastern Europe by the Germans during World War I. Acoustic shock waves were sent underground, and the seismograph measured the time it took for the signals to return to the surface, as well as their strength upon return. These data were then analyzed to map out underground structures. In the 1990s, a combination of seismic and computer technology was used to create sophisticated three-dimensional diagrams of underground geology.

Measurement while drilling, which involved the use of advanced sensors near the drill bit, could provide detailed information on geological formations without interrupting the drilling process to retrieve rock samples. Computers were used to analyze the data.

In the 1980s, the techniques of horizontal drilling and changing direction while drilling began. Horizontal drilling aids in discovery, facilitates access to reservoirs under certain conditions, and increases productivity. The practice has been used to create gas storage wells that yield gas production six times greater than vertical wells. Directional drilling uses a steerable motor behind the drill bit to change the trajectory of drilling according to information obtained from sensors near the drill bit. Coiled tubing that is flexible enough to bend, yet rigid enough to push equipment through a borehole, is used to analyze conditions in non-vertical wells. Coiled tubing technology was also used to rework damaged wells rather than redrill them. Other developments in drilling centered on improvements in equipment. More powerful drilling motors, improved sensing equipment, and new drilling fluids that were more efficient in lubricating and cooling drilling equipment improved the efficiency of oil exploration efforts. Because of these and other techniques, the average cost of finding and producing oil per barrel decreased about 60 percent in inflation-adjusted terms from 1985 to 1995.

Horizontal drilling was necessary to access natural gas trapped in shale. Hydrofracturing pumps highly pressurized water into the drill hole, letting the water break up the shale, releasing the natural gas. The technology was enabling the United States to become a leader in natural gas production.

The industry made use of various techniques of enhanced oil recovery to boost productivity by reaching partially depleted oil reservoirs. Common methods included the injection of air, water, steam, or chemicals into underground reservoirs to put more pressure on the oil, making it easier to pump it to the surface.

Advances in the design and construction of drilling rigs allowed companies to operate deeper wells both on and offshore. In 1918, the deepest wells were 6,000 feet, and by 1930, they were 10,000 feet deep. In the early 1990s, ultra-heavy rigs allowed drilling up to 25,000 feet. Another advance allowed offshore drillers to operate in water that was deeper than ever before. Tender-assisted drilling, with a semi-submersible rig tethered to the ocean floor by cables, gave increased stability while permitting drilling in waters up to 3,000 feet deep.

INDUSTRY LEADERS

Saudi Arabian Oil Company. Saudi Arabian involvement in the oil industry began modestly. In 1933, Standard Oil of California (Chevron) won the first and only concession to explore for oil in Saudi Arabia. It established the California-Arabian Standard Oil Company (Casoc) with joint partner Texaco to begin oil production. In 1944, Casoc was renamed the Arabian-American Oil Company (Aramco). To market the expanding Saudi production in the Western Hemisphere, Socal and Texaco invited Jersey Standard (Exxon) and Socony-Vacuum (Mobil) into Aramco to become partners. By 1948, Socal, Texaco, and Jersey Standard each owned 30 percent of the company, while the remaining 10 percent was held by Socony-Vacuum.

In 1973, the Saudi government acquired a 25 percent share in Aramco, which was raised to 60 percent in 1974. In 1980, Saudi Arabia bought the remaining shares of the Aramco from the U.S. owners, although it was not until 1988 that Aramco was formally nationalized as the Saudi Arabian Oil Co., retroactive to 1976. The 100 percent Saudi-owned company is often referred to as Saudi Aramco. Saudi Minister of Petroleum and Minerals Hisham Nazar was appointed chairman, and a Saudi had been president of the company since 1983. Many Americans continued to serve in the technical management of the company in the late 1980s.

In 1993, the Saudi Arabian Marketing and Refining Company (Samarec), which had been formed in 1988 primarily to serve the domestic market, was merged into

Saudi Aramco. This created a single integrated national oil company to serve domestic as well as international markets. Prior to the merger, Aramco's payroll was 47,000 and Samarec's was 12,000. In 1995, Saudi Aramco's President and CEO Ali Naimi was appointed Saudi Arabia's minister of oil, indicating the importance of Aramco to the country's oil industry.

In the early 2000s, state-owned Saudi Arabian Oil Company was the sole producer in the world's leading oil producing country and was the world's largest petroleum company. It owned roughly 260 billion barrels worth of oil reserves, which accounted for nearly one-fourth of global oil reserves. The firm owned all reserves and handled all oil and gas production in Saudi Arabia, except for shared production of the Saudi portion of the Neutral Zone. The company had expanded into refining and marketing activities, although foreign companies continued to own a share of some Saudi refineries. In 2004 the company's production supplied more than 10 percent of world demand. Oil exports contributed between 90 and 95 percent of Saudi Arabia's total export earnings and between 70 and 80 percent of government revenues in 2004, with about 40 percent of the country's GDP based on petroleum exports.

National Iranian Oil Company. Iranian Prime Minister Muhammad Mussadegh nationalized the operations of Anglo–Iranian Oil, which became BP in 1954, in 1951, creating the National Iranian Oil Company (NIOC). NIOC took over ownership of the resources and production facilities, but since it was inexperienced at management and overseas marketing, the state-owned enterprise signed an agreement in 1954 with the eight-member Iranian Oil Participants (IOP) consortium. Under the terms of this agreement, the IOP provided management services and purchased and distributed the output, with NIOC recognized as the operator. The IOP was forced to cease operations in Iran during the 1979 Iranian Revolution.

In the mid-1990s, NIOC began to subcontract production of new oil and gas fields in Iran to foreign companies. When TOTAL S.A. signed a contract to develop the Sirri offshore oil field in 1995, it was the first foreign oil company allowed to return to Iran following the 1979 revolution. Two years later, NIOC contracted with TOTAL, Petronas of Malaysia, and Russia's Gazprom in a US$2 billion project to develop the massive South Pars natural gas field. As OPEC's second largest oil producer, NIOC produced roughly 3.8 billion b/d in 2004 and controlled 9 percent of the world's oil reserves. NIOC's oil earnings constituted 40 to 50 percent of Iran's government revenues and 80 percent of export earnings.

NIOC directly controlled all oil production, while natural gas production was handled by its National Iranian Gas Co. affiliate, and both were under the control of the Ministry of Oil. National Iranian Drilling Co., a subsidiary of NIOC, conducted exploration for oil and gas.

China Petroleum & Chemical Corp. Immediately after the founding of the People's Republic of China in 1949, the China Petroleum & Chemical Corp. (Sinopec Corp.) was established to exploit the estimated 29 million tons of the country's oil reserves. The company held a monopoly on China's petroleum industry until the formation of the China National Offshore Oil Corp. in 1982, and the China National Petrochemical Corporation in 1983. China Petrochemical restructured in 2000, forming Sinopec Corporation, which was a vertically integrated energy and chemical company. This company announced that the restructuring was "to diversify the ownership structure, abide by the rules of the market economy, and establish a modern enterprise system." With proven reserves of 3.3 billion barrels of crude oil and 2.9 trillion cubic feet of gas, Sinopec posted 2003 sales of US$51.25 billion, a significant increase over 1993 sales of US$6 billion.

Petróleos Mexicanos. Petróleos Mexicanos (Pemex) was formed in 1938 as the result of the first nationalization of foreign oil company properties in a non-Communist country. Lacking expertise and capital, the new company could not maintain significant production, and oil had to be imported until major oil discoveries were made in 1972.

Pemex was essentially a decentralized public agency of the Mexican government. The company was involved in the production and sales of petrochemicals as well as all oil and gas exploration, production, refining, transportation, storage, and sales. Exploration and production accounted for 38 percent of 1996 total revenues of US$29.4 billion. In the early 2000s, Pemex was responsible for about 7 percent of Mexico's total export profits. Pemex held a 5 percent stake in Repsol S.A., a major oil and gas company in Spain and a leading oil company in Europe. In 2003 Petróleos Mexicanos held proven oil reserves of 17.1 billion barrels and natural gas reserves of 15 tcf (trillion cubic feet). The company reported US$55.92 billion in sales in 2003.

BP PLC. BP began as British Petroleum in Iran, where oil served as BP's primary source of income and held a monopoly on production for decades. The company was gradually squeezed out of Iran as the oil industry there was nationalized, and the firm began production elsewhere. BP made major oil discoveries in Alaska's Prudhoe Bay in 1969 and in the North Sea in 1970, and these two regions remained BP's primary sources of oil and gas. Alaskan oil accounted for more than 50 percent of BP's global crude oil production, while British territory in the North Sea accounted for about one-third of BP's production. BP also operated or had interests in oil fields in other countries, including Australia, Colombia, Indonesia, and Venezuela. In addition to oil and gas exploration and production, BP was also a major refiner and marketer of petroleum products and manufacturer of chemicals and plastics.

British Petroleum became BP Amoco after it merged with Amoco in 1998. The company became the world's largest private sector petroleum company when it bought Atlantic Richfield Company in 2000. In 2004 BP had proven reserves of 18.4 billion barrels of oil. Sales in 2004 reached US$285 billion, with net earnings of about US$1.57 billion. BP produced 1.9 million barrels of crude oil and 8.6 billion cubic feet of natural gas per day in 2004. By 2007, it reported sales of US$281 billion.

Exxon Mobil Corporation. Originally Standard Oil of New Jersey (Jersey Standard), the company's origin was as the holding company of the Standard Oil firm. Until 1911, it held nearly half of the former monopoly's net value. At that time a Supreme Court ruling broke up the company. The largest of the companies created after the disbandment of the Standard Oil Trust, Jersey Standard rapidly expanded its overseas production and marketing activities. By 1954, it had become the largest oil company in the world. In 1972, the company changed its name to Exxon to end confusion with other companies still using the Standard Oil name.

Exxon's slide from prominence began in the 1970s as nationalization of oil assets that had been held previously by producing companies reduced the company's access to oil. With its reserves shrinking, Exxon's dependence on crude oil for the bulk of its sales slowed the company's growth, allowing Shell to gradually replace it as the world's leading oil company during the 1980s. A further blow to the company's reputation and its balance sheet was the notorious *Exxon Valdez* oil spill off the coast of Alaska in 1989. By 1992, the disaster had cost Exxon more than US$6 billion for criminal damages and cleanup. In mid-1994, a federal jury ruled that the company and the tanker's captain had caused the disaster through recklessness and fined Exxon US$5 billion. The company formally appealed this judgment in 1997, and in 2001, a U.S. Circuit Court of Appeals found the fine excessive and mandated that the Alaskan state court lower it.

Prior to its 1999 merger with Mobil, Exxon Corp. was the world's second largest private sector petroleum company after Royal Dutch/Shell. Exxon usurped Royal Dutch/Shell as the world leader when the US$83 billion deal with Mobil was completed. By 2003, however, Exxon Mobil had slipped to second place, behind BP. In 2004, Exxon Mobil had proven reserves of 21.2 billion barrels of oil equivalent and sales of US$263.9 billion. By 2007, it had sales in excess of US$404 billion.

Royal Dutch/Shell Group of Companies. Royal Dutch/Shell is the world's third largest private sector petroleum and natural gas company. It was created in 1907 as a partnership between the Dutch company Royal Dutch Petroleum, with 60 percent participation, and the British company Shell Transport and Trading, with 40 percent. These two companies continued to exist as independent entities based in The Hague, Netherlands, and London, England, respectively.

Royal Dutch/Shell's crude oil production was almost evenly divided among Europe, Africa, the Middle East, East Asia, and the Western Hemisphere. The leading sources of Royal Dutch/Shell's global production were its operations in the United States, the United Kingdom and its North Sea fields, Nigeria, Oman, and Malaysia. Royal Dutch/Shell was also a leader in natural gas production in the Netherlands and the United States, which were large gas producers. As of 2000, gas reserved equaled 56.2 tcf. Other leading natural gas-producing countries for Royal Dutch/Shell were Canada, Malaysia, the United Kingdom, and Brunei. Sales in 2004 totaled US$201.7 billion, and the firm employed 119,000 workers. By 2007, its sales were at approximately US$355.8 billion.

Venezuela nationalized all oil holdings in 1975, paying US$1 billion for the assets. Prior to nationalization, foreign companies produced about 70 percent of Venezuela's oil, although the state had been a 50 percent partner in their operations since 1945. In 1977, Petróleos de Venezuela SA (PDVSA) was created as a holding company of subsidiaries that replaced the former companies. Exxon's operations became the subsidiary Lagoven, Royal Dutch/Shell's became Maraven, and operations of other smaller companies were combined into the subsidiaries Memeven and Corpoven. The oil companies continued to operate their former possessions by contract for fees, and thus PDVSA was able to continue to take advantage of their expertise.

The exploration launched in the 1980s by PDVSA yielded oil reserves that nearly doubled the country's known reserves. In the late 1980s, after oil prices fell, PDVSA accelerated its diversification. It remained an integrated petroleum company but also became involved in coal and bitumen production, petrochemicals, and fertilizers. In 2004 the company's proven reserves were estimated at 77.2 billion barrels of oil, which was the largest amount outside of the Middle East, and 147.1 tcf of natural gas.

Despite being subject to OPEC quotas, Venezuela's crude oil production rose during the 1990, reaching 3.14 million b/d by 2000. To reach a planned increase in production to 6.5 million b/d by 2006, PDVSA needed about US$40 billion in new investment. Consequently, the firm began offering foreign oil companies the opportunity to return to Venezuela and help PDVSA improve extraction from existing fields. A late 1997 round of bidding brought US$2 billion in contract payments from international oil firms.

Petroleum production fell up to 25,000 b/d in 2003 after protestors threatened the government of President Hugo Chavez and threw the country into civil turmoil. As a result, almost all of Venezuela's exports were temporarily halted. According to company statistics, however, production was normalized by later that year, reaching about 3.25 million b/d of crude oil.

The United States was Venezuela's leading export market, primarily through the U.S.-based CITGO gasoline company, which PDVSA acquired in 1990. During 1997, Venezuela surpassed Saudi Arabia as the largest oil exporter to the United States, with a market share of 18 percent. Sales in 2000 grew 64.4 percent to US$53.6 billion, while earnings soared 156 percent to US$7.21 billion. Revenues dropped in 2002 to US$42.58 billion. The firm's oil reserves had totaled 77.2 billion barrels in 2004 and were second only to those held in the Middle East.

TOTAL S.A. With operations in more than 100 countries and reserves of 11.4 billion barrels, TOTAL, based in France, is one of the world's largest integrated oil companies. Total Fina was formed in 1999 through the merger of France's Total and PetroFina in Belgium. The new company bought France-based Elf Aquitaine in 2000 and was renamed TOTAL S.A. in 2003. Sales in 2004 exceeded US$166.2 billion. By 2007, sales were reported to be US$233.8 billion.

MAJOR COUNTRIES IN
THE INDUSTRY

The Russian Federation. In the early 2000s Russia owned the world's largest reserves of natural gas and the eighth largest reserves of oil. In addition, Russia was the world's largest exporter of natural gas and the second largest exporter of oil. Production of oil surged during the 1980s when the Soviet Union intensified exploitation of its oilfields in Western Siberia. However, output slowed after peaking at 12.5 million b/d in 1988, which was blamed on unrealistic state-mandated production levels that had exhausted the USSR's major oil fields. After the collapse of the Soviet Union in 1991, Russian oil production was thrown into chaos, and by 1996 production fell to about 6 million b/d. In 1999 the situation began to

change when world oil prices surged and the Russian economy began to improve. By 2004, total production had risen almost 40 percent to about 9.27 million b/d. This made Russia the second largest producer of crude oil after Saudi Arabia. Improvements in upstream techniques at older oilfields, as well as other production efficiencies, contributed to higher outputs.

In 2003, about 70 percent of the Russian oil industry was controlled by five companies: Yukos and Sibneft, which merged that year to create YukosSibneft, Russia's largest oil company; LUKoil; Surgutneftegaz; and Tyumen Oil, which merged with British Petroleum that year to create TNK-BP. About 150 small and medium size companies shared the rest of the oil industry in Russia. The picture differed sharply for the natural gas industry, however. One state-controlled company, Gazprom, produced almost 90 percent of Russia's natural gas and held almost one-third of the world's reserves. Gazprom was also Russia's biggest earner of hard currency. Strict domestic regulations, however, had a negative impact on the company's profits.

While Russia exported more than 70 percent of its crude oil production in the early 2000s, infrastructure problems prevented producers from meeting their export goals. Much of Russia's oil must be shipped long distances by rail, greatly increasing costs. The December 2001 opening of the Baltic Pipeline System (BPS), which carried oil from West Siberia to a new port at Primorsk, on the Gulf of Finland just north of St. Petersburg, gave Russia a direct outlet to European markets. The pipeline handled about 1 million b/d in late 2004, and output was expected to increase to 1.2 million b/d in 2005. In addition, Russia announced in 2004 that it would build a Far Eastern Pipeline from Angarsk in southern Siberia to Nakhodka on the Sea of Japan. The 2,500 mile pipeline would cost between US$15 billion and US$18 billion with capacity for 1.6 million b/d.

Russia's natural gas industry was also held back by infrastructure. Many of the country's oil companies sat on natural gas reserves that were not exploited because Gazprom controlled the pipeline network, limiting access to export markets. If third-party access to the pipeline network were achieved, natural gas exports could significantly increase. During the early 2000s, Gazprom became more interested in diversifying its exports, shifting trade from Eastern Europe to the European Union, Turkey, Japan, and other Asian markets. Construction of a proposed natural gas pipeline from Russia to Finland and Great Britain via the Baltic Sea was scheduled to begin in 2007, but in 2005 Gazprom announced that the project's start would be delayed to 2010.

Saudi Arabia. The discovery of oil on the island nation of Bahrain in 1931 suggested that oil could be found on the

Saudi Arabian mainland and convinced Saudi King Ibn Saud to offer a concession to the foreign firm Socal (Chevron). Oil in large quantities was not discovered until 1938. By 1940, Saudi oil production reached 20,000 b/d, and Saudi Arabia became a significant producer. In 1976, the country overtook the United States as the world's second largest oil producer behind the Soviet Union.

The country reached its highest production levels in 1980 when it registered 9.9 billion b/d of oil. Of that total, it exported 9.2 billion b/d, recording US$101.8 billion in exports, but OPEC production quotas kept Saudi Arabia's production down after 1980. By 1985, production dropped to 3.2 billion b/d. Following the 1990 Iraqi invasion of Kuwait, however, Saudi Arabia boosted its production from 5.3 million b/d to 7.5 million b/d. After reaching 9.12 million b/d in 2000, production fell to 8.2 million b/d, which continued to be the largest production level in the world, in 2001. Total oil production, including liquid natural gas, averaged 10 million b/d in early 2003, when Saudi Arabia implemented its spare production capacity to help offset losses from Venezuela, Nigeria, and Iraq, but its OPEC quota was cut later that year to 7.9 b/d. In 2004 Saudi Arabia's capacity was estimated at between 10.5 and 11 million b/d. Saudi Arabia's proven oil reserves were 261.9 billion barrels in 2004. Saudi officials announced that they planned to increase production to 12.5 million b/d moving into the 2010s.

Most of Saudi Arabia's oil production took place in the eastern part of the country, along the Persian Gulf coast and offshore. However, discoveries were made in the northwest near the Jordanian border and the Red Sea coast. Since 1987, Saudi Aramco had rights to explore anywhere in the Kingdom.

Long a major exporter to the United States, Saudi Arabia was also a key supplier to Europe and Japan. By the early 2000s, however, Venezuela, Canada, and Mexico had increased their exports to the United States. As a result, Saudi Arabia stepped up exports to Asia, which by 2004 accounted for about 60 percent of Saudi Arabia's crude oil exports. Despite slipping to second place in the U.S. export market, Saudi Arabia hoped to maintain or expand its position as a key supplier to the United States.

The United States. The United States was a major oil exporter until the 1940s, but beginning in 1948, U.S. imports of crude petroleum and refined oil products exceeded exports. The country was the world's leading oil producer, reaching a peak of 89.64 million b/d in 1970 before declining to 8.77 million b/d in 1974, when the Soviet Union surpassed the United States as the leading oil producer. Production remained fairly stable

into the mid-1980s, but began to fall in the late 1980s and early 1990s, with only 8.585 million b/d produced in 1993. By 1997, production had fallen further, to less than 7 million b/d, positioning the United States as the third largest oil producer, trailing Saudi Arabia and Russia. The United States remained in third place in 2000, with crude oil production of 5.83 million b/d, and by 2003 production had dropped to about 5.7 million b/d. The Energy Information Administration (EIA) reported that this downward trend was expected to continue, while natural gas output was expected to climb. The country's leading oil-producing states were Alaska, Texas, Louisiana, California, and Oklahoma. U.S. crude oil reserves at the beginning of 2005 totaled 21.9 billion barrels.

While U.S. oil production declined significantly from 1985 to 2003, consumption remained high. Most of this demand was attributed to the transportation sector. In the first 10 months of 2004, U.S. oil consumption averaged 20.4 million b/d compared to 20 million b/d in 2003. Total petroleum consumption in 2005 was expected to grow 1.4 percent.

In 1993, the United States produced more natural gas than oil by value for the first time. By 1999, the United States accounted for 23.2 percent of worldwide natural gas production, behind only Russia, which accounted for 23.7 percent of production. U.S. natural gas reserves in 2004 were the sixth largest in the world, totaling 187 tcf. Production of dry natural gas was expected to reach about 19.1 tcf in 2005, but demand was expected to grow. Consumption had reached about 22 tcf in 2004, and was projected to rise 3.7 percent in 2005. To meet growing demand, the United States relied on imports, primarily from Canada. However, Canada's increasing domestic use had the potential to reduce its export levels of natural gas in the 2010s. As the United States sought additional import sources, it had begun expanding liquid natural gas (LNG) facilities that were expected to significantly increase LNG imports by 2007. In the early 2000s, most LNG imports came from Trinidad and Tobago, Algeria, and Qatar.

Iran. Iran has been a major world producer and exporter of oil since the 1920s. All of Iran's oil and gas production had been monopolized by the state-owned National Iranian Oil Co. Iranian oil production reached a peak of 6.02 million b/d in 1974. It stood at 5.24 million b/d on the eve of the 1979 revolution, a period of political and economic upheaval that disrupted production and exports. The outbreak of the Iran-Iraq War in 1980 severely damaged Iran's oil-producing facilities, and production plummeted to 1.32 million b/d in 1981. Production increased gradually during the 1980s and accelerated after the end of the war in 1988 but remained limited by OPEC quotas. In 2004, Iran reported proven oil reserves of 132 billion barrels. The country's oil production capacity was estimated to be about 3.9 million b/d in early 2005, making it the world's second largest producer. Spurred in large part by a sharp increase in domestic production, Iran hoped to double national oil production by 2015 with the help of substantial foreign investment for much-needed modernizations to its facilities.

Natural gas production in Iran continued to grow rapidly through the late 1990s and early 2000s. Production surpassed pre-Iran-Iraq War levels by the end of the war in 1988 and continued to rise during the late 1980s and 1990s. In 2005, Iran was second only to Russia in natural gas reserves, with 940 tcf. Although Iran was the leading exporter of natural gas among OPEC countries in the 1970s, it was no longer a significant exporter. With almost half of its total energy needs supplied by natural gas, Iran's domestic demand accounted for most of its natural gas production. Because it had enormous undeveloped reserves, however, it had the potential to become a major natural gas exporter. The country had announced that it would spend billions of dollars in the late 2000s and early 2010s to boost natural gas production.

Mexico. Mexico, a leading oil producer and exporter in the 1920s, nationalized its petroleum industry in 1938. Following nationalization, the industry began serving the growing domestic market as demand grew faster than supply. For a time Mexico even had to import small amounts of oil. Mexico disappeared from the world market for several decades before becoming a dominant producer in the late 1970s. A major exploration drive had revealed large new reserves beginning in 1972, however, and by 1974 the country resumed exporting oil. Production grew from 500,000 b/d in 1972 to 1.9 million b/d in 1980 as Mexico re-established itself as a major oil-producing country on the strength of reserves located on the southern shore of the Gulf of Mexico. Increase in domestic demand, however, decreased 2003 exports to approximately 1.78 million b/d. The vast majority of Mexico's oil is exported to the United States.

With production estimated at 3.8 million b/d, Mexico ranked as the fourth leading oil producer worldwide in 2003, but dropped to fifth place in 2004. Estimates of Mexico's crude oil reserves were revised downward in late 2002 to about 15.7 billion barrels and fell further in 2005 to an estimated 14.6 billion barrels. However, the country's ultimate potential reserves, including liquid natural gas, were expected to be as high as 40.6 billion barrels. In 2004 Mexico had proven natural gas reserves of 15 tfc.

All oil and gas exploration and production, both inshore and offshore, was conducted by the state-owned company Petróleos Mexicanos (Pemex). In 2003, about one-third of Mexico's federal budget came from Pemex revenues. While no foreign companies had equity in Mexican production, in the early 2000s Pemex began to offer contracts to foreign companies. The North American Free Trade Agreement (NAFTA) also allowed U.S. and Canadian firms greater participation in Mexico's oil industry. In 2004, Mexican President Vincent Fox proposed several reforms in the energy sector, including proposals to allow private investment and foreign participation in the oil and natural gas industries. He also proposed changes in how Pemex is taxed. It was uncertain, however, whether such measures would receive sufficient legislative support to be enacted.

Canada. Before 2002, Canada was not among the top 20 countries with proven reserves. However, by early 2005 it ranked second in the world with 178.8 billion barrels, more than 95 percent of which was in the Alberta oil sands deposits that had been excluded previously from estimates of crude reserves. Although exploitation of oil sands greatly boosted Canada's production, it is much more costly to extract oil from sand fields than from conventional deposits, which has led to controversy about the potential growth of oil sands production. Some analysts have warned that high production costs could limit growth in the industry, but the EIA predicted that oil sands production would increase significantly in the 2010s. Canada also has considerable offshore oil reserves, which it planned to develop more extensively through the early 2000s. Production at the Hibernia field off the coast of Newfoundland began in 1997, and another Atlantic field, Terra Nova, began operations in 2002 that averaged 134,000 b/d in 2003. Exploitation of offshore fields in the Pacific, however, was held up by a federal ban that prevents offshore drilling. If this ban is lifted, offshore drilling could begin there by 2010. In 2004, Canada was the seventh largest oil producer with total oil production of 3.1 million b/d. It was also the world's seventh largest oil consumer, using 2.3 million b/d. More than 99 percent of Canada's crude oil exports are sold to the United States.

Canada ranked as the world's third largest producer of natural gas in 2002, but its proven reserves stood at only 56.1 trillion cubic feet in early 2005. At that rate, according to the EIA, Canada will deplete its natural gas reserves in about 8.6 years. Canada is a major supplier of natural gas to the United States, accounting for about 16 percent of U.S. consumption in 2003.

BIBLIOGRAPHY

British Petroleum PLC. Company Statistics, 2004. Available from www.bp.com.

Clark, Nicola. "Libya Signs Energy Exploration Deal with Shell." *The New York Times,* 26 March 2004.

Dougherty, Carter. "China, Seeking Oil and Foothold, Brings Funds for Africa's Riches." *The Boston Globe,* 22 February 2004.

DeHaemer, Christian. "How to Profit From the Natural Gas Boom: New Technology Makes Natural Gas a Viable Replacement for Oil." 8 October 2008. Available from www.istockanalyst.com.

"Drilling More Helps—a Little." *USA Today,* 13 June 2008.

Francis, David R. "Has Global Oil Production Peaked?" *Christian Science Monitor,* 29 January 2004.

"Hoover's Company Capsules." *Hoover's Online,*2008. Available from www.hoovers.com.

Itano, Nicole. "Proposal to Limit Oil and Coal Projects Draws Fire." *The New York Times,* 24 March 2004.

Krueger, Jessica. *U.S. Oil Stakes in West Africa.* Center for Strategic and International Studies, Washington, D.C., 2002. Available from www.csis.org.

McNulty, Sheila. "Gulf of Mexico Output Still at Only Half Capacity," 7 October 2008. Available from www.ft.com.

"Oil Market Remains Oversupplied After Cut: Khatibi." *NIOC News,* 15 November 2008. Available from www.nioc.ir.

Palmeri, Christopher. "Industry Outlook 2001—Energy." *Business Week,* 2 January 2001. Available from www.businessweek.com.

Roberts, Dexter, and Mark L. Clifford. "China: Hungry for Energy." *Business Week,* 24 December 2001. Available from www.businessweek.com.

Romero, Simon. "Energy of Africa Draws the Eyes of Houston." *The New York Times,* 23 September 2003.

Schoof, Renee. "U.S. Taps Canada's Oil Sands—But at What Cost?" McClatchy Washington Bureau, 12 October 2008. Available from www.mcclatchydc.com.

Sengupta, Soomini. "The Making of an African Petrostate." *The New York Times,* 18 February 2004.

Sinopec Corp. Company Information and Statistics, 2004. Available from english.sinopec.com.

Starobin, Paul. "An Opportunity for Russian Oil?" *Business Week,* 3 December 2001. Available from www.businessweek.com.

St. Clair, Neil. "Mixed Reviews After Oil and Natural Gas Industry Address Public." 7 October 2008. Available from news10.now.com.

Trop, Jaclyn. "Oil Falls But Not Price of Petro-Based Goods." *The Detroit News,* 11 November 2008.

U.S. Department of Energy, Energy Information Administration. Country Analyses and Briefs, 2003–2004. Available from www.eia.doe.gov.

————. *International Energy Outlook 2004.* Available from www.eia.doe.gov.

"Venezuela Urges OPEC Output Cut," 3 September 2008. Available from www.reuters.com.

Walt, Vivenne. "Why the Energy Crisis Will Outlast the Credit Crisis," 15 November 2008. Available from www.conservationvalue.blogspot.com.

SIC 2911

PETROLEUM REFINING

NAICS CODE(S)

324110. Petroleum refiners transform crude oil into such fuels as gasoline, kerosene, distillate fuel oils, and residual fuel oils. Refined petroleum products are also used in lubricants and a wide number of chemical applications. (See also **Petroleum and Natural Gas, Crude.**)

INDUSTRY SNAPSHOT

After nearly a century of extraordinary growth, the world petroleum refining industry struggled to adapt to a harsh economic climate in the 1990s. Global production of refined petroleum products leveled off at about 65 million barrels per day (b/d) in the early 1990s. Growth accelerated again in the mid-1990s to more than 70 million b/d, due largely to rapid growth in emerging markets, especially in East Asia. The Asian financial crisis that began in late 1997, however, combined with the beginning of a recession in Japan to slow demand for refined products like gasoline. Global production hovered in the 75 billion b/d range in 1998 and 1999. Production levels surged again in 2000 due to a stronger economy in Asia, as well as economic prosperity in North America and Europe. However, worldwide recessionary conditions began to undercut demand again at the start of the twenty-first century. In 2003, worldwide consumption hit 78.1 million b/d, with Asia and the Pacific Rim accounting for the highest growth percentages. In addition, 2003 marked the highest prices since the early 1980s.

Furthermore, there were slight changes to the industry in 2003, with little more than a 1 percent change up or down in North America and Europe, according to *Euromonitor.* The market in Germany, for instance, declined 1 percent to 122.4 metric tons from 2002 and was expected to decline another 8 percent in 2008. The petroleum market in France fell 1.5 percent to 92.8 metric tons. Transportation was the main consumer of petroleum products, and diesel was the largest market sector at 41.9 metric tons with projected growth to 100 metric tons by 2008. In the United Kingdom, the total market had fallen 0.5 percent to 79.1 metric tons, with diesel dominating at 25.2 metric tons. Declines were expected in 2008 to a total volume of 74.4 metric tons. In contrast to Europe, the U.S. market reported an increase of 1.4 percent to 7.05 billion barrels in 2003, with slight anticipated growth the following year as motor gasoline remaining the biggest market sector. By 2008, the sector was projected to hold more than 43 percent of the refined petroleum market for a total value of US$3.4 billion.

Further consolidation among companies and higher profits for the largest companies were industry trends of the mid-2000s. In addition, in an effort to overcome its image as an enemy of the environment, research was underway to make the industry "green" and environmentally friendly. Innovations were expected to have a major impact on the petroleum industry. Industry leader BP, for example, was running a "Beyond Petroleum" campaign, having garnered more than 18 percent of the solar power market in 2003, along with other green research investments. In 2004 and early 2005, global demand greatly outpaced supply, which raised prices to record levels. However, record high oil prices did not cause the expected decrease in demand, primarily due to low interest rates and a spike in economic activity worldwide, especially in China. Global oil production grew 3.4 percent in 2004 to 71.7 million b/d.

ORGANIZATION AND STRUCTURE

No industry has epitomized the term "monopoly capitalism" better than the oil industry. For example, the U.S. 1890 Sherman Antitrust Act was in large part inspired by the overwhelming monopolistic power of John D. Rockefeller's Standard Oil trust. Even in the 2000s, almost a century after the breakup of Standard Oil, the offspring of that early conglomerate—Exxon Mobil and ChevronTexaco—remained among the largest corporations in the world, dominating all aspects of the oil industry. With their massive integrated supply, production, and distribution systems, leading oil companies were involved in a myriad of industry activities, including resource extraction, manufacturing, and distribution.

Petroleum refining was considered part of the "downstream" side of the oil business. In addition to refining, downstream operations included transportation (mostly via pipelines) of crude oil to refineries and refined oil products to wholesalers, distributors, and retailers. The "upstream" side of the business involved all aspects of finding and recovering crude oil, including exploration, geological studies, testing, drilling, and extraction. Integrated companies, which were referred to as the "majors" and included Exxon Mobil, Royal Dutch/Shell, BP, and ChevronTexaco, carried out upstream and downstream operations. Raw materials obtained by the upstream arm of the corporation were transferred to the refiner, which in turn supplied the finished products to company-owned wholesalers and retailers.

Competing with the major companies in the late 1990s were numerous small integrated and nonintegrated companies, or "independents." Some of these independents, such as Atlantic Richfield and Phillips Petroleum,

were integrated international corporations in their own right, although their numbers dwindled in the early 2000s due to industry consolidation. For example, BP Amoco, which subsequently shortened its name to BP, acquired Atlantic Richfield in 2000. In addition, a merger of Phillips Petroleum and Conoco created ConocoPhillips in August 2002. Most of the remaining independents were regional companies specializing in refining. Prominent independents like Ashland Oil and Valero Energy Corp. played an important role in the refining industry, but were not at the same level as the majors.

Petroleum refineries converted crude oil into a variety of products. Most of these products, such as fuel, were distributed in the form in which they were to be used, although some products were used in the manufacture of other products such as plastics. The most common refining technique was distillation, or fractionating. Heated crude oil was pumped into the bottom of a distillation tower where the lighter oil portions, or fractions, vaporized. The fractions cooled as they rose and condensed into liquids that flowed back down and were re-vaporized. This process was repeated until the desired degree of purity was achieved. Heavier fractions, such as fuel and diesel oils, condensed at higher temperatures and were tapped from the lower part of the tower, while lighter, value-added products like kerosene, gasoline, and butane condensed at lower temperatures and were taken from the top.

More sophisticated refineries conducted additional processing of distilled products, applying various combinations of pressure, heat, or chemical catalysts to break down heavy molecules into light ones. These various processes, termed "cracking," were used to create cleaner, more efficient fuels and oils such as high-octane gasoline and lubricants. Catalytic cracking, for instance, used a powdered chemical catalyst to increase the gasoline yield by converting heavy fractions to light ones, while hydrocracking added hydrogen to produce products with reduced carbon to hydrogen ratios. Other processes included thermal cracking, hydrofining, reforming, and alkalization.

The chief products made from these processes included the so-called "light products," including the lightest fractions, such as liquefied petroleum gas (LPG), gasoline, aviation fuel, and petroleum solvents; the middle distillates, including kerosene, heating oil, waxes, and diesel fuel; and the heaviest fractions, including asphalts (bitumens) and residual fuel oil used in industry and power generation. The type of products a given refinery produced depended more on geographical location, customer demand, and seasonal needs than technical capability.

In addition to fuels and oils, refineries produced "intermediate" products such as ethanol, styrene, ethyl chloride, butadiene, and methanol. These intermediates were mostly used in the manufacture of plastics, but they were also used for antifreeze, synthetic fibers and rubbers, and detergents.

BACKGROUND AND DEVELOPMENT

Petroleum was, quite literally, the fuel that drove modern industrial society, supplying nearly one-half of the world's energy. Automobiles, tractors, trucks, aircraft, and ships were powered by petroleum derivatives, including gasoline, kerosene, and diesel oil. Homes and offices were heated by fuel oil and natural gas or by petroleum-generated electricity. Plastics, paints, fertilizers, insecticides, soaps, and synthetic rubber all used petroleum as a raw material. Even synthetic fibers in clothing were derived from petroleum products.

Petroleum began to be used in ancient times to waterproof boats and repair roads. It also served as a medicine, an ointment, an incendiary, and an illuminant. Serious exploitation of petroleum did not begin until the 1850s, however, when the rising price of lamp oil, which was derived from whale blubber, prompted a search for a cheap and convenient substitute.

In 1854, a young New York lawyer named George Bissell and some partners formed the world's first petroleum company—the Pennsylvania Rock Oil Company—and began exploiting oil seeps (underground deposits of oil and gas that escape to the surface) around Titusville, Pennsylvania, where the world's first well was drilled in 1859. Soon after, numerous small operators sprang up throughout the United States, distilling kerosene from crude oil, distributing it in barrels, and selling it by the gallon in retail stores. Oil production began in Russia at about the same time. For the rest of the century, the United States and Russia dominated world production.

In the United States, the era of independent oil producers was short-lived. Most of the nation's refineries were bought by John D. Rockefeller, who by the late 1870s exercised almost complete control over the industry. The Rockefeller monopoly eventually fell victim to the Sherman Antitrust Act (1890), and in 1911, after years of wrangling, Rockefeller's Standard Oil trust was separated into 34 distinct companies.

The rise of the oil industry was closely tied to the emergence of the automobile. While Rockefeller was consolidating control over the U.S. petroleum industry, a Belgian inventor named Etienne Lenoir was developing the first internal combustion engine. By 1885 the first gasoline-powered vehicles hit the road in Germany, and by 1899, more than 30 different manufacturers were producing and selling motor vehicles in the United States. Gasoline, once a useless by-product of the refining process, suddenly became a valuable commodity. The growing popularity of the automobile and the development of an automated production system by Henry Ford in 1914 ensured a growing market for gasoline, which through 1997 accounted for 42.3 percent of total U.S. consumption of refined oil products and 28.4 percent of world consumption.

By the late 1930s, the United States held a dominant position in the international trade of oil and refined petroleum products. Outside the United States, only the Dutch/British conglomerate Royal Dutch Shell and Britain's Anglo-Persian Oil Company, which became British Petroleum, were able to compete with the five major U.S. oil companies (Exxon, Mobil, Chevron, Texaco, and Amoco). Known as the "Seven Sisters," these powerful companies had complete control of the oil fields, refineries, pipelines, and tankers.

The dynamic growth of the U.S. refining industry in the 1920s and 1930s was fueled by vast reserves of petroleum and natural gas as well as by the development of advanced thermal and catalytic oil-cracking processes, which in turn stimulated the growth of the petrochemical industry. With the advent of World War II, demand for fuels of all types—especially aviation gasoline—surged, leading to a simultaneous expansion of refinery capacity.

After the war, rapid economic growth and pent-up consumer demand kept the refineries running at full capacity. Cheap oil began pouring out of the Middle East, which led quickly to the rapid replacement of fuels like coal with petroleum, and the proliferation of automobiles in western Europe, North America, and Japan. Demand for gasoline especially soared, and from 1951 to 1970 the oil industry reported annual growth rates of 7 percent per year, with world production increasing from 12 to 46 million barrels per day (b/d). At the same time, industry growth in Europe and Japan began to narrow the U.S. lead in petroleum refining. By the 1970s, many other oil-producing nations, such as Saudi Arabia, Iran, Canada, and Venezuela, were also refining petroleum on a large scale.

Starting in the late 1970s, growth in world demand for refined petroleum products slowed considerably and even fell in 1979 for the first time since the Great Depression. The slowdown was precipitated initially by the 1973 Arab oil embargo, which spurred many oil-consuming nations to seek ways to offset the influence of the Organization of Petroleum Exporting Countries (OPEC) on prices and production. Europe and Japan, in particular, accelerated development of alternative sources of energy and attempted to increase the energy efficiency of automobiles.

By the early 1990s, global production of refined petroleum products was roughly 65 million b/d, nearly

80 percent of which was in the form of fuel. Gasoline alone accounted for nearly 27 percent of production worldwide and more than 40 percent of U.S. production. Distillate and residual fuel oil accounted for another 47 percent of world production. Jet fuel accounted for 6.1 percent, liquefied petroleum gases for 3.6 percent, kerosene for 2.5 percent, and lubricants for 1.1 percent of the remainder.

The petroleum refining industry, especially in North America, faced uncertainty with simultaneous declining profits and increasing costs. In the United States, profits fell to a five-year low in 1992 while the costs of upgrading and research rose 8.3 percent at the same time. As the decade progressed, prospects did not brighten. Following an average decline of 4.8 percent in sales by integrated international refineries over five years, sales in 1996 fell 6 percent. These trends were repeated in most of the industrialized world, pushing many of the major oil companies and larger independents to focus more attention on rapidly industrializing countries in Southeast Asia and Latin America.

For small independents, international expansion was not an option, and many went out of business. The number of refineries in the United States fell from 319 in 1980 to 202 in 1992. Twelve more refineries, all with capacities of less than 50,000 b/d, shut down in 1992 due to relentless financial pressure. Although the problems of small U.S. refiners were aggravated by a recession in the early 1990s, the most difficult problem they faced was the Clean Air Act (CAA). While the large, integrated companies were able to procure the capital necessary for plant reconfigurations, product reformulation, and research and development, the smaller refineries were faced with greater investments on a per-barrel basis and found it extremely difficult to obtain the funds necessary to compete.

In November 1992, the CAA called for the 39 U.S. cities with the highest carbon monoxide levels to use oxygenated gasoline in winter months, causing much misery for the refining industry. In 1995, the nine cities with the worst levels—Baltimore, Chicago, Hartford, Houston, Los Angeles, Milwaukee, New York, Philadelphia, and San Diego—were required to begin using gasoline that fully met the CAA's Phase I specifications. This reformulated gasoline was required to have a minimum oxygen content of 2 percent by weight with a maximum aromatics content not to exceed 25 percent (including a maximum of 1 percent benzene by volume), and no heavy metals. Nitrogen-oxide levels were to remain the same or less than 1990 levels, and tailpipe emissions of volatile organic compounds and toxins were to be reduced 15 percent.

These regulations could not have come at a worse time for refiners. Not only were margins shrinking as overall demand fell, but the quality of crude oil inputs also was declining just as the demand for higher quality outputs increased. This situation created an additional cost pressure as more refiners had to make investments to process the low-grade crude. Moreover, the new regulations hampered the ability to change products between seasons, geographical areas, and applications, pushing up costs everywhere. The cost of implementing the Phase I reformulations was expected to run refiners alone between US$3 billion and US$5 billion. As U.S. refiners faced four more major amendments of the Clean Air Act that were slated to go into effect by the early twenty-first century, they estimated compliance costs would as high as US$20 billion.

The difficulties within the refining industry were not confined to the United States. In Canada, petroleum refiners reeled under the impact of slumping demand, overcapacity, and increasingly strict environmental controls. During the first six months of 1991, Canada's leading oil companies—Imperial Oil, Shell Canada, and Petro-Canada—posted losses, and by 1992, all had announced plant closures. The onset of the Asian financial crisis in late 1997 decreased demand for petroleum products worldwide, providing additional hurdles for refiners.

While the CAA affected only the refining industry in the United States, a global regulatory threat was acknowledged in December 1997 when an international climate change conference held in Kyoto, Japan, produced the Kyoto Protocol on Climate Change to curb the emission of greenhouse gases, most of which resulted from the use of refined petroleum. By May 1998, the European Union had signed the protocol, but the treaty faced considerable opposition in the United States, especially with the Republican control of the U.S. Congress.

The difficult operating environment for refining companies in the 1990s led to a series of mergers, acquisitions, and alliances that profoundly changed the shape of the entire industry. In February of 1996, British Petroleum and Mobil entered into a joint venture that merged the two companies' European refining and marketing operations, creating an entity in the top three in both gasoline and lubricants in Europe. In 1997 alone, the two companies expected to save US$100 million to US$150 million by eliminating redundant operations and cutting overlapping staff.

Similar cost savings were expected from other collaborations. Texaco and Royal Dutch/Shell combined their downstream operations in the western and midwestern United States in 1997. They extended the venture into a coast-to-coast refining and marketing enterprise through a 1998 joint venture with Saudi Arabian Oil Company involving downstream operations in the eastern United

States and along the Gulf Coast. This arrangement among the three companies included 12 refineries and control of 11.4 percent of overall U.S. refinery capacity. Although no refineries were expected to be closed as a result of the joint venture, pretax savings were expected to run as high as US$800 million.

Consolidation continued into the late 1990s as oil giants remained focused on cutting costs. The 1999 merger that formed Exxon Mobil had resulted in cost savings of US$4.6 billion by 2001. The deal also helped to boost sales to US$232.7 billion in 2000, making Exxon Mobil the largest company in the United States, as well as the world, a position previously held by Royal Dutch/Shell. The firm's US$17.7 billion in profits that year were the highest ever recorded in U.S. business history. Other major deals included the US$57 billion merger of British Petroleum and Amoco Corp. to form BP Amoco in 1998, as well as the US$26.8 billion stock purchase of Atlantic Richfield by BP Amoco in 2000, which subsequently became BP. The consolidation made British Petroleum the second leading global oil company, but also resulted in economies of scale worth an estimated US$6 billion. In 2001, Chevron and Texaco joined forces to create ChevronTexaco Corp., the second largest oil company in the United States and the fourth largest in the world. The world's fifth largest integrated oil player was also the result of consolidation. Total Fina Elf was formed in 2000 when Total Fina, itself the result of a 1999 merger between France-based Total and Belgium-based PetroFina, acquired Elf Aquitaine, also based in France.

The industry was also beset by strict new environmental regulations that required enormous investments in research and facilities in the 1990s. Strict regulations, such as the Clean Air Act Amendments of the 1990s, were enacted in the United States, resulting in a spate of refinery closures and the collapse of some small independents. Similar problems faced refiners around the world, and one of the most dramatic shakeouts in the history of the oil business occurred in the 1990s. Once the tumult subsided, however, the survivors were more fit and prosperous than ever.

In many cases, firms like Exxon Mobil had agreed to divest a portion of their refining operations to gain regulatory approval for their deals. As a result, independent refining firms like Valero Energy Corp. were able to increase their capacity by purchasing these refineries. In addition, many leading refiners, particularly in the United States, continued to grow larger by following a consolidation trend that mirrored the activities of the largest oil companies. Valero, the largest independent oil refiner in the United States with 2001 sales of nearly US$15 billion and earnings of US$564 million, acquired

Ultramar Diamond Shamrock at the end of 2001, increasing its number of refineries from 6 to 12 and upping its combined production capacity to 2 million barrels per day. The US$9.8 billion acquisition of Tosco by Phillips Petroleum was considered the largest downstream deal of 2001. In fact, although the value of total global energy merger and acquisition activity fell from US$264.4 billion in 2000 to US$243.5 billion in 2001, the value of downstream mergers and acquisitions, boosted by the major U.S. deals, grew from US$19.9 billion to US$35.4 billion over the same time.

Of the 761 refineries in operation in 2000, 158 were located in the United States, 95 in China, 35 in Japan, 33 in Russia, and 17 each in India, Germany, and Italy. North America led the world in refining capacity, followed by Asia and Western Europe. Refiners remained concerned about the costs associated with adhering to increasingly stringent environmental regulations like the Kyoto Protocol and later phases of the Clean Air Act despite reporting improved profit margins in 2000 and 2001 that were due to improved economic conditions in Asia, which bolstered demand; prosperous economies in both North America and Asia, and aggressive cost cutting efforts. However, the catalyst sector of the petroleum refining industry expected to benefit from these regulations. The catalyst market was worth US$1.1 billion in 2000, and anticipated growth was estimated to be nearly 4 percent per year through 2005. The June 2001 issue of *The Oil and Gas Journal* reported that growth in catalysts was largely the result of "increasing demand for reformulated and other, less-polluting gasoline mandated by the Clean Air Act Amendments of 1990, plus new regulations calling for reductions in sulfur content in gasoline and diesel fuel."

CURRENT CONDITIONS

By 2003, despite the highest prices in two decades, worldwide consumption had hit 78.1 million b/d, with Asia and the Pacific Rim accounting for the highest growth. China alone commanded more than 40 percent of the growth in total market demand worldwide. Russia was a leader in production with more than 40 percent of worldwide growth since the late 1990s. Global oil reserves were estimated at 1.15 billion barrels. By mid-2004, crude prices had reached more than US$40 per barrel and by mid-2005, had soared to more than US$50 per barrel, almost doubling since 2001, and had hit a record of nearly US$140 per barrel in 2008.

Producers in 2005 were under tremendous political pressure from consuming nations to bring down oil prices and were pumping close to capacity, enabling refiners and other buyers to boost supplies in times of increased demand. Despite an increase in the flow of oil, inadequate capacity at U.S. refineries was a major factor in the gas problem of the mid-2000s, and sites for new refineries were proposed while the U.S. increasingly relied on imported gas. Beginning in 1976, demand for gas in the U.S. had grown about 33 percent, but no new refineries had been constructed. Approximately 325 refineries existed in the U.S. in 1981 with only about 150 remaining as of the mid-2000s. However, due to the expansion of existing plants, capacity had fallen only 11 percent. The International Energy Agency predicted an increase in global demand of 1.81 million b/d during 2005, an increase from earlier forecasts due to increased demand in China and North America.

In the mid-2000s, the industry was taking a proactive role in environmentally friendly manufacturing and production practices. Industry giant BP led the way in 1997, and by 2003 had the image of a paradoxically green refiner, with wildly successful "Beyond Petroleum" and "BP on the Street" campaigns. Royal Dutch/Shell had success as well with ad campaigns showcasing the company's respect for marine environments. However, ExxonMobil moved more slowly than BP and Royal Dutch/Shell, so the time the company started running its own green ads in 2004, Exxon products and services were boycotted in some countries.

As worldwide focus moved increasingly toward environmentally friendly industry practices, refiners were anxiously watching the U.S. Environmental Protection Agency's policies for clean diesel that were set to go into effect in 2006. Among other concerns was that of the potential lack of available supply of pure diesel, making compliance with new regulations prohibitively difficult.

When Hurricanes Gustav and Ike struck the U.S. Gulf Coast and refineries were shut down in 2008, Americans experienced a "double whammy." Rice University Energy Specialist Ken Medlock reportedly acknowledged that the U.S. Department of Energy reported the "lowest gasoline inventories since 1967" following the two hurricanes.

RESEARCH AND TECHNOLOGY

For many years, the driving force behind innovations in petroleum refining technology was cost reduction. Increasing yields and purity and boosting efficiency were the focus of industry research and development. However, in the 1990s environmental concerns that were promoted by industry self interest and government regulation became increasingly important. These two considerations—cutting costs and reducing environmental damage—were not always at odds with one another, and often overlapped. Operational integrations that improved heat transfer efficiency or reduced energy requirements saved money and were beneficial to the environment.

The search for an efficient means to produce the complex reformulated gasoline mandated by the U.S. Clean Air Act was one aspect of pollution prevention that prompted several technological advances involving four-carbon compounds, including butylene, isobutane, and isobutylene. Less harmful than the six-carbon aromatics like benzene that were previously used in gasoline, these compounds could be combined with methanol to form oxygenates, which could provide the oxygen needed in the new gasoline standard. Of these possible oxygenates, methyl tertiary butyl ether (MTBE), which was a combination of isobutylene and methanol, was most promising.

Among the technologies developed was a system that integrated the isomerization of n-butene to isobutylene with an MTBE catalytic distillation process. This highly versatile system also allowed ethanol to be substituted for methanol to produce ethyl tertiary butyle ether (ETBE). Substituting the five-carbon compound isoamylene for isobutylene enabled production of tertiary amyl butyl ether (TAME), which was also expected to be important in future gasoline formulations and boasted an even higher octane content than MTBE.

As in other industries, the ability of computers to rapidly record, compile, and recall enormous volumes of data resulted in rapid improvements in efficiency. Computers could measure, monitor, and control refinery processes with pinpoint precision, while their modeling and diagramming capabilities made it possible to develop new processes more quickly and refine existing ones. With the help of increasingly sophisticated computers, petroleum refiners were expected to be able to develop more efficient, less toxic fuels and create new, high-value-added products.

The ability to develop a safer, more diverse range of products was essential for the survival of the petroleum refining industry. With demand for refined products in the developing world unlikely to offset continued slow growth in industrialized countries and with rapid development of alternative energy sources, the oil industry's dominance of the world energy market was expected to decline at the beginning of the twenty-first century. Only by changing and adapting could the industry expect to enjoy success in the 2000s.

WORKFORCE

Petroleum refining has not been a labor-intensive industry. Most of the processes involved could be implemented using a complex array of machinery rather than personnel. Operations were monitored and controlled by computers that in turn were operated and monitored by skilled technicians. Refinery workers analyzed data, adjusted machinery as necessary, repaired equipment, and checked output. Mechanical engineers improved and developed new machinery. Chemical engineers analyzed and monitored the cracking processes. Scientists worked to develop new techniques and products. The overall level of skill required for refinery workers necessitated that management, at least at the plant level, was frequently drawn from the engineering ranks and thus had a better understanding of, and relationship with, employees.

The increasing automation and streamlining of refining operations in the early 1990s by most refiners along with the merging of downstream operations in the later 1990s resulted in a steady reduction in the labor force. Amoco alone dropped 8,500 workers from its payroll in 1992, and dozens of other companies followed suit. Plant closures and downsizing resulted in large numbers of workers being laid off in many countries, with no prospects of rehiring.

Nevertheless, this restructuring had its positive side. In 1993, a trend-setting three-year arrangement was made in the United States between the major oil refiners and the Union of Oil, Chemical, and Atomic Workers. According to the *Monthly Labor Review,* the deal "struck a new balance between the union's goal of improved wages and benefits, safety concerns, and a national health care program and the companies' desire to contain costs and retain operational flexibility." Meanwhile, in Great Britain, BP sought to revitalize itself by giving individuals more responsibility and replacing hierarchically structured departments with smaller, more flexible teams that had open, informal lines of communication. Similar initiatives were launched by Canada's Imperial Oil, which earned a reputation for supporting education and innovative employee assistance programs. However, as large refining firms continued to consolidate in an effort to cut costs and as the number of refineries continued to dwindle in the early 2000s, employment prospects in petroleum refining were not encouraging.

INDUSTRY LEADERS

BP plc. While Exxon and Shell competed for dominance of the oil industry in the mid-1990s, Britain's largest company, British Petroleum (BP), quietly held its position as the world's third largest international oil company. By 2007, the company was number one worldwide, with sales of more than US$281 billion and a daily capacity of 3.4 million oil barrels.

Another leading oil refining and marketing company in the mid-1990s was Chicago-based Amoco, the fifth largest U.S. oil company with revenues of US$31.9 billion in 1997. The bulk of Amoco's total sales was derived from its refining, marketing, and transportation operations. Amoco supplied products to approximately 9,300 gasoline retail outlets in the eastern, midwestern, and southeastern United States. In the mid-1990s, Amoco was restructured to cut expenses and increase flexibility by making individual business units more autonomous. North America accounted for about 87 percent of company revenues, and the company began placing more emphasis on overseas markets, particularly newly opened markets, such as China.

The 1998 merger of British Petroleum and Amoco pushed Shell further down the list among the largest oil companies in the world. BP Amoco found itself as the second largest company, a position it cemented in 2000 with its purchases of Atlantic Richfield and Burmah Castrol. Eventually, the name Amoco was dropped from the BP name. Sales in 2001 grew 18.5 percent to US$175.4 billion, while earnings surged 32.5 percent to US$8 billion, US$2.2 billion of which was attributed to U.S. refining and marketing operations. With more than 107,000 employees, BP was the leading producer of oil and gas in the United States, and its refining capacity totaled 2.9 million b/d. Plans in 2002 included boosting refining operations in Germany by acquiring a controlling stake in Veba Oil. In 2003 the company had an interest in TNK-Russia.

Exxon Mobil Corporation. The brainchild of John D. Rockefeller, Exxon began in 1882 as the Standard Oil Company of New Jersey (Jersey Standard), which was part of the mammoth Standard Oil Trust. The largest of the companies created after the trust was disbanded in 1911, Jersey Standard rapidly expanded its overseas production and marketing activities. By 1954 it had become the largest oil company in the world. In 1972 the company changed its name to Exxon to end confusion with other companies still using the Standard Oil name.

As the offshoot of Standard Oil, Exxon Corporation spent most of the 1990s vying with Shell for the number one spot in the industry. By 2007, Exxon was the world's oil leader, posting sales of approximately US$404.55 billion. Unlike Shell, Exxon's control over vast stocks of crude oil meant that its earnings from refining and marketing were barely one-third of earnings from the production of crude.

Exxon's slide from preeminence began in the 1970s as nationalization of oil assets previously held by producing companies reduced the company's access to oil. With its reserves shrinking, Exxon's dependence on crude oil for the bulk of its sales slowed the company's growth, allowing Shell to replace it as the world's leading oil company during the 1980s. A further blow to the company's reputation and its balance sheet was the notorious *Exxon Valdez* oil spill off the coast of Alaska in 1989. By 1992 the disaster had cost Exxon more than US$6 billion in criminal damages and cleanup costs. In mid-1994, a federal jury found that the company and the tanker's captain had caused the disaster through recklessness and fined Exxon US$5 billion. The company formally appealed this judgment in 1997, and in 2001 a U.S. Circuit Court of Appeals found the fine excessive and mandated that the Alaskan state court lower the fine.

Mobil Corporation, another company generated from the breakup of the Standard Oil Trust, recorded sales of US$58.4 billion in 1997. The world's fourth largest oil company, Mobil owned more than 20 refineries in 12 countries and operated about 18,400 service stations in more than 90 countries. Refining and marketing operations accounted for US$55.01 billion in sales.

When Exxon and Mobil merged to form Exxon Mobil in 1999, a new industry leader was born. In the 1990s, Exxon focused on lowering costs and selling non-strategic assets. After the merger, Exxon Mobil considered the U.S. market to be mature and concentrated its refining and marketing investments in the Asia/Pacific region and the newly-opened markets of Eastern Europe in an effort to cut costs. After reaching a peak of US$232.7 billion in revenues in 2000, sales declined 6.8 percent to US$212.9 billion the following year. After reaching an unprecedented US$17.7 billion in 2000, earnings also declined to US$15.5 billion in 2001. Exxon Mobil's refining capacity was roughly 6 million b/d and the company reported 123,000 employees.

Royal Dutch/Shell Group. Royal Dutch/Shell Group was created by the partnership of Netherlands-based Royal Dutch Petroleum and Great Britain-based Shell Transport and Trading parent companies that shared a 60–40 interest in the group's holding companies. In 1997, Shell's two joint ventures with Texaco and Saudi Arabian Oil Company combined to form the largest refining and marketing operation in the United States. The venture ran 12 refineries that handled 11.4 percent of overall U.S. refinery capacity and almost 26,000 gas stations that had a 17.5 share of the U.S. market. Shell's refining, marketing, and transporting activities accounted for about 80 percent of its total business in 1997, with the company deriving 46 percent of its sales from Europe, 22 percent from the United States, 19 percent from Asia, and the remaining 13 percent from other countries in the Western Hemisphere. In the late 1990s, however, downstream activities like refining and marketing, particularly in the United States, were largely overlooked in favor of upstream ventures.

After decades of being in second place behind Exxon, Shell emerged in the 1990s as the world's largest petroleum and natural gas company with 1997 sales of US$128.7 billion and 47 refineries. However, by 2003, the company had slipped to number three.

Shell was the leading employer in the industry with 101,000 employees in more than 100 countries worldwide. By 2000, however, the firm's work force had fallen to 90,000. Sales in 2001 fell 9.3 percent to US$135 billion, but by 2003 they had risen to US$201.7 billion. Group leadership alternated between the two parent companies, which maintained headquarters in The Hague and London. For the most part, however, Shell's overseas subsidiaries operated almost entirely independently of the parent companies and were giant international corporations in their own right. By 2007, the company reported sales of US$355.8 billion.

In 2001, only US$500 million of Shell's US$10.8 billion in earnings was attributable to U.S. refining and marketing operations. To augment its presence in this area, in 2002 the firm acquired the oil refining operations of Motiva and Equilon from ChevronTexaco. However, some analysts believed the firm was late in taking advantage of the industry's improved profit margins, which had already begun to decline as a recession continued in the United States.

ChevronTexaco Corp. Formed by the 2001 merger of California-based Chevron and New York-based Texaco, ChevronTexaco was the fourth largest integrated oil company in the world in 2008. To gain regulatory approval for the merger, ChevronTexaco agreed to sell its Motiva and Equilon oil refining operations to Royal Dutch/Shell. The company's Caltex Petroleum subsidiary was responsible for the majority of the firm's remaining refining operations, which had been a joint venture between Chevron and Texaco. The company reported 2007 sales of US$220.91 billion.

Texaco was founded in 1902 by "Buckskin Joe" Cullinan as The Texas Company to exploit oil discoveries in Texas and reapidly expanded around the world. In 1936, it formed Caltex with Standard of California, and the two companies used their combined resources to market their products overseas and to exploit Standard's discoveries in Saudi Arabia. In the 1930s, The Texas Company became the first oil company to operate service stations in the United States.

Renamed Texaco in 1959, the company lost ground to other oil companies as U.S. wells dried up in the 1960s and 1970s and overseas supplies were lost to third world nationalizations. The company's position was further undermined in 1983 when it purchased Getty Oil for US$8.6 billion only to find out that Getty had already agreed to an acquisition by Pennzoil. Ordered to pay Pennzoil US$10.53 billion in damages, Texaco sought bankruptcy protection in 1987, agreeing to a US$3 billion settlement with Pennzoil later that year. In 1988, the company sold Texaco Canada, which was followed by the sale of its West German subsidiary and 2,500 unprofitable gas stations. By 1989, Texaco had recovered sufficiently to launch a refining and marketing joint venture, Star Enterprise, with Saudi Arabian Oil Company (Saudi Aramco).

In the 1990s Texaco's 50-50 refining and marketing joint venture with Chevron—Caltex Petroleum—began upgrading refineries and improving its marketing network in the Asia-Pacific region. Texaco's U.S. refining and marketing businesses were operated within joint ventures with Royal Dutch/Shell and Saudi Aramco. Texaco had divested its non-core chemical operations in the 1990s to focus its resources on petroleum.

Chevron, another one-time Standard Oil subsidiary, was originally named the Standard Oil Company of California (Socal) and like many of its other ex-Standard stable mates, quickly established itself as a major international company. In the 1930s, Socal had been awarded drilling concessions to oil fields in Bahrain and Saudi Arabia that proved so vast that the company brought in Texaco to help market the crude. The two companies formed Caltex (California Texas Oil Company), which remained a prime source of revenue for both companies throughout the remainder of the century. Renamed Chevron in 1984, the company engaged in extensive restructuring in the early 1990s, announcing plans in 1993 to sell refineries in Texas and Pennsylvania, while simultaeously building a refinery in Thailand and expanding refineries in Singapore and Korea. Further restructuring in 1997 resulted in the sale of a refinery and 450 service stations in the United Kingdom to Royal Dutch/Shell.

Chevron proudly announced the exciting potential for its Blind Faith well in the Gulf of Mexico. "First oil from Blind Faith is another milestone in Chevron's efforts to tap the vast deepwater energy resources in the Gulf of Mexico," Chevron North America Exploration and Production President Gary Luquette explained. Chevron had the largest presence in the Gulf of Mexico, where the company projected production levels of up to 70,000 b/d to help the United States meet demand for oil.

Total S.A. Total S.A. was the largest oil company in France with 2004 revenues of US$166.2 billion and derived more than one-half of its sales from downstream operations. Total had reserves of 11.1 barrels of oil, 28 refineries, and more than 16,000 Total, Elf, or Fina brand gas stations in more than 100 countries, primarily in Europe and Africa. Formerly majority-owned by the French government, Elf was fully privatized by 1996 and was aggressively seeking acquisitions in the mid-1990s, mainly for its chemicals unit, which was responsible for about 20 percent of overall revenues.

Total operated refineries throughout Europe as well as 4,763 service stations in Europe, 2,345 in Africa, and 771 elsewhere in 1997. The French government held a substantial stake in Total for a long period of the company's history, but by 1997 the government's interest was less than 1 percent. After acquiring Belgium's Petrofina in 1999, Total changed its name to Total Fina. The following year, Total Fina acquired Elf Aquitaine to form Total Fina Elf S.A., the fifth largest oil firm in the world. The merger resulted in sales growth of 153 percent to US$107.89 billion, while earnings soared 324 percent to US$6.5 billion. The company reported 45,500 employees and 2007 sales of US$233.825.

MAJOR COUNTRIES IN THE INDUSTRY

Petroleum refining was one of the first industries to become truly international in scope. Originally concentrated in or near the oil fields, the industry shifted to the major consuming nations to avoid the dangers of political instability in producing nations. Inexpensive oil and larger crude tankers made this move feasible. OPEC's inability to sustain high prices for its crude oil led exporting nations to build large refineries in their own countries and invest in existing refining operations in industrialized countries. Saudi Arabia's Arabian-American Oil Company (Aramco), for example, gained control over 50 percent of Texaco's refining business in Texas. In addition, Pemex, Mexico's state-owned oil company, entered a joint venture in 1993 with Shell Oil Company to upgrade Shell's refinery in Deer Park, Texas. Meanwhile, U.S. firms were building facilities in Southeast Asia and Africa, while Shell was adding capacity in the Pacific Rim and Latin America.

Global production of refined petroleum products in 2004 was 71.72 million b/d. North America led refinery production, followed by the Asia-Pacific region, Europe, the Middle East, Central and South America, the former Soviet Union, and Africa. The largest single producer was the United States, followed by Russia, Japan, and China. Consumption of refined petroleum products followed a similar pattern, although demand exceeded production in both North America and Asia. The United States, the Russian Federation, and Japan accounted for 40 percent of global consumption in the mid-1990s, although China's use had increased dramatically by the end of the decade. China's oil imports, including refined petroleum products, grew from less than 30 metric tons in 1998 to nearly 70 metric tons in 2000. China was considered a key growth market for petroleum refiners with energy consumption levels second only to the United States and projected 4 percent growth in consumption annually through the early 2000s.

Aaron Brady, an analyst with Cambridge Energy Research Associates, confirmed that no oil refineries had been built in the United States since the 1970s. However, plans for a new refinery in South Dakota were awaiting approval in mid-2008 and Motiva announced plans to double the capacity of its Port Arthur, Texas, refinery, making it the largest U.S. refinery. These plans, along with expanded global capacity, could help meet the annual 1 percent increase in demand.

Although dozens of U.S. refineries were shut during the 1990s and early 2000s, overall U.S. production and capacity did not drop significantly because expansion and upgrading of remaining facilities picked up the slack. In many cases, refineries were sold by U.S. companies to foreign "upstream" operations seeking to diversify. Moreover, because the difficulties of the petroleum industry in the United States were paralleled in other leading producers, especially Canada and western Europe, the U.S. share of the world market remained stable throughout the 1990s. U.S. crude oil distillation capacity totaled 16.5 million b/d in the early 2000s, compared to 6.7 million b/d in Russia, 4.9 million b/d in Japan, and 4.3 million b/d in China. Given the relative saturation of North American and European petroleum markets, leading U.S. refiners focused increasing attention on new markets in eastern Europe and Southeast Asia in the late 2000s.

BIBLIOGRAPHY

"BP Releases 'Statistical Review of World Energy 2004.'" *EERE Network News,* 16 June 2004.

"Chevron Announces First Oil From Blind Faith Field in Gulf of Mexico." Chevron Press Releases, 12 November 2008. Available from www.chevron.com.

Davidson, Paul. "Oil Refineries Can't Keep Pace With Demand." *USA Today,* 13 June 2008.

Draper, Deborah J., ed. *Business Rankings Annual.* Detroit: Thomson Gale, 2004.

"Energy Markets Turbulent But Strong in 2003." BP, 15 June 2004. Available from www.bp.com.

Flakus, Greg. "Fuel Shortage in Parts of US Caused by Shut Down of Refineries During Hurricanes." *Voice of America News,* 20 September 2008. Available from www.voanews com.

"Global Output Struggles to Meet Demand." *World Oil,* February 2005.

Greenberg, Karl. "Gas Companies Blend Profits, Messages of Saving Nature." *Brandweek,* 21 June 2004.

———. "More Green than Ever Before (Petrol)." *Brandweek,* 23 June 2003.

"Hoover's Company Capsules." *Hoover's Online,* 2008. Available from www.hoovers.com.

"IEA Raises Global Demand Forecast." *Global Markets,* 14 March 2005.

"International Trade Statistics." World Trade Organization, 2003. Available from www.wto.org.

Lazich, Robert S., ed. *Market Share Reporter.* Detroit: Thomson Gale, 2004.

Lorenzetti, Maureen. "Lower Expectations." *Oil and Gas Journal,* 23 September 2002.

"M&A Value Dropped in 2001." *Oil Daily,* 17 January 2002.

McHardy, Daniel. "Is U.S. Financial Crisis a Hurdle for Refinery Project?" *New Brunswick business Journal,* 2 October 2008. Available from www.nbbusinessjournal.canadaeast.com..

"Oil Giants Face New Competition For Future Supply." *The Wall Street Journal,* 19 April 2005.

"Petroleum Refining in France, Germany, UK, US." *Euromonitor,* August 2004. Available from www.euromonitor.com.

Roberts, Dexter, and Mark L. Clifford. "China: Hungry for Energy." *Business Week,* 24 December 2001. Available from www.businessweek.com.

Schwartz, Nelson D. "Inside the Head of BP." *Fortune,* 26 July 2004.

"Steep Weekly Rises in U.S. Oil Supply Cuts Price 4.8 Percent." *The New York Times,* 28 April 2005.

"US Sales." *Oil and Gas Journal,* 4 June 2001.

PROFESSIONAL SERVICES

───────■───────

ACCOUNTING, AUDITING, AND BOOKKEEPING SERVICES

NAICS CODE(S)

541211. Industry firms furnish accounting, bookkeeping, and related auditing services to organizations and individuals. Although accounting firms may offer data processing as part of their service, companies that provide strictly financial data processing services, such as corporate payroll, are treated separately in **Data Processing Services.**

INDUSTRY SNAPSHOT

Accounting, auditing, and bookkeeping are three dimensions of a single, broad industry. Together, they provide businesses and individuals with the financial information they need to maintain stability as well as to gauge and interpret fiscal health. Accountants and auditors perform a range of functions, such as financial record keeping and analysis, business advising, and auditing, for diverse employers or clients, including large corporations, non-profit organizations, government agencies, small companies, and wealthy individuals. In contrast, bookkeepers typically work in small firms, performing the financial record keeping for the companies for whom they work. Additional duties of bookkeepers may include the production of financial statements and reports, preparation of bank deposits and payroll checks, purchasing, and invoicing.

The rapid globalization of the accounting industry has accompanied the general globalization of commerce as major accountancy firms have grown from small national partnerships to multinational enterprises. Four large multinational accounting and auditing firms dominated the industry in 2005. The "Big Four," ranked in order by most recent fiscal year (2009 or 2010) global revenue, were Deloitte LLP with revenues of US$26.6 billion, PricewaterhouseCoopers with US$26.6 billion, Ernst & Young International with US$21.3 billion, and KPMG International with US$20.1 billion.

The biggest change to hit the financial sector in decades was the Sarbanes-Oxley Act of 2002, which resulted from several large corporate scandals involving Enron, Arthur Andersen, and WorldCom. The Act defined criminal and civil penalties for securities violations; required auditors to be independent of their clients; and increased the amount of disclosure required regarding financial statements, insider trading, and executive compensation. Accounting firms were forced to separate their auditing business from their consulting business in order to comply with the Act's independence requirements. The Act's rules also have meant an increase in the requirements of firms and its auditors, which in turn have meant increased costs. These increases have led many companies to leave the Big Four accounting firms, and in 2004, each of the Big Four lost more customers than they gained.

The accountancy boards that oversee training are almost entirely domestic bodies. This has created a profession represented largely by national bodies that meet the needs of domestic bodies or sectors of it. Accounting firm specialties may include auditing, taxation, insolvency, or forensic accounting. Other dynamics include in-house work for companies or organizations in the private, public, or voluntary sectors. Each accounting specialty has different training requirements. The International Federation of Accountants function was to focus on educating accountants to work in their own national

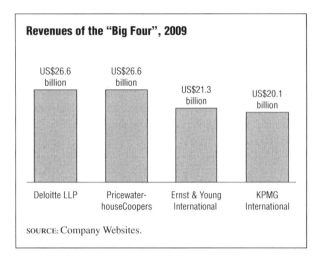

Revenues of the "Big Four", 2009

US$26.6 billion — Deloitte LLP

US$26.6 billion — Pricewater-houseCoopers

US$21.3 billion — Ernst & Young International

US$20.1 billion — KPMG International

SOURCE: Company Websites.

environment. The biggest challenge was to keep accountants up to date in a changing world. Consequently, the Federation provided training focused on continuing education and life-long training.

The mortgage meltdown of the mid-to-late 2000s found the accounting industry once again near the swirl of controversy. Firms such as New Century Mortgage, one of the largest subprime lenders in the U.S. before going bankrupt in 2007, employed Big Four accounting firms as auditors. Fortunately, the accounting firms have weathered the downturn with their reputations in much better shape than was the case during the recession of the early 2000s. The increased regulatory attention focused on the accounting industry may have played a role in that. Accounting firms, academia, and professional associations all noted an improved quality of accounting work since the scandals with firms such as Enron and WorldCom. The close public scrutiny served to improve performance.

ORGANIZATION AND STRUCTURE
Most accounting firms are structured as partnerships rather than as corporations. In a corporation, the shareholders own the company but are financially liable only for the value of their vested interest. In a partnership, the partners are considered the firm's owners and bear unlimited personal liability for the firm. In most cases, firms are structured as partnerships for tax benefits because partnerships are not required to disclose profits. Accountants and auditors often draw criticism for the structure of their firms. Critics argue that accountants, who owe their existence to public laws and are charged with the dissemination of financial information, should disclose more information about their businesses than they were required to do in the early twenty-first century. Most large accounting firms, with many national and international offices, have structures similar to cooperatives, with each firm treated as

a member of the organization and as a separate and independent legal entity.

Four major fields of accounting are defined by the U.S. Department of Labor: public accounting, management accounting, government accounting and auditing, and internal auditing.

Public accountants provide clients with a variety of accounting, tax, auditing, and consulting services. While most public accountants specialize in one area, they may work for large accounting firms that provide the full spectrum of services. Public accountants may also be involved with forensic accounting. They generally have a strong understanding of law and may be involved in the investigation of white-collar crimes, bankruptcies, and contract disputes. Legislation enacted in 2002 restricted the advice public accountants are allowed to give to their clients if they are also involved with auditing their clients' financial statements.

Management accountants are also known by a host of other names, such as cost accountants, industrial accountants, corporate accountants, and private accountants. Generally, they work directly for a company or organization, providing the information necessary for internal management to make operating decisions for their companies, including those relating to costs, performance, budgets, and asset management.

Government accountants and auditors are public sector workers who ensure that government agencies, the private sector, and individuals meet the requirements of regulations and taxation. Internal auditors are responsible for checking the accuracy of their organizations' financial records. Their work has increasingly involved the auditing and control of information technology systems used within a company.

In the 1990s, accounting professionals moved increasingly toward the management consulting side of the industry. However, outsourced consulting services were being scaled back even before the Enron scandal of 2002 because of problems in perceived, actual, or potential conflicts of interest between those hired from auditing firms to check the books of corporations and issue financial reports and those who stood to make lucrative gains by working closely with corporate insiders as management consultants.

Accounting involves all management functions of an organization, including purchasing, manufacturing, wholesaling, retailing, and a variety of marketing and transportation activities. Senior accountants—or controllers armed with financial and accounting knowledge of their business—are often selected as production or marketing executives. Accounting firms rely on two major financial statements—the income statement and the balance sheet—to interpret the financial health of businesses. To obtain these statements, accountants analyze, record, quantify, accumulate, summarize, classify, report, and interpret numerous financial events and their cumulative effect on the organization. Accounting firms help clients make informed business decisions by evaluating an organization's performance and by indicating the possible financial implications of various business plans. Solid accounting practices are thus regarded as essential ingredients in the successful operation of almost all organizations and economies.

Industry Standards and Regulations. Each field of accounting has its own certification procedure, although participation is not always mandatory. The accounting industry is supervised by a number of governmental boards in each country, with increasing calls for a set core of international standards and regulations. This was particularly the case after the industry shake-up following the failure of Enron.

In the United States, accounting rules and standards are set by the Financial Accounting Standards Board (FASB). In the United Kingdom, oversight of the industry is handled by the Accounting Standards Committee (ASC). Working on a more global scale, The International Accounting Standards Board (IASB) independently sets accounting standards and is based in London, England. Board members come from nine countries around the world, but they often are representatives of regions or of several countries. Additionally, the World Trade Organization's (WTO) Council of Trade in Services, one of the WTO's three main subcouncils, established The Committee on Financial Services, which reviews and makes suggestions regarding the global trade of financial services and examines regulatory developments affecting this group. In 2002, the World Trade Organization began a round of negotiations to examine and improve worldwide accounting standards and practices.

Such committees are responsible for defining the rules and processes that accountants and auditors must follow in order to present a clear and honest picture of financial situations. Most of these committees also serve as the disciplinary bodies responsible for dealing with abuses or transgressions of acceptable accounting practices.

Off-balance-sheet financing, bizarre acquisition accounting, and numerous other accounting abuses, such as the creation of offshore partnerships to hide losses and debts, were cited by critics as indications of substantial flaws in industry practices. Furthermore, the industry has been long troubled by auditors' affiliations with the companies that they audit. Auditors, while formally appointed by a company's shareholders, typically report their findings to managers, even when the company's financial records suggest fraudulent practices. Moreover, when accounting firms

also serve clients in a management consulting capacity, the potential for additional conflicts of interest becomes readily apparent. Consequently, the industry has searched for better ways to guarantee impartiality.

One solution called for tougher enforcement of auditing and accounting procedures. In 1997, in light of costly litigation fees that were continuously paid by major accounting firms, the U.S. Securities and Exchange Commission (SEC) initiated auditing requirements that demanded notification if an auditor discovered any uncorrected illegal acts. Steps had been taken already in United Kingdom in the late 1980s and 1990s to address similar issues. The Financial Reporting Review Panel, a sister body to the industry's rule-making organization, was given significant power to deter fraudulent accounting practices. For example, the panel can publicly reprimand companies whose adherence to accepted standards and principles is deemed too liberal.

However, the biggest regulatory change to affect this industry in many years was the Sarbanes-Oxley Act of 2002. Initiated to restore faith in the system following several huge financial scandals, the Act has had a huge impact on the accounting industry and corporations. Highlights include:

- Boards of Directors must have five financially literate members, including two that must have been or still are CPAs;

- It is unlawful for an auditing firm to also provide its client with non-audit services, including bookkeeping, design of financial systems, appraisals or valuations, management functions or human resource services, brokerage or investment advice, or actuarial services;

- Auditing firms conducting more than 100 audits each year must be inspected annually, while all others require inspection every three years; and

- The Securities and Exchange Commission has the power to recognize the generally accepted accounting principles to be used as determined by an independent standard-setting body and is responsible for keeping these standards current and appropriately in line with international standards.

Great Britain specifically had tightened its accounting standards after scandals in the late 1980s and early 1990s. However, all countries were talking about reform in the wake of the U.S. scandals. Increasing levels of globalization in the world economy in the 2000s furthered the efforts of international organizations such as the International Accounting Standards Board (IASB) to create a single set of accounting standards applicable around the world.

BACKGROUND AND DEVELOPMENT

Accounting, auditing, and bookkeeping services developed to meet several needs. Businesses needed to track economic activity to determine and improve their economic health and to fulfill financial obligations, while stockholders and creditors, such as banks, required reliable financial information on companies to allow them to make informed business decisions. The public accounting profession began to serve these dual needs.

The roots of the modern accounting industry can be traced back more than 100 years to the formation of the auditing business and the development of generally accepted accounting principles (GAAP). These rules became increasingly necessary with the rise of multinational corporations and the introduction of complicated tax laws. However, as some industry critics pointed out in 2002, the multiple conflicting ways in which GAAP rules were interpreted have often produced misleading and incompatible financial statements, which heightened the need for more globally accepted and implemented standards.

By the beginning of the twenty-first century, the leading accounting firms had become high-tech marvels, providing not only auditing services, valuations, and tax-planning strategies to the world's largest corporations, but also guidance in areas such as risk management, mergers and acquisitions, corporate financing, and production. In 2002, projections were that this blend would change. Following the Enron crisis, an irate U.S. public and Congress demanded greater transparency in industry practices and better precautions to ensure that the types of conflicts of interest that had seriously jeopardized the financial health of a number of U.S. corporations would no longer be permitted.

The waters of high finance are potentially treacherous. Several events in the 1980s began to cast an unfavorable light on the giants of the accounting industry. "On both sides of the Atlantic," according to the *Economist,* accountants "found it hard to resist accounting wheezes urged on companies by clever advisors keen to boost reported earnings per share. In Britain, fiddles of this sort were easier because accounting standards were too flexible. But even in America, with more rigid standards, auditors were buffeted by managers insisting on flattering figures in their accounts." Criticism subsequently erupted when several major corporations went bankrupt, causing substantial losses for many bewildered and unsuspecting investors. Favorable audit reports frequently have preceded the financial collapse of firms, which called into question the integrity of auditing practices. Over a decade before the Enron scandal was the U.S. savings and loan crisis of the late 1980s, when many institutions went bankrupt despite having received clean economic bills of health.

The late twentieth and early twenty-first centuries brought additional turmoil as many people suspected that auditors' affiliations with managers had caused them to overlook shady financial records at the expense of shareholders to whom auditors are bound to report accurate information. This resulted in record numbers of malpractice lawsuits being filed against accounting firms. The accounting profession responded by re-examining legal and ethical issues, and the pace of these inquiries accelerated significantly in 2002.

Toward the end of the 1990s, several large multinational accounting firms, known worldwide as the Big Six, dominated the industry and generated a substantial amount of total industry revenue. Although their corporate names and identities varied somewhat depending on the location of their headquarters, in the United States, the Big Six included Price Waterhouse, Coopers & Lybrand, KPMG, Arthur Andersen, Ernst & Young, and Deloitte & Touche. In the early 1990s, uncontested dominance by the Big Six accounting firms was balanced somewhat by the fast growth of small firms. However, by the end of the decade, global corporations re-emerged as the fastest growing in the industry, outpacing their smaller counterparts worldwide and swallowing them up in record numbers.

Operations of the Big Six firms in the international arena increased faster than their U.S. operations did due to the rapid expansion of the world marketplace. The nations of Eastern Europe and the Commonwealth of Independent States moved quickly to privatize their accounting industries and update them to meet international standards, creating a very competitive environment for the large multinational accounting firms. Moreover, despite Asian economic turmoil in 1997 and 1998, major industry players continued their efforts to develop a strong presence in Asia in the late 1990s.

By the end of the twentieth century, mergers and acquisitions had become another trend very much at the forefront of the industry. While the Big Six proceeded to acquire smaller firms, merger proposals within the Big Six remained rampant. A planned merger between Ernst & Young and KPMG was abandoned in 1998, even as Coopers & Lybrand and Price Waterhouse simultaneously moved forward with their merger plans. However, not all industry players greeted such news with open arms. The *Financial Times* reported that the Coopers & Lybrand–Price Waterhouse deal received chilly reception from European Union regulators, who suspected that the merger, which the firms claimed would stimulate competition and benefit clients, actually would mainly benefit the firms' partners. The deal nonetheless cleared regulatory hurdles, and by 2001, PricewaterhouseCoopers had become the largest U.S. firm offering auditing and accounting, tax services, and management advisory services (MAS).

As markets opened in former Communist nations and developing countries in the late twentieth century, accounting firms found tremendous opportunities for growth by capitalizing on these largely untapped markets. While these countries worked quickly to update their systems of accounting and financial management to align them with international standards, major multinational firms mobilized en masse to set up shop in these emerging markets. However, while growth in these markets accelerated in the late 1990s, a great deal of uncertainty remained as to whether and when these ventures would begin to generate substantial profits.

Lawsuits and Liability. As a competitive business, the members of the accounting industry battle each other several ways. However, litigation in the form of fraud lawsuits, which progressively had threatened accounting firms from the 1980s through the early twenty-first century, continued to be a concern that united all members of the profession. In fact, major U.S. firm Laventhol and Horwath succumbed to bankruptcy under a barrage of lawsuits, prompting some analysts to speculate that one of the Big Six might follow. By early 2002, Arthur Andersen executives were scrambling to prevent a similar fate for their firm. In recognition of this increased threat, five of the Big Six created limited liability partnerships in the 1990s to shield their partners from mistakes made by their peers.

In addition, many firms began to take steps such as client screening and peer review to ensure greater quality control. During the 1990s, the industry readjusted, with some accounting firms dropping clients that were in high-risk categories. Some accounting firms would no longer accept new clients that posed potential risks, such as fledgling companies preparing for an initial public offering. Nevertheless, lawsuits continued to haunt the industry at the beginning of the twenty-first century. In addition, to reduce legal costs and avoid the federal court system, accounting firms sometimes pursued alternative dispute resolution methods, particularly mediation and arbitration.

The intense competition of the 1980s led to permanent changes in the accounting industry. Faced with shrinking profit margins in their core businesses, accounting firms moved into new areas of business in the late 1980s in an effort to pump up revenues. This trend accelerated through the 1990s. The Big Six increasingly shifted their focus to information control and assurance, corporate financing, human resources consulting, and entrepreneurial services, in which firms offered financial advising and operating strategies for international expansion to companies seeking to capitalize on a booming global economy and emerging markets.

The major focus of new revenue in the accounting industry in the late 1990s was predominately in consulting. Major firms restructured to incorporate the lucrative consulting arena and, in many cases, focused their consulting expertise along industry lines. Arthur Andersen was one of the first of the large firms to move into the consulting arena. The company created Andersen Consulting in the 1970s and broadened its products and services considerably. Andersen Consulting developed a specialty in systems consulting and helped many of the world's corporate leaders create systems within their organizations.

While the transition into consulting was successful for Andersen, it was not without controversy. For example, enormous internal debate arose when Arthur Andersen decided to reorganize in the late 1980s into two autonomous affiliates—Arthur Andersen, the tax and audit division providing small-scale consulting services, and Andersen Consulting, providing large-scale systems consulting—to comprise Andersen Worldwide. The massive changes took their toll on some older partners who liked the traditional way of doing things and who watched their influence within the firm diminish. However, by 1997, consulting at Andersen Worldwide outpaced traditional accounting services, with US$6.1 billion in global revenue and annual growth of 25 percent at Andersen Consulting, compared to US$5.2 billion in revenue and an annual growth of 13 percent at Arthur Andersen. The divisions between these two entities grew, leading to disputes over the leadership position at Andersen Worldwide. In 1998, these divisions culminated in Andersen Consulting's secession from the parent company to become a completely separate entity that was renamed "Accenture" in 2000.

Although the trend toward industry dominance by a few large multinational firms was expected to continue, the top auditing and accounting firms had hardly retained their positions by sticking to established formulae. Indeed, the Big Five rapidly expanded their services in the late 1990s, most notably into the fields of financial planning and consulting, including information technology consulting, as corporations sought increasingly high-tech solutions to management and control problems and tasks.

In light of the accounting industry's rapid globalization in the late twentieth and early twenty-first centuries, as well as the numerous accounting scandals that came to light in the early part of the century, one of the predominant issues facing the industry was the need for national and international coordination of accounting standards, principles, and practices. Furthermore, issues of professional ethics were fiercely contested in the opening years of the new millennium. This was especially the case as accounting and auditing improprieties and dubious practices increasingly were uncovered after the collapse of multinational energy giant Enron, which had become the largest energy trading company and was the seventh-largest company in the United States by 2001. Enron's downfall arguably was brought on, or at least exacerbated, by devious accounting methods and the highly suspect procedures of the Andersen staff members who performed Enron's audits. The Enron failure, involving a write-off of more than US$1 billion in investment losses and a US$1.2 billion drop in equity for shareholders, was the largest bankruptcy case ever in the United States as of 2001.

In addition, in the early 2000s, the rapidly accelerating pace of bankruptcy filings by previously profitable corporations, such as retail giant Kmart and telecommunications firm Global Crossing, appeared similarly linked to improper accounting and auditing practices by staff from some of the industry's largest firms. This sparked motivation both inside and outside the industry for a worldwide review of accounting and auditing standards, and also increased demands for new industry norms, a more transparent work ethic, and greater diligence in the oversight functions performed by national and international bodies, including the industry's own professional associations.

A rapid turnaround in this trend toward consulting already was occurring in the United States by the time of the Enron scandal, however. Most large auditing and accounting firms, anxious to distance themselves from perceptions of impropriety, took pains to spin off their consulting arms around the beginning of the millennium. As firms began to outgrow the national standards and governing bodies to which they were bound, calls increased for a clear, concise, global accounting language that was easily understood worldwide and applicable across national boundaries. In early 2002, different nations adhered to different accounting principles, making measurements of profits and assets derived from the same set of information disparate across nations, complicating the accurate appraisal and comparison of companies' financial standings. Consequently, efforts were underway in regional and international forums, including the World Trade Organization, to develop common global standards and practices for the industry.

Another concern of the accounting industry in the early twenty-first century was the way in which firms that use conventional accounting principles account for intangible assets, such as research and development and employee talent. Critics have noted that immediate posting of substantial amounts invested by companies in intangibles, such as human resource development, does not present an accurate picture of a company's financial

health because potential substantial returns are not taken into account.

Federal officials were preparing to propose a series of regulatory changes to enhance U.S. competitiveness overseas, attract foreign investment, and give U.S. investors a broader selection of foreign stocks. A timetable was reportedly being prepared that would permit U.S. companies to shift to international rules that are set by a foreign organization and allow more latitude when reporting earnings. Foreign accounting standards were considered to be weak in some important areas. However, following the failure of Arthur Andersen and Enron, a shift to international standards was expected to eliminate the conflict of interest rules involving limitations on auditors and creditors performing accounting and consulting work for the same client. Consequently, the Sarbanes-Oxley Act of 2002 created an oversight board. Changes allegedly reflected the trend to pushing for global markets that were considered to be essential to protect Americans as they increasingly sought foreign investment opportunities. In the decade ending November 2007, U.S. holdings of foreign stock increased to US$4.3 trillion from US$1.2 trillion.

By 2005, the accounting industry was dominated by a small number of major multinational firms, known as the "Big Four"—the same corporations as the earlier Big Six and Big Five, with the exception of Coopers Lybrand, which in 1998 had merged with PriceWaterhouse to become PricewaterhouseCoopers, and Arthur Andersen, which had crumbled in the widely-publicized accounting scandals of the early 2000s. Together, clients of the Big Four (PricewaterhouseCoopers, Deloitte Touche Tohmatsu, Ernst & Young, and KPMG) included the vast majority of large corporations in most markets worldwide. However, an increase in costs caused by the new regulations appeared to be the primary motivation for more companies to leave the Big Four than to be brought on as new customers by the end of 2004. Managers were also thought to want better access to the top accountants in those firms handling their finances. Small accounting and auditing firms offered lower costs and increased access over that available from the large firms.

The trend toward mergers and consolidation in many industries in the mid-2000s was expected to occur in the accounting, auditing, and bookkeeping services industry as well. In 2004, there were approximately 45,000 firms in the industry, and according to *The Practical Accountant*, by 2014, fewer than 23,000 were expected to still be in operation. In addition, traditional accounting practices continued to become increasingly specialized along industry lines as accounting firms recognized the more varied and focused needs of companies in different industries and began to offer niche services in specialty areas, such as construction, manufacturing, and real estate.

In addition to the changing needs caused by the improving economy and new tax laws, such as the *Jobs and Growth Tax Relief Reconciliation Act of 2003,* the industry was subject to increased governance and oversight. After the fall of powerhouse Arthur Andersen, for example, Congress passed the Sarbanes-Oxley Act as an industry regulator. The Public Company Accounting Oversight Board was set up to examine accounting firms either annually or every three years, depending on the size of the company. In the event that the Board discovered anything wrong, the company would be given up to a year to correct the problem without disciplinary action or publicity.

CURRENT CONDITIONS

The U.S. accounting industry, like that of other nations, continues to work to integrate its standards into a global norm to deal with the realities of a globalizing economy. In October 2010, it was announced that the group responsible for developing the global standards, the International Accounting Standards Board (IASB) aimed to complete its convergence projects with the U.S. Financial Accounting Standards Board (FASB) by the middle of 2011. In the wake of the late 2000s financial crisis, the G-20 had asked the groups to step up their coordination efforts. The G-20 is a group of economic representatives of 19 nations plus the European Union which meets to discuss global economic issues. IASB chairman Sir David Tweedie noted that the standards for financial statement presentation were proving controversial, but that the two boards involved (IASB and FASB) were continuing to work. He also denied reports in the press that the convergence project was in danger of falling apart. The boards were also beginning to consider timing issues of when, once agreed upon, the new standards would take effect.

In November 2010, the World Congress of Accountants met in Malaysia. More than 6,000 delegates representing 134 countries attended, a new record. Attendees included accountants, regulators, government officials, and corporate leaders. There were 183 speakers representing over 40 nations. Among the ideas discussed were the effects of increasing globalization on the field. Globalization was creating tremendous need for accounting services in the economically emerging nations such as China. As this rapid growth has continued right through the late 2000s, the demand is likely to continue to grow.

WORKFORCE

With the increasing requirements imposed by new regulations in the industry, the employment outlook was very positive well into the first decade of the twenty-first century. As global commerce flourished and became more complex, and as technology increasingly worked its way into the accounting and auditing sector, this industry was expected to experience a drop in some service functions and dramatic growth in others. The industry needed to reposition itself to reflect changing workforce needs, especially as corporate mergers and acquisitions continue, as bankruptcies accelerate, and as new software and Internet-based solutions for tax preparation and business management become available.

During the 1990s, employees of most auditing and accounting firms were hired based on their knowledge of three traditional departments: audit, tax, and consulting. Changes in the consulting side of the industry accelerated in consideration of industry problems that followed the failure of Enron and the legal problems of Arthur Andersen. Few large firms were expected to continue their practice of including management consulting as a sideline business, no matter how formidably wealth-producing, because the risks of lawsuits increased with greater public and official oversight of the industry.

According to the U.S. Department of Labor's Bureau of Labor Statistics, in 2008, approximately 1.3 million accountants and auditors worked in U.S. private and government positions. About 24 percent worked for companies specializing in accounting, tax, payroll, and bookkeeping services. About 8 percent of U.S. accountants and auditors was self-employed, down from 12 percent in 2000. Employment for the field as a whole is expected to grow by 22 percent from 2008 to 2018, faster than the average of all other occupations. Helping drive this expected growth would be increasing numbers of new businesses as well as new financial laws and regulations for businesses to deal with. In May 2008, median annual earnings of accountants and auditors were US$59,430. Proper education, such as an accounting degree, and in some cases certification, such as a Certified Public Accountant (CPA) or Certified Management Accountant (CMA) designation, are important ways to qualify for employment consideration.

Corporate clients of auditing and accounting firms tended to hire staff from their auditing companies, which potentially offered the former an inside edge on the best ways to profit from particular methods of accounting. This practice, however, was likely to be stopped, or at least be greatly dampened, as a variety of measures was proposed early in 2002 to require a two-year waiting period before an outsourced staff member of an auditing or accounting firm who had performed a corporate audit could be hired directly by that corporation.

In an effort to curb their costs and help make their clients' services more affordable, in the late 1990s some certified public accounting (CPA) firms turned to accounting "paraprofessionals" to deal with their staffing needs without adversely affecting their billing rates.

Paraprofessionals do not hold a CPA title, but they have basic accounting skills. Some possess a knowledge of bookkeeping, while others have associate's degrees in accounting, and many have bachelor's degrees in accounting. Some paraprofessionals continue their education and eventually earn a CPA. The use of paraprofessionals provides significant payroll savings for accounting firms. Paid at a lower wage than other accountants in the profession, paraprofessionals are generally part-time workers. As a result, the firms pay much less in fringe benefit costs and have the luxury of scheduling more work during peak periods, such as prior to tax deadlines, while paying for fewer non-billable hours.

According to the findings of the Accounting and Corporate Regulatory Authority, accounting graduates in Singapore were especially attracted to the Big Four accounting firms. Deloitte, Ernst & Young, KPMG, and PricewaterhouseCoopers found it was easier for them than for their smaller counterparts to recruit new hires. Approximately 1,000 accounting professionals graduated from universities in the region each year. Women accounted for about 70 percent of the graduates, but only 35 percent of them went on to gain the experience and post-graduate qualifications necessary to become public accountants. The Accounting and Corporate Regulatory Authority concluded that the results indicated that there was a problem retaining female accountants. It urged the Big Four accounting firms to review their practices in order to improve their retention of female accountants in the profession.

Women in the Accounting Profession. Since the mid-1980s, the number of accounting graduates from colleges in the United States has been evenly divided between men and women. By 2002, almost 57 percent of graduates were women according to the American Institute of Certified Public Accountants. The "Management of an Accounting Practice" survey conducted in 1996 revealed that women accounted for 51.3 percent of new hires in the United States. The survey found that the percentage of women owners of accounting firms had risen to 15.5 percent, but a substantial disproportion of men to women in the upper ranks of the profession continued to be noted. The scarcity of women in the upper echelons of the industry was the subject of considerable debate at the end of the twentieth century. Some industry analysts attributed the disproportionately small number of women at the top of the industry to a higher rate of female attrition as women took sabbaticals to raise their families, resulting in proportionately fewer women than men available for

promotion. Significant numbers of accountants interested in working in more family-friendly jobs have found work in the industrial sector or in other financial-service organizations where work options may be more flexible and hours more predictable. As accountancy positions in the industry's top-tier firms became increasingly demanding, accountants looking for greater flexibility were more likely to seek smaller firms or open a private practice. However, some studies indicated that women were not dropping out of accounting in significantly greater numbers than men. In fact, the female turnover rate in accounting firms was only slightly higher than the male turnover rate in the late 1990s—19 percent for women, compared to 18 percent for men.

Although the working hours at a typical accounting firm can be difficult for anyone to manage, some analysts viewed the female exodus from the industry as the effect of institutional bias against women. Nonetheless, the number of women entering the accounting field almost tripled between the late 1960s and the end of the twentieth century. By contrast, the proportion of men entering the accounting profession steadily declined from 1977 through the late 1990s, despite a mild upturn registered at the start of the 1990s.

KPMG did make efforts to better retain women professionals. The firm had been selected by *Working Mother* magazine as one of the 100 best companies for working mothers. A Women's Advisory Board at the firm held networking and training events, and the firm also offered flexible schedules so workers could better balance work and home lives.

INDUSTRY LEADERS

As noted, the massive shift toward consulting posed serious ethical considerations for auditing practices by the early 2000s. As accounting firms took a more active role in the financial strategies of corporate management, the ability of the same firm to gauge the financial outcome of that strategy objectively and accurately became dubious. Furthermore, with the advances in information technology and tax-preparation automation, which was a specialty of some computer outsourcing firms, tax-preparation fees at accounting firms continued to decline, leading the larger accounting and auditing firms to add business and technology services, such as management consulting, to their menu of products. As the International Accounting Standards Committee (IASC) moved closer to a complete international model, however, "traditional" accounting practices were expected to regain their footing. Early in 2002, in order to offset lost revenues as industry leaders shied away from the consulting services they had been offering, industry professionals called for increases in premiums and the price of audits, as well as in other areas. After the passage of the Sarbanes-Oxley Act in July 2002, service fees increased more than 25 percent. By the end of 2003, at least three of the Big Four had raised premiums or dropped between 200 and 500 clients that were deemed too risky, costing those firms millions of dollars in lost revenues. However, despite the regulatory changes, the Big Four continued to amass a large share of industry receipts through 2010.

Deloitte Touche Tohmatsu. The global group of member firms that makes up Deloitte Touche Tohmatsu has its foundations in England, Scotland, and Japan. In 1845, William Welch Deloitte established an office in London and in 1893, a U.S. office. George A. Touche formed his accounting firm in 1898, and quickly opened a New York office in 1900. Both companies expanded their enterprises, forming partnerships along the way. In 1968, Iwao Tomita, founding Partner of Tohmatsu Awoki & Co., later Tohmatsu & Co., started operations in Tokyo, and by 1975, the company was part of Touche's international network of partner firms. A merger of the Deloitte and Touche firms in 1990 created Deloitte & Touche, and in 1993, the international organization was named Deloitte Touche Tohmatsu. By 2003, the company had branded itself as simply Deloitte.

For the fiscal year 2004, Deloitte Touche Tohmatsu reported US$16.4 billion in sales. The company had 115,000 employees in 148 countries and expected its most aggressive growth to come from China and India. By 2010, the company reported revenues of US$26.6 billion and 170,000 employees worldwide. Approximately 49 percent of revenue came from the Americas; 37 percent from EMEA (Europe, Middle East, Africa); and 14 percent from Asia Pacific. Deloitte was the only one of the original Big Six accounting firms that had not divested itself of its consulting operations.

PricewaterhouseCoopers. With its beginning firmly entrenched in the United Kingdom in the 1800s, the PricewaterhouseCoopers of the first decade of the 2000s came into being in 1998 with the merger of Pricewaterhouse and Coopers & Lybrand. The firm reported 2004 revenues of US$16.3 billion, with over 122,000 employees in 144 countries. Approximately 42 percent of the employees worked in Europe, 25 percent in North America and the Caribbean, and 16 percent in Asia, with the remaining spread among South America, Australia, and Africa. The company acknowledged that less than 11 percent of its partners were women, despite having an evenly balanced distribution of male and female

employees. At the end of 2004, the company stated that it was working to improve those figures and that 22 percent of its new partners were women in 2004. By 2010, the firm, now going by the name PwC, claimed that its member firms performed services for 415 of the Fortune Global 500 companies. In 2010, revenues were US$26.6 billion, and PwC reported 160,000 employees.

Ernst & Young International. Although the founders of what became Ernst & Young never met, they each founded their companies in the United States in the early 1900s and died within days of each other. Arthur Young & Co. was founded in Chicago in 1906, while A.C. Ernst and his brother Theodore started Ernst & Ernst in Cleveland in 1903. The firms did not merge until 1989. At the end of 2004, the company reported 100,000 employees in 140 countries and revenues of US$14.5 billion. By 2010, global revenues reached US$21.3 billion, and the firm had 141,000 employees.

KPMG International. With a home base in The Netherlands, KPMG is the only one of the Big Four not headquartered in the United States. Formed in 1997 with the merger of Peat Marwick International and Klynveld Main Goerdeler, the company had 2009 revenues of US$20.11 billion and 140,000 employees in 146 countries.

MAJOR COUNTRIES IN THE INDUSTRY

The United States was the de facto headquarters of the international accounting industry. Although KPMG's head office was in The Netherlands, each of the Big Four maintained a strong presence in the United States. However, for most of these firms, non-U.S. operations had emerged as leading sources of income and were the expected sources for the greatest amounts of new growth. An article in the September 2008 *CPA Journal* emphasized the need for U.S. accounting education to teach the next generation of accountants how to function in a global environment in which international accounting standards would be central.

The United Kingdom, the birthplace of many of today's largest accounting firms, is the home of the International Accounting Standards Board (IASB), which is responsible for establishing most of the regulations followed by companies doing business globally.

The logistics of the accountancy profession in places such as China make it difficult for firms to operate at the level they are accustomed to in nations with more developed accounting systems. Firms with operations in these areas were spending a large part of their resources on training and recruiting professionals. However, many accounting firms were looking at China and India as new areas for growth. In other developing countries, the accounting industry suffered from a severe shortage of available resources and adequate training for accounting professionals.

BIBLIOGRAPHY

"About Tenet Healthcare." Tenet Healthcare Corporation, 12 November 2010. Available from http://www.tenethealth.com.

"Accountants Urged to Look Beyond Financials." *Web CPA,* 11 November 2010. Available from http://www.webcpa.com.

Amaefule, Everest. "VP asks to Harmonize Accounting Formats." *Punch,* 23 July 2008. Available from http://www.Punchng.com.

Beekum, Rakeesh. "Small Accounting Firms Still Have a Competitive Edge." The South African Institute of Chartered Accountants, 14 July 2008. Available from www.saica.co.za.

Brazma, Alvis. "Retail Accounting: Accounting Tasks Made Simpler," 13 July 2008. Available from http://www.bestsyndications.com.

Cohn, Michael. "FASB and IASB Rejigger Convergence Plans." *Web CPA,* 29 October 2010. Available from http://www.webcpa.com.

Collins, Shane, "Layoffs Create More Competitive Job Market Graduates Struggle." *The Rebel Yell,* 14 July 2008. Available from http://www.unlvrebelyell.com.

"Deloitte announces aggregate revenue results of US$26.6 billion." Deloitte press release, 13 September 2010. Available from http://www.deloitte.com.

"Ernst & Young at a glance." Ernst & Young, 12 November 2010. Available from http://www.ey.com.

"Facts & Figures." PriceWaterhouseCoopers, 12 November 2010. Available from http://www.pwc.com.

"Hoover's Company Capsules." *Hoover's Online,* 2008. Available from http://www.hoovers.com.

Krantz, Matt. "More Firms Flee Big Four Accountants." *USA Today,* 26 September 2004. Available from http://www.usatoday.com.

Labaton, Stephen. "Accounting Plan would Allow Use of Foreign Rules." *The New York Times,* 5 July 2008. Available from http://www.nytimes.com.

Lee, Jessica C. "Fallen Giants: Collapse of Big Companies Creates More Scrutiny on Outside Auditors, Internal Management." *Orange County Business Journal,* 21 July 2008.

Nagpal, Sahil. "Accounting Graduates Aim For Big Four Firms." Top News Network, 11 July 2008. Available from http://www.topnews.in.

Newing, Rod. "Business and Mobility Give You the Edge." *Financial Times,* 16 June 2008. Available from http://www.FT.com.

Ramesh, M. "KPMG Sees Big Market in Financial Reporting Standards." *The Hindu Business Line,* 11 July 2008. Available from http://www.thehindubusinessline.com.

Rudov, Cornell. "Industry Back to Profession." *The Practical Accountant,* June 2004.

"Sarbanes-Oxley's Footprint." *Crain's New York Business,* 24 September 2007.

Solnik, Claude. "It's ladies first all across the accounting industry." *Long Island Business News,* January 19-25, 2007.

"Survival of the Fittest." *The Practical Accountant,* April 2004.

U.S. Department of Labor, Bureau of Labor Statistics. *Occupational Outlook Handbook, 2010-11,* "Accountants and Auditors." Available from http://www.bls.gov.

"USA Regulations: Sarbanes-Oxley in Brief." *Country ViewsWire,* 19 September 2002.

"Who We Are." KPMG, 12 November 2010. Available from http://www.kpmg.com.

Zarb, Bert J., and Philip Jagolinzer. "What Are Students Taught in International Accounting Courses?" *The CPA Journal,* September 2008.

SIC 7311

ADVERTISING AGENCIES

NAICS CODE(S)

541810. Advertising agencies produce promotional campaigns and individual advertisements in all media, including print, broadcast, and the Internet. Besides creative work (written copy, artwork, graphics, and Web design), they have expanded their services to include public relations, marketing strategy, and interactive (Internet-based) advertising and market research.

INDUSTRY SNAPSHOT

In truly volatile times, only the strong survive. Many agencies fell victim to troubling economic times. Advertising professionals and budgets have typically been among the first cuts to be made when clients are struggling to keep their businesses going strong. The Adweek U.S. Agency of the Year for 2008 survived losing a US$300 million Saturn account in 2007 and ended up facing rounds of layoffs. Optimism, dedication and hard work were all necessary components for Goodby, Silverstein to turn things around. As a result, the agency grew from 350 employees to 500. Its client roster also expanded to include Sprint. Hyundai, the NBA, and Frito Lay's Cheetos brand. During a fantastic four weeks, four of its exciting new clients signed on and brought the agency US $2.4 billion in business.

After suffering what *ADWEEK* dubbed "one of the worst industry downturns ever" during the early years of the first decade of the 2000s, the advertising industry began to stabilize in 2003 along with the rest of the U.S. economy. In addition to the aftermath of the September 11, 2001, terrorist attacks on the United States, the global industry weathered other storms, including the U.S.-led war with Iraq and outbreaks of severe acute respiratory syndrome (SARS), and was looking forward to better times. Revenue results from 2004 showed that the industry was continuing on its upward trend, although few agencies had yet to reach pre-2001 levels. Forecasts for the industry's performance were positive. Growth was expected to be steady and measured, with Asia being the region where most growth was expected, particularly in China.

During the early years of the first decade of the 2000s, cost-conscious advertisers began focusing on more targeted advertising approaches, including customer relationship management (CRM), to ensure more of a return on their advertising dollar. CRM is a process that attempts to bring together many fragments of information about customers, sales, marketing effectiveness, responsiveness, and market trends to help businesses use technology and human resources to gain insight into the behavior of customers and the value of those customers. Buying decisions have become more influenced by the availability of purchase-related information, and major purchases, such as automobiles, can be carried out interactively, over the World Wide Web. As a result, the specifics of customer wants and needs became key to the industry. The era of tailored customer engagements had begun.

In an attempt to compensate for a dearth of new accounts and worldwide cutbacks by advertisers during the early years of the first decade of the 2000s, new technologies and outlets were used. New business models such as program repurposing, the use of multiple media platforms, and the emergence of interactive TV began to reshape the focus of advertising. Broad-based mass marketing was replaced by more highly focused campaigns designed to target specific consumers. New technological developments allowed advertisers to use e-mail alerts to market directly to pre-selected audiences. By gathering specific data about the particular interests and buying habits of segments of the consumer population and then directing pitches to them, advertisers began to shift from a shotgun approach to a narrower, and supposedly more efficient, strategy.

More demands were made on advertising agencies with the introduction of digital video recorders that gave viewers the ability to fast-forward through television commercials at will. Unlike VCRs, digital recorders store programs on a hard drive instead of a videotape. Initially, analysts projected that such devices would doom television advertising. In some instances, however, such as the Super Bowl of 2002, TiVo, the leading maker of digital video recorders, found that its viewers used the replay option more often for commercials than for the game itself.

High usage of technology pushed Goodby, Silverstein & Partners into the digital age. The 2006 *ADWEEK* U.S Agency of the Year was representative of award-winners who preferred working with pencil and pen but changed how they do business. The agency successfully met its challenge to prove to former and potential clients

that there was a capability for keeping up with changing times. Key to that effort was hiring talent with a wider skills set plus adding digital production and animation studios in-house.

In a 2007 interview with *ADWEEK*, ad industry legend Hal Riney observed that computers and MBAs had relegated advertising to middle management. As a result, ads had become retail-focused and lacked continuity. Riney believed that restricting creativity by focusing on financial issues and strategic briefs has hurt the advertising industry.

According to Scott Goodson, founder and CEO of Strawberry Frog and 2007 Global Future Marketing Summit Chair, there are three key components for the new agency model: ideas, value, and talent. Uniting these components results in a more significant culture where. By creating value through great ideas, agencies are then able to charge top dollar for their work.

ORGANIZATION AND STRUCTURE

Advertising is one of the basic components of marketing. Advertising agencies promote their clients' products, services, and/or ideas through a variety of media outlets, including newspapers, magazines, television, radio, cinema, and billboards. The use of advertising and advertising agencies has spread from a concentration in consumer goods and retailing to virtually all business sectors. Modern full-service agencies provide a wide variety of services to advertisers, including strategy formulation, copywriting, artwork preparation and acquisition, booking of reproduction services, production of television and radio broadcasts, Internet campaigns and research, media selection and buying, market research, trade merchandising, and public relations. Larger agencies may add market research, sales promotion, direct marketing, and public relations to their services, whereas smaller agencies may employ outside specialists for these tasks.

Media advertising is known in the industry as "above-the-line" marketing. Although activities such as direct marketing and sales promotion are often derisively called "below-the-line" advertising because they often employ no creative element, full-service agencies became increasingly involved in such practices in the latter decades of the twentieth century.

Regulation. The National Advertising Division of the Council of Better Business Bureaus was created by the advertising industry in 1971 to provide a system of voluntary self-regulation and as a pre-emptive measure to minimize government intervention in the industry. In the United States, the Federal Trade Commission is responsible for monitoring and regulating advertising.

This combined voluntary and government imposed regulation restricts or bans advertising of particular products, such as tobacco, alcoholic beverages, medicine, and drugs in some or all mediums. In Europe, an EU directive banning tobacco advertising throughout the European Union became law on July 30, 1998. The tobacco industry and the German government challenged the legality of the law, arguing that the European Union could not regulate single-market issues, an assertion with which the European Court of Justice agreed. The court acknowledged that advertising crosses national boundaries, for example, in printed publications. The commission revised a draft directive to prohibit trans-border tobacco advertising and promotion. Tobacco advertising on television is banned in the European Union by a separate law, the *Television Without Frontiers Directive,* which also prohibits the sponsorship of television programs by tobacco companies. The following eight EU countries ban tobacco advertising: Belgium, Denmark, Finland, France, Ireland, Italy, Portugal, and Sweden. The United Kingdom and the Netherlands have announced plans to introduce national legislation to ban such advertising. In 2000, the United States Supreme Court ruled against further government restrictions on cigarette advertising and upheld a ruling that the Food and Drug Administration lacked explicit authority to regulate tobacco.

Li Fang Wu, assistant secretary general for the Chinese Advertising Association, observed that government restrictions in China prevent ads from making fun of the government, as well as certain social programs. Punishment for inappropriate ads may be removal from broadcast, or fines of up to five times the cost of media time.

BACKGROUND AND DEVELOPMENT

Several economic and social factors contributed synergistically to the proliferation of advertising agencies in the nineteenth century. As the Industrial Revolution resulted in expanded production, advertising was used to sell the increased output. The idea of people being content with what they needed was slowly and inexorably replaced with the psychological and sociological concept that a need could be created in the minds of the consumer through advertising. Once that need was established, manufacturers could produce a supply of goods to meet the perceived, and yet very real demand, of a consumer society driven to fulfill its wants as well as its needs.

The democratization of the press and the explosion of both the number and circulation of magazines combined with an increase in the educational level in the Western world to further expand the value of agencies. Early ad copy was typically verbose and used typography for emphasis because of technological limitations. Catchy

slogans and jingles—often coupled with artwork, including trademarks and logos—proliferated as companies competed to secure customers for their products. The early twentieth century brought an increased emphasis on graphic, as well as conceptual, content.

Until the early nineteenth century, all advertisers arranged their own promotions. Rynell and Son, established in 1812 in London, was one of the earliest advertising agencies. Volney Palmer, a newspaper editor, founded America's first advertising agency in the mid-1800s. Instead of buying space for clients and preparing their ads, however, Palmer's firm represented newspapers and sold space in them to advertisers. N.W. Ayer and Son, another U.S. firm, is considered the first client-based agency. Newspapers soon became the primary advertising vehicle, and in spite of the development of many new media formats over the years, newspapers continued to hold the largest share of the global advertising market through the 1990s, despite the emergence of electronic mass media vehicles like radio and television.

As the consumer society became sated, and markets for mundane items, such as detergents, matured and stagnated, advertising took on the role of repackaging the old into the new. It could drive a mass culture to new wants, new desires to have the "new and improved" versions, at least in perception if not in fact, of products it had come to consider "household names."

The spate of mergers and acquisitions in the late 1990s and early years of the first decade of the 2000s that transformed the structure of the global advertising industry is similar to consolidation maneuvers that took place in the late 1980s. The trend's roots go back to the 1961 foundation of Interpublic Group, a holding company organized to buy and manage individual advertising agencies. Marketing conglomerates patterned after Interpublic proliferated in the late 1980s, which saw the formation and ascent of such "mega-agencies" as Omnicom Group, WPP Group, and Euro RSCG Worldwide. Although these groups offered their clients comprehensive services, some combinations caused conflicts of interest as mergers brought competing advertisers under the same umbrella organization. Advertising organizations worked hard to assure their clients that their campaigns would be treated with confidentiality, pointing to their operation of each acquired agency as an autonomous agency. Some advertisers still shifted their accounts to other agencies.

More and more, clients have started to initiate another type of consolidation. Related efforts involved consolidating global media planning and media buying accounts. In 2006, Mediaedge:cia had three major clients—Campbell Soup, Colgate-Palmolive, and Ikea—consolidate all of their global business. Such moves can bring in substantial earnings for agencies. It is also noteworthy that Mediaedge:cia won the Campbell Soup account, worth an estimated US$400 million a year, without participating in a review process. The agency responded to Campbell's request for them to draft a plan indicating how it would handle the new business. A decision was made to award the account one month after presentation.

Along with consolidation, globalization was changing the face of the industry. The internationalization of advertising agencies in the twentieth century was often dependent on their clients' global expansion. As automakers, oil companies, and consumer goods manufacturers established overseas operations, they often took their domestic agencies with them.

As globalization and consolidation shifted the size, reach, and character of new and existing multinationals, they were forced to reach a balance between overall global consistency in their firm's international strategy and the specifics required by adaptation to local or regional cultures. Most corporations that were traditionally centralized began exploring strategies for local adaptation, and those that were traditionally decentralized moved toward integration and broadened their focus to include regional oversight. To achieve these goals, multinationals adopted a multiple-tier system in which overarching international strategy was determined by headquarters, and the regional/local groups determined regional/local tactics.

The top global brands began to influence the makeup of agencies as they demanded that advertising services be localized. This change reflected their realization that local differences be addressed despite the continuing globalization, not just of their specific industry, but of the world economy itself. Budget constraints, brought on by the softening of the global economy, led advertisers to seek more certainty that their message would be presented to an audience more likely to be open to its suggestions. Covering narrower segments of a market, whether determined by geography or demographics, became more important for branding than communications aimed at the masses. Consolidation in the media industry also allowed advertisers to buy diverse marketing packages from one conglomerate.

The World Wide Web, which introduced the world of "dot-com" to the advertising matrix in the mid-1990s, had a tremendous potential for advertising. Nevertheless, because it could not guarantee how many consumers would see an advertisement, it proved quirky and difficult to quantify in its nascent stages. However, by the late 1990s, advances in online tracking technology had helped to elevate online advertisements to a widely accepted, cutting-edge medium.

The years bracketing the turn of the millennium were marked by agency consolidation and globalization in the world's advertising market. Multinational advertising conglomerates that included more than one network controlled 58.6 percent of global agency business in 2000 when the worldwide gross income was US$40.46 billion (including direct marketing and sales promotion). The top three firms, accounting for 42.1 percent of total worldwide advertising industry revenues, were Interpublic, with 15.8 percent (US$6.38 billion); Omnicom, with 13.9 percent (US$5.63 billion); and WPP Group with 12.4 percent (US$5.01 billion). These three firms also accounted for 45 percent of the US$18.94 billion in total revenues the U.S. advertising industry secured in 2001. U.S. sales for Interpublic totaled US$3.64 billion (19.2 percent); Omnicom, US$2.73 billion (14.4 percent); and WPP US$2.25 billion (11.9 percent).

As the twenty-first century dawned, agencies were tending toward centralized media strategy and planning with decentralized media implementation and measurement effectiveness. All major agencies had established independent media-buying companies. In addition, agencies were increasingly unbundling their services, separating media, direct marketing, and specialist support departments. The International Advertising Association research on global best practices in marketing and advertising in 2000 identified some trends it believed would shape global brand management.

- Consolidation will continue across the industry, although agency mergers will reach a point of diminishing returns. A convergence of agency and media resources will result from this consolidation trend.

- The rapid pace and ubiquity of technology will lead to the digitization of all creative work.

- The world will continue to shrink, even though it will be no less diverse; successful brands will have both global and local appeal.

- Wireless communications will enable an "anytime, anywhere" knowledge exchange, and no geographic market will have an exclusive on talent.

- Change will be the only constant.

CURRENT CONDITIONS

In his company's 2004 annual report, the CEO of industry giant WPP, Martin Sorrell, stated that the industry was seeing a rise after the recessionary forces that had affected it until 2003. Sorrell expected growth in Asia, a growing Americanization, the Olympics in Beijing, retail concentration, and a demand for internal communication to aid the industry in its recovery.

In addition to demanding more competitive fees from agencies during the mid-years of the first decade of the 2000s, corporate marketers began to concentrate more on quantitative results, which some advertising industry players admitted they were hard pressed to provide. Some observers argued that this heightened level of scrutiny, which emphasized testing and analysis, was severely hindering the all-important creative process.

Forecasts for the industry were positive in mid-2004, calling for steady and measured growth; no significant spikes were on the horizon. In addition, predictions from industry leaders varied somewhat. On the more conservative end of the spectrum, *Advertising Age* reported that ZenithOptimedia anticipated a 5.7 percent increase in U.S. industry spending in 2004, followed by a 3.8 percent increase in 2005. Specifically, newspaper advertising was expected to achieve growth of 4 percent, followed by outdoor advertising (4.8 percent) and magazine spending (6 percent). By comparison, Universal McCann Senior Vice President and Director of Forecasting Robert Coen projected that the U.S. advertising industry would grow 6.5 percent in 2004, followed by 7.3 percent in 2005.

Citing additional forecasts from ZenithOptimedia, *Advertising Age* further indicated that Europe held the potential to surpass the United States in advertising spending during 2005, as the former finally began to experience a more substantial level of economic recovery. Largely on the strength of Germany and the United Kingdom, ad spending in Europe was forecast to reach 4.2 percent in 2004 and 4 percent in 2005.

One important global market during the middle of the first decade of the 2000s was Asia. Asian advertising agencies were on solid footing, despite what some observers considered a difficult 2003. However, estimates regarding growth in the region varied. In its 14 May 2004 issue, *Campaign* discussed a report from Initiative Futures that placed Asia-Pacific (not including Japan) advertising expenditure growth at 7.4 percent for 2003. More optimistic was a report from Paris-based Recma that estimated annual growth at 14.3 percent. The two reports were somewhat different in that Recma included billings for Japan. In addition, the methodology used to compile Recma's report was criticized by a number of industry players as being somewhat subjective. In any case, with its booming economy and increased levels of investment by multinational corporations, China was expected to make the Asian market an attractive one for advertisers for years to come.

Some technological developments were expected to have an impact on the industry. For example, the growth in digital television meant that viewers have more control over content: they can skip television ads. As a result, some companies were creating branded programs. For example, Deloitte Touche Tohmatsu reported that it created a 30-minute music video program that viewers could select; the Coca-Cola brand appeared throughout the show.

Industry experts noted a move to turn away from lengthy reviews starting in 2005. This meant clients were more frequently moving their business from one shop to another without seeking ideas from multiple shops. Contributing factors included hard costs and soft costs. Those costs included travel expenses and lost work hours, respectively. Substantial savings resulted, because reviews typically cost US$100,000 or more.

Ubiquitous Media Chairman Bob Schmidt proclaimed the potential for promoting usage of alternative media. Options included his successful attempts to advertise on airport carrousels. Clients with budgets between US$50 million and US$150 million were ideal. Schmidt utilized his background and experiences as a founding partner in a major advertising firm to enhance interest in supplementing traditional media plans by coming up with creative alternatives.

Clients and prospects applauded R/GA's ability to integrate tech know-how and the creative process. At the heart of big ideas were breakthrough applications, according to Nick Law, R/GA's North American chief creative officer. They did that with the NikePlus and its design-your-own shoe NikeID application. Furthermore, the agency created the Nike Women Rockstar Workout with pop star Rihanna enabling visitors to craft their own experience. They could also learn dance moves from Rihanna's "S.O.S." music video. Last but certainly not least, visitors could find out where to purchase the Nike Women' clothing worn in the video.

By 2007, advances in the digital age were blurring content distribution lines and causing concerns related to intellectual property protection. In the past, marketers frequently paid additional compensation for extending the use of campaigns into new geographical regions. This does not operate the same way for new digital directions. According to Rick Kurnit, a partner in the Frankfurt Kurnit & Selz law firm in New York, the digital environment provided multiple opportunities for using agency generated content. The announcement that Geico's cavemen, from the auto insurance company's popular ad campaign, were set to appear in a TV sitcom pilot caused *ADWEEK* writer Noreen O'Leary to wonder what might happen if writers sent them on a high speed car chase. *ADWEEK* writer Steve McClellan reported that Brent Poer, senior vice president of MediaVest USA's connectivetissue unit, posed the following question for consideration if the pilot is picked up and a related show cancelled later: Was it the brand or the creative concept that failed? The show actually was picked up, well promoted, poorly viewed, critically panned and subsequently cancelled shortly after initial episode was aired.

O'Leary also pointed out that even before the digital era soared along, the advertising industry was losing out with traditional repurposing of ideas. In its first year of sales, US$4.99 Easy Button novelty items earned the marketer US$7.5 million in unanticipated sales. Although it was adapted from the McCann Erikson Staples ad campaign, the advertising firm did not profit from the unanticipated Easy Button sales. Such cases are cause for concern and debate in an industry where many agencies are locked into traditional work-for-hire agreements.

The global media agency Mindshare was credited with being a great resource for creating integrated mobile sponsorships. Rather than buying ads on shows where competitors spent more money or had special sponsorships in place, Mindshare came up with innovative approaches. For example, The Nextel Cup series of NASCAR races saw integration of broadcast commercials with ancillary content on the World Wide Web and mobile. As a result, consumers were able to obtain more information about the racing circuit plus see interviews featuring drivers and commentators.

INDUSTRY LEADERS

Omnicom Group. Operating as a strategic holding company for three of the world's leading advertising agency brands, New York-based Omnicom was the number-one ranked advertising company in the world according to *Ad Age*. Operating BBDO Worldwide, DDB Worldwide, and TBWA Worldwide to serve its global advertising clients, Omnicom was also operating seven national agencies to serve its U.S. clients, five media services companies (including an asset bartering company and branded-entertainment television production company), and 160 other diversified marketing services companies (including public relations, customer relationship management, and specialty industry communications). Omnicom was also the highest-ranked advertising-related company on the *Forbes* Top 2000 Global Companies list of 2005, ranking at 380 overall. The company employed 68,000 people in 2008 and had revenues of US$13.4 billion in 2008.

Omnicom was involved in a trademark controversy regarding usage of the trademark Fuse. Fuse, an award-winning sports marketing agency with approximately 35 employees, demanded Omnicom discontinue usage of its trademark. When Omnicom refused to do so, Fuse proceeded with litigation seeking an order to prohibit usage. Omnicom failed to report why it chose to use the Fuse name. It had attempted to acquire Fuse as far back as 2000 and was aware of its existence.

With global industry giants for clients, such as Pepsi, FedEx, and VISA, BBDO Worldwide is Omnicom's largest agency, operating 345 offices in 76 countries by mid-2005. This business unit reported gross income of US$1.24 billion in 2003 (up 16.4 percent from 2002). Founded in 1891, the name BBDO is derived from the

name first used in 1928: Batten, Barton, Durstine & Osborn.

DDB Worldwide Communications, created as Ned Doyle, Mac Dane, and Bill Bernbach in 1949, had more than 200 offices in approximately 90 countries by 2009. DDB merged with another independent agency, Needham Harper Worldwide, in 1986, creating a global company under the Omnicom Group's umbrella. In 1997, amid a series of acquisitions, DDB Worldwide launched a joint venture with movie director Spike Lee. In 1998, the agency introduced a new "unified strategic-thinking process" for the agency. The process is based on a framework of "six springboards." They are brand foundations, communications planning, media selection, integrated communication, creative, and evaluation. In 1999 the company acquired Hoffman Reiser Schalt (now Reiser Schalt DDB) of Germany and, as it attempted to broaden its global reach, bought a large stake in Brazil's DPZ in 2000. Sales exceeded the US$1 billion mark in 2004, up over the previous two years, but not yet reaching 2001's level of US$1.245 billion. In January 2005, *ADWEEK* named DDB the global advertising agency of the year.

TBWA Worldwide, like its sister agencies, was headquartered in New York City, but operated globally. In 2005 it was present in 75 countries operating 237 offices. Major clients included McDonalds, adidas, Apple, Nissan, and Sony PlayStation. In 2004, sales for this business unit were on the rise over the previous two years, reaching US$837.9 million, but had not yet reached 2001 levels of US$954.6 million. By 2009, it had 267 offices in 77 countries and approximately 12,000 employees worldwide.

TBWA account leaders and creatives work side by side with media planners from the OMD Omnicom sister shop. The pilot project reflected how agencies are connecting media planning and creative efforts. It was expected to move on to Asia and become a model for servicing clients by offering numerous media options.

TBWA was named the 2008 Global Agency of the Year by *Advertising Age* and *ADWEEK*. It continued to be applauded for its innovative efforts in 2009 when *Fast Company* named it as 24th on its list of "The World's 50 Most Innovative Companies." TBWA was only one in a trio of marketing communications companies on the list.

WPP Group plc. WPP Group's 112,000 employees in more than 100 countries provided communications services to more than 300 companies listed on the *Fortune* Global 500 list. Based in London, the group's largest agency brands include Ogilvy & Mather, JWT, Young & Rubicam, and since March 2005, Grey Worldwide. Billings in 2004 for the group were approximately US$35.7 billion, with 39 percent coming from North America, 26 percent from

Continental Europe, 17 percent from the United Kingdom, and 18 percent from the rest of the world. For 2009, it reported sales of US$10.8 billion.

New York-based Ogilvy & Mather (O&M) was founded in 1948 and first hit its stride in 1950 with its eye-patched "Hathaway Man," an advertising tool for dress shirts that ran for the next 25 years. Founder David Ogilvy took on legendary status, and his book *Ogilvy on Advertising* became an industry textbook. O&M eventually merged with its former parent company, the British group Mather & Crowther. Sales reached an estimated US$706 million in 2003, an increase of nearly 20 percent from 2002. In 2000, Ogilvy Interactive, the interactive division of the advertising firm, and AsiaNet Corp. formed Ogilvy AsiaNet to provide Web development and advertising services in Hong Kong, Korea, Taiwan, and China. The company had changed its strategic focus to emphasize global clients, and by the end of 2004, O&M had a 50-50 split of global versus national clients.

JWT (formerly J. Walter Thomson) has had many of its global clients for a long time; Ford has been a client for over 60 years, while Unilever has been a client for more than 100 years. Founded in 1846 as an agency to sell advertising space in religious magazines, the company was purchased by J. Walter Thomson in 1877, who soon realized that he could make money designing ads for his publications. Developing the first creative department, he is considered to be the father of modern advertising. For 2008, JWT had revenues of US$3.7 billion and 9,000 employees.

The Interpublic Group of Companies Inc. Another New York-based advertising giant, Interpublic had 43,000 employees working in 130 countries in 2005. Formed in 1961, Interpublic was the first advertising holding company, and in 2005 operated under five divisions: McCann Worldgroup (home to global services subsidiaries, including McCann Erickson), the FCB Group (including Foote, Cone & Belding Worldwide), The Partnership (independent agencies), Constituent Management Group (marketing services), and Interpublic Alligned Companies. Total group sales were almost US$6.2 billion in 2006. For 2008, sales were US$7 billion with approximately 45,000 employees.

McCann WorldGroup, which changed its name from McCann Erickson WorldGroup in 2003, recorded US$1.22 billion in gross income in 2003 (up 3.7 percent from 2002). McCann is the lead agency in the Interpublic Group and is considered to be the first agency to consolidate second-string agencies and diversify into less traditional areas of marketing and public relations. Its partners are The Lowe Group and Foote, Cone & Belding Worldwide. McCann Erickson was founded in 1930

and had major long-term accounts that included Standard Oil (now Exxon) and Coca-Cola. Marion Harper, who led McCann Erickson for more than 30 years, founded Interpublic in 1961 as a holding company for an expanding family of autonomous agencies. The concept was shaky at the start but began to catch on in the 1970s, grew in the 1980s, and was the global standard by the 1990s.

Publicis Groupe S.A. Paris-based Publicis Groupe S.A. was the world's fourth-largest communications group in 2004, the number-one agency in Europe, and the number-three in the United States. It is an advertising and communications firm that operates three major global networks, Publicis Worldwide, Leo Burnett Worldwide, and Saatchi & Saatchi. The company also has a healthcare communications network, combining Nelson Communications with the healthcare activities of the Publicis and Saatchi & Saatchi networks. In addition, Publicis owns Zenithmedia, a joint venture with Cordiant Communications, and Optimedia, a wholly owned subsidiary. The firm offers a range of services to companies in 100 countries, with a particular strength in France, Germany, the United Kingdom, Spain, Italy, and North America. In 2005 Publicis employed 38,610 people across 1,000 agencies in 110 countries, and had revenues of approximately US$4.7 billion. For 2008, earnings were approximately US$6.6 billion with 43,808 employees.

Founded in Chicago in the midst of the Depression with eight employees and three clients, by 2005 Leo Burnett Worldwide was the second-ranked agency in the United States, but it also had significant global interests; it operated 95 offices in 83 countries. The company is well known for establishing a number of international brand icons, including the Jolly Green Giant and the Marlboro Man. Burnett's parent company, The Leo Group, merged with the MacManus Group in January 2000 to form Bcom3. Dentsu acquired a 20 percent stake in the new company in March 2000. However, when Bcom3 was acquired the Publicis Groupe in 2002, Leo Burnett became a unit of Publicis. The company's sales reached US$826 million in 2004.

Zenith became the first US shop to eliminate its media buying, planning, and research departments. This move was viewed as a positive step toward breaking down silos, forcing specialists in different disciplines to work more closely together to create integrated client strategies. The idea to create restructured groups, called biospheres, was actually inspired by a client. Verizon approached Zenith with a proposal about creating a team-focused group dedicated exclusively to its business. This approach put more emphasis on clients by placing them at the center.

Dentsu. In 2005, Dentsu remained Japan's leading ad agency, as well as the leading global agency brand. Employees totaled 5,800 by March 2005, with 2004 sales of more than US$2.7 billion. During the early years of the first decade of the 2000s, Dentsu controlled more than 20 percent of the Japanese market and almost half of prime television ad slots. A 15 percent interest in Publicis Groupe, as well as a partnership with U.S.-based Young & Rubicam, has given Dentsu an international presence. In 2004 the agency was strengthening its foothold throughout Asia. It completed an initial public offering on the Tokyo Stock Exchange in 2001. For 2008, earnings were reported at US$20.7 billion with 17,000 employees.

In a speech at the New Year's Back-to-Work Ceremony, Dentsu President & COO Tatsuyo Takashima declared that the new corporate slogan for 2009 would be "Good Innovation." The slogan referenced more than just a focus on technology. It also related to ideas and entrepreneurship.

Havas. France's Havas began as the country's first press agency in 1835. In 1975, the holding company format was adopted, and the company's name changed to Eurocom. This was later changed to Havas in 1996. Euro RSCG is the company's global brand and has a network of 230 agencies in more than 75 countries. It is composed primarily of two divisions: the main above-the-line network Euro RSCG, and approximately 76 below-the-line agencies, grouped in 1999 as the Sales Machine. Havas employs approximately 14,400 people. By 2008, the company earned US$2.2 billion with 14,438 employees.

By June of 2005, Havas's Chairman and CEO Alain de Pouzilhac had spent months battling corporate raider Vincent Bolloré, who had increased his share in the company to 20 percent. Industry analysts were also watching for a takeover of Havas.

Havas soared in 2006 to experience actual growth in its revenue for the first time in five years. This achievement was largely attributed to excellent performance in net new business combined with acclaimed award-winning creativity.

MAJOR COUNTRIES IN THE INDUSTRY

The United States. The United States remained the largest market for advertising in the mid-years of the first decade of the 2000s. In its "60th Annual Agency Report," *Advertising Age* reported that in 2003, U.S. advertising and media agencies achieved domestic revenues of US$10.66 billion, an increase of 3.7 percent from the previous year. At US$9.15 billion, advertising agencies accounted for the bulk of industry revenues, up

3.4 percent from 2002. This paltry growth was a direct result of the demand for more competitive fees by corporate marketers, which served to reduce agency profits.

The global market research firm Euromonitor reported that the top five agencies in the United States accounted for more than 76 percent of the market in 2003. These leading agencies were Interpublic, Omnicom, WPP, Havas, and Publicis. Television advertising was the most prominent sector, taking almost 40 percent of ad spending.

A weak U.S. dollar worked to the advantage of U.S. agencies with global operations, as they were able to earn revenues in comparatively stronger foreign currencies. According to *Advertising Age,* the leading 457 advertising and media agencies in the United States saw revenues from international operations climb more than 6 percent in 2003, reaching US$9.88 billion. In all, U.S. agencies saw total worldwide revenues climb nearly 5 percent in 2003, reaching US$20.54 billion.

Japan. As of 2003, Japan was the world's second-largest market in terms of advertising expenditures. That year, expenditures grew 2 percent. ZenithOptimedia indicated that Japan was poised for 3 percent growth in 2004 and 1.5 percent in 2005, which was substantial after several years of virtually no growth. The Ministry of the Economy reported that revenue grew 1.2 percent in April 2005, with employment in the industry also increasing 1.9 percent, providing the second month of increases. The increases were considered the result of consumer spending hikes following a period of economic downturn.

During the early years of the first decade of the 2000s, advertising expenditures in Japan reached US$46 billion. Television was the largest sector with 34 percent of the total market, and Internet, or interactive, advertising was the smallest sector with 1 percent. The major media outlets in Japan are newspapers, magazines, and television. There is little cable penetration. Japan has the world's highest literacy rate, and 99 percent of Japanese households have newspaper delivery. Japan's newspapers have the world's largest total circulation. Magazines are also widely read in Japan, and more than 200 new magazines are started each year. Many Japanese magazines focus on fashion or consumer life. The Japanese allot more broadcast time for television commercials than Americans do, and 15-second commercials are more common in Japan. Commercials are customarily low-key and employ a soft-sell approach. Beautiful imagery, fantasy elements, and humor are popular techniques. The consumer is sought by indirect messages that appeal to the emotions. The specific benefits of a product are rarely mentioned, and the name of the sponsor is sometimes not even given until the end of the commercial.

China. According to the May 14, 2004, issue of *Campaign,* Market research firm Initiative Futures reported that China was an increasingly important market heading into the second half of the first decade of the 2000s. Although the nation was sixth overall in worldwide advertising expenditures early in the decade, by 2003 it had climbed to third place, behind the United States and Japan. All of the major international advertising firms are present in China. As *Campaign* noted, "All eyes remain fixed on China, where players say there is no sign of a slowdown in investment by multinationals. Instead, adspend for the market will continue to rise as the country ascends the priority list of aspiring global companies."

Television advertising takes the largest single portion of the Chinese advertising market. China's regular television viewing population is 84 percent of its 1.2 billion people. Major articles sold on television include toiletries, foodstuffs, pharmaceuticals, liquor, and home electronics. Television stations in big markets (Beijing, Guangzhou, and Shanghai) require advertisers to book and pay for specific spots two to ten months in advance. A highly charged debate continues between isolationist policy-makers who consider foreign investment a threat to China's economic security and their rivals who see closer ties with the world as the key to financial strength.

For 2007, China's media spending was expected to hit US$14 billion. This soaring expenditure did not mean everything was ideal for advertising agencies. One 20-year multinational agency network veteran indicated how important China had become to the success of agency networks, coupled with the great difficulty of serving as a company CEO in that country. Challenges include labor-intensive requests, speeded up progression from review to production, and average agency relationships lasting less than three years.

France. In 2003, global agencies dominated France's advertising industry, although two of the top agencies were headquartered in the country: Havas and Publicis. Havas led the market with a 24 percent marketshare. *Euromonitor* projected slow growth of only 2 percent up to 2008, with most ad spending remaining with the press.

Havas and Publicis Conseil continued to be the most creative advertising agencies in France during 2003, followed by TBWA\Paris. In terms of billing, Havas Advertising led with EU434.3 million, followed by Publicis Groupe (EU313.8 million), and TBWA France (EU 12.5 million). French Art Directors' Club President Remi Babinet indicated that due to the country's relative reluctance to embrace new or entrepreneurial approaches, it was difficult for small, emerging players to find success in France in comparison to other European countries. To further the concentration of agencies in the country, in

2005 analysts were predicting that a takeover of Havas was inevitable.

The United Kingdom. The market growth for advertising services in the United Kingdom has resulted in the growing size and strength of the local advertising industry. Also, British advertising has a reputation as one of the world's most effective and creative. With the United Kingdom's use of innovative techniques, campaigns tend to be memorable. Advertisements in the United Kingdom range from subtle to outrageous in order to grab attention and provoke a response. This comes from the years when all television advertising came at the end of a program; such sustained periods of advertising required them to be highly "watchable." However, most ad spending was done with the press, which accounted for 50 percent of the market's advertising value in 2003.

After a period of consolidation in the 1990s, the U.K. advertising industry experienced increasing cross-ownership, internationalization, and a centralizing of accounts by major clients. Nonetheless, creative strength has been maintained by granting autonomy to groups within the major advertising companies. As brands and products mature from a regional to a national, international, and global focus, U.K. advertising companies have expanded their clientele worldwide. In 2003, France's Publicis Group was the leader in the U.K. market, according to Euromonitor. Along with Germany, the United Kingdom was expected to propel Europe past the United States in advertising expenditures in 2005, as the region finally experienced a period of long-awaited economic recovery.

Germany. Most large German advertising agencies are dominated by their U.S. subsidiaries, branches, or affiliates. BBDO Germany, subsidiary to the U.S. agency, was Germany's largest agency in 2003, according to Euromonitor. To increase their competitiveness, many German full-service agencies have entered into partnership arrangements with other domestic and foreign advertising firms, especially from the United States, Great Britain, France, Italy, and Switzerland.

BIBLIOGRAPHY
"60th Annual Agency Report; Revenue for U.S. Ad, Media Agencies Gains 3.7 Percent to $10.7 Billion." *Advertising Age,* 19 April 2004.
"2009: Moving Forward Under A New Corporate Slogan: 'Good Innovation.'" *Dentsu,* 5 January 2009. Available from www.dentsu.com.
"Agency of the Future: Change the Model, Change the World." *ADWEEK,* 5 March 2007.
"Asian Agencies: Asia's Rising Stars." *Campaign,* 16 July 2004.
Baar, Aaron. "Review Fatigue Leads to Rise in Handoffs." *ADWEEK,* 5 February 2007.

"Digital Television Puts the Viewer in Control." *TMT Trends: A Focus on Media and Entertainment,* July 2004. Available from www.deloitte.com.

"France: Who's Big and Who's Clever." *Campaign,* 18 June 2004.

"Major Market Profiles: Advertising in France, Germany, UK, and USA (Executive Summaries)." *Euromonitor,* October 2004. Available from www.euromonitor.com.

McClellan, Steve. "Network Trumps Rivals with Big Ideas and Global Wins, Often Sans Pitches." *ADWEEK,* 26 February 2007.

McMains, Andrew. "Network Pulls Together to Post Impressive Growth, Produce Stellar Creative." *ADWEEK,* 8 January 2007.

Morrissey, Brian. "A Potent Tech-Creative Combo Fuels Its Rise to the Top." *ADWEEK,* 22 January 2007.

O'Leary, Noreen. "The Lay of the Land." *ADWEEK,* 5 February 2007.

———. "Where Do We Go From Here? The Recession Is Behind Us, but the Ad Industry Now Faces New Worries." *ADWEEK,* 22 December 2003.

———. "Your Big Idea, Their Next Big Thing." *ADWEEK,* 12 March 2007.

Parpis, Eleftheria. "Shop Transformed Itself for the Digital Age without Skipping a Creative Beat." *ADWEEK,* 8 January 2007.

Remson, Adam. "Bob Schmidt Is Everywhere." *ADWEEK,* March 2007.

"TBWA Worldwide Named to Fast Company Magazine's List of the World's 50 Most Innovative Companies." TBWA\, 12 February 2009. Available from tbwaworld.com.

Voight, Joan. "Riney Laments the Decline of His Agency, Industry." *ADWEEK,* 8 January 2007.

Wentz, Laurel, and Normandy Madden. "Global, 2002 Outlook." *Advertising Age,* 7 January 2002.

Whipp, Lindsay. "Japan's Service Sector Grows as Spending Rises." *Bloomberg News,* 24 June 2005. Available from www.iht.com.

"World: Media Analysis—Asia-Pacific Media Agencies Ride Out the Recession." *Campaign,* 14 May 2004.

"Zenith Media Realignment Puts Clients in the Center." *ADWEEK,* 12 March 2007.

"Zenith Spending Forecast Shows Growth but No Surge; U.S. Up Slightly; Shift Continues to Unmeasured." *Advertising Age,* 19 July 2004.

SIC 8711

ENGINEERING SERVICES

NAICS CODE(S)

541330. Engineering firms provide professional engineering services on a contract or hourly basis. Such services include system and structure analysis, specification, design, and project management. Many engineering services are integrated with construction activities. For discussion of the construction industry, see also the chapter entitled **Construction Materials and Services**.

INDUSTRY SNAPSHOT

Among the many changes taking place in the engineering services industry—such as consolidation and pricing structure shifts—diversification emerged as one of the most important, particularly due to the economic downturn and construction slump of the early years of the first decade of the 2000s. The number of design-build firms, those which offered both engineering and construction services, grew throughout the late 1990s and early years of the first decade of the 2000s as clients, including those in the public sector, became increasingly comfortable with the design-build concept. By 2003 many companies in the industry were looking to diversify not only products and services, but also location, expanding their focus to international markets. Globalization had become almost a prerequisite for participation and success in the industry.

The forecast for design-build firms beyond the midyears of the first decade of the 2000s was for growing demand from sectors as diverse as transportation networks, water treatment plants, and automotive manufacturing.

The leaders in the construction industry continued to be VINCI and Bouygues of France. Employing engineers in almost every category, the leading engineering firms were involved in major projects around the world. This sector had become truly international in its focus.

ORGANIZATION AND STRUCTURE

Engineering encompasses a variety of disciplines concerned with the design of structures, devices, machines, and other elements of modern industrial society. Major sectors of the engineering industry include civil engineering, mechanical engineering, electrical engineering, petroleum engineering, and industrial engineering.

The civil engineering field is primarily concerned with the design and construction of public works such as bridges, dams, and other large facilities, while mechanical engineering tackles the area of machine, system, and tool design, including plumbing and ventilation systems. A somewhat related discipline is industrial engineering, which studies designs, methods, and processes for effective and efficient production. Electrical engineers, on the other hand, study the technology of electricity for the purpose of determining the design and application of electricity in power generation and distribution, machine operation, and communications.

Associations. Major associations developed in the nineteenth century to bring together engineers and engineering firms involved in similar areas of work and study. Principal engineering associations in the United States include the American Society of Civil Engineers (ASCE), the American Society of Mechanical Engineers (ASME), and the Institute of Electrical and Electronics Engineers (IEEE).

Quality Standards and Assessments. Quality certification is an issue of growing importance to many establishments involved in providing engineering services. While some engineering standards have long been in place, customers in various markets have increasingly demanded significant assurances that a supplier's goods will be of a certain quality. As a result, individual companies using engineering services, in addition to professional organizations, have begun to articulate more exacting quality standards and to require that engineers anywhere along the production chain be versed in such standards. Initiatives to meet these demands include quality certification from the International Organization for Standardization (ISO), which confers certification on companies worldwide that meet various requirements for process regularity and product specifications.

BACKGROUND AND DEVELOPMENT

The engineering industry's various branches of study developed at different periods in the evolution of the world's industrial landscape. Many forms of engineering trace their roots to the Industrial Revolution that began in Europe in the latter eighteenth century and continued in the United States through the mid-nineteenth century. A flurry of new inventions during that period, such as the steam engine, triggered demand for new manufacturing machinery, transportation equipment, roads, bridges, canals, and sanitation systems. Fulfilling this demand were designs by individuals who became the forebears of mechanical, civil, and industrial engineering. Later, when electric lights and other electrical applications were pioneered in the late nineteenth century, the field of electrical engineering was born.

Civil engineers have long been central figures in the construction of bridges and roads. In the eighteenth and nineteenth centuries the major advances in this field of study originated in Europe, especially in France, which boasted the leading schools of engineering education in the world. As Daniel L. Schodek noted in *Landmarks in American Civil Engineering,* "French institutions maintained the leadership in formalizing an approach to engineering education based on scientific principles . . . it was the French system that primarily influenced formal education in civil engineering in America." By the beginning of the twentieth century, a recognizable civil engineering profession was thriving in the United States and elsewhere. The arrival of the automobile accelerated the construction of highways, tunnels, and overpasses, all of which required the talents of civil engineers.

Electrical engineering advanced through the invention of the vacuum tube by Lee De Forest in 1907. This vacuum tube (called a triode) spurred the creation of various devices that could transmit an electrical signal.

As telephone and radio developed, electrical engineering grew as well. During the twentieth century, government and wartime spending subsidized many engineering achievements. Advances in computers, space technology, and the development of the integrated circuit all contributed to the explosive growth in the electrical engineering industry in the latter part of the 1900s.

The entire international engineering industry in the late 1990s was buoyed by a sense of optimism brought about by robust market conditions. Engineering firms in the United States led the industry in the late 1990s largely because of their continued success in securing international business through local subsidiaries. In 1997 for instance, U.S. design firms garnered more than US$25.4 billion of the US$32.7 billion in total world billings. This strong market, however, did foster some problems, such as the growing shortage of skilled professionals, a trend which steadily boosted compensation and benefits.

Other firms around the world also took note of international opportunities in the late 1990s. Europe established itself as the top regional design market in 1997, posting US$2.4 billion in billings. In second place, Asia reported US$1.7 billion in billings, while the Middle East (US$610.9 million), Latin America (US$576.5 million), Canada (US$419.4 million), North/Central Africa (US$334.8 million), the Caribbean Islands (US$114.8 million), and Antarctic/Arctic (US$21 million) followed. The billing figure for Asia showed a dramatic jump in 1997, but the Asian currency crisis that began in Thailand and reverberated throughout the region signaled that 1998 wouldn't be nearly as lucrative. In the meantime, once Asia's design market cooled off, other regions, particularly Latin America and the Middle East, picked up the slack.

The engineering industry of the late 1990s underwent fundamental change. Consolidation increased the level of globalization, which created large enterprises with increasingly international operations, as well as some niche players. The industry also began moving away from cost-reimbursable contracts to fixed price, lump sum, and turnkey design-build contracts. Such arrangements benefited firms that contracted engineering services by providing, in effect, a price cap on how much a project cost. These arrangements also gave the engineering firm greater autonomy and incentive to complete projects in timely and affordable ways. Another major industry shift occurred because clients of design firms were increasingly operating on a global scale; as a result, they began wanting design firms to deliver more than mere designs, *Engineering News Record* noted. This trend prompted many firms that were purely engineering in scope to add construction capabilities to their offerings.

A particularly bright spot for the engineering services industry was the long-moribund market for power plants, particularly in Latin America. In some cases, rejuvenated demand for power plant design more than doubled individual firms' revenues from that sector. Also, demand for cogeneration system design by industrial firms, which improves power production efficiency by deriving more energy from the same amount of resources, continued to grow, and many of the world's nuclear plants, which had fallen into disfavor in many developed economies, were in dire need of upgrade.

An issue of concern for U.S. firms in the late 1990s was the professional liability of engineers for tort actions brought against them for alleged flaws in design work. The average firm turned down US$190,000 worth of work in 1996 due to professional liability concerns; according to the Association of Consulting Engineers Council, fewer than 20 percent of the claims made against design professionals in the late 1990s had merit, based on a survey of 866 firms. In 1996 only 9 percent of the firms surveyed did not carry professional liability insurance, which cost, on average, 2.31 percent of gross annual revenues.

Uncertainty about U.S. government funding for engineering research prompted more than 100 scientific, mathematical, and engineering societies to issue a statement in 1997 calling upon the U.S. Congress and the Clinton administration to double federal investments in research over the next decade, beginning in fiscal year 1999, which began September 30, 1998. In the late 1990s, according to the American Society of Mechanical Engineers, the U.S. Department of Defense was funding about 40 percent of all federally funded engineering research. In fiscal year 1998, US$40.7 billion was devoted to mechanical engineering-related programs in the U.S. federal budget; of that amount, the Defense Department funded US$33.5 billion, followed by the National Aeronautical and Space Administration (US$4.1 billion), and the Department of Energy (US$1.3 billion).

Firms in the United States continued to be leaders of the international engineering world in 2000. According to *Engineering News Record,* the top 500 U.S. design firms collectively posted US$35.1 billion in U.S. design billings in 2000, an increase of 8.1 percent from the year earlier. However, international market billings for this group fell 3 percent to US$7.6 billion. This was partially due to continued uncertainty regarding the instability of many markets in southeast Asia. China, however, was viewed as an increasingly friendly market.

The top 200 global design firms, as ranked by *Engineering News Record,* generated US$16.1 billion in international revenues in 2000. The petroleum market accounted for the largest segment, with US$4.14 billion in revenues, or 25.7 percent of the total. Second was transportation, which generated US$3.17 billion, or 19.7 percent. Third was building, with US$1.63 billion in revenues, or 10.2 percent. Power accounted for US$1.56 billion, while industrial secured US$1.54 billion, and water generated US$1.12 billion. Sewer/wastewater, hazardous waste, manufacturing, and telecommunications all brought in less than US$1.0 billion. In 2000, 168 U.S. firms reported an average profit of 7.1 percent, while 10 firms reported a loss. Internationally, 156 firms reported an average profit of 6.7 percent, while 11 reported losses.

Consolidation throughout the late 1990s and early years of the first decade of the 2000s created several new industry leaders. The merger of Nedeco and Nethconsult, both comprised of several small Dutch operations, boosted Nedeco to second place on *Engineering News Record*'s list of the leading international design firms. The largest firm in that ranking, AMEC, owes its large size to its late 1990s purchase of AGRA Ltd., located in Canada. France-based engineering and construction behemoth Technip acquired Coflexip, a sub-sea engineering and construction firm also headquartered in France, in 2001. The merger, which joined France's two largest engineering and construction companies, created one of the leading engineering and construction firms in all of Europe and one of the world's top five oil and gas engineering organizations. Annual revenues for Technip-Coflexip were predicted to reach US$4 billion in 2002.

Design-build firms gained increasing prominence in the early years of the first decade of the 2000s, particularly in the United States. While global revenues for the 100 largest design-build firms grew only 3.7 percent, to US$58.24 billion, in 2000, design-build revenues in the United States jumped 22.3 percent, reaching US$39.89 billion. According to *Engineering News Record,* although total international design-build sales dropped more than 22 percent, to US$18.35 billion, in 2000, "the trend is clearly away from project-by-project management and toward management of larger construction programs for clients."

CURRENT CONDITIONS

As the U.S. economic recovery seemed established by 2005, the need for skilled engineers was growing, particularly in the aerospace industry. Although product design engineers were in high demand by many industry sectors by 2004, overall growth was below the average for all other industries, due in part to the internationalization of engineering. Project work was being bid on by companies from all over the world.

Those in the engineering services industry understood that to remain viable and competitive in down markets, there must be diversification—not only of products and services, but also of geography. International growth in the mid-years of the first decade of the 2000s was a factor for the major industry players, no matter the home country. Of the reported US$249.3 billion in revenues of the top 25 global construction firms, US$87.8 billion was earned outside of the home country. The Design-Build Institute of America expected that design-build companies would increase their share of the U.S. nonresidential construction market from 35 percent to 45 percent by 2005, and that most of the commercial work would use design-build services by that time.

A trend in the architectural segment of the design-build industry was in the rehabbing of old, urban buildings. Termed "adaptive reuse," the rethinking and revisioning of older buildings can not only save the structures from demolition, but also build up communities through revitalizing an area. Such buildings generally have the advantage of having major systems already in place, which lowers the costs involved.

By the mid-years of the first decade of the 2000s, PLM was emerging as a new must-have technology for design engineers; according to independent research firm Gartner, PLM would be absolutely necessary by 2007 if a company intended to stay afloat. An acronym for product lifecycle management, PLM was software that offered a way for a company's products and services to be managed from start to finish in an automated, accountable, quality-process-control fashion.

In 2008, ASME held a "Global Summit on the Future of Mechanical Engineering." A major related conclusion was the necessity for engineers to be assertive leaders "in developing solutions that foster a cleaner, healthier, safer and sustainable world." An article in ASME's "flagship publication," *Mechanical Engineering,* spotlighted in the January 2009 issue, that engineers had skills related to processes identified as key parts of resource utilization.

RESEARCH AND TECHNOLOGY

All branches of the engineering industry have been profoundly affected by the rise of computers and technological innovations in the 1980s, 1990s, and the first decade of the 2000s.

In an April 28, 2009 speech presented for the 146th annual meeting of the National Academy of Science, U.S. President Barak Obama revealed plans for the Advanced Research Projects-Energy-Agency. Its focus will be to "conduct high risk, high-reward research, and seek to place a market-based cap on carbon emissions and make renewable energy more profitable." American Society of Mechanical Engineers (ASME) President Thomas

Barlow classified the effort as an "historic level for scientific funding" in a letter sent to the White House.

Computers. Computers continued to increase in importance to engineers in dramatic fashion. As computer hardware and software capabilities have grown, a larger share of complex design problems has been resolved using computers, according to *Design News.* Moreover, software has grown more accessible and easier to use for design engineers. Computer workstations with two or more processors on board were the latest trend in hardware systems by the late 1990s. These systems essentially allowed engineers to run two separate, high-power computing operations at once.

The Internet. Some observers credited the Internet as the most important technical innovation to sweep the industry since computer-aided design (CAD) software became mainstream in the 1980s. Benefits of using the Internet for engineers include improved collaboration among engineers, manufacturers, and vendors; increased access to crucial, up-to-date data; and efficient reuse of information.

Prototyping. Rapid prototyping (RP) increases predictability and improves surface finishing. This technology allows engineers to transform their virtual designs in CAD programs to physical models. It allows for early verification of product designs and quick production of prototypes for testing. According to *New Technology Week,* RP includes a variety of technologies, ranging from numerical-control machining techniques to "computer-aided, design-driven solid free form fabrication that does not require human intervention." The United States led this field in the late 1990s, but Germany and Japan were also planning to bolster the use of RP systems. Europe and Japan used RP more than the United States in medical applications, with surgical planning and the creation of artificial limbs the leading uses.

Virtual Design. According to *Mechanical Engineering,* manufacturing and engineering firms around the globe have begun building products using virtual reality. Early adopters have already found that these techniques can significantly reduce the time involved with the design cycle, decrease the need to build actual prototypes and models, and ultimately increase the product's market acceptance and penetration. What's more, the components of the system—computer-aided design (CAD), computer-aided manufacturing (CAM), computer-aided engineering (CAE), and industrial design geometry—can be shared across computer networks, where they can be analyzed and changed if required.

Solid Modeling. In *Design News,* Paul E. Teague noted that software developers across the globe were touting the potential for solid modeling to revolutionize engineering.

Using three-dimensional solid modeling software, engineers can review designs online and change them without affecting production schedules. In other words, engineers can visualize the product at each step along the design route, long before making a physical prototype. Solid modeling allows for early troubleshooting to identify problems while they can still be corrected inexpensively. It also allows engineers to generate drawings quickly, and it allows a change in one part to be reflected automatically in the entire assembly.

Fluid Power. According to *Design News,* in the late 1990s, engineers in the fluid-power industry—particularly those in industrial automation, as well as automotive and mobile equipment design—expected to see increased demand for hydraulic valves and controllers that are compatible with fieldbus technology. According to The Fieldbus Foundation, fieldbus is "an all-digital, serial, two-way communications system that interconnects measurement and control equipment such as sensors, actuators and controllers." Nevertheless, the trend toward increased use of fieldbus technology in hydraulics likely will be quite gradual, primarily because there is no agreement on the protocols or standards those components must meet.

Composites. Some industry observers believe that engineers of the future will have vast new materials options to choose from for designs. Materials scientists have made important advances in the development of composite materials that accentuate the positive aspects and blunt the negative characteristics of materials. Europe, which is at the forefront of composite technology, and other industry participants, are expected to continue to investigate new composite materials that will free engineers from previous constraints in design. Before it was acquired by Germany's Daimler Benz in the late 1990s, Chrysler Corporation unveiled a car with a body made entirely of plastic. Also on the horizon was greater use of a new kind of plastic polymer, called thermoplastic elastomers, which has properties similar to rubber and is more oil resistant than other similar products. According to *Design News,* plastics will continue to replace metal in automotive applications.

WORKFORCE

In 2002 there were 1.48 million engineering jobs in the United States, according to the U.S. Bureau of Labor Statistics. These were further broken out by engineering specialty:

- electrical–292,000;
- civil–228,000;
- mechanical–215,000;
- industrial–194,000;

- aerospace–78,000;
- computer hardware–74,000;
- environmental–47,000;
- chemical–33,000;
- materials–24,000;
- nuclear–16,000;
- petroleum–14,000;
- biomedical–7,600;
- mining and geological–5,200;
- marine–4,900;
- agricultural–2,900;
- all others–243,000

Jobs in engineering were expected to grow slower than average for all other occupations in the period up to 2012, although some sectors, such as environmental engineering, are expected to have faster than average growth. Some slowdown was determined to be due to the increased use of engineers in other countries.

Income varied by the type of discipline. For example, at the highest end were petroleum engineers, earning a mean income of US$83,370 in 2002, while the lowest end was held by agricultural engineers who earned a median of US$50,700.

The industry continued to be male dominated, both in the workforce and in academia. According to U.S. Census data, the number of female engineers had been slowly increasing, having risen from 5.8 percent of all engineers in 1983 to 10.6 percent in 1999. In 2000, the largest percentage of women engineers were in the categories of computer engineering (27.5 percent) and environmental engineering (22.2 percent), while the lowest sectors were marine engineering (5.1 percent) and petroleum engineering (6.3 percent). Income figures showed a strong disparity between genders. China had more female engineers than the United States, claiming about 37 percent of the engineering workforce.

Civil engineering in Africa was faced with challenges impacting how the profession functioned on that continent. Writing for *Africa News Service* in April 2007, Lukong Pius Nyuylime shared insights about those challenges. They included poor knowledge of mission, lack of confidence in local engineers, clash of political and technical interest, no patriotism, and no incisive socio-economic environment.

The American Society of Civil Engineers has created an exciting online destination. One visit to ASCEville.org will enhance awareness of the role civil engineering plays in a modern world. There are many educational and interactive opportunities for exploration. Contents include activity guides, handouts, success stories and labs involving repairing civil engineering structures. The site was also a great resource for historical data and career field insights.

Writer Alan S. Brown shared several self-proclaimed "snapshots of changes sweeping the engineering world" in a June 2005 *Mechanical Engineering* feature story. Those "snapshots" shared distinctive but representative case studies starring Elkay, Barry-Wehmiller, GM, and TRW. An important conclusion was that "access to offshore services makes many companies more competitive." For example, establishing business relationships based on hiring low-wage Indian workers was mutually beneficial. Fortunes were saved on projects utilizing new software programs because Indian workers had a strong work ethic, took their education seriously from a young age, and were eager to work long hours doing tedious jobs. Brown acknowledged that "advances in communications and software" greatly supported offshore usage practices. The Internet and transoceanic fiber optic cables made large file transfer near or far virtually effortless. CAD software facilitated collaboration between engineering teams no matter where they were physically located in the world. Instead of hiring low-level engineers, a growing number of U.S. companies were finding using offshore engineers was a more practical and cost-efficient alternative. In some cases, Indian engineers were brought to the United States and allowed to work in a foreign land. If sent back home later, they returned with knowledge and insights about the company to share with others when they were trained to work on the job.

INDUSTRY LEADERS

VINCI. Created in 1899 by French engineers, VINCI was the leading global contractor according to *Engineering News-Record*. The company was providing engineering services to the following industries: transportation infrastructure, energy infrastructure, manufacturing, and telecommunications. VINCI was the leading civil engineering firm in France and was a major player globally. In 2008 its revenues were approximately US$25 billion and the company employed more than 72,000 people. By 2007 VINCI planned to recruit 12,000 French employees on permanent contracts to address an anticipated dramatic increase in spending through 2013.

VINCI led the Apion Kleos consortium. The Greek government chose this concession as its preferred bidder for its biggest motorway concession project. This project called for the financing, design, construction, and repair of a toll roadway between Athens and Tsakona, Greece. The project strengthened VINCI's position in Greece, where it already operated the Rion-Antirion Bridge. It was both the biggest construction worksite and concession VINCI ever won outside of France.

Bouygues SA. Founded in Paris in 1952, by 2005 Bouygues was one of the world's largest companies offering construction services, with its civil engineering and public works segment beginning operation in 1965. Bouygues was parent to the world's leading roadworks company, Colas. In 2005 it was working on such projects as the Grand Hotel Intercontinental de Paris, the Groene Hart tunnel in the Netherlands, Tangier harbor in Hong Kong, and the Masan Bay bridge in South Korea. Bouygues employed 115,411 people working in about 80 countries. The company was a major employer in Africa, which accounted for 44.3 percent of its approximately 52,000-member workforce outside of France. Bouygues' revenues in 2005 were nearly US$32 billion. By 2007, the employees added up to 137,500 with 2008 sales of US $46.1.

The company made large investments in research and development. In 2005 it was working on such projects as the use of robots on worksites to increase productivity, acoustics and vibrations, low temperature asphalt, and environmentally friendly warm-mix asphalt.

Halliburton Co. A provider of products and services to the oil and gas industry, Texas-based Halliburton offers engineering and construction services through its KBR (Kellogg, Brown, and Root) division. This division provides services to the chemical manufacturing and energy industries, and is also involved in infrastructure construction. The company provides civil engineering, nuclear engineering, weapons engineering, marine engineering, and petroleum engineering services. In 2009 Halliburton employed more than 50,000 people in over 70 countries. There were 60,000 people in the KBR division working in 43 countries.

In 2007 Halliburton defended the work of its Halliburton Products & Services Ltd. subsidiary in Iran. U.S. law prohibits citizens and operations to do business directly with Iran. Foreign subsidiaries are permitted to do work there as long as the subsidiary acts as an independent agent. That means it must function in this regard separately from the parent company. The U.S. Senate Subcommittee on Interstate, Commerce, Trade, and Tourism questioned how Halliburton had operated based on evidence including a 2004 report on CBS News' 60 Minutes program. The program suggested that Halliburton shared office space plus telephone and fax lines with its subsidiary. Halliburton Vice President and Corporate Secretary Sherry Williams denied the accusations. Furthermore, Williams claimed that Halliburton had sought advice from three outside law firms plus federal regulators about the work the subsidiary might perform in Iran.

A positive 2007 announcement reflected that Halliburton won three Hart's E & P meritorious engineering achievement awards. Halliburton won the awards for three outstanding technologies. SuperFill surge reduction system allows wellbore fluids to enter the casing freely and exit the drillpipe during casing running operations, effectively reducing surge pressures. AssetPlanner software helps industry members meet the challenges of numerous production demands; health, safety and environmental mandates; and return-on-investment goals by accelerating and optimizing development plans for new or mature fields. The ReFlexRite multilateral system provides a re-entry multilateral solution that allows lateral branches to be added to existing single horizontal wells.

Founded in 1919, Brown and Root Inc. began operating as a subsidiary of Halliburton in 1962. In 1996 it split into three entities, one of which was named Brown and Root Engineering and Construction (BREC). That year, the Houston, Texas-based company posted revenues of US$4.1 billion, with a payroll of 36,000 employees. With operations in more than 60 countries, about two-thirds of its business was conducted outside of the United States. When Halliburton acquired Dresser Industries in 1998, BREC was merged with Dresser's MW Kellogg division to form Kellogg Brown and Root.

In August 2009, Halliburton proudly proclaimed that Total had awarded it a contract of US $140 million for deepwater drilling support and finishing up other Angola offshore activities. Contractual obligations would involve approximately three deepwater rigs during a period of three years. "Halliburton has aligned its people and processes to deliver engineered fluid solutions customized to maximize wellborne value to our customers, and we look forward to executing and adding value to Total's operations," stated Barold Vice President Jeff Miller. Barold is a Halliburton product service line.

Bechtel Group. Bechtel Group of San Francisco, California, continued to be one of the world's leading engineering, construction, and management companies. The firm of 40,000 employees working in 40 countries posted US$17.4 billion in revenues in 2004. The majority (89 percent) of Bechtel's revenues were due to international contracts. The firm's specialties include roads and rail systems, airports and seaports, power plants, pipelines, and telecommunications. By 2008, the company had 44,000 employees with sales of US $31.4 billion. The company was founded in 1898 when it was involved with grading railway beds. By 1931, the company was helping with the building of the Hoover Dam.

On July 30, 2009, Bechtel was a key player in a good news story. Chevron shared the news about its decision to bestow "a major front-end engineering and design (FEED) contract for the first phase of the Wheatstone natural gas development in northwest Australia." Contract components include two liquefied natural gas (LNG) processing trains plus one domestic gas plant.

Fluor Corp. One of the largest engineering, procurement, construction and maintenance service firms in the world is Fluor Corp., an engineer-contractor based in Irving, Texas. Fluor posted US$9.38 billion in sales in 2004 and had more than 35,000 employees. In 2005 the company had offices in more than 25 countries. Fluor relies most heavily on petroleum and industrial engineering markets, as well as the hazardous waste engineering sector. International projects bring in nearly one-third of revenues. In 2005 Fluor's projects included providing engineering support for the modernization of a KoSa plant; front-end engineering and design for the Ju'Aymah gas plant in Saudi Arabia; and engineering, construction and procurement services on the Trans-Alaska Pipeline. Fluor reported revenues of US$14.1 billion in 2006.

In May 2007 Fluor announced that it was selected to provide engineering, procurement, construction management, and pre-commissioning services to Saudi International Petrochemical Co. Ltd. for an acetyls complex in Jubail, Saudi Arabia. The billion-dollar contract involved a main plant, set to manufacture acetic acid and vinyl acetate monomer, a high-end specialty plastic for clients, and a new utilities plant.

CH2M Hill Companies Ltd. CH2M Hill provides engineering and construction services including procurement, engineering and management assistance. In 2009 the company employed more than 25,000 people working in regional offices around the world. CH2M Hill remained "committed to developing people through challenging projects." As a result of impressive growth in many company areas, CH2M planned to focus recruitment efforts on a variety of industries, including the water, transportation, environmental, and industrial sectors. The firm's Applied Sciences Laboratory does a range of environmental and industrial testing. CH2M Hill was providing such environmental services as ecosystem management, human health and ecological risk assessment, and brownfield and remediation services. The company also managed large nuclear projects. Revenues for 2006 were approximately US$4.5 billion. That reflected an increase of 27 percent from 2005. CH2M earned its rankings of No. 5 and No. 38 on *Engineering News Record*'s list of Top 500 Design Firms and Top 400 Contractors, respectively. The company's growth as "a market force in the federal area," especially in the area of nuclear waste services, also was noted. On the international scene, CH2M was a leader in a program management joint venture for the estimated US$6 billion 2012 London Olympics.

CH2M Hill was chosen to manage the design of an advanced water purification facility for Oxnard, California. It will provide the city with reclaimed water suitable for using with landscape and agricultural irrigation, industrial process water, and groundwater recharge. This project was part of the City of Oxnard's Groundwater Recovery

Enhancement and Treatment program. Plans called for the initial phase to be fully operational by year end 2009.

CH2M Hill received a contract from Fort Hills Energy L.P. to provide engineering and procurement services for the Infrastructure Utilities Work for the Fort Hills Project Mine and Upgrader sites. The sites were located in Alberta's Athabasca oil sands area and Edmonton, respectively.

On September 1, 2009, the man who joined CH2M Hill as its 148th employee and served as CEO from 1991 to 2008 died after a long cancer battle. Ralph R. Peterson was heralded as "a sustainable development thought leader in the engineering and construction industry." Peterson's many noteworthy achievements included that he "executed a global growth and diversification strategy that developed an industry-leading portfolio of businesses and services."

MAJOR COUNTRIES IN THE INDUSTRY

By 2005 the engineering field had become truly international. Large-scale projects were contracted out in various parts to companies from around the world. Of the top 150 design firms, almost all of them did some business internationally. The same was true of the top 250 construction firms.

In the United States, there were accusations that FEMA awarded US$3.6 billion worth of Hurricane Katrina contracts to companies with poor credit histories and bad paperwork. No-bid contracts for cleanup work were issued to firms including Bechtel Group, CH2M Hill Companies, and Fluor Corp. Investigators were checking to see if the significant waste to taxpayers had also violated federal law.

France was home to several of the world's largest engineering and construction companies in terms of revenues. The United States continued to lead the way in environmental engineering services and design services.

In an August 19, 2009, article for the *Deccan Herald,* writer Pradeesh Chandran discussed dynamics of engineering outsourcing and its relationship to future automotive and aerospace growth or expansion opportunities in India. A Dataquest survey obtained results reflecting that engineering design and service exports were expected to be "next big thing in India's march towards becoming a global knowledge powerhouse." Furthermore, a Booz Allen Hamilton study for Nasscom results showed marked growth in transitioning services to India and China. This growth led to a forecast of even more growth soaring to US $30 billion for the engineering service industry by 2010.

BIBLIOGRAPHY

"'ASCEville': Where Civil Engineering meets Awesome!" American Society of Civil Engineers, 21 July 2008. Available from www.asce.org.

"ASME Commends President Obama for Commitment to Research, Innovation and Education." ASME, 6 May 2009. Available from www.asme.org.

————. "Manufacturers Embrace the Environmental Mandate." ASME, 30 December 2008. Available from www.asme.org.

Angelo, William J. "Grabbing the Lucrative Adaptive Reuse Market." *Design Build,* July 2004.

Brown, Alan S. "Where the Engineers Are." *Mechanical Engineering,* June 2005. Available from www.memagazine.org.

"CH2M Hill Hires Nearly 900 Professionals in Q1 2007." *PR Newswire,* 25 April 2007.

"CH2M Hill Receives Infrastructure Utilities Contract for Fort Hills Oil Sands Project." *PR Newswire,* 30 April 2007.

Chandram, Pradeesh. "Infosys to Focus on engineering services for growth." *Deccan Herald,* 19 August 2009. Available from www. deccanherald.com.

"Chevron Moves Wheatstone Project in Australia Closer to Commercialization." Chevron, 30 July 2009. Available from www.Chevron.com.

"Engineering and Construction Services in France, Germany, UK, US." *Euromonitor,* October 2004. Available from www.euromonitor.com.

Fischbach, Amy Florence. "The Top 40 Electrical Design Firms." *EC&M,* 1 May 2004.

"Fluor Wins $1-Billion Contract for Acetyls Complex in Jubail, Saudi Arabia." *Business Wire,* 9 May 2007.

"Halliburton Awarded Contract to Provide Fluid Services to Total in Angola." Halliburton, 11 August 2009. Available from www.halliburton.com.

"Halliburton Defends its Dealings: Subsidiary's Work in Iran Was Not Against Law, Executive Contends." *Houston Chronicle,* 1 May 2007.

"Halliburton Wins Three Engineering Achievement Awards." Houston, Tex.: Halliburton Co., 30 April 2007. Available from www.halliburton.com.

"Hoover's Company Capsules." *Hoover's Online,* 2007. Available from www.hoovers.com.

Jones, Brad. "CH2M Hill Chosen to Design Advanced Water Purification Facility for the City of Oxnard." CH2M HILL, 25 April 2007. Available from www.ch2m.com.

Kerman, Sophie, and Andrew Noel. "Vinci First-Quarter Sales Climb 27% on Tolls, Road Building." *Bloomberg News,* 2 May 2007. Available from www.bloomberg.com.

Kross, Robert. "You Need Desktop PLM." *Design News,* 2 June 2003.

Lazich, Robert S., ed. *Market Share Reporter.* Detroit: Thomson Gale, 2004.

Lemyze, Christine. "PLM's Time Has Come." *Design News,* 2 June 2003.

Marketwire. "CH2M Hillrsquo;s Long Term Former CEO and Chairman Ralph R. Peterson Passes Away." 2 September 2009. Available from in.sys-con.com.

"More than a third [of] Chinese Engineers Are Female." *People's Daily Online,* 5 November 2004. Available from www.english. people.com.

Nyuylime, Lukong Pius. "Civil Engineering—Real Challenge Is Quality." *Africa News Service,* 12 April 2007.

"Product Development MEs, EEs Bask in Sunshine." *Design News,* 14 July 2004.

Reina, Peter, and Gary J. Tulacz. "Global Firms Increase Their Local Presence." *Engineering News Record,* 23 July 2001. Available from www.enr.com.

"Research & Stats." Society of Women Engineers, July 2005. Available from www.swe.org.

Rosta, Paul B. "Total 2003 Revenue Exceeds $53 Billion." *Design Build,* July 2004.

Rubin, Debra K. "CH2M Hill's Formula for Success: Fly High but Stay Grounded." *ENR,* 12 March 2007.

Schodek, Daniel L. *Landmarks in American Civil Engineering.* Cambridge, Mass.: MIT Press, 1987.

"Top 200 Environmental Firms 2004." *Engineering News Record,* 2004. Available from www.enr.com.

"Top Global Contractors 2004." *Engineering News Record,* 2004. Available from www.enr.com.

"Top Global Design Firms 2004." *Engineering News Record,* 2004. Available from www.enr.com.

Tulacz, Gary J. "Design Firms Break Out of the Mold." *Engineering News Record,* 16 April 2001. Available from www.enr.com.

———. "Design-Build Trends Draw a Wealth of Work . . . and Competitors." *Engineering News Record,* 19 June 2000. Available from www.enr.com.

———. "The Top 100." *Engineering News Record,* 18 June 2001. Available from www.enr.com.

"VINCI, Preferred Bidder for a Second Motorway Concession in Greece." VINCI, 11 May 2007. Available from www.vinci.com.

Yen, Hope. "Probe: Katrina Contracts Given to Companies with Poor Credit Histories, Bad Paperwork." *Times Record News,* 23 April 2007. Available from www.timesrecordnews.com.

SIC 8111

LEGAL SERVICES

NAICS CODE(S)

541110. The legal services industry includes offices of lawyers and other legal advisers and services.

INDUSTRY SNAPSHOT

In the middle of the first decade of the 2000s, the legal services industry was growing. The top eight firms listed on *American Lawyer*'s 2004 "Global 100" list had revenues of more than US$1 billion each in 2003. Four of these firms were based in the United Kingdom, with the other four based in the United States. The top 100 firms around the world had aggregate earnings of almost US$48.2 billion.

Consolidation has created larger, more competitive firms with bigger profits. Mid-sized firms continued to find themselves squeezed out by mega-firms with dozens of offices housing thousands of fee earners. Law firms also are seeing greater profits from their embrace of high technology resources including software and the Internet. These resources allow attorneys to deliver services more efficiently, and cut down on the number of employees

needed for case work, thereby resulting in significant cost savings, as well as increased client satisfaction.

The American Bar Association (ABA) claimed to be the largest voluntary professional organization in the world. It was founded in 1878 by a group of 100 lawyers to provide some national uniformity to their profession in the U.S. At that time, lawyers trained under other lawyers as apprentices, rather than having formal law school training. As of 2009, the ABA had more than 400,000 members. Its focus had expanded to include accreditation of law schools and building public understanding of "the importance of the rule of law" throughout the world.

The hiring of diversity managers was becoming a new law firm trend. Many firms were hiring full-time diversity managers. These experts served in a variety of roles. The roles included advising during the staff hiring process, recruiting, professional development, and review processes. An Altman Weil survey found only 15 percent of the diversity managers participating in their research study had been employed by their firms for more than three years. Almost one-third of them had only been on board for less than a year.

Legal services offshoring was another trend gaining in popularity and practice. The soaring costs of legal services in both the United States and Europe were leading many companies to send legal work to countries with lower costs such as India. According to research findings reported by ValueNotes, offshoring for legal services vendors was expected to have growth rates ranging anywhere from 30 to 100 percent. There were concerns about the legal services that would be provided because some industry experts estimated not more than 15 percent of the approximately 79,000 lawyers graduating from more than 400 colleges in India every year were capable of ensuring the high-quality work clients desired.

ORGANIZATION AND STRUCTURE

United States. In the United States, lawyers (also called attorneys) serve as advocates and advisers in both civil and criminal cases. Lawyers generally are required to have a four-year undergraduate degree plus a three-year graduate degree from an accredited law school, and also must pass a written examination to be admitted to practice in any state. Because of a number of scandals involving lawyers beginning in the 1970s—notably Watergate—by 1997, 48 states required that the examination include a section on professional ethics.

Lawyers who pass the exam may be employed as individual practitioners, as employees of a law firm, as government employees, as employees of businesses, or as legal services attorneys (in civil cases) or public defenders (in criminal cases), representing those who can't afford to hire an attorney. In the early 1960s, the U.S. Supreme Court determined that all defendants in felony cases have the right to an attorney; in 1974, the federal government established the Legal Services Corporation, a private nonprofit corporation that represents the indigent in civil cases, even though such representation is not legally required. Lawyers also can become judges, magistrates, or hearing officers, who hear cases and render decisions. In the United States, all licensed lawyers may argue in a courtroom, unlike the system in the United Kingdom.

In addition to lawyers, there are many other paraprofessional personnel who assist in providing legal services. Paralegals, who assist lawyers by doing research, investigating facts, and preparing legal documents, are usually college graduates, but they do not need special licensing or examinations. Law clerks assist judges in research or in writing documents. Title examiners, abstractors, and searchers assist real estate or bank attorneys in determining the legal status of property being bought and sold, by examining public and private records.

Most U.S. law firms are structured as partnerships in which senior attorneys own the company and share in the profits. Some firms may also divide partner status into various ranks, with the highest rank culminating in full partnership. Partner status is typically conferred on lawyers after they've been with a firm for a number of years based on such considerations as seniority, their level of annual billings, and their success rate in trials.

The globalization of the legal services industry has created an increasing demand for firms that can seamlessly take care of all of a client's needs under one single establishment. A growing number of accounting firms have been pushing the ABA and state bar associations to allow multidisciplinary partnerships (MDPs). These certified public accountants (CPAs) want to offer legal services in addition to their financial and business service offerings. Accounting firms are the biggest employers of attorneys worldwide. At least three of the Big Four accounting firms were affiliated with or had acquired law practices in many nations, allowing them to offer legal services. However, accounting firms are not allowed to own law firms in the United States, even though this is common in many countries in Latin America, Europe, and other parts of the world.

Many of those in the legal profession have a number of concerns regarding MDPs. They believe that confidentiality, independent judgment and advice, and loyalty to clients could be compromised if firms were allowed to offer both accounting and legal services. They also question whether there really is a demand among clients for seamless access to all professional services. Another concern is that MDPs that provide legal services will pose increased competition to the legal services industry.

According to *Accounting Horizons,* the ABA organized the Commission on Multidisciplinary Practice (MDP

Commission) to examine and make recommendations on the issue of enabling lawyers to become partners and share fees with non-lawyers, including accountants, stockbrokers, and financial planners. After the MDP commission heard testimony and conducted open hearings on the matter, it recommended unanimously that the Model Rules of Professional Conduct (MRPC) be amended to permit MDPs. In August 1999, the ABA deferred voting on the recommendation, dependent on further study. The MDP Commission instituted more hearings and again proposed its recommendation, but the ABA voted against it in July 2000. However, the MRPC is strictly advisory, and individual states are free to adopt, change, or ignore it. A number of states have been holding their own debates on MDPs, and it is likely that the ABA will take another look at the MDP issue in the future.

ABA President Carolyn B. Lamm announced the launch of a diversity commission she created to address glass ceiling related issues. The commission plans to sponsor regional programs. These programs will be set up similar to sessions held jointly by Lamm's own firm, White & Case, and the National Asian Pacific American Bar Association. A major goal is to "emphasize building networks in which lawyers who already have overcome barriers to advancement can share with aspiring lawyers the strategies and understanding that worked for them." In addition, the commission has been charged to review diversity summit findings and recommendations from an event held in June 2009. It was organized by ABA immediate Past President Thomas Wells, Jr., and Oregon Court of Appeals Judge Ellen F. Rosenblum was appointed to chair the Commission.

Writing for the *Jacksonville Financial News & Daily Record* (FL), Brian Wargo shared insights about Las Vegas legal aid services and the high demand for people in need of those services. The information served as a case study for what was happening with Nevada Legal Services and other similar agencies elsewhere. "It's terrible to say but when the economy is bad, our business is good and we don't see any slacking in the demand for our services," said Nevada Legal Services Executive Director Anna Marie Johnson. The economy's impact was felt when poor situations caused an increase from 9 percent in 2008 to 17 percent in 2009. Nevada State Bar President Kathleen England claimed changing economic times also made it difficult to bring in first rate lawyers for pro bono work.

Europe and Canada. England, Wales, Scotland, and Northern Ireland each have distinct court systems and bodies of law. However, all of these countries divide professionals who provide legal services into two categories: barristers, who hold exclusive rights to argue in the higher courts; and solicitors, who meet with clients and provide advice to them. Generally, these two coordinate their efforts for the client. France maintains a similar division, dividing advocates into *avocats* (the equivalent of barristers) and *avouets* (the equivalent of solicitors). English barristers belong to one of four Inns at Court, which are combinations of a school and a professional organization. French law students must decide whether to follow a career path as a judge or a lawyer. Canada combines qualities of numerous legal systems, by requiring that lawyers complete college and law school, pass an examination, and serve an "articling period" of apprenticeship to another lawyer.

Canadian Attorney-General Chris Bentley proposed a U.S.$60 million budget increase to support "struggling" Ontario, Canada, legal aid. The response was "added support of defense lawyers from Ottawa, Brockville and Halton, and Niagara regions" to Bentley's four-year phase-in plan. A massive Ontario boycott was gaining momentum after approximately 700 lawyers participated in actions reflecting being upset about "legal aid's eroding fee structure." A Refugee Lawyers Association resolution expressed the sentiments of many others when it stated, "Although this increase in funding is welcome, it is not adequate."

BACKGROUND AND DEVELOPMENT

Written codes of law date back at least to 1700 B.C., when the Babylonian king Hammurabi had his kingdom's laws carved on a huge column of stone. His code contained hundreds of categories of offenses for which punishment was in kind; that is to say, the crime of the transgressor was enacted upon him or her as punishment. For instance, if a builder cut corners and a house collapsed, killing the owner's son, the builder's son would be executed. The Judeo-Christian Ten Commandments, probably dating to around 1300 B.C., drew heavily from Hammurabi's code and served as the basic framework for many modern Western laws. The first law school might have been based in Bologna, Italy, around 1150 A.D. Students would hire a teacher to explain the Roman law; one teacher, Irnenius, was so popular that he had to hire other teachers to assist him, thus setting up the first law faculty. By the time of the reign of Henry II in England (1154-89), a person brought before a court could appoint an advocate to plead a case.

In 1215, King John of England signed the Magna Carta ("great charter"), which gave his subjects basic legal rights such as freedom of religion and the right to a fair trail. The Magna Carta served as the foundation of the Anglo-American law system. In the United States, the Constitution and its Bill of Rights were influenced by the Magna Carta and embodied one of the first examples of modern law. However, many other countries derive their legal systems from Roman law, such as the Napoleonic Code in France. In countries whose laws are based on the Anglo-American system or Roman law, which includes most of Western Europe, there is also a well-established system of trained specialists who provide legal advice and services. Many other countries have their own unique legal systems, based on indigenous law (some African countries, for example) or religious law (Islamic countries). In these countries, the system of trained lawyers and judges prevalent in Western countries might instead consist of tribal heads or religious leaders. However, in the late twentieth century, these systems were increasingly influenced by the Western legal systems.

CURRENT CONDITIONS

United States. The top law practices in the multi-billion dollar U.S. legal services industry have a worldwide presence. Some employ thousands of attorneys, and revenues were increasing at an annual rate of 8 to 10 percent. Firms with expertise in intellectual property and high technology issues are finding success, as well as those that specialize in mergers and acquisitions. The United States is becoming an increasingly litigious society, and the overabundance of attorneys has led to fierce competition. While there are still high-priced lawyers serving an elite clientele, the average American has no problem attaining legal representation, thanks to the growing number of lawyers, along with the increasing availability of low-cost legal services.

Legal trends identified by *Crain's Detroit Business* included non-compete clause interpretation, mediation, class-action suits, and intellectual property disputes. In addition, there was an upswing of specialized niche firms, dubbed "boutiques" by those in the industry. Another popular trend in the first decade of the 2000s was prepaid legal service insurance plans. Both business owners and individuals can pay a low monthly fee and can access basic legal services on an as-needed basis. Using this type of service eliminates costly retainer fees for consumers who may have normally done without legal services due to the high cost. Services provided in prepaid legal insurance plans often include home purchases or sales, will preparation, and legal consultation by telephone.

Analysis of the 2006-2007 *NALP Directory of Legal Employers* revealed that major law firms employ one associate for every partner, with an overall ratio of lawyers to partners of 2.19. Formerly known as the National Association for Law Placement, the NALP represented more than 132,000 lawyers in more than 1,500 law offices nationwide, primarily those with more than 100 lawyers. Among cities with the highest representation in the directory, lawyer/partner ratios ranged from a low of 1.6 in Milwaukee to a high of 3.16 in New York.

Although industry experts believed it would not happen for some time, some lawyers expressed concern about implementation of a tax on legal services. This tax would also include services offered by private counsel. It was viewed as a means to align the tax base and the economy.

U.S. Circuit Court Judge Jean Johnson discussed why it was important for fellow Florida Bar Association members to meet "pro bono requirements." The minimum standard annually was 20 hours or US$350 donated to a legal aid organization. Additional hours spent on more extensive cases were eligible to be used for meeting hours during the next two years. After noting her judicial district had not been good about meeting past pro bono obligations, Johnson issued a call to action stressing need to fulfill pro bono obligations.

United Kingdom. Financial markets experienced economic challenges from many fronts in 2008. The United Kingdom's "Magic Circle firms" continued to be industry leaders. Notable among them were Clifford Chance, Freshfields Buckhouse Deringer, Linklaters, and Allen & Overy. Within the United Kingdom, the industry was highly fragmented, impacted by many mergers and acquisitions. U.S. firms stood out in areas related to restructuring and high yield sections, according to "Legal 500."

Corporate services made up the largest share of the legal market in the United Kingdom, according to the market research firm Euromonitor, and the segment was expected to account for 36 percent of the market by 2008. Most law practices for private practice chose to head their organizations in London.

Legal Services Minister Bridget Prentice said that new kinds of business structures would continue to increase the choices of models for delivering legal services. Firms owned and managed by non-lawyers providing legal services would enable this progression. The Legal Services Bill, introduced in Parliament in November 2006, was believed to be a key enabler. The bill called for an independent oversight regulator, the Legal Services Board, and was expected to get Royal Assent in summer 2007. Implementation was expected to occur two to three years following Royal Assent.

The Journal reported that several boutique and specialty practices hung their shingles. Notable among them were "niche firms," such as Major Family Law and Sharon Langridge Employment, which had been praised by peers acknowledging future potential.

France. Having grown 14 percent in a year to reach a value of US$18.4 billion in 2003, the market for French legal services was expected to show continued rapid growth, according to Euromonitor, growing another 40 percent by 2008.

Based on revenues, about half of all activity dealt with real estate, construction, sales, and leases. Family

instruments and deeds of succession accounted for 33 percent of revenues.

France's ratio of one lawyer to every 2,000 citizens is significantly lower than that of other European countries. No Franco-French law practices exist that have more than one hundred partners. An expanding number of U.S. and U.K. law firms have set up shop in France since the late 1990s, and many now boast bigger Paris offices than those of the top French law practices. The big players in the French legal services industry are those practices with ties to the Big Four accounting firms, including Fidal with its association with KPMG and HDS Ernst & Young. However, some of these law firms have seen attorneys and clients leave for foreign competition. Specialized, smaller practices still thrive, mainly in the capital and corporate finance sectors. Seeing this trend, domestic firms are reevaluating firm management.

According to "The Legal 500 2009," leading and mid-size law firms in France had a good year in 2008. Many firms had a stronger posting for 2008 than 2007. Nonetheless, the global economy problems had an impact on how law would be practiced in the future. Some established international firms were reviewing past practices while newer ones took the risk of opening up shop. There were also many "lateral moves" among members of prominent firms and Freshfields Bruckhaus Deringer LLP lost significant finance practice partners. In addition, top boutiques with specialities were acknowledged to be shining stars to watch soar more in years ahead.

Italy. A number of London's top law firms have entered into Italy's domestic market, but a downward trend is likely due to slowness in the securities market, as well as continuing debt issues. Italy's top two indigenous practices are Gianni, Origoni, Grippo & Partners, and Pavia e Ansaldo.

In September 2009, Clifford Chance rehired a man to be partner who had departed in April. As reported by Julia Berris, "Clifford Chance's Italian practice has suffered a number of key losses in recent months." It was noted by Clifford Chance Italy Managing Partner Charles Adams that "appointment of Lucio Bonavitacola to the partnership further strengthens our regulatory team."

Spain. Madrid and Barcelona are home to most of Spain's top law practices. The country's legal services market is made up of international firms, independent law practices, and multidisciplinary partnerships. Spain's successful economic expansion since the mid-1980s has resulted in a sophisticated and vibrant market. Despite downturns in the global economy, Spanish law firms are continuing to thrive. Increased activity in the private sector has resulted in stronger demand for attorneys, especially in the fields of international trade, property litigation, and labor.

Russia and the CIS. Russia's 1998 currency crisis caused a number of the country's Western law practices to shut down or significantly cut back on staff. However, *The World Legal Forum* noted that in the early years of the first decade of the 2000s, the Russian economic climate seemed to be improving. Many international firms in Russia do work in the energy sector. Higher oil prices and increased foreign investment in the energy market have also led to cautious optimism. President Vladimir Putin's reform agenda also has helped, including the introduction of a number of pro-investor bills and the modernization of Russia's tax system. Most indigenous Russian firms have difficulty competing with foreign firms, particularly in international matters, because they do not have global practices. However, several domestic firms get significant referral business. These firms include Alrud and Pepeliaev and Goltsblat & Partners. The largest foreign law practices in Russia were: Linklaters CIS; Freshfields Bruckhaus Deringer; LeBoeuf, Lamb, Greene & MacRae LLP; and White & Case LLC.

Hong Kong. The legal services sector in Hong Kong is made up of two types of legal professionals, barristers and solicitors. Barristers are litigation and advocacy specialists, while solicitors undertake general practice. Barristers must receive instruction from solicitors to perform services for clients, the majority of which are related to criminal cases, shipping, intellectual property, construction, personal injuries, and landlord-tenant disputes.

When it comes to allowing foreign attorneys to participate in its legal services industry, Hong Kong is the most favorable jurisdiction in Asia, according to the Hong Kong Trade Development Council. By the end of July 2001, there were approximately 39 foreign firms, and more than 500 foreign solicitors were practicing in Hong Kong. Mainland China is the biggest export market for Hong Kong's legal sector, since most demand comes from both Hong Kong and foreign corporations that are currently investing in or are planning to invest in China.

Legal professionals in Hong Kong will benefit from China's bilateral agreement with the United States over accession to the World Trade Organization (WTO). They offer expert knowledge of Chinese law and their client base in China is strong. These factors, among others, make for a bright outlook for Hong Kong's legal services industry. However, by the mid-years of the first decade of the 2000s, the market was considered be "over lawyered," leading to intense competition. In 2004, U.K.-based Denton Wilde Sapte left the market altogether.

China (mainland). *The American Lawyer* reported that, although China's ties to the West had been mainly via Hong Kong, its legal sector was increasingly seen as standing tall on its own. Many Western law firms gave up on establishing offices in mainland China after the government imposed more restrictions on citizens after the Tiananmen Square incidents in 1989. However, the Chinese government's willingness to bring about a more modernized financial infrastructure in the late 1990s brought a number of foreign law practices to the country. By the early years of the first decade of the twenty-first century, more than one hundred firms had opened offices inside the mainland. China's admission to the World Trade Organization (WTO) is another significant factor in the expansion of foreign firms into China. However, heavy restrictions still plague Western firms in China. For example, they are prohibited from hiring Chinese attorneys and are forbidden to practice Chinese law.

In February 2007, MWE China Law Offices announced it had established a strategic alliance with McDermott Will & Emery. McDermott was one of the world's top 25 law firms. MWE China Law Offices agreed to serve as a separate law firm and provide more quality services for its clients with support from its U.S. partner. McDermott operated nine offices in the United States and five offices in Europe.

Japan. In the early 1990s, only a small number of Western lawyers worked in Japan, reported *The American Lawyer*. They were mainly employed by Japanese corporations looking to purchase assets in the United States and Europe. The late 1990s burst of Japan's economic bubble reversed the situation, and Western companies began lining up to buy weakened Japanese assets at reduced costs. As a result, British and U.S. firms added lawyers to their Japan-based operations and began to influence Japan's legal services industry with Western legal and cultural practices. However, restrictions still abound for Western firms. Japan prohibits mergers between Japanese and foreign law firms. Although they are allowed to share office space, they must keep the partnership structure and billing separate. Within the industry itself, many mergers had occurred between law firms.

South Korea. Due to the economic ties between the two countries, many lawyers in South Korea are trained in the United States. However, the qualification process in South Korea remained much more rigorous, with more people unable to pass the bar exam than people able to pass.

In an interview with Nam Jeong-ho at oongangdaily.joins.com, White and Case LLP CEO Hugh Verrier discussed dynamics related to "the opening of Korea's legal service market." Verrier admitted that the Korean law firms opposed the open market evolution. After fruitful discussions, Verrier remained optimistic and confident about arriving at a point "where Korean law firms are equally connected to the global legal community." Verrier stated White and Case had maintained a strong presence in Korea and Asia for many years. "We have two dozen Korean-speaking lawyers, including Korean partners in New York City," Verrier claimed.

RESEARCH AND TECHNOLOGY

Readers of novels by Charles Dickens will recall how long-suffering legal clerks were responsible for preparing court documents by hand, as well as sifting through dusty court files and yellowing books to conduct research on cases. In many ways, this was still the state of legal research until the 1970s. Prior to the development of word processing equipment, legal secretaries had the agonizing task of typing documents on manual, and later electric, typewriters, and were forced to retype entire documents if a lawyer decided to add an extra paragraph. Research was conducted by law students, paralegals, and newly graduated lawyers at firms, using paper indexes to books of court opinions and statutes. With the development of desktop and laptop computers, plus online research services, the field of legal research and document preparation was changed drastically, so that research that would have taken hours or even days to conduct by hand became the work of a few minutes on a computer. Lawyers who had left all of their document preparation and research to their staffs began to do much more of this work on their own computers.

In the late 1960s, the Ohio State Bar Association decided to put state case law onto a computer, allowing users to locate cases by typing in a word or phrase. In 1973, LEXIS-NEXIS, the first commercial, full-text online legal information service, was created by Ohio's Mead Corporation, originally providing case law for only three states (New York, Ohio, and Missouri). Because personal computers were not available to the general public at the time, users of the service had to go to courthouses that had special terminals, or purchase terminals at an extremely high cost. Shortly afterward, the West Publishing Company of Minnesota introduced a similar service, WEST-LAW. West had the advantage of already being the publisher of volumes of federal and state laws and court opinions. LEXIS-NEXIS and WESTLAW thus began a rivalry for the lucrative legal research market that continued through the next three decades.

By the late 1990s, both LEXIS-NEXIS and WEST-LAW had become key components of multibillion-dollar businesses, and almost every lawyer and law student in the United States had easy access to the two services via personal computers. In 1994 LEXIS-NEXIS was purchased by London-based publisher Reed Elsevier plc, and in 1996 West Publishing and WESTLAW joined

Minnesota's Thomson Corporation (as parts of the new West Group). The two companies vied for the law student market, knowing that these students (who received unlimited free access) were likely to keep their preferred service once they graduated and became paying customers. Both LEXIS-NEXIS and WESTLAW provided access to thousands of full-text databases of state, federal, and international statutes, cases, law and business journals, and news sources. They also had established Internet-based services for attorneys practicing in specialized fields. By 2000, LEXIS-NEXIS had more than 3 billion documents accessible via books, CD-ROMs, and on the Internet. Subscribers numbered more than 2 million, and 2000 sales growth was 29.9 percent. Along with Lexis.com, which offers legal data on the World Wide Web, the company's online products include a legal directory, jurisdictional and citation services, legal research information, and a legal filing service, all available under various other brand names.

By the end of the twentieth century, the Internet had made a major impact on both law firms and users of legal services. The average person can now use various Web sites to perform routine legal research, download legal forms, and handle many of their basic legal needs, all without having to consult an attorney. If hiring a lawyer becomes inevitable, free Internet services can help with the selection process. For example, Lawyers.com offers profiles of 420,000 attorneys worldwide to help users find the right legal counsel for their needs.

Law practices are growing increasingly reliant on the Internet. By the mid-years of the first decade of the 2000s, such technologies were becoming increasingly necessary to legal firms. In particular, Web-based technologies such as portals and extranets were seeing exponential growth into 2004, allowing many legal services to be conducted completely electronically, including hearings. Attorneys can perform case research, market their practices, and communicate with clients and their fellow lawyers, all by going online. Transport of documents can be done via encrypted e-mail at speeds surpassing traditional means. Firms in multiple locations can access data in case files and law libraries via password-protected intranets. Digital courtrooms are another popular online trend. This technology allows for virtual meetings of judges, juries, expert witnesses, and the like, resulting in significant cost savings for courthouses. Videoconferencing software and technology is likely to pave the way for trials to be held over the Internet.

The Internet also is being used in law schools to supplement coursework and allow students easier access to their professors. In addition, the ABA investigated opportunities for law schools to offer students credit for distance learning.

An internal survey of independent provider law found debt collection was "the most requested legal service for second quarter of 2009." From April to June 2009, approximately 574,000 requests were made to Pre-Paid Legal Services with 46,073 relating to debt collection. This top position was both anticipated and expected to continue for a long time. Pre-Paid Legal Services was a pioneer in industry marketing, designing and underwriting legal service plans.

WORKFORCE

Demand for lawyers was expected to continue growing through 2012 at about the average rate for all professions. A majority of the lawyers operated in the United States, and about three-quarters of them worked in private or solo practices. Others held jobs in government offices, banks, insurance companies, real estate agencies, and other firms including not-for-profit organizations.

Demand for paralegals was expected to rise beyond the average rate through 2012, as these workers increasingly take on a number of legal tasks previously carried out only by attorneys.

According to the ABA's Commission on Women in the Profession report called "Visible Invisibility: Women of Color in Law Firms," conditions were extremely poor for minority females in U.S. law firms with 25 or more lawyers. Nearly half of the women of color reported experiencing demeaning comments or harassment compared to only 3 percent of white men. Regarding retention, 53 percent of women of color remained at law firms while 72 percent of white males chose to remain.

A National Association for Law Placement (NALP) study evaluated female partners at law firms. The research found an average of 17.3 female partners at firms throughout the United States. The number of female law school graduates was about 49 percent annually. They still, however, trailed behind their male counterparts in climbs up the corporate ladder to arrive at partner ranks or high-profile management jobs in law firms.

Writing for *The Lawyer*, Luke McLeod-Roberts revealed that Allen & Overy had launched a "career development scheme" focused on enhancing associate communication skills related to their clients and colleagues. Part of what made the program distinctive was its admitted focus on "softer skills" and women. McLeod-Roberts claimed that the percentage of female partners at major firms of Allen & Overy, Slaughter and May, and Freshfields Bruckhaus Deringer was 15, 19 and 12 respectively. Clifford Chance and Linklater' percentage of female partners was also approximately 15. As Allen & Overy Associate Director of HR Sasha Hardman acknowledged, "It's really important for our success as a business that we look at ways to retain and develop talented women." The number of new female Allen & Overy partners increased from 18 percent to 40 percent of lawyers gaining partner status.

Managing partners at nearly every firm were finding it difficult to decide how to divide their time between managing the firm and practicing law. Partners and associates of diverse firms agreed there was a fundamental necessity for balancing being a lawyer with leadership duties. Some firms opted not to have a managing partner as part of their structure. There also were firms that functioned by relegating a lot of the recommendation- and decision-making responsibilities to committees.

INDUSTRY LEADERS

Clifford Chance LLP. In 2009, London-based Clifford Chance continued to be among the top ranked law firms worldwide. It maintained 29 offices in 20 countries in the Americas, Asia, Europe, and the Middle East. Clifford Chance offered services around six global practice areas: banking and finance, capital markets, corporate (including mergers and acquisitions), litigation and dispute resolution, real estate, tax, pensions, and employment. The practice came into being by way of a merger in 2000 with Punder Vohard Weber & Axster of Germany, and U.S. firm Rogers & Wells. Clients include Siemens, Pfizer, and Citigroup.

In 2007 Clifford Chance announced that it had signed a contract with offshore vendor Integreon. In 2009, near its home base and abroad, Clifford Chance was proud to play an active role in its communities. All employees were encouraged to be actively involved in pro bono service for arts and charitable projects.

Skadden, Arps, Slate, Meagher & Flom LLP. Founded in 1948, New York-based Skadden, Arps was the second-highest ranked law firm in the world on both *The Lawyer* and *The American Lawyer* global 100 lists in 2004. In 2005, the company had approximately 4,400 employees, including about 1,700 lawyers, working in 20 offices throughout the world. The practice has provided legal counsel for almost one-half of the *Fortune* 250 industrial and service companies, and specializes in mergers and acquisitions, bankruptcy, and securities.

Freshfields Bruckhaus Deringer. By 2009, Freshfields had approximately 2,500 lawyers practicing in 27 centers in Europe, Asia, the Middle East, and the United States. The London-based Freshfields prided itself in "providing business law advice of the highest quality." Freshfields lawyers practiced in such areas as antitrust, competition and trade; corporate, mergers and acquisitions, and securities; dispute resolution; employment, pensions and benefits; finance; information technology; real estate; and tax.

In April 2007, Freshfields announced that it had advised on the largest IPO to date. The retail portion of this global offering involving China CITIC Bank was more than 220 times oversubscribed, while the institutional portion was also significantly oversubscribed. Total proceeds from the IPO were US$5.4 billion and will exceed US$6.2 billion if an over-allotment option is exercised in full.

Linklaters. Specializing in commercial law, London-based Linklaters had 30 offices in 23 countries, including the world's major financial centers, in 2007. Of the firm's more than 2,000 lawyers, about 55 percent worked outside of the United States. The company's legal services cover core practice areas such as asset finance, banking, mergers and acquisitions, intellectual property, restructuring and insolvency, and tax.

In 2009, Linklaters' commitment to "community investment" earned exceptional recognition when the firm earned distinction as "the first ever law firm in the United Kingdom to achieve the prestigious Bitc "CommunityMark." That award is a national honor endorsed by Prime Minister Gordon Brown and HRH Prince of Wales. Linklaters takes pride in having set an example by being the initial law firm to commit one percent of partners' pre-tax income to charity. The firm also claims to have launched the practice of giving one paid day off per year for staff to volunteer.

Baker & McKenzie. One of the world's largest law firms, Baker & McKenzie has approximately 3,900 attorneys practicing in approximately 70 offices in 39 countries. The Chicago-based firm had offices throughout Asia, Europe, the Middle East, Latin America, and North America. It continued to be the most global of all U.S. firms. Fee income for the fiscal year of 2009 was approximately US$2.11 billion. The practice's main areas of expertise include tax and international trade. In 1999, Baker & McKenzie named a woman to its top partner slot, becoming one of the first major law firms to do so. The firm, founded in 1949, had about 1,300 partners by 2009.

Allen & Overy LLP. Allen & Overy's theme is "Justice Around the World." It uses a tree analogy to describe its focus: "Broad International Cover with Deep Local Roots." In 2009, its international legal practice employed approximately 5,000 staff in 31 major centers throughout the world. Clients included BT Group, Equitable Life Assurance Society, Merrill Lynch, Shell Chemicals, and Virgin Mobile. Allen & Overy advises private clients on commercial trust, partnership, property, and tax issues. Based in London, the firm was founded in 1930, gaining fame when it worked for King Edward VIII during his abdication. Allen & Overy expanded globally beginning in 1978 when it opened offices in Dubai and then Brussels.

In September 2009, Allen & Overy announced it received special honors at the 2009 China Law & Practice Awards Ceremony. Notable among them were two awards related to restructuring. In remarks, Allen & Overy Managing Partner of Mainland China Simon Black stated this demonstrated our integrated HK/mainland practice is winning work and recognition.

Jones Day. As one of the largest practices in the world, Jones Day was also one of the oldest. It was founded in 1893 in Cleveland, Ohio. The practice offers legal counsel to more than half of the *Fortune* 500 companies. In 2009, Jones Day employed in excess of 2,400 lawyers in 32 locations including major centers of business and finance worldwide. Major clients included General Motors, IBM, and Texas Instruments.

In 2007, for the third consecutive year, Jones Day announced that its partner Bernard Amory was named regulatory communications lawyer of the year by the Who's Who Legal Awards. The award selection process reviewed thousands of nominations from clients and private practice professionals in the course of an ongoing research process to identify the pre-eminent lawyer and firm in each of 27 practice areas covered in *The International Who's Who of Business Lawyers of 2007*. The resource was a compendium edition of all the individual Who's Who legal publications released in April.

BIBLIOGRAPHY

"ABA President Carolyn B. Lamm Creates New Diversity Commission to Share Success Strategies with Lawyers Challenging the Glass Ceiling." American Bar Association, 4 August 2009. Available from www.abanet.org.

"About Clifford Chance." Clifford Chance, 2009. Available from www.cliffordchance.com.

"About Us." Allen & Overy, 2009. Available from www.allenovery.com.

"About Us." Freshfields Bruckhaus Deringer LLP, 2009. Available from www.freshfields.com.

"About Us." Linklaters, 2009. Available from www.linklaters.com.

Allen & Overy's China Practice Scoops Three 2009 CLP Awards." 24 September 2009. Available from www.allenovery.com.

Ankeny, Robert. "On the Docket." Crain's Detroit Business, 2 February 2004.

Barksdale, Titan. "Proposed Tax on Legal Services is Floated: Lawyers Express Opposition; Legislator Says It Won't Happen Anytime Soon." Winston-Salem Journal, 28 January 2007.

"Collecting debts tops lists of legal services: 2nd Quarter Data Released." The Duncan Banner-McClatchy-Tribune, 14 September 2009. Available from www.tradingmarkets.com.

Frank, Kimberly E., et al. "CPAs' Perceptions of the Emerging Multidisciplinary Accounting/Legal Practice." Accounting Horizons, March 2001.

"Freshfields Advises on the World' Largest IPO This Year to Date." Freshfields Bruckhaus Deringer LLP, 27 April 2007. Available from www.freshfields.com.

Gannon, Joyce. "Firms Teach Women Lawyers Importance of Networking to Climbing Law Firm Ladder." Pittsburgh Post-Gazette, 18 October 2006.

Heilman, Dan. "Hiring Diversity Managers–a New Law Firm Trend." Minnesota Lawyer, 5 March 2007.

"Hoover's Company Capsules." Hoover's Online, 2007. Available from www.hoovers.com.

Jeong-ho, Nam. "Open legal market brings global opportunities." Korea JoongAng Daily, 24 September 2009. Available from joongangdaily.joins.com.

Johnson, Glen. "Legal Services Offshoring: Hype Vs. Reality." The America s Intelligence Wire, 3 January 2007.

"Jones Day Partner Bernard Amory Named Regulatory Communications Lawyer of the Year for the Third Consecutive Year." Jones Day, April 2007. Available from www.jonesday.com.

"Key Facts & Figures." Baker & McKenzie, August 2009. Available from www.bakernet.com.

"Law Firm Leverage Varies with Firm Size and Location." Daily Record, 5 February 2007.

"The Lawyer Global 100: The World's Elite Law Firms 2004." The Lawyer, November 2004. Available from www.thelawyer.com.

"The Legal 500 2009." 2009. Available from www.legal500.com.

"Legal Services in Australia, China, France, Germany, Japan, South Korea, UK, US." Euromonitor, October 2004. Available from www.Euromonitor.com.

Makin, Kirk. "Legal-aid boycott now affects entire province." Globe and Mail (Toronto), 19 September 2009. Available from www.theglobeandmail.com.

McLeod-Roberts, Luke. "Allen & Overy Teaches Female Associates to Communicate." The Lawyer, 14 September 2009. Available from www.thelawyer.com.

Pribek, Jane. "ABA Reports Women of Color Still Having a Tough Time in Large Law Firm Environment." Wisconsin Law Journal, 22 November 2006.

"Recommended Law Firms and Lawyers Worldwide." The Legal 500, 16 July 2005. Available from www.legal500.com.

Solnik, Claude. "When it Comes to Law Firm Management, It's Whatever Works, Baby." Long Island Business News, 12 January 2007.

"UK Government: Make Legal Services More Accessible to Consumer Says Bridget Prentice." Europe Intelligence Wire, 26 March 2007.

U.S. Bureau of the Census. Service Annual Survey. Washington, 2004. Available from www.census.gov.

U.S. Bureau of Labor Statistics. "National Occupational Employment and Wage Data." Occupational Employment Statistics. Washington, D.C., 2004. Available from http://stats.bls.gov.

"US Law Firm Marches Into China." Alestron, 1 February 2007.

Wargo, Brian. "Economy Boosts Demand for Free Legal Aid." The Jacksonsville Financial News & Daily Record, 18 September 2009. Available from www.jaxdailyrecord.com.

World Legal Forum. Country Overview, 2001. Available from www.worldlegalforum.co.uk.

"Your Guide to the Region's Top Lawyers." The Journal, 25 September 2009. Available from www.nebusiness.co.uk.

MANAGEMENT CONSULTING SERVICES

NAICS CODE(S)

541611. Management consultants provide administrative, strategic, and technical advice and training to organizations in the public and private sectors. Examples of these services include financial planning, organizational planning, marketing advice, information technology consulting, human resource planning, and logistics advice. Some industry firms also provide management accounting and auditing services (see also **Accounting, Auditing, and Bookkeeping Services**). Others specialize in various forms of information technology planning and systems management (see also **Information Technology Services**).

INDUSTRY SNAPSHOT

The management consulting industry is highly fragmented and polarized. Participants vary widely in size, type, and specialization, with the majority of firms being either extremely large or extremely small. Management consulting services range from general management advice to technology development and from financial advising to strategy implementation. The industry is also characterized by its broad scope and increasingly blurred functional boundaries. Barriers to entry are low, the industry remains largely unregulated, and no certification requirements exist for becoming a management consultant. However, consultants can obtain an internationally recognized Certified Management Consultant (CMC) designation. Members must adhere to a strict code of professional conduct.

The industry's revenues are concentrated primarily among large U.S. and Western European consulting and accounting firms. However, while the United States weighs in with the largest presence in the industry, the U.S. market continues to mature. Accordingly, opportunities for market growth exist in emerging markets in Eastern Europe, the Commonwealth of Independent States, Latin America, and the Pacific Rim. Most large U.S. and European firms are shifting their revenue bases abroad, increasing integration of the world market.

For many years, an attractive feature of the industry was its stability and durability. Consulting was considered largely recession-proof by many analysts because during times of economic decline, businesses tend to look to consulting firms for restructuring advice and financial planning. When the dot-com bubble burst and recessionary economic conditions took hold in North America and Europe, however, growth in worldwide management consulting revenues began to slow. After several difficult years, the industry appeared to be recovering by 2004, with industry revenues at US$125 billion, according to Kennedy Information Research Group. In an October 2008 *Business Economics* article, Andrew Gross and Jozsef Poor, two business professors, estimated the size of the global market to be over US$150 billion in 2005 and US$210 billion in 2007. IBM Global Services was the leading firm, with almost US$57 billion in revenue.

However, the popping of the subprime mortgage bubble and resulting global recession left the industry enduring another downturn in the late 2000s. A number of consultants reportedly left the field to work in executive positions in other industries. With consulting firms starting to hire again in 2010, many of these were looking for an opportunity to return to the field. In the United Kingdom, 67 percent of consultancies had increased staff in the first half of 2010. In the United States, the Department of Labor's Bureau of Labor Statistics expected the consulting industry to be among the fastest growing between 2008 and 2018. Despite this growth, competition for jobs was expected to be stiff, because many people aspire to work in the field.

ORGANIZATION AND STRUCTURE

In the large, mature U.S. and Western European markets, demand is concentrated largely in the private sector. However, the trend for growth in the United States has been in the government and health care. In new, emerging markets, including central and Eastern Europe, India, and Asia, public sector institutions, including government bodies and international organizations, account for larger proportions of the demand. In particular, national governments in these regions are among the most rapidly growing client base because they utilize consulting firms to increase economic competitiveness. China has accounted for the most growth in the Asia Pacific region.

The global management consulting industry is composed of six major industry sectors: information technology (IT), human resources, strategy, operations, finance and accounting, and marketing and sales. An increasingly competitive consulting sector, IT includes companies that use computer and telecommunications technologies to solve business problems, create or seize business opportunities, and address business and management issues surrounding the implementation and integration of new technologies such as electronic commerce, technology needs assessment, and change management. Growth in many of these types of consulting companies has increasingly come from outsourcing. Numerous IT consultants have evolved beyond merely offering consulting services and have become full-service firms, with many traditional IT firms forming their own consulting subsidiaries. Alliances with providers are becoming common. IT consultants may consult with a company to determine its IT needs; purchase, install and integrate the recommended software and hardware; and eventually operate the system for the client.

Human resources firms in this group plan, develop, and implement programs that help managers motivate and compensate employees, as well as develop their ability to achieve corporate objectives. Examples include total quality management, team building, competency modeling, job analysis, benefits packaging, diversity planning, and pension funding. According to an October 2008 article in *Business Economics*, this sector accounted for 12 percent of the global management consulting market in 2007.

Strategy consultants help managers and directors develop and implement comprehensive, deliberate, strategic plans for improving an organization's competitive position or furthering its corporate mission. Such services often include growth and Internet strategies, acquisition and divestment advice, restructuring planning, and implementation of privatization.

Recent trends have shown clients to be tired of strategy in itself. They have become increasingly sophisticated consumers of strategy consulting services, and are looking for results that can be implemented quickly. Clients have become more results-driven with the result being a greater desire for compensation to consultants being tied to these results.

Operations consultants help managers improve production methods and business processes to increase efficiency and effectiveness. Activities include materials requirements planning, inventory planning and control, statistical quality control, customer relationship management (CRM), and project scheduling. This sector of the consulting industry is expected to have the largest growth rate in the 2010s.

Finance and accounting consultants advise managers on financial management, investment, and reporting to help them maximize the value of their organizations and ensure their future viability. Examples include shareholder value studies, treasury management, financial planning and risk management, and financial market review.

Marketing and Sales consultants provide managers with information and advice to help them maintain or increase market share. Thesr services include market analysis and segmentation, new market entry/positioning, product research, and new product development.

Traditionally, firms have billed their clients on an hourly basis, charging anywhere from US$100 to more than US$500 per hour. However, in the 1990s, a growing number of consultants, especially small firms, began to generate substantial fees based on performance for projects with a measurable outcome. Those fees could be as much as 70 percent. Recognizing the importance of results and accountability, these firms began accepting payment based on the clients' realized results. This practice was criticized because it could raise ethical concerns. For example, consultants accepting performance-based fees might be tempted to advise clients in such a manner as to encourage greater short-term results, neglecting the long-term stability of the company. To offset this potential danger, many consulting firms included members of the clients' management staff on the consulting team.

During the economic slowdown in North America and Europe in the early 2000s, the industry returned to traditional billing practices. According to a 2001 issue of *Consultants News,* performance-based pricing in the management consulting industry declined 50 percent between 1999 and 2000. The shift was due, in part, to the need for clients concerned about containing costs to obtain specific price quotes before hiring consultants.

Major suppliers of management consulting services are a diverse, competitive, and rapidly consolidating group. Firms differ along a number of ways, including organization type, organization size, area(s) of expertise, degree of specialization, clients and industries served, geographic presence, and global reach. The five major types of suppliers are consulting firms, "Big Four" accounting firms, computer software and hardware companies, independent businesses, and consulting divisions of large businesses and government organizations.

The sole or primary business of a consulting firm is the delivery of management advice and assistance. The majority of consulting firms are small, with annual billings of less than US$5 million. High profit potential, growing demand for management consulting services, and low barriers to entry fueled an influx of small firms and individual practitioners during the 1990s. Although fewer in number, large consulting firms, which are typically defined as those with annual revenues exceeding US$1 billion, account for a significant portion of global industry revenues. Fourteen firms met this criteria in 2001, many of whom derived a significant proportion of their revenues outside their home countries.

A shrinking number of mid-sized firms, generating between US$5 million and US$1 billion in revenues, operated successfully in the early 2000s. Limited global reach coupled with significant overhead costs make it increasingly difficult for mid-sized firms to maintain a foothold in this highly competitive market. Industry sources predicted that these firms would slowly be forced out of the market by large competitors looking to diversify service lines and expand access to international markets. Mid-sized firms are prime candidates for mergers and takeovers because of ready access to local and regional markets as well as having well-established client bases. The highest proportion of mid-sized firms operate in Europe.

The "Big Four" accounting firms are the four largest accounting and audit firms in the world—Pricewater houseCoopers, Ernst & Young, Deloitte Touche Tohmatsu, and KPMG International. Arthur Andersen was part of this group, which was formerly known as the Big Five, until Anderson was convicted for obstructing justice in the case against Enron. Prior to its demise, it spun off Andersen Consulting, which became autonomous from its parent in 2000 and changed its name to Accenture. In the late 2000s, Accenture had become the world's largest technology and management consulting company.

During the 1960s, when markets for traditional accounting services began to mature, the "Big Four" began to diversify into management consulting services, primarily focusing on the IT and financial services segments of the market. Like Andersen, the Big Five firms granted increasing autonomy to consulting divisions throughout the 1990s. In fact, under increasing pressure from U.S. federal regulators who were unhappy about potential conflicts of interest inherent in a company offering auditing as well as consulting services, Ernst & Young sold its consulting arm to France's Cap Gemini Group in 2000. KPMG spun off its consulting activities as KPMG Consulting the following year.

Consultants from the computer software and hardware companies were among the newest management consultants. In the early 1990s, large IT firms, including computer vendors, systems integrators, and software developers, began diversifying into management consulting when competition for core services intensified. A handful of these companies developed substantial management consulting practices, including Electronic Data Systems (EDS), International Business Machines (IBM), Digital Equipment Corporation (DEC), Unisys Corporation, and Sema Group. Most of these companies either bought into the market through formal mergers and acquisitions or gained access through informal alliances and loose networks with consulting organizations.

Independent Practitioners. The group of independent consultants is the most internationally diverse of the consultants. Local independent consultants were among the first to respond to demand in new markets and continued to play a significant role as markets have grown and matured. The lack of regulatory agencies to monitor professional competence along with the minimal start-up costs allows almost anyone to enter the market. Such businesses consist mainly of entrepreneurs, laid-off business professionals, former large-firm consultants, industry specialists, and, increasingly, university professors.

Internal consulting divisions began to spring up within large business and government organizations during the 1970s. For the most part, they provided management advice to various divisions within the organization. During the 1980s, internal divisions expanded their client bases beyond the parent company. In the early stages of growth in eastern Europe, Asia, and other markets, internal consultants to national and government organizations were among the first groups to offer management consulting advice.

BACKGROUND AND DEVELOPMENT

The origins of the management consulting services industry can be traced to "time and motion" studies performed in the United States in the 1880s. Around that time, Frank and Lillian Gilbreth improved methods for laying bricks by eliminating unnecessary steps or "motions" in the process. Frank W. Taylor similarly increased productivity in the U.S. steel industry by identifying and timing individual elements involved in various processes and pinpointing sources of inefficiency.

Business schools prepared students to be qualified consultants and provided business research to the management consulting field. In 1881, Arthur D. Little established the first management consulting firm in Cambridge, Massachusetts, bearing his name. The company quickly became a viable business and held a leadership position for more than 100 years. The first U.S. collegiate business school, the Wharton School, was also founded in 1881 in Cambridge, Massachusetts. Nearly two decades later, in 1900, the first graduate school of business opened, Dartmouth Amos Tuck School, followed by the Harvard Business School in 1908. The first European school, the Institute European d'Administration (INSEAD), opened in Fontainebleau, France, in 1957.

During the first half of the twentieth century, a contingent of small consulting firms and enterprising individuals began to advise businesses in the United States and Europe, primarily on matters of industrial productivity. These early consultants developed methods for saving time and other resources and applied them universally across businesses and industries. Some of the better known firms that were started during this period include Booz Allen and Hamilton (United States, 1914); Buck Consultants (Belgium, 1917); Orga SRL (Italy, 1925); McKinsey and Company (United States, 1926); Gherzi Management Consultants (Switzerland, 1929); Van de Bunt Management Consultants (The Netherlands, 1933); B.W. Berenschot (The Netherlands, 1938); PA Consulting (Great Britain, 1943); and Bossard (France, 1956).

A number of significant events that accelerated and influenced the development of the management consulting industry occurred in the 1960s. U.S. accounting firms began to expand into management consulting around this time. Within 10 years, these firms captured significant shares of the U.S. management consulting market and began to move into international markets. Toward the end of the decade, large consulting firms began to diversify service lines and also expanded into international markets. For the most part, global expansion involved establishing highly autonomous foreign offices that were staffed by local consultants who understood local business environments.

In 1963, Bruce Henderson founded the Boston Consulting Group (BCG) in Cambridge, Massachusetts, which operated as the first "pure strategy" consulting firm. Henderson developed several management tools, including "the growth share matrix" and "the experience curve," which were used in strategic planning to assess a company's competitive position or its individual business units. BCG's success had a number of long-term ramifications for the industry. It catalyzed the development of a long string of strategy "boutiques," many of which were founded by former BCG consultants and demonstrated how new management theories and business methodologies could create a competitive advantage for a management consulting firm. Finally, BCG's aggressive recruiting of MBA graduates drove up salaries for entry-level management consultants.

The 1980s were a period of tremendous growth, expansion, turbulence, and change. Thousands of business professionals laid off during massive downsizings in the major U.S. industries joined the growing ranks of consultants. U.S. consulting industry revenues doubled between 1980 and 1985 and doubled again within the following two to three years. Meanwhile the European market had grown 50 percent, fueled by demand for information technology consulting and assistance with privatization. Small local firms and individual consultants began to open in new markets around the world. Large consulting firms rushed to establish an early foothold in promising new markets in the United States and Europe. As a result the global market became larger and more integrated.

Eastern Europe and Asia were the fastest-growing new markets in the 1990s. Large Japanese corporations and Asian organizations emerged as major new clients, along with world organizations and governments in eastern and central Europe. The breakup of the Soviet Union led to increased demand for political risk studies, industrial infrastructure analyses, legal system assessments, and investment/market analysis in the former Soviet nations. Ongoing development in Poland, Romania, and other transition economies in Eastern Europe fueled the region's demand. As the dominant U.S. market continued to mature, most major U.S. firms concentrated their efforts on acquiring firms in the new markets to establish themselves in potentially lucrative areas without facing the cultural barriers typically involved in establishing new ventures.

Bolstering explosive industry growth in the mid-to-late 1990s was the Y2K (year 2000) computer problem. Consultants were contracted en masse to help businesses reconfigure their computing environments to be compatible with four-digit dating systems. This massive global project involved consultants in information technology, systems implementation, financial planning, and strategy.

The management consulting industry also became increasingly polarized during the 1990s. Large firms continued to grow by diversifying service lines to meet industry-specific needs, recruiting heavily to meet skyrocketing demand, and acquiring mid-sized firms and IT suppliers. These industry leaders evolved into "mega-service providers," or "one-stop-shopping centers," in order to secure profitable contracts with multinational corporations whose needs were as broad as their geographic bases. In addition, small firms and individual practitioners, such as business school professors and business technology experts, began entering the industry in record numbers. These niche practices usually focused on specific business concerns, such as operational strategies, and specific practices, such as electronic commerce.

Complex contracts involving large integrated teams of consultants and clients emerged in the late 1990s. The consulting activities of large firms shifted from "formulation" to "implementation," as the role of management consultants evolved from "management advisor" to "management tool." With this growing emphasis on implementation, especially in the area of IT consulting, the management consulting industry became increasingly difficult to define. Services ranging from customized software development to traditional strategic planning advice were bought and sold under the management consulting label. Important boundaries between management consulting, accounting, and computer/telecommunications fields began to break down, and the leading firms in these fields consolidated rapidly.

Major industry mergers and acquisitions during this period included the 1998 merger of Price Waterhouse and Coopers & Lybrand to form PricewaterhouseCoopers, which reduced the Big Six accounting firms to the Big Five. Two years later, Paris, France-based Capgemini Group bolstered its industry standing from eighth place to third place by acquiring the consulting operations of Ernst & Young for US$11 billion. Also in 2000, United Kingdom-based PA Consulting Group, Ltd., paid US$96 million for Hagler Bailly, a U.S.-based consulting firm. In September 2000, Hewlett-Packard attempted to purchase the IT consulting arm of PricewaterhouseCoopers, but the US$17 billion stock deal fell through the following month due to unstable IT market conditions.

An unprecedented level of cutbacks and layoffs dominated the U.S. and U.K. management consulting landscape early in the twenty-first century. The electronic commerce boom of the late 1990s had fostered an environment in which most leading consultancies were forced to compete with upstart Internet consultancies like Scient and Viant not only for business from clients looking to develop Internet strategies, but also for a rapidly shrinking pool of qualified employees. When the electronic commerce market began to slow and the North American economy softened in 2000, many firms found themselves overloaded with highly paid employees. As a result, to offset revenue growth slowdowns caused by the weak economy, many firms cut staff in the interest of profitability. In an effort to remain competitive, however, many companies also started discounting their fees as well as cutting their typical annual fee increases.

Demand for management consulting services remained strong in areas like continental Europe, where the Internet had arrived more slowly and where deregulation of certain industries was taking place. In the long term, some industry analysts expected Latin America as well as the Asia-Pacific region to offer substantial growth opportunities.

The absence of mandatory certification requirements and lack of enforceable industry standards continued to be prominent concerns within the industry. The increasing number of business relationships between management consulting firms and IT suppliers was considered to be a conflict of interest that could bias consultant recommendations regarding IT products. Another pressing issue is the conflict between accounting firms' auditing activities, which require absolute objectivity, and their management consulting activities, which increasingly became long term and high contact. "Relationship consulting," in which consulting firms work with clients over a period of several years to monitor and ensure progress on the implementation of ideas, has been a growing trend that added to this dilemma. Dialogue and legislative action related to conflict-of-interest issues throughout the 1990s came to a head late in the decade when the U.S. Securities and Exchange Commission (SEC) took aim at Big Five auditors, especially KPMG, to ensure independence from consulting clients. Rival firms took notice and began to spin off or sell divisions.

Like KPMG Consulting and Ernst & Young, Accenture also split from its accounting parent. However, this break was more closely tied to the perception by Anderson consultants that the slowly growing auditing business was eating into the profits garnered by Anderson Consulting, which had reported double-digit growth during the 1990s. Along with newly earned independence, KPMG Consulting and Accenture gained access to additional capital via public offerings, a new phenomenon among the upper echelon of management consultants.

Following a period of decline during the weak economy of the early 2000s, the management consulting industry appeared to be recovering by mid-2004. Industry revenues were US$119 billion in 2003, increasing to US$125 billion in 2004. While some leading firms such as Accenture experienced noteworthy growth during 2004, other large players such as Capgemini reported slower sales growth. Overall, pricing for consulting services remained steady during the mid-2000s, although conditions were ripe for improvement.

During the early 2000s, consulting firms that focused heavily on strategy rather than on technology suffered the most. For example, The Boston Consulting Group reported relatively stable revenues, but McKinsey & Co. reported declines of approximately 12 percent from 2000 to 2003. When the economy fell into a slump, consulting firms suddenly competed for a dwindling number of contracts that were far less profitable than they had been. As competition increased, consulting firms had to be more competitive with their fees.

Heading into the mid-2000s, the technology market showed promise for consultants, especially in the areas of wireless technology, project management, and security/reliability. However, leading corporations, especially those that had experienced significant losses during the dot-com boom, emerged from the early 2000s with more skepticism of management consultants. Entering the mid-2000s, the corporate sector was more focused on measurable results from investments in consulting services. Institute of Management Consultants USA Inc. Chairman Norman Eckstein indicated that large companies were seeking partnership-like arrangements with consultants. In addition, the biggest consulting firms were reducing the number of projects and employing fewer consultants on a short-term basis to appease corporate clients.

Moving into the second half of the 2000s, the management consulting industry was leaner and arguably more efficient than ever before. Although some observers had questioned the viability of some industry leaders during the early 2000s, it appeared that management consultants would continue to have a large role in the corporate sector. As explained in *The Economist,* "Independent strategic advice may be in greater demand given the growing calls for good corporate governance and scrutiny of conflicts of interest."

CURRENT CONDITIONS

With the field pared back and ready for growth after the early 2000s, the short-lived upswing was disappointing.

The growth that came soon disappeared in the late 2000s with another global economic downturn. As the early 2000s recession was noted for the dot-com bust, the new one was noted for subprime mortgages and a general freezing of credit markets. Businesses became nervous in this environment and greatly curtailed spending. In a 2008 survey of senior executives at consultancies by the Chartered Management Institute, some 42 percent said that the availability of credit would create a problem for them in the coming year. Some 72 percent also forecast a drop in training and development at their firm.

Niches that were thought to provide some protection against adverse economic conditions included health care and alternative energy. Aging populations in North America, Japan, and Europe promise to help keep the health sector active, while environmental concerns do the same for the alternative energy field. The downturn in developed nations also reinforced the trend of consulting firms looking for growth in the emerging markets such as China and India, where economic development continued at a rapid rate. However, there are also barriers to consultancies easily taking advantage of these new markets. For instance, in Asia, there are established domestic networks that must be negotiated in order to do business successfully, and these can vary from nation to nation.

Signs of industry improvement arrived in 2010. In the United Kingdom, the Management Consultancies Association reported that in the first half of the year, most private sector sources of revenue were performing well, and that financial services and manufacturing were looking particularly strong. Demand from the public sector, however, continued to be weak.

Management consulting, particularly at the large firms, retained its attraction to new graduates looking for employment. Universum World's 2010 Most Attractive Employers index saw the Big Four holding four of the top five positions in the best business employers category. While Internet giant Google held the top spot in the poll, KPMG was second, Ernst & Young third, PricewaterhouseCoopers fourth, and Deloitte fifth. The list is based on surveys of almost 130,000 students at leading academic institutions in the world's twelve top economies.

RESEARCH AND TECHNOLOGY

Research has always been a key aspect of the management consulting industry. Consultants spend a significant portion of their time identifying, understanding, and developing tools to help clients address business and management issues. From the industry's inception in the 1880s until the early 1960s, research and development consisted largely of industrial productivity studies. In 1963, the Boston Consulting Group shifted the industry's research focus to strategic planning when it developed the growth share matrix and the experience curve.

During the 1980s, management research and consulting advice concentrated on quality improvement. Tools and techniques like total quality management, continual quality improvement, and quality circles were developed and sold to businesses in the United States and Europe. The hub of research shifted in the 1990s toward re-engineering and change management. Management consultants during this period generally developed ways to better integrate business, human, and technological processes. At the end of the twentieth century, firms had focused on information technology-based consulting and systems implementation, particularly as they related to the Internet and electronic commerce. As the corporate climate has become more dependent upon sophisticated and efficient technological and communications systems, the management consulting industry has shifted a substantial portion of its research efforts into this specialized field of knowledge.

Each major shift in the focal point that emerges from the consulting industry's research efforts, such as productivity, strategy, quality, and integration, creates a surge of growth in the industry. New firms enter the market as specialists in the "hottest" areas, diversifying into other areas as revenues grow and client bases expand. Large firms add new service lines or acquire existing niche companies to capitalize on the increased demand.

Business schools play an important role in the research and development of new consulting approaches. Ongoing research at these institutions and the ensuing reports provide a constant flow of information and ideas for consultants to apply to their work. Professors of management and senior partners at large firms market their consulting services by publishing management articles and research results in leading business and industry journals.

Advances in IT facilitate expansion and globalization of large consulting practices, enabling firms to build barriers to entry at the top tier of the industry. Extensive telecommunications networks and sophisticated computer technologies permit large firms to mobilize worldwide teams and resources. Moreover, electronic storage and retrieval capabilities allow firms to store, build upon, and readily access massive amounts of knowledge and experience.

WORKFORCE

After a period of intense recruitment in the late 1990s, management consulting firms began to downsize their employee ranks. For instance, Accenture laid off four percent of its workforce and asked hundreds of employees in the United States, Asia, and Europe to take a leave of absence in 2001. PricewaterhouseCoopers also reduced its workforce and cut the pay of its U.S. consulting employees

by seven percent. Similarly, Cap Gemini cut four percent of its workforce in the United States, Britain, and Scandinavia, and KPMG Consulting laid off seven percent of its staff. As a result of these moves, between October of 2000 and October of 2001 the worldwide consulting industry reported a decrease of nearly five percent from a total of 600,000 employees to 572,000 employees.

A rebound eventually came, and during the fiscal year ended February 2005, the U.S. Department of Labor Bureau of Labor Statistics (BLS) indicated that the management consulting industry had added 30,300 new jobs in the prior year. During 2004, Accenture added 17,000 employees and doubled its staff to 10,000 in India alone.

According to the BLS, by 2008 the United States employed approximately one million management, scientific, and technical consultants on a wage and salary basis. Employment was projected to increase by 83 percent between 2008 and 2018, more than in any other industry. A large number of people eager to work in this field was expected to keep competition for openings keen, however.

Employers in this diverse, highly communicative, idea-based industry seek out primarily intelligent, creative, presentable employees with a diverse and well-rounded knowledge base. Along with traditional needs, such as financial planning and growth strategies that require a substantial amount of formal business training, firms look for people with industry-specific knowledge. Consultants are often involved in system installation and development of global networks, for which technical knowledge is a primary asset, with basic writing and people skills. As a result, firms have broadened their recruiting efforts from the top tier of business schools and begun to seek employees who have training in computers, sciences, and the liberal arts. Firms look primarily for consultants with the most distinguished pedigrees, which allows them to justify higher fees. Most major industry players maintain business units whose sole function is to recruit, hire, and train employees.

The life of a management consultant is notoriously arduous, involving a substantial amount of time away from home. However, what consultants lose in free time and effort they make up for in salary, which typically ranges from US$35,000 to US$125,000 for new hires. Partners tend to make between US$120,000 and US$500,000. Bonuses become increasingly larger portions of the salary as people move up the ranks of a firm. At some firms, those occupying the senior levels account for close to 25 percent of the firms' total salary expense. Among the highest salaries are those for leading management "gurus," many of whom were professors at leading business universities. Self-employed consultants or those working for small firms generally earn substantially lower salaries than those working for large firms.

The ranks of self-employed consultants and small consulting firms are often comprised of laid-off or retired business professionals, former consultants for large firms, and academics. Most consultants in these categories are specialists in their industry or practice area.

INDUSTRY LEADERS

McKinsey and Company. McKinsey and Company opened its first office in Chicago, Illinois, in 1926 and its first foreign office in London in 1959. McKinsey remained primarily a strategy consultancy firm, bucking the industry trend toward IT specialization. McKinsey's growth in the late 1990s had been concentrated in Russia, Eastern Europe, China, and India.

McKinsey is considered one of the most prestigious management-consulting firms in the world. As a generalist firm, McKinsey engages a broad range of clients and offers a diversified portfolio of services, although the bulk of its work is concentrated in the areas of strategy and organization. McKinsey is particularly well known for its efficient data gathering and its extensive and frequent reporting.

The company invests heavily in internal research and development, spending approximately US$50 million annually researching, recording, and communicating business information and theory. Its centralized database of information provides its offices around the world with ready access to key corporate and business information. McKinsey's conservative environment is exemplified by a traditional "up or out" worker policy, in which employees who fail to move up in the company are dismissed. This policy is aided by the firm's extensive employee training. McKinsey's conservative but prestigious atmosphere has fostered many well-known international business figures and high-ranking government officials.

Accenture Ltd. Accenture (formerly Andersen Consulting) posted revenues of more than US$21.55 billion in fiscal 2010 and reported about 204,000 employees. It has offices and operations in more than 200 cities in 53 countries. Operations are highly decentralized with ownership and control of foreign offices vested in local professionals. Accenture's services are arranged into 19 industry groups within the five operating groups of Communications and High Tech, Financial Services, Health and Public Service, Products, and Resources. The firm's client list includes 94 of the *Fortune* Global 100 and more than three-fourths of the *Fortune* Global 500.

Andersen Consulting became a dominant player in the global market in 1989, when it was established as a separate business unit from Arthur Andersen. Andersen Consulting restructured its organization in 1997 into 127 specialized industry units, along with units for outsourcing and knowledge management. In 1998, Andersen Consulting voted to split completely from Arthur Andersen, which had been renamed Andersen Worldwide. Wanting to separate itself from what it viewed as the less lucrative auditing business of its parent, the consultancy earned full autonomy from Andersen Worldwide in 2000, at which time Anderson Consulting changed its name to Accenture. The firm completed its initial public offering the following year.

Deloitte Touche Tohmatsu. Having dropped the word "International" from its name in 1997, Deloitte acknowledged its solid reputation as a global company. Deloitte Consulting, which focuses on strategic planning, IT, and financial management consulting, is the largest unit of Deloitte, accounting for about 25 percent of its sales. In fiscal 2010, the Deloitte Touche Tohmatsu network became the world's largest private professional services network with 170,000 employees across more than 140 nations. The firm planned to hire 250,000 new people by 2015.

BearingPoint Inc. As the former consulting division of accounting giant KPMG International, BearingPoint became a separate subsidiary in 1999. It officially separated from its parent in 2000 and launched an initial public offering in February 2001. In 2002, the company hired many former U.S. employees of Andersen Consulting and acquired Andersen's business consulting businesses in Hong Kong, China, Australia, Sweden, Norway, Finland, Switzerland, Singapore, Korea, Spain, Japan, and France. The company changed its name from KPMG Consulting to BearingPoint and began trading on the New York Stock Exchange in 2002.

By 2005, the company employed 16,000 people in 200 offices in 39 countries. It concentrates primarily on business and technology strategy as well as technology services, including systems design, architecture, applications implementation, network infrastructure, systems integration, and managed services. According to BearingPoint Chairman and CEO Rod McGeary in the February 2005 issue of *Consulting Magazine* online, the company was the market leader in China and expected that country to be an area for international growth.

Microsoft and Bearing Point announced in August 2008 that they had united to create a risk-based compliance solution incorporating Microsoft technology. It included helping organizations identify areas of risk, accessing and remediating control deficiencies, and strengthening compliance without compromising profitability. Microsoft's software connected users with Bearing Point's leadership in business strategy, management consulting, and systems integration. The Bearing Point Enterprise Governance, Risk and Compliance solution had evolved from its initial public sector focus to being capable of extending across many industries.

In November 2008, the NYSE suspended trading of BearingPoint stock when the price dropped to US$0.07 per share. In March 2009, Bearing Point announced a plan to sell its business units to competitors PricewaterhouseCoopers and Deloitte, as well as other private buyers.

IBM Global Services. IBM Global Services is the world leader in technology consulting and services and is among the largest providers of business consulting and systems integration. In 2002, IBM purchased the consulting arm of the largest accountancy in the world, PricewaterhouseCoopers, following the economic slowdown and corporate accounting scandals of the early 2000s. PwC Consulting, the consulting subsidiary of PricewaterhouseCoopers, had been pursued by several suitors, including Hewlett-Packard. A business segment of IBM, the company earned more than US$45 billion in 2004 and employed more than 175,000 people. By 2007, IBM Global Services was estimated to be the largest player in the global management consulting market with almost US$57 million in revenues.

A.T. Kearney. A.T. Kearney was founded in 1926 when McKinsey and Company spun off a segment of its operations. After being acquired by EDS's Management Consulting Services in 1995, A.T. Kearney doubled in size and emerged as one of the world's premier consulting firms, particularly in the automotive industry. The acquisition by EDS substantially enhanced the firm's industry expertise and greatly benefited its information technology consulting, the area from which A.T. Kearney derives the bulk of its revenue. However, integration difficulties took their toll on the firm's performance throughout the late 1990s.

A.T. Kearney operated in North and South America, Europe, and Asia and was quickly moving into emerging markets in Argentina, Brazil, Russia, India, and Turkey. Sales in 2000 reached US$1.3 billion, 65 percent of which were derived from international operations. By 2003, the firm's revenues had fallen to US$846 million, down almost 16 percent from 2002. Revenues fell again in 2004, to US$806 million, with losses of US$10 million. According to *The Financial Times* this prompted parent EDS to enter into talks for a buyout by partners. In July 2010, the firm, with 2,700 employees, ended merger discussions it had participated in with Booz & Co.

Capgemini. Based in Paris, France, management consultant Cap Gemini catapulted from eighth place to third place among the largest management consultancies in the world when it paid US$11 billion for the consulting arm of Ernst & Young in 2000, forming Cap Gemini Ernst & Young. On April 15, 2004, the company shortened its name to Capgemini. The purchase, which was the largest

in industry history at that time, boosted Capgemini's North American operations to roughly 33 percent of total sales.

Founded in 1967, Capgemini has become the largest IT consultant in Europe. The firm offers IT consulting services, particularly for systems integration and software development, as well as corporate strategy development and implementation. As of 2010, the firm had over 106,000 employees in more than 35 countries.

Booz Allen Hamilton Inc. Booz Allen Hamilton, a management and technology consulting firm founded in 1914, concentrates on large international businesses and on government contracts to a greater extent than its competition. A large proportion of its operations are in U.S. defense and military contracts, followed by local, state, federal, and foreign government consulting. The firm generated over US$5 billion in revenues in 2009 and had approximately 23,000 employees in more than 30 countries. Operations were divided into two business niches focused on government clients and the commercial sector.

PA Consulting Group Ltd. PA Consulting was founded in 1943 in the United Kingdom and was the largest consulting firm worldwide in 1970. Faltering revenues in the 1980s were exacerbated by recession in the early 1990s. Despite its drop in rank, PA Consulting remained a formidable competitor in the international management consulting market. The company had a strong focus on change management.

Roland Berger Strategy Consultants GmbH. Three-quarters owned by Deutsche Bank, Roland Berger Strategy Consultants is the largest management consulting firm of European origin. Since its establishment as Roland Berger & Partners in 1967 by Roland Berger, the firm has grown to about 2,000 employees in 2009. Its core European markets were Germany, the United Kingdom, and France.

The company has grown quickly with an emphasis on innovation and expansion strategy consulting. The firm acquired IPG, a British strategy consultant, in 1999, and in 2000, Roland Berger & Partners changed its name to Roland Berger Strategy Consultants to better reflect its specialization.

MAJOR COUNTRIES IN THE INDUSTRY

From the industry's inception through the present, the United States has hosted the world's largest management consulting firms. However, along with the business climate in general, the consulting industry was becoming more global in focus during the 2000s. Outsourcing (the transfer of management to a third party, which may or may not be offshore) and offshoring (the transfer of work to another country to a company's facility or to a third party) were two hotly discussed topics throughout the world. The issue was especially of concern in North America, where everything from manufacturing jobs to computer programming and customer service tasks were being sent to countries with lower labor costs, such as China and India.

Ernst & Young LLP was one of the leading global consultancy that helped companies to successfully implement and manage outsourcing initiatives. Ernst & Young accomplished this through its Business Risk Services unit, which helped companies perform risk assessments, engage in strategic planning, manage licensing, improve operational processes, evaluate third-party vendors, and more. Ernst & Young worked with organizations to help them outsource specific functional elements or entire processes. Accenture was another leading global consulting enterprise that assisted companies to use outsourcing as part of a strategy to maximize performance. In the mid-2000s, Accenture began offering consulting services in outsourcing business processes, applications, and technology infrastructures. Infosys, which is a leading Indian outsourcing services provider specializing in IT, formed its own U.S.-based consulting subsidiary in April 2004. The firm was led by a team of business consulting heavyweights, including CEO Stephen Pratt, who in 2003 was dubbed one of the world's top 25 consultants by *Consulting Magazine.*

In addition to advising clients regarding offshoring, some consulting firms engaged in a variation of the practice by moving their headquarters to foreign locations. Critics, including unions and government officials, argued that this was a tactic to avoid federal and state tax payments. In the June 21, 2004, issue of *Computerworld,* Illinois State Comptroller Dan Hynes questioned the move of Accenture's headquarters to Bermuda. Although the company insisted that it paid its U.S. taxes, Hynes characterized the company an expatriate, and argued that it was "unfair and unpatriotic" to award state contracts to the consulting giant. Hynes drafted a bill that was introduced to the Illinois legislature to prevent expatriate firms from receiving state contacts. Other states passed or considered similar measures.

In November 2010, anti-offshoring sentiment in the U.S. was expected to decrease in the wake of a trip to India by President Barack Obama. He said India was a job creator for the United States, and returned with free trade deals that he said would create 50,000 new U.S. jobs.

The European Union is the other major player in the management consulting industry. According to European Federation of Management Consulting Associations (FEACO), the size of the market reached US$117 billion in 2008, 8.2 percent growth over 2007. Germany was the largest market, followed by the United Kingdom, Spain, and France. Management consulting was considered to be the most popular career choice for European engineering and business students.

Many analysts considered China to be one of the most exciting emerging markets, along with other emerging Asia Pacific nations. While Hong Kong is clearly the leading center of consulting activity in the region, with more than 100 international and local management consulting companies, many firms are moving into mainland China, particularly Beijing, to take advantage of growing opportunities there. As state control of industry segments continues to diminish, consultancy firms are expected to have a lucrative market. Major international firms such as McKinsey, PricewaterhouseCoopers, and Accenture had already begun establishing themselves in the region.

BIBLIOGRAPHY

"About Us." Bearing Point, 15 November 2010. Available from bearingpoint.com.

"About Us." Capgemini, 15 November 2010. Available from http://www.capgemini.com.

Agarwal, Surabhi. "Software Firms Optimistic after Obama Visit, US Poll Outcome." Livemint.com, 15 November 2010. Available from http://www.livemint.com.

"Big Four Challenge Google's Attractive Employer Status." *Consulting Times,* October 2010. Available from http://www.consulting-times.com.

"Consultant, Heal Thyself." *Economist,* 2 November 2002.

"Deloitte Ascends to Become the Largest Private Professional Services Organization Worldwide." Deloitte press release, 5 October 2010. Available from http://www.deloitte.com.

"European Consulting Market 2008 Shows Sustained Growth." FEACO, 15 November 2010. Available from http://www.feaco.org.

"Fact Sheet." Booz Allen Hamilton, 15 November 2010. Available from http://www.boozallen.com.

"Fact Sheet—Q4 Fiscal 2010." Accenture, 15 November 2010. Available from newsroom.accenture.com.

Gross, Andrew C., and Jozsef Poor. "The Global Management Consulting Sector." *Business Economics,* October 2008.

Jones-Bonbrest, Nancy. "Organization Woman." *Baltimore Sun,* 16 July 2008. Available from http://www.baltimoresun.com.

Koudsi, Suzanne. "Consultants: Who Are We?" *Fortune,* 3 September 2001.

London, Simon. "EDS in Talks to Sell AT Kearney." *The Financial Times,* 26 February 2005.

"Managing the Next Generation Workforce." Next Step Growth, 2008. Available from http://www.nextstepgrowth.com.

Michaels, Adrian. "Deloitte Holds Fast on Keeping Its Consultancy." *The Financial Times,* 1 July 2001. Available from news.ft.com.

"Microsoft Corp. and BearingPoint Inc. Alliance." TAXI, The Creative Finder, 7 August 2008. Available from http://www.designtaxi.com.

"Multi-Generational Workforce Requires New Management Strategies to Attract and Engage Top Talent." PR Web, 16 July 2008. Available from http://www.prweb.com.

Nemko, Marty. "Best Careers 2009: Management Consultant." *US News* & *World Report* Careers blog, 11 December 2008. Available from money.usnews.com.

Newing, Rod. "Recruitment: Leavers Look for Way Back in as Others Ponder an Exit."*Financial Times*, 14 November 2010. Available from http://www.ft.com.

"NYSE Suspends BearingPoint." *Consulting Magazine,* 18 November 2008. Available from http://www.consultingmag.com.

"Profitability Elusive for Many Firms." *Consultants News,* 2001.

Purcell, Margaret A. "Ask an Outside Consultant." *Star-Tribune* (Minneapolis), 14 July 2008. Available from http://www.startribune.com.

"Statement from A.T. Kearney." A.T. Kearney news release, 5 July 2010. Available from http://www.atkearney.com.

"Stronger growth for UK consulting sector." *Consulting Times,* October 2010. Available from http://www.consulting-times.com.

Verton, Dan. "Illinois Moves to Blacklist Accenture." *Computerworld,* 21 June 2004.

"Winners' Curse; Management Consultants." *The Economist,* 21 July 2001.

SIC 7360

PERSONNEL SERVICES

NAICS CODE(S)

5613. Personnel services link job seekers with employers under various arrangements. By far the most common form is through temporary staffing, wherein the employee is paid by the personnel service to work temporarily for another firm needing assistance. Other types of personnel services include employment agencies, which seek to place job seekers in permanent positions, and recruitment agencies, which also contract to fill permanent positions, but typically perform more screening—and sometimes searching—to find employment candidates who meet certain criteria.

INDUSTRY SNAPSHOT

The American Staffing Association's annual economic analysis for 2009 had an overall positive outlook projecting more "growth" for the future. Staffing industry changes were believed to be reflective of the overall economy. Thus, as the Association pointed out, it was considered to be "a coincident economic indicator and a leading employment indicator." Although economic conditions were volatile, future projections still called for better than average industry expansion. This was excellent news for staffing, which constantly continued to be a major part of the employment services industry.

The U.S. Bureau of Labor statistics projected an increase of 692,000 jobs between 2006 and 2016, according to an American Staffing Association Staffing Statistics report. This positive projections realization would mean it achieved ranking of "second largest job-growth industry in the U.S." Futhermore, the American Staffing Association noted that while the U.S. staffing industry "contracted" in 2008, it rebounded to grow faster than the overall economy due to "the flexibility factor."

Manpower, Inc.'s March 29, 2007, Annual Talent Shortage Survey findings claimed 41 percent of employers throughout the world were experiencing difficulty in filling jobs. Openings that were particularly challenging to fill included sales representatives, skilled manual trades people, and technicians. Technician areas included technical workers for the areas of production/operations, engineering, and maintenance. Manpower surveyed nearly 37,000 employees across 27 countries and territories as a follow-up to a 2006 survey. Sales representatives were listed as the most difficult position to fill in the United States, Japan, Hong Kong, Taiwan, Singapore, New Zealand, Ireland, and Peru. Other jobs on the 2007 "Hot Jobs" to fill list included engineers, accounting and finance staff, laborers, production operators, drivers, management/executives, and machinists/operators.

The industry experienced phenomenal growth during the 1990s, as average daily employment increased steadily from 0.98 million jobs in 1991 to a record 2.54 million in 2000. However, conditions changed in the wake of an economic recession that was exacerbated by the terrorist attacks against the United States on September 11, 2001. Subsequently, daily staffing fell to 2.18 million workers in 2001 and 2.06 million workers in 2002. Overall, the American Staffing Association (ASA) reported that 739,000 contract and temporary staffing jobs were lost as a result of the 2001 economic recession. After peaking in the third quarter of 2000, contract and temporary staffing levels declined through the first quarter of 2002, falling 28 percent before conditions started to improve.

According to Adecco S.A., the world's largest employment services company, the United States, United Kingdom, Italy, France, Spain, Switzerland, Canada, and Australia were among the world's largest staffing markets, accounting for the majority of global staffing demand. Euromonitor, an international market research firm, was expecting the market for employment services in China to grow by a staggering 160 percent between 2003 and 2008.

In the third quarter of 2009, a national U.S. survey resulted in data showing there were projections for "hiring to remain stable in Q3 2009 as compared to Q2 2009." Data of this type indicated there was a "hesitancy among employers," according to Manpower Inc. President for the Americas Jonas Prising.

Manpower's global Employment Outlook Survey results for the third quarter of 2009 showed potential employees would experience "more of the same sluggish hiring pace seen during the first half of the year." Worldwide projections took into account employer expectations that "they will hold on to the staff they have."

Manpower"s Employment Outlook Survey for fourth quarter 2009 projected challenging times worldwide for people searching for jobs. The strongest hiring plans areas were emerging markets of India and Brazil. Others with related potential included Columbia, Peru, China, and Canada. Weak areas included the United States, Spain, Japan, and Mexico.

ORGANIZATION AND STRUCTURE

Origins and Development. The personnel services industry originated in the early to mid-twentieth century from three key developments: (1) government agencies that were created to combat unemployment, grounded on the emergence of unemployment as a social problem in industrial society; (2) demand during and immediately after World War II for temporary clerical work, originally when permanent employees were sick or on vacation; and (3) executive search firms, or so-called headhunters, who were sought to help companies recruit highly qualified personnel. While other kinds of organizations also evolved with and from these developments, in terms of revenues and influence, for-profit temporary staffing agencies have assumed paramount stature.

During the 1990s, temp services grew large enough that their volume of job placements could be measured as a percentage of national labor forces, although, as of the late 1990s, in no country did that percentage exceed 5 out of every 100 workers. In 1997 the Netherlands was estimated to have the highest proportion of temporary staffing in its labor force, with 3 percent of all Dutch workers employed by temporary services. France ranked second with 2 percent, followed by the United States and the United Kingdom, which were even at 1.8 percent. Temporary staffing was estimated to account for 0.5 percent of the working populations in both Germany and Japan.

The personnel services industry has its roots in the clerical staffing business, but the industry has broadened its spectrum of placements to include factory workers on up to top executives. In early 2001, office and clerical positions accounted for slightly more than 20 percent of all temporary and contract positions, according to the ASA. About 35 percent of workers were employed in the industrial sector, followed by professional and management (21 percent), information technology (9.3 percent), health care (7.8 percent), and technical (6.4 percent).

By 2004, highly skilled professionals such as accountants, attorneys, biochemists, and engineers were the fastest-growing category of temporary workers. In fact, at the largest staffing enterprises, these workers constituted up to one-third of placements. Marketing professionals were another emerging occupational group within the temp industry.

The biggest development impacting the personnel services industry during the early years of the first decade of the 2000s was the 2001 economic recession, which led to the loss of 739,000 contract and temporary staffing positions, according to the ASA. Contract and temporary staffing levels reached a high point in the third quarter of 2000 and then declined through the first quarter of 2002, falling 28 percent before any signs of improvement appeared. This mirrored trends in the larger U.S. job market, which lost 2.7 million jobs between March 2001 and August 2003, based on figures from the U.S. Department of Labor's Bureau of Labor Statistics (BLS).

Sales in the temporary help sector continue to make up the biggest share of revenue in the personnel services industry. Sales in this sector increased more than threefold between 1990 and 2000, reaching a record US$63.6 billion. However, the economic recession caused industry sales to decrease US$7.4 billion in 2001, to US$56.2 billion. After declining to US$55.2 billion in 2002, sales improved with the larger economy, reaching US$56.3 billion in 2003.

In July of 2003, a conference was hosted by Adecco at the London Business School to explore temporary staffing in a number of countries. At the conference, Hiroshi Saito, a management professor at Kanto Gakuen University in Tokyo, touched upon a number of important developments that were benefiting the temporary staffing industry in Japan. One major trend was the gradual relaxation of government restrictions on temporary employment agencies, which were first allowed in Japan during 1985.

According to an article in *Japan Press Weekly,* the nation's temporary workforce doubled from 1999 to 2002 as the Japanese government allowed temporary staffing in a growing number of industries. As of April 1, 2004, restrictions on the use of manufacturing workers were lifted. Although many manufacturing firms had already worked around these restrictions by outsourcing assembly lines to so-called external service providers, the development was expected to further industry growth.

At the London Business School conference, Saito explained that Japan was home to approximately 500,000 temporary employees in 2003, 66 percent of whom held clerical jobs, followed by information technology workers holding 12 percent of the jobs, and technical and engineering positions holding 10 percent. The remainder worked in a variety of other fields.

In 2003 approximately 75 percent of Japan's temporary workforce consisted of young adults, 70 percent of whom were women. Although staffing companies like Adecco were preparing to capitalize on the growing use of temporary workers in Japan, some observers were critical of this trend. Opponents argued that Japanese firms were maximizing profits at the expense of the nation's youngest workers, who found well paying, permanent full-time positions hard to come by.

Logistics of Personnel Placement. Personnel services conduct their businesses in a variety of ways, but all successful ones must be able to do two things: obtain employer contracts to place employees and recruit qualified workers to fill open slots. Finding employer contracts involves marketing the service via advertisements, direct marketing, and sometimes word of mouth. Effective marketing requires that personnel services be aware of potential clients' needs, which may be very specific, and that the service convey an image of competence and cost-effectiveness to sway an employer to use that particular service.

At least equally important is a personnel service's need to recruit satisfactory workers, since if an agency earns a reputation with a customer for supplying unqualified help, it will in all likelihood lose that account. Most of the world's large agencies perform one or more stages of screening to ensure they hire employees who will meet their clients' expectations. The minimal screening usually involves completion of a conventional job application form to collect such data as work history and educational background, followed by some form of personal interview with the applicant. Most firms also administer a variety of tests, some general and some job-specific, to better ascertain applicants' skills. Examples of such tests include general math and reading quizzes, typing tests, computer software proficiency exams, and job-specific questionnaires. The largest companies have developed proprietary software for evaluating candidates' aptitudes. When applicants lack the necessary skills, some agencies offer training services. In addition, once a worker has been placed in a position, most temp services perform some form of follow-up with the employer to determine whether it was a successful match.

Workers placed through temporary services are employed by the agency rather than the client. In countries without universal health insurance, such as the United States, often this means the temporary worker receives no insurance benefits, although temp services may offer benefits to varying degrees. Employers usually pay for the temp service on an hourly basis, and a portion of this fee becomes the worker's wage, with a share taken by the agency as well. Some agencies may charge additional flat fees for their services.

Because staff placement demands an understanding of the work being contracted, many firms, especially smaller ones, elect to specialize within certain markets. Specialization also allows larger companies to market a more

easily identifiable service—for example, experienced computer programmers, rather than generic "temps"—to potential customers. This sort of specialization is probably most extensive in Europe and the United States in the industry's health care segment, which supplies trained workers to serve as nurses' aides and in-home health care assistants. Many other specialties exist, though, including legal staffing, scientific services, and computer specialists.

To the extent a personnel firm offers specialized services, it may operate in either a commodity-like market or a premium-service market. Generalized services in major markets, such as France, the United Kingdom, and the United States, are usually commodity services and operate on relatively tight margins. Specialized, particularly technical, services can charge substantially more for their workers and tend to experience wider profit margins.

The degree of specialization also signifies the barriers that exist to enter a given market. To be credible to their customers, the most specialized firms must have individuals on their recruiting and placement staff who are highly experienced in the targeted field (e.g., a scientific staffing agency requires in-house scientists who evaluate applicants and work with customers). Building this level of expertise represents a substantial barrier to entry and helps preserve such specialty companies from price competition. At the same time, in the commodity markets for general office and light industrial help, which require only very broad skills, the entry barriers are low, but the ability to set favorable pricing—and hence, often profitability—is minimal.

CURRENT CONDITIONS

Industry Status. In 2004, Adecco estimated that the industry's revenues were US$400 billion worldwide, with employee leasing and independent contractors (US$200 billion) representing the largest category. At US$140 billion, temporary staffing was the next largest category, followed by the US$30 billion search and placement services segment. These market share figures do not include penetration rates. In 2003 penetration rates in the United Kingdom were the highest at 3.8 percent, while rates in the Netherlands were 3.3 percent, followed by 2.4 percent in France, 1.7 percent in the United States, and 1.1 percent in Japan and Portugal.

According to the Bureau of Labor Statistics, employment services were expected to grow at an annual average rate of 3.8 percent through 2014, creating nearly 1.6 million new jobs. Furthermore, the U.S. staffing industry was expected to grow faster by adding more jobs than any other industry during the next decade. The Remedy Temp Quarterly Labor Forecast showed an expected year-over-year increase of 4 percent in demand for temporary workers during the third quarter of 2006.

In Europe, most agency-placed employment occurs in the manufacturing sector, with most temporary work going to young, mostly low-skilled workers. An interesting anomaly in the personnel industry occurs in Spain. Here more than 30 percent of the country's total employed workforce is under temporary contract, with 76 percent citing an inability to find permanent employment as the reason. In Germany and Switzerland, most temporary work was being undertaken as a means to obtain employment training.

In the United Kingdom, the number of workers supplied via temporary agencies increased 250 percent between 1992 and 2001. By mid-2004, Great Britain was home to more than half of Europe's temporary employees. Around this time, regulatory changes were made to protect the employment rights of U.K. temporary workers. However, *Management Today* indicated that the changes did little to specify the stance of agency employees in such areas as maternity leave and unfair dismissal. Additionally, while the revisions required agencies to sign contracts with their employees, certain exceptions left the nature of agency staff's contractual relationships unclear, in terms of whether they worked for the temporary agency or the client company. Euromonitor valued the employment services market in the United Kingdom at about US$43 billion in 2003, with the temporary help sector accounting for 93 percent of the total market. In the temporary sector, the IT, computing, and telecommunications fields provided the most jobs. The industry remains highly fragmented with the majority of the 10,000 employment services offices being single-office agencies. In France, the market was valued at US$21.9 billion in 2003, with more than 40 percent of the market being attributed to construction-related jobs.

Changes were on the horizon in Europe during the mid-years of the first decade of the 2000s. One major development was the European agency workers directive. Published by the European Commission in 2002, the directive "aims to allow temporary agency workers employment conditions that are equally favourable to those available to a permanent worker in the same job and in the same company," according to a July 2004 *BusinessEurope.com* article. Scheduled to become law in 2006, the directive is only applicable to temporary workers who are provided via an agency and who have worked a minimum of six weeks.

In Asia, employment service market values were growing. In Japan, the industry was valued at US$20.6 billion, with temporary staffing accounting for almost 94 percent of the market. The industry was not quite so big in China, and was valued at about US$1.24 billion in 2003. However, that figure represented a 20.7 percent growth beyond 2002, and the market was expected to grow by 160 percent in the five years leading up to 2008.

Recruitment services took the lion's share of the market, accounting for 63 percent of the market's value. State-run agencies were still dominant in China, but the number of private agencies was on the rise.

By June 2006, one trend was for foreign recruitment firms to use acquisition and other methods to enter the Chinese market. For example, America-based Monster bought shares in China's first online recruitment operator, ChinaHR.com. Randstad of Holland invested in a Shanghai human resource firm. Britain's largest recruitment firm started its China operations in Shanghai after its acquisition of St. George's Harvey Nash human resources service firm.

By May 2007, Taneesha Kulshrestha, in an article in *The Financial Express,* reported that only 9 percent of Indian employers expressed difficulty in filling positions due to lack of suitable talent, compared to 41 percent of employers throughout the world. Other countries where shortages were not so severe included Ireland, the Netherlands, and China.

Indian companies were starting to hold more recruitment firms accountable for attrition and job-hopping of employees. Attrition across some sectors such as retail and banking had jumped by substantial percentages. Changes in payment for recruitment utilizing a "33-33-33 fees model" meant 33 percent was paid when the mandate reached a recruitment firm, 33 percent was given when an offer letter was accepted by an employee, and 33 percent was paid when an employee came on board.

Industry Trends. While most people using personnel services, particularly temporary placement services, are young, the aging population in many countries was affecting the personnel services industry. Many labor markets were expected to shrink due to falling birthrates, with the average age of the workforce expected to rise to 41 years by 2005. However, while the total size of the working population was decreasing in Europe, it was showing small gains in the United States. These gains were attributed to the trend for Americans to retire later, while Europeans were retiring earlier.

Employers in Japan and Singapore led the way with plans to retain older workers. There were retention strategies for reportedly 83 percent and 53 percent respectively of the employers in those countries. Manpower suggested that laws and incentive programs in these countries that promoted recruiting and retaining workers 50 or older were contributing factors. In the United States, only 18 percent of employers reported having a recruitment strategy.

With the globalization of economies came the globalization of the world's labor force, and the personnel industry giants provided an increasing amount of service directed at this "internationalization" by giving placed employees a consistency of working conditions and terms as they moved from one country to another. Governments have been increasingly favoring policies that allow for the inflow of temporary, specialized labor, rather than permanent status.

Declines have been seen in the demand for unskilled or low-skilled labor. Rapid changes in technology have been the primary influencer behind this trend. In addition, the growing number of service-oriented jobs has been related to a rise in the need for so-called "social skills." Most personnel agencies were seeing the need to place more educated people, and many were offering training services to upgrade the skills of the client's employees.

Temporary employment often can be seen as an indication of the economic health, since companies are able to quickly adapt to changes in demand by increasing or decreasing their reliance on temporary workers. Since the 1970s, the most significant growth in temporary staffing services has taken place during the early stages of economic recovery, according to the American Staffing Association (ASA).

In its *Annual Economic Analysis of the Staffing Industry,* released in mid-2004, the ASA cited figures from the W.E. Upjohn Institute for Employment Research indicating that the most important reason for hiring temporary help was to assist in times of unanticipated increases in business. Almost half of companies said that they use temporary employees to fill the shoes of absent permanent employees, or to fill a job vacancy until a permanent worker is hired. Temporary workers also are used by companies for special projects, just-in-time production practices, and seasonal needs, and are often screened as possible permanent hires.

Heading into the middle of the first decade of the 2000s, one major trend that was unfolding in the personnel services industry was the so-called "emergent workforce," a term used by staffing firm Spherion Corp. to describe a segment of workers who value such things as performance-based rewards, a high degree of control over their careers, and growth opportunities. Comprising an estimated 31 percent of the U.S. workforce in 2004, Spherion projected that emergent workers would account for a growing portion of the workforce heading into the late years of the decade. By 2007, expectations called for this group to constitute more than half of all U.S. employees.

Along these lines, during the middle of the decade, a growing number of U.S. workers, especially professionals, were opting to forego traditional employment arrangements in lieu of contract or project-based employment, which offered more flexibility and time with family. These desires became more important for many Americans in the wake of the September 11, 2001, terrorist attacks, which forced many people to evaluate the things that mattered most in their lives. While IT and accounting professionals had pursued these types of arrangements for some time, by 2004 lawyers, biochemists, and even marketing professionals were doing so.

By 2006 many companies and recruitment firms were signing "no-poaching" agreements. This prevented parties from stealing employees from client companies. Some avoided unethical practices by not hiring clients' employees and making those who approached the firms progress through the traditional recruitment process.

Another trend was for companies to use head-hunters to hire "laterals." These placements were defined by Sujata Dutta Sachdeva of *The Economic Times* as being for employees with 18 months or more of experience. Companies tended to prefer them because they required less training than employees new to their fields, otherwise known as "freshers."

By March 2007, remuneration packages for temporary workers in the Indian job market were catching up to permanent ones. An exclusive preview from *The Economic Times,* citing data from the latest TeamLease salary survey, showed a14 percent growth in salaries for temps in 2006. In addition, salary increments for temps in the manufacturing sector had increased to 17 percent in 2006, up from 14 percent in 2005.

The Daily Press stated that American Staffing Association 2009 data showed there was a "temporary position trend" moving throughout the country. It was reported that the "demand for temporary and contract employees increased markedly from July to August." The fact that 216,000 jobs were lost nationally in August reflected trends spotlighted in U.S. Department of Labor data, according to *The Daily Press.*

The Federal Reserve's "beige book" shared insights about "pace of layoffs," according to Jeff Harrington of the St. Petersburg Times. They had "slowed" per observations. It was also noted that "few contacts outside of temporary staffing noted any plans to expand payrolls in the near term."

The increasing amount of Las Vegas temp jobs was something economists viewed as a potential "early indicator" reflecting an economic turnaround, according to *Las Vegas Sun* business reporter Nicole Lucht. The American Staffing Association concluded that temp agencies' employment growth had remained virtually static for first and second quarters of 2009. On average, there were 1.9 million temp workers employed each day for the period of April through June.

In the *Occupational Outlook Handbook, 2008-09 Edition,* a brief industry job outlook reflected moderate decline by 7 percent until 2016. This decline was largely attributed to "the proliferation of personal computers." They enabled workers to perform duties themselves rather waiting for others to do so.

INDUSTRY LEADERS

Adecco SA. The biggest human resource services agency overall worldwide, Adecco ranked as "the world leader in workforce solutions." This Switzerland-registered firm, through its Adecco Group Network, united more than 700,000 associates with business clients utilizing a network exceeding 33,000 employees and 6,600 offices. Thanks to a multinational management team, it maintains a presence in more than 70 countries and territories worldwide. It is a valued resource for both temporary and permanent placement of workers in the industrial, clerical, and technical fields. Staffing services also encompass professional and white-collar employees in fields such as accounting, information technology, and engineering. Adecco manages its services through professional business lines such as Adecco Engineering & Technical; Adecco Finance; Adecco Legal; Adecco Information Technology; Adecco Medical & Science; Adecco Sales, Marketing & Events; and Adecco Human Capital Solutions. In addition, Adecco's Lee Hecht Harrison Services division was the third-largest outplacement company in the world in 2005. In early 2006, Adecco bought German staffing firm DIS Deutscher Industrie Service.

Adecco was established through the merging of Adia of Switzerland and Ecco of France in 1996. The world's largest privately held staffing firm, TAD Resources International, was added to the fold in 1997. Begun in Cambridge, Massachusetts, in 1956, TAD had revenues of US$1.2 billion by the time of its acquisition. In 1999 the firm acquired the information technology and staffing firm Delphi, and also acquired one of the largest personnel services companies in Japan, Career Staff. The year 2000 saw Adecco merge with North American giant Olsten Temporary Staffing, which operated 1,400 offices in 14 countries by 1999.

In 2004, North American group CEO Julio Arrieta and Chief Financial Officer Felix Weber resigned when the company's operations in this region were embroiled in an accounting scandal that prompted investigations by U.S. and Swiss officials, including the U.S. Securities and Exchange Commission. Problems seemed to be related more to poor accounting procedures than to anything more sinister, but company chairmanJohn Bowmer resigned in June 2004.

When it comes to earning distinction as a great employer for seniors, Adecco has consistently been rated among the best. Futhermore, Adecco Group North America has been ranked in the top 50 six times for AARP's "Best Employer for Workers Over 50." In September 2009, its most recent ranking at spot 20 on the list was acknowledged. In the same news release, Adecco claimed it was meeting demand described by the Bureau of Labor Statistics regarding the unemployment rate for workers more than 55 years old being 6.8 percent. The

entire workforce comparable figure was 9.7 percent. Adecco's Renaissance Program worked with targeted focus of training and placing mature workers and retirees.

Manpower Inc. A huge and highly-respected staffing firm, Milwaukee, Wisconsin-based Manpower operated 4,300 offices in 68 countries in 2005. The company's sales for 2006 were approximately US$17.6 billion. Most of Manpower's sales come from placing workers in industrial, office, and professional positions. In 2005 the company placed 3 million people in temporary or contract positions with 400,000 client companies. Manpower's subsidiary Right Management offered career transition and organizational consulting services.

Founded in Milwaukee in 1948, Manpower opened its first franchised office location in 1954. In 1955 it began its international growth, opening a Canadian office and then expanding into Europe the next year. By 1965 the company was operating in more than 30 countries. Since 2000 Manpower has shown significant growth through acquisitions, acquiring Elan Group, Jefferson Wells International, and Right Management Consultants in the first four years of the first decade of the 2000s.

Randstad Holding N.V. Headquartered in the Netherlands, Randstad established itself as the temporary employment services market leader in Belgium, Germany, the Netherlands, Poland, and the Southeastern United States. Randstad focuses on "work solutions." Employees are encouraged to think of the agency as a means to find companies where their skills and talents can become further developed, benefiting everyone. Employers are connected with "priceless people" with the ability to increase market place rankings and business value. The company offers a wide range of staffing services via five service lines: staffing, in-house services, professionals, search & placement, and HR solutions. It acquired an industry innovator, the Netherlands-based Vedior, for approximately US$5.1 billion in 2008.

Randstad announced that it acquired an additional 23 percent of the capital of the Chinese HR services provider Talent Shanghai. It previously acquired a stake in May 2006. Randstad now owns 47 percent of the capital. Talent Shaghai delivers a complete range of human resource management services including recruitment, executive search, and graduate placement services.

Kelly Services Inc. Founded in 1946 and headquartered in Troy, Michigan, Kelly Services operated company-owned offices in 32 countries and territories by 2007. By 2008, it was placing 650,000 people into temporary positions annually. These positions were wide-ranging, including accountants, call center workers, substitute teachers, engineers, physicians, information technology specialists, legal professionals, industrial workers, clerical, scientific professionals, and more. Sales for 2008 exceeded US$5.5 billion.

In April 2007, Kelly Services President and CEO Carl Camden discussed his company's "leadership role among business, labor, and civic organizations committed to making health care reform a reality." Kelly Services was a founding member of the "Better Health Care Together" campaign, which issued four "common sense principles for achieving a new American health care system by 2012" in 2007.

Also in 2007, Kelly Services launched the 2007 Virtual Kelly Job Expo. It was cited as being an industry first in Australia. Open from May 18 through 27, it offered a new, high-tech way to conveniently search for jobs. Kelly Services Country Manager James Bowmer described it as combining old methods of expos and fairs with job boards and online searches. The Job Expo effectively offered alternatives for people who were not available to attend traditional fairs.

In recognition of "world-class outstanding performance in 2008,"Intel Corporation awarded its Supplier Continuous Quality Improvement (SCQI) award to Kelly Services. Only 14 suppliers were chosen for 2008 to join a special class of suppliers receiving Intel's highest honor for those special companies involved in a distinctive "strategic partnership." Requirements for SCQI candidates included ability "to demonstrate basic compliance to the Electronic Industry Code of Conduct and Intel's Green Sustainability Program." Kelly Services was named a SCQI winner for the fourth time in six years.

BIBLIOGRAPHY

"About Us." Kelly Services, 4 March 2009. Available from www.kellyservices.com.

"Adecco Honored by AARP as a 'Best Employer for Workers Over 50'." Adecco,10 September 2009. Available from www.adecco.com.

American Staffing Association. "Staffing Statistics." 4 September 2009. Available from www.americanstaffing.net.

Anderson, Adam. "Randstad Professionals US Company Description." 2009. Available from www.hoovers.com.

Berchem, Steven P. "The Bright Spot. ASA's Annual Economic Analysis of the Staffing Industry." *Staffing Success,* May-June 2004.

Berkhout, Ernest E., and Marko J. van Leewen. "International Database on Employment and Adaptable Labour (IDEAL)." Randstad, May 2004. Available from www.randstad.com.

Bernstein, James. "CEO of U.S. Unit of Temp Agency Adecco Resigns Amid Accounting Problems." *Newsday,* 17 January 2004.

Callahan, Sean. "Temp Staffing Takes Hold in Marketing." *B to B,* 9 February 2004.

Davies, Claire. "Focus On: Employment Law Changes." *BusinessEurope.com,* July 2004.

"Engineering and Industrial Jobs at the Kelly Services Online Job Expo." Available from www.ferret.com.au.

"Foreign Recruitment Firms Eye China Market." *Alestron,* 16 June 2006.

"Global Manpower Employment Outlook Survey Reveals Continued Weak Hiring Ahead But More Employers Are Saying They Will Hold On to Current Staff in the Third Quarter." 9 June 2009. Available from www.manpower.com.

Gurchiek, Kathy. "Employers Not Feeling the Love Toward Older Workers." Society for Human Resource Management, 21 May 2007. Available from www.shrm.org.

Harrington, Jeff. "Industries in Southeast stabilizing, Federal Reserve report shows." *St. Petersburg Times* (FL), 9 September 2009. Available from www.tampabay.com.

"Hoover's Company Capsules." *Hoover's Online,* 2007. Available from www.hoovers.com.

"Job Openings a Good Sign." *Daily Press* (VA), 7 September 2009. Available from www.dailypress.com.

Johnson, Joan. "Staffing Services Growing Faster than Economy." *Colorado Springs Business Journal,* 23 June 2006.

"Kelly Services CEO Urges Reform to Cover Nation's 45 Million Uninsured." InsuranceNewsNet.com, Inc., 23 April 2007. Available from http://insurancenewsnet.com.

"Kelly Services, Inc. Receives Intel's Prestigious Supplier Continuous Quality Improvement Award." Available from ir.kellyservices.com.

Kulshrestha, Taneesha. "India's Talent Resources Better than Global Peers." *The Financial Express,* 22 May 2007. Available from www.financialexpress.com.

Lucht, Nicole. "Spike in temporary jobs could be positive sign for economy." 11 September 2009. Available from www.lasvegassun.com.

"Manpower Employment Outlook Survey Indicates U.S. Hiring Pace is Still Sluggish Data Suggests Employment Downturn May Level off During Q3 2009." Manpower, Inc. Available from www.manpower.com.

"Manpower Employment Outlook Survey Indicates World's Labor Markets Will Still Be Challenged in Fourth Quarter 2009, but Many Headed in the Right Direction." Manpower, 8 September 2009. Available from www. manpower.com.

"Manpower Inc. Annual Talent Shortage Survey Reveals Sales Representatives, Skilled Trades People and Technicians Top Most Wanted List Globally." Manpower Inc., 29 March 2007. Available from www.manpower.com.

Rajawat, K. Yatish, and Chhavi Dang. "Now, Cos Look to Fix Attrition Liability on Recruitment Firms." *The Economic Times,* 21 September 2006.

"Randstad Increases Ownership in Talent Shanghai to 70 Percent." Randstad Holding nv, 23 May 2007. Available from www.ir.randstad.com.

"Recruitment Agencies: Why Randstad?" Randstad Holding nv, 2009. Available from www.us.randstad.com.

Sachdeva, Sujata Dutta. "Lateral Placements: Head-hunters' Delight." *The Economic Times,* 26 February 2006.

"Secure Rights of Temporary Workers." *Japan Press Weekly,* 25 February 2003. Available from www.japan-press.co.jp.

Sinha, Vivek. "Temps Are Now Getting their Money's Worth." *The Economic Times,* 27 March 2007.

Thottam, Jyoti, et al. "When Execs Go Temp." *Time,* 26 April 2004.

U.S. Department of the Census, Bureau of Labor Statistics. "Occupational Outlook Handbook, 2008–2009 Edition." 2009. Available from www.bls.gov.

"Workplace Rights a Temporary Fix." *Management Today,* May 2004.

RETAIL AND WHOLESALE TRADE

AUTOMOBILE DEALERS

NAICS CODE(S)

441110, 441120. The world's car dealerships sell new and used cars and light trucks to the general public. They include manufacturer franchises and independent retailers. New car franchises also often perform repair services, including manufacturer-authorized repairs. For more details on trends affecting the broader automotive industry, see also the topics **Motor Vehicles** and **Motor Vehicle Parts and Accessories.**

INDUSTRY SNAPSHOT

Globally, the retail car industry remains highly fragmented. There are very few big players, with most dealerships being independent used car dealers or franchisers of the major car brands. The industry is highly dependent on economic trends, with disposable income levels greatly dictating purchasing levels and patterns. Some markets remain virtually untapped. In mature markets, industry participants were continuing to use incentives to lure customers' purchases.

In the United States, the new car market is experiencing a surprisingly quick recovery of health after a very difficult recession that saw both Chrysler and General Motors (GM), an icon of U.S. industry, file for bankruptcy. The manufacturing and retail sides of the car industry are tightly linked, and this period also saw many dealerships lose their franchise as the automakers, particularly GM, sought to reduce the number of dealers. By the second half of 2010, however, the big three companies GM, Ford, and Chrysler, began posting strong sales growth over year-before levels. The federal government,

which poured US$80 billion of public "bail out" money into the industry during the recession, planned to sell the ownership stake it acquired back to private investors. Steven Rattner, who headed the White House auto task force, claimed in a Fox Business Network interview that the sale would make back more than half the rescue money.

The current "next big thing" in the industry continues to be electric and hybrid gas/electric cars, though it remains to be seen whether Americans will fully embrace this change. Sales of electrics and hybrids may be a better fit for China, which the world's top car manufacturers see as a major growth area. The number of car owners in China increased from 50 million in 2008 to 63 million in 2009. The Chinese economy is growing rapidly, and with a population of over one billion, the potential for sales growth is tremendous. Xu Changming, director of the Information Resource Development Department in China's State Information Center, noted that with the expected growth in car ownership, it would be difficult to rely on oil, so there is an urgent need to develop alternative-energy cars.

Regarding the possibility of Chinese car makers selling in the United States, China's Deputy Minister of Commerce, Ma Xiuhong, told the *Detroit Free Press* that Chinese automakers did not have the dealer relationships in order to successfully make major plans for moving to the United States. The newspaper noted, however, that several Chinese automakers planned to export vehicles to the United States. Chrysler's partner, Chery Automobile, was cited.

According to the *Detroit Free Press,* owners of the oldest GM-affiliated dealership in India expected an increase in sales among first-time buyers with the Chevrolet Spark. The minicar was believed to be well suited to India's roads and developing economy. GM has sold the Chevrolet brand in India since 2003. For September 2010

967

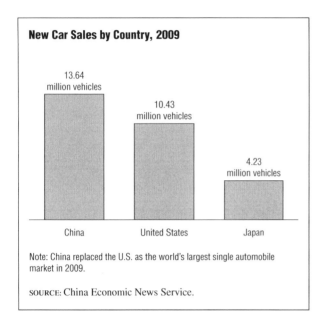

New Car Sales by Country, 2009

13.64 million vehicles

10.43 million vehicles

4.23 million vehicles

China   United States   Japan

Note: China replaced the U.S. as the world's largest single automobile market in 2009.

SOURCE: China Economic News Service.

grant car loans as a service to their customers and as a source of additional revenue and profit. Many more dealers also furnish maintenance and repair services, typically to customers of the dealership or to owners of cars from the dealership's franchised line.

Pricing. Pricing has long been a debated issue in auto retailing, and it is one that regained attention as the new superstores eschewed negotiable pricing in their outlets. As in many retail trades, new car retailers priced their products based in part on a manufacturer's suggested rates and in part on other factors including current demand and incentive programs which usually resulted in cars selling at less than the manufacturer's suggested level. Sometimes the disparity between a car's list price and its usual selling price could be great.

A major determinant in traditional pricing had also been buyer negotiation—more often termed haggling— based on what the buyer might know about the dealer's costs or prices of competitive products. Thanks to the Internet, consumers increasingly have access and pay attention to information about dealers' costs, the value of various option packages, and the average mark-up on car prices to cover dealer costs and profit. This information gives consumers considerable bargaining power and has helped keep prices—and consequently, dealer profits—low compared to earlier periods.

GM reported sales in India as being 8,617 units, up 13 percent over the same month in 2009. The most popular models were the Chevy Beat, Spark, and Tavera.

ORGANIZATION AND STRUCTURE

While the central function of car dealerships is selling cars, dealerships often engage in two related business lines: financing and repairs. Small dealerships usually do not have resources to offer financing, but larger chains may

Traditional used car pricing usually involved a similar process of negotiation. However, with used cars, the cost and market value could be much more ambiguous. Factors such as a used car's age, condition, and relative popularity figured into its valuation, and while published "book" values were available for comparison, the procedure might be cloaked in much greater subjectivity in comparison to new car pricing. The murkiness of used car valuation is, in part, what made the used car side of the business more profitable, as dealers often had flexibility to mark up trade-ins and other acquisitions at much higher rates than new cars. However, it also led to some abuses, notably when consumers were unaware of the average market price for a car (or the exact condition of all its components) and a dealer convinced him or her to pay much more than it was worth.

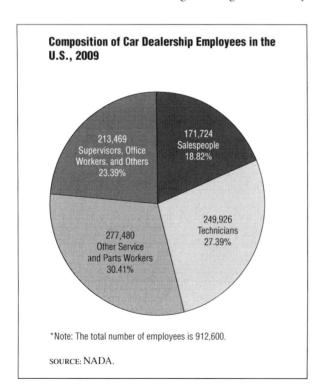

Composition of Car Dealership Employees in the U.S., 2009

213,469 Supervisors, Office Workers, and Others 23.39%

171,724 Salespeople 18.82%

277,480 Other Service and Parts Workers 30.41%

249,926 Technicians 27.39%

*Note: The total number of employees is 912,600.

SOURCE: NADA.

New Car Franchises. Compared to other retail businesses, car dealerships were unusually dependent on manufacturers in that new cars in Japan, Western Europe, and North America were sold almost exclusively by companies that had been granted one or more dealership franchises by manufacturers. All of the world's leading automakers thus regulated, with increasing scrutiny, the number and type of retailers that sold their products. Some manufacturers watched with discomfort as consolidators purchased the businesses that had been granted franchises. A notable dispute erupted in 1997 between Republic Industries Inc., parent company of AutoNation, and the automakers Honda and Toyota. The manufacturers attempted to ban Republic from acquiring more than a certain number of their franchise holders within certain markets and over a specific time frame. Toyota, for example, mandated a nine-month waiting period between acquisitions of its franchises and imposed maximum limits of seven separate Toyota franchises and three Lexus franchises per retailer.

New car dealership franchises were usually granted along the lines of the manufacturers' different marketing divisions. This means, for instance, that General Motors Corporation issued separate licenses to market different lines, such as Chevrolet and Pontiac; in other words, a Chevrolet-brand dealer did not automatically have rights to sell Pontiac models.

Since the late 1990s, automakers both in the United States and abroad have sought to derive a more-efficient cost structure from auto retailing. For example, in the United Kingdom, car manufacturers were redrawing their marketing districts in order to grant a wider geographic market to a fewer number of dealers. Similar moves were made in the United States by the country's Big Three (Ford, General Motors, and DaimlerChrysler). The recession that began in 2007 saw a reinforcement of this trend. An increasing number of import-franchised dealerships, including those of autos from Japan, Europe, and South Korea, have helped offset this trend.

Used Car Dealers. While new car dealers often marketed used cars as well, including many that were traded in during the purchase of new cars, used car firms exclusively dealt in previously owned vehicles. These cars were obtained from wholesalers, auctions, or private individuals. As a result, used car dealers were considered independent, required no license from manufacturers, and were able to sell any make and any model.

BACKGROUND AND DEVELOPMENT

Automotive retailing throughout the world underwent rapid transformation in the 1990s. In major markets—such as those of Japan, Western Europe, and the United States—the widely fragmented retail structures began to give way to larger, consolidated dealerships. Although new auto demand was relatively flat during the mid-1990s, squeezing already tight profit margins at dealerships and North American dealerships were posting higher levels of sales and earnings than ever before by the end of the decade. Fueled by these sales, the number of dealerships in the United States grew to 22,007 in 2000, compared to 22,004 in 1999. Although the addition of three dealerships may appear insignificant at first

glance, the increase was important as it marked the first such upswing in the United States since 1986. Between 1992 and 1997, the total number of car dealers in the United States had declined by about four percent.

Drawing the most attention in the decade, perhaps, was the rise of dealership consolidators and so-called superstore chains, which assembled an extensive line of new or, more often, used cars in a customer-friendly sales environment. The superstores, which originated in the United States with such chains as AutoNation USA and CarMax, were based on mass merchandising's category-killer concept, first pioneered in the United States by the likes of Toys "R" Us, and later refined by such chains as Home Depot and Office Depot. The goal of these chains was to combine in one place a wide selection of popular merchandise—theoretically, everything falling under a particular retail category—that might otherwise be sold by several separate traditional retailers. CarMax, launched by the Circuit City electronics chain, and its counterparts sought to bring economies of scale to the traditionally local and decentralized automotive retail sector. The same was the goal of dealer consolidators, which acquired a large number of dealerships in targeted markets instead of creating a unified brand image for all their outlets. They then merged back-office administrative operations, including ordering and advertising, while usually keeping the local name and image of the dealerships.

Critics of these chains pointed out that the revenue growth of many consolidators and superstores resulted solely from the rapid accumulation of new sales outlets, such as AutoNation's acquisition of nearly 400 stores in less than 16 years. Because operations like AutoNation had yet to prove their ability to operate any more profitably than their more traditional rivals in the late 1990s, skeptics disagreed over the impact these dealer groups would have on the industry.

Consolidation did appear to pay off for the largest industry players, however, and profitability proved to be a key issue for car dealers in the late 1990s. After the value of manufacturing was subtracted, about one-fourth of the average new car's retail price was left to cover dealer costs and profit. On the slim margins typical of the late 1990s, profits averaged just one to two percent of a car's sales price. Many industry watchers, including manufacturers and the emerging consolidators, speculated that room for considerable efficiency gains existed in car distribution that would allow a much higher share of the dealer mark-up to go toward profits. Fewer and larger dealerships would be able to achieve economies of scale and offer buyers better service for the buck. This belief underpinned the business philosophy of the consolidators.

Fueled by low unemployment and high consumer confidence, auto markets in Western Europe and North

America reached near record levels in both sales and production in the late 1990s and early 2000s. Although many dealers expected to see a softening of new car sales in 2001 as economic conditions weakened, just the opposite proved to be true. The catalyst for this turnaround was the decision by General Motors to launch a zero-interest financing campaign for new car buyers. The success of the "Keep America Rolling" program, which was put in place to boost sales after the September 11, 2001, terrorist attacks against the United States, prompted other auto-makers to follow suit. As a result, what had been predicted to be a bleak year for dealers emerged as the second-best sales year in industry history. Dealers found themselves in the unique position of being able to reap the benefits of the expensive marketing campaign, while not having to eat the associated costs, which did undercut earnings for most major car manufacturers in 2001.

With the dawn of the twenty-first century, the Internet had become an important marketing tool for car dealers. According to data compiled by J.D. Power and Associates, a growing number of car dealer Web sites attracted a total of more than eight million visitors a month by 2001. Research Web sites, such as those operated by Kelley Blue Book, secured roughly 20 million monthly visitors that year. These numbers reflected the fact that although few vehicle purchasers actually completed the transaction online, most used the Internet to research their purchases before contacting a dealer. Predictions that the Internet would replace traditional dealers, as businesses began to sell directly to consumers via the Internet, proved false. Instead, most of the online players who survived the dot-com melt-down of 2000 worked directly with traditional dealers by directing online shoppers either to dealer Web sites or dealer showrooms.

Globally, the retail industry for automobiles remained highly fragmented, although consolidation was beginning to occur and appeared likely to continue due to increased capital requirements of dealerships, limited options open to dealers to exit the business, and manufacturer strategy to strengthen brand identity by consolidating franchised dealers.

With only 3 percent of its population owning cars by 2004, China came to be recognized as an industry growth leader in terms of sales and a potential wellspring of future growth. Major manufacturers were vying for opportunities to establish facilities in the country.

In the years leading up to the 2007 global recession, car sales in Europe were already sluggish. In Europe's largest market, Germany, purchasers once noted for replacing their cars often and buying only the best were driving cars that averaged eight years old. In France, car sales were also down 1.3 percent in 2004.

In the United States, the automotive industry remained the largest sector of the retail industry in 2004, with total sales of approximately US$1 trillion. This equated to about one-quarter of all U.S. retail sales. According to a 2005 study by the National Automobile Dealers Association (NADA), franchised new car dealers sold 16.86 million new vehicles in 2004, worth US$714 billion, and 20 million used vehicles, 11.8 million of which were retailed and 7.9 million of which were wholesaled. Dealers watched interest rates rise in the middle of 2004. Coupled with rising inventory expenses, dealers expected that profits would subsequently decrease.

Industry consolidation slowed in the U.S. during 2004, but continued with the number of dealerships reaching 21,640, down from a high of 25,150 in 1987. However, dealerships in 2004 were larger, selling greater volumes; in 2004, 6,490 dealerships sold more than 750 new vehicles each per year, whereas, in 1985, there were only 3,850 dealerships with sales that high.

Hybrid model vehicles, which use both gas and electric power, were beginning to find demand from both environmentally aware consumers and high mileage drivers. While sticker prices of hybrids remained a factor, it was expected that prices would drop as the technology developed.

By 2007, there was a growth in import dealerships in some of the strongest U.S. domestic markets. According to *The Dallas Morning News,* import dealers were "getting bigger and better" while becoming the largest group of area auto retailers. Many of the import dealerships were striving to improve their service departments and offering heightened levels of customer service including vehicle delivery services and concierges.

In its 2007 Market Data Dealer Data report, *Automotive News* shared significant financial and census findings. By 2006, the average U.S. dealership's net pre-tax profit amounted to 1.5 percent of total sales, per the NADA. The number of import-exclusive U.S. dealerships rose by 223 in 2006 to 6,127. Overall there were 21,761 new-vehicle dealerships in the United States at the beginning of 2007.

CURRENT CONDITIONS

The recession that struck the globe between 2007 and 2009 fell heavily on the auto industry. From 2008 to 2009, franchised U.S. new car dealer light vehicle sales dropped from 13.2 to 10.4 million units. Coming to the industry's aid in 2009 was a 3.5 percent increase in used car sales and 1.9 percent increase in service and parts sales as drivers endeavored to make do with older cars.

Also coming to the industry's aid in the recession was the federal government. A "Cash for Clunkers" trade-in program was enacted to boost new vehicle sales. The U.S. government also injected US$80 billion of public funds into the industry, actually acquiring a majority ownership in General Motors (GM). The government then led GM to cut its less popular brands, further consolidate its dealer network and focus on smaller, more fuel-efficient vehicles.

Despite being politically unpopular, the government bailout bore fruit as the auto industry began a rapid, V-shaped, recovery from recession. In September 2010, Ford, GM, and Chrysler posted sales growth of 40 percent, 11 percent, and 61 percent, respectively, over September 2009, when the Cash for Clunkers program ended. The NADA Optimism Index of new dealers, which dropped below 80 during the recession, hit 154 in the second quarter of 2010. This index measures the optimism of dealers about profitability for the coming quarter.

Franchised dealership consolidation continued during the recession, with a net of 1,550 dealerships closing in 2009. That figure was expected to drop to 500 in 2010. To give some perspective on where this long-term trend toward fewer and larger dealers has led the industry, in 1990, 6,330 dealerships in the U.S. had sales of fewer than 150 new vehicles per year. In 2010, there were only 4,682 dealers in that category.

Among the rest of the fallout from the recession, private equity group Cerberus Capital Management saw its 80 percent ownership stake in Chrysler Corporation disappear in a 2009 bankruptcy. While it still owns Chrysler Financial, that firm is no longer affiliated with its namesake car manufacturer.

Globally, emerging markets, such as China and India, remain the focus of growth projections. Car ownership is expected to reach 75 million in China by 2011, with the country surpassing Japan as the world's second largest car market. In 2009, China accounted for 22 percent of world volume in new car sales.

Among products, fuel-efficient hybrid and electric cars are poised for growth. The Nissan Leaf, an all-electric car, and Chevy Volt, a primarily electric car, debuted in the United States in 2010. More than 20 additional models were expected in U.S. showrooms in the following three years. Skeptics question whether the U.S. market will truly embrace these. Even with tax credits being offered by the government, the cars remain expensive compared to traditional models and the range before requiring recharging is limited.

In a political victory for U.S. auto dealers, the 2010 financial regulation legislation passed by Congress exempted dealership financing of cars from new oversight by the Consumer Financial Protection Bureau, which will oversee loans made by traditional banks.

RESEARCH AND TECHNOLOGY

AutoCheckMate developed a cost-saving technology that photographs vehicles when they are left for service. Two versions of the system track vehicle information that is available on a Web site. One version utilizes a hand-held camera and digital camera combination to record information that includes vehicle identification numbers. The other version is designed for high-volume dealerships. It uses a hand-held scanner, sensors, and up to 16 cameras to obtain vehicle data.

Drive Technology Group, Inc. developed its Drive-Way software product, with which dealerships could buy a license from Reynolds and Reynolds, the largest vendor of dealer management systems. This allows the product to access the dealership's system in order to extract, encrypt, and submit data securely. Rather than using a modem, DriveWay uses a dealership's high-speed network and bandwidth. Drive Technology offered this at a time when Reynolds and Reynolds decided to shut down access to modems that had been used to maintain dealership systems.

Research continues into making electric vehicles more affordable and viable as an alternative to traditional cars. Installing a network of public car charging stations is one area that has been targeted for investment and growth. ECOtality, a San Francisco firm, has won a US$115 million federal contract to install 15,000 of its charging stations in 16 metro areas by September 2011. Coulomb Technologies, a rival, has a US$15 million government contract to install 2,600 public as well as 2,000 home chargers. The government's plan is to have a network of charging points across the country, one that will make U.S. consumers more open to driving electric and hybrid vehicles.

WORKFORCE

After years with more than one million total employees, dealership closings helped push total 2009 employment down to 912,600 in the United States, according to industry group NADA. Of these, 171,724 were salespeople; 249,926 were technicians; 277,480 were other service and parts workers; and 213,469 were supervisors, office workers, and others. The average dealership had 49 employees and a yearly payroll of US$2,354,000.

According to the U.S. Bureau of Labor Statistics, auto dealership employees worked longer hours than those in most other industries. Sales employees often have to deal with stress due to the competitive nature of their work. Sales employees also need strong communication skills in dealing with customers. Those who are successful may be promoted into supervisory and management positions. Service techs are often graduates of automotive training programs. They need basic reading and math skills in order to work with technical manuals and tools. Techs may begin their career in apprentice or trainee positions.

Average weekly earnings for nonsupervisory workers in dealerships were US$609 in 2008, higher than the average for retail industries and comparable to that of all private industries, which is US$608. Total employment at dealerships is expected to decline by six percent between 2008 and 2018, due to continuing consolidation, but a high turnover rate means that there are likely to be openings for job seekers.

Only 3 percent of dealership employees were in unions or under union contracts as of 2008, compared to 14 percent in all industries.

INDUSTRY LEADERS

AutoNation Inc. Fort Lauderdale, Florida-based AutoNation, which has roots as a waste disposal company dating to the 1980s, rose quickly in the mid-1990s to become the world's largest and most controversial automotive retailer. Under the leadership of H. Wayne Huizenga, also the founder of Waste Management, AutoNation embarked upon a string of dealership acquisitions. Simultaneously, the firm bought up a number of the largest car rental firms in both the United States and Europe.

AutoNation was reputed for buying out franchise dealerships at substantially higher valuations than had ever before been seen in the industry, particularly during its first years of 1995-1997. Indeed, when Ford Motor Company endeavored a small-scale experiment in buying out a few of its own dealers, it found that dealers were unwilling to accept Ford's conventional buyout offer because they apparently wanted sums on par with AutoNation's high-stakes acquisitions. Although AutoNation was by no means the only aggressive consolidator in the United States, it came to symbolize the tumult facing the industry. In early 1998, a leading auto industry trade journal featured an issue with extensive treatment of how smaller dealers were responding to competitors like AutoNation. Most sentiments were against the consolidation trend, although some industry executives expressed the surprising view that nearby superstores were helping their conventional businesses because their heavy advertising and novelty attracted more car shoppers to a central area, many of whom also browsed traditional dealerships along the way.

By the beginning of the twenty-first century, AutoNation had divested its car rental holdings and closed its 23 used car megastores. Believing that it had grown too quickly, the firm decreased its number of dealerships from 290 in 1999 to 282 in 2000. Franchises were pared from 395 to 375 over the same period, with 358 reported in 2004. During 2004, the company retailed 650,000 new and used cars of 35 different brands. As of 2005, AutoNation was ranked 112th in the *Forbes* 500.

By 2007, AutoNation reported owning 254 new car franchises in more than 16 states with approximately 25,000 employees. It also offered high-tech sales policies and online sales options through its AutoNation.com and individual dealer Web sites. Additional AutoNation offerings included maintenance and repair services, auto parts, and vehicle financing and insurance.

As the economy slowed in 2007, so did AutoNation's performance. First quarter 2007 profit from continuing operations fell 15.4 percent to US$82.9 million. Revenue was down 3.8 percent from the same quarter in 2006, to approximately US$4.4 billion, while operating income fell 7.3 percent to US$187.4 million.

Results continued to reflect difficult conditions in 2009. Revenue declined to US$10.8 billion from US$13.4 billion in 2008. In the annual report for 2009, the firm expressed a belief that 2010 would continue to be challenging but that new vehicle sales would gradually improve. This appeared to be borne out by September 2010 new vehicle sales which increased by 35 percent over September 2009.

Penske Automotive Group Inc. Penske Automotive Group, headquartered in Bloomfield Hills, Michigan, was founded by Marshall Cogan as United Auto Group in 1990. The company became one of the United States' largest consolidators. Focusing primarily on the luxury car market, in 2002, the company acquired Sytner Group, one of the U.K.'s leading luxury car retailers. By March 2005, Synter operated 87 franchises. In January 2005, United also purchased a remaining 50 percent interest in Tulsa Auto Collection, six dealerships originally owned by the Ford Motor Company. By 2007, the firm operated 314 retail automotive franchises, representing 41 different brands and 26 collision repair centers. It employed nearly 16,000 workers at its 169 franchised U.S. dealerships and 145 international dealerships. In May 2007, United Auto announced it had acquired the Classic Automotive Group in Austin, Texas. The acquisition represented four new franchises that were anticipated to add US$300 million in annualized revenue to the company's operations. In July of that year, the company changed its name to Penske Automotive Group. As of October 2010, the company operated 325 retail auto franchises, including 152 outside the U.S., most of which are in the United Kingdom.

Sonic Automotive Inc. One of the fastest growing dealership groups at the turn of the twenty-first century, Sonic Automotive became one of the largest car retailers in the United States. Bruton Smith founded the firm in 1997 with five dealerships. A member of the Fortune 500 and the Russell 2000 stock index, Sonic operated 145 franchises at 122 locations in 2010, as well as 26 collision repair centers. Total revenue for 2009 was US$6.1 billion.

CarMax Inc. A publicly traded spin-off of the United States' Circuit City Stores Inc., CarMax was credited with introducing the no-haggling, wide-selection, customer-friendly superstore concept to the auto retail industry. By 2004, it was the United States' largest dealer of used cars. Founded in 1993, the used car chain grew much more slowly and attracted less media attention than groups such as AutoNation, but during the 1990s, it forged a solid position in a number of U.S. regional markets, primarily in the southeast. Among the amenities it offered were fixed pricing, somewhat akin to grocery stores' so-called everyday low pricing; snacks; and recreation areas for children. The group doubled its outlets from 20 in 1998 to more than 40 in 2001 and 63 by March 2005. Some of these units sold new cars as well as the typical selection of used cars that were less than six years old with fewer than 60,000 miles.

By 2007, CarMax had earned the distinction of being a *Fortune* 500 company. In 2010, the company was named to *Fortune's* "100 Best Companies to Work For" list for the sixth straight year. CarMax operated 103 used car superstores, reporting fiscal 2010 revenue of US$7.5 billion, up from US$7 billion in 2009. CarMax's inventory of more than 25,000 used and new cars, with customer ratings and reviews, was available on the company Web site.

European Motor Holdings plc/Inchcape plc. European Motor Holdings was founded in 1991 when a group of nine motor retail businesses joined forces. The following year, the group purchased Casemount Holdings Ltd., which evolved into its motor services arm. Eight more dealerships were added that year as well. Normand Motor Group Ltd., which included 16 dealer franchises throughout southeastern and northwestern England, was acquired in 1994. Two years later, European Motor bought Telford Motor Auctions. The firm secured exclusive rights to import and distribute the Perodua, a compact vehicle manufactured in Malaysia, in 1997. This marked the first import of Malaysian vehicles into the United Kingdom.

By 2005, European Motor Holdings operated 37 franchises, all of European-make cars, at 34 locations throughout the United Kingdom. By 2006, European Motor Holdings owned and operated 50 dealerships in the United Kingdom and continued serving as the sole distributor for Perodua economy cars. In January 2007, European Motor Holdings was acquired by global auto distributor and retailer Inchcape. As of 2010, Inchcape was the market leader in 13 of the 26 markets it operated in across Europe, Africa, Asia, Australia, and South America. Inchcape sales revenue for 2009 was US$8.8 billion.

Zhongsheng Group Holdings Ltd. China's dealership industry is fragmented and underdeveloped, with the average dealer buying only 70 vehicles per year. Zhongsheng Group Holdings Ltd, one of the leading national dealers, announced a plan in 2010 to expand by buying stakes in several other firms in the auto sales and service market.

Zhongsheng focuses on the luxury end of the market and is working to create a "one-stop" business model with new vehicle sales, part sales, repair and maintenance, accessories, and other auto-related products and services.

Group 1 Automotive Group, Inc. Houston-based Group 1 is the fourth-largest dealership group in the United States. It owns and operates 136 franchises at 101 dealerships in the United States and United Kingdom. In addition, it is responsible for approximately 25 collision service centers. Its dealerships offer new and used cars, plus light trucks through 32 different brands. Group 1 also offers financing plans, maintenance, and repair services, and it sells replacement parts.

MAJOR COUNTRIES IN THE INDUSTRY

United States. Sales of new vehicles in the United States fell 21 percent in 2009 to 10.4 million units. The average price increased slightly to US$28,966 from US$28,350 in 2008. Among the stronger performers were Crossover utility vehicles (CUVs), which declined 5.5 percent, considerably less than the drop in most other major categories. Almost 9.1 million used vehicles were sold through new car dealers retail operations in 2009, at an average price of US$14,976.

By the end of 2009, the automobile population in the United States was approximately 239 million light vehicles. This figure had been increasing an average of two percent per year for the prior decade. NADA estimated the average age of vehicles on U.S. roads to be 10.2 years.

Car dealerships remained large employers. Estimates put the employee count at nearly 1.18 million for 2008, with about 23 percent being retail salespersons, two percent being sales managers, 18 percent being service techs, and 15 percent being office and administrative workers.

The year 2010 has been referred to as the year of the auto recall, with the United States on track for more recalls than any year since 2004. With many measures of auto quality and safety on the upswing, this situation may represent automakers becoming more proactive about potential problems.

Japan. A languishing economy and end of major government incentives conspired to create difficulty for the Japanese auto market in 2010. Domestic sales of new cars, trucks and buses were down 4.1 percent in September 2010 from September 2009. According to Honda executive vice president Koichi Kondo, the fourth quarter of 2010 could see auto sales down as much as 30 percent from 2009 figures.

Another development in the Japanese auto industry is that production has begun to move into other parts of

Asia. To take advantage of lower costs, by 2011 both Nissan and Mitsubishi planned to be importing cars into Japan that were built in Thailand. The activities being outsourced included not only assembly but parts production as well.

BIBLIOGRAPHY

"2007 Market Data Dealer Data." *Automotive News,* 14 May 2007.

"Auto Dealers Urge Congress to Make Available Data on Totaled Vehicles." *Insurance Journal,* 11 April 2007. Available from http://www.insurancejournal.com.

"Annual Report." AutoNation, 2009. Available from http://corp.autonation.com.

"Annual Report." CarMax, 2010. Available from http://www.carmax.com.

"Annual Report." Penske Automotive, 2009. Available from http://www.penskeautomotive.com.

Bell, Claes. "Auto Dealer Exemption from Financial Regulation Bill a Done Deal." *Cars Blog,* 25 June 2010. Available from www.bankrate.com.

Belsie, Laurent. "Toyota recall October 2010: Lots of Recalls. Better Cars?" *Christian Science Monitor,* 21 October 2010.

Box, Terry. "Import Dealerships Surge Ahead." *The Dallas Morning News,* 26 April 2007.

"Car Dealers Worried U.S. FTA May Bring Used Autos." *Digital Chosunilbo* (English Edition), 2 May 2007. Available from http://www.english.chosun.com.

"Car ownership in China expected to overtake Japan next year." *People's Daily Online,* 31 May 2010. Available from http://english.peopledaily.com.cn.

"Car Retailer Down 15.4 Percent As Sales Lag in Key Markets." *South Florida Sun–Sentinel,* 27 April 2007.

"CarMax Launches Customer Ratings and Reviews on carmax.com." *PR Newswire,* 23 April 2007.

"Chinese Automotive Market." *Mercer Management Consulting,* 2010. Available from http://www.altassets.com.

"Company Profile." Zhongsheng Group, 2010. Available from http://www.zs-group.com.

"Corporate Overview." Group 1 Automotive, 2010. Available from http://www.group1corp.com.

"Corporate Profile." Sonic Automotive, 2010. Available from http://www.sonicautomotive.com.

Eckhoff, Jeff. "Iowa's Cut-Off Auto Dealers See Glimmers of Sunshine." *Des Moines Register,* 17 October 2010.

"Ford Sales Rise 40 Percent, Chrysler Up 61 Percent as Industry Rebounds." *Automotive News,* 1 October 2010. Available from http://www.autoweek.com.

Gaudio, Thomas. "Controlling Damage Costs at Dealerships." *NJBIZ,* 30 April 2007. Available from http://www.njbiz.com.

"General Motor's India's September Sales grow by 13 Percent at 8617 units." *PR URGENT,* 15 October 2010. Available from http://www.prurgent.com.

Gopwani, Jewel. "Small Car Is a Big Deal for Dealers." *Detroit Free Press,* 13 May 2007.

"Hoover's Company Capsules." *Hoover's Online,* 2007. Available from http://www.hoovers.com.

"Investors Relations page." *Inchcape,* 2010. Available from http://www.inchcape.com.

Kisiel, Ralph. "Tech Firm Offers Way to Tap Dealer Data." *Automotive News,* 14 May 2007.

Merx, Katie. "China's Cars to Reach U.S. Gradually." *Detroit Free Press,* 17 May 2007.

Osburn, Chaz. "Dealers Saved by 0 Percent." *Automotive News,* 21 January 2002.

Ovide, Shira. "Rattner on GM Bailout: Taxpayer Hit Won't Be More than $10-$20 Billion." *Wall Street Journal blogs,* 15 October 2010. Available from blogs.wsj.com.

Ramsey, Mike. "Bumpy Road for Electrics." *Wall Street Journal,* 17 October 2010.

Sawyers, Arlena. "Acquisitions Alter Dealership Ranking." *Automotive News,* 23 April 2001.

Smith, Rebecca. "Scouting Sites for an Electric Future." *Wall Street Journal,* 20 October 2010.

Takahashi, Yoshio. "Japan Auto Sales Down." *Wall Street Journal,* 1 October 2010.

Tierney, Christine. "Automakers Hope Paris Auto Show Revives European Sales." *The Detroit News,* 21 September 2004. Available from http://www.aiada.org.

"Top 10 Numbers." *Automotive News,* 14 April 2003.

"UPDATE: Cerberus Plans Revival of Chrysler Financial—Sources." *Wall Street Journal,* 24 September 2010.

U.S. Department of the Census, Bureau of Labor Statistics. "Career Guide to Industries, Automobile Dealers", 2010-2011. Available from http://www.bls.gov.

Webster, Sarah A. "Car Dealer on a Roll." *Detroit Free Press,* 29 May 2007.

———. "Dealers Hope Customers Will Start Coming Back." *Detroit Free Press,* 15 May 2007.

"Zhongsheng Group to buy into mainland auto sale and service firms." *Steel Guru,* 11 October 2010. Available from http://www.steelguru.com.

SIC 5961

CATALOG AND MAIL-ORDER SERVICES

NAICS CODE(S)

454113. The catalog and mail-order industry, also known as non-store retailing or home shopping, sells products and services through television, catalog, online services, and direct mail. Certain firms have sizable mail-order operations in addition to other activities, such as manufacturing finished goods or store retailing, and may also be discussed under those categories.

INDUSTRY SNAPSHOT

Catalog and mail-order houses encompass companies that market products through all non-store retail channels, including catalogs, mail, radio, computer, and television. The three major non-store retailing markets, in descending order of size, are consumer, business, and charity.

Providing customers with a means to shop directly from their homes and offices, catalog and mail-order services continue to play a role in the retail industry. Although the glory days of the paper-based catalog may have gone, the globalization of the marketplace and decreases in the time consumers have for shopping have breathed new life into the industry. Coupled with the growing acceptance and use of the Internet by consumers, changes are being seen as traditional catalog providers have supplemented their sales channels with the Internet. The growth of television around the world and into new, developing markets has also brought with it the use of this medium as a sales tool. Home shopping television networks are proving highly successful, and are spreading around the globe.

According to the Direct Marketing Association's *Multichannel Marketing in the Catalog Industry* report, print was still king. Catalog companies' Internet sales were estimated at 39 percent of total direct sales in 2005. That estimate compared to 38 percent in 2004. An impressive survey finding revealed that 74 percent of respondents considered their catalogs to still be their primary sales vehicle.

While speaking at the National Catalog Advocacy & Strategy Forum, U.S. Postal Service President of Shipping and Mailing Services Robert Bernstock made some startling observations. Notable among them was the one about "the business model is broken" regarding the catalog industry. Bernstock pledged support to turn things around after a major "relook at the whole structure" took place.

ORGANIZATION AND STRUCTURE

Although large retailers, such as the United States' JC Penney Company, typically maintain an inventory warehouse, most industry participants keep little, if any, inventory on hand. When a customer orders a product, the retailer contacts a wholesale supplier that ships the item to the retailer or directly to the customer—an arrangement referred to as just-in-time inventory. Because they refrain from traditional retail purchasing, manufacturing, and inventory management activities, many non-store retailers are essentially marketing companies. Some catalog companies, for instance, simply assemble a group of complementary products manufactured by other firms and market those items in a catalog. Similarly, many direct-mail and broadcast-media retailers essentially act as middlemen, selling products that are manufactured and stored by wholesalers.

The benefits of non-store retailing are numerous. In the case of catalog and direct-mail marketing, retailers enjoy more efficient access to markets. Indeed, tailored customer lists allow companies to carefully target select segments of the market. Besides advantages associated with segmented marketing, mail-order retailers typically

enjoy reduced fixed costs that would otherwise be incurred by operating a retail store or using face-to-face or telemarketing sales techniques. Expenses in the areas of rent, inventory, and payroll are all reduced in the catalog and mail-order industry. Furthermore, mail-order companies have access to much larger geographic markets than do many retail establishments.

A chief drawback of non-store retailing, however, can be high advertising costs. The expense of producing and delivering catalogs, fulfilling orders, and serving customers often leaves retailers with slim profit margins (or losses if response to a promotional effort is poor). Retailers often expect only 0.5 percent to 3 percent of recipients of advertising to actually respond to a solicitation by mail. The problem is compounded in many regions, particularly Europe, by high postal rates and restrictions on mail advertisements that increase mailing costs. High shipping expenses are also a drawback, particularly for large or heavy goods like appliances and furniture.

Because of high mail and shipping costs, cross-border sales by catalog and mail-order houses remain limited. Nevertheless, some firms have successfully entered world markets. Sales between the United States and the European Union, for instance, increased throughout the 1990s on the strength of increasingly uniform markets. The 2002 adoption of the single united currency, the euro, was expected to increase sales even more dramatically. The most exportable mail-order products in the 1990s, in order of revenue size, were information, education, and collectible products. Several U.S. firms successfully marketed specialty U.S. products in Asian countries. Overseas mail-order firms also enjoyed increased success in the United States. Firms that instituted successful exporting ventures to the U.S. market in the 1990s included Aer Rianta, Bertelsmann AG, Jelmoli, Moore Ltd., Patrimonium, Quelle, and Otto Versand.

The International Direct Mail Advisory Council, created by the Universal Postal Union, a division of the United Nations, promotes cooperation between the public and private sectors to advance the mail-order industry worldwide. The organization conducts studies on the direct-mailing conditions throughout the world and has established an advisory council made up of mail-order companies. The council's immediate goals included standardizing addresses and mailing customs.

BACKGROUND AND DEVELOPMENT

A Venetian book merchant, Aldus Manutius, provided one of the first mail-order services in 1498, selling Greek and Latin books through a catalog. Later, American Benjamin Franklin was credited for starting the modern mail-order industry in 1744 with a direct-mail offer in the United States. He produced a mail-order catalog bearing this promise: "Those persons who live remote, by sending their orders and money to said B. Franklin, may depend on the same justice as if present." Mail-order techniques were well-suited to the fragmented North American population. In 1863, in fact, the U.S. Congress authorized the issuance of a discount stamp for mailers of "printed matter and manuscripts," known as second-class mail. It also issued a third-class stamp for "bulk mailers." Several large U.S. companies pioneered mass mail-order techniques, relying heavily on direct mail to promote their businesses. Sears, Roebuck and Co., which introduced innovative mail-order catalogs in the early 1900s, became one of the most effective practitioners of direct marketing.

Three of the largest mail-order houses that gained prominence in the early 1900s were Sears, Montgomery Ward (founded in 1872), and Spiegel (founded in 1865). Similar but smaller organizations emerged in other parts of the world. In Japan, for example, department stores like Mitsukoshi and Takashimaya began marketing to rural customers through catalogs in the late nineteenth century. These and other industry pioneers usually offered general merchandise at low prices. They often manufactured their own products and counted on large-scale advertising to generate high sales volumes. Such operations continued to experience moderate sales growth throughout the mid-1900s and even started to gain appeal in Germany, the United Kingdom, and a few other nations. Growth in Japan, though, was squelched until 1972 by a government edict that restricted direct advertising. In the 1980s a variety of technological, demographic, and financial developments converged to cause explosive growth in catalog and mail-order sales.

Technological advances that catapulted many competitors to success in the 1980s included computers and software that increased marketing efficiency and improved customer service. Computer systems that became popular during the early 1980s allowed competitors to manage and manipulate large amounts of consumer data. They were also used to track and manage inventory more effectively. When a customer ordered a product, the mail-order house could electronically alert its warehouse, or its supplier, and quickly ship the product. Inexpensive desktop computer systems allowed small, specialty non-store retailers to more easily compete with larger firms on a national scale.

Other factors contributed to the increased profitability of the industry as well. Credit card systems eased payment problems, for instance. Some analysts contend that the non-store retail industry benefited most from pivotal demographic changes that developed over the course of the 1980s. One of the most important shifts was the rise in the percentage of working women, elderly people, and dual-

income households in the United States, Japan, and Europe. Those market groups vastly increased their level of mail-order buying during the decade.

Worldwide consumer catalog and mail-order sales alone stood at US$176 billion in 1996, up from US$150 billion in 1993, according to *Direct Marketing*. Germany represented the largest market for catalog shopping, while the United States led in overall mail-order and catalog sales, according to an *Advertising Age* report. Although the growth rates slowed in more mature markets such as the United States, Germany, and Japan, in the mid- to late 1990s they remained steady. Emerging economies, however, experienced far more dramatic increases in mail-order sales growth. Chile's sales shot up by 300 percent in 1996, while India's rose by 20 percent, and the Czech Republic's by 25 percent.

The high-growth consumer products of the mid- to late 1990s included animal care merchandise, books, computer hardware and software, wine and liquor, and gardening products. In the business sector, they included stationery products, computer hardware and software, and medical supplies. Items that experienced lower growth during this period were video cassettes, cosmetics, physical fitness products, and audio recordings.

With a flooded retail store market in mature industrial countries, some industry observers believed that these retailers, some of whom have already invested in powerful customer databases, will turn to the mail-order business to boost their sales and increase store traffic. As a consequence, they forecast possible mergers of retailers and mail-order companies, so that retailers can combine their strong databases with successful mail-order operations.

Moreover, Sigmund Kiener, a member of the managing board of Quelle Group, argued in *Direct Marketing* that for mail-order companies to remain successful in the late twentieth and early twenty-first century, they would have to provide more diverse products or services and they would also have to distinguish themselves from other companies. With advanced information networking systems in place, companies can expand their product lines quite easily. Kiener urged that companies must invest in umbrella brands with strong name recognition that span several product or service categories, in order to build their corporate identities. Marketing research will continue to play an important role in mail-order and catalog business, because companies will require catalogs and mail-order literature that target individual customers. Finally, Kiener identifies developing a multinational customer base as another challenge the industry must face. When approaching international markets, however, companies must target a keenly defined market sector in order to succeed.

Along these lines, mail-order and catalog companies began to switch from general advertisements and solicitations to more specific and individualized ones or market their products to specific niches. Using new technology such as customer databases that track shopping and ordering habits, mail-order houses can produce catalogs geared directly to the individual tastes of customers. As a result, companies maximize the response to their advertisements and reduce expenses for wasted advertisements.

The mail-order and catalog industry, however, had concerns toward the end of 2001 when lethal doses of anthrax were sent through the mail to unsuspecting individuals. As the anthrax was believed to be tainting other letters that it came in contact with, 66 percent of the respondents surveyed said they preferred to receive less unsolicited mail during the time of crisis. Another 45 percent were worried about chemicals and viruses being sent through the mail in addition to anthrax, according to research performed by CLT Research. Approximately 38 percent of those surveyed said they would miss receiving catalogs if they were no longer sent in the mail. The industry was looking at different ways to send materials, including the use of transparent envelopes and plastic wrapping for catalogs. Where wrapping was a necessity, it was determined that the sender's address and an endorsement by a group such as the Ad Council would increase the chances that recipients would open the mail.

While analysts expected that television shopping would constitute the direct-marketing distribution channel of the future, by the mid-1990s it proved to have a more modest impact. The television mail-order industry emerged during the 1980s in the United States and spread to Europe and Japan by the early 1990s. The two giants of this segment were QVC and Home Shopping Network (HSN), but their sales remained well below predictions in the early 1990s. For example, these two stations reported around US$3 billion in combined revenues in 1996, in contrast to forecasts that the industry would gross US$10 billion by 1996 and US$100 billion by 2003.

A study by Jupiter Media Metrix indicated that interactive TV (iTV) technology would soon have home shopping viewers make their purchases via remote control devices, rather than calling in by telephone to order showcased products. By 2005, iTV shopping programs were expected to garner sales of US$3.4 billion and were predicted to demonstrate cost savings for home shopping networks, enabling them to cut down on call centers.

With the popularity of the Internet in the mid- to late-1990s, mail-order houses and general retailers alike set up Web sites to market their products. With millions of Internet users throughout the world, companies saw great potential for sales. Security concerns and tax uncertainties hindered the industry. Some users remained wary of providing their credit card numbers on the Internet, fearing hackers might intercept them, which led to the creation of secure servers that scramble confidential information. Various government agencies also wrangled over how to tax Internet commerce. Nevertheless, Internet commerce continued to grow. Moreover, some online marketers achieved great success, especially Amazon.com, which had its first-ever profitable quarter ending December 31, 2001, with profits of US$5 million. Sales in Japan, France, Germany, and the United Kingdom increased by 81 percent to a total of US$262.4 million.

Online shopping was also expected to increase during the 2001 holiday season, due in part to the reluctance of consumers to travel and deliver gifts in person in the wake of the terrorist attacks on the United States on September 11, 2001, according to *InfoWorld. Business Week Online* reported that online sales in the European market were expected to increase by 50 percent during the 2001 holiday season, reaching as much as US$8.6 billion. Germany and the United Kingdom were likely to lead the pack and account for 65 percent of online holiday shopping. France was expected to demonstrate only 8 percent, and Italy and Spain were projected to weigh in at very low percentages. Internet shopping also gained popularity in Scandinavia but was expected to amount to only 9 percent of holiday sales.

In 2001, the number of Europeans using the Internet grew approximately 40 percent to 140 million. In Europe, 36 percent of households were online, compared to 55 percent in the United States. Online consumers appeared to feel more confident and secure about shopping on the Web, and concerns about credit card theft, privacy issues, and fraud had lessened. This was in part due to the majority of online selling being handled by trusted brick-and-mortar retailers, given that a large number of dot-com companies were no longer in business.

DMA Vice President of Information and Special Projects Ann Zeller had discussions with *Bottom Line* about the *DMA/Catalog Age State of the Catalog/Interactive Report 2004.* Zeller indicated that in spite of challenging early years in the first decade of the twenty-first century, forces such as consumer Internet and e-mail acceptance and improved minimal cost technology in IT and telephony were laying the groundwork for a much stronger catalog industry. Report findings showed nearly 30 percent of catalogers' online sales were incremental or new customer sales that would not have been acquired without their Web sites.

While online shopping and e-retailing showed momentum, catalogs were not likely to go away, and direct-mail strategies of catalogers were still solid. *Business Week* reported that Coldwater Creek, a catalog seller of apparel for women, found that the best way to attract users to its Web site was not through banner ads but by using its own catalog and other traditional direct marketing strategies to lure consumers online. E-mail campaigns and banner ads are significantly less expensive than mailing catalogs, which can cost up to US$1 a customer, assuming the company is taking advantage of volume discounts. However, according to research compiled by Shop.org, catalog-based e-retailers were consistently more profitable than Internet-only stores or Web sites of brick-and-mortar retailers. The catalog industry sites using direct marketing methods spent only about US$14 to acquire new Web-based customers, while traditional retailers spent US$34 and Web-only e-retailers spent US$55.

Besides online services, other emerging mail-order media in the mid-1990s included CD-ROM systems on personal computers, in-flight ordering systems on commercial jets, and screen-based telephones. Although the future of the industry was unclear, many industry participants envisioned a global retail industry dominated by direct advertising and mail-order media that was made possible by low-cost, interactive, electronic information systems. Pricewaterhouse Coopers estimated that worldwide online and interactive television sales would top US$350 billion by 2010.

The industry also faced the challenge of reducing waste because of its approximately 100 billion advertising pieces mailed annually throughout the world. As a result, company practices were perceived by some as environmentally unsound. With growing consumer environmental awareness in Western Europe, the United States, and Japan, consumers voiced strong concern for the environment, calling for the reduction of advertisement and packaging and patronizing companies that espoused similar environmental sensibilities. Environmental legislation mandating the use of recycled—and often more expensive—paper by advertisers proliferated. Some countries in Europe simply outlawed mail advertisements that were not specifically requested by the recipient. To shed this negative image and to save money, some mail-order companies started to reduce the amount of paper used by viewing on-screen before printing, verifying addresses before mailing advertisements, using recycled paper and recycling paper, and publicizing a commitment to environmental protection.

ForestEthics, a San Francisco-based environmental advocacy organization, threatened to go public with a "blacklist" of cataloguers that it believed were practicing harmful eco practices. Among the names mentioned were Land's End, JC Penney, and L.L. Bean. During a March 2004 American Forest Products Association Paper Week conference seminar, ForestEthics accused the companies of not using enough recycled material and instead using too much pulp fiber sourced from endangered forests.

CURRENT CONDITIONS

Although the world's largest retail market is the United States, the largest catalog retailer continued to thrive as Germany's Otto Group. However, the increased use of the Internet for home shopping, as well as suitable distribution channels, had made it possible to be successful in this industry on a global basis. The largest catalog companies often provide catalogs and Web sites that are directed to specific countries or regional markets around the world. The industry continued to experience consolidation, particularly among companies that had experienced difficulty adapting from a pure catalog format to one that included the Internet.

Around the world, traditional catalog providers were seeing increasing competition from other forms of home shopping providers. Dell Inc. sells its computers directly to consumers, avoiding any middlemen or retailers by using direct-selling methods, including its Internet site. Dell had sales in 2005 of more than US$49 billion. HSN started in the home shopping business in 1977 selling product over the radio. By 2004, the company had become the fourth-largest cable network in the United States and was using television, catalogs, and the Internet to create sales of US$2.4 billion. HSN also operated home shopping services in Germany, Japan, and China.

Online auction provider eBay was also providing consumers with a way to shop from home. Although the company itself generates revenues through advertising and listing fees, eBay earned revenues of almost US$3.3 billion on gross merchandise volume of US$34.2 billion in 2004. The company had 135.5 million registered users, of which 56.1 million were considered active. Amazon.com also showed that hard-copy material was not needed at all for direct selling. Started in 1995, the company reached profitability in 2004, although it had incurred significant debt on its way to becoming the world's most diverse retailer.

In its conference call for the 17th Annual DM Catalog on the Road, the Direct Marketing Association encouraged catalog industry professionals to be more proactive than reactive. The major focus for the one-day intensive workshop was described as "actively discussing actionable strategies to help strengthen your business." Challenges were categorized as being due to "the low dollar, postal increase and high fuel costs biting into profits" of catalog industry principles.

RESEARCH AND TECHNOLOGY

In the mid- to late 1990s, catalog and mail-order companies were increasingly moving their computer systems toward client/server architecture, with relational databases and distributed processing. Information database systems allowed companies to produce highly specific catalogs and marketing materials, tailored to smaller groups and individuals. Companies expected to eventually be able to print a set of catalogs for niche markets, each featuring a different product mix and marketing message. On the distribution end, just-in-time inventory practices assumed a primary role in helping companies to maintain profit margins through lower fixed costs and better customer service.

Industry observers anticipated that new advertising media would drive the evolution of the mail-order industry. Some expected that these new mail-order channels would eclipse sales made through traditional broadcast, print, and telephone media by the early years of the first decade of the 2000s. The burgeoning multimedia environment, which was expected eventually to integrate video, telecommunications, optical disc technology, and personal computers, would result in consumer-controlled, interactive advertising. Advertisers would be forced to adjust their marketing techniques as consumers gained greater control in choosing which ads and media they internalize. To that end, pilot interactive television systems were already available in some countries. Finally, advancements in recycled paper, printing technology, and ink would help the direct-mail segment move toward reduced waste and lower production costs.

WORKFORCE

The catalog and mail-order industry offers relatively meager employment opportunities in relation to retail businesses with similar sales volumes. While the workforce in this industry was expected to grow at a faster pace than employment in most other retail sectors, throughout the first decade of the 2000s, advances in automation and information systems, particularly in Europe and the United States, could curtail job growth as companies eliminated labor-intensive positions. The greatest job opportunities in the giant North American mail-order industry were expected to be in the areas of computer programming and information system management, as companies sought to integrate and streamline customer, inventory, and financial information.

The National Retail Federation (NRF) urged the U.S. Congress to approve legislation authorizing creation of Association Health Plans to help small business meet the rising cost of employee health insurance. In 2004, the NRF was the world's largest retail trade association, with membership including all retail formats and distribution channels, including department, specialty, discount, catalog, Internet, and independent stores, as well as the industry's key trading partners and establishments, and more than 23 million employees. In April 2004, the NRF applauded the Bush administration's decision to reject a trade case filed by the AFL-CIO against labor

conditions in China that called for high tariffs to be imposed on all merchandise imported from China.

Internet searches revealed that salaries for professionals working in the industry were very broad-ranging and inconsistent. Entry level positions could be as low as US$8 per hour. On the other hand, top corporate executives might receive high salaries. Related information to these findings was anonymously shared by some Hanover Direct employees who posted survey responses on line.

INDUSTRY LEADERS

Otto GmbH & Co. KG. The Otto Group (formerly Otto Versand) earned its title as the world's largest mail-order group. It was also dubbed as being the world's number two, following Amazon, in B2C (business-to-consumer) online trade. Based in Hamburg, Germany, the company was selling a variety of merchandise including sporting goods, appliances, and clothing by operating in 19 countries in Europe, North America, and Asia. It had about 123 subsidiaries. The Otto Group was organized into the four business segments of multi-channel retail, financial services, services, and wholesale. The company produces more than 600 print catalogs per year, and customers can also purchase goods via the Internet and CD-ROM. Otto owns a number of German travel agencies and was a majority stakeholder in the U.S.-based Crate & Barrel retail chain. It also controls Actebis Holding, a major distributor of computers in the European market. Executive board chairman Michael Otto's family stayed in the mix by owning the majority of Otto and separately controlling Spiegel, the U.S. catalog company. Preliminary figures put the company's fiscal 2005 sales at more than US$18 billion, with more than 50 percent coming from sources outside of Germany. However, the mail order segment of the business had experienced the same declines facing the rest of the industry in Germany.

Otto announced plans to launch a new fashion branded catalog in summer 2007. The catalog, called *Oli,* is targeted at an affluent, youthful market. It will offer "high-street fashion" plus lots of fashionable accessories.

In March 2007, Otto launched *Montage,* a catalog and online women's wear home-shopping service also targeted at an affluent market. Plans called for publication of nine seasonal catalogs for the brand, exceeding a traditional model of two catalog seasons per year.

In keeping with its aspirations to revitalize the UK business, Otto restructured marketing operations. Colin Webb, the former Boots and Norwich Union marketing chief, was named UK group commercial director.

Amazon.com. Amazon.com was launched on the Internet in 1995. It operates retail Web sites based in the United States, the United Kingdom, Germany, Japan, Canada,

France, and China. Having started as an online book seller, these sites had grown to provide consumers with a wide selection of products, including clothing, electronics, entertainment products, toys, gourmet foods, jewelry, and household products. The company also provides an online marketplace for third-party sellers. In 2004, Amazon.com had sales revenues of more than US$6.9 billion, of which about 56 percent came from U.S.-based sales. However, international sales showed the highest growth rate for the company, increasing by more than 53 percent over 2003 levels. Amazon.com was turning a net profit at the end of 2004, but it was only its second year of doing so since its inception. In 2005, Amazon announced plans to help Sears Canada recreate its Internet-based sales offering, and the company also added Macy's Department Store products to its list of offerings.

In 2007 Amazon announced the opening of its Major League Baseball Fan Shop at www.amazon.com/mlb. There, fans of all ages could find books, jerseys, hats, collectibles, toys, and novelties linked to their favorite team. The standard free shipping offers were available.

Amazon also unveiled its plans to employ 450 people at its Irish support center. Plans called for that staff to focus on helping customers on its British and French Web sites. They would handle orders, e-mails and telephone calls from customers who use www.amazon.co.uk and www.amazon.fr.

Even in troubled economic times, online retailers experienced expected growth in the midst of uncertainty. Writing for InternetRetailer.com, Mark Brohan reported that e-commerce sales saw moderate "single-digit rate" of growth. Furthermore, when Internet sales increased, comparable sales at stores saw a decrease. For 2008, Brohan concluded that positive movement in Internet sales attributed to 20 percent of growth for total retail sales. Amazon.com continued to be a standout successful case study for Internet retailers. In times when many others were literally closing up shop, Brohan acknowledged that Amazon opened 28 new Internet stores since 2007. In addition, more than 5 percent of its revenue was spent on technology and content. Brohan attributed a major part of Amazon's success to its focus on overseas expansion and new merchandising category diversification. For 2008, the company reported sales of approximately US$19.2 billion and 20,700 employees.

Lands' End. Founded by Gary Comer, Lands' End was the world's top direct seller of apparel in 2005. Lands' End focused on marketing its clothing primarily through its flagship catalog and specialty catalogs. The company also boasts approximately 16 full price and outlet stores in the United States, 3 outlet stores in the United Kingdom and 1 outlet store in Japan. In addition, Land's End has been developing a growing online presence, with Web sites based in the United States, the United Kingdom, Japan, Germany, France, and Ireland. Owned by Sears, Roebuck, which was purchased by Kmart in 2005, Lands' End products can also be found in approximately 370 Sears stores. Geared mainly toward middle-aged consumers, Lands' End also sells home goods, luggage, accessories, and corporate gift items. The company has reduced production of catalogs in favor of an expanded global Web presence. In both 2002 and 2003, sales totaled almost US$1.6 billion, and total net income was nearly US$67 million. Since having a new owner, Lands' End does not disclose sales or provide information about its overall Internet sales. The company employs about 5,500 year-round employees and seasonal employees. The most recent total for seasonal employees was 7,000. In 2005, the company cut 375 jobs and closed a call center due to heavier use of the Internet for orders. Top competitors are L.L. Bean, The Gap, and Spiegel.

In a move reflecting high-tech savvy, Land's End introduced a new proactive chat feature on it Web site in the summer of 2006. The www.landsend.com site tracks visitors' movements on the site. After shoppers spend a long time on pages or go back and forth between them, the system alerts a pop-up to ask if they want to talk with a live person for assistance. By December 2006, 7 percent of eligible site visitors had taken advantage of the offer.

Land's End took advantage of its business relationship by adding new merchandise and store-in-store boutiques within 100 Sears stores. It also added baby clothing and women's intimate apparel into its merchandising mix.

Land's End made the decision to expand its holiday catalog offerings to include some of Sears' big ticket items, including 42-inch plasma TVs for US$2,000. This decision was met with mixed reviews when some critics expressed dissatisfaction with the company's move away from only selling its classic clothing. The move was believed to be evidence of the impact the company's mostly new management team was having on Land's End since the Sears' takeover.

A creative promotion for its Land's End Business Outfitters offered to provide makeovers to three companies in the summer of 2007. Companies were urged to visit www.makeover.landsend.com to enter their story and possibly receive a makeover for their employees. Land's End Business Outfitters apparel experts will work with the selected three companies to develop an apparel program especially suited to their needs. Options include uniforms, business suits, polo shirts, and khakis.

Lands' End launched two noteworthy, especially focused Web sites in 2009. They targeted female swimsuit shoppers and kids searching for cool backpacks to make them stand out at school. The interactive sites were launched in May 2009 and the summer of 2009 respectively. "The Island" featured "a fashion show runway format" designed to provide multiple product views from distinct angles. "Packland" enables customer selection of "four online environments, — namely jungle, ocean, fantasy world or spy lab." It also offers a special innovative "social shopping feature" where custom backpack designs can be e-mailed to others.

L.L. Bean Inc. Based in Freeport, Maine, L.L. Bean was founded in 1912 by Leon Leonwood Bean and is controlled by its founder's descendants. In the beginning, it started as a one-room operation selling the single product called "the Maine Hunting Shoe." In 1967, L.L.'s grandson, Leon Gorman, took over the company as president. Gorman assumed the role of chairman of the board in 2001 and passed company leadership to Chris McCormick. McCormick became the first non-family member ever to hold the position.

The company specializes in outdoor specialty merchandise. L.L. Bean sells mainly via more than 61 catalogs with special formats delivered to the United States and more than 140 countries. Internet-based orders were continuing to rise in numbers rapidly. The company has a retail store in Freeport, Maine, that is open 24 hours, 365 days a year, and welcomes more than 3 million visitors annually. In addition, it has factory stores in the United States and Japan. L.L. Bean's merchandise is made up of more than 16,000 items and includes outdoor clothing as well as household furniture. Sales in 2004 were estimated at approximately US$1.4 billion and the company employed 3,900 people. L.L. Bean made the news in May 2004 when it filed lawsuits against four companies for allegedly using pop-up ads that appeared when customers visited the L.L. Bean Web site. According to *Dow Jones Business News,* L.L. Bean Vice President for E-commerce Mary Lou Kelley said the only legitimate windows that would pop up on the company's Web site would be one-question customer surveys.

In 2007, L.L. Bean shared many exciting plans for the future while celebrating its 95th anniversary. The company is investing more than US$90 million in its Freeport hometown for several projects including developing a retail complex and parking structure in conjunction with partner Berensen Associates scheduled for completion in 2008. L.L Bean also planned to open three new stores in 2007 in Connecticut, New York, and Massachusetts. An additional five stores were scheduled to open in 2008. Net sales for 2006 were US$1.54 billion, marking a 4.6 percent increase over the previous year's US$1.47 billion. The regular workforce in Maine increased by 400 positions for a total of more than 4,350 employees. L.L. Bean's board of directors approved a 7.5 percent bonus for more than

4,900 eligible employees. These employees were listed on both regular and temporary rosters and had worked a minimum of 1,000 hours during the 2006 calendar year and were actively employed through December 2006. Major competition includes Bass Pro Shops, Spiegel, and Land's End.

Eric Wilson previewed the new "L. L. Bean Signature Collection" set to debut in March 2010. It was created by Alex Carleton, the new company creative director and acclaimed founder of Rogues Gallery. Signature Collection pieces will include tailored linen blazers and madras shirtdresses. Contrary to the approach competitor Woolrich has taken with its "Woolrich W. M." higher priced label, plans call for the new L.L. Bean line to stay in the price range of its classic line. "This is for modern, everyday dressing. My goal is not to challenge you. My goal is to make your life better," Wilson stated.

JC Penney Corporation Inc. In the early years of the first decade of the 2000s, J.C. Penney ran one of the top catalog operations in the United States, but its chain of department stores, numbering more than 1,000, was suffering from competition from discount stores such as Wal-Mart and Target. In 2004, J.C. Penney sold its nearly 2,800-unit Eckerd drugstore chain (formerly constituting 45 percent of the company's sales) to The Jean Coutu Group (stores and support facilities in 13 northeastern and mid-Atlantic states) and CVS (southern stores and Eckerd's pharmacy and mail order businesses) for US$4.5 billion. Sales in 2002 totaled approximately US$32 billion while annual net income totaled some US$98 million. Employees in 2002 numbered 229,000. Fiscal 2005 sales were US$18.4 billion, of which US$2.74 billion was from catalog/Internet sales. Internet sales accounted for 30 percent of the total catalog/Internet sales amount and were the fastest growing segment, having increased by 32 percent over 2004 levels. J.C. Penney posted revenue of US$19.9 billion in 2006. It also reported operating 1,033 department stores throughout the United States and Puerto Rico. In addition, the company boasted of having one of the largest apparel and home furnishing sites on the Internet at www.jcpenney.com, as well as the nation's largest general merchandise catalog business. J.C. Penney had approximately 155,000 employees. By 2009, the company reported US$18.5 in sales and 147,000 employees.

Hanover Direct. Based in Edgewater, New Jersey, Hanover Direct sends out approximately 200 million catalogs annually. The firm sells home fashions through its *Domestications* and *The Company Store* catalogs; and men's and women's clothing via its *International Male* and *Silhouettes* catalogs. Hanover Direct also offers options for youth and special market shoppers such as *Company Kids* and *Scandia Down.* The company did sell gifts through the *Gump's By Mail* catalog, but it sold this division in early 2005. All catalogs have linked Web sites.

Hanover Direct has had its share of struggles, including a US$233.3 million loss in 2003. In the fourth quarter of 2003, it did show a quarterly profit of US$364,000 after losing US$16.6 million three months earlier. Thomas Shull resigned in May 2004 as Hanover Direct chairman, chief executive, and president. *According to Knight-Ridder/ Tribune Business News,* the action came after the company revealed, in regulatory filings, information alleging Shull and several other top executives had cashed in on more than US$3 million in special bonuses provided in case they lost their jobs through a change in ownership. William Wachtel, a managing partner of Wachtel & Masyr LLP law firm and Hanover Board of Directors member, took over as chairman. He was also a manager of Chelsey Direct LLC, which gained a controlling interest in Hanover in November 2003. Major competition comes from Federated, Otto Versand, and Williams-Sonoma.

MAJOR COUNTRIES IN THE INDUSTRY

United States. In 2000, a study by the Direct Marketing Association (DMA) reported that, despite the sluggishness of the economy at the time, catalog sales in the United States were expected to increase at more than two times the rate of overall growth in the retail sector. The study predicted that 2001 would see US$120 billion in catalog sales, an increase of 8.9 percent beyond the US$110.2 billion generated in 2000. This prediction seemed to have come true in the United States, where many had been predicting the death of catalogs with the growing presence of the Internet. In 2003, the global market research firm Euromonitor valued the mail-order and home shopping market at US$207.5 billion. In 2005, *Investor's Business Daily* was reporting that rather than being the source of death for the catalog industry, the Internet was actually helping it grow. The catalog industry was supplementing their marketing efforts by providing online catalogs in addition to their hardcopy counterparts. Although catalogs remain the core business of these firms, the Internet allows them to weather the storm of slowdowns in the economy and higher postal rates.

Catalogers have looked to lessen costs and streamline operations by lessening the number of pages in their offerings, reducing the weight or size of the pages, and making changes in catalog style. They have also explored using freestanding inserts in newspapers, alternative delivery methods, telemarketing, and home shopping to keep them in the black. Euromonitor was predicting that year-on-year growth for the mail order and home shopping industry would be between 4 percent and 10.3 percent in the years leading up to 2008. Internet-based

sales were expected to be the area showing the highest growth, with sales expected to reach US$161 billion by 2008, an increase of almost 24 percent over 2003 levels. In the United States, the mail order and home shopping industry remained highly fragmented.

Europe. According to the European Mail Order and Distance Selling Trade Association (EMOTA), the number of firms in Europe with established mail-order operations exceeds 2,000. As of 2004, the European mail-order industry had sales of just below 50 billion euro and average per capita sales of approximately 130 euro, and it employed about 300,000 people. Although the mail-order industry was set up as international in structure, barriers do exist because of differences in European countries regarding taxation, postal service distribution, international payment, and differences in legislation. Sales to purchasers in other European countries were only about 3 percent; however, transition to the euro, although it was anticipated to take some time, was expected to broaden the reach of mail-order companies and avoid the high cost of converting currencies.

According to research group Mintel, of the home shopping industry in Europe, catalog shopping had dropped from a once-high of 53 percent of the market to 25 percent in 2004. Internet-based shopping had overtaken it as the leading form, capturing a 32 percent market share; however, catalog shopping still exceeded it in terms of value. As a percentage of all retail sales, catalog sales were still low at 3 percent, and this was expected to decline to 2 percent by 2009.

United Kingdom. Valued at US$28.6 billion in 2003, the U.K. mail-order and home-shopping market differed from the U.S. market in that in the United Kingdom, general mail order accounted for the largest market share (60 percent), whereas in the United States, the Internet was the largest source for the industry. Great Universal Stores was the nation's industry leader, taking 22.5 percent of the market, according to Euromonitor. Together with Otto Versand and Littlewoods, these three leading companies controlled 60 percent of the market. The market was expected to experience huge growth in the period up to 2008, with growth rates predicted to exceed 48 percent.

Germany. German consumers showed a preference for using catalogs to do their home shopping. Of the total market, valued at almost US$60 billion in 2003, almost 68 percent came from catalog shopping, with the market expected to be valued at almost US$81 billion by 2008. Market leader KarstadtQuelle—created as the result of a merger between Germany's leading department store and leading mail-order company—held 13 percent of the market in 2003.

Japan. In Japan the mail-order sector started in the 1950s and achieved double-digit yearly growth during the 1980s. Growth slowed in the early 1990s, but the market continued to expand, while the general retail market remained sluggish. Japanese consumers liked the convenience of home shopping and the fact that mail-order firms often sold goods at lower prices than traditional outlets. The country's parcel delivery system allowed companies to enter the market without the need for proprietary delivery services.

By the end of the twentieth century, 8 million out of the total population of 125 million Japanese were online, according to statistics from International Data Corp., and that number was forecast to reach 32 million by 2003. In Japan, Internet shopping was expected to rise from US$2 billion in sales in 1998 to US$45 billion by 2003. The recession caused the Japanese to spend less, but they still were actively buying on U.S.-based Web sites to save money on imported merchandise. A study by *Nikkei Weekly* showed that 39 percent of new Internet users are female. Japanese purchase many of the same goods via the Internet that Americans do, but the country's e-commerce industry has yet to grow as quickly as that of the United States, due in part to high telephone rates.

In December 2001, Japanese retailer Sumitomo Corp. announced a joint venture with Otto Versand to pool their resources in the online mail-order sector, according to *European Report.* Called Sumisho Hermes General Service Inc., the new company was divided 51 percent and 49 percent between Sumitomo and Otto Versand. The two companies have worked together since the establishment of Otto-Sumisho in 1986, which sells Otto Versand catalog merchandise in Japan and manages Eddie Bauer products there as well.

BIBLIOGRAPHY

"About JCPenney." J. C. Penney Corporation Inc., 2007. Available from www.jcpenney.net.

"Amazon.com Opens Support Base in Ireland for British, French Web Customers." *Yahoo! Finance,* 23 April 2007. Available from biz.yahoo.com.

"Amazon.com Pays Tribute to America's Pastime with a New Destination for Baseball Fans." *Business Wire,* 2 April 2007.

"Are Your Employees Dressed for Success?" *PR Newswire,* 20 March 2007.

Borck, James R. "Fighting the Grinch." *InfoWorld,* 26 October 2001. Available from www.infoworld.com.

Bresada, Alexandra. "Company Profile: J.C. Penney Corp." *Hoover's Online,* 2009. Available from www.hoovers.com.

Brohan, Mark. "Online Retailing Weathered the Storm in 2009 and Finished as the Retail Market's Only Growth Driver." June 2009. Available from www. internetretailer. com.

"Chairman Quits Edgewater, N.J.-Based Mail-Order Firm." *Knight-Ridder Business Tribune News,* 7 May 2004.

"Coaxing with Catalogs." *Business Week,* 6 August 2001.

"Dead Man Walking: Spiegel Sell-Off Begins." *Catalog Age,* 29 April 2004.

"DMA Catalog on the Road 2009-Overview." January 2009. Available from www.the-dma.org.

"Eco Group to Launch Catalog 'Blacklist'" *Catalog Age,* 29 April 2004.

"Eddie Bauer, in Need of a New Image, Goes Casual with an Outdoor Twist." *Knight-Ridder/Tribune Business News,* 14 May 2004.

Hajewski, Doris. "Filling a Bigger Wish List: Lands' End Finds New Beginning in Cross-Merchandising with Sears." 10 December 2006.

"Hanover Direct Today." Hanover Direct, 2009. Available from www.hanoverdirect.com.

"Home shopping catalogue sales overtaken by Internet." *Screen Pages,* 2005. Available from www.screenpages.com.

Ihlwan, Moon. "A Gold Mine Called Home Shopping." *BusinessWeek Online,* 5 November 2001. Available from www.businessweek.com.

Kiener, Sigmund. "The Future of Mail-order." *Direct Marketing,* January 1995.

"Lands' End Sends Kids Packing." Marketing Vox, 3 August 2009. Available from www.marketingvox.com.

"L.L. Bean Reports 2006 Net Sales Results." L.L. Bean Inc., 9 March 2007. Available from www.llbean.com.

"L.L. Bean Sues 4 Cos for Pop-Up Ads Linked to Web Site." *Dow Jones Business News,* 17 May 2004.

Magill, Ken. "Catalogers Say Books Are Still Primary Sales Drivers: DMA." *Direct,* 12 December 2006.

"Mail Order and Home Shopping in France, Germany, UK and USA." *Major Market Profiles,* 2004. Available from www.euromonitor.com.

"Mail Order: Sumitomo-Otto Versand Joint Venture." *European Report,* 12 December 2001.

"Mail Order Survives, Thrives." *Investor's Business Daily,* February 2005. Available from www.the-dma.org.

Nolan, Kelly. "Is There No Ending to Lands' Offerings?" 8 January 2007.

"Otto Group and Hagebau Combine Forces in Direct Order DIY Sales." Otto Group, 2 April 2007. Available from www.ottogroup.com.

"Otto Targets Affluent Youth Fashion Market." *Marketing Week,* 5 April 2007.

Pierce, Rachel. "Company Profile: Amazon.com." *Hoover's Online,* 2009. Available from www.hoovers.com.

Shearman, J. Craig. "Retailers Urge Passage of AHP Legislation." National Retail Federation, 13 May 2004. Available from www.nrf.com.

———. "Retailers Welcome Bush Rejection of China Trade Sanctions." National Retail Federation, 28 April 2004. Available from www.nrf.com.

Tierney, Jim. "Live From the ACMA Forum: Catalog Industry Broken." 21 May 2009. Available from multichannelmerchant.com.

Wilson, Eric. "L. L. Bean Tries on a New Look." *The New York Times,* 20 August 2009. Available from www.nytimes.com.

Zeller, Ann. "Five Questions: On the Current State of the
    Catalog Industry." Direct Marketing Association, 2005.
    Available from www.the-dma.org.

SIC 5411

GROCERY STORES

NAICS CODE(S)

445110. Retail grocers purvey a broad line of fresh, frozen, canned, and other prepackaged foods. Many of these stores also carry a variety of nonfood items such as health and beauty aids, paper goods, and cleaning supplies, but food and beverages make up the majority of their product lines and sales volumes. Excluded from this discussion are convenience stores and specialty food shops, such as butchers and produce markets.

INDUSTRY SNAPSHOT

Within the world's largest economies, the grocery retailing industry remained fiercely competitive, slimly profitable, and dominated by a few multibillion-dollar companies in each national market. Not only were grocery stores competing with each other, they also were having to stave off restaurants and other prepared-food vendors for a share of consumers' food budgets. The global recession had actually helped some retailers in this fight by causing consumers in the most affected countries to eat out less.

Despite the recession, grocery retailers continued to experiment with home delivery of groceries, marketing the service to busy professionals or senior citizens especially, although the service was not expected to replace traditional shopping in the foreseeable future. Many larger grocers have also included conveniences such as in-store pharmacies, which are perceived as a customer convenience and

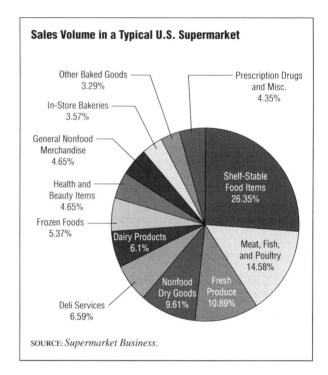

SOURCE: *Supermarket Business.*

also garner higher profit margins than food products. Some larger grocers tried to increase sales by creating multiple service outlets, including mini banking centers.

According to food and grocery industry research firm IGD, China, the second largest grocery retail market in the world, has gained considerable ground on the largest market, the United States. Based on total annual sales data to the end of 2010, the United States remains first with US$1 trillion, while China is second with US$832 billion. Rounding out the top five are Japan at US$543 billion, India at US$439 billion, and France at US$323 billion. Projecting figures to 2014, IGD expected China to take the top spot with US$1.2 trillion and the U.S. to be second at US$1.17 trillion. India was also expected to overtake Japan at the third position, and Russia was expected to displace France in fifth. These predicted changes reflect the ongoing trend of rapid growth in developing economies of the world relative to the mature economies of the United States, Western Europe, and Japan.

Growth in online grocery shopping continues to be a closely watched industry driver. IGD reports that as of 2009, 13 percent of adults had shopped for groceries on the Internet, which marked a 63 percent increase over 2006. In the United Kingdom, where acceptance of online grocery shopping has been more rapid than in the United States, IGD estimated that sales had increased 85 percent since 2006. Nonetheless, online shopping remains a drop in the bucket of all grocery sales. Market intelligence firm Synovate's 2009 global grocery shopping survey reports that only one percent of all respondents practiced it.

Largest Grocery Retail Markets in the World, 2010	
	In billions of U.S. dollars
U.S.	$1,000
China	$ 832
Japan	$ 543
India	$ 439
France	$ 323
Russia	$ 293
Brazil	$ 291
United Kingdom	$ 268
Germany	$ 252
Italy	$ 205
SOURCE: IGD.	

ORGANIZATION AND STRUCTURE

Business Structure. Three business set-ups describe the world's major food retailing enterprises: corporate chains, affiliated independent stores, and retailer-owned cooperatives. Corporate chains are the simplest because their retail outlets are fully owned or controlled by the corporate parent. Such chains generally show the highest degree of homogeneity across stores and regions. Individual outlets may also be franchised to local or regional owners, but they usually follow a rigid formula for operations and marketing, and they procure stock through prescribed corporate channels.

Like corporate chains, independent affiliates and retailer-owned cooperatives may share a common retail identity, but ownership and control vary considerably. Independent affiliates are groups of independently owned stores that purchase at least part of their goods, which may include a common private label, through a central wholesaler. The wholesaler generally provides goods to independent stores at lower prices than small retailers would otherwise be able to obtain in their small-volume purchases. The independents choose whether to include this affiliation in their names and marketing. In the trade, the term "independent" can describe small operations of up to ten stores. Among affiliated independents, then, the corporation of prominence is often not any of the retailers; instead it's the wholesaler with which the independent stores affiliate. (See also **Wholesalers.**)

Retailer-owned cooperatives, also known as buying groups, go one step further than affiliated independents. These independent stores affiliate with a central buying organization and also own shares of it. As with affiliates, the voluntary retail members choose whether to market the common identity in their stores. Because they own the buying group, the retailers also share in any profits or losses the buying groups incur, and, depending on their size, may have administrative clout with the buying group's management. In this sense, the buying group is a joint venture among all its members.

In practice, distinctions often blur the various types because of crossover activities. A corporate chain may distribute merchandise on the side to independent stores or affiliates; a wholesaler or buying group might open or acquire retail outlets. These models also do not take into account the simplest form—independent, unaffiliated stores. Although in many places they are numerically prevalent over any other form, few such operations could be considered major participants in the industry.

Store Formats. In leading countries, most of the industry's sales occur in supermarkets, which in the trade are defined as having US$2 million or more in annual sales. Supermarkets also are characterized by offering a full line of food, including fresh produce, meats, frozen foods, and dry packaged and canned goods, as well as diverse nonfood items such as cosmetics, toiletries, and cleaning goods. Many also offer in-store food preparation services, especially deli counters and bakeries. Supermarkets range in size from approximately 30,000 to 70,000 square feet.

Hypermarkets are largely a European format of massive, all-in-one stores that include a full department store with a complete grocery line, and often a gas station and other service amenities. The quintessential European hypermarkets, such as those by Carrefour S.A. of France, which is credited with pioneering the concept in the 1970s, may be upwards of 300,000 square feet in size.

Supercenters in the United States, although smaller and more limited in scope, are somewhat analogous to European hypermarkets. Wal-Mart experimented with the hypermarket concept with a 225,000-square-foot store, but it met a lackluster reception from U.S. consumers. The consensus in U.S. retailing is that the hypermarket format is unlikely to attract much following in the near future, due to already vibrant retail trade in many of the product groupings such as a large store would offer. The supercenter, ranging from 100,000 to 200,000 square feet, was Wal-Mart's solution. Like hypermarkets, supercenters include extensive food selection comparable to that of the largest supermarkets. These offerings are coupled with a general line of housewares, linens, discount apparel, toys, small electronics, and hardware.

Deep-discount stores, also known as limited assortment stores, offer no-frills merchandise at prices ranging from 5 percent to 25 percent less than that of name brand merchandise available through conventional stores. Led by such chains as Germany's Aldi Einkauf GmbH, these discounters may sell only private-label and off-brand products and may not stock a full or even consistent line of groceries. The physical store tends to be austere as well. The leading European chains leave their groceries in boxes on wood pallets rather than stocking them on shelves.

General-line grocery stores are numerically predominant in most places of the world, even while in the industrial economies they make up a relatively small percentage (as little as 20 percent) of industry sales. These stores may offer only a limited line of the most common produce items, no fresh meats, and a small selection of the most commonly used canned, frozen, and prepackaged goods. On the smaller end, the distinction may begin to blur with that of convenience stores. General grocery stores are often independent or small regional chains and, in some markets, are highly vulnerable to loss of sales to—or acquisition by—supermarkets and other larger format retailers.

Product Share. By product category, according to *Supermarket Business,* the typical U.S. supermarket obtains 26.35 percent of its sales volume from shelf-stable food items; 14.58 percent from meat, fish, and poultry; 10.89 percent from fresh produce; 9.61 percent from nonfood dry goods; 6.59 percent from deli services; 6.1 percent from dairy products; 5.37 percent from frozen foods; 4.65 percent from health and beauty items; 4.65 percent from general nonfood merchandise such as audio and video supplies, toys, periodicals, and photographic goods; 3.57 percent from in-store bakeries; 3.29 percent from other baked goods; and the remaining 4.35 percent from prescription drugs and other miscellaneous items.

Private-label, or store-brand, goods garner an estimated three percent of all grocery sales in Japan. In the United States, individual chains report that private labels generate an average of 20 percent of unit sales; this figure is not fully comparable, however, because that percentage is not based on industry sales as a whole. In Europe, private labels account for up to 50 percent of sales by some chains, most notably in the United Kingdom, although national averages are more in the range of 20 to 40 percent. Despite their low-cost, low-quality connotation in markets such as the United States, private labels in Europe are sometimes used to market premium merchandise. This practice varies widely, however, and more often than not the private label is used to market value-oriented product lines.

Market Forces. A variety of economic and demographic factors influence the industry's fortunes:

- **Demand fluctuation.** Economists describe the demand for basic grocery staples as inelastic. That is, groceries are consumed at relatively fixed rates regardless of cyclical economic conditions or modest price fluctuations. Demand for premium or luxury foods, conversely, tends to be more susceptible to demand swings, as consumers become more or less willing to part with their money for what is perceived as desirable but unnecessary. In some cases, premium goods are the most profitable for retailers, but private-label or store-brand staples may also be quite profitable.

- **Disposable income.** For obvious reasons, the maintenance and growth of consumers' disposable income is closely tied to the continuing and expanding sales of all but the most basic groceries.

- **Consumer confidence.** In a broader sense, consumer confidence is also a factor to the extent that consumers may not have more money than before, but they may be more willing to spend from existing incomes or credit lines if they perceive economic health. Consumer confidence typically moves with the business cycle, rising during good times and falling during recessions.

- **Competition.** The number, scope, and physical dispersion of stores in a given locality dictate the competitive environment. Stores compete mainly on price, convenience, and the range of products and services they offer. In less saturated markets, such as those of Eastern Europe and parts of Asia, one grocery store may possess a local monopoly for consumers of average or less than average means, while upper-income consumers may have additional choices. Particularly in industrial economies, grocery retailers increasingly compete with food service establishments, such as full-service restaurants (see also **Restaurants**), fast food chains, and eat-in coffee and bakery shops, for consumers' food purchases.

- **Local demographics.** Although competitive strategies such as aggressive pricing or acquisition can fuel short-term growth, an expanding local population is often a requisite for the long-term sales health of individual grocery stores. In addition, especially in competitive retail climates, stores must be in tune with local buying preferences in order to stock the most saleable product mix.

- **Location.** Finally, related to both demographics and competition, is a store's physical location relative to residential centers and competing venues. Optimal location is within short driving or walking distance from a large share of the intended customer base and near other retail or entertainment attractions to benefit from the convenience of cross-purpose shopping patterns. However, grocers must be far enough from direct competitors or other outlets of the same chain so as not to over- saturate the market. Likewise, ease of access, such as ample free parking, also is important and has been a selling point for some recent European suburban store openings.

BACKGROUND AND DEVELOPMENT

In the latter half of the 1990s, Europe's combination of market saturation in the West, market development in the transition economies of the East, and lagging retail sales had made the continent a hotbed for merger activities. Some European chains, such as those in Germany, actually experienced declining domestic sales. Therefore, acquisitions were a key to survival for many industry players.

In the United States, the Federal Trade Commission (FTC) in 1999 and 2000 halted several mergers, which would have made supermarket chains anti-competitive. Prior to 1999, the FTC generally examined mergers on a store-by-store basis. However, when in December 1999 Royal Ahold N.V. terminated its acquisition of Pathmark stores because of FTC opposition, the grocery merger climate cooled. Only months later, in June 2000, the FTC filed an injunction to block Kroger from buying 74

Winn-Dixie grocery stores in Texas and Oklahoma, claiming the purchase would have given Kroger a 33 percent market share in Fort Worth, Texas.

Saturated domestic markets increasingly portend foreign expansion for the most robust of these chains and acquisition by competitors for the less dynamic players. Perhaps no place has felt the brunt of the industry's appetite for expansion more than Latin America, where European and U.S. interests have gobbled up local chains and built new retail outlets, voraciously, in search of fast sales growth. These foreign chains have descended on Latin America with cookie-cutter success formulas and competitive savvy and, in the process, are stimulating indigenous firms to modernize and compete. For example, Grupo Pao de Acucar SA, Brazil's largest domestic grocery chain and second largest to Carrefour of France, responded to uninvited foreign suitors and competitors by opening that country's first 24-hour hypermarket and implementing sweeping technological upgrades and logistical improvements. However, the foreign grocery conquistadors have already been confronted with the downside of such rapid expansion: a Brazilian economic slowdown in 1997 diminished short-term returns and caused more than one European grocery concern to scale down its ambitious growth plans. The competitive climate was similar in Asia.

Further promising to recolor the global supermarket landscape entering the twenty-first century was the foray by U.S. discount giant Wal-Mart Stores Inc. (the world's largest retailer in terms of sales) into the supermarket arena with its supercenter format. A scaled-down version of the European hypermarket, Wal-Mart's supercenters combined a full-service grocery department with an extensive line of housewares, clothing, toys, and other nonfood merchandise, at highly competitive pricing. Wal-Mart's threat was by no means confined to its home country, either. As of 1998, it had outlets in eight countries. By 2001, Wal-Mart had 1,100 locations in nine countries outside the United States. Its 1997 purchase of a 21-store German chain heralded its entrance into the already crowded western European field, although the move was seen by some analysts as a jumping point for penetration of the less saturated eastern European market. The popularity of shopping clubs, such as Sam's Club (a Wal-Mart sister company) and Costco, also grew through the 1990s and into the first decade of the 2000s, creating more competition for the traditional grocery supermarkets.

In markets where it has expanded, Wal-Mart has often proven detrimental to local grocers, according to *Chief Executive*. In the first five years after the opening of a new Wal-Mart, other area grocery stores lost between 8 and 17 percent in annual sales. Wal-Mart continued to look for ways to expand internationally, as did most other large grocery chains, with mergers with and

acquisitions of existing grocery companies being the most used method for growth. Most future growth was expected to occur in Eastern and Southern Europe and Asia, particularly China and India.

With the coming of the new millennium, perhaps the single greatest market of opportunity for food retailers lay in China, where an immense population, a briskly expanding economy, and a relative dearth of Western-style retail venues attracted growth-oriented merchants. Similar market conditions occurred elsewhere in Asia, notably Indonesia and to a lesser extent India, but these economies were decidedly less robust than China's. Among leading companies, Carrefour, Royal Ahold, and Wal-Mart were best poised for substantial expansion in China, although it was likely that local retail powerhouses would also emerge.

CURRENT CONDITIONS

According to 2010 research from IGD, the top 10 retail grocery markets, in terms of value, were the United States, China, Japan, India, France, Russia, Brazil, United Kingdom, Germany, and Italy. U.S.-based giant Wal-Mart continued to dominate the industry on a world scale, followed by Carrefour of France, Metro Group of Germany, Tesco of the United Kingdom, and Schwarz Group of Germany.

Over the past decade, large-scale retailers, particularly those in the United Kingdom and the United States, have made sizable gains in cost efficiency through technological innovation and tight organizational control. These cost-cutting measures, often motivated by lean economic conditions, caused some U.S. observers to question whether such parsimony is not hurting sales by restricting the product line too tightly or by decreasing the level of customer service. It was likely, though, that because of their close ties to profitability, these practices would persist in firms that had adopted them and would continue spreading to the grocery chains of Asia, central and eastern Europe, and Latin America.

In Europe, moves to liberalize laws restricting merchants' hours in the Netherlands and Germany were expected to boost sales in those nations, enabling consumers to make more convenience trips to stores. While largely unregulated in the United States, longer store hours are a relatively new phenomenon in many parts of Europe. Nevertheless, as the continent seeks to rejuvenate its commercial sector, these and other traditional prohibitions on retail activities were expected to continue to be challenged in the political arena.

An ongoing consumer trend in Europe, as in much of the developed world, is a rapidly aging population. By 2050, the average age of the European population will be about 48. The impact of this long-run trend on grocers means stores will likely sell fewer food products and expand space for health and beauty products within an already growing non-food sales space.

The Economic Research Service branch of the U.S. Department of Agriculture reported that the U.S. population had not only become more ethnically diverse, it was also better educated and wealthier. The aging of the Baby Boomer population makes for an aging market as well. In the mid-years of the first decade of the 2000s, the explosion of different diets (such as low-carb diets), which were expected to grow sales of such branded foods exponentially into 2006; more attention to nutrition labels, coupled with a general interest in healthier eating and so-called whole foods; and desire for convenience prompted U.S. grocery stores to change or expand their product lines.

While burgeoning size has been a hallmark of grocery stores for a number of years, smaller niche stores have begun to flourish as well. Some focus on specific types of food products, such as organics, while others focus on specific customer populations. Ethnic food stores are one of the fastest growing niches, according to the U.S. Bureau of Labor Statistics.

The recession that began in 2007 has been felt in the grocery business. *Progressive Grocer*'s 63rd Annual Consumer Expenditures Study found that U.S. supermarket sales of US$437 billion in 2009 marked only a 1.6 percent gain over 2008. This marked the first time in five years that the rate of sales growth for the industry had fallen from the prior year's rate.

RESEARCH AND TECHNOLOGY

The industry requires advanced technology for a host of logistical concerns, including inventory tracking and ordering systems, frequent customer discount programs, and transportation management.

Integrated computer systems are the logistical lifeblood of modern supermarket chains. One interlinked system often tallies customers' orders at the register, tracks for inventory movement, and orders new stock from suppliers. Newer systems may also maintain a customer profile database for marketing and promotional uses. These computers are based on a 1980s innovation known as efficient consumer response (ECR), a theory of just-in-time inventory management that employs technology to minimize standing inventories (and, consequently, costs) while ensuring maximal breadth of stock on hand at any given time. In other words, ECR's goal is to make every item the store carries available at any time yet supplied in tightly controlled quantities based on purchasing patterns, so the store is never overstocked on any item and has no excess of unmoving inventory. The detailed information on inventory patterns that these systems collect also serves to aid

central planners to allocate resources differently, based on store-specific purchase trends.

A growing factor in grocery retailing is the use of the Internet. Some major chains, particularly in Britain, France, and the United States, have made strong offerings of Internet-based services. Some chains simply list online the locations of their outlets and other general information, but the more daring have begun to offer ordering services via the Internet or affiliate with Internet vendors to do so. Some observers have speculated wildly that the Internet spelled doom for conventional retailing, as customers could place orders directly from wholesalers or manufacturers at lower prices and remove the retail go-between. However, after failures of Internet grocers in the 1990s, that industry began a comeback in the first decade of the 2000s. Safeway had reported that its online sales had doubled between 2002 and 2004. Online grocery sales reached about US$2.4 billion in the United States. Safeway was using the Internet grocery technology of Tesco of the United Kingdom. Tesco was a success story in the online grocery shopping business. By 2010, more than 300,000 orders were being placed at its online site each week. Also for 2010, it was expected that online grocery shopping in Europe would reach the US$100 billion mark, or 10 percent of all grocery purchases. Based on interviews with 6,000 consumers in six countries, the report stated that Europeans found the produce fresher than when it was purchased in grocery stores and liked the convenience of online buying.

In 2009, Tesco announced a plan to open a network of "dark stores" in the United Kingdom. These are laid out as full-scale supermarkets in areas with inexpensive real estate. Instead of being open to the public, they are used exclusively by Tesco staff to fill and deliver online orders. Tesco further announced a plan in 2010 to expand its online services to China, the Czech Republic, and Poland.

Americans have been less receptive to online grocery shopping. In October 2000, Priceline.com's Web House Club Inc., which enabled shoppers to collect bids on up to 600 grocery items, failed in the food manufacturing segment. Although the service had attracted some two million members, manufacturers were reluctant to absorb the losses from selling at lower prices. Their reluctance was credited to the unsuitability of the Internet buying concept to the sale of perishable goods, high costs in opening and operating grocery stores, and the expense of grocery stores' major fixed assets such as trucks, equipment and fixtures, and warehouses.

Although the Priceline.com model was less than successful in the grocery industry, some grocers continued to explore online grocery buying possibilities, which could either be individual store-based or rooted in a large supermarket chain. For instance, in 2010, Sears entered the online grocery market, expanding its online presence to include home delivery of groceries through its Kmart stores in selected markets, including New York City.

Though online grocery shopping remains in its infancy in the United States, it was growing rapidly. A 2009 Nielsen study found that between 2004 and 2008, online consumer packaged goods (CPG) sales increased between 25 and 30 percent.

The British chain Safeway Plc., formerly part of U.S. giant Safeway Inc., began to deploy new logistical tracking technology, using a positioning system to monitor its delivery trucks. The system provided detailed information about the location and status of all its fleet. The chain then used the information to redirect shipments around traffic congestion, determine exactly when stock would arrive at a given location, and monitor the performance of its drivers. The chain expected to recoup the US$2.5 million system's annual operating expenses of US$570,000 within the first year of use.

New to the industry in 2002 was a self-service technology that its makers postulated would curtail long supermarket lines. The most commonly-used system was Montreal-based Optimal Robotics' U-Scan Express, which combined a touch-sensitive video display, a barcode scanner, an ATM-like payment device, scales, and a surveillance camera to enable customers to check themselves out. The system enabled customers with few items, typically 15 or fewer, to scan their own groceries, compute discounts and coupons, and pay with check, cash, or credit cards. The system entered retail stores in 1998, and by 2002 had become commonplace, particularly among larger retailers. Whether this sort of technology dramatically quickened checkout lines was uncertain, but it clearly offered potential to reduce staff overheads of retailers.

A different kind of self-service technology promised to be perhaps more efficient for shoppers and retailers alike. In Britain, South Africa, and the United States, among other places, experiments were conducted with several types of "scan-as-you-go" technologies. Rather than waiting until the end of a shopping trip to account for all items a customer selects, these systems employed handheld scanners or other monitors to track each item from the moment the customer first picked it up. Depending on the system's sophistication, it might either provide a final sales receipt to be paid at a register or automatically debit the shopper's pre-established account. In either case, these systems also provided special shoplifting deterrents. In fact, they allowed more detailed tracking of merchandise than almost any other transaction method.

Some retail chains have begun touting the use of reusable shopping bags to their customers. Kroger held an open online design contest for reusable shopping bags. In 2009, Kroger sold an average of almost 13,000 reusable shopping bags per day. Each bag reportedly has the potential to save 1,000 plastic bags over its lifetime.

WORKFORCE

According to the U.S. Bureau of Labor Statistics, grocery stores employed 2.5 million people in the United States in 2008, making it one of the largest of industries by employment. Sales and related occupations, such as cashiers, made up 42 percent of jobs. Stock clerks and order fillers made up 17 percent. In 2008, nonsupervisory workers earned an average of US$340 per week in grocery stores, compared to US$608 in all private sector industries. This disparity reflects the large number of entry level and part-time workers in grocery retailing.

Grocery stores are typically open more days and hours than other types of businesses. Employees are often needed in the evenings and on weekends, and employers often offer flexible scheduling that changes from week to week. For many of the jobs, such as cashiers, stockers and baggers, the work can be repetitive, marked by long hours of standing. Additionally, dealing with customers can become hectic and stressful at times.

Typically, supermarket employees were hired into entry-level positions that required little or no previous experience. In 2008, 29 percent of employees were between 16 and 24 years of age, compared to 13 percent in all industries. Entry-level grocery employees generally need a good appearance and attitude since their jobs often include being a first line of contact with customers. Cashiers need basic arithmetic skills and stock clerks and baggers must be in good enough shape to do crouching and lifting. Many employers prefer to fill cashier positions with high school graduates. Most employees are trained on the job and may be advanced to jobs with increasing responsibilities over time.

Grocery store managers have needed increasing levels of technical skill, as their jobs often include responsibility for millions of dollars in annual sales and hundreds of employees. They use complex software applications to control inventory, manage expenses, and perform other vital functions. Companies often look for graduates of universities, colleges, or technical institutes with retail-related degrees to fill the ranks of manager training programs, although there is also considerable promotion from within the ranks of store employees.

Twenty-two percent of U.S. grocery store employees belong to unions or are under union contracts. This is above the average of other industries, which is 14 percent. Chain grocery store employees are the most likely to be unionized.

Total employment in grocery stores is not expected to grow significantly from 2008 to 2011. Nonetheless, first-time and part-time job seekers, especially, are likely to find job openings because of high turnover within this industry. Additionally, employment of food preparation and serving employees, such as in bakery departments, is expected to grow faster than average as these departments are experiencing increasing popularity with customers.

MAJOR COUNTRIES IN THE INDUSTRY

France. According to IGD, 2009 was a tough year for French grocery retailers, with 2010 expected to be the same. Hypermarkets, which account for much of grocery sales in France, have mostly been experiencing slow growth due to economic challenges and the market being fairly saturated. The major firms are responding with innovations to the hypermarket concept that hold promise of reinvigorating it. These include changes in design layout to create a greater "store within a store" feel, more shopper interaction and self service options, and "drive" services that allow the customer to place an order online and pick up the goods at a drive-through point. All the major French firms had drives in action for the first time in 2010. Industry giant Carrefour plans to have them at 175 of its French locations by 2013.

Major players in France in addition to Carrefour include Centers Distributeurs E Leclerc, ITM Enterprises, Casino, and the Auchan Group. As in a number of leading markets, France regulates construction of large-scale hypermarkets; they are often located outside of city centers. As in other European countries, saturated domestic markets are proving a catalyst for international expansion by French firms.

Carrefour S.A. Carrefour S.A. is Europe's leading retailer and the second leading retailer in the world. In 2009, Carrefour operated more than 8,000 stores across France, Europe, Asia, and Latin America. As of 2009, sales were approximately US$119 billion and the company employed over 450,000 people. Carrefour's leading position was secured in Europe when it merged with food retailer Promodés in 2000. That year, the company's net sales leaped by more than 62 percent of its 1996 sales, with 59.5 percent coming from France, 13.8 percent from Spain, 13.5 percent from Brazil, 5.9 percent from Argentina, 2.9 percent from Taiwan, and the remaining 4.3 percent from elsewhere. After 1996, the company upped its share in other European grocery concerns and, as its sales results showed, aggressively pursued foreign expansion, though subsequent foreign-market uncertainties caused Carrefour to proceed with caution.

In 1997, a stall in the Brazilian economy and the broader Asian financial crisis sparked worries among investors and analysts that Carrefour would be adversely affected. Nonetheless, the firm pressed ahead with new store openings in China, Indonesia, South Korea, and Taiwan, but scaled back plans for Thailand and Latin America. Carrefour sold off its stake in the U.S.-based Office Depot in 1997.

Since CEO Lars Olofsson took over in 2009, the firm has sought to grow its market share in France, which accounts for 40 percent of its sales, by cutting prices and promoting its brand. In the first half of 2010, the firm posted a net profit of US$104 million. Global objectives included improving operations in its Brazilian hypermarkets and strengthening its presence in China.

ITM Enterprises SA (Intermarche). ITM Enterprises SA is a group of approximately 2,000 independent grocers known as Les Mousquetaires, 1,800 of which are in France. ITM buys and distributes merchandise for its members, offering them purchasing power and a distribution system they would not otherwise have. The firm specializes in low prices, proximity, and "people friendly" store sizes (usually under 2,500 square meters). ITM is the majority owner of the supermarket chain Intermarche. In 2008, the company reported revenues of US$49 billion. After barely testing the waters of major cross-border expansion in the mid-1990s, in 1997 Intermarche led a Switzerland-based buying group that purchased a 75 percent share in the large German chain Spar Handels AG, which had recently acquired 36 stores from another leading French retailer, Promodés. In addition to giving Intermarche control of Spar Handels' retail operations, the move made the Intermarche group Europe's largest food distributor. As of 2010, Intermarche has its own store brand presence in France, Belgium, Portugal, Poland, Bosnia, and Romania.

Germany. As of 2010, the German grocery market was valued by industry research firm IGD at US$252 billion, the ninth largest in the world. This was down from a seventh place showing in 2006 at US$236 billion. Projections to 2014 show Germany holding on to the ninth position with US$264 billion.

The country faced a 1998 increase in Germany's value-added tax, which rose one percentage point to 16 percent. This was followed by an economic downturn in the early years of the 2000s. As a result, German consumers turned their preferences to discount grocery outlets. Discounter ALDI used its philosophy of purchasing cheap site land, selling its own brands, and keeping employee counts limited to bring its market share to 40 percent of the German market by the mid-2000s.

According to a 2007 ACNielsen report, Germany was the cheapest country in Europe for international grocery products. France had a heavily regulated market with many rules resulting in higher cost for consumers. An abundance of discounters in Germany was limiting price increases. A French government report revealed that "maxi-discount" stores had a 30 percent market share of the retail food sector in Germany, compared to 13 percent in France.

As the global recession tightened its grip in 2008, inflation was felt in Germany as well. The average grocery bill increased 4.7 percent over the course of the year. Consumers often switched to the cheapest offerings available. Prices had stabilized by the end of the year, but consumers seemed to be sticking to their economizing behavior by shopping less often and buying in bulk. This practice presented a threat to small, independent grocers.

ALDI Group. Begun in Essen, Germany, in 1948, ALDI had grown to become an international grocery store chain by 2009, with more than 9,400 stores in 14 countries, including 11 other European nations, the United States, and Australia. The stores were noted for discounted, ALDI-branded product offerings and a no-frills approach to product display. Customers must pay for bags and place a deposit for shopping carts, products are displayed on crates and in boxes, and the number of staff is kept to a minimum. Remaining privately owned, the company's revenues were reported to be approximately US$69 billion in 2009, marking 4.6 percent growth over 2008, about 40 percent of the German market.

Metro AG. Once the second largest retailer in the world behind Wal-Mart, Metro AG's global position had fallen by 2005 but it still remained high. As of 2010, it employed some 300,000 people at over 2,100 locations in 34 nations in Europe, Africa, and Asia. Its 2009 year-end sales figure was US$107 billion. Of this total, 61 percent was from outside Germany. The company began an efficiency and value enhancement program in 2009 to improve customer orientation and achieve higher growth by 2012. Expansion is ongoing or planned in Kazakhstan, Ukraine, Egypt, and China.

Tengelmann Warenhandelsgesellschaft KG. Tengelmann Group, a 143 year-old multi-sector retailer, reported 2009 sales of US$3.6 billion from its 660 Kaiser's and Tengelmann supermarket locations. Tengelmann was also the largest shareholder in the A&P Supermarket chain in the United States.

Japan. Japan, the world's third largest grocery market in 2010 at US$543 billion, is projected to slip to fourth place by 2014 at US$566 billion. This is happening within the backdrop of an economy that has been sluggish since the 1990s, changing consumer buying patterns from a quality-only orientation to somewhat more of a value-oriented approach—yet one that was still highly brand conscious. Retailers, some unaccustomed to the notion of price competition, struggled to adjust to this new paradigm. They responded by introducing private label lines, by increasing imports of cheaper, foreign goods, and by reducing operating overheads to finance price slashing. By 2003, almost 15 percent of Japanese consumers' spending was on groceries, and they were showing an increasing preference for discount grocery retailers. Euromonitor predicted the strong potential influence of foreign retailers on the discount grocery market.

As with much of Japan's economy, retailers participated in markedly complex, multi-level distribution arrangements that industry analysts have seen as obstacles to new innovation and improved profitability. Some chains began to streamline procurement and distribution, but efficiency gains in this area continue to be an issue in the short term.

As with other leading countries, Japan continued to experience consolidation of its grocery chains as less competitive enterprises were acquired by a few leading retail conglomerates, whose financials also had not been consistently robust. A number of Japanese firms continued to make retailing inroads in China, where they had advantages of physical and cultural proximity over European and U.S. competitors.

Ito-Yokado Co. Ltd. A conglomerate of convenience stores, supermarkets, restaurants, department and specialty stores, and manufacturing, Ito-Yokado remained one of Japan's leading retailers as of 2010. In addition to holding more than 10,000 7-Eleven stores (as well as being majority owner of the world-wide franchisor of the 7-Eleven brand), the company operated 175 supermarkets in Japan. The firm struggled as consumer spending in Japan languished with the global recession, announcing job cuts at its home office in 2010 and posting an operating loss for the first half of the year of US$39 million.

The Netherlands.

Royal Ahold N.V. Once one of the world's largest food retailers, Royal Ahold remained a significant force in the industry with locations primarily in Europe and the United States. Its Albert Heijn subsidiary was the top food retailer in the Netherlands. In 2003, the company faced an accounting scandal after it overstated earnings in the United States. At this point, Ahold entered its self-described "Road to Recovery," restructuring itself around its core food business by selling its Spanish winery stake and divesting itself of its supermarkets in South America and Asia. In early 2005, Ahold sold its chain of convenience stores in the United States and began selling some of its Bi-Lo, Food

City, and Bruno's supermarkets. For 2009, Ahold posted sales of US$39 billion and had 206,287 employees. Also in 2009, the company announced a reorganizing of both its European and North American operations. The stated intent is to create a sharper focus on customer needs and simplify and standardize processes as the firm seeks to achieve profitable growth.

United Kingdom. The U.K. grocery sector has been growing since the 1990s. As of 2009, research firm IGD estimated that 52 percent of retail spending was for food and groceries. According to *Euromonitor,* this growth was not expected to slow, with the large grocery store chains of Tesco and ASDA maintaining their dominant positions in the country. The U.K. grocery market's value for 2010 was about US$267 billion. This puts it in eighth position among world grocery markets, down from sixth in 2006; the United Kingdom market was leapfrogged in the world rankings by fast-growing Russia and Brazil. The United Kingdom was projected to retain its eighth position in 2014 with a value of US$311 billion.

Tesco Plc. Tesco remained the U.K.'s largest grocery retailer, with sales of US$86 billion for fiscal 2010 in its 4,881 stores. While the United Kingdom accounted for 68 percent of Tesco's sales, 15.3 percent came from other European countries and 14.8 percent from Asia. The company is also a leader in the promotion of online grocery sales, with the company handling over 300,000 such orders each week.

In the *Independent,* Edel Kennedy discussed dynamics related to supermarket giants charging customers in the South twice what they charged Northern shippers for the same goods. The findings showed extreme differences between prices charged to locations that were no more than 33 miles apart. The National Consumer Agency was conducting a series of surveys after making the decision to look at the situation in more depth. A price survey of Tesco and Dunnes by the Irish *Independent* was credited with enhancing awareness of the problem.

Asda. Taking over second place from Sainsbury in the United Kingdom, Asda uses Wal-Mart style pricing, advertising, and display to promote its grocery business, while introducing an increasing line of non-grocery items to its stores. Bought by Wal-Mart in 1999, Asda was originally formed by a group of farmers in Yorkshire. In 2010, the company operated 370 stores and 23 depots in the United Kingdom and employed over 170,000 people. Asda was also seeking to grow its online business, launching a new non-food online business, Asda Direct, in 2008.

J Sainsbury Plc. Once second among U.K. grocery chains, 140 year-old Sainsbury lost its position to Wal-Mart-managed Asda. In an attempt to recover lost profit, the company is focusing its marketing strategy on providing great quality food at fair prices in its 537 supermarkets and 335 convenience stores, offering many of its own private label products. In 2004, the company sold its U.S. grocery business, Shaw's supermarkets. As of 2010, Sainsbury had 150,000 employees and a U.K. market share of 16 percent.

Writing for *The Daily Telegraph,* David Litterick shared comparisons between the United Kingdom's economic plight in the early 1990s and 2008. Differences were very evident when comparing Tesco and Sainsbury. Tesco's turnover had reversed to more than twice that of Sainsbury. These changes made it hard for investors to decide whether to buy, sell, or hold supermarket stock.

United States. The U.S. grocery market remains the largest in the world as of 2010, with an estimated value just over US$1 trillion. However, by 2014, China was expected to push the United States into second place. As of 2008, there were some 85,200 grocery stores in the United States, with 25,900 being convenience stores.

Industry-wide, grocers in the United States had witnessed a decline in their net-profit-after-taxes figures. After reaching their highest levels since 1980 in 2001-2002 at 1.36 percent of sales, this figure had fallen to 0.88 in 2003-2004. Due to this economic decline, there was also a decline in new store openings and major store remodelings. The global recession that began in 2007 and had been acutely felt in the United States only added to the competitive pressures, and most new store openings were attributed to the giants in the industry, with most store closings reported by the smaller chains, those operating between 10 and 100 stores.

U.S. grocery chains were comparatively less internationalized than their European counterparts. In a few cases, such as with Safeway in Britain, U.S. chains once held foreign operations and sold them. However, other than trade within North America and with the recent exception of Wal-Mart, U.S. food stores were noticeably absent from foreign markets. Within the U.S. market, Wal-Mart was the top grocery retailer, followed by Kroger, Safeway, Costco, SUPERVALU, and Sam's Club, based on 2007 sales.

Wal-Mart Stores Inc. Considered the greatest challenge facing the U.S. grocery industry, Wal-Mart's grocery sales reached 49 percent of its total revenue of US$401 billion in 2009. This was up from 28 percent in 2005. Wal-Mart's push to increase its presence in the grocery sector caused a reduction in margins and reduced the market share of many other industry players. Supermarket consultant David Livingston, in summing up the situation faced by Wal-Mart's competitors, noted the difficulty of competing on price and added "you've got to do something else," such as offer superior customer service. Wal-Mart continues its international expansion, having purchased Asda, the United Kingdom's second largest grocery chain, Supermercados Amigo in Puerto Rico, and Bompreo supermarkets in Brazil.

The Kroger Company. Second place Kroger was once the United States' largest grocer, a position it lost to Wal-Mart. In fiscal 2009, the company had sales of US$76.7 billion. It had 2,468 supermarkets, 777 convenience stores, 374 jewelry stores, and 334,000 employees. The company also manufactures and processes some of the food it sells. Founded in 1883, Kroger operates under a variety of names in addition to its own. These include Ralph's, Smith's, Food4Less, and many others.

In its efforts to thwart competition, Kroger had been reducing prices faster than it was able to reduce cost, and was thus seeing declines in its profit margins. The company's management is seeking growth from expansion of its number of stores by way of "in-market" acquisitions.

Safeway Inc. Safeway garnered sales of US$40.1 billion in 2009, down from US$44.1 billion in 2008. As of 2010, the company operated 1,725 stores, primarily in the Western, Midwestern, and Mid-Atlantic regions of the United States and in Western Canada. It also held a 49 percent stake in the 115-store Mexican chain, Casa Ley. Safeway operated several regional supermarket companies, including The Vons Companies in Southern California; Dominick's Supermarkets; Alaska's largest retailer, Carr-Gottstein Foods; eastern U.S. grocer Genuardi's Family Markets; and Randall's Food Markets. It also owned more than half of e-retailer Groceryworks.

Faced with an increasingly competitive grocery environment, in 2003, Safeway developed a new long-term strategy intended to differentiate itself by, for example, establishing industry-leading quality standards for perishable goods. As of 2009, the firm claimed to have made substantial progress and to be in a stage of the plan involving lowering everyday prices to achieve parity with key competitors.

BIBLIOGRAPHY
Brand-Williams, Oralandar. "Officials: E. Coli Outbreak May Spread." *The Detroit News,* 27 June 2008.
"Carrefour reports market share gains in France." *Yahoo! Finance.* 31 August 2010. Available from http://finance.yahoo.com.
Chanil, Debra, and Meg Major. "Inside the Marketbasket." *Progressive Grocer,* September 2010.
Fackler, Martin. "Japan Goes From Dynamic to Disheartened." *New York Times,* 16 October 2010.
"Free Factsheets." IGD, 2010. Available from http://www.igd.com.
"Hoover's Company Capsules." *Hoover's Online,* 2010. Available from http://www.hoovers.com.
Intermarche Company Web site. 2010. Available from http://www.intermarche.com.
Kennedy, Edel. "Shoppers Fleeced by Cross-Border Price Gap." *Independent,* 17 June 2008.
Klingholz, Reiner. "Europe's Real Demographic Challenge." *Policy Review,* October/November 2009.
"Kroger Fact Book." The Kroger Company, 2009. Available from http://www.thekrogerco.com.
"Kroger Urging Customers to Pare Plastic Bag Use." *Progressive Grocer,* 7 April 2010. Available from http://www.progressivegrocer.com.
Litterick, David. "Sainsbury: Is it Time To Buy, Sell or Hold?" 19 June 2008. Available from Telegraph.co.uk.
Painter, Steve. "In grocery sales, Wal-Mart sacks competition." *Northwest Arkansas News,* 21 June 2009.
Rastello, Sandrine. "French Struggle to Cope with Some of Europe's Highest Food Prices." *International Herald Tribune,* 18 June 2008.
Ritter, Ian. "Kroger Proves Recession Doesn't Stop Grocery Shopping." CBS Business Network, 12 March 2009. Available from http://www.bnet.com.
"Safeway Annual Report." Safeway. 2009. Available from http://www.safeway.com.
"Sears Begins Grocery Deliveries." *Progressive Grocer,* 13 June 2010. Available from http://www.progressivegrocer.com.
"SPAIN:Intermarche Owner Quiet on Exit Talk." *just-food,* 2 July 2009. Available from http://www.just-food.com.
"Tengelmann Group Announces Positive Results." Tengelmann Group. 26 August 2010. Available from http://tengelmann.de.
"Tesco Case Study." DaveChaffey.com blog, 2008. Available from http://www.davechaffey.com.
"Tesco to Open Customer-Free 'Dark Stores.'" *The Daily Telegraph,* 6 December 2009.
U.S. Census Bureau, Department of Labor Statistics. "Career Guide to Industries." 2010-2011. Available from http://www.bls.gov.
Wallace, Richard. "Does Format Innovation Hold the Key to Growth in France?" IGD, 8 May 2010. Available from http://www.igd.com.
Wiesenfeld, David. "In the Future, Your Kids Won't Shop the Way You Do." *Progressive Grocer,* 7 September 2009. Available from http://www.progressivegrocer.com.

SIC 7514

PASSENGER CAR RENTAL

NAICS CODE(S)

532111. Car rental firms provide short-term use of automobiles and light trucks to consumers and businesses.

INDUSTRY SNAPSHOT

In some respects, the car rental industry is less traditional in makeup than other industries, although it remains a major player in the world market. Its initial development was primarily a U.S. phenomenon, and U.S.-owned companies have continued to dominate the industry.

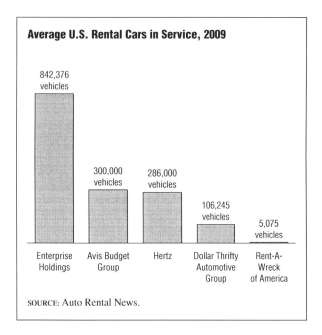

Average U.S. Rental Cars in Service, 2009

842,376 vehicles — Enterprise Holdings

300,000 vehicles — Avis Budget Group

286,000 vehicles — Hertz

106,245 vehicles — Dollar Thrifty Automotive Group

5,075 vehicles — Rent-A-Wreck of America

SOURCE: Auto Rental News.

Small European companies opened, primarily after World War II, but most eventually became affiliates or subsidiaries of the U.S. firms.

The twenty-first century has been a challenging one for the industry. The terrorist attacks against the United States on September 11, 2001, and the ensuing sluggish economy contributed to declining revenues and fleet sizes during the early 2000s. For example, in the United States, the rental car fleet fell from a high of 1.83 million vehicles in 2000 to 1.64 million vehicles in 2002. However, by 2004 the car rental industry was showing improvement, with revenues increasing to US$17.4 billion from US$16.45 billion in 2003.

It was not long, however, before a new recession arrived in the late 2000s. According to *Auto Rental News,* U.S. industry revenue fell more than US$1 billion from 2008 to 2009. In response, the industry tightened its belt. Enterprise Holdings, the largest North American car company, had its first ever "companywide" layoffs. For the industry as a whole, the U.S. Department of Labor reported over 25,000 lost jobs from the downturn. Companies also shrank their fleets and kept older cars longer. *USA Today* noted that the average mileage on rental cars rose from about 16,000 in 2006 to over 25,000 during the recession. Some rental rates were raised as well, increasing an average of US$20 a day between 2007 and 2008. Decreasing fleet sizes for most car rental companies and a drop in consumer demand were cited as reasons for the increase.

As of 2010, these various efforts appeared to have borne fruit. Industry earnings had improved, and firms were increasing their new car purchases, with Hertz

having purchased 80,000 new cars in the fourth quarter of 2009 alone, for example, in order to lower the average mileage of its fleet back to normal levels.

The 2007 Rental Car Satisfaction Study released by J.D. Power and Associates showed that customers had become less satisfied with airport car rentals. Several automakers had reduced the number of vehicles they made available to car rental companies, which resulted in a decrease in affordable and fuel-efficient cars on rental car lots. Avis, Enterprise, and Hertz began to offer limited time special deals, such as 50 percent rate cuts, for their customers. Others, including National and Alamo, offered reduced prices for add-on options, such as navigation systems. Some car rental agencies also offered their customers deals with no expiration dates.

ORGANIZATION AND STRUCTURE

At the peak of post-World War II industry development, most major car rental corporations were owned by large conglomerates. For a time, Ford Motor Company wholly owned Hertz Corporation and Budget Rent A Car Corp., General Motors controlled 81.5 percent of the National Car Rental System, and a Chrysler Corp. holding company owned Thrifty Rent-A-Car System and Dollar Rent-A-Car System. Vendors primarily operated under franchise or license agreements with privately owned, individual car rental locations. Adjustments to keep pace with the global economy in the industry resulted in the end of such alignments by the end of the twentieth century. By 1997, Hertz, Dollar, and Thrifty were traded publicly. Avis continued to be primarily a public corporation, but Cendant Corporation owned a 20 percent share, and Republic Industries, known for its sprawling auto dealership empire, owned Alamo, National Car Rental, and Spirit Rent-A-Car. Enterprise, which dominated the industry along with Hertz, stood alone as a private company.

The relationship between car rental and air travel was not accidental. The car rental industry had blossomed after World War II when commercial air travel became increasingly common, and car rental entrepreneurs capitalized on the need for convenient ground transportation for business travelers. In the late 1970s and early 1980s the airline industry was deregulated, which dramatically increased air travel and stimulated the car rental industry. As airlines competed for business with lowered fares, air travel became affordable for countless travelers who previously had been grounded by budget constraints.

In the 1970s and 1980s, car rental companies quickly capitalized on the growth in air travel by increasing the size of rental car fleets and the number of rental agency outlets. As more car rental companies entered the field, it became necessary for each to distinguish itself either by price or by service. Many companies specialized in niche markets, such as corporate, leisure, or insurance replacement. Others emphasized geographic coverage, focusing on local, national, or international operations.

The economic downturn of the 1990s caused a shift in the industry, particularly among those companies that catered to corporate accounts. The ability to quickly move supply to meet demand became the single factor that dictated a company's future. Consumers insisted on new cars, inexpensive prices, and good service, while the auto industry was unable to continue supplying car rental companies with large numbers of "program" cars. Those companies that could overcome supply issues through implementation of good management techniques, shrewd pricing schemes, and large distribution systems tended to thrive.

Attrition did not completely thin the ranks of small firms, but competition led to an increase in the mergers and acquisitions that had restructured the industry by the mid-1990s. At the end of the twentieth century, several major car rental firms that had been owned by automobile manufacturers began to be traded publicly. Emphasis was placed on service and convenience that could be provided to customers through increased automation, better reservation and delivery systems, and huge worldwide fleets. Corporate service contracts were negotiated with sharp pencils in hand, and the resulting improvements in cash flow improved the health of the industry as a whole.

By the end of the century, most car rental firms filled niches within the industry. Some catered primarily, but not exclusively, to corporate accounts, and some addressed the needs of individuals seeking a rental car for personal reasons. Large firms expanded their businesses, keeping track of their growing fleets with the help of sophisticated reservations systems and high-speed computers.

In November 2010, BMW announced a plan to begin an hourly car rental program in Munich, Germany, with which customers could reserve any BMW model by phone, on the Internet, or in person; BMW envisioned this service as a way consumers could rent its more expensive models for use on special occasions. Another interesting development in Europe was the expected growth of the car-sharing industry. Firms provided customers with a card, which could then be used to procure short-term use of a large fleet of various types of vehicles, allowing customers to pay only for the amount of drive time needed, with no monthly commitments. Zipcar brought the car sharing model to the United States as well, but it remains to be seen just how much Americans will embrace it.

BACKGROUND AND DEVELOPMENT

The car rental business grew out of classic American entrepreneurial spirit. In September 1918, 22-year-old Walter L. Jacobs took wrench and brush in hand and repaired and repainted a dozen Model T Fords and proceeded to use them to open a car rental operation in Chicago. Within five years, Jacobs had expanded his operation to the point that annual revenues neared US$1 million. Jacobs' company attracted the attention of General Motors Corporation, which purchased the company three years later along with John Hertz's Yellow Truck company.

Hertz became the first car rental company to open rental offices at railroad stations, which was a logical step, since the train was the predominant mode of travel in the 1920s. Hertz was also the first to allow advance reservations. In 1932, Hertz opened a facility at Chicago's Midway airport, becoming the first car rental agency to capitalize on the potential needs of air travelers. With the advent of jet travel in 1953, two-thirds of Hertz's customers were travelers, 70 percent of whom were business travelers. Further analysis of the industry showed that in the 1950s, 60 percent of car rental customers had arrived at their rental locations by air, while only 30 percent had traveled by rail. Hertz and other rental firms altered their business strategies accordingly.

The emergence of Avis, Hertz's closest early competitor, was almost entirely a consequence of the post-World War II establishment of the airline industry as the primary mode of commercial travel. As early as 1946, Warren E. Avis, a World War II Army Air Corps flyer and Detroit auto dealer, was confident that the airlines were about to become the preferred transportation mode worldwide. Capitalizing on the fact that no car rental agency had an airport operation with a fleet of cars (Hertz's pioneer efforts consisted only of an airport office), Avis opened the Avis Airlines Rent-A-Car System offices at Miami Airport and at Detroit's Willow Run Airport. The immediately successful fledgling business grew steadily and Avis built a network of independent local operators, each licensed to do business at airports under the Avis name. New York, Chicago, Dallas, Washington, Los Angeles, and Houston soon joined the Avis System.

In an ongoing effort to carry his business to his customers, Warren Avis opened numerous downtown locations serving major hotels and office buildings in 1948. By 1954, the Avis System boasted 185 locations in the United States, 10 in Canada, and 1 in Mexico, as well as working agreements with local rent-a-car companies in England, France, Germany, Ireland, Italy, Scotland, and Switzerland. That same year, Avis was sold to Richard Robie, who expanded the company's corporate-owned locations to another 16 cities, developed the first nationwide plan for one-way car rentals, and began distribution of the company's own charge card.

Increases in international travel prompted car rental companies to expand beyond national boundaries. By

1955, Hertz operated in Ireland, Switzerland, Canada, and France, as well as in 227 U.S. airports and at more than 20 domestic railroad stations. In 1957, the Hertz facility at Orly Airport in Paris was the first on-site car rental operation at an international European airport. Additional Hertz locations quickly appeared in Spain, Belgium, Denmark, Germany, the Netherlands, New Zealand, Aruba, Australia, the Ivory Coast, Guatemala, Iceland, Japan, Kenya, and Tobago.

Car rental companies dramatically increased their fleets to meet domestic and international growth. In 1958, Hertz spent more than US$60 million for nearly 18,000 vehicles, which was the single largest purchase of cars to that time. Within five years, the Hertz fleet grew to 85,000 vehicles in 386 cities in 73 countries. As the industry grew, the disposition of used cars became a challenge. Typically, rental fleets were renewed on a nine- to 15-month basis, with retired cars sold from the fleets through the offices of various wholesaling firms. As car rental fleets grew in size, however, used car wholesale markets became glutted and prices became depressed. To remedy this, Avis opened its own retail car sales operation, selling most of the used cars in its fleet to individual buyers. By the 1970s, the public considered used cars sold by Avis and other leading car rental companies to be bargains. As new car prices escalated, late-model used cars became increasingly attractive to buyers. By 1987, Avis was retailing about 50,000 cars annually from over 100 used car sales locations nationwide.

Deregulation of the airline industry began in phases in 1978, and with it came the biggest challenge to date for car rental companies. Airlines allowed increased competition; not only did flights become available to almost any worldwide destination, but new airlines were also founded. With the flood of new competition, airlines offered attractive fares to encourage people to fly to more places. As air passenger volumes surged, car rental companies had to follow the marketing precedent set by the airlines. To encourage loyalty from their customers, car rental companies offered bonus "points" to stimulate repeat business. In 1972, Hertz introduced the #1 Club Gold, which listed members in a data file that included license, address, and credit card information that could be accessed instantly to allow customers the convenience of renting a car without having to wait in line and fill out forms. In 1991, Hertz expanded the club to include Canadian travelers. In 1992, the club included Europe; in 1993, it included Australia; and in 1994, Japan, Singapore, and Hong Kong.

Sharply higher oil prices, the 1981-82 air traffic controller's strike, and competitive pricing combined in the 1980s to make it difficult for car rental companies to raise prices to cover inflation-driven cost increases. With more players in a heightened competitive environment, customer service became the primary focus. Customers began to routinely demand no-hassle reservations and easy car drop-off and were not satisfied if these features were a perk provided only to favored customers. In response, Hertz became the first car rental company to offer express service for car returns, as well as instant returns and self-service returns. Avis then introduced Avis Express service at major airports around the country, helping to speed harried customers through airport terminals. The Avis service allowed deplaning customers to bypass the terminal counter and go directly to an Avis shuttle bus or Avis Express facility where completed agreements and pre-assigned cars awaited them. In 1983, the system was extended, and Avis was able to produce a printed rental agreement within seconds at any Avis rental counter throughout Europe. In 1984, Avis opened the first automated self-service return system in the industry, using third-generation "Wizard" computer terminals. Not to be outdone, Hertz introduced computerized driving directions (CDD) and offered car seats for children, hand controls for the physically challenged, and portable cellular phones. To further enhance their customer's feeling of security, Hertz established a 24-hour emergency road service, which was another example of the emphasis on customer service that characterized industry development at the end of the twentieth century.

A general economic downturn in the 1990s put pressure on pricing, making it difficult for companies to raise rates. At the same time, customers were demanding better service, including easier reservation, pick-up and drop-off procedures, and frequent customer rewards. The ensuing economic resurgence proved to be a mixed blessing. As the economy improved, the auto industry experienced a rise in car sales. Manufacturers were able to sell every car they produced, and special program sales to agencies dropped off dramatically. For example, General Motors reduced the number of cars it supplied to car rental companies nearly 50 percent between model year 1992 and model year 1994, dropping from 795,000 to 400,000 cars delivered to car rental agencies.

The industry sought innovative approaches beyond the classic expansion and consolidation that had stabilized industries. In the 1990s, the opportunity for expansion was dramatic. The economies of the former Communist-bloc nations were opening, and political instability throughout the world was relatively low. In the mid-1990s, Hertz opened four locations in the Commonwealth of Independent States (the former Soviet Union). When the Channel Tunnel connecting the United Kingdom and France was opened, Hertz became the first car rental company to serve the entire European Union.

Small car rental agencies began to reassert themselves at the turn of the century. Ranked third in overall fleet size, Alamo Rent-A-Car entered the European market in 1987 when it acquired airport sites in England. In the mid-1990s, Alamo teamed with local firms to acquire additional locations in Germany. Prior to the German acquisition, which more than doubled its European presence, Alamo operated at 35 locations in six European countries. To make its increased global offering even more attractive to customers, Alamo announced a partnership with Hilton Hotel Corporation in 1994, enabling its customers to earn Hilton Honors points when they rented a car. Expansion was ongoing in 1994 and 1995, as Alamo added airport locations in Prague, Czech Republic; Amsterdam, The Netherlands; Zurich and Geneva, Switzerland; Frankfurt, Munich, and Dusseldorf, Germany; Brussels, Belgium; and Manchester, Norwich, and Southampton, United Kingdom. In 1994, Alamo became one of the last major car rental companies to adopt the policy of reviewing customers' driving records to determine whether to rent them a car. (A customer with three bad driving citations or one drunk driving conviction within the previous two years was not eligible to rent a car.) Similar policies had been introduced by Hertz and Avis in 1993, and Alamo also found driver screening to be a necessary step to reduce liability insurance costs.

At the end of the twentieth century and beginning of the twenty-first century, globalization became increasingly important to rental car companies as the travel industry experienced sharp increases in global travel. As traditional car rental customers and business travelers traveled abroad more frequently, rental car companies expanded to meet the needs of world travelers seeking familiar companies and service when away from home. Technological advances, particularly in communications, enabled car rental companies worldwide to efficiently book rental cars and increase their profitability.

In 2000, more than 1.8 million cars and trucks were available for rental in the United States. Car rental rates had begun to grow 5 to 7 percent annually in the 1990s. Corporate travel rates were negotiated between major firms, and car rental suppliers became increasingly lucrative. Additional revenues were generated as major car rental companies invested in various revenue/yield management systems. Hertz, Dollar, Thrifty, Budget, and Avis car rental were traded publicly, forcing executive management teams to focus sharply on improving shareholder value. Airline travel increased several percentage points each year, and conservative estimates predicted that the car rental industry would keep pace. At the same time, the increasing globalization of the world's economies gave rental firms catering to business interests an incentive to increase their presence worldwide.

At the turn of the century, large distribution systems, large fleets, and computerized reservation and management systems kept major industry players profitable. Hertz lost its ranking as number one in the industry, despite managing to produce increased revenue with a smaller fleet than first place Enterprise Rent-A-Car. Although they swapped position depending on whether they were ranked internationally by revenues, fleet size, or personnel totals, the top four car rental firms in the early 2000s were Enterprise, Hertz, ANC Rental Corp., and Avis. They were followed closely by Budget Rent A Car, Dollar Rent A Car, the rapidly growing Thrifty Rent A car, and U-Save Auto Rental.

In 1995, Chrysler reorganized its Thrifty and Dollar units into one autonomous company to make them more attractive for purchase. Thriving as the Dollar Thrifty Automotive Group, Inc., and bolstered by Dollar's affiliation with Eurocar, three years later Dollar/Thrifty ignored their former parent's intent and remained independent. Alamo Rent A Car Inc. flirted with the possibility of buying General Motors' National Car Rental System. Instead, National was sold in 1995 to auto sales giant Republic Industries. Two years later, Alamo also found itself under the Republic Industries umbrella. Hertz and Avis continued to trade publicly, but Avis enjoyed, as well as exploited, a close relationship with Cendant, which owned 20 percent of Avis stock. In March 2000, Hertz merged with Ford Motor Co. and became a wholly owned subsidiary of the automaker. Enterprise, the only car rental giant to function as a private company with privately held stock, steadily challenged Hertz for industry dominance, and in 2000 surpassed Hertz's sales by US$500 million, although Enterprise had only 30 more airport locations nationwide than its rival.

After weathering difficult years during the early 2000s, which were marked by a drop in business travel following the terrorist attacks against the United States on September 11, 2001, the car rental industry appeared to be poised for better times as it moved the mid-2000s. In its March 1, 2004, issue, *Travel Weekly* reported that "despite the war in Iraq, SARS and travel jitters, the industry's financial situation remained stable in 2003 as car companies maintained tight fleets, controlled costs and generally managed to avoid rate-cutting."

According to *Auto Rental News,* the U.S. fleet of rental cars fell from a high of 1.83 million vehicles in 2000 to 1.62 million by 2003 before rising to 1.66 million in 2004. U.S. industry revenues fell from a high of US$19.4 billion in 2000 to US$18.2 billion in 2001 and US$16.4 billion in 2002. From there, revenue improved to US$16.5 billion in 2003 and US$17.6 billion in 2004.

The world leader in the industry continued to be the United States. Vehicles were available at 17,663 car rental locations in 2004. The company leader in the industry, supplying almost 30.5 percent of all cars, was Enterprise, followed by Hertz (21 percent), Vanguard (12 percent), Avis (11 percent), and Budget (six percent). Avis and Budget were owned by Cendant Corporation. Euromonitor predicted that the U.S. industry would grow more than 20 percent between 2004 and 2008, and the leisure market would remain the largest sector of the industry, accounting for about 40 percent of all rentals.

Car rentals have always been closely tied to travel. In 2004, France continued to be the most popular destination in the world, with more than 76 million visitors. Euromonitor valued the car rental industry in France at almost US$2 billion in 2003, with almost 59 percent of rentals for leisure travel. This sector was expected to grow nine percent by 2008. In France, Hertz, Avis Europe, and Europcar dominated the market, and each holding a share between 20 and 22 percent.

The United Kingdom ranked sixth in the world as a tourist destination, and the car rental industry was valued at US$1.98 billion in 2003, which was almost the same as France. However, in the United Kingdom, more than 54 percent of cars were rented by business travelers. Hertz, Avis Europe, National, and Enterprise dominated the U.K. car rental market. The industry was expected to grow 11.8 percent between 2004 and 2008, with most cars continuing to be rented by domestic corporate customers.

In early 2004, reservations and car rentals in parts of Europe were more than 2003 levels, with leisure rentals doing especially well in the United Kingdom, France, and Italy. However, a decline in rates was the result of pressure from car rental brokers, which resulted in losses for industry leaders in 2003. For example, Avis lost EU$47.4 million that year. In 2004, Avis Europe continued to express concerns over the downward pressure being exerted on profit margins. Fierce competition and increased customer and broker use of the Internet to book rentals was cited as the cause.

In July 2004, when business travel had not increased, small car rental companies in Finland had reported difficulties because large rental companies were taking leisure market share from them. In addition, changes in automobile taxes caused car values to fall sharply, which was expected to cause many small Finnish firms to shut their doors following the summer 2004 car rental season.

CURRENT CONDITIONS

Although at one time almost all the major car rental companies had been owned by vehicle manufacturers,

by 2005, only Hertz in the United States and Europcar International in France were owned by manufacturers (Ford and Volkswagen, respectively). Manufacturers originally had used car rental subsidiaries to regulate the sales cycle of new car purchasing. According to Perot Systems, companies had shifted their focus to profitability, customer service, branding, and globalization. The car rental industry had become more concerned with cost containment and revenue growth while they tried to provide customers with a wide selection of vehicles with added amenities. The use of the Internet to book rentals had grown rapidly. Companies had also become increasingly focused on establishing brand identity in new markets and had concentrated on more niche marketing to customer groups defined by use—leisure, corporate, replacement, and truck rentals.

Refueling became controversial in the mid- to late 2000s. If customers did not return their rental cars with full gas tanks, they had been charged per gallon refueling prices well above the going rate at the local gas stations. In June 2008, Hertz had the highest refueling charges at US$7.99 per gallon, but said it would adjust fuel policies for rental throughout United States and Canada.

Car rental agencies began to increase prices the way the airlines had in the late 2000s. Up to 20 percent could be added to the rental rate for optional add-ons, such as navigational systems and refueling costs. Hertz announced in July 2008 that it would institute a system for customers who returned cars without full gas tanks, charging them a US$6.99 service fee in addition to the cost for gas at local gas station rates.

Enterprise had led the way in effectively adding hybrids into its rental fleet, offering 4,000 hybrids in its fleet of 1.1 million vehicles. Among the hybrids, Asian makes were the most popular in the late 2000s. The Toyota Prius was the top choice at rental firms. Consequently other automotive manufacturers, including Kia, Mazda, and Hyundai were developing high-fuel efficient cars.

As in many industries, China's fast growing economy created the anticipation of growth for auto rental and leasing. A December 2008 report from Beijing Lian Long Consulting, Ltd. projected that revenue in the industry would quadruple to US$40 billion by 2018. There were already some 3,000 auto rental companies in China, but most were small, with 80 percent having fleets of fewer than 50 cars. This left open the possibility of not only growth in China's market but also consolidation.

In the United States, the American Car Rental Association reported that in September 2010 the Graves Amendment was under assault from some members of the U.S. Congress. The Graves Amendment repealed state "vicarious liability" laws which could hold a car rental company responsible for damages caused by its customers, for example, even in cases where the rental company was not negligent.

RESEARCH AND TECHNOLOGY

Once the increase in air travel had made the rental car industry characteristically competitive, the implementation of technology became crucial for various rental companies. Technology in car rental was typically equated with efficient reservations and vehicle distribution. In 1971, Hertz introduced a centralized reservation and data center to run its global point-of-sales reservation system. The Oklahoma City-based center operated 24 hours a day, 365 days a year. By 1993, the center was handling more than 100,000 phone calls and more than 80,000 preprinted messages per day. The investment Hertz made in the raw computing power necessary to support the operation was enhanced by the addition of a high-speed data communications network that allowed 33 Hertz claims management offices in ten states to process insurance claims.

One year after Hertz automated car reservations, Avis introduced the Wizard System. Wizard was even more comprehensive than the Hertz system, and in 1972, Avis had the first and largest computer-based, online, real-time, global rental, reservation, and management information system in the industry. Hardware and software enhancements in 1979 and 1984 kept Wizard ahead of the competition. The third-generation Wizard computer terminal, which was introduced in 1984, included Rapid Return, an automated check-in service available to Avis customers at major airports and key downtown locations in the United States. Use of Rapid Return meant that an Avis customer could enter a vehicle number, mileage, and fuel level into a stand-alone computer terminal and receive a completed transaction record, or receipt, in less than one minute.

In 1998, the Wizard System continued to provide Avis with a significant technological advantage beyond its competitors. In enhanced form, it was state-of-the-art technology for nearly 30 years after its introduction, partly because of its comprehensive range of applications. The Wizard not only performed reservation and rental counter functions and vehicle inventory control, but also flagged cars for preventive maintenance services. It recorded buyers of Avis used cars and transmitted the information to computers of car manufacturers in case of a safety recall. It was an excellent worldwide management information system and could produce reports tailored to corporate customer specifications for accounting and cost control purposes on demand, then deliver them electronically to the client company's own computer. Avis

offices in countries around the world used Wizard to communicate 24 hours a day, seven days a week using the computer network. By 2010, the name had come to be used in marketing, with each of Avis' member customers receiving a "Wizard Number" designed to give them faster reservation and rentals.

The largest of the car rental companies had integrated communications technology into their businesses, allowing shorter advance booking time, computerized maps for customers, 24-hour customer service call centers, and improved marketing information. Information technology and satellite tracking systems improved car rental service and fleet availability at the beginning of the twenty-first century as companies could predict their customers' needs with increased accuracy and estimate the number and type of available fleet cars. The information technology available to car rental companies was put to the test during the last two weeks of September 2001, when as many as 100,000 cars had been displaced as air travelers scrambled to rent cars to make it to destinations thousands of miles from their grounded airplanes. By using the Internet to communicate and track vehicles, rental franchises were able to effectively return the cars to their proper locations.

Global positioning satellites had also become more commonplace in the car rental industry and benefited the customers as well as the rental company. For example, Budget installed NavLynx Telematics in its cars and used the system as a marketing tool, boasting that its customers would never be lost again. An added use was discovered in December 2000 when the company was able to locate a car stolen from its Toronto fleet after it was driven to Calgary, Alberta, Canada, 2,000 miles from its last known location.

In lieu of technology and in an effort to supplement lesser technologies, some car rental companies began to appeal to customers through a variety of customer-friendly product offerings. National introduced the Emerald Club, which allowed its customers to bypass the rental counter and select their cars personally without the need to process paperwork. Choice Rental and Quick Rent enhanced the experience of other National customers, and the company's Handheld Return Service gave each customer a human interface to speed car returns at airports. Thrifty used a high-tech approach similar to that of Avis and contracted with SABRE Direct Connect and Apollo's Inside Link to provide communication technology. Enterprise began to advertise "we'll pick you up" service improving customer convenience by literally bringing the rental vehicle to the customer's doorstep.

By the mid-2000s, some industry observers were critical of the industry's use of technology to track vehicles, especially for enforcing geographic restrictions and maximum speeds driven. However, proponents argued that technology like GPS systems was necessary to monitor corporate assets and ensure driver safety because such technology made it possible for rental car companies to locate stolen vehicles or determine if a renter was driving in a region where auto insurance did not apply. In support of tracking measures, industry leaders acknowledged that technology was typically used to notify companies when customers were violating rental contracts.

In 2010, Hertz teamed with IBM and Mindshare Technologies to create a new level of customer service analysis. The system they developed gathered customer feedback from Internet surveys, emails, and text messages for real time analysis and action. The system placed feedback into categories such as staff courtesy issues and mechanical issues in order to make it easier to note patterns and address issues. It flags comments that request a callback from a manager, a process used to be done manually.

WORKFORCE

Jobs in the automotive rental industry were most commonly entry-level positions at which an employee could work up to management or ownership of a franchise. The U.S. Department of Labor predicted that the demand for counter and rental clerks, which includes auto rental clerks, would grow from 2008 to 2018 by 3 percent, slower than the average of other occupations. However, high turnover in entry-level positions was expected to create a favorable environment for job opportunities. Although jobs were available throughout the United States as well as worldwide, the majority of jobs were located in metropolitan areas and near airports, where the need for car rental sites was the greatest. The average wage for automotive rental and leasing clerks in May 2009 was US$12.37 per hour.

Although entry-level rental clerks were typically required to have only a high school diploma, they were required to be knowledgeable about the company and its services and procedures. Most of the larger car rental companies developed training programs for new employees, including information about the company as well as customer service, although training programs varied greatly in thoroughness and longevity. Some employers trained new employees with a series of videotapes, brochures, books, and pamphlets, while others had formal classroom programs which ranged in duration from a few days to weeks.

Car rental company employees were typically expected to work evenings, nights, and weekend hours but had flexible schedules and could be part- or full-time employees. Full-time employees usually received benefits, such as insurance and paid holidays and vacations.

According to the U.S. Bureau of Labor Statistics, working conditions in the rental industry were usually pleasant, and most stores and service establishments were clean, well lighted, and temperature-controlled. However, the job also required long hours of standing, and customer contact could be constant and stressful.

INDUSTRY LEADERS

Enterprise Holdings. Still privately owned by its founding family, the Taylors, in 2010, Enterprise Holdings was the largest car rental company worldwide in terms of fleet size. It was also ranked number 24 on the Forbes 500 Largest Private Companies in America list. Enterprise was started in 1957 as "Executive Leasing" by Jack Taylor, a World War II Navy fighter pilot and former sales manager at a St. Louis, Missouri, Cadillac dealership. The firm originally provided only executive leasing services, but in the early 1960s, Taylor expanded the business to include short-term car rentals and extended his operation in other cities. In 1961, Enterprise had 1,000 lease cars in its automotive fleet. By 1969, it had 5,000 lease cars, and by 1973, an additional 1,000 rental units were in service. The company also diversified to include non-automotive-related businesses.

In 1976, Enterprise established a special fleet leasing company to handle large commercial accounts. The following year, Enterprise reported more than 10,000 lease cars. In the 1970s and 1980s, rental and leasing operations grew substantially, with the rental operation directed largely at the "home city" rental market. This market was comprised of two broad segments: the replacement segment, whose customers needed a car due to an accident, mechanical repair, or theft, and the discretionary segment, whose customers needed a car for short business and leisure trips and other special occasions. As a service to property and casualty adjusters, Enterprise operated Claims Connection, which allowed adjusters to arrange for rental cars with a single phone call. By the 1990s, Enterprise had become the largest rental car company in the United States in fleet size and number of locations. Company officials boasted that their rates were as much as 30 percent lower than most airport rental car companies and that they served customers from more than 2,000 offices near where people lived and worked. In 1990, Enterprise had 100,000 rental units and 30,000 lease units. By 1998, the company had 300,000 rental units in service, which was impressive when compared to the 30,000 units Enterprise had in 1986 or the 5,000 available in 1980.

By 2004, the Enterprise fleet had grown to more than 600,000 cars and sales totaled US$7.4 billion. The company had about 6,000 locations in the United States, Canada, the United Kingdom, Germany, and Ireland, and employed more than 57,000 workers. In 2010 Enterprise reported annual revenue of US$12.1 billion with 68,000 employees.

Enterprise announced plans to implement a rental transaction system that was projected to cut internal energy consumption 5 million kilowatt-hours as the company completed its transition from PCs to thin clients in the summer of 2008. The move was expected to save approximately US$500,000 annually and reduce carbon dioxide emissions 6.5 million pounds per year.

In August 2007, the Taylor family, owners of Enterprise Holdings, acquired both National Car Rental and Alamo Rent A Car. These entities continued operating under their own brands. Between the Enterprise, National, and Alamo brands, Enterprise Holdings' combined auto fleet was 1.1 million as of 2010.

Alamo Rent A Car. Alamo was founded in 1974, initially serving primarily Florida locations with a fleet of 1,000 cars. In slightly over 20 years, Alamo grew to include 217 domestic outlets and 180 international offices. Although early corporate expansion was conservative, an aggressive growth plan was put into place in 1980 that set a pace for the rest of the twentieth century. Alamo was the rental car industry's success story of the 1990s with 15 million annual reservations, 1,000 locations, and a 322,000-car fleet, exceeded in number only by Enterprise and Hertz.

National Car Rental. National Car Rental was formed in 1947 by the amalgamation of 24 independent car rental operators. In 1961, National was purchased by LTV Corporation, which sold it in 1969 to Household International Inc., a Chicago-based conglomerate. In 1974, National was a wholly owned subsidiary of Household, but it was sold in 1986 to an investment group that included General Motors (GM). National eventually became GM property outright when the latter became the major shareholder in the investment group. GM held National until 1995, when it agreed to sell it to another group of investors for a price reported to be between US$1.25 and US$1.5 billion. The sale to William E. Lobeck and partners thwarted a bid by Alamo Rent A Car to acquire National as the former attempted to challenge Hertz for the top spot in airport car rentals. National went on to acquire Canada's Tilden Rent-A-Car System, Ltd. in the summer of 1996. Early in 1997, National became a wholly owned subsidiary of Republic Industries, but continued to pursue market expansion aggressively. In the spring of 1998, the company took over Australia's DASFLEET Rentals, which had been owned by the Australian government. By that time, National served customers in 132 countries from 3,000 locations, and had over

200,000 vehicles in its automotive fleet, 145,000 of which were in the United States and Canada.

The Hertz Corporation. Considered the founder of the car rental industry, Hertz traced its origins to a Chicago car rental operation established by Walter L. Jacobs in 1918. After the company recorded revenues of US$1 million, it was sold to a series of holding companies and partnerships, each of which furthered growth. Jacobs first sold the company to John Hertz, president of Yellow Cab and Yellow Truck and Coach Manufacturing Company. The rental business, then called the Hertz Drive-Ur-Self System, was acquired in 1926 by General Motors Corporation at the same time that GM bought Hertz's Yellow Truck operation. This General Motors affiliation continued until 1953, when the Omnibus Corporation purchased the several Hertz properties. Omnibus promptly divested itself of its bus interests in order to concentrate on car and truck renting and leasing. In 1954 the company was renamed the Hertz Corporation and was listed for the first time on the New York Stock Exchange.

In 1954, the new corporation bought Metropolitan Distributors, a pioneer in New York truck leasing. Metropolitan Distributors dated to World War I and was the largest concern of its kind located in any single city. After 13 years of operation, in 1967, it was purchased by RCA. Although a wholly owned subsidiary of RCA Corporation, Hertz operated as a separate entity, with its own management and board of directors. In 1985, Hertz joined UAL, Inc., and in 1987, Hertz was sold to Park Ridge Corporation, which had been formed by Ford Motor Company and some members of Hertz senior management for the exclusive purpose of purchasing Hertz. The next year, Volvo North America Corporation joined Ford and Hertz management as an investor in the Park Ridge Corporation, and in 1993, Park Ridge and Hertz merged. In 1994, Ford purchased the outstanding shares of Hertz and made it an independent, wholly owned subsidiary of Ford. By the late 1990s, the company's Worldwide Reservation Center handled approximately 40 million phone calls and delivered approximately 30 million reservations annually, a total that had increased steadily over the previous decade.

As a car rental pioneer, Hertz was the first company to offer car rentals in places other than backstreet garages. It was first to market "fly-drive" rentals, pairing the use of a rental car with specific flights. As early as 1926, Hertz had introduced a credit card, calling it a "National Credential" card, and using it to facilitate billing for regular customers. A little over 30 years later, in 1959, the "National Credential" card became the Hertz International AUTO-matic Charge Card.

Hertz also was first to provide customers with Computerized Driving Directions (CDD), which were detailed directions to local destinations, complete with distance figures and approximate drive times. This service proved so popular that by the end of the century it had been made available in the United States, Canada, Australia, and throughout Europe.

In 2000, Hertz lost its number one ranking in the industry in terms of revenue and transactions to Enterprise, whose sales exceeded Hertz's US$4 billion. In 2004, Enterprise continued to outpace Hertz. Owned by the Ford Motor Company, Hertz was a leader among the world's car rental companies in 2004. With a fleet of 525,000 vehicles at 7,200 locations in 150 countries, Hertz had more "firsts" and led in more categories than any competitor worldwide. Hertz continued to provide customers with a wide variety of current model cars for short-term rental—daily, weekly, or monthly—at airports, in downtown and suburban business centers, in residential areas, and at resort locales.

In the mid- to late 2000s, Hertz expanded its fleet to include more environmentally friendly vehicles. Hertz purchased 3,400 Toyota Prius cars to increase the number of hybrids in its fleet. The company also increased its subcompact and compact fleets 30 percent through June 2008. At the same time, concern for child safety in cars was increasing, and AAA and Hertz joined forces to make booking car seats easy. Hertz announced plans to allow customers with a valid AAA membership to reserve up to two car seats during the summer of 2008.

In 2005, Ford sold Hertz to a private equity group. As of 2010, Hertz operated some 8,100 locations in 147 countries around the world. According to Auto Rental News, it was the third largest car rental company in the U.S. market, with 2009 revenue of US$3.3 billion and a domestic fleet numbering 286,000.

Avis Budget Group (formerly Cendant Corporation). Former real estate and travel services conglomerate Cendant Corporation was the world leader in the general use car rental business, operating the Avis and Budget brands. The company's vehicle services division also included fleet services and car parking lot subsidiaries, although the company sold its PHH Arval fleet management business and its Wright Express fuel card business in February 2005. The vehicle services division accounted for 31 percent (US$6.13 billion) of Cendant's total revenues of US$19.79 billion, with the rental car section accounting for 22 percent (US$4.35 billion) of total revenues.

At the end of 2004, Cendant owned and operated 1,080 of the approximately 4,900 car rental locations that made up the Avis System worldwide and franchised an additional 850 locations. Avis locations accounted for

about 13 percent (US$2.57 billion) of Cendant's revenues. Cendant owned or franchised 2,170 Budget-branded car rental locations of the 3,070 in the Budget system at the end of 2004. The vast majority of revenues from both brands came from airport locations. However, the company reported increased revenue from the use of its cars as replacements in insurance claims. In 2004, Cendant strengthened its ties with State Farm Insurance, and was working to form similar alliances with other insurance carriers using replacement cars.

Avis Rent A Car System Inc. Ranked by total revenue and volume of rental transactions, Avis Rent A Car was the second largest general use car rental business in the world in 2005. Warren E. Avis, who correctly anticipated the need for car rental agencies at airports, founded Avis in 1946. Avis Airlines Rent-A-Car System steadily expanded into major city airports around the country. In 1948, Warren Avis pressed for expansion that included downtown locations serving hotels and office buildings. As he began to establish a national reputation for quality service, Avis dropped "airlines" from the company name. In 1954, Avis sold the business to Boston-based car rental agent Richard Robie for US$8 million. Over the next two years, Robie expanded the company's corporate-owned locations to 16 cities, developed the first nationwide plan for one-way car rentals, and began distribution of the company's own charge card.

Business expansion caused a severe capital drain, however. In 1956, Robie sold the company to British investors headed by Amoskeag Company, which formed Avis, Inc., to acquire the assets of the Avis System and created Avis Rent A Car System, Inc., as a wholly owned subsidiary to conduct business operations.

Steady growth continued into the 1960s as Avis expanded into car leasing; developed various car rental enhancements; and added operations in Austria, Belgium, Norway, Spain, and elsewhere. Using electronic data processing equipment, Avis established the industry's first central billing charge card system for corporate accounts. In 1962, the company was sold to New York-based investment bankers Lazard Freres, changed advertising agencies, and adopted the now-familiar advertising slogan, "We're only number two. We try harder," which was the first time an advertiser admitted to not being the biggest in the market. It was a ploy that proved to be an enormous motivator for Avis employees.

In 1965, revenues reached US$74.5 million, and ITT Corporation acquired Avis. Over the next several years, Avis moved to strengthen its position in the international market by increasing corporate-owned operations instead of franchised operations, and by 1973, Avis had surpassed its competitors in Europe. Avis began to operate as a public company in 1972, when ITT was ordered to divest itself of certain businesses. It went public with the sale of 48 percent of its total outstanding shares, and a court-appointed trustee held the balance of the shares. Having been owned by several companies over ten years, Avis was sold in 1987 to its 11,500 employees for US$1.75 billion and was administered through an employee stock ownership plan (ESOP).

In 1991, Hertz filed a lawsuit against Avis, alleging false advertising claims that were based on a survey Hertz believed used questionable methods. The suit was settled in favor of Hertz in early 1992, but Avis paid no damages. By 1993, the company had paid off over 82 percent of its ESOP acquisition debt and planned to retire the debt completely in 1995. In 1993, the company had a fleet of rental vehicles in 138 countries. Avis owned 8.8 percent of Avis Europe, which was the market leader in Europe.

By 2004, the Avis fleet numbered about 200,000 vehicles, down from 220,000 vehicles in 2001. Revenue totals were US$2.5 billion in 2002, down from more than US$3.4 billion in 2001. Although it boasted more than 1,700 locations in the United States, Canada, Puerto Rico, the U.S. Virgin Islands, Argentina, Australia, and New Zealand, most of Avis' business continued to come from its U.S. operations. Cendant's 20 percent ownership of the company was considered to be positive, and as the new century approached, Avis looked forward to exploring ways that Cendant could help the company increase its market share. In 2001, Cendant purchased all the outstanding Avis shares, and Avis became a wholly owned subsidiary of Cendant. In 2006, Cendant stockholders approved a name change to Avis Budget Group. For 2009, Avis and Budget together were ranked as the second largest U.S. car rental firm by Auto Rental News, with annual revenues of US$3.9 billion, a fleet of 300,000, and 2,100 locations.

Budget Rent A Car System Inc. Acquired by Cendant in 2002, Budget Rent A Car was one of the largest car rental operations in the United States in the mid-2000s. While it lacked the market share of Avis, Hertz, or Enterprise, with almost 1,900 locations worldwide in 2005 Budget was one of the best-known brand names in the industry. At the end of the twentieth century Budget reported huge growth. In 1996, the company had purchased Van Pool Services, Inc. (VPSI) from Chrysler Corporation, acquiring the U.S. leader in commuter van pooling services. In a later transaction, Budget acquired Pentagon Express, another van pool service company. The Budget Group, Inc., was formed in 1997, when Budget Rent A Car was acquired by Team Rental Group, Inc. In 2002, the company's assets in the United States, Canada, Latin America, the Caribbean, Australia, and New Zealand were sold to Cendant and the remaining worldwide assets were sold to Avis Europe Plc.

Avis Europe Plc. Avis Europe was a leading car rental company in 2010, with operations in Europe, Africa, the Middle East, and Asia, operating the Avis and Budget brands under an exclusive licensing deal from Avis Budget Group in the United States. Under the Avis brand, Avis Europe had 2,900 locations in 110 countries and operated 1,050 locations in 65 countries under the Budget brand. The company shared marketing and technology initiatives with Avis Budget Group. Established in 1965 as a division of Avis Inc., Avis Europe was taken private in 1989, but in 1997 was re-listed on the London Stock Exchange. In 1997, the company acquired the license for the Avis brand in Asia, and subsequently had major licensee agreements in Greece, Germany, France, and the Netherlands. In 2003, the company acquired many of the assets of Budget. Sales revenue for Avis Europe was about US$1.6 billion in 2009, down from US$1.8 billion in 2008.

Europcar International. Europcar was founded in Paris in 1949 and was acquired by Renault in 1970. The company began to expand in Europe acquiring Budget's operations in Italy in 1974. In 1988, Volkswagen bought one-half of the company, with the other half purchased by Wagon-Lits. Accor acquired Wagon-Lits in 1992, and by 1999 had sold its share of Europcar to Volkswagen, making the latter the sole owner.

European investment company Eurazeo acquired Europcar in 2006. Europcar was operating a fleet of over 190,000 vehicles and employed a workforce of 7,000 by 2009, making it Europe's leading car rental company. Europcar had operations in Europe, the Middle East, Africa, the Asia-Pacific region, the Caribbean, Mexico, Central America, and South America. The company's revenues were approximately US$2.6 billion in 2009.

In September 2008, Europcar and Enterprise Holdings formed a strategic commercial alliance. Together their global network encompasses a fleet of more than 1.2 million vehicles.

Europcar became the first European company to be awarded Green Charter certification, marking the company's commitment to sustainable development and focus on addressing climate change issues. After receiving this recognition in June 2008, Europcar acknowledged that it had been renting green cars for more than ten years. The Green Charter, established in 2007, consisted of commitments in four key areas: "green" fleet, fleet maintenance, initiatives to raise awareness, and internal processes related primarily to fleet purchasing.

Dollar Thrifty Automotive Group Inc. Operating under the brands Dollar Rent A Car and Thrifty Rent A Car, the Dollar Thrifty Automotive Group was listed by Auto

Rental News as the fourth largest U.S. rental car company in 2009, with US$1.5 billion in revenue, a fleet of 106,200, and 600 locations. The two brands came under one company umbrella in 1995.

Thrifty's operation was founded in 1958. Dollar Rent A Car was founded in Los Angeles in 1966. Chrysler acquired Thrifty in 1989, then purchased Dollar and integrated it into the Chrysler Pentastar Transportation Group in 1990, where it remained until Pentastar was renamed Dollar Thrifty. The Dollar Thrifty Automotive Group (DTAG) first traded publicly in 1997. As of November 2010, the Avis Budget Group was pursuing an acquisition of Dollar Thrifty.

Rent-a-Wreck. In a triumph of low technology, a small but very stable company, with the iconoclastic name Rent-a-Wreck of America, Inc., determined that substantial cost-savings could be passed to customers if the rented cars were good quality, mechanically sound, older vehicles. Not precisely "wrecks," these cars nonetheless lacked aesthetic appeal compared to the brand-new vehicles offered by the competition, but the ugly ducklings proved very popular. Although Rent-a-Wreck was small in comparison to Hertz and Avis, with US$32 million annual revenues and a fleet of 5,100 vehicles in 2009, the company had recorded over 35 years of successful operation and had expanded into such markets as Norway, Sweden, and Denmark.

BIBLIOGRAPHY

"Avis Budget Group Reports Results For Fourth Quarter And Full Year 2009." Avis Budget Group press release, 10 November 2010. Available from http://www.avisbudgetgroup.com.

"BMW Plans to Test Short-Term Car Rentals in Munich." *Auto Rental News,* 3 November 2010. Available from http://www.autorentalnews.com.

"Car Rental Companies Set to Further Rebound in 2004." *Travel Weekly,* 1 March 2004.

"Company Fact Sheets." Enterprise Holdings, 10 November 2010. Available from http://www.enterpriseholdings.com.

"Deep Analysis & Strategic Consultancy Research Report on China's Auto Rental & Lease Chain Industry." *Research and Markets,* 10 November 2010. Available from http://www.researchandmarkets.com.

Elliott, Christopher. "ACTIF Speaks Out for its Members—Recent Attack on Rental Industry for Use of Vehicle Tracking Technology." *Auto Rental News,* 4 February 2004. Available from http://www.fleet-central.com.

"Europcar Awarded First Ever Green Charter." Breaking Travel News, 20 June 2008. Available from http://www.breakingtravelnews.com.

"Hertz Corporate Profile." Hertz Corporation 10 November 2010. Available from http://www.hertz.com.

"Hertz Teams With IBM and Mindshare Technologies to Analyze Customer Feedback." *Auto Rental News,* 27 October 2010. Available from http://www.autorentalnews.com.

"Hoover's Company Capsules." *Hoover's Online,* 2008. Available from http://www.hoovers.com.

Hunter, Elissa. "Business Travel Survey 2008." Breaking Travel News, 9 June 2008. Available from http://www.btnonline.

Jonas, David. "Fuel Prices, Stinging Car Renters, Impacting Contracts." Travel Management, 26 June 2008. http://www.management.travel/news.php?cid=car-rental-fuel-costs.Jun-08.26.

"Legislative Updates." American Car Rental Association, 10 November 2010. Available from http://www.acraorg.com.

"Major Market Profiles: Car Rental in US (UK, France, Germany)." *Euromonitor,* October 2004. Available from http://www.euromonitor.com.

McSherry, Mark. "Smaller Cars Help Hertz Weather Gasoline Storm." Reuters, 1 July 2008. Available from http://www.reuters.com.

Mitchell, Jacqueline. "Best Deals on Rental Cars." *Forbes,* 13 June 2008. Available from http://www.forbes.com.

Nunez, Jessica. "Car Rental Rates Rise With Costs." *The Detroit News,* 28 June 2008.

"Our Company." Avis Europe, 10 November 2010. Available from http://www.avis-europe.com.

"Research & Statistics." *Auto Rental News,* 10 November 2010. Available from http://www.autorentalnews.com.

Reitz, Stephanie. "Government Sues Ex-Cendant Chairman, Seeking $22 M." *Business Week,* 19 June 2008. Available from http://www.businessweek.com.

Stancavage, John. "Avis Deal May Face FTC Issue, Report Says." *Tulsa World,* 9 November 2010. Available from http://www.tulsaworld.com.

Stoller, Gary. "Rental Car Industry Starts to Emerge from the Perfect Storm." *USA Today,* 6 April 2010. Available from http://www.usatoday.com.

Thibodeau, Patrick. "IT Sees the Light on Green Computing." *Computerworld,* 30 June 2008.

Tier, Benjamin. "Hertz Expands Green Fleet," 25 June 2008. Available from http://carrentals.co.uk.

———. "Hertz Launches Child Safety Campaign," 3 July 2008. Available from http://www.carrentals.co.uk.

U.S. Department of Labor, Bureau of Labor Statistics. "Occupational Outlook Handbook: Counter and Rental Clerks.", 2010-2011. Available from http://www.bls.gov.

White, Martha C. "Car Rental Agencies Using Add-Ons to Lift Returns." *The New York Times,* 24 June 2008.

"Where the Avis, Dollar Thrifty Saga Goes From Here." *Auto Rental News,* 13 October 2010. Available from http://www.autorentalnews.com.

SIC 5812

RESTAURANTS

NAICS CODE(S)

722110. Restaurants are involved in retail sale of prepared foods and beverages for on-site or immediate consumption, and include fast-food restaurants, diners, refreshment stands, and full-service restaurants. Caterers and institutional food service establishments are also included in this category.

2009 Restaurant Revenues

	In billions of U.S. dollars
McDonalds Corp.	$22.7
Compass Group	$20.7
Sodexo	$19.8
Yum Brands	$10.8
Starbucks	$ 9.8
Darden Restaurants	$ 7.2

SOURCE: *Fortune*.

INDUSTRY SNAPSHOT

While most restaurants are single units, independently owned and operated, the majority of industry revenues are dominated by large chains such as McDonald's and Yum! Brands. McDonald's was the world's leading restaurant in terms of sales with US$22.7 billion in 2009. Yum! Brands, which owns KFC and Taco Bell, among other brands, was the world leader that year in number of restaurants at 37,080.

A difficult economic environment hurt the restaurant industry in 2009, particularly in the developed markets such as the United States. Writing in *Nation's Restaurant News,* Sarah Lockyer called 2009 "one of the worst years on record." High unemployment in the United States caused consumers to trim back expenses, which included eating at home more and eating out less. Full service restaurants were hit particularly hard. Technomic, a Chicago food consulting firm, expected 2010 to mark an improvement, but with significant challenges remaining as long as unemployment in the United States remained elevated.

Emerging nations such as China and India represented potential growth areas for restaurant firms. This was due to overall market saturation as well as economic difficulties in the developed markets. Yum! Brands, which earned 30 percent of its profit from China in 2009, expects that figure would grow to 40 percent by 2015. In "The Economist" magazine, Yum's chief financial officer Rick Carucci referred to China as "the biggest growth opportunity for the industry this century."

The industry continues to face public relations challenges as relates to the health of its offerings and the obesity epidemic in nations such as the United States. While many chains have begun offering healthier menu choices, they have little control over whether customers will actually choose them. A 2010 health reform bill passed by the U.S. Congress called for restaurant chains with 20 or more outlets to post calorie counts on the menu. While it remains to be seen what effect this will have on customer behavior, the possibility of further regulation worries many in the industry.

For an industry where fresh food is a key ingredient for success, the tomato salmonella scare was a major crisis in 2008. Writing for *The Boston Globe,* Mike Stobbe and Seth Borenstein analyzed the crisis and its impact on the restaurant industry. Restaurant chains, including McDonald's, decided to toss fresh tomatoes before later returning them to their food choices. Substantial money was lost as a result. Restaurant chains as a rule decided to be cautious while the federal government sorted through the problem. The timing for announcements was widely debated. Some experts felt they were too late because problems were winding down, while others believed they were too soon because health inspectors had not pinned down the source of contamination. Some critics argued that the problem was less severe than the last big tomato scare in 2006. Restaurants did not stop serving tomatoes then.

The Technomic Information Services' 2008 Top 100 Fast-Casual Restaurant Report identified and analyzed four key characteristics with an ongoing influence on fast-casual menus and continuing growth opportunities. They were exceptional flavor and spice profiles, high-quality ingredients, regional ethnic cuisines, and, fresh and healthy inspirations.

ORGANIZATION AND STRUCTURE

Traditionally, the restaurant industry has consisted of two main sectors: full-service restaurants (including family restaurants, casual dining establishments, dinner houses, and grill-buffets) and quick service restaurants (QSR), also known as fast-food restaurants. The QSR sector typically serves hamburgers, chicken, sandwiches, pizza, Mexican dishes, and breakfast and snack items. The National Restaurant Association (NRA) of the United States breaks the industry down further into restaurants that provide full menus with table service, limited menus with table service, and limited menus without table service. Of establishments with a limited menu and providing table service, most are small, independently owned operations.

The restaurant industry is a mature industry, and in many countries, such as the United States and in Western Europe, competition is very tough as many markets are saturated. In addition, restaurants must compete with expanded supermarket offerings that include a vast array of frozen foods, deli foods, and other fully or partially prepared meals for at-home dining. As a result, many large restaurant companies have turned to acquisition to expand their menu offerings, to increase their number of locations, and to capture market share in a region or niche that previously was unavailable to them.

Franchising. Since the 1970s, the growth of franchising has propelled the growth of the larger restaurant industry.

The popularity of franchising stems from the parent company's ability to expand without as much expense, as start-up costs are usually paid by whoever purchases the franchise. In addition to a license fee and equipment and stock purchases, the local owner, or franchisee, pays the franchiser royalties based on sales. For the person buying into a well-known franchise, this is an extremely low-risk investment, when compared with independent eating establishments, which do not have an established clientele to be tapped. However, franchise owners lose flexibility. Independent restaurant owners can plan their own menus, avoid royalty expenses, and run their business as they see fit. Franchises are restricted by terms of the franchise agreement. Ultimately, independent restaurant owners—who rely largely on "word-of-mouth," local newspapers, and radio spots for their advertising—find it nearly impossible to compete against the huge, national marketing budgets of the large chains that advertise heavily on television and through promotional tie-ins with movies and sports.

The degree of franchising offered throughout the restaurant industry varies. Some companies, such as Subway, prefer nearly all their outlets to be operated by franchisees, while Darden (Red Lobster, Olive Garden, Longhorn Steakhouse, Bahama Breeze, Capital Grille and Seasons 52) does not offer franchising domestically in the United States. Others strive for a combination; in 2009, 81 percent of McDonald's restaurants were franchises. The franchisor may also change the percentage of its company- versus franchisee-operated locations as part of restructuring efforts or to better position its brands. For example, *Fortune* reported that Tricon Global Restaurants, later known as Yum! Brands, shuttered franchisees in England where sales had slumped and opened company-owned restaurants in France, Holland, and Germany to spur franchisee interest there. "Part of the trick for any large franchise operator is to allow local flexibility while maintaining quality control and a central marketing message."

BACKGROUND AND DEVELOPMENT

Although the restaurant industry consists primarily of small, local, independently owned diners and cafés, the number of well-known, large, mega-chain restaurants has continued to increase. Contributing to this growth was the increased number of single-person households and single-parent families, as well as the increasing numbers of working women throughout the world. Less time was allotted for meal preparation and convenience became more important. Since the early 1970s, franchised eating places have almost tripled their share of the market, from 15 percent of industry volume to about 43 percent in the mid-1990s.

Several factors contributed to the expansion of the restaurant industry. Restaurants were considered easy business ventures by anyone who could cook; thus, there was a proliferation of new restaurants. However, half these ventures fail or change management every five years, according to the U.S. Small Business Administration.

Most growth in the restaurant industry, however, is due to the increase in franchised establishments, both fast-food and casual dining. In particular, the late twentieth century saw tremendous growth in the global expansion of American brands, such as McDonald's, KFC, Starbucks, and Applebee's. Since its beginnings in 1997, when PepsiCo spun off its fast-food chains—KFC, Pizza Hut, and Taco Bell—to form Tricon Global Restaurants, Tricon opened more than 5,100 restaurants, nearly 63 percent of which were outside the United States. According to an article in *Fortune,* the U.S. mega-chains tailored their menus to reflect local customs and tastes when opening new locations abroad. For example, KFC (formerly Kentucky Fried Chicken) serves tempura crispy strips in Japan, potatoes and gravy in northern England, rice and soy sauce in Thailand, and potato-and-onion croquettes in Holland.

By the late 1990s, competition cooled down in mature markets as some analysts warned that the chain restaurant market was saturated—especially the fast-food segment. As a result, some restaurant chains announced their plans to reduce their expansion, in contrast to the ambitious multinational expansion plans touted by leading chains in the early and mid-1990s. In addition, with the influx of independent and regional dinner house and casual dining restaurants, veteran operations such as T.G.I. Friday's, Bennigan's, and Applebee's started to recast their images and refocus their restaurants to differentiate themselves from the competition. T.G.I. Friday's began as primarily a singles bar and evolved into a family-oriented casual dining restaurant that still has strong bar sales. Other such restaurants followed this pattern, trying to offer something unique and attempting to strike a balance between their bar and restaurant facets.

Restaurants and their investors gravitated toward themed formats in the late 1980s and early 1990s, as the popularity of these restaurants surged among consumers. However, by the latter part of the 1990s, some theme restaurants proved to be largely a fad as the sales of some of the largest operations such as Planet Hollywood began to wilt and investors pulled out.

In the mid-1990s, restaurants and supermarkets introduced prepared foods for carry-out service or what they termed "home meal replacements" (HMR). These allowed customers to enjoy freshly cooked foods in the convenience of their own homes. This trend boded well with the proliferation of VCRs, TVs, computers, and other electronic entertainment devices in homes around the world. HMR sales rose to US$50 billion in 1997, up 13 percent from 1996, and were expected to climb to US$170 billion by 2005. Other product and service trends of the mid to late 1990s were salad bars/dinner buffets, specialized menus (e.g., health food and vegetarian), and home delivery. The continued rise in single-parent families, single-person households, and dual income households fueled the growth of the industry worldwide, especially in mature industrialized countries. Restaurants reported that more than 50 percent of their revenues came from carry-out sales.

There was a sharp downturn in the U.S. tourism and hospitality sectors after the terrorist attacks of September 11, 2001. September 11 also had a negative impact on the foodservice industry in the United Kingdom, as reported by Foodservice Intelligence. The United Kingdom and parts of Western Europe also had to deal with outbreaks of foot-and-mouth disease (FMD), a highly contagious disease affecting livestock such as cattle, sheep, and pigs. A February 2001 outbreak in Great Britain spread into parts of Ireland, France, and the Netherlands, resulting in the destruction of more than 4 million animals. Nearly a year later, in January 2002, officials announced that Britain was rid of the disease. Despite these problems, Foodservice Intelligence believed long-term growth of the British restaurant industry would not be adversely impacted. Perhaps a more serious, long-term issue for the U.K. restaurant industry is avoiding a general stagnation of the restaurant dining experience by failing to provide new and innovative concepts to attract customers.

Entirely different from FMD, although often lumped together in the public's mind, were the outbreaks of bovine spongiform encephalopathy (BSE), also known as mad cow disease, that plagued Britain, parts of Europe, and Japan in the early years of the first decade of the twenty-first century. Both FMD and BSE altered the eating habits of Europeans in the affected countries, and caused a decline in tourism, according to *Nation's Restaurant News*. One British analyst estimated a 10 percent decline in beef sales in the United Kingdom in 2001 as more people turned to white meat and fish.

McDonald's was particularly hard hit by BSE: its European sales faltered so much that by late 2000, worldwide profits were adversely affected, according to *The Wall Street Journal*. Ironically, as consumer confidence gradually reappeared toward beef products in Europe, infected cows were discovered in Japan in the fall of 2001. In addition, although McDonald's uses Australian and New Zealand rather than Japanese-raised beef in its Japanese restaurants, consumers there were avoiding all beef. In the fourth quarter of 2001, sales dropped more than 10 percent from the same period the previous year.

At the onset of the twenty-first century, the sandwich became the fastest growing item in the U.S. restaurant industry—particularly in the fast-food and "fast-casual" dining establishments. Long regarded as a humble food item, sandwiches from companies such as Cosi, Briazz, Corner Bakery Cafe, and Panera Bread, and even traditional fast-food chains such as Arby's, were elevated to near-gourmet stature with handmade breads and imaginative combinations of fillings using high quality ingredients. Even burger behemoth McDonald's tried to get into the game by test launching five different deli-style sandwiches under the Oven Selects name. By 2004, the sandwich market was valued at US$17 billion, up seven percent from the previous year. The rise of the sandwich was attributed to consumers' waning interest in burgers and fries in favor of healthier options, combined with the desire for quick, on-the-go meals. What has made sandwiches so attractive to restaurateurs is the premium price they command: compared to a 99-cent burger, sandwiches can cost four dollars or more. However, consumers do not seem to mind the higher prices. In fact, a study by Technomic reported that U.S. sales of custom-made sandwiches were growing 15 percent annually, dramatically outpacing the three percent sales growth rate for burgers and steaks.

Another emerging concept in the early twenty-first century was the "fast-casual" restaurant, which, like fast-food chains, does not have a dining room wait staff and therefore has no tipping. However, the fast-casual restaurant offers a higher-quality menu than the fast-food chains.

CURRENT CONDITIONS

The leading restaurants in the global restaurant business are U.S.-based, and the largest restaurant market is also the United States. According to the National Restaurant Association, 2010 U.S. industry revenues were about US$580 billion, an average of US$1.6 billion each day. There were an estimated 945,000 U.S. restaurants and 12.7 million workers, making the industry one of the largest private employers. According to MRSI, a marketing research company based in Ohio, by 2005 there were about eight million restaurants worldwide. The industry remains highly competitive, with the number of restaurants exceeding consumer demand.

Industry Trends.

Go Healthy. The explosion of health-conscious diets, from the low-carb to the low-fat and all points in between, caused restaurants of all types to reinvent their menus. In fast-food, restaurants were busily adding salads and special sandwiches to the menu, or retooling classic favorites to suit different dieters. For example, at McDonald's children could choose apples over fries or milk over soda pop with a Happy Meal. Vegetarian meal options were also on the rise. Concern over climbing obesity rates in the developed world and the possibility of increased government regulation will likely keep this trend current.

Workforce. Rising health care costs and the possibility of government mandates for employee insurance also concern the industry. For example, San Francisco restaurants were forced to comply with a requirement that restaurants with more than 20 workers spend a minimum amount on employees' health care. In response, restaurant owners raised their prices or tacked on surcharges to pay the new health care costs that amounted to US$1.17 for every hour most employees work.

Multi-brand Restaurants. Another trend in the fast-food industry is the multi-brand restaurant concept, where two to three recognized brands sell food side by side under the same roof. This may be done through the use of separate counters, so the restaurant looks like a mini food court, or one brand may dominate the menu and offer a few favorites of another brand. For example, Yum!—the leading multi-branding restaurateur with its three major fast-food chains—sells its Personal Pan Pizzas at the drive-thru windows of some Taco Bell and KFC stores. Multi-branding has proven successful because it provides additional convenience and food choices for customers, while allowing companies a way to introduce multiple brands to an area that they may not otherwise target due to the high cost of property or low population levels. Instead of building and maintaining two or three separate units, the company operates one store.

Contract Food Service. The global food service market relies on institutions, corporations, and organizations that outsource their food operations. The world's largest food service provider is Compass Group PLC of Britain, followed by France's Sodexho. U.S.-based Aramark Worldwide Corp. is a distant third in the industry with operations that are largely focused in the United States. According to data from Merrill Lynch and reported by *The Wall Street Journal,* 37 percent of institutions around the world worked with contract food service companies rather than an in-house food staff. The United States was the largest market for the industry with 55 percent of institutions turning to outsourced food services. Organizations often outsource their cafeteria and catering needs, rather than relying on an in-house staff, because large food service companies, such as Compass or Sodexho, are usually less expensive solutions. Such companies obtain ingredients more cheaply due to global buying power, and costs are kept lower since food service employees are generally paid less and with fewer benefits than their corporate counterparts. Another benefit in outsourcing to a large, multinational company, such as Compass or Sodexho, is that many organizations

operate in multiple countries and prefer to work with a single, global food service provider for all their locations.

RESEARCH AND TECHNOLOGY

The Information Age has seen increased use of computer and telecommunications technology in the restaurant industry, such as vibrating paging systems given to wait-staff and patrons to indicate when food or tables were ready. The use of sophisticated computer technology has continued into the twenty-first century to provide greater convenience and speed to the customer in the hopes of boosting sales as well as to increase staff efficiency through the use of wireless systems. Many European restaurants use wireless applications, and the concept is growing in the United States. At an Irving, Texas, facility of Nokia, a cellular phone manufacturer, foodservice giant Sodexho is introducing a cashless payment system that takes advantage of the fact that most of Nokia's employees carry cell phones. Cafeteria customers use their cell phones as a "speed-pay" device by scanning them in front of a specially designed reader at the cafeteria's entrance. At checkout, the order is rung up and the customer scans his or her phone again at a second reader to process the payment to a pre-authorized credit card account.

At some McDonald's locations, employees are using "wearable computers" so that when the drive-up window line becomes too long, waitstaff are alerted and can take orders from customers waiting in line, entering the order on a portable device that transmits it to the kitchen. Other types of wireless systems allow managers to keep tabs on a location when they are on the road. Alerts are sounded if building doors are unlocked or if a freezer door remains open, and some devices even offer video feeds of restaurant activity. The Internet was also being used more frequently by customers to select restaurants; MRSI research indicated that 45 percent of 25 to 34 year olds had used the Internet to find out about restaurants to which they had never been.

In 2008, Israeli firm Conceptic introduced an e-menu system that allowed diners to view and read about menu offerings as well as order from a touch-screen positioned at each table in the restaurant. It remains to be seen whether such devices will catch on, but they have been installed at restaurants in Israel, South Africa, Belgium, and France.

INDUSTRY LEADERS

Compass Group PLC. One of the world's largest food-service companies, UK-based Compass operated in more than fifty countries as of 2010. The company reported revenue of US$11.2 billion for the first six months of 2010, and US$20.5 billion for all of fiscal 2009. The company employed more than 386,000 people worldwide. Compass Group provides contract foodservice to corporations, hospitals, educational institutions, and retailers, as well as at entertainment venues, airports, and railway stations in the United States, Europe, and in emerging markets in Asia and South America.

Founded in 1941 as Factory Canteens Limited, Compass Group got its start feeding munitions workers. In the 1960s, after a period of acquisition and mergers, Factory Canteens emerged as Grand Metropolitan Catering Services, which became Compass Services in 1984 and Compass Group in 1987. Throughout the 1990s, a number of acquisitions and mergers occurred as Select Service Partner (part of SAS Airlines), Canteen Vending, Eurest International, SHRM, and Restaurant Associates joined Compass Group. In 1998, Compass Group was awarded its first global contract, to provide foodservice operations for Philips. In 2000, Compass Group merged with the hospitality company Granada Group to become Granada:Compass, but a year later it was demerged and re-listed as Compass Group. In 2002, Seiyo Food Systems Inc. of Japan became a wholly owned subsidiary of Compass Group. Compass Group was named the Official Catering Services Supplier for the 2002 Olympic and Paralympic Winter Games in Salt Lake City, Utah. In 2004, Compass became food service provider for the French National Rail Company, as well as becoming the first foreign company to provide passenger food service on trains in China. In 2009, Compass acquired KIMCO Corporation in the U.S. and Plural Group in Germany.

Sodexho, Inc. Founded in 1966 in Marseille, France, Sodexho Alliance was an extension of the Bellon family's 60-year background in maritime catering to cruise ships and luxury ocean liners. Initially focusing on staff restaurants, schools, and hospitals, it has become one of the world's leading contract food services providers. Revenues for 2009 were US$20.3 billion. Employing 380,000 people, the company had operations in 80 countries in 2010. In 2001, Sodexho Alliance purchased Sodexho Marriott Services, a leading food service company in the United States, to be its North American subsidiary. In 2008, the company changed its name from Sodexo Alliance to Sodexo. The company refers to itself as a provider of "quality of daily life" solutions to businesses, and in addition to food services provides such services as facilities management and what it calls "motivation solutions," such as employee benefits and incentives.

McDonald's Corporation. Serving more than 60 million customers a day worldwide, in 117 countries, McDonald's ranks as the largest restaurant company in the world. Worldwide sales totaled US$22.7 billion in 2009, of which about 68 percent was sales from company-operated restaurants, and the remainder was from franchise fee revenues. Globally, 35 percent of revenues were derived from the United States and 41

percent from Europe. Its brand name is one of the most highly recognized in the world, along with Coca-Cola.

McDonald's first opened in San Bernadino, California in 1948. The original owners, Dick and Mac MacDonald, signed a franchise agreement along with machine salesman Ray Kroc. In 1961, Kroc bought out the MacDonald brothers for US$2.7 million. McDonald's golden arches first appeared in 1962; Ronald McDonald also made his first appearance that year. In 1967, McDonald's opened its first restaurants outside the United States, with locations in Canada.

Throughout the 1970s, McDonald's restaurants grew by more than 500 per year. Also during the 1970s, items such as the Egg McMuffin and McDonald's Happy Meals were added. In 1978, McDonald's became the largest single-brand restaurant chain in the United States based on number of locations when it overtook Kentucky Fried Chicken, now known as KFC. At the time, McDonald's had 4,465 restaurants in the United States, 236 more than KFC. Throughout the 1980s, U.S. sales growth slowed to about five percent annually due to increased domestic competition. In response, McDonald's added "value menus" and new products to appeal to health-conscious consumers. In the mid to late 1990s, McDonald's entered into a partnership agreement with Wal-Mart and formed alliances with Amoco and Chevron to place McDonald's retail outlets at selected locations. Through a joint venture with the Food Service Administration of the Moscow City Council, McDonald's opened its first restaurants in Russia during the 1990s. Its first restaurant, the Moscow-McDonald's, was "rubles only" and served approximately 50,000 customers per day.

In the late 1990s, McDonald's held its position as the world's leading restaurant chain, but its market share declined. In addition to increased competition, the company's rampant expansion in the 1990s eroded its profits. Critics argued that the company failed to introduce any successful new products in the decade to entice new customers and ensure repeat visits. Observers also charged that McDonald's supersaturated the market with its chains, especially in the United States.

Starting in the late 1990s, McDonald's began acquiring other chains to diversify its business as a result of the increasingly burger-saturated market in the United States. In 1998, McDonald's bought Chipotle Mexican Grill. In December 1999, it acquired Boston Chicken Inc.'s 751 units for US$173.5 million, when Boston Chicken was in the midst of bankruptcy proceedings. McDonald's initially planned to convert many of Boston Chicken's units to McDonald's or one of its partner brands, but after closing about 100 units, it decided to see if new life could be breathed into the chain and planned to open 40 units in 2002, including sites in Australia and Canada.

In 2003, McDonald's began a revitalization strategy in an attempt to improve its financial standing and move in line with consumer preferences. New food lines were introduced, including breakfast and salad products, and the company began to modernize many of its store designs, hoping to have system-wide sales increases of three percent to five percent during 2005.

Richmond, Virginia, area businessman Chris Coleson stepped into the national spotlight after major news media told the story of about a life-changing diet of almost exclusively McDonald's food. Coleson lost approximately 80 pounds in 200 days eating mainly McDonald's salads, wraps, and apples. Also in 2008, McDonald's unveiled the most complete global packaging redesign in its history. In 2009, McDonald's McCafe coffee drinks, designed to compete with Starbucks and other up-market coffee offerings, went national in the United States. McCafe fruit smoothies and frappes were added to the menu in 2010.

Burger King Corporation. Founded in 1954 by David Edgerton and James McLamore, as of 2010, Burger King had more than 12,000 restaurants in 76 countries. Of these restaurants, approximately 90 percent were owned and operated by independent franchisees. Revenues for fiscal 2009 were US$2.5 billion.

Until 2002, Burger King was a private subsidiary of London-based Diageo PLC, which formed out of a 1997 merger between Grand Metropolitan PLC (GrandMet) and Guinness PLC (brew and alcohol producer and publisher). GrandMet was a food, liquor, and retailing giant begun in London in the early 1920s. Some of GrandMet's most visible brands included Green Giant, Pillsbury, Burger King, and Haagen-Dazs. In 2002, Diageo sold the company to TPG for US$1.5 billion.

After its founding in Miami, Florida, Burger King began catering to families in the postwar years, offering a simple menu of moderately priced, broiled burgers. The chain expanded rapidly, and in 1967, the two founders sold the company to Pillsbury, which GrandMet acquired in 1988. Attempting to turn the tide of slower sales, the company renewed focus on Burger King's core menu and cut prices and costs. The company also began new advertising campaigns such as "It Just Tastes Better" in 1998.

Jumping on the health-conscious trend current in the industry, in 2008, Burger King announced availability of the new Burger King Kids Meal featuring BK Apple Fries and Kraft Macaroni & Cheese. The innovative fries were fresh-cut skinless red apples sliced to resemble French fries. The new meal launch was supported by a major advertising and marketing campaign introducing "Little King," son of the Burger King icon. It was also linked to Burger King sponsorship of Jonas Brothers' "Burning Up" tour.

In October 2010, Burger King was sold to an affiliate of 3G Capital for roughly US$4 billion, with Bernardo Hees becoming Burger King's CEO and Alexandre Behring, 3G Capital's Managing Partner, becoming co-Chairman of the Board. Prior Chairman and CEO John Chidsey continued as co-Chairman.

Yum! Brands Inc. With 37,080 restaurants in more than 110 countries, Louisville, Kentucky-based Yum! Brands was larger than McDonald's in terms of locations. Sales in foreign countries have been on the rise, with the company reporting that China was the fastest growing and most profitable country for the company after the United States. In 1997, PepsiCo Inc. spun off its popular restaurant division as Tricon Global Restaurants, which owned Pizza Hut, KFC (Kentucky Fried Chicken), and Taco Bell. Tricon later became Yum! In 2009, Yum!, which also owned A&W All-American Food Restaurants and Long John Silver's restaurants, reported US$10.8 billion in revenue and over 1 million employees. Of its total revenues, 87 percent came from sales from company-operated restaurants, with the remainder coming from franchise and license fees.

Tony Sagami discussed how Pizza Hut and KFC adapted to the Chinese culture to produce huge demand in China and Asia as a whole. YUM! Brands has more than 2,000 KFCs and 300 Pizza Huts in China. A.C. Nielsen discovered KFC is the top brand in China. Sagami notes that YUM! Brands' success is linked to an ability "to take advantage of the Chinese's passion for American products." Being masters of a "localization strategy" is another ingredient in a recipe for foreign success. The packaging retains an American flavor, but food adapts effectively to Asian culture. For example, chicken satay pizza is popular at Pizza Huts in Kualu Lumpur. Customers can stop by another restaurant in the chain for pizza with a can of tuna on top in Thailand or sea eel in Shanghai. Sagami said it was also true that smaller portions are served and restaurants are believed to be upscale.

KFC Corporation. In the early twenty-first century, KFC (then known as Kentucky Fried Chicken), founded by Colonel Harland Sanders in 1952, dominated the world fast-food chicken market. In 2010, KFC operated over 20,000 restaurants, of which about 75 percent were in the 109 countries in which it operated outside of its home base in the United States. About 23 percent of its restaurants were owned and operated by the company, with the rest being franchised. Although KFC is best known for its Original Recipe and Extra Crispy fried chicken, the company also introduced KFC's Rotisserie Gold chicken and chicken sandwiches in the U.S., which have appealed to increasingly health-conscious consumers. In other countries, the menu is more focused on chicken sandwiches and chicken strips, with overall choice being reflected by local tastes.

Pizza Hut. Pizza Hut originated in 1958 in Wichita, Kansas, founded by two college-age brothers. It expanded over the following decades with restaurants in Russia, France, the United Kingdom, Australia, and Hong Kong. As of 2010, it operated almost 10,000 restaurants in over 90 countries. About 22 percent of the restaurant units were operated by the company, with the remainder being franchised. It was named a top 10 franchise in 2009 by *Entrepreneur*. As of the first quarter in 2008, Yum! Brands had 140 Pizza Huts in 35 cities plus 33 KFC restaurants in nine cities in India.

Taco Bell. Founded in 1962 by Glen Bell, who passed away in 2010, Taco Bell grew to become the United States' leading Mexican-themed fast-food restaurant, with more than 5,600 restaurants in the United States serving some 36.8 million customers per week. Twenty-two percent of restaurants were company operated. At the onset of the twenty-first century, the company launched the "Think Outside the Bun" ad campaign to compete head-on with hamburger-oriented fast-food chains. Part of the campaign included offering products with premium ingredients, such as steak, to boost the appeal of its menu to more consumers, while still retaining low prices.

Wendy's/Arby's Group Inc. Wendy's was founded by Dave Thomas in 1969 in Columbus, Ohio. He named the restaurant after his daughter. Its second location opened in 1970, and its first franchise was sold in 1972. The company went public in 1976 and by the end of the year counted 500 locations. By 1978, there were 1,000. In January 2002, Wendy's lost its founder and long-time pitchman when Thomas died of liver cancer at the age of 69. Thomas had appeared in hundreds of Wendy's commercials, representing a down-to-earth spokesman to whom many Americans felt they could relate. In 2008, Wendy's combined with sandwich restaurant Arby's to form one firm. As of 2010 it was the third largest quick service restaurant company in the U.S. with more than 10,000 restaurants and some US$12 billion in annual sales.

Doctor's Associates Inc. (Subway Restaurants). Subway, the world's leading chain of submarine sandwich restaurants, was founded by 17-year-old Fred DeLuca and family friend Peter Buck in 1965 as a submarine sandwich counter in Bridgeport, Connecticut. By 1974, there were 16 units throughout the state and Subway started offering franchising opportunities. In February 2001, Subway opened its 1,000th international location in Australia. Subway became the largest U.S. restaurant chain based on number of units when it took over the top spot from McDonald's at the end of 2001, until Yum! took that spot at the top. As of 2010, Subway,

owned by Doctor's Associates Inc. of Milford, Connecticut, had 33,667 units in 92 countries, all of which were held by franchisors (except for one which was being used as a testing facility). Also in 2010, *Entrepreneur* magazine ranked Subway as the number-one franchise opportunity for the 17th time in 23 years.

Darden Restaurants Inc. Darden Restaurants traces its origin to Bill Darden's opening of *The Green Frog*, a 25-seat luncheonette in Waycross, Georgia in 1938. Considered the world's largest company-owned and operated full-service restaurant firm, the company operated all its 1,800 restaurants; none were franchised. However, the company did license its Red Lobster brand to a Japanese firm which had 38 such restaurants in Japan. The current company was formed from the 1995 spin-off of General Mills' restaurant holdings, and included the restaurant chains Red Lobster, Olive Garden, Bahama Breeze, and Smokey Bones BBQ. The first Red Lobster was opened in Florida in 1968. Red Lobster dominates the U.S. seafood restaurant sector, while Olive Garden leads U.S. casual Italian-themed restaurants. Darden reported US$7.11 billion in sales for fiscal 2010, a 1.4 percent decrease from fiscal 2009. Darden announced a plan in 2010 with Americana Group to open Red Lobster, Olive Garden, and Longhorn Steakhouse restaurants in the Middle East.

Brinker International Inc. One of the world's largest casual dining companies, Brinker International Inc. reported US$2.9 billion in revenues in fiscal 2010, down from US$3.3 billion in fiscal 2009. Based in Dallas, Texas, Brinker operated a system-wide total of more than 1,700 units that included Chili's Grill & Bar, Romano's Macaroni Grill, and Maggiano's Little Italy.

Applebee's International Inc./DineEquity. Applebee's, headquartered in Lenexa, Kansas, operated over 1,990 casual dining restaurants in the United States and in 15 countries as of 2010. In 2007, it was acquired by DineEquity for approximately US$2.1 billion, becoming a wholly owned subsidiary. DineEquity's plan was to franchise a considerable proportion of Applebee's company-owned units. For 2009, total revenues for DineEquity, which includes IHOP restaurants, were US$1.4 billion.

Starbucks Corporation. Founded in Seattle, Washington, in 1971, Starbucks was operating more than 16,000 locations in over 50 countries including the United States by 2010. In addition to its stores, the company sells its products in grocery stores through an affiliation with Kraft Foods, and to corporate foodservice suppliers. Approximately 53 percent of its stores were company-owned as of 2009, with the remainder licensed. Revenues for fiscal 2009 for company-operated stores were US$8.2

billion. Total revenues were US$9.8 billion, down six percent from 2008.

In October 2010 Starbucks announced a partnership with Yahoo! to offer customized news, entertainment, and lifestyle content to its customers through the Starbucks Digital Network. The network will be free and accessible through in-store Wi-Fi.

Whitbread Group plc. The United Kingdom's biggest full-service restaurant group, Whitbread is also the United Kingdom's largest hospitality provider, operating hotels and health and fitness clubs. Its 1,000-unit restaurant segment includes such brands as pub restaurants Brewers Fayre and Beefeater, and it is also the owner of the Costa chain of coffee shops, the largest in the United Kingdom. The company operates about 500 Pizza Hut locations under a joint venture agreement with Yum! Brands, and American T.G.I. Friday's restaurants under agreement with Carlson. Whitbread had company-wide revenues of approximately US$2.2 billion in fiscal 2010.

Autogrill S.p.A. Clothing family Bennetton controls Italy-based food concession operator Autogrill. It was founded as a small bar in Milan in 1928. Growing organically and through acquisition, in 2010, it was the world's leading operator of concessions for travellers, with 5,300 outlets in 1,249 locations in 42 countries. The concessions are located primarily in airports, railway stations and along highways in 15 countries in Europe, North America and the Pacific region. Revenues for 2009 were US$7.9 billion, with 66 percent coming from food and beverage sales. The company employed 67,000 people.

MAJOR COUNTRIES IN THE INDUSTRY

The United States. The United States was the world's largest market for restaurants and many of the world's largest restaurant chains hail from this country. In 2008, there were 546,300 privately owned food service and drinking places nationwide. About 47 percent of these were limited service eating establishments such as fast-food restaurants. Full service restaurants made up about 39 percent.

More than 70 percent of all restaurants are single unit, independently owned enterprises, with most having fewer than 20 employees. *The Washington Post* reported that Americans spend US$110 billion annually on fastfood. Each day, roughly 25 percent of the U.S. adult population can be found at a fast-food outlet and 90 percent of children aged three to nine eat at McDonald's at least once a month.

In 2000, the number of meals eaten in the home began to increase for the first time in a decade, while restaurant meals declined. Further evidence of the increase of in-home meals, and a general move away from fastfood—burgers in particular—may also be seen by the fact that in 1996, the top 100 U.S. fast-food restaurants increased their number of locations by 6.1 percent. However, this growth rate dropped dramatically, so that by 2000, the companies added only one percent more locations, according to data collected by Chicago foodconsulting firm Technomic Inc. and reported by *The Wall Street Journal*. Although hamburgers are the item of choice for most U.S. fast-food consumers, 2000 sales for fast-food chicken items grew faster than those for burgers or pizza. Chicken sales increased 5 percent to US$11.4 billion, while burger sales grew 4.7 percent to US$46.0 billion, and pizza sales rose 4.4 percent to US$24.5 billion, as reported by *The Wall Street Journal*.

The "Great Recession" that began in 2007 reinforced this trend of Americans eating out less, and a major focus of U.S. restaurant chains' growth and plans for the future involved spreading out beyond geographic borders. There were many opportunities to serve their food abroad while faced with economic challenges at home. Arriving in countries with less competition and enhanced appreciation for products that were novelties added to the excitement to venture out. Brinker International set a "long-term vision to achieve ranking as the dominant, global casual-dining restaurants portfolio company." In 2007, Brinker signed development agreements for expansion into several countries from Australia to Turkey. "Trends continue to be in our favor," said McDonald's Corp. president, Ralph Alvarez. Finding the right location continues to be McDonald's biggest challenge. It already has more than 17,500, or approximately 56 percent of its restaurants, outside the U.S. Since 2006, Burger King opened 34 restaurants in 14 Brazil cities.

European Union. The European market has shown a shift in consumer preferences toward processed products, convenience foods, and snack foods, as well as concern for nutritional, health, and environmental problems. According to *Nation's Restaurant News*, American fastfoods are changing the way Europeans eat, and there is also a greater similarity between French and American meals at the fine-dining level. Overall, McDonald's continued to lead the restaurant industry in Europe, though other domestic and international chains have gnawed away at the company's market share. While nearly all German restaurants are small restaurants and pubs as opposed to large chains, U.S.-style chain restaurants such as McDonald's are popular there, as they are in France.

United Kingdom. The U.K. restaurant industry was reported to be weathering the economic downturn well, according to a 2009 Harden's food guide. Closures in London over the trailing 12 months were reported to be

64, the fewest since the year 2000, while openings were a healthy 121, up eight percent from the prior year. Many cafés and bars had been part of mergers and acquisitions in the early to middle years of the first decade of the 2000s, with many brewers selling their pubs.

Several other issues have had an effect on the U.K. food service industry, such as a *Licensing Act* revision in 2005 allowing pubs to apply for longer opening hours and increased restrictions on smoking in pubs that serve prepared food.

The UK Borders Agency published a list of company names and employers to crack down on illegal activities involving people-smuggling. Fines were issued to five restaurants. Home Secretary Jacqui Smith almost concurrently announced plans to aggressively change the way immigration issues were handled. The approximately 7,500 UKBA officers and staff would be reorganized into 70 to 80 immigration teams.

Japan. Ongoing economic difficulties in Japan have led to consolidation as companies sought to remain profitable in an environment characterized by severe competition. Because many Japanese people live far from where they work, and because many live in small apartments, eating out is often a necessity. In addition, young people often postpone marriage in favor of the single life. As a result, the Japanese restaurant industry grew fast and changed dramatically after 1969, when it became possible for foreign companies to invest in Japan. Restaurants from abroad began investing in the Japanese market. Fast-food restaurants such as McDonald's and KFC are popular, as are casual- dining establishments such as Denny's.

Throughout the 1970s, family restaurants enjoyed a period of great popularity as places to gather for a variety of social reasons, from business meetings to birthday celebrations. From 1975 to 1985, chains began targeting market needs, spawning take-out businesses such as Hokka Lunch Box, tavern rooms such as Murasaki, and coffee bars. Next came luxurious French restaurants and delivery businesses, including Domino's franchises. Since 1985, the industry has organized itself around specific types of restaurants, including luxury, specialty-oriented, unique, group-oriented, family-oriented, natural food, and entertainment-oriented venues.

At the onset of the twenty-first century, family restaurants sought to reinvigorate their image from places with mediocre service and outdated, overpriced food choices. Japan's popular new franchises target 20- and 30-something customers and feature contemporary menu formats such as *yakiniku* (Korean barbecued meat and vegetables); *kaiten-sushi* (sushi served via a conveyor belt); *izakaya* (Japanese pub cuisine); *shabu shabu* (Japanese-style boiled beef); and ramen (Chinese noodles).

According to *The Nikkei Weekly,* restaurant companies that operate multiple restaurant formats, particularly those in the mid-range sector, were an emerging trend in the Japanese restaurant industry and were expected to be successful. For example, Tokyo-based Kiwa Corp.'s various restaurant formats include casual Chinese fare, a Peking duck eatery with a theme-park-like setting, and a European-style restaurant. Foreign cuisine is popular in Japan, as an increasing number of Japanese have traveled abroad. Another multi-format restaurant company is Global-Dining Inc., whose concepts include Monsoon Cafe (offering Southeast Asian food), La Boheme (Italian), Zest (Tex-Mex), Tableaux (multinational), and Gonpachi (izakaya cuisine).

China. China's economic growth rate at the beginning of the twenty-first century has been extraordinarily high, reaching 13 percent in 2007. The 2008 rate of nine percent was the lowest in seven years. Many restaurant firms in other nations, such as the U.S., saw China's emerging market as ground for lucrative expansion. One chain that made inroads into China was Yum! Brands. It began opening its KFC restaurants there in the late 1980s. Franchising was a relatively new option in China, but took off as businesspeople witnessed the success of McDonald's and KFC in the country. Yum! Brands had 3,434 locations in China at the end of the 2000s.

BIBLIOGRAPHY
"3G Capital Completes Acquisition of Burger King Holdings, Inc. " Burger King News Release, 19 October 2010. Available from http://www.bk.com.
"About Us." Applebee's website, 2010. Available from www.applebees.com.
"About Us." Subway, 2010. Available from http://www.subway.com.
"About Us." Wendy's Arby's Group, 2010. Available from www.wendysarbys.com.
Alleyne, Richard. "Restaurant industry remains buoyant despite recession." *The Daily Telegraph,* 20 August 2009. Available from http://www.telegraph.co.uk.
"Annual Report." Brinker International, 2010. Available from http://www.brinker.com.
"Annual Report." McDonald's, 2009. Available from http://www.aboutmcdonalds.com.
"Annual Report." Starbucks, 2009. Available from http://www.starbucks.com.
"Annual Report." Whitbread, 2009. Available from www.whitbread.co.uk.
"Annual Report." Yum! Brands, 2009. Available from http://www.yum.com.
Bristow, Michael. "China's Economic Growth Slows." *BBC News,* 22 January 2009. Available from news.bbc.co.uk.
Browning, Eliza. "Would You Pay $190 for a Burger?" ABC News, 18 June 2008. Available from abcnews.go.com
"Burger King Corp. Introduces New Nutritionally Balanced Kids meal as Part of BK Positive Steps Nutrition Program." 30 June 2008. Available from http://investor.bk.com/.

Carroll, Jill, and Shirley Leung. "U.S. Consumption of French Fries is Sliding as Diners Opt for Healthy." *The Wall Street Journal*, 20 February 2002. Available from www.wsj.com.

"Closed for Business: KFC Shutters Two Most Historic Restaurants. " KFC News Release, 6 October 2010. Available from http://www.kfc.com.

Collison, Kevin. "Applebee's Goes Bold With Stand on Environment." *The Kansas Star*, 10 June 2008. Available from http://www.redorbit.com.

"E-Menu: The Future of Restaurant Technology." *ISRAEL21cdotcom*, 3 March 2008. Available from http://www.youtube.com.

"Facts at a Glance." National Restaurant Association, 2010. Available from www.restaurant.org.

"Fact Sheet: Starbucks Digital Network, in partnership with Yahoo!" Starbucks News Release, 20 October 2010. Available from http://www.starbucks.com.

"Fast-Casual Chains Continue to Out Perform Other Restaurants, says Technomic." *BusinessWire*, 19 June 2008.

Friedman, Amanda Mosle. "Monetary Shift Spells Unity in 'Euro-land.'" *Nation's Restaurant News*, 6 August 2001.

Fulks, Tricia. "Tomatoes Making a Come back After Nationwide Scare." *Charleston Daily Mail*, 19 June 2008.

"Glen W. Bell Jr., Founder of Taco Bell, Passes Away at 86. " Taco Bell News Release, 17 January 2010. Available from http://www.tacobell.com.

"Hoover's Company Capsules." *Hoover's Online*, 2008. Available from http://www.hoovers.com.

"Interim Report." Compass Group, 2010. Available from http://compass-group.com.

"Investor Overview." DineEquity, 2010. Available from www.dineequity.com.

"Investor Relations Highlights." Autogrill, 2010. Available from www.autogrill.com.

James, Andrea. "Call of the Siren: Starbucks to Expand Presence in Europe." *Seattle Post-Intelligencer*, 12 June 2008.

"Labor Force Survey." Japanese Director General for Policy Planning & Statistical Research and Training Institute, August 2010. Available from http://www.stat.go.jp.

Leung, Shirley. "Fast-food Chains Upgrade Menus, and Profits, with Pricey Sandwiches." *The Wall Street Journal*, 5 February 2001. Available from http://www.wsj.com.

———. "Tricon Raises 2002 Earnings Outlook On Higher Sales and Multi-Branding." *The Wall Street Journal*, 11 February 2002. Available from http://www.wsj.com.

Liddle, Alan J. "2000 Top 100." *Nation's Restaurant News*, 26 June 2000. Available from http://www.nrn.com.

———. "New Concepts Trump Old-Style Family Restaurants." *The Nikkei Weekly*, 16 July 2001.

McCoy, Laura. "Restaurants Add Health Costs to Menus." *AARP Bulletin*, May 2008.

"Our Company." Starbucks, 2010. Available from www.starbucks.com.

Papiernik, Richard L. "Industry Sales for 2002 Projected to Hit $407B." *Nation's Restaurant News*, 7 January 2002.

Payne, Samantha. "Five Restaurants Fined in Crackdown on Illegal Workers." Kent Online, 19 June 2008. Available from http://www.kentonline.co.uk.

"Pizza Hut Recognized by Indian Consumers." *The Business Journals*, 18 June 2008. Available from http://www.louisville.bizjournals.com.

"PizzaHut.com Tops in the Industry: Tracking $Two Billion in Sales." Pizza Hut news release, 20 April 2010. Available from http://www.pizzahut.com.

"Profile." *Sodexo Group*, 2010. Available from http://www.sodexo.com.

Sagami, Tony. "YUM! Brands Taking Over in China." EMediaWire, 19 June 2008. Available from www.emediawire.com.

Shallwani, Pervaiz. "Africa's Rich, Bold Flavors Are Popping up in American Restaurants." *Detroit Free Press*, 18 June 2008.

Stobbe, Mike, and Seth Borenstein. "Why Did Food Sellers Treat Tomatoes Like Hot Potatoes?" *The Boston Globe*, 10 June 2008. Available from http://www.boston.com.

"Top 100 Companies Ranked by US Foodservice Revenues." *Nation's Restaurant News*, 28 July 2004.

"Triarc and Wendy's Complete Merger Transaction." *Wendy's News Release*, 29 September 2008. Available from http://www.wendysarbys.com.

U.S. Bureau of Labor Statistics. "Career Guide to Industries, Food Services and Drinking Places", 2010-2011. Available from http://www.bls.gov.

"US Restaurants Push Abroad." Drover's CattleNetwork,17 June 2008. Available from http://www.cattlenetwork.com.

Williams, Reed. "McDonald's Diet Gains National Attention." *Times Dispatch*, 18 June 2008.

SIC 5311

RETAIL DEPARTMENT STORES, VARIETY STORES AND GENERAL MERCHANDISE STORES

NAICS CODE(S)

452111, 452112, 452990, 452910. Department stores carry a diverse line of nonfood merchandise, including general wearing apparel (suits, coats, and dresses), home furnishings (furniture, floor coverings, curtains, draperies, linens, and major household appliances), and housewares (table and kitchen appliances, dishes, and utensils). Many department stores offer their own credit lines and various supplemental services as well. Variety stores carry a diverse line of goods in the low-price range. General merchandise stores carry goods similar to department stores, but normally have fewer than 50 employees. For discussion of food retailing, see **Grocery Stores**.

INDUSTRY SNAPSHOT

The retail industry, the second largest industry in the United States in terms of number of establishments and number of employees, enjoyed unprecedented gains in

World's Largest General Retailers, 2009	
	Revenue, in millions of U.S. dollars
Wal-Mart Stores	$408,214
Carrefour S.A	$121,452
Target Corp.	$ 65,327
Sears Holdings	$ 44,043
Marks and Spencer Group LLC	$ 14,100
PPR S.A.	$ 19,600

SOURCE: *Fortune.*

the late 1990s and through 2000. In part, this was due to strong consumer confidence, low interest rates, and high employment levels. Between 1994 and 2000, the retail industry grew rapidly. By late 2000, however, as the United States and much of Europe and Asia were experiencing recession, and retailers began to feel the effects of the sluggish global economy, a slowdown in manufacturing, high consumer debt, and job layoffs. The unstable economic environment following the 2001 terrorist attacks, coupled with the rise of Wal-Mart and other discount retailers, pushed many retailers over the financial edge.

By the middle of the first decade of the twenty-first century, as economic recovery was well under way and the retail landscape had improved, the landscape had changed forever. Consumers around the world were showing a preference for discount shopping and a shopping format that allowed them to buy all their goods under one roof—clothes, housewares, electronics, personal items and food. Major department store chains had merged to gain economies of scale in an effort to compete against discounters such as Wal-Mart, or had divested themselves of some businesses in an effort to focus on their core retail undertakings. By the end of 2004, the leading retailer of any kind in the world was U.S.-based Wal-Mart. France's Carrefour followed, the company credited with giving the world the hypermarket format.

In response to marketing pressures, stores restructured internal organizations and changed marketing patterns. Where they could, stores also took advantage of the same new technology that had changed their marketing environment. Department stores were particularly quick to embrace advanced computer technology. The ability to centralize operations, have a complete and up-to-date status of inventory, and get an accurate reading of items purchased were only a few of the data-related advantages offered by computerized point-of-sale systems. Retailers were able to reduce not only their paperwork but also the lead times necessary to update stock. Particularly in the

United States, improved logistics led to a shift from stand-alone stores offering personalized shopping assistance to mega-chains, which were able to bring identical merchandise into nearly identical mall stores at competitive prices. In addition, by the mid-2000s, global online shopping from nearly every retail store was common place. This created an opportunity for more sales and less overhead costs as "virtual stores" became popular.

Writing for *The Bulletin,* published in Bend, Oregon, in a June 16, 2008, article Jeff McDonald shared insights about developer's struggles to attract more national retailers around new big-box stores. Many national retailers were deciding not to expand due to financial stress and economic-linked challenges. "If they have strong demographics to support new stores, they are moving forward cautiously. It is not as aggressive as 2005 and 2006," David Arredondo, vice president of development for C.E. John, explained. C.E. John develops, manages, and invests in commercial real estate throughout the western United States.

Writing for *Dow Jones Newswires* on June 13, 2008, Karen Talley concluded that department stores will be faced with making a choice between raising prices and hoping consumers accept it or watching their margins get cropped by inflation. Some retail consultants believe world financial markets are positioning to play a role in higher import costs.

BACKGROUND AND DEVELOPMENT

The modern department store has it roots in the U.S. mail-order catalog business that flourished in the nineteenth century. With catalogs offering quality merchandise at competitive prices, the United States pioneered the concept of self-service retailing. The first true "department" stores may have been the general stores and trading posts that sprang up in the small towns of the frontier United States, supplying locals with every necessity from sewing needles to plowshares. In the East, New York City saw the first urban department stores establish themselves as early as 1846. Although their primary business came from the city's elite, early urban merchants wanted to expand operations to people of all classes. While accepted marketing practices of the time consisted of holding goods behind a counter and bringing them forth on request, these new outlets openly displayed merchandise on floor racks to encourage browsing. Parallel retail development had occurred in a number of European countries by the mid-nineteenth century, but the global significance of the U.S. retail industry probably owes its existence to steady growth and westward settlement—which happened to come at a time that U.S. families on the East Coast were being introduced to the availability of heretofore unimagined luxuries and conveniences.

Richard Sears, who had the innovative concept of expanding mail-order business into catalog sales—and eventually into retail outlets—is credited with the creation of the modern department store. In 1886, Sears, then a railroad station agent, bought a shipment of watches. He proceeded to mail out these watches to purchasers, and the R.W. Sears Watch Company was born. Sears advertised for a watchmaker to help him support the growing business, and in 1887 Sears hired Alvah C. Roebuck. Their early catalogs advertised only watches and jewelry. However, in 1889 the pair sold the watch business in a move that was a precursor to real growth. After two years without an established company identity, in 1891 a new mail-order firm came into being, and, in 1893 that firm formally became Sears, Roebuck and Company. In 1896 the company produced its first general catalog and brought low prices and money-back guarantees to its primary customer base—farmers who had previously been vulnerable to the idiosyncrasies of local general stores.

The success of Sears and other pioneer U.S. department stores caught the attention of the global industry. Similar operations sprung up around the world, often from widely diverse beginnings. In the United Kingdom, a Russian refugee named Michael Marks sold out of an open stall in the market square in Leeds until 1894, when he formed a partnership with cashier Tom Spencer. Marks and Spencer broke new ground for retailers by buying directly from manufacturers, eliminating the middleman and reducing cost of goods and time to market at the same time. In Japan, Takshimaya had been a clothing retail outlet as early as 1831. In 1922, the company initiated full department store operations. G. J. Coles & Coy, the forerunner to today's Coles Myer, was a variety store that expanded to serve remote areas throughout Australia. As other major department stores followed a similar pattern of expansion, the largest stores in each nation often based development specifically on the U.S. department store concept. Both Coles Myer and Japan's Ito-Yokado blatantly modeled their businesses after U.S.-style stores, and they were not alone.

The concept of large scale, organized credit service began in 1911, when Sears offered payment plans to farmers for large mail-order purchases. By the 1920s, layaway installment plans were common, and their practicality was emphasized by the lean years of the Depression and wartime shortages. In a time when plastic credit cards were not part of the world's culture, the introduction of department store charge plates not only made purchasing easier for budget-conscious customers, but at the same time these store cards, usable only in the issuing store, were a great incentive to customer loyalty.

In the affluent years following World War II, most department stores turned to upscale clients and merchandise, relegating low-end bargains to "bargain basements" and occasional sales. This created a marketing gap into which discount operations such as Kmart (an outgrowth of S. S. Kresge's "five and dime" stores) quickly moved to fill. In 1962, Wal-Mart came on the scene, with expansion remaining slow (only 15 stores) until the company went public in 1970. By 1980, the company had grown to include 276 stores in 11 states with revenues of US\$1 billion. Rapid growth began in the 1980s at the end of which the company had grown to 1,400 stores with revenues of US\$26 billion. Once it had such large buying power behind it, the company was able to introduce just-in-time ordering of merchandise. In its efforts to keep prices low, Wal-Mart established a computer-based inventory system that monitored sales of individual products and thus inventory. When inventory levels got low, the computer system would advise suppliers to ship out more product. Wal-Mart cut down on its storage needs and did not find itself faced with product consumers did not want. This was to revolutionize the retail industry and make it increasingly difficult for smaller companies to remain competitive as they did not have the ability to demand just-in-time delivery.

By the 1980s, department stores were suffering from their earlier marketing errors. Beset by newer department stores, specialty stores, discounters, and mail-order houses, the classic firms went through a testing time of leveraged buyouts, mergers, and acquisitions. Surviving stores adjusted in-house operations to reduce cost and broaden their customer bases and in doing so lost portions of their traditional market. This state of flux continued into the 1990s, when yet another new competitor was introduced—technology. By 2000 it became evident the survivors of the retail industry had recognized the potential of e-commerce.

Shifts in market positions during the first half of the 1990s prompted retailers to adopt several competitive countermeasures. They experimented with downsizing and consolidation, merchandise mix changes, more consumer services, and greater use of advanced technologies, such as quick response systems, to control inventory costs and increase productivity. Electronic data interchange (EDI) allowed purchasing departments to institute store warehousing with a minimum of hard copy paper trail. Malls, which surrounded retail department stores with competing specialized retail outlets, also provided the same department stores with a ready supply of shoppers. Foreign markets, particularly those in emerging nations such as China, India, and smaller countries on the Pacific

Rim and in Latin America, beckoned. In 1998, the United States' National Retail Federation was salivating at the prospect of a reopened China and urged its membership to lobby the government for retention of China's most-favored-nation (MFN) trade status.

Several demographic changes during the 1990s also contributed to a shift in retail strategies. The typical retail customer of the 1990s was significantly different than the retail customer of the preceding decade. One striking change was the decline in the number of households composed of married couples. In 1980, married households comprised 60.8 percent of the retail market segment. By 1991, this percentage had decreased to 55.3 percent. Not surprisingly, during this same period, the number of people living alone increased. This demographic shift influenced buying habits and forced retailers to respond with appropriate marketing and products. The renewed popularity of catalog sales may have been caused, in part, by the busy schedules of individuals living alone or in single-parent households, but these were not the full-line catalogs of the previous century. Approaching 2000, the catalog image had changed. No longer did the price conscious, commodity-crammed tome represent the direction of the market. In fact, 1992 saw patriarch Sears mail out its last full-line catalog. Instead, catalogs, even those that covered relatively broad product lines, began to have an "image." Dime-store-like wares were sold from convenient, pocket-sized booklets, by firms like Fingerhut and Lillian Vernon. In 1998, it was easy for stay-at-home shoppers to glance at exterior catalog format and differentiate immediately between offerings of rugged outerwear that came from Eddie Bauer and L.L. Bean and the seductive lingerie available through Victoria's Secret. Catalogs proved a good way to globalize a retail market as well. Curio shops in Europe used their charm to capitalize on U.S. fascination for travel and things from abroad, even as U.S. companies extended their mailings to include an increasingly broader geographical area.

In the 1990s, the population's increasing familiarity with the Internet combined with an increase in the number of teenagers and young adults, and analysts predicted that the first years of the twenty-first century would represent a boom for "storeless" shopping. Direct retail sales, which included telemarketing and temporary exhibits with door-to-door sales, topped US$22 billion in 1997. Interactive television shopping channels and Internet retail pages both anticipated increased business as the year 2000 approached. By 1997, television-based shopping had hit a plateau at a disappointing US$4.5 billion annually. The relatively poor performance of television shopping networks was tied to the sequential nature of its offerings. It simply took a long time to shop that way. On the Internet, however, a click of the mouse placed the

shopper in the store he favored, a second click put the desired product in a "shopping cart," and a final click confirmed the purchase. In the late 1990s, department store Web pages could be both an enticement to investigate a store itself and a convenient place to shop online. In 1997, the fledgling Internet marketing industry stood at US$2.4 billion annually and was growing rapidly, fueled by the popularity of retail pages belonging to specialty bookstores and computer manufacturers.

One reaction to competition of any kind caused the retail industry to seek new ways to advertise product. Critics referred to the marketing tactics of the late 1990s as a "promotion frenzy." Certainly, the number and frequency of in-store sales increased dramatically between 1980 and 2000. Virtually anything that could serve as a differentiator was tried. Newspaper coupons offered discounts. Stores opened at odd hours. Christmas and other holiday sales began months in advance of the festival date. Nordstrom department stores capitalized on its upscale status, advertising almost excessive customer care. Other stores remained regional, marketing to the audience they knew best—and did so with some success. Restricting themselves to the south central United States, Dillard's Inc. and rival Proffitt's Inc. perked along quietly, together taking away US$10 billion or US$12 billion each year from larger national rivals.

Sometimes the differentiator was something bizarre. Ultimate among upscale promoters, giant retailer Neiman Marcus sold one-of-a-kind collectibles, extravaganza events, and monogrammed jet planes—all available through either store or catalog. Other times, the difference was something understated and conservative. Harrod's in Oxford Street, Knightsbridge, and London, simply displayed the best goods for the best people, insisting on proper attire for shoppers and refusing to sell to those of whom it did not approve. Although Harrod's-sponsored duty-free shops graced airports around the world, sedately presiding at its traditional Knightsbridge address, this paragon of upscale stores bore an unexportable level of prestige.

Until the latter part of the twentieth century, few retailers attempted to expand into foreign markets. However, the easing of investment restrictions in some foreign countries and the emerging trend of establishing affiliated firms in other markets characterized this new era in retailing. In the mid-1990s, the countries with the largest department stores were the United States, Japan, Great Britain, Australia, and France. Of these stores, those catering to increasingly global markets included Marks & Spencer Plc., Ito-Yokado, J.C. Penney, and Coles Myer. Responding to increasing pressure from rival retail outlets, television and the Internet, industry voices pressed for further global expansion to exploit an untapped world market made up of audiences less vulnerable to high-technology competition.

As the year 2000 approached, it became increasingly apparent that those retail stores and chains that were in good economic health were those that combined increased value for money spent with a newly awakened customer consciousness. Stores that developed their own "store brands"—various private label lines of goods—also enjoyed greater assurance of repeat customers.

By the early years of the first decade of the twenty-first century, consumer trends leaned toward frugality and value. As consumers sought more value, they tended to abandon department stores in favor of discount stores. In the late 1990s and early years of the first decade of the 2000s, consumers also flocked to warehouse and wholesale clubs, which feature products sold in bulk at much lower prices. By the end of 2001, warehouse clubs claimed a US$70 billion share of an already tight retail industry. Warehouse shopping outlets grew at a rate of 10 percent annually, twice as fast as the rest of the retail industry.

The U.S. economy, in a recession since the first quarter of 2001, resulted in a slowdown of manufacturing, rising energy prices, job layoffs, and rising consumer debt, all of which posed challenges to the retail industry. The industry was plagued with a number of bankruptcies, most notably Montgomery Ward, Ames Department Stores, Casual Male Corp., eToys, Bradlees, Stern's, and Kmart. Not bankrupt, but facing difficulty and closures in 2002 were J.C. Penney, Nordstrom Inc., Saks Inc., Microwarehouse, and Big Lots Inc.

Montgomery Ward filed for bankruptcy in 2001 for the second time in just two years, and closed all 258 locations. The sluggish 2000 holiday shopping season failed to provide enough earnings to keep the company from bankruptcy. Bradlees Corp. closed its 105 retail locations the same year, when the chain could not keep pace with Wal-Mart and Target in the New England states. Kohl's department stores bought 15 of the closed locations and Wal-Mart and Home Depot snatched up 10. Months later, Stern's, owned by Federated Department Stores, closed all locations in February 2001.

Kmart filed for Chapter 11 bankruptcy protection early in 2002, after two lackluster holiday shopping seasons and several years of economic instability. The company had upgraded some 100 stores nationwide to Super Kmarts, adding full service grocery and perishable items. However, the expansion could not address the company's inefficiency and instability. At the same time Kmart announced the bankruptcy filings, it also began examining which underperforming stores would close, and before emerging from Chapter 11 in May 2003, Kmart had closed 600 stores.

CURRENT CONDITIONS

During the years 2003 and 2004, the global economy seemed on an upswing, although some countries were still facing economic downturns. Global retailers as a whole were performing better. According to research by Deloitte Touche Tohmatsu, only 6 percent of retailers had reported a net loss in 2003, while more than twice that amount had reported losses in 2001. This improvement had led to an increase in the number of mergers and acquisitions around the world. Perhaps most striking was Kmart's emergence from bankruptcy and its subsequent merger with Sears. Other prominent acquisitions included the May Department Stores' purchase of Marshall Field's in the U.S. and the purchase by Baroness Retail of Debenhams in the United Kingdom.

Retailers were facing new marketing challenges. Developed countries were finding their populations aging, and as a result started designing programs specifically targeting this segment of the market. Consumers were also becoming more accepting of the Internet as a source for their shopping, a trend seen to even greater degree in Europe than in North America. This trend toward online shopping was considered the result of consumers feeling stretched for time, a condition also being reflected in their preference for retailers that provided them with all their shopping needs under one roof. The lines were continuing to be blurred between the various retail sectors. Department stores had merged with grocery stores to form hypermarkets. Wholesalers were being cut out of the middle through the formation of warehouse clubs. This change in store format was being encouraged further by the increasing preference for discount shopping by consumers around the world, a trend expected to continue.

While many U.S. companies continued to find growth through expansion domestically, there was a continuing trend of many large retailers to expand globally. China was considered by most analysts and retail managers to be the area of the world that held the most growth potential. Having begun to allow foreign ownership and investment, the country was positioned for rapid expansion of its market. In 2004, the government removed restrictions requiring foreign investors to partner with existing Chinese companies; foreigners could open stores independently and were no longer restricted in terms of the number of stores they opened. Having established itself as a major exporter of many of the goods produced for sale in the discount stores of foreign markets, China offered retailers a ready domestic source of product and growing amounts of disposable income in the domestic population.

While total U.S. retail industry revenues climbed 6 percent to US$300.1 billion, department stores were down by 1 percent over the previous year. By 2008, the world had entered the second recession in a decade and job loss reached unprecedented highs as industries laid off thousands. The housing boom of the mid-2000s stalled as foreclosure rates reached all time highs. Non-essential spending tapered off and discount stores became the shopping standard to millions worldwide. Even shopping trends were deeply impacted. The "Black Friday" pre-Christmas rush that had launched the Christmas shopping frenzy of the mid-decade years, took noticeable hits in both 2008 and 2009 as shoppers refused to spend money that they did not have. Holiday spending is largely a credit game that helps the struggling economy by allowing consumers to purchase items and pay over time with increased interest. If the consumer doesn' shop, then the credit is halted and stores suffer losses as they have already purchased their inventories.

RESEARCH AND TECHNOLOGY

Christine Dugas writing for *USA Today* reported there was a steady and alarming rise in shoplifting at many retail chains. Retail and law enforcement experts agreed there was an increase in shoplifting during the U.S. economic slow period. University of Florida Professor of Criminology Richard Hollinger pointed out that both employee theft and shoplifting were up. According to the National Retail Federation, of 116 retailers surveyed about shoplifting, 74 percent claimed they experienced an increase in incidents in 2007 over 2006. Retail theft cost about US$40.5 billion annually.

Point-of-sale systems used a variety of computerized features to improve the accuracy and efficiency of store operations, including electronic invoicing from wholesaler to dealer, shelf stocking by the use of bar-coded stickers, and cycle accounting—which replaced massive annual inventory taking by utilizing portable minicomputers to regularly rotate department counts. The use of "quick-response" systems grew rapidly in the 1990s. A quick-response system usually involved a strategic alliance between a retailer and manufacturer and used electronic data interchange (EDI) to issue invoices and payments. EDI permitted system users to track consumer purchasing patterns, further enhancing the process of supply and demand. The greatest benefits of all quick-response systems included prompt inventory turnover, with fewer out-of-stock situations, speedy customer response capability, and reduced overall operating costs.

Coles Myer, an Australian store, and Japan's Ito-Yokado led the industry in utilization of electronic scanning, and by the late 1990s optical barcode scanners had become commonplace. May Department Stores upgraded its investment and inventory systems, a move that it believed promoted better communication and greater

efficiency in restocking its stores. J.C. Penney implemented a state-of-the-art, automated merchandise replenishment system. Penney's variation on factory materials requirement planning (MRP) triggered orders based on projected sales demand, so that stores were constantly stocked with basic merchandise items.

The technology used every day in other industries was quickly embraced by the retail world. Communication by satellite allowed corporate buyers worldwide to communicate easily with department managers. Point-of-sale computer inquiries facilitated customer check cashing, layaway, and package pickup—and virtually all other cross-store communications once handled by pneumatic tube or manual labor.

WORKFORCE

As of 2004, the retail trade division in the United States represented about 12.6 percent of all establishments and employed 11.7 percent of all workers. In April 2005, almost 15 million Americans worked in the retail industry, down from a high of 16 million in December 2000, with the average non-supervisory worker earning US$12.08 per hour. Many stores compensated their salespeople using hourly wages, commissions, or a combination of the two. The majority of employees in retail were clerks or managers. Typically, benefits were very limited in smaller retail stores. The larger retailers and department stores typically were comparable to other employers and may have included health insurance, vacation time, and other paid time off.

INDUSTRY LEADERS

Wal-Mart Stores Inc. Wal-Mart is not only the largest retailer of any sort in the world, it is also one of the world's biggest companies, ranking 12th on *Fortune* magazine's list of the 2,000 largest global companies in 2005. Wal-Mart is best known for its operation of large discount stores. Including Wal-Marts, Sam's Clubs, and Wal-Mart Supercenters in the count, the company had more than 8,500 stores around the world in 2009, of which 70 percent were in the United States. Outside the United States, company stores flourished in Argentina (11 stores), Brazil (149), Canada (262), China (43), Germany (91), South Korea (16), Mexico (679), Puerto Rico (54), and the United Kingdom (267). Much of the company's growth in the first decade of the twenty first century was the result of the acquisition of existing companies in each country. The company owned about 37 percent of Japanese retail chain Seiyu by the start of 2005, and had plans to exercise warrants bringing its ownership level to 70 percent by 2007.

Wal-Mart founder Samuel Walton opened the first Wal-Mart in Rogers, Arkansas, in 1962. By the end of that decade, Walton and his brother operated 18 Wal-Mart stores and 15 Ben Franklin franchises in small towns throughout Arkansas, Missouri, Kansas, and Oklahoma. Wal-Mart went public in 1970. Initially trading over the counter, in 1972 the company was listed on the New York Stock Exchange. In 1983, Wal-Mart opened its first three Sam's Wholesale Clubs and began its expansion into bigger city markets. In 1987, the company introduced a new merchandising concept that Walton called Hypermart USA. Hypermarts combined grocery stores and general merchandise markets with services such as restaurants, banking, and videotape rental. Capitalizing on hypermart success, the company introduced several of its own brands, including Sam's American Choice product line, which included beverages, colas, and fruit drinks, and Great Value, initially used for a line of 350 packaged food items in its superstore centers. By 2009, over 50 percent of their revenue was generated by the grocery business. In 1970, Wal-Mart sales were US$44 million. By January 2005, they totaled more than US$285.2 billion, of which US$56.3 billion was from international operations. By 2009, Wal-Mart reported sales of US$408.2 billion and over 2.1 million employees.

PPR S.A. PPR Group (formerly known as Pinault-Printemps-Redoute) began in the timber industry in 1963, but through its expansion policy, the company found itself focusing on retail and luxury goods in 2003. After buying 44 percent of Gucci in 1999 of which it owned almost 100 percent by 2005, the company began to withdraw from its business-to-business lines and from consumer credit. In 2004, the company posted sales of approximately US$30.6 billion, of which 60 percent was derived from its retail division. With a large stable of luxury brands including, Stella McCartney, Yves Saint Laurent, Alexander McQueen, Balenciaga, Boucheron, and Bottega Veneta, PPR has a presence in 65 countries, 56 percent of its revenues are derived from outside of its home base of France. For 2009, the company reported US$19.6 billion in sales.

Target Corp. Target stores anchor the Target Corporation's retail empire. Formerly Dayton-Hudson, Target Corp. was the number two discount retailer in the United States in 2010, second only to Wal-Mart. With more than 1,300 stores, Target had US$46.8 billion in sales and controlled about 9 percent of the market. By 2009, the company's reported sales figure rose to US$64.9 billion with 351,000 employees and 1,743 locations.

J.L. Hudson's men's clothing store was established in 1881 in Detroit, Michigan, by owner Joseph L. Hudson. In 10 years (by 1891) Hudson's had become the largest U.S. retailer of men's clothing. Diversifying to include all sorts of apparel and household furnishings after World War II, both Hudson's and Minnesota's Dayton stores (founded in 1902) realized that the suburbs would soon replace city centers as major shopping areas. In parallel efforts, the two retailers began to build suburban shopping centers in the Detroit and Minneapolis areas. In 1956, Dayton built the world's first, fully enclosed shopping mall, Southdale, in Edina (a suburb of Minneapolis, Minnesota). Two years earlier, in 1954, Hudson's opened Northland Shopping Center in Southfield, Michigan, at that time the largest shopping center in the world. The corporation's low-end and specialty merchandising began in 1962, when Hudson's opened its first Target discount store and, four years later, when B. Dalton Bookstores were created, again by Hudson's.

In 1969, the Dayton-Hudson Corporation was formed by the merger of Dayton Department Stores and J.L. Hudson'. Hoping to emulate the success of Target stores, in 1978 the corporation bought California-based Mervyn's, department stores and throughout the next two decades extended Mervyn's locations across the country. In 1990, the next Dayton-Hudson acquisition was the prestigious, century-and-a-half-old Marshall Field's department store—one of Chicago's biggest retailers. With the help of Marshall Field's, Dayton-Hudson pioneered retailing's entry into the new world of "infomercials." Its 30-minute program, called "Marshall Field's Presents," aired in 30 national markets—despite serving only six of those markets. After failing to turn around the companies, Target sold both Mervyn's and Marshall Field's in 2004.

Marks and Spencer Group LLC. Tracing its roots back to a Leeds, England market stall in 1884, in 2010 the department store chain Marks & Spencer operated 600 stores and served 10 million customers each week. In addition, the company franchised 295 stores in 40 countries or territories in Europe, the Middle East, Asia, and the Far East. The company entered the Canadian market in the 1970s but failed to gain a strong foothold in this market. By 1999, it had closed all its Canadian-based stores. Marks & Spencer continued to struggle financially and began to sell off some of its non-U.K.-based assets, including 220 Brooks Brothers clothing stores in the United States and its stores in France. In 2004, it reported revenues of approximately US$15.2 billion with U.K.-based sales up 3.8 percent. In late May 2005, company executives announced that profits had fallen by almost 20 percent. Industry experts were claiming that this was because the stores were increasingly being seen as having old-fashioned product lines, with women's fashions being particularly hard hit. The company was experiencing mild increases in sales of its food lines, and was planning expansion in this area. For 2009, the reported sales were US$14.1 billion with 77,864 employees.

Kmart Corporation and Sears, Roebuck and Co.

Sears, Roebuck began in Minnesota in 1886 with Richard W. Sears and his R.W. Sears Watch Company. In two years' time, Sears had published his first mail order catalog, an 80-page document advertising watches and jewelry. In two more years, the catalog had grown to 322 pages and included some full-line items—clothes, jewelry, and durable goods such as sewing machines and bicycles. For the next hundred years, Sears catalogs brought modern retail products to every region of the country. By the mid-1960s, Sears posted US$1 billion in monthly sales, but in 1991 a national recession and intense competition caused Sears serious difficulties. Earnings for the entire year of 1991 were just US$200 million. The following year, the Sears catalog was no more, and the company began a process of reconstruction and reorganization that was still ongoing in 1998.

In a remarkable turnaround, the company repositioned its automotive services to concentrate on tire and battery replacement, rather than general repairs. It opened new HomeLife furniture stores to provide space in the main stores for clothes, and it introduced a new cosmetic line. In the 1990s, it operated HomeLife, Sears, Parts America, National Tire and Battery, Orchard Supply Hardware, and other retail stores in the United States, in addition to catalog and Sears stores in Canada, and Sears stores in Mexico. In 1992, it was estimated that one in thirty Americans had worked for Sears in some capacity at some time. Company sales totaled US$54.83 billion in 1994. However, when profit margins narrowed, Sears looked to restructure again, aiming the new reorganization at methods that would improve dollar returns for corporate shareholders. Employee counts were reduced, and stores were remodeled to increase customer appeal. In the summer of 1998 Sears continued to downsize. The company sold its interest in Britain's prestigious Selfridges Department Store, as well as its British Shoe business, and planned to opt out of the United Kingdom's Freemans mail order system. Domestically, Sears divested itself of several other successful—but tangential—operations, including Allstate Insurance, Dean Witter financial services, and its Discover credit card.

In 2004, Sears had nearly 2,400 Sears-branded and affiliated stores in Canada and the United States. That year, the company posted revenues of US$36.1 billion, down 12 percent from the previous year when it had acquired Land's End. Sales continued to decline, even as competitors were bouncing back.

In March 2005, Sears joined with Kmart Corporation, making the combined company the third largest U.S. retailer. Kmart faced stiff competition from Wal-Mart and after attempting to redefine its niche, the company filed for bankruptcy in 2002. In 2003, it emerged from bankruptcy

and began a major restructuring plan for its then 2,100 stores. In 2004, Kmart's store count had dropped to almost 1,500 stores, 400 of which it was planning to convert to the Sears name.

Kmart operates in the United States, Canada, Puerto Rico, and the Czech Republic. The corporation grew from a Detroit five-and-dime store, opened in 1899 by Sebastian Kresge. Kresge enjoyed quick success, selling jewelry, housewares, and personal goods. By 1912, there were 85 Kresge stores producing annual sales of US$10.3 million. In the late 1950s, food grew into the largest single department at the Kresge stores, and in 1962, the first Kresge discount store was opened and baptized "Kmart." The Kmart stores were an instant success; by 1963, there were 63 facilities, and by 1966 that number had increased to 122.

The late 1970s, however, witnessed the rise of new competitors with more inviting stores and specialty stores that took over Kmart's share of the firm's staples, such as sporting goods, drugs, and personal grooming items. Changes in public taste showed up in lagging profits, which sank 28 percent in 1980. Kmart responded by remodeling existing stores and stocking them with more fashionable merchandise and installing a computer system to monitor inventories, orders, and shipments. In the mid-1980s, Kmart added several celebrity spokespeople to its payroll, including actress Jaclyn Smith, racecar driver Mario Andretti, and caterer Martha Stewart. Despite Martha Stewart's legal troubles in 2004, including a conviction for lying about stock sales, Kmart was committed to the Martha Stewart Everyday brand, a series of products that was instrumental in the rise of Kmart sales in the 1990s. Profits for 1987 rose 19 percent, and by 2001 total sales reached US$37.03 billion, but the discounter continued to struggle for market share. In the 1990s, Wal-Mart made decisive inroads into Kmart's customer base, and the firm continued to lose sales to niche stores as well. Kmart management concluded that the chain needed to diversify its product line to offer one-stop shopping across the traditional retail boundaries. Kmart's plan was to convert many of its existing stores to Big Kmart outlets, which featured a limited grocery line in addition to general merchandise, and Super Kmart stores, which offered an extensive line of groceries along with amenities like a bakery, a deli, and in-store banking. The new formats also highlighted trendier merchandise in contrast to the chain's established product line, which was viewed by some as dowdy and unfashionable.

Medill News Service's Gabrielle Tompkins consulted with industry analysts and shared their concerns about Sears Holding after its first quarter 2008 big loss. Morning Star's Kimberly Picciola believed that Sears' problems were due to struggles with its merchandising and inventory management. Gimme Credit's Carol Lewenson felt that the goal of making the merged Kmart and Sears into a retail success has become increasingly less achievable.

Carrefour S.A. In 2004, the largest retailer outside of the United States was France's Carrefour S.A., which had 6,000 stores worldwide. By size, Carrefour was only behind Wal-Mart. Carrefour's 2003 sales reached more than US$88.47 billion, drawn from overseas operations in Argentina, Brazil, Portugal, Spain, Taiwan, and the United States, as well as its Paris headquarters. Established in 1959, Carrefour was considered the originator of the 100,000-square-foot hypermarket that became its trademark in Europe and other parts of the world. Carrefour hypermarkets offered produce, groceries, clothing, consumer goods, and household appliances in a large, open marketplace environment. Globally, the hypermarkets provided a variety of products and services: minimarkets, gasoline, insurance, home improvements, furniture and electrical appliances, vacation packages, and credit cards. The company also operated a number of discount stores and invested in a variety of products from frozen foods to real estate. Carrefour's interests extended to a number of U.S. retailers, including involvement with Office Depot and PetSmart. Its sales rose to US$113.8 billion with 495,000 employees in 2009.

MAJOR COUNTRIES IN THE INDUSTRY

United States. In 2010, the United States continued to hold the dominant position in the retail industry. Eight of the top 10 retail companies of all types globally were American. Wal-Mart was simply the largest retailer of any kind, anywhere, and was the largest retail employer as well, employing 2.1 million people around the world at the start of 2010. *Forbes Global* listed Wal-Mart as the world's largest public corporation by revenue. The department stores market was valued by Euromonitor to be worth US$118.4 million in 2004, with variety stores adding a further US$412.1 billion. With 32.8 percent of the warehouse and superstore market in 2003, Wal-mart's next four biggest competitors could not match it in terms of sales, even if one was to combine all their sales. However, they were multi-billion dollar companies in their own rights. In fact, Costco was actually bigger than Wal-Mart as a wholesale club operator, beating out Wal-Mart's Sam's Club stores. Target Corporation was the country's second-ranking discount retailer, operating in 47 U.S. states in 2005 and was ranked at number 30 on the *Fortune* 500 as of 2010. In terms of the department store sector of the retail industry, this remained somewhat consolidated in the United States in 2003, with the top five players (Sears Roebuck,

J.C. Penney, Federated, The May Department Stores, and Dillard's) accounting for 64.6 percent of the market. Size seemed to matter to the management of the department store sector, with mergers and acquisitions of smaller stores continuing. However, the market was expected to experience several more years of declining sales. Much of this decline would be the result of the increasing influence of discount stores on the marketplace. Variety stores, such as Wal-Mart and Target, were expected to remain the largest market sector.

According to Sandra M. Jones of *Business 2.0,* only a few of the approximately three dozen retailers reporting May 2008 numbers said the U.S. economic stimulus checks helped sales. Wal-Mart was among them. Economist Scott Hoyt expects the tax rebates scheduled for July arrival to "provide a bridge to the crucial back-to-school and holiday seasons."

Maria Halkias of *The Dallas Morning News* observed that there was a trend evolving for luxury department stores to become involved in projects overseas. Major developers throughout the world were contacting Neiman Marcus, Saks Fifth Avenue, Barneys New York, Lord & Taylor, and Bloomingdale's. In May 2008, Macy's responsibly named a new corporate-level position of president for international retail development and announced plans to explore opportunities outside the United States for its Bloomingdale's and Macy's stores. U.S. mall developers established major shopping centers elsewhere. Taubman, based in Michigan, was building 600,000 square feet of retail space in Maceo, China, which was considered to be a larger gaming market than Las Vegas. Simon Property Group already owned approximately 50 European shopping centers plus eight premium outlet centers in Japan, South Korea, and Mexico. Its international projects under construction included three in Italy and four in China.

Japan. Throughout the 1990s, it appeared unlikely that there would be any significant growth in the number of Japanese department stores, although the *Large Store Law* attempted to regulate their development. Under this law, any store with more than 500 but less than 1,000 square meters was permitted to be opened only by notification to the government. Large-scale stores were allowed to stay open until 8:00 p.m. Additionally, such stores could stay open until 9:00 p.m. up to 60 days per year and could close only 24 days per year without reporting to the government. The Japanese department store industry was expected to continue to compete on the basis of differentiation between stores and companies. Thus, the number of department stores was limited, and each was encouraged to retain its own identity. Any significant increase in Japanese domestic competition seemed unlikely. The only danger was to Japanese department stores, like Takashimaya, that limited business to the top end of the consumer market. These were challenged by leading superstore retailers—notably Ito-Yokado—which were steadily improving retail product quality. The superstores were larger, more diverse, and arguably more efficient than the traditional department store, and lacked only the tradition itself that earmarked the older firms.

However, the 1990s also saw the deregulation of Japan's retail industry. Initially foreign investors entered the market through joint ventures with existing Japanese companies, but by the end of the 1990s, foreign companies were setting up on their own. Membership clubs offered by Costco and hypermarkets introduced by France's Carrefour caught the attention of consumers. In 2002, Wal-Mart bought controlling interest in The Seiyu Ltd. Although Seiyu was a grocery chain, Walmart's variety store format was sure to take effect on the company.

The late 1990s and early years of the first decade of the 2000s brought much disruption to Japan's retail sector. Like its counterparts in the United States, department stores faced steep competition from discounters. However, by 2003, both large department stores and discounters faced continuing problems, with sales declines expected to continue through 2008. The department store sector in Japan was highly concentrated, with the top three companies (Daimaru, Takashimaya, and Mitsukoshi) accounting for 71.8 percent of the market. Japanese consumers prefer large hypermarkets, very large commercial enterprises that are a combination of a department store and a supermarket. The global market research firm Euromonitor was predicting that hypermarkets would overtake department stores as the largest sector in the retail industry in Japan, making up 42.8 percent of the market by 2008.

As reported by *The Yomiuri Shimbun,* more Japanese retailers were beginning to carry plus sizes. This move was in response to increasing numbers of men and women searching for clothing considered large by Japanese standards. Marui department stores, targeting young consumers seeking brand names, expanded its inventory to carry up to size 23. The chain also carries trendy footwear in sizes up to 26.5 and fashion rings in large sizes. Marui's Kita-Senju, Tokyo store has the largest selection of large-size clothes.

Toru Fujioka, writing for Bloomberg News, reported that Japanese department store sales fell in virtually every category. Categories with drops were led by luxury goods. "Many consumers nowadays have various purchasing venues such as online shopping making it increasingly difficult to gauge actual consumption," Morgan Stanley's Takehiro Sato explained.

France. The French consumer continued to have a love affair with department stores—two in particular: Rallye and Galeries Lafayette. Together these two companies controlled more than three-quarters of the department store retail market in France in 2002. The Galeries Lafayette store in Paris had the highest sales volume of any retailer in Europe. Valued at US$10.4 billion in 2003, the market was expected to continue on its upward swing, increasing 14 percent by 2008.

The French company Carrefour is attributed with the creation of the hypermarket, where a supermarket is placed under the same roof as a department store. This concept has been copied successfully by many other companies, including Wal-Mart and Target, and has been responsible for turning Carrefour into the second largest retailer in the world.

United Kingdom. As in many other developed countries, the department store sector continued to face intense competition from discount retailers in the mid-years of the first decade of the 2000s. Once the leading retailer in the United Kingdom, Marks & Spencer had been forced to sell off most of its overseas ventures in the late 1990s and early years of the decade. The year 2005 found it struggling with declining sales and profits, and a lackluster consumer image.

However, other industry players were showing signs of growth and expansion. Debenhams, noted for its fashion departments, showed sales increases of more than 9 percent in 2003, and was a franchisor of stores in the Middle East, Indonesia, Denmark, Sweden, Iceland, and the Czech Republic. In 2005, it planned to open new stores in Saudi Arabia and Dubai, as well as Cyprus and Indonesia. John Lewis Partnership, so named because its 63,000 permanent staff members are partners in the business, operated 26 high-end department stores in 2005, and owned the high-end grocery store chain Waitrose. Despite their success, the Allders department store chain of 45 stores fell into bankruptcy in early 2005 after it failed to find a buyer for its company. In the following months, other major chains bought up some locations while many others closed their doors.

The British department store market, which was valued by *Euromonitor* at US$13.6 billion in 2003, was expected to grow by 10.8 percent through 2010. Although Wal-Mart had made major inroads into the market through its purchase of grocery chain ASDA, consumers seemed reluctant to accept the Wal-Mart brand name as it was seen to promote an American lifestyle on the British consumer. However, ASDA was gradually converting its format over to the hypermarket style popular in the United States, and most of the company's advertising mimicked that presented in the United States.

China. With its huge population and increasing openness to foreign investment, China was being actively pursued by retailers. Although in 2003 its department store market was worth about half that of the U.S., the market was expected to grow from US$58.2 billion to US$102.5 billion by 2008. The market remained highly fragmented, with the five leading companies being domestic. As a group, Shanghai No.1 Department Store, Dashang, Beijing Hualian, Shanghai Yuyuan, and Beijing Wangfujing held less than 12 percent of the market. Foreign companies were making major inroads in the wholesale club market of the retail trade. Wal-Mart entered the Chinese marketplace in 1996 and by 2005 was operating 40 supercenters, three Sam's Clubs and two Neighbourhood Markets. Having already become a source of manufacturing for the goods many foreign retailers sell, China has a ready supply of domestically produced products to feed into its growing retail marketplace.

BIBLIOGRAPHY

"2005 Global Powers of Retailing." Deloitte Touche Tohmatsu, January 2005. Available from www.deloitte.com.

Burrows, Dan. "Carrefour Sales Up, Cuts Forecast." *WWD*, 9 July 2004.

———. "Discounters Don't Disappoint." *WWD*, 20 February 2004.

Desjardins, Doug. "Style Inhabits the Unlikeliest Places." *DSN Retailing Today*, 5 April 2004.

Draper, Deborah J., ed. *Business Rankings Annual*. Detroit: Thomson Gale, 2004.

Dugas, Christine. " More Consumers, Workers Shoplift as Economy Slows." *USA Today*, 18 June 2008.

"Engineering and Construction Services in Australia, China, France, Germany, Japan, South Korea, UK, US." *Euromonitor*, August 2004. Available from http://www.majormarketprofiles.com.

Fujioka, Toru. "Japan's Retail Sales Rise at Slowest Pace Since July." 29 May 2008. Available from Bloomberg.com.

Halkias, Maria. "U.S. Luxury Department Stores Being Drawn Overseas." *The Dallas Morning News*, 25 May 2008.

Hogsett, Don. "Penney Sees Profits Soar 173 Percent." *Home Textiles Today*, 24 May 2004.

"Hoover's Company Capsules." *Hoover's Online*, 2008. Available from www.hoovers.com.

Howell, Debbie. "Kmart's Got Cash, But Then What?" *DSN Retailing Today*, 19 July 2004.

"International Trade Statistics." World Trade Organization, 2003. Available from www.wto.org.

Jacobson, Greg. "Will Sears Grand Be Part of the Solution?" *MMR*, 11 August 2003.

Jones, Sandra. "How Sears Came Down with Seasonal Disorder." *Business 2.0*, July 2004.

———. "May Retail Sales Rise as Tax Rebate Checks Help, Shoppers Unite." *Chicago Tribune*, 6 June 2008.

Kalish, Ira. "Global Consume Jones, Sandra M. "May Retail Sales Rise as Tax Rebate Checks Help, Shoppers Unite." *Chicago Tribune*, 6 June 2008.

"Kmart and Martha Stewart Living Omnimedia Have Agreed to Extend Through 2009 Their Long-Term Distribution Agreement for the Everyday Label." *DSN Retailing Today*, 17 May 2004.

"Kmart: Martha Stewart Still 'Valued Brand Partner.'" *DSN Retail Fax*, 19 July 2004.

Lazich, Robert S., ed. *Market Share Reporter*. Detroit: Thomson Gale, 2004.

Moses, Alexandra R. "Kmart Files for Chapter 11 Bankruptcy Protection After Key Supplier Cuts Off Shipments." *Detroit Free Press*, 22 January 2002.

"A New Era In Japan's Retailing Market: Deregulation Paves the Way for Inroads by Foreign Groups." The Japan Society of Northern California, 2004. Available from www.usajapan.org.

"Retailers Warm Up To Plus-Size Clientele." *The Yomiuri Shimban*. 16 June 2008.

Sears, Roebuck and Co. "Sears: Historical Chronology." Sears, Roebuck and Co., 2002. Available from www.sears.com.

Talley, Karen. "Inflation Seen as Next Issue Retailers Must Fight." *Dow Jones Newswires*, 13 June 2008.

Tompkins, Gabrielle. "Sears Continue to Disappoint." *Medill News Service*, 3 June 2008.

Vargas, Melody. "U.S. Retail Sales Rise 6.3 Percent Over Last Year," 14 July 2004. Available from retailindustry.about.com.

"The WWD List: Broadline Leaders." *WWD*, 6 May 2004.

SIC 5000, 5100

WHOLESALERS

NAICS CODE(S)

42. The broad wholesale industry generally serves as an intermediary between commercial buyers and sellers of commodities and merchandise. A common example is buying a manufacturer's products and selling them to a retailer. The industry consists of three types of firms: wholesale merchants, manufacturers' sales branches or sales offices, and agents or brokers. Wholesale merchants buy merchandise for resale to three types of resellers: retailers, contractors or professional business users, and other wholesalers. The second group of wholesalers, manufacturers' sales offices, includes separate sales subsidiaries or sales offices maintained by manufacturing, refining, or mining enterprises for the purpose of marketing their products. The third group includes firms that act as agents or brokers in buying merchandise for, or selling merchandise to, individuals or companies on a commission basis.

INDUSTRY SNAPSHOT

With the implementation of automated ordering, shipping, and inventory control systems, wholesalers were able to increase their output and revenues without having to increase their workforces. This technology made the industry more efficient and cost effective, thus saving money for the end consumer. To remain competitive, wholesalers offered retailers the convenience of dealing with one supplier by forming consortia that allowed companies offering complementary products to cooperatively supply their array of goods. In addition, wholesalers started to stock and maintain inventories on their customers' sites, which created an extra value to the customers doing business with wholesalers. Such an emphasis on value derived in part from a trend in retailing toward eliminating wholesale agreements and dealing directly with manufacturers. The U.S. wholesale industry remained one of the largest and most advanced in the world, with US\$4.2 trillion in 2007 revenues, an 8.6 percent increase over 2006.

The wholesale industry continued to grow much faster than the U.S. economy during the global economic recession. In 2007, revenues shot up 3.7 percent through wholesale distribution channels, more than the U.S. Gross Domestic Product (GDP) rates. Because of the wholesale-distributor relationship of providing value to the customer, profitability remained at an all time high.

Wholesalers not only buy and sell goods, they also provide a wide range of services designed to add value and facilitate smooth functioning of the market. For retail clients, wholesalers anticipate their needs and demands and stock large quantities of goods at locations convenient to the retailer. Wholesalers assemble shipments, deliver merchandise, extend credit, service goods sold, assist with sales promotion and publicity, and provide marketing information and sales assistance. In support of retailers, they also offer billing, collections, and record keeping services. For the manufacturer, wholesalers buy, sell, and store merchandise, finance production by purchasing in advance, and reduce risk by screening customers and providing market information.

Wholesalers are a key link between manufacturers and the marketplace—a position that historically gave them enormous power over both their customers and their suppliers. Their ability to anticipate consumer needs and demands, combined with their purchasing power and wide distribution abilities, made many wholesalers much more than mere "middlemen." Wholesalers could influence retail buying decisions, create new markets, and make or break a new product. They were so powerful that producers often had to adjust manufacturing priorities, product design and development, and marketing strategies in accordance with the wishes of their wholesale customers. However, manufacturers and retailers were not resigned to the power of the wholesalers. By the 1990s, major manufacturers and retailers alike were actively seeking ways to bypass wholesalers, a movement facilitated by new advancements in transportation and delivery systems, heightened

competition, falling prices, and computerized technologies. Retail giant Wal-Mart started a retail revolution when it demanded just-in-time delivery from suppliers. The rise of electronic commerce in the late 1990s prompted many industry analysts to predict that the Internet would eventually eliminate the need for traditional distributors. However, by the first few years of the 2000s, most experts had come to view the Internet as a distribution management tool, albeit an unpredictable one.

Under pressure from suppliers and customers, wholesalers saw their market gradually eroded by alternative channels of distribution such as warehouse clubs, mail order, and giant retailers that dealt directly with manufacturers. Costco Wholesale Corporation, for example, buys the majority of its merchandise directly from manufacturers and sells to business and consumer members, earning revenues of more than US\$48 billion in 2004. Manufacturers, eager to increase their profit margins, welcomed these new distribution channels, as did price-conscious consumers. This trend was particularly evident in consumer goods, a market that was simultaneously shrinking for wholesalers while also accounting for increased portions of their total sales. These changes were not only apparent in the United States, but also throughout Europe, Canada, and Japan.

Faced with these challenges, wholesalers were forced to reexamine their competitive strategies, and they began to reorient their services and product mix. Many wholesalers determined that in order to survive, they would have to provide value-added services, improve productivity, expand geographically, diversify into new product lines, enlarge existing lines, and develop new markets. Rising competition prompted strategic alliances and consolidation among the largest wholesale and distribution firms. Although the total number of wholesalers continued to fall in the mid-years of the first decade of the 2000s, the market for small niche players that could target specialized needs remained open, and overall employment was expected to rise.

Bloomberg News reported that U.S. wholesalers' inventories rose at rates that exceeded forecast in April. Forecasts issued by economists had projected that wholesale inventories would rise 0.4 percent. Wholesalers were determined to account for approximately a quarter of all business stockpiles. *Bloomberg News* survey findings showed inventories of durable goods increased 1.1 percent and nondurable products increased by 1.7 percent.

ORGANIZATION AND STRUCTURE

Virtually all goods sold in all but the most underdeveloped economies pass through at least one wholesaler. Although under increasing pressure from newly emergent economic and technological forces, the wholesale industry was still one of the largest and most diverse sectors in the economies of most countries.

The trend toward integration of manufacturing, retailing, and wholesaling functions in many industries can make it difficult to develop an accurate overall picture of the wholesale industry. Despite the emergence of some very large global companies, the industry remains extremely fragmented. The wholesale industry sells everything from raw materials such as petroleum, minerals, and forest products, to manufactured goods such as packaged food, automobiles, and consumer electronics. Wholesalers obtain the products they sell from manufacturers, mining operations, agricultural concerns, and other wholesalers. Consequently, the level of wholesale trade activity depends on a wide variety of factors, including the health of the economy, international commodity prices, and the rates of growth in employment, income, investment, and trade. Moreover, because wholesalers sell to each other, sales figures generated by the industry are not equivalent to the value of goods it actually handles.

The largest group in the industry is wholesale merchants. This group accounted for roughly 60 percent of all sales and 85 percent of all firms in both the United States and Canada. With the possible exception of Japan, which maintains a rather complicated distribution system compared to most industrial countries, the parallels between wholesale industries in different nations suggest that wholesale merchants accounted for similar shares in other countries.

Wholesale merchants, also known as jobbers, include a number of subcategories such as industrial distributors, voluntary group wholesalers, exporters, importers, cash-and-carry wholesalers, drop shippers, truck distributors, retailer cooperative warehouses, terminal elevators, cooperative buying associations, assemblers, buyers, and cooperatives engaged in the marketing of farm products. Merchant wholesaling firms are the primary distribution channel for all major products carried by wholesalers, with the exception of motor vehicles and parts.

Merchants are distinguished from brokers because they actually buy and take ownership of the goods they distribute, whereas brokers do not. Agents and commission brokers sell goods on a commission basis and tend to be more specialized than merchant wholesalers. Auction companies, manufacturing agents, food brokers, and import/export agents and brokers all fall into the category of agents and brokers. The types of products most often sold by agents and brokers include farm products, food, petroleum products, apparel, and dry goods.

Manufacturers' sales subsidiaries, on the other hand, are often indistinguishable from merchants in that they also usually "buy" the products they sell from their parent company. Because major international industries such as petroleum refining and automobile manufacturing

maintain their own wholesalers, these types of firms, though small in number, account for a sizable portion of total wholesale sales. They are also prominent in the international realm of wholesaling. For example, foreign-owned wholesale establishments in Canada amounted to less than 5 percent of all firms in the late 1990s. However, because these firms were concentrated in the petroleum, automotive, machinery and equipment, hardware, and plumbing and heating products sectors, they accounted for 27 percent of the industry's sales. Of that, about half was generated by U.S.-owned establishments.

The chief function of wholesale merchants is to sell goods to trading establishments; industrial, commercial, institutional, farm, or construction contractors; or professional business users. The chief function of brokers is to bring buyer and seller together. In addition to selling or setting up deals, wholesale establishments often carry out a wide range of other functions including carrying inventory; extending credit; assembling, sorting, and grading goods in large lots; breaking bulk and redistribution into smaller lots; delivery; refrigeration; and various types of promotion such as advertising and label design. Wholesalers may also service, repair, or lease the products they handle.

The number of functions an individual wholesale firm carries out is influenced by several factors, such as the characteristics of the products it sells, the end user, and the structure of the industry in which it sells. Full-service wholesalers such as electrical, pharmaceutical, and hardware wholesalers generally perform all the marketing functions and carry an extensive product line. Limited-function wholesalers carry a more narrow product line and don't include such services as credit or merchandise delivery. Manufacturers' sales subsidiaries usually offer the same mix of functions as full-service wholesale merchants, and are owned by large companies that frequently modify their products and require rapid, accurate information on sales. Sometimes, manufacturers' subsidiaries also sell competitors' products. To be successful, a wholesaler must find the right mix of functions and be able to offer them at a cost lower than its suppliers or customers could achieve on their own.

Specialization in a specific product group such as resources, consumer goods, or industrial goods, is common among all wholesalers whether they are multibillion-dollar nationwide organizations, such as the U.S. companies SUPERVALU and C&S Wholesale Grocers, or small rack jobbers that stock and service individual displays or counters at different stores.

Many establishments classified as wholesalers also sell directly to consumers and other businesses. These firms include businesses selling office and store furniture, lumber and building materials, farm supplies, fuel oil, and all types of machinery and equipment. In some cases, the same outlet may conduct what can be considered wholesale and retail activities at the same time by offering different prices depending on the buyer's status. Resellers, for example, may not have to pay sales tax, whereas an end user may be required to do so. Wholesalers may also own separate retail subsidiaries or divisions that conduct retail trade fed by the company's wholesale operations.

Size is a valued asset in the wholesale industry. The efficiency of both individual companies and the industry as a whole is determined by such factors as economies of scale, links with producers, and the ability to provide customers with the best prices, service, convenience, and quality. Size gives wholesalers buying clout with suppliers and allows them to spread fixed costs over a wider sales base. In the United States and Canada, the industry tends to be more concentrated. The sheer physical size of both nations makes it essential for wholesale firms to be able to capture the economies of scale and resources needed to collect and distribute goods efficiently.

The tendency toward large firms is especially evident in the wholesaling of consumer products, where multi-billion-dollar enterprises with strong links to retailers dominate such sectors as food, pharmaceuticals, motor vehicles and parts, hardware supplies, and building products. Major wholesaling firms in this segment often have their own network of corporate stores, franchises, or company-sponsored retail dealerships. In other cases, leading consumer product wholesalers capture markets by forging close links with independent retail chains, franchises, or cooperatives. These structures often prove extremely successful, taking market share away from both the large retailers and the wholesalers with their own retail outlets. For example, 85 percent of retail hardware outlets in Canada are independents associated with a single wholesaler, Home Hardware. To reach these retailers, manufacturers have to sell through Home Hardware. Moreover, by avoiding direct involvement in the retail business, these wholesale firms do not risk offending their clients by directly competing with them. The competitive advantages enjoyed by firms operating in this manner have caused an increasing number of major retailers to convert their own stores into franchises and focus on wholesaling.

Only in the field of industrial products—where the main customers are other businesses and trade contractors—does size play a less prominent role. Because of the diverse range of products they handle and the need for good product knowledge and service, industrial goods wholesalers frequently specialize. Consequently, market share for individual companies is relatively low. Nonetheless, large companies also play a role in this market,

particularly in the heavy equipment, farm machinery, electrical, plumbing and heating equipment, and paper products sectors. Vertical integration with manufacturers of these products is also common among some larger firms.

Although the scales are tilted heavily in favor of large firms, many small wholesalers are able to compete successfully by carving out exclusive market niches. High levels of specialization, in-depth product knowledge, and personalized service help smaller wholesalers find and maintain customers. Importing is one area where smaller companies are able to thrive by taking advantage of the rising number of independent boutiques and gift shops that specialize in unique and unusual items from around the world. Major retailers also turn increasingly to wholesalers to handle their import requirements. As global trading patterns evolved and manufacturing became more specialized, wholesalers with knowledge of foreign markets and services were likely to gain an edge on those who relied solely on domestic suppliers.

The implementation of the U.S.-Canadian Free Trade Agreement and later the North American Free Trade Agreement (NAFTA)—a pact between the United States, Canada, and Mexico—opened new markets for wholesalers in these countries. U.S. and Canadian wholesalers began to expand into each other's countries and into Mexico. The primary impediment to the establishment of foreign affiliates was investment restrictions in certain countries.

In contrast to the wholesale industries in North America and Europe, which placed a premium on size, efficiency, and economies of scale, Japan's distribution system was extraordinarily complex and inefficient. In 2002 there were 380,000 wholesaler stores in Japan and nearly 1.2 million retailers—both down significantly from the mid-1990s. The Japanese distribution network was diverse and complicated, differing for each product by the size of the producer and end retailer or user. Japan had a greater number of retailers and wholesalers per capita than any other country in the world, and small retail outlets—so-called mom-and-pop shops—accounted for the majority of consumer shopping.

In the early 1980s, in spite of its success in manufacturing and its apparent modernity, much of Japan's cultural and social life remained rooted in its agricultural past. Unlike Western cities with their identifiable core and surrounding suburbs, large Japanese cities resembled an assemblage of small villages, each with their own business districts and close community ties. This village structure was reflected in the distribution system, with numerous small wholesalers supplying numerous small retailers within very narrowly defined geographic regions.

Further complicating the Japanese system were the high price of land and restrictive laws that prevented large stores from being opened without approval from neighboring small merchants. With one in five Japanese employed in the distribution system, small merchants were a powerful political force capable of stalling any attempts by the government to give more leeway to large businesses. Moreover, with price coordination pervasive in Japan, consumers had no incentive to favor large stores over small stores, since even "discount prices" were almost identical. As a result, according to Charles J. McMillan in *The Japanese Industrial System*, pricing and retailing strategies largely regulate the relationships in distribution channels. For consumers, this meant that Japanese prices were frequently among the highest in the world because of the many layers in the distribution channel. McMillan argued that alleged dumping by Japanese manufacturers in overseas markets had more to do with the greater efficiency of foreign distribution systems than with any deliberate attempt by Japanese manufacturers to gain market share.

By the 1990s, signs of change became evident in the Japanese distribution system. Pressure from foreign exporters and rising consumer dissatisfaction with inflated prices led to increased efforts to modernize the system, particularly on the part of manufacturers, importers, and large department stores. According to a report released by Japan's Economic Planning Agency, the simplification of Japan's distribution system in the late 1990s was considered a key factor in the decrease in consumer prices in both 1998 and 1999. The impetus for reform in the distribution industry was "heated competition among discount businesses in a number of industries," according to a July 2000 article in *Yomiuri Shimbun*.

In many developing countries, the system of wholesale trade is highly fragmented. Small companies deliver a variety of goods to retailers, selection often being dependent on availability and bargaining ability. Many distribution systems are still government controlled, with inefficiencies in terms of networks, labor, and product flow.

BACKGROUND AND DEVELOPMENT

In its most rudimentary form, wholesaling referred to the buying of goods from the manufacturer or producer and the subsequent selling of those goods to retail stores and other businesses, which in turn sold them to the public. Wholesaling also involved buying goods from other wholesalers and reselling them to yet other wholesalers. It could involve buying goods from one supplier, exchanging those goods for goods from another supplier,

and then selling the newly acquired goods. This "middleman" function evolved largely because of the great differences in needs, market size, and product availability in different regions of the world.

Although primitive forms of wholesaling may have existed as far back as the first urban civilizations of the Middle East, the world's first true wholesalers and distributors were probably the ancient Phoenicians. Like the Dutch and the British after them, this seafaring people built a civilization based almost entirely on trade. From ancient Britain to Judea, the Phoenicians transported and traded the goods of the ancient world. By the time of the Romans, trade had become even more geographically extensive. According to M.P. Charlesworth in *Trade-Routes and Commerce of the Roman Empire*, Roman business people had journeyed to Ireland and traveled to the edge of the Baltic Sea, made contact with the Scythians of the Tauric Chersonese, conducted transactions with the Chinese traders beyond the lonely Stone Tower of Tashkurgan, traded in the markets of India, and exchanged goods with the Aethiopians.

Unlike modern wholesalers, these early traders seldom specialized. They left Rome carrying whatever commodity they thought would be in demand elsewhere and traded it in some distant market for another product that could be expected to yield a profit in Rome or could be traded elsewhere for yet another product. Trade continued in much the same fashion for centuries. Slave traders in the eighteenth century operated in a similar way, buying stocks of inexpensive cloth and jewelry in England, exchanging it for slaves in Africa, reselling those slaves at a substantial profit in the Americas, then buying cotton and other goods for resale in the home market at even greater profits.

Although all contemporary trading professions descended from these early merchants, those that most closely resembled them, according to James E. Vance, Jr. in *The Merchant's World: The Geography of Wholesaling*, were the wholesalers. Wholesaling was the driving force behind the expansion of the mercantile economy, opening up new continents and pushing into frontier areas. Not surprisingly, the art of wholesaling was perfected in the new nations of North America. Faced with scattered, thinly spread populations, yet desiring to achieve a standard of living comparable to that enjoyed by their European brethren, North Americans organized an efficient, large-scale wholesale trading system that Vance ranked among the outstanding accomplishments of the North Americans during the nineteenth century. This system was nonexistent in Europe, where an increased demand for specialized products prior to the Industrial Revolution was largely met by a rise in the numbers of local artisans. North America's different conditions led instead to an expansion of trade.

Relatively large middle classes of petty merchants, small manufacturers, and professionals quickly rose to meet the demands of frontiersmen for new products. These merchants shipped goods to the interior and often settled branches of the family close to the frontier to ensure that trade was efficient and profitable.

During the Industrial Revolution, the wholesaling that had risen out of conditions peculiar to North America became an economic necessity for all industrializing nations. Production was highly concentrated. Quantities of manufactured goods needed far surpassed the levels achieved by the small manufacturers and artisans of the past. Demand, on the other hand, was dispersed throughout the nation, even throughout the world. Inevitably, wholesalers sprang up in England, Germany, and France, as well as in North America, to meet the demands of consumers for the products of the new age. With the proliferation of goods, specialization emerged and modern wholesaling was born.

Wholesaling was an essential component of the industrial economy. Wholesalers linked buyers and sellers, adding economic value through efficient performance of selling and physical distribution. By selling efficiently, wholesalers made it possible for even small manufacturers to reach out to customers and helped all manufacturers to reach more distant markets. As the link between producer and customer, wholesalers were best equipped to perform many crucial marketing functions such as new product introduction, in-store merchandising, sales support, order taking and processing, customer service, training, returns processing, and problem solving. Other valuable services the wholesaler could provide included local stocking, consolidated shipments with the orders of many suppliers, and shorter delivery times. All of these factors placed enormous power in the hands of the wholesaler—power that helped the industry grow rapidly, often at a rate that exceeded overall national economic and population growth rates. They also prompted a growing movement towards integration and consolidation, a movement well underway by the mid-twentieth century as successful regional wholesalers expanded their reach, acquired other wholesalers, and built stronger ties with manufacturers and retail outlets.

Since 1970, the wholesale industry continued to expand more rapidly than the overall economy. Canadian statistics show that annual growth in the wholesale portion of the gross domestic product (GDP) in constant 1986 dollars averaged 4.5 percent per year from 1971 to 1981, compared to 3.8 percent for the Canadian economy as a whole. The first real setback for wholesalers did not come until the 1981-1982 recession when sales, employment, and the number of establishments declined relative to the previous year's levels. To survive the recession, many wholesalers restructured, dropped marginal product lines,

reduced staff, and shut down warehouses. Consolidation intensified as larger firms ate up smaller ones.

This restructuring made wholesalers even more competitive during the boom years of the mid-1980s. Growth in wholesale trade accelerated at an annual average of 8.6 percent in Canada. This was compared to 4.3 percent for the Canadian economy as a whole. By 1988, the Canadian wholesale industry's share of their total GDP had increased to 5.5 percent—a rate of growth matched in most other leading economies. Growth slowed at the end of the decade but continued at better than 2 percent through 1994. During the 1980s, the industry also increased capital investments. Real expenditure increases by wholesalers in Canada, for example, were 22 percent in 1983 and 25 percent in 1984. Most of these investments were aimed at improving the efficiency and quality of customer services; they also went into machinery and equipment purchases, such as computer technology. Overall real capital expenditures declined in 1985 but continued to increase through the remainder of the decade.

With the onset of the recession at the end of the 1980s, expenditures again fell while mergers, consolidations, and restructuring once again increased. From 1987 to 1993, the number of U.S. wholesaling firms declined from 364,000 to only 280,000, a 25 percent drop. Wholesale companies suffered not only from reduced overall demand, but also from increasing competition from alternative channels of distribution such as warehouse clubs and discount stores. These additional pressures may have accounted for the industry's accelerated adjustments and restructuring. By 1992, alternative channels of distribution—direct manufacturer-to-retailer sales, warehouse clubs, discount stores, and home center stores—accounted for 24 percent of the wholesale market.

In the mid-1990s the wholesale industry continued to play a vital role in global distribution. The U.S. industry alone posted sales of approximately US$2.3 trillion in 1996, up from US$2.2 trillion in 1995. In real terms, however, wholesalers had gained little ground since 1988, although low inflation rates had benefited the industry's growth. In 1997 the top 10 companies in the industry recorded combined sales of about US$136.3 billion.

Wholesalers started to adopt electronic data interchange (EDI) technology during this period. EDI is a standardized electronic transmission system that wholesalers use for orders, reports, and payments. While most large firms used EDI to some degree, the prohibitive cost of installing and operating an EDI system prevented widespread implementation of the technology by the industry's many small wholesalers. However, as new technology became less expensive in the late 1990s, smaller firms found themselves better able to afford the increasingly necessary upgrades.

The wholesale industry grew more customer oriented in the mid to late 1990s. However, many wholesale companies lacked the selection that customers wanted, so wholesalers providing complementary services began to collaborate, forming consortia to offer customers a wider array of products. Wholesale consortia allow customers the convenience and efficiency of doing business with just one supplier.

Studies in the United States showed that wholesalers, despite their low-tech portrayal at times, were on the vanguard of the technological revolution and grew at a faster rate than all other industries in the country. Between 1989 and 1994, the industry's sales grew by 15 percent, in contrast to the manufacturing and housing industries, which respectively expanded by 11.4 and 10.2 percent during the same period. The industry's implementation of technology for ordering, shipping, and inventory control allowed it to increase its output by 23 percent without expanding its employee ranks, according to *Business Week*.

Furthermore, using EDI, the industry successfully reduced its lead times, shipping its products to customers in shorter amounts of time. Wholesalers used methods such as frequent shipment, and just-in-time delivery or continuous replenishment arrangements to bring about these decreased lead times. With the advances in technology, manufacturers could track consumer tastes and preferences directly from the retailer's cash register. Customers could transmit an order directly to the supplier via fax or e-mail and have the goods delivered to their door the next day. At the same time, advances in production technology made it possible for manufacturers to develop short-run, customized production lines tailored specifically to the needs of a single customer. However, while the wholesale industry embraced technology, some of its clients were able to use technology to circumvent wholesalers. Local market knowledge, direct customer contact, and links with suppliers—all once privileges of the wholesaler—could now be achieved by retailers and manufacturers without the wholesaler's intervention.

Despite the industry's growth and its increased efficiency, wholesalers continued to face greater competition from alternative forms of distribution. The trend toward alternative channels of distribution appeared first in the United States but quickly spread to Canada. In Europe and Japan, where markets were more tradition-bound and strictly regulated, these new developments had less impact on the industry. Nevertheless, even in Japan, discount stores and warehouse clubs made rapid gains due to loosening regulations and the growing demand of consumers for prices that better reflected the strength of

the yen in the early to mid-1990s. While Japan's prices had always been well above world averages, the rising yen exacerbated these differences—differences that were painfully obvious to the increasing numbers of Japanese traveling overseas.

Direct manufacturer-to-retail arrangements constituted the most formidable challenge to the industry in the mid to late 1990s. These arrangements usually took the form of strategic alliances between manufacturers and major retail chain stores, warehouse clubs, discount stores, and home center stores. Other alternative channels included mail order, catalog sales, and direct sales from manufacturer to industrial user or from retailer to industrial users.

Product lines sold through alternative distribution channels included consumer durables such as sports equipment, toys, jewelry, furniture, and electrical appliances, as well as nondurables such as clothing. Large retail chains and club stores with direct links to suppliers were another major source of competition for wholesalers, particularly smaller firms. The rapid expansion of superstores. such as Wal-Mart, Kmart, and Target. drained business from many independent retailers and convenience stores, forcing them to close down and taking away the livelihood of local wholesalers. These superstores had the buying power to negotiate directly with manufacturers and eliminate the need for the wholesale intermediary.

Another factor contributing to the erosion of the wholesaler's position within the supply chain was the deregulation and increased efficiency of the transportation industry. Deregulation reduced costs, while new computer technologies facilitated precise tracking and scheduling, as well as order taking and processing. With shipping companies like United Parcel Service guaranteeing delivery anywhere in the world within 48 hours, suppliers could easily afford to bypass distributors and ship directly to customers. Furthermore, technological advances made it possible for customers to enter orders via electronic data interchange, eliminating the need for the distributor to take orders. Freight consolidation software and sophisticated new materials handling systems reduced the need for local stocking.

Trade accords, such as the North American Free Trade Agreement (NAFTA) and the General Agreement on Tariffs and Trade (GATT), offered wholesalers the possibility of expanding more rapidly into new markets. These agreements called for the gradual reduction and ultimate elimination of tariffs and other trade barriers on a plethora of goods by the early years of the first decade of the 2000s. Wholesalers, especially large ones, viewed these accords as avenues for compensating for lost market share domestically. For example, Canadian wholesalers looked forward to access to the huge U.S. market, while U.S. wholesalers positioned themselves for expansion into Mexico and Canada.

GATT, by reducing restrictions on trade and business in many countries, including the European Union, the United States, and Japan, facilitated increased efficiency of existing foreign affiliates and made it easier to establish new ones. Competitive wholesalers operating in this new international economic environment were presented with a wide range of opportunities to increase their market share. By investing in newer technologies and opening export markets, successful wholesalers could strengthen their position and institute the additional value-added services needed to fend off the challenge posed by the alternative distribution channels.

Globalization was a key force in wholesale trade during the late 1990s. By 1998, roughly 20 percent of sales reported by U.S. merchant wholesalers were attributed to products manufactured internationally. Some analysts expected international goods to account for nearly 30 percent of U.S. merchant wholesaler sales by 2003. As the industry grew increasingly global, wholesalers began to focus on reducing costs and improving efficiency, turning to new technology to enhance inventory management. Wholesalers implemented warehouse automation, bar code scanning, and other data collection and identification technologies during the late 1990s to achieve these ends. To improve inventory management, many wholesalers relied on integrated supply: they owned and managed inventories at their customers' facilities. The integrated wholesaler/vendor supply market was forecast to reach US$11 billion by the early years of the first decade of the 2000s, compared to US$700 million in 1994, according to the *U.S. Industry and Trade Outlook.*

U.S. companies began to pursue global expansion via acquisitions and mergers in the late 1990s. In 1998 U.S. wholesalers completed 86 international deals, according to *Mergers & Acquisitions.* Avnet Inc., a leading U.S.-based electronics distributor, made several international acquisitions in the late 1990s, including electronics components distributor Eurotronics B.V. On the domestic front, the firm also purchased Marshall Industries, another leading North American electronics distributor in October 1999. Bolstered by its new holdings, Avnet usurped Arrow Electronics in 2000 as the largest electronics distributor in North America.

Several noteworthy deals also took place among U.S. pharmaceutical suppliers in the early years of the first decade of the 2000s. For example, Cardinal Health Inc., the second largest drug wholesaler in the United States, paid US$2.1 billion for Bindley Western Drug Co., the fifth largest industry player, in 2001. A few months after that deal was completed, Bergen Brunswig and AmeriSource merged in a US$7 billion deal to form Amerisource Bergen, then the largest U.S. drug wholesaler with US$35 billion in annual revenues and a 29 percent share of the drug distribution market. When the deals were complete, the firms began reducing their number of distribution centers in an effort to streamline operations and cut expenses.

Wholesalers remained optimistic about doing business in China at the turn of the century. China began to open its market up to wholesale enterprises in the late 1990s with the launching of the country's first distribution center. Not only did this benefit domestic distributors, it also boded well for foreign investors trying to gain access to China's market, according to *Nikkei Weekly.* Japanese companies in particular were optimistic about the wholesale distribution center because they had found it difficult to obtain wholesale licenses in the past. China's entrance into the World Trade Organization in 2001 promised further opportunities to international wholesalers looking to expand into Asia.

CURRENT CONDITIONS

By 2007, the wholesale industry was valued at US$4.2 trillion, nearly a 50 percent increase from 2003's US$2.9 trillion. The consolidation that began at the end of the twentieth century continued throughout the first decade of the twenty-first century, largely due to globalization, e-commerce, and cost issues. However, a newer trend was for smaller, more regional companies to merge, in order to claim and serve a particular niche, rather than to compete against the huge corporations. Wholesalers offer their customers flexibility, fast response, consistent service, as well as local availability. This relationship creates an environment that allows wholesale distribution to be the most significant channel to market for manufacturers as well as the most important part in the supply chain to customers. Because of this, overall employment was expected to remain healthy. According to the Bureau of Labor Statistics, employment for the wholesale industry as a whole was projected to rise 11 percent between 2002 and 2012. According to the *National Association of Wholesaler-Distributors,* the industry employs about 1 out of 20 private sector workers throughout the U.S. In fact, studies show that the wholesale distribution industry has contributed more than 25 percent of the U.S. economy's total productivity gains over the past 15 years. Total employment in the industry grew in 2007 for the fourth consecutive year, to 5.2 million within the U.S.

Certain segments of the wholesaling industry appeared ripe for consolidation in the early 2000s. For example, the largest 250 industrial distributors in the United States held only a 15 percent share of the industrial distribution market there in 2001, according to

Industrial Distribution. Many analysts believed this market fragmentation would likely prompt future mergers and acquisitions as the leading players sought to increase their market share. While small firms able to offer specialized services would likely survive, analysts believed midsized players would eventually be squeezed out of the market, many via buyouts by industry leaders.

In addition, e-commerce was no longer seen as a threat to the industry. Instead, it was considered to be a useful tool. For example, Pembroke Consulting forecast that by 2008, the wholesale industry would attribute one-third of annual revenues to online orders. On the positive side, customers would more frequently take some of the work on themselves, because they would be able to do more research online. This self-education would better prepare them to buy, which would reduce both cost and hassle for the wholesaler. Prices also would stabilize as a result. On the negative side, an informed consumer can be a demanding and inflexible consumer. Customers in various market segments were expected to use their research to bypass the wholesaler entirely and go straight to the manufacturers.

In 2004, the wholesale trade in Canada had total sales in excess of US$355 billion in 2004, with food accounting for 17 percent of the total, motor vehicles 16 percent, and machinery and equipment 9 percent. In the United States, 2004 merchant wholesale sales were valued at US$3.34 trillion, with food accounting for 12.4 percent, pharmaceuticals and sundries at 9 percent, and professional and commercial equipment at 8.7 percent.

In China, as in many other developing nations, the wholesale distribution system remained extremely fragmented. Despite the country's huge potential consumer base and the increasing amount of foreign investment, wholesale markets are divided up on a regional basis, with about 60 percent of the wholesalers operating in all markets being state-owned. By 2004, these markets were still dominated by the traditional booth method of trading whereby prices were determined over the counter and so did not always reflect supply and demand relationships. The country also continued to use a cash payment method rather than payment through a central banking system as done in developed countries. China's wholesale industry was also plagued by a lack of standardization in terms of product distribution, leading to huge inefficiencies in manpower and waste in product.

The British clothing chain Primark dropped all three of its suppliers in Southern India after learning they subcontracted work to children. This move came after a TV station pulled "The Devil Wears Primark" from its schedules. The documentary was scheduled to expose low-cost high street fashion sources and prompt reform in many of the Indian clothing factories. Primark grew to become Britain's second largest clothing chain with discount fashions possible by sourcing out almost its entire range to low cost suppliers in Asia. Primark distanced itself from the questionable vendors. It also set up Primark Better Lives Foundation to provide financial assistance to organizations improving the lives of young people.

RESEARCH AND TECHNOLOGY

Research and development in the wholesale industry focused almost entirely on the development of computer-based systems to improve inventory control, communications, logistics, and overall efficiency. For wholesalers, however, technology was a dual-edged sword. While technology made it possible for wholesalers to streamline their operations, improve efficiency, and increase their overall competitiveness, it also made it possible for suppliers and customers to develop alternative channels of distribution that bypassed the wholesalers. A study co-sponsored by Canada's Ministry of Industry, Science and Technology found that the communications and wholesale industries were more likely than any other service industries to introduce computer-based technologies. Usage in the wholesale industry was above average in 24 of the 29 technologies examined, and wholesalers led the way in implementation of computerized order entry, computerized inventory control, and electronic data interchange.

Some industry analysts predicted that electronic commerce via the Internet would replace EDI, and that it might eventually even eliminate the need for traditional distribution companies. However, by the early years of the first decade of the 2000s, most experts had come to view Internet technology as another distribution tool. According to Richard Trombly in *Industrial Distribution*, "the birth of e-commerce brought with it the threat of disintermediation. Many experts predicted that distributors would be removed from the supply chain. For many reasons, this never came to pass. Like integrated supply, vendor managed inventory, catalog houses and retail competition, e-commerce is now just one of the facts of business for distributors."

Because wholesaling is such an information-intensive business, it is imperative that wholesalers implement the latest computer technology in order to compete successfully. From orders and invoices to stock-keeping units and freight bills, huge volumes of data flow through the industry. By taking advantage of information technology, including electronic commerce tools, wholesalers are better able to manage their operations, operate with lower inventory and fewer warehouse locations, and improve customer services.

Wholesalers who led the way in the implementation of sophisticated computer data processing, communication systems, and other innovations were the large wholesaling firms operating in the industrial and resource sectors, as well as the leading food distributors. With their close links to suppliers, these firms were more easily able to obtain the capital required for investment in leading-edge technology than their smaller rivals. An example of this technology is efficient consumer response (ECR), a just-in-time restocking system keyed to customer buying patterns. ECR required a significant investment in sophisticated scanning technology, and although it threatened to squeeze the wholesaling profits made on inventory stocked in warehouses, it was considered a necessary investment by the suppliers and customers who did business with wholesalers.

Although smaller companies were slower to enter the computer age, by the mid-1990s, declining costs and increasing capabilities made it easier for them to benefit from the new distribution technologies. More wholesalers in the United States, Canada, and elsewhere began to mechanize and automate their warehouse operations, use computers to improve inventory control, and coordinate just-in-time systems with manufacturers and customers. In the United States and Europe, some large wholesalers operated fully automated facilities by the late 1990s.

INDUSTRY LEADERS

In an industry that has more than a million companies operating worldwide, generates sales in excess of US$10 trillion, and handles every known product, leadership is invariably confined within specific product sectors. Within individual sectors, large companies dominate the market, often accounting for 50 percent or more of sales while representing 1 percent or less of the total number of companies active in the sector. The world's largest wholesale companies are primarily U.S. firms, the largest of which deal in groceries, information technology, and pharmaceuticals.

Ingram Micro. The largest wholesaler of information technology products in the world, Santa Ana, California-based Ingram Micro supplies 280,000 products to about 165,000 retailers throughout 150 countries globally. In the United States, the company was selling to such giants as OfficeMax, Office Depot, CompUSA, and Amazon.com. Products include desktop and laptop computers, monitors, printers, CD-ROM drives, storage devices, and other related merchandise. The firm buys its products from almost 1,400 suppliers, including such leading hardware and software manufacturers as IBM, Hewlett-Packard, Microsoft, Xerox, NEC/Mitsubishi, and Canon. Begun in California in 1979, the company grew to achieve its global position through a series of

acquisitions and mergers in North America, Europe, the Asia-Pacific and Latin America. In 2004, the company improved its position in the Asia-Pacific region substantially when it acquired Tech Pacific of Singapore, one of the area's largest technology distributors and the only IT distributer in Asia. In Australia, Ingram Micro is the largest computer distributer. Ingram reported sales of US$35.05 billion in 2008 and employed 15,000 people.

Writing for ARN News, Nadia Cameron revealed the inside story about Ingram's partnership with Intersell resulting in the launch of a Web-based license tracking tool to help resellers manager their software annuity business. The tool is called License Tracker and makes it possible for resellers to oversee software licenses from nine of Ingram's vendors. It is a welcome addition to the Intersell TechLink4U platform. Other platform applications include website building, marketing campaign and quoting. An exclusive arrangement was signed in 2006 between Ingram and Intersell. The Techlink4U platform was launched in October 2006. In 2007, they joined forces with Cisco, Intel, Microsoft and Level Platforms to create MSP, a group dedicated to education regarding managed services.

In May 2008, the management software systems firm RedPrairie stated Ingram was implementing its Workforce Management application to improve productivity and gain new capabilities with visibility into labor throughout distribution network. Ingram Senior Vice President Operations Terry Tysseland was enthusiastic about the decision due to RedPrarie's track record with others and the "rigorous" pilot trial where the solution turned out to be functionally rich with features for improved workforce productivity.

McKesson. McKesson Corporation, with sales of US$106.6 billion for 2009, is the largest wholesale distributor of pharmaceuticals, health and beauty products, and medical supplies in North America with a workforce of 32,000 people. By 2005, the company was distributing approximately one-third of all the pharmaceuticals in the United States, and was ranked fifteenth on the Fortune 500 listing. San Francisco-based McKesson distributes the products of more than 3,000 pharmaceutical manufacturers and medical-surgical supply developers to more than 25,000 pharmacies, and also distributes its products to 50,000 hospitals, health care clinics and physician practices. In 2005 the company's largest customer, Rite Aid Corporation, accounted for 7 percent of its sales, while in total, its top ten customers accounted for 49 percent. The company's Canadian subsidiary is the largest pharmaceutical distributor in Canada, and it also owned 49 percent of Mexico's leading distributor, Nadro.

Writing for *Bloomberg News,* Elizabeth Amon reported lawsuit suit news involving McKesson. According to Connecticut Attorney General, Richard Blumenthal, the company conspired with First DataBank to inflate average prices for pharmaceuticals. The complaint charged McKesson with manipulating the drug market and increasing its market share at the expense of taxpayers and consumers. Federal and state agencies used average wholesale prices when setting reimbursement rates for medicines. As a result, health care providers could increase profits by prescribing drugs supplied by McKesson. Blumenthal believed that millions of dollars were due to compensate for McKesson's actions. Company spokesperson Larry Kurtz, said McKesson would vigorously defend itself.

Franz Haniel (Celesio AG). In 2004, Franz Haniel & Cie. GmbH of Germany owned 60 percent of Europe's largest pharmaceutical distributor, Celesio AG. The company earned revenues of more than US$28.1 billion in fiscal year 2009. The acquisition of DocMorris, Germany's best known pharmacy brand, was a major one. The company announced a change in focus to target trading and services. In addition to wholesale, it also operates over 2,200 pharmaceutical retailers in seven countries. The Haniel Group has more than 46,000 employees and a presence in more than 14 countries.

AmerisourceBergen. AmerisourceBergen Corp. was created in August 2001 from the merger of Orange, California-based Bergen Brunswig and Valley Forge, Pennsylvania-based AmeriSource, two leading U.S. pharmaceutical distributors. The deal created an industry giant with sales of US$77.05 billion and just over 10,000 employees in 2009. AmerisourceBergen supplies approximately 25,000 health care facilities, pharmacies, and grocery stores with pharmaceuticals and related merchandise.

In the late 1990s, Bergen Brunswig had ranked among the world's top ten wholesalers with sales of US$11.6 billion. In 1998 Bergen Brunswig agreed to be purchased by rival Cardinal Health. However, concerns raised by the U.S. Federal Trade Commission (FTC) prompted Cardinal to rescind its offer. A similar deal between AmeriSource and McKesson was also nixed after the FTC raised regulatory issues.

SUPERVALU. SUPERVALU Inc., the world's third-largest food wholesaler in 2010, supplies 3,200 grocery retailers in the United States with the products of more than 500 manufacturers through the company's 24 distribution centers. For 2008, SUPERVALU reported sales of US$44 billion with over 192,000 employees. In the late 1990s, the Minneapolis-based firm helped its clients compete against chains by providing services in all phases of store operations, from accounting to choosing store locations. Besides distributing national and brand name products, it also manufactured its own line of products. The biggest threat to SUPERVALU was

not that its customers, mainly independent grocers, might set up their own distribution systems, but that they would fall victim to the big price-busting grocery chains. In response, the company expanded into retail in order to boost sales and generate more volume for its wholesaling business. The move into retail also was an effort to reduce SUPERVALU's reliance on the low-margin food wholesaling industry in which margins averaged 1 percent, compared to 5 percent for the retail food industry, which is also considered low-margin.

SUPERVALU is adding its own "Wild Harvest" brand of organic foods to the aisles of stores in its family. The line of moderately priced quality products may help people to think differently about organics. According to The Daily Green.com Web site, SUPERVALU Brand Manager Adam Graham was asked about tofu French fries. Graham wants customers seeking good tasting familiar products to find what they are looking for with the "Wild Harvest" line featuring 168 items. SUPERVALU hopes the line will also inspire people who never tried organics to do so.

School educators and students were thrilled to receive the 2008 SUPERVALU Best Kept School Award for their work with school grounds and wider community. Ballykeel Primary School excelled as the overall winner. Approximately 200 schools from across Northern Ireland entered the competition. Judges had been actively reviewing schools and their practices to discover the tidiest and most environmentally active schools since March 2008. BallyKeel, with 319 students, stood out with a scheme to grow fresh vegetables and provide summer bedding for elderly people in the community. In addition to a monetary prize, all category winners received a personalized sign and perpetual crystal trophy.

Idaho Statesman reporter Joe Estrella shared the news about SUPERVALU's announcement regarding plans to lay off 80 employees with its Finance department in Boise. Another 30 Finance employees were expected to be let go from the SUPERVALU Minneapolis Headquarters. Cognizant was contracted to handle outsourcing of accounts payable and vendor management operations to India. SUPERVALU announced its commitment to assist affected employees whether they moved to other company jobs and sites or left completely. The June 2008 announcement recalled a November 2007 announcement when 180 information technology jobs were target for outsourcing to India.

BIBLIOGRAPHY

Amon, Elizabeth. "McKesson, Halliburton, Siemens, REFCO, Merck in Court News." *Bloomberg News,* 30 May 2008. Available from www.bloomberg.com.

"Annual Benchmark Report for Wholesale Trade: January 1992 Through January 2005: A Detailed Summary for

Wholesale Sales, Inventories, and Purchases." *Current Business Reports,* U.S. Census Bureau, March 2005. Available from www.census.gov.

"Best Kept Award for Bally Keel PS." *Ballymena Times,* 17 June 2008.

Cameron, Nadia. "Ingram Launches Software License 6/Tracker." *ARN News,* 28 May 2008. Available from www.arn_net.com.

"Course is Set for Further Growth." Haniel, 28 April 2008. Available from www.haniel.com.

Draper, Deborah J., ed. *Business Rankings Annual.* Detroit: Thomson Gale, 2004.

Eyriey, Nick. "Forbidden Fruit." *Office Products International,* October 2003.

Fein, Adam J. "The Road to Opportunity in Wholesale Distribution," 2004. Available from www.naw.org.

Fein, Adam J. "The State of the Wholesale Distribution Industry," 2008. Available from www.naw.org.

"Hoover's Company Capsules." *Hoover's Online,* 2008. Available from www.hoovers.com.

"International Trade Statistics." World Trade Organization, 2003. Available from www.wto.org.

Lazich, Robert S., ed. *Market Share Reporter.* Detroit: Thomson Gale, 2004.

McMillan, Charles J. *The Japanese Industrial System.* Berlin: Walter de Gruyter, 1984.

"Organics Get More Mainstream." *The Daily Green,* 21 May 2008. Available from www.thedailygreen.com.

Parsley, William A. "A Tip of the Hat," National Association of Wholesaler- Distributors, 2004. Available from www.naw.org.

"Primark Sacks Child-Labour Wholesalers." 17 June 2008. Available from www.female_first.co.UK.

Robertson, Jack. "Payment Terms Remain Sticky Issue in China." *EBN,* 1 December 2003.

Smock, Douglas A. "Distributors: Times Are Changing." *Purchasing,* 6 May 2004.

Sullivan, Laurie. "Distribution." *EBN,* 7 July 2003.

"The Tenth Five-Year Plan of Retail and Wholesale Industry and its Development." *China Daily,* 2005. Available from bizchina.chinadaily.com.cn.

Trombly, Richard. "A Direct Threat." *Industrial Distribution,* March 2002. Available from www.manufacturing.net.

Truttman, Renee. "Ingram Micro Selects RedPrarie for Workforce Management Solution." ThomasNet News, 15 May 2008. Available from news.thomasnet.com.

U.S. Department of Labor, Bureau of Labor Statistics. "Wholesale Trade." *Career Guide to Industries,* 27 February 2004.

"Value-added Services Drive Distributor Sales." *Purchasing,* 15 April 2004.

Wholesale Trade. Statistics Canada, January 2002. Available from www.statcan.ca.

"Wholesalers Inventories Grew Faster in April Than Forecasters Expected." *The New York Times,* 7 June 2008. Available from www.nytimes.com.

TEXTILES, APPAREL, AND LEATHER

———————— ■ ————————

SIC 2300

APPAREL

NAICS CODE(S)

315. Usually from purchased textiles, apparel makers cut and assemble fabrics into all types of finished clothing. Footwear is not discussed here. For discussion of leather apparel, see **Leather Goods and Accessories,** and for more information on textile production, see **Textile Mills.**

INDUSTRY SNAPSHOT

The global apparel industry is one of the most important sectors of the worldwide economy in terms of financial investment, revenue generated, import and export trade, and employment. The apparel market represents a substantial area of consumer spending, but in the last decades of the twentieth century, there was a pronounced migration of its mass production from higher-wage industrial economies to lower cost labor markets in the developing world. In an effort to cut costs and increase revenue, from the mid-1990s into the 2010s, apparel manufacturers in industrial nations continued to seek countries with low-cost labor for production. Developing economies in Asia, Africa, and South America received the bulk of these production contracts. Simultaneously, apparel companies in developed economies began reducing their domestic workforces as a direct result of outsourcing labor to countries with no minimum wage pay scale and a large workforce from which to draw. Meanwhile, apparel firms that could not compete with low-cost manufacturers either merged with larger companies, diversified, or closed.

By 2007, the European Union was the world's largest textile exporter, followed by China, Hong Kong, the United States, Japan, South Korea, Taiwan, India, Turkey, and Pakistan. World trade in apparel was highly regulated through the late twentieth century, but the movement away from trade barriers in the 1990s and early 2000s profoundly affected the industry, paving the way—in the view of many analysts—for China to rapidly become the world's dominant player. In 2002, 70 percent of all growth in apparel imports to the United States came from China and Vietnam. According to the American Textile Manufacturers Institute (ATMI), China's share of the U.S. import market, averaging about nine percent in the 1990s when quotas were in effect, skyrocketed to 53 percent in 2003 after several categories of clothing were removed from quota requirements. This trend intensified after 2005, when remaining trade quotas expired. Indeed, by 2006, China had captured 65 percent of the global market in total apparel exports, with US$8,260.9 billion. The U.S. government reinstated the quotas on two categories of textile imports (body-supporting garments such as bras and synthetic filament fabric) from China in July 2005, after the two countries failed to reach an agreement following four rounds of talks in Beijing.

Due to various anti-sweatshop campaigns, many major apparel retailers and brand name manufacturers became increasingly aware that ensuring decent working conditions in production facilities could affect their reputation in the eyes of consumers as well as the corporate bottom line. Leading categories in the global apparel industry include outerwear; men's shirts; women's blouses and shirts; men's pants; and women's coats, jackets, suits, skirts, and vests. In 2007, a group of U.S. senators proposed Senate Bill 367, titled the Decent

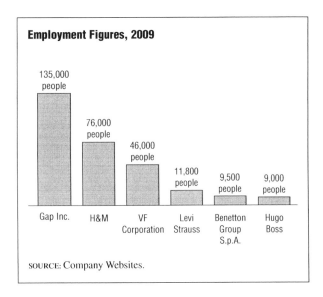

Employment Figures, 2009

135,000 people — Gap Inc.
76,000 people — H&M
46,000 people — VF Corporation
11,800 people — Levi Strauss
9,500 people — Benetton Group S.p.A.
9,000 people — Hugo Boss

SOURCE: Company Websites.

Working Conditions and Fair Competition Act, to ban the sale in the United States of imported goods made in sweatshop factories. This bill, sponsored by groups like the National Labor Committee and the United Steelworkers of America, was designed to prohibit the import, export, and sale of goods made in factories or workshops that violate core labor standards, as well as to prohibit the procurement of sweatshop goods by the United States government. As of the end of 2010, the bill had not become law.

ORGANIZATION AND STRUCTURE

The international apparel industry has three primary sectors: designers or jobbers, manufacturers, and retailers. Designers or jobbers develop apparel items by purchasing materials, designing concepts, developing prototypes, and hiring manufacturers. Manufacturers mass produce the apparel items based on the samples created by the designers. Finally, retailers market the clothing to the public. A host of different relationships and arrangements may exist among these three sectors. For example, a designer may produce only clothing concepts and prototypes then contract manufacturers to mass produce them. The designer might sell its products directly to a number of retailers. On the other hand, a designer might not only produce concepts and prototypes but also operate a retail or direct marketing business and therefore outsource only the manufacturing. Major companies may include divisions corresponding to all three of these sectors.

The International Apparel Federation (IAF) is the leading federation for apparel manufacturers, their associations, and the supporting industry with over 150,000 companies in more than 40 countries. It represents over 20 million employees around the world. The IAF is dedicated to the advancement of the apparel industry worldwide. In addition, leading apparel-producing countries have their own trade associations, many of which are also members of the IAF. One of the major associations is the American Apparel and Footwear Association (AAFA) that was established in 2000 through a merger of the American Apparel Manufacturing Association (AAMA) and the Footwear Industry America (FIA). By 2010, AAFA members accounted for more than US$225 billion in annual U.S. sales. Euratex, the European Apparel and Textile Confederation, works with European apparel producers to improve manufacturing and sales. Euratex's objective is to promote the interests of its members and to provide structure for the European Union, the largest world market for textile and clothing products.

Trade Agreements. To ensure fair trade around the world, the international community, including leading apparel producers, importers, and exporters, has implemented multilateral trade agreements. Two of the most important ones for the global apparel industry are the General Agreement on Tariffs and Trade (GATT) and the North American Free Trade Agreement (NAFTA). GATT, a renegotiation of an existing trade pact by the same name, resulted from the Uruguay Round talks from 1986 to 1994 and took effect in 1994. The agreement mandated the reduction and gradual elimination of tariffs that hinder foreign competition. In particular, GATT required the phasing out of textile and apparel import quotas by 2005. Further, GATT replaced the Multifiber Arrangement (MFA), which permitted quota restraints, with the Agreement on Textiles and Clothing (ATC). The ATC allows countries to select the quota categories they want to phase out. A Textiles Monitoring Body (TMB) oversees the implementation of commitments and prepares reports for major reviews pertaining to GATT, MFA, and NAFTA. The agreement also has provision for special treatment to certain categories of countries, such as those which have not been MFA members since 1986, new entrants, smaller suppliers, and least developed countries. GATT also established the World Trade Organization to serve as a permanent organization for the development of fair, systematic global trade policies.

Founded in 1995, the World Trade Organization (WTO) governs trade between nations participating in the Uruguay Round of Multilateral Trade Negotiations. The organization's objective is to liberalize trade and ensure stable and fair trading conditions for participating members. Based in Geneva, Switzerland, the WTO allows any country to challenge the trade policies of any other country before its tribunal, the Dispute Settlement Body. The WTO consists of 153 members, representing more than 97 percent of the world trade, including countries from all around the world as well as leading apparel producers such as the United States, the European Union, Japan, India, and Singapore. China joined the WTO in December 2001.

Implemented in 1994, the North American Free Trade Agreement (NAFTA) superseded the Canada-United States Free Trade Agreement, and gradually reduced and ultimately eliminated tariffs among North American countries, making way for substantially freer trade by 2005. NAFTA consists of agreements between the United States and Canada as well as bilateral agreements with Mexico. Besides phasing out tariffs, NAFTA also established temporary trade quotas to protect the participating countries from price dumping and other disruptive practices while the agreement was being implemented. As of 2007, NAFTA represented the largest trade bloc in the world. As an outgrowth of NAFTA, the North American Agreement on Labor Cooperation was established to improve working conditions in the U.S., Canada, and Mexico. The agreement provides oversight mechanisms to ensure that labor laws are being enforced in all three countries. As a last resort for non-enforcement of the labor law, the agreement provides the ability to invoke trade sanctions.

The African Growth and Opportunity Act (AGOA), which went into effect in 2000, created a special trading agreement between the United States and 41 sub-Saharan African nations that allowed these countries duty-free access to U.S. markets for several categories of consumer goods, including apparel. Initially set to expire in 2008, the United States Congress passed the AGOA Acceleration Act in 2004, which extended the legislation to 2015. There was a special apparel provision, which permitted lesser-developed nations to employ foreign fabric in the garment exports, which was to expire in 2007. However, it was extended through 2012. As a result of AGOA, U.S. exports of clothing from sub-Saharan Africa reached over US$17 million in goods in 2008, and the U.S. imported US$81.4 million in favor of the AGOA countries.

Changes in the Industry. By the mid-1990s, new factors began to influence the success of clothing manufacturers. Producers contended that worker productivity does not solely determine a company's competitiveness. Instead, according to *WWD,* competitiveness is determined by the overall productivity and efficiency of the company. Therefore, industry observers expected to see significant restructuring in the apparel industry, including the implementation of information technology, in order to achieve this kind of productivity.

Manufacturers in the early 2000s also noted changes in consumer preferences in economically developed regions such as the United States, the European Union,

and Japan, where consumers demanded value and quality instead of the lowest price or a particular brand, as they did in previous decades. Even in developing markets, brand loyalty had weakened, as consumers were exposed to an array of competing brands. In addition, apparel makers found that the most stable demand for products around the world was for high-priced luxury and fashion items. Analysts recommended that producers discontinue the practice of manufacturing clothing seasonally and produce it instead by the product category.

Moreover, manufacturers in high-wage economies, including France, Germany, the United States, and Japan, continued to outsource much of their production of apparel items from their domestic market to lower-wage economies in developing countries with no minimum wage legislation and an eager workforce. France depended on manufacturers in Spain and North Africa, while Germany outsourced to Eastern Europe and Turkey for lower-cost production. In addition to Latin America, the United States relied on countries across the globe, such as India and Singapore, for low-wage manufacturing. Finally, Japan contracted manufacturers in developing Asian countries. Since investment in apparel manufacturing equipment remained small relative to other industries, apparel firms could shift production from country to country with little investment.

Another trend among clothing manufacturers was the formation of alliances among the countries involved in the apparel production process. This trend broke with earlier patterns of going from economy to economy in search of the lowest production costs. Such alliances were intended to create a stronger bond between the apparel firms and the countries that manufacture the clothing.

Besides internationalizing production, apparel firms in industrial countries sought to expand cross-border trade of their goods. This was necessary as the markets matured in many of the major apparel-producing countries, leaving them with few available channels of expansion. Consequently, apparel firms from the United States, France, Germany, Italy, Japan, and other maturing countries started to market their products in places such as South Korea, Russia, and Turkey, as well as South America.

At the start of the twenty-first century, apparel manufacturers and retailers were struggling with a changing global economy and looking at strategies such as licensing, consolidation, and global expansion to stay afloat. Leading U.S. department store chains Bradlees and Montgomery Ward both went out of business in 2000, and U.S. clothing manufacturers C.L. Fashions and Bugle Boy shut down as well. J.C. Penney Company was forced to close a number of its stores due to declining sales, and Marks and Spencer, the largest apparel retailer in the United Kingdom, experienced a significant decrease in profits. Retailers looking to expand included Sweden's H&M (Hennes & Mauritz), which in 2009 had about 2,000 stores in 37 countries. Japan's Fast Retailing, with (as of 2010) 808 stores in Japan, and 136 stores in foreign markets, has been expanding into the United States, United Kingdom, and China. Designers hit with the high cost of manufacturing were looking at ways to survive through licensing strategies. Mossimo avoided bankruptcy when it signed a three-year, US$1 billion agreement with Target. Polo Ralph Lauren, Calvin Klein, and Giorgio Armani, along with other designers, cut back on licensing agreements in hopes of attaining higher quality assurance and a faster product turnaround.

The apparel industry continued to face the problem of clothing producers' reliance on sweatshop labor. Sweatshops force employees, including children, to work long hours for low wages and to endure unsafe working conditions. While sweatshop conditions are often thought only to exist in developing countries, they also occur in major industrial nations such as the United States. Developing Asian countries such as the Philippines, Malaysia, Thailand, and Vietnam also contain sweatshops. Some of the operations deceive Western apparel firms by having front businesses and coercing employees to remain silent. In 1998, a number of major apparel firms in the United States and nongovernment organization (NGO) participants in the Apparel Industry Partnership put forth a code of conduct through the Fair Labor Association to monitor and certify companies that meet its standards. The Netherlands' Clean Clothes Campaign, the United Kingdom's Ethical Trading Initiative, and Australia's Fair Wear campaign were among other global initiatives established to help bring attention to and end substandard labor practices in the garment industry.

CURRENT CONDITIONS

The textile and apparel industry was becoming more and more global in the mid- to late 2000s. India and China were seeing an exceptional number of fashion designers open new stores in their countries. Other countries whose textile and apparel industries were picking up included Egypt and Israel, where an agreement made with the United States in 2004 allowed finished products manufactured in specific regions in Egypt duty-free access to the U.S. market. According to *WWD,* Israeli exports of apparel-related items to Egypt, including woven and knitted fabric, packing materials, and chemicals for washing and dyeing, increased by more than 300 percent to about US$93 million in

2005, compared to less than US$30 million in 2004. The textile industry was already an important part of the Egyptian economy, and as of 2009, it accounted for 25 percent of the country's total industry and 30 percent of all jobs. Egypt exports an average of 305,000 tons of cloth and garments annually, 80 percent of which goes to the United States (US$876 million), and 20 percent of which goes to the European Union and Arab countries (US$223 million).

By the late 2000s, the largest apparel manufacturers and exporters were countries primarily from the Asia-Pacific region, which included China, Hong Kong, Philippines, Malaysia, Indonesia, Bangladesh, Sri Lanka, Pakistan, Thailand, and India. The total global apparel industry revenue was US$1,252.8 billion. The Asia Pacific region constituted the largest amount of production and trade worldwide, 35.40 percent. Europe represented 29.40 percent, the United States represented 22.3 percent, and the rest of the world 12.9 percent. China had captured 65 percent of the global market in terms of apparel exports with over US$8.2 billion. In 2009, U.S. spending on clothing and shoes reached US$326 billion.

RESEARCH AND TECHNOLOGY

With government and industry funding, apparel manufacturers and retailers around the world, but especially in the United States, Japan, and the United Kingdom, have researched ways of developing communications and network systems to improve contact between apparel customers and manufacturers. The goals of the research are to track consumer trends more carefully and to offer consumers custom-tailored garments in a short amount of time. The apparel industry has short product life cycles, tremendous product variety and unpredictable demand, and long and inflexible supply processes. Some of its major contributors are significant consolidation in retail, increasing use of electronic commerce, and wholesale trade.

In addition to developing communications networks, designers and manufacturers began to implement computer-aided design software into the production process in order to produce fast, accurate clothing designs. Also, to increase productivity and to avoid relying on sweatshops for low-cost production, manufacturers invested more in plant automation. In the mid-1990s, researchers sought to create sensors to enable automated cutting and sewing as well as machinery to perform intricate weaving and sewing. Moreover, developers also moved to integrate all aspects of the apparel production process into a cohesive and systematic computer-integrated manufacturing program as opposed to separate applications for design, manufacturing, and marketing. Laser technology was also being used for finishing work, including appliqués, labels, badges, and other types of decoration.

The move toward e-tailing, or selling on the Internet, gave new life to many industries, and the garment industry was no exception. Online apparel sales continued to increase. Another technological advance affecting the industry was the virtual dressing room. Clothing buyers could use a virtual model, custom built to their specifications, to try on an outfit and then make their purchase with a touch of a button.

INDUSTRY LEADERS

Levi Strauss & Co. Based in San Francisco, Levi Strauss (founded in 1853) was the number one manufacturer of brand name apparel in the world. With a market presence in more than 110 countries was organized into three regional divisions: Americas, Europe, and Asia Pacific. The company has sold jeans and sportswear under the brand names of Levi's, Levi Strauss Signature, Denizen, and Dockers. In 2009, approximately 50 percent of its revenue came from outside the United States. Its goal in the next decade was to expand the brands in China, India, Russia, and Brazil. In 2008, company revenue was US$4.303 billion, with 11,400 employees worldwide. Major competition came from VF, Gap, and Tommy Hilfiger.

VF Corp. With about 27 percent of the U.S. market, VF Corporation was the number one jeans manufacturer in the world. Its jeans brand names include Wrangler, Rider, Lee, and Rustler. Other apparel lines include Jansport, Nautica, Eagle Creek, Vans, and North Face. In 2009, VF acquired the Splendid and Ella Moss brands. Though most of its sales came from jeans, the company also offered knitwear, outdoor gear, heavy-duty work clothes, children's clothing, and men's and women's clothing (VF sold its lingerie line to Fruit of the Loom in 2006). Sales in 2009 were US$7.2 million, and the company employed 46,600 people. That year, growth in Asia increased the company's revenue by 28 percent. VF Corp.'s primary competitors were Gap, Levi Strauss, and Sears.

Benetton Group S.p.A. This Italian company specialized in casual clothing for men, women, and children, which it sold in 120 countries. Benetton, which produced over 150 million apparel items annually, sold its wares through department stores and 6,000 franchised stores with the Benetton name, as well as company-owned and franchised megastores. Its brands include United Colors of Benetton, Sisley, and Playlife. The company also sold accessory items such as sunglasses, watches, and shoes. Sales for Benetton in 2009 reached 2,049 million euro,

and the company employed over 9,500 people. Major competition came from Gap, H&M, and Inditex.

Hugo Boss AG. Based in Germany, Hugo Boss was the key maker of designer executive wear in the early twenty-first-century. With sales in 110 countries, Hugo Boss owns 330 retail stores with over 1,000 stores owned by franchises around the world. The company designed and licensed its clothing, fragrances, and accessories through its namesake shops and other retail stores all over the world. Hugo Boss also made casual clothes and moved into the women's wear market. The company employed just over 9,000 workers in 2009. Total revenue in 2009 was 104.0 million euro.

Gap Inc. Based in San Francisco, The Gap ran 3,076 stores worldwide by 2009, and remains the largest specialty apparel retailer in the United States. Primarily in the United States, the company also has retail outlets in Japan, Germany, France, and Canada. The company's Gap stores specialize in casual clothes for both men and women. Other chains were Old Navy, Banana Republic, Piperlime, Athleta, babyGap, GapMaternity, and Gap-Kids. The company also added an intimate apparel brand called GapBody. The Gap employed 135,000 people in 2009. Revenue for 2009 totaled approximately US$14.5 billion.

H&M. Started in 1947, Sweden-based H&M (Hennes & Mauritz) designs and sells inexpensive but fashionable clothing for men, women, teenagers and children. By 2010, the majority of its clothing is manufactured in Asia and Europe, including China, Turkey, India, Bangladesh, and Egypt. By 2009, H&M operated about 2,000 stores in 37 countries with more than 76,000 employees. Sales were about SEK 118,300 million in 2009.

MAJOR COUNTRIES IN THE INDUSTRY

China. Since China began its open-up policy and reform in the late 1970s, its garment industry has grown at a rate of 15.7 percent annually. The output between 1990 and 1995 totaled 30 billion garment items, equaling the total for the previous 40 years. Since 1994, China has remained the largest producer and exporter of apparel worldwide. The total volume of exports makes up one-sixth of the world total. Apparel production in China totaled 670 million pieces in 1978. By 2000 this figure had risen to 11.6 billion, demonstrating a yearly increase of 14 percent. Exports of garments in 2000 totaled US$36.1 billion, 50 times the rate in 1978. By 2002, China had 45,000 garment businesses that produced more than 310 pieces of clothing every second, making a profit of US$60,000 every minute. China's exports of textiles and apparel were valued at US$1,252.8 billion in 2006.

United States. By the beginning of the twenty-first century, the United States retail industry was undergoing significant changes, with many retailers shutting down their businesses, filing for bankruptcy, closing unprofitable stores, and consolidating. Garment manufacturers were expected to feel a substantial impact from this trend, which was characterized by a reduction in sales due to the elimination of distributors and decreasing profits as failed retailers reduced inventory with heavy mark-downs.

According to the U.S. Department of Labor's 2009 survey of U.S. Consumer Unit Expenditures, the average annual apparel and services expenditure was 3.8 percent of the consumer's annual income, averaging US$1,881. However, consumer spending on clothing and shoes alone reached about US$326 billion in 2009, which, as a share of disposable personal income, was the lowest ever in U.S. history, at only 2.98 percent. Spending on clothing as a share of income has been on a steady decline for the last two decades, compared to 1950, when spending on clothing was 9 percent of income. As a direct result of increased global competition for imported clothing, advances in manufacturing technology, and increased worker productivity, clothing is less expensive both in inflation-adjusted prices and as a share of disposable income.

U.S. apparel retailers and catalogers increasingly established sales outlets overseas to sell their products. The largest export categories were home furnishings and men's outerwear. Men's and boys' trousers were the dominant products exported to Canada, Japan, and the European Community. Mexico was a major player in the growth of U.S. garment imports, with the United States taking advantage of quota and duty provisions allowed by the North American Free Trade Agreement (NAFTA). Over two-thirds of Mexican imports were made up of components that originated in the United States. On the other hand, Asian imports employed virtually no U.S. components.

European Union. The European Union (EU) includes key industry players such as France, Italy, Germany, and the United Kingdom—major producers and exporters and important importers of apparel items. In 2006, after enlargement to 27 member nations, the EU textile and apparel industry employed about 2.5 million people in about 220,000 enterprises. Textile and clothing turnover in 2006 was 190 billion euros (about US$262.5 billion).

Italy. In terms of employment, production, sales, and consumption, Italy was by far the largest player in

the EU apparel industry in the early to mid-2000s, according to a report published by the EU in 2004. Italy, however, has been impacted by the global financial crisis along with nearly every other country. In 2009, the Italian government created a US$2 billion fund to help support small to medium-sized companies in danger of closing due to the poor economy. A percentage of that is available to fashion houses which are major employers. The main support is a tax credit to ease the production of apparel samples and collections. There has been a slump in the demand for fashion, but the Italian government is committed to saving the endangered "Made in Italy" fashion sector and generates conditions to allow companies to be more competitive in international markets. In 2009, Italy reported a US$67.2 billion in revenue from the apparel industry.

France. France's apparel industry in 2008 employed just over 82,000 workers—a significant decrease from approximately 270,000 workers in the late 1990s. In 2001, apparel turnover was valued at US$15.8 billion; consumption that year, however, was about US$36.6 billion. Consequently, France had to import a large amount of clothing items to meet internal demand. France also was a key exporter of apparel products: between 1995 and 2001, France's export market increased 31 percent. In 2001, some 41 percent of France's clothing exports were to non-EU nations. By 2003, however, the French textile and apparel industry faced both increased competition from Asia and a decline in domestic consumer spending. Between 2002 and 2003, clothing and textile consumption in France dropped about 1 percent in value. According to the U.S. Commercial Service, total French textile and apparel imports to the U.S. amounted to US$11.89 billion in 2009, with exports reaching US$15.8 billion.

Germany. Germany's apparel industry faced declining sales in the late 1990s. The country's apparel manufacturers convened often to devise a way out of the industry's slump. Critics of the German industry attributed its lackluster performance to the industry's emphasis only on quality, which brought it success in the 1970s and 1980s but failed to win new customers or retain old ones in the 1990s. Failures were also cited at the retail level. Analysts called for greater commitment to customer satisfaction to pull the industry out of its quagmire. In addition, observers recommended more advertising and further foreign market penetration.

According to EU statistics, Germany represented the largest clothing and outerwear market in the European Union in 2009 with a total consumption of about 51 billion euros. Germans spend less than 5 percent of their disposable income on clothing. The German clothing industry is the second largest consumer industry there, exceeded by the food and beverage industry. In 2009, Germany was the third largest producer of apparel in the EU. According to the Goethe Institute, a slowdown in domestic spending affected the German apparel industry more than the rise in cheap imports. As a result, some German manufacturers turned to niche products, such as specialized socks for individuals suffering from some types of skin diseases, like athlete's foot. Designer fashions, too, became better established in the world market as leading German brands such as Hugo Boss, Willy Bogner, and Strenesse established themselves in the global fashion market. Men's wear is expected to become the most dynamic as more men become fashion-conscious. In 2008, the German textile and clothing industry recorded a decrease in production, turnover, and employment. Production decreased by 3.4 percent to 10.8 billion Euros with an 11.1 billion Euros in turnovers. In addition, the apparel industry reduced its workforce in 2008 by 4.6 percent to 65,155 employees.

United Kingdom. Another important market, the United Kingdom employed about 150,000 workers in the apparel industry in 2007. According to EU data, clothing and textile industries combined produced US$13.4 billion. Though Britain has not historically been a major export market for apparel, exports grew 44 percent from 1995 to 2001.

Market analysis company Key Note reported that Marks and Spencer, the United Kingdom's biggest single clothing retailer, shocked the industry in September 1999 with its announcement that it would stop sourcing the majority of its apparel from the United Kingdom and would terminate contracts with a number of key suppliers without notice. By the beginning of the twenty-first century, this decision had resulted in the closing of several large factories and job losses in the thousands. The high cost of labor and an inability to compete with lower-wage countries contributed to a bleak outlook for the UK apparel industry.

BIBLIOGRAPHY

"2009 Annual Report." VF Corporation. Available from http://www.vfc.com.

"2009 Annual Report." Levi Strauss. Available from http://www.levistrauss.com.

"Adapting to Shifting Trade Winds." *WWD*, 19 September 2006.

Clothing Expenditures: Share of Disposable Income 1929-2009; March 2010. Available from http://seekingalpha.com.

"Ethiopia: The Next Sourcing Hot-Spot?" *just-style.com*, 1 March 2007.

"Hoover's Company Capsules." *Hoover's Online*, 2007. Available from http://www.hoovers.com.

"Japan Looks to Revival of Exports." *WWD*, 20 March 2007.

Kaiser, Amanda, and Katherine Bowers. "Smaller World." *WWD*, 12 December 2006.

Tucker, Ross. "Duty Free Zones Spur Growth in Egypt." *WWD*, 12 December 2006.

U.S.: Senate Bill Bans Imported Sweatshop Goods." *just-style.com*, 24 January 2007.

SIC 2386, 3151

LEATHER GOODS AND ACCESSORIES

NAICS CODE(S)

315292, 315992. This segment of the broader global leather industry produces various forms of leather apparel, including gloves, jackets, vests, and hats, and miscellaneous accessories such as belts, purses, and bags.

INDUSTRY SNAPSHOT

The global leather apparel industry produces within two broad categories: light leather and heavy leather. The category of light leather usually refers to the tanned skins that come from smaller animals and reptiles, known simply as skins, while the heavy leather distinction refers to leather that comes from larger species of animals, often called hides. Most apparel and accessories crafted by this industry come in both light and heavy leather styles, with heavy generally being the more valuable form.

ORGANIZATION AND STRUCTURE

Trade Reforms. The 1990s saw important developments in the arena of world trade, including renewed emphasis on broadening the scope of liberalized trade. Two key trade agreements that had potential to rejuvenate the leather industry were concluded in the first half of the decade: the General Agreement on Tariffs and Trade (GATT) and the North American Free Trade Agreement (NAFTA). Both agreements eased market access to many of the world's leading economies, covering a wide range of merchandise. GATT stipulated a gradual phase-out of all protective tariffs and quotas with complete elimination by 2005.

In North America, NAFTA was passed in 1994. It also called for a gradual reciprocal phase-out of tariffs placed on leather exports and imports between Mexico and the United States. Concurrently, members of the European Union continued to make strides throughout the decade toward unifying their respective economies. This initiative culminated in the 1999 rollout of monetary union, or the Euro, among a majority of the EU member states. In the long term, Europe's economic unification

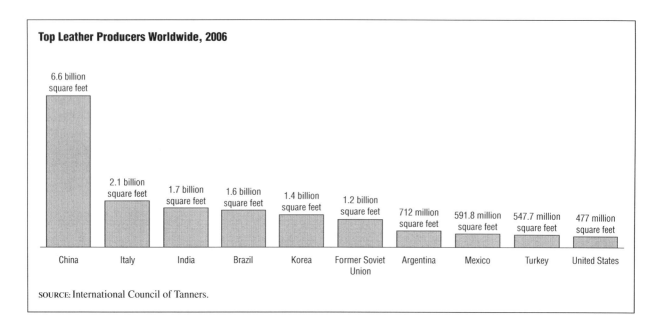

Top Leather Producers Worldwide, 2006

- China: 6.6 billion square feet
- Italy: 2.1 billion square feet
- India: 1.7 billion square feet
- Brazil: 1.6 billion square feet
- Korea: 1.4 billion square feet
- Former Soviet Union: 1.2 billion square feet
- Argentina: 712 million square feet
- Mexico: 591.8 million square feet
- Turkey: 547.7 million square feet
- United States: 477 million square feet

SOURCE: International Council of Tanners.

was expected to make market entry in its numerous distinct nations easier for exporters to the region. In addition, the establishment of the World Trade Organization (WTO) in 1995 provided nations with a cooperative forum for the creation and implementation of trade agreements and policies. Its membership grew to 147 nations in 2004, including many developing countries. The 1995 WTO Agreement on Agriculture promoted reforms centering on fair, market-oriented trading systems, detailing specific commitments to reduce support and protection in the areas of domestic support, export subsidies, and market access, and through the establishment of strengthened and more operationally effective GATT rules and disciplines.

In 2005, the United States and Australia entered into a Free Trade agreement that would eliminate tariffs between the two countries over a ten-year process. In 2003, leather goods (including footwear), accounted for .08 percent of the U.S. industrial exports to Australia, totaling US$9.5 million. Australia's exports to the United States totaled US$9.6 million that same year. The initial tariff elimination made 94 percent of the exports duty-free immediately, with the remaining 6 percent to be phased out over 10 years.

In 2009, the United States and the Republic of Korea entered into the U.S.-Korea Free Trade Agreement where, after a period of phasing out the tariffs, the industrial trade, which includes all leather goods imported and exported, will be 100 percent duty-free. In the 2006-2008 years, the leather products exported to Korea from the U.S. averaged US$16.1 million, while Korean exports to the U.S. averaged US$36.3 million annually.

The United States-Central America Free Trade Agreement of 2005 includes signatures from the United

States, Costa Rica, Dominican Republic, El Salvador, Guatemala, Honduras, and Nicaragua. Footwear, leather, and leather goods accounted for nearly two percent of the U.S. exports to Central America and the Dominican Republic in 2003, for a total of US$144 million. Central American and Dominican exports to the U.S. in 2003 were US$189 million, or 4.4 percent of the area's total industrial exports to the U.S. The Free Trade Agreement will phase out all tariffs in this sector within 10 years of the signing.

Production Process. The process of manufacturing gloves and leather apparel involves more or less the same number of major stages. Dependent upon their unique qualities, however, the number and types of operations performed within each stage can vary widely. The major manufacturing stages are tanning of hides and skins; finishing and dyeing; leather preparation; and garment making, including cutting, closing, stitching, and "laying off."

Types of Gloves and Mittens. Several types of light and heavy leathers enter into the production of gloves and mittens. Certain dress gloves, for instance, are produced from kidskins. Kidskins come from milk-fed baby goats that are raised in a delicate manner to protect against bruises and scratches, guaranteeing smoothness and a resilient quality uncommon to most gloves. Many are brush-dyed to ensure that the inside of the gloves remains white. Traditionally worn on formal and semiformal evening occasions, kidskin gloves enjoy a reputation as the aristocrats of glove wear.

Mocha leather is used for both men's and women's gloves, and when finished takes on the appearance of a fine silky velvet. This type of leather comes from black longhair sheep, native to Asia and Africa, whose skin is tanned with alum or formaldehyde. At first, mocha gloves, desired for their thickness and weight, were produced for men only. Later they were shaved, skived (a leather industry term referring to the operation of cutting leather more or less horizontally to reduce its thickness), or friezed (which refers to the process of removing the epidermis or grain layer by scraping with a hand-held knife and, later, by automated machine) to a fine thinness deemed acceptable for both men's and women's wear. Mocha leather is preferred for its durability, and, from a manufacturer's standpoint, for the ease with which it is dip-dyed or brush-dyed.

Suede gloves, of Swedish origin, come from kidskin or milk-fed baby lambs. Most are finished with a nap on the flesh side of their skin. Compared to other leathers, suede is the thinnest and most perishable of all. For glove manufacturers, suede is highly desired for its adaptability to all colors in brush-dyeing.

Capeskin leather, named for its Cape Town, South Africa, port of embarkment, is made from small African sheep. It possesses a sturdy, lightweight quality, with a very fine grain that when finished is soft to the touch and pliable. Buffing provides it with a glossy fashionable finish.

Pigskin leather made from wild Mexican or South American Peccary boars is the finest of all pigskin leathers. Domestic U.S. pigs, in comparison, are raised primarily for meat, and produce a hide fit only for luggage and upholstery. However, unregulated hunting depleted the numbers of Peccary boars, and the Mexican government eventually had to take steps to limit their killing. Peccary leather produces a soft glove, with a distinctive grain pattern owing to the pattern of its hair follicles arranged in detached lines of three.

Goatskin is tanned with sumac to produce a distinctive leather-grain glove. Goatskin gloves come from leather obtained from South America, South Africa, India, and Spain. Possessing strong and durable characteristics, goatskin is used mostly for men's gloves. Cabretta leather is obtained from a species of haired sheep native to certain provinces in Brazil. This type of skin was used mainly for shoe leather until the 1930s when it became available in glove form. Cabretta, close in appearance to Capeskin and very durable, is produced with a smooth, bright, glossy finish. Gloves made from lambskin leather come from young sheep that have grown beyond the milk-fed stage, having eaten grasses and grains that considerably change the character of their skin. Lambskin is not as fine, resilient, and durable as kidskin gloves or suede.

Buckskin, deerskin, reindeer, calfskin, bovine, and horsehide form the major group of heavy leathers used in glove making. As a group they are known for their durability, heaviness, warmth, and pliable nature. Tanned to be washable, they are mostly manufactured as men's work gloves. Heavy hides are also put to use in the production of leather apparel and handbags.

BACKGROUND AND DEVELOPMENT

The leather goods and accessories industry is highly dependent on overall economic health and consumer spending. From 1989 to 1999, the major regions of economic growth—the developed economies of the United States, Western Europe, and Japan—still had not resumed earlier levels of demand despite economic recoveries. Demand strengthened somewhat, beginning in 2000 and the first half of 2001, as markets for light leather began to recover. The global market for leather clothing and accessories was generally disappointing in 2002 and 2003, however, due to tepid economic growth and the impact of Severe Acute Respiratory Syndrome (SARS), which temporarily disrupted global trade. On the other hand, production of hides and skins increased, particularly in developing countries. Prices for hides and skins, however, declined through this period due primarily to falling demand in developed countries, which are the primary import markets for leather items.

One particular region exerting a significant downward impact on the production of light leather finished products consisted of the former planned economies of Eastern Europe and the new states that emerged from the breakup of the former Soviet Union. Throughout the region, economic conditions in general were in a state of prolonged decline or stagnation in the 1990s. Formerly producing a substantial amount of leather goods and accessories, these nations saw their production plummet 26.2 percent from 428.4 million square meters in 1991 to 316 million square meters in 1999 as government subsidies dried up and as local consumers were unable to sustain demand in the harsh transition to market economies.

Significant changes occurred in the industry after the 1990s. The world leather export market faced dramatic shifts with the shifting global economy during the first decade of the twenty-first century. Total global export value in the leather industry was valued at US$128 billion in 2005. Then it jumped to US$140.5 billion in 2006, US$157.5 billion in 2007, and US$168.8 billion in 2008, before taking a sizeable drop in 2009 to US$145.1 billion. The value of the import market for leather goods globally followed the same trend as the exports. The import market worldwide was valued at US$137.5 billion in 2005, US$150 billion in 2006,

US$166.8 billion in 2007, US$177.95 billion in 2008, and US$150.4 billion in 2009.

A pronounced trend that gained momentum beginning in the late 1950s was the shift in all leather producing activities from developed to developing economic regions. Not without periods of difficulty, much of this shift transpired due to a post-World War II climate of liberalized world trade jointly initiated by political authorities in the developed countries. Indicative of their export orientation, developing regions or countries such as Mexico, China, Korea, and Turkey, with a significant presence in the world leather industry, typically maintained a final leather product manufacturing capacity that exceeded domestic consumption. While many factors are responsible for these changes, environmental regulation was one of the major reasons for the migration of leather processing from the developed countries to developing countries. Between 1977 and 1996, global production of leather increased by 12.7 percent. Production in developing countries, especially of goat and sheep skins, grew 49.3 percent, while in developed countries it dropped by 7.5 percent. During the same period, developing countries' market share increased from 35.6 percent to 47.2 percent. Asia's production jumped some 94 percent during this period, while production in most developed countries declined. For example, North America's production dropped 12.1 percent while Europe's diminished by 16 percent from 1977 to 1996. Although production declined, net exports of bovine raw hides and skins from developed countries nearly tripled during the same period. Even in the area of leather-making machinery production—an activity once dominated solely by developed countries, particularly Italy and Germany—challenges emerged from countries such as China, India, South Korea, Taiwan, and Thailand.

Because developed regions account for a major share of finished leather product consumption met through developing country exports, the state of industry conditions in these markets determines the health of the industry overall. In particular, the direction of macroeconomic variables such as per capita income and consumer expenditure are critical. The uneven economic recoveries of Europe and the United States in the mid- to late 1990s showed signs of improved consumer spending; however, in Japan and parts of Southeast Asia, economic downturns quashed consumer purchase levels. For the developing countries involved in the export production of finished leather goods, this translated into an acute period of global competition manifested by increasing overcapacity, frequent exchange rate adjustments to stimulate trade, and worsening unemployment.

From 1999 to 2001, bovines yielded almost 11.0 billion square feet of light leather, of which 56 percent was used for shoes. Sheep and goat hides yielded 4.5 billion square feet of leather, most of which was used for clothing and accessories. According to the Food and Agricultural Organization of the United Nations (FAO), world production of bovine hides and skins increased by roughly 10 percent from the mid-1980s to 1999, with developing nations accounting for most of this growth. Asian nations, where tanning operations expanded significantly, produced more hides and skins than any other region by the early 2000s. World output of sheepskins rose by four percent during this period, while production of goatskins increased by more than 70 percent. In developing countries, goatskin output rose by about 76 percent, and it increased in developed countries by 15 percent.

In 2002, world bovine hide production was estimated by the FAO at a record 5.8 billion tons, an increase of two percent from 2001, when production fell by 1.7 percent. Production grew again in 2003, by an estimated 1.5 percent. The increase was considerably higher in developing countries, where higher rates of animal slaughter occurred. According to data from the International Council of Tanners, some 3.3 billion square feet of leather were used to make garments in 2000, which accounted for 18 percent of leather used throughout the world that year.

In general, international leather prices increased by 2 percent in 2000 and in the first part of 2001, reflecting larger exports from European countries that were still insufficient to match import demand. Exports also grew among developing nations, which positioned themselves for increasingly significant roles in international trade as tariffs and other restrictions began to be phased out according to GATT and World Trade Organization agreements. China's growing prominence in the market contributed to substantial export growth in the late 1990s and early 2000s. Between 1992 and 2000, U.S. imports of leather clothing from China increased by almost 300 percent. Chinese imports accounted for more than 95 percent of the entire American leather clothing market in 2000. Even though the shipments of leather products into the United States dropped considerably in the last half of 2000s, China has still maintained its prominence in the industry. Between July 2007 and July 2010, according to Homeland Security, shipments of leather items entering the United States fell from 16,196 shipments to 11,654 shipments in 2010. During this same period, China exported globally 65,980 shipments of leather goods.

Besides issues of international trade, productivity improvements were foremost in the strategies of developed country firms. The redeployment of manufacturing equipment and workstations into "rink" or horseshoe-shaped production processes, gained momentum in firms in developed countries. The rink system was structured around a teamwork concept so that instead of an operator being assigned to a specific task, a worker might become proficient in any number of operations while the team was also responsible for all final inspections. The United Nations Industrial Development Organization (UNIDO) reported "prodigious" per-operator productivity gains that jumped by 20 percent or more, a reduction in the amount of manufacturing floor space devoted to output time, higher quality products, and a marked decline in the product rejection rate.

On the political front, there was also speculation that the anti-cruelty to animals political sympathies championed by animal rights activists, mostly in Western Europe and the United States, might impart a dampening effect on leather consumption, as they had already on fur purchasing. Vegans and animal rights activists promote a full boycott on the use of all items made from leather, believing that the trend of wearing animal hides is unnecessary and cruel to animals. Groups such a PETA (People for the Ethical Treatment of Animals) call for boycotts and encourage the use of alternative man-made materials.

From the early 1980s through the early 2000s, distinct regional trends in light leathers manufacturing occurred, with the bovine light leather trade expanding around 9.4 percent per year sustained by a strong demand for leather and leather products. The most pronounced trend was noted by the progressive emergence of Asia's industry presence, surpassing Latin America as the principal exporting region of light bovine leather while remaining a primary supplier of sheep and goat leather among developing countries. In the same period, precipitous declines in the regions of the former planned economies of Eastern Europe and the Commonwealth of Independent States overshadowed the mild upturn in production levels in traditionally dominant Western Europe. Meanwhile, modest declines in North America were offset by a marked upward trend in South America.

The dramatic regional declines noted in the former planned economies of Eastern Europe and in the new states making up the Commonwealth of Independent States occurred in both the light and heavy leather industries. Of the two, light leather production was hit the hardest. The sharpest declines were recorded in regional leaders Poland, the Czech Republic, and Slovakia. On an annual basis, these three countries accounted for 40 to 50 percent of the region's light leather manufacturing. While their respective market shares remained fairly stable, actual production levels tapered sharply along with those of neighboring transition economies. To secure the confidence of international financial institutions, political authorities in

Poland and the Czech Republic pledged to combat inflationary tendencies through fiscal austerity and the pursuit of tight monetary policies that kept interest rates high.

Rise of Developing Economies. A pronounced trend that gained momentum after the late 1950s was the shift in all leather producing activities from developed to developing countries. Though not without periods of difficulty, much of this shift transpired due to a post-World War II climate of liberalized world trade jointly initiated and adhered to by political forces in the developed countries. As the production of light and heavy leather products in the Commonwealth of Independent States and Eastern Europe was expected to progress along a downward course, the continued ascendancy of the developing countries appeared more probable.

The rapid emergence of developing regions in the leather goods and accessories industry made some producers in developed regions nervous. In 1996, the European leather goods industries committee filed a complaint with the European Commission, which regulates trade and competition, about the massive influx of leather goods imported into the region from China, which had by 1999 become the world's largest leather-exporting country. Such complaints were likely to result in some form of anti-dumping legislation designed to protect Europe's manufacturers from the threat of over-importing after remaining trade quotas regulating the global clothing market were removed in 2005.

Indicative of their export orientation, developing countries with a significant presence in the world leather industry typically maintained a final leather product manufacturing capacity that exceeded domestic consumption. The shift of final leather products from developed to developing countries was connected to the labor-intensive nature of leather apparel production. Since both developed and developing countries faced more or less the same material and overhead costs, developing countries were able to produce with a substantial cost advantage because of comparatively low-wage labor. In more than a few instances, firms in developed countries chose to relocate parts or all of their final leather production process to developing nations. During years in which U.S. exports of leather apparel rose steadily, much of those exports included parts shipped to less developed countries, especially Mexico, for final assembly before shipment back into the United States for consumption. Similar developing country outward processing arrangements were a common practice undertaken by firms in the European Union.

CURRENT CONDITIONS

According to figures from the International Council of Tanners, the world's top leather producers through 2006 were China (6.6 billion square feet), Italy (2.1 billion square feet) and India (1.7 billion square feet), followed by Brazil (1.6 billion square feet), Korea (1.4 billion square feet), the former Soviet Union (1.2 billion square feet), Argentina (712 million square feet), Mexico (591.8 million square feet), Turkey (547.7 million square feet), and the United States (477 million square feet).

By the end of the 2000s, the major end use of all leather produced in the world was footwear, accounting for 52 percent (11.9 billion square feet) of worldwide leather use. Furniture was responsible for 14 percent, followed by automotive uses (10.2 percent), garments (10 percent), gloves (4.4 percent), and other leather products (9.4 percent).

RESEARCH AND TECHNOLOGY

Prior to the 1980s, the general trend in the manufacture of leather products centered on incremental refinements in the existing techniques to enhance productivity. Some of these included the strategic redeployment of machinery and workers to significantly reduce an item's output time and the introduction of labor-saving equipment such as automatic stackers and hide hoists. Many other techniques concentrated on research and product development devoted to leather processing with solvent tanning and the use of synthetic materials.

By the 1980s and 1990s, major technological developments swept through the leather products industry, making previous developments seem minor in comparison. In the leather preparation stage, one critical operation centered on a multipurpose machine known as the "drum." Made from wood, it is used for a wide variety of operations such as chemically removing hair from the hide or skin, coloring or dyeing, lubricating, and leather softening. Although in its outward appearance the subsequent drum looked much like its predecessors from the 1890s, it had been transformed at the close of twentieth century to a high-tech, precision-engineered piece of equipment inside. Powered by electromechanical means, the drum is equipped with complex process instrumentation, programmed and controlled by a microprocessor, and sometimes even linked to personal computers. The late-twentieth-century drum contained systems allowing for the quick discharge and re-circulation of leather processing liquors. Unlike earlier versions, it was constructed with pegs that tended to stretch and draw hides in a manner that positively enhanced the efficiency of chemical treatments. In the early 1990s, UNIDO estimated that more than 90 percent of global hide production was processed using the wooden drum. It also reported that newer alternative systems made from stainless steel and polymer were being used.

By the early 2000s, improvements in the tanning process made it possible to soften low-quality skins sufficiently to use them in high-quality garments. Stamping and printing technologies allowed manufacturers to make inexpensive skins resemble luxury materials such as snakeskin or alligator skin. Since, according to FTC labeling guidelines, any product made of animal hide can be labeled as genuine leather, these new technologies enabled producers to use the hide from any type of animal. Other developments in the tanning and preparations stages were in hide splitting, shaving, and drying operations. In through-feed splitting operations, a hide is inserted in one side of a machine and comes out on the opposite side in two layers. The splitting operation acts to cut the grain or top epidermis from the body of the skin, producing a porous quality that makes it more flexible for downstream processing. In former times, it could take up to four laborers to operate the splitting machine, but by the 1990s, the operation was performed by a continually sharpened band-knife. The introduction of microprocessor controls to this application made it easier to program and monitor for splitting thickness.

Shaving machines are activated using microprocessor controls to bring about a higher degree of accuracy, instantaneous change of thickness, and greater control over undesirable leather ribbing (once caused by shaving machine vibrations). One of the most critical operations performed in leather processing, leather drying is a balanced operation in which care has to be exercised to dispose of all excess water while still ensuring that the leather remains flexible and soft. Natural air-drying has been traditionally considered the best method; however, from a business standpoint it is very time consuming. Subsequently, factory air-flow drying came to be the standard method. In the mid-1980s, an energy-saving dehumidification drying process was developed in France that incorporated a controlled closed-circuit energy recovery system using heat pumps. Subsequent approaches to drying included the use of infrared radiation or microwave energy. A major advantage of microwave drying is that it evaporates water without raising the temperature of the leather, which may detract from its softness. When drying leathers, it is common to stretch or "toggle" them to prevent area loss. Previously a labor-intensive operation, labor-saving toggle machines were introduced in which hides are stacked horizontally to ensure membrane flexibility.

In the product development stage, advances in microprocessor technology affected leather cutting and stitching operations in developed countries. Traditionally, finished leather materials were cut manually. Swing beam presses were then introduced, later augmented by traveling head presses, through which layers of material were fed by conveyor under a computer-automated cutting head. Computer programs were later developed to determine the nesting of leather components in order to minimize material waste and to detect surface imperfections.

Microcomputer-controlled sewing machines were diffused throughout the developed final leather products industry in the 1980s, which led to significant labor savings. Sewing machines received different stitching instructions from preprogrammed data input devices while the operator's role consisted of simply loading, unloading, and initiating the stitching sequence. Programming was conducted either on a separate digitizing unit or on one attached to the machine to allow for direct input. Because they significantly reduced both the amount of required operator training time and the number of tasks previously performed, these new machines ushered in a period of pronounced skill loss in the labor force. Because of their higher capital intensity and productivity-enhancing impact, it was wondered whether they might stem the process of shifting final leather production processes to developing countries, which tend to rely more heavily on manual labor.

Ecological concerns also affect the world's leather industry. In developed countries, research efforts were directed to finding suitable replacements for chrome in tanning operations, and in leather processing and finishing operations, there was a move away from using solvent-based chemicals in favor of water-based alternatives. The passage of stringent environmental legislation in developed countries accelerated the search for environmentally friendly manufacturing processes. However, progress was slow, as escalating tariffs discouraged producers from investing in environmentally sustainable technologies, according to the World Trade Organization. Although no directly comparable data are available, the costs of compliance in developed countries generally were much higher than in developing countries. For instance, the cost of treating solid residues from processing hides and skins in developed countries could be as much as four times higher than in many developing countries because of tighter pollution limits, higher transportation and waste site costs, and higher labor costs. Tanning processes cause environmental problems by producing solid residue and large volumes of toxic effluent. The problem of correcting for environmental pollution has not been resolved as much as it has been displaced to developing countries where authorities—under pressure to attract and maintain foreign investment—have been reluctant to pass or enforce environmental legislation. However, the problems seem to be escalating among developing countries intent on being a part of the world leather trade industry while maintaining as high a profit margin as possible. In 2009, in Kanpur—the self-proclaimed "Leather City of the World"—pollution levels were so high that despite an industry crisis, the pollution control board decided to seal only 49 of its 404 high-polluting

tanneries. Then, in November 2009 it was discovered that one of Uganda's main leather producing companies was dumping its waste water in a wetland adjacent to Lake Victoria.

MAJOR COUNTRIES IN THE INDUSTRY

African Countries. African countries have 20 percent of the world's cattle, sheep and goats but produce only 14.9 percent on the world's hides and skins market. Their exports of hides and skins had fallen in the first half of the 2000s. At a time when other developing countries had substantially increased their share of the world footwear production in relation to already developed countries, African nations had only a modest increase. Import penetration of their domestic leather footwear markets by other developing countries is estimated at 73.3 percent. This huge gap between resources and production shows considerable potential of the African leather industry. Not only would this bring income to the trading economy in Africa, but becuse leather is a renewable source, it also would provide employment all along the production chain.

China and Korea. In 2006, world leather production was boosted by increases in China and the Republic of Korea. When expressed in terms of its regional market share in light leather, Asia's ascending status was clear. China ranked first in world production of leather, and Korea was fifth. China's export market also grew dramatically during the early to mid-2000s. Taking advantage of cheap labor and improved production technologies, China's leather industry was able to offer quality clothing at prices low enough to serve even moderate-income consumers. About half of China's leather garment exports to the United States in 2000 were made from pigskin, which is much cheaper to produce than most other types of leather but is relatively coarse. With advanced stamping and printing techniques, however, Chinese manufacturers were able to make relatively low-quality skins soft enough to be sewn into fashionable clothing. Indeed, prices became so attractive that, by 2000, leather apparel was increasingly seen by U.S. consumers as a mass-market product instead of a luxury item. From 1998 to 2006, the amount of leather production trade in China grew by more than 50 percent. However, between 2008 and 2010, China's market share had dropped by 2.24 percent.

Hong Kong has emerged in the last part of the 2000s into a leather production super power. Ranking right behind China, between October 2008 and October 2010, Hong Kong had over 46,870 shipments exported. While in 2010, Hong Kong's market share dropped 3.15 percent.

Italy. Italy was the dominant country in the European Union in the leather industry and ranked as the number-two leather producer in the world. In 2006, Italy produced 214.7 million square meters (66 percent) of Europe's leather. It was also the world's largest importer of bovine hides; 68 percent of the hides processed in Italy in 2005 were bovine. Of the leather produced in Italy in the mid-2000s, 46.7 percent was used for footwear, followed distantly by furniture upholstery (24.6 percent), leather goods (12.8 percent), garments and gloves (6.7 percent), car interiors (4.7 percent), and other uses (4.5 percent). A majority of the 168 million pounds of leather exported from Italy in 2005 went to Hong Kong. China was the second largest market for Italian leather exports, followed by Romania and Austria.

India. In 2006, India ranked third in the world in leather production, after China and Italy, and employed some 2.5 million people, about 30 percent of them women. A report by Exim Bank in India projected another one million jobs would be added in the industry by 2011. By 2005, annual production was valued at about US$4 billion, with exports earning about US$2.4 billion in 2005. Sixty-eight percent of leather exports were shipped to Europe, and 12 percent to the United States. Hong Kong and China were also big markets for Italian leather exports, and Russia was emerging as another important market. The ANCI reported a 54.2 percent growth in exports to Russia in 2006, amounting to US$107.9 million in goods.

Faced with increasing competition from cheaper markets, Indian leather companies hoped to increase their share of the American market by improving the quality of their products. By 2003, India was importing about 20 percent of its finished skins from high-quality producers in Italy, Portugal, and Africa. Producers were also upgrading manufacturing and finishing equipment. The Indian leather industry (including shoes) grew 17 percent in 2004. India expected to double the value of its leather exports by 2010.

India has the world's largest cattle population and the second largest livestock population. However, due to the predominance of the Hindu religion, in which cows are considered sacred, strict laws about slaughterhouses exist. In the past, the leather manufacturing industry was dominated by Muslims, although the journal reported this may change as others see the profitability of the business.

United States. Within North America, the United States led the region in light leather production by a small margin and was the fifth largest leather producer in the world. Because of expedited U.S. feedlot production, cattle grown in a relatively short time period yield a higher average weight per hide than most other countries. Many U.S. light leather apparel producers and glove and mitten manufacturers did not survive the competitive challenge posed by foreign imports. Many thus decided to relocate production to developing regions where labor costs were considerably lower. Even U.S. light leather tanners met their domestic demand for finished leather products by sourcing them overseas, mostly to South Korea and China.

According to the U.S. Census Bureau, total U.S. shipments of leather and allied products equaled US$5.3 billion in 2007, up from US$3.4 billion in 2004. California was the highest producing state, followed by Missouri and Texas. In 2000, the United States imported US$1.7 billion of leather apparel—a whopping 71 percent increase from the previous year. Handbags alone accounted for US$1.2 billion. Since 2000, leather apparel in the United States has been increasingly marketed to middle income consumers. Discount chains such as Target, Kmart, and Wal-Mart offer a range of products, including bomber jackets, skirts, jeans, and halter tops priced from US$39.99 to US$109.99.

According to U.S. International Trade Administration statistics, the United States exported US$78.9 million of leather clothing in 2004, an increase of 22.5 percent from the previous year. Top destinations were Japan, the United Kingdom, Italy, Canada, Mexico, and Germany. In addition, the country exported US$124.1 million of miscellaneous leather products, up 43.6 percent from 2003. U.S. imports of leather apparel, which declined by 13.5 percent in value from 2003 to 2004, still far surpassed exports at a total of US$1.197 billion. China was the leading supplier, followed by Italy and India. Imports of other leather products totaled US$390 million.

Russia. The leather industry in Russia experienced a 14 percent growth rate between 2002 and 2005, according to the European Commission. The value of the market in 2005 was reported at 125 million euros and output of finished leather at factories in Russia was growing. By 2006, Russia production was up to 1.2 billion square feet.

Brazil. Brazil's light leather production totals accounted for nearly all South America's market share by 2006. Because much of its final leather goods output was produced for export to developed countries, and its labor costs were on the rise, it remained unclear whether Brazil could maintain its advantage against lower labor cost countries such as China, Indonesia, and Vietnam. In terms of heavy leather global production, South America experienced significant growth. Brazil managed to continue as a major force despite some slippage. Rising demand for automobile upholstery accounted for a significant portion of Brazil's increase in leather output in the 2000s, and shoe manufacture also consumed much of

Brazil's leather. Nevertheless, the country exported US$3.5 million of leather apparel and accessories in 2003. By 2006, Brazil had risen to fourth place among leather producers globally.

BIBLIOGRAPHY

Foreman, Katya. "Europe's Hot Category: Leather Goods Brands in Retail Growth Push." *WWD*, 26 March 2007.

"Leather Statistics." International Council of Tanners, 2010. Available from http://www.tannerscouncilct.org.

"News." *Russian Leathernet*, 15 April 2007. Available from http://www.leathernet.ru.

Zargani, Luisa. "Russian, Japanese Buyers Drive Mipel." *WWD*, 2 April 2007.

SIC 2200

TEXTILE MILLS

NAICS CODE(S)

313. Textile mills produce a vast range of finished and intermediate textile products, but production centers on broadwoven fabrics from cotton, wool, and other natural and man-made fibers. These textiles are used in such diverse applications as clothing, household linens, furniture, and motor vehicle interiors. Certain industry firms also perform textile finishing by applying chemicals and processes to purchased fabrics. (See also **Apparel.**)

INDUSTRY SNAPSHOT

At the close of the first decade of the twenty-first century, the global textile industry was valued at approximately 157 billion pounds of textile fibers annually. However, the textile industry in the United States and other developed countries faced some severe challenges, requiring significant restructuring of manufacturing priorities and operations. From the 1980s to the late 1990s the international competitiveness of the textile industry in developed countries, where labor costs were higher than in the developing world, steadily improved more efficient machinery was introduced. However, this increased productivity that was a result of automation led to accelerating layoffs of textile workers and rapidly increasing mill closures throughout the decade, as fewer people were needed to produce the same—or even greater—volumes of goods.

In addition, the global financial crisis that began in late 2007 and the Asian crisis of 1997-1998 on the textile industry in developed countries continued to have a substantial impact. Although the price of Asian textiles fell significantly during the crises, developed countries were importing them in increasing numbers, contributing to a

decline in the textile industries in some developed countries, including the United States. In 2001 at least 100 U.S. textile mills closed and between 60,000 and 75,000 U.S. textile workers were laid off. The situation was even worse in 2003, when a total of 99,400 apparel and textile workers in the United States lost their jobs. By 2010, polyester fibers held a 47 percent market share, up from 22 percent in 1999. However, as some economists believed that the recession was beginning to subside in 2010, an annual growth rate of 3 percent in the textile fibers segment and 4 percent in the polyester fibers segment was projected through 2015. Polyester fibers' growth in the market share was at 22 percent in 1999 and 47 percent by 2010.

After heavily investing in costly new and more efficient technology and equipment, U.S. textile mills found it difficult to compete with the lower-priced textile imports from Asia in the early 2000s. In response, many U.S. mills shifted production to emphasize such non-apparel textiles as home furnishings and industrial textiles, reduced their workforces, merged with other companies, forged tighter links with apparel and other end-use manufacturers, sought opportunities to shift production to sites in the developing world, or closed their doors. Many U.S. textile mill centers that had been flourishing, especially in the South, were forced to diversify. Some sought opportunities in new manufacturing and service industries in order to re-hire laid off workers and start to grow again.

Despite the problems introduced by the Asian financial crisis Asia's textile business at the start of the new millennium was showing renewed strength. Asia, which was responsible for the vast majority of the world's broadwoven cotton milling, continued to shape the global textile industry. In particular, China remained a towering competitor. The burgeoning Chinese economy was a powerhouse in textile milling and supported thriving industries in textile machinery used in textile mills, as well as apparel, the biggest end market for milled textiles. China has been the world's largest producer of woven cotton textiles since the 1980s, a position that was strengthened by the Chinese economic boom that began in the 1990s. The Asian financial crisis of the late 1990s dampened China's intra-region trade but did not diminish the volume of its textile exports. When China joined the World Trade Organization in December 2001, its position as the dominant player in the international textile industry was further assured.

European textile manufacturers have adapted their fashion outlook after being "hammered" by their Asian competition. An article by Sally McGrane on July 3, 2008, in *Time* magazine described the "smart fabrics and interactive textiles" pioneered in the United States that were becoming part of the European market. For example, uniforms worn by firefighters look ordinary, but are made of high-tech fabrics that track the wearer's vital signs. The new uniforms can also provide GPS readings to indicate the wearer's location in a burning building. According to McGrane, the European Commission is spending US$63 million to develop the special materials, creating new market opportunities.

According to Euratex Research and Development (R&D) manager Lutz Walter, fitting applications to markets was increasingly important to the industry, although approval and pricing were critical considerations. For example, the high value in the medical field cannot be realized until devices are approved. That approval can take 10 years. The industry has to gauge the market carefully to determine a price for high-tech apparel, such as baby clothes that can detect sudden infant death syndrome, that will appeal to consumers while still making a profit for the companies. European Commission-funded teams have created some unique prototypes with limited commercial availability, including a tank top that could monitor cardiac patients.

Massachusetts-based Venture Development Corp. forecast that the approximately US$550 million of revenue in 2008 could double by 2010. The European clothing and textile industry was estimated to be US$326 billion.

ORGANIZATION AND STRUCTURE

Global Patterns of Production and Consumption. While China continued to be the world's largest producer of textiles in the early 2000s, Japan, the United States, and the European Union were the world's largest consumers of textile products. Textile mills around the globe produced fabric from either natural raw material fibers, such as cotton, wool, silk, and flax, or two principal types of manufactured fibers: artificial fibers (previously called cellulosic) and synthetic fibers (previously called non-cellulosic). Consumer demand for end-use products containing fabric significantly impacted intermediate levels and types of fabric production.

The textile milling and production process involves a variety of operations, including opening and cleaning, carding, spinning, weaving, knitting, and finishing. Textile mills purchase production machinery from textile machinery manufacturers that were historically responsible for introducing advanced machinery. Innovations in equipment, as in most industries, tends to save labor and to waste less material, creating significant reductions in unit costs.

Firms of all sizes in developed and developing countries alike produce broadwoven fabrics, which are woven on wide looms. In developed nations, the textile industry tends to be dualistic in nature, as a large number of small

and medium-sized firms produce a limited range of fabrics and account for a relatively small proportion of output, while a few large firms produce a wider range of fabrics and a disproportionate share of output. Whether a country is developed or developing, the textile industry in a particular country is shaped by such diverse factors as the complexity of products produced; available capital; the skill level, sophistication, and wages of workers; the degree of vertical integration; industry concentration levels in the country; the overall importance of the industry to the country's entire economy; and the country's degree of participation in the international market.

The Production Process. The production of textile fibers and fabrics is a multistage sequence involving opening and cleaning, carding, weaving, and wet processing. Firms that transform cotton fiber, for example, into broadwoven fabric employ a wide range of machines, equipment, and workers to perform a variety of operations. In addition to broadwoven fabrics, the textile industry produces weft, lace, and warp knit fabrics, mainly in circular form. The textile industry also comprises carpet and rug production as well as yarn-spinning mills and plants producing man-made fibers.

The production of cotton fabric is integral to the success of the textile industry worldwide and involves many of the same steps as the production of fabric from other fibers. First, opening-room machinery loosens cotton layers taken from bales of cotton and reduces them into smaller pieces before delivering the fiber to cleaning machines for further processing. If the cotton fibers are not properly selected or are imprecisely fed, production efficiency is reduced and quality suffers. In the second, or carding, stage, a machine called a "card" disentangles and collects the cotton fibers to prepare for the next phase, weaving. In the weaving phase, looms weave the cotton fibers into fabric. Finally, the fabric is subjected to a multi-step, wet-processing phase that involves preparation by separating the fabric from the loom and removing natural contaminants; dye is added to color the fabric; and finishing, with the addition of such enhancements as durable press, water repellency, stability, mothproofing, soil resistance, and flame-proofing.

Not all woven-cotton fabrics pass through the entire wet-processing chain. For instance, surgical goods undergo intensive preparation yet require no dyeing or finishing. Only the preparation and finishing steps are necessary for certain yarn-dyed goods. In general, the fabric's fiber content and intended end-use determine which wet-processing procedures the fabric will undergo.

Throughout many developed countries, electronic monitoring systems were implemented first on weaving machines but soon expanded to provide efficiency data broken down by department, shift, weaver and fixer sets, style sets, and machine levels. Because of the systems' memory capability, electronic monitoring systems eliminate the need to read pick clocks at the end of each shift. Moreover, system stops are recorded and classified within weft, warp, and mechanical categories, enabling managers and technicians to easily pinpoint and rectify problem areas.

Global Institutional Framework. In the years immediately following World War II, most textile trade was governed by bilateral agreements that limited the volume of textiles one country could send to another. The United States and Great Britain repeatedly met challenges from the Asian textile producers in the post-war period with protectionist measures typically involving complicated rules and high tariffs. Over time, bilateral agreements were negotiated that somewhat reduced the tendency to place other non-quota restrictions on trade and offered some promise of advancing a more open trading climate. Nevertheless, many countries were unwilling to live with quotas, especially where cotton textile exports were a principal source of hard currency. In addition, because bilateral agreements were negotiated on a country-by-country basis, they were very time- and energy-consuming to design and implement.

As alternatives to bilateral arrangements, multilateral frameworks were established to govern world trade in the second half of the twentieth century. The first such agreement was the 1948 General Agreement on Tariffs and Trade (GATT). A series of renegotiated and updated GATTs followed approximately every five years, culminating in the 1986 to 1994 Uruguay Round of GATT negotiations which established the World Trade Organization (WTO) on January 1, 1995. After that, WTO members met regularly in a General Council; three main subcouncils, including the Council for Trade in Goods, or Goods Council, that governed international trade in textiles; and in a number of committees and other groups. As of April 23, 2004, 147 nations were members of the WTO, which had replaced the GATT as the formal, institutionalized body of international trade practices and policies, but followed a revised and significantly expanded set of GATT rules.

From the outset, GATT's overriding aim was to "liberalize world trade and place it on a secure basis." GATT was internally structured with a code of rules for conducting international trade, using an international forum for settling trade disputes. Despite the stated intentions of GATT, various departures from the rules were commonplace, especially for textiles. In general, GATT resulted in a more liberalized trade climate for textiles emerged among developed countries in North America and Western Europe in the early post-war years.

However, during the 1950s the textile trade relationship progressively deteriorated between these countries and Japan, the socialist countries of Eastern Europe, and the less industrialized countries of the world.

In 1960 textile trade effectively was separated from GATT's fundamental principle of fostering liberalized trade with the adoption of an "Avoidance of Market Disruption" clause. This provision allowed countries to impose import restrictions if a potential increase in imports was expected to have a negative impact; if a particular country's textile imports were identified as the source of a problem, which under GATT rules would be considered discriminatory; and if a sizable price difference existed between inexpensive textile imports and comparable goods in a domestic market.

In February 1962, 19 major trading countries signed on the Long Term Arrangement Regarding Cotton Textiles (LTA), which, under GATT, remained in effect for several five-year periods, each followed by a new round of negotiations. Under the terms of the LTA, import countries were allowed to return to bilateral agreements and unilateral restraints. By 1973, 82 countries had signed the LTA. One unforeseen consequence was that many exporting countries merely switched over to the quota-free production of manufactured fibers. U.S. textile producers attempted to include manufactured fibers under the LTA but were unsuccessful. Instead, a separate treaty was negotiated in 1974 called the Arrangement Regarding International Trade in Textiles, later referred to as the Multifiber Arrangement (MFA).

Cotton textiles eventually were phased into the MFA during a second round of negotiations (MFA II), when several new provisions were added that had not been part of the LTA. These provisions included the creation of a multilateral textile surveillance board to monitor implementation of the MFA, stricter rules for determining market disruption claims, and an allowance for growth in quota levels at a rate of 6 percent annually instead of the 5 percent permitted under the earlier LTA. MFA II also featured greater flexibility in quota arrangements, such as the "swing" provision that permitted the transfer of a quota from one category to another, the "carry forward" clause that allowed an exporting country to borrow against next year's quota, and the "carry over" clause which allowed an exporting country to add unused quota onto the limits for the following year. MFA II was followed by MFA III, which was in force from 1982 to July 1986.

MFA IV originally was to be in force from August 1986 to July 1991 but was extended to 1994 before being superseded by the 1995 Agreement on Textiles and Clothing (ATC) that included a mechanism for phasing out bilateral quotas. As early as 1986, developing countries were pushing to phase out the MFA itself but were rebuffed by the powerful U.S. textile lobby, according to Dr. Sri Ram Khanna, an international consultant on the Asian textile industry. The failure to achieve a phase-out of quotas at that time led the developing countries to set up the Geneva-based International Textiles and Clothing Bureau, one of whose main tasks was to create a coordinated plan to liberalize textile trade.

One of the most significant developments affecting the international textiles industry was the Uruguay Round of GATT, a series of multilateral negotiations conducted by GATT member states from 1986 to 1994, which ultimately led to the creation of the World Trade Organization. The Uruguay Round addressed multiple trade disagreements associated with the MFA treaty and reestablished a climate of quota-free liberalized trade that impacted the textile industry. The International Textiles and Clothing Bureau played an instrumental role in influencing the MFA phase-out of the 1994 GATT accord. The 1995 Agreement on Textiles and Clothing (ATC) that resulted from the Uruguay Round replaced the earlier MFA arrangements and was designed to eliminate bilateral quotas completely over a 10-year period.

The ATC represented a marked departure from past similar agreements. The document contained procedural guidelines to resolve longstanding points of contention, such as the integration of MFA quotas and other "gray area" textile measures, the administration of quota phase-outs during the transition period, transition safeguards, the circumvention of quotas, and reciprocity between developed and developing countries for all categories of textiles. It also established the Textiles Monitoring Body or Board (TMB) to referee the quota phase-out process.

The TMB, an 11-member committee set up under the WTO's Council for Trade in Goods (Goods Council), was responsible for monitoring the quota phase-out integration. The TMB also functioned as a standing textile dispute resolution body for the phase-out transition period. Near the end of each phase-out stage, the TMB had to prepare a comprehensive report on the progress and degree of compliance with the ATC's overall goal of trade liberalization.

The textile trade integration process established by the Uruguay Round, which went into effect on January 1, 2005, entirely eliminated the quota system. The phase-out process was structured in four stages, each allowing progressively higher quotas of textile imports up to the point when quotas were completely eliminated. At the start of the phase-out process, small suppliers, who accounted for less than 1.2 percent of all textile quotas in December 1991, were allowed to move immediately to the second-stage quota rate. Members operating with "gray area" quotas, who could not be justified under

MFA or GATT rules, had to officially notify the TMB, conform their quotas to GATT rules, and eventually phase out quotas through the self-destruct mechanism built into the transition process.

Despite the objections of the United States, exporting countries continued to administer transition quotas. However, administrative procedures were subjected to mutual consultation between exporter and importer governments, and a circumvention clause, which was added under pressure from the powerful U.S. textile lobby, targeted specific remedial action against imports that arrived through unlawful channels. The circumvention clause specified a penalty of entry denial in cases of transshipment violations, quota debits for rerouting, legal action for declarations of false origin, and a penalty of new quotas for false declarations of fiber type or quantity shipped or false description of goods. All remedial action had to follow strict rules of evidence.

The transition safeguards provision of the ATC was intended to protect an importing country's domestic textile industry against rising imports. The action to prevent damage, however, had to be applied against all countries rather than an individual country. During the 10-year transition period, MFA-like quotas were permissible on individual countries only under close scrutiny. The ATC's reciprocity clause, backed by the European textile producers, obligated WTO members to promote improved access to textile markets by undertaking tariff reductions; to agree to limit tariff ceilings; and to eliminate non-tariff barriers by streamlining customs, administrative, and licensing procedures. This clause also ensured the implementation of fair trade policies, forbid dumping and anti-dumping procedures and subsidies, and called for the protection of intellectual property rights. Finally, discrimination against textile imports as a means of retaliating against general trade policy disputes was prohibited.

Employment. The extremely hazardous and undesirable working conditions of the early textile mills in the United States and England, coupled with the long hours, which typically were 14-hour workdays, sparked the first labor strikes and efforts to form unions in the United States beginning in the 1830s as well as in Europe during the nineteenth century. Attempts by U.S. mill laborers to unionize were only partially successful, however, despite the large number of strikes and walkouts by textile workers, including young New England women in the mills of Lowell and other rapidly growing northern industrial towns. As new groups of immigrants arrived in the United States from Ireland and French Canada, ready to work for lower wages than the native-born workers would accept, mill owners profited, replacing the local residents with immigrants when the mills reopened after the Civil War.

Similarly, beginning in the 1880s countless "sweatshops" sprang up in U.S. cities where garment workers, typically Italian, Jewish, and Chinese immigrants, toiled for long hours under miserable conditions, often with little hope for improving their working conditions and pay due to the waves of new immigrants arriving on U.S. shores who could easily replace them. The first successful apparel workers union, the International Ladies' Garment Workers' Union, was founded in New York City in 1900.

Additional groups of immigrants began to take jobs in the mills in the final decades of the nineteenth century and the beginning of the twentieth century. Lowell, Massachusetts, for example, became home to immigrants representing over 40 ethnic groups, including Greeks, Poles, Italians, Swedes, Portuguese, Armenians, Lithuanians, Jews, and Syrians, who followed the French Canadians and the Irish into the mills. What had started out as a somewhat paternalistic working environment, where young local women lived in communal boardinghouses on mill property, became an increasingly cutthroat operation where workers' needs and interests were neglected by those who owned and ran the mills.

In 1912 general strikes among mill workers in Lowell finally produced results. Led by union organizers from the Industrial Workers of the World (IWW), the Lowell strikes resulted in a 10-cent raise for mill workers, similar to the results of strikes by textile mill workers in other New England cities. However, the strikes also convinced some mill owners to relocate in the South. Organizing effective labor unions in the textile mills of the United States has continued to be a challenging endeavor because mill owners generally were able to utilize the influxes of immigrants as sources of inexpensive labor. Even at the start of the twenty-first century, the percentage of unionized U.S. textile mill workers was very low compared to other U.S. industries, which was reflected in the somewhat lower-than-average wages for textile mill workers. In October 2001 the average hourly wage for U.S. textile workers was US$11.36, just 13 cents per hour more than in October 2000, according to the U.S. Bureau of Labor Statistics.

Concern among consumers worldwide about poor working conditions and wages in many textile and apparel jobs of multinational corporations in developing countries grew through the 1990s and early years of the 2000s. This led to international activism on behalf of workers in developing countries. For example, many activists increased their efforts to curb the use of child labor in the carpeting industries of countries like India and Pakistan and to ensure that working conditions for employees in multinational firms like Nike are monitored and improved. In the late twentieth century, U.S. and European consumers increased selective boycotting to promote improved pay structures and working conditions for foreign laborers in such plants.

Growing attempts to unionize labor in the textile industries of developing countries offered promise that working conditions and wages among the world's poorest industrial laborers would gradually improve. For example, union activity in Nigeria, Africa's largest country, grew in strength over a 20-year period of industrial restructuring beginning in the late 1970s. The National Union of Textile, Garment, and Tailoring Workers of Nigeria (NUTGTWN) helped reorganize an industry that was rapidly expanded and modernized thanks to Nigeria's burgeoning oil industry. In North America, however, the North America Free Trade Agreement (NAFTA) caused an outflow of textile and apparel jobs to such developing countries as Costa Rica, Honduras, and Mexico, costing many U.S. textile workers their jobs, exemplifying the complexity of situations in the international textile industry that cannot be fully addressed by international boycotts or unionization alone. Since the late twentieth century, multinational corporations increasingly have relocated their production to plants in the developing world. This has led to growth in the economies of some developing countries, but increasing numbers of workers were lost their jobs at some of the former textile-producing giants of the developed world. On the other hand, some of this relocation of production activity benefited U.S. workers. For example, by relocating their apparel production operations to Mexico but requiring that U.S.-produced yarns and fabrics be used in manufacturing apparel, U.S. companies arguably have kept a number of textile-milling jobs in the United States that otherwise might have been lost.

In general, however, employment in the global textile industry paralleled the drop in production growth rates in the late twentieth century. The average annual growth in textile employment from 1963 to 1973 was 3.2 percent for developing countries. That figure dropped to 1.1 percent for the period between 1973 and 1990. By the late 1990s, approximately 608,000 workers were employed in the U.S. textile industry. However, that figure fell significantly and steadily over the next several years in response to the greater technological efficiency of milling machinery and the competitive challenge of Asian textile imports. By October 2001 the number of textile workers in the United States had fallen to approximately 456,700, some 383,600 of whom were production workers. The unemployment rate for U.S. textile workers that month was 9.4 percent, a full 4 percentage points higher than the general U.S. unemployment rate of 5.4 percent. In 2003, U.S. textile mills employed only 241,300 workers, eliminating 38,400 jobs. Between 1990 and 2003, employment in U.S. textile mills fell by 49 percent. By 2010, there were 422,000 employees in the U.S. textile industry, making it one of the largest manufacturing employers in the United States.

BACKGROUND AND DEVELOPMENT

Although textiles have been produced since prehistoric times, the modern era of textile production using capitalist methods took root in England with the Industrial Revolution that began in the 1700s. Toward the end of the 1600s, a growing volume of cotton textiles was being imported to England from India, which was then a British colony, the result of British legislation passed in 1690. Indian fabric appealed to English urban tastes but competed with England's own fledgling textile industry. The British Parliament, whose members reasoned that the British textile industry could develop best if isolated from outside competition, soon banned Indian cottons. This marked the start of a long period of significant growth in the production of British textiles during the eighteenth and nineteenth centuries, first through cottage industries and later through the use of advanced techniques and equipment in an growing number of large industrial plants.

Advancement of the British textile industry was assisted by British manufacturers willing to offer cash rewards to textile machine inventors who created more productive machines. In 1733 John Kay (1704–64) developed the mechanical flying shuttle, which for the first time allowed a single worker to weave cotton fabric in widths that exceeded the length of an adult person's arm. Before this invention, production of broadwoven cotton fabrics required two workers moving a shuttle back and forth to insert thread. However, Kay's flying shuttle exerted backward pressure on spinners to supply the necessary level of yarn, a difficult if not impossible task. This problem was soon corrected by the inventions of a spinning jenny, which was a carding machine that introduced the simultaneous spinning of multiple threads, by John Hargreaves in 1764; a water frame, introduced by Sir Richard Arkwright in 1771, which spun cotton fiber into thread; and especially the spinning mule invented by Samuel Crompton in 1779, which yielded strong, fine-quality yarns able to withstand the rigors of the weaving process. Around the same time, and in a complementary manner, Eli Whitney's 1793 invention of the cotton gin enabled cotton fibers to be separated from cotton plants much faster than by the previous hand method, addressing the industry's need for more raw material to keep up with advanced spinning technologies.

The development of new spinning and weaving techniques profoundly altered how cotton textiles were produced. Unlike the inferior machines and less productive techniques used in the cottage industry, these new technologies required larger industrial structures and a close proximity to water to generate mechanical power. Most importantly, these technologies enabled industrial textile manufacturers in the early days of the modern factory system to produce cotton textiles at a lower unit cost and to drive rural cottage industry rivals, and later each other, to ruin. Arkwright was the first industrial capitalist to establish a series of English textile mills, and his plants employed from 150 to 600 workers, many of them children. Arkwright's 1795 power-loom was initially greeted with hostility and resistance by hand-loom weavers fearing for their livelihood, blocking its widespread introduction until 1810.

Although England continued to maintain a commanding lead in textile technological developments, a similar pattern of factory-based textile production soon spread across the United States and Europe. Two groundbreaking developments that occurred in the United States in 1793 were the invention of Whitney's cotton gin and the opening of Samuel Slater's cotton mill in what would later become Pawtucket, Rhode Island. Slater, who had apprenticed at one of Arkwright's mills in England, emigrated to the United States after memorizing the complete plans for a water-powered machine for spinning yarn, which he quickly constructed in 1790. Together with his partners Almy and Brown, Slater also designed and built new power-driven equipment for carding and spinning cotton. Slater's mill was the first of many mechanized, water-powered mills to appear in the Northeastern United States over the next several decades.

The U.S. textile industry began developing in earnest with the War of 1812 between the United States and Britain. The war placed unprecedented demand on the fledgling U.S. industry to produce cloth and blankets for the U.S. military. Aided by exhaustive embargoes placed on foreign products, the U.S. textile industry grew significantly during the war, culminating in 170 mills by the war's end. Ironically, the transfer (or theft) of power-loom technology developed in England played a critical role in the early success of the U.S. textile industry.

In 1826 Lowell, Massachusetts, became the first planned industrial city, with more than a mile of textile mills built along the banks of the Merrimack River that supplied water power to the new industrial site. By 1850 six miles of canals had been built in Lowell to power the city's rapidly growing textile plants that included 40 mill buildings and 320,000 spindles, as well as 10,000 looms, which was equal to the 10,000 textile workers employed there. By 1890 some 15,000 workers ran the looms and machines that produced the ever-growing yards of fabric in this young U.S. city, although by that time Fall River, Massachusetts, had surpassed Lowell in terms of the number of laborers employed in the textile industry (19,000) and in its status as the U.S. city with the highest production of textiles.

The nineteenth century brought about tremendous economic upheaval in England, Europe, and the United States. Refinements in existing textile technologies augmented productivity as the cotton textile industry spurred industrial development in a number of countries. Assisted by high tariffs levied on imported textiles in 1816, which were increased in 1824 and 1828, the United States pursued a protectionist policy of import substitution that shielded its textile industry from external competition. Southern cotton, cultivated and picked by slave labor brought to North America from the Caribbean and Africa, provided the raw material for textile production in the North where the textile industry was concentrated in the ante-bellum years. The growing reliance of the U.S. textile industry on cotton produced by slave labor contributed to the underlying conditions that led to the U.S. Civil War in the 1860s.

By 1860, on the eve of the Civil War, cotton textile production had grown to become one of the leading manufacturing industries in the United States. Besides the protective tariff structure, the industry was also helped by rapid population growth, diffusion of the power loom, a burgeoning transportation infrastructure that significantly reduced transportation costs and increased profits, and a sustained increase in per-capita income.

By 1900 Great Britain and the United States reigned supreme among the developed countries in cotton textile production. Canada and several countries in Western Europe also made significant progress in developing their textile industries. Most textile industries were nurtured through deliberate government intervention. By 1913, the United States and Western Europe produced about 85 percent of the world's cotton textiles.

In the 1920s and 1930s extensive mill closings in northern U.S. cities produced widespread layoffs. Between 1890 and 1930, the center of textile manufacturing in the United States shifted from the cities of New England to the South where newly built textile mills took over the critical role played for several generations by the New England mills.

During World War I, world cotton textile production grew rapidly as production increased by 90 percent. Between 1918 and 1929, however, developed countries experienced a decline in the relative share of textile output because of increasing competition from Japan. Shortly after World War I, Japan began an impressive drive to develop its cotton textile industry by concentrating on export growth. By 1933 Japan had displaced Great Britain and the United States as the leading exporter of cotton textile products. The example set by Japan also served as a model for other developing Asian countries, which pursued a similar growth strategy to gain entry into the world cotton textile market.

Japan's success prompted retaliatory moves by the United States and Great Britain. In 1932 Britain enacted protective measures to limit Japan's access to its textile markets. Other industrialized countries followed suit, and by 1936 Japanese exports of cotton textiles were subject to quota restrictions in 40 of the 106 markets in which Japan's textile producers participated. U.S. textile producers brought their concerns about Japanese export penetration to the U.S. Tariff Commission, which drew up the first unilateral voluntary export restraint (VER) agreement. Although the VER proved ineffective in stemming Japan's export tide, Japanese and U.S. textile trade associations managed to negotiate a bilateral pact that limited Japan's exports through 1940.

During World War II, the developed countries responded to competitive textile threats by resorting to protectionist measures. This response set the pattern for the increasingly hostile textile trade climate over the next half century. Left untouched by the destruction of World War II, the U.S. and British cotton textile industries were uniquely positioned to recapture their leadership status in world textile markets after the war. The textile industries in most other developed countries did not survive the war, while Japan's suffered particularly serious damage. However, Japan's textile industry recovered rapidly and by 1953 once again was surpassing the United States and Great Britain in exports of cotton textiles. During this period, Hong Kong, South Korea, Pakistan, and India became increasingly industrialized and positioned themselves as significant players in the world market.

After a vibrant period of steady growth and rising employment from 1953 to 1973, worldwide levels of textile employment and production (broadwoven cotton textiles being no exception) entered a protracted period of worldwide decline from 1973 to 1990. A GATT study pinpointed the erosion of consumer demand in developed countries as a major factor underlying the downturn. The reduced demand created a glut of textile products that in turn resulted in a global trend of textile overcapacity. Developing countries were hit particularly hard since much of their textile output was produced for export to the developed countries. From 1963 to 1973, the average annual growth rate in world textile production was 4.5 percent, with developing countries reporting a 5.5 percent growth rate. However, from 1973 to 1990 the worldwide average annual growth rate plummeted to

1.1 percent, with growth in developing countries falling to 2.8 percent for the same period.

Technological advances in the production of cotton broadwoven fabric, such as computer automation introduced from the 1960s through the 1990s, significantly improved the efficiency and profitability of textile mills. In the opening and cleaning stage, for example, computers were installed to select the most desirable combination of cotton bales for the specific end product. Bale pluckers and automatic feeds could be programmed to retrieve a set quantity of fiber from the bales, making it possible to process more than 1,000 pounds of fiber per hour while assuring a homogeneous blend, a performance far superior to any achieved with manual feeding. Automated blending contributed to more evenly distributed variations in fiber characteristics, more uniform processing, improved fabric quality, lower raw material costs, and reduced costs in labor. Automated equipment in the opening department was completely controlled by microprocessors, delivering well-opened stock via chute feeds to the cards and eliminating the need for picker laps and their transportation. Using automated equipment, masses of cotton fiber were gradually opened to progressively smaller tufts without ever being compressed.

Prior to the 1960s, card operations reached a processing range of 4 to 18 pounds per hour depending on the type and quality of cotton fiber used and the desired purity level and nep (one or more entangled fibers) count. In the early 1970s modified carding technology was introduced, improving processing speed to an average of 50 pounds per hour. By 1980 high-production cards commonly operated at processing speeds of 100 to 250 pounds per hour. The direct feeding of cotton sheets to the card via chutes led to the automation of the cardroom. Compared to earlier lap-fed cards, chute feeding offered numerous advantages, including the elimination of such run-out problems as fabric damage caused by lap ends jerking the feed roll, more constant feed rates, higher operating efficiency, more uniform yard-to-yard weights, reductions in labor costs and error, improved dust and trash removal, lower maintenance and production costs, and reductions in operating space. However, because chute feeding lacked blending capability, manufacturers had to use additional blending machinery. Other carding improvements, including the use of electronic clutches, solid state circuitry, DC motors, microprocessors, and minicomputers, allowed increased precision and higher efficiency.

Weaving technology also improved, with shuttleless looms such as the rapier/projectile, air-jet, and water-jet looms. Subsequent refinements began to displace shuttle looms in the 1970s. Textile firms took advantage of shuttleless looms to reduce labor costs while producing a higher-quality product. Besides their higher speed and productivity, shuttleless looms are superior to shuttle looms for safety and environmental reasons. Shuttleless looms ended the problem of errant shuttles striking and injuring workers and operate without the noise-producing checking motion of conventional, shuttle-weaving machines. Rapier looms incorporate insulated covers into their design, further reducing noise levels. In 2000 there were 2,864 shuttle looms in the United States, but by the end of 2002 this number had fallen to 1,949. The number of shuttleless looms, which had climbed to 51,556 in 2000, fell to 39,472 by the end of 2002.

The new looms achieve greater productivity primarily because of their faster, more reliable weft insertion systems and greater machine width. Early shuttleless looms used large weft packages creeled in by the weaver, eliminating the need for support labor such as magazine tenders. Later developments in shuttleless weaving technology incorporated such features as automatic pick finders, which make repairs less time-consuming, and self-lubrication, which reduces parts' wear and maintenance downtime. The precision-wound, flat-cheese type of weft package is a peripheral device developed and used with shuttleless looms. It was invented because weft insertion speeds of shuttleless looms triggered a problem of weft breaks when the weft yarn was unwound from its package. The precision-wound, flat-cheese weft package unwinds a length of yarn from the weft package prior to picking and thus lowers the quality requirements for weft packages and permits the use of weaker, previously unacceptable yarns.

Aside from shuttleless looms and related innovations, another notable characteristic of more recent weaving machines is a greater reliance on electronics. Electronic monitoring systems alert weavers and technicians to operational stoppages. The telemechanique system distinguishes between weft, warp, and mechanical stoppages and identifies their causes. By the 1980s, push-button control and electronic weft-stop motions had become standard features of most weaving looms.

In less than a century, from 1900 to 1986, textile mill production of raw cotton fiber recorded a fivefold increase in volume. Cotton remained the predominant world fiber, although its relative share among all fibers fell from 81 percent in 1900 to just 45 percent by 1986. As cotton use declined, consumption of manufactured fibers climbed from 12.3 percent in 1950 to 49.8 percent in 1986. The relative decline in the production of cotton textile fabrics compared to fabrics of manufactured fibers, however, was partially a result of the displacement of cotton in established end uses. In addition, changes in the respective shares of cotton and manufactured fibers reflected growth in income and population, fluctuations in the relative prices of raw materials and end products, and developments in processing technology. The substitution of manufactured fibers for natural fibers grew fastest in developed countries, initially fueled by manufacturing economics. By the late 1980s chemical synthetics, such as rayon, accounted for roughly 85 percent of consumption of manufactured fibers. In the 1990s, growing attention from the high-fashion world also encouraged a shift to man-made fibers.

By the late 1990s the global textile industry experienced highly divergent conditions and results by region and sometimes even by quarter. The Asian financial crisis of 1997, caused by the currency devaluation and structural adjustment required by the International Monetary Fund, reduced the demand for textiles within affected countries, including Thailand, Indonesia, and South Korea, both for domestic sales and for manufacture as finished export goods. At the same time, the Asian crisis drove prices down and made Asian textiles, which often already enjoyed a cost advantage over textiles produced in Europe and the United States, even more affordable abroad. Consequently, major importers like the United States increased their trade deficits in textiles by snapping up less expensive imports from Asia. A concurrent drop in U.S. textile exports to Asia for finishing and assembly swelled the U.S. trade deficit as well.

The late 1990s recession in Asia prompted an atmosphere of reengineering, with Asian countries updating or reorganizing their textile industries and seeking new markets in western Europe or the United States. In the late 1990s, Bangladesh began privatizing its government-owned textile mills. India weighed the benefits and disadvantages of drawing upon increased government support to underpin its textile industry. Sri Lanka fought a fierce battle in textiles as leakage from the foreign-owned textile plants in its free trade zone created havoc in the country's domestic textile and garment market. Japan's efforts were targeted at updating its textile technology since many Japanese factories were considerably out of date.

In 1997 the United States and China signed an historic textile-trade agreement that assured U.S. access to Chinese textile markets. In return, China was granted a slightly higher U.S. import quota. The agreement, prompted by a huge trade disparity between the United States and China in the textile industry, was widely hailed. While Chinese economists predicted that lowering restrictions to U.S. textile goods would force some state-run Chinese textile mills out of business, China flourished under this agreement and became a member of the World Trade Organization in December 2001.

CURRENT CONDITIONS

In 2005, international trade in textiles and apparel was valued at approximately US$495 billion. China alone controlled 10.6 percent of the trade in textiles and 47.1 percent in the apparel market. With international trade quotas on textiles lifted as of January 2005, many analysts predicted that China's share of the global market would soon reach 50 percent, with its share of the U.S. market at 70 percent. China's dominance in the industry, some analysts feared, would push many small developing nations out of the market altogether.

Because of lower-priced textile imports from Asia, the future viability and direction of the textile industry in developed countries like the United States has been called into question. Prospects for increased profitability might be closely tied to new regional and cross-regional trade liberalization agreements. For example, the Caribbean Basin Initiative (CBI), the Andean Trade Preference Expansion Act introduced to the U.S. Senate in 2001, and the African Growth and Opportunities Act (AGOA), part of the U.S. Trade and Development Act of 2000, aimed to establish new multilateral frameworks for improved international textile trade between the United States and various partner countries. European textile and apparel producers have also attempted to create greater trade opportunities through multilateral agreements with Eastern European and North African producers and markets. AGOA has had some success. Between 1999 and the beginning of 2005, Africa's share of the U.S. textile and apparel market increased from 0.95 percent to 2.5 percent. Nevertheless, China's rapidly growing industry threatened to eradicate this foothold, causing Kenya Apparel Manufacturers and Exports Association chairman Jas Bedi to voice concern that if left unchecked, China could "drive the whole world out of business."

Developing countries also sought new trade relationships in the textile industry with fellow developing nations as well as established industrialized states. For instance, in early 2002 India's Synthetic and Rayon Textiles Exports Promotion Council (SRTEPC) announced its intention to increase the number of sub-Saharan countries with which Indian textile manufacturers would be trading in order to increase the volume of Indian exports. The move was expected to improve the climate for Indian textile manufacturing and trade and help counteract the negative effects of a worldwide drop in cotton prices in 2001 and the January 2002 imposition of a 10 percent increase in import duties on raw cotton to India that was expected to make Indian textiles less competitive on the global market. Cross-border joint ventures and partnerships also were used to improve trade opportunities between the textile industries of more developed and less developed countries, both within and across geographical regions.

In terms of textile imports, Western Europe was the world's largest regional consumer in 2000, accounting for more than one-third of the world's textile imports. Asia was a close second, with a regional share of over 30 percent of world textile imports. North America followed, accounting for about 13 percent of the world's textile imports. Latin America, the Central/Eastern Europe/Baltic/CIS region, the Middle East, and Africa each accounted for less than one-tenth of the world's textile imports.

Pakistan's textile industry was under pressure from skyrocketing fuel prices and unremitting power outages that some thought might lead to its collapse. Because the textile industry is a major source of exports as well as a significant employer, a downturn could have a major impact on the country's economy. In the first eight months of the 2007–08 fiscal year, textiles accounted for approximately 70 percent of Pakistan's exports. The sector also contributed 8.5 percent to the gross domestic product and with 15 million employees, accounted for almost 40 percent of the country's manufacturing work force. Industry officials, however, feared large scale layoffs would be necessary. About half of the textile industry in Pakistan generated power through gas run generators, leading to concern that related price increases could cause shut downs.

In June 2008, Sri Lanka was warned by the European Union that rights abuses were "deficiencies" as the country attempted to renew a bilateral trade deal. Sri Lanka was given until the end of October 2008 to renew the deal, knowing that a lapse in the deal would have a negative impact on textile workers. Textiles, mainly shipped to the United States and Europe, have been a significant part of Sri Lanka's economy for a long time. There are major concerns about human rights in Sri Lanka linked to some allegations that the government was doing nothing to prevent killings and torture. Trade Minister G.L. Peiris told Reuters in an interview in June 2008 that Sri Lanka had rejected some allegations and stated the military was attempting to improve its rights record.

In 2000, textiles and garments comprised 95 percent of Bangladesh's exports of industrial goods. For Laos, they comprised 93 percent; for Cambodia, 83 percent; for Pakistan, 73 percent; for Sri Lanka, 71 percent; for Nepal, 61 percent; and for India, 30 percent. The industry employed about 1.8 million workers in Bangladesh, as well as 1.4 million in Pakistan and 250,000 in Sri Lanka. After 2002, however, many textile manufacturing countries were forced to downsize. Indonesia closed 835 factories in 2002 alone and curtailed operations in 767

others. Fifty factories closed in Guatemala and 200 closed in Mexico. According to a working paper from the International Textile, Garment, and Leather Workers Federation, most of the 150 factories planning to open in Mexico in the early 2000s instead chose to locate in China. The El Salvador government reported the loss of 6,000 textile jobs in 2004, while in the first two months after WTO quotas expired in 2005, 18 additional textile and garment factories in Central America closed, eliminating 10,000 jobs. According to the *New York Times* only India, Pakistan, and Brazil may have textile industries strong enough to continue competing successfully against China.

While textile producing countries braced for massive changes that could threaten the very survival of their industries, analysts pointed out that consumers in importing countries would enjoy significant savings as of 2005. In the United States, for example, consumers could save about US$6 billion once quotas were lifted on clothing.

Four leading Taiwan textiles manufacturers and blue sign accreditation process participants banded together for the European Outdoor Show in Freidrichschafen, Germany. Everest Textile, and Singtex Industrial Co., Ltd. were scheduled to share insights about working to produce more environmentally-friendly outdoor clothing. Their event was appropriately named "The Four Textile Dragons of Taiwan." Blue sign Accreditation Process had reportedly gained popularity, by enhancing recognition of companies and enabling them to distinguish themselves from Chinese producers through quality, innovation, and sustainable business practices.

MAJOR COUNTRIES IN THE INDUSTRY

China. The growing dominance of China in the early 2000s profoundly influenced the global textile industry and was expected to play an increasingly significant role after remaining WTO quotas expired in 2005. After some quotas in the U.S. market were abolished in early 2002, China's exports to the United States, including textiles and garments, grew between 300 and 500 percent that year alone. In some categories, U.S. imports of Chinese textiles and finished goods rose 600 percent, and in 2004 textiles contributed to a record US$162 billion trade deficit with China, the largest U.S. deficit ever with a single country. China's exports to the European Union rose by 164 percent in 2002, and by more than 500 percent in just the first four months of 2005. At the same time, textile and finished goods exports from other producers plummeted. From January 2002 to March 2003, for example, U.S. imports of textile-made luggage from the Philippines and Thailand fell by 54 percent and 48 percent respectively, while imports from China grew by 664 percent. Despite calls from the European Union and the United States to limit textile and apparel exports, China said in 2005 that it would not reduce global shipments, valued at about US$100 billion, but that higher costs for raw materials and labor would slow growth in this sector.

Since textiles and clothing account for up to 95 percent of industrial exports in some Asian economies, China's growth caused considerable concern about the future viability of the textile industry in poor countries. It was widely believed that after 2005 China would capture about 50 percent of the global textile and apparel market, and by 2007 would account for 70 percent of U.S. textile and garment imports. Because of China's dominance in this market, as many as 30 million textile industry jobs in smaller developing countries were at stake.

The European Union. The European Union, the second-largest exporter of textiles in the early years of the 2000s, had about 177,000 textile and clothing companies in 2002 and employed more than 2 million people. Textiles alone accounted for 70,000 firms and employed just over 1 million workers. Exports to non-European countries were valued at 25.49 billion euros (approximately US$32.63) in 2000, and grew slightly to 25.59 euros (about US$32.76) in 2003. High labor costs also affected the industry, causing some manufacturers to relocate from relatively high-wage countries like Germany to low-wage countries like Poland or Romania. Ten of these former Eastern-Bloc nations, however, joined the European Union in May 2004. In 2001, Italy was the major player in the EU textile industry, with 31 percent of the EU market. Next was the United Kingdom with 15 percent, followed by Germany with 14 percent, France with 13 percent, Spain with 9 percent, and Portugal with 6 percent. Turkey was another important European manufacturer. Turkey produced 893,000 tons of cotton yarn and 1,590 million meters of cotton fabric in 2001, with textile exports valued at about US$10.3 billion.

Although high labor costs hurt the European clothing industry, Europe remained more competitive in textiles because the industry was less labor-intensive than garment manufacturing and could more effectively use new technologies to increase productivity. At the beginning of the twenty-first century, Europe had a trade surplus in textiles, mainly because it exported fabrics to Eastern Europe and North Africa to be made into clothing that was then re-imported to Europe. In 2003, the United States remained the European Union's single most important export market for textiles, buying about 10 percent of its total textile exports that year compared to 12 percent in 2000.

The United States. The U.S. textile industry, struggling with plant closings and high labor costs, closed more than 50 textile plants and eliminated 10 percent of jobs in 2003. Among those companies was Pillotex, which in 2000 had been one of the country's largest textile manufacturers. Its closure, which eliminated 6,000 jobs, was blamed on inexpensive imports. In 2003, U.S. textile imports increased 6 percent, reaching about US$17 billion, while exports rose by 1 percent. Textile production (including yarn, thread, fabric, and finishing) was valued at US$39.8 billion in 2003, representing an 8 percent drop from the previous year. Textile corporate sales, which gained 3 percent in 2002, fell 3 percent in 2003 to US$47 billion. Exports of textile mill products were valued at US$10.5 billion in 2000 and remained relatively stable through 2003. Exports rose in 2004, exceeding US$11.6 billion. By 2009, the U.S. textile industry was valued at US$63 billion and projected to grow by 6 percent in 2010. The United States was the third-largest global exporter of textile products in 2009, at US$14 billion. Following the closings and layoffs earlier in the decade, in 2009 and 2010 there were 12 U.S. textile plant expansions.

The primary consumers of U.S.-produced textiles and apparel in the early years of the 2000s were Mexico, Canada, Honduras, the Dominican Republic, El Salvador, and Japan. U.S. exports to neighboring countries increased significantly after implementation of the North American Free Trade Agreement (NAFTA) in 1994. In 2000, for example, U.S. exports of textile mill products to Mexico showed an increase of 33.6 percent over the prior year, although U.S. apparel exports to Mexico decreased by 4.4 percent. U.S. textile and apparel exports to Canada showed a similar pattern with a 2.5 percent gain over 1999, while U.S. apparel exports to Canada declined by 0.7 percent in one year. In 2002, the U.S. Bureau of Labor Statistics reported that the value of U.S. textile exports to Mexico grew by 3.5 percent, reaching US$3.2 billion. Exports to Canada during that period rose 3.4 percent, with a value of US$2.6 billion. At the beginning of the first decade of the 2000s, end uses for the fabric produced in U.S. textile mills included apparel, 36 percent; home furnishings, 16 percent; floor coverings, 25 percent; and industrial or other uses, 23 percent.

The increasingly favorable trade climate between the United States and Caribbean nations created by the Caribbean Basin Initiative (CBI) improved U.S. textile and apparel exports to CBI nations dramatically in just one year. U.S. textile exports to CBI countries in 2000 were valued at US$947 million, up 35.5 percent from the prior year, and apparel exports were valued at US$4.09 billion, up 14 percent. In 2001, CBI nations together were the second-largest market for U.S. textile exports. As of 2005, more than 70 percent of garments manufactured in Central America were produced from U.S. fabric and yarn.

A Texas state grant supplemented efforts to bring Santana Textiles to South Texas. The company is the world's fifth-largest denim producer. Texas agreed to invest US $1.65 million from the Texas Enterprise Fund into Santana's new manufacturing plant in Edinburg. The plan will create 800 new jobs and US $170 million in capital investment. Santana operates four plants in Brazil, where it is headquartered, and one in Argentina.

INDUSTRY LEADERS

Coats Holdings Ltd., formerly Coats Viyella, was the largest company in the world producing sewing thread and craft materials at the beginning of the twenty-first century. As of 2004, the U.K.-based firm had almost finished divesting its Viyella business, which focused on clothing and home furnishings, and was concentrating exclusively on Coats, which manufactures industrial and craft thread. Sales in 2009 exceeded US$1.4 billion, and the company reported a workforce of over 20,600 people. Coats had manufacturing plants in more than 65 countries, distributing its products in 150 countries worldwide.

Unifi Inc. was the world's largest producer of textured yarns, particularly multi-filament nylon and polyester yarns, for use in apparel, home furnishings, upholstery, automotive and industrial materials, hosiery, and sewing threads. In 2009, Unifi, based in Greensboro, North Carolina, posted sales of US$553.6 million, down from 2008's revenue of S$713.3. UNIFI's *Repreve,* a 100 percent recycled yarn made at its Yadkinville plant, enabled the company to report its first profitable quarter in five years in 2008. The company's product line includes "value-added specialty yarns" that make up 10 percent of its sales, which is expected to increase due to consumer demand for sustainable products.

The largest U.S. textile firms in 2004 were Mohawk Industries, with revenues of US$5.3 billion in 2009; Milliken, a textiles and chemical company with revenues in 2008 estimated at US$2.5 billion; and Springs Industries, whose 2003 revenues were an estimated US$2.5 billion. Another leading company, Westpoint Stevens, filed for bankruptcy in 2003 and as of 2005 was expecting to be acquired by an investment group led by W.L. Ross. Westpoint's 2003 revenues were US$1.64 billion. Burlington Industries, with revenues of US$993 million in 2002, also filed for bankruptcy and was purchased by Ross in 2003 for US$614 million. Interface, with 2004 revenues of US$881.7 million, is the world's leading producer of commercial carpet. Top European textile companies include Sara

Lee Courtaulds, created in 2000 when the Sara Lee Corporation acquired U.K.-based Courtaulds Textiles.

WORKFORCE

The effects of rapid globalization and the elimination of trade barriers have not been positive for vast numbers of workers and consumers in developing countries or for workers in developed countries who have been displaced as multinational companies outsource to take advantage of low labor costs.

Employment figures in the U.S. textile industry continued to fall at the beginning of the twenty-first century. The most serious losses came in 2001 when textile industry employment fell by 13 percent. The three states with the most textile workers in 2001 were North Carolina, with 97,700 employees; South Carolina, with 56,400 employees; and Gerogia, with 39,700 employees. The average U.S. textile employee worked 41.5 hours per week in 1997 but by October 2001 was working only 39.6 hours. By 2009, the industry employed 422,000 workers, a significant drop from the 1997 level of 607,500. However, even in the face of rising unemployment rates nationwide, the textile industry was one of the largest manufacturing employers in the United States.

According to Mickey Powell in the June 2008 *Martinsville Bulletin,* after Spring Industries and other companies told the West Piedmont Workforce Investment Board and Patrick Henry Community College about a shortage of people with high-level manufacturing technician skills, the college added two training programs to its curriculum. The Martinsville-Henry County Economic Development Corp. views these programs as "a way of developing an existing, trained pool of labor."

RESEARCH AND TECHNOLOGY

Technological advances in wet processing toward the end of the twentieth century focused on reducing energy consumption and curtailing water usage in response to rising energy costs and increasingly stringent government regulation of water pollutants. In most developed countries, the textile industry has ranked among the industrial leaders in cutting energy consumption requirements when compared to other industries. Since dyeing and finishing together accounted for more than three-fourths of all energy consumed in cotton fabric production, due to the energy needed to evaporate water and solvents from fabric, the wet-processing stage was singled out for energy-saving innovations. Washers were designed with counter-current water flows to curtail both energy consumption and chemical usage. Systems designed to recycle water and recover heat were incorporated into washers. In addition, solvent removal equipment was redesigned to eliminate wetting and drying steps, and newer dryers featured heat recovery and reuse designs. Improved dyeing technology required lower liquor ratios and allowed faster dyeing with less energy and fewer chemicals. Finishing machines were built for increased speed and lower "pickup" levels using hard roll pads or foam applications, and tenter frames became more energy efficient through improved air flow.

Man-Made Fibers and Fabrics. The demand for new fabrics and more functionality is a driving force in research. While flax, a natural fiber, has been woven into linen for at least 7,000 years, and cotton has been produced almost as long, the first man-made fiber, rayon, was invented only at the start of the twentieth century. In 1910, the American Viscose Company brought together two different chemicals and methods of manufacturing to create two types of rayon: viscose and cuprammonium. Nearly 100 years later, viscose rayon was the only type still produced in the United States. The Celanese Corporation started commercial production of the next man-made fiber, acetate, in the United States in 1924. Nylon was introduced in 1939, making the E. I. du Pont de Nemours & Company Inc. world famous. At the beginning of the twenty-first century nylon was second only to polyester as the synthetic fiber most commonly used in the United States.

In the middle of the twentieth century, acrylic was produced commercially by E. I. du Pont de Nemours, the same company that had been responsible for starting commercial production of polyester fiber in the United States in 1953. In 1954 the Celanese Corporation began producing triacetate fiber in the United States, although domestic U.S. production of triacetate stopped in 1985. Spandex, whose filaments can stretch at least 100 percent then spring back to the original, was first produced commercially in the United States by E. I. du Pont de Nemours in 1959. Two years later, Hercules Incorporated began commercial production of polyolefin/polypropylene in the United States. In 1966 polyolefin became the first fiber in the world to win the Nobel Prize. By 2006, no other fiber had yet managed to do the same.

Micro fibers, which have less than one denier per filament, were first produced commercially in the United States in 1989 by E. I. du Pont de Nemours. Micro fibers (or microdenier) are the world's thinnest fibers and are finer even than silk. According to *Fabric History,* "To relate it to something more familiar—A human hair is more than 100 times the size of some micro fibers." Microfibers have been produced from a wide range of synthetic fibers, including polyester, nylon, and acrylic.

At the turn of the millennium, the world's most popular synthetic fibers were super fabric polyester; rayon, the world's least expensive fabric to produce; viscose, a more expensive type of rayon; Polartec, favored by hikers, campers, and upholstery makers; Lycra and spandex; nylon and Pewlon; Elite, an Italian elastic; and Tencel, a strong, silky fiber made from wood pulp. Tencel is the trade name given to lyocell, a man-made fiber first produced commercially in the United States in 1993 by Courtalds Fibers. Lyocell comes from trees grown expressly for this fiber whose wood is processed in an environmentally friendly way by spinning the solvent and recycling the dissolving agent. Tencel is considered the first "natural" man-made fabric, manufactured without a chemical combination like acetate or polyester are made.

Research by such companies as DuPont and the Japanese giant, Toray, is leading the world further into the production of man-made fibers. In mid-1998, DuPont premiered Tactel, a thread designed with the fashion world in mind. Tactel is smooth, non-wrinkling, opalescent, and soft. In June 1998 Royal Dutch/Shell and Korea-based SK Chemicals announced production of Corterra, a knittable, stretchy material that can be dyed a wide variety of colors. It was initially used in underwear and athletic wear, replacing the coarser and less breathable spandex/nylon blends. In the late 1990s, the Finnish company Kultratrurve OY used a century-old English patent to become the first to spin fabric from peat. The resulting cloth, which was static resistant, hypoallergenic, warmer and lighter than wool, and inexpensive to produce, was anticipated to have a healthy future in medical dressings, wound care, and fabrics, fleeces, and felts for clothing and furniture.

In 2001 innovative experimental and commercial fabrics were being created by the Fosshield Technology Division of the Foss Manufacturing Co. in Hampton, New Hampshire. Company researchers, meshed synthetic fibers with silver, a natural antimicrobial agent, to create a polyester Fossfibre bicomponent fiber embedded with AgION, an inorganic zeolite based on silver. This fiber offered promising new possibilities for the production of hospitality, medical, travel, and sanitary materials. According to *Textiles World* in a December 2001 article, Fossfibre with AgION is especially useful because it contains no drugs, and bacteria therefore cannot develop a resistance to it. Furthermore, products created with this new fiber, such as the Fosshield antimicrobial cleansing wipes (a durable, no woven wipe that can be used in the home by consumers to clean any non-fabric surface) can be washed and rewashed many times without losing their antimicrobial properties.

While production of traditional woven textiles has continued to decline in the United States, production of technical textiles that are used primarily in industries has grown. In North Carolina, which is the largest textile-producing state, the number of nonwoven fabric mills increased by 30 percent from 1993 to 2003, while employment grew by 9 percent.

Fiber Recycling. As consumer consciousness about protecting the environment has grown, increased interest in product recycling has led to research to recycle fibers and fabrics into new materials. Researchers have found new ways to recycle fibers like wool and to determine how wear-damaged fibers can be reprocessed. Creative uses have also been found for non-fiber products, recycling them into materials to create apparel and other textiles. For example, a fleecy sweatshirt can be created from 25 large soda bottles by spinning plastic fibers, then pressing, chewing, and spinning them again into Polartec or one of its sibling fabrics.

New Fabric Finishes, Colors, and Treatments. Not only are new fibers under development, but new finishes also are being researched to update familiar cloths. For example, researchers in the 1990s experimented with cross-pollinations from carpet, upholstery, and even tire manufacturers to create new apparel textile enhancements. Certain silks have benefited from a Teflon bath, and linen infused with Lycra is more wrinkle resistant and more wearable than traditional linen. By the late 1990s enzymatic dyeing had become one of the most promising new widely used technologies. Traditional chemical or natural dyes could leave fabric stiff with dye or create colors that fade, and some more vibrant colors, such as red and orange, had been linked to health problems. However, fabrics washed with certain enzymes are measurably softer and smoother, accepting dyes more readily. Enzymatic treatments affect almost all properties of a fabric, including its tensile strength, shearing, bending, compression, and surface.

During the ITMA Asia & CITME 2008, BASF was selected to discuss its innovative ecological solutions that ensure zero "add-on" of formaldehyde to textiles while fulfilling the highest quality standards. Standard sources of formaldehyde can be replaced by BASF's formaldehyde-free Helizarin pigment printing system and other solutions. BASF also offers the Helizarin ECOSOFT Printing Systems as an eco-efficient printing solution and has pioneered resin finishing that allows clothes to look fresh without ironing. This distinctive finishing offers comfort to consumers and reduces energy usage since clothes do not need ironing. A disadvantage was considered to be that the fabrics finished with resin lose tensile and tearing strengths.

Cognis, a German ingredients supplier, created the innovative technology used by Skineez Skincarewear for its product line that has been called a "fusion of cosmetics and textiles." Skineez provides shaping underwear

with active ingredients designed to fight against cellulite while products are worn. After a successful launch in Europe, the underwear impregnated with skin care actives made its debut as a silhouette-slimmer alternative in June 2008 at U.S. Macy's stores. The line is part of a new class of products called Cosmeto-textiles. Other examples on the market include products from Lytess, such as anti-bacterial underwear, moisturizing vests, and anti-cellulite jeans. The France-based firm Mulliez has created some garments that are designed to hold in perspiration and body odor until they are washed.

Mass Customization. One of the most exciting recent developments in the textile industry was the trend for mass customization that started in the mid-1990s. Heralded by analysts as a new industry paradigm, mass customization combines the technologies and efficiencies of mass production with the marketing appeal of custom products. Using integrated computer networks, manufacturers can rapidly take and fulfill custom orders for textiles, theoretically without the high costs associated with traditional custom-manufacturing.

The apparel market appeared especially conducive to mass customization. For example, with mass customization a consumer would be able to place an order for a custom-designed pair of jeans from a local store and have the jeans made to order to be delivered within days. A 1998 study conducted by Auburn University in collaboration with industry giants such as DuPont expected future use of 3-D scanners that could record the exact body measurements of apparel customers. More information from the customer would add information on design and fabric options, and the order would be submitted to a textile and apparel factory in real time. The study also modeled future possibilities giving end users access to a textile mill's production capabilities in order to request exact fabrics, clothing styles, upholstery, carpets, with the customer's preferences, including their preferred fit (tight, loose, relaxed, elastic), recorded on a magnetic card. While the demand for mass-customization might not supplant conventional product demand, mass-customized apparel could represent an important new niche market in the twenty-first century.

In an article for ESPN Sports on June 10, 2001, Jim Wilkie revealed that NASCAR had selected the same material used to make military armor for its race cars. Tegris is a flexible fiberglass or carbon fiber alternative that wears away in a highly desirable fashion that NASCAR prefers in case remnants are left on the track. NASCAR reportedly learned about the material created by Milliken in 2007. Applications for the polypropylene composite have thus far included the aero splitter on the front and part of right side panel of NASCAR's Car of Tomorrow (COT).

BIBLIOGRAPHY

American Textile Manufacturers Institute. "ATMI Urges Congress, Administration to Adopt More Equitable Textile Trade Policies," 7 February 2002. Available from www.atmi.org.

———. "Quick Facts about U.S. Textiles," 2004. Available from www.atmi.org.

———. "Textile Companies." Available from www.atmi.org (accessed 7 February 2002).

———. "Textile Industry Year-End Trade and Economic Report," 2 January 2002. Available from www.atmi.org.

Becker, Elizabeth. "Textile Quotas to End Soon, Punishing Carolina Mill Towns." *New York Times,* 2 November 2004.

———. "U.S. Quiet on China Trade Tax, but Europe Welcomes It." *New York Times,* 14 December 2004.

Becker, Elizabeth, and David Barboza. "Free of Quota, China Textiles Flood the U.S." *New York Times,* 10 March 2005.

Bharati, Vivek. "Managing Change: Gaping Holes in Textile Sector." *The Financial Express,* 27 February 2004. Available from fecolumnists.expressindia.com.

Bird, Katie. "Cosmeto-textiles Hit the US Market Via Macy's. 24 June 2008. Available from www.cosmeticsdesign.com.

Buschle-Diller, Gisela, et al. "Effect of Enzymatic Treatment on Dyeing and Finishing of Cellulosic Fibers." *National Textile Center Annual Report,* 1997.

Canadian Textiles Institute. "The Textile Industry: Fact Sheet," 2000. Available from http://phx.corporate-ir.net.

Current Filing Report, September 20, 2010. Available from www.textiles.ca.

De Silva, Dalton. "Sri Lanka: Government Selects Textiles as Priority Industry." *South Asian Business Analyst,* November 1997.

Ellis, Kristi. "Revised Labor Report Hits Industry Harder." *Women's Wear Daily,* 9 February 2004.

European Union Textiles and Clothing Statistics. 2 February 2005. Available from http://europa.eu.int.

Fabric History. www.fabriclink.com (accessed 22 January 2002).

Goodman, Peter S., and Blustein, Paul. "A New Pattern is Cut for Global Textile Trade." *Washington Post,* 17 November 2004, p. A1.

"Industry Report Underscores Grim Conditions in 2003." *Textile World,* January 2004. Available from www.textileworld.com.

"International Business: European Softens China Stance." *New York Times,* 16 March 2005.

"Interview—EU Raises Rights Abuses in Sri Lanka Trade Talks." Reuters,12 June 2008. Available from in. reuters.com.

Kearney, Neil. "What Future for Textiles and Clothing Trade After 2005?" International Textile, Garment, and Leather Workers Federation, 2 September 2003. Available from www.itglwf.org.

Lange, Mark. *Economic Outlook for U.S. Cotton.* National Cotton Council of America, 27 September 2001. Available from www.cotton.org.

Lazich, Robert S., ed. *Market Share Reporter, 2002.* Farmington Hills, MI: Gale Group/Thomson Learning, 2002.

Luke, John E. "Will Productivity Save U.S. Textiles?" *Fibre World,* November 2001. Available from www. textileindustries.com.

McGrane, Sally. "Smarter Clothes." *Time,* 3 July 2008. Available from www.time.com.

Mulama, Joyce. "International Labour Day in Kenya: A Murky Future for Textile Workers." *News from Africa,* 5 May 2005. Available from http://www.newsfromafrica.org.

Nelson, Valerie J. "By Design: With The Softness of Silk and the Strength of Polyester, Tencel . . . " *Los Angeles Times* (17 October 1996): 2.

"Pakistan Textile Sector Staggers Under Double Blow." *Economic Times: India Times,* 3 July 2008. Available from economictimes.indiatimes.com.

Powell, Mickey. "PHCC Plans Two New Certificate," 17 June 2008. Available from www.Martinsvillebulletin.com.

Rodie, Janet Bealer. "Quality Fabric of the Month: Microbes Begone!" *Textiles World,* December 2001. Available from www.textileindustries.com.

Shetty, Aarti. "Prices Rocket Following 10% Import Duty Hike on Raw Cotton." *The Financial Express* (New Delhi), 14 January 2002. Available from new.financialexpress.com.

Soras, Constantine G. "Fed Rates Hit 40-Year Low." *Textiles World,* December 2001. Available from www. textileindustries.com.

Stengg, Werner. *The Clothing and Textile Industry in the EU: A Survey,* June 2001. Available from europa.eu.int.

"Taiwan Textiles to take Eco-Message to Europe," 3 July 2007. Available from www.ecotextile.com.

"Texas Enterprise Fund Helps Land Santana Textiles." *Austin Business Journal,* 3 July 2008. Available from www. bizjournals.com.

Textile Federation. "Newsclip—Africa Growth & Opportunity Act." www.texfed.co.za (accessed 11 January 2002).

"Theme of BASF: 'Putting FUTURE into Textiles,'" 2 July 2008. Available from www.fibre2fashion.com.

Thompson, Ginger. "International Business: Fraying of a Latin Textile Industry." *New York Times,* 25 March 2005.

Trivedi, Vijay. "Synthetic Textile Exporters to Tap Sub-Saharan Regions." *The Financial Express* (New Delhi), 14 January 2002. Available from new.financialexpress.com.

"UNIFI Banks On Green," 3 July 2008. Available from digtriad.com.

Union of Needletrades, Industrial and Textile Employees (UNITE!). "UNITE: A New Union with a Long History." www.uniteunion.org (accessed 7 February 2002).

"USA: Textile Chief Blames Asian Imports for Troubles," accessed 13 January 2002 at www.just-style.com.

U.S. Department of Commerce/International Trade Administration. *U.S. Industry & Trade Outlook 2000.* The McGraw-Hill Companies, 2000.

U.S. Department of Commerce, Office of Textiles and Apparel. *Andean Pact; Bolivia; Colombia; Ecuador; Peru; Proposed Legislation: Bill to Renew and Expand Andean Trade Preferences Could Provide Opportunities for U.S. Fabric and Yarn Exports,* 17 December 2001. Available from web. otexa.ita.doc.gov.

———. *China: China's Accession to the WTO,* 14 December 2001. Available from web.otexa.ita.doc.gov.

———. *Sub-Saharan Africa: The African Growth and Opportunity Act Provides New Opportunities for U.S. Yarn and Fabric Sales,* 4 June 2001. Available from web.otexa.ita. doc.gov.

————. *Trade Data: U.S. Imports and Exports of Textiles and Apparel.* Available from otexa.ita.doc.gov.

U.S. Department of Labor, Bureau of Labor Statistics. "Textile, Apparel, and Furnishings Occupations," www.bls.gov.

————. "Textile Mill Products," www.bls.gov.

Valenti, Catherine. "Textile Industry Unraveling: Increased Competition, Economic Woes Plague U.S. Textile Industry." ABC News, 30 November 2001. Available from more. abcnew.go.com.

Waldrep, G. C. III. *Southern Workers and the Search for Community: Spartanburg County, South Carolina.* Urbana and Chicago, IL: University of Illinois Press, 2000.

Wang, Peter W. K. "What's Latest with World Textile Significance." TransWorld Information, 2004. Available from www.ttnet.net.

Wilkie, Jim. "COT 'Shielded' on Right-Side Door Panel, Splitter." ESPN, 10 June 2008. Available from sports.espn.go.com.

World Trade Organization. "International Trade Statistics 2003." Available from www.wto.org.

————. "Textiles." Available from www.wto.org.

————. "Trading into the Future: The Introduction to the WTO; The Agreements—Textiles: Back in the Mainstream," www.wto.org.

————. "The WTO," www.wto.org.

TRANSPORTATION AND DEFENSE EQUIPMENT

———■———

SIC 3721

AIRCRAFT

NAICS CODE(S)

336411. The global aircraft industry manufactures new and rebuilt aircraft for the commercial and general aviation markets. For discussion of military aircraft, see also **Defense and Armaments**.

INDUSTRY SNAPSHOT

Civil aircraft production is dominated by the commercial market, supplying the jets and turboprops used by the world's passenger and cargo airlines. As of the end of 2010, just two manufacturers—Boeing in the United States and Airbus S.A.S. in France—have controlled nearly the entire global market for commercial aircraft for well more than a decade. This lead was secured primarily by manufacturing medium and large jets for 100 or more passengers, the industry's most lucrative and capital-intensive segments. Aircraft manufacturers noted the rising demand for large-capacity, wide-body planes and expected that the average number of seats per plane would increase to 240 by 2015. They expected that Asian countries would help drive this trend with a 356-seat average capacity per plane by 2015. In October 2007, Airbus introduced the A380 with over 5,146 square feet of floor space to become 49 percent larger than its closest competitor. If fashioned in the typical three-class configuration, the A380 can carry 525 passengers, or 853 in an all-economy class configuration.

The huge costs and risks of aircraft manufacturing encouraged business consolidation and a proliferation of international joint ventures in what has been termed a "borderless industry." Few countries could be considered self-sufficient in production, and even for those that could, most competitors in the industry pursue multiple cross-border ventures in order to keep costs down and draw on the special competencies and efficiencies of firms around the globe.

Globally, the industry experienced continued growth in the early 2000s. Boeing's World Air Cargo Forecast predicted an annual expansion rate of 6.2 percent through 2023, tripling the levels of overall air traffic. Strong growth was reported in international trade, with the most reported in the Asia-Pacific region. Traffic in North America and within Europe was expected to realize below average increases. The U.S. firms Cessna Aircraft Co. and Raytheon led the continuing strong surge in sales in the general aviation segment. The U.S. industry reached US$147 billion in 2003 sales. That year, Boeing, with about 280 units, and Airbus, with about 300 units, produced a combined US$33 billion in aircraft. These had a per-unit value of US$50 million or more, according to *Fortune*. For the first half of 2004, the companies delivered a combined 312 aircraft.

In 2006, according to *Flight International*, only 112 regional aircraft were produced and the "booming business aviation sector" was considered to be a major source for generating revenues. According to researchers from the Teal Group, US$421 billion in aircraft will be built by 2012.

In their study released in May 2007, the Teal Group projected global deliveries of 999 business jets

Aerospace and Defense Industry Leaders, 2008

	Revenue, in billions of U.S. dollars
EADS (Airbus)	$63.3
Boeing	$60.9
United Technologies	$58.7
Lockheed Martin	$42.7
Honeywell International	$36.6
Northrop Grumman	$33.9
BAE Systems	$30.6
General Dynamics	$29.3
Raytheon	$23.2
Finmeccanica	$23.0
Aviation Industry Corp. of China	$21.7
Bombardier	$19.7

SOURCE: *Fortune.*

and 14 executive jetliners in the Boeing BBJ and Airbus A319CJ category. Those aircraft were modified for executive use and typically purchased by the heads of state or large corporations. In addition, the Teal Group projected deliveries of 30 regional jets similarly adapted for corporate or government use. Then in June 2009, the Teal Group forecast production of 2,909 regional aircraft worth an estimated US$65.9 billion between 2009 and 2018. The prediction calls for 1,732 regional jets valued at US$46.9 billion, and 1,177 turboprops worth US$19 billion. Referring to the previous decade as "the glory days" for the airline industry, the study shows that the projected numbers represent an 8 percent decline from 1999 to 2008. According to Richard Aboulafia, Teal Group's vice president, "production during that time totaled 3,563 aircraft worth US$71.7 billion, comprising 2,791 jets worth US$61.1 billion, and 722 turboprops worth US$10.6 billion."

ORGANIZATION AND STRUCTURE

Although the field includes all types of aircraft—including large transports, hang gliders, rotary-wing aircraft (such as helicopters), and balloons—a few conglomerates specializing in civil transports and military aircraft dominate the global aircraft industry. Since most modern aircraft are incredibly complex (the Boeing 747, for example, has 6 million parts), a worldwide network of approximately 400 subcontractors supplies major structures and subassemblies, such as wings and fuselages, to manufacturers of finished aircraft. These subcontractors are supplied, in turn, by up to 4,000 firms that manufacture components or raw materials. Parts that differentiate a product, or those strongly identified with a company, are usually produced in-house due to their strategic and competitive importance.

A strong customer base and careful order book management are needed in order to recoup high development costs for airliners or large business jets. Standards for safety, quality, and value, among other things, are obviously crucial. To break even on the design and manufacture of a new airliner, for example, the following things must transpire to achieve goals. An aircraft company must receive an order for, receive the money for, and provide delivery of hundreds of airliners globally. Because that process can take years, many orders fall through. Thus, the industry gauges not just orders and transactions but completed orders, and otherwise has made an art of order book management. In 2001 alone, Airbus experienced 101 order cancellations (90 percent of which were due to company bankruptcies). Some of these cancellations may yet reenter the Airbus order book and become part of the company's healthy backlog.

The industry is not only cyclical, it relies on a small number of consumers, mostly airlines and governments. Due to long lead times and backlogs, airlines may hastily buy aircraft in advance of their true needs to keep from missing out on model availability in future periods or to avoid availability at much higher prices.

Airline specifications and regulations also affect the design, marketing, and sales of passenger aircraft. Because safety is a highly visible priority in aviation, no civilian operator would readily buy an aircraft that has not been certified by an agency such as the Federal Aviation Administration (FAA) in the United States, the Civil Aviation Authority (CAA) in the United Kingdom, or the Interstate Aviation Committee (IAC) in the Commonwealth of Independent States (CIS). In 1993 the Airbus A330 became the first aircraft to be certified simultaneously in the United States and Europe. To enhance the marketability of their aircraft, Airbus and Boeing also sought extended range certification. This extension would allow flights on routes within 180 minutes' flying time of diversion airports, rather than 60 minutes, the standard for most twin-engine aircraft. Boeing and Airbus accomplished this objective for their 777 and A330 models.

For general aviation, the 1990s were a period of consolidation. Companies either streamlined their production (as in the case of Beech Aircraft Corp.), were acquired by large conglomerates (for example, the business jet operations of British Aerospace were acquired by Raytheon Co.), or both (Cessna was acquired by Textron). In 1997 two of the industry's largest producers, Boeing Company and McDonnell Douglas Corporation, merged. Other well-known companies, such as Piper Aircraft Corp. and Fairchild Aircraft in the United States, as well as Fokker N.V. of the Netherlands, filed for bankruptcy during this period.

Ultralight aviation grew out of a hang gliding resurgence in the 1970s. In 1976 a U.S. adventurer attached a golf-cart engine to a hang glider, creating an inexpensive way to go aloft. Like the earliest flying machines, ultralights and homebuilts—sophisticated craft that come in a kit for home assembly—became the province of tinkerers and serious amateurs. These small machines made aviation more affordable and more accessible for its proponents. They are available for a fraction of the cost of factory-built aircraft (typically less than US$5,000) and are governed by a different set of FAA standards (such as a 254 lb. total weight limit and a five-gallon fuel tank limit). In the mid-1990s approximately 10,000-15,000 ultralights were in existence in the United States. Although not as lucrative as other segments, the ultralight/homebuilt industry has been both the source and beneficiary of many innovations. Less-developed countries such as Peru have actually used ultralights as military training craft.

Rotorcraft, helicopters, and similar craft accounted for about 3 percent of the civil aircraft market in the late 1990s. At that time, worldwide drops in military spending negatively affected the civil helicopter market, for the military dumped its surplus rotorcraft into the civil market, reducing sales. In the civil helicopter sector, Bell Helicopter-Textron shared healthy fractions of the market with Eurocopter, MD Helicopters, and Robinson (which eschewed turbines for piston engines in its entire product line). Total civil helicopter deliveries averaged approximately 500 units per year with a value of US$1 billion in the late 1990s. In the early 2000s, analysts expected slightly less favorable results, especially for rotorcraft manufacturers that failed to specialize in niche markets or had not managed to merge with, or been acquired by, other producers.

With an aging fleet and handicapped by older aircraft-manufacturing technology, the CIS had the potential to become an important market for aircraft. China was expected to surpass Japan as the largest international aircraft market early in the twenty-first century. Eastern Europe, Asia, and the Pacific Rim, along with China, were expected to be growth markets. Similarly, demand in Central and South America rose for aircraft makers.

Asian carriers in particular seemed promising. Boeing predicted that they would purchase US$232 billion in new aircraft by the year 2010; indeed, the world market was predicted to be worth US$857 billion. The long-term commitment required by aerospace developers seemed philosophically compatible with traditional Asian business strategy. The region has a large market and a large supply of skilled workers—crucial in an industry with high quality standards. Joint ventures have proliferated in the region, as local manufacturers sought experience and American and European firms sought a competitive

marketing edge. Singapore, Indonesia, Taiwan, China, and South Korea all have aircraft manufacturing programs. However, the lingering recession in Japan and in other Far East countries in the early 2000s was thought to be an unfavorable factor in the growth of demand for new aircraft.

BACKGROUND AND DEVELOPMENT

Long before aircraft with viable commercial applications were developed, aviation was the province of dreamers and idealists. The quest for flight has been documented as early as the first century in Ovid's tale of Daedalus and Icarus; according to mythology, Icarus made wings of wax and bird feathers, flew too close to the sun, and died. The brothers Joseph Michelle and Jacques Etienne Mongolfier introduced a passenger-carrying hot air balloon in France in 1783. Military tacticians, always searching for the "high ground," employed the balloon as an observation post as early as 1794 during the battle of Maubeuge in France. Not surprisingly, in 1910 a form of balloon called an airship, or dirigible, was the first aircraft to be used for commercial aviation.

Numerous isolated eccentrics tinkered with gliders in the nineteenth century. Before falling to his death in 1896, Otto Lilienthal studied birds and found the secret of flight to be in the curved wing. He and the Scottish engineer Percy Pilcher, who was also killed experimenting with gliders, laid the foundation for the Wright brothers' invention of the airplane at the turn of the twentieth century. Lilienthal also received credit for manufacturing the first aircraft for sale, the Lilienthal Type 11 glider.

Many others had sought to build powered aircraft, too often constructing machines with flapping wings, called "ornithopters." On December 17, 1903, bicycle makers Orville and Wilbur Wright earned credit as the first to produce an aircraft capable of powered, sustained, and controlled flight. Such a lofty honor had been coveted around the world. Thus, the early development of the "flying machine" was hindered by bickering and fierce legal battles. For example, Gabriel Voisin, who along with his brother, Charles, was the first to build aircraft in France on a commercial basis, scoffed at the influence of both the Wright brothers and other aviation pioneers.

A company founded by Glenn Curtiss made the first commercial sale of an aircraft in 1909 to the Aeronautic Society of New York. In the same year, one of the Wright brothers succeeded in meeting U.S. Army specifications for an aircraft and sold it to the government for US$30,000. The Wrights promptly sued Curtiss for patent infringement, virtually freezing the development of the aircraft industry in the United States until World

War I. After the war, U.S. Army war surplus Curtiss JN-4 "Jenny" trainers, along with the de Havilland Moth, manufactured in Great Britain, would carry the postwar barnstorming craze across the country. The Piper Cub, introduced in 1937, quickly became the best-selling one-engine plane of all time in general aviation.

Although Leonardo da Vinci had sketched a helicopter design in 1483, the first sustained helicopter flight was not achieved until 1935, with a coaxial model built by Louis Breguet and René Dorand in France. Within the next five years, Igor Sikorsky had perfected a single-rotor type of helicopter in the United States, opening the door for many practical applications.

The early companies formed by the pioneers eventually merged with and were acquired by larger concerns. For example, the Wright Company, formed in 1909 when a group of New York investors bought the Wright brothers' patents for US$100,000 in cash, was sold to another group in 1915. That group then merged with the Glenn L. Martin companies to form the Wright-Martin Aircraft Corporation, which later became the Wright Aeronautical Company, which merged in 1929 with the Curtiss Aeroplane and Motor Company to form the Curtiss-Wright Corporation, controlled by North American Aviation.

Larger conglomerates dependent upon government support continued to dominate the aircraft industry throughout World War II and the postwar period. The First World War had demonstrated the possibilities of aircraft in wartime; by World War II, aircraft had become an integral part of modern warfare. Many of the phenomenal advancements in aircraft design—jet engines, swept-back wings, electronic flight controls, and composite materials—were funded by governments in wartime. Air Force One, a Boeing 747 that serves as both the U.S. president's air transport and mobile command post in the event of a war, illustrates how important aircraft have become to national security. The technological improvements in military aircraft have been accompanied by a proportional increase in their price tags; a typical 1945 fighter plane cost about US$51,000 (or about US$430,000 in 1998 dollars). By the 1990s, the F-16 jet fighter, a staple of the U.S. Air Force, was selling for approximately US$25 million.

Two new airliners developed in the 1960s, the wide-body ("jumbo") jet and the supersonic transport (SST), met with much different degrees of success. The Boeing 747, the first jumbo jet, which started service on February 9, 1969, was warmly welcomed and widely purchased. Meanwhile, economic and environmental concerns caused the United States to cancel its SST program. The Anglo-French SST (the Concorde) and the Soviet SST (the Tu-144) entered service in 1976 and 1977, respectively. Due to high fuel costs and other concerns, the airlines did not

embrace the Concorde, and production ceased in 1979. Meanwhile, in the Soviet Union a series of disastrous crashes halted development and production of the Tu-144.

Asian countries, such as South Korea, Malaysia, Vietnam, Indonesia, and the Philippines, ordered numerous new planes as their economies grew rapidly in the mid-1990s. However, economic problems began to plague East Asian countries in the late 1990s, causing devaluations of their currencies and forcing them to reconsider their aircraft orders and projects. In early 1998 Philippine Airlines canceled its order of four 747-400 planes from Boeing. Latin America also emerged as a thriving market for the aircraft industry, with orders for US$4 billion worth of planes announced in 1997. Because of their growing economies, Asian and South American countries made up the largest new growth markets for such aircraft. However, South Korea, Indonesia, Malaysia, and even Japan experienced shrinking economies in the late 1990s, leaving short-term expansion of the East Asian market far from certain.

Though constantly under the threat of quick market erosion, from the mid-1990s through 2001 the industry reported fairly strong sales overall. Results differed considerably by segment. By the end of that period, a cyclical slowdown—evident early in 2001 with apparent airline overcapacity and confirmed in late 2001 with the September 11 terrorist attacks—all but guaranteed contraction in the aircraft industry in 2002. The attacks spurred a heavy round of aircraft order cancellations worldwide in the following months. In 2002 some of the cancellations were rescinded as passenger traffic recovered. This prompted some analysts to quietly call for a modest recovery in many segments in 2003. Passenger bookings subsequently rebounded, and excess plane capacity was absorbed or retired, even as the SARS scare in Asia and the instability of many world regions also contributed to the decline of passenger air travel.

CURRENT CONDITIONS

Taking into account other factors, commercial sales were accurately predicted to rise in the 2000s due to the need to replace older, less fuel-efficient aircraft that did not meet new international noise and emissions standards. During a climate-change conference in Kyoto, Japan, United Nations participants laid the groundwork for much stricter aircraft emission regulations to take effect in the early 2000s, under the Kyoto Protocol. The European Union established its own standards, which mandated a 16 percent reduction of nitrous oxide emissions from all new-model engines beginning in 2000 and from all other models beginning in 2006. In 2003, a bill was proposed in the U.S. Senate that allocated several million dollars to reduce both emissions and noise. As a result of the new standards, aircraft producers expected additional orders for new planes and new engines. Airbus expected a need for 782 new aircraft each year into 2020.

During the early 2000s growth was being driven by the need to replace older aircraft and by fleet expansion in developing countries. As the popular Boeing 747s used by many airlines approached the end of their operational lives, manufacturers started offering replacement models, such as Boeing's 777 and Airbus' A340 and A330. In 2001 the U.S. aerospace industry alone generated US$50 billion in sales of civil aircraft (commercial and general aviation), engines, and parts. This represented a 13 percent increase in aircraft shipments and a 4.2 percent growth in civil sector business. In fact, industry analysts predicted that the Asian market would account for about a fifth of sales through 2005. Major manufacturers, such as Boeing and Airbus, received contracts from airlines around the world, so many that in 2003, for example, Boeing had a 1,100 plane order backlog, and Airbus had a 1,500 plane order backlog.

Richard L. Collins pointed out in a January 2007 *Flying* magazine article that "airplane selling is a highly competitive business." Collins discussed issues related to the trend for more experienced pilots to buy used aircraft. Those issues included having cash for "major and expensive surprises," design features such as glass cockpits being available only in new models, and how the aircraft's engine operates during flight.

Turboprops are the only player in the market to enjoy steady growth during the close of the first decade of the twenty-first century. This is directly related to the escalating cost of jet fuel. Of the smaller regional aircraft, Embraer has emerged as the number one player with 56 percent of the market share, replacing Bombadier who fell from 72 percent in 2003 to 31 percent in 2009.

RESEARCH AND TECHNOLOGY

In the wake of the September 11, 2001, terrorist attacks, the U.S. government, on an interim basis, issued orders to the airlines to ensure that existing cockpit doors on commercial aircraft would be locked at all times and secured with extra bars and barriers. It also immediately went a step further, developing a standard redesigned, reinforced cockpit door that the airlines were required to install on all aircraft by 2003.

With an annual research budget exceeding US$1 billion for its aeronautical division, the U.S. National Aeronautics and Space Administration (NASA) contributes substantially to advances in aircraft technology. NASA has assisted the general aviation industry in the United States in such areas as developing new wing and blade designs—including the civil tiltrotor project—and

cockpit technology for business and commuter aircraft. NASA plans to develop aircraft that meet the world's new environmental and safety standards.

Boeing is another leading aircraft technology researcher. Each year the company devotes between US$1.5 billion and US$1.8 billion for research and development. In the mid-1990s, the majority of the company's research funds went to developing its 777. In the early 2000s, with the delivery of its 777s, Boeing turned to refining its existing aircraft and designing new planes. In cooperation with NASA and several universities, Boeing began to develop a blended-wing-body (BWB) plane. The BWB's advantages include superior fuel economy, lower production costs, greater capacity, and greater range than the conventional aircraft of the 1990s. The BWB's prodigious capacity comes from the design of the wings, which hold seats for passengers. Researchers estimate that the plane could be ready by 2015. Meanwhile, Boeing plans to meet the fast-approaching requirements for environmentally friendly aircraft with its 717-200, which features reduced emissions and lower noise levels than its rivals. Test flights of the 717-200 began in early 1998.

In the mid-1990s United States and Russian researchers jointly studied the possibility of developing new supersonic civil aircraft. Although supersonic projects had largely ceased in 1978, both countries had renewed their interest. The U.S. component of the research team consisted of NASA, Boeing, Rockwell-Collins, Pratt & Whitney, and General Electric. The Russian component of the team included Tupolev, the developer of the Tu-144 supersonic jet. The collaborators basically went to work rebuilding the plane's engine in order to use the plane to study the ozone layer and sonic-boom problems.

In contrast to the huge government-sponsored research programs of the aerospace conglomerates, the research and development (R&D) efforts of the makers of ultralights and "kit planes," designed to be assembled by the user, were lean but smart. The popular kit designs offered by Burt Rutan and others in the 1970s offered advanced materials such as exotic composites, plastic foams, and fiberglass and epoxy laminates. Also featured in these designs were canards, small wings placed at the nose of the aircraft, and winglets, fins at the end of the main wing, both of which increased efficiency and stability. Computer modeling enabled designers to incorporate the most advanced wing shapes into designs to be built at home. At least one company has adopted these technologies to produce an inexpensive, six-passenger business turboprop (less than US$1 million, compared to US$3 million and up for competitors).

The Gossamer Condor was a significant experimental aircraft. In 1977 it enabled the first human-powered flight. In 1986 came perhaps Rutan's greatest achievement—the

Voyager, the first aircraft to circle the world without refueling. By the early 2000s, Rutan's conceptions of light-weight craft with intercontinental range had found a military application in the U.S. armed forces—highly capable drones, used effectively during the hostilities in Afghanistan. High-altitude drones with extended range were also expected to acquire satellite-like global or regional communications roles in the new century. Rutan's designs and principles have found their civil application in the Beech Starship, a small business turboprop, and in a small jet fighter/trainer.

Instrumentation is another area of continuing research. A computerized display of flight information, the Electronic Flight Information System (EFIS), has promised to improve the decision-making abilities of pilots by providing an integrated, improved display of navigational, meteorological, and aircraft performance information in the cockpit. State-of-the-art airliners and business craft such as the Boeing 757 and 767, the Airbus A-310, and the Beech Starship are equipped with this system.

The Global Positioning Satellite (GPS) system, first developed for use by the U.S. military, relies on groupings of satellites to provide extremely precise location information (including altitude) to receiving units within airplanes—some small enough to be handheld and inexpensive enough to be used by the general aviation market. However, the units' small size and accuracy have caused concern about their potential misuse in armaments.

Environmental groups in the United States, Europe, and Australia have focused on noise pollution. At the turn of the century, the U.S. Airport Noise and Capacity Act of 1990 had forced U.S. airlines to make their fleets meet quieter noise specifications. Smaller business jets were exempt from this rule. The International Civil Aviation Organization (ICAO) imposed similar standards.

Heavily congested airports have suggested the need for 600-800 seat, ultra-high-capacity aircraft (UHCA or VLCT, very large commercial transport). Airbus began research on such a project, estimated to cost between US$6 billion and US$8 billion. Boeing also began research for its proposed UHCA, the 747-X. The potential market for these aircraft was projected at between 400 and 500 aircraft by 2010. In the early 2000s, Boeing studied development of smaller capacity, but higher speed, transports than the proposed UHCAs.

A concept for a 300-seat supersonic airliner, dubbed the "Orient Express," has been the subject of a study group comprised of engineers and others from Boeing, Aerospatiale, British Aerospace, Japan Aircraft Development Corp., Tupolev, and Alenia. Traveling at Mach 3, or three times the speed of sound, the aircraft would cut travel time between Tokyo and Los Angeles to 4 hours, from the current 10. Fares were projected to eventually fall to a level just 20 percent higher than those for conventional flight.

Two types of vertical takeoff and landing (VTOL) aircraft also were being developed to serve inner-city airports. Ishida Corp. of Japan (in collaboration with U.K. and U.S. firms) is developing the 14-passenger TW-68. With wings that rotate 90 degrees, the craft would allow vertical takeoff and landing. Due to traffic congestion, Boeing projected a need for thousands of civil tiltrotor aircraft (such as the Bell/Boeing V-22) in the first few decades of the new century.

The Polytechnic of Turin announced it is leading an EU-funded project to develop an intercity aircraft designed to use fuel cell technology for the propulsion system and hydrogen storage. The technologies will also have applications involving replacing on board electrical systems with larger "more electric" or "all-electric" aircraft. Related advantages for the technology included low noise and emissions. The Environmentally Friendly Inter City Aircraft powered by Fuel Cells (ENFICA-FC) project is receiving funding from the EU as part of its aeronautics and space priority of the Sixth Framework Programme (FP6).

WORKFORCE

Aircraft companies worldwide employ a vast and skilled labor force, albeit one accustomed to volatility. Aircraft manufacturers strive for stability in employee rosters, although this is seldom possible over the long term in such a cyclical industry. Due to training costs and other investments in labor, such as security clearances, manufacturers had tended to resist dismissing workers, but this pattern has changed as companies like Boeing have been apt to change head counts quickly in order to maintain the bottom line. As manufacturers' fortunes rise and fall, aircraft workers have seen job cuts in the tens of thousands followed by thousands of new hires. The industry likewise has an extensive and active trade union membership and a history of strikes.

Due to the complexity of manufacturing aircraft, the low-unit volumes, and the demand for customization of the finished product, few manufacturers have found labor-saving automation to be cost-effective except in limited applications, such as computer-aided design (or "paperless design"), which was first used extensively in creating the prototype of the B-2 stealth bomber.

Aerospace workers often earn high salaries in relation to other industries, but wages have been under severe pressure as a result of wavering profits and fierce competition. Boeing factory workers in St. Louis, for instance, secured an average wage of US$24.50 an hour as part of their 2001 contract. This amounted to an average gain of 7 percent over the previous rates, which had been in effect since a contentious 1996 pact. However, wage gains in some places were offset by heavy layoffs at Boeing in 2001 and 2002 in the midst of the U.S. recession and skittish demand for aircraft following the September 11, 2001, terrorist attacks. Boeing, in particular, has been an aggressive negotiator with its workers, and has relocated and outsourced many skilled jobs to lower-wage markets like China and Russia. In an earlier cost-cutting measure, Boeing sold a major machining facility to the British company GKN plc, a move that fueled labor concerns over offshore control.

Workers at Canada's Bombardier plants have been more strident in their bid to raise salaries and benefits. In 2002, Montreal-based members of the International Association of Machinists and Aerospace Workers (IAM) went on strike to demand a 5 percent annual wage increase, a retirement age of 58, and greater security against the outsourcing of jobs. Historically, Canadian aerospace workers have earned less than some of their counterparts in the advanced market economies. In 2002, Airbus employees in France also campaigned for a higher wage boost than the 2.5 percent offered by management.

Boeing employees faced pension check problems when their payments were stopped after they were transferred to United Space Alliance (USA), a joint venture with Lockheed Martin Corp. Through USA 1998 e-mail employees were promised that they would be entered into their plan in addition to current plan. Boeing reportedly paid some employees for a few months and then stopped sending checks plus made request for reimbursement. As published in the *Orlando Sentinel,* the official Boeing response was that the mix-up had been caused by a coding error resulting in payment to employees who were not entitled to receive Boeing benefits.

On February 3, 2007, production employees walked off the job at four of Airbus' German factories. The action was reportedly in opposition to what their union claimed might be the elimination of up to 8,000 of the 19,000 Airbus jobs in Germany.

There was a trend for outsourcing manufacturing to low-cost countries. Bombardier opened a plant in Mexico to make flight controls and electrical harnesses. It also announced plans to move some of its fuselage work on the Q400 to China.

In 2007, Embraer was forced to recruit 2,000 more workers to overcome productions and increase deliveries. This move came after experiencing challenges involving some of its leading suppliers and those at its own facilities. In 2006, Embraer took over a production facility in Brazil for the wings of the Embraer 190/195 jets. Kawasaki Heavy Industries had previously handled the facility.

INDUSTRY LEADERS

Boeing. By many measures Boeing Company is one of the world's largest aircraft producers. Its net earnings in 2004 were US$1.8 million, a one-year increase of 160 percent, on revenues of US$52.4 billion. In 2004, Boeing won a key contract to sell its new 787 to Northwest Airlines, Airbus' third-largest customer. The advantages cited as reasons for choosing the 787 were operating economies. The 787 consumed 20 percent less fuel and cost 10 percent less to operate than other liners of similar size. In 2005, the company announced 193 orders from 16 airlines for its 787, which Boeing claims has 32 percent less associated maintenance costs than its rival, the Airbus A330. Boeing was third in the defense aircraft industry, but in terms of commercial market share it trailed Airbus by a very thin margin. In 2008, Boeing reported sales of approximately U.S.$60.9 billion and 159,648 in 2010 employees. According to James Gunsalus, writing for *International Herald Tribune*, Boeing projected profit forecasts of US$4.55 to US$4.75 a share in 2007 and US $5.55 to US $5.75 a share in 2008.

Boeing had its origins in the Pacific Aero Products Company, incorporated in Seattle in 1916 by William Edward Boeing, who soon renamed it the Boeing Airplane Company. In 1928 Boeing Airplane, Boeing Air Transport (a subsidiary airline formed earlier), and engine manufacturer Pratt & Whitney were merged to form the United Aircraft and Transport Corporation. The Air Mail Act of 1934 disintegrated the large conglomerates of the day, such as United Aircraft and Transport, which by then had merged its airline acquisitions to form United Airlines. The Boeing Airplane Company emerged as an independent entity.

Outside the civil aircraft sector, Boeing established interests in the fields of data communications (Boeing Computer Services, 1970), artificial intelligence (Carnegie Group, 1984), and defense electronics (ARGOSystems, 1987). Throughout its history Boeing has been a large supplier of military planes and remains one of the world's largest defense contractors.

In 1997 Boeing dramatically increased its hold on the aircraft market by acquiring one of its leading competitors, McDonnell Douglas Corporation, formerly the third-largest manufacturer of airplanes. With the merger, Boeing controlled about 50 percent of the aircraft industry. McDonnell Douglas had been formed by the 1967 merger of The McDonnell Company and Douglas Aircraft, makers of such illustrious transports as the DC-3 (named C-47 by the U.S. military). For a time during the 1950s, Douglas had produced over half of the world's airliners.

The Boeing 737, the best-selling aircraft in history, has dominated the medium-size, medium-range category and, in the late 1990s, remained Boeing's top model. The most profitable lines for Boeing have been its jumbo jets, such as the 747, and the smaller, 130- to 150-seat planes, like the 737-300. However, since the 1990s both of these lines have faced formidable competition from Airbus.

A new plant opened in Everett, Washington, as Boeing was set to deliver its 787 Dreamliner in 2008. As of May 2007, there were about 568 firm orders from 44 airlines earning distinction as fastest-selling airplane in the history of aviation. Boeing had been faced with challenges linked to delivery delays of composite parts built by different suppliers throughout Asia, Europe, and North America. Industry analysts revealed that investment in the aircraft was approximately US $10 billion. The product launch added more than US$70 billion to Boeing's order backlog. In 2006, Boeing launched a new group known as the Green Team, created to concentrate on designs to reduce fuel usage, develop low-cost environmentally-friendly planes.

Airbus. Airbus S.A.S. is a French company held jointly by manufacturers from four nations. One of the world's two largest makers of planes, it was conceived in the 1960s as Europe's answer to the United States' domination of the large commercial transport market. France and Great Britain had discussed such a venture as early as 1965. However, Britain dropped out of the project due to political disputes. In 1969 the West Germans agreed to partner with France to build the A300, a wide-body, twin-engine airliner. The French company Aerospatiale agreed to hold 37.9 percent of the consortium. In 1971 Construcciones Aeronauticas SA (CASA) of Spain joined Aerospatiale, taking on a 4.2 percent share, and Deutsche Airbus (since 1992 wholly owned by Daimler-Benz) assumed another 37.9 percent share. British Aerospace joined in 1979 and held a 20 percent share of the consortium. Associate members Fokker (Dutch) and Belairbus (Belgian) also have participated in some projects. As of 2003, the European Aeronautic Defence and Space Company (EADS) owned 80 percent of Airbus, and BAE SYSTEMS owned the remaining 20 percent. Airbus had its maiden flight for A380 in 2005 and planned on introducing it in 2007 for hub airports. In addition, Airbus announced plans to build a mid-size A350 plane by 2010. It would be based on the A330 platform and compete directly against Boeing's forthcoming 787 Dreamliner. The company's main aircraft assembly plant is located in Toulouse, France.

In 2004 Airbus booked 370 orders and sales of US$34.4 billion, triple the company's 1997 earnings of US$11.6 billion. Such gains represented substantial inroads in market share. The company claimed 52.7 percent gross market share by number of aircraft units. Its greatest announcement during the mid-2000s was its assembly of the largest aircraft in aviation history, the double-decker Airbus A380, capable of carrying more than 550 passengers. As of 2004, Airbus had 139 orders and commitments for the new model. With the launch of the company's new A350, Airbus had twelve models, including the wide-body twin-engine jets A300 and A310; the single-aisle twin-engine jets A319, A320, and A321; and the four-engine jet A340. Airbus also has developed the A3XX, a super-jumbo jet capable of transporting more than 600 passengers, which it expected to be the main driver of its sales in the twenty-first century. In 2005, Airbus reported sales of approximately US$26.4 billion and 55,000 employees. By February 2007, the company was planning to cut US$2.7 billion from annual costs by 2010 in order to pay for development of its A350. In 2008, the company had a revenue of US$36.45 billion with a workforce of 52,000.

A substantial amount of orders for A350XWB were received from the Middle East and Latin America. Qatar Airways and Columbia's Avianca agreed to buy 80 and 70 of the aircraft respectively. Since 1990, Airbus has been the industry leader of Latin American orders for new aircraft at an estimated 54 percent.

Airbus announced its plans to establish a new delivery center for its aircrafts in Tianjin, North China. Airbus' China branch claimed that in excess of 3,000 A320 aircrafts have been in service for more than 190 airlines globally. They have total time of flight of 50 million hours. More than 5,000 aircrafts were ordered with 32 aircrafts being produced monthly.

Airbus adopted Abaqus Finite Element Analysis (FEA) software from SIMULIA as its preferred solution for static non-linear FEA. SIMULIA is the Dassault Systemes brand for realistic simulation. Dassault agreed to provide software and related services to Airbus sites in Toulouse, France; Filton, UK; Hamburg/Bremen, Germany; and Getafe, Spain. Airbus plans to use the Abaqus FEA software for supporting development of advanced virtual testing methods.

Bombardier Inc. Based in Montreal, Bombardier was the world's third-largest commercial aircraft maker as of 2006 and specialized in regional airplanes. With sales of approximately US$19.7 billion for fiscal year ending January 31, 2008, and 59,760 employees, Bombardier controls the largest percentage of the market in this segment. In 2001 it took in 230 new orders and, among the major producers, was likely the least affected by the downturn that year. The company's leading planes include the Canadair Regional Jet (CRJ) and the de Havilland Dash-8. It is also one of the two largest makers of business jets including Challenger and Learjet.

Substantial improvements were incorporated into the interior design of CRJ NextGen aircraft. They included enlarged passenger windows for increased over-all viewing area. In addition, overhead bins were modified to accommodate larger roller bags and LED lighting was utilized to brighten the cabin. Bombardier Regional Aircraft President Steven Ridolfi said that this "new interior will enhance passenger experience and we have lowered the operating costs to airlines."

According to *Flight International,* Bombardier was "under pressure to revitalise its offering with a new generation of products" following canceling the launch of its CSeries. The company announced plans to spend the same level of research and development funding for this series in the 2007 to 2008 financial year as it had in 2006 to 2007. The launch decision was postponed and service entry target set for 2013. In 2008, they signed a deal with Lufthansa for delivery of 60 aircraft and 30 options in their C-series.

Flight International also reported that Bombardier was reaping the benefits of a resurgence in orders for the Dash 8 turboprop represented by its Q Series. In 2004, the turboprops represented about 15 percent of regional aircraft market orders. By 2006, that percentage was approximately two-thirds with Bombardier experiencing many Q Series orders.

Embraer. The Brazilian manufacturer Embraer-Empresa Brasileira de Aeronautica, created in 1969, makes small regional jets and turboprop transports, of which it is the second-largest producer after Bombardier. Cancellations and low order volume hit the firm especially hard in 2001. At that time, orders declined by 90 percent from the previous year. The year 2000 had been a banner year for orders, though, so some drop-off was expected. Embraer expected to deliver a total of 135 planes in 2002 and only slightly more in 2003. That year, the company reported US$2.1 billion in sales. Like many other smaller manufacturers, the company has performed significant subcontract work, specifically on the McDonnell Douglas MD-11 and the Boeing 777. The company also produces military aircraft in cooperation with Alenia and Aermacchi in the AMX program. Embraer reported sales of approximately US$3.8 billion in 2006. In 2007, Embraer planned to increase deliveries across its ranges resulting in second quarter output rising by 60 percent in excess of the first quarter to 40 aircraft. This would enable the company to meet its 2007 full-year target of 165 to 170 aircraft *Flight International* claimed.

Embraer launched the Advanced Range (AR) versions of its Embraer 170 and Embraer 175 aircraft. These versions were designed with current and potential customer requirements for increased range and operating flexibility in mind. Northwest Airlines was the launch customer for Embraer 175 AR. December 2008 was set as the target certification date for the new versions.

MAJOR COUNTRIES IN THE INDUSTRY

United States. The United States has been a world leader since the dawn of aviation in the early 1900s. In the late 1990s, the United States produced about 60 percent of the world's aircraft, led primarily by the Boeing Corp. but also by companies such as Cessna, Raytheon, and Bell Helicopter. The United States is both the world's largest producer of and the world's largest market for civil aircraft: more than half of all flights originate or terminate within the country. The United States remained the world leader in 2004, with more than 5,200 passenger aircraft delivered, valued at US$412.7 billion. The U.S. aerospace industry started 2005 off well, with most domestic companies showing profit increases. Raytheon's net income rose 30 percent, with aircraft sales showing an 18 percent increase. In 1951 the United States produced 80 percent of the world's airliners, a figure that declined to about 60 percent in the twenty-first century with the ascent of Airbus and regional manufacturers such as Bombardier. The FAA predicted that the U.S. contribution to the worldwide commercial fleet would rise to 7,419 by 2009.

Approximately 80 percent of active civil U.S. aircraft are classified as general aviation aircraft; the United States accounts for 75 percent of the world's estimated 322,630 fixed-wing (as opposed to rotary-wing) general aviation aircraft, excluding the Commonwealth of Independent States and China. The country's greatest difficulties have been in the rotary wing sector, particularly helicopters and piston-engine aircraft, both of which have suffered considerable trade deficits. Despite these deficits, the United States remains the world's top exporter of aircraft, especially to Asia and the European Union.

France. France is a major competitor of the United States in both the commercial and general aviation markets. In 2004, France delivered 482 passenger aircraft with $57.7 billion. By 2001, the country's industry leader Airbus S.A.S. captured 50.2 percent of the commercial airliner market in terms of numbers and 61.0 percent net market share in terms of value. France also competes strongly in the general aviation market, with its piston-engine planes and helicopters.

State-owned Aerospatiale, which owned a 37 percent share of Airbus, was created in 1970 through the merger of Sud-Aviation, Nord-Aviation, and SEREB. The company is a member of several international joint ventures relating to military and civil transports, and has begun manufacturing planes in the United States. Another notable French company is Dassault-Breguet, which introduced the first of its highly successful line of Mirage fighters in 1955. The company's Falcon series of business jets also is well respected. However, France's insistence on government-owned aircraft companies plagued its industry in the late 1990s. Airbus is now the only major competitor to commercial industry leader Boeing. In the late 1990s, its other shareholders called upon the French government to allow it to become a single corporate entity in order to continue competing as strongly as possible against Boeing.

Germany. In the late 1990s and early 2000s, Germany played a central role in many European joint ventures, such as Airbus and Eurocopter. That helped explain why, in 2004, Germany's sales in aircraft were US$96.6 billion for 989 passenger aircraft delivered. Part of the German aerospace conglomerate Messerschmitt-Bolkow-Blohm GmbH (MBB) can be traced to a company Willy Messerschmitt founded in 1923, which produced sport planes, gliders, and military craft such as the Bf 109 and the world's first operational jet fighter, the Me 262. The company now manufactures helicopters and business aircraft and is a member of various joint ventures. Daimler-Benz AG, Germany's largest manufacturer, which owns MBB as well as Deutsche Aerospace, took over a former Soviet plant in Dresden and has refurbished it to repair existing Soviet-built aircraft and manufacture sections of new Western aircraft such as the Fokker 100. Daimler-Benz also owns a large share of Airbus.

China. China represented an expanding market for aircraft and also was a minor producer, mainly to meet its own domestic demand. According to a Chinese government forecast issued in 2001, the country was expected to buy 400 new aircraft between 2001 and 2005 in order to support a projected passenger load of 100 million a year. As of 2000, China had 67 million passengers on its planes, making it the world's sixth-largest market in terms of volume. In 2004, China delivered 1,790 passenger aircraft woth $241.7 billion, as reported in Airbus' *Global Market Forecast 2004-2023.*

Two state-led manufacturing consortia lead China's production, China Aviation Industry (AVIC) I and II. Both produce civil aircraft, but AVIC II is more heavily involved in defense transport. According to *Xinhua Economic News,* the Chinese government announced its plans to start development of aircraft with a takeoff weight of more than 100 tons or exceeding 150 seats. It also planned to advance efforts related to key techniques in design, manufacturing and testing. China aimed to accelerate the development and manufacture of its first turbofan regional airliner, the ARJ-21, and produce a range of indigenous regional jets.

In May 2007, The People's Bank of China issued a set of commemorative coins featuring their country's new-generation fighter aircraft, the Jian-10. The issuance consisted of 10,000 gold coins with a face value of US$19.5 each. Shenzhen Guobao Mint produced the coins. China Gold Coin was set to distribute them.

China sent mixed signals to potential manufacturing partners and suppliers around the world. It engaged most of the world's leading aircraft makers in partnership talks, but several of these projects were stalled by government policies. The Chinese airlines, for their part, have been eager to order foreign-built planes, but even some of these orders have been delayed by government interventions. One reason may be that the government has been divided over whether to protect the domestic industry or gain access to the resources of the world's largest aircraft manufacturers. Regional jets are expected to be one of the most demanded items in the Chinese market in the first two decades of the twenty-first century.

Japan. Japan is home to a medium-sized contingent of aircraft manufacturers that serve mostly as subcontractors to larger producers like Boeing and Embraer. The result for Japan was passenger aircraft delivered of US$106.4 billion in 2004, placing it fifth among the world's aircraft producing countries. Mitsubishi Heavy Industries, Kawasaki Heavy Industries, and Fuji Heavy Industries have cooperated in the development of the Boeing 777, which may explain that airplane's strong Asian sales. Flight instruments, electronic control components, and carbon fiber for the tail section have all been supplied by Japanese companies.

In the early 2000s Japanese firms sought to take a more central role in building medium-to-large regional craft, jets with between 80 and 110 seats, and had a number of design concepts in early testing. Analysts have estimated that the Japanese industry still lags 10 years behind that of the United States.

Asia Pacific. The Asia Pacific region was expected to show significant growth, and was viewed by the European Aeronautic Defence & Space (EADS) consortium as one of its top three markets in 2005. That same year, Airbus announced that India would be purchasing 570 aircraft over the next 20 years to meet the demand of its expanding market. Boeing also announced in April 2005 that the company would focus marketing efforts on Asian carriers. The country's aviation industry was growing rapidly, and a number of new airlines opened during the early 2000s. In the Airbus *Global Market Forecast 2004-2023,* the report stated that "China and India have the potential to reshape the travel industry."

BIBLIOGRAPHY

"Airbus Chooses SIMULIA Software." *Airline Industry Information,* 22 May 2007.

"Airbus Employees Strike at Four German Plants." *International Herald Tribune,* 3 February 2007.

"Airbus Orders Take Off in Middle East, Latin America." Cargo News Asia, 31 May 2007. Available from http:/www.cargonewsasia.com.

"Airbus Sees Strong Cargo Market." *The Journal of Commerce Online,* 30 March 2004.

"Airbus to Set Up New Delivery Center in Tianjin." *Alestron,* 24 May 2007.

Bernstein, Mark. "Four Years from Launch, What's the Buzz on the A380." *World Trade,* April 2004.

"Boeing: A Comeback in the Air." *Business Week Online,* 13 April 2005.

"Boeing Commercial Airplanes." *Airfinance Journal,* April 2005.

"Bombardier Boosts Income, Revenue on Strong Aircraft Sales." 30 May 2007. Available from http://atwonline.com.

"Bombardier Introduces Next Generation Family of Regional Jets." 31 May 2007. Available from http://www.sys-con.com.

"Bright Outlook in 2004." *Airline Business,* 1 February 2004.

"China to Buy 400 Aircraft in Five Years." *Alestron,* 3 July 2001.

"China to Expand Civil Aircraft Industry in 2006–2010 Period Beijing, May 15 (CEIS)—China's Civil Aircraft Industry Will Expand Through Independent Innovation and International Cooperation, According to the Government's 11th Five-Year Plan for the Development of Industry." *Xinhua Economic News,* 15 May 2007.

"China to Issue Fighter Aircraft Commemorative Coins." *Xinhua News Agency,* 28 May 2007.

"Clear Policy Sought on Emissions." *Flight International,* 22 May 2007.

Collins, Richard. "Why You Should Buy a New Airplane." *Flying,* January 2007.

"Component Tracking." *Flight International,* 13 April 2004.

Done, Kevin. "Embraer Recruits 2,000." *The Financial Times,* 16 May 2007.

Draper, Deborah J., ed. *Business Rankings Annual.* Detroit: Thomson Gale, 2004.

"EADS Consolidates in Asia Pacific." *Australasian Business Intelligence,* 13 January 2005.

"EU Project to Develop First Fuel-Cell Aircraft." *Cordis,* 31 May 2007. Available from http://cordis.europa.eu

"Embraer Boosts E-Jet Endurance." *Flight International,* 22 May 2007.

"Embraer Launches Advanced Range Version of Two Models." *Airline Industry Information,* 23 May 2007.

Flores, Jackson. "Forecasts." *Flight International,* 27 April 2004.

"German Antimonopoly Agency Allows JV to Convert A320 Planes." *Russia & CIS Business and Financial Newswire,* 21 May 2007.

Global Market Forecast 2004-2023. Airbus S.A.S., 2004-2005. Available from http://www.airbus.com.

Gunsalus, James. "Boeing's 787s Enter Final-Assembly Phase." *Detroit Free Press,* 22 May 2007.

Holmes, Stanley. "Crunch Time for Boeing; As an August Deadline Looms for the 787 Dreamliner, Company Executives Insist on It's On Target, Despite Supplier Delays." *Business Week Online,* 22 May 2007.

"Hoover's Company Capsules." *Hoover's Online,* 2004. Available from http://www.hoovers.com.

"India Will buy 570 Aircraft–Forecast." *Airline Industry Information,* 22 June 2005.

Kingsley-Jones, Max. "Production." *Flight International,* 13 December 2004.

Lazich, Robert S., ed. *Market Share Reporter.* Detroit: Thomson Gale, 2004.

Morrison, Murdo. "Believing in Bombardier." *Flight International,* 3 April 2007.

Morrison, Murdo, and Helen Massy-Bresford. "Bombardier's Bet." *Reed Business Information,* 6 March 2007.

Napier, David H. "2001 Year-End Review and 2002 Forecast: An Analysis." Aerospace Industries Association, 2002. Available from http://www.aia-aerospace.org.

Schneider, Andrew C. "U.S. Companies Still Like Russia." *Kiplinger Business Forecasts,* 8 May 2007.

"Senate Bill Would Promote Quiet Aircraft Technology." *Noise Regulation Report,* April 2003.

Sobie, Brendan. "Supersonic Transports." *Flight International,* 6 July 2004.

Solon, Daniel. "Business Jet Market Gets a Lift From Climb in Corporate Earnings: Studies Predict Thousands of Planes, Worth Billions of Dollars, Will Be Delivered in the Next Few Years." *International Herald Tribune,* 22 May 2007.

Taylor, Alex. "Lord of the Air." *Fortune,* 10 November 2003.

"Teal Group Analysts Predict that 6,743 Commercial Aircraft, Valued at $421 Billion, Are to Be Built Between 2003 and 2012." *Airfinance Journal,* September 2003.

"Teal Predicts 2,909 Regional Aircraft Worth US$65.9 Billion to be Built in 2009-2018." Teal Group Corporation, 15 June 2009. Available at www.tealgroup.com.

"U.S. Aerospace Industry Statistics." International Trade Administration, 1989-2009.

"U.S. Firms Start Year Well." *Flight International,* 3 May 2005.

Wessel, Harry. "Pensions Lost in Space: Boeing Employees Transferred to United Space Alliance Were Promised Pensions — Until Now." *Orlando Sentinel,* 27 February 2007.

SIC 3480

DEFENSE AND ARMAMENTS

NAICS CODE(S)

33299. The armaments industry designs and manufactures the world's military equipment and accessories, including air, sea, and ground weapons. Examples of industry products range from military handguns and grenade launchers to planes, missiles, and tanks. Nuclear weapons are not discussed in this section. Certain firms in this industry also produce for the commercial aerospace sector; for more information on these activities, see also **Aircraft Manufacturing.**

INDUSTRY SNAPSHOT

In the 1980s, toward the end of the Cold War, global military spending peaked at more than US$1.36 trillion. It leveled off at about US$800 billion in the mid-1990s, due primarily to massive reductions in the post-Cold War era. Boosted by the U.S. war on terror and increased defense budgets in China and India, world military

Sales Figures of Industry Leaders, 2009

US$60.9 billion — Boeing
US$31.98 billion — General Dynamics
US$34.9 billion — BAE
US$45.18 billion — Lockheed Martin
US$56.6 billion — European Aeronautic Defense and Space Company

SOURCE: Hoover's Online.

spending rose for a sixth consecutive year to reach US$1.04 trillion in 2004, which equaled 2.6 percent of global gross domestic product. The United States remains, by far, the world's principal weapons producer and broker and is home to a number of leading manufacturers that arm many nations throughout the world. The country accounted for nearly half of all military expenditures in 2004. Russia also retains its position as the world's second largest armament manufacturer, followed by the European Union and China. By 2009, the total for global military spending had reached US$1.53 trillion, or 2.7 percent of the global gross domestic product. U.S. spending was at US$661 billion in 2009, 43 percent of the world's share.

The three basic arms industry segments are land weapons (ordnance), aircraft, and ships. The military equipment industry was helped in the 1990s by the post-Gulf War rearmament in the Middle East as well as the prolonged peacekeeping mission in the former Yugoslavia for which the United States, France, Germany, the United Kingdom, and other participating countries required defense equipment. Continued confrontation between the United States and Iraq kept defense spending a priority in the United States into the late 1990s. The September 11, 2001, terrorist attacks against the United States, subsequent military action in Afghanistan, and the U.S.-led war with Iraq in 2003, resulted in spending increases that lasted well into the 2000s.

ORGANIZATION AND STRUCTURE

In 2004 global military expenditures, excluding nuclear weapons and certain aerospace equipment and systems,

totaled about US$1.04 trillion, with the United States accounting for nearly half of that figure at $US455 billion. Global arms sales, however, declined for the third year in a row, to US$25.6 billion in 2003. The majority of those arms were purchased by the U.S. federal government to supply its armed forces. These purchases were made by nearly every country in the world, and rebel groups as well. Major arms-consuming regions outside of North America included the European Union, the Middle East, Commonwealth of Independent States, and east and central Asia. Developing nations accounted for a little over two-thirds of the global arms export market. The decline in arms sales in the early to mid-2000s was attributed to the growth of protectionist policies in developed countries and an unstable international economy which had developing nations upgrading existing weapons systems rather than purchasing new ones.

The United States and the Soviet Union dominated the arms industry during the last half of the twentieth century. The United States made slightly over 50 percent of worldwide arms sales in 2000, about US$18.6 billion in all. Russia retained the vast majority of the Soviet Union's military might after the Soviet state was dismantled in the early 1990s. Moving into the twenty-first century, the former rivals continued to design the world's leading weapons systems, many of which were produced throughout the world. Certain systems manufactured outside the United States have been under licensing agreements with U.S.-based developers. Significant portions of U.S. weapons, for example, were manufactured under license in Italy and Japan. Many weapons have also been produced in the Commonwealth of Independent States (CIS), which is a voluntary economic organization that includes all Soviet states except the three Baltic republics, as well as France, Germany, and a few other nations.

The arms industry in the early 1990s represented the culmination of a century of industry volatility. Indeed, arms industry statistics, which can be difficult to pin down accurately, have historically experienced wild fluctuations within the global political landscape. The entire industry can be depressed one year, and within a few months experience a robust turnaround as the result of a major regional conflict that has boosted sales. Arms sales vary greatly according to procurement budgets set by political bodies in specific countries.

In the 1990s there was a nearly invisible shift in the defense industry structure, at least in the United States, where service industries assumed an increasingly important role. The change was due to the growing importance of information technology for modern weapons design. By the end of the decade, service workers—employees who install, maintain, troubleshoot, operate, and integrate hardware and software systems—accounted for almost three out of four of U.S. Defense Department contract jobs, up 50 percent from 1984 levels. IT companies BDM, SAIC, and Computer Sciences Corporation became major suppliers to the American military.

Weapons Types. The three basic arms industry segments are ordnance, or land weapons; aircraft; and ships, including destroyers, submarines, carriers, and smaller ships. Land weapons include artillery, land vehicles, and small arms such as rifles and hand grenades. Major categories of artillery, or heavy weapons, include cannon, which typically fire low-velocity exploding projectiles; mortars, which fire shells in a high arcing trajectory; howitzers, which fire a variety of shells; and rocket launchers. Land weapons also include anti-aircraft weapons and missiles, which account for a comparatively large proportion of weapons expenditures worldwide.

Types of missiles include guided, which are directed by remote control or internal mechanisms; surface-to-surface, including small tactical and larger strategic missiles; air-launched; and surface-to-air. Leading U.S. missile systems in the 1990s included the AIM-9M Sidewinder and AIM-7F Sparrow air-to-air missiles; the RGM-84A Harpoon antiship system; the TOW-2 antitank missile; and the Patriot antimissile system. Equivalent Russian missiles included the Aphid, Atoll, and Apex air-to-air missiles; the Styx antiship system; and the Spigot and Spandrel antitank missiles. Italy, the United Kingdom, and France had similar missile systems.

Land vehicles include tanks, personnel and equipment carriers and transports, and other armed and unarmed vehicles. The dominant armored vehicle in the mid-1990s was the U.S. M1A1 Abrams battle tank. Developed at a cost of US$20.4 billion, each tank cost about US$4.4 million to produce and was designed to absorb direct hits from certain armor-piercing shells. The high-tech M1 was powered by a turbine engine that allowed the massive vehicle to cruise at 60 miles per hour while a damper allowed the operator of the 120 mm cannon to fire laser-aimed projectiles with high accuracy. The tank was also equipped with infrared sights for night vision. The M1's peers included the Russian-designed T-80 and T-72, as well as tanks built in Germany (the Leopard series), the United Kingdom (Challenger, Chieftan, and Vickers), and France (AMX-30B2), among others.

Major weapons in the aircraft segment include the U.S. F-22, F-16 Falcon, F-15 Eagle, and F/A-18 Hornet—all fighter/attack jets. Similar Russian planes were the aging MIG-29 Fulcrum, Su-27 Flanker, and Su-24 Fencer. North Atlantic Treaty Organization (NATO) contributions to the fighter jet segment have included the

Mirage (France) and the Tornado (United Kingdom, Germany, and Italy). In addition to these fighters were larger craft such as the U.S. C-17 airlift-type plane and the B-2 (Stealth) Bomber. Also included in the aircraft group are helicopters, among the most respected of which has been the U.S. UH-60 Blackhawk developed in the early 1990s.

BACKGROUND AND DEVELOPMENT

Organized warfare was first recorded around 3500 B.C. following the first settlements of Western civilization. As communities expanded to accommodate growing herds and populations, conflicts rose between neighboring villages. Crude weapons, such as catapults and hunting tools, were used throughout the period. It was not until about A.D. 1300, particularly with the invention of gunpowder, that more advanced weaponry evolved. After pikes and longbows were introduced in the fourteenth century, for example, the French invented the cannon in the fifteenth century. The first ship-borne cannon was introduced in the sixteenth century, and breakthrough inventions like the rifled gun barrel followed in the 17th and 18th centuries. Despite advances, weapons remained crude by modern standards until later in the eighteenth century.

By the eighteenth century artillery had become a staple of every serious war machine. Soldiers were usually armed with guns, and horse-drawn cannons were common. However, up to that time, the arms industry was relatively undeveloped, as most armies expected their soldiers to supply their own weapons and ammunition. The onset of the Industrial Revolution in Europe changed the arms industry during the early 1800s. The ability to effectively make more complex and expensive weapons made it necessary for governments to assume a greater role in purchasing arms. The result was competition among many nations to design and build the most destructive weapons. That competition culminated in the early twentieth century with the creation of advanced weapons such as tanks, armored personnel carriers, flame throwers, and even military aircraft.

New weapons developed during the late 19th and early 20th centuries radically changed the concept of war and battle. It suddenly became possible, for example, to transport soldiers rapidly over water, land, and through the air, and for ships to do battle without ever coming in sight of their adversary. Similarly, long-range cannon, missiles, bombers, and jets effectively reduced the capacity of ground and sea troops to defend a position. Importantly, the introduction of atomic explosive devices in 1945 had a momentous impact on the concept of warfare, and therefore, on the arms industry. That development contributed to a new phenomenon in the global weapons industry: the world arms trade became dominated by two nuclear superpowers, the United States and the Soviet Union.

The Cold War. Beginning in the 1950s the arms industry was influenced by Cold War politics and the ensuing arms race between the United States and the Soviet Union. Immediately after World War II, the United States came to dominate armament production in the non-Communist sphere. For more than a decade, the United States was effectively the sole supplier of major weapons to the free world. Besides equipping its own forces, the United States outfitted armies throughout Western Europe and much of Latin America, Asia, the Middle East, and parts of Africa. At one point in the early 1950s, in fact, the United States was shipping nearly US$15 billion worth of military equipment and services annually to war-torn Western European nations alone. The United States began to cede its monopoly on the Western military market during the late 1950s. By the early 1960s the United States still controlled about 40 percent of the total global arms export market, while other NATO countries were supplying more than 15 percent and the rest were served primarily by Eastern Bloc nations. Nonetheless, the United States continued to be the leading global arms manufacturer, supplying more than 90 percent of all noncommunist arms.

Between the 1950s and the 1980s the two countries became engaged in a heated competition to develop the most deadly and feared conventional and nuclear weapons. Massive investments by both nations in arms technology produced a dazzling array of high-tech weaponry that tested the limits of human ingenuity. By the 1980s, in fact, both countries and their allies had amassed enough firepower to destroy civilization many times over. The acronym MAD (mutually assured destruction) was coined to describe the military stalemate or balance of power that existed between the Eastern and Western blocs.

The Cold War intensified during the 1950s and 1960s as the Soviet Union continued to amass military might along with the United States and its allies. Like the United States, the Soviet Union sustained its dominant lead over other nations of the world through intense research and development expenditures, including those related to aerospace initiatives. The Soviet Union was initially slow to enter the arms export market; between 1968 and 1972, it exported a total of about US$25 billion of arms to foreign countries compared to about US$55 billion exported by the United States. However, it significantly increased foreign sales in the 1970s and 1980s, exporting US$175 billion worth of weapons between 1973 and 1982 compared to about US$115 billion shipped by U.S. arms manufacturers. In contrast,

all other nations combined exported less than US$100 billion between 1973 and 1982. Meanwhile, the United States and the Soviet Union each budgeted hundreds of billions of dollars annually for their own defense.

The global defense industry boomed during the 1980s as the United States launched its final drive to end the Cold War. In the mid-1980s the U.S. government increased its military procurement budget and began investing aggressively in the research and development of a new generation of nuclear and non-nuclear weapons and defense systems. The result was explosive industry growth as the U.S. arms procurement budget ballooned to a peacetime record of about US$115 billion annually. The Soviet Union had little choice but to try to match the challenge and sustain the balance of power. By the late 1980s, however, the United States was close to winning the arms race as it made plans to begin developing its costly and controversial "Star Wars" missile defense system.

Meanwhile, other nations began to increase their sales and purchases of arms. In 1987 global defense spending reached an all-time high of approximately US$1.15 trillion for defense equipment and armaments. The arms export market of all markets, except the United States and the Soviet Union, had grown to about US$70 billion by 1988. U.S. and Soviet arms producers continued to dominate the overall industry because of demand in their home countries, but the export market outside of those nations was increasingly available to arms suppliers. By the mid-1980s the United States and the Soviet Union were supplying about 20 percent and 30 percent, respectively, of the arms export market. Other NATO countries controlled about 30 percent of the market, and the remaining 20 percent was met by other nations.

With the end of Cold War and the collapse of the Soviet Union, world weapons production decreased significantly. The declines eventually leveled out, due to Middle East rearmament after the Gulf War and the Western intervention in the war in the former Yugoslavia. By the end of the decade, some producing nations were reporting increases again. A major shift in the 1990s came when the developing world took the lead in arms imports, with total world arms imports rising from 35 to 57 percent between 1989 and 1999. Another trend was the consolidation of the industry by a wave of mergers and acquisitions in the last half of the decade. Consolidation that began in the United States moved to Western Europe. Similar consolidation was seen as inevitable in the overly large industries of Russia and China as well.

After the Cold War, there was a trend for multinational military operations in the 1990s. Global defense spending dropped continuously from its apex in 1987, reaching a post-Cold War peak in 1998. Expenditures rose again between 1998 and 2000 to approximately US$798 billion, an increase of about 5 percent. Most of the world's military powerhouses slashed their defense budgets drastically in the 1990s and early 2000s, although the administration of President George W. Bush requested significant defense increases for the first half of the 2000s in response the war in Afghanistan and the war against terrorism. The Stockholm International Peace Institute suggested that the plans for military growth of some nations could result in increased global procurement expenditures in the later 2000s.

Although defense has historically been a domestic industry, more governments have begun to expand armament sources to include foreign companies. By 1999, for example, the United States was eighth on the list of the world's top importers, purchasing a significant US$800 million in arms from the United Kingdom, Germany, Israel, Australia, and the Netherlands.

The reasons for the trend are varied. For example, the cost of producing modern, high-tech military technology has skyrocketed, and few nations besides the United States or possibly Russia are able to support the costs of a domestic industry that provides for all defense needs. A single 1972 F-16 cost US$30 million in 1996, which was still substantially less than F-22s, which were expected to cost US$100 million each, according to figures released by *The Economist.* If domestic companies cannot afford to produce weapons, a government must purchase them elsewhere. Similarly, if a government cannot purchase all weapons produced by a domestic firm, that firm must seek foreign markets. France has even claimed that arms exports are necessary to maintain its trade balance.

As an alternative to individual governments producing their own defense equipment, certain countries have organized joint ventures to share development and manufacturing costs. In 2001, France, Germany, Italy, Spain, Sweden, and the United Kingdom launched the European Technology Acquisition Programme (ETAP). ETAP was an unprecedented agreement that joined both governments and specific industries in the development of new aircraft. In 2001 U.S. defense contractor Raytheon and the French Thales announced that their national regulators had approved a joint venture for the production of new radar systems and command and control centers.

Cross-border cooperation between defense companies brought advantages as well as problems. Besides dispersing the prohibitive costs of armament production, multinational defense projects also ensure that participating nations possess uniform, interoperable equipment. This is vital at a time when coalitions of countries such as NATO and United Nations troops cooperate in peacekeeping or other missions. Such operations function more smoothly when all participants have compatible technology and equipment. A substantial share of the costs to bring new members into NATO result from technological upgrades of the military equipment of those nations to make them compatible. However, technology exchange can also be an obstacle to cooperation when different nations view export controls on technology differently. For example, tensions arose between the United States, which works to prevent its state-of-the-art weaponry from reaching unstable regions or so-called rogue states, and its European allies, who are often willing to make such exports to keep home companies commercially viable.

As companies turned to the world market, there was an increase of competition for weapons sales. In the ensuing struggle for survival during the mid-1990s, the global defense industry endured a wave of consolidation. Boeing acquired defense industry leader McDonnell Douglas, and Rolls-Royce purchased U.S. defense firm Allison. In November 1999, U.K. giant British Aerospace merged with Marconi Electronic Systems to form BAE Systems. A pan-European merger of Matra BAe Dynamics, Aerospatiale Matra Missiles, and Alenia Marconi Systems' missile division resulted in MBDA, the second largest missile company in the world. Intense consolidation of the European market was expected to continue and to sweep through Russian and Chinese defense firms too.

CURRENT CONDITIONS

According to a report issued by the London-based International Institute for Strategic Studies in March 2010, the total spent on global defense budgets rose from US$1.3 trillion in 2006 to US$1.5 trillion in 2009. The United States led with spending of US$661 billion, nearly half of the total figure.

During the mid-2000s, the defense industry was benefiting from the U.S.-led war with Iraq and Afghanistan. The war began with a massive military assault on the city of Baghdad in March 2003, as the Bush administration sought to free Iraq from dictator Saddam Hussein and uncover weapons of mass destruction. The invasion was followed by a long-term military presence; by October 2010, the U.S. military had roughly 48,000 troops in Iraq and had reported more than 4,430 casualties and nearly 32,000 wounded. All other nations had withdrawn their troops.

Unlike the nation's first war with Iraq during the early 1990s, which was fought largely from the air, soldiers involved in Operation Iraqi Freedom in the 2000s faced significant combat on the ground from well-armed opposition forces. In its June 17, 2004, issue, *The New York Times* noted: "By the time of the coalition invasion, Iraq had one of the largest conventional arms stockpiles in the world. According to one American military estimate, this included three million tons of bombs and bullets; millions of AK-47s and other rifles, rocket launchers and mortar tubes; and thousands of more sophisticated arms like ground-to-air missiles. Much of the arsenal was stored in vast warehouse complexes, some of which occupied several square miles. As war approached, Iraqi commanders ordered these mountains of munitions to be dispersed across the country in thousands of small caches."

Although the Baghdad invasion called for a significant share of armaments, defense contractors already were benefiting from increased spending on weapons before the assault. For example, in its February 2003 issue, *Aviation Week & Space Technology* reported that the Department of Defense had modified an existing contract with leading defense contractor Raytheon to include 167 additional Tactical Tomahawk missiles for US$224.5 million. In addition, the publication revealed that the U.S. military had tentative plans to purchase about 2,200 PAC-3 interceptor missiles from Lockheed Martin, as well as 1,400 Patriot PAC-2 GEM+ missiles from Raytheon.

By late 2003, Congress had approved President Bush's request for US$87 billion in funding for operations in Iraq and Afghanistan. Of this total, US$67 billion was earmarked for military spending. Heading into the mid-2000s, U.S. defense contractors and related industries stood to benefit from increasing levels of defense spending. From 2001 to 2004, U.S. defense spending increased more than 35 percent as the nation sought to modernize its fighting forces. The U.S.-led war with Iraq in 2003 made defense spending a top priority.

The February 9, 2004, issue of *Aviation Week & Space Technology,* provided information from Pentagon Comptroller Dov Zakheim that revealed that US$74.9 billion was marked for procurement in the Fiscal 2005 defense budget, Plans were in place to obtain "42 F/A-18E/Fs, 24 F/A-22s, 14 C-17s and 11 V-22s. Another US$68.9 billion is tagged for research and development. A total of US$2 billion, a 32 percent increase, will go for unmanned aerial vehicle (UAV) production including four Global Hawks (with long-lead funding for six more), nine Predators (among them two of the faster, larger B-models) and 24 Shadow-200s. Another US$1.6 billion is earmarked for precision weaponry."

In a news release preview, Strategic Affairs Manager Roberto Mangabeira Unger revealed that Brazil's National Defense Plan projected establishing partnerships with countries like Russia and France to build a state-of-the-art weapons industry. Unger added that the partnerships must include a significant element of research and development in Brazil. In April 2008, Brazil had reached out to Russia and signed an agreement to jointly develop jet fighters.

RESEARCH AND TECHNOLOGY

Government spending on research and technology declined during the late 1990s along with the overall global reduction in defense spending. Nevertheless, a vast amount of technology developed near the end of the Cold War was introduced during that period. Most notable were new generation aircraft and missile systems developed by the United States and its allies. The U.S. government, in fact, continued to spend heavily on weapons research and development during the early 1990s, although expenditures declined 50 percent by the mid-1990s. In 1994, for example, the United States was completing development of its new stealth fighter jets, the F-22, the F/A-18E/F fighter, and the Joint Strike Fighter. Other aircraft that were in the works in 2001 were the V-22 Osprey Aircraft and the C-17 Transport Aircraft. Similarly, the United States introduced innovative and costly stealth aircraft—the B-2 bomber and the F-117A fighter jet, as well as the F-22—in the mid-1990s.

In addition to the most technologically advanced jets and bombers in the world, the United States also introduced the world's most advanced helicopters in the early 1990s. The principal helicopter under development throughout the 1990s was the RAH-66 Comanche, a highly advanced, armored reconnaissance unit that far surpassed any helicopter being developed elsewhere in the world. Of lesser but still impressive technological prowess was the AW-64 Apache Attack Helicopter. This jet-powered machine was capable of cruising through battlefields at high speeds and simultaneously launching a barrage of cannon fire, rockets, and laser-guided missiles in multiple directions. The Apache's fatal Hellfire missile system allowed a pilot to unleash an armor-piercing missile that was aimed and guided by a soldier on the ground, allowing the Apache pilot to seek other targets.

In addition to high-tech weaponry developed late in the Cold War, some of the most advanced defense devices included high-flying planes and satellite systems that gathered intelligence and helped ground forces communicate. Advanced military imaging satellites used by both Commonwealth of Independent States and Western forces, for example, were capable of reading a car's license plate from space. In addition, early warning satellite systems could quickly detect launched missiles and relay their flight patterns to observers on the ground. Similarly, the U.S.-bred Airborne Warning & Control System (AWACS) could monitor and control air and land combat from a plane in the air.

In the mid-1990s numerous projects under development by companies throughout the world manifested the ongoing trend toward high-tech space age weaponry. One example was work done in the United States on a new breed of non-lethal weapons designed to incapacitate, but not necessarily kill, the enemy. Although they were considered at least a decade away from actual use in the field, the weapons showed great promise, and manufacturers and the U.S. government were investing in their development. Among the many non-lethal technologies under development were optical munitions, which used isotropic and directed radiators to generate a high-powered, multi-dimensional, visible light source that could disrupt enemy sensors, among other applications. Similarly, high-power microwave projectiles could be used to disable enemy information systems. Other non-lethal weapons being created in the mid-1990s included laser dye rods, which created an intense flash and blinded personnel and optical sensors; pulsed chemical lasers, which created a high-pressure "plasma blast wave" that incapacitated people and destroyed materials; and acoustic bullets that caused blunt-object trauma rather than ripping the skin and vital organs.

In September 2005, the U.S. military planned to mount microwave guns on armored vehicles in Iraq. Officially called Active Denial Systems, the new weapons would be used for subduing mobs of insurgents that operated in close proximity to civilians. Developed at the Air Force Research Laboratory in New Mexico, the weapons produced a burning sensation beneath the skin when directed at a target, which subsided when the target moved away from the energy beam, and did no physical damage. The military planned to name armored vehicles equipped with the devices as "Sheriffs."

In September 2008, while speaking at the U.S. Air Force Association's annual conference, Acting Air Force Secretary Michael Donley called the failure to award a US$35 billion 179 aerial refueling plane contract "a missed opportunity." Consequently, the military was left with an unclear path to replace its aging tanker fleet. Defense Secretary Robert Gates cancelled bidding from Boeing and Northrup Grumman, requesting a "cooling off" period between the rivals.

According to Robert Fox, the Jane's Information Group's *Defence Industrial Quarterly* survey showed the United States and the United Kingdom at top of the list for defense spending. The United States spent US$696.30 billion annually, while the United Kingdom US$79.27 billion annually. Fox analyzed dynamics and pointed out many defense related items were not purchased entirely or primarily for "strictly tactical or strategic reasons." Furthermore, Fox concluded that the

report's highlight was "the tripling in two years of defense budgets" for China, Russia, and India.

INDUSTRY LEADERS

The Boeing Company. The Boeing Company was the third-largest defense company in the world in 2008 with sales of nearly US$60.9 billion. Boeing's position in this sector generates 51 percent of the company's total revenue. Boeing owes its position to acquisitions of the McDonnell Douglas Corporation in 1997 and Rockwell's defense and aerospace business in 1996. In 2001 Boeing acquired the satellite operations of Hughes Electronics. Boeing manufactured the F-15 Eagle fighter-bomber, the F/A-18 Hornet strike bomber, and an array of other fighter, bomber, and transport aircraft. About 60 percent of its sales came from commercial aircraft like the 737, the 747, and the 767. Boeing has 71,000 employees working in the defense sector.

General Dynamics. General Dynamics, also of the United States, was another key arms manufacturer in the mid-2000s that was the fifth largest defense contractor globally. In late 2004, General Dynamics consisted of four principle divisions: Information Systems and Technology (battlespace information networks, data acquisition/processing, advanced electronics, and management systems); Combat Systems (land and amphibious combat machines and systems, including power trains, turrets, armored vehicles, gun systems, and munitions); Aerospace (mid-size, large cabin, and ultra-long-range business aircraft); and Marine Systems (submarines, surface combatants, auxiliary ships, and large commercial vessels). In the mid-1990s General Dynamics started acquiring related businesses, including Lockheed Martin's armament unit and Teledyne's vehicle systems division. General Dynamics was a defense industry leader throughout the 1980s and early 1990s. After posting revenues of US$10.17 billion in 1990, however, the company experienced a rapid decline in orders from the military. However, by the mid-1990s General Dynamics' sales began to stabilize. By 2001 sales had reached US$12.2 billion, a 17 percent increase over 2000. Sales rose more than 15 percent in 2004, to US$19.2 billion. By 2009, General Dynamics revenue was at US$31.98 billion, with a workforce of 91,200 in 2010.

According to the *Charlotte Business Journal,* General Dynamics Armament and Technical Products awarded Goodrich Corp. a production contract. Goodrich then agreed to provide scanner modules and other items for the U.S. Army joint services lightweight standoff chemical agent detector system. This system employs infrared detection methods to search for and identify chemical-agent vapor clouds. Operators hear audible or visual alarms allowing personnel to either avoid contaminated areas or dress in protective gear. Both companies involved in the arrangement were headquartered in Charlotte, North Carolina.

Max Jarman revealed that the Land Warrior program was revived as part of the U.S. Army's US$160 billion Future Combat Systems modernization program. The Pentagon had cancelled the US$3 billion program in 2007. At that time, concerns were expressed about the cost and weight of the Internet-based integrated communications system. Initially, the Army deployed approximately 400 systems. A US$70 million contract awarded to General Dynamics C4 Systems was for another 900 systems to equip the 5th Brigade, 2nd Infantry Division, Stryker Brigade Combat Team. The new version of the system utilizes a Stryker armored combat vehicle as a communications base. An additional benefit is that the new system weighed 7.2 pounds as opposed to the original 10 pounds.

General Dynamics delivered a new nuclear power attack submarine to the Navy in August 2008, eight months ahead of schedule. It was built by General Dynamics Electric Boat subsidiary. The latest addition was called "New Hampshire." It is the fifth ship of Virginia Class which is the Navy's major class of combatant ships. "Like the previous ships of the class, New Hampshire has been designed specifically to incorporate emergent technologies that will provide new capabilities to meet new threats," explained Electric Boat President John Casey. The company, in partnership with Northrop Grumman Shipbuilding, received contracts to build the first 10 submarines of a planned 30-ship Virginia Class under a team agreement dividing the construction workload between the two shipyards.

In 2008, the U.S. Government sued General Dynamics, who agreed to pay US$4 million to settle the claim that a General Dynamics unit in Glen Cove, New York fraudulently billed the government for defectively manufactured parts used in U.S. military aircraft and submarines. The unit involved closed in 2004.

BAE Systems. BAE Systems, formerly British Aerospace, was Europe's largest defense contractor in 2004. The company was formed by the merger of British Aerospace and Marconi Electronic Systems in November 1999. British Aerospace was a long-time leader in global defense markets, distinguished by its products such as the Hawk, Tornado, Gripen, and Harrier fighter jets. Moreover, the company will develop the state-of-the-art Eurofighter. BAE also built missiles, electronic defense systems, naval vessels, commercial aircraft, space systems, and a wide range of ordnance and ammunition. The company was the core of the United Kingdom's defense

industry. It garnered revenues of US$14.4 billion in 2000, 0.2 percent over 1999. Sales were US$17.5 billion in 2004, up 17.5 percent from the previous year. BAE agreed to acquire the United Kingdom's Alvis, a manufacturer of armored vehicles, in mid-2004. BAE reported sales of US$34.9 billion in 2009 with a workforce of over 107,000.

The U.S. Army awarded a US$5 million contract for Air Warrior Flexible Body Armor to BAE Systems. This special armor increases freedom of movement at flight controls. In addition, it improves mobility to operate aircraft systems safely. An added bonus was that the armor could be upgraded for added protection against rifle bullets by inserting the Small Arms Protective Insert Plates.

Lockheed Martin Corporation. U.S.-based Lockheed Martin Corporation, the largest defense contractor in the world, develops and manufactures aerospace products and systems, submarine-launched ballistic missiles, and defense electronics. Products and services included those related to aircraft, missiles, space, electronics, and aerospace design and support. The company reported that in 2000, about 19 percent of its sales were attributable to its aeronautical segment that builds combat and airlift aircraft, such as the F-22 fighter, the Joint Strike Fighter, and the C-130J transport for the military. Roughly 67 percent came from missiles and space systems. Lockheed assumed a lead in the global defense industry in the mid-1990s as a result of strong demand for several of its technologies. Sales rose from about US$9.8 billion in 1991 to nearly US$24 billion in 2001 because of the company's diversification and penetration of new defense markets, including the Middle East and Asia. In 2000, the company sold its subsidiary Hanford Corporation. During the early 2000s, the U.S. government accounted for about 70 percent of Lockheed's sales, which reached US$35.5 billion in 2004, up 11.6 percent over the previous year. According to the *Philadelphia Business Journal*, Lockheed Martin won a contract to manage the supply of auto parts for the military's vehicles, which would generate US$5.6 billion by 2018. The company reported US$45.18 billion in sales and 140,000 employees for 2009.

European Aeronautic Defense and Space Company. The European Aeronautic Defense and Space Company (EADS) is the world's second largest aerospace/defense company, after Boeing. It was formed in July 2000 with the merger of three firms: DaimlerChrysler Aerospace of Germany, Aerospatiale Matra of France, and Construcciones Aeronauticas SA (CASA) of Spain. In addition to commercial aircraft, EADS manufactures military planes, helicopters, missiles, defense satellites, and electronics.

Company sales grew 19.5 percent between 1999 and 2000, reaching about US$18.3 billion. In 2001, EADS entered a joint project with five other European companies to develop manned and unmanned military aircraft. By 2009, sales were US$56.6 billion, up from 2004's US$43.32 billion. In 2009, they had a workforce of 119,500.

MAJOR COUNTRIES IN THE INDUSTRY

United States. The United States's large defense budget and its control of export markets made it the undisputed leader in the arms industry throughout the 2000s. In addition to sales of major weapons systems, such as the M1A1 Abrams Main Battle Tank kits and a wide variety of missiles, the United States also exported significant numbers of spare parts, components, and weapons upgrades to other nations, and also provided service and training.

In 2001 alone, about one-third of the United States' US$302 billion defense budget went to defense contractors for procurement, research, or development. That sum also accounted for about 37 percent of world military expenditures in 2000. As a consequence of the September 11, 2001, terrorist attacks against the United States, President George W. Bush requested a defense budget of US$379 billion in 2003.

By the mid-2000s, about 3.5 percent of the U.S. gross domestic product went to defense spending, an increase from 2.9 percent in 2000. The United States's US$401.7 billion defense budget for fiscal year 2005 was 7 percent higher than the estimated 2004 levels of US$375.3 billion, and 10 percent higher than actual 2003 levels of US$365.3 billion. In addition to an overall defense spending increase of 35 percent from 2001 to 2004, the Bush Administration doubled spending related to missile defense systems during the same timeframe.

Besides accounting for roughly half of global arms purchases, the United States controlled just over 50 percent of the global arms export market during the early 2000s. Its share, valued at almost US$18.6 billion in 2000, was up almost US$6 billion from 1999 largely on the strength of a purchase of 80 F-16 aircraft by the United Arab Emirates. Its dominance of the export market stemmed from the marketing savvy of the U.S. government and U.S. arms manufacturers, as well as the technological superiority of its weapons. That technological edge was honed with hundreds of billions of dollars of research and development into new weapons over several decades.

Although the U.S. defense industry stumbled during the global weapons industry downturn of the early and mid-1990s, its future seemed secure entering the new century. By 1999, the U.S. accounted for 64 percent of the world's arms exports, an all-time record. According to the U.S. State Department, U.S. exports went to more than 154 of the world's 190 independent nations in 2000. The United States has sustained criticism abroad for its large defense trade surplus, which persists because the U.S. Congress has at times mandated that defense equipment be domestically produced. In 1999, for example, the United States imported US$2 billion in armaments from the European Union, but exported US$15 billion worth of weapons to the European Union.

The U.S. government, which strictly regulates arms exports by U.S. manufacturers, officially views arms transfers or exports as a legitimate instrument of U.S. foreign policy. The goals of its arms sales decisions were to help U.S. allies defend themselves and remain compatible with U.S. forces, promote regional stability in areas of critical interest to the United States, ensure that U.S. forces would retain their technological superiority over potential adversaries, and enhance the ability of U.S. arms makers to sustain a long-term technology and manufacturing advantage.

According to an August 2004 Congressional Research Service (CRS) report, in 2003 the United States ranked first with US$14.5 billion in global arms transfer agreements, followed by Russia (US$4.3 billion), Germany (US$1.4 billion), France (US$1 billion), Italy (US$600 million), China (US$300 million), and the United Kingdom (US$100 million). All other European countries accounted for US$2.3 billion in arms transfers, and a combination of other countries accounted for US$1.1 billion.

The United States also ranked first in actual worldwide arms deliveries in 2003 (US$13.6 billion). The United Kingdom was ranked second at US$4.7 billion, followed by Russia at US$3.4 billion. France and Germany both recorded deliveries valued at US$1.2 billion, followed by China (US$500 million) and Italy (US$100 million). All other European countries accounted for US$2.4 billion in deliveries, and a combination of other countries accounted for US$1.6 billion.

According to *The Times of India,* an impressive US$962 million contract had been secured by India, the world's largest arms importer, for the United States to supply six C1303 "Super Hercules" aircraft for use by Indian special forces. India had already bought the U.S. warship *USS Trenton* in 2007 for US$49 million. By September 11, 2008, other deals were close to being secured. One of them, that required clearance before signing, involved eight Boeing P-8I long-range maritime reconnaissance aircraft. Competition from Russia, France, and Italy to supply arms and armament to India was expected to be intense.

The U.S. government was collaborating with NATO to send a Defense Department envoy to Georgia in light of that country's war with Russia, according to Assistant Secretary of State Daniel Fried. Plans included analyzing how the US$1 billion economic aid package pledged by the U.S. government should be utilized to provide appropriate military assistance.

The Russian Federation. With control of 70 percent of the former Soviet Union's weapons industry, Russia remained the second largest player in the global armament industry during the early 2000s, even though its production, sales, and exports stood well below 1980s figures. In 1995 Russia reported exports of US$2.5 billion, which were well below Cold War levels, but between 1998 and 2000 the Russian defense industry boosted production to about 18.7 percent of 1991 levels (the last year of Soviet production). It had reported sales worth US$4 billion in 2000. Exports accounted for about 60 percent of the industry's business from 1999 to 2000. During the early 2000s, Russia's main arms customers were China and India, which together accounted for 70 percent of Russia's 2000 sales. Agreements with Iran were expected to increase significantly after 2001. Russia's own military spending totaled US$56 billion in 1999.

Russia has specialized in inexpensive, durable weapons, but was facing increasing competition, especially from its partners in the Confederation of Independent States (CIS), such as the Ukraine. Market pressures were expected to result in a wave of mergers, acquisitions, and bankruptcies that would shrink, but also toughen the Russian industry. Nonetheless, deep skepticism remained in some quarters about the ability of many Russian firms to survive in the free market. To become competitive, the industry will have to cultivate export markets—in 2001 the Russian government expected to purchase no more than 30 percent of its production capacity. Russian industry will also have to overcome meager product lines. During the early 2000s, two-thirds of all sales came from combat aircraft, such as the MIG fighter. As of 2004, many developing nations were reluctant to acquire more advanced weapons systems from Russia due to concerns about the country's inability to provide adequate levels of support and training, as well as quality spare parts.

According to an Itar-Tass report in the *IPR Strategic Business Information Database,* Russia's arms exports were more than US$5 billion mark in 2003. The increase, which was attributed to continued overall growth of military product sales, was from US$4.2 billion in 2002 and US$3.2 billion in 2001. China and India continued to be Russia's principal trading partners during the mid-2000s, although military products were exported to a total of 52 countries. According to Russian export agency Rosoboroneksport, trade was increasing with partners in Southeast Asia, including Vietnam, Malaysia, and Indonesia. One significant deal between Russia and China was the sale of 24 Su-30 MKK multi-fighter aircraft in 2003, for US$1 billion.

During the mid-2000s, Russia devoted 2.6 to 2.7 percent of its gross domestic product to defense spending. According to the August 24, 2004, issue of Russia's *St. Petersburg Times,* the country's 2005 budget included a 28 percent increase in defense spending to 528 billion rubles from 411 billion rubles in 2004 and 93 billion rubles in 1999. Russia's increased spending had been devoted primarily to improving conditions within the military rather than to upgrading weapons systems.

China. China is another important player in the global arms production market. The country established itself as a major player in the arms industry during the 1970s and 1980s when it began producing and later designing its own arms, although many of its designs were simply takeoffs of Soviet-built equipment. In that period, China was the leading arms exporter among developing nations, shipping nearly US$15 billion of weapons abroad between 1978 and 1988. In the early 1990s Chinese arms exports shrank nearly 70 percent between 1990 and 1993 after its biggest customer, Iraq, was defeated in the Persian Gulf War. Between 1997 and 1999, China exported arms worth US$2 billion to a variety of nations in Asia, Africa, and the Middle East. China had a military budget of US$36.5 billion in 1999.

By the late 1990s China maintained a large defense equipment labor force with 3 million workers in 1,000 factories. However, many of those plants were located in remote rural areas and as a result, they were unable to engage in international trade for the most part. Poor-quality equipment and an uneducated labor force also hurt the industry. The Chinese government began addressing such problems in 1998 when it inaugurated a reorganization of its defense production sector. Ultimately, however, many companies were expected to shut down and the industry streamlined. China had achieved success in building advanced armament, such as its multiple-warhead nuclear missiles, as well as its M-9 and M-11 ballistic missiles. However, the bulk of the country's output remained old-model weapons lacking modern technical advances. Unlike other Asian countries, China remained cut off from the Western technology of the European Union and the United States. Instead, China's only defense technology trading partner was Russia, but China's low procurement budget and Russia's insistence on not selling the country its most advanced equipment left China far behind its neighbors in assembling a technologically up-to-date weapons arsenal.

In 2003, the value of China's arms transfers fell to US$300 million, its lowest level since 1996. China mainly supplied light weapons and small arms to countries such as Africa. In addition, the country was more focused on upgrading its own military force than on selling weapons, namely missiles, to other nations.

European Union. The European Union (E.U.) was a world leader in armament production and exportation, second only to the United States. In 1999, led by France, the United Kingdom, and Germany, the E.U. controlled 22.5 percent of the global defense equipment exports. In the 1990s, the fragmented European defense industry had to be consolidated to compete on the world market with the U.S. defense juggernaut. A good deal of streamlining occurred in the early 2000s. British Aerospace merged with Marconi Electronic Systems to become BAE Systems in 1999, while Daimler Chrysler Aerospace, Aerospatiale Matra, and CASA merged to form the EADS aerospace powerhouse in 2000. In late 2001, the governments of the United Kingdom, Germany, France, Sweden, Italy, and Spain agreed to form ETAP, a project to coordinate aircraft development led by firms from the six nations. The same year, three European firms merged to form MBDA. Called the first pan-European defense company, MBDA was jointly owned by BAE Systems, EADS, and Finmeccanica. The European Union was also the leading arms importing region in 1999 at 29 percent, a 59 percent increase from 1998.

By the early 2000s, some industry observers were concerned about the future of Europe's defense industry. Amidst great global demand for U.S. weapons, and a reduction in arms producers in the Near East, European firms continued to form joint ventures with one another, as in the case of the Eurofighter project. Additionally, the Joint Strike fighter was evidence that European firms were working collaboratively with the United States on some projects. In order to survive, Europe was expected to put increased emphasis on the development of its own cutting-edge weaponry. In the December 23, 2002, issue of *Country ViewsWire,* Daniel Keohane of the Centre for European Reform expressed the opinion that more multinational defense projects were a solution to the region's woes.

United Kingdom. The United Kingdom, which traditionally vied with France to be the leading weapon maker in the European Union, was also a leading global arms exporter. The United Kingdom ranked second behind the United States in worldwide arms deliveries in 2003, with US$4.7 billion in sales, based on a Congressional Research Service (CRS) report. Although the country produces some weapons under license from U.S. companies, it was also recognized as a technical innovator,

particularly in aerospace-related weaponry. Much of the country's defense industry activity was carried out through BAE Systems, formerly British Aerospace, a large, diversified company primarily engaged in defense-related businesses. With privatization of the industry and expanding global projects, the United Kingdom expected its industry to thrive much the same as U.S. companies. Between 1997 and 1999 the United Kingdom was Europe's leading arms importer, purchasing about US$6.6 billion worth of military equipment. Its total military budget for 2000 was US$34 billion.

France. France's production, procurement expenditures, and exports made it one of the E.U.'s leaders in the arms industry. According to a CRS report, in 2003 France ranked fourth in global arms transfer agreements (US$1 billion). Along with Germany, France ranked fourth in actual worldwide arms deliveries that year, with deliveries valued at US$1.2 billion.

During the mid-1990s, France was able to maintain its leadership status despite cutbacks in domestic procurement budgets and falling exports. France's defense-related workforce also plummeted to about 250,000 in the mid-1990s. The French defense industry had revenues totaling about US$11 billion in 2000 and a workforce of 157,000. Between 1997 and 1999, France imported about US$1.3 billion in defense equipment, which was one of the lowest import rates in Europe. Between 1999 and 2000, French exports plunged by 30 percent to US$2.4 billion, the lowest level since 1994. Its defense production fell by 9 percent during the same period. Between 1991 and 2001, according to the Conseil des industries de defence francaises, France's defense spending dropped 17 percent. In 2000 France's defense budget stood at US$27.3 billion, down about US$4 billion from 1997.

The French arms industry was long dominated by a dozen large companies, partly government owned, that had benefited since the 1960s from a government emphasis on investments in defense technology. In 2000, however, France ended strict government control of arms production and sales to the country's armed forces when it opened the bidding process for French contracts to other European companies.

Germany. In 2003, Germany ranked third in global arms transfer agreements (US$1.4 billion). Along with France, the country ranked fourth in actual worldwide arms deliveries that year, with deliveries valued at US$1.2 billion.

Germany was the European Union's second largest arms manufacturer in the late 1990s and its leading exporter. The German arms industry re-emerged during the 1950s and 1960s and developed a reputation for design innovation. Like their peers, most German arms makers experienced domestic defense cutbacks and reduced arms exports in the mid-1990s. In 2000 Germany's defense budget totaled US$23.3 billion, down from US$35 billion in the late 1990s. Equipment procurement accounted for less than US$4.1 billion of that year's budget. German defense equipment manufacturers announced they would follow U.K. producers in consolidating operations and working more with the United States to remain competitive in the 2000s.

BIBLIOGRAPHY

BAE Systems Receives $5 Million Contract from U.S. Army for Air Warrior Flexible Body Armor." *MarketWatch,* 15 September 2008.

Blanche, Ed. "Iran Goes Shopping." *Jane's Defence Weekly,* 21 March 2001.

"Brazil to Rebuild Its Weapons Industry." *PR Inside,* September 2008. Available from PR-inside.com.

Chamberlin, Jeffrey. *Comparisons of U.S. and Foreign Military Spending: Data from Selected Public Sources.* Washington, D.C.: Congressional Research Service, Library of Congress, 28 January 2004.

Cook, Nick. "BAE Systems Rocky Ride to Global Status," *Interavia Business & Technology,* June 2001.

———. "Europeans Plan Future Air Programmes," *Jane's Defence Weekly,* 28 November 2001.

"Defense Mergers At All-Time High." *CDIs Weekly Defense Monitor,* 3:26, 8 July 1999. Available from www.cdi.org.

"EU Industry: Cooperation on Arms Purchases Needed, Says Study." *Country ViewsWire,* 23 December 2002.

"European Industry Looks Ahead," *Jane's Defence Industry,* 1 January 2001.

Firestone, David. "Lawmakers Back Request by Bush on Funds for Iraq." *The New York Times,* 18 October 2003.

Foss, Christopher F. "Pan-European Defence Company is Ratified." *Jane's Defence Weekly,* 2 January 2002.

Fox, Robert. "Time for a Real Review of Defence Spending," 4 September 2008. Available from guardian.co.uk.

Freinberg, Tony, and Sean Rayment. "Microwave Gun to be Used by US Troops on Iraq Rioters." *The Telegraph,* 19 September 2004. Available from www.telegraph.co.uk.

Galeotti, Mark. "Russia's Arms Bazaar." *Jane's Intelligence Review,* 1 April 2001.

"General Dynamics Delivers Submarine Ahead of Schedule." *Washington Business Journal,* 28 August 2008.

"General Dynamics Nabs Army Deal for Land Warrior System," 12 September 2008. Available from azcentral.com.

"Global Arms Market Surges." *Periscope Daily Defense News Capsules,* 4 September 2001.

"Global Arms Sales." *Interavia Business & Technology,* 30 September 2004.

"Global Arms Sales Down for the Third Year in a Row." *Federation of American Scientists Press Release,* 1 September 2004. Available from www.fas.org.

"Global Military Spending Unaffected By Recession" *USA Today,* 2 March 2010.

"Globalized Weaponry." *In Focus,* Interhemispheric Resource Center, and Institute For Policy Studies, 5:16, June 2000. Available from www.foreignpolicy-infocus.org.

"Goodrich Lands Contract with General Dynamics Unit." *Charlotte Business Journal,* 15 September 2008.

Grimmett, Richard F. "Conventional Arms Transfers to Developing Nations, 1993-2000." Washington, D.C.: Congressional Research Service, Library of Congress, 16 August 2001.

———. "Conventional Arms Transfers to Developing Nations, 1996-2003." Congressional Research Service, 26 August 2004.

Holmes, Stanley, "A Call to Arms Awakens Defense." *Business Week,* 1 October 2001, p. 62.

Hoover, Kent. "Bush Boosts Defense, Tech R&D, Reduces Other Areas." *Business First-Columbus,* 30 March 2001.

Keller, William W. *Arm in Arm.* New York: Basic Books, 1995.

Koch, Andrew "Consolidation Will Allow Technology to Spread." *Jane's Defence Weekly,* 15 August 2001.

Lewis, J.A.C. "Cash Benefit of France's Export Sales in Doubt." *Jane's Defence Weekly,* 10 May 2000.

———. "French Arms Exports Drop 30 Percent." *Jane's Defence Weekly,* 16 January 2002.

"Lockheed Martin to Help Military Meet Auto Parts Needs." *Philadelphia Business Journal,*12 September 2008.

"Long March To Modernisation." *Jane's Defence Weekly,* 11 September 2001.

Mann, Paul. "NATO's Transatlantic Market Pits Politics Versus Business." *Aviation Week & Space Technology,* 21 May 2001.

Markusen, Ann. "The Case Against Privatizing National Security." Council for Foreign Relations, July 2001.

"Military Spending on Rise." The Associated Press, 8 June 2005.

Morocco, John D. "European Nations To Team Up On Next-Generation Technology." *Aviation Week & Space Technology,* 18 June 2001.

Mulholland, David. "Global Arms Sales up in 2000, Russia Moves to Second Place." *Jane's Defence Weekly,* 29 August 2001.

———. "New Anti-terrorism Crusade May Bolster Industry." *Jane's Defence Weekly,* September 19, 2001.

Nicoll, Alexander. "France to Open Door on Defence Contracts." *Financial Times,* 21 May 2001.

"Official: Tanker Contract 'a missed opportunity.'" *International Herald Tribune,* 15 September 2008.

Office of Management and Budget. "Overview of the President's 2005 Budget." Washington, D.C.: Executive Office of the President of the United States, 19 September 2004. Available from www.whitehouse.gov.

Pronina, Lyuba. "Budget Bolsters Defense." *St. Petersburg Times* (Russia), 24 August 2004.

"Raytheon and Thales Team up." *Jane's Defence Weekly,* 1 August 2001.

Robinson, Dan. "US Officials See Difficult Period in US-Russia Relations," 9 September 2008. Available from newsVOA.com.

"Russia: First Time—Arms Exports Reach 5BN Dollars." *IPR Strategic Business Information Database,* 27 January 2004.

Schneider, Greg, "There'll Always Be An Arms Industry." *The Washington Post,* 21 May 2001.

SIPRI Yearbook 2001: Armaments Disarmament and International Security. Oxford: Oxford University Press, 2001.

"U.S. Wants to Be India's No. 1 Partner in Defense." *The Times of India,* 11 September 2008.

Velocci, Anthony L., Jr. "Consolidation Juggernaut Yet To Run Its Course." *Aviation Week & Space Technology,* December 3, 2001.

———. "U.S. Primes Buoyed by Weapons Purchasing." *Aviation Week & Space Technology,* 3 February 2003.

Wall, Robert, "New Arms Policies Seen Altering Warfare." *Aviation Week & Space Technology,* 3 September 2001.

———. "New Patriot Missiles Ready for Combat." *Aviation Week & Space Technology,* 3 February 2003.

Wall, Robert, David A. Fulghum, and Alexey Komarov. "Russian Defense Industry Struggles With Reform." *Aviation Week & Space Technology,* 20 August 2001.

White, Deborah. "Iraq War Facts, Results & Statistics at October 30, 2010. " *About.com,* 19 November 2010.

"World Military Spending Topped $1 Trillion in 2004," *Reuters,* 7 June 2005.

"World Military Expenditures and Arms Transfers 1999-2000." U.S. Department of State, Bureau of Verification and Compliance, October 2001.

Wright, Evan. "How Much Is That Uzi in the Window?" *The New York Times,* 17 June 2004.

SIC 3714

MOTOR VEHICLE PARTS AND ACCESSORIES

NAICS CODE(S)

336399. The automotive parts industry manufactures motor vehicle parts and accessories. For motor vehicles or passenger car bodies see **Motor Vehicles,** and for automotive tire production see **Tires and Inner Tubes.**

INDUSTRY SNAPSHOT

The global motor vehicle parts and accessories industry, which was valued at US$900 billion in 2004, is a relative newcomer to the global marketplace. The industry became international in scope as major car manufacturers turned away from direct manufacture of auto parts in favor of heavy reliance on auto parts suppliers to develop major car components. This happened for the simple reason that many auto parts could be made more cheaply off-site by suppliers than by the large automakers themselves. In 1988, no global automotive parts suppliers existed, but within a decade about 50 very large companies manufactured or assembled various automotive systems for sale to the world's major automotive manufacturers, and by the mid-2000s the industry was quite fragmented. Some analysts who observed the ongoing flux in the industry projected that the number of major systems suppliers would shrink to as few as 16 by 2008.

The performance of the automotive parts industry is tied directly to the performance of the automobile industry. This fact, along with rising prices for materials and interest rates, made the future of many suppliers uncertain in the mid-2000s. Auto parts suppliers were continually faced with demands of the auto manufacturers, who were their largest customers, to lower prices and increase quality. As a result, auto parts manufacturers struggled to maintain consistent profit margins, despite increased demand and favorable market conditions. In 2004, while some companies were posting record profit increases, many others were posting the opposite. By 2004, major companies were outsourcing overseas to remain viable and competitive.

ORGANIZATION AND STRUCTURE

At the beginning of the twenty-first century, auto parts suppliers operated in the power-train, chassis, body, interior, and electronic segments. Some companies specialized in subsets of these commodity areas (e.g., brakes and safety systems), but the major categories remained identifiable. The auto parts industry also had two primary sectors: the original equipment (OE) sector, which included parts for the car manufacturers, and the aftermarket parts sector, which included replacement parts for cars and trucks. The major OE players were distinguished by product and customer base. Tier One suppliers were those that produced parts sold directly to automakers, while Tier Two suppliers sold parts to Tier One companies, and Tier Three suppliers sold the raw materials used to manufacture parts to Tier Two and Tier One operations.

Sales of original equipment parts were dependent on many factors, including the size, number, and complexity of any given car or truck market, and the number of parts and accessories that OE car manufacturers produced themselves. Parts were distributed through new car dealers, oil companies, major parts distributors, and small jobbers. Common products included wheels, bodies, frames, axles, transmissions, transaxles, bearings, valves, springs, bumpers, brakes, fuel injectors, seats, seat belts, airbags, and cushioning and safety padding materials. In the early 1980s, OE suppliers often signed annual contracts with auto manufacturers covering only the current model year. By the 1990s, multi-year contracts were being written, sometimes for the life of the vehicle. The late 1990s consolidation of the supplier industry was reinforced by the actions of the automakers themselves, who dealt with a few technologically advanced OE suppliers worldwide. Sometimes this limitation of supplier numbers became extreme. In the early 1990s, Chrysler made the decision to reduce its 2,500 suppliers fewer than 750 primary suppliers over the next several years.

By 1997, Chrysler had reduced its supplier count to 1,200, with an ultimate goal of just 150 major suppliers.

The aftermarket parts segment of the auto parts market tends to be more stable and subject to fewer fluctuations than the OE segment, although some OE suppliers also sell to the aftermarket. Aftermarket parts consist primarily of items that could be described as consumable, subject to the daily wear and tear of vehicle operation, such as spark plugs, piston rings, brake pads, rotors, batteries, oil and gas filters, shock absorbers, struts, springs, exhaust systems, wiper blades, and air filters. During recessions, OEM demand usually drops, but sales in the aftermarket had remained level and frequently strengthened during economic downturns, largely because financially strapped car owners tended to fix and repair cars rather than buy new. The major threat to the aftermarket parts industry was the increasingly high level of quality in original parts. Obviously, original equipment that lasts longer has a negative effect on demand for replacement parts. Aftermarket parts traditionally were sold through service stations, general and specialized repair shops, tire stores, department stores, dealers, auto parts stores, and discount stores, but in 1998 they began to be sold through electronic home shopping. Analysts expected the aftermarket business to maintain moderate long-term growth, but eventual consolidation echoing the consolidation of OE suppliers was likely, especially in the United States.

The OE and aftermarket parts manufacturers shared an ability to make specialized parts that required a high level of technical skill. Because they could spread the costs of research and design, as well as tool and die costs, over many different contracts, "outside" auto parts manufacturers held an important cost advantage over the parts divisions of the automakers that frequently was supplemented by the lower cost of non-union labor. These cost factors gave outside firms significant influence in the design and engineering of new parts for upcoming car models, as car manufacturers depended on suppliers to help keep costs low and technological advances high.

BACKGROUND AND DEVELOPMENT

The early development of the auto parts industry was closely linked to the growth of the automobile early in the twentieth century. As the production of automobiles increased, so did the need for automotive parts. For many decades, the automotive parts industry served a limited number of models, which allowed parts makers to concentrate their efforts on producing mass quantities of a small assortment of components. In the 1970s, however, as Japan began exporting vehicles to the United States, the variety of models began to expand. The

following decade, the popularity of small trucks began to surge. As a result, parts makers found themselves having to increase the number of parts they offered, while reducing the quantities of each part manufactured. Although the broadened automotive parts market increased sales for many auto parts makers, it also undercut earnings growth due to the costs associated with manufacturing a more diverse group of parts. The industry growth also prompted many new players to enter the market, increasing competition.

The auto parts industry began to grow in earnest during the late 1980s and early 1990s, when many major car manufacturers began to rely more heavily on auto parts suppliers to develop major car components, mainly because many auto parts could be made more cheaply off-site by suppliers than by the automakers themselves. These suppliers were often forced by the car manufacturers, who were their largest customers, to endure price freezes or reductions. The parts makers responded by cutting the costs of their own business operations. In the mid-1990s parts suppliers had eliminated many of their extraneous costs, but needed further cost reductions that could not be accomplished through traditional approaches and strategies. Chrysler and General Motors (GM) helped their parts suppliers with two innovative and cost-effective methods to meet the competitive cost challenges for the late 1990s.

Chrysler Corporation gave many of its parts suppliers responsibility for complete component system building within a target price that was set by Chrysler, while still maintaining high quality and features. If the suppliers reduced costs below target levels, then enhancements had to be added to their systems. If parts supplier costs exceeded target levels, then savings had to be found elsewhere in the system without cutting back on enhancements or quality. Chrysler was guaranteed substantial cost savings that they shared with the parts suppliers in the form of incentives to pursue additional operational goals that ultimately benefited Chrysler. Although the pressure on parts suppliers was tremendous, the resulting synergistic relationship between parts suppliers and the auto company enhanced the competitive strength of all involved.

Following Chrysler's innovation, General Motors devised a plan dispatching teams of engineers, designers, and purchasing cost accountants to meet with teams of employees at the parts manufacturers' plants. Under the direction of GM Worldwide Purchasing Director, Dr. J. Ignacio Lopez (who was later indicted for theft of GM trade secrets), week-long meetings called PICOS (purchased input concept optimization for suppliers) were held to help suppliers rid their operations of inefficiencies and bottlenecks. These joint GM and parts supplier teams were intended to be close-knit efforts to find solutions to parts supplier production problems. However, some parts suppliers did not welcome GM's efforts to view proprietary cost information, and Lopez's tendency to view cost as a primary criterion forced many suppliers to choose between operating at a loss and dropping out of competition. Lopez, who was dubbed the "Inquisitor" (a derogatory term used to describe Lopez given his more manipulative policies), made few friends among suppliers, especially those who had spent many years working with GM to develop a specific project, only to lose the resulting contract to a competing supplier whose lower bid did not need to include the cost of development. For these and other embittered suppliers, it was particularly ironic that, after Lopez departed, the suppliers' international competitive positions actually had been strengthened by his methods. The early, desperate haste to cut costs and streamline operations ultimately had its reward, and the resulting lean and mean suppliers were well-positioned to bid for new contracts at GM and around the world.

As the auto supply industry gained prominence in the 1990s, auto manufacturers began looking for suppliers to do more than just build parts as they sought sources capable of design, engineering, integration, and global delivery. The motivation for this search was a simple desire to control costs. Because they were not as heavily unionized as the automakers, many suppliers could operate for less cost. In the early 1990s, for example, the Big Three U.S. automotive companies (GM, Ford, and Chrysler) paid more than US$42 per hour in labor costs, while supplier Lear Seating and ITT Automotive paid US$12 and US$14 per hour, respectively. It was understandable that Ford found it practical to sell its seat assembly line to Lear in November 1993 for approximately US$600 million. In May 1994 Chrysler turned its seat cover operations over to Johnson Controls and its wiring assembly plants to Yazaki. General Motors divested itself of no fewer than 41 parts operations between 1993 and 1994. Toyota already was manufacturing less than 25 percent of its own parts, compared to GM's 47 percent, and the success of the Japanese model served as further incentive to global auto manufacturers to use the growing parts industry.

Also affecting the auto parts industry during the 1990s was the increase in the number of standard features on many models. Air conditioning, tilt steering, stereo radios, power windows, power door locks, and power seats all helped increase sales for car manufacturers and parts suppliers alike. By the early 1990s, almost 94 percent of all U.S. cars were delivered with air conditioning, up from 76 percent a decade earlier. Automatic transmissions were installed in 89 percent of all cars, a less dramatic rise (from 82 percent) possibly dampened by increased use of standard transmissions on sport-utility vehicles. Power side windows were on 79 percent of all U.S. cars, almost twice that of the early 1980s. Stereo radios were frequently standard, and drivers in 2000 looked for CD players and CD changers to take the place of cassette players in luxury models. As each new feature was developed for an automobile, it entered the parts market as well. Antilock brakes, aluminum wheels, and airbags became familiar options. In spite of controversy surrounding their use, by the end of the twentieth century driver and passenger airbags were relatively standard, and side-impact airbags were expected to follow suit. In addition, increased safety consciousness continued to encourage high demand for anti-lock braking systems (ABS) on cars and trucks.

By the mid-1990s, "quality" had become a buzzword throughout the global auto parts industry. Notably, with quality as the primary standard of measurement, an international comparative study of 71 auto parts manufacturers by Andersen Consulting found that 13 had attained a level of world-class production. Only 3 of the 13 were in the United States. Monitoring the internal defect rate of parts failing their first inspection at a given OEM identified incoming defects in parts provided by smaller auto parts manufacturers. Similar checks followed part development, and the final link in the chain was the customer, who voiced a complaint if faulty parts passed through earlier inspection points. Analysis showed the Japanese to be consistently at the top of the quality supply chain, and the United Kingdom and Italy were consistently at the bottom.

Car manufacturing plants for all countries acted as quality control to prevent customers from receiving defective parts with some success. The number of incoming defects generally was roughly four to five times the number of final customer complaints. U.S. car companies were particularly good at screening the bad parts from their cars out of necessity, with incoming defects found in 6,100 parts per million in relation to 262 customer complaints per million parts.

Automakers traditionally evaluated the quality of auto parts by counting the number of bad parts per million. In turn, the suppliers providing those auto parts were assigned ratings, and all automakers and suppliers sought zero-defect ratings. To attract more business, suppliers eventually began to use the ratings designations and quality awards as marketing tools, and automakers began to expect more. For example, BMW reduced its number of annual supplier awards to just three winner categories: most innovative idea, best economic idea, and best environmental idea. No longer was quality considered something deserving of a prize or even comment because the highest quality was demanded and assumed, therefore, to exist. With all suppliers providing product that was absolute top-quality, any contest between them was moot.

Along with general quality issues and industry-mandated efficiency of operation, automotive parts manufacturers in the United States had another, more specific, target. ISO 9000 standards of quality and efficient operation were familiar in Europe and the U.S. Big Three automobile manufacturers (Chrysler, Ford, General Motors) added a superset: QS 9000. For major suppliers, it was mandatory to be QS 9000 compliant, or in some cases to be working on QS 9000 compliance, to do business with the Big Three. Although return on investment was alleged to be threefold, since becoming QS compliant frequently carried a price tag of well over US$100,000, only companies able to invest that amount in a gamble on possible future business could continue to operate independently.

Competition, cost cutting, and consolidation characterized the auto parts industry as the year 2000 approached. Automakers long had attempted to reduce manufacturing costs, improve efficiencies, and streamline production, which put pressure on parts suppliers to make substantial cost reductions in their operations. The parts suppliers in turn sought to improve their own production techniques for greater profit from their own operations. Cost cutting, new managerial techniques, and production efficiencies were key to survival for many parts manufacturers in an increasingly volatile marketplace. Forced to be cost conscious to be competitive, many auto parts companies followed the automakers in an attempt to adopt successful Japanese production techniques. Just-in-time manufacture, statistical process controls, *kanban* systems, and core competencies became parts issues just as they had become car issues. In the mid- to late 1990s, Japanese firms established numerous "transplant" operations in North America and Europe that further influenced rival domestic firms. The impact of Asian parts makers also was felt as their increasing presence combined with that of East European parts makers forced Western European suppliers into a more global focus.

Globalization had profound implications for the worldwide auto parts industry. Only those systems integrators capable of responding to a world market could survive. Before consolidation in the global automotive parts industry reached its peak, Japan had approximately 2,100 auto parts suppliers serving nine original equipment manufacturers (OEMs). Europe had about 2,300 suppliers serving 18 OEMs, and the United States had 10,000 suppliers serving three OEMs and foreign transplants. In the late 1990s, however, those numbers began to shrink as manufacturers struggled to cope with the increasingly global nature of the automotive industry.

Small suppliers, unable to meet the needs of global systems integrators, began to fall by the wayside. Those that survived focused on the needs of a higher tier of larger suppliers, rather than attempting to do business directly with the automakers. Estimates suggested that more than 50 percent of Tier One suppliers would be out of business by 2000 and that those remaining in business would have been forced to cut their production costs between 18 and 24 percent in order to compete successfully. Approximately 1,400 Tier One suppliers went out of business in the late 1990s, and the attrition of global, mega-suppliers was just as severe as for the smaller firms. Industry analysts anticipated that fewer than 25 parts and systems firms would be global players by 2002 and only 18 would still be in operation by 2005.

The oft-mentioned consolidation that characterized the automotive supplier industry in the late 1990s was orchestrated, in part, by a number of highly profitable venture-capital, "buyout" firms that saw opportunity both in "spinoff" auto parts manufacturers, such as Visteon and Delphi, and in the independent market. Positioning themselves as intermediaries, these firms purchased attractive but struggling parts companies, matched them with other, frequently larger, companies, and then resold them. Often the purchased companies remained in operation for some time, held by a financing firm that oversaw operational streamlining. Whether the target-company was resold or nursed to profitability and held—even for as long as 11 or 15 years—the end result was earnings for the buyout firm. If capital was available, it was an undeniably attractive way to go. In 1998, one financier was simultaneously exploring five such deals in Europe and several more in the United States.

In addition to economic-based mergers, consolidation allowed global auto parts suppliers to position themselves to better serve customers internationally. For instance, the Perkings Group Companies in Great Britain formed a joint venture with Ishikawajima-Shibaura Machine Company of Japan to manufacture at least 50,000 diesel engines per year by 2000. United Technologies Automotive entered into a joint venture with Dongfeng-Citroen Automobile of China to make harnesses and body wiring. Italy's Magneti Marelli and the U.S.-based TRW Inc. entered into an agreement to produce air-bag sensors for the Italian industry. These and other consolidations brought production directly to the consumer. Germany's Mann+Hummel Automotive sought to increase its presence and name recognition in the U.S. market by acquiring the North American operations of Geiger Technic Inc., based in Kalamazoo, Michigan. Similarly, the Degussa Corporation of Quebec, Canada, opened a million-unit catalyst emissions control plant in Puebla, Mexico, and the United States' CDI Corporation opened a new office in Paris.

Increased demand as automotive manufacturers outsourced the manufacture of more and more car components meant that OEM parts production was proportionately on the rise. Gross sales mounted increasingly, which seemed to indicate satisfactory business growth. Even the almost excessive number of mergers and acquisitions could be described as symptomatic of healthy worldwide expansion on the part of the acquiring companies. Unfortunately, however, even as sales increased, profitability was decreasing. In the mid-1990s auto suppliers reported a peak profit margin of 8.2 percent, but by 1998–1999 auto suppliers suddenly found themselves looking at margins that were narrower than they had been since the early 1990s. Returns on investment decreased, and ratios of debt to assets increased.

Financial conditions created a pattern that the Automotive Consulting Group of Ann Arbor, Michigan, called the "Lopez Effect," which referred to the huge gap that had formed between successful "best-in-class" suppliers and struggling firms. There seemed to be no middle ground of modestly successful companies without a huge global presence reporting comfortable profitability. These extreme levels of supplier success were attributed to the ruthless buying patterns endorsed by Ignacio Lopez during his tenure with General Motors and their impact on suppliers who were forced to reduce operations to bare-bones essentials in order to meet GM's pricing demands. Suppliers that survived the experience, and companies who emulated them even without having done business with Lopez, were the companies whose profitability appeared stable and whose market presence seemed most assured. Those that continued to operate in a "pre-Lopez" mode, without trimming the fat from their operations, failed with almost predictable regularity.

The Lopez Effect, the need for global presence, carefully orchestrated buyouts, and the demand for high quality product, combined to make the end of the twentieth century difficult for many supplier firms. However, the end result, like that of the Lopez Effect alone, seemed to be the evolution of a limited number of stable, profitable, highly efficient, high-quality systems-integrating companies.

Auto manufacturers anticipated that modular assembly would be the wave of the future, which dealt another blow to small suppliers without the wherewithal to develop complete component systems that included steering column assemblies, power trains, and entire dash board and electrical systems instead of individual parts to be used on automaker assembly lines. This trend was reflected in the decision by Ford Motor Company to hand control of its Batavia, Ohio-based transmission plant over to a German transmission supplier in 1999.

Industry consolidation continued in 1999 as Lear Corp., Johnson Controls Inc., TRW Inc., and Dana Corp. used acquisitions to position themselves among the largest automotive suppliers in the world, with more than US$10 billion in sales. The largest mergers of the year included the purchase of United Kingdom-based LucasVarity PLC, the industry's nineteenth largest player, by TRW for US$6.5 billion and the purchase of United Technologies Automotive, ranked fifteenth among global auto parts leaders, by Lear Corp. for US$2.3 billion. Ten of the 25 largest auto parts makers in 2000 were based in North America, reporting combined sales of US$113 billion. Sales for the remaining 15 industry leaders, 11 of which were based in Europe and four of which were based in Japan, totaled US$95 billion. The greater success of the small number of North American firms was at least partially the result of heightened consolidations levels.

The automotive parts industry, particularly in North America and Europe, was characterized by sluggish sales, poor earnings, and layoffs in 2001. As weakened economies took their toll on the automotive industry, demand for automotive parts began to diminish. Even in times of economic prosperity, however, growth in markets like North America and Europe was projected to be less than 2 percent. As with the automobile industry, most analysts believed that the majority of future growth in the automotive parts industry would take place in emerging markets, such as Eastern Europe, Latin America, and Asia-Pacific.

CURRENT CONDITIONS

The U.S. aftermarket segment of the industry was valued at US$250 billion in 2004, according to the Automotive Aftermarket Industry Association. According to *Euromonitor,* the U.S. aftercare and accessories market was dominated by the replacement parts segment, which in 2003 accounted for US$72.6 billion of the US$123.5 billion total market. Of this amount, the top five companies controlled 46.1 percent, revealing the fragmented nature of the industry and the likelihood of consolidation. In Europe, aftermarket business was profitable, but declining. Datamonitor expected European revenues to drop gradually during the mid-2000s, for a total decline of about 1 percent by 2008. Critical factors for the industry included lower volumes of replacement parts and competitive pricing.

Suppliers continued to do business with decreasing numbers of small supply companies. A contemporary survey suggested that a majority of suppliers made this move based on price and product delivery as well as quality, but the end result was an overall improvement in parts quality. In addition, the total number of Tier Two and Tier Three suppliers was reduced, and survival of the fittest became reality. In 2004, the strongest companies were those that were not dependent on the Big Three automakers, which collectively reported falling sales.

The industry moved progressively toward consolidation as a result of the pressure of increasing costs for auto companies and suppliers alike. By 2004, for example, average steel costs were 29 to 75 cents per pound, an increase of between 11 and 45 percent. Suppliers were no longer able to pass along added costs resulting from rising prices of steel, plastic, and aluminum. OEMs demanded more capacity, designing, and engineering responsibilities from the suppliers, but due to their own need to cut costs, they were not prepared to help suppliers pay for the added services and capabilities. In fact, a study from Alix Partners found that the supplier industry was suffering major setbacks, with up to 17 percent of companies in danger of bankruptcy by 2006. While some companies, such as Denso that had huge profit increases, were doing well, combined 2003 losses from other companies were in the multi-billion dollar range. Industry leaders like Delphi were turning to offshore outsourcing, particularly to China, India, and other developing countries in Asia, to trim costs and stay afloat.

In order to increase delivery times to customers in Australia and New Zealand, Pratt & Whitney Canada established a new parts distribution centre in Sydney, Australia. Company Vice President for Customer Support Maria Delia Posta explained that the opening of this site was part of an after market strategy to expand the company's global footprint.

In September 2008, General Automotive Company and SenCer announced their Advanced Composite Technology (ACT) joint venture. ACT's main purpose was "to develop, commercialize and market SenCer's ground breaking Ultra Temp ceramic composite materials for accelerating the development of energy efficient, environmentally friendly fuel cell technologies." As part of the joint venture, General Automotive's oxygen sensors would be further developed and marketed.

In September 2008, Hyundai announced plans to create a US$1.3 million social activity fund in Russia that would include car maintenance education, an internship at Hyundai plants, and a road safety campaign. The company also introduced The Five Star Quality Evaluation System to assure quality control and worker safety. Hyundai's plant in St. Petersburg, Russia, was scheduled to begin operating in 2011.

RESEARCH AND TECHNOLOGY

High levels of competition, automaker insistence on high quality, and an increasingly sophisticated end-user market resulted in aggressive research and development in the industry. In 1997, Robert Bosch GmbH, although firmly established in the industry, invested over US$1.8 billion in research and development and dedicated 14,000 employees to research. Since the mid-1990s, its R&D expenditures

increased at a steady rate of well over US$2 million annually, and the company's focus on "smart" restraint systems suggested there would be no slackening of effort in the future. Bosch's Automotive Occupancy Sensing (AOS) system, under development in 1998, used infrared and ultrasonic sensors to check front seat occupancy and prevent unnecessary air-bag deployment. Future enhancements to the system were expected to aid in the use of anti-theft devices, adjustments to seat and headrest positions, mirror dimming, communication, and determining a driver's wakefulness, as well as safer and more efficient use of air bags and driver and passenger restraints.

Accidental injury and even death involving air-bag use caused many parts companies to explore ways to improve air-bag deployment. Existing air-bag systems combined optical, ultrasound capacity, and weight sensors to trigger air-bag use, but passenger injuries suggested that "smarter" air-bags were needed. Atlantic Research Corporation developed Variflow inflators capable of accommodating increasingly advanced sensor information. They and other corporations worked in an environment that added side-impact air bags to driver- and passenger-seat devices.

As more computer technology was introduced into the automobile, Information, Communications, Entertainment and Safety (ICES) centers were bundled together by parts manufacturers into space-age, driver/passenger friendly units. Visteon demonstrated an ICES installation in 1998 that provided everything from a navigation guide and climate control to in-car Internet access. Driven by Intel's Pentium processor and running on Microsoft software, the unit increased driver safety by operating entirely on voice commands—not unlike the computers providing navigation guides and climate control to the fictional *Enterprise* of Gene Roddenberry's *Star Trek*. Analysts predicted that the use of electronic systems in cars would grow from 15 percent to 20 percent of total vehicle content by 2010.

Laser tail lights, new-formula finishing compounds, and continued focus on ABS braking systems characterized the car-owner-friendly direction of many new developments. United Technologies Automotive utilized surface acoustic wave technology in hand-held remote vehicle entry systems, which was the first time such technology had been used outside the aerospace industry. These convenient sending units allowed drivers to unlock their cars from several feet away without fumbling for keys and represented just a small part of UTC's nearly US$2 billion annual R&D expenditure.

Less showy examples of supplier technological advances abounded. Auto manufacturers and parts suppliers had long been required to consider steel, aluminum, or composites as the three basic options for material use in component construction. Steel was favored because it was economical to use in high volumes, reasonable in cost, recyclable, and had good crash properties. Nevertheless, steel had its share of weaknesses, including high tooling costs and material weight, as well as the need to treat it to prevent rust.

Aluminum and composites could be used in many different parts and accessories because of strength and weight characteristics. Aluminum could reduce weight as much as 50 percent, and used familiar manufacturing processes, had good surface qualities, and was easy to recycle. However, aluminum piece cost was high, the metal was difficult to repair, apt to dent and scratch, and had poor formability. Manufacturers were attracted by low tooling costs, good formability, and reparability of composites, with up to 15 percent mass savings, rust resistance, and low-volume vehicle choice. However, composites were expensive, sensitive to high oven temperatures, could produce surface irregularities, and were not readily recyclable.

When metals were the material of choice, some form of welding process had to be used to build the part. A few automobile and parts manufacturers were hesitant to implement high-tech lasers for welding. Motoman and Progressive Tool and Industries Company estimated that reluctance to use laser welding was costing them between US$100 and US$200 per vehicle. The advantages of laser welding over spot welding included reduction in vehicle weight by as much as 200 pounds, stronger weld bodies, and rust prevention. Laser welding also saved time. Finishing a wheel well with spot welding could take up to three minutes, while finishing it with a laser weld took just 32 seconds and produced a 15 percent stronger bond. State-of-the-art laser technology in the mid-1990s was called Nd-YAG, (neodymium yttrium-aluminum garnet). GM, Toyota, and Honda were quick to embrace the concept, but conservatism on the part of plant managers slowed worldwide implementation of Nd-YAG technology.

Bharatbook.com acknowledged that there was an "increasing use of power-hungry options in modern cars," including heated seats and quick-defrost glass. These types of options placed tremendous demands on automotive charging systems, resulting in technology and specifications for components used in starters and alternators (collectively known as rotating electrics) becoming more advanced. The complexity of passenger cars and light trucks resulted in an increase of different alternators and starters.

Advances in computer-aided design (CAD) and computer-aided manufacture (CAM) helped drive the automotive and supplier industries in the 1990s. Solid modeling and life-sized graphics gave way to computer designs that were created entirely at a computer workstation. Corporate investment in computer use and training could be high, but computers were becoming common in the industry by the early 1990s.

Nonetheless, enhancements to computer use occurred. In addition to on-board computing in automobiles themselves, which made life easier for automobile driver, passenger, and repair department, the role of the designer also was facilitated by new software applications and hardware availability. The Standard for the Exchange for Product Model Data (STEP) was a universal computer language that provided information on specific auto parts to computer design programs such as CATIA and Unigraphics. The language was designed to eliminate the need for suppliers to maintain more than one engineering system, even if they served multiple customers, which meant that GM, Ford, Chrysler, BMW, Mercedes-Benz, Porsche, and Opel all endorsed STEP.

The Partnership for a New Generation of Vehicles (PNGV), formed in 1994 between the U.S. government and its three largest auto manufacturers, required assistance from the U.S. auto parts industry. The goal of the partnership was the development of a new supercar. The prototype vehicle was expected to get 80 miles to the gallon, seat six, and cost no more than US$15,000. About 200 suppliers were involved with the project by 1995, channeling resources and brainpower to help introduce the new car to the world by 2004. It was expected that the new car would be 40 percent lighter than cars of the mid-1990s and would make heavy use of composite materials. The project received a boost in 1998, when U.S. President Bill Clinton's budget increased funding to PNGV 22 percent to US$277 million. The U.S. Department of Energy received the largest chunk of the federal windfall (US$164 million), as development costs continued to be shared by the government and the auto industry. In 1998, PNGV research and development was refocused to concentrate on four key automobile systems: hybrid electric vehicle drives, direct injection engines, fuel cells, and increasingly lightweight materials. Spin-off from PNGV research placed the United States in an enviable position when the Kyoto Protocol on Global Warming of 1997 required the United States to dramatically reduce carbon dioxide emissions within ten years. Efforts associated with PNGV promised the availability of mass-marketed "clean" electric vehicles well within that timeframe. Also affecting research efforts was the zero-emission vehicle law passed in California, which required 10 percent of each automaker's vehicles sold in that state to have zero-emissions by 2004.

INDUSTRY LEADERS

Robert Bosch GmbH. Based in Stuttgart, Germany, Bosch, a name long-identified in Germany with the automotive industry, held its leading place among global automotive suppliers with sales of approximately US$30 billion in 2000, which reflected 7 percent growth over 1999. By 2004, Bosch reported US$54.6 billion in sales, a 19.6 percent increase over 2003. Automotive parts accounted for roughly 70 percent of total revenues. By 2006, sales had increased to US$57.6 billion and the company had 258,000 employees.

Bosch traditionally dedicated a significant portion of its earnings to research and development. This aggressive approach to new technology and innovation assured Bosch continued presence in the world market as it introduced various road handling improvements, voice recognition systems, and even devices to avoid collisions. Major Bosch systems included antilock braking and fuel injection and various auto electronics components, including starters and alternators. In 1998, Bosch offerings included a high-pressure accumulator injection system for diesel engines and advanced mobile radio telephone technology, as well as the first car radio that could be used to make telephone calls.

At the end of the twentieth century, Bosch subsidiaries and business affiliations were in 131 countries, and 130 of their production plants were outside Germany. This extensive globalization was hardly accidental, as Bosch had opened its first foreign office in the nineteenth century, establishing a factory in the United States that had exceeded its domestic plants in capacity in the years before World War I. In 2004, Bosch increased automotive production 5 percent, most of which was attributed to demand in China and elsewhere in Asia.

Visteon Corporation. Formerly Ford Automotive Components Group, which had included Ford Glass Division, Ford Climate Control Division, and divisions producing electronic controls, systems, trim, and engine accessories, Visteon Corporation was spun off from Ford Motor Company in 2000 as the second largest automotive parts supplier in the world, a position it retained in 2003. The group had been operating as an independent division of Ford since the late 1990s. The second largest manufacturer of automobiles and auto parts in the world, Ford had viewed the reorganization of all wholly owned parts suppliers into a single entity as the most logical way to prepare for the increased incorporation of electronics into motor vehicles. Because the company structure already was in place, Visteon began with 79,000 hand-picked employees, all veterans of Ford's international success. In 2004, Visteon employed 70,200 people.

Despite efforts to extend its global reach, less than 30 percent of sales came from operations outside North America in 2004. Ford Motor Company continued to account for 82 percent of Visteon's revenues, which fell 4

percent to US$18.7 billion that year. Its heavy reliance on Ford, which suffered several setbacks in the early 2000s due to negative publicity surrounding accidents related to the Firestone tires that were standard equipment on the popular Ford Explorer sport-utility vehicle, contributed to Visteon's decline for the year. The first quarter of 2005 looked promising for the company, however. Visteon announced results of $5 billion for the first quarter, including record aftermarket and non-Ford revenues of US$1.7 billion for a 30 percent increase. By 2007, Visteon reported revenues of US$11.3 billion and 41,500 employees. Pardus Capital Management controlled 23 percent of Visteon.

Delphi Corporation. Based in Troy, Michigan, Delphi Corporation, formerly Delphi Automotive Systems, was the world's largest and most comprehensive automotive parts manufacturer with 190,000 employees working in 31 countries. The firm was formerly known as the General Motors Corporation Automotive Components Group Worldwide (ACGW) and was spun off into an autonomous subsidiary in the mid-1990s. In 1997, the transfer of Delco from Hughes Electronics (another General Motors subsidiary) provided Delphi with a significant increase in total sales and a strong presence in the electronics portion of the supplier industry. When that deal was completed, Delphi's products included steering systems, chassis systems, thermal systems, energy and engine management systems, electric systems, and interior lighting systems. While nearly three-fourths of the company's sales were to North American customers, Europe, the Middle East, and Africa accounted for about 20 percent of total sales, and South America (including Mexico) and the Pacific Rim represented substantial, growing markets.

In 1999, GM spun Delphi off completely, and sales for the newly independent firm grew 8.3 percent that year to US$22.4 billion. Sales reached record levels in 2000 but tumbled 10.5 percent in 2001 to US$26.1 billion as a recession softened the global auto parts industry. By 2004, Delphi was back up to US$28.6 billion in sales. While General Motors continued to account for 70 percent of Delphi's revenues, the firm also sold its products to a huge portfolio of international automakers, including Fiat, Mercedes-Benz, Hyundai, Audi, Volkswagen, Daewoo, Skoda, Rover, Honda, Renault, Mitsubishi, Toyota, DaimlerChrysler, Ford, Isuzu, Suzuki, and SEAT. In 2005, Delphi filed for Chapter 11 bankruptcy.

Delphi manufacturing facility positioning reflected continuing growth outside the United States. The company was in direct operation of 78 plants in North America, but operated 63 in Europe, the Middle East and Africa; 55 in Mexico and South America; and 12 in

Asia-Pacific locations. The company reported US$22.3 billion ins sales and 169,500 employees.

While the development of Delphi in its incarnation as General Motors Corporation Automotive Components Group Worldwide had closely followed the development of General Motors Corporation (see **Motor Vehicles**), the growth of its electronic subsidiary, Delco, is worth independent examination. Delco was originally founded in 1912 by C. F. Kettering, the inventor of the electric starter, and the company originally built starters for Cadillac motor cars. General Motors acquired Delco in 1936 and quickly expanded its product line to include radios. Delco's first car radios were built for Chevrolet and were strictly aftermarket items that were installed as dealer options. Through the 1930s and 1940s, Delco concentrated its manufacturing efforts on a variety of car radio products to satisfy the expanding automotive and home electronics markets. In 1956 the company developed the high-power transistor, which spawned the development of a variety of experimental products, including an in-dash portable radio and the prototype of a 45-rpm automobile record player that anticipated the automobile CD changer. Delco's ready market for automotive components and radios grew with GM automobile sales, which provided a stable and profitable source of income. During the 1960s and 1970s, Delco began production of AM/FM stereos and introduced new power and automotive-control systems.

Denso Corporation. Nippondenso had changed its name to the more international Denso Corporation in the late 1990s. Denso was one of Japan's largest manufacturers of auto parts, although the majority of the company's plants were located outside Japan. Due to weaker demand in North America and Europe, sales in 2001 fell 10.6 percent to US$15.9 billion as earnings tumbled 18 percent to US$481 million. By 2004, however, sales were up to US$24.3 billion. In part because of its extensive global presence, Denso boasted an employee base close to 86,000 in 2001 and 96,000 in 2004. In 2007, it reported revenues of US $30.6 billion with 112,262 employees.

Denso sold a variety of products to manufacturers worldwide, ranging from air conditioners and heating units to anti-lock braking systems and fuel systems. Toyota Motor Corp., its former parent, still owned 23 percent of the firm in 2007.

Johnson Controls Inc. With 2004 sales of US$26.5 billion and earnings of US$817.5 million, Johnson Controls was a leader in the global automotive parts industry. That year, the company's employee base totaled 123,000. Johnson Controls was founded by Professor Warren Johnson in 1885. Initially existing to manufacture and

market Johnson's own invention (the thermostat), 100 years later the company boasted worldwide leadership in two lines of business: building controls and automotive systems. In spite of the emphasis on "controls" suggested by its name, Johnson's automotive division was the dominant corporate revenue-producer. More than 40 percent of Johnson's total sales came from business with the U.S. Big Three, for which the company provided seating, various interior systems, and batteries. As of 2007, Johnson reported US$39.6 billion and 140,000 employees.

Lear Corporation. The largest supplier of car seats in the world, Lear Corporation also manufactured floor and acoustic systems, instrument panels, and other interior products, including headliners and door panels. Employing 111,000 people around the world, Lear marketed to Volvo, BMW, Fiat, Saab, and Volkswagen, in addition to the United States' Big Three. In spite of a growing global presence, in the late 1990s more than half of Lear's sales were to Ford and GM. Expanding through acquisitions and mergers since its 1917 founding as American Metal Products, Lear accelerated this growth process in the latter years of the century, securing Empetek, Dunlop-Cox, Keiper Car Seating, and ITT Automotive in 1997 and buying two privately-held Italian firms (Gruppo Pianfe S.r.L and Strapazzini S.r.L.) in 1998. Lear also paid US$2.3 billion in 1999 for United Technologies Automotive. Global sales rose 7.7 percent to US$16.96 billion in 2004, while earnings skyrocketed 11 percent to US$422.2 million. Lear employed more than 110,000 people in 34 countries. For 2007, the company reported sales of US$16 billion while the company employed more than 91,000 employees. It had more than 200 facilities in 34 countries and maintained its status as a global car seat market leader.

TRW Automotive Holdings Corp. TRW was founded in 1901 as the Cleveland Cap Screw Company. Within a few years, the company was producing most of the engine valves supplied to the burgeoning automotive industry. Mass production of engine valves allowed the company to flourish until the Great Depression in the United States forced it to diversify, developing products for the aviation industry. A joint venture with Ramo-Wooldridge Corporation to build the intercontinental ballistic missile led to the merger that formed Thompson Ramo Wooldridge, renamed TRW in 1965.

In the 1980s, TRW returned to its core businesses with an exclusive contract with Ford Motor Company to supply airbags. The company expanded its European manufacturing capacity by opening plants in France, the United Kingdom, and Brazil. Further European expansion included the acquisition of 92 percent of the Czech Republic's largest auto engine valve and steering systems maker and participating in joint ventures with companies such as Italy's Magneti Marelli.

After purchasing LucasVarity plc in 1999 for US$7 billion in one of the largest acquisitions in industry history, Toledo, Ohio-based TRW Inc. found itself competing with the leading firms in the global auto parts industry that had US$10 billion or more in revenues. LucasVarity was formed in 1996 via a merger between Lucas Industries plc and Varity Corporation. Prior to its takeover by TRW, a lion's share (40 percent) of Lucas's US$6.56 billion in international sales came from braking systems used in Mercedes-Benz and Ford vehicles, as well as Korea's Kia automobiles. As a result, the merger strengthened TRW's international operations by giving it access to the European braking systems sector. In 2004, private investment group Blackstone purchased the company from TRW, renaming it TRW Automotive Holdings Corp.

Product lines for TRW included restraint systems and controls, steering and suspension systems, electronics, and engine components and engineered fasteners. Automotive parts accounted for roughly 60 percent of sales, which fell to US$12.01 billion in 2004. Net income for 2004 was $29 million. TRW employed approximately 60,000 people worldwide, primarily in Europe and North America. By 2007, the company reported net income of US$14.7 billion and 66,300 billion employees.

Dana Corporation. Dana Corporation was founded in 1904 in Toledo, Ohio, by Clarence Spicer, whose fascination for mechanical design led him to question the bicycle drive methodology that operated automobiles at the beginning of the twentieth century. Experimenting with a propeller shaft drive, Spicer designed universal joints which allowed the spin of the drive shaft to be governed by the engine and then reverse direction and turn wheels on an axle set at right angles to the shaft. Less than 100 years later, Dana Corporation, which was named for an early CEO, operated facilities in 30 separate countries, employed 97,300 people, and grossed more than US$12.4 billion in revenues. By 2004, Dana's sales were US$9.1 billion (13 percent more than in 2003), and its workforce had shrunk to 46,000. Continuing to manufacture axles and driveshafts, Dana also sold piston rings, filters, bearings and sealing products, brake and chassis products, and thermal and fluid management systems to automakers around the world. In 2006, Dana filed for Chapter 11 bankruptcy and later evolved into Dana Corporation Holding company.

Valeo SA. One of the largest automotive parts operations in Europe, Paris-based Valeo operated in 26 countries, including the United States, Germany, Argentina, the United Kingdom, Brazil, China, South Korea, Spain,

India, Japan, Poland, Tunisia, and Turkey. Primarily a manufacturer of engine cooling systems, clutches, and friction material, Valeo reported revenues of US$12.8 billion in 2004, up just over 11 percent from the previous year, and employed more than 62,000 people. By 2008, the company acknowledged plans to analyze the impact of "the brutal deterioration of automotive production." Valeo had 122 plants, 61 R&D centers, and 9 distribution centers, and reported 59,700 employees in 28 countries worldwide.

During the acquisition frenzy of the late 1990s, Valeo acquired ITT Electrical Systems for US$1.7 billion. After watching its new electrical systems arm struggle to stay afloat, Valeo placed the U.S.-based unit under Chapter 11 bankruptcy protection in 2001. Shortly thereafter, in response to slowing demand for auto parts, Valeo announced its intent to cut 5,000 jobs worldwide in 2002. Valeo Service also distributed the company's products to the automotive aftermarket.

MAJOR COUNTRIES IN THE INDUSTRY

Japan. U.S. trade with Japan was filled with controversy during the latter years of the twentieth century. Toyota Corporation and other Japanese car manufacturers were under considerable scrutiny as they attempted to purchase a greater number of auto parts from outside their country. The Japanese-U.S. trade agreement of the mid-1990s, known as the U.S.-Japan Auto Framework Agreement, sought to improve the balance of trade. In fact, U.S. auto parts exports to Japan increased 20 percent in 1996, although exports to Japan were less than 5 percent of U.S. automotive parts exports. A joint venture between Toyota and General Motors called New United Motor Manufacturing Inc. (NUMMI), was run by Toyota and provided a boost to as many as 35 auto parts manufacturers in the mid-1990s. These companies exported approximately US$80 million in auto parts to Japan in 1995, where five years earlier the export total had been just US$2 million. An ITT study done in 1997 reported that Japanese firms held nearly 15 percent of the world auto parts market.

Economic turmoil in Japan undercut auto production there, and as a result auto parts production in Japan declined 5.8 percent in 1998 to US$118.7 billion (12.46 trillion yen). This decline was in line with *The Automobile Parts Industry Facing the 21st Century* report released in the mid-1990s by the Japan Auto Parts Industries Association (JAPIA), which forecast slow growth in auto parts sales through 2005. The projected decrease was blamed on cyclical economic patterns, exchange rate uncertainty, increased overseas competition, and a fall in exports from Japan as companies moved operations closer to their markets. Market growth was expected to come from expanding foreign markets and increases in the domestic replacement parts market. Suppliers were encouraged to develop strategic alliances with foreign producers to maintain competitiveness, to control the manufacturing and supply cost of auto parts, and to work with companies to develop a standardization system for their vehicle parts. The Japanese government also was given specific responsibility to support an "International Division of Labor," as well as the Japanese small business sector, which included 92 percent of the entire auto parts business in the country according to JAPIA.

The Japanese government also was given a proactive role in enhancing labor/management relations, particularly in the areas of retaining aging workers and training new employees, including the rising numbers of women in the industry. To encourage company innovation, the government took interest in intellectual property and patent right protection. At the same time, the Japan Ministry of International Trade and Industry (MITI) helped the country's six minicar producers agree on standardization of engines, electronics, transmissions, braking systems, and heating and air conditioning systems. These manufacturers included Honda, Mitsubishi Motors, Suzuki, Daihatsu, and Fuji Heavy Industries. This was a significant advantage to parts manufacturers, since there were approximately 4 million minicars on Japanese roads, with 75,000 new vehicle registrations annually, according to the Ministry of Transportation and the Japan Automobile Manufacturers Association.

Some analysts suggested that low volume production would prevent Japanese suppliers from being part of the exclusive list of auto parts survivors that were predicted to emerge in the early 2000s. However, 4 of the top 25 auto parts suppliers in 2000 were based in Japan. In addition, a newly emerging component of the parts market promised to improve the Japanese industry outlook significantly. Increasing use of electronic systems and subsystems in new cars provided a natural market for Japan's traditional high-technology strength.

The United States. Although both the original equipment and the auto parts replacement market remained stable in the late 1990s, the recession of the early 2000s was expected to undermine original equipment production and possibly favor the auto parts replacement market as increasingly cost conscious individuals would likely keep their vehicles longer. Earlier estimates had suggested that 49 percent of total U.S. sales would come from under-car parts, 14 percent from drive train parts, and 13 percent from engine parts and cooling systems, but the challenge to keep manufacturing lean and maximize profit was the same. According to *Euromonitor,* by 2008

the market was expected to grow 18.8 percent, reaching US$146.7 billion.

Consolidation, acquisition, and foreign expansion had all underlined efforts of U.S. suppliers to ensure continued success through global presence. The North American Free Trade Agreement (NAFTA) offered additional support to the U.S. aftermarket, since tariffs were reduced on parts exported to Mexico and Canada. Trade agreements with Japan focused particularly on the balance of trade in auto parts and other items related to automobile manufacture. Under pressure to do so, Japan bought more parts from the United States in the late 1990s, but Japan also increased its transplant presence in North America, skewing the balance of trade in another way.

In September 2008, U.S. Auto Parts Network, the leading online provider of aftermarket auto parts and accessories, announced that it had entered an agreement to purchase the assets of Smart Trac. In addition to basic education and helpful tips, U.S. Auto planned to integrate its parts catalogue into the site, enhancing it with diverse data.

The European Union. To counter the increased presence of U.S. and Japanese manufacturers, European parts makers prepared to expand the European Union's common market by eliminating all barriers to trade by the 2010s. European manufacturers worked to downsize and streamline processes, occasionally emulating the lean manufacturing processes of their Japanese counterparts. Carrying globalization from the Old to the New World, European companies also increased investments in the U.S. market. According to *Euromonitor,* the market in France was expected to grow 9 percent to a value of 3.4 billion euros by 2008, with engines and transmissions being the largest sector. The market in Germany was expected to grow 28 percent by 2008, to a value of 77 billion euros. Finally, the U.K. market was expected to grow 4.8 percent by 2008, with transmission and braking systems as the largest sector.

More than 100 North American motor vehicle parts members took part in a joint industry reception held in September 2008 for Automechanika Frankfurt hosted by the U.S. Consul General at the U.S. Embassy. The reception united the Automotive Aftermarket Industry Association (AAIA), the Automotive Aftermarket Suppliers Association (AASA), the Motor & Equipment Manufacturers Association (MEMA), the Overseas Automotive Council (OAC), and the Specialty Equipment Market Association in conjunction with U.S. commercial service as sponsors. "We are working together to promote export of U.S. products to Germany, Europe and the world," explained Anthony Cardez, executive director of OAC.

China's auto exports to Europe were expected to increase dramatically by 2018, including the Great Wall's Wingle pickup, the first Chinese-built pickup truck to be exported to Europe. The auto parts aftermarket had been typically dominated by suppliers operating satellite factories of some automakers, leaving a small market share for independent parts suppliers. Overall, following market liberalization in 2003 and appreciation of the euro has resulted in the European Aftermarket reporting growth that exceeded other regions.

BIBLIOGRAPHY

"100+ North American Parts Suppliers Participated in Automechanika Reception." *Automotive Aftermarket Suppliers Association,* 17 September 2008. Available from www.aftermarketsuppliers.org.

"Auto Parts Makers Go Global." *AutoTrends,* December 2001. Available from www.jama.org.

"Auto Parts Suppliers Must Cut Costs." *United Press International,* 20 November 2003.

"Automotive Aftercare and Accessories in France, Germany, UK, US." *Euromonitor,* August 2004. Available from www.majormarketprofiles.com.

Automotive Aftermarket Industry Association. "U.S. Motor Vehicle Aftermarket Increased 3 Percent in 2003." *AAIA 2004/2005 Aftermarket Factbook,* 2004. Available from www.apaa.org.

Cole, August. "Delphi Echoes Automakers' Gloom." *CBS MarketWatch,* 10 December 2001. Available from www.marketwatch.com.

Content, Thomas. "Auto Parts Suppliers' Share Prices Shift Into High Gear." *Knight Ridder/Tribune Business News,* 1 December 2003.

———. "Industry Analysts Predict Strong 2004 Sales for Auto Parts Suppliers." *Knight Ridder/Tribune Business News,* 6 January 2004.

Dana Corporation Fact Sheet. Dana Corporation, 2005.

Donnelly, Paul. "Logistics Management Is Mission Critical When Parts Manufacturers Go Offshore." *World Trade,* March 2004.

Draper, Deborah J., ed. *Business Rankings Annual.* Detroit: Thomson Gale, 2004.

Fitzgerald, Craig. "Three Point Landing." *Automotive Industries,* May 2004.

"General Automotive Announces Joint Venture Operating Terms." *MarketWatch,* 2 September 2008. Available from www.marketwatch.com.

"A Glimpse at the European Auto Parts Aftermarket," 30 September 2008. Available from news.cens.com.

"Global Market Review of Starter Motors and Alternators—Forecasts to 2014." Bharat Book Bureau, 30 September 2008. Available from www.bharatbook.com.

"Hoover's Company Capsules." *Hoover's Online,* 2008. Available from www.hoovers.com.

Hyun-cheol, Kim. "Hyundai on Charm Campaign in Russia." *Korea Times,* 24 September 2008. Available from www.koreatimes.co.kr.

"India to Become a Hub of Auto Parts." *Asia Africa Intelligence Wire,* 31 August 2003.

"Industry Trends." Automotive Parts & Accessories Association, 2004. Available from www.apaa.org.

"International Trade Statistics." 2003. Available from www.wto.org.

Lazich, Robert S., ed. *Market Share Reporter.* Detroit: Thomson Gale, 2004.

Martinez, Nate. "Japanese Aftermarket Firm Trust/G. Reddy Files for Bankruptcy," 10 September 2008. Available from www.printthis.clickability.com.

"Pratt & Whitney Canada Establishes New Parts Distribution Centre in Sydney, Australia." *MarketWatch,* 18 September 2008. Available from www.marketwatch.com.

Sherefkin, Robert. "Euro Doesn't Spur US Supplier Buys." *Automotive News Europe,* 28 June 2004.

———. "Study Sees Tough Time for Suppliers." *Automotive News,* 7 June 2004.

———. "U.S. Share of Auto Parts Business Expected to Fall 18 Percent." *Crain's Detroit Business,* 22 March 2004.

"U.S. Auto Parts Network, Inc. Announces Acquisition of Auto Information and Advice Website," 30 September 2008. Available from www.itnewsonline.com.

"U.S. Auto Parts Suppliers Face a Hit from NAFTA Next Year." *The Kiplinger Letter,* 8 April 2004.

"Valeo Press Release." 2 October 2008. Available from www.valeo.com.

Valeo S.A. SWOT Analysis. Datamonitor, April 2005.

"Visteon Announces First Quarter 2005 Results." Visteon Corporation, 27 April 2005.

Wrigley, Al. "Auto Parts Suppliers Looking Offshore to Escape '201' Hike." *American Metal Market,* 29 January 2003.

SIC 3711

MOTOR VEHICLES

NAICS CODE(S)

336111. One of the largest sectors of the global economy, the automobile industry manufactures passenger cars, trucks, commercial cars, and buses. Included in this discussion are firms that build chassis and passenger car bodies. Some industry companies also manufacture motor vehicle parts (see **Motor Vehicle Parts and Accessories**).

INDUSTRY SNAPSHOT

In the mid-2000s, the worldwide leader in the motor vehicle industry was the United States, followed closely by Japan and Germany. The top six companies in the industry accounted for more than half of global sales, although the rest of the industry's companies were steadily gaining market share on General Motors, Toyota, Ford, Chrysler, Volkswagen, and Honda. Although the three mature world markets—Japan, North America, and western Europe—continued to account for the majority of global motor vehicle production and sales, nearly all of the industry's future growth was projected to come from emerging markets in the Asia-Pacific region, Latin America, the Middle East, and eastern Europe.

Due to increasing globalization, the saturation of mature markets, and economic decline in North America and Europe, the automobile industry worldwide is characterized by intense competition. As a result, most major manufacturers restructured operations in an effort to speed product development, reduce costs, and improve production efficiency. In addition, many manufacturers began to outsource, shifting production facilities to developing countries to take advantage of less expensive labor, reduce exposure to currency fluctuations, and avoid trade restrictions. Automakers also have been forced to lower prices, trim their ranks, and slow or stop production to deal with waning demand for new vehicles. Added difficulty for automotive manufacturers was the rise in steel prices, which increased 30 to 40 percent in 2004. Automakers and suppliers were both seeing reductions in profits as a result.

At the same time, the growing worldwide environmental movement has prompted automakers to increase research and development expenditures in an effort to build commercially viable electric and electric-gas hybrid vehicles and to make their cars fully recyclable. In the mid-2000s, Toyota was leading the way with its gas-electric hybrid Prius sedan. According to the Alliance of Automobile Manufacturers (AAM), 2004 "Tier 2" vehicle models were almost 100 percent cleaner than those of three decades before. In fact, more than one-third of all new vehicles met the strict mandatory 2009 standards five years early. R.L. Polk & Company reported that registrations for hybrid electric vehicles in the United States were 81 percent higher in 2004 than in 2003, with 83,153 registered new vehicles. The Toyota Prius captured 64 percent of that market, with 53,761 new registrations followed by the Honda Civic Hybrid that had 31 percent of the market with 25,586 registered hybrid cars in 2004.

The auto industry worldwide was struggling to survive in 2008. Automakers were facing drastic changes, including massive layoffs of salaried employees and plant closings as sales expectations plummeted. However, Dartmouth's Tuck School of Business Professor Richard D'Aveni observed, "This is the straw that is breaking the camel's back for something that has been happening for the past 25 years."

ORGANIZATION AND STRUCTURE

The global automobile market can be divided into six segments: three mature markets and three relatively new markets that reflect emerging economies. Western Europe, North America, and Japan continued their longtime

dominance of the industry in the mid-2000s. However, Eastern Europe, the Pacific Rim (excluding Japan), and Latin America were rapidly developing a secondary consumer market.

Mature Markets. In 2004, the three mature markets combined controlled more than 85 percent of the world's motor vehicle production and sales. Japan and Europe gained in market share during the early 2000s. The major difference between U.S. and foreign markets was that producers in the United States and Canada sold the majority of vehicles produced within the domestic market, while manufacturers in Japan exported more than 40 percent of their total production. In 2004, 61,387,595 vehicles were sold worldwide, 5.5 percent more than in 2003, according to *Automotive News.*

North America. Dominated throughout the latter part of the twentieth century by General Motors (GM), Ford Motor Company, and DaimlerChrysler, the U.S. car market was characterized not so much by an industry drive to increase total sales, but rather was reflected by the Big Three's intense competition with foreign manufacturers for market share. In the 1970s, U.S. automakers held 90 percent of the domestic passenger car market. By 2000, this figure had plunged to 54 percent due to the growing popularity of "transplant cars" (foreign cars made in U.S. plants) and imports. The rapid growth in sales of light trucks, which over the 10 years ending in 1992 doubled to 5 million units and increased an additional 50 percent to a record 7.9 million units in 2004, helped U.S. manufacturers regain some of their lost market share. In fact, in 2004 more than one-half of all new vehicle sales were trucks. Truck sales were increased in part by the extreme popularity of sport-utility vehicles, but standard pickups, compact pickups, and vans added to the total. The Big Three had held a dominant 79 percent share of the U.S. light truck market in 2000, but that number had fallen from a high of nearly 85 percent. The popularity of sport-utility vehicles (SUVs) manufactured by rivals, such as Toyota and Honda, had allowed those firms to steal domestic light truck market share from the Big Three. By 2004, GM and Ford continued to hold around 24 percent of the world market for motor vehicles, losing about 1.5 percent market share from 2003. The numbers improved when North American automakers' stakes in foreign automakers were included. GM Daewoo in South Korea sold just over 900,000 units in 2004, and Ford had a 34 percent controlling stake in Mazda.

Japan. Domestic car and truck sales in Japan totaled 3.96 million units in 2004, reflecting a slowdown of 1.6 percent, according to Datamonitor. Demand for passenger cars fell 0.8 percent, and demand for trucks fell 5.8

percent. Sales growth in the Japanese domestic market was limited by a fluctuating economy in the 1990s that included national recessions punctuated by weak recoveries, unfavorable currency exchange rates, and a culture that considered cars a luxury rather than a necessity. However, global sales in Japan accounted for 30.9 percent of the worldwide market, a gain of almost 1 percent from 2003. The Japanese automotive market was dominated by six large domestic producers: Toyota, Nissan, Honda, Mitsubishi, Mazda, and Suzuki.

Western Europe. The European automobile market, traditionally restricted to include seven major western industrialized nations, expanded into two major marketing segments in the 1990s as the Communist bloc collapsed. However, traditional leaders like Germany, which produced more than 9.5 million vehicles in 2004, continued to dominate the market. Germany was the third largest automobile producer in the world. France, with Renault and PSA Peugeot-Citroen SA, and Italy with Fiat S.p.A., were also major producers in the global automotive market. The largest automakers in eastern and central Europe positioned themselves to deal with continued growth and increased competition as the eastern and central European markets grew rapidly. In addition, several companies established joint ventures with or acquired controlling interest in other companies for broader market presence.

Emerging Markets.

Asia-Pacific. The Asia-Pacific region, excluding Japan, was perhaps the most volatile emerging market in the 1990s. Sales to this part of the world in 1991 were only 4 million units, but increased to 6 million units by 1996 and 8 million units by 2000.

Economic reforms during the 1990s were expected to increase buying power and open markets to international competition in China and India, the two most populous nations on earth. In China, the potential increase of automobiles on the road was staggering, with growth estimated to start at 5 million units and increase to 40 million by the year 2000. Chinese domestic manufacturers struggled with a possible overcapacity problem in 1997, when government subsidies were contingent upon meeting high manufacturing quotas. Nevertheless, analysts called for continuing high market growth, although results might be adjusted below original expectations. In 2004, Chinese automakers increased global market share to 3.8 percent, but sales slowed to 7.4 percent growth. The slowdown, which was in contrast to the segment's 36.5 percent growth in 2003, was attributed to credit restrictions imposed by the Chinese government. Exponential growth was possible in India, where about 950 million people had fewer than 6 million registered automobiles in 1998. However, immediate expansion of the Indian market was

thwarted in the late 1990s by a combination of economic and trade issues. Not only did India impose a 40 percent tariff on automotive imports, but in late 1997 the country also began to require potential importers to follow a 50 percent "local content" rule. At the same time, most Indian manufacturers had joined with Japanese and South Korean automakers that were suffering domestic economic upheavals. However, India held 1 percent of the global market, and sales passed 600,000 units, led by Tata Motors Ltd. and Mahindra & Mahindra, who were two of the three fasted growing automakers according to *Automotive News*.

Indonesia, Taiwan, and the Philippines also struggled with slow economies. However, South Korea, the largest emerging market in the Asia-Pacific region, recovered from a significant drop in 1998 production to become the world's seventh largest producer of vehicles, with a production level of 2.8 million units in 1999. The recovery was due primarily to the success of Hyundai Motor Company, the largest carmaker in South Korea, and the ninth largest automaker in the world with sales of more than 3 million units. South Korean vehicle exports reached US$31.8 billion by December 2004, representing 12.6 percent of the country's overall exports according to the *Asia Africa Intelligence Wire*. Thailand's automotive industry had also reported gains, and production was expected to exceed 1 million units in 2005. The Thai Automotive Industry Association reported that vehicle exports through September 2004 were more than 236,000, an increase over 2003.

Foreign manufacturers increased their presence in the Asia-Pacific region despite a small domestic market for new cars. Ford and GM (the United States); Daewoo and Hyundai (Korea); Mitsubishi (Japan); and Fiat, Mercedes, BMW, Peugeot, and Volkswagen (Europe) all sought part of the market, even though any success in the Pacific was relative. For example, in the 18 months between January 1997 and June 1998, South Korea, which was arguably one of the more Westernized of the Pacific Rim nations, purchased fewer imported cars from all sources than the number of cars it had exported to the United States in just over two weeks. To bolster the economy, the Asia Pacific Economic Cooperation (APEC) forum sought to achieve free trade throughout the Asia-Pacific region by 2010 for industrialized countries. Developing nations were expected to follow suit by 2020. However, in the late 1990s, the Asian automobile economy temporarily appeared to be of greater significance as an exporter than as a consumer.

Eastern Europe. As Communism fell in Eastern Europe several large markets were restructured. Purchasing power remained low as the recovery took hold, but some areas showed evidence of pent-up demand for

Western goods, including automobiles. Analysts predicted that most domestic firms, formerly protected from competition, would either cease to exist or be acquired by established foreign automakers. By 1993, German automakers Bayerische Motoren Werke (BMW) and Volkswagen, as well as U.S. giant General Motors, had established transplants in Eastern Europe. The Eastern European market for automobiles, supported by 280 million consumers in the Commonwealth of Independent States alone, was anticipated to grow to 6 million units annually by 2010.

Latin America. Competitors in the Latin American market sold 2 million vehicles annually in the early 1990s. Economic reforms in Mexico, Argentina, Chile, Venezuela, and Brazil provided a combined market of 125 million consumers. By mid-2004, Chile had imported more than 56,000 automobiles valued at US$465 million, a 15 percent growth over the same period in 2003. Primary exporters to Chile included Japan and South Korea. Although some automakers were reluctant to commit major financial resources in Latin America due to lingering concerns about political instability, the Big Three U.S. automakers, as well as Volkswagen and a few other European manufacturers, established production facilities in Mexico and Brazil. The main advantage of Latin American production was an abundance of inexpensive labor, and the North American Free Trade Agreement (NAFTA), which reduced trade barriers between the United States, Canada, and Mexico, and was expected to make Mexico even more attractive to producers from the United States and Canada. Accordingly, Mexico's production levels grew steadily throughout the 1990s, reaching a high of 1.5 million in 1999 when it was the tenth-largest producer of motor vehicles in the world.

BACKGROUND AND DEVELOPMENT

The development of the automobile was truly international as individuals from many countries contributed innovations that led to the features and production methods used to build cars. The first self-propelled vehicle was a three-wheeler powered by steam invented by Frenchman Nicholas Joseph Cugnot in 1769. Nearly a century later, Belgian Etienne Lenoir invented the first internal combustion engine. The first gasoline-powered vehicles were constructed by Germans Karl Benz and Gottlieb Daimler in 1885, and Armand Peugeot offered the first motorized vehicles for public sale in France four years later.

In the United States, brothers Charles and Frank Duryea of Massachusetts worked from Benz's designs to create their own gasoline-powered automobile in the early 1890s. By 1899, approximately 30 different manufacturers produced and sold various types of motor vehicles in the United States. In 1914, U.S. inventor Henry Ford, who built his first car in 1896, perfected an automated production system that revolutionized the industry. Ford's assembly line had moving belts that produced four times as many Model Ts as the year before and provided for ongoing reduced prices while adding new features to the car. By 1920, half of all the cars on the road worldwide were Model Ts. Many other well-known U.S. manufacturers came into existence at this time as well, including Buick, Cadillac, Chrysler, Oldsmobile, Packard, and Studebaker.

Many innovations were made in the worldwide automobile industry in the late 1920s, including automatic transmissions. Manufacturers began to focus on styling, aerodynamics, and fuel efficiency. Although personal car production came to a virtual halt during World War II as most countries devoted all industrial capacity to national defense, the war brought improvements to the industry with better assembly line production. During World War II women workers began to be accepted in factories. Postwar prosperity and pent-up demand led to a booming worldwide automobile market.

The automobile industry followed a typical pattern of globalization with the largest producers in each nation first exporting products and then gradually moving sales and production operations to lucrative overseas markets. The United States' Ford Motor Company had the very earliest success in reaching the markets of Western Europe. Ford began assembling cars in the United Kingdom in 1911, and became Great Britain's largest automaker by 1914. Ford began exporting to Japan in 1925 and built plants in several major European nations after World War II. General Motors followed a slightly different route, establishing an export company in 1911 to handle overseas sales before entering the Japanese market in 1927. After World War II, GM expanded its European operations by purchasing existing companies, such as Vauxhall in the United Kingdom and Opel in Germany.

The first imports to the U.S. market included exotic European luxury and sports cars, including Rolls Royce, Mercedes, Jaguar (which was later purchased by Ford Motor Company), and Porsche. Until the 1960s, imports accounted for less than 0.5 of all U.S. auto sales. Led by Volkswagen and its popular Beetle model, imports improved their foothold in the U.S. market, rising from a 10 to 15 percent share between 1968 and 1970. The oil crises of the 1970s increased the price of fuel and led many consumers to seek small, fuel-efficient, foreign cars through the end of the 1980s. Japanese manufacturers were most successful in anticipating the demand for fuel economy, and quickly gained market share at the expense of U.S. producers. Design, quality, price, and economy of operation combined to increase foreign market share, and in 1998 nearly 40 percent of cars and 18 percent of trucks were made outside the United States. Ironically, in the late 1990s luxury cars had become some of the most popular imports.

Throughout the 1990s, tough competition and minimal growth caused restructuring throughout the North American market. Automakers struggled to reduce new product development time and, to counter a perceived German and Japanese competitive advantage, improve quality, while still containing costs. Competitors throughout the U.S.-Canadian market also were affected by passage of NAFTA as North American producers gained access to inexpensive labor and the rapidly growing Mexican market, while domestic content requirements decreased the prospects of car producers from other parts of the world.

The dominance of the United States' Big Three automotive companies faded in the 1990s, while Japanese manufacturers began to enjoy huge success before being forced to maintain similar market share under the auspices of a volatile and occasionally shaky domestic economy. The recovery of the mid-2000s was followed by a more generalized Pacific Rim recession in the late 1990s, although Japanese overseas efforts continued to prosper. The proliferation of transplant auto companies reshaped the industry, but no single event equaled the impact of the merger of automotive giants Chrysler Corporation and Daimler-Benz AG.

The Daimler-Chrysler merger would have been noteworthy in any industry for the complete secrecy in which initial talks and various planning stages took place. The May 1998 merger announcement took the auto world by total surprise and led to immediate speculation that an overall industry restructure was on the horizon. Small international automakers looked with interest or concern for possible overtures from major manufacturers who sought to compete with Daimler-Chrysler's unprecedented world presence. The Daimler-Chrysler merger was considered a "merger of equals" with products that did not overlap. Daimler-Benz contributed luxury cars and Chrysler manufactured a variety of smaller passenger cars, trucks, and utility vehicles. Combined sales were expected to reach US$130 billion, placing the company into the economic stratosphere of Ford and GM.

In one stroke, the balance of the auto industry was changed, as rivals began pursuing consolidation in an effort to remain competitive. In 1999, Ford added the car operations of Volvo to its increasingly global mix of holdings, and later bought Land Rover. GM acquired a portion of Suzuki, as well as of Subaru. Renault paid US$5.4 billion for a 37 percent share of Nissan. In

addition, Volkswagen bought Italian luxury sports carmaker Automobili Lamborghini SpA and Rolls Royce Cars of Britain. South Korean leader Hyundai Motor Co. bought Kia Motors Corp. and Asia Motors Corp. Not to be outdone, DaimlerChrysler itself also participated in merger and acquisition activity, purchasing a controlling share of Mitsubishi Motors. The value of automotive mergers and acquisitions reached an industry record of US$71.3 billion in 1999. As the cash reserves of major automakers dwindled, merger and acquisition spending slowed to US$22 billion in 2000.

Less dramatic industry activity included the economic consolidation of the European Union, which reduced some trade restrictions and provided Japanese competitors with new opportunities to establish a presence in the western European market. The resulting increase in competition encouraged European manufacturers, who in many cases continued to lag behind North American and Japanese automakers in terms of quality and production efficiency, to remain competitive by modernizing facilities and restructuring operations.

The North American automotive industry boomed in 1999 and 2000, bolstered by favorable economic conditions, including the lowest unemployment rate in decades, the growth of personal income levels, and a high level of consumer confidence. Sales in the United States grew 3.6 percent to reach a record 17.5 million units in 2000. However, the Big Three continued to lose ground to rivals like Toyota and Honda, who were largely responsible for the 5 percent global market share loss by the Big Three between 1997 and 2000. This was due at least in part to efforts by Japanese car makers to expand their product lines to more closely resemble those of the Big Three.

CURRENT CONDITIONS

Recessions in North America and Europe began taking a toll on the automotive industries in those regions in early 2001. Oversupply in North America prompted auto manufacturers to shut down assembly plants for days and, in some cases, weeks, during the first quarter of the year. Immediately following the terrorist attacks on the United States on September 11, 2001, automotive sales tumbled. When analysts began predicting that U.S. unit sales would fall nearly 6 percent to 16.5 million, General Motors (GM) launched a successful no-interest financing program, dubbed "Keep America Rolling." The free financing appealed to increasingly cost conscious consumers, and when sales at GM began to rebound, other carmakers began to launch their own special promotions. In 2005, GM hit the jackpot again by offering its employee-pricing program to all buyers, which resulted in sales increases of 47 percent in June

2005, the company's best year since 1986, according to *The Detroit Free Press.* Following GM's success, Ford and Chrysler offered similar plans in mid-2005. An overall increase of 15.9 percent in U.S. automotive sales was primarily a result of the GM program.

In early 2005, overseas automakers continued to gain U.S. market share. Sales of cars and light trucks in April 2005 totaled 1,504,332, an increase of 5.7 percent over April 2004. However, GM and Ford continued to lose market share, as did all U.S. automakers. While Chrysler posted substantial sales increases, and new GM and Ford vehicles were selling well, the Big 3 U.S. auto companies overall lost market share, bringing them to about 43 percent of the domestic market. Japanese companies were gaining rapidly as Nissan North America reported a gain of almost 32 percent, Toyota Motor Sales U.S.A. increased sales almost 26 percent, and American Honda Motor Co. climbed 18 percent. In 2007, DaimlerChrysler sold the Chrysler Group to private equity firm Cerberus Capital Management. By 2008, the Big Three were in serious trouble, and appealed to the U.S. Congress for loans to keep them operational.

As of the mid-2000s, some manufacturers in the industry were considering increasing or beginning a build-to-order (BTO) segment. There would be fewer such vehicles, but buyers would pay a premium to custom design their vehicles. In addition, cars would not be built on uncertain industry forecasts but on known demand. By the late 2000s, it was uncertain if the industry as a whole would move in this direction.

RESEARCH AND TECHNOLOGY

Issues of general ecology and global warming continued to drive the development of alternative fuel vehicles. Automakers resisted the demand of buyers and government for many years, citing the high cost of fuel cells and business and marketing risks involved, but legislative changes worldwide forced investment in the technology. In the United States, under the Alternative Motor Fuels Act of 1988, manufacturers of alternate-fuel vehicles were to be included "favorably" in the Corporate Average Fuel Economy program, and otherwise encouraged to build environmentally-friendly vehicles. The State of California passed a law requiring any automaker that sold more than 5,000 vehicles annually in the state to guarantee 2 percent Zero Emission Vehicles (ZEV) by 1998 and 10 percent ZEV by 2003, emitting no harmful substances into the atmosphere. Electric vehicles presented the most feasible technology for meeting California standards, and manufacturers worldwide began investigating ways to produce a practical electric car. Early models were unpopular because of slow cruising speeds and lack of

performance, but by the end of the century electric car production began to be realistic.

Nissan's electric R'nessa was able to reach 80 kilometers per hour (km/h) in 12 seconds, with a maximum speed of 120 km/h. In 1998, an electric race car debuted at the Le Mans race in France. Toyota combined an internal combustion engine with an electric motor-driven car to reduce pollutants without sacrificing automobile performance. The same year, GM introduced a number of ecofriendly concept cars at the North American International Auto Show, the most notable of which was the Parallel Hybrid performance car. By 2001, Toyota and Honda were selling gas-electric hybrid vehicles at the retail level. The four-door Toyota Prius, priced in the low US$20,000s, got 55 miles per gallon (mpg) on city roads, while the two-door Honda Insight, priced between US$15,000 and US$16,000, boasted 70 mpg on highways.

Alternative fuel vehicles were not limited to passenger cars. In Germany, the Mercedes Nebus (new electric bus) was developed in the laboratories of Daimler-Benz, and a dual-fuel conversion system was developed allowing Isuzu trucks to take advantage of clean-burning natural gas. In addition, Daimler-Benz partnered with Ford Motor Company to produce Ballard Power System's proton exchange membrane fuel cell.

With worldwide landfill space rapidly filling, another research issue of increasing importance to the industry was automobile recycling. By the 1990s, the U.S. automobile industry alone consumed 23 million tons of steel, plastic, and other materials annually, and only 75 percent of these materials were reclaimed. By the mid-2000s, automotive manufacturers had improved recycling significantly. According to the Alliance of Automobile Manufacturers, "Today, 95 percent of cars retired from active use each year are processed for recycling, with about 75 percent of a car's material content (steel, aluminum, copper, etc.) eventually being recycled for raw materials use, including material that goes back into the manufacturing of new parts for new automobiles." The most difficult recycling challenge for automakers was plastic, since an average car could contain 100 different formulations that had to be labeled and sorted in order to be reused. German automaker BMW took a progressive approach toward recycling that anticipated even the most stringent environmental standards in its domestic market. BMW's "design for disassembly" program was expected to result in the first fully recyclable car. In addition, the company formed partnerships with German automobile dismantling firms to create its own recycling infrastructure.

In 1992, the Big Three formed the United States Council for Automotive Research (USCAR) in order to cooperatively develop generic, fundamental technologies that would permit them to bring vehicles to market quickly with less cost to customers and less impact on the environment. U.S. government antitrust regulations prevented the automakers from working on specific vehicles or discussing pricing issues, but the initiative enabled automakers to share the cost and risk associated with the "pre-competitive" development of new technologies. Some USCAR initiatives included

- new composite materials,
- increased emphasis on computer-aided design (CAD) and manufacturing (CAM),
- occupant safety,
- advanced batteries, and
- automobile recycling

The Big Three automakers joined 250 companies and government organizations in experimenting with Intelligent Vehicle Highway Systems (IVHS). IVHS covered a wide range of high-technology devices intended to automate different aspects of automobile operation. IVHS research included equipping cars with radar to prevent collisions, installing transponders to track commercial vehicles, and developing satellite-linked navigation systems for automobiles.

Along with incorporating environmental regulations and new technology into their practices, motor vehicle manufacturers also developed several new production practices during the 1990s. Automakers in the United States and Europe, following the lead of those in Japan, formed partnerships with suppliers in order to ensure product quality and reduce costly parts inventories. They reorganized workflow in their plants into tightly coordinated phases known as "just-in-time" or "lean" production, which adapted the Japanese manufacturers' *kanban* system. In addition, manufacturing workers were empowered to form teams and to provide input on improving product quality and production efficiency.

By the mid-2000s, computer chips were being incorporated in many new vehicle designs. From regulating safety features to emissions, computers were an indispensable addition for the industry. According to the Alliance of Automobile Manufacturers (AAM), the computer technology in standard motor vehicles in 2004 was an average of 1,000 times more powerful than the computer technology used to guide the Apollo 11 lunar mission.

WORKFORCE

The intense global competition of the 1990s produced increased emphasis on productivity and cost reduction. Worldwide, automakers reacted by reducing their labor forces, often outsourcing certain types of work to maintain continued levels of production. Japanese automakers were forced to rethink their traditional policy of lifetime employment, and some began implementing layoffs.

In the United States, nearly all workers at Ford, Chrysler, and GM manufacturing plants were represented by the United Auto Workers (UAW) union. The decline in UAW membership from a 1979 peak of 1.5 million to 769,685 in 1998 reflected reductions in the overall automobile industry. Responding to changes in the auto industry as a whole, UAW leaders maintained their traditional positions on some issues but tried to adapt to automakers' emerging needs as the unions saw the need to cooperate with manufacturers to ensure that unionized companies were able to retain market share. For example, the UAW asked for a greater voice in decisions affecting product quality. The arrival of Japanese transplants in the United States presented a further challenge to Japanese automakers and the UAW. Initially, these new plants screened workers carefully and offered self-directed team environments in order to discourage union activity. Despite such efforts, however, most transplant operations were unionized within a few years.

Managers in the automobile industry in North America and Europe faced significant changes in the nature of their jobs. In the 1990s, many automakers reworked product development processes to include representatives from marketing and manufacturing as well as design and engineering. These and other operational changes required coordination and teamwork across functional and geographic boundaries. From quality-oriented shop floor team meetings to full-scale executive retraining, members of the industry reorganized to allow a flow of information from the bottom up.

In 2004, the U.S. motor vehicle industry directly employed 1.3 million people. According to the Alliance of Automotive Manufacturers, when jobs dependent on the industry are included, that number soars to 13.3 million employees. Workers in the global automobile industry earned vastly different wages depending on the country in which they were employed. Germany, France, the United States, Canada, and Japan routinely paid employees four to nine times as much as workers were paid in developing countries of Latin America and the Pacific Rim. The high cost of health care and other benefits, as well as the influence of labor unions, contributed to high labor costs in more affluent nations. By the 1990s, global automakers were eager to locate new plants in areas with low wage rates, and older plants in more expensive areas were likely to be closed.

Only 13 percent of executive positions in the auto industry were held by women in the late 2000s. A study by Paragon Leadership International found that "poor work-life balance was a primary reason for few women in executive positions. In addition, women were not promoted as quickly as men were.

INDUSTRY LEADERS

General Motors Corporation. General Motors was incorporated in 1908 by William C. Durant and initially manufactured cars under the Oldsmobile and Buick nameplates. Between 1909 and 1920, GM had acquired more than 30 companies. The company's vehicle base eventually grew to include Chevrolet, Pontiac, Cadillac, GMC, Saturn, and Buick. GM had purchased stakes in several overseas manufacturers to continue to broaden its reach, and by the mid-1990s owned 50 percent of Swedish automaker Saab-Scania and 37.5 percent of the Japanese automaker Isuzu. The firm also held a 12 percent share of the western European market, mostly through sales in Germany and the United Kingdom.

Throughout the 1990s, GM was criticized for maintaining a bloated payroll, failing to outsource its component businesses to lower-cost contractors to the extent other car companies had, and operating seven distinct U.S. marketing divisions along with various international brands. GM also suffered from lower employee productivity and slower production times than its conmpetition. All of these issues seemed to come to a head in mid-1998 when the UAW called a strike at a metal stamping plant in Flint, Michigan. Within weeks, the work stoppage had idled nearly a third of GM's workforce and caused losses in the billions. At issue was the company's decision not to invest in previously planned upgrades to the unproductive Flint plant. The union claimed the issues involved worker health and safety as well as the threat of subcontracting the plant's work, all issues that were covered under a 1996 agreement. Eventually, GM settled the strike without gaining many concessions from the union, which did pledge to improve the plant's productivity and hold off some other disputes until 1999 contract talks. Shortly afterward, GM also announced modest internal reforms, but nothing on the scale many believed necessary. In 2001, the firm announced plans to lay off 10 percent of its North American workforce in 2002. The company discontinued the Oldsmobile brand in 2004.

General Motors was the world's largest manufacturer of automobiles, in terms of revenue and unit production in the mid-2000s. In 2004, GM led the industry in sales of trucks and SUVs, and had passed Toyota in car sales. Sales in 2004 were US$193.5 billion, and income was US$2.8 billion. The company realized market share gains in several regions around the world, including Latin America, Africa, the Middle East, and China. The European market reported losses due to intense competition. General Motors' profits were also affected by US$5.2 billion in healthcare expenses in 2004, which was reflected by about US$1,500 per vehicle sold. For 2005, General Motors posted a loss as US$10.6 billion. Sales in 2007 were US$182,347 million with approximately 266,000 employees.

In October 2008 GM Chairman and CEO Rick Wagoner and President Fritz Henderson announced company plans for workplace reductions through employee retirement incentive programs that resulted in a reduction of 5,000 salaried employees. In addition, according to *The Detroit Free Press,* a leading auto economist considered that GM was in need of an "economic 911" that required a US$15-billion industry bail out. The company had appealed to the U.S. Congress for a loan in November 2008.

Chrysler AG. Chrysler was founded by Walter P. Chrysler in 1925 and grew rapidly during the early years of the automobile industry. The company went through several cycles of crisis and recovery, with the most notable example coming in the late 1970s when Chrysler President Lee Iacocca convinced the U.S. Congress to pass the US$1.5 billion Chrysler Loan Guarantee Act to save the company from bankruptcy. A major factor in Chrysler's recovery was the 1983 introduction of the Caravan/Voyager minivan, a utilitarian vehicle that appealed to families and went unchallenged by competitors for many years. The product eventually accounted for 25 percent of Chrysler's sales and 66 percent of its profits, and its success enabled the company to repay its loans ahead of schedule. Chrysler further improved its position in the growing light truck market by purchasing American Motors Corporation (AMC) and its popular Jeep line in 1987.

In 1998, on the eve of a "merger-of-equals" with Daimler-Benz, Chrysler struggled with minor quality problems that became all the more noticeable because of direct competition with quality-conscious Toyota and Honda. The company also appeared to stagnate slightly in terms of productivity, inventory, and market share. Just as Daimler took advantage of Chrysler's worldwide presence and broader automobile product line, Chrysler in 1998 was ripe for Daimler's historical attention to detail and aggressive policies of growth. However, a new management team did not begin to restructure Chrysler operations until late 2000 when the company was losing millions of dollars each quarter.

The merger created DaimlerChrysler and created the industry's third largest player, sparking an unprecedented wave of industry consolidation by rivals seeking to complete with the new global giant. The company's brands included Dodge, Jeep, and Mercedes. Daimler-Chrysler's sales grew 12 percent in 2004, reaching US$192.3 billion. At the end of 2004, the company employed 384,723 people worldwide. After admitting its discontent with its merger with Chrysler, Daimler sold its stake to private equity firm Cerberus Capital Management in 2007. The company was renamed Chrysler LLC.

Ford Motor Company. Henry Ford, who had perfected assembly-line production, established Ford Motor Company in 1903. The company introduced its first product, the Model A, later that year, and in 1908 followed with the Model T, which dominated the industry for the next 18 years. In 1913 Ford pioneered the moving assembly line for production of 1914 model automobiles. Ford later expanded to include the Lincoln and Mercury nameplates. The company purchased 25 percent of Japanese automaker Mazda (then called Toyo Kogyo) in 1979, and held 10 percent of Kia Motors in South Korea, 100 percent of British luxury-sport manufacturer Jaguar, and 75 percent of Aston Martin, also of the United Kingdom. The Ford family continued its active participation in the daily operation of the company into the twenty-first century. When CEO Jac Nasser resigned in 2001, William Clay Ford Jr., great-grandson of Henry Ford, took the helm as executive chairman, while Alan Mulally assumed the duties of president and CEO.

Negative publicity surrounding accidents related to the Bridgestone/Firestone tires used on Ford Explorers troubling the company at the beginning of the twenty-first century. In addition, the Escape, Ford's small sport-utility vehicle, was recalled several times after its initial release. Ford's 28.9 share of the U.S. light truck market reflected the company's focus on SUVs, compared to 19.1 percent of the domestic passenger automobile market it held in 2000. To shore up its position in the global market, Ford spent a considerable portion of its cash reserves on foreign acquisitions in the late 1990s and early 2000s, paying US$6 billion for the passenger car division of Volvo in 1999 and acquiring Land Rover shortly thereafter.

Early in 2002, the firm announced plans to cut 35,000 jobs, shut down five plants, and discontinue four vehicles by 2005. In 2004, Ford employed a total of 324,864 employees, a 1 percent decrease from 2003 that was attributed to capacity reductions and improvement in manufacturing efficiency. Ford's restructuring plan sought to return the company to a profitable status. According to TradingMarkets.com, Ford sought to return the company to a profitable status through restructuring, including "dropping models and consolidating production lines." In addition, Ford eliminated one-third of its North American jobs and sold Aston Martin in 2007 as well as Jaguar and Land Rover in 2008 to Tata Motors. The third largest automotive manufacturer in the world in 2007, Ford Motor Company posted US$172.5 billion in sales.

Toyota Motor Corporation. Toyota was founded in 1926 by Sakichi Toyoda, whose entrepreneurial experience began with the manufacture of looms. Sakichi's son Kiichiro Toyoda moved the family company into the automobile business in 1933, and in 1937 took it public under the name Toyota. The company was forced to retool to make trucks during World War II and suffered financial difficulties for several years afterward. It returned to prosperity during Japan's economic recovery in the 1950s, and

successfully entered the U.S. market in 1965. By 1970 Toyota was the fourth largest automobile manufacturer in the world. The company opened its first production plant in the United States in 1984 through a US$1.5 billion joint venture with General Motors. Although the alliance seemed unlikely, the New United Motor Manufacturing Inc. (NUMMI) plant offered benefits to both companies. The experience allowed Toyota to begin U.S. production cautiously during a time of increasing protectionism, while providing a better understanding of U.S. labor relations. It gave GM insight to high-quality Japanese production methods. Already exporting a number of passenger models, including the 4Runner, Camry, Celica, Corolla, and Tercel, Toyota moved into the luxury car line in 1989 with the Lexus. In the next decade, the continued appeal of the Lexus combined with an across-the-market popularity of luxury vehicles to enhance Toyota's global position.

Like other Japanese producers, Toyota was hurt by the mid-1990s rise in the value of the Japanese yen in relation to the U.S. dollar, which made Japanese products less affordable in overseas markets, as well as by several periods of national recession. In response, Toyota began an extensive cost-cutting program and increased its commitment to building transplants around the world. Foreign sales grew increasingly important to Toyota's business strategy. In the late 1990s, Toyota held 32 percent of the Japanese market, over 16 points ahead of its nearest competitor, and continued to dominate the U.S. import market. The Toyota Camry was the third best selling car in the United States, trailing the Ford Taurus and Honda Accord. With US$20 billion in cash reserves, Toyota entered the twenty-first century as one of the strongest performers in the automotive industry.

Japan's largest and the world's fourth largest automaker, Toyota posted sales of US$172.7 billion in 2005, a 5.6 percent increase over 2004. The company sold 6.7 million units and competed directly with the Big Three for North American market share. Toyota introduced several trucks and sport-utility vehicles in 2000. That year, its share of the U.S. light truck market reached 7.6 percent, while its share of the U.S. passenger automobile market totaled 11 percent. In 2005, Toyota was close to capturing 15 percent of the global market overall, and was gaining on General Motors to become the industry leader by 2008. During the mid-2000s, its gas and electric hybrid Prius sedan was sweeping the European and U.S. markets. By March 2008, the company reported sales of US$262.4 billion, although global economic conditions later that year caused the company to report its first loss ever.

Honda Motor Company Ltd. Honda began in 1928 as an automobile repair shop in Hamamatsu, Japan. Founder Soichiro Honda saw his facilities destroyed during World

War II, but the company recovered by producing motor-cycles in the late 1940s. Honda expanded into car and truck production in the 1960s and began exporting to the United States. Since the Honda Civic and Accord models were more fuel efficient than U.S. cars, Honda's sales boomed during the oil crises of the 1970s. The company joined the movement into the luxury segment with the Acura line in 1986. Honda purchased 20 percent of the United Kingdom's Rover in 1990, but was later outbid for controlling interest in that company by BMW. In 1992, Honda established a presence in China through a joint venture to produce motorcycles there.

In the late 1990s, Honda exported roughly half of the units it produced. Dependence on U.S. sales left Honda particularly vulnerable to currency fluctuations in the early part of the decade, prompting Honda to expand its manufacturing operations in North America. A large number of units were produced by North American transplant operations, and the popular Honda Accord was outsold only by the Ford Taurus in the United States. Although the company produced commercial vehicles, virtually all exported units were the Acord, Acura, Civic, and Prelude passenger cars. In 2000, Honda held a 10 percent share of the U.S. passenger car market, ahead of Big Three rival Daimler-Chrysler. It began gaining ground in the light trucks sector at beginning of the twenty-first century with a new CR-V sport utility vehicle and the Odyssey minivan. The firm's Acura luxury division also began to perform well at about the same time.

Honda Motor Company, Japan's third largest auto-maker, ranked sixth in global sales with US$80.7 billion in 2005. The company, which in addition to its automotive business was the world's largest producer of motorcycles and small engines, posted a profit of US$4.5 billion that year. By March 2008, Honda reported US$178.96 in sales with 121,229 employees.

Nissan Motor Co. Ltd. Nissan was founded in Tokyo in 1911 as Kwaishinsha Motor Car Works by Hashimoto Masujiro. In 1925 the name was changed to DAT Motors, which meant "fast rabbit" in Japanese. The company introduced a small car called Datsun in 1931, and then organized its small vehicle operations separately as Nissan Motors in 1933. The company entered the U.S. market in 1958 as Datsun and gained market share quickly in the 1960s with high-quality, low-cost vehicles. In 1981 it began a slow and costly name change back to Nissan in the United States, about the time it began to establish transplants in overseas markets. Like other leading Japanese automakers, Nissan introduced a luxury line, Infiniti, in 1989. In 1990, Nissan took over Fuji Heavy Industries, the Japanese producer of Subaru automobiles. The auto manufacturer was hurt in the mid-

1990s by a recession at home and unfavorable currency exchange rates, which eventually prompted the firm's decision to partner with Renault.

The second largest car maker in Japan, Nissan had continued the cost cutting measures it launched in 1999 under new CEO Carlos Ghosen, who took over that year shortly after France's Renault acquired a controlling 37 percent stake in Nissan. By 2004, Renault's share in Nissan had risen to 45 percent. Ghosen's Nissan Revival Plan called for the reduction of 21,000 jobs by 2003, an unprecedented number of layoffs for a Japanese firm. Part of that plan included the shutdown of three plants, the last of which was bulldozed in 2001. Nissan had announced plans to move production of its Maxima sedan from Japan to the United States. Sales in 2004 reached US$70 billion, representing 23 percent growth from 2003. That year the company employed 123,748. By March 2008, Nissan reported sales at US$109,010.

Regie Nationale des Usines Renault SA. Renault was founded in 1898 near Paris by Louis Renault, and produced the world's first sedan in 1899. Renault had produced trucks and planes for Germany during the occupation of France, and at the end of World War II, Louis Renault was accused of collaboration with the enemy and died in prison. The French government had taken over the company in 1945, but had reduced its share in the company from 26 percent to 16 percent in 2003. Renault entered the U.S. market by purchasing 46 percent of American Motors Corporation in 1979. When the venture proved unprofitable, posting a net loss of US$1.5 billion by 1984, Renault sold its stake in AMC to Chrysler. To regain its corporate health, Renault exited the U.S. market, and in the early 1990s laid off 50,000 workers, modernizing several plants. Renault also invested in the Asian market, purchasing a 37 percent share in Nissan in 1999 and took over the company's leadership. The firm's decision in 1999 to expand operations outside France proved a wise one, particularly after its European market share began to fall By the mid-2000s, Renault owned 44 percent of Nissan. The firm remained focused on small and mid-sized automobiles.

Renault was the second largest automaker in France with 11 percent of the European market in 2000, behind Peugeot, which boasted a 13 percent share. Sales in 2004 totaled US$55.5 billion, reflecting growth of almost 18 percent, and profits grew 55 percent to US$4.8 billion. By 2006, the company reported US$54.8 in sales.

Volkswagen AG. Volkswagen began in 1937, when Ferdinand Porsche received financial backing from Adolf Hitler to produce an affordable "people's car" in Germany. Although production was delayed until after World War II, by the 1950s the company had launched its popular microbus and had started building plants overseas. In the 1960s the unpretentious Volkswagen Beetle gained popularity as a counterculture symbol in the United States, eventually becoming the best selling car in the world. In 1978, Volkswagen opened the first transplant factory in the United States, although the location closed 10 years later. By the mid-1990s, Volkswagen was the sales leader in Europe and controlled 50 percent of the growing Chinese market, but its U.S. market share was less than 1 percent. In addition, Volkswagen's 1990 investment in the Czechoslovakian automaker Skoda ensured that it would take advantage of the economic recovery in Eastern Europe.

In 1998, Volkswagen introduced an updated version of its beloved Beetle. More luxurious in interior design and slated for a more affluent market than the ubiquitous "Bug" of the postwar years, the new Beetle took its audience by storm. Like its predecessor, it was undeniably cute, but it was slightly larger than the old version, much more expensive, and boasted such amenities as standard air conditioning. By 2006, the company reported US$138.362 sales.

The largest automaker in Europe, Volkswagen AG posted sales of US$121.3 billion in 2004, an increase of almost 11 percent from 2003. Volkswagen was one of the largest employers in the industry with 336,800 workers worldwide. Although its most popular vehicles included the Beetle, Jetta, and Passat, Volkswagen also owned luxury lines, including Rolls Royce, Bentley, Audi, and Lamborghini.

Fiat S.p.A. Fiat traces its corporate beginnings from articles of association of the "Societa Anonima Fabbrica Italiana Torino," signed in 1899. Giovanni Agnelli was a member of the society's board of directors. The company grew steadily, and during World War I manufactured more than 1,000 vehicles for the Italian army. By 1920, Agnelli was chairman of the Societa and promptly adopted Henry Ford's assembly line to keep automobile costs within an acceptable consumer range. Fiat continued to manufacture a broad variety of passenger cars and commercial vehicles, including a number of sports and racing models. In 1945 Agnelli died, but the company's momentum carried it through the years following Italy's defeat in World War II, and the Agnelli family retained ownership of approximately 30 percent of the corporation through 2002. By the mid-1980s, Fiat had continued to introduce a large number of new models of affordable passenger cars each year, along with traditional luxury sports models, including Alfa Romeo, Maserati, and Ferrari. In 1988, Fiat's Termoli 3 plant was opened, billed as the most highly automated car factory in the world.

In the late 1990s, Fiat controlled 14 percent of the European market, but was highly dependent on the sheltered Italian sector. To extend its reach beyond Western Europe, the firm agreed to sell a 20 percent share of the company to General Motors in exchange for a 6 percent stake in the North American giant. Sales in 2005 grew 4.5 percent to US$66.1 billion. Sales of Italian commercial vehicles dropped 2.4 percent overall during the year, but Fiat Auto reported a 0.6 percent increase, selling 17,565 vehicles and raising its market share to 40.1 percent.

MAJOR COUNTRIES IN THE INDUSTRY

Japan. In response to protectionist sentiments and changing economic conditions, every major Japanese manufacturer built production facilities in the United States in the 1980s. These remote manufacturing locations became commonly known as "transplants." By 1993 50 percent of the vehicles sold in the U.S. market by Japanese companies were produced in the United States. This mirrored the worldwide trend of locating production facilities closer to final markets, which helped automakers avoid tariffs and quotas, reduce exposure to currency fluctuations, take advantage of inexpensive labor, and understand local market conditions.

In the mid-1990s, the effect of Japan's manufacturers on the global market was increasing even as its domestic market was in transition. In 1997 Japanese automakers exported 4.55 million units, representing more than 40 percent of total output, although exports had declined steadily for nearly a decade as more production facilities moved overseas. In mid-decade, imports to the Japanese domestic market passed the 10 percent mark for the first time, as U.S. sales supplemented those of European cars.

The Japanese domestic market faced a recession in the early 1990s and another economic downturn at the end of the decade. Complications were created for Japanese automakers as the yen rose against the U.S. dollar, making Japanese products relatively more expensive in the U.S. market, and then fell, resulting in instability for the Japanese economy and impacting business worldwide. By 2004, sales were back up, with the most popular models being the Honda Odyssey and Toyota Sienna minivans and the subcompact Nissan Cube. The global market improved slightly from 2003, although Japanese domestic sales were down. Japanese companies held 30.9 percent of the global market based on number of units sold in 2004.

These difficult market conditions combined to place extraordinary pressure on the profitability of Japanese automakers in the 1990s. In response, Japanese producers raised prices, continued to shift production to overseas markets, and reevaluated some of the basic business philosophies that had contributed to past success. The factors that had differentiated the Japanese automobile industry included a high level of worker involvement; cooperative labor-management relations; extremely loyal employees, who tended to remain with a single company for the duration of their careers; a strong commitment to quality; and early implementation of just-in-time production processes. In addition, Japanese automakers were closely linked to suppliers through a *keiretsu* (group affiliation) system. However, in the face of declining profitability, Japanese automakers increasingly loosened *keiretsu* ties and purchased parts from outside suppliers, overhauled lean production systems, offered less variety in order to control costs, and reevaluated the nature of their responsibility toward employees.

Actual Japanese motor vehicle exports to the United States declined significantly throughout the 1990s, from 3.4 million units in 1986 to 1.6 million units in 2004. Total exports to North America were 1,726,465, about 3.4 percent less than in 2003. Conversely, production in U.S.-based Japanese auto plants rose over the same period, surpassing 4 million units by 2004. The North American plants of Japanese automakers accounted for 63 percent of U.S. automotive sales in 2000, compared to less than 12 percent in 1986. Transplant manufacturing served the dual purpose of reducing manufacturing costs and increasing marketability of product by reducing the stigma of foreign manufacture.

Japanese exports to Europe, however, rose 10 percent to 1,275,229, a gain attributed in *Automotive News* to the weakening yen against the euro. The improved market in Europe resulted in an overall increase of 4.2 percent in Japanese exports to 4,957,663. Toyota Motor Corporation was responsible for exports of more than 800,000 units, and the company expected an increase of another 12 percent to more than 900,000 during 2005.

The United States. The United States, in the form of the Big Three automakers, dominated the industry in the early 2000s, but was evolving. With an increased focus on popular and profitable pickup trucks and sport-utility vehicles, the United States lost 3 percent of its domestic passenger car market share, which in 1998 had been 61.1 percent. Domestic car production dropped to 6.9 million units, reflecting decreased sales of all passenger cars except luxury models. In contrast, sales of new trucks increased to a record 7.1 million units. In the late 1990s, six of the top ten vehicles in the United States were trucks, sport-utility vehicles, or vans. The Alliance of Automobile Manufacturers reported that in 2004, 58 percent of new vehicles were light trucks, with sales of new trucks reaching 7.9 million. For the first time, light trucks outsold passenger cars in all 50 states.

With 31 automobile manufacturers competing in the U.S. market in the early 1990s, the country was genuinely open market for automobiles. Additional manufacturers entered the market as the decade wore on and small international companies flexed their wings. In 2000, Toyota and Honda held more of the U.S. passenger car market than Big Three rival DaimlerChrysler, but the Big Three continued to dominate the domestic light truck market. Companies reporting the largest growth were Hyundai, Volkswagen, Kia, Mitsubishi, and BMW.

In response to the proliferation of transplants in the United States and the resulting confusion about the national origin of automobiles sold in the U.S. market, the U.S. Congress passed a content labeling law in 1994. All new vehicles sold in the United States were required to bear a label stating the percentage of the car's value contributed by parts of U.S. or Canadian origin, the city and country where the car was assembled, the two countries that contributed the greatest value of parts to the car, and the country of origin for the engine and transmission. Although some Japanese manufacturers felt that the law unfairly linked all vehicles of a certain model together regardless of where they were produced, some German automakers predicted that consumers would be pleased to learn that their new vehicle was 100 percent German. By 1996, transplants, which were known as the International Auto Sector (IAS), had generated nearly 1.3 million jobs in the United States. As transplant influence and presence grew, voices rose suggesting that they should be fully integrated into the economy and viewed in the same light as the traditional U.S. Big Three manufacturers.

The European Union. Taken collectively, European car manufacturers enjoyed a good deal of success in the late 1990s. Porsche held an initial lead in corporate growth with an annual increase of more than 70 percent. The merger of Daimler-Benz with Chrysler allowed Daimler, which was already Germany's largest company, to increase its standing in the global market. Audi and BMW reported strong market gains, as did Jaguar, which was a wholly owned subsidiary of Ford Motor Company. Saab held its own, although Volvo struggled in the late 1990s. Volkswagen, already a powerful presence in the car market, introduced the popular redesigned Beetle. By the mid-2000s, European automakers had retained 33.5 percent of the global sales market.

German luxury automakers had been unprepared for Japanese luxury car's strong showing in the U.S. market in the early 1990s. BMW responded by purchasing British manufacturer Rover to diversify into small cars and sport-utility vehicles, and later added the quintessential luxury car manufacturer Rolls Royce to its portfolio. BMW also began increasing exports to Japan, as did Audi and Mercedes-Benz, and all three began to attract younger clients, increasing their sales in Japan by 34 percent between 1991 and 2001.

Germany's strong environmental movement led the country to adopt the strictest environmental standards in Europe, leaving the German automobile industry well positioned as environmental standards rose around the world. German automakers developed the first luxury compacts in response to protests by environmental groups against large cars, and they initiated the most advanced programs in the world for automobile recycling, even as Mercedes (Daimler-Benz) worked to enhance its electric car offering.

South Korea. International focus remained on the emerging industrial economies in the Pacific Rim. China and India offered huge consumer potential, but South Korea emerged as the auto-producing nation of the late 1990s. Kia, Daewoo, and, in particular Hyundai, pursued international markets with increasing success.

In the mid-1990s, Hyundai, the dominant Korean automobile producer, clung to a growth rate of just 0.6 percent and planned to lay off 8,000 employees, representing approximately 17 percent of its total workforce. In 1998, Hyundai's U.S. sales increased 28 percent higher over 1997, and Kia doubled its emerging U.S. sales in the same time frame. Daewoo, South Korea's third-largest automaker, considered late summer 1998 as a target date to begin exporting their product to the United States. These marketing strategies served to counter and even nullify the effects of a sagging domestic economy. Total South Korean automotive exports reached 1.63 million vehicles in 2001.

BIBLIOGRAPHY

"America's Automobile Industry." Alliance of Automotive Manufacturers, 2004. Available from www.autoalliance.org.

"Business in Asia Today." *Asia Africa Intelligence Wire,* 14 December 2004.

Butters, Jamie. "Ford, Chrysler to Follow GM's Discount Lead." *The Detroit Free Press,* 6 July 2005.

"China's Auto Imports Rise 35% in Value in First 8 Months," 30 September 2008.

Connelly, Mary, and Lindsay Chappell. "Crisis Could Hit Chrysler Revival." *Automotive News Europe,* 3 May 2004.

"Current Statistics." Japan Automobile Manufacturers Association, July 2004. Available from www.japanauto.com.

Dawson, Chester. "An Endurance Test for Japanese Carmakers." *Business Week,* 26 April 2004.

———. "Nissan: Saying Sayonara." *BusinessWeek,* 24 September 2001.

Draper, Deborah J., ed. *Business Rankings Annual.* Detroit: Thomson Gale, 2004.

"Economic Slowdown Accelerating Auto Industry's Slide." TradingMarkets.com, 25 September 2008. Available from www.tradingmarkets.com.

"Fiat Auto Increases Market Share in Commercial Vehicles" *Europe Intelligence Wire,* 8 March 2005.

Flint, Jerry. "Broken Lights." *Forbes Global,* 7 June 2004.

———. "Smug No More." *Forbes,* 10 May 2004.

"Ford Motor Company SWOT Analysis." *Datamonitor,* 2005.

Green, Jeff. "Industry Outlook 2001: Autos." *Business Week,* 8 January 2001.

Higgins, Tim. "Cuts at Chrysler: More Will Lose Jobs: Plant to Close Early," *The Detroit Free Press,* 24 October 2008.

"Hoover's Company Capsules." *Hoover's Online,* 2008. Available from www.hoovers.com.

Hughes, Elizabeth Blish. "Women Power Players in the Auto Industry," 8 September 2008. Available from sify.com.

"Industry Report: Automobile Industry." *US Business Reporter,* 2001. Available from www.activemedia-guide.com.

"International Trade Statistics." World Trade Organization, 2003. Available from www.wto.org.

"Is BTO the Auto Industry's Answer to Poor Profitability?" *Just-Auto.com,* 26 July 2004. Available from just-auto.com.

Japan Automobile Manufacturers Association. "Gas Prices Climb Gradually in Japan." *Japan Auto Trends,* July 2004.

Jewett, Dale. "Toyota Gains on GM in Global Race." *Automotive News,* 16 May 2005.

Lazich, Robert S., ed. *Market Share Reporter.* Detroit: Thomson Gale, 2004.

"Light Truck Country." Alliance of Automobile Manufacturers, 2005.

Merx, Katie. "Without Bailout, Huge Job Loss Soon." *The Detroit Free Press,* 24 October 2008.

"Middle East: Seismic Change in Middle East Consumer Patterns." IPR Strategic Business Information Database, 25 July 2004.

"New Vehicles Now 99 Percent Cleaner." Alliance of Automotive Manufacturers, 27 May 2004. Available from www.autoalliance.org.

"R.L. Polk Says HEV Registrations Increased 81 Percent in 2004." *Electric and Hybrid Vehicles Today,* 27 April 2005.

Stoddard, Haig. "Suddenly Vulnerable." *Ward's Auto World,* 1 May 2004.

Teahen, John K., Jr. "April: Japan's Big 3 Were Hot, But the U.S. Big 2 Were Not." *Automotive News,* 9 May 2005.

"Thailand: Government Drives Auto Industry Globalisation." JustAuto.com, 29 November 2004. Available from justauto.com.

Tierney, Christine. "Japanese to Cut Car Production." *The Detroit News,* 17 November 2008.

"Today's Automobile: A Computer on Wheels." Alliance of Automotive Manufacturers, 22 March 2004. Available from www.autoalliance.org.

"Vehicle Imports Increase 23% in May." *The America's Intelligence Wire,* 23 June 2004.

"Ward's Reports Estimated Production." *PR Newswire Industry News,* 30 July 2004.

Webster, Sarah A. "Ford's MyKey is Like a Parent for New Drivers." *The Detroit Free Press,* 7 October 2008.

Woodward, Chris. "Auto Firms Suffer Globally," *USA Today,* 24 October 2008.

Yamaguchi, Yuzo. "Japan Exports to N.A. Fall 3.4% in 2004; Success of Prius Hybrid, Scion Put Toyota Up 3.9%." *Automotive News,* 7 February 2005.

SIC 3731

SHIPBUILDING AND REPAIR

NAICS CODE(S)

336611. The shipbuilding and repair industry is made up of government and privately owned (commercial) shipyards that build and repair various types of ships, lighters, and barges. These vessels may be self-propelled or may require towing by another vessel. For discussion of transportation services via ship, see also **Water Transportation**.

INDUSTRY SNAPSHOT

At the close of the first decade of the twenty-first century, Asian shipbuilders remained the clear leaders in the shipbuilding and repair industry, with South Korea, China, and Japan holding rank as three of the the top four, and the European Union (EU) slipping in at number three. United States shipyards lagged considerably behind Asia, mainly due to years of Asian government subsidies to the region's shipyards. Contention over worldwide subsidies, rising global labor and construction costs, mergers, joint ventures and other collaborative relationships, and a shrinking pool of qualified workers were key issues.

As of May 2005, orders for oil tankers and bulk carriers fell from the previous year by 35 and 16 percent, respectively, but containership contracts rose nearly 70 percent as the result of increased trade in the Asia Pacific region. Demand for large containerships stagnated by the

mid-2000s as ship owners waited to see if world trade would make use of all the new ships that would enter service beginning in 2006, as reported by Bruce Barnard in *The Journal of Commerce Online*. However, the market for smaller ships was still performing well, as the need for ships to service large vessels grew.

As of April 2007, most U.S. shipyards were enjoying a booming business while repair yards were struggling to survive. More and more navy ships were being kept out at sea for longer periods of time. Consequently, maintenance dollars were being moved to operating accounts. In addition, large steel jobs were being sent overseas.

Additional concerns became apparent when the Metal Trades Department of the AFL-CIO sued the coast guard for allowing domestic shipyards to use preassembled foreign ship parts and engines. The suit claimed that the coast guard ignored Jones Act requirements that ships moving between U.S. ports be built in the United States.

By 2008, the global shipbuilding industry was dominated by South Korea's "big three" builders, that together produced more ships than the rest of the global building industry combined. In order of rank in 2008, South Korea carried 50.6 percent, followed by China at 34.4 percent, the European Union at 5.7 percent, Japan at 3.7 percent, the Philippines at 1.5 percent, and the remainder of builders at 4.1 percent.

Momentum was evident for the concept of a "green passport" for ships. The document, formulated by members of the Marine Environment Protection Committee in 2003, would contain an inventory of all materials potentially hazardous to human health or the environment used in the construction (and subsequent operation) of a ship. It would be produced by the shipyard during the construction stage and passed on to the purchaser of the vessel. The document format would record subsequent changes in equipment and materials, and successive owners of the ship would be required to maintain the accuracy of the "passport." The final owner would be responsible for delivering it, along with the vessel, to the recycling yard.

ORGANIZATION AND STRUCTURE

The International Maritime Organization (IMO), a special agency within the United Nations, adopts maritime conventions to improve maritime safety and prevent pollution. The IMO also intervenes in legal issues, such as liability and compensation, and works to promote marine traffic. Members of the IMO comprised most of the world's shipping nations, or about 164 governments, by 2004. The IMO's budget for 2004-05 was more than US$84 million. Member contributions are based on the size of the country's merchant fleet. Top contributors to

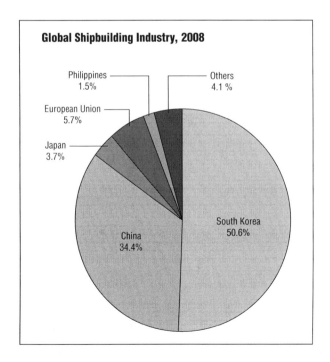

Global Shipbuilding Industry, 2008

Philippines 1.5%
Others 4.1 %
European Union 5.7%
Japan 3.7%
China 34.4%
South Korea 50.6%

the IMO as of 2005 included Panama, Liberia, the Bahamas, Greece, the United Kingdom, and Japan.

Recognizing that technological advances can be a key component to increasing marine safety and reducing pollution, the IMO's Technical Cooperation and Facilitation, Maritime Safety, Legal, and Marine Environment Protection committees devise technical resolutions to address these issues. Resolutions and recommendations are then presented to the IMO's governing body, which is made up of an assembly of representatives from its 164 governments. The assembly typically meets every two years.

CURRENT CONDITIONS

The shipbuilding industry has shifted eastward over the past three decades. Western Europe's shipbuilders lost market share first to Japan, then to South Korea, and more recently to China. The primary reasons for the European Union's decline in the industry was due to Asian government subsidies to the shipbuilding industry and the advanced building techniques perfected by South Korean builders. Losing the ability to compete on pricing, European yards were forced to specialize, focusing on gas and chemical tankers, and cruise ships. In 2001, the European Commission, which regulates competition in the European Union, asked for support for European subsidies from the European Union's General Affairs Council in order to bring the European Union in line with the Organization for Economic Cooperation and Development (OECD) agreement to end subsidies and other forms of aid to shipbuilders and repairers. The agreement was opposed by the United Kingdom, Denmark, Sweden, the Netherlands, and Finland. The United States opted not to participate in the agreement.

By 2002 tensions between the European Union and South Korea were rising, as the European Union accused its Asian competitor of price dumping, or pricing a vessel at less than fair market value in order to undercut other builders. When negotiations between the two parties broke down, the European Union filed a complaint with the World Trade Organization (WTO) in October 2002. According to the European Union, by selling ships below production cost, South Korea was destroying Europe's shipbuilding industry by causing layoffs and bankruptcies. Nevertheless, some industry observers argued that the European Union's maritime status was improving, and that its claims were somewhat misleading since many European-owned vessels fly so-called "flags of convenience," which hide true national affiliations. In March 2005, the WTO gave South Korea 90 days to end the questioned shipbuilding subsidies.

Fierce competition, government subsidies, overcapacity, high labor, and production costs, and an Asian financial crisis all contributed to decreasing revenues among most commercial shipbuilders worldwide. The worldwide practice of government subsidies contributed to an artificial pricing market for the industry and led to price dumping. This in turn created a kind of domino effect among shipbuilders and repairers. By May 2005, orders for containerships had declined.

By the mid-2000s, Asian shipyards continued to produce the bulk of the world's large commercial vessels—tankers and bulk carriers. South Korea, the world's shipbuilding leader, received orders for 159 ships from 26 countries during the first quarter of 2004 alone, with compensated gross tons (cgt) ordered reaching a record 5.26 million, up 31 percent from the same period in 2003. South Korea completed nearly US$4.5 billion worth of ships during the first three months of 2004, a number that was expected to reach or exceed US$12 billion by the year's end. South Korea's record-breaking pace continued through the first half of the year, by which time it had received orders for 256 new vessels, contributing to a backlog of 847 vessels.

Malaysia vowed to strengthen its capacity and capability of shipbuilding and ship repair under the recently launched Third Industrial Master Plan. This effort was among the five strategic thrusts for long-term growth and viability of the marine transport subsector. Related areas of concentration were aimed at enhancing domestic capabilities in building and repair as well as intensifying and upgrading engineering skills, strengthening infrastructure and support facilities, strengthening institutional support, and expanding activities in the fabrication of offshore structures.

European yards remained the largest producers of cruise ships and ferries. Lagging far behind in this sector, U.S. yards continued to focus primarily on military contracts, with only a few yards competing for international commercial contracts. In early 1998 the largest private U.S. shipyard, Virginia-based Newport News Shipbuilding Inc., announced that it would stop building commercial ships altogether and would focus instead on navy contracts. Late in 2001, Newport News was acquired by Northrop Grumman Corp. in a deal valued at US$2.6 billion. Northrop combined the two shipbuilding divisions, forming a US$4 billion shipbuilding enterprise named Northrop Grumman Newport News. As of mid-2004, the unit was one of only two entities capable of designing and building nuclear-powered submarines.

In March 2007, Russian President Vladimir Putin signed the decree "on the open joint-stock company Amalgamated Shipbuilding Corporation." Under the presidential decree, the Centre for Shipbuilding and Ship Repair Technology was established by Russia's Central Shipbuilding Technology Research Institute (St. Petersburg). Main activities will focus on "development and implementation of new-research-intensive shipbuilding and ship repair technologies; technological support for the design, construction, technical maintenance, repairs and disposal of ships and vessels in Russia and abroad; the design and technical upgrade of the production assets of shipbuilding and ship repair centres; the design and production of ship fittings and shipbuilding engineering output; the development, production and supply of specialized equipment and technological fittings."

The future of Canadian shipbuilding and repair remained uncertain after new Prime Minister Stephen Harper was sworn into office. Industry insiders were excited about Harper's statement calling for three Canadian-made icebreakers capable of promoting the country's goals for protecting Canada's sovereignty in the Arctic. There was speculation that the icebreakers, whether armed or not, would be assigned to the Canadian Coast Guard. Because the Coast Guard is in charge of enforcing northern shipping rules, the proposed move was thought to be less threatening than having the role assigned to navy vessels.

Leading U.S. shipbuilders were primarily engaged in servicing military (navy) contracts. As a result, they have not been active participants in the commercial sector until recent years. Reports show that without drastic improvements in labor and production efficiency, increased use of technology, changes in management culture, and the removal of global government subsidies, the U.S. industry is not likely substantially to increase its market position in the foreseeable future.

A clarion call was issued for "lean enterprise" to be practiced by the shipbuilding and repair industry. This involved trimming costs, simplifying production lines, and cutting down on inventory, all with the goal of reducing turnaround time and eliminating waste. Empire, a Norfolk industrial supply house, began following lean guidelines in 2005 after it was requested to do so by its largest customer, Northrop Grumman Newport News, according to an article in the *Virginian-Pilot*. The navy was also reportedly trying to become "lean" with related methods resulting in a savings of more than US$230 million in fiscal year 2005.

RESEARCH AND TECHNOLOGY

As safety, pollution, and competition became increasingly important issues, improvements in ship design and capacity, yard and port expansion projects, and new government and international programs were implemented. Typical vessel capacity expanded rapidly during the closing decades of the twentieth century. For example, in the 1960s typical capacity was 1,000 TEUs (twenty-foot equivalent units). By the 1970s it was 2,000 TEUs, by the 1980s it had increased to between 3,000 and 4,000 TEUs, and by the late 1990s vessels of 6,000 TEUs, with

the capacity to carry 8,000 TEUs, were common. In 1998 South Korea announced its intention to build 8,000-TEU containerships. The vessels would be constructed by Samsung Heavy Industries, one of the country's leading shipbuilders. Samsung's proposals called for vessels of 345 meters in length, 45.3 meters in width, draft of 27.0 meters, and a deadweight of 150,000 tons. To increase fuel efficiency and loading capacity, the hull design was to be 5 percent lighter in size-to-weight ratio than the 6,000-TEU vessels of its Japanese competitors. Samsung was working with a German firm to run tests of the structural integrity of their new hull design. The vessels would be powered by a 93,000 hp diesel engine and would be able to reach a speed of 25 knots. Samsung expected the new vessels to be in production by 2000. A U.S. Army Corps of Engineers study reported that by the end of 1999, some 34 percent of the global box ship fleet would be made up of more than 300 vessels of 4,000 TEUs or more. One German study estimated the cost of the 8,000-TEU vessel to be US$110 million to US$120 million.

In response to the need for ports capable of handling ever-increasing amounts of cargo and supersized vessels, in early 1998 the port of Hong Kong announced its plans to increase the port's capacity. In 1997 Hong Kong handled 14.5 million TEUs of containers and retained its position as the world's busiest container port. Its 1998 capacity was forecast to reach nearly 16 million TEUs of containers, a 7.5 percent increase in container traffic from the previous year. The Hong Kong Port Development Board chairman noted in *World Trade* that port expansion was necessary to keep up with industry changes, notably increasing vessel sizes and the formation of large shipping consortia.

It is generally agreed that the building of even larger container ships is inevitable. Vessels of 10,000 TEU and above are being designed, and there is no engine power constraint for craft of this size.

Ranked second in the world among leading shipbuilding nations, China announced a similar port expansion project as part of its strategy to turn Shanghai into an international shipping center. Included in the US$633 million expansion plan is dredging a harbor channel to accommodate deep-draught container vessels. Dredging is expected to be completed by 2020. Other waterways would be dredged as well for container traffic into the Jiangsu and Hubei provinces. Construction would also begin on the country's largest and most state-of-the-art shipyard at Waigaoqiao, in the Pudong New Area of Shanghai.

WORKFORCE

BAE Systems Ship Repair President Al Krekich expressed his concerns about the graying of his industry's workforce.

His remarks were shared during the "Momentum in Shipbuilding and Repair" panel discussion at the Propeller Club of the United States' Maritime Industry Advocacy Group international convention. One of the industry's biggest emerging challenges was recruiting young people. The average age of the estimated 800 workers at BAE Systems' Norfolk shipyard was 50. That was younger than estimates for the Norfolk Naval Shipyard in Portsmouth. According to an article in the *Virginian-Pilot,* Krekich said that "an injection of youth" was needed in order for the industry to keep moving forward.

Another convention panel member, Maritime Industry Consultants Principal John Graykowski, said that retention of workers was also a major concern. Graykowski strongly advised establishing a "national shipbuilding university" to produce highly trained workers capable of working with technological advances that could also contain costs. Shipbuilders Council of America President Alan Walker said that many shipyards created apprentice programs for training younger employees, but noted that the United States was not viewed as promoting the kinds of skills needed for shipyard work.

INDUSTRY LEADERS

South Korea During the mid-2000s, South Korea's top shipbuilders were Hyundai Heavy Industries Co. Ltd. and Samsung Heavy Industries Co. Ltd. Daewoo Heavy Industries Co. Ltd., a leader during the early 2000s, was exiting the shipbuilding industry. As reported by *The Journal of Commerce Online,* orders at South Korean shipyards were full until the end of 2007, and some orders were being taken for 2008 delivery.

Hyundai Heavy Industries Co. Ltd. (HHI) As of 2010, Hyundai Heavy Industries (HHI) enjoyed status as the largest shipbuilder in the world. HHI formerly was a subsidiary of the Hyundai Group, a large diversified conglomerate, but in February 2002 it became an independent enterprise. This involved HHI's takeover of the Hyundai Mipo Dockyard and Hyundai Samho Heavy Industries. In 2004, HHI employed almost 26,000 workers across six business divisions. In addition to the shipbuilding division, these included construction equipment, electro/electric systems, engine and machinery, industrial plant and engineering, and offshore and engineering. HHI's 2004 revenue from new orders was US$9.35 billion, 4.7 percent less than US$9.8 billion in 2003. The company anticipated solid revenue growth in 2005 due to price increases implemented after dramatic increases in steel costs and increased demand for containerships and tankers. For 2008, HHI reported sales of US$27.03 billion and 25,240 employees. Its shipbuilding division made tankers, bulk carriers, containerships, and high-tech gas and chemical carriers.

Samsung Heavy Industries Inc. (SHI) South Korea's Samsung Heavy Industries (SHI) was an affiliate of the Samsung Group, a conglomerate with holdings in machinery, electronics, chemicals, finance, and motor engines. SHI was the second largest shipbuilder in the world, and a part of the "big three" shipbuilders of South Korea. SHI focuses mainly on shipbuilding and offshore business, but also competes in the construction equipment market. In addition to ship automation and building automation systems, SHI designs and manufactures large passenger ships, liquified natural gas (LNG) carriers, shuttle tankers, and drill ships. In 2004 SHI reported US$4.46 billion in annual sales and employed 8,572 people. By 2005 annual sales had increased to US$5.47 billion. It announced plans to establish a joint venture with Malaysia Marine and Heavy Engineering (MMHE) to repair LNG carriers. The joint venture aims to tap into the LNG ship repair market following an increase in orders to construct these carriers. To be capitalized at US$1 million, the Kuala Lumpur-based firm was established as 30 percent owned by SHI and 70 percent owned by MMHE. SHI has overseas facilities, including a Chinese factory devoted to the production of ship blocks. By 2008, revenues had increased to US$8.4 billion with a workforce of 12,481. In 2009, SHI was contracted to build *Utopia* , a residential cruise ship that will be the largest passenger ship ever built in Asia.

Daewoo Heavy Industries Ltd. (DHI) Daewoo Heavy Industries (DHI) was a leading Korean shipbuilder during the early 2000s. By mid-2004 its parent company, the Daewoo Group, was spinning DHI off as an independent company. In addition, DHI had divested its automobile and shipbuilding units, with the latter going to Australian interests. From this point forward, DHI operated the following divisions: construction equipment, industrial vehicles, machine tools, factory automation systems, diesel engines, and defense systems. The company's shipbuilding business unit once produced LNG carriers, submarines, double-hulled crude-oil tankers, bulk carriers, and containerships. DHI realized a revenue of US$4.1 billion in 2007.

Japan. In 2004, the Shipbuilder's Association of Japan (SAJ) included 19 members with combined orders of eight million tons. Among the members were seven major companies, most of which had broad-ranging non-marine business sectors. The shipbuilding segments alone of these seven companies made up approximately 11 percent of their total corporate sales. The 11 other SAJ members were medium-sized firms that relied on marine-related contracts. For them, the shipbuilding and repair segment comprised 86 percent of their total corporate sales.

Mitsubishi Heavy Industries Ltd. (MHI) As with many of Japan's leading shipbuilders, MHI is a fully diversified conglomerate. MHI's business units cover aeronautics, industrial plants and equipment, and steel construction and shipbuilding, to name just a few. In 2003 shipbuilding represented about 8 percent of MHI's US$21.6 billion in revenues, behind machinery manufacturing and power systems. MHI's shipbuilding sector includes containerships, LNG carriers, very large crude carriers (VLCC), and marine pollution and offshore production structures and equipment. In 2007, MHI gained a revenue of US$38.1 billion and had a workforce of 63,500.

Kawasaki Heavy Industries Ltd. (KHI) Kawasaki (KHI) was another of Japan's leading shipbuilders, with 2008 sales of US$15.08 billion and more than 30,500 employees. KHI has two shipyards, Sakaide and Kobe, both more than 100 years old. KHI's shipbuilding expertise covers bulk carriers, tankers, LNG carriers, high-speed ferries, research submersibles, containerships, and liquid petroleum gas (LPG) carriers. In addition, KHI supplies a variety of marine equipment and engines. Like Mitsubishi Heavy Industries, KHI is a diversified conglomerate with business units covering environmental products, industrial plants, aeronautics, general purpose engines, construction, and civil engineering in addition to its shipbuilding and marine engineering business unit.

MAJOR COUNTRIES IN THE INDUSTRY

South Korea. In 2002 South Korea edged ahead of Japan to become the world's largest shipbuilder. That year, the *Journal of Commerce Online* reported that South Korea achieved a market share of 31.8 percent, ahead of Japan's 31.7 percent. Although the world-leader position has shifted between the two nations, by 2003 South Korea retained its position ahead of other countries with 16 million gross tons in new orders, keeping its lead over Japan. During the first half of 2003, Korea's orders for new ships increased 171 percent from the previous year, and by the end of 2003 Korea held 43 percent of the global market. At 232 vessels—7.8 million tons—this half-year total surpassed the country's figures for all of 2002. By comparison, Japan received orders totaling 4.99 million tons between January and August of 2003, up 13 percent from the same period the previous year. During the first half of 2004, South Korea continued at a record pace, recording orders for 256 new vessels—9.06 million tons—an increase of more than 16 percent from 2003. By 2008, South Korea had continued its dominance of the market with 50.6 percent, and orders totally 12.4 million tons. This dominance is largely attributed to South Korea's advanced shipbuilding technology in perfecting the block construction technique, the strong work ethic

of its workers, and the efficiency and high productivity of its yards.

South Korean shipyards expanded capacities in the 1990s. As of early 2001, they were able to exploit a depreciation of the won and boost their business to a point where they reported a three-year backlog. Korean construction includes tankers and bulk carriers, roll-on/roll-off (ro/ro) vessels, car carriers, containerships, chemical carriers, and others. Most of Korea's shipbuilding industry is located in the South Kyongsang province and comprises approximately 80 shipbuilding firms that construct, salvage, or repair a variety of vessels. Korean shipbuilders, like most in the Asian shipbuilding nations, rely heavily on computer-aided design (CAD), or computer-aided design/computer-aided manufacturing (CAD/CAM) and automation of facilities.

High-speed ferries, supersized containerships, and liquefied natural gas carriers were particular highlights of Korean shipbuilding. Importantly, Korea pioneered the world's first double-hulled tanker, a significant contribution given that international conventions now require that single-hulled oil tankers be replaced by double-hulled vessels. Both the Korean government and the industry itself invested heavily in technology and automation to improve efficiency, contain costs, and meet production schedules. To further spur industry growth, the Korean government plans to expand its shipbuilding and repair facilities and to create nearly 30 new ports. By 2011, South Korea expects to double its seaport capacity to accommodate 560 million tons of freight per year. Despite such positives, the Asian financial crisis of the late 1990s hit Korean shipbuilders especially hard, causing several to file for bankruptcy.

China. Although it trailed its Asian counterparts in the early 2000s, China experienced explosive growth by the mid-2000s and surged to second place in production. In order to reach its goal of becoming the world's shipbuilding leader by 2015, China was investing billions of dollars to improve its position. After allowing foreign investment in its ports in March 2002, China benefited from US$2.2 billion in investments that year, followed by an estimated US$3.6 billion in 2003. This effort was met with significant results. From a paltry share of only 0.8 percent in 1982, China saw its stake in the global shipbuilding market increase to 12.6 percent by the end of 2003. That year, orders for new vessels increased 173 percent, and the nation completed a record 6 million deadweight tons (dwt). This was an increase of 46 percent from 2002, surpassing forecasts of a 5 million dwt increase.

As of May 2005, shipbuilders in the province of Shandong in east China held orders for 120 ships totaling

US$566 million, as reported by *Xinhua News Agency.* China's shipbuilding industry is led by the China State Shipbuilding Corp. (CSSC) and the China Shipbuilding Industry Corp. By 2010, CSSC was expected to complete the world's largest shipyard. Located at the mouth of the Yangtze River on the Shanghai coast, the new yard will be capable of producing up to 12 million deadweight tons per year. Although the new shipyard, along with its burgeoning economy, would go far to help China achieve its goal of world shipbuilding dominance, industry analysts revealed a number of significant challenges. These included falling shipping container rates, the competitiveness of Chinese currency in comparison to the U.S. dollar, a possible containership glut, and productivity issues at China's state-operated companies. In 2008, China carried 34.4 percent of the production market with 8.4 million tons.

Europe. In 2003, the European Union indicated that its shipbuilding world market share fell drastically during the early 2000s, from 19 percent in 2000 to 13 percent in 2001. In 2002, a 50 percent drop in orders caused the European Union's market share to decline even more, to 7 percent, which then rose slightly to 8.7 percent by the end of 2003. By 2008, the rate had slipped yet again to 5.7 percent of the market.

Although the European Union attributed a significant amount of its market share decline to alleged price dumping by Korean companies, some industry observers argued that conditions were not as bad as the European Union claimed. In June 2003 the *Journal of Commerce Online* said that "Europe is strengthening its position as a maritime power with dominant market positions in almost every sector from tankers and bulk carriers, to cruise liners, containerships and liquefied gas carriers."

In addition to mentioning European-owned vessels flying under the flags of other nations and European interests in such shipping industry leaders as A.P. Moller, the article went on to explain that German banks were "Europe's 'unseen' shipowners," who "have built up a massive fleet of container vessels for charter thanks to investors seeking a tax-efficient home for their savings. This is a big business with charter tonnage now accounting for nearly 50 percent of the fleet of the world's top 30 liner shipping companies."

The late 1990s brought increased consolidation and collaboration among European yards in an effort to remain competitive. Drastic workforce reductions throughout the European Union were common. By 1996, European shipyard employment was about 113,000 and further reductions during 1998 were expected. In 1998, Germany, Poland, Spain, and Denmark were expected to experience the greatest additional reductions in labor. The employment picture was more optimistic for Norway, the

Netherlands, and Italy. Northern European countries had higher wages on average than their southern counterparts. There were also strong contrasts in work hours, ranging from an annual working hour rate of 1,400 to about 2,300 hours. In the 1960s, the Netherlands shipbuilding workforce numbered around 50,000 workers. That figure has dropped to about 10,000 employees in 100 shipyards with only 4,000 being employed in building oceangoing ships.

In 2007, plans were announced to merge the three U.K. yards still in the business of building surface warships into one operation. Industry insiders predicted that the deal would lead to an even split of ownership between two companies, VT Group and BAE Systems, but that BAE would control more than 50 percent of the voting rights. BAE and VT yards are slated to do most of the work on two 65,000-metric ton aircraft carriers for the Royal Navy. According to Nick Chaffey, global head of defense at PA Consulting, consolidation in naval shipbuilding is not a European phenomenon. It is considered to be a global issue that is even beginning to affect the United States. Chaffey also noted that current actions are helping to prepare for the period somewhere between 2015 and 2020 when orders from the British will likely dive.

Japan. Fourth-place Japan saw new ship contracts double during the first quarter of 2004, rising from 1.2 million compensated gross tons (cgt) to almost 2.5 million cgt. By the early 2000s, South Korea had pulled ahead of Japan to lead the shipbuilding industry. According to Korea's Ministry of Commerce, Industry and Energy, the nation's research and development technologies have given it an edge over Japan in terms of being able to build more customized vessels for its customers, whereas Japan has produced more standard-feature ships.

Japanese shipbuilders had previously managed to maintain their lead over South Korea, in spite of the Asian financial crisis of the late 1990s. This was partially due to differences in how both nations obtained construction materials. Japanese shipbuilders relied on domestic suppliers for such high-end additions as equipment, whereas Korean companies strongly relied on imports of machinery and steel. Japanese yards also relied heavily on high technology, particularly computer-aided design and drafting, and Japan's largest shipbuilders were broadly diversified conglomerates with subsidiaries in heavy engineering sectors.

Japan, like the other leading shipbuilding nations, witnessed a decline in prices despite an overall increase in the world's shipbuilding orders. By the end of 2000, employment in the shipbuilding industry was 85,000, and further workforce reductions were expected, reflecting a global trend. Japan finished 2003 with a 28 percent global market share. By 2008, Japan's percentage had slipped dramatically to 3.7 percent of the industry.

The United States. During the early 2000s, the U.S. shipbuilding industry ranked tenth in the world in terms of tonnage built. Productivity in the maritime industry is quite low compared to other large manufacturing sectors such as the aerospace and automobile industries. Shipbuilding in the United States has historically been considered a strategic industry, supporting both military and commercial interests. As of 2002, the U.S. shipbuilding and repair industry consisted of about 250 private companies and five publicly owned and operated repair yards. U.S. shipbuilding and repair revenues totaled US$10.2 billion in 1998. About 10 percent of the companies accounted for 85 percent of these revenues. The shipyards on the East and Gulf coasts account for more than 80 percent of the revenues for the entire industry.

Lack of technological innovation and automation, failure to upgrade worker skills, and a lack of collaborative partnerships among yards, combined with complicated and inefficient management hierarchies all contributed to the United States' low market share. In contrast, Asian yards excelled at using new technologies, regularly upgrading workers' skills, developing collaborative ventures, and maintaining flatter, less complex management hierarchies. Outside forces, particularly foreign government subsidies, price dumping, and overcapacity, further contributed to the problem. At the turn of the century, efforts were also under way to streamline yard operations and increase efficiency by means of technology and flatter management structures.

In 2003 the U.S. shipbuilding industry, and some 2,000 workers, benefited from a defense appropriations bill that included more than US$1 billion to build two new ships at Northrop Grumman's Avondale shipyard. Despite this good news, the overall outlook for U.S. shipbuilders paled in comparison to those in Asia.

In 2006 industry insiders applauded the navy's new system of awarding ship repair contracts. The "multiship, multioption" allows shipyards to win contracts to maintain a class of ships. This process replaced the former single-ship awards. The navy also made it possible to generate more money for shipbuilding with its quest to build a 313-ship fleet. A reduction in naval fleet size, from approximately 600 ships in the late 1980s to roughly 275 by the 2000s, hurt big shipbuilders and smaller suppliers. Diversification was considered to be a key strategy for survival. Reduction in the navy's maintenance budget, however, created cause for concern.

BIBLIOGRAPHY

Bangsberg, P.T. "Record China Shipbuilding in 2003." *Journal of Commerce Online*, 12 January 2004.

———. "Shipbuilding Boom Cools for S. Korea Yards." *Journal of Commerce Online*, 6 January 2004.

Barnard, Bruce. "Big Box Ship Orders Slow." *Journal of Commerce Online*, 3 May 2005.

"Canadian Shipbuilding & Repair: The Most Uncertain of Times." *Canadian Sailings* (13 March 2006).

"China Breaks Ground for World's Largest Shipyard." *World Trade* (March 2004).

Chuter, Andrew. "And Then There Was One." *Defense News* (23 April 2007). Available from www.defensenews.com.

"Container Ship Orders Decline." *The Journal of Commerce* (9 May 2005).

"Flexibility is Key When Work Drops: Hampton Rubber Has Found Ways to Diversify Into New Lines of Work." *Daily Press,* 13 March 2007.

"Flying Start to Year for World's Top Builders." *Journal of Commerce Online*, 13 May 2003.

Glass, Jon W. "Executive Says Recruiting is a Challenge in Ship Repair Industry." *Virginian-Pilot*, 13 October 2006.

Glass, P. "U.S. Repair Yard Hit Hard by Competition." *Workboat* (April 2007).

McWilliams, Jeremiah. "Author Urges Ship Repair Industry to Get 'Lean'." *Virginian-Pilot,* 9 March 2006.

"Move to Strenghten Shipbuilding, Repair Sector." *Business Times* (8 August 2006).

"Recycling of Ships." London: International Maritime Organization, 4 April 2007. Available from www.imo.org.

"Russia's Putin Signs Decrees on Shipbuilding Corporation, Ship Repair Centre." *BBC Monitoring International Reports,* 22 March 2007.

"Samsung Heavy to Form Ship Repair Joint Venture in Malaysia." *AsiaPulse* (23 January 2006).

SIC 3743

TRAIN EQUIPMENT

NAICS CODE(S)

336510. Railroad equipment manufacturers build the world's passenger and freight transit equipment, including subway trains and street cars, locomotives, railcars, and parts and equipment used to run railroad systems.

INDUSTRY SNAPSHOT

In the early years of the first decade of the 2000s, freight car manufacturing across the globe declined, falling from 75,685 cars in 1998 to 34,247 cars in 2001. Railcar demand from 2001 to 2003 was dismal, the lowest in twenty years. The outlook was improving in the middle of the decade, however, especially as the industry consolidated further. According to the Railway Supply Institute, North America had ordered 20,315 new cars through the third quarter of 2004. This was an increase from 19,770 orders the previous quarter. Tank cars, box cars, non-articulated platform flat cars, and aluminum gondola cars were in the highest demand. At the same time, locomotive production continued its tradition of steady growth, fueled by developments that increased efficiency. Besides new trains and infrastructure, many countries sought safer methods of controlling and monitoring railroads. Therefore, information and technology firms began to develop and market computerized signal and communication systems for the railroad industry.

Railroad companies also invested money in new railroad equipment to lure commercial and freight clients to areas where train use had decreased over the years, such as in the United States. New technologies available to railroads included more durable yet lighter-weight freight trains capable of traveling 80 miles per hour, as well as electronic tracking systems to ensure safety on the railroad. In addition, the industry was focusing on the development of more environmentally friendly cars and locomotives in the mid-years of the first decade of the 2000s.

Emerging economies such as those of China, South Korea, and Indonesia began expanding and improving railway systems and contracting railroad equipment manufacturers to produce advanced machinery to carry their transportation systems into the next century. The United States also started to upgrade its passenger and freight railroad equipment, and South American countries such as Brazil took measures to improve railroad transportation as well. By the mid-years of the first decade of the 2000s, China's booming market also caused increased demand in this sector.

Several industry insiders and analysts, including 65-year industry veteran Norman W. Seip and Thomas D. Simpson of the Railway Supply Institute, felt more good times were in store for railroads and related industries. However, as Simpson pointed out, "The new railroad freight car building industry has been a cyclical one with spectacular highs and industry-sapping lows." Although some suppliers remained anxious about the future, builders were enjoying exploring their opportunities.

The demand for switchers was tremendous. As a result, there were many designs and opportunities for small companies normally linked to rebuilding. A new generation of switchers was distinguished by microprocessor engine controls enabling them to replace more efficient four-axle units in many Class I or largest operating railroad yards.

Economic Planning Associates (EPA), a consulting and market research firm, issued a freight car forecast calling for delivery of 69,000 railcars and intermodal platforms in 2007. The forecast was "based on opening year backlogs and further growth in orders." Furthermore, EPA expectations for 2008 included continued demand for a number of car types, a revival of demand for coal cars, boxcars and intermodal equipment, plus an increase in tank car production capacity with support deliveries of 70,500 units.

ORGANIZATION AND STRUCTURE

Although the organization of the railroad industry varied by country, the role of the railroad equipment manufacturer remained largely the same in each context: it sold equipment such as locomotives, signal systems, and railcars to the railroad operators, whether owned and operated by a government or a monopoly and whether for freight or passengers. Railroad leasing companies and other manufacturers and producers who relied on railroads might also purchase train equipment.

In the mid-1990s, railroad operators began working more closely with equipment manufacturers in order to ensure high standards of reliability and performance were met as increasingly complex technology came on-line, according to *International Railway Journal.* Since many train lines crossed national boundaries, notably in Europe, railroad operators realized they had to procure equipment compatible with different national railroad systems. In Germany, for example, Deutsche Bahn (DB) worked closely with Siemens and other manufacturers to develop the InterCity Express 2.2 and the InterCity Express Tilting trains to meet the railroad's standards for smoother, more comfortable, and more efficient travel.

Based in Alexandria, Virginia, the Railway Progress Institute (RPI) represented the global railroad industry and served more than 100 members. Originally called the Railway Business Association, the RPI served both freight and passenger railroads, and the association's key objectives included the following: promoting a free enterprise system of railroads throughout the world, advancing high-speed train penetration and light rail systems in urban cities, and representing its members' interests.

BACKGROUND AND DEVELOPMENT

Inventors developed early railroad equipment in the first part of the nineteenth century. The English engineer Richard Trevithick built the first steam engine in 1802, which did not run on tracks and reached a maximum speed of 6 miles per hour. The following year, Trevithick developed a locomotive designed for tracks, which weighed more than six tons and could reach speeds of only about 2 miles per hour, taking four hours to get to the end of the 8 miles of track Trevithick laid for the train.

In 1814 another engineer, George Stephenson, built a five-ton steam engine that could pull eight cars loaded with 30 tons of cargo. Stephenson designed this train for a mine in England and went on to build a number of other trains, including his 1825 "Locomotion," which became the first passenger train. The Locomotion traveled a 16-mile track from Stockton to Darlington, England.

In the middle of the century, the rest of Europe and the United States began installing railroads and purchasing steam engines from the British company founded by Stephenson. Countries such as the Netherlands, Germany, France, and the United States imported trains from Britain during the early years of the railroad equipment industry. The United States alone purchased about 100 steam engines from Britain between 1829 and 1841.

In Asia, the United States, and the United Kingdom, railroad equipment manufacturers supplied these countries with their first locomotives at the turn of the century. However, by the 1920s, Japan began to produce its own trains, and by 1935 Japan had manufactured 687 locomotives. Later in the century, Japan became a major proponent of the railroad, creating the world's first high-speed railway in 1964, which stretched about 257 miles across the country and reached speeds of 100 miles per hour.

Throughout the 1970s, 1980s, and 1990s, the prosperity and prospects of the railroad equipment manufacturing industry depended on the overall economics of the countries in question. In the stable and even flourishing economies of Europe, the United States, and China, railroad manufacturers experienced heightened demand and solid growth in the 1990s as they received new contracts to produce equipment for the modernization of old railroad systems. Several large railroad companies in the United States, including Amtrak and Union Pacific Corp., as well as city and state transit authorities, ordered high-speed trains and electronic tracking systems. Europe continued to expand its high-speed railway production, including new orders for locomotives from British Rail. In addition, China forged ahead in the creation of the Eurasia Continental railroad system.

However, in the turbulent economies of South Korea and Thailand, which experienced devaluations of currencies and mushrooming debt in the mid-1990s, demand slumped and existing contracts were reevaluated. South Korea's new president, Kim Dae-jung, called for the review of the country's 412-kilometer Supertrain project because of its escalating construction costs. Furthermore, Thailand halted production of its Skytrain project, which would have eased Bangkok's notorious traffic problems, when it terminated its contract with the developer, Hopewell Co. When construction stopped in August of 1997, Hopewell had built only 20 percent of the railroad.

In the global market, Germany, Canada, France, the United States, Japan, and China led the world in railroad equipment manufacturing in the mid-1990s. To remain competitive, companies in the industry had to accommodate railroad operators and restricted budgets and funding. Railroad operators in Europe pressured manufacturers to provide low-cost—low cost to purchase, operate, and maintain—railroad equipment, forcing manufacturers to seek lower prices from their sub-suppliers. *Railway Age* reported that in some cases, railcar costs dropped by 30 percent between 1994 and 1997, spurring on production of light-weight, flexible, more durable, and more efficient equipment.

Of the technologies produced to meet these economic pressures, the self-propelled diesel railcar was one of the most successful in the mid-1990s. Leading models included the RegioSprinter from Siemens, Talent from Bombardier and Talbot, Dieseltreibwagen from GEC Alsthom, and RegioShuttle from Daimler-Benz. North American railroad operators began considering adopting this kind of railroad equipment as well in the mid-1990s.

The locomotive sector of the industry experienced significant changes in the mid-1990s with the introduction of new locomotive technologies. During this period, railroads adopted diesel locomotive alternator and electric traction motor technology. In addition, self-propelled railcar technology began replacing its locomotive-hauled counterpart, and electric locomotives continued to supplant diesel trains. In 1995, the world locomotive fleet included 94,000 diesel locomotives, down 12 percent from 1992, and 53,000 electric locomotives, up 5 percent from 1992.

Since a new locomotive ran about US$200,000 in the mid-1990s and yearly maintenance and fuel costs totaled US$300,000, many railroad operators turned to rebuilding and remanufacturing equipment instead of purchasing new trains. As a result, locomotive replacement sales slackened in the early 1990s. However, with the new, more powerful, and more fuel-efficient locomotives, manufacturers hoped to entice railroad operators once again. In 1995, *International Railway Journal* reported that shipments of locomotives totaled US$9.2 billion.

Enhanced performance of newer diesel-electric locomotives pushed locomotive sales to near record levels in the early years of the first decade of the 2000s, particularly in North America. Although most major North American railroads had finished replacing aging fleets by 2000, "a wholesale building bust doesn't appear imminent," wrote a *Railway Age* columnist in July of 2000. "Robust domestic railroad traffic driven by a healthy economy and a growing export market should keep builders' order books filled for at least the next few years." However, most major North American railroad companies did plan to reduce locomotive orders in the coming years, particularly as the North American economy weakened.

Light-rail systems without trolley wires made their way to North America in 2001. Bombardier delivered three Talent diesel-electric light-rail vehicles to Ottawa, Ontario, for service scheduled to begin in 2002. In the United States, at roughly the same time, New Jersey Transit began working on converting an unused 32-mile Conrail track into a light-rail line. When construction was completed, the line would make use of 20 Adtranz diesel-electric cars.

Asia remained an important market in the railroad equipment industry in the early years of the first decade of the 2000s. Foreign competition began to make its way into China as the market for imported goods began to open there. German and Chinese officials continued to work together on plans for a 26-mile magnetic levitation (maglev) train in Shanghai, capable of reaching speeds of 340 mph. If completed, the train was expected to be the first public transit system in the world to make use of maglev technology. China also remained involved in the development of the Eurasia Continental Bridge, which would connect Rotterdam, The Netherlands, to the Jiangsu Province of China, with both roads and railways. In addition, improved economic conditions in Thailand prompted transportation officials to examine ways to resurrect the Hopewell mass transit system, which had been suspended due to a recession.

CURRENT CONDITIONS

Railcar demand was falling in the early years of the first decade of the 2000s, accompanied by falling prices, which in 2003 were 20 percent lower than those at the beginning of the decade. According to *Railway Age,* from mid-2001 to mid-2003, railcar builders suffered the lowest demand in nearly 20 years, producing only about 30,000 units, less than one-third of the industry's capability. In addition, in order to redesign cars to meet stricter 286 horsepower (hp) truck technology requirements, railcar manufacturers were set to lose an additional amount per railcar of up to US$2,000. While the future was looking up by the middle of the decade, it was still predicted that this segment would experience consolidation on a large scale. Things looked brighter in 2005, as the freight-car industry saw orders rise steadily. As reported in *Trains Magazine,* more than 20,000 new freight cars were ordered during the third quarter of 2004 alone, up 3 percent from the second quarter and three times the amount from third quarter 2003. Because of high demand, manufacturers showed a backlog of more than 61,000 cars. Demand for covered hoppers, flatcars, and aluminum gondolas was greatest, as carriers worked to meet demand and replace aging equipment. The industry saw strength in North America and Europe, as well as in emerging markets.

In Europe, the Paris Transit Authority hired Alstom and Bombardier to build 805 metro cars in a multi-year contract worth roughly US$584 million. Plans called for the new cars to replace roughly 40 percent of the existing fleet operated by Paris Transit. Alstom and Bombardier also agreed to jointly supply 10 tilting trains, worth US$120 million, to Swiss Railways. In addition, Alstom secured a US$118 million contract to build 100 electric railcars for French National Railway, and Bombardier won a US$76 million contract to refurbish 60 three-car trains for Netherlands Railways. Danish State Railways awarded a US$579 million contract to Italy-based Breda for 83 four-car diesel trains.

China and Russia were both considered potential growth markets by several railroad equipment industry analysts. China's extensive railway system was in need of extensive upgrades, as was Russia's. According to the U.S. Foreign and Commercial Service in Moscow, more than 33 percent of electric locomotives and 50 percent of diesel locomotives in Russia were in need of replacement in the early years of the first decade of the 2000s. Competition in these markets was expected to intensify as Japanese, European, and U.S. manufacturers all attempted to gain market share. Iran was emerging as a growth area as well. In 2005 German and Chinese companies were competing to work with the Tail Transportation Industry Company (Rtico) on a $680 million contract to develop a third metro line in Tehran. The project included electrical work, signaling and utilities, as well as the manufacture of rolling stock, for which Bombardier of Canada was bidding as well.

RESEARCH AND TECHNOLOGY

The 1990s brought the railroad equipment industry new technology to improve railroad travel efficiency and safety. Some of the most prominent advances included intelligent trains and tracking systems, high-speed trains, and safety equipment. Intelligent trains and tracking systems used computer and digital communications technology, which create a train and track system controlled by computers that have a strong communication link with railroad monitors. Some researchers sought to integrate Global Positioning System (GPS) satellites into railroad communications systems. This technology helped eliminate human error in railroad transportation because the computer system could automatically stop a train if an impending collision was miles away.

New high-speed train technology started to emerge in the mid-1990s that would allow trains to travel up to 150 miles per hour and contain advanced operation and track systems to ensure safety at high speeds. The faster high-speed trains, those that travel more than 110 miles per hour, required non-electric locomotives in order to reach maximum speeds and accelerate quickly. In addition, non-electric locomotives alleviated the need to install expensive electric locomotive infrastructure. In the late 1990s, the California High-Speed Rail Authority launched a US$25 million plan to develop one of the first high-speed railway lines in the United States. In November of 2000, the U.S. Federal Railroad Administration also began conducting research on T-16, a former Amtrak car refitted with technology that allowed it to test performance at speeds as high as 160 mph.

New safety equipment being developed included innovative warning systems, more reliable signal systems, and techniques for making trains more conspicuous. The first kind of safety device consisted of signals using light and sound to alert drivers of approaching trains. Researchers were trying to determine what kinds of signals would provide enough advanced warning for motorists. In order to make locomotives more conspicuous, researchers experimented with alternating lights combined with standard headlights, as well as advanced horn systems and reflectors on train cars to make them more visible.

Although researchers began experimenting with tilting train technology in the mid-1960s, it did not emerge as a viable alternative until the mid-1990s because economic problems plagued major researching countries, such as Germany, leading to slow progress when research terminated between 1975 and 1986. However, in 1987 research resumed and demonstrated that tilting wheels could lead to more efficient regional transportation. Tilting trains required only minimal modification of existing infrastructure and could smoothly handle curves at higher speeds than conventional trains because of the tilting technology. Tilting trains also worked well in large urban areas and on railroad lines shared with slower trains such as freight trains, according to *International Railway Journal*. However, critics pointed out that tilting trains could not travel as quickly as high-speed trains on specially built tracks. In addition, the tilting could cause more wear on the outer part of the rail, requiring more frequent track repair and maintenance, and tilting wheels might cost more to repair than conventional wheels because they contain more parts. Nonetheless, railroad operators, such as Deutsche Bahn (DB), began upgrading with this technology. By the early years of the first decade of the 2000s, DB wanted to operate 120 tilting trains, which would constitute the largest fleet of tilting trains in Europe. Other countries developing tilting trains in the late 1990s included Italy, Switzerland, Finland, and Spain.

In the freight train sector, DB decided to move its freight car technology into the twenty-first century by having new intelligent freight cars built. DB opted for this technology to remain competitive with other modes of transport and to improve freight train safety and reliability. Intelligent freight cars contain technology to replace antiquated railroad practices and procedures such as shouting messages, transmitting data by hand, loading and unloading cars manually, and performing safety checks without the aid of technology. In the mid-1990s, DB tested 20 intelligent freight cars with hopes of implementing the technology by the beginning of the next decade.

The first decade of the 2000s brought attention to the polluting effects of railways. With focus on noise pollution reduction, the European Commission was hopeful that computer-aided engineering would prove helpful in designing a quieter train system. In terms of air pollution, at the end of 2003 in North America, in an effort to develop less polluting units, a hybrid switching locomotive was being tested by RailPower Technologies, Railserve, and Chevron. Named the "Green Kid," the 1,000 horsepower (hp) hybrid locomotive was intended to reduce air pollution to levels significantly lower than those of traditional units.

INDUSTRY LEADERS

Bombardier. In May of 2001, Adtranz was acquired by Montreal, Quebec-based Bombardier Inc. Prior to its takeover of Adtranz, Bombardier ranked fourth in the world and first in North America for manufacturing subway cars, light-rail vehicles, monorails, and high-speed trains. Upon completion of the merger, Bombardier became the largest rail transportation equipment maker in the world, in addition to being the third largest aircraft manufacturer worldwide. Rail transportation equipment accounted for roughly 40 percent of the firm's US$10.7 billion in sales in 2001. By 2004, the company reported US$16 billion in revenue from all divisions. Bombardier had earnings of US$19.7 billion in fiscal year 2009.

The Swiss/German joint venture ABB Daimler-Benz Transportation (Adtranz) led the world in railcar production in the late 1990s. Formed in 1996, Adtranz manufactured a complete line of railroad equipment, including railroad control systems, locomotives, high-speed trains, passenger trains, trams, subway trains, and people movers. The company operated in about 50 countries throughout the world with a strong presence in Europe and an expanding presence in Asia and South America. Bombardier competed with the likes of Boeing and Airbus in aircraft manufacturing.

In the fall of 2006, there was news of a Bombardier partnership with March Networks of Canada. The companies united to develop an advanced, onboard mobile security system for passenger railcars. It was set to become part of Bombardier's SEKURFLO product line.

Bombardier was happy to share updates reflecting the popularity of the light rail vehicles and trams of its

Flexity family. Several cities ordered the advanced vehicle designs. Frankfurt am Main was notable among them with its order of 146 Flexity Swift vehicles. The transport operator Stockholm SL (AB Storstockholms Lokaltrafik) aimed to increase its Flexity Swift fleet of 22 bi-directional vehicles by another nine such vehicles. Delivery on the order was set for August 2008. The low-floor vehicles, 30 meters in length, carry a maximum of 212 passengers.

Bombardier announced its plans to bid for an opportunity to sell approximately 1,000 rail cars in India annually during the course of three years. Doing so would support efforts to reduce city traffic by building more metro networks. Bombardier Asian passengers division President Kristian Mikkelsen stated India appeared to be a long term market. The company had been awarded a contract including order for 424 coaches to New Delhi Metro.

Alstom. Alstom was another of the world's leading railroad equipment producers. It was initially a joint venture between France's Alcatel Alsthom and the United Kingdom's Marconi plc. Alstom specialized in the production of high-speed train and power generation equipment, including signaling devices. In the 1990s, Alstom continued to thrive, receiving major contracts to manufacture railroad equipment from around the world. Some of the company's key contracts included supplying high-speed trains for a Florida state transportation project and developing new trains for Amtrak in conjunction with Bombardier. Alstom also collaborated with the Korea High-speed Railway Construction Authority in South Korea's Supertrain project. Through a multitude of acquisitions, rail transportation operations at Alstom grew 12 percent annually between 1995 and 2000. In November of 2000, Alstom forged a joint venture with the Electro-Motive Division of General Motors Corp., one of the largest makers of diesel-electric locomotives in the world, to offer locomotive maintenance services on a global scale. Sales for all divisions in 2004 were US$20.5 billion. The firm employed more than 75,000 workers across the globe in 2004. Construction industry leader Bouygues owned approximately one-quarter of Alstom. By 2008, sales added up to US $26.7 billion with 76,000 employees.

In March 2007, Alstom President and CEO Patrick Kron signed two contracts with the Chinese Ministry of Railways. They call for Alstom and Datong Electric Locomotives to supply 500 Co-Co electric freight locos for heavy haul routes. The first 10 Prima locos will be assembled at Belfort and Alstom will supply components for the next 190 to be assembled at Datong where the remaining 300 will be built.

PRO BAHN awarded Alstom its "Rail Passenger Award 2007" for its innovative and passenger-friendly trains. The award acknowledged construction of 42 electric multiple units of type ET 474.3 delivered to S-Bahn Hamburg in a consortium with Bombardier. The dual-current trains can be operated in both a DC network of suburban trains and the AC network of the long-distance trains. They are equipped with both a lateral shoe gear and a roof pantograph. The trains can obtain their traction energy either from a lateral third rail or from an overhead line.

Siemens. A diversified industrial company, Siemens AG was also a world leader in railroad equipment production. The Germany-based Siemens provided interfaces between the electrical and mechanical parts of a train's drive system, as well as between trains and railroad signal equipment. The company developed technology for freight, local, and long-distance trains. Moreover, Siemens built the world's largest electronic microcomputer interlocking system for the Dutch National Railroad. Siemens strengthened its position in the railroad equipment industry in 1996 with the acquisition of locomotive manufacturer Krupp AG and a joint venture with driver-less train producer Lagardere Groupe. In 2004, the company reported overall sales of US$93.4 billion. At the turn of the twenty-first century, Siemens made significant inroads into Brazil, where its orders grew 36 percent between 1999 and 2000, and China, where it secured a US$22 million signaling and operation contract for a new metro line in Guangzhou. The firm also exported 12 light-rail cars from its plant in Sacramento, California, to Venezuela, marking the first export of new light-rail vehicles from the United States in 70 years.

Growth was evident by Siemens' decision to expand its main light rail vehicle manufacturing facility. The company subsequently booked orders for propulsion systems on three major car-building contracts. By 2008, it boasted sales of US$111.7 billion with an employee roster of 427,000.

In April 2007, Siemens announced that the Spanish railway company Renfe would run its high-speed Velaro train on a line of 650 kilometers. The world's fastest series production train was scheduled to travel from Madrid to Barcelona. Its design featured drive system components and technical modules in the Velaro mounted on the bottom of rail cars. The result was about 20 percent more passenger space than locomotive-hauled trains. Velaro sleeps 404 people in the three classes of Club, Preferente and Turista. A special feature allows seats to be rotated in the direction of train travel. Siemens agreed to deliver 26 Velaro trains to Renfe and assume responsibility for maintenance during a 14-year period.

Trinity Industries Inc. Trinity Industries, based in Dallas, Texas, is an industrial company with operations in five business segments, including railcars. In 2004, Trinity earned almost US $2.2 billion in revenues, showing sales growth of more than 50 percent. By the third quarter of 2004, Trinity's order backlog was 19,800 cars, the company's highest since 1999. Trinity was the largest supplier of freight and tank railcars in Europe and in the United States. The company operated manufacturing facilities in Mexico and Romania.

Trinity Industries Chairman, President and CEO Timothy R. Wallace reported receiving orders for 10,012 railcars in North America during the second quarter of 2006. As a result, the company shipped 6,233 cars. On June 30, Trinity's backlog of undelivered cars was 29,320, an increase of more than 3,700 from March 30.

The Greenbrier Companies. Headquartered in Lake Oswego, Oregon, Greenbrier is a supplier of equipment and services to the railroad industry, primarily in North America, and manufactures and refurbishes freight wagons in the European market. The company owns a lease fleet of approximately 10,000 railcars. It also performs management services for approximately 125,000 railcars. In 2004, Greenbrier earned $729.5 million in revenue, an increase of more than 65 percent over 2003. In 2004, Greenbrier's Polish manufacturing company, Wagony Swidnica, was awarded a large order from the Iraqi Coalition Provisional Authority. The Polish company, acquired by Greenbrier in 1998, employed 900 workers in the lower Silesia region of Poland. Greenbrier was also capitalizing on emerging markets in China, entering into two long-term cooperation agreements with Chinese railcar maker Zhuzhou Rolling Stock Works. In April 2007, Greenbrier reported owning approximately 10,000 railcars and performed management services for approximately 135,000 railcars. By 2009, the respective numbers changed to owning a fleet of 8,600 railcars and managing approximately 138,000 others. Approximately 80 percent of sales came from within U.S.

MAJOR REGIONS IN THE INDUSTRY

Europe. European railways, while seeing their share of the transportation market shrink in past years, still carried 30 percent of the continent's goods in 2005, as reported in the *Economist*. Railways from Eastern Europe were taking advantage of opportunities from legislation designed to bring new operators and private funding. European companies remained among top industry leaders during the mid-years of the first decade of the 2000s.

German companies produced locomotives and train cars, as well as signal and track systems, making the country an important manufacturer of railroad equipment. The country's level of production sank in the mid-1990s after peaking in 1992. In 1996, German output remained about 28 percent below its 1990 level. Nonetheless, Germany continued to lead the world in exports of railroad equipment with US$1.2 billion of export sales in the mid-1990s. The country's primary customers included the Netherlands, the Russian Federation, Switzerland, China, and Hungary. Germany worked to expand its reach in China in the late 1990s. In the early years of the first decade of the 2000s, German and Chinese officials continued to work together to create a 26-mile, 340 mph maglev (magnetic levitation) train, the first public transit system in the world to make use of maglev technology, in Shanghai.

Since railroad equipment is essential to French mass transportation and since one of the leading producers is based in France, the country plays an instrumental role in the global railroad equipment industry. Like other leading manufacturers, France's output dropped considerably in the mid-1990s. In 1996, France's output fell 29 percent beneath its 1990 level. Neverthelesss, France ranked as the world's fourth-largest exporter of railroad equipment and the country recorded US$644.2 million in proceeds from its exports in 1995. The United Kingdom constituted the country's main market for railroad equipment, accounting for 45 percent of France's train exports with US$292.3 million. France also exported railroad products to Germany, Belgium-Luxembourg, Chile, and the United States.

In the early years of the first decade of the 2000s, France began to invest heavily in its rail-based mass transportation system. For example, the Paris Transit Authority awarded Alstom and Bombardier a US$584 million contract to build 805 metro cars over several years; by 2005, the new cars were expected to replace roughly 40 percent of the existing fleet operated by Paris Transit. In addition, the French National Railway hired Alstom to build 100 electric railcars for US$118 million.

China. China emerged as an important market in the railroad equipment industry in the early years of the first decade of the 2000s. Foreign competition began to make its way into the Republic as the market for imported goods began to open there. Along with its work with German officials on a high-speed maglev train in Shanghai, China also remained involved in the development of the Eurasia Continental Bridge, which will use roads and railways to connect Rotterdam, The Netherlands, to the Jiangsu Province of China.

Canada. Canada's role as a railroad equipment exporter increased rapidly in the 1990s, and the value of its exports almost doubled in just five years. Between 1991 and 1995,

Canada's exports climbed from US$458 million to US$965 million, propelling Canada into its position as the world's second-largest exporter. By far, the country's leading trading partner in 1995 was the United States, with US$892 million worth of imports, accounting for 92 percent of Canada's exports. Other importers of Canadian railroad equipment included Turkey (US$35 million), the United Kingdom (US$11 million), Saudi Arabia (US$10 million), and Indonesia (US$4 million). The United States remained Canada's largest trading partner in the early years of the first decade of the 2000s. In 2001, Canada became the first North American nation to make use of light-rail systems without trolley wires when Bombardier delivered three Talent diesel-electric light-rail vehicles to Ottawa, Ontario; service was scheduled to begin in 2002. Bombardier, the industry's top company, was actively working on contracts with developing areas overseas during the middle of the decade.

United States. Although the U.S. rail system is comparatively underdeveloped compared to those of Western Europe and Japan, railroad equipment production grew substantially in the 1990s. Between 1992 and 1995, the country's production level shot up by 54 percent, and between 1994 and 1995 it increased by 11 percent. Although the U.S. railroad equipment market expanded in the 1990s with the aid of a Congressional mandate to research and implement high speed train networks throughout the country, overall demand remained small. Therefore, U.S. manufacturers turned to other markets to sell products. The country's biggest markets in 1995 were Canada with US$548.7 million in imports and Mexico with US$67.2 million. In other trade, U.S. manufacturers targeted Chile, Romania, Swaziland, and Turkmenistan as strong export markets. In 1998, U.S. producers planned to ship US$30 million worth of railroad equipment to Chile and US$50 million worth to Romania. U.S. manufacturers also sought to supply railroad equipment to Swaziland and Turkmenistan, which were starting to develop railroad systems.

Reflecting a global drop in the number of freight cars manufactured during the late 1990s and the early years of the first decade of the 2000s, the U.S. rail car fleet fell by roughly 19,000 cars between 1999 and 2000. The locomotive fleet experienced a more modest drop of 228 cars over the same time period. In the early years of the first decade of the 2000s, the nation bought roughly US$20 billion in railway equipment and supplies annually and employed more than 150,000 workers in more than 500 U.S. businesses. By 2005, manufacturing and transportation revenues were improving for the North American rail industry.

The Class I market was credited with driving growth as a result of the California Air Resources Board and

Texas Commission on Environmental Quality regulations in urban rail yards. Furthermore, *Railway Age* Executive Editor Marybeth Luczak claimed the U.S. Environmental Protection Agency was another key influence on growth. Luczak believed that Tier 3 proposals, with a 2012 deadline, would be issued in 2007. Those regulations were expected to target the switchers.

Three companies involved in the "Responsible Care" program, the U.S. chemical industry's performance initiative to reduce emissions and improve worker safety, united to reduce emissions and improve worker safety plus work on a joint project team. The team focus centered around creating a "next generation tank car" for transportation of highly hazardous chemicals. Dow Chemical, Union Pacific, and Union Tank Car formed the trio.

A possible technology malfunction caused major concern for Metro and other transit systems using similar signals. The National Transportation Safety Board issued letters expressing related cautions and recommendations. On June 22, 2009, a track circuit system failed to recognize an approaching train. Consequently nine people were killed and 80 injured. Major areas with similar track circuits include Atlanta, Boston, and San Francisco.

Japan. Japan's railroad equipment industry emerged around 1917 when engine manufacturers such as Hitachi, Kawasaki, Osaka, and Mitsubishi produced the country's first domestically made locomotives. Japan quickly blossomed into Asia's leading manufacturer of locomotives, as well as a major supplier of railroad equipment to Asia and Northern Africa. In 1995 Japan was the world's fifth leading exporter of railroad equipment. Its largest external market was Egypt, which imported equipment valued at US$123.6 million. The United States imported US$70 million of railroad equipment, and assorted Asian countries bought about US$20.4 million worth of equipment. Japan has the largest railway system of any of the other leading economies. In the late 1990s, the Japanese government began working with Chinese authorities to establish the Japan-China Railways Council to facilitate the exchange of railway technologies, and to increase trade between the two countries. This work continued into the first decade of the 2000s.

BIBLIOGRAPHY

"2006 Freight Car Orders Soar." *Railway Age,* February 2007.

"Alstom Receives Pro-Bahn Rail Passenger Award 2007." *Railway Gazette,* 16 March 2007. Available from www.railwaygazette.com.

"Alstom Signs Chinese Contracts." *Railway Gazette,* 1 April 2007. Available from www.railwaygazette.com.

Briginshaw, David. "Bombardier Addresses Overcapacity." *Railway Age,* June 2004.

Chatterjee, Saikat. "Bombardier May Sell 1,000 Rail Cars in India on Growth Surprise." *Bloomberg News*, 29 September 2009. Available from www.bloomberg.com.

Daniels, Nancy. "Company Profile: Trinity Industries, Inc." *Hoover's Online*, 2009. Available at www.hoovers.com.

Dorsch, Jeff. "Company Profile: The Greenbrier Companies." *Hoover's Online*, 2009. Available at www.hoovers.com.

"EPA Forecast: 69,000 New RailCars in 2007." *Railway Age*, March 2007.

"Flexity—Success Story in European Cities." Bombardier Inc., 15 April 2007. Available from www.bombardier.com.

"Freight-Car Orders Climb in 2004: Builders Increase Pace of Deliveries, But Backlog at Recent High." *Trains Magazine*, February 2005.

"Germans and Chinese Compete for Metro Work; Rtico to Incorporate Foreign Assistance." *MEED Middle East Economic Digest,* 4 March 2005.

"Greenbrier and Boston Transit Announce Iraqi Freight Car Order for Poland." *PR Newswire*, 17 June 2004.

"Greenbrier in Chinese Freight-Car Deals." *The Journal of Commerce Online*, 15 December 2004.

Harrison, E. Hunter. "CN." *The Journal of Commerce,* 10 January 2005.

"Hoover's Company Capsules." *Hoover's Online*, 2007. Available from www.hoovers.com.

"Huffing and Puffing." *Economist*, 28 May 2005.

"Industry Outlook: Railroads Demand Limits on Hazmat Liability." *Railway Age*, July 2006.

"Industry Outlook: Tank Cars, the Next Generation." *Railway Age,* September 2006.

Judge, Tom. "Heavy-Haul Hammer Test." *Railway Age*, April 2003.

Kruglinski, Anthony. "A Veteran Railroad Supplier Looks Ahead." *Railway Age*, September 2006.

———. "'Bob the Carbuilder' Speaks Out." *Railway Age,* July 2003.

———. "Railcar Production: Looking for a Sign." *Railway Age,* September 2001.

Lazich, Robert S., ed. *Market Share Reporter*. Detroit: Thomson Gale, 2004.

Luczak, Marybeth. "Cleaner, Greener Locomotives." *Railway Age,* February 2007.

Oliver, Lynett. "Corporate Profile: Alstom." *Hoover's Online*, 2009. Available from www.hoovers.com.

"Rail Update: Supply Briefs for Trinity Industries." *Railway Age,* September 2006.

"Siemens Grows in Sacramento, Adds Propulsion Orders." *Railway Age,* September 2006.

"Siemens: Innovation News." Siemens AG, 5 April 2007. Available from www.siemens.com.

Simpson, Thomas D. "Will the Good Times Continue?" *Railway Age,* July 2006.

"Transit Briefs: Canada." *Railway Age,* October 2006.

Vantuono, William C. "New Power Plays to Watch." *Railway Age,* August 2006.

———. "Power Play." *Railway Age,* July 2000.

TRANSPORTATION SERVICES

AIR TRANSPORTATION

NAICS CODE(S)

481. Air transportation providers include commercial airlines that offer scheduled and non-scheduled domestic and international flights, air freight transportation (air courier), and the operation of airports and terminals. (See also SIC 3721, **Aircraft Manufacturing.**

INDUSTRY SNAPSHOT

According to the International Air Transport Association (IATA), the worldwide air transportation industry served 1.6 billion passengers annually in 2004, a number that was projected to increase to 2.3 billion by the end of the decade. Employment levels were projected to increase from 28 million workers to 31 million workers during the same time. The freight segment of the industry transported two-fifths of the world's goods by value in the mid-2000s.

Following the September 11, 2001, terrorist attacks against the United States, the industry suffered severe declines in traffic and revenue. Many companies restructured, merged, or went bankrupt. In addition, the Severe Acute Respiratory Syndrome (SARS) epidemic in Asia and the war in Iraq slowed passenger travel. Despite soaring fuel costs, in 2004 the industry had returned to pre-2001 passenger and cargo levels, with an industry profit of US$3.2 billion reported early in the year. By mid-year, passenger traffic had increased 20 percent and cargo traffic had increased 13 percent. China and India were expected to have the highest rates of passenger growth between 2004 and 2008.

Analysts were concerned that high fuel costs that were continuing to rise would cause the industry to become unprofitable. The top three passenger airlines each reported losses in 2004. Air cargo services continued to experience growth, with industry leader FedEx showing a 1 percent growth in net income. Airport and terminal expansion continued worldwide, with many operating companies exploring the option of privatization. The ongoing drop in import demand in the United States resulted in a change of focus for Asian-based airlines, which decreased market exposure in North America in favor of European routes. Simultaneously, an increasing number of manufactures were choosing to transport their products by sea rather than by air.

Most major airlines sell tickets via Internet transactions either directly or through special travel web sites. Many also use e-ticketing, which is designed to alleviate the risk for passengers of carrying and potentially misplacing a conventional paper ticket. By 2003, *Forrester Research* reported that the vast majority of all airline tickets were issued online, with revenues totaling billions of dollars. The industry shared the goal of total e-ticketing by 2007.

The crisis in the global airline industry was vividly illustrated by Emma Clarke, who described "carcasses of hundreds of abandoned planes scattered across the arid lands of southwest United States." Companies with substantial parts of their fleets not in use included American Airlines, Delta Airlines, Northwest Airlines, and United Airlines. Major reasons were cited as rising fuel costs and reduced demand for seats. The aircraft were being parked at maintenance and storage centers known as "aircraft boneyards." "If the airline industry keeps on going in the direction that it is headed, there will be a couple of hundred airplanes here in the next 12 to 18 months," according to Mike Potter, who oversees operations of an aircraft graveyard in the Mojave Desert near Los Angeles,

California. Furthermore, the Association of Asia Pacific Airlines (AAPA) predicted that some airlines would not survive difficult economic times through 2009. AAPA Director-General Andrew Herdman explained that Asian carriers were facing the challenges of ongoing turbulence even while exploring long-term goals and future growth.

Strong orders for the mid-2000s sustained the industry into 2008, with approximately 1,200 new aircraft that reflected an increase of approximately 15 percent after 2007. Delivery of new aircraft was expected to peak by 2010, with US$300 billion in sales predicted by 2018. In addition, a large inventory of used jets were for sale and the private jet market continued to thrive in the late 2000s.

The airline industry was modifying standard practices in the late 2000s. Passengers began to be charged a fee for checking their all luggage and having to pay more for oversized bags than in the past. Travel Industry Association (TIA) President and CEO Roger Dow said that the "air travel crisis has hit a tipping point—more than 100,000 travelers each day are voting with their wallets by choosing to avoid trips." In addition, results of a TIA survey led Dow to conclude that "landmark research should be a wake-up call to the United States policy leaders that the time for meaningful air system reform is now."

According to International Air Transport Association (IATA) estimates, at least 24 carriers stopped service in 2008 as a result of increased fuel expenses. IATA Chief Executive Officer Giovanni Bisignani reasoned that budget airlines were more likely to suffer in tough economic times because jet fuel expenses were a high percentage of costs.

ORGANIZATION AND STRUCTURE

The global air transportation industry includes passengers, mail, and freight carriers. Companies in this industry operate scheduled and nonscheduled air service over local, regional, national, and international routes with single-engine and multi-engine aircraft. The industry is divided into three sectors: air passenger services, air cargo services, and general aviation.

Air passenger service includes scheduled passenger transportation, as well as support activities, such as maintenance of aircraft; training of pilots, flight attendants, ticket agents, and ground crews; maintenance of computerized reservation and accounting equipment; and food preparation.

Air cargo (freight) services include transportation of mail, business and manufacturing commodities, food, and livestock. On a cost-per-mile basis, air cargo transport costs are higher than truck, water, and rail transport. However, sending freight by air allows shippers to reduce product inventories, handling costs, and warehouse expenses.

General aviation includes non-airline, nonmilitary aviation concerns such as fixed-base operators, flight schools, tour and recreational operators, and corporate flight departments. About half of all hours flown in general aviation are attributed to commercial activities or business aircraft, including chartered passenger and cargo flights, sky advertising, crop dusting, and mapping for geographic information systems. Business flying includes corporate and individually owned aircraft and accounts for about one-third of total general aviation flying time. A variety of aircraft is used for business flying, including helicopters, single and twin engine planes, and jets, ranging in cruising speed from 150 to 500 miles per hour. The flexibility of corporate and private aircraft allows salespeople, executives, and other frequent travelers to avoid inconvenient airline schedules and to access regions that are often difficult to reach by commercial flights.

In 2006, there were 33 mainline air carriers with large passengers jets (more than 90 seats) and 81 regional carriers that use smaller piston, turboprop, and regional aircraft (up to 90 seats) as well as 25 all-cargo carriers. The U.S. Bureau of Labor Statistics reported that job opportunities are more extensive for regional and low-cost carriers and predicted that hourly and salaried jobs would increase 7 percent between 2006 and 2016.

Economic Indicators. Three key measures in analyzing an airline's profitability are:

- passenger revenues per revenue passenger mile (the total number of seats occupied by paying passengers on all flights multiplied by the number of total miles flown);

- load factor realized (revenue passenger miles divided by available seat miles); and

- operating costs per available seat mile (all compensation, fuel, and other operating costs divided by the available seat miles).

Airline seats are counted among a company's assets. When an airline seat is not filled on a flight, that is unused capacity, and the potential revenue from that seat is lost. The break-even point for an airline was reached when approximately 60 percent of its seats were filled. Airline seats had become a commodity by the late 2000s, despite companies' attempts to differentiate themselves in terms of on-time service, convenient routes and flight schedules, and frequent-flier programs. Thus, price competition can be intense, and airlines are often forced to operate close to, and sometimes below, the break-even point.

Airlines make large capital investments in fixed assets, such as aircraft, computerized reservation systems, and baggage and cargo handling equipment. These investments, which are important for profitability, often account for more than 60 percent of a company's total assets and can be purchased outright with cash, financed with long-term debt, or leased. Because airplanes and equipment are expensive, leasing remained significant for airline companies through the 2000s. By leasing, airlines reduce the cost of expensive equipment, including the newest passenger jets. Some leases are operating leases, in which required payments are shown in the notes of a company's financial statements. Others are called capital leases, which appear as both assets and liabilities on a company's balance sheet.

Operating costs per available seat mile also figure into airline profitability. A significant cost to any airline is fuel. A one-cent change in the cost of fuel can increase or decrease consolidated industry operating profits up to US$100 million, which is another reason airlines lease newer aircraft. New aircraft are significantly more fuel efficient and thus less expensive to operate. Other costs include salaries, which are often up to 40 percent of a carrier's costs, and property and liability insurance premiums which can increase considerably if an unusually high number of accidents occur.

In addition, when the economy is strong, air traffic usually increases. For example, the troubled U.S. economy along with a reduction in air service to the Caribbean lowered prospects for the 2008–09 winter tourist season. "Every seat we lose is an opportunity for a tourist to come to the Caribbean," acknowledged Caribbean Hotel Association President and Co-chair of the Caribbean Tourism Development Company Enrique De Marchena Kaluche. However, discount airline JetBlue was only one of five major carriers providing service to increased capacity and Air Tran began direct service from Baltimore, Maryland, to San Juan, Puerto Rico, in December 2008

BACKGROUND AND DEVELOPMENT

Air Passenger Services. Germany was the first country to offer air passenger service with hydrogen-filled dirigibles in 1910. In 1914 the United States became the first country to offer scheduled passenger service. However, it was difficult for airlines to profit by carrying passengers until 1925, when the Kelly Air Mail Act provided U.S. government subsidies to help companies like United, American, and Delta make it through tough times.

In the 1920s and 1930s, European governments were able to develop an extensive airline system. While airmail delivery was neither as sophisticated nor as efficient as in the United States, European passenger service was actually more sophisticated. Great Britain had a commercial air route to India by 1929 that was quickly followed by a well-developed mail, freight, and passenger service to many foreign countries.

Significant advances in operations, navigation, weather forecasting, and aerodynamics helped the air transportation industry grow rapidly between 1920 and 1939. The

introduction of the DC-3, which was the first large, modern passenger aircraft, put Europe, Asia, and North America within reach of Great Britain. The DC-3 included metal construction, dependable and efficient engines, variable-pitch propellers, and a retractable landing gear.

During and after World War II, international passenger flight continued to develop. Long-range, four-engine aircraft were built after the war. Passengers were more comfortable in the new planes' fully pressurized cabins and were put at ease knowing that the airplanes were equipped with advanced instrumentation that usually allowed safe flight through storms and heavy winds.

By 1958, flight by passenger plane had become the most common form of long-distance travel, superseding travel on ocean liners and railroads. In 1970, wide-body jumbo jets began service. Passenger travel at supersonic speeds was introduced with service on the French Concorde in 1976.

Air Cargo Services. Before World War I, many countries had used aircraft to deliver mail. After the war, air transportation services were developed. In 1918 the U.S. War Department provided the U.S. Post Office with planes and pilots, leading to the country's first scheduled air service. The Kelly Air Mail Act helped motivate private carriers to deliver mail under contract, often in open-cockpit, single-engine planes. The Air Commerce Act of 1926 hastened the development of radio navigation and airports by making government agencies responsible for the management of ground-based radar and terminal facilities.

Shipping of mail and commodities by air began in the 1920s. A few firms offered all cargo schedules around the U.S. Great Lakes. In the late 1920s, U.S. automobile manufacturer Henry Ford began to use a private airline to carry his company's freight. As larger aircraft came into service in the 1930s, the air cargo business expanded, but it provided much less revenue than passenger travel and mail delivery. Before World War II, cut flowers, fashion clothing, machinery parts, pharmaceuticals, jewelry, and live animals were common freight because they had a high value, an uncommon size, or were highly perishable. After the war, the advent of larger aircraft resulted in the formation of several all-cargo carriers, mostly to fill the worldwide need for goods of all kinds. Planes could literally carry tons of goods, from coal to construction equipment. Pressurized cabins allowed longer-range livestock delivery. By 1950, complete automobiles, heavy machinery, and frozen foods were commonly transported. Advances in container technology enabled small shipments to be packaged in large containers for easier handling and less risk of theft. Worldwide delivery of overnight mail became a reality in the 1970s, with air cargo companies competing with national postal services for business.

The International Airline Transport Association (IATA) announced the third consecutive drop in international freight traffic in August 2008. According to IATA CEO Giovanni Bisignani, the "three-month decline, led by weakness in Asia-Pacific markets, is a clear indication that global trade is slowing." Furthermore, Chantelle Benjamin acknowledged that a slowdown in the second quarter of 2008 meant there was a weakening of air freight markets before passenger markets.

General Aviation. Worldwide economic growth after World War II led to the development of more formidable business and commercial flying in many countries. In the 1960s, single and twin-engine aircraft were produced with turboprop engines. Fully pressurized business jets allowed faster and more economical flight at high altitudes. Typical business aircraft seated up to 15 passengers and were flown by professional pilots.

Regulation. The air transportation industry is regulated nationally and internationally. In 1926 the U.S. Air Commerce Act set standards for planes and pilots that helped the development of commercial and civil aviation. In 1938 the U.S. Civil Aeronautics Authority assumed regulatory duties but was divided in 1940 into the Civil Aeronautics Board and the Civil Aeronautics Administration. Together, these agencies were responsible for setting industry regulations, accident investigation, airline development, and the enforcement of safety standards. In 1958 the U.S. Federal Aviation Agency took on many of these duties and developed a standard military and civil air navigation and air traffic control system. The agency was renamed the Federal Aviation Administration (FAA) in 1967, at which time it became part of the U.S. Department of Transportation.

The U.S. National Transportation Safety Board assumed accident investigations from the Civil Aeronautics Board, which was disbanded in 1978. An body of the United Nations, the International Civil Aviation Organization (ICAO), was formed in 1947. It continued to be responsible for developing the world's navigation, safety, and dependability standards, as well as being the international body responsible for resolving legal issues.

In the mid-1940s, the U.S. government sought to create a global airline industry. The Chicago Conference brought the nations of the world together to achieve this goal, but the result was just the opposite. Other nations were apprehensive that U.S. carriers would dominate worldwide airline travel if operating rights and fares were determined purely by market forces, and subsequently, many nations protected their private carriers through

extensive controls over entry and pricing in international markets. The Bermuda Agreement between the United States and Great Britain in 1946 granted international operating authority only through bilaterally negotiated treaties. As a result, entry into international markets was greatly restricted, and international traffic rights were only granted when full reciprocity between countries had been achieved.

The activities of the International Air Transport Association (IATA) also delayed free-market flying and industry deregulation. Members of IATA met periodically to set pricing standards for specified regions, which resulted in regional cartels that looked to the IATA to set prices. IATA conferences regularly set tariffs for many international bilateral agreements. Pooling agreements, which divided the revenues of two bilateral nation carriers equally and ensuring one carrier did not profit more than another, were also anticompetitive. Competition was easily stifled in such an international climate.

The U.S. government became increasingly frustrated with the anticompetitive activities of IATA and the international airline industry. The United States opposed the 1955 IATA tariff schedule and the 1962 IATA proposal, which attempted to increase rates for roundtrip air travel. Compromises were made only after many European nations proposed to ban all U.S. carriers from landing in their respective countries. This climate continued throughout the 1960s and into the 1970s. The United States believed a consumer-friendly, competitive international market was best for the world, while other countries favored industry-centered, protectionist policies. Until 1978, the global airline industry was basically a worldwide cartel. After 1978, deregulation, privatization, and bilateral treaties had completely transformed this segment of the world economy. Free-trade forces, rather than protectionist policies, ruled the international skies.

During U.S. President Jimmy Carter's administration in the late 1970s, the United States cracked the uncompetitive hammerlock of the international airline industry with three major initiatives of domestic deregulation, the "Open Skies Policy," and the IATA "Show Cause" order. Alfred Kahn, a highly influential proponent of free domestic airline markets who came to be regarded as the father of U.S. airline deregulation policy, was appointed chairman of the Civil Aeronautics Board in 1977. The Airline Deregulation Act of 1978 reflected the pro-consumer, highly competitive stance that the United States advocated internationally. Under the Act, route structures and price setting became the decisions of the domestic carriers, not the U.S. government. A "hub and spoke" route system was quickly created, as well as the right to expand internationally. The U.S. carriers fine-tuned their domestic routes, creating a stronger link into their international flights.

The Open Skies Policy, officially known as the "Policy for the Conduct of International Air Transportation," resulted in treaties with 20 nations that increased the number of agreements between U.S. and non-U.S. carriers. The strong, deregulated system in the United States was better able to handle an increase in international traffic. The "Show Cause" order, which effectively ended IATA's ability to create and maintain international regional cartels, weakened the ability of IATA to set international airline prices. U.S. carriers increased traffic on the routes subject to the new liberalized agreements. They confidently decreased traffic on those routes that were more regulated. These actions by the U.S. government greatly encouraged other governments to adopt similar free market policies and the protectionist policies slowly disappeared.

The increase in international airline competition was felt in several ways. The creation of more liberalized bilateral trade agreements gave U.S. airlines greater access to many international markets. The number of international gateways increased, as did the level of competition. The location of the gateways also changed. For instance, in the U.S.–European market, the New York City gateway that had been traditional since 1978 gave way to new inland gateways, including Atlanta and Dallas by 1988. These new gateways also allowed U.S. airlines to gain competitive advantages over the European carriers. U.S. carriers also established hub systems in certain locations, making them formidable competitors not only to domestic rivals but also to their foreign counterparts. For example, American Airlines was dominant in Dallas, Delta in Atlanta, and United in Newark at the end of the twentieth century.

There has been a shift in the competitive struggle among U.S. carriers for international traffic as well. Before U.S. deregulation in 1978, carriers such as Eastern, Pan Am, and TWA were allowed by the U.S. government to establish strong international routes at the expense of weak domestic routes. Conversely, American, Delta, and United were permitted to develop their domestic routes at the expense of weak international ones. U.S. policy at the time was to not let any carrier have a competitive advantage in both domestic and international routes. After deregulation, domestic carriers with strong, established routes in the United States made attractive partners to foreign carriers who were eager to sign bilateral route agreements to gain access to the U.S. market. The strong, large domestic carriers, specifically American, Delta, and United, retained their domestic hub and spoke systems. Freed to establish domestic systems after 1978, U.S. international carriers became less attractive to potential foreign partners and were less competitive internationally. Lacking a strong series of national routes, such as the hub and spoke system developed by the national airlines, the U.S. international carriers were not able to feed their international routes.

The result was that the strong U.S. domestic carriers bought the international routes of their more international or regional siblings, such as TWA, Eastern, and Pan Am. Unfortunately, it was not soon enough for the latter two carriers to avoid bankruptcy. The shifting and reinvestment that took place within the United States for rights to international markets increased the international competitiveness of U.S. carriers as a group.

In response to Carter administration policies, other nations agreed that government ownership and protectionism placed their carriers at an international disadvantage. Chile and New Zealand deregulated domestic airlines soon after U.S. changes. Canada followed in 1988, with Australia, South Korea, and Japan deregulating in 1990. In 1987 Europe implemented a three-year plan to increase international service by developing access routes to regional airports for commuter carriers within the European Community.

In 1995 the International Chamber of Commerce (ICC) reported that of 150 airlines worldwide, 70 had majority government ownership, 20 had minority government ownership, and 60 had no government-held shares. It was clear that privatization of international carriers proceeded quickly and was another solution to the problem of inefficient operations. Airlines often became more competitive when they were relieved of the burdens of state-run management and began to have access to capital markets. It was clear that the trend in the late 1980s and during the 1990s was that governments increasingly relinquished control of their airlines, selling off all or part of them to private investors, many of which were nonnationals.

Complete privatization of British Airways and Japan Air Lines became a reality in 1987, as it had for Mexicana in 1988 and Air Canada in 1989. The Netherlands reduced its 55 percent share in KLM to 38 percent by between 1986 and 1992, Germany's share of Lufthansa fell from 65 percent to 51 percent in 1989; and Brazil trimmed its holdings in VASP. As of 2001, there was an extensive list of airlines in the process of full or partial privatization, including SAS, Sabena, Alia, Sudan Airways, Air-India, Pakistan International, and Air New Zealand.

In 1995, the International Chamber of Commerce saw fit to recommend that in all countries, state aid to airlines be absolutely minimized. The ICC asserted that state ownership or assistance typically had distorted the market and was detrimental to airlines and users, that government shareholders often interfered in management issues. In addition, state aid needed to be strictly limited in time and scope to be available only in exceptional circumstances and on a transitional basis.

Nevertheless, in the late 1990s, outside the United States, partial or majority state ownership remained the rule, not the exception, especially in Asia, Africa, the Middle East, and Europe. In 1995 in the European Union, governments held between 90 and 100 percent of five major carriers. Several important Asian airlines were between 55 and 100 percent owned by their respective governments.

Deregulation resulted in mergers that strongly influenced the international airline industry. For example, USAir and Piedmont; Northwest and Republic; TWA and Ozark; American and AirCal; USAir and PSA Continental, Frontier, and People Express; Texas Air and Eastern; and Delta and Western merged in the United States. U.S. hubs were strengthened by this consolidation, which appeared also to be the impetus for a number of mergers outside the United States, including British Airways and British Caledonian; Swissair and Crossair; British Airways and Brymon Airlines; Lufthansa and Interflug; KLM, NLM Cityhopper, and Netherlines; Transavia and Martinair; and Air France, UTA, AirInter, and TAT.

Strategic alliances grew in the international airline industry, as many firms pursued economies of scale while retaining domestic status. In 1995, 136 airlines worldwide had formed more than 280 alliances, whether involving joint sales and marketing, joint passenger and cargo flights, code-sharing, joint frequent-flier plans, management contracts, catering, or joint ventures to handle maintenance and cargo handling.

British Airways and United created a joint marketing program in which they shared price promotions, gate space, and codes. British Airways also established an alliance with Air Russia, a new carrier serving Europe, Moscow, North America, and Asia. Schedules, marketing, and even managers were shared by Lufthansa and Air France to protect their market shares.

Cross-holding arrangements and minority ownership between international airlines had also developed following the U.S. initiatives of the late 1970s. Some of them included Air New Zealand (20 percent owned by Quantas, 7.5 percent by American, 7.5 percent by JAL); America West (20 percent owned by Ansett); Austrian (10 percent owned by Swissair, 10 percent by Lufthansa, 1.5 percent by Air France); Continental (18.4 percent owned by SAS); Delta (5.7 percent owned by Singapore Airlines, 5.7 percent by Swissair), LAN Chile (30 percent owned by SAS), Northwest (11.1 percent owned by KLM); and Sabena (20 percent owned by KLM, 20 percent owned by British Airways).

Computerized reservation systems (CRSs) provide significant competitive advantages to their owners. They have been increasingly used as strategic weapons in the war for passengers by restricting access and display of industry information in certain markets. Carriers that are too small to develop their individual CRSs have banded together to form them. In Asia, Cathay Pacific, China Airlines, Malaysia Airlines, Singapore Airlines, and Philippine Airlines created the Abacus CRS. Air Canada and Canadian Pacific consolidated their CRSs to create the Gemini system, which interfaced with United's Apollo system. Lufthansa, Air France, SAS, Iberia, and seven other carriers developed Amadeus. British Airways, KLM, Alitalia, Aer Lingus, Swissair, and four other carriers formed Galileo. USAir and four of the Galileo carriers also bought half interest in United's Apollo, which was later absorbed by Galileo.

Airlines hubs were was increasing in the international airline industry, generally following the experience of the U.S. domestic market. Hubs are like a wheel and spoke system on a bicycle. Each carrier funnels its routes (spokes) into a group of major regional airports (hubs) that are strategically placed within the country. Direct flights between small cities are mostly eliminated in favor of flights to major points, the hubs, that provide a route to other destinations. Most carriers have kept their hubs unattractive to competitors by operating near-monopolies; the competition has generally been among hub locations. Carriers that dominate hubs have more power over pricing, landing slots, and gate spaces than carriers that simply serve the location with a few daily flights. Large economies of scale can be generated by having multiple hub locations, leading to increased globalization of the international airline industry.

Some factors continued to inhibit competition in the international airline industry. Capacity constraints, which are caused by insufficient landing slots, slow growth of additional airports, and shortages in air traffic control systems, have caused barriers to entry that impeded further competition and improved the prospects of monopolies. International traffic rights that favored some carriers over others were also an anticompetitive factor as carriers with access to tightly restricted markets often gained competitive advantages over carriers without favored access. Mounting antitrust problems generated from mergers and international alliances had created an increased concentration of carriers. In addition, ongoing governmental prevention of free-market competition in favor of protecting domestic carriers—or at least the "national" airline—through tariffs, bilateral agreements, landing rights, or price restrictions also threatened to return the industry to its historically anticompetitive status.

In the late 1990s, international airlines continued to move toward smoke-free cabins on transatlantic and transpacific flights. In 1990 smoking was banned on all U.S. domestic flights except to Hawaii, Alaska, and flights over six hours long. No-smoking policies were rapidly extended to all commercial airline flights. Air Canada was the first airline to ban smoking on all of its international flights. In the United States, American, Continental, Northwest, TWA, United, and USAir were among the first to ban smoking on transatlantic flights. In 1995, Delta followed Air Canada's lead, banning smoking on all of its international flights and in all its lounges. Northwest banned smoking on its flights to London, Paris, Frankfurt, and Hong Kong as did Qantas on its flights from North America to Australia and New Zealand.

Although some airlines acquired new planes to replace old ones, the industry consistently retained its older fleet. Most older jets wound up in the fleets of smaller, upstart airlines, increasing the industry's overall capacity and eroding profits. To combat unrestrained and imprudent capacity expansions, airlines around the world began to rely more heavily on their alliances. Ironically, no sooner had the prospect of much freer global competition emerged, than such alliances were found to mitigate the need for larger fleets. In 1997 United, Lufthansa, SAS, Air Canada, Thai Airways, and Varig formed the Star Alliance, which worked cooperatively toward their individual objectives. Other alliances included Delta, Swissair, Sabena, Austrian Airlines, American Airlines, and British Airways.

The European Union (EU) implemented airline deregulation, which reached its final stage among the EU countries in April 1997. Government involvement in the European airline industries had bred inferior service, bureaucratic management, high labor costs, and low productivity, according to many critics. Airlines in Germany and the United Kingdom quickly privatized to compete in the newly deregulated market and quickly reported strong profits. However, airlines in countries like France and Italy continued to be largely state-owned and struggled in the new business climate. While deregulation had reduced the degree of government involvement in the industry and opened up EU markets to competitors from other countries, by 1998 new airlines had emerged and established airlines began moving into new markets.

In the late 1990s, domestic and established airlines held a substantial advantage over newcomers and had carved out a market presence, but limited capacity at airports had resulted in competition below most analysts' expectations. Predation, when airlines lowered their fares to intentionally incur losses, which forced other airlines to lower their fares and also incur losses, combined with a lack of new airplanes to hinder the success of new airlines. Large, established airlines had more abundant capital and sometimes used predation to drive new airlines entrants out of business.

Deregulation also began in Asia in the late 1990s. Japan overturned its long-standing policy and permitted new airlines to form and compete in the Japanese market. However, the country's flight slot shortage left newcomer Skymark with few flights to offer. Furthermore, Japan Airlines started a bargain subsidiary, which increased Skymark's competition. Meanwhile, with the sale of 33 percent of its shares in 1997, China Eastern became China's first publicly-traded airline. China Airlines then announced it would sell off part of its shares that were owned by the government. However, the financial crisis in Asia during the late 1990s had a negative impact on the airline industry, including deregulation. With bad debt and depreciating currency haunting the region in 1997, Asian airlines reported a 24 percent drop in profits. South Korea's Korean Air Lines led the way with US$700 million in losses.

Some of the key concerns the industry grappled with in the early 2000s included safety, security, and competition. Two crashes in the United States in the late 1990s put safety and security on center stage. In 1996 Valujet had to suspend its flights for three months following the crash of Flight 592 in the Florida Everglades. The crash also led to increased inspection of all small airlines by the Federal Aviation Administration (FAA) as well as new regulations for outsourcing maintenance and the installation of smoke detectors and fire extinguishers in cargo compartments.

Later that year, the explosion of TWA Flight 800 shortly after takeoff from John F. Kennedy Airport in New York raised suspicions of terrorism and resulted in the implementation of a number of expensive and time-consuming preventive measures. The airlines were forced to begin running some luggage through costly and sophisticated explosives detectors and all baggage on domestic flights had to be matched with passengers. Investigators ultimately concluded that a fire in the fuel tank was responsible for the crash of the TWA flight, and in May 2001 the FAA issued rulings that required significant changes for the design, maintenance, and operation of airplane fuel tanks to prevent another such explosion.

In spite of publicity about crashes, calls for more competition and new entrants rang out steadily in the late 1990s and early 2000s. In the United States, Congress and the Department of Transportation suggested that the industry needed more competition from new airlines even though small U.S. airlines like ValuJet, Air South, and Vanguard remained unprofitable in the mid- to late 1990s. However, in Europe, new airlines began sprouting up after a wave of deregulation throughout the region. Belgium's Virgin Express was one of the most successful of the new entrants.

The airline industry's success strategy had been to increase traffic faster than capacity and to expand unit revenues faster than costs. However, by 2001 recessions in the United States, Japan, and several Far Eastern countries and declining demand for air travel had caused a decline in airline profits worldwide before the September 11, 2001, terrorist attacks against the United States. The decline in air travel was aggravated by the industry's efforts to increase capacity before achieving an increase in traffic. For the 270 airlines that belonged to the International Air Transport Association (IATA), the first year-to-year decline in traffic since 1991 occurred in 2001, and as air travel decreased, so did profits.

In the aftermath of the September 11, 2001, terrorist attacks, the U.S. airline industry's security measures were scrutinized and were found lacking, especially for domestic flights. The U.S. Congress reacted by creating the Transportation Security Administration (TSA) in late 2001 and was given control of U.S. airport security in 2002. The TSA instituted new security measures at all U.S. airports and by the middle of 2003, all commercial airplanes were required to have more secure cockpit doors. During the time it took for the new doors to be installed on passenger planes, locks and security bars were added to most cockpit doors and movement to and from the cockpit was restricted. U.S. airline pilots tried to get approval to arm themselves with handguns, but the idea was rejected by the TSA in May 2002. According to the chairman of the TSA, "Specially trained air marshals should be the only armed officers on board." Although the number of air marshals flying on U.S. flights was increasing, there may never be a marshal for every flight.

Taking all accident causes into consideration the IATA reported that by the mid-2000s the rate of airline accidents had been reduced more than 50 percent since the mid-1980s. In addition, new aircraft were 75 percent quieter and 70 percent more fuel-efficient than the first commercial jet aircraft. Approximately 1.6 billion passengers and 40 percent of the world's freight was carried by the air transportation industry in the mid-2000s.

Global airline alliances were further strengthened by initiatives like the U.S. open skies agreements that were negotiated beginning in the mid-1990s. These alliances liberalized air traffic with Asia and Oceania, as well as between the United States and South America and Europe. The United States provided an antitrust exemption and a code-sharing clause in those agreements to make them more palatable to other nations. In August 2004, China's Civil Aviation Administration signed an agreement with the U.S. Department of Transportation that had the potential to become an open skies agreement in 2006, adding 14 weekly passenger flights between the two countries.

CURRENT CONDITIONS

At the April 2005 Air Finance Conference in New York, IATA Director General and CEO Giovanni Bisignani

announced that high fuel prices were making the air industry unprofitable. "The fuel bill has risen from US$44 billion in 2003 [to] US$63 billion last year. If oil averages at US$43 per barrel for 2005, the bill will be US$76 billion. And that would leave us with an industry loss of US$5.5 billion for 2005 and over US$40 billion for the period of 2001 to 2005," said Bisignani. He further stated that labor costs, which were extremely difficult to reduce, accounted for 18 and 38 percent of operating costs in Asia and the United States, respectively. Bisignani indicated the need for the industry to eliminate complex technical processes that did not add value for the consumer, such as e-ticketing that could save the industry US$3 billion per year. The industry was further burdened in the United States by taxes on tickets, which had risen from 7 percent to 26 percent between 1972 and 2004, as well as costs for security measures that had reached US$5.6 billion. According to Bisignani, governments should allow the airline industry to conduct business globally, allowing cross-border capitalization and mergers.

The trend for privatization of airports that had begun in the late 1980s was expected to continue. Short term, long term, and perpetual contracts for designing, financing, owning and operating airport facilities by the private sector were being signed by municipal and state governments. For example, in 2004, Toyko's Narita Airport Authority was privatized, and Hong Kong, Thailand, and India were studying the possibility of privatizing airports.

According to the IATA, passenger traffic had increased 7.3 percent for the year ended February 28, 2005, and all global regions had reported growth. Much of this growth was attributed to economic expansion, intense competition that had driven down airfares, and recovery from the effects of Severe Acute Respiratory Syndrome (SARS) in 2003. Growth in passenger traffic was the strongest in Latin American (13.6 percent), Africa (11.2 percent), and the Middle East (11.1 percent). However, global growth from 2004 to 2008 was expected to be 6 percent annually, with China and India expected to have the highest rates of passenger growth. Growth in the Asia/Pacific region had been slow, partly due to the effects of a devastating earthquake under the Indian Ocean and resulting tsunami on December 26, 2004, that took the lives of at least 126,000 people and left 800,000 homeless in Sumatra, Thailand, Sri Lanka, and India.

In 2005, the industry was still dealing with increased security requirements following the September 11, 2001, terrorist attacks against the United States. While the requirements for strengthened cockpit doors had been met, the list of restricted and banned items allowed in personal belongings carried on by passengers continued to evolve. In addition, the industry was still working to balance data privacy issues with the requirements by many nations to supply passenger data and to streamline and improve baggage screening.

The IATA reported that air cargo had a 6.5 percent annual growth rate by the end of February 2005, with the Middle East showing a 17.6 percent growth rate and Latin America showing a decline of 2.7 percent. Despite the overall growth, rising fuel costs were expected to negate comparable growth in profits. The growth rate for this sector was expected to be 6 percent annually between 2004 and 2008, with China and India expected to have the most rapid growth.

In all, global air traffic overall increased 15 percent in 2004, but hull loss, which monitors air accidents, declined to make the year the safest on record. The goal of the IATA Operational Safety Audit, the first global standard for safety audits, was to increase this decline to 25 percent by 2006. The U.S. Federal Aviation Administration (FAA) was exploring the possibility of reversing its downgrade of the Philippine aviation safety rating in the first quarter of 2009. The downgrade had prevented Philippine-based carriers from expanding into the United States.

In April 2005, thousands watched as the largest passenger jet to date, the Airbus A380, took off for its maiden test flight. In December 2004, Airbus announced that the project was US$1.9 billion over budget. The company, which was owned by Netherlands-based EADS and the U.K.'s BAE Systems, had secured 154 orders by the time of the test flight, although it claimed to need 250 orders to break even. Airbus determined that future growth would come from having large planes that could offer passengers inexpensive seats on flights to major international cities. United States-based rival Boeing had determined that the future was in short-haul flights and decided to concentrate on mid-sized aircraft.

A reduction of 8.1 percent in domestic flights was expected in the fourth quarter of 2008, which translated to a loss of 25 million seats. As people traveled less by air, airports were expected to be less crowded and fares were expected to drop through the 2008 holiday season. In addition, budget cuts and web conferencing had a negative impact on business air travel. Passenger enplanements at 143 U.S. airports were projected to decline 1.6 percent in 2008, 6.8 percent in 2009, and 1.8 percent in 2010. With fewer air passengers, airport growth was predicted to be minimal. Boeing and Airbus received substantial orders from American Airlines and US Airways to replace existing capacity rather than to expand their fleets.

In an attempt to cut costs, the airline industry dropped the 5 percent commission paid by the airlines to travel agents beginning on November 1, 2008. The IATA proposed that passengers pay a transaction fee or service charge directly to the travel agents, some of whom opposed the policy.

RESEARCH AND TECHNOLOGY

In the late 1990s, Boeing Corporation debuted the world's largest twin-engine jet, able to fly 4,000 miles and to carry upwards of 370 passengers. Called the Boeing 777, its engines had the same diameter as the fuselage of a Boeing 737. The 777 was the last new aircraft production design of the twentieth century. The jet cost Boeing US$4 billion to develop and was the largest commercial project for Boeing since the company had introduced the 747 a quarter of a century earlier. Boeing collaborated with United Airlines, American Airlines, Delta, All Nippon Airways, British Airways, Cathay Pacific, Japan Airlines, and Qantas to create 777, which was the first time such an effort was undertaken to design an airplane. The aircraft's design allowed flexibility for passenger seating, galleys, and toilets that could be moved by airline employees to meet the cabin needs of particular routes. The aircraft was also the first to be totally designed by a computer. Design engineers, tooling specialists, and production experts used computer-aided design to pre-assemble a prototype aircraft online. Using this new technology, expensive reworking of the aircraft was virtually eliminated.

In the early 2000s, Boeing began vying with the European consortium Airbus Industrie to build a super jumbo jet capable of flying more than 500 passengers at a time. The increased demand for international travel in the late 1990s, coupled with the shortage of landing spots at crowded airports, especially in Asia, added to the pressure placed on manufacturers to design bigger planes that, by carrying more passengers, would place fewer traffic demands on airports. However, Boeing and other manufacturers did not concentrate on building a next-generation supersonic passenger aircraft, especially after the crash of an Air France Concorde in July 2000 outside Paris that killed 113 people. Officials said they believed a metal strip on the runway from another jet ruptured a tire and sent debris hurtling toward the fuel tank, triggering a fire and a fuel leak. After the crash, all Concordes were grounded for more than 15 months to be revamped for greater safety. A British Airways Concorde was flying its first passenger flight following the crash was on September 11, 2001, and the plane was in the air as the terrorist attacks against the United States began. Economic conditions, increasing maintenance costs, and low passenger numbers combined to end Concorde service in November 2003.

Advances in satellite technology were also making air travel safer, quicker, and more profitable for transatlantic and transpacific carriers. The U.S. military began using global positioning system (GPS) receiver technology in the early 1980s and came to be used to improve commercial air navigation. A satellite navigation system was designed to increase the capacity of airports in Asia, where air travel was increasing faster than in any other part of the world in the late 1990s and early 2000s. Traffic in Asia was expected to double between 1995 and 2005, spurred by the retirement of out-of-date air traffic control systems.

In the late 2000s, GPS systems kept aircraft over the Pacific separated by 60 miles, 12 times the minimum distance required over land. When air traffic is heavy, many flights have to be diverted, which wastes fuel and time. With GPS, airplanes are watched by groups of orbiting satellites, and pilots know the exact location of their own and other aircraft. Using GPS, planes are able to fly the shortest route with increased safety rather than using a predetermined flight path that might be hundreds of miles out of the way. Precision landings are expected to be easier at airports without a full complement of instrumentation or equipment. Flights over China and Russia also became safer and faster. In the United States, a GPS network became fully operational in 1997. The U.S. system was expected to enhance the nation's radar system, helping pilots to land more easily and safely in bad weather and fly direct routes between cities.

The air cargo segment of the airline industry was growing at a faster pace than comparable segments in shipping and railways. At the same time, efforts were underway by the airline industry to improve and increase their cargo sectors to offset the decrease in passengers.

WORKFORCE

In 2002, the air transportation industry employed approximately 559,000 people in the United States. Although pilots and flight attendants had the highest profile in the industry, 34.3 percent of the total number of industry employees were in office and administrative support. Pilots, copilots, and flight engineers made up 11.9 percent of the workforce, and flight attendants accounted for 17.4 percent. The remainder included mechanics, cargo handlers, and cleaning staff. The median annual salary for a pilot in 2002 was US$126,840, while a flight attendant earned a median of US$43,200, and a cargo handler earned US$23,890. CollegeGrad.com predicted a 12 percent increase in salaries between 2002 and 2012, below the 16 percent expected for all industries combined.

In the wake of the terrorist attacks against the United States on September 11, 2001, U.S. military forces, principally National Guard troops, were immediately dispatched to assist existing airport security personnel in their duties. Within several months, however, when strict screening procedures were in place, the military presence in airports became far less visible. Meanwhile, Congress

took the responsibility for airport preflight and security screening from the airlines and placed it with the newly created Transportation Security Agency (TSA). The TSA, with an expected workforce of 35,000 to 40,000 employees, was predicted to be the largest U.S. government agency begun since the 1960s. However, Congress also provided that airlines might be permitted to go back to their previous methods of contracting out screening/security services within three years of the placement of the TSA security inspectors.

A source of contention in the U.S. airline industry is the FAA's 35-year-old policy requiring pilots of commercial aircraft with 30 or more seats to retire once they reach the age of 60. This policy was justified partially by a 1981 National Institutes of Health study that found that the accident rate for pilots older than 60 had an increased accident rate after age 60. Airline pilots, including the Professional Pilots Federation, had challenged the findings, arguing that they have to pass physical examinations every six months to continue flying. Pilots considered the policy to be an age discrimination and civil rights issue because they are the only workers in the United States who are forced to retire upon reaching a certain age. The FAA had been criticized earlier about the policy, but U.S. courts often deferred to the agency to set its own standards. Pilots of small U.S. commuter airlines and the FAA's own pilots are allowed to fly past 60, while Great Britain and other countries have raised age limits from 60 to 65. However, the Airline Pilots Association, the United States' largest pilot union, had supported the FAA's rule since 1980. A spokesperson for that union agreed that 60 was an arbitrary cutoff but said that the early to mid-60s is the appropriate range for mandatory retirement because of the demanding career and lifestyle of a pilot.

Salaries continued to be a hot issue in the industry in the late 2000s. Within days after passenger flights resumed following the terrorist attacks of September 11, 2001, travel traffic dipped significantly, and large airline layoffs followed. This resulted in more decreases in salaries that already had been cut in the previous few years. As a major operating cost of any airline, salaries can represent more than 40 percent of total airline costs. Many of the world's major carriers are unionized, and before deregulation, carriers were willing to let the unions bargain for higher salaries and benefits because they could pass on such higher costs to the flying public as higher fares. Since deregulation, however, many airlines came to realize that they could not operate competitively within such high salary structures, especially when competing against nonunionized regional and discount carriers. The airlines tried to hire new employees at lower rates and have granted stock options and other incentives to existing employees in lieu of higher salaries. In addition, bankruptcy filings have enabled the airlines to renegotiate labor agreements.

In 1994, UAL Corp., parent of United Airlines, sold 55 percent of its stock to company pilots and machinists in exchange for US$4.9 billion in wage and productivity concessions, which made it the United States' largest employee-owned corporation and the largest employee-owned airline worldwide. The buyout of UAL was an alternative to cuts in jobs and operations badly needed to enable the airline to compete with regional low-cost carriers. U.S. government and labor leaders hailed this new level of employee control as evidence of a new spirit of cooperation between management and labor. Employees were given four seats on the company's board of directors. Management was prevented by contract from laying off workers or selling assets that would have a detrimental effect on jobs. In the late 1990s, similar airline/employee agreements were created around the world, including Air France Group, which planned to sell shares to its employees as part of its privatization efforts.

The airline industry remained heavily unionized in some countries in the late 1990s, especially in North America and Europe. Company executives of airlines trying to restructure in deregulated environments have criticized unions, arguing that the unions' inflexibility interfered with the competition and modernization of airlines. Nonetheless, unions continued to play a strong role in the industry as the formation of global airline alliances spurred the move to global unionization. The Star Solidarity Alliance, representing 210,000 workers, formed after multinational airlines teamed up to create the Star Alliance. The International Transport Workers Federation (ITF) then coordinated the Union Solidarity coalition to benefit airline workers worldwide through the sharing of information and strategies.

INDUSTRY LEADERS

AMR Corporation. American Airlines, the largest scheduled passenger airline worldwide, grew from the consolidation of companies owned by the Aviation Corporation (AVCO). AVCO, formed in 1929, had acquired enough small transportation companies by 1930 to form a coast-to-coast network called American Airways. In 1934 American Airways developed a more integrated route system and became American Airlines. By the late 1930s, American had supplanted United as the leading U.S. airline. In May 1982, a plan for reorganization under the newly established AMR Corporation was approved at the American Airlines annual meeting. In 2001 AMR acquired the assets of TWA. With American and regional carriers, American Eagle and American Connection (the largest regional system in the world), AMR managed a total active fleet of more than 1,000 aircraft in 2007. The company

reported 2007 revenues of more than US$22.9 billion and 85,500 employees.

UAL Corporation. United began the first scheduled service in the United States in 1926 as Varney Airlines. Varney, along with Pacific Air Transport and National Air Transport, eventually merged with Boeing Air Transport, which included the Boeing Company and Pratt and Whitney. United Airlines was created as a management company for Boeing's airline division, becoming an independent business when Boeing Air Transport was dissolved. On July 12, 1994, stockholders approved the airline's plan to turn over 53 percent of the company's ownership to its employees in exchange for wage concessions. However, one of the major changes in the reorganization of 2003 was the transfer of company ownership from the employees and the elimination of the employee ownership plan.

United Airlines, a subsidiary of the UAL Corporation, ranked second in the industry, despite its reorganization under bankruptcy protection in 2003. In 2007, the company had sales of US$20.1 billion. United served more than 200 destinations worldwide in approximately 30 countries and two U.S. territories, and reported about 55,000 employees. United Express regional feeder service, operated by independent contractors, had approximately 280 aircraft.

Delta Air Lines Inc. Delta Air Lines was founded in Macon, Georgia in 1924 as Huff-Daland Dusters. The world's first crop-dusting service, Huff-Daland was created to combat a boll weevil infestation of cotton fields. In 1928 C. E. Woolman and two partners bought the company and renamed it Delta Air Service. Their 1952 purchase of Chicago and Southern Airlines made them the fifth largest U.S. airline at the time. Delta began international service to Asia in 1987, and by 1989 international traffic provided 11 percent of their revenues.

Delta had experienced more than its share of turbulence that resulted in a decision to merge with Northwest Airlines. Following a six-month investigation, the U.S. Justice Department approved the merger in 2008, clearing the way for creating the world's largest airline. Regulators reflected that the proposed merger "is likely to produce substantial and credible efficiencies that will benefit U.S. consumers and is not likely to substantially lessen competition." Furthermore, the expected cost savings from combining airport operations, information technologies, and other efficiencies were projected to result in reduced prices for fliers. Both carriers had announced plans to cut jobs in early 2008, but as of June 30, 2008, the airlines had reported a combined total of 85.071 full-time employees. The airlines combined income for 2007 was US$31.7 billion.

Delta reported US$103 million in charges linked to job cuts (US$95 million) and closure of some airport facilities (US$8 million).

Japan Airlines Corp. Japanese Air Lines was formed in 1951 by a group of bankers led by Seijiro Yanagito. The Allies had not permitted the airline to use Japanese flight crews until well after the end of World War II, so the airline leased pilots as well as equipment from Northwest Airlines. In 1953 the airline was reorganized as Japan Air Lines (JAL), with ownership split 50/50 between the government and the public. JAL expanded quickly, covering Asia, Europe, and later the United States. In 1987 the government of Japan sold its stake in the airline to the public, ending nationalization of the air transport industry in Japan and opening overseas routes to JAL's main competitor, All Nippon Airways.

JAL was the product of a late 2004 merger between Japanese Airlines, which had become Japan's leading airline and the country's third largest airline, Japan Air Systems. With 210 destinations in 35 countries, the company posted 2007 revenues of approximately US$19.6 billion and employed more than 53,000 people. Its fleet was estimated to include more than 270 aircraft.

British Airways plc. British Airways (BA) was formed in 1935 as a merger of three private U.K. airlines: Hillman's Airways, Spartan Air Lines, and United Airways. In 1939 the airline was combined with Imperial Airways to form the state-owned British Overseas Airways Corporation (BOAC). In 1972 BOAC was merged with another state airline, British European Airways (BEA), to form British Airways. British Airways, in partnership with Air France, began offering supersonic passenger service on the Concorde in 1976. In 1987 the airline was sold to the public and then purchased British Caledonian, which had been its chief competitor in the United Kingdom. In 2003, British Airways retired its fleet of seven Concordes, citing high maintenance costs, low passenger numbers, and overall economic conditions.

The airline made alliances with airlines in Europe, Asia, and North America to increase traffic and bring down costs. In the early 2000s, British Airways owned 25 percent of US Airways and shared flight codes, frequent-flyer plans, and merged travel lounges, which reduced costs for both companies. By tying bonuses to profit performance, BA retained cost-conscious employees, who helped the airline increase productivity 65 percent since 1985 and cut costs almost US$950 million between 1994 and 1997.

British Airways (BA) earned US$16.7 billion in revenue in 2007, employed 43,501 people to serve approximately 150 destinations in 75 countries, and operated more than 240 aircraft.

Air France–KLM Group. Air France was founded in 1933 through the merger of Air Union, Société Générale de Transport Aerien, Compagnie Internationale de Navigation Aerienne, Air Orient, and Compagnie Aeropostale and was nationalized in 1945. Ranked second in Europe in the global air transportation industry following the merger between Air France and Air France Europe, the company reported US$13.7 billion in 2003 revenue. Headquartered in Paris, it served about 180 destinations with more than 380 aircraft with some routes focused on regional travel. In 1976 Air France began flying supersonic Concorde aircraft from Paris to Dakar to Rio de Janeiro. In 1977 it began offering Concorde service from Paris to New York. The French government owned 99 percent of the company's stock until the late 1990s, it began privatizing it through pilot and employee stock options that diminished the government's share to 44 percent by 2003.

In May 2004, the first international merger of two major European airlines occurred when Air France acquired Dutch airline KLM. The merger was expected to make the company the largest in the world in terms of revenues and the third largest in terms of passenger traffic. Each airline continued to operate separately and KLM remained in Dutch control with 51 percent of it voting rights held by the state and two foundations, which would enable it to retain its foreign landing rights.

Deutsche Lufthansa AG. Deutsche Lufthansa (DLH) was created by the Weimar Republic in 1926 when it merged Deutsche Aero Lloyd and Junkers Luftverkehr. By 1931 DLH was Europe's most comprehensive air route network. Operations ceased after World War II until 1954, when the Allies permitted Deutsche Lufthansa to recapitalize. Lufthansa started small, with only domestic routes, but by 1958 it was had nonstop routes between Germany and New York. Lufthansa gradually expanded its routes to include Cairo, Tokyo, Prague, and other world capitals.

In the early 1990s, the airline faced declining yields, strong competition, and overcapacity in many markets as well as long vacations, high wages, and short workweeks for employees. However, management was able to consolidate many of its subsidiaries and holdings while improving its relationship with labor. An aggressive privatization and restructuring program helped DLH rebound from a 1991 loss of US$300 million to report profits of more than US$300 million in 1996. The government, which in the 1990s was concentrating on reunification with East Germany, did not have the resources to rebuild a failing airline and agreed to a privatization program that reduced government holdings from 52 to 35 percent. The company reduced its costs 15 percent and its employees 17 percent through employee attrition, a new pension plan, responsible labor contracts, new information technologies, and organizational changes resulted in a 31 percent increase in productivity, a modernized fleet, and a reduction in debt.

Contrary to trends followed by many of its competitors, Lufthansa announced plans to slightly increase its flight service for the winter of 2008. The expanded route network would include 194 destinations in 79 countries compared to 188 destinations in winter 2007. A total of 13,402 Lufthansa flights per week would be scheduled compared to 13,272 during same time in 2007.

With US$22 billion in revenue in 2004, Lufthansa was the number three airline in Europe and the number two cargo airline worldwide. The airline reported carrying 50.9 million passengers and 1.7 million tons of cargo and mail with a fleet of 377 aircraft. In March 2005, Lufthansa acquired Swiss International Airlines, which added 80 aircraft to the total fleet.

FedEx Corporation. Founded in 1971 as Federal Express, FedEx was originally conceived in a college term paper. In 1973, the company began service in 25 cities with a fleet of 14 small aircraft. In the mid-1980s, FedEx opened a European hub and generated US$2 billion in one year. In early 2000, FDX diversified into customs brokerage with the purchase of Tower Group International, which eventually formed the core of a new subsidiary, FedEx Trade Networks Inc. The trading unit also provided trade consulting and international transportation and logistics services. In April, FDX changed its name to FedEx Corp., and the core express delivery business took on the moniker FedEx Express.

FedEx specialized in overnight delivery of packages, documents, and heavy freight, and was the top express transportation company worldwide. With 2008 sales of US$38 billion, the company's 290,000 employees handled 3.5 million shipments daily to more than 220 countries and territories, using 675 aircraft to serve airports around the world. Its delivery divisions included FedEx Express, FedEx Ground, FedEx Freight, and FedEx Custom.

In 2008, FedEx took delivery of the first Airbus 380 Freighter, with plans to have nine more of the aircraft by 2011. The plane will be able to carry more than 330,000 pounds (150 metric tons) within 40,000 cubic feet (1,100 cubic meters) and will have a range of 11,100 kilometers (approximately 5,994 nautical miles).

BAA plc. In 2005 BAA, the world's leading airport company, owned and operated seven of the largest airports in the United Kingdom, including Heathrow, the world's busiest international airport. The company also has interest in or management contracts with ten airports outside of the country, and manages the retail operations of U.S.-based Baltimore-Washington International and Boston Logan International airports. The company manages

airport operations as a whole, including passenger and baggage screening, fire services, runways and lighting, catering, parking, and flight information systems. The company was privatized in 1987. By 2004, its earnings were almost US$3.6 billion and it employed 12,533 people. By 2006 when it was acquired by Spanish infrastructure manager Ferrovail, the company reported 15,377 employees.

After the longest public inquiry in the history of British planning, BAA received approval to add a fifth terminal at Heathrow Airport in London, England. Prior to beginning construction, the company was required to build a railhead and steelbar factory to reduce the amount of construction traffic on local roadways. In addition, two rivers had to be diverted. The terminal, which is scheduled to be completed in 2011, will be able to handle an additional 30 million passengers. In April 2005, the company created Global Airport Services to develop and operate duty-free retailing at non-BAA airports.

BIBLIOGRAPHY
"Air Industry Information," 26 April 2005. Available from www.collegegrad.com.
"Airbus A380 Set for Maiden Flight." *BBC News*, U.K. edition, 27 April 2005. Available from news.bbc.co.uk.
"Airport Executives Plead for More Time." *Airwise News*, 23 May 2002. Available from news.airwise.com.
Benjamin, Chantelle. "Global Slowdown Hurts Air Freight Volumes." Available from www.businessday.co.
"China, US Sign Air Traffic Expansion Plan." *Airwise News*, 2 August 2004. Available from news.airwise.com.
Clarke, Emma. "Airline Crisis Stokes Boneyard Boom," 8 October 2008. Available from www.cnn.com.
DeLollis, Barbara, and Barbara Hansen. "Decrease in Flights Troubles the Caribbean." *USA Today*, 27 June 2008.
"Delta to Record $103 Million in Charges." *The Detroit Free Press, 9 June 2008.*
"Domestic Carriers Queue Up to Develop Dedicated Cargo Hubs." *Economic Times*, 29 September 2008. Available from economictimes.indiatimes.com.
Draper, Deborah J., ed. *Business Rankings Annual.* Detroit: Thomson Gale, 2004.
Elliott, Christopher. "5 Reasons to Travel During the Holidays." 8 October 2008. Available from www.cnn.com.
"FAA Issues New Fuel Tank Rules." *Airwise News,* 8 May 2001. Available from news.airwise.com.
"Global Air Traffic Up 20 Percent." *Airwise News,* 28 July 2004. Available from news.airwise.com.
"Hoover's Company Capsules," *Hoover's Online,* 2008. Available from www.hoovers.com.
International Air Transport Association. "Industry Statistics," 2004. Available from www.iata.org.
———. "Press Releases," 2004, 2005. Available from www.iata.org.
"International Trade Statistics," 2003. Available from www.wto.org.
Jordan, Lara Jakes. "Justice Approves Delta-Northwest Airline Merger." 29 October 2008. Available from ap.google.com.
Lavell, Tom, and Steve Rothwell. "Air Berlin Cuts Fleet, China Flights; Shares Slump." *Bloomberg News,* 18 June 2008. Available from www. bloomberg.com.

"Lufthansa Offers Customers Attractive Timetable," 2 October 2008. Available from konzern.lufthansa.com.

"Major Market Profiles (USA, Germany, France, and UK)." *Euromonitor International,* October 2004. Available from www. euromonitor.com.

Maxon, Terry. "DIFW, Other U.S. Airports Likely to see Little Growth in Passengers." *Dallas News,* 7 October 2008. Available from www.dallasnews.com.

Osborn, Graeme. "Freedom to Fly." *Flight International,* 11 March 2003.

"Passengers to Bear the Brunt as Airlines Get Ready to Scrap Travel Agents' Commission." *Indiana Express,* 8 October 2008. Available from www.indianexpress.com.

Putzger, Ian. "US Woes Force Airlines to Focus on Europe." Available from www.cargonewsasia.com.

Sharkey, Joe. "Forecast for Business Jets Eases Off on Exuberance." *The New York Times,* 6 October 2008. Available from www. nytimes.com.

"Soaring Prices Ground Travel," 12 June 2008. Available from www.rollingout.com.

"Some Airlines Will Not Survive Global Financial Crisis: Industry Group," 3 October 2008. Available from ap.google.com.

Tait, Leonie. "US Airlines: Keepin' It Simple." *Euromonitor International,* 10 March 2005. Available from www.euro monitor.com.

"Transportation in Canada 2003: Annual Report," 17 May 2004. Transport Canada. Available from www.tc.gc.ca.

"TSA Chief Rules Out Cockpit Guns." *Airwise News,* 21 May 2002. Available from news.airwise.com.

Ubac, Michael Lim. "RP Expects FAA to Upgrade Safety Rating." *Philippine Daily Inquirer,* 8 October 2008.

U.S. Department of Labor, Bureau of Labor Statistics. 8 October 2008. Available from www.bls.gov.

Yang, John. "Securing the Skies: Secure Cockpits, Air Marshals Still in Future." *ABC News,* 7 February 2002. Available from abcnews.com.

SIC 4311

POSTAL SERVICES

NAICS CODE(S)

4911. The world's postal and package delivery services are performed primarily by government agencies, although similar services are increasingly performed by private sector corporations, sometimes categorized as courier services. (See also **Trucking and Courier Services.**)

INDUSTRY SNAPSHOT

The global postal services industry is one of the largest international networks in the world. According to the Universal Postal Union (UPU), by 2009 some 96 percent of the world had postal service. Organizations with postal services operations—typically governmental bodies, but increasingly, non-public entities—handle billions of mailing items, including letters, packages, bills, and advertising, throughout the world each year. According to the UPU, in 2009 the industry employed 5.5 million people worldwide and handled more than 444 billion letters and parcels annually.

The level of mail volume tends to correlate directly with the overall level of economic activity in a country. Accordingly, a surge in growth within the postal services industry, especially in international mailing, has accompanied the increasing globalization of commerce. Many postal organizations have invested heavily to establish global infrastructures. Moreover, the concentration of this market sector is opening. While industrialized countries still lead this industry, developing countries such as China, India, and Brazil were increasing substantially in the mid- to late 2000s.

Postal services in advanced nations face substantial challenges from competing technologies. Fax machines, electronic mail and messaging systems, electronic funds transfers, Internet-based services and electronic commerce, and other communications technologies have sliced into traditional postal business. In a few regions, these technologies are still in their infancy but guarantee increased competition in the near future. However, within the United States, these technological advances are cutting a wide swath through the U.S. Postal Service (USPS) business.

In an Associated Press story from November 2010 the USPS reported a loss of US$8.5 billion in 2009, even following dramatic steps to stem the financial loss, including cutting over 105,000 full time jobs. The USPS reported income of US$67.1 billion for the fiscal 2009 year ending September 30, but total expenses exceeded US$70 billion, with the service required to post a US$5.5 billion payment for future retiree health benefits. The blame is two-fold, with a slumping economy that has impacted postal systems worldwide, but the main contributor to this decline was the increased volume of Internet use for every day communication and business transactions. First-class mail, consisting of letters and cards, as well as bills, payments, and like items, which had produced more than half of the postal revenue, had fallen sharply during the last half of the first decade of the 2000s. In 2008, there was a 4.8 percent decline, followed by an 8.6 percent decline in 2009, and an additional 6.6 percent drop by 2010.

Postmaster General John Potter, retiring at the end of 2010, had created a 10-year recovery plan for the U.S. postal system, including moving to a five-day work schedule. However, parts of the plan require action and approval by Congress and the president.

ORGANIZATION AND STRUCTURE

Postal facilities range from enormous processing centers that handle several million items a day and employ thousands of

Postal Workers Worldwide

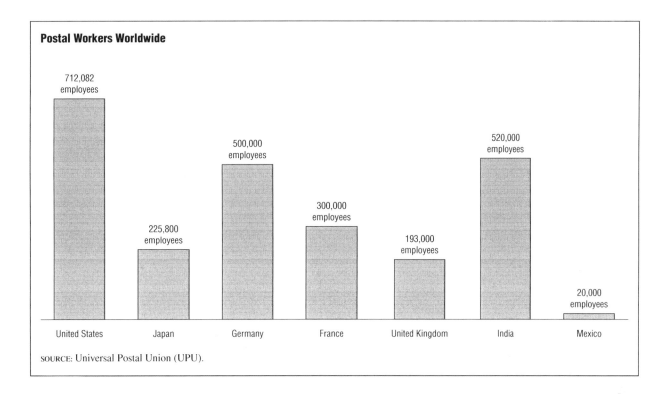

712,082
employees

500,000
employees

520,000
employees

300,000
employees

225,800
employees

193,000
employees

20,000
employees

United States   Japan   Germany   France   United Kingdom   India   Mexico

SOURCE: Universal Postal Union (UPU).

people to small kiosks with one part-time employee. The efficient management of postal operations in countries like the United States and Germany requires the organization of large transport fleets, extensive property management, the supervision of hundreds of thousands of employees, and the implementation and maintenance of advanced information technologies.

Some governmental postal organizations, like the United States Postal Service (USPS), are required by law to break even financially, so they use their so-called profits as an impetus to implement new technologies and improve overall service. Typical measurements used to determine a postal administration's service level include the percentage of on-time deliveries, customer surveys, and the balance sheet. Because labor and transportation expenses constitute the bulk of a postal operation's operating costs, the search for labor-cutting technologies and efficiency management has been among the top priorities of postal service companies and agencies worldwide.

The three basic components of postal delivery services are letters, parcels, and express. Letters are distinguished from parcels either by weight (documents) or by contents (goods). Express service includes both letters and parcels and is characterized by speed of delivery. Postal administrators generally have a monopoly on letter services, while parcel and express services are offered in competition with private carriers. The production process for postal services can be divided into five stages: collection, sorting for destinations, transportation, final sorting, and delivery of mail.

Postal administrators also offer financial services, which can be categorized as postal payment, such as money orders and postal orders; girobank, including mortgage and foreign currency; savings bank; and other payments such as pensions, welfare services, licenses, and taxation. In some cases, postal administrators historically also have had authority over the telecommunications sector in their nations, but many industrialized countries were reorganizing their telecommunications services into separate entities in the early twenty-first century.

Universal Postal Union. An enterprise as important and complex as the exchange of international mail requires a broad framework of rules and regulations among nations. In the mid-nineteenth century, most large European countries signed at least a dozen individual treaties for foreign mail. Given different currencies and units of measurement, these agreements required detailed accounts that were extraordinarily elaborate and perplexing. At one point there were more than 1,200 different postal rates in effect in Europe.

In 1863 a conference held in Paris to standardize those agreements was attended by 15 European and U.S. postal administrations. However, it became obvious that bilateral treaties between individual countries would not work and that a single treaty governing the international post was needed. In 1874 the representatives of 22 postal administrations met in Switzerland and signed the Treaty of Berne. Initially known as the General Postal Union, this international collaboration was renamed the Universal Postal

Union (UPU) in 1878. It has retained this name into the twenty-first century.

By 2010, some 191 nations belonged to the UPU, which on July 1, 1948, became a specialized agency of the United Nations (UN). Any UN member state can belong to the UPU, which is funded through member contributions according to a variegated rate scale. Other sovereign states not belonging to the United Nations can join the UPU if at least two-thirds of the UPU member states assent. The UPU works together with other UN agencies and international organizations in order to carry out its objectives. Governed by the Universal Postal Congress, which performs legislative functions, and by two councils, the Postal Operations Council and the Council of Administration, the UPU set a strategic plan for 2000 to 2004. Approved by the Universal Postal Congress and known as the Beijing Postal Strategy, the plan's main objectives, in summary:

- To ensure customers' global postal access for goods and messages;

- To make delivery services more reliable, secure, and efficient;

- To become more cost effective;

- To respond better to postal customers;

- To integrate technological, regulatory, and economic changes by reforming and developing postal services; and,

- To increase collaboration among postal stakeholders.

In 2009 the countries of the UPU had more than 660,000 postal outlets and collectively delivered 438 billion pieces of mail in the letter classification per year. In addition, the UPU reported that it processes 6 billion parcels annually.

About two-thirds of national post offices worldwide also offered financial services, with over half offering savings bank options as well as checking, bill-pay centers, and mortgage and insurance centers. The UPU has a formal agreement to cooperate with the World Savings Bank Institute (WSBI). In situations where natural catastrophes or armed conflict have disrupted normal social life, including regular mail delivery services, the UPU assists by setting up humanitarian services and short-term arrangements to reconnect broken postal links.

In accordance with its mandate, the UPU was to create a single domain for exchanging postal items and for unobstructed freedom of transit within that domain. Each UPU member country has pledged to respect the inviolability of mail in transit and to convey it by the most rapid means of transport used for its own domestic mail delivery. UPU rules govern weight specifications, size limits, and conditions of acceptance for international mail. Historically, the UPU also standardized the basic rates that member countries could charge for delivering

postal items within the UPU's territory. Over the years, however, its stated rates have been used as guidelines rather than fixed rules, and postal administrators have had increased freedom to set rates for international mail.

The UPU also provides technical assistance for the modernization of postal administrations, especially those in the least developed nations. Aid includes recruiting and dispatching experts, granting vocational fellowships, and setting up national training schools for postal workers and management. Funding comes from both the UPU budget and the contributions of developed nations. The UPU has also promoted stamp collecting through the promulgation of a code of ethics and a variety of other activities, including philatelic studies and the dispatch of stamp experts to postal administrations.

In 2006, approximately five years after establishing the Quality of Service Fund (QSF), UPU tapped into that fund to underwrite 279 projects. Those projects were focused on improving postal services in developing and least advanced countries with estimated costs of US$39.6 million. The UPU annual budget was approximately US$29 million, 60 percent of which was earmarked for projects in developing countries. Although most projects focused on one country, the QSF also had financed 13 regional projects allowing countries to pool their resources.

On March 8, 2007, Thomas Gallagher reported in *Traffic World* that the International Air Transport Association and UPU had agreed to collaborate on ways to "harmonize standards and procedures to improve coordination between airlines, postal administrations and third party handlers to pave the way for consistent and accurate reporting of mail movement status." Both groups also agreed to expand their usage of Electronic Data Interchange.

BACKGROUND AND DEVELOPMENT

The ancient Romans developed a highly efficient postal system, known as the *cursus publicus,* that served and connected far-flung territorial holdings. Relay stations were placed at frequent intervals along the empire's roads, and men, chariots, and about 40 horses were kept at each station. According to some accounts, the messengers of these relay systems were so efficient that they could cover more than 170 miles in 24 hours—a speed not achieved again in Europe until the nineteenth century. After the collapse of the Roman Empire in the fifth century, this postal system decayed.

Relay systems with post houses were first developed in China around 1000 B.C. and were also used extensively in the Americas by the Mayan and Incan civilizations. When Marco Polo visited China in the thirteenth century, he found a postal system far in advance of anything Europe had at the time. According to Polo's account, 10,000 post houses existed in China, with one placed every 25 to 30 miles. Besides numerous horsemen, foot runners lived in villages three miles apart. They wore girdles hung with bells to alert the relay runner waiting at the next station.

Increases in literacy during the European Renaissance and the invention of Gutenberg's printing press in 1450 gave new momentum to the creation of more widespread and more complex postal services. The trend toward more powerful nation-states, however, resulted in government-run systems that eventually displaced private carriers. In 1477, Louis XI set up a Royal Postal Service in France that employed 230 mounted couriers. In England, Henry VIII created a Master of the Posts position to maintain regular postal service along the main roads from London in 1516. Initially, these state-run services only served the government. Before long, however, the revenue-producing potential of postal services for public use was recognized.

Although states sought to keep their postal monopolies, keen entrepreneurs nevertheless found opportunities to introduce services that governments were not providing. As letter-carrying became profitable, private businesses sprang up to exploit the market. Most postal businesses were purely local, although some, like that of the Parr family in Austria, created nationwide enterprises. Under the patronage of the Habsburg Empire, the Taxis family built up the most famous, most extensive system. Their service grew throughout the sixteenth century until it covered most of Europe and employed nearly 20,000 couriers. The Taxis service lasted until the late nineteenth century in Germany.

In 1680, William Dockwra established a postal service in England that was more efficient than that of many cities in the twenty-first century. He opened 450 receiving stations in different parts of London, and messengers called for mail every hour. Letters and packages were carried to sorting offices, and the hour of receipt and initial letter of the sorting office was stamped on each piece of mail. According to one account, as many as 12 deliveries were made each day in business districts, and four to eight daily deliveries were made in residential areas, resulting in huge demand. Two years later, however, the government sued Dockwra for infringing on the state monopoly and closed down his service, only to reopen it later, but with no compensation to Dockwra.

The early nineteenth century publication in Great Britain of *Post Office Reform: Its Importance and Practicability* by Rowland Hill was a milestone in postal history. Hill's study demonstrated two crucial points: (1) the intricate rate system in place inflated costs by requiring huge amounts of paperwork and staff, and (2) the collection of money payments on delivery, another enormous cost, could be eliminated. Hill recommended that a uniform postage rate be instituted at a penny for each half-ounce,

with a minimum of four pence. Furthermore, rather than have the addressee pay the cost upon delivery, the sender would be responsible for prepaying the cost by attaching postage stamps. The wisdom of Hill's proposals was quickly grasped, and his reforms were introduced into the British postal system in 1840. Hill's ideas quickly spread to other countries, and both Switzerland and Brazil began issuing postage stamps in 1843. Hill was knighted for his efforts.

The advances in transportation technology that took place in the nineteenth and twentieth centuries profoundly impacted postal systems worldwide. As rail services became widespread, specially adapted railway cars became moving post offices for sorting and canceling stamps, thus greatly accelerating mail delivery. Regular airmail flights began in the United States in 1918, and the first regular international service, between Paris and London, was inaugurated a year later.

In many countries, post offices offer financial services to the public, often to the chagrin of private competitors. Until the early 1990s, many commercial banks ignored the threat of post office banks. However, when post offices started promoting financial services more aggressively, finding new customers and luring customers away from banks, their attitudes changed. Post office managers invested in financial service operations to make up for lost revenues in mail-handling and telecommunications services, which slowly were being opened to competition, and to replace revenues lost in the worldwide transition to such technological innovations as electronic mail (e-mail), electronic bill-paying services, electronic funds transfers (EFTs), and e-commerce. Profitable financial services offered through post offices, however, garnered considerable criticism from the private sector in some parts of the world. Private bankers have protested that in many countries, postal groups are subsidized by governments and thus pose unfair competition.

By the end of the twentieth century, the most crucial issues for national post offices included privatization and growing competition from privately owned postal delivery services, such as United Parcel Service (UPS), Federal Express (FedEx), DHL Worldwide Express, and Airborne Express. Many industry analysts noted that commercial pressures had caused a liberalization of the international mail market. At the end of the twentieth century, many public sector postal organizations were considering or actively shifting segments of their business to the private sector to more easily stave off competition from their private counterparts. However, while the European Union tried to usher its member states toward a more competitive industry, many nations appeared to be succeeding in slowing privatization efforts in order to avoid breaking up their post office monopolies. Nonetheless, given the enormous growth potential identified in this sector, the struggle for dominance among private postal corporations and their governmental counterparts continued to characterize the industry in the early years of the twenty-first century.

The opposition of national post offices to greater competition was evident in actions taken by various government-supported postal services against private remailers. Remailers' services make economic sense when, for example, cost or quality considerations make posting mail to Holland from France rather than from Germany more cost and/or time-effective. For instance, a remailer could ship mail from Germany to Holland in bulk, thus avoiding German postal charges, and then post all of the mail in France. State post offices tried to use the rules of the UPU to justify turning back incoming mail from remailers. The German Bundespost went further, claiming that a letter with a return address in Germany would have to be posted in Germany. Most governmental postal administrations, however, recognized the increasingly competitive atmosphere as an irreversible trend and took steps to diversify their services to regain market share previously lost to private competitors and increasing their own competitive standing.

Postal administrations at the start of the twenty-first century continued to face problems of competition from the private sector despite attempts by some government postal services to reorganize and, in some cases, to operate independently of the public treasury. The United States Postal Service (USPS) situation exemplifies the constraints post offices may operate under as they attempt to separate from federal government control and function more autonomously. In 1970 the U.S. Congress abolished the Post Office Department through the Postal Reorganization Act and simultaneously established the USPS, which began operations on July 1, 1971. However, Congress left in place a host of regulatory and legislative restrictions. A Postal Rate Commission reviews prices and retains full power to rule on any postal rate increase. The USPS was subject to vociferous Congressional opposition to post office closures and to the political power of hundreds of thousands of active and retired postal employees. Additionally, under the 1970 legislation, the USPS was required to continue to provide universal service by not allowing any one class of mail or group of customers to subsidize another. However, the USPS has fully taken advantage of subsequent legislation that has allowed the it to enter into joint ventures, and has agreements with postal operations in a wide range of countries, including Brazil, Chile, Mexico, Canada, the United Kingdom, China, and Japan.

In a concerted effort to update operations to meet increased competition presented by new technologies, many postal administrations have attempted to gain an edge on the market by engaging in cooperative arrangements with businesses outside the postal industry. The USPS, for example, made a landmark agreement at the beginning of the twenty-first century with Federal Express, one of its largest private competitors, by teaming up with FedEx to offer more streamlined express mail services with time-guaranteed deliveries. The service started in March 2001 in Charlotte, North Carolina. In 1997 the United Kingdom's Royal Mail, the letter division of the U.K. Post Office, entered into a joint venture with Microsoft Corporation to provide electronic mail service to its customers. The Dutch postal and telecommunications group, Koninklijke PTT Nederland, acquired TNT Express Worldwide, highlighting a trend that industry analysts expected to continue in the 2010s as European post offices merged with logistics companies.

Moreover, in order to combat intense competition, many national post offices have seriously considered privatization. The United Kingdom's Post Office, one of the nation's largest employers, was the subject of privatization considerations for several years. After planning to sell substantial portions of Royal Mail and Parcelforce in the late 1990s, the British government decided that its postal operations would remain in the public sector. Germany, in contrast, went ahead with plans to privatize its postal bank, Deutsche Postbank. Switzerland's postal services implemented a major diversification strategy and heavily diversified its financial services at the close of the twentieth century. In Italy, the postal administration, which employed 200,000 at the end of the 1990s but was viewed as one of Europe's least efficiently run postal services, prepared for a major transformation of its organizational structure by becoming a joint stock company. Industry analysts expected the trend toward privatization would increasingly affect postal services throughout the developed world.

CURRENT CONDITIONS

According to the UPU, in 2003 some 96 percent of the world had postal service, with 81 percent receiving their mail at home and 15 percent having to collect their mail from a postal outlet. The remaining 4 percent without service were located primarily in Africa. By 2009, domestically, 177 billion pieces of mail were processed annually with 584 million pieces processed each day. Globally, there were 438 billion pieces of mail processed. There were an estimated 6 billion parcels processed globally in 2009.

Since the end of the 1980s, most postal services have been decreasing their number of outlets, resulting in a 15 percent decline in the total number of outlets. In spite of the worst economic slump since the Great Depression, the UPU reported that mail and express service was rebounding. In 2008, global postal revenue reached US$324 billion, a sizable increase from US$265 billion reported in 2003. By 2009, there were approximately 660,000 post offices around the world and approximately 5.5 million employees, according to the UPU.

Increasingly, postal operators have been expanding their product offerings to include logistics services; hybrid mail, where e-mail messages are sent to the postal outlet, printed, and delivered to the recipient; and online services, including e-mail, e-commerce, and e-banking. Competition from new technologies was expected to continue, with the use of e-mail and cellular phone use and its related text messaging capabilities on the increase. Many postal organizations were also offering a variety of government-related services. Italy's Poste Italiane, for example, was using its customer access to offer passport application and immigration application services. Poste Italiane was reportedly the first European postal service to sell postage via the Internet. With approximately 14,000 branches by 2009, the USPS announced plans to offer mobile phones and Poste Italiane-branded products in addition to its own calling plans and services on the Vodafone network. It was similar to another Vodafone deal in Italy with French retailer Carrefour. In the United Kingdom, customers could pay their utility bills, purchase foreign currency, renew their car licenses, and purchase a variety of gifts and stationary at their local post office. Many U.K. post offices are also the local shop for newspapers, bread, and milk.

Although the handling of mail was still predominantly monopolized by governments by 2005, regulations were changing to allow competition. For example, member countries of the European Union were scheduled to end their monopolies by 2009, allowing private carriers to enter the market by handling increasingly smaller postal weights. According to the UPU, by 2003 some 94 percent of its member countries faced competition from non-public entities. In terms of domestic service, 80 percent competed with letter mail, while 85 percent competed with parcel mail. The numbers were higher in terms of international mail, with 85 percent facing competition from letter mail and 90 percent from parcel mail. Many postal organizations were forming alliances with courier companies. For example, the USPS signed an agreement with FedEx, giving the latter responsibility for handling air transport of mail, replacing the services offered by commercial airlines. FedEx's existing market knowledge and infrastructure offered advantages to both parties. FedEx also had shipping agreements with France's La Poste, and the Trinidad and Tobago Postal Corporation.

In the international mail market, industry participants expected the most growth into 2008 to occur in Europe and the Commonwealth of Independent States (CIS), countries of the former USSR. Many analysts believed that China represented the greatest potential market for postal administrations as a result of the country's massive population, rapid modernization, emergence as a formidable economic

power, and reacquisition of the business center Hong Kong. China offered a lucrative potential market to the world's postal organizations. Accordingly, many major international companies were continuing to invest in the Asian-Pacific region. UPS was overhauling its infrastructure in an effort to strengthen its operations, while DHL Worldwide Express was expecting service increases of about 30 percent annually, and TNT Express Worldwide was purchasing transportation networks.

RESEARCH AND TECHNOLOGY

Perhaps the best way to understand the role of technology in postal operations is to follow a letter from pickup to final delivery in a highly automated postal system. In the advanced Canadian system, the process included the following steps:

- *Receiving*—Mail is picked up from letter boxes and unloaded at the receiving dock of the nearest mail processing plant.

- *Preparing*—Bags are opened and unloaded. Any undersized, oversized, or irregular items are segregated from standard letters.

- *Canceling*—At the processing plant, a canceller automatically faces the letter mail and cancels it with a date stamp.

- *Encoding*—A multi-line optical character reader (MLOCR) scans the postal code and compares it with the address to determine whether the code is accurate. An optical character reader (OCR) reads postal codes that are typed or laser printed. The MLOCR or OCR then applies vertical barcodes used to separate letters into sorting bins.

In some plants, if the MLOCR cannot read a postal code, a video encoding system (VES) identifier barcode is printed on the back. The image of the front is sent to a video-coding desk where a coder types in the postal code, which is stored in memory, and the letter is fed once more into the MLOCR. The MLOCR matches the stored postal code with the VES identifier bar, and the correct barcodes are printed on the front.

- *Consolidation*—The mail is consolidated for shipping to the downstream (processing for delivery) plants.

- *Dispatching*—Mail going outside an area is transported via trucks, vessels, or airlines to the appropriate mail processing location.

- *Receiving*—Mail is received at the downstream plant, primarily in containers inside larger bins from the originating plants.

- *Preparing*—Incoming mail from the originating plants is grouped by delivery areas.

- *Sorting*—The letter sorting machine reads the bar codes supplied by the MLOCR and OCR. The machine directs each letter to one of many destination bins.

- *Dispatching*—Mail is dispatched to stations and letter carrier deposits.

- *Delivery*—Mail is delivered by letter carriers or via community mail centers, postal boxes, rural mail boxes, or general delivery.

Because postal service has traditionally required so many workers, introducing labor-saving technology is the key to implementing efficiencies and controlling costs. Since most USPS expenditures go toward labor costs, automating the mailing process has been a major priority in the United States. Most emerging technologies are in the electronics field. For example, by the late 1990s the USPS had developed a postal machine that could read up to 30 percent of handwritten addresses on envelopes, with an projected success rate of 100 percent shortly thereafter. At the time this project was the driving force of a US$4 billion automation program that was aimed at eliminating thousands of letter-sorting jobs. The USPS, Canada, and France also participated in a cooperative agreement to test a new global electronic courier service, PostECS, which was anticipated to ensure the security of official documents transmitted over the Internet. To follow and trace mail through every step of its processing and delivery, post offices began using tiny radio transmitters, or tags, affixed to pieces of mail. In addition to these innovations, postal administrations have incorporated electronic certification, authentication, encryption, and even electronic postmarks into their already highly automated systems and procedures.

Even before the anthrax scare struck the United States, Britain, and Pakistan in the closing months of 2001, the U.S. Mailing Industry Task Force, representing both public and private mailing enterprises, including the USPS, advanced several recommendations to improve security in the industry. These included the recommendation to create "intelligent mail," whereby "a unique, digital stamp for each piece of mail would make it possible to track and trace mail," according to the USPS's 2001 annual report.

With the world's major courier companies able to track packages through their systems, customers increasingly demanded a method of tracking and tracing letter mail sent by regular post. The USPS created the CONFIRM system in which mailers include two bar codes on their mail which then allow the customer to track where the mail is in the system.

The Centre of Enterprises with Public Participation (CEEP) expressed concern about the progress of European countries toward full liberalization. CEEP requested that the European Parliament and the Council guarantee "sustainable funding" along with its postal services directive based on the European Commission's October 2006 proposal. CEEP referenced a 120-page study conducted by Oxford-based consultancy OXERA and funded by nine public postal operators on universal service funding mechanisms in the postal sector. The study pointed to several regulatory policy questions that needed to be addressed before the market was fully liberalized.

WORKFORCE

Having reached its peak at the start of the 1990s, the number of people employed globally by the postal service declined almost 20 percent by 2003, from a high of 6.2 million employees to 5 million employees. By 2010, there were 5.5 million postal employees worldwide processing 438 billion letters annually.

Around the world, labor-management relations have plagued the postal services industry and generated significant negative publicity. In January 2005, French postal workers walked out to protest the opening of the system to outside competition. In November 2004, postal workers in Belgium and Italy took part in a general strike to protest their governments' economic policies. The emphasis on higher productivity and cost saving has not helped labor-management relations in the postal services of many developed countries, including the United States where the USPS in 2003 employed more than 729,000 persons. The main U.S. postal unions have complained of increasingly poor working conditions. In the late 1990s, some employees reported being overloaded with tasks during their regular working hours but then being harassed working overtime. By the beginning of the twenty-first century, U.S. postal workers had filed more than 100,000 grievances against the USPS. Workers also complained of physical hardships. Letter sorting operators, for example, complained that typing ZIP codes of several digits at a rate of one per second for 45 minutes without a break led to carpal tunnel syndrome.

Some critics of the U.S. postal unions, however, maintained that U.S. postal workers were coddled. Under civil service rules, as many as five years could pass before a worker would be fired, even for just cause. Major mailers, angered with increasingly high postal rates, charged that even where automation had eliminated the need for workers, redundant workers remained on the job, doing very little. Post office supervisors, charged with keeping mail flowing, claimed that some postal workers would call in sick to avoid putting in a day's work.

Labor-management friction, combined with the often hectic atmosphere of postal operations, was more serious, leading to the seemingly ubiquitous threat of physical violence in the workplace, which sometimes proved fatal. A rash of shootings at post offices in the United States in the 1990s perpetuated existing fears of workplace violence and generated substantial negative publicity for the U.S. postal industry, including the caricaturing of disgruntled postal workers. However, statistically speaking, postal employees were at no greater risk of exhibiting violent behavior, which some referred to as "going postal," than employees in other jobs in the United States. Recognizing the harmful effects of such an atmosphere on both a tangible and a financial level, postal administrators have tried diligently to improve labor-management relations.

MAJOR COUNTRIES IN THE INDUSTRY

The United States. The U.S. mailing industry is a significant part of the nation's infrastructure and economy. According to the UPU, the industry employed 712,082 people in 2009. Operating income was down US$3.8 billion in 2009, partly due to a failing economy and the obligatory pre-funding of pension and healthcare liabilities through 2017. About 177 billion pieces of mail are delivered to more than 150 million addresses annually. While the number of addresses increase annually (900,000 between 2008 and 2009), the amount delivered per person is on a steady decline. The quasi-independent USPS, successor to the former government-run Postal Department, delivered more than 46 percent of the world's mail volume in 2004, employing more than 707,000 people. By 2009, the USPS had revenues of US$68.09 billion and had delivered more than 177 billion pieces of mail to more than 150 million addresses in 2010.

The USPS also faced significant threats and challenges. Shortly after the September 11, 2001, terrorist attacks against the United States, the USPS was hit by the potentially devastating threat posed by several anthrax-laced or anthrax-containing letters sent through the public mail system. Two postal employees died of anthrax infections and several others were contaminated with the deadly virus. In response, the USPS had to rapidly mount a campaign in which at least nine anthrax-contaminated postal units and branches were temporarily closed, decontaminated, and later reopened; 267 postal hub facilities linked to the Washington, D.C., and Trenton, New Jersey, mail-processing facilities where anthrax was discovered were tested and retested; about 16,000 postal employees in New York, New Jersey, Florida, and Washington, D.C., who were potentially exposed to the anthrax virus, were tested for anthrax infection and given prophylactic antibiotics; all postal employees were offered flu injections, since early symptoms of anthrax closely resemble those of the flu; and special security measures were put in place to

detect the presence of biochemical contaminants in the mail-processing system and to irradiate and sanitize mail.

The emergency response to the anthrax scare, the USPS's endeavors to prevent future anthrax attacks, and the necessity of rebuilding postal facilities and assets destroyed at or near the World Trade Center site would cost unanticipated millions of dollars, prompting the USPS to request a special allocation from the U.S. Congress in early 2002 to help offset these extraordinary expenses. In addition, the USPS expected that an increase in the cost of first-class postage would be required to help balance its books. In March 2002 the decision was officially made to raise the price of a first-class stamp from 34 cents to 37 cents (US$0.34 to US$0.37), a change that would go into effect a few months later. Nevertheless, the national recession that began around the time of the September 11 terrorist attacks, coupled with a significant drop in mailing volumes after the start of the anthrax attacks (and an associated 6.6 percent decrease in U.S. postal revenues for September and an 8 percent to 10 percent decrease for October, according to Union Network International), contributed to a loss of income for the USPS of US$1.7 billion for the fiscal year ending September 30, 2001.

Despite the major challenges it faced, the USPS continued to be one of the world's largest mailing operations in 2010. The organization ran 36,400 postal outlets that processed 177 billion pieces of mail. It is the second largest civilian employer in the United States (excluding the federal government) behind Wal-Mart.

Legislation passed by the U.S. Congress that has significantly impacted postal operations in the United States and around the world included annual allocations from the U.S. federal government to the Postal Service Fund to pay for free and reduced-rate mail. In 2001 this totaled US$96 million, including US$67 million to cover the costs of free mail for the blind and for U.S. voters living overseas. In 2003, there were 56.8 million pieces of free mail for the blind and handicapped out of a total 424.9 million pieces of mail. In 2004, industry analysts pointed out that substantial rate increases were necessary because the USPS was legally required to financially break at worst, which it had not done for the first three years of the decade. Increased competition from the US$20 million Internet postal industry, of which Stamps.com was the clear market leader, was another challenge for the USPS.

In July 2006, USPS announced plans to establish a "Global Business" unit. This came at a time when private and public sector leaders were working together more and more to meet postal industry demands. The global business focus brings all international postal efforts into one unit covering operations, transportation, finance, planning, information technology, account management, and postal relations. Related predictions called for an increase of its US$1.9 billion annual share of the international shipping market. USPS Vice President of Network Operations Management Paul Vogel was named as the head of the new unit. Vogel was already involved with USPS effort to release international and military air mail rates from the Department of Transportation, which allegedly were much higher than they would be if the USPS could bid out related shipments in the same manner it does for domestic mail.

Northrop Grumman received a US$874.6 million fixed-price contract from USPS to provide 100 Flats Sequencing Systems (FSS). The FSS were designed to advance automating the flats mail stream. That stream included large envelopes, catalogs, and magazines. FSS production units at were set to be in operation beginning in 2008, with the remaining installations to be completed by 2010.

The USPS also entered a long-term contract with United Airlines for the transportation of domestic mail from the spring of 2007 through September 30, 2011. Among passenger carriers, United Airlines was already ranked as the number-one carrier of international mail.

In addition, the USPS agreed to combine its eight primary international mail offerings into four categories familiar to U.S. customers. Beginning May 14, 2007, U.S. customers would be able to utilize Priority Mail and Express Mail packaging for items with foreign and domestic destinations. These products were named Express Mail International, Priority Mail International, and First-Class Mail International. The premium international service continued to be known as Global Express Guaranteed.

USPS officials told its Board of Governors about plans to have one technology capable of continuously tracking mail and providing customers with feedback by 2011. The "Intelligent Mail" system would rely on one standardized intelligent 65-bar code used on each piece or container of mail. The technology would make it possible for business customers to monitor the progress of mail as it moved from arrival at a postal facility to delivery at its destination. Related tasks would be automated for optimal service.

The USPS announced that all of its Priority and Express Mail packages were made of 100 percent recyclable paper. This impacted the approximately 500 million packages were used each year, with an estimated value of US$6 billion. Related changes in processes and practices called for rewriting contracts with approximately 200 suppliers requiring they revise composition of paper provided to USPS. New packages reportedly included 60 separate material components and 1,400 individual ingredients.

As part of its effort to offer convenient service options for its customers, USPS contracted with private operators offering hours that expanded service opportunities. Controversy arose related to the USPS decision to let Full

Gospel Interdenominational Church in Manchester, New Hampshire, operate a "Sincerely Yours Inc." outlet as the only post office in the downtown area. U.S. District Court Judge Dominic J. Squatrito ruled that religious displays in area where postal products were sold inappropriately endorsed Christianity and recruited outsiders to join the church in advancing its mission. It was deemed inappropriate for the church to exhibit religious items while conducting duties for the USPS or U.S. government.

A price increase took effect in May 2007 for stamps and other products. A "Forever Stamp" was introduced that could be used forever on first-class mail letters even if postage increases occurred in the future. The stamps were priced at 41 cents (US$0.41) each. By 2010, stamps for first-class mail cost 44 cents (US$0.44). A request by the USPS to increase the cost of a first-class stamp in 2011 was rejected by the Postal Regulatory Commission on the basis that the USPS could not justify the requested increase.

Germany. The postal and telecommunications system in Germany was completely reorganized in the early 1990s, and by the late 1990s the *Postdienst* postal service enterprise was operating as its own public enterprise. *Postdienst* further poised itself for enormous international expansion by acquiring the world's leading express delivery company in terms of cross-border deliveries, DHL Worldwide Express, just before the turn of the century. The German postal service Deutsch Post AG, which also was the largest postal service provider in Europe as of 2009, reported US$82.85 billion in revenues and employed more than 500,000 people worldwide. They deliver approximately 70 million pieces of mail throughout Germany six days a week.

France. The second ranked postal operator in Europe, and third worldwide, France's La Poste is a public enterprise under autonomous management. In 2002, the company handled 25 billion domestic letters and more than 1 billion international letters 2002. La Poste reported US$28.36 billion in revenue in 2008 with over 300,000 employees, making it France's second largest employer. In 2006, the European Commission recommended that France end the unlimited guarantee given to La Poste in its capacity as a public body by the end of 2008. Such a move would be part of its monitoring of existing state aid schemes under the EC Treaty. The unlimited guarantee gave La Poste an advantage over its competitors when obtaining financing, while distorting competition for a market in the process of becoming liberalized.

United Kingdom. Royal Mail Holdings of the United Kingdom became a public limited company owned by the British government in 2001, operating under the brand names Royal Mail, Post Office, and ParceForce Worldwide.

One of the United Kingdom's leading businesses, Royal Mail employed nearly 193,000 workers in 2009 and had sales of approximately US$6.2 billion. By 2009, the organization was processing 79 million items each day. The company has a market share of 90 percent, and the remaining 10 percent is privately owned. Parcelforce Worldwide was the United Kingdom's leading carrier of time-critical packages. By 2006, it was estimated that Royal Mail delivered more than 2 billion letters on behalf of their competition under deals allowing private companies to collect, sort, and hand mail to Royal Mail for delivery. The business market was believed to hold most promise for growth where 10 customers accounted for 20 percent of total market and 100 for 40 percent of that market. Non-postal services provided by Royal Mail include home and auto insurance, savings accounts, mortgages, and broadband and phone services, as well as passport and tax services.

India. In the developing world, India has one of the largest volume mail services, although it was showing dramatic declines in volume. Domestic letter volume dropped from 13.6 billion items in 2001 to 8.7 billion items in 2003. By 2009, India Post had more than 155,000 post offices serving 1.3 billion citizens. India Post claims to be the largest postal system worldwide, with more than 520,000 employees.

In 2006, India Post announced plans for incorporating a "one-stop-shop" approach enabling customers to make all of their routine bill payments, including service tax and road tax. After achieving success as a collection point for citizens filing income tax returns, India Post planned to enhance its offerings of information access and other services to customers by making them available through its service centers. These services, which included banking and savings plans, as well as life insurance, were expected to total nearly 50 percent of India Post's profits.

Upgrading technology was the focus of substantial investment by India Post in 2007. The Department of Post also identified three core services for future investment: parcels, financial services, and logistics. Revenues were expected to increase substantially based on efforts related to logistics. After technology upgrades were completed at all post offices, the Department of Post planned to increase ancillary services, such as its "instant money order scheme" and "postal retail."

Other Major Countries in the Industry. The Japanese postal system, Japan Post, was made a public corporation wholly owned by the government in April 2003. The company planned to divide along product and service lines before fully privatizing. In 2004, Japan Post reported about US$12 billion in sales and employed more than 271,000 people. Plans were announced for Japan Post to become privatized on October 1, 2007, into a holding company and

four service firms: Japan Post Service, Japan Post Insurance, Japan Post Bank, and Japan Post Network. In January 2006, Japan Post Corp. was established by Japan Post as a preparatory company for the privatization and will transfer to the holding company. The plan was to move forward quickly, but with the new government Democratic Party of Japan, the plan was halted until October 2011. Estimated profits were predicted to be in the yen 500 billion to yen 600 billion range up to fiscal year 2011. The overall workforce was approximately 225,800 in 2009.

China established the "China Post Group," which separated regulatory functions of the former State Post Bureau from its business activities. The China Post Group also united the China Postal Air Freight Corporation and the China Postal Savings Bank. China Postal Group had registered capital of US$11.5 billion in 2007. It planned to restructure linked businesses, including mail delivery services, in addition to the issuing of stamps. In the latter half of the first decade of the 2000s, China Post had linked banking and other financial services, including insurance.

In the Pacific Rim, national postal administrations had been working to modernize their operations to embrace the international market. The New Zealand Post, a leader in postal reform reported annual sales of US$932.8 million in 2006-2007, with 1.84 million delivery points. After successfully revitalizing its own services, it helped Malaysia to restructure its postal unit and provided advice to the government of South Korea on postal service modernization. The primary emphasis of both endeavors was cutting labor costs and increasing productivity by implementing more efficient management methods and integrating new technologies into postal operations.

In March 2006, *The Economist* reported on the status of Sepomex, Mexico's state-owned postal system. Sepomex only had one automated mail sorting machine. Letters and parcels were still frequently delivered via bicycle. There were only 20,000 employees serving approximately 103 billion people. Nevertheless, Sepomex managed to retain 60 percent of Mexico's postal market, sharing the remaining percentage with private companies. Government claims that 95 percent of the mail was delivered within target times ranging from 1 to 10 days were questioned. In 2010, the *Consumer Postal Council* reported that Sepomex was handling approximately 700 million pieces of mail annually, or seven letters per Mexican citizen per year. Due to the widespread distrust of Sepomex, more than 4,000 private, and more expensive, delivery and courier companies had emerged to meet consumer needs. As of 2007, Sepomex had 19,665 employees, a decrease of 10,000 from 1987, with fleet of 1,000 trucks. Sepomex reported revenue for 2007 of US$61.3 million, and the average pay for its mail carriers was US$3,500 annually.

BIBLIOGRAPHY

Boyd, John D. "Global Ambitions: USPS Picks Vogel to Lead New Global Business Unit; European Postal Services Seek Complete Deregulation." *Traffic World,* 24 July 2006.

"China Bifurcates Postal Services." *PTI—The Press Trust of India Ltd.,* 1 December 2006.

"Editorial: Partners to a Point: Postal Services, Proselytizing Don't Mix." *Sacramento Bee,* 30 April 2007.

Friedman, Daniel. "USPS Reaches Key Milestone in Green Purchases." FederalTimes Web site, 22 May 2007. Available from federaltimes.com.

Gallagher, Thomas L. "IATA Gets Technology Help." *Traffic World,* 8 March 2007. Available from www.trafficworld.com.

———. "USPS Seeks International Growth." *Traffic World,* 27 March 2007.

"Hoover's Company Capsules." *Hoover's Online,* 2007. Available from www.hoovers.com.

"India Post Plans Diversification." *The Times of India,* 17 November 2006.

Knight Ridder Tribune Business News. "Japan Post Eyes [yen]587 Bil. FY11 Profit." *Yomiuri Shimbun,* 25 April 2007.

Lazich, Robert S., ed. *Market Share Reporter.* Detroit: Thomson Gale, 2004.

Michaels, Adrian, and Andrew Parker. "Mobile Tie-Up Poste Italiane to Lift Slow Growth." *The Financial Times,* 5 April 2007.

Milner, Mark. "Postal Services: Message to Ministers: Future of Royal Mail Requires Judgment of Solomon: A Year of Competition Strengthened the Business—But the Future is Uncertain." *The Guardian,* 29 December 2006.

Mishra, Ashish Kumar. "India Post Gets Tech Savvy to Take on Competition." *Economic Times,* 18 January 2007.

Montgomery Research. *Pushing the Envelope: Achieving High Performance in a Competitive Postal Environment,* 30 April 2004. Available from www.accenture.com.

"New Postal Contract Signed Between United Airlines and USPS." *Airline Industry Information,* 2 April 2007.

"Northrop Grumman Gets Big USPS Contract." *ePostal News,* 12 March 2007.

"On Mexican Time; Mexico's Postal Services." *The Economist,* 25 March 2006.

Postal Freedom Index. Consumer Postal Council. Available from www.postalconsumers.org.

"Postal Rates, Delivery Delays." *The Kiplinger Letter,* 9 July 2004.

"Postal Services: France Called On to Withdraw La Poste's Unlimited Guarantee." *European Report,* 5 October 2006.

"Red Ink: U.S. Postal Service Lost $8.5 Billion Last Year." *Associated Press,* 12 November 2010. Available from www. syracuse.com.

Seth, Yogima. "India Post Plans Diversification." *The Times of India,* 17 November 2006.

Union Network International. "Anthrax Attack Update: Postal Unions Lobby U.S. Congress for Funds to Respond to Crisis," 8 November 2001. Available from www.union-network.org.

Universal Postal Union. "Global Postal Sector 2009." Available from www.upu.int.

———. "Worldwide Postal Network in Figures," January 2004. Available from www.upu.int.

"UPS Claims QSF Fund a Success." *ePostal News,* 1 May 2006.

"USPS Combines International Mail Services Into Familiar Brands." *Direct,* 25 April 2007.

"USPS: Don't Forget That Stamps Cost More Now." *Sun–News,* 18 May 2007.

"USPS Eyes 2009 for Total Intelligent Mail Adoption." *Direct,* 11 January 2007.

RAIL TRANSPORTATION

NAICS CODE(S)

4821. Companies in this industry sector are involved with the line-haul transportation of passengers and freight via rail systems (except passenger transportation by rail within or around specific urban centers—see SIC 4100 **Local, Suburban Transit and Interstate Highway Passenger Transit**). Industry firms also conduct support activities related to the operation of rail terminals for line-haul passengers and freight, yards, sidings, and switching. Not included in this heading are **Railway Construction** (SIC 1629), and the **Manufacture of Rail Equipment** (SIC 374).

INDUSTRY SNAPSHOT

Almost every country in the world has a rail system, although the degree to which it is put to use for passenger rather than freight use can vary dramatically. How the industry is regulated, and even the size of the track used, can often be as individual as the country. The industry is typically divided between freight and passenger operations, and within passenger operations it is subdivided into local and long distance (high-speed) services. This industry discussion focuses on freight and long-distance

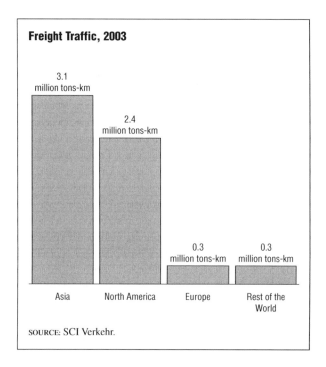

Freight Traffic, 2003

3.1 million tons-km — Asia
2.4 million tons-km — North America
0.3 million tons-km — Europe
0.3 million tons-km — Rest of the World

SOURCE: SCI Verkehr.

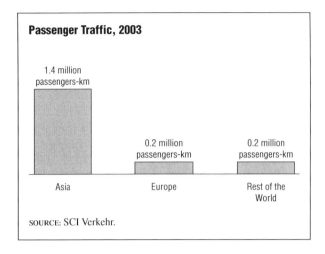

Passenger Traffic, 2003

1.4 million
passengers-km

0.2 million
passengers-km

0.2 million
passengers-km

Asia   Europe   Rest of the
World

SOURCE: SCI Verkehr.

passenger services and their complimentary services, including terminals and switching.

By 2003, about 746,000 miles of rail lines were being used to transport freight and people between cities, across countries, and increasingly, across nations. By 2010, there were approximately 233,000 miles of railroad tracks within the United States. According to the United Nations, the world population was expected to grow from 6.1 billion to 8.9 billion people between 2000 and 2050. As a result, the need for efficient, economical, and environmentally friendly means of transport for the growing population and the products they consume was resulting in technological advances in the speed of trains, the weight of cargo that could be carried, the efficiency of train fueling systems, and the computerization of the logistics behind moving mass numbers of people and products.

By the mid-2000s, the railway industry was looking up, thanks to the substantial increase in "intermodalism," the seamless combination of various modes of transport, such as trains, boats, and trucks, to ship freight. In intermodal transport, freight is shipped in trailers or containers that can be directly interchanged between different modes of transportation. In the United States, intermodal traffic went from only 3 million containers in 1980 to over 8 million in 2009, and, according to the Association of American Railroads (AAR), intermodal traffic set records in most of those years.

ORGANIZATION AND STRUCTURE

According to *Worldwide Rail Market,* published for the German rail equipment manufacturing firm Vossloh AG, there were almost 746,000 miles (1.2 million kilometers)of rail lines around the world by 2005. SCI Verkehr GmbH, a German rail consulting company, reported that the longest network could be found in Asia (with approximately 284,000 miles of track), followed by North

America (approximately 194,000 miles), Europe (162,000 miles), Latin America (67,000 miles), Africa (56,000 miles), and Australia/Pacific (39,500 miles). However, how these rail lines were used varied significantly by region. For example, the primary use of rail lines in North America was for freight, which resulted in primarily single-track lines with relatively few rail crossings. In Europe, lines are used for both passenger and freight and travel through large urban centers, requiring more complicated organizational and safety structures to function.

Most countries regulate their rail industries through government-run organizations. For example, in the United States, the Federal Railroad Administration, under the Department of Transportation, is responsible for safety legislation. The International Union of Railways (known as the UIC), located in Paris, had 162 members in 2005, including all rail transport and infrastructure managers in Europe, and most major railways in the remainder of the world. The organization was working to develop international transport by rail and was preparing standards, regulations, and recommendations to achieve that goal.

Trends in the growth and mobility of the world's population, as well as increases in the amount of trade between countries, have led to increased cooperation with other transportation industries, regional trade agreements, privatization, railroad mergers, and transportation innovations. In North America, the U.S.-Canadian Free Trade Agreement, signed in 1988, resulted in Class I railroads on both sides of the border accelerating their connections in each other's territories. Both the United States and Canada expanded into Mexico in the early 1990s. For example, in 1991 a joint venture between Burlington Northern (BN) and the Mexican corporation Grupo Protexa S.A. produced Protexa Burlington International (PBI), an innovative rail-barge link between Galveston, Texas, and Mexican Gulf ports. Two years later, the Canadian National Railway began connecting with PBI via BN to deliver Canadian grain to Mexico. Territorial expansion was further increased both by a wave of rail mergers in the United States in the mid-1990s and by the North American Free Trade Agreement (NAFTA), which diminished most trade barriers between the United States, Canada, and Mexico.

According to a 2010 study by Roland Berger Strategy Consultants on behalf of the Association of European Rail Industry (UNIFE), the total world market annually for the rail supply industry was estimated at US$164.248 billion in 2007, with a projected annual growth rate of 2 to 2.5 percent over the next decade. The 2016 projected volume was expected to reach US$210.785 billion.

With trade between the United States and Canada creating a north-south orientation, railroads shifted their east-west systems accordingly. The two countries began sharing track, rail beds, and operations on both sides of the border. U.S. railroads, for example, gained entry to Canada through interline agreements with Canadian railroads, such as the Atchison, Topeka, and Santa Fe Railway Company (Santa Fe) interline connection with the Canadian National Railway Company's Grand Trunk line at Chicago. In essence, railroads could finally provide complete service from Mexico to Canada.

Under an agreement with Mexico's government, NAFTA allowed Canadian and U.S. railroads to market their services in Mexico, operate unit trains with their own locomotives, construct and own terminals, and finance rail infrastructure. The agreement did not, however, allow full foreign ownership of a Mexican transportation firm. While pre-cleared containers and boxcars could cross the border into Mexico, neither Canada nor the United States was permitted to handle their own shipments into Mexico. Mexican law required foreign railroad operators to turn shipments over to Ferrocarriles Nacionales de Mexico (FNM), Mexico's national railway. Neither Mexico nor the United States allowed locomotives from the other nation to cross the border. Power units, therefore, had to be switched at border terminals, such as Laredo or Brownsville, Texas, a policy that helped trucking firms capture about 75 percent of all U.S. southbound trade with Mexico.

Southern Pacific (SP), which was later acquired by Union Pacific (UP), invested directly in Mexico's infrastructure with Mexican partner Ferropuertos (rail ports). SP developed a network of distribution centers at Mexican rail ports that enabled timely unloading. In 1993, it completed construction on an intermodal facility at Monterey that was operated by Mexican firms.

In Europe, a spirit of cooperation was spurred by the establishment of the European Union in 1993 and led to the creation of a pan-European rail network. Prior to the formation of the EU, national and state-run railways had traditionally refused to collaborate. Cooperative efforts were initiated in 1991 when European transport ministers, in an effort to improve intermodal links, adopted standard measurements for containers and other units used by rail transport industries. Previously, non-standardized shipping lots and container sizes used throughout Europe had been a major problem for the transport and distribution industries.

Four different rail gauges and seven different types of loading gauges on European railroads had hampered any previous opportunity for an interconnecting system. Rail systems had been especially outdated in Spain, Portugal, Greece, and Ireland where truck and loading gauges were not standardized, signaling systems were mismatched, bridge and tunnel dimensions varied, power lines used uneven voltage, and track slope and curve gradients differed.

EU directives called for increased rail use to reduce truck traffic on Europe's overly congested and polluted roadways. In the early 1990s, trucks accounted for 70 percent of all freight movement in the European Union. A goal was set to assess an 8 percent increase in cross-border intermodal traffic hauled by a combination of trucks, railways, and barges no later than 1997. The EU plan called for a pan-European combined transport network including an investment of US$2.5 billion in new rail, terminals, boxcars, and locomotives to boost multimodal transport across the borders of member nations. A planned 30,000 kilometers of high-speed track to be built in two phases was scheduled for completion by 2005. About US$590 million was earmarked for high-speed rail links to connect the northern route (Paris-London-Brussels-Amsterdam-Cologne) with the southern route (Seville-Barcelona-Lyon-Turin-Milan-Venice). Further connections would be made with Tarvisio and Trieste, Italy; Madrid, Spain; and Lisbon and Oporto, Portugal.

EU directives also called for approximately US$120 billion to be spent on developing and implementing high-speed passenger rail systems. Eurotunnel, the Anglo-French channel-tunnel consortium, developed "Le Shuttle" service, connecting London with Paris and Brussels through the Channel Tunnel. Often dubbed the "Chunnel," service began in November 1994 and made it possible for passengers to travel between London and Paris in three hours and between London and Brussels in three hours and 15 minutes.

Gauge unification was completed on the United Kingdom-Benelux-Italy and Germany-Spain-Portugal routes in the early 1990s. Completion of a rail link between Munich, Germany, and Verona, Italy, via a tunnel through the Brenner Pass was targeted for completion in the early 2000s. Other links on the EU's list of priority Trans-European Networks included the Betuwe project, a US$4 billion, 75-mile rail freight corridor that was expected to carry between 60 and 65 million tons of freight a year on Nederlandse Spoorwegen Cargo. The corridor connected Rotterdam, the world's largest port, to the German railway network. The Betuwe line was officially opened in June, 2007.

Rail operations in many other countries continued to be government owned and operated, particularly in some of the less industrialized Asian nations. Passenger fares were subsidized, making rail travel inexpensive. Typically, densely populated nations increased funding on railway projects to develop programs to extend and update rail networks. In 1994, South Korea undertook a 432-kilometer high-speed rail project, the first phase of which was completed in 2004. The network, which linked Seoul with the southern port of Pusan, was the largest outside Japan at the time. In Thailand, rail networks were built to connect Bangkok to major regional centers. In Taiwan, the Taiwan High Speed Rail system was opened in 2007, connecting Taipei and Kaohsiung. Indonesia developed viable rail service between Bandung and Jakarta. Given the limitations of truck service, that line was considered by shippers to be the best way to transport such goods as garments and textiles. Plans also called for a mass transit system in Jakarta. In 2002, Vietnam developed a US$10.6 billion modernization plan for its railway system in Hanoi. Scheduled upgrades included a railway line to Ho Chi Minh City.

In China, the need to develop better rail networks became synonymous with continued economic growth. About 70 percent of China's goods were transported on 34,000 miles of track. Recognizing that overly subsidized and outmoded railroads had stalled railway development, the Chinese government called for the industry's privatization. China's first railway corporation was formed in 1993 when the Guangzhou railway bureau of the ministry was converted into Guangzhou Railway. Chinese officials examined France's TGV, Germany's ICE, Japan's "bullet train," and Sweden's X2000 rail systems and inadvertently set off a rash of competitive bidding by foreign train manufacturers seeking to do business with China. Although the Ministry of Railways (MOR) did not privatize the Chinese railway network, it did reorganize the system into two fairly independent entities, North Loric and South Loric, which oversaw a total of 14 regional units. Between 1998 and 2002, the MOR planned to spend roughly US$29.6 billion refurbishing and extending its 50,000 miles of rail.

In 1992, China officially inaugurated the Eurasia land bridge, a rail link extending over 6,700 miles from Lianyungang, China, to Rotterdam, the Netherlands, through Kazakhstan, Uzbekistan, Kyrgyzstan, Tajikistan, Russia, Belarus, Poland, and Germany. It was the second transcontinental railway after the Trans-Siberian Express Railway (TSER). By that time, China's biggest project was the 2,370-kilometer Beijing-Kowloon line. Extending south to Canton, the rail freight system line connected Beijing to Hong Kong by 1997 and connected more than 4,400 freight stations in China.

Efforts in Russia involved upgrading the Trans-Siberian Express Railway (TSER), which had almost 67 various railroad gauges. A 50-50 joint venture partnership between the Russian Ministry of Railways and the U.S. maritime arm of CSX Corporation (Sea-Land Services) set up a land bridge rail service that utilized the 7,000-mile Trans-Siberian Railroad. A computer system to trace containers moving within the rail system was installed, and more than 3,400 railcars were dedicated to the service. In 1994, Sea-Land began offering two weekly express block train departures between Rotterdam and Moscow. The routing moved through Brest, Poland, on the Russian border where it switched from the Western rail gauge to the Russian gauge, then on to a rail terminal in Moscow. The Moscow terminal was designed to operate on a hub-and-spoke concept to consolidate shipments onto feeder block trains going to Vostochny on Russia's east coast. Service continued from Moscow to Yekaterinburg, Russia; Alma Ata, Kazakhstan; Tashkent, Uzbekistan; and to Vostochny and Vladivostok in eastern Russia.

Sea-Land also established rail service from the Russian port of Novorossiysk on the Black Sea to the region's interior, allowing increases in rail volume and greater demand for container shipment from Japan, India, the United States, and several Mediterranean countries. Plans to privatize Russia's railroad network were launched in the early 2000s, with the first stage completed in October 2003 with the formation of the Joint Stock Company (JSC) Russian Railways.

BACKGROUND AND DEVELOPMENT

The earliest railroads, which were built in Europe in the eighteenth century, employed rail that guided wagons with specially shaped wheels. The first great railway successes occurred in Great Britain. The big push for railroad development came in 1823 when English inventor George Stephenson introduced steam power for railroad freight service for the Yorkshire, England-based Stockton & Darlington Railway. Dubbed Locomotion No. 1, the service could haul 35 cars at 12 miles an hour. The government insisted on uniform gauges and on laws regarding brakes and safety standards.

France built its first railway line in 1828. Belgium, Germany, Italy, the Netherlands, and Russia all had networks in operation by the 1830s. Most railroads adopted the British standard, with the exception of railways in Spain and Portugal. Although European railroads were primarily state-owned, Russian lines were not nationalized until 1919 during the communist revolution.

Because canal transportation was the most common method of moving freight, rail transportation in the United States did not begin to develop rapidly until the 1830s, when population centers began to increase in the West. In July 1862 President Abraham Lincoln signed the Pacific Railroad Act, authorizing the Central Pacific and the Union Pacific railroads to build the first railroad line from the Atlantic to the Pacific coasts. The project was completed in 1869. By 1900, the U.S. network of rail lines had reached nearly 200,000 miles of track.

A multitude of technical advances that spurred industry development occurred in the decades following the Civil War. However, this rapid expansion of the U.S. rail industry resulted in a series of discriminatory rate wars as well as abuses and corruption. As a result, the U.S. government, under the Interstate Commerce Act of 1887, made the railroads the first industry to be regulated by a federal agency. With the passage of the Transportation Act of 1920, the Interstate Commerce Commission gained complete authority over every area of railroading.

In Canada, rail service began in 1836 and had expanded to 6,960 miles by 1880. In 1881, as part of an agreement under which the province of British Columbia entered the Canadian Confederation, Canada formed the Canadian Pacific Railway Company and completed its transcontinental railway. The Canadian National Railway Company (CN) was organized in 1922 to take over several railroads that had gone bankrupt because of years of speculative railway building. In 1987, the government was forced to deregulate its railroads, making it possible for them to bargain for rates with shippers and to compete successfully with deregulated U.S. railroads. Until the early 1990s, however, revenues were pressured, resulting in a weak business outlook. To streamline operations, CN announced it wanted to sell roughly 20 percent of its eastern and central network by 1995 and another third to short-line operators. Canadian Pacific (CP), which ranked third among North American railroads in miles of track but seventh in revenue-ton miles in 1992, received permission in 1993 to sell or abandon most of its rail operations from Sherbrooke, Quebec, to Saint John, New Brunswick. In late 1993, both railroads were allowed to share a 300-mile line between Quebec and Ontario where the carriers previously had been operating parallel tracks a few miles apart. Both railroads outlined terms of a merger that would meld marketing and administrative functions and share tracks and rail yards.

Asian countries with significant railroad systems included India, China, and Japan. India's system was built in the 1850s and patterned after the British model, using a different gauge. China began building railroads in the 1870s but had only 7,500 miles in operation by 1920. Under Communist rule, the People's Republic of China increased its total track length to 32,600 miles. Japan built its first lines in the 1870s.

The invention of cars, trucks, and airplanes as alternate forms of transportation seriously challenged the railroad industry, and by the early 1970s the industry's share of traffic had dropped to 37 percent. In particular, the increased use of trucking created stiff competition for freight payloads. By the mid-1970s, 10 U.S. railroads had declared bankruptcy. The Railroad Revitalization and Regulatory Reform Act of 1976 was passed to revitalize the industry. With the formation of the federally subsidized Consolidated Rail (Conrail), portions of six bankrupt Northeast railroads were successfully restructured as a single viable freight system.

In 1980, under the Stagger Rail Act, the U.S. government began to deregulate and ease restrictions on the rail industry, allowing carriers to abandon unprofitable lines, redirect resources to buy new equipment, and rebuild tracks in profitable corridors. The Act also freed railroads to negotiate rates directly with customers. The result was an expansion of the railroad industry and an investment of nearly US$160 billion in track and equipment. Nonetheless, by 1987, after spending billions on modernizing track and rolling stock, the government privatized Conrail.

Privatization and liberalization efforts continued into the 1990s. While the railroad industries in the United States and Japan had been privatized in the 1980s, many European players did not begin to move away from government involvement until the mid-1990s. For example, the United Kingdom's British Rail became a private company in the mid-1990s, and other countries like Germany contemplated implementing similar privatization programs.

In the 1990s, the United States had the largest network of rail mileage, followed by Europe. The total rail mileage in Canada, Mexico, and Central America combined amounted to one-third of that in the United States. The 10 leading companies in the railroad transportation industry reported combined sales of more than US$118.9 billion in 1996. That year, the *International Railway Journal* estimated that annual capital investment in the industry exceeded US$50 billion worldwide. Germany led in railroad capital investment with plans of pumping US$10 billion annually into the industry through 2001, while China had the second most ambitious investment program with roughly US$6 billion allocated to the railroad industry in 1996.

Later in the decade, the European Union took steps to create a freight rail "freeway." The countries initially involved in the agreement included Germany, the Netherlands, Austria, and Italy. In mid-1997, key organizations for rail transport users and railroads, including the Community of European Railways and the International Union of Road-Rail Transport Companies, supported the EU's plan to establish these rail freeways. EU governments determined that the corridor between these four countries constituted one of the highest-volume corridors in Europe, and that a rail freeway would bring about accelerated transportation to and from Germany and ports on the Mediterranean by increasing freight speeds to 50 kph (31 mph) and eliminating delays when crossing national boundaries. Similarly, the planned Trans-Asia Railway Project was expected to connect Malaysia, Thailand, Cambodia, Laos, Vietnam, and China, as well as to expand passenger and cargo traffic.

Intermodalism, which is the planning and coordinating of the entire transport trip from ship to train to truck, contributed to industry growth in Europe, the United

States, and other world markets as one of the fastest growing segments of the industry in the mid- to late 1990s. Because truck transportation cost nearly twice as much as freight railroad services, new double-stack railcars offered an economic alternative with single carriers being able to move more boxes at one time, making the cost less expensive. Consequently, distinctions between rail and trucking companies became blurred in some areas as trucking firms and railroads began working together, providing complementary services and no longer competing with each other. Trains carried freight over long distances, while trucks worked the profitable short-haul lanes that fed into rail hubs. Leading railroads, such as Deutsche Bahn, UP, and CSX, offered intermodal services.

Intermodalism also gave rise to third-party coordinators who planned the transport of goods through the various modes of transportation needed. Railroads increased their use of these third-party retailers or "middlemen" who dealt directly with importers and exporters in the late 1990s. Intermodal marketing companies (IMCs), which marketed rail services and provided shippers with door-to-door services, became leading sources for intermodal shipments for railroads. France and Germany introduced intermodal freight systems with their Kombiverkehr and Intercontainer services. Under these arrangements, the dispatching customer controlled the entire chain, including delivery and collection at the receiving end.

Global rail freight volume grew 1.8 percent in 2000, according to Paris, France-based International Transport Union. Global passenger travel grew less than 1 percent, although the popularity of high-speed trains in Europe accounted for 2.3 percent passenger traffic growth. Rail-based freight traffic in Europe rose 7 percent, while intermodal freight traffic increased 8 percent. According to the *International Railway Journal,* European freight transported via rail had fallen from 21 percent in 1970 to 8 percent by the late 1990s. In the middle of the decade, Britain privatized its railway operations, which led to the creation of Railtrack, a private company.

In North America, consolidation stopped when the U.S. Surface Transportation Board (STB) banned railroad mergers for a 15-month period starting in March 2000. Canadian National Railway and Burlington Northern Santa Fe, which had announced their intent to merge into North American Railways Inc. in December of 1999, appealed the mandate. However, the U.S. Court of Appeals found in favor of the STB in July of 2000. Rather than endure a delay that would likely last two years, the firms cancelled their merger plans.

Privatization and deregulation of the world's railroads continued as European countries, such as the United Kingdom and Germany, and Latin American countries, such as Mexico, worked to reduce government involvement in their transportation industries, including railroads. Even Russia was on the privatization bandwagon, announcing in 2001 its intent to privatize the Russian State Railways via a reform project that would take place over the following decade.

Despite growth in passenger and freight traffic, the European Commission launched a rail freight revitalization program in 2001 in an effort to increase rail freight traffic throughout the European Union. The European rail industry was also impacted by the collapse of Rail-track. Performance problems, including several fatalities, coupled with a growing debt load were cited as reasons for the refusal of the British government to continue subsidizing Railtrack in 2001. Many industry analysts believed that Britain would create a non-profit entity that would possibly be overseen by the Strategic Rail Authority to replace Railtrack. Shortly after Railtrack's demise became public, the Strategic Rail Authority announced its intent to increase its capital investment in the national rail network in an effort to increase passenger traffic 40 to 50 percent and freight traffic 80 percent.

France was unique among the largest European players for resisting such privatization efforts, despite the financial hardships of its state railway operator, Société Nationale des Chemins de Fer Français (SNCF). According to the June 2001 issue of *The Economist,* the European Commission pressured France to split its track and rail operations for two reasons: to foster transparency in financial reporting and to allow competition in the track segment. In 2001, Reseau Ferre de France (RFF), a state-owned firm which paid SNCF to manage the French rail network, struggled with a debt load of € 22.8 billion, which required interest payments of € 2.4 billion annually. The European Commission began calling for the French government to reduce support for its national rail network and allow competition on at least some segments of its lines.

The advent of rail "freeways," was marked by the European Commission's creation of a rail freeway connecting German, Austrian, Dutch, and Italian ports, facilitating smooth transport between those countries. Finally, more countries began adopting high-speed trains that were capable of traveling more than 180 kilometers per hour (110 miles per hour) to ease highway traffic congestion and reduce environmental degradation. Germany, France, and Japan led this movement. In fact, both France and Japan boasted high-speed trains, known as TGVs, capable of traveling at an average speed of 360 kph (190 mph) by 2001.

In North America, despite the ban on outright mergers from the U.S. Surface Transportation Board, strategic alliances between the North American railroad industry leaders, including UP, BNSF, CSX, CN, CP, and Grupo Transportacion Ferroviaria Mexicana (TFM), continued to unfold. For example, CP established an office in

Mexico City due to the success of its joint service with UP and three Mexican railways. CN, UP, and TFM began offering intermodal service that connected Montreal, Toronto, and Detroit, with Houston and Laredo, Texas, and Mexico City in 2001. Also that year, UP and Norfolk Southern extended their intermodal service to include Miami and Jacksonville, Florida.

CURRENT CONDITIONS

With the world's population projected to grow from its 2002 level of 6.2 billion people to 8.9 billion people by 2050, the need for an increasingly efficient means of transporting these people and the goods they produce and require grows. Deregulation of industries and the dismantling of trade barriers have resulted in huge increases in the amount of international trade. According to Deutsche Bank, since the mid-1970s the amount of exports rose from 10 to 25 percent in 30 years. The ability of existing rail structures to cope with this problem continued to be a concern in 2005. Rail networks were faced with environmental issues as well as decreasing amounts of space for expansion in many countries, particularly in and around major urban centers. According to research conducted for Vossloh AG, the rail transport industry had been undergoing a renaissance since the mid-1990s as railways held two major advantages over other modes of transport in terms of meeting increasing trade and passenger transport demands. First, almost every medium-sized town in the world has a rail station to connect it to other centers. Second, compared to the use of roads and airports, railways remained relatively underused (although problems existed in many major urban centers). Railways remained one of the best methods of mass transportation of people and goods. Advances in technology were also helping to improve the efficiency of systems, with faster trains being developed, and increases in the ability to manage the logistics of transportation.

After the terrorist attacks against the United States in 2001, safety was also a primary concern. The industry turned to developing security plans and features. The Railway Alert Network (RAN), linked to the Surface Transportation Information Sharing and Analysis Center, was developed to collect and disseminate security information to the industry. In the mid-2000s, RAN was recognized by the U.S. government as one of the most successful security systems in any private industry.

According to SCE Verkehr of Germany, by 2003 Asia was the leader in the share of freight traffic transported (in tons/kilometer) with 3.1 million tons/km. This was followed by North America (2.4 million), Europe (0.3 million), and the rest of the world (0.3 million). In terms of passenger traffic (in passengers/km), the figures are notable for the absence of North America as a distinct region with its own listing. By

2003, Asia was transporting 1.4 million passengers/km, Europe 0.2 million, and the rest of the world (including North America, Africa, Australia, and Africa) 0.2 million.

Europe, North America, and the Asia/Pacific held the majority of rail markets as of 2010. However, with the dynamic growth expected in population and technology, the Asia/Pacific region was projecgted to surpass North America by 2016. With the exception of Japan and South Korea, most of the railways in Asia maintained simple infrastructures in 2005. However, in Europe the focus was expected to be on the improvement of existing systems, including the increase of rail speed, in an effort to prepare for the expansion of the European Union and the resulting expected increase in trade. In addition, the need to standardize the rail gauges between borders created an upswing in rail business as well.

In North America, 20.5 percent of the revenues of the nation's freight rail systems came from the transport of coal, which accounted for 43.6 percent of the tonnage shipped, according to the Association of American Railroads (AAR). North America was expected to devote more resources to the addition of high-speed passenger rail lines between major centers. In the United States, Amtrak began operating the Acela Express between Boston and New York and Washington, D.C., and New York in 2000. Five years later, in 2005, the trains were carrying 9,000 to 10,000 passengers each weekday and were capable of reaching speeds of up to 150 miles per hour. The future of North American rail lines may be the JetTrain, which was expected to reach speeds of up to 160 miles per hour in the busy Toronto-Montreal corridor in Canada.

Rail transport is also on the rise in Africa, the Middle East, and other areas of the Americas. These countries have sustained high population growth rates, but were expected to remain small compared to their larger counterparts in terms or market volumes. However, as of 2010, large metro projects had been started in Argentina, India, and the United Arab Emirates. Many countries that have had little to no exposure to a rail system as of 2010 were expected to develop markets with significant rail transport projects in the 2010s. For example, Saudi Arabia was creating a major rail infrastructure in their Mineral Railway, Saudi Landbridge, and Mecca-Medina high speed line at the end of the first decade of the 2000s.

Other key trends in the industry included the continued growth of intermodalism, the seamless combination of various modes of transport, such as trains, boats, and trucks, to ship freight. By the middle of the first decade of the 2000s, intermodal transportation was experiencing the highest growth in the United States, having emerged from the depressed economy of the early years of the 2000s in good shape. By 2003 there were 9.9 million intermodal trailers in the United States, and industry analysts expected that intermodal service would drive the railroad industry's growth for several years. As of 2004, for the first time, intermodal represented the highest source of the U.S. industry's revenue, at 22 percent. Containers were about three-fourths of the total intermodal volume in the mid-2000s.

By the mid-2000s, North American freight rail capacity was reaching its limit. In the United States, there were 142,000 miles of rail in 2004. Despite the transfer of freight shipping to truck operators, railroads continued to handle the bulk of freight shipping in the United States, with 42 percent of intercity freight, according to the AAR. To help meet demand, Union Pacific and CSX, as well as other railroad operators, were accelerating production and re-working operating plans to meet the increasing, strained demand. Canada was also beginning to suffer similar system stress in 2004. According to AAR, freight demand was projected to increase nearly 70 percent by 2020.

According to jpost.com, Army Radio reported a dramatic increase in the number of passengers riding on trains in Israel. Approximately 8.8 million train tickets were sold in the second quarter of 2008, reflecting an increase of 14 percent over the same period in 2007. The Army Radio report stated that the average number of train travelers rose between April and July to 131,500 per month for an increase of 11 percent compared to the same time in 2007. Three new stations had been opened by the Transportation Ministry at Modi in Central, Canei Aviv, and Kiryat.

RESEARCH AND TECHNOLOGY

In 2005, work continued on the development of magnetically levitated (maglev) trains, which would mean increased speeds, safety, and reliability, as well as lower maintenance because the drive system would be independent of wheel-and-rail friction. In December 2003, a maglev train reached speeds of 581 kilometers per hour (361 mph) during Japanese testing. Although the technology has been around since the 1960s, little had been done to develop it commercially. However, in 2003, a maglev line opened to connect Shanghai with Pudong Airport. By July 2004, 1 million people had taken the maglev, which had reached speeds of 501 kilometers per hour. By December 2004, Germany was working on developing a maglev system. As of 2010, several countries were proposing or developing their own maglev systems to ease road congestion or other rail system congestion and improve high speed travel. Among those in development in 2010 were the London to Glasgow line in the United Kingdom; the Sydney to Illawarra, Australia, maglev line, which is expected to cut the two hour commute to 20 minutes; the Tokyo to Nagoya to Osaka

bullet train, which is expected to open in 2025; the Shanghai to Hangzhou, China, line, which is expected to be completed by 2013; and a line connecting Mumbai to Delhi, India.

France developed the Train à Grande Vitesse (TGV) in 1981, which led to a US$10 billion investment in its TGV-Atlantique 325, a train capable of speeds up to 515.3 kph. By 2001, France and Japan had each developed TGVs with average speeds of 360 kph (190 mph). A TGV test train set a record for fastest wheeled train in 2007 when it reached 357.2 mph. In 2009, the Chinese CRH service Harmony Express surpassed the previous records of passenger rail transport on the Wuhan-Guangzhou High Speed Railway.

In 2003, the World Congress on Railway Research reported that the new technologies in the field of railway research included developments in energy consumption, reducing diesel exhaust, electronic braking, track design and train control systems. With the increase in traffic on rail systems, the advancement of computer monitoring and control systems continued to be significant.

On August 7, 2008, results were announced by Bombardier for the Grona Taget (Green Train) Project. That research, development, and demonstration project originated in 2005 and was set to run through 2010 or 2011. The project focused on developing new high speed trains designed especially for the Nordic countries' special technical guidelines and traffic requirements. The Bombardier Regina train was used as the test vehicle. On July 23, 2008, the test train set a new speed record of 295 kph and reduced travel time from Stockholm to Gothenburg, Sweden, by 15 minutes. The two new "ECO4" products were tested on the train were the modern engine technology and assistance system as known as the Bombardier MITRAC Permanent Magnet Motor and Bombardier EBI Drive 50 Driver, respectively. Principal partners of the Green Train project included Banverket, the Swedish Railway Administration, and Bombardier Transportation.

The *Casper Star-Tribune* reported that the Wyoming Department of Transportation had launched a high-speed train feasibility study after obtaining US$200,000 from the government. Plans under consideration called for a line traveling south from Casper to Cheyenne, down Colorado's Front Range and ending in Albuquerque, New Mexico. TransSystems of Minneapolis, Minnesota, completed a detailed report in July 2008 that examined every aspect of the proposed route, including tracks, grade, curvature, and alignment. Colorado launched its own study in April 2008 that would continue for approximately one year and a half. New Mexico had purchased the right of way for existing tracks running from about 40 miles south of Albuquerque to Trinidad, Colorado.

INDUSTRY LEADERS

East Japan Railway Company. East Japan Railway Company (JR East), the largest passenger railway company in the world and one of the seven regional passenger companies resulting from the 1987 break-up of Japan's state-owned Japan National Railway, was a leader in the industry with 2009 revenues of US$32.32 billion, a sizeable increase over 2003 levels. With history dating back to 1872, the company served about 59 million people in the Kanto and Tohoku regions of Japan with 6.169 million customers annually in the Tokyo area via 4,680 miles of track. Three bullet train networks operated between Tokyo and Nagano, Niigata, and Morioka. In 2008, JR East reported approximately 61,900 employees.

Deutsche Bahn Group. In 2007, Deutsche Bahn Aktiengesellschaft (DB), Europe's largest railway, reported sales of US$42.7 billion, an increase over 2003 levels. In 2009, the company carried approximately 2 billion people by rail through 5,665 stations. The firm's cargo division, which merged with the cargo operations of Nederlandse Spoorwegen in 1999, carried 282.3 million tons of freight in 2003. Incorporated in 1951, the company was owned by the German government, although officials had been working to privatize Deutsche Bahn since the mid-1990s. The company had been decreasing its workforce since it reached a peak of 602,000 in 1948. Employee numbers were reduced to 498,000 in 1960; 398,000 in 1970; 288,768 in 1996; and 229,000 in 2006.

Since the beginning of the 1980s, managers from the private sector had been appointed to Deutsche Bahn's board. The end of civil service status for the company's management was designed to lead to greater commercial orientation for the company. This objective was only partially attained, since government policy did not allow DB the necessary freedom of action in the early 1990s. Movements to end the bureaucratic status of the railroad were driven by the reunification of Germany, the accompanying takeover of the East's Deutsche Reichsbahn (another large German railroad transportation company), and the development of the European Union transport policy. The unification treaty called for the ultimate technical and organizational merger of the two railways. In May 2010, Duetsche Bahn bid on and won the UK-based transport company, Arriva. That merger became effective August 2010.

Société Nationale des Chemins de Fer Français. Government-owned Société Nationale des Chemins de Fer Français (SNCF) was France's largest passenger and freight rail network and the second largest in Europe, with a market share in 2002 of 20.5 percent. Approximately 50 percent of SNCF's traffic was international. The company reported sales of US$28.3 billion in 2003. Its well-known TGV trains were able to reach speeds of 250 mph. SNCF employed 180,000 people around the globe.

Union Pacific. U.S.-based Union Pacific was formed by the passage of the Pacific Railroad Act of 1862. The act called for the creation of a public corporation, Union Pacific Railroad Company, to build a railroad from Nebraska to the California-Nevada border. The railroad's completion supplied a critical impetus to the growth of the West, which quickly developed into a land of pioneers. The company's acquisition of Southern Pacific in 1996 secured its position as the U.S. leader.

Union Pacific (UP) was the largest railroad company in the United States in 2008, with 32,012 miles of track, sales of US$18 billion, and an employee base of more than 50,000 people. In 2005, UP's largest customer was APL, a steamship company, followed by General Motors. The company's primary role was the transportation of freight.

CSX Corp. CSX had its origins in the Baltimore and Ohio Railroad (B&O), which was formed in 1827. After several consolidations and mergers, the railroad was incorporated as CSX Corp. in 1978, when it began to diversify into fiber-optics, natural resources, and water transportation. However, due to low profits and a stagnant stock performance, the company undertook a major restructuring program, selling its telecommunications and oil and gas businesses and putting the money back into its own outstanding common stock. In the late 1990s, the firm acquired a 42 percent stake in Conrail. Rival Norfolk Southern purchased the remaining 58 percent.

By 2005, CSX had become the largest operator of rail networks in the eastern United States. In 2009, with 22,000 miles of rail concentrated in the United States, CSX Corp. provided rail transportation and distribution services in 23 states in the East, Midwest, and South; the District of Columbia; and two Canadian provinces. Revenues were US$8 billion in 2009, and the company reported 35,847 employees. Growing intermodal operations were handled by the CSX Intermodal unit. By 2009, the company reported sales of US$9.041 million and 30,000 employees.

MAJOR COUNTRIES IN THE INDUSTRY

United States. In a cover story for *Barron's*, Jay Palmer provided an overview of the "The Big Seven" U.S. railways, indicating that Union Pacific and Burlington Northern in the West, CSX and Norfolk Southern in the East, and Canadian National, Canadian Pacific, and Kansas City

Southern, had been doing very well since being deregulated in 1978. These railroads handled approximately 90 percent of the nation's freight rail traffic.

In the United States, although major passenger routes existed, the rail system was primarily used for freight, accounting for 40 percent of all freight transportation, according to the Association of American Railroads. By 2009, rail moved 47.2 percent of all coal in the country and 8.2 percent of the grain or other farm-related products. In 2005, the United States was the world leader for freight moved by rail. In a 2010 report by the Association of American Railroads, freight railroad operators garnered about US$46.1 billion in revenues in 2009, using 8.24 million containers, 1.64 million trailers and employing more than 183,000 people. The efforts of U.S. railroads to significantly reduce rates and substantially enhance service quality made the United States freight rail system the most productive in the world. However, the National Railroad Passenger Corporation (Amtrak), which had been federally subsidized to forestall losses since inaugurating service in 1971, encountered significant problems in the late 1990s, including sluggish traffic and revenues, declining federal subsidies, and deteriorating locomotives. Almost totally owned by the U.S. Department of Transportation, in 2005 the company continued to face continuing threats for an end to its subsidies.

Paul Darst reported on August 10, 2008, in *The State Journal* that industry and state officials said some businesses were depending on the railways as "a viable way" for transporting their goods to and from the marketplace. According to American Association of Railroads spokesman Tom White, U.S. railroad companies had record-breaking years in 2006 and 2007. The economic downturn had taken its toll beginning with the last quarter of 2007, resulting in stagnant railroad industry growth. White explained that the high cost of fuel in the late 2000s was making trains great alternatives, adding that trains were three to four times more fuel-efficient than tractor-trailers.

The *Ann Arbor News* on August 11, 2008, reported that Amtrak was experiencing some challenges due to demands faced by travel increases. The number of train passengers increased 13.9 percent in July 2008 over July 2007. The *Ann Arbor News* concluded that the overcrowding on many trains was a result of the backlogged infrastructure problems that prevented expanded service. Passenger counts also showed increases on previously well-traveled routes, such as the line from Washington, D.C., to Boston. Consequently, Congress overwhelmingly passed legislation that had the potential to increase Amtrak's funding 33 percent or more in the 2008-09 fiscal year. Another significant piece of legislation was a grant program to encourage individual states to expand their rail offerings. Amtrak faced major infrastructure challenges with an aging network of bridges, tracks, and tunnels. In addition, some of the overhead wiring providing electrical power to the trains also needed replacing.

"There's two railroads out there," Amtrak President Alex Kummant revealed. "There's the one we run everyday, and there's the one everybody imagines is out there."

According to WallaceFarmer.com, National Corn Growers Association President Ron Litterer submitted written comments to the Federal Surface Transportation Board on behalf of all U.S. corn growers. The association expressed concerns about the railroad industry's request to stop shipping anhydrous ammonia, which is an important component for some fertilizers. Litterer said the Association "believes that only Congress has the authority to change the railroads' obligation." Daryl Haack of the Association's action team, believed that the railroads were actually trying to have anhydrous ammonia reclassified because it was an inhalation hazard, making railways the potentially safest way to haul the ammonia.

The Russian Federation. In an interview given to the Euro-Asian Transport Union in September 2004, G.M. Fadeev, minister of railways of the Russian Federation, noted that 81 percent of the total cargo turnover and 39.4 percent of the passenger turnover was handled by the country's rail system. Fadeev estimated that by 2010, the amount of cargo transit in Russia would reach 70 to 80 million tons per year, five times the amount that was moved in 2004. To improve its rail system, the country invested in advanced container terminals using computerized management systems. The Russian Federation joined with the railway authorities of Germany, Poland, Belarus, and the Commonwealth of Independent States (CIS) to introduce a fast-track container block train between Moscow and Berlin. Further investment was planned for a Moscow-Smolensk-Brest rail link to provide increased integration with western European railways. Due to a 17.2 percent increase in rail freight traffic in 1999, the Ministry of Railways was able to post a US$1 billion profit. Coal was to be the most common commodity transported, followed by construction materials, iron and manganese ore, ferrous metals, and timber. In 2009, the 17 regional railways covered a total of 85,500 kilometers and employed 950,000 people.

The Trans-Siberian Railroad between Moscow and the Russian Far East, Mongolia, China, and the Sea of Japan, which was built between 1891 and 1916, became the longest continuous railroad in the world. In the early 1990s, efforts to upgrade the Trans-Siberian Express Railway (TSER), which used 67 different gauges of rail, were begun through a joint venture between the Russian Ministry of Railways and U.S.-based Sea-Land Services. To make access possible to the 7,000-mile Trans-Siberian Railroad, Sea-Land set up a land bridge rail service. In the mid-1990s, Russia and Finland began constructing a US$68 million railroad connecting the two countries to carry 6 million tons of cargo annually. Extending 600 kilometers (370 miles), the new railroad was expected to transport up to 28 million tons per year.

India. India's first railroads were built in the 1850s. Although they were intended to emulate British standards, India's rail network did not equal Western standards. Instead, Indian lines were built extensively in broad gauge (1.66 meter) and in meter gauge. After nationalizing the entire system in 1947, the Indian government substantially increased its investment by improving the rail system. As of 2002, some 37,900 miles of railroads were operated in India, making it the third largest system in the world. There were direct rail connections from Bombay to all parts of India. Rail service was also available at India's major seaports. In the late 1990s, Indian Railways continued to operate under traditional management practices and experienced strong demand in excess of capacity for both passengers and freight. The railroad expected to remain competitive for long-distance transit and transport, even if India's plans to sustain a modern highway system were successful.

China. As of 2009, China operated the world's second most extensive rail network, with about 53,438 miles of track. Approximately 60 percent of all freight traffic in China was transported by rail, as was 35 percent of passenger traffic. Although rail was introduced in China as early as the 1870s, only 7,500 miles were in operation by 1920. The network became much more extensive when the Communists took control in 1949. Recognizing that its network was outmoded, the government called for its privatization in 1994. However, it initially formed its first railway corporation, the Guangzhou Railway Corp., in 1993. Recognizing the need for fast and efficient rail systems, Chinese officials began examining high-speed rail networks being developed in France, Germany, Japan, and Sweden. China also began courting international investors, including the World Bank, to fund its railroad projects, despite reports that the country's passenger and cargo traffic declined 39 percent in 1996. China planned to build 6,000 kilometers of electric railways between 2001 and 2005 as part of the Ministry of Railroad's plan to connect China with Russia, Tibet, Eastern Europe, and Southwest Asia. In addition, China's entrance to the World Trade Organization early in the twenty-first century opened the Chinese rail market to increased competition. As a result, China was considered a key growth market by many analysts. In 2004, rail car demand had reached nearly three times actual capacity.

In August 2008, www.companiesandmarkets.com announced the availability of its China Transportation Sector Analysis. It found that the railway was still the most popular mode of transportation for freight, totaling 55.2 percent of the market. Low cost was credited as being the reason for railways' popularity as a means of transportation for domestic cargo. China's railway network was expected to grow to 100,000km by the end of 2010 and to 120,000 by 2020. The main growth sector will be in freight transport to meet the growing demand.

Germany. In the mid-1990s, Germany operated the world's fifth most extensive rail network. Subsequent developments in Germany's rail system made it a leader in rail technology, particularly the intercity express (ICE), which traveled at a top speed of 280 kph. In 1993, ICE service was inaugurated between Berlin, Munich, Frankfurt, and Stuttgart. The development of Intercargo Express trains proved that containers up to 32 twenty-foot equivalent units (TEUs) could be transported at top speeds of up to 100 mph. ICE trains began traveling between Bremen in the north to Stuttgart in the south, reducing regular transport times by two hours. Through 2001, Germany planned to invest US$10 billion a year to develop and implement ICE train service connecting major cities throughout the country and to introduce additional high-speed railways throughout Germany. These investments were considered necessary to prepare the railroad industry for privatization. Privatization plans continued in 2005.

Canada. The Canadian Transportation Safety Board indicated that public education in combination with improved visibility and signage at railway crossings caused a drop in the number of accidents at the crossings. The number of accidents at railroad crossings reportedly went down 75 percent from 826 incidents in 1980 to 209 in 2007. Major efforts were planned to address trespassers and suicides. In 2007, 82 people were hit on Canadian tracks, and 57 of them were killed by the accidents. Regardless of the number, those accidents have a long-term affect on anyone who sees them. Edmonton Locomotive Engineer and Peer Support Volunteer with CN Rail and the Teamsters Union Ted Ermet reported a recurring nightmare of "driving his train around a corner to find a school bus stuck on the tracks." Ermet has tried to organize meetings of traumatized train crew members with professional counselors following an accident. In July 2008, Transport Canada issued a public request for proposals. The request offered a maximum of US$382,000 over four-and-a-half years to develop a suicide reduction program related to rail lines. The program would operate jointly with the Washington-based Federal Railroad Administration, which announced a US$1 million grant to Operation Lifesavers in July 2007 aimed at reducing trespassing fatalities along rail lines.

BIBLIOGRAPHY

"AAR Statement on New York Times Article on Grade Crossing Safety." Association of American Railroads, 11 July 2004. Available from www.aar.org.

"All Aboard! Travelers Turn to Passenger Trains as Gas Prices Increase." *The Ann Arbor News*, August 11, 2008. Available from blog.mlive.com.

Bangsberg, P.T. "One-Track Mind." *The Journal of Commerce,* 31 May 2004.

"Bombardier: Green Train Project in Sweden Demonstrates the Future of High Speed Trains in Nordic Countries." Bombardier press release, 7 August 2008. Available from www.marketwatch.com.

"China: An $8 Billion Market." *Railway Age,* July 2001.

"China Transportation Sector Analysis (2006–2007): www. companiesand markets.com Adds New Report." *PR-Inside.com,* 11 August 2008. Available from www.pr-inside.com.

"CSX 2009 Annual Report." CSX Corporation, Inc. Available from phx.corporate-ir.net.

Darst, Paul. "Companies Turn to Tracks for Shipping." *The State Journal,*10 August 2008.

Draper, Deborah J., ed. *Business Rankings Annual.* Detroit: Thomson Gale, 2004.

"Freight Rail Security Plan Emphasizes Timely Intelligence." Association of American Railroads, 5 May 2004. Available from www.aar.org.

Gallagher, John. "Running Out of Track." *Traffic World,* 21 June 2004.

"Hoover's Company Capsules." *Hoover's Online,* 2008. Available from www.hoovers.com.

"International Trade Statistics." 2003. World Trase Organization. Available from www.wto.org.

Kaufman, Lawrence H. "Mexico: Land of Opportunity." *Railway Age,* February 2001.

Leenan, Maria, Mark Doing, Karl Strang, and Nicolas Wille. "Worldwide Rail Market." Vossloh AG, October 2003. Available from www.vossloh.de.

"Market and Investment Volumes in Railway Technology in Central and Eastern Europe." Vossloh AG press release, 2004. Available from www.vossloh.de

"Ministers of Transport from European and Asian Countries: A Look into the Future." Euro-Asian Transport Union. Available from www.eatu.org.

"North American Freight Railroad Statistics." Association of American Railroads, 2002.

Palmer, Jay. "Tickets to Riches." *Barron's,* 4 August 2008. Available from online.barrons.com.

"Rail Freight Traffic Up from Last Year." Association of American Railroads, 22 July 2004. Available from www.aar.org.

"Railroads Announce Surge in Intermodal and Carload Freight." Association of American Railroads, 14 May 2004. Available from www.aar.org.

"Railroads Say 'You're Hired!'" Association of American Railroads, 28 April 2004. Available from www.aar.org.

"Railroads Want to Quit Hauling Anhydrous Ammonia." Wallaces Farmer Web site, 6 August 2008. Available from wallacesfarmer.com.

"Transportation Ministry Reports 14% Rise in Train System Users." *The Jerusalem Post,* 11 August 2008. Available from www.jpost.com.

"Tres Grand Void; French Railways." *The Economist,* 2 June 2001.

U.S. Foreign & Commercial Service. "The Russian Railway Sector," June 2000. Available from www.bisnis.doc.gov.

Vantuono, William C. "Betting on a Breakthrough." *Railway Age,* December 2003.

Worldwide Rail Market Study: Status quo and Outlook 2016. Association of European Rail Industry. Available from www. unife.org.

"Wyoming: Good Investment in High-Rail Study." 9 August 2008. Available from www.trib.com.

SIC 4210

TRUCKING AND COURIER SERVICES

NAICS CODE(S)

484. The broad category of trucking and courier services includes three distinct subsets: (1) local trucking services, which may include storage facilities; (2) long-distance trucking services; and (3) courier services, except those by air. Many industry firms specialize in just one or two of these areas. A portion of the industry competes with services offered by government-sponsored and private postal delivery services. For more information, see also **Postal Services**.

INDUSTRY SNAPSHOT

Trucking services encompass three broad market sectors: truckload (TL), less-than-truckload (LTL), and small package (courier). In the United States, they also are classified by three general groupings: Interstate Commerce Commission (ICC)-regulated trucking, non-ICC intercity trucking, and non-ICC local trucking. Trucking companies primarily compete amongst themselves, although barge, steamship, railroad, and airline services are also regarded as competitors.

After a few dismal years at the beginning of the twenty-first century, the trucking and courier services industry was looking up in 2005, as manufacturers began to produce and ship more freight to meet increasing demand of a growing world marketplace and to handle the increasing volume of international trade resulting from improvements in the economies of developing countries and easing of trade barriers. However, cost increases related to higher wages, compliance upgrades, and fuel costs were digging into profits.

Recent Courier Services Employment Figures

DHL International GmbH	500,000 employees
United Parcel Service	408,000 employees
FedEx	280,000 employees
Yamato	169,836 employees
TNT N.V.	154,500 employees

SOURCE: Company Websites.

Consolidation was occurring at a rapid pace, although the industry remained highly fragmented, with the largest players accounting for small percentages of the total market in each country.

Additionally, in order to stay competitive, the trucking industry was evaluating the need to invest in equipment and technology. Intermodal transportation, in which freight is shipped in trailers or containers that can be directly interchanged between trucks, boats, and trains, also was growing as the preferred shipping model across industries. The trucking industry in the mid-2000s was under new regulations regarding safety and security, emissions, training, and taxes. By 2005, trucking was still regulated by individual country governments, although in the United States, trucking safety was regulated federally, while licensed and monitored by individual states.

In 2008, PRWeb reported that Global Industry Analysts, Inc., noted the industry had evolved from offering transportation to supplying a range of services to meet the needs of different industries. For example, trucking industries became one-stop providers for integrated transportation and logistics services. Technological innovations had greatly enhanced the ability of the trucking industry to gain customer confidence while reducing administrative and processing costs. Global Industry Analysts went on to say that the trend was for "sustained cooperation with other modes of transportation for meeting specific delivery requirements as cost efficiencies."

The trucking industry has struggled along with the rest of the world in the recession at the close of the first decade of the twenty-first century. Fuel prices remained high, so the cost of running the trucks did not decline, but interstate transport must continue regardless. Another issue facing the trucking industry at the close of the decade was the growing age of its drivers. In 2006, the U.S. trucking industry employed 1.8 million drivers of heavy trucks. A large percentage of these drivers were reaching retirement age. The percentage of new employees or potential new drivers was not been keeping pace with retirements. By 2005, there was an estimated 20,000 driver shortfall in the long-haul sector, and by 2014, that number was expected to increase to 111,000. Employee turnover was also extremely high. By 2005, the turnover rate was a record 136 percent for the industry's largest carriers, meaning that for every 100 new drivers hired, 136 quit their jobs.

ORGANIZATION AND STRUCTURE

Truckload (TL) freight is the largest segment in the trucking business in terms of tonnage. These loads, which usually fill an entire truck, primarily are hauled directly from sender to receiver. The freight they haul can range anywhere from raw materials to finished products.

Less-than-truckload (LTL) freight, defined as shipments weighing less than 10,000 pounds, usually goes through a five-step process: local pick-up, sorting at a terminal facility, line haul, sorting at a destination terminal, and local delivery. LTL carrier operations and small package carriers use regional or national networks, sophisticated sorting terminals, and local pick-up and delivery service. Many LTL carriers historically handled packages as a component of their LTL business, but much of this traffic was served by specialized package carriers.

Courier services, also known as small package services, are provided by such companies as United Parcel Service (UPS) and Federal Express (FedEx) in the United States and include two- to three-day ground delivery, as well as expedited next-day delivery. Group transportation has played an increasingly important role in small package and express letter services, sometimes called couriers, thereby blurring the distinction between ground and air services. FedEx, while considered an air carrier for classification purposes, owns and operates an enormous truck fleet, not only for local pick-up and delivery, but also in lieu of aircraft for the line-haul portions of shorter trips. Similarly, UPS utilizes air and rail intermodal services to expedite its traditional ground carrier traffic. Likewise, Roadway Services, a traditional LTL player, operates Roadway Express, which serves both the ground delivery and air express package markets.

The industry is further divided based on driver/ownership. Companies that transport goods for payment are for-hire carriers, companies that own a fleet are private carriers, and individual owner-operators own or lease the tractor (truck) and haul goods using other's trailers.

BACKGROUND AND DEVELOPMENT

The trucking industry has its roots in Great Britain where, in the 1870s, vans were hauled by steam engines. In 1885 Karl Benz invented a gasoline-powered internal-combustion automobile that spurred the development of a similarly powered load-carrying vehicle produced in 1896 by Gottlieb Daimler. In 1892, Frenchman Maurice Le Blance introduced a steam-powered cartage vehicle specifically for commercial users. In the United States, the Automobile Club of America staged a contest in 1903 to test the durability and speed of heavy hauling trucks. The event's success resulted in a flourishing industry. By 1908, 4,000 trucks were on the road in the United States. When World War I started in 1914, 300,000 trucks were in service, and by the end of the war in 1918, a million were in use. During World War I the U.S. Army rapidly added to its truck fleet.

While early trucks resembled horse-drawn wagons, by 1915 they included roofs, roll-down curtains, windshields, doors, and side windows, and by the 1930s most truck cabs were entirely enclosed. The semi-trailer, with the truck's front end resting on the rear portion of the hauling truck tractor, became commonplace by the 1920s. In the early 1930s the diesel engine was introduced. Trucks continued to develop rapidly as a result of their prominent role in World War II.

Between the late 1920s and the early 1930s, the trucking industry in the United States was dominated by large numbers of itinerant owner-operators. The industry became increasingly unstable, unreliable, and chaotic. To correct the problem, in 1933 the National Industrial Recovery Act (NRA) was introduced to bring together two organized groups of trucking officials to agree to a code of fair competition. The groups proposed a code in which trucking firms would be subject to maximum hours of labor and minimum wages for all employees. The resulting Motor Carriage Act of 1934 provided safety regulations for interstate carriers, as well as economic regulation of for-hire carriers under the authority of the Interstate Commerce Commission (ICC), a regulatory agency that had been formed in the late nineteenth century.

The ICC required that operators of for-hire trucks wishing to carry freight across state lines had to be licensed by the ICC. Licenses were granted only if the need for additional truck capacity could be provided. Cargo types were also limited, with some commodities, such as food, being highly restricted. Only farmer cooperative truckers or truckers operating private carriers were exempt. Rate bureaus were formed to research and analyze costs to establish competitive trucking rates. A U.S. Justice Department antitrust exemption gave regulated trucking firms the right to collectively set rates subject to the ICC's approval.

In 1980, the U.S. Congress passed the Motor Carrier Act, a trucking deregulation bill that increased competition among trucking firms by limiting collective rate setting, easing entry restrictions, and all but eliminating the ICC's authority to set rates. The act also stimulated competition by allowing unregulated private trucking firms, which had been forbidden to carry other firms' freight, to transport freight from wholly owned subsidiaries of their parent companies. Elimination or modification of the circuitous routing and empty backhauls characteristic of the regulated environment made the trucking industry much more efficient, lowering trucking rates and benefiting both shippers and consumers.

Passage of the bill signaled a major victory for those who had for decades opposed the cartel behavior of the ICC, the trucking industry, and organized labor. Deregulation was estimated to save shippers US$5 billion annually. This legislative act paved the way for new trucking firms to enter the market and set lower rates. The ICC also loosened its route setting and commodities restrictions. While large trucking firms have since faced tough competition, deregulation has resulted in a competitive industry with thousands of new trucking firms in business.

The deregulation wave of the 1980s, however, left the intricate web of controls on U.S. intrastate trucking almost untouched. In all but eight states, restrictions on truck weight and size on interstate highways, combined with prescribed rates and routes, continued to circumscribe the industry. With deregulation, shippers around the world found they could employ the entire gamut of transportation modes to meet their shipping needs. Many manufacturers found trucking to be the most attractive option when production was behind schedule or if low train tunnels along certain routes made shipping certain products by rail impossible. For shippers who needed to meet steamship schedules, trucks offered a faster and more flexible option than rail. Additionally, shippers needing to transport small quantities found LTL services appealing. LTL trucking companies could consolidate small shipments from a number of different companies into a single truckload. Prior to LTL shipping companies, shippers had to persuade truckers to bend their schedules to accommodate their production cycles. Many companies had to rely on their own private fleets for local and regional delivery. Meeting tight delivery schedules was next to impossible.

From a U.S. manufacturer's perspective, the biggest advance in the trucking industry came when truckers began forming alliances with railroads in 1990. For example, J.B. Hunt Transport Inc. and Schneider National formed alliances with Conrail, Norfolk Southern, Southern Pacific, Union Pacific, and Burlington Northern. Such alliances offered manufacturers the speed and flexibility of trucks and the low cost of rail service. As a result, trucking companies began to utilize equipment that accommodated intermodal containers rather than tractor trailers so that containerized cargo could be easily moved between both transportation modes.

The Intermodal Surface Transportation Efficiency Act (ISTEA) of 1991 aimed to reduce paperwork by forcing states to adopt uniform measures, such as making fuel tax payments to a single state. In 1994 an International Fuel Tax Agreement and the International Registration Plan were also designed to fit the single-state payment/registration pattern. In total, these various uniformity measures were estimated to save carriers between US$500 million and US$1 billion annually in administrative costs.

During the Clinton administration, the U.S. government moved to consolidate its bureaucracy, resulting in the closure of the 108-year-old ICC in 1994. Some of its functions were transferred to the jurisdiction of a new agency called the Commerce Board, which operated under the U.S. Department of Transportation.

The U.S. trucking industry reported record levels in both production and earnings in the late 1990s. According to the U.S. Bureau of the Census, motor carrier revenue grew 7.8 percent in 1998, reaching US$187.4 billion. Local trucking activities, which grew 12.8 percent, accounted for US$66.9 billion of the total, while long-distance trucking, which grew 5.2 percent, brought in the remaining US$120.5 billion. Nearly every segment of the trucking and courier services industry in 1998 experienced considerable growth. As demand grew, companies found themselves facing driver shortages, which prompted them to offer higher pay and better equipment to drivers.

During this time, the trucking industry began to transform itself from a narrowly defined industry into a flexible one, ready to provide a number of services to meet clients' changing cargo-transport needs. Large trucking services with national and international delivery capabilities, as well as small niche services, were in the best position to capitalize on the industry's changes in the late 1990s. Medium-size services struggled to find their place in the global trucking market with less potential for growth because they were unable to provide the geographic coverage of the large companies or the specialized services of the small companies. This transformation resulted from deregulation in the European Union and the United States during the early to mid-1990s, which allowed trucking services to concentrate on the needs of shippers. Previously, the industry generally had operated under rigid policies that forced shippers to adapt to trucking services.

Globalization of the trucking industry increased, due in part to trade accords such as NAFTA, as well as the expansion of trade blocs like the European Union. In addition to providing trucking services to destinations throughout the world, trucking fleets started to expand their operations internationally by forming alliances with trucking companies and freight forwarders in other countries. However, even though NAFTA created seamless trade between the United States and Canada, it failed to bring about liberalized trucking between Mexico and the United States, and trucking companies began to pressure the government to remove the restrictions.

The European Union also began implementing policies to create smooth trade among its 15 member countries and to convert its regionalized and fragmented trucking industry into a large complex industry on par with the U.S. industry. Because the European Union's freight rail service was fragmented and costly to use, trucking accounted for about 85 percent of the region's freight transport. Nevertheless, restrictions there hampered the trucking industry. Major trading countries, such as France and Spain, imposed bans on trucks hauling most kinds of freight on Sundays and holidays, in part to ease road congestion and to appease domestic drivers who wanted Sundays off and were concerned that foreign drivers would deliver on Sundays without such restrictions. Other countries, such as Belgium and Luxembourg, planned to implement similar measures in the late 1990s. These restrictions affected the United Kingdom the most because about 60 percent of U.K. exports to the European Union were transported by truck. With pressure from the various factions involved in the dispute, the European Commission began to consider developing a sweeping policy for all member countries.

Another prominent trend in the industry was the ongoing development of intermodal transportation (the integration of various modes of transportation such as truck, train, and aircraft). Many of the industry's largest players, including UPS, Nippon Express, and FedEx, had already adopted multiple modes of transportation by the late 1990s, having fleets of planes and trucks. This change in the structure of the industry reduced the distinction between less-than-truckload and truckload transport services and was expected to blur the distinction completely by the early 2000s. In addition, in an effort to remain competitive, trucking companies began offering a full spectrum of logistics operations to customers, including basic transportation (local, regional, truckload, less-than-truckload, and air freight), inventory management and warehousing, light assembly, and state-of-the-art information systems.

Furthermore, some companies that shipped products began to reduce and eliminate their inventories in the late 1990s to cut storage costs, which made transportation even more important. Shippers relied on trucking services to transport their products quickly and to meet strict deadlines in order to reduce their inventories. Similar to their air-express counterparts, trucking companies introduced single-rate, one-bill, seamless door-to-port or door-to-door scheduled delivery worldwide.

The trucking industry also began to make use of the Internet in the late 1990s, as companies set up Web sites to market their services and to allow customers to place orders and check on order status and prices. By 1998 most of the major trucking companies provided their clients with tracking capabilities at their Web sites, so individual and business customers waiting for deliveries could check the status of those deliveries online.

The rise of electronic commerce in the late 1990s had a profound impact on some of the industry's largest players, particularly those in the United States, where the Internet revolution had taken hold. UPS had been allowing clients to track shipments online since the mid-1990s. In the late 1990s rival FedEx determined that UPS had gained an advantage in Internet-based shipping partly because it focused on deliveries to residences, which increased as consumers began buying books, CDs, computers, software, and a multitude of other products over the Internet. In January 1999, in an effort to compete with UPS, which had a fleet of 13,500 trucks, FedEx established FedEx Home Delivery to handle its new residential ground delivery operations. Online shopping grew to roughly US$4 billion over the holiday season of 1999, at which time FedEx handled shipping for only 10 percent of all goods sold online, compared to the 55 percent handled by UPS.

The economy was uncertain at the turn of the century. Many small players had already crumbled under the combined pressure of slowing demand and higher operating expenses. More than 1,300 small U.S.-based trucking firms shut their doors in 2000. Demand for transportation and shipping services began to tumble, according to *Logistics Management & Distribution Report,* as the multitude of businesses that had increased production for the flourishing economy of the late 1990s found themselves burdened with surplus inventories in 2000. Compounding the problem was a surge in oil costs, reflected in the price of diesel fuel used by trucks. By late 2000, diesel fuel rates in the United States had reached an average of US$1.65 per gallon, which was a 73 percent increase over prices in the late 1990s.

Logistics grew increasingly important to the trucking and courier services industry in the early 2000s. In one instance, UPS was able to use its expertise in logistics to oversee the transport and delivery of 4.5 million vehicles to 6,000 North American automobile dealers for Ford Motor Company. By following just-in-time principles, UPS was able to reduce delivery time 25 percent and reduced inventory requirements at Ford, saving the automaker roughly US$240 million. A similar project for National Semiconductor Corp. proved equally successful. According to a May 2001 article in *Business Week,* UPS designed and constructed a National Semiconductor warehouse in Singapore that uses "a delivery process that is efficient and automated, almost to the point of magic." Once new products, such as computer chips, are manufactured and sent to the Singapore warehouse, "it is UPS's computers that speed the box of chips to a loading dock, then to truck, to plane, and to truck once again. In just 12 hours, the chips will reach one of National's customers, a PC maker half a world away in Silicon Valley. Throughout the journey, electronic tags embedded in the chips will let the customer track the order with accuracy down to about three feet." In a two-year period, UPS logistics services cut National Semiconductor's shipping and inventory management expenses an estimated 15 percent. By 2001, small trucking companies were offering similar just-in-time services to their clients.

Despite these technological and operational advances, the industry remained susceptible to economic

conditions. When the slowing North American economy entered a recession in 2001, trucking and courier services firms like UPS and FedEx began to feel the pinch. The economic downturn that eventually spread to Europe and Asia undercut freight volumes as businesses shipped less inventory. At the same time, diesel fuel costs soared, reaching rates nearly 75 percent higher than those of the late 1990s. By the middle of the first decade of the 2000s, industry analysts made it clear that shippers were going to have to shoulder much of the rising cost of transportation, as trucking rates would have to increase exponentially to cover rising operating costs, from fuel to equipment to driver salaries.

Tension between Mexican and U.S. road freight officials escalated as U.S. authorities continued denying Mexican freight trucks access to U.S. destinations, despite a previous agreement that borders would be open as of January 1, 2000. In 2001, the NAFTA International Tribunal ruled that the United States was in violation of its NAFTA obligations. Those opposed to allowing Mexican freight trucks into the United States argued that Mexican trucks were unsafe and that U.S. jobs would be lost to foreign competition. Eventually, Mexican trucking association Canacar began calling for the cancellation of all NAFTA policies relating to road freight. Heated negotiations continued into 2002.

CURRENT CONDITIONS

Private trucking reported a surge in the early 2000s due to such factors as strict security regulations in the wake of worldwide instability and threat of terrorism and war, which made increased oversight of the trucking industry necessary. In addition, the higher cost of private trucking was going down. According to the National Private Truck Council, the freight carried by private trucking companies was expected to grow 50 percent by 2020. Of the US$462 billion in revenues for intercity trucking, private trucking accounted for about 60 percent in 2002. As of 2003, there were 33,000 companies with private fleets of at least 10 vehicles.

High diesel prices continued to be a problem, as prices in the United States averaged US$3.18 per gallon by mid-November 2010. According to the American Trucking Associations, fuel accounts for about 25 percent of a trucking company's operating costs, and therefore increased prices were cutting into profits. India, Sri Lanka, Malaysia, Thailand, and Indonesia had all increased fuel prices in 2005, causing some truckers to hold demonstrations and work slowdowns. In April 2005, the Road Haulage Association in Great Britain, where truckers pay some of the world's highest fuel prices, was calling for a reduction of tax levels on fuel prices.

Also around the world, drivers continued to face increased regulation on driving hours. In the United States, the Federal Motor Carrier Safety Administration issued new rules to shorten driving hours and required compliance by January 2004. As of 2010, long-haul drivers are limited to 11 hours of actual driving within a 14 hour period, after which they must have a 10-hour rest period. Federal regulations do not require drivers to sleep, just that they must have 10 hours of down time. Keeping track of a driver's hours is a required by the Hours of Service (HOS) regulation. Drivers must keep a log book containing a grid outlining each 24-hour period in 15-minute increments. They must specify where and when they stopped between shifts and what duties they performed, along with their name, truck number, company information, and any other pertinent information. Authorities can ask to review a log book at any time for inspection. In lieu of an actual log book, motor carriers may utilize an electronic on-board recorder to record the driver''s hours. In April 2005, Britain introduced legislation to decrease the average number of hours a driver could work in a week from 55 to 48. This legislation was proposed after a BBC report that the Road Haulage Association claimed that an extra 45,000 drivers were going to be needed in order to meet demand.

Advances in satellite navigation and logistics technologies were increasing efficiencies in the industry. In a further effort to reduce costs and maintain efficiency, the industry was consolidating. The biggest news in 2003 was the merging of Yellow Corp. and Roadway Corp. The US$1.1 billion merger resulted in a new company valued at approximately US$6 billion, with a command of about 60 percent of the LTL market. With the 2002 shutdown of competitor Consolidated Freightways, the only other unionized carrier was ABF Freight System, valued at US$1.3 billion.

In the courier segment of the trucking industry, Transport Canada indicated several important trends that were facing the industry. First, mergers and acquisitions were expected to continue as companies worked to establish intermodal forms of transport for packages in order to remain competitive. In addition, Transport Canada anticipated that postal services around the world would continue to partner with courier companies to increase their services in the face of declines in the volume of letter mail.

Increases in sales via the Internet were also having an impact on courier services, as they continued to be the distributor of choice for many sales companies. Furthermore, increased international shipping was occurring as trade liberalized around the world and the economies of developing countries improved.

RESEARCH AND TECHNOLOGY

The escalating importance of transportation and logistics to business in the 1990s placed greater demands on fleet managers than ever before. The greatest impact in the streamlining of business was new information technology. In the early 1990s, satellite systems were introduced to the industry to track vehicles along routes and to determine package status via combinations of barcode scanning and wireless transmission of shipment data. By the late 1990s, this technology was standard for almost all trucking companies.

In 1991 UPS completed the construction of an US$80 million computer and telecommunications center in Mahwah, New Jersey, which served as the cornerstone of its global computer network. The center was part of the company's US$1.5 billion investment in a five-year plan to develop state-of-the-art high technology to drive its delivery network. In 1993 UPS installed a satellite earth station to provide a direct satellite link between the United States and Germany. By having its own earth station, UPS reduced the potential for transmission failures and allowed package tracking data to move more reliably between the two countries.

UPSnet was a cost-efficient and highly reliable global telecommunications fiber-optic network that linked 1,200 UPS distribution sites in 1992, including 80 international locations. The network was a vital component of UPS' international expansion in the air express delivery business. The system provided immediate access to information for tracking international shipments, expediting customs clearance, billing and delivery confirmation, and electronically capturing and transmitting signatures.

UPS' proprietary International Shipments Processing System (ISPS) was an integrated network designed to process and track parcels moving within the company's international shipping network. It provided electronic shipment information directly to U.S. and Canadian customs bureaus prior to the arrival of shipments and was able to monitor the precise status and location of packages clearing customs in more than 180 countries and territories. The system had many benefits, including reduced transit time, improved reliability of package and document transport, and lowered service costs. It also simplified the import-export shipment process and replaced manual document preparation and key-entry tasks.

Some trucking companies, such as OTR Express, employed sophisticated computer systems to track customers and their shipping trends in order to expedite service. One such system developed by Ohio-based Roberts Express involved a two-way satellite network, an automated shipment and control system, and personalized Customer Assistance Teams. The system allowed rapid customer response by tracking the nearest truck via satellite and an in-house computer system. By utilizing its computer network, the trucking firm was able to make pickup or reach its destinations within 15 minutes of the promised delivery time.

In 1994 the U.S. National Highway Traffic Safety Administration (NHTSA) developed technology called the Autonomous Driver Alertness Monitor (ADAM) to curtail fatigue-related accidents. An NHTSA study found that out of 6.5 million crashes in 1990, approximately 57,000 were caused by drowsiness. When a driver blinks repetitively, ADAM sets off a loud noise or flashing light to jolt the driver. The monitors could either be placed on drivers' eyeglasses or on seatbelts. To help prevent driver fatigue, some trucking firms also used the Princeton Logistics System, a computerized dispatch program that assists long-haul drivers in selecting backhaul loads that will shorten their drive home. Many companies used "team driving," with two drivers sharing the driving and the mileage-based pay. The advantage was to maximize productivity and time by keeping the truck moving.

Safety and environmental issues have also greatly impacted the industry. For example, trucks equipped with anti-lock brakes became more commonplace. In the United States, drivers who haul freight long distance are required to take periodic, random alcohol and drug tests to ensure they are free of judgment-impairing substances when they are behind the wheel. The U.S. Department of Transportation and the Federal Highway Administration established 0.04 percent blood alcohol concentration level at or above which a CMV driver is considered to be driving under the influence of alcohol. German truck manufacturers Freightliner and Daimler-Benz tested a second generation of truck design that uses an interactive video computer system. Called Vector, the system videotapes the highway as the truck is moving; interprets data, such as speed and traffic; and directs the truck to travel at a certain speed. Application of this technology was not expected to reach the marketplace until the twenty-first century. Meanwhile, other designs addressing fuel consumption, emissions standards, and engines were being tested in order to meet tougher standards imposed by the Clear Air Act and to allow trucks to operate more efficiently and profitably.

Global Industry Analysts reported that trucking firms began to reduce spending in 2008 based on "the slowdown of truck-dependent industries." They predicted a drop in capital investment in the U.S. trucking sector in fall 2008 that would create a tighter trucking capacity. The long-term result could be less trucking capacity when demand returns.

WORKFORCE

Truck driving jobs typically require a high school education with some college for candidates 18 years of age with inter-state driving clearance. Federal Motor Carrier Safety Regulations require truck drivers to be 21 years of age or older, have minimal 20/40 vision, and good

hearing. Many companies also require an ability to read and speak English.

Beginning truck drivers generally received informal training, and several trucking companies, such as C.R. England, have driving schools. Many learn by riding with and observing experienced drivers. Given the shortages in the industry, job opportunities in trucking were abundant and expected to increase in both the United States and Europe at the beginning of the 2010s.

Long hours on the road, weeks away from home, nonunion wages at nonunion trucking companies, and the cramped quarters of the sleeper cab have all been cited as drawbacks of trucking industry employment. Truckers have complained about being forced to load and unload freight themselves or having to pay out of their own pockets for extra help at the dock, a practice termed "lumping." Such complaints have caused many trucking companies to focus on shorter regional markets, typically 250 to 500 miles in length, and to form partnerships with railroads to offer intermodal service.

Employees at some large carriers have been forced to accept wage cuts. In some cases, wage negotiations with trade unions have spurred bitter management-labor showdowns and strikes, with work rules and health, welfare, and pension benefits nominally at issue. Most notable was the 1997 UPS labor strike in which UPS eventually sued the International Brotherhood of Teamsters for US$50 million, claiming the strike had been illegal. The strike was resolved on terms that favored the union, and some analysts predicted that the result would cause labor costs to increase for all unionized LTL companies. In 1998 the Teamsters announced their plans to seek similar employee compensation packages for other major companies: Yellow Freight System, Roadway Express, Consolidated Freightways, and ABF Freight System. Some companies reported losing business to non-unionized competition because of their ability to offer lower rates.

On September 3, 2008, the ATA introduced ATA Business Solutions, a suite of information products, business tools, services, training programs, and conferences created to address critical issues affecting trucking-related companies. ATA President and CEO Bill Graves explained that the focus was on making targeted companies "more profitable and efficient in today's difficult economic times." The solutions were developed and approved by top industry professionals to address diverse industry segments from owner-operators to companies with large fleets to delivery services.

A report from the Department of Labor and Industries, issued in 2008, revealed some of the highest rates of workplace injuries in Washington State. "Preventing Injuries in the Trucking Industry Focus" put tips to help employers reduce common workplace hazards in the spotlight. The report examined occurrences from 1997 to 2005. Findings showed the Washington trucking industry had US$265 million in claims each year for muscular skeletal disorders, including injury to muscles, tendons, and joints.

On August 29, 2008, in *Fleet Owner,* Sean Kilcarr that the impact of a "one-of-a-kind online alcohol and drug database" for commercial drivers of trucks. A 2007 Arkansas law required the database to be established and mandated that employers must search it prior to hiring a commercial driver. The "eGovernment" services provider, Olathe, won the contract to develop "The Online Commercial Driver Alcohol and Drug Testing Result Database." It was launched in January 2008 and subsequent results showed more than 5,100 commercial driver records had been searched and 263 positive test results were reported to the database. J.B. Hunt participated in the lobbying process for the database and wanted to broaden its use of online systems throughout the United States. "Drivers are the most important people at our company and this services helps to ensure they are safe vehicle operators," acknowledged Davis Whiteside, J.B. Hunt's senior director of compliance.

INDUSTRY LEADERS

Courier Services.

United Parcel Service Inc. (UPS). UPS was founded in August 1907 in Seattle, Washington, when teenagers Jim Casey and Claude Ryan started a telephone message service called the American Messenger Company. The boys soon found themselves delivering small parcels for local department stores. In 1952 the company expanded to include small package delivery within a 150-mile radius of specific metropolitan areas, with the first being Los Angeles. The company's first international operation came in 1975, with service to Ontario, Canada. In 1976 service was initiated within West Germany, and by 1985 service had expanded to six other European countries. An important milestone was reached in 1987 when UPS became the first package delivery service in history to deliver to every address in the United States and Puerto Rico. That year the company also expanded its international service to Japan and parts of Canada. In 1988, UPS acquired Italian service partner Alimondo, providing UPS with 40 facilities throughout Italy. That same year its International Air Service delivery network extended to 41 countries. UPS also announced the acquisition of Asian Courier System (ACS), a Hong Kong-based carrier, and Britain's Arkstar Limited and its subsidiaries, including Atlasair Parcel Service Ltd., providing UPS with a network of 19 branches throughout Britain. In 1991, UPS introduced Euro-Expedited Service, a pan-European ground package and freight delivery service, as an economical alternative to air express. By 1992 UPS was the largest package distribution company in the world.

With sales of US$45.3 billion and roughly 408,000 employees worldwide, United Parcel Service (UPS) was the largest package shipper in the world in 2009. The Atlanta, Georgia-based company moved approximately 15 million packages per business day to 6.1 million customers across the United States and to more than 200 countries and territories. It has a fleet of approximately 93,600 vehicles and about 600 aircraft. The company did not separate the revenue earned from trucking versus that earned from other forms of transport, including air, as much of its courier services involves a variety of transport forms for each delivery.

In 2003, the company announced plans to spend US$600 million dollars to improve its pickup and delivery processes. Considered the most technologically savvy of the world's largest shipping firms, UPS used such systems as UPSnet, with more than 500,000 miles of communications lines, as well as a satellite that tracked hundreds of thousands of packages each day and connected roughly 1,300 UPS distribution plants in 46 different nations.

In August 2008, UPS Freight reported that its heavy-freight division had dramatically improved transit times, including more than 1,200 traffic lanes. The company reported that it had reduced shipping times for more than 10,000 lanes during the prior 18 months. UPS Freight announced improvements in lines starting in the Midwest, Northeast, and Mid-Atlantic.

A UPS sustainability report issued in 2008 showed that UPS missed meeting a goal that it had set in 2002. Spokeswoman Elizabeth Rasberry acknowledged the goal should have been met in 2007, but added that business had "changed considerably during that time." In the meantime, UPS had implemented Package Flow Technology, which eliminated approximately 30 million miles from its delivery routes, saving the company 3 million gallons of gas.

UPS provided permanent part-time package handlers with fully paid healthcare benefits. Employees also received discounts of 22 percent on Verizon Wireless services and up to 40 percent on Dell and Panasonic products. Part-time employees at some locations received tuition assistance up to US$3,000 per year as well as adoption assistance.

FedEx. Founded in 1971, the Federal Express concept was originally conceived in a Yale University term paper written by company founder Fred Smith Federal Express specializes in overnight delivery of packages, documents, and heavy freight, and was a top express transportation company worldwide. Its delivery divisions include FedEx Express, FedEx Ground, FedEx Freight, and FedEx Custom.

In 1973 the Memphis, Tennessee-based company began service in 25 cities with a fleet of 14 small aircraft. In the mid-1980s, Federal Express opened its European hub and generated US$2 billion in one year alone. Although the company was experiencing losses in the international arena in the 1990s, its total sales were US$11.5 billion and it employed more than 126,000 people. Shortly after Federal Express bought ground shipper Caliber System in the late 1990s, the company consolidated all operations under a new parent company named FDX Corporation.

In early 2000, FDX diversified into customs brokerage with the purchase of Tower Group International, which eventually formed the core of a new subsidiary, FedEx Trade Networks Inc. The trading unit also provided trade consulting and international transportation and logistics services. In April 2000, FDX changed its name to FedEx Corp., and the core express delivery business took on the name FedEx Express. Ground delivery operations were renamed FedEx Ground. To expand its less-than-truckload freight operations, the firm paid US$1.2 billion for American Freightways Corporation in December 2000. FedEx merged American Freightways with former Caliber unit Viking Freight into its FedEx Freight arm. As part of the deal, FedEx assumed US$250 million in American Freightways' debt, which concerned some analysts because FedEx was already spending billions of dollars each year maintaining its costly infrastructure.

In 2008, FedEx faced legal challenges, including a nationwide lawsuit demanding the federal pension benefits reserved for employees. FedEx was also looking at ways to improve its business model. If FedEx decided to reinvent itself, the result would be a new way of doing business that gave it an edge over its competitors. Major areas of discussion included whether FedEx should deal with drivers in the same way it handled other employees, which would give drivers the same tax benefits, insurance, vacations, and overtime pay as other employees. There was much debate about whether FedEx should implement Teamsters' model or await legal case resolutions. Another possible alternative was for the FedEx chairman to utilize efforts to move toward multi route drivers instead of payroll workers.

According to the September 2, 2008, edition of the *Memphis Business Journal,* the International Brotherhood of Teamsters sent a letter to Fed Ex shareholders, asking for support to remove company Chairman Fred Smith, saying he was "incapable of providing rigorous, independent oversight" of the board. The union expressed severe concern about Smith's ability to function due to the dual duties of CEO and chairman. It was the union's goal to organize FedEx mechanics and ground drivers. The union disputed the classification of these drivers as independent contractors. FedEx claimed its employees had rejected third-party representation many times.

In August 2008, FedEx announced that it planned to launch next day business service throughout Mexico. FedEx Express Nacional was set to launch in late 2008. FedEx planned to add 180 employees to the 1,000 already on the payroll in Mexico.

FedEx boasted 2008 sales of US$38 billion. The company's 290,000 employees handled approximately 3.5 million shipments each day to more than 220 countries and territories, using more than 44,000 ground delivery vehicles and 675 aircraft. The company does not differentiate between revenues earned by truck transport and that earned through air or other means.

DHL International GmbH. Owned by the German Deutsche Post, DHL International was a global leader in international express shipping. Begun in 1969 as an air shipper of paper from San Francisco, California, to Hawaii, the company was soon expanding globally. It exceeded the dreams of founding entrepreneurs Adrian Dalsey, Larry Hillblom, and Robert Lynn. By the end of 2002, Deutsche Post owned the company, and in 2003 the parent company merged its other acquisitions into DHL. India's Twenty Four Seven convenience stores were partners with DHL, making the delivery service accessible any time of day at those stores. The consolidation was viewed as a continuation of outstanding services offered by the partners. By 2009, the company had solidified its status in the industry by offering services to more than 220 countries and territories. DHL had a network of approximately 4,700 offices with 500,000 employees. Its fleet consisted of approximately 76,200 vehicles and approximately 420 aircraft.

TNT N.V. Although it is the primary manager of the postal system of the Netherlands, TNT is a world leader in the express delivery and logistics businesses. What began in Australia in 1946 as a single truck operation had grown by 1996 to an international firm large enough to acquire the postal service of the Netherlands, which had started the privatization process in 1989. Through a series of joint ventures and acquisitions, by 2010 the firm had grown to employ more than 154,500 people, and had revenues of more than US$14.19 billion.

Yamato. Founded in 1919 by young entrepreneur Koshin Kogura, Yamato was the first courier service in Tokyo. Yamato Transport Co. Ltd. was the forerunner of private parcel delivery service in Japan, and in 2004 it marked two decades as that country's market. A strong domestic service included home moving, delivery of refrigerated goods, and facsimile transmission, Yamato had links with UPS in the United States that allowed the company to make deliveries in 200 countries outside Japan. By the end of its fiscal year in March 2008, Yamato employed about 169,836 workers and brought in approximately US$14 billion per year.

Trucking Companies.

Nippon Express. Nippon Express Co. Ltd. (Nittsu) was Japan's leading general transportation company. Founded in the 1930s, Nittsu assumed full responsibility for the door-to-door, worldwide delivery of all types of goods, including electronic components, oil refinery equipment, and fine arts. Because of opening markets in the European Union, Nittsu had been developing its European trucking network and improving its warehouse facilities. In addition to trucking services, the company offered rail and air transport services through its subsidiaries. Nittsu reported annual revenues of more than US$14 billion as of 2009.

Schneider National. In 2008, one of the largest truckload carriers in the United States was privately owned Schneider National. Based on annual revenue, Schneider was the third largest trucking company in the United States at that time with a fleet of about 14,000 tractors, 40,000 trailers, and approximately 11,000 intermodal carriers. The company also had a strong presence in Canada and Mexico. Founded in 1935, Schneider grew through a series of acquisitions over the years, first by acquiring the right to transport in various states, and then throughout North America.

Wal-Mart named Schneider National as the 2007 Intermodal Carrier of the Year on the basis of "overall dedication to customer service, operational excellence and the ability to offer creative solutions" to the chain in support of its complex needs.

J.B. Hunt Transport Services Inc. Begun in 1969 with five trucks and seven refrigerated trailers, by 2007 the company operated 1,800 trucks (tractors) and provided trucking services to the United States, Canada, and Mexico. By 2009, annual revenues reached over US$3 billion, and the company employed over 16,000 people with a fleet of over 12,000 trucks and 47,000 trailers and containers.

YRC Worldwide. After a series of acquisitions, YRC Worldwide continued to work under a series of brand names, including Yellow Transportation, Roadway, New Penn, and Reimer Express. The 2003 acquisition of Roadway doubled the size of the company. In 2008, the company reported revenues of US$8.94 billion and 55,000 employees. The company was the leader in less-than-truckload (LTL) transportation in the United States, consolidating freight from various suppliers in order to improve cost efficiencies for customers.

MAJOR COUNTRIES IN THE INDUSTRY

United States. The U.S. trucking industry remained the world's strongest throughout the first decade of the 2000s. *Euromonitor* indicated that the U.S. trucking market increased from US$468.2 billion in 2002 to US$490 billion in 2003. Of this total, 66.2 percent came from intercity trucking, which was expected to remain the largest sector through 2008, growing to 67.2 percent of the market. In 2001, approximately 70 percent of trade crossing the U.S.–Canadian border was transported via truck. *Euromonitor* predicted increases of 14 percent by 2007 from a 2003 value of US$484.6 billion. Eighty percent of all communities in the United States relied exclusively on trucks to deliver all fuel, clothing, medicine, and consumer goods. The trucking industry has a workforce of approximately 10 million. There are over 500,000 interstate motor carriers and 93 percent of the carriers operate fleets of 20 or fewer trucks.

European Union. The European Union's trucking industry was strong in the late 1990s as trucks continued to ship more than 80 percent of the region's cargo because European railroads were largely regulated during that period. Deregulation of Western Europe's trucking industry occurred with the establishment of the European Union in 1993, which also brought a change in rules dictating cabotage. Non-national trucking carriers began to be allowed to pick up and backhaul cargo throughout the European Union. Internal spot checks replaced systematic stops at customs at borders, thereby speeding up traffic flow and preventing long border delays.

These new rules were not welcomed by all EU member nations, however. Germany, a main transit route for cargo traveling to and from Turkey, the Netherlands, and Belgium, opposed the rules, saying that increased truck traffic would result in congestion, pollution, and road damage. Nonetheless, the German market (along with the U.K. market) was predicted to increase more than 20 percent between 2003 and 2008, according to *Euromonitor.* Switzerland was the most vocal opponent of truck traffic. Its central European location made the country the main transit route for truck movement to and from Italy, the Balkans, Turkey, and the Middle East, which had forced laws requiring trucks to only travel its roads during the daytime. The Swiss also had passed a referendum to prohibit all through-truck traffic as of 2004, after which time all cargo was required to travel via rail.

China. Trucking started to play a greater role in shipping cargo in China in the 1990s. The country's trucking industry remained small in the 1980s, accounting for about 6 percent of China's freight traffic, but by the early 1990s trucking's share had risen to 13.6 percent. Although trucking services cost more than train services, Chinese companies preferred trucking services because of problems with the country's railroads, including train delays, insufficient availability, and lost and damaged goods. In addition, trucks provided more reliable service that was less prone to damage, and China's highway expansion during this period helped the trucking industry prosper. In 1997 China resumed control of Hong Kong, which also had a strong trucking industry that accounted for 25 percent of the province's total annual freight volume. Although many analysts considered China a key growth market for international trucking and courier services players, the market remained fairly closed in the early 2000s.

BIBLIOGRAPHY

American Trucking Associations. "ATA Advocates Realistic Solution to Freight Transportation Challenges," 22 May 2003. Available from www.truckline.com.

———. "ATA Truck Tonnage Index Shows 5.4 Percent Increase in April," 28 May 2003. Available from www.truckline.com.

———. "Facts About Trucking," February 2002. Available from www.truckline.com.

———. "Trucking Will Dominate Freight Movement." *U.S. Freight Transportation Forecast to 2014,* 7 March 2003.

"American Trucking Associations Introduces ATA Business Solutions." *Market Watch,* 3 September 2008.

Arndt, Michael. "Industry Outlook 2001: Transportation." *Business Week,* 2 January 2001.

"Canadian Courier Market Size, Structure and Fleet Analysis Study." Transport Canada, 2003. Available from www.tc.gc.ca.

Curry, Sheree. "Out of Work? Get Part-time Work and Benefits" *Main Street,* 26 August 2008. Available from http://www.mainstreet.com/print/4073.

Davidson, Laurence Viele, and Bob Van Voris. "In Driver Lawsuit, FedEx Stands to Lose Money, Business Model." *St. Paul Pioneer Press,* 23 August 2008. Available from www.airlinepilotforums.com.

DHL. "From Humble Beginnings to Global Market Leader," 2008. Available from www.dhl.com.

Draper, Deborah J., ed. *Business Rankings Annual.* Detroit: Thomson Gale, 2004.

"FedEx Introduces Next-Day Service in Mexico." *Atlanta Business Chronicle,* 28 August 2008.

Gelinas, Tom. "Competition!" *Fleet Equipment,* May 2004.

Haddad, Charles. "UPS vs. FedEx: Ground Wars." *Business Week,* 21 May 2001.

Hannon, Dave. "Lack of Investment Could Shrink Trucking Capacity." *Purchasing,* 3 September 2008. Available from www.goliath.ecnext.com.

Harrington, Lisa H. "NAFTA and Trucking." *Transportation & Distribution,* September 2001.

Henry, John. "Trucking Industry Thrives Despite New Regulations." *Arkansas Business,* 12 July 2004.

"Hoover's Company Capsules." *Hoover's Online,* 2008. Available from www.hoovers.com.

"Intermodal, Truck Freight Seen Weakening." *Bulk Transporter,* April 2005. Available from bulktransporter.com.

"International Trade Statistics." World Trade Organization, 2003. Available from www.wto.org.

Kilcarr, Sean. "Arkansas Offers Real-Time Drug Test Results." *FleetOwner,* 29 August 2008.

Lazich, Robert S., ed. *Market Share Reporter.* Detroit: Thomson Gale, 2004.

"Modern Bulk Transporter's Annual Gross Revenue Report 2003: Operating Ratios Deteriorate Further." *Modern Bulk Transporter,* May 2004.

"Report: Trucking Industry Draws High Workplace Injuries, Costs." *Tacoma Daily Index,* 2 September 2008.

"Rising Fuel Costs Continue to Challenge the Trucking Industry, According to a New Report by Global Industry Analysts, Inc." *PRWeb* 1 September 2008. Available from www.PRWeb.com.

"Schneider National Selected as Wal-Mart's Intermodal Carrier of the Year." *Supply Chain Market,* 19 August 2008.

Schulz, John D. "Trucking's Good News, Bad News." *The Journal of Commerce,* 31 May 2004.

———. "Trucking's Private Renaissance?" *Traffic World,* 3 May 2004.

"A Shifting Delivery Model Leads to Higher Emissions, Energy Use for UPS." GreenBiz Web site, 3 September 2008. Available from www.greenbiz.com.

"Supply Chain a Key to UPS Growth, Says CEO." *Journal of Commerce Online,* 14 July 2004.

Tanzer, Andrew. "Chinese Walls." *Forbes,* 11 November 2001.

"Teamsters Solicit Shareholders to Oust Smith as FedEx Chairman." *Memphis Business Journal,* 2 September 2008.

"Truck Recruitment in High Gear." *BBC News: UK Edition,* 26 May, 2004. Available from news.bbc.co.uk.

"Truckers Traveling Rough Road." *Logistics Management & Distribution Report,* May 2001.

"Trucking in France, Germany, UK, US." *Euromonitor,* October 2004. Available from www.majormarketprofiles.com.

"Twenty Four Seven Ties Up with DHL." *News Center,* 22 August 2008. Available from www.Moneycontrol.com.

"UPS Freight Says It Improved Transit Times." Best Way Technologies Web site, 25 August 2008. Available from www.bestwaytech.com.

SIC 4400

WATER TRANSPORTATION

NAICS CODE(S)

483. Industry firms transport freight and passengers on the open seas and inland waters. The freight segment is also commonly known as the merchant marine. Maritime transportation companies also furnish such services as lighterage (floating inter-locking barges), towing and tugboating, and canal and marina operation. For further information about water transportation vessels, see also **Shipbuilding.**

INDUSTRY SNAPSHOT

Merchant fleets of every nation carry merchandise between ports throughout the world in direct competition with each other. Intermodal ships, which deliver goods using two or more transport modes, primarily

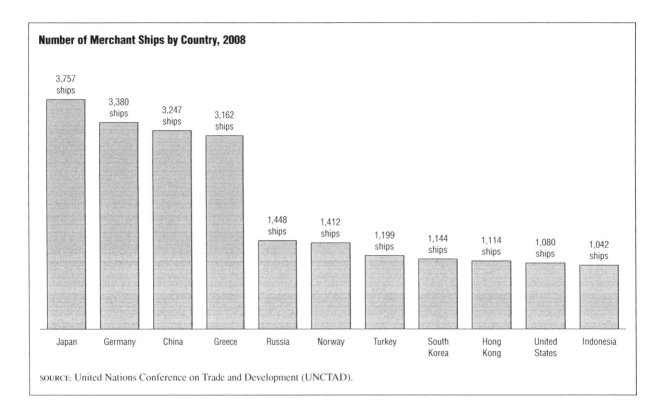

Number of Merchant Ships by Country, 2008

Japan: 3,757 ships; Germany: 3,380 ships; China: 3,247 ships; Greece: 3,162 ships; Russia: 1,448 ships; Norway: 1,412 ships; Turkey: 1,199 ships; South Korea: 1,144 ships; Hong Kong: 1,114 ships; United States: 1,080 ships; Indonesia: 1,042 ships

SOURCE: United Nations Conference on Trade and Development (UNCTAD).

consist of containerships, roll-on/roll-off (ro/ro) vessels, and container/barge carriers. General cargo ships include breakbulk vessels, partial container ships, and other ships designed to carry non-containerized cargo. Primary U.S. operators include CSX (Sea-Land Service Inc.), American President Lines (APL), and Seabulk International Inc.

According to the United Nations Conference on Trade and Development (UNCTAD), the world seaborne trade increased by 3.6 percent in 2008 to reach 8.17 billion tons. In 2009, according to the United States Maritime Administration (MARAD), the total world merchant fleet had expanded by 6.7 percent to 1.19 billion deadweight tons (dwt). Oil tankers (2.7 percent increase) and dry bulk carriers (7 percent increase) made up the bulk of the world fleet, which continued to increase over previous years. By 2003, the average age of a ship was 12.5 years, with 27.7 percent of ships reported to be 20 years or older. General cargo ships had the oldest average age of 17.4 years. Most markets showed increases in the volumes transported during 2003, with the volume of crude oil increasing 3.4 percent, and bulk products, including iron ore and coal, increased 9.1 percent. However, by 2008, the global economic crisis had impacted the shipping industry as well as nearly every other global industry. Poor credit abroad brought about a reduced demand for goods and shipping services and led to decelerated growth in international seaborne commerce.

Simultaneously, delivery of new vessels was on the rise as a result of orders placed before the financial crisis

when the industry was expecting continued high growth rates in demand. A potential future crisis could be created by a surge of oversupply and a tumbling freight rate. Combined with a maritime security crisis, the industry could face a critical situation in the future. Based on data from Lloyd's Register, UNCTAD reported that of the 30,228 ships registered by January 31, 2003, Greece was the world leader in terms of the number of vessels domiciled (the home of the parent company, or owner, of the ship), accounting for 19.52 percent of the world's ships. Greece was followed by Japan, with 13.6 percent; Norway, with 7.57 percent; China, with 5.77 percent; the United States, with 5.54 percent; and Germany with 5.31 percent.

According to 2006 MARAD statistics, the U.S. merchant fleet comprised 465 total ships with 13.273 million combined deadweight tons (DWT). The majority were tanker ships, with a total of 97, followed by 76 container ships, and 27 ro/ro ships. By 2004, the total combined fleet of the world's top 20 countries was 28,650 vessels, with a combined DWT of 821.7 million. The number of worldwide container ports grew by approximately 4 percent to reach 506 million twenty foot equivalent units (TEUs) in 2008. Mainland China ports accounted for nearly 22.6 percent of the total world container shipping ports.

Steamship lines worldwide have employed various means to improve their productivity, increase sailing frequencies and port coverage, and reduce costs.

Registered Shipping Vessels by Type, 2005

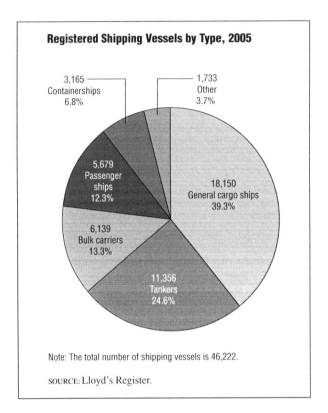

Note: The total number of shipping vessels is 46,222.

SOURCE: Lloyd's Register.

Common methods have included vessel sharing agreements, slot and terminal rationalization arrangements, and the introduction of new technologies. Shipping lines also have relied on shipping conferences, which are groups of carriers that service particular trade routes, to facilitate cooperative arrangements and establish rates, although the importance of such conferences had begun to decline in the first decade of the twenty-first century. Conferences lessened the need for individual lines to build new ships when serving new routes. Intra-industry cooperation also enabled steamship lines to overcome the double hurdle of overcapacity and declining world petroleum demand.

In the mid-2000s, many Massachusetts seaside communities began asking the state to subsidize the construction of piers and docks for ferry services connecting cities and towns on Massachusetts Bay. Water transportation was projected to be a large part of the region's future. "It's not just an alternative from transportation that takes cars off the road, but it also brings people in and stimulates the local economy," according to Louis Elisa, director of the state's Seaport Advisory Council, which subsidizes municipal ferry projects. Gloucester Mayor Carolyn Kirk expressed the desire for her city's harbor to be converted from an under-utilized resource to a revenue source.

Rising shipping costs were expected to reduce some of the advantages of inexpensive labor in China.

Outsourcing of manufacturing to China was probably already underway in 2008, according to Jeff Rubin and Benjamin Tal of CIBC, a Canadian bank. The cost to ship a standard 40-foot container to the U.S. East Coast from Shanghai had nearly tripled, which minimized the already small profits for Chinese exports.

ORGANIZATION AND STRUCTURE

Cargo vessels constitute the largest component of water transportation. Depending on their design, they might haul general cargo (finished and unfinished goods), dry bulk, or liquid bulk. These vessels are structured as common carriers available for public use to provide transportation for passengers or cargo and operate on regular timetables and port rotations.

Containerized vessels are designed to be highly efficient. Containers used to haul cargo need less labor and time to load and unload than breakbulk (noncontainerized) vessels. The containerized category consists of intermodal ships, including roll-on/roll-off (ro/ro) vessels, and container/barge carriers. Ro/ros make it possible for cargo stored in containers to be passed over ramps through doors in the ship's , while cars, trucks, and other vehicles could be driven on and off the vessel's aft (rear).

The five trade lanes that account for the vast majority of U.S. international ocean liner shipments are United States-northern Europe, United States-Asia, United States-Mediterranean, United States-South America, and United States-Australia. These trade lanes have varied in their characteristics. Containerized shipping was concentrated in three trade lanes: Asia-North America, Asia-Europe, and Europe-North America. The northern Europe and Asia trades have been the largest in volume and value.

Some dry bulk commodities, such as grain, lumber, cement, potash, coal, and ore, cannot be containerized and are shipped in vessels specially designed for those cargo types. Many have special hoisting devices that assist in unloading. Liquid bulk, such as crude oil and refined petroleum, is transported in tankers, which require such special features as cofferdams that separate the tanks to prevent leakage, expansion trunks, mechanical venting, and steam heating to reduce oil viscosity in cold weather.

Beyond vessel design, a prominent feature of international liner shipping is the existence of carrier conferences, an affiliation permitted in almost all countries. The characteristics of concerted activity and partial immunity from competition and antitrust laws are common to such conferences worldwide. Members of a conference enter into an agreement under which they consent to fix and maintain rates to be charged by the members of the conference. Most nations recognize the conference system but differ in their respective laws and regulations.

The European Union gives antitrust immunity to conference carriers alone. In Europe, conferences are free to organize themselves as their members see fit and may limit membership. By limiting membership, closed conferences are better able to control capacity and thereby exert greater influence over rates than open conferences. Australia provides partial antitrust immunity and exempts only rate fixing, pooling or apportioning of business, cargo restrictions, decisions on conference membership, loyalty agreements, and practices essential to the conference service and of overall benefit to exporters. Likewise, Canada grants conference carriers block antitrust immunity, but independent carriers are subject to competition laws. As in Australia, Canadian policy holds that discussion agreements between conferences and independents are illegal. Japan has granted the broadest exemption in that all ocean liner and non-liner transporters in domestic and foreign trades receive blanket antitrust exemption. Although the United States continues to recognize the existence of conferences, the passage of the Ocean Shipping Reform Act of 1998 (OSRA) took away much of the commercial power of conferences operating in the United States. Members can no longer be required to adhere to conference rates and restrictions cannot be placed on the service agreements members negotiate. In addition, conferences cannot require members to disclose the rates they charge.

The International Maritime Organization (IMO), an agency of the United Nations, began in 1958 when it was determined that there was a need for an international body to regulate safety in the shipping industry. In 1960, the IMO created a new version of the International Convention for the Safety of Life at Sea (SOLAS). In 1973, the IMO created the Convention for the Prevention of Pollution from Ships covering accidental and operational oil pollution, as well as pollution by chemicals, goods in packaged form, sewage, garbage, and air pollution. However, how these conventions are implemented varies from country to country.

The Chinese government reported that the country had the world's fourth largest maritime fleet. In addition, five Chinese ports had been listed among the world's top 10 for throughputs (the quantity of raw material processed for any given time). According to the Ministry of Transport's Director of Water Transport Song Dexing, China's water transport industry had made significant progress beginning in 1978. Growth in the water transportation industry in the mainland port throughput as well as in container throughput helped China maintain top ranking in the world for five successive years, with Shanghai rated as the world's largest port. The top 10 liner companies included The China Shipping Company and China Shipping Container Lines Company.

BACKGROUND AND DEVELOPMENT

Transportation of goods over water is as ancient as civilization, but did not come to full fruition as an industry until explorers seeking new trade routes for cargo opened sea routes from Europe to Asia and the Americas. To accommodate increased trade volumes, large merchant ships had to be built. Spanish carracks, which held some 1,600 tons of cargo, and later, galleons, became the forerunners of the full-rigged ships that dominated trade during the seventeenth and nineteenth centuries.

Clipper ships began to be used in the nineteenth century. Carrying passengers as well as cargo, these ships became known for their speed, some traveling as fast as 18 to 20 knots. Even with the introduction of the steamship in the mid-nineteenth century, some clipper ships continued to post the fastest speeds of all ships for a time. By the late nineteenth century, however, clipper ships began to be replaced with Britain's adaptation of iron-hulled steamships.

The steamship radically transformed ocean shipping and led to the creation of steam-powered liner systems. By the twentieth century, mechanically propelled vessels had replaced nearly all sail-powered cargo ships. With the exception of wind-driven dhows (Arabian boats with triangular sails) and junks in Asia, by 1960, almost 60 percent of all commercial ships were powered by diesel engines, 30 percent by steam turbine, and the rest by steam-reciprocating engines. Nuclear power, which proved impractical for commercial purposes, came into use in military ships in the 1960s.

The seas remained territory mainly for cargo carrying lines, however. With increases in global trade in the mid-twentieth century, the seas soon became crowded with cargo vessels operated by both large and small corporations. Vessels were redesigned to allow for transporting mixed cargo and accommodating bulk commodities, such as grains, mineral ores, coal, and oil. Until the late 1960s and early 1970s, these general cargo or breakbulk, ships were widely used by the liner trades. After a truckload or boxcar load of cargo was delivered to the pier, breakbulk ships were loaded by breaking the truckload or boxcar load into small quantities that were lifted onto the ship with a sling and boom and stowed in the cargo hold. This process was fairly labor-intensive, costly, and time consuming.

To become more efficient and accommodate large payloads, cargo ships were extensively redesigned. In the late 1960s, containerized vessels were introduced that were capable of hauling cargo in 20- and 40-foot containers. These large metal boxes could be placed on a tractor-trailer chassis, loaded at the exporter's plant, sealed, shipped by truck or train to the port, lifted onto the container ship by a dockside crane, and stacked in specially designed slots. The container itself was then unloaded at the destination. This could be accomplished without directly handling the cargo inside the container. Vessels were specifically designed or adapted to carry these containers. A roll-on/roll-off design made it possible for containers to be passed over ramps and through doors in the ships' sides while cars, trucks, and other vehicles could be driven on and off the vessel. Containerized ships, which accommodate containers filled by consolidators or shippers, were designed to receive cargo with cranes or special hoisting equipment.

The use of containers had the greatest impact on the cost of labor. In 1960, in-port labor costs accounted for 80 percent of the total cost of a typical voyage. With containerized shipments, average handling time per voyage fell from 157 hours to 31 hours, reducing cargo-handling costs between 80 and 65 percent. With steamship lines introducing containerization on all of the major trade routes, many turned to intermodal services whereby containers could be lifted on and off trucks, railroad cars, and steamships, allowing for seamless shipping over land and water. Intermodal services minimized bottlenecks in port as cargo was transferred between modes of transportation. Such efficiencies allowed the development of just-in-time production methods that turned transportation into an important part of a coordinated warehousing/production logistical system.

Supertankers, carrying 24,900 deadweight tons (DWT), were first built in 1949. After the Suez Canal was closed by the Egyptian government during the 1956 crisis, larger and more efficient tankers, many of which were constructed by the Japanese, were built to haul 100,000 tons around the Cape of Good Hope, bypassing the Canal. Tankers were adapted to meet increasing demands for hauling crude oil when they could not keep pace with supertankers. Even larger tankers, known as large crude carriers, capable of accommodating 250,000 to 275,000 tons, also were being built. Eventually, the success of these large vessels led to the development of ultra-large crude carriers boasting capacities up to 400,000 tons. In the 1990s, even larger vessels were being developed, and special consideration was added to protect tankers against oil spills in case of collision.

Tugboats, which were originally called towboats, were introduced to help large vessels navigate harbors and channels. Utilizing standard engines, they were able to generate enormous towing and pushing power due to a very large, slowly rotating propeller. Refrigerated fishing boats capable of catching, processing, and freezing fish while at sea were another development in vessel design. Water taxis, including hovercraft, which make use of air pressure to ride just above the surface of the water, and hydrofoils, which skim along the surface of the water while the hydrofoils remain submerged, have also come into use. Hydrofoils can move up to 50 knots due to the hydrodynamic advantage gained by having the vessel's

hull out of the water while the foils remain submerged, powered by individual engines and motors.

The passage of the Ocean Shipping Reform Act of 1998 (OSRA) was a momentous event for commercial shipping. OSRA completely altered how service contracts between carriers and shippers were negotiated and regulated. It freed carriers to negotiate rates without interference from shipping conferences. The effect of the Act was almost instantaneous. During the first year it was in effect, the Federal Marine Commission reported more than 141,000 service contracts. With the international maritime industry in a period of growth and ferment that lasted into the 2000s, government regulatory bodies worldwide continued their attempts to guide the industry's development. OSRA ushered in a new era in regulation, the most significant of which was the influence on regulators in other countries as well.

International shipping was seriously affected by the economic troubles and subsequent financial collapse in several Asian nations in the late 1990s. By 1999, conditions had apparently improved. International shipping reached a record high of 5.23 billion tons, according to the United Nations Conference on Trade and Development (UNCTAD). However, the 1.3 percent growth rate was the lowest in more than a decade.

By 1999, world surplus tonnage had decreased to 23.7 DWT, or 3 percent of the world fleet, the lowest in the 1990s. By the end of the decade, although demand for maritime transportation of freight was threatening to overtake supply, price competition was driving rates down. In 2000 the industry rallied, and rates jumped to their highest levels in 30 years, enabling both container shipping firms and dry bulk carriers to realize profits. Larger firms, such as Nippon Yusen Kaisha, had recovered from the 1990s downturn and reported highly profitable years in the early 2000s. Consolidation continued, the most notable of which was the acquisition of Sea-Land Service Inc. by the A.P. Moller-Maersk Line in 1999. The most profitable shipping concerns became those that were part of a conglomerate corporation that also operated concerns in related fields including shipbuilding, intermodal transportation, and freight handling. Such shipping lines included Hyundai and Hanjin of Korea, Mitsui OSK and K Line of Japan, P&O Nedlloyd of the United Kingdom, and Hapag-Lloyd of Germany.

Shipping Conferences. Shipping conferences, or associations of ocean carriers operating in specific trades, played a major role in freight-carrying steamship lines. After the first conference was formed in 1875 to serve the Calcutta-England trade, the number of conferences grew rapidly. Conferences were primarily formed to counter and avoid the rate wars that had resulted from rapid increases in tonnage transported between 1860 and 1880. Shipping companies competed for business by building ships of increasing speed and size to realize greater economies of scale. National policies of most large trading nations favored the development of a strong national flag merchant fleet. Every major power in Europe, as well as Japan, Brazil, and some of the British dominions, employed subsidies to expand, protect, and control merchant shipping.

Conferences were formed to promote cooperation among conference members. In general, they:

- agreed upon a common tariff to minimize price competition;

- attempted to control the supply of available shipping space by agreeing on sailing schedules and the amount of tonnage available;

- often employed a revenue or cargo-sharing pool;

- made rebates or loyalty payments to reward shippers who made extensive use of conference ships; and

- attempted to keep new competitors from entering the trade (or convinced them to join the conference).

The operation of conferences in the early twentieth century prompted two major investigations of the system. In 1909, the British Royal Commission concluded that the conference system was warranted and a deferred rebate system should be accepted. From 1912 to 1914, the U.S. Congress conducted a major investigation of conferences, concluding that while conference agreements were used to restrain competition among the conference members, there were certain advantages to the conference system. Among these benefits were improved service arising from greater stability of rates and greater regularity of sailings that occurred as conference members coordinated their schedules.

By rationalizing sailing dates and ports of call, conference carriers were able to reduce costs. In turn, stable rate levels promoted investment in newer and more efficient ships. Disadvantages included the monopolistic nature of the conference, the possibility of earning excess profits, indifference to cargo delivery, arbitrary policies for settling claims, failure to give adequate notice of rate changes, and retaliation and discrimination against shippers. It was believed that large volume shippers received better rates and service. As a result, the U.S. Congress passed the Shipping Act of 1916, which offered limited acceptance of the conference system. The Shipping Act provided conferences with antitrust immunity, while maintaining a major regulatory role in seaborne transportation for government agencies. To get around the more burdensome portions of the law, yet ensure the stability and effectiveness of its business-friendly aspects,

conferences began to use a dual-rate contract system that awarded shippers who signed requirements or loyalty contracts with lower tariff rates. By the end of the 1950s, more than 60 conferences and thousands of shippers used some form of dual-rate contract.

In the wake of the 1961 amendment, further calls for reform were fueled by carrier complaints about delays in the FMC's approval process for conference agreements, application of vague standards for approval, and loss of predictability in regulatory decision-making. As newcomers crowded into the U.S. trades, many routes became heavily overrun, contributing to a growing instability of rates and service. Moreover, intense competition led several established carriers to offer shippers informal and illegal rebates on published rates.

The Shipping Act of 1984 replaced the Shipping Act of 1916 and its amendments, focusing on unjust discrimination between shippers and attempting to harmonize the objectives of facilitating an efficient ocean transportation system while controlling the potential abuses and disadvantages allegedly inherent in the conference system. After much debate on the effects of allowing discriminatory pricing for ocean shipping services, the 1984 Act specifically authorized service contracts as a compromise between carrier and shipper interests. In exchange, however, Congress removed the antitrust immunity for dual-rate contracts, making carriers and conferences file these contracts confidentially with the FMC, which in turn would make public a summary of these contracts. The idea was to block the conferences' ability to abuse their market position.

While the 1984 legislation was intended to augment competition, opponents continued to argue that conferences were actually legalized cartels and should not be exempt from any antitrust laws. They maintained that competition in the open market should be encouraged to stimulate creative pricing and that subsidies by foreign governments to their own national shipyards should also be abolished, making U.S. shipyards more competitive. Buyers of steamship services, particularly those transporting large volumes, argued that they had the legal right to negotiate prices and service levels based on fair market value and that foreign companies do not operate under these constraints.

One example of the tremendous power of the conferences was the operation of the Trans-Atlantic Agreement (TAA), which was formed in 1992. Nearly 70 percent of the steamship lines carrying freight on the North Atlantic entered into TAA's price-setting pact to increase rates on a route that was losing revenues due to diminished trade between the United States and Europe. The rates agreed upon by TAA members caused an uproar among shippers, who claimed that the conference caused freight rates to rise 54 percent in one year, and that no alternative means of transportation existed. Similar ongoing complaints lodged against the TAA by shippers have resulted in nearly continuous investigation of conference practices by the FMC and the European Commission.

The Ocean Shipping Reform Act of 1998 (OSRA), the long-awaited revision of the Shipping Act of 1984, went into effect in May 1999. Among other provisions, the new law changed the nature of service contracts between carriers and their customers. They were no longer public documents but confidential agreements that were not open even to fellow conference members. Consequently, carriers would be able to negotiate their rates independent of conference rate structures. Under OSRA, conferences were prohibited from requiring members to disclose their rates. The philosophy behind the prohibition was to free prices from being set by conferences, giving shippers greater flexibility in negotiating favorable rates. With their power to determine the rates for specific routes stripped away, at least for U.S. trade, conferences, and the monopolistic practices they represented to some, were expected to slowly disappear or to evolve into shippers associations or similar marketing organizations.

CURRENT CONDITIONS

Throughout 2000 and 2001 the Canadian Parliament tried unsuccessfully to hammer out its own legislation based on the U.S. model. Following OSRA's lead, bodies such as the European Union and the Organization for Economic Cooperation and Development (OECD) came out in favor of doing away with antitrust exemptions for shipping conferences and replaced those industry agreements with confidential individual service contracts. The U.S. Federal Maritime Commission (FMC) also played a key international role, repeatedly taking action to end Japanese port regulations that discriminated against non-Japanese carriers. In 1997 the FMC fined Japanese ships entering U.S. harbors, resulting in reform to the Japanese port regulations in 1998. However, in August 2001 the FMC reopened and expanded its investigation when it became evident that discrimination had not ended.

In 2001, the bottom fell out of the industry and rates plummeted, with containership prices plunging 15 percent. A crude oil tanker that had earned US$65,000 a day in March 2001 could earn only US$16,000 a day the following June. The crash sent shockwaves through the industry, causing American Eagle Tankers to call off an initial public offering and Overseas Shipholding Group to cancel a US$150 million stock offering.

Following the terrorist attacks against the United States on September 11, 2001, the U.S. Congress passed the Maritime Transportation Security Act of 2002, canceling its visa procedure for crew members. The Act was intended to ensure the safety of the maritime industry, citing the need to verify that a visa actually belongs to the person using it. The cost to implement these security measures was a major concern to shipping companies. The International Labor Organization of the United Nations supported the U.S. action, seeking ways to protect and identify maritime workers while protecting their rights. However, a lack of international agreement on the standards to be used for biometric technology was delaying resolution of the issue. Its full provisions went into effect in mid-2004. The regulation required vessels and ports to conduct vulnerability assessments and develop security procedures that included passenger and baggage screening, security patrols, and the installation of surveillance equipment.

The loss of the oil tanker *Prestige* off the Spanish coast in November 2002 had a significant effect on the shipping industry. Carrying 77,000 tons of heavy fuel, the ship began to list in severe weather and started leaking its load. Spanish, French, and Portuguese authorities would not allow the ship to be brought into shore and after limping out to sea, the ship sank. The result was an ecological disaster, with approximately 250 miles of polluted Spanish, Portuguese, and French coastline. The Spanish government estimated that US$9.9 billion would be needed to clean up the coast. The incident raised several serious concerns in addition to the environmental effects. First, the *Prestige* had not been inspected in 12 months, highlighting the low rate of inspection in many countries. France and Spain stated that single-hull ships would not be allowed to sail within 200 miles of their shores. The European Union set plans in motion to phase out and eventually ban single-hull vessels. Spain sued the American Bureau of Shipping, which led to the U.S. government instituting a law to ban single-hulled ships by 2005. At the time of the accident, there were 5,500 single-hull vessels in operation, compared to 2,500 ships with double hulls. Also at issue was the need for the development of places of refuge for vessels in distress.

According to Lloyd's Register, in January 2005, the worldwide merchant marine industry included 46,222 registered shipping vessels totaling 597.7 million gross tons. These included 18,150 general cargo ships, 11,356 tankers, 6,139 bulk carriers, 5,679 passenger ships, and 3,165 containerships, as well as 1,733 other types of vessels.

The United Nations Conference on Trade and Development (UNCTAD), reported that as of 2008, the market had shifted in terms who the countries owning merchant ships. Japan led the world with 3,757 ships, followed by Germany (3,380), China (3,247), Greece (3,162), Russia (1,448), Norway (1,412), Turkey (1,199), South Korea (1,144), Hong Kong (1,114), the United States (1,080), and Indonesia (1,042). Growth in the industry was expected to continue, mainly due to the economic performance of the United States, Japan, and China.

In Boston, Massachusetts, an editorial in *The Boston Globe* p July 24, 2008, supported the development of the waterfront and the inner harbor, citing the Lovejoy Water Shuttle Terminal in Boston's North Station. Lovejoy had great unrealized potential, offering "strong rail connections, good access for disabled people, and easy proximity to businesses and attractions, including TD Banknorth Garden." The owner of the water shuttle terminal, the Massachusetts Department of Conservation and Recreation, was reportedly amenable to a water shuttle service at Lovejoy Wharf, and acknowledged the need to join forces with water transit experts in the state's Executive Office of Transportation to create a plan to incorporate the Lovejoy terminal into Boston's water transportation network.

On July 23, 2008, Evergreen Marine Corporation, of Taiwan, signed an agreement to maintain service between Asia and Baltimore through 2018, based on an expected increase in shipping between Asia and the U.S. East Coast. The agreement was dependent on the expansion of the Panama Canal by 2014, which would allow Evergreen's largest ships to use the Canal. Evergreen, the second largest shipping line in Baltimore, is the only one serving Baltimore directly from Asia.

Dramatic increases in the cost of fuel, combined with a peak season surcharge in 2008, resulted in increases between 25 and 30 percent over 2007 shipping rates for cargo between the United States and India, although the rates remained lower than they had been in 2006. The increase was expected to be reflected in revenues for 2008 holiday sales.

WORKFORCE

The Baltic and International Maritime Council/International Shipping Federation (BIMCO/ISF) reported in its *2005 Manpower Update* that there were about 721,000 sailors, with 586,000 needed, and 466,000 officers, with 476,000 needed. According to BIMCO/ISF, these figures reflected a continuing trend for a surplus of sailors and shortage of officers. Recruitment increased steadily during the 1990s, until it was diminished by the Asian financial crisis. Although the size of the world fleet increased 1 percent per year between 1995 and 2000, labor needs were offset as older ships were phased out and new vessels that required small crews were introduced. There had been a steady change in the nationality of the global workforce during the 1990s as well. The number of seafarers from the Organization for Economic Cooperation and Development (OECD) nations, which were primarily in the European Union, Japan, and North America, dropped from 31.5

percent of the total workforce in 1995 to 27.5 percent in 2000. By 2004, UNCTAD was reporting that Asia was providing 60 percent of the world's sailors, with the largest supplier being the Philippines, followed by Indonesia, Turkey, China and India.

According to the U.S. Bureau of Labor Statistics (BLS), employment in the U.S. water transportation sector fell gradually from about 211,000 in 1980 to 175,000 in 1995 before increasing in 2000, eventually reaching 201,000. However, according the BLS, by 2008, that number had significantly decreased to more than 81,000. Nonetheless, in 2000, water transportation workers comprised only 4 percent of the total U.S. transportation workforce, an increase of 3 percent over 1980. The water transportation occupation sector was projected to grow by 15 percent, faster than the average between 2008 and 2018. The *2010–2011 National Occupational Employment and Wage Estimates* issued by the BLS reported that 32,900 sailors and marine oilers employed in the industry earned a mean annual salary of US$34,390. Captains, mates, and pilots numbered about 33,100 and earned a mean annual salary of US$61,960. There were about 11,500 ship engineers employed in 2010, earning US$60,690.

In the mid-2000s, some schools began to offer career technical training in industry-related classes as the need to replace the aging population of merchant marine sailors was recognized. San Diego, California's Sweetwater School District, for example, offered a Regional Occupational Program course in Maritime Services at their high school to prepare students to work immediately in full-time maritime positions after graduation.

INDUSTRY LEADERS

A.P. Moller-Maersk Group. Danish-owned A.P. Moller-Maersk Group was founded in 1904 as A/S Dampskibsselskabet Svendborg (The Steamship Company of Svendborg) by Peter Maersk Moller and his son, Arnold Peter Moller. In 2002, the company was ranked as the largest container shipping company in the world by the United Nations. The company purchased P&O Nedlloyd in 2005 and changed its container-shipping segment name to Maersk Line. In 2008, A.P. Moller-Maersk had over 500 container vessels, as well as tankers, liners/container vessels (Maersk Sealand), bulk carriers, supply ships, special vessels, and drilling rigs, totaling nearly 12 million DWT. The company had ordered 34 ships in June and July 2008 for delivery by 2012. With offices in more than 135 countries and approximately 115,000 employees worldwide, the company reported 2009 revenues of approximately US$47.694 billion. The group included various subsidiaries that specialized in various types of shipping, including Maersk Sealand (container shipping), Maersk Tankers and Maersk Gas Carriers (tanker shipping), and Maersk Bulk (bulk shipping).

Maersk Line, the company's cargo liner service, has linked the United States with Asia since 1975 with fast, fully containerized ships operating on a fixed weekly schedule. In 1999 it was expanded greatly by Moller's acquisition for US$800 million of the international liner business of Sea-Land Service Inc. in a deal that included all of Sea-Land's vessels, containers, container terminals, and some leases. The takeover was the largest deal to that date in the consolidation of the shipping industry. Sea-Land's 70 containerships boosted Maersk's fleet to approximately 180 vessels and made the new firm, Maersk Sealand, twice as large as its nearest competitor in the container shipping business. By 2002, Maersk Sealand was providing service between the United States and Asia, Northern Europe, the Middle East/Mediterranean, and eastern and western Africa; Europe and the Middle East, Asia, eastern and western Africa; Asia and the Middle East and eastern and western Africa; and Japan and Indonesia and Thailand.

Maersk projected global growth for the industry to be between 7 and 8 percent annually in 2008, with trade in Asia growing even more. The company's Asia Pacific Chief Executive Jesper Praestensgaard regarded the purchase of ships as an investment that will last 25 to 30 years. He also acknowledged that oil prices in the late 2000s were causing decreased consumption and increased overhead in typical transportation costs.

Mediterranean Shipping Company S.A. Mediterranean Shipping Company (MSC) was founded by Gianluigi Aponte in 1970 in landlocked Geneva, Switzerland. MSC was the second largest container ship company in the world in 2010, with 414 container vessels and a capacity of 1,638,962 TEUs. MSC's success is based on customer focus and being cost efficient with an ability to react quickly to market trends because it is a privately owned company. The company also operates the MSC Cruises, which is the third largest cruise group in the world. The number of MSC employees is estimated at 29,000, operating in 270 ports worldwide on six continents, with revenues estimated at US$3 billion per year. In 2007, the MSC line was named shipping line of the year for the sixth time in 11 years, an achievement not matched by any other line. MSC has also ordered 11 new ships that will be able to carry up to 15,000 TEUs, which will make them some of the largest container vessels in the world.

Royal P&O Nedlloyd N.V. Founded in 1837, Royal P&O Nedlloyd (P&O) grew into a major transport company. The company's history goes back to the era of the steamship, when its founders started trade links between

northern Europe and the Mediterranean/Balkan region. In December 1996, P&O Containers and Nedlloyd Lines merged to form P&O Nedlloyd. By 2005, it operated in 18 countries, with port operations being the fastest growing segment of the company. P&O was the leading provider of ferry service in the United Kingdom, with a fleet of 26 ships. In 2004, one-third of its revenues of more than US$6.7 billion came from its port business, one-third came from its ferry business, and approximately one-sixth came from its container shipping business. In 2004, the 50-50 joint venture P&O had with Royal Nedlloyd, P&O Nedlloyd, became a public entity that was traded on the Amsterdam Exchange, for which P&O retained 25 percent of the shares. The new company was renamed Royal P&O Nedlloyd, and was the third largest container company in the world at the time of its creation. In 2005, A.P. Moller-Maersk Group purchased P&O Nedlloyd. At the time of the takeover, P&O Nedlloyd had a fleet of 156 vessels that called at 217 ports in 99 countries. The company's 2004 revenues were reported at US$6.7 billion.

Mitsui O.S.K. Lines Ltd. Mitsui O.S.K. Lines Ltd.(MOL) was founded in 1884 as Osaka Shosen Kaisha, launching an "express" service that traveled between Yokohama and New York in less than 26 days. By 2005, the company was Japan's largest marine transportation company, with the largest merchant fleet in the world. The company operated containerships and car and truck carriers, as well as dry bulk carriers that transported a huge variety of products. including electrical goods, iron ore, liquefied natural gas, and crude and refined petroleum products. The MOL Group also managed ports and operated tugboats, ferries, and cruise ships. MOL's revenues in March 2004 were more than US$9.4 billion and the MOL Group reported 9,626 employees in March 2008. Revenues were up 16.4 percent in 2008 over 2007.

MOL assessed additional fees on goods transported to the United States and Canada from Vietnam beginning on September 1. The increase was blamed on delays at ports, which port representatives claimed was unfounded because the situation had been corrected. Saigon city officials agreed that the fees were unreasonable, but only Maersk removed its fees.

Nippon Yusen Kaisha Line. Nippon Yusen Kaisha Line (NYK) was established in Tokyo in 1885. The line responded to changing market forces in the mid-1990s by entering into an alliance with NOL of Singapore, Hapag-Lloyd AG of Germany, and P&O Containers of the United Kingdom in 1995. In 1998, NYK inaugurated a containership service for trade with the United States and Europe and opened a branch in Taipei, Taiwan. Two years later, the firm opened NYK Logistics in the Peoples Republic of China.

NYK's core businesses by 2005 were container transport, tramp shipping, and passenger cruise ships. The company boasted the largest liner fleet in Japan and the largest fleet of car and truck carriers in the world. NYK was a leader for the development of Pacific trade routes by incorporating the Panama and Suez Canals as short cuts. The company's Asia East Coast Express (AEX) service, which used the Suez Canal, connected Southeast Asia to ports on the U.S. East Coast within 22 days. Its Singapore California Express connected Singapore to the U.S. West Coast within 16 to 18 days. Its 2000 profits of US$290 million were more than double its results for 1999.

By 2007, the company's revenues had reached nearly US$26 billion with about 55,000 employees worldwide. It had a fleet of 776 major vessels by 2008, with offices in 240 locations in 27 countries.

HAPAG-Lloyd AG. HAPAG-Lloyd's (Hapag) dates back to the mid-nineteenth century when the Hamburg-Amerikanische Packetfahrt-Actien-Gesellschaft (the Hamburg-American Steamship Co.) was founded in 1847, and Norddeutscher Lloyd (North German Lloyd) was founded in 1857. The two companies were formed as passenger lines and were the leading German ship lines for both passenger and cargo service through the first half of the twentieth century. In 1930, the two formed the Hapag-Lloyd Union and merged in 1970 to form Hapag-Lloyd. Shortly after that, Hapag established the TRIO Group, which was a global cooperative venture with four other companies, NYK and Mitsui O.S.K. Lines of Japan and Overseas Containers Ltd. and Ben Line of the United Kingdom. The formation of the TRIO group was the largest in the history of shipping and resulted in the replacement of 60 vessels with the group sharing 19 giant containerships. The next two-and-a-half decades were difficult for the company, which was affected by a downturn in shipping caused by a surplus of tonnage and economic issues. By 1991, Hapag was reporting profits. The firm was reorganized in 1994 to streamline operations. By the time it celebrated its 150th anniversary in 1997, it was shipping about 1.1 million 20-foot containers annually with profits of US$48 million, for a 23 percent jump from 1996.

German tourism giant Touristik Union National (TIU) bought a controlling share of HAPAG-Lloyd in 1998. As of 2002, the company reported US$4 billion in revenue. In 2004 the shipping company accounted for 19 percent of its TIU's revenues of US$24 billion. In 2007, the company ordered eight new containerships with 8,730 TEUs. Germanischer Lloyd awarded Hapag-Lloyd a "GL Excellence—5 Stars" certificate based on "particularly high standards of safety and security, quality, labour protection and environmental protection." It was the first such award

worldwide. In 2008, TUI announced its intention to sell its entire stake in Hapag-Lloyd shipping by the end of the year. Industry speculation predicted a sale price of close to US$5.9 billion.

Hanjin Shipping Company Ltd. Hanjin Shipping Company Ltd. of South Korea was established in 1977 as Hanjin Container Lines. It opened its first international route in 1978, serving the Middle East with one vessel capable of carrying 750 TEUs. In 1979, Hanjin began to serve the Pacific-Southwest and in 1983 provided all-water service to the U.S. East Coast, as well as between South Korea and Japan. In 1988, the company merged with Korea Shipping Corp. and became Hanjin Shipping Company Ltd. By 1991, the company had begun its Pendulum Service between the United States and Europe through Asia. Trans-Atlantic service was initiated in 1995, as was Mediterranean service. Hanjin, DSR, and Cho Yang Lines USA Inc. consolidated their shipping resources in 1996, creating a combined fleet of 70 vessels with a capacity of 194,000 TEUs. In 2001 Hanjin was the second largest shipping company in the world in containership loading tonnage. In November 2001, Hanjin formed the United Alliance with COSCO Container Lines, Senator Lines, K Line, and Yang Ming Marine for international trade. As of 2009, the company owned approximately 200 ships that transported over 100 million tons of cargo annually.

China Ocean Shipping (Group) Company. China Ocean Shipping (Group) Company (COSCO), the state-owned shipping company of China, was founded in 1961 and began service between China and the United States in 1982. COSCO's U.S. East Coast and Gulf Coast service utilized a fleet of eight container vessels, five of which had a capacity of 1,500 TEUs and three of which had a 1,200 TEU capacity. The company served the U.S. West Coast with a fleet of six vessels that had a combined capacity of 2,500 TEUs.

Throughout the mid- to late 1990s, COSCO increased its role in global maritime trade. The company reversed its traditional position as an independent carrier and entered into a space-sharing agreement with K Line and Yang Ming Line on its Asia-Europe routes in 1996. This agreement was officially renewed in 1998. In 1997, COSCO announced that it was expanding its service to include trans-Atlantic routes, which challenged the dominance of the TAA. COSCO again shed its independent status when it joined the Westbound Pacific Stabilization Agreement (WSTA) in 1998 in what appeared to be leading up to the company's entering a shipping conference. In 2005, the company reported revenues of US$17 billion, although it does not usually make its financial status public and had a merchant fleet of 600 vessels with an annual capacity of 270 million tons.

BIBLIOGRAPHY

"Analysts Predict Higher Rates." *Journal of Commerce,* 15 March 2004.

Ardizzone, Sally. "Program Preps Students for Career as Merchant Marines." *San Diego Business Journal,* 10 March 2003.

"As Tankers Tank, Shipping Tempts Markets." *Journal of Commerce,* 10 July 2001.

The Baltic and International Maritime Council "Publication of the BIMCO/ISF 2005 Manpower Update," 2 February 2005. Available from www.bimco.org.

Barnard, Bruce. "Mergers, Acquisitions Roil Industry." *Journal of Commerce,* 25 April 2000.

Berkenkopf, Katren. "Hamburg: Hapag's Aggressive Approach." *Lloyds List,* 28 April 2000.

Bonney, Joseph. "Strength in Numbers." *Journal of Commerce,* 13 August 2001.

"China Claims Fourth Largest Maritime Fleet." *India Times,* 4 August 2008. Available from www.economictimes.indiatimes.com.

"Container Shipping Growth." *Toronto Star,* 21 July 2008. Available from www.thestar.com.

Damas, Philip, "Who's Making Money?" *American Shipper,* 1 July 2000.

Damas, Philip, and Chris Gillis. "Inside the Maersk Machine." *American Shipper,* March 2001.

Damas, Philip, Chris Gillis, and Robert Mottley. "Maritime Flags Unravel." *American Shipper,* 1 March 2000.

Draper, Deborah J., ed. *Business Rankings Annual.* Detroit: Thomson Gale, 2004.

Dupin, Chris. "The Bottom Line." *Journal of Commerce,* 28 May 2001.

———. "Compatible Regimes?" *Journal of Commerce,* 6 November 2000.

———. "Mending Fences." *Journal of Commerce,* 5 November 2001.

———. "OECD Rekindles Antitrust Issue." *Journal of Commerce,* 7 January 2002.

Edmonson, R.G. "FMC Renews Japan Port Probe." *Journal of Commerce,* 13 August 2001.

Freudmann, Aviva. "Carrier Shifts Focus Back to Transport." *Journal of Commerce,* 25 February 2000.

———. "Conference, 5 Ship Lines Are Fined US$7 Million." *Journal of Commerce,* 18 May 2000.

———. "Traditional Ro-Ro Ships Becoming Endangered." *Journal of Commerce,* 16 February 2000.

Giovanetti, Geoffrey N. "Is Ocean Freight Becoming a Commodity?" *Journal of Commerce,* 7 June 2004.

"Hoover's Company Capsules." *Hoover's Online,* 2004. Available from www.hoovers.com.

"International Trade Statistics," World Trade Organization, 2003. Available from www.wto.org.

Koenig, Robert. "Preussag Shuffles the Deck." *Journal of Commerce,* 26 June 2000.

McCandish, Laura. "Shipping Line to Extend Port Pact." *Baltimore Sun,* 23 July 2008. Available from www.baltimoresun.com.

Manoj, P. "Cargo Freight Rates to the U.S. Rise 25–30%." *LiveMint The Wall Street Journal,* 3 August 2008. Available from www.livemint.com.

Mitchell, Carlyle L. "Canada's Ocean Industries: Contribution to the Economy 1988—2000." Department of Fisheries and Ocean, September 2003. Available from www.dfo-mpo.gc.ca.

Mongelluzzo, Bill. "A Surfeit of Services." *Journal of Commerce,* 10 May 2004.

Pandya, Nick. "Rise: Cool Companies: No. 39: The Maersk Company Limited." *Guardian* (London), 2 September 2000.

Pei, Jianfeng. "OSRA Credited with Positive Effects on Ocean Shipping." *Purchasing,* 24 August 2000.

Peterkofsky, Roy I. "How to Make It Work." *Journal of Commerce,* 19 April 2004.

"Review of Maritime Transport, 2007." United Nations Conference on Trade and Development (UNCTAD Secretariat), 2007. Available from www.unctad.org.

Richardson, Paul. "Who's Next to Be Merged?" *Journal of Commerce,* 29 March 2000.

Rosenberg, Steven. "Seaside Communities Moving to Put Water Routes to Work for Visitors and Commuters." *The Boston Globe,* 31 July 2008.

"Shipping Costs Could Slow China's Boom." *Minneapolis Star Tribune,* 13 August 2008. Available from www.startribune.com.

"Shipping Lines Posing Unreasonable Fees." *Thanh Nein News,* 7 August 2008. Available from www.thanhniennews.com/.

Tirschwell, Peter M. "FMC Defines Ocean Common Carrier." *Journal of Commerce,* 9 May 2000.

———. "Time Is Money." *Journal of Commerce,* 31 May 2004.

Tower, Courtney. "Canada Readies Maritime Reform." *Journal of Commerce,* 29 March 2000.

———. "Canadian Shippers Demand OSRA–like Law." *Journal of Commerce,* 18 July 2001.

"UN Agency Launches Talks on New Identification System for Maritime Workers." *UN News Centre,* 6 June 2003. Available from www.un.org.

U.S. Department of Transportation Maritime Administration. "Maritime Statistics," 2004. Available from www.marad.dot.gov.

"What's Up, Dock?" *The Boston Globe,* 24 July 2008. Available from www.savetheharbor.org.

UTILITIES AND PUBLIC SERVICES

———————■———————

ELEMENTARY AND SECONDARY SCHOOLS

NAICS CODE(S)

611110. Elementary and secondary schools furnish academic training for students between the ages of about 5 to 17. Courses of study usually are offered in age-level divisions (commonly known as grades in the United States), and schools generally subdivide younger and older groups of students into elementary and secondary schools, respectively. Public and private institutions are included within this category. The industry includes parochial schools and military academies that provide academic courses, as well as secondary schools that provide both academic and technical courses.

INDUSTRY SNAPSHOT

Most experts, government officials, and the general public agree that effective education is necessary for a nation's economic health. The world's industrialized nations, including the United States, France, Germany, Japan, and the United Kingdom, typically invest heavily in public education. In contrast, education in the developing world, while often a recognized priority of governments and families, receives considerably less financial support from the government, with significant variation by nation and region. Consequently, economic opportunities for young people just out of secondary school are extremely variable around the world. In turn, weak economic growth in any part of the world can result in a surge of immigration to more affluent nations, which eventually leads to higher costs for administering, operating, and maintaining schools in those countries whose populations were growing.

To compete in an increasingly global economy, national, regional, and local school officials and administrators in many countries examine educational operations in other economically successful countries. As a result, international studies of education and efforts to compile truly comparative educational statistics across nations have increased noticeably. For example, in 2004 the United Nations Educational, Scientific, and Cultural Organization (UNESCO) published worldwide education statistics in the "Global Education Digest," which compared educational systems, trends, goals, and standards. The study reported a significant correlation between a country's income and its emphasis on education at any level, with average time spent in formal schooling ranging from 4 to 17 years. In addition, the study found that 10 percent of students in 35 countries repeat primary grades, and in 38 countries repeat secondary grades.

Concern over developing a future workforce capable of meeting employer needs has led numerous educational institutions and employers to develop collaborative programs to train students for twenty-first century jobs. The result has been enhanced programs for teaching math and science, along with reading and writing; new emphasis on managerial skills, such as communication, decision making, and problem solving; and efforts to improve the variety and quality of vocational and technical skills-training programs. In many countries, school systems increasingly have emphasized training in computer literacy to give elementary and secondary school students the necessary skills and hands-on experience for computer use not only in college, but in their careers.

Although educators around the world share the need to keep pace with changes in the global economy and rapid changes in technology, approaches to improvements in education have varied widely across countries. While the United States has clung to a "single-ladder" approach to education, with essentially one course of elementary and secondary study taken by all students, other nations have seen advantages in offering more specialized education to students beginning at an earlier age. For example, Germany has endorsed early differentiation between vocational and pre-university preparation. In the United Kingdom, the number of comprehensive secondary schools, which somewhat resemble U.S. public high schools by including students on all academic paths, was growing around the turn of the millennium. In addition, egalitarian, "progressive" education was being supplanted by more orthodox schooling in some parts of the United Kingdom in the late 1990s. However, the British continued to emphasize official testing in order to evaluate schools, determine student achievement, and steer students in academic or vocational directions. In France students are assured of carefully legislated curricula designed to provide equal opportunities to all students. Once reserved for the academic elite, the coveted French *baccalauréat* has been subdivided into academic and vocational tracks and is awarded to all students who successfully complete their secondary studies. Japanese legislation outlaws educational discrimination based on ability or potential and students are trained identically throughout elementary school with their achievement more closely related to parental example and expectation than to any particular government education policy. The Japanese have provided very little specialized vocational education, but Japanese schools methodically support a strict work ethic for students.

ORGANIZATION AND STRUCTURE

Internationally, elementary and secondary school systems encompass a wide variety of institutions, including:

- Government-funded elementary and secondary schools (known as "public" schools in the United States);

- Self-standing, publicly or privately funded kindergartens;

- Privately funded day schools, boarding schools, and secondary finishing schools;

- Religiously affiliated schools (some of which are known as "parochial," or parish-supported, schools);

- Charter schools (publicly subsidized and supervised but independently run schools);

- Vocational high schools;

- Military academies;

- College preparatory schools;

- Visual and/or performing arts academies;

- Schools for students with special needs such as physical, behavioral, emotional, learning, psychological, and/or other mental handicaps or disabilities;

- Online, Internet-based schools; and

- Home schools.

In many countries governed by parliamentary systems, national government departments, such as ministries of education, youth, and sports, set the tone for the development and implementation of educational policy and/or for evaluating the success of schools. In the United States, the Department of Education is similar to a ministry in that educational policy decisions are often made in this executive agency and then supported through specific education laws enacted by the U.S. Congress. The president, as the chief executive, presents educational initiatives and guidelines, which others in the executive and legislative develop. However, U.S. education policy is often diluted by state governments, who until the twenty-first century were allowed wide jurisdiction for setting educational standards, finalizing details, and funding educational programs.

Government support of educational costs varies widely around the world. In some countries, especially in the developing world, school fees and textbook costs are borne by the parents of students which often makes schooling inaccessible to those on the lower end of the socioeconomic scale, even where the government supports some of the physical infrastructure and/or basic furnishings. Consequently, universal access to education is limited because many students lack the resources to attend school.

A wide range of public and private school options are available to students at the elementary and secondary levels in the United Kingdom. The United States offers similar, if fewer options than are available in the United Kingdom. Most other countries have small numbers of students enrolled in private academies in proportion to government-supported schools. While private schools in the United States frequently are day schools, in Great Britain and on the European continent many non-government school pupils live in residential houses attached to the schools.

Vocational Training. Many European and emerging Pacific Rim countries provide highly specialized vocational education to high school students through combinations of apprenticeship systems, on-the-job training, and traditional academic learning. Almost all countries outside the United States offer specific vocational paths of study that are available to students well before graduation from secondary school.

The level of sophistication for vocational training in the United States has grown gradually, frequently involving school-to-work partnerships with business and industry. Despite the appeal that U.S. higher education has for to foreign students, the competitive position of U.S. workers declined in the 1990s in some industry sectors, especially in comparison to workers in some European and Pacific Rim countries. Critics suggested that this resulted from a lack of support in the United States for vocational training and education programs.

Germany's vocational training system in particular has been highly acclaimed worldwide, and is given much credit for Germany's economic success. The German system is unique because of the intense interconnection of business and education that is not apparent in most other industrialized nations. Although the percentage of students seeking admittance into German vocational training programs fell in the early 1990s, the system has been considered to be highly successful. Businesses benefit from a supply of well-qualified workers and can fine-tune vocational training to specific needs. Graduates benefit because on-the-job training provides them with experience in the workplace and marketable skills. Nevertheless, in the late 1990s critics claimed that the German vocational training system produced an excess of skilled blue-collar workers when the need for such workers was decreasing. Rapid changes in technology made it difficult to keep up with current needs as the system was reformed, but efforts continued in the twenty-first century to increase the system's flexibility and responsiveness to Germany's changing workforce requirements.

BACKGROUND AND DEVELOPMENT

Growth of Education and Literacy. Schooling has a broad and varied history through the ages as education came to have the complex structure of the late 2000s. Economic development does not occur without the development of a nation's human resources. Thus, the development of education in the United States as one of the foremost economies of the world, illustrates challenges faced by other countries as they educate their children and youth. (See also *World Education Encyclopedia,* published by the Gale Group-Thompson Learning.)

Development of U.S. Public Schooling. Compulsory, "normal," and free public education was developed and expanded in the United States as the country rapidly industrialized during the nineteenth century. Prior to the early 1800s, education was not regulated and often was home-based. Children were taught the rudiments of reading, writing, and mathematics, although some education provided a classical education that included the study of Latin and Greek. An educational middle ground where the average pupil could be given the basic foundation for a liberal arts education was not typically available. However, this began to change as the population grew and the United States became more industrialized and urbanized.

Horace Mann (1796–1859) was a prominent U.S. social reformer, educator, and statesman who, according to Susan Ritchie, "greatly advanced the cause of universal, free, non-sectarian public schools." Mann believed that

"while other reforms were remedial, education was preventative [*sic*]." Education therefore took priority over other arenas for social development and reform. Viewing education, intelligent voting, and religious freedom as the primary supports of American liberties, Mann, who was trained as a lawyer and served for three years in the Massachusetts Senate before becoming secretary of the Massachusetts Board of Education in 1837, advocated the spread of educational opportunity to the general population.

As a member of the Massachusetts Board of Education, Mann provided greater funding for schools in Massachusetts and laid the groundwork for secularizing religious schools, making public schooling available to everyone. He also enhanced teacher training programs and argued for more humane forms of discipline in schools. Mann was an educator at heart during his lifetime regardless of the social or political arena in which he worked, whether as a state senator, a U.S. congressman, or as the first president of Antioch College in Yellow Springs, Ohio. According to Ritchie, Mann regarded the "importance of universal public education as the means for the creation of a just society."

After the concept of free education for all children had been firmly established and public schools had begun to spread across the growing United States during the first half of the 1800s, educators shifted their attention to enhancing the quality of education. At first American common schools were similar to those in Europe, often consisting of one room and one teacher who taught students ranging in age from 6 to about 13. Older children generally were needed at home to work on the family farm or business, and rarely attended school. In fact, in rural and frontier areas older boys occasionally raided and terrorized small schools, priding themselves on "breaking them up" and sometimes running beleaguered instructors out of town. In the minds of some (especially adult male community members), females were expected to be only barely literate, and advanced education for girls was deemed unnecessary, undesirable, or even unhealthy. In the early one-room schoolhouses, each child was instructed separately rather than in a group or grade and progressed through a series of books, moving from one grade to the next as the requisite work was completed. It was not unusual for a student to be in a third reader, for example, while still struggling with a math primer. The predominant method of education was modeled on Johann Pestalozzi's theories that emphasized first-hand observation of actual objects rather than the rote memorization of facts.

By the late 1800s, however, many attitudes concerning universal schooling had changed, and growing support for public schools that was accessible to all was apparent. Moreover, ideas were introduced for the type of education most beneficial to developing a democratic citizenry and an actively growing workforce that would meet the needs of the country's expanding industrial economy and increasingly diverse population.

By the 1880s the United States was experiencing an influx of millions of new immigrants that rapidly expanded the urban population and created new challenges for the common schools, including how to provide the greatest amount of education to the largest number of children in the shortest amount of time. Schools had to accommodate larger classes, higher enrollments, and new teaching practices. To make it possible for one teacher to instruct many students, differences between the students had to be eliminated as much as possible. Children began to be grouped on the basis of age, and curricula were developed for specific age groups.

The teaching methods of German philosopher and psychologist Johann Herbart were imported from Europe by educators to meet the challenge of increased population. Herbart believed that effective education was predicated on instruction and that the building blocks were the materials of instruction, or the subject matter. Schools in Europe and the United States that were influenced by Herbart's theories were teacher- and curriculum-centered rather than child-centered. To many educators, the most attractive component of Herbart's theory was the idea of a lesson plan, whose very existence suggested that instruction could be provided systematically to all students. Herbart's emphasis on the importance of motivating students to learn was a new concept in the 1880s. By the turn of the twentieth century, streamlined teaching methods and broader-based curricula had become standard.

Another educator who substantially transformed American philosophical and educational thought and practice in the late 1800s and early 1900s was John Dewey (1859–1952). Trained as a philosopher and experienced in teaching at the secondary and university levels, Dr. Dewey strongly believed in applying the principles of the scientific method to the study of human thinking and progress. According to Richard Field, at the end of the nineteenth century, Dewey developed an "empirically based theory of knowledge that was in concert with the then developing American school of thought known as pragmatism." This led to the establishment of an experimental laboratory school at the University of Chicago, where Dewey tested his pedagogical theories and published his first important educational study, *The School and Society,* in 1899. Moving to Columbia University in New York in 1904, Dewey continued teaching, philosophical research and writing, and social action, producing many well-regarded studies and treatises, including *How We Think* in 1910 (revised in 1933) and *Democracy and Education* in 1916. Besides making crucial contributions to American educational theory and practice, Dewey worked actively during his lifetime for other social reforms, such as women's suffrage and the unionization of American teachers. According to Field, Dewey's educational "stressed the need for an open-ended,

flexible, and experimental approach to problems of practice aimed at the determination of the conditions for the attainment of human goods and a critical examination of the consequences of means adopted to promote them, an approach that he called the 'method of intelligence'."

The "progressive education" movement of the 1920s in the United States, inspired in large measure by Dewey's work and leadership, aimed to make creative and socially useful education available to everyone. To some degree, Dewey and other proponents of progressive education were reacting to the testing movement that had begun in the 1910s after the first scale for measuring intelligence was published by Alfred Binet in 1905. By the 1920s children were given increasing numbers of intelligence quotient (IQ) and achievement tests, and growing numbers of schools and classrooms grouped students by ability and intelligence, which combined to work against the basic tenets of progressive education that all children were capable of learning and of developing their natural potential when given the right educational environment.

Progressive teaching in the 1920s and 1930s did much to improve scholarship by eliminating the rigid categorization and isolation of subjects, but educators were teaching each subject in relation to others, which uncovered a downside of progressive education. Practical difficulties associated with child-centered classes and the Piagetian need for children to learn "at their own pace," along with a tendency to equate "progressive" with "permissive," enthusiasm for progressive education lessened, bringing a return to more traditional learning methods and goals. However, discoveries about student learning and creatively sparking student interest continued to influence teaching methods for the remainder of the twentieth century and into the twenty-first century. A number of late twentieth century educational developments in the United States were profoundly shaped by Dewey's philosophy and work. According to the University of Vermont's John Dewey Project in Progressive Education, "Open classrooms, schools without walls, cooperative learning, multiage approaches, whole language, the social curriculum, experiential education, and numerous forms of alternative schools all have important philosophical roots in progressive education."

Several political developments led to heavy criticism of schools in the United States in the 1950s and 1960s. In the 1954 landmark court case, *Brown v. The Board of Education of Topeka,* the U.S. Supreme Court's decision to end the concept of "separate but equal" educational opportunities for students of different racial or ethnic backgrounds, struck down the legal basis for segregation in public schools. Resistance to that court decision left schools in the middle of a bitter and often violent debate that included questions of whether busing students from one district to schools in another district was a viable way to encourage equitable educational outcomes.

Schools in the United States, which most of the Western world had expected would dominate the post-war scientific world, became a battleground during the Cold War after the Soviet Union launched Sputnik, the first satellite. The "new math" and "new science" that were introduced in the late 1950s and early 1960s were direct responses to the fear that the United States was losing its technological preeminence to the Soviet Union.

During the 1970s improved educational strategies were focused on accommodating those students with special needs. Special education classes and resource rooms were added to schools to provide those students with special educational requirements led to "mainstreaming" students with handicaps and learning challenges into general classroom settings.

By the 1980s, a country's educational success was measured by the contributions its graduates made to the workforce, and thus the economy, of the country. The globalization of industry may have meant that specific companies were functioning in multiple national environments, but ensuring the availability of local human resources continued to be essential to the economic success of each nation.

Since a direct, causal relationship between school spending and academic results is difficult to establish, many U.S. school districts needed to find ways to gauge the effectiveness of their educational spending. Site-based reporting was developed at Fordham University and nationally distributed by Coopers and Lybrand and became available to school districts in the 1990s. Using this evaluation system allowed school districts to set benchmarks that determined where expenditures were either excessive or falling short of the norm.

The school-age population rapidly increased at the end of the twentieth century as immigration increased, which combined with a "baby boomlet" of children of baby boomers caught U.S. educators by surprise. By the 1999–2000 school year 92,012 public elementary and secondary schools were operating in the United States. Schools offering regular education programs accounted for the majority, with 84,902, while 1,947 offered special education; 1,048 focused on vocational education; and 4,115 were alternative schools. About 89,599 of these schools reported teaching a total of 46.9 million students, with 98 percent of them in regular public schools, which in Mississippi, New Hampshire, and North Dakota were the only kind of schools available. The largest student populations were in California, Florida, Illinois, New York, and Texas, each of which had more than 2 million students in public schools. In contrast, the District of

Columbia and Wyoming each reported having fewer than 100,000 public school students.

Approximately 28,000 of the 110,000 schools operating in the United States in the mid-1990s were nonprofit private institutions, including religiously affiliated schools and tax-exempt, independent schools. Another 7,000 tax-paying, private academic schools and 4,000 private, vocational schools were outside the mainstream of U.S. public school systems. By 1998 these "charter," or PSA schools— privately run institutions subject to state regulation—had increased dramatically in number.

In the 1990s U.S. public schools employed approximately 6 million people, or about 30 percent of all civilian government employees. Rapidly escalating costs of special education and other services were a financial burden to schools. Educational allocations had grown to such an extent that they were at risk of being cut when the federal government began to take serious steps to balance the national budget. In the late 1990s federal expenditures for U.S. public elementary and secondary schools reached US$290 billion annually, or nearly 4 percent of the gross domestic product (GDP), making education a major U.S. national budget item. However, the national budget proposed by President George W. Bush in March 2002 included significant cuts in spending on many elementary and secondary school programs, according to the National Priorities Project, a U.S. non-profit, activist group collaborating with local grassroots organizations to clarify national budget issues for ordinary citizens.

The U.S. Department of Education reported in the early 1990s that 60 percent of preschoolers attended private preschools, while 7 percent of all secondary school students were enrolled in private institutions. Because of the extremely high total enrollment in U.S. schools, the overall percentage growth of enrollment in private schools increased slowly, but by the mid-1990s private-school attendance had risen to nearly 9 percent. Students at all grade levels who came from high-income families were more likely to go to private school, although the increase in the number of charter schools began to affect this pattern in the late 1990s. However, enrollment in private church-supported schools did not always fit any socio-economic pattern. Statistics from the early 1990s indicated that the majority of preschool, kindergarten, elementary, and secondary students attending church-related schools were from low- to middle-income families.

By the fall of 1999, about 27,223 private elementary and secondary schools were operating in the United States. These schools fell into three main categories: Catholic schools (most of them parochial, or parish-based, schools); other religious schools; and non-sectarian schools. Non-Catholic religious schools represented almost half of these private schools, or 49 percent. Catholic schools were second-most numerous, at 30 percent of the total, while nonsectarian schools accounted for 22 percent of the private schools in operation at that time. The southern United States had the largest share of private schools (30 percent), while the West had the smallest share (20 percent). Sixty-one percent of private schools offered elementary grades only, while 30 percent featured a combination of elementary and secondary grades and just 9 percent were secondary-only schools. Of the private schools operating in fall 1999, most (82 percent) were offering regular programming. The remainder specialized in Montessori techniques, special education, vocational and/or technical training, alternative approaches, early childhood programs, or other special emphases. The private schools taught more than 5 million elementary and secondary students in the fall of 1999. All together, students attending private school represented about 10 percent of all elementary and secondary students in the United States.

In the 1990s, U.S. economists voiced concern that a weak school system was hurting the ability of the United States to compete in the global economy. Despite modest improvements in some test scores, U.S. students continued to rank behind many of their international peers in science and math. Large financial outlays for education in the United States too often failed to make any significant impact on the quality of education. To improve educational results, new methods were introduced that focused on the importance of competition and pushed schools to be innovative, discarding seemingly ineffective rules and regulations. Interest in charter schools and home schooling in the late 1990s and early-2000 years grew as parents sought alternatives to more traditional forms of public and private education. This has prompted U.S. federal, state, and local government officials and school administrators to reconsider how public funds for education may best be allocated and to examine possible viable alternatives to public schooling.

One response to the challenge to improve the educational system in the United States was the voucher system, which allowed parents to receive government money to send their children to the public or private school that could best meet their children's needs. Citing free-market principles, proponents presented the voucher system as a way to create competition in an educational marketplace and exert pressure for educational and financial reform. Magnet schools, which were designed to draw talented students to public schools with challenging curricula, were another approach to stimulate interest in public schools. Magnet schools were intended to stop the accelerating outflow of students from public school systems to private schools, especially in some of the more financially challenged urban areas.

Charter schools allowed parents, teachers, businesses, and organizations to organize a school. They were

public schools with requirements to meet publicly developed standards and could not discriminate in admissions. However, charter schools were independent of traditional school systems. Charter schools could provide new incentives for school districts to become more dynamic and entrepreneurial, especially since some had backing from for-profit corporations. As an alternative to voucher systems, charter schools encouraged at least limited competition, although they were not immediately accepted. An advantage of charter schools was the freedom to develop unique and optimal curricula with only one central governing board. The continued existence of any charter school was based on a performance contract, and performance monitoring ideally allowed for the disbanding of any school that did not meet standards. However, charter schools also had the potentially undesirable effect of diverting attention and financial support from crumbling and under-funded public schools that, in the absence of charter schools, might have had a better chance of receiving very necessary fiscal and community support for repairs and reform.

Some U.S. school districts, such as Madison County Schools in Huntsville, Alabama, had opened schools only for ninth grade. These schools were opened to reduce overcrowding in high schools, but the separations of 14- and 15-year-old students from upper levels of high school eased the transition to high school as well. A total of 185 ninth-grade-only schools were open in the United States in the 2005–06 school year, up from 127 for the 1999–2000 school year.

U.S. strategies for reforming elementary and secondary education programs at the beginning of the twenty-first century included compensatory education programs for disadvantaged students and programs to provide students from all socioeconomic categories access to English-language skills, basic literacy and math skills, and other prerequisites to high-level thinking and problem-solving skills. Wide discrepancies often existed in U.S. educational offerings and the quality of public schools from one state to another as well as from one school district to another, so the potential was great for public dissatisfaction in the United States, where parents and students considered private schools an increasingly desirable alternative. The choice of a private school over a public school depended on a variety of factors, including satisfaction with local public schools, family income, private school tuition, and sometimes the availability of public schooling for students of certain ages, such as preschoolers, since publicly funded preschools did not exist in many parts of the United States. By the late 2000s, some public school districts were beginning to consider adding pre-schools classes in their schools.

At the end of the twentieth century, the United States was not alone in critically assessing its school systems.

Stimulated by the concern that students would not be prepared to meet future workforce needs, national governments, private industry, and many public and private organizations and agencies worldwide directed their attention to improving the quality of education.

In 2000 a series of international tests of student achievement known as the Program for International Student Assessment (PISA) began. PISA was designed to measure the skills of 15-year-olds in literacy for reading, mathematics, and science, as well as in general and interdisciplinary skills. The first assessment was administered in 2000 and focused on measuring reading literacy. In 2003 the second cycle of PISA will be administered to test mathematics literacy in particular, and in 2006 the third cycle will highlight science literacy. All three categories of literacy, however, were scheduled to be tested during each round of testing.

Because PISA is primarily an assessment of students in the Organization for Economic Cooperation and Development (OECD) countries, which typically are economically developed nations, less will be known from this series of tests than may be gathered through other international assessments and statistical projects undertaken by more global, education-related organizations and agencies like UNESCO or the World Bank.

Initial results of the first cycle of PISA demonstrated significant differences in learning achievement across countries, even in the developed world. In the 27 OECD countries and four non-OECD countries whose testing results were compared by the National Center for Education Statistics in "Highlights from the 2000 Program for International Student Assessment," girls significantly outperformed boys in reading literacy. This was especially true in Finland and Latvia, where the average scores of girls and boys on the combined reading literacy tests varied by more than 50 percent. Other countries with strong gender differences in reading literacy were New Zealand and Norway, where girls did better than boys by more than an average 40 percent. In all countries except the Republic of Korea and Brazil, the average score difference between girls and boys in reading was at least 20 percent, with girls scoring higher than the boys. However, fewer significant gender differences were found in mathematics and science results.

In mathematics literacy, boys outperformed girls in 13 of the 27 OECD countries, as well as in Brazil, although no significant gender disparity was found in the United States. Average score differences approached 30 percent in favor of boys in Austria, the Republic of Korea, and Brazil. In the science literacy test, very few significant gender differences showed up in the testing results. Males scored significantly higher than females in science only in Austria, Denmark, and the Republic of

Korea. In New Zealand and Latvia, girls outperformed boys in the science assessment.

In the mid-1990s an OECD study on educational achievement in 21 industrial countries showed the United States leading all countries in the proportion of population that had earned a college or university degree. This was no small achievement, since other OECD countries also performed well. In most of the countries in the study, more than half of the adult population had completed high school. In Germany, Norway, Switzerland, and the United States, more than 80 percent of the population had earned high school diplomas. Historical U.S. graduation rates serve to intensify the significance of these figures. In the nineteenth century, less than 3 percent of Americans graduated from high school, and graduation rates remained at less than 50 percent until the middle of the twentieth century. By 1997 approximately 83 percent of U.S. students either held a high school diploma or had completed secondary school equivalency requirements.

Opinions varied widely as to how the United States was performing in terms of educational quality compared to other industrialized nations at the end of the twentieth century. Studies in the early 1990s found that 75 percent of U.S. students scored below proficiency levels in mathematics, while the average 10- to 11-year-old in Japan and Russia tested two years ahead of his or her peers in the United States. An OECD study conducted a few years later suggested that while 14-year-old Americans lagged in math, their reading and science levels matched those of children of the same age in France.

However, according to comparative educational statistics provided by the U.S. Department of Education, U.S. students in the 1990s compared favorably to their counterparts in other large industrialized nations in reading, but unfavorably in mathematics and science. Test scores indicated that U.S. schoolchildren were holding their own in reading and writing, and the U.S. Department of Education reported improvement in scientific and technological skills as well. Other internal evaluations also suggested that some achievement levels were improving. Standard Achievement Tests (SATs) given in the latter part of the twentieth century to high school students in the United States demonstrated a significant upward trend in student performance. Seventy-four percent more students scored above the benchmark level 650 in 1996 than in 1981, most of which could be traced to the influx of Asian-American students, who performed unusually well on the tests. However, even with the testing scores of Asian Americans removed, a 57 percent improvement was still shown.

Instruction in the arts, especially music, were found to have other educational value for students. For example, the non-profit, New York-based VH1 Save The Music Foundation discovered that teaching music helps students with development in many ways. The Foundation provided elementary schools with instruments and reported that benefits included cognitive development, self-discipline, self-esteem, critical thinking, spatial reasoning, reading, and math. In addition, the National Assembly of State Agencies reported that students with major arts involvement performed at a higher level on standardized achievement tests than students with low arts involvement.

International Futures. As industrialized countries continued to struggle to improve educational opportunities for their children and youth, transition and developing economies face yet more strenuous challenges to introduce their students to the skills necessary to succeed in a rapidly globalizing economy. In Russia, for example, students found themselves with more choices of dress and behavior than during the Cold War, and schools even began to pay attention to individual spiritual growth, which would have been anathema under the Communist regime. However, with the breakdown of the Soviet economic system, government agencies had limited funds available to outfit and maintain schools and pay teachers' salaries. The result has been that fewer educational opportunities may be found in certain parts of Russia now than were available during the Cold War days. Similarly, in parts of the developing world like sub-Saharan Africa where funds from the richer countries of the world were once plentiful through international development assistance programs, allocations for economic and social development programming from some major international donors were substantially redirected to other geographical regions and budget needs after the end of the Cold War. This has placed responsibility for the continued development of educational programs in such places as Africa more squarely on the shoulders of regional and national government leaders, which created a risk to the children and youth of some of the world's most impoverished nations. Additionally, the structural adjustment programs of the International Monetary Fund (IMF) of the late twentieth century further delayed economic prosperity in many poor countries and has often jeopardized the well-being of students in those nations.

As governments worldwide attempted to improve education in the twenty-first century, many were unable or unwilling to provide the necessary funds to develop high-quality school systems that featured access to all. Parents around the world therefore often considered private institutions as an educational alternative for their children.

CURRENT CONDITIONS

According to U.S. Census data from 2002, there were more than 53 million school-aged children between 5 and 17

years old, about 48.1 million of whom were enrolled in public schools. Schools received revenues of approximately US$8,552 per student in 2002, with the highest revenue per student in New York State at US$13,230 and the lowest in Utah at US$6,054. By the 2003–2004 school year, the median revenue figure across the U.S. had risen to US$9,764 per student, with the District of Columbia rising to the highest level at US$13,947. The total revenue figure for public schools during the 2004–2005 school year was estimated at more US$508 billion, while total expenditures were US$495 billion.

Homeschooling in the United States was evolving and becoming accepted by educators. As of 2004, there were approximately 75,000 public schools in the United States. According to *Market Share Reporter,* New York City had the largest school district in terms of enrollment, with 1.1 million students. In second place was Los Angeles with 747,000, followed by Chicago with 442,000; Miami-Dade County, Florida, with 364,000; Broward County, Florida, with 263,000; and Clark County, Nevada with 255,000. Other major districts were located in Houston and Philadelphia. According to the National Center for Education Statistics, enrollment in public schools was expected to increase 5 percent by 2013, while private school enrollment was expected to increase 7 percent. Statistics were unavailable for homeschoolers, but a 2003 study reported that approximately 1.1 million students were homeschooled. Funding for the U.S. public school system was becoming bleak in many states, which were either forced to cut their budgets in the mid-2000s and/or had funding cut by the state.

The need for some type of education reform has been debated for decades. Some call for a "back to basics" approach, while others want to prepare students to be able to compete for jobs in a global economy. Still others advocate "educating the whole child." One of the more recent examples began in 2002, when President Bush signed the No Child Left Behind Act (NCLB) into law, which was intended to ensure the adequate education of every child in public school. NCLB required annual testing on basic skills in language and math for third through eighth grades, adding science by 2012. Tutoring was to be paid by the government for students deemed "at risk," but funding was not available in the mid- to late 2000s. If students did not achieve specified benchmarks of learning and scores did not consistently improve, the schools themselves were penalized financially and were required to fund outside tutoring for students or were expected to allow students to transfer to other schools, or both.

In 2004, achievement deficits were reported at 6,000 schools under NCLB, and some analysts projected that the number could swell to one-third of the public schools in the country by 2006. Proponents of NCLB said that the worth of educating every child was being affirmed and that substandard or underachieving schools would no longer be able to maintain the status quo. Critics of NCLB pointed to the fallacy that tests and learning are the same, that the costs were excessive and that the federal government had given itself too much local control.

The American Federation of Teachers (AFT) had been active in the testing debate since launching its "Reclaim Your Classroom" campaign. The Texas AFT has protested the amount of time teachers lose during a school year to benchmarking, exam prep, administration, and other aspects of testing. The Texas AFT wanted teachers to document instructional time they lose during an academic year, with a goal "to end the confusing, duplicative demands of testing tied to different state and federal accountability systems. The AFT had improved data usage to enhance teaching and learning experiences, with the "Making Data Work for You" project as a collaboration of national unions, as well as state and local affiliates focused on helping educators analyze data and determine its appropriate use.

In 2008, school administrators faced additional challenges as they tried to maintain quality bus service for their districts as fuel costs rose, increasing 35 percent from the end of 2007 through July 2008. For example, in Garden City, Michigan, bus service was eliminated for extra curricular activities on Saturdays. In Montgomery County, Maryland, outside Washington, D.C., Superintendent Jerry Weast received permission from the school board to increase the distance students could walk to school if gasoline prices create "exigent circumstances," according to Robin Leeds of the National School Transportation Association.

Asian languages, especially Chinese and Japanese were beginning to find a place in schools in the late 2000s. For example, in Michigan, a strip mall in Novi, a suburb of Detroit, is the location for the state's only year-round Japanese school. Annual tuition for attending the Koby International Academy was US$10,000 in 2008. Students enjoy small class sizes and the experiences of reading, writing, and solving math problems in Japanese. Approximately 95 percent of the school's families stay in Michigan three to five years, and Japanese parents want their children to fit in with their peers when they return to Japan. Other families want their children to be familiar their Japanese heritage and culture. Children are typically enrolled in classes that meet after public schools end for the day and on weekends.

RESEARCH AND TECHNOLOGY

As knowledge of the world expands and as information processing technology improves, public schools have come under increasing pressure to thoroughly prepare students for the information age. Interactive learning began in the latter part of the twentieth century when tape recorders began to be introduced in some classrooms and was further developed as computer labs were installed in the schools of some industrialized countries beginning in the late 1960s. In addition, the growth of educational software packages, the use of the Internet, and videoconferencing equipment and programs in schools enhanced the technology curriculum.

Teaching and learning in the information age demanded new methods to prepare students to meet new technology. The move into the computer age has been expensive for school districts. Significant initial costs are associated with acquiring and maintaining computer hardware and associated software. Wiring, cabling, telephone lines, and technical support, in addition to required continual upgrades of information technology, can far exceed initial investments.

Class size was the subject of debate in the early twenty-first century. According to the American Educational Research Association, three countries conducted studies with diverse results. University of London Institute of Education researchers determined that "students tend to be on task more of the time in smaller classes." With the addition of just five classes, there were decreases in the odds that students would remain on task by approximately 25 percent. The study found that students at both elementary and secondary levels benefited from smaller class sizes. Another study at the University of Wisconsin demonstrated that smaller classes not only provided more engaging learning environment than larger classes, but also allowed students a greater share of their teacher's attention. However, a study of Hong Kong schools, which had larger classes than schools in the United States, found that the level of student involvement did not change with class size.

A study by the National Council on Teacher Quality found that elementary school teachers were not effectively prepared by education school to teach math. A federal panel had previously attributed the widespread difficulty U.S. students had with fractions to elementary schools. The difficulty later prevented the students from mastering more complicated subjects, such as algebra, later on.

WORKFORCE

According to the National Education Association, the estimated total number of instructional staff in the United States during the 2004–2005 school year was almost 3.54 million, about 25 percent of whom were male. About 1.82 million of the total staff were elementary school teachers, 1.29 million were secondary school teachers, more than 245,000 were nonsupervisory instructional staff, slightly more than 186,000 were principals. The average elementary teacher earned US$47,487, and a secondary school teacher earned US$48,000.

Elementary and secondary schools provided diverse job opportunities at different skill levels. Overall, the education level of most workers in the industry was high. For example, at the beginning of the twenty-first century, a bachelor's degree that included significant coursework in educational methods, theory, and psychology was required to be a teacher in an elementary school, and substantial coursework in a specific subject area was required or middle and high school teachers. States required prospective teachers to intern in an active classroom with a mentor as part of their coursework. Many school districts were beginning to assign mentors to new teachers. In Germany most teachers at the enc of the twentieth century spent five years in college before taking examinations and being assigned a mentor for two years of practical training. They sat for additional exams before being allowed to seek employment. In Japan teachers completed a four-year undergraduate program emphasizing academic specialization and then were mentored during their first years of teaching.

The educational services sector was the second largest industry in the United States in 2002, providing about 12.7 million jobs. Workers in the industry were employed various components of education and its related services, from counseling students to driving school buses to serving cafeteria lunches. However, most occupations were professional, including administrative, managerial, service, and other workers. Teachers accounted for half of all employment in education. By the fall of 1999, about 395,317 full-time equivalent (FTE) teachers were providing instruction to U.S. elementary and secondary students in private schools alone, with 38 percent of those teachers working in Catholic schools, 39 percent employed in other religious schools, and 24 percent working in nonsectarian schools.

Teachers in the United States were not protected by unions until the middle of the twentieth century, but 41 percent of elementary and secondary teachers and educations services workers either were union workers or were covered by union contracts by the 1990s. In contrast, only 18 percent of workers in all other industries combined were in unions or covered by union contracts. The American Federation of Teachers (AFT) and the National Education Association (NEA) were the largest teachers' unions in the United States at the beginning of the twenty-first century.

Internationally, average salaries for education-related employees, including school administrators, teachers, counselors, and librarians often are significantly higher than the average salaries for other occupations. In the United States, however, educators' salaries are sometimes noticeably lower than salaries for other professionals, such as doctors and lawyers. Teacher earnings increase with additional education and length of service. Educational services employees who worked a traditional school year from September to June had the opportunity to earn additional money during the summer when regular classes were not in session.

Variations in Teacher Workloads. Compared to school systems in many other industrialized nations, teachers in the United States spend very little structured time sharing information with each other about students, teaching materials, or teaching techniques. Generally, the U.S. teacher's time at school is spent with students, either teaching academic subjects or monitoring playgrounds and lunchrooms. However, any districts have begun to include time in the school year for teachers to collaborate and attend in-service educational opportunities.

In a number of Asian countries, the situation is quite different than in the United States. An study of Asian educational practices in the early 1990s found that teachers in Beijing could not believe that the teaching workload in U.S. schools was as high as it actually was. Asian teachers wondered how U.S. teachers found time to prepare lessons, collaborate about methodology, grade papers, and work with individual students. Teachers in China, as in other Asian nations, only teach three or four hours each day, spending the rest of their workday managing other aspects of their students' education. Teachers in Europe also spend time outside the classroom, averaging just 18 hours of direct classroom instruction per week in the late 1990s. In contrast, U.S. teachers usually spent 25 hours in direct classroom instruction during a five-day school week, and elementary school teachers faced students 30 or more hours each week. A typical workweek for teachers in the United States included 36.5 hours in the classroom in addition to approximately 11 hours a week spent on miscellaneous duties, including grading papers and preparing lesson plans.

MAJOR COUNTRIES IN THE INDUSTRY

Every country in the world provides some form of education to their children. Some countries are much better than others in providing substantial government funding for schools. Traditional knowledge may be imparted informally through "bush" schools to village youth in Sierra Leone or formally with training in advanced computing technology and mathematics is provided through a *Gymnasium* to urban secondary students in Germany.

Regardless of the method, everyone in the world believes in teaching their children the values of their society, the principles they believe will contribute to their children's healthy development, and the skills necessary to negotiate the adult world. All countries benefit greatly from educating their children and youth, raising children to become adults who can contribute to the growth of the economy and benefit society.

Simultaneously, a number of countries stand out in dedicating significant public and private financial and human resources to developing, outfitting, and maintaining schools and educational programs. The teaching methods and educational theories of these countries are often imported by other countries around the world, which has resulted in a few countries whose emphasis on education has been significant and influential.

Japan. Japan provides a comprehensive approach to primary education for nearly all of the nation's school-age children. Children begin elementary school at age 6 and at age 12 begin middle school. Attendance is compulsory through the lower level of secondary school for six years of elementary school and three years of middle school covering the ages 6 to 15 years. After that time attendance is not required, although about 97 percent of students who graduate from middle school do attend high school, or *kotogakko*. About 90 percent of all students in Japan graduate from high school. The majority of high schools are public, although about 30 percent of Japanese high school students attend private schools.

Enrollment in high school is a competitive exercise, with admission based on a combination of student grades and achievement test scores. Achievement test scores are sent to the schools where a student has applied but are never shown to the students. Because exams play such an important role in student advancement, many students' after-school hours are spent in special tutorial programs called *juku* rather than on social or recreational activities as in other countries. Pure vocational education is rare in Japan, although a growing number of students pursue some kind of vocational training. Japanese schools teach hard work, which leads to high student academic achievement. The education system was being reviewed to allow more independent teaching styles.

United Kingdom. Education in the United Kingdom is characterized by an unusual range of choices, including public or private school. Other decisions include which public or private school and whether the educational focus should be vocational or academic. Every child between the ages of 5 and 16 in Great Britain must attend school of some sort, or between ages 4 and 16 in Northern Ireland. Many students begin at schools funded and administered by local education authorities

(LEAs). The remainder attend schools that U.S. pupils would term "private," that are funded by private individuals, but are called "public" in the United Kingdom since they are owned and administered by the general public rather than by the state. Whether deemed "public" or "private," these independently operated schools function as a business, with teachers and headmasters in control of the school budget.

A very large proportion of British children begin their schooling at age 3 or 4, attending nursery schools or "reception classes" in elementary schools that prepare them for primary school. At age 5 in Great Britain, or age 4 in Northern Ireland, children attend a primary school, where they remain until approximately age 11. Most students continue to secondary schools that accept all students regardless of background or ability and require no testing as a prerequisite for entry. However, those students who choose to complete their education in public schools must first pass demanding entrance examinations at the school of their choice, whether they seek admission to a publicly funded "grammar school" or to ancient and prestigious institutions. Although tuition is costly, students who attend "public" schools are typically affluent and the price rarely discourages enrollment. Even those parents who must scrape and save to enroll their children in the more prestigious academies consider the social and academic opportunity afforded by attendance at these schools to be worth the expense. School pride associated with public secondary schools is intense, whether or not the school in question is well known internationally. The phenomenon of students from multiple generations of families attending the same private school is not an unusual one, and indeed some private institutions have been preparing young scholars for several centuries.

Whether or not students attend a fee-based public school, U.K. parents have a choice when selecting secondary schools. State schools are under close governmental scrutiny. Exams are administered to students at ages 7, 11, 14, and 16, to establish the performance of the school as well as to evaluate individual students. In addition, schools undergo intense school inspections that evaluate the school, teaching staff, and administrative staff on a wide variety of criteria. Exam results, along with school truancy records and school inspection reports, are open to public view and are used by parents as a guide to select the best state school for their children.

Completion of secondary schooling, whether in state or public schools, is indicated by two stages of examinations. At age 16, students take the main state examination for each subject they have studied. These are the famous "O-level" exams, and performance on them generally dictates whether or not a student will continue vocational training or go on to university. Admission to the university is predicated on satisfactory completion of a fixed number of advanced, or "A-level" exams, which are administered after about two additional years of study. In 1988 the General Certificate of Education (GCE) that had been awarded on completion of O-level testing was replaced with the General Certificate of Secondary Education (GCSE). Students on a course of advanced study that is considered vocational compared to the pure academics measured by A-levels (drama, business studies) may use their secondary school diplomas to enter universities offering comparable areas of study. Regardless of the educational track, this means that British students attending university—Oxford, Cambridge, or the less exclusive regional "red-brick" colleges—begin their collegiate studies approximately two years ahead of their U.S. counterparts.

Businesses in the United Kingdom have been encouraged to help improve schools, particularly in vocational education, and the British government has established a national curriculum for use in state schools. The tests that measure the success of this curriculum has become part of an aggressive monitoring of schools. It is not impossible for a dissatisfied education inspector to mandate wholesale staff dismissal and replacement, or more commonly, to advise the replacement of an underachieving school's headmaster or headmistress.

France. Public education in France is highly centralized. The country is divided into a number of geographically-based education districts, called "academies." Each academy is headed by a rector who reports directly to the Minister of National Education, Research, and Technology. The French educational system was set up to ensure uniformity, and presumably quality, in education throughout the country, but critics have claimed the system is inflexible and precludes local citizens from voicing their opinions on educational problems.

Ten years of public school attendance are mandated from ages 6 to 16, but in reality most children attend school for at least a dozen years. It is possible for a child to be in school for 16 years prior to enrolling in a university. Public education is free, although about one-sixth of French elementary schoolchildren and one-fifth of secondary students attend private schools, about 95 percent of which are Roman Catholic. Primary and elementary training is divided into preschool (pre-elementary) training for toddlers through age 6, primary school (*école primaire*) for students aged 6 through 11, and secondary school (*collège*) attended by students aged 12 to 15. Four years of *collège* culminates in the *brevet de collège* diploma, following the successful completion of the final two years of coursework and acceptable performance on the timed, written examination in French, history-geography, and

mathematics that concludes this level of their secondary studies.

Most French students also take advantage of a second cycle of secondary education, or *lycée*. Students entering the *lycée* either select a three-year course of study leading to the General Baccalaureate, which provides entrance to the university, or to one of two types of technical training programs: the three-year Technological Baccalaureate program that opens the way to post-secondary schools of technology, professional, or arts studies; or the Professional Baccalaureate program that leads directly to a job or to on-the-job training after two years of study.

Germany. Although a strong national standard of education exists in Germany, each German state controls an educational system distinct from that of the other states. A permanent national commission is responsible for providing uniformity in curriculum, requirements, and standards imposed largely through textbook selection, but the implementation of these standards varies from state to state. Private schools exist in Germany, but since public education, including university study, is free and exceedingly high in standard, the number of private schools is quite small.

German students are required to attend school from ages 6 to 18. Kindergartens are available to nurture and support the development of children of preschool age (3 to 5 years old). However, kindergartens are not part of the German state school system, and parents frequently must contribute to their cost of operation. The 12 years of mandatory state school attendance consists of 9 or 10 years of full-time attendance, depending on the state, and the remaining years either consist of full-time studies or are divided between school and on-the-job training. Students are asked at an early age to identify their academic or vocational goals. Elementary education, or *Grundschule,* lasts six years in Berlin and Brandenburg and four years elsewhere in the country, followed by a two-year orientation phase, *Orientierungsstufe* in many parts of Germany.

Students begin to diverge even further from each other in their courses of study after elementary school. About one-fourth of German secondary students go on to the *Hauptschule,* a secondary general school for grades 5 through 9, or 7 through 9, depending on the length of elementary education a student has had. A student who has successfully completed *Hauptschule,* which covers basic academic training in addition to introductory vocational studies, earns a school-leaving certificate that permits admittance to a vocational apprenticeship program that lasts two to three years. Some graduates go on to complete tenth grade, and if they earn especially high grades, they may receive a more prestigious school-leaving certificate. Students may also choose to attend a vocational training school following *Hauptschule.*

Two-fifths of German secondary students attend the *Realschule* instead of the *Hauptschule* for grades 5 through 10. The *Realschule* is designed to prepare students for such occupations as mid-level administrators and managers, service workers, and civil servants. One to three years of study in a full-time vocational school known as a *Berufsfachschule* is also possible for students who complete *Hauptschule* or *Realschule.* About one-fourth of German secondary students enter the *Gymnasium* directly after elementary school. Several kinds of *Gymnasium* exist, but the emphasis remains on academic subjects. After a total of 12 or 13 years of schooling, students in the *Gymnasium* sit for the *Abitur* examinations, which open the door to university studies.

Certain alternatives exist in some parts of Germany, including the *Gesamtschule,* a form of post-elementary school that allows students a broader, less tracked education than the traditional split between vocational and academic studies. About 13 percent of German secondary students attend the *Gesamtschule.* Germany also provides special schools known as *Sonderschulen* to educate disabled students.

BIBLIOGRAPHY

American Federation of Teachers, 2004. Available from www.aft.org.

Boser, Ulrich. "A New Law Is Put to the Test." *U.S. News & World Report,* 22 March 2004.

Broughman, Stephen, and Lenore A. Colaciello. "Private School Universe Survey: 1999–2000," *NCES Statistical Analysis Report,* NCES 2001–330. Washington, DC: National Center for Education Statistics, Office of Educational Research and Improvement, U.S. Department of Education, August 2001. Available from nces.ed.gov.

Field, Richard. "John Dewey (1859–1952)." In *The Internet Encyclopedia of Philosophy,* 2001. Available from www.iep.utm.edu.

"Global Education Digest 2004: Comparing Education Statistics Across the World." United Nations Educational, Scientific, and Cultural Organization, 2004. Available from www.uis.unesco.org.

John Dewey Project on Progressive Education. "A Brief Overview of Progressive Education." College of Education and Social Services, University of Vermont, 2002. Available from www.uvm.edu.

"International Studies Add to Body of Class-Size Research." *American Teacher,* 1 May 2008.

Lazich, Robert S., ed. *Market Share Reporter.* Detroit: Thomson Gale, 2004.

Lewis, Shawn D. "Preserving Culture." *The Detroit News,* 17 July 2008.

Marlowe-Ferguson, Rebecca, and Christopher Lopez, eds. *World Education Encyclopedia, Second Edition.* Farmington Hills, Michigan: The Gale Group-Thomson Learning, 2001.

National Center for Education Statistics. "1.1 Million Homeschooled Students in the United States in 2003."

Washington, DC: U.S. Department of Education, 2003. Available from nces.ed.gov.

———. "Common Core of Data: Information on Public Schools and School Districts in the United States." Washington, DC: U.S. Department of Education, 2002. Available from nces.ed.gov.

———. *Highlights from the 2000 Program for International Student Assessment (PISA),* NCES 2002–116. Washington, DC: Office of Educational Research and Improvement, U.S. Department of Education, 2002. Available from nces.ed.gov.

———. "International Comparisons in Education." Washington, DC: Office of Educational Research and Improvement, U.S. Department of Education, 2002. Available from nces.ed.gov.

———. *Outcomes of Learning: Results from the 2000 Program for International Student Assessment of 15-Year-Olds in Reading, Mathematics, and Science Literacy,* NCES 2002–115. Washington, DC: U.S. Department of Education, 2002.

———. "Overview of Public Elementary and Secondary Schools and Districts: School Year 1999–2000," *NCES Statistical Analysis Report,* NCES 2001–339R. Washington, DC: U.S. Department of Education, September 2001. Available from nces.ed.gov.

———. "Projections of Education Statistics to 2013." Washington, DC: U.S. Department of Education, 2004. Available from nces.ed.gov.

Nicholls, Cheryl. "Art Education Helps Children Thrive." *African American Family,* August 2008.

OECD. *Education at a Glance: OECD Indicators 2001 Edition.* Organization for Economic Co-operation and Development, 2001. Available from oecdpublications.gfi-nb.com.

"Proposed FY2003 Budget and Analysis: States and Local Governments to Lose Funding for Many Programs." National Priorities Project, 2002. Available from www.nationalpriorities.org.

Purdon, Gwen. "Schools Cutting Bus Service Because of Fuel Prices." *USA Today,* 10 July 2008.

"Rankings & Estimates: Rankings of the States 2004 and Estimates of School Statistics 2005." National Education Association, June 2005. Available from www.nea.org.

Ritchie, Susan. "Horace Mann." In *Dictionary of Unitarian and Universalist Biography,* 2001. Available from www25.uua.org.

Rose, Mike. "Standardized Spring." *American Teacher,* March 2008.

"Testing, Testing." *Community Care,* 20 May 2004.

UNESCO Institute for Statistics. "Quest 2001, Survey 2001 Electronic Questionnaire and Manuals." United Nations Educational, Scientific, and Cultural Organization, 2001. Available from www.uis.unesco.org.

U.S. Department of Labor, Bureau of Labor Statistics. "Educational Services." *Career Guide to Industries, 2004–05 Edition.* Available from www.bls.gov.

White, Elizabeth, "9th-Grade-Only Schools a Success." *The Detroit Free Press,* 24 August 2008.

Williams, Candice, and Karen Bouffard. "School of Choice: Parents opt to Teach Kids at Home for Growing List of Reasons." *The Detroit News,* 10 September 2008.

World Development Indicators 2001. Washington, DC: The World Bank, 2001.

Zuckerbrod, Nancy. "Teacher Education Schools Flunk Math." *The Detroit News,* 27 June 2008.

SIC 4911, 4920

ENERGY

NAICS CODE(S)

22111. The world's energy industry produces, transmits, and distributes electricity and natural gas. Electric power generation may be derived by any number of methods, including burning fossil fuels, harnessing wind or water motion, or energy from nuclear reactions. Often several separate companies or organizations are involved in the production and distribution chain, which includes everything from initial production to delivery to end users. Various firms and public utilities specialize in certain phases of energy production, while others integrate several production steps. For example, some firms may generate electricity and sell it to distributors that resell it to the public. Similarly, natural gas companies may operate pipelines feeding the distribution companies that then provide natural gas to end users in businesses and private residences.

INDUSTRY SNAPSHOT

The International Energy Agency reported that 41.6 percent of the total worldwide energy supply in 2002 came from non-coal and non-oil sources, up from 30 percent in 1973. Non-oil sources included natural gas, nuclear, hydro, combustible renewables, waste, wind and solar. Most electricity was still being produced using coal, but there was a growing use of natural gas and nuclear power in some countries. Alternative renewable forms of electricity generation were continuing to make inroads, with many investments in wind, geothermal and combustible renewable sources.

On a global basis, 16.1 trillion kilowatt hours of electricity was supplied in 2002. The countries producing the most electricity were the United States, China and Japan, all of which were large consumers. U.S., German, British and Japanese electric utilities dominated the industry, and the European-based companies showed the strongest signs of globalization, with France exporting more electricity than any other country. Total consumption of electricity worldwide was projected to reach 16.4 trillion kilowatt hours (kwh) by 2010, 18.5 trillion kwh by 2015, 20.7 trillion kwh by 2020, and 23.1 trillion kwh by 2025. Total consumption of energy generation fuels, on the other hand, was projected to reach 193.6 quadrillion btu by 2010, 213.9 by 2015, 235.5 by 2020, and 258.6 by 2025.

More than 96 trillion cubic feet of natural gas was produced globally in 2003, with the most growth occurring in the countries of the former Soviet Union since 1976. Russia, Canada and Norway were the world' leading exporters, and although the United States was the second largest producer, it was had to import natural gas to meet demand.

The leading companies in the natural gas industry hold or have held monopolistic control over domestic distribution rights in the United Kingdom, Japan, the Netherlands, France, and Germany, as have companies in the United States and other countries that were involved in worldwide exploration for or production of natural gas. In 2004, gas reserves totaled 6.1 quadrillion cubic feet worldwide, 90 percent of which was controlled by the top 20 countries, accounting for more than 5.4 quadrillion cubic feet.

The vast majority of the energy industry's growth is expected to come from emerging markets in developing nations, including Asian, Latin American, and Eastern European countries, where large pent-up demand exists for energy, or where existing power plants need to be updated, with China, Latin America, and Africa reporting the biggest annual increases in demand. The energy needs of developing nations, coupled with widespread global initiatives to deregulate the electric and gas industries and privatize state-owned companies, were increasing competition in an industry that was once considered to be necessarily monopolistic.

The Detroit Free Press reported that high gas prices in mid-2008 were affecting several areas of the economy, concluding that "loss of wealth could be a double whammy for the U.S. economy." and that short term as well as long term effects could include a decrease in spending that would impede productive growth as firms shifted their "focus from increasing worker efficiency to reducing energy costs."

By 2008, heating and cooling costs were increasing throughout the world. While poor economic conditions led to downsizing and budget cuts, utility bills were becoming increasingly difficult for struggling families to pay without sacrifices and struggles. Individuals and groups were speaking out in protest and governments sometimes reacted by enacting laws that restricted increases.

ORGANIZATION AND STRUCTURE

The electric and gas industries can effectively be divided into seven market regions: United States–Canada; Western Europe; Japan; Asia–Pacific, excluding Japan; Eastern Europe and the former Soviet Union; Latin America; and the Middle East and Africa. In the more developed regions, there is generally a surplus of power, while the underdeveloped regions, especially Latin America and the Asia–Pacific region where demand for power was not met, were expected to experience the vast majority of growth for the electric and gas industries. The Energy Information Administration predicted electricity demand in developing countries would grow at more than twice the rate of growth in industrialized countries between 1995 and 2020.

Electric Services. Every country typically has its own electric power industry structure, which had been solidified in the first half of the twentieth century in more developed countries. While traditional national and regional markets continued to exist in the late 1990s, deregulation and privatization of utilities were rapidly changing the organization of the electric power industry. By the early 1990s, private capitalization of independent power projects had set the stage for a new global business environment. A surplus of power in developed countries like the United States and the United Kingdom, which were in the throes of utility deregulation, and power demand from developing countries in Asia-Pacific and Latin American markets characterized this environment regionally. While Western European utilities had joined in some of the conglomerates providing power in emerging markets, the independent power movement began in the United States and the United Kingdom, where utilities facing deregulation, competition, and fixed returns had turned to external markets for higher profits.

In the United States, regulation and deregulation began to substantially change the power industry in 1978 when the Public Utility Regulatory Policies Act was adopted to encourage conservation by allowing non-regulated independent producers to generate electricity that could be sold to utilities. The Act created an independent power industry that grew faster than expected, with independent producers responsible for half of the generating capacity that went on line during the 1980s. The 1992 Energy Policy Act granted the industry wholesale transmission or "wheeling of power" rights, allowing utilities to buy energy from utilities across state lines in 1993. The Act also enabled states to permit retail wheeling, or transportation, of power to individual businesses and consumers. Between the late 1980s and early 2000s, the U.S. Federal Regulatory Energy Commission (FERC) approved roughly 850 wholesaler power transmission permits.

In the late 1990s, states were moving toward deregulating their retail electricity markets. According to Strategic Energy Ltd., by April 1998 California, Rhode Island, Massachusetts, and Pennsylvania had opened their retail markets to competition. In addition, Montana, Nevada, Kansas, Illinois, New Hampshire, Maine, and Oklahoma had passed retail wheeling legislation to allow consumers to purchase energy directly from providers and were completing the transition to competitive markets. By early 1998, 11 states had opted to test deregulation with pilot programs that allowed some customers to participate in limited retail choice experiments as a prelude to retail competition, and legislative or regulatory activity had taken place in the remaining 29 states. In the early

2000s, many states suspended plans to open their energy markets to competitions following highly-publicized problems with retail deregulation in California, including widespread blackouts.

Between 1988 and 1991, Great Britain largely completed privatizing its electricity industry, except the nuclear power segment. The government's public monopoly responsible for generation and transmission of power in England and Wales was separated into two generating companies, PowerGen PLC and National Power, and a transmission company, National Grid Co. Efforts to privatize the natural gas industry moved slowly, and by 1994 plans had been made to deregulate the local gas industry in 1996 when some British Gas PLC customers were allowed to choose their gas supplier.

By 1998, the privatization efforts in the United Kingdom had resulted in an average decrease of 21 percent in residential electricity bills in England and Wales. In mid-1998, British ministers announced plans to overhaul the country's electricity industry again. The ruling Labour Party hoped to reform wholesale trading arrangements in the national electricity pool, which they believed had unduly favored growth in gas-fired power plants and had caused the country to go beyond its pollution targets. Ministers proposed tighter restrictions for future gas-fired power plants in order to preserve a market for British coal while the new trading arrangements were introduced. In May 1999, the United Kingdom became the first country to grant all of its residential and commercial gas and electricity consumers the right to choose their utilities.

Natural Gas. Since the mid-1980s, the natural gas regulatory climate in the United States has changed dramatically. In 1985, FERC issued an order requiring pipelines to become open-access carriers for both gas producers and users, turning pipeline companies into transportation services. In November 1993, FERC Order 633, which was aimed at reducing regulation and encouraging competition, took effect, making local utilities responsible for their natural gas supplies from well head to consumer. Additionally, pipeline companies were no longer allowed to sell gas directly to customers and had to utilize a marketing unit. As a result, pipeline companies abandoned their sales operations and developed gas market affiliates to serve as intermediaries.

BACKGROUND AND DEVELOPMENT

Development of the Electric Power Industry. The technological developments leading to the birth of the electric power industry were international in scope. In 1831 Englishman Michael Faraday and American Joseph

Henry independently discovered the induction principle that paved the way for the development of the electric generator, which in turn made possible the widespread and economical production and distribution of electric power. However, the necessary technology was not available for the electric power industry for another 50 years, but by the 1850s generators were being manufactured commercially in several countries. In 1870 the first practical generator capable of producing a continuous electric current was built by Belgian manufacturer Zenobe Theophile Gramme.

Most historians credit U.S. inventor and entrepreneur Thomas Alva Edison for the electric power industry. Edison was determined to utilize electricity to provide an improved, less expensive means of lighting than arc-lighting and manufactured gas. According to Milton A. Chase in *Electric Power: An Industry at a Crossroads,* Edison's goal was to compete with the gas industry that had been established 50 years earlier. After Edison developed the electric incandescent lamp for commercial use, he pioneered the electric power industry, beginning with a New York power company, in order to sell electricity to those who purchased his incandescent bulbs. Consequently, Edison is widely acknowledged as the creator of the first successful system to produce, distribute, and utilize electric power.

In January 1882 the first public power station, which used an electric generator began operating in London for demonstration purposes. That same year in the state of New York, Edison supervised the installation of the world's first permanent, commercial central power system. Both stations employed direct-current (DC) systems that were ineffective for transmitting power long distances. Edison's New York power station, which used coal-fired boilers to produced steam that ran generators, became a model for franchised Edison Electric Light operations in other U.S. cities.

Initially, Edison's companies were limited by the DC system to selling power to areas in close proximity to central power stations. The first practical alternating-current (AC) generator was built in Germany and served Frankfurt beginning in 1891. In 1892 Edison sent his assistant, Samuel Insull, to oversee what in the next decade would become the electric powerhouse Commonwealth Edison. That same year Edison's firm merged with the Thomson-Houston company, which was a proponent of AC power, to become General Electric Company. Insull, who was from England, advanced the use of the AC system and created the model for the power industry that came to be used by the Edison operations by the turn of the century. Insull also pioneered a build-and-grow strategy for utilities that became cost effective once power producers diversified their customer base to diffuse the peak load of electricity demand. Insull also

became a strong proponent of electric utility monopolies, public relations, and advertising.

During the first years of the twentieth century, technological developments led to ever-increasing capacities generated by turbine motors. Insull and others perpetuated the grow-and-build strategy that encouraged AC electricity use with technological advances in turbines and high-voltage transmission systems. Utilities were thus able to open new plants and serve more customers based on the theory that lower consumer costs and unlimited business growth could be expected along with growing use and evolving improvements in turbine technology. Another component of Insull's strategy was to use holding companies to finance the construction of power plants. In addition to providing financial backing, the holding company system provided management and engineering expertise that could be used to employ system interconnections while holding companies acquired small systems. The number of new holding companies peaked in the United States in 1924, when 20 corporations controlled 61 percent of the U.S. commercial generating capacity. During the 1920s, some of those holding companies exploited speculative investment trends and concocted schemes for utilities to control huge power domains that were controlled by a limited number of shareholders with just a few shares of a preferred stock at the highest level of what some called a pyramid ownership system.

During the 1920s the largest percentage of electric power was produced by hydroelectric power plants. The two principal sources for power generators were hydro and thermal, with the former creating power from generators turned by water and the latter using generators powered by steam. The early hydroelectric plants were the most cost effective plants of their time, but technological advances by the 1930s made thermal generation the system of choice.

By the early 1930s, 10 holding companies controlled about three-quarters of the United States' power industry. The grasp of the holding companies on the electric utility industry was pried loose following the Great Depression and a federal investigation into the abuse of holding companies, which had caused overexpansion and financial problems for establishments such as Insull's pyramid of companies. Three of Insull's largest firms went into receivership in 1932 and he was indicted on federal charges. He fled to Europe, but returned to the United States in 1934, and was acquitted on three counts of embezzlement and fraud before returning to Europe to live out his days in rich seclusion. When the Holding Company Act of 1935 was passed, it abolished leveraged holding companies and stripped apart monopolies not connected by contiguous service territory. The landscape of the utilities industry in the United States was settled by

New Deal legislation that created federal utilities, such as the Tennessee Valley Authority (TVA), and rural electric authorities.

By the time the Holding Company Act was passed in the United States, other industrialized countries had also begun to regulate their growing utility industries. In 1935 the Canadian province of Quebec established an Electrical Commission to regulate electric distribution services and rates. As early as 1926, Great Britain enacted the Electricity (Supply) Act, which restructured the industry and oversaw construction of a national power transmission grid. By 1932, Japan, which was engaged in war with mainland China, began operating under a revised Electric Utility Industry Law that gave the country's leaders the final word on such matters as mergers and rates. After World War II, economic and political conditions encouraged the establishment of national power systems in Canada, the United Kingdom, France, and new Communist countries, while only a few private or semi-private systems developed in such countries as Japan and West Germany. The United States, meanwhile, had the world's most heterogeneous industry, consisting of numerous private companies and government utilities, as a result of legislation and New Deal reforms.

Build-and-grow strategies went unchallenged in the United States until the late 1960s when utilities faced high operating costs. In the 1970s the proper mix of generating fuel was debated worldwide. Through the 1950s, many nations had relied largely on hydroelectric power, but it proved inadequate for growing industrial needs. Coal had been a long-standing fossil fuel for thermal generation, although the fuel of choice shifted to oil after prices declined in the 1960s, and then to nuclear generation in the early 1970s. During the late 1970s concerns about the safety of nuclear energy caused a shift back to coal, and falling oil and natural gas prices in the 1980s changed the situation. Nuclear power fell increasingly out of favor after dangerous leaks at Three Mile Island in the United States in 1979 and at the Soviet Union's Chernobyl plant in 1986, although an increase in the number of nuclear plants in France and a lack of fossil fuels in Japan helped solidify nuclear power's importance in those countries.

Development of the Natural Gas Industry. The first discoveries of natural gas were made in Iran between 6000 and 2000 B.C. These gas "seeps" are thought to have been struck by lightning, fueling the "eternal fires" of the ancient Persians who embraced a fire-worshipping religion. Natural gas was discovered in China as early as 900 B.C., and by 200 B.C. the ancient Chinese, who were the first people known to utilize natural gas for industrial uses, created a system of bamboo poles through

which gas was piped. The gas was burned to dry rock salt and manufacture salt. Manufactured gas was discovered in 1609 by Belgian chemist and physician Jan Baptista van Helmont who noticed that a "spirit," which he called "gas," escaped from coal when heated. Natural gas was not discovered in Europe until 1659. During the late eighteenth and early nineteenth centuries, William Murdock, a British engineer who became known as the father of the gas industry, successfully lit his home with gas manufactured (or distilled) from coal, lit the outside of a factory with gaslight, and installed 900 gaslights in cotton mills.

Murdock's work, along with that of other inventors sparked the interest of German businessman Frederick Albert Winsor, who received a British patent to manufacture gas on a substantial scale in 1804. In London, Winsor and his business partners were responsible for the first public street lighting with gas in 1807. They were also responsible for the first gas company, which was formed in 1812. Manufactured gas remained the primary fuel for illuminating streets and houses in Europe for most of the next two centuries. In 1812 the first U.S. gas company provided street lighting services in Baltimore, and in 1836 the first Canadian gas company followed suit in Montreal.

Discoveries of natural gas reserves in the United States resulted in substantial development of the gas industry, with the earliest discovery reported in West Virginia in 1775. During the 1820s gunsmith William Aaron Hart developed the first natural gas well in the United States (in Fredonia, New York) and subsequently piped gas to nearby buildings, where it was used for lighting. By the end of the Civil War, about 300 U.S. manufactured gas distribution companies had been formed, and in 1865 the first company known to have distributed natural gas was founded in Fredonia.

In the 1870s, the first long-distance pipeline carried gas 25 miles (a very short distance in modern practice) to Rochester, New York, and the first iron pipeline transported natural gas about 5 miles to customers in Pennsylvania. However, Edison's electric light, and the electric power industry he helped develop, nearly wiped out the natural gas industry in the 1880s. Although manufactured gas was increasingly used for cooking and heating water during the last quarter of the nineteenth century, the natural gas industry in the United States remained localized around gas fields due to the limitation for pipeline transmission. In 1890 a technological breakthrough resulted in the invention of a leak-proof pipeline couple, but construction and other restrictions kept pipelines from extending more than 100 miles. By 1925, all of the 3.5 million natural gas customers in the United States continued to be within a few hundred miles of gas fields.

The U.S. natural gas industry received a much-needed boost during the early twentieth century, when major reserves were discovered in Texas, Oklahoma, and Louisiana. Between 1906 and 1920, natural gas production more than doubled to 800 billion cubic feet per year. The industry grew rapidly after long-distance transmission of gas became practical in the late 1920s after the introduction of seamless, electrically welded steel pipelines that could carry gas under great pressure and in great quantities. In 1927 the largest reserve in the United States was discovered in Kansas, and was found to extend into Texas and Oklahoma. Between 1927 and 1931 more than 10 major natural gas pipeline systems were constructed in the country. By the 1930s, natural gas was transmitted from Texas fields to Midwestern cities, and numerous cities began switching from the more expensive manufactured gas to natural gas, which was increasingly used for heating as well as cooking and water heating purposes. Pipelines constructed after World War II were longer and wider in diameter, and the rapid discovery of new reserves in the United States continued through the 1960s, while production increased at a substantial pace between the mid-1950s and the mid-1970s.

Until well into the 1950s, natural gas was not available in substantial quantities in most European nations, which continued to rely largely on manufactured gas. "Associated" natural gas found during oil drilling was often considered a nuisance and was flared or burned away. In 1956 a major gas field was discovered in North Africa, and a later major engineering project resulted in the development of a pipeline running from Algeria to the Mediterranean Sea and to Sicily, crossing the sea where it is more than 610 meters deep in some places. The largest European gas field was discovered in 1959 on the Dutch coast. New discoveries in the 1960s led to robust expansion of the European natural gas industry, particularly in the Netherlands and the Soviet Union. During the mid-1960s Great Britain also became a major player in the industry after it discovered and began to produce sizable quantities of natural gas from reserves beneath the North Sea. In 1971 the largest gas field in Asia was discovered in the North Sumatra basin of Indonesia.

The largest known gas field in the world, Urengoy, was discovered in the Soviet Union in 1966 in the West Siberian region of the Arctic Circle and began production in 1978. Subsequent discoveries of major fields in the Arctic Circle followed. Beginning in the 1970s, the Soviet Union built the longest gas transmission lines, including the Northern Lights system that links Eastern Europe with Siberian gas fields in the Arctic Circle, crossing 700 rivers and the Ural Mountains. In 1983 the Soviet Union surpassed the United States in gas production and became the world's leading producer of natural gas.

In the United States during the late 1960s and early 1970s, consumption exceeded reserve discovery. During the same period crude oil shortages helped promote natural gas as a significant source of world energy, although a fear of low reserves diminished the popularity of natural gas during the late 1970s. Since the 1980s, natural gas has been popular because it has the advantages of being a relatively clean burning fuel that is free of the soot, carbon monoxide, and nitrogen oxides associated with other fossil fuels that have been used to power electric generators. Many plants built in the 1990s were designed to be powered by natural gas. Worldwide, in the early 1990s the greatest known reserves in history were available, and nations that had previously relied on manufactured gas turned increasingly to the less-expensive natural gas. Producing countries were exporting greater quantities of the natural gas by pipeline and in liquid natural gas (LNG) form by tanker ship to plants where the liquid was reconverted to gas form.

In the late 1990s, the electric and gas utilities were still largely a consortium of national utility industries, although conditions were slowly beginning to change as privatization and reform efforts swept the globe. The resulting competition between companies and across national boundaries reinvigorated what had been a apathetic and established collection of energy companies. Historically monopolistic, the electric and gas power industries were in a state of global transition in the last decade of the twentieth century. In the United States, for instance, deregulation in the electric power industry began in 1998. However, while the United Kingdom had already successfully deregulated its electric power industry by the late 1990s, many other European Union countries, including Germany, resisted E.U. mandates to allow competition in the industry. When faced with an E.U. deadline to allow competition by February 1999, Germany finally began to open its markets. By the end of the year, German electricity prices, which for years had been among the highest in Europe, had fallen roughly 50 percent.

CURRENT CONDITIONS

It was highly debated whether U.S. President Barack Obama would be able to keep campaign promises to balance energy management while addressing climate change. Promoting a cleaner and greener environment had appeared to be a major campaign goal that had the potential to result in more jobs for U.S. citizens. After the November 2008 U.S. presidential election, it was apparent that there were other issues Obama might need to address that would delay the promised focus on climate change. According to *The New York Times*, Obama had confirmed his continued commitment to reducing carbon dioxide emissions 80 percent b 2050, developing innovative energy-saving technology, investing US$150 billion to reduce oil imports, creating jobs, and reversing global warming.

Electricity. Coal generated the most electricity at 39 percent of the total, followed by natural gas with 19.1 percent, nuclear with 16.6 percent, hydro with 16.1 percent, oil with 7.2 percent and other sources, including geothermal, wind, combustible renewables, and waste, with 1.9 percent.

According to the International Energy Association (IEA), global electricity supply in 2002 was more than 16.1 trillion kilowatt hours (kwh). The largest electricity producing country worldwide was the United States, which produced almost a quarter of global production. However, U.S. consumption required substantial imports to meet demand. China followed in terms of production, with 10.2 percent of world production, and Japan was third, with 6.8 percent of the total. France continued to export the most electricity, while Italy and Germany remained the largest importers.

U.S., German, British, and Japanese electric utilities dominated the top rankings, with European companies showing the strongest signs of globalization. Total consumption of electricity worldwide was projected to reach 16.4 trillion kwh by 2010, 18.5 kwh by 2015, 20.7 kwh by 2020, and 23.1 kwh by 2025. Total consumption of energy generation fuels, on the other hand, was projected to reach 193.6 quadrillion btu by 2010, 213.9 quadrillion btu by 2015, 235.5 quadrillion btu by 2020, and 258.6 quadrillion btu by 2025.

The United States, France, and Japan remained the world's biggest producers of nuclear electricity, producing 30.3, 16.4 and 11.1 percent of the total in 2003, respectively. However, only 20 percent of the U.S.'s total domestic electricity was generated by nuclear power, while in France nuclear power accounted for 78 percent, by far the highest in the world. Canada produced 13.1 percent of the world's hydro electric power, followed by China with 10.8 percent and Brazil with 10.7 percent. Almost all of Norway's electric power was generated by hydro.

At the June 23, 2008, meeting of the Economic Club of Detroit, Mike Morris, president and CEO of American Electric Power, said that the U.S. needed environmental plans to meet future energy challenges. He observed that the American predisposition to waste energy should be addressed in particular, indicating that renewable energy was a viable solution that should be explored.

Portions of the United States' and Canada's power systems are joined via gas transmission lines and electric power networks. Canadian government-owned electric utilities, such as Ontario Hydro, which operated as a private business, have traditionally exported surplus power to northeastern U.S. states.

Natural Gas. According to the IEA, worldwide gross production of natural gas in 2003 was 96.02 trillion cubic feet. OECD countries accounted for 41.5 percent of global production, the countries of the former USSR 28.2 percent, Asia 10.3 percent, the Middle East 9.4 percent, Africa 5.5 percent, Latin America 4.4 percent, and all other non-OECD European countries 0.7 percent. Non-OECD nations reported substantial increases in natural gas produced between 1976 and 2003, especially in countries that had been part of the former Soviet Union. Although in 2003 the world's second largest producer of natural gas, behind the Russian Federation, was the United States, it remained a net importer of gas. Russia, Canada, and Norway were the largest exporters of natural gas. The Energy Information Administration projected total worldwide production of natural gas to reach 105.5 trillion cubic feet by 2010, 118.5 trillion cubic feet by 2015, 134.5 trillion cubic feet by 2020, and 151 trillion cubic feet by 2025.

The leading companies in the natural gas industry held or formerly held monopolistic control over domestic distribution rights, including those in the United Kingdom, Japan, the Netherlands, France, and Germany, as well as companies from the United States and other countries that were involved in worldwide exploration for or production of natural gas. In 2004, the world had 6.1 quadrillion cubic feet in natural gas reserves, almost 90 percent, or more than 5.4 quadrillion cubic feet, of which was controlled by the top 20 countries.

In an effort to deregulate the industry, California was the first of the United States to allow customers of its three leading electric utilities to choose providers. State legislators also instituted price caps on allowable charges, but the effort backfired when gas and oil prices soared. Unable to pass along price increases to consumers, California utilities struggled to buy the resources they needed to fuel power generation. As a result, California's largest utility, Pacific Gas and Electric, filed for bankruptcy protection in 2001, from which it finally emerged in 2004. To make matters worse, stringent guidelines that slowed new power plant construction contributed to power shortages that caused blackouts. These problems prompted several other U.S. states to delay deregulation, although almost half had at least started the process. All members of the European Union were required to fully open their electric power markets and roughly 20 percent of natural gas markets in each country had to be deregulated by 2005.

The *International Energy Outlook 2004* predicted that global electricity consumption would double by

2025. Of the fuels used to generate electricity, oil and nuclear power were expected to decrease, while the use of renewable sources and natural gas were expected to increase. As of 2003, however, nuclear generation of electricity continued to be strong, with 441 reactors worldwide and more than 30 being built. Renewable sources, such as hydropower and wind power had experienced the fastest growth into the mid-2000s and were projected to grow 57 percent by the 2030s. As with most energy sources, the majority of the growth in this segment was anticipated to come from developing countries like China and India, which were planning or building renewable energy plants in 2003. The use of natural gas to generate electricity was expected to double.

Natural gas consumption for all uses was projected to jump a staggering 70 percent. Reserves, which were approximately 6.1 quadrillion cubic feet, increased for the ninth consecutive year in 2004. In fact, according to *International Energy Outlook,* "outside the United States, the world has produced less than 10 percent of its total estimated natural gas endowment and carries more than 30 percent as remaining reserves." The growing popularity of natural gas, particularly as a source of electric power, fueled consolidation of gas and electric utilities from the beginning of the twenty-first century and into the 2000s. This industry convergence also was the result of increased competition, which prompted utilities to seek economies of scale.

RESEARCH AND TECHNOLOGY

Energy research in the 1990s focused on high-efficiency, environmentally friendly, pollution-free vehicles, fuel sources, and power generators. In 1998, automakers worldwide pledged to begin building cleaner cars, offering them for sale across the United States starting with the 1999 model year. Cleaner cars were scheduled to be available in late 1998 in the Northeast in accordance with air quality standards adopted in 1992 that required a certain percentage of low-emission vehicles by 1998. Development of electric vehicles was continued by all the major automakers, with Ford, General Motors, Honda, Nissan, and Toyota all offering electric vehicles or hybrid electric vehicles for sale in the 1998 model year, according to the Electric Vehicle Association of America. Government-sponsored research in Japan in the late 1990s included vehicles powered by electricity, compressed natural gas, and methane, as well as research on fuel cell that converted chemical energy from fuel directly into electricity onboard.

Japan's Agency of Natural Resources and Energy also had made substantial research investments in a wide range of power generating technologies, including fuel cells; photovoltaic generators, using solar batteries; wind generators; and geothermal power generators, a type of clean and domestically available energy produced by using heat from the earth's interior that cause hot springs, geysers, and heated groundwater. By the late 1990s geothermal plants existed in Japan, the United States, Italy, New Zealand, Iceland, and Mexico. The 1997 Asian financial crisis prompted Indonesia to postpone construction of at least eight geothermal plants.

Coal, historically a dominant fuel for thermal generation, was expected to maintain about a 36 percent share of the electricity generation market through 2020, as a result of clean coal technologies that improved generating efficiency and reduced the amount of carbon dioxide produced by coal-fired generators. With increased interest in renewable resources, including wind machines, photovoltaic systems, and geothermal technologies, the Edison Electric Institute predicted an increasing number of electric utilities that would begin employing more economically viable methods of power generation from renewable resources early in the twenty-first century.

WORKFORCE

By the early 1990s, U.S. utilities had already been through several rounds of cost reductions. Major power producers, including Pacific Gas and Electric Company and Southern Company in the United States, Ontario Hydro in Canada, and British Gas PLC in Great Britain, were reducing staff. In 1994, for instance, British Gas PLC announced that it would cut 25,000 jobs over five years in response to tighter profit margins, increased competition, and rate regulation. In addition, in late 1999 Duke Energy launched a series of layoffs designed to cut costs. Throughout the 2000s, industry consolidation among both gas and electric utilities continued providing opportunities to achieve economies of scale through layoffs and other cost reduction measures.

INDUSTRY LEADERS

United States. The largest electricity generator in 2005 in the United States was American Electric Power Company Inc. (AEP), which was founded in New York in 1906 as American Gas & Electric Company, owned more than 36,000 megawatts (MW) of power and had 5 million customers in 11 states. Its generating capacity was largely powered by coal. The company was also a leading marketer of natural gas, natural gas liquids, coal and oil. AEP reported US$14.1 billion in 2004 revenues and about 20,000 employees.

Exelon Corporation was a major distributor of electricity in the United States with 2007 sales of US$18.9 billion and 17,800 employees. The company's markets included the Chicago and Philadelphia areas where it served approximately 5.4 million customers. Exelon had several subsidiaries, including Commonwealth Edison.

Pacific Gas and Electric Corp. served about 5.1 million electric and 4.3 million natural gas customers in northern and central California. The company was also actively involved in generating electricity and procuring natural gas. When California legislators deregulated the industry, they included price caps that resulted in Pacific Gas and Electric being unable to offset rising energy prices with rate increases. Consequently, the company filed for bankruptcy protection in 2001. In early 2002, the state of California filed suit against PG&E, alleging that the holding company was to blame for the utility's financial ruin. PG&E emerged from bankruptcy in 2004 and reported sales of US$13.2 billion in 2007 and 20,000 employees by 2008.

Duke Energy Corporation was created in June 1997 through the merger of Duke Power Company in Charlotte, North Carolina, and PanEnergy Corp. in Houston, Texas. In 2004, Duke Energy provided electric and gas service to millions of customers in the South and Midwest. The company reported 2007 sales of US$12.7 billion and 17,800 employees.

Germany. In 2004, E.ON AG, which was the result of the 2000 merger of VEBA Group and VIAG Group, remained the largest investor-owned energy services provider in the world. The company had focused its attention on its electricity and gas holdings. The E.ON Energie subsidiary supplied 14 million electricity and gas customers in Central Europe. Its acquisition of Ruhrgas in 2003 brought it Germany's market leader in natural gas distribution, and a European Union leader with a 7,000 mile pipeline system throughout Europe. E.ON UK (formerly PowerGen) was the second largest energy supplier in the United Kingdom. E.ON also owns utility operations in Kentucky, and had stakes in plants in Texas and Argentina. The company reported approximately 70,000 employees and revenues of US$66.5 billion.

RWE AG, a global energy company, reported more than 120 million customers across Europe and North America in 2005. In late 2008, the company acquired 50 percent of Agrinergy and was focused on developing the latter company's Clean Development Mechanism. In 2004, RWE AG reported 2004 revenues of nearly US$56 billion and had almost 98,000 employees.

Japan. The Tokyo Electric Power Company (TEPCO), which was one of the world's largest energy companies, could trace its roots to the first Japanese electricity utility, Tokyo Electric Lighting Company that had been founded in the 1880s. TEPCO was incorporated in 1951, the year the Japanese electric power industry was reprivatized after being held under government monopoly control during World War II. After its incorporation, TEPCO relied largely on hydroelectric generation of power well into the 1960s. Pilot nuclear power plants went on-line in 1966, and after pollution reached critical stages in the late 1960s, the company discontinued coal-fired generators temporarily. TEPCO began shifting away from oil-fired generation during the 1970s, and increasingly began to rely on nuclear power, which by 1991 accounted for 28 percent of the company's total power generation.

In 1991 TEPCO was the world's largest user of liquefied natural gas (LNG) and liquefied petroleum gas (LPG), which it was buying from suppliers worldwide. The company was heavily involved in research and development that had allowed it to achieve the world's lowest levels of sulfur dioxide and carbon dioxide emissions. The company also developed and displayed a prototype electric car in the early 1990s. In the late 1980s it became involved in an optical digital fiber network that led to the creation of a TEPCO cable television system in 1989.

In mid-1998 TEPCO became the first Japanese participant in a World Bank prototype carbon fund designed to reduce the amount of greenhouse gases. It was essentially an emissions trading scheme, similar to the one offered to "dirty" U.S. power plants as part of the Clean Air Act Amendments of 1990. Essentially, the World Bank planned to use the carbon fund to finance costs associated with various types of greenhouse gas reduction strategies. The amount of greenhouse gases reduced by the projects earned the company "carbon offsets," or credits, that could be used by the utility to offset emissions by their dirtier plants. The utility also could sell any offsets to other companies who needed them to meet regulatory emissions requirements.

TEPCO had 43.9 million customers in 2007. As Japan has deregulated its electricity industry, TEPCO has faced increasing competition, leading to diversification into other industries like local and long-distance telephone services. The company's wide range of business activities resulted in a name change to the TEPCO Group. The company posted revenues of almost US$42 billion and employed more than 52,500 workers in 2007.

United Kingdom. British Gas PLC was incorporated in 1986 with the privatization of the government-owned British Gas Corporation, which reversed a 1949 action that had nationalized utilities. Until February 1997, British Gas PLC was the largest integrated gas supply operation in the world and was among the United Kingdom's 20 largest companies. In 1997 the company's shareholders approved the spin-off of British Gas into two companies: BG Group PLC, which concentrated on gas transportation, exploration, and production, and Centrica, for local distribution. The impetus for the split had begun in 1996, with the demonopolization and separation of transportation and usage operations from the other gas industry businesses in preparation for competitive markets. With 2.7 million customers, BG Group had 2007 sales of US$16.6 billion and nearly 5,000 employees.

Centrica markets gas, electricity, and telecommunications services in England, Wales, and Scotland using several brand names, including British Gas, Nwy Prydain, and Scottish Gas, respectively. Its subsidiary, Centrica Energy, handles upstream gas production, electricity generation, and wholesale gas sales. With the European market expected to be open to competition by 2007, Centrica had established a joint venture energy supply company in Belgium and began to operate Luseo Energia in Spain in 2003 to serve the small- to medium-sized business market for electricity. In North America, Centrica offered natural gas and electricity services to the deregulated Canadian market under the Direct Energy brand, while the United States subsidiary, Energy America, supplied natural gas and electricity to customers in Ohio, Michigan, and Pennsylvania. In 2004, Centrica posted revenues of almost US$32 billion, and employed more than 42,000 people.

Following privatization in 1986, British Gas was no longer restricted geographically to the United Kingdom and its offshore waters, and by 1989 the company had made significant investments in foreign oil and gas assets worldwide. By 1990 British Gas had acquired interests in exploration and production companies, including Acre Oil and part of Texas Eastern North Sea; Tenneco international subsidiaries with exploration and production operations in the North Sea, Africa, and Latin America; a 51 percent interest in Canada's Bow Valley Industries; Consumer's Gas Co., Canada's largest natural gas distributor and an experienced developer of natural gas vehicles; and a small stake in a Spanish utility. By then, the company had spent US$2 billion on acquisitions and held nearly 7 trillion cubic feet of natural gas reserves in 18 countries. In 1992 British Gas entered the South American market and formed a consortium to buy Argentina's gas distribution company MetroGas.

Scottish Power provided electricity and gas service to more than 6 million customers in the United Kingdom and the United States, earning the company revenues of US$10.7 billion in 2004. In the United States, PacifiCorp had capacity of more than 8,300 megawatts generated from coal, hydro, wind, gas-fired combustion turbines, and geothermal sources. The company was operating its regulated business in Oregon, Washington, Wyoming, California, Utah, and Idaho, as well as wind and thermal

energy facilities. It provided natural gas marketing and storage in the United States through the PPM Energy subsidiary.

Canada. Hydro-Quebec, Ontario Power Generation, and Hydro One were government-owned companies run as businesses. Hydro-Quebec and its subsidiaries are comprised of about two-thirds hydroelectric plants and one-third generation plants. Ontario Power, in contrast, generated most of its electricity from nuclear and fossil fuel-based power plants, while Hydro One distributed power throughout Ontario. Hydro One and Ontario Power Generation were created when Ontario Hydro was split into two separate entities in 2000 in response to the Ontario government's legislation—the Energy Competition Act—calling for the creation of a competitive electricity market by 2000. Hydro-Quebec had 2004 sales of more than US$8.8 billion, with 3.6 million customers, while Hydro One, with 1.2 million customers, posted roughly US$3.1 billion in sales. Revenues at Ontario Power Generation grew 9.8 percent in 2003 to reach US$4 billion.

Ontario Hydro and Hydro-Quebec trace their roots to the late nineteenth century when Canadian water was first harnessed in order to mass-produce power. Ontario Hydro's lineage stems from the first major generating station in Ontario, which was built to use the power of Niagara Falls. In 1914 Ontario Hydro purchased its first generating station and built its first power plant. By 1922 Ontario Hydro was the largest utility in the world after completing its first major power station, Queenston-Chippawa, which was then the largest generator in the world and has since been renamed Sir Adam Beck-Niagara Generation Station No. 1. During the 1950s the company turned to the St. Lawrence River and harnessed its power in a joint project with the state of New York. Ontario Hydro constructed an experimental nuclear plant in 1962 and completed its first major nuclear power plant in 1971, by which time the company had enough excess generating capacity to supply electricity to the northeastern United States. Ontario Hydro was incorporated as a government corporation in 1974, and since then had faced growing concerns regarding fossil fuel shortages and environmental damage caused by its operations. Faced with a surplus of power, Ontario Hydro lost US$2.8 billion in 1993. In 1994 the company announced it would cut its generating capacity 8.4 percent and retire one unit at its Bruce nuclear plant by 1995, two years ahead of schedule.

Hydro-Quebec's began with the construction of Quebec's first large dam and the formation of Montreal Light, Heat and Power Company (MLHPC) in 1901. In 1944, the Quebec Hydro-Electric Commission was created and took over the assets of MLHPC, with demand for power fueled primarily by the defense industry. During the 1950s the company used its first bond offering to U.S. markets to finance its Bersimis River project. During the 1960s, Hydro-Quebec acquired numerous private electricity distribution companies, including rural cooperatives, municipal systems, and non-government companies. From the 1970s through the 1990s, Hydro-Quebec's power projects ran into increasing opposition from Native American and environmentalist groups. Of major concern was the James Bay project, which began in 1971 and was completed in 1985, with a system of 41 dams and dykes. In 1987 Hydro-Quebec began James Bay II, which was also known as the Great Whale project and was designed to place a hydroelectric plant on the Great Whale River and sparked international environmentalist opposition.

In December 1992 Maurice F. Strong, who had served as secretary general of the United Nations' 1992 Earth Summit, became chairman of Ontario Hydro, which by that time had been labeled by environmentalists as one of Canada's leading polluters. In the mid-1990s, increasing numbers of North American utilities cut costs by promoting conservation and buying electricity from independent power producers, and Hydro Quebec's earnings fell as a result of excess generating capacity, declining sales, and a sizable debt. Ontario Hydro cancelled plans to expand generating capacity more than 40 percent in 25 years. In 1994 Hydro-Quebec announced plans to cut development of hydroelectric plants in lieu of reduced agreements to sell power to U.S. utilities. Additionally, the company pushed back its completion date for the Great Whale project from 2001-2002 to 2002-2004.

The Russian Federation. Unified Energy System of Russia (UES) is a publicly traded company, although 53 percent of it was still owned by the government in 2004. By 2005, UES was operating 440 electric power stations with a capacity of more than 197,000 MW, including 21,000 MW at nuclear power plants. Deregulation of the industry was expected to be completed in 2006, at which time the company's distribution and power generation assets were to be separated.

France. The SUEZ Group was the tenth largest electricity producer in the world, operating in more than 130 countries, and the sixth-largest gas producer, handling 20 percent of the Atlantic's liquefied natural gas market. SUEZ also provided water and waste management services. The company was one of the largest employers in the world's energy and services industry with almost 87,000 employees in 2004. SUEZ reported revenues of US$55 billion in 2004.

MAJOR COUNTRIES IN THE INDUSTRY

The United States. Although traditionally regionally based, since 1999 the energy industry in the United States had witnessed a trend toward large, global energy firms consolidating the market and value chain.

In September 1997, three energy companies—France's Total, Russia's Gazprom, and Malaysia's Petronias—had inked an agreement with the Iranian National Petroleum Company to develop 2 billion cubic feet per day in reserves from the South Pars field, which held about 40 percent of Iran's natural gas reserves. In 2000, Italy's Eni and National Iranian Oil reached a US$3.8 billion deal to further develop South Pars.

While residential consumers dominated the electrical market in the United States, industrial users were the largest users of natural gas, accounting for 38.1 percent of the total 2003 market volume of 8.1 trillion cubic feet. Demand had grown slowly over 2002 levels because of increasing prices. Although by 2003 the top five U.S. gas utility companies continued to account for 21.4 percent of the total market, the trend since 1999 was away from regional utilities and toward larger, global companies managing the gas along its entire route from source to end user. This trend was reported by *Euromonitor* to be the response to manage the risks associated with the energy market. In 2003, Texas and California were the biggest consumers of natural gas, accounting for 280 billion cubic feet (bcf) and 200 bcf, respectively. The country' market was expected to grow to a volume of 22.8 trillion cubic feet by 2008.

The United States was the largest energy producing country in the world, as well as the world's largest consumer. The market's size had grown to 3.4 trillion kwh by 2003, and *Euromonitor* predicted growth of 7.3 percent by 2008. Consumption varied across the country depending on climate, regulations, and industrial development, but residential use was expected to dominate total market share. The country' largest electricity distributor in 2004 was Exelon Corporation in the Chicago and Philadelphia areas. The production of electricity through nuclear, fossil fuel, hydro, or other alternate sources remained a highly fragmented component of the energy industry in the United States in 2003. Most of the country's renewal electrical energy was produced in the South and West, where the climate favored the industry.

Historically, Canada was a major exporter of natural gas to the United States. Between 1986 and 1993, imports of natural gas into the United States rose from 689 billion cubic feet annually to 2.1 trillion cubic feet, primarily as a result of the 1992 completion of Canada's Iroquois pipeline system. The three Canada-to-U.S. gas transportation corridors grew dramatically each year between 1989 and 1997. The three corridors experienced more growth in the capacity to deliver gas between 1990 and 1997 than any of the other seven major interregional transportation corridors. In 1998 the Northern Border system was extended into the Midwest from Montana, adding 650 million cubic feet per day in natural gas capacity. As a result, imports from Canada grew nearly 9 percent in 1999. The Maritimes and Northeast line, completed in December of 1999, added 400 million cubic feet per day in capacity, and the Alliance Pipeline, connecting North Dakota and Chicago in December 2000, boosted capacity by another 1.3 billion cubic feet.

The U.S. electric power industry contained a wide range of entities, although in the late 1990s it continued to be dominated by investor-owned utility monopolies that had historically provided service to large and consolidated markets. As of March 1998, there were 223 investor-owned utilities in the United States, compared with 4,132 independent, or non-utility, power producers. The remainder of power providers included such diverse sources as publicly owned utilities, federal utilities, and cooperatives. The power marketer, an independent middleman that buys and sells wholesale electricity at market prices but lacks its own generation, transmission, or distribution capacity, was a new class of power provider made possible by deregulation. U.S.-based Enron Corp., the energy marketing and trading giant that underwent a highly publicized bankruptcy in 2001, was an example of such a firm. As a result of the Enron scandal, which centered around questionable accounting practices utilized by the firm, some analysts began to question the viability of other energy marketers operating without generation, transmission, or distribution capacity.

In the fall of 2008, after leading the U.S. House of Representatives Energy and Commerce Committee for decades, U.S. Congressman John Dingell, a Democrat from Michigan, was replaced by fellow Democrat Henry Waxman. After representing Michigan for 52 years, Dingell was the House's most experienced leader with 52 years of service. The coalition supporting Waxman believed it was "time for a change" and stronger support for renewables and innovative energy alternatives lied ahead.

Asia-Pacific. Key power-producing nations of the Asia-Pacific region included China and India, while Indonesia and Malaysia were the area's leading natural gas producers. In 2000 the largest natural gas field in China, with estimated reserves of more than 7 trillion cubic feet, was discovered in the Tarim Basin.

Japan. Japan boasts some of the world's largest energy utilities in terms of assets and revenues. A leading consumer and importer of natural gas, Japan lacks substantial mineral resources, which created a high demand for

new power plant construction, particularly nuclear capacity, throughout the 1990s. In the mid-1990s, Japan was primarily a closed market with utility monopolies, although privatization was being considered. In January 1996, the Japanese electricity industry was in turmoil when the Electric Utility Industry law was drastically modified as the first step to decreasing customer's bills. Independent power producers moved into the market later in 1996, offering rates lower than the electric monopolies, giving Japan a taste of how low prices can go in a competitive marketplace. As in Europe, electric power and gas companies in Japan began moving into one another's markets as deregulation efforts continued into the early 2000s.

While slightly smaller geographically than the state of California, in 2004 Japan was the world's fourth largest energy market and second largest importer, behind the United States. The country imported about 97 percent of its natural gas needs, all in liquid natural gas form. Japan has the highest energy costs in the OECD, which is the reason often cited for Japan's urban areas not being well served by natural gas distribution lines. The three companies that dominated the Japanese market were Tokyo Gas, Chubu Gas, and Osaka Gas. In 2002, Japan generated 1.04 trillion kwh of electricity, 62 percent of which was produced from thermal means, 28 percent from nuclear, and 8 percent from hydro. Japan planned to increase the amount of electricity produced using nuclear power 30 percent by 2011.

China. Between 1979 and 1996 only 10 percent of China's electric power industry investment was foreign. With 1.2 billion people in the late 1990s, China was the world's most populous nation, and electricity consumption there was forecast to grow 5.8 percent per year through 2020. In 2004, China remained the second largest user of energy in the world after the United States and the world's second largest producer of hydro electricity with 1.1 trillion kilowatt hours, or 10.8 percent of world production, in 2003.

An oversupply of electricity was created when the government closed inefficient plants and led to a slowdown in new electric generation construction until 2003. That year, the economy grew suddenly, and with this growth came increased electrical demand. As a result, the government approved the construction of 30 large electric power plants that would add an additional 22 gigawatts of power to the system. In the late 1990s China broke ground on the Three Gorges Dam project, which was anticipated to become the largest hydroelectric station in the world, with a projected total capacity of 18.2 gigawatts upon completion in 2009. Embezzlement charges related to the multi-billion financing of the project led to court cases and prison sentences for nearly 100 individuals in

2000, but work on the dam continued. Another large project involving the construction of 25 generating stations on the Yellow River was also proceeding.

China has not historically been a major user of natural gas, which in 2004 accounted for only 3 percent of the energy used in the country. However, the Chinese government was expanding the use of natural gas, given that its had 53.3 trillion cubic feet of reserves, with plans to double its use by 2010.

Europe. In the years preceding 1949, most European gas had been manufactured from coal, but during the 1950s and 1960s coal became too costly and processes were created to convert less expensive oil feedstock to a coal-gas equivalent. In the 1960s, natural gas arrived in substantial quantity in the United Kingdom for the first time. In 1964 the country entered into a 15-year contract to buy gas from Algeria and began receiving liquefied natural gas (LNG) by tanker. In 1966 natural gas was discovered under the North Sea, leading to an enormous conversion program to transform the country's system and appliances from manufactured to natural gas.

In contrast to Asian markets, Western European power companies operated in a market with substantial power reserves during the early 1990s. Nonetheless, private power projects—as opposed to government-regulated or owned utilities—began to attract increased interest in Europe, as did private financing of new generating capacity. An increasing number of governments made their national power industries more competitive based on the successes of other companies. As deregulation spread, competition and the number of private power projects increased. Projects included new power plants, the purchase and updating of existing plants, and cogeneration projects that were designed to provide heat and power to industrial customers.

By the late 1990s, Europe's electricity markets had become increasingly integrated following a 1997 directive adopted by the European Union that provided independent power producers greater access to power networks in other countries. Cross-border investments were made in the European electricity market, and regional power pools emerged. For example, Sweden, Finland, and Norway operated a joint electricity pool in Scandinavia in the late 1990s.

The European Union agreed on a timetable in the late 1990s to deregulate Western European gas markets, the first phase of which was scheduled for completion in August 2000. The region's principal natural gas producing countries in 1999 included the northwestern European nations of Norway and the Netherlands, which held the area's largest reserves, and the United Kingdom. Leading natural gas consumers included Germany, which was a major importer, the United Kingdom, Italy, the Netherlands, and France. Its key electric power producers in 1999 included Germany, France, and the United Kingdom, Italy, and Spain. In the early 2000s, deregulation caused increased intertwining of E.U. electricity and natural gas industries, as well as the increasing use of natural gas in electric power generation.

Eastern Europe was rich in natural gas, with 37.3 percent of the world's reserves, one-third of which were located in Russia and an additional 2 percent located in Turkmenistan. In Eastern Europe, substantial expansion plans from the 1980s had given way to plans to update existing plants that were often inefficient fossil fuel-burning or nuclear plants. The electric industries of Eastern Europe and the former Soviet Union were quite distinct from those in other parts of the world, where electricity capacity strained to keep up with demand. In this region, electricity was an overdeveloped resource with no shortage in capacity, but the industry suffered from outdated technology that made production inefficient and harmful to the environment. However, natural gas consumption was projected to grow from 28.1 trillion cubic feet in 1999 to 37.5 trillion cubic feet in 2020.

Germany. In 2002, Germany was ranked as the fifth largest energy consumer in the world and the largest consumer of electricity in Europe. With few resources other than coal, the country must import most of its energy needs. However, coal was used to generate more than 50 percent of the country's electricity, with nuclear power accounting for an additional 28 percent. The government had been increasing the amount of energy used that was generated from renewable sources. By 2050, Germany expected half of its demand to be met by these sources. Germany's electric and natural gas industries have been deregulated, and although open to competition, still remain highly concentrated. In 2003, there were 900 energy companies operating in Germany's electric market, four of which controlled 73 percent of the electric distribution business in the country: RWE Power, EnBW, E.On, and Vattenfall. *Euromonitor* expected growth to remain slow to 2008 due to a downturn in the economy, with industry consuming the most electricity. In the German natural gas industry, most resources were imported from Russia. Ruhrgas, a subsidiary of energy giant E.On, controlled 43 percent of Europe's second largest gas market in 2003.

The Netherlands. Natural gas is responsible for meeting half of the Netherland's total energy needs, the highest percentage of natural gas use for any country in the world. In 1998 the Netherlands produced 2.8 trillion cubic feet of natural gas. Reserves in 2001 were 63 trillion cubic feet, about 1.2 percent of the world total. The public/private company Nederlandse Gasunie, which was 50 percent government-owned, served the 97 percent of Dutch homes heated by natural gas. Esso and Shell each controlled 25 percent of the company, which purchased, transported, and marketed the country's natural gas.

Russia. The principal electric power producing country in Eastern Europe was Russia, which accounted for 5.7 percent of world production in 1999. Russia also was the world's largest producer of natural gas that year, accounting for 23.7 percent of world production, although Uzbekistan was one of the top ten global natural gas producers. In the early 1990s, Russia overtook the United States as the leading natural gas producer. In 2005, the country had the world's largest natural gas reserves, was the leading exporter of gas, and had the third largest domestic gas market. In 2004 Russia's gas production was 222.4 trillion cubic feet, with reserves of 1,680 trillion cubic feet. However, growth in the industry had remained modest following the collapse of the Soviet Union as a result of aging gas fields, a lack of pipelines to use for export, and government regulations. The country's energy strategy, released in 2003, predicted only 1.3 percent growth by 2010.

By 2005, Russia had more than 440 thermal and hydroelectric power plants and 31 nuclear reactors, capable of generating a total of 205.6 gigawatts of power. Thermal power—oil, natural gas, and coal—were used to generate approximately 63 percent of Russia's electrical supply. However, the government planned to increase hydro and nuclear production so fossil fuels could be exported. More than half of the country's nuclear reactors were of the same design as the one used in the Chernobyl plant in the Ukraine, site of the world's worst nuclear accident. Almost half of Russian nuclear reactors were between 21 and 30 years old in 2005, and in need of upgrading or rebuilding since the working life of a reactor was 30 years.

Latin America. By the late 1990s, privatization had been adopted or considered in every Latin American country. The region's leading electricity providers in the late 1990s were Brazil and Mexico, while the leading natural gas producer was Venezuela, with known reserves of 147 trillion cubic feet as of the early 2000s. Brazil was undoubtedly the largest economy of the region, and was expected to account for 77 percent of the growth in the region's electricity consumption by 2020. Central and South America led the developing world in privatization of the electricity sector. In 1997 Brazil followed in the footsteps of Chile and Argentina by selling state-owned utility assets to private investors. Gas use in Latin America was expected to increase roughly 7.5 percent each year through 2020, causing many leading utilities to begin expanding pipeline networks and increasing use of

existing lines. In early 2000, for example, Brazil's state-owned Petrobras contracted for increased natural gas deliveries from Bolivia via an existing pipeline.

The Middle East and Africa. The Middle East and Africa had substantial natural gas reserves in the late 1990s. At the time, gas was substituted for oil domestically to allow for more oil exports. In the Algeria was the area's leading natural gas producer, while Iran and Saudi Arabia were the area's largest consumers. Four of the top five countries with natural gas reserves were in the Middle East and Africa in 2001, including Iran, with 15.4 percent of the world's reserves; Qatar, with 7.5 percent; United Arab Emirates, with 4 percent; and Saudi Arabia, with 4 percent. Algeria claimed about 3 percent of global natural gas reserves, while Nigeria had 2.3 percent and Iraq had 2.1 percent.

Algeria. In 2002 Algeria, the second largest country in Africa, was the fifth leading producer of natural gas in the world, with 2.8 trillion cubic feet. A major gas exporter, most natural gas was sent to Europe and the United States. The two government-owned companies that dominated the industry were Sonatrach, which was responsible for production and wholesale distribution, while Sonelgaz controlled distribution to retail markets. The government was planning to open the retail market to foreign investors, but price liberalizations set for 2005 were met by mass protests following a record cold spell in Algeria. Most of the country's electrical production remained gas fired.

Canada. By 2005, Canada remained one of the United States' most important sources for energy imports. In 2002, the country was the third-largest producer of natural gas behind Russia and the United States. Canada's natural gas pipeline network is very tied into the U.S., and almost all of its exports went there. In terms of electricity, Canada produces the majority of it through hydro generation (it was the world's largest hydro electric producer in 2005. It maintains an integrated trading network with the United States, importing about as much as it exports. The countries's electrical power grids are so intertwined, that in 2003, North America's largest blackout plunged more than 50 million people into darkness, affecting most of Ontario, Ohio, New York, and Chicago.

BIBLIOGRAPHY

"About Us." American Electric Power, 2004. Available from www.aep.com.

Broder, John M. "Obama Affirms Climate Change Goals." *The New York Times*, 18 November 2008. Available from www.nytimes.com.

"Can Deregulated Energy Markets Provide a Diverse and Secure Energy Supply?" Ernst & Young, January 2005. Available from www.ey.com.

"The Changing Structure of the Electric Power Industry 2000: An Update." *International Energy Outlook 2000.* Energy Information Administration, U.S. Department of Energy. Available from www.eia.doe.gov.

"Country Analysis Briefs." Energy Information Administration, U.S. Department of Energy, 2005. Available from www.eia.doe.gov.

"Hoover's Company Capsules." *Hoover's Online,* 2008. Available from www.hoovers.com.

"International Energy Outlook 2004," Energy Information Administration, U.S. Department of Energy, April 2004. Available from www.eia.doe.gov.

Ivanovich, David, and Stewart Powell. "Waxman Wins Bid to Lead Energy Committee," 20 November 2008. Available from www.chron.com.

"Key World Energy Statistics." International Energy Agency, 2004. Available from www.iea.org.

Lazich, Robert S., ed. *Market Share Reporter.* Detroit: Thomson Gale, 2004.

Miller, Rich, and Matthew Benjamin. "At Issue: Energy and Economy Americans Watching Their Wealth Slip Away." *The Detroit Free Press,* 15 June 2008.

Morris, Mike. "Energy: The Next U.S. Challenge." *Vital Speeches of the Day,* September 2008.

"Natural Gas." *International Energy Outlook 2001.* Energy Information Administration. Available from www.eia.doe.gov.

Palmeri, Christopher. "Industry Outlook 2001—Energy." *Business Week,* 2 January 2001.

Roberts, Dexter, and Mark L. Clifford. "China: Hungry for Energy." *Business Week,* 24 December 2001.

"RWE and Agrinergy Establish Key Partnership" RWE, 18 November 2008. Available from www.rwe.com.

Schwankhaus, Dieter. "Success of Wind Power: A Question of State and Federal Subsidies?" Ernst & Young, 2004. Available from www.ey.com.

SIC to NAICS Conversion Guide

*The following listing cross-references four-digit 1987 Standard Industrial Classification (SIC) codes with six-digit 1997 North American Industry Classification System (NAICS) codes. Because the systems differ in specificity, some SIC categories correspond to more than one NAICS category. Please refer to the **Introduction** under "About Industry Classification" for more information.*

AGRICULTURE, FORESTRY & FISHING

0111   Wheat *see* NAICS 111140: Wheat Farming

0112   Rice *see* NAICS 111160: Rice Farming

0115   Corn *see* NAICS 111150: Corn Farming

0116   Soybeans *see* NAICS 111110: Soybean Farming

0119   Cash Grains, NEC *see* NAICS 111130: Dry Pea and Bean Farming; NAICS 111120: Oilseed (except Soybean) Farming; NAICS 111150: Corn Farming; NAICS 111191: Oilseed and Grain Combination Farming; NAICS 111199: All Other Grain Farming

0131   Cotton *see* NAICS 111920: Cotton Farming

0132   Tobacco *see* NAICS 111910: Tobacco Farming

0133   Sugarcane and Sugar Beets *see* NAICS 111991: Sugar Beet Farming; NAICS 111930: Sugarcane Farming

0134   Irish Potatoes *see* NAICS 111211: Potato Farming

0139   Field Crops, Except Cash Grains, NEC *see* NAICS 111940: Hay Farming; NAICS 111992: Peanut Farming; NAICS 111219: Other Vegetable (except Potato) and Melon Farming; NAICS 111998: All Other Miscellaneous Crop Farming

0161   Vegetables and Melons *see* NAICS 111219: Other Vegetable (except Potato) and Melon Farming

0171   Berry Crops *see* NAICS 111333: Strawberry Farming; NAICS 111334: Berry (except Strawberry) Farming

0172   Grapes *see* NAICS 111332: Grape Vineyards

0173   Tree Nuts *see* NAICS 111335: Tree Nut Farming

0174   Citrus Fruits *see* NAICS 111310: Orange Groves; NAICS 111320: Citrus (except Orange) Groves

0175   Deciduous Tree Fruits *see* NAICS 111331: Apple Orchards; NAICS 111339: Other Noncitrus Fruit Farming

0179   Fruits and Tree Nuts, NEC *see* NAICS 111336: Fruit and Tree Nut Combination Farming; NAICS 111339: Other Noncitrus Fruit Farming

0181   Ornamental Floriculture and Nursery Products *see* NAICS 111422: Floriculture Production; NAICS 111421: Nursery and Tree Production

0182   Food Crops Grown Under Cover *see* NAICS 111411: Mushroom Production; NAICS 111419: Other Food Crops Grown Under Cover

0191   General Farms, Primarily Crop *see* NAICS 111998: All Other Miscellaneous Crop Farming

0211   Beef Cattle Feedlots *see* NAICS 112112: Cattle Feedlots

0212   Beef Cattle, Except Feedlots *see* NAICS 112111: Beef Cattle Ranching and Farming

0213   Hogs *see* NAICS 112210: Hog and Pig Farming

0214   Sheep and Goats *see* NAICS 112410: Sheep Farming; NAICS 112420: Goat Farming

0219   General Livestock, Except Dairy and Poultry *see* NAICS 112990: All Other Animal Production

0241   Dairy Farms *see* NAICS 112111: Beef Cattle Ranching and Farming; NAICS 112120: Dairy Cattle and Milk Production

0251   Broiler, Fryers, and Roaster Chickens *see* NAICS 112320: Broilers and Other Meat-Type Chicken Production

0252   Chicken Eggs *see* NAICS 112310: Chicken Egg Production

0253   Turkey and Turkey Eggs *see* NAICS 112330: Turkey Production

0254   Poultry Hatcheries *see* NAICS 112340: Poultry Hatcheries

0259   Poultry and Eggs, NEC *see* NAICS 112390: Other Poultry Production

0271 Fur-Bearing Animals and Rabbits *see* NAICS 112930: Fur-bearing Animal and Rabbit Production

0272 Horses and Other Equines *see* NAICS 112920: Horse and Other Equine Production

0273 Animal Aquaculture *see* NAICS 112511: Finfish Farming and Fish Hatcheries; NAICS 112512: Shellfish Farming; NAICS 112519: Other Animal Aquaculture

0279 Animal Specialties, NEC *see* NAICS 112910: Apiculture; NAICS 112990: All Other Animal Production

0291 General Farms, Primarily Livestock and Animal Specialties *see* NAICS 112990: All Other Animal Production

0711 Soil Preparation Services *see* NAICS 115112: Soil Preparation, Planting and Cultivating

0721 Crop Planting, Cultivating and Protecting; NAICS 481219: Other Nonscheduled Air Transportation; NAICS 115112: Soil Preparation, Planting, and Cultivating

0722 Crop Harvesting, Primarily by Machine *see* NAICS 115113: Crop Harvesting, Primarily By Machine

0723 Crop Preparation Services For Market, except Cotton Ginning *see* NAICS 115114: Postharvest Crop Activities (except Cotton Ginning)

0724 Cotton Ginning *see* NAICS 115111: Cotton Ginning

0741 Veterinary Service For Livestock *see* NAICS 541940: Veterinary Services

0742 Veterinary Services for Animal Specialties *see* NAICS 541940: Veterinary Services

0751 Livestock Services, Except Veterinary *see* NAICS 311611: Animal (except Poultry) Slaughtering NAICS 115210: Support Activities for Animal Production

0752 Animal Specialty Services, Except Veterinary; NAICS 115210: Support Activities for Animal Production; NAICS 812910: Pet Care (except Veterinary) Services

0761 Farm Labor Contractors and Crew Leaders *see* NAICS 115115: Farm Labor Contractors and Crew Leaders

0762 Farm Management Services *see* NAICS 115116: Farm Management Services

0781 Landscape Counseling and Planning *see* NAICS 541690: Other Scientific and Technical Consulting Services; NAICS 541320: Landscape Architectural Services

0782 Lawn and Garden Services *see* NAICS 561730: Landscaping Services

0783 Ornamental Shrub and Tree Services *see* NAICS 561730: Landscaping Services

0811 Timber Tracts *see* NAICS 111421: Nursery and Tree Production; NAICS 113110: Timber Tract Operations

0831 Forest Nurseries and Gathering of Forest Products; NAICS 111998: All Other Miscellaneous Crop Farming; NAICS 113210: Forest Nurseries and Gathering of Forest Products

0851 Forestry Services *see* NAICS 115310: Support Activities for Forestry

0912 Finfish *see* NAICS 114111: Finfish Fishing

0913 Shellfish *see* NAICS 114112: Shellfish Fishing

0919 Miscellaneous Marine Products *see* NAICS 114119: Other Marine Fishing; NAICS 111998: All Other Miscellaneous Crop Farming

0921 Fish Hatcheries and Preserves *see* NAICS 112511: Finfish Farming and Fish Hatcheries; NAICS 112512: Shellfish Farming

0971 Hunting, Trapping, and Game Propagation *see* NAICS 114210: Hunting and Trapping

MINING INDUSTRIES

1011 Iron Ores *see* NAICS 212210: Iron Ore Mining

1021 Copper Ores *see* NAICS 212234: Copper Ore and Nickel Ore Mining

1031 Lead and Zinc Ores *see* NAICS 212231: Lead Ore and Zinc Ore Mining

1041 Gold Ores *see* NAICS 212221: Gold Ore Mining

1044 Silver Ores *see* NAICS 212222: Silver Ore Mining

1061 Ferroalloy Ores, Except Vanadium *see* NAICS 212234: Copper Ore and Nickel Ore Mining; NAICS 212299: Other Metal Ore Mining

1081 Metal Mining Services *see* NAICS 213114: Support Activities for Metal Mining; NAICS 541360: Geophysical Surveying and Mapping Services

1094 Uranium-Radium-Vanadium Ores *see* NAICS 212291: Uranium-Radium-Vanadium Ore Mining

1099 Miscellaneous Metal Ores, NEC *see* NAICS 212299: Other Metal Ore Mining

1221 Bituminous Coal and Lignite Surface Mining *see* NAICS 212111: Bituminous Coal and Lignite Surface Mining

1222 Bituminous Coal Underground Mining *see* NAICS 212112: Bituminous Coal Underground Mining

1231 Anthracite Mining *see* NAICS 212113: Anthracite Mining

1241 Coal Mining Services *see* NAICS 213113: Support Activities for Coal Mining

1311 Crude Petroleum and Natural Gas *see* NAICS 211111: Crude Petroleum and Natural Gas Extraction

1321 Natural Gas Liquids *see* NAICS 211112: Natural Gas Liquid Extraction

1381 Drilling Oil and Gas Wells *see* NAICS 213111: Drilling Oil and Gas Wells

1382 Oil and Gas Field Exploration Services *see* NAICS 541360: Geophysical Surveying and Mapping

Services; NAICS 213112: Support Activities for Oil and Gas Field Exploration

1389 Oil and Gas Field Services, NEC *see* NAICS 213112: Support Activities for Oil and Gas Field Exploration

1411 Dimension Stone *see* NAICS 212311: Dimension Stone Mining and Quarry

1422 Crushed and Broken Limestone *see* NAICS 212312: Crushed and Broken Limestone Mining and Quarrying

1423 Crushed and Broken Granite *see* NAICS 212313: Crushed and Broken Granite Mining and Quarrying

1429 Crushed and Broken Stone, NEC *see* NAICS 212319: Other Crushed and Broken Stone Mining and Quarrying

1442 Construction Sand and Gravel *see* NAICS 212321: Construction Sand and Gravel Mining

1446 Industrial Sand *see* NAICS 212322: Industrial Sand Mining

1455 Kaolin and Ball Clay *see* NAICS 212324: Kaolin and Ball Clay Mining

1459 Clay, Ceramic, and Refractory Minerals, NEC *see* NAICS 212325: Clay and Ceramic and Refractory Minerals Mining

1474 Potash, Soda, and Borate Minerals *see* NAICS 212391: Potash, Soda, and Borate Mineral Mining

1475 Phosphate Rock *see* NAICS 212392: Phosphate Rock Mining

1479 Chemical and Fertilizer Mineral Mining, NEC *see* NAICS 212393: Other Chemical and Fertilizer Mineral Mining

1481 Nonmetallic Minerals Services Except Fuels *see* NAICS 213115: Support Activities for Non-metallic Minerals, (except Fuels); NAICS 541360: Geophysical Surveying and Mapping Services

1499 Miscellaneous Nonmetallic Minerals, Except Fuels *see* NAICS 212319: Other Crushed and Broken Stone Mining and Quarrying; NAICS 212399: All Other Non-Metallic Mineral Mining

CONSTRUCTION INDUSTRIES

1521 General Contractors-Single-Family Houses *see* NAICS 233210: Single-Family Housing Construction

1522 General Contractors-Residential Buildings *see* NAICS 233320: Commercial and Institutional Building Construction; NAICS 233220: Multi-Family Housing Construction

1531 Operative Builders *see* NAICS 233210: Single-Family Housing Construction; NAICS 233220: Multi-Family Housing Construction; NAICS 233310: Manufacturing and Light Industrial Building Construction; NAICS 233320: Commercial and Institutional Building Construction

1541 General Contractors-Industrial Buildings and Warehouses *see* NAICS 233320: Commercial and Institutional Building Construction; NAICS 233310: Manufacturing and Light Industrial Building Construction

1542 General Contractors-Nonresidential Buildings, Other than Industrial Buildings and Warehouses *see* NAICS 233320: Commercial and Institutional Building Construction

1611 Highway and Street Construction, Except Elevated Highways *see* NAICS 234110: Highway and Street Construction

1622 Bridge, Tunnel, and Elevated Highway Construction *see* NAICS 234120: Bridge and Tunnel Construction

1623 Water, Sewer, Pipeline, and Communications and Power Line Construction *see* NAICS 234910: Water, Sewer and Pipeline Construction; NAICS 234920: Power and Communication Transmission Line Construction

1629 Heavy Construction, NEC *see* NAICS 234930: Industrial Nonbuilding Structure Construction; NAICS 234990: All Other Heavy Construction

1711 Plumbing, Heating, and Air-Conditioning *see* NAICS 235110: Plumbing, Heating and Air-Conditioning Contractors

1721 Painting and Paper Hanging *see* NAICS 235210: Painting and Wall Covering Contractors

1731 Electrical Work *see* NAICS 561621: Security Systems Services (except Locksmiths); NAICS 235310: Electrical Contractors

1741 Masonry, Stone Setting and Other Stone Work *see* NAICS 235410: Masonry and Stone Contractors

1742 Plastering, Drywall, Acoustical and Insulation Work *see* NAICS 235420: Drywall, Plastering, Acoustical and Insulation Contractors

1743 Terrazzo, Tile, Marble, and Mosaic Work *see* NAICS 235420: Drywall, Plastering, Acoustical and Insulation Contractors; NAICS 235430: Tile, Marble, Terrazzo and Mosaic Contractors

1751 Carpentry Work *see* NAICS 235510: Carpentry Contractors

1752 Floor Laying and Other Floor Work, NEC *see* NAICS 235520: Floor Laying and Other Floor Contractors

1761 Roofing, Siding, and Sheet Metal Work *see* NAICS 235610: Roofing, Siding, and Sheet Metal Contractors

1771 Concrete Work *see* NAICS 235420: Drywall, Plastering, Acoustical and Insulation Contractors; NAICS 235710: Concrete Contractors

1781 Water Well Drilling *see* NAICS 235810: Water Well Drilling Contractors

1791 Structural Steel Erection *see* NAICS 235910: Structural Steel Erection Contractors

1793 Glass and Glazing Work *see* NAICS 235920: Glass and Glazing Contractors

1794 Excavation Work *see* NAICS 235930: Excavation Contractors

1795 Wrecking and Demolition Work *see* NAICS 235940: Wrecking and Demolition Contractors

1796 Installation or Erection of Building Equipment, NEC *see* NAICS 235950: Building Equipment and Other Machinery Installation Contractors

1799 Special Trade Contractors, NEC *see* NAICS 235210: Painting and Wall Covering Contractors; NAICS 235920: Glass and Glazing Contractors; NAICS 562910: Remediation Services; NAICS 235990: All Other Special Trade Contractors

FOOD & KINDRED PRODUCTS

2011 Meat Packing Plants *see* NAICS 311611: Animal (except Poultry) Slaughtering

2013 Sausages and Other Prepared Meats *see* NAICS 311612: Meat Processed From Carcasses

2015 Poultry Slaughtering and Processing *see* NAICS 311615: Poultry Processing; NAICS 311999: All Other Miscellaneous Food Manufacturing

2021 Creamery Butter *see* NAICS 311512: Creamery Butter Manufacturing

2022 Natural, Processed, and Imitation Cheese *see* NAICS 311513: Cheese Manufacturing

2023 Dry, Condensed, and Evaporated Dairy Products *see* NAICS 311514: Dry, Condensed, and Evaporated Dairy Product Manufacturing

2024 Ice Cream and Frozen Desserts *see* NAICS 311520: Ice Cream and Frozen Dessert Manufacturing

2026 Fluid Milk *see* NAICS 311511: Fluid Milk Manufacturing

2032 Canned Specialties *see* NAICS 311422: Specialty Canning; NAICS 311999: All Other Miscellaneous Food Manufacturing

2033 Canned Fruits, Vegetables, Preserves, Jams, and Jellies *see* NAICS 311421: Fruit and Vegetable Canning

2034 Dried and Dehydrated Fruits, Vegetables, and Soup Mixes *see* NAICS 311423: Dried and Dehydrated Food Manufacturing; NAICS 311211: Flour Milling

2035 Pickled Fruits and Vegetables, Vegetables Sauces and Seasonings, and Salad Dressings *see* NAICS 311421: Fruit and Vegetable Canning; NAICS 311941: Mayonnaise, Dressing, and Other Prepared Sauce Manufacturing

2037 Frozen Fruits, Fruit Juices, and Vegetables *see* NAICS 311411: Frozen Fruit, Juice, and Vegetable Processing

2038 Frozen Specialties, NEC *see* NAICS 311412: Frozen Specialty Food Manufacturing

2041 Flour and Other Grain Mill Products *see* NAICS 311211: Flour Milling

2043 Cereal Breakfast Foods *see* NAICS 311920: Coffee and Tea Manufacturing; NAICS 311230: Breakfast Cereal Manufacturing

2044 Rice Milling *see* NAICS 311212: Rice Milling

2045 Prepared Flour Mixes and Doughs *see* NAICS 311822: Flour Mixes and Dough Manufacturing from Purchased Flour

2046 Wet Corn Milling *see* NAICS 311221: Wet Corn Milling

2047 Dog and Cat Food *see* NAICS 311111: Dog and Cat Food Manufacturing

2048 Prepared Feed and Feed Ingredients for Animals and Fowls, Except Dogs and Cats *see* NAICS 311611: Animal (except Poultry) Slaughtering; NAICS 311119: Other Animal Food Manufacturing

2051 Bread and Other Bakery Products, Except Cookies and Crackers *see* NAICS 311812: Commercial Bakeries

2052 Cookies and Crackers *see* NAICS 311821: Cookie and Cracker Manufacturing; NAICS 311919: Other Snack Food Manufacturing; NAICS 311812: Commercial Bakeries

2053 Frozen Bakery Products, Except Bread *see* NAICS 311813: Frozen Bakery Product Manufacturing

2061 Cane Sugar, Except Refining *see* NAICS 311311: Sugarcane Mills

2062 Cane Sugar Refining *see* NAICS 311312: Cane Sugar Refining

2063 Beet Sugar *see* NAICS 311313: Beet Sugar Manufacturing

2064 Candy and Other Confectionery Products *see* NAICS 311330: Confectionery Manufacturing from Purchased Chocolate; NAICS 311340: Non-Chocolate Confectionery Manufacturing

2066 Chocolate and Cocoa Products *see* NAICS 311320: Chocolate and Confectionery Manufacturing from Cacao Beans

2067 Chewing Gum *see* NAICS 311340: Non-Chocolate Confectionery Manufacturing

2068 Salted and Roasted Nuts and Seeds *see* NAICS 311911: Roasted Nuts and Peanut Butter Manufacturing

2074 Cottonseed Oil Mills *see* NAICS 311223: Other Oilseed Processing; NAICS 311225: Fats and Oils Refining and Blending

2075 Soybean Oil Mills *see* NAICS 311222: Soybean Processing; NAICS 311225: Fats and Oils Refining and Blending

2076 Vegetable Oil Mills, Except Corn, Cottonseed, and Soybeans *see* NAICS 311223: Other Oilseed Processing; NAICS 311225: Fats and Oils Refining and Blending

2077 Animal and Marine Fats and Oils *see* NAICS 311613: Rendering and Meat By-product Processing; NAICS 311711: Seafood Canning; NAICS 311712: Fresh and Frozen Seafood Processing; NAICS 311225: Fats and Oils Refining and Blending

2079 Shortening, Table Oils, Margarine, and Other Edible Fats and Oils, NEC *see* NAICS 311225: Fats and Oils Refining and Blending; NAICS 311222: Soybean Processing; NAICS 311223: Other Oilseed Processing

2082 Malt Beverages *see* NAICS 312120: Breweries

2083 Malt *see* NAICS 311213: Malt Manufacturing

2084 Wines, Brandy, and Brandy Spirits *see* NAICS 312130: Wineries

2085 Distilled and Blended Liquors *see* NAICS 312140: Distilleries

2086 Bottled and Canned Soft Drinks and Carbonated Waters *see* NAICS 312111: Soft Drink Manufacturing; NAICS 312112: Bottled Water Manufacturing

2087 Flavoring Extracts and Flavoring Syrups NEC *see* NAICS 311930: Flavoring Syrup and Concentrate Manufacturing; NAICS 311942: Spice and Extract Manufacturing; NAICS 311999: All Other Miscellaneous Food Manufacturing

2091 Canned and Cured Fish and Seafood *see* NAICS 311711: Seafood Canning

2092 Prepared Fresh or Frozen Fish and Seafoods *see* NAICS 311712: Fresh and Frozen Seafood Processing

2095 Roasted Coffee *see* NAICS 311920: Coffee and Tea Manufacturing; NAICS 311942: Spice and Extract Manufacturing

2096 Potato Chips, Corn Chips, and Similar Snacks *see* NAICS 311919: Other Snack Food Manufacturing

2097 Manufactured Ice *see* NAICS 312113: Ice Manufacturing

2098 Macaroni, Spaghetti, Vermicelli, and Noodles *see* NAICS 311823: Pasta Manufacturing

2099 Food Preparations, NEC *see* NAICS 311423: Dried and Dehydrated Food Manufacturing; NAICS 111998: All Other Miscellaneous Crop Farming; NAICS 311340: Non-Chocolate Confectionery Manufacturing; NAICS 311911: Roasted Nuts and Peanut Butter Manufacturing; NAICS 311991: Perishable Prepared Food Manufacturing; NAICS

311830: Tortilla Manufacturing; NAICS 311920: Coffee and Tea Manufacturing; NAICS 311941: Mayonnaise, Dressing, and Other Prepared Sauce Manufacturing; NAICS 311942: Spice and Extract Manufacturing; NAICS 311999: All Other Miscellaneous Food Manufacturing

TOBACCO PRODUCTS

2111 Cigarettes *see* NAICS 312221: Cigarette Manufacturing

2121 Cigars *see* NAICS 312229: Other Tobacco Product Manufacturing

2131 Chewing and Smoking Tobacco and Snuff *see* NAICS 312229: Other Tobacco Product Manufacturing

2141 Tobacco Stemming and Redrying *see* NAICS 312229: Other Tobacco Product Manufacturing; NAICS 312210: Tobacco Stemming and Redrying

TEXTILE MILL PRODUCTS

2211 Broadwoven Fabric Mills, Cotton *see* NAICS 313210: Broadwoven Fabric Mills

2221 Broadwoven Fabric Mills, Manmade Fiber and Silk *see* NAICS 313210: Broadwoven Fabric Mills

2231 Broadwoven Fabric Mills, Wool (Including Dyeing and Finishing) *see* NAICS 313210: Broadwoven Fabric Mills; NAICS 313311: Broadwoven Fabric Finishing Mills; NAICS 313312: Textile and Fabric Finishing (except Broadwoven Fabric) Mills

2241 Narrow Fabric and Other Smallware Mills: Cotton, Wool, Silk, and Manmade Fiber *see* NAICS 313221: Narrow Fabric Mills

2251 Women's Full-Length and Knee-Length Hosiery, Except Socks *see* NAICS 315111: Sheer Hosiery Mills

2252 Hosiery, NEC *see* NAICS 315111: Sheer Hosiery Mills; NAICS 315119: Other Hosiery and Sock Mills

2253 Knit Outerwear Mills *see* NAICS 315191: Outerwear Knitting Mills

2254 Knit Underwear and Nightwear Mills *see* NAICS 315192: Underwear and Nightwear Knitting Mills

2257 Weft Knit Fabric Mills *see* NAICS 313241: Weft Knit Fabric Mills; NAICS 313312: Textile and Fabric Finishing (except Broadwoven Fabric) Mills

2258 Lace and Warp Knit Fabric Mills *see* NAICS 313249: Other Knit Fabric and Lace Mills; NAICS 313312: Textile and Fabric Finishing (except Broadwoven Fabric) Mills

2259 Knitting Mills, NEC *see* NAICS 315191: Outerwear Knitting Mills; NAICS 315192: Underwear and Nightwear Knitting Mills; NAICS 313241: Weft Knit Fabric Mills; NAICS 313249: Other Knit Fabric and Lace Mills

2261 Finishers of Broadwoven Fabrics of Cotton *see* NAICS 313311: Broadwoven Fabric Finishing Mills

2262 Finishers of Broadwoven Fabrics of Manmade Fiber and Silk *see* NAICS 313311: Broadwoven Fabric Finishing Mills

2269 Finishers of Textiles, NEC *see* NAICS 313311: Broadwoven Fabric Finishing Mills; NAICS 313312: Textile and Fabric Finishing (except Broadwoven Fabric) Mills

2273 Carpets and Rugs *see* NAICS 314110: Carpet and Rug Mills

2281 Yarn Spinning Mills *see* NAICS 313111: Yarn Spinning Mills

2282 Yarn Texturizing, Throwing, Twisting, and Winding Mills *see* NAICS 313112: Yarn Texturing, Throwing and Twisting Mills; NAICS 313312: Textile and Fabric Finishing (except Broadwoven Fabric) Mills

2284 Thread Mills *see* NAICS 313113: Thread Mills; NAICS 313312: Textile and Fabric Finishing (except Broadwoven Fabric) Mills

2295 Coated Fabrics, Not Rubberized *see* NAICS 313320: Fabric Coating Mills

2296 Tire Cord and Fabrics *see* NAICS 314992: Tire Cord and Tire Fabric Mills

2297 Nonwoven Fabrics *see* NAICS 313230: Nonwoven Fabric Mills

2298 Cordage and Twine *see* NAICS 314991: Rope, Cordage and Twine Mills

2299 Textile Goods, NEC *see* NAICS 313210: Broadwoven Fabric Mills; NAICS 313230: Nonwoven Fabric Mills; NAICS 313312: Textile and Fabric Finishing (except Broadwoven Fabric) Mills; NAICS 313221: Narrow Fabric Mills; NAICS 313113: Thread Mills; NAICS 313111: Yarn Spinning Mills; NAICS 314999: All Other Miscellaneous Textile Product Mills

APPAREL & OTHER FINISHED PRODUCTS MADE FROM FABRICS & SIMILAR MATERIALS

2311 Men's and Boys' Suits, Coats and Overcoats *see* NAICS 315211: Men's and Boys' Cut and Sew Apparel Contractors; NAICS 315222: Men's and Boys' Cut and Sew Suit, Coat, and Overcoat Manufacturing

2321 Men's and Boys' Shirts, Except Work Shirts *see* NAICS 315211: Men's and Boys' Cut and Sew Apparel Contractors; NAICS 315223: Men's and Boys' Cut and Sew Shirt, (except Work Shirt) Manufacturing

2322 Men's and Boys' Underwear and Nightwear *see* NAICS 315211: Men's and Boys' Cut and Sew Apparel Contractors; NAICS 315221: Men's and

Boys' Cut and Sew Underwear and Nightwear Manufacturing

2323 Men's and Boys' Neckwear *see* NAICS 315993: Men's and Boys' Neckwear Manufacturing

2325 Men's and Boys' Trousers and Slacks *see* NAICS 315211: Men's and Boys' Cut and Sew Apparel Contractors; NAICS 315224: Men's and Boys' Cut And Sew Trouser, Slack, And Jean Manufacturing

2326 Men's and Boys' Work Clothing *see* NAICS 315211: Men's and Boys' Cut and Sew Apparel Contractors; NAICS 315225: Men's and Boys' Cut and Sew Work Clothing Manufacturing

2329 Men's and Boys' Clothing, NEC *see* NAICS 315211: Men's and Boys' Cut and Sew Apparel Contractors; NAICS 315228: Men's and Boys' Cut and Sew Other Outerwear Manufacturing; NAICS 315299: All Other Cut and Sew Apparel Manufacturing

2331 Women's, Misses', and Juniors' Blouses and Shirts *see* NAICS 315212: Women's and Girls' Cut and Sew Apparel Contractors; NAICS 315232: Women's and Girls' Cut and Sew Blouse and Shirt Manufacturing

2335 Women's, Misses' and Junior's Dresses *see* NAICS 315212: Women's and Girls' Cut and Sew Apparel Contractors; NAICS 315233: Women's and Girls' Cut and Sew Dress Manufacturing

2337 Women's, Misses' and Juniors' Suits, Skirts and Coats *see* NAICS 315212: Women's and Girls' Cut and Sew Apparel Contractors; NAICS 315234: Women's and Girls' Cut and Sew Suit, Coat, Tailored Jacket, and Skirt Manufacturing

2339 Women's, Misses' and Juniors' Outerwear, NEC *see* NAICS 315999: Other Apparel Accessories and Other Apparel Manufacturing; NAICS 315212: Women's and Girls' Cut and Sew Apparel Contractors; NAICS 315299: All Other Cut and Sew Apparel Manufacturing; NAICS 315238: Women's and Girls' Cut and Sew Other Outerwear Manufacturing

2341 Women's, Misses, Children's, and Infants' Underwear and Nightwear *see* NAICS 315212: Women's and Girls' Cut and Sew Apparel Contractors; NAICS 315211: Men's and Boys' Cut and Sew Apparel Contractors; NAICS 315231: Women's and Girls' Cut and Sew Lingerie, Loungewear, and Nightwear Manufacturing; NAICS 315221: Men's and Boys' Cut and Sew Underwear and Nightwear Manufacturing; NAICS 315291: Infants' Cut and Sew Apparel Manufacturing

2342 Brassieres, Girdles, and Allied Garments *see* NAICS 315212: Women's and Girls' Cut and Sew Apparel Contractors; NAICS 315231: Women's and Girls'

Cut and Sew Lingerie, Loungewear, and Nightwear Manufacturing

2353 Hats, Caps, and Millinery *see* NAICS 315991: Hat, Cap, and Millinery Manufacturing

2361 Girls', Children's and Infants' Dresses, Blouses and Shirts *see* NAICS 315291: Infants' Cut and Sew Apparel Manufacturing; NAICS 315223: Men's and Boys' Cut and Sew Shirt (except Work Shirt) Manufacturing; NAICS 315211: Men's and Boys' Cut and Sew Apparel Contractors; NAICS 315232: Women's and Girls' Cut and Sew Blouse and Shirt Manufacturing; NAICS 315233: Women's and Girls' Cut and Sew Dress Manufacturing; NAICS 315212: Women's and Girls' Cut and Sew Apparel Contractors

2369 Girls', Children's and Infants' Outerwear, NEC *see* NAICS 315291: Infants' Cut and Sew Apparel Manufacturing; NAICS 315222: Men's and Boys' Cut and Sew Suit, Coat, and Overcoat Manufacturing; NAICS 315224: Men's and Boys' Cut and Sew Trouser, Slack, and Jean Manufacturing; NAICS 315228: Men's and Boys' Cut and Sew Other Outerwear Manufacturing; NAICS 315221: Men's and Boys' Cut and Sew Underwear and Nightwear Manufacturing; NAICS 315211: Men's and Boys' Cut and Sew Apparel Contractors; NAICS 315234: Women's and Girls' Cut and Sew Suit, Coat, Tailored Jacket, and Skirt Manufacturing; NAICS 315238: Women's and Girls' Cut and Sew Other Outerwear Manufacturing; NAICS 315231: Women's and Girls' Cut and Sew Lingerie, Loungewear, and Nightwear Manufacturing; NAICS 315212: Women's and Girls' Cut and Sew Apparel Contractors

2371 Fur Goods *see* NAICS 315292: Fur and Leather Apparel Manufacturing

2381 Dress and Work Gloves, Except Knit and All-Leather *see* NAICS 315992: Glove and Mitten Manufacturing

2384 Robes and Dressing Gowns *see* NAICS 315231: Women's and Girls' Cut and Sew Lingerie, Loungewear, and Nightwear Manufacturing; NAICS 315221: Men's and Boys' Cut and Sew Underwear and Nightwear Manufacturing; NAICS 315211: Men's and Boys' Cut and Sew Apparel Contractors; NAICS 315212: Women's and Girls' Cut and Sew Apparel Contractors

2385 Waterproof Outerwear *see* NAICS 315222: Men's and Boys' Cut and Sew Suit, Coat, and Overcoat Manufacturing; NAICS 315234: Women's and Girls' Cut and Sew Suit, Coat, Tailored Jacket, and Skirt Manufacturing; NAICS 315228: Men's and Boys' Cut and Sew Other Outerwear Manufacturing; NAICS 315238: Women's and Girls' Cut and Sew Other Outerwear Manufacturing; NAICS 315291: Infants' Cut and Sew Apparel Manufacturing; NAICS 315999: Other Apparel Accessories and Other Apparel Manufacturing; NAICS 315211: Men's and Boys' Cut and Sew Apparel Contractors; NAICS 315212: Women's and Girls' Cut and Sew Apparel Contractors

2386 Leather and Sheep-Lined Clothing *see* NAICS 315292: Fur and Leather Apparel Manufacturing

2387 Apparel Belts *see* NAICS 315999: Other Apparel Accessories and Other Apparel Manufacturing

2389 Apparel and Accessories, NEC *see* NAICS 315999: Other Apparel Accessories and Other Apparel Manufacturing; NAICS 315299: All Other Cut and Sew Apparel Manufacturing; NAICS 315231: Women's and Girls' Cut and Sew Lingerie, Loungewear, and Nightwear Manufacturing; NAICS 315212: Women's and Girls' Cut and Sew Apparel Contractors; NAICS 315211: Men's and Boys' Cut and Sew Apparel Contractors

2391 Curtains and Draperies *see* NAICS 314121: Curtain and Drapery Mills

2392 Housefurnishings, Except Curtains and Draperies *see* NAICS 314911: Textile Bag Mills; NAICS 339994: Broom, Brush and Mop Manufacturing; NAICS 314129: Other Household Textile Product Mills

2393 Textile Bags *see* NAICS 314911: Textile Bag Mills

2394 Canvas and Related Products *see* NAICS 314912: Canvas and Related Product Mills

2395 Pleating, Decorative and Novelty Stitching, and Tucking for the Trade *see* NAICS 314999: All Other Miscellaneous Textile Product Mills; NAICS 315211: Men's and Boys' Cut and Sew Apparel Contractors; NAICS 315212: Women's and Girls' Cut and Sew Apparel Contractors

2396 Automotive Trimmings, Apparel Findings, and Related Products *see* NAICS 336360: Motor Vehicle Fabric Accessories and Seat Manufacturing; NAICS 315999: Other Apparel Accessories, and Other Apparel Manufacturing; NAICS 323113: Commercial Screen Printing; NAICS 314999: All Other Miscellaneous Textile Product Mills

2397 Schiffli Machine Embroideries *see* NAICS 313222: Schiffli Machine Embroidery

2399 Fabricated Textile Products, NEC *see* NAICS 336360: Motor Vehicle Fabric Accessories and Seat Manufacturing; NAICS 315999: Other Apparel Accessories and Other Apparel Manufacturing; NAICS 314999: All Other Miscellaneous Textile Product Mills

LUMBER & WOOD PRODUCTS, EXCEPT FURNITURE

2411 Logging *see* NAICS 113310: Logging

2421 Sawmills and Planing Mills, General *see* NAICS 321912: Cut Stock, Resawing Lumber, and Planing; NAICS 321113: Sawmills; NAICS 321918: Other Millwork (including Flooring); NAICS 321999: All Other Miscellaneous Wood Product Manufacturing

2426 Hardwood Dimension and Flooring Mills *see* NAICS 321918: Other Millwork (including Flooring); NAICS 321999: All Other Miscellaneous Wood Product Manufacturing; NAICS 337215: Showcase, Partition, Shelving, and Locker Manufacturing; NAICS 321912: Cut Stock, Resawing Lumber, and Planing

2429 Special Product Sawmills, NEC *see* NAICS 321113: Sawmills; NAICS 321912: Cut Stock, Resawing Lumber, and Planing; NAICS 321999: All Other Miscellaneous Wood Product Manufacturing

2431 Millwork *see* NAICS 321911: Wood Window and Door Manufacturing; NAICS 321918: Other Millwork (including Flooring)

2434 Wood Kitchen Cabinets *see* NAICS 337110: Wood Kitchen Cabinet and Counter Top Manufacturing

2435 Hardwood Veneer and Plywood *see* NAICS 321211: Hardwood Veneer and Plywood Manufacturing

2436 Softwood Veneer and Plywood *see* NAICS 321212: Softwood Veneer and Plywood Manufacturing

2439 Structural Wood Members, NEC *see* NAICS 321912: Cut Stock, Resawing Lumber, and Planing; NAICS 321214: Truss Manufacturing; NAICS 321213: Engineered Wood Member (except Truss) Manufacturing

2441 Nailed and Lock Corner Wood Boxes and Shook *see* NAICS 321920: Wood Container and Pallet Manufacturing

2448 Wood Pallets and Skids *see* NAICS 321920: Wood Container and Pallet Manufacturing

2449 Wood Containers, NEC *see* NAICS 321920: Wood Container and Pallet Manufacturing

2451 Mobile Homes *see* NAICS 321991: Manufactured Home (Mobile Home) Manufacturing

2452 Prefabricated Wood Buildings and Components *see* NAICS 321992: Prefabricated Wood Building Manufacturing

2491 Wood Preserving *see* NAICS 321114: Wood Preservation

2493 Reconstituted Wood Products *see* NAICS 321219: Reconstituted Wood Product Manufacturing

2499 Wood Products, NEC *see* NAICS 339999: All Other Miscellaneous Manufacturing; NAICS 321920: Wood Container and Pallet Manufacturing; NAICS 321999: All Other Miscellaneous Wood Product Manufacturing

FURNITURE & FIXTURES

2511 Wood Household Furniture, Except Upholstered *see* NAICS 337122: Nonupholstered Wood Household Furniture Manufacturing

2512 Wood Household Furniture, Upholstered *see* NAICS 337121: Upholstered Wood Household Furniture Manufacturing

2514 Metal Household Furniture *see* NAICS 337124: Metal Household Furniture Manufacturing

2515 Mattresses, Foundations, and Convertible Beds *see* NAICS 337910: Mattress Manufacturing; NAICS 337121: Upholstered Wood Household Furniture Manufacturing

2517 Wood Television, Radio, Phonograph and Sewing Machine Cabinets *see* NAICS 337129: Wood Television, Radio, and Sewing Machine Cabinet Manufacturing

2519 Household Furniture, NEC *see* NAICS 337125: Household Furniture (except Wood and Metal) Manufacturing

2521 Wood Office Furniture *see* NAICS 337211: Wood Office Furniture Manufacturing

2522 Office Furniture, Except Wood *see* NAICS 337214: Nonwood Office Furniture Manufacturing

2531 Public Building and Related Furniture *see* NAICS 336360: Motor Vehicle Fabric Accessories and Seat Manufacturing; NAICS 337127: Institutional Furniture Manufacturing; NAICS 339942: Lead Pencil and Art Good Manufacturing

2541 Wood Office and Store Fixtures, Partitions, Shelving, and Lockers *see* NAICS 337110: Wood Kitchen Cabinet and Counter Top Manufacturing; NAICS 337212: Custom Architectural Woodwork, Millwork, and Fixtures; NAICS 337215: Showcase, Partition, Shelving, and Locker Manufacturing

2542 Office and Store Fixtures, Partitions Shelving, and Lockers, Except Wood *see* NAICS 337215: Showcase, Partition, Shelving, and Locker Manufacturing

2591 Drapery Hardware and Window Blinds and Shades *see* NAICS 337920: Blind and Shade Manufacturing

2599 Furniture and Fixtures, NEC *see* NAICS 339113: Surgical Appliance and Supplies Manufacturing; NAICS 337127: Institutional Furniture Manufacturing

PAPER & ALLIED PRODUCTS

2611 Pulp Mills *see* NAICS 322110: Pulp Mills; NAICS 322121: Paper (except Newsprint) Mills; NAICS 322130: Paperboard Mills

2621 Paper Mills *see* NAICS 322121: Paper (except Newsprint) Mills; NAICS 322122: Newsprint Mills

2631 Paperboard Mills *see* NAICS 322130: Paperboard Mills

2652 Setup Paperboard Boxes *see* NAICS 322213: Setup Paperboard Box Manufacturing

2653 Corrugated and Solid Fiber Boxes *see* NAICS 322211: Corrugated and Solid Fiber Box Manufacturing

2655 Fiber Cans, Tubes, Drums, and Similar Products *see* NAICS 322214: Fiber Can, Tube, Drum, and Similar Products Manufacturing

2656 Sanitary Food Containers, Except Folding *see* NAICS 322215: Non-Folding Sanitary Food Container Manufacturing

2657 Folding Paperboard Boxes, Including Sanitary *see* NAICS 322212: Folding Paperboard Box Manufacturing

2671 Packaging Paper and Plastics Film *see* NAICS 322221: Coated and Laminated Packaging Paper and Plastics Film Manufacturing; NAICS 326112: Unsupported Plastics Packaging Film and Sheet Manufacturing

2672 Coated and Laminated Paper, NEC *see* NAICS 322222: Coated and Laminated Paper Manufacturing

2673 Plastics, Foil, and Coated Paper Bags *see* NAICS 322223: Plastics, Foil, and Coated Paper Bag Manufacturing; NAICS 326111: Unsupported Plastics Bag Manufacturing

2674 Uncoated Paper and Multiwall Bags *see* NAICS 322224: Uncoated Paper and Multiwall Bag Manufacturing

2675 Die-Cut Paper and Paperboard and Cardboard *see* NAICS 322231: Die-Cut Paper and Paperboard Office Supplies Manufacturing; NAICS 322292: Surface-Coated Paperboard Manufacturing; NAICS 322298: All Other Converted Paper Product Manufacturing

2676 Sanitary Paper Products *see* NAICS 322291: Sanitary Paper Product Manufacturing

2677 Envelopes *see* NAICS 322232: Envelope Manufacturing

2678 Stationery, Tablets, and Related Products *see* NAICS 322233: Stationery, Tablet, and Related Product Manufacturing

2679 Converted Paper and Paperboard Products, NEC *see* NAICS 322215: Non-Folding Sanitary Food Container Manufacturing; NAICS 322222: Coated and Laminated Paper Manufacturing; NAICS 322231: Die-Cut Paper and Paperboard Office Supplies Manufacturing; NAICS 322298: All Other Converted Paper Product Manufacturing

PRINTING, PUBLISHING, & ALLIED INDUSTRIES

2711 Newspapers: Publishing, or Publishing and Printing *see* NAICS 511110: Newspaper Publishers

2721 Periodicals: Publishing, or Publishing and Printing *see* NAICS 511120: Periodical Publishers

2731 Books: Publishing, or Publishing and Printing *see* NAICS 512230: Music Publishers; NAICS 511130: Book Publishers

2732 Book Printing *see* NAICS 323117: Book Printing

2741 Miscellaneous Publishing *see* NAICS 511140: Database and Directory Publishers; NAICS 512230: Music Publishers; NAICS 511199: All Other Publishers

2752 Commercial Printing, Lithographic *see* NAICS 323114: Quick Printing; NAICS 323110: Commercial Lithographic Printing

2754 Commercial Printing, Gravure *see* NAICS 323111: Commercial Gravure Printing

2759 Commercial Printing, NEC *see* NAICS 323113: Commercial Screen Printing; NAICS 323112: Commercial Flexographic Printing; NAICS 323114: Quick Printing; NAICS 323115: Digital Printing; NAICS 323119: Other Commercial Printing

2761 Manifold Business Forms *see* NAICS 323116: Manifold Business Form Printing

2771 Greeting Cards *see* NAICS 323110: Commercial Lithographic Printing; NAICS 323111: Commercial Gravure Printing; NAICS 323112: Commercial Flexographic Printing; NAICS 323113: Commercial Screen Printing; NAICS 323119: Other Commercial Printing; NAICS 511191: Greeting Card Publishers

2782 Blankbooks, Loose-leaf Binders and Devices *see* NAICS 323110: Commercial Lithographic Printing; NAICS 323111: Commercial Gravure Printing; NAICS 323112: Commercial Flexographic Printing; NAICS 323113: Commercial Screen Printing; NAICS 323119: Other Commercial Printing; NAICS 323118: Blankbook, Loose-leaf Binder and Device Manufacturing

2789 Bookbinding and Related Work *see* NAICS 323121: Tradebinding and Related Work

2791 Typesetting *see* NAICS 323122: Prepress Services

2796 Platemaking and Related Services *see* NAICS 323122: Prepress Services

CHEMICALS & ALLIED PRODUCTS

2812 Alkalies and Chlorine *see* NAICS 325181: Alkalies and Chlorine Manufacturing

2813 Industrial Gases *see* NAICS 325120: Industrial Gas Manufacturing

2816 Inorganic Pigments *see* NAICS 325131: Inorganic Dye and Pigment Manufacturing; NAICS 325182: Carbon Black Manufacturing

2819 Industrial Inorganic Chemicals, NEC *see* NAICS 325998: All Other Miscellaneous Chemical Product Manufacturing; NAICS 331311: Aluminum Refining; NAICS 325131: Inorganic Dye and Pigment Manufacturing; NAICS 325188: All Other Inorganic Chemical Manufacturing

2821 Plastics Material Synthetic Resins, and Nonvulcanizable Elastomers *see* NAICS 325211: Plastics Material and Resin Manufacturing

2822 Synthetic Rubber *see* NAICS 325212: Synthetic Rubber Manufacturing

2823 Cellulosic Manmade Fibers *see* NAICS 325221: Cellulosic Manmade Fiber Manufacturing

2824 Manmade Organic Fibers, Except Cellulosic *see* NAICS 325222: Noncellulosic Organic Fiber Manufacturing

2833 Medicinal Chemicals and Botanical Products *see* NAICS 325411: Medicinal and Botanical Manufacturing

2834 Pharmaceutical Preparations *see* NAICS 325412: Pharmaceutical Preparation Manufacturing

2835 In Vitro and In Vivo Diagnostic Substances *see* NAICS 325412: Pharmaceutical Preparation Manufacturing; NAICS 325413: In-Vitro Diagnostic Substance Manufacturing

2836 Biological Products, Except Diagnostic Substances *see* NAICS 325414: Biological Product (except Diagnostic) Manufacturing

2841 Soaps and Other Detergents, Except Specialty Cleaners *see* NAICS 325611: Soap and Other Detergent Manufacturing

2842 Specialty Cleaning, Polishing, and Sanitary Preparations *see* NAICS 325612: Polish and Other Sanitation Good Manufacturing

2843 Surface Active Agents, Finishing Agents, Sulfonated Oils, and Assistants *see* NAICS 325613: Surface Active Agent Manufacturing

2844 Perfumes, Cosmetics, and Other Toilet Preparations *see* NAICS 325620: Toilet Preparation Manufacturing; NAICS 325611: Soap and Other Detergent Manufacturing

2851 Paints, Varnishes, Lacquers, Enamels, and Allied Products *see* NAICS 325510: Paint and Coating Manufacturing

2861 Gum and Wood Chemicals *see* NAICS 325191: Gum and Wood Chemical Manufacturing

2865 Cyclic Organic Crudes and Intermediates, and Organic Dyes and Pigments *see* NAICS 325110: Petrochemical Manufacturing; NAICS 325132: Organic Dye and Pigment Manufacturing; NAICS

325192: Cyclic Crude and Intermediate Manufacturing

2869 Industrial Organic Chemicals, NEC *see* NAICS 325110: Petrochemical Manufacturing; NAICS 325188: All Other Inorganic Chemical Manufacturing; NAICS 325193: Ethyl Alcohol Manufacturing; NAICS 325120: Industrial Gas Manufacturing; NAICS 325199: All Other Basic Organic Chemical Manufacturing

2873 Nitrogenous Fertilizers *see* NAICS 325311: Nitrogenous Fertilizer Manufacturing

2874 Phosphatic Fertilizers *see* NAICS 325312: Phosphatic Fertilizer Manufacturing

2875 Fertilizers, Mixing Only *see* NAICS 325314: Fertilizer (Mixing Only) Manufacturing

2879 Pesticides and Agricultural Chemicals, NEC *see* NAICS 325320: Pesticide and Other Agricultural Chemical Manufacturing

2891 Adhesives and Sealants *see* NAICS 325520: Adhesive and Sealant Manufacturing

2892 Explosives *see* NAICS 325920: Explosives Manufacturing

2893 Printing Ink *see* NAICS 325910: Printing Ink Manufacturing

2895 Carbon Black *see* NAICS 325182: Carbon Black Manufacturing

2899 Chemicals and Chemical Preparations, NEC *see* NAICS 325510: Paint and Coating Manufacturing; NAICS 311942: Spice and Extract Manufacturing; NAICS 325199: All Other Basic Organic Chemical Manufacturing; NAICS 325998: All Other Miscellaneous Chemical Product Manufacturing

PETROLEUM REFINING & RELATED INDUSTRIES

2911 Petroleum Refining *see* NAICS 324110: Petroleum Refineries

2951 Asphalt Paving Mixtures and Blocks *see* NAICS 324121: Asphalt Paving Mixture and Block Manufacturing

2952 Asphalt Felts and Coatings *see* NAICS 324122: Asphalt Shingle and Coating Materials Manufacturing

2992 Lubricating Oils and Greases *see* NAICS 324191: Petroleum Lubricating Oil and Grease Manufacturing

2999 Products of Petroleum and Coal, NEC *see* NAICS 324199: All Other Petroleum and Coal Products Manufacturing

RUBBER & MISCELLANEOUS PLASTICS PRODUCTS

3011 Tires and Inner Tubes *see* NAICS 326211: Tire Manufacturing (except Retreading)

3021 Rubber and Plastics Footwear *see* NAICS 316211: Rubber and Plastics Footwear Manufacturing

3052 Rubber and Plastics Hose and Belting *see* NAICS 326220: Rubber and Plastics Hoses and Belting Manufacturing

3053 Gaskets, Packing, and Sealing Devices *see* NAICS 339991: Gasket, Packing, and Sealing Device Manufacturing

3061 Molded, Extruded, and Lathe-Cut Mechanical Rubber Products *see* NAICS 326291: Rubber Product Manufacturing for Mechanical Use

3069 Fabricated Rubber Products, NEC *see* NAICS 313320: Fabric Coating Mills; NAICS 326192: Resilient Floor Covering Manufacturing; NAICS 326299: All Other Rubber Product Manufacturing

3081 Unsupported Plastics Film and Sheet *see* NAICS 326113: Unsupported Plastics Film and Sheet (except Packaging) Manufacturing

3082 Unsupported Plastics Profile Shapes *see* NAICS 326121: Unsupported Plastics Profile Shape Manufacturing

3083 Laminated Plastics Plate, Sheet, and Profile Shapes *see* NAICS 326130: Laminated Plastics Plate, Sheet, and Shape Manufacturing

3084 Plastic Pipe *see* NAICS 326122: Plastics Pipe and Pipe Fitting Manufacturing

3085 Plastics Bottles *see* NAICS 326160: Plastics Bottle Manufacturing

3086 Plastics Foam Products *see* NAICS 326150: Urethane and Other Foam Product (except Polystyrene) Manufacturing; NAICS 326140: Polystyrene Foam Product Manufacturing

3087 Custom Compounding of Purchased Plastics Resins *see* NAICS 325991: Custom Compounding of Purchased Resin

3088 Plastics Plumbing Fixtures *see* NAICS 326191: Plastics Plumbing Fixtures Manufacturing

3089 Plastics Products, NEC *see* NAICS 326122: Plastics Pipe and Pipe Fitting Manufacturing; NAICS 326121: Unsupported Plastics Profile Shape Manufacturing; NAICS 326199: All Other Plastics Product Manufacturing

LEATHER & LEATHER PRODUCTS

3111 Leather Tanning and Finishing *see* NAICS 316110: Leather and Hide Tanning and Finishing

3131 Boot and Shoe Cut Stock and Findings *see* NAICS 321999: All Other Miscellaneous Wood Product Manufacturing; NAICS 339993: Fastener, Button, Needle, and Pin Manufacturing; NAICS 316999: All Other Leather Good Manufacturing

3142 House Slippers *see* NAICS 316212: House Slipper Manufacturing

3143 Men's Footwear, Except Athletic *see* NAICS 316213: Men's Footwear (except Athletic) Manufacturing

3144 Women's Footwear, Except Athletic *see* NAICS 316214: Women's Footwear (except Athletic) Manufacturing

3149 Footwear, Except Rubber, NEC *see* NAICS 316219: Other Footwear Manufacturing

3151 Leather Gloves and Mittens *see* NAICS 315992: Glove and Mitten Manufacturing

3161 Luggage *see* NAICS 316991: Luggage Manufacturing

3171 Women's Handbags and Purses *see* NAICS 316992: Women's Handbag and Purse Manufacturing

3172 Personal Leather Goods, Except Women's Handbags and Purses *see* NAICS 316993: Personal Leather Good (except Women's Handbag and Purse) Manufacturing

3199 Leather Goods, NEC *see* NAICS 316999: All Other Leather Good Manufacturing

STONE, CLAY, GLASS, & CONCRETE PRODUCTS

3211 Flat Glass *see* NAICS 327211: Flat Glass Manufacturing

3221 Glass Containers *see* NAICS 327213: Glass Container Manufacturing

3229 Pressed and Blown Glass and Glassware, NEC *see* NAICS 327212: Other Pressed and Blown Glass and Glassware Manufacturing

3231 Glass Products, Made of Purchased Glass *see* NAICS 327215: Glass Product Manufacturing Made of Purchased Glass

3241 Cement, Hydraulic *see* NAICS 327310: Cement Manufacturing

3251 Brick and Structural Clay Tile *see* NAICS 327121: Brick and Structural Clay Tile Manufacturing

3253 Ceramic Wall and Floor Tile *see* NAICS 327122: Ceramic Wall and Floor Tile Manufacturing

3255 Clay Refractories *see* NAICS 327124: Clay Refractory Manufacturing

3259 Structural Clay Products, NEC *see* NAICS 327123: Other Structural Clay Product Manufacturing

3261 Vitreous China Plumbing Fixtures and China and Earthenware Fittings and Bathroom Accessories *see* NAICS 327111: Vitreous China Plumbing Fixture and China and Earthenware Fitting and Bathroom Accessories Manufacturing

3262 Vitreous China Table and Kitchen Articles *see* NAICS 327112: Vitreous China, Fine Earthenware and Other Pottery Product Manufacturing

3263 Fine Earthenware (Whiteware) Table and Kitchen Articles *see* NAICS 327112: Vitreous China, Fine Earthenware and Other Pottery Product Manufacturing

3264 Porcelain Electrical Supplies *see* NAICS 327113: Porcelain Electrical Supply Manufacturing

3269 Pottery Products, NEC *see* NAICS 327112: Vitreous China, Fine Earthenware, and Other Pottery Product Manufacturing

3271 Concrete Block and Brick *see* NAICS 327331: Concrete Block and Brick Manufacturing

3272 Concrete Products, Except Block and Brick *see* NAICS 327999: All Other Miscellaneous Nonmetallic Mineral Product Manufacturing; NAICS 327332: Concrete Pipe Manufacturing; NAICS 327390: Other Concrete Product Manufacturing

3273 Ready-Mixed Concrete *see* NAICS 327320: Ready-Mix Concrete Manufacturing

3274 Lime *see* NAICS 327410: Lime Manufacturing

3275 Gypsum Products *see* NAICS 327420: Gypsum and Gypsum Product Manufacturing

3281 Cut Stone and Stone Products *see* NAICS 327991: Cut Stone and Stone Product Manufacturing

3291 Abrasive Products *see* NAICS 332999: All Other Miscellaneous Fabricated Metal Product Manufacturing; NAICS 327910: Abrasive Product Manufacturing

3292 Asbestos Products *see* NAICS 336340: Motor Vehicle Brake System Manufacturing; NAICS 327999: All Other Miscellaneous Nonmetallic Mineral Product Manufacturing

3295 Minerals and Earths, Ground or Otherwise Treated *see* NAICS 327992: Ground or Treated Mineral and Earth Manufacturing

3296 Mineral Wool *see* NAICS 327993: Mineral Wool Manufacturing

3297 Nonclay Refractories *see* NAICS 327125: Nonclay Refractory Manufacturing

3299 Nonmetallic Mineral Products, NEC *see* NAICS 327420: Gypsum and Gypsum Product Manufacturing; NAICS 327999: All Other Miscellaneous Nonmetallic Mineral Product Manufacturing

PRIMARY METALS INDUSTRIES

3312 Steel Works, Blast Furnaces (Including Coke Ovens), and Rolling Mills *see* NAICS 324199: All Other Petroleum and Coal Products Manufacturing; NAICS 331111: Iron and Steel Mills

3313 Electrometallurgical Products, Except Steel *see* NAICS 331112: Electrometallurgical Ferroalloy Product Manufacturing; NAICS 331492: Secondary Smelting, Refining, and Alloying of Nonferrous Metals (except Copper and Aluminum)

3315 Steel Wiredrawing and Steel Nails and Spikes *see* NAICS 331222: Steel Wire Drawing; NAICS 332618: Other Fabricated Wire Product Manufacturing

3316 Cold-Rolled Steel Sheet, Strip, and Bars *see* NAICS 331221: Cold-Rolled Steel Shape Manufacturing

3317 Steel Pipe and Tubes *see* NAICS 331210: Iron and Steel Pipes and Tubes Manufacturing from Purchased Steel

3321 Gray and Ductile Iron Foundries *see* NAICS 331511: Iron Foundries

3322 Malleable Iron Foundries *see* NAICS 331511: Iron Foundries

3324 Steel Investment Foundries *see* NAICS 331512: Steel Investment Foundries

3325 Steel Foundries, NEC *see* NAICS 331513: Steel Foundries (except Investment)

3331 Primary Smelting and Refining of Copper *see* NAICS 331411: Primary Smelting and Refining of Copper

3334 Primary Production of Aluminum *see* NAICS 331312: Primary Aluminum Production

3339 Primary Smelting and Refining of Nonferrous Metals, Except Copper and Aluminum *see* NAICS 331419: Primary Smelting and Refining of Nonferrous Metals (except Copper and Aluminum)

3341 Secondary Smelting and Refining of Nonferrous Metals *see* NAICS 331314: Secondary Smelting and Alloying of Aluminum; NAICS 331423: Secondary Smelting, Refining, and Alloying of Copper; NAICS 331492: Secondary Smelting, Refining, and Alloying of Nonferrous Metals (except Copper and Aluminum)

3351 Rolling, Drawing, and Extruding of Copper *see* NAICS 331421: Copper (except Wire) Rolling, Drawing, and Extruding

3353 Aluminum Sheet, Plate, and Foil *see* NAICS 331315: Aluminum Sheet, Plate, and Foil Manufacturing

3354 Aluminum Extruded Products *see* NAICS 331316: Aluminum Extruded Product Manufacturing

3355 Aluminum Rolling and Drawing, NEC *see* NAICS 331319: Other Aluminum Rolling and Drawing

3356 Rolling, Drawing, and Extruding of Nonferrous Metals, Except Copper and Aluminum *see* NAICS 331491: Nonferrous Metal (except Copper and Aluminum) Rolling, Drawing, and Extruding

3357 Drawing and Insulating of Nonferrous Wire *see* NAICS 331319: Other Aluminum Rolling and Drawing; NAICS 331422: Copper Wire Drawing; NAICS 331491: Nonferrous Metal (except Copper and Aluminum) Rolling, Drawing, and Extruding; NAICS 335921: Fiber Optic Cable Manufacturing; NAICS 335929: Other Communication and Energy Wire Manufacturing

3363 Aluminum Die-Castings *see* NAICS 331521: Aluminum Die-Castings

3364 Nonferrous Die-Castings, Except Aluminum *see* NAICS 331522: Nonferrous (except Aluminum) Die-Castings

3365 Aluminum Foundries *see* NAICS 331524: Aluminum Foundries

3366 Copper Foundries *see* NAICS 331525: Copper Foundries

3369 Nonferrous Foundries, Except Aluminum and Copper *see* NAICS 331528: Other Nonferrous Foundries

3398 Metal Heat Treating *see* NAICS 332811: Metal Heat Treating

3399 Primary Metal Products, NEC *see* NAICS 331111: Iron and Steel Mills; NAICS 331314: Secondary Smelting and Alloying of Aluminum; NAICS 331423: Secondary Smelting, Refining and Alloying of Copper; NAICS 331492: Secondary Smelting, Refining, and Alloying of Nonferrous Metals (except Copper and Aluminum); NAICS 332618: Other Fabricated Wire Product Manufacturing; NAICS 332813: Electroplating, Plating, Polishing, Anodizing, and Coloring

FABRICATED METAL PRODUCTS, EXCEPT MACHINERY & TRANSPORTATION EQUIPMENT

3411 Metal Cans *see* NAICS 332431: Metal Can Manufacturing

3412 Metal Shipping Barrels, Drums, Kegs and Pails *see* NAICS 332439: Other Metal Container Manufacturing

3421 Cutlery *see* NAICS 332211: Cutlery and Flatware (except Precious) Manufacturing

3423 Hand and Edge Tools, Except Machine Tools and Handsaws *see* NAICS 332212: Hand and Edge Tool Manufacturing

3425 Saw Blades and Handsaws *see* NAICS 332213: Saw Blade and Handsaw Manufacturing

3429 Hardware, NEC *see* NAICS 332439: Other Metal Container Manufacturing; NAICS 332919: Other Metal Valve and Pipe Fitting Manufacturing; NAICS 332510: Hardware Manufacturing

3431 Enameled Iron and Metal Sanitary Ware *see* NAICS 332998: Enameled Iron and Metal Sanitary Ware Manufacturing

3432 Plumbing Fixture Fittings and Trim *see* NAICS 332913: Plumbing Fixture Fitting and Trim Manufacturing; NAICS 332999: All Other Miscellaneous Fabricated Metal Product Manufacturing

3433 Heating Equipment, Except Electric and Warm Air Furnaces *see* NAICS 333414: Heating Equipment (except Electric and Warm Air Furnaces) Manufacturing

3441 Fabricated Structural Metal *see* NAICS 332312: Fabricated Structural Metal Manufacturing

3442 Metal Doors, Sash, Frames, Molding, and Trim Manufacturing *see* NAICS 332321: Metal Window and Door Manufacturing

3443 Fabricated Plate Work (Boiler Shops) *see* NAICS 332313: Plate Work Manufacturing; NAICS 332410: Power Boiler and Heat Exchanger Manufacturing; NAICS 332420: Metal Tank (Heavy Gauge) Manufacturing; NAICS 333415: Air-Conditioning and Warm Air Heating Equipment and Commercial and Industrial Refrigeration Equipment Manufacturing

3444 Sheet Metal Work *see* NAICS 332322: Sheet Metal Work Manufacturing; NAICS 332439: Other Metal Container Manufacturing

3446 Architectural and Ornamental Metal Work *see* NAICS 332323: Ornamental and Architectural Metal Work Manufacturing

3448 Prefabricated Metal Buildings and Components *see* NAICS 332311: Prefabricated Metal Building and Component Manufacturing

3449 Miscellaneous Structural Metal Work *see* NAICS 332114: Custom Roll Forming; NAICS 332312: Fabricated Structural Metal Manufacturing; NAICS 332321: Metal Window and Door Manufacturing; NAICS 332323: Ornamental and Architectural Metal Work Manufacturing

3451 Screw Machine Products *see* NAICS 332721: Precision Turned Product Manufacturing

3452 Bolts, Nuts, Screws, Rivets, and Washers *see* NAICS 332722: Bolt, Nut, Screw, Rivet, and Washer Manufacturing

3462 Iron and Steel Forgings *see* NAICS 332111: Iron and Steel Forging

3463 Nonferrous Forgings *see* NAICS 332112: Nonferrous Forging

3465 Automotive Stamping *see* NAICS 336370: Motor Vehicle Metal Stamping

3466 Crowns and Closures *see* NAICS 332115: Crown and Closure Manufacturing

3469 Metal Stamping, NEC *see* NAICS 339911: Jewelry (including Precious Metal) Manufacturing; NAICS 332116: Metal Stamping; NAICS 332214: Kitchen Utensil, Pot, and Pan Manufacturing

3471 Electroplating, Plating, Polishing, Anodizing, and Coloring *see* NAICS 332813: Electroplating, Plating, Polishing, Anodizing, and Coloring

3479 Coating, Engraving, and Allied Services, NEC *see* NAICS 339914: Costume Jewelry and Novelty Manufacturing; NAICS 339911: Jewelry (including Precious Metal) Manufacturing; NAICS

339912: Silverware and Plated Ware Manufacturing; NAICS 332812: Metal Coating, Engraving, and Allied Services (except Jewelry and Silverware) to Manufacturing

3482   Small Arms Ammunition *see* NAICS 332992: Small Arms Ammunition Manufacturing

3483   Ammunition, Except for Small Arms *see* NAICS 332993: Ammunition (except Small Arms) Manufacturing

3484   Small Arms *see* NAICS 332994: Small Arms Manufacturing

3489   Ordnance and Accessories, NEC *see* NAICS 332995: Other Ordnance and Accessories Manufacturing

3491   Industrial Valves *see* NAICS 332911: Industrial Valve Manufacturing

3492   Fluid Power Valves and Hose Fittings *see* NAICS 332912: Fluid Power Valve and Hose Fitting Manufacturing

3493   Steel Springs, Except Wire *see* NAICS 332611: Steel Spring (except Wire) Manufacturing

3494   Valves and Pipe Fittings, NEC *see* NAICS 332919: Other Metal Valve and Pipe Fitting Manufacturing; NAICS 332999: All Other Miscellaneous Fabricated Metal Product Manufacturing

3495   Wire Springs *see* NAICS 332612: Wire Spring Manufacturing; NAICS 334518: Watch, Clock, and Part Manufacturing

3496   Miscellaneous Fabricated Wire Products *see* NAICS 332618: Other Fabricated Wire Product Manufacturing

3497   Metal Foil and Leaf *see* NAICS 322225: Laminated Aluminum Foil Manufacturing for Flexible Packaging Uses; NAICS 332999: All Other Miscellaneous Fabricated Metal Product Manufacturing

3498   Fabricated Pipe and Pipe Fittings *see* NAICS 332996: Fabricated Pipe and Pipe Fitting Manufacturing

3499   Fabricated Metal Products, NEC *see* NAICS 337215: Showcase, Partition, Shelving, and Locker Manufacturing; NAICS 332117: Powder Metallurgy Part Manufacturing; NAICS 332439: Other Metal Container Manufacturing; NAICS 332510: Hardware Manufacturing; NAICS 332919: Other Metal Valve and Pipe Fitting Manufacturing; NAICS 339914: Costume Jewelry and Novelty Manufacturing; NAICS 332999: All Other Miscellaneous Fabricated Metal Product Manufacturing

INDUSTRIAL & COMMERCIAL MACHINERY & COMPUTER EQUIPMENT

3511   Steam, Gas, and Hydraulic Turbines, and Turbine Generator Set Units *see* NAICS 333611: Turbine and Turbine Generator Set Unit Manufacturing

3519   Internal Combustion Engines, NEC *see* NAICS 336399: All Other Motor Vehicle Parts Manufacturing; NAICS 333618: Other Engine Equipment Manufacturing

3523   Farm Machinery and Equipment *see* NAICS 333111: Farm Machinery and Equipment Manufacturing; NAICS 332323: Ornamental and Architectural Metal Work Manufacturing; NAICS 332212: Hand and Edge Tool Manufacturing; NAICS 333922: Conveyor and Conveying Equipment Manufacturing

3524   Lawn and Garden Tractors and Home Lawn and Garden Equipment *see* NAICS 333112: Lawn and Garden Tractor and Home Lawn and Garden Equipment Manufacturing; NAICS 332212: Hand and Edge Tool Manufacturing

3531   Construction Machinery and Equipment *see* NAICS 336510: Railroad Rolling Stock Manufacturing; NAICS 333923: Overhead Traveling Crane, Hoist, and Monorail System Manufacturing; NAICS 333120: Construction Machinery Manufacturing

3532   Mining Machinery and Equipment, Except Oil and Gas Field Machinery and Equipment *see* NAICS 333131: Mining Machinery and Equipment Manufacturing

3533   Oil and Gas Field Machinery and Equipment *see* NAICS 333132: Oil and Gas Field Machinery and Equipment Manufacturing

3534   Elevators and Moving Stairways *see* NAICS 333921: Elevator and Moving Stairway Manufacturing

3535   Conveyors and Conveying Equipment *see* NAICS 333922: Conveyor and Conveying Equipment Manufacturing

3536   Overhead Traveling Cranes, Hoists, and Monorail Systems *see* NAICS 333923: Overhead Traveling Crane, Hoist, and Monorail System Manufacturing

3537   Industrial Trucks, Tractors, Trailers, and Stackers *see* NAICS 333924: Industrial Truck, Tractor, Trailer, and Stacker Machinery Manufacturing; NAICS 332999: All Other Miscellaneous Fabricated Metal Product Manufacturing; NAICS 332439: Other Metal Container Manufacturing

3541   Machine Tools, Metal Cutting Type *see* NAICS 333512: Machine Tool (Metal Cutting Types) Manufacturing

3542   Machine Tools, Metal Forming Type *see* NAICS 333513: Machine Tool (Metal Forming Types) Manufacturing

3543 Industrial Patterns *see* NAICS 332997: Industrial Pattern Manufacturing

3544 Special Dies and Tools, Die Sets, Jigs and Fixtures, and Industrial Molds *see* NAICS 333514: Special Die and Tool, Die Set, Jig, and Fixture Manufacturing; NAICS 333511: Industrial Mold Manufacturing

3545 Cutting Tools, Machine Tool Accessories, and Machinists' Precision Measuring Devices *see* NAICS 333515: Cutting Tool and Machine Tool Accessory Manufacturing; NAICS 332212: Hand and Edge Tool Manufacturing

3546 Power-Driven Handtools *see* NAICS 333991: Power-Driven Hand Tool Manufacturing

3547 Rolling Mill Machinery and Equipment *see* NAICS 333516: Rolling Mill Machinery and Equipment Manufacturing

3548 Electric and Gas Welding and Soldering Equipment *see* NAICS 333992: Welding and Soldering Equipment Manufacturing; NAICS 335311: Power, Distribution, and Specialty Transformer Manufacturing

3549 Metalworking Machinery, NEC *see* NAICS 333518: Other Metalworking Machinery Manufacturing

3552 Textile Machinery *see* NAICS 333292: Textile Machinery Manufacturing

3553 Woodworking Machinery *see* NAICS 333210: Sawmill and Woodworking Machinery Manufacturing

3554 Paper Industries Machinery *see* NAICS 333291: Paper Industry Machinery Manufacturing

3555 Printing Trades Machinery and Equipment *see* NAICS 333293: Printing Machinery and Equipment Manufacturing

3556 Food Products Machinery *see* NAICS 333294: Food Product Machinery Manufacturing

3559 Special Industry Machinery, NEC *see* NAICS 333220: Rubber and Plastics Industry Machinery Manufacturing; NAICS 333319: Other Commercial and Service Industry Machinery Manufacturing; NAICS 333295: Semiconductor Manufacturing Machinery; NAICS 333298: All Other Industrial Machinery Manufacturing

3561 Pumps and Pumping Equipment *see* NAICS 333911: Pump and Pumping Equipment Manufacturing

3562 Ball and Roller Bearings *see* NAICS 332991: Ball and Roller Bearing Manufacturing

3563 Air and Gas Compressors *see* NAICS 333912: Air and Gas Compressor Manufacturing

3564 Industrial and Commercial Fans and Blowers and Air Purification Equipment *see* NAICS 333411: Air Purification Equipment Manufacturing; NAICS

333412: Industrial and Commercial Fan and Blower Manufacturing

3565 Packaging Machinery *see* NAICS 333993: Packaging Machinery Manufacturing

3566 Speed Changers, Industrial High-Speed Drives, and Gears *see* NAICS 333612: Speed Changer, Industrial High-Speed Drive, and Gear Manufacturing

3567 Industrial Process Furnaces and Ovens *see* NAICS 333994: Industrial Process Furnace and Oven Manufacturing

3568 Mechanical Power Transmission Equipment, NEC *see* NAICS 333613: Mechanical Power Transmission Equipment Manufacturing

3569 General Industrial Machinery and Equipment, NEC *see* NAICS 333999: All Other General Purpose Machinery Manufacturing

3571 Electronic Computers *see* NAICS 334111: Electronic Computer Manufacturing

3572 Computer Storage Devices *see* NAICS 334112: Computer Storage Device Manufacturing

3575 Computer Terminals *see* NAICS 334113: Computer Terminal Manufacturing

3577 Computer Peripheral Equipment, NEC *see* NAICS 334119: Other Computer Peripheral Equipment Manufacturing

3578 Calculating and Accounting Machines, Except Electronic Computers *see* NAICS 334119: Other Computer Peripheral Equipment Manufacturing; NAICS 333313: Office Machinery Manufacturing

3579 Office Machines, NEC *see* NAICS 339942: Lead Pencil and Art Good Manufacturing; NAICS 334518: Watch, Clock, and Part Manufacturing; NAICS 333313: Office Machinery Manufacturing

3581 Automatic Vending Machines *see* NAICS 333311: Automatic Vending Machine Manufacturing

3582 Commercial Laundry, Drycleaning, and Pressing Machines *see* NAICS 333312: Commercial Laundry, Drycleaning, and Pressing Machine Manufacturing

3585 Air-Conditioning and Warm Air Heating Equipment and Commercial and Industrial Refrigeration Equipment *see* NAICS 336391: Motor Vehicle Air Conditioning Manufacturing; NAICS 333415: Air Conditioning and Warm Air Heating Equipment and Commercial and Industrial Refrigeration Equipment Manufacturing

3586 Measuring and Dispensing Pumps *see* NAICS 333913: Measuring and Dispensing Pump Manufacturing

3589 Service Industry Machinery, NEC *see* NAICS 333319: Other Commercial and Service Industry Machinery Manufacturing

3592 Carburetors, Pistons, Piston Rings and Valves *see* NAICS 336311: Carburetor, Piston, Piston Ring and Valve Manufacturing

3593 Fluid Power Cylinders and Actuators *see* NAICS 333995: Fluid Power Cylinder and Actuator Manufacturing

3594 Fluid Power Pumps and Motors *see* NAICS 333996: Fluid Power Pump and Motor Manufacturing

3596 Scales and Balances, Except Laboratory *see* NAICS 333997: Scale and Balance (except Laboratory) Manufacturing

3599 Industrial and Commercial Machinery and Equipment, NEC *see* NAICS 336399: All Other Motor Vehicle Part Manufacturing; NAICS 332999: All Other Miscellaneous Fabricated Metal Product Manufacturing; NAICS 333319: Other Commercial and Service Industry Machinery Manufacturing; NAICS 332710: Machine Shops; NAICS 333999: All Other General Purpose Machinery Manufacturing

ELECTRONIC & OTHER ELECTRICAL EQUIPMENT & COMPONENTS, EXCEPT COMPUTER EQUIPMENT

3612 Power, Distribution, and Specialty Transformers *see* NAICS 335311: Power, Distribution, and Specialty Transformer Manufacturing

3613 Switchgear and Switchboard Apparatus *see* NAICS 335313: Switchgear and Switchboard Apparatus Manufacturing

3621 Motors and Generators *see* NAICS 335312: Motor and Generator Manufacturing

3624 Carbon and Graphite Products *see* NAICS 335991: Carbon and Graphite Product Manufacturing

3625 Relays and Industrial Controls *see* NAICS 335314: Relay and Industrial Control Manufacturing

3629 Electrical Industrial Apparatus, NEC *see* NAICS 335999: All Other Miscellaneous Electrical Equipment and Component Manufacturing

3631 Household Cooking Equipment *see* NAICS 335221: Household Cooking Appliance Manufacturing

3632 Household Refrigerators and Home and Farm Freezers *see* NAICS 335222: Household Refrigerator and Home and Farm Freezer Manufacturing

3633 Household Laundry Equipment *see* NAICS 335224: Household Laundry Equipment Manufacturing

3634 Electric Housewares and Fans *see* NAICS 335211: Electric Houseware and Fan Manufacturing; NAICS 333414: Heating Equipment (except Electric and Warm Air Furnaces) Manufacturing

3635 Household Vacuum Cleaners *see* NAICS 335212: Household Vacuum Cleaner Manufacturing

3639 Household Appliances, NEC *see* NAICS 335212: Household Vacuum Cleaner Manufacturing; NAICS 333298: All Other Industrial Machinery Manufacturing; NAICS 335228: Other Household Appliance Manufacturing

3641 Electric Lamp Bulbs and Tubes *see* NAICS 335110: Electric Lamp Bulb and Part Manufacturing

3643 Current-Carrying Wiring Devices *see* NAICS 335931: Current-Carrying Wiring Device Manufacturing

3644 Noncurrent-Carrying Wiring Devices *see* NAICS 335932: Noncurrent-Carrying Wiring Device Manufacturing

3645 Residential Electric Lighting Fixtures *see* NAICS 335121: Residential Electric Lighting Fixture Manufacturing

3646 Commercial, Industrial, and Institutional Electric Lighting Fixtures *see* NAICS 335122: Commercial, Industrial, and Institutional Electric Lighting Fixture Manufacturing

3647 Vehicular Lighting Equipment *see* NAICS 336321: Vehicular Lighting Equipment Manufacturing

3648 Lighting Equipment, NEC *see* NAICS 335129: Other Lighting Equipment Manufacturing

3651 Household Audio and Video Equipment *see* NAICS 334310: Audio and Video Equipment Manufacturing

3652 Phonograph Records and Prerecorded Audio Tapes and Disks *see* NAICS 334612: Prerecorded Compact Disc (Except Software), Tape and Record Reproducing; NAICS 512220: Integrated Record Production/Distribution

3661 Telephone and Telegraph Apparatus *see* NAICS 334210: Telephone Apparatus Manufacturing; NAICS 334416: Electronic Coil, Transformer, and Other Inductor Manufacturing; NAICS 334418: Printed Circuit/Electronics Assembly Manufacturing

3663 Radio and Television Broadcasting and Communication Equipment *see* NAICS 334220: Radio and Television Broadcasting and Wireless Communications Equipment Manufacturing

3669 Communications Equipment, NEC *see* NAICS 334290: Other Communication Equipment Manufacturing

3671 Electron Tubes *see* NAICS 334411: Electron Tube Manufacturing

3672 Printed Circuit Boards *see* NAICS 334412: Printed Circuit Board Manufacturing

3674 Semiconductors and Related Devices *see* NAICS 334413: Semiconductor and Related Device Manufacturing

3675 Electronic Capacitors *see* NAICS 334414: Electronic Capacitor Manufacturing

3676 Electronic Resistors *see* NAICS 334415: Electronic Resistor Manufacturing

3677 Electronic Coils, Transformers, and Other Inductors *see* NAICS 334416: Electronic Coil, Transformer, and Other Inductor Manufacturing

3678 Electronic Connectors *see* NAICS 334417: Electronic Connector Manufacturing

3679 Electronic Components, NEC *see* NAICS 334220: Radio and Television Broadcasting and Wireless Communications Equipment Manufacturing; NAICS 334418: Printed Circuit/Electronics Assembly Manufacturing; NAICS 336322: Other Motor Vehicle Electrical and Electronic Equipment Manufacturing; NAICS 334419: Other Electronic Component Manufacturing

3691 Storage Batteries *see* NAICS 335911: Storage Battery Manufacturing

3692 Primary Batteries, Dry and Wet *see* NAICS 335912: Dry and Wet Primary Battery Manufacturing

3694 Electrical Equipment for Internal Combustion Engines *see* NAICS 336322: Other Motor Vehicle Electrical and Electronic Equipment Manufacturing

3695 Magnetic and Optical Recording Media *see* NAICS 334613: Magnetic and Optical Recording Media Manufacturing

3699 Electrical Machinery, Equipment, and Supplies, NEC *see* NAICS 333319: Other Commercial and Service Industry Machinery Manufacturing; NAICS 333618: Other Engine Equipment Manufacturing; NAICS 334119: Other Computer Peripheral Equipment Manufacturing; NAICS 335129: Other Lighting Equipment Manufacturing; NAICS 335999: All Other Miscellaneous Electrical Equipment and Component Manufacturing

TRANSPORTATION EQUIPMENT

3711 Motor Vehicles and Passenger Car Bodies *see* NAICS 336111: Automobile Manufacturing; NAICS 336112: Light Truck and Utility Vehicle Manufacturing; NAICS 336120: Heavy Duty Truck Manufacturing; NAICS 336211: Motor Vehicle Body Manufacturing; NAICS 336992: Military Armored Vehicle, Tank, and Tank Component Manufacturing

3713 Truck and Bus Bodies *see* NAICS 336211: Motor Vehicle Body Manufacturing

3714 Motor Vehicle Parts and Accessories *see* NAICS 336211: Motor Vehicle Body Manufacturing; NAICS 336312: Gasoline Engine and Engine Parts Manufacturing; NAICS 336322: Other Motor Vehicle Electrical and Electronic Equipment Manufacturing; NAICS 336330: Motor Vehicle Steering and Suspension Components (except Spring) Manufacturing; NAICS 336340: Motor Vehicle Brake System Manufacturing; NAICS 336350: Motor Vehicle Transmission and Power Train Part Manufacturing; NAICS 336399: All Other Motor Vehicle Parts Manufacturing

3715 Truck Trailers *see* NAICS 336212: Truck Trailer Manufacturing

3716 Motor Homes *see* NAICS 336213: Motor Home Manufacturing

3721 Aircraft *see* NAICS 336411: Aircraft Manufacturing

3724 Aircraft Engines and Engine Parts *see* NAICS 336412: Aircraft Engine and Engine Parts Manufacturing

3728 Aircraft Parts and Auxiliary Equipment, NEC *see* NAICS 332912: Fluid Power Valve and Hose Fitting Manufacturing; NAICS 336413: Other Aircraft Part and Auxiliary Equipment Manufacturing

3731 Ship Building and Repairing *see* NAICS 336611: Ship Building and Repairing

3732 Boat Building and Repairing *see* NAICS 811490: Other Personal and Household Goods Repair and Maintenance; NAICS 336612: Boat Building

3743 Railroad Equipment *see* NAICS 333911: Pump and Pumping Equipment Manufacturing; NAICS 336510: Railroad Rolling Stock Manufacturing

3751 Motorcycles, Bicycles, and Parts *see* NAICS 336991: Motorcycle, Bicycle, and Parts Manufacturing

3761 Guided Missiles and Space Vehicles *see* NAICS 336414: Guided Missile and Space Vehicle Manufacturing

3764 Guided Missile and Space Vehicle Propulsion Units and Propulsion Unit Parts *see* NAICS 336415: Guided Missile and Space Vehicle Propulsion Unit and Propulsion Unit Parts Manufacturing

3769 Guided Missile Space Vehicle Parts and Auxiliary Equipment, NEC *see* NAICS 336419: Other Guided Missile and Space Vehicle Parts and Auxiliary Equipment Manufacturing

3792 Travel Trailers and Campers *see* NAICS 336214: Travel Trailer and Camper Manufacturing

3795 Tanks and Tank Components *see* NAICS 336992: Military Armored Vehicle, Tank, and Tank Component Manufacturing

3799 Transportation Equipment, NEC *see* NAICS 336214: Travel Trailer and Camper Manufacturing; NAICS 332212: Hand and Edge Tool Manufacturing; NAICS 336999: All Other Transportation Equipment Manufacturing

MEASURING, ANALYZING, & CONTROLLING INSTRUMENTS

3812   Search, Detection, Navigation, Guidance, Aeronautical, and Nautical Systems and Instruments *see* NAICS 334511: Search, Detection, Navigation, Guidance, Aeronautical, and Nautical System and Instrument Manufacturing

3821   Laboratory Apparatus and Furniture *see* NAICS 339111: Laboratory Apparatus and Furniture Manufacturing

3822   Automatic Controls for Regulating Residential and Commercial Environments and Appliances *see* NAICS 334512: Automatic Environmental Control Manufacturing for Regulating Residential, Commercial, and Appliance Use

3823   Industrial Instruments for Measurement, Display, and Control of Process Variables; and Related Products *see* NAICS 334513: Instruments and Related Product Manufacturing for Measuring Displaying, and Controlling Industrial Process Variables

3824   Totalizing Fluid Meters and Counting Devices *see* NAICS 334514: Totalizing Fluid Meter and Counting Device Manufacturing

3825   Instruments for Measuring and Testing of Electricity and Electrical Signals *see* NAICS 334416: Electronic Coil, Transformer, and Other Inductor Manufacturing; NAICS 334515: Instrument Manufacturing for Measuring and Testing Electricity and Electrical Signals

3826   Laboratory Analytical Instruments *see* NAICS 334516: Analytical Laboratory Instrument Manufacturing

3827   Optical Instruments and Lenses *see* NAICS 333314: Optical Instrument and Lens Manufacturing

3829   Measuring and Controlling Devices, NEC *see* NAICS 339112: Surgical and Medical Instrument Manufacturing; NAICS 334519: Other Measuring and Controlling Device Manufacturing

3841   Surgical and Medical Instruments and Apparatus *see* NAICS 339112: Surgical and Medical Instrument Manufacturing

3842   Orthopedic, Prosthetic, and Surgical Appliances and Supplies *see* NAICS 339113: Surgical Appliance and Supplies Manufacturing; NAICS 334510: Electromedical and Electrotherapeutic Apparatus Manufacturing

3843   Dental Equipment and Supplies *see* NAICS 339114: Dental Equipment and Supplies Manufacturing

3844   X-Ray Apparatus and Tubes and Related Irradiation Apparatus *see* NAICS 334517: Irradiation Apparatus Manufacturing

3845   Electromedical and Electrotherapeutic Apparatus *see* NAICS 334517: Irradiation Apparatus Manufacturing; NAICS 334510: Electromedical and Electrotherapeutic Apparatus Manufacturing

3851   Ophthalmic Goods *see* NAICS 339115: Ophthalmic Goods Manufacturing

3861   Photographic Equipment and Supplies *see* NAICS 333315: Photographic and Photocopying Equipment Manufacturing; NAICS 325992: Photographic Film, Paper, Plate and Chemical Manufacturing

3873   Watches, Clocks, Clockwork Operated Devices and Parts *see* NAICS 334518: Watch, Clock, and Part Manufacturing

MISCELLANEOUS MANUFACTURING INDUSTRIES

3911   Jewelry, Precious Metal *see* NAICS 339911: Jewelry (Including Precious Metal) Manufacturing

3914   Silverware, Plated Ware, and Stainless Steel Ware *see* NAICS 332211: Cutlery and Flatware (except Precious) Manufacturing; NAICS 339912: Silverware and Plated Ware Manufacturing

3915   Jewelers' Findings and Materials, and Lapidary Work *see* NAICS 339913: Jewelers' Material and Lapidary Work Manufacturing

3931   Musical Instruments *see* NAICS 339992: Musical Instrument Manufacturing

3942   Dolls and Stuffed Toys *see* NAICS 339931: Doll and Stuffed Toy Manufacturing

3944   Games, Toys, and Children's Vehicles, Except Dolls and Bicycles *see* NAICS 336991: Motorcycle, Bicycle, and Parts Manufacturing; NAICS 339932: Game, Toy, and Children's Vehicle Manufacturing

3949   Sporting and Athletic Goods, NEC *see* NAICS 339920: Sporting and Athletic Good Manufacturing

3951   Pens, Mechanical Pencils, and Parts *see* NAICS 339941: Pen and Mechanical Pencil Manufacturing

3952   Lead Pencils, Crayons, and Artist's Materials *see* NAICS 337127: Institutional Furniture Manufacturing; NAICS 325998: All Other Miscellaneous Chemical Product Manufacturing; NAICS 339942: Lead Pencil and Art Good Manufacturing

3953   Marking Devices *see* NAICS 339943: Marking Device Manufacturing

3955   Carbon Paper and Inked Ribbons *see* NAICS 339944: Carbon Paper and Inked Ribbon Manufacturing

3961   Costume Jewelry and Costume Novelties, Except Precious Metals *see* NAICS 339914: Costume Jewelry and Novelty Manufacturing

3965 Fasteners, Buttons, Needles, and Pins *see* NAICS 339993: Fastener, Button, Needle and Pin Manufacturing

3991 Brooms and Brushes *see* NAICS 339994: Broom, Brush and Mop Manufacturing

3993 Signs and Advertising Specialties *see* NAICS 339950: Sign Manufacturing

3995 Burial Caskets *see* NAICS 339995: Burial Casket Manufacturing

3996 Linoleum, Asphalted-Felt-Base, and Other Hard Surface Floor Coverings, NEC *see* NAICS 326192: Resilient Floor Covering Manufacturing

3999 Manufacturing Industries, NEC *see* NAICS 337127: Institutional Furniture Manufacturing; NAICS 321999: All Other Miscellaneous Wood Product Manufacturing; NAICS 316110: Leather and Hide Tanning and Finishing; NAICS 335121: Residential Electric Lighting Fixture Manufacturing; NAICS 325998: All Other Miscellaneous Chemical Product Manufacturing; NAICS 332999: All Other Miscellaneous Fabricated Metal Product Manufacturing; NAICS 326199: All Other Plastics Product Manufacturing; NAICS 323112: Commercial Flexographic Printing; NAICS 323111: Commercial Gravure Printing; NAICS 323110: Commercial Lithographic Printing; NAICS 323113: Commercial Screen Printing; NAICS 323119: Other Commercial Printing; NAICS 332212: Hand and Edge Tool Manufacturing; NAICS 339999: All Other Miscellaneous Manufacturing

TRANSPORTATION, COMMUNICATIONS, ELECTRIC, GAS, & SANITARY SERVICES

4011 Railroads, Line-haul Operating *see* NAICS 482111: Line-Haul Railroads

4013 Railroad Switching and Terminal Establishments *see* NAICS 482112: Short Line Railroads; NAICS 488210: Support Activities for Rail Transportation

4111 Local and Suburban Transit *see* NAICS 485111: Mixed Mode Transit Systems; NAICS 485112: Commuter Rail Systems; NAICS 485113: Bus and Motor Vehicle Transit Systems; NAICS 485119: Other Urban Transit Systems; NAICS 485999: All Other Transit and Ground Passenger Transportation

4119 Local Passenger Transportation, NEC *see* NAICS 621910: Ambulance Service; NAICS 485410: School and Employee Bus Industry; NAICS 487110: Scenic and Sightseeing Transportation; NAICS 485991: Special Needs Transportation; NAICS 485999: All Other Transit and Ground

Passenger Transportation; NAICS 485320: Limousine Service

4121 Taxicabs *see* NAICS 485310: Taxi Service

4131 Intercity and Rural Bus Transportation *see* NAICS 485210: Interurban and Rural Bus Lines

4141 Local Bus Charter Service *see* NAICS 485510: Charter Bus Industry

4142 Bus Charter Service, Except Local *see* NAICS 485510: Charter Bus Industry

4151 School Buses *see* NAICS 485410: School and Employee Bus Industry

4173 Terminal and Service Facilities for Motor Vehicle Passenger Transportation *see* NAICS 488490: Other Support Activities for Road Transportation

4212 Local Trucking Without Storage *see* NAICS 562111: Solid Waste Collection; NAICS 562112: Hazardous Waste Collection; NAICS 562119: Other Waste Collection; NAICS 484110: General Freight Trucking, Local; NAICS 484210: Used Household and Office Goods Moving; NAICS 484220: Specialized Freight (except Used Goods) Trucking, Local

4213 Trucking, Except Local *see* NAICS 484121: General Freight Trucking, Long-Distance, Truckload; NAICS 484122: General Freight Trucking, Long-Distance, Less Than Truckload; NAICS 484210: Used Household and Office Goods Moving; NAICS 484230: Specialized Freight (except Used Goods) Trucking, Long-Distance

4214 Local Trucking with Storage *see* NAICS 484110: General Freight Trucking, Local; NAICS 484210: Used Household and Office Goods Moving; NAICS 484220: Specialized Freight (except Used Goods) Trucking, Local

4215 Couriers Services Except by Air *see* NAICS 492110: Couriers; NAICS 492210: Local Messengers and Local Delivery

4221 Farm Product Warehousing and Storage *see* NAICS 493130: Farm Product Storage Facilities

4222 Refrigerated Warehousing and Storage *see* NAICS 493120: Refrigerated Storage Facilities

4225 General Warehousing and Storage *see* NAICS 493110: General Warehousing and Storage Facilities; NAICS 531130: Lessors of Mini-warehouses and Self Storage Units

4226 Special Warehousing and Storage, NEC *see* NAICS 493120: Refrigerated Storage Facilities; NAICS 493110: General Warehousing and Storage Facilities; NAICS 493190: All Other Warehousing and Storage Facilities

4231 Terminal and Joint Terminal Maintenance Facilities for Motor Freight Transportation *see* NAICS 488490: Other Support Activities for Road Transportation

4311 United States Postal Service *see* NAICS 491110: Postal Service

4412 Deep Sea Foreign Transportation of Freight *see* NAICS 483111: Deep Sea Freight Transportation

4424 Deep Sea Domestic Transportation of Freight *see* NAICS 483113: Coastal and Great Lakes Freight Transportation

4432 Freight Transportation on the Great Lakes-St. Lawrence Seaway *see* NAICS 483113: Coastal and Great Lakes Freight Transportation

4449 Water Transportation of Freight, NEC *see* NAICS 483211: Inland Water Freight Transportation

4481 Deep Sea Transportation of Passengers, Except by Ferry *see* NAICS 483112: Deep Sea Passenger Transportation; NAICS 483114: Coastal and Great Lakes Passenger Transportation

4482 Ferries *see* NAICS 483114: Coastal and Great Lakes Passenger Transportation; NAICS 483212: Inland Water Passenger Transportation

4489 Water Transportation of Passengers, NEC *see* NAICS 483212: Inland Water Passenger Transportation; NAICS 487210: Scenic and Sightseeing Transportation, Water

4491 Marine Cargo Handling *see* NAICS 488310: Port and Harbor Operations; NAICS 488320: Marine Cargo Handling

4492 Towing and Tugboat Services *see* NAICS 483113: Coastal and Great Lakes Freight Transportation; NAICS 483211: Inland Water Freight Transportation; NAICS 488330: Navigational Services to Shipping

4493 Marinas *see* NAICS 713930: Marinas

4499 Water Transportation Services, NEC *see* NAICS 532411: Commercial Air, Rail, and Water Transportation Equipment Rental and Leasing; NAICS 488310: Port and Harbor Operations; NAICS 488330: Navigational Services to Shipping; NAICS 488390: Other Support Activities for Water Transportation

4512 Air Transportation, Scheduled *see* NAICS 481111: Scheduled Passenger Air Transportation; NAICS 481112: Scheduled Freight Air Transportation

4513 Air Courier Services *see* NAICS 492110: Couriers

4522 Air Transportation, Nonscheduled *see* NAICS 621910: Ambulance Services; NAICS 481212: Nonscheduled Chartered Freight Air Transportation; NAICS 481211: Nonscheduled Chartered Passenger Air Transportation; NAICS 487990: Scenic and Sightseeing Transportation

4581 Airports, Flying Fields, and Airport Terminal Services *see* NAICS 488111: Air Traffic Control; NAICS 488119: Other Airport Operations; NAICS 561720: Janitorial Services; NAICS

488190: Other Support Activities for Air Transportation

4612 Crude Petroleum Pipelines *see* NAICS 486110: Pipeline Transportation of Crude Oil

4613 Refined Petroleum Pipelines *see* NAICS 486910: Pipeline Transportation of Refined Petroleum Products

4619 Pipelines, NEC *see* NAICS 486990: All Other Pipeline Transportation

4724 Travel Agencies *see* NAICS 561510: Travel Agencies

4725 Tour Operators *see* NAICS 561520: Tour Operators

4729 Arrangement of Passenger Transportation, NEC *see* NAICS 488999: All Other Support Activities for Transportation; NAICS 561599: All Other Travel Arrangement and Reservation Services

4731 Arrangement of Transportation of Freight and Cargo *see* NAICS 541618: Other Management Consulting Services; NAICS 488510: Freight Transportation Arrangement

4741 Rental of Railroad Cars *see* NAICS 532411: Commercial Air, Rail, and Water Transportation Equipment Rental and Leasing; NAICS 488210: Support Activities for Rail Transportation

4783 Packing and Crating *see* NAICS 488991: Packing and Crating

4785 Fixed Facilities and Inspection and Weighing Services for Motor Vehicle Transportation *see* NAICS 488390: Other Support Activities for Water Transportation; NAICS 488490: Other Support Activities for Road Transportation

4789 Transportation Services, NEC *see* NAICS 488999: All Other Support Activities for Transportation *see* NAICS 487110: Scenic and Sightseeing Transportation, Land; NAICS 488210: Support Activities for Rail Transportation

4812 Radiotelephone Communications *see* NAICS 513321: Paging; NAICS 513322: Cellular and Other Wireless Telecommunications; NAICS 513330: Telecommunications Resellers

4813 Telephone Communications, Except Radiotelephone *see* NAICS 513310: Wired Telecommunications Carriers; NAICS 513330: Telecommunications Resellers

4822 Telegraph and Other Message Communications *see* NAICS 513310: Wired Telecommunications Carriers

4832 Radio Broadcasting Stations *see* NAICS 513111: Radio Networks; NAICS 513112: Radio Stations

4833 Television Broadcasting Stations *see* NAICS 513120: Television Broadcasting

4841 Cable and Other Pay Television Services *see* NAICS 513210: Cable Networks; NAICS 513220: Cable and Other Program Distribution

4899 Communications Services, NEC *see* NAICS 513322: Cellular and Other Wireless Telecommunications; NAICS 513340: Satellite Telecommunications; NAICS 513390: Other Telecommunications

4911 Electric Services *see* NAICS 221111: Hydroelectric Power Generation; NAICS 221112: Fossil Fuel Electric Power Generation; NAICS 221113: Nuclear Electric Power Generation; NAICS 221119: Other Electric Power Generation; NAICS 221121: Electric Bulk Power Transmission and Control; NAICS 221122: Electric Power Distribution

4922 Natural Gas Transmission *see* NAICS 486210: Pipeline Transportation of Natural Gas

4923 Natural Gas Transmission and Distribution *see* NAICS 221210: Natural Gas Distribution; NAICS 486210: Pipeline Transportation of Natural Gas

4924 Natural Gas Distribution *see* NAICS 221210: Natural Gas Distribution

4925 Mixed, Manufactured, or Liquefied Petroleum Gas Production and/or Distribution *see* NAICS 221210: Natural Gas Distribution

4931 Electric and Other Services Combined *see* NAICS 221111: Hydroelectric Power Generation; NAICS 221112: Fossil Fuel Electric Power Generation; NAICS 221113: Nuclear Electric Power Generation; NAICS 221119: Other Electric Power Generation; NAICS 221121: Electric Bulk Power Transmission and Control; NAICS 221122: Electric Power Distribution; NAICS 221210: Natural Gas Distribution

4932 Gas and Other Services Combined *see* NAICS 221210: Natural Gas Distribution

4939 Combination Utilities, NEC *see* NAICS 221111: Hydroelectric Power Generation; NAICS 221112: Fossil Fuel Electric Power Generation; NAICS 221113: Nuclear Electric Power Generation; NAICS 221119: Other Electric Power Generation; NAICS 221121: Electric Bulk Power Transmission and Control; NAICS 221122: Electric Power Distribution; NAICS 221210: Natural Gas Distribution

4941 Water Supply *see* NAICS 221310: Water Supply and Irrigation Systems

4952 Sewerage Systems *see* NAICS 221320: Sewage Treatment Facilities

4953 Refuse Systems *see* NAICS 562111: Solid Waste Collection; NAICS 562112: Hazardous Waste Collection; NAICS 562920: Materials Recovery Facilities; NAICS 562119: Other Waste Collection; NAICS 562211: Hazardous Waste Treatment and Disposal; NAICS 562212: Solid Waste Landfills; NAICS 562213: Solid Waste Combustors and

Incinerators; NAICS 562219: Other Nonhazardous Waste Treatment and Disposal

4959 Sanitary Services, NEC *see* NAICS 488119: Other Airport Operations; NAICS 562910: Remediation Services; NAICS 561710: Exterminating and Pest Control Services; NAICS 562998: All Other Miscellaneous Waste Management

4961 Steam and Air-Conditioning Supply *see* NAICS 221330: Steam and Air-Conditioning Supply

4971 Irrigation Systems *see* NAICS 221310: Water Supply and Irrigation Systems

WHOLESALE TRADE

5012 Automobiles and Other Motor Vehicles *see* NAICS 421110: Automobile and Other Motor Vehicle Wholesalers

5013 Motor Vehicle Supplies and New Parts *see* NAICS 441310: Automotive Parts and Accessories Stores; NAICS 421120: Motor Vehicle Supplies and New Part Wholesalers

5014 Tires and Tubes *see* NAICS 441320: Tire Dealers; NAICS 421130: Tire and Tube Wholesalers

5015 Motor Vehicle Parts, Used *see* NAICS 421140: Motor Vehicle Part (Used) Wholesalers

5021 Furniture *see* NAICS 442110: Furniture Stores; NAICS 421210: Furniture Wholesalers

5023 Home Furnishings *see* NAICS 442210: Floor Covering Stores; NAICS 421220: Home Furnishing Wholesalers

5031 Lumber, Plywood, Millwork, and Wood Panels *see* NAICS 444190: Other Building Material Dealers; NAICS 421310: Lumber, Plywood, Millwork, and Wood Panel Wholesalers

5032 Brick, Stone and Related Construction Materials *see* NAICS 444190: Other Building Material Dealers; NAICS 421320: Brick, Stone and Related Construction Material Wholesalers

5033 Roofing, Siding, and Insulation Materials *see* NAICS 421330: Roofing, Siding, and Insulation Material Wholesalers

5039 Construction Materials, NEC *see* NAICS 444190: Other Building Material Dealers; NAICS 421390: Other Construction Material Wholesalers

5043 Photographic Equipment and Supplies *see* NAICS 421410: Photographic Equipment and Supplies Wholesalers

5044 Office Equipment *see* NAICS 421420: Office Equipment Wholesalers

5045 Computers and Computer Peripheral Equipment and Software *see* NAICS 421430: Computer and Computer Peripheral Equipment and Software Wholesalers; NAICS 443120: Computer and Software Stores

5046 Commercial Equipment, NEC *see* NAICS 421440: Other Commercial Equipment Wholesalers

5047 Medical, Dental, and Hospital Equipment and Supplies *see* NAICS 421450: Medical, Dental and Hospital Equipment and Supplies Wholesalers; NAICS 446199: All Other Health and Personal Care Stores

5048 Ophthalmic Goods *see* NAICS 421460: Ophthalmic Goods Wholesalers

5049 Professional Equipment and Supplies, NEC *see* NAICS 421490: Other Professional Equipment and Supplies Wholesalers; NAICS 453210: Office Supplies and Stationery Stores

5051 Metals Service Centers and Offices *see* NAICS 421510: Metals Service Centers and Offices

5052 Coal and Other Minerals and Ores *see* NAICS 421520: Coal and Other Mineral and Ore Wholesalers

5063 Electrical Apparatus and Equipment Wiring Supplies, and Construction Materials *see* NAICS 444190: Other Building Material Dealers; NAICS 421610: Electrical Apparatus and Equipment, Wiring Supplies and Construction Material Wholesalers

5064 Electrical Appliances, Television and Radio Sets *see* NAICS 421620: Electrical Appliance, Television and Radio Set Wholesalers

5065 Electronic Parts and Equipment, Not Elsewhere Classified *see* NAICS 421690: Other Electronic Parts and Equipment Wholesalers

5072 Hardware *see* NAICS 421710: Hardware Wholesalers

5074 Plumbing and Heating Equipment and Supplies (Hydronics) *see* NAICS 444190: Other Building Material Dealers; NAICS 421720: Plumbing and Heating Equipment and Supplies (Hydronics) Wholesalers

5075 Warm Air Heating and Air-Conditioning Equipment and Supplies *see* NAICS 421730: Warm Air Heating and Air-Conditioning Equipment and Supplies Wholesalers

5078 Refrigeration Equipment and Supplies *see* NAICS 421740: Refrigeration Equipment and Supplies Wholesalers

5082 Construction and Mining (Except Petroleum) Machinery and Equipment *see* NAICS 421810: Construction and Mining (except Petroleum) Machinery and Equipment Wholesalers

5083 Farm and Garden Machinery and Equipment *see* NAICS 421820: Farm and Garden Machinery and Equipment Wholesalers; NAICS 444210: Outdoor Power Equipment Stores

5084 Industrial Machinery and Equipment *see* NAICS 421830: Industrial Machinery and Equipment Wholesalers

5085 Industrial Supplies *see* NAICS 421830: Industrial Machinery and Equipment Wholesalers; NAICS 421840: Industrial Supplies Wholesalers

5087 Service Establishment Equipment and Supplies *see* NAICS 421850: Service Establishment Equipment and Supplies Wholesalers; NAICS 446120: Cosmetics, Beauty Supplies, and Perfume Stores

5088 Transportation Equipment and Supplies, Except Motor Vehicles *see* NAICS 421860: Transportation Equipment and Supplies (except Motor Vehicles) Wholesalers

5091 Sporting and Recreational Goods and Supplies *see* NAICS 421910: Sporting and Recreational Goods and Supplies Wholesalers

5092 Toys and Hobby Goods and Supplies *see* NAICS 421920: Toy and Hobby Goods and Supplies Wholesalers

5093 Scrap and Waste Materials *see* NAICS 421930: Recyclable Material Wholesalers

5094 Jewelry, Watches, Precious Stones, and Precious Metals *see* NAICS 421940: Jewelry, Watch, Precious Stone, and Precious Metal Wholesalers

5099 Durable Goods, NEC *see* NAICS 421990: Other Miscellaneous Durable Goods Wholesalers

5111 Printing and Writing Paper *see* NAICS 422110: Printing and Writing Paper Wholesalers

5112 Stationery and Office Supplies *see* NAICS 453210: Office Supplies and Stationery Stores; NAICS 422120: Stationery and Office Supplies Wholesalers

5113 Industrial and Personal Service Paper *see* NAICS 422130: Industrial and Personal Service Paper Wholesalers

5122 Drugs, Drug Proprietaries, and Druggists' Sundries *see* NAICS 422210: Drugs, Drug Proprietaries, and Druggists' Sundries Wholesalers

5131 Piece Goods, Notions, and Other Dry Goods *see* NAICS 313311: Broadwoven Fabric Finishing Mills; NAICS 313312: Textile and Fabric Finishing (except Broadwoven Fabric) Mills; NAICS 422310: Piece Goods, Notions, and Other Dry Goods Wholesalers

5136 Men's and Boys' Clothing and Furnishings *see* NAICS 422320: Men's and Boys' Clothing and Furnishings Wholesalers

5137 Women's Children's and Infants' Clothing and Accessories *see* NAICS 422330: Women's, Children's, and Infants' Clothing and Accessories Wholesalers

5139 Footwear *see* NAICS 422340: Footwear Wholesalers

5141 Groceries, General Line *see* NAICS 422410: General Line Grocery Wholesalers

5142 Packaged Frozen Foods *see* NAICS 422420: Packaged Frozen Food Wholesalers

5143 Dairy Products, Except Dried or Canned *see* NAICS 422430: Dairy Products (except Dried or Canned) Wholesalers

5144 Poultry and Poultry Products *see* NAICS 422440: Poultry and Poultry Product Wholesalers

5145 Confectionery *see* NAICS 422450: Confectionery Wholesalers

5146 Fish and Seafoods *see* NAICS 422460: Fish and Seafood Wholesalers

5147 Meats and Meat Products *see* NAICS 311612: Meat Processed from Carcasses; NAICS 422470: Meat and Meat Product Wholesalers

5148 Fresh Fruits and Vegetables *see* NAICS 422480: Fresh Fruit and Vegetable Wholesalers

5149 Groceries and Related Products, NEC *see* NAICS 422490: Other Grocery and Related Product Wholesalers

5153 Grain and Field Beans *see* NAICS 422510: Grain and Field Bean Wholesalers

5154 Livestock *see* NAICS 422520: Livestock Wholesalers

5159 Farm-Product Raw Materials, NEC *see* NAICS 422590: Other Farm Product Raw Material Wholesalers

5162 Plastics Materials and Basic Forms and Shapes *see* NAICS 422610: Plastics Materials and Basic Forms and Shapes Wholesalers

5169 Chemicals and Allied Products, NEC *see* NAICS 422690: Other Chemical and Allied Products Wholesalers

5171 Petroleum Bulk Stations and Terminals *see* NAICS 454311: Heating Oil Dealers; NAICS 454312: Liquefied Petroleum Gas (Bottled Gas) Dealers; NAICS 422710: Petroleum Bulk Stations and Terminals

5172 Petroleum and Petroleum Products Wholesalers, Except Bulk Stations and Terminals *see* NAICS 422720: Petroleum and Petroleum Products Wholesalers (except Bulk Stations and Terminals)

5181 Beer and Ale *see* NAICS 422810: Beer and Ale Wholesalers

5182 Wine and Distilled Alcoholic Beverages *see* NAICS 422820: Wine and Distilled Alcoholic Beverage Wholesalers

5191 Farm Supplies *see* NAICS 444220: Nursery and Garden Centers; NAICS 422910: Farm Supplies Wholesalers

5192 Books, Periodicals, and Newspapers *see* NAICS 422920: Book, Periodical and Newspaper Wholesalers

5193 Flowers, Nursery Stock, and Florists' Supplies *see* NAICS 422930: Flower, Nursery Stock and Florists' Supplies Wholesalers; NAICS 444220: Nursery and Garden Centers

5194 Tobacco and Tobacco Products *see* NAICS 422940: Tobacco and Tobacco Product Wholesalers

5198 Paint, Varnishes, and Supplies *see* NAICS 422950: Paint, Varnish and Supplies Wholesalers; NAICS 444120: Paint and Wallpaper Stores

5199 Nondurable Goods, NEC *see* NAICS 541890: Other Services Related to Advertising; NAICS 422990: Other Miscellaneous Nondurable Goods Wholesalers

RETAIL TRADE

5211 Lumber and Other Building Materials Dealers *see* NAICS 444110: Home Centers; NAICS 421310: Lumber, Plywood, Millwork, and Wood Panel Wholesalers; NAICS 444190: Other Building Material Dealers

5231 Paint, Glass, and Wallpaper Stores *see* NAICS 422950: Paint, Varnish, and Supplies Wholesalers; NAICS 444190: Other Building Material Dealers; NAICS 444120: Paint and Wallpaper Stores

5251 Hardware Stores *see* NAICS 444130: Hardware Stores

5261 Retail Nurseries *see* NAICS 444220: Nursery and Garden Centers; NAICS 453998: All Other Miscellaneous Store Retailers (except Tobacco Stores); NAICS 444210: Outdoor Power Equipment Stores

5271 Mobile Home Dealers *see* NAICS 453930: Manufactured (Mobile) Home Dealers

5311 Department Stores *see* NAICS 452110: Department Stores

5331 Variety Stores *see* NAICS 452990: All Other General Merchandise Stores

5399 Miscellaneous General Merchandise Stores *see* NAICS 452910: Warehouse Clubs and Superstores; NAICS 452990: All Other General Merchandise Stores

5411 Grocery Stores *see* NAICS 447110: Gasoline Stations with Convenience Stores; NAICS 445110: Supermarkets and Other Grocery (except Convenience) Stores; NAICS 452910: Warehouse Clubs and Superstores; NAICS 445120: Convenience Stores

5421 Meat and Fish (Seafood) Markets, Including Freezer Provisioners *see* NAICS 454390: Other Direct Selling Establishments; NAICS 445210: Meat Markets; NAICS 445220: Fish and Seafood Markets

5431 Fruit and Vegetable Markets *see* NAICS 445230: Fruit and Vegetable Markets

5441 Candy, Nut, and Confectionery Stores *see* NAICS 445292: Confectionery and Nut Stores

5451   Dairy Products Stores *see* NAICS 445299: All Other Specialty Food Stores

5461   Retail Bakeries *see* NAICS 722213: Snack and Nonalcoholic Beverage Bars; NAICS 311811: Retail Bakeries; NAICS 445291: Baked Goods Stores

5499   Miscellaneous Food Stores *see* NAICS 445210: Meat Markets; NAICS 722211: Limited-Service Restaurants; NAICS 446191: Food (Health) Supplement Stores; NAICS 445299: All Other Specialty Food Stores

5511   Motor Vehicle Dealers (New and Used) *see* NAICS 441110: New Car Dealers

5521   Motor Vehicle Dealers (Used Only) *see* NAICS 441120: Used Car Dealers

5531   Auto and Home Supply Stores *see* NAICS 441320: Tire Dealers; NAICS 441310: Automotive Parts and Accessories Stores

5541   Gasoline Service Stations *see* NAICS 447110: Gasoline Stations with Convenience Stores; NAICS 447190: Other Gasoline Stations

5551   Boat Dealers *see* NAICS 441222: Boat Dealers

5561   Recreational Vehicle Dealers *see* NAICS 441210: Recreational Vehicle Dealers

5571   Motorcycle Dealers *see* NAICS 441221: Motorcycle Dealers

5599   Automotive Dealers, NEC *see* NAICS 441229: All Other Motor Vehicle Dealers

5611   Men's and Boys' Clothing and Accessory Stores *see* NAICS 448110: Men's Clothing Stores; NAICS 448150: Clothing Accessories Stores

5621   Women's Clothing Stores *see* NAICS 448120: Women's Clothing Stores

5632   Women's Accessory and Specialty Stores *see* NAICS 448190: Other Clothing Stores; NAICS 448150: Clothing Accessories Stores

5641   Children's and Infants' Wear Stores *see* NAICS 448130: Children's and Infants' Clothing Stores

5651   Family Clothing Stores *see* NAICS 448140: Family Clothing Stores

5661   Shoe Stores *see* NAICS 448210: Shoe Stores

5699   Miscellaneous Apparel and Accessory Stores *see* NAICS 448190: Other Clothing Stores; NAICS 448150: Clothing Accessories Stores

5712   Furniture Stores *see* NAICS 337122: Nonupholstered Wood Household Furniture Manufacturing; NAICS 337110: Wood Kitchen Cabinet and Counter Top Manufacturing; NAICS 337121: Upholstered Wood Household Furniture Manufacturing; NAICS 442110: Furniture Stores

5713   Floor Covering Stores *see* NAICS 442210: Floor Covering Stores

5714   Drapery, Curtain, and Upholstery Stores *see* NAICS 442291: Window Treatment Stores; NAICS

451130: Sewing, Needlework, and Piece Goods Stores; NAICS 314121: Curtain and Drapery Mills

5719   Miscellaneous Homefurnishings Stores *see* NAICS 442291: Window Treatment Stores; NAICS 442299: All Other Home Furnishings Stores

5722   Household Appliance Stores *see* NAICS 443111: Household Appliance Stores

5731   Radio, Television, and Consumer Electronics Stores *see* NAICS 443112: Radio, Television, and Other Electronics Stores; NAICS 441310: Automotive Parts and Accessories Stores

5734   Computer and Computer Software Stores *see* NAICS 443120: Computer and Software Stores

5735   Record and Prerecorded Tape Stores *see* NAICS 451220: Prerecorded Tape, Compact Disc, and Record Stores

5736   Musical Instrument Stores *see* NAICS 451140: Musical Instrument and Supplies Stores

5812   Eating and Drinking Places *see* NAICS 722110: Full-Service Restaurants; NAICS 722211: Limited-Service Restaurants; NAICS 722212: Cafeterias; NAICS 722213: Snack and Nonalcoholic Beverage Bars; NAICS 722310: Foodservice Contractors; NAICS 722320: Caterers; NAICS 711110: Theater Companies and Dinner Theaters

5813   Drinking Places (Alcoholic Beverages) *see* NAICS 722410: Drinking Places (Alcoholic Beverages)

5912   Drug Stores and Proprietary Stores *see* NAICS 446110: Pharmacies and Drug Stores

5921   Liquor Stores *see* NAICS 445310: Beer, Wine and Liquor Stores

5932   Used Merchandise Stores *see* NAICS 522298: All Other Non-Depository Credit Intermediation; NAICS 453310: Used Merchandise Stores

5941   Sporting Goods Stores and Bicycle Shops *see* NAICS 451110: Sporting Goods Stores

5942   Book Stores *see* NAICS 451211: Book Stores

5943   Stationery Stores *see* NAICS 453210: Office Supplies and Stationery Stores

5944   Jewelry Stores *see* NAICS 448310: Jewelry Stores

5945   Hobby, Toy, and Game Shops *see* NAICS 451120: Hobby, Toy and Game Stores

5946   Camera and Photographic Supply Stores *see* NAICS 443130: Camera and Photographic Supplies Stores

5947   Gift, Novelty, and Souvenir Shops *see* NAICS 453220: Gift, Novelty, and Souvenir Stores

5948   Luggage and Leather Goods Stores *see* NAICS 448320: Luggage and Leather Goods Stores

5949   Sewing, Needlework, and Piece Goods Stores *see* NAICS 451130: Sewing, Needlework, and Piece Goods Stores

5961 Catalog and Mail-Order Houses *see* NAICS 454110: Electronic Shopping and Mail-Order Houses

5962 Automatic Merchandising Machine Operator *see* NAICS 454210: Vending Machine Operators

5963 Direct Selling Establishments *see* NAICS 722330: Mobile Caterers; NAICS 454390: Other Direct Selling Establishments

5983 Fuel Oil Dealers *see* NAICS 454311: Heating Oil Dealers

5984 Liquefied Petroleum Gas (Bottled Gas) Dealers *see* NAICS 454312: Liquefied Petroleum Gas (Bottled Gas) Dealers

5989 Fuel Dealers, NEC *see* NAICS 454319: Other Fuel Dealers

5992 Florists *see* NAICS 453110: Florists

5993 Tobacco Stores and Stands *see* NAICS 453991: Tobacco Stores

5994 News Dealers and Newsstands *see* NAICS 451212: News Dealers and Newsstands

5995 Optical Goods Stores *see* NAICS 339115: Ophthalmic Goods Manufacturing; NAICS 446130: Optical Goods Stores

5999 Miscellaneous Retail Stores, NEC *see* NAICS 446120: Cosmetics, Beauty Supplies, and Perfume Stores; NAICS 446199: All Other Health and Personal Care Stores; NAICS 453910: Pet and Pet Supplies Stores; NAICS 453920: Art Dealers; NAICS 443111: Household Appliance Stores; NAICS 443112: Radio, Television, and Other Electronics Stores; NAICS 448310: Jewelry Stores; NAICS 453998: All Other Miscellaneous Store Retailers (except Tobacco Stores)

FINANCE, INSURANCE, & REAL ESTATE

6011 Federal Reserve Banks *see* NAICS 521110: Monetary Authorities-Central Banks

6019 Central Reserve Depository Institutions, NEC *see* NAICS 522320: Financial Transactions Processing, Reserve, and Clearing House Activities

6021 National Commercial Banks *see* NAICS 522110: Commercial Banking; NAICS 522210: Credit Card Issuing; NAICS 523991: Trust, Fiduciary, and Custody Activities

6022 State Commercial Banks *see* NAICS 522110: Commercial Banking; NAICS 522210: Credit Card Issuing; NAICS 522190: Other Depository Intermediation; NAICS 523991: Trust, Fiduciary, and Custody Activities

6029 Commercial Banks, NEC *see* NAICS 522110: Commercial Banking

6035 Savings Institutions, Federally Chartered *see* NAICS 522120: Savings Institutions

6036 Savings institutions, Not Federally Chartered *see* NAICS 522120: Savings Institutions

6061 Credit Unions, Federally Chartered *see* NAICS 522130: Credit Unions

6062 Credit Unions, Not Federally Chartered *see* NAICS 522130: Credit Unions

6081 Branches and Agencies of Foreign Banks *see* NAICS 522293: International Trade Financing; NAICS 522110: Commercial Banking; NAICS 522298: All Other Non-Depository Credit Intermediation

6082 Foreign Trade and International Banking Institutions *see* NAICS 522293: International Trade Financing

6091 Nondeposit Trust Facilities *see* NAICS 523991: Trust, Fiduciary, and Custody Activities

6099 Functions Related to Deposit Banking, NEC *see* NAICS 522320: Financial Transactions Processing, Reserve, and Clearing House Activities; NAICS 523130: Commodity Contracts Dealing; NAICS 523991: Trust, Fiduciary, and Custody Activities; NAICS 523999: Miscellaneous Financial Investment Activities; NAICS 522390: Other Activities Related to Credit Intermediation

6111 Federal and Federally Sponsored Credit Agencies *see* NAICS 522293: International Trade Financing; NAICS 522294: Secondary Market Financing; NAICS 522298: All Other Non-Depository Credit Intermediation

6141 Personal Credit Institutions *see* NAICS 522210: Credit Card Issuing; NAICS 522220: Sales Financing; NAICS 522291: Consumer Lending

6153 Short-Term Business Credit Institutions, Except Agricultural *see* NAICS 522220: Sales Financing; NAICS 522320: Financial Transactions Processing, Reserve, and Clearing House Activities; NAICS 522298: All Other Non-Depository Credit Intermediation

6159 Miscellaneous Business Credit Institutions *see* NAICS 522220: Sales Financing; NAICS 522293: International Trade Financing; NAICS 522298: All Other Non-Depository Credit Intermediation

6162 Mortgage Bankers and Loan Correspondents *see* NAICS 522292: Real Estate Credit; NAICS 522390: Other Activities Related to Credit Intermediation

6163 Loan Brokers *see* NAICS 522310: Mortgage and Other Loan Brokers

6211 Security Brokers, Dealers, and Flotation Companies *see* NAICS 523110: Investment Banking and Securities Dealing; NAICS 523120: Securities Brokerage; NAICS 523910: Miscellaneous Intermediation; NAICS 523999: Miscellaneous Financial Investment Activities

6221 Commodity Contracts Brokers and Dealers *see* NAICS 523130: Commodity Contracts Dealing; NAICS 523140: Commodity Brokerage

6231 Security and Commodity Exchanges *see* NAICS 523210: Securities and Commodity Exchanges

6282 Investment Advice *see* NAICS 523920: Portfolio Management; NAICS 523930: Investment Advice

6289 Services Allied With the Exchange of Securities or Commodities, NEC *see* NAICS 523991: Trust, Fiduciary, and Custody Activities; NAICS 523999: Miscellaneous Financial Investment Activities

6311 Life Insurance *see* NAICS 524113: Direct Life Insurance Carriers; NAICS 524130: Reinsurance Carriers

6321 Accident and Health Insurance *see* NAICS 524114: Direct Health and Medical Insurance Carriers; NAICS 525190: Other Insurance and Employee Benefit Funds; NAICS 524130: Reinsurance Carriers

6324 Hospital and Medical Service Plans *see* NAICS 524114: Direct Health and Medical Insurance Carriers; NAICS 525190: Other Insurance and Employee Benefit Funds; NAICS 524130: Reinsurance Carriers

6331 Fire, Marine, and Casualty Insurance *see* NAICS 524126: Direct Property and Casualty Insurance Carriers; NAICS 525190: Other Insurance and Employee Benefit Funds; NAICS 524130: Reinsurance Carriers

6351 Surety Insurance *see* NAICS 524126: Direct Property and Casualty Insurance Carriers; NAICS 524130: Reinsurance Carriers

6361 Title Insurance *see* NAICS 524127: Direct Title Insurance Carriers; NAICS 524130: Reinsurance Carriers

6371 Pension, Health, and Welfare Funds *see* NAICS 523920: Portfolio Management; NAICS 524292: Third Party Administration for Insurance and Pension Funds; NAICS 525110: Pension Funds; NAICS 525120: Health and Welfare Funds

6399 Insurance Carriers, NEC *see* NAICS 524128: Other Direct Insurance Carriers (except Life, Health, and Medical)

6411 Insurance Agents, Brokers, and Service *see* NAICS 524210: Insurance Agencies and Brokerages; NAICS 524291: Claims Adjusters; NAICS 524292: Third Party Administrators for Insurance and Pension Funds; NAICS 524298: All Other Insurance Related Activities

6512 Operators of Nonresidential Buildings *see* NAICS 711310: Promoters of Performing Arts, Sports and Similar Events with Facilities; NAICS 531120: Lessors of Nonresidential Buildings (except Mini-warehouses)

6513 Operators of Apartment Buildings *see* NAICS 531110: Lessors of Residential Buildings and Dwellings

6514 Operators of Dwellings Other Than Apartment Buildings *see* NAICS 531110: Lessors of Residential Buildings and Dwellings

6515 Operators of Residential Mobile Home Sites *see* NAICS 531190: Lessors of Other Real Estate Property

6517 Lessors of Railroad Property *see* NAICS 531190: Lessors of Other Real Estate Property

6519 Lessors of Real Property, NEC *see* NAICS 531190: Lessors of Other Real Estate Property

6531 Real Estate Agents and Managers *see* NAICS 531210: Offices of Real Estate Agents and Brokers; NAICS 813990: Other Similar Organizations; NAICS 531311: Residential Property Managers; NAICS 531312: Nonresidential Property Managers; NAICS 531320: Offices of Real Estate Appraisers; NAICS 812220: Cemeteries and Crematories; NAICS 531390: Other Activities Related to Real Estate

6541 Title Abstract Offices *see* NAICS 541191: Title Abstract and Settlement Offices

6552 Land Subdividers and Developers, Except Cemeteries *see* NAICS 233110: Land Subdivision and Land Development

6553 Cemetery Subdividers and Developers *see* NAICS 812220: Cemeteries and Crematories

6712 Offices of Bank Holding Companies *see* NAICS 551111: Offices of Bank Holding Companies

6719 Offices of Holding Companies, NEC *see* NAICS 551112: Offices of Other Holding Companies

6722 Management Investment Offices, Open-End *see* NAICS 525910: Open-End Investment Funds

6726 Unit Investment Trusts, Face-Amount Certificate Offices, and Closed-End Management Investment Offices *see* NAICS 525990: Other Financial Vehicles

6732 Education, Religious, and Charitable Trusts *see* NAICS 813211: Grantmaking Foundations

6733 Trusts, Except Educational, Religious, and Charitable *see* NAICS 523920: Portfolio Management; NAICS 523991: Trust, Fiduciary, and Custody Services; NAICS 525190: Other Insurance and Employee Benefit Funds; NAICS 525920: Trusts, Estates, and Agency Accounts

6792 Oil Royalty Traders *see* NAICS 523999: Miscellaneous Financial Investment Activities; NAICS 533110: Owners and Lessors of Other Non-Financial Assets

6794 Patent Owners and Lessors *see* NAICS 533110: Owners and Lessors of Other Non-Financial Assets

6798 Real Estate Investment Trusts *see* NAICS 525930: Real Estate Investment Trusts

6799 Investors, NEC *see* NAICS 523910: Miscellaneous Intermediation; NAICS 523920: Portfolio Management; NAICS 523130: Commodity Contracts Dealing; NAICS 523999: Miscellaneous Financial Investment Activities

SERVICE INDUSTRIES

7011 Hotels and Motels *see* NAICS 721110: Hotels (except Casino Hotels) and Motels; NAICS 721120: Casino Hotels; NAICS 721191: Bed and Breakfast Inns; NAICS 721199: All Other Traveler Accommodations

7021 Rooming and Boarding Houses *see* NAICS 721310: Rooming and Boarding Houses

7032 Sporting and Recreational Camps *see* NAICS 721214: Recreational and Vacation Camps

7033 Recreational Vehicle Parks and Campsites *see* NAICS 721211: RV (Recreational Vehicle) Parks and Campgrounds

7041 Organization Hotels and Lodging Houses, on Membership Basis *see* NAICS 721110: Hotels (except Casino Hotels) and Motels; NAICS 721310: Rooming and Boarding Houses

7211 Power Laundries, Family and Commercial *see* NAICS 812321: Laundries, Family and Commercial

7212 Garment Pressing, and Agents for Laundries *see* NAICS 812391: Garment Pressing and Agents for Laundries

7213 Linen Supply *see* NAICS 812331: Linen Supply

7215 Coin-Operated Laundry and Drycleaning *see* NAICS 812310: Coin-Operated Laundries and Drycleaners

7216 Drycleaning Plants, Except Rug Cleaning *see* NAICS 812322: Drycleaning Plants

7217 Carpet and Upholstery Cleaning *see* NAICS 561740: Carpet and Upholstery Cleaning Services

7218 Industrial Launderers *see* NAICS 812332: Industrial Launderers

7219 Laundry and Garment Services, NEC *see* NAICS 812331: Linen Supply; NAICS 811490: Other Personal and Household Goods Repair and Maintenance; NAICS 812399: All Other Laundry Services

7221 Photographic Studios, Portrait *see* NAICS 541921: Photographic Studios, Portrait

7231 Beauty Shops *see* NAICS 812112: Beauty Salons; NAICS 812113: Nail Salons; NAICS 611511: Cosmetology and Barber Schools

7241 Barber Shops *see* NAICS 812111: Barber Shops; NAICS 611511: Cosmetology and Barber Schools

7251 Shoe Repair Shops and Shoeshine Parlors *see* NAICS 811430: Footwear and Leather Goods Repair

7261 Funeral Services and Crematories *see* NAICS 812210: Funeral Homes; NAICS 812220: Cemeteries and Crematories

7291 Tax Return Preparation Services *see* NAICS 541213: Tax Preparation Services

7299 Miscellaneous Personal Services, NEC *see* NAICS 624410: Child Day Care Services; NAICS 812191: Diet and Weight Reducing Centers; NAICS 532220: Formal Wear and Costumes Rental; NAICS 812199: Other Personal Care Services; NAICS 812990: All Other Personal Services

7311 Advertising Agencies *see* NAICS 541810: Advertising Agencies

7312 Outdoor Advertising Services *see* NAICS 541850: Display Advertising

7313 Radio, Television, and Publishers' Advertising Representatives *see* NAICS 541840: Media Representatives

7319 Advertising, NEC *see* NAICS 481219: Other Nonscheduled Air Transportation; NAICS 541830: Media Buying Agencies; NAICS 541850: Display Advertising; NAICS 541870: Advertising Material Distribution Services; NAICS 541890: Other Services Related to Advertising

7322 Adjustment and Collection Services *see* NAICS 561440: Collection Agencies; NAICS 561491: Repossession Services

7323 Credit Reporting Services *see* NAICS 561450: Credit Bureaus

7331 Direct Mail Advertising Services *see* NAICS 541860: Direct Mail Advertising

7334 Photocopying and Duplicating Services *see* NAICS 561431: Other Business Service Centers (including Copy Shops)

7335 Commercial Photography *see* NAICS 481219: Other Nonscheduled Air Transportation; NAICS 541922: Commercial Photography

7336 Commercial Art and Graphic Design *see* NAICS 541430: Graphic Design Services

7338 Secretarial and Court Reporting Services *see* NAICS 561410: Document Preparation Services; NAICS 561492: Court Reporting and Stenotype Services

7342 Disinfecting and Pest Control Services *see* NAICS 561720: Janitorial Services; NAICS 561710: Exterminating and Pest Control Services

7349 Building Cleaning and Maintenance Services, NEC *see* NAICS 561720: Janitorial Services

7352 Medical Equipment Rental and Leasing *see* NAICS 532291: Home Health Equipment Rental; NAICS 532490: Other Commercial and Industrial Machinery and Equipment Rental and Leasing

7353 Heavy Construction Equipment Rental and Leasing *see* NAICS 234990: All Other Heavy Construction; NAICS 532412: Construction, Mining and Forestry Machinery and Equipment Rental and Leasing

7359 Equipment Rental and Leasing, NEC *see* NAICS 532210: Consumer Electronics and Appliances Rental; NAICS 532310: General Rental Centers; NAICS 532299: All Other Consumer Goods Rental; NAICS 532412: Construction, Mining and Forestry Machinery and Equipment Rental and Leasing; NAICS 532411: Commercial Air, Rail, and Water Transportation Equipment Rental and Leasing; NAICS 562991: Septic Tank and Related Services; NAICS 532420: Office Machinery and Equipment Rental and Leasing; NAICS 532490: Other Commercial and Industrial Machinery and Equipment Rental and Leasing

7361 Employment Agencies *see* NAICS 541612: Human Resources and Executive Search Consulting Services; NAICS 561310: Employment Placement Agencies

7363 Help Supply Services *see* NAICS 561320: Temporary Help Services; NAICS 561330: Employee Leasing Services

7371 Computer Programming Services *see* NAICS 541511: Custom Computer Programming Services

7372 Prepackaged Software *see* NAICS 511210: Software Publishers; NAICS 334611: Software Reproducing

7373 Computer Integrated Systems Design *see* NAICS 541512: Computer Systems Design Services

7374 Computer Processing and Data Preparation and Processing Services *see* NAICS 514210: Data Processing Services

7375 Information Retrieval Services *see* NAICS 514191: On-Line Information Services

7376 Computer Facilities Management Services *see* NAICS 541513: Computer Facilities Management Services

7377 Computer Rental and Leasing *see* NAICS 532420: Office Machinery and Equipment Rental and Leasing

7378 Computer Maintenance and Repair *see* NAICS 443120: Computer and Software Stores; NAICS 811212: Computer and Office Machine Repair and Maintenance

7379 Computer Related Services, NEC *see* NAICS 541512: Computer Systems Design Services; NAICS 541519: Other Computer Related Services

7381 Detective, Guard, and Armored Car Services *see* NAICS 561611: Investigation Services; NAICS 561612: Security Guards and Patrol Services; NAICS 561613: Armored Car Services

7382 Security Systems Services *see* NAICS 561621: Security Systems Services (except Locksmiths)

7383 News Syndicates *see* NAICS 514110: New Syndicates

7384 Photofinishing Laboratories *see* NAICS 812921: Photo Finishing Laboratories (except One-Hour); NAICS 812922: One-Hour Photo Finishing

7389 Business Services, NEC *see* NAICS 512240: Sound Recording Studios; NAICS 512290: Other Sound Recording Industries; NAICS 541199: Other Legal Services; NAICS 812990: All Other Personal Services; NAICS 541370: Surveying and Mapping (except Geophysical) Services; NAICS 541410: Interior Design Services; NAICS 541420: Industrial Design Services; NAICS 541340: Drafting Services; NAICS 541490: Other Specialized Design Services; NAICS 541890: Other Services Related to Advertising; NAICS 541930: Translation and Interpretation Services; NAICS 541350: Building Inspection Services; NAICS 541990: All Other Professional, Scientific and Technical Services; NAICS 711410: Agents and Managers for Artists, Athletes, Entertainers and Other Public Figures; NAICS 561421: Telephone Answering Services; NAICS 561422: Telemarketing Bureaus; NAICS 561439: Private Mail Centers; NAICS 561431: Other Business Service Centers (including Copy Shops); NAICS 561491: Repossession Services; NAICS 561910: Packaging and Labeling Services; NAICS 561790: Other Services to Buildings and Dwellings; NAICS 561599: All Other Travel Arrangement and Reservation Services; NAICS 561920: Convention and Trade Show Organizers; NAICS 561591: Convention and Visitors Bureaus; NAICS 522320: Financial Transactions, Processing, Reserve and Clearing House Activities; NAICS 561499: All Other Business Support Services; NAICS 561990: All Other Support Services

7513 Truck Rental and Leasing, Without Drivers *see* NAICS 532120: Truck, Utility Trailer and RV (Recreational Vehicle) Rental and Leasing

7514 Passenger Car Rental *see* NAICS 532111: Passenger Cars Rental

7515 Passenger Car Leasing *see* NAICS 532112: Passenger Cars Leasing

7519 Utility Trailer and Recreational Vehicle Rental *see* NAICS 532120: Truck, Utility Trailer and RV (Recreational Vehicles) Rental and Leasing

7521 Automobile Parking *see* NAICS 812930: Parking Lots and Garages

7532 Top, Body, and Upholstery Repair Shops and Paint Shops *see* NAICS 811121: Automotive Body, Paint, and Upholstery Repair and Maintenance

7533   Automotive Exhaust System Repair Shops *see* NAICS 811112: Automotive Exhaust System Repair

7534   Tire Retreading and Repair Shops *see* NAICS 326212: Tire Retreading; NAICS 811198: All Other Automotive Repair and Maintenance

7536   Automotive Glass Replacement Shops *see* NAICS 811122: Automotive Glass Replacement Shops

7537   Automotive Transmission Repair Shops *see* NAICS 811113: Automotive Transmission Repair

7538   General Automotive Repair Shops *see* NAICS 811111: General Automotive Repair

7539   Automotive Repair Shops, NEC *see* NAICS 811118: Other Automotive Mechanical and Electrical Repair and Maintenance

7542   Carwashes *see* NAICS 811192: Car Washes

7549   Automotive Services, Except Repair and Carwashes *see* NAICS 811191: Automotive Oil Change and Lubrication Shops; NAICS 488410: Motor Vehicle Towing; NAICS 811198: All Other Automotive Repair and Maintenance

7622   Radio and Television Repair Shops *see* NAICS 811211: Consumer Electronics Repair and Maintenance; NAICS 811213: Communication Equipment Repair and Maintenance; NAICS 443112: Radio, Television and Other Electronics Stores

7623   Refrigeration and Air-Conditioning Services and Repair Shops *see* NAICS 443111: Household Appliance Stores; NAICS 811310: Commercial and Industrial Machinery and Equipment (except Automotive and Electronic) Repair and Maintenance; NAICS 811412: Appliance Repair and Maintenance

7629   Electrical and Electronic Repair Shops, NEC *see* NAICS 443111: Household Appliance Stores; NAICS 811212: Computer and Office Machine Repair and Maintenance; *see* NAICS 811213: Communication Equipment Repair and Maintenance; NAICS 811219: Other Electronic and Precision Equipment Repair and Maintenance; NAICS 811412: Appliance Repair and Maintenance; NAICS 811211: Consumer Electronics Repair and Maintenance

7631   Watch, Clock, and Jewelry Repair *see* NAICS 811490: Other Personal and Household Goods Repair and Maintenance

7641   Reupholster and Furniture Repair *see* NAICS 811420: Reupholstery and Furniture Repair

7692   Welding Repair *see* NAICS 811490: Other Personal and Household Goods Repair and Maintenance

7694   Armature Rewinding Shops *see* NAICS 811310: Commercial and Industrial Machinery and Equipment (except Automotive and Electronic) Repair and Maintenance; NAICS 335312: Motor and Generator Manufacturing

7699   Repair Shops and Related Services, NEC *see* NAICS 561622: Locksmiths; NAICS 562991: Septic Tank and Related Services; NAICS 561790: Other Services to Buildings and Dwellings; NAICS 488390: Other Support Activities for Water Transportation; NAICS 451110: Sporting Goods Stores; NAICS 811310: Commercial and Industrial Machinery and Equipment (except Automotive and Electronic) Repair and Maintenance; NAICS 115210: Support Activities for Animal Production; NAICS 811212: Computer and Office Machine Repair and Maintenance; NAICS 811219: Other Electronic and Precision Equipment Repair and Maintenance; NAICS 811411: Home and Garden Equipment Repair and Maintenance; NAICS 811412: Appliance Repair and Maintenance; NAICS 811430: Footwear and Leather Goods Repair; NAICS 811490: Other Personal and Household Goods Repair and Maintenance

7812   Motion Picture and Video Tape Production *see* NAICS 512110: Motion Picture and Video Production

7819   Services Allied to Motion Picture Production *see* NAICS 512191: Teleproduction and Other Post-Production Services; NAICS 561310: Employment Placement Agencies; NAICS 532220: Formal Wear and Costumes Rental; NAICS 532490: Other Commercial and Industrial Machinery and Equipment Rental and Leasing; NAICS 541214: Payroll Services; NAICS 711510: Independent Artists, Writers, and Performers; NAICS 334612: Prerecorded Compact Disc (Except Software), Tape, and Record Manufacturing; NAICS 512199: Other Motion Picture and Video Industries

7822   Motion Picture and Video Tape Distribution *see* NAICS 421990: Other Miscellaneous Durable Goods Wholesalers; NAICS 512120: Motion Picture and Video Distribution

7829   Services Allied to Motion Picture Distribution *see* NAICS 512199: Other Motion Picture and Video Industries; NAICS 512120: Motion Picture and Video Distribution

7832   Motion Picture Theaters, Except Drive-In *see* NAICS 512131: Motion Picture Theaters, Except Drive-In

7833   Drive-In Motion Picture Theaters *see* NAICS 512132: Drive-In Motion Picture Theaters

7841   Video Tape Rental *see* NAICS 532230: Video Tapes and Disc Rental

7911   Dance Studios, Schools, and Halls *see* NAICS 713990: All Other Amusement and Recreation Industries; NAICS 611610: Fine Arts Schools

7922   Theatrical Producers (Except Motion Picture) and Miscellaneous Theatrical Services *see* NAICS

561310: Employment Placement Agencies; NAICS 711110: Theater Companies and Dinner Theaters; NAICS 711410: Agents and Managers for Artists, Athletes, Entertainers and Other Public Figures; NAICS 711120: Dance Companies; NAICS 711310: Promoters of Performing Arts, Sports, and Similar Events with Facilities; NAICS 711320: Promoters of Performing Arts, Sports, and Similar Events without Facilities; NAICS 512290: Other Sound Recording Industries; NAICS 532490: Other Commercial and Industrial Machinery and Equipment Rental and Leasing

7929   Bands, Orchestras, Actors, and Other Entertainers and Entertainment Groups *see* NAICS 711130: Musical Groups and Artists; NAICS 711510: Independent Artists, Writers, and Performers; NAICS 711190: Other Performing Arts Companies

7933   Bowling Centers *see* NAICS 713950: Bowling Centers

7941   Professional Sports Clubs and Promoters *see* NAICS 711211: Sports Teams and Clubs; NAICS 711410: Agents and Managers for Artists, Athletes, Entertainers, and Other Public Figures; NAICS 711320: Promoters of Performing Arts, Sports, and Similar Events without Facilities; NAICS 711310: Promoters of Performing Arts, Sports, and Similar Events with Facilities; NAICS 711219: Other Spectator Sports

7948   Racing, Including Track Operations *see* NAICS 711212: Race Tracks; NAICS 711219: Other Spectator Sports

7991   Physical Fitness Facilities *see* NAICS 713940: Fitness and Recreational Sports Centers

7992   Public Golf Courses *see* NAICS 713910: Golf Courses and Country Clubs

7993   Coin Operated Amusement Devices *see* NAICS 713120: Amusement Arcades; NAICS 713290: Other Gambling Industries; NAICS 713990: All Other Amusement and Recreation Industries

7996   Amusement Parks *see* NAICS 713110: Amusement and Theme Parks

7997   Membership Sports and Recreation Clubs *see* NAICS 713910: Golf Courses and Country Clubs; NAICS 713940: Fitness and Recreational Sports Centers; NAICS 713990: All Other Amusement and Recreation Industries

7999   Amusement and Recreation Services, NEC *see* NAICS 561599: All Other Travel Arrangement and Reservation Services; NAICS 487990: Scenic and Sightseeing Transportation, Other; NAICS 711190: Other Performing Arts Companies; NAICS 711219: Other Spectator Sports; NAICS 713920: Skiing Facilities; NAICS 713940: Fitness

and Recreational Sports Centers; NAICS 713210: Casinos (except Casino Hotels); NAICS 713290: Other Gambling Industries; NAICS 712190: Nature Parks and Other Similar Institutions; NAICS 611620: Sports and Recreation Instruction; NAICS 532292: Recreational Goods Rental; NAICS 487110: Scenic and Sightseeing Transportation, Land; NAICS 487210: Scenic and Sightseeing Transportation, Water; NAICS 713990: All Other Amusement and Recreation Industries

8011   Offices and Clinics of Doctors of Medicine *see* NAICS 621493: Freestanding Ambulatory Surgical and Emergency Centers; NAICS 621491: HMO Medical Centers; NAICS 621112: Offices of Physicians; NAICS 621111: Offices of Physicians (except Mental Health Specialists)

8021   Offices and Clinics of Dentists *see* NAICS 621210: Offices of Dentists

8031   Offices and Clinics of Doctors of Osteopathy *see* NAICS 621111: Offices of Physicians (except Mental Health Specialists); NAICS 621112: Offices of Physicians, Mental Health Specialists

8041   Offices and Clinics of Chiropractors *see* NAICS 621310: Offices of Chiropractors

8042   Offices and Clinics of Optometrists *see* NAICS 621320: Offices of Optometrists

8043   Offices and Clinics of Podiatrists *see* NAICS 621391: Offices of Podiatrists

8049   Offices and Clinics of Health Practitioners, NEC *see* NAICS 621330: Offices of Mental Health Practitioners (except Physicians); NAICS 621340: Offices of Physical, Occupational, and Speech Therapists and Audiologists; NAICS 621399: Offices of All Other Miscellaneous Health Practitioners

8051   Skilled Nursing Care Facilities *see* NAICS 623311: Continuing Care Retirement Communities; NAICS 623110: Nursing Care Facilities

8052   Intermediate Care Facilities *see* NAICS 623311: Continuing Care Retirement Communities; NAICS 623210: Residential Mental Retardation Facilities; NAICS 623110: Nursing Care Facilities

8059   Nursing and Personal Care Facilities, NEC *see* NAICS 623311: Continuing Care Retirement Communities; NAICS 623110: Nursing Care Facilities

8062   General Medical and Surgical Hospitals *see* NAICS 622110: General Medical and Surgical Hospitals

8063   Psychiatric Hospitals *see* NAICS 622210: Psychiatric and Substance Abuse Hospitals

8069   Specialty Hospitals, Except Psychiatric *see* NAICS 622110: General Medical and Surgical Hospitals; NAICS 622210: Psychiatric and Substance Abuse

Hospitals; NAICS 622310: Specialty (except Psychiatric and Substance Abuse) Hospitals

8071 Medical Laboratories *see* NAICS 621512: Diagnostic Imaging Centers; NAICS 621511: Medical Laboratories

8072 Dental Laboratories *see* NAICS 339116: Dental Laboratories

8082 Home Health Care Services *see* NAICS 621610: Home Health Care Services

8092 Kidney Dialysis Centers *see* NAICS 621492: Kidney Dialysis Centers

8093 Specialty Outpatient Facilities, NEC *see* NAICS 621410: Family Planning Centers; NAICS 621420: Outpatient Mental Health and Substance Abuse Centers; NAICS 621498: All Other Outpatient Care Facilities

8099 Health and Allied Services, NEC *see* NAICS 621991: Blood and Organ Banks; NAICS 541430: Graphic Design Services; NAICS 541922: Commercial Photography; NAICS 621410: Family Planning Centers; NAICS 621999: All Other Miscellaneous Ambulatory Health Care Services

8111 Legal Services *see* NAICS 541110: Offices of Lawyers

8211 Elementary and Secondary Schools *see* NAICS 611110: Elementary and Secondary Schools

8221 Colleges, Universities, and Professional Schools *see* NAICS 611310: Colleges, Universities, and Professional Schools

8222 Junior Colleges and Technical Institutes *see* NAICS 611210: Junior Colleges

8231 Libraries *see* NAICS 514120: Libraries and Archives

8243 Data Processing Schools *see* NAICS 611519: Other Technical and Trade Schools; NAICS 611420: Computer Training

8244 Business and Secretarial Schools *see* NAICS 611410: Business and Secretarial Schools

8249 Vocational Schools, NEC *see* NAICS 611513: Apprenticeship Training; NAICS 611512: Flight Training; NAICS 611519: Other Technical and Trade Schools

8299 Schools and Educational Services, NEC *see* NAICS 611512: Flight Training; NAICS 611692: Automobile Driving Schools; NAICS 611710: Educational Support Services; NAICS 611691: Exam Preparation and Tutoring; NAICS 611610: Fine Arts Schools; NAICS 611630: Language Schools; NAICS 611430: Professional and Management Development Training Schools; NAICS 611699: All Other Miscellaneous Schools and Instruction

8322 Individual and Family Social Services *see* NAICS 624110: Child and Youth Services; NAICS 624210: Community Food Services; NAICS

624229: Other Community Housing Services; NAICS 624230: Emergency and Other Relief Services; NAICS 624120: Services for the Elderly and Persons with Disabilities; NAICS 624221: Temporary Shelter; NAICS 922150: Parole Offices and Probation Offices; NAICS 624190: Other Individual and Family Services

8331 Job Training and Vocational Rehabilitation Services *see* NAICS 624310: Vocational Rehabilitation Services

8351 Child Day Care Services *see* NAICS 624410: Child Day Care Services

8361 Residential Care *see* NAICS 623312: Homes for the Elderly; NAICS 623220: Residential Mental Health and Substance Abuse Facilities; NAICS 623990: Other Residential Care Facilities

8399 Social Services, NEC *see* NAICS 813212: Voluntary Health Organizations; NAICS 813219: Other Grantmaking and Giving Services; NAICS 813311: Human Rights Organizations; NAICS 813312: Environment, Conservation and Wildlife Organizations; NAICS 813319: Other Social Advocacy Organizations

8412 Museums and Art Galleries *see* NAICS 712110: Museums; NAICS 712120: Historical Sites

8422 Arboreta and Botanical or Zoological Gardens *see* NAICS 712130: Zoos and Botanical Gardens; NAICS 712190: Nature Parks and Other Similar Institutions

8611 Business Associations *see* NAICS 813910: Business Associations

8621 Professional Membership Organizations *see* NAICS 813920: Professional Organizations

8631 Labor Unions and Similar Labor Organizations *see* NAICS 813930: Labor Unions and Similar Labor Organizations

8641 Civic, Social, and Fraternal Associations *see* NAICS 813410: Civic and Social Organizations; NAICS 813990: Other Similar Organizations; NAICS 921150: American Indian and Alaska Native Tribal Governments; NAICS 624110: Child and Youth Services

8651 Political Organizations *see* NAICS 813940: Political Organizations

8661 Religious Organizations *see* NAICS 813110: Religious Organizations

8699 Membership Organizations, NEC *see* NAICS 813410: Civic and Social Organizations; NAICS 813910: Business Associations; NAICS 813312: Environment, Conservation, and Wildlife Organizations; NAICS 561599: All Other Travel Arrangement and Reservation Services; NAICS 813990: Other Similar Organizations

8711 Engineering Services *see* NAICS 541330: Engineering Services

8712 Architectural Services *see* NAICS 541310: Architectural Services

8713 Surveying Services *see* NAICS 541360: Geophysical Surveying and Mapping Services; NAICS 541370: Surveying and Mapping (except Geophysical) Services

8721 Accounting, Auditing, and Bookkeeping Services *see* NAICS 541211: Offices of Certified Public Accountants; NAICS 541214: Payroll Services; NAICS 541219: Other Accounting Services

8731 Commercial Physical and Biological Research *see* NAICS 541710: Research and Development in the Physical Sciences and Engineering Sciences; NAICS 541720: Research and Development in the Life Sciences

8732 Commercial Economic, Sociological, and Educational Research *see* NAICS 541730: Research and Development in the Social Sciences and Humanities; NAICS 541910: Marketing Research and Public Opinion Polling

8733 Noncommercial Research Organizations *see* NAICS 541710: Research and Development in the Physical Sciences and Engineering Sciences; NAICS 541720: Research and Development in the Life Sciences; NAICS 541730: Research and Development in the Social Sciences and Humanities

8734 Testing Laboratories *see* NAICS 541940: Veterinary Services; NAICS 541380: Testing Laboratories

8741 Management Services *see* NAICS 561110: Office Administrative Services

8742 Management Consulting Services *see* NAICS 541611: Administrative Management and General Management Consulting Services; NAICS 541612: Human Resources and Executive Search Consulting Services; NAICS 541613: Marketing Consulting Services; NAICS 541614: Process, Physical, Distribution, and Logistics Consulting

8743 Public Relations Services *see* NAICS 541820: Public Relations Services

8744 Facilities Support Management Services *see* NAICS 561210: Facilities Support Services

8748 Business Consulting Services, NEC *see* NAICS 611710: Educational Support Services; NAICS 541618: Other Management Consulting Services; NAICS 541690: Other Scientific and Technical Consulting Services

8811 Private Households *see* NAICS 814110: Private Households

8999 Services, NEC *see* NAICS 711510: Independent Artists, Writers, and Performers; NAICS 512210: Record Production; NAICS 541690: Other Scientific and Technical Consulting Services;

NAICS 512230: Music Publishers; NAICS 541612: Human Resources and Executive Search Consulting Services; NAICS 514199: All Other Information Services; NAICS 541620: Environmental Consulting Services

PUBLIC ADMINISTRATION

9111 Executive Offices *see* NAICS 921110: Executive Offices

9121 Legislative Bodies *see* NAICS 921120: Legislative Bodies

9131 Executive and Legislative Offices, Combined *see* NAICS 921140: Executive and Legislative Offices, Combined

9199 General Government, NEC *see* NAICS 921190: All Other General Government

9211 Courts *see* NAICS 922110: Courts

9221 Police Protection *see* NAICS 922120: Police Protection

9222 Legal Counsel and Prosecution *see* NAICS 922130: Legal Counsel and Prosecution

9223 Correctional Institutions *see* NAICS 922140: Correctional Institutions

9224 Fire Protection *see* NAICS 922160: Fire Protection

9229 Public Order and Safety, NEC *see* NAICS 922190: All Other Justice, Public Order, and Safety

9311 Public Finance, Taxation, and Monetary Policy *see* NAICS 921130: Public Finance

9411 Administration of Educational Programs *see* NAICS 923110: Administration of Education Programs

9431 Administration of Public Health Programs *see* NAICS 923120: Administration of Public Health Programs

9441 Administration of Social, Human Resource, and Income Maintenance Programs *see* NAICS 923130: Administration of Social, Human Resource, and Income Maintenance Programs

9451 Administration of Veteran's Affairs, Except Health Insurance *see* NAICS 923140: Administration of Veteran's Affairs

9511 Air and Water Resource and Solid Waste Management *see* NAICS 924110: Air and Water Resource and Solid Waste Management

9512 Land, Mineral, Wildlife, and Forest Conservation *see* NAICS 924120: Land, Mineral, Wildlife, and Forest Conservation

9531 Administration of Housing Programs *see* NAICS 925110: Administration of Housing Programs

9532 Administration of Urban Planning and Community and Rural Development *see* NAICS 925120: Administration of Urban Planning and Community and Rural Development

9611 Administration of General Economic Programs *see* NAICS 926110: Administration of General Economic Programs

9621 Regulations and Administration of Transportation Programs *see* NAICS 488111: Air Traffic Control; NAICS 926120: Regulation and Administration of Transportation Programs

9631 Regulation and Administration of Communications, Electric, Gas, and Other Utilities *see* NAICS 926130: Regulation and Administration of Communications, Electric, Gas, and Other Utilities

9641 Regulation of Agricultural Marketing and Commodities *see* NAICS 926140: Regulation of Agricultural Marketing and Commodities

9651 Regulation, Licensing, and Inspection of Miscellaneous Commercial Sectors *see* NAICS 926150: Regulation, Licensing, and Inspection of Miscellaneous Commercial Sectors

9661 Space Research and Technology *see* NAICS 927110: Space Research and Technology

9711 National Security *see* NAICS 928110: National Security

9721 International Affairs *see* NAICS 928120: International Affairs

9999 Nonclassified Establishments *see* NAICS 999990: Unclassified Establishments

NAICS to SIC Conversion Guide

The following listing cross-references six-digit 1997 North American Industry Classification System (NAICS) codes with four-digit 1987 Standard Industrial Classification (SIC) codes. Because the systems differ in specificity, some NAICS categories correspond to more than one SIC category.

AGRICULTURE, FORESTRY, FISHING, & HUNTING

111110   Soybean Farming *see* SIC 0116: Soybeans

111120   Oilseed (except Soybean) Farming *see* SIC 0119: Cash Grains, NEC

111130   Dry Pea and Bean Farming *see* SIC 0119: Cash Grains, NEC

111140   Wheat Farming *see* SIC 0111: Wheat

111150   Corn Farming *see* SIC 0115: Corn

111150   Corn Farming *see* SIC 0119: Cash Grains, NEC

111160   Rice Farming *see* SIC 0112: Rice

111191   Oilseed and Grain Combination Farming *see* SIC 0119: Cash Grains, NEC

111199   All Other Grain Farming *see* SIC 0119: Cash Grains, NEC

111211   Potato Farming *see* SIC 0134: Irish Potatoes

111219   Other Vegetable (except Potato) and Melon Farming *see* SIC 0139: Field Crops, Except Cash Grains, NEC; SIC 0161: Vegetables and Melons

111310   Orange Groves *see* SIC 0174: Citrus Fruits

111320   Citrus (except Orange) Groves *see* SIC 0174: Citrus Fruits

111331   Apple Orchards *see* SIC 0175: Deciduous Tree Fruits

111332   Grape Vineyards *see* SIC 0172: Grapes

111333   Strawberry Farming *see* SIC 0171: Berry Crops

111334   Berry (except Strawberry) Farming *see* SIC 0171: Berry Crops

111335   Tree Nut Farming *see* SIC 0173: Tree Nuts

111336   Fruit and Tree Nut Combination Farming *see* SIC 0179: Fruits and Tree Nuts, NEC

111339   Other Noncitrus Fruit Farming *see* SIC 0175: Deciduous Tree Fruits; SIC 0179: Fruits and Tree Nuts, NEC

111411   Mushroom Production *see* SIC 0182: Food Crops Grown Under Cover

111419   Other Food Crops Grown Under Cover *see* SIC 0182: Food Crops Grown Under Cover

111421   Nursery and Tree Production *see* SIC 0181: Ornamental Floriculture and Nursery Products; SIC 0811: Timber Tracts

111422   Floriculture Production *see* SIC 0181: Ornamental Floriculture and Nursery Products

111910   Tobacco Farming *see* SIC 0132: Tobacco

111920   Cotton farming *see* SIC 0131: Cotton

111930   Sugarcane Farming *see* SIC 0133: Sugarcane and Sugar Beets

111940   Hay Farming *see* SIC 0139: Field Crops, Except Cash Grains, NEC

111991   Sugar Beet Farming *see* SIC 0133: Sugarcane and Sugar Beets

111992   Peanut Farming *see* SIC 0139: Field Crops, Except Cash Grains, NEC

111998   All Other Miscellaneous Crop Farming *see* SIC 0139: Field Crops, Except Cash Grains, NEC; SIC 0191: General Farms, Primarily Crop; SIC 0831: Forest Nurseries and Gathering of Forest Products; SIC 0919: Miscellaneous Marine Products; SIC 2099: Food Preparations, NEC

112111   Beef Cattle Ranching and Farming *see* SIC 0212: Beef Cattle, Except Feedlots; SIC 0241: Dairy Farms

112112   Cattle Feedlots *see* SIC 0211: Beef Cattle Feedlots

112120   Dairy Cattle and Milk Production *see* SIC 0241: Dairy Farms

112210 Hog and Pig Farming *see* SIC 0213: Hogs

112310 Chicken Egg Production *see* SIC 0252: Chicken Eggs

112320 Broilers and Other Meat-Type Chicken Production *see* SIC 0251: Broiler, Fryers, and Roaster Chickens

112330 Turkey Production *see* SIC 0253: Turkey and Turkey Eggs

112340 Poultry Hatcheries *see* SIC 0254: Poultry Hatcheries

112390 Other Poultry Production *see* SIC 0259: Poultry and Eggs, NEC

112410 Sheep Farming *see* SIC 0214: Sheep and Goats

112420 Goat Farming *see* SIC 0214: Sheep and Goats

112511 Finfish Farming and Fish Hatcheries *see* SIC 0273: Animal Aquaculture; SIC 0921: Fish Hatcheries and Preserves

112512 Shellfish Farming *see* SIC 0273: Animal Aquaculture; SIC 0921: Fish Hatcheries and Preserves

112519 Other Animal Aquaculture *see* SIC 0273: Animal Aquaculture

112910 Apiculture *see* SIC 0279: Animal Specialties, NEC

112920 Horse and Other Equine Production *see* SIC 0272: Horses and Other Equines

112930 Fur-bearing Animal and Rabbit Production *see* SIC 0271: Fur-Bearing Animals and Rabbits

112990 All Other Animal Production *see* SIC 0219: General Livestock, Except Dairy and Poultry; SIC 0279: Animal Specialties, NEC; SIC 0291: General Farms, Primarily Livestock and Animal Specialties

113110 Timber Tract Operations *see* SIC 0811: Timber Tracts

113210 Forest Nurseries and Gathering of Forest Products *see* SIC 0831: Forest Nurseries and Gathering of Forest Products

113310 Logging *see* SIC 2411: Logging

114111 Finfish Fishing *see* SIC 0912: Finfish

114112 Shellfish Fishing *see* SIC 0913: Shellfish

114119 Other Marine Fishing *see* SIC 0919: Miscellaneous Marine Products

114210 Hunting and Trapping *see* SIC 0971: Hunting, Trapping, and Game Propagation

115111 Cotton Ginning *see* SIC 0724: Cotton Ginning

115112 Soil Preparation, Planting and Cultivating *see* SIC 0711: Soil Preparation Services; SIC 0721: Crop Planting, Cultivating and Protecting

115113 Crop Harvesting, Primarily By Machine *see* SIC 0722: Crop Harvesting, Primarily by Machine

115114 Postharvest Crop Activities (except Cotton Ginning) *see* SIC 0723: Crop Preparation Services For Market, except Cotton Ginning

115115 Farm Labor Contractors and Crew Leaders *see* SIC 0761: Farm Labor Contractors and Crew Leaders

115116 Farm Management Services *see* SIC 0762: Farm Management Services

115210 Support Activities for Animal Production *see* SIC 0751: Livestock Services, Except Veterinary; SIC 0752: Animal Specialty Services, Except Veterinary; SIC 7699: Repair Shops and Related Services, NEC

115310 Support Activities for Forestry *see* SIC 0851: Forestry Services

MINING

211111 Crude Petroleum and Natural Gas Extraction *see* SIC 1311: Crude Petroleum and Natural Gas

211112 Natural Gas Liquid Extraction *see* SIC 1321: Natural Gas Liquids

212111 Bituminous Coal and Lignite Surface Mining *see* SIC 1221: Bituminous Coal and Lignite Surface Mining

212112 Bituminous Coal Underground Mining *see* SIC 1222: Bituminous Coal Underground Mining

212113 Anthracite Mining *see* SIC 1231: Anthracite Mining

212210 Iron Ore Mining *see* SIC 1011: Iron Ores

212221 Gold Ore Mining *see* SIC 1041: Gold Ores

212222 Silver Ore Mining *see* SIC 1044: Silver Ores

212231 Lead Ore and Zinc Ore Mining *see* SIC 1031: Lead and Zinc Ores

212234 Copper Ore and Nickel Ore Mining *see* SIC 1021: Copper Ores; SIC 1061: Ferroalloy Ores, Except Vanadium

212291 Uranium-Radium-Vanadium Ore Mining *see* SIC 1094: Uranium-Radium-Vanadium Ores

212299 Other Metal Ore Mining *see* SIC 1061: Ferroalloy Ores, Except Vanadium; SIC 1099: Miscellaneous Metal Ores, NEC

212311 Dimension Stone Mining and Quarry *see* SIC 1411: Dimension Stone

212312 Crushed and Broken Limestone Mining and Quarrying *see* SIC 1422: Crushed and Broken Limestone

212313 Crushed and Broken Granite Mining and Quarrying *see* SIC 1423: Crushed and Broken Granite

212319 Other Crushed and Broken Stone Mining and Quarrying *see* SIC 1429: Crushed and Broken Stone, NEC; SIC 1499: Miscellaneous Nonmetallic Minerals, Except Fuels

212321 Construction Sand and Gravel Mining *see* SIC 1442: Construction Sand and Gravel

212322 Industrial Sand Mining *see* SIC 1446: Industrial Sand

212324 Kaolin and Ball Clay Mining *see* SIC 1455: Kaolin and Ball Clay

212325 Clay and Ceramic and Refractory Minerals Mining *see* SIC 1459: Clay, Ceramic, and Refractory Minerals, NEC

212391 Potash, Soda, and Borate Mineral Mining *see* SIC 1474: Potash, Soda, and Borate Minerals

212392 Phosphate Rock Mining *see* SIC 1475: Phosphate Rock

212393 Other Chemical and Fertilizer Mineral Mining *see* SIC 1479: Chemical and Fertilizer Mineral Mining, NEC

212399 All Other Non-Metallic Mineral Mining *see* SIC 1499: Miscellaneous Nonmetallic Minerals, Except Fuels

213111 Drilling Oil and Gas Wells *see* SIC 1381: Drilling Oil and Gas Wells

213112 Support Activities for Oil and Gas Field Exploration *see* SIC 1382: Oil and Gas Field Exploration Services; SIC 1389: Oil and Gas Field Services, NEC

213113 Support Activities for Coal Mining *see* SIC 1241: Coal Mining Services

213114 Support Activities for Metal Mining *see* SIC 1081: Metal Mining Services

213115 Support Activities for Non-metallic Minerals, (except Fuels) *see* SIC 1481: Nonmetallic Minerals Services Except Fuels

UTILITIES

221111 Hydroelectric Power Generation *see* SIC 4911: Electric Services; SIC 4931: Electric and Other Services Combined; SIC 4939: Combination Utilities, NEC

221112 Fossil Fuel Electric Power Generation *see* SIC 4911: Electric Services; SIC 4931: Electric and Other Services Combined; SIC 4939: Combination Utilities, NEC

221113 Nuclear Electric Power Generation *see* SIC 4911: Electric Services; SIC 4931: Electric and Other Services Combined; SIC 4939: Combination Utilities, NEC

221119 Other Electric Power Generation *see* SIC 4911: Electric Services; SIC 4931: Electric and Other Services Combined; SIC 4939: Combination Utilities, NEC

221121 Electric Bulk Power Transmission and Control *see* SIC 4911: Electric Services; SIC 4931: Electric and Other Services Combined; SIC 4939: Combination Utilities, NEC

221122 Electric Power Distribution *see* SIC 4911: Electric Services; SIC 4931: Electric and Other

Services Combined; SIC 4939: Combination Utilities, NEC

221210 Natural Gas Distribution *see* SIC 4923: Natural Gas Transmission and Distribution; SIC 4924: Natural Gas Distribution; SIC 4925: Mixed, Manufactured, or Liquefied Petroleum Gas Production and/or Distribution; SIC 4931: Electric and Other Services Combined; SIC 4932: Gas and Other Services Combined; SIC 4939: Combination Utilities, NEC

221310 Water Supply and Irrigation Systems *see* SIC 4941: Water Supply; SIC 4971: Irrigation Systems

221320 Sewage Treatment Facilities *see* SIC 4952: Sewerage Systems

221330 Steam and Air-Conditioning Supply *see* SIC 4961: Steam and Air-Conditioning Supply

CONSTRUCTION

233110 Land Subdivision and Land Development *see* SIC 6552: Land Subdividers and Developers, Except Cemeteries; SIC 1521: General Contractors-Single-Family Houses; SIC 1531: Operative Builders

233220 Multi-Family Housing Construction *see* SIC 1522: General Contractors-Residential Buildings, Other Than Single-Family; SIC 1531: Operative Builders

233310 Manufacturing and Light Industrial Building Construction *see* SIC 1531: Operative Builders; SIC 1541: General Contractors-Industrial Buildings and Warehouses

233320 Commercial and Institutional Building Construction *see* SIC 1522: General Contractors-Residential Buildings, Other Than Single-Family; SIC 1531: Operative Builders; SIC 1541: General Contractors-Industrial Buildings and Warehouses; SIC 1542: General Contractors-Nonresidential Buildings, Other than Industrial Buildings and Warehouses

234110 Highway and Street Construction *see* SIC 1611: Highway and Street Construction, Except Elevated Highways

234120 Bridge and Tunnel Construction *see* SIC 1622: Bridge, Tunnel, and Elevated Highway Construction

234910 Water, Sewer and Pipeline Construction *see* SIC 1623: Water, Sewer, Pipeline, and Communications and Power Line Construction

234920 Power and Communication Transmission Line Construction *see* SIC 1623: Water, Sewer, Pipeline, and Communications and Power Line Construction

234930 Industrial Nonbuilding Structure Construction *see* SIC 1629: Heavy Construction, NEC

234990 All Other Heavy Construction *see* SIC 1629: Heavy Construction, NEC; SIC 7353: Heavy Construction Equipment Rental and Leasing

235110 Plumbing, Heating and Air-Conditioning Contractors *see* SIC 1711: Plumbing, Heating, and Air-Conditioning

235210 Painting and Wall Covering Contractors *see* SIC 1721: Painting and Paper Hanging; SIC 1799: Special Trade Contractors, NEC

235310 Electrical Contractors *see* SIC 1731: Electrical Work

235410 Masonry and Stone Contractors *see* SIC 1741: Masonry, Stone Setting and Other Stone Work

235420 Drywall, Plastering, Acoustical, and Insulation Contractors *see* SIC 1742: Plastering, Drywall, Acoustical and Insulation Work; SIC 1743: Terrazzo, Tile, Marble, and Mosaic Work; SIC 1771: Concrete Work

235430 Tile, Marble, Terrazzo and Mosaic Contractors *see* SIC 1743: Terrazzo, Tile, Marble, and Mosaic Work

235510 Carpentry Contractors *see* SIC 1751: Carpentry Work

235520 Floor Laying and Other Floor Contractors *see* SIC 1752: Floor Laying and Other Floor Work, NEC

235610 Roofing, Siding, and Sheet Metal Contractors *see* SIC 1761: Roofing, Siding, and Sheet Metal Work

235710 Concrete Contractors *see* SIC 1771: Concrete Work

235810 Water Well Drilling Contractors *see* SIC 1781: Water Well Drilling

235910 Structural Steel Erection Contractors *see* SIC 1791: Structural Steel Erection

235920 Glass and Glazing Contractors *see* SIC 1793: Glass and Glazing Work; SIC 1799: Special Trade Contractors, NEC

235930 Excavation Contractors *see* SIC 1794: Excavation Work

235940 Wrecking and Demolition Contractors *see* SIC 1795: Wrecking and Demolition Work

235950 Building Equipment and Other Machinery Installation Contractors *see* SIC 1796: Installation or Erection of Building Equipment, NEC

235990 All Other Special Trade Contractors *see* SIC 1799: Special Trade Contractors, NEC

FOOD MANUFACTURING

311111 Dog and Cat Food Manufacturing *see* SIC 2047: Dog and Cat Food

311119 Other Animal Food Manufacturing *see* SIC 2048: Prepared Feed and Feed Ingredients for Animals and Fowls, Except Dogs and Cats

311211 Flour Milling *see* SIC 2034: Dried and Dehydrated Fruits, Vegetables, and Soup Mixes; SIC 2041: Flour and Other Grain Mill Products

311212 Rice Milling *see* SIC 2044: Rice Milling

311213 Malt Manufacturing *see* SIC 2083: Malt

311221 Wet Corn Milling *see* SIC 2046: Wet Corn Milling

311222 Soybean Processing *see* SIC 2075: Soybean Oil Mills; SIC 2079: Shortening, Table Oils, Margarine, and Other Edible Fats and Oils, NEC

311223 Other Oilseed Processing *see* SIC 2074: Cottonseed Oil Mills; SIC 2076: Vegetable Oil Mills, Except Corn, Cottonseed, and Soybeans; SIC 2079: Shortening, Table Oils, Margarine, and Other Edible Fats and Oils, NEC

311225 Fats and Oils Refining and Blending *see* SIC 2074: Cottonseed Oil Mills; SIC 2075: Soybean Oil Mills; SIC 2076: Vegetable Oil Mills, Except Corn, Cottonseed, and Soybeans; SIC 2077: Animal and Marine Fats and Oils; SIC 2079: Shortening, Table Oils, Margarine, and Other Edible Fats and Oils, NEC

311230 Breakfast Cereal Manufacturing *see* SIC 2043: Cereal Breakfast Foods

311311 Sugarcane Mills *see* SIC 2061: Cane Sugar, Except Refining

311312 Cane Sugar Refining *see* SIC 2062: Cane Sugar Refining

311313 Beet Sugar Manufacturing *see* SIC 2063: Beet Sugar

311320 Chocolate and Confectionery Manufacturing from Cacao Beans *see* SIC 2066: Chocolate and Cocoa Products

311330 Confectionery Manufacturing from Purchased Chocolate *see* SIC 2064: Candy and Other Confectionery Products

311340 Non-Chocolate Confectionery Manufacturing *see* SIC 2064: Candy and Other Confectionery Products; SIC 2067: Chewing Gum; SIC 2099: Food Preparations, NEC

311411 Frozen Fruit, Juice, and Vegetable Processing *see* SIC 2037: Frozen Fruits, Fruit Juices, and Vegetables

311412 Frozen Specialty Food Manufacturing *see* SIC 2038: Frozen Specialties, NEC

311421 Fruit and Vegetable Canning *see* SIC 2033: Canned Fruits, Vegetables, Preserves, Jams, and Jellies; SIC 2035: Pickled Fruits and Vegetables, Vegetables Sauces and Seasonings, and Salad Dressings

311422 Specialty Canning *see* SIC 2032: Canned Specialties

311423 Dried and Dehydrated Food Manufacturing *see* SIC 2034: Dried and Dehydrated Fruits, Vegetables, and Soup Mixes; SIC 2099: Food Preparations, NEC

311511 Fluid Milk Manufacturing *see* SIC 2026: Fluid Milk

311512 Creamery Butter Manufacturing *see* SIC 2021: Creamery Butter

311513 Cheese Manufacturing *see* SIC 2022: Natural, Processed, and Imitation Cheese

311514 Dry, Condensed, and Evaporated Dairy Product Manufacturing *see* SIC 2023: Dry, Condensed, and Evaporated Dairy Products

311520 Ice Cream and Frozen Dessert Manufacturing *see* SIC 2024: Ice Cream and Frozen Desserts

311611 Animal (except Poultry) Slaughtering *see* SIC 0751: Livestock Services, Except Veterinary; SIC 2011: Meat Packing Plants; SIC 2048: Prepared Feed and Feed Ingredients for Animals and Fowls, Except Dogs and Cats

311612 Meat Processed From Carcasses *see* SIC 2013: Sausages and Other Prepared Meats; SIC 5147: Meats and Meat Products

311613 Rendering and Meat By-product Processing *see* SIC 2077: Animal and Marine Fats and Oils

311615 Poultry Processing *see* SIC 2015: Poultry Slaughtering and Processing

311711 Seafood Canning *see* SIC 2077: Animal and Marine Fats and Oils; SIC 2091: Canned and Cured Fish and Seafood

311712 Fresh and Frozen Seafood Processing *see* SIC 2077: Animal and Marine Fats and Oils; SIC 2092: Prepared Fresh or Frozen Fish and Seafoods

311811 Retail Bakeries *see* SIC 5461: Retail Bakeries

311812 Commercial Bakeries *see* SIC 2051: Bread and Other Bakery Products, Except Cookies and Crackers; SIC 2052: Cookies and Crackers

311813 Frozen Bakery Product Manufacturing *see* SIC 2053: Frozen Bakery Products, Except Bread

311821 Cookie and Cracker Manufacturing *see* SIC 2052: Cookies and Crackers

311822 Flour Mixes and Dough Manufacturing from Purchased Flour *see* SIC 2045: Prepared Flour Mixes and Doughs

311823 Pasta Manufacturing *see* SIC 2098: Macaroni, Spaghetti, Vermicelli, and Noodles

311830 Tortilla Manufacturing *see* SIC 2099: Food Preparations, NEC

311911 Roasted Nuts and Peanut Butter Manufacturing *see* SIC 2068: Salted and Roasted Nuts and Seeds; SIC 2099: Food Preparations, NEC

311919 Other Snack Food Manufacturing *see* SIC 2052: Cookies and Crackers; SIC 2096: Potato Chips, Corn Chips, and Similar Snacks

311920 Coffee and Tea Manufacturing *see* SIC 2043: Cereal Breakfast Foods; SIC 2095: Roasted Coffee; SIC 2099: Food Preparations, NEC

311930 Flavoring Syrup and Concentrate Manufacturing *see* SIC 2087: Flavoring Extracts and Flavoring Syrups NEC

311941 Mayonnaise, Dressing, and Other Prepared Sauce Manufacturing *see* SIC 2035: Pickled Fruits and Vegetables, Vegetables Sauces and Seasonings, and Salad Dressings; SIC 2099: Food Preparations, NEC

311942 Spice and Extract Manufacturing *see* SIC 2087: Flavoring Extracts and Flavoring Syrups NEC; SIC 2095: Roasted Coffee; SIC 2099: Food Preparations, NEC; SIC 2899: Chemicals and Chemical Preparations, NEC

311991 Perishable Prepared Food Manufacturing *see* SIC 2099: Food Preparations, NEC

311999 All Other Miscellaneous Food Manufacturing *see* SIC 2015: Poultry Slaughtering and Processing; SIC 2032: Canned Specialties; SIC 2087: Flavoring Extracts and Flavoring Syrups NEC; SIC 2099: Food Preparations, NEC

BEVERAGE & TOBACCO PRODUCT MANUFACTURING

312111 Soft Drink Manufacturing *see* SIC 2086: Bottled and Canned Soft Drinks and Carbonated Waters

312112 Bottled Water Manufacturing *see* SIC 2086: Bottled and Canned Soft Drinks and Carbonated Waters

312113 Ice Manufacturing *see* SIC 2097: Manufactured Ice

312120 Breweries *see* SIC 2082: Malt Beverages

312130 Wineries *see* SIC 2084: Wines, Brandy, and Brandy Spirits

312140 Distilleries *see* SIC 2085: Distilled and Blended Liquors

312210 Tobacco Stemming and Redrying *see* SIC 2141: Tobacco Stemming and Redrying

312221 Cigarette Manufacturing *see* SIC 2111: Cigarettes

312229 Other Tobacco Product Manufacturing *see* SIC 2121: Cigars; SIC 2131: Chewing and Smoking Tobacco and Snuff; SIC 2141: Tobacco Stemming and Redrying

TEXTILE MILLS

313111 Yarn Spinning Mills *see* SIC 2281: Yarn Spinning Mills; SIC 2299: Textile Goods, NEC

313112 Yarn Texturing, Throwing and Twisting Mills *see* SIC 2282: Yarn Texturizing, Throwing, Twisting, and Winding Mills

313113   Thread Mills *see* SIC 2284: Thread Mills; SIC 2299: Textile Goods, NEC

313210   Broadwoven Fabric Mills *see* SIC 2211: Broadwoven Fabric Mills, Cotton; SIC 2221: Broadwoven Fabric Mills, Manmade Fiber and Silk; SIC 2231: Broadwoven Fabric Mills, Wool (Including Dyeing and Finishing); SIC 2299: Textile Goods, NEC

313221   Narrow Fabric Mills *see* SIC 2241: Narrow Fabric and Other Smallware Mills: Cotton, Wool, Silk, and Manmade Fiber; SIC 2299: Textile Goods, NEC

313222   Schiffli Machine Embroidery *see* SIC 2397: Schiffli Machine Embroideries

313230   Nonwoven Fabric Mills *see* SIC 2297: Nonwoven Fabrics; SIC 2299: Textile Goods, NEC

313241   Weft Knit Fabric Mills *see* SIC 2257: Weft Knit Fabric Mills; SIC 2259: Knitting Mills, NEC

313249   Other Knit Fabric and Lace Mills *see* SIC 2258: Lace and Warp Knit Fabric Mills; SIC 2259: Knitting Mills, NEC

313311   Broadwoven Fabric Finishing Mills *see* SIC 2231: Broadwoven Fabric Mills, Wool (Including Dyeing and Finishing); SIC 2261: Finishers of Broadwoven Fabrics of Cotton; SIC 2262: Finishers of Broadwoven Fabrics of Manmade Fiber and Silk; SIC 2269: Finishers of Textiles, NEC; SIC 5131: Piece Goods, Notions, and Other Dry Goods

313312   Textile and Fabric Finishing (except Broadwoven Fabric) Mills *see* SIC 2231: Broadwoven Fabric Mills, Wool (Including Dyeing and Finishing); SIC 2257: Weft Knit Fabric Mills; SIC 2258: Lace and Warp Knit Fabric Mills; SIC 2269: Finishers of Textiles, NEC; SIC 2282: Yarn Texturizing, Throwing, Twisting, and Winding Mills; SIC 2284: Thread Mills; SIC 2299: Textile Goods, NEC; SIC 5131: Piece Goods, Notions, and Other Dry Goods

313320   Fabric Coating Mills *see* SIC 2295: Coated Fabrics, Not Rubberized; SIC 3069: Fabricated Rubber Products, NEC

TEXTILE PRODUCT MILLS

314110   Carpet and Rug Mills *see* SIC 2273: Carpets and Rugs

314121   Curtain and Drapery Mills *see* SIC 2391: Curtains and Draperies; SIC 5714: Drapery, Curtain, and Upholstery Stores

314129   Other Household Textile Product Mills *see* SIC 2392: Housefurnishings, Except Curtains and Draperies

314911   Textile Bag Mills *see* SIC 2392: Housefurnishings, Except Curtains and Draperies; SIC 2393: Textile Bags

314912   Canvas and Related Product Mills *see* SIC 2394: Canvas and Related Products

314991   Rope, Cordage and Twine Mills *see* SIC 2298: Cordage and Twine

314992   Tire Cord and Tire Fabric Mills *see* SIC 2296: Tire Cord and Fabrics

314999   All Other Miscellaneous Textile Product Mills *see* SIC 2299: Textile Goods, NEC; SIC 2395: Pleating, Decorative and Novelty Stitching, and Tucking for the Trade; SIC 2396: Automotive Trimmings, Apparel Findings, and Related Products; SIC 2399: Fabricated Textile Products, NEC

APPAREL MANUFACTURING

315111   Sheer Hosiery Mills *see* SIC 2251: Women's Full-Length and Knee-Length Hosiery, Except Socks; SIC 2252: Hosiery, NEC

315119   Other Hosiery and Sock Mills *see* SIC 2252:, Hosiery, NEC

315191   Outerwear Knitting Mills *see* SIC 2253: Knit Outerwear Mills; SIC 2259: Knitting Mills, NEC

315192   Underwear and Nightwear Knitting Mills *see* SIC 2254: Knit Underwear and Nightwear Mills; SIC 2259: Knitting Mills, NEC

315211   Men's and Boys' Cut and Sew Apparel Contractors *see* SIC 2311: Men's and Boys' Suits, Coats and Overcoats; SIC 2321: Men's and Boys' Shirts, Except Work Shirts; SIC 2322: Men's and Boys' Underwear and Nightwear; SIC 2325: Men's and Boys' Trousers and Slacks; SIC 2326: Men's and Boys' Work Clothing; SIC 2329: Men's and Boys' Clothing, NEC; SIC 2341: Women's, Misses, Children's, and Infants' Underwear and Nightwear; SIC 2361: Girls', Children's and Infants' Dresses, Blouses and Shirts; SIC 2369: Girls', Children's and Infants' Outerwear, NEC; SIC 2384: Robes and Dressing Gowns; SIC 2385: Waterproof Outerwear; SIC 2389: Apparel and Accessories, NEC; SIC 2395: Pleating, Decorative and Novelty Stitching, and Tucking for the Trade

315212   Women's and Girls' Cut and Sew Apparel Contractors *see* SIC 2331: Women's, Misses', and Juniors' Blouses and Shirts; SIC 2335: Women's, Misses', and Junior's Dresses; SIC 2337: Women's, Misses', and Juniors' Suits, Skirts and Coats; SIC 2339: Women's, Misses', and Juniors' Outerwear, NEC; SIC 2341:

Women's, Misses, Children's, and Infants' Underwear and Nightwear; SIC 2342: Brassieres, Girdles, and Allied Garments; SIC 2361: Girls', Children's, and Infants' Dresses, Blouses, and Shirts; SIC 2369: Girls', Children's, and Infants' Outerwear, NEC; SIC 2384: Robes and Dressing Gowns; SIC 2385: Waterproof Outerwear; SIC 2389: Apparel and Accessories, NEC; SIC 2395: Pleating, Decorative and Novelty Stitching, and Tucking for the Trade

315221 Men's and Boys' Cut and Sew Underwear and Nightwear Manufacturing *see* SIC 2322: Men's and Boys' Underwear and Nightwear; SIC 2341: Women's, Misses, Children's, and Infants' Underwear and Nightwear; SIC 2369: Girls', Children's and Infants' Outerwear, NEC; SIC 2384: Robes and Dressing Gowns

315222 Men's and Boys' Cut and Sew Suit, Coat, and Overcoat Manufacturing *see* SIC 2311: Men's and Boys' Suits, Coats and Overcoats; SIC 2369: Girls', Children's and Infants' Outerwear, NEC; SIC 2385: Waterproof Outerwear

315223 Men's and Boys' Cut and Sew Shirt, (except Work Shirt) Manufacturing *see* SIC 2321: Men's and Boys' Shirts, Except Work Shirts; SIC 2361: Girls', Children's and Infants' Dresses, Blouses and Shirts

315224 Men's and Boys' Cut And Sew Trouser, Slack, And Jean Manufacturing *see* SIC 2325: Men's and Boys' Trousers and Slacks; SIC 2369: Girls', Children's and Infants' Outerwear, NEC

315225 Men's and Boys' Cut and Sew Work Clothing Manufacturing *see* SIC 2326: Men's and Boys' Work Clothing

315228 Men's and Boys' Cut and Sew Other Outerwear Manufacturing *see* SIC 2329: Men's and Boys' Clothing, NEC; SIC 2369: Girls', Children's and Infants' Outerwear, NEC; SIC 2385: Waterproof Outerwear

315231 Women's and Girls' Cut and Sew Lingerie, Loungewear, and Nightwear Manufacturing *see* SIC 2341: Women's, Misses, Children's, and Infants' Underwear and Nightwear; SIC 2342: Brassieres, Girdles, and Allied Garments; SIC 2369: Girls', Children's and Infants' Outerwear, NEC; SIC 2384: Robes and Dressing Gowns; SIC 2389: Apparel and Accessories, NEC

315232 Women's and Girls' Cut and Sew Blouse and Shirt Manufacturing *see* SIC 2331: Women's, Misses', and Juniors' Blouses and Shirts; SIC 2361: Girls', Children's and Infants' Dresses, Blouses and Shirts

315233 Women's and Girls' Cut and Sew Dress Manufacturing *see* SIC 2335: Women's, Misses'

and Junior's Dresses; SIC 2361: Girls', Children's and Infants' Dresses, Blouses and Shirts

315234 Women's and Girls' Cut and Sew Suit, Coat, Tailored Jacket, and Skirt Manufacturing *see* SIC 2337: Women's, Misses' and Juniors' Suits, Skirts and Coats; SIC 2369: Girls', Children's and Infants' Outerwear, NEC; SIC 2385: Waterproof Outerwear

315238 Women's and Girls' Cut and Sew Other Outerwear Manufacturing *see* SIC 2339: Women's, Misses' and Juniors' Outerwear, NEC; SIC 2369: Girls', Children's and Infants' Outerwear, NEC; SIC 2385: Waterproof Outerwear

315291 Infants' Cut and Sew Apparel Manufacturing *see* SIC 2341: Women's, Misses, Children's, and Infants' Underwear and Nightwear; SIC 2361: Girls', Children's and Infants' Dresses, Blouses and Shirts; SIC 2369: Girls', Children's and Infants' Outerwear, NEC; SIC 2385: Waterproof Outerwear

315292 Fur and Leather Apparel Manufacturing *see* SIC 2371: Fur Goods; SIC 2386: Leather and Sheep-Lined Clothing

315299 All Other Cut and Sew Apparel Manufacturing *see* SIC 2329: Men's and Boys' Clothing, NEC; SIC 2339: Women's, Misses' and Juniors' Outerwear, NEC; SIC 2389: Apparel and Accessories, NEC

315991 Hat, Cap, and Millinery Manufacturing *see* SIC 2353: Hats, Caps, and Millinery

315992 Glove and Mitten Manufacturing *see* SIC 2381: Dress and Work Gloves, Except Knit and All-Leather; SIC 3151: Leather Gloves and Mittens

315993 Men's and Boys' Neckwear Manufacturing *see* SIC 2323: Men's and Boys' Neckwear

315999 Other Apparel Accessories and Other Apparel Manufacturing *see* SIC 2339: Women's, Misses' and Juniors' Outerwear, NEC; SIC 2385: Waterproof Outerwear; SIC 2387: Apparel Belts; SIC 2389: Apparel and Accessories, NEC; SIC 2396: Automotive Trimmings, Apparel Findings, and Related Products; SIC 2399: Fabricated Textile Products, NEC

LEATHER & ALLIED PRODUCT MANUFACTURING

316110 Leather and Hide Tanning and Finishing *see* SIC 3111: Leather Tanning and Finishing; SIC 3999: Manufacturing Industries, NEC

316211 Rubber and Plastics Footwear Manufacturing *see* SIC 3021: Rubber and Plastics Footwear

316212 House Slipper Manufacturing *see* SIC 3142: House Slippers

316213   Men's Footwear (except Athletic) Manufacturing *see* SIC 3143: Men's Footwear, Except Athletic

316214   Women's Footwear (except Athletic) Manufacturing *see* SIC 3144: Women's Footwear, Except Athletic

316219   Other Footwear Manufacturing *see* SIC 3149: Footwear, Except Rubber, NEC

316991   Luggage Manufacturing *see* SIC 3161: Luggage

316992   Women's Handbag and Purse Manufacturing *see* SIC 3171: Women's Handbags and Purses

316993   Personal Leather Good (except Women's Handbag and Purse) Manufacturing *see* SIC 3172: Personal Leather Goods, Except Women's Handbags and Purses

316999   All Other Leather Good Manufacturing *see* SIC 3131: Boot and Shoe Cut Stock and Findings; SIC 3199: Leather Goods, NEC

WOOD PRODUCT MANUFACTURING

321113   Sawmills *see* SIC 2421: Sawmills and Planing Mills, General; SIC 2429: Special Product Sawmills, NEC

321114   Wood Preservation *see* SIC 2491: Wood Preserving

321211   Hardwood Veneer and Plywood Manufacturing *see* SIC 2435: Hardwood Veneer and Plywood

321212   Softwood Veneer and Plywood Manufacturing *see* SIC 2436: Softwood Veneer and Plywood

321213   Engineered Wood Member (except Truss) Manufacturing *see* SIC 2439: Structural Wood Members, NEC

321214   Truss Manufacturing *see* SIC 2439: Structural Wood Members, NEC

321219   Reconstituted Wood Product Manufacturing *see* SIC 2493: Reconstituted Wood Products

321911   Wood Window and Door Manufacturing *see* SIC 2431: Millwork

321912   Cut Stock, Resawing Lumber, and Planing *see* SIC 2421: Sawmills and Planing Mills, General; SIC 2426: Hardwood Dimension and Flooring Mills; SIC 2429: Special Product Sawmills, NEC; SIC 2439: Structural Wood Members, NEC

321918   Other Millwork (including Flooring) *see* SIC 2421: Sawmills and Planing Mills, General; SIC 2426: Hardwood Dimension and Flooring Mills; SIC 2431: Millwork

321920   Wood Container and Pallet Manufacturing *see* SIC 2441: Nailed and Lock Corner Wood Boxes and Shook; SIC 2448: Wood Pallets and Skids; SIC 2449: Wood Containers, NEC; SIC 2499: Wood Products, NEC

321991   Manufactured Home (Mobile Home) Manufacturing *see* SIC 2451: Mobile Homes

321992   Prefabricated Wood Building Manufacturing *see* SIC 2452: Prefabricated Wood Buildings and Components

321999   All Other Miscellaneous Wood Product Manufacturing *see* SIC 2421: Sawmills and Planing Mills, General; SIC 2426: Hardwood Dimension and Flooring Mills; SIC 2429: Special Product Sawmills, NEC; SIC 2499: Wood Products, NEC; SIC 3131: Boot and Shoe Cut Stock and Findings; SIC 3999: Manufacturing Industries, NEC

PAPER MANUFACTURING

322110   Pulp Mills *see* SIC 2611: Pulp Mills

322121   Paper (except Newsprint) Mills *see* SIC 2611: Pulp Mills

322121   Paper (except Newsprint) Mills *see* SIC 2621: Paper Mills

322122   Newsprint Mills *see* SIC 2621: Paper Mills

322130   Paperboard Mills *see* SIC 2611: Pulp Mills

322130   Paperboard Mills *see* SIC 2631: Paperboard Mills

322211   Corrugated and Solid Fiber Box Manufacturing *see* SIC 2653: Corrugated and Solid Fiber Boxes

322212   Folding Paperboard Box Manufacturing *see* SIC 2657: Folding Paperboard Boxes, Including Sanitary

322213   Setup Paperboard Box Manufacturing *see* SIC 2652: Setup Paperboard Boxes

322214   Fiber Can, Tube, Drum, and Similar Products Manufacturing *see* SIC 2655: Fiber Cans, Tubes, Drums, and Similar Products

322215   Non-Folding Sanitary Food Container Manufacturing *see* SIC 2656: Sanitary Food Containers, Except Folding; SIC 2679: Converted Paper and Paperboard Products, NEC

322221   Coated and Laminated Packaging Paper and Plastics Film Manufacturing *see* SIC 2671: Packaging Paper and Plastics Film, Coated and Laminated

322222   Coated and Laminated Paper Manufacturing *see* SIC 2672: Coated and Laminated Paper, NEC; SIC 2679: Converted Paper and Paperboard Products, NEC

322223   Plastics, Foil, and Coated Paper Bag Manufacturing *see* SIC 2673: Plastics, Foil, and Coated Paper Bags

322224   Uncoated Paper and Multiwall Bag Manufacturing *see* SIC 2674: Uncoated Paper and Multiwall Bags

322225   Laminated Aluminum Foil Manufacturing for Flexible Packaging Uses *see* SIC 3497: Metal Foil and Leaf

322231   Die-Cut Paper and Paperboard Office Supplies Manufacturing *see* SIC 2675: Die-Cut Paper and Paperboard and Cardboard; SIC 2679: Converted Paper and Paperboard Products, NEC

322232   Envelope Manufacturing *see* SIC 2677: Envelopes

322233   Stationery, Tablet, and Related Product Manufacturing *see* SIC 2678: Stationery, Tablets, and Related Products

322291   Sanitary Paper Product Manufacturing *see* SIC 2676: Sanitary Paper Products

322292   Surface-Coated Paperboard Manufacturing *see* SIC 2675: Die-Cut Paper and Paperboard and Cardboard

322298   All Other Converted Paper Product Manufacturing *see* SIC 2675: Die-Cut Paper and Paperboard and Cardboard; SIC 2679: Converted Paper and Paperboard Products, NEC

PRINTING & RELATED SUPPORT ACTIVITIES

323110   Commercial Lithographic Printing *see* SIC 2752: Commercial Printing, Lithographic; SIC 2771: Greeting Cards; SIC 2782: Blankbooks, Loose-leaf Binders and Devices; SIC 3999: Manufacturing Industries, NEC

323111   Commercial Gravure Printing *see* SIC 2754: Commercial Printing, Gravure; SIC 2771: Greeting Cards; SIC 2782: Blankbooks, Loose-leaf Binders and Devices; SIC 3999: Manufacturing Industries, NEC

323112   Commercial Flexographic Printing *see* SIC 2759: Commercial Printing, NEC; SIC 2771: Greeting Cards; SIC 2782: Blankbooks, Loose-leaf Binders and Devices

323112   Commercial Flexographic Printing *see* SIC 3999: Manufacturing Industries, NEC

323113   Commercial Screen Printing *see* SIC 2396: Automotive Trimmings, Apparel Findings, and Related Products; SIC 2759: Commercial Printing, NEC; SIC 2771: Greeting Cards; SIC 2782: Blankbooks, Loose-leaf Binders and Devices; SIC 3999: Manufacturing Industries, NEC

323114   Quick Printing *see* SIC 2752: Commercial Printing, Lithographic; SIC 2759: Commercial Printing, NEC

323115   Digital Printing *see* SIC 2759: Commercial Printing, NEC

323116   Manifold Business Form Printing *see* SIC 2761: Manifold Business Forms

323117   Book Printing *see* SIC 2732: Book Printing

323118   Blankbook, Loose-leaf Binder and Device Manufacturing *see* SIC 2782: Blankbooks, Loose-leaf Binders and Devices

323119   Other Commercial Printing *see* SIC 2759: Commercial Printing, NEC; SIC 2771: Greeting Cards; SIC 2782: Blankbooks, Loose-leaf Binders and Devices; SIC 3999: Manufacturing Industries, NEC

323121   Tradebinding and Related Work *see* SIC 2789: Bookbinding and Related Work

323122   Prepress Services *see* SIC 2791: Typesetting; SIC 2796: Platemaking and Related Services

PETROLEUM & COAL PRODUCTS MANUFACTURING

324110   Petroleum Refineries *see* SIC 2911: Petroleum Refining

324121   Asphalt Paving Mixture and Block Manufacturing *see* SIC 2951: Asphalt Paving Mixtures and Blocks

324122   Asphalt Shingle and Coating Materials Manufacturing *see* SIC 2952: Asphalt Felts and Coatings

324191   Petroleum Lubricating Oil and Grease Manufacturing *see* SIC 2992: Lubricating Oils and Greases

324199   All Other Petroleum and Coal Products Manufacturing *see* SIC 2999: Products of Petroleum and Coal, NEC; SIC 3312: Steel Works, Blast Furnaces (Including Coke Ovens), and Rolling Mills

CHEMICAL MANUFACTURING

325110   Petrochemical Manufacturing *see* SIC 2865: Cyclic Organic Crudes and Intermediates, and Organic Dyes and Pigments; SIC 2869: Industrial Organic Chemicals, NEC

325120   Industrial Gas Manufacturing *see* SIC 2813: Industrial Gases; SIC 2869: Industrial Organic Chemicals, NEC

325131   Inorganic Dye and Pigment Manufacturing *see* SIC 2816: Inorganic Pigments; SIC 2819: Industrial Inorganic Chemicals, NEC

325132   Organic Dye and Pigment Manufacturing *see* SIC 2865: Cyclic Organic Crudes and Intermediates, and Organic Dyes and Pigments

325181   Alkalies and Chlorine Manufacturing *see* SIC 2812: Alkalies and Chlorine

325182   Carbon Black Manufacturing *see* SIC 2816: Inorganic Pigments; SIC 2895: Carbon Black

325188   All Other Inorganic Chemical Manufacturing *see* SIC 2819: Industrial Inorganic Chemicals,

NEC; SIC 2869: Industrial Organic Chemicals, NEC

325191 Gum and Wood Chemical Manufacturing *see* SIC 2861: Gum and Wood Chemicals

325192 Cyclic Crude and Intermediate Manufacturing *see* SIC 2865: Cyclic Organic Crudes and Intermediates, and Organic Dyes and Pigments

325193 Ethyl Alcohol Manufacturing *see* SIC 2869: Industrial Organic Chemicals, NEC

325199 All Other Basic Organic Chemical Manufacturing *see* SIC 2869: Industrial Organic Chemicals, NEC; SIC 2899: Chemicals and Chemical Preparations, NEC

325211 Plastics Material and Resin Manufacturing *see* SIC 2821: Plastics Material Synthetic Resins, and Nonvulcanizable Elastomers

325212 Synthetic Rubber Manufacturing *see* SIC 2822: Synthetic Rubber

325221 Cellulosic Manmade Fiber Manufacturing *see* SIC 2823: Cellulosic Manmade Fibers

325222 Noncellulosic Organic Fiber Manufacturing *see* SIC 2824: Manmade Organic Fibers, Except Cellulosic

325311 Nitrogenous Fertilizer Manufacturing *see* SIC 2873: Nitrogenous Fertilizers

325312 Phosphatic Fertilizer Manufacturing *see* SIC 2874: Phosphatic Fertilizers

325314 Fertilizer (Mixing Only) Manufacturing *see* SIC 2875: Fertilizers, Mixing Only

325320 Pesticide and Other Agricultural Chemical Manufacturing *see* SIC 2879: Pesticides and Agricultural Chemicals, NEC

325411 Medicinal and Botanical Manufacturing *see* SIC 2833: Medicinal Chemicals and Botanical Products

325412 Pharmaceutical Preparation Manufacturing *see* SIC 2834: Pharmaceutical Preparations; SIC 2835: In Vitro and In Vivo Diagnostic Substances

325413 In-Vitro Diagnostic Substance Manufacturing *see* SIC 2835: In Vitro and In Vivo Diagnostic Substances

325414 Biological Product (except Diagnostic) Manufacturing *see* SIC 2836: Biological Products, Except Diagnostic Substances

325510 Paint and Coating Manufacturing *see* SIC 2851: Paints, Varnishes, Lacquers, Enamels, and Allied Products; SIC 2899: Chemicals and Chemical Preparations, NEC

325520 Adhesive and Sealant Manufacturing *see* SIC 2891: Adhesives and Sealants

325611 Soap and Other Detergent Manufacturing *see* SIC 2841: Soaps and Other Detergents, Except

Specialty Cleaners; SIC 2844: Perfumes, Cosmetics, and Other Toilet Preparations

325612 Polish and Other Sanitation Good Manufacturing *see* SIC 2842: Specialty Cleaning, Polishing, and Sanitary Preparations

325613 Surface Active Agent Manufacturing *see* SIC 2843: Surface Active Agents, Finishing Agents, Sulfonated Oils, and Assistants

325620 Toilet Preparation Manufacturing *see* SIC 2844: Perfumes, Cosmetics, and Other Toilet Preparations

325910 Printing Ink Manufacturing *see* SIC 2893: Printing Ink

325920 Explosives Manufacturing *see* SIC 2892: Explosives

325991 Custom Compounding of Purchased Resin *see* SIC 3087: Custom Compounding of Purchased Plastics Resins

325992 Photographic Film, Paper, Plate and Chemical Manufacturing *see* SIC 3861: Photographic Equipment and Supplies

325998 All Other Miscellaneous Chemical Product Manufacturing *see* SIC 2819: Industrial Inorganic Chemicals, NEC; SIC 2899: Chemicals and Chemical Preparations, NEC; SIC 3952: Lead Pencils, Crayons, and Artist's Materials; SIC 3999: Manufacturing Industries, NEC

PLASTICS & RUBBER PRODUCTS MANUFACTURING

326111 Unsupported Plastics Bag Manufacturing *see* SIC 2673: Plastics, Foil, and Coated Paper Bags

326112 Unsupported Plastics Packaging Film and Sheet Manufacturing *see* SIC 2671: Packaging Paper and Plastics Film, Coated and Laminated

326113 Unsupported Plastics Film and Sheet (except Packaging) Manufacturing *see* SIC 3081: Unsupported Plastics Film and Sheet

326121 Unsupported Plastics Profile Shape Manufacturing *see* SIC 3082: Unsupported Plastics Profile Shapes; SIC 3089: Plastics Products, NEC

326122 Plastics Pipe and Pipe Fitting Manufacturing *see* SIC 3084: Plastic Pipe; SIC 3089: Plastics Products, NEC

326130 Laminated Plastics Plate, Sheet, and Shape Manufacturing *see* SIC 3083: Laminated Plastics Plate, Sheet, and Profile Shapes

326140 Polystyrene Foam Product Manufacturing *see* SIC 3086: Plastics Foam Products

326150 Urethane and Other Foam Product (except Polystyrene) Manufacturing *see* SIC 3086: Plastics Foam Products

326160   Plastics Bottle Manufacturing *see* SIC 3085: Plastics Bottles

326191   Plastics Plumbing Fixtures Manufacturing *see* SIC 3088: Plastics Plumbing Fixtures

326192   Resilient Floor Covering Manufacturing *see* SIC 3069: Fabricated Rubber Products, NEC; SIC 3996: Linoleum, Asphalted-Felt-Base, and Other Hard Surface Floor Coverings, NEC

326199   All Other Plastics Product Manufacturing *see* SIC 3089: Plastics Products, NEC; SIC 3999: Manufacturing Industries, NEC

326211   Tire Manufacturing (except Retreading) *see* SIC 3011: Tires and Inner Tubes

326212   Tire Retreading *see* SIC 7534: Tire Retreading and Repair Shops

326220   Rubber and Plastics Hoses and Belting Manufacturing *see* SIC 3052: Rubber and Plastics Hose and Belting

326291   Rubber Product Manufacturing for Mechanical Use *see* SIC 3061: Molded, Extruded, and Lathe-Cut Mechanical Rubber Products

326299   All Other Rubber Product Manufacturing *see* SIC 3069: Fabricated Rubber Products, NEC

NONMETALLIC MINERAL PRODUCT MANUFACTURING

327111   Vitreous China Plumbing Fixture and China and Earthenware Fitting and Bathroom Accessories Manufacturing *see* SIC 3261: Vitreous China Plumbing Fixtures and China and Earthenware Fittings and Bathroom Accessories

327112   Vitreous China, Fine Earthenware and Other Pottery Product Manufacturing *see* SIC 3262: Vitreous China Table and Kitchen Articles; SIC 3263: Fine Earthenware (Whiteware) Table and Kitchen Articles; SIC 3269: Pottery Products, NEC

327113   Porcelain Electrical Supply Manufacturing *see* SIC 3264: Porcelain Electrical Supplies

327121   Brick and Structural Clay Tile Manufacturing *see* SIC 3251: Brick and Structural Clay Tile

327122   Ceramic Wall and Floor Tile Manufacturing *see* SIC 3253: Ceramic Wall and Floor Tile

327123   Other Structural Clay Product Manufacturing *see* SIC 3259: Structural Clay Products, NEC

327124   Clay Refractory Manufacturing *see* SIC 3255: Clay Refractories

327125   Nonclay Refractory Manufacturing *see* SIC 3297: Nonclay Refractories

327211   Flat Glass Manufacturing *see* SIC 3211: Flat Glass

327212   Other Pressed and Blown Glass and Glassware Manufacturing *see* SIC 3229: Pressed and Blown Glass and Glassware, NEC

327213   Glass Container Manufacturing *see* SIC 3221: Glass Containers

327215   Glass Product Manufacturing Made of Purchased Glass *see* SIC 3231: Glass Products, Made of Purchased Glass

327310   Cement Manufacturing *see* SIC 3241: Cement, Hydraulic

327320   Ready-Mix Concrete Manufacturing *see* SIC 3273: Ready-Mixed Concrete

327331   Concrete Block and Brick Manufacturing *see* SIC 3271: Concrete Block and Brick

327332   Concrete Pipe Manufacturing *see* SIC 3272: Concrete Products, Except Block and Brick

327390   Other Concrete Product Manufacturing *see* SIC 3272: Concrete Products, Except Block and Brick

327410   Lime Manufacturing *see* SIC 3274: Lime

327420   Gypsum and Gypsum Product Manufacturing *see* SIC 3275: Gypsum Products; SIC 3299: Nonmetallic Mineral Products, NEC

327910   Abrasive Product Manufacturing *see* SIC 3291: Abrasive Products

327991   Cut Stone and Stone Product Manufacturing *see* SIC 3281: Cut Stone and Stone Products

327992   Ground or Treated Mineral and Earth Manufacturing *see* SIC 3295: Minerals and Earths, Ground or Otherwise Treated

327993   Mineral Wool Manufacturing *see* SIC 3296: Mineral Wool

327999   All Other Miscellaneous Nonmetallic Mineral Product Manufacturing *see* SIC 3272: Concrete Products, Except Block and Brick; SIC 3292: Asbestos Products; SIC 3299: Nonmetallic Mineral Products, NEC

PRIMARY METAL MANUFACTURING

331111   Iron and Steel Mills *see* SIC 3312: Steel Works, Blast Furnaces (Including Coke Ovens), and Rolling Mills; SIC 3399: Primary Metal Products, NEC

331112   Electrometallurgical Ferroalloy Product Manufacturing *see* SIC 3313: Electrometallurgical Products, Except Steel

331210   Iron and Steel Pipes and Tubes Manufacturing from Purchased Steel *see* SIC 3317: Steel Pipe and Tubes

331221   Cold-Rolled Steel Shape Manufacturing *see* SIC 3316: Cold-Rolled Steel Sheet, Strip, and Bars

331222   Steel Wire Drawing *see* SIC 3315: Steel Wiredrawing and Steel Nails and Spikes

331311 Aluminum Refining *see* SIC 2819: Industrial Inorganic Chemicals, NEC

331312 Primary Aluminum Production *see* SIC 3334: Primary Production of Aluminum

331314 Secondary Smelting and Alloying of Aluminum *see* SIC 3341: Secondary Smelting and Refining of Nonferrous Metals; SIC 3399: Primary Metal Products, NEC

331315 Aluminum Sheet, Plate, and Foil Manufacturing *see* SIC 3353: Aluminum Sheet, Plate, and Foil

331316 Aluminum Extruded Product Manufacturing *see* SIC 3354: Aluminum Extruded Products

331319 Other Aluminum Rolling and Drawing, *see* SIC 3355: Aluminum Rolling and Drawing, NEC; SIC 3357: Drawing and Insulating of Nonferrous Wire

331411 Primary Smelting and Refining of Copper *see* SIC 3331: Primary Smelting and Refining of Copper

331419 Primary Smelting and Refining of Nonferrous Metals (except Copper and Aluminum) *see* SIC 3339: Primary Smelting and Refining of Nonferrous Metals, Except Copper and Aluminum

331421 Copper (except Wire) Rolling, Drawing, and Extruding *see* SIC 3351: Rolling, Drawing, and Extruding of Copper

331422 Copper Wire Drawing *see* SIC 3357: Drawing and Insulating of Nonferrous Wire

331423 Secondary Smelting, Refining, and Alloying of Copper *see* SIC 3341: Secondary Smelting and Refining of Nonferrous Metals; SIC 3399: Primary Metal Products, NEC

331491 Nonferrous Metal (except Copper and Aluminum) Rolling. Drawing, and Extruding *see* SIC 3356: Rolling, Drawing, and Extruding of Nonferrous Metals, Except Copper and Aluminum; SIC 3357: Drawing and Insulating of Nonferrous Wire

331492 Secondary Smelting, Refining, and Alloying of Nonferrous Metals (except Copper and Aluminum) *see* SIC 3313: Electrometallurgical Products, Except Steel; SIC 3341: Secondary Smelting and Refining of Nonferrous Metals; SIC 3399: Primary Metal Products, NEC

331511 Iron Foundries *see* SIC 3321: Gray and Ductile Iron Foundries; SIC 3322: Malleable Iron Foundries

331512 Steel Investment Foundries *see* SIC 3324: Steel Investment Foundries

331513 Steel Foundries (except Investment) *see* SIC 3325: Steel Foundries, NEC

331521 Aluminum Die-Castings *see* SIC 3363: Aluminum Die-Castings

331522 Nonferrous (except Aluminum) Die-Castings *see* SIC 3364: Nonferrous Die-Castings, Except Aluminum

331524 Aluminum Foundries *see* SIC 3365: Aluminum Foundries

331525 Copper Foundries *see* SIC 3366: Copper Foundries

331528 Other Nonferrous Foundries *see* SIC 3369: Nonferrous Foundries, Except Aluminum and Copper

FABRICATED METAL PRODUCT MANUFACTURING

332111 Iron and Steel Forging *see* SIC 3462: Iron and Steel Forgings

332112 Nonferrous Forging *see* SIC 3463: Nonferrous Forgings

332114 Custom Roll Forming *see* SIC 3449: Miscellaneous Structural Metal Work

332115 Crown and Closure Manufacturing *see* SIC 3466: Crowns and Closures

332116 Metal Stamping *see* SIC 3469: Metal Stamping, NEC

332117 Powder Metallurgy Part Manufacturing *see* SIC 3499: Fabricated Metal Products, NEC

332211 Cutlery and Flatware (except Precious) Manufacturing *see* SIC 3421: Cutlery; SIC 3914: Silverware, Plated Ware, and Stainless Steel Ware

332212 Hand and Edge Tool Manufacturing *see* SIC 3423: Hand and Edge Tools, Except Machine Tools and Handsaws; SIC 3523: Farm Machinery and Equipment; SIC 3524: Lawn and Garden Tractors and Home Lawn and Garden Equipment; SIC 3545: Cutting Tools, Machine Tool Accessories, and Machinists' Precision Measuring Devices; SIC 3799: Transportation Equipment, NEC; SIC 3999: Manufacturing Industries, NEC

332213 Saw Blade and Handsaw Manufacturing *see* SIC 3425: Saw Blades and Handsaws

332214 Kitchen Utensil, Pot and Pan Manufacturing *see* SIC 3469: Metal Stamping, NEC

332311 Prefabricated Metal Building and Component Manufacturing *see* SIC 3448: Prefabricated Metal Buildings and Components

332312 Fabricated Structural Metal Manufacturing *see* SIC 3441: Fabricated Structural Metal; SIC 3449: Miscellaneous Structural Metal Work

332313 Plate Work Manufacturing *see* SIC 3443: Fabricated Plate Work (Boiler Shops)

332321 Metal Window and Door Manufacturing *see* SIC 3442: Metal Doors, Sash, Frames, Molding, and

Trim Manufacturing; SIC 3449: Miscellaneous Structural Metal Work

332322 Sheet Metal Work Manufacturing *see* SIC 3444: Sheet Metal Work

332323 Ornamental and Architectural Metal Work Manufacturing *see* SIC 3446: Architectural and Ornamental Metal Work; SIC 3449: Miscellaneous Structural Metal Work; SIC 3523: Farm Machinery and Equipment

332410 Power Boiler and Heat Exchanger Manufacturing *see* SIC 3443: Fabricated Plate Work (Boiler Shops)

332420 Metal Tank (Heavy Gauge) Manufacturing *see* SIC 3443: Fabricated Plate Work (Boiler Shops)

332431 Metal Can Manufacturing *see* SIC 3411: Metal Cans

332439 Other Metal Container Manufacturing *see* SIC 3412: Metal Shipping Barrels, Drums, Kegs and Pails; SIC 3429: Hardware, NEC; SIC 3444: Sheet Metal Work; SIC 3499: Fabricated Metal Products, NEC; SIC 3537: Industrial Trucks, Tractors, Trailers, and Stackers

332510 Hardware Manufacturing *see* SIC 3429: Hardware, NEC; SIC 3499: Fabricated Metal Products, NEC

332611 Steel Spring (except Wire) Manufacturing *see* SIC 3493: Steel Springs, Except Wire

332612 Wire Spring Manufacturing *see* SIC 3495: Wire Springs

332618 Other Fabricated Wire Product Manufacturing *see* SIC 3315: Steel Wiredrawing and Steel Nails and Spikes; SIC 3399: Primary Metal Products, NEC; SIC 3496: Miscellaneous Fabricated Wire Products

332710 Machine Shops *see* SIC 3599: Industrial and Commercial Machinery and Equipment, NEC

332721 Precision Turned Product Manufacturing *see* SIC 3451: Screw Machine Products

332722 Bolt, Nut, Screw, Rivet, and Washer Manufacturing *see* SIC 3452: Bolts, Nuts, Screws, Rivets, and Washers

332811 Metal Heat Treating *see* SIC 3398: Metal Heat Treating

332812 Metal Coating, Engraving, and Allied Services (except Jewelry and Silverware) to Manufacturing *see* SIC 3479: Coating, Engraving, and Allied Services, NEC

332813 Electroplating, Plating, Polishing, Anodizing, and Coloring *see* SIC 3399: Primary Metal Products, NEC; SIC 3471: Electroplating, Plating, Polishing, Anodizing, and Coloring

332911 Industrial Valve Manufacturing *see* SIC 3491: Industrial Valves

332912 Fluid Power Valve and Hose Fitting Manufacturing *see* SIC 3492: Fluid Power Valves and Hose Fittings; SIC 3728: Aircraft Parts and Auxiliary Equipment, NEC

332913 Plumbing Fixture Fitting and Trim Manufacturing *see* SIC 3432: Plumbing Fixture Fittings and Trim

332919 Other Metal Valve and Pipe Fitting Manufacturing *see* SIC 3429: Hardware, NEC; SIC 3494: Valves and Pipe Fittings, NEC; SIC 3499: Fabricated Metal Products, NEC

332991 Ball and Roller Bearing Manufacturing *see* SIC 3562: Ball and Roller Bearings

332992 Small Arms Ammunition Manufacturing *see* SIC 3482: Small Arms Ammunition

332993 Ammunition (except Small Arms) Manufacturing *see* SIC 3483: Ammunition, Except for Small Arms

332994 Small Arms Manufacturing *see* SIC 3484: Small Arms

332995 Other Ordnance and Accessories Manufacturing *see* SIC 3489: Ordnance and Accessories, NEC

332996 Fabricated Pipe and Pipe Fitting Manufacturing *see* SIC 3498: Fabricated Pipe and Pipe Fittings

332997 Industrial Pattern Manufacturing *see* SIC 3543: Industrial Patterns

332998 Enameled Iron and Metal Sanitary Ware Manufacturing *see* SIC 3431: Enameled Iron and Metal Sanitary Ware

332999 All Other Miscellaneous Fabricated Metal Product Manufacturing *see* SIC 3291: Abrasive Products; SIC 3432: Plumbing Fixture Fittings and Trim; SIC 3494: Valves and Pipe Fittings, NEC; SIC 3497: Metal Foil and Leaf; SIC 3499: Fabricated Metal Products, NEC; SIC 3537: Industrial Trucks, Tractors, Trailers, and Stackers; SIC 3599: Industrial and Commercial Machinery and Equipment, NEC; SIC 3999: Manufacturing Industries, NEC

MACHINERY MANUFACTURING

333111 Farm Machinery and Equipment Manufacturing *see* SIC 3523: Farm Machinery and Equipment

333112 Lawn and Garden Tractor and Home Lawn and Garden Equipment Manufacturing *see* SIC 3524: Lawn and Garden Tractors and Home Lawn and Garden Equipment

333120 Construction Machinery Manufacturing *see* SIC 3531: Construction Machinery and Equipment

333131 Mining Machinery and Equipment Manufacturing *see* SIC 3532: Mining Machinery and Equipment, Except Oil and Gas Field Machinery and Equipment

333132 Oil and Gas Field Machinery and Equipment Manufacturing *see* SIC 3533: Oil and Gas Field Machinery and Equipment

333210 Sawmill and Woodworking Machinery Manufacturing *see* SIC 3553: Woodworking Machinery

333220 Rubber and Plastics Industry Machinery Manufacturing *see* SIC 3559: Special Industry Machinery, NEC

333291 Paper Industry Machinery Manufacturing *see* SIC 3554: Paper Industries Machinery

333292 Textile Machinery Manufacturing *see* SIC 3552: Textile Machinery

333293 Printing Machinery and Equipment Manufacturing *see* SIC 3555: Printing Trades Machinery and Equipment

333294 Food Product Machinery Manufacturing *see* SIC 3556: Food Products Machinery

333295 Semiconductor Manufacturing Machinery *see* SIC 3559: Special Industry Machinery, NEC

333298 All Other Industrial Machinery Manufacturing *see* SIC 3559: Special Industry Machinery, NEC; SIC 3639: Household Appliances, NEC

333311 Automatic Vending Machine Manufacturing *see* SIC 3581: Automatic Vending Machines

333312 Commercial Laundry, Drycleaning, and Pressing Machine Manufacturing *see* SIC 3582: Commercial Laundry, Drycleaning, and Pressing Machines

333313 Office Machinery Manufacturing *see* SIC 3578: Calculating and Accounting Machines, Except Electronic Computers; SIC 3579: Office Machines, NEC

333314 Optical Instrument and Lens Manufacturing *see* SIC 3827: Optical Instruments and Lenses

333315 Photographic and Photocopying Equipment Manufacturing *see* SIC 3861: Photographic Equipment and Supplies

333319 Other Commercial and Service Industry Machinery Manufacturing *see* SIC 3559: Special Industry Machinery, NEC; SIC 3589: Service Industry Machinery, NEC; SIC 3599: Industrial and Commercial Machinery and Equipment, NEC; SIC 3699: Electrical Machinery, Equipment, and Supplies, NEC

333411 Air Purification Equipment Manufacturing *see* SIC 3564: Industrial and Commercial Fans and Blowers and Air Purification Equipment

333412 Industrial and Commercial Fan and Blower Manufacturing *see* SIC 3564: Industrial and Commercial Fans and Blowers and Air Purification Equipment

333414 Heating Equipment (except Electric and Warm Air Furnaces) Manufacturing *see* SIC 3433: Heating Equipment, Except Electric and Warm Air Furnaces; SIC 3634: Electric Housewares and Fans

333415 Air-Conditioning and Warm Air Heating Equipment and Commercial and Industrial Refrigeration Equipment Manufacturing *see* SIC 3443: Fabricated Plate Work (Boiler Shops); SIC 3585: Air-Conditioning and Warm Air Heating Equipment and Commercial and Industrial Refrigeration Equipment

333511 Industrial Mold Manufacturing *see* SIC 3544: Special Dies and Tools, Die Sets, Jigs and Fixtures, and Industrial Molds

333512 Machine Tool (Metal Cutting Types) Manufacturing *see* SIC 3541: Machine Tools, Metal Cutting Type

333513 Machine Tool (Metal Forming Types) Manufacturing *see* SIC 3542: Machine Tools, Metal Forming Type

333514 Special Die and Tool, Die Set, Jig, and Fixture Manufacturing *see* SIC 3544: Special Dies and Tools, Die Sets, Jigs and Fixtures, and Industrial Molds

333515 Cutting Tool and Machine Tool Accessory Manufacturing *see* SIC 3545: Cutting Tools, Machine Tool Accessories, and Machinists' Precision Measuring Devices

333516 Rolling Mill Machinery and Equipment Manufacturing *see* SIC 3547: Rolling Mill Machinery and Equipment

333518 Other Metalworking Machinery Manufacturing *see* SIC 3549: Metalworking Machinery, NEC

333611 Turbine and Turbine Generator Set Unit Manufacturing *see* SIC 3511: Steam, Gas, and Hydraulic Turbines, and Turbine Generator Set Units

333612 Speed Changer, Industrial High-Speed Drive, and Gear Manufacturing *see* SIC 3566: Speed Changers, Industrial High-Speed Drives, and Gears

333613 Mechanical Power Transmission Equipment Manufacturing *see* SIC 3568: Mechanical Power Transmission Equipment, NEC

333618 Other Engine Equipment Manufacturing *see* SIC 3519: Internal Combustion Engines, NEC; SIC 3699: Electrical Machinery, Equipment, and Supplies, NEC

333911 Pump and Pumping Equipment Manufacturing *see* SIC 3561: Pumps and Pumping Equipment; SIC 3743: Railroad Equipment

333912 Air and Gas Compressor Manufacturing *see* SIC 3563: Air and Gas Compressors

333913 Measuring and Dispensing Pump Manufacturing *see* SIC 3586: Measuring and Dispensing Pumps

333921 Elevator and Moving Stairway Manufacturing *see* SIC 3534: Elevators and Moving Stairways

333922 Conveyor and Conveying Equipment Manufacturing *see* SIC 3523: Farm Machinery and Equipment; SIC 3535: Conveyors and Conveying Equipment

333923 Overhead Traveling Crane, Hoist, and Monorail System Manufacturing *see* SIC 3531: Construction Machinery and Equipment; SIC 3536: Overhead Traveling Cranes, Hoists and Monorail Systems

333924 Industrial Truck, Tractor, Trailer, and Stacker Machinery Manufacturing *see* SIC 3537: Industrial Trucks, Tractors, Trailers, and Stackers

333991 Power-Driven Hand Tool Manufacturing *see* SIC 3546: Power-Driven Handtools

333992 Welding and Soldering Equipment Manufacturing *see* SIC 3548: Electric and Gas Welding and Soldering Equipment

333993 Packaging Machinery Manufacturing *see* SIC 3565: Packaging Machinery

333994 Industrial Process Furnace and Oven Manufacturing *see* SIC 3567: Industrial Process Furnaces and Ovens

333995 Fluid Power Cylinder and Actuator Manufacturing *see* SIC 3593: Fluid Power Cylinders and Actuators

333996 Fluid Power Pump and Motor Manufacturing *see* SIC 3594: Fluid Power Pumps and Motors

333997 Scale and Balance (except Laboratory) Manufacturing *see* SIC 3596: Scales and Balances, Except Laboratory

333999 All Other General Purpose Machinery Manufacturing *see* SIC 3569: General Industrial Machinery and Equipment, NEC; SIC 3599: Industrial and Commercial Machinery and Equipment, NEC

COMPUTER & ELECTRONIC PRODUCT MANUFACTURING

334111 Electronic Computer Manufacturing *see* SIC 3571: Electronic Computers

334112 Computer Storage Device Manufacturing *see* SIC 3572: Computer Storage Devices

334113 Computer Terminal Manufacturing *see* SIC 3575: Computer Terminals

334119 Other Computer Peripheral Equipment Manufacturing *see* SIC 3577: Computer Peripheral Equipment, NEC; SIC 3578:

Calculating and Accounting Machines, Except Electronic Computers; SIC 3699: Electrical Machinery, Equipment, and Supplies, NEC

334210 Telephone Apparatus Manufacturing *see* SIC 3661: Telephone and Telegraph Apparatus

334220 Radio and Television Broadcasting and Wireless Communications Equipment Manufacturing *see* SIC 3663: Radio and Television Broadcasting and Communication Equipment; SIC 3679: Electronic Components, NEC

334290 Other Communication Equipment Manufacturing *see* SIC 3669: Communications Equipment, NEC

334310 Audio and Video Equipment Manufacturing *see* SIC 3651: Household Audio and Video Equipment

334411 Electron Tube Manufacturing *see* SIC 3671: Electron Tubes

334412 Printed Circuit Board Manufacturing *see* SIC 3672: Printed Circuit Boards

334413 Semiconductor and Related Device Manufacturing *see* SIC 3674: Semiconductors and Related Devices

334414 Electronic Capacitor Manufacturing *see* SIC 3675: Electronic Capacitors

334415 Electronic Resistor Manufacturing *see* SIC 3676: Electronic Resistors

334416 Electronic Coil, Transformer, and Other Inductor Manufacturing *see* SIC 3661: Telephone and Telegraph Apparatus; SIC 3677: Electronic Coils, Transformers, and Other Inductors; SIC 3825: Instruments for Measuring and Testing of Electricity and Electrical Signals

334417 Electronic Connector Manufacturing *see* SIC 3678: Electronic Connectors

334418 Printed Circuit/Electronics Assembly Manufacturing *see* SIC 3661: Telephone and Telegraph Apparatus; SIC 3679: Electronic Components, NEC

334419 Other Electronic Component Manufacturing *see* SIC 3679: Electronic Components, NEC

334510 Electromedical and Electrotherapeutic Apparatus Manufacturing *see* SIC 3842: Orthopedic, Prosthetic, and Surgical Appliances and Supplies; SIC 3845: Electromedical and Electrotherapeutic Apparatus

334511 Search, Detection, Navigation, Guidance, Aeronautical, and Nautical System and Instrument Manufacturing *see* SIC 3812: Search, Detection, Navigation, Guidance, Aeronautical, and Nautical Systems and Instruments

334512 Automatic Environmental Control Manufacturing for Regulating Residential, Commercial, and Appliance Use *see* SIC 3822:

Automatic Controls for Regulating Residential and Commercial Environments and Appliances

334513 Instruments and Related Product Manufacturing for Measuring Displaying, and Controlling Industrial Process Variables *see* SIC 3823: Industrial Instruments for Measurement, Display, and Control of Process Variables; and Related Products

334514 Totalizing Fluid Meter and Counting Device Manufacturing *see* SIC 3824: Totalizing Fluid Meters and Counting Devices

334515 Instrument Manufacturing for Measuring and Testing Electricity and Electrical Signals *see* SIC 3825: Instruments for Measuring and Testing of Electricity and Electrical Signals

334516 Analytical Laboratory Instrument Manufacturing *see* SIC 3826: Laboratory Analytical Instruments

334517 Irradiation Apparatus Manufacturing *see* SIC 3844: X-Ray Apparatus and Tubes and Related Irradiation Apparatus; SIC 3845: Electromedical and Electrotherapeutic Apparatus

334518 Watch, Clock, and Part Manufacturing *see* SIC 3495: Wire Springs; SIC 3579: Office Machines, NEC; SIC 3873: Watches, Clocks, Clockwork Operated Devices and Parts

334519 Other Measuring and Controlling Device Manufacturing *see* SIC 3829: Measuring and Controlling Devices, NEC

334611 Software Reproducing *see* SIC 7372: Prepackaged Software

334612 Prerecorded Compact Disc (Except Software), Tape and Record Reproducing *see* SIC 3652: Phonograph Records and Prerecorded Audio Tapes and Disks; SIC 7819: Services Allied to Motion Picture Production

334613 Magnetic and Optical Recording Media Manufacturing *see* SIC 3695: Magnetic and Optical Recording Media

ELECTRICAL EQUIPMENT, APPLIANCE, & COMPONENT MANUFACTURING

335110 Electric Lamp Bulb and Part Manufacturing *see* SIC 3641: Electric Lamp Bulbs and Tubes

335121 Residential Electric Lighting Fixture Manufacturing *see* SIC 3645: Residential Electric Lighting Fixtures; SIC 3999: Manufacturing Industries, NEC

335122 Commercial, Industrial, and Institutional Electric Lighting Fixture Manufacturing *see* SIC 3646: Commercial, Industrial, and Institutional Electric Lighting Fixtures

335129 Other Lighting Equipment Manufacturing *see* SIC 3648: Lighting Equipment, NEC; SIC 3699: Electrical Machinery, Equipment, and Supplies, NEC

335211 Electric Houseware and Fan Manufacturing *see* SIC 3634: Electric Housewares and Fans

335212 Household Vacuum Cleaner Manufacturing *see* SIC 3635: Household Vacuum Cleaners; SIC 3639: Household Appliances, NEC

335221 Household Cooking Appliance Manufacturing *see* SIC 3631: Household Cooking Equipment

335222 Household Refrigerator and Home and Farm Freezer Manufacturing *see* SIC 3632: Household Refrigerators and Home and Farm Freezers

335224 Household Laundry Equipment Manufacturing *see* SIC 3633: Household Laundry Equipment

335228 Other Household Appliance Manufacturing *see* SIC 3639: Household Appliances, NEC

335311 Power, Distribution, and Specialty Transformer Manufacturing *see* SIC 3548: Electric and Gas Welding and Soldering Equipment; SIC 3612: Power, Distribution, and Specialty Transformers

335312 Motor and Generator Manufacturing *see* SIC 3621: Motors and Generators; SIC 7694: Armature Rewinding Shops

335313 Switchgear and Switchboard Apparatus Manufacturing *see* SIC 3613: Switchgear and Switchboard Apparatus

335314 Relay and Industrial Control Manufacturing *see* SIC 3625: Relays and Industrial Controls

335911 Storage Battery Manufacturing *see* SIC 3691: Storage Batteries

335912 Dry and Wet Primary Battery Manufacturing *see* SIC 3692: Primary Batteries, Dry and Wet

335921 Fiber Optic Cable Manufacturing *see* SIC 3357: Drawing and Insulating of Nonferrous Wire

335929 Other Communication and Energy Wire Manufacturing *see* SIC 3357: Drawing and Insulating of Nonferrous Wire

335931 Current-Carrying Wiring Device Manufacturing *see* SIC 3643: Current-Carrying Wiring Devices

335932 Noncurrent-Carrying Wiring Device Manufacturing *see* SIC 3644: Noncurrent-Carrying Wiring Devices

335991 Carbon and Graphite Product Manufacturing *see* SIC 3624: Carbon and Graphite Products

335999 All Other Miscellaneous Electrical Equipment and Component Manufacturing *see* SIC 3629: Electrical Industrial Apparatus, NEC; SIC 3699: Electrical Machinery, Equipment, and Supplies, NEC

TRANSPORTATION EQUIPMENT MANUFACTURING

336111 Automobile Manufacturing *see* SIC 3711: Motor Vehicles and Passenger Car Bodies

336112 Light Truck and Utility Vehicle Manufacturing *see* SIC 3711: Motor Vehicles and Passenger Car Bodies

336120 Heavy Duty Truck Manufacturing *see* SIC 3711: Motor Vehicles and Passenger Car Bodies

336211 Motor Vehicle Body Manufacturing *see* SIC 3711: Motor Vehicles and Passenger Car Bodies; SIC 3713: Truck and Bus Bodies; SIC 3714: Motor Vehicle Parts and Accessories

336212 Truck Trailer Manufacturing *see* SIC 3715: Truck Trailers

336213 Motor Home Manufacturing *see* SIC 3716: Motor Homes

336214 Travel Trailer and Camper Manufacturing *see* SIC 3792: Travel Trailers and Campers; SIC 3799: Transportation Equipment, NEC

336311 Carburetor, Piston, Piston Ring and Valve Manufacturing *see* SIC 3592: Carburetors, Pistons, Piston Rings and Valves

336312 Gasoline Engine and Engine Parts Manufacturing *see* SIC 3714: Motor Vehicle Parts and Accessories

336321 Vehicular Lighting Equipment Manufacturing *see* SIC 3647: Vehicular Lighting Equipment

336322 Other Motor Vehicle Electrical and Electronic Equipment Manufacturing *see* SIC 3679: Electronic Components, NEC; SIC 3694: Electrical Equipment for Internal Combustion Engines; SIC 3714: Motor Vehicle Parts and Accessories

336330 Motor Vehicle Steering and Suspension Components (except Spring) Manufacturing *see* SIC 3714: Motor Vehicle Parts and Accessories

336340 Motor Vehicle Brake System Manufacturing *see* SIC 3292: Asbestos Products; SIC 3714: Motor Vehicle Parts and Accessories

336350 Motor Vehicle Transmission and Power Train Part Manufacturing *see* SIC 3714: Motor Vehicle Parts and Accessories

336360 Motor Vehicle Fabric Accessories and Seat Manufacturing *see* SIC 2396: Automotive Trimmings, Apparel Findings, and Related Products; SIC 2399: Fabricated Textile Products, NEC; SIC 2531: Public Building and Related Furniture

336370 Motor Vehicle Metal Stamping *see* SIC 3465: Automotive Stamping

336391 Motor Vehicle Air Conditioning Manufacturing *see* SIC 3585: Air-Conditioning and Warm Air Heating Equipment and Commercial and Industrial Refrigeration Equipment

336399 All Other Motor Vehicle Parts Manufacturing *see* SIC 3519: Internal Combustion Engines, NEC; SIC 3599: Industrial and Commercial Machinery and Equipment, NEC; SIC 3714: Motor Vehicle Parts and Accessories

336411 Aircraft Manufacturing *see* SIC 3721: Aircraft

336412 Aircraft Engine and Engine Parts Manufacturing *see* SIC 3724: Aircraft Engines and Engine Parts

336413 Other Aircraft Part and Auxiliary Equipment Manufacturing *see* SIC 3728: Aircraft Parts and Auxiliary Equipment, NEC

336414 Guided Missile and Space Vehicle Manufacturing *see* SIC 3761: Guided Missiles and Space Vehicles

336415 Guided Missile and Space Vehicle Propulsion Unit and Propulsion Unit Parts Manufacturing *see* SIC 3764: Guided Missile and Space Vehicle Propulsion Units and Propulsion Unit Parts

336419 Other Guided Missile and Space Vehicle Parts and Auxiliary Equipment Manufacturing *see* SIC 3769: Guided Missile Space Vehicle Parts and Auxiliary Equipment, NEC

336510 Railroad Rolling Stock Manufacturing *see* SIC 3531: Construction Machinery and Equipment; SIC 3743: Railroad Equipment

336611 Ship Building and Repairing *see* SIC 3731: Ship Building and Repairing

336612 Boat Building *see* SIC 3732: Boat Building and Repairing

336991 Motorcycle, Bicycle, and Parts Manufacturing *see* SIC 3751: Motorcycles, Bicycles, and Parts; SIC 3944: Games, Toys, and Children's Vehicles, Except Dolls and Bicycles

336992 Military Armored Vehicle, Tank, and Tank Component Manufacturing *see* SIC 3711: Motor Vehicles and Passenger Car Bodies; SIC 3795: Tanks and Tank Components

336999 All Other Transportation Equipment Manufacturing *see* SIC 3799: Transportation Equipment, NEC

FURNITURE & RELATED PRODUCT MANUFACTURING

337110 Wood Kitchen Cabinet and Counter Top Manufacturing *see* SIC 2434: Wood Kitchen Cabinets; SIC 2541: Wood Office and Store Fixtures, Partitions, Shelving, and Lockers; SIC 5712: Furniture Stores

337121 Upholstered Wood Household Furniture Manufacturing *see* SIC 2512: Wood Household Furniture, Upholstered; SIC 2515: Mattresses, Foundations, and Convertible Beds; SIC 5712: Furniture Stores

337122 Nonupholstered Wood Household Furniture Manufacturing *see* SIC 2511: Wood Household Furniture, Except Upholstered; SIC 5712: Furniture Stores

337124 Metal Household Furniture Manufacturing *see* SIC 2514: Metal Household Furniture

337125 Household Furniture (except Wood and Metal) Manufacturing *see* SIC 2519: Household Furniture, NEC

337127 Institutional Furniture Manufacturing *see* SIC 2531: Public Building and Related Furniture; SIC 2599: Furniture and Fixtures, NEC; SIC 3952: Lead Pencils, Crayons, and Artist's Materials; SIC 3999: Manufacturing Industries, NEC

337129 Wood Television, Radio, and Sewing Machine Cabinet Manufacturing *see* SIC 2517: Wood Television, Radio, Phonograph and Sewing Machine Cabinets

337211 Wood Office Furniture Manufacturing *see* SIC 2521: Wood Office Furniture

337212 Custom Architectural Woodwork, Millwork, and Fixtures *see* SIC 2541: Wood Office and Store Fixtures, Partitions, Shelving, and Lockers

337214 Nonwood Office Furniture Manufacturing *see* SIC 2522: Office Furniture, Except Wood

337215 Showcase, Partition, Shelving, and Locker Manufacturing *see* SIC 2426: Hardwood Dimension and Flooring Mills; SIC 2541: Wood Office and Store Fixtures, Partitions, Shelving, and Lockers; SIC 2542: Office and Store Fixtures, Partitions Shelving, and Lockers, Except Wood; SIC 3499: Fabricated Metal Products, NEC

337910 Mattress Manufacturing *see* SIC 2515: Mattresses, Foundations, and Convertible Beds

337920 Blind and Shade Manufacturing *see* SIC 2591: Drapery Hardware and Window Blinds and Shades

MISCELLANEOUS MANUFACTURING

339111 Laboratory Apparatus and Furniture Manufacturing *see* SIC 3821: Laboratory Apparatus and Furniture

339112 Surgical and Medical Instrument Manufacturing *see* SIC 3829: Measuring and Controlling Devices, NEC; SIC 3841: Surgical and Medical Instruments and Apparatus

339113 Surgical Appliance and Supplies Manufacturing *see* SIC 2599: Furniture and Fixtures, NEC; SIC 3842: Orthopedic, Prosthetic, and Surgical Appliances and Supplies

339114 Dental Equipment and Supplies Manufacturing *see* SIC 3843: Dental Equipment and Supplies

339115 Ophthalmic Goods Manufacturing *see* SIC 3851: Ophthalmic Goods; SIC 5995: Optical Goods Stores

339116 Dental Laboratories *see* SIC 8072: Dental Laboratories

339911 Jewelry (including Precious Metal) Manufacturing, *see* SIC 3469: Metal Stamping, NEC; SIC 3479: Coating, Engraving, and Allied Services, NEC; SIC 3911: Jewelry, Precious Metal

339912 Silverware and Plated Ware Manufacturing *see* SIC 3479: Coating, Engraving, and Allied Services, NEC; SIC 3914: Silverware, Plated Ware, and Stainless Steel Ware

339913 Jewelers' Material and Lapidary Work Manufacturing *see* SIC 3915: Jewelers' Findings and Materials, and Lapidary Work

339914 Costume Jewelry and Novelty Manufacturing *see* SIC 3479: Coating, Engraving, and Allied Services, NEC; SIC 3499: Fabricated Metal Products, NEC; SIC 3961: Costume Jewelry and Costume Novelties, Except Precious Metals

339920 Sporting and Athletic Good Manufacturing *see* SIC 3949: Sporting and Athletic Goods, NEC

339931 Doll and Stuffed Toy Manufacturing *see* SIC 3942: Dolls and Stuffed Toys

339932 Game, Toy, and Children's Vehicle Manufacturing *see* SIC 3944: Games, Toys, and Children's Vehicles, Except Dolls and Bicycles

339941 Pen and Mechanical Pencil Manufacturing *see* SIC 3951: Pens, Mechanical Pencils and Parts

339942 Lead Pencil and Art Good Manufacturing *see* SIC 2531: Public Building and Related Furniture; SIC 3579: Office Machines, NEC; SIC 3952: Lead Pencils, Crayons, and Artist's Materials

339943 Marking Device Manufacturing *see* SIC 3953: Marking Devices

339944 Carbon Paper and Inked Ribbon Manufacturing *see* SIC 3955: Carbon Paper and Inked Ribbons

339950 Sign Manufacturing *see* SIC 3993: Signs and Advertising Specialties

339991 Gasket, Packing, and Sealing Device Manufacturing *see* SIC 3053: Gaskets, Packing, and Sealing Devices

339992 Musical Instrument Manufacturing *see* SIC 3931: Musical Instruments

339993 Fastener, Button, Needle, and Pin Manufacturing *see* SIC 3131: Boot and Shoe Cut Stock and Findings; SIC 3965: Fasteners, Buttons, Needles, and Pins

339994   Broom, Brush and Mop Manufacturing *see* SIC 2392: Housefurnishings, Except Curtains and Draperies; SIC 3991: Brooms and Brushes

339995   Burial Casket Manufacturing *see* SIC 3995: Burial Caskets

339999   All Other Miscellaneous Manufacturing *see* SIC 2499: Wood Products, NEC; SIC 3999: Manufacturing Industries, NEC

WHOLESALE TRADE

421110   Automobile and Other Motor Vehicle Wholesalers *see* SIC 5012: Automobiles and Other Motor Vehicles; SIC 5013: Motor Vehicle Supplies and New Parts

421130   Tire and Tube Wholesalers *see* SIC 5014: Tires and Tubes

421140   Motor Vehicle Part (Used) Wholesalers *see* SIC 5015: Motor Vehicle Parts, Used

421210   Furniture Wholesalers *see* SIC 5021: Furniture

421220   Home Furnishing Wholesalers *see* SIC 5023: Home Furnishings

421310   Lumber, Plywood, Millwork, and Wood Panel Wholesalers *see* SIC 5031: Lumber, Plywood, Millwork, and Wood Panels; SIC 5211: Lumber and Other Building Materials Dealers

421320   Brick, Stone and Related Construction Material Wholesalers *see* SIC 5032: Brick, Stone and Related Construction Materials

421330   Roofing, Siding, and Insulation Material Wholesalers *see* SIC 5033: Roofing, Siding, and Insulation Materials

421390   Other Construction Material Wholesalers *see* SIC 5039: Construction Materials, NEC

421410   Photographic Equipment and Supplies Wholesalers *see* SIC 5043: Photographic Equipment and Supplies

421420   Office Equipment Wholesalers *see* SIC 5044: Office Equipment

421430   Computer and Computer Peripheral Equipment and Software Wholesalers *see* SIC 5045: Computers and Computer Peripheral Equipment and Software

421440   Other Commercial Equipment Wholesalers *see* SIC 5046: Commercial Equipment, NEC

421450   Medical, Dental and Hospital Equipment and Supplies Wholesalers *see* SIC 5047: Medical, Dental, and Hospital Equipment and Supplies

421460   Ophthalmic Goods Wholesalers *see* SIC 5048: Ophthalmic Goods

421490   Other Professional Equipment and Supplies Wholesalers *see* SIC 5049: Professional Equipment and Supplies, NEC

421510   Metals Service Centers and Offices *see* SIC 5051: Metals Service Centers and Offices

421520   Coal and Other Mineral and Ore Wholesalers *see* SIC 5052: Coal and Other Minerals and Ores

421610   Electrical Apparatus and Equipment, Wiring Supplies and Construction Material Wholesalers *see* SIC 5063: Electrical Apparatus and Equipment Wiring Supplies, and Construction Materials

421620   Electrical Appliance, Television and Radio Set Wholesalers *see* SIC 5064: Electrical Appliances, Television and Radio Sets

421690   Other Electronic Parts and Equipment Wholesalers *see* SIC 5065: Electronic Parts and Equipment, Not Elsewhere Classified

421710   Hardware Wholesalers *see* SIC 5072: Hardware

421720   Plumbing and Heating Equipment and Supplies (Hydronics) Wholesalers *see* SIC 5074: Plumbing and Heating Equipment and Supplies (Hydronics)

421730   Warm Air Heating and Air-Conditioning Equipment and Supplies Wholesalers *see* SIC 5075: Warm Air Heating and Air-Conditioning Equipment and Supplies

421740   Refrigeration Equipment and Supplies Wholesalers *see* SIC 5078: Refrigeration Equipment and Supplies

421810   Construction and Mining (except Petroleum) Machinery and Equipment Wholesalers *see* SIC 5082: Construction and Mining (Except Petroleum) Machinery and Equipment

421820   Farm and Garden Machinery and Equipment Wholesalers *see* SIC 5083: Farm and Garden Machinery and Equipment

421830   Industrial Machinery and Equipment Wholesalers *see* SIC 5084: Industrial Machinery and Equipment; SIC 5085: Industrial Supplies

421840   Industrial Supplies Wholesalers *see* SIC 5085: Industrial Supplies

421850   Service Establishment Equipment and Supplies Wholesalers *see* SIC 5087: Service Establishment Equipment and Supplies

421860   Transportation Equipment and Supplies (except Motor Vehicles) Wholesalers *see* SIC 5088: Transportation Equipment and Supplies, Except Motor Vehicles

421910   Sporting and Recreational Goods and Supplies Wholesalers *see* SIC 5091: Sporting and Recreational Goods and Supplies

421920   Toy and Hobby Goods and Supplies Wholesalers *see* SIC 5092: Toys and Hobby Goods and Supplies

421930   Recyclable Material Wholesalers *see* SIC 5093: Scrap and Waste Materials

421940 Jewelry, Watch , Precious Stone, and Precious Metal Wholesalers *see* SIC 5094: Jewelry, Watches, Precious Stones, and Precious Metals

421990 Other Miscellaneous Durable Goods Wholesalers *see* SIC 5099: Durable Goods, NEC; SIC 7822: Motion Picture and Video Tape Distribution

422110 Printing and Writing Paper Wholesalers *see* SIC 5111: Printing and Writing Paper

422120 Stationery and Office Supplies Wholesalers *see* SIC 5112: Stationery and Office Supplies

422130 Industrial and Personal Service Paper Wholesalers *see* SIC 5113: Industrial and Personal Service Paper

422210 Drugs, Drug Proprietaries, and Druggists' Sundries Wholesalers *see* SIC 5122: Drugs, Drug Proprietaries, and Druggists' Sundries

422310 Piece Goods, Notions, and Other Dry Goods Wholesalers *see* SIC 5131: Piece Goods, Notions, and Other Dry Goods

422320 Men's and Boys' Clothing and Furnishings Wholesalers *see* SIC 5136: Men's and Boys' Clothing and Furnishings

422330 Women's, Children's, and Infants' Clothing and Accessories Wholesalers *see* SIC 5137: Women's Children's and Infants' Clothing and Accessories

422340 Footwear Wholesalers *see* SIC 5139: Footwear

422410 General Line Grocery Wholesalers *see* SIC 5141: Groceries, General Line

422420 Packaged Frozen Food Wholesalers *see* SIC 5142: Packaged Frozen Foods

422430 Dairy Products (except Dried or Canned) Wholesalers *see* SIC 5143: Dairy Products, Except Dried or Canned

422440 Poultry and Poultry Product Wholesalers *see* SIC 5144: Poultry and Poultry Products

422450 Confectionery Wholesalers *see* SIC 5145: Confectionery

422460 Fish and Seafood Wholesalers *see* SIC 5146: Fish and Seafoods

422470 Meat and Meat Product Wholesalers *see* SIC 5147: Meats and Meat Products

422480 Fresh Fruit and Vegetable Wholesalers *see* SIC 5148: Fresh Fruits and Vegetables

422490 Other Grocery and Related Product Wholesalers *see* SIC 5149: Groceries and Related Products, NEC

422510 Grain and Field Bean Wholesalers *see* SIC 5153: Grain and Field Beans

422520 Livestock Wholesalers *see* SIC 5154: Livestock

422590 Other Farm Product Raw Material Wholesalers *see* SIC 5159: Farm-Product Raw Materials, NEC

422610 Plastics Materials and Basic Forms and Shapes Wholesalers *see* SIC 5162: Plastics Materials and Basic Forms and Shapes

422690 Other Chemical and Allied Products Wholesalers *see* SIC 5169: Chemicals and Allied Products, NEC

422710 Petroleum Bulk Stations and Terminals *see* SIC 5171: Petroleum Bulk Stations and Terminals

422720 Petroleum and Petroleum Products Wholesalers (except Bulk Stations and Terminals) *see* SIC 5172: Petroleum and Petroleum Products Wholesalers, Except Bulk Stations and Terminals

422810 Beer and Ale Wholesalers *see* SIC 5181: Beer and Ale

422820 Wine and Distilled Alcoholic Beverage Wholesalers *see* SIC 5182: Wine and Distilled Alcoholic Beverages

422910 Farm Supplies Wholesalers *see* SIC 5191: Farm Supplies

422920 Book, Periodical and Newspaper Wholesalers *see* SIC 5192: Books, Periodicals, and Newspapers

422930 Flower, Nursery Stock and Florists' Supplies Wholesalers *see* SIC 5193: Flowers, Nursery Stock, and Florists' Supplies

422940 Tobacco and Tobacco Product Wholesalers *see* SIC 5194: Tobacco and Tobacco Products

422950 Paint, Varnish and Supplies Wholesalers *see* SIC 5198: Paint, Varnishes, and Supplies; SIC 5231: Paint, Glass, and Wallpaper Stores

422990 Other Miscellaneous Nondurable Goods Wholesalers *see* SIC 5199: Nondurable Goods, NEC

RETAIL TRADE

441110 New Car Dealers *see* SIC 5511: Motor Vehicle Dealers (New and Used)

441120 Used Car Dealers *see* SIC 5521: Motor Vehicle Dealers (Used Only)

441210 Recreational Vehicle Dealers *see* SIC 5561: Recreational Vehicle Dealers

441221 Motorcycle Dealers *see* SIC 5571: Motorcycle Dealers

441222 Boat Dealers *see* SIC 5551: Boat Dealers

441229 All Other Motor Vehicle Dealers *see* SIC 5599: Automotive Dealers, NEC

441310 Automotive Parts and Accessories Stores *see* SIC 5013: Motor Vehicle Supplies and New Parts; SIC 5531: Auto and Home Supply Stores

441310 Automotive Parts and Accessories Stores *see* SIC 5731: Radio, Television, and Consumer Electronics Stores

441320 Tire Dealers *see* SIC 5014: Tires and Tubes; SIC 5531: Auto and Home Supply Stores

442110 Furniture Stores *see* SIC 5021: Furniture; SIC 5712: Furniture Stores

442210 Floor Covering Stores *see* SIC 5023: Home Furnishings; SIC 5713: Floor Covering Stores

442291 Window Treatment Stores *see* SIC 5714: Drapery, Curtain, and Upholstery Stores; SIC 5719: Miscellaneous Homefurnishings Stores

442299 All Other Home Furnishings Stores *see* SIC 5719: Miscellaneous Homefurnishings Stores; SIC 5722: Household Appliance Stores

443111 Household Appliance Stores *see* SIC 5999: Miscellaneous Retail Stores, NEC; SIC 7623: Refrigeration and Air-Conditioning Services and Repair Shops; SIC 7629: Electrical and Electronic Repair Shops, NEC

443112 Radio, Television, and Other Electronics Stores *see* SIC 5731: Radio, Television, and Consumer Electronics Stores; SIC 5999: Miscellaneous Retail Stores, NEC; SIC 7622: Radio and Television Repair Shops

443120 Computer and Software Stores *see* SIC 5045: Computers and Computer Peripheral Equipment and Software; SIC 5734: Computer and Computer Software Stores; SIC 7378: Computer Maintenance and Repair

443130 Camera and Photographic Supplies Stores *see* SIC 5946: Camera and Photographic Supply Stores

444110 Home Centers *see* SIC 5211: Lumber and Other Building Materials Dealers

444120 Paint and Wallpaper Stores *see* SIC 5198: Paint, Varnishes, and Supplies; SIC 5231: Paint, Glass, and Wallpaper Stores

444130 Hardware Stores *see* SIC 5251: Hardware Stores

444190 Other Building Material Dealers *see* SIC 5031: Lumber, Plywood, Millwork, and Wood Panels; SIC 5032: Brick, Stone and Related Construction Materials; SIC 5039: Construction Materials, NEC; SIC 5063: Electrical Apparatus and Equipment Wiring Supplies, and Construction Materials; SIC 5074: Plumbing and Heating Equipment and Supplies (Hydronics); SIC 5211: Lumber and Other Building Materials Dealers; SIC 5231: Paint, Glass, and Wallpaper Stores

444210 Outdoor Power Equipment Stores *see* SIC 5083: Farm and Garden Machinery and Equipment; SIC 5261: Retail Nurseries, Lawn and Garden Supply Stores

444220 Nursery and Garden Centers *see* SIC 5191: Farm Supplies; SIC 5193: Flowers, Nursery Stock, and

Florists' Supplies; SIC 5261: Retail Nurseries, Lawn and Garden Supply Stores

445110 Supermarkets and Other Grocery (except Convenience) Stores *see* SIC 5411: Grocery Stores

445120 Convenience Stores *see* SIC 5411: Grocery Stores

445210 Meat Markets *see* SIC 5421: Meat and Fish (Seafood) Markets, Including Freezer Provisioners; SIC 5499: Miscellaneous Food Stores

445220 Fish and Seafood Markets *see* SIC 5421: Meat and Fish (Seafood) Markets, Including Freezer Provisioners

445230 Fruit and Vegetable Markets *see* SIC 5431: Fruit and Vegetable Markets

445291 Baked Goods Stores *see* SIC 5461: Retail Bakeries

445292 Confectionery and Nut Stores *see* SIC 5441: Candy, Nut, and Confectionery Stores

445299 All Other Specialty Food Stores *see* SIC 5451: Dairy Products Stores; SIC 5499: Miscellaneous Food Stores

445310 Beer, Wine and Liquor Stores *see* SIC 5921: Liquor Stores

446110 Pharmacies and Drug Stores *see* SIC 5912: Drug Stores and Proprietary Stores

446120 Cosmetics, Beauty Supplies, and Perfume Stores *see* SIC 5087: Service Establishment Equipment and Supplies

446120 Cosmetics, Beauty Supplies, and Perfume Stores *see* SIC 5999: Miscellaneous Retail Stores, NEC

446130 Optical Goods Stores *see* SIC 5995: Optical Goods Stores

446191 Food (Health) Supplement Stores *see* SIC 5499: Miscellaneous Food Stores

446199 All Other Health and Personal Care Stores *see* SIC 5047: Medical, Dental, and Hospital Equipment and Supplies; SIC 5999: Miscellaneous Retail Stores, NEC

447110 Gasoline Stations with Convenience Stores *see* SIC 5411: Grocery Stores; SIC 5541: Gasoline Service Stations

447190 Other Gasoline Stations *see* SIC 5541: Gasoline Service Stations

448110 Men's Clothing Stores *see* SIC 5611: Men's and Boys' Clothing and Accessory Stores

448120 Women's Clothing Stores *see* SIC 5621: Women's Clothing Stores

448130 Children's and Infants' Clothing Stores *see* SIC 5641: Children's and Infants' Wear Stores

448140 Family Clothing Stores *see* SIC 5651: Family Clothing Stores

448150 Clothing Accessories Stores *see* SIC 5611: Men's and Boys' Clothing and Accessory Stores; SIC

5632: Women's Accessory and Specialty Stores; SIC 5699: Miscellaneous Apparel and Accessory Stores

448190 Other Clothing Stores *see* SIC 5632: Women's Accessory and Specialty Stores; SIC 5699: Miscellaneous Apparel and Accessory Stores

448210 Shoe Stores *see* SIC 5661: Shoe Stores

448310 Jewelry Stores *see* SIC 5944: Jewelry Stores; SIC 5999: Miscellaneous Retail Stores, NEC

448320 Luggage and Leather Goods Stores *see* SIC 5948: Luggage and Leather Goods Stores

451110 Sporting Goods Stores *see* SIC 5941: Sporting Goods Stores and Bicycle Shops; SIC 7699: Repair Shops and Related Services, NEC

451120 Hobby, Toy and Game Stores *see* SIC 5945: Hobby, Toy, and Game Shops

451130 Sewing, Needlework and Piece Goods Stores *see* SIC 5714: Drapery, Curtain, and Upholstery Stores; SIC 5949: Sewing, Needlework, and Piece Goods Stores

451140 Musical Instrument and Supplies Stores *see* SIC 5736: Musical Instrument Stores

451211 Book Stores *see* SIC 5942: Book Stores

451212 News Dealers and Newsstands *see* SIC 5994: News Dealers and Newsstands

451220 Prerecorded Tape, Compact Disc and Record Stores *see* SIC 5735: Record and Prerecorded Tape Stores

452110 Department Stores *see* SIC 5311: Department Stores

452910 Warehouse Clubs and Superstores *see* SIC 5399: Miscellaneous General Merchandise Stores; SIC 5411: Grocery Stores

452990 All Other General Merchandise Stores *see* SIC 5331: Variety Stores; SIC 5399: Miscellaneous General Merchandise Stores

453110 Florists *see* SIC 5992: Florists

453210 Office Supplies and Stationery Stores *see* SIC 5049: Professional Equipment and Supplies, NEC; SIC 5112: Stationery and Office Supplies; SIC 5943: Stationery Stores

453220 Gift, Novelty and Souvenir Stores *see* SIC 5947: Gift, Novelty, and Souvenir Shops

453310 Used Merchandise Stores *see* SIC 5932: Used Merchandise Stores

453910 Pet and Pet Supplies Stores *see* SIC 5999: Miscellaneous Retail Stores, NEC

453920 Art Dealers *see* SIC 5999: Miscellaneous Retail Stores, NEC

453930 Manufactured (Mobile) Home Dealers *see* SIC 5271: Mobile Home Dealers

453991 Tobacco Stores *see* SIC 5993: Tobacco Stores and Stands

453998 All Other Miscellaneous Store Retailers (except Tobacco Stores) *see* SIC 5261: Retail Nurseries, Lawn and Garden Supply Stores; SIC 5999: Miscellaneous Retail Stores, NEC

454110 Electronic Shopping and Mail-Order Houses *see* SIC 5961: Catalog and Mail-Order Houses

454210 Vending Machine Operators *see* SIC 5962: Automatic Merchandising Machine Operator

454311 Heating Oil Dealers *see* SIC 5171: Petroleum Bulk Stations and Terminals; SIC 5983: Fuel Oil Dealers

454312 Liquefied Petroleum Gas (Bottled Gas) Dealers *see* SIC 5171: Petroleum Bulk Stations and Terminals; SIC 5984: Liquefied Petroleum Gas (Bottled Gas) Dealers

454319 Other Fuel Dealers *see* SIC 5989: Fuel Dealers, NEC

454390 Other Direct Selling Establishments *see* SIC 5421: Meat and Fish (Seafood) Markets, Including Freezer Provisioners; SIC 5963: Direct Selling Establishments

TRANSPORTATION & WAREHOUSING

481111 Scheduled Passenger Air Transportation *see* SIC 4512: Air Transportation, Scheduled

481112 Scheduled Freight Air Transportation *see* SIC 4512: Air Transportation, Scheduled

481211 Nonscheduled Chartered Passenger Air Transportation *see* SIC 4522: Air Transportation, Nonscheduled

481212 Nonscheduled Chartered Freight Air Transportation *see* SIC 4522: Air Transportation, Nonscheduled

481219 Other Nonscheduled Air Transportation *see* SIC 0721: Crop Planting, Cultivating and Protecting; SIC 7319: Advertising, NEC; SIC 7335: Commercial Photography

482111 Line-Haul Railroads *see* SIC 4011: Railroads, Line-haul Operating

482112 Short Line Railroads *see* SIC 4013: Railroad Switching and Terminal Establishments

483111 Deep Sea Freight Transportation *see* SIC 4412: Deep Sea Foreign Transportation of Freight

483112 Deep Sea Passenger Transportation *see* SIC 4481: Deep Sea Transportation of Passengers, Except by Ferry

483113 Coastal and Great Lakes Freight Transportation *see* SIC 4424: Deep Sea Domestic Transportation of Freight; SIC 4432: Freight Transportation on the Great Lakes-St. Lawrence Seaway; SIC 4492: Towing and Tugboat Services

483114   Coastal and Great Lakes Passenger Transportation *see* SIC 4481: Deep Sea Transportation of Passengers, Except by Ferry; SIC 4482: Ferries

483211   Inland Water Freight Transportation *see* SIC 4449: Water Transportation of Freight, NEC; SIC 4492: Towing and Tugboat Services

483212   Inland Water Passenger Transportation *see* SIC 4482: Ferries; SIC 4489: Water Transportation of Passengers, NEC

484110   General Freight Trucking, Local *see* SIC 4212: Local Trucking Without Storage; SIC 4214: Local Trucking with Storage

484121   General Freight Trucking, Long-Distance, Truckload *see* SIC 4213: Trucking, Except Local

484122   General Freight Trucking, Long-Distance, Less Than Truckload *see* SIC 4213: Trucking, Except Local

484210   Used Household and Office Goods Moving *see* SIC 4212: Local Trucking Without Storage; SIC 4213: Trucking, Except Local; SIC 4214: Local Trucking with Storage

484220   Specialized Freight (except Used Goods) Trucking, Local *see* SIC 4212: Local Trucking Without Storage; SIC 4214: Local Trucking with Storage

484230   Specialized Freight (except Used Goods) Trucking, Long-Distance *see* SIC 4213: Trucking, Except Local

485111   Mixed Mode Transit Systems *see* SIC 4111: Local and Suburban Transit

485112   Commuter Rail Systems *see* SIC 4111: Local and Suburban Transit

485113   Bus and Motor Vehicle Transit Systems *see* SIC 4111: Local and Suburban Transit

485119   Other Urban Transit Systems *see* SIC 4111: Local and Suburban Transit

485210   Interurban and Rural Bus Lines *see* SIC 4131: Intercity and Rural Bus Transportation

485310   Taxi Service *see* SIC 4121: Taxicabs

485320   Limousine Service *see* SIC 4119: Local Passenger Transportation, NEC

485410   School and Employee Bus Industry *see* SIC 4119: Local Passenger Transportation, NEC; SIC 4151: School Buses

485510   Charter Bus Industry *see* SIC 4141: Local Bus Charter Service; SIC 4142: Bus Charter Service, Except Local

485991   Special Needs Transportation *see* SIC 4119: Local Passenger Transportation, NEC

485999   All Other Transit and Ground Passenger Transportation *see* SIC 4111: Local and Suburban Transit; SIC 4119: Local Passenger Transportation, NEC

486110   Pipeline Transportation of Crude Oil *see* SIC 4612: Crude Petroleum Pipelines

486210   Pipeline Transportation of Natural Gas *see* SIC 4922: Natural Gas Transmission; SIC 4923: Natural Gas Transmission and Distribution

486910   Pipeline Transportation of Refined Petroleum Products *see* SIC 4613: Refined Petroleum Pipelines

486990   All Other Pipeline Transportation *see* SIC 4619: Pipelines, NEC

487110   Scenic and Sightseeing Transportation, Land *see* SIC 4119: Local Passenger Transportation, NEC; SIC 4789: Transportation Services, NEC; SIC 7999: Amusement and Recreation Services, NEC

487210   Scenic and Sightseeing Transportation, Water *see* SIC 4489: Water Transportation of Passengers, NEC; SIC 7999: Amusement and Recreation Services, NEC

487990   Scenic and Sightseeing Transportation, Other *see* SIC 4522: Air Transportation, Nonscheduled; SIC 7999: Amusement and Recreation Services, NEC

488111   Air Traffic Control *see* SIC 4581: Airports, Flying Fields, and Airport Terminal Services; SIC 9621: Regulations and Administration of Transportation Programs

488119   Other Airport Operations *see* SIC 4581: Airports, Flying Fields, and Airport Terminal Services; SIC 4959: Sanitary Services, NEC

488190   Other Support Activities for Air Transportation *see* SIC 4581: Airports, Flying Fields, and Airport Terminal Services

488210   Support Activities for Rail Transportation *see* SIC 4013: Railroad Switching and Terminal Establishments; SIC 4741: Rental of Railroad Cars; SIC 4789: Transportation Services, NEC

488310   Port and Harbor Operations *see* SIC 4491: Marine Cargo Handling; SIC 4499: Water Transportation Services, NEC

488320   Marine Cargo Handling *see* SIC 4491: Marine Cargo Handling

488330   Navigational Services to Shipping *see* SIC 4492: Towing and Tugboat Services; SIC 4499: Water Transportation Services, NEC

488390   Other Support Activities for Water Transportation *see* SIC 4499: Water Transportation Services, NEC; SIC 4785: Fixed Facilities and Inspection and Weighing Services for Motor Vehicle Transportation; SIC 7699: Repair Shops and Related Services, NEC

488410   Motor Vehicle Towing *see* SIC 7549: Automotive Services, Except Repair and Carwashes

488490   Other Support Activities for Road Transportation *see* SIC 4173: Terminal and Service Facilities for Motor Vehicle Passenger Transportation; SIC 4231: Terminal and Joint Terminal Maintenance Facilities for Motor Freight Transportation; SIC 4785: Fixed Facilities and Inspection and Weighing Services for Motor Vehicle Transportation

488510   Freight Transportation Arrangement *see* SIC 4731: Arrangement of Transportation of Freight and Cargo

488991   Packing and Crating *see* SIC 4783: Packing and Crating

488999   All Other Support Activities for Transportation *see* SIC 4729: Arrangement of Passenger Transportation, NEC; SIC 4789: Transportation Services, NEC

491110   Postal Service *see* SIC 4311: United States Postal Service

492110   Couriers *see* SIC 4215: Couriers Services Except by Air; SIC 4513: Air Courier Services

492210   Local Messengers and Local Delivery *see* SIC 4215: Couriers Services Except by Air

493110   General Warehousing and Storage Facilities *see* SIC 4225: General Warehousing and Storage; SIC 4226: Special Warehousing and Storage, NEC

493120   Refrigerated Storage Facilities *see* SIC 4222: Refrigerated Warehousing and Storage; SIC 4226: Special Warehousing and Storage, NEC

493130   Farm Product Storage Facilities *see* SIC 4221: Farm Product Warehousing and Storage

493190   All Other Warehousing and Storage Facilities *see* SIC 4226: Special Warehousing and Storage, NEC

INFORMATION

511110   Newspaper Publishers *see* SIC 2711: Newspapers: Publishing, or Publishing and Printing

511120   Periodical Publishers *see* SIC 2721: Periodicals: Publishing, or Publishing and Printing

511130   Book Publishers *see* SIC 2731: Books: Publishing, or Publishing and Printing

511140   Database and Directory Publishers *see* SIC 2741: Miscellaneous Publishing

511191   Greeting Card Publishers *see* SIC 2771: Greeting Cards

511199   All Other Publishers *see* SIC 2741: Miscellaneous Publishing

511210   Software Publishers *see* SIC 7372: Prepackaged Software

512110   Motion Picture and Video Production *see* SIC 7812: Motion Picture and Video Tape Production

512120   Motion Picture and Video Distribution *see* SIC 7822: Motion Picture and Video Tape Distribution; SIC 7829: Services Allied to Motion Picture Distribution

512131   Motion Picture Theaters, Except Drive-In *see* SIC 7832: Motion Picture Theaters, Except Drive-In

512132   Drive-In Motion Picture Theaters *see* SIC 7833: Drive-In Motion Picture Theaters

512191   Teleproduction and Other Post-Production Services *see* SIC 7819: Services Allied to Motion Picture Production

512199   Other Motion Picture and Video Industries *see* SIC 7819: Services Allied to Motion Picture Production; SIC 7829: Services Allied to Motion Picture Distribution

512210   Record Production *see* SIC 8999: Services, NEC

512220   Integrated Record Production/Distribution *see* SIC 3652: Phonograph Records and Prerecorded Audio Tapes and Disks

512230   Music Publishers *see* SIC 2731: Books: Publishing, or Publishing and Printing; SIC 2741: Miscellaneous Publishing; SIC 8999: Services, NEC

512240   Sound Recording Studios *see* SIC 7389: Business Services, NEC

512290   Other Sound Recording Industries *see* SIC 7389: Business Services, NEC; SIC 7922: Theatrical Producers (Except Motion Picture) and Miscellaneous Theatrical Services

513111   Radio Networks *see* SIC 4832: Radio Broadcasting Stations

513112   Radio Stations *see* SIC 4832: Radio Broadcasting Stations

513120   Television Broadcasting *see* SIC 4833: Television Broadcasting Stations

513210   Cable Networks *see* SIC 4841: Cable and Other Pay Television Services

513220   Cable and Other Program Distribution *see* SIC 4841: Cable and Other Pay Television Services

513310   Wired Telecommunications Carriers *see* SIC 4813: Telephone Communications, Except Radiotelephone; SIC 4822: Telegraph and Other Message Communications

513321   Paging *see* SIC 4812: Radiotelephone Communications

513322   Cellular and Other Wireless Telecommunications *see* SIC 4812: Radiotelephone Communications; SIC 4899: Communications Services, NEC

513330 Telecommunications Resellers *see* SIC 4812: Radiotelephone Communications; SIC 4813: Telephone Communications, Except Radiotelephone

513340 Satellite Telecommunications *see* SIC 4899: Communications Services, NEC

513390 Other Telecommunications *see* SIC 4899: Communications Services, NEC

514110 New Syndicates *see* SIC 7383: News Syndicates

514120 Libraries and Archives *see* SIC 8231: Libraries

514191 On-Line Information Services *see* SIC 7375: Information Retrieval Services

514199 All Other Information Services *see* SIC 8999: Services, NEC

514210 Data Processing Services *see* SIC 7374: Computer Processing and Data Preparation and Processing Services

FINANCE & INSURANCE

521110 Monetary Authorities-Central Banks *see* SIC 6011: Federal Reserve Banks

522110 Commercial Banking *see* SIC 6021: National Commercial Banks; SIC 6022: State Commercial Banks; SIC 6029: Commercial Banks, NEC; SIC 6081: Branches and Agencies of Foreign Banks

522120 Savings Institutions *see* SIC 6035: Savings Institutions, Federally Chartered; SIC 6036: Savings institutions, Not Federally Chartered

522130 Credit Unions *see* SIC 6061: Credit Unions, Federally Chartered; SIC 6062: Credit Unions, Not Federally Chartered

522190 Other Depository Intermediation *see* SIC 6022: State Commercial Banks

522210 Credit Card Issuing *see* SIC 6021: National Commercial Banks; SIC 6022: State Commercial Banks; SIC 6141: Personal Credit Institutions

522220 Sales Financing *see* SIC 6141: Personal Credit Institutions; SIC 6153: Short-Term Business Credit Institutions, Except Agricultural; SIC 6159: Miscellaneous Business Credit Institutions

522291 Consumer Lending *see* SIC 6141: Personal Credit Institutions

522292 Real Estate Credit *see* SIC 6162: Mortgage Bankers and Loan Correspondents

522293 International Trade Financing *see* SIC 6081: Branches and Agencies of Foreign Banks; SIC 6082: Foreign Trade and International Banking Institutions; SIC 6111: Federal and Federally Sponsored Credit Agencies; SIC 6159: Miscellaneous Business Credit Institutions

522294 Secondary Market Financing *see* SIC 6111: Federal and Federally Sponsored Credit Agencies

522298 All Other Non-Depository Credit Intermediation *see* SIC 5932: Used Merchandise Stores; SIC 6081: Branches and Agencies of Foreign Banks; SIC 6111: Federal and Federally Sponsored Credit Agencies; SIC 6153: Short-Term Business Credit Institutions, Except Agricultural; SIC 6159: Miscellaneous Business Credit Institutions

522310 Mortgage and Other Loan Brokers *see* SIC 6163: Loan Brokers

522320 Financial Transactions Processing, Reserve, and Clearing House Activities *see* SIC 6019: Central Reserve Depository Institutions, NEC; SIC 6099: Functions Related to Deposit Banking, NEC; SIC 6153: Short-Term Business Credit Institutions, Except Agricultural; SIC 7389: Business Services, NEC

522390 Other Activities Related to Credit Intermediation *see* SIC 6099: Functions Related to Deposit Banking, NEC; SIC 6162: Mortgage Bankers and Loan Correspondents

523110 Investment Banking and Securities Dealing *see* SIC 6211: Security Brokers, Dealers, and Flotation Companies

523120 Securities Brokerage *see* SIC 6211: Security Brokers, Dealers, and Flotation Companies

523130 Commodity Contracts Dealing *see* SIC 6099: Functions Related to Deposit Banking, NEC; SIC 6221: Commodity Contracts Brokers and Dealers; SIC 6799: Investors, NEC

523140 Commodity Brokerage *see* SIC 6221: Commodity Contracts Brokers and Dealers

523210 Securities and Commodity Exchanges *see* SIC 6231: Security and Commodity Exchanges

523910 Miscellaneous Intermediation *see* SIC 6211: Security Brokers, Dealers, and Flotation Companies; SIC 6799: Investors, NEC

523920 Portfolio Management *see* SIC 6282: Investment Advice; SIC 6371: Pension, Health, and Welfare Funds; SIC 6733: Trusts, Except Educational, Religious, and Charitable; SIC 6799: Investors, NEC

523930 Investment Advice *see* SIC 6282: Investment Advice

523991 Trust, Fiduciary and Custody Activities *see* SIC 6021: National Commercial Banks; SIC 6022: State Commercial Banks; SIC 6091: Nondeposit Trust Facilities; SIC 6099: Functions Related to Deposit Banking, NEC; SIC 6289: Services Allied With the Exchange of Securities or Commodities, NEC; SIC 6733: Trusts, Except Educational, Religious, and Charitable

523999 Miscellaneous Financial Investment Activities *see* SIC 6099: Functions Related to Deposit Banking, NEC; SIC 6211: Security Brokers, Dealers, and Flotation Companies; SIC 6289: Services Allied With the Exchange of Securities or Commodities, NEC; SIC 6792: Oil Royalty Traders; SIC 6799: Investors, NEC

524113 Direct Life Insurance Carriers *see* SIC 6311: Life Insurance

524114 Direct Health and Medical Insurance Carriers *see* SIC 6321: Accident and Health Insurance; SIC 6324: Hospital and Medical Service Plans

524126 Direct Property and Casualty Insurance Carriers *see* SIC 6331: Fire, Marine, and Casualty Insurance; SIC 6351: Surety Insurance

524127 Direct Title Insurance Carriers *see* SIC 6361: Title Insurance

524128 Other Direct Insurance Carriers (except Life, Health, and Medical) *see* SIC 6399: Insurance Carriers, NEC

524130 Reinsurance Carriers *see* SIC 6311: Life Insurance; SIC 6321: Accident and Health Insurance; SIC 6324: Hospital and Medical Service Plans; SIC 6331: Fire, Marine, and Casualty Insurance; SIC 6351: Surety Insurance; SIC 6361: Title Insurance

524210 Insurance Agencies and Brokerages *see* SIC 6411: Insurance Agents, Brokers, and Service

524291 Claims Adjusters *see* SIC 6411: Insurance Agents, Brokers, and Service

524292 Third Party Administration for Insurance and Pension Funds *see* SIC 6371: Pension, Health, and Welfare Funds; SIC 6411: Insurance Agents, Brokers, and Service

524298 All Other Insurance Related Activities *see* SIC 6411: Insurance Agents, Brokers, and Service

525110 Pension Funds *see* SIC 6371: Pension, Health, and Welfare Funds

525120 Health and Welfare Funds *see* SIC 6371: Pension, Health, and Welfare Funds

525190 Other Insurance and Employee Benefit Funds *see* SIC 6321: Accident and Health Insurance; SIC 6324: Hospital and Medical Service Plans; SIC 6331: Fire, Marine, and Casualty Insurance; SIC 6733: Trusts, Except Educational, Religious, and Charitable

525910 Open-End Investment Funds *see* SIC 6722: Management Investment Offices, Open-End

525920 Trusts, Estates, and Agency Accounts *see* SIC 6733: Trusts, Except Educational, Religious, and Charitable

525930 Real Estate Investment Trusts *see* SIC 6798: Real Estate Investment Trusts

525990 Other Financial Vehicles *see* SIC 6726: Unit Investment Trusts, Face-Amount Certificate Offices, and Closed-End Management Investment Offices

REAL ESTATE & RENTAL & LEASING

531110 Lessors of Residential Buildings and Dwellings *see* SIC 6513: Operators of Apartment Buildings; SIC 6514: Operators of Dwellings Other Than Apartment Buildings

531120 Lessors of Nonresidential Buildings (except Mini-warehouses) *see* SIC 6512: Operators of Nonresidential Buildings

531130 Lessors of Mini-warehouses and Self Storage Units *see* SIC 4225: General Warehousing and Storage

531190 Lessors of Other Real Estate Property *see* SIC 6515: Operators of Residential Mobile Home Sites; SIC 6517: Lessors of Railroad Property; SIC 6519: Lessors of Real Property, NEC

531210 Offices of Real Estate Agents and Brokers *see* SIC 6531: Real Estate Agents and Managers

531311 Residential Property Managers *see* SIC 6531: Real Estate Agents and Managers

531312 Nonresidential Property Managers *see* SIC 6531: Real Estate Agents and Managers

531320 Offices of Real Estate Appraisers *see* SIC 6531: Real Estate Agents and Managers

531390 Other Activities Related to Real Estate *see* SIC 6531: Real Estate Agents and Managers

532111 Passenger Cars Rental *see* SIC 7514: Passenger Car Rental

532112 Passenger Cars Leasing *see* SIC 7515: Passenger Car Leasing

532120 Truck, Utility Trailer and RV (Recreational Vehicle) Rental and Leasing *see* SIC 7513: Truck Rental and Leasing, Without Drivers; SIC 7519: Utility Trailer and Recreational Vehicle Rental

532210 Consumer Electronics and Appliances Rental *see* SIC 7359: Equipment Rental and Leasing, NEC

532220 Formal Wear and Costumes Rental *see* SIC 7299: Miscellaneous Personal Services, NEC; SIC 7819: Services Allied to Motion Picture Production

532230 Video Tapes and Disc Rental *see* SIC 7841: Video Tape Rental

532291 Home Health Equipment Rental *see* SIC 7352: Medical Equipment Rental and Leasing

532292 Recreational Goods Rental *see* SIC 7999: Amusement and Recreation Services, NEC

532299 All Other Consumer Goods Rental *see* SIC 7359: Equipment Rental and Leasing, NEC

532310 General Rental Centers *see* SIC 7359: Equipment Rental and Leasing, NEC

532411 Commercial Air, Rail, and Water Transportation Equipment Rental and Leasing *see* SIC 4499: Water Transportation Services, NEC; SIC 4741: Rental of Railroad Cars; SIC 7359: Equipment Rental and Leasing, NEC

532412 Construction, Mining and Forestry Machinery and Equipment Rental and Leasing *see* SIC 7353: Heavy Construction Equipment Rental and Leasing; SIC 7359: Equipment Rental and Leasing, NEC

532420 Office Machinery and Equipment Rental and Leasing *see* SIC 7359: Equipment Rental and Leasing, NEC; SIC 7377: Computer Rental and Leasing

532490 Other Commercial and Industrial Machinery and Equipment Rental and Leasing *see* SIC 7352: Medical Equipment Rental and Leasing; SIC 7359: Equipment Rental and Leasing, NEC; SIC 7819: Services Allied to Motion Picture Production; SIC 7922: Theatrical Producers (Except Motion Picture) and Miscellaneous Theatrical Services

533110 Owners and Lessors of Other Non-Financial Assets *see* SIC 6792: Oil Royalty Traders; SIC 6794: Patent Owners and Lessors

PROFESSIONAL, SCIENTIFIC, & TECHNICAL SERVICES

541110 Offices of Lawyers *see* SIC 8111: Legal Services

541191 Title Abstract and Settlement Offices *see* SIC 6541: Title Abstract Offices

541199 Other Legal Services *see* SIC 7389: Business Services, NEC

541211 Offices of Certified Public Accountants *see* SIC 8721: Accounting, Auditing, and Bookkeeping Services

541213 Tax Preparation Services *see* SIC 7291: Tax Return Preparation Services

541214 Payroll Services *see* SIC 7819: Services Allied to Motion Picture Production; SIC 8721: Accounting, Auditing, and Bookkeeping Services

541219 Other Accounting Services *see* SIC 8721: Accounting, Auditing, and Bookkeeping Services

541310 Architectural Services *see* SIC 8712: Architectural Services

541320 Landscape Architectural Services *see* SIC 0781: Landscape Counseling and Planning

541330 Engineering Services *see* SIC 8711: Engineering Services

541340 Drafting Services *see* SIC 7389: Business Services, NEC

541350 Building Inspection Services *see* SIC 7389: Business Services, NEC

541360 Geophysical Surveying and Mapping Services *see* SIC 1081: Metal Mining Services; SIC 1382: Oil and Gas Field Exploration Services; SIC 1481: Nonmetallic Minerals Services Except Fuels; SIC 8713: Surveying Services

541370 Surveying and Mapping (except Geophysical) Services *see* SIC 7389: Business Services, NEC; SIC 8713: Surveying Services

541380 Testing Laboratories *see* SIC 8734: Testing Laboratories

541410 Interior Design Services *see* SIC 7389: Business Services, NEC

541420 Industrial Design Services *see* SIC 7389: Business Services, NEC

541430 Graphic Design Services *see* SIC 7336: Commercial Art and Graphic Design; SIC 8099: Health and Allied Services, NEC

541490 Other Specialized Design Services *see* SIC 7389: Business Services, NEC

541511 Custom Computer Programming Services *see* SIC 7371: Computer Programming Services

541512 Computer Systems Design Services *see* SIC 7373: Computer Integrated Systems Design; SIC 7379: Computer Related Services, NEC

541513 Computer Facilities Management Services *see* SIC 7376: Computer Facilities Management Services

541519 Other Computer Related Services *see* SIC 7379: Computer Related Services, NEC

541611 Administrative Management and General Management Consulting Services *see* SIC 8742: Management Consulting Services

541612 Human Resources and Executive Search Consulting Services *see* SIC 7361: Employment Agencies; SIC 8742: Management Consulting Services; SIC 8999: Services, NEC

541613 Marketing Consulting Services *see* SIC 8742: Management Consulting Services

541614 Process, Physical, Distribution and Logistics Consulting *see* SIC 8742: Management Consulting Services

541618 Other Management Consulting Services *see* SIC 4731: Arrangement of Transportation of Freight and Cargo; SIC 8748: Business Consulting Services, NEC

541620 Environmental Consulting Services *see* SIC 8999: Services, NEC

541690 Other Scientific and Technical Consulting Services *see* SIC 0781: Landscape Counseling and Planning; SIC 8748: Business Consulting Services, NEC; SIC 8999: Services, NEC

541710 Research and Development in the Physical Sciences and Engineering Sciences *see* SIC 8731: Commercial Physical and Biological Research; SIC 8733: Noncommercial Research Organizations

541720 Research and Development in the Life Sciences *see* SIC 8731: Commercial Physical and Biological Research; SIC 8733: Noncommercial Research Organizations

541730 Research and Development in the Social Sciences and Humanities *see* SIC 8732: Commercial Economic, Sociological, and Educational Research; SIC 8733: Noncommercial Research Organizations

541810 Advertising Agencies *see* SIC 7311: Advertising Agencies

541820 Public Relations Services *see* SIC 8743: Public Relations Services

541830 Media Buying Agencies *see* SIC 7319: Advertising, NEC

541840 Media Representatives *see* SIC 7313: Radio, Television, and Publishers' Advertising Representatives

541850 Display Advertising *see* SIC 7312: Outdoor Advertising Services; SIC 7319: Advertising, NEC

541860 Direct Mail Advertising *see* SIC 7331: Direct Mail Advertising Services

541870 Advertising Material Distribution Services *see* SIC 7319: Advertising, NEC

541890 Other Services Related to Advertising *see* SIC 5199: Nondurable Goods, NEC; SIC 7319: Advertising, NEC; SIC 7389: Business Services, NEC

541910 Marketing Research and Public Opinion Polling *see* SIC 8732: Commercial Economic, Sociological, and Educational Research

541921 Photographic Studios, Portrait *see* SIC 7221: Photographic Studios, Portrait

541922 Commercial Photography *see* SIC 7335: Commercial Photography; SIC 8099: Health and Allied Services, NEC

541930 Translation and Interpretation Services *see* SIC 7389: Business Services, NEC

541940 Veterinary Services *see* SIC 0741: Veterinary Service For Livestock; SIC 0742: Veterinary Services for Animal Specialties; SIC 8734: Testing Laboratories

541990 All Other Professional, Scientific and Technical Services *see* SIC 7389: Business Services, NEC

MANAGEMENT OF COMPANIES & ENTERPRISES

551111 Offices of Bank Holding Companies *see* SIC 6712: Offices of Bank Holding Companies

551112 Offices of Other Holding Companies *see* SIC 6719: Offices of Holding Companies, NEC

ADMINISTRATIVE & SUPPORT, WASTE MANAGEMENT & REMEDIATION SERVICES

561110 Office Administrative Services *see* SIC 8741: Management Services (Except Construction Management Services)

561210 Facilities Support Services *see* SIC 8744: Facilities Support Management Services

561310 Employment Placement Agencies *see* SIC 7361: Employment Agencies; SIC 7819: Services Allied to Motion Picture Production; SIC 7922: Theatrical Producers (Except Motion Picture) and Miscellaneous Theatrical Services

561320 Temporary Help Services *see* SIC 7363: Help Supply Services

561330 Employee Leasing Services *see* SIC 7363: Help Supply Services

561410 Document Preparation Services *see* SIC 7338: Secretarial and Court Reporting Services

561421 Telephone Answering Services *see* SIC 7389: Business Services, NEC

561422 Telemarketing Bureaus *see* SIC 7389: Business Services, NEC

561431 Other Business Service Centers (including Copy Shops) *see* SIC 7389: Business Services, NEC; SIC 7334: Photocopying and Duplicating Services

561439 Private Mail Centers *see* SIC 7389: Business Services, NEC

561440 Collection Agencies *see* SIC 7322: Adjustment and Collection Services

561450 Credit Bureaus *see* SIC 7323: Credit Reporting Services

561491 Repossession Services *see* SIC 7322: Adjustment and Collection Services; SIC 7389: Business Services, NEC

561492 Court Reporting and Stenotype Services *see* SIC 7338: Secretarial and Court Reporting Services

561499 All Other Business Support Services *see* SIC 7389: Business Services, NEC

561510 Travel Agencies *see* SIC 4724: Travel Agencies

561520 Tour Operators *see* SIC 4725: Tour Operators

561591 Convention and Visitors Bureaus *see* SIC 7389: Business Services, NEC

561599 All Other Travel Arrangement and Reservation Services *see* SIC 4729: Arrangement of Passenger Transportation, NEC; SIC 7389: Business

Services, NEC; SIC 7999: Amusement and Recreation Services, NEC; SIC 8699: Membership Organizations, NEC

561611 Investigation Services *see* SIC 7381: Detective, Guard, and Armored Car Services

561612 Security Guards and Patrol Services *see* SIC 7381: Detective, Guard, and Armored Car Services

561613 Armored Car Services *see* SIC 7381: Detective, Guard, and Armored Car Services

561621 Security Systems Services (except Locksmiths) *see* SIC 1731: Electrical Work; SIC 7382: Security Systems Services

561622 Locksmiths *see* SIC 7699: Repair Shops and Related Services, NEC

561710 Exterminating and Pest Control Services *see* SIC 4959: Sanitary Services, NEC; SIC 7342: Disinfecting and Pest Control Services

561720 Janitorial Services *see* SIC 4581: Airports, Flying Fields, and Airport Terminal Services; SIC 7342: Disinfecting and Pest Control Services; SIC 7349: Building Cleaning and Maintenance Services, NEC

561730 Landscaping Services *see* SIC 0782: Lawn and Garden Services; SIC 0783: Ornamental Shrub and Tree Services

561740 Carpet and Upholstery Cleaning Services *see* SIC 7217: Carpet and Upholstery Cleaning

561790 Other Services to Buildings and Dwellings *see* SIC 7389: Business Services, NEC; SIC 7699: Repair Shops and Related Services, NEC

561910 Packaging and Labeling Services *see* SIC 7389: Business Services, NEC

561920 Convention and Trade Show Organizers *see* SIC 7389: Business Services, NEC

561990 All Other Support Services *see* SIC 7389: Business Services, NEC

562111 Solid Waste Collection *see* SIC 4212: Local Trucking Without Storage; SIC 4953: Refuse Systems

562112 Hazardous Waste Collection *see* SIC 4212: Local Trucking Without Storage; SIC 4953: Refuse Systems

562119 Other Waste Collection *see* SIC 4212: Local Trucking Without Storage; SIC 4953: Refuse Systems

562211 Hazardous Waste Treatment and Disposal *see* SIC 4953: Refuse Systems

562212 Solid Waste Landfills *see* SIC 4953: Refuse Systems

562213 Solid Waste Combustors and Incinerators *see* SIC 4953: Refuse Systems

562219 Other Nonhazardous Waste Treatment and Disposal *see* SIC 4953: Refuse Systems

562910 Remediation Services *see* SIC 1799: Special Trade Contractors, NEC; SIC 4959: Sanitary Services, NEC

562920 Materials Recovery Facilities *see* SIC 4953: Refuse Systems

562991 Septic Tank and Related Services *see* SIC 7359: Equipment Rental and Leasing, NEC; SIC 7699: Repair Shops and Related Services, NEC

562998 All Other Miscellaneous Waste Management *see* SIC 4959: Sanitary Services, NEC

EDUCATIONAL SERVICES

611110 Elementary and Secondary Schools *see* SIC 8211: Elementary and Secondary Schools

611210 Junior Colleges *see* SIC 8222: Junior Colleges and Technical Institutes

611310 Colleges, Universities and Professional Schools *see* SIC 8221: Colleges, Universities, and Professional Schools

611410 Business and Secretarial Schools *see* SIC 8244: Business and Secretarial Schools

611420 Computer Training *see* SIC 8243: Data Processing Schools

611430 Professional and Management Development Training Schools *see* SIC 8299: Schools and Educational Services, NEC

611511 Cosmetology and Barber Schools *see* SIC 7231: Beauty Shops; SIC 7241: Barber Shops

611512 Flight Training *see* SIC 8249: Vocational Schools, NEC; SIC 8299: Schools and Educational Services, NEC

611513 Apprenticeship Training *see* SIC 8249: Vocational Schools, NEC

611519 Other Technical and Trade Schools *see* SIC 8243: Data Processing Schools; SIC 8249: Vocational Schools, NEC

611610 Fine Arts Schools *see* SIC 7911: Dance Studios, Schools, and Halls; SIC 8299: Schools and Educational Services, NEC

611620 Sports and Recreation Instruction *see* SIC 7999: Amusement and Recreation Services, NEC

611630 Language Schools *see* SIC 8299: Schools and Educational Services, NEC

611691 Exam Preparation and Tutoring *see* SIC 8299: Schools and Educational Services, NEC

611692 Automobile Driving Schools *see* SIC 8299: Schools and Educational Services, NEC

611699 All Other Miscellaneous Schools and Instruction *see* SIC 8299: Schools and Educational Services, NEC

611710 Educational Support Services *see* SIC 8299: Schools and Educational Services, NEC; SIC 8748: Business Consulting Services, NEC

HEALTH CARE & SOCIAL ASSISTANCE

621111   Offices of Physicians (except Mental Health Specialists) *see* SIC 8011: Offices and Clinics of Doctors of Medicine; SIC 8031: Offices and Clinics of Doctors of Osteopathy

621112   Offices of Physicians, Mental Health Specialists *see* SIC 8011: Offices and Clinics of Doctors of Medicine; SIC 8031: Offices and Clinics of Doctors of Osteopathy

621210   Offices of Dentists *see* SIC 8021: Offices and Clinics of Dentists

621310   Offices of Chiropractors *see* SIC 8041: Offices and Clinics of Chiropractors

621320   Offices of Optometrists *see* SIC 8042: Offices and Clinics of Optometrists

621330   Offices of Mental Health Practitioners (except Physicians) *see* SIC 8049: Offices and Clinics of Health Practitioners, NEC

621340   Offices of Physical, Occupational, and Speech Therapists and Audiologists *see* SIC 8049: Offices and Clinics of Health Practitioners, NEC

621391   Offices of Podiatrists *see* SIC 8043: Offices and Clinics of Podiatrists

621399   Offices of All Other Miscellaneous Health Practitioners *see* SIC 8049: Offices and Clinics of Health Practitioners, NEC

621410   Family Planning Centers *see* SIC 8093: Specialty Outpatient Facilities, NEC; SIC 8099: Health and Allied Services, NEC

621420   Outpatient Mental Health and Substance Abuse Centers *see* SIC 8093: Specialty Outpatient Facilities, NEC

621491   HMO Medical Centers *see* SIC 8011: Offices and Clinics of Doctors of Medicine

621492   Kidney Dialysis Centers *see* SIC 8092: Kidney Dialysis Centers

621493   Freestanding Ambulatory Surgical and Emergency Centers *see* SIC 8011: Offices and Clinics of Doctors of Medicine

621498   All Other Outpatient Care Facilities *see* SIC 8093: Specialty Outpatient Facilities, NEC

621511   Medical Laboratories *see* SIC 8071: Medical Laboratories

621512   Diagnostic Imaging Centers *see* SIC 8071: Medical Laboratories

621610   Home Health Care Services *see* SIC 8082: Home Health Care Services

621910   Ambulance Service *see* SIC 4119: Local Passenger Transportation, NEC; SIC 4522: Air Transportation, Nonscheduled

621991   Blood and Organ Banks *see* SIC 8099: Health and Allied Services, NEC

621999   All Other Miscellaneous Ambulatory Health Care Services *see* SIC 8099: Health and Allied Services, NEC

622110   General Medical and Surgical Hospitals *see* SIC 8062: General Medical and Surgical Hospitals; SIC 8069: Specialty Hospitals, Except Psychiatric

622210   Psychiatric and Substance Abuse Hospitals *see* SIC 8063: Psychiatric Hospitals; SIC 8069: Specialty Hospitals, Except Psychiatric

622310   Specialty (except Psychiatric and Substance Abuse) Hospitals *see* SIC 8069: Specialty Hospitals, Except Psychiatric

623110   Nursing Care Facilities *see* SIC 8051: Skilled Nursing Care Facilities; SIC 8052: Intermediate Care Facilities; SIC 8059: Nursing and Personal Care Facilities, NEC

623210   Residential Mental Retardation Facilities *see* SIC 8052: Intermediate Care Facilities

623220   Residential Mental Health and Substance Abuse Facilities *see* SIC 8361: Residential Care

623311   Continuing Care Retirement Communities *see* SIC 8051: Skilled Nursing Care Facilities; SIC 8052: Intermediate Care Facilities; SIC 8059: Nursing and Personal Care Facilities, NEC

623312   Homes for the Elderly *see* SIC 8361: Residential Care

623990   Other Residential Care Facilities *see* SIC 8361: Residential Care

624110   Child and Youth Services *see* SIC 8322: Individual and Family Social Services; SIC 8641: Civic, Social, and Fraternal Associations

624120   Services for the Elderly and Persons with Disabilities *see* SIC 8322: Individual and Family Social Services

624190   Other Individual and Family Services *see* SIC 8322: Individual and Family Social Services

624210   Community Food Services *see* SIC 8322: Individual and Family Social Services

624221   Temporary Shelter *see* SIC 8322: Individual and Family Social Services

624229   Other Community Housing Services *see* SIC 8322: Individual and Family Social Services

624230   Emergency and Other Relief Services *see* SIC 8322: Individual and Family Social Services

624310   Vocational Rehabilitation Services *see* SIC 8331: Job Training and Vocational Rehabilitation Services

624410   Child Day Care Services *see* SIC 7299: Miscellaneous Personal Services, NEC; SIC 8351: Child Day Care Services

ARTS, ENTERTAINMENT, & RECREATION

711110   Theater Companies and Dinner Theaters *see* SIC 5812: Eating and Drinking Places; SIC 7922: Theatrical Producers (Except Motion Picture) and Miscellaneous Theatrical Services

711120   Dance Companies *see* SIC 7922: Theatrical Producers (Except Motion Picture) and Miscellaneous Theatrical Services

711130   Musical Groups and Artists *see* SIC 7929: Bands, Orchestras, Actors, and Other Entertainers and Entertainment Groups

711190   Other Performing Arts Companies *see* SIC 7929: Bands, Orchestras, Actors, and Other Entertainers and Entertainment Groups; SIC 7999: Amusement and Recreation Services, NEC

711211   Sports Teams and Clubs *see* SIC 7941: Professional Sports Clubs and Promoters

711212   Race Tracks *see* SIC 7948: Racing, Including Track Operations

711219   Other Spectator Sports *see* SIC 7941: Professional Sports Clubs and Promoters; SIC 7948: Racing, Including Track Operations; SIC 7999: Amusement and Recreation Services, NEC

711310   Promoters of Performing Arts, Sports, and Similar Events with Facilities *see* SIC 6512: Operators of Nonresidential Buildings; SIC 7922: Theatrical Producers (Except Motion Picture) and Miscellaneous Theatrical Services; SIC 7941: Professional Sports Clubs and Promoters

711320   Promoters of Performing Arts, Sports, and Similar Events without Facilities *see* SIC 7922: Theatrical Producers (Except Motion Picture) and Miscellaneous Theatrical Services; SIC 7941: Professional Sports Clubs and Promoters

711410   Agents and Managers for Artists, Athletes, Entertainers and Other Public Figures *see* SIC 7389: Business Services, NEC; SIC 7922: Theatrical Producers (Except Motion Picture) and Miscellaneous Theatrical Services; SIC 7941: Professional Sports Clubs and Promoters

711510   Independent Artists, Writers, and Performers *see* SIC 7819: Services Allied to Motion Picture Production; SIC 7929: Bands, Orchestras, Actors, and Other Entertainers and Entertainment Groups; SIC 8999: Services, NEC

712110   Museums *see* SIC 8412: Museums and Art Galleries

712120   Historical Sites *see* SIC 8412: Museums and Art Galleries

712130   Zoos and Botanical Gardens *see* SIC 8422: Arboreta and Botanical or Zoological Gardens

712190   Nature Parks and Other Similar Institutions *see* SIC 7999: Amusement and Recreation Services, NEC; SIC 8422: Arboreta and Botanical or Zoological Gardens

713110   Amusement and Theme Parks *see* SIC 7996: Amusement Parks

713120   Amusement Arcades *see* SIC 7993: Coin Operated Amusement Devices

713210   Casinos (except Casino Hotels) *see* SIC 7999: Amusement and Recreation Services, NEC

713290   Other Gambling Industries *see* SIC 7993: Coin Operated Amusement Devices; SIC 7999: Amusement and Recreation Services, NEC

713910   Golf Courses and Country Clubs *see* SIC 7992: Public Golf Courses; SIC 7997: Membership Sports and Recreation Clubs

713920   Skiing Facilities *see* SIC 7999: Amusement and Recreation Services, NEC

713930   Marinas *see* SIC 4493: Marinas

713940   Fitness and Recreational Sports Centers *see* SIC 7991: Physical Fitness Facilities; SIC 7997: Membership Sports and Recreation Clubs; SIC 7999: Amusement and Recreation Services, NEC

713950   Bowling Centers *see* SIC 7933: Bowling Centers

713990   All Other Amusement and Recreation Industries *see* SIC 7911: Dance Studios, Schools, and Halls; SIC 7993: Coin Operated Amusement Devices; SIC 7997: Membership Sports and Recreation Clubs; SIC 7999: Amusement and Recreation Services, NEC

ACCOMODATION & FOODSERVICES

721110   Hotels (except Casino Hotels) and Motels *see* SIC 7011: Hotels and Motels; SIC 7041: Organization Hotels and Lodging Houses, on Membership Basis

721120   Casino Hotels *see* SIC 7011: Hotels and Motels

721191   Bed and Breakfast Inns *see* SIC 7011: Hotels and Motels

721199   All Other Traveler Accommodations *see* SIC 7011: Hotels and Motels

721211   RV (Recreational Vehicle) Parks and Campgrounds *see* SIC 7033: Recreational Vehicle Parks and Campsites

721214   Recreational and Vacation Camps *see* SIC 7032: Sporting and Recreational Camps

721310   Rooming and Boarding Houses *see* SIC 7021: Rooming and Boarding Houses; SIC 7041: Organization Hotels and Lodging Houses, on Membership Basis

722110 Full-Service Restaurants *see* SIC 5812: Eating and Drinking Places

722211 Limited-Service Restaurants *see* SIC 5499: Miscellaneous Food Stores; SIC 5812: Eating and Drinking Places

722212 Cafeterias *see* SIC 5812: Eating and Drinking Places

722213 Snack and Nonalcoholic Beverage Bars *see* SIC 5461: Retail Bakeries; SIC 5812: Eating and Drinking Places

722310 Foodservice Contractors *see* SIC 5812: Eating and Drinking Places

722320 Caterers *see* SIC 5812: Eating and Drinking Places

722330 Mobile Caterers *see* SIC 5963: Direct Selling Establishments

722410 Drinking Places (Alcoholic Beverages) *see* SIC 5813: Drinking Places (Alcoholic Beverages)

OTHER SERVICES

811111 General Automotive Repair *see* SIC 7538: General Automotive Repair Shops

811112 Automotive Exhaust System Repair *see* SIC 7533: Automotive Exhaust System Repair Shops

811113 Automotive Transmission Repair *see* SIC 7537: Automotive Transmission Repair Shops

811118 Other Automotive Mechanical and Electrical Repair and Maintenance *see* SIC 7539: Automotive Repair Shops, NEC

811121 Automotive Body, Paint, and Upholstery Repair and Maintenance *see* SIC 7532: Top, Body, and Upholstery Repair Shops and Paint Shops

811122 Automotive Glass Replacement Shops *see* SIC 7536: Automotive Glass Replacement Shops

811191 Automotive Oil Change and Lubrication Shops *see* SIC 7549: Automotive Services, Except Repair and Carwashes

811192 Car Washes *see* SIC 7542: Carwashes

811198 All Other Automotive Repair and Maintenance *see* SIC 7534: Tire Retreading and Repair Shops; SIC 7549: Automotive Services, Except Repair and Carwashes

811211 Consumer Electronics Repair and Maintenance *see* SIC 7622: Radio and Television Repair Shops; SIC 7629: Electrical and Electronic Repair Shops, NEC

811212 Computer and Office Machine Repair and Maintenance *see* SIC 7378: Computer Maintenance and Repair; SIC 7629: Electrical and Electronic Repair Shops, NEC; SIC 7699: Repair Shops and Related Services, NEC

811213 Communication Equipment Repair and Maintenance *see* SIC 7622: Radio and Television Repair Shops; SIC 7629: Electrical and Electronic Repair Shops, NEC

811219 Other Electronic and Precision Equipment Repair and Maintenance *see* SIC 7629: Electrical and Electronic Repair Shops, NEC; SIC 7699: Repair Shops and Related Services, NEC

811310 Commercial and Industrial Machinery and Equipment (except Automotive and Electronic) Repair and Maintenance *see* SIC 7623: Refrigeration and Air-Conditioning Services and Repair Shops; SIC 7694: Armature Rewinding Shops; SIC 7699: Repair Shops and Related Services, NEC

811411 Home and Garden Equipment Repair and Maintenance *see* SIC 7699: Repair Shops and Related Services, NEC

811412 Appliance Repair and Maintenance *see* SIC 7623: Refrigeration and Air-Conditioning Services and Repair Shops; SIC 7629: Electrical and Electronic Repair Shops, NEC; SIC 7699: Repair Shops and Related Services, NEC

811420 Reupholstery and Furniture Repair *see* SIC 7641: Reupholster and Furniture Repair

811430 Footwear and Leather Goods Repair *see* SIC 7251: Shoe Repair Shops and Shoeshine Parlors; SIC 7699: Repair Shops and Related Services, NEC

811490 Other Personal and Household Goods Repair and Maintenance *see* SIC 3732: Boat Building and Repairing; SIC 7219: Laundry and Garment Services, NEC; SIC 7631: Watch, Clock, and Jewelry Repair; SIC 7692: Welding Repair; SIC 7699: Repair Shops and Related Services, NEC

812111 Barber Shops *see* SIC 7241: Barber Shops

812112 Beauty Salons *see* SIC 7231: Beauty Shops

812113 Nail Salons *see* SIC 7231: Beauty Shops

812191 Diet and Weight Reducing Centers *see* SIC 7299: Miscellaneous Personal Services, NEC

812199 Other Personal Care Services *see* SIC 7299: Miscellaneous Personal Services, NEC

812210 Funeral Homes *see* SIC 7261: Funeral Services and Crematories

812220 Cemeteries and Crematories *see* SIC 6531: Real Estate Agents and Managers; SIC 6553: Cemetery Subdividers and Developers

812220 Cemeteries and Crematories *see* SIC 7261: Funeral Services and Crematories

812310 Coin-Operated Laundries and Drycleaners *see* SIC 7215: Coin-Operated Laundry and Drycleaning

812321 Laundries, Family and Commercial *see* SIC 7211: Power Laundries, Family and Commercial

812322 Drycleaning Plants *see* SIC 7216: Drycleaning Plants, Except Rug Cleaning

812331   Linen Supply *see* SIC 7213: Linen Supply; SIC 7219: Laundry and Garment Services, NEC

812332   Industrial Launderers *see* SIC 7218: Industrial Launderers

812391   Garment Pressing and Agents for Laundries *see* SIC 7212: Garment Pressing, and Agents for Laundries

812399   All Other Laundry Services *see* SIC 7219: Laundry and Garment Services, NEC

812910   Pet Care (except Veterinary) Services *see* SIC 0752: Animal Specialty Services, Except Veterinary

812921   Photo Finishing Laboratories (except One-Hour) *see* SIC 7384: Photofinishing Laboratories

812922   One-Hour Photo Finishing *see* SIC 7384: Photofinishing Laboratories

812930   Parking Lots and Garages *see* SIC 7521: Automobile Parking

812990   All Other Personal Services *see* SIC 7299: Miscellaneous Personal Services, NEC; SIC 7389: Business Services, NEC

813110   Religious Organizations *see* SIC 8661: Religious Organizations

813211   Grantmaking Foundations *see* SIC 6732: Education, Religious, and Charitable Trusts

813212   Voluntary Health Organizations *see* SIC 8399: Social Services, NEC

813219   Other Grantmaking and Giving Services *see* SIC 8399: Social Services, NEC

813311   Human Rights Organizations *see* SIC 8399: Social Services, NEC

813312   Environment, Conservation and Wildlife Organizations *see* SIC 8399: Social Services, NEC; SIC 8699: Membership Organizations, NEC

813319   Other Social Advocacy Organizations *see* SIC 8399: Social Services, NEC

813410   Civic and Social Organizations *see* SIC 8641: Civic, Social, and Fraternal Associations; SIC 8699: Membership Organizations, NEC

813910   Business Associations *see* SIC 8611: Business Associations; SIC 8699: Membership Organizations, NEC

813920   Professional Organizations *see* SIC 8621: Professional Membership Organizations

813930   Labor Unions and Similar Labor Organizations *see* SIC 8631: Labor Unions and Similar Labor Organizations

813940   Political Organizations *see* SIC 8651: Political Organizations

813990   Other Similar Organizations *see* SIC 6531: Real Estate Agents and Managers; SIC 8641: Civic, Social, and Fraternal Associations; SIC 8699: Membership Organizations, NEC

814110   Private Households *see* SIC 8811: Private Households

PUBLIC ADMINISTRATION

921110   Executive Offices *see* SIC 9111: Executive Offices

921120   Legislative Bodies *see* SIC 9121: Legislative Bodies

921130   Public Finance *see* SIC 9311: Public Finance, Taxation, and Monetary Policy

921140   Executive and Legislative Offices, Combined *see* SIC 9131: Executive and Legislative Offices, Combined

921150   American Indian and Alaska Native Tribal Governments *see* SIC 8641: Civic, Social, and Fraternal Associations

921190   All Other General Government *see* SIC 9199: General Government, NEC

922110   Courts *see* SIC 9211: Courts

922120   Police Protection *see* SIC 9221: Police Protection

922130   Legal Counsel and Prosecution *see* SIC 9222: Legal Counsel and Prosecution

922140   Correctional Institutions *see* SIC 9223: Correctional Institutions

922150   Parole Offices and Probation Offices *see* SIC 8322: Individual and Family Social Services

922160   Fire Protection *see* SIC 9224: Fire Protection

922190   All Other Justice, Public Order, and Safety *see* SIC 9229: Public Order and Safety, NEC

923110   Administration of Education Programs *see* SIC 9411: Administration of Educational Programs

923120   Administration of Public Health Programs *see* SIC 9431: Administration of Public Health Programs

923130   Administration of Social, Human Resource and Income Maintenance Programs *see* SIC 9441: Administration of Social, Human Resource and Income Maintenance Programs

923140   Administration of Veteran's Affairs *see* SIC 9451: Administration of Veteran's Affairs, Except Health Insurance

924110   Air and Water Resource and Solid Waste Management *see* SIC 9511: Air and Water Resource and Solid Waste Management

924120   Land, Mineral, Wildlife, and Forest Conservation *see* SIC 9512: Land, Mineral, Wildlife, and Forest Conservation

925110   Administration of Housing Programs *see* SIC 9531: Administration of Housing Programs

925120   Administration of Urban Planning and Community and Rural Development *see* SIC 9532: Administration of Urban Planning and Community and Rural Development

926110   Administration of General Economic Programs *see* SIC 9611: Administration of General Economic Programs

926120   Regulation and Administration of Transportation Programs *see* SIC 9621: Regulations and Administration of Transportation Programs

926130   Regulation and Administration of Communications, Electric, Gas, and Other Utilities *see* SIC 9631: Regulation and Administration of Communications, Electric, Gas, and Other Utilities

926140   Regulation of Agricultural Marketing and Commodities *see* SIC 9641: Regulation of Agricultural Marketing and Commodities

926150   Regulation, Licensing, and Inspection of Miscellaneous Commercial Sectors *see* SIC 9651: Regulation, Licensing, and Inspection of Miscellaneous Commercial Sectors

927110   Space Research and Technology *see* SIC 9661: Space Research and Technology

928110   National Security *see* SIC 9711: National Security

928120   International Affairs *see* SIC 9721: International Affairs

999990   Unclassified Establishments *see* SIC 9999: Nonclassified Establishments

Geographic Index

General Index

A

AAR (Association of American Railroads), 1153, 1158, 1161

A.B. Dick Company (office machines), 572

AB Electrolux, 227, 232, 233–234

AB InBev (Belgian brewery), 411–412

ABB Daimler-Benz Transportation (Adtranz), 1123–1124

ABB Group (Switzerland), 261, 543, 567

ABBA Optical, 743

Abbott Laboratories, 62, 117–118, 121

ABC Clinical Guide to Herbs (American Botanical Council), 100

ABC Radio Networks, Inc., 679, 682, 684

ABC Television Networks, 717

Abdullah, Halimah, 831

ABI Pay-TV markets, 595

ABIQUIM (Brazilian chemical association) study, 84

Abitibi-Consolidated Inc., 855, 856, 857

Accenture Ltd. (formerly Anderson Consulting), 172, 956

ACCO Brands Corp., 575

Accor SA (Paris, hotel operator), 313

Accounting, auditing, bookkeeping services, **915–924**
    background/development, 918–921
    countries in the industry, 923–924
    current conditions, 921
    industry leaders, 922–923

    industry snapshot, 915–916
    organization/structure, 916–917
    workforce, 921–922

Accounting and Corporate Regulatory Authority, 922

Accounting Standards Committee (ASC, UK), 917

Ackley Manufacturing and Sales, 762

Acott, Mike, 177

Ad Age magazine, 929

Adams, Judith, 289

Adams Media Research, 598

Adecco SA staffing company, 960–961, 964

Adelphi Communications, 600, 601

Adherence Technologies (pharmaceuticals), 124

Adhesives and sealants, **47–53**
    background/development, 48–49
    countries in the industry, 52–53
    current conditions, 49–50
    industry leaders, 51–52
    industry snapshot, 47
    organization/structure, 47–48
    research and technology, 50–51

ADI (austempered ductile iron), 768

Adidas-Salomon AG, 345

ADSL (asymmetric digital subscriber lines), 706

Advance disposal fees (glass/plastic containers), 498

Advanced Micro Devices (AMD), 273

Advanced Photo System (APS) cameras, 262, 266

Advanced Research Projects Agency (ARPA, U.S.), 629

Advanced Television Advisory Commission (FCC), 240

Advertising Age magazine, 928, 929, 931

Advertising agencies, **924–932**
    background/development, 926–927
    countries in the industry, 931–932
    current conditions, 927–929
    industry leaders, 929–931
    industry snapshot, 924–925
    organization/structure, 925–926

Advertising Agency of the Year Award (2008), 924

ADWEEK magazine, 924, 925, 928, 929

AEG-Kanis, 536

Aer Rianta mail-order, 975

Aerospatiale Matra Missiles, 1081

Affiliated Computer Services, Inc., 162–163

Africa
    accounting, auditing, bookkeeping firms, 923
    agriculture industry data, 2–5, 7, 16, 22–23, 26
    air transport industry, 1136
    All Africa Conference of Churches, 102
    apparel industry, 1037
    auto parts industry, 1096
    book publishing industry, 587
    chemical industry data, 84, 87, 92
    civil engineering industry, 937

1299

International Newspapers Advertising and Marketing Executives, 640

International Olympic Committee (IOC), 326

International Organization for Standardization (ISO), 934

International Paper Company (IP), 225, 852, 856, 862, 876, 881

The International Political Economy of Coffee (Lucier), 425

International Railway Journal, 1120, 1121, 1123, 1156, 1157

International Scientific Committee for Tuna and Tuna-Like Species in the North Pacific Ocean (2002), 28

International Standardization Organization (ISO), 89–90, 168, 488, 625, 747, 773

International Steel Group, 777

International Telecommunication Union (ITU), 691, 697–698, 700, 702, 703

International Time Recording Company, 170

International Trade Administration, 237, 239, 760

International Trade Commission (ITC), 237, 508, 772–773

International Union of Pure and Applied Chemistry (IUPAC), 89

International Union of Railways, 1153

International Union of Road-Rail Transport Companies, 1156

International Video Federation (IVF), 348

The International Who's Who of Business Lawyers, 948

Internet & American Life Project survey, 637

Internet Network Information Center (InterNIC), 628

Internet Protocol (IP) PBX systems, 692

Internet Protocol Television (IPTV), 688

Internet services, **624–635**
  background/development, 629
  countries in the industry, 635
  current conditions, 629–630
  industry leaders, 631–635
  industry snapshot, 624–625
  online gambling operations, 298–299
  online legal services, 946–947
  online publications, 665–666
  online radio, 679
  organization/structure, 625–629
  research and technology, 630–631

InternetRetailer.com, 980

Interpublic Group of Companies Inc., 927, 930

Interstate Aviation Committee (IAC, CIS), 1068

Interstate Banking and Branching Efficiency Act (1994), 359

Interstate Commerce Commission (ICC), 1163, 1165

Intrernational Organization of Standardization (ISO), 650

Investor's Business Daily, 982

IP (Internet protocol) applications and systems, 688

iPad (Apple tablet), 649, 654

Iranian Oil Participants (IOP) consortium, 899

Iraq Petroleum Company, 894

Ireland
  advertising agencies, 926
  beer industry data, 405, 409
  catalog/mail-order services, 980
  elementary/secondary schools, 1195
  glass industry, 499
  iron and steel foundries, 765
  legal services, 942–943
  logging industry, 225
  metal can industry, 787
  metals mining industry, 850
  newspaper industry, 638
  nonresidential building construction, 208
  passenger car rentals, 995, 1000
  personnel services, 959
  restaurants, 1007
  telecommunications services, 700
  television broadcasting stations, 713
  textile industry, 1054
  tire industry, 519
  tobacco industry, 467

Irish Association of Health Stories, 100

Irishenco Construction Company (Ireland), 185

Iron and steel foundries, **764–770**
  background/development, 765–767
  current conditions, 767–768
  industry leaders, 769–770
  industry snapshot, 764–765
  organization/structure, 765
  research and technology, 768–769
  workforce, 769

Iron and Steel Statistics Bureau (ISSB), 796

ISDN (integrated service digital network), 704, 706

Ishibashi, Shojiro, 521

Ishikawajima- Shibaura Machine Company, 1092

Ishikawajima-Harima Heavy Industries Company, 187

Ispat International, 777

Israel
  book publishing industry, 586
  credit card industry, 383
  defense and armaments industry, 1081
  elevator industry, 528
  forestry industry, 39
  hotel industry, 312
  newspaper industry, 644
  soft drinks/bottled water industry, 461
  telecommunications services, 700
  video industry, 353

Isuzu Motors Ltd., 543

Italy, 406
  advertising agencies, 926, 930
  apparel industry, 1039, 1041, 1042
  asphalt manufacturing, 81
  auto parts industry, 1092, 1098
  bridge projects, 185
  cable-television industry, 596
  catalog/mail-order services, 976
  cement industry, 191
  commercial printing industry, 678
  commodity futures exchange, 379
  credit industry, 384
  defense and armaments industry, 1078, 1079, 1081
  electronics industry, 254
  food packaging industry, 556
  furniture industry, 479, 480, 481
  glass industry, 497
  grocery stores, 987
  hand tools/hardware industry, 758
  heating and cooling equipment, 569
  industrial machinery industry, 553
  iron and steel foundries, 768
  leathers goods/accessories, 1046, 1048, 1050
  legal services, 943, 944
  management consulting services, 952
  metals, primary nonferrous, 801, 804
  motion picture industry, 324
  office furniture industry, 492
  office machinery, 575
  ophthalmic goods, 736, 742, 743
  passenger car rentals, 995, 998
  periodical publishers, 663, 665
  postal services, 1147
  power-generating equipment, 536, 5454
  radio markets, 686
  rail transportation, 1156
  shipbuilding/repair industry, 1118
  soaps/detergents industry, 134, 138
  soft drinks/bottled water industry, 451
  steel industry, 776
  telecommunications services, 700

train equipment industry, 1126
vending machine industry, 560
video tape rental and retail, 354
watch industry, 278, 279, 281, 284
wholesale industry, 1027, 1030
wine industry data, 411, 413
World Aquaculture Society, 21
Yamiuri Giants, 332

Japan Airlines Corp., 1133, 1140
Japan Auto Parts Industries Association (JAPAI), 1098
Japan Automobile Manufacturers Association (JAMA), 1099
Japan Chemical Week journal, 111
Japan Clock and Watch Association (JCWA), 279
Japan National Railway, 1160
Japan Paper Association, 877
Japan Tobacco and Salt Public Corporation, 474
Japan Tobacco International, Inc., 467, 474
The Japanese Industrial System (McMillan), 1028
J.B. Hunt Transport Services Inc., 1172
JC Penney Corporation Inc., 975, 978, 981, 1017, 1039–1040
JCB International Co. Inc., 389
Jefferson Wells personnel services, 964
Jehovah's Witnesses, anti-gambling rules, 296
Jelmoli mail-order, 975
JennAir, 229
Jersey Standard (Exxon), 898
Jeweler's Circular Keystone magazine, 279
Jewish Heritage Days, 288
Jobs, Steve, 147, 157, 319
Jobs and Growth Tax Relief Reconciliation Act (2003), 921
John, C.E., 1015
John Dewey Project in Progressive Education, 1188
John Wiley & Sons' (publisher), 588, 589, 591
Johnson, Anna Marie, 942
Johnson, Magic, 329
Johnson & Johnson, 127, 132, 743, 745, 751
Johnson Controls Inc., 1091, 1093, 1097
Joint Technical Committee 1 (JTC1), 650
Jones, Fletcher, 172
Jones Day legal services, 948
Jones Radio Network, 685
JooJoo tablet, 654
Jordan, Michael, 329, 331

Journal of Agriculture and Food Chemistry, 431
Journal of Biomedical Materials Research Part A, 750
The Journal of Commerce Online, 1113
Journal of Forestry, 223
Journal of Public Health (Canada), 144
The Journal of the American Medical Association (JAMA), 731
JoyFest (Christian entertainment), 288
JP Morgan Chase, 357, 361, 364, 389
Jupiter Media Metrix, 977
Justice Department (U.S.), 197–198, 382, 535
JWT advertising, 930

K

Kahney, Leander, 157
Kaiser Permanente Colorado, 491
Kajima Corporation, 207, 208
Kamyr AB (Sweden), 880
Kansai Paint Co. Ltd., 111, 114–115
Kansas City Board of Trade, 372
Kansas City Star newspaper, 646
Kao Corporation (Japan, soaps/detergents), 137
Kawasaki Heavy Industries Ltd., 544, 1073
Kawasaki Steel, 774
Kay, John, 1056
Kaypro computer manufacturer, 148
Kellogg Brown & Root, Inc., 207
Kellogg Company, 417–418, 419, 420, 422, 865
Kelly Air Mail Act (U.S.), 1131
Kelly Services Inc., 964–965
Kentucky Fried Chicken, 440, 459, 1005, 1006, 1008, 1010–1011
Kenya Apparel Manufacturers and Exports Association, 1059
"Kids Getting Older Younger" theory (KGOY), 341
Kiener, Sigmund, 976
Killer Loop brand sunglasses, 742
Kimberly-Clark, 881
Kimberly Process (diamond) Certification Scheme (KPCS), 839
Kimble Glass, Inc., 501–502
KIMCO Corporation, 1009
Kindred Healthcare, 117
King, Stephen, 581, 583
Kingdom Holding Company (Saudi Arabia), 393
Kirin Brewery Company, Limited, 412
Kiseleva, Angela, 142
KitchenAid, 229

Klaussner Furniture Industries, Inc., 483
Klic, Karl, 673
Klynveld Main Goerdeler accounting, 923
Kmart Corporation, 343, 461, 920, 980, 989, 1016, 1018, 1021–1022, 1030, 1050
KMI Corporation, 697
Knight Ridder, 638, 646
Koch Industries, 876
Kodansha Ltd. Publishers, 585
KONE Corporation, 525, 527–528, 529, 530, 532
Konica Corporation, 265, 266
Koninklijke BAM Groep (Royal BAM), 207
Konrad, David, 152
Koop, C. Everett, 470
Korea Exchange (KRX), 377–378
Korea High-Speed Railway Construction Authority, 1124
Korea Press Foundation, 637
Korea Semiconductor Industry Association (KSIA), 276
Korea Tobacco, 467
Korean Society for Journalism and Communication Studies, 637
KPMG International accounting firm, 915, 918, 922, 923, 944, 951, 953
Kraft, Foods Inc., 417, 418, 423, 430–431
Krekich, Al, 1115–1116
Kresge Department Store, 1–16
Kroger Company, 428, 986, 989, 993
Kronos, Inc., 576
Krow, Gary, 165
KSkyB, 328
Kuang Yuang Industrial Company, 763
Kubota Corporation (Japan), 544
Kumagai Gumi Co. Ltd., 215
Kumar, Arun, 499
Kyocera Corporation (Japan), 254
Kyoto Protocol on Climate Change (1997), 50, 897, 907, 1070

L

La Ley legal periodicals (Argentina), 663
La Quinta lodging, 306
La-Z-Boy, Inc., 483
Labor, Department of (U.S.), 230, 872
Labor costs, glass industry, 498
Lafare SA (building materials group), 181, 202
Lafarge North America, 193–194

Metal oxide semiconductor (MOS) memory, 271

Metal Suppliers (e-commerce), 775

Metals, primary nonferrous, **800–809**
background/development, 802–805
current conditions, 805–806
industry snapshot, 800–801
organization/structure, 801–802
research and technology, 806–809

MetalSite (e-commerce), 775

Methyl tertiary butyl ether (MTBE). *See* Petroleum refining

Metro AG, 991

Metro International publishers, 643

Mexico
agricultural chemical industry, 78
auto parts industry, 1092, 1096
beer industry data, 409
book publishing industry, 582, 583, 587
cement manufacturing, 191
cereal industry, 417, 418
chemical industry data, 90
commercial printing industry, 674, 677–678
crude petroleum/natural gas, 894, 899, 903
fabricated rubber industry, 512
fabricated structural metal industry, 796
furniture industry, 484
gemstone mining industry, 837
greeting cards industry, 606, 612
grocery stores, 993
horticultural products exports, 2
industrial inorganic chemicals, 87
industrial machinery industry, 553
iron and steel foundries, 770
laundry equipment, commercial, 561
leathers goods/accessories, 1046
legal services, 948
metals, primary nonferrous, 801, 803, 804
motion picture industry, 323
motor vehicle industry, 1103
office furniture industry, 489, 492
paperboard mills, 876
periodical publishers, 663
petroleum refining, 912
plastics industry, 505
postal services, 1146, 1151
pumps, measuring and dispensing, 561
rail transport, 1153
rail transportation, 1156
real estate industry, 395
service machines industry, 561
soft drinks/bottled water industry, 453, 458, 462–463
steel industry, 777

surgical/medical equipment, 746
telecommunications services, 702
television broadcasting stations, 715
textile industry, 1060
tobacco industry, 468, 472
toy manufacturing, 336
train equipment industry, 1125
wine industry data, 411

Meyer, Phillip, 638

MFA (Multifiber Arrangement), 1038, 1053

MGM MIRAGE, 300–301

Miami Herald newspaper, 646

Michelin, AndrŌ and Edouard, 517, 521

Michelin Tires, 509, 517, 519–520

Michigan Optometric Association, 740

Microbreweries, 405

Microsoft Corporation, 147, 148, 151, 167, 317, 386, 595, 598, 618, 627, 649–650, 655–656, 1033

Microsoft Disk Operating System (MS-DOS), 649, 651, 655

Microsoft Network (MSN), 632

Microsoft Windows Operating System (OS), 650, 652

Middle East
agricultural industry data, 2, 4, 19
air transport industry, 1136
aircraft industry, 1074
apparel industry, 1040
auto parts industry, 1096
book publishing industry, 586–587
chemical industry data, 85, 92, 103
commercial printing industry, 673
computer development, 150
crude petroleum/natural gas, 893, 894–895, 900
defense and armaments industry, 1078, 1080
elevator industry, 532
energy industry, 1210
engineering services, 934
fertilizer industry data, 72
flour/milling operations, 142, 143
glass industry, 495, 497
legal services, 948
motor vehicle industry, 1101, 1107
nonresidential building construction, 203
ophthalmic goods, 742
paper industry, 852
petroleum refining, 912
plastics industry, 505
soft drinks/bottled water industry, 459, 463
sports teams and promoters, 332
steel industry, 774
television broadcasting stations, 712
textile industry, 1060

trucking industry, 1172
video tape rental and retail, 350
wholesale industry, 1028

Mikli, Alain, 735

Military & Aerospace magazine, 256

Millennium Development Goals (UN), 705

Milliken textiles, 1062

Mindanao Economic Development Council (Philippines), 24

Mindshare advertising, 929

MindSpring, 632

Mine Improvement and New Emergency Response Act (MINER Act, 2006), 846

Mine Safety and Health Administration (MSHA, U.S.), 831, 846

Miner, Robert, 657

Mineral Commodity Summaries (U.S. Geological Survey), 846

Mini-disc (MD) players, 236

Mining, coal, **823–833**
background/development, 826–827
countries in the industry, 830–833
current conditions, 827–828
historical background, 826–827
industry leaders, 829–830
industry snapshot, 823–824
organization/structure, 824–826
research and technology, 828–829

Mining, gemstone, **833–842**
background/development, 837–838
countries in the industry, 840–842
current conditions, 838–839
industry leaders, 839–840
industry snapshot, 833–834
organization/structure, 834–837

Mining, metal, **844–850**
background/development, 845–846
countries in the industry, 849–850
current conditions, 846–848
industry leaders, 848–849
industry snapshot, 844–845
organization/structure, 845

Mining Bureau (U.S. Bureau of Mines), 845

Mining Enforcement and Safety Administration (MESA), 846

Mining Journal magazine, 828

Ministry of Agriculture and Rural Development (MARD, Vietnam), 6

Ministry of International Trade and Industry (Japan), 238

Minnesota Mining and Manufacturing Company (3M), 48, 51

Minolta Corporation, 264, 265

Miramax studios, 319

The Mirror newspaper (UK), 637

National Association of Home Builders (NAHB), 212, 213, 234

National Association of Industrial and Office Parks (NAIOP), 394

National Association of PET Container Resources (NAPCOR), 507

National Association of Realtors, 392

National Association of Wholesaler-Distributors magazine, 1031

National auto rental, 994

National Automatic Merchandising Association (NAMA), 560

National Automobile Dealers Association (NADA), 970, 971

National Basketball Association (NBA), 326, 328, 329

National Bioethics Advisory Commission (NBAC), 61

National Broadcasting Company (NBC), 680, 713

National Cable & Communications Association, 595

National Car Rental, 994, 997, 999, 1001

National Catalog Advocacy & Strategy Forum, 975

National Chemical Industry Association (Mexico), 87

National Commission on Chemical Safety, 84

National Commodity and Derivative Exchange, 376

National Directory of Magazines, 661

National Education Association (NEA), 1193–1194

National Electrical Code (U.S.), 248

National Electrical Manufacturers Association, 258

National Emission Standards for Hazardous Air Pollutants (NESHAP), 481

National Energy Policy (NEP, U.S.), 832

National Energy Technology Center (U.S.), 541

National Eye Institute (NEI), 741

National Football League (NFL), 326, 331

National Futures Association (NFA), 370

National Green Building Standard, 234

National Hand Tool Corporation, 762

National Health Service (NHS, UK), 732, 733

National Highway Traffic and Safety Administration (NHTSA), 511, 512, 519, 1169

National Hockey League (NHL), 326, 331, 333

National Indian Gaming Commission, 299

National Industrial Recovery Act (NRA), 1165

National institute for Occupational Safety and Health (NIOSH), 32

National Institute of Biodiversity (Costa Rica), 99–100

National Institute of Standards and Technology (NST), 625

National Iranian Drilling Company, 899

National Iranian Oil Company, 899

National Labor Committee, 1038

National Library of Medicine, 615

National Lubricating Grease Institute (NLGI), 887

National Marine Fisheries Service (U.S.), 21, 25

National Milling Company (NAMILCO), 140

National Mining Association, 831

National Newspaper Publisher Association, 645

National Oceanic and Atmospheric Administration, 27

National Oil Corporation of Libya, 897

National Park Service (U.S.), 44, 529

National Petrochemical and Refiners Association, 890

National Public Radio (NPR), 679, 680–681, 686

National Restaurant Association (NRA), 1005, 1007

National Retail Federation (NRF), 979

National Science Foundation (NSF), 187

National Starch and Chemical, 51–52

National Stock Exchange of India, 369

National Tobacco Corporation (China), 467

National Transportation Safety Board (U.S.), 1132

National Union Electric Corporation (U.S.), 238–239

National Union of Textile, Garment and Tailoring Workers of Nigeria (NUTGTWN), 1055

Nations Restaurant News magazine, 1005

Natta, Giulio, 511

Natural gas. *See* Petroleum and natural gas, crude

Natural Resources Defense Council (U.S.), 785

Nature's Path (cereals), 420

Natuzzi of Italy (furniture), 480

Natuzzi S.p.A. (furniture), 484

Naylor, Rosamond, 21

Nazareth Health Care System (Kentucky), 732

NBC Universal Inc., 321, 597, 598, 600

NEA (National Education Association), 1193–1194

NEC (Nippon Electric Company, Japan), 156, 275, 573, 574, 1033

Nedeco Engineering, 935

Needham Harper Worldwide, 929

Nehustan elevator company (Israel), 528

NeoCon 2009 (office furniture showcase), 492

Nepal Department of Drug Administration, 96

Nestlé SA, 418, 425, 429–434

Nestle Waters North America, 455

Net PC (Microsoft-Intel collaboration), 151

Netflix, Inc., 347, 352–353, 597

Nethconsult Engineering, 935

Netherlands

    accounting, auditing, bookkeeping firms, 923

    advertising agencies, 926

    aircraft industry, 1068

    apparel industry, 1040

    beer industry data, 409

    cable-television industry, 596

    commercial printing industry, 674

    credit industry, 384

    defense and armaments industry, 1081

    energy industry, 1209–1210

    engineering services, 935, 938

    fabricated structural metal industry, 800

    Foreign Investment Agency, 393

    grocery stores, 987, 991–992

    horticultural products exports, 2

    information retrieval services, 614, 621

    management consulting services, 952

    metal can industry, 783–784

    passenger car rentals, 996

    periodical publishers, 662, 663, 669

    personnel services, 960, 961

    rail transportation, 1156

    railroad equipment industry, 1121

    real estate industry, 395

    restaurants, 1006

    roadway project, 183

    shipbuilding/repair industry, 1118

    soft drinks/bottled water industry, 451

TRIPS (Agreement on Trade-Related Aspects of Intellectual Property Rights), 100

Trized Properties, Inc., 398

Trombly, Richard, 1032

Trucking and courier services, **1163–1173**
background/development, 1164–1167
countries in the industry, 1170–1173
current conditions, 1167–1168
industry leaders, 1170–1172
industry snapshot, 1163–1164
organization/structure, 1164
research and technology, 1168–1169
workforce, 1169–1170

Trump Entertainment Resorts, Inc., 301

"TRUSTe" global initiative, 626

TRW Automotive Holdings Corp., 1092, 1093, 1097–1098

TSA (Transportation Security Administration), 1136, 1138

Tsutaya (Japan video operations), 353

Tully's Mountain View Coffee Co., 429

Tunnel construction. *See* Bridge, tunnel, elevated highway construction

Turkey
apparel industry, 1037, 1039
auto parts industry, 1098
credit card industry, 380
fabricated structural metal industry, 798
flour/milling operations, 143
hand tools/hardware industry, 758
industrial machinery industry, 556
iron and steel foundries, 768
leather goods/accessories, 1046, 1048
management consulting services, 957
metals mining industry, 850
newspaper industry, 644
soft drinks/bottled water industry, 459
telecommunications services, 700
textile industry, 1061
trucking industry, 1172

Turkish Petroleum Company, 894

The Tussauds Group, 293

TV Guide, 645

TWA airlines, 1135, 1139

Twain, Mark, 607

Tweedie, David, 921

Twitter, 627, 654

Tyco Electronics, 252, 254

Tyco Healthcare, 753

U

UAL Corporation (United Airlines), 1129, 1135, 1139

Ubiquitous Media, 928

Ukraine
coal mining industry, 828
metals mining industry, 850
steel industry, 774
telecommunications services, 698

Ultramar Diamond Shamrock oil, 908

UMI/Data Times, 616

Unbox Video Downloads, 347

UNESCO (United Nations Educational, Scientific, and Cultural Organizations), 1185, 1191

Unilever, 131, 133, 135–136, 441–442, 458

Union Camp Corporation paper packaging, 868

Union of Concerned Scientists (2006 report), 220

Union of Oil, Chemical and Atomic Workers, 910

Union Pacific Corporation, 1121

Union Pacific Railroad (U.S.), 1155, 1160

Uniroyal, 514

Unisys Corporation, 951

United Airlines, 1129, 1135

United Auto Workers (UAW) union, 1106

United Kingdom (UK)
accounting, auditing, bookkeeping firms, 917, 923–924
advertising agencies, 926, 928, 930, 931
air transport industry, 1133, 1140, 1141
aircraft industry, 1068
amusement parks, 289
apparel industry, 1040, 1043
asphalt manufacturing, 181
auto parts industry, 1093, 1097, 1098
automobile dealers, 969
banking/insurance industry, 362, 368
beer industry data, 405
biotech industry, 54, 55, 56, 64–65
book publishing industry, 579, 583, 588, 592–593
cable television industry, 597, 602, 603
catalog/mail-order services, 976, 977, 979, 982
cereal products, 417, 418, 422
Civil Aviation Authority, 1068
coal mining industry, 828
coffee industry, 430, 431, 434

commercial printing industry, 674, 675, 678
credit industry, 383, 384, 390
crude petroleum/natural gas, 900
defense and armaments industry, 1078, 1079, 1081, 1087
electricity consumption, 247
electronics manufacturing, 253
elementary and secondary schools, 1185, 1195–1196
energy industry, 1201, 1202, 1205–1206
Ethical Trading Initiative, 1040
Financial Futures Exchange, 372
folding paperboard boxes, 865
Forestry Commission, 224
gambling and gaming industry, 295, 296–297, 301–302
glass industry, 497, 501
greeting cards industry, 606, 607, 609, 612
grocery stores, 984, 986, 988, 992
hand tools/hardware industry, 758
Highways Agency, 188
Homewise agency research study, 228
hospital industry, 733–734
hotel industry, 314
industrial machinery industry, 553, 556
information retrieval services, 614, 620–621, 623
inorganic industrial chemicals, 81
iron and steel foundries, 765, 768, 769, 770
IT industry, 174
laundry equipment, commercial, 561
legal services, 941, 942–943, 944
lubricaing oils and greases, 888, 891
management consulting services, 950, 953
metal cans industry, 786–787, 790–791
metals, primary nonferrous, 804
metals mining industry, 846
motion picture industry, 317
newspaper industry, 637, 638, 639, 642, 648
office furniture industry, 492
office machinery, 571
paper industry, 856, 857
paperboard cartons and boxes, 869
paperboard mills, 876
passenger car rentals, 995, 997, 998, 1000
periodical publishers, 662, 663, 665, 669
personnel services, 960, 961, 962
petroleum refining, 904, 912
postal services, 1146, 1150–1151

hydroelectric power generators, 538

industrial inorganic chemicals, 80, 85–86

industrial machinery industry, 553, 556, 558

information retrieval services, 615, 618, 619, 622

Internet services, 629

iron and steel foundries, 765, 767, 769

IT industry, 173–174

Kelly Air Mail Act, 1131

laundry equipment, commercial, 561

leather goods/accessories, 1045–1046, 1048, 1050

legal services, 941–942, 948

liquor industry data, 405, 406–407

livestock production, 11–12, 17

logging industry, 218

lubricating oils and greases, 888–889

management consulting services, 949, 950, 952

metal cans industry, 782, 783, 785–786, 790, 792

metals, primary nonferrous, 801, 804, 806, 807, 808

metals mining industry, 844, 848

motion picture industry, 321–322

motor vehicle industry, 1106, 1111

motors/generator industry, 255, 261

National Bioethics Advisory Commission, 61

New Deal, 183

newspaper industry, 637, 638, 640, 646, 647

nonresidential building construction, 203, 207–208

office furniture industry, 486, 487, 488–489, 492

office machinery, 571, 573, 575, 577

old corrugated box recycling, 863

ophthalmic goods, 735–739, 743

orange production, 10

organic chemical industry, 95

packaged software industry, 649, 659–660

paint and coatings industry, 115–116

paper industry, 851, 853, 855, 856, 857, 859

paperboard containers and boxes, 861, 862–864, 867, 868, 869

paperboard mills, 872–878

passenger car rental, 994, 998, 1000

periodical publishers, 662, 663, 668

personnel services, 959, 961

petroleum refineries, 908

pharmaceutical industry, 117, 128–129

photographic equipment production, 265, 269

plastics industry, 502, 507, 508

postal services, 576, 606, 975, 1142–1143, 1146, 1149–1150

power-generating equipment, 535

pulp mills, 878–879, 884

pumps, measuring and dispensing, 561

radio market, 678, 686–687

rail transportation, 1153, 1160–1161

rapid prototyping (RP) technology, 936

real estate industry, 394, 398–399

recycling industry, 498, 506

regulations limiting CFCs, 229

renewable energy sources, 534

residential construction, 210, 211–212, 216–217

Resource Conservation and Recovery Act, 83, 108–109, 645

restaurants, 1005, 1007, 1012

retail industry, 1014–1015, 1017, 1022

sanitary food containers, 865

semiconductor industry, 271

Sherman Antitrust Act, 905, 906

shipbuilding/repair industry, 1115, 1119

soaps/detergent industry, 132, 138

soft drinks/bottled water industry, 450, 453–454, 458, 462

sports clubs and promoters, 327–328, 330

steel industry, 780

steel mills, 771

surgical/medical equipment, 746, 748, 749, 751, 753

telecommunications equipment, 695

telecommunications services, 698, 700, 701, 710

television broadcast services, 712–713, 715, 722–723

textile industry, 1051, 1053, 1057, 1061–1062

tire manufacturers, 514

tobacco industry, 465, 467–468, 476–477

toy manufacturing, 336, 337–338, 340, 345

Trade Act (1974), 650

traditional medicines data, 97

train equipment industry, 1120, 1121, 1125, 1126

trucking industry, 1172

vending machine industry, 560

video tape rental and retail, 353

watch industry, 278

wholesale industry, 1025, 1026, 1027, 1030, 1032, 1033

wind energy industry, 540, 542

wine industry data, 404–405, 406, 409, 410

Works Progress Administration, 183

World Aquaculture Society, 21

United States Agency for International Development (USAID), 361, 427–428

United States Council for Automotive Research (USCAR), 1105

United States Forest Service, 35

United States Surgical Corporation (USSC), 745, 747

United Steelworkers of America, 1038

United Steelworkers Union (USW), 765, 776

United Technologies Corporation (UTC), 525, 529, 531, 568–569, 1092, 1093, 1094, 1097

UNIVAC I computer, 150, 573

Universal Copyright Convention (1952), 581, 650

Universal Corporation (tobacco drying business), 466

Universal McCann, 928

Universal Postal Congress, 1144

Universal Postal Union, 975

Universal Postal Union (UPU), 975, 1142, 1143–1144

Universal Studios, 288, 290, 293, 321

University of Tokyo, 259

Unix-related operating system, 650

UPM Changshu paper mill, 876

UPM-Kymmene of Finland, 857, 876

U.S. Agency for International Development (USAID), 22

U.S. Airport Noise and Capacity Act (1990), 1072

U.S.-Australia Free Trade Agreement, 1044

U.S. Auto Parts Network, 1099

U.S. Bureau of Mines, 845

U.S.-Canada Free Trade Agreement, 1027, 1153

U.S.-Central America Free Trade Agreement, 1044

U.S. Civil Aeronautics Administration, 1132

U.S. Clean Air Act, 83, 541

U.S. Construction Trends report, 204

U.S. Corrugated and Paperboard Boxes Industry, 875

U.S. Department of Agriculture (USDA) aquaculture data, 22, 25
citrus production projections, 7